SUBJECT-MATTER INDEX

OF

PATENTS FOR INVENTIONS

ISSUED BY THE

UNITED STATES PATENT OFFICE

FROM

1790 TO 1873, INCLUSIVE.

VOLUME I.

COMPILED AND PUBLISHED UNDER THE DIRECTION OF

M. D. LEGGETT,

COMMISSIONER OF PATENTS.

WASHINGTON:
GOVERNMENT PRINTING OFFICE.
1874.

INDEX OF PATENTS

ISSUED FROM

THE UNITED STATES PATENT OFFICE

FROM 1790 TO 1873, INCLUSIVE.

Invention.	Inventor.	Residence.	Date.	No.
A.				
Abdominal and back supporter and truss combined.	R. J. Cundiff	Lynchburgh, Va	June 7, 1870	103, 992
Abdominal and spinal supporter	J. C. Zachos	New York, N. Y	July 16, 1872	129, 202
Abdominal and uterine supporter	J. A. Campbell	Lima, N. Y	Apr. 10, 1841	2, 041
Abdominal and uterine supporter	E. J. Harding	Saint Louis, Mo	Mar. 24, 1868	75, 902
Abdominal and uterine supporter combined	Z. Waters	Bloomington, Ill	July 27, 1869	93, 144
Abdominal supporter	M. G. Briggs	Boston, Mass	Feb. 6, 1872	123, 326
Abdominal supporter	H. B. Conant	Geneva, Wis	Aug. 2, 1853	9, 896
Abdominal supporter	E. Dexter	Quincy, Ill	June 5, 1866	55, 252
Abdominal supporter	M. Faloon	Bloomington, Ill	June 16, 1868	78, 946
Abdominal supporter	S. S. Fitch	New York, N. Y	Mar. 19, 1850	7, 186
Abdominal supporter	L. D. Fleming	Newark, N. J	Dec. 31, 1845	4, 336
Abdominal supporter	J. Funkhouser	Rockingham County, Va	Oct. 6, 1868	82, 702
Abdominal supporter	E. K. Gale	New York, N. Y	Mar. 14, 1846	4, 425
Abdominal supporter	B. A. Grover	Momence, Ill	July 5, 1859	24, 630
Abdominal supporter	J. W. Gurley	Petersburgh, Va	July 22, 1873	141, 137
Abdominal supporter	E. J. Harding	Saint Louis, Mo	Feb. 2, 1869	86, 539
Abdominal supporter	E. J. Harding	Saint Louis, Mo	July 15, 1873	140, 778
Abdominal supporter	W. Henderson and J. Greenawalt.	Pittsburgh, Pa	June 25, 1867	66, 022
Abdominal supporter	S. L. Hockert	Milwaukee, Wis	Sept. 8, 1868	82, 001
Abdominal supporter	J. W. Hood	Mount Sterling, N. Y	Dec. 11, 1847	5, 395
Abdominal supporter	I. J. H. Howard	San Francisco, Cal	June 24, 1862	35, 683
Abdominal supporter	H. R. and G. W. Hubbard	Middletown, Conn	Apr. 17, 1849	6, 353
Abdominal supporter	A. F. Jennings	Sherman, N. Y	Aug. 25, 1868	81, 510
Abdominal supporter	A. T. Kirk	Chicago, Ill	May 28, 1872	127, 352
Abdominal supporter	M. L. Knapp	Painesville, Ohio	Jan. 28, 1851	7, 916
Abdominal supporter	A. I. Lonsbury	Somerville, Tenn	Nov. 11, 1851	8, 515
Abdominal supporter	M. M. Merrill	Boston, Mass	July 8, 1873	140, 585
Abdominal supporter	J. M. Milligan	New Albany, Ind	Feb. 10, 1857	16, 602
Abdominal supporter	J. A. Morrell	Chicago, Ill	Mar. 17, 1868	75, 695
Abdominal supporter	M. W. O'Meara	New York, N. Y	Mar. 12, 1850	7, 175
Abdominal supporter	J. L. Porter	Kirksville, Mo	May 25, 1869	90, 389
Abdominal supporter	M. F. Potter	Kaneville, Ill	May 18, 1869	90, 191
Abdominal supporter	J. V. Richardson	Milwaukee, Wis	Aug. 29, 1871	118, 645
Abdominal supporter	H. H. Thompson	Washington, D. C	Nov. 22, 1864	45, 193
Abdominal supporter	J. Thompson	Milwaukee, Wis	Nov. 19, 1867	71, 246
Abdominal supporter	A. B. Weaver	Carthage, Ind	Sept. 27, 1859	25, 597
Abdominal supporter	J. White, S. N. Marsh, and H. Smith.	Canajoharie, N. Y	Sept. 28, 1843	3, 289
Abdominal supporter	W. M. Young	Trempealeau County, Wis	Dec. 24, 1867	72, 710
Abdominal supporter and corsets combined	S. A. Moody	New York, N. Y	May 3, 1864	42, 591
Abrading and polishing wheel	E. C. Merrill	Charleston, Vt	Dec. 7, 1869	97, 671
Abrasion, Form of rubbing surfaces for regulating.	C. Schiele	Frankfort, Germany	May 21, 1850	7, 385
Abrasive powder	J. Russell	Bath, Me	Jan. 22, 1867	61, 363
Accelerating washer	M. Cass	Caroline, N. Y	Aug. 29, 1827	....
Accelerating wheel-head	D. H. Tuttle	Williamson, N. Y	May 17, 1824	....
Accordeon	A. Faas	Philadelphia, Pa	Aug. 12, 1856	15, 511
Accordeon	E. Prics	New York, N. Y	June 21, 1864	43, 226
Accordeon	C. F. Zimmerman	Philadelphia, Pa	July 10, 1866	56, 319
Accordeon	C. F. Zimmermann	Philadelphia, Pa	Aug. 2, 1870	106, 018
Accordeon, &c	F. Goetze and D. Müller	New York, N. Y	Oct. 28, 1873	144, 025
Accordeon, Construction of	A. Faas	Philadelphia, Pa	June 13, 1854	11, 062
Accordeon, Method of tuning	E. A. Robbins	Rochester, N. Y	June 12, 1855	13, 044
Accordeon, Musical notation for	C. F. Zimmermann	Philadelphia, Pa	Jan. 3, 1871	110, 719
Accordeon-strap	C. F. Zimmermann	Philadelphia, Pa	Jan. 29, 1867	61, 698
Accordeon, Valve of	C. M. Zimmermann	Philadelphia, Pa	July 22, 1856	15, 401
Accordeons, &c., Tuning reeds of	M. and N. Schneider	New Orleans, La	Sept. 27, 1845	4, 212
Accoucheur's chair	N. W. Smith	Shutesbury, Mass	Oct. 16, 1849	6, 795
Account-indicator, Commercial	C. Brunschwiler	New York, N. Y	June 29, 1869	91, 905
Accouterments, Cavalry	J. K. Mizner	Detroit, Mich	Jan. 16, 1866	52, 064
Accouterments, Mode of slinging	W. D. Mann	Detroit, Mich	Dec. 8, 1863	40, 849
Acetate of copper or verdigris, Manufacture of	S. Dempsey	New York, N. Y	Feb. 4, 1813	....
Acid, and in the application of the same for various useful purposes, Production and manufacture of carbonic.	S. Stevens	New York, N. Y	Aug. 27, 1867	68, 321
Acid and other liquids, Apparatus for concentrating sulphuric.	J. Hughes	Brooklyn, N. Y	May 28, 1867	65, 227
Acid and other vessels, Cap to prevent the bursting of carbonic.	J. Matthews	New York, N. Y	Apr. 22, 1873	138, 171
Acid and paint from material used to purify gas, Manufacture of.	J. Hughes	Stapleton, N. Y	May 28, 1872	127, 350
Acid and phosphates, Manufacture of phosphoric	T. A. Genth	Philadelphia, Pa	Aug. 2, 1859	24, 931
Acid and water-proof composition for coating cloth.	H. W. Johns	New York, N. Y	May 10, 1870	102, 824

Index of patents issued from the United States Patent Office from 1790 *to* 1873, *inclusive*—Continued.

Invention.	Inventor.	Residence.	Date.	No.
Acid, Apparatus for concentrating sulphuric	D. Ashworth and R. Eaton	Woburn. Mass	May 26, 1868	78, 352
Acid, Apparatus for generating carbonic	W. H. Bate	East Somerville, Mass	Dec. 20, 1870	110, 190
Acid, Apparatus for generating carbonic	B. Bates	Baltimore, Md	Apr. 5, 1870	101, 415
Acid, Apparatus for generating carbonic	L. Kimball	Bradford, Mass	June 11, 1872	127 893
Acid, Apparatus for making nitric	P. O'Reilly	Providence, R. I	Mar. 24, 1857	16, 879
Acid, Apparatus for making sulphuric	S. Ravenel	Charleston, S. C	Apr. 25, 1871	114, 042
Acid, Apparatus for producing sulphurous	M. Hatschek	Pesth, Hungary	Mar. 22, 1870	101, 011
Acid as a substitute for other solid acids, Preparing phosphoric.	E. N. Horsford	Cambridge, Mass	Apr. 22, 1856	14, 722
Acid by lime decomposition, Margaric, stearic, and oleic.	H. Seybert and L. Vanuxem	Philadelphia, Pa	Aug. 16, 1830	....
Acid compound for use in baking and cooking	J. E. Lauer	New York, N. Y	Feb. 19, 1867	62, 277
Acid, Concentrating apparatus for sulphuric	W. T. Clough	Newark, N. J	July 1, 1856	15, 222
Acid concentrating-pan, Sulphuric	P. Marcelin and J. Saunders	Greenpoint, N. Y	Apr. 28, 1868	77, 202
Acid, Concentrating sulphuric	D. Ashworth and R. B. Eaton	Woburn, Mass	Mar. 19, 1867	62, 919
Acid, Concentrating sulphuric	J. D. Loftus	Chelsea, Mass	Jan. 1, 1867	60, 759
Acid for dyeing woolens, &c., Mixing	H. Young	Rochester, N. Y	Nov. 19, 1833	....
Acid for extinguishing fire, Mode of collecting and storing carbonic.	E. Thayer	Worcester, Mass	Nov. 16, 1869	97, 001
Acid from carboys, Apparatus for discharging	W. Gee	New York, N. Y	Oct. 24, 1871	120, 259
Acid from oil-refineries, Mode of recovering spent.	L. S. Fales	New York, N. Y	Nov. 23, 1869	97, 182
Acid from petroleum-refinery, Mode of utilizing the waste.	R. M. Smith	Baltimore, Md	May 17, 1864	42, 803
Acid generator, fountain, and other vessels, Carbonic.	J. Matthews	New York, N. Y	May 13, 1873	138, 908
Acid in liquids, Apparatus for ascertaining the amount of.	H. Twitchell	Cincinnati, Ohio	Feb. 15, 1870	99, 976
Acid, Manufacture of acetic	C. J. T. Burcey	Black Rock, Conn	Sept. 12, 1871	118, 788
Acid, Manufacture of acetic	A. and M. Pirz	East New York, N. Y	Mar. 2, 1869	87, 365
Acid, Manufacture of boracic	F. Gutzkow	San Francisco, Cal	Mar. 25, 1873	137, 072
Acid, Manufacture of citric	W. K. Johnston	Memphis, Tenn	May 24, 1870	103, 340
Acid, Manufacture of nitric	H. M. Baker	Williamsburgh, N. Y	Oct. 11, 1870	108, 090
Acid, Manufacture of pyroligneous	M. E. Converse and A. T. Atherton.	Rindge, N. H., and Lowell, Mass.	May 26, 1868	78, 264
Acid, Manufacture of pyroligneous	A. H. Emery	New York, N. Y	Aug. 8, 1865	49, 247
Acid, Manufacture of solid fatty	L. A. De Milly	Paris, France	Sept. 8, 1868	81, 884
Acid, Manufacture of stearic	E. De Bassano and A. Brudeun.	Brussels, Belgium	Aug. 27, 1861	33, 135
Acid, Manufacture of stearic	F. C. A. Bock	Copenhagen, Denmark	June 29, 1869	92, 004
Acid, Manufacture of sulphuric	L. Chandor	St. Petersburg, Russia	May 31, 1864	42, 985
Acid, Manufacture of sulphuric	D. E. Contaret	Roxbury, Mass	June 13, 1854	11, 050
Acid, Manufacture of sulphuric	C. Hinrichs	New York, N. Y	Sept. 7, 1852	9, 249
Acid, Manufacture of sulphuric	D. Jackson	Walworth, England	Aug. 13, 1872	130, 432
Acid, Manufacture of sulphuric	A. Monnier	Camden, N. J	Aug. 11, 1857	17, 976
Acid, Manufacture of sulphuric	J. Saunders	Brooklyn, N. Y	Nov. 25, 1873	144, 928
Acid, Manufacture of sulphuric	J. Smith and J. R. Savage	Philadelphia, Pa	Feb. 16, 1864	41, 647
Acid, Manufacture of sulphuric	A. H. Tait	New York, N. Y	Feb. 9, 1869	86, 881
Acid, Manufacture of sulphuric	E. Thomson and W. H. Greene	Philadelphia, Pa	Sept. 23, 1873	143, 202
Acid, Manufacture of sulphuric and hydrochloric	H. M. Baker	Washington, D. C	Jan. 26, 1869	86, 200
Acid, Manufacture of sulphurous	N. P. Akin	Philmont, N. Y	May 21, 1872	127, 008
Acid, Manufacture of sulphurous	P. Marcelin	New York, N. Y	Feb. 13, 1872	123, 713
Acid, Manufacture of sulphurous	P. Marcelin and E. Ende	New Orleans, La	June 12, 1860	28, 678
Acid, Method of manufacturing sulphuric	J. Hargreaves	Paterson, N. J	Aug. 24, 1839	1, 303
Acid, Method of purifying acetic	A. A. Fesquet	Marseilles, France	Aug. 30, 1864	44, 053
Acid, Obtaining pure sulphurous	J. Albrecht	New Orleans, La	June 29, 1858	20, 755
Acid on sheet-iron, Method of neutralizing	E. A. Harvey	Wilmington, Del	May 8, 1866	54, 538
Acid, Pan for concentrating sulphuric	P. Marcelin and J. Saunders	Greenpoint, N. Y	May 12, 1868	77, 826
Acid phosphate of lime, Method of preparing	E. N. Horsford	Cambridge, Mass	Apr. 14, 1868	76, 763
Acid, Process for making sulphuric	B. Bell	Boston, Mass	Nov. 7, 1811	....
Acid, Process for making sulphuric	H. Holland	Westfield, Mass	Dec. 27, 1859	26, 588
Acid, Purifying acetic	J. F. Cavarly	Flushing, N. Y	Dec. 5, 1871	121, 586
Acid, Purifying acetic	T. L. Olden	Brooklyn, N. Y	Mar. 8, 1870	100, 553
Acid, Purifying pyroligneous	C. F. Binder	Philadelphia, Pa	June 20, 1871	116, 142
Acid, Purifying pyroligneous or acetic	C. C. Parsons	New York, N. Y	Feb. 23, 1869	87, 193
Acid to cane-juice, Method of applying sulphurous	T. Byrne	Baton Rouge, La	Sept. 4, 1860	29, 860
Acid used in refining petroleum, Process of recovering the.	R. G. Loftus	Chelsea, Mass	June 14, 1864	43, 157
Acids, Apparatus for manufacturing fatty	M. Werk	Cincinnati, Ohio	Oct. 5, 1858	21, 711
Acids, Evaporating and concentrating sulphuric and other.	W. T. Clough	Newark, N. J	June 18, 1872	127, 957
Acids from leather, Removing	M. W. Fry	Guyandotte, W. Va	Nov. 4, 1873	144, 328
Acids, Mode of preparing vegetable	N. S. Allison and B. Kugler	Philadelphia, Pa	June 5, 1812	....
Acids, Preparing wooden vessels for holding	W. Archdeacon	Chicago, Ill	July 16, 1872	129, 204
Acids, Process for purifying pyroligneous and acetic.	C. C. Parsons	New York, N. Y	Nov. 9, 1869	96, 721
Acids, Receivers or carboys for the manufacture of muriatic and other.	A. Baumgarten	New York, N. Y	Aug. 3, 1869	93, 270
Acids, Separating oleic and stearic	J. S. Gwynne	Pittsburgh, Pa	Sept. 3, 1846	4, 735
Acids, Treatment of fatty	J. C. Appenzeller	Cincinnati, Ohio	Jan. 25, 1859	22, 691
Acoustic apparatus	D. D. Stelle	New Brunswick, N. J	Feb. 14, 1860	27, 165
Acoustic auricle	E. G. Hyde	Irvington, N. J	Jan. 27, 1857	16, 485
Acoustic drum	S. Sawyer	Boston, Mass	Oct. 24, 1834	....
Acupuncture instrument	A. R. Brown	Litchfield, Mich	Jan. 1, 1867	60, 917
Acupuncture instrument	A. R. Brown	Albion, Mich	Dec. 15, 1868	84, 854
Acupuncture instrument	G. Herrick	Albion, Mich	Apr. 26, 1870	102, 262
Acupuncture instrument, Mold for making	A. R. Brown	Albion, Mich	Oct. 6, 1868	82, 686
Adding and registering numbers, Instrument for	N. Spofford and C. Corliss	Haverhill, Mass	June 23, 1868	79, 272
Adding and subtracting register	H. A. House	Bridgeport, Conn	Nov. 29, 1870	109, 619
Adding figures, Instrument for	C. Corliss	Haverhill, Mass	June 23, 1868	79, 272
Adding numbers, Instrument for	J. B. Newbrough	Saint Louis, Mo	June 21, 1859	24, 481
Adding-machine	I. W. Arndt	Green Bay, Wis	Apr. 12, 1859	23, 537
Adding-machine	J. Ballou	Cincinnati, Ohio	Mar. 13, 1860	27, 418
Adding-machine	B. B. Brown	Delaware, Ohio	Oct. 19, 1869	95, 876
Adding-machine	J. T. Campbell	Rockville, Ind	Aug. 9, 1859	24, 990
Adding-machine	G. W. Chapin	Brooklyn, N. Y	Feb. 8, 1870	99, 533
Adding-machine	G. W. Chapin	Brooklyn, N. Y	Sept. 6, 1870	106, 999
Adding-machine	G. B. Fowler	Chicago, Ill	July 14, 1863	39, 222
Adding-machine	J. Groesbeck	Philadelphia, Pa	Mar. 1, 1870	100, 288

Index of patents issued from the United States Patent Office from 1790 *to* 1873, *inclusive*—Continued.

Invention.	Inventor.	Residence.	Date.	No.
Adding-machine	E. M. Hamilton	New York, N. Y	July 18, 1871	117, 169
Adding-machine	J. Harris, jr	Roxbury, Mass	Jan. 1, 1861	31, 016
Adding-machine	A. L. Hatfield	Lewisburgh, Pa	Sept. 26, 1854	11, 7[illegible]6
Adding-machine	I. G. Hubbs	New York, N. Y	Aug. 19, 1856	15, 565
Adding-machine	M. C. Jeffers	New York, N. Y	Sept. 29, 1863	40, 105
Adding-machine	D. Kohler	Sunbury, Pa	June 6, 1834	....
Adding-machine	F. T. Leilich	Frederick, Md	Aug. 23, 1870	106, 701
Adding-machine	G. Lindervos	Point Arena, Cal	June 24, 1873	140, 146
Adding-machine	D. R. Nelson	Jackson, Ohio	Apr. 24, 1860	28, 006
Adding-machine	J. B. Newbrough	Saint Louis, Mo	Sept. 28, 1858	21, 621
Adding-machine	N. Ockerland	New York, N. Y	July 26, 1870	1[illegible]5, 717
Adding-machine	V. Parks	Fort Wayne, Ind	Mar. 5, 1867	62, 677
Adding-machine	H. Parmelee	Philadelphia, Pa	Jan. 25, 1870	99, 226
Adding-machine	S. Pool	Chapel Hill, N. C	Sept. 23, 1873	143, 184
Adding-machine	T. Rossiter	New Haven, Conn	Aug. 3, 1869	93, 350
Adding-machine	N. S. Saxton	Riverhead, N. Y	Nov. 13, 1855	13, 800
Adding-machine	C. E. Spear	Gardiner, Me	Aug. 30, 1870	106, 881
Adding-machine	A. M. Stephenson	Manteno, Ill	Mar. 25, 1873	137, 107
Adding-machine	T. T. Strode	Mortonville, Pa	Oct. 2, 1860	30, 264
Adding-machine	T. T. Strode	Mortonville, Pa	Aug. 1, 1865	49, 168
Adding-machine	E. A. Swain	New York, N. Y	Jan. 11, 1870	98, 720
Adding-machine	F. F. Warner	Chicago, Ill	Dec. 27, 1870	110, 520
Adding-machine	C. H. Webb	New York, N. Y	Mar. 10, 1868	75, 3[illegible]2
Adding-machine	C. Winter	Piqua, Ohio	Apr. 12, 1859	23, 637
Addometer	J. Burns	New York, N. Y	Aug. 24, 1858	21, 243
Addometer	L. N. Nutz	Alton, Ill	Aug. 17, 1858	21, 236
Address-case for railway-car	S. W. Downey	Piedmont, W. Va	Jan. 28, 1868	73, 881
Address printing-machine	H. Julien	Ottawa, Canada	July 28, 1868	80, 285
Addresses, &c., Machine for printing	J. A. Barrington	Fredericktown, Ohio	June 14, 1859	24, 364
Addresses on newspapers, &c., Apparatus for printing.	J. A. Campbell	Georgetown, Canada	Jan. 17, 1860	26, 831
Addresses on newspapers, &c., Apparatus for printing.	G. Hutchison	Allegheny, Pa	Sept. 6, 1859	25, 337
Addresses on newspapers, &c., Apparatus for printing.	C. K. Marshall	Vicksburgh, Miss	Nov. 1, 1859	25, 974
Addresses on newspapers, Machine for printing	N. Bowlus	Middletown, Md	May 1, 1860	28, 059
Addresses on newspapers, Machine for printing	S. D. Carpenter	Madison, Wis	May 5, 1857	17, 194
Addresses on newspapers, Machine for printing	E. P. Day	New York, N. Y	June 6, 1854	11, 022
Addresses on newspapers, Machine for printing	D. B. Tiffany and S. W. Soule	Xenia, Ohio, and Milwaukee, Wis.	Mar. 20, 1860	27, 580
Addresses on newspapers, &c., Machine for printing.	J. A. Campbell	Buffalo, N. Y	Jan. 20, 1863	37, 432
Addresses on newspapers, &c., Machine for printing.	R. W. and D. Davis	Yellow Springs, Ohio	Sept. 6, 1859	25, 319
Addresses on newspapers, &c., Machine for printing.	D. Fuller	Cherry Valley, Ill	Sept. 15, 1863	39, 913
Addresses on newspapers, &c., Machine for printing.	J. C. Gaither	Somerset, Pa	Apr. 7, 1868	76, 433
Addresses on newspapers, &c., Machine for printing.	J. Lord	Pawtucket, Mass	Sept. 7, 1858	21, 429
Addresses on newspapers, &c., Machine for printing.	A. H. Nordyke	Richmond, Ind	Mar. 1, 1859	23, 107
Addresses on newspapers, &c., Machine for printing.	M. and C. Peck and R. W. Wright.	New Haven and Orange, Conn.	Jan. 12, 1864	41, 234
Addresses on newspapers, &c., Printing	H. Moeser	Pittsburgh, Pa	June 24, 1851	8, 175
Addresses on newspapers, &c., Printing	S. W. Soule	Cincinnati, Ohio	Oct. 2, 1860	30, 259
Addressing letters	J. S. Brown	Washington, D. C	Sept. 9, 1862	36, 393
Addressing-machine	W. H. Clague and R. B. Randall	Rochester, N. Y	Dec. 19, 1871	121, 931
Addressing-machine	F. A. Darling	Fayetteville, N. Y	Apr. 8, 1873	137, 599
Addressing-machine	G. A. Davison	Montana, Iowa	July 4, 1871	116, 567
Addressing-machine	R. Dick	Buffalo, N. Y	May 7, 1867	64, 502
Addressing-machine	G. Gibbons	Meriden, Conn	Aug. 10, 1869	93, 527
Addressing-machine	S. Holton	Middlebury, Vt	Feb. 25, 1873	136, 323
Addressing-machine	J. McFatrick	Lena, Ill	Oct. 4, 1870	108, 038
Addressing-machine	J. K. Rukenbrod	Salem, Ohio	Dec. 12, 1871	121, 900
Addressing-machine	N. E. and G. W. Warren	Cleveland, Ohio, and Hillsdale, Mich.	Apr. 4, 1865	47, 142
Addressing-machine, Feed-rack for	W. H. Henderson and W. H. Snider.	Lena, Ill	July 13, 1869	92, 444
Addressing-machine, Newspaper	H. A. Gage	Manchester, N. H	July 9, 1861	32, 763
Addressing-machine, Newspaper	C. K. Marshall	New Orleans, La	Feb. 9, 1869	86, 680
Addressing-machine, Newspaper	P. O'Conner	Youngstown, Ohio	Apr. 25, 1871	114, 032
Addressing newspapers, &c., Apparatus for	W. M. Doty	New York, N. Y	Jan 26, 1864	41, 369
Addressing newspapers, &c., Machine for	J. Battey	Honeoye Falls, N. Y	Jan. 17, 1860	26, 827
Addressing newspapers, &c., Machine for	G. Schuh	Madison, Ind	Apr. 26, 1859	23, 787
Addressing newspapers, &c., Printing-press for	G. Henderson	Allegheny, Pa	Sept. 6, 1859	25, 363
Adhesive material	A. J. Russell	New York, N. Y	Apr. 2, 1861	31, 909
Adjustable bit	F. Jonas	Burlington, Iowa	Apr. 1, 1873	137, 373
Adjustable box for arbors, &c	B. D. and H. E. Kay	Fall River, Mass	Nov. 10, 1868	83, 859
Adjustable bracket	J. H. Davis	Chillicothe, Mo	July 13, 1869	92, 519
Adjustable bracket	J. B. Morrison	Brooklyn, N. Y	Aug. 26, 1873	142, 263
Adjustable chair	A. Chase	North Weare, N. H	June 11, 1861	32, 511
Adjustable chair	R. A. Thompson	Beaver Falls, Pa	Dec. 3, 1872	133, 550
Adjustable chair	T. Weaver	Harrisburgh, Pa	Jan. 10, 1865	45, 887
Adjustable clamp	W. G. Floyd	Brooklyn, E. D., N. Y	Mar. 6, 1866	52, 983
Adjustable clamp	C. S. Meeker	New Haven, Conn	June 1, 1869	90, 768
Adjustable gage	R. E. Jones	New York, N. Y	Jan. 26, 1869	86, 308
Adjustable hanger	R. A. Stratton	Philadelphia, Pa	May 12, 1863	38, 539
Adjustable miter	P. A. Snyder	Jersey City, N. J	Dec. 18, 1866	60, 646
Adjustable press	N. C. Stiles	Middletown, Conn	Nov. 24, 1868	84, 313
Adjustable seat	I. Cook	Saint Louis, Mo	Mar. 3, 1868	74, 993
Adjustable seat	B. N. Hemenway	Rockland, Me	July 16, 1872	129, 560
Adjustable seat	L. Postawka	Cambridge, Mass	Apr. 4, 1871	113, 342
Adjustable seat-fastener	W. T. Thornton	Belleville, Mich	Dec. 3, 1867	71, 821
Adjustable spring	A. Roff	Southport, Conn	July 7, 1868	79, 778

Index of patents issued from the United States Patent Office from 1790 *to* 1873, *inclusive*—Continued.

Invention.	Inventor.	Residence.	Date.	No.
Adjustable table	O. C. Dodge	Brooklyn, N. Y	Nov. 20, 1860	30,671
Adjustable wrench	A. Hotchkiss	Sharon, Conn	May 4, 1852	8,922
Adjustable wrench	J. Magee	Usquepaugh, R. I	Dec. 28, 1869	98,393
Adjustable wrench	A. Sedgwick	Poughkeepsie, N. Y	Sept. 25, 1866	58,306
Advertiser, Balloon	E. L. Moodie	New York, N. Y	Mar. 18, 1873	136,930
Advertising-album	W. S. Gavan	Savannah, Ga	Dec. 19, 1871	122,005
Advertising-album	G. W. Hawes	New York, N. Y	Oct. 24, 1871	120,260
Advertising-apparatus	A. Berthoud	New York, N. Y	Nov. 26, 1861	33,772
Advertising-apparatus	W. Hebdon	New York, N. Y	Nov. 15, 1870	109,208
Advertising-apparatus	J. A. Royce	Lee, Mass	July 9, 1867	66,637
Advertising-apparatus, Panoramic	J. Berthoud	Paris, France	Nov. 18, 1862	36,937
Advertising-box to lamp and other posts, Clamp for securing.	P. McCosker	Pittsburgh, Pa	Sept. 30, 1873	143,365
Advertising-cabinet, Electric	H. W. McAllister	Chicago, Ill	May 30, 1871	115,494
Advertising-calendar	J. D. Parsons	Albany, N. Y	May 11, 1869	90,017
Advertising-carriage	W. C. Harris, A. R. Roseman, and H. B. Hutchins.	Philadelphia, Pa	Feb. 18, 1868	74,530
Advertising-device	I. Beziegler	Philadelphia, Pa	Apr. 30, 1872	126,367
Advertising-device	H. H. Browne	Mount Vernon, N. Y	June 16, 1868	78,923
Advertising-device	A. Davis	Lowell, Mass	Oct. 8, 1867	69,637
Advertising-device	J. E. Emery	Albany, N. Y	Apr. 4, 1871	113,409
Advertising-device	C. Peabody and P. H. Delaney	Detroit, Mich	Dec. 8, 1868	84,707
Advertising-device	R. F. Rankin	Columbus, Ohio	June 29, 1869	92,137
Advertising-device	W. Raphael	Saint Louis, Mo	July 30, 1872	130,070
Advertising-device	W. H. Reiff	Philadelphia, Pa	Apr. 25, 1871	114,198
Advertising-device	W. S. Webb	Providence, R. I	Feb. 23, 1869	87,228
Advertising-directory	B. F. Stillwell	San Francisco, Cal	Nov. 17, 1863	40,648
Advertising-frame	D. G. Howell	Danby, N. Y	Feb. 8, 1870	99,675
Advertising-frame	B. S. Moulton	Danvers, Mass	Oct. 15, 1872	132,314
Advertising frame	W. H. Sadler and J. M. Drysdale	Baltimore, Md	Apr. 13, 1869	88,910
Advertising-frame	J. Sonnedecker	Cincinnati, Ohio	May 5, 1868	77,545
Advertising-frame, Electro-magnetic	J. Brooks	Boston, Mass	Dec. 14, 1869	97,756
Advertising-lamp	E. Boesch	San Francisco, Cal	Mar. 21, 1871	112,890
Advertising-lantern	T. L. Wright	New York, N. Y	Dec. 12, 1871	121,923
Advertising-machine	I. W. Sylvester	New York, N. Y	June 25, 1867	66,055
Advertising-medium, Ornamental	J. O. Belknap	New Orleans, La	July 11, 1871	116,799
Advertising, Mode of	E. Wiebé	Brooklyn, N. Y	Nov. 15, 1859	26,136
Adz	P. H. Bradley	Portland, Me	Aug. 24, 1869	93,957
Æolian-attachment	G. W. Ingalls	Concord, N. H	Dec. 23, 1851	8,608
Æolian-attachment, &c., Manner of adjusting the pitch of reeds for.	C. Horst	New Orleans, La	Sept. 27, 1845	4,210
Aërated liquids, Draft-pipe for	O. F. Stedman	Westfield, N. Y	Jan. 7, 1873	134,710
Aërated liquids, Mode of preparing	P. H. Vander Weyde	Philadelphia, Pa	Feb. 4, 1868	74,175
Aërated water, Manufacture of	G. McCoy	New York, N. Y	Apr. 23, 1867	64,019
Aërating and mixing substances, Apparatus for	E. L. Pratt	Boston, Mass	Nov. 6, 1866	59,449
Aërating liquid, Apparatus for	E. L. Pratt	Boston, Mass	Sept. 10, 1867	68,788
Aërating liquid, Apparatus for	T. Warker	New York, N. Y	Apr. 8, 1862	34,916
Aërating water	C. D. Simons and J. J. Riondel	Charleston, S. C	Aug. 16, 1810	....
Aërator, Flame	C. L. Browne	Washington, D. C	May 12, 1868	77,799
Aërial car	O. Abbruzzo	St. Margherita, Italy	July 21, 1868	80,107
Aërial car	I. W. Forbes	La Porte, Ind	July 16, 1872	129,401
Aërial car	F. Just and A. Koellener	Buffalo, N. Y	Oct. 10, 1865	50,365
Aërial car	A. P. Keith	Easton, Mass	Mar. 1, 1870	100,415
Aërial car	E. Oakes	Richmond, Ind	Aug. 30, 1870	106,862
Aërial carriage and way	D. Towse	Pittsburgh, Pa	Dec. 10, 1867	71,921
Aërial carriage and way	D. Towse	Pittsburgh, Pa	Dec. 10, 1867	71,922
Aërial carriage and way	D. Towse	Pittsburgh, Pa	Dec. 10, 1867	71,923
Aërial machine	L. C. Crowell	West Dennis, Mass	June 3, 1862	35,437
Aërial machine	J. A. Elston	Elston Station, Mo	Aug. 13, 1867	67,739
Aërial machine	A. Kinsella	Cascades, Wash	June 3, 1862	35,453
Aërial navigator	T. Moy and R. E. Shill	London and Mile End, England.	Nov. 26, 1872	133,381
Aërial navigator	Z. Stone	Kinsmans, Ohio	May 12, 1868	77,850
Aërial railway	J. A. A. Fountaine	New York, N. Y	Feb. 5, 1867	61,824
Aërial railway	R. Montgomery	New York, N. Y	Sept. 11, 1866	57,949
Aërial ship	M. Braun	Cape Vincent, N. Y	Feb. 8, 1870	99,629
Aërial transit, Method of	R. A. Cheesebrough	New York, N. Y	Feb. 1, 1870	99,406
Aërostat	S. Andrews	Perth Amboy, N. J	July 5, 1864	43,449
Aërostats or balloons of various forms, Manner of directing the course of.	M. Muzzi	Bologna, Italy	Oct. 16, 1844	3,799
Aërostatic jack	A. V. Ojeda	San Francisco, Cal	Aug. 29, 1871	118,475
Afghan	D. Bickford	Boston, Mass	July 21, 1868	80,122
Agare Americana, Machine for dressing the leaves of.	E. J. y Patrullo	Merida, Mexico	Apr. 23, 1861	32,143
Agare-plant, Machine for dressing the leaves of the.	E. J. y Patrullo	Merida, Mexico	Mar. 5, 1861	31,616
Age to wine, Process of imparting	J. Searle	San Francisco, Cal	July 11, 1865	48,728
Ageing alcoholic liquors and producing vinegar, Apparatus for.	R. D. Turner	New York, N. Y	Mar. 4, 1873	136,470
Ageing alcoholic liquor	H. Purdy	Burlington, Iowa	Oct. 18, 1870	108,388
Ageing alcoholic liquors, Mode of	J. L. Martin	Baltimore, Md	May 21, 1867	64,990
Ageing and mixing liquors, Apparatus for	S. C. Bruce	New York, N. Y	Jan. 9, 1872	122,513
Ageing and purifying spirits	J. M. Crafts	Boston, Mass	July 28, 1868	80,459
Ageing and refining wine and liquor, Apparatus for.	R. D. Turner	New York, N. Y	Sept. 24, 1867	69,275
Ageing-apparatus for whisky and other spirits	J. P. Greeley	Boston, Mass	Nov. 29, 1870	109,611
Ageing-apparatus for whisky and other spirits	W. P. Martin	Millersburgh, Ky	Oct. 12, 1869	95,703
Ageing liquors and spirits and for producing aromatic ethers, Process for.	C. L. Fleischmann	Washington, D. C	May 4, 1869	89,748
Ageing liquors, Apparatus for	R. D. Turner	New York, N. Y	July 16, 1872	129,440
Ageing liquors, Apparatus for mixing and	S. C. Bruce	New York, N. Y	Dec. 28, 1869	98,226
Ageing spirits	A. Caldwell	Lexington, Ky	Sept. 27, 1870	107,658
Ageing spirits, Apparatus for	E. L. Morse	Saint Louis, Mo	July 13, 1869	92,633
Ageing spirits, Apparatus for	P. M. Papin	Saint Louis, Mo	May 18, 1869	90,120
Ageing spirituous liquors, Apparatus for	R. D. Turner	New York, N. Y	Oct. 19, 1869	96,056
Ageing whisky and other spirits, Apparatus for	J. Peiffer and S. Richards	Valonia, Pa	Mar. 7, 1871	112,485
Ageing wine	F. Haeck	Brussels, Belgium	Dec. 4, 1866	60,179
Ageing wine and liquor, Apparatus for	A. Luquet and P. Huerne	San Francisco, Cal	May 14, 1872	126,722

Index of patents issued from the United States Patent Office from 1790 *to* 1873, *inclusive*—Continued.

Invention.	Inventor.	Residence.	Date.	No.
Ageing wine and spirits, Apparatus for	S. C. Bruce	New York, N. Y	Feb. 9, 1869	86, 640
Ageing wines and liquors	A. Luquet	San Francisco, Cal	Mar. 11, 1873	136, 741
Agitating and heating substances, Apparatus for	G. Nebeker	Wilmington, Del	June 26, 1866	55, 886
Agitating and kneading substances, Apparatus for.	W. Adamson	Philadelphia, Pa	Apr. 18, 1865	47, 264
Agricultural boiler	C. M. Cloud	Grinnell, Iowa	Sept. 2, 1873	142, 326
Agricultural boiler	F. Farquhar	Richmond, Ind	May 3, 1870	102, 671
Agricultural boiler	J. H. Haviland, G. W. Cronk, and J. F. Autisdel.	Janesville, Wis	Nov. 19, 1872	133, 097
Agricultural boiler	P. H. Inman and C. B. Withington.	Janesville, Wis	Jan. 16, 1872	122, 723
Agricultural boiler	H. A. Mears	Rockford, Ill	June 24, 1873	140, 213
Agricultural boiler	H. A. Mears	Rockford, Ill	Dec. 16, 1873	145, 517
Agricultural boiler	J. Murdock	South Carver, Mass	Nov. 14, 1871	120, 894
Agricultural boiler	D. R. Prindle	East Bethany, N. Y	July 7, 1868	79, 685
Agricultural boiler and steamer	R. S. Hazen, sr	Calmus, Iowa	Sept. 3, 1872	130, 996
Agricultural digger	A. L. Kennedy	Philadelphia, Pa	Nov. 8, 1870	109, 019
Agricultural fork	T. Beale	New Milford, Ill	Mar. 5, 1867	62, 594
Agricultural fork	C., A., and C. N. Clow	Port Byron, N. Y	Dec. 8, 1857	18, 804
Agricultural forks, shovels, and hoes, Handle of	R. M. Hine	Throopsville, N. Y	Oct. 28, 1856	15, 976
Agricultural implements, Blade for	W. Scott	Floyd Court-House, Va	Dec. 30, 1873	146, 026
Agricultural implements, Combined	L. Lehmann	Monee, Ill	Nov. 15, 1870	109, 226
Agricultural implements, Combined	C. R. Rand	Dubuque, Iowa	Feb. 14, 1871	111, 871
Agricultural implements, Disk for	E. T. Bussell	Indianapolis, Ind	June 11, 1872	127, 677
Agricultural implements mounted on wheels, Leveling attachment to.	B. F. Cook	Olema, Cal	Nov. 12, 1867	70, 804
Agricultural machine	H. Cowing	New Orleans, La	Aug. 4, 1868	80, 795
Agricultural steam-apparatus	E. C. Bellinger	Barnwell District, S. C	Nov. 19, 1833	....
Agricultural steam-boiler	L. S. Robbins	New York, N. Y	May 26, 1868	78, 235
Agriculture	V. Pardee	Trenton, N. Y	Feb. 6, 1829	....
Air and gas, Apparatus for mixing	T. C. Hopper	Philadelphia, Pa	Dec. 12, 1871	121, 719
Air and gas engine	A. H. De Villeneuve	Paris, France	Mar. 19, 1872	124, 671
Air and gas engine	D. Dick	Meadville, Pa	Apr. 9, 1867	63, 619
Air and gas engine	J. F. Haskins	Fitchburgh, Mass	July 16, 1872	129, 337
Air and gas engine	O. Trossin	Berlin, Germany	July 22, 1873	141, 189
Air and liquid cooler	D. E. Somes	Washington, D. C	Mar. 29, 1870	101, 392
Air and making ice, Apparatus for cooling	T. D. Kingan	Indianapolis, Ind	Dec. 16, 1873	145, 659
Air and other substances, Cooling	D. E. Somes	Washington, D. C	Nov. 12, 1867	70, 909
Air and steam engine	F. B. Blanchard	Waterville, Me	July 10, 1855	13, 209
Air and steam engine, Combined	O. M. Stillman	Westerly, R. I	Aug. 9, 1864	43, 803
Air and steam for actuating engine, Process for mixing.	W. M. Storm	New York, N. Y	Apr. 5, 1853	9, 654
Air and steam jet to promote combustion	G. M. Copeland	Brooklyn, N. Y	Feb. 26, 1867	62, 397
Air and supplying boilers therewith, Heating	G. E. Hibbard	Fond du Lac, Wis	Dec. 16, 1873	145, 568
Air and water warming apparatus for dwellings	L. C. St. John	Buffalo, N. Y	Oct. 7, 1851	8, 413
Air, Apparatus for compressing	W. Arthur	Brooklyn, N. Y	July 25, 1865	48, 886
Air, Apparatus for compressing	J. B. J. Mignon and S. H. Rouart.	Paris, France	Mar. 19, 1867	63, 075
Air, Apparatus for navigating the	C. McDermott	Monticello, Ark	Nov. 12, 1872	133, 046
Air, Apparatus for navigating the	W. F. Quimby	Stanton, Del	Nov. 26, 1861	33, 797
Air, Apparatus for purifying and cooling	A. S. Lyman	New York, N. Y	Jan. 19, 1864	41, 309
Air, Apparatus for removing dust and gas from	J. D. Whelpley and J. J. Storer	Boston, Mass	Mar. 6, 1866	53, 068
Air, Apparatus for supplying a continuous flow of	B. Rouquayrol	Paris, France	Mar. 20, 1866	53, 385
Air, Apparatus for transmitting power by the medium of.	H. Call	Concord, N. H	Aug. 24, 1869	93, 964
Air, Apparatus for transmitting power by the medium of.	H. Call	Concord, N. H	Jan. 18, 1870	98, 846
Air apparatus, Fresh	J. McNeven	New York, N. Y	Sept. 14, 1869	94, 905
Air bath, Compressed	P. T. Ware	Toronto, Canada	May 8, 1866	54, 655
Air bath, Hot and cold	S. M. Landis	Philadelphia, Pa	May 14, 1867	64, 677
Air-blast engine	J. Grimm	Saint Louis, Mo	Oct. 26, 1869	96, 223
Air-brake	T. Luce	Richmondville, Mich	Sept. 10, 1872	131, 286
Air-brake and signal, Steam-power	G. Westinghouse, jr	Pittsburgh, Pa	Mar. 5, 1872	124, 404
Air-brake for car	L. H. Dwelley	Dorchester, Mass	Nov. 28, 1865	51, 158
Air-brake for railway-car	C. Fogelberg	Boston, Mass	May 28, 1872	127, 332
Air-brake for railway-car	T. O. Ward	Paw Paw, Mich	Jan. 30, 1872	123, 312
Air-brake, Locomotive	G. Westinghouse, jr	Pittsburgh, Pa	Oct. 28, 1873	144, 005
Air-brake, Steam	G. Westinghouse, jr	Pittsburgh, Pa	Mar. 5, 1872	124, 405
Air-brake, Steam-power	H. L. McAvoy	Baltimore, Md	Apr. 29, 1873	138, 339
Air-brake, Steam-power	G. Westinghouse, jr	Pittsburgh, Pa	Jan. 23, 1872	123, 067
Air by exhaust-steam, Method of heating	A. C. Fletcher	New York, N. Y	May 19, 1863	38, 637
Air by steam, Apparatus for heating	J. Hollingsworth	Chicago, Ill	June 5, 1860	28, 578
Air-chamber	R. Creuzbaur	Travis County, Texas	June 18, 1861	32, 595
Air-compressing apparatus	B. T. Babbitt	New York, N. Y	May 17, 1870	103, 121
Air-compressing apparatus	B. T. Babbitt	New York, N. Y	Nov. 12, 1872	133, 004
Air compressing apparatus	F. S. Dumont	New York, N. Y	Apr. 27, 1869	89, 390
Air-compressing apparatus	G. D. Emerson	New York, N. Y	Aug. 20, 1872	130, 627
Air-compressing apparatus	J. Ericsson	New York, N. Y	Dec. 30, 1873	146, 055
Air-compressing apparatus	R. S. Pardée	San Diego, Cal	Oct. 14, 1873	143, 634
Air-compressing apparatus	J. S. Patric	Victor, N. Y	Apr. 18, 1865	47, 328
Air-compressing apparatus	J. S. Patric	Rochester, N. Y	Oct. 17, 1871	120, 094
Air-compressing apparatus	J. B. Waring	South Norwalk, Conn	July 16, 1872	129, 631
Air-compressing apparatus, Hydraulic	M. Hey	Philadelphia, Pa	Apr. 26, 1870	102, 397
Air-compressing apparatus, Hydraulic	C. Moore	Jersey City, N. J	July 1, 1873	140, 524
Air-compressing apparatus, Hydraulic	W. D. Seal	Washington, D. C	June 14, 1870	104, 362
Air-compressing engine	J. F. Haskins	Fitchburgh, Mass	Aug. 6, 1872	130, 296
Air-compressor	H. H. Day	New York, N. Y	Nov. 11, 1873	144, 390
Air-compressor	H. P. Fairfield	Boston, Mass	Sept. 2, 1873	142, 452
Air-compressor, Hydraulic	M. Hey	Philadelphia, Pa	July 25, 1871	117, 285
Air-compressor, Hydraulic	W. E. Prall	Washington, D. C	Nov. 7, 1871	120, 597
Air-compressor or blower	L. Chase	Portland, Me	Aug. 12, 1873	141, 762
Air-compressor or blower	L. Chase	Portland, Me	Sept. 30, 1873	143, 329
Air-condensing and storing by the pressure of water, Apparatus for.	J. Cochrane	New York, N. Y	July 23, 1872	129, 791
Air-condensing apparatus	H. J. Bailey	Pittsburgh, Pa	Jan. 14, 1868	73, 283
Air-condensing apparatus	H. Moore	Bangall, N. Y	Mar. 3, 1868	75, 042
Air-condensing apparatus	J. S. Patric	Rochester, N. Y	Oct. 17, 1871	120, 095
Air-cooling and ice-manufacturing machine	J. Kraffert	Hoboken, N. J	Dec. 27, 1870	110, 573

Index of patents issued from the United States Patent Office from 1790 *to* 1873, *inclusive*—Continued.

Invention.	Inventor.	Residence.	Date.	No.
Air-cooling apparatus	T. D. Kingan	Indianapolis, Ind	July 1, 1873	140, 375
Air-cooling apparatus	N. S. Shaler	Newport, Ky	May 30, 1865	47, 991
Air-cooling process	E. H. Grant	Washington, D. C	Feb. 16, 1869	87, 041
Air-cooling ventilator	F. Villard	Mount Eaton, Ohio	May 29, 1866	55, 180
Air-cushion for doors	J. W. Wetmore	Erie, Pa	Sept. 2, 1873	142, 540
Air cylinder, Compressed	G. W. W. Goodwyn	New Orleans, La	Mar. 1, 1870	100, 282
Air-draft, Subignis	S. Randall	Providence, R. I	Mar. 12, 1811	....
Air-engine	W. Alworth	Scranton, Pa	May 28, 1872	127, 137
Air-engine	J. B. Atwater	Chicago, Ill	Mar. 13, 1866	53, 097
Air-engine	D. Bickford	Boston, Mass	June 6, 1865	48, 043
Air-engine	J. R. Cameron	Pittsburgh, Pa	Nov. 12, 1867	70, 800
Air-engine	P. Chick	Taunton, Mass	Dec. 18, 1866	60, 474
Air-engine	W. Denkmann	Washington, D. C	Dec. 16, 1862	37, 155
Air-engine	J. Ericsson	New York, N. Y	Nov. 4, 1851	8, 481
Air-engine	J. Ericsson	New York, N. Y	July 31, 1855	13, 348
Air-engine	J. Ericsson	New York, N. Y	Apr. 15, 1856	14, 690
Air-engine	J. Ericsson	New York, N. Y	Dec. 14, 1858	22, 287
Air-engine	J. Ericsson	New York, N. Y	Oct. 9, 1860	30, 306
Air-engine	E. Langen and N. A. Otto	Cologne, Prussia	Aug. 13, 1867	67, 659
Air-engine	F. J. Laubereau	Paris, France	Apr. 10, 1849	6, 301
Air-engine	J. J. E. Lenoir	Paris, France	Mar. 19, 1861	31, 722
Air-engine	R. Lord	Pawtucket, Mass	Sept. 17, 1861	33, 308
Air-engine	A. S. Lyman	New York, N. Y	Feb. 28, 1854	10, 576
Air-engine	T. McDonough	Middletown, Conn	Sept. 23, 1856	15, 771
Air-engine	H. Messer	Roxbury, Mass	Jan. 6, 1863	37, 299
Air-engine	D. Myers	Chicago, Ill	Nov. 15, 1870	109, 338
Air-engine	J. R. Napier and W. J. M. Rankine.	Glasgow and Govan Parish, Great Britain.	Sept. 19, 1854	11, 696
Air-engine	H. Norman and C. F. Dietrich	New Orleans, La	Feb. 25, 1873	136, 259
Air-engine	H. M. Paine	Worcester, Mass	Nov. 30, 1858	22, 219
Air-engine	J. R. Peters	New York, N. Y	Nov. 18, 1862	36, 964
Air-engine	B. F. Rice	Clinton, Mass	Apr. 5, 1859	23, 495
Air-engine	A. K. Rider	New York, N. Y	Jan. 17, 1871	111, 088
Air-engine	A. K. Rider	New York, N. Y	Oct. 24, 1871	120, 325
Air-engine	P. Shaw	East Abington, Mass	May 2, 1854	10, 868
Air-engine	O. M. Stillman	Stonington, Conn	June 26, 1860	28, 910
Air-engine	O. M. Stillman	Stonington, Conn	June 26, 1860	28, 911
Air-engine	S. Wilcox, jr	Westerly, R. I	May 3, 1859	23, 876
Air-engine	S. Wilcox, jr	Westerly, R. I	Nov. 20, 1860	30, 700
Air-engine	S. Wilcox, jr	Westerly, R. I	Nov. 20, 1860	30, 701
Air-engine	S. Wilcox, jr	Westerly, R. I	Sept. 19, 1865	50, 061
Air engine	A. O. Wilcox	Philadelphia, Pa	July 19, 1853	9, 871
Air-engine	J. A. Woodbury, J. Merrill, and G. Patten.	Winchester, Boston, and Charlestown, Mass.	May 17, 1853	9, 739
Air-engine	J. A. Woodbury, J. Merrill, and G. Patten.	Winchester and Boston, Mass.	Oct. 4, 1853	10, 081
Air engine and motor	P. A. Ensign	Adrian, Mich	Oct. 2, 1866	58, 397
Air engine, Compressed	D. Bickford	Westerly, R. I	May 15, 1860	28, 248
Air engine, Compressed	A. M. Smith	Chicago, Ill	Aug. 8, 1871	117, 825
Air engine, Compressed	W. M. Storm	Troy, N. Y	Sept. 23, 1851	8, 380
Air engine, Compressed	W. C. Turnbull	Baltimore, Md	Apr. 17, 1860	27, 938
Air engine, Condensed	A. Parsey	London, England	July 31, 1847	5, 205
Air-engine or fan-blower	G. C. Hawkins	Boston, Mass	Jan. 10, 1871	110, 915
Air-engines, Air-compressing apparatus for	J. McLeish	Philadelphia, Pa	Dec. 10, 1872	133, 713
Air-engines, Method of distributing the air over the heating and cooling surfaces of.	E. Buckup	New York, N. Y	July 2, 1850	7, 470
Air-flue register	W. L. McDowell	Philadelphia, Pa	Feb. 8, 1870	99, 692
Air flue with the chimney-pipes, Descending	J. Macomber	Greenwich, N. Y	Nov. 19, 1811	....
Air for illuminating purposes, Apparatus for carbonizing.	W. A. Simonds	Boston, Mass	June 21, 1864	43, 264
Air for illuminating purposes, Apparatus for carbonizing.	W. A. Simonds	Boston, Mass	Oct. 4, 1864	44, 560
Air for preserving animal and vegetable substances, Mode of drying and purifying.	E. D. Brainard	Albany, N. Y	July 16, 1867	66, 786
Air for use in the arts, Heating	J. A. Morrell	New York, N. Y	Sept 2, 1873	142, 497
Air from cases, Apparatus for expelling	D. Clavidge	Indianapolis, Ind	May 15, 1866	54, 686
Air from liquors on tap, Method of excluding	A. F. Boyd	Muskingum County, Ohio	Apr. 21, 1857	17, 073
Air-furnace for melting ores and refining and heating iron with stone-coal.	T. Gregg	Connellsville, Pa	Mar. 16, 1814	....
Air, gas, &c., Apparatus for compressing	S. Bidwell	Philadelphia, Pa	Nov. 8, 1864	44, 930
Air-heater	W. Sage	Durham, Conn	Feb. 20, 1855	12, 425
Air heater and cooler	L. Perkins	London, England	July 10, 1866	56, 338
Air-heater and steam-condenser, Compound	B. F. Sturtevant	Jamaica Plain, Mass	Feb. 22, 1870	100, 240
Air-heater and steam-condenser, Compound	B. F. Sturtevant	Jamaica Plain, Mass	Feb. 22, 1870	100, 241
Air-heater and steam-condenser, Compound	B. F. Sturtevant	Jamaica Plain, Mass	Feb. 22, 1870	100, 242
Air-heater, Tubular	R. R. Hawley	Normal, Ill	Sept. 1, 1868	81, 781
Air-heating apparatus, Compressed	H. Bushnell	New Haven, Conn	July 1, 1873	140, 466
Air-heating furnace	J. Barker	Baltimore, Md	July 7, 1846	4, 622
Air-heating furnace	J. Barker	Baltimore, Md	Feb. 8, 1848	5, 436
Air-heating furnace	E. Barrow	New York, N. Y	Dec. 11, 1845	4, 301
Air-heating furnace	R. L. Bate	Adrian, Mich	Apr. 1, 1862	34, 856
Air-heating furnace	J. Bradley	Saint Albans, Vt	June 24, 1844	3, 636
Air-heating furnace	W. Bryent	Boston, Mass	Oct. 24, 1854	11, 847
Air-heating furnace	H. Bushnell	Hartford, Conn	Mar. 27, 1849	6, 238
Air-heating furnace	P. H. Carman	Brooklyn, N. Y	June 29, 1869	91, 908
Air-heating furnace	G. Chilson	Boston, Mass	Nov. 19, 1850	7, 780
Air-heating furnace	R. T. Crane	Chicago, Ill	Mar. 20, 1860	27, 530
Air-heating furnace	D. Culver	Hartford, Conn	May 15, 1847	5, 114
Air-heating furnace	H. A. Engels	Cincinnati, Ohio	Feb. 12, 1850	7, 082
Air-heating furnace	C. Fowler	Hartford, Conn	July 10, 1829	....
Air-heating furnace	G. Fox	Hartford, Conn	Mar. 10, 1843	2, 994
Air-heating furnace	J. D. Green and E. Ivers	Philadelphia, Pa	Jan. 6, 1857	16, 348
Air-heating furnace	W. H. Harris	Grand Rapids, Mich	Sept. 22, 1863	40, 033
Air-heating furnace	C. R. Harvey	New York, N. Y	Jan. 24, 1854	10, 447
Air-heating furnace	J. P. Hayes	Philadelphia, Pa	June 22, 1858	20, 640
Air-heating furnace	W. Hickok	New York, N. Y	May 15, 1847	5, 118
Air-heating furnace	T. D. Ingersoll	Monroe, Mich	Mar. 30, 1858	19, 781
Air-heating furnace	A. Janes	New York, N. Y	Aug. 9, 1845	4, 140

Index of patents issued from the United States Patent Office from 1790 *to* 1873, *inclusive*—Continued.

Invention.	Inventor.	Residence.	Date.	No.
Air-heating furnace	J. Liddle	New York, N. Y	Aug. 26, 1856	15, 613
Air-heating furnace	J. MacGregor, jr	Wilton, N Y	Mar. 5, 1850	7, 143
Air-heating furnace	E. D. Norcross	Augusta, Me	Feb. 24, 1852	8, 758
Air-heating furnace	J. S. Sumner	Newton, Mass	Mar. 5, 1872	124, 229
Air-heating furnace	J. H. Sutton	Honesdaie, Pa	Mar. 13, 1855	12, 533
Air-heating furnace	J. M. Thatcher	Bergen, N. J	Nov. 19, 1867	71, 244
Air-heating furnace	O. Tiffany	New York, N. Y	Mar. 20, 1849	6, 205
Air-heating furnace	G. W. Wilson	Chelsea, Mass	Feb. 28, 1865	46, 601
Air-heating furnace	G. W. Wilson	Chelsea, Mass	June 11, 1867	65, 784
Air-heating furnace	J. M. Wilson	Philadelphia, Pa	Sept. 2, 1873	142, 363
Air-heating pipe, Connecting the joints of	J. Young	Franklin Furnace, Ohio	Mar. 7, 1854	10, 617
Air in dwellings, &c., Mode of securing pure and wholesome.	D. E. Somes	Washington, D. C	Oct. 11, 1864	44, 671
Air in heated apartments, Apparatus to effect the hydration of.	P. J. Schopp	Louisville, Ky	May 31, 1870	103, 665
Air, Keeping air-springs supplied with	S. G. Randall	Middlebury, Vt	Apr. 5, 1859	23, 497
Air, Machine for blowing uniform currents of	J. Griffin	Harpersfield, N. Y	Mar. 1, 1859	23, 084
Air, Moistening, cooling, and warming	D. E. Somes	Washington, D. C	Feb. 5, 1867	61, 886
Air-navigating apparatus	T. Green	New York, N. Y	Aug. 12, 1873	141, 785
Air of rooms with antiseptic vapors, Apparatus for impregnating the.	A. J. Sax	Paris, France	June 20, 1865	48, 352
Air or gas engine	P. Shearer	Reading, Pa	Sept. 3, 1861	33, 215
Air, Paper reservoir for compressed	C. W. Wailey	New Orleans, La	Sept. 1, 1868	81, 713
Air-pipe, Furnace	J. P. Dawson	Des Moines, Iowa	July 9, 1872	128, 864
Air-power	S. Morey	Philadelphia, Pa	Apr. 8, 1812	....
Air, Process for cooling	D. E. Somes	Washington, D. C	Oct. 3, 1865	50, 286
Air-purifying apparatus in the manufacture of fertilizers.	J. E. Cox	Cincinnati, Ohio	Mar. 29, 1870	101, 353
Air-register	H. F. Hayden	Washington, D. C	Dec. 19, 1871	121, 942
Air-register	E. A. Tuttle	Brooklyn, N. Y	Nov. 14, 1871	120, 912
Air-spring	G. M. Alsop	Philadelphia, Pa	Sept. 23, 1862	36, 498
Air-spring	J. Corriston	Sandusky, Ohio	Oct. 13, 1868	83, 043
Air-spring for railway-cars	P. G. Gardiner	New York, N. Y	June 1, 1869	90, 657
Air spring for railway-cars, &c., Compressed	L. Bissell	Newark, N. J	Oct. 11, 1841	2, 307
Air-springs, Automatic vent-opener for	J. Walther	Brooklyn, N. Y	May 27, 1873	139, 346
Air-supplying apparatus	H. W. Adams	Philadelphia, Pa	Dec. 27, 1870	110, 414
Air-tight box, case, &c	J. G. Staunton	Buffalo, N. Y	Jan. 3, 1865	45, 766
Air-tight can	C. Barry	Philadelphia, Pa	Aug. 18, 1868	81, 243
Air-tight can	W. J. Gordon	Philadelphia, Pa	Mar. 16, 1869	87, 840
Air-tight jar	G. M. Ramsey	New York, N. Y	Nov. 19, 1867	71, 215
Air-tight vessel, Constructing	T. C. Taylor	Philadelphia, Pa	Feb. 27, 1866	52, 909
Air to air-chambers, Mode of supplying	P. H. Vander Weyde	Philadelphia, Pa	Aug. 21, 1866	57, 412
Air to be used as a motive-power, Apparatus for heating and cooling.	W. Hidden and J. Reeves	New York, N. Y	Aug. 10, 1858	21, 133
Air to furnaces, Applying heated	J. Silsbe	Tyrone, N. Y	Aug. 8, 1837	343
Air-trap for steam and other enginery	G. W. Blake	New York, N. Y	July 13, 1869	92, 571
Air, Treating diseases by condensed	O. Stone	Rochester, N. Y	Oct. 24, 1865	50, 641
Air with gasoline, Apparatus for charging	B. Pickering	Milton, Ohio	Dec. 11, 1866	60, 417
Air with hydrocarbon vapors, Apparatus for charging.	H. M. Paine	Newark, N. J	Feb. 23, 1869	87, 192
Air with hydrocarbon vapors, Machine for charging.	H. B. Myer	Cleveland, Ohio.	Feb. 27, 1866	52, 876
Alarm:				
See Bell alarm.				
Blast-furnace alarm.				
Box-alarm.				
Burglar-alarm.				
Clock-alarm.				
Door-bell alarm.				
Electric-alarm.				
Electric fire and burglar alarm.				
Electro-magnetic alarm.				
Electro-magnetic house-alarm.				
Electro-magnetic temperature-alarm.				
Fire-alarm.				
Fog-alarm.				
Hat-body-machine alarm.				
High-water alarm.				
Hotel-alarm.				
House-alarm.				
Leak-alarm.				
Letter-box alarm.				
Lock-alarm.				
Locomotive-engine alarm.				
Low-water alarm.				
Milk-boiler alarm.				
Money-drawer alarm.				
Nautical alarm.				
Overflow-alarm.				
Pickpocket-alarm.				
Pocket-alarm.				
Portable alarm.				
Portable-box alarm.				
Portable burglar-alarm.				
Pressure-alarm.				
Railway-alarm.				
Railway-switch alarm.				
Railway-telegraph alarm.				
Steam-alarm.				
Steam-boiler alarm.				
Steam-pressure alarm.				
Switch-alarm.				
Target-alarm.				
Thill-alarm.				
Tidal alarm.				
Till-alarm.				
Till-lock alarm.				
Time-alarm.				
Vessel-alarm.				

Index of patents issued from the United States Patent Office from 1790 *to* 1873, *inclusive*—Continued.

Invention.	Inventor.	Residence.	Date.	No.
Alarm-attachment	J. H. Thorp	New York, N. Y	Dec. 6, 1870	109, 971
Alarm-gage for steam-boiler	J. Whitmore	Lowell, Mass	July 27, 1858	21, 040
Alarm-gage for steam-boiler, Steam and water	G. W. Grader and B. F. Cowan	Memphis, Tenn	Dec. 14, 1858	22, 287
Alarm-lock	S. A. Andrews	Farmers' Valley, Wis	Sept. 18, 1866	58, 043
Alarm-lock	F. Brewster	Cleveland, Ohio	Mar. 16, 1869	87, 905
Alarm-lock	G. N. Bruster	Factoryville, N. Y	May 19, 1863	38, 556
Alarm-lock	J. Cone	Yellow Springs, Ohio	June 24, 1856	15, 168
Alarm-lock	A. B. Crane	Newton, Mass	July 16, 1872	129, 213
Alarm-lock	C. Fleischel	New York, N. Y	June 15, 1852	9, 019
Alarm-lock	E. Herbster	Chicago, Ill	May 4, 1869	89, 762
Alarm-lock	H. L. Hervey	Windsor, Conn	Feb. 9, 1858	19, 295
Alarm-lock	H. L. Hervey	Windsor, Conn	Apr. 13, 1858	19, 926
Alarm-lock	B. F. Irvine and T. A. Hitchcock.	North La Crosse, Wis	Dec. 7, 1869	97, 513
Alarm-lock	H. Lockwood	New York, N. Y	Apr. 12, 1859	23, 591
Alarm-lock	C. E. Pierce	New York, N. Y	Sept. 26, 1871	119, 403
Alarm-lock	J. S. and R. Porter	Waterford, N. Y	Mar. 5, 1867	62, 683
Alarm-lock	C. Schnepf	Marietta, Ohio	Oct. 31, 1871	120, 541
Alarm-lock	N. Seubert	Syracuse, N. Y	June 1, 1869	90, 962
Alarm-lock	N. Seubert	Syracuse, N. Y	Aug. 24, 1869	94, 137
Alarm-lock	T. P. Sink	Fairton, N. J	Dec. 6, 1870	109, 954
Alarm-lock	G. J. Swingle	Davenport, Iowa	Jan. 30, 1872	123, 305
Alarm-lock	J. T. Taylor	Newnan, Ga	Oct. 17, 1871	120, 125
Alarm-lock	J. H. Thorp	New York, N. Y	Mar. 21, 1871	112, 987
Alarm-lock	S. I. Trask	Guilford Centre, N. Y	Feb. 5, 1856	14, 209
Alarm-lock	O. D. Warner	Bristol, Conn	Jan. 19, 1869	86, 116
Alarm-lock	J. W. Wells	Pittsburgh, Pa	Sept. 7, 1858	21, 457
Alarm-lock	J. Ziegler	Baltimore, Md	Apr. 10, 1860	27, 856
Alarm-lock, Burglar	N. Cheek	Chapel Hill, N. C	Aug. 4, 1868	80, 599
Alarm-lock, Burglar	D. Edwards	McConnellsville, Ohio	Aug. 12, 1840	1, 722
Alarm-lock, Burglar	S. T. Heminway	Saratoga Springs, N. Y	Jan. 7, 1868	73, 182
Alarm-lock, Burglar	A. Isensee	Indianapolis, Ind	Jan. 28, 1868	73, 897
Alarm-lock, Burglar	G. Jacobs	Washington, D. C	June 25, 1867	66, 090
Alarm-lock, Electrical	F. Girard	Havana, Cuba	Mar. 14, 1871	112, 585
Alarm-lock for doors	A. Iske	Lancaster, Pa	Jan. 7, 1868	73, 013
Alarm-lock for money-drawers	G. Kimball	Cleveland, Ohio	Oct. 18, 1870	108, 303
Alarm-lock for tills	D. K. Miller	Bernville, Pa	Apr. 16, 1867	63, 922
Alarm-lock for tills	C. Tucker	Bloomington, Ill	May 7, 1867	64, 598
Album	A. Hathaway	Charlestown, Mass	Aug. 6, 1867	67, 540
Album-case	C. E. Rankin	New York, N. Y	May 6, 1862	35, 173
Album-clip	C. Weil	New York, N. Y	Mar. 29, 1864	42, 134
Album, Construction of	J. D. Mets	Dubuque, Iowa	Apr. 4 1865	47, 120
Album, Machine for cutting the front edge of photographic.	S. D. Burlock	Philadelphia, Pa	Dec. 6, 1864	45, 314
Album, Photograph	J. F. Tapley	Springfield, Mass	Aug. 9 1870	106, 232
Album, Photographic	J. W. Beackley	Philadelphia, Pa	May 31 1864	42, 922
Album, Photographic	E. D. Griggs	Waterbury, Conn	May 20, 1862	35, 310
Album, Photographic	F. R. Grunel	Geneva, Switzerland	May 14, 1861	32, 287
Album, Photographic	W. Matthews	New York, N. Y	July 29, 1862	36, 011
Album, Photographic	E. Maynard	Washington, D. C	Aug. 2, 1864	43, 696
Album, Photographic	J. D. Mets	Dubuque, Iowa	July 21, 1863	39, 300
Album, Photographic	J. D. Mets	Dubuque, Iowa	Nov. 24, 1863	40, 702
Album, Photographic	C. E. Prétat	New York, N. Y	Nov. 1, 1864	44, 890
Album, Photographic	J. F. Tapley	Springfield, Mass	Mar. 16, 1869	87, 804
Album, Photographic	R. Van Velthoven	Philadelphia, Pa	Oct. 30, 1866	59, 323
Album, Photographic	R. Van Velthoven and J. H. Hazzard.	Philadelphia, Pa	Oct. 17, 1865	50, 521
Album, Porcelain and card	J. C. Spooner	Springfield, Mass	Mar. 20, 1866	53, 354
Album, Stereoscope and photographic	J. Q. A. Tresize	Zanesville, Ohio	Nov. 17, 1863	40, 654
Albumen and prussiate of potash from blood, Manufacture of.	A. H. Hirsh	Chicago, Ill	Nov. 28, 1865	51, 181
Albumen from blood, Process of purifying and decoloring.	P. Jacques	Paris, France	Dec. 21, 1869	98, 165
Albumen, Manufacture of	G. Bourgado	New York, N. Y	Sept 6, 1870	107, 158
Albumen, Preparation of	G. Bourgado	New York, N. Y	Aug 9, 1870	107, 112
Albumen, Process for manufacturing	J. M. Fuchs	New York, N. Y	Dec 24, 1867	72, 625
Alcohol and other pure distillates, Manufacture of	J. F. Collins	New York, N. Y	Jan. 1, 1867	60, 835
Alcohol and other spirits, Manufacture of	J. F. Collins	New York, N. Y	Nov 20, 1866	59, 891
Alcohol and spirits, Purifying	C. C. Parsons	New York, N. Y	June 14, 1870	104, 343
Alcohol, Apparatus for heating by vapor of	T. K. Anderson	Painted Post, N. Y	Feb 13, 1849	6, 107
Alcohol, Apparatus for purifying	C. J. Falkmann	London, Great Britain	Nov 7, 1865	50, 884
Alcohol, Apparatus for rectifying	A. A. Foubert and J. G. Béquet	St. Helier, England, and Paris, France.	Oct. 24, 1865	50, 668
Alcohol, Apparatus for rectifying	H. Lamotte	London, England	Oct. 23, 1866	59, 149
Alcohol, Apparatus for rectifying	M. Thompson	Saint Louis, Mo	Aug 9, 1864	43, 805
Alcohol, &c., Distillation of	A. Fries	Cincinnati, Ohio	July 11, 1865	48, 711
Alcohol for burning-fluid, Carbonated	S. Casey	Lebanon, Me	Mar 17, 1834	....
Alcohol from apples, Extracting	A. Wolcott	East Bloomfield, N. Y	Oct. 6, 1835	....
Alcohol from common spirits by steam, Extracting	A. and N. Wolcott	Bloomfield, N. Y	Mar 19, 1827	....
Alcohol from olefiant gas, Mode of manufacturing	E. A. Cotelle	Paris, France	Feb 23, 1864	41, 685
Alcohol from water and other heavier fluids, Separating.	B. F. Greenough	Cincinnati, Ohio	Dec. 20, 1853	10, 349
Alcohol from whisky, Apparatus for separating	A. V. H. Webb	New York, N. Y	Aug. 28, 1841	2, 234
Alcohol, Method of treating grain for the manufacture of.	W. M. Watson	Tonica, Ill	Dec. 5, 1865	51, 369
Alcohol, Process for purifying	L. Atwood	Boston, Mass	Aug. 23, 1853	9, 951
Alcohol, &c., Process of purifying	C. C. Parsons	New York, N. Y	July 13, 1869	92, 640
Alcohol, &c., Process of treating maize, barley, and other cereals for the manufacture of.	A. Fleischmann	Olmütz, Moravia, Austria	July 12, 1864	43, 555
Alcoholic and other spirits, Apparatus for treatment of.	R. D. Turner	New York, N. Y	Feb. 14, 1871	111, 791
Alcoholic liquid, Apparatus for concentrating and analyzing.	F. Haeck	Brussels, Belgium	Nov. 8, 1864	45, 002
Alcoholic liquid, Process of purifying and refining	F. Schleifer	San Francisco, Cal	July 27, 1869	93, 127
Alcoholic spirits from tomatoes, Manufacture of	J. S. Williams	Cinnaminson, N. J	Nov. 24, 1868	84, 455
Alcoholic spirits, Manufacture of	J. Neely and S. Allen	Buckingham County, Va	May 28, 1867	65, 108
Alcoholic spirits, Manufacture of	I. J. Rolfe and J. Rogers	Nevada City, Cal	Feb. 6, 1872	122, 423
Alcoholic spirits, Manufacture of	M. Thompson	Saint Louis, Mo	June 28, 1864	43, 348

Index of patents issued from the United States Patent Office from 1790 *to* 1873, *inclusive*—Continued.

Invention.	Inventor.	Residence.	Date.	No.
Alcohometer	H. Guth	New York, N. Y	June 28, 1859	24, 556
Ale and beer cooler	J. Mackintire	Somerville, Mass	Sept. 2, 1856	15, 662
Ale and beer, Cooling	M. Reynolds	New York, N. Y	Apr. 19, 1870	102, 041
Ale, beer, and water cooler	I. Erskine	Bowling Green, Ohio	Nov. 26, 1872	133, 362
Ale, beer, and water cooler	L. J. Wolf	Philadelphia, Pa	May 25, 1869	90, 415
Ale, beer, &c., Apparatus for cooling	F. Zeitz	Philadelphia, Pa	June 7, 1870	103, 955
Ale, beer, &c., Apparatus for fermenting	A. W. Lake	Adams, N. Y	Jan. 26, 1869	86, 234
Ale, Brewing	C. Clifford	Adams, N. Y	Apr. 23, 1867	63, 994
Ale, Pneumatic apparatus for drawing	H. Andes	Wilkesbarre, Pa	Oct. 12, 1869	95, 628
Alembic, Vaporous	C. Merot	Philadelphia, Pa	Nov. 5, 1818	....
Alizarine, Process of preparing	C. Graebe and C. Liebermann	Frankfort-on-the-Main and Berlin, Prussia.	Oct. 5, 1869	95, 465
Alkali-can	C. Barry	Philadelphia, Pa	Oct. 13, 1868	82, 914
Alkali-can	P. Hickey	Philadelphia, Pa	Mar. 17, 1868	75, 547
Alkali-can, Caustic	E. A. Thomas	Philadelphia, Pa	Apr. 24, 1866	54, 230
Alkali from marine salt and kelp, Extracting	J. Nazro		Jan. 6, 1797	....
Alkalies. acids, and salts, Package for caustic	J. H. Seibert	Philadelphia, Pa	Feb. 6, 1872	123, 544
Alkalies, acids, &c., Package for	J. H. Seibert	Philadelphia, Pa	Mar. 19, 1872	124, 859
Alkalies, acids, &c., Package for putting up caustic	J. H. Seibert	Philadelphia, Pa	June 18, 1872	128, 176
Alkalies, &c., Box, can, or vessel for putting up caustic.	H. Pemberton and B. Heinemann.	Allegheny and Natrona, Pa	Apr. 30, 1867	64, 251
Alkalies, Box for preserving	G. Thompson	East Tarentum, Pa	Sept. 15, 1857	18, 214
Alkalies, Box for putting up caustic	H. Pemberton	Allegheny City, Pa	Nov. 27, 1866	60, 051
Alkalies, Device for putting up caustic	G. Thompson	East Tarentum, Pa	Oct. 21, 1856	15, 957
Alkalies, Encasing caustic	G. W. Humphrey	Pompey, N. Y	Mar. 25, 1873	137, 137
Alkalies for making soap, Putting up	J. W. Wylé	Philadelphia, Pa	Oct. 7, 1873	143, 430
Alkalies, Manufacture of caustic	L. Prang	Boston, Mass	May 29, 1866	55, 158
Alkalies, Manufacture of phosphates of the	B. Tanner	New Brighton, England	Feb. 13, 1872	123, 743
Alkalies, Metal can for putting up	H. Everett	Philadelphia, Pa	Aug. 20, 1867	67, 859
Alkalies, Method of putting up caustic	T. C. Taylor	Philadelphia, Pa	Feb. 27, 1866	52, 910
Alkalies, Mode of preparing carbonated and caustic	K. Lieber	Charlottenberg near Berlin, Prussia.	Dec. 15, 1868	85, 015
Alkalies, Packing caustic	W. H. Balmain	Saint Helens, Great Britain	Dec. 20, 1870	110, 189
Alkalies, Preservation of caustic	J. Seiberling	Philadelphia, Pa	Aug. 14, 1860	29, 625
Alkalies, Process for recovering waste	H. M. Baker	Rochester, N. Y	Apr. 24, 1866	54, 093
Alkalies, Process of manufacturing caustic	H. Pemberton	East Tarentum, Pa	Feb. 8, 1859	22, 888
Alkalies, Putting up	J. Reakirt	Philadelphia, Pa	July 7, 1868	79, 599
Alkalies, Putting up caustic	J. Reakirt	Philadelphia, Pa	Jan. 26, 1869	86, 319
Alkalies, Putting up caustic	T. C. Taylor	Philadelphia, Pa	Feb. 6, 1866	52, 465
Alkalies, Putting up caustic	E. A. Thomas	Philadelphia, Pa	June 30, 1863	39, 080
Alkalies, Recovering waste	G. Howland	Brunswick, N. Y	Aug. 25, 1863	39, 653
Alkaline carbonates, Manufacture of	L. Chandor	New York, N. Y	July 14, 1863	39, 213
Alkaline carbonates, Manufacture of	H. De Grousilliers	Berlin, Germany	Oct. 21, 1873	143, 755
Alkaline chromates, Manufacture of	R. A. Tilghman	Philadelphia, Pa	Oct. 31, 1848	5, 897
Alkaline liquors used in treating straw, wood, &c., Method of saving and utilizing the.	S. Pettebone	Niagara Falls, N. Y	Dec. 3, 1867	71, 783
Alkaline silicates, Manufacture of	T. Elkenton	Philadelphia, Pa	July 7, 1863	39, 135
Alkaline solution, Process for evaporating	C. Heaton	New York, N. Y	Mar. 20, 1866	53, 298
Alkaline solution, Apparatus for evaporating and calcining.	M. L. Keen and H. Burgess	Royer's Ford, Pa	Feb. 7, 1865	46, 244
Alkaline solutions from treating straw, Re-using	J. H. Dugan	Bloomfield, N. J	Dec. 9, 1873	145, 409
Alloy	E. Martin	Waterbury, Conn	Aug. 23, 1859	25, 206
Alloy	F. P. Pfeiffer	Philadelphia, Pa	Aug. 14, 1866	57, 184
Alloy	W. Schrier	Logansport, Ind	May 17, 1870	103, 089
Alloy	H. W. Wright	Glastenbury, Conn	Aug. 5, 1873	141, 529
Alloy, Bronze	G. M. Levi and C. M. Künzel	Brussels & Liege, Belgium.	Nov. 14, 1871	120, 984
Alloy-composition	T. Brown	Georgetown, N. Y	Dec. 9, 1856	16, 170
Alloy, Flux for treating	E. Mourier and J. F. E. Vallent.	Paris, France	Mar. 3, 1857	16, 771
Alloy for dentists' use	M. M. Johnston	New York, N. Y	Nov. 26, 1867	71, 307
Alloy for filtering oils and for the manufacture of paint, cement, &c., Metallic.	J. Webster	Birmingham, Great Britain	Sept. 7, 1869	94, 532
Alloy for forming eyelets	G. B. Brayton	Boston, Mass	May 25, 1869	90, 337
Alloy for hardening iron	H. L. Macker and G. W. Marston.	Boston and Cambridge, Mass.	Nov. 19, 1872	133, 237
Alloy for harness-trimming, &c., Metal	A. A. Randall	South Braintree, Mass	Dec. 21, 1869	98, 107
Alloy for journal-boxes, &c	G. W. Disman	Chesterville, Ohio	Oct. 15, 1867	69, 783
Alloy for journal-boxes	T. Firth	Cincinnati, Ohio	May 1, 1855	12, 788
Alloy for journal-boxes	J. Garratt, sr	Indianapolis, Ind	Aug. 14, 1855	13, 427
Alloy for journal-boxes and bearings, Metallic	G. Sherman	Memphis, Tenn	Aug. 7, 1860	29, 525
Alloy for lining water-coolers, tanks, &c	Z. E. Fobes	Troy, N. Y	Jan. 16, 1872	122, 716
Alloy for making plates and sheets	J. D. Grüneberg	Spring Mills, N. J	Nov. 26, 1867	71, 479
Alloy for making water-meter	J. S. Barden	Providence, R. I	Sept. 21, 1869	94, 936
Alloy for mold-board and other parts of plow	O. F. Burton	Jersey City, N. J	Feb. 12, 1867	61, 997
Alloy for plow mold-board, Metallic	S. L. Madge	Toledo, Ohio	Jan. 18, 1870	98, 874
Alloy for points of lightning-rods	S. Spratt	Cincinnati, Ohio	Jan. 8, 1850	7, 008
Alloy for preventing friction in machinery	W. H. Saunders	Carroll County, Tenn	Jan. 2, 1872	122, 408
Alloy for producing ornamental coatings on metals.	H. Aiken	Philadelphia, Pa	Apr. 1, 1873	137, 279
Alloy for sabots of projectiles	T. Taylor	Washington, D. C	July 27, 1869	93, 137
Alloy for sheet-metal	T. D. Jackson	Brooklyn, N. Y	Oct. 31, 1848	5, 895
Alloy for the manufacture of metal sheet, foil, &c	L. Brandeis	Brooklyn, N. Y	Nov. 5, 1867	70, 513
Alloy for the manufacture of plow mold-board	W. Magee	Jamaica, N. Y	Sept. 19, 1871	119, 091
Alloy for the manufacture of spoons and forks	H. W. Wright	Taunton, Mass	May 12, 1868	77, 793
Alloy for tubing	J. S. Barden	Providence, R. I	Sept. 21, 1869	94, 935
Alloy, Journal-box	J. Fidler	New Albany, Ind	Sept. 30, 1856	15, 804
Alloy, Journal-box	B. F. Lawton	Troy, N. Y	Aug. 21, 1855	13, 465
Alloy, Journal-box	B. F. Lawton	Troy, N. Y	Aug. 21, 1855	13, 466
Alloy, Metallic	H. B. Babcock	New York, N. Y	June 5, 1849	6, 502
Alloy, &c., Metallic composition for fusible	B. Wood	Nashville, Tenn	Mar. 20, 1860	27, 590
Alloy of aluminium	M. G. Farmer	Salem, Mass	Apr. 28, 1863	38, 301
Alloy of aluminium	M. G. Farmer	Salem, Mass	Sept. 6, 1864	44, 086
Alloy of copper and tin	A. E. Lavroff	St. Petersburg, Russia	Aug. 22, 1871	118, 372
Alloy of copper for bearings	C. J. A. Dick	Pittsburgh, Pa	Apr. 9, 1872	125, 549
Alloy of copper, zinc, and aluminium	J. Baur	New York, N. Y	Oct. 27, 1863	40, 388
Alloy of iron, zinc, and nickel	O. Boyden	Newark, N. J	May 27, 1851	8, 114
Alloy of manganese	E. Savage	West Meriden, Conn	Jan. 18, 1870	99, 007
Alloy of manganese, Manufacture of	E. Savage	West Meriden, Conn	Apr. 26, 1870	102, 324

Index of patents issued from the United States Patent Office from 1790 *to* 1873, *inclusive*—Continued.

Invention.	Inventor.	Residence.	Date.	No.
Alloy of metals in forming water-pipes, &c., Art of ufacturing and uniting.	W. A. Shaw	New York, N. Y	Dec. 31, 1867	72, 919
Alloy of nickel, zinc, and copper	H. W. Wright	Glastenbury, Conn	Aug. 5, 1873	141, 530
Alloy or bell-metal	H. L. Macker	Boston, Mass	Aug. 27, 1872	130, 814
Alloy or bronze	G. M. Levi and C. M. Küzel	Brussels and Liege, Belgium	May 23, 1871	115, 220
Alloy or metallic compound for bearings, &c	C. Adams	Pittsburgh, Pa	Nov. 5, 1872	132, 744
Alloy to imitate precious metals, Metallic	L. Sibert	Staunton, Va	Mar. 15, 1870	100, 937
Alloy to imitate silver, &c	H. L. Macker	Boston, Mass	Jan. 23, 1872	122, 901
Alloy to imitate silver	A. Schmitte and H. A. Levallois	Paris, France	Nov. 19, 1867	71, 072
Alloy to resemble silver	A. E. P. Baudvin	Paris, France	Sept. 16, 1873	142, 760
Alloys of aluminium and vulcanite, Combination of	N. C. Fowler	Yarmouth Port, Mass	Feb. 14, 1865	46, 347
Alloying copper, iron, &c., by cementation, Mode of.	M. Sorel	Paris, France	Sept. 17, 1838	924
Allumettes, Machine for making paper	B. B. Lehman	Lebanon, Pa	Mar. 26, 1867	63, 265
Almanac, Perpetual	W. Gibson	Lanark, Scotland	Oct. 10, 1865	50, 430
Almond-peeling machine	H. Wathew	Philadelphia, Pa	Oct. 30, 1866	59, 324
Alphabet block	S. L. Hill	Williamsburgh, N. Y	Nov. 13, 1866	59, 603
Alphabet-block	E. H. Muldaur	Dover, Del	July 8, 1873	147, 722
Alphabet-frame	E. B. Nourse	Eaton, Ohio	Oct. 2, 1866	58, 463
Alphabeticon	J. H. R. Reffelt	Hoboken, N. J	Jan. 2, 1866	51, 864
Altiscope	J. Clark	Philadelphia, Pa	Mar. 13, 1866	53, 115
Altitude-instrument	H. Colby	New York, N. Y	Feb. 22, 1870	100, 119
Altitude of the sun, Instrument for taking	F. Yeiser	Lexington, Ky	Feb. 8, 1859	22, 913
Alum and fertilizers from mineral phosphates, Manufacture of.	P. Spence	Newton Heath, Manchester, Great Britain.	Dec. 13, 1870	110, 084
Alum from lignite, Mode of making	G. Troost	Philadelphia, Pa	Mar. 3, 1817	....
Alum-making, Preparing clay for	H. D. Pochin	Salford, England	Oct. 21, 1856	15, 934
Alum, Porous	H. Pemberton	Allegheny City, Pa	Oct. 6, 1868	82, 747
Alum, Process for manufacturing	J. H. Wurtz	New York, N. Y	Oct. 22, 1859	7, 737
Alumina, alum, and other aluminous substances, Manufacture of sulphate of.	H. Pemberton	Allegheny City, Pa	Jan. 1, 1867	60, 780
Alumina, Manufacture of acetate of	G. T. Lewis	Philadelphia, Pa	Oct. 30, 1866	59, 238
Alumina, Manufacture of sulphate of	H. Pemberton	Allegheny City, Pa	May 19, 1868	78, 005
Alumina, Manufacture of sulpho-acetate of	G. T. Lewis	Philadelphia, Pa	Oct. 30, 1866	59, 239
Alumina, Process of manufacturing sulphate of	M. J. Funcke	Eichelskamp, Prussia	Jan. 23, 1841	1, 945
Alumina, Treatment of sulphate of	A. A. Croll	London, England	May 28, 1867	65, 175
Aluminium and calomel, Manufacture of	L. T. Corbelli and V. Raitti	Florence, Tuscany, and Modena.	Oct. 26, 1858	21, 923
Aluminium, Apparatus for and method of casting.	J. B. Bean	Baltimore, Md	Sept. 3, 1867	68, 548
Aluminium, Electro-deposition of	J. A. Jeançon	Newport, Ky	July 15, 1873	140, 924
Aluminium, Preparation of	L. T. Corbelli and V. Raitti	Florence, Tuscany, and Modena.	Oct. 26, 1858	21, 922
Aluminium with vulcanite and other materials, Combining.	N. C. Fowler	Yarmouth, Mass	Feb. 7, 1865	46, 230
Amalgam and mercury from ore-pulp, Machine for collecting.	Z. Wheeler	San Francisco, Cal	July 14, 1863	39, 251
Amalgam, Device for straining gold and silver	T. Varney	San Francisco, Cal	Mar. 18, 1862	34, 708
Amalgam for coating harness-trimmings, &c	H. L. Macker	Boston, Mass	Feb. 13, 1872	123, 712
Amalgam, Process for refining	W. Brückner	San Francisco, Cal	Mar. 21, 1865	46, 875
Amalgam, Separating and collecting gold and silver.	S. W. Wood	Cornwall, N. Y	Feb. 9, 1864	41, 565
Amalgamating and collecting gold and silver	H. W. Adams and W. S. Worthington.	New York and Newtown, N. Y.	Feb. 16, 1864	41, 588
Amalgamating and collecting gold and silver from ore, Apparatus for.	W. P. Parrott and J. J. Bordman.	Boston, Mass	June 11, 1867	65, 593
Amalgamating-apparatus	W. H. Butler	Chicago, Ill	Sept. 19, 1865	49, 975
Amalgamating-apparatus	J. N. Phelps	New York, N. Y	Oct. 18, 1864	44, 775
Amalgamating-apparatus, Method of elevating the mercury in.	O. Hofmann	Ellsworth, Nev	July 2, 1872	128, 623
Amalgamating gold and silver	A. K. Eaton	New York, N. Y	Apr. 4, 1854	10, 734
Amalgamating gold and silver	S. Longman	Brooklyn, N. Y	Aug. 17, 1858	21, 204
Amalgamating gold and silver	I. M. Phelps	Chicago, Ill	July 11, 1871	116, 865
Amalgamating gold and silver	G. B. Simpson	Washington, D. C	Feb. 6, 1866	52, 456
Amalgamating gold and silver, Apparatus for	J. S. Diltz	Mount Ophir, Cal	Mar. 1, 1864	41, 763
Amalgamating gold and silver, Apparatus for	R. McCully	Philadelphia, Pa	Feb. 23, 1869	87, 276
Amalgamating gold and silver, Apparatus for	J. Oliver	Ophir, Cal	Nov. 12, 1872	132, 919
Amalgamating gold and silver, Apparatus for	H. H. Scoville and P. W. Gates	Chicago, Ill	Sept. 20, 1864	44, 343
Amalgamating gold and silver, Apparatus for	J. J. Storer	Boston, Mass	Nov. 1, 1864	44, 898
Amalgamating gold and silver, Machine for	A. B. Crosby	Boston, Mass	Feb. 28, 1865	46, 546
Amalgamating gold and silver, Machine for	J. C. Dickey	Saratoga Springs, N. Y	Nov. 22, 1864	45, 144
Amalgamating gold and silver, Machine for	J. Hoeniger	New York, N. Y	July 15, 1862	35, 876
Amalgamating gold and silver, Machine for	T. Varney	San Francisco, Cal	July 15, 1862	35, 904
Amalgamating gold and silver, Process of	A. B. Paul and J. L. Wood	San Francisco and Independence, Cal.	Oct. 19, 1869	95, 931
Amalgamating gold and silver, Process of	J. Tunbridge	Newark, N. J	Dec. 16, 1873	145, 603
Amalgamating gold and silver, Process of	J. N. Wyckoff	New York, N. Y	Oct. 3, 1865	50, 296
Amalgamating gold and silver ores, Apparatus for.	L. E. Rivot	Paris, France	Jan. 28, 1868	73, 839
Amalgamating gold and silver ores, Process of	P. T. G. Stockman	Brooklyn, N. Y	Dec. 5, 1871	121, 554
Amalgamating gold and silver with lead, Apparatus for.	H. L. Fulton	Chicago, Ill	June 5, 1866	55, 273
Amalgamating gold in tailings, Apparatus for	T. A. Pratt	Marysville, Cal	Nov. 28, 1871	121, 296
Amalgamating gold, Machine for	F. N. Du Bois	Chicago, Ill	Apr. 15, 1862	34, 948
Amalgamating gold, &c., Process for	F. N. Du Bois	Black Hawk, Colo	Apr. 3, 1866	53, 590
Amalgamating gold, Process for	C. C. Knowles	Lowell, Mass	Aug. 6, 1850	7, 546
Amalgamating gold, &c., shaking and rocking table for.	A. Behr and W. J. Ward	Black Hawk, Colo	Apr. 25, 1865	47, 384
Amalgamating gold with mercury	M. Foreman and J. R. Mathewson.	Philadelphia, Pa	Sept. 18, 1866	58, 088
Amalgamating-machine	M. B. Dodge	Black Hawk Point, Colo	May 3, 1864	42, 568
Amalgamating-machine	E. Heath	San Francisco, Cal	Feb. 17, 1863	37, 688
Amalgamating machine, Gold and silver	Z. Wheeler	San Francisco, Cal	Dec. 8, 1863	40, 874
Amalgamating ores, Apparatus for	A. Bassett	Virginia, City, Nev	Jan. 22, 1867	61, 383
Amalgamating ores, Apparatus for	J. Tunbridge	Newark, N. J	Dec. 12, 1871	121, 827
Amalgamating ores, &c., Apparatus for	G. D. Wyckoff	Oil City, Pa	Mar. 19, 1872	124, 873
Amalgamating ores of silver, Process of	W. R. Frink	Virginia City, Nev	Aug. 30, 1864	43, 983
Amalgamating ores of the precious metals, Method of	F. Libben	New York, N. Y	July 2, 1861	32, 686
Amalgamating ores, Process for	W. F. Stewart	Austin, Nev	Dec. 20, 1864	45, 534
Amalgamating-pan	S. W. Bullock	Elizabeth, N. J	June 27, 1865	48, 480

Index of patents issued from the United States Patent Office from 1790 *to* 1873, *inclusive*—Continued.

Invention.	Inventor.	Residence.	Date.	No.
Amalgamating-pan	I. S Parke	Virginia City, Nev	Oct. 14, 1873	143, 635
Amalgamating-pan, &c., Composition for coating	C. H. Golding	Virginia City, Nev	Jan. 16, 1866	52, 040
Amalgamating-pan for gold and silver ores	I. S. Parke	Virginia City, Nev	Apr. 18, 1871	113, 791
Amalgamating-riffle	J. S. Briggs	Michigan Bluffs, Cal	Mar. 1, 1859	23, 072
Amalgamating the precious metals	J. B. Beers	San Francisco, Cal	Aug. 20, 1867	67, 842
Amalgamating the precious metals	H. J. Smith	Boston, Mass	July 9, 1867	66, 529
Amalgamating the precious metals	L. R. Streeter	Lowell, Mass	May 29, 1855	12, 988
Amalgating the precious metals and preventing the loss of mercury.	J. S. Phillips	San Francisco, Cal	May 16, 1871	114, 848
Amalgamating the precious metals, Apparatus for	J. B. Atwater	Chicago, Ill	Dec. 15, 1863	40, 894
Amalgamating the precious metals, Apparatus for	E. J. Fraser	San Francisco, Cal	Apr. 30, 1872	126, 196
Amalgamating the precious metals, Machine for	E. Coleman	San Francisco, Cal	Aug. 18, 1863	39, 550
Amalgamating the precious metals, Mode of	C. A. Seely	New York, N. Y	May 2, 1865	47, 577
Amalgamating the precious metals, Polishing ore to aid in.	I. W. Forbes	LaPorte, Ind	May 30, 1871	115, 293
Amalgamation, Cleaning pulverized ore so as to aid.	I. W. Forbes	LaPorte, Ind	May 30, 1871	115, 294
Amalgamation, Composition for preparing gold and silver ores for.	W. Gluyas	San Francisco, Cal	Oct. 11, 1859	25, 787
Amalgamation of gold and silver	A. B. Crosby	Greene, Me	Sept. 26, 1871	119, 264
Amalgamation, Preparing ores for	A. B. Paul	San Francisco, Cal	Nov. 19, 1872	133, 172
Amalgamator	S. F. Ambler	Brooklyn, N. Y	Feb. 4, 1862	34, 286
Amalgamator	J. B. Atwater	Chicago. Ill	July 25, 1865	48, 887
Amalgamator	J. and E. W. Barker	Baltimore, Md	Jan. 18, 1859	22, 616
Amalgamator	J. A. Bertola	New York, N. Y	Oct. 20, 1857	18, 485
Amalgamator	J. C. Brewster	New York, N. Y	Feb. 8, 1870	99, 630
Amalgamator	J. A. Brock	Chicago, Ill	May 1, 1860	28, 136
Amalgamator	E. Brown	Chicago, Ill	Oct. 23, 1866	58, 981
Amalgamator	G W. Carter	San Francisco, Cal	Feb. 7, 1860	27, 035
Amalgamator	F. P. Cavanah	Pioneer Mills, N. C	May 3, 1859	23, 881
Amalgamator	S. F. Charles	Dahlonega, Ga	Sept. 25, 1866	58, 335
Amalgamator	T. J. Chubb	Brooklyn, N. Y	Aug. 8, 1865	49, 232
Amalgamator	T. J. Chubb	Brooklyn, N. Y	Aug. 6, 1867	67, 498
Amalgamator	A. M. Church	Augusta, Ga	Jan. 25, 1859	22, 704
Amalgamator	M. H. Collins	Chelsea, Mass	Nov. 21, 1865	51, 021
Amalgamator	F. W. Crosby	New York, N. Y	Mar. 26, 1867	63, 221
Amalgamator	J. Curtis	New York, N. Y	Dec. 28, 1835	....
Amalgamator	J. Curtis	New York, N. Y	Dec. 28, 1835	....
Amalgamator	J. Curtis	New York, N. Y	Dec. 28, 1835	....
Amalgamator	G. S. Curtis and T. Tripp	Chicago, Ill	Apr. 17, 1866	54, 062
Amalgamator	A. G. Day	New York, N. Y	Sept. 26, 1865	50, 101
Amalgamator	L. Eddleblute	Garden Valley, Cal	Dec. 27, 1859	26, 576
Amalgamator	J. W. Evans	New York, N. Y	June 3, 1856	15, 037
Amalgamator	G. B. Field	New York, N. Y	Aug. 27, 1867	68, 175
Amalgamator	A. L. Fleury	New York, N. Y	Jan. 14, 1868	73, 241
Amalgamator	J. B. Forrissier	New York, N. Y	June 25, 1867	66, 142
Amalgamator	S. Fountain	Silver City, Nev	Apr. 28, 1868	77, 183
Amalgamator	W. M. Fuller	Chicago, Ill	Apr. 10, 1866	53, 805
Amalgamator	S. Gardiner, jr	New York, N. Y	Oct. 9, 1855	13, 645
Amalgamator	H. A. Gaston	Austin, Nev	Mar. 27, 1866	53, 435
Amalgamator	H. A. Gaston	Nevada City, Cal	Sept. 3, 1867	68, 359
Amalgamator	P. W. Gates	Chicago, Ill	Oct. 24, 1865	50, 572
Amalgamator	W. Gluyas	San Francisco, Cal	Aug. 7, 1860	29, 545
Amalgamator	A. W. Hall	New York, N. Y	Sept. 6, 1864	44, 140
Amalgamator	A. W. Hall	New York, N. Y	Feb. 28, 1865	46, 560
Amalgamator	I. T. Halsted	Fredonia, N. Y	July 25, 1865	48, 930
Amalgamator	H. Halvorson	North Cambridge, Mass	Oct. 17, 1865	50, 534
Amalgamator	E. Hamilton	Chicago, Ill	Feb. 27, 1866	52, 846
Amalgamator	T. Hansbrow	Sacramento, Cal	Oct. 27, 1863	40, 406
Amalgamator	K. Hazen	Brooklyn, N. Y	Sept. 6, 1859	25, 333
Amalgamator	F. G. Hesse	San Francisco, Cal	Oct. 8, 1867	69, 564
Amalgamator	F. G. Hesse	San Francisco, Cal	Nov. 12, 1867	70, 839
Amalgamator	J. M. Hill	Angel's Camp, Cal	Jan. 1, 1861	31, 063
Amalgamator	H. L. Hopkins	San Francisco, Cal	Sept, 27, 1864	44, 422
Amalgamator	A. Horn	Silver City, Nev	Nov. 19, 1867	71, 011
Amalgamator	A. Horn	Silver City, Nev	Aug. 4, 1868	80, 739
Amalgamator	R. W. Howard	Warwick, R. I	June 18, 1867	65, 912
Amalgamator	W. H. Howland	San Francisco, Cal	Oct. 25, 1859	25, 933
Amalgamator	W. W. Hubbell	Philadelphia, Pa	Oct. 8, 1867	69, 672
Amalgamator	A. Hunter	San Francisco, Cal	May 7, 1867	64, 534
Amalgamator	S. Johnson	San Francisco, Cal	Apr. 13, 1869	88, 963
Amalgamator	W. Kendrick	New York, N. Y	May 29, 1866	55, 114
Amalgamator	E. N. Kent	New York, N. Y	Dec. 4, 1855	13, 879
Amalgamator	J. Kenyon	Black Hawk, Colo	July 19, 1864	43, 589
Amalgamator	I. W. Knox	San Francisco, Cal	Apr. 24, 1860	27, 990
Amalgamator	G. C. Langtry and G. Emmett	Gold Hill, Nev	Feb. 20, 1872	123, 918
Amalgamator	G. A. Mariner and J. Kune	Chicago, Ill	Oct. 6, 1868	82, 730
Amalgamator	L. G. Marshall	San Francisco, Cal	Jan. 7, 1862	34, 115
Amalgamator	F. Maxson	San Francisco, Cal	Oct. 18, 1859	25, 840
Amalgamator	G. E. Mills	New York, N. Y	June 26, 1860	28, 885
Amalgamator	F. Morris	San Francisco, Cal	Mar. 25, 1873	137, 088
Amalgamator	G. M. Norton	San Francisco, Cal	Sept. 18, 1860	30, 085
Amalgamator	A. F. W. Partz	Wurtsborough, N. Y	July 14, 1863	39, 240
Amalgamator	A. B. Paul	Nevada, Cal	Aug. 27, 1861	33, 159
Amalgamator	C. C. Peck	Black Hawk, Colo	Feb. 21, 1865	46, 492
Amalgamator	C. C. Peck	Black Hawk, Colo	Nov. 21, 1865	51, 079
Amalgamator	W. Robbins and E. Swasey	Hindsdale, Ill., and Buckport, Me.	Apr. 21, 1868	77, 097
Amalgamator	J. A. Robinson, jr	San Francisco, Cal	Jan. 22, 1867	61, 463
Amalgamator	D. E. Rose	Cincinnati, Ohio	Jan. 15, 1867	61, 262
Amalgamator	H. P. Russ	San Francisco, Cal	Mar. 22, 1859	23, 313
Amalgamator	H. H. Scoville, jr	Chicago, Ill	May 30, 1865	48, 030
Amalgamator	A. J. Senatz and G. W. Knowlton.	Sacramento, Cal	Apr. 30, 1867	64, 258
Amalgamator	G. B. Simpson	Washington, D. C	Apr. 17, 1866	54, 028
Amalgamator	R. and W. T. Smith	Carondelet, Mo	Apr. 7, 1868	76, 538
Amalgamator	L. Solomon	New York, N. Y	Dec. 7, 1858	22, 245
Amalgamator	J. T. Staats	New York, N. Y	Mar. 13, 1866	53, 194

Index of patents issued from the United States Patent Office from 1790 *to* 1873, *inclusive*—Continued.

Invention.	Inventor.	Residence.	Date.	No.
Amalgamator	S. Standish	Pacheco, Cal	Jan. 15, 1867	61, 274
Amalgamator	A. M. Stetson	San Francisco, Cal	Aug. 26, 1856	15, 619
Amalgamator	G. Stevens	San Francisco, Cal	June 29, 1869	91, 878
Amalgamator	C. C. Stevenson	Gold Hill, Nev	Apr. 19, 1870	102, 177
Amalgamator	W. L. Strong	San Francisco, Cal	May 7, 1867	64, 458
Amalgamator	S. G. Sturges	Newark, N. J	Sept. 18, 1866	58, 149
Amalgamator	A. Swazey	Chicago, Ill	Nov. 5, 1867	70, 646
Amalgamator	J. Thomson	Gibsonville, Cal	May 25, 1869	90, 409
Amalgamator	T. Tripp	Chicago, Ill	Apr. 17, 1866	54, 074
Amalgamator	T. Tripp and G. S. Curtis	Chicago, Ill	Apr. 17, 1866	54, 075
Amalgamator	T. Tripp and G. S. Curtis	Chicago, Ill	Apr. 17, 1866	54, 076
Amalgamator	T. Varney	San Francisco, Cal	July 12, 1864	43, 535
Amalgamator	Z. Wheeler	San Francisco, Cal	Nov. 29, 1864	45, 289
Amalgamator	J. D. Whelpley and J. J. Storer	Boston, Mass	Sept. 11, 1866	58, 010
Amalgamator	J. White	Bangor, Me	Aug. 28, 1860	29, 837
Amalgamator	S. E. Woodworth	Murphy's, Cal	Apr. 9, 1861	32, 022
Amalgamator	S. E. Woodworth and J. S. Wethered.	San Francisco, Cal	Nov. 27, 1860	30, 781
Amalgamator	J. N. Wickoff and T. M. Fell	Brooklyn, N. Y., and Melvin Mines, Va.	Nov. 27, 1860	30, 783
Amalgamator and concentrator	G. Johnston and E. G. Smith	Auburn, Cal	July 9, 1867	66, 499
Amalgamator and ore-concentrator	J. Scott	San Francisco, Cal	May 24, 1870	103, 377
Amalgamator and ore-crusher	J. Burrell	Central City, Colo	Jan. 28, 1862	34, 238
Amalgamator and ore-mill	A. B. Paul	Silver City, Nev	May 13, 1862	35, 253
Amalgamator, Cylindrical	T. M. Fell	New York, N. Y	Jan. 1, 1867	60, 709
Amalgamator, Electrical	J. H. Rae	Syracuse, N. Y	Oct. 13, 1868	83, 091
Amalgamator for collecting gold and silver	J. A. Bertola	New York, N. Y	July 29, 1862	35, 987
Amalgamator for collecting gold and silver	J. S. and H. Curtis	Chicago, Ill	Feb. 23, 1869	87, 248
Amalgamator for gold and silver	W. H. Deviar	Valley Township, Mo	Mar. 18, 1862	34, 673
Amalgamator for gold and silver	P. G. Gardiner	New York, N. Y	Oct. 4, 1864	44, 525
Amalgamator for gold and silver	W. A. Palmer	San Francisco, Cal	Nov. 18, 1862	36, 963
Amalgamator for gold and silver	T. Varney	San Francisco, Cal	Dec. 16, 1862	37, 185
Amalgamator for gold and silver, Electro-magnetic.	A. B. Paul	San Francisco, Cal	June 1, 1869	90, 777
Amalgamator for gold and silver, Voltaic	J. H. Rae	Syracuse, N. Y	Feb. 20, 1872	123, 932
Amalgamator for ores of gold and silver	W. M. Fuller	Chicago, Ill	Dec. 24, 1867	72, 626
Amalgamator, Gold	W. Ball	Chicopee, Mass	Sept. 9, 1851	8, 344
Amalgamator, Gold	H. Brevoort	San Francisco, Cal	Aug. 30, 1859	25, 242
Amalgamator, Gold	R. H. Collyer	New York, N. Y	June 6, 1854	11, 034
Amalgamator, Gold	A. K. Eaton	New York, N. Y	Nov. 6, 1860	30, 567
Amalgamator, Gold	J. H. Fisher	Placerville, Cal	Feb. 2, 1858	19, 246
Amalgamator, Gold	D. Leibee	Middletown, Ohio	Jan. 1, 1856	14, 023
Amalgamator, Gold	A. S. Wright	San Francisco, Cal	Aug. 15, 1854	11, 541
Amalgamator, Gold	J. N. Wickoff and T. M. Fell	Brooklyn, N. Y., and Orange Mines, Va.	July 26, 1859	24, 902
Amalgamator, Gold and silver	H. W. Adams	New York, N. Y	Nov. 29, 1864	45, 214
Amalgamator, Gold and silver	H. Bolthoff	Burlington, Iowa	Mar. 7, 1865	46, 632
Amalgamator, Gold and silver	M. Laflin	Chicago, Ill	Mar. 5, 1867	62, 639
Amalgamator, Gold and silver	H. Pietsch	New York, N. Y	Jan. 7, 1862	34, 072
Amalgamator, Ore	J. M. Beath	San Francisco, Cal	Dec. 20, 1864	45, 468
Amalgamator, Re-immersing	J. R. Miller	Fredericksburgh, Va	July 2, 1850	7, 478
Amalgamator, Shoe for	J. H. Bullock	Gold Hill, Nev	May 12, 1868	77, 868
Ambrotypes, Method of mounting	J. S. McClure	Mobile, Ala	Nov. 1, 1859	25, 977
Ambulance	G. W. Arnold	Morgantown, W. Va	Apr. 5, 1864	42, 152
Ambulance	C. Britain	Saint Joseph, Mich	Aug. 11, 1863	39, 460
Ambulance	J. M. Hayward	Boston, Mass	May 16, 1865	47, 719
Ambulance	B. Howard	New York, N. Y	June 27, 1865	48, 404
Ambulance	E. R. McKean	Washington, D. C	Oct. 11, 1864	44, 643
Ambulance	M. Pinner	New York, N. Y	Jan. 27, 1863	37, 518
Ambulance	D. H. Rucker, J. E. Allen, and J. S. Smith.	Washington, D. C	Nov. 6, 1866	59, 459
Ambulance	W. Slatter	Allegheny City, Pa	May 30, 1865	47, 992
Ambulance	A. W. Süs	New York, N. Y	Aug. 18, 1863	39, 595
Ammonia-engine	C. Fellier	Paris, France	Dec. 12, 1871	121, 909
Ammonia-gas engine	E. Lamm	New Orleans, La	Mar. 12, 1872	124, 495
Ammonia, Manufacture of	A. Paraf	Thann, France	Aug. 6, 1867	67, 447
Ammonia, Manufacture of carbonate of	S. R. Divine	New York, N. Y	Jan. 26, 1869	86, 142
Ammonia, sulphur, and other products from gas-lime, Preparation of.	R. J. Everett	Bridgeport, Conn	June 4, 1872	127, 470
Ammoniacal and other liquids, Apparatus for evaporating.	L. S. Fales	New York, N. Y	July 27, 1869	93, 072
Ammoniacal-gas engine	E. Lamm	New Orleans, La	July 19, 1870	105, 581
Ammoniacal-gas engine	W. H. Laubach	Philadelphia, Pa	May 28, 1872	127, 250
Ammoniacal-gas engine	W. H. Smith and F. V. De Coppet	New Orleans, La	July 29, 1873	141, 242
Ammoniacal-gas-engine feeder	E. Lamm	New Orleans, La	Dec. 5, 1871	121, 527
Ammunition box, Military	J. J. Hirschbuhl	Louisville, Ky	Feb. 18, 1862	34, 423
Ammunition for fire-arms, Fixed	G. Conover	Middletown, Conn	Feb. 23, 1864	41, 684
Ammunition holder for cartridge-box, Fixed	J. W. Cochran	New York, N. Y	Mar. 17, 1868	75, 625
Ammunition holder for cartridge-box, Fixed	J. W. Cochran	New York, N. Y	Mar. 17, 1868	75, 626
Ammunition in chests and boxes, Packing	F. L. Hagadorn	Baltimore, Md	Nov. 26, 1867	71, 298
Amputating-apparatus	G. W. Griswold	Carbondale, Pa	Jan. 17, 1854	10, 435
Amulet, Metal	E. West		May 19, 1809	
Anæsthetics, Instrument for administration of	O. Willson	Aurora, Ill	Dec. 10, 1867	71, 934
Anchor	W. J. Armstrong and C. Browne	Brooklyn, N. Y	Nov. 5, 1867	70, 498
Anchor	A. B. Babbitt	Taunton, Mass	May 23, 1871	115, 011
Anchor	E. I. Barlow	San Francisco, Cal	Nov. 30, 1869	97, 342
Anchor	A. Bradford	Raynham, Mass	Mar. 1, 1864	41, 754
Anchor	C. F. Brown	Warren, R. I	May 22, 1866	54, 847
Anchor	C. F. Brown	Warren, R. I	Jan. 26, 1869	86, 206
Anchor	C. A. Chamberlin	Allegheny City, Pa	Apr. 19, 1864	42, 346
Anchor	C. A. Chamberlin	Pittsburgh, Pa	July 11, 1871	116, 806
Anchor	C. A. Chamberlin	Philadelphia, Pa	Sept. 16, 1873	142, 769
Anchor	G. Coffin	Jamaica Plains, Mass	June 27, 1865	48, 370
Anchor	T. L. Dalton	New York, N. Y	Jan. 6, 1857	16, 356
Anchor	P. Dinzey	Bartholomew, West Indies	June 12, 1866	55, 593
Anchor	J. D. Greene	Cambridge, Mass	Apr. 13, 1869	88, 781
Anchor	R. V. D. Guinon	Brooklyn, N. Y	Apr. 3, 1855	12, 622
Anchor	J. W. Habberley	South Malden, Mass	Oct. 13, 1868	82, 940
Anchor	Z. Hall	Dennis, Mass	Nov. 25, 1873	144, 901

Index of patents issued from the United States Patent Office from 1790 to 1873, inclusive—Continued.

Invention.	Inventor.	Residence.	Date.	No.
Anchor	F. Howes	Boston, Mass	Dec. 22, 1868	85, 228
Anchor	W. M. Hughes	San Francisco, Cal	Feb. 28, 1871	112, 247
Anchor	C. T. Julius	Philadelphia, Pa	Jan. 1, 1867	60, 903
Anchor	W. A. Kentish	New York, N. Y	May 2, 1848	5, 547
Anchor	F. J. Latham	New York, N. Y	Aug. 21, 1866	57, 339
Anchor	A. H. Law	San Francisco, Cal	May 17, 1870	103, 205
Anchor	G. A. Lloyd and C. A. Stewart	San Francisco, Cal	July 9, 1867	66, 665
Anchor	G. A. Lloyd and C. A. Stewart	San Francisco, Cal	Oct. 12, 1869	95, 698
Anchor	C. E. Marshall	Digby, Nova Scotia	Oct. 17, 1865	50, 542
Anchor	F. Martin	Marseilles, France	Mar. 19, 1861	31, 726
Anchor	E. P. McCarthy and J. Johnston.	San Francisco, Cal	Dec. 1, 1868	84, 565
Anchor	E. R. C. Morgan	Mumbles, South Wales	June 21, 1864	43, 273
Anchor	J. W. Morgan	Saltney, Great Britain	Apr. 20, 1869	89, 232
Anchor	G. Norton	Boston, Mass	Feb. 23, 1869	87, 109
Anchor	G. C. Pattison	Baltimore, Md	Jan. 24, 1871	111, 144
Anchor	G. C. Pattison	Baltimore, Md	Jan. 24, 1871	111, 145
Anchor	G. C. Pattison	Baltimore, Md	Sept. 18, 1866	58, 128
Anchor	G. C. Pattison	Baltimore, Md	Feb. 2, 1869	86, 439
Anchor	G. C. Pattison	Baltimore, Md	May 3, 1870	102, 583
Anchor	G. C. Pattison	Baltimore, Md	May 3, 1870	102, 584
Anchor	D. C. Pierce	Clayton, N. Y	Jan. 7, 1868	73, 035
Anchor	D. C. Pierce	Clayton, N. Y	Jan. 7, 1868	73, 036
Anchor	W. H. Porter	Great Britain	Mar. 18, 1842	2, 497
Anchor	C. W. Roeden	San Francisco, Cal	Nov. 24, 1868	84, 304
Anchor	J. W. Russell and D. Joline	Tottenville, N. Y	Jan. 28, 1868	73, 758
Anchor	W. W. Smith	Newcastle-on-Tyne, England.	Feb. 4, 1873	135, 450
Anchor	E. Snell	London, Great Britain	Aug. 29, 1869	49, 688
Anchor	W. Williams	Saint Louis, Mo	Mar. 16, 1858	19, 659
Anchor	F. Wittram	San Francisco, Cal	June 9, 1868	78, 852
Anchor	F. Wittram	San Francisco, Cal	Apr. 27, 1869	89, 454
Anchor and life-preserver, Combined floating	J. Humphries	Washington, D. C	Mar. 16, 1858	19, 638
Anchor, Apparatus for working	A. Campbell	Jersey City, N. J	July 3, 1860	28, 965
Anchor-ball	H. W. Harkness	Bristol, Conn	Aug. 24, 1858	21, 298
Anchor-cable of iron-clad vessels, Means for the protection of.	I. Newton	New York, N. Y	Feb. 9, 1864	41, 530
Anchor, Cast-iron	J. S. Stoddard	Palmyra, N. Y	July 2, 1836	....
Anchor, Cat-block for freeing a ship's	G. W. Duncan	Bath, Me	Apr. 28, 1863	38, 356
Anchor, Compound	S. N. Miller	West Roxbury, Mass	June 29, 1852	9, 076
Anchor, Floating	G. L. Baker	Astoria, N. Y	Feb. 12, 1867	61, 983
Anchor, Floating drag or	A. F. Lewis	Shopiere, Wis	Aug. 22, 1854	11, 555
Anchor for animal	P. H. Raiford	Houston, Tex	June 8, 1869	91, 042
Anchor, Grappling	A. S. and T. J. Trafton	Portsmouth, N. H	Mar. 30, 1869	88, 346
Anchor shackle, Second	G. Gilmour	Chelsea, Mass	Mar. 10, 1857	16, 821
Anchor shackle, Second	T. Leavitt	Malden, Mass	Jan. 3, 1860	26, 684
Anchor, Ship's	N. P. Isaacs and J. Raisbach	New York, N. Y	July 5, 1845	4, 096
Anchor-stock	J. L. Hanly	San Francisco, Cal	May 14, 1867	64, 762
Anchor-stopper	G. H. Babcock	Providence, R. I	Aug. 7, 1866	56, 873
Anchor-stopper, Cat-head	W. H. Barker	Windsor, Nova Scotia	Dec. 13, 1870	109, 998
Anchor-stopper, Cat-head	P. H. Jackson	New York, N. Y	Nov. 27, 1855	13, 847
Anchor-tripper	T. L. Baylies	Richmond, Ind	Apr. 19, 1859	23, 654
Anchor-tripper	S. R. Bryant	New York, N. Y	Feb. 27, 1855	12, 435
Anchor-tripper	E. Davidson	Providence, R. I	Jan. 23, 1866	52, 143
Anchor-tripper	G. Gibson	Port Richmond, N. Y	Dec. 5, 1865	51, 305
Anchor-tripper	B. H. Heitmann	Hoboken, N. J	May 16, 1865	47, 720
Anchor-tripper	H. Higgins	Orleans, Mass	Jan. 10, 1860	26, 765
Anchor-tripper	J. B. Holmes	New York, N. Y	Apr. 28, 1857	17, 182
Anchor-tripper	J. B. Hopkins	Dennis Port, Mass	Apr. 6, 1869	88, 571
Anchor-tripper	W. Stacey	Kittery, Me	Dec. 27, 1864	45, 649
Anchor, Water	N. W. Wheeler	Brooklyn, N. Y	June 11, 1867	65, 625
Anchor-well and anchor	R. and T. Winans	Baltimore, Md	Jan. 29, 1861	31, 276
Anchors, Making and fagoting	J. Tucker and J. Judge	Washington, D C	Nov. 19, 1829	....
Anchors, Means for casting	J. Evans, jr	Millbridge, Me	Aug. 13, 1867	67, 741
Anchors, Mode of recovering lost	C. B. Whittemore	Boston, Mass	Sept. 3, 1867	68, 402
Anchoring stationary machinery	S. Boone	Le Gros, Ind	Aug. 20, 1867	67, 943
Andiron	J. T. Dee and I. Murray	Fredericktown, Mo	Apr. 30, 1872	126, 273
Andiron	W. Dexter	Winchester, Conn	May 17, 1814	....
Andiron	J. B. Logan	Blountville, Tenn	Mar. 27, 1860	27, 640
Andiron	W. Pye	New York, N. Y	Nov. 16, 1821	....
Andiron	J. B. Sargent	New Britain, Conn	Aug. 17, 1858	21, 218
Andiron	J. Stickney	Baltimore, Md	May 4, 1805	....
Andiron and fire-place	F. Passy	Paris, France	June 23, 1868	79, 253
Andiron and fire-place	J. Sweet	Berkshire, Mass	Feb. 26, 1811	....
Andiron-bars	J. Cochran	Batavia, N. Y	July 1, 1836	....
Andirons, Construction of	J. R. Remington	Lowndes County, Ala	May 16, 1846	4, 523
Andirons, Construction of	E. Smylie	New York, N. Y	July 12, 1843	3, 170
Andirons, Construction of feet of brass	J. Griffiths	New York, N. Y	Mar. 15, 1827	....
Andirons, Manufacturing	W. Wilson	Greenfield, Mass	May 16, 1832	....
Andirons, Pedestal feet for	E. Smylie	New York, N. Y	Feb. 1, 1827	....
Andirons, Preparing and finishing	E. Smylie	New York, N. Y	Feb. 22, 1827	....
Anemometer	G. R. Stuntz	Superior, Wis	Feb. 4, 1862	34, 321
Anemometer, Electrical	F. S. Baldwin	Saint Louis, Mo	July 1, 1873	140, 340
Angle-instrument	B. Dearborn	Boston, Mass	Apr. 29, 1808	....
Angle-iron cutter	A. McGuffie	Buffalo, N. Y	Dec. 9, 1873	145, 437
Angle-iron, Machine for bending	D. Bell	Buffalo, N. Y	Dec. 15, 1863	40, 899
Angle-protractor	H. Taylor	United States Navy	Dec. 20, 1864	45, 535
Angles, Gage for determining	E. C. C. Kellogg	Hartford, Conn	Nov. 13, 1866	59, 721
Angler's combined float and sinker	J. W. Hoard	Providence, R. I	Dec. 12, 1854	12, 060
Angler's float	J. A. Terrell	Bloomfield, Ky	Feb. 2, 1869	86, 609
Angler's reel	W. H. Bradley	New York, N. Y	Sept. 22, 1868	82, 377
Angling-fly	J. Mullaly	New York, N. Y	May 20, 1873	139, 180
Angling-reel	C. L. Noe	Bergen Point, N. J	Jan. 28, 1873	135, 283
Angulometer, Plane	E. Thayer	Worcester, Mass	Aug. 26, 1862	36, 312
Aniline colors	G. E. C. Delaire	Paris, France	July 30, 1861	32, 965
Aniline colors, Compound of	E. Zinssmann	New York, N. Y	Mar. 24, 1868	76, 031
Aniline colors for dyeing and printing, Method of preparing.	A. S. L. Leonhardt	Berlin, Prussia	Sept. 12, 1865	49, 958

Index of patents issued from the United States Patent Office from 1790 *to* 1873, *inclusive*—Continued.

Invention.	Inventor.	Residence.	Date.	No.
Aniline colors, Manufacture of	P. Monnet	Lyons, France	Sept. 2, 1862	36, 357
Aniline colors, Preparation of	J. Renard	Lyons, France	July 31, 1860	29, 424
Aniline colors, Producing	P. Monnet	Lyons, France	Sept. 2, 1862	36, 356
Aniline red, Manufacture of	C. and A. Clemm	Philadelphia, Pa., and Manheim, Baden.	Oct. 10, 1865	50, 335
Anilines, Manufacture of coloring-matter from	P. Chevalier	Lyons, France	Mar. 13, 1866	53, 241
Animal and bird trap	A. T. Latta	Camden, S. C	July 14, 1868	79, 987
Animal and bird trap	G. C. Stamper	Pella, Iowa	June 23, 1868	79, 154
Animal and game trap	J. H. Richardson	Westport, Mo	May 2, 1871	114, 343
Animal and insect trap	W. W. Hannah	Hudson, N. Y	July 29, 1873	141, 346
Animal and vegetable substances, Apparatus for drying and curing.	M. J. Stein	New York, N. Y	Mar. 26, 1872	124, 982
Animal and vegetable substances, Apparatus for packing.	F. Stabler	Baltimore, Md	Mar. 20, 1866	53, 355
Animal and vegetable substances for curing meat, tanning, &c., Apparatus for decomposing.	D. Bruce	Rossville, N. Y	Jan. 22, 1867	61, 315
Animal-cage trap	S. W. Rice	Roseburgh, Oreg	Apr. 15, 1873	137, 864
Animal-cage, Wheel for	G. R. Peckham	Worcester, Mass	Sept. 1, 1868	81, 678
Animal-carcass scraping-machine	R. C. Tompkins	New York, N. Y	Nov. 11, 1873	144, 579
Animal-cleaning machine	C. D. Wheeler	New York, N. Y	Nov. 29, 1859	26, 313
Animal deposits in streets, Apparatus for preventing.	E. Berlinger	New York, N. Y	Nov. 12, 1872	133, 007
Animal-dosing instrument	O. Barker	Brooklyn, N. Y	Mar. 22, 1870	100, 967
Animal-fats, Treating	H. Mége	Paris, France	Dec. 30, 1873	146, 012
Animal-fetter	M. E. Burlingame	Willett, N. Y	July 29, 1862	35, 991
Animal-fetter	M. E. Burlingame	Willett, N. Y	Aug. 1, 1865	49, 081
Animal-gag	W. H. H. Hallock	Mattituck, N. Y	Oct. 17, 1871	120, 062
Animal-marking instrument	J. S. Bodle	Mechlenburg, N. Y	Mar. 5, 1867	62, 596
Animal matter, Apparatus for treating and drying.	W. C. Marshall	New York, N. Y	Apr. 8, 1873	137, 699
Animal matter, Drying and disintegrating	C. C. Coe	Hartford, Conn	Aug. 19, 1873	141, 853
Animal matter, Machine for cutting and grinding	A. Smith	Cincinnati, Ohio	Nov. 26, 1867	71, 544
Animal matter, oil, &c., Drying and deodorizing	M. J. Stein	New York, N. Y	June 4, 1872	127, 670
Animal matter, Process and apparatus for treating and drying.	C. G. Bruce and M. J. Stein	New York, N. Y	Oct. 15, 1872	132, 243
Animal matter, Process and apparatus for treatment of.	M. J. Stein	New York, N. Y	Nov. 5, 1872	132, 873
Animal matters, Mode of salting	C. Payne	South Lambeth, England	Sept. 11, 1841	2, 247
Animal or other power to propel machinery, Constructing machine for applying.	I. F. Moore	Falmouth, Va	May 4, 1841	2, 073
Animal-power	J. J. Adgate	Liberty, N. Y	Apr. 28, 1868	77, 236
Animal-power	H. Bolton	Elizabethtown, Canada	Jan. 23, 1872	122, 907
Animal-power	H. F. Carpenter	Polo, Ill	Sept. 24, 1872	131, 498
Animal-power	J. R. Deyo	Sterling, Ill	Apr. 9, 1872	125, 444
Animal-power	J. C. Gentry	Philadelphia, Pa	Dec. 14, 1830	....
Animal-power	J. B. Hall	Cheshire, N. Y	Nov. 23, 1869	97, 193
Animal-power	W. Patterson	Oneonta, N. Y	Aug. 8, 1871	117, 922
Animal-power	C. M. and G. Richards	Harpersville, N. Y	May 9, 1865	47, 659
Animal-power	H. Rosameyer, jr	Allegheny City, Pa	June 11, 1872	127, 800
Animal-power	T. Starr	New Lisbon, Ohio	Dec. 1, 1868	84, 590
Animal-power	M. G. Wood	Church Corners, Mich	Oct. 24, 1871	120, 357
Animal-power, Adjustable	N. Potter	East Troy, Pa	Feb. 28, 1871	112, 179
Animal-power apparatus	O. M. Brock	Monroeton, Pa	Jan. 10, 1871	110, 892
Animal-power, Endless chain for	G. N. Palmer	Greene, N. Y	June 3, 1873	139, 604
Animal-power, Machine for applying	J. Dearborn	Seabrook, N. H	May 21, 1867	64, 951
Animal-power, Propelling machinery by	S. Cooper	Augusta County, Va	Apr. 12, 1830	....
Animal-power to mechanical purposes, Applying	W. E. Arnold	Chatham, Conn	May 7, 1831	....
Animal-seizing device	D. Fasig	Rowsburg, Ohio	May 11, 1869	89, 922
Animal-shearing apparatus	C. A. J. Lengelée	Paris, France	Mar. 25, 1873	137, 220
Animal-shoeing stock	J. Sinclair	Davenport, Iowa	Nov. 11, 1862	36, 920
Animal substances, Separating fatty matter from	H. A. Amelung	Chicago, Ill	Jan. 27, 1863	37, 482
Animal-tether	T. N. Wheeler	Blue Earth City, Minn	July 5, 1870	105, 018
Animal-trap	A. J. Adams	Portland, Oreg	Apr. 28, 1868	77, 157
Animal-trap	H. Adams	Erie County, Pa	Aug. 10, 1833	....
Animal-trap	S. L. Allen	Cinnaminson, N. J	July 16, 1872	129, 203
Animal-trap	H. L. Anderson	Smithville, Ind	Apr. 9, 1867	63, 603
Animal-trap	C. Angle	Hazel Green, Mich	June 28, 1870	104, 684
Animal-trap	J. Annis	Galva, Ill	Oct. 18, 1864	44, 763
Animal-trap	S. M. Armstead	Grand Haven, Mich	Dec. 31, 1867	72, 713
Animal-trap	H. H. C. Arnold	Burlington, Kans	Feb. 27, 1872	124, 027
Animal-trap	H. H. C. Arnold	Nicholasville, Ky	Dec. 2, 1873	145, 082
Animal-trap	S. Arnold	Silver Springs, Tenn	June 21, 1870	104, 406
Animal-trap	S. Arnold	Silver Springs, Tenn	Aug. 2, 1870	105, 880
Animal-trap	S. Ayres	Worcester, Mass	Jan. 12, 1869	85, 780
Animal-trap	H. J. Baddeley	Napa, Cal	Dec. 3, 1872	133, 557
Animal-trap	L. V. Badger	Chicago, Ill	July 9, 1867	66, 550
Animal-trap	J. W. Bagby	Northcutt's Store, Ky	Aug. 31, 1869	94, 173
Animal-trap	H. Bagley	Mechanicsville, Iowa	Mar. 29, 1864	42, 063
Animal-trap	F. P. Baker	Boston, Mass	Sept. 7, 1869	94, 464
Animal-trap	L. J. Baker	East Machias, Me	Dec. 5, 1865	51, 283
Animal-trap	W. Ball	Oregon, Mo	Aug. 9, 1870	106, 107
Animal-trap	G. T. Barker	Pittsfield, Mass	May 12, 1863	38, 458
Animal-trap	G. Barr	Clatskanie, Oreg	Nov. 12, 1872	132, 948
Animal-trap	T. J. Belford	Worthington, Ohio	Feb. 16, 1869	87, 022
Animal-trap	H. Belmer	Cincinnati, Ohio	Aug 13, 1867	67, 709
Animal-trap	J. Biddle	Edinburgh, Pa	Aug. 29, 1871	118, 581
Animal-trap	W. Biddle	Pittsburgh, Pa	July 12, 1839	1, 238
Animal-trap	W. J. and H. L. Biddle	New Madison, Ohio	Feb. 18, 1868	74, 658
Animal-trap	T. Bingham	Stockport, Ohio	Jan. 5, 1869	85, 634
Animal-trap	A. S. Blake	Waterbury, Conn	Apr. 26, 1859	23, 750
Animal-trap	J. Blame	Mount Pleasant, Md	Dec. 14, 1869	97, 755
Animal-trap	J. L. Brabyn	New York, N. Y	Apr. 6, 1858	19, 825
Animal-trap	L. B. Bradley	Watertown, Conn	Aug. 28, 1855	13, 483
Animal-trap	J. W. Bradway	Akron, Ind	Mar. 31, 1863	38, 024
Animal-trap	J. Branch	Mooers, N. Y	Sept. 14, 1869	94, 708
Animal-trap	A. C. Briant	Lafayette, Ind	Feb. 25, 1868	74, 886
Animal-trap	W. W. Brigg	Home, Tenn	June 20, 1871	116, 017
Animal-trap	A. Brown	Bridgeport, Oreg	Dec. 21, 1869	98, 023
Animal-trap	E. Brown	Wayne, Mich	May 4, 1869	89, 626

Index of patents issued from the United States Patent Office from 1790 *to* 1873, *inclusive.*—Continued.

Invention.	Inventor.	Residence.	Date.	No.
Animal-trap	G. W. Brown	Sacramento, Cal	Dec. 3, 1867	71, 693
Animal-trap	M. D. Brown	Newburgh, Tenn	Nov. 28, 1871	121, 324
Animal-trap	D. R. Bruton	Thomasville, N. C	June 29, 1869	92, 010
Animal-trap	A. Burnham	Montague, Mass	May 19, 1863	38, 559
Animal-trap	M. Butler	Vernon, Ind	Feb. 25, 1868	74, 887
Animal-trap	L. W. Buxton	Nashua, N. H	Apr. 24, 1860	27, 967
Animal-trap	J. Caffrey	Paradise Township, Pa	Jan. 2, 1855	12, 125
Animal-trap	A. Campbell	Oxford, Ind	Sept. 1, 1868	81, 596
Animal-trap	W. H. Campbell	Brooklyn, N. Y	July 10, 1866	56, 175
Animal-trap	C. R. Capps	Illiopolis, Ill	Feb. 25, 1868	74, 889
Animal-trap	H. C. Case	Pekin, Ill	Mar. 8, 1870	100, 599
Animal-trap	W. F. Caswell	Raynham, Mass	July 25, 1865	48, 905
Animal-trap	R. Chadwick	Nantucket, Mass	July 30, 1861	32, 961
Animal-trap	La F. C. Chamberlin	Osawatomie, Kan	Mar. 12, 1872	124, 417
Animal-trap	J. W. Churchill	Pittston, Pa	Aug. 15, 1865	49, 378
Animal-trap	J. W. Churchill	Pittston, Pa	Nov. 26, 1867	71, 364
Animal-trap	G. E. Clarke	Racine, Wis	Dec. 26, 1865	51, 777
Animal-trap	G. E. Clarke	Racine, Wis	Dec. 4, 1866	60, 143
Animal-trap	G. E. Clarke	Racine, Wis	Aug. 27, 1867	68, 046
Animal-trap	W. J. Clarkson	Gourdin's Depot, N. E. R. R., S. C.	Feb. 1, 1870	99, 293
Animal-trap	J. J. Cline	High Hill, Ohio	Apr. 14, 1868	76, 713
Animal-trap	D. Cole	Orwell, Pa	Aug. 28, 1866	57, 480
Animal-trap	W. F. Collier	Worcester, Mass	Feb. 15, 1870	99, 995
Animal-trap	I. N. Connell	Spencer's Station, Ohio	Aug. 20, 1867	67, 959
Animal-trap	J. Coombe	San José, Cal	Feb. 6, 1872	123, 381
Animal-trap	J. F. Coppock	Dexter, Iowa	Oct. 10, 1871	119, 826
Animal-trap	J. Ccsolowsky	Titusville, Pa	Nov. 8, 1870	109, 112
Animal-trap	G. G. Cottrell	Sharon, Conn	June 5, 1866	55, 245
Animal-trap	H. H. Cottrill	Vinton Station, Ohio	Mar. 9, 1869	87, 548
Animal-trap	W. Cover	Jenner's Cross Roads, Pa	Jan. 7, 1868	72, 979
Animal-trap	R. S. Craig	Cincinnati, Ohio	Nov. 7, 1854	11, 887
Animal-trap	E. H. Crane	Jonesville, Mich	July 5, 1864	43, 396
Animal-trap	J. Curtis	Saint Charles, Minn	Oct. 15, 1867	69, 777
Animal-trap	E. A. C. Da Silva	New York, N. Y	Feb. 11, 1873	135, 732
Animal-trap	A. W. Davis	South Haven, Mich	Nov. 19, 1872	133, 082
Animal-trap	G. H. Davis	Patten, Me	Jan. 30, 1872	123, 089
Animal-trap	W. H. Davis	Lexington, Ind	Dec. 24, 1867	72, 461
Animal-trap	J. M. Dearborn	Boston, Mass	Mar. 3, 1868	74, 998
Animal-trap	H. D. Deming and P. G. Walker.	Delmar, Pa	Mar. 5, 1861	31, 651
Animal-trap	J. Dildine	Limestoneville, Pa	Dec. 10, 1872	133, 836
Animal-trap	S. F. Dimock	Spencer, Ohio	Nov. 27, 1866	59, 980
Animal-trap	M. W. Drake	Owasso, Mich	Aug. 3, 1869	93, 185
Animal-trap	U. H. Duparck	Albion, Mich	Sept. 13, 1864	44, 168
Animal-trap	A. J. Eddy and J. B. Wilber	Winnesheik County and Howard County, Iowa.	Dec. 13, 1864	45, 399
Animal-trap	A. Edwards	Chicago, Ill	Sept. 5, 1865	49, 735
Animal-trap	A. Ellis and O. Albertson	Salem, Ind	July 31, 1866	56, 735
Animal-trap	A. Ellis and O. Albertson	Salem, Ind	Dec. 24, 1867	72, 470
Animal trap	J. W. Ells	Pittsburgh, Pa	Apr. 13, 1869	88, 778
Animal-trap	J. H. Elward	Polo, Ill	Jan. 9, 1866	51, 933
Animal-trap	J. P. Emswiler	Knightstown, Ind	June 25, 1867	66, 007
Animal-trap	S. F. Estell	Richmond, Ind	Oct. 16, 1866	58, 795
Animal-trap	S. F. Estell	Richmond, Ind	Nov. 20, 1866	59, 762
Animal-trap	S. F. Estell	Richmond, Ind	Aug. 18, 1868	81, 265
Animal-trap	S. F. Estell	Chicago, Ill	Feb. 4, 1873	135, 534
Animal-trap	E. B. Everitt	West Meriden, Conn	June 14, 1870	104, 293
Animal-trap	O. S. Ewing	Rome, Tenn	Nov. 14, 1871	120, 953
Animal-trap	J. B. Fairchild	Covington, Ky	June 12, 1866	55, 478
Animal-trap	L. Faris	Princetown, Ohio	Feb. 23, 1869	87, 159
Animal-trap	T. Fell	New York, N. Y	Oct. 3, 1871	119, 592
Animal-trap	W. A. Fenn	Rochester, N. Y	Apr. 27, 1869	89, 300
Animal-trap	A. C. Flanders	Owatonna, Minn	June 15, 1869	91, 427
Animal-trap	J. M. Flautt	Reedsburgh, Wis	Dec. 27, 1864	45, 595
Animal-trap	F. Flora	Pierce, Ohio	Jan. 28, 1873	135, 268
Animal-trap	H. Foust	Mill Village, Pa	Oct. 3, 1871	119, 594
Animal-trap	F. Fox	Meadville, Pa	June 21, 1870	104, 570
Animal-trap	A. A. Fradenburg	Nevada City, Cal	May 22, 1866	54, 885
Animal-trap	D. M. Francisco	Three Rivers, Mich	Dec. 5, 1871	121, 608
Animal-trap	S. Frisbie and H. C. Hart	Unionville, Conn	Apr. 9, 1872	125, 449
Animal-trap	A. Frost	Seymour, Ind	June 11, 1867	65, 661
Animal-trap	H. S. Frost	Watertown, Conn	Oct. 31, 1871	120, 375
Animal-trap	C. G. Frushour	La Gro, Ind	Oct. 19, 1869	95, 893
Animal-trap	S. Gibson	Martic Township, Pa	July 13, 1858	20, 873
Animal-trap	W. S. Gitchell	Peru, Ind	Feb. 28, 1865	46, 557
Animal-trap	J. Gould	Clinton, Pa	June 3, 1873	139, 572
Animal-trap	J. W. Greene	Chillicothe, Mo	Jan. 7, 1873	134, 539
Animal-trap	H. Hackman, jr	Pequea, Pa	June 16, 1857	17, 570
Animal-trap	J. Haddleton	Rochester, N. Y	Sept. 24, 1867	69, 089
Animal-trap	J. H. Hair	Galesburgh, Ill	June 17, 1873	140, 036
Animal-trap	W. R. Hampton	Fairfield, Ill	Nov. 29, 1870	109, 614
Animal-trap	B. F. Hancock	Monroe, Wis	Apr. 28, 1868	77, 372
Animal-trap	G. Haneline	Akron, Ohio	Aug. 10, 1869	93, 533
Animal-trap	G. R. Harding	Manchester, Va	Oct. 17, 1871	120, 063
Animal-trap	B. and D. H. Harnish	Lancaster and Pequea, Pa	Apr. 2, 1872	125, 290
Animal-trap	G. Hart	Granger, Ohio	Sept. 1, 1857	18, 092
Animal-trap	G. L. Hart	New Britain, Conn	Jan. 17, 1871	110, 973
Animal-trap	G. L. and H. C. Hart	Unionville, Conn	Oct. 18, 1864	44, 721
Animal-trap	S. H. and H. C. Hart	Unionville, Conn	Feb. 14, 1871	111, 841
Animal-trap	D. Harwood	Dutch Flat, Cal	July 20, 1869	92, 823
Animal-trap	E. E. Haughwout	New York, N. Y	Apr. 5, 1870	101, 459
Animal-trap	E. Hause and L. Kelley	Tecumseh, Mich	July 18, 1871	117, 072
Animal-trap	C. Henert	Washington, D. C	June 22, 1869	91, 744
Animal-trap	J. Herr	Carbondale, Ill	June 8, 1869	91, 131
Animal-trap	N. T. Hersch	Round Hill, Pa	June 7, 1870	104, 031
Animal-trap	J. M. Hill	Cisne, Ill	Feb. 20, 1872	123, 779
Animal-trap	T. M. Hill	Richmond, Ind	Nov. 3, 1868	83, 633
Animal-trap	S. Hoke	Union City, Ind	Oct. 29, 1867	70, 336

Index of patents issued from the United States Patent Office from 1790 *to* 1873, *inclusive*—Continued.

Invention.	Inventor.	Residence.	Date.	No.
Animal-trap	J. W. Hollingsworth	Seymour, Ind	Oct. 16, 1866	58, 826
Animal-trap	J. W. Hollingsworth	Salem, Ind	May 21, 1867	64, 869
Animal-trap	A. A. Hotchkiss	Sharon, Conn	Feb. 14, 1871	111, 745
Animal-trap	J. W. F. How	Douglas County, Oreg	Mar. 28, 1871	113, 168
Animal-trap	J. W. F. How	Canyonville, Oreg	Mar. 19, 1872	124, 821
Animal-trap	N. S. Howell	Tualitin, Oreg	Nov. 14, 1871	120, 877
Animal-trap	S. Huffman	Westfield, Ill	Feb. 25, 1868	74, 759
Animal-trap	J. Hughson	Buffalo, N. Y	Sept. 7, 1869	94, 496
Animal-trap	W. Huntington	Howell, Mich	Dec. 17, 1867	72, 396
Animal-trap	B. Illingworth	Freeport, Ill	Oct. 22, 1867	70, 093
Animal-trap	L. E. Ingersoll	Columbus, Pa	June 11, 1872	127, 887
Animal-trap	G. Irwin	Elizabethtown, Ky	July 9, 1867	66, 592
Animal-trap	W. B. Jarvis	Washington, N. C	Feb. 23, 1869	87, 173
Animal-trap	C. Jillson	Worcester, Mass	Nov. 16, 1858	22, 078
Animal-trap	S. F. Jones	Saint Paul, Ind	May 1, 1866	54, 361
Animal-trap	P. W. King	Lowville, N. Y	May 5, 1868	77, 622
Animal-trap	A. Kinkead	Greenwich, Ohio	June 7, 1864	43, 030
Animal-trap	G. W. Kintz	Rochester, N. Y	Mar. 16, 1869	87, 945
Animal-trap	T. B. Kirby	Flowerfield, Mich	Sept. 8, 1868	82, 008
Animal-trap	S. Knight	Adel, Iowa	Dec. 12, 1865	51, 463
Animal-trap	J. Kohler	Cincinnati, Ohio	July 7, 1868	79, 577
Animal-trap	J. O. Kopas	Washington, D. C	Apr. 19, 1870	102, 134
Animal-trap	J. O. Kopas and G. W. Bauer	Washington, D. C	Apr. 19, 1870	102, 133
Animal-trap	J. Krummenauer	New York, N. Y	Mar. 4, 1873	136, 378
Animal-trap	G. F. Lampkin	Georgetown, Ky	July 9, 1872	128, 802
Animal-trap	W. S. Lawrence	Winchester, Ky	Jan. 21, 1873	135, 134
Animal-trap	D. A. Leach	Bloomington, Ind	Sept. 23, 1873	143, 169
Animal-trap	H. Lee	Oberlin, Ohio	Feb. 12, 1867	61, 941
Animal-trap	J. A. Lee	Chattanooga, Tenn	Nov. 3, 1868	83, 642
Animal-trap	W. W. Leech	Pittsburgh, Pa	Feb. 25, 1868	74, 762
Animal-trap	H. S. Lesher	Galesburgh, Ill	Sept. 1, 1868	81, 798
Animal-trap	L. Lewis	Tuskegee, Ala	Feb. 13, 1872	123, 633
Animal-trap	J. Liming	Philadelphia, Pa	Dec. 22, 1863	41, 012
Animal-trap	W. D. Lindsley	Eudora, Kans	June 14, 1870	104, 172
Animal-trap	N. M. Linton	Wilmington, Ohio	Nov. 19, 1867	71, 188
Animal-trap	C. Long	Newark, Ohio	May 23, 1871	115, 222
Animal-trap	J. H. Lord	San Francisco, Cal	Apr. 26, 1870	102, 411
Animal-trap	A. M. Lovett	Zanesville, Ohio	Mar. 18, 1873	136, 842
Animal-trap	J. N. Lowrance	Montezuma, Ill	July 16, 1872	129, 415
Animal-trap	N. B. Lucas	Jersey County, Ill	Apr. 11, 1848	5, 508
Animal-trap	W. Luker	Kalamazoo, Mich	Nov. 16, 1869	96, 821
Animal-trap	H. F. Lushbaugh and O. Z. Hurd	Mount Pulaski, Ill	Nov. 24, 1868	84, 291
Animal-trap	C. C. Lyman	Edenborough, Pa	Dec. 17, 1867	72, 211
Animal-trap	C. C. Lyman	Edenborough, Pa	Mar. 24, 1868	75, 777
Animal-trap	M. W. Lyman	Chicago, Ill	Mar. 15, 1870	100, 779
Animal-trap	M. W. Lyman	Chicago, Ill	Mar. 19, 1872	124, 838
Animal-trap	J. Manchester	New York, N. Y	Feb. 4, 1868	74, 105
Animal-trap	J. Manchester	New York, N. Y	Oct. 19, 1869	95, 920
Animal-trap	H. Mansfield	Warsaw, Ind	Aug. 20, 1867	67, 893
Animal-trap	T. E. Marable	Petersburgh, Va	Nov. 22, 1870	109, 530
Animal-trap	M. B. Marshall	Draw Bridge, Md	Mar. 10, 1868	75, 438
Animal-trap	D. J. Martin	Covington, Ohio	July 23, 1867	66, 980
Animal-trap	A. A. Mattern	Morrison, Ill	June 25, 1872	128, 233
Animal-trap	A. J. Matthews	Hartwell, Ga	June 10, 1873	139, 800
Animal-trap	R. B. May	Murfreesborough, Tenn	Feb. 25, 1873	136, 330
Animal-trap	J. C. McClamroch	Edina, Mo	May 26, 1868	78, 306
Animal-trap	W. McClure	Sinking Spring, Ohio	Oct. 13, 1868	83, 074
Animal-trap	C. Melone	Lawrence, Kans	Mar. 13, 1866	53, 164
Animal-trap	J. Merchen	Brookville, Ind	June 17, 1873	139, 967
Animal-trap	J. B. Merriman and G. B. Lewis	Plantsville, Conn	Nov. 8, 1870	109, 035
Animal-trap	G. W. Merritt and H. S. Gibbs	Norwalk, Conn	Jan. 26, 1869	86, 175
Animal-trap	O. Metcalf	Salem, Ind	Jan. 14, 1868	73, 254
Animal-trap	L. Meyer	Saint Louis, Mo	June 11, 1872	127, 701
Animal-trap	J. H. Miller	Vernon, Ind	Jan. 21, 1868	73, 625
Animal-trap	W. Miller	Chicopee, Mass	Feb. 25, 1868	74, 842
Animal-trap	J. H. Mooney and G. A. Lloyd	San Francisco, Cal	Sept. 26, 1871	119, 237
Animal-trap	L. Moore	Baraboo, Wis	July 13, 1869	92, 631
Animal-trap	W. Morris	Elkhart City, Ill	Apr. 9, 1867	63, 651
Animal-trap	J. Nampel	Freeport, Ill	Nov. 16, 1869	96, 946
Animal-trap	W. H. Newby	Seymour, Ind	May 1, 1866	54, 393
Animal-trap	J. Newell	Ypsilanti, Mich	Feb. 27, 1872	124, 149
Animal-trap	A. Newton	Darby Creek, Ohio	Aug. 30, 1870	106, 858
Animal-trap	G. A. Norman	Baltimore, Md	May 20, 1873	139, 182
Animal-trap	H. S. North and J. O. Couch	Middletown, Conn	June 28, 1859	24, 573
Animal-trap	H. Ogborn	Richmond, Ind	Nov. 19, 1867	71, 206
Animal-trap	E. Oliver	New York, N. Y	Dec. 13, 1870	110, 065
Animal-trap	E. Oliver	New York, N. Y	Feb. 14, 1871	111, 771
Animal-trap	D. J. Owen	Springville, Pa	Apr. 27, 1869	89, 429
Animal-trap	D. J. Owen	Springville, Pa	May 31, 1870	103, 767
Animal-trap	D. J. Owen	Springville, Pa	Apr. 29, 1873	138, 275
Animal-trap	G. W. Pagett	Adams Township, Ind	May 2, 1865	47, 563
Animal-trap	G. J. Parham	Harrodsburgh, Ind	Nov. 26, 1867	71, 321
Animal-trap	J. C. Parish	Petersburgh, Va	Feb. 7, 1871	111, 673
Animal-trap	W. Patterson	Waukegan, Ill	July 16, 1872	129, 295
Animal-trap	H. Pattison	Duck Creek, Ill	June 15, 1869	91, 363
Animal-trap	R. L. Payne	Halifax, Va	Nov. 2, 1858	21, 978
Animal-trap	J. D. Pell	New York, N. Y	Mar. 21, 1871	112, 844
Animal-trap	S. Pence	Eaton, Ohio	Oct. 8, 1867	69, 695
Animal-trap	L. V. Percival and J. Link	United States Army	Sept. 20, 1870	107, 532
Animal-trap	D. N. Phelps	San Leandro, Cal	Sept. 25, 1866	58, 2[illegible]6
Animal-trap	T. S. Phillips	Casadaga, N. Y	Oct. 8, 1867	69, 583
Animal-trap	O. Pier	Harmony, N. Y	June 27, 1854	11, 175
Animal-trap	D. Pittman	Fort Madison, Iowa	June 4, 1861	32, 486
Animal-trap	C. Polley	Shelbyville, Tenn	Sept. 7, 1869	94, 642
Animal-trap	H. Polley	San Francisco, Cal	Dec. 5, 1871	121, 468
Animal-trap	H. W. Prouty	Boston, Mass	Sept. 15, 1868	82, 246
Animal-trap	J. Quigley	Winona, Minn	May 28, 1861	32, 434
Animal-trap	S. S. Rain	Lowville, N. Y	Sept. 10, 1867	68, 651

Index of patents issued from the United States Patent Office from 1790 *to* 1873, *inclusive*—Continued.

Invention.	Inventor.	Residence.	Date.	No.
Animal-trap	S. S. Rain	Lowville, N. Y	July 7, 1868	79, 686
Animal-trap	N. Rasmussen	Chicago, Ill	Oct. 3, 1871	119, 645
Animal-trap	S. Reed	Whitestown, Pa	Jan. 14, 1868	73, 384
Animal-trap	W. N. Reed	Washington, D. C	Sept. 21, 1869	94, 975
Animal-trap	E. Reichard	Washington, Mo	Oct. 13, 1868	83, 094
Animal-trap	J. H. Reisinger	Vinton, Ohio	May 5, 1868	77, 657
Animal-trap	F. Reuthe	Hartford, Conn	May 12, 1857	17, 297
Animal-trap	F. Renthe	Hartford, Conn	Aug. 24, 1858	21, 302
Animal-trap	J. H. Richardson	Westport, Mo	Sept. 13, 1870	107, 292
Animal-trap	T. L. Rivers	Saint Louis, Mo	May 19, 1868	78, 015
Animal-trap	J. Rollins	Kingston, Tenn	Mar. 26, 1872	124, 976
Animal-trap	B. F. Sanford	Galesburgh, Ill	Dec. 5, 1865	51, 356
Animal-trap	J. Sebroy	Fortville, Ind	Nov. 5, 1867	70, 624
Animal-trap	H. Seehausen	Memphis, Tenn	Jan. 25, 1870	99, 245
Animal-trap	T. Shailer	Haddam, Conn	May 10, 1844	3, 580
Animal-trap	J. Sherman	New Oxford, Pa	Sept. 1, 1868	81, 829
Animal-trap	T. Silliman	Three Rivers, Mich	Nov. 26, 1867	71, 543
Animal-trap	T. Silliman	Three Rivers, Mich	Apr. 27, 1869	89, 352
Animal-trap	R. Simpson	Port Jefferson, Ohio	Oct. 29, 1867	70, 370
Animal-trap	J. A. Sinclair	Woodsfield, Ohio	Feb. 18, 1868	74, 617
Animal-trap	G. Slusser	Hillsborough, Ohio	Aug. 14, 1860	29, 627
Animal-trap	B. C. Smith	Pekin, Ill	July 11, 1871	117, 005
Animal-trap	B. F. Smith	Philadelphia, Pa	Oct. 14, 1873	143, 727
Animal-trap	E. B. Smith	Marietta, Ohio	June 30, 1868	79, 506
Animal-trap	O. R. Smith	Elgin, Minn	Aug. 11, 1868	81, 023
Animal-trap	V. O. and J. R Spencer	Mansfield, Pa	Feb. 7, 1860	27, 080
Animal-trap	E. Sprague and G. C. Belt	Bridgeton, Ind	June 28, 1870	104, 896
Animal-trap	W. A. Stack	Hillsborough, Md	Nov. 10, 1868	84, 013
Animal-trap	W. L. Starr	Columbus, Ohio	Mar. 31, 1868	76, 289
Animal-trap	J. J. St. Ledger	Philadelphia, Pa	Mar. 30, 1869	88, 526
Animal-trap	A. Storm	Brooklyn, N. Y	Feb. 5, 1867	61, 889
Animal-trap	J. N. Stow and R. Loop	Camden, Ohio	Apr. 25, 1871	114, 062
Animal-trap	Z. Swope	Lancaster, Pa	Aug. 16, 1859	25, 224
Animal-trap	J. Teed	Tompkins, N. Y	Apr. 16, 1867	63, 961
Animal-trap	A. C. Thomas	Camp Charlotte, Ohio	Feb. 11, 1868	74, 256
Animal-trap	J. S. Thompson	Sycamore, Ill	Feb. 11, 1868	74, 451
Animal-trap	N. S. Thompson	Germantown, Ohio	Jan. 21, 1868	73, 475
Animal-trap	W. Tinsley	New York, N. Y	Feb. 7, 1860	27, 083
Animal-trap	R. Tompkins	Clarksville, Tenn	Nov. 23, 1869	97, 248
Animal-trap	J. Trainer	Rural Dale, Ohio	Oct. 22, 1867	70, 133
Animal-trap	J. Trainer	Vinton Station, Ohio	May 19, 1868	78, 029
Animal-trap	C. S. Trevitt	Washington, D. C	Oct. 22, 1867	70, 134
Animal-trap	R. M. Turner	Woodland, Mich	Sept. 7, 1858	21, 454
Animal-trap	J. L. Tusten	Winona, Miss	Nov. 9, 1869	96, 744
Animal-trap	T. B. Van Pelt	Westport, Mo	July 20, 1869	92, 911
Animal-trap	C. B. Veroneo	Athens, Ga	Apr. 4, 1871	113, 371
Animal-trap	G. S. Walker	Erie, Pa	Aug. 22, 1871	118, 309
Animal-trap	S. Ward	Richmond, Ill	Sept. 24, 1867	69, 279
Animal-trap	A. L. Waring	Coshocton, Ohio	Oct. 13, 1868	83, 011
Animal-trap	A. Warner	Cleveland, Ohio	Sept. 23, 1862	36, 543
Animal-trap	J. Westcott	Patchogue, N. Y	Oct. 15, 1867	69, 878
Animal-trap	L. Wetmore	Tioga County, Pa	July 12, 1859	24, 771
Animal-trap	J. Wheelock	San Francisco, Cal	Mar. 7, 1865	46, 741
Animal-trap	J. P. Wigal	Henderson, Ky	Jan. 14, 1868	73, 418
Animal-trap	H. Y. Wildey	Philadelphia, Pa	Oct. 2, 1860	30, 269
Animal-trap	J. M. Wilkinson	Bloomington, Tenn	Sept. 2, 1873	142, 362
Animal-trap	W. T. Williams	New York, N. Y	Feb. 19, 1861	31, 504
Animal-trap	J. P. Wilson	Frankfort, N. Y	Jan. 31, 1860	27, 017
Animal-trap	G. Wolf	Williamsport, Md	Apr. 24, 1866	54, 241
Animal-trap	J. J. Wood	North Manchester, Ind	Sept. 27, 1870	107, 844
Animal-trap	R. E. Wood	Santa Cruz, Cal	Nov. 29, 1870	109, 789
Animal-trap	W. J. Woodside	Zanesville, Ohio	Apr. 28, 1868	77, 341
Animal-trap	W. Wright	Philadelphia, Pa	June 19, 1860	28, 820
Animal-trap	H. D. Wrightson	Queenstown, Md	Mar. 7, 1871	112, 403
Animal-trap	C. Zaiser	Newark, N. J	Feb. 11, 1868	74, 264
Animal-trap adjustable platform	J. Thomas	West Chester, Pa	June 26, 1849	6, 554
Animal-trap and seed-safe combined	S. V. Greer	Rocky Hill Station, Ky	July 15, 1873	140, 773
Animal-trap, Construction of	M. H. Biddle	Mount Carmel, Ill	Oct. 5, 1858	21, 647
Animal-trap, Construction of	E. Hill	Cincinnati, Ohio	Oct. 5, 1858	21, 676
Animal-trap, Device for setting	I. Miller	Bryan, Ohio	Sept. 10, 1867	68, 776
Animal-trap, Manufacture of	C. Jillson	Worcester, Mass	Jan. 6, 1857	16, 335
Animal-trap, Self-setting	H. B. Myers	Schoolcraft, Mich	Feb. 14, 1865	46, 379
Animal-trap wheel	W. F. Collier	Worcester, Mass	June 13, 1871	115, 933
Animal-trap wheel	B. B. and J. R. Hill	Worcester, Mass	July 4, 1871	116, 592
Animals against flies, Lotion for protecting	J. Greene	Providence, R. I	Oct. 24, 1871	120, 191
Animals, Apparatus for relieving choked	G. Clump	Hamden, Conn	Apr. 21, 1868	76, 998
Animals, Apparatus for taming wild	P. R. Sanderson	Caledonia, N. Y	Dec. 10, 1867	71, 914
Animals, Brand for marking	H. Thompson	Hector, N. Y	Apr. 30, 1867	64, 263
Animals, Device for catching	W. L. Hopper	Monmouth, Ill	Aug. 27, 1867	68, 197
Animals, Device for catching and holding domestic	H. V. Van Etten	Auburn, N. Y	Dec. 29, 1868	85, 413
Animals from railways, Apparatus for removing	L. Montgilion	Elk Ridge Landing, Md	Feb. 13, 1849	6, 113
Animals from the heat of the sun, Mode of protecting.	C. Elveena	New York, N. Y	Sept. 18, 1866	58, 081
Animals, Instrument for administering balls to	T. H. Bex	Syracuse, N. Y	June 17, 1873	139, 856
Animals, Slings for raising	F. Hohorst	New York, N. Y	Feb. 18, 1873	136, 059
Ankle-brace	J. S. Niswander	Oakland, Cal	Mar. 21, 1871	112, 952
Ankle-brace	S. B. Sherer	Aurora, Ill	Apr. 7, 1868	76, 353
Ankle-brace joint	E. E. Howe	Boston, Mass	Aug. 20, 1872	130, 639
Ankle or knee guard	H. A. Hall	Boston, Mass	May 12, 1868	77, 728
Ankle-supporter	R. Cunningham	Chicago, Ill	Mar. 20, 1866	53, 276
Ankle supporter and filler	S. Silberschmidt	Baltimore, Md	Oct. 7, 1873	143, 537
Ankles, Surgical apparatus for fractured or injured	G. W. Yerger	Philadelphia, Pa	Mar. 20, 1849	6, 214
Annealing and hardening metals, Process for	J. N. Lauth	Pittsburgh, Pa	Oct. 29, 1872	132, 675
Annealing and swaging castings, Method of	E. B. Wilson	Westminster, England	Sept. 17, 1861	33, 315
Annealing-apparatus	J. Worcester	Newport, Ky	Sept. 25, 1860	30, 174
Annealing-box	J. C. Lewis	Sharpsburgh, Pa	May 1, 1866	54, 376
Annealing car-wheels	A. L. Mowry	Cincinnati, Ohio	May 7, 1861	32, 252
Annealing cut nails	J. McCarty	Reading, Pa	June 11, 1861	32, 525

Index of patents issued from the United States Patent Office from 1790 *to* 1873, *inclusive*—Continued.

Invention.	Inventor.	Residence.	Date.	No.
Annealing-furnace	E. Bennett	Philadelphia, Pa	July 11, 1865	48, 761
Annealing-furnace	J. J. Eagleton	New York, N. Y	May 20, 1856	14, 908
Annealing-furnace	T. F. Hammer	Branford, Conn	Jan. 9, 1872	122, 604
Annealing-furnace	H. W. Moore	Bridgeport, Conn	Oct. 9, 1866	58, 666
Annealing-furnace	W. R. Thomas	Catasaqua, Pa	Jan. 14, 1868	73, 407
Annealing-furnace for sheet-iron, &c	J. Malone	Temperanceville, Pa	May 22, 1866	55, 014
Annealing-furnace, Nail and tack	E. G. Paull	Fair Haven, Mass	Apr. 13, 1869	88, 805
Annealing-furnace, Plowshare	W. M. Watson	Tonica, Ill	Feb. 6, 1872	123, 528
Annealing hollow iron-ware	D. Stuart	Philadelphia, Pa	Sept. 27, 1853	10, 057
Annealing metal, Process and apparatus for	J. M. Bottum	New York, N. Y	Nov. 16, 1869	96, 874
Annealing pot and saucer	J. Hibell	Nechells, England	July 7, 1868	79, 759
Annotto, Solution of	A. Macphail	Jersey City, N. J	June 7, 1864	43, 034
Annunciator	J. S. Birch	New York, N. Y	Dec. 1, 1868	84, 474
Annunciator	J. Capron	New York, N. Y	Dec. 27, 1870	110, 547
Annunciator	M. L. Deering	New York, N. Y	Jan. 2, 1866	51, 809
Annunciator	C. H. Greenleaf	Franconia, N. H	July 9, 1872	128, 724
Annunciator	C. H. Greenleaf	Franconia, N. H	Aug. 19, 1873	141, 927
Annunciator	H. Gross and G. S. Zingling	Tiffin, Ohio	Nov. 5, 1867	70, 552
Annunciator	H. Horsfall	New York, N. Y	Oct. 31, 1856	50, 709
Annunciator	S. F. Nichols	Trappe, Md	May 28, 1872	127, 185
Annunciator	A. Rankin	Philadelphia, Pa	Feb. 17, 1863	37, 706
Annunciator and fire-alarm, Hotel	E. A. Hill	Chicago, Ill	Apr. 25, 1871	114, 007
Annunciator, Electric	J. B. Shannon	Philadelphia, Pa	June 11, 1872	127, 931
Annunciator, Electric	G. W. Shawk	Cleveland, Ohio	June 10, 1873	139, 826
Annunciator, Electric	A. Storer	Cleveland, Ohio	Aug. 19, 1873	141, 898
Annunciator, Electric hotel	W. W. Foot	Saybrook, Ohio	June 24, 1873	140, 129
Annunciator, Electric vote	T. B. Doolittle	Bridgeport, Conn	Oct. 14, 1873	143, 679
Annunciator, Electro-magnetic	C. S. Bulkley	New York, N. Y	Nov. 15, 1853	10, 226
Annunciator, Electro-magnetic	J. Capron	New York, N. Y	Aug. 15, 1871	117, 979
Annunciator, Electro-magnetic	C. E. Chinnock	New York, N. Y	Feb. 20, 1872	123, 808
Annunciator, Electro-magnetic	E. Gray	Chicago, Ill	Aug. 22, 1871	118, 231
Annunciator, Electro-magnetic	W. Humans	Cambridge, Mass	Mar. 4, 1873	136, 518
Annunciator, Electro-magnetic	W. N. McInnis	Northumberland, Pa	Mar. 29, 1870	101, 372
Annunciator, Electro-magnetic	G. W. Shawk and A. Storer	Cleveland, Ohio	Mar. 4, 1873	136, 465
Annunciator for hotels, &c., Electro-magnetic	O. Hagendorf	New York, N. Y	Dec. 17, 1872	134, 053
Annunciator for railway-carriage	M. H. Ford	Boston, Mass	May 8, 1849	6, 442
Annunciator for signals in hotels, &c., Electro-magnetic.	C. S. Bulkley	Macon, Ga	Oct. 29, 1850	7, 739
Annunciator, Hotel	J. Bale	Buffalo, N. Y	Feb. 27, 1855	12, 433
Annunciator, Hotel	J. H. H. Bennett	Hunt's Hollow, N. Y	Dec. 17, 1861	33, 926
Annunciator, Hotel	W. H. Hale	Worcester, Mass	Apr. 22, 1856	14, 719
Annunciator, Hotel	W. Horsfall	New York, N. Y	Oct. 4, 1853	10, 071
Annunciator, Hotel	H. B. Porter	Chicago, Ill	Nov. 19, 1867	71, 214
Annunciator, Hotel	L. J. Vansands	Chicago, Ill	Oct. 5, 1869	95, 620
Annunciator, Hotel electrical	H. B. Porter	Chicago, Ill	Dec. 28, 1869	98, 296
Annunciator, Magnetic	J. Blackie	Washington, D. C	July 26, 1864	43, 633
Annunciator or bell-telegraph	J. Garvey	New York, N. Y	Nov. 19, 1850	7, 783
Annunciators, Electro-magnetic hotel	G. B. Scott	Brooklyn, N. Y	Jan. 9, 1872	122, 664
Annunciator, Speaking-tube	R. May	New York, N. Y	July 2, 1872	128, 552
Annunciator, Speaking-tube	D. Rousseau	New York, N. Y	June 10, 1873	139, 818
Ant-destroying composition	J. D. Dennis	Gilroy, Cal	June 8, 1869	91, 094
Ant-destroying process	J. J. Dulany and H. Dreyer	Oakland, Tex	Oct. 28, 1873	144, 075
Ant-obstructing device	E. Rooks	Trenton, Tenn	Feb. 14, 1871	111, 875
Ant-trap	T. G. Ames	Kosse, Tex	Apr. 1, 1873	137, 336
Ant-trap	G. W. Cottingham and J. S. Menefee.	Texana, Tex	Aug. 7, 1860	29, 468
Ant-trap	L. Rubarth	Davilla, Tex	July 15, 1873	140, 954
Anthracene, Apparatus for preparing	J. C. F. Cheever	New York, N. Y	Sept. 17, 1872	131, 393
Anthracene, Apparatus for preparing	H. J. Fenner and F. Versmann.	Greenwich and London, England.	Apr. 30, 1872	126, 277
Anthracene, Manufacture of	H. J. Fenner and F. Versmann.	Greenwich and London, England.	Aug. 27, 1872	130, 909
Anthracite and other fuel, Promoting combustion of.	P. Davis	Baltimore, Md	July 29, 1834	....
Anti-attrition compound	E. Mott	Philadelphia, Pa	Oct. 4, 1817	....
Anti-friction axle and journal-box	J. H. Carkeet	Montgomery, Ala	Dec. 31, 1867	72, 796
Anti-friction box	J. L. Dutton, sr	Philadelphia, Pa	Dec. 20, 1859	26, 483
Anti-friction box	D. A. Morris	Pittsburgh, Pa	Mar. 21, 1854	10, 676
Anti friction box	G. T. Parry	Spring Garden, Pa	Aug. 2, 1853	9, 912
Anti-friction box	J. L. Parry	Philadelphia, Pa	Nov. 9, 1869	96, 720
Anti-friction box and axle	J. Harris, jr	Boston, Mass	Feb. 22, 1848	5, 452
Anti-friction box for axles, &c	W. Rowan	Belfast, Ireland	Oct. 9, 1845	4, 226
Anti-friction box for hubs and rotary bearings	E. Fisk and J. C. Green	Fayette, Me	Nov. 14, 1835	....
Anti-friction box for shafting	J. McIlvain	Churchville, Md	Dec. 29, 1868	85, 393
Anti-friction press	A. H. Emery	New York, N. Y	Sept. 11, 1860	29, 960
Anti-friction roller for shafting	W. E. Wilcox	Peoria, Ill	June 22, 1869	91, 695
Anti-friction washer	U. H. Reed, J. Lake, and L. Sisson.	North Easton, Mass	Nov. 17, 1868	84, 067
Anti-friction wheel for belt-gearing	D. Eldredge	Philadelphia, Pa	Aug. 29, 1865	49, 614
Anti-stream boat	W. Wadsworth	Hartford, Conn	July 17, 1806	....
Anvil	O. and S. E. Brigham	Fitchburg, Mass	Feb. 3, 1857	16, 525
Anvil	L. Kirkup	Brooklyn, N. Y	Jan. 1, 1867	60, 745
Anvil	C. Peters and W. Fetter	Trenton, N. J., and Bucks County, Pa.	May 4, 1852	8, 925
Anvil	C. H. Schadt	New York, N. Y	Feb. 12, 1861	31, 410
Anvil and hammer	C. Josselyn	Pembroke, Mass	Oct. 9, 1816	....
Anvil and vise combined	J. D. Barton, F. S. Rogers, and D. Fisher.	Kalamazoo, Mich	July 17, 1866	56, 346
Anvil and vise combined	R. D. Chandler	Fairhaven, N. J	June 29, 1869	91, 909
Anvil, Apparatus for polishing	M. Fisher and J. Norris	Trenton, N. J	Oct. 4, 1853	10, 066
Anvil-block	S. Van Tiers	Hanover Iron Works, Pa	Mar. 19, 1836	....
Anvil, Centering	J. Adt	Waterbury, Conn	July 7, 1863	39, 193
Anvil-clamp for holding ties while being upset by hand-forging.	N. P. Quick	Carmel, N. Y	July 20, 1869	92, 881
Anvil-cutter	V. A. Dunn	West Peru, Me	Mar. 10, 1868	75, 395
Anvil for forming horseshoe-calks	R. Saylor and E. T. Rhodes	Marshall, Mich	Dec. 1, 1868	84, 583
Anvil for making horseshoes	A. S. Wilkinson	Pawtucket, R. I	July 10, 1866	56, 311
Anvil for repairing T-rails, Vise	S. Mason and E. M. Davis	Michigan City, Ind	Apr. 6, 1858	19, 861
Anvil for swaging horse shoe-calks	P. Badore	Montpelier, Vt	Dec. 18, 1866	60, 610

Index of patents issued from the United States Patent Office from 1790 *to* 1873, *inclusive*—Continued.

Invention.	Inventor.	Residence.	Date.	No.
Anvil-last	D. Bainbridge	Philadelphia, Pa	Oct. 11, 1870	108, 231
Anvil-making machine	J. Taylor	Shade Gap, Pa	Jan. 31, 1844	3, 418
Anvil on which to rivet trunks	W. D. Burnett	Newark, N. J	Dec. 18, 1866	60, 617
Anvils and the top and bottom parts of hammers, &c., Manufacture of.	D. Foster	Sheffield, England	Oct. 5, 1869	95, 517
Apiary	W. Faulkner	Vevay, Ind	Feb. 4, 1868	74, 065
Apparel, Machine for incising button-holes and embossing and printing articles of.	S. S. Stone	Troy, N. Y	Aug. 23, 1864	43, 932
Apparel, &c., Manufacture of seamless felt wearing.	S. M. Perkins	Springfield, Pa	Jan. 25, 1853	9, 557
Apparel, Means for stiffening articles of wearing	J. Sloan	Philadelphia, Pa	Feb. 11, 1868	74, 250
Apparel, Perforated wearing	H. E. Smith	New York, N. Y	Nov. 2, 1869	96, 358
Apparel, Safety-attachment for pocket of	A. Arnemann	Guttenberg, Iowa	Sept. 18, 1868	81, 862
Apparel, shoes, &c., Fastening wearing	R. Judson and W. H. Lynch	Matteawan, N. Y	Mar. 24, 1868	75, 924
Apparel, Waist-band for wearing	Z. Wolfsbruck	New York, N. Y	Apr. 14, 1868	76, 871
Apple and other fruit, Grinding	B. Churchell	Buckfield, Me	Dec. 9, 1825	....
Apple and other fruit, Machine for stringing dried	S. T. Sanford	Fall River, Mass	Feb. 11, 1863	37, 708
Apple and vegetable knife	A. Kimber	Muncie, Ind	June 30, 1872	129, 966
Apple-bin	S. S. and G. W. Cole	Canton, Ill	Aug. 30, 1864	43, 973
Apple-butter stirrer	G. W. Collins	West Lebanon, Pa	Aug. 26, 1873	142, 208
Apple cutter and corer	J. Wroten	Salisbury, Md	Sept. 26, 1865	50, 197
Apple cutting and coring machine	C. Darling	Utica, N. Y	July 1, 1856	15, 224
Apple cutting and coring machine	A. F. Ledbetter	Westminster, N. C	Mar. 1, 1859	23, 095
Apple-cutting machine	A. Glendening	Loudoun County, Va	Sept. 9, 1824	....
Apple gathering and cleansing machine	E. Wells	Duxbury, Vt	Dec. 6, 1831	....
Apple-gathering device	H. F. Wadhams	South Dansville, N. Y	Apr. 2, 1867	63, 584
Apple-gathering instrument	E. Tyler	Hancock, Ill	Nov. 7, 1865	50, 859
Apple-grinder	J. R. Dean	Augusta Township, Ohio	Apr. 5, 1832	....
Apple-grinder	C. F. D. Jones, jr	New Hartford, N. Y	Aug. 13, 1872	130, 505
Apple-grinder and corn-sheller	E. Harris, J. Newton, W. Webster, and J. W. Dart.	Truxton, N. Y	Mar. 10, 1832	....
Apple-grinding machine	R. Butterworth	Trenton, N. J	Sept. 5, 1865	49, 714
Apple-grinding machine	I. T. Carpenter	Martin's Ferry, Ohio	Jan. 24, 1860	26, 892
Apple-grinding machine	D. D. Demarest	New Milford, N. Y	Jan. 14, 1829	....
Apple-grinding machine	C. H. Weeks	Paris, N. Y	Apr. 9, 1827	....
Apple-grinding machine	T. I. Wells	New York	Aug. 25, 1840	1, 739
Apple-grinding mill	W. O. Hickok	Harrisburgh, Pa	Nov. 20, 1855	13, 839
Apple-grinding mill	F. B. Hunt	Westfield, Ind	July 26, 1853	9, 876
Apple-grinding mill	L. McKee	Hagerstown, Md	Feb. 26, 1861	31, 553
Apple-grinding mill, Hand	R. P. Clark	Johnstown, N. Y	Sept. 13, 1859	25, 385
Apple grinding or grating machine	J. Farnham	Tioga, N. Y	June 28, 1825	....
Apple-mill	S. Keeler	Lancaster, Pa	Jan. 27, 1863	37, 510
Apple-mill	G. S. Rust	Chester, Ill	Feb. 23, 1864	41, 723
Apple-mill, &c., Convertible	G. S. Rust	Chester, Ill	Aug. 12, 1862	36, 171
Apple-mill, Grinding-cylinder for	J. Shaefer	Lancaster, Pa	Aug. 9, 1859	25, 050
Apple-packing machine	H. B. Gill	Ogden, N. Y	May 6, 1862	35, 199
Apple-parer	W. A. C. Oaks	Reading, Pa	July 22, 1873	141, 070
Apple-pulping machine	G. Clayton	Marshallton, Pa	June 6, 1871	115, 705
Apple-quarterer	C. E. Billings	Warren, Vt	Dec. 8, 1868	84, 791
Apple-rake	E. Hart	Berlin, Conn	Dec. 31, 1812	....
Apple-sauce	A. R. Davis	Cambridge, Mass	Feb. 9, 1869	86, 649
Apple-seed gatherer	R. Brusie	Cleveland, Ohio	July 2, 1867	66, 211
Apple steaming and mashing machine	J. Dimm	Greenwood, Pa	Dec. 1, 1837	499
Apples and shelling corn, Grinding	M. Morehouse	Butler County, Ohio	Jan. 23, 1834	....
Apples, Apparatus for expressing juice from	G. R. Burt	Perry, N. Y	Jan. 23, 1872	122, 878
Apples, corn, bark, &c., Grinding	G. Parmalee	Reading, Conn	Mar. 4, 1830	....
Apples, Cutting and coring	G. C. Wright	Le Roy, Ohio	June 26, 1860	28, 935
Apples, Drying and preserving	M. P. Smith	Baltimore, Md	Nov. 8, 1870	109, 068
Apples, Grinding	A. Dean	Jerusalem, N. Y	Mar. 15, 1859	23, 231
Apples, Machine for gathering	S. Laning	Camden, N. J	Nov. 1, 1830	....
Approach-gate	S. H. Cole	East Enterprise, Ind	Aug. 16, 1870	106, 330
Approach-opening gate	R. Brinkerhoff	Mansfield, Ohio	May 28, 1861	32, 407
Approach-opening gate	S. Cole	Rochester, N. Y	May 5, 1857	17, 202
Approach-opening gate	W. T. Cole	Reed, Ohio	Sept. 24, 1861	33, 338
Approach-opening gate	R. E. House	Binghamton, N. Y	Jan. 13, 1857	16, 386
Approach-opening gate	C. A. Howard	Pontiac, Mich	Sept. 29, 1857	18, 283
Approach-opening gate	G. W. McGill	Buffalo, N. Y	May 19, 1857	17, 335
Approach-opening gate	W. G. Philips	Newport, Del	Dec. 9, 1856	16, 187
Approach-opening gate	E. Woodruff	Elizabethtown, N. J	Apr. 3, 1855	12, 652
Aquaria	E. D. Davis	Brooklyn, N. Y	Nov. 9, 1858	22, 019
Aquaria, Construction of	J. Chilcott and J. Scrimgeour	Brooklyn, N. Y	Oct. 5, 1858	21, 719
Aquarium	J. A. Cutting	Boston, Mass	Mar. 12, 1861	31, 657
Aquarium	H. Shlarbaum	New York, N. Y	Jan. 1, 1861	31, 040
Aqueduct	J. Osborn	Mount Carmel, Conn	Sept. 4, 1860	29, 906
Aqueduct-coupling	J. Aldrich	Lake Village, N. H	Jan. 16, 1866	52, 010
Aqueduct, Earthen or clay tube for	J. Ramsey	Burke, Vt	Apr. 4, 1810	....
Aqueduct formed of water-proof lime, Water or gas	J. M. Benham	Bridgewater, N. Y	Oct. 1, 1830	....
Aqueduct or water-conductor, Elevating	J. Clapp	Greenfield, Mass	Nov. 16, 1811	....
Aqueduct-pipe	T. B. Armistead	Bloomfield, N. Y	Apr. 15, 1830	....
Aqueduct-pipe, Composition for	G. Myers	Bridgewater, N. Y	Mar. 28, 1844	3, 514
Aqueduct-pipe, Making	T. B. Robbins	Stockbridge, Mass	Mar. 19, 1821	....
Aqueduct supply-pipe, Construction of	J. H. Thorndike	Boston, Mass	July 1, 1844	3, 650
Aqueducts of water-proof lime, Making	J. M. Benham	Bridgewater, N. Y	Aug. 29, 1827	....
Arastra	J. C. Davis	Alameda County, Cal	Apr. 8, 1862	34, 881
Arastra	S. E. Woodworth and J. S. Wethered.	Murphy's and San Francisco, Cal.	June 11, 1861	32, 548
Arbor, Expansion	H. C. Taylor	Marquette, Mich	June 25, 1872	128, 260
Arbor, Grape, &c	J. O. Altick	Dayton, Ohio	Mar. 19, 1867	62, 989
Arbor or fence-post	J. P. Dorman	Galesburgh, Ill	Nov. 30, 1869	97, 367
Arch, Construction of	F. Alsip	North McGregor, Iowa	Nov. 7, 1871	120, 608
Arch-girder	J. Bevan	New York, N. Y	May 21, 1850	7, 374
Arch, tunnel, &c., Construction of	G. T. Lape	Summit, N. Y	Sept. 1, 1868	81, 797
Arched structure	C. Henderson	London, England	Apr. 18, 1871	113, 881
Archil, Preparation of	J. Eberhardt	Philadelphia County, Pa	June 27, 1854	11, 194
Archil, Preparation of	L. Jarosson	New York, N. Y	June 15, 1852	9, 027
Architecture, Naval	J. Bowdlear	Roxbury, Mass	Oct. 20, 1863	40, 321
Architecture, Naval	C. Hoxie	New York	Feb. 11, 1834	....
Area of irregular figures, Mode of finding the	T. Wood	Smithfield, Ohio	July 22, 1839	1, 256
Arithmetic, Art of teaching	O. H. Shaw	Richmond, Va	Apr. 16, 1831	....

Index of patents issued from the United States Patent Office from 1790 *to* 1873, *inclusive*—Continued.

Invention.	Inventor.	Residence.	Date.	No.
Arithmetical frame	H. K. Bugbee	New York, N. Y	July 12, 1864	43, 545
Arithmetical frame	E. T. Curtis	Calumet, Mich	Aug. 26, 1873	142, 151
Arithmetical sum setter	A. W. Price	Detroit, Mich	Apr. 23, 1872	126, 123
Arithmometer	T. Hill	Waltham, Mass	Nov. 24, 1857	18, 692
Arithmometer for adding	O. L. Castle	Upper Alton, Ill	Nov. 24, 1857	18, 675
Arithmometer for addition	O. L. Castle	Upper Alton, Ill	Nov. 2, 1858	21, 941
Ark, Safety	W. Hollins	Baltimore, Md	May 4, 1824	....
Arm and hand, Artificial	B. F. Palmer	Philadelphia, Pa	Jan. 11, 1859	22, 576
Arm and hand, Artificial	T. Uren	New York, N. Y	Jan. 31, 1865	46, 158
Arm and hand, Artificial	T. Uren	New York, N. Y	Jan. 31, 1865	46, 159
Arm, Artificial	J. Condell	Morristown, N. Y	July 11, 1865	48, 659
Arm, Artificial	E. Cotly	Washington, D. C	Oct. 27, 1863	40, 397
Arm, Artificial	H. A. Kimball and A. J. Lawrence.	Philadelphia, Pa	May 23, 1865	47, 835
Arm, Artificial	J. H. Koeller	New York, N. Y	July 19, 1864	43, 590
Arm, Artificial	J. H. Koeller	New York, N. Y	Oct. 11, 1864	44, 638
Arm, Artificial	D. W. Kolbe	Philadelphia, Pa	Nov. 15, 1864	45, 052
Arm, Artificial	M. Lincoln	Malden, Mass	Aug. 11, 1863	39, 487
Arm, Artificial	A. McOmber	Schenectady, N. Y	Jan. 1, 1867	60, 921
Arm, Artificial	J. Peterson	Canoga, N. Y	Mar. 7, 1865	46, 696
Arm, Artificial	E. Spellerberg	Philadelphia, Pa	Apr. 26, 1864	42, 515
Arm, Artificial	E. Spellerberg	Philadelphia, Pa	Nov. 28, 1865	51, 238
Arm, Artificial	I. Stoffel	Washington, D. C	Jan. 10, 1865	45, 876
Arm, Artificial	I. Stoffel	Washington, D. C	Aug. 28, 1866	57, 594
Arm, Artificial	T. Uren	New York, N. Y	May 30, 1865	48, 002
Arm-chair, Folding	H. S. Golightly and C. S. Twitchell.	New Haven, Conn	June 28, 1864	43, 366
Arm-chair, Folding	W. C. Goodwin	Hamden, Conn	Jan. 21, 1862	34, 204
Arm-rest and paper-cutter, Combined	C. B. Dickinson	Brooklyn, N. Y	May 26, 1868	78, 192
Arm-rest, Compositor's	C. L. Alexander	Washington, D. C	May 28, 1872	127, 208
Arm-rest, Penman's	J. B. Withey	Lexington, Mich	May 26, 1868	78, 250
Arm-support for keyed instrument	L. Buchbuger	Chicago, Ill	Nov. 29, 1870	109, 582
Arms, Slinging	O. E. Woods	Philadelphia, Pa	May 15, 1866	54, 807
Arms-supporter for riflemen	S. Kinman	Humboldt, Cal	Feb. 14, 1865	46, 365
Arms-supporter, India-rubber	H. Greentree	Baltimore, Md	Dec. 12, 1871	121, 868
Armillary sphere	H. Bryant	Hartford, Conn	Sept. 10, 1872	131, 148
Armlet	A. S. Potter	Providence, R. I	Apr. 9, 1872	125, 407
Arm-pit shield	W. E. Beames	New York, N. Y	Oct. 22, 1872	132, 348
Arm-pit shield	J. Sibley	New York, N. Y	Sept. 16, 1873	142, 875
Armor, Defensive	C. H. Hudson	Roxbury, Mass	Sept. 27, 1864	44, 426
Armor for marine and other batteries, Defensive	J. B. Eads	Saint Louis, Mo	July 14, 1863	39, 218
Armor for ship	T. Whitby	Lambeth, England	Sept. 3, 1867	68, 474
Armor for ship, Defensive	M. L. Callender and N. W. Northrup.	New York and Greene, N. Y.	May 27, 1862	35, 412
Armor for ships and other batteries, Defensive	C. W. S. Heaton	Belleville, Ill	Apr. 14, 1863	38, 206
Armor for ships and other batteries, Defensive	R. H. Jewett	Mount Sterling, Ill	Feb. 17, 1863	37, 695
Armor for ships and other batteries, Defensive	R. Montgomery	New York, N. Y	Feb. 10, 1863	37, 633
Armor for ships and other batteries, Defensive	W. W. W. Wood	Philadelphia, Pa	Sept. 23, 1862	36, 546
Armor for ships, batteries, &c., Defensive	G. B. Manley	Danville, Pa	Jan. 13, 1863	37, 402
Armor for ships, Construction of the defensive	W. Rumbold	Saint Louis, Mo	July 15, 1862	35, 895
Armor for ships, Metallic defensive	W. Ballard	New York, N. Y	June 24, 1862	35, 665
Armor for water and land batteries, Defensive	J. L. Jones	Saint Louis, Mo	Apr. 15, 1862	35, 001
Armor, Metallic defensive	B. B. Hotchkiss	Sharon, Conn	Aug. 12, 1862	36, 152
Armor, Naval defensive	G. M. Mowbray	Titusville, Pa	Sept. 9, 1862	36, 439
Armor plate, Defensive	E. Cox	Covington, Ky	May 27, 1862	35, 364
Armor-plate, Defensive	M. Wappich	Sacramento, Cal	Mar. 3, 1863	37, 836
Armor-plate for land or marine battery	F. P. Dimpfel	Philadelphia, Pa	Aug. 4, 1863	39, 384
Armor-plate for marine or other batteries, Means of connecting metallic.	T. Shaw	Philadelphia, Pa	May 13, 1862	35, 279
Armor-plate for ships and other batteries	B. T. Babbitt	New York, N. Y	Jan. 13, 1863	37, 380
Armor-plate for vessels	J. F. Winslow	Troy, N. Y	May 27, 1862	35, 407
Armor-plate, Ships'	H. H. Warden	New York, N. Y	Feb. 25, 1862	34, 539
Armor-plates, Means of affixing defensive	E. Brady	Philadelphia, Pa	Mar. 3, 1863	37, 807
Armor-plates, Mode of protecting	M. Bernabé	Toulon, France	Jan. 15, 1867	61, 143
Armor-plates, Pile for	J. Jeavons	Sheffield, England	Dec. 13, 1870	110, 143
Armor-plates, Press for bending ships'	E. Sauer	New York, N. Y	Mar. 24, 1863	37, 982
Armor-plates to marine batteries, Means of affixing defensive.	O. G. Stillman	Fabius, N. Y	Nov. 25, 1862	37, 013
Armor-plates to vessels, Attaching	J. Rusch	New York, N. Y	May 20, 1862	35, 353
Armor, Ships' defensive	S. D. Carpenter	Madison, Wis	May 23, 1865	47, 796
Armor to navigable vessels and water batteries, Means of attaching.	J. B. Love	Philadelphia, Pa	Oct. 22, 1861	33, 532
Armored can	W. F. Thompson	Toledo, Ohio	May 7, 1872	126, 502
Armor-plating for vessels	G. J. Gunther	London, England	Nov. 24, 1868	84, 418
Army stretcher	J. J. Smith	Philadelphia, Pa	Sept. 8, 1863	39, 840
Arrow-spring	J. B. Cleaveland	Indianapolis, Ind	Aug. 15, 1871	118, 108
Articulator	E. T. Starr	Philadelphia, Pa	May 19, 1868	78, 151
Artillery and mining blasting	T. P. Shaffner	Louisville, Ky	Dec. 18, 1866	60, 572
Artillery, Carriage for field	D. Cobb	Boston, Mass	Apr. 25, 1808	....
Artillery carriages, Wheel for flying	J. D. Murphy	Baltimore, Md	Apr. 3, 1860	27, 733
Artillery, Field	S. W. Wood	Cornwall, N. Y	May 7, 1872	126, 607
Artist's stretcher	J. E. Todd	Middletown, Conn	Sept. 18, 1866	58, 154
Artist's stretching-frame	J. F. Carroll	South Boston, Mass	July 21, 1868	80, 135
Artist's materials, Apparatus for drying	G. D. Jones	New York, N. Y	Dec. 11, 1866	60, 382
Arts, Composition of matter for various uses in the	C. L. Coombs	Washington, D. C	Aug. 24, 1869	94, 080
Asbestus and obtaining useful products therefrom, Treating.	J. S. Rosenthal	Philadelphia, Pa	Aug. 20, 1872	130, 663
Asbestus and other fibrous minerals, Treating	C. A. Stevens	New York, N. Y	Mar. 14, 1871	112, 650
Asbestus and other mineral fibers for useful purposes, Treating.	C. A. Stevens	New York, N. Y	Mar. 14, 1871	112, 649
Asbestus for the production of textile fiber, Treatment of.	J. S. Rosenthal	Philadelphia, Pa	Aug. 6, 1872	130, 245
Asbestus, Treating	J. S Rosenthal	Philadelphia, Pa	Aug. 13, 1872	130, 538
Asbestus Use and application of	J. Scott	Philadelphia, Pa	Nov. 26, 1835	... ...
Asbestus yarn	J. S. Rosenthal	Philadelphia, Pa	Aug. 13, 1872	130, 537
Ash-bin	W. W. Chase	Springfield, N. H	July 28, 1868	80, 451
Ash-box	G. Dunlop	Williamsburgh, N. Y	Sept. 24, 1872	131, 607
Ash-box	J. Kee and J. Sloan	Philadelphia, Pa	Apr. 24, 1866	54, 173

Index of patents issued from the United States Patent Office from 1790 *to* 1873, *inclusive*—Continued.

Invention.	Inventor.	Residence.	Date.	No.
Ash-box and sifter	H. D. Rogers	Cincinnati, Ohio	Mar. 1, 1870	100, 452
Ash-hopper	P. Zimmerman	Sylvan, Pa	Aug. 3, 1869	93, 388
Ash-house	M. Hall, jr	Osborn, Ohio	Dec. 17, 1867	72, 290
Ash-leach	J. W. Kernodle and A. H. Haun.	Lebanon, Ind	June 17, 1873	139, 963
Ash-leach	D. T. Miller	Woodbury, Pa	Apr. 9, 1872	125, 607
Ash-leach	S. A. Porter	Prescott, Wis	Feb. 16, 1864	41, 638
Ash-leaching apparatus	P. Perdew and A. W. Brinkerhoff.	Syracuse, Ohio	May 20, 1856	14, 925
Ash-pan	J. A. Lawson	Troy, N. Y	June 16, 1863	38, 902
Ash-pan	C. H. Low	Cleveland, Ohio	Nov. 9, 1869	96, 711
Ash-pan cleaner, Locomotive	A. O. Denio	Wilmington, Del	Aug. 12, 1873	141, 769
Ash-pan drawer and lifter	J. Morrison, jr	Troy, N. Y	June 20, 1865	48, 299
Ash-pan, Locomotive	L. H. Dee	Grand Junction, Iowa	July 12, 1870	105, 317
Ash-pan, Locomotive	H. A. Stoddard	Springfield, Mass	Sept. 6, 1870	107, 117
Ash-screen	E. C. Jenkins, jr	Worcester, Mass	Jan. 24, 1871	111, 126
Ash-screen and coal-hod combined	T. J. Thurston	Lewiston, Me	Aug. 11, 1868	81, 037
Ash-screen and commode	J. C. Morrell	Manchester, England	Mar. 11, 1873	136, 609
Ash-shovel	R. J. S. Thompson	Washington, Pa	Mar. 15, 1870	100, 952
Ash-shovel and sifter	W. C. McGill	Cincinnati, Ohio	Feb. 23, 1869	87, 186
Ash-sifting shovel	A. M. Olds	Chicago, Ill	Sept. 5, 1865	49, 781
Ash-tub or leach	C. Roop	Middletown, Pa	July 9, 1867	66, 636
Ashes, Apparatus for leaching	E. Williams	Westfield, N. Y	Jan. 9, 1838	529
Ashes, Leaching	G. Clement	Canandaigua, N. Y	June 10, 1837	228
Ashes, Manufacturing	J. Bellows, jr., and E. White		Dec. 29, 1804	
Ashlar-cutting	W. Boulton	Tompkinsville, N. Y	July 26, 1870	105, 633
Asparagus-plant, Utilizing the products of the	J. P. Gage and J. C. Gilbert	New York, N. Y	Oct. 7, 1862	36, 608
Asphalt pipe, Manufacture of	A. Müller	Jersey City, N. J	Oct. 21, 1873	143, 922
Asphalt, Treating	P. Barthel	Frankfort-on-the-Main, Germany.	Feb. 18, 1873	135, 879
Asphaltum, Process for burning	S. Stevens	Washington, D. C	Apr. 9, 1872	125, 497
Astronomical instrument	C. Emmanuel	Paris, France	Jan. 17, 1865	45, 954
Astronomical instrument	H. Glover	New York, N. Y	Nov. 16, 1858	22, 075
Astronomical machine	J. Swaim	Philadelphia, Pa	June 29, 1833	
Atmosphere, Apparatus for moistening	J. G. Garland	Biddeford, Me	July 1, 1873	140, 410
Atmosphere-cooler	M. J. Kelly	Chicago, Ill	Oct. 18, 1864	44, 731
Atmosphere of apartments, Boiler for hydrating the.	P. I. Schopp	Louisville, Ky	Oct. 12, 1869	95, 735
Atmospheric engine	E. and J. Prentis	Baltimore, Md	June 22, 1824	
Atmospheric engine	S. E. Tuttle	Evansville, Wis	Mar. 12, 1872	124, 520
Atmospheric lubricator, Self-feeding	J. Sutton	New York, N. Y	Nov. 6, 1855	13, 769
Atmospheric motive-power	W. Jones	New Albany, Ind	Mar. 5, 1872	124, 361
Atmospheric motive-power	W. Jones	New Albany, Ind	July 16, 1872	129, 567
Atmospheric propelling-engine, Talbot's	E. A. Talbot	Dublin, Ireland	June 21, 1828	
Atmospheric regulator for stove, furnace, &c	B. Holly	Seneca Falls, N. Y	July 13, 1858	20, 919
Atmospheric steam-engine	J. Mead and M. Kitchell	Lebanon, Ohio	July 27, 1829	
Atmospheric steam-engine, Two-cylinder	W. Willis	Charleston, S. C	Nov. 14, 1826	
Atmospheric transportation	R. H. Gilbert	Washington, D. C	Feb. 8, 1870	99, 663
Atomizer	J. J. Essex	Newport, R. I	June 27, 1871	116, 286
Atomizer	C. P. Janes	Boston, Mass	June 6, 1871	115, 615
Atomizer	H. D. Lockwood	Charlestown, Mass	Aug. 1, 1871	117, 651
Atomizer	H. D. Lockwood	Charlestown, Mass	May 28, 1872	127, 356
Atomizer-bulb	H. D. Lockwood	Charlestown, Mass	Apr. 29, 1873	138, 416
Atomizer for administering medicine	J. Sheedy	New York, N. Y	Sept. 21, 1869	95, 152
Atomizer, Liquid	H. Kraut	Saint Louis, Mo	July 7, 1868	79, 764
Atomizer or vaporizer	J. N. Gerard	New York, N. Y	Sept. 23, 1873	143, 070
Atomizer, Steam	I. P. Leete	Philadelphia, Pa	Oct. 25, 1870	108, 710
Atomizing apparatus	A. M. Shurtleff	Boston, Mass	Mar. 16, 1869	87, 978
Atomizing apparatus for surgical use	A. M. Shurtleff	Boston, Mass	Mar. 24, 1868	75, 991
Atomizing, Drying and concentrating liquid substance by.	S. R. Percy	New York, N. Y	Apr. 9, 1872	125, 406
Atomizing, inhaling, and injecting liquids and gases, Apparatus for.	W. R. Leonard	New York, N. Y	Apr. 23, 1872	125, 965
Atomizing liquids, Apparatus for	A. M. Shurtleff	Boston, Mass	Mar. 3, 1868	75, 208
Atomizing liquids, Apparatus for	A. M. Shurtleff	Boston, Mass	May 2, 1871	114, 482
Atomizing-tube	C. H. Eccleston	Oxford, N. Y	Sept. 10, 1867	68, 614
Atomizing-tube	T. J. Holmes	Malden, Mass	Aug. 23, 1870	106, 587
Atomizing-tube	W. L. Leach	Boston, Mass	Jan. 5, 1869	85, 596
Atomizing-tube	A. M. Shurtleff	Boston, Mass	Dec. 18, 1866	60, 580
Auger	J. Blake	East Pepperell, Mass	Apr. 17, 1860	27, 946
Auger	J. Brownell	Otsego, N. Y	May 16, 1815	
Auger	L. Colt	Niagara Falls, N. Y	Aug. 11, 1868	80, 915
Auger	R. Cook	Saratoga Springs, N. Y	June 17, 1851	8, 162
Auger	K. Curtiss	Winchester, Conn	Apr. 22, 1856	14, 752
Auger	R. French	Derby, Conn	July 20, 1843	3, 181
Auger	E. C. Gillette	Richfield, British Columbia	Mar. 14, 1865	46, 854
Auger	C. L. Griswold	Chester, Conn	May 30, 1865	47, 946
Auger	W. Hale	Champlain, N. Y	Feb. 7, 1807	
Auger	J. M. Hathaway	New York, N. Y	Sept. 4, 1860	29, 883
Auger	T. Hofstatter, jr	New York, N. Y	Mar. 12, 1867	62, 849
Auger	R. H. Hopkins	Hinsdale, N. H	June 21, 1870	104, 457
Auger	M. Howe	New York	Apr. 2, 1814	
Auger	C. Hoxie		July 12, 1804	
Auger	W. A. Ives	New Haven, Conn	Aug. 28, 1860	29, 793
Auger	W. A. Ives	New Haven, Conn	Oct. 12, 1869	95, 803
Auger	W. A. Ives	New Haven, Conn	Feb. 7, 1871	111, 648
Auger	R. Jennings	Deep River, Conn	Jan. 30, 1855	12, 318
Auger	W. Jones	Portsmouth, Va	June 12, 1835	
Auger	W. Jones	Portsmouth, Va	June 15, 1835	
Auger	A. C. Kasson	Milwaukee, Wis	Jan. 15, 1867	61, 208
Auger	P. Kavanagh	Canarsie, N. Y	Sept. 10, 1872	131, 279
Auger	T. C. Keith	Valley Falls, R. I	Mar. 12, 1867	62, 754
Auger	R. M. Lafferty and E. P. Smith.	Three Rivers, Mich	Sept. 12, 1871	118, 806
Auger	E. G. Lamson	Windsor, Vt	Jan. 16, 1866	52, 056
Auger	H. T. Love	Vermillion Township, Kan	Nov. 7, 1865	50, 887
Auger	J. A. McGee	New York, N. Y	Dec. 10, 1867	72, 065
Auger	C. Monson	Moscow, Wis	June 14, 1870	104, 335
Auger	H. T. Moody	Newburyport, Mass	May 29, 1866	55, 144

Index of patents issued from the United States Patent Office from 1790 *to* 1873, *inclusive*—Continued.

Invention.	Inventor.	Residence.	Date.	No.
Auger	A. Newton, L. B. Smith, and E. Sanford.	Meriden, Conn	Mar. 27, 1847	5, 036
Auger	I. T. Payne	Chester, Conn	Mar. 10, 1868	75, 454
Auger	N. B. Phelps	Rochester, N. Y	Dec. 27, 1859	26, 613
Auger	H. Pitcher	Fond du Lac, Wis	Aug. 29, 1871	118, 552
Auger	H. Pitcher	Fond du Lac, Wis	Mar. 26, 1872	126, 076
Auger	T. M. Richardson	Stockton, Me	Sept. 28, 1869	95, 379
Auger	N. C. Sanford	Meriden, Conn	Sept. 23, 1862	36, 534
Auger	N. C. Sanford	Meriden, Conn	June 16, 1868	79, 012
Auger	J. H. Schreiner	Philadelphia, Pa	Aug. 17, 1826	....
Auger	J. Swan	Seymour, Conn	May 30, 1871	115, 541
Auger	A. C. Vaughan	Philadelphia, Pa	Mar. 31, 1868	76, 278
Auger	B. Walch	Frederick, Md	Jan. 17, 1871	111, 099
Auger	C. Wardwell	Painesville, Ohio	Apr. 20, 1869	89, 097
Auger	S. Wood	Worcester, Mass	Nov. 1, 1859	25, 990
Auger and gimlet	O. Percival	East Haddam, Conn	Oct. 14, 1835	....
Auger and reamer combined	O. W. Townsend	Fond du Lac, Wis	Feb. 21, 1871	111, 990
Auger, Annular	R. Stewart	Elmira, N. Y	Apr. 10, 1866	53, 896
Auger-bit	A. L. Andrews	Bristol, Conn	June 21, 1870	104, 404
Auger-bit	W. A. Ives	New Haven, Conn	June 1, 1869	90, 755
Auger-bit	H. C. Lewis	Essex, Conn	June 1, 1869	90, 759
Auger-bit	J. C. Mills	Rochester, N. Y	Feb. 21, 1871	112, 065
Auger-bit	H. L. Shailer	Deep River, Conn	Mar. 16, 1869	87, 796
Auger-bit	R. A. Whitmore	De Witt, Ark	Nov. 5, 1872	132, 883
Auger-bit die, Construction of	R. N. Watrous	Elmira, N. Y	Aug. 8, 1871	117, 838
Auger-bit, Expanding	A. Weeks	South Boston, Mass	Aug. 11, 1857	18, 003
Auger-bits, Device for re-setting old	C. W. Beals	Greig, N. Y	Aug. 1, 1871	117, 594
Auger-bits, Machine for bending the lips of	J. Swan	Seymour, Conn	Mar. 15, 1870	100, 816
Auger-bits, Machine for forming	W. A. Ives	New Haven, Conn	Mar. 19, 1872	124, 683
Auger-bits, Machine for forming	J. Swan	Seymour, Conn	July 29, 1873	141, 401
Auger-bits, Machine for forming lips of	J. Swan	Seymour, Conn	June 27, 1871	116, 509
Auger-bits, Machine for making	W. W. Grier and R. H. Boyd	Hutton, Pa	May 22, 1866	54, 893
Auger-bits, Machine for making	J. Swan	Seymour, Conn	Apr. 21, 1868	76, 955
Auger-bits, Manufacture of	J. Swan	Seymour, Conn	July 14, 1868	80, 027
Auger-bits, Method of forming spur-lip for	W. A. Ives	New Haven, Conn	Feb. 28, 1871	112, 255
Auger-blanks, Die for swaging the ends of	R. Jennings	Deep River, Conn	June 12, 1866	55, 498
Auger, Boring and withdrawing	J. Snyder	Tuscarora, N. Y	June 1, 1830	....
Auger, Combined convex and concave	N. C. Sanford	Meriden, Conn	Mar. 27, 1849	6, 221
Auger, Double-podded center-screw	E. L'Hommedieu	Saybrook, Conn	July 31, 1809	....
Auger, Earth	G. H. Baisley and G. Wilson	Hamilton, Mo	July 15, 1873	140, 756
Auger, Earth	W. H. Beach and C. W. Hanson.	Hamburg, Iowa	Feb. 4, 1873	135, 509
Auger, Earth	E. H. Clark	Appleton, Wis	Oct. 28, 1873	143, 963
Auger, Earth	W. Cole	Milan, Tenn	Nov. 11, 1873	144, 510
Auger, Earth	G. G. Collins and J. A. Morrison	Philo, Ill	Jan. 14, 1873	134, 734
Auger, Earth	W. T. Cooley	Chicago, Ill	Sept. 30, 1873	143, 276
Auger, Earth	A. J. Dine	Xenia, Ind	May 7, 1867	64, 503
Auger, Earth	X. Earle	Depere, Wis	May 21, 1872	126, 941
Auger, Earth	S. Emery	Cameron, Mo	Aug. 26, 1873	142, 218
Auger, Earth	W. H. Gates	Perry Township, Iowa	Oct. 1, 1872	131, 872
Auger, Earth	T. C. Harris	Dresden, Iowa	Nov. 5, 1872	132, 830
Auger, Earth	H. P. Haskin	Roscoe, Ill	Oct. 8, 1872	132, 072
Auger, Earth	N. H. Lindley	Bridgeport, Conn	July 18, 1871	117, 180
Auger, Earth	T. Orchard	Sacramento, Cal	Apr. 25, 1871	114, 185
Auger, Earth	C. D. Pierce	Lawrence, Kans	Aug. 12, 1873	141, 664
Auger, Earth	S. Pope	Covington County, Miss	Mar. 22, 1870	101, 160
Auger, Earth	I. N. Pyle	Cameron, Mo	Nov. 12, 1872	132, 980
Auger, Earth	W. H. Salyer	Corning, Iowa	Aug. 19, 1873	141, 892
Auger, Earth	J. B. Smith	Memphis, Tenn	Mar. 4, 1873	136, 555
Auger, Earth	A. Sorg and S. C. Bollman	Decatur, Ind	June 24, 1873	140, 226
Auger, Earth	H. C. Stouffer	Canfield, Ohio	Dec. 24, 1872	134, 324
Auger, Earth	H. C. Stouffer	Canfield, Ohio	Mar. 18, 1873	137, 036
Auger, Earth	I. M. West	Summit, Nebr	Apr. 8, 1873	137, 744
Auger, Earth	B. F. White and S. R. Owen	Stewartsville, Mo	Feb. 13, 1872	123, 755
Auger, Earth	J. Wilson	Cameron, Mo	Oct. 29, 1872	132, 611
Auger, Earth	I. Yeazel	Clark County, Ohio	Mar. 19, 1872	124, 711
Auger, Earth-boring	A. Crafts and E. Weeks	Auburn, Ohio	Nov. 20, 1849	6, 880
Auger, Earth-boring	J. W. Heath	Memphis, Tenn	Mar. 31, 1868	76, 188
Auger, Earth-boring	W. W. Jilz	Hamilton, Mo	Aug. 1, 1871	117, 542
Auger, Earth-boring	W. W. Jilz	St. Joseph, Mo	July 16, 1872	129, 283
Auger, Earth-boring	A. A. McMahen	Oxford, Miss	July 12, 1859	24, 749
Auger, Earth-boring	G. Page	Baltimore, Md	May 3, 1839	1, 140
Auger, Excavating	J. Buck	Bucksport, Me	Feb. 5, 1850	7, 067
Auger, Expanding	C. Meyer	Fond du Lac, Wis	Mar. 29, 1859	23, 381
Auger finishing-tool	R. Jennings	Deep River, Conn	July 3, 1866	56, 058
Auger for barrels, Shredding	A. Kelly	Sharpsburgh, Pa	July 6, 1869	92, 195
Auger for boring boxes	R. L. Priester	Souder's Station P. O., Md.	Nov. 14, 1871	120, 827
Auger for boring earth	J. M. Cooper	Newbern, Ala	Oct. 7, 1842	2, 807
Auger for boring guns, pistols, &c	D. Pettibone	Philadelphia, Pa	Feb. 12, 1814	....
Auger for boring guns, Twisted screw	W. Holmes	Winchester, N. H	Apr. 4, 1820	....
Auger for boring hubs of wheels, Set	S. Caldwell	Windham, Conn	Nov. 20, 1826	....
Auger for boring large holes	N. J. Lampman	Coxsackie, N. Y	Apr. 8, 1835	....
Auger for boring-machine	G. Flautt	Cavetown, Md	Feb. 12, 1850	7, 083
Auger for boring post-holes	C. Hoxie	Hudson, N. Y	July 26, 1824	....
Auger for boring square holes	A. S. Perrine	Louisville, Ky	Mar. 1, 1870	100, 440
Auger for boring wood	G. W. Low	Chillicothe, Ohio	Feb. 9, 1864	41, 517
Auger for cutting rotary tenons	G. Taylor and G. H. Burger	Worthington, Ohio	Aug. 30, 1859	25, 289
Auger for wood	M. Morris	Broad Brook, Conn	Nov. 30, 1858	22, 195
Auger-gage	S. L. Lyford	Portland, Me	May 29, 1866	55, 132
Auger-gage	A. Stowel	....	Feb. 14, 1833	....
Auger-gage	W. E. Whiting	Providence, R. I	Feb. 11, 1868	74, 466
Auger-gimlet, &c	W. Spangler	Harper's Ferry, Va	July 11, 1854	11, 280
Auger-gimlet, &c., Single-twist	W. N. Clark	Chester, Conn	Jan. 31, 1845	3, 899
Auger, Ground	D. Ring	Damariscotta, Me	Apr. 4, 1865	47, 172
Auger-handle	D. W. George	Minnesota City, Minn	Sept. 28, 1869	95, 220
Auger-handle	S. W. Hemenway	Lansing, Iowa	May 20, 1873	139, 066
Auger-handle	T. C. Hendry	Union Point, Ga	Oct. 20, 1868	83, 156
Auger-handle	G. W. Herring	Bangor, Me	Nov. 30, 1869	97, 398
Auger-handle	W. A. Ives	New Haven, Conn	Oct. 11, 1870	108, 267

Index of patents issued from the United States Patent Office from 1790 *to* 1873, *inclusive*—Continued.

Invention.	Inventor.	Residence.	Date.	No.
Auger-handle	W. A. Ives	New Haven, Conn	Jan. 10, 1871	110, 920
Auger-handle	F. B. Pease	Ontario Centre, N. Y	Sept. 2, 1873	142, 410
Auger-handle	S. T. Peat	Florence, N. J	July 13, 1869	92, 541
Auger-handle	H. D. Pennoyer	Athens, N. Y	July 28, 1868	80, 365
Auger-handle	L. L. Pollard	Worcester, Mass	July 23, 1861	32, 890
Auger-handle	N. C. Sanford	Meriden, Conn	June 17, 1856	15, 147
Auger-handle	G. Sanford	Ellenville, N. Y	Oct. 1, 1850	7, 688
Auger-handle	W. W. Simrell	Great Bend, Pa	Aug. 19, 1862	36, 240
Auger-handle	D. Y. Smith	Joliet, Ill	Sept. 19, 1865	50, 045
Auger-handle	D. Y. Smith	Joliet, Ill	Dec. 10, 1867	72, 099
Auger-handle	J. Swan	Seymour, Conn	Apr. 21, 1868	76, 956
Auger-handle	J. Swan	Seymour, Conn	Dec. 14, 1869	97, 830
Auger-handle	G. H. Talbot	Boston, Mass	Dec. 11, 1855	13, 925
Auger-handle	A. Thayer	Malden Bridge, N. Y	Dec. 3, 1850	7, 815
Auger-handle, &c	D. C. Stone	Wawarsing, N. Y	Mar. 12, 1845	3, 949
Auger-handle fastening	W. N. Clark	Chester, Conn	July 28, 1857	17, 868
Auger-handle fastening	G. H. Hubbard	Shelburne Falls, Mass	Mar. 6, 1855	12, 484
Auger-handles and braces, Socket for	A. H. McKinley	Higginsport, Ohio	Aug. 16, 1853	9, 939
Auger-handles, Shank-socket for	J. M. Horton	Albany, N. Y	July 8, 1862	35, 856
Auger, Hollow	G. F. Almy	Delphos, Ohio	Aug. 12, 1873	141, 745
Auger, Hollow	A. Bauman and O. O. Witherell.	Toledo, Ohio	Jan. 24, 1871	111, 167
Auger, Hollow	F. Beals and M. Smith	New Haven, Conn	Jan. 9, 1866	51, 911
Auger, Hollow	H. T. Bean, J. C. Freeman, and D. B. Mills.	Palestine, Ill	Dec 7, 1869	97, 590
Auger, Hollow	J. H. Beauregard	Sandy Hill, N. Y	Dec. 29, 1868	85, 423
Auger, Hollow	C. S. Bonney	Syracuse, N. Y	Aug. 2, 1870	105, 896
Auger, Hollow	G. E. Booth	Seymour, Conn	May 7, 1867	64, 478
Auger, Hollow	A. Brush	East Constable, N. Y	Jan. 7, 1868	73, 162
Auger, Hollow	C. L. Campbell	Binghamton, N. Y	May 10, 1864	42, 639
Auger, Hollow	W. A. Clark	Woodbridge, Conn	Feb. 2, 1869	86, 364
Auger, Hollow	W. A. Clark	Woodbridge, Conn	Aug. 17, 1869	93, 808
Auger, Hollow	W. A. Clark	Woodbridge, Conn	Dec. 12, 1871	121, 707
Auger, Hollow	A. Conant	Pepperville, Mass	June 11, 1829	....
Auger, Hollow	C. W. Corr	Carlinville, Ill	Feb. 25, 1873	136, 138
Auger, Hollow	A. F. Cushman	Hartford, Conn	Aug. 30, 1870	106, 919
Auger, Hollow	J. Deming	Salem, Ohio	Dec. 3, 1872	133, 570
Auger, Hollow	M. L. Edwards	Salem, Ohio	Dec. 3, 1872	133, 573
Auger, Hollow	O. A. Essig	Canton, Ohio	May 6, 1873	138, 623
Auger, Hollow	E. W. Fawcett, E. W. Silver, and J. Deming.	Salem, Ohio	Sept. 23, 1873	143, 132
Auger, Hollow	R. Gaylord	Seymour, Conn	July 21, 1863	39, 284
Auger, Hollow	D. George	Granville, Ohio	Mar. 28, 1848	5, 487
Auger, Hollow	S. P. Gilbert	Racine, Wis	Apr. 2, 1861	31, 883
Auger, Hollow	A. B. Hendryx	Seymour, Conn	Feb. 25, 1862	34, 497
Auger, Hollow	M. Isbell	New Haven, Conn	May 7, 1867	64, 423
Auger, Hollow	W. A. Ives	New Haven, Conn	Oct. 13, 1868	82, 957
Auger, Hollow	S. Katz	Bossardsville, Pa	Aug. 8, 1871	117, 784
Auger, Hollow	F. Kraus	Philadelphia, Pa	Mar. 31, 1868	76, 205
Auger, Hollow	J. Lefeber	Cambridge City, Ind	Oct. 2, 1866	58, 436
Auger, Hollow	J. McClure	Rockland, Me	Oct. 9, 1866	58, 658
Auger, Hollow	G. M. Nye and A. T. Haviland	Elmira, N. Y	May 22, 1860	28, 400
Auger, Hollow	J. L. Parker	Harrisonburgh, Va	Apr. 14, 1868	76, 804
Auger, Hollow	H. J. Rickard	Rochester, N. Y	May 18, 1869	90, 195
Auger, Hollow	J. H. Smith	Pineville, Pa	July 17, 1866	56, 459
Auger, Hollow	J. M. Smith	Seymour, Conn	June 5, 1866	55, 382
Auger, Hollow	G. N. Stearns	Syracuse, N. Y	Sept. 8, 1863	39, 841
Auger, Hollow	G. N. Stearns	Syracuse, N. Y	Aug. 27, 1872	130, 8[illegible]6
Auger, Hollow	J. Swan	Seymour, Conn	Sept. 19, 1871	119, 096
Auger, Hollow	I. H. Van Wie	Clarksville, N. Y	July 26, 1870	105, 744
Auger, Hollow	J. Ward	New York, N. Y	Jan. 1, 1867	60, 972
Auger, Hollow	A. Wyckoff	Elmira, N. Y	July 12, 1859	24, 773
Auger, Hollow	A. Wyckoff	Elmira, N. Y	Apr. 3, 1866	53, 722
Auger, Hollow	A. Wyckoff and L. F. Stevens.	Elmira, N. Y	Mar. 12, 1861	31, 694
Auger, Hollow	E. Young	Amanda, Ohio	Jan. 1, 1867	60, 985
Auger, Ice	W. A. Clark	New Haven, Conn	June 10, 1873	139, 769
Auger-lips, Machine for forming	J. Swan	Seymour, Conn	May 20, 1873	139, 091
Auger, Mining	J. Hobart	Dubuque, Iowa	May 23, 1846	4, 531
Auger, Mining	P. Nichols	Boston, Mass	May 18, 1810	....
Auger or bit	E. L'Hommedieu	Saybrook, Conn	Feb. 11, 1835	....
Auger or bit, Expanding	L. H. Gibbs	Washington, D. C	July 17, 1855	13, 261
Auger, Peat	N. Aubin	Montreal, Canada	Jan. 25, 1870	99, 129
Auger, Post	C. Adams	Pittsburgh, Pa	Oct. 20, 1868	83, 233
Auger, Post	J. Armstrong	Bucyrus, Ohio	July 13, 1869	92, 504
Auger, Post	H. W. Caswell	Yarmouth, Me	Mar. 19, 1867	63, 016
Auger, Post	Z. S. Cracraft	Lacon, Ill	Oct. 5, 1869	95, 566
Auger, Post	J. B. Drapar	Salem, Ill	Nov. 3, 1868	83, 611
Auger, Post	H. C. Partridge and J. Preston.	Bainbridge, N. Y	Jan. 25, 1870	99, 227
Auger, Post	G. Seeger and C. H. Shaffer	Clark's Hill, Ind	Dec. 21, 1869	98, 196
Auger, Post	S. S. and J. G. Sherman	McHenry, Ill	July 6, 1869	92, 214
Auger, Post	A. Vaughan	Chicago, Ill	June 15, 1869	91, 387
Auger, Post-hole	A. Burton	Chicago, Ill	Apr. 14, 1868	76, 598
Auger, Post-hole	A. R. Clark	Albia, N. Y	Aug. 22, 1871	118, 196
Auger, Post-hole	S. W. Corbin	Bainbridge, N. Y	Mar. 2, 1869	87, 470
Auger, Post-hole	I. Hart	Clarksburgh, W. Va	Aug. 31, 1869	94, 412
Auger, Post hole	S. C. Horton	Tarrytown, N. Y	Feb. 2, 1869	86, 400
Auger, Post-hole	J. Killgore, G. D. Clapsaddle, and E. Smart.	Arcola, Ill	June 11, 1867	65, 577
Auger, Post-hole	J. M. Leeds and J. E. Hallowell.	Kokomo, Ind	Jan. 23, 1866	52, 180
Auger, Post-hole	T. Luson	Sharon, Wis	June 4, 1867	65, 400
Auger, Post-hole	S McCray	Woodstock, Ill	Sept. 10, 1867	68, 638
Auger, Post-hole hollow	S. H. Yocum	Tipton, Ind	Mar. 31, 1868	76, 132
Auger, Pump, and spur-bits	R. French	Derby, Conn	Nov. 11, 1834	....
Auger, Screw	D. Bassett	Derby, Conn	Mar. 18, 1829	....
Auger, Screw	E. L'Hommedieu	Norwich, Conn	July 17, 1816	....
Auger, Screw	P. Williamson	New York, N. Y	Sept. 9, 1833	....
Auger, Serpentine-screw	G. Shelter	York, Pa	Sept. 10, 1829	....
Auger, Serpentine-screw	G. Shelter	York, Pa	Mar. 21, 1831	....
Auger shafts, Coupling for earth	G. W. Irwin and T. A. Cox	Champaign County, Ill	July 8, 1873	140, 710

Index of patents issued from the United States Patent Office from 1790 *to* 1873, *inclusive*—Continued.

Invention.	Inventor.	Residence.	Date.	No.
Auger-shank, Method of attaching cutting-lips to.	N. S. White and A. Denio	Shaftsbury, Vt	Dec. 21, 1858	22, 394
Auger, &c., Ship	I. W. Hoagland	Jersey City, N. J	Mar. 20, 1855	12, 551
Auger, Single-twist	E. L'Hommedieu	Saybrook, Conn	Oct. 1, 1830	....
Auger, Single-twist spiral-screw	N. C. Sanford	Meriden, Conn	Aug. 8, 1834	....
Auger, Slotting	P. Cunningham	Eckley, Pa	Sept. 1, 1868	81, 607
Auger, Spiral-screw	A. Newton	Meriden, Conn	Aug. 8, 1834	....
Auger, Spoke-tenon	W. Morehouse	Buffalo, N. Y	Jan. 14, 1862	34, 159
Auger-stock	W. T. Barnes	Buffalo, N. Y	Apr. 3, 1849	6, 256
Auger-stock	S. C. Norcross	Norway, Me	Aug. 25, 1863	39, 669
Auger-strap	S. Gore	Sheshequin, Pa	July 20, 1825	....
Auger, Submarine	N. Blake	Ira, N. Y	Apr. 20, 1852	8, 882
Auger to bore square holes, &c	C. Jackson	Otsego County, N. Y	Feb. 14, 1818	....
Auger, Tube	R. Thomas	Richmond County, N. C	May 29, 1819	....
Auger, Tubular	J. A. Reynolds	Elmira, N. Y	Jan. 13, 1857	16, 399
Auger-twisting machine	W. L. Aldrich and W. Evans	Norwich and Seymour, Conn.	Aug. 6, 1867	67, 395
Auger, Undermining	P. Sheldon	Jamestown, N. Y	Oct. 7, 1873	143, 535
Auger, Well	E. Altman	Hamilton, Mo	Jan. 31, 1871	111, 300
Auger, Well	J. B. Christian	Hamburg, Iowa	Sept. 17, 1872	131, 427
Auger, Well	J. Y. Goode	Water Valley, Miss	Dec. 7, 1869	97, 501
Auger, Well	J. and T. J. Ingels	Atchison, Kans	Nov. 15, 1870	109, 214
Auger, Well	H. R. King	Poplar Bluff, Ark	Oct. 17, 1871	120, 076
Auger, Well	A. A. McMahen	Oxford, Miss	Apr. 13, 1869	88, 891
Auger, Well	W. L. Payne	Topeka, Kans	Sept. 23, 1873	143 181
Auger, Well	F. Spees	Tabor, Iowa	Feb. 20, 1872	123, 847
Auger, Well	W. H. Stone	Pattonsburgh, Mo	July 11, 1871	116, 883
Auger, Well	J. Wilson and G. H. Baisley	Hamilton, Mo	July 5, 1870	105, 021
Auger, Well-boring	P. Ollom	Muncie, Ind	Feb. 19, 1867	62, 216
Augers and bits, Manufacture of	J. Swan	Seymour, Conn	June 9, 1868	78, 769
Augers and boring-bits, Process for making	C. Whitehouse	Bridgtown, England	June 15, 1869	91, 503
Augers and spiral conveyors, Packing	J. Mattison	Oswego, N. Y	Nov. 2, 1869	96, 455
Augers, Casting screw	J. Carl and J. W. Heath	Grenada, Miss	Aug. 21, 1860	29, 668
Augers, Coupling-device for earth-boring	A. J. and G. Heine	Frémont, Nebr	July 16, 1872	129, 027
Augers, Coupling for earth-boring	T. Orchard	Lincoln, Cal	Dec. 6, 1870	109, 930
Auger, Device for fastening cutter of hollow	W. A. Clark	Bethany, Conn	July 12, 1859	24, 722
Augers, Die for making	E. L'Hommedieu	Chester, Conn	Aug. 29, 1854	11, 613
Augers, Die for making	E. H. Tracy	Meriden, Conn	July 4, 1865	48, 633
Augers, Die for manufacturing	S. A. Smith	Essex, Conn	Mar. 4, 1873	136, 391
Augers, Handle-fastening for	J. M. Hathaway	New York, N. Y	Aug. 21, 1860	29, 692
Augers, Machine for cutting down	E. O. and E. Carrington	Wallingford, Conn	July 2, 1867	66, 297
Augers, Machine for finishing the lips and points of.	W. P. Maxson	Elmira, N. Y	Nov. 19, 1872	133, 238
Augers, Machine for grinding and cutting down	E. O. and E. Carrington	West Meriden, Conn	Apr. 7, 1868	76, 301
Augers, Machine for making	I. Tower	Rochester, N. Y	Mar. 1, 1864	41, 822
Augers, Machine for regulating the twist and diameter of screw.	N. C. Sanford and L. P. Smith	Meriden, Conn	Apr. 10, 1849	6, 305
Augers, Machine for swaging the head of screw	R. Jennings	Deep River, Conn	July 31, 1866	56, 869
Augers, Machine for turning the lips of	R. Cook	Shelburne Falls, Mass	Mar. 27, 1855	12, 583
Augers, Machinery for manufacturing double-twist screw.	E. L'Hommedieu and R. N. Watrous.	Chester, Conn	July 24, 1838	851
Augers, Manufacture of	J. Swan	Seymour, Conn	Aug. 20, 1867	68, 012
Augers, Manufacturing screw	W. Field	Pawtucket, R. I	Apr. 15, 1840	1, 553
Augers, Means for operating earth	W. H. Beach and C. N. Hanson.	Hamburg, Iowa	Feb. 4, 1873	135, 510
Augers, Means for operating earth	J. B. Christian	Hamburg, Iowa	May 13, 1873	138, 788
Augers, Method of attaching expansible cutting-lips to.	N. Clare and J. Quigly	Malden, N. Y	Apr. 6, 1858	19, 829
Augers, Method of manufacturing	G. G. Griswold	Chester, Conn	Apr. 1, 1856	14, 561
Augers, Method of securing the cutters to the spindles of.	C. L. Barnes	New York, N. Y	Aug. 17, 1858	21, 179
Augers, Method of using the common screw	O. Stetson and W. Sebree	Georgetown, Ky	Dec. 11, 1810	....
Augers, Mold for casting	W. Evans and R. E. Hayden	Seymour, Conn	Apr. 6, 1869	88, 559
Augers, Tenoning	W. A. Clark	Bethany, Conn	June 12, 1860	28, 653
Augers to handles, Attaching	E. Broad	Saint Anthony, Minn	Jan. 8, 1869	90, 919
Augers to handles, Attaching	M. S. Brooks	Chester, Conn	Oct. 28, 1851	8, 464
Augers to handles, Attaching	C. W. Cotton	Shelburne Falls, Mass	Mar. 20, 1855	12, 575
Augers to handles, Attaching	J. E. Larkin	Ballston Spa, N. Y	Nov. 19, 1850	7, 785
Augers to handles, Attaching	H. W. Olney	Allegheny, Pa	Nov. 7, 1865	50, 838
Augers to sinker for boring artesian well, Mode of uniting.	W. Morris	Kanawaha County, Va	Sept. 4, 1841	2, 243
Augers, Turning any number of	H. Branch	New York	Aug. 7, 1826	....
Augers, Twisting-machine	O. Snow	Meriden, Conn	May 13, 1834	....
Aural instruments	C. G. Page	Washington, D. C	Nov. 20, 1860	30, 688
Automatic brake	J. Wilkinson	Baltimore, Md	Jan. 1, 1861	31, 047
Automatic brake for machinery	T. Stebins	San Francisco, Cal	Oct. 8, 1872	132, 113
Automatic folding-gate	J. B. Mahana	Benson, Vt	Jan. 10, 1865	45, 842
Automatic gate	W. W. Burson	Rockford, Ill	Nov. 10, 1868	83, 923
Automatic gate	J. B. Cotton	Dayton, Ohio	Aug. 30, 1870	106, 917
Automatic gate	G. C. Crum	Barr's Store, Ill	July 1, 1873	140, 479
Automatic gate	L. S. Deming	Newington, Conn	Sept. 8, 1863	39, 798
Automatic gate	B. F. Dickey	Marshall, Michigan	July 13, 1869	92, 430
Automatic gate	J. S. Elkins and J. T. Green	Marquette, Wis	June 19, 1866	55, 623
Automatic gate	L. Filson	Bushnell, Ill	Apr. 29, 1873	138, 238
Automatic gate	J. W. Foster	Racine, Wis	Apr. 28, 1863	38, 304
Automatic gate	J. S. Fort	Kenton, Ohio	Aug. 19, 1873	141, 925
Automatic gate	C. E. Gillespie	Edwardsville, Ill	June 10, 1873	139, 742
Automatic gate	E. Harter	Dowagiac, Mich	Oct. 6, 1868	82, 831
Automatic gate	N. Long	Muncie, Indiana	Apr. 22, 1873	138, 033
Automatic gate	G. McKnight	Hebron, N. Y	Nov. 15, 1864	45, 063
Automatic gate	H. W. Miskimen	Kingston Mines, Ill	Dec. 10, 1861	33, 896
Automatic gate	T. J. Murphy	Rochester, N. Y	Dec. 1, 1868	84, 569
Automatic gate	G. W. Olbert and W. Young	Barr's Store, Ill	Oct. 21, 1873	143, 839
Automatic gate	M. Orewiler	Bucyrus, Ohio	Sept. 27, 1870	107, 801
Automatic gate	J. G. Page	Rockford, Ill	Aug. 7, 1866	56, 987
Automatic gate	J. P. Ponce	Mayfield, Cal	Apr. 29, 1873	138, 283
Automatic gate	J. H. Schenck	Chicago, Ill	June 26, 1866	55, 914
Automatic gate	P. A. Spicer and M. Crossman	Marshall, Mich	July 26, 1870	105, 735
Automatic gate	G. B. Stevenson	Upper Sandusky, Ohio	Apr. 15, 1873	137, 971
Automatic gate	J. E. Stong	Newton Brook, Canada	Aug. 19, 1873	141, 960
Automatic gate	E. Waterbury	Stamford, Conn	Nov. 12, 1861	33, 723

Index of patents issued from the United States Patent Office from 1790 *to* 1873, *inclusive*—Continued.

Invention.	Inventor.	Residence.	Date.	No.
Automatic gate	E. P. Wheeler	Corinth, Miss	Oct. 7, 1873	143, 551
Automatic gate	S. Whitaker	Bel Air, Md	May 3, 1870	102, 741
Automatic gate	W. I. Wooster	Harvard, Ill	Mar. 18, 1873	136, 892
Automatic gate	S. J. Wright	Ellsworth, N. Y	Apr. 30, 1867	64, 394
Automatic gate for railway-crossing	G. B. Pullinger	Philadelphia, Pa	Dec. 18, 1855	13, 956
Automatic hoop	L. W. Taylor	Weathersfield, Vt	June 1, 1869	90, 700
Automatic lubricator	J. Dreyfus	New York, N. Y	May 21, 1867	64, 956
Automatic lubricator	E. Von Jeinsen	Omaha, Nebr	July 5, 1870	105, 147
Automatic press	P. Hayden	Pittsburgh, Pa	Sept. 12, 1865	49, 877
Automatic register	S. Rigler	Ottawa, Ill	Dec. 10, 1867	72, 084
Automatic regulator	J. M. Osgood	Somerville, Mass	Nov. 1, 1864	44, 884
Automatic rope-skipper	J. Hoffmann	Waterbury, Conn	July 1, 1873	140, 503
Automatic switch	S. Hodkinson	Louisville, Ky	May 4, 1869	89, 578
Automatic ventiiator	M. E. Mead	Darien Depot, Conn	May 18, 1869	90, 180
Automatic ventilator	B. F. Prentis	Benwood, W. Va	Oct. 11, 1870	108, 185
Auxiliary engine to be used in supplying steam-boilers with water, Manner of arranging the parts of.	J. Cochrane	Baltimore, Md	Apr. 16, 1845	4, 003
Auxiliary table	J. Blake	Scranton, Pa	Mar. 23, 1869	88, 121
Auxiliary table	E. Johnson	McLean County, Ill	Apr. 29, 1873	138, 406
Awl	S. Babbitt	Brazil, Ind	July 12, 1870	105, 161
Awl	S. Babbitt	Brazil, Ind	Aug. 1, 1871	117, 501
Awl	R. Egan	Brooklyn, N. Y	Apr. 25, 1865	47, 403
Awl	T. Kenney	Lynn, Mass	May 2, 1871	114, 446
Awl	G. K. Mellor	Woonsocket, R. I	Dec. 24, 1872	134, 214
Awl	S. E. Totten	Brooklyn, N. Y	June 18, 1867	65, 843
Awl and punch, Belt	W. J. Innis	Providence, R. I	Nov. 15, 1859	26, 107
Awl and similar tools, Handle for	D. H. Chamberlain	Boston, Mass	May 30, 1848	5, 609
Awl and tool	H. Aiken	Franklin, N. H	Apr. 13, 1858	19, 901
Awl, Belt	S. Y. Beach	Seymour, Conn	May 25, 1869	90, 485
Awl, Belt	F. I. Palmer	Youngstown, Ohio	Apr. 5, 1870	101, 655
Awl, Centering	D. A. Wilcox	Woodstock, Vt	Aug. 17, 1869	93, 937
Awl, Centering	N. Woodbury	Woodstock, Vt	June 22, 1869	91, 806
Awl-drill, &c., Setting	E. B. Bigelow and S. P. Brigham.	West Boyleston Township, Mass.	Jan. 27, 1835	....
Awl for heel-machine	H. H. Bigelow	Worcester, Mass	Mar. 28, 1871	113, 008
Awl, Grafting	D. B. Oliver	Cambria, N. Y	Nov. 22, 1870	109, 442
Awl-haft	W. Campbell	Gilsum, N. H	July 1, 1836	....
Awl-haft	D. H. Chamberlain	Boston, Mass	Apr. 3, 1849	6, 261
Awl-haft	N. S. Clement	Worcester, N. Y	Apr. 21, 1857	17, 078
Awl-haft	L. H. Farnsworth	Hudson, Mass	June 16, 1868	78, 947
Awl-haft	B. James	Worcester, Mass	Apr. 15, 1856	14, 704
Awl-haft	E. Martin	Grafton, Mass	Mar. 21, 1843	3, 014
Awl-haft	D. M. Smith	Gilsum, N. H	Oct. 25, 1832	....
Awl-haft	D. M. Smith	Gilsum, N. H	Mar. 31, 1836	....
Awl-handle	N. S. Clement	New Britain, Conn	Mar. 19, 1867	62, 938
Awl-handle	D. R. Wight	Sturbridge, Mass	Mar. 24, 1868	76, 020
Awl handle, Brad	H. L. Barker	Hartford, Conn	Feb. 6, 1866	52, 443
Awl holder and extractor, Pegging	H. Huston	Cannonsburgh, Pa	Sept. 8, 1863	39, 815
Awl, Lasting	C. K. Bradford	Lynnfield, Mass	Oct. 1, 1867	69, 395
Awl-making die	J. P. Blake	Rockville, Mass	Apr. 13, 1869	88, 837
Awl, Pegging	G. B. Paine	Montpelier, Vt	Feb. 16, 1869	87, 062
Awl, Shoemakers'	B. I. Lane	South Framingham, Mass	Apr. 17, 1860	27, 913
Awl-sockets, &c	H. Aiken	Dracut, Mass	Dec. 16, 1833	....
Awl, Tying-up	N. W. Baker	Lynn, Mass	June 22, 1869	91, 593
Awls to hafts, Method of attaching	D. Pierce	Montague, Mass	Aug. 13, 1838	882
Awning	W. Armstrong	Milwaukee, Wis	June 14, 1864	43, 081
Awning	G. H. Bancroft	Philadelphia, Pa	May 7, 1867	64, 399
Awning	J. C. Bowe	Urbana, Ohio	Nov. 13, 1866	59, 548
Awning	H. A. Bowman	Worcester, Mass	Apr. 27, 1869	89, 462
Awning	J. Boyle	New York, N. Y	Feb. 18, 1873	135, 966
Awning	S. Chace	Providence, R. I	Oct. 11, 1859	25, 723
Awning	G. W. Gerau	Brooklyn, N. Y	Apr. 15, 1873	137, 772
Awning	W. Hildebrand	Fort Wayne, Ind	Nov. 8, 1870	109, 007
Awning	E. E. Laumont	New York, N. Y	Oct. 17, 1865	50, 479
Awning	W. Matthews	Orange, N. J	June 11, 1872	127, 781
Awning	S. Miller and J. S. McClellan	Champaign County, Ohio	Nov. 12, 1867	70, 880
Awning	S. Miller and J. S. McClellan	Champaign County, Ohio	Nov. 26, 1867	71, 509
Awning	J. Sebo	Wilmington, Del	May 25, 1844	3, 594
Awning	L. G. Sert and C. L. Schurr	Baltimore, Md	Oct. 25, 1870	108, 639
Awning	H. Sykes	New York, N. Y	Oct. 7, 1873	143, 542
Awning	J. A. Pain	Clyde, N. Y	Apr. 10, 1866	53, 859
Awning	N. Poulson	Washington, D. C	Sept. 8, 1868	82, 032
Awning	R. P. Pratt	Hartford, Conn	Oct. 13, 1868	83, 090
Awning	T. G. Tyler	New York, N. Y	Sept. 29, 1868	82, 569
Awning	J. B. Watkins	New Bedford, Mass	Aug. 19, 1862	36, 251
Awning, Adjustable	L. Yenne and C. Schneider	New York, N. Y., and Newark, N. J.	Sept. 20, 1870	107, 584
Awning and fan for horses' heads	H. L. Byrd	Baltimore, Md	Sept. 13, 1870	107, 333
Awnmg and reflector	J. Corduan	Brooklyn, N. Y	May 2, 1865	47, 524
Awning, device for operating	A. Thalhofer	South Bend, Ind	June 28, 1870	104, 900
Awning-fixture	E. Peach	Utica, N. Y	July 31, 1860	29, 599
Awning for animals	S. Moffit	Minneapolis, Minn	Apr. 4, 1871	113, 323
Awning for car, &c	J. H. Monce	New York, N. Y	July 26, 1870	105, 829
Awning for horse and dray	J. Nelson	Cincinnati, Ohio	Sept. 25, 1855	13, 600
Awning fcr horse-car	M. C. Battey	Washington, D. C	Nov. 17, 1868	84, 160
Awning-frame	H. Hilliard	Brooklyn, N. Y	July 5, 1870	105, 076
Awning-frame	J. W. Loane	Baltimore, Md	May 7, 1872	126, 556
Awning-frame	H. Stephens	New York, N. Y	Aug. 26, 1873	142, 291
Awning-frame	C. Werner	Charleston, S. C	Nov. 29, 1870	109, 694
Awning-frame, Adjustable	L. Yenne	New York, N. Y	May 3, 1870	102, 642
Awning-frame for horses, attachable to harness	N. Pullman	New Oregon, Iowa	Sept. 29, 1857	18, 300
Awning frame, Shade	J. Drechsler	New York, N. Y	Dec. 3, 1872	133, 572
Awning frame, Window	J. A. Allen	Philadelphia, Pa	Apr. 29, 1873	138, 223
Awning, metal	W. O. Pa. isen	New York, N. Y	Apr. 27, 1858	20, 085
Awning, Shop	W. H. Bakewell	New York, N. Y	Mar. 23, 1852	8, 817
Awning-slide	J. Boyle	New York, N. Y	Oct. 29, 1872	132, 559
Awning-slide	T. F. Darcy	New York, N. Y	Feb. 27, 1872	124, 037

Index of patents issued from the United States Patent Office from 1790 *to* 1873, *inclusive*—Continued.

Invention.	Inventor.	Residence.	Date.	No.
Awning, Street-car	C. B. Turnbull	Washington, D. C	July 15, 1873	140, 972
Awning-windlass	I. Walter	Cincinnati, Ohio	Feb. 27, 1872	124, 178
Awning, Window	C. C. Moore	New York, N. Y	Dec. 5, 1871	121, 650
Awning, Window	J. B. Wheeden	Baltimore, Md	July 6, 1869	92, 239
Awnings, Painting striped	C. E. Wheeler	Boston, Mass	May 13, 1873	138, 773
Ax	J. H. Beidler	Adrian, Mich	Aug. 10, 1869	93, 585
Ax	D. W. Colburn	Laomi, Ill	July 9, 1867	66, 563
Ax	J. Franklin	Springfield, Ohio	Nov. 2, 1869	96, 416
Ax	J. W. Hilton and R. W. Green	Bradford, Pa	Sept. 1, 1868	81, 635
Ax	A. H. Jumper	Sunman, Ind	Aug. 31, 1869	94, 318
Ax	H. Mann	Bellefonte, Pa	June 3, 1862	35, 480
Ax	W. Peabody	Orono, Me	Aug. 22, 1871	118, 266
Ax	E. Quast	Freedom, Mo	Nov. 16, 1869	96, 937
Ax	B. Smith	Canton, Conn	Nov. 2, 1832	....
Ax and hook combined, Grubbing	P. W. Norris	Detroit, Mich	Feb. 15, 1870	99, 784
Ax and pick, Ice	J. N. Bunnell	Unionville, Conn	Dec. 6, 1870	109, 867
Ax-bit-blank bar	J. Lippincott	Pittsburgh, Pa	Dec. 22, 1868	85, 110
Ax-bit-blank machine	E. Bartholomew	Mill Hall, Pa	June 20, 1871	116, 011
Ax-bits, Machine for forming	L. Chapman	Collinsville, Conn	June 1, 1869	90, 726
Ax-bits, Manufacture of	C. Blair	Collinsville, Conn	Aug. 17, 1869	93, 666
Ax blanks, Method of making	J. W. Ells	Pittsburgh, Pa	Sept. 3, 1867	68, 423
Ax, Chopping	T. Merriam	Waterloo, Wis	Apr. 12, 1864	42, 303
Ax-dressing machinery	J. Mackey	Napanock, N. Y	Aug. 29, 1848	5, 736
Ax-dressing machinery	E. K. Root	Collinsville, Conn	Aug. 22, 1848	5, 731
Ax for wood-splitting machine	J. H. Silkman	Milwaukee, Wis	Jan. 23, 1866	52, 216
Ax, Grinding	H. Mann	Bellefonte, Pa	Aug. 17, 1869	93, 727
Ax, Hand	E. H. Meigs	East Berlin, Conn	Aug. 11, 1868	80, 868
Ax-handle	J. M. Sears	Vandalia, Ill	May 30, 1871	115, 532
Ax-handle	B. D. Stevens	Decorah, Iowa	June 2, 1868	78, 550
Ax-handle fastening	J. E. Emerson	San Francisco, Cal	Apr. 10, 1860	27, 784
Ax-handle guard	L. B. Hoit	Cedar Falls, Iowa	July 12, 1870	105, 205
Ax-handle shield	B. Butler	Saint Johnsbury Centre, Vt.	Jan. 26, 1869	86, 130
Ax-handles, Mode of securing	G. W. Simonds	Lynnfield, Mass	July 10, 1866	56, 281
Ax, hatchet, &c	D. Hinman	Winchester, Conn	Nov. 2, 1832	....
Ax-helve	W. Morehouse	Buffalo, N. Y	Apr. 11, 1865	47, 214
Ax-helves, Metal cap for	A. W. Porter	Saint Johnsville, N. Y	July 17, 1860	29, 192
Ax-making machine	E. F. Hurd	Johnsonville, N. Y	Aug. 14, 1866	57, 142
Ax making machine	E. F. Hurd	Hoosick Falls, N. Y	Nov. 21, 1871	121, 172
Ax-making machine	C. Hutchins	East Douglass, Mass	Mar. 3, 1857	16, 732
Ax-making machine	J. Simmons	Cohoes, N. Y	Mar. 1, 1853	9, 601
Ax-making machine	I. W. Turne	Baltimore, Md	Nov. 4, 1842	2, 841
Ax-making process	J. Orelup	Ballston Spa, N. Y	June 8, 1852	9, 000
Ax, Oval	A. Collins	Winsted, Conn	Oct. 25, 1832	....
Ax, Oval	S. Hyde	Williamsburgh, Mass	Jan. 29, 1830	....
Ax, Oval	S. Hyde	Williamsburgh, Mass	Mar. 2, 1831	....
Ax-pole, Making	D. P. Estep	Pittsburgh, Pa	Oct. 14, 1856	15, 880
Ax-poll blank	W. Bunton	Pittsburgh, Pa	Oct. 12, 1869	95, 646
Ax-poll swaging-machine	R. Blake and A. Carpenter	Scranton, Pa	May 4, 1869	89, 623
Ax-polls, Machine for making	R. H. Cole	Saint Louis, Mo	June 16, 1857	17, 556
Ax-polls, Machine for making	G. Reynolds	Manchester, N. H	July 20, 1858	20, 957
Ax-polls, Machine for punching	R. Blake	Scranton, Pa	Aug. 11, 1868	80, 900
Ax-shaving machine	H. C. Reynolds	Manchester, N. H	Aug. 6, 1867	67, 584
Ax, Stone	W. C. Peckham	Troy, Ohio	Oct. 29, 1872	132, 540
Ax-testing machine	W. Hunt	East Douglass, Mass	Sept. 2, 1856	15, 656
Axes, Attaching handles to	T. H. Tyndale	Belleville, Ill	May 25, 1869	90, 412
Axes, Attaching handles to	H. C. Wooding	Wallingford, Conn	June 5, 1866	55, 437
Axes, Die for forming the eyes of pick	H. L. Lowman	New York, N. Y	Nov. 27, 1866	60, 022
Axes, Forging	D. Hinman	Canton, Conn	June 29, 1833	....
Axes, Forging	E. Shaw	Canton, Conn	June 29, 1833	....
Axes, hammers, &c., Manufacture of	F. C. Curie	Lancaster, Pa	Sept. 29, 1868	82, 607
Axes, &c., Hardening	J. N. Rockwell	Napanock, N. Y	June 23, 1857	17, 639
Axes, hatchets, &c., Method of punching the eyes of	E. K. Root	Collinsville, Conn	Dec. 10, 1838	1, 027
Axes, hoes, scythes, pitch-forks, &c., Making	J. P. Hazard	Washington County, R. I	Aug. 9, 1833	....
Axes, hoes, scythes, pitch-forks, &c., Making	J. F. Mackie	New York	Nov. 19, 1833	....
Axes, hoes, scythes, pitch-forks, &c., Making	L. Olds	Oneonta, N. Y	July 9, 1833	....
Axes, Machine for making	J. Pratt, jr	Charlemont, Mass	May 16, 1832	....
Axes, Machine for manufacturing	D. C. Stone	Napanock, N. Y	Apr. 21, 1838	699
Axes, Machinery for hammering heads of	L. Dodge	Waterford, N. Y	May 1, 1866	54, 311
Axes, Machinery for making	H. D. Morris	Baldwinsville, N. Y	Aug. 31, 1869	93, 232
Axes, Making	J. L. Lewis	Pittsburgh, Pa	Mar. 13, 1866	53, 155
Axes, Manufacture of	J. Lippincott	Pittsburgh, Pa	Feb. 21, 1860	27, 227
Axes, Manufacture of	J. Lippincott	Pittsburgh, Pa	July 23, 1867	66, 978
Axes, Manufacture of	H. C. Reynolds	Manchester, N. H	Aug. 1, 1865	49, 156
Axes, Manufacturing	H. D. Morris	Baldwinsville, N. Y	Jan. 11, 1870	98, 789
Axes, Manufacturing	E. K. Root	Canton, Conn	Mar. 30, 1836	....
Axes, Manufacturing	E. Shaw and R. H. Burk	Canton, Conn	Nov. 3, 1831	....
Axes, Manufacturing and forming the eyes of	M. D. Whipple	Douglass, Mass	Jan. 31, 1833	....
Axes, Method of manufacturing	G. Palmer and C. W. Hubbard	Pittsburgh, Pa	Aug. 22, 1871	118, 264
Axes, Method of securing helves in	H. N. and J. C. Bill	Willimantic, Conn	July 25, 1854	11, 350
Axes, Mode of making	J. Alley, sr	Pise, Ind	Apr. 9, 1829	....
Axes, picks, &c., Fastening handles to	J. Stewart	Saint Cloud, Minn	Aug. 18, 1868	81, 308
Axes, &c., Sharpening	J. Shotwell		Mar. 16, 1799	....
Axes, Shears for the manufacture of	L. Dodge	Cohoes, N. Y	Apr. 2, 1861	31, 927
Axes to handles, Fastening	W. H. Livingston	New York, N. Y	Sept. 25, 1860	30, 146
Axes to handles, Mode of attaching	J. Stewart	Money Creek, Minn	Oct. 29, 1867	70, 284
Axes, Step or gudgeon, Vertical	J. Andrews	Dinwiddie County, Va	Aug. 11, 1817	....
Axle:				
See Anti-friction.				
Car.				
Carriage.				
Carriage-wheel.				
Divided.				
Grindstone.				
Iron.				
Locomotive.				
Mail.				
Metallic.				

Index of patents issued from the United States Patent Office from 1790 to 1873, inclusive—Continued.

Invention.	Inventor.	Residence.	Date.	No.
Axle—Continued. *See* Movable. Trussed. Tubular. Vehicle. Wagon. Wheat-drill. Wheel. Wooden				
Axle	J. Elmire	Martic Township, Pa	Aug. 18, 1868	81, 079
Axle	E. Finn	Berlin, Wis	Dec. 15, 1868	84, 940
Axle	S. D. Littlefield	Burlington, Wis	Oct. 1, 1867	69, 350
Axle	W. Nevins	Falmouth, Me	Oct. 1, 1867	69, 362
Axle	J. D. Smith	Schuylerville, N. Y	May 18, 1869	90, 317
Axle	H. T. Tichenor	Fort Branch, Ind	Aug. 27, 1867	68, 130
Axle	H. W. Tilton	Walpole, Mass	June 29, 1869	91, 987
Axle	H. G. Weibling	Denver City, Col	Jan. 20, 1863	37, 479
Axle and axle-box	D. Wigger	New York, N. Y	Nov. 12, 1867	70, 928
Axle and bolster coupling	G. Brown	Carlisle, N. Y	Nov. 21, 1848	5, 932
Axle and gudgeon, Mode of making boxes for	I. Babbit	Boston, Mass	July 17, 1839	1, 252
Axle and its bearing	R. R. McGregor	Covington, Tenn	Apr. 19, 1870	102, 025
Axle and journal-box lubricator	J. B. G. M. F. Piret	Paris, France	Aug. 2, 1870	105, 977
Axle and journal, Lubricating	W. Kenworthy and J. H. Pollitt	Birmingham, Pa	June 6, 1871	115, 618
Axle and other spindles, Lubricator for	W. H. Harvey	Bangor, Me	Oct. 31, 1871	120, 515
Axle and shaft	W. H. Hawley	Utica, N. Y	Nov. 2, 1869	96, 318
Axle, Attaching draft-pole to	E. C. Smith	Birmingham, Conn	Nov. 27, 1866	60, 075
Axle bearing, Railway-car	W. E. Wilcox and T. H. Wills	Peoria and Beardstown, Ill	July 27, 1869	93, 151
Axle-blanks, Tool for finishing	H. E Forrest	Cambridgeport, Mass	Jan. 14, 1873	134, 742
Axle-box	S. F. Allen	Chicago, Ill	Sept. 4, 1866	57, 657
Axle-box	S. Barker	Harttord, Conn	Sept. 24, 1867	69, 160
Axle-box	J. Bevin	Unadilla Forks, N. Y	Apr. 8, 1856	14, 639
Axle-box	W. A. Boyden	Altoona, Pa	Nov. 19, 1867	71, 125
Axle-box	H. Brady	Factoryville, N. Y	Aug. 20, 1867	67, 946
Axle-box	G. Brill	Philadelphia, Pa	Mar. 19, 1867	62, 931
Axle-box	N. Campbell	Brooklyn, N. Y	Apr. 16, 1867	63, 783
Axle-box	H. L. Castile	Memphis, Tenn	May 15, 1860	28, 253
Axle-box	J. Christy	Philadelphia, Pa	Jan. 16, 1866	52, 029
Axle-box	C. Cook	Winsted, Conn	Sept. 5, 1865	49, 726
Axle-box	D. Dalzell	South Egremont, Mass	Aug. 16, 1870	106, 469
Axle-box	D. Dalzell	South Egremont, Mass	July 25, 1871	117, 390
Axle-box	L. A. Dochez	New York, N. Y	Dec. 31, 1867	72, 821
Axle-box	D. H. Dotterer	Philadelphia, Pa	Apr. 3, 1866	53, 588
Axle-box	D. H. Dotterer	Philadelphia, Pa	June 18, 1867	65, 797
Axle-box	D. H. Dotterer	Philadelphia, Pa	May 30, 1871	115, 449
Axle-box	W. B. Fahnestock	Lancaster, Pa	Mar. 30, 1858	19, 762
Axle-box	A. A. Freeman	Philadelphia, Pa	Apr. 2, 1867	63, 379
Axle-box	A. Goodyear, 2d	Hamden, Conn	July 4, 1871	116, 702
Axle-box	E. P. Haskell	New Bedford, Mass	Nov. 17, 1868	84, 185
Axle-box	J. B. Hendricks	Clayton, Ill	Sept. 14, 1869	94, 823
Axle-box	J. T. Henry	New Haven, Conn	Jan. 16, 1872	122, 829
Axle-box	H. Howson	Philadelphia, Pa	Nov. 2, 1858	21, 998
Axle-box	J. J. Lahaye and J. E. Wooten	Reading, Pa	July 5, 1870	105, 096
Axle box	B. P. Lamason	Milton, Pa	Sept. 24, 1867	69, 225
Axle-box	F. Leppens	Hartford, Conn	Nov. 13, 1866	59, 616
Axle-box	J. Lightner	Roxbury, Mass	Nov. 21, 1848	5, 935
Axle-box	I. S. Lister	Philadelphia, Pa	June 23, 1868	79, 238
Axle-box	J. S. Lister	Philadelphia, Pa	Feb. 9, 1869	86, 679
Axle-box	E. Lockwood	Bordentown, N. J	Sept. 5, 1865	49, 772
Axle-box	D. Metz	Washington, D. C	Nov. 2, 1869	96, 337
Axle-box	M. V. Miller and G. Henry	Manchester, Pa., and Steubenville, Ohio.	Aug. 7, 1866	56, 977
Axle-box	J. Montgomery	Harrisburgh, Pa	May 15, 1866	54, 753
Axle-box	C. M. Oliver	Port Carbon, Pa	Nov. 13, 1866	59, 632
Axle-box	B. M. Pearne and L. Coville	Oxford, N. Y	July 14, 1868	79, 916
Axle-box	P. Philippi	Beardstown, Ill	Feb. 19, 1867	62, 221
Axle-box	H. B. Pitner	La Porte, Ind	Dec. 10, 1867	72, 079
Axle-box	W. H. Pollard	Seneca Falls, N. Y	June 4, 1867	65, 428
Axle-box	W. F. Rippon	Providence, R. I	May 15, 1866	54, 775
Axle-box	O. H. P. Robinson	Bellport, N. Y	Mar. 13, 1866	53, 186
Axle-box	H. B. Rowley	Rushville, N. Y	Nov. 27, 1866	60, 064
Axle-box	W. H. Saunders	Hastings, N. Y	Dec. 2, 1856	16, 153
Axle-box	A. E. Smith	Bronxville, N. Y	Mar. 11, 1856	14, 415
Axle-box	A. E. Smith	Bronxville, N. Y	Jan. 27, 1857	16, 499
Axle-box	W. Stechschult	Glandorf, Ohio	Mar. 15, 1864	41, 945
Axle-box	J. Stephenson	New York, N. Y	July 25, 1865	49, 005
Axle-box	L. Wakefield	Minneapolis, Minn	Mar. 23, 1869	88, 242
Axle-box	S. A. Wing and L. G Johnston	Greenfield Centre, N. Y	Sept. 5, 1871	118, 770
Axle-box, &c	D. Cumming	Sorrel Horse, Pa	July 27, 1858	20, 991
Axle-box alarm and lubricator, Car	O. Evans	Saint Paul, Minn	Jan. 28, 1873	135, 213
Axle-box and hanger	D. H. Dotterer	Philadelphia, Pa	Aug. 13, 1867	67, 638
Axle-box and hub	G. Leverich	Elizabethport, N. J	Feb. 2, 1869	86, 558
Axle-box and sleeve, Vehicle-wheel	W. H. Cowell	Columbus, Ohio	Aug. 12, 1873	141, 699
Axle-box and spindle	J. Bower	Lafayette, Ind	Jan. 14, 1873	134, 725
Axle-box, Anti-friction	P. Seyl, P. Fischer, and P. Brenner.	Chicago, Ill	July 18, 1871	117, 211
Axle-box bearing	A. B. Allen	Rutland, Vt	Mar. 30, 1869	88, 356
Axle box, Car	W. G. Beattie	Nine Elms, England	Dec. 17, 1872	134, 026
Axle box, Car	J. E. Bering	Newburgh, N. Y	Dec. 2, 1873	145, 146
Axle box, Car	J. W. Cochran	New York, N. Y	Nov. 2, 1858	21, 943
Axle box, Car	W. W. Crane	Auburn, N. Y	May 13, 1873	138, 794
Axle box, Car	J. C. Creed	Omaha, Nebr	Jan. 12, 1869	85, 793
Axle box, Car	J. M. Dodge	Newark, N. J	Mar. 4, 1873	136, 424
Axle box, Car	D. H. Dotterer	Philadelphia, Pa	Sept. 5, 1871	118, 701
Axle box, Car	H. G. Downs	Seneca Falls, N. Y	Jan. 7, 1873	134, 594
Axle box, Car	W. Ebbit	New York, N. Y	Mar. 18, 1862	34, 674
Axle box, Car	C. T. Fay	San Francisco, Cal	Feb. 18, 1873	135, 977
Axle box, Car	S. F. Gates	Cambridge, Mass	Apr. 29, 1873	138, 242
Axle box, Car	J. T. Hagerty	Camp Point, Ill	Feb. 15, 1870	99, 882

Index of patents issued from the United States Patent Office from 1790 *to* 1873, *inclusive*—Continued.

Invention.	Inventor.	Residence.	Date.	No.
Axle box, Car	J. Harris	Dorchester, Mass	Dec. 10, 1867	71, 873
Axle box, Car	C. A. Haskins	Chicago, Ill	May 28, 1872	127, 163
Axle box, Car	G. H. Henfield	San Francisco, Cal	Jan. 7, 1868	73, 183
Axle box, Car	H. H. Hill and G. M. Sargent	Moline, Ill	July 29, 1873	141, 350
Axle box, Car	J. Hogan	South Boston, Mass	Aug. 26, 1873	142, 104
Axle box, Car	W. B. Howe	Troy, N. Y	Oct. 21, 1873	143, 763
Axle box, Car	W. R. Hunter	Erie, Pa	Jan. 26, 1869	86, 230
Axle box, Car	J. G. Johnson	Elkton, Md	Dec. 9, 1873	145, 425
Axle box, Car	J. Kinzer	Pittsburgh, Pa	Jan. 28, 1873	135, 343
Axle box, Car	J. J. Labaye	Reading, Pa	July 4, 1871	116, 721
Axle box, Car	G. F. Lynch	Milwaukee, Wis	Oct. 11, 1870	108, 277
Axle box, Car	W. J. Mauker	Sedalia, Mo	Apr. 29, 1873	138, 265
Axle box, Car	H. E. Marchand	Pittsburgh, Pa	May 27, 1873	139, 322
Axle box, Car	W. J. L. Moulton	San Francisco, Cal	Dec. 2, 1873	145, 227
Axle box, Car	D. Muzzey	Saint Albans, Vt	Nov. 25, 1873	145, 004
Axle box, Car	A. H. Nathan and M. Thornton.	Macon, Ga	May 12, 1868	77, 831
Axle box, Car	W. G. Parr	Normal, Ill	Oct. 10, 1871	119, 877
Axle box, Car	C. Pinder and D. C. Robinson	Lowell, Mass	Oct. 29, 1867	70, 356
Axle box, Car	L. Schulze	Chicago, Ill	Oct. 14, 1873	143, 592
Axle box, Car	M. Sessions and D. Muzzey	Saint Albans, Vt	Dec. 19, 1871	122, 069
Axle box, Car	T. B. Stewart	Wethersfield, Conn	Nov. 19, 1867	71, 241
Axle box, Car	T. B. Stewart	Hartford, Conn	Mar. 5, 1872	124, 227
Axle box, Car	W. Stone	Hollidaysburgh, Pa	Nov. 26, 1867	71, 422
Axle box, Car	J. E. Uhl	Renovo, Pa	May 6, 1873	138, 717
Axle box, Car	S. Ustick	Philadelphia, Pa	Mar. 4, 1873	136, 472
Axle box, Car	S. Ustick	Philadelphia, Pa	Aug. 26, 1873	142, 302
Axle box, Car	S. Ustick	Philadelphia, Pa	Aug. 26, 1873	142, 303
Axle box, Car	J. L. Vauclain	Lafayette, Ind	July 9, 1861	32, 803
Axle box, Car	W. W. Whitaker	Gloversville, N. Y	Sept. 3, 1873	142, 752
Axle box, Car	J. Whitaker and S. S. Cook	Woonsocket, R. I	Dec. 30, 1873	146, 116
Axle box, Car	C. Williams	Adrian, Mich	Oct. 31, 1871	120, 473
Axle box, Carriage	A. G. Baker and G. M. Ennis	New Bedford, Mass	Jan. 4, 1870	98, 543
Axle box, Carriage	G. B. Durkee	Alden, N. Y	May 17, 1870	103, 161
Axle box, Carriage	L. R. Dye	Cranberry, N. J	Sept. 6, 1871	107, 170
Axle box, Carriage	E. W. Ives	Hamden, Conn	Apr. 25, 1871	114, 148
Axle box, Carriage	D. Jewett	Lynn, Mass	Apr. 19, 1870	102, 127
Axle box, Carriage	J. Jones and J. and J. Dunkerly	Paterson, N. J	Apr. 22, 1873	138, 091
Axle box, Carriage	F. B. Morse	Plantsville, Conn	Jan. 9, 1872	122, 635
Axle box, Carriage	A. E. Smith	Bronxville, N. Y	Feb. 8, 1870	99, 607
Axle box, Carriage	P. R. Stage	Greensburgh, Ind	Nov. 26, 1872	133, 494
Axle box, Carriage	W. Stechschult	Glandorf, (Ottawa Post-Office,) Ohio.	Nov. 29, 1864	45, 279
Axle box, Carriage	E. M. Stratton	New York, N. Y	Apr. 1, 1856	14, 579
Axle box, Carriage	F. Wood	Bridgeport, Conn	Oct. 24, 1865	50, 648
Axle-box cover	W. S. Auchincloss	New York, N. Y	May 15, 1866	54, 666
Axle-box cover	W. H. Fitz Gerald	Brooklyn, N. Y	Apr. 25, 1871	114, 122
Axle-box cover	F. Grinnell	Meadville, Pa	June 8, 1869	91, 115
Axle-box cover	F. K. Hain	Renova, Pa	Oct. 9, 1866	58, 640
Axle-box cover, Car	D. Cowley	Erie, Pa	Dec. 13, 1870	110, 117
Axle-box cover, Car	R. McDowell	Lambertville, N. J	Mar. 19, 1867	63, 070
Axle-box cover, Railway	E. Moyel and J. Howell	Wyandotte, Kans	May 20, 1873	139, 179
Axle-box for car-trucks	W. Loughridge	Weverton, Md	Nov. 15, 1864	45, 058
Axle-box for journal of railway-cars	O. N. French	New London, Conn	July 15, 1851	8, 220
Axle-box for locomotives, Driving	J. W. Goff	Providence, R. I	Feb. 2, 1869	86, 390
Axle-box for lubricating railway rolling-stock, &c	P. F. Aerts	London, England	Aug. 2, 1859	24, 914
Axle-box for railway-cars	D. Jewett	Lynn, Mass	May 26, 1868	78, 210
Axle-box for railway-cars	D. S. Wood	Albany, N. Y	Mar. 22, 1864	42, 037
Axle-box for railway-cars, Replaceable	W. D. Arnett	Cincinnati, Ohio,	May 27, 1856	14, 981
Axle-box for vehicles	C. H. Allen	Saint Louis, Mo	Oct. 28, 1873	143, 950
Axle-box for vehicles	S. F. Green	Croton Falls, N. Y	Sept. 29, 1863	40, 100
Axle box from pedestal, Disconnecting car	W. D. Arnett	Chicago, Ill	June 15, 1858	20, 535
Axle-box guide	R. Hitchcock	Springfield, Mass	Apr. 30, 1867	64, 316
Axle-box lid	J. Bristow	Detroit, Mich	Sept. 21, 1869	94, 943
Axle-box, Lubricating	T. S. Speakman	Camden, N. J	Apr. 12, 1870	101, 933
Axle-box lubricator	C. D. Flynt	New York, N. Y	June 18, 1872	128, 135
Axle-box lubricator	C. Meziex	New York, N. Y	June 30, 1863	39, 059
Axle-box lubricator	S. S. Putnam	Dorchester, Mass	Nov. 2, 1869	96, 348
Axle-box lubricator	C. M. Ried	Greensborough, Ala	Feb. 16, 1869	87, 069
Axle-box lubricator	J. and W. Shackleton	Cleveland, Ohio	Dec. 10, 1872	133, 895
Axle-box lubricator, Car	M. C. Hubbard	Philadelphia, Pa	Mar. 16, 1869	87, 777
Axle-box lubricator, Car	J. Trent	Brooklyn, N. Y	Mar. 12, 1872	124, 642
Axle-box lubricator, Car	S. Ustick	Philadelphia, Pa	Apr. 30, 1872	126, 349
Axle-box lubricator, Car	S. Ustick	Philadelphia, Pa	Apr. 30, 1872	126, 350
Axle-box lubricator, Car	S. Ustick	Philadelphia, Pa	Apr. 30, 1872	126, 351
Axle-box lubricator, Carriage	S. S. Putnam	Dorchester, Mass	Nov. 20, 1866	59, 779
Axle-box lubricator, Carriage and wagon	W. W. Crane	Auburn, N. Y	Nov. 26, 1872	133, 417
Axle box, Railway	C. B. Boynton	Saint Paul, Minn	Nov. 12, 1867	70, 793
Axle box, Railway	A. Higley	South Bend, Ind	Feb. 2, 1869	86, 543
Axle box, Railway	J. J. Lahaye	Reading, Pa	May 8, 1866	54, 563
Axle box, Railway	H. Rice	Concord, N. H	Apr. 3, 1860	27, 738
Axle box, Railway	S. T. Shelley	Louisville, Ky	Jan. 10, 1865	45, 870
Axle box, Railway	J. B. Sutherland	Detroit, Mich	May 16, 1871	114, 877
Axle box, Railway	J. Wardrobe, C. D. B. Fisk, J. F. Curtis, and G. Fetley.	Carlin, Nev	Dec. 13, 1870	110, 093
Axle-box, Railway-car	R. N. Allen	Cleveland, Ohio	Mar. 23, 1858	19, 741
Axle-box, Railway-car	W. S. Auchincloss	Wilmington, Del	Dec. 5, 1871	121, 572
Axle-box, Railway-car	R. Brewer	New York, N. Y	June 10, 1873	139, 655
Axle-box, Railway-car	W. Campbell	Clinton, Iowa	Aug. 17, 1869	93, 858
Axle-box, Railway-car	W. Davis and C. Macan	Elizabethport and Rahway, N. J.	June 29, 1869	91, 919
Axle-box, Railway-car	G. W. and J. C. Geisendorff	Indianapolis, Ind., and Cincinnati, Ohio.	Feb. 9, 1858	19, 290
Axle-box, Railway-car	J. Harris	Dorchester, Mass	Jan. 3, 1860	26, 673
Axle-box, Railway-car	C. W. Harvey	Buffalo, N. Y	Jan. 14, 1873	134, 801
Axle-box, Railway-car	R. Levington	Monroe, Mich	Oct. 14, 1851	8, 428
Axle-box, Railway-car	M. McCammon	Chicago, Ill	Oct. 12, 1869	95, 705
Axle-box, Railway-car	D. R. Perkinpine	Philadelphia, Pa	Mar. 18, 1856	14, 468

Index of patents issued from the United States Patent Office from 1790 *to* 1873, *inclusive*—Continued.

Invention.	Inventor.	Residence.	Date.	No.
Axle-box, Railway-car	W. W. Simrell	Great Bend, Pa	July 29, 1862	36, 033
Axle-box, Railway-car	L. Stevens	Fitchburgh, Mass	May 31, 1859	24, 245
Axle-box, Railway-car	J. Tull and S. Norris	Philadelphia, Pa	July 3, 1847	5, 180
Axle-box, Railway-car	W. E. Wilcox	Peoria, Ill	June 22, 1869	91, 804
Axle-box, Railway-car	W. E. Wilcox	Peoria, Ill	July 27, 1869	93, 150
Axle-box roller	G. W. and J. C. Geisendorff	Indianapolis, Ind., and Cincinnati, Ohio.	Feb. 6, 1855	12, 347
Axle-box, sand-band, and casing for carriage-wheel hub, Combined.	M. McNalley	Houston, Tex	Dec. 26, 1871	122, 185
Axle-box, Self-acting lubricator for	E. von Jeinsen	Omaha, Nebr	July 5, 1870	105, 146
Axle-box, Street-car	J. Stephenson	New York, N. Y	June 4, 1872	127, 524
Axle-box, Street-car	A. Wright	Saint Louis, Mo	Nov. 12, 1872	133, 073
Axle-box, Vehicle	C. Ahrenbeck	Navasota, Tex	June 11, 1872	127, 821
Axle-box, Vehicle	W. A. Clark	New Haven, Conn	Sept. 9, 1873	142, 556
Axle-box, Vehicle	C. F. Gillette	Sparta, Wis	Feb. 19, 1873	62, 126
Axle-box, Vehicle	I. Halloway	New York, N. Y	Jan. 3, 1860	26, 672
Axle-box, Vehicle	J. Reilly	Racine, Wis	Feb. 12, 1868	62, 068
Axle-box, Vehicle	O. P. Rice	New York, N. Y	Sept. 30, 1873	143, 300
Axle-box, Vehicle	J. P. Smith	Terre Haute, Ind	Mar. 11, 1873	166, 778
Axle-box, Vehicle-wheel	D. Dalzell	South Egremont, Mass	July 9, 1872	128, 861
Axle-box, Wagon	A. E. Smith	Bronxville, N. Y	Sept. 11, 1866	57, 987
Axle-box washer	W. K. Foster	Cambridgeport, Mass	Oct. 22, 1867	70, 082
Axle boxes, Attachment to car	D. A. Hopkins	Jersey City, N. J	June 10, 1873	139, 791
Axle boxes, Boring carriage	A. Broad	Salisbury, Conn	June 14, 1809	....
Axle boxes, Casting carriage	S. Williamson	Cincinnati, Ohio	July 7, 1863	39, 189
Axle-boxes, Core for casting	W. H. Hawley	Utica, N. Y	Aug. 9, 1870	106, 265
Axle-boxes, Device for making core for	H. Kellogg	Milford, Conn	Sept. 3, 1872	131, 007
Axle boxes, Elastic check for car	J. Stephenson	New York, N. Y	June 4, 1872	127, 523
Axle-boxes, Fastening cover to	J. O. Clute and P. Kinney	Albany, N. Y	Mar. 31, 1863	38, 032
Axle-boxes from carriage-hubs, Apparatus for removing.	C. Searle	Brooklyn, N. Y	Aug. 17, 1869	93, 911
Axle-boxes from sand and dust, Device for protecting.	C. D. Seys	Nokomis, Ill	Feb. 13, 1872	123, 582
Axle-boxes, Gage for setting	T. Scott	Saint Paul, Minn	Apr. 29, 1873	138, 347
Axle-boxes, Machine for forming lining for	H. Kellogg	Milford, Conn	Nov. 26, 1872	133, 450
Axle boxes, Machine for lining carriage	H. Kellogg	Milford, Conn	Nov. 26, 1872	133, 449
Axle-boxes, Machinery for dressing	W. Hamilton	Allegheny City, Pa	May 5, 1863	38, 385
Axle-boxes, Making	A. E. Smith	Bronxville, N. Y	May 8, 1860	28, 207
Axle boxes, Manufacture of carriage	W. J. Parmelee	Fort Plain, N. Y	Apr. 1, 1873	137, 475
Axle-boxes, Oil reservoir for	E. von Jeinsen and J. M. McDonald.	San Francisco, Cal	Apr. 4, 1871	113, 599
Axle-brace for carriages, Adjustable	T. O. Rogers	Elmira, N. Y	Feb. 2, 1858	19, 264
Axle-clip for carriage-work	M. Seward	New Haven, Conn	July 19, 1864	43, 607
Axle-clip trimming and straightening die	E. H. Plant	Plantsville, Conn	July 19, 1870	105, 595
Axle-clips, Mode of making	H. M. Beecher	West Meriden, Conn	Aug. 12, 1873	141, 625
Axle coupling, Car	D. F. Fetter	New York, N. Y	Jan. 11, 1870	98, 681
Axle coupling, Carriage	G. F. Smith	Plantsville, Conn	Aug. 18, 1868	81, 115
Axle-coupling, Divided	C. A. Nutting	Macon, Ga	June 4, 1872	127, 637
Axle fitting and setting apparatus	J. Cunningham	Rochester, N. Y	Nov. 8, 1870	109, 115
Axle-forging die	J. Harrington	Bridgeport, Conn	May 23, 1871	115, 196
Axle-forming die	J. Nicol	Auburn, N. Y	Jan. 18, 1870	98, 878
Axle-gage	A. J. and A. H. Beach	Linden, Mich	Jan. 28, 1868	73 867
Axle-gage	J. Birkett	Tazewell County, Ill	July 6, 1869	92, 148
Axle-gage	R. C. Kelly	Brandon, Wis	Aug. 16, 1870	106, 373
Axle-gage	G. Luedke	Princeton, Wis	Dec. 28, 1869	98, 280
Axle-gage	H. W. Spaulding	Chelsea, Vt	June 6, 1871	115, 778
Axle-gage	R. K. Vestal	Santa Cruz, Cal	Apr. 4, 1871	113, 598
Axle-gage	D. C. Witsell	Carrollton, Pa	May 30, 1871	115, 549
Axle-grease	J. J. Barrett	Chillicothe, Ohio	Oct. 6, 1868	82, 675
Axle-head	R. E. Bean	Franklin, N. H	Oct. 6, 1868	82, 680
Axle journal and box, Railway-car	O. Robirds	Saint Louis, Mo	Aug. 3, 1869	93, 348
Axle journal-lubricator, Carriage	G. W. Parsons	Harrisburgh, Pa	Nov. 27, 1866	60, 049
Axle, Lubricating	J. Ives	Mount Carmel, Conn	May 2, 1871	114, 298
Axle-lubricating compound	G. M. Denison	Essex, Conn	Nov. 7, 1871	120, 631
Axle-lubricator	G. P. Blaisdell	North Easton, Mass	Dec. 13, 1870	110, 002
Axle-lubricator	G. A. Brannan	Baltimore, Md	Feb. 4, 1873	135, 517
Axle-lubricator	J. F. Hinman	Battle Creek, Mich	Nov. 24, 1863	40, 692
Axle-lubricator	J. E. Mowerson and C. S. D. Baun.	Westwood, N. J	Apr. 9, 1872	125, 477
Axle-lubricator	E. Sawyer	Hollow Square, Ala	Mar. 29, 1870	101, 384
Axle-lubricator	E. W. Smith	Waterbury, Conn	July 23, 1872	129, 760
Axle-lubricator	M. Soellinger and H. Noetzli	Keokuk, Iowa	Feb. 20, 1872	123, 949
Axle-lubricator	J. L. Sorber	Chillicothe, Ohio	Apr. 7, 1868	76, 541
Axle-lubricator	H. Thurlow	Skaneateles, N. Y	Jan. 17, 1871	111, 095
Axle-lubricator	H. S. Weaver	Irwin Station, Pa	Aug. 1, 1871	117, 581
Axle-lubricator	J. L. Winslow	Portland, Me	Dec. 1, 1868	84, 667
Axle-lubricator	J. Worden	Normal, Ill	Sept. 1, 1868	81, 858
Axle-lubricator, and mode of attaching it to axle	L. Adams	Amherst, Mass	Feb. 18, 1868	74, 476
Axle-lubricator, Automatic railway	M. Egan	Ogdensburgh, N. Y	Nov. 6, 1855	13, 749
Axle lubricator, Car	J. Barber	Bridesburgh, Pa	Dec. 5, 1871	121, 575
Axle lubricator, Car	J. E. Bering	Newburgh, N. Y	Dec. 23, 1873	145, 834
Axle lubricator, Car	G. A. Brannan	Baltimore, Md	Aug. 13, 1872	130, 470
Axle lubricator, Car	W. P. Burrow	Norfolk, Va	Feb. 20, 1872	123, 865
Axle lubricator, Car	J. W. Cochran	New York, N. Y	May 25, 1858	20, 331
Axle lubricator, Car	J. W. Cochran	New York, N. Y	Oct. 5, 1858	21, 652
Axle lubricator, Car	J. W. Cochran	New York, N. Y	June 1, 1858	20, 406
Axle lubricator, Car	J. S. Eggleston	Auburn, N. Y	Sept. 3, 1872	131, 087
Axle lubricator, Car	T. C. Hargrave	Boston, Mass	May 3, 1864	42, 577
Axle lubricator, Car	T. C. Hargrave	Boston, Mass	May 3, 1864	42, 578
Axle lubricator, Car	B. P. La Mothe	New York, N. Y	June 7, 1864	43, 033
Axle lubricator, Car	J. Lichtenstein	Baltimore, Md	Nov. 22, 1870	109, 525
Axle lubricator, Car	T. J. Mooers	Blossburgh, Pa	Jan. 11, 1870	98, 701
Axle lubricator, Car	J. R. Morris	Houston, Tex	Jan. 7, 1873	134, 696
Axle lubricator, Car	W J. L. Moulton	San Francisco, Cal	Dec. 2, 1873	145, 226
Axle lubricator, Car	W. Painter	Baltimore, Md	Apr. 16, 1872	125, 841
Axle lubricator, Car	T. H. Paul	Frostburgh, Md	Mar. 12, 1872	124, 618
Axle lubricator, Car	J. S. Sanson	Morrisania, N. Y	Jan. 2, 1872	122, 495
Axle lubricator, Car	T. Sayles	Chicago, Ill	Sept. 20, 1870	107, 631

Index of patents issued from the United States Patent Office from 1790 *to* 1873, *inclusive*—Continued.

Invention.	Inventor.	Residence.	Date.	No.
Axle lubricator, Car	T. R. Timby	Tarrytown, N. Y	Jan. 28, 1873	135, 386
Axle lubricator, Car	S. Ustick	Philadelphia, Pa	Apr. 30, 1872	126, 352
Axle lubricator, Car	E. von Jeinsen	Omaha, Nebr	Aug. 2, 1870	106, 086
Axle lubricator, Car	R. Vose and J. M. Evans	New York, N. Y	May 28, 1872	127, 391
Axle lubricator, Car	I. P. Wendell	Philadelphia, Pa	Jan. 24, 1871	111, 287
Axle lubricator, Car	M. W. Woodruff	Camillus, N. Y	May 7, 1872	126, 508
Axle lubricator, Carriage	H. F. Phillips	Auburn, N. Y	Apr. 1, 1873	137, 479
Axle lubricator, Carriage	C. Polley	Scott, Ohio	Sept. 20, 1864	44, 338
Axle lubricator, Carriage	S. S. Putnam	Dorchester, Mass	Feb. 4, 1868	74, 134
Axle-lubricator plug	A. C. Garratt	Hanover, Mass	Jan. 16, 1855	12, 238
Axle lubricator, Railway	W. Clough	Madison, Ind	Mar. 30, 1858	19, 750
Axle lubricator, Railway-car	C. Hyatt	Buffalo, N. Y	Nov. 1, 1870	108, 789
Axle lubricator, Railway-car	I. P. Wendell	Philadelphia, Pa	Jan. 24, 1871	111, 286
Axle lubricator, Vehicle	J. S. Eggleston	Auburn, N. Y	Jan. 2, 1872	122, 374
Axle lubricator, Vehicle	L. H. Fisher	Walpole, Mass	Dec. 10, 1872	133, 769
Axle lubricator, Wagon	W. Loewenstein	Keokuk, Iowa	Apr. 29, 1873	138, 263
Axle lubricator, Wagon	C. A. Wakefield	Pittsfield, Mass	June 13, 1871	115, 914
Axle-nut and axle	C. Thomas	Boston, Mass	June 28, 1870	104, 901
Axle-nut die	A. B. Candee and L. S. Taylor	Hamden and Southington, Conn.	June 2, 1868	78, 576
Axle-nut lubricator	D. Dalzell	South Egremont, Mass	May 28, 1872	127, 313
Axle-nuts, Method of manufacturing	S. Vanstone	Providence, R. I	June 28, 1870	104, 984
Axle or journal lubricator	R. V. Laney	Cumberland, Md	Mar. 12, 1872	124, 595
Axle or shaft	G. Foster	Brooklyn, N. Y	Dec. 13, 1859	26, 425
Axle-roller	W. S. Mackintosh	Pittsburgh, Pa	June 16, 1868	78, 984
Axle-rolling machine	W. P. Porter	Pittsburgh, Pa	Mar. 10, 1868	75, 457
Axle-set	H. R. Ladd	Orwell, Ohio	Mar. 9, 1869	87, 571
Axle-shafts, &c., Coating the bearing of boxes for	W. Peters	Baltimore, Md	July 22, 1862	35, 976
Axle-skein	D. and J. Gray	Wayland, N. Y	June 24, 1862	35, 676
Axle-skein	H. C. Kochensperger	Thornville, Ohio	Jan. 2, 1872	122, 391
Axle-skein	L. Mayhew	Saratoga Springs, N. Y	Dec. 27, 1870	110, 579
Axle-skein	L. Mayhew	Greenfield, N. Y	Apr. 4, 1871	113, 681
Axle-skein	L. Mayhew	Greenfield, N. Y	Aug. 22, 1871	118, 377
Axle-skein	L. Mayhew	Rock City Falls, N. Y	Oct. 24, 1871	120, 303
Axle-skein	H. F. Phillips	Auburn, N. Y	Aug. 18, 1863	39, 617
Axle-skein	E. Rooks	Trenton, Tenn	Nov. 9, 1869	96, 620
Axle-skein	G. Schreyer	Columbus, Ohio	May 4, 1869	89, 602
Axle-skein	T. S. Sleeper	Binghamton, N. Y	Sept. 28, 1869	95, 279
Axle skein and box	G. E. Clarke	Racine, Wis	May 5, 1868	77, 585
Axle-skein, Malleable-iron	A. J. Alston	Allegheny City, Pa	Dec. 24, 1872	134, 189
Axle-skein, Reversible	A. F. Smith	Aiken, Tex	Apr. 16, 1872	125, 762
Axle-skein setter	J. Burt	Sturgis, Mich	Aug. 4, 1868	80, 594
Axle-skein, Steel	A. J. Alston	Allegheny City, Pa	Dec. 24, 1872	134, 188
Axle-skein, Truss-brace attachment for	O. Vanorman	Fond du Lac, Wis	July 16, 1872	129, 258
Axle-skein, Truss-brace for	O. Vanorman	Fond du Lac, Wis	Dec. 5, 1871	121, 692
Axle-skein mold, Machine for preparing	J. G. Holt	Chicago, Ill	June 5, 1866	55, 295
Axle-spindles to skeins, Device for fitting	C. L. Campbell	Binghamton, N. Y	Sept. 28, 1869	95, 319
Axle-spindles to skeins of wagons, Machine for fitting	C. L. Campbell	Binghamton, N. Y	Oct. 9, 1866	58, 714
Axle thimble-skein	W. D. Baughn	Milford, Mich	Nov. 26, 1867	71, 264
Axle thimble-skein	M. Ehrgott	Pittsburgh, Pa	Mar. 9, 1869	87, 652
Axle thimble-skein	J. A. Williams	Elizabeth, Ill	Oct. 8, 1867	69, 735
Axle-tourniquet.	J. Strong	....	Jan. 29, 1801	....
Axletree	C. E. Buck	Racine, Wis	Jan. 21, 1868	73, 575
Axletree	R. Haslup	Baltimore, Md	Feb. 24, 1831	....
Axletree	J. W. Whitney	Buffalo, N. Y	Sept. 5, 1848	5, 753
Axletree	J. W. Wilkie	Auburn, N. Y	Mar. 26, 1867	63, 347
Axletree	J. W. Wilkie	Auburn, N. Y	Mar. 26, 1867	63, 348
Axletree-arm	D. Philips	Sharon, Pa	Feb. 3, 1852	8, 707
Axletree, hub, and spoke	G. Wilkinson	White Creek, N. Y	Dec. 6, 1831	....
Axletree safety-carriage machine, Double	E. G. Fitch	Blakely, Ala	Feb. 7, 1829	....
Axletrees, Diminishing friction in	B. Hinkley	Fayette, Me	Apr. 14, 1835	....
Axletrees, Machine for turning	W. H. Heffley	Rochester, Ind	Aug. 16, 1870	106, 364
Axletrees, Mode and machinery for setting	T. Fessenden	Boston, Mass	Sept. 25, 1837	410
Axletrees, Reduced friction-roller	F. Rees	Clarksville, Ga	Apr. 14, 1832	....
Axletrees, Setting	J. N. Arvin and S. H. Perkins	Valparaiso, Ind	July 17, 1860	29, 132
Axle-turning machine	G. S. Knight	Syracuse, N. Y	Aug. 20, 1867	67, 886
Axle-turning machine	A. F. Moore	Florence, Ind	Mar. 28, 1871	113, 078
Axle-turning machine	A. F. Moore	Florence, Ind	Apr. 1, 1873	137, 316
Axle-turning machine	R. Zeider	El Paso, Ill	Aug. 20, 1872	130, 782
Axle-washer	A. E. Smith	Bronxville, N. Y	July 24, 1855	13, 327
Axle-wheel	C. J. Crane	Burr Oak, Mich	Oct. 24, 1865	50, 655
Axles and shafts, Bearing for	W. H. Hovey	Hartford, Conn	Dec. 10, 1850	7, 819
Axles, Connecting skeins with	A. Combs	Farmington, Ohio	May 14, 1850	7, 363
Axles, Constructing	J. Montgomery	New York, N. Y	Nov. 21, 1871	121, 187
Axles, Gage for making	P. Geiser	Waynesborough, Pa	July 20, 1869	92, 817
Axles, Grease-box for	J. M. Smart	New York, N. Y	Nov. 6, 1849	6, 854
Axle, Machine for rolling shoulder on	W. Van Anden	Poughkeepsie, N. Y	Aug. 22, 1854	11, 596
Axles, Mode of lubricating	J. F. Stevenson and T. B. Hammer.	McKeesport, Pa	Mar. 18, 1862	34, 704
Axles of machinery, Anti-friction device for	N. Beilly, C. Durand, G. H. Mesnard, and Z. Poirier.	France, England, and South Lambeth, England.	Oct. 9, 1866	58, 739
Axles or journals, Mode of preventing the heating of	E. D. Murfey	New York, N. Y	Nov. 15, 1870	109, 237
Axles, Preventing friction on	T. S. and T. S. Minniss	Meadville, Pa	Feb. 15, 1859	22, 971
Axles, Splicing-bar for	J. E. Balderston	Philadelphia, Pa	Jan. 21, 1862	34, 189
Axles to vehicles, Mode of attaching	W. Gray and H. E. Porter	Hebron, Conn	Apr. 28, 1868	77, 185
B.				
Baby-chair	P. Henrichs	Erie, Pa	Jan. 7, 1873	134, 668
Baby-chair	C. Holtz	New York, N. Y	Mar. 16, 1869	87, 933
Baby chair and table	J. Kopp	Bridgeport, Conn	Dec. 11, 1866	60, 389
Baby creeper or walker	P. Hurd	Croton, Mich	Mar. 10, 1868	75, 274
Baby-holder	R. Hale	Chicago, Ill	Jan. 28, 1868	73, 801
Baby-jumper	W. Berg and M. Stephan	Canton, Ohio	June 8, 1869	90, 985
Baby-jumper	S. G. Bigelow	Silver Lake, Ind	Nov. 12, 1872	133, 008
Baby-jumper	J. H. Coldwell	Poughkeepsie, N. Y	Mar. 31, 1868	76, 053
Baby-jumper	J. A. De Frame	New York, N. Y	Apr. 16, 1861	32, 109
Baby-jumper	J. P. Faulks	Glasgow, Mo	Aug. 29, 1871	118, 599

Index of patents issued from the United States Patent Office from 1790 *to* 1873, *inclusive*—Continued.

Invention.	Inventor.	Residence.	Date.	No.
Baby-jumper	W. Gibson	Fort Wayne, Ind	June 26, 1866	55,849
Baby-jumper	D. M. Holmes	Westchester, N. Y	Sept. 17, 1872	131,349
Baby-jumper	A. H. Mason	Binghamton, N. Y	Sept. 10, 1867	68,637
Baby-jumper	C. Rich	Poughkeepsie, N. Y	Oct. 13, 1868	82,992
Baby-jumper	E. Rice	Elizabethtown, N. J	Oct. 28, 1851	8,478
Baby-jumper	A. F. Spooner	Sterling, Ill	Apr. 22, 1873	138,209
Baby-jumper	J. P. Thompson	Philadelphia, Pa	Oct. 2, 1866	58,510
Baby-jumper	E. L. Warner	Oxford, Conn	July 5, 1870	105,149
Baby-jumper	M. J. Wellman	New York, N. Y	Mar. 31, 1857	16,942
Baby-jumper	J. E. Wells	Chicago, Ill	Aug. 13, 1872	130,397
Baby jumper and cradle	R. Ashe	Somerville, Mass	July 23, 1867	67,153
Baby jumper and cradle, Combined	G. H. Mellen	Chicago, Ill	June 30, 1868	79,534
Baby jumper and rocker	B. Beach	Meriden, Conn	Sept. 28, 1869	95,183
Baby jumper and supporter	H. Frankfurth	Utica, N. Y	Dec. 3, 1861	33,833
Baby jumper and swing	S. T. McDougall	New York, N. Y	July 5, 1864	43,420
Baby jumper and walker	J. H. Coldwell	New York, N. Y	Aug. 30, 1864	43,972
Baby jumper and walker	L. O. Colvin	Newark, N. J	Sept. 3, 1872	131,083
Baby jumper, couch, and carriage	J. S. Brown	Green Point, N. Y	Nov. 27, 1860	30,717
Baby-swing	J. Wolf	Cleveland, Ohio	Dec. 26, 1865	51,772
Baby-swing	J.H.Wygant and R.P. Paulison	Hackensack, N. J	May 21, 1872	127,134
Baby-tender	J. S. Brown	New York, N. Y	May 17, 1864	42,745
Baby-tender	A. H. Carson and A. Brown	Newport, R. I., and Troy, N. Y.	Apr. 25, 1871	113,979
Baby-tender	L. Limerick	Louisville, Ky	May 7, 1867	64,432
Baby-tender	S. M. Simonds	Lynn, Mass	Mar. 28, 1871	113,103
Baby-tender	A. Wheeler	Newton, Mass	Sept. 1, 1863	39,766
Baby-tender	C. N. Ziegler	Grafton, Ohio	Jan. 9, 1872	122,546
Baby-tender, Locomotive	J. C. Smith	Boston, Mass	Apr. 3, 1849	6,247
Baby traveling and toilet chair	E. Hoare	Dedham, Mass	May 16, 1871	114,818
Baby-walker	P. W. Clark	Paw Paw, Mich	June 25, 1872	128,361
Baby-walker	J. Erikson	Madison, Wis	Aug. 5, 1873	141,431
Baby-walker	G. Enell	Guttenburgh, N. J	May 7, 1872	126,452
Baby-walker	F. A. Geisler	Bristol, R. I	Sept. 22, 1868	82,304
Baby-walker	J. C. Goulding	Trenton, N. J	Nov. 23, 1869	97,078
Baby-walker	C. Maschmann	Watertown, N. Y	June 20, 1871	116,073
Baby-walker	P. Pallissard	Aroma, Ill	June 12, 1866	55,529
Baby-walker	P. H. Randolph	Leavenworth City, Kans	Nov. 30, 1869	97,315
Baby-walker	J. Rohr	Batesville, Ind	Nov. 19, 1867	71,220
Baby-walker	J. Thomas	Brooklyn, N. Y	Mar. 17, 1857	16,862
Baby-walker	C. D. and J. A. Westlake	Laurel, Md	Mar. 19, 1872	124,706
Baby walker and cradle	J. H. Brown	New York, N. Y	Jan. 2, 1866	51,795
Baby walker and hanging chair	L. O. Colvin	Newark, N. J	July 11, 1871	116,813
Baby walker and jumper	E. Y. Robbins	Cincinnati, Ohio	Dec. 2, 1856	16,150
Baby-walker, Willow	J. E. Kauffman	Osborn, Ohio	June 25, 1872	128,230
Back and abdominal supporter	J. Ford	Salem, Oreg	Mar. 31, 1868	76,070
Back-band fastener	D. L. McGregor	Charlestown, Mass	Dec. 17, 1867	72,312
Back-band hook	H. Beagle	Philadelphia, Pa	Nov. 29, 1870	109,572
Back-band hook	H. Beagle, jr	Philadelphia, Pa	Oct. 3, 1871	119,556
Back-band hook	W. McKerahan	Allegheny City, Pa	Feb. 9, 1869	86,852
Back-band hook	J. Straus	Saint Louis, Mo	June 3, 1873	139,524
Back-band hook	S. Ward	Princeton, Ind	Feb. 26, 1867	62,513
Back-band hook	S. Ward	Princeton, Ind	Mar. 9, 1869	87,737
Back-band hook and buckle	S. Ward	Princeton, Ind	Sept. 3, 1872	131,139
Back-band hook for plow-harness	N. Warlick	Chambers County, Ala	Oct. 28, 1856	15,993
Back-band strap, Self-adjusting and vibrating	R. Jancovins	Newark, N. J	June 1, 1858	20,434
Back-brace	E. P. Banning, jr	New York, N. Y	Mar. 12, 1872	124,473
Backgammon and checker board	E. O. Goodwin	Bristol, Conn	Nov. 25, 1856	16,116
Backgammon-board	N. B. Williams	New York, N. Y	Mar. 16, 1869	87,895
Backlash for mill-gearing	J. L. Post	Ashley, Ill	Oct. 18, 1870	108,515
Backlash in machinery, Device for preventing	J. L. Post	Ashley, Ill	Mar. 14, 1871	112,736
Backlash in machines driven by gearing, Means for preventing.	G. H. Babcock, J. P. Manton, and J. Boyd.	Providence, R. I	Oct. 12, 1869	95,757
Backlash in mills, Device for preventing	A. B. Rider	Fairfield, Ill	June 25, 1872	128,327
Backlash spring for machinery	H. W. Bachman	McLean, Ill	Oct. 22, 1872	132,347
Back-log boiler for ranges, &c	B. Hunter	Philadelphia, Pa	Mar. 26, 1872	124,899
Back-pad press	E. W. Harlow	Hastings, Mich	Jan. 24, 1871	111,119
Bacon and ham box or case	M. W. Brown	New York, N. Y	Oct. 18, 1870	108,322
Bacon, ham, and shoulders, Mode of curing	W. G. Bell	Charlestown, Mass	Nov. 30, 1869	97,268
Badge, Campaign	H. C. Griggs	Waterbury, Conn	Oct. 27, 1868	83,486
Badge, Fastening for policeman's	T. Kirkpatrick	New York, N. Y	Aug. 30, 1870	106,942
Badge for hats, Illuminated	W. J. Scott	Albany, N. Y	Jan. 9, 1872	122,665
Bag: *See* Broom-bag. Carpet-bag. Dash-board bag. Feed-bag. Floating bag. Fruit-gathering bag. Grain-bag. Guano-bag. Horse nose-bag. Ice-bag. Mail-bag. Packing-bag. Paper-bag. Phosphate-bag. Saddle-bag. Striking-bag. Tobacco-bag. Tobacco-packing bag. Traveling-bag. Woven bag.				
Bag and shoe-string fastener	J. H. Weeden	Waterbury, Conn	Sept. 21, 1869	94,987
Bag-clasp	E. L. Dickey	Chicago, Ill	Feb. 18, 1868	74,517
Bag-clasp fastener	A. H. Balch and W. D. E. Nelson.	Montreal, Canada	Apr. 18, 1871	113,834
Bag-fastener	W. P. Brooks	Fairmount, Minn	May 1, 1866	54,287
Bag-fastener	W. H. Brown	Worcester, Mass	Aug. 7, 1866	56,894

Index of patents issued from the United States Patent Office from 1790 *to* 1873, *inclusive*—Continued.

Invention.	Inventor.	Residence.	Date.	No.
Bag-fastener	S. R. Bush	Bush's Mill, Ohio	Nov. 18, 1873	144, 738
Bag-fastener	L. H. Colborn	Chicago, Ill	May 5, 1868	77, 587
Bag-fastener	S. C. Dix	Neponset, Ill	Apr. 12, 1870	101, 837
Bag-fastener	F. H. Drake	Kenosha, Wis	Mar. 24, 1868	75, 877
Bag-fastener	A. C. Fletcher	New York, N. Y	July 25, 1865	48, 122
Bag-fastener	C. A. Haring	Peoria, Ill	Oct. 26, 1869	96, 229
Bag-fastener	C. J. Huntington	Rockford, Ill	Feb. 2, 1869	86, 403
Bag-fastener	W. P. Maxson	Albion, Wis	May 24, 1859	24, 133
Bag-fastener	J. Miller	Ovid, Mich	June 4, 1867	65, 499
Bag-fastener	C. H. Nye	Vineland, N. J	Oct. 27, 1868	83, 534
Bag-fastener	D. Overholtzer	Polo, Ill	Jan. 7, 1868	73, 193
Bag-fastener	S. P. Parmly	New Orleans, La	June 15, 1869	91, 362
Bag-fastener	G. H. Peacock	Fairport, N. Y	Apr. 21, 1868	76, 941
Bag-fastener	E. Romans	La Porte, Ind	Nov. 5, 1867	70, 620
Bag-fastener	G. C. Setchell and C. L. Taylor	Norwich, Conn	Dec. 26, 1871	122, 135
Bag-fastener	A. M. Wright	Safe Harbor, Pa	July 30, 1867	67, 393
Bag-fastener	W. Zeller and R. Lechner	Lebanon County and Berks County, Pa.	Sept. 24, 1867	69, 295
Bag fastener or tie	D. B. Baker	Rollersville, Ohio	June 11, 1867	65, 632
Bag-filler	W. H. and J. G. Mitchell	Circleville, Ohio	May 14, 1872	126, 732
Bag-filler	A. J. Olney	Van Buren, Ind	July 6, 1869	92, 347
Bag-filling and weighing-machine	C. A. Whelan and C. F. Wakely	Madison, Wis	Jan. 3, 1871	110, 707
Bag-frame	W. T. Mercereau	Newark, N. J	Apr. 24, 1866	54, 190
Bag-frame	A. J. Sessions	Bristol, Conn	June 12, 1866	55, 543
Bag-frame bending-machine	G. Havell	Newark, N. J	Nov. 9, 1869	96, 695
Bag, grain, &c., tie	G. W. Osborn	Parkville, Mich	Oct. 4, 1870	107, 952
Bag-holder	I. Allen	Manchester, N. Y	July 4, 1871	116, 661
Bag-holder	O. Barnett and A. D. Brooks	Dartford, Wis	Sept. 12, 1871	118, 897
Bag-holder	C. J. Barney	Edgartown, Mass	Dec. 4, 1866	60, 121
Bag-holder	B. S. Boydston	Richmond, Ind	July 9, 1867	66, 554
Bag-holder	E. Boynton	Palmyra, Wis	June 28, 1870	104, 698
Bag-holder	C. D. Brainerd	Danville, Vt	Dec. 31, 1867	72, 788
Bag-holder	J. B. Brown	Washington, D. C	Jan. 7, 1873	134, 637
Bag-holder	J. M. Burke	Dansville, N. Y	Jan. 4, 1870	98, 553
Bag-holder	S. P. Clemons	Dansville, N. Y	Jan. 5, 1869	85, 643
Bag-holder	J. N. Collins	Menasha, Wis	Aug. 31, 1869	94, 283
Bag-holder	G. E. Corbin	Saint Johns, Mich	Sept. 4, 1866	57, 683
Bag-holder	J. S. Corbin	Ann Arbor, Mich	July 25, 1865	48, 911
Bag-holder	L. Crofoot	Pavilion, N. Y	Jan. 5, 1869	85, 511
Bag-holder	L. Crofoot	Pavilion, N. Y	Feb. 22, 1870	100, 123
Bag-holder	L. Crofoot	Pavilion, N. Y	Aug. 13, 1872	130, 489
Bag-holder	D. Culver	Kingston, Pa	July 2, 1872	128, 598
Bag-holder	G. Dare	Auburn, N. Y	May 25, 1869	90, 344
Bag-holder	G. W. Dungan and W. Wasson	Genoa, Nev	Feb. 13, 1872	123, 684
Bag-holder	E. C. Fairchild	Sunderland, Mass	Mar. 3, 1868	75, 138
Bag-holder	E. A. Fisher	Morganville, N. Y	June 8, 1869	91, 004
Bag-holder	L. H. Gano	Milwaukee, Wis	Mar. 12, 1867	62, 741
Bag-holder	N. A. Geisinger	Coopersburgh, Pa	Oct. 21, 1873	143, 897
Bag-holder	E. N. Giles	Brownville, N. Y	Sept. 10, 1872	131, 267
Bag-holder	C. F. Gillett	Sparta, Wis	Apr. 10, 1866	53, 809
Bag-holder	C. F. Gillett	Sparta, Wis	July 17, 1866	56, 402
Bag-holder	F. Godfrey	Grand Rapids, Mich	Apr. 12, 1864	42, 283
Bag-holder	O. Hanks	Cincinnati, Ohio	Apr. 2, 1867	63, 383
Bag-holder	T. Harding	Springfield, Ohio	Oct. 22, 1867	69, 989
Bag-holder	A. V. Heyden	Milwaukee, Wis	Feb. 26, 1867	62, 332
Bag-holder	C. W. Hills and O. F. Woodruff	Morrison, Ill	Jan. 30, 1866	52, 288
Bag-holder	J. H. Hollidge	Washington, D. C	July 30, 1872	130, 051
Bag-holder	G. G. Hollinger	Mount Joy, Pa	Aug. 6, 1872	130, 130
Bag-holder	J. Hunter and H. M. Clayton	Ashland, Pa	May 13, 1873	138, 752
Bag-holder	E. L. Lyon	Steamburgh, N. Y	May 14, 1872	126, 723
Bag-holder	J. McPhail	Charles City, Iowa	Nov. 16, 1869	96, 941
Bag-holder	J. Melcher	Minneapolis, Minn	May 28, 1867	65, 105
Bag-holder	P. Meyers	Stoutsville, Ohio	Feb. 16, 1869	87, 059
Bag-holder	C. K. Mitchell	Greenville, Mich	July 11, 1871	116, 981
Bag-holder	L. W. Morlan	New Lisbon, Ohio	June 6, 1865	48, 083
Bag-holder	E. S. Moulton	Plymouth, Mich	July 9, 1867	66, 614
Bag-holder	J. V. H. Nott	Guilderland, N. Y	Dec. 4, 1866	60, 233
Bag-holder	A. M. Olds	Glenmont, Wis	Aug. 20, 1861	33, 097
Bag-holder	J. H. Park	White House, N. J	May 5, 1868	77, 648
Bag-holder	J. I. Peyton and C. N. S. Wallach.	Washington, D. C	Apr. 27, 1869	89, 500
Bag-holder	R. Ramsey	New Wilmington, Pa	Feb. 21, 1865	46, 498
Bag-holder	E. Reynolds	Corunna, Mich	Nov. 28, 1865	51, 220
Bag-holder	S. S. Rockwell	Lansing, Mich	Apr. 3, 1866	53, 681
Bag-holder	J. Roseborough, jr	South Hermitage, Pa	June 18, 1872	128, 073
Bag-holder	N. N. Rugg	Geneva, Ill	June 22, 1869	91, 568
Bag-holder	W. H. Smith	Sparta, Wis	July 31, 1866	56, 819
Bag-holder	W. H. Starry	Middletown, Ohio	Nov. 13, 1866	59, 677
Bag-holder	G. W. Striker	Iowa Falls, Iowa	Sept. 23, 1873	143, 194
Bag-holder	G. D. Sweigert	Martic Township, Pa	May 3, 1870	102, 616
Bag-holder	A. D. Swogger	Worth, Pa	Dec. 27, 1870	110, 511
Bag-holder	C. H. Thomas	Williamsburgh, Ohio	July 22, 1873	141, 186
Bag-holder	T. J. Trapp	Williamsport, Pa	July 4, 1871	116, 777
Bag-holder	T. J. Trapp	Williamsport, Pa	Aug. 13, 1872	130, 547
Bag-holder	L. Turner	Cedar Rapids, Iowa	July 2, 1867	66, 424
Bag-holder	I. Vance and C. Rogers	Pittsburgh, Pa	May 21, 1872	127, 122
Bag-holder	D. S. Wing	Rome, N. Y	Nov. 29, 1870	109, 788
Bag-holder	J. and T. R. Yaggy	Plainfield, Ill	Apr. 14, 1868	76, 686
Bag-holder and conveyor	C. K. Hostetter	East Donegal Township, Pa	Dec. 18, 1860	30, 943
Bag holder and elevator, Combined	G. H. Smith	Des Moines, Iowa	Apr. 14, 1863	38, 183
Bag holder and filler	A. M. Darling	Davenport, Iowa	Nov. 26, 1867	71, 286
Bag holder and filler	W. F. Lum	Waterloo, Wis	Dec. 5, 1871	121, 529
Bag holder and filler, Combined	W. F. Lum	Waterloo, Wis	Mar. 14, 1871	112, 727
Bag-holder and measure	G. E. Randall	Yaphank, N. Y	Aug. 2, 1864	43, 706
Bag-holder and scale	W. Zimmerman	Lebanon, Pa	Nov. 9, 1869	96, 759
Bag-holder and scales, Combined	W. Zimmerman	Lebanon, Pa	Mar. 7, 1871	112, 522
Bag-holder and truck, Combined	J. Hewitt	Albany, N. Y	May 28, 1872	127, 346
Bag-holder and truck, Combined	H. A. Reid	Beaver Dam, Wis	Apr. 20, 1869	89, 077

Index of patents issued from the United States Patent Office from 1790 *to* 1873, *inclusive*—Continued.

Invention.	Inventor.	Residence.	Date.	No.
Bag-holder and truck, Combined	P. C. Van Brocklin	Paris, Canada	Jan. 9, 1872	122, 685
Bag-holder, Hopper for	W. Wasson and G. W. Dungan.	Genoa, Nev	July 16, 1872	129, 633
Bag holding and filling machine	J. Agate	Cuba, N. Y	Sept. 2, 1862	36, 328
Bag-holding apparatus	J. S. Lehman	Mount Joy, Pa	Feb. 11, 1868	74, 232
Bag-holding device and truck	J. S. Lehman	Mount Joy, Pa	Sept. 15, 1868	82, 132
Bag-lock	H. Ahrend	Newark, N. J	June 3, 1873	139, 526
Bag-lock	E. L. Gaylord	Bridgeport, Conn	Aug. 6, 1872	130, 209
Bag-lock	B. Steinmetz	Paris. France	Sept. 13, 1870	107, 422
Bag-machine	N. Biedinger	Cincinnati, Ohio	July 1, 1873	140, 242
Bag-machine, Pasting-apparatus for	S. E. Pettee	Mansfield, Mass	Nov. 30, 1858	22, 199
Bag-mouth fastener	T. K. Reed	North Bridgewater, Mass.	Feb. 28, 1865	46, 587
Bag-string fastener	E. B. Southwick	Mendon, Mich	Jan. 4, 1870	98, 527
Bag-string inserter	W. J. Cussen	Richmond, Va	June 4, 1872	127, 579
Bag-tie	J. W. Bates	Glencoe, Minn	Oct. 20, 1868	83, 240
Bag-tie	J. W. Blackstone	Darlington, Wis	July 2, 1872	128, 526
Bag-tie	J. Bowers	Brookville, Ill	Sept. 24, 1872	131, 593
Bag-tie	J. Brannihr and D. H. Rhodes	Hempstead and Baldwinsville, N. Y.	Mar. 11, 1873	136, 637
Bag-tie	D. Dick and O. W. Preston, jr	Corning, N. Y	Dec. 15, 1868	84, 998
Bag-tie	J. W. H. Doubler	Darlington, Wis	Apr. 16, 1872	125, 795
Bag-tie	L. H. Gano	Milwaukee, Wis	Mar. 3, 1868	75, 008
Bag-tie	L. H. Gano	New York, N. Y	Feb. 9, 1869	86, 745
Bag-tie	J. J. Gordon	Flint, Mich	Dec. 3, 1867	71, 739
Bag-tie	J. Grimes	Alexandria, Va	Oct. 29, 1867	70, 201
Bag-tie	D. B. Hall	Bucksport, Me	Apr. 2, 1867	63, 510
Bag-tie	C. P. and W. H. Markham	Rogersville, N. Y	May 30, 1871	115, 336
Bag-tie	J. C. Meloy	Hastings, Minn	Nov. 2, 1869	96, 459
Bag-tie	L. Morehouse	Barton, Wis	Mar. 5, 1867	62, 667
Bag-tie	G. Murray	Waterloo, N. Y	May 11, 1869	90, 013
Bag-tie	T. H. Russell	Lebanon, N. H	Apr. 30, 1872	126, 157
Bag-tie	E. Truslow	New York, N. Y	June 30, 1868	79, 414
Bag-turning machine	J. Martin	New York, N. Y	Mar. 18, 1873	136, 926
Bags, Clasp for fastening	W. H. Cloud, A. L. Hatfield, and C. H. Burdick.	Tremont, Ohio	Apr. 6, 1858	19, 830
Bags, Holding and filling	G. E. Randall	Yaphank, N. Y	June 13, 1865	48, 208
Bags, Machinery for turning	W. V. Gee	New Haven, Conn	Dec. 4, 1860	30, 808
Bags and sacks, Machine for holding open	J. Robinson	New Wilmington, Pa	Sept. 9, 1862	36, 423
Bags and sacks, Manufacture of	W. B. Carlock	New York, N. Y	July 3, 1849	6, 566
Bags, sacks, &c., Fastening	A. B. Wood, jr	Ovid, Mich	Nov. 1, 1864	44, 907
Bags while being filled, Machine for holding	J. H. Morris	Niles, Mich	Sept. 3, 1861	33, 209
Bagasse, Drying	G. Merrick	New Orleans, La	Apr. 10, 1845	3, 994
Bagasse-drying-machine	J. H. Dakin	Baton Rouge, La	May 21, 1850	7, 375
Bagasse-drying-machine	S. H. Gilman	Cincinnati, Ohio	Oct. 28, 1851	8, 466
Bagasse for fuel, Preparing	J. M. Frink	Coral, Ill	May 26, 1863	38, 667
Bagasse-furnace	J. Amick	Assumption Parish, La	Apr. 19, 1870	101, 968
Bagasse-furnace	A. JnChapman	Bayou Goula, La	Nov. 22, 1859	26, 162
Bagasse-furnace	F. Daunoy	Carrollton, La	Dec. 21, 1858	22, 353
Bagasse-furnace	C. A. Desobry	Plaquemine, La,	Sept. 6, 1859	25, 322
Bagasse-furnace	C. A. Desobry	Plaquemine, La	June 19, 1860	28, 741
Bagasse-furnace	J. M. Frink	Coral, Ill	May 26, 1863	38, 666
Bagasse-furnace	S. H. Gilman	New Orleans, La	Dec. 4, 1855	13, 873
Bagasse-furnace	S. H. Gilman	New Orleans, La	Aug. 5, 1856	15, 481
Bagasse-furnace	S. H. Gilman	New Orleans, La	Jan. 10, 1860	26, 759
Bagasse-furnace	A. Hager and Y. Allyn	Baton Rouge and New Orleans, La.	May 6, 1856	14, 812
Bagasse-furnace	J. M. Jones and J. M. Charpentier.	New Orleans and Saint Mary's Parish, La.	Sept. 18, 1860	30, 107
Bagasse-furnace	J. M. Jones and J. M. Charpentier.	New Orleans and Pattersonville, La.	Oct. 23, 1860	30, 477
Bagasse-furnace	G. M. Longacre	New Orleans, La	July 21, 1857	17, 842
Bagasse-furnace	C. Neames	New Orleans, La	Feb. 14, 1860	27, 146
Bagasse-furnace	E. Skelly	Plaquemine, La	June 15, 1858	20, 591
Bagasse-furnace	A. Stillman	New York, N. Y	May 1, 1855	12, 807
Bagasse-furnace	M. Thompson	New York, N. Y	Dec. 15, 1857	18, 874
Bagasse-furnace	L. Tregre	Parish of Saint John the Baptist, La.	July 5, 1859	24, 675
Bagatelle	M. Redgrave	Cincinnati, Ohio	May 30, 1871	115, 357
Bagatelle game and apparatus	W. Evers	San Francisco, Cal	Dec. 12, 1871	121, 767
Bagatelle-table	W. Evers	San Francisco, Cal	Sept. 10, 1872	131, 259
Baggage-check	V. W. Blanchard	Bridport, Vt	Jan. 7, 1868	72, 965
Baggage check	F. X. Bellerive	Plattsburgh, N. Y	July 4, 1871	116, 667
Baggage-check	M. N. Coe	Water Valley, Miss	Mar. 12, 1872	124, 418
Baggage-check	L. O. Cottle	Cedar Rapids, Iowa	Jan. 23, 1872	122, 994
Baggage-check	L. O. Cottle	Cedar Rapids, Iowa	Dec. 24, 1872	134, 257
Baggage-check	J. M. Curless	Cedar Rapids, Iowa	July 29, 1873	141, 205
Baggage-check	E. Flather	Bridgeport, Conn	Jan. 14, 1868	73, 315
Baggage-check	C. E. Ingalls	Boston, Mass	Feb. 13, 1872	123, 703
Baggage-check	J. H. McAlvin	Cedar Rapids, Iowa	May 7, 1872	126, 559
Baggage-check	G. F. Newcomb	New Haven, Conn	June 14, 1870	104, 339
Baggage-check	E. H. Paine	Louisville, Ky	Nov. 24, 1868	84, 372
Baggage-check	W. D. Richardson	Springfield, Ill	Oct. 6, 1863	40, 186
Baggage-check	H. S. Ross	Buffalo, N. Y	May 26, 1868	78, 394
Baggage-check	G. C. Thomas	Brooklyn, N. Y	Mar. 20, 1866	53, 360
Baggage-check	G. C. Thomas	Brooklyn, N. Y	Feb. 19, 1867	62, 300
Baggage-check, Folding	E. H. Graves	Chicago, Ill	Sept. 7, 1869	94, 487
Baggage-check, Railway	F. H. Furniss and F. R. Myers.	Cleveland, Ohio	Jan. 20, 1863	37, 441
Baggage-director	T. M. Richardson	Searsport, Me	July 2, 1861	32, 718
Bail, Detachable tipping	J. Keith	Brooklyn, N. Y	Dec. 7, 1869	97, 519
Bail-car	W. D. Mason and A. T. Rice.	Chicago, Ill	Apr. 5, 1870	101, 483
Bail hooks or eyes, Machine for forming pot	J. Miller	Washington, Pa	Oct. 27, 1868	83, 522
Bail, Machine for forming wire	J. P. Van Bramer	Galesburgh, Ill	Sept. 19, 1871	119, 204
Bail-making machine	H. C. Wilder	Ashby, Mass	Aug. 25, 1868	81, 447
Bailing-press	P. K. Dederick	Albany, N. Y	Oct. 29, 1872	132, 639
Bailing-wheel for raising water from the hold of steam-boats, &c.	H. D. Forbes	New York, N. Y	May 26, 1843	3, 107
Bait and vegetable cutter	Z. G. Greenleaf	Bath, Me	Feb. 18, 1868	74, 682
Bait mill for fisherman	S. Hamblin	Taunton, Mass	Mar. 29, 1870	101, 260
Bait or meat cutter	N. Richardson	Gloucester, Mass	Jan. 21, 1868	73, 464

Index of patents issued from the United States Patent Office from 1790 *to* 1873, *inclusive*—Continued.

Invention.	Inventor.	Residence.	Date.	No.
Baker	C. H. Beeman, 2d	North Fairfax, Vt	Feb. 11, 1868	74, 282
Baker	J. T. Davy	Troy, N. Y	Feb. 12, 1845	3, 910
Baker and boiler, Combined	W. H. Miller	Brandenburgh, Ky	Mar. 7, 1871	112, 479
Baker and roaster, Double-reflecting	S. Hasey	Rensselaerville, N. Y	Dec. 28, 1832	....
Baker and roaster, Economical	P. Willcox	Springfield, Mass	Sept. 25, 1831	....
Baker, Coal-heating	J. D. Wheelock	Mayville, Wis	June 17, 1856	15, 155
Baker, Custard and cake	C. L. Sweatt and G. A. Huntoon	Fisherville, N. H	Jan. 17, 1871	111, 012
Baker, Metal	J. St. John	Hudson, N. Y	Sept. 30, 1834	....
Baker, Portable	J. H. Jackson	United States Army	Apr. 26, 1864	42, 535
Baker, Reflecting	L. B. Olmsted	Binghamton, N. Y	Jan. 20, 1836	....
Baker, Reflecting	W. Taintor and H. S. Orton	Porter County, Ind	Aug. 9, 1845	4, 145
Baker, Reflecting tin	W. Prescott	Boston, Mass	May 24, 1832	....
Baker, Steam	P. F. Wilcox	Springfield, Mass	Sept. 3, 1834	....
Baker, Tin	N. D. Whiten	New York, N. Y	Oct. 10, 1835	....
Baker, Tin	G. Williston	New London, Conn	Jan. 11, 1831	....
Baker's table	A. S. Maxwell	Dixon, Ill	Oct. 18, 1870	108, 373
Bake-pan	W. Beach	Philadelphia, Pa	Dec. 16, 1856	16, 226
Bake-pan	W. B. Chamberlin	Westfield, N. J	Aug. 26, 1873	142, 144
Bake-pan	J. Chase, jr	Watertown, N. Y	Mar. 17, 1868	75, 524
Bake-pan	W. A. Daggett	South Vineland, N. J	Oct. 1, 1872	131, 745
Bake-pan	R. D. McDonald	Jersey City, N. J	Nov. 26, 1872	133, 377
Bake-pan	J. G. Metsker	Logansport, Ind	Sept. 16, 1873	142, 928
Bake-pan	B. F. Miller	New York, N. Y	Oct. 8, 1861	33, 444
Bake-pan, Perforated	C. M. Cooney	Washington, D. C	July 21, 1868	80, 147
Baking and cooking, Apparatus for	W. G. Ruggles	Worcester, Mass	May 18, 1858	20, 304
Baking and roasting apparatus	T. J. T. Cummings	Fort Wayne, Ind	Mar. 5, 1872	124, 256
Baking-apparatus	J. P. Hayes	Boston, Mass	Jan. 30, 1849	6, 063
Baking-frame	T. C. Riddell	Wilmington, Del	Oct. 15, 1867	69, 939
Baking-iron	E. Skinner	Sandwich, N. H	Oct. 1, 1830	....
Baking-mold	G. Wingate	Boston, Mass	Nov. 25, 1873	144, 939
Baking or burning pan	W. Burtus	New York, N. Y	Nov. 7, 1820	....
Baking or cooking	A. Stowell	Medford, Mass	Dec. 14, 1830	....
Baking-pan	R. G. Elder	New York, N. Y	Jan. 28, 1868	73, 703
Baking-pan	A. Heminway and W. A. Daggett.	Landis Township, N. J	May 10, 1870	102, 938
Baking-pan	G. W. Mitchell	New York, N. Y	Oct. 15, 1867	69, 830
Baking-pan	W. Moran	Jersey City, N. J	June 25, 1872	128, 238
Baking-pan	S. W. Rogers	Harwich, Mass	Dec. 15, 1868	84, 908
Baking-pan	C. T. Smith	Jersey City, N. J	Nov. 11, 1873	144, 417
Baking-pan	S. West	Trenton, N. J	Nov. 13, 1866	59, 732
Baking-pan, Cover for	W. C. Davis	Cincinnati, Ohio	Nov. 3, 1863	40, 461
Baking pan, Potato	A. Jones	Lebanon, N. H	May 2, 1871	114, 444
Baking-powder	G. A. Mariner and J. Fish	Chicago, Ill	Dec. 13, 1864	45, 419
Baking-powder	J. Stowell	Charlestown, Mass	Nov. 16, 1869	96, 994
Baking powder, Bread	J. G. Copping and J. Weideman	Clinton, Iowa	Oct. 14, 1873	143, 580
Baking-powder, &c., Manufacture of acid phosphates for use in.	N. B. Rice	East Saginaw, Mich	Jan. 3, 1871	110, 680
Baking-powder, Putting up	G. F. Wilson	Providence, R. I	Sept. 5, 1871	118, 768
Baking kitchen, Steam	S. Smith	Herkimer County, N. Y	June 11, 1811	....
Balance	I. Bisbee	Richmond, Mo	Dec. 24, 1867	72, 593
Balance	H. W. Catlin	Burlington, Vt	Dec. 15, 1863	40, 906
Balance	H. A. Clum	Rochester, N. Y	Mar. 28, 1865	46, 992
Balance	B. Dearborn	Boston, Mass	Mar. 24, 1819	....
Balance	N. Griffing	New York, N. Y	Apr. 8, 1835	....
Balance	S. Harris	Philadelphia, Pa	July 7, 1863	39, 145
Balance	J. B. Hendricks	Clayton, Ill	Feb. 13, 1872	123, 564
Balance	W. S. How	Cincinnati, Ohio	Aug. 9, 1870	106, 163
Balance	C. Howlett	Hartford, Conn	May 6, 1862	35, 155
Balance	G. W. King	Georgetown, D. C	Sept. 6, 1870	107, 182
Balance	C. C. Marsh	New York, N. Y	Oct. 10, 1871	119, 871
Balance	L. A. Mátos	Philadelphia, Pa	June 2, 1868	78, 532
Balance	A. Y. McDonald	Dubuque, Iowa	Mar. 6, 1866	53, 020
Balance	G. R. Moore	Brattleborough, Vt	Jan. 6, 1844	3, 396
Balance	B. Morrill	Boscawen, N. H	May 26, 1843	3, 111
Balance	E. C. Pickering	Boston, Mass	Nov. 4, 1873	144, 286
Balance	S. A. Rogers	Geneva, N. Y	July 31, 1817	....
Balance	R. Shaler	Madison, Conn	Nov. 28, 1865	51, 226
Balance	J. Vaughn	Rutland, Vt	May 6, 1836	....
Balance, Aeromatic	J. A. Gridley	Southampton, Mass	Mar. 26, 1861	31, 802
Balance and scale-beam for weighing, Platform	J. D. Dale	Lansingburgh, N. Y	Aug. 30, 1838	899
Balance, Columbian	W. Granger	Middlebury, Vt	Sept. 8, 1810	....
Balance, Compensating spring	O. C. Squyer	West Dresden, N. Y	May 8, 1860	28, 212
Balance, Compound lever	J. B. Whetmore	Bush, N. Y	Feb. 27, 1832	....
Balance, Computing spring	S. R. P. Camp	New York, N. Y	June 7, 1870	103, 977
Balance, Constructing	D. Rogers	Auburn, N. Y	July 13, 1824	....
Balance, Construction of platform	A. Dole	Bangor, Me	July 18, 1840	1, 699
Balance, Dearborn's	S. Blaisdel	Lancaster, Ohio	Oct. 10, 1827	....
Balance, Dearborn's	U. West and D. Loring	New York, N. Y	Aug. 23, 1831	....
Balance, Double-scale	T. Fairbanks	Saint Johnsbury, Vt	Mar. 13, 1849	6, 169
Balance, Eagle	L. Jencks and H. Dexter	Killingly, Conn	Nov. 24, 1834	....
Balanced elevator	C. B. Sawyer	Fitchburgh, Mass	June 14, 1864	43, 136
Balance-elevator	C. B. Sawyer	Fitchburgh, Mass	May 24, 1870	103, 375
Balance for counter, &c	E. Hibbard	Lunenburgh, Vt	Nov. 7, 1835	....
Balance for detecting counterfeit coin	H. Maranville	Clinton, Ohio	Jan. 13, 1857	16, 390
Balance for detecting counterfeit money	F. J. Herpers	Newark, N. J	Dec. 29, 1857	18, 973
Balance for detecting spurious coin	J. Allender	New London, Conn	Nov. 27, 1855	13, 840
Balance for weighing, Platform	B. Bull	New York, N. Y	Mar. 3, 1837	133
Balance for weighing, Platform	B. Morison	Milton, Pa	Mar. 17, 1838	641
Balance-gate	W. C. Van Hoesen	Leeds, N. Y	Apr. 20, 1852	8, 894
Balance, Hydrostatic	J. O. Bandissin	Saint Louis, Mo	May 10, 1864	42, 722
Balance, Hydrostatic	S. Squire	Brooklyn, N. Y	Jan. 10, 1860	26, 795
Balance in combination with a knife, Spring	G. H. Smith	Greenwood, Iowa	Sept. 14, 1858	21, 520
Balance or fly wheel applied to machinery	J. Ordroman	....	Apr. 26, 1819	....
Balance or scale-beam	S. E. Winslow	Philadelphia, Pa	July 31, 1840	1, 708
Balance-pendulum lock	R. Gaines	Georgetown, D. C	Mar. 17, 1806	....
Balance-pendulum lock	S. Goodwin and R. Gaines	Baltimore, Md., and Georgetown, D. C.	Jan. 22, 1806	....
Balance pivot-gate	D. Brown	Hampden, Me	Apr. 26, 1870	102, 365

Index of patents issued from the United States Patent Office from 1790 to 1873, inclusive—Continued.

Invention.	Inventor.	Residence.	Date.	No.
Balance-platform	A Bliss	Benson, Vt	June 12, 1835	....
Balance, Platform	C. Crain and E. L. Wemple	Madison, N. Y	Apr. 8, 1840	1, 546
Balance-platform	I. Gay	Dunstable, N. H	Jan. 14, 1833	....
Balance, Platform	J. Gibbs	Newark, Ohio	Sept. 12, 1846	4, 757
Balance, Platform	S. L. Hay	Boston, Mass	July 14, 1834	....
Balance, Platform	J. Horton	Madrid, N. Y	July 2, 1836	....
Balance, Platform	T. Y. Jennings	Geneve, Ohio	Nov. 10, 1841	2, 339
Balance, Platform	C. P. Ladd	Strasburgh, Vt	May 17, 1836	....
Balance-platform	J. B. Maag	New York, N. Y	Feb. 19, 1833	....
Balance, Platform	R. L. McCollum	Rochester, N. Y	Dec. 31, 1838	1, 048
Balance-platform	B. Morison	Milton, Pa	Jan. 13, 1833	....
Balance-platform	B. Morison	Milton, Pa	Dec. 31, 1833	....
Balance, Platform	J. M. Peck	Strasburgh, Vt	May 17, 1836	....
Balance, Platform	D. M. Smyth	New York, N. Y	Apr. 10, 1855	12, 698
Balance, Portable	A. Dole	Bangor, Me	Dec. 23, 1841	2, 397
Balance, Safety-valve spring	T. S. Ray and S. E. Cleveland	Buffalo, N. Y	Dec. 5, 1865	51, 350
Balance, Self-indicating	Z. W. and O. Avery	Bethany, Pa	May 12, 1857	17, 252
Balance, Spring	W. G. Barker	Detroit, Mich	Aug. 6, 1867	67, 482
Balance, Spring	E. P. Beckwith	New London, Conn	Jan. 16, 1855	12, 249
Balance, Spring	J. H. and R. H. Bull	New York, N. Y	Sept. 20, 1844	3, 752
Balance, Spring	N. Burnham	Norwalk, Ohio	July 15, 1862	35, 869
Balance, Spring	W. A. Crowell	Salisbury, Conn	June 26, 1860	28, 838
Balance, Spring	D. C. Lawrence	Cedar Falls, Iowa	Apr. 29, 1862	35, 125
Balance, Spring	J. K. O'Neil	Kingston, N. Y	May 22, 1866	54, 941
Balance, Spring	H. Saloshinsky	New York, N. Y	June 13, 1865	48, 211
Balance, Spring	W. B. Snyder	Lakeville, Conn	Feb. 28, 1865	46, 592
Balance, Steelyard	E. and T. Fairbanks	Saint Johnsbury, Vt	Feb. 10, 1837	120
Balance, Steelyard	E. and T. Fairbanks	Saint Johnsbury, Vt	Feb. 10, 1837	121
Balance, Weighing	R. Eastman	Concord, N. H	Mar. 13, 1849	6, 174
Balance, Weighing	B. Morison	Milton, Pa	Feb. 16, 1837	129
Balance, Weighing and price	A. M. Maynard	Savoy, Mass	Nov. 25, 1873	144, 914
Balance for quick weighing, Pendulum	B. Fenn	Hartford, Ohio	Mar. 29, 1853	9, 635
Balance-weight	S. Harris	Philadelphia, Pa	Dec. 4, 1866	60, 184
Balance-wheel	E. S. Pierce	Hartford, Conn	Nov. 19, 1867	71, 212
Balance-wheel	H. Randall	Scott, N. Y	Oct. 1, 1872	131, 782
Balance-wheel	F. W. Wild	Baltimore, Md	Apr. 25, 1871	114, 240
Balance-wheels, &c., Mode of hanging	J. Brinkerhoff	Auburn, N. Y	Mar. 31, 1863	38, 025
Balancing vertical reciprocating masses	W. F. Durfee	Bridgeport, Conn	Mar. 21, 1871	112, 792
Balcony, Portable	E. Balmforth	Danbury, Conn	Dec. 17, 1872	133, 962
Baldric	V. Price	New York, N. Y	Feb. 28, 1871	112, 180
Bale-band shears	A. H. Daniels	Manchester, N. H	Mar. 2, 1869	87, 328
Bale-band stretcher	L. J. Anderson	Water Valley, Miss	Feb. 6, 1872	123, 374
Bale-band stretcher	F. M. Logue	Satartia, Miss	Aug. 5, 1873	141, 447
Bale-band tightener	P. C. Ingersoll	Greenpoint, N. Y	June 25, 1867	66, 087
Bale-fastener	A. C. Fletcher	New York, N. Y	Jan. 28, 1868	73, 791
Bale-fastening	T. B. Bunting	New York, N. Y	Sept. 11, 1866	58, 018
Bale-fastening	W. M. Irvine	Montgomery, Ala	Aug. 25, 1868	81, 374
Bale fastening, Cotton	T. McIntire	Franklin Furnace, Ohio	July 17, 1860	29, 185
Bale-fastening, Wire	E. S. Lenox	New Brighton, N. Y	Dec. 21, 1869	98, 169
Bale, Hay, straw, &c	L. Dodge	Waterford, N. Y	Mar. 26, 1872	125, 031
Bale-hook	R. T. Yardley	Baltimore, Md	Sept. 19, 1871	119, 213
Bale-hoop, Cotton	J. McMurtry	Lexington, Ky	Feb. 23, 1858	19, 437
Bale-hoop fastening	R. Dillon	New York, N. Y	Feb 26, 1867	62, 400
Bale-hoop, Fastening	J. F. Milligan	Saint Louis, Mo	Mar. 13, 1866	53, 230
Bale-hoop fastening	J. Reese	Pittsburgh, Pa	Feb. 5, 1867	61, 868
Bale-hoop-straightening machine	C. Hughes	New Orleans, La	Oct. 9, 1860	30, 322
Bale-hoop tie	G. Brodie	Plum Bayou, Ark	July 11, 1871	116, 925
Bale-hoops, Clasps for cotton	A. C. Richard	Newtown, Conn	Sept. 14, 1858	21, 517
Bale-hoops, Coupling for	J. Agnew	Columbia, S. C	Aug. 31, 1858	21, 305
Bale hoops, Machine for tightening and securing compressed.	R. S. Adams	Loyd, N. Y	May 15, 1866	54, 810
Bale-hoops, Tool for fastening	E. A. Jeffery	Corning, N. Y	June 21, 1859	24, 464
Bale-label	N. C. Jones	New York, N. Y	Aug. 11, 1868	80, 967
Bale, Metallic band for binding	W. Field	Providence, R. I	Aug. 17, 1858	21, 190
Bale-raft, Cotton	T. Byrne	New York, N. Y	Nov. 28, 1865	51, 140
Bale-tag, Cotton	E. A. Locke	Boston, Mass	May 24, 1864	42, 860
Bale-tie	L. Arnold	Galveston, Tex	Nov. 26, 1872	133, 349
Bale-tie	A. Barbarin	New Orleans, La	Aug. 27, 1867	68, 149
Bale-tie	S. Brett	New York, N. Y	June 6, 1871	115, 692
Bale-tie	G. Brodie	Plum Bayou, Ark	Sept. 16, 1873	142, 894
Bale-tie	F. G. Brown	Brenham, Tex	Dec. 19, 1871	121, 988
Bale-tie	J. T. Butler	New Orleans, La	Jan. 9, 1872	122, 563
Bale-tie	L. Carter	Huntsville, Ala	Dec. 2, 1873	145, 091
Bale-tie	F. Cook	New Orleans, La	Nov. 26, 1872	133, 412
Bale-tie	F. Cook	New Orleans, La	Feb. 4, 1873	135, 526
Bale-tie	F. Cook	New Orleans, La	May 6, 1873	138, 479
Bale-tie	F. Cook	New Orleans, La	May 6, 1873	138, 480
Bale-tie	F. Cook	New Orleans, La	Sept. 16, 1873	142, 772
Bale-tie	F. Cook	New Orleans, La	Sept. 30, 1873	143, 223
Bale-tie	F. Cook	New Orleans, La	Dec. 23, 1873	145, 847
Bale-tie	J. S. Davis	Louisville, Ky	Oct. 17, 1871	120, 045
Bale-tie	D. K. Dedrick	Albany, N. Y	Feb. 11, 1873	135, 700
Bale tie	J. W. Gurley	Petersburgh, Va	Dec. 17, 1872	134, 052
Bale-tie	J. L. Haigh	New York, N. Y	Aug. 6, 1872	130, 218
Bale-tie	J. W. Hedenberg	Chicago, Ill	Apr. 8, 1873	137, 549
Bale-tie	J. Holmes and J. C. H. Slack	Manchester, England	Apr. 4, 1871	113, 518
Bale-tie	H. A. House	Bridgeport, Conn	Dec. 10, 1872	133, 858
Bale-tie	E. P. Jones	Shell Mound, Miss	June 10, 1873	139, 675
Bale-tie	W. A. Jordan	New Orleans, La	Aug. 23, 1870	106, 698
Bale-tie	W. A. Jordan	New Orleans, La	Sept. 6, 1870	107, 058
Bale-tie	H. Lampson	London, England	May 28, 1867	65, 239
Bale-tie	J. McMurtry	Lexington, Ky	Sept. 16, 1873	142, 803
Bale-tie	D. L. Miller	Madison, N. J	Apr. 9, 1872	125, 474
Bale tie	W. Parsons	Palmyra, N. Y	Jan. 23, 1872	122, 907
Bale-tie	J. E. Perkins	San Francisco, Cal	Mar. 7, 1871	112, 375
Bale-tie	M. Quin	Galveston, Tex	Feb. 18, 1873	135, 938
Bale-tie	J. F. Rusling	Lawrenceville, Pa	Oct. 17, 1871	120, 104
Bale-tie	S. O. Ryder	New York, N. Y	Apr. 2, 1867	63, 563

Index of patents issued from the United States Patent Office from 1790 *to* 1873, *inclusive*—Continued

Invention.	Inventor.	Residence.	Date.	No.
Bale-tie	J. L. Sheppard	Charleston, S. C	Aug. 22, 1871	118, 286
Bale-tie	W. C. Stiff	Birmingham, England	July 10, 1873	140, 556
Bale-tie	C. Swett	Copiah County, Miss	July 16, 1872	129, 186
Bale-tie	J. D. Van Benthuysen	New Orleans, La	Oct. 29, 1866	70, 295
Bale-tie	N. S. Walker	Liverpool, England	Oct. 15, 1872	132, 223
Bale-tie	F. Watkins	London Works, Birmingham, England.	Apr. 25, 1871	114, 236
Bale-tie and straining-lever	J. C. Coit	Cheraw, S. C	Jan. 16, 1872	122, 813
Bale-tie and straining-lever	J. C. Coit	Cheraw, S. C	July 23, 1872	129, 715
Bale-tie, Band or hoop	E. J. Beard	Saint Louis, Mo	July 15, 1873	140, 873
Bale-tie clamp	T. D. Leonard	Waco, Tex	Nov. 18, 4873	144, 776
Bale tie, Cotton	G. W. Adams	New Orleans, La	Feb. 20, 1872	123, 853
Bale tie, Cotton	A. S. Armstrong	New Orleans, La	June 10, 1873	139, 754
Bale tie, Cotton	A. Barbarin	New Orleans, La	Aug. 27, 1867	68, 148
Bale tie, Cotton	J. W. Barnum	New Orleans, La	Nov. 5, 1867	70, 503
Bale tie, Cotton	J. W. Barnum	New Orleans, La	Mar. 31, 1868	76, 141
Bale tie, Cotton	J. W. Barnum	New Orleans, La	Mar. 31, 1868	76, 142
Bale tie, Cotton	J. W. Barnum	New Orleans, La	Mar. 31, 1868	76, 143
Bale tie, Cotton	J. W. Barnum	New Orleans, La	Mar. 31, 1868	76, 144
Bale tie, Cotton	J. W. Barnum	New Orleans, La	Mar. 31, 1868	76, 145
Bale tie, Cotton	J. W. Barnum	New Orleans, La	Mar. 31, 1868	76, 146
Bale tie, Cotton	E. J. Beard	Saint Louis, Mo	July 30, 1872	129, 917
Bale tie, Cotton	G. N. Beard	Saint Louis, Mo	Aug. 13, 1867	67, 707
Bale tie, Cotton	G. N. Beard	Saint Louis, Mo	May 11, 1869	89, 844
Bale tie, Cotton	G. N. Beard	Saint Louis, Mo	Dec. 27, 1870	110, 539
Bale tie, Cotton	G. N. Beard	Saint Louis, Mo	Sept. 30, 1873	143, 319
Bale tie, Cotton	G. N. Beard	Saint Louis, Mo	Dec. 9, 1873	145, 273
Bale tie, Cotton	G. Brodie	Plum Bayou, Ark	Feb. 27, 1872	123, 976
Bale tie, Cotton	G. Brodie	Jefferson County, Ark	July 30, 1872	129, 925
Bale tie, Cotton	A. G. Buford	Water Valley, Miss	Nov. 11, 1873	144, 502
Bale tie, Cotton	W. J. Carroll	Natchez, Miss	May 16, 1871	114, 760
Bale tie, Cotton	J. S. Carson	Brook Haven, Miss	Mar. 9, 1869	87, 541
Bale tie, Cotton	W. Chambers	New Orleans, La	July 12, 1870	105, 172
Bale tie, Cotton	W. Chambers	New Orleans, La	Dec. 6, 1870	109, 804
Bale tie, Cotton	M. D. Cheek	Clarendon, Ark	Aug. 27, 1867	68, 167
Bale tie, Cotton	M. R. Clark	Columbia, S. C	Oct. 18, 1870	108, 450
Bale tie, Cotton	R. W. Cobb	Helena, Ala	July 8, 1873	140, 575
Bale tie, Cotton	B. Coleman	Louisville, Ky	Mar. 5, 1867	62, 610
Bale tie, Cotton	F. Cook	New Orleans, La	May 6, 1873	138, 481
Bale tie, Cotton	F. Cook	New Orleans, La	May 6, 1873	138, 482
Bale tie, Cotton	F. Cook	New Orleans, La	May 6, 1873	138, 483
Bale tie, Cotton	F. Cook	New Orleans, La	May 6, 1873	138, 484
Bale tie, Cotton	F. Cook	New Orleans, La	June 10, 1873	139, 777
Bale tie, Cotton	F. Cook	New Orleans, La	June 24, 1873	140, 246
Bale tie, Cotton	F. Cook	New Orleans, La	July 15, 1873	140, 766
Bale tie, Cotton	F. Cook	New Orleans, La	Aug. 19, 1873	142, 001
Bale tie, Cotton	T. Cromer	Galveston, Tex	Sept. 23, 1873	143, 124
Bale tie, Cotton	W. Crone	Galveston, Tex	Aug. 5, 1873	141, 494
Bale tie, Cotton	J. Crookes	Saint Louis. Mo	June 8, 1869	91, 091
Bale tie, Cotton	J. B. Dunn	Petersburgh, Va	Feb. 4, 1868	74, 059
Bale tie, Cotton	N. T. Edson	New Orleans, La	Sept. 17, 1867	68, 859
Bale tie, Cotton	H. Fassmann	New Orleans, La	Jan. 29, 1867	61, 527
Bale tie, Cotton	H. Fassmann	New Orleans, La	Feb. 5, 1867	61, 727
Bale tie, Cotton	H. Fassmann	New Orleans, La	Feb. 19, 1867	62, 188
Bale tie, Cotton	H. Fassmann	New Orleans, La	Mar. 3, 1868	75, 140
Bale tie, Cotton	W. D Field	Providence, R. I	May 6, 1873	138, 492
Bale tie, Cotton	W. D. Field	Providence, R. I	June 17, 1873	140, 024
Bale tie, Cotton	A. C. Fletcher	New York, N. Y	Feb. 4, 1868	74, 070
Bale tie, Cotton	E. A. Franklin	Brenham, Tex	May 14, 1872	126, 687
Bale tie, Cotton	E. Garrett	New Orleans, La	May 24, 1859	24, 112
Bale tie, Cotton	A. J. Going	Clinton, La	Apr. 1, 1873	137, 301
Bale tie, Cotton	J. M. Goldsmith	Boston, Mass	Sept. 30, 1873	143, 343
Bale tie, Cotton	R. S. Goodgion	Goodgion's Factory, S. C	Aug. 6, 1872	130, 293
Bale tie, Cotton	J. H. Gridley	Washington, D. C	Oct. 23, 1866	59, 007
Bale tie, Cotton	J. W. Hedenberg	Chicago, Ill	Mar. 10, 1868	75, 267
Bale tie, Cotton	C. G. Johnsen	New Orleans, La	July 11, 1871	116, 964
Bale tie, Cotton	E. P. Jones	Sun Flower County, Miss	Oct. 25, 1870	108, 600
Bale tie, Cotton	B. Kimball	Saint Louis, Mo	Oct. 21, 1873	143, 911
Bale tie, Cotton	J. Knight	Louisville, Ky	Feb. 12, 1867	61, 040
Bale tie, Cotton	R. G. Latting	New Orleans, La	Dec. 18, 1866	60, 528
Bale tie, Cotton	R. G. Latting	New Orleans, La	Jan. 15, 1867	61, 217
Bale tie, Cotton	R. H. Lecky	Allegheny City, Pa	Oct. 29, 1867	70 230
Bale tie, Cotton	Z. W. Lee	Blakely, Ga	Oct. 16, 1866	58, 844
Bale tie, Cotton	Z. W. and E. D. Lee	Blakely, Ga	July 3, 1860	28, 991
Bale tie, Cotton	L. Littlejohn	New York, N. Y	Aug. 13, 1867	67, 777
Bale tie, Cotton	E. T. Mainwaring	Tipton, England	Jan. 1, 1869	90, 761
Bale tie, Cotton	M. F. Maury	New Orleans, La	May 28, 1867	65, 102
Bale tie, Cotton	O. K. McClean	New Orleans, La	Sept. 16, 1873	142, 802
Bale tie, Cotton	J. R. McClintock and J. Cumberland.	New Orleans, La	May 23, 1871	115, 225
Bale tie, Cotton	J. I. McComb	Liverpool, England	Oct. 23, 1866	59, 152
Bale tie, Cotton	J. B. McDonald	Louisville, Ky	June 8, 1869	91, 034
Bale tie, Cotton	J. McMurtry	Lexington, Ky	Oct. 2, 1866	58, 445
Bale tie, Cotton	W. McNabb	Clapton, England	May 14, 1872	126, 645
Bale tie, Cotton	H. B. Merritt	Saint Louis, Mo	Nov. 5, 1867	70, 452
Bale tie, Cotton	I. H. Merritt	Cincinnati, Ohio	Apr. 10, 1866	53, 851
Bale tie, Cotton	J. F. Milligan	Saint Louis, Mo	July 30, 1867	67, 334
Bale tie, Cotton	J. F. Milligan	Saint Louis, Mo	Sept. 24, 1867	69, 113
Bale tie, Cotton	J. F. Milligan	Saint Louis, Mo	Nov. 29. 1870	109, 748
Bale tie, Cotton	H. T. Minor, jr	Savannah, Ga	July 16, 1872	129, 157
Bale tie, Cotton	S. J. Mitchell	Saint Louis, Mo	Aug. 27, 1867	68, 225
Bale tie, Cotton	W. M. Morris	Washington County, Miss.	Apr. 6, 1869	88, 727
Bale tie, Cotton	C. Mudge	New Orleans, La	Jan. 7, 1868	73, 026
Bale tie, Cotton	T. C. Oakman	Paterson, N. J	June 15, 1869	91, 361
Bale tie, Cotton	D. G. Olmstead	Vicksburgh, Miss	Mar. 23, 1858	19, 707
Bale tie, Cotton	W. Onions	Saint Louis, Mo	June 5, 1866	55, 353
Bale tie, Cotton	W. Onions	Saint Louis, Mo	Nov. 6, 1866	59, 443
Bale tie, Cotton	W. Onions	Saint Louis, Mo	May 14, 1867	64, 696

Index of patents issued from the United States Patent Office from 1790 *to* 1873, *inclusive*—Continued.

Invention.	Inventor.	Residence.	Date.	No.
Bale tie, Cotton	W. J. Orr	Charlotte, N. C	Sept. 2, 1873	142, 505
Bale tie, Cotton	C. J. Paine	Painesville, Ohio	Sept. 24, 1867	69, 120
Bale tie, Cotton	J. W. Petty	New Orleans, La	Mar. 5, 1867	62, 559
Bale tie, Cotton	J. L. Phillips	Washington County, Miss	Jan. 7, 1868	73, 034
Bale tie, Cotton	F. Quarles	Waco, Tex	Nov. 18, 1873	144, 793
Bale tie, Cotton	W. C. Ramsay	Wadesborough, N. C	Apr. 8, 1873	137, 570
Bale tie, Cotton	J. Reese	Pittsburgh, Pa	Feb. 26, 1867	62, 365
Bale tie, Cotton	J. Reinecker	New Orleans, La	Feb. 12, 1867	62, 069
Bale tie, Cotton	G. Ricker	Covington, Ky	Mar. 12, 1867	62, 777
Bale tie, Cotton	E. S. Roberts	Columbus, Ga	Mar. 10, 1868	75, 461
Bale tie, Cotton	J. W. Rogan	Memphis, Tenn	Jan. 25, 1870	99, 239
Bale tie, Cotton	S. Rogers	Pittsburgh, Pa	Apr. 30, 1867	64, 255
Bale tie, Cotton	G. A. Seaver	New Orleans, La	Oct. 23, 1866	59, 141
Bale tie, Cotton	G. A. Seaver	New York, N. Y	May 12, 1868	77, 770
Bale tie, Cotton	D. M. Sechler	Cincinnati, Ohio	Mar. 19, 1867	63, 105
Bale tie, Cotton	J. L. Sheppard	Charleston, S. C	Oct. 15, 1867	69, 849
Bale tie, Cotton	J. L. Sheppard	Charleston, S. C	Mar. 17, 1868	75, 705
Bale tie, Cotton	J. L. Sheppard	Charleston, S. C	Feb. 27, 1872	124, 090
Bale tie, Cotton	J. A. Shone	Holly Springs, Miss	Aug. 11, 1868	81, 018
Bale tie, Cotton	D. S. Skinner	Providence, R. I	Sept. 24, 1872	131, 573
Bale tie, Cotton	D. S. Skinner	Providence, R. I	Dec. 16, 1873	145, 536
Bale tie, Cotton	W. M. Smith	Augusta, Ga	Dec. 14, 1869	97, 977
Bale tie, Cotton	W. M. Smith	Augusta, Ga	Feb. 15, 1870	99, 964
Bale tie, Cotton	J. R. Speer	Pittsburgh, Pa	Nov. 26, 1867	71, 338
Bale tie, Cotton	H. D. Starr	Texana, Tex	Sept. 2, 1873	142, 527
Bale tie, Cotton	C. Swett	Vicksburgh, Miss	Oct. 23, 1866	59, 144
Bale tie, Cotton	C. Swett	Copiah County, Miss	July 16, 1872	129, 187
Bale tie, Cotton	C. Swett	Copiah County, Miss	July 16, 1872	129, 188
Bale tie, Cotton	C. Swett	Copiah County, Miss	July 16, 1872	129, 189
Bale tie, Cotton	C. Swett	Copiah County, Miss	July 16, 1872	129, 190
Bale tie, Cotton	C. Swett	Copiah County, Miss	July 16, 1872	129, 191
Bale tie, Cotton	W. Trowbridge	New Orleans, La	Mar. 10, 1868	75, 319
Bale tie, Cotton	J. W. Truman	Macon, Ga	Sept. 24, 1867	69, 274
Bale tie, Cotton	C. Ulmer	Mobile, Ala	July 30, 1867	67, 231
Bale tie, Cotton	C. W. Wailey	New Orleans, La	Oct. 15, 1867	69, 870
Bale tie, Cotton	J. S. Wallis	New Orleans, La	May 4, 1869	89, 612
Bale tie, Cotton	L. Weil	New York, N. Y	Dec. 30, 1873	145, 037
Bale-tie fastener	R. S. Sayre	Stilesborough, Ga	Dec. 10, 1872	133, 803
Bale-tie fastener, Wire	C. Brown	New York, N. Y	May 7, 1872	126, 515
Bale-tie for cotton, Iron	C. C. Bier	New Orleans, La	June 26, 1860	28, 825
Bale-tie for cotton, Iron	W. Boyd	New Orleans, La	Aug. 30, 1859	25, 240
Bale-tie for cotton, Iron	P. Davey	Portsmouth, Ohio	Sept. 25, 1860	30, 126
Bale-tie for cotton, Iron	W. S. Loughborough	Rochester, N. Y	May 8, 1860	28, 187
Bale-tie for cotton, Iron	J. Nuttall	New Orleans, La	May 10, 1859	23, 940
Bale-tie for cotton, Iron	W. Stewart	Natchez, Miss	May 1, 1860	28, 1[illegible]0
Bale-tie for cotton, Iron	C. W. Wailey	Lexington, Ky	Mar. 27, 1860	27, 660
Bale-tie for cotton, Metallic	J. Aiken	Natchez, Miss	May 1, 1860	28, 044
Bale-tie for cotton, Metallic	T. Cook	New Orleans, La	Mar. 2, 1858	19, 490
Bale-tie for cotton, Metallic	T. Guyol	New Orleans, La	Jan. 28, 1868	73, 713
Bale-tie for cotton, &c., Wire	D. McComb	Memphis, Tenn	Aug. 13, 1872	130, 519
Bale-tie, Hoop	J. F. Milligan	Saint Louis, Mo	July 23, 1872	129, 851
Bale-tie lock	J. Wheelock	San Francisco, Cal	Nov. 2, 1869	96, 521
Bale-tie, Machine for fastening	J. Adams	New Orleans, La	June 18, 1867	65, 856
Bale-tie, Metallic	I. C. Plant	Macon, Ga	Aug. 24, 1858	21, 272
Bale-tie, Wire	O. Macdaniel	New York, N. Y	Mar. 26, 1867	63, 166
Bale-tie, Wire	E. S. Lenox	New York, N. Y	July 9, 1872	128, 803
Bale ties, Device for forming	J. McClean	New Orleans, La	Dec. 9, 1873	145, 357
Bale-ties, Device for making	M. N. Coe	Madison Parish, La	Dec. 12, 1871	121, 756
Bale ties, Machine for adjusting cotton	M. Martin	Charlotte, N. C	May 9, 1871	114, 581
Bales already formed, Press for compressing	F. F. Cornell, jr., and E. M. Wight.	New York, N. Y	Feb. 5, 1867	61, 719
Bales and packages, Fastening band on	H. Knowles	New York, N. Y	Mar. 1, 1859	23, 092
Bales, &c., Clasp for fastening bands on cotton	H. Knowles	New York, N. Y	Aug. 16, 1859	25, 125
Bales, Fastening for cotton	J. W. Evans	New York, N. Y	Aug. 21, 1860	29, 683
Bales, Fastening for metallic bands for cotton	W. Minor	Houma, La	Oct. 27, 1857	18, 514
Bales, Fastening for metallic bands of cotton	C. J. Provost	Sardis, Ala	Sept. 29, 1857	18, 299
Bales, Fastening iron bands on cotton	C. G. Wells	Galveston, Tex	Apr. 5, 1859	23, 518
Bales, Fastening metal hoops on cotton	J. T. Butler	Natchez, Miss	Nov. 15, 1859	26, 087
Bales, Fastening of metallic band for cotton	O. C. Evans	New York, N. Y	Mar. 26, 1861	31, 848
Bales, &c., Hoop-fastening for cotton	E. Davidson	Batesville, Ark	Aug. 9, 1859	24, 995
Bales, Hoop fastening for cotton	G. J. Widrig	Memphis, Tenn	Apr. 12, 1859	23, 632
Bales, Hoop-lock for cotton	E. V. Fassman	New Orleans, La	Apr. 18, 1865	47, 288
Bales, Iron tie for cotton	G. N. Beard	Saint Louis, Mo	July 16, 1861	32, 818
Bales, Iron tie for cotton	J. J. McComb	New Orleans, La	Jan. 29, 1861	31, 252
Bales, Label for cotton	P. H. Taylor	New Orleans, La	Mar. 1, 1870	100, 467
Bales, Lock for cotton	A. P. Merrill, jr	Natchez, Miss	May 22, 1860	28, 392
Bales, Machine for preparing hay for pressing into	O. and C. Waste	Cameron, Ill	Nov. 29, 1864	45, 285
Bales, &c., Machine for tightening and securing metallic band for cotton.	G. W. Penniston	North Vernon, Ind	Aug. 31, 1858	21, 360
Bales, &c., Mark-holder for	P. Fitch	Brooklyn, N. Y	Apr. 28, 1863	38, 363
Bales, &c., Mark-holder for	H. W. Goodrich and E. A. Locke.	Chelsea and Boston, Mass.	Apr. 28, 1863	38, 365
Bales, &c., Metallic band-fastening for	A. O. Broad	Louisville, Ky	June 9, 1857	17, 485
Bales, Metallic band for cotton	R. W. Fenwick	Washington, D. C	Sept. 25, 1860	30, 133
Bales, &c., Mode of attaching labels to	E. A. Locke	Boston, Mass	Sept. 29, 1863	40, 109
Bales, Mode of securing metal hoops on cotton	J. McMurtry	Fayette County, Ky	Apr. 10, 1860	27, 866
Bales of cotton and other fibrous materials, Non-elastic band for.	D. McComb	Memphis, Tenn	June 17, 1856	15, 142
Bales of cotton, &c., Incorrodible mark or label for.	H. D. Mears	Washington, D. C	Sept. 15, 1863	39, 944
Bales of goods, Machine for roping	R. Dillon	New York, N. Y	Feb. 22, 1848	5, 451
Bales of hay, Constructing	O. and C. Waste	Cameron, Ill	Nov. 29, 1864	45, 284
Bales of merchandise, Mode of fastening	T. W. Reilly	New Orleans, La	Dec. 15, 1863	40, 983
Bales, Pressing cotton, &c., into	S. A. Clemens	Granby, Conn	Sept. 3, 1850	7, 612
Bales, Securing iron bands on cotton	C. W. Pyle	Galveston, Tex	Sept. 27, 1859	25, 584
Bales, Securing metallic band on cotton	P. C. Ingersoll	Green Point, N. Y	May 18, 1858	20, 311
Bales, Tightening rope on cotton	C. Wilson	Brooklyn, N. Y	Feb. 19, 1861	31, 505
Baling cotton	C. Colahan	Alton, Ill	Jan. 29, 1867	61, 517
Baling cotton, &c	B. W. Collier	Oxford, Miss	Apr. 16, 1872	125, 721

Index of patents issued from the United States Patent Office from 1790 *to* 1873, *inclusive*—Continued.

Invention.	Inventor.	Residence.	Date.	No.
Baling cotton, Band for	H. W. Oliver, jr	Pittsburgh, Pa	Mar. 31, 1868	76, 238
Baling cotton, Hoop-lock for	F. Quant	Painesville, Ohio	Nov. 28, 1865	51, 214
Baling cotton, &c., Metallic band for	J. Downes	Handsworth, England	Nov. 7, 1871	120, 727
Baling device, Hay	L. Doty	Frankfort, Ill	Aug. 12, 1873	141, 636
Baling hay	R. Wakeman and J. L. Ballance	Port Deposit, Md	July 10, 1866	56, 294
Baling hay, &c., Machine for	E. Dorr	Rockford, Ill	July 12, 1864	43, 482
Baling hay, &c., Mode of	E. Dorr	Rockford, Ill	July 12, 1864	43, 481
Baling, Machine for cutting and preparing hay for	S. Colahan	Cleveland, Ohio	Mar. 28, 1865	46, 993
Baling manure	H. C. Babcock	Hartford, Conn	July 2, 1872	128, 454
Baling, Metallic band for	G. Brodie	Little Rock, Ark	Mar. 22, 1859	23, 291
Baling-press	J. M. Albertson	New London, Conn	Dec. 15, 1868	84, 982
Baling-press	J. M. Albertson	New London, Conn	Dec. 7, 1869	97, 471
Baling-press	J. M. Albertson	New London, Conn	June 17, 1873	139, 849
Baling-press	W. J. Arrington	Louisville, Ga	Aug. 15, 1871	117, 962
Baling-press	H. A. Ashley	Springfield, Ohio	Oct. 30, 1866	59, 309
Baling-press	S. J. Austin	Freeport, Me	Sept. 17, 1867	68, 935
Baling-press	C. J. Barney	Rockport, Ind	May 7, 1872	126, 435
Baling-press	H. W. Baumann	Memphis, Tenn	Aug. 12, 1873	141, 622
Baling-press	J. Berkeley	Washington, Tex	Jan. 12, 1869	85, 783
Baling-press	A. P. Boren	Greensborough, N. C	May 18, 1869	90, 152
Baling-press	G. Brodie	Plum Bayou, Ark	Sept. 19, 1871	119, 009
Baling-press	C. B. Brooks	Auburn, Me	June 13, 1865	48, 151
Baling-press	C. Brown and D. L. Miller	Buffalo, N. Y., and Madison, N. J.	Sept. 1, 1868	81, 745
Baling-press	M. Brunner, jr	Fremont, Ohio	Sept. 17, 1872	131, 424
Baling-press	H. K. Burnett	Poughkeepsie, N. Y	Mar. 18, 1873	136, 965
Baling-press	S. P. Cady	Hastings, Mich	Sept. 10, 1872	131, 250
Baling-press	N. Chapman	Milford, Mass	Apr. 13, 1869	88, 846
Baling-press	N. Chapman	Hopedale, Mass	Oct. 3, 1871	119, 573
Baling-press	M. D. Cheek	Clarendon, Ark	Mar. 12, 1867	62, 815
Baling-press	M. D. Cheek	Memphis, Tenn	Dec. 29, 1868	85, 365
Baling-press	M. D. Cheek	Memphis, Tenn	Aug. 23, 1870	106, 660
Baling-press	C. C. Converse	New York, N. Y	Sept. 18, 1866	58, 222
Baling-press	W. M. Conner	Burlington, Ky	July 22, 1873	141, 035
Baling-press	J. S. Cook	West Groton, Mass	Nov. 21, 1871	121, 087
Baling-press	F. F. Cornell, jr	New York, N. Y	May 23, 1865	47, 800
Baling-press	F. F. Cornell, jr	New York, N. Y	June 20, 1865	48, 261
Baling-press	F. F. Cornell, jr	New York, N. Y	Feb. 5, 1867	61, 718
Baling-press	T. J. Corning	San José, Cal	Feb. 28, 1871	112, 224
Baling-press	T. J. Corning	San José, Cal	Nov. 14, 1871	120, 942
Baling-press	W. P. Craig	Milton, Ky	July 4, 1865	48, 523
Baling-press	D. Cumming, jr	New York, N. Y	Apr. 7, 1868	76, 407
Baling-press	P. K. Dederick	Greenbush, N. Y	Apr. 13, 1869	88, 775
Baling-press	P. K. Dederick	Greenbush, N. Y	Feb. 1, 1870	99, 295
Baling-press	P. K. Dederick	Albany, N. Y	Feb. 1, 1870	99, 296
Baling-press	P. K. Dederick	Albany, N. Y	Feb. 1, 1870	99, 297
Baling-press	W. Deering	Louisville, Ky	Nov. 23, 1869	97, 176
Baling-press	L. Dodge	Waterford, N. Y	Oct. 17, 1871	120, 048
Baling-press	G. Duncan	San Francisco, Cal	Nov. 1, 1870	108, 772
Baling-press	D. Dunn	Lewisport, Ky	Sept. 1, 1868	81, 612
Baling-press	C. J. Emmett	New York, N. Y	Oct. 5, 1869	95, 447
Baling-press	D. A. Fanghaenel	Kansas City, Mo	July 16, 1872	129, 119
Baling-press	G. F. Felton	De Pere, Wis	Apr. 23, 1872	125, 944
Baling-press	C. V. Fleetwood and E. W. Morton.	Vincennes, Ind	Mar. 22, 1864	42, 046
Baling-press	D. Frisbie and S. C. Goodsell	New Haven, Conn	May 8, 1866	54, 644
Baling-press	G. B. Garlinghouse	North Madison, Ind	Aug. 27, 1867	68, 062
Baling-press	C. W. Gillis	San Antonio, Tex	Nov. 20, 1866	59, 832
Baling-press	J. H. Godwin	Scotland Neck, N. C	Aug. 27, 1867	68, 182
Baling-press	W. Golding	New Orleans, La	Apr. 23, 1872	125, 890
Baling-press	J. Gorham	Bairdstown, Ga	Dec. 3, 1867	71, 740
Baling-press	J. B. Gridley	Louisville, Ky	Apr. 10, 1866	53, 917
Baling-press	G. F. Grund	Fremont, Ohio	Apr. 9, 1872	125, 454
Baling-press	T. D. Guthrie, jr	Galva, Ill	Oct. 8, 1867	69, 657
Baling-press	J. Harder	Lock Haven, Pa	July 14, 1863	39, 230
Baling-press	J. K. Harris	Allensville, Ind	Aug. 26, 1862	36, 297
Baling-press	J. K. Harris	Allensville, Ind	June 23, 1863	38, 963
Baling-press	G. W. Hart	Aurora, Ind	Nov. 21, 1865	51, 043
Baling-press	H. F. Hicks	Grand View, Ind	June 27, 1865	48, 487
Baling-press	P. Higdon	Lewisport, Ky	Aug. 24, 1869	94, 110
Baling-press	D. H. Hill	Union Springs, Ala	Jan. 12, 1869	85, 822
Baling-press	E. Hill	Hamilton, Ill	Nov. 22, 1870	109, 515
Baling-press	G. H. Hoke and J. A. Brown	Elizabeth, Ind	Oct. 15, 1867	69, 807
Baling-press	G. D. Howe	Lewisport, Ky	Dec. 11, 1866	60, 376
Baling-press	A. J. Hunt	Walla Walla, Wash	July 16, 1872	129, 477
Baling-press	F. A. Huntington and J. F. Carter.	San Francisco, Cal	May 7, 1872	126, 394
Baling-press	W. Iler	Shreveport, La	Sept. 27, 1870	107, 688
Baling-press	W. R. King	Chicago, Ill	Dec. 4, 1866	60, 196
Baling-press	W. R. King	Chicago, Ill	Apr. 16, 1872	125, 741
Baling-press	L. W. Liles	Roanoke, Ala	May 7, 1872	126, 405
Baling-press	C. Locher	Oroville, Cal	Aug. 23, 1870	106, 703
Baling-press	T. E. Marable	Petersburgh, Va	Oct. 24, 1871	120, 297
Baling-press	E. J. Marsters	Shaw's Flat, Cal	June 7, 1870	103, 907
Baling-press	A. W. Mason	Station 2, (P. and G. R. R.,) Fla.	Apr. 23, 1872	125, 971
Baling-press	D. L. Miller	Madison, N. J	July 7, 1863	39, 158
Baling-press	J. F. Milligan	Saint Louis, Mo	Oct. 13, 1868	83, 079
Baling-press	W. H. Morris	Troy, Tenn	Aug. 13, 1872	130, 524
Baling-press	B. L. and T. H. B. Myers	Washington, N. C	May 7, 1872	126, 480
Baling-press	G. W. Nutter	Santa Cruz, Cal	Aug. 2, 1870	106, 075
Baling-press	G. C. Paine	San Francisco, Cal	Apr. 4, 1865	47, 124
Baling-press	W. H. H. Peairs	Olathe, Kans	Nov. 28, 1871	121, 408
Baling-press	P. Philip and P. J. Stophilbeen	Hudson and Schodack, N. Y.	Apr. 5, 1864	42, 223
Baling-press	J. Price, jr	Petaluma, Cal	Sept. 1, 1863	39, 748
Baling-press	A. J. Purviance	Mount Zion, Iowa	July 2, 1867	66, 388
Baling-press	J. Randolph	Huntsville, Tex	Jan. 2, 1872	122, 406

Index of patents issued from the United States Patent Office from 1790 *to* 1873, *inclusive*—Continued.

Invention.	Inventor.	Residence.	Date.	No.
Baling-press	B. Roberts	Clintondale, N. Y	Feb. 23, 1864	41, 722
Baling-press	J. W. Roberts	New Monmouth, N. J	June 14, 1864	43, 132
Baling-press	C. H. Robinson	Bath, Me	Jan. 10, 1865	45, 863
Baling-press	J. B. Root	New York, N. Y	Dec. 30, 1873	146, 096
Baling-press	C. H. Schnelle	Saint Louis, Mo	May 7, 1872	126, 415
Baling-press	J. S. Schofield	Macon, Ga	Feb. 13, 1872	123, 734
Baling-press	I. S. Schuyler	New York, N. Y	May 6, 1862	35, 203
Baling-press	L. Seeberger and N. Levy	Cincinnati, Ohio	July 17, 1866	56, 456
Baling-press	G. W. Serrin	Memphis, Tenn	Apr. 21, 1868	77, 108
Baling-press	W. B. Smith	Aberdeen, Ind	July 2, 1867	66, 404
Baling-press	B. F. Stroud	Marshall, Tex	May 10, 1870	102, 879
Baling-press	E. Taylor	Memphis, Tenn	Apr. 7, 1868	76, 548
Baling-press	J. P. Taylor	Hudson City, N. J	Sept. 10, 1872	131, 232
Baling-press	J. P. Taylor and J. R. Baker	Hudson City and Jersey City, N. J.	Nov. 5, 1867	70, 649
Baling-press	C. H. Thatford	Jamaica, N. Y	Feb. 27, 1866	52, 911
Baling-press	H. H. Tift	Mystic, Conn	June 15, 1869	91, 495
Baling-press	J. D. Towner and G. J. Harris	Murfreesborough, Tenn	Oct. 24, 1871	120, 347
Baling-press	I. P. Walker	Milwaukee, Wis	July 4, 1871	116, 650
Baling-press	E. R. Wallace	Jonesville, S. C	Feb. 21, 1871	111, 993
Baling-press	F. B. Wallin	Saugatuck, Mich	May 14, 1872	126, 853
Baling-press	J. P. White	New York, N. Y	Sept. 5, 1865	49, 815
Baling-press	J. I. Williams	Meridian, Miss	Oct. 2, 1866	58, 526
Baling-press	G. Winship	Atlanta, Ga	Nov. 4, 1873	144, 245
Baling-press	P. W. Yarrell	Graysburgh, N. C	Oct. 1, 1872	131, 805
Baling-press, Beater	F. F. Cornell, jr	New York, N. Y	Feb. 5, 1867	61, 717
Baling-press, Beating-device for	L. C. Field	Galesburgh, Ill	July 4, 1865	48, 621
Baling-press, Broom-corn	W. J. Willson	Coles County, Ill	Aug. 16, 1870	106, 440
Baling-press, Construction of	F. F. Cornell, jr	New York, N. Y	Nov. 7, 1865	50, 798
Baling press, Cotton	B. D. Gullett	Amity City, La	Feb. 2, 1869	86, 532
Baling press, Cotton	W. Norman	Van Buren, Ark	Oct. 31, 1865	50, 772
Baling-press, Hand-power	P. C. Ingersoll	Green Point, N. Y	Nov. 25, 1873	144, 982
Baling press, Hand-power	W. R. Newman	Galesburgh, Ill	Nov. 29, 1870	109, 653
Baling press, Hay and cotton	E. Buel	Silver Creek, N. Y	Apr. 20, 1869	89, 022
Baling press, Hay and cotton	P. K. Dederick	Albany, N. Y	Oct. 29, 1872	132, 566
Baling-press, Horizontal	J. D. Wilber	Pleasant Plains, N. Y	May 2, 1865	47, 591
Baling short-cut hay, &c	C. Brown	Buffalo, N. Y	Aug. 27, 1867	68, 282
Baling short-cut hay and straw	S. W. Adwen	Rochester, N. Y	June 8, 1869	91, 057
Baling short-cut hay and straw	W. Hadwin	Rochester, N. Y	Feb. 20, 1872	123, 824
Baling short-cut hay or straw	C. Brown	New York, N. Y	Apr. 16, 1872	125, 786
Baling short-cut hay or straw	W. Hadwin	Rochester, N. Y	Feb. 28, 1871	112, 140
Ball:				
See Base-ball.				
Billiard-ball.				
Cannon-ball.				
Cat-ball.				
Copper ball.				
Croquet-ball.				
Foot-ball.				
Loaded ball.				
Mast-ball.				
Minie-ball.				
Musket-ball.				
Nine-pin ball.				
Pop-corn ball.				
Puddle-ball.				
Puddlers' ball.				
Rifle-ball.				
Rubber ball.				
Ball alley	J. D. Patrick	San Francisco, Cal	Oct. 8, 1867	69, 581
Ball-alley	J. D. Patrick	San Francisco, Cal	Sept. 1, 1868	81, 676
Ball-and-socket joint	R. R. and J. Craig	Nevada, Cal	Dec. 28, 1869	98, 234
Ball-and-socket joint	W. P. Haskins	Mendota, Ill	Oct. 29, 1867	70, 334
Ball-and-socket joint	E. Maynard	Washington, D. C	Jan. 26, 1869	86, 173
Ball-and-socket joint	M. W. St. John	Leonardsville, N. Y	June 30, 1868	79, 408
Ball-and-socket joint	M. W. St. John	Leonardsville, N. Y	Aug. 26, 1873	142, 293
Ball-brace	H. S. Bartholomew	Bristol, Conn	May 21, 1861	32, 347
Ball holder, Billiard-table	H. W. Collender	New York, N. Y	Oct. 7, 1873	143, 500
Ball-joint, Detachable	H. Breevort	Brooklyn, N. Y	Apr. 14, 1868	76, 706
Ball, Loaded	W. Hunt	New York, N. Y	Aug. 10, 1848	5, 701
Ball-motor, Rotating	D. A. Drasch	St. Egidi, Austria	Dec. 22, 1868	85, 220
Ball-players, Base for	E. D. Taylor	Hornellsville, N. Y	Mar. 3, 1868	75, 076
Ball rounding and polishing machine	J. L. Knowlton	Philadelphia, Pa	Aug. 1, 1865	49, 122
Ball tally-board, Base	T. L. Canary	Brownsburgh, Ind	Sept. 1, 1868	81, 598
Balls and shot by pressure, Machine for making	T. Bruff	Washington, D. C	Oct. 5, 1808	......
Balls, Apparatus for hardening copper	A. Weldon	Chicago, Ill	July 29, 1873	141, 247
Balls, &c., Machine by which the centrifugal force is controlled in throwing.	J. Martin	Louisville, Ky	Aug. 3, 1840	1, 713
Balls or mandrels, Machine for turning	W. Newsham	Philadelphia, Pa	Mar. 8, 1870	100, 654
Balls or shot, Machine for manufacturing	L. Magers	Baltimore, Md	Nov. 13, 1840	1, 855
Balls, shot, &c., Machine for throwing	R. McCarty	New York, N. Y	Dec. 31, 1838	1, 043
Balls, shot, &c., of lead, Casting	D. Pettibone	Philadelphia, Pa	Nov. 10, 1819	......
Balls, springs, &c., Manufacture of	A. R. Davis	Cambridge, Mass	June 9, 1863	38, 813
Ballast-box for vessel, Deck	T. Fowler	Richmond Valley, N. Y	Feb. 11, 1862	34, 358
Balloon	J. H. Connell	Lexington, Ky	Nov. 17, 1863	40, 608
Balloon	J. P. Gage	New York, N. Y	Mar. 8, 1859	23, 163
Balloon	M. Nelson	New York, N. Y	May 21, 1861	32, 378
Balloon	T. L. Shaw	Omaha City, Nebr	Feb. 10, 1863	37, 667
Balloon	J. J. Sherman	Albany, N. Y	Aug. 27, 1861	33, 165
Balloon	A. G. Wright	Santa Cruz, Cal	Dec. 27, 1864	45, 665
Balloon, Advertising	W. F. Browne	New York, N. Y	Nov. 11, 1873	144, 436
Balloon and appendage	H. Bell	London, England	Mar. 26, 1850	7, 207
Balloons, Arrangement for mooring and managing	J. W. Brewer	Cincinnati, Ohio	July 11, 1854	11, 248
Balloon, Federal	M. McFarland		Oct. 28, 1799	......
Balloon, Locomotive	P. Haenlein	Mainz, Germany	Aug. 27, 1872	130, 915
Balloon, Marine	C. W. Sykes	Suffield, Conn	Sept. 11, 1866	57, 996
Ballot-box	G. L. Bailey	Portland, Me	May 22, 1860	28, 339
Ballot-box	A. Cummings	New York, N. Y	May 18, 1858	20, 256

Index of patents issued from the United States Patent Office from 1790 *to* 1873, *inclusive*—Continued.

Invention.	Inventor.	Residence.	Date.	No.
Ballot-box	G. A. Frébault	Paris, France	Aug. 23, 1870	106, 682
Ballot box	J. Gamber	Petersburgh, Pa	Aug. 19, 1873	141, 872
Ballot-box	J. A. Hill	Bloomington, Iowa	Aug. 6, 1850	7, 545
Ballot-box	S. C. Jollie	New York, N. Y	Oct. 5, 1858	21, 684
Ballot-box	J. A. McPherson	Troy, N. Y	Jan. 24, 1865	46, 012
Ballot-box	J. P. Outcalt	Lancaster, Ohio	Feb. 25, 1868	74, 932
Ballot-box, Registering	J. S. Savage	Kingston, N H	Aug. 26, 1873	142, 124
Ballot-boxes, Apparatus for detecting fraud in	M. I. Shinn	Richmond, Ind	Oct. 23, 1860	30, 503
Balm	S. G. Wallis	Waterford, Pa	July 21, 1868	80, 101
Balsam, Lavender	E. Bartlette	New York, N. Y	June 29, 1833	....
Baluster-cutting machine	P. J. Frantze, M. Tillesen, and J. A. Gregersen.	Chicago, Ill	July 29, 1873	141, 214
Balusters, Construction of sheet-metal	G. Fischer	New York, N. Y	Feb. 16, 1869	86, 977
Bamboo, cane, and other fibrous plants, Mode of treating.	C. Heaton	New York, N. Y	July 2, 1867	66, 338
Bamboo-fiber, Process of preparing	L. S. Robbins and J. A. Southmayd.	New York, N. Y., and Elizabeth, N. J.	Mar. 2, 1869	87, 432
Bamboo or cane fiber, Manufacture of flock from	L. S. Robbins and J. A. Southmayd.	New York, N. Y., and Elizabeth, N. J.	Mar. 2, 1869	87, 433
Bananas and plantains, Manufacture from	J. Fry	New Orleans, La	July 27, 1869	93, 075
Band and fastener, Package	F. R. Hunt	Leavenworth, Kans	Mar. 18, 1873	137, 000
Band and skirt-hoop attachment	A. K. Young	Boston, Mass	Aug. 19, 1862	36, 253
Band, Anti-interfering	W. Hall and J. R. Clifford	Boston, Mass	Sept. 8, 1868	81, 998
Band-clasp, Elastic	J. C. Arms	Northampton, Mass	Oct. 15, 1872	132, 230
Band-clasp, Elastic	A. Scheydecker	Amsterdam, N. Y	Sept. 20, 1870	107, 550
Band-comb	E. Brown	Wappinger's Falls, N. Y	Mar. 4, 1873	136, 358
Band-comb	D. N. Ropes	Orange, N. J	Dec. 2, 1873	145, 071
Band-coupling	S. Moulton	Hartford, Conn	July 2, 1867	66, 244
Band-cutter	W. C. Barr and E. J. Hunkins	Macon City, Mo	Oct. 5, 1869	95, 414
Band-cutter	A. Zwiebel	Burlington, Wis	Apr. 27, 1869	89, 372
Band-cutter and thrashing-machine attachment	S. C. Myers and J. McCauley	McAllisterville, Pa	Aug. 29, 1871	118, 634
Band-cutter, spreader, and feeder, Automatic	W. H. H. Youngs	Waverly, Iowa	Dec. 20, 1870	110, 324
Band-cutting fork'	D. Arnold	West Lodi, Ohio	Apr. 23, 1872	125, 926
Band-cutting fork	D. Arnold	Clyde, Ohio	Nov. 26, 1872	133, 396
Band-cutting knife, Straw	F. Coulon	Rockford, Ill	Mar. 31, 1868	75, 055
Band-cutting machine	W. U. Hoover	Macomb, Ill	June 20, 1865	48, 280
Band-drawer	B. W. Field	Ferrisburgh, Vt	Apr. 20, 1869	89, 136
Band, Endless	L. Binns	Bradford, England	Oct. 21, 1873	143, 743
Band-fastening	D. E. Hall	Detroit, Mich	Jan. 19, 1869	85, 929
Band-fastening, Metallic	A. Barbarin	New Orleans, La	Oct. 9, 1866	58, 574
Band for bundle	C. Perley	New York, N. Y	Aug. 15, 1865	49, 435
Band for machinery	J. H. Clifton	New Castle, Pa	May 22, 1860	28, 350
Band for machinery, Driving	C. M. Reullier	Paris, France	Aug. 5, 1862	36, 110
Band, Gripe	E. White and J. H. Warren	French Corral, Cal	Apr. 17, 1866	54, 048
Band hook, Back	C. Wack	Evansville, Ind	July 28, 1868	80, 373
Band-knife	F. Coulon	Rockford, Ill	June 20, 1871	116, 027
Band, Machine	S. J. Whitton	Coleraine, Mass	May 10, 1870	102, 898
Band-perforating machine, Metal	A. Leland	Philadelphia, Pa	Mar. 13, 1866	53, 228
Band-puller	H. M. Wait	Woodstock, Ill	July 21, 1868	80, 251
Band-tie	J. I. Peyton	Washington, D. C	July 18, 1871	117, 202
Band-tightener	G. Brodie	Jefferson County, Ark	Jan. 30, 1872	123, 228
Band-tightener	F. M. Lottridge	Portland, Me	Dec. 14, 1869	97, 784
Band-twisting machine, Jack	J. Collier	Morenci, Mich	Oct. 27, 1868	83, 465
Bands, clamps, &c., Fastening for attaching the ends of.	E. Carter	Norwalk, Conn	Sept. 28, 1869	95, 322
Bands, Clasp for metallic or other flexible	A. C. Richard	Newtown, Conn	Oct. 19, 1858	21, 848
Bands, Composition for making self-cementing	E. M. Carrington	New York, N. Y	Jan. 12, 1869	85, 790
Bands, Contracting wrought-iron	E. Cooper	Richmond, Va	Mar. 16, 1833	....
Bands, Guiding endless belt or apron	S. Sawyer	Boston, Mass	Mar. 30, 1833	....
Bands, Hoop-lock for securing the ends of metallic	P. C. Ingersoll	Green Point, N. Y	Mar. 15, 1859	23, 249
Bands, Machine for making endless	L. Binns	Bradford, England	Dec. 9, 1873	145, 386
Bands, Machine for re-rolling metallic	C. W. Chapman	Liverpool, England	Mar. 11, 1873	136, 585
Bands, Machine for trimming metallic	J. G. Merrill	Boston, Mass	Oct. 8, 1872	131, 962
Bands, &c., Making iron-keyed	E. Cooper	Richmond, Va	Sept. 14, 1826	....
Bands, &c., Method of joining sheet-metal	W. Painter	Baltimore, Md	Sept. 5, 1865	49, 782
Bands of iron, Clasp for the ends of	C. Warner	New York, N. Y	Mar. 15, 1859	23, 281
Bands or belts, Making gutta-percha	C. Hancock	Grosvenor Place, England	May 23, 1848	5, 590
Bandage	N. Jensen	Washington, D. C	Dec. 14, 1858	22, 293
Bandage for preternatural enlargements	A. R. Brown	Albion, Mich	Nov. 24, 1868	84, 255
Bandage, Obstetrical	M. Willis	Rochester, N. Y	Mar. 26, 1861	31, 843
Bandage, pad, &c., for cure or relief of hernia, &c.	R. Thompson	Columbus, Ohio	July 29, 1837	315
Bandage, Supporting	E. F. Hofmann	New York, N. Y	Mar. 16, 1869	87, 932
Bandage, Suspensory	E. Heaton	New Haven, Conn	May 14, 1867	64, 766
Bandage, Suspensory	W. H. Phelps	Boston, Mass	May 12, 1868	77, 757
Bandage, Suspensory	J. L. Taylor	New York, N. Y	Apr. 12, 1870	101, 941
Bandbox	G. H. Dickerman	Boston, Mass	Jan. 4, 1859	22, 493
Bandboxes, Machine for cutting the top and bottom of.	B. Mestayer	New York, N. Y	Nov. 13, 1821	....
Bandboxes, Manufacture of	W. Tabele	New York, N. Y	Oct. 9, 1849	6, 783
Bandelore	J. L. Haven and C. Hettrick	Cincinnati, Ohio	Nov. 20, 1866	59, 745
Banding and ornamental binding, Raised	D. K. Van Vechten	New York, N. Y	Dec. 12, 1820	....
•Banding, Machine	C. Lenzmann	Brooklyn, N. Y	Dec. 1, 1857	18, 753
Banjo	L. Brown	Baltimore, Md	Apr. 6, 1869	88, 541
Banjo	F. P. Dobson	New York, N. Y	Apr 6, 1869	88, 555
Banjo	G. C. Dobson and W. McDonnell.	Boston, Mass	May 25, 1869	90, 350
Banjo	H. C. Dobson	New York, N. Y	July 16, 1867	66, 810
Banjo	H. C. Dobson	New York, N. Y	Mar. 4, 1873	136, 491
Banjo	J. Field	New York, N. Y	May 11, 1869	89, 923
Banjo	F. W. Harlass	New York, N. Y	Aug. 15, 1865	49, 401
Banjo	E. B. Mansfield	Boston, Mass	May 28, 1872	127, 179
Banjo	J. Mayberger	New York, N. Y	Dec. 24, 1867	72, 517
Banjo	G. Mein	Williamsburgh, N. Y	Aug. 28, 1866	57, 540
Banjo	J. S. Stiles	Springfield, Vt	July 22, 1873	141, 182
Banjo	G. Teed	New York, N. Y	Apr. 8, 1862	34, 913
Banjo	W. B. Tilton	New York. N. Y	Apr. 24, 1866	54, 264
Banjo	S. F. Van Hagen	Albany N. Y	Oct. 18, 1859	25, 872
Bank and other lock	W. Johnson	Milwaukee, Wis	June 29, 1858	20, 716
Bank and safe lock	S. T. Bacon	Boston, Mass	July 12, 1859	24, 710

Index of patents issued from the United States Patent Office from 1790 *to* 1873, *inclusive*—Continued.

Invention.	Inventor.	Residence.	Date.	No.
Bank and safe lock	W. Hall	Boston, Mass	Oct. 16, 1845	4, 236
Bank and safe, Safety-lock for	M. R. Stephenson and O. Edwards.	Boston, Mass	July 9, 1844	3, 651
Bank-bills, &c., Clasp for	C. Perley	New York, N. Y	Aug. 9, 1864	43, 792
Bank-check	A. Man	Brooklyn, N. Y	Sept. 3, 1867	68, 448
Bank-check, &c	A. C. Paqnet	Philadelphia, Pa	May 16, 1871	114, 963
Bank-check canceler	W. M. Simpson	Newark, N. J	Feb. 16, 1858	19, 384
Bank-checks, &c., Preventing and detecting the alteration of.	S. Crane	Dalton, Mass	Aug. 22, 1871	118, 204
Bank-lock	S. S. Burlingame	Warwick, R. I	Oct. 19, 1858	21, 862
Bank-lock	J. H. Crygier	New York, N. Y	Nov. 22, 1853	10, 265
Bank-lock	F. Denzler	New York, N. Y	Feb. 20, 1855	12, 403
Bank-lock	L. Derby	New York, N. Y	Nov. 2, 1858	21, 947
Bank-lock	W. Hall	Boston, Mass	June 27, 1854	11, 158
Bank-lock	A. C. Harig and D. C. Stoy	Louisville, Ky	July 25, 1854	11, 374
Bank-lock	W. Johnson	Milwaukee, Wis	Aug. 2, 1859	24, 975
Bank-lock	L. H. Miller	Providence, R. I	Oct. 5, 1858	21, 689
Bank-lock	C. G. Mueller	Charleston, S. C	Apr. 3, 1855	12, 647
Bank-lock	T. P. Murphy	New York, N. Y	May 31, 1853	9, 757
Bank-lock	H. Ritchie	Newark, N. J	Apr. 3, 1849	6, 252
Bank-lock	D. M. Smith	Springfield, Vt	Apr. 3, 1849	6, 272
Bank-lock	L. Yale, jr	Newport, N. Y	July 12, 1853	9, 853
Bank-lock	L. Yale	Newport, N. Y	Feb. 28, 1854	10, 584
Bank-lock	L. Yale	Newport, N. Y	May 22, 1855	12, 932
Bank-lock, Powder-proof	W. Hall	Boston, Mass	July 29, 1851	8, 257
Bank-note	J. M. Batchelder	Cambridge, Mass	Feb. 3, 1863	37, 561
Bank-note	J. Gibson, jr	Albany, N. Y	Oct. 3, 1871	119, 599
Bank-note	J. Murdock	New York, N. Y	Mar. 26, 1861	31, 820
Bank-note, bond, revenue-stamp, &c	G. W. Casilear	Washington, D. C	Feb. 15, 1870	99, 757
Bank-note, bond, revenue-stamp, &c	J. Duthie	New York, N. Y	Apr. 9, 1872	125, 550
Bank-note plates, Method of engraving	G. W. Casilear	Washington, D. C	May 6, 1873	138, 613
Bank-note plates, Method of engraving	G. W. Casilear	Washington, D. C	May 6, 1873	138, 614
Bank-notes against forgery, Use of type in guarding	A. Brewster	Hartford, Conn	July 15, 1816	....
Bank-notes, bills, &c., Blank for	P. Hannay	Washington, D. C	Aug. 5, 1856	15, 486
Bank-notes by lithography, Preventing counterfeit of.	F. Peabody and J. Dixon	Salem, Mass	Apr. 20, 1832	....
Bank-notes, &c., Device to prevent counterfeiting	M. C. Lea	Philadelphia, Pa	Apr. 21, 1863	38, 231
Bank-notes, Etching the end-piece of	H. S. Tanner	Philadelphia, Pa	July 1, 1815	....
Bank-notes, Formation of	G. Murray	Philadelphia, Pa	Mar. 23, 1822	....
Bank-notes from being counterfeited, Method of preventing.	C. D. Scropyan	New Haven, Conn	Jan. 8, 1856	14, 069
Bank notes, Graphic-plate for	J. Meere	Philadelphia, Pa	July 1, 1815	....
Bank-notes, Manufacture of	A. C. Carey	Lynn, Mass	Apr. 10, 1860	27, 857
Bank-notes, Manufacturing	G. T. Jones	Cincinnati, Ohio	May 15, 1866	54, 834
Bank-notes, &c., Mode of detecting counterfeited	L. Heath	Boston, Mass	July 2, 1867	66, 337
Bank-notes, Mode of making	J. P. Puglia	Philadelphia, Pa	Aug. 13, 1822	....
Bank-notes, &c., Mode of preventing the counterfeiting of.	I. Rehn	Philadelphia, Pa	Apr. 28, 1863	38, 335
Bank-notes, papers, &c., Self-cementing band for holding.	E. M. Carrington	New York, N. Y	Aug. 25, 1868	81, 339
Bank-notes, &c., Preventing the counterfeiting of	S. Beer	New York, N. Y	Dec. 1, 1868	84, 606
Bank-notes, &c., Preventing the counterfeiting of	C. D. Scropyan	New York, N. Y	June 2, 1857	17, 473
Bank-notes, Process of manufacturing	G. T. Jones	Cincinnati, Ohio	July 9, 1867	66, 500
Bank-notes, &c., Shears for cutting	S. P. Ruggles	Boston, Mass	Jan. 5, 1858	19, 046
Bank-notes to prevent counterfeiting, Mode of preparing.	G. T. Jones	Cincinnati, Ohio	May 15, 1866	54, 835
Bank-notes when cut, Table to hold	F. G. Johnson	Brooklyn, N. Y	Feb. 28, 1854	10, 575
Bank or other bills, Universal vitriolic test for making.	A. Brewster	Hartford, Conn	July 11, 1808	....
Bank, vault, and safe lock	J. Oxnard	Portland, Me	Apr. 10, 1845	3, 990
Banks, Mode of preventing forgery on	N. Sylvester	New York, N. Y	July 12, 1824	....
Banks, vaults, safes, &c., Lock for	M. R. Stephenson and O. Edwards.	Boston, Mass	Apr. 17, 1844	3, 546

Bar:
See Axle-bit blank bar.
Boring-bar.
Calk-bar.
Chain cross-bar.
Claw-bar.
Clevis-bar.
Core-bar.
Crow-bar.
Draft-bar.
Draw-bar.
Equalizing-bar.
Fire-bar.
Fish-bar.
Furnace-grate bar.
Grate-bar.
Harvester-finger bar.
Horseshoe-bar.
Insect-bar.
Iron-bar.
Iron and steel bar.
Lifting-bar.
Metal bar.
Metallic bar.
Miners' bar.
Mosquito-bar.
Nut-bar.
Pinch-bar.
Railway-bar.
Rolled-bar.
Sand-bar.
Shaker-bar.
Shifting-bar.
Shutter-bar.
Sickle-bar.

Index of patents issued from the United States Patent Office from 1790 *to* 1873, *inclusive*—Continued.

Invention.	Inventor.	Residence.	Date.	No.
Bar—Continued. *See* Skylight-bar. Slide-bar. Spike-bar. Splinter-bar. Stove-bar. Tamping-bar. Tapered bar. Tenter-bar. Tie-bar. Toe-calk bar. Trace safety-bar. Vehicle side-bar. Wrench-bar.				
Bar-room register	J. McNamee	Easton, Pa	June 10, 1862	35, 566
Bar-straightening machine	G. Lauder	Pittsburgh, Pa	May 28, 1867	65, 242
Bars and tubes, Machine for bending	A. Harris	Minneapolis, Minn	Dec. 31, 1872	134, 428
Bars or plates of metal, Machinery for rolling tapering.	J. Holmes	Pittsburgh, Pa	July 18, 1865	48, 868
Barbers' and dental chair	M. Leidecker	Rochester, N. Y	May 3, 1870	102, 688
Barbers' and dental chair	M. Leidecker and P. Cron	Rochester N. Y	Nov. 3, 1868	83, 644
Barbers' chair	A. Abel	New York, N. Y	Mar. 8, 1870	100, 487
Barbers' chair	A. Abel	New York, N. Y	Mar. 19, 1872	124, 713
Barbers' chair	N. W. Bonney	Lewiston, Me	Mar. 5, 1867	62, 523
Barbers' chair	F. J. Coates	Cincinnati, Ohio	Dec. 3, 1872	133, 566
Barbers' chair	J. N. Ewald	Frankfort, Ind	June 18, 1872	128, 029
Barbers' chair	A. Gerdes and J. Reiché	New York, N. Y	Oct. 6, 1868	82, 704
Barbers' chair	P. Haberstich	Dayton, Ohio	Feb. 18, 1873	135, 986
Barbers' chair	C. Kaestner	Chicago, Ill	June 2, 1868	78, 525
Barbers' chair	H. Perry	Bethel, Me	July 16, 1872	129, 423
Barbers' chair	A. Schwaab	New York, N. Y	Feb. 18, 1873	136, 009
Barbers' chair	J. and J. Stock	New York, N. Y	May 5, 1868	77, 548
Barbers' chair and stool	H. Remick	Portsmouth, N. H	Sept. 19, 1865	50, 032
Barbers' check-holder	G. W. Hoglen	Dayton, Ohio	Sept. 17, 1872	131, 499
Barge and army boat, Portable safety	S. C. Batchelor	Cincinnati, Ohio	Jan. 20, 1841	1, 935
Barge-coupling ratchet	W. W. Patterson and E. Bishop	Pittsburgh, Pa	Feb. 7, 1871	111, 564
Barges, Construction of	A. Snyder	Freeport, Pa	Apr. 16, 1872	125, 700
Barges in river, Steering apparatus for	M. Lytle	Allegheny, Pa	Sept. 13, 1859	25, 429
Barges, Unloading coal	W. A. Wright	East Haven, Conn	May 6, 1873	138, 727
Barilla from tobacco-stems, &c., Manufacturing	G. Easterly	Richmond, Va	Feb. 5, 1810	....
Bark and corn grinding mill	C. Parker	Meriden, Conn	Nov. 25, 1837	484
Bark and dye-wood, Machine for cutting	H. Haight, jr., and H. White	Stamford, Conn	Apr. 11, 1825	....
Bark and dye-woods, Machine for grinding	O. Pease and A. Donalds	Norfolk, Conn	Mar. 18, 1808	....
Bark and grain, Mill for grinding	V. Birely	Frederick, Md	July 11, 1842	2, 716
Bark and leaves of various trees, Mode of extracting filamentous matter similar to silk, cotton, &c., from the.	A. C. Vautier	Paris, France	Oct. 22, 1861	33, 551
Bark and other materials, Apparatus for making extracts from.	J. W. Jones	Cumberland, Md	Apr. 14, 1868	76, 775
Bark and other materials, Apparatus for leaching	G. A. Starkweather	Waymart, Pa	Mar. 16, 1869	87, 984
Bark, &c., Apparatus for, and mode of, packing ground.	J. Lyon	Philadelphia, Pa	Jan. 5, 1815	....
Bark, Apparatus for preparing quercitron	J. Andrews	Philadelphia, Pa	July 15, 1816	....
Bark breaking and rossing machine	J. W. Burdwin and G. S. Tillinghast.	Morrisville, N. Y	Mar. 19, 1872	124, 788
Bark-breaking machine	N. Sears	Hudson, N. Y	Oct. 31, 1820	....
Bark-crusher	B. Irving	New York, N. Y	Dec. 22, 1868	85, 172
Bark cutting and grinding machine	J. Warrell		Mar. 17, 1802	....
Bark-extracts, Apparatus for manufacturing	W. Maynard	Salem, Mass	Sept. 12, 1871	118, 956
Bark for exportation, Grinding and packing	J. Richardson and B. Stout	Bucks County, Pa	June 6, 1812	....
Bark for tanning and other purposes, Process of extracting the strength of.	J. Brainer and W. H. Burridge.	Cleveland, Ohio	Apr. 8, 1862	34, 873
Bark from tree, Tool for splitting	E. Michaels	Palermo, Me	Aug. 28, 1866	57, 542
Bark from willows, &c., Machine for removing	L. A. Beardsley	South Edmeston, N. Y	June 26, 1860	28, 824
Bark from wood, Mode of separating	J. Maitre	Chatillon, France	Dec. 31, 1867	72, 873
Bark-grinding machine	A. Bull	Caroline, N. Y	Mar. 27, 1828	....
Bark-grinding machine	M. Hurd	Augusta, N. Y	May 3, 1831	....
Bark-grinding mill	B. A. Beardsley	Sangerfield, N. Y	Feb. 4, 1843	2, 944
Bark-grinding mill	A. Lindsey	Canton, Me	Dec. 26, 1845	4, 335
Bark-leach	S. B. Patterson	Bridgeport, Ct	Mar. 17, 1868	75, 571
Bark-leaching apparatus	H. C. Crowell	Morgan, Ohio	Feb. 14, 1871	111, 730
Bark-leaching apparatus	C. Korn	Wurtsborough, N. Y	Dec. 3, 1867	71, 765
Bark, Machine for breaking and grinding	C. Tobey	Hudson, N. Y	May 7, 1807	....
Bark, Machine for rossing	R. Healy	Swanton Falls, Vt	June 9, 1863	38, 861
Bark, Machine for separating the qualities of	J. Brakeley	New York, N. Y	June 5, 1860	28, 554
Bark, Machine for shaving	M. Winger	Lancaster County, Pa	Nov. 29, 1859	26, 317
Bark, Manufacture of quercitron	M. Winger	Ephratah, Pa	Oct. 25, 1870	108, 669
Bark-mill	C. Churchman and G. Martin, jr.	Upper Chichester, Pa	July 16, 1813	....
Bark-mill	O. Coogan	Pittsfield, Mass	Oct. 24, 1871	120, 246
Bark-mill	J. G. Curtis	Emporium, Pa	Apr. 19, 1870	101, 984
Bark-mill	J. Elliott	Philadelphia, Pa	May 24, 1822	....
Bark-mill	C. Foss	Madison, Ohio	Oct. 25, 1826	....
Bark-mill	L. Gale	Berkshire County, Mass	Mar. 20, 1811	....
Bark-mill	L. Gale	Lenox, Mass	May 16, 1815	....
Bark-mill	J. T. Gifford	Veteran, N. Y	Feb. 27, 1832	....
Bark-mill	C. H. Green and R. Montgomery	Sangerfield, N. Y	Sept. 30, 1831	....
Bark-mill	J. Helenbrook	Olean, N. Y	Feb. 14, 1871	111, 744
Bark-mill	L. N. Hermance	Kingston, N. Y	June 7, 1870	103, 881
Bark-mill	D. Humberd and G. Downs	McConnellstown, Pa	Mar. 27, 1832	....
Bark-mill	M. Hurd	Augusta, N. Y	Feb. 1, 1830	....
Bark-mill	C. Korn	Wurtsborough, N. Y	Oct. 4, 1870	107, 923
Bark-mill	R. Montgomery and L. W. Harris.	Sangerfield, N. Y	Aug. 12, 1840	1, 714
Bark-mill	A. P. Norton and M. Owen	Sangerfield, N. Y	June 25, 1845	4, 090
Bark-mill	J. Olds	Meriden, Conn	Apr. 18, 1814	....
Bark-mill	G. E. Palen and F. P. Avery	Tunkhannock, Pa	Jan. 24, 1871	111, 239
Bark-mill	T. W. Pryor	Philadelphia, Pa	May 21, 1805	....
Bark-mill	I. Scudder	Prattsville, N. Y	Oct. 25, 1845	4, 237

Index of patents issued from the United States Patent Office from 1790 *to* 1873, *inclusive*—Continued.

Invention.	Inventor.	Residence.	Date.	No.
Bark-mill	R. H. Shultis	Ellenville, N. Y	May 17, 1870	103, 246
Bark-mill	F. Stamm	East Lampeter, Pa	Jan. 31, 1871	111, 397
Bark-mill	W. Tansley	Salisbury Centre, N. Y	May 29, 1860	28, 518
Bark-mill	W. Tansley	Salisbury Centre, N. Y	Oct. 18, 1864	44, 756
Bark-mill	W. Tansley	Salisbury Centre, N. Y	Dec. 14, 1869	97, 989
Bark-mill	N. S. Thomas	Painted Post, N. Y	Aug. 8, 1865	49, 319
Bark-mill	E. and J. Trask	Sangerfield, N. Y	Nov. 22, 1821	
Bark-mill	J. Trask, A. Seabury, and W. Young.	Sangerfield, N. Y	Apr. 17, 1833	
Bark-mill	M. Winger	Ephratah, Pa	May 17, 1864	42, 811
Bark-mill, Cast-iron	W. Torrey	Westbrook, Me	Sept. 13, 1827	
Bark-mill, Feed-regulator for	B. Irving	New York, N. Y	Feb. 9, 1869	86, 675
Bark, Mill for breaking and grinding tanners'	J. Montgomery	Sangerfield, N. Y	May 29, 1828	
Bark-mill for grinding farmers' bark	M. Beecher	Remson, N. Y	Sept. 27, 1844	3, 767
Bark, Mode of grinding	J. Markley		July 19, 1794	
Bark, Obtaining coloring-matter from oak	C. Hinrichs	New York, N. Y	Aug. 7, 1860	29, 489
Bark-planing machine	J. Brakeley	New York, N. Y	Mar. 19, 1861	31, 697
Bark, Preparation of quercitron	J. Elliott	Philadelphia, Pa	Aug. 20, 1822	
Bark rosser and breaker	G. S. Tillinghast and J. W. Burdwin.	Morrisville, N. Y	Dec. 20, 1870	110, 403
Bark-rossing machine	J. Cowie	Portland, Me	Sept. 15, 1863	39, 888
Bark-rossing machine	C. Gilpin and J. T. Hill	Cumberland, Md	July 2, 1872	128, 612
Bark-rossing machine	J. Martin and G. W. Wilson	Morenci, Mich	Aug. 5, 1873	141, 448
Bark-rossing machine	B. F. Taber	Buffalo, N. Y	Jan. 27, 1863	37, 530
Bark-shaving machine	M. Winger	Ephratah, Pa	Oct. 25, 1870	108, 668
Barkers' mill	J. Rumsay		Aug. 26, 1791	
Barley-fork	F. Dunn	Pulaski, N. Y	Mar. 1, 1870	100, 382
Barley-fork	M. C. Remington	Auburn, N. Y	May 14, 1867	64, 798
Barley, Machine for making pearl	A. Wulze	Saint Louis, Mo	May 3, 1859	23, 879
Barley machine, Pearl	W. Rickard	Chicago, Ill	Feb. 18, 1868	74, 595
Barley or gavel fork	D. P. Sharp	Ithaca, N. Y	May 3, 1870	102, 598
Barley-shelling machine	H. Handschy	Bridgeville, Ohio	Sept. 5, 1834	
Barn-door fastening	D. N. Minor	Bridgewater, Mich	Oct. 30, 1866	59, 248
Barn-fork, Manufacture of	C. T. Beebe	Jackson, Mich	Dec. 19, 1871	121, 983
Barn-shovel, &c., Sheet-iron	J. Brower	Berks County, Pa	Feb. 19, 1819	
Barn, Stock	J. Tyler	New Carlisle, Ohio	Aug. 2, 1870	106, 095
Barometer	P. Armand le comte de Fontaine-Moreau.	London, England	Aug. 20, 1846	4, 702
Barometer	H. A. Clum	Auburn, N. Y	May 29, 1860	28, 454
Barometer	H. A. Clum	Auburn, N. Y	Apr. 16, 1861	32, 050
Barometer	A. H. Emery and J. Johnson	New York, N. Y., and Saco, Me.	June 11, 1872	127, 752
Barometer	E. F. Hamann	Collikoon, N. Y	Sept. 18, 1860	30, 061
Barometer	W. R. Hopkins	Geneva, N. Y	Jan. 27, 1841	1, 951
Barometer	J. T. Large	Brooklyn, N. Y	July 16, 1861	32, 836
Barometer	G. V. Mooney	New York, N. Y	May 30, 1865	47, 971
Barometer	J. Thomson	Wayne, Ill	Feb. 9, 1864	41, 549
Barometer	T. R. Timby	Medina, N. Y	Nov. 3, 1857	18, 560
Barometer	L. Woodruff	Ann Arbor, Mich	June 5, 1860	28, 626
Barometer, Mercurial	G. Tagliabue	New York, N. Y	July 5, 1859	24, 674
Barometer, Mercurial	T. R. Timby	Worcester, Mass	Oct. 28, 1862	36, 872
Barometer, Self-recording	D. Peelor	Johnstown, Pa	Apr. 4, 1871	113, 693
Barrack, Portable	M. F. Brantingham	Sangamond County, Ill	May 12, 1857	17, 256
Barrel	E. H. Cady	Grand Rapids, Mich	May 24, 1870	103, 298
Barrel	P. H. Griswold	Grand Rapids, Mich	July 19, 1870	105, 565
Barrel	T. Hanvey	Elma, N. Y	Dec. 20, 1870	110, 232
Barrel	S. Harris	Kilburn, England	Nov. 1, 1864	44, 864
Barrel	G. M. Huntley	Grand Rapids, Mich	Aug. 30, 1870	106 827
Barrel	H. G. Porter	Grand Rapids, Mich	Apr. 26, 1870	102, 432
Barrel	H. G. Porter	Grand Rapids, Mich	Feb. 14, 1871	111, 868
Barrel	H. G. Porter	Grand Rapids, Mich	Dec. 26, 1871	122, 133
Barrel	S. Roberts	Cleveland, Ohio	May 14, 1861	32, 340
Barrel	J. Tomlinson	Goderich, Ontario, Canada	Oct. 3, 1871	119, 546
Barrel	D. H. Waters	Grand Rapids, Mich	Dec. 14, 1869	97, 840
Barrel	D. H. Waters	Grand Rapids, Mich	Dec. 14, 1869	97, 841
Barrel	J. W. Westen	New York, N. Y	Dec. 13, 1870	110, 096
Barrel	H. Willard	Grand Rapids, Mich	Apr. 12, 1870	101, 956
Barrel	H. Willard	Grand Rapids, Mich	Apr. 26, 1870	102, 346
Barrel	H. Willard	Grand Rapids, Mich	Apr. 26, 1870	102, 347
Barrel	H. Willard	Grand Rapids, Mich	May 10, 1870	103, 000
Barrel	H. Willard	Grand Rapids, Mich	Mar. 21, 1871	112, 875
Barrel	H. Willard	Grand Rapids, Mich	Feb. 25, 1873	136, 196
Barrel, Amalgamating	J. Brodie	San Francisco, Cal	July 5, 1864	43, 462
Barrel, Amalgamating	J. B. Johnson	San Francisco, Cal	July 12, 1864	43, 507
Barrel and box elevator	E. and J. E. Blake	Chicopee, Mass	Aug. 15, 1871	118, 097
Barrel and cask for containing oil, &c	A. Pelletier	Washington, D. C	Jan. 21, 1868	73, 643
Barrel and cask closing apparatus	A. Koegler	Newark, N. J	Dec. 26, 1871	122, 177
Barrel and keg	E. Johnson, jr., and G. W. Ansly.	Cleveland, Ohio	May 31, 1864	42, 949
Barrel and keg	J. Merrill	Boston, Mass	Oct. 2, 1866	58, 452
Barrel and keg making machinery	N. Goodall and L. Tainter	Watertown, N. Y	June 9, 1828	
Barrel and other cylindrical package	H. Willard	Grand Rapids, Mich	Nov. 14, 1871	120, 920
Barrel and other vessel	J. A. Frey, J. Allen, and G. D. Smith.	Washington, D. C	Apr. 17, 1866	53, 970
Barrel and tank, Cement for coating oil	I. Waterman	London, Canada	July 4, 1871	116, 651
Barrel, Ash	T. H. Kane	New York, N. Y	Dec. 24, 1872	134, 145
Barrel beveling and crozing machine	H. A. Crossley	Cleveland, Ohio	May 24, 1870	103, 303
Barrel-carriage	W. Furley	Smithsburgh, Md	Oct. 30, 1849	6, 826
Barrel, Cast-iron	A. Putnam, jr	Saratoga Springs, N. Y	Feb. 7, 1871	111, 679
Barrel-chamfering machine	J. Tilley	West Troy, N. Y	Dec. 10, 1861	33, 908
Barrel chamfering and crozing machine	T. M. Adams and T. B. Luce	Linden, Mich	Dec. 13, 1830	110, 106
Barrel chamfering and crozing machine	A. H. Crozier and C. Carrier	Oswego, N. Y	Aug. 10, 1858	21, 117
Barrel chamfering, beveling, and howeling machine.	S. Widerman	Elysville, Md	Apr. 23, 1842	2, 583
Barrel-cleaning apparatus	I. Pfeiffer	New York, N. Y	Dec. 7, 1869	97, 688
Barrel, Core	R. Cartwright	Chicago, Ill	Apr. 26, 1870	102, 220
Barrel-cover	C. Bird	Dorchester, Mass	Nov. 12, 1867	70, 789
Barrel-cover	G. Hunt	Wawayanda, N. J	Apr. 8, 1873	137, 683

Index of patents issued from the United States Patent Office from 1790 *to* 1873, *inclusive*—Continued.

Invention.	Inventor.	Residence.	Date.	No.
Barrel-cover	H. Steiger	Washington, D. C	May 10, 1864	42, 699
Barrel creasing and beveling machine	A. H. Crozier	Oswego, N. Y	July 4, 1854	11, 211
Barrel cresset	J. F. Little	Lockport, N. Y	July 23, 1867	67, 062
Barrel crozing and chamfering machine	J. Greenwood	Rochester, N. Y	June 4, 1872	127, 478
Barrel crozing and chamfering machine	C. Murdock	Ellenville, N. Y	June 2, 1868	78, 470
Barrel crozing and chamfering machine, Tool for	H. Martin	Louisville, Ky	Feb. 1, 1859	22, 813
Barrel crozing and howeling machine	E. and B. Holmes	Buffalo, N. Y	July 28, 1868	80, 481
Barrel-crozing machine	H. De Bus and G. Johnson	Cincinnati, Ohio	Feb. 11, 1868	74, 319
Barrel-crozing machine	J. Ellis	South Brooks, Me	July 16, 1872	128, 955
Barrel-crozing machine	J. Maley	Middletown, Ohio	Dec. 1, 1868	84, 500
Barrel-crozing machine	H. Nelson	Lake Village, N. H	Apr. 5, 1870	101, 650
Barrel-crozing machine	J. Solter	Baltimore, Md	Oct. 22, 1872	132, 377
Barrel-dressing	C. Titus	Union, Me	July 14, 1868	80, 032
Barrel dressing and crozing machine	W. Brown	Saint Louis, Mo	July 29, 1873	141, 317
Barrel-dressing machine	L. Wirthlin	Saint Louis, Mo	Aug. 25, 1863	39, 696
Barrel, Drying	S. Gibbons	Binghamton, N Y	Aug. 27, 1867	68, 181
Barrel-fastening	E. T. Gilmore	New York, N. Y	Dec. 12, 1871	121, 865
Barrel-filler	S. C. Catlin	Cleveland, Ohio	Dec. 20, 1870	110, 201
Barrel-filler	F. Stitzel	Louisville, Ky	Nov. 8, 1870	109, 071
Barrel-filler	L. H. Watson	Pittsburgh, Pa	Apr. 18, 1871	113, 954
Barrel-filler, Automatic	S. C. Catlin	Cleveland, Ohio	June 25, 1870	99, 159
Barrel-filler, Self-closing	H. A. Webber and C. Reifsnyder.	Chicago, Ill	Dec. 5, 1865	51, 372
Barrel-filling apparatus	H. A. Webber and C. Reifsnyder.	Chicago, Ill	Dec. 5, 1865	51, 370
Barrel-filling apparatus	H. A. Webber and C. Reifsnyder.	Chicago, Ill	Dec. 5, 1865	51, 371
Barrel-filling apparatus, Automatic self-closing	W. S. Payne	Petroleum Centre, Pa	Sept. 10, 1867	68, 649
Barrel-filling apparatus with whistling indicator	H. S. Phillips	Sewickley, Pa	Nov. 16, 1869	96, 933
Barrel-filling device	F. Stitzel	Louisville, Ky	Nov. 21, 1871	121, 134
Barrel-filling machine	J. L. Stewart	Philadelphia, Pa	Nov. 8, 1870	109, 151
Barrel, Flour	W. H. Towers	New York, N. Y	May 1, 1866	54, 444
Barrel for beer, &c, Construction of	M. Hawe	Albany, N. Y	Jan. 17, 1871	111, 058
Barrel for carbon-oil	B. Hackett	Pittsburgh, Pa	Jan. 19, 1864	41, 340
Barrel for cooling fluids	G. Verplaetse	New York, N. Y	Mar. 2, 1869	87, 447
Barrel for holding oil	J. A. Bassett	Salem, Mass	Apr. 18, 1865	47, 273
Barrel for holding petroleum	L. Day and H. Chapman	Buffalo, N. Y	Oct. 31, 1865	50, 694
Barrel for holding petroleum	G. W. Williamson	Gouldsborough, Pa	Aug. 1, 1865	49, 202
Barrel for holding petroleum and other oils	J. Holland	Conshohocken, Pa	Feb. 14, 1865	46, 359
Barrel for petroleum, &c	J. S. Lipps	Brooklyn, N. Y	Sept. 4, 1866	57, 738
Barrel-handle	M. S. Scofield	Stamford, Conn	Dec. 27, 1870	110, 502
Barrel-handling device for stores	G. M. Moore	Farmington, Ill	Aug. 27, 1872	130, 931
Barrel-head	J. B. Barsaloux	Saint Louis, Mo	June 27, 1871	116, 398
Barrel-head	J. A. Cook	Oswego, N. Y	Mar. 16, 1869	87, 760
Barrel head	W. W. Crooker	Waukegan, Ill	Nov. 5, 1872	132, 752
Barrel-head	R. B. De Bare	Philadelphia, Pa	Oct. 4, 1870	107, 885
Barrel-head	G. W. Gilbert	Radnor, Pa	Nov. 28, 1865	51, 260
Barrel-head	L. L. Gilliland	Dayton, Ohio	June 13, 1865	48, 168
Barrel head	S. S. Gray	Boston, Mass	July 25, 1871	117, 274
Barrel-head	A. Hanvey	Steubenville, Ohio	Aug. 1, 1871	117, 536
Barrel-head	A. Hanvey	Steubenville, Ohio	Oct. 14, 1873	143, 571
Barrel-head	G. Righter	Radnor, Pa	July 20, 1869	92, 885
Barrel-head	J. McCammon	Dayton, Ohio	Jan. 23, 1866	52, 182
Barrel-head	J. W. Taylor	Ashland, Va	Aug. 20, 1872	130, 600
Barrel-head	C. W. Saladee	Saint Catharine's, Canada	Apr. 16, 1872	125, 694
Barrel-head	J. W. Taylor	Ashland, Va	June 17, 1873	140, 095
Barrel-head	M. L. Thompson	Flemington, N. J	Oct. 22, 1867	70, 050
Barrel-head	M. L. Thompson	Flemington, N. J	Aug. 11, 1868	80, 886
Barrel-head, Adjustable	P. Rink and J. Docherty	Wertsville, N. J	July 14, 1868	79, 919
Barrel-head, Adjustable	A. C. Yawger	Newark, N. J	Aug. 4, 1868	80, 582
Barrel head and tap	G. Weaver and H. N. Allen	Boston, Mass	Dec. 22, 1868	85, 260
Barrel-head-centering device	J. J. Ralya	Cleveland, Ohio	Aug. 12, 1873	141, 816
Barrel-head circling and beveling machine	W. H. Doane	Cincinnati, Ohio	June 24, 1862	35, 674
Barrel-head-cutter	P. Chase	Peoria, Ill	Jan. 11, 1870	98, 666
Barrel-head cutting and beveling tool	W. Watkins	Crete, Ill	May 12, 1863	38, 520
Barrel-head-cutting machine	A. H. Crozier	Oswego, Ill	Mar. 20, 1855	12, 543
Barrel-head-cutting machine	W. Manning	Rouse's Point, N. Y	Mar. 2, 1858	19, 509
Barrel-head-cutting machine	J. H. Mattison	Scriba, N. Y	Mar. 2, 1858	19, 510
Barrel-head-cutting machine	J. B. Stanhope	Philadelphia, Pa	Mar. 26, 1872	124, 917
Barrel-head-cutting machine	C. R. Tompkins	Rochester, N. Y	Feb. 21, 1865	46, 508
Barrel-head-cutting machine	W. L. Young	Muscatine, Iowa	Feb. 20, 1855	12, 452
Barrel-head-cutting machinery	C. B. Hutchinson	Waterloo, N. Y	Feb. 1, 1853	9, 565
Barrel-head-dressing machine	W. Trapp	Elmira, N. Y	Aug. 23, 1864	43, 933
Barrel-head-dressing machine	P. Welch	Oswego, N. Y	Jan. 12, 1864	41, 248
Barrel-head machine	A. Benster	Detroit, Mich	Jan. 26, 1864	41, 356
Barrel-head machine	J. B. Dougherty	Rochester, N. Y	Sept. 17, 1867	68, 856
Barrel-head machine	B. Fitch	Mooers, N. Y	May 18, 1858	20, 261
Barrel-head machine	C. B. Hutchinson	Auburn, N. Y	Sept. 11, 1860	30, 024
Barrel-head machine	H. L. McNish	Lowell, Mass	Oct. 9, 1860	30, 378
Barrel-head machine	W. Mickle	Oneonta, N. Y	May 31, 1870	103, 762
Barrel-head machine	J. S. Thompson	Glen's Falls, N. Y	Feb. 20, 1866	52, 772
Barrel-head machinery, Method of connecting the beveling-knives in circular cutting.	W. Bevard	Muscatine, Iowa	Jan. 12, 1858	19, 066
Barrel-head-making machine	A. Cutter	Boston, Mass	Oct. 11, 1870	108, 115
Barrel-head-manufacturing machine	L. B. Batcheller	Rochester, N. Y	Apr. 3, 1860	27, 682
Barrel-head-rounding machine	O. Redmond	Rochester, N. Y	Dec. 1, 1868	84, 509
Barrel-head-sawing machine	P. I. Steere	Cheshire, Mass	May 3, 1853	9, 699
Barrel-head-turning machine	J. J. Ralya	Cleveland, Ohio	Apr. 18, 1871	113, 795
Barrel-heads, Apparatus for rounding and beveling	J. P. Heacock	Marlborough, Ohio	Mar. 7, 1854	10, 594
Barrel-heads, Charring	J. D. Copenhaver	Martinsburgh, W. Va	Sept. 13, 1370	107, 339
Barrel-heads, Cutter for	W. H. Bennette	Utica, N. Y	Oct. 31, 1865	50, 677
Barrel-heads, Machine for chamfering	J. Greenwood	Rochester, N. Y	June 21, 1859	24, 458
Barrel-heads, Machine for cutting	A. H. Crozier	Oswego, N. Y	July 13, 1858	20, 864
Barrel-heads, Machine for cutting both bevels simultaneously on.	A. D. Stewart	Bennington, Vt	July 20, 1858	20, 962
Barrel-heads, Machine for forming	P. H. Lawler and J. B. Dougherty.	Spencerport and Rochester, N. Y.	Aug. 27, 1861	33, 153
Barrel-heads, Machine for making	E. Greenlee	Summerhill, Pa	Aug. 30, 1864	43, 985

Index of patents issued from the United States Patent Office from 1790 *to* 1873, *inclusive*—Continued.

Invention.	Inventor.	Residence.	Date.	No.
Barrel-heads, Machine for making	J. Greenwood	Rochester, N. Y	Mar. 7, 1865	46, 661
Barrel-heads, Machine for making	G. Schlcemer	Greenfield, Wis	Jan. 30, 1872	123, 201
Barrel-heads, Machine for manufacturing	N. W. Robinson	Keesville, N. Y	May 6, 1856	14, 829
Barrel-heads, Machine for planing	G. R. Hay	Cleveland, Ohio	Jan. 16, 1872	122, 828
Barrel-heads, Machinery for dressing	T. Shepard	Oswegatchie, N. Y	Nov. 27, 1849	6, 912
Barrel-heads, Making	J. L. Kilgore	Cleveland, Ohio	Nov. 18, 1873	144, 771
Barrel-heads, Method of securing	G. W. Banker	Medford, Mass	June 12, 1860	28, 712
Barrel-heads, Method of securing	J. T. Tomkins	New York, N. Y	Jan. 3, 1865	45, 771
Barrel-heads, shingles, &c., Machine for sawing	J. B. Dougherty	Rochester, N. Y	Mar. 10, 1863	37, 885
Barrel-heads, Submerging	N. B. Cleveland	Waupun, Wis	Feb. 21, 1860	27, 256
Barrel-header	C. B. Pettengill	Hebron, Me	Apr. 8, 1873	137, 567
Barrel-header	L. S. Thompson	Spencerport, N. Y	July 16, 1872	129, 375
Barrel-header	C. F. Weaver and J. W. Goss	Rochester, N. Y	July 30, 1872	130, 090
Barrel heading, circling, and beveling machine	R. Grotz	Chicago, Ill	Jan. 14, 1868	73, 321
Barrel-headings, Machine for jointing	W. Trapp	Elmira, N. Y	Aug. 23, 1864	43, 935
Barrel-headings, Machine for sawing	C. J. Holman	Chicago, Ill	Dec. 24, 1867	72, 639
Barrel-heater	A. E. Salisbury and S. S. Steel	Martin, Ohio	May 6, 1873	138, 531
Barrel-hoop	J. B. Dougherty	Rochester, N Y	Sept. 1, 1863	39, 720
Barrel-hoop	J. B. Dougherty	Rochester, N. Y	Oct. 13, 1863	40, 250
Barrel-hoop	H. Ogborn	Richmond, Ind	Nov. 25, 1873	144, 920
Barrel-hoop	H. W. C. Tweddle	Allegheny, Pa	Oct. 23, 1866	59, 097
Barrel-hoop	H. Willard	Grand Rapids, Mich	July 15, 1873	140, 862
Barrel-hoop-chamfering device	H. Pelsue	East Wallingford, Vt	May 17, 1864	42, 790
Barrel-hoop-crimping machine	M. Reed	Rochester, N. Y	May 3, 1864	42, 597
Barrel-hoop-cutting machine	J. Dobbins	Litchfield, Mich	July 21, 1868	80, 154
Barrel-hoop-cutting machine	A. Goodyear	Springport, Mich	Aug. 14, 1866	57, 120
Barrel-hoop-dressing machine	A. McAlpine	Pittston, Pa	Jan. 15, 1867	61, 226
Barrel-hoop lock	J. Chase	Orange, Mass	Feb. 11, 1868	74, 305
Barrel-hoop loosener and nail extractor	C. F. Dean	Saint Johnsbury, Vt	Jan. 26, 1869	86, 285
Barrel-hoop-sawing machine	G. H. Shearer	Bay City, Mich	Dec. 24, 1867	72, 551
Barrel-hoops, Box for steaming	J. L. Gage	Rochester, N. Y	Apr. 23, 1872	126, 047
Barrel-hoops, Machine for dressing	J. T. Forsyth	Wheeling, W. Va	Sept. 29, 1868	82, 613
Barrel-hoops, Machine for making splints for	J. B. Dougherty	Rochester, N. Y	Feb. 23, 1864	41, 688
Barrel-hoops, Metal clasp for	D. M. Lawrence	Washington, D. C	Mar. 19, 1867	62, 964
Barrel-hoops, Staple for securing ends of	H. Ogborn	Richmond, Indiana	July 1, 1873	140, 430
Barrel, keg, and pail, Combined	G. W. Banker	New York, N. Y	June 13, 1871	115, 807
Barrel-lifter	L. H. Goff	Saint Albans, Vt	Sept. 4, 1866	57, 819
Barrel-lining composition	B. H. Howell	New York, N. Y	May 23, 1865	47, 825
Barrel-lining composition	H. W. C. Tweddle	Pittsburgh, Pa	Aug. 7, 1866	57, 016
Barrel lining, Oil	W. R. Bree	Pottsville, Pa	Aug. 20, 1867	67, 947
Barrel lining, Oil	M. G. Huntley	Grand Rapids, Mich	Nov. 21, 1871	121, 106
Barrel-machine	R. W. George	Richmond, Me	June 7, 1864	43, 074
Barrel-machine	P. H. Lawler	Rochester, N. Y	Oct. 9, 1866	58, 729
Barrel-machine	W. R. and E. Middleton	Cleveland, Ohio	May 2, 1871	114, 321
Barrel-machine	A. Wyckoff	Elmira, N. Y	Dec. 19, 1865	51, 643
Barrel, Machine for compressing the cylinder of cask upon its head to form a tight.	W. Reid	West Arlington, Vt	June 5, 1866	55, 363
Barrel-machinery	S. Andrews	Perth Amboy, N. J	Feb. 12, 1850	7, 077
Barrel-machinery	H. Baker	Cortland, N. Y	Oct. 16, 1866	58, 754
Barrel-machinery	H. S. Higgens	Graham, Ind	Nov. 7, 1854	11, 894
Barrel-machinery	M. T. Kennedy	New Brighton, Pa	Aug. 6, 1872	130, 224
Barrel-machinery	T. Molinier	New Orleans, La	Feb. 10, 1847	4, 966
Barrel-machinery	R. Murdock	Rochester, N. Y	June 12, 1849	6, 523
Barrel-machinery	G. W. Pierce	Holly, N. Y	Oct. 24, 1865	50, 625
Barrel-machinery	W. Trapp, jr	Dryden, N. Y	Oct. 1, 1845	4, 218
Barrel-making	L. Raymond	Rockland, Del	Jan. 21, 1868	73, 461
Barrel-making machine	W. and M. Adams	Ogden, N. Y	Jan. 24, 1828	......
Barrel-making machine	S. J. Arnold and A. F. Clark	Raymondsville, N. Y	Sept. 1, 1868	81, 575
Barrel-making machine	H. Baker	McLean, N. Y	July 30, 1844	3, 683
Barrel-making machine	W. Brown	Saint Louis, Mo	Aug. 17, 1869	93, 855
Barrel making machine	W. Brown	Saint Louis, Mo	July 9, 1872	128, 786
Barrel-making machine	S. Roberts	Cleveland, Ohio	Apr. 1, 1862	34, 847
Barrel-making machinery	I. Crossett	East Bennington, Vt	July 1, 1844	3, 648
Barrel-making machinery	H. P. Hall	Akron, N. Y	July 15, 1873	140, 776
Barrel-making machinery	G. W. Livermore	Cambridgeport, Mass	Mar. 21, 1854	10, 680
Barrel, Metallic	J. I. Bard	New Orleans, La	Jan. 16, 1872	122, 796
Barrel, Metallic	J. A. Frey	New York, N. Y	June 11, 1867	65, 741
Barrel, Metallic oil	E. Parker	Philadelphia, Pa	July 19, 1864	43, 625
Barrel, Oil	R. N. Allen	Cleveland, Ohio	Jan. 20, 1863	37, 427
Barrel-opening tool	D. Snedeker	New York, N. Y	May 8, 1860	28, 208
Barrel-opening tool	T. J. Phillips	Washington, D. C	Jan. 28, 1868	73, 923
Barrel or cask	C. H. Carver	Taunton, Mass	Sept. 11, 1866	57, 863
Barrel or cask	C. T. Provost	New York, N. Y	Aug. 27, 1867	68, 234
Barrel or cask	S. Shea	Corry, Pa	Jan. 29, 1867	61, 690
Barrel or kibble, Lime	F. K. Winsor	Hillsdale, Mich	June 7, 1870	103, 953
Barrel-packer	T. Burns	Williamsburg, N. Y	Apr. 11, 1865	47, 253
Barrel-packer	W. H. Glasgow	New York, N. Y	Mar. 15, 1859	23, 243
Barrel-pitching apparatus	J. W. Brady	Baltimore, Md	Dec. 20, 1870	110, 193
Barrel-pitching apparatus	A. A. C. Klancke	Washington, D. C	Dec. 20, 1870	110, 373
Barrel-pitching apparatus	R. Rosochacki	Cleveland, Ohio	Mar. 22, 1870	101, 166
Barrel-pitching apparatus	L. Schulze	Louisville, Ky	Aug. 30, 1870	106, 964
Barrel-pitching apparatus	G. Sichler	New York, N. Y	June 17, 1873	139, 976
Barrel-pitching apparatus	W. C. Vollmer and R. Rosochaiki	Cuyahoga County, Ohio	July 16, 1872	128, 987
Barrel-pitching furnace	H. Shlandeman	Decatur, Ill	June 25, 1872	128, 329
Barrel-pitching machine	D. Myers	Baltimore, Md	Dec. 26, 1871	122, 128
Barrel-pitching machine	A de Witzleben	Washington, D. C	Aug. 8, 1871	117, 936
Barrel-roller	S. G. Hill	Muscatine, Iowa	May 28, 1872	127, 236
Barrel-rolling apparatus	L. L. Hyatt and A. G. Hüpfel	New York and Morrisania, N. Y.	Apr. 15, 1871	113, 771
Barrel rolling device	H. W. Stephenson	Cincinnati, Ohio	Apr. 25, 1865	47, 465
Barrel-rolling tongs	M. W. Ingle	Indianapolis, Ind	Mar. 7, 1871	112, 462
Barrel-setting-up apparatus	W. B. Elliott	Corning, N. Y	Mar. 29, 1870	101, 242
Barrel-stand and keg-holder	C. N. Cass	Winchester, Ill	July 8, 1873	140, 573
Barrel-stand, Movable	P. J. Skinner	Oswego, N. Y	Jan. 14, 1868	73, 395
Barrel-stave	C. Murdock	Hartford, Conn	June 1, 1869	90, 679
Barrel stave-dressing machine	J. J. Ralya	Allegheny City, Pa	Nov. 26, 1867	71, 326
Barrel-stave jointer	M. Randolph	Saint Louis, Mo	July 16, 1867	66, 737

Index of patents issued from the United States Patent Office from 1790 *to* 1873, *inclusive*—Continued.

Invention.	Inventor.	Residence.	Date.	No.
Barrel staves and heads, Machine for shaving, jointing, and forming.	B. Langdon and W. Mowry	Washington County, N. Y	June 20, 1811	....
Barrel-support	T. W. Claussen	Mars Bluff, S. C	Mar. 4, 1873	136, 416
Barrel, tank, and cask for transporting acid and petroleum.	J. B. Davenport	New York, N. Y	Aug. 29, 1871	118, 438
Barrel-tapping	W. Boynton	Auburn, N. Y	Aug. 7, 1866	56, 889
Barrel tapping-piece	A. Zinsser	New York, N. Y	Mar. 24, 1868	76, 030
Barrel-tightening strap	S. Macferren	Philadelphia, Pa	Dec. 20, 1870	110, 255
Barrel-transporter	J. Griffing	Ipswich, Mass	July 1, 1873	140, 364
Barrel-trussing machine	J. Reid	Allegheny City, Pa	Oct. 29, 1872	132, 601
Barrel-trussing machine	P. Welch	Saint Louis, Mo	Dec. 6, 1870	109, 854
Barrel-vent	R. C. Fleming	Philadelphia, Pa	June 2, 1868	78, 447
Barrel, Ventilated flour	T. Pearsall	Smithborough, N. Y	June 27, 1854	11, 200
Barrel-washer	A. Muntzenberger	Kenosha, Wis	Nov. 25, 1873	145, 003
Barrel-washing machine	J. Peacock	Rockford, Ill	Mar. 13, 1866	53, 177
Barrel-washing machine	J. Peacock	Rockford, Ill	Aug. 27, 1867	68, 311
Barrel-washing machine	T. Reynolds	Yonkers, N. Y	May 24, 1870	103, 371
Barrels and casks, Apparatus for pitching beer and other.	W. Vogt	Louisville, Ky	July 11, 1871	116, 896
Barrels and casks, Coating for oil	S. H. Titus	Saint Louis, Mo	Nov. 25, 1862	37, 018
Barrels and casks during the process of pitching, Apparatus for agitating and cooling.	D. Cammerer	Cincinnati, Ohio	June 21, 1870	104, 421
Barrels and firkins, Adjustable head for	H. D. Rumsey	Homer, N. Y	Feb. 4, 1868	74, 150
Barrels and casks, Machine for distributing pitch in	B. J. Stukenborg	Cincinnati, Ohio	July 4, 1871	116, 772
Barrels and packages, Construction of	C. Green	Wilmington, Del	Mar. 1, 1870	100, 286
Barrels, and placing them in tiers or rows, Machine for hoisting.	G. B. Vroom and S. Kinzie	Jersey City, N. J., and Brooklyn, N. Y.	Jan. 22, 1861	31, 197
Barrels, Apparatus for aerating beer	J. Metzger	East Cambridge, Mass	May 16, 1871	114, 839
Barrels, Apparatus for lifting	J. S. Brewer	Chicago, Ill	Feb. 28, 1871	112, 214
Barrels, casks, &c., Apparatus for pitching and coating.	L. Shulze	Baltimore, Md	Dec. 6, 1870	109, 948
Barrels, Apparatus for pitching beer, &c	H. Reutti and P. Winklehaus	Hamilton, Ohio	Apr. 19, 1870	102, 156
Barrels, &c., Apparatus for rolling and handling	S. Longley	Cincinnati, Ohio	June 3, 1856	15, 042
Barrels, &c., Apparatus for steaming and cleaning	A. K. Lee	Galveston, Tex	May 3, 1873	138, 810
Barrels, &c., Applying solution to the interior and exterior of oil.	J. O. Woodruff	Auburn, N. Y	Oct. 24, 1865	50, 649
Barrels, Automatic plug for	T. Windle and J. H. Dorst	New Albany, Ind	Jan. 26, 1869	86, 196
Barrels, boxes, &c., Machine for lifting and carrying.	J. W. Babcock	Chicopee, Mass	Feb. 18, 1873	135, 958
Barrels, &c., Bush for	D. F. Fetter	New York, N. Y	June 22, 1869	91, 618
Barrels, Bushing for	D. F. Fetter	New York, N. Y	Feb 19, 1867	62, 189
Barrels, casks, &c., Apparatus for pitching	L. Schulze	Baltimore, Md	May 30, 1871	115, 530
Barrels, casks, &c., Machine for pitching	G. Meyer	Quincy, Ill	Jan. 21, 1873	135, 139
Barrels, casks, &c., Metallic hoop for	W. Wilson, jr	Wilmington, Del	June 27, 1865	48, 497
Barrels, Cleansing and purifying beer	W. Harvey	Waterville, N Y	Apr. 2, 1872	125, 193
Barrels, Composition for coating oil	D. Ahl	Newville, Pa	Dec. 6, 1864	45, 379
Barrels, Composition for coating oil	J. G. Thompson	Carbondale, Pa	Mar. 7, 1865	46, 734
Barrels, Composition for lining	A. C. Dunn	New York, N. Y	May 29, 1866	55, 073
Barrels, Composition for lining	L. Held	Harlem, N. Y	June 27, 1865	48, 398
Barrels, &c., Composition for lining oil	J. Baur	Brooklyn, N. Y	June 6, 1865	48, 041
Barrels, &c., Composition for lining oil	F. Becker	Scranton, Pa	Mar. 10, 1863	37, 848
Barrels, Composition for lining oil	W. Budd and J. L. Husband	Philadelphia, Pa	Mar. 7, 1865	46, 636
Barrels, Composition for lining oil	H. Loewenberg	New York, N. Y	Apr. 25, 1865	47, 496
Barrels, Composition for lining oil	J. P. Schenck, jr	Matteawan, N. Y	Jan. 1, 1867	60, 944
Barrels, Composition for lining oil	G. W. Williamson	Goldsborough, Pa	July 12, 1864	43, 552
Barrels, Composition for lining petroleum	J. Fox	Philadelphia, Pa	May 23, 1865	47, 810
Barrels, Composition for lining petroleum	R. Price	Jersey City, N. J	Aug. 1, 1865	49, 152
Barrels, Connection for floating	R. W. Park	Pittsburgh, Pa	May 3, 1864	42, 594
Barrels, Construction of	G. St. George, jr	New York, N. Y	Aug. 27, 1867	68, 322
Barrels, Cresset for heating	J. S. Thompson and M. J. Seymour.	Glen's Falls, N. Y	Mar. 29, 1859	23, 410
Barrels, Device for tilting	J. C. Curran	Philadelphia, Pa	Aug. 3, 1869	93, 180
Barrels, Elastic cement for lining petroleum	J. J. K. Boote and W. A. Gibson	Cleveland, Ohio	Apr. 4, 1871	113, 485
Barrels, &c., Fermentation guard for	A. P. Gardner	Moscow, Pa	Dec. 23, 1873	145, 860
Barrels, &c., for containing petroleum, Composition for lining.	H. Preuss	New York, N. Y	Jan. 10, 1865	45, 857
Barrels for holding oil, &c., Process for lining	J. Baur	New York, N. Y	Mar. 28, 1865	46, 988
Barrels for holding petroleum, Composition for lining.	H. Loewenberg	New York, N. Y	Jan. 24, 1865	46, 060
Barrels for petroleum, &c., Composition for lining	L. Francis	New York, N. Y	Feb. 28, 1865	46, 554
Barrels from bursting, Safety-plug to prevent	R. Bridge	Paterson, N. J	Mar. 6, 1866	52, 957
Barrels from leaking, Method of preventing oil	D. Ahl	Newville, Pa	Jan. 17, 1865	45, 902
Barrels, &c., from leaking, Method of preventing oil	G. T. Parry and W. S. Warner	Philadelphia, Pa	Jan. 10, 1865	45, 855
Barrels, Gage for filling	W. H. Noyes	Boston, Mass	June 5, 1860	28, 637
Barrels, Head-lining for	G. A. Reed	New York, N. Y	Mar. 11, 1873	136, 763
Barrels impervious to oil, &c., Composition for rendering.	G. R. Percy	New York, N. Y	Jan. 24, 1865	46, 021
Barrels impervious to petroleum, Process of rendering.	J. Baur	Brooklyn, N. Y	Aug. 8, 1865	49, 215
Barrels, &c., Implement for rolling, guiding, and controlling.	B. V. Tamplin	Peoria, Ill	Apr. 22, 1873	138, 055
Barrels, kegs, &c., Tool to be used in the manufacture of.	W. G. Burr	Mount Pleasant, N. Y	Oct. 12, 1839	1, 367
Barrels, &c., Lining	G. Arnd	New York, N. Y	June 21, 1864	43, 172
Barrels, Lining for oil	R. V. Jones	Canton, Ohio	Aug. 21, 1866	57, 333
Barrels, Lining for petroleum	W. H. Stone	Brooklyn, N. Y	May 2, 1865	47, 581
Barrels, &c., Lining petroleum	T. O. Oliver	New York, N. Y	Apr. 18, 1865	47, 363
Barrels, Lock for securing stamp upon	J. L. Harley	Baltimore, Md	Sept. 6, 1870	107, 176
Barrels, Machine for chamfering and crozing	J. H. Mattison	Scriba, N. Y	Oct. 12, 1858	21, 769
Barrels, Machine for chamfering and crozing	P. Welch	Oswego, N. Y	Jan. 12, 1864	41, 249
Barrels, Machine for crozing and chamfering	H. Littlejohn	Troy, N. Y	Mar. 1, 1859	23, 097
Barrels, Machine for crozing, chamfering, and beveling.	W. M. Arnall	Sperryville, Va	Oct. 5, 1858	21, 718
Barrels, Machine for cutting the locks in hoops for	F. C. La Riviere	Minneapolis, Minn	June 4, 1867	65, 491
Barrels, Machine for finishing the inside of	E. Greenlee	Summer Hill, Pa	Dec. 4, 1860	30, 811
Barrels, Machine for forcing hoops on	J. Greenwood	Rochester, N. Y	Dec. 30, 1873	145, 942
Barrels, &c., Machine for forming	J. Rees	Elk Horn Grove, Ill	Oct. 5, 1858	21, 725

Index of patents issued from the United States Patent Office from 1790 *to* 1873, *inclusive*—Continued.

Invention.	Inventor.	Residence.	Date.	No.
Barrels, Machine for leveling the staves in	E. and B. Holmes	Buffalo, N. Y	July 28, 1868	80, 482
Barrels, Machine for making plugs for	L. H. Dwelley	Dorchester, Mass	Nov. 13, 1866	59, 567
Barrels, Machine for sawing heading for	P. Welch	Oswego, N. Y	Apr. 5, 1864	42, 244
Barrels, Machine for setting staves in	C. B. Hutchinson	Auburn, N. Y	Mar. 19, 1867	63, 052
Barrels, Machine for setting up	A. Cutter	Boston, Mass	Oct. 11, 1870	108, 113
Barrels, Machine for setting up	A. G. Mack	Rochester, N. Y	Jan. 1, 1861	31, 026
Barrels, &c., Machine to be used in combination with improved iron truss-hoop in the manufacture of.	J. H. Bruner and R. H. Thompson.	Mitford and Granville, Ohio	Nov. 12, 1842	2, 852
Barrels, Machinery for making	C. Ruggles	Huron, Ohio	Nov. 18, 1873	144, 635
Barrels, Making	P. Werum	Berlin, Ohio	Aug. 25, 1863	39, 694
Barrels, Manufacturing	J. Cole and S. Miller	Washington County, Ohio	Sept. 29, 1831	....
Barrels, Manufacturing	J. Squier	Salina, N. Y	Jan. 21, 1835	....
Barrels, Manufacturing oil	B. Springer	Henry County, Ind	Apr. 27, 1832	....
Barrels, Mechanism for heading	J. Grifling	Ipswich, Mass	Mar. 11, 1873	136, 595
Barrels, Metallic head for	S. Lewis	Rochester, N Y	Dec. 20, 1864	45, 507
Barrels, Method of boring gun	H. Peeler	Boston, Mass	Feb. 6, 1849	6, 088
Barrels, Method of making	S. Roberts	Cleveland, Ohio	Oct. 16, 1860	30, 425
Barrels, Method of making	S. Roberts	Cleveland, Ohio	Feb. 26, 1861	31, 558
Barrels, Method of securing bush for bung to	T. Summerfield	New York, N. Y	May 23, 1865	47, 877
Barrels, Mode of chamfering and crozing	J. H. Mattison	Scriba, N. Y	Oct. 3, 1857	18, 549
Barrels, Mode of manufacturing	G. W. Banker	Medford, Mass	Oct. 11, 1859	25, 784
Barrels, Mode of pitching	J. F. T. Halbeck and M. Gottfried.	Chicago, Ill.	May 3, 1864	42, 580
Barrels, Mode of repairing	E. W. Gillman	Hunter's Point, N. Y	June 30, 1868	79, 340
Barrels of oil, &c., Instrument for ascertaining the amount of water, &c., in.	G. Tagliabue	New York, N. Y	May 5, 1863	38, 427
Barrels, Pitching	W. Anheuser	Saint Louis, Mo	Apr. 4, 1871	113, 480
Barrels, Pitching	J. P. Benoit	Detroit, Mich	Oct. 26, 1869	96, 076
Barrels, Raising liquid from	E. Cook	Rochester, N. Y	Apr. 30, 1872	126, 267
Barrels, Self-acting tilt for	I. Hudson and W. Winshall	Stockport, Great Britain	Sept. 27, 1870	107, 779
Barrels, &c., Skid for elevating and lowering	C. Brosius	Hancock, Md	Feb. 18, 1868	74, 493
Barrels, Skid for supporting	W. W. Doane and W. P. Barr	Brewer, Me	Oct. 16, 1866	58, 787
Barrels to contain petroleum, coal-oil, &c., Preparing.	L. S. Robbins	New York, N. Y	May 3, 1864	42, 598
Barrels to hold oil, petroleum, &c., Preparing	H. Wurtz	New York, N. Y	Feb. 21, 1865	46, 518
Barrels to render them oil-tight, Coating	A. H. Hook and J. H. Darlington	New York, N. Y	June 7, 1864	43, 025
Barrels water and oil tight, Composition for making	T. Schumann and C. G. Frash	New York, N. Y	July 5, 1864	43, 433
Barrels with glue, Process of lining oil	E. W. Leggett	New York, N. Y	Oct. 21, 1873	143, 770
Barrels with sheet-metal, Mode of lining	T. R. Cook	Saratoga Springs, N. Y	Nov. 5, 1867	70, 414
Barrow and cultivator, Combined wheel	L. Treffitz and G. H. Shimpert	Pinckneyville, Ill	Jan. 5, 1869	85, 709
Barrow and garden-plow, Combined wheel	J. D. O'Callaghan	Calhoun, Ga	Oct. 12, 1869	95, 718
Barrow and hand-plow combined, Wheel	B. G. Fitzhugh	Frederick, Md	Oct. 17, 1871	119, 973
Barrow and step-ladder combined, Wheel	H. J. Evans	Christieville, Canada	Sept. 26, 1871	119, 339
Barrows and trucks, Tubular frame of wheel	B. W. Tuthill	New York, N. Y	Dec. 12, 1871	121, 916
Barrow and turnip-drill, Combined	A. M. Newland	Olivet, Mich	Nov. 8, 1870	109, 041
Barrow, Coal	P. K. Dederick	Albany, N. Y	Apr. 26, 1870	102, 376
Barrow, Construction of wheel	N. Tufts, 2d	Charlestown, Mass	Sept. 13, 1824	....
Barrow, Drill	G. Colby	Fayetteville, Pa	June 12, 1849	6, 520
Barrow, Dumping wheel	G. H. Kanmacher	Chicago, Ill	May 21, 1872	127, 065
Barrow frame, Wheel	B. W. Tuthill	Oregon City, Oreg	Jan. 3, 1871	110, 698
Barrow, Hand	M. S. Schofield	Stamford, Conn	Jan. 18, 1870	99, 009
Barrow, Horse wheel	J. Rowley	Pittsford, N. Y	Nov. 1, 1825	....
Barrow trays, Machine for making wheel	E. Breed	Jamestown, N. Y	Aug. 6, 1872	130, 273
Barrow, Truck	J. J. Richardson	Marion, S. C	Jan. 21, 1873	135, 157
Barrow, Wheel	N. Cronkite	Milford, N. Y	May 24, 1870	103, 430
Barrow, Wheel	D. B. Ellis	Ypsilanti, Mich	Nov. 12, 1867	70, 821
Barrow, Wheel	J. Ennis	Columbus, Ga	Oct. 18, 1870	108, 341
Barrow, Wheel	J. Gehr	Clear Spring, Md	Nov. 7, 1871	120, 736
Barrow, Wheel	C. R. Hight	Geneva, Ill	Aug. 6, 1872	130, 129
Barrow, Wheel	C. C. Johnson	Springfield, Vt	Jan. 19, 1869	86, 077
Barrow, Wheel	J. M. and J. L. Jones	Paris and Lexington, Ky	Oct. 21, 1873	143, 767
Barrow, Wheel	H. Lawrence	New York, N. Y	July 18, 1871	117, 085
Barrow, Wheel	H. Lawrence	New York, N. Y	July 18, 1871	117, 086
Barrow, Wheel	E. B. Marshall	Atlanta, Ga	Oct. 20, 1868	83, 189
Barrow, Wheel	W. McKibbin	San Francisco, Cal	Oct. 24, 1871	120, 159
Barrow, Wheel	W. F. Newcombe	Cleveland, Ohio	May 19, 1868	78, 003
Barrow, Wheel	P. Noling	Woodside, Wis	Oct. 12, 1869	95, 717
Barrow, Wheel	C. and C. Nutting, jr	San Francisco, Cal	Nov. 19, 1872	133, 170
Barrow, Wheel	F. Parkerson	Philadelphia, Pa	Mar. 31, 1868	76, 241
Barrow, Wheel	R. M. Reynolds	East Saginaw, Mich	Oct. 4, 1870	107, 053
Barrow, Wheel	N. C. Sanford	Meriden, Conn	June 6, 1865	48, 101
Barrow, Wheel	J. B. Schneider	Kankakee, Ill	June 10, 1873	139, 823
Barrow, Wheel	B. W. Tuthill	Oregon City, Oreg	Sept. 28, 1869	95, 288
Barrow, Wheel	J. J. Van Kersen	Kalamazoo, Mich	Dec. 27, 1864	45, 658
Barrow, Wheel	J. G. Weir	Pittsburgh, Pa	Dec. 28, 1869	98, 324
Baryta, Manufacture of	C. M. T. Du Motay	Paris, France	Nov. 11, 1873	144, 517
Baryta, Manufacture of artificial sulphates of	J. Philip	Hamburg, Germany	Nov. 7, 1871	120, 771
Barytes, Process of preparing sulphate of	W. M. Page and E. B. Krausse	Saint Louis, Mo	Sept. 15, 1868	82, 154
Base-ball, Apparatus for playing parlor	F. C. Lebring	Hoboken, N. J	Feb. 4, 1868	74, 154
Base-ball, India-rubber	H. A. Alden	Matteawan, N. Y	July 7, 1868	79, 719
Base-ball table	W. Buckley	New York, N. Y	Aug. 20, 1867	67, 951
Base-balls, Manufacture of	H. A. Alden	Matteawan, N. Y	Dec. 17, 1867	72, 355
Basin	H. H. Craigie	New York, N. Y	Mar. 12, 1867	62, 734
Basin, Overflow	H. Boyd	New York, N. Y	Mar. 12, 1867	62, 812
Basin-plug	W. S. Carr	New York, N. Y	June 4, 1867	65, 343
Basin-trap	H. H. Craigie	New York, N. Y	Dec. 7, 1869	97, 482
Basin with waste-pipe attachment	G. C. Miller and J. H. Coates	Goshen and New York, N. Y	Mar. 15, 1870	100, 782
Basins, Means for draining	L. R. Comstock	Philadelphia, Pa	July 8, 1873	140, 577
Basins, Press for forming metal	G. Murray	Cambridge, Mass	Dec. 5, 1865	51, 342
Basket	E. Beecher	Plymouth, Conn	Aug. 30, 1864	44, 039
Basket	L. W. Beecher	Westville, Conn	Sept. 28, 1869	95, 185
Basket	W. H. Carpenter	New York, N. Y	Aug. 24, 1869	94, 075
Basket	E. B. Cole	Huntington, Mass	Dec. 12, 1871	121, 758
Basket	J. Graham	Vassar, Mich	June 18, 1872	128, 036
Basket	W. C. Higgins	North Blandford, Mass	Apr. 1, 1873	137, 368
Basket	H. C. Jones	Dowagiac, Mich	Dec. 11, 1866	60, 383

Index of patents issued from the United States Patent Office from 1790 *to* 1873, *inclusive*—Continued.

Invention.	Inventor.	Residence.	Date.	No.
Basket	H. C. Jones	Dowagiac, Mich	Aug. 11, 1868	80, 825
Basket	H. C. Jones	Dowagiac, Mich	Aug. 6, 1872	130, 135
Basket	H. C. Jones	Dowagiac, Mich	Aug. 6, 1872	130, 136
Basket	H. C. Jones	Dowagiac, Mich	Aug. 6, 1872	130, 137
Basket	H. C. Jones	Dowagiac, Mich	Aug. 6, 1872	130, 138
Basket	H. C. Jones	Dowagiac, Mich	Aug. 6, 1872	130, 139
Basket	H. C. Jones	Dowagiac, Mich	Dec. 17, 1872	133, 941
Basket	H. C. Jones	Dowagiac, Mich	Sept. 2, 1873	142, 343
Basket	E. B. Lyman	Waterbury, Conn	Sept. 5, 1865	49, 774
Basket	L. Marble	Vassar, Mich	Jan. 7, 1862	34, 088
Basket	S. P. P. Miller	Beaver, Pa	May 5, 1868	77, 516
Basket	J. R. Park	Marlborough, N. Y	May 1, 1860	28, 105
Basket	S. I. Russell	Chicago, Ill	Dec. 10, 1872	133, 892
Basket	S. M. Sherman	Fort Dodge, Iowa	Aug. 20, 1861	33, 106
Basket	T. R. Sherry	Newark, N. J	July 4, 1865	48, 595
Basket	H. E. Tower	Worthington, Mass	Mar. 5, 1872	124, 231
Basket	H. E. Tower	Worthington, Mass	Mar. 5, 1872	124, 232
Basket	B. F. Tuthill	Chicago, Ill	June 27, 1871	116, 374
Basket	A. Van Riper	Washington Tp., N. J	Aug. 21, 1847	5, 247
Basket	G. Z. and W. A. Van Riper	Lagrange, Mich	Feb. 27, 1866	52, 914
Basket	R. B. Wheeler	Dowagiac, Mich	Oct. 29, 1872	132, 703
Basket	S. H. Wheeler	Niles, Mich	July 22, 1873	141, 023
Basket and bird-cage, Combined hanging	S. Vanstone	Providence, R. I	Apr. 15, 1873	137, 980
Basket braiding block	G. O. Gillette	Streetsborough, Ohio	Aug. 20, 1872	130, 711
Basket' Clothes	L. and A. C. Carman	McCoy's Station, Ohio	Sept. 20, 1870	107, 446
Basket, Cotton	R. L. Myers	Washington, N. C	Dec. 21, 1869	98, 091
Basket, Cover for fruit	J. C. Ingham and C. Colby	Benton Harbor, Mich	July 22, 1873	141, 142
Basket, Extension	A. Norman	Rochester, N. Y	Mar. 30, 1869	88, 327
Basket-finishing machine	F. H. Brown	Chicago, Ill	Oct. 29, 1867	70, 318
Basket, Flower	G. Gunther	New York, N. Y	June 13, 1865	48, 171
Basket, Folding	A. M. Olds	New York, N. Y	Jan. 28, 1868	73, 749
Basket for berries	S. R. Wilmot	Brooklyn, N. Y	May 14, 1861	32, 324
Basket for feeding tarred corn-cobs to furnace	E. Bimm	Dayton, Ohio	May 28, 1867	65, 157
Basket for grinding tile	P. C. Reniers	Pittsburgh, Pa	Sept. 21, 1869	94, 977
Basket for house-plant	A. P. Eastman	Washington, D. C	Mar. 7, 1871	112, 433
Basket for railway-car, Bracket	J. L. Howard	Hartford, Conn	May 25, 1869	90, 543
Basket for tile-grinder	P. C. Reniers	Pittsburgh, Pa	Dec. 13, 1870	110, 072
Basket-form	A. F. Scow	Chicago, Ill	May 13, 1873	138, 765
Basket-form	A. F. Scow	Chicago, Ill	May 20, 1873	139, 025
Basket, Form-block for	W. H. Carpenter	New York, N. Y	Aug. 11, 1868	80, 910
Basket-former	H. C. Jones	Dowagiac, Mich	Mar. 28, 1871	113, 058
Basket-forming	T. and J. Churchill	Detroit, Mich	Dec. 27, 1864	45, 585
Basket, Fruit	L. Carpenter	Saint Joseph, Mich	May 3, 1870	102, 488
Basket, Grain	H. C. Jones	Dowagiac, Mich	Apr. 15, 1873	137, 845
Basket, Grain	H. C. Jones	Dowagiac, Mich	Apr. 15, 1873	137, 846
Basket, Grain	H. C. Jones	Dowagiac, Mich	Sept. 2, 1873	142, 341
Basket, Grain	H. C. Jones	Dowagiac, Mich	Sept. 2, 1873	142, 342
Basket, Grain	H. C. Jones	Dowagiac, Mich	Dec. 16, 1873	145, 573
Basket-handle, Fastening	A. Faas	Philadelphia, Pa	June 23, 1857	17, 621
Basket-handle, Metallic	O. A. North	New Britain, Conn	Nov. 19, 1872	133, 168
Basket, Hanging	C. C. Hibbert	Lynn, Mass	Mar. 19, 1872	124, 817
Basket, Hanging	J. H. O'Neil	Cleveland, Ohio	Apr. 12, 1870	101, 907
Basket, Hanging	D. Sherwood	Lowell, Mass	Nov. 16, 1869	96, 977
Basket, Lady's work	S. Ainsworth	Saratoga Springs, N. Y	Dec. 27, 1864	45, 571
Basket, Lady's work	R. V. Jones	Canton, Ohio	May 25, 1869	90, 553
Basket-machine	M. Shaffer	La Fayette, Ind	Dec. 28, 1869	98, 424
Basket-machine	G. Storer	New Britain, Conn	Feb. 12, 1867	62, 085
Basket-machine	J. B. Sweetland and E. C. Goodrich.	Pontiac, Mich	Dec. 12, 1865	51, 491
Basket-making machine	F. H. Brown	Chicago, Ill	Oct. 22, 1867	70, 072
Basket-making machine	J. Moore and S. W. Day	Oak Creek, Wis	Jan. 14, 1873	134, 920
Basket, Metallic	A. Schenck	Chicago, Ill	Aug. 4, 1863	39, 426
Basket or dish, Table	J. Gibson, jr	Albany, N. Y	Sept. 19, 1871	119, 086
Basket, Peach	H. Carpenter	Brooklyn, N. Y	Oct. 27, 1868	83, 459
Basket-protector	P. Eley	New York, N. Y	Apr. 4, 1865	47, 096
Basket, Reticule wicker	J. Venet	New York, N. Y	Dec. 14, 1869	97, 836
Basket, Reticule wicker	J. Venet	New York, N. Y	Apr. 16, 1872	125, 706
Basket, Silver-plate cake and fruit	R. Gleason, jr	Dorchester, Mass	June 17, 1856	15, 127
Basket-splint	I. F. Wilcox	Streetsborough, Ohio	Nov. 28, 1871	121, 304
Basket-splint machine	A. and G. Van Riper	Bergen County, N. J	Oct. 2, 1847	5, 319
Basket-splints, Machine for riving	W. I. Horton	La Grange, Ala	Nov. 29, 1859	26, 268
Basket, Stave	H. C. Jones	Dowagiac, Mich	Mar. 28, 1871	113, 059
Basket-stuff-cutting machine	C. Jordan	Wrentham, Mass	Mar. 22, 1870	101, 021
Basket, Trout	P. R. Ridgway	Boston, Mass	July 16, 1872	129, 592
Basket, Water-proof	G. M. Allerton	Dover Plains, N. Y	Oct. 22, 1872	132, 428
Basket-weaving machine	F. H. Brown	Chicago, Ill	Sept. 10, 1867	68, 695
Basket-weaving machine	F. H. Brown	Chicago, Ill	Oct. 1, 1867	69, 309
Basket, Weighing	C. Renno and P. Landenberger	New York, N. Y	Nov. 23, 1869	97, 119
Basket, Wine	J. Roussillon	Epernay, France	Mar. 21, 1871	112, 852
Basket, Wire	D. Sherwood	Lowell, Mass	Feb. 18, 1873	135, 943
Basket, Work	T. V. Hobbs	Chicago, Ill	June 3, 1873	139, 508
Baskets, Apparatus for casting metal for metallic	W. H. Trissler	Dunkirk, N. Y	July 9, 1872	128, 928
Baskets, Construction of	J. A. H. Ellis	Springfield, Vt	Apr. 7, 1857	16, 970
Baskets for catching eels, Method of making	J. Downs	Belleport, N. Y	Apr. 25, 1843	3, 056
Baskets, Form-block for shaping	H. Carpenter	New York, N. Y	Dec. 31, 1867	72, 797
Baskets, Form or mold on which wooden slats, &c., are made into.	J. A. H. Ellis	Springfield, Vt	Mar. 31, 1857	16, 953
Baskets, Machine for braiding open-work	F. H. Brown	Chicago, Ill	Oct. 29, 1867	70, 160
Baskets, Machine for cutting material for	L. J. Bridgeman	Rock Stream, N. Y	Sept. 27, 1870	107, 654
Baskets, Machine for dressing willow for	E. K. Root	Hartford, Conn	Oct. 16, 1866	58, 958
Baskets, Machine for forming	E. S. Jeffery	New Haven, Conn	July 18, 1865	48, 869
Baskets, Machinery for forming	J. W. Millet	Bachelorsville, N. Y	May 2, 1865	47, 602
Baskets, Making splits for	J. S. Borden	Shrewsbury, N. J	June 29, 1833	....
Baskets, Manufacture of stave	H. C. Jones	Dowagiac, Mich	Mar. 15, 1870	100, 902
Baskets, Means for manufacturing	E. Bredt	New York, N. Y	June 20, 1865	48, 255
Baskets, Means of manufacturing	J. D. and J. T. Shuler	Lockport, N. Y	May 13, 1862	35, 265
Baskets, Method of manufacturing	L. Marble	Vassar, Mich	July 5, 1859	24, 699
Baskets, Preparing moss for ornamental	J. W. Shiveley	Saratoga Springs, N. Y	Apr. 30, 1873	126, 237

Index of patents issued from the United States Patent Office from 1790 *to* 1873, *inclusive*—Continued.

Invention.	Inventor.	Residence.	Date.	No.
Baskets, Tool for manufacturing splint	A. Baker	Templeton, Mass	Feb. 2, 1858	19, 229
Bat for cricket, &c	P. Caminoni	New York, N. Y	May 24, 1864	42, 834
Bat, Spring	G. W. Hill	Deep River, Conn	Oct. 30, 1866	59, 313
Bath:				
See Air-bath.				
Bird-bath.				
Combination bath.				
Compressed-air bath.				
Cot-bath.				
Cot elastic bath.				
Electrical bath.				
Electro-magnetic bath.				
Foot-bath.				
Galvanic bath.				
Immersion-bath.				
Medicated bath.				
Medicated shampoo bath.				
Mineral bath.				
Parlor bath.				
Photographic bath.				
Portable bath				
Shower-bath.				
Steam-bath.				
Swimming-bath.				
Vapor-bath.				
Ventilated bath.				
Warm bath.				
Zincing and tinning bath.				
Bath and wash-stand	R. Cooper	Georgetown, D. C	Jan. 31, 1871	111, 321
Bath-boiler	E. H. Chapman and T. M. Hammett.	Philadelphia, Pa	Dec. 31, 1867	72, 798
Bath-chamber	G. F. Foote	Middletown, N. Y	Dec. 10, 1872	133, 702
Bath, Confluent pipe for	H. Jones	Philadelphia, Pa	Apr. 12, 1870	101, 884
Bath-house, Portable	J. Gourlay	Escanaba, Mich	May 5, 1868	77, 480
Bath, Portable	E. J. Knowlton	Ann Arbor, Mich	Mar. 1, 1870	100, 297
Bath-room	H. G. Covel	Brooklyn, N. Y	Dec. 24, 1872	134, 258
Bath-room rack	M. A. H. Saurman	Philadelphia, Pa	Nov. 10, 1868	83, 884
Bath-seat, Portable	A. P. Young	Providence, R. I	Aug. 16, 1870	106, 445
Bath-tub	L. Bagger	Washington, D. C	June 17, 1873	139, 995
Bath-tub	A. Barrows	Philadelphia, Pa	Oct. 12, 1869	95, 633
Bath-tub	C. A. Blessing	Philadelphia, Pa	Aug. 31, 1869	94, 385
Bath-tub	A. Brady	New York, N. Y	June 7, 1864	43, 002
Bath-tub	A. C. Brownell	Brooklyn, N. Y	Apr. 7, 1868	76, 298
Bath-tub	J. Carroll	New York, N. Y	May 28, 1867	65, 172
Bath-tub	J. C. Clapp	Homer, N. Y	Oct. 22, 1867	69, 968
Bath-tub	E. F. Cook	Omaha, Nebr	Feb. 9, 1864	41, 486
Bath-tub	E. J. Knowlton	Ann Arbor, Mich	Jan. 28, 1868	73, 906
Bath-tub	J. H. Mercer	New York, N. Y	Mar. 3, 1868	75, 180
Bath-tub	J. L. Mott	New York, N. Y	Sept. 27, 1853	10, 049
Bath-tub	A. R. Robb	Brooklyn, N. Y	July 9, 1872	128, 755
Bath-tub	M. A. Stevens	Hartford, Conn	June 22, 1869	91, 785
Bath-tub, Combination	A. C. Brownell	Brooklyn, N. Y	May 24, 1870	103, 293
Bath-tub eduction-tube	W. H. Walton	Philadelphia, Pa	Oct. 5, 1869	95, 542
Bath tub, Electrical	J. Kidder	New York, N. Y	Jan. 9, 1866	51, 948
Bath tub, Electro-medical	S. Russell, jr	New York, N. Y	June 10, 1873	139, 819
Bath tub, Magnetic	J. R. Anderson	New York, N. Y	June 18, 1872	128, 094
Bath-tub, Plug-socket	R. C. Scrimgeour	Brooklyn, N. Y	Apr. 8, 1873	137, 726
Bath-tub, Portable	R. McCully	Philadelphia, Pa	Mar. 23, 1869	88, 154
Bath-tub, Portable	J. P. Rider	Brooklyn, N. Y.	July 6, 1869	92, 364
Bath-tub, Portable	G. Wheeler	New York, N. Y	Nov. 19, 1872	133, 276
Bath-tub, Portable India-rubber	J. W. Ramsay and D. Wilson	Grafton, Va	Sept. 4, 1860	29, 914
Bath-tubs, Flask for molding	J. Demarest	Mott Haven, N. Y	Aug. 28, 1855	13, 514
Bath-tubs, Sheet-metal lining for	C. A. Blessing	Philadelphia, Pa	July 28, 1868	80, 441
Bathing-apparatus	H. Bachmann and J. Ehrenfried.	Lancaster, Pa	Jan. 26, 1833	....
Bathing-apparatus	D. Brumley	New York, N. Y	Nov. 19, 1833	....
Bathing-apparatus	G. I. Byrd and P. Milne	New York, N. Y	June 17, 1840	1, 636
Bathing-apparatus	C. Escudier	Pattersonville, La	Jan. 18, 1859	22, 636
Bathing-apparatus	W. Hensler	Milwaukee, Wis	Mar. 1, 1864	41, 771
Bathing-apparatus	J. Ingram	New York, N. Y	Oct. 8, 1867	69, 675
Bathing-apparatus	F. Kraemer	Brooklyn, N. Y	Aug. 10, 1858	21, 138
Bathing-apparatus	L. Lefebvre	New Orleans, La	Apr. 21, 1857	17, 102
Bathing-apparatus	J. K. O'Neil	Kingston, N. Y	Aug. 11, 1857	17, 979
Bathing-apparatus	G. Scholl	New Philadelphia, Ohio	Sept. 5, 1871	118, 750
Bathing-apparatus	J. C. Schooley	Cincinnati, Ohio	Apr. 2, 1861	31, 912
Bathing-apparatus	C. Schultz and T. Warker	New York, N. Y	Oct. 17, 1865	50, 499
Bathing-apparatus	W. T. Street	Frankford, Pa	May 10, 1870	102, 878
Bathing-apparatus	C. Venn	Kastnersville, Canada	Oct. 31, 1871	120, 555
Bathing-apparatus	W. G. Young	Baltimore, Md	Dec. 16, 1845	4, 309
Bathing apparatus, Rectum	C. B. Verenee	Athens, Ga	July 11, 1871	116, 895
Bathing-apparatus, Safety	W. H. Pitt	Philadelphia, Pa	Dec. 22, 1868	85, 126
Bathing-dress	O. Morse	Concord, Mass	Feb. 23, 1869	87, 107
Bathing, Life-line for sea	W. T. Street	Frankford, Pa	Dec. 1, 1868	84, 592
Bathing-machine	L. Desens	Paris, France	Dec. 6, 1864	45, 368
Bathing-machine	W. Merritt	New York, N. Y	Feb. 1, 1814	....
Bathing vessel, Warm	D. Harrington	Centreville, Va	Oct. 4, 1813	....
Baton, Alarm	J. F. Haskins	Fitchburgh, Mass	May 30, 1871	115, 464
Baton, Police	S. Beery and J. W. McDonald	Urbana, Ohio, and Houston, Tex.	Oct. 14, 1873	143, 610
Baton, Police	C. Kast	Williamsport, Pa	Mar. 28, 1871	113, 061
Baton, Police	H. C. Richard	Pottsville, Pa	June 20, 1871	116, 097
Batter and egg stirrer and beater	H. Muth	Cincinnati, Ohio	Oct. 22, 1872	132, 483
Batter-cup	B. Wieland	Orangeville, Ill	July 25, 1865	49, 019
Batter-machine	E. Yerby	Washington, D. C	July 27, 1858	21, 042
Batter-mixer	A. Burdick	Middletown, Conn	June 18, 1872	128, 013

Index of patents issued from the United States Patent Office from 1790 *to* 1873, *inclusive*—Continued.

Invention.	Inventor.	Residence.	Date.	No.
Batter-pot	E. A. Jeffery	New York, N. Y	Feb. 7, 1871	111, 548
Battery:				
See Carbon battery.				
Centrifugal battery.				
Chain-shot battery.				
Electric battery.				
Electro battery.				
Electro-magnetic battery.				
Electro-medical battery.				
Electrotyping battery.				
Field battery.				
Floating battery.				
Fuse-firing battery.				
Galvanic battery.				
Gun battery.				
Non-freezing battery.				
Physiological battery.				
Platoon battery.				
Portable body battery.				
Sap battery.				
Self-acting battery.				
Ship's battery.				
Stamp battery.				
Stamping battery.				
Thermo-electric battery				
Traveling battery.				
Voltaic battery.				
Battery-current manipulator	J. Kidder	New York, N. Y	Nov. 7, 1871	120, 750
Battery, Galvanic	A. L. Nolf	New York, N. Y	Sept. 2, 1873	142, 502
Battery, Traveling	C. Perley	New York, N. Y	Feb. 24, 1863	37, 766
Batting and wadding	S. Baxendale	Boston, Mass	Dec. 11, 1866	60, 324
Batting-machine feed-mechanism	W. Fuzzard	Malden, Mass	Aug. 16, 1864	43, 845
Batting, Machine for making	F. W. Bloodgood	New York, N. Y	Dec. 16, 1873	145, 615
Batting or wadding, Fibrous	J. T. Stoddard	Plymouth, Mass	Feb. 23, 1864	41, 727
Battledore	M. Cregen	Chicago, Ill	Aug. 1, 1871	117, 518
Bayonet	F. W. Alexander	Baltimore, Md	Nov. 15, 1864	45, 009
Bayonet	A. Mills	United States Army	Mar. 29, 1870	101, 297
Bayonet and bayonet-fastening, Spade	F. Chillingworth and I. Merrill	Springfield, Mass	Apr. 16, 1872	125, 720
Bayonet-attachment	W. Hoffman	Washington, D. C	Apr. 18, 1865	47, 303
Bayonet-attachment	C. Howard	New York, N. Y	May 15, 1866	54, 728
Bayonet-attachment	J. W. Neil	Brooklyn, N. Y	Jan. 7, 1873	134, 608
Bayonet-attachment	P. A. Oliver	Elizabeth, N. J	July 30, 1867	67, 210
Bayonet-shank	H. Waters	Northbridge, Mass	June 21, 1864	43, 247
Bayonet, Drill	T. Wahlfelt	Stockholm, Sweden	Aug. 1, 1871	117, 702
Bayonet-fastening	J. N. Ward	United States Army, New York, N. Y.	Dec. 15, 1857	18, 876
Bayonet fastening, Saber	C. A. McEvoy	Richmond, Va	Oct. 30, 1860	30, 539
Bayonet-guard, Removable	J. G. Ernst	York, Pa	Aug. 5, 1862	36, 081
Bayonet-scabbard	E. Rice	Cambridge, Mass	May 21, 1872	127, 104
Bayonet scabbard and guard	J. G. Ernst	York, Pa	Dec. 23, 1862	37, 222
Bayonet-scabbard, Frog for	W. Hoffman	Solano County, Cal	May 8, 1860	28, 175
Bayonet-scabbards, Machine for cutting out	H. D. Smith	New York, N. Y	June 30, 1863	39, 074
Bayonet-scabbards, Manufacture of	E. Gaylord	Chicopee, Mass	May 15, 1860	28, 269
Bayonet, Sliding	J. Jenkinson	Brooklyn, N. Y	July 1, 1862	35, 760
Bayonet-socket	B. Burton	Brooklyn, N. Y	Oct. 7, 1873	143, 495
Bayonet-socket	A. Willson	New York	June 11, 1814	....
Bayonet-sockets, Turning	J. Humphreys	Millburgh, Mass	Feb. 23, 1864	41, 704
Bayonet, Spade	S. S. Alexander	Philadelphia, Pa	June 22, 1869	91, 586
Bayonet, Spade	E. Rise	United States Army	June 22, 1869	91, 564
Bayonet, Spade	W. S. Wetmore	London, England	Dec. 26, 1871	122, 206
Bayonet, Steel scabbard for	J. E. Emerson	Trenton, N. J	Aug. 19, 1862	36, 209
Bayonets, Scabbard for trowel	F. Chillingworth	Springfield, Mass	Dec. 1, 1868	84, 612
Bead-forming die for sheet-metal vessel	S. R. Wilmot	Bridgeport, Conn	July 10, 1866	56, 313
Bead-miters, Machine for cutting	R. F. Thompkins	New York, N. Y	July 13, 1869	92, 491
Beads, Manufacturing metallic	J. R. Wendt	Boston, Mass	Feb. 10, 1857	16, 631
Beading-machine, Sheet-metal-ware	C. E. Marchand	Alliance, Ohio	June 10, 1873	139, 681
Beading moldings, &c., Plane for	S. C. Howes	South Chatham, Mass	Nov. 3, 1863	40, 483
Beading-tool and circular shears, Combined	J. F. Flanders	Newburyport, Mass	Jan. 2, 1849	5, 994
Beam	R. J. Gatling	Indianapolis, Ind	Nov. 16, 1869	96, 793
Beam and girder	J. Montgomery	Croton Landing, N. Y	Oct. 20, 1868	83, 196
Beam and girder, Wrought-iron	A. Pollak	Philadelphia, Pa	June 5, 1855	13, 025
Beam and scale, Movable suspended	S. Wallis		Sept. 21, 1801	....
Beam, Composite	W. W. Lummus	Lynn, Mass	June 17, 1873	139, 902
Beam, Corrugated	R. Montgomery	New York, N. Y	Sept. 25, 1855	13, 599
Beam, Corrugated	S. J. Seely	New York, N. Y	May 10, 1864	42, 692
Beam engine, Triangular	N. W. Wheeler	Brooklyn, N. Y	Jan. 16, 1866	52, 101
Beam-engines, Parallel motion for	J. M. Thompson	Taunton, Mass	July 11, 1854	11, 252
Beam-fagot	H. T. Buffington, jr	Buffalo, N. Y	Sept. 29, 1868	82, 487
Beam, Floor	W. W. Lummus	Lynn, Mass	June 17, 1873	139, 903
Beam, Floor	W. W. Lummus	Lynn, Mass	June 17, 1873	139, 904
Beam, floor, and ceiling, Fire-proof	I. Hodgson and W. H. Brown	Indianapolis, Ind	May 30, 1871	115, 472
Beam, Hollow	J. W. Cremin	New York, N. Y	Dec. 26, 1871	122, 230
Beam, Metal	J. K. Ingalls	Brooklyn, N. Y	June 10, 1856	15, 113
Beam, Metal	J. Merrill	Boston, Mass	May 14, 1867	64, 783
Beam, Metal	R. Montgomery	New York, N. Y	Apr. 14, 1868	76, 795
Beam, Metallic	L. Holms	Paterson, N. J	Mar. 22, 1870	101, 015
Beam or girder for fire-proof structure	W. W. Hughes	Philadelphia, Pa	Jan. 17, 1871	111, 063
Beam, Plow	J. S. Hall	Manchester, Pa	Feb. 22, 1859	23, 024
Beam, Scale	A. B. Davis	Philadelphia, Pa	Feb. 26, 1861	31, 534
Beam, Sheet-metal	R. Montgomery	New York, N. Y	July 12, 1853	9, 842
Beams and columns, Connection for wrought-iron	A. Bonzano	Phœnixville, Pa	July 1, 1873	140, 455
Beams, Connecting rigidly the ends of metal	S. Nowlan	New York, N. Y	Apr. 13, 1858	19, 945
Beams, Construction of fagots for	W. W. Miller	Safe Harbor, Pa	Oct. 22, 1867	70, 011
Beams, Construction of fagots for	G. Walters and T. Shaffer	Phœnixville, Pa	Oct. 15, 1867	69, 872
Beams, Machine for shearing the ends of	J. M. Cornell	New York, N. Y	Aug. 13, 1872	130, 486
Beams, Manufacture of corrugated	R. Montgomery	New York, N. Y	May 31, 1859	24, 299
Beams or girders, Mode of preparing fagots for manufacturing wrought	G. Walters and T. Shaffer	Phœnixville, Pa	Dec. 17, 1867	72, 246

Index of patents issued from the United States Patent Office from 1790 *to* 1873, *inclusive*—Continued.

Invention.	Inventor.	Residence.	Date.	No.
Beaming-machine	A. Hill	Hinsdale, Mass	May 6, 1805	....
Beaming-machine	J. Ladd		July 17, 1801	....
Bean-pot lifter and carrier	G. F. Foss	East Boston, Mass	Apr. 28, 1868	77, 182
Bean-puller	S. W. Moore	Albion, N. Y	June 25, 1867	66, 034
Bean-puller	S. R. Niles	Rawsonville, Mich	Aug. 11, 1868	80, 994
Bean-pulling machine	J. Baxter	North Greece, N. Y	May 3, 1864	42, 548
Bean pulling machine	J. Day	Murray, N. Y	Nov. 10, 1857	18, 576
Bean-pulling machine	S. R. Niles	Rawsonville, Mich	Apr. 20, 1869	89, 164
Beans, Machine for cleaning and assorting	R. Read	Brockport, N. Y	Mar. 11, 1862	34, 645
Bearing and packing	E. D. Murfey	New York, N. Y	Aug. 1, 1871	117, 558
Bearing and packing material	E. D. Murfey	New York, N. Y	Dec. 27, 1870	110, 582
Bearing and packing material	E. D. Murfey	New York, N. Y	Dec. 27, 1870	110, 583
Bearing and packing, Saturating fibrous materials and powdered substances for.	E. D. Murfey	New York, N. Y	Oct. 11, 1870	108, 285
Bearing, Anti-friction	A. Hall	Tiffin, Ohio	Sept. 10, 1872	131, 162
Bearing, Compensation	L. Smith	Buffalo, N. Y	Apr. 17, 1855	12, 732
Bearing, End-thrust	C. Perley	New York, N. Y	Feb. 24, 1863	37, 765
Bearing for machinery	C. B. Richards	Hartford, Conn	Aug. 1, 1871	117, 682
Bearing for machinery, Anti-friction	J. Harden	Chicago, Ill	Jan. 14, 1868	73, 245
Bearing for machinery, Lubricating	L. H. Olmstead	Stamford, Conn	Jan. 21, 1868	73, 459
Bearing for machinery, Self oiling and adjusting	T. S. Brown	Poughkeepsie, N. Y	Dec. 18, 1866	60, 616
Bearing-step and vertical shaft	F. A. Gardner	Danbury Conn	Apr. 18, 1871	113, 867
Bearing-surface and journal for machinery	J. Wharton	Philadelphia, Pa	Aug. 15, 1871	118, 086
Bearing-surfaces in machinery, Material for	J. Schieder	New York, N. Y	Dec. 13, 1870	110, 163
Bearing, Thrust	A. W. Case	South Manchester, Conn	June 2, 1868	78, 428
Bearings and journals, Material for	E. D. Murfey	New York, N. Y	Nov. 15, 1870	109, 239
Bearings, Composition for	E. D. Murfey	New York, N. Y	Nov. 1, 1870	108, 931
Bearings, Composition for coating	P. J. Kelly	New York, N. Y	Nov. 8, 1870	109, 018
Bearings for machinery, Casting	H. F. and G. S. Snyder and W. N. Jones.	Williamsport, Pa	Dec. 29, 1868	85, 341
Bearings of machinery, &c., Metallic composition for.	I. S. Hill and J. Dixon	Boston and Taunton, Mass	Jan. 31, 1845	3, 896
Bearings, &c., Rubber compound for	P. J. Kelly	New York, N. Y	June 27, 1871	116, 322
Beater and compressing press	G. Ertel	Quincy, Ill	Feb. 4, 1873	135, 533
Beater or power press, Operating	C. Nelson	Newburgh, N. Y	June 19, 1866	55, 779
Beater-press	J. Cory	Chicago, Ill	Feb. 11, 1873	135, 780
Beater-press	P. K. Dederick	Albany, N. Y	July 4, 1865	48, 619
Beater-press	S. R. Dummer	New York, N. Y	Jan. 30, 1866	52, 275
Beater-press	G. Ertel	Liberty, Ill	Dec. 31, 1867	72, 728
Beater-press	L. C. Field	Galesburgh, Ill	Aug. 1, 1865	49, 193
Beater-press	F. Frey	Liberty, Ill	Feb. 27, 1872	124, 047
Beating, bruising, and cutting substances, Mach. for	A. Britz	Philadelphia, Pa	July 18, 1816	....
Bed, Air	J. R. Hamilton	Portland, Oregon	July 16, 1867	66, 706
Bed, Air	J. Scott	Philadelphia, Pa	Oct. 18, 1853	10, 139
Bed and bed-bottom	J. W. C. Peters and W. A. Le Row.	Chicago, Ill	Oct. 25, 1870	108, 622
Bed and bedstead, Invalid	S. S. Brown	Woonsocket, R. I	Mar. 2, 1869	87, 463
Bed and chair, Combination of camp	S. G. Crane	Rochester, N. Y	July 16, 1861	32, 822
Bed and chair, Combined	G. A. Keene	Lynn, Mass	July 3, 1860	29, 038
Bed and crib, Sofa	S. Chapin	Cincinnati, Ohio	Mar. 21, 1865	46, 879
Bed and cushion spring	D. E. Somes	Washington, D. C	Oct. 12, 1869	95, 848
Bed and frame, Spring	W. Z. Cooke	Hartford, Conn	Feb. 18, 1873	135, 892
Bed and knapsack, Atmospheric air	C. Linden	Eden Township, Ill	Oct. 7, 1862	36, 618
Bed and lounge spring	F. Fraps	Springfield, Mass	July 30, 1867	67, 186
Bed and musical-instrument board combined	J. McDonald	New York, N. Y	Nov. 23, 1869	97, 101
Bed and seat bottom	W. F. Clark	Mount Pleasant, Iowa	Sept. 12, 1871	118, 908
Bed and seat spring	J. P. Chamberlin	North Abington, Mass	May 16, 1871	114, 923
Bed and seat spring	J. P. Chamberlin	North Abington, Mass	Dec. 19, 1871	121, 990
Bed and seat spring, Means of securing	J. D. Eleston	Canaan, Conn	Sept. 8, 1868	81, 991
Bed and sofa	W. H. Schwalbe	New York, N. Y	Sept. 1, 1868	81, 691
Bed attachment, Invalid	N. Teal	Kendallville, Ind	Aug. 6, 1867	67, 610
Bed, berth, and car-seat spring	N. S. Whipple	Detroit, Mich	Oct. 5, 1869	95, 622
Bed-boat or life-preserver	J. Stevenson	Philadelphia, Pa	Feb. 20, 1855	12, 450
Bed bottom	J. R. Abbe	Providence, R. I	May 15, 1866	54, 658
Bed-bottom	P. Agger	Cincinnati, Ohio	Sept. 12, 1871	118, 834
Bed bottom	I. T. Allen	New York, N. Y	Jan. 24, 1860	26, 878
Bed-bottom	J. Allen	Pughtown, Pa	Apr. 21, 1868	76, 968
Bed-bottom	J. H. Allyn	Whitesborough, N. Y	Mar. 21, 1871	112, 765
Bed-bottom	P. Anderson	Chicago, Ill	Sept. 9, 1873	142, 549
Bed bottom	C. D. Austin	Amsterdam, N. Y	Feb. 27, 1872	124, 109
Bed-bottom	A. S. Babbit	Keeseville, N. Y	Jan. 29, 1867	61, 595
Bed bottom	D. Babcock	Seneca Falls, N. Y	July 9, 1867	66, 549
Bed-bottom	H. Barber	Juneau, Wis	Dec. 23, 1862	37, 210
Bed-bottom	J. J. Baxter	Grand Rapids, Mich	Mar. 16, 1869	87, 752
Bed-bottom	S. W. Beach	Niles, Mich	May 1, 1866	54, 281
Bed-bottom	A. H. Bell	Cedar Falls, Iowa	Jan. 14, 1873	124, 839
Bed-bottom	V. Bell	Seville, Ohio	July 5, 1870	105, 028
Bed-bottom	V. Bell	Seville, Ohio	Feb. 14, 1871	111, 807
Bed-bottom	H. Benedict	Philadelphia, Pa	Jan. 16, 1872	122, 698
Bed-bottom	H. Benedict	Philadelphia, Pa	July 8, 1873	140, 571
Bed-bottom	C. E. Best	Jordan, N. Y	Feb. 19, 1867	62, 248
Bed-bottom	R. F. Billings	Portland, Me	Aug. 23, 1859	25, 170
Bed-bottom	A. Bingham	Talladega, Fla	Aug. 23, 1859	25, 171
Bed-bottom	A. Bingham	Newtonville, Mass	Nov. 12, 1867	70, 687
Bed-bottom	D. E. Bishop	Baltimore, Md	Apr. 16, 1872	125, 783
Bed-bottom	C. D. Blinn	Port Hudson, Mich	May 23, 1865	47, 789
Bed-bottom	J. Blythe	Lafayette, Ind	May 19, 1863	38, 551
Bed-bottom	P. Boesen and M. Bedessem	Kenosha, Wis	Feb. 18, 1873	135, 965
Bed-bottom	L. M. Bolles	Cooperstown, N. Y	Oct. 8, 1867	69, 617
Bed-bottom	A. T. Boon and J. H. Bell	Galesburgh, Ill	May 11, 1869	89, 912
Bed-bottom	W. Bowen	Dayton, Mich	Mar. 8, 1870	100, 491
Bed-bottom	B. R. Boynton	Keeseville, N. Y	Sept. 3, 1867	68, 551
Bed-bottom	F. S. Bradley	New Haven, Conn	Feb. 11, 1868	74, 293
Bed-bottom	C. Bradway	Maquoketa, Iowa	July 20, 1869	92, 787
Bed-bottom	W. R. Briggs	Boston, Mass	Jan. 25, 1870	99, 056
Bed-bottom	C. A. Brighom	Cleveland, Ohio	Apr. 13, 1869	88, 773
Bed-bottom	E. L. Brockett	Nelson, Ohio	June 17, 1873	140, 005
Bed-bottom	J. Bromiley	Pawtucket, R. I	Sept. 20, 1864	44, 279

Index of patents issued from the United States Patent Office from 1790 *to* 1873, *inclusive*—Continued.

Invention.	Inventor.	Residence.	Date.	No.
Bed-bottom	C. M. Brown	Aurora, Ill	Mar. 27, 1866	53, 519
Bed-bottom	J. H. Brown	Hudson, Wis	Feb. 18, 1868	74, 660
Bed-bottom	D. W. Burbank	New York, N. Y	June 12, 1866	55, 462
Bed-bottom	E. L. Bushnell	Poughkeepsie	Oct. 18, 1870	108, 447
Bed-bottom	L. W. Buxton	Nashua, N. H	May 8, 1860	28, 233
Bed-bottom	L. W. Buxton	Nashua, N. H	Aug. 7, 1860	29, 540
Bed-bottom	D. M. Bye	Roanoke, Ind	Sept. 28, 1869	95, 192
Bed-bottom	E. G. Cameron	Ashtabula, Ohio	Feb. 11, 1873	135, 774
Bed-bottom	J. B. Campbell	Cincinnati, Ohio	Feb. 26, 1867	62, 315
Bed-bottom	S. A. Canfield	Carlstadt, N. J	May 1, 1866	54, 292
Bed-bottom	F. Carré	Paris, France	Nov. 7, 1865	50, 883
Bed-bottom	E. Caswell	Lyons, N. Y	Mar. 17, 1868	75, 519
Bed-bottom	W. A. Chamberlin	Alexander, N. Y	May 26, 1868	78, 184
Bed-bottom	D. G. Chapin	Galena, Ill	Dec. 3, 1867	71, 700
Bed-bottom	A. D. Chase	Reading, Pa	Aug. 7, 1866	57, 039
Bed-bottom	P. G. Chase	Berlin, Wis	May 23, 1865	47, 797
Bed-bottom	J. Christie	Lowell, Mich	Oct. 6, 1868	82, 800
Bed-bottom	H. M. Clark	West Meriden, Conn	Apr. 23, 1867	63, 993
Bed-bottom	I. A. Clippinger and S. S. Pratt	Newton, Iowa	Feb. 8, 1870	99, 636
Bed-bottom	H. A. Coats	Wellsville, N. Y	Feb. 25, 1867	62, 395
Bed-bottom	D. C. Colby	Washington, D. C	July 9, 1867	66, 564
Bed-bottom	G. T. Comins	Lowell, Mass	Dec. 9, 1862	37, 085
Bed-bottom	H. M. Conklin	Syracuse, N. Y	Oct. 8, 1867	69, 632
Bed-bottom	W. F. Converse	Harrison, Ohio	July 2, 1861	32, 683
Bed-bottom	H. Cook and C. E. Simmons	Waukegan, Ill	Dec. 24, 1867	72, 605
Bed-bottom	W. Cooke	New York, N. Y	May 28, 1872	127, 152
Bed-bottom	H. A. Cooke	Charlestown, Mass	Dec. 12, 1865	51, 427
Bed-bottom	H. A. Cooke	Charlestown, Mass	July 9, 1867	66, 567
Bed-bottom	A. W. Cramer	Honesdale, Pa	Aug. 23, 1870	106, 666
Bed-bottom	C. Croley	Dayton, Ohio	May 28, 1867	65, 061
Bed-bottom	M. C. Cronk	Auburn, N. Y	Dec. 12, 1865	51, 429
Bed-bottom	L. M. Crosby and E. G. Cameron.	Ashtabula, Ohio	Nov. 25, 1873	144, 959
Bed-bottom	S. H. Crossman	Battle Creek, Mich	Mar. 13, 1866	53, 121
Bed-bottom	R. H. Cutter	Cleveland, Ohio	Sept. 10, 1867	68, 612
Bed-bottom	J. D. F. Dahl	Milwaukee, Wis	May 12, 1868	77, 720
Bed-bottom	J. and S. Danner	Canton, Ohio	Apr. 23, 1867	63, 998
Bed-bottom	W. F. Daugherty	Mount Pleasant, Iowa	Oct. 15, 1867	69, 779
Bed-bottom	G. B. and C. B. Davis	Freeport, Ill	Oct. 23, 1866	58, 994
Bed-bottom	J. W. Davis	Washington, D. C	Feb. 5, 1867	61, 724
Bed-bottom	J. Decamp	Cincinnati, Ohio	Sept. 28, 1869	95, 329
Bed-bottom	P. Demeure and A. Mauritz	New York, N. Y	Sept. 13, 1853	10, 010
Bed-bottom	L. L. and A. J. Deming and R. Alden.	Erie, Pa	Nov. 28, 1871	121, 279
Bed-bottom	H. Doebele	Philo, Ohio	Aug. 6, 1867	67, 420
Bed-bottom	G. H. Dow	Freeport, Ill	June 11, 1867	65, 731
Bed-bottom	J. Dreusike	Cincinnati, Ohio	Sept. 24, 1867	69, 193
Bed-bottom	J. Dreusike	New York, N. Y	Oct. 28, 1873	143, 970
Bed-bottom	F. B. Duffey	Sparta, Wis	Oct. 2, 1866	58, 394
Bed-bottom	S. Dunlap	Rome, Ga	June 8, 1869	90, 999
Bed-bottom	A. M. Dye	Clinton, Ill	Dec. 27, 1859	26, 575
Bed-bottom	W. H. Elliot	Plattsburgh, Pa	Aug. 10, 1858	21, 123
Bed-bottom	T. Falloon	Lyons, N. Y	May 22, 1866	54, 877
Bed-bottom	M. Falloon	Bloomington, Ill	Mar. 21, 1871	112, 912
Bed-bottom	J. S. Farrington	Wilwaukee, Wis	June 11, 1867	65, 556
Bed-bottom	H. E. Ficket and J. W. Summers.	Glen's Falls, N. Y	Nov. 22, 1859	26, 228
Bed-bottom	E. S. Field	Hartford, Conn	Sept. 10, 1872	131, 158
Bed-bottom	D. Fitzgerald	New York, N. Y	Apr. 16, 1867	63, 790
Bed-bottom	J. P. Flanders and S. K. Wells	Burlington, Vt	Oct. 29, 1867	70, 330
Bed-bottom	J. H. Fletcher	Lowell, Mass	May 22, 1866	54, 879
Bed-bottom	J. Flinn	Philadelphia, Pa	July 31, 1866	56, 740
Bed-bottom	H. A. and A. Follett	Smithfield, R. I	Aug. 6, 1867	67, 521
Bed-bottom	D. Frankfoder	Wakarusa, Ind	July 1, 1873	140, 492
Bed-bottom	D. Frankfoder and G. W. McGeorge.	Wakarusa, Ind	Nov. 19, 1872	133, 090
Bed-bottom	S. B. Freeman	Burlington, Iowa	Oct. 18, 1870	108, 470
Bed-bottom	S. B. Freeman	Fort Wayne, Ind	Nov. 18, 1873	144, 754
Bed-bottom	G. Frey	New York, N. Y	Dec. 8, 1863	40, 831
Bed-bottom	F. S. Frost	West Cambridge, Mass	July 9, 1867	66, 481
Bed-bottom	J. C. Fry	Sidney, Ohio	Feb. 25, 1868	74, 812
Bed-bottom	E. K. Garretson and W. Fulghum.	Winchester, Ind	May 6, 1873	138, 630
Bed-bottom	C. Gense	Fouilloy, France	Apr. 15, 1873	137, 909
Bed-bottom	G. L. Gerard	New Haven, Conn	Mar. 26, 1867	63, 153
Bed-bottom	G. L. Gerard	New Haven, Conn	Sept. 15, 1868	82, 218
Bed-bottom	E. and O. W. Gibbs	Richland Centre, Wis	June 9, 1868	78, 732
Bed-bottom	C. F. Gillette	Sparta, Wis	Apr. 2, 1867	63, 500
Bed-bottom	E. T. Gilmore	Westborough, Mass	May 14, 1872	126, 801
Bed-bottom	S. Gissinger	Pittsburgh, Pa	Oct. 3, 1871	119, 600
Bed-bottom	S. Gissinger	Pittsburgh, Pa	Mar. 5, 1872	124, 205
Bed-bottom	W. Graham	Sharpsburgh, Pa	Nov. 19, 1872	133, 093
Bed-bottom	J. S. Grant	Sidney Centre, Me	Sept. 3, 1867	68, 499
Bed-bottom	B. Gregg	Bennington, Vt	Aug. 11, 1868	80, 944
Bed-bottom	B. Gregg	Bennington, Vt	Oct. 4, 1870	108, 018
Bed-bottom	F. C. Gridley	Hudson, Wis	Jan. 28, 1868	73, 799
Bed-bottom	B. Griffin	Lawrence, Mass	June 8, 1858	20, 486
Bed-bottom	B. Griffin	Lawrence, Mass	Aug. 13, 1867	67, 647
Bed-bottom	F. C. Hagen	Cuba, N. Y	June 29, 1869	91, 931
Bed-bottom	H. J. Hale	Indianapolis, Ind	Oct. 6, 1868	82, 829
Bed-bottom	C. H. Hall	Binghamton, N. Y	May 21, 1867	64, 973
Bed-bottom	R. L. Hall	Lowell, Mass	Sept. 26, 1865	50, 118
Bed-bottom	R. L. Hall	Lowell, Mass	Oct. 2, 1866	58, 545
Bed-bsttom	W. M. Hamilton	Wenona, Ill	Sept. 29, 1868	82, 521
Bed-bottom	J. W. Hampton	Mount Pleasant, Iowa	Oct. 24, 1871	120, 271
Bed-bottom	J. W. Hampton	Mount Pleasant, Iowa	Sept. 17, 1872	131, 438
Bed-bottom	P. C. Hard	Wadsworth, Ohio	Feb. 25, 1873	136, 158

Index of patents issued from the United States Patent Office from 1790 *to* 1873, *inclusive*—Continued.

Invention.	Inventor.	Residence.	Date.	No.
Bed-bottom	C. H. Hardy	Charlestown, Mass	May 7, 1867	64, 528
Bed-bottom	J. Harper	Hillsborough, Iowa	Sept. 17, 1872	131, 397
Bed-bottom	J. J. Harris	Pewamo, Mich	Mar. 2, 1869	87, 489
Bed-bottom	H. P. Hart	New Woodstock, N. Y	Apr. 12, 1859	23, 573
Bed-bottom	W. J. Haswell	Waverly, N. Y	Dec. 11, 1866	60, 368
Bed-bottom	R. Hatch	Strafford, Vt	Aug. 30, 1859	25, 263
Bed-bottom	L. K. Hawes	Whitewater, Wis	Mar. 31, 1868	76, 677
Bed-bottom	A. R. Henderson and J. Ford	Andover, N. Y	May 22, 1866	54, 902
Bed-bottom	P. Hinkle	San Francisco, Cal	July 21, 1868	80, 176
Bed-bottom	A. Hitchcock	Wayne County, Mich	May 8, 1866	54, 545
Bed bottom	B. Hitchcock	Waukegan, Ill	Apr. 14, 1868	76, 633
Bed-bottom	S. Hobbs	Wilmot, Ohio	Sept. 12, 1871	118, 804
Bed-bottom	E. C. Holden and E. L. Brockett	Owatonna, Minn	May 18, 1869	90, 171
Bed-bottom	E. F. Holloway and J. W. Hudelson.	Knightstown, Ind	Sept. 4, 1866	57, 720
Bed-bottom	B. Holmes	New York, N. Y	Feb. 18, 1873	135, 989
Bed-bottom	E. Hopkins	Newaygo, Mich	June 14, 1870	104, 310
Bed-bottom	D. Hoskins	Philadelphia, Pa	Sept. 13, 1870	107, 261
Bed-bottom	T. Howe	Cambridgeport, Mass	June 13, 1854	11, 054
Bed-bottom	Z. Howe	Lowell, Mich	Aug. 27, 1867	68, 078
Bed-bottom	E. Hoyt	Stamford, Conn	Nov. 25, 1873	144, 906
Bed-bottom	B. R. Hundley	Lynchburgh, Ohio	June 13, 1854	11, 066
Bed-bottom	M. A. Hunt	Cincinnati, Ohio	Apr. 29, 1873	138, 252
Bed-bottom	W. R. S. Hunter	Blackberry Station, Ill	June 16, 1868	78, 876
Bed-bottom	P. C. Ingersoll	Green Point, N. Y	Oct. 31, 1865	50, 713
Bed-bottom	W. B. Ingersoll	New York, N. Y	July 2, 1867	66, 350
Bed-bottom	H. L. Isham	Plattsburgh, N. Y	Oct. 1, 1867	69, 441
Bed-bottom	R. V. Jenks and W. A. Miller	Paterson, N. J	June 13, 1871	115, 863
Bed-bottom	S. C. Jennings	Wantoma, Wis	Aug. 6, 1867	67, 554
Bed-bottom	C. Johnson	Chicago, Ill	Nov. 7, 1871	120, 587
Bed-bottom	F. G. Johnson	Brooklyn, N. Y	Jan. 10, 1865	45, 832
Bed-bottom	W. Jones	Berlin, Wis	May 15, 1866	54, 737
Bed-bottom	B. D. Joslin and R. A. Newhall	North Brownville, Mich	May 12, 1868	77, 738
Bed-bottom	W. B. Judson	Poughkeepsie, N. Y	Jan. 10, 1871	110, 854
Bed-bottom	J. F. Keeler	Cleveland, Ohio	May 12, 1857	17, 282
Bed-bottom	C. A. Kellogg	Elyria, Ohio	July 24, 1866	56, 570
Bed-bottom	A. W. Kendrick	Xenia, Ohio	Mar. 24, 1868	75, 926
Bed-bottom	M. Kohn	Hartford, Conn	Nov. 21, 1871	121, 111
Bed-bottom	S. E. Lanphear and H. H. Blair	Brunswick, Ohio	June 19, 1866	55, 678
Bed-bottom	S. L. Leach	Corry, Pa	June 24, 1873	140, 284
Bed-bottom	F. Leadbetter	Plymouth, Mich	Nov. 5, 1867	70, 583
Bed-bottom	R. Leavitt	Cambridge, Mass	Aug. 24, 1858	21, 263
Bed-bottom	G. D. Leonard	Chicago, Ill	Oct. 10, 1871	119, 862
Bed-bottom	G. D. Leonard	Chicago, Ill	May 21, 1872	126, 970
Bed-bottom	C. P. Loeser	Hartford, Conn	Jan. 1, 1867	60, 913
Bed-bottom	R. O. Lowrey	Salem, N. Y	Mar. 16, 1869	87, 948
Bed-bottom	J. Lynn and J. R. Crowell	Seneca Falls, N. Y	May 8, 1866	54, 567
Bed-bottom	J. I. Mabbett	Titusville, Pa	Nov. 5, 1867	70, 448
Bed-bottom	J. I. Mabbett	Titusville, Pa	Apr. 14, 1868	76, 785
Bed-bottom	D. P. Mahan	Antioch, Cal	Dec. 17, 1872	134, 079
Bed-bottom	D. Manuel	Boston, Mass	Feb. 19, 1867	62, 213
Bed-bottom	D. Manuel	Boston, Mass	Mar. 19, 1867	63, 066
Bed-bottom	J. S. Martin	Mount Pleasant, Iowa	July 16, 1872	129, 152
Bed-bottom	A. Matson	Brockville, N. Y	June 29, 1869	92, 074
Bed-bottom	N. Maxey	Plymouth, Ind	Jan. 21, 1868	73, 622
Bed-bottom	A. and W. P. McBride	Lowell, Mich	Aug. 10, 1869	93, 632
Bed bottom	S. McDonald	Cincinnati, Ohio	Aug. 6, 1867	67, 442
Bed-bottom	A. D. McMaster	Rochester, N. Y	Dec. 5, 1871	121, 647
Bed-bottom	B. F. S. Monroe	Utica, N. Y	Jan. 25, 1859	22, 742
Bed-bottom	T. B. Moore	Bridesburgh, Pa	Mar. 12, 1867	62, 871
Bed-bottom	T. B. Moore and G. De Bow	Bridesburgh, Pa	June 9, 1868	78, 753
Bed-bottom	M. Morehouse	Boscobel, Wis	Mar. 29, 1870	101, 376
Bed-bottom	T. H. B. Morehouse	Lansing, Mich	Dec. 19, 1871	122, 048
Bed-bottom	A. W. Morse	Eaton, N. Y	Feb. 22, 1859	23, 064
Bed-bottom	L. Mudge	Springfield, Ohio	Nov. 26, 1867	71, 504
Bed-bottom	M. M. Murray	Cincinnati, Ohio	Mar. 19, 1872	124, 847
Bed-bottom	R. B. Nevens	Lowell, Mass	Sept. 10, 1867	68, 645
Bed-bottom	J. N. Newell	Adrian, Mich	May 17, 1870	103, 226
Bed-bottom	L. L. Newman	East Saginaw, Mich	Aug. 2, 1870	106, 074
Bed-bottom	J. M. Noble	Delhi, Iowa	May 25, 1858	20, 362
Bed-bottom	A. W. Obermann	Chicago, Ill	Aug. 27, 1872	130, 858
Bed-bottom	T. L. Odell and J. C. Hudson	Iowa Falls, Iowa	Feb. 11, 1873	135, 724
Bed-bottom	H. Ogborn and A. W. Kendrick	Richmond, Ind., and Brooklyn, N. Y.	Feb. 11, 1873	135, 725
Bed-bottom	H. Ogborn and A. W. Kendrick	Richmond, Ind., and Brooklyn, N. Y.	Feb. 11, 1873	135, 835
Bed-bottom	H. Ogborn and A. W. Kendrick	Richmond, Ind., and Brooklyn, N. Y.	Feb. 18, 1873	135, 933
Bed-bottom	H. Ogborn and A. W. Kendrick	Richmond Ind., and Brooklyn, N. Y.	Mar. 4, 1873	136, 382
Bed-bottom	O. S. Osgood	Burlington, Iowa	Dec. 28, 1869	98, 401
Bed-bottom	O. S. Osgood	Burlington, Iowa	Aug. 30, 1870	106, 954
Bed-bottom	O. S. Osgood	Burlington, Iowa	May 9, 1871	114, 704
Bed-bottom	O. S. Osgood	Mount Pleasant, Iowa	Oct. 24, 1871	120, 315
Bed-bottom	H. H. Palmer	Rockford, Ill	Jan. 2, 1866	51, 856
Bed-bottom	H. H. Palmer	Rockford, Ill	Jan. 15, 1867	61, 242
Bed-bottom	B. Partello	Detroit, Mich	July 20, 1869	92, 878
Bed-bottom	J. D. Patton	Davenport, Iowa	Aug. 28, 1866	57, 560
Bed-bottom	E. M. Payne	Waverly, N. Y	Aug. 14, 1866	57, 181
Bed-bottom	T. Payne	Grand Rapids, Mich	June 15, 1869	91, 259
Bed-bottom	S. Pearson	Cincinnati, Ohio	Aug. 15, 1865	49, 434
Bed-bottom	C. Penfield	New Britain, Conn	Feb. 4, 1873	135, 580
Bed-bottom	S. E. Pettee	Bethlehem, Pa	Feb. 5, 1867	61, 757
Bed-bottom	J. Potter	Portland, Me	Feb. 4, 1868	73, 997
Bed-bottom	J. Potter	Portland, Me	Jan. 4, 1870	98, 520
Bed-bottom	J. H. Power	Burlington, Iowa	Jan. 23, 1872	123, 046
Bed-bottom	J. D. Pratt	Cleveland, Ohio	Nov. 2, 1869	96, 346
Bed-bottom	A. M. Pugh	Bucyrus, Ohio	Jan. 19, 1869	85, 960

Index of patents issued from the United States Patent Office from 1790 *to* 1873, *inclusive*—Continued.

Invention.	Inventor.	Residence.	Date.	No.
Bed-bottom	E. W. Quincy	Peoria, Ill	July 1, 1873	140,387
Bed-bottom	R. Rakestraw	Wyoming, Ill	Feb. 11, 1873	135,844
Bed-bottom	H. B. Ramsey	Rockville, Ind	July 2, 1872	128,562
Bed-bottom	T. Raser	Genesee, Ill	Oct. 1, 1867	69,366
Bed-bottom	C. D Read	Burlington, Vt	July 2, 1867	66,390
Bed-bottom	C. D. Read	Burlington, Vt	May 18, 1869	90,303
Bed-bottom	E. P. Read	Chicago, Ill	Dec. 12, 1871	121,728
Bed-bottom	E. P. Read	Chicago, Ill	Dec. 12, 1871	121,729
Bed-bottom	C. V. Reeder	San José, Cal	July 1, 1873	140,540
Bed-bottom	J. Reynolds, jr	Cincinnati, Ohio	Aug. 20, 1872	130,746
Bed-bottom	G. Richardson	Milwaukee, Wis	Aug. 23, 1870	106,726
Bed-bottom	G. Richardson	Milwaukee, Wis	Sept. 5, 1871	118,745
Bed-bottom	J. Rickard and J. Cook	Philadelphia, Pa	Mar. 19, 1867	62,973
Bed-bottom	E. R. Rison	Kinmundy, Ill	Sept. 4, 1866	57,770
Bed-bottom	G. W. Robbins	Fond du Lac, Wis	Aug. 6, 1867	67,585
Bed-bottom	G. W. Robinson	Galesburgh, Ill	June 27, 1871	116,354
Bed-bottom	W. W. Robinson	Ripon, Wis	Jan. 2, 1866	51,866
Bed-bottom	O. A. A. Rouillion	New York, N. Y	Nov. 5, 1861	33,685
Bed-bottom	J. Rouse	Dowagiac, Mich	May 15, 1866	54,779
Bed-bottom	C. Ruprecht	Cleveland, Ohio	July 30, 1872	130,077
Bed-bottom	F. Russell	Otselic, N. Y	Sept. 14, 1858	21,519
Bed-bottom	R. S. Sanborn	Ripon, Wis	Sept. 26, 1865	50,108
Bed-bottom	R. S. Sanborn	Ripon, Wis	Oct. 9, 1866	58,679
Bed-bottom	C. H. Sawyer	Hollis, Me	Dec. 19, 1865	51,624
Bed-bottom	F. Schimming	Philadelphia, Pa	Apr. 10, 1866	53,888
Bed-bottom	A. Schlingman	Alexandria, Ohio	Jan. 7, 1868	73,052
Bed-bottom	C. A. Scott	Aurora, Ill	Mar. 27, 1866	53,492
Bed-bottom	D. A. Scott	Cincinnati, Ohio	Apr. 9, 1872	125,490
Bed-bottom	D. A. Scott	Cincinnati, Ohio	Sept. 3, 1872	131,122
Bed-bottom	D. A. Scott and J. E. Burdge	Cincinnati, Ohio	Nov. 19, 1867	71,225
Bed-bottom	W. H. Sears	Cheshire, Conn	Sept. 23, 1873	143,190
Bed-bottom	H. G. Seekins	Elyria, Ohio	July 10, 1866	56,278
Bed-bottom	G. W. Seidler	Hartford, Conn	Oct. 31, 1865	50,738
Bed-bottom	T. J. Sheears	Ypsilanti, Mich	July 15, 1873	140,955
Bed-bottom	I. N. Sheets	Jefferson, Ohio	July 28, 1868	80,312
Bed-bottom	J. H. Sherman	Galesburgh, Ill	Nov. 7, 1871	120,599
Bed-bottom	C. E. Simmons and H. Cook	Waukegan, Ill	Dec. 3, 1867	71,654
Bed-bottom	P. P. Simmons	Davenport, Iowa	Apr. 21, 1868	77,113
Bed-bottom	W. W. Skaats	Cincinnati, Ohio	Sept. 23, 1873	143,035
Bed-bottom	E. Small	Dennisport, Mass	July 30, 1867	67,362
Bed-bottom	E. Smith, jr., and A. Chase	Worcester, Mass	Aug. 21, 1866	57,395
Bed-bottom	H. T. Smith	Washington, D. C	Feb. 6, 1872	123,520
Bed-bottom	H. T. Smith	Washington, D. C	May 28, 1872	127,278
Bed-bottom	J. G. Smith	Battle Creek, Mich	Aug. 7, 1866	57,003
Bed-bottom	J. J. Smith	Philadelphia, Pa	Oct. 13, 1868	83,001
Bed-bottom	J. L. Smith	Lowell, Mass	Jan. 29, 1861	31,264
Bed-bottom	N. Smith and E. S. Field	Hartford, Conn	Sept. 10, 1872	131,187
Bed-bottom	R. A. Smith	East Weare, N. H	Dec. 5, 1871	121,473
Bed-bottom	S. A. Smith	Monroe, Wis	Dec. 3, 1867	71,804
Bed-bottom	W. C. Smith	Warrensburgh, Mo	Oct. 19, 1869	95,945
Bed-bottom	S. L. Southard	Rock Island, Ill	Feb. 4, 1868	74,162
Bed-bottom	C. B. Spencer	Hastings, Minn	Sept. 3, 1872	131,034
Bed-bottom	C. B. Spencer	Hastings, Minn	Nov. 25, 1873	145,023
Bed-bottom	J. Sperry	Charleston, Ill	Mar. 29, 1870	101,326
Bed-bottom	D. Sporo	Sharon, Wis	Nov. 6, 1866	59,470
Bed-bottom	O. W. Stanford	Lebanon, Ohio	Jan. 12, 1869	85,866
Bed-bottom	W. Stenger and A. Beyrnheimer.	Jefferson, Ohio	July 2, 1867	66,410
Bed-bottom	W. Stickney	Lockport, N. Y	Aug. 6, 1867	67,604
Bed-bottom	W. Stickney	Lockport, N. Y	Sept. 17, 1867	68,912
Bed-bottom	W. H. Tambling	Berlin, Wis	Oct. 16, 1860	30,432
Bed-bottom	W. H. Tambling	Mazo Manie, Wis	Apr. 14, 1868	76,674
Bed-bottom	J. V. Taylor	La Cygne, Kans	July 15, 1873	140,856
Bed-bottom	P. Taylor and W. A. Gove	Pawtucket, R. I., and Charlestown, Mass.	June 5, 1866	55,390
Bed-bottom	D. M. Thomas	Dowagiac, Mich	Feb. 5, 1867	61,775
Bed-bottom	L. Thomas and J. A. Kurtz	Pittsburgh, Pa	Jan. 23, 1872	123,062
Bed-bottom	E. C. Thompson	New York, N. Y	Jan. 31, 1871	111,402
Bed-bottom	T. P. Thompson	Charlestown, Mass	June 18, 1867	65,964
Bed-bottom	L. B. Tinkham	Lawrence, Mass	Apr. 26, 1859	23,813
Bed-bottom	J. Tinney	Westfield, N. Y	Apr. 4, 1871	113,596
Bed-bottom	J. E. Todd	Middletown, Conn	Jan. 9, 1866	51,981
Bed-bottom	A. M. Tomb	Lyons, N. Y	Jan. 2, 1866	51,882
Bed-bottom	A. M. Tomb	Lyons, N. Y	June 25, 1867	66,057
Bed-bottom	M. B. Towslee	Pewamo, Mich	June 20, 1871	116,237
Bed-bottom	W. H Trissler	Dunkirk, N. Y	Oct. 22, 1872	132,422
Bed-bottom	C. B. Tucker	Cambridgeport, Mass	May 16, 1865	47,757
Bed-bottom	C. B. Tucker and L. S. Babbitt.	Chicago, Ill	Aug. 20, 1867	67,930
Bed-bottom	E. W. Tucker	Lowell, Mich	Apr. 3, 1866	53,706
Bed-bottom	H. Tucker	Newton, Mass	Sept. 9, 1862	36,429
Bed-bottom	A. Turnbull	New Britain, Conn	June 25, 1872	128,438
Bed-bottom	A. Turnbull	New Britain, Conn	Apr. 1, 1873	137,511
Bed-bottom	A. Turnbull and R. L. Webb	New Britain, Conn	Apr. 9, 1872	125,421
Bed-bottom	P. Ulmer	Charlestown, Mass	Oct. 2, 1860	30,267
Bed-bottom	C. Valkmar	New York, N. Y	Dec. 6, 1870	109,852
Bed-bottom	C. Van Deusen	Clarksville, N. Y	Oct. 10, 1871	119,727
Bed-bottom	B. C. Vanduzen	Cincinnati, Ohio	Mar. 18, 1873	137,039
Bed-bottom	W. W. Wait	Richmond, Ind	Mar. 8, 1870	100,569
Bed-bottom	H. B. Walbridge	Toledo, Ohio	Mar. 10, 1868	75,321
Bed-bottom	C. Walker	Chester, Vt	Apr. 28, 1868	77,339
Bed-bottom	J. C. Walker and W. Lapish	Burlington, Iowa	Nov. 28, 1871	121,437
Bed-bottom	C. D. Walkes	Elyria, Ohio	Dec. 14, 1869	97,997
Bed-bottom	W. Weaver	Phœnixville, Pa	Feb. 5, 1867	61,901
Bed-bottom	P. W. Webster and W. H. Prescott.	Concord, N. H	July 30, 1867	67,238
Bed-bottom	C. Weed	Boston, Mass	May 21, 1867	65,028
Bed-bottom	F. Wellhouse	Leavenworth, Kans	July 16, 1872	129,074
Bed-bottom	A. S. Wells	New Britain, Conn	Apr. 1, 1873	137,398

Index of patents issued from the United States Patent Office from 1790 *to* 1873, *inclusive*—Continued.

Invention.	Inventor.	Residence.	Date.	No.
Bed-bottom	A. West	Burlington, Iowa	Nov. 3, 1868	83, 809
Bed-bottom	C. W. White	Cincinnati, Ohio	June 18, 1867	65, 9[illegible]5
Bed-bottom	G. Widdicomb	Grand Rapids, Mich	Nov. 9, 1869	96, 750
Bed-bottom	N. O. Wilcox	Omaha, Nebr	May 13, 1873	138, 971
Bed-bottom	J. W. Wilder	New York, N. Y	Nov. 5, 1867	70, 663
Bed-bottom	J. D. Wilkinson	Plattsburgh, N. Y	Mar. 24, 1868	75, 820
Bed-bottom	D. S. Williams	Coldwater, Mich	Dec. 10, 1867	71, 933
Bed-bottom	H. W. Williams	Stowe, Vt	Nov. 5, 1867	70, 489
Bed-bottom	N. J. Willis	Waltham, Mass	Jan. 22, 1867	61, 374
Bed-bottom	J. E. Wilsey and D. Forbes	Chicago, Ill	Aug. 7, 1866	57, 031
Bed-bottom	L. Wilson	Ovid, N. Y	Nov. 26, 1867	71, 352
Bed-bottom	D. Winder	Cincinnati, Ohio	Oct. 11, 1859	25, 780
Bed-bottom	S. J. Wingate	Decatur, Ill	Jan. 7, 1868	73, 218
Bed-bottom	W. Workman and C. F. Swain	Ripon, Wis	Aug. 1, 1865	49, 189
Bed-bottom	E. Yeoman	Waukegan, Ill	Aug. 13, 1867	67, 698
Bed-bottom, Adjustable	E. Hoag	Coxsackie, N. Y	May 25, 1869	90, 449
Bed-bottom and chair spring	A. H Knapp	Newton Centre, Mass	Jan. 28, 1868	73, 905
Bed-bottom and mattress spring fastener	J. S. Barnum	Topeka, Kans	Apr. 6, 1869	88, 602
Bed-bottom and seat	E. C. Cross	Lime Rock, Conn	Jan. 8, 1867	61, 001
Bed-bottom and sofa, Spring	W. D. Adams	Poughkeepsie, N. Y	Mar. 26, 1872	124, 927
Bed-bottom connection	F. Metz	Lyons, N. Y	Apr. 10, 1866	53, 853
Bed-bottom, Folding	F. C. Payne	New York, N. Y	Mar. 29, 1864	42, 108
Bed-bottom frame	J. W. C. Peters	Chicago, Ill	July 2, 1872	128, 504
Bed-bottom frame	J. E. Whittlesey and J. W. C. Peters.	Chicago, Ill	Oct. 15, 1872	132, 226
Bed bottom, Invalid	J. D. Brunner	Doylestown, Pa	Dec. 31, 1872	134, 460
Bed bottom, Invalid	C. A. Tousley	Battle Creek, Mich	Nov. 26, 1872	133, 502
Bed bottom, Invalid	C. A. Tousley	Battle Creek, Mich	Mar. 4, 1873	136, 562
Bed bottom, Invalid	S M. Wilkes	Staunton, Va	Sept. 17, 1872	131, 488
Bed-bottom or cushion, Spring	H E. Maker	Newton, (Upper Falls,) Mass.	Apr. 27, 1869	89, 321
Bed-bottom, Paper	J. B. Crane	Dalton, Mass	Jan. 17, 1871	110, 958
Bed-bottom, seat, &c., Spring	C. Fich	Poughkeepsie, N. Y	Feb 21, 1871	111, 974
Bed-bottom slat	J. N. Dennett	Bath, Me	Aug. 21, 1860	29, 679
Bed-bottom, sofa, and chair-seat, Spring	C. Rich	Poughkeepsie, N. Y	June 27, 1871	116, 529
Bed-bottom, Spring	E. Adler	New York, N. Y	Dec. 23, 1856	16, 310
Bed-bottom, Spring	J. H. Almond	Louisville, Ky	Jan. 26, 1869	86, 120
Bed-bottom, Spring	C. L. Ames and A. H. Frost	Chicago, Ill	Oct. 7, 1873	143, 397
Bed-bottom, Spring	S. B. Andrews	Chicago, Ill	Apr. 2, 1872	125, 250
Bed-bottom, Spring	C. F. Baade	Brooklyn, N. Y	Aug. 16, 1870	106, 316
Bed-bottom, Spring	H. D W. Bailey	Sterling, Ill	Sept. 13, 1870	107, 213
Bed-bottom, Spring	J. Bailey and J. Decamp	Cincinnati, Ohio	Apr. 3, 1860	27, 680
Bed-bottom, Spring	F. P. Baldwin and C. T. Segar	Utica, N. Y	Oct. 10, 1871	119, 688
Bed-bottom, Spring	J. Barnes	New York, N. Y	Aug. 2, 1864	43, 662
Bed-bottom, Spring	J. Barnes	New York, N. Y	Feb. 20, 1866	52, 658
Bed-bottom, Spring	J. Barnes	New York, N. Y	July 17, 1866	56, 484
Bed-bottom, Spring	W. W. Bartlett	Portland, Me	June 21, 1870	104, 538
Bed-bottom, Spring	L. M. Bates	Cleveland, Ohio	Apr. 4, 1871	113, 385
Bed-bottom, Spring	A. B. Batey	Binghamton, N. Y	Dec. 10, 1867	71, 840
Bed-bottom, Spring	B. F. Bennett	Lockport, N. Y	Nov. 13, 1866	59, 546
Bed-bottom, Spring	E. R. Benton	Cleveland, Ohio	May 24, 1859	24, 091
Bed-bottom, Spring	C. H. Berry	East Somerville, Mass	Dec. 28, 1869	98, 339
Bed-bottom, Spring	G. Bevis	Rochester, N. Y	Jan. 26, 1864	41, 358
Bed-bottom, Spring	C. Bigeon	Cincinnati, Ohio	Jan. 16, 1872	122, 798
Bed-bottom, Spring	C. C. Bisbee	Rochester, N. Y	Aug. 2, 1859	24, 924
Bed-bottom, Spring	H. E. Bissell	Hartford, Conn	Sept. 14, 1869	94, 701
Bed-bottom, Spring	H. H. Blair and S. Barry	Brunswick, Ohio	May 6, 1873	138, 472
Bed-bottom, Spring	A. M. Blake	Canton, Ohio	Jan. 28, 1868	73, 770
Bed-bottom, Spring	O. Blake	Peru, Ind	May 31, 1870	103, 548
Bed-bottom, Spring	S. F. Bouton and N. P. Ames	Chicago, Ill	Feb. 25, 1868	74, 747
Bed-bottom, Spring	J. B. Bowditch	New Haven, Conn	Apr. 4, 1865	47, 086
Bed-bottom, Spring	L. R. Bradbury	Charlestown, Mass	Apr. 7, 1868	76, 296
Bed-bottom, Spring	C. B. Bristol	New Haven, Conn	June 12, 1866	55, 574
Bed-bottom, Spring	D. C. Bronson	Great Bend, Pa	May 24, 1870	103, 425
Bed-bottom, Spring	S. M. Brooks	Memphis, Tenn	Aug. 2, 1870	106, 028
Bed-bottom, Spring	S. M. Brooks	Burlington, Conn	Aug. 27, 1872	130, 788
Bed-bottom, Spring	G A. Brown	Kalamazoo, Mich	Oct. 6, 1868	82, 687
Bed-bottom, Spring	G. W. Brown	Buffalo, N. Y	Sept. 16, 1873	142, 895
Bed-bottom, Spring	G. Brownlee	Princeton, Ind	Aug. 15, 1871	117, 976
Bed-bottom, Spring	G. Brownlee	Princeton, Ind	Feb. 27, 1872	124, 032
Bed-bottom, Spring	J. N. Bull	Springfield, Mass	Apr. 19, 1870	102, 089
Bed-bottom, Spring	G. E. Burt	Harvard, Mass	July 9, 1872	128, 704
Bed-bottom, Spring	I. Bush	Indianola, Iowa	Feb. 18, 1873	135, 885
Bed-bottom, Spring	M. Cahill	Kalamazoo, Mich	July 26, 1870	105, 636
Bed-bottom, Spring	J. B. Campbell	Cincinnati, Ohio	Mar. 1, 1870	100, 2[illegible]6
Bed-bottom, Spring	G. O Capen	Providence, R. I	May 17, 1870	103, 138
Bed-bottom, Spring	A. H. Ceiley	Springfield, Mass	Jan. 25, 1870	99, 058
Bed-bottom, Spring	C. L. Chadeayne	Yonkers, N. Y	Oct. 5, 1869	95, 564
Bed-bottom, Spring	N. W. Clark	Clarkston, Mich	May 14, 1872	126, 675
Bed-bottom, Spring	A. Cole	Lockport, N. Y	July 17, 1866	56, 373
Bed-bottom, Spring	A. Cole	Mishawaka, Ind	Dec. 28, 1869	98, 230
Bed-bottom, Spring	A. Cole	Manamuskin, N. J	Mar. 7, 1871	112, 323
Bed-bottom, Spring	J. Collins	Grand Rapids, Mich	June 29, 1869	91, 913
Bed-bottom, Spring	W. N. Cook	Grand Rapids, Mich	Oct. 19, 1869	95, 880
Bed-bottom, Spring	W. Z. Cooke	New Britain, Conn	Oct. 1, 1872	131, 743
Bed-bottom, Spring	J. L. Cooper and E. A. Monroe	Elmira, N. Y	June 1, 1869	90, 820
Bed-bottom, Spring	J. Coover	Chambersburgh, Pa	Feb. 23, 1858	19, 410
Bed-bottom, Spring	D. V. Crandall	Chicago, Ill	July 11, 1871	116, 815
Bed-bottom, Spring	W. S. Crippen	Grand Rapids, Mich	Apr. 26, 1870	102, 231
Bed-bottom, Spring	A. C. Crondal	New York, N. Y	Feb. 9, 1864	41, 488
Bed-bottom, Spring	L. Cutler	Springfield, Mass	July 5, 1870	104, 938
Bed-bottom, Spring	J. and S. Danner	Canton, Ohio	June 14, 1864	43, 104
Bed-bottom, Spring	J. and S. Danner	Canton, Ohio	Sept. 11, 1866	57, 875
Bed-bottom, Spring	G. W. Dow	Lynn, Mass	June 16, 1857	17, 605
Bed-bottom, Spring	J. F. Duffy and W. P. Frailey	Chicago, Ill	May 17, 1870	103, 030
Bed-bottom, Spring	C. H. Dunks	Detroit, Mich	Feb. 5, 1870	99, 765
Bed-bottom, Spring	C. H. Dunks	New York, N. Y	Sept. 2, 1873	142, 377

Index of patents issued from the United States Patent Office from 1790 *to* 1873, *inclusive*—Continued.

Invention.	Inventor.	Residence.	Date.	No.
Bed-bottom, Spring	S. Dunlap	Rome, Ga	Mar. 4, 1873	136, 494
Bed-bottom, Spring	B. F. Ells	Dayton, Ohio	Mar. 1, 1870	100, 385
Bed-bottom, Spring	W. J. Emens	Louisville, Ky	Feb. 18, 1868	74, 675
Bed-bottom, Spring	B. C. English and F. Fraps	Springfield, Mass	Apr. 7, 1868	76, 425
Bed-bottom, Spring	E. E. Everitt	Philadelphia, Pa	Sept. 24, 1867	69, 198
Bed-bottom, Spring	M. Faloon	Bloomington, Ill	Apr. 5, 1870	101, 600
Bed-bottom, Spring	A. H. Fatzinger	New York, N. Y	Sept. 13, 1870	107, 348
Bed-bottom, Spring	J. A. Fegan	Brooklyn, N. Y	Mar. 2, 1869	87, 403
Bed-bottom, Spring	E. S. Field	Hartford, Conn	May 6, 1873	138, 490
Bed-bottom, Spring	E. S. Field	Hartford, Conn	May 6, 1873	138, 491
Bed-bottom, Spring	C. D. Flynt	New York, N. Y	Sept. 24, 1872	131, 675
Bed-bottom, Spring	E. Foster	Hartford, Conn	Apr. 13, 1858	19, 922
Bed-bottom, Spring	F. B. Franklin	Appleton, Wis	Mar. 4, 1862	34, 570
Bed-bottom, Spring	A. Frazee and L. W. Smith	Canandaigua, N. Y	July 31, 1866	56, 741
Bed-bottom, Spring	M. Freeman	Chicago, Ill	Aug. 20, 1872	130, 574
Bed-bottom, Spring	T. J. Gaffney and C. H. Dunks	Detroit, Mich	Oct. 27, 1868	83, 373
Bed-bottom, Spring	C. Gammel	Utica, N. Y	June 3, 1873	139, 567
Bed-bottom, Spring	J. C. Gaston	Cincinnati, Ohio	Feb. 16, 1869	86, 916
Bed-bottom, Spring	G. L. Gerard	New Haven, Conn	May 4, 1869	89, 651
Bed-bottom, Spring	J. E. Gillespie	Trenton, N. J	Dec. 20, 1864	45, 487
Bed-bottom, Spring	C. Glenn	Allegheny City, Pa	Dec. 6, 1870	109, 889
Bed-bottom, Spring	R. A. Goodyear	Binghamton, N. Y	June 22, 1869	91, 738
Bed-bottom, Spring	L. Granger	Memphis, Mich	June 16, 1868	78, 956
Bed-bottom, Spring	G. C. Grut	Milwaukee, Wis	Sept. 21, 1869	95, 105
Bed-bottom, Spring	G. C. Grut	Chicago, Ill	Oct. 3, 1871	119, 602
Bed-bottom, Spring	S. M. Guest	Chicago, Ill	Mar. 12, 1872	124, 436
Bed-bottom, Spring	C. Hacker	Euphemia, Ohio	Oct. 27, 1868	83, 489
Bed-bottom, Spring	H. Hard	Akron, Ohio	Nov. 21, 1871	121, 169
Bed-bottom, Spring	H. Hard	Akron, Ohio	July 30, 1872	130, 043
Bed-bottom, Spring	G. W. Hardy	Grand Rapids, Mich	Sept. 10, 1872	131, 165
Bed-bottom, Spring	P. J. Harvey	Chicago, Ill	Feb. 11, 1868	74, 353
Bed-bottom, Spring	W. W. Hawk	Detroit, Mich	Dec. 31, 1872	134, 430
Bed-bottom, Spring	W. Haworth	Canton, Ohio	June 1, 1869	90, 840
Bed-bottom, Spring	C. E. Hendrick	Chicopee, Mass	July 16, 1872	128, 960
Bed-bottom, Spring	E. Hennessey	Waterville, Me	Oct. 1, 1861	33, 417
Bed-bottom, Spring	H. A. Hight, sr	Fort Wayne, Ind	Dec. 30, 1873	146, 072
Bed-bottom, Spring	E. B. Hill	Grand Rapids, Mich	Feb. 7, 1871	111, 646
Bed-bottom, Spring	E. B. Hill and E. Van Valkenburg.	Grand Rapids, Mich	Sept. 2, 1873	142, 391
Bed-bottom, Spring	F. D. Hill	Poughkeepsie, N. Y	July 9, 1872	128, 867
Bed-bottom, Spring	P. Hill	Millport, N. Y	Sept. 12, 1871	118, 856
Bed-bottom, Spring	S. H. Hine	Sedan, Ind	Feb. 27, 1872	123, 994
Bed-bottom, Spring	C. and M. Hogeboom and L. Van Vleck.	Winslow, Ill	Aug. 31, 1869	94, 207
Bed-bottom, Spring	R. Holden	New York, N. Y	Jan. 3, 1860	26, 675
Bed-bottom, Spring	O. Howe	Cambridgeport, Mass	Nov. 19, 1861	33, 741
Bed-bottom, Spring	T. Howe	Cambridgeport, Mass	Mar. 1, 1870	100, 408
Bed-bottom, Spring	H. F. Howell	Mount Pleasant, Iowa	June 18, 1872	128, 043
Bed-bottom, Spring	W. C. Hubbard	Hubbardston, Mich	July 4, 1871	116, 712
Bed-bottom, Spring	L. Hull	Charlestown, Mass	May 21, 1872	127, 057
Bed-bottom, Spring	L. Hull	Charlestown, Mass	Sept. 17, 1872	131, 447
Bed-bottom, Spring	F. A. Huntington	San Francisco, Cal	Dec. 17, 1867	72, 202
Bed-bottom, Spring	H. L. Huntington	Chicago, Ill	Nov. 19, 1867	71, 014
Bed-bottom, Spring	J. Johnson	Hartford, Conn	July 9, 1872	128, 886
Bed-bottom, Spring	T. W. Johnston	Richmond, Me	Mar. 8, 1870	100, 635
Bed-bottom, Spring	J. S. Judson	Austin, Minn	Nov. 4, 1873	144, 338
Bed-bottom, Spring	W. B. Judson	Poughkeepsie, N. Y	Dec. 27, 1870	110, 471
Bed-bottom, Spring	J. B. Kelley and N. P. Kingsley.	Brandon, Vt	Oct. 13, 1868	82, 960
Bed-bottom, Spring	E. S. Kimball	Springfield, Mass	Dec. 21, 1869	98, 069
Bed-bottom, Spring	B. F. Kingman and M. V. B. Shepard.	Chicago, Ill	July 14, 1868	79, 839
Bed-bottom, Spring	S. P. Kittle	Brooklyn, N. Y	Nov. 21, 1865	51, 061
Bed-bottom, Spring	A. Kneppler	East New York, N. Y	July 27, 1869	93, 096
Bed-bottom, Spring	J. P. Knowles	Lockport, N. Y	July 1, 1862	35, 763
Bed-bottom, Spring	S. Landgraf	New York, N. Y	Oct. 29, 1872	132, 673
Bed-bottom, Spring	H. Lathrop	Utica, N. Y	Nov. 8, 1864	44, 962
Bed-bottom, Spring	G. Lightfoot	Elgin, Ill	Jan. 2, 1872	122, 325
Bed-bottom, Spring	T. Linfoot	Cincinnati, Ohio	Feb. 6, 1866	52, 426
Bed-bottom, Spring	S. Logan	Greenville, Pa	Jan. 9, 1872	122, 618
Bed-bottom, Spring	G. W. Loomis	Hartford, Conn	Mar. 22, 1870	101, 029
Bed-bottom, Spring	G. E. Lord	Utica, N. Y	Jan. 31, 1865	46, 119
Bed-bottom, Spring	J. E. Lord	Quincy, Ill	Feb. 28, 1871	112, 158
Bed-bottom, Spring	R. O. Lowrey	Saratoga Springs, N. Y	Feb. 11, 1868	74, 388
Bed-bottom, Spring	H. E. Maker	South Framingham, Mass	Nov. 5, 1872	132, 844
Bed-bottom, Spring	C. F. Manuel and D. M. Leonard	La Crosse, Wis	May 16, 1871	114, 355
Bed-bottom, Spring	D. Manuel	Boston, Mass	Jan. 26, 1869	86, 169
Bed-bottom, Spring	F. N. Marvin	Birmingham, Conn	Sept. 3, 1872	131, 107
Bed-bottom, Spring	W. D. Mason, C. H. Jacobus, and R. Millen.	New York, N. Y., and Newark, N. J.	Sept. 24, 1872	131, 621
Bed-bottom, Spring	F. B. Mattson	Rockford, Ill	Feb. 23, 1869	87, 184
Bed-bottom, Spring	E. W. Maxson	Scranton, Pa	Jan. 31, 1871	111, 362
Bed-bottom, Spring	W. McArthur	Philadelphia, Pa	June 7, 1870	104, 048
Bed-bottom, Spring	J. J. McCormick	Paterson, N. J	Apr. 30, 1861	30, 235
Bed-bottom, Spring	S. B. McCracken	Detroit, Mich	May 26, 1868	78, 223
Bed-bottom, Spring	W. C. McGill	Cincinnati, Ohio	Nov. 18, 1873	144, 688
Bed-bottom, Spring	R. W. McIntyre	Oregon, Wis	Nov. 5, 1872	132, 728
Bed-bottom, Spring	D. McMurchy	Jeffersonville, Ind	May 21, 1872	126, 977
Bed-bottom, Spring	W. H. Meriwether	New Braunfels, Tex	Aug. 8, 1854	11, 484
Bed-bottom, Spring	A. E. Miller	Arcadia, Ohio	Nov. 26, 1872	133, 329
Bed-bottom, Spring	J. Moore	Tarentum, Pa	Aug. 24, 1869	94, 020
Bed-bottom, Spring	G. W. Morrill	Sterling, Ill	July 20, 1869	92, 740
Bed-bottom, Spring	W. A. Morse and D. S. Bean	Boston, Mass	June 19, 1860	28, 766
Bed-bottom, Spring	C. W. Mutell	Springfield, Mass	May 31, 1870	103, 646
Bed-bottom, Spring	A. W. Newell	Bradford, Pa	Jan. 28, 1868	73, 744
Bed-bottom, Spring	C. W. Northrup	Utica, N. Y	Sept. 30, 1873	143, 373
Bed-bottom, Spring	H. Ogborn and A. W. Kendrick	Richmond, Ind., and Brooklyn, N. Y.	Jan. 23, 1872	122, 906
Bed-bottom, Spring	M. Ohmer	Dayton, Ohio	Apr. 27, 1869	89, 494

Index of patents issued from the United States Patent Office from 1790 *to* 1873, *inclusive*—Continued.

Invention.	Inventor.	Residence.	Date.	No.
Bed-bottom, Spring	B. J. Oleff	Milwaukee, Wis	Dec. 3, 1867	71, 634
Bed-bottom, Spring	B. H. Otis	Havana, Ill	Jan. 9, 1872	122, 645
Bed-bottom, Spring	W. Owen and S. Harter	Pierceton, Ill	Mar. 12, 1872	124, 507
Bed-bottom, Spring	M. Le Page	Woodhaven, N. Y	Aug. 13, 1867	67, 776
Bed-bottom, Spring	H. H. Palmer	Rockford, Ill	Nov. 24, 1868	84, 300
Bed-bottom, Spring	E. Parker	Plymouth, Conn	Apr. 23, 1872	126, 081
Bed-bottom, Spring	L. E. Payne	Disco, Mich	Feb. 9, 1864	41, 533
Bed-bottom, Spring	J. F. Peck	Springfield, Mass	May 25, 1869	90, 384
Bed-bottom, Spring	E. Perry	Hopkinton, Mass	Aug. 24, 1869	94, 025
Bed-bottom, Spring	C. B. Pickett	Delaware, Ohio	Sept. 10, 1872	131, 180
Bed-bottom, Spring	M. Pierce	Winona, Minn	Oct. 29, 1867	70, 355
Bed-bottom, Spring	J. Pollitt	Edon, Ohio	Aug. 12, 1873	141, 726
Bed-bottom, Spring	J. Potter	Portland, Me	July 27, 1869	93, 118
Bed-bottom, Spring	J. H. Potts	Ottumwa, Iowa	Mar. 22, 1870	101, 161
Bed-bottom, Spring	S. Puffer	Oxford, N. Y	July 9, 1872	128, 905
Bed-bottom, Spring	J. H. Quackenbush	Luddington, Mich	Dec. 20, 1870	110, 284
Bed-bottom, Spring	J. Ralston	Mansfield, Ohio	Nov. 12, 1872	132, 982
Bed-bottom, Spring	B. Rear	Toronto, Canada	Jan. 28, 1868	73, 755
Bed-bottom, Spring	S. H. Reeves	New York, N. Y	May 6, 1873	138, 529
Bed-bottom, Spring	G. Reneky and S. Kiess	Edgerton, Ohio	Nov. 17, 1868	84, 069
Bed-bottom, Spring	M. A. Richardson	Sherman, N. Y	May 14, 1872	126, 743
Bed-bottom, Spring	G. B. Richmond	Charlestown, Mass	May 31, 1870	103, 658
Bed-bottom, Spring	G. W. Robbins	Dubuque, Iowa	May 9, 1871	114, 712
Bed-bottom, Spring	M. Roberts	Saint Paul, Minn	July 24, 1866	56, 678
Bed-bottom, Spring	M. Rosenberg and H. Scheuerle	New York, N. Y	Nov. 13, 1860	30, 635
Bed-bottom, Spring	H. Russell and M. S. Fuller	Nashville, Mich.	Dec. 1, 1868	84, 581
Bed-bottom, Spring	I. M. Russell	Lewiston, Me	Dec. 7, 1869	97, 706
Bed-bottom, Spring	W. P. Sadler	Springfield, Ill	May 7, 1872	126, 579
Bed-bottom, Spring	G. E. Safford	New York, N. Y	June 15, 1858	20, 609
Bed-bottom, Spring	A. L. Sawyer and W. Baldwin	Detroit, Mich	May 26, 1868	78, 397
Bed-bottom, Spring	G. Schott	New York, N. Y	Nov. 17, 1863	40, 645
Bed-bottom, Spring	C. Schroder	New York, N. Y	Oct. 14, 1856	15, 900
Bed-bottom, Spring	C. Schroder	New York, N Y	Feb. 23, 1858	19, 473
Bed-bottom, Spring	D. A. Scott	Cincinnati, Ohio	July 6, 1869	92, 375
Bed-bottom, Spring	D. A. Scott	Cincinnati, Ohio	June 21, 1870	104, 504
Bed-bottom, Spring	D. A. Scott and J. E. Burdge	Cincinnati, Ohio	Feb. 4, 1868	74, 153
Bed-bottom, Spring	W. S. Seaman	Milwaukee, Wis	Aug. 20, 1872	130, 753
Bed-bottom, Spring	J. L. Secomb	Detroit, Mich	Feb. 15, 1870	99, 790
Bed-bottom, Spring	J. L. Secomb	Chicago, Ill	June 18, 1872	128, 175
Bed-bottom, Spring	J. L. Secomb	Chicago, Ill	Jan. 7, 1873	134, 614
Bed-bottom, Spring	D. N. Sellig	New York, N. Y	Apr. 5, 1870	101, 526
Bed-bottom, Spring	I. A. Sergeant	Springfield, Ohio	Apr. 26, 1859	23, 786
Bed-bottom, Spring	M. Shepard	Chicago, Ill	July 26, 1870	105, 853
Bed-bottom, Spring	E. G. Sherman	Forestville, N. Y	Apr. 29, 1873	138, 348
Bed-bottom, Spring	P. Sisson	Brant, N. Y	Aug. 25, 1868	81, 422
Bed-bottom, Spring	C. I. Skow	Racine, Wis	May 17, 1870	103, 249
Bed-bottom, Spring	H. Smith and J. Potter	Groveton, N. H., and Portland, Me.	Feb. 21, 1871	112, 085
Bed-bottom, Spring	H. T. Smith	Washington, D. C	Oct. 6, 1857	18, 357
Bed-bottom, Spring	G. Speckner	Madison, Wis	May 9, 1871	114, 618
Bed-bottom, Spring	W. D. Spencer and E. Parker	New Britain, Conn	Apr. 1, 1873	137, 498
Bed-bottom, Spring	W. Starke	Chicago, Ill	Apr. 29, 1873	138, 446
Bed-bottom, Spring	E. Steinel	Amsterdam, N. Y	Dec. 3, 1867	71, 808
Bed-bottom, Spring	J. Stengel	Croton, Mich	Dec. 7, 1869	97, 720
Bed-bottom, Spring	C. S. Stevens	Portland, Me	May 24, 1870	103, 521
Bed-bottom, Spring	J. Stevens	Lowell, Mass	Apr. 23, 1861	32, 165
Bed-bottom, Spring	P. Stovall	Newman, Ga	Oct. 25, 1870	108, 650
Bed-bottom, Spring	R. Tattershall	Beloit, Wis	Mar. 10, 1868	75, 490
Bed-bottom, Spring	R. Tattershall	Beloit, Wis	Apr. 19, 1870	102, 182
Bed-bottom, Spring	J. C. Taylor	Ann Arbor, Mich	May 19, 1868	78, 026
Bed-bottom, Spring	H. L. Thistle	New York, N. Y	Jan. 22, 1861	31, 196
Bed-bottom, Spring	S. A. Thompson and C. T. Kendrick.	Manchester, Mich., and Brooklyn, N. Y.	Apr. 22, 1873	138, 056
Bed-bottom, Spring	J. D. Tifft	Cuyahoga Falls, Ohio	Jan. 14, 1868	73, 268
Bed-bottom, Spring	L. L. Tingley	Pawtucket, R. I	May 1, 1866	54, 443
Bed-bottom, Spring	C. H. Triphagen	Pewamo, Mich	Aug. 8, 1871	117, 830
Bed-bottom, Spring	H. Tucker	Cambridgeport, Mass	July 3, 1855	13, 188
Bed-bottom, Spring	F. Tyler	Cleveland, Ohio	Aug. 9, 1859	25, 063
Bed-bottom, Spring	S. E. Tyler	Beloit, Wis	July 7, 1868	79, 705
Bed-bottom, Spring	P. Ulmer	New York, N. Y	Oct. 4, 1859	25, 689
Bed-bottom, Spring	M. and L. Van Vleck	Monroe, Wis	Apr. 26, 1870	102, 337
Bed-bottom, Spring	A. Walker	New Haven, Conn	Dec. 31, 1867	72, 943
Bed-bottom, Spring	N. Warlick	Chambers Court-House, Ala	Nov. 16, 1858	22, 098
Bed-bottom, Spring	D. P. Webster	Upper Gilmanton, N. H	Aug. 14, 1866	57, 229
Bed-bottom, Spring	D. P. Webster and H. W. Ladd	Philadelphia, Pa	Apr. 23, 1867	64, 175
Bed-bottom, Spring	D. P. Webster and H. W. Ladd	Upper Gilmanton, N. H., and Philadelphia, Pa.	Sept. 10, 1867	68, 818
Bed-bottom, Spring	O. H. Weed	Charlestown, Mass	Aug. 27, 1867	68, 268
Bed-bottom, Spring	W. Wells	Salem, Mass	Mar. 8, 1870	100, 698
Bed-bottom, Spring	G. Widdicomb	Grand Rapids, Mich	Dec. 17, 1867	72, 350
Bed-bottom, Spring	N. J. Willis	Boston, Mass	Feb. 27, 1866	52, 937
Bed-bottom, Spring	N. J. Willis	Boston, Mass	June 23, 1868	79, 285
Bed-bottom, Spring	J. E. Wilsey and D. Forbes	Chicago, Ill., and Scotland, Great Britain.	July 31, 1866	56, 844
Bed-bottom, Spring	G. Wilson	Chicago, Ill	Oct. 3, 1871	119, 487
Bed-bottom, Spring	S. Winslow	Charlestown, Mass	Jan. 19, 1869	85, 980
Bed-bottom, Spring	W. H. Woodworth	Pewamo, Mich	Oct. 17, 1871	120, 142
Bed-bottom, Spring	E. E. Worden and H. Wilms	Brandon, Vt	Feb. 25, 1868	74, 872
Bed-bottom, Spring	A. W. Wright	Bunker Hill, Ill	Apr. 7, 1868	76, 575
Bed-bottom, Spring	E. L. Wright	Sterling, Ill	June 20, 1871	116, 250
Bed-bottom spring	W. Wright	New York, N. Y	Dec. 19, 1854	12, 111
Bed-bottom spring	L. M. Bates	Newark, Ohio	Apr. 23, 1867	63, 985
Bed-bottom spring	L. M. Bates	Jackson, Mich	Oct. 5, 1869	95, 553
Bed-bottom spring	T. A. Carl	Nashville, Tenn	Nov. 8, 1870	108, 966
Bed-bottom spring	J. P. Chamberlin	Abington, Mass	Dec. 21, 1869	98, 146
Bed-bottom spring	H. R. Crampton	Lockport, N. Y	Sept. 18, 1860	30, 049
Bed-bottom spring	W. C. T. Davidson	Hannibal, Mo	Feb. 6, 1872	123, 335
Bed-bottom spring	M. W. Farber	Mount Pleasant, Iowa	May 23, 1871	115, 043

Index of patents issued from the United States Patent Office from 1790 *to* 1873, *inclusive*—Continued.

Invention.	Inventor.	Residence.	Date.	No.
Bed-bottom spring	M. Flanigan	Detroit, Mich	Mar. 23, 1869	88,153
Bed-bottom spring	O. F. A. Faulkner	Mount Pleasant, Iowa	July 16, 1872	129,218
Bed-bottom spring	J. Fox	Albion, Mich	Nov. 9, 1869	96,686
Bed-bottom spring	J. P. Haskins	Saratoga Springs, N. Y.	Aug. 20, 1872	130,579
Bed-bottom spring	H. Ingraham	Naples, N. Y	Nov. 22, 1870	109,413
Bed-bottom spring	J. Johnson	Northampton County, N. C	July 16, 1867	66,849
Bed-bottom spring	P. W. Kniskern	Fort Smith, Ark	Nov. 9, 1869	96,706
Bed-bottom spring	G. Koenig	Plymouth, Mich	Jan. 7, 1868	73,188
Bed-bottom spring	F. F. Lahm	Chicago, Ill	Nov. 2, 1869	96,446
Bed-bottom spring	J. M. Losie	Indianapolis, Ind	Sept. 8, 1868	82,012
Bed-bottom spring	A. McDaniel	Dubuque, Iowa	Sept. 8, 1868	81,923
Bed-bottom spring	E. D. Merriam and S. Aldrich	La Grange, Ohio	Aug. 27, 1867	68,098
Bed-bottom spring	W. H. Miller	Hannibal, Mo	Jan. 30, 1872	123,279
Bed-bottom spring	H. Ogborn and A. W. Kendrick	Richmond, Ind., and Brooklyn, N. Y.	Mar. 11, 1873	136,665
Bed-bottom spring	B. Partello	Detroit, Mich	Mar. 23, 1869	88,070
Bed-bottom spring	J. F. Peck	Springfield, Mass	Nov. 22, 1870	109,445
Bed-bottom spring	D. Punchies	Plymouth, Mich	Nov. 13, 1866	59,649
Bed-bottom spring	H. M. Scott	Portland, Me	Nov. 22, 1859	26,235
Bed-bottom spring	H. G. Seekins	Elyria, Ohio	Mar. 26, 1867	63,313
Bed-bottom spring	A. E. Thayer	Philadelphia, Pa	Apr. 25, 1871	114,225
Bed-bottom spring	J. A. Van Wert and A. Crooley	Elmira, N. Y	July 15, 1873	140,975
Bed-bottom, Spring-slat	J. S. Vanhorn and W. H. Pack	Jersey City, N. J	Aug. 18, 1868	81,120
Bed-bottom, Woven-wire	G. Richardson	Milwaukee, Wis	Aug. 29, 1871	118,644
Bed-bottoms, Foundation for spring	D. Manuel	Dedham, Mass	Nov. 30, 1869	97,306
Bed-bottoms, Means of securing springs to slats of	Z. S. Cracraft	Lacon, Ill	Nov. 17, 1868	84,092
Bed-bottoms, seats, &c., Connection of springs for	C. Rich	Poughkeepsie, N. Y	May 10, 1870	102,867
Bed-bottoms, Spring-fastener for	D. A. Scott	Cincinnati, Ohio	Apr. 22, 1873	138,203
Bed-bottoms, Spring-holder for	R. Lapham	New York, N. Y	Nov. 20, 1868	59,799
Bed-bottoms, Spring-slat for	J. M. French	East Cambridge, Mass	Dec. 12, 1865	51,433
Bed-brace, Spring	H. D. Bolt	Elmira, N. Y	May 18, 1869	90,229
Bed-bug destroyer	B. Garrand	Maryville, Tenn	Mar. 12, 1836	....
Bed-bug destroyer	R. Sealy	New York, N. Y	June 20, 1823	....
Bed-bug destroying compound	E. Hooper	Diamond Springs, Cal	Oct. 8, 1872	132,080
Bed-bug exterminator	C. L. Fowell	Corsicana, Tex	June 3, 1873	139,562
Bed-bug trap	J. A. Clark	Georgetown, D. C	June 13, 1829	....
Bed-bug trap	E. B. Lake	Bridgeport, N. J	Aug. 21, 1866	57,338
Bed-bug trap	W. Tapper	New York, N. Y	Dec. 12, 1865	51,493
Bed-bug trap for bedsteads	C. Legab	Pittsburgh, Pa	Apr. 15, 1873	137,936
Bed-bugs and other vermin, Compound for destroying.	P. Seebald	New York, N. Y	June 23, 1868	79,151
Bed-bugs by steam, Destroying	T. Miller	Newburgh, N. Y	Nov. 19, 1833	....
Bed-bugs by steam, Destroying	B. Overman	Greensborough, N. C	June 22, 1832	....
Bed, Camp	W. S. G. Baker	Baltimore, Md	Dec. 17, 1861	33,924
Bed, Camp	L. Hutchins	Norwich, Conn	Oct. 28, 1862	36,783
Bed, Canopy	I. E. Palmer	Montville, Conn	Jan. 31, 1860	27,007
Bed, chair, &c., Spring-bottom for	G. W. Griswold	Abington, Pa	Oct. 29, 1861	33,622
Bed, Child's	M. E. J. Marr	Jefferson, La	Apr. 7, 1868	76,336
Bed-clothes clamp	W. Fisher	Ripon, Wis	Dec. 11, 1866	60,351
Bed-clothes clamp	A. Storm	Rutland, Vt	Sept. 10, 1867	68,668
Bed-clothes clasp	F. A. Rockwell	Ridgefield, Conn	Feb. 12, 1850	7,088
Bed-clothes, Device for securing	G. Inwood	San Francisco, Cal	Mar. 30, 1869	88,298
Bed-clothes, Frame for supporting	G. A. McLane	Chicago, Ill	Mar. 5, 1872	124,213
Bed-clothes holder	M. D. Brooks	Albany, N. Y	Oct. 15, 1867	69,898
Bed-clothes holder	J. B. Munson	Bailey Hollow, Pa	June 9, 1868	78,756
Bed-clothes retainer	J. Brikenhead	Canton, Mass	June 20, 1871	116,013
Bed-clothes retainer, Child's	M. L. Thompson	Brooklyn, N. Y	Nov. 28, 1865	51,270
Bed, Conical spring	W. J. and A. E. Lyman	East Hampton, Mass	Sept. 18, 1835	....
Bed-cord	S. Albro	Buffalo, N. Y	July 3, 1860	28,950
Bed-cord tightener	A. B. Stroup	Waldron, Ind	Apr. 10, 1860	27,844
Bed, Cot	C. W. Irwin	Saint Louis, Mo	Oct. 22, 1861	33,527
Bed, Cot	L. B. Morse	Athol, Mass	Feb. 4, 1873	135,573
Bed-cushion and other upholstering	H. H. Barnes	Hoosick Falls, N. Y	Jan. 10, 1871	110,820
Bed, Elastic-spring	A. G. Hull	New York, N. Y	Oct. 1, 1831	....
Bed elevator, Invalid	D. S. Dunning	New York, N. Y	June 16, 1857	17,558
Bed, Inclosed folding spring	L. Derome	San Francisco, Cal	Jan. 18, 1870	98,932
Bed, Extension	F. Menzer	San Francisco, Cal	Apr. 5, 1870	101,489
Bed, Folding	F. C. Payne	New York, N. Y	Apr. 28, 1868	77,311
Bed, Folding	L. Whitehead, sr	Brooklyn, N. Y	Mar. 28, 1871	113,231
Bed, Folding	W. Wright	Bloomfield, N. J	Nov. 14, 1871	120,924
Bed, Folding box	A. G. Bayles	New York, N. Y	Nov. 19, 1872	133,137
Bed for ships and hospitals	B. F. McAlhatten	New York, N. Y	Mar. 4, 1862	34,583
Bed, Fracture	M. M. Latta	Goshen, Ind	Aug. 21, 1866	57,340
Bed-frame	S. Springer	Chicago, Ill	Mar. 29, 1870	101,327
Bed-frame and attachment	J. M. Farnham	Hartford, Conn	July 16, 1872	129,121
Bed frame, Military and civic	T. S. Lambert	Peekskill, N. Y	Apr. 15, 1862	34,971
Bed foundation	W. A. N. Long	Fisherville, N. H	Mar. 26, 1861	31,850
Bed, Hospital	H. Conway	Dayton, Ohio	Feb. 18, 1868	74,669
Bed, Hospital	E. Gray	Cuyahoga Falls, Ohio	Apr. 14, 1868	76,747
Bed, Hospital	I. Waller	Cleveland, Ohio	Mar. 5, 1872	124,398
Bed, Invalid	G. H. Clark	Pontiac, Mich	Sept. 15, 1857	18,189
Bed, Invalid	J. Crosby	Manchester, N. H	Aug. 23, 1864	43,900
Bed, Invalid	S. D. Hopkins	Staunton, Va	Aug. 24, 1852	9,215
Bed, Invalid	R. H. Mathews	Painesville, Ohio	Feb. 28, 1865	46,569
Bed, Invalid	J. N. Morrison	Philadelphia, Pa	Sept. 22, 1863	40,056
Bed-key, Ratchet	W. M. Gray	Brooklyn, N. Y	Dec. 10, 1867	71,871
Bed-lounge	A. F. Benten	San Francisco, Cal	Sept. 5, 1871	118,677
Bed-lounge	E. and F. Boese and A. Neuberger.	Chicago, Ill	Jan. 5, 1869	85,560
Bed-lounge	J. Brader	New York, N. Y	Mar. 28, 1871	113,012
Bed-lounge	H. S. Carter	Chicago, Ill	Mar. 1, 1870	100,257
Bed-lounge	H. Closterman	Cincinnati, Ohio	June 11, 1872	127,741
Bed-lounge	J. L. Cox	Manchester, N. H	Sept. 8, 1868	81,880
Bed-lounge	R. H. Cutter	Cleveland, Ohio	Jan. 29, 1867	61,610
Bed-lounge	G. Hartzell	Philadelphia, Pa	Apr. 8, 1873	137,677
Bed-lounge	G. Hartzell and J. P. Reifsneider.	Philadelphia, Pa	June 6, 1871	115,732
Bed-lounge	C. H. Hildreth	Chicago, Ill	June 11, 1872	127,693

Index of patents issued from the United States Patent Office from 1790 *to* 1873, *inclusive*—Continued.

Invention.	Inventor.	Residence.	Date.	No.
Bed-lounge	A. N. Hornung	La Porte, Ind	Sept. 3, 1872	131, 002
Bed-lounge	F. H. Lamb	Ravenna, Ohio	Jan. 2, 1872	122, 469
Bed-lounge	S. Kennedy	Allegheny City, Pa	Dec. 17, 1872	133, 992
Bed-lounge	J. D. Pratt	Cleveland, Ohio	July 16, 1867	66, 883
Bed-lounge	J. D. Pratt	Cleveland, Ohio	Oct. 27, 1868	83, 544
Bed-lounge	V. Ven Dissen	New York, N. Y	Apr. 4, 1871	113, 372
Bed-lounge	B. F. Walton	Philadelphia, Pa	June 27, 1871	116, 514
Bed-lounge	B. C. Wilkins	Elgin, Ill	Dec. 28, 1869	98, 325
Bed-lounge	L. Wunsch, H. Stuhlreyer, and J. Schwarz.	Cincinnati, Ohio	May 14, 1872	126, 862
Bed-lounges, Mode of constructing	E. P. Curtiss and H. H. Hendee.	Buffalo, N. Y	Feb. 9, 1869	86, 820
Bed, Office	A. J. Vawter	Indianapolis, Ind	July 14, 1868	80, 038
Bed or cradle guard	J. J. Roll	Newark, N. J	Feb. 18, 1873	136, 097
Bed-pan	E. M. Chaffee	Providence, R. I	Sept. 17, 1867	68, 954
Bed-pan attachment for invalid beds	S. G. Welling	New Rochelle, N. Y	May 12, 1868	77, 937
Bed-pan. Female syringe	A. Rittenhouse	Philadelphia, Pa	Sept. 22, 1868	82, 349
Bed, Parlor	M. Crosby	Boston, Mass	Sept. 19, 1871	119, 079
Bed, Parlor	H. Goodrich	Stoneham, Mass	May 28, 1872	127, 338
Bed-pins, Device in machine for manufacturing	H. Gross	Tiffin, Ohio	Sept. 23, 1856	15, 763
Bed-pins, Machine for making	C. Goddard	Edinburgh, Ohio	May 2, 1854	10, 859
Bed-pins, Machine for making	W. McBride	Bristolville, Ohio	Feb. 28, 1854	10, 577
Bed, Portable camp	P. N. Ouroussoff	St. Petersburg, Russia	May 28, 1867	65, 262
Bed, Portable folding	G. N Seidler	Hartford, Conn	Apr. 2, 1861	31, 936
Bed-rail fastener	J. Lemman	Cincinnati, Ohio	Sept. 20, 1870	107, 618
Bed, Rolling	J. Krisch and C. Thoener	New York, N. Y	Apr. 4, 1871	113, 307
Bed-sacking, Mode of tightening	J. K. Simpson	Boston, Mass	Aug. 10, 1827	....
Bed-seats, &c., Elastic support for	J. Perry	Brooklyn, N. Y	Nov. 7, 1865	50, 840
Bed-seat for invalids	G. H. Waterhouse	East Sagus, Mass	May 7, 1872	126, 599
Bed, Secret	C. F. Bowers	Boston, Mass	Mar. 24, 1868	75, 849
Bed-slat, Spring	P. C. Ingersoll	Green Point, N. Y	Dec. 17, 1867	72, 398
Bed, Sofa	S. Blair	New Haven, Conn	June 27, 1848	5, 646
Bed, Sofa	E. B. Bowditch	New Haven, Conn	Oct. 18, 1853	10, 125
Bed, Sofa	W. Brown	Worcester, Mass	Aug. 18, 1868	81, 065
Bed, Sofa	E. N. G. Childs	Cincinnati, Ohio	July 16, 1872	129, 528
Bed, Sofa	M. Crosby	Boston, Mass	May 21, 1872	127, 029
Bed, Sofa	E. N. Doring	New York, N. Y	Dec. 9, 1873	145, 404
Bed, Sofa	S. Graves	North Weymouth, Mass	Mar. 5, 1872	124, 265
Bed, Sofa	G. Knell	Philadelphia, Pa	Oct. 24, 1871	120, 283
Bed, Sofa	F. Krater	Pittsburgh, Pa	May 28, 1872	127, 171
Bed, Sofa	J. Needham	Morrisania, N. Y	Mar. 15, 1870	100, 789
Bed, Sofa	F. C. Payne	New York, N. Y	May 3, 1870	102, 702
Bed, Sofa	J. J. Russ	Worcester, Mass	June 14, 1870	104, 358
Bed, Sofa	J. J. Russ	Worcester, Mass	Aug. 20, 1872	130, 664
Bed, Sofa	C. C. Schmitt	New York, N. Y	Apr. 4, 1871	113, 576
Bed, Sofa	B. L. Southack	New York, N. Y	Feb. 23, 1869	87, 216
Bed, Sofa	J. Werner	New York, N. Y	Sept. 12, 1871	118, 994
Bed, sofa, and lounge bottom	R. Jennings	Racine, Wis	Nov. 26, 1872	133, 371
Bed, sofa, &c., Spring	W. Lord	San Francisco, Cal	Aug. 2, 1870	106, 069
Bed, sofa, &c., Spring	J. Sears	Cortland, N. Y	Dec. 20, 1870	110, 293
Bed, Spiral-spring	M. F. Moody and B. Eastman	Northampton, Mass	Apr. 13, 1836	....
Bed, Spring	L. Andersen	Chicago, Ill	Oct. 4, 1870	107, 995
Bed, Spring	B. Barstow	Westfield, Mass	July 18, 1871	117, 036
Bed, Spring	O. C. Campbell	Omaha, Nebr	Apr. 1, 1873	137, 287
Bed, Spring	J. H. Crane	Charlestown, Mass	Apr. 3, 1860	27, 709
Bed, Spring	S. Elder	Buffalo, N. Y	Apr. 23, 1861	32, 126
Bed, Spring	J. M. Farnham	Hartford, Conn	Nov. 14, 1871	120, 865
Bed, Spring	J. Fisk	Augusta, Me	July 27, 1869	92, 949
Bed, Spring	J. French	Ware, Mass	Aug. 25, 1831	....
Bed, Spring	C. Gentil	New York, N. Y	Nov. 11, 1862	36, 902
Bed, Spring	B. S. Harrington	Boston, Mass	July 10, 1866	56, 216
Bed, Spring	L. Hull	Charlestown, Mass	Mar. 29, 1870	101, 267
Bed, Spring	J. Johnson	Hartford, Conn	Aug. 15, 1871	118, 018
Bed, Spring	J. Johnson	Hartford, Conn	Nov. 14, 1871	120, 881
Bed, Spring	S. P. Kittle	Newark, N. J	Dec. 7, 1869	97, 521
Bed, Spring	W. W. and G. F. Ladd	Chelsea, Mass	Feb. 15, 1870	99, 779
Bed, Spring	N. Meson	Lincoln, Mass	Feb. 7, 1871	111, 554
Bed, Spring	W. P. Miller	Marysville, Cal	June 9, 1863	38, 834
Bed, Spring	G. H. Pool	New York, N. Y	Jan. 1, 1867	60, 782
Bed, Spring	F. W. Shapleigh and M. J. Colman.	Boston, Mass	July 30, 1867	67, 359
Bed, Spring	S. Smith and J. H. Gill	Williamsburgh. N. Y	Oct. 21, 1873	143, 854
Bed, Spring	S. Stout	Tremont, Ill	June 3, 1873	139, 627
Bed, Spring	D. E. Taylor	Charlton, Mass	Mar. 25, 1873	137, 260
Bed, Spring	C. Van Dyeck	Nashville, Tenn	Oct. 1, 1867	69, 514
Bed, Spring	I. E. Webster	Buffalo, N. Y	Apr. 2, 1872	125, 357
Bed-spring	J. H. Baker and A. Doney	Saratoga Springs, N. Y	Mar. 11, 1873	136, 692
Bed-spring	H. Beyrodt	Louisville, Ky	June 30, 1868	79, 302
Bed-spring	H. Chandler	Bennington, Vt	Sept. 12, 1871	118, 906
Bed-spring	H. F. Clark	Lowell, Mich	Aug. 11, 1868	80, 808
Bed-spring	W. C. Cook	Appleton, Wis	May 21, 1861	32, 352
Bed-spring	D. V. Crandall	Canton, Iowa	Apr. 3, 1866	53, 579
Bed-spring	D. V. Crandall	Chicago, Ill	Apr. 25, 1871	114, 112
Bed-spring	D. T. Gale	Fort Wayne, Ind	Nov. 8, 1870	108, 998
Bed-spring	F. J. Gardner	Washington, N. C	Nov. 30, 1869	97, 386
Bed-spring	D. F. Haasz	Philadelphia, Pa	July 9, 1867	66, 490
Bed-spring	E. S. Hayward	Roxbury, Mass	Nov. 19, 1867	71, 169
Bed-spring	H. N. Hemingway	Rochester, N. Y	Dec. 8, 1868	84, 824
Bed-spring	J. Hyde	Troy, N. Y	Sept. 3, 1867	68, 442
Bed-spring	W. W. Jones	Philadelphia, Pa	Nov. 25, 1873	144, 984
Bed-spring	G. B. Markham	Plymouth, Mich	Aug. 27, 1867	68, 224
Bed-spring	P. C. Morehous	Hannibal, Mo	Jan. 23, 1872	123, 036
Bed-spring	M. M. Murray	Cincinnati, Ohio	Dec. 3, 1872	133, 663
Bed-spring	S. D. Newbro	Lansing, Mich	Sept. 27, 1859	25, 557
Bed-spring	A. W. Obermann	Chicago, Ill	June 21, 1870	104, 633
Bed-spring	F. R. Smith	Bennington, Vt	May 6, 1873	138, 589
Bed-spring	L. Smith	Foxborough, Mass	May 22, 1866	55, 021
Bed-spring	C. Rich	Poughkeepsie, N. Y	Aug. 30, 1870	106, 980
Bed-spring	N. B. White	South Dedham, Mass	July 3, 1866	56, 132

Index fo patents issued from the United States Patent Office from 1790 *to* 1873, *inclusive*—Continued.

Invention.	Inventor.	Residence.	Date.	No.
Bed-spring attachment	A. Smith	Boston, Mass	Oct. 15, 1872	132, 328
Bed-spring fastening	D. Mannel	Boston, Mass	Mar. 5, 1867	62, 653
Bed-spring guide	A. C. Stich	Kalamazoo, Mich	Oct. 22, 1867	70, 041
Bed-springs, Device for forming the eyes of	N. B. White	South Dedham, Mass	Oct. 23, 1866	59, 145
Bed-springs, Device for forming spiral	E. L. Bushnell	Poughkeepsie, N. Y	Aug. 8, 1871	117, 860
Bed-springs, Machine for coiling	M. Van Pleck	Albany, N. Y	Mar. 21, 1871	112, 868
Bed ventilating, cooling, or warming device	D. E. Somes	Washington, D. C	Feb. 8, 1870	99, 722
Bed, Wardrobe	F. C. Payne and A. Reid	New York, N. Y	Apr. 12, 1859	23, 604
Beds, cushions, &c., Filling for	G. C. Barney	Chicago, Ill	June 2, 1868	78, 412
Beds, Feathers for	G. Schott	New York, N. Y	Sept. 13, 1864	44, 223
Beds, Head-rest for	B. F. Walton	Jersey City, N. J	Mar. 4, 1873	136, 395
Beds, Instrument for stirring straw and husk	C. A. Richardson	Waterville, Me	Apr. 1, 1856	14, 574
Beds, Manufacturing wood to be used as a substitute for curled hair in stuffing.	W. Baker	Utica, N. Y	May 30, 1842	2, 654
Beds, mattresses, &c., Filling for	J. C. Wightman	Newton, Mass	Dec. 2, 1873	145, 140
Beds, Means of ventilating, cooling, and warming.	D. E. Somes	Washington, D. C	Nov. 16, 1869	96, 989
Beds, Mode of warming	P. Lannay	Baltimore, Md	Nov. 11, 1823	....
Beds, Mosquito canopy for	W. B. Ellis	Boston, Mass	Feb. 23, 1869	87, 154
Beds or lounges, Converting the backs of car-seats into	H. B. Myer	Buffalo, N. Y	Sept. 19, 1854	11, 699
Beds, Palm-leaf for stuffing	J. C. Smith	Cambridgeport, Mass	Apr. 3, 1835	....
Beds, seats, &c., Expanding bottom for	E. K. Garretson	Ottawa, Ill	Aug. 25, 1868	81, 358
Beds, sofas, &c., Spring foundation for	J. H. Crane	Charlestown, Mass	Feb. 7, 1860	27, 037
Beds to tents, Attaching	E. Lynch	Buffalo, N. Y	Jan. 28, 1862	34, 258
Bedstead	W. R. Bacall	Boston, Mass	Aug. 6, 1867	67, 397
Bedstead	T. B. Baldwin	Marshall, Tex	Aug. 8, 1871	117, 724
Bedstead	J. H. Barth	Indianapolis, Ind	Jan. 10, 1854	10, 418
Bedstead	W. Bell	Lexington, Ky	Nov. 7, 1826	....
Bedstead	R. Belt	Centreville, Ky	Feb. 22, 1831	....
Bedstead	J. H. Belter	New York, N. Y	Aug. 19, 1856	15, 552
Bedstead	B. F. Berry	Utica, N. Y	Apr. 22, 1835	....
Bedstead	G. Beurer	Brooklyn, N. Y	Feb. 11, 1868	74, 193
Bedstead	W. H. Bramble	Springfield, Ohio	Apr. 19, 1859	23, 659
Bedstead	W. E. Briggs	Sparta, Wis	Aug. 13, 1872	130, 355
Bedstead	S. Caro	Washington, D. C	Dec. 31, 1872	134, 359
Bedstead	J. C. Climo	Philadelphia, Pa	Mar. 17, 1868	75, 527
Bedstead	J. C. Climo	Philadelphia, Pa	June 9, 1868	78, 647
Bedstead	G. G. Cochran	Brooklyn, N. Y	May 14, 1867	64, 632
Bedstead	E. Coleman	New Bedford, Mass	Oct. 31, 1834	....
Bedstead	N. Colver	Boston, Mass	Apr. 24, 1849	6, 386
Bedstead	I. Cooper	Baltimore, Md	Feb. 22, 1825	....
Bedstead	J. R. Coxe	Philadelphia, Pa	Oct. 16, 1812	....
Bedstead	H. B. Coyle	Philadelphia, Pa	May 28, 1872	127, 312
Bedstead	C. W. Curtiss	New Haven, Conn	Dec. 12, 1842	2, 881
Bedstead	S. Davis	Catskill, N. Y	Dec. 29, 1826	....
Bedstead	W. Deckman	Canton, Ohio	Aug. 21, 1860	29, 678
Bedstead	I. Deyo	Naples, N. Y	June 6, 1871	115, 716
Bedstead	C. P. Dorman	Galesburgh, Ill	Nov. 14, 1865	50, 920
Bedstead	D. E. Dugan	Springville, Pa	Dec. 7, 1869	97, 619
Bedstead	E. Eaton	Cincinnati, Ohio	Sept. 27, 1859	25, 563
Bedstead	I. Eaton	Mount Gilead, Va	Dec. 31, 1833	....
Bedstead	S. Espach	Cincinnati, Ohio	Dec. 27, 1859	26, 577
Bedstead	D. M. Estey	Brattleborough, Vt	Nov. 16, 1869	96, 787
Bedstead	H. H. Evarts	Chicago, Ill	Feb. 22, 1870	100, 133
Bedstead	F. G. Ford	Bridgeton, N. J	Mar. 25, 1873	137, 191
Bedstead	A. Foster	New York, N. Y	July 2, 1861	32, 687
Bedstead	W. Gambel	Baltimore, Md	Aug. 25, 1831	....
Bedstead	C. H. Gould	Concord, N. H	Sept. 2, 1856	15, 648
Bedstead	J. R. Guy	Springfield, Ohio	Oct. 11, 1859	25, 732
Bedstead	T. Q. Hall	Indianapolis, Ind	June 14, 1870	104, 143
Bedstead	J. Harding	Detroit, Mich	Sept. 28, 1869	95, 223
Bedstead	J. Hart	Lebanon, Ky	Mar. 3, 1840	1, 504
Bedstead	J. Henfrey	United States Army	Sept. 23, 1862	36, 519
Bedstead	F. Hesz	Cincinnati, Ohio	June 12, 1855	13, 034
Bedstead	P. Hinds	Kendall's Mill's, Me	June 16, 1857	17, 569
Bedstead	B. Hinkley	Utica, N. Y	July 5, 1848	5, 656
Bedstead	B. Hinkley	Troy, N. Y	Dec. 25, 1849	6, 972
Bedstead	B. Hinkley	Troy, N. Y	Dec. 11, 1855	13, 969
Bedstead	B. Hinkley	Troy, N. Y	July 26, 1859	24, 873
Bedstead	J. Hoert	New York, N. Y	May 28, 1867	65, 222
Bedstead	J. Horner	New Brunswick, N. J	July 30, 1867	67, 304
Bedstead	E. Howe, jr	Brooklyn, N. Y	Aug. 26, 1856	15, 609
Bedstead	T. Howe	Cambridgeport, Mass	July 17, 1855	13, 265
Bedstead	S. Huddleston	Cottage Grove, Ind	July 1, 1856	15, 235
Bedstead	B. Humphreville and J. King	Morristown, N. J	Dec, 17, 1834	....
Bedstead	W. Huntress	South Berwick, Me	June 10, 1856	15, 076
Bedstead	S. Hyde	Arcadia, N. Y	May 2, 1828	....
Bedstead	H. Ingraham	Naples, N. Y	Aug. 3, 1869	93, 305
Bedstead	R. Jenkins	Covington, Ky	June 5, 1860	28, 582
Bedstead	D. H. Jennings and J. Bounds	Bridgeport, Conn	June 22, 1869	91, 749
Bedstead	G. A. Jeremiah	New York, N. Y	Mar. 14, 1871	112, 716
Bedstead	W. B. Johns	United States Army	June 1, 1858	20, 435
Bedstead	L. J. Johnson	Cleveland, Ohio	July 25, 1871	117, 424
Bedstead	B. Judd	New London, Conn	May 25, 1832	....
Bedstead	C. Kniseley	Meadville, Pa	June 16, 1836	....
Bedstead	L. C. Kuhn	....	Aug. 10, 1791	....
Bedstead	M. Lally	East Palestine, Ohio	May 30, 1871	115, 485
Bedstead	N. Lamphear	Monmouth, Ill	June 29, 1858	20, 723
Bedstead	J. Leigh	Edgefield, S. C	Aug. 7, 1860	29, 498
Bedstead	J. Maguire	Philadelphia, Pa	Jan. 15, 1836	....
Bedstead	D. Mannel	Lancaster, Pa	Apr. 14, 1863	38, 202
Bedstead	R. Martin	Chicago, Ill	Feb. 23, 1869	87, 273
Bedstead	R. Maxwell	Tucker County, Va	Oct. 19, 1858	21, 841
Bedstead	J. McClintic	Chambersburgh, Pa	Nov. 2, 1825	....
Bedstead	S. McQuerns and B. M. Lyon	Abbeville, S. C	Mar. 8, 1859	23, 222
Bedstead	J. C. Merritt	West Point, N. Y	June 14, 1870	104, 182
Bedstead	C. Messenger	Warren, Ohio	July 26, 1859	24, 880
Bedstead	R. Miller	Glasgow, Ky	May 23, 1834	....
Bedstead	A. Moon	Bristol, Wis	July 1, 1856	15, 249

Index of patents issued from the United States Patent Office from 1790 *to* 1873, *inclusive*—Continued.

Invention.	Inventor.	Residence.	Date.	No.
Bedstead	E. Morris	Burlington, N. J	Dec. 9, 1873	145, 305
Bedstead	J. Morris	Derby, Conn	July 8, 1843	3, 162
Bedstead	C. F. Nahmmacher	Pittsburgh, Pa	June 13, 1871	115, 836
Bedstead	L. Newcomb, jr	New Bedford, Mass	Nov. 11, 1851	8, 516
Bedstead	S. Oberholzer	Wheaton, Ill	Apr. 30, 1872	126, 226
Bedstead	H. D. Olds	Cedar Rapids, Iowa	May 13, 1873	138, 756
Bedstead	D. O'Leary	Hubbard, Ohio	Aug. 20, 1872	130, 655
Bedstead	H. Pace, sr	Cincinnati, Ohio	Dec. 10, 1846	4, 880
Bedstead	I. Pedrick	Bridgeton, N. J	May 21, 1867	64, 901
Bedstead	J. E. Pencille	Lockport, N. Y	July 13, 1869	92, 643
Bedstead	C. Perley	New York, N. Y	Feb. 27, 1866	52, 879
Bedstead	D. Powles	Baltimore, Md	Oct. 31, 1821	....
Bedstead	D. U. Pratt	Cleveland, Ohio	Feb. 3, 1863	37, 589
Bedstead	P. Prettyman	Georgetown, Del	Mar. 31, 1834	....
Bedstead	P. Prettyman	Georgetown, Del	Sept. 26, 1835	....
Bedstead	B. S. Pringle	Barnesville, Ga	Sept. 4, 1860	29, 913
Bedstead	H. B. Ramsey	Rockville, Ind	Oct. 25, 1870	108, 729
Bedstead	D. C. Raub	Saint Louis, Mo	May 6, 1873	138, 582
Bedstead	H. Reisinger	York, Pa	Aug. 18, 1832	....
Bedstead	L. W. Roath	Lexington, Ohio	Aug. 4, 1868	80, 668
Bedstead	R. Roberts	Saint Paul, Ind	Nov. 5, 1867	70, 618
Bedstead	E. Rogers and M. Pearson	Essex County, Mass	June 11, 1829	....
Bedstead	A. Rothwell	Washington, D. C	July 2, 1867	66, 398
Bedstead	I. Russell	Dedham, Mass	Sept. 16, 1851	8, 358
Bedstead	H. W. Sabin	Canandaigua, N. Y	July 1, 1851	8, 190
Bedstead	D. W. Smead	Peru, Ill	Oct. 19, 1852	9, 347
Bedstead	J. J. Smith and J. H. Pugh	Philadelphia, Pa	Aug. 26, 1856	15, 621
Bedstead	G. Snowden	Hudson, N. J	Feb. 14, 1871	111, 785
Bedstead	N. W. Speers	Cincinnati, Ohio	Apr. 27, 1858	20, 097
Bedstead	S. Springer	Chicago, Ill	Dec. 12, 1871	121, 734
Bedstead	A. Stark	Topeka, Kans	Aug. 22, 1865	49, 568
Bedstead	W. St. Charles	Fairmont, Va	June 8, 1858	20, 518
Bedstead	W. B. Stewart	Brooklyn, N. Y	Aug. 27, 1867	68, 255
Bedstead	W. L. Thomas	Middlebury, Ohio	Apr. 7, 1868	76, 553
Bedstead	P. Thompson	Springfield, Ohio	Apr. 5, 1859	23, 513
Bedstead	W. S. Todd	Mechanicsville, Iowa	Sept. 14, 1858	21, 527
Bedstead	C. Van Noy	Lexington, Ky	Jan. 10, 1832	....
Bedstead	G. Vaughan, jr	Philadelphia, Pa	Sept. 18, 1833	....
Bedstead	S. Walker	Boston, Mass	Mar. 20, 1860	27, 585
Bedstead	T. Wall	Jones' Station, Ohio	June 5, 1860	28, 621
Bedstead	W. M. Ward and P. Bennage	Eureka, Ill	Sept. 22, 1868	82, 457
Bedstead	C. A. Warner	Bristol, Conn	June 29, 1858	20, 750
Bedstead	W. White	Portsmouth, Va	Sept. 25, 1855	13, 607
Bedstead	H. K. Whitner	Philadelphia, Pa	Mar. 9, 1869	87, 742
Bedstead	S. Willard	Cincinnati, Ohio	Aug. 1, 1854	11, 449
Bedstead	P. Williamson	Baltimore, Md	Dec. 6, 1821	....
Bedstead	P. Williamson	Baltimore, Md	Oct. 17, 1822	....
Bedstead	D. Witt	Hubbardston, Mass	Feb. 9, 1869	86, 892
Bedstead	B. F. Woodside	Atlanta, Ga	Aug. 20, 1867	68, 023
Bedstead	W. Zaiser	Cincinnati, Ohio	Nov. 19, 1850	7, 791
Bedstead	J. P. Zeller	South Bend, Ind	Apr. 9, 1872	125, 653
Bedstead, Adjustable	W. O. Reid	Vienna, N. C	Mar. 1, 1870	100, 324
Bedstead, Adjustable bolster for	J. Hofmann	Chicago, Ill	May 16, 1871	114, 819
Bedstead, Alarm	J. C. House	Lowville, N. Y	July 17, 1855	13, 263
Bedstead and bed-bottom	F. G. Ford	Baltimore, Md	Feb. 14, 1871	111, 832
Bedstead and bed-bottom	E. Krieghoff	Rochester, N. Y	July 9, 1867	66, 598
Bedstead and bed for the sick and lame	J. Baily	Philadelphia, Pa	Mar. 18, 1825	....
Bedstead and cot	V. L. Baker	Richmond, Va	Aug. 2, 1870	105, 885
Bedstead and crib, Folding	R. S. Titcomb	Gloversville, N. Y	Dec. 10, 1867	72, 122
Bedstead and crib, Folding	R. S. Titcomb	Gloversville, N. Y	Apr. 28, 1868	77, 334
Bedstead and lounge	J. Dourson	Columbus, Ohio	Dec. 28, 1869	98, 359
Bedstead and lounge	R. Jewell	New York, N. Y	Apr. 12, 1870	101, 882
Bedstead and mattress	E. Cherrington	Boston, Mass	Nov. 23, 1835	....
Bedstead and quilting-frame	J. Park	Joliet, Ill	Sept. 8, 1868	81, 936
Bedstead and sacking-bottom, Portable	S. Whitmarsh	Northampton, Mass	Oct. 8, 1850	7, 712
Bedstead and sofa or chair	J. S. McCurdy	New York, N. Y	June 29, 1869	92, 075
Bedstead and spring bed-bottom	W. McArthur	Philadelphia, Pa	Jan. 31, 1871	111, 364
Bedstead and table	G. Wilson	Chicago, Ill	Sept. 20, 1870	107, 580
Bedstead and table combined	O. Lafreniere	New York, N. Y	Sept. 15, 1863	39, 933
Bedstead and table fastener	J. M. Baird	Wheeling, W. Va	May 3, 1870	102, 473
Bedstead and trunk combined	F. Boissard and S. Conrath	New York, N. Y	Aug. 27, 1861	33, 128
Bedstead and wardrobe combined	J. A. Morgan	Bloomfield, Iowa	Mar. 12, 1872	124, 609
Bedstead, Barrack or hospital	C. S. Snead	Louisville, Ky	Dec. 14, 1869	97, 981
Bedstead, Bisected	P. Breasted	Green County, N. Y	Feb. 21, 1826	....
Bedstead, Book-case	E. Putnam	Boston, Mass	Sept. 1, 1868	81, 687
Bedstead-bottom	S. E. Hartwell	New York, N. Y	Oct. 26, 1858	21, 878
Bedstead-bottom	G. Schott	New York, N. Y	Dec. 26, 1865	51, 755
Bedstead-bottom	J. C. Stuck	Boston, Mass	Aug. 2, 1864	43, 719
Bedstead-bottom, Spring	G. Schott and J. Loudon	New York, N. Y	June 7, 1859	24, 333
Bedstead, Bureau	D. Arnaud	Boston, Mass	Dec. 1, 1868	84, 466
Bedstead, Bureau	W. F. Browne	New York, N. Y	Aug. 27, 1872	130, 789
Bedstead, Bureau	L. Derome	San Francisco, Cal	Mar. 31, 1863	38, 035
Bedstead, Bureau	F. Hoffman	New York, N. Y	Oct. 26, 1858	21, 926
Bedstead, Bureau	H. W. Kingman	New York, N. Y	Oct. 12, 1844	3, 792
Bedstead, Bureau	A. Parker	New York, N. Y	July 21, 1868	80, 208
Bedstead, Bureau	F. C. Payne	New York, N. Y	Nov. 1, 1864	44, 887
Bedstead, Bureau	E. Shackford and D. Arnaud	Boston, Mass	Apr. 14, 1868	76, 664
Bedstead, Bureau	M. Sulzbacher	New York, N. Y	Feb. 18, 1868	74, 628
Bedstead, Bureau	H. L. Thistle	New York, N. Y	May 10, 1859	23, 960
Bedstead, Bureau	D. Trefry	Boston, Mass	June 22, 1869	91, 688
Bedstead, Bureau	E. Whitney	Boston, Mass	July 14, 1857	17, 818
Bedstead, bureau, and stand combined	A. and L. A. Parker	Girard, Kans	Apr. 4, 1871	113, 692
Bedstead, Cabinet	S S. Burr	Dedham, Mass	Oct. 26, 1869	96, 196
Bedstead, Cabinet	S. S. Burr	Boston, Mass	Sept. 26, 1871	119, 312
Bedstead, Cabinet	W. H. Dutton	Philadelphia, Pa	Apr. 7, 1868	76, 423
Bedstead, Cabinet	M. Crosby	Boston, Mass	June 18, 1872	127, 962
Bedstead, Cabinet	S. C. Maine	Boston, Mass	June 15, 1869	91, 244
Bedstead, Cabinet	A. J. Roberts	Boston, Mass	July 26, 1870	105, 850

Index of patents issued from the United States Patent Office from 1790 *to* 1873, *inclusive*—Continued.

Invention.	Inventor.	Residence.	Date.	No.
Bedstead, Cabinet	D. T. Robinson	Boston, Mass	Aug. 10, 1869	93, 556
Bedstead, Cabinet	W. H. and L. Young	Boston, Mass	July 7, 1868	79, 622
Bedstead, Camp	E. J. Evericks	Paris, France	Mar. 1, 1870	100, 386
Bedstead, Camp	C. Fostensen, H. Iverson, and C. J. Skow.	Racine, Wis	July 11, 1865	48, 671
Bedstead, Camp	W. A. Mauran	Boston, Mass	Aug. 20, 1861	33, 124
Bedstead, Camp	A. D. McCoy	Alexandria, La	Dec. 27, 1870	110, 485
Bedstead, Camp	A. Polino	Paris, France	Dec. 10, 1861	33, 901
Bedstead, Camp	W. C. Shaw and J. Stalcup	Philadelphia, Pa., and Wilmington, Del.	Sept. 10, 1850	7, 633
Bedstead, Camp	J. White	Cleveland, Ohio	Nov. 12, 1861	33, 724
Bedstead, Canopy	A. M. Rodgers	Brooklyn, N. Y	Mar. 22, 1870	101, 165
Bedstead, chair, secretary, and wardrobe	W. Reckards	New York, N. Y	May 12, 1868	77, 841
Bedstead-clamp	T. B. Gregory	Champaign, Ill	Sept. 27, 1870	107, 774
Bedstead combined with other furniture, Wardrobe	H. R. and J. L. Plimpton	Hampton County, Mass	Mar. 25, 1856	14, 514
Bedstead, Cot	S. Clark	New York, N. Y	Mar. 23, 1836	....
Bedstead, Cot	P. Williamson	Baltimore, Md	Nov. 11, 1830	....
Bedstead cord-pin	J. T. Bever	Hainesville, Mo	July 19, 1859	24, 788
Bedstead crib-attachment	E. F. Bryan	Savannah, Ga	Jan. 14, 1873	134, 847
Bedstead crib-attachment	F. Ryder	Great Falls, N. H	Aug. 13, 1872	130, 443
Bedstead crib-attachment	B. Snyder	Philadelphia, Pa	June 10, 1873	139, 829
Bedstead crib-attachment	M. W. Tarbell and J. H. P. Inslee.	Jersey City, N. J	Feb. 25, 1873	136, 280
Bedstead crib-attachment	H. R. Tracy	New York, N. Y	Feb. 25, 1868	74, 865
Bedstead crib-attachment	J. H. L. Wilson	Auburn, Kans	Apr. 4, 1871	113, 382
Bedstead, Double-tenon draw-key	S. Cooper	Chambersburgh, Pa	Nov. 5, 1825	....
Bedstead drapery fastening	G. W. Watrous	Hartford, Conn	July 19, 1859	24, 837
Bedstead drapery fastener or suspender	R. B. Pullan	Cincinnati, Ohio	June 18, 1861	32, 585
Bedstead, Drum-sacking	H. Wilbur	Newburyport, Mass	June 16, 1828	....
Bedstead, Easy-draft	P. T. Walcott	Monmouth County, N. J	Jan. 6, 1812	....
Bedstead, Elevated	D. Burnett	Bedford Station, N. Y	Aug. 6, 1867	67, 494
Bedstead, Expanding	N. Cross	New York, N. Y	Dec. 16, 1862	37, 153
Bedstead, Extension	C. S. Debow	New York, N. Y	Apr. 18, 1846	4, 463
Bedstead, Extension	J. Holzman	New York, N. Y	July 23, 1867	67, 055
Bedstead, Extension	A. Iske	Lancaster, Pa	Nov. 10, 1863	40, 564
Bedstead, Extension	F. Menzer	San Francisco, Cal	Feb. 1, 1870	99, 455
Bedstead, Fan ventilating	F. Moore	Panola, Miss	Oct. 23, 1860	30, 492
Bedstead-fastener	D. Babcock	Seneca Falls, N. Y	Feb. 3, 1863	37, 560
Bedstead-fastener	J. C. Cline	Philadelphia, Pa	May 5, 1868	77, 457
Bedstead-fastener	J. Doering	Philadelphia, Pa	Apr. 6, 1869	88, 617
Bedstead-fastener	E. S. Earley	Philadelphia, Pa	Apr. 20, 1869	89, 209
Bedstead-fastener	J. Janeway	Indianapolis, Ind	Aug. 4, 1868	80, 743
Bedstead-fastener	A. B. Sheaffer	Ephrata, Pa	May 24, 1870	103, 511
Bedstead-fastener	H. Swinford	Mifflinburgh, Pa	Jan. 18, 1870	99, 030
Bedstead-fastener	H. S. Wing	Plattsburgh, N. Y	May 18, 1869	90, 320
Bedstead-fastening	J. W. Adams	Boston, Mass	Sept. 10, 1846	4, 748
Bedstead-fastening	E. H. Badger	Petersburgh, Va	Apr. 3, 1826	....
Bedstead-fastening	J. M. Baird	Wheeling, W. Va	Oct. 7, 1873	143, 431
Bedstead-fastening	G. W. Baker	Cochranton, Pa	May 24, 1859	24, 085
Bedstead-fastening	D. Ball	Sandy Hill, N. Y	Apr. 16, 1842	2, 562
Bedstead-fastening	D. Ball	Albany, N. Y	Apr. 10, 1847	5, 060
Bedstead-fastening	E. R. Ball	Kalamazoo, Mich	Apr. 4, 1854	10, 731
Bedstead-fastening	E. T. Barlow	San Francisco, Cal	Aug. 29, 1871	118, 424
Bedstead-fastening	J. Barnes	Burlington, Vt	Apr. 20, 1869	89, 116
Bedstead-fastening	W. S. Bartle	Newark, N. Y	Jan. 29, 1867	61, 504
Bedstead-fastening	C. E. Bander	Cleveland, Ohio	Jan. 18, 1853	9, 541
Bedstead-fastening	G. W. Baynes, T. Hinty, and M. Jackson.	Glenville, Va	Aug. 16, 1853	9, 931
Bedstead-fastening	A. Bechtol	Berkeley Springs, Va	Oct. 9, 1860	30, 286
Bedstead-fastening	W. Bell	Lexington, Ky	Feb. 15, 1838	606
Bedstead-fastening	J. Benjamen	Naples, N. Y	July 26, 1870	105, 771
Bedstead-fastening	J. Bodefer	Cincinnati, Ohio	Apr. 10, 1855	12, 693
Bedstead-fastening	L. G. Bradford	Plymouth, Mass	Sept. 3, 1872	130, 973
Bedstead-fastening	L. G. Bradford	Plymouth, Mass	Feb. 25, 1873	136, 301
Bedstead-fastening	C. Bradway	Maquoketa, Iowa	Nov. 30, 1869	97, 270
Bedstead-fastening	H. Branch	New York, N. Y	Apr. 18, 1832	....
Bedstead-fastening	J. Brooke	Baltimore, Ohio	May 15, 1849	6, 451
Bedstead-fastening	G. Burket	Croghan, Ohio	June 8, 1858	20, 478
Bedstead-fastening	L. W. Buxton	Nashua, N. H	Apr. 5, 1859	23, 525
Bedstead-fastening	W. H. Carter	Candor, N. Y	Sept. 6, 1870	106, 997
Bedstead-fastening	A. N. and A. Case	Gustavus, Ohio	Mar. 1, 1853	9, 598
Bedstead-fastening	W. Clark	Weymouth, Ohio	Mar. 9, 1858	19, 544
Bedstead-fastening	C. S. Comins	Lowell, Mass	Jan. 3, 1871	110 632
Bedstead-fastening	C. C. Coolidge	Boston, Mass	May 7, 1850	7, 339
Bedstead-fastening	A. S. Dalbey	Richmond, Ind	Feb. 16, 1869	86, 909
Bedstead-fastening	J. Doering	Philadelphia, Pa	Sept. 13, 1864	44, 167
Bedstead-fastening	J. Drayton	Buffalo, N. Y	Sept. 26, 1854	11, 722
Bedstead-fastening	M. Elder	Mansfield, Ohio	Jan. 22, 1850	7, 035
Bedstead-fastening	W. H. Elliot	New York, N. Y	Nov. 20, 1866	59, 794
Bedstead-fastening	W. H. Elliot	New York, N. Y	Nov. 20, 1866	59, 795
Bedstead-fastening	W. H. Elliot	New York, N. Y	Nov. 20, 1866	59, 825
Bedstead fastening	W. H. Elliot	New York, N. Y	Aug. 3, 1869	93, 188
Bedstead-fastening	J. W. Elstun	Indianapolis, Ind	May 28, 1872	127, 226
Bedstead-fastening	H. C. Ernst	Vandalia, Ill	Feb. 23, 1841	1, 991
Bedstead-fastening	B. Essig	Sacramento, Cal	Mar. 10, 1868	75, 254
Bedstead-fastening	E. E. Everitt	Philadelphia, Pa	Mar. 29, 1859	23, 359
Bedstead-fastening	S. Fahs and A. H. Lochman	York, Pa	Oct. 30, 1847	5, 342
Bedstead-fastening	C. H. Fessenden	Candor, N. Y	Mar. 22, 1870	100 993
Bedstead-fastening	J. R. Finley and L. Martin	Delphi, Ind	Apr. 16, 1872	125, 801
Bedstead-fastening	J. Fowler	Pittsburgh, Pa	July 11, 1842	2, 715
Bedstead-fastening	S. A. Frayer	Coxsackie, N. Y	June 6, 1871	115, 725
Bedstead-fastening	P. H. Frelinghousen	Jonestown, Pa	Feb. 19, 1867	62, 262
Bedstead fastening	E. I. Gazzam	Pittsburgh, Pa	Jan. 23, 1846	4, 360
Bedstead fastening	C. M. Gilbert	Philadelphia, Pa	Apr. 17, 1866	53, 972
Bedstead-fastening	C. M. Gilbert	Philadelphia, Pa	Sept. 22, 1868	82, 305
Bedstead-fastening	C. M. Gilbert	Philadelphia, Pa	May 14, 1872	126, 630
Bedstead-fastening	E. F. Gilbert	Lyons, N. Y	Oct. 18, 1870	108, 472
Bedstead-fastening	S. Goetz	Reed's Mills, Ohio	Feb. 7, 1871	111, 528

Index of patents issued from the United States Patent Office from 1790 *to* 1873, *inclusive*—Continued.

Invention.	Inventor.	Residence.	Date.	No.
Bedstead-fastening	E. G. Gory	Cincinnati, Ohio	Mar. 19, 1872	124, 735
Bedstead-fastening	A. Grillet	Philadelphia, Pa	July 26, 1870	105, 798
Bedstead-fastening	H. Gross	Hoboken, N. J	Jan. 2, 1872	122, 457
Bedstead-fastening	J. Guild	Cincinnati, Ohio	Dec. 20, 1843	3, 387
Bedstead-fastening	S. Harris	Philadelphia, Pa	Dec. 23, 1856	16, 276
Bedstead-fastening	J. Haslet and C. Devitt	Irville, Ohio	May 9, 1846	4, 508
Bedstead-fastening	J. C. Helme	Wilkesbarre, Pa	June 27, 1848	5, 649
Bedstead-fastening	B. Hinkley	Utica, N. Y	Dec. 9, 1846	4, 878
Bedstead-fastening	W. Hinman	Elkhart, Ind	Apr. 15, 1856	14, 660
Bedstead-fastening	E. G. Hopkins	Pen Yan, N. Y	Nov. 15, 1859	26, 104
Bedstead-fastening	S. Hovey	Painesville, Ohio	Aug. 28, 1849	6, 674
Bedstead-fastening	R. Hubbard	Milton, Ind	May 15, 1860	28, 276
Bedstead-fastening	J. C. and F. J. Jackson	Rochester, N. Y., and Danbury, Conn.	May 5, 1868	77, 491
Bedstead-fastening	L. L. Jackson	Paterson, N. J	Aug. 13, 1867	67, 766
Bedstead-fastening	J. C. Jeffries	Mount Vernon, Ind	June 28, 1859	24, 562
Bedstead-fastening	J. Johnson	Geneseo, N. Y	June 29, 1852	9, 073
Bedstead-fastening	W. Johnston	Appleton, Wis	Mar. 3, 1868	75, 025
Bedstead-fastening	W. Johnston	Appleton, Wis	Dec. 15, 1868	84, 949
Bedstead-fastening	J. A. and A. F. Jones	Lexington, Ky	Aug. 1, 1848	5, 689
Bedstead-fastening	S. Jones	San Francisco, Cal	June 11, 1872	127, 694
Bedstead-fastening	J. R. Kain and S. Lewis	Tiffin, Ohio	May 6, 1851	8, 076
Bedstead-fastening	L. Kent	Dorset, Vt	Sept. 12, 1838	911
Bedstead-fastening	J. Knipe	New York, N. Y	Jan. 8, 1842	2, 415
Bedstead-fastening	J. Lemman	Cincinnati, Ohio	Oct. 2, 1866	58, 437
Bedstead-fastening	S. Lewis	Tiffin, Ohio	June 27, 1848	5, 650
Bedstead-fastening	S. Lewis	Tiffin, Ohio	Nov. 18, 1856	16, 093
Bedstead-fastening	S. Lewis	Tiffin, Ohio	Dec. 13, 1864	45, 417
Bedstead-fastening	J. Maguire	Trenton, N. J	Feb. 19, 1867	62, 212
Bedstead-fastening	J. F. Mancha	Ridgely, Md	Jan. 28, 1873	135, 279
Bedstead-fastening	P. Maulding and J. W. Fraley	Marshall, Tex	Aug. 16, 1870	106, 382
Bedstead-fastening	I. M. May	Anderson, Ind	Sept. 14, 1858	21, 511
Bedstead-fastening	L. May	Columbus, Ga	May 28, 1872	127, 255
Bedstead-fastening	P. McIntyre	Norwich, Conn	May 25, 1869	90, 568
Bedstead-fastening	I. McLaughlin	Sunderland, Vt	Apr. 28, 1836	
Bedstead-fastening	W. H. McPherson	Nashville, Tenn	Dec. 12, 1871	121, 726
Bedstead-fastening	W. E. Merrill and T. Tupper	Nashua, N. H	Dec. 13, 1853	10, 313
Bedstead-fastening	E. Mets and W. B. Geddes	Rochester, N. Y	Nov. 22, 1870	109, 538
Bedstead-fastening	P. Miles	New Haven, Conn	May 15, 1860	28, 326
Bedstead-fastening	H. Miller	South Bend, Ind	Aug. 7, 1849	6, 630
Bedstead-fastening	J. E. Milliken	Bridgeton, Me	Mar. 10, 1868	75, 445
Bedstead-fastening	T. W. Moore	New York, N. Y	Nov. 14, 1871	120, 893
Bedstead-fastening	T. W. Moore	New York, N. Y	June 11, 1872	127, 786
Bedstead-fastening	J. Morrison	McArthurstown, Ohio	Oct. 29, 1850	7, 743
Bedstead-fastening	J. Moulton	Ossipee, N. H	Dec. 11, 1849	6, 940
Bedstead-fastening	I. W. Moyer	Utica, N. Y	May 15, 1847	5, 117
Bedstead fastening	H. B. Nash	Kingsbury, N. Y	Dec. 4, 1847	5, 387
Bedstead-fastening	A. S. Newnouse	Richmond County, Ga	June 15, 1852	9, 034
Bedstead-fastening	T. O'Keefe	Appleton, Wis	June 1, 1869	90, 776
Bedstead-fastening	J. P. Owen	Norwalk, Ohio	Dec. 11, 1849	6, 944
Bedstead-fastening	C. H. Parker	New Geneva, Pa	June 11, 1850	7, 428
Bedstead-fastening	M. Pechman	New York, N. Y	May 14, 1867	64, 699
Bedstead-fastening	G. Porter	Cincinnati, Ohio	Dec. 30, 1833	
Bedstead-fastening	P. Post	New Haven, Conn	June 12, 1838	780
Bedstead-fastening	R. M. Price	Leesville, Ohio	Apr. 18, 1871	113, 925
Bedstead-fastening	W. H. Price	Philadelphia, Pa	Jan. 3, 1854	10, 378
Bedstead-fastening	C. D. Purdy	La Porte, Ind	Jan. 1, 1869	90, 780
Bedstead-fastening	C. D. Purdy	La Porte, Ind	Sept. 27, 1870	107, 812
Bedstead fastening	R. Ramsey	Wilmington, Pa	Feb. 19, 1850	7, 107
Bedstead-fastening	A. H. Rennie	Binghamton, N. Y	Mar. 19, 1867	63, 095
Bedstead-fastening	J. Richman	Lancaster, Ohio	Dec. 28, 1832	
Bedstead-fastening	O. Robinson	Rochester, N. Y	Dec. 28, 1858	22, 456
Bedstead-fastening	A. Roda	Rochester, N. Y	Jan. 24, 1860	26, 924
Bedstead-fastening	J. Rodefer	Cincinnati, Ohio	Dec. 18, 1839	1, 431
Bedstead-fastening	W. H. Sabin	New Milford, Pa	May 12, 1840	1, 603
Bedstead-fastening	J. D. Sanborn	Bennington, N. Y	Apr. 3, 1849	6, 275
Bedstead-fastening	J. C. Santee	Hughesville, Pa	Jan. 24, 1865	46, 029
Bedstead-fastening	J. Scheplor	Lambertville, N. J	Feb. 14, 1871	111, 878
Bedstead-fastening	A. Schlingman	West Alexandria, Ohio	Apr. 30, 1867	64, 257
Bedstead-fastening	I. A. Sergeant	Hamilton, Ohio	July 13, 1852	9, 122
Bedstead-fastening	W. Shaw	Clarion, Pa	Mar. 30, 1852	8, 845
Bedstead-fastening	W. Shaw	Clarion, Pa	Aug. 17, 1852	9, 203
Bedstead-fastening	J. Simpson	Newark, Ohio	Apr. 2, 1872	125, 342
Bedstead-fastening	H. T. Smith	Washington, D. C	Aug. 14, 1860	29, 628
Bedstead-fastening	I. Smith	Chagrin Falls, Ohio	Oct. 25, 1845	4, 243
Bedstead-fastening	J. J. Smith	Philadelphia, Pa	Mar. 29, 1864	42, 120
Bedstead-fastening	W. Stevens	Tarentum, Pa	Dec. 7, 1869	97, 722
Bedstead-fastening	J. M. Stewart	Newark, N. J	Aug. 6, 1872	130, 328
Bedstead-fastening	R. H. St. John	Columbus, Ohio	July 11, 1854	11, 305
Bedstead-fastening	D. Hotlemeyer	Hancock, Md	May 29, 1849	6, 483
Bedstead-fastening	G. Sugg and W. Metz	Chicago, Ill	Apr. 23, 1867	64, 048
Bedstead-fastening	G. Sugg and W. Metz	Chicago, Ill	Mar. 2, 1869	87, 380
Bedstead-fastening	W. Swift and W. Ottiwell	New Bedford, Mass	Sept. 11, 1828	
Bedstead-fastening	E. S. Taylor	Cleveland, Ohio	Mar. 1, 1853	9, 604
Bedstead fastening	J. Taylor	Macon, Ga	Sept. 4, 1849	6, 687
Bedstead-fastening	J. C. Turner	Newark, N. J	June 7, 1870	104, 082
Bedstead-fastening	J. H. Waite	Orange, Mass	Sept. 6, 1870	107, 131
Bedstead-fastening	J. B. Wardwell	Georgetown, D. C	June 18, 1867	65, 970
Bedstead-fastening	C. Wolf	Rochester, N. Y	June 10, 1873	139, 844
Bedstead-fastening	C. Wolf	Rochester, N. Y	Sept. 16, 1873	142, 973
Bedstead-fastening	C. Wolf	Rochester, N. Y	Dec. 2, 1873	145, 266
Bedstead-fastening	E. S. Wright	Buffalo, N. Y	July 6, 1858	20, 839
Bedstead-fastening	J. W. Yothers	Spruce Grove, Pa	Oct. 30, 1855	13, 736
Bedstead-fastening	N. Zins	Evansville, Ind	Nov. 30, 1869	97, 468
Bedstead, Fastening of cast-iron	A. C. Semple	New York, N. Y	Feb. 23, 1858	19, 451
Bedstead-fastening, Plug	J. J. Smith	Philadelphia, Pa	June 7, 1859	24, 361
Bedstead, Folding	C. P. Alling, jr	Sylvan, Wis	Nov. 24, 1868	84, 337
Bedstead, Folding	D. Bach and K. Krenkel	New York, N. Y	Feb. 28, 1860	27, 263

Index of patents issued from the United States Patent Office from 1790 to 1873, inclusive—Continued.

Invention.	Inventor.	Residence.	Date.	No.
Bedstead, Folding	V. Baker	Weedsport, N. Y	July 11, 1848	5,662
Bedstead, Folding	A. G. Bayles, J. W. H. Carroll, and Y. D. Miner.	New York and Williamsburgh, N. Y.	May 13, 1873	138,840
Bedstead, Folding	J. Binder	Chelsea, Mass	Jan. 15, 1850	7,014
Bedstead, Folding	T. B. Bleecker	New York, N. Y	Apr. 17, 1847	5,072
Bedstead, Folding	W. H. Buel	Laughlintown, Pa	Feb. 15, 1870	99,755
Bedstead, Folding	S. S. Burr	Dedham, Mass	Feb. 18, 1868	74,494
Bedstead, Folding	E. Cotty	Brooklyn, N. Y	May 1, 1860	28,127
Bedstead, Folding	M. Crosby	Boston, Mass	Oct. 18, 1870	108,457
Bedstead, Folding	J. H. Durand	Kalamazoo, Mich	Oct. 3, 1865	50,300
Bedstead, Folding	A. M. Dye	Clinton, Ill	Oct. 9, 1860	30,304
Bedstead, Folding	T. G. Gifford	New York, N. Y	Feb. 15, 1870	99,847
Bedstead, Folding	H. Gill	Dedham, Mass	Apr. 22, 1862	35,018
Bedstead, Folding	S. Gillespie	New York, N. Y	Feb. 28, 1860	27,284
Bedstead, Folding	M. B. Goodell	Worcester, Mass	Mar. 23, 1869	88,158
Bedstead, Folding	J. C. Fall and A. C. Richards	Cincinnati, Ohio	July 5, 1870	105,069
Bedstead, Folding	T. B. Horkins	Bristol, Pa	May 11, 1869	89,993
Bedstead, Folding	H. H. Hill	Pontiac, Ill	Oct. 29, 1872	132,576
Bedstead, Folding	B. Hinkley	Troy, N. Y	Feb. 17, 1857	16,647
Bedstead, Folding	J. Housiaux	Washington, D. C	June 9, 1863	38,827
Bedstead, Folding	T. Howe	Cambridgeport, Mass	Apr. 3, 1866	53,620
Bedstead, Folding	J. A. Johnston	Antrim, Ohio	May 12, 1857	17,281
Bedstead, Folding	J. L. Killgore	Wilmington, Del	Apr. 8, 1873	137,690
Bedstead, Folding	J. P. Koch	New York, N. Y	Dec. 27, 1859	26,598
Bedstead, Folding	K. Kunkel	New York, N. Y	Feb. 21, 1871	112,053
Bedstead, Folding	W. C. Lutz	Jacob's Church, Va	Feb. 28, 1860	27,299
Bedstead, Folding	S. H. Mapes	Almond, N. Y	Oct. 1, 1867	69,457
Bedstead, Folding	J. Müller	Philadelphia, Pa	Apr. 13, 1869	88,977
Bedstead, Folding	J. Müller	Philadelphia, Pa	Dec. 7, 1869	97,545
Bedstead, Folding	F. C. Payne	New York, N. Y	Dec. 24, 1861	34,009
Bedstead, Folding	J. L. Roberts	Dorchester, Mass	July 26, 1864	43,656
Bedstead, Folding	G. D. Sargent	Boston, Mass	Dec. 11, 1860	30,888
Bedstead, Folding	G. Sickels	Boston, Mass	Nov. 2, 1869	96,356
Bedstead, Folding	W. Stoddard	Hingham, Mass	Apr. 3, 1855	12,656
Bedstead, Folding	J. Sutter	New York, N. Y	May 3, 1864	42,601
Bedstead, Folding	T. S. Thorson	Chicago, Ill	Dec. 17, 1872	134,111
Bedstead, Folding	J. Turner	Cambridgeport, Mass	Jan. 3, 1871	110,697
Bedstead, Folding	J. B. Wickersham	New York, N. Y	June 2, 1857	17,460
Bedstead, Folding and cot	E. M. Payne	Waverly, N. Y	Jan. 29, 1867	61,681
Bedstead, Folding bureau	D. B. Maynard	Worcester, Mass	Dec. 22, 1868	85,232
Bedstead, Folding bureau or wardrobe	A. E. Botter	New York, N. Y	Dec. 20, 1853	10,351
Bedstead, Folding case	E. Whitney	Lynn, Mass	Sept. 18, 1860	30,101
Bedstead, Folding iron	H. F. Vandenhove	New York, N. Y	Nov. 3, 1857	18,565
Bedstead, Folding metallic	W. Gardner	New York, N. Y	Dec. 9, 1862	37,094
Bedstead for the sick	N. Richardson	Boston, Mass	Sept. 9, 1835	....
Bedstead for the sick	A. Smith	Milo, N. Y	July 12, 1830	....
Bedstead for the sick and wounded	D. Anthony	Adams, Mass	Sept. 15, 1834	....
Bedstead for the sick and wounded	W. S. Wolf	New York, N. Y	July 15, 1834	....
Bedstead for the sick and wounded	W. Woolley	New York, N. Y	Aug. 30, 1834	....
Bedstead for the sick, Elevating	D. Bancroft	Grafton, Vt.	Oct. 12, 1830	....
Bedstead, Fracture	E. Daniels	Owego, N. Y	Apr. 9, 1861	31,958
Bedstead-frame	J. M. Farnham	Hartford, Conn	Nov. 30, 1869	97,375
Bedstead, Hammock	I. M. Kilner	Chester, Great Britain	June 11, 1872	127,892
Bedstead, Hospital	J. D. Cochran	Milford, N. H	Sept. 27, 1864	44,399
Bedstead, Hospital	A. Iske	Lancaster, Pa	Aug. 15, 1865	49,412
Bedstead, Hospital	A. Iske	Lancaster, Pa	Apr. 28, 1868	77,193
Bedstead, Hospital	J. Sebo	Wilmington, Del	July 1, 1862	35,782
Bedstead, Hospital	J. Sebo	Wilmington, Del	May 26, 1863	38,700
Bedstead, Invalid	T. Arnold	Mobile, Ala	May 29, 1855	12,940
Bedstead, Invalid	C. S. Baker	Manchester, N. H	Oct. 22, 1867	69,958
Bedstead, Invalid	I. F. Baker	West Yarmouth, Mass	Sept. 2, 1862	36,332
Bedstead, Invalid	A. W. Barker	Suffolk County, Mass	Mar. 5, 1850	7,131
Bedstead, Invalid	H. N. Blair	Troy, Pa	Dec. 31, 1872	134,456
Bedstead, Invalid	A. Bray	Chicopee, Mass	June 3, 1873	139,493
Bedstead, Invalid	I. Buckman	South Woodstock, Vt	Apr. 17, 1849	6,314
Bedstead, Invalid	A. W. Chase	Ann Arbor, Mich	May 15, 1860	28,254
Bedstead, Invalid	C. M. Clinton and E. J. Morgan.	Ithaca, N. Y	Apr. 8, 1873	137,596
Bedstead, Invalid	H. Cordes	Belleville, N. J	July 17, 1866	56,376
Bedstead, Invalid	O. G. Cosby	Richmond, Va	Apr. 15, 1873	137,828
Bedstead, Invalid	E. Daniels	Union, N. Y	May 29, 1855	12,944
Bedstead, Invalid	B. Eastman	Philadelphia, Pa	July 17, 1855	13,253
Bedstead, Invalid	I. T. Forbes	Coburg, Canada	Aug. 29, 1854	11,605
Bedstead, Invalid	F. G. Ford	Washington, D. C	June 13, 1871	115,948
Bedstead, Invalid	O. P. Furman	Addison, N. Y	Nov. 22, 1864	45,151
Bedstead, Invalid	J. H. Gibson	McDonough, N. Y	Mar. 6, 1866	52,988
Bedstead, Invalid	S. Grantz	Beaver Creek, Md	Jan. 3, 1860	26,666
Bedstead, Invalid	G. W. Grote	Saint Catharine's, Canada	Apr. 22, 1873	138,083
Bedstead, Invalid	W. A. Guyer	New York, N. Y	July 10, 1866	56,211
Bedstead, Invalid	P. W. Hardwick	Wayne County, Ind	May 8, 1866	54,533
Bedstead, Invalid	W. Heath	Bath, Me	Nov. 13, 1866	59,600
Bedstead, Invalid	W. Heath	Bath, Me	Jan. 7, 1868	73,008
Bedstead, Invalid	W. Heath	Bath, Me	Mar. 10, 1868	75,265
Bedstead, Invalid	W. Heath	Bath, Me	May 23, 1871	115,054
Bedstead, Invalid	J. R. Hill	Goshen, Ohio	Mar. 22, 1864	41,996
Bedstead, Invalid	W. S. Hill	Manchester, N. H	Mar. 27, 1866	53,533
Bedstead, Invalid	E. Hutchinson	Manchester, N. H	June 12, 1866	55,496
Bedstead, Invalid	L. J. Johnson	Norwich, Conn	May 11, 1869	89,868
Bedstead, Invalid	M. Johnson	Colebrook, N. H	Oct. 27, 1863	40,413
Bedstead, Invalid	S. P. Johnson	Portland, Me	Nov. 12, 1867	70,722
Bedstead, Invalid	J. Karney	Cincinnati, Ohio	Oct. 23, 1849	6,814
Bedstead, Invalid	C. G. Kuhn	New York, N. Y	May 21, 1872	127,070
Bedstead, Invalid	I. H. Latourandais	Flint Hill, Va	May 1, 1847	5,100
Bedstead, Invalid	D. D. Marsh	Sunapee, N. H	June 16, 1868	78,986
Bedstead, Invalid	J. Massey	New York, N. Y	Sept. 17, 1867	68,892
Bedstead, Invalid	T. A. McFarland	Erie, Pa	July 25, 1871	117,440
Bedstead, Invalid	D. Merrill	Worcester, Mass	Feb. 9, 1864	41,526
Bedstead, Invalid	G. Miller	Fremont, Ohio	Feb. 2, 1858	19,254

Index of patents issued from the United States Patent Office from 1790 *to* 1873, *inclusive*—Continued.

Invention.	Inventor.	Residence.	Date.	No.
Bedstead, Invalid	J. H. Oerter	New York, N. Y	Feb. 7, 1871	111, 561
Bedstead, Invalid	M. A. Ormsbee	Fair Haven, Vt	July 11, 1871	116, 861
Bedstead, Invalid	J. Parker	Liverpool, England	June 15, 1858	20, 580
Bedstead, Invalid	B. Pollard	Dutch Flat, Cal	Oct. 1, 1872	131, 903
Bedstead, Invalid	S. Puffer	Oxford, N. Y	Mar. 6, 1866	53, 041
Bedstead, Invalid	W. O. Reid	Vienna, N. C	Jan. 31, 1871	111, 380
Bedstead, Invalid	J. Robinson	Madison Station, Miss	July 8, 1873	140, 646
Bedstead, Invalid	W. W. Rowles and A. J. Russell	Baltimore, Md	Mar. 24, 1868	75, 983
Bedstead, Invalid	A. J. Russell	Baltimore, Md	June 28, 1870	104, 774
Bedstead, Invalid	A. J. Russell	Baltimore, Md	May 23, 1871	115, 108
Bedstead, Invalid	H. A. Scott	Winchester, N. H	Apr. 9, 1872	125, 491
Bedstead, Invalid	H. A. Scott	Winchester, N. H	July 23, 1872	129, 754
Bedstead, Invalid	H. A. Scott	Winchester, N. H	Dec. 17, 1872	134, 008
Bedstead, Invalid	J. Sebo	Wilmington, Del	Sept. 30, 1862	36, 578
Bedstead, Invalid	H. O. Sheidley	Republic, Ohio	Oct. 11, 1859	25, 766
Bedstead, Invalid	F. H. Smith and W. F. Wood	North Hebron, N. Y	July 6, 1869	92, 380
Bedstead, Invalid	G. Smith	Stratford, Canada	May 30, 1870	115, 371
Bedstead, Invalid	W. Swift	Brooklyn, N. Y	Feb. 14, 1860	27, 169
Bedstead, Invalid	W. Swift	Brooklyn, N. Y	Nov. 24, 1863	40, 716
Bedstead, Invalid	C. D. Van Allen	New York, N. Y	Apr. 25, 1854	10, 840
Bedstead, Invalid	F. M. Webster	Newport, Ky	May 8, 1849	6, 433
Bedstead, Invalid	C. Woolley	New York, N. Y	Apr. 16, 1842	2, 567
Bedstead, Invalid and fracture	T. McIlroy	New York, N. Y	Nov. 19, 1867	71, 196
Bedstead, Iron	J. Bayston and G. W. Nicholson	Chicago and Naperville, Ill.	Mar. 30, 1869	88, 435
Bedstead, Iron	J. M. French	East Cambridge, Mass	Dec. 16, 1862	37, 163
Bedstead, Iron folding	J. Biberthaler	New York, N. Y	July 26, 1859	24, 853
Bedstead-joint	L. G. Bradford	Plymouth, Mass	Dec. 6, 1870	109, 799
Bedstead-key	J. Blake and D. Cushing	Providence, R. I	Dec. 14, 1830	....
Bedstead-key	H. Stein	New York, N. Y	Aug. 20, 1872	130, 671
Bedstead, Lounge	B. Cerf	New York, N. Y	Jan. 2, 1866	51, 802
Bedstead, Lounge	F. C. Payne	New York, N. Y	Aug. 15, 1871	118, 047
Bedstead, Lounge	H. H. Reichert	New York, N. Y	July 9, 1872	128, 908
Bedstead, lounge, and chair	S. A. Skinner	Bristol, Vt	Sept. 9, 1862	36, 441
Bedstead-machine	A. Stedman	Pittsford, N. Y	Jan. 16, 1835	....
Bedstead, Metallic	J. Carey	Brooklyn, N. Y	May 27, 1862	35, 414
Bedstead, Metallic	M. Lefferts	New York, N. Y	Apr. 15, 1856	14, 668
Bedstead, Metallic portable	J. Homer	New York, N. Y	Jan. 28, 1818	....
Bedstead, Metamorphosic alleviator	J. Lowe	Vienna, N. Y	Oct. 25, 1830	....
Bedstead, Metamorphosic alleviator	J. Lowe	Whitesborough, N. Y	Nov. 21, 1831	....
Bedstead or chair, Hospital	W. Woolley	New York, N. Y	Sept. 28, 1831	....
Bedstead or cot	H. W. Ladd	Chelsea, Mass	Sept. 20, 1870	107, 509
Bedstead, Parlor	F. E. Coffin	Boston, Mass	Jan. 24, 1871	111, 108
Bedstead, Parlor	F. E. Coffin	Boston, Mass	June 3, 1873	139, 454
Bedstead, Parlor	M. Crosby	Boston, Mass	Nov. 10, 1868	83, 936
Bedstead, Parlor	M. Crosby	Boston, Mass	Oct. 4, 1870	107, 881
Bedstead, Parlor	J. A. Morgan	Bloomfield, Iowa	Aug. 31, 1869	94, 431
Bedstead, Parturient invalid	J. N. Robbins	Troy, Mo	Oct. 20, 1831	....
Bedstead, Portable	F. Cotton	Brooklyn, N. Y	Jan. 25, 1859	22, 706
Bedstead, Portable	J. Daley	Baltimore, Md	May 14, 1827	....
Bedstead, Portable	S. Willard	Cincinnati, Ohio	July 25, 1854	11, 398
Bedstead, Portable cot	W. C. Betts	New York, N. Y	May 11, 1852	8, 934
Bedstead, Portable cot	A. McDonough	Philadelphia, Pa	July 10, 1849	6, 588
Bedstead, Portable folding	H. W. Eastman	Baltimore, Md	Apr. 9, 1861	31, 962
Bedstead, Portable folding-chair	G. H. Cottam	Hampton Road, England	Apr. 25, 1854	10, 825
Bedstead, Portable invalid	Z. C. Favor	Chicago, Ill	Apr. 20, 1858	19, 987
Bedstead put together with right and left screws	T. B. Smith	Troy, N. Y	Oct. 11, 1824	....
Bedstead-rail	C. Robinson	Cambridgeport, Mass	Apr. 27, 1858	20, 092
Bedstead-rail attachment	J. Shaefer	Lancaster, Pa	May 6, 1862	35, 182
Bedstead-rail fastening	J. P. Allen	Manchester, Mass	Nov. 3, 1841	2, 326
Bedstead-rails, Apparatus for cutting screws on	J. R. Kain	Tiffin, Ohio	Nov. 22, 1853	10, 254
Bedstead-rails, Apparatus for cutting screws on	H. Smith	Norwalk, Ohio	Nov. 22, 1853	10, 261
Bedstead-rails, Machine for cutting screws on	H. Gross and W. Campbell	Tiffin City, Ohio	Apr. 1, 1851	8, 019
Bedstead rails, Machine for cutting screws on	J. Lindly	Cynthiana, Ky	June 20, 1838	797
Bedstead-rails, Machine for cutting screws on	J. P. Owens	Norwalk, Ohio	Nov. 22, 1853	10, 257
Bedstead-rails, Manner of cutting tenons and boring holes in.	T. Cole	Greensburgh, Ind	Nov. 12, 1841	2, 356
Bedstead, Revolving rail and round tenon	G. Post	Auburn, N. Y	Oct. 11, 1828	....
Bedstead, sacking-bottom, &c	D. Powles	Baltimore, Md	Jan. 26, 1827	....
Bedstead, Sacking-bottom for	I. Cooper	Johnstown, Pa	Oct. 7, 1844	3, 778
Bedstead, Secret	W. Woolley	New York, N. Y	May 17, 1830	....
Bedstead, Secret or sofa	W. Woolley	New York, N. Y	Oct. 3, 1831	....
Bedstead, Secretary	E. E. and M. G. Briggs	Boston, Mass	Feb. 16, 1869	86, 901
Bedstead, Secretary	G. Gage	Kendall's Mills, Mo	July 24, 1860	29, 265
Bedstead, Sectional	C. Page	North Danvers, Mass	Dec. 13, 1853	10, 315
Bedstead, seat, &c	C. T. Frost	Medfield, Mass	June 8, 1869	90, 941
Bedstead-slat	A. S. and O. H. Drisko	Boston, Mass	July 5, 1870	104, 944
Bedstead-slat	S. Hickock	Buffalo, N. Y	Dec. 22, 1857	18, 902
Bedstead-slat	T. Howe	Cambridgeport, Mass	Sept. 27, 1859	25, 569
Bedstead-slat	O. H. Weed	Charlestown, Mass	Feb. 11, 1868	74, 262
Bedstead-slat	D. Wehrle	Williamsville, N. Y	Sept. 10, 1872	131, 198
Bedstead-slat holder	F. G. Ford	Philadelphia, Pa	Nov. 7, 1871	120, 734
Bedstead-slats, Elastic loop for suspending	C. Robinson	Cambridgeport, Mass	June 30, 1857	17, 695
Bedstead, Sliding sofa	G. Wode	New York, N. Y	June 12, 1838	782
Bedstead so constructed as to be easily removable in case of fire, &c.	W. Gilman and W. Jackson	....	Mar. 19, 1804	....
Bedstead, Sofa	J. J. Anderson	Boston, Mass	Feb. 2, 1869	86, 344
Bedstead, Sofa	W. P. Barclay	Chicago, Ill	Oct. 13, 1868	83, 025
Bedstead, Sofa	J. Beiersdorf	Chicago, Ill	July 1, 1873	140, 453
Bedstead, Sofa	C. H. Berry	East Somerville, Mass	Dec. 10, 1867	71, 957
Bedstead, Sofa	F. Boeger	Philadelphia, Pa	Jan. 16, 1866	52, 020
Bedstead, Sofa	K. Borren	New York, N. Y	Apr. 26, 1859	23, 806
Bedstead, Sofa	E. B. Bowditch	New Haven, Conn	July 24, 1849	6, 607
Bedstead, Sofa	E. B. Bowditch	New Haven, Conn	Feb. 26, 1850	7, 116
Bedstead, Sofa	J. Brada	New York, N. Y	Jan. 14, 1873	134, 843
Bedstead, Sofa	E. Brady	New York, N. Y	May 2, 1865	47, 512
Bedstead, Sofa	J. C. Butler	Albany, N. Y	May 10, 1870	102, 769
Bedstead, Sofa	W. Clowes	Hartwood, N. Y	June 24, 1843	3, 140

Index of patents issued from the United States Patent Office from 1790 *to* 1873, *inclusive*—Continued.

Invention.	Inventor.	Residence.	Date.	No.
Bedstead, Sofa	F. Cotton	Brooklyn, N. Y	Feb. 23, 1864	41, 682
Bedstead, Sofa	J. Dourson	Columbus, Ohio	Mar. 23, 1869	88, 146
Bedstead, Sofa	J. Dourson	Columbus, Ohio	Feb. 13, 1872	123, 620
Bedstead, Sofa	J. C. Emery	Concord, N. H	June 20, 1848	5, 641
Bedstead, Sofa	A. D. Farrell	New York, N. Y	May 2, 1843	3, 072
Bedstead, Sofa	W. Farson	Philadelphia, Pa	Jan. 18, 1870	98, 858
Bedstead, Sofa	W. Farson	Philadelphia, Pa	Oct. 31, 1871	120, 374
Bedstead, Sofa	W. Farson	Philadelphia, Pa	Oct. 22, 1872	132, 392
Bedstead, Sofa	S. S. Gilliland and J. R. Wagoner.	Dayton, Ohio	May 17, 1853	9, 726
Bedstead, Sofa	N. M. Graw	New York, N. Y	Dec. 10, 1838	1, 030
Bedstead, Sofa	C. F. Grundin	Boston, Mass	June 17, 1873	139, 952
Bedstead, Sofa	J. T. Hammitt	Philadelphia, Pa	Mar. 16, 1852	8, 800
Bedstead, Sofa	J. B. Harlow	Portland, Me	Feb. 11, 1873	135, 643
Bedstead, Sofa	D. B. Hubbard	Wheeling, W. Va	Aug. 22, 1871	118, 368
Bedstead, Sofa	C. F. H. Huff	New York, N. Y	May 9, 1871	114, 684
Bedstead, Sofa	J. Irwin	Philadelphia, Pa	May 11, 1858	20, 206
Bedstead, Sofa	F. Keller	New York, N. Y	Aug. 1, 1865	49, 120
Bedstead, Sofa	J. Kena	Brooklyn, N. Y	Nov. 14, 1865	50, 939
Bedstead, Sofa	J. S. Kenyon	Webster City, Iowa	July 3, 1866	56, 064
Bedstead, Sofa	P. J. Larson	Chicago, Ill	Dec. 16, 1873	145, 508
Bedstead, Sofa	E. Lord	Portland, Me	Dec. 24, 1872	134, 210
Bedstead, Sofa	E. Lord	Portland, Me	Dec. 23, 1873	145, 741
Bedstead, Sofa	E. Lovell	Saint Louis, Mo	Aug. 26, 1873	142, 249
Bedstead, Sofa	M. Sulzbacher	New York, N. Y	Mar. 1, 1870	100, 464
Bedstead, Sofa	T. J. Magee	Cincinnati, Ohio	Sept. 8, 1863	39, 863
Bedstead, Sofa	T. J. Magee	Cincinnati, Ohio	Dec. 8, 1863	40, 848
Bedstead, Sofa	C. F. Martine	Boston, Mass	June 6, 1854	11, 026
Bedstead, Sofa	C. F. Martine	Boston, Mass	Sept. 3, 1867	68, 373
Bedstead, Sofa	M. K. Maximilian	New York, N. Y	Sept. 1, 1868	81, 659
Bedstead, Sofa	J. M. Meschutt	New York, N. Y	July 23, 1841	2, 185
Bedstead, Sofa	S. Millet	New York, N. Y	Aug. 8, 1854	11, 488
Bedstead, Sofa	J. Needham	New York, N. Y	Aug. 20, 1846	4, 703
Bedstead, Sofa	F. C. Payne	New York, N. Y	June 23, 1863	38, 978
Bedstead, Sofa	J. F. C. Peikhardt	New York, N. Y	Feb. 21, 1860	27, 234
Bedstead, Sofa	J. R. Penniman	Boston, Mass	Aug. 22, 1827	....
Bedstead, Sofa	J. F. C. Pickhardt	New York, N. Y	May 8, 1866	54, 592
Bedstead, Sofa	J. Pratt, 3d	Hartford, Conn	Apr. 1, 1842	2, 530
Bedstead, Sofa	H. H. Reichert	New York, N. Y	Apr. 23, 1872	126, 088
Bedstead, Sofa	J. A. Robson	New York, N. Y	Nov. 20, 1849	6, 893
Bedstead, Sofa	S. R. Roscoe	Obion County, Tenn	May 14, 1867	64, 799
Bedstead, Sofa	S. R. Roscoe	Obion, Tenn	Sept. 8, 1868	81, 949
Bedstead, Sofa	H. S. Rose	Bath, N. Y	Mar. 13, 1866	53, 188
Bedstead, Sofa	C. Rossow	Chicago, Ill	May 13, 1873	138, 819
Bedstead, Sofa	R. Scarritt	Saint Louis, Mo	Oct. 8, 1850	7, 707
Bedstead, Sofa	L. Schaefer	Cleveland, Ohio	Sept. 3, 1867	68, 389
Bedstead, Sofa	J. Schafer	New York, N. Y	Mar. 19, 1872	124, 765
Bedstead, Sofa	A. Schwaab	New York, N. Y	Sept. 7, 1869	94, 656
Bedstead, Sofa	G. Sickels	Middletown, Conn	Dec. 4, 1844	3, 845
Bedstead, Sofa	B. L. Southack	New York, N. Y	Oct. 20, 1868	83, 333
Bedstead, Sofa	J. K. Stockton	New York, N. Y	Feb. 25, 1873	136, 276
Bedstead, Sofa	C. Street	Cincinnati, Ohio	Apr. 1, 1873	137, 5[illegible]5
Bedstead, Sofa	C. F. Tauchert	Cincinnati, Ohio	Dec. 17, 1872	134, 016
Bedstead, Sofa	W. H. Tendler	Cambridge, Mass	May 31, 1859	24, 267
Bedstead, Sofa	W. H. Tendler	Cambridge, Mass	Apr. 10, 1860	27, 871
Bedstead, Sofa	W. H. Tendler and J. F. Moeshlin.	Cambridge, Mass	Aug. 28, 1860	29, 832
Bedstead, Sofa	W. Walcutt	New York, N. Y	Mar. 26, 1872	124, 990
Bedstead, Sofa	A. Walker	New Haven, Conn	June 29, 1852	9, 083
Bedstead, Sofa	A. G. Warren	Norwich, Conn	May 28, 1850	7, 404
Bedstead, Sofa	J. Werner	New York, N. Y	Apr. 7, 1868	76, 570
Bedstead, Sofa	S. M. and S. A. Winn	San Francisco, Cal	Oct. 7, 1873	143, 553
Bedstead, sofa, and settee	F. Breckels	New York, N. Y	Apr. 7, 1834	....
Bedstead, sofa, settee, &c	J. P. Allen	Manchester, Mass	May 19, 1832	....
Bedstead, Spring	J. Böhmer	Saint Louis, Mo	Apr. 20, 1869	89, 119
Bedstead, Spring	W. H. Kimball and A. J. French	Lynn, Mass	Sept. 2, 1856	15, 658
Bedstead, Spring	N. Houghton	New York, N. Y	Feb. 25, 1862	34, 500
Bedstead, Spring	R. Lapham	New York, N. Y	June 19, 1866	55, 680
Bedstead, Spring	D. R. Lightner	Bucyrus, Ohio	Sept. 4, 1860	29, 892
Bedstead, Spring	J. B. McClanathan	Horicon, Wis	Feb. 13, 1866	52, 585
Bedstead, Spring	N. M. Phillips	New York, N. Y	Mar. 16, 1858	19, 649
Bedstead, Spring	C. F. Spencer	Rochester, N. Y	Mar. 29, 1859	23, 404
Bedstead, Spring	S. H. Tift	Morrisville, Vt	Oct. 16, 1866	58, 914
Bedstead, Spring	W. Woods and E. Smith	Worcester, Mass	May 2, 1865	47, 594
Bedstead-spring	E. F. Dunaway	Cincinnati, Ohio	Aug. 22, 1871	118, 351
Bedstead-spring	E. F. Dunaway	Cincinnati, Ohio	Aug. 22, 1871	118, 352
Bedstead-spring	D. Manuel	Newton, Mass	Dec. 12, 1865	51, 516
Bedstead, Spring-bottom for	A. Foote	North Blandford, Mass	June 24, 1856	15, 209
Bedstead, Spring-bottom for	R. Hatch	Strafford, Vt	Dec. 29, 1857	18, 968
Bedstead, Spring cot	F. C. Hall	Baltimore, Md	Apr. 9, 1872	125, 389
Bedstead, Steam spring	C. T. Young	North Chelmsford, Mass	Dec. 29, 1857	18, 008
Bedstead, Tent	A. D. McCoy	New Orleans, La	Feb. 12, 1867	62, 049
Bedstead-tester	F. Layaux	Monroe, La	Aug. 30, 1870	106, 842
Bedstead, Toilet	G. V. Leicester	Boston, Mass	Nov. 9, 1869	96, 599
Bedstead, Trunk	R. C. Dubois	Washington, D. C	Apr. 19, 1870	102, 098
Bedstead, Ventilating	H. W. Henley	New York, N. Y	Jan. 24, 1860	26, 946
Bedstead-vetilating attachment	J. H. Martin	Hartford, N. Y	Aug. 16, 1864	43, 857
Bedstead, Wardrobe	R. M. Austin	Philadelphia, Pa	June 4, 1872	127, 546
Bedstead, Wardrobe	W. R. Bagnall	Chelsea, Mass	Oct. 1, 1867	69, 304
Bedstead, Wardrobe	C. L. Barritt	Brooklyn, N. Y	June 24, 1873	140, 109
Bedstead, Wardrobe	W. Berg	New York, N. Y	Feb. 28, 1860	27, 329
Bedstead, Wardrobe	S. S. Burr	Boston, Mass	Aug. 30, 1870	102, 776
Bedstead, Wardrobe	S. S. Burr and L. Pierce	Dedham and Charlestown, Mass.	Sept. 7, 1869	94, 560
Bedstead, Wardrobe	J. Byrnes	Chicago, Ill	May 6, 1873	138, 610
Bedstead, Wardrobe	A. Dietz	New Orleans, La	Dec. 13, 1864	45, 393
Bedstead, Wardrobe	J. F. Dodge	Nashua, N. H	July 19, 1870	105, 556
Bedstead, Wardrobe	J. Eby	Muncie, Ind	Apr. 11, 1865	47, 197

Index of patents issued from the United States Patent Office from 1790 to 1873, inclusive—Continued.

Invention.	Inventor.	Residence.	Date.	No.
Bedstead, Wardrobe	Z. C. Favor	Boston, Mass	Apr. 2, 1838	668
Bedstead, Wardrobe	T. L. Fortune	Weston, Mo	July 5, 1864	43, 4[illegible]5
Bedstead, Wardrobe	R. W. Frost	New York, N. Y	Apr. 1, 1873	137, 3[illegible]6
Bedstead, Wardrobe	E. Hunter and D. Van Sickle	Chicago, Ill	May 27, 1873	139, 316
Bedstead, Wardrobe	S. C. Maine	Boston, Mass	Mar. 19, 1867	63, 065
Bedstead, Wardrobe	W. H. Pease	Dayton, Ohio	Oct. 6, 1863	40, 184
Bedstead, Wardrobe	J. F. C. Pickhardt	New York, N. Y	Aug. 13, 1867	67, 797
Bedstead, Wardrobe	C. Robbins	Chicago, Ill	Feb. 23, 1858	19, 449
Bedstead, Wardrobe	J. Smith	Chicago, Ill	Apr. 8, 1873	137, 628
Bedstead, Wardrobe	A. A. Young	Boston, Mass	Oct. 27, 1868	83, 432
Bedstead, Wardrobe or bureau	J. S. McCurdy	New York, N. Y	Apr. 14, 1857	17, 047
Bedstead, Windlass	C. Adams	Boston, Mass	Feb. 26, 1825	....
Bedstead, Windlass	L. Foster	Boston, Mass	Feb. 16, 1824	....
Bedstead, Windlass	L. Foster	Boston, Mass	June 25, 1824	....
Bedstead, Windlass	T. Lamb	Washington, D. C	Nov. 13, 1840	1, 856
Bedsteads and attaching and stretching sackings, Manner of fastening.	M. Gregg	Philadelphia, Pa	Mar. 25, 1840	1, 526
Bedsteads, Attaching curtain-posts to	T. Early	Williamson County, Tenn	Jan. 8, 1839	1, 062
Bedsteads, Attaching cutters for cutting screws on rails of.	J. Zimmer	Tiffin, Ohio	Dec. 23, 1851	8, 6[illegible]0
Bedsteads, Bed-bug protector for	S. Clarke	New York, N. Y	July 3, 1866	56, 0[illegible]8
Bedsteads, Bevel-grooved and dovetail joints for	J. Mitchel	Harrisburgh, Pa	Jan. 11, 1826	....
Bedsteads, Boring and cutting screws on	J. Guild	Cincinnati, Ohio	Oct. 29, 1846	4, 829
Bedsteads, Constructing	C. J. Fountain, J. F. Adams, and G. F. Hillyer.	New York, N. Y	Apr. 20, 1839	1, 129
Bedsteads, Constructing	S. P. Smith	Salina, N. Y	Oct. 26, 1838	990
Bedsteads, Constructing and cording	M. Engle	Easton, Pa	Apr. 24, 1840	1, 562
Bedsteads, Construction of	O. R. Herbert	Mount Pleasant, N. J	July 14, 1824	....
Bedsteads, Construction of	J. F. Hollister	Plano, Ill	May 2, 1871	114, 439
Bedsteads, Cutting screws on rails of	S. Lewis	Tiffin, Ohio	Sept. 26, 1848	5, 812
Bedsteads, Machine for cutting screws of screw	P. Williams	Towanda, Pa	Feb. 16, 1837	126
Bedsteads, Machine for cutting screws on	O. Parkhurst and D. Bullock	Cohoes, N. Y	July 10, 1855	13, 225
Bedsteads, Machine for cutting screws on posts and rails of.	O. Thornley	Lebanon, Ind	Oct. 7, 1851	8, 414
Bedsteads, Machine for cutting screws on rails and posts of.	J. P. Owen	Norwalk, Ohio	Mar. 16, 1852	8, 806
Bedsteads, Machine for cutting screws on rails of	S. Lewis	Rochester, N. Y	Oct. 7, 1851	8, 416
Bedsteads, Machine for cutting screws on rails of	J. Lindley	Cynthiana, Ky	Oct. 10, 1840	1, 816
Bedsteads, Machine for cutting screws on rails of	J. Thompson	Cynthiana, Ky	July 29, 1841	2, 1[illegible]8
Bedsteads, Machinery for cutting screws in	J. Garside and H. J. Betjeman	Harrison, Ohio	Aug. 28, 1849	6, 668
Bedsteads, Machinery for cutting screws in the posts and rails of.	W. F. Converse, R. H. Penny, and R. S. Hannaford.	Harrison, Ohio	Dec. 31, 1844	3, 872
Bedsteads, Machinery for cutting screws on rails of	W. F. Converse and J. Burdge	Cincinnati, Ohio	Apr. 24, 1849	6, 387
Bedsteads, Machinery for cutting screws on rails of	S. Lewis	Tiffin, Ohio	Apr. 9, 1850	7, 264
Bedsteads, Making and stretching the sacking of	W. S. Anderson	Shelbyville, Tenn	June 4, 1838	765
Bedsteads, Mortise and tenon for	W. H. Elliot	New York, N. Y	Apr. 14, 1868	76, 611
Bedsteads, sofas, chairs, &c., Raising or inclining the various parts of.	E. Cherrington	Boston, Mass	Feb. 9, 1839	1, 078
Bedsteads, Spiral spring for	W. L. Beardsley	Binghamton, N. Y	Nov. 29, 1870	109, 573
Bedsteads, Table attachment for	D. Bull	Amboy, Ill	Sept. 17, 1867	68, 948
Bedsteads, Table attachment for	E. D. W. Hatch	Chicago, Ill	Apr. 20, 1869	89, 146
Bedsteads, Tester-frame for	J. C. Davis	Montgomery, Ala	Dec. 31, 1867	72, 814
Bedsteads, Tightening sacking-bottoms of	B. Bosworth	Fayette County, Ky	Dec. 14, 1839	1, 429
Bedsteads, Tightening sacking-bottoms of	J. Hart	Nicholasville, Ky	June 21, 1839	1, 185
Bedsteads to appartments, Application of	J. B. Brown	Boston, Mass	Oct. 9, 1866	58, 590
Bee-feeder	J. M. Beebe	Casadaga, N. Y	Mar. 26, 1867	63, 135
Bee-feeder	P. Miller, jr	Fredonia, N. Y	Mar. 23, 1869	88, 158
Bee-feeder	E. J. Peck	Linden, N. J	Apr. 30, 1872	126, 229
Bee-feeder	C. C. Van Deusen	Sprout Brook, N. Y	July 5, 1870	105, 144
Bee-feeding apparatus	E. Buel	Silver Creek, N. Y	Jan. 29, 1867	61, 514
Bee-feeding device	W. Brown	Shelbyville, Ind	June 21, 1859	24, 516
Bee-hive	D. L. Addair	Hawesville, Ky	Aug. 27, 1867	68, 141
Bee-hive	L. Adams	Mason City, Ill	Dec. 9, 1873	145, 324
Bee-hive	G. C. Aiken	Nashua, N. H	Feb. 15, 1859	22, 924
Bee-hive	L. W. and S. W. Albee	South Charlestown, N. H	Aug. 21, 1866	57, 272
Bee-hive	C. C. Aldrich	Morristown, Minn	Apr. 9, 1872	125, 427
Bee-hive	T. R. Allen	Syracuse, N. Y	Dec. 8, 1868	84, 788
Bee-hive	H. Alley	Wenham, Mass	June 18, 1872	128, 005
Bee-hive	W. J. Andrews	Columbia, Tenn	June 11, 1867	65, 629
Bee-hive	J. H. Andrews	Almont, Mich	Aug. 25, 1863	39, 622
Bee-hive	E. S. Armstrong	Jerseyville, Ill	Dec. 12, 1871	121, 837
Bee-hive	D. Arndt	West Middletown, Pa	May 9, 1846	4, 502
Bee-hive	D. Arndt	Zanesville, Ohio	Aug. 21, 1860	29, 6[illegible]8
Bee-hive	W. B. Arndt	Nova, Ohio	Nov. 5, 1872	132, 787
Bee-hive	D. J. Arnold	Brownville, Nebr	Sept. 24, 1872	131, 589
Bee-hive	R. Arnold	Suffolk, Va	Dec. 20, 1870	110, 332
Bee-hive	R. Arnold	Suffolk, Va	Sept. 12, 1871	118, 894
Bee-hive	T. Atkinson	Memphis, Tenn	May 11, 1869	89, 841
Bee-hive	T. Atkinson	Memphis, Tenn	Aug. 10, 1869	93, 395
Bee-hive	E. S. Bacon	Albion, N. Y	Aug. 28, 1860	29, 753
Bee-hive	A. C. Badgley	Earleville, Ill	Oct. 29, 1867	70, 313
Bee-hive	C. W. Banks	Baltimore, Md	Oct. 1, 1872	131, 7[illegible]0
Bee-hive	S. D. Barber and J. Wolf	Mattoon, Ill	Jan. 4, 1870	98, 544
Bee-hive	E. Bartholomew	Cleveland, Ohio	Nov. 22, 1859	26, 154
Bee-hive	N. P. Bassett	Fulton, N. Y	Aug. 4, 1868	80, 587
Bee-hive	J. H. Bassler	Pine Grove, Pa	June 8, 1869	90, 984
Bee-hive	H. A. Bathurst	Clearfield, Pa	Dec. 12, 1871	121, 840
Bee-hive	H. Baughman	Columbus, Ohio	May 26, 1868	78, 253
Bee-hive	E. B. Beach	West Meriden, Conn	Apr. 21, 1868	76, 976
Bee-hive	D. S. Bear	Toledo, Iowa	Feb. 18, 1868	74, 487
Bee-hive	C. Beard	Waynesborough, Va	Jan. 16, 1872	122, 697
Bee-hive	E. Beard	New Sharon, Me	Feb. 25, 1836	....
Bee-hive	J. M. Beebe	Casadaga, N. Y	Nov. 12, 1867	70, 7[illegible]2
Bee-hive	J. M. Beebe	Casadaga, N. Y	Aug. 6, 1872	130, 101
Bee-hive	J. Bebe	Carrolltown, Pa	Nov. 8, 1870	108, 900
Bee-hive	B. Benton	Weesaw, Mich	Nov. 7, 1871	120, 698
Bee-hive	H. Berix	Petersburgh, Ohio	June 15, 1869	91, [illegible]
Bee-hive	T. F. Bingham	Gowanda, N. Y	Nov. 17, 1863	40, 600

Index of patents issued from the United States Patent Office from 1790 *to* 1873, *inclusive*—Continued.

Invention.	Inventor.	Residence.	Date.	No.
Bee-hive	T. F. Bingham	Gowanda, N. Y	Jan. 5, 1864	41, 052
Bee-hive	T. F. Bingham	Gowanda, N. Y	Aug. 9, 1864	43, 756
Bee-hive	T. F. Bingham	Gowanda, N. Y	Oct. 30, 1866	59, 169
Bee-hive	T. F. Bingham	Gowanda, N. Y	Oct. 30, 1866	59, 170
Bee-hive	J. S. Black	Bloomfield, Ky	May 15, 1860	28, 249
Bee-hive	W. Black	Harrisburgh, Pa	Jan. 26, 1869	86, 128
Bee-hive	E. Blake	Hartford County, Me	Nov. 16, 1820	....
Bee-hive	A. Blood, sr	Norfolk, Va	Nov. 16, 1858	22, 059
Bee-hive	E. Booth	Springfield, Mass	Nov. 28, 1842	2, 861
Bee-hive	H. C. Boyers	Danville, Iowa	July 19, 1864	43, 564
Bee-hive	A. Bradshaw	Rantoul, Ill	Jan. 31, 1871	111, 310
Bee-hive	J. Bradt	La Porte, Ind	Nov. 18, 1862	36, 938
Bee-hive	J. Bradt	La Porte, Ind	July 3, 1866	55, 998
Bee-hive	N. Brasher	Green's Fork, Ind	July 31, 1860	29, 356
Bee-hive	F. Brewer	Waynesville, Mo	Mar. 7, 1871	112, 317
Bee-hive	L. C. Bristol and C. T. Alverson	Victor, N. Y	Oct. 9, 1866	58, 585
Bee-hive	J. F. Broomfield	Richmond, Ky	May 16, 1871	114, 912
Bee-hive	G. A. Brown and F. A. McCallen.	Russellville, Ky	Jan. 10, 1871	110, 894
Bee-hive	J. S. Brown	Washington, D. C	July 29, 1856	15, 457
Bee-hive	L. Brown	Pontiac, N. Y	Oct. 20, 1863	40, 323
Bee-hive	P. Brown	Taylorville, Ill	Sept. 10, 1872	131, 247
Bee-hive	A. M. Brubaker and B. R. Witmer.	Millersville, Pa	Mar. 11, 1873	136, 642
Bee-hive	S. R. Bryant	Waterford, Pa	Oct. 2, 1860	30, 202
Bee-hive	S. R. Bryant	Waterford, Pa	Feb. 12, 1861	31, 369
Bee-hive	W. Bryant	Nashville, Tenn	Dec. 21, 1842	2, 890
Bee-hive	B. F. Bucklin	Cuyahoga Falls, Ohio	Jan. 23, 1872	122, 990
Bee-hive	R. Bullard	Litchfield, Mich	June 4, 1861	32, 463
Bee-hive	D. S. Burget	Martinsburgh Borough, Pa	July 5, 1870	105, 037
Bee-hive	J. Burnham	York, Mich	Nov. 7, 1871	120, 709
Bee-hive	T. Burris	Fieldon, Ill	Aug. 15, 1865	49, 375
Bee-hive	H. Burton	Richview, Ill	Sept. 1, 1868	81, 747
Bee-hive	R. P. Buttles	Mansfield, Pa	Feb. 9, 1869	86, 729
Bee-hive	G. Calvert	Upperville, Va	Nov. 1, 1853	10, 196
Bee-hive	G. Calvert	Upperville, Va	June 22, 1869	91, 712
Bee-hive	D. M. Calvin	East Fallowfield, Pa	Apr. 8, 1873	137, 530
Bee-hive	D. M. Calvin	East Fallowfield, Pa	Dec. 2, 1873	145, 048
Bee-hive	J. A. Cameron	Memphis, Tenn	Feb. 9, 1869	86, 643
Bee-hive	P. Campbell	Carrolltown, Pa	Dec. 14, 1869	97, 759
Bee-hive	A. Canniff	Fort Scott, Kans	Oct. 8, 1872	132, 052
Bee-hive	H. F. Carpenter	Greencastle, Pa	June 7, 1870	103, 978
Bee-hive	J. I. Cassel and W. Quin	Eaton, Ohio	Apr. 14, 1868	76, 602
Bee-hive	J. Chase	Ripley, Ohio	July 21, 1868	80, 138
Bee-hive	E. Y. Chevalier	Fort Wayne, Ind	Aug. 5, 1862	36, 070
Bee-hive	J. B. Child	Lee Centre, Ill	Apr. 10, 1866	53, 785
Bee-hive	W. R. Clark	Piqua, Ohio	Oct. 18, 1864	44, 707
Bee-hive	W. R. Clark	Piqua, Ohio	Nov. 7, 1871	120, 624
Bee-hive	W. R. Clark	Piqua, Ohio	Nov. 26, 1872	133, 355
Bee-hive	G. H. Clarke	East Washington, N. H	Jan. 8, 1856	14, 051
Bee-hive	G. H. Clarke	East Washington, N. H	Mar. 1, 1859	23, 078
Bee-hive	A. Claypool	Weston, Ohio	Jan. 24, 1871	111, 107
Bee-hive	H. Clipp	Orange, Ind	Apr. 2, 1867	63, 472
Bee-hive	A. Clow	Waterford, Pa	Apr. 16, 1861	32, 101
Bee-hive	J. Coats	Camden, Ohio	Oct. 29, 1867	70, 167
Bee-hive	A. F. Cobb	Chapel Hill, Mo	Apr. 21, 1868	76, 999
Bee-hive	T. S. Collins and H. Senseman	Tremont, Ohio	Nov. 14, 1871	120, 858
Bee-hive	D. Collom	Tallmadge, Ohio	Aug. 31, 1869	94, 186
Bee-hive	A. Colton	Pittsfield, Vt	Dec 31, 1845	4, 343
Bee-hive	O. Colvin	Belvidere, Ill	Jan. 15, 1867	61, 164
Bee-hive	R. Colvin	Baltimore, Md	Dec. 3, 1861	33, 826
Bee-hive	P. Compton	Sullivansville, N. Y	May 19, 1868	78, 062
Bee-hive	A. V. Conklin	Bennington, Ohio	Oct. 20, 1868	83, 257
Bee-hive	G. E. Conwell	Knoxville, Iowa	Dec. 31, 1867	72, 805
Bee-hive	H. B. Cooper	Memphis, Tenn	Feb. 22, 1870	100, 015
Bee-hive	S. and J. D. Cope	Damascusville, Ohio	Feb. 12, 1844	3, 439
Bee-hive	E. Corner	Columbus, Ohio	Dec. 24, 1861	34, 034
Bee-hive	W. Courtney	Richview, Ill	Dec. 31, 1867	72, 808
Bee-hive	W. Courtney	Richview, Ill	May 10, 1870	102, 917
Bee-hive	E. Cox	Monroe, Wis	July 16, 1867	66, 680
Bee-hive	J. H. Crandell	Upper Marlborough, Md	Apr. 20, 1869	89, 129
Bee-hive	S. B. Cranford	Upper Marlborough, Md	Aug. 10, 1869	93, 418
Bee-hive	L. H. Critchfield	Shreeve, Ohio	Oct. 5, 1869	95, 436
Bee-hive	W. F. Cunningham	Middletown, Ky	July 16, 1872	129, 464
Bee-hive	S. Cuplin	Iowa Falls, Iowa	July 28, 1868	80, 395
Bee-hive	J. Croner	Cross Creek Village, Pa	June 29, 1869	92, 018
Bee-hive	S. Cuplin	Iowa Falls, Iowa	Nov. 24, 1868	84, 415
Bee-hive	S. Cuplin	Iowa Falls, Iowa	Jan. 31, 1871	111, 434
Bee-hive	S. Cuplin	Iowa Falls, Iowa	Nov. 14, 1871	120, 944
Bee-hive	J. A. Cutting	Haverhill, N. H	June 24, 1844	3, 638
Bee-hive	E. J. Danavan	Indianapolis, Ind	Nov. 1, 1870	108, 893
Bee-hive	R. Daniels and G. P. Cobb	Woodstock, Vt	Mar. 12, 1861	31, 658
Bee-hive	J. W. Davidson	Rome, Ohio	Sept. 17, 1842	2, 777
Bee-hive	E. Davis	Noblesville, Ind	Sept. 6, 1870	107, 012
Bee-hive	O. Davis	Newton, Iowa	July 7, 1868	79, 734
Bee-hive	S. Davis	Claremont, N. H	July 26, 1853	9, 883
Bee-hive	S. T. Davis	Millersville, Pa	Apr. 15, 1873	137, 831
Bee-hive	A. Decker	Fairfield County, Ohio	July 30, 1845	4, 129
Bee-hive	L. Defenbaugh	Kokomo, Ind	Dec. 19, 1865	51, 566
Bee-hive	J. H. Dennis	Boston, Mass	Jan. 24, 1854	10, 445
Bee-hive	J. Detrick and W. B. Niven	Bellefontaine, Ohio	June 13, 1871	115, 941
Bee-hive	A. Deweese	Oak Mills, Kans	Apr. 1, 1873	137, 348
Bee-hive	A. F. Dickey	Benford's Store, Pa	Dec. 5, 1871	121, 597
Bee-hive	W. M. Dickinson	Goshen, Ind	May 26, 1863	38, 660
Bee-hive	E. W. Diefendorf	Moniteau, Mo	Aug. 29, 1871	118, 520
Bee-hive	L. J. Diehl	Butler, Ind	Dec. 16, 1873	145, 634
Bee-hive	W. W. Dodson and J. B. Bray	Lynnville, Tenn	Dec. 19, 1871	121, 999
Bee-hive	G. Dofler	Frederick, Md	Mar. 4, 1843	2, 986

Index of patents issued from the United States Patent Office from 1790 *to* 1873, *inclusive*—Continued.

Invention.	Inventor.	Residence.	Date.	No.
Bee-hive	J. Donnel	Davenport, Iowa	Feb. 24, 1863	37, 741
Bee-hive	D. Dougal and W. Truxal	Butler, Pa	Sept. 3, 1861	33, 189
Bee-hive	J. A. Douglass	Altoona, Pa	Nov. 8, 1870	108, 984
Bee-hive	B. Douthett	Pittsburgh, Pa	Nov. 17, 1868	84, 052
Bee-hive	J. A. Dugdale	Selma, Ohio	July 31, 1849	6, 622
Bee-hive	H. N. Dunham and B. Addington.	Centreville, Ind	Sept. 7, 1869	94, 583
Bee-hive	A. P. Durant	Athens, Ohio	Dec. 8, 1868	84, 805
Bee-hive	J. and H. A. Earhart	Campbellstown, Pa	Nov. 8, 1864	44, 943
Bee-hive	M. Easley	Rush, Ill	June 1, 1869	90, 735
Bee-hive	G. Eason	Lyons, N. Y	Sept. 22, 1868	82, 298
Bee-hive	J. R. East	Fincastle, Tenn	Nov. 18, 1873	144, 750
Bee-hive	H. Eddy	North Bridgewater, Mass	Sept. 19, 1854	11, 691
Bee-hive	D. Edge	Saint Mary's, Ill	Oct. 27, 1868	83, 479
Bee-hive	J. C. Edwards	Cattleville, Mo	Sept. 26, 1871	119, [illegible]36
Bee-hive	W. T. Eisenhart	Doylestown, Pa	Nov. 13, 1866	59, 569
Bee-hive	W. A. Elam	Milan, Tenn	Nov. 23, 1869	97, 067
Bee-hive	A. E. Ellis	Friendsville, Ill	Oct. 9, 1866	58, 624
Bee-hive	W. J. Elvin	North Madison, Ind	June 30, 1868	79, 454
Bee-hive	C. Embrey	Williamsport, Md	Oct. 11, 1870	108, 244
Bee-hive	R. G. Emerson	Fair Haven, Ill	May 12, 1863	38, 475
Bee-hive	M. Engel	Easton, Pa	Apr. 15, 1840	1, 555
Bee-hive	T. S. Engledow	Cedar Falls, Iowa	Jan. 19, 1869	86, 063
Bee-hive	T. S. Engledow	Cedar Falls, Iowa	Jan. 10, 1871	110, 909
Bee-hive	D. H. Farnam	Litchfield, Conn	May 20, 1842	2, 633
Bee-hive	H. A. Farnam	South Bend, Ind	Dec. 26, 1871	122, 242
Bee-hive	I. B. Farquhar	Bloody Run, Pa	June 1, 1869	90, 649
Bee-hive	O. Field	Independence, Iowa	Sept. 15, 1868	82, 101
Bee-hive	J. T. Fife	Tyner City, Ind	Dec. 8, 1868	84, 812
Bee-hive	H. Filson	Monongahela City, Pa	July 20, 1869	92, 947
Bee-hive	S. Fink	Lindsey, Ohio	Feb. 6, 1872	123, 470
Bee-hive	J. E. Finley	Memphis, Tenn	Nov. 6, 1866	59, 377
Bee-hive	J. E. Finley	Memphis, Tenn	May 4, 1869	89, 644
Bee-hive	J. E. Finley	Enon, Ohio	June 15, 1869	91, 321
Bee-hive	C. Finn	Des Moines, Iowa	May 3, 1870	102, 526
Bee-hive	C. Finn	Des Moines, Iowa	Apr. 15, 1873	137, 834
Bee-hive	G. J. Flansburgh	Bethlehem, N. Y	Feb. 16, 1869	86, 913
Bee-hive	W. A. Flanders	Sharon, Vt	Oct. 25, 1853	10, 152
Bee-hive	W. A. Flanders	Cleveland, Ohio	Mar. 6, 1860	27, 4[illegible]8
Bee-hive	W. A. Flanders	Shelby, Ohio	July 14, 1863	39, 221
Bee-hive	W. A. Flanders	Shelby, Ohio	Apr. 5, 1864	42, 181
Bee-hive	W. A. Flanders	Shelby, Ohio	May 7, 1867	64, 515
Bee-hive	W. A. Flanders	Shelby, Ohio	May 5, 1868	77, 473
Bee-hive	H. H. Flick	Lavansville, Pa	Sept. 21, 1869	95, 100
Bee-hive	E. A. Floyd	Macomb, Ill	June 4, 1867	65, 367
Bee-hive	M. D. Fogel	Alpha, Ohio	Feb. 25, 1868	74, 810
Bee-hive	S. P. Forgy	Allensville, Ky	Aug. 4, 1868	80, 716
Bee-hive	T. H. Forster	Indianapolis, Ind	June 7, 1870	104, 011
Bee-hive	T. A. Frakes	Middletown, Ill	May 17, 1870	103, 166
Bee-hive	A. Francis and I. Carlisle	Chandlersville, Ohio	Nov. 28, 1842	2, 862
Bee-hive	A. H. Frank	Buffalo, N. Y	Dec. 27, 1864	45, 598
Bee-hive	E. P. French	Nashua, N. H	May 11, 1858	20, 202
Bee-hive	J. J. and A. J. Frey	Hook's Point, Iowa	Mar. 23, 1869	88, 157
Bee-hive	J. D. Fulkerson	Unity, Ohio	July 1, 1844	3, 646
Bee-hive	A. Fuller	Plymouth, Ind	May 1, 1866	54, 325
Bee-hive	P. J. Furlong	Galen, N. Y	June 1, 1858	20, 417
Bee-hive	G. G. Gabrion	Olive, Mich	Nov. 8, 1870	108, 997
Bee-hive	J. C. Gaston	Cincinnati, Ohio	Nov. 10, 1868	83, 952
Bee-hive	J. C. Gaston	Cincinnati, Ohio	Feb. 16, 1869	86, 915
Bee-hive	J. Gatschets	York Township, Ohio	Nov. 19, 1867	70, 989
Bee-hive	A. W. Geaheart	Beallsville, Ohio	Feb. 14, 1860	27, 122
Bee-hive	D. Gebhart	Sallamonia, Ind	Apr. 18, 1871	113, 870
Bee-hive	G. Gebhart	Lebanon, Pa	Feb. 20, 1843	2, 967
Bee-hive	E. Gerry	Garden City, Minn	Apr. 1, 1873	137, 433
Bee-hive	A. Gilmore	Wayne, Me	June 5, 1849	6, 494
Bee-hive	R. Gipson	Shelby, Ohio	May 31, 1864	42, 995
Bee-hive	J. H. Gisler	Saint Louis, Mo	Feb. 28, 1871	112, 139
Bee-hive	J. W. Gladding	Normal, Ill	Dec. 6, 1870	109, 888
Bee-hive	J. W. Gladding	Normal, Ill	Jan. 9, 1872	122, 598
Bee-hive	L. L. Goodwin	Toronto, Ind	Nov. 15, 1870	109, 201
Bee-hive	J. Gould	Grinnell, Iowa	Jan. 11, 1870	98, 761
Bee-hive	F. Grabbe	North Topeka, Kans	Sept. 24, 1872	131, 610
Bee-hive	G. Graffham	Lawrenceville, Ill	July 24, 1866	56, 551
Bee-hive	M. Graham	Coshocton, Ohio	July 27, 1869	93, 081
Bee-hive	J. H. Graves	Rochester, N. Y	Feb. 10, 1863	37, 622
Bee-hive	A. Gray	Reiley, Ohio	Nov. 26, 1867	71, 381
Bee-hive	D. S. Gray	Onarga, Ill	July 11, 1865	48, 768
Bee-hive	J. C. Gray	Frankfort, Ind	Feb. 19, 1861	31, 454
Bee-hive	W. Green	Kinzua, Pa	Sept. 1, 1863	39, 729
Bee-hive	S. V. Greer	Glasgow, Ky	June 4, 1872	127, 479
Bee-hive	H. Grems	Westmoreland, N. Y	Mar. 8, 1870	100, 524
Bee-hive	D. M. Griffith	Alum Bank, Pa	June 13, 1871	115, 843
Bee-hive	D. L. Grover	Groton, N. Y	July 1, 1873	140, 497
Bee-hive	E. Grumman	Norwalk, Conn	May 26, 1842	2, 645
Bee-hive	J. A. Gruver	West Union, Iowa	July 7, 1863	39, 142
Bee-hive	D. M. Gunn and C. L. Cain	Oskaloosa, Iowa	Oct. 15, 1861	33, 484
Bee-hive	D. M. Gunn and C. L. Cain	Oskaloosa, Iowa	Dec. 2, 1862	37, 039
Bee-hive	H. Gushee and J. G. Dawes	San Francisco, Cal	Oct. 11, 1859	25, 731
Bee-hive	M. Guthrie	Clifton, Iowa	Nov. 13, 1866	59, 593
Bee-hive	W. H. Hall	Wallingford, Conn	Dec. 27, 1839	1, 446
Bee-hive	H. A. Hannum	Cazenovia, N. Y	Feb. 3, 1863	37, 576
Bee-hive	H. A. Hannum	Cazenovia, N. Y	Nov. 8, 1864	44, 949
Bee-hive	J. S. Harbison	Sacramento, Cal	Jan. 4, 1859	22, 500
Bee-hive	J. S. Harbison	Sacramento, Cal	Dec. 13, 1859	26, 431
Bee-hive	W. Harden	Chariton, Iowa	Sept. 20, 1864	44, 305
Bee-hive	H. S. Harned and F. S. Elliott	Boonesborough, Iowa	Feb. 28, 1871	112, 244
Bee-hive	J. H. Harper	Washington, D. C	Aug. 5, 1862	36, 088
Bee-hive	J. Harper	Hillsborough, Iowa	Feb. 21, 1865	46, 467

Index of patents issued from the United States Patent Office from 1790 *to* 1873, *inclusive*—Continued.

Invention.	Inventor.	Residence.	Date.	No.
Bee-hive	J. Harris	Belmont County, Ohio	Jan. 27, 1843	2,929
Bee-hive	J. Harris	New Carlisle, Ind	May 27, 1862	35,426
Bee-hive	E. Harrison	Springfield, Ohio	Oct. 1, 1867	69,428
Bee-hive	A. H. Hart	Stockbridge, Wis	Aug. 13, 1867	67,649
Bee-hive	A. H. Hart	Appleton, Wis	July 2, 1872	128,619
Bee-hive	S. Hart	New Haven, N. Y	Mar. 26, 1845	3,971
Bee-hive	N. D. Hartley and M. L. Morehouse.	Quincy, Ill	Feb. 12, 1861	31,384
Bee-hive	G. R. Hartman	Fort Wayne, Ind	July 9, 1861	32,769
Bee-hive	H. Harvey	Meriden, Ill	June 13, 1871	115,849
Bee-hive	C. Hastings	Dowagiac, Mich	Jan. 7, 1868	73,096
Bee-hive	B. S. and E. H. Haviland	Fort Dodge, Iowa	May 21, 1867	64,864
Bee-hive	R. Hawkins	Beallsville, Pa	Apr. 24, 1860	27,980
Bee-hive	T. Hawkins	Auburn, N. Y	July 10, 1866	56,219
Bee-hive	J. Hazen	Bethlehem, N. Y	Sept. 2, 1862	36,349
Bee-hive	J. Hazen	Bethlehem, N. Y	July 2, 1867	66,336
Bee-hive	J. Heacock	Marlborough, Ohio	June 4, 1867	65,381
Bee-hive	H. L. Heckman	Brooklyn, Iowa	Jan. 24, 1871	111,204
Bee-hive	Z. R. Henck	Port Royal, Pa	Oct. 12, 1842	2,814
Bee-hive	J. H. Hendrick	Clinton, Ill	Dec. 26, 1865	51,716
Bee-hive	J. H. Hendrick	Clinton, Ill	Oct. 1, 1867	69,431
Bee-hive	J. H. Hendrick	Clinton, Ill	Jan. 31, 1871	111,451
Bee-hive	E. E. Henegan	Downsville, Wis	July 8, 1873	140,702
Bee-hive	W. M. Henry	Leo, Ind	Aug. 1, 1871	117,539
Bee-hive	W. Henschen	Hennepin County, Minn	Apr. 4, 1865	47,109
Bee-hive	D. Herman	Bigler Post-Office, Pa	Dec. 5, 1865	51,315
Bee-hive	J. M. Hicks	Indianapolis, Ind	Sept. 6, 1870	107,047
Bee-hive	J. N. Hieronymus	Fairbury, Ill	Dec. 5, 1871	121,618
Bee-hive	J. Hiestand	Palestine, Ill	Nov. 5, 1867	70,436
Bee-hive	S. O. Higgason	Union City, Tenn	Apr. 23, 1872	126,055
Bee-hive	H. Hiser	Wooster, Ohio	June 27, 1842	2,692
Bee-hive	G. T. Hixson	Gallipolis, Ohio	Sept. 24, 1872	131,613
Bee-hive	H. Hodgson	Fremont, Ohio	Feb. 13, 1866	52,571
Bee-hive	A. Hogg	Rutland, Ohio	Sept. 22, 1863	40,038
Bee-hive	I. Honeywell	Toledo, Iowa	Feb. 11, 1868	74,362
Bee-hive	J. S. Hooton	New Carlisle, Ind	June 30, 1868	79,471
Bee-hive	T. P. Hornbrook	Wheeling, Va	May 21, 1861	32,367
Bee-hive	J. and W. H. Horsman	New London, Ind	July 30, 1872	130,052
Bee-hive	W. S. Hough	Galt, Canada	Nov. 25, 1873	144,847
Bee-hive	J. M. Hubbard	Canterbury, N. H	Feb. 5, 1836	....
Bee-hive	H. O. Hughes	Judson, Mo	Dec. 8, 1868	84,826
Bee-hive	P. and S. Hurst	Orrville, Ohio	July 9, 1872	128,883
Bee-hive	S. Hutchinson	North Lewisburgh, Ohio	July 2, 1867	66,348
Bee-hive	W. Hyde	Emery, Ohio	Aug. 7, 1860	29,491
Bee-hive	S. Ide	East Shelby, N. Y	Apr. 2, 1861	31,890
Bee-hive	C. R. Isham	Peoria, N. Y	Jan. 30, 1872	123,104
Bee-hive	J. A. Jackson	Macon, Mich	Feb. 11, 1868	74,369
Bee-hive	J. Jacobs	Yellow Springs, Ohio	Dec. 27, 1859	26,591
Bee-hive	J. Jacobs	Columbus, Ohio	Sept. 25, 1860	30,143
Bee-hive	Z. L. Jacobs	Hebron, Conn	Apr. 9, 1867	63,641
Bee-hive	A. E. James	Point Pleasant, Va	Jan. 6, 1844	3,398
Bee-hive	E. L. Jinnett	Vermillion County, Ill	Mar. 19, 1861	31,719
Bee-hive	C. and A. Jones	Santa Anna, Ill	Apr. 18, 1871	113,892
Bee-hive	E. Jones	Amsterdam, N. Y	Feb. 12, 1845	3,911
Bee-hive	J. Jones	Galway, N. Y	May 12, 1842	2,618
Bee-hive	R. Jones	Cedarville, Ill	Oct. 29, 1867	70,338
Bee-hive	S. M. Judd	Danbury, Conn	Mar. 30, 1836	....
Bee-hive	J. J. Justin	Milwaukee, Wis	July 10, 1866	56,230
Bee-hive	H. C. Keith	Ancona, Ill	Feb. 26, 1867	62,425
Bee-hive	W. J. Kelly	Commerce, Mich	Mar. 21, 1871	112,813
Bee-hive	S. Kelly	Washington, D. C	Dec. 8, 1857	18,815
Bee-hive	A. Kelsey	Westport, Mo	Mar. 31, 1857	16,926
Bee-hive	W. R. Kelsey	Big Steam Point, N. Y	May 9, 1846	4,501
Bee-hive	L. Kennedy	Hartford, Conn	Feb. 9, 1864	41,513
Bee-hive	W. Kennedy	Roxbury, Mass	June 21, 1864	41,211
Bee-hive	K. P. Kidder	Burlington, Vt	Apr. 13, 1858	19,931
Bee-hive	K. P. Kidder	Burlington, Vt	June 26, 1860	28,871
Bee-hive	K. P. Kidder	Burlington, Vt	Mar. 17, 1863	37,915
Bee-hive	K. P. Kidder	Burlington, Vt	May 14, 1867	64,773
Bee-hive	H. A. King	Nevada, Ohio	Sept. 8, 1868	82,006
Bee-hive	H. A. King	New York, N. Y	Mar. 26, 1872	124,962
Bee-hive	H. A. King	New York, N. Y	Sept. 10, 1872	131,168
Bee-hive	H. A. King and J. Loughmaster.	Seal, Ohio	Nov. 24, 1863	40,725
Bee-hive	H. A. and N. H. King and F. S. Walker.	Nevada, Ohio	Oct. 10, 1865	50,367
Bee-hive	I. King	Germantown, Ohio	Nov. 10, 1868	83,861
Bee-hive	W. R. King	Shelbyville, Ky	May 9, 1871	114,690
Bee-hive	E. N. Kingsley	Minneapolis, Minn	Sept. 11, 1866	57,924
Bee-hive	W. T. Kirkpatrick	Tamaroa, Ill	Dec. 14, 1869	97,933
Bee-hive	A. H. Klepper	Muscatine, Iowa	Sept. 26, 1871	119,366
Bee-hive	E. J. Kline	Kirkville, Iowa	May 12, 1868	77,832
Bee-hive	W. Kraiss	Fairview, Pa	Apr. 30, 1867	64,334
Bee-hive	L. Kramer	Point Pleasant, Pa	May 14, 1867	64,675
Bee-hive	E. Kretchmer	Pleasant Grove, Iowa	Nov. 13, 1866	59,614
Bee-hive	E. Kretchmer	Pleasant Grove, Iowa	July 23, 1867	67,123
Bee-hive	E. Kretchmer	Coburg, Iowa	May 6, 1873	138,661
Bee-hive	J. Lamborn	Marshallton, Pa	Aug. 26, 1845	4,168
Bee-hive	J. C. and R. R. Lander	Mazo Manie, Wis	Nov. 24, 1868	84,286
Bee-hive	L. L. Langstroth	Philadelphia, Pa	Oct. 5, 1852	9,300
Bee-hive	J. Lash	Mount Vernon, Nebr	Aug. 9, 1864	43,779
Bee-hive	D. Latchaw	Barkeyville, Pa	Feb. 13, 1872	123,632
Bee-hive	D. Latchaw	Barkeyville, Pa	Aug. 5, 1873	141,443
Bee-hive	A. S. Layton	Yellville, Ark	Feb. 9, 1869	86,765
Bee-hive	W. M. Lee	Rosendale, Wis	Oct. 15, 1861	33,486
Bee-hive	W. M. Lee	Rosendale, Wis	Aug. 25, 1863	39,660
Bee-hive	J. K. Leedy	Woodstock, Va	July 12, 1859	24,745
Bee-hive	J. Leffel and E. Harrison	Springfield, Ohio	Sept. 27, 1870	107,792

Index of patents issued from the United States Patent Office from 1790 *to* 1873, *inclusive*—Continued.

Invention.	Inventor.	Residence.	Date.	No.
Bee-hive	G. W. Leffingwell	Columbus, Wis	July 23, 1867	66, 977
Bee-hive	W. Lehman	Lexington, Mo	Feb. 4, 1873	135, 566
Bee-hive	V. Leonard	Springfield, Pa	June 4, 1867	65, 402
Bee-hive	V. Leonard	Springfield, Pa	Sept. 3, 1867	68, 759
Bee-hive	V. Leonard	Springfield, Pa	Aug. 16, 1870	106, 377
Bee-hive	C. P. Lloyd	Portsmouth, Ohio	Feb. 12, 1867	61, 043
Bee-hive	B. Lockrone	Somerset, Ohio	Oct. 27, 1868	83, 514
Bee-hive	J. Longgrear and J. E. Clark	Rolla, Mo	Aug. 13, 1872	130, 511
Bee-hive	D. Lootbourrow	Hillsborough, Iowa	Jan. 7, 1873	134, 687
Bee-hive	R. Lovett	Canton, Ohio	Mar. 29, 1864	42, 093
Bee-hive	J. J. Lower	Tennessee, Ill	Dec. 24, 1867	72, 651
Bee-hive	G. W. Lowry	Lavansville, Pa	Nov. 9, 1869	96, 712
Bee-hive	O. Mack	Gilsum, N. H	Apr. 22, 1835	....
Bee-hive	S. Maitland	Fort Wayne, Ind	Aug. 28, 1860	29, 799
Bee-hive	H. Markham	Henderson, Ill	Feb. 23, 1864	41, 711
Bee-hive	G. Marsh	Steamburgh, N. Y	Feb. 28, 1871	112, 262
Bee-hive	J. S. Marshall	West Greenville, Pa	Apr. 22, 1862	35, 031
Bee-hive	J. R. Martin	Martinsburgh, Ind	Dec. 17, 1867	72, 308
Bee-hive	R. Martin	Fairfield, Ohio	May 19, 1840	1, 612
Bee-hive	C. R. C. Masten and A. D. Van Vlack.	Pleasant Valley, N. Y	Jan. 19, 1869	86, 023
Bee-hive	T. H. Mathews	Rushville, Ill	Aug. 23, 1864	43, 921
Bee-hive	J. Mathius	Pemberton, Ohio	Oct. 8, 1867	69, 569
Bee-hive	J. A. McAnulty	Gilpin, Pa	Jan. 31, 1871	111, 466
Bee-hive	T. F. McCafferty	Columbus, Ohio	Mar. 30, 1869	88, 315
Bee-hive	S. McClanathan	Warren, Ill	Mar. 24, 1863	38, 012
Bee-hive	H. M. McClellan	York, Pa	Dec. 1, 1857	18, 757
Bee-hive	J. McDonald	Buffalo, Ohio	June 23, 1868	79, 243
Bee-hive	N. McGonnigle	Allegheny, Pa	July 31, 1860	29, 394
Bee-hive	C. McGrew	Bloomington, Ill	Feb. 12, 1867	62, 051
Bee-hive	S. D. McLean	Sunny Slope, Tenn	June 4, 1872	127, 498
Bee-hive	J. D. Meador	Independence, Mo	Feb. 2, 1869	86, 569
Bee-hive	J. Meese, sr	Milton, Ohio	Jan. 31, 1860	27, 004
Bee-hive	G. W. Merchant	La Porte, Ind	Sept. 25, 1866	58, 276
Bee-hive	M. Metcalf	Grand Rapids, Mich	July 30, 1861	32, 952
Bee-hive	J. F. Metherd and S. Young	Union City, Ind	Mar. 28, 1871	113, 187
Bee-hive	J. Milholland and B. Crane	Chandlersville, Ohio	Apr. 29, 1842	2, 592
Bee-hive	G. Miller	Battle Ground, Wash	Sept. 30, 1873	143, 295
Bee-hive	J. Miller	Lexington, Ohio	Nov. 6, 1843	3, 325
Bee-hive	O. Miller	Girard, Pa	Apr. 2, 1861	31, 900
Bee-hive	W. D. Miller	Mad River, Ohio	Sept. 1, 1843	3, 246
Bee-hive	N. C. Mitchell	Caledonia, Ohio	Feb. 18, 1868	74, 709
Bee-hive	J. Montgomery	Union City, Tenn	Jan. 4, 1870	98, 612
Bee-hive	F. Moore	Carrollton, Ohio	June 9, 1868	78, 813
Bee-hive	J. E. Moore	Bridgewater, Pa	Feb. 20, 1872	123, 924
Bee-hive	S. C. Moore	Pattonsburgh, Mo	Aug. 8, 1871	117, 914
Bee-hive	W. L. Moorhead and T. D. Howell.	Lanesville, Ohio	Feb. 16, 1843	2, 953
Bee-hive	S. Morrill	Dixfield, Me	Feb. 4, 1834	....
Bee-hive	S. Morrill	Dixfield, Me	Jan. 16, 1835	....
Bee-hive	M. Morton	Gallatin, Mo	Apr. 5, 1870	101, 647
Bee-hive	W. T. Mosher	Poplar Ridge, N. Y	Aug. 27, 1872	130, 932
Bee-hive	A. R. Moulton	Fall Branch, Tenn	Sept. 10, 1872	131, 296
Bee-hive	M. D. Mulford, jr	New Providence, Iowa	July 31, 1866	56, 782
Bee-hive	E. F. Mulkey and J. Case	Tamaroa, Ill	Aug. 27, 1872	130, 933
Bee-hive	A. Mutersbaugh	Lewinsville, Va	Nov. 7, 1871	120, 766
Bee-hive	P. M. Myers, J. W. Walser, and J. Spangler.	Canton, Ohio	May 7, 1867	64, 557
Bee-hive	S. C. Myers	Mount Pleasant, Pa	July 22, 1839	1, 255
Bee-hive	B. F. Nave	Fort Wayne, Ind	Sept. 29, 1868	82, 628
Bee-hive	J. Neal	Orleans, Iowa	Jan. 28, 1868	73, 915
Bee-hive	J. Newman and N. Brown	Rossville, Ill	Mar. 18, 1873	136, 933
Bee-hive	C. S. Newsom	Gallipolis, Ohio	Apr. 16, 1872	125, 837
Bee-hive	P. Nicolle	Lindsay, Canada	Mar, 28, 1871	113, 084
Bee-hive	A. Niebel	Tiffin, Ohio	Oct. 27, 1868	83, 532
Bee-hive	E. O'Connor	Philadelphia, Pa	Oct. 17, 1871	119, 991
Bee-hive	H. Ogborn	Richmond, Ind	Mar. 22, 1864	42, 017
Bee-hive	L. M. Olden	Pana, Ill	Nov. 26, 1867	71, 405
Bee-hive	O. Osmundson	Mission, Ill	Apr. 20, 1869	89, 067
Bee-hive	J. N. Outten	Caseyville, Ky	Sept. 29, 1868	82, 634
Bee-hive	J. A. Paddock and J. S. Estep	Cass County, Ill	July 6, 1869	92, 348
Bee-hive	S. E. Paine and W. Kerr	Xenia, Ill	Feb. 13, 1872	123, 724
Bee-hive	J. W. Palmer	Port Republic, Va	Nov. 1, 1859	25, 979
Bee-hive	J. W. Palmer and J. K. Leedy	Port Republic and Tom's Brook, Va.	Oct. 9, 1860	30, 341
Bee-hive	L. Parker	Winterset, Iowa	Apr. 28, 1863	38, 328
Bee-hive	E. Parks	Wheatfield, N. Y	July 22. 1845	4, 116
Bee-hive	J. L. Patourel	Chandlersville, Ohio	June 11, 1841	2, 122
Bee-hive	J. M. Patton	Tipton, Iowa	Feb. 11, 1868	74, 415
Bee-hive	C. Pawling	New Pittsburgh, Ohio	Oct. 14, 1856	15, 894
Bee-hive	J. Pearson	West Milton, Ohio	Feb. 2, 1869	86, 441
Bee-hive	R. Pearson	Appleton, Wis	Aug. 3, 1869	93, 340
Bee-hive	T. W. Peirce	Minneapolis, Minn	Mar. 27, 1866	53, 475
Bee-hive	H. Penoyer	Centralia, Ill	Feb. 28, 1865	46, 584
Bee-hive	E. Pepple	Canton, Ohio	June 24, 1843	3, 141
Bee-hive	P. O. Peterson	Oakland, Cal	May 14, 1872	126, 739
Bee-hive	E. W. Phelps	Elizabeth, N. J	Nov. 9, 1858	22, 030
Bee-hive	W. H. Pierson	West Jersey, Ill	Oct. 16, 1866	58, 881
Bee-hive	H. A. Pitts	Winthrop, Me	Sept. 25, 1841	2, 268
Bee-hive	J. F. Pool	Monroe, Wis	Aug. 18, 1868	81, 206
Bee-hive	C. H. Potter	Philadelphia, Pa	June 4, 1872	127, 513
Bee-hive	W. Powers	Youngstown, Ohio	Mar. 8, 1859	23, 192
Bee-hive	I. C. Pratt	Morton, Ill	Dec. 18, 1860	30, 984
Bee-hive	J. P. Praul	Pleasant Hill, Ill	Feb. 16, 1869	87, 003
Bee-hive	J. M. Price	Buffalo Grove, Iowa	Mar. 22, 1870	101, 039
Bee-hive	J. S. Procter	Franklin, Ky	Dec. 26, 1871	122, 279
Bee-hive	T. Prosser	Birmingham, Pa	June 8, 1858	20, 508
Bee-hive	E. D. Pugh	Fort Plain, Iowa	Sept. 12, 1871	118, 972

Index of patents issued from the United States Patent Office from 1790 *to* 1873, *inclusive*—Continued.

Invention.	Inventor.	Residence.	Date.	No.
Bee-hive	R. Ramsay	New Wilmington, Pa	Jan. 7, 1862	34, 094
Bee-hive	D. R. Read	Lawrence, Kans	Apr. 18, 1871	113, 928
Bee-hive	E. B. Redfield and E. C. Hubbard.	White's Corners and Water Valley, N. Y.	June 15, 1869	91, 266
Bee-hive	B. H. Reece	Marion, Iowa	July 15, 1862	35, 892
Bee-hive	O. P. Reeve	Tipton, Iowa	Jan. 10, 1865	45, 859
Bee-hive	O. P. Reeve and C. C. Parker	Central City, Mo	Aug. 8, 1871	117, 815
Bee-hive	J. L. Reid	Van Wert, Ohio	Aug. 12, 1862	36, 169
Bee-hive	S. B. Replogle	Martinsburgh, Pa	July 21, 1868	80, 091
Bee-hive	O. Reynolds	Webster, N. Y	Dec. 4, 1844	3, 841
Bee-hive	O. Reynolds	Webster, N. Y	July 31, 1847	5, 211
Bee-hive	O. Reynolds	Webster, N. Y	June 4, 1861	32, 484
Bee-hive	W. Reynolds and J. V. Brooks	Lexington, Ill	Mar. 28, 1871	113, 207
Bee-hive	D. Rice	Richfield, Ill	Aug. 12, 1873	141, 818
Bee-hive	J. C. Rich	Penfield, N. Y	Mar. 4, 1843	2, 988
Bee-hive	S. L. Richardson	Webster City, Iowa	Dec. 29, 1868	85, 401
Bee-hive	J. E. Richey and C. Hotchkiss	Van Wert, Ohio	Mar. 15, 1864	41, 942
Bee-hive	J. Robb	Lewistown, Pa	Dec. 31, 1845	4, 340
Bee-hive	W. H. Roberts	Campbell's Station, Tenn	June 18, 1872	128, 070
Bee-hive	H. G. Robertson	Greenville, Tenn	Jan. 29, 1856	14, 168
Bee-hive	G. A. Robinson	Mount Pulaski, Ill	July 27, 1869	93, 009
Bee-hive	J. M. Robnett	Centralia, Ill	June 1, 1869	90, 873
Bee-hive	S. Rogers and A. J. Mason	Butler, Ind	Sept. 24, 1872	131, 628
Bee-hive	S. Rogers and A. J. Mason	Butler, Ind	Aug. 26, 1873	142, 281
Bee-hive	H. F. Rohm	West Providence, Pa	Sept. 20, 1870	107, 548
Bee-hive	H. F. Rohm	West Providence, Pa	Sept. 20, 1870	107, 628
Bee-hive	J. Rohrer	Middletown, Pa	Oct. 8, 1861	33, 451
Bee-hive	A. I. Root and M. Andrews	Medina, Ohio	June 18, 1872	128, 072
Bee-hive	J. E. Ross	Mount Sidney, Va	July 8, 1842	2, 707
Bee-hive	D. Rudolph	Sugar Grove, Ohio	Mar. 3, 1868	75, 201
Bee-hive	W. A. Ruth	Wyoming, Del	Nov. 29, 1870	109, 672
Bee-hive	H. W. Sabin	Gorham, N. Y	Jan. 15, 1846	4, 355
Bee-hive	A. Sanburn	Carthage, Ohio	Mar. 26, 1845	3, 972
Bee-hive	B. D. Sanders	Holliday's Cove, Va,	Oct. 27, 1857	18, 523
Bee-hive	M. R. Sanders	Cambria Township, Pa	Nov. 14, 1871	120, 899
Bee-hive	J. D. Sanderson	Stetson, Me	Dec. 14, 1858	22, 309
Bee-hive	R. Sanford	Marion, N. Y	Nov. 23, 1869	97, 124
Bee-hive	W. K. Sawyer	Three Oaks, Mich	Aug. 1, 1871	117, 690
Bee-hive	G. C. Schneider	Adrian, Mich	Oct. 6, 1868	82, 880
Bee-hive	H. Scovell and J. C. Banker	Waseca, Minn	Sept. 24, 1872	131, 632
Bee-hive	N. B. Sebring	Metamora, Ohio	May 18, 1869	90, 199
Bee-hive	B. F. See	Monroe, Ohio	Jan. 19, 1869	86, 037
Bee-hive	P. J. Severson	Knowersville, N. Y	Feb. 25, 1868	74, 854
Bee-hive	D. and A. M. Shaeffer	Centreville, Iowa	Dec. 31, 1867	72, 918
Bee-hive	H. M. Shaffer	Bucyrus, Ohio	Oct. 2, 1860	30, 255
Bee-hive	M. B. Shaw	Zionsville, Iowa	June 18, 1872	127, 991
Bee-hive	E. N. Shedd	Three Oaks, Mich	Sept. 21, 1869	95, 151
Bee-hive	T. Shields	Hillsborough, Ohio	Oct. 6, 1868	82, 757
Bee-hive	S. P. Shipley	Olena, Ohio	June 16, 1868	78, 898
Bee-hive	J. Shoe	Pleasant Hill, Ohio	Dec. 8, 1868	84, 774
Bee-hive	J. Sholl	New York, N. Y	Nov. 9, 1839	1, 402
Bee-hive	J. H. Shook	Normal, Ill	Oct. 14, 1873	143, 643
Bee-hive	S. A., F. J., and J. B. Short, and J. Kile.	Decatur, Ala	Mar. 7, 1871	112, 388
Bee-hive	W. P. Shortridge	Easton, Mo	Sept. 12, 1871	118, 822
Bee-hive	S. Shrock	New Philadelphia, Pa	Nov. 10, 1868	84, 010
Bee-hive	H. P. Simmons and A. J. King	Paterson and Hudson, N. J	Feb. 4, 1873	135, 493
Bee-hive	N. Simpson	Pomeroy, Ohio	May 21, 1867	65, 020
Bee-hive	W. Y. Singleton	Springfield, Ill	Feb. 18, 1868	74, 618
Bee-hive	L. S. Sisson	West Edmeston, N. Y	Jan. 10, 1871	110, 937
Bee-hive	G. Slusser	Hillsborough, Ohio	Aug. 13, 1867	67, 680
Bee-hive	A. J. Smith	Decorah, Iowa	Oct. 15, 1861	33, 499
Bee-hive	A. J. Smith	Wayland, Mich	Aug. 22, 1865	49, 563
Bee-hive	A. J. Smith and H. C. Reed	Decorah, Iowa	Mar. 31, 1868	76, 258
Bee-hive	G. W. Smith, N. B. Vosburgh, A. J. Kramer, and W. L. Winter.	Linn County, Iowa	Aug. 4, 1863	39, 451
Bee-hive	J. L. Smith	Liberty Centre, Ohio	Sept. 27, 1870	107, 732
Bee-hive	J. W. Smith	Iowa Point, Kans	Jan. 6, 1863	37, 363
Bee-hive	M. S. Snow	Forestville, N. Y	Mar. 24, 1868	75, 804
Bee-hive	C. E. Spaulding	Theresa, N. Y	May 11, 1869	89, 896
Bee-hive	C. J. Sperry and L. Chandler	New London, Minn	Sept. 30, 1873	143, 307
Bee-hive	G. Spinney	Saugus, Mass	Sept. 26, 1865	50, 179
Bee-hive	O. Sprague	Fulton, Ill	Mar. 28, 1865	47, 047
Bee-hive	N. A. Springer	Pontiac, Ill	Nov. 22, 1870	109, 557
Bee-hive	H. Staggs	Topeka, Kans	Jan. 9, 1872	122, 542
Bee-hive	U. Stanbury	Plymouth, Ind	Oct. 20, 1868	83, 335
Bee-hive	T. Stanly	Farmington, Conn	Dec. 9, 1811	....
Bee-hive	T. Stanly	Farmington, Conn	Jan. 6, 1812	....
Bee-hive	S. Stansberry	Knoxville, Tenn	Mar. 2, 1858	19, 520
Bee-hive	R. P. Starbuck	Gallatin, Mo	May 18, 1869	90, 203
Bee-hive	J. H. Starr	Middleburgh, N. Y	Nov. 6, 1866	59, 471
Bee hive	J. B. Staunton	Ellicottsville, N. Y	May 28, 1872	127, 281
Bee-hive	J. G. Staunton	Ellicottsville, N. Y	Nov. 19, 1872	133, 128
Bee-hive	M. J. Stearnes	Galesville, Wis	Feb. 7, 1871	111, 696
Bee-hive	S. D. Stearns and G. Ellsworth.	Weston, Ohio	Sept. 12, 1871	118, 827
Bee-hive	S. Stevens	New Carlisle, Ind	May 14, 1867	64, 806
Bee-hive	S. Stevens	Terre Coupee, Ind	June 15, 1869	91, 492
Bee-hive	A. J. Sternberg	Butler, Ind	Sept. 9, 1873	142, 748
Bee-hive	H. A. Stidger	Carrollton, Ohio	Feb. 18, 1868	74, 627
Bee-hive	M. Stillwell	Manlius, N. Y	Oct. 22, 1861	33, 548
Bee-hive	J. H. Stockwell	Bronson, Mich	Oct. 21, 1873	143, 937
Bee-hive	O. Stoddard	Busti, N. Y	Aug. 15, 1848	5, 714
Bee-hive	L. M. Stoops	Grand View, Ind	Oct. 27, 1868	83, 565
Bee-hive	J. B. Strickler	Milford, Ill	Jan. 6, 1863	37, 310
Bee-hive	H. Stump	Adel, Iowa	Dec. 6, 1864	45, 358
Bee-hive	A. J. Surles	Florence, Ga	Mar. 18, 1851	7, 991
Bee-hive	C. Suydam	Lambertville, N. J	Nov. 18, 1845	4, 272

Index of patents issued from the United States Patent Office from 1790 *to* 1873, *inclusive*—Continued.

Invention.	Inventor.	Residence.	Date.	No.
Bee-hive	D. H. Swartz	Lancaster, Ohio	Jan. 24, 1871	111, 273
Bee-hive	J. Sweet	Bethlehem, Mass	Apr. 11, 1810	....
Bee-hive	J. Tallman	Clayton, Ill	Sept. 22, 1868	82, 363
Bee-hive	P. Taltavull	Washington, D. C	Oct. 26, 1858	21, 912
Bee-hive	L. and M. Taylor and E. Cox	Jordan, Wis	Feb. 13, 1866	52, 622
Bee hive	S. Taylor	Burlington, Me	Oct. 9, 1866	58, 696
Bee-hive	H. R. Terry	Edinborough, Pa	Nov. 5, 1861	33, 668
Bee-hive	J. H. Thomas	Rochester, N. Y	July 2, 1867	66, 415
Bee-hive	J. H Thurston	Rainsborough, Ohio	Nov. 17, 1868	84, 232
Bee-hive	S. Titcomb	Farmington, Me	Apr. 10, 1849	6, 285
Bee-hive	R. S. Torrey	Bangor, Me	June 7, 1859	24, 342
Bee-hive	R. S. Torrey	Bangor, Me	Aug. 3, 1869	93, 372
Bee-hive	H. A. Tozier	Littleton, Me	Oct. 9, 1866	58, 697
Bee-hive	J. Tritt	New Richmond, Ohio	Dec. 19, 1871	122, 080
Bee-hive	S. Trumbull	Suffield, Conn	Apr. 6, 1842	2, 539
Bee-hive	H. Tuller	Ash Grove, Ill	June 2, 1868	78, 621
Bee-hive	E. B. Turnipseed	Columbia, S. C	Oct. 18, 1870	108, 536
Bee-hive	G. V. Umbaugh	Lima, Ohio	Mar. 23, 1869	88, 235
Bee-hive	T. S. Underhill	Saint Johnsville, N. Y	Dec. 13, 1859	26, 452
Bee-hive	J. H. Valentine	Sparta, Ill	July 1, 1862	35, 791
Bee-hive	J. T. Vanduzer	Tyrone, N. Y	Dec. 27, 1864	45, 657
Bee-hive	A. C. Varela	Washington, D. C	Dec. 24, 1867	72, 572
Bee-hive	F. Varin	Huntsville, Ala	Nov. 7, 1871	120, 799
Bee-hive	S. Vreeland	Cuba, N. Y	July 20, 1869	92, 913
Bee-hive	E. Walker	Indianapolis, Ind	Dec. 27, 1870	110, 517
Bee-hive	F. R. Walker	Waterford, Pa	May 7, 1861	32, 259
Bee-hive	S. H. Walker	Somerville, Tenn	May 31, 1859	24, 251
Bee-hive	W. W. Walker	Nettle Lake, Ohio	Jan. 13, 1863	37, 414
Bee-hive	N. W. Walton and J. L. Cuningham.	Pennsborough, W. Va	Sept. 2, 1873	142, 537
Bee-hive	W. Wambach	Indianapolis, Ind	Jan. 24, 1871	111, 283
Bee-hive	P. S. Ward	Millville, Iowa	Oct. 21, 1862	36, 740
Bee-hive	W. Warren	Three Oaks, Mich	May 5, 1863	38, 431
Bee-hive	J. Wash	Mount Sterling, Ill	July 3, 1866	56, 127
Bee-hive	J. Wash	Mount Sterling, Ill	Apr. 21, 1868	77, 139
Bee-hive	D. G. Watt	Lawrence, Kans	June 29, 1869	91, 885
Bee-hive	C. Webb	Wallingford, Conn	May 4, 1841	2, 079
Bee-hive	T. Webb	Buda, Ill	Jan. 12, 1869	85, 878
Bee-hive	J. M. Weeks	Salisbury, Vt	June 30, 1836	....
Bee-hive	J. M. Weeks	Salisbury, Vt	July 1, 1841	2, 151
Bee-hive	J. H. Welty	Mount Carroll, Ill	Apr. 28, 1863	38, 340
Bee-hive	G. R. West	Fairfield, Ohio	Apr. 20, 1844	3, 554
Bee-hive	W. L. West	Elmira, N. Y	Feb. 8, 1859	22, 908
Bee-hive	J. Wheeldon	Greensburgh, Ind	Jan. 3, 1871	110, 809
Bee-hive	J. Wheeldon	Greensburgh, Ind	Nov. 14, 1871	120, 918
Bee-hive	C. Wheeler	Little Valley, N. Y	June 20, 1845	4, 087
Bee-hive	C. Wheeler	Little Valley, N. Y	May 9, 1854	10, 877
Bee-hive	G. Wheeler	Little Valley, N. Y	July 3, 1849	6, 576
Bee-hive	G. T. Wheeler	Mexico, N. Y	Nov. 22, 1870	109, 477
Bee-hive	W. Whitcomb	Grafton, Vt	Sept. 19, 1846	4, 763
Bee-hive	J. C. White	Huntsville, Ala	Feb. 13, 1872	123, 654
Bee-hive	M. F. White	Mount Pleasant, Iowa	June 21, 1870	104, 521
Bee-hive	A. Whitman, jr	Londonderry, Vt	Nov. 6, 1834	....
Bee-hive	H. H. Whitney	Waterford, Pa	Apr. 30, 1861	32, 217
Bee-hive	C. Wiggins	Fayette County, Pa	Feb. 27, 1827	....
Bee-hive	J. W. Winder	Cincinnati, Ohio	May 31, 1870	103, 697
Bee-hive	T. H. Windle	Wagontown, Pa	Aug. 10, 1858	21, 163
Bee-hive	A. Wilkinson	Greensburgh, Ind	Jan. 24, 1871	111, 289
Bee-hive	C. Williams	Weston, Mo	Aug. 28, 1860	29, 848
Bee-hive	J. Williams	Bean's Station, Tenn	May 7, 1872	126, 605
Bee-hive	R. A. Williams	Colusa, Cal	Dec. 6, 1870	109, 986
Bee-hive	S. C. Williams	Shenandoah County, Va	May 14, 1823	....
Bee-hive	H. K. Wilson	Barboursville, Ky	Apr. 16, 1872	125, 776
Bee-hive	F. Wolfersberger	Plymouth, Ohio	May 12, 1842	2, 617
Bee-hive	J. Wood	Alert, Ohio	Jan. 12, 1869	85, 884
Bee-hive	A. E. Woodhull	Spencer, Mich	Dec. 26, 1871	122, 302
Bee-hive	R. H. Woodside	Coultersville, Ill	Apr. 8, 1873	137, 645
Bee-hive	F. Woodward	Sacramento City, Cal	Aug. 13, 1861	33, 059
Bee-hive	A. T. Wright	Oskaloosa, Iowa	June 16, 1863	38, 925
Bee-hive	A. T. Wright	New Vienna, Ohio	June 4, 1867	65, 522
Bee-hive	A. T. Wright	New Vienna, Ohio	Jan. 5, 1869	85, 716
Bee-hive	A. T. Wright	New Vienna, Ohio	Jan. 12, 1869	85, 885
Bee-hive	A. T. Wright	Oskaloosa, Iowa	Aug. 26, 1873	142, 318
Bee-hive	J. M. Youart	Indianapolis, Ind	Feb. 15, 1870	99, 994
Bee-hive	V. Zimmerman	Morris, Ill	Sept. 22, 1868	82, 372
Bee-hive and management of bees	A. Alley	Cincinnati, Ohio	Aug. 26, 1831	....
Bee-hive and management of bees	E. Britton	Little Falls, N. Y	Sept. 9, 1831	....
Bee-hive and management of bees	P. Munch	Putnam, Ohio	July 27, 1831	....
Bee-hive and management of bees	L. H. Parish	Brighton, N. Y	Aug. 6, 1834	....
Bee-hive for raising queen-bees	J. Davis	Indianapolis, Ind	Nov. 23, 1869	97, 055
Bee-hive honey-box	H. M. Johnson and C. M. Barker	Marshall and Albion, Mich.	Jan. 7, 1873	134, 674
Bee-hive honey-box	E. C. Lewis	Glasgow, Mo	Nov. 14, 1871	120, 885
Bee hive miller-trap	T. L. Gray	Thomasville, Tenn	Dec. 21, 1869	98, 052
Bee-hive portal, Moth-proof	E. Beard	Salem, Iowa	Mar. 10, 1868	75, 349
Bee-hive protector	A. S. Johnson	Waupun, Wis	Oct. 27, 1868	83, 388
Bee-hive slide	E. Beard	Charlestown, Mass	Mar. 12, 1830	....
Bee-hives, Closing and opening the entrance to	G. Upham	Hebron, Ohio	May 1, 1845	4, 018
Bee-hives, Comb frame for	W. Kenyon	Crawfordsville, Ind	Feb. 6, 1872	123, 483
Bee-hives, Comb-frame for	M. Metcalf	Grand Rapids, Mich	Jan. 14, 1862	34, 157
Bee-hives, Compound to be used in	T. F. McCafferty	Forest, Ohio	Aug. 27, 1867	68, 221
Bee-hives, Entrance to	J. E. Dalton and T. Stevens	New Vienna, Ohio	Apr. 9, 1850	7, 258
Bee-hives, Feed-box of	J. D. Egleston	Canaan, Conn	Jan. 27, 1857	16, 474
Bee-hives, Fumigator for	A. R. Denlinger	Gordonsville, Pa	June 17, 1873	139, 881
Bee-hives, Machine for making comb-guide for	H. A. King	New York, N. Y	May 23, 1871	115, 066
Bee-hives, Moth-fly trap for	J. D. Meador	Independence, Mo	Sept. 1, 1868	81, 808
Bee-hives, Moth-trap for	L. Gates	Pleasant Hill, Mo	Mar. 18, 1873	136, 911
Bee-hives, Moth-trap for	R. Haven	Perrysville, Ind	Sept. 24, 1861	33, 347

Index of patents issued from the United States Patent Office from 1790 *to* 1873, *inclusive*—Continued.

Invention.	Inventor.	Residence.	Date.	No.
Bee-hives, Moth-trap for	W. J. Hazen	Bethany, Pa	Nov. 12, 1861	33, 704
Bee-hives, Moth-trap for	E. W. Phelps	Newark, Ohio	Apr. 6, 1852	8, 585
Bee-hives, Surplus honey-boxes in	H. Moon and D. C. Turner	Red Creek, N. Y	Aug. 25, 1868	81, 398
Bee-hives, Swarm-indicator for	W. W. Snell	Rushford, Minn	Oct. 24, 1865	50, 639
Bee-hives, Use of slides in	N. Potter	Buffalo, N. Y	Mar. 11, 1851	7, 970
Bee-hives, Working the doors of	J. Case	Selma, Ohio	Nov. 19, 1850	7, 779
Bee-hiving device	C. Cutler	Tonawanda, N. Y	May 21, 1861	32, 357
Bee-house	D. Burbank	Lexington, Ky	Nov. 9, 1869	96, 668
Bee-house	W. Carter	Saint Louis, Mo	Dec. 15, 1868	84, 994
Bee-house	C. Decker	New Michigan, Ill	Oct. 20, 1868	83, 263
Bee-house	D. S. Gray	Onargo, Ill	Feb. 2, 1869	86, 528
Bee-house	W. Groves	Harrisburgh, Pa	June 12, 1835	....
Bee-house	J. W. Wood	Alden, Ill	Nov. 29, 1870	109, 702
Bee house and hive	W. M. Simpson	Davidsburgh, Mich	Apr. 28, 1868	77, 222
Bee-houses and bee-hives and the management thereof, Construction of.	J. Searle	Hill, N. H	Jan. 20, 1838	580
Bee-keepers' protecting-mask	L. C. Huff	Sonina, Ala	July 1, 1873	140, 417
Bee-moth instrument	R. P. Battles	Mansfield, Pa	Nov. 23, 1869	97, 161
Bee-moth trap	G. Fletcher, sr	Greensburgh, Ind	Mar. 26, 1850	7, 212
Bee-palace	L. Hamlin	Kerkersville, Ohio	July 13, 1844	3, 664
Bee-protector	J. Cory	Holden, Mo	June 28, 1870	104, 832
Bee-protector	T. D. Howell	Zanesville, Ohio	Dec. 15, 1843	3, 379
Bee-separator	J. H. Starr	Middlebush, N. Y	Aug. 8, 1865	49, 314
Bees, Composition for stupefying	A. Y. Rozenbury	Waterloo, Ind	May 23, 1871	115, 107
Bees, House for the management of	M. A. Glass	Independence, Iowa	July 4, 1871	116, 700
Bees, Mode of managing honey	F. Kelsey	Lockport, N. Y	Aug. 26, 1828	....
Bees, Trellis for propagating	A. Simons	Fairfield, Iowa	Aug. 18, 1868	81, 220
Beef and vegetable cutter, Dried	W. and J. T. Bird	Flemington, N. J	Dec. 5, 1865	51, 288
Beef-cutter	B. Meeker	Brooklyn, N. Y	Oct. 21, 1815	....
Beef cutter, Dried	D. W. Goble	Newark, N. J	July 9, 1850	7, 489
Beef cutter, Dried	C. J. and D. C. Holmes	Stafford Springs, Conn	Dec. 28, 1869	98, 263
Beef, Machine for cutting smoked	S. R. Kneeland	....	Oct. 9, 1810	
Beef, Manufacture of chipped	C. L. Tucker	Chicago, Ill	July 20, 1869	92, 907
Beef, &c., Method of preparing	B. F. Stephens	Brooklyn, N. Y	June 8, 1869	91, 176
Beef or cold-slaw shaving or cutting machine	H. Bangs	New York, N. Y	Apr. 28, 1831	....
Beef, salted, Mode of making and curing	W. A. Tomlinson	New York, N. Y	Dec. 14, 1830	....
Beef-spreader	F. Tesh	Johnstown, Pa	Jan. 9, 1855	12, 222
Beef-steak and other meat, Machine for mangling	R. McCorkell	Warsaw, Minn	Oct. 25, 1864	44, 811
Beef-steak chopper	E. Atkins	Monroe, La	July 16, 1872	128, 997
Beef-steak crusher	J. J. Doyle	Sharon, Conn	Nov. 14, 1865	50, 921
Beef-steak crusher	H. Thompson	Concord, N. H	Sept. 14, 1869	94, 852
Beef-steak cutter and mangler	D. C. Thompson	Ischua, N. Y	Dec. 8, 1868	84, 718
Beef-steak cutters, Die for forming	H. Thompson	Concord, N. H	June 27, 1871	116, 372
Beef-steak for broiling, Device for preparing	W. A. Clark	Woodbridge, Conn	Apr. 4, 1871	113, 260
Beef-steak for cooking, Preparing	T. G. Stagg	New York, N. Y	Oct. 22, 1850	7, 735
Beef-steak, Machine for preparing	A. M. Bond	Concord, N. H	May 2, 1871	114, 396
Beef-steak mangle	J. Locke	Lewisburgh, Pa	Aug. 29, 1871	118, 542
Beef-steak, paring apples, and sharpening knives, Machine for pressing.	B. F. Alexander	Glen Hope, Pa	Oct. 31, 1865	50, 671
Beef-steak preparer	I. C. Nichols	Union, N. Y	Aug. 6, 1867	67, 568
Beef-steak tenderer	J. S. Morris	Mosiertown, Pa	Nov. 4, 1873	144, 216
Beer	G. W. La Baw	Jersey City, N. J	Feb. 16, 1864	41, 626
Beer, alcohol, &c., cooler and condenser	J. Frageser	New York, N. Y	June 19, 1866	55, 746
Beer, ale, and other fermented liquors, Manufacture of.	J. Firmenich	Buffalo, N. Y	Sept. 14, 1869	94, 880
Beer, ale, &c., Apparatus for preserving	R. Eickemeyer	Yonkers, N. Y	Sept. 22, 1868	82, 394
Beer, ale, &c., cooler	T. Bergner and S. Zeisse	Philadelphia, Pa	May 23, 1871	115, 018
Beer, ale, &c., on draught by means of carbonic-acid gas, Preserving and delivering.	T. Ahrens	Louisville, Ky	Aug. 2, 1870	106, 019
Beer, ale, porter, &c., Composition for the manufacture of.	T. Hawks	Rochester, N. Y	June 16, 1868	78, 874
Beer, ale, &c., Process of "hopping"	W. S. Haight	Waterford, N. Y	July 16, 1867	66, 833
Beer and ale on draught, Preserving	C. E. Haynes	Boston, Mass	Nov. 8, 1870	109, 126
Beer and liquid cooler	T. Gründmann	Cleveland, Ohio	Mar. 15, 1870	100, 752
Beer and mash cooler	C. Wise and B. Loeffler	New York, N. Y	May 7, 1867	64, 614
Beer and other liquids, Cooler for	J. Chollar and C. W. Cunningham.	Washington, D. C	July 18, 1865	48, 791
Beer and other liquids, Cooler for	J. J. Märki	Richmond, Ind	Dec. 7, 1869	97, 540
Beer and other liquids, Cooler for	G. B. Turrell	New York, N. Y	Dec. 22, 1868	85, 190
Beer and other liquids on draught, Apparatus for cooling and discharging.	J. M. Heiss	Baltimore, Md	June 20, 1871	116, 053
Beer and other liquids on draught, Cooling and preserving.	J. M. Heiss	Baltimore, Md	May 30, 1871	115, 468
Beer and water cooler	C. Geenen	New Orleans, La	Feb. 6, 1872	123, 390
Beer and water cooler	F. Wagner	Philadelphia, Pa	July 9, 1872	128, 768
Beer and water cooler	J. Weinberger	New Orleans, La	Mar. 12, 1872	124, 465
Beer and wine, Cooler for preserving	F. Loesch	Buffalo, N. Y	Dec. 30, 1873	145, 955
Beer and yeast, Manufacture of	L. Pasteur	Paris, France	July 22, 1873	141, 072
Beer, Apparatus for manufacture of	G. Habich	Roxbury, Mass	June 8, 1858	20, 488
Beer, Apparatus for preserving	C. Pholmann	Lanesville, Ky	May 24, 1870	103, 498
Beer, Apparatus for preserving and forcing	E. C. Kransnick	Saint Louis, Mo	Nov. 25, 1873	144, 987
Beer, Apparatus for raising	J. L. Treat	New York, N. Y	Apr. 13, 1869	88, 927
Beer, Brewing	C. Abresch	New York, N. Y	Nov. 23, 1869	97, 143
Beer, Brewing spruce	W. Bezeau	Philadelphia, Pa	June 13, 1815	....
Beer, Composition for making	S. Hinds	Montrose, Pa	May 11, 1831	....
Beer, &c., Compound for clarifying	C. Hefft	Pekin, Ill	July 23, 1872	129, 732
Beer-cooler	J. Agate	Pittsford, N. Y	July 14, 1868	79, 931
Beer-cooler	J. Agate	Pittsford, N. Y	June 1, 1869	90, 716
Beer-cooler	J. Boyle	Roxbury, Mass	May 17, 1859	24, 004
Beer-cooler	D. Cammerer	Cincinnati, Ohio	Mar. 19, 1867	63, 013
Beer-cooler	D. Cammerer	Cincinnati, Ohio	Sept. 29, 1868	82, 593
Beer-cooler	J. Chandless	New York, N. Y	Feb. 11, 1873	135, 683
Beer-cooler	H. C. Dart	New York, N. Y	May 18, 1869	90, 242
Beer-cooler	H. C. Dart	New York, N. Y	July 13, 1869	92, 429
Beer-cooler	R. Dreher	Milwaukee, Wis	Apr. 16, 1872	125, 668
Beer-cooler	H. Ellerbrock and C. Mahler	Baltimore, Md	Feb. 6, 1872	123, 465
Beer-cooler	J. Fallows	Philadelphia, Pa	Nov. 3, 1868	93, 702
Beer-cooler	A. Fischer	New York, N. Y	Mar. 20, 1866	53, 285

Index of patents issued from the United States Patent Office from 1790 *to* 1873, *inclusive*—Continued.

Invention.	Inventor.	Residence.	Date.	No.
Beer-cooler	A. Foubert	Buffalo, N. Y	Jan. 9, 1872	122, 592
Beer-cooler	J. Fragcser	New York, N. Y	Dec. 17, 1861	33, 967
Beer-cooler	G. Fuchs and J. Luigart	Logansport, Ind	June 9, 1868	78, 659
Beer-cooler	J. Geemen	Chicago, Ill	Nov. 10, 1868	83, 953
Beer-cooler	W. Gee	New York, N. Y	Aug. 23, 1870	106, 686
Beer-cooler	J. Gimlich	Pittsfield, Mass	May 27, 1873	139, 310
Beer-cooler	P. H. Griffin	Albany, N. Y	Dec. 31, 1867	72, 731
Beer-cooler	V. Haeffner	Dobb's Ferry, N. Y	Jan. 20, 1863	37, 443
Beer-cooler	G. M. Haszinger	Vicksburgh, Miss	June 13, 1871	115, 850
Beer-cooler	C. W. Haug	New York, N. Y	Jan. 24, 1871	111, 203
Beer-cooler	H. Heimerle	Buffalo, N. Y	Dec. 31, 1867	72, 733
Beer-cooler	J. Herget	Saint Louis, Mo	Sept. 11, 1866	57, 900
Beer-cooler	N. Hiemenz	Buffalo, N. Y	May 12, 1868	77, 732
Beer-cooler	A. Hitscherich	Milwaukee, Wis	Nov. 9, 1869	96, 590
Beer-cooler	J. Hoefer	New York, N. Y	May 23, 1865	47, 823
Beer-cooler	C. Jones	Brooklyn, N. Y	May 24, 1859	24, 124
Beer-cooler	E. Kraft	Tyrone, Pa	Dec. 24, 1872	134, 208
Beer-cooler	J. M. Otto	Brooklyn, N. Y	June 4, 1872	127, 639
Beer-cooler	A. Pfund	New York, N. Y	June 17, 1873	140, 073
Beer-cooler	H. Pietsch and M. Walter	Milwaukee, Wis	Apr. 6, 1869	88, 584
Beer-cooler	A. D. Puffer	Somerville, Mass	Nov. 24, 1868	84, 439
Beer-cooler	T. L. Rankin and C. W. Grassmuck.	New Richmond, Ohio, and Peru, Ill.	Dec. 29, 1868	85, 477
Beer-cooler	H. Rensch	Quincy, Ill	Nov. 27, 1866	60, 059
Beer-cooler	A. F. Rick	Chicago, Ill	Apr. 22, 1873	138, 195
Beer-cooler	C. L. Ridgway	Boston, Mass	Aug. 29, 1871	118, 646
Beer-cooler	W. Rese	Saint Louis, Mo	Apr. 3, 1866	53, 682
Beer-cooler	D. Sager	Albany, N. Y	June 28, 1864	43, 342
Beer-cooler	A. W. and J. Sangster	Buffalo, N. Y	Apr. 16, 1867	63, 947
Beer-cooler	F. Schmidt	Milwaukee, Wis	Apr. 29, 1873	138, 289
Beer-cooler	L. Schulze	Louisville, Ky	Oct. 13, 1868	83, 099
Beer-cooler	P. Schweikhart	Buffalo, N. Y	May 7, 1867	64, 452
Beer-cooler	H. Shlaudeman	Decatur, Ill	May 5, 1868	77, 664
Beer-cooler	H. Steubing	New York, N. Y	Oct. 6, 1863	40, 200
Beer-cooler	F. Streubel and A. Roos	New York, N. Y	Oct. 22, 1861	33, 549
Beer-cooler	M. Tschirgi and L. Kammüller.	Dubuque, Iowa	Aug. 14, 1866	57, 221
Beer-cooler	G. B. Turrell	New York, N. Y	July 16, 1861	32, 845
Beer-cooler	F. Uhrland	Buffalo, N. Y	Sept. 19, 1865	50, 055
Beer-cooler	G. Waters	Cincinnati, Ohio	Sept. 19, 1865	5[illegible], 056
Beer-cooler	G. Winter	Buffalo, N. Y	Oct. 27, 1868	83, 431
Beer-cooler	J. Yates and E. Deuell	Brooklyn, N. Y	Nov. 17, 1868	84, 244
Beer-cooler for beer on draught	H. Sell	New York, N. Y	Mar. 14, 1871	112, 742
Beer-cooler, Portable	E. C. Bundy	Oneonta, N. Y	Mar. 15, 1870	100, 852
Beer-cooler tap-holder attachment	J. H. Fisher	Chicago, Ill	Sept. 23, 1873	143, 068
Beer-drawing attachments for casks, &c	S. Marks	San Francisco, Cal	Oct. 28, 1873	144, 119
Beer-elevator	A. H. Ladner and T. F. Fenlin	Philadelphia, Pa	June 28, 1870	104, 742
Beer, Factitious	F. Luedke	New York, N. Y	Sept. 25, 1860	30, 147
Beer, Fermenting-tun for	A. Hammer	Philadelphia, Pa	Jan. 2, 1855	12, 160
Beer-forcing apparatus	W. H. Otto and P. Korper	Tremont, Pa	Feb. 13, 1872	123, 639
Beer-fountain, Portable	D. Gay	Bath, Me	Apr. 24, 1849	6, 393
Beer from casks, Hydro-pneumatic apparatus for raising.	R. Sealy	New York, N. Y	Aug. 31, 1844	3, 725
Beer from barrels, Apparatus for forcing	J. Devlin	Brooklyn, N. Y	May 28, 1872	127, 156
Beer from barrels, Apparatus for forcing	J. Devlin	Brooklyn, N. Y	Nov. 19, 1872	133, 084
Beer, &c., from barrels, Apparatus for forcing	J. Devlin	Brooklyn, N. Y	June 17, 1873	139, 882
Beer from malt and Indian meal, Manufacture of	J. Singer	Chicago, Ill	Aug. 25, 1863	39, 685
Beer-glass, &c., Froth-arrester for	J. Winkler	Hudson City, N. J	Nov. 17, 1868	84, 242
Beer-hopping apparatus	W. S. Haight	Waterford, N. Y	June 30, 1868	79, 342
Beer, Machine for mashing and boiling wort for	J. and M. Stark	Buffalo, N. Y	Jan. 7, 1868	73, 056
Beer, Making	H. L. Bowker	Boston, Mass	Sept. 12, 1871	118, 901
Beer, Making	J. S. Bressler	Milwaukee, Wis	Mar. 6, 1866	53, 078
Beer, Making	E. J. Krause	Lancaster, Pa	June 27, 1865	48, 413
Beer, Making spruce	J. Williams	Cambridge, Mass	Feb. 17, 1820	....
Beer, Manufacture of	C. C. Haley	Troy, N. Y	Oct. 29, 1872	132, [illegible]74
Beer, Manufacture of lager	J. Schneider	Williamsburgh, N. Y	July 17, 1866	56, 453
Beer, Manufacture of small	O. F. Green and J. E. Clark	Saint Louis, Mo	Sept. 22, 1868	82, 401
Beer, Manufacturing spruce	G. Jones	Boston, Mass	Jan. 27, 1832	....
Beer-material, Concentrated	F. G. Rietsch	Rudoletz, Austria	Feb. 3, 1852	8, 708
Beer-mug	W. C. King	Pittsburgh, Pa	Dec. 30, 1873	146, 078
Beer on draught, Apparatus for preserving	J. W. Moore	Bellefonte, Pa	Aug. 19, 1873	141, 944
Beer or ale by re-brewing, Restoring sour or musty	M. Granger	Lowville, N. Y	Jan. 11, 1832	....
Beer, Pine-apple	G. Rivera	Cambridgeport, Mass	Feb. 11, 1868	74, 429
Beer-powder	J. McKellar	Thomaston, Me	May 15, 1860	28, 289
Beer-preserver and cooler	J. Lorenz	Hamilton, Ohio	May 23, 1871	115, 072
Beer, Preserving	A. Adametz	New York, N. Y	Sept. 2, 1873	142, 428
Beer-preserving apparatus	W. Dietrichsen	Newark, N. J	May 25, 1869	90, 349
Beer-preserving apparatus	A. F. W. Neynaber	Philadelphia, Pa	May 29, 1866	55, 151
Beer-preserving cellar	R. Schmid	Chicago, Ill	Mar. 16, 1869	87, 878
Beer, Root or tonic	B. Bates	Baltimore, Md	Apr. 4, 1871	113, 617
Beer, Vegetable	S. Whiton	Hartford, Conn	Mar. 21, 1846	4, 430
Beer, &c., vessel	W. Compton	New York, N. Y	Oct. 30, 1866	59, 188
Beer, water, and other liquids, Apparatus for cooling and purifying.	J. P. Gruber	New York, N. Y	Feb. 22, 1870	100, 027
Beer while on draught, Preserving	D. Wernz	New York, N. Y	Nov. 13, 1866	59, 690
Beer with cold air, Apparatus for preserving and forcing.	F. Blucher	Mascoutah, Ill	Dec. 5, 1871	121, 577
Beer-wort, &c., Method of cooling	O. P. Lewis	Cincinnati, Ohio	Oct. 25, 1870	108, 606
Belaying-cleat	J. Bangs	South Dennis, Mass	Feb. 25, 1868	74, 789
Belaying cleat	C. S. H. Foster	Deer Isle, Me	Dec. 15, 1868	84, 873
Belaying-cleat	H. Ryder	Somerville, Mass	Oct. 8, 1872	131, 974
Belaying-cleat for boat	W. W. Andrews	Warrensville, Ohio	Oct. 21, 1862	36, 696
Bell	A. G. Bevin	East Hampton, Conn	June 1, 1869	90, 811
Bell	W. Fletcher	New York, N. Y	June 1, 1869	90, 654
Bell	W. Hoyt	Brookville, Ind	Mar. 3, 1825	....
Bell	J. Kintz	West Meriden, Conn	Apr. 19, 1870	102, 016
Bell	J. Regester	Baltimore, Md	Mar. 14, 1871	112, 631
Bell	J. S. Tibbets	Evansville, Ind	Aug. 4, 1863	39, 433
Bell	H. Tyler	Utica, N. Y	Oct. 20, 1826	....

Index of patents issued from the United States Patent Office from 1790 *to* 1873, *inclusive*—Continued.

Invention.	Inventor.	Residence.	Date.	No.
Bell, Æolian chiming	H. Herrmann	New York, N. Y	Feb. 7, 1871	111, 537
Bell, Alarm	S. C. Bond	Hainesville, Ill	May 9, 1871	114, 521
Bell, Alarm	L. F. Bruce	Bridgeport, Conn	Aug. 3, 1869	93, 168
Bell, Alarm	L. Holmes	Paterson, N. J	May 18, 1869	90, 173
Bell, Alarm	T. and G. A. Pemberton	Birmingham, England	Apr. 19, 1870	102, 035
Bell, Alarm	C. Penfield	New Britain, Conn	Jan. 12, 1869	85, 760
Bell, Alarm	W. M Preston	Roxbury, N. Y	Apr. 2, 1872	125, 328
Bell, Alarm	C. A. Slack	Frenchtown, N. J	Feb. 9, 1869	86, 876
Bell, Alarm	C. Wiley	Hannibal Centre, N. Y	Mar. 23, 1869	88, 106
Bell alarm, Door	C. C. Gerhardt and G. S. Lander.	Wyandotte, Kans	Apr. 16, 1872	125, 731
Bell and bell wheel, Rotating	J. Regester	Baltimore, Md	July 13, 1869	92, 470
Bell and burglar-alarm, Door	D. L. Collins	Antwerp, N. Y	Nov. 20, 1866	59, 820
Bell and burglar-alarm, Door	E. H. Crane	Burr Oak, Mich	June 26, 1866	55, 823
Bell and burglar-alarm, Door	M. A. Genung	Granville, Ohio	June 17, 1862	35, 603
Bell and caster-stand, Call	F. A. Blatterlien	West Meriden, Conn	Nov. 8, 1870	109, 101
Bell and gong striking apparatus	C. and G. M. Stevens	Boston, Mass	May 21, 1872	126, 992
Bell and slop-bowl, Call	N. Lawrence	Taunton, Mass	June 28, 1870	104, 859
Bell and table-caster, Combined	H. A. Dierkes	New York, N. Y	Dec. 7, 1869	97, 617
Bell and vessel, Call	N. Lawrence	Taunton, Mass	Aug. 30, 1870	106, 840
Bell attachment	A. E. Taylor	Ogdensburgh, N. Y	Oct. 23, 1860	30, 509
Bell attachment, Alarm	A. Sherwood	Auburn, N. Y	Aug. 26, 1873	142, 287
Bell, Call	H. H. Abbe	East Hampton, Conn	Jan. 2, 1866	51, 784
Bell, Call	E. C. Barton	East Hampton, Conn	Aug. 20, 1872	130, 690
Bell, Call	N. L. Bradley	West Meriden, Conn	Aug. 25, 1863	39, 697
Bell, Call	E. G. Cone	East Hampton, Conn	Oct. 27, 1868	83, 468
Bell, Call	H. A. Dierkes	New York, N. Y	Aug. 8, 1871	117, 871
Bell, Call	H. A. Dierkes	New York, N. Y	Mar. 26, 1872	125, 029
Bell, Call	H. A. Dierkes and J. Fretts	New York, N. Y	Mar. 21, 1871	112, 907
Bell, Call	W. H. Nichols	East Hampton, Conn	July 16, 1867	66, 874
Bell, Call	W. H. Nichols	East Hampton, Conn	Aug. 27, 1872	130, 818
Bell, Call	E. Parker	West Meriden, Conn	Mar. 29, 1864	42, 107
Bell, Call	D. W. Sexton	East Hampton, Conn	May 3, 1864	42, 604
Bell, Call	H. Stratton	West Meriden, Conn	Feb. 11, 1873	135, 860
Bell, Call	H. A. Thompson	Hartford, Conn	June 5, 1866	55, 392
Bell, Call	C. Volger	Wilmington, Del	June 20, 1871	116, 241
Bell, Car	A. Borrowman	New York, N. Y	Apr. 16, 1867	63, 843
Bell, Car	J. Sweeney	New York, N. Y	Nov. 27, 1866	60, 083
Bell, Cast-iron	E. G. Cone	East Hampton, Conn	Aug. 6, 1867	67, 500
Bell, Ceremonial	J. H. Smith	Keokuk, Iowa	Jan. 10, 1871	110, 875
Bell, Chime and alarm	G. R. Meneely	West Troy, N. Y	Jan. 2, 1872	122, 397
Bell, Cow or sheep	S. Newton		Dec. 22, 1804	
Bell-crank	M. C. Ames	Hartford, Conn	May 7, 1872	126, 369
Bell, Door	W. Allport	New Britain, Conn	Dec. 29, 1868	85, 352
Bell, Door	W. Allport	New Britain, Conn	Apr. 12, 1870	101, 609
Bell, Door	H. D. Blake	New Britain, Conn	Apr. 9, 1872	125, 530
Bell, Door	F. Blakemore	Philadelphia, Pa	July 2, 1872	128, 458
Bell, Door	A. T. Brooks	New Britain, Conn	Dec. 31, 1867	72, 791
Bell, Door	A. T. Brooks	New Britain, Conn	June 30, 1868	79, 308
Bell, Door	N. F. Cone	La Crosse, Wis	Sept. 8, 1863	39, 796
Bell, Door	N. F. Cone	La Crosse, Wis	Feb. 23, 1864	41, 683
Bell, Door	J. P. Connell	Kensington, Conn	Mar. 21, 1871	112, 903
Bell, Door	J. P. Connell	Kensington, Conn	June 18, 1872	127, 959
Bell, Door	J. P. Connell	Kensington, Conn	Oct. 15, 1872	132, 199
Bell, Door	M. L. Delavan and J. Dyson	New Britain, Conn	July 23, 1867	67, 030
Bell, Door	M. A. Genung	Granville, Ohio	Mar. 10, 1863	37, 863
Bell, Door	E. H. Goldman and D. W. Hisey.	Kansas, Ill	May 24, 1870	103, 446
Bell, Door	T. Lyons	Hartford, Conn	Aug. 11, 1868	80, 983
Bell, Door	W. T. Munger	New Britain, Conn	June 20, 1871	116, 082
Bell, Door	W. H. Nichols	Chatham, Conn	Jan. 30, 1866	52, 365
Bell, Door	W. H. Nichols	East Hampton, Conn	Sept. 22, 1868	82, 434
Bell, Door	C. S. Nickelson	Canton, N. Y	Oct. 24, 1865	50, 616
Bell, Door	O. A. North	New Britain, Conn	Apr. 27, 1869	89, 331
Bell, Door	O. B. Oakley and H. Rosekrans	San Francisco, Cal	Sept. 1, 1868	81, 672
Bell, Door	M. B. Ogden	Fond du Lac, Wis	Aug. 23, 1864	43, 924
Bell, Door	C. Penfield	New Britain, Conn	July 30, 1867	67, 212
Bell, Door	C. Penfield	New Britain, Conn	Jan. 12, 1869	85, 759
Bell, Door	C. W. Saladee	Circleville, Ohio	Mar. 16, 1869	87, 794
Bell, Door	E. B. Sims	Antwerp, N. Y	Sept. 16, 1873	142, 953
Bell, Door	A. A. Stuart	Cedar Rapids, Iowa	May 20, 1873	139, 206
Bell, Door	A. L. Swan	Cherry Valley, N. Y	Nov. 19, 1872	133, 269
Bell, Door	A. Turnbull	New Britain, Conn	June 13, 1865	48, 242
Bell, Door	W. H. Watrous	Hartford, Conn	Mar. 20, 1866	53, 366
Bell, Door and alarm	G. O. Lackey	Akron, Ohio	Oct. 25, 1870	108, 708
Bell, Diving	J. A. Weisse	New York, N. Y	Apr. 27, 1869	89, 453
Bell, Electro-magnetic alarm	M. G. Farmer	Salem, Mass	May 4, 1852	8, 920
Bell, Electro-magnetic alarm	C. Williams, jr., and J. Redding	Somerville and Charlestown, Mass.	Feb. 7, 1871	111, 707
Bell, Electro-magnetic fog	A. Barbarin and B. F. Simms	New Orleans, La	July 15, 1856	15, 323
Bell, Enameled	F. Raymond	Woodhaven, N. Y	June 29, 1869	92, 095
Bell, Fog	A. C. Rand and R. R. Johnson	Buffalo, N. Y	Apr. 13, 1858	19, 949
Bell for doors, Alarm	E. Barton	East Hampton, Conn	Sept. 9, 1862	36, 436
Bell for fire-engines, Alarm	J. P. Parke	Philadelphia, Pa	Dec. 19, 1808	
Bell for horses	J. Barton	Cairo, N. Y	Mar. 18, 1834	....
Bell for horses, Alarm chime	C. Kirchkof	Newark, N. J	Sept. 29, 1863	40, 108
Bell, Gong	I. A. Bevin	Chatham, Conn	Oct. 9, 1866	58, 580
Bell, Gong	L. S. Carpenter	East Hampton, Conn	Apr. 20, 1869	89, 024
Bell, Gong	H. A. Foss	New Britain, Conn	May 28, 1872	127, 333
Bell-head, Rotary	S. M. and W. M. Fulton	Pittsburgh, Pa	Nov. 30, 1869	97, 383
Bell-holder, Stationary	S. Croll	Philadelphia, Pa	Feb. 14, 1871	111, 729
Bell, Horse	J. Barton	Middle Haddam, Conn	Feb. 14, 1854	10, 532
Bell, House	H. Barton	East Hampton, Conn	Oct. 9, 1866	58, 576
Bell, House	J. Barton	East Hampton, Conn	June 15, 1858	20, 538
Bell, House	A. L. Swan	Cherry Valley, N. Y	Dec. 26, 1871	122, 200
Bell, House	A. Turnbull	New Britain, Conn	June 12, 1866	55, 558
Bell joint	B. P. Walker	Wolverhampton, England	May 4, 1869	89, 820
Bell-lever box	B. W. Hopper	Astoria, N. Y	Jan. 8, 1869	91, 019

Index of patents issued from the United States Patent Office from 1790 *to* 1873, *inclusive*—Continued.

Invention.	Inventor.	Residence.	Date.	No.
Bell-levers, Attaching caps to bases of	E. W. Brettel	Elizabeth, N. J	Aug. 2, 1870	105, 900
Bell, Locomotive alarm	B. Briscoe	Detroit, Mich	Mar. 2, 1869	87, 462
Bell-machinery for hotels, &c	T. D. Jackson and A. Judson	Rochester, N. Y	Oct. 17, 1846	4, 816
Bell, Magnetic alarm	A. Eckert	Trenton, Ohio	Oct. 10, 1854	11, 780
Bell or gong, Door	H. H. Abbe	Chatham, Conn	July 11, 1865	48, 637
Bell or gong, Door	A. G. Dexter	San Francisco, Cal	June 13, 1865	48, 234
Bell, Portable house	A. W. Hale	New Britain, Conn	Aug. 31, 1858	21, 335
Bell, Pressure	J. Barton	Middle Haddam, Conn	Apr. 8, 1856	14, 593
Bell-pull	S. Bonsall and L. Hillebrand	Philadelphia, Pa	Mar. 3, 1868	75, 118
Bell-pull	S. Bonsall and L. Hillebrand	Philadelphia, Pa	Dec. 15, 1868	84, 998
Bell-pull	C. J. Bradbury	Boston, Mass	Feb. 28, 1860	27, 330
Bell-pull	J. Garvey and M. H. Kimball	San Francisco, Cal	Nov. 3, 1868	83, 622
Bell-pull	J. Garvey and M. H. Kimball	San Francisco, Cal	Nov. 3, 1868	83, 623
Bell-pull	H. Homer	New York, N. Y	Sept. 5, 1865	49, 757
Bell-pull	W. T. Munger	New Britain, Conn	June 10, 1873	139, 687
Bell, Pull	W. M. Preston	Roxbury, N. Y	Aug. 20, 1872	130, 742
Bell-pull	J. J. C. Smith	Somerville, Mass	Jan. 18, 1870	99, 020
Bell-pull	A. L. Swan	Cherry Valley, N. Y	Nov. 7, 1871	120, 682
Bell-pull	A. L. Swan	Cherry Valley, N. Y	Aug. 19, 1873	142, 057
Bell-pull, Noiseless	J. F. Cory	New York, N. Y	Nov. 3, 1868	83, 606
Bell pulls and trips, Construction of	S. L. Covell, jr	Troy, N. Y	July 16, 1867	66, 801
Bell-ringer, Automatic	E. N. Scherr	Philadelphia, Pa	Mar. 1, 1859	23, 118
Bell-ringer, Steam	W. H. Beach	Chicago, Ill	Apr. 19, 1864	42, 428
Bell-ringer, Steam	G. B. Snow	Buffalo, N. Y	June 11, 1872	127, 933
Bell-ringer, Steam	J. West and O. M. Parker	Quincy, Ill	June 25, 1872	128, 441
Bell-ringer, Steam	J. West and O. M. Parker	Quincy, Ill	Jan. 7, 1873	134, 719
Bell-ringing apparatus	J. R. Baird	Vincennes, Ind	Nov. 17, 1857	18, 623
Bell-ringing apparatus	J. Harrison	Troy, N. Y	Aug. 28, 1860	29, 784
Bell-ringing apparatus	R. Kinsley	Springfield, Mass	June 11, 1861	32, 520
Bell-ringing apparatus for locomotive, Automatic	J. S. Lamar	Augusta, Ga	July 9, 1872	128, 801
Bell-rope supporter	W. C. Marshall	Hartford, Conn	Aug. 10, 1869	93, 461
Bell-ropes, Eye for railway-car	W. M. Walton	Newark, N. J	Dec. 21, 1869	98, 130
Bell, Self-adjusting fog	H. L. De Zeng	Geneva, N. Y	Aug. 26, 1856	15, 605
Bell, Sheet-steel	J. E. Tencate	Pittsburgh, Pa	Jan. 9, 1872	122, 679
Bell, Signal	G. F. and D. H. Benckert	Philadelphia, Pa	Oct. 11, 1859	25, 714
Bell, Signal	J. A. Woodward	Philadelphia, Pa	Nov. 15, 1859	26, 137
Bell, Signal or alarm	G. H. Hoagland	Port Jervis, N. Y	July 21, 1857	17, 836
Bell strap, Cow	J. H. and A. Hughs	Wautoma, Wis	Dec. 19, 1871	122, 020
Bell, Table or call	A. W. Turner	New York, N. Y	Jan. 30, 1866	52, 344
Bell to straps, Attaching	D. W. Welch	Middle Haddam, Conn	Aug. 10, 1869	93, 652
Bell-yoke attachment	C. H. Meneely	Troy, N. Y	May 9, 1871	114, 585
Bells and adjustable clappers for ringing fog	D. Jones, jr	Saint John, New Brunswick.	Nov. 27, 1849	6, 915
Bells, &c., Apparatus for sounding house	J. Corduan	Brooklyn, N. Y	Mar. 29, 1859	23, 353
Bells by steam, Ringing	G. B. Snow	Buffalo, N. Y	July 11, 1854	11, 307
Bells, Casting	A. Jusberg	Galva, Ill	Aug. 27, 1867	68, 206
Bells, Constructing and hanging	E. Dewey	New York, N. Y	Apr. 10, 1839	1, 114
Bells, Construction and tone of	R. Leslie	....	Feb. 2, 1793	....
Bells, Device for ringing street-car	C. Carr	Boston, Mass	Apr. 5, 1870	101, 580
Bells, Die for making	A. Patterson	Birmingham, Pa	Mar. 5, 1867	62, 678
Bells, Electro-magnetic machine for ringing	C. Robinson	New York, N. Y	Dec. 6, 1864	45, 347
Bells for cows, &c., Brazing and bronzing	S. Booth	Berlin, Conn	June 1, 1832	....
Bells, Hanging	G. E. Baker	Waukegan, Ill	July 10, 1866	56, 160
Bells, Hanging	H. Belfied	Philadelphia, Pa	Apr. 12, 1859	23, 639
Bells, Hanging	T. H. Bell	Washington, D. C	Apr. 17, 1860	27, 880
Bells, Hanging	J. Currier	Boston, Mass	Jan. 23, 1834	....
Bells, Hanging	N. G. Du Bois	Brooklyn, N. Y	Jan. 12, 1858	19, 082
Bells, Hanging	G. Equillon	Paris, France	Oct. 26, 1869	96, 092
Bells, Hanging	S. Fuller	Boston, Mass	Dec. 26, 1833	....
Bells, Hanging	G. W. Hildreth	Lockport, N. Y	June 19, 1855	13, 089
Bells, Hanging	M. R. Jones	Troy, N. Y	Mar. 19, 1872	124, 685
Bells, Hanging	A. Laroÿe	Sas Slykens, near Ostend, Belgium.	Mar. 21, 1871	112, 932
Bells, Hanging	A. Lynar	New York, N. Y	Dec. 24, 1819	....
Bells, Hanging	G. R. Meneely	West Troy, N. Y	Sept. 7, 1858	21, 422
Bells, Hanging	G. R. Meneely	West Troy, N. Y	Oct. 9, 1860	30, 338
Bells, Hanging	J. Russell	New York, N. Y	Oct. 10, 1829	....
Bells, Hanging	E. W. Vanduzen	Cincinnati, Ohio	Oct. 23, 1866	59, 098
Bells, Hanging	E. W. Vanduzen	Cincinnati, Ohio	Oct. 23, 1866	59, 099
Bells, Hanging	J. B. Young	Harper's Ferry, Va	July 4, 1854	11, 236
Bells, Hanging door	J. O. Harris	Ottawa, Ill	June 21, 1864	43, 2[illegible]3
Bells, Hanging house	E. Stetson	New Bedford, Mass	Aug. 17, 1843	3, 226
Bells, Machine for making wire	R. W. Norton	New Haven, Conn	Aug. 30, 1870	106, 951
Bells, Machinery for operating fog	J. Haynes	Pembroke, Me	Apr. 2, 1861	31, 886
Bells, Machinery for ringing fog	A. Morse	Portland, Me	Aug. 27, 1861	33, 156
Bells, Manufacture of corrugated	G. S. Saxton	Saint Louis, Mo	Dec. 17, 1867	72, 422
Bells, Manufacture of cow	G. C. Albaugh	Louisville, Ky	Feb. 26, 1861	31, 521
Bells, Manufacture of cow	W. T. and L. B. Tibbals	Cobalt, Conn	Aug. 31, 1869	94, 453
Bells, Method of making smoke	J. S. and T. B. Atterbury	Pittsburgh, Pa	Aug. 14, 1866	57, 063
Bells, Mold for casting	E. Jones	Troy, N. Y	Dec. 18, 1855	13, 948
Bells, Molding	W. H. Davis	Brooklyn, N. Y	Sept. 15, 1868	82, 094
Bells, Molding and casting	B. Hanks	Albany, N. Y	Nov. 4, 1816	....
Bells on steamers, Mode of operating pilot	J. R. Hopkins	Lincoln, Me	Nov. 17, 1857	18, 641
Bells or other hollow castings, Machine for turning or plaining the inside of.	O. Jones	Troy, N. Y	Oct. 4, 1870	107, 918
Bells, Ringing	J. Harrison	New York, N. Y	Mar. 8, 1864	41, 843
Bells, Ringing	J. Harrison	New York, N. Y	Aug. 6, 1867	67, 537
Bells, Ringing	J. Harrison	East Hampton, Conn	May 20, 1873	139, 147
Bells, Ringing	B. Kitt	Cincinnati, Ohio	June 5, 1860	28, 586
Bells, Ringing	T. V. Stran	New Albany, Ind	June 29, 1852	9, 081
Bells, Ringing	P. L. Weimer	Lebanon, Pa	July 23, 1867	67, 006
Bells, Ringing fixed	A. Carson	New York, N. Y	Dec. 6, 1853	10, 300
Bells to straps, Mode of attaching horse	J. Barton	Middle Haddam, Conn	Feb. 21, 1854	10, 539
Bells to their yokes, Attaching	G. R. Meneely	West Troy, N. Y	July 28, 1868	80, 422
Bells, &c., Tuning	A. Patterson	Birmingham, Pa	Nov. 26, 1867	71, 322
Bellows	J. Arndt	Wheeling, Va.	Mar. 2, 1858	19, 475
Bellows	W. T. Barnes	Buffalo, N. Y	Apr. 24, 1849	6, 400

Index of patents issued from the United States Patent Office from 1790 *to* 1873, *inclusive*—Continued.

Invention.	Inventor.	Residence.	Date.	No.
Bellows	L. Bishop	Readsborough, Vt.	Dec. 22, 1831	....
Bellows	R. Boeklen and L. Planer	Brooklyn and New York, N. Y.	June 16, 1863	38, 880
Bellows	J. Bowden	Mitcham, England	July 10, 1869	56, 335
Bellows	J. and W. Bowden	Bushwick, N. Y	Feb. 25, 1868	74, 884
Bellows	G. Bushnell	Schodack, N. Y	Oct. 1, 1867	69, 401
Bellows	G. W. Dalbey	Wheeling, W. Va	Nov. 14, 1865	50, 912
Bellows	G. L. Dimpfel	New York, N. Y	May 23, 1834	....
Bellows	J. Dixon	Pittsborough, N. C	June 11, 1827	....
Bellows	J. Drake	....	May 19, 1794	....
Bellows	C. L. English	Cincinnati, Ohio	Nov. 19, 1867	71, 060
Bellows	C. D. Everett	Cleveland, Ohio	June 25, 1872	128, 378
Bellows	E. Field	Cincinnati, Ohio	July 10, 1866	56, 199
Bellows	A. F. Jones	New York, N. Y	Aug. 8, 1871	117, 783
Bellows	J. B. and J. A. Maxwell	Allegheny, Pa	Feb. 7, 1860	27, 062
Bellows	A. Miller and U. Faris	Red Rock, Iowa	Apr. 9, 1872	125, 605
Bellows	W. Pilcher	Chicago, Ill	Aug. 19, 1873	141, 888
Bellows	J. Robe	Morgantown, Va	Apr. 17, 1834	....
Bellows	J. Rumsay	....	Aug. 26, 1791	....
Bellows	J. H. Snyder	Rockford, Ill	Dec. 5, 1871	121, 678
Bellows	L. U. Stuart	Brooklyn, N. Y	Feb. 11, 1862	34, 380
Bellows, Application of steam to work	J. Stevens, jr	....	Aug. 26, 1791	....
Bellows, Blacksmith's	J. F. Cory and H. C. Webb	Brooklyn, E. D., N. Y	May 31, 1870	103, 720
Bellows by steam, Working	M. Bell	Antis Township, Pa	Apr. 24, 1838	705
Bellows, Double	W. Lillie	Edwards, N. Y	June 2, 1845	4, 066
Bellows, Elastic piston	H. Dotterer	Philadelphia, Pa	May 1, 1810	....
Bellows, Flexible sides for	A. F. Jones	New York, N. Y	Apr. 30, 1872	126, 214
Bellows, Foot	H. Neumeyer	Macungie, Pa	Oct. 25, 1864	44, 814
Bellows for blasting foundries, furnac s, forges, &c., Triangular.	W. S. Jacks	New York, N. Y	Apr. 4, 1829	....
Bellows for blow-pipes	H. Cassell and W. F. Semple	Fredericktown, Ohio	Feb. 25, 1862	34, 479
Bellows for furnaces and forges, Pump	I. Jennings	New York, N. Y	Sept. 20, 1808	....
Bellows for furnaces, &c., Construction of	H. Dotterer	Philadelphia, Pa	Apr. 14, 1825	....
Bellows for furnaces, Mode of operating	H. Crumlish	Buffalo, N. Y	Oct. 7, 1873	143, 439
Bellows for furnaces or forges, Working	J. W. Godfrey	....	May 25, 1803	....
Bellows for musical instruments	M. Smith	New Haven, Conn	Feb. 25, 1851	7, 947
Bellows for pumping ships, Pendulum	B. Wynkoop	....	June 26, 1797	....
Bellows for reed-instruments	I. T. Packard	Campello, Mass	Sept. 28, 1852	9, 290
Bellows for smiths' and furnace fires	J. R. Morrison	Springfield, Ohio	Dec. 23, 1834	....
Bellows, Forge	H. Dotterer	Philadelphia, Pa	Feb. 16, 1809	....
Bellows, Forge	W. Thompson	Detroit, Mich	Apr. 17, 1860	27, 936
Bellows, Hand	J. Grennell	Springfield, Mass	Aug. 3, 1838	872
Bellows, Making	J. J. Eddy	Providence, R. I	Sept. 9, 1825	....
Bellows, Making japanned	R. B. Richardson	Philadelphia, Pa	Aug. 22, 1817	....
Bellows-nozzle from burning, Preserving	J. Dodge, jr	Saint Albans, Vt	Jan. 20, 1824	....
Bellows or blowing-machine	E. Brady	Mount Pleasant, N. Y	Apr. 3, 1828	....
Bellows-pipe, Welding	A. Pearsall	Nashville, Tenn	Aug. 31, 1858	21, 359
Bellows, Reciprocating	J. S. Butler and A. J. Stucker	Siver City, Idaho	July 13, 1869	92, 580
Bellows, Rotary	J. Darling	Adrian, Mich	May 23, 1846	4, 533
Bellows, Rotary	H. Phinney	Kingston, N. Y	Jan. 29, 1867	61, 684
Bellows, Rotary	A. Savage and H Killam	Scottsville, N. Y	Nov. 24, 1843	3, 350
Bellows, Sand	J. W. Hendley	Washington, D. C	July 24, 1866	56, 558
Bellows, Smith's	J. P. Hemmingsen	Marshalltown, Iowa	Mar. 2, 1869	87, 412
Bellows, Smith's	A. Holmes	Pomfret, N. Y	Mar. 23, 1818	....
Bellows, Smith's	M. Loomis	Worcester, N. Y	May 2, 1848	5, 544
Bellows, Smith's	G. H. Peek	East Hamburgh, N. Y	May 3, 1870	102, 704
Bellows, Steam	J. Eastman	Bath, N. H	Apr. 8, 1831	....
Bellows-tub	A. H. McPharin	Huntingdon, Pa	June 11, 1829	....
Bellows, Windworm for blacksmith's	C. F. Conrad	Adrian, Mich	Dec. 31, 1867	72, 721
Bellows, Wooden	B. and J. Tyler	Claremont, N. H	Feb. 1, 1817	....
Belly-band fastener	C. H. Horne	Astoria, Oreg	Nov. 30, 1869	97, 401
Belt and band fastening	G. D. Young	Plymouth, Mass	Jan. 29, 1856	14, 175
Belt and band of rubber and metal, Driving	L. Sterne	London, England	Aug. 3, 1869	93, 364
Belt attachment for machinery, Slack	J. W. Howard	Greenville, Ala	Oct. 19, 1869	95, 903
Belt, Cartridge	W. B. Hayden	Columbus, Ohio	Jan. 31, 1871	111, 450
Belt, Chain	W. M. Julian and M. Kidnocker	Tarlton, Ohio	Jan. 12, 1869	85, 830
Belt-clamp	E. Ainsworth	Wilmington, Del	Oct. 14, 1873	143, 604
Belt-clasp	A. D. Ansell	Hartford, Conn	July 18, 1865	48, 784
Belt-clasp	J. Chenoweth and J. McLain	Auglaize County, Ohio	Oct. 8, 1867	69, 628
Belt-clasp	G. Churchill	Hartford, Conn	Jan. 18, 1859	22, 624
Belt-clasp	G. Cuppers	New York, N. Y	Apr. 5, 1864	42, 170
Belt-clasp	P. Harlow	Hudson, Mass	Feb. 12, 1867	61, 935
Belt-clasp	E. Hatch	Charlestown, Mass	Feb. 11, 1868	74, 354
Belt-clasp	J. H. Hawes and G. H. Bliss	Boston and West Stockbridge, Mass.	Apr. 28, 1868	77, 282
Belt-clasp	O. Kromer and C. Ohlemacher	Sandusky, Ohio	Nov. 20, 1866	59, 914
Belt-clasp	I. N. Plotts	New York, N. Y	Nov. 7, 1865	50, 841
Belt-clasp	T. W. Porter	Boston, Mass	Mar. 24, 1868	75, 970
Belt-clasp	J., S. A., G. E., and F. F. Reading.	Birmingham, England	Mar. 24, 1868	75, 976
Belt-clasp	J. T. Senn	Troy, Ala	Nov. 12, 1872	133, 061
Belt-clasp	A. M. Smith	Rochester, N. Y	June 29, 1852	9, 080
Belt clasp	C. Towns	Cleveland, Ohio	Feb. 16, 1869	87, 081
Belt-clasp, &c	G. F. White and H. Chamberlain.	Hornsey and London, England.	Oct. 30, 1866	59, 332
Belt-clasp for machinery	H. G. Ellsworth	Auburn, N. Y	Mar. 28, 1854	10, 692
Belt-clasp, Leather	L. Sanders	Brooklyn, N. Y	Mar. 4, 1873	136, 549
Belt coupling	T. H Corbett	Brooklyn, N. Y	Nov. 27, 1855	13, 843
Belt-coupling	C. Fairfax, jr	Cincinnati, Ohio	Aug. 21, 1860	29, 684
Belt-coupling	S. Green	Grand Rapids, Mich	Mar. 23, 1858	19, 735
Belt-coupling	R J. Jordon	Elkhart, Ind	July 30, 1867	67, 197
Belt-coupling	C. W. T. Krausch	Philadelphia, Pa	Apr. 28, 1868	77, 295
Belt-coupling	W. Leas	Kokomo, Ind	Jan. 23, 1866	52, 178
Belt-coupling	W. Leas	Kokomo, Ind	July 31, 1866	56, 767
Belt-coupling	T. S. Livermore	Leicester, Mass	June 23, 1868	79, 239
Belt-coupling	J. Mattix	Kokomo, Ind	Aug. 7, 1866	56, 966
Belt-coupling	T. McMullen	Osgood, Ind	Aug. 25, 1868	81, 391
Belt-coupling	S. Metzler	Naperville, Ill	June 25, 1861	32, 637

Index of patents issued from the United States Patent Office from 1790 *to* 1873, *inclusive*—Continued.

Invention.	Inventor.	Residence.	Date.	No.
Belt-coupling	A. C. G. Rathburn and A. M. Comstock.	Lyme, Conn	Feb. 7, 1865	46,264
Belt-coupling	T. Rüdiger	Oberle's Corners, Minn	June 1, 1869	90,876
Belt-coupling	E. Thayer	New York, N. Y	Jan. 8, 1867	61,118
Belt-coupling	J. L. Thomas	Newburgh, Ohio	Feb. 11, 1868	74,449
Belt-coupling	H. Underwood	New York, N. Y	Oct. 28, 1862	36,814
Belt coupling, Round	W. S. Jarboe	New York, N. Y	Oct. 1, 1872	131,879
Belt-cutter	M. G. Goodale	Lowell, Mass	Nov. 12, 1867	70,711
Belt-cutting machine	H. D. Smith	New York, N. Y	Oct. 13, 1863	40,287
Belt-cutting machine, Round	J. C. Foster	New London, Conn	June 13, 1871	115,949
Belt, Driving	W. Clissold	Dudbridge, England	Aug. 27, 1861	33,133
Belt, Driving	W. R. Colton	Syracuse, N. Y	Feb. 4, 1873	135,409
Belt, Driving	M. J. Haines	Bristol, England	Apr. 16, 1867	63,883
Belt, Driving	A. Schpakowsky	St. Petersburg, Russia	Dec. 23, 1873	145,907
Belt, Driving	T. R. White and W. G. Bedford	Philadelphia, Pa	June 25, 1867	66,111
Belt, Endless	H. Richards and J. A. Traut	New Britain, Conn	Sept. 29, 1868	82,640
Belt, Endless driving	J. F. Reigart	Washington, D. C	Dec. 9, 1873	145,447
Belt-fastener	G. M. Beardsley	Fenton, Mich	Aug. 25, 1868	81,331
Belt-fastener	S. S. Bolton	Big Rapids, Mich	Dec. 6, 1870	109,798
Belt-fastener	A. Hyde	Springfield, Mass	July 1, 1873	140,419
Belt-fastener	W. C. James	Fishersville, N. H	July 18, 1871	117,175
Belt-fastener	C. Liebrich and L. Uitting	Philadelphia, Pa	Jan. 20, 1863	37,453
Belt-fastener	M. Olmsted	Alum Creek, Tex	Nov. 28, 1872	121,405
Belt-fastener	C. O. Pike	North Leverett, Mass	Dec. 17, 1867	72,325
Belt-fastener	D. Wigger	New York, N. Y	Nov. 12, 1867	70,930
Belt-fastener	F. G. Wilson	Nashua, N. H	Dec. 15, 1868	84,925
Belt-fastening	G. W. Blake	Pepperell, Mass	Apr. 24, 1860	28,033
Belt-fastening	G. W. Blake	East Pepperell, Mass	Mar. 26, 1861	31,859
Belt-fastening	G. A. Brown	Reading, Mich	Sept. 12, 1871	118,785
Belt-fastening	M. W. Costolo	Boston, Mass	Dec. 19, 1865	51,561
Belt-fastening	A. Fickett	Rochester, N. Y	Aug. 23, 1859	25,187
Belt-fastening	W. Frazier	Hartford, Conn	Dec. 20, 1859	26,488
Belt-fastening	J. W. Hicks	Laurel, Md	Dec. 12, 1871	121,781
Belt-fastening	T. Kennedy	Mount Carmel, Conn	Sept. 15, 1868	82,227
Belt-fastening	G. Koeb and L. Houcke	Springfield, Ohio	Mar. 30, 1869	88,307
Belt-fastening	J. C. Merritt	West Point, N. Y	Aug. 27, 1872	130,816
Belt-fastening	H. Norfolk	Vicksburgh, Miss	Apr. 2, 1872	125,213
Belt-fastening	J. E. Richard	Columbia, S. C	Apr. 22, 1873	138,194
Belt-fastening	T. Ruediger	Carver County, Minn	Feb. 4, 1873	135,492
Belt-fastening	E. Schmeltz	New York, N. Y	Mar. 17, 1868	75,704
Belt-fastening	G. V. Sheffield and B. Whitcomb.	Worcester, Mass	Dec. 24, 1867	72,690
Belt-fastening	S. J. Sherman	Brooklyn, N. Y	Dec. 18, 1866	60,579
Belt-fastening	P. Subit	Boston, Mass	Oct. 7, 1873	143,474
Belt-fastening	A. Whiteley	Springfield, Ohio	Feb. 5, 1856	14,213
Belt for polishing, Endless	J. A. Traut	New Britain, Conn	Mar. 26, 1867	63,341
Belt for the body, Electric	J. E. Bazault	Paris, France	Mar. 26, 1872	125,[illegible]06
Belt-gearing	J. H. Butler	Hampden, Me	Jan. 17, 1871	110,955
Belt-gearing	G. B. Hamlin	Willimantic, Conn	Oct. 11, 1870	108,259
Belt-gearing	G. B. Hamlin	Willimantic, Conn	Sept. 10, 1872	131,268
Belt-gearing	G. C. Howard	Philadelphia, Pa	Feb. 28, 1871	112,145
Belt-gearing, Idler for	T. Bell and J. F. Hillerich	Louisville, Ky	Aug. 5, 1873	141,417
Belt guide	L. R. Jenkins	Philadelphia, Pa	Sept. 11, 1866	57,917
Belt-guide	C. P. Leavitt	New York, N. Y	Aug. 9, 1870	106,179
Belt-hole cover	T. P. Rodgers	Taunton, Mass	Oct. 28, 1873	144,144
Belt-hole scupper	B. L. Wood	Taunton, Mass	Nov. 18, 1873	144,816
Belt-hook	F. J. Jones	Detroit, Mich	Mar. 31, 1868	76,082
Belt-hook	F. E. Oliver	New York, N. Y	Oct. 6, 1863	40,182
Belt-hook	H. L. Peirce	Taunton, Mass	Apr. 27, 1869	89,499
Belt-hook	C. G. Sargent	Graniteville, Mass	Dec. 15, 1868	84,968
Belt-hook	E. F. Sherman	Chicopee, Mass	July 21, 1868	80 227
Belt hook, pliers, and punch	N. E. Hale	Nashua, N. H	Sept. 27, 1859	25,567
Belt-joining clasp	B. D. Randleman	Port Louisa, Iowa	July 21, 1868	80,219
Belt joining or splicing	J. Ashworth	Lewiston, Me	Jan. 26, 1869	86,123
Belt-knife	H. Blake	East Pepperell, Mass	Aug. 11, 1868	80,899
Belt-knives, Manufacture of	B. F. Radford	Hyde Park, Mass	Dec. 19, 1871	121,963
Belt-lacer	J. K. Priest and W. Earl, jr	Nashua, N. H	Aug. 25, 1868	81,537
Belt-lacing	H. A. Alden	Matteawan, N. Y	July 31, 1860	29,348
Belt-lacing	H. C. Babcock	Cincinnati, Ohio	Nov. 12, 1867	70,775
Belt-lacing device	D. P. Davis	New York, N. Y	Dec. 3, 1867	71,713
Belt-lacing gage	H. Gould	Minneapolis, Minn	May 6, 1873	138,639
Belt-lacing, Machine for cutting	B. F. Sanborn	Boston, Mass	Sept. 11, 1866	57,976
Belt-lacing tool	J. M. Stamp	Grass Valley, Cal	Mar. 8, 1870	100,686
Belt, Lady's safety	M. G. Porter	Charlestown, Mass	Feb. 1, 1870	99,347
Belt, Lady's waist	J. M. Flagg	Providence, R. I	Feb. 6, 1872	123,471
Belt-lap cutter	C. S. Robinson	Concord, N. H	Feb. 12, 1867	62,073
Belt, Machine	T. F. Snover	Oconto, Wis	May 12, 1868	77,847
Belt on pulley, Apparatus for shifting	P. J. Zier	Pittsburgh, Pa	Feb. 6, 1872	123,543
Belt or girdle, Waist	M. I. Findley	New York, N. Y	May 26, 1868	78,367
Belt, Pulley	L. R. Faught	Philadelphia, Pa	Oct. 15, 1872	132,205
Belt-replacer	W. C. Bridges	Michigan City, Ind	Apr. 19, 1870	101,978
Belt-rivet	C. Frank	Cincinnati, Ohio	Apr. 2, 1867	63,497
Belt-riveting tool	M. D. Lawrence	Flintville, Wis	Aug. 20, 1872	130,646
Belt, Safety	N. Downing	Brooklyn, N. Y	Oct. 29, 1861	33,579
Belt-shifter	S. Forsythe	San Francisco, Cal	July 23, 1872	129,806
Belt-shifter	W. E. Leighton	Pembroke, Me	Apr. 12, 1870	101,745
Belt-shifter	J. E. Mutchler	Grand Rapids, Mich	Oct. 18, 1870	108,379
Belt-shifter	T. P. Rogers	Taunton, Mass	Aug. 27, 1872	130,870
Belt-shifter	W. H. H. Sisum	Newark, N. J	May 21, 1872	127,109
Belt-shifter	W. H. H. Sisum	Newark, N. J	Apr. 18, 1871	113,939
Belt shifter and tightener	B. O'Bryan	Marietta, Pa	June 24, 1873	140,299
Belt-shifter for machinery	L. J. Knowles	Warren, Mass	July 7, 1857	17,743
Belt-shifting apparatus	O. H. Wade	East Bridgewater, Mass	Oct. 14, 1873	143,736
Belt-shifting device	A. M. Freeland	New York, N. Y	Aug. 27, 1867	68,061
Belt-shifting device	W. Sellers	Philadelphia, Pa	Dec. 16, 1862	37,180
Belt-shipper	E. Buck	Vincennes, Ind	June 30, 1868	79,443
Belt-shipper	T. W. Frost	Dorchester, Mass	Apr. 14, 1868	76,739
Belt-shipper	J. C. Goar	Monterey, Cal	Aug. 14, 1860	29,587

Index of patents issued from the United States Patent Office from 1790 *to* 1873, *inclusive*—Continued.

Invention.	Inventor.	Residence.	Date.	No.
Belt-shipper	J. C. Goar	Jamaica Plain, Mass	Oct. 21, 1862	36, 707
Belt-shipper	J. S. Otis	Leeds, Mass	Jan. 3, 1871	110, 674
Belt-shipper	T. P. Rodgers	Taunton, Mass	Sept. 15, 1863	39, 956
Belt-shipper for mules	W. H. Saltmarsh	Waltham, Mass	Dec. 24, 1867	72, 686
Belt-splice	G. E. Burt	Harvard, Mass	July 30, 1872	129, 928
Belt-splice point finisher	J. C. McLaren	Montreal, Canada	Dec. 13, 1870	110, 060
Belt-stop for machinery, Traveling	T. E. Baden	Washington, D. C	July 26, 1870	105, 765
Belt-stretcher	S. Rogers	Pittsburgh, Pa	Jan. 9, 1866	51, 970
Belt-stud	D. M. Weston	Boston, Mass	Apr. 14, 1868	76, 861
Belt-tension apparatus	S. E. Jewett	Haverhill, Mass	July 22, 1873	141, 004
Belt-tightener	J. Albertson and D. W. Marmon	Richmond, Ind	Jan. 2, 1872	122, 345
Belt-tightener	H. C. Allyn	Falls Village, Conn	Apr. 16, 1872	125, 780
Belt-tightener	J. W. Batcheller	Oregon, Mo	Jan. 23, 1872	122, 932
Belt-tightener	M. C. Chambelin and A. Clawson.	Plain View, Minn	Feb. 8, 1870	99, 634
Belt-tightener	L. Funke	Champion Mills, N. Mex	Jan. 23, 1872	122, 943
Belt-tightener	J. M. Hawley	Holton, Ind	Sept. 10, 1867	68, 625
Belt-tightener	J. A. and H. A. House	Brooklyn, N. Y	June 23, 1863	39, 015
Belt-tightener	J. M. King	Quincy, Minn	Dec. 15, 1868	85, 012
Belt-tightener	R. N. Meriam	Worcester, Mass	Nov. 9, 1869	96, 718
Belt-tightener	J. Nichols	Fond du Lac, Wis	Dec. 20, 1864	45, 5 4
Belt-tightener	S. Patton	Chatsworth, Ill	Aug. 18, 1868	81, 285
Belt-tightener	M. Peatt	Dexter, Mich	Nov. 19, 1867	71, 052
Belt-tightener	J. Pinnell	Pittston, Pa	Dec. 24, 1872	134, 309
Belt-tightener	G. W. Runk	Franklin, La	Jan. 24, 1871	111, 257
Belt-tightener	W. Sellers	Haverhill, Mass	Dec. 23, 1873	145, 908
Belt-tightener	T. G. Stansberry	Medora, Ill	Sept. 3, 1867	68, 465
Belt-tightener	A. N. Woodard	Fenton, Mich	Apr. 19, 1870	102, [illegible]74
Belt-tool	D. A. J. Lamson	Cherry Valley, Mass	Sept. 15, 1857	18, 206
Belt, Waist	A. R. Boylson	Chicago, Ill	Nov. 17, 1868	84, 082
Belt, Waist	J. H. Vogt and G. Dietzel	New York, N. Y	Mar. 11, 1873	136, 685
Belt, Woven endless	S. W. Baker	Providence, R. I	Oct. 22, 1861	33, 510
Belts, Composition to prevent the slipping of machine.	I. F. Eaton	Boston, Mass	May 17, 1870	103, 034
Belts, Connecting and disconnecting machinery by means of.	T. A. Madison	Terre Haute, Ind	May 31, 1859	24, 220
Belts, Fastening driving	J. C. Desumeur, C. and E. Dudin, and L. Delacourt.	Guise, France	Dec. 5, 1871	121, 452
Belts, Manufacture of India-rubber	A. H. Hook	New York, N. Y	Apr. 26, 1870	102, 268
Belts, Shifting	M. Wells	Brooklyn, N. Y	Feb. 2, 1858	19, 272
Belts, Tightening and guiding	C. K. Myers	Pekin, Ill	Dec. 14, 1869	97, 955
Belts together, Machine for drawing	E. F. Miller and B. Gardner	Williamsburgh and Hampshire County, Mass.	Oct. 24, 1865	50, 609
Belts, Tool for mending	G. W. Miller	West Meriden, Conn	Aug. 4, 1868	80, 756
Belts, Tool for use in lacing	F. W. Du Bois	New York, N. Y	May 13, 1873	138, 740
Belting	C. J. Fay	Philadelphia, Pa	June 18, 1867	65, 895
Belting	H. Lemaistre	Brussels, Belgium	Mar. 17, 1868	75, 554
Belting	W. P. Powers	North La Crosse, Wis	Aug. 26, 1873	142, 272
Belting	T. Standring	Fort Richmond, N. Y	Sept. 1, 1868	81, 823
Belting	H. Underwood	New York, N. Y	Apr. 10, 1860	27, 846
Belting, Apparatus for forming rubber	T. J. Mayall	Roxbury, Mass	Dec. 27, 1859	26, 603
Belting, Artificial leather	S. M. Allen	Woburn, Mass	Jan. 21, 1868	73, 427
Belting, Artificial leather	S. M. Allen	Woburn, Mass	July 21, 1868	80, 048
Belting, Composition for stuffing	J. Haseltine	Warren, N. H	Aug. 13, 1867	67, 766
Belting-conveyer	J. Campbell	Saint Louis, Mo	Sept. 1, 1863	39, 716
Belting, Elastic	D. C. Gately	Newtown, Conn	Mar. 13, 1860	27, 440
Belting, Elastic	J. and S. Peatfield	Ipswich, Mass	Mar. 13, 1860	27, 471
Belting, Fastening for machine	L. Smith	Buffalo, N. Y	Nov. 17, 1857	18, 659
Belting, Fastening leather	E. Osgood	Bangor, Me	May 10, 1853	9, 710
Belting, Finishing vulcanized India-rubber	C. McBurney	Boston, Mass	June 13, 1871	115, 880
Belting for driving machines	M. A. Strouvelle	Saint Louis, Mo	Sept. 17, 1867	69, 042
Belting for machinery	S. M. Allen	Woburn, Mass	Mar. 13, 1866	53, 095
Belting for machinery	J. H. Clifton	Newcastle, Pa	Aug. 16, 1859	25, 096
Belting, hose, &c., Manufacture of	W. A. Torrey	Mont Clare, N. J	July 10, 1866	56, 292
Belting, India-rubber	B. F. Lee	New York, N. Y	Dec. 20, 1859	26, 549
Belting, Lap-joint for	H. Underwood	New York, N. Y	Feb. 9, 1858	19, 318
Belting, Leather	W. Strevell, S. B. Wells, and G. B. Kerper.	Jersey City, N. J., and New York, N. Y.	Jan. 28, 1868	73, 848
Belting, Machine	J. H. Cheever	New York, N. Y	Sept. 28, 1858	21, 596
Belting, Machine	V. Fountain, jr	Castleton, N. Y	Dec. 17, 1867	72, 181
Belting, Machine	W. H. Gates	Louisville, Ky	Jan. 1, 1867	60, 713
Belting, Machine	T. J. Mayall	Boston, Mass	Feb. 7, 1860	27, 060
Belting, Machine	J. Montgomery	New York, N. Y	June 22, 1869	91, 656
Belting, Machine	H. Taylor	Trenton, N. J	Jan. 26, 1864	41, 405
Belting, Machine	J. G. Street	Brooklyn, N. Y	Apr. 26, 1870	102, 447
Belting, Machine for cutting solid leather	T. J. Dickerson and O. B. Warren.	Auburn, N. Y	Nov. 14, 1871	120, 948
Belting, Machine for making India rubber	R. Hale	Roxbury, Mass	May 5, 1857	17, 216
Belting, Machine for making rubber	T. J. Mayall	Roxbury, Mass	Jan. 31, 1860	27, 001
Belting, Machine for making rubber	T. J. Mayall	Roxbury, Mass	Apr. 3, 1860	27, 730
Belting, Machine for removing rivets from	H. F. Crafts and W. Updegraff	Williamsport, Pa	Sept. 10, 1872	131, 152
Belting, Making rubber	D. C. Gately	Newtown, Conn	Nov. 22, 1859	26, 178
Belting, Manufacture of	J. B. Crane	Dalton, Mass	June 18, 1867	65, 879
Belting, Manufacture of	C. E. Smith	Philadelphia, Pa	May 31, 1859	24, 243
Belting, Manufacture of caoutchouc	D. C. Gately	Newtown, Conn	Dec. 20, 1859	26, 489
Belting, Manufacture of elastic	S. T. Parmelee	Edinburgh, Scotland	Apr. 26, 1859	23, 779
Belting, Manufacture of India-rubber	D. C. Gately	Newtown, Conn	Dec. 27, 1859	26, 580
Belting, Manufacture of India-rubber	D. C. Gately	Newtown, Conn	Jan. 3, 1860	26, 669
Belting, Manufacture of leather	G. O. Clark and F. G. Slemmer	Philadelphia, Pa	Dec. 10, 1872	133, 698
Belting, Manufacture of machine	J. H. Clifton	Newcastle, Pa	Aug. 16, 1859	25, 095
Belting, Manufacture of machine	G. and D. Hurn	London, England	Feb. 9, 1869	86, 755
Belting, Manufacture of paper	J. B. Crane	Dalton, Mass	Nov. 24, 1868	84, 263
Belting, Manufacture of round	M. Jewell	Hartford, Conn	June 15, 1858	20, 564
Belting, Manufacture of rubber	A. O. Bourn and I. F. Williams.	Providence and Bristol, R. I	Apr. 4, 1871	113, 486
Belting, Manufacture of rubber	G. P. Dodge	London, England	Jan. 15, 1867	61, 173
Belting, Manufacture of rubber	D. C. Gately	Newtown, Conn	Nov. 29, 1859	26, 264
Belting, Manufacture of rubber	D. C. Gately	Newtown, Conn	Nov. 29, 1859	26, 265
Belting, Manufacture of vulcanized rubber	D. C. Gately and J. B. Forsyth	Newtown, Conn., and Boston, Mass.	Aug. 5, 1873	141, 433

Index of patents issued from the United States Patent Office from 1790 *to* 1873, *inclusive*—Continued.

Invention.	Inventor.	Residence.	Date.	No.
Belting, Manufacturing rubber	D. C. Gately	Newtown, Conn	Jan. 31, 1860	26, 982
Belting, Metal	W. P. Powers	North La Crosse, Wis	Nov. 30, 1869	97, 312
Belting, Mode of	B. Chester	New York, N. Y	Dec. 22, 1857	18, 941
Belting, Mode of forming joints in India-rubber	J. McDougall	Masonville, Mich	Oct. 11, 1859	25, 749
Belting, Mold for making cushioned	S. W. Tyler	Troy, N. Y	May 2, 1871	114, 371
Belting or banding, Machine for	T. J. Mayall	Roxbury, Mass	Nov. 24, 1863	40, 699
Belting or banding, Manufacture of India-rubber	J. H. Cheever	Boston, Mass	Mar. 11, 1856	14, 389
Belting, Round	A. Holbrook, jr	Providence, R. I	June 18, 1872	128, 040
Belting, Rubber	D. C. Gately	Newtown, Conn	Nov. 22, 1859	26, 177
Belting, Rubber-coated rubber	P. Jewell, jr	Hartford, Conn	July 16, 1867	66, 848
Belting, Splicing	J. W. Lyder and H. Shevo	Alliance, Ohio	June 23, 1868	79, 136
Belting, Splicing	N. E. Smith	East Cleveland, Ohio	July 2, 1867	66, 261
Belting, Vulcanized India-rubber	D. C. Gately	Newtown, Conn	Oct. 27, 1868	83, 374
Bench:				
See Carpenter's bench.				
Clothes-wringer bench.				
Corn-husking bench.				
Currier's bench.				
Cutter-bench.				
Folding bench.				
Folding wash-bench.				
Laundry-bench.				
Revolving bench.				
Saw-bench.				
Shoemaker's bench.				
Sleigh-bench.				
Wash-bench.				
Work-bench.				
Bench, Carpenter's	J. W. Mahan	Lexington, Ill	Mar. 25, 1856	14, 511
Bench-clamp	C. W. Clapp	Wappinger's Falls, N. Y	Mar. 11, 1856	14, 390
Bench-clamp	G. Cooper	Hartford, Conn	Mar. 20, 1860	27, 592
Bench-clamp	O. L. Fenner	Rochester, N. Y	Nov. 30, 1869	97, 376
Bench-dog	A. K. and H. P. Hood	Lowell, Mass	Mar. 12, 1867	62, 748
Bench-dog	C. P. Whitman	Charlemont, Mass	Aug. 29, 1871	118, 662
Bench-drill	C. G. Miller	Brattleborough, Vt	May 26, 1868	78, 309
Bench-hook	D. Boyce	North Providence, R. I	Sept. 23, 1873	143, 054
Bench-hook	R. Frisbie	Middletown, Conn	July 10, 1860	29, 070
Bench-hook	A. Hotchkin	Schenevus, N. Y	Oct. 16, 1855	13, 678
Bench-hook	J. Humphreys	Chicopee Falls, Mass	Apr. 27, 1869	89, 483
Bench-hook	W. B. Kean	Worcester, Mass	Aug. 13, 1850	7, 565
Bench-hook	J. W. McGill	New York, N. Y	May 14, 1872	126, 644
Bench-hook	H. M. Putnam	Fitchburgh, Mass	June 20, 1871	116, 220
Bench-hook	H. J. Skinner	Dunkirk, N. Y	June 7, 1870	104, 069
Bench-hook	C. H. Weston	Lowell, Mass	Oct. 2, 1866	58, 519
Bench-hook	E. B. White	Nashua, N. H	Mar. 9, 1858	19, 595
Bench hook and clamp	E. P. Woods and A. E. Blood	Lowell and Lynn, Mass	June 27, 1865	48, 498
Bench-hook, Carpenter's	L. F. Noe	New York, N. Y	Aug. 14, 1866	57, 176
Bench-hook, Joiner's	P. P. Cowles	Cabotville, Mass	June 6, 1848	5, 619
Bench hook or dog	C. T. Crane	Lowell, Mass	May 28, 1867	65, 060
Bench-hook, Socket for	J. Sawyer	South Royalston, Mass	Feb. 28, 1854	10, 579
Bench or table	L. D. Hubbard	Worcester, Mass	Apr. 7, 1868	76, 459
Bench-pin	H. Gabelmann	Fort Scott, Kans	May 10, 1870	102, 802
Bench-pin	T. J. W. Porter	Grand Rapids, Mich	Jan. 12, 1869	85, 850
Bench-plane, Bit-fastening for cast-iron	W. S. Loughborough	Victor, N. Y	Apr. 4, 1854	10, 748
Bench-plane bit, Manner of securing	C. W. Seely and B. F. Locke	Wellington, Ohio	June 7, 1859	24, 335
Bench-rest	J. D. Spiller	Concord, N. H	June 5, 1855	13, 016
Bench-shears	J. Hill	Charlotte, Mich	Aug. 17, 1869	93, 715
Bending and folding sheet-metal, Machine for	J. B. and L. C. Clark	Plantsville, Conn	Dec. 14, 1869	97, 762
Bending and hardening springs, Machine for	C. A. Coggeshall	Bridgeport, Conn	July 6, 1869	92, 268
Bending-brake for sheet-metal	F. Yaesché	Springfield, Mass	Aug. 15, 1871	118, 090
Bending circles, Machine for	W. Boyd	Hartford, N. Y	June 2, 1868	78, 418
Bending corrugated plates of metal, Apparatus for	R. Montgomery	New York, N. Y	June 3, 1862	35, 496
Bending-device	W. Malick	Tidioute, Pa	Dec. 31, 1867	72, 874
Bending-device for wood	E. Lacey	Chicago, Ill	Jan. 24, 1871	111, 218
Bending-machine	L. H. Beckwith	Port Jervis, N. Y	Sept. 3, 1867	68, 340
Bending-machine	J. Forbes	Halifax, Canada	Sept. 12, 1871	118, 920
Bending-machine	E. D. and W. K. Gird	Cedar Lake, N. Y	Mar. 19, 1867	63, 034
Bending-machine	H. S. Golightly and C. S. Twitchell.	New Haven, Conn	Aug. 10, 1869	93, 612
Bending-machine	G. Huntington	Norwichville, Canada	Oct. 15, 1867	69, 916
Bending-machine	S. W. Kimble	Springfield, Ill	Oct. 28, 1873	144, 109
Bending-machine	D. Pierce	Almont, Mich	Nov. 23, 1869	97, 113
Bending-machine	L. Raymond	New York, N. Y	Aug. 25, 1857	18, 058
Bending-machine	W. Richardson and L. B. Müller	Baltimore, Md	Jan. 28, 1868	73, 837
Bending-machine	J. J. H. Sercombe	New London, Wis	May 10, 1870	102, 975
Bending-machine	H. Winter	Honesdale, Pa	May 3, 1870	102, 641
Bending-machine	J. N. Woodward	Aurora, Ill	Sept. 17, 1867	69, 060
Bending-machine chain, Timber	L. Heywood	Gardner, Mass	Mar. 13, 1860	27, 447
Bending-machine clamp, Wood	J. B. Van Horn	Trenton, N. J	June 30, 1868	79, 530
Bending-machine for corrugated metal plates	A. Johnson	Brooklyn, N. Y	July 26, 1870	105, 805
Bending machine, Metal	W. W. Cumberland	Newark, N. J	Dec. 12, 1854	12, 053
Bending machine, Metal	C. H. Delamater	New York, N. Y	Aug. 4, 1863	39, 382
Bending machine, Metal	W. C. Eiseman	Pittsburgh, Pa	Feb. 27, 1872	124, 123
Bending machine, Metal	S. Hall	New York, N. Y	Feb. 26, 1867	62, 327
Bending machine, Metal	J. Noland	Philadelphia, Pa	Dec. 24, 1867	72, 669
Bending machine, Metal	R. Potts	Chatham, N. Y	Oct. 15, 1867	69, 936
Bending machine, Metallic-plate	E. L. Gaylord	Terrysville, Conn	Oct. 3, 1857	18, 542
Bending machine, Metallic-plate	E. L. Gaylord	Terrysville, Conn	Aug. 18, 1857	18, 011
Bending machine, Metallic-plate	D. Howell	Louisville, Ky	Jan. 12, 1858	19, 090
Bending machine, Metallic-plate	J. Perry	Plymouth Hollow, Conn	Aug. 18, 1857	18, 019
Bending machine, Sheet-metal	R. Brady	New York, N. Y	Jan. 8, 1856	14, 049
Bending machine, Sheet-metal	G. W. Burling	Trenton, N. J	Oct. 28, 1856	15, 964
Bending machine, Sheet-metal	J. Eppley	York, Pa	May 16, 1848	5, 571
Bending machine, Sheet-metal	J. M. Grove and H. Hedrick	Anderson, Ind	July 28, 1868	80, 348
Bending machine, Sheet-metal	C. C. Hare	Kansas City, Mo	Apr. 19, 1870	102, 001
Bending machine, Sheet-metal	R. B. McConnell	Evansville, Ind	Apr. 2, 1872	125, 317
Bending machine, Sheet-metal	W. J. McLea	Leroy, N. Y	Jan. 5, 1869	85, 531
Bending machine, Sheet-metal	A. Shepard	New Britain, Conn	Dec. 8, 1868	84, 714

Index of patents issued from the United States Patent Office from 1790 *to* 1873, *inclusive*—Continued.

Invention.	Inventor.	Residence.	Date.	No.
Bending machine, Sheet-metal	W. Webster	Morrisania, N. Y	Mar 28, 1854	10, 713
Bending machine, Sheet-metal	A. W. and P. A. Whitney	Woodstock, Vt	Oct. 20, 1868	83, 347
Bending machine, Sheet-metal	J. Wright	Plantsville, Conn	Jan. 20, 1857	16, 456
Bending machine, Timber	J. D. Sarven	Maury County, Tenn	Jan. 20, 1857	16, 453
Bending machine, Volute-spring	R. Miller	Pittsburgh, Pa	Aug. 23, 1870	106, 603
Bending machine, Wire-screw eye	N. C. Perry	Chester, Conn	Aug. 23, 1870	106, 720
Bending machine, Wood	A. Bailey	Gardiner, Me	Oct. 11, 1859	25, 711
Bending machine, Wood	C. F. Beverly	Lancaster, Ohio	Oct. 13, 1857	18, 379
Bending machine, Wood	T. Blanchard	Boston, Mass	May 4, 1858	20, 137
Bending machine, Wood	I. W. Bowers	Boston, Mass	Jan. 21, 1868	73, 493
Bending machine, Wood	D. F. Breed	Valparaiso, Ind	Jan. 21, 1868	73, 496
Bending machine, Wood	D. Catchpole and J. Havens	Geneva and Auburn, N. Y	Oct. 1, 1867	69, 313
Bending machine, Wood	A. Chubb	Painesville, Ohio	Feb. 22, 1859	23, 012
Bending machine, Wood	E. A. Conner	Metropolis, Ill	Mar. 14, 1871	112, 553
Bending machine, Wood	J. Conner	Richmond, Ind	Feb. 18, 1868	74, 668
Bending machine, Wood	M. F. Connett	Evansville, Ind	July 11, 1865	48, 661
Bending machine, Wood	J. A. Dann	New Haven, Conn	Apr. 23, 1867	63, 997
Bending machine, Wood	V. De Lyon and V. Werner	Canton, Miss	Apr. 27, 1869	89, 387
Bending machine, Wood	O. Evans	Alliance, Ohio	June 5, 1866	55, 264
Bending machine, Wood	S. C. and E. O. Fink	Indianapolis, Ind	Sept. 10, 1867	67, 621
Bending machine, Wood	J. Fipps	New Albany, Ind	Nov. 8, 1870	108, 992
Bending machine, Wood	J. Fishbaugh	Tiffin, Ohio	May 1, 1866	54, 316
Bending machine, Wood	R. Fitts, jr	Fitchburgh, Mass	Mar. 2, 1869	87, 404
Bending machine, Wood	J. W. Griffiths	Brooklyn, N. Y	Jan. 2, 1866	51, 826
Bending machine, Wood	O. W. Griffiths	Charlestown, Mass	Apr. 2, 1872	125, 130
Bending machine, Wood	G. Gustafson	Chicago, Ill	Oct. 10, 1871	119, 702
Bending machine, Wood	J. Hale	Somerville, Mass	Apr. 21, 1868	77, 036
Bending machine, Wood	J. S. Hall	Jeffersonville, Ind	Aug. 25, 1868	81, 365
Bending machine, Wood	H. Hanna	Columbus, Ohio	Dec. 9, 1873	145, 416
Bending machine, Wood	E. C. Harris	New York, N. Y	Feb. 27, 1866	52, 944
Bending machine, Wood	E. P. Haskell	Harlan, Ind	Dec. 9, 1862	37, 096
Bending machine, Wood	L. Heywood	Gardner, Mass	Dec. 17, 1867	72, 292
Bending machine, Wood	L. Heywood	Gardner, Mass	Dec. 17, 1867	72, 293
Bending machine, Wood	L. Heywood	Gardner, Mass	Aug. 4, 1868	80, 627
Bending machine, Wood	M. V. B. Howe	Gardner, Mass	Jan. 28, 1868	73, 720
Bending machine, Wood	P. Hurm	Hamilton, Ohio	Aug. 1, 1865	49, 109
Bending machine, Wood	S. Keeler	Lancaster, Pa	June 13, 1865	48, 181
Bending machine, Wood	S. U. King	Windsor, Vt	Oct. 24, 1865	50, 601
Bending machine, Wood	S. Kingsland	Lyndon, Wis	July 22, 1862	35, 983
Bending machine, Wood	J. Klahr	Bernville, Pa	Dec. 10, 1867	71, 886
Bending machine, Wood	G. Kriebel	Hosensack, Pa	Oct. 24, 1865	50, 602
Bending machine, Wood	E. Lacey	Chicago, Ill	Sept. 12, 1871	118, 864
Bending machine, Wood	J. P. Selzelter	Lancaster, Pa	Feb. 21, 1865	46, 479
Bending machine, Wood	C. Leseberg	Cincinnati, Ohio	Mar. 19, 1872	124, 753
Bending machine, Wood	W. P. Letchworth	Buffalo, N. Y	Aug. 18, 1868	81, 095
Bending machine, Wood	J. C. Lucas	Newark, N. J	June 16, 1868	78, 983
Bending machine, Wood	A. Luckhaupt	Columbus, Ohio	Oct. 1, 1861	33, 395
Bending machine, Wood	O. Marland	Boston, Mass	Feb. 14, 1871	111, 855
Bending machine, Wood	A. F. Marshall	Black River, N. Y	Sept. 5, 1871	118, 736
Bending machine, Wood	J. W. Martin	Philadelphia, Pa	Feb. 15, 1870	99, 925
Bending machine, Wood	E. G. Matthews	Oakham, Mass	Apr. 25, 1871	114, 171
Bending machine, Wood	H. McDonald	Union Springs, N. Y	Jan. 22, 1861	31, 182
Bending machine, Wood	H. McDonald	Shortsville, N. Y	Oct. 21, 1871	120, 305
Bending machine, Wood	H. McDonald	Shortsville, N. Y	Oct. 24, 1871	120, 306
Bending machine, Wood	J. McMichael	Philadelphia, Pa	Dec. 20, 1870	110, 262
Bending machine, Wood	J. F. Melcher	Bloomington, Ill	Sept. 15, 1868	82, 247
Bending machine, Wood	J. Merrill	Boston, Mass	Oct. 13, 1868	83, 078
Bending machine, Wood	E. Mets	Rochester, N. Y	June 30, 1868	79, 489
Bending machine, Wood	L. E. Minott	Sheboygan, Wis	Aug. 1, 1871	117, 663
Bending machine, Wood	C. Moyer, jr	Coopersburgh, Pa	Oct. 16, 1866	58, 873
Bending machine, Wood	C. L. Nelson and O. Bostwick	Burlington, Vt	Mar. 27, 1860	27, 672
Bending machine, Wood	J. Newman	Falmouth, Me	July 31, 1866	56, 788
Bending machine, Wood	H. H. Nichols	Keeseville, N. Y	Sept. 21, 1869	95, 037
Bending machine, Wood	H. Ocorr	Sheboygan, Wis	Sept. 26, 1871	119, 393
Bending machine, Wood	J. Phillips	Chicago, Ill	Oct. 24, 1871	120, 321
Bending machine, Wood	J. H. Preston	Jefferson City, Mo	Sept. 21, 1869	95, 042
Bending machine, Wood	C. Prudden	Philadelphia, Pa	Apr. 17, 1866	54, 012
Bending machine, Wood	N. Purdy	Milwaukee, Wis	May 4, 1869	89, 790
Bending machine, Wood	J. N. Ray	Indianapolis, Ind	Dec. 13, 1864	45, 457
Bending machine, Wood	J. N. Ray	Indianapolis, Ind	May 1, 1866	54, 405
Bending machine, Wood	T. D. Roberts	Middletown, N. Y	Dec. 5, 1865	51, 353
Bending machine, Wood	E. Robinson	Raynham, Mass	Oct. 8, 1861	33, 467
Bending machine, Wood	A. Rogers	Painesville, Ohio	Mar. 20, 1860	27, 568
Bending machine, Wood	W. H. Ryan	Louisville, Ky	Aug. 2, 1864	43, 745
Bending machine, Wood	J. P. Schmucker	Ashland, Ohio	Oct. 2, 1866	58, 488
Bending machine, Wood	F. Seidle and S. Eberly	Mechanicsburgh, Pa	July 10, 1860	29, 107
Bending machine, Wood	F. Smith and P. Swope	Tiffin, Ohio	Feb. 28, 1865	46, 591
Bending machine, Wood	A. G. Snyder	Ashtabula, Ohio	Mar. 16, 1869	87, 981
Bending machine, Wood	J. K. B. Solomon	Rigglesville, Pa	Aug. 30, 1870	106, 880
Bending machine, Wood	A. P. Spaulding and E. Pierce	Westminster, Mass	Sept. 11, 1860	30, 004
Bending machine, Wood	H. E. Stager	Milwaukee, Wis	Jan. 9, 1866	51, 978
Bending machine, Wood	O. W. Stearns	Lebanon, N. H	July 2, 1867	66, 409
Bending machine, Wood	E. J. Updegraff	York, Pa	Apr. 8, 1856	14, 636
Bending machine, Wood	D. B. Wedden	Newark, N. J	Oct. 16, 1860	30, 404
Bending machine, Wood	J. L. Whipple and E. Trowbridge.	Detroit, Mich	May 28, 1872	127, 396
Bending machine, Wood	W. D. Williams	Raleigh, N. C	May 3, 1870	102, 637
Bending machinery, Wood	R. Fitts, jr	Fitchburgh, Mass	Aug. 5, 1862	36, 082
Bending machinery, Wood	J. Hann	Frenchtown, N. J	July 6, 1869	92, 187
Bending-mandrel	C. French	Seymour, Conn	Apr. 7, 1868	76, 432
Bending metal	C. H. Schubens	Newark, N. J	May 7, 1867	64, 585
Bending metals edgewise, Machine for	G. W. Brown	Galesburgh, Ill	May 25, 1869	90, 492
Bending mold-boards, Adjustable die for	J. H. Franklin	Avoca, Wis	Sept. 6, 1870	107, 032
Bending several pieces of wood of unequal lengths at once, Method of.	H. A. Barnard	Moline, Ill	Mar. 9, 1858	19, 538
Bending sheet-metal	J. Wright	Harmar, Ohio	Feb. 26, 1856	14, 332
Bending sheet-metal, Plier for	M. Rothschild	Harrisburgh, Pa	Feb, 18, 1868	74, 601
Bending sheet-metal, Roller for	D. Newton	Southington, Conn	Mar. 10, 1857	16, 804

Index of patents issued from the United States Patent Office from 1790 *to* 1873, *inclusive*—Continued.

Invention.	Inventor.	Residence.	Date.	No.
Bending timber, Method of	E. Green and M. Blackslee	Litchfield, Conn	Mar. 20, 1822	....
Bending timber, Retaining-strap for	L. E. Minott	Sheboygan, Wis	Aug. 1, 1871	117, 664
Bending wood	T. Blanchard	Boston, Mass	Dec. 18, 1849	6, 951
Bending wood, Method of	T. Blanchard	Boston, Mass	Oct. 21, 1856	15, 944
Bending wood, Method of	R. Fitts	New Ipswich, N. H	Jan. 4, 1859	22, 529
Bending wood, Method of	E. A. and C. Kilburn	Burlington, Vt	Oct. 7, 1856	15, 851
Bending wood, Method of	J. C. Morris	Cincinnati, Ohio	Mar. 11, 1856	14, 405
Bending wooden hoops, Machine for	J. Dobbins	Waterloo, Mich	Nov. 6, 1866	59, 369
Benzine from hydrocarbon, Apparatus for removing.	H. J. Berg	Butler, Pa	Aug. 24, 1869	93, 952
Benzine, Purifying	G. Lupton	Indianapolis, Ind	Dec. 13, 1870	110, 054
Benzole-light	H. M. Paine	Worcester, Mass	July 13, 1852	9, 119
Benzole-vapor apparatus	C. Cunningham	Nashua, N. H	Mar. 13, 1855	12, 535
Benzole-vapor apparatus	O. P. Drake	Boston, Mass	Aug. 30, 1853	9, 967
Berry-box	T. Mabbett, jr	Vineland, N. J	Jan. 14, 1868	73, 352
Berry-box	C. Reese	Baltimore, Md	Apr. 23, 1872	126, 087
Berry-boxes, Machine for cutting	C. Colby	South Pass, Ill	Aug. 27, 1867	68, 171
Berth for railway-cars, Sleeping	A. Judson	Newark, N. J	July 21, 1868	80, 184
Berth for railway-cars, Sleeping	D. M. Lawrence	Cincinnati, Ohio	Nov. 9, 1858	22, 025
Berth for railway-cars, Sleeping	D. L. Long	Dayton, Ohio	Aug. 23, 1859	25, 205
Berth for ships, Oscillating	I. A. Chomel	New York, N. Y	June 17, 1873	140, 014
Berth for vessels, Oscillating	B. Weisker	New York, N. Y	Aug. 5, 1873	141, 614
Berth-knee former	D. Taylor	East Boston, Mass	June 6, 1854	11, 005
Berth lock, Sleeping-car	T. A. Bissell	Detroit, Mich	Dec. 23, 1873	145, 835
Berth, Movable	N. W. Wheeler	Brooklyn, N. Y	Apr. 25, 1865	47, 481
Berth, Oscillating	L. D. Newell	New York, N. Y	Sept. 10, 1872	131, 223
Berth, Oscillating ship's	T. S. Brown	Philadelphia, Pa	Aug. 28, 1860	29, 763
Berth, Ship's	I. A. Chomel	New York, N Y	Aug. 27, 1872	130, 792
Berth, Ship's	J. Evans	Denver, Colo. Ter.	Apr. 16, 1872	125, 729
Berth, Ship's	H. Getty	Brooklyn, N. Y	Aug. 25, 1857	18, 044
Berth, Ship's	J. Monroe	New York, N. Y	July 6, 1869	92, 204
Berth, Sleeping-car	B. F. Manier	Green Island, N. Y	Apr. 4, 1871	113, 539
Berth, Sleeping-car	W. B. Snow	Chicago, Ill	Feb. 25, 1868	74, 773
Berth, Sleeping-car	W. B. Snow	Chicago, Ill	May 17, 1870	103, 097
Berth, Step for	S. E. Siegel	New York, N. Y	July 9, 1872	128, 761
Berth, Vessel	B. Weisker	New York, N. Y	June 3, 1873	139, 638
Berths for vessels, Method of constructing	H. King	New York, N. Y	Sept. 4, 1841	2, 240
Berths, Step-attachment for	E. Hoyt and E. P. Whitney	Stamford, Conn	Mar. 12, 1867	62, 850
Bessemer-converter bottom	A. L. Rothman	Joliet, Ill	Sept. 3, 1872	131, 120
Bessemer or Kelly converter, Compound for lining bottom of.	J. E. Atwood	Pittsburgh, Pa	May 13, 1873	138, 760
Bessemer plant	A. L. Rothman	Joliet, Ill	Nov. 19, 1872	133, 258
Beton, Hydraulic	J. Drevet	Paris, France	May 21, 1872	126, 940
Bevel	L. D. Howard	Saint Johnsbury, Vt	Nov. 5, 1867	70, 570
Bevel, Adjustable	E. A. Bell	Meriden, Conn	Apr. 25, 1871	114, 096
Bevel, Adjustable	W. C. Ellis	Springfield, Mass	Mar. 21, 1871	112, 793
Bevel, Adjustable	L. D. Howard	Saint Johnsbury, Vt	Feb. 14, 1871	111, 746
Bevel, Adjustable	J. A. Traut	New Britain, Conn	May 9, 1871	114, 626
Bevel and tapering gage	D. H. Tierney	New York, N. Y	June 16, 1868	79, 032
Bevel and try square	J. Graham	Ludlow, Vt	Nov. 5, 1867	70, 547
Bevel, Carpenter's	L. Bailey and S. D. Sargent	New Britain, Conn	Mar. 19, 1872	124, 779
Bevel, Carpenter's	H. Fairbanks and I. J. Robinson.	Saint Johnsbury, Vt	Mar. 11, 1873	136, 714
Bevel, Carpenter's	W. H. Laughlin	Quincy, Ill	July 23, 1872	129, 737
Bevel, Carpenter's	S. D. Sargent	Hartford, Conn	July 22, 1873	141, 081
Bevel, Carpenter's adjustable	I. J. Robinson and H. Fairbanks.	Saint Johnsbury, Vt	Apr. 9, 1872	125, 617
Bevel, Protracting	W. W. Branch, jr	Madison, Ohio	Mar. 27, 1866	53, 397
Bevel-rest	J. E. Seavey	Kennebunkport, Me	Dec. 30, 1873	146, 027
Bevel, square, rule, &c., Combined	J. D. Otstot	Springfield, Ohio	July 5, 1870	105, 121
Bevel-turning gage	J. W. Moore	Worcester, Mass	Sept. 21, 1869	94, 968
Beverage	G. Beck	Rochester, N. Y	July 3, 1866	55, 983
Beverage	A. Cochard	Port Richmond, N. Y	Jan. 31, 1865	46, 081
Beverage	W. Davis	Portland, Me	June 4, 1867	65, 475
Beverage	W. H. Goss	Boston, Mass	June 22, 1869	91, 621
Beverage	E. G. Holland	Union Springs, N. Y	May 29, 1866	55, 106
Beverage	A. C. Howell	Vienna, N. J	June 27, 1865	48, 405
Beverage	J. H. Kenyon	Sempronius, N. Y	Apr. 10, 1866	53, 834
Beverage	C. Nessi	San Francisco, Cal	Nov. 16, 1869	96, 928
Beverage	S. B. Shaw	West Randolph, Mass	July 6, 1869	92, 376
Beverage	H. Smith and H. F. Snow	Dover, N. H	July 17, 1866	56, 458
Beverage	C. Sussegger	New York, N. Y	June 19, 1866	55, 737
Beverage and sirup from mustang grape	J. C. Wood	Larissa, Tex	June 11, 1872	127, 944
Beverage cooling and dispensing apparatus	J. Matthews	New York, N. Y	May 6, 1873	138, 671
Beverage from sour or bitter oranges	P. G. Pearson	Jacksonville, Fla	Apr. 27, 1869	89, 430
Beverage, Medicated	W. W. Timmons	Rahway, N. J	Feb. 2, 1869	86, 471
Beverage or champagne mead	A. S. Taylor	San Francisco, Cal	Aug. 16, 1870	106, 428
Beverage, Tonic	J. Mayer	Cleveland, Ohio	Jan. 26, 1869	86, 172
Beverages, Composition for	R. F. Brown	Provincetown, Mass	Oct. 19, 1869	95, 980
Beverages for medicinal and other purposes, Manufacture of.	E. N. Horsford	Cambridge, Mass	June 14, 1870	104, 311
Bias-cutter	J. H. Goodfellow	Troy, N. Y	Sept. 13, 1870	107, 248
Bias-cutting device	G. Moore	Scotch Plains, N. J	Jan. 14, 1873	134, 918
Bias-marking device	G. Moore	Scotch Plains, N. J	Jan. 14, 1873	134, 919
Bib, Child's	A. L. Thomson	Hudson City, N. J	May 2, 1871	114, 366
Bib, Compression	W. Young	Easton, Pa	July 18, 1871	117, 233
Bidet or hip-bath	D. Gibbons	Rochester, N. Y	Nov. 14, 1871	120, 961
Bier	D. Fitzgerald	New York, N. Y	May 19, 1863	38, 575
Bier	W. Scarlett	Aurora, Ill	Oct. 2, 1860	30, 251
Bilge and keel of vessels, Block for supporting	F. Grice	Washington, D. C	Feb. 20, 1849	6, 120
Bilge and leakage water indicator for ship or other vessel.	R. Shaler	Madison, Conn	Aug. 26, 1856	15, 624
Bilge-block for docking ships	P. Burgess	Brooklyn, N. Y	Apr. 19, 1864	42, 345
Bilge-boat, Solid	D. Brader	Beach Haven, Pa	Apr. 9, 1872	125, 435
Bilge-water and for the ventilation of vessel, Apparatus for the discharge of.	J. Briggs	Louisville, Ky	Oct. 27, 1863	40, 394
Bilge-water &c., Apparatus for elevating and discharging.	N. Hodge	North Adams, Mass	Oct. 19, 1852	9, 344

Index of patents issued from the United States Patent Office from 1790 *to* 1873, *inclusive*—Continued.

Invention.	Inventor.	Residence.	Date.	No.
Bilge-water, Device for discharging	J. A. Miller	Paducah, Ky	Feb. 11, 1873	135, 656
Bilge-water gage	J. R. Barry	Philadelphia, Pa	Sept. 27, 1864	44, 385
Bilge-water gage	W. P. Kirkland	San Francisco, Cal	July 31, 1866	56, 763
Bilge-water gage, Vessel	C. McCloskey	East Cambridge, Mass	June 4, 1872	127, 422
Bilge-ways	S. Thomas	New York, N. Y	Oct. 10, 1829	....
Bill and currency holder	G. B. Isham	Burlington, Vt	July 7, 1863	39, 148
Bill and note holder	G. K. Snow	Watertown, Mass	Oct. 21, 1862	36, 734
Bill-folding gage	A. J. Marshall	Buffalo, N. Y	Oct. 15, 1872	132, 166
Bill-holder	A. Buswell	San Francisco, Cal	Mar. 24, 1863	37, 949
Bill-holder	J. A. M. Collins	Keokuk, Iowa	Dec. 29, 1868	85, 367
Bill-holder	E. F. French	Franklin, Vt	Mar. 17, 1857	16, 829
Bill-holder	G. Moulton	Cambridge, Mass	Aug. 27, 1867	68, 305
Bill-holder	G. W. Palmer	Boston, Mass	Mar. 27, 1855	12, 604
Bill-holder	C. T. Wakeley	Madison, Wis	Feb. 7, 1865	46, 282
Bill of credit	J. Golder	Philadelphia, Pa	Sept. 26, 1835	....
Bill of exchange	C. C. Wright	New York, N. Y	June 19, 1835	....
Bill of fare	W. A. Bury	Grosse Isle, Mich	May 8, 1860	28, 152
Bill of fare, Apparatus for displaying	J. Faye	Philadelphia, Pa	Aug. 23, 1864	43, 904
Bill-of-fare frame	C. Gloyd	Wynant, Ohio	Oct. 9, 1860	30, 311
Bill-register	J. N. Ayres	Stamford, Conn	Aug. 24, 1852	9, 211
Billiard and bagatelle table	W. A. Clark	Boston, Mass	Sept. 21, 1869	95, 084
Billiard and dining table	H. W. Collender	New York, N. Y	Apr. 21, 1868	77, 001
Billiard and dining table	F. E. Held	Chicago, Ill	Mar. 1, 1870	100, 401
Billiard and other game tables, Mode of constructing.	W. E. Bond	Cleveland, Ohio	Aug. 3, 1869	93, 272
Billiard and other tables, Device for leveling	B. W. Bull	New York, N. Y	Aug. 16, 1870	106, 317
Billiard and other tables, and for other purposes, Fabric for bed of.	L. A. Grill	New York, N. Y	July 11, 1871	116, 951
Billiard-ball	J. W. Hyatt, jr	Albany, N. Y	Oct. 10, 1865	50, 359
Billiard-ball, Vulcanite	W. H. Lippincott	Pittsburgh, Pa	May 12, 1868	77, 823
Billiard-balls and other articles, Compositions for	J. W. Hyatt, jr	Albany, N. Y	Apr. 14, 1868	76, 765
Billiard-balls and other composition articles, Manufacture of.	L. D. Benjamin, P. Wayne, and A. Stone.	Albany, N. Y	Apr. 4, 1871	113, 272
Billiard-balls, knife-handles, and other articles, Process of coating.	J. W. Hyatt, jr	Albany, N. Y	May 16, 1871	114, 945
Billiard-balls, &c., Method of coating	J. W. Hyatt, jr	Albany, N. Y	Apr. 6, 1869	88, 634
Billiard-board, Portable	L. C. Prindle	Chicago, Ill	Aug. 13, 1872	130, 389
Billiard-counter	H. Ball	Walpole, N. H	July 6, 1869	92, 247
Billiard-cue	G. Bevitt	Madison, Wis	Jan. 23, 1866	52, 128
Billiard-cue	C. Coan and A. R. Burdick	Chicago, Ill., and Racine, Wis.	Oct. 8, 1872	132, 054
Billiard-cue	C. H. Gould	New York, N. Y	June 25, 1867	66, 147
Billiard-cue	H. C. Griffin	Franklin, N. H	Mar. 24, 1868	75, 751
Billiard-cue	M. V. Ingersoll	Norwalk Bridge, Conn	Aug. 9, 1870	106, 166
Billiard-cue	C. Leicht	New York, N. Y	May 27, 1856	14, 964
Billiard-cue	J. N. McIntire	New York, N. Y	Oct. 27, 1868	83, 397
Billiard-cue	L. Nemetz	New York, N. Y	Mar. 4, 1873	136, 535
Billiard-cue	H. Platts	Ithaca, N. Y	June 3, 1873	139, 519
Billiard-cue	O. C. Wilbur, jr	Coventry, R. I	Apr. 9, 1872	125, 643
Billiard-cue, Apparatus for chalking	D. F. Shaw	Elkhart, Ind	Aug. 3, 1869	93, 356
Billiard-cue chalk-holder	J. Jenkinson	Brooklyn, N. Y	Dec. 3, 1867	71, 621
Billiard-cue clamp	O. D. Benjamin	Toledo, Ohio	Nov. 25, 1873	144, 824
Billiard-cue, Clamp for gluing the tip on	S. Gissinger	Lawrenceville, Pa	Dec. 18, 1866	60, 503
Billiard-cue, Clamp for leathering	E. Brunswick	Chicago, Ill	Apr. 2, 1867	63, 465
Billiard-cue, Composition tip for	A. Wetherbee	Waltham, Mass	Nov. 10, 1868	84, 036
Billiard-cue cutter	F. R. Gardner	Cleveland, Ohio	Aug. 27, 1872	130, 912
Billiard-cue, Fastening for the tip of	O. C. Wilbur, jr	Providence, R. I	Jan. 10, 1871	110, 883
Billiard-cue, Press for attaching leathers to	W. L. Aldrich	Atlanta, Ga	Feb. 14, 1860	27, 093
Billiard-cue rack	E. Brunswick	Chicago, Ill	Jan. 7, 1868	72, 969
Billiard-cue rack	V. A. Buschmann	Baltimore, Md	May 5, 1868	77, 452
Billiard-cue tip	H. W. Collender	New York, N. Y	Jan. 4, 1859	22, 491
Billiard-cue tip	G. W. Dickinson	Saratoga Springs, N. Y	Nov. 4, 1873	144, 324
Billiard-cue tip	J. H. Green	Christiansburgh, Iowa	Aug. 30, 1859	25, 257
Billiard-cue tip	J. A. Veazie	Boston, Mass	Dec. 10, 1867	71, 925
Billiard-cue tip and fastener	E. B. Stocking	Binghamton, N. Y	Apr. 2, 1867	63, 575
Billiard-cue trimmer	H. Pernot	New York, N. Y	Mar. 3, 1868	75, 049
Billiard-cues true, Machine for cutting ends of	J. Glynn and M. Borowsky	Placerville, Cal	July 5, 1859	24, 625
Billiard-cushion	H. A. Alden	Matteawan, N. Y	Apr. 29, 1873	138, 356
Billiard-cushion	A. Bassford	New York, N. Y	Jan. 22, 1867	61, 308
Billiard-cushion	J. Berlien	Chicago, Ill	Feb. 1, 1870	99, 393
Billiard-cushion	J. Berlien	Chicago, Ill	Jan. 21, 1870	104, 542
Billiard-cushion	H. W. Collender	New York, N. Y	Nov. 26, 1867	71, 282
Billiard-cushion	M. Delaney	New York, N. Y	Aug. 15, 1871	117, 995
Billiard-cushion	J. G. H. Meyer	San Francisco, Cal	Oct. 1, 1872	131, 890
Billiard-cushion	W. St. Martin	Cincinnati, Ohio	May 27, 1873	139, 434
Billiard-cushion	J. Syrcher	Buffalo, N. Y	Nov. 10, 1863	40, 580
Billiard-cushion	J. Wagner	Detroit, Mich	Apr. 23, 1872	126, 113
Billiard-cushion	W. K. Winant	Brooklyn, N. Y	Aug. 10, 1858	21, 159
Billiard-cushion, India-rubber	C. L. Richards	New York, N. Y	Mar. 22, 1870	101, 163
Billiard-cushion, Lining	L. Wacker	Buffalo, N. Y	July 8, 1862	35, 851
Billiard-cushion of rubber and gutta-percha	J. Murphy	New York, N. Y	Sept. 26, 1871	119, 391
Billiard-game keeper	G. Miller and J. Reichert	New York, N. Y	Aug. 21, 1866	57, 443
Billiard-game register	E. Holmes and H. C. Roome	New York, N. Y	Mar. 9, 1869	87, 674
Billiard-game register	W. A. Hough	Saint Johnsville, N. Y	Apr. 27, 1869	89, 408
Billiard-game register, Electro-magnetic	G. A. Webster	Elgin, Ill	Aug. 15, 1871	118, 082
Billiard-indicator	M. Gootman	New York, N. Y	Jan. 16, 1866	52, 041
Billiard-indicator	B. Schmitz	Brooklyn, N. Y	Jan. 10, 1865	45, 868
Billiard-light	W. St. Martin	Cincinnati, Ohio	Feb. 25, 1873	136, 275
Billiard-marker	W. H. Newell	Hudson City, N. J	Aug. 15, 1871	118, 044
Billiard-register	H. I. Behrens	New York, N. Y	Feb. 8, 1859	22, 849
Billiard-register	G. W. Earl and J. H. Hawley	Kalamazoo, Mich	Apr. 23, 1867	64, 000
Billiard-register	L. Godefroy	Pulaski, Tenn	Dec. 26, 1871	122, 167
Billiard-register	R. H. Ingersoll	Washington, D. C	Feb. 6, 1866	52, 417
Billiard-register	O. W. Kellogg and H. R. Hill	Ripon, Wis	Oct. 2, 1866	58, 429
Billiard-register	I. Kling	Seymour, Ind	June 23, 1868	79, 233
Billiard-register	J. Lee	Galesburgh, Ill	July 23, 1872	129, 670
Billiard-register	M. McCay	Topeka, Kans	Dec. 24, 1872	134, 211
Billiard-register	G. Simpson and R. M. Taylor	Waterbury, Vt	May 14, 1867	64, 718

Index of patents issued from the United States Patent Office from 1790 *to* 1873, *inclusive*—Continued.

Index of patents issued from the United States Patent Office from 1790 *to* 1873, *inclusive*—Continued.

Invention.	Inventor.	Residence.	Date.	No.
Binder for papers, Temporary	M. A. Shepard	Lebanon, Ill	Sept. 10, 1872	131, 229
Binder, Temporary	J. F. Adams	Irvington, N. Y	Sept. 10, 1872	131, 203
Binder, Temporary	W. H. Barnard	Washington, D. C	June 17, 1873	139, 998
Binder, Temporary	D. Dunton	Carpentersville, Ill	Mar. 25, 1873	137, 131
Binder, Temporary	G. W. Emerson	Chicago, Ill	July 7, 1868	79, 560
Binder, Temporary	T. J. Gaffney and A. P. Williams	Cincinnati, Ohio	Dec. 3, 1872	133, 580
Binder, Temporary	N. M. Shaffer	New York, N. Y	Jan. 14, 1868	73, 261
Binder's board, Machine for cutting	J. A. Elder	Westbrook, Me	Oct. 11, 1853	10, 122
Binding-folder	J. B. Nichols	Lynn, Mass	Aug. 29, 1854	11, 615
Binding-folder	E. P. West	Jersey City, N. J	May 13, 1873	138, 772
Binding-guide	J. S. McCurdy	New York, N. Y	Feb. 26, 1856	14, 322
Binding-guide	G. W. White	New York, N. Y	Sept. 24, 1872	131, 583
Binding, Metallic	T. B. De Forest	Birmingham, Conn	Nov. 20, 1866	59, 895
Binnacle	E. S. Ritchie	Brookline, Mass	June 27, 1865	48, 443
Bird-bath	T. W. Van Tassel	Washington, D. C	Aug. 10, 1869	93, 503
Bird-cage	H. C. W. Battermann	New York, N. Y	July 23, 1861	32, 855
Bird-cage	G. J. Bolz, M. Grebner, and J. M. Jagel.	New York, N. Y	Oct. 31, 1871	120, 483
Bird-cage	T. H. Bradley	Saint Louis, Mo	July 12, 1870	105, 164
Bird-cage	G. F. J. Colburn	Newark, N. J	Jan. 4, 1870	98, 562
Bird-cage	G. F. J. Colburn	Newark, N. J	Jan. 25, 1870	99, 164
Bird-cage	G. Günther	New York, N. Y	Apr. 29, 1873	138, 396
Bird-cage	G. Günther	New York, N. Y	Jan. 5, 1869	85, 523
Bird-cage	G. Günther	New York, N. Y	Mar. 7, 1871	112, 449
Bird-cage	E. Hutchinson	New York, N. Y	Nov. 25, 1873	144, 907
Bird-cage	E. B. Jewett	Buffalo, N. Y	Nov. 26, 1872	133, 372
Bird-cage	J. C. Jewett and J. Vogt	Buffalo, N. Y	Sept. 21, 1869	95, 116
Bird-cage	O. Lindemann	New York, N. Y	Feb. 4, 1873	135, 567
Bird-cage	J. Maxheimer	New York, N. Y	June 3, 1862	35, 459
Bird-cage	J. Maxheimer	New York, N. Y	Apr. 6, 1869	88, 654
Bird-cage	J. Maxheimer	New York, N. Y	Dec. 23, 1873	145, 886
Bird-cage	G. J. Munschauer	Buffalo, N. Y	Mar. 11, 1873	136, 611
Bird-cage	C. L. Osborn	Brooklyn, N. Y	Apr. 14, 1863	38, 177
Bird-cage	C. L. Osborn	Brooklyn, N. Y	Feb. 28, 1865	46, 579
Bird-cage	C. L. Osborn	New York, N. Y	Aug. 4, 1868	80, 561
Bird-cage	G. R. Osborn	Bridgeport, Conn	Sept. 27, 1870	107, 802
Bird-cage	G. R. Osborn and B. A. Drayton	Morrisania, N. Y	July 30, 1872	129, 980
Bird-cage	G. R. Osborn and B. A. Drayton	Morrisania, N. Y	Dec. 17, 1872	134, 094
Bird-cage	W. Staehlen	Brooklyn, N. Y	Sept. 3, 1861	33, 216
Bird-cage	J. H. Williams	New York, N. Y	May 25, 1869	90, 619
Bird-cage, Bath-tub for	G. T. and G. E. Peters	Jersey City, N. J	May 6, 1873	138, 692
Bird-cage bottom	O. Lindemann	New York, N. Y	Nov. 7, 1871	120, 755
Bird-cage bracket	A. D. Judd	New Haven, Conn	May 16, 1871	114, 948
Bird-cage, Construction of	G. Günther	New York, N. Y	Apr. 2, 1872	125, 288
Bird-cage, Construction of	G. R. Osborn and B. A. Drayton	New York, N. Y	May 9, 1871	114, 593
Bird-cage, Feed-cup for	G. Günther	New York, N. Y	Nov. 26, 1872	133, 442
Bird-cage hook	J. Bradbury	Berlin, Conn	Nov. 7, 1871	120, 569
Bird-cage hook	D. McArthur	New Haven, Conn	Nov. 5, 1872	132, 840
Bird-cage hook	J. M. Spring	New Britain, Conn	Apr. 18, 1871	113, 808
Bird-cage, Manufacture of	G. Günther	New York, N. Y	June 4, 1872	127, 598
Bird-cage, Manufacture of	J. Hepp	New York, N. Y	Mar. 12, 1872	124, 576
Bird-cage mat	O. Lindemann	New York, N. Y	Jan. 2, 1872	122, 472
Bird-cage mat	C. S. Scheuck	New York, N. Y	May 2, 1871	114, 345
Bird-cage mat	J. A. Singer	New York, N. Y	Apr. 4, 1871	113, 461
Bird-cage musical attachment	G. Günther	New York, N. Y	July 17, 1866	56, 407
Bird-cage, Paper for bottom of	J. H. Singer	New York, N. Y	Feb. 7, 1871	111, 579
Bird-cage, Rod for construction of	J. H. Williams	New York, N. Y	Jan. 1, 1869	90, 906
Bird-cage, Spring-perch for	E. Aldom	New York, N. Y	Dec. 12, 1871	121, 742
Bird, Decoy	N. Wales	Boston, Mass	Feb. 11, 1868	74, 458
Bird-house	H. Miller	Johnston, R. I	May 3, 1870	102, 573
Bird-house, Metallic	H. Miller	Cranston, R. I	Apr. 14, 1868	76, 648
Bird-house, Metallic	J. Murdock	Jersey City, N. J	Mar. 16, 1869	88, 799
Bird-trap	S. M. Brooks	Memphis, Tenn	May 10, 1870	102, 761
Bird-trap	R. Rex	Charles City, Iowa	Sept. 12, 1865	49, 923
Bird-trap	J. S. Stone and G. W. Chamberlin.	Fitchburgh, Mass	Oct. 20, 1868	83, 220
Biscuit and crackers, Machine for making and baking.	B. F. Mason	Kennebunkport, Me	July 6, 1839	1, 221
Biscuit and sugar-bread, Making	E. Treadwell	New York, N. Y	May 18, 1826	....
Biscuit, Apparatus for making scroll	A. Exton	Trenton, N. J	Jan. 16, 1866	52, 036
Biscuit-board	I. R. Shank	Buffalo, Va	July 26, 1859	24, 890
Biscuit-board and flour-chest	D. E. Bryer	Logansport, Ind	Aug. 30, 1864	44, 040
Biscuit-cutter	S. E. Clapp	Cambridge, Mass	May 5, 1868	77, 583
Biscuit-cutting machine	J. and S. Turner	Toronto, Canada	Mar. 25, 1873	137, 114
Biscuit-machine	A. Exton	Trenton, N. J	Aug. 27, 1861	33, 136
Biscuit-machine, Scroll	A. Exton	Trenton, N. J	Jan. 30, 1866	52, 278
Biscuit-making machine	W. Liddle	New Orleans, La	Sept. 21, 1815	....
Biscuit, Manufacture of	C. D. and C. D. Boss, jr	New London, Conn	Oct. 11, 1870	108, 097
Biscuit, Manufacture of sweet	H. Even	Pekin, Ill	Apr. 15, 1873	137, 766
Biscuit-pan	J. C. Milligan	Brooklyn, N. Y	Nov. 9, 1869	96, 605
Biscuit-pan	J. C. Milligan	Brooklyn, N. Y	Apr. 5, 1870	101, 490
Bistouries	C. C. Brown	Washington, D. C	Oct. 10, 1865	50, 330
Bisulphites, Apparatus for the manufacture of	W. J. Turner	Bradford, England	Feb. 20, 1872	123, 799
Bit:				

See Adjustable bit.
Auger-bit.
Ax-bit.
Boring-bit.
Brace-bit.
Bridle-bit.
Carving-machine bit.
Center-bit.
Countersink-bit.
Curb-bit.
Doweling-bit.
Drill-bit.
Driving-bit.
Expansive bit.

Index of patents issued from the United States Patent Office from 1790 *to* 1873, *inclusive*—Continued.

Invention.	Inventor.	Residence.	Date.	No.
Bit—Continued.				
See Extension-bit.				
Horse-training bit.				
Joint-bit.				
Ox-bit.				
Plane-bit.				
Safety-bit.				
Screw-cutting bit.				
Spring-bit.				
Upper-jaw bit.				
Weaning-bit.				
Bit	H. S. Shepardson	Shelburne, Mass	Feb. 27, 1872	124, 089
Bit and auger	C. Whitehouse	Bridgtown, England	Apr. 6, 1869	88, 760
Bit and auger die	J. Swan	Seymour, Conn	Nov. 16, 1869	96, 847
Bit and drill brace	G. G. Parker and W. P. Dodge	Prospect, N. Y	Mar. 21, 1871	112, 842
Bit and other tools, Device for holding	W. H. Barber	Greenfield, Mass	May 24, 1864	42, 827
Bit and tap, Combined	S. A. Smith	New Haven, Conn	Oct. 12, 1869	95, 846
Bit-braco	C. H. Amidon	Greenfield, Mass	May 21, 1867	64, 931
Bit-brace	Q. S. Backus	Miller's Falls, Mass	Nov. 5, 1872	132, 791
Bit-brace	C. L. Butler	Greenfield, Mass	Nov. 16, 1869	96, 881
Bit-brace	W. Cleveland	Lawrence, Mass	Mar. 7, 1871	112, 419
Bit-brace	J. W. Craig	Knoxville, Ill	June 9, 1868	78, 652
Bit-brace	C. M. Daboll	New London, Conn	Mar. 24, 1868	75, 870
Bit brace	W. P. Dolin	Charlottesville, Va	Jan. 17, 1871	110, 960
Bit-brace	S. F. Fenn	Middletown, Conn	Dec. 3, 1867	71, 727
Bit-brace	J. S. Fray	Bridgeport, Conn	Aug. 20, 1872	130, 709
Bit-braco	R. French	Seymour, Conn	Mar. 21, 1871	112, 799
Bit-brace	S. B. Hill	Chicopee, Mass	Apr. 14, 1868	76, 632
Bit-braco	W. A. Ives	New Haven, Conn	Mar. 16, 1869	87, 940
Bit-brace	W. A. Ives	New Haven, Conn	Feb. 7, 1871	111, 649
Bit-braco	J. T. Lyman	Jeffersonville, Ind	Apr. 4, 1871	113, 680
Bit-brace	C. Morrill	New York, N. Y	Dec. 10, 1861	33, 899
Bit-brace	O. Peck	Southington, Conn	May 8, 1866	54, 650
Bit-brace	W. E. Bereau	Oakland, Cal	Dec. 16, 1873	145, 524
Bit-brace	F. P. Pfleghar	New Haven, Conn	Mar. 17, 1868	75, 699
Bit-brace	H. W. Porter	Rothsville, Pa	July 7, 1857	17, 769
Bit-brace	J. Rice	Prairie Creek, Ind	Jan. 9, 1872	122, 652
Bit-brace	C. O. Richey	Aurora, Ind	June 5, 1866	55, 364
Bit-brace	S. C. Rundlett	Portland, Me	Apr. 28, 1868	77, 219
Bit-brace	W. F. Seavey	Portland, Me	July 23, 1867	67, 139
Bit-brace	H. S. Shepardson	Shelburne Falls, Mass	Mar. 1, 1870	100, 458
Bit-brace	G. Stackpole	Portland, Me	Sept. 23, 1862	36, 538
Bit-brace	G. Stackpole	New York, N. Y	Apr. 2, 1867	63, 438
Bit-brace	C. H. Stockbridge	Whateley, Mass	Feb. 19, 1867	62, 232
Bit-brace	I. C. Tate	New London, Conn	May 19, 1868	78, 157
Bit-brace	C. Whitus	Philadelphia, Pa	Apr. 9, 1872	125, 642
Bit-brace	F. A. Wood	Jersey City, N. J	Dec. 1, 1868	84, 523
Bit-brace	W. H. Woods	San Francisco, Cal	Apr. 9, 1867	63, 684
Bit to brace, Fastener of	E. Smith	Norwich, N. Y	Aug. 17, 1852	9, 209
Bit brace for boring obliquely to the stock	C. C. Plaisted	Chicopee, Mass	July 28, 1857	17, 891
Bit-brace wrench	D. Wilcox	Ansonia, Conn	Mar. 2, 1869	87, 531
Bit-fastening	H. Lettington	Norwich, N. Y	May 13, 1856	14, 876
Bit for cutting out cylindrical plugs of wood	C. W. Saladee	Columbus, Ohio	May 26, 1857	17, 395
Bit for cutting washers	H. Pennie	Buffalo, N. Y	Sept. 6, 1859	25, 348
Bit grinding and polishing machine	J. Swan	Seymour, Conn	Feb. 15, 1870	99, 970
Bit-holder	B. B. Hill	Chicopee, Mass	Sept. 29, 1857	18, 282
Bit-holder	B. B. Hill and S. W. Adams	Chicopee, Mass	Jan. 5, 1858	19, 028
Bit-holder	C. H. Stockbridge	Northampton, Mass	Nov. 10, 1868	84, 015
Bit holder	D. H. Whittemore	Worcester, Mass	Apr. 20, 1858	20, 010
Bit-holder	J. Winkelhouse	New York, N. Y	Sept. 21, 1869	95, 060
Bit-holder for bit-stock	L. C. Rodier	Springfield, Mass	Aug. 30, 1864	44, 047
Bit in brace, Device for holding	G. Benjamine	Avoca, N. Y	June 9, 1857	17, 479
Bit in brace, Securing	O. Peck	Windsor, Vt	Feb. 23, 1864	41, 718
Bit in brace, Securing	W. Wimmer	Elizabethport, N. J	May 22, 1866	54, 990
Bit in socket, Device for holding	C. F. Hunter	Adrian, Mich	Oct. 27, 1863	40, 412
Bit in stock, Method of securing	D. Kelly	Grand Rapids, Mich	Dec. 16, 1862	37, 196
Bit in stock, Method of securing	W. Tucker	Blackstone, Mass	Mar. 22, 1859	23, 326
Bit in stock, Mode of securing	A. C. Moore	Wilmington, Vt	Mar. 31, 1857	16, 931
Bit or auger in its stock or handle, Method of fastening.	L. Winslow	Rochester, N. Y	Nov. 25, 1862	37, 022
Bit or boring tool	B. Sanderson	Derby Line, Vt	May 19, 1863	38, 633
Bit or drill holder	A. J. Smith	Lynn, Mass	July 7, 1857	17, 770
Bit or drill stock	D. H. Chamberlain	Boston, Mass	Oct. 26, 1852	9, 353
Bit or drill stock	D. H. Chamberlain	Boston, Mass	Feb. 7, 1854	10, 499
Bit-stock	A. S. Alden	Chicopee, Mass	Mar. 16, 1869	87, 816
Bit-stock	C. H. Amidon	Greenfield, Mass	Oct. 3, 1865	50, 214
Bit-stock	C. H. Amidon	Greenfield, Mass	Jan. 14, 1868	73, 279
Bit-stock	M. Andrews	Bridgewater, Mass	Apr. 24, 1847	5, 087
Bit-stock	Q. S. Backus	Miller's Falls, Mass	Nov. 5, 1872	132, 790
Bit-stock	H. S. Bartholomew	Bristol, Conn	May 24, 1870	103, 281
Bit-stock	C. H. Clark	Pittsfield, Mo	Aug. 2, 1870	105, 906
Bit-stock	J. F. Cory	New York, N. Y	June 25, 1861	32, 618
Bit-stock	A. P. Daboll	New London, Conn	June 17, 1873	139, 876
Bit-stock	B. Darling	Bridgewater, Mass	Oct. 20, 1868	83, 261
Bit-stock	S. W. Davis	Wilmington, Del	Aug. 18, 1868	81, 260
Bit-stock	O. Ellsworth	Boston, Mass	Sept. 25, 1866	58, 234
Bit-stock	L. Feely	Rochester, N. Y	Dec. 30, 1873	146, 056
Bit-stock	D. P. Foster	Waltham, Mass	May 4, 1869	89, 755
Bit-stock	D. P. Foster	Waltham, Mass	Mar. 29, 1870	101, 251
Bit-stock	A. D. Goodell	Florence, (Northampton,) Mass.	July 14, 1868	79, 825
Bit-stock	A. D. Goodell	Miller's Falls, Mass	June 10, 1873	139, 667
Bit-stock	A. D. Goodell	Miller's Falls, Mass	July 29, 1873	141, 345
Bit-stock	D. W. Goodell	Northampton, Mass	Nov. 28, 1865	51, 173
Bit-stock	R. S. Hildreth	South Adams, Mass	Feb. 1, 1870	99, 317
Bit-stock	I. Holliday	South Brooklyn, N. Y	May 24, 1870	103, 462
Bit-stock	S. U. King	Windsor, Vt	July 7, 1863	39, 150
Bit-stock	C. E. Lombard	Springfield, Mass	Oct. 17, 1865	50, 481

Index of patents issued from the United States Patent Office from 1790 *to* 1873, *inclusive*—Continued.

Invention.	Inventor.	Residence.	Date.	No.
Bit-stock	W. Lyon	Deep River, Conn	Oct. 23, 1860	30,487
Bit-stock	C. Manson	Boston, Mass	May 2, 1871	114,314
Bit-stock	W. H. McCoy	Erving, Mass	Aug. 15, 1871	118,039
Bit-stock	D. A. Newton	New York, N. Y	Oct. 28, 1873	144,123
Bit-stock	M. V. Nobles	Rochester, N. Y	June 20, 1865	48,346
Bit-stock	W. W. S. Orbeton	Haverhill, Mass	Oct. 30, 1866	59,254
Bit-stock	H. S. Pratt	Brooklyn, N. Y	Oct. 1, 1872	131,829
Bit-stock	G. Richards	Richmond Centre, Wis	Oct. 27, 1868	83,410
Bit-stock	C. B. Rose	Sunderland, Mass	Apr. 16, 1867	63,944
Bit-stock	C. B. Rose	Sunderland, Mass	Sept. 15, 1868	82,251
Bit-stock	S. Sawyer	Erving, Mass	Aug. 15, 1871	118,058
Bit-stock	W. H. Sible	Harrisburgh, Pa	Mar. 9, 1869	87,715
Bit-stock	A. W. Smith	Manchester, N. H	Jan. 2, 1866	51,874
Bit stock	R. D. O. Smith	Washington, D. C	Sept. 8, 1868	82,041
Bit-stock	N. Spofford	Haverhill, Mass	Nov. 1, 1859	25,984
Bit-stock	A. Stanley	New Britain, Conn	Nov. 30, 1869	97,455
Bit-stock	O. G. Stratton	Greenfield, Mass	Aug. 11, 1868	81,031
Bit-stock	A. W. Streeter	Shelburne Falls, Mass	Jan. 8, 1867	61,113
Bit-stock	J. Taylor	Hebron, Conn	June 30, 1836	....
Bit-stock	O. H. Taylor	Brooklyn, N. Y	Sept. 8, 1868	82,044
Bit-stock	O. H. Taylor	Brooklyn, N. Y	Nov. 2, 1869	96,505
Bit-stock	F. M. and J. W. Thompson	Greenfield, Mass	Feb. 23, 1869	87,309
Bit-stock	J. W. and F. M. Thompson	Greenfield, Mass	Sept. 15, 1868	82,179
Bit-stock	C. P. Whitman	Charlemont, Mass	Aug. 23, 1870	106,754
Bit-stock and wrench	S. S. Hout and B. B. Beers	New Fairfield, Conn	July 19, 1859	24,807
Bit stock, Composition	A. Phelps	Marlborough, Conn	Oct. 10, 1829	....
Bit stock, Drill	H. B. Williams	Cincinnati, Ohio	May 13, 1873	138,973
Bit-stock fastener	C. P. Whitman	Charlemont, Mass	Nov. 16, 1869	97,010
Bit-stock, Method of constructing	A. W. Streeter	Shelburne Falls, Mass	Mar. 31, 1857	16,938
Bit to brace, Attaching	O. Peck	Windsor, Vt	Aug. 4, 1863	39,419
Bit to brace, Attaching	O. Peck	Windsor, Vt	Oct. 13, 1863	40,275
Bit to brace, Device for attaching	S. U. King	Windsor, Vt	June 8, 1858	20,495
Bitting attachment	S. V. R. York	Antwerp, N. Y	Apr. 28, 1868	77,235
Bitters and sauce bottle tube, Manufacture of	J. B. Lyon	Pittsburgh, Pa	Dec. 17, 1872	133,947
Bitters, Cider	T. P. Devor	Millerstown, Pa	July 30, 1872	129,937
Bitters, Stomach	M. Becker	Philadelphia, Pa	Sept. 7, 1869	94,466
Bitumen and clay, Combining	P. Lea	Goliad, Tex	Sept. 24, 1872	131,690
Bitumen, ore, &c., Compound of	P. Lea	Goliad, Tex	Nov. 11, 1873	144,396
Blackboard	H. L. Andrews	Chicago, Ill	Sept. 15, 1868	82,062
Blackboard	M. F. Cowdery	Sandusky, Ohio	Feb. 6, 1872	123,456
Blackboard	M. F. Cowdery	Sandusky, Ohio	Feb. 6, 1872	123,457
Blackboard	W. H. Jockel	New York, N. Y	July 13, 1869	92,533
Blackboard	F. G. Johnson	New York, N. Y	Dec. 3, 1872	133,583
Blackboard	J. Reber	Nebraska, Ohio	Nov. 4, 1873	144,289
Blackboard	T. J. Thorp	Buffalo, N. Y	Jan. 21, 1873	135,019
Blackboard, Adjustable	P. W. Moeller	New York, N. Y	Nov. 25, 1873	144,917
Blackboard and map-case	W. C. Herider	Miami Town, Ohio	Sept. 22, 1863	40,035
Blackboard, Composition	R. W. Young	Rising Sun, Ind	Apr. 25, 1871	114,246
Blackboard, &c., Composition for covering	N. V. Evans	Winslow, Ind	Jan. 16, 1872	122,763
Blackboard, Composition for covering	J. B. Rowell	Lynn, Mass	Aug. 7, 1860	29,552
Blackboard for school	W. Arronquier	Worcester, Mass	Dec. 10, 1867	71,946
Blackboard, &c., Liquid slating for forming	W. W. Dudley	Centreville, Ind	Aug. 30, 1870	106,923
Blackboard-rubber	J. F. Bigger and W. A. Pugh	Rushville, Ind	Jan. 9, 1872	122,511
Blackboard-rubber	P. B. Horton	San Francisco, Cal	Nov. 18, 1873	144,674
Blackboard, slate, &c., Composition for forming	W. A. Reason	Chicago, Ill	Sept. 27, 1864	44,456
Blackboard-wiper	P. Perry	Waterford, N. Y	Sept. 30, 1862	36,589
Blacking	J. McCrellish	Philadelphia, Pa	Nov. 20, 1866	59,851
Blacking	W. F. Quinby	Wilmington, Del	Aug. 28, 1866	57,567
Blacking	L. R. Rockwood	Worcester, Mass	Feb. 22, 1859	23,065
Blacking	A. Tomlinson	Cincinnati, Ohio	Oct. 31, 1865	50,780
Blacking and brush holder	E. H. Sweetser	Salem, Mass	Mar. 26, 1872	124,984
Blacking and brush holder	E. H. Sweetser	Salem, Mass	Aug. 13, 1872	130,450
Blacking and polish, Boot and shoe	H. A. Reams	Durham, N. C	Mar. 19, 1872	124,760
Blacking-apparatus and boot-rack combined	J. M. McMaster	Rochester, N. Y	Sept. 12, 1871	118,809
Blacking apparatus, Boot	H. H. Dodge	Georgetown, D. C	Mar. 6, 1866	52,977
Blacking apparatus, Boot	J. Vandercar	Brooklyn, N. Y	Feb. 18, 1868	74,637
Blacking block, Boot and shoe	F. G. Harding	Boston, Mass	June 2, 1857	17,431
Blacking, Boot and shoe	J. H. Patterson	Glen's Falls, N. Y	Sept. 26, 1871	119,239
Blacking-box	J. S. Brooks	Rochester, N. Y	Aug. 8, 1865	49,224
Blacking-box	R. Cadle	Shawneetown, Ill	Mar. 23, 1869	88,128
Blacking-box	J. H. Doughty	New York, N. Y	Mar. 14, 1865	46,783
Blacking-box	C. H. Gatchell	Oldtown, Me	Nov. 23, 1869	97,072
Blacking-box	E. M. Gates	Watertown, N. Y	Sept. 12, 1871	118,924
Blacking-box	W. L Gilroy	Philadelphia, Pa	Dec. 22, 1868	85,084
Blacking-box	S. R. Sinclaire	New York, N. Y	Nov. 14, 1871	120,907
Blacking-box	H. Smith	Haddonfield, N. J	Jan. 30, 1872	123,204
Blacking-box	T. H. Spencer	Providence, R. I	Aug. 21, 1866	57,401
Blacking-box	A. M. Utley	Watertown, N. Y	Nov. 21, 1871	121,069
Blacking-box	J. Van Santvoord	Mount Vernon, N. Y	Oct. 31, 1871	120,554
Blacking-box and brush	C. E. Yager	Hudson, N. Y	Aug. 30, 1870	106,909
Blacking-box and holder	G. H. Monroe	Cincinnati, Ohio	June 21, 1864	43,221
Blacking-box, Construction of	T. H. Spencer	Providence, R. I	May 12, 1868	77,778
Blacking-box cover	J. B. Shaler	Brooklyn, N. Y	Apr. 22, 1873	138,102
Blacking-box, Foot-rest for	J. H. Porter	New York, N. Y	Oct. 11, 1864	44,656
Blacking-box handle-attachment	T. S. Robinson	New York, N. Y	June 25, 1867	66,173
Blacking-box holder	C. R. Bacon and G. D. Clark	Newark, N. J	Feb. 11, 1868	74,276
Blacking-box holder	W. A. Field	Boston, Mass	Apr. 16, 1867	63,876
Blacking-box holder	R. R. Forrest	Washington, Pa	Aug. 13, 1872	130,419
Blacking-box holder	C. E. S. Jelliffe	Williamsburgh, N. Y	Aug. 1, 1865	49,115
Blacking-box holder	H. B. Hammon	Bristolville, Ohio	Aug. 3, 1869	93,196
Blacking-box holder	J. W. Lewis	Providence, R. I	Jan. 1, 1861	31,065
Blacking-box holder	T. K. Payson	New York, N. Y	Nov. 12, 1867	70,892
Blacking-box holder	J. H. Rector and A. Sweetland	Syracuse, N. Y	July 26, 1864	43,645
Blacking-box holder	N. H. Talbot	North Easton, Mass	July 25, 1871	117,481
Blacking-box holder	G. W. Taylor	Springfield, Vt	Jan. 1, 1867	60,962
Blacking-box holder	A. Wilder	Calais, Me	Jan. 8, 1867	61,128
Blacking-box holder	S. T. Wyman	Lynn, Mass	Dec. 16, 1873	145,544
Blacking-box, Implement for holding	W. and J. Cairns	Jersey City, N. J	Jan. 13, 1857	16,374

Index of patents issued from the United States Patent Office from 1790 *to* 1873, *inclusive*—Continued.

Invention.	Inventor.	Residence.	Date.	No.
Blacking-box, Manufacture of	G. W. Bentley	New York, N. Y	May 9, 1865	47, 676
Blacking box, Shoe	G. H. Wetjen	New York, N. Y	Sept. 12, 1871	118, 995
Blacking-case	C. E. Brown	Northampton, Mass	Apr. 9, 1867	63, 700
Blacking-case	W. P. Huges	Rochester, N. Y	July 16, 1872	129, 137
Blacking-case	G. H. Rice	Norwalk, Conn	Apr. 8, 1873	137, 722
Blacking case and closet	J. McFerran	Philadelphia, Pa	Feb. 18, 1868	74, 705
Blacking-case and night-chair, Combined	J. H. Doughty	New York, N. Y	July 24, 1866	56, 535
Blacking case, Boot	E. S. Carter	Keokuk, Iowa	Mar. 13, 1866	53, 111
Blacking-case, Portable	A. W. Overbaugh	New York, N. Y	May 21, 1867	64, 899
Blacking-dish and knife	E. L. Bolster	Waterbury, Conn	June 11, 1867	65, 637
Blacking for leather	S. Adams	Cleveland, Ohio	May 30, 1842	2, 660
Blacking for leather, &c	I. B. Merrill	Dexter, Me	Apr. 21, 1868	77, 069
Blacking for leather, Oil	S. S. Allen	Richmond, Ind	Nov. 10, 1868	83, 817
Blacking for leather, Oil	O. K. Tripp	Rochester, N. Y	Oct. 24, 1871	120, 348
Blacking for shoes, &c	J. L. Sneed	Frankfort, Ky	Nov. 18, 1873	144, 801
Blacking-fount	C. Künstler	Brooklyn, N. Y	Sept. 28, 1869	95, 357
Blacking, Japan-paste	H. Lake	San Francisco, Cal	Jan. 28, 1868	73, 730
Blacking, Leather	A. D. Strong	Ashtabula, Ohio	Aug. 12, 1873	141, 829
Blacking leather, Composition for	J. Engelhardt	Carbondale, Pa	Apr. 21, 1868	76, 897
Blacking machine, Boot and shoe	M. A. Myer	Decatur, Ill	Feb. 5, 1867	61, 755
Blacking machine, Mold	B. S. Benson	Baltimore, Md	Oct. 27, 1868	83, 448
Blacking, Manufacture of	R. Bartholow	Cincinnati, Ohio	Apr. 4, 1865	47, 082
Blacking, Manufacture of	G. W. Corey	Port Jervis, N. Y	Feb. 6, 1866	52, 391
Blacking, Manufacture of	J. L. Lucas	Saratoga Springs, N. Y	Oct. 11, 1870	108, 271
Blacking, Metal-founder's	J. C. Sellars	Birkenhead, England	June 30, 1868	79, 504
Blacking, Metal-founder's	J. C. Sellars	Birkenhead, England	May 16, 1871	114, 978
Blacking, Packing shoe	C. Herold	Pittsburgh, Pa	Aug. 27, 1872	130, 917
Blacking, Shoe and stove	J. Breinig	Allentown, Pa	Sept. 10, 1872	131, 245
Blacking-spreader	H. S. Kerr	Philadelphia, Pa	Apr. 23, 1872	125, 894
Blacking-spreader	H. S. Kerr	Philadelphia, Pa	May 7, 1872	126, 399
Blacking, Water-proof	D. L. Pickard	Rochester, N. Y	Oct. 10, 1865	50, 383
Blacksmith's butteris	E. Bacher	Findlay, Ohio	Oct. 8, 1872	132, 044
Blacksmith, Foot-lifter for	T. C. Williams	Warrenton, Mo	Apr. 4, 1871	113, 379
Blacksmith's furnace for burning anthracite coal	E. Nichols and J. Augur	Hamden and New Haven, Conn.	Aug. 21, 1839	1, 293
Blacksmith's hardy	C. F. Moore	Snedikerville, Pa	Aug. 1, 1871	117, 665
Blacksmith's hearth	J. Cavender	Milton, Ohio	Aug. 27, 1861	33, 132
Blacksmiths, Mode of blowing and striking for	S. Hoyt and E. Pierce	Pultney, N. Y	Mar. 3, 1827	....
Blacksmith's striker	G. Bell	Martinsburgh, W. Va	June 25, 1867	66, 118
Blacksmith's striker	D. S. Blue	Fort Seneca, Ohio	Nov. 27, 1855	13, 841
Blacksmith's striker	H. Kendall	East Dorset, Vt	May 12, 1857	17, 284
Blacksmith's tool	S. J. Forbes	Marshalltown, Iowa	Oct. 10, 1871	119, 837
Blacksmith's tool	T. B. and L. W. Kelly	Hammondsburgh, Pa., and Brunswick, Ohio.	Nov. 25, 1862	37, 000
Blacksmith's tool	J. F. Kernon	Saugerties, N. Y	Mar. 5, 1872	124, 362
Black-washing mold	G. Ross	Newport, Ky	May 3, 1864	42, 600
Bladder, Machine for crumbling stone in	J. L. Hannah	New York, N. Y	Aug. 19, 1834	....
Blade-case and attaching-pin, Combined	W. L. Bowser	Moncton, New Brunswick	Feb. 9, 1869	86, 637
Blank clip for swingletree, Method of forming	M. Loughran	Pittsburgh, Pa	July 11, 1865	48, 699
Blanks, Machine for nicking screw	J. C. Rhodes	East Bridgewater, Mass	Nov. 10, 1863	40, 588
Blanket	M. V. Nobles	Elmira, N. Y	Feb. 27, 1872	124, 007
Blanket-fastener	L. C. Chase	Boston, Mass	Oct. 15, 1867	69, 768
Blanket, Horse	S. W. Baker	Providence, R. I	Feb. 25, 1868	74, 742
Blankets and overcoats, Sling for carrying	J. Short	Salem, Mass	Apr. 15, 1862	35, 002
Blankets, &c., Machine for making	J. Getzendannar	Frederick County, Md	Sept. 30, 1814	....
Blast and cupola furnace	D. W. Hendrickson	Red Bank, N. J	June 17, 1873	139, 891
Blast and cupola furnace	F. Lawrence	Philadelphia, Pa	Sept. 2, 1873	142, 482
Blast and cupola furnace for melting iron	J. Pattarson	Warwick, N. Y	June 13, 1831	....
Blast and draft of furnace, forge, &c., Mode of managing.	A. Collins	Ulster, N. Y	Dec. 31, 1838	1, 054
Blast and puddling furnace for making wrought-iron direct from the ore, Combined rotary.	J. Neville	Jersey City, N. J	Apr. 29, 1873	138, 429
Blast-apparatus	B. F. Sturtevant	West Roxbury, Mass	July 13, 1869	92, 490
Blast-apparatus for furnace	R. A. Smith	Newburyport, Mass	Nov. 15, 1870	109, 356
Blast apparatus for puddling and other furnaces, Hot.	P. Hoop, jr., and R. Hoop	Berlin Cross Roads, Ohio	Oct. 27, 1868	83, 382
Blast apparatus, Hot	J. J. Pierce	Sharpsville, Pa	June 7, 1870	103, 923
Blast apparatus, Steam	G. A. Jasper	Charlestown, Mass	Oct. 4, 1864	44, 533
Blast for furnace used in smelting iron, &c., Apparatus for heating the.	J. Player	Norton, England	June 11, 1867	65, 600
Blast for iron and other furnaces	F. A. T. de Beauregard	Paris, France	Jan. 22, 1867	61, 323
Blast for smelting iron-ore, Furnace	T. Gregg	Connellsville, Pa	May 22, 1832	....
Blast-furnace	E. B. Andrews	Lancaster, Ohio	Oct. 7, 1873	143, 487
Blast-furnace	G. Atkins	Sharon, Pa	July 13, 1869	92, 505
Blast-furnace	J. G. Blunt	Leavenworth, Kans	Apr. 15, 1873	137, 884
Blast-furnace	F. Büttgenbach	Düsseldorf, Germany	Nov. 25, 1873	144, 829
Blast-furnace	I. B. B. Case	Toledo, Ohio	Sept. 12, 1871	118, 905
Blast-furnace	H. Davies	Newport, Ky	Dec. 12, 1871	121, 762
Blast-furnace	J. F. Harris	Fort Edward, N. Y	June 25, 1872	128, 304
Blast-furnace	D. W. Hendrickson	New York, N. Y	Apr. 23, 1867	64, 012
Blast-furnace	D. W. Hendrickson	Red Bank, N. J	Apr. 1, 1873	137, 366
Blast-furnace	W. Kelly	Eddyville, Ky	Jan. 20, 1857	16, 444
Blast-furnace	B. Kugler	Philadelphia, Pa	June 2, 1836	....
Blast-furnace	F. W. Lurmann	Osnabruck, Prussia	Nov. 5, 1867	70, 447
Blast-furnace	J. H. McKernan	Indianapolis, Ind	Jan. 23, 1872	123, 035
Blast-furnace	P. P. Parrott	Greenwood Iron-Works, N. Y.	Aug. 20, 1872	130, 590
Blast-furnace	J. Pattison	New York, N. Y	Dec. 10, 1872	133, 718
Blast-furnace	W. Raschette	St. Petersburg, Russia	June 21, 1864	43, 274
Blast-furnace	S. C. Salisbury	New York, N. Y	Apr. 24, 1866	54, 215
Blast-furnace	J. Steece	Lawrence County, Ohio	May 16, 1833	....
Blast-furnace	I. Tyson, jr	Baltimore, Md	Apr. 18, 1834	....
Blast-furnace	S. Wilkes	Hammondsville, Ohio	Sept. 8, 1857	18, 167
Blast-furnace	H. Wissenborn	New York, N. Y	Feb. 3, 1857	16, 560
Blast-furnace	J. V. Woodhouse	Mine La Motte, Mo	June 3, 1873	139, 489
Blast-furnace	W. Wright and G. Brown	Newcastle-upon-Tyne, England.	Aug. 12, 1856	15, 541
Blast-furnace, Air-heating pipe for	S. and J. Thomas	Catasauqua, Pa	Nov. 22, 1859	26, 212

Index of patents issued from the United States Patent Office from 1790 *to* 1873, *inclusive*—Continued.

Invention.	Inventor.	Residence.	Date.	No.
Blast-furnace alarm-apparatus	E. Davis	Millerton, N. Y	May 27, 1873	139, 300
Blast-furnace, Apparatus for charging	W. A. Miles	Salisbury, Conn	Nov. 12, 1872	132, 974
Blast-furnace, Apparatus for feeding	L. S. Goodrich	Waverly, Tenn	May 30, 1871	115, 305
Blast-furnace, Apparatus for feeding	L. S. Goodrich	Waverly, Tenn	July 23, 1872	129, 813
Blast-furnace, &c., Apparatus for heating air for	H. Davies	Portsmouth, Ohio	Oct. 22, 1861	33, 521
Blast-furnace, Apparatus for opening and closing the top of.	J. Thomas	Parryville, Pa	May 24, 1870	103, 391
Blast-furnace, Appendage to blast-pipe of	J. L. Agnew	Negaunee, Mich	July 27, 1869	93, 032
Blast furnace, Arrangement of pipes for hot	J. Young	Franklin Furnace, Ohio	Aug. 2, 1853	9, 908
Blast-furnace breast-plate	R. A. Fisher	San Francisco, Cal	July 22, 1873	141, 043
Blast-furnace charging-apparatus	J. H. Collins	Edgehill, Pa	Sept. 24, 1872	131, 667
Blast-furnace charging-apparatus	W. A. Miles	Salisbury, Conn	Aug. 20, 1872	130, 652
Blast-furnace cinder-plate	S. W. Harris	Albany, N. Y	Sept. 2, 1873	142, 463
Blast-furnace, Combination of a double traveling hearth with.	L. Sibert	Wookstock, Va	Nov. 20, 1849	6, 894
Blast-furnace, Construction and mode of working	H. Bessemer	London, England	July 25, 1871	117, 246
Blast-furnace, Construction of	S. Chubbuck and J. Briggs	Wareham, Mass	Jan. 9, 1841	1, 926
Blast-furnace, Fluxing	C. Shunk	Armstrong County, Pa	Feb. 12, 1856	14, 257
Blast-furnace for making iron	D. W. Hendrickson and J. P. McLean.	New York, N. Y	Sept. 3, 1867	68, 565
Blast-furnace for smelting iron, &c	S. W. Harris	Albany, N. Y	Sept. 2, 1873	142, 464
Blast-furnace for smelting metal	J. Barker	Baltimore, Md	Apr. 20, 1837	172
Blast-furnace hearth	G. Poe	Elk Ridge Landing, Md	June 23, 1838	804
Blast-furnace hopper	D. Bauman	Parryville, Pa	May 28, 1872	127, 214
Blast-furnace, Hot-air	R. Long	Chillicothe, Ohio	Dec. 10, 1867	72, 056
Blast furnace, Hot	A. Burtenshaw	Hope Furnace, Ohio	Mar. 29, 1870	101, 223
Blast-furnace, Method of heating	T. W. Bakewell	Cincinnati, Ohio	Nov. 6, 1855	13, 743
Blast-furnace, Oven or furnace for heating the blast of.	T. Whitwell	Stockton-on-Tees, England	July 9, 1867	66, 543
Blast-furnace, Oven or stove for heating the blast of.	J. M. Hartman	Philadelphia, Pa	July 26, 1870	105, 378
Blast-furnaces, Collecting and using the waste gases from.	J. E. A. B. De Langlade	Bordeaux, France	Mar. 19, 1872	124, 796
Blast-furnace to steam-boiler, Mode of applying the waste heat of.	M. Bell	Antis, Pa	June 10, 1840	1, 630
Blast-generator	C. C. Lloyd	Philadelphia, Pa	Apr. 17, 1849	6, 341
Blast-generator	W. H. Place	New York, N. Y	Feb. 4, 1862	34, 331
Blast-generator, Hydraulic	A. F. W. Partz	New York, N. Y	June 2, 1857	17, 447
Blast-heating furnace	H. Hamilton	Youngstown, Ohio	July 13, 1869	92, 526
Blast-heating furnace or oven	G. H. Lagorce	Newcastle, Pa	June 13, 1871	115, 870
Blast in furnace, Mode of heating	C. C. Alger	Stockbridge, Mass	June 30, 1838	819
Blast in furnace, Mode of heating air for hot	J. Jones	York, Pa	Dec. 10, 1838	1, 033
Blast, Method of generating air	I. J. Hendryx	New York, N. Y	Feb. 17, 1857	16, 645
Blast of furnace, Application of steam to	C. Foss	Madison, Ohio	Aug. 2, 1826	....
Blast oven for iron-furnace, Hot	S. and J. Thomas	Hokendauqua, Pa	June 1, 1869	90, 796
Blast oven for metallurgic furnace, Hot	T. Whitwell	Stockton-on-Tees, England	Aug. 27, 1872	130, 885
Blast oven, Hot	R. E. Brown	Saint Louis, Mo	Feb. 2, 1864	41, 421
Blast oven, Hot	D. and J. Campbell and S. Raymond.	Middletown, Pa	Sept. 14, 1869	94, 709
Blast oven, Hot	J. Fraggett	Youngstown, Ohio	May 31, 1870	103, 597
Blast oven, Hot	J. Player	Philadelphia, Pa	May 31, 1870	103, 651
Blast oven, Hot	J. Young	Portsmouth, Ohio	Sept. 3, 1872	131, 143
Blast oven or furnace, Hot	E. M. Furguson	Brady's Bend, Pa	Apr. 5, 1870	101, 449
Blast-oven pipe, Hot	J. K. McLanahan	Hollidaysburgh, Pa	July 23, 1872	129, 744
Blast-pipe for conveying heated air and gas to furnace.	R. Cook	Saratoga Springs, N. Y	Mar. 26, 1850	7, 211
Blast-producing chair, Rotary	L. R. Breisach	New York, N. Y	Feb. 16, 1858	19, 343
Blast-regulator	A. Kipp, jr	Sing Sing, N. Y	Aug. 16, 1864	43, 856
Blast, smelting, and cupola furnace	S. C. Salisbury	New York, N. Y	Mar. 23, 1869	88, 083
Blasts, &c., Machine for blowing	P. W. Mackenzie	Jersey City, N. J	Jan. 2, 1855	12, 165
Blastic compound	L. Buchholtz	Richmond, Va	Aug. 19, 1856	15, 551
Blasting by electrical currents	C. Stowell	Concord, Mass	Oct. 28, 1862	36, 824
Blasting by electricity	T. P. Shaffner	Louisville, Ky	Dec. 19, 1865	51, 671
Blasting by electricity	T. P. Shaffner	Louisville, Ky	Dec. 19, 1865	51, 674
Blasting-charge	G. Werlich	Watertown, Wis	Aug. 3, 1869	93, 379
Blasting-compound	M. Nowak	Williamsburgh, N. Y	May 24, 1864	42, 869
Blasting logs	M. Cooke	Sacramento City, Cal	May 3, 1870	102, 503
Blasting, Method of	N. Cadwallader	Birchville, Cal	May 29, 1866	55, 055
Blasting, Nitro-glycerine compound for	J. Horsley	Cheltenham, England	Dec. 28, 1869	98, 382
Blasting, Package of powder-charges for	H. M. Boies	Scranton, Pa	Nov. 11, 1873	144, 434
Blasting-plug	G. H. Felt	New York, N. Y	Feb. 27, 1866	52, 836
Blasting-plug	J. H. Holsey	Butler, Ga	Oct. 31, 1871	120, 438
Blasting-plug	J. H. Holsey	Butler, Ga	July 8, 1873	140 628
Blasting-plug	C. Monson	New Haven, Conn	Oct. 3, 1865	50, 263
Blasting-plug	D. Shoemaker	Kittaning Township, Pa	Sept. 16, 1873	142, 948
Blasting-powder	H. Biebuyck	Brussels, Belgium	Oct. 7, 1862	36, 599
Blasting-powder	W. and E. Fehleisen	Cilli City, Austria	Jan. 29, 1867	61, 659
Blasting-powder	W. H. Jackson	Salem, Mass	Mar. 23, 1869	88, 171
Blasting-powder	F. A. Jaeckel	Buckan-Magdeburg, Prussia.	May 24, 1864	42, 913
Blasting-powder	A. Murtineddu	Marseilles, France	May 12, 1857	17, 291
Blasting-powder	P. A. Oliver	New York, N. Y	July 14, 1868	80, 004
Blasting-powder	W. Silver, jr	Pittston, Pa	Nov. 22, 1853	10, 260
Blasting-powder	W. Silver, jr	Wapwallopen, Pa	July 1, 1856	15, 257
Blasting-powder	W. R. Thomas and M. Emanuel, jr.	Catasauqua, Pa	Mar. 11, 1862	34, 654
Blasting-powder, Composition for	W. R. Thomas and M. Emanuel, jr.	Catasauqua, Pa	Apr. 9, 1861	32, 016
Blasting-powder, Composition for	W. R. Thomas and M. Emanuel, jr.	Catasauqua, Pa	Dec. 9, 1862	37, 117
Blasting-powder, Compound for	A. T. Rand	New York, N. Y	Oct. 29, 1867	70, 359
Blasting-powder, Machine for making	W. Silver	Bloomsburgh, Pa	Apr. 6, 1869	88, 674
Blasting-purposes, Tamping-device for	J. Shoemaker	Putneyville, Pa	Oct. 18, 1870	108, 397
Blasting rock	G. C. Bunsen	Belleville, Ill	May 30, 1865	47, 925
Blasting rock	M. Shaw	New York, N. Y	June 3, 183[illegible]	....
Blasting rock, &c	C. Monson	New Haven, Conn	Apr. 1, 1851	8, 011
Blasting rock, Chemical composition for	C. Seidel	New York, N. Y	Feb. 12, 1867	61, 957
Blasting rock, Explosive composition for	E. Callow	London, England	Feb. 17, 1852	8, 734
Blasting rock, Implement for	C. F. Brown	Warren, R. I	July 11, 1854	11, 250

Index of patents issued from the United States Patent Office from 1790 *to* 1873, *inclusive*—Continued.

Invention.	Inventor.	Residence.	Date.	No.
Blasting rock, Loading the boring for	E. Gilbert	Rochester, N. Y	July 22, 1823	....
Blasting rock, Making cartridges for	J. B. Ives	Lebanon, Pa	July 17, 1826	....
Blasting rock, Method of	J. Brodie and S. H. Wheeler	San Francisco, Cal	Oct. 8, 1872	131, 995
Blasting rock, Method of	I. Whitcomb	Hingham, Mass	July 29, 1873	141, 248
Blasting rock, Mode of	J. Gilleland	Athens, Ga	Dec. 4, 1860	30, 809
Blasting rock, Plug for	J. D. Buckley and S. F. Mosher	Schagticoke, N. Y	May 17, 1859	24, 006
Blasting rock, timber, &c	J. Norton	Cork, Ireland	Aug. 8, 1854	11, 508
Blasting rock under water, Apparatus for	J. B. Eads	Saint Louis, Mo	Jan. 27, 1857	16, 473
Bl sting rock under water	B. Maillefert	New York, N. Y	Mar. 2, 1852	8, 776
Blasting-squib	S. H. Daddon	Saint Clair, Pa	Sept. 30, 1873	143, 396
Blasting, Tamping-plug for	E. Gomez	New York, N. Y	Apr. 26, 1870	102. 250
Blasting, &c., Treating explosive compounds to render them safe for.	E. A. L. Roberts	Titusville, Pa	May 20, 1873	139, 192
Bleached fabric, Process for dechlorinating	I. A. Roth	Philadelphia, Pa	Oct. 4, 1853	10, 095
Bleaching	J. B. Fuller	Norwich, Conn	June 25, 1867	66, 013
Bleaching	J. G. Kientzle	Montgomery County, Pa	Oct. 8, 1818	....
Bleaching and cleaning cloth	C. H. Farnham	Norwich, Conn	Aug. 15, 1835	....
Bleaching and cleaning vegetable fiber	E. T. Rice	New York, N. Y	Feb. 22, 1870	100, 071
Bleaching and cleansing textile fabric, Apparatus for.	S. Barlow	Middleton, England	May 27, 1862	35, 357
Bleaching and disinfecting	P. Marcelin	New York, N. Y	Apr. 9, 1872	125, 469
Bleaching and dyeing yarn, cloth, and other textile fabrics, Method of.	I. C. Colton and A. M. Hastings	Buffalo and Rochester, N. Y.	Mar. 5, 1867	62, 612
Bleaching and removing stains, Liquid for	M. E. Tompkins	Brooklyn, N. Y	Nov. 26, 1867	71, 426
Bleaching animal and vegetable fiber	C. M. E. du Motay and C. R. Maréchal.	Metz, France	Aug. 28, 1866	57, 649
Bleaching-apparatus	C. T. Appleton	Roxbury, Mass	Apr. 17, 1855	12, 709
Bleaching-apparatus	E. A. Combs	Monroe, Wis	July 14, 1868	79, 955
Bleaching-apparatus	J. Meyer	Bay Ridge, N. Y	May 17, 1864	42, 782
Bleaching-apparatus	M. Pierce	Norwich, Conn	Nov. 8, 1845	4, 257
Bleaching-apparatus	I. A. Roth and J. Lea	Philadelphia County, Pa	May 9, 1854	10, 894
Bleaching cane-juice, Apparatus for	W. A. Jordan	New Orleans, La	Apr. 2, 1867	63, 527
Bleaching cloth, yarn, &c., Process of	W. Luther	Niagara Falls, N. Y	Jan. 28, 1868	73, 733
Bleaching cotton and linen yarn, &c	J. Kendall	Leominster, Mass	Aug. 22, 1817	....
Bleaching cotton and woolen fabric	J. Jenning	Plainville, Conn	Dec. 28, 1869	98, 387
Bleaching cotton goods by steam	A. Milne and D. S. Deane	Clinton, N. Y	July 14, 1813	....
Bleaching cotton, linen, &c	J. B. Green	Portsmouth, N. H	May 29, 1832	....
Bleaching dark soaps and "foots"	O. Loew	New York, N. Y	Mar. 29, 1870	101, 283
Bleaching fabrics, Apparatus for	L. Mendelson	New York, N. Y	Aug. 8, 1871	117, 796
Bleaching fatty substances	F. F. Mayer	New York, N. Y	Aug. 6, 1861	32, 005
Bleaching fibrous materials, Process of	H. M. Baker	Rochester, N. Y	Oct. 16, 1866	58, 935
Bleaching fibrous substances, Process for	J. Short	New York, N. Y	Jan. 23, 1866	52, 250
Bleaching ivory, bone, &c	D. K. Tuttle	New York, N. Y	Jan. 12, 1869	85, 875
Bleaching linen, cotton, &c., Apparatus for	L. W. Wright	United States	Mar. 3, 1838	622
Bleaching-liquors, Manufacture of	H. Deacon	Widnes, England	May 27, 1873	139, 239
Bleaching oil, paraffine, wax, &c., Apparatus for	C. Adams	Philadelphia, Pa	Feb. 13, 1866	52, 509
Bleaching palm-leaf, straw, &c	F. Perrin	Cambridge, Mass	July 31, 1866	56, 860
Bleaching paper-pulp and drying paper, Apparatus for.	L. Dodge	Waterford, N. Y	July 31, 1866	56, 732
Bleaching-powder, Manufacture of	H. Deacon	Widnes, England	Aug. 22, 1871	118, 210
Bleaching-powder, Manufacture of	T. Gray	Union Road, England	Mar. 19, 1867	63, 036
Bleaching-powder, sulphate, &c., Manufacture of	H. Deacon	Widnes, England	Dec. 5, 1871	121, 595
Bleaching-powder, Treating mixed gases containing chlorine for the production of.	H. Deacon	Widnes, England	Aug. 22, 1871	118, 212
Bleaching, Preparation of cloth and vegetable fiber for.	G. W. Billings	New York, N. Y	Mar. 14, 1865	46, 774
Bleaching-process	A. R. Arrott	Saint Helen's, England	Sept. 13, 1864	44, 250
Bleaching-process	J. A. Roth	Philadelphia, Pa	Nov. 18, 1856	16, 100
Bleaching-process	B. Schmidt	New York, N. Y	Jan. 12, 1869	85, 860
Bleaching rags, Apparatus for	H. Loring	Boston, Mass	June 5, 1855	13, 008
Bleaching resin	A. K. Lee	Galveston, Tex	May 27, 1873	139, 402
Bleaching-safe	C. W. Shiveley	Peru, Ind	Jan. 14, 1873	134, 941
Bleaching straw goods	A. M. Rosbugh	Panora, Iowa	May 10, 1870	102, 868
Bleaching thread, yarn, &c., Apparatus for	J. E. Clarner	Pawtucket, R. I	Nov. 15, 1870	109, 177
Bleaching with sulphur-fumes, Apparatus for	A. J. Crosby and O. W. Crow	Bluffton, Ind	Feb. 25, 1868	74, 898
Bleaching wool	J. Watteau	Antwerp, Belgium	Dec. 5, 1871	121, 564
Bleaching wool, yarn, &c	E. H. Haserick	Lake Village, N. H	July 23, 1872	129, 819
Blind, Apparatus for setting and copying music for the.	E. Marquis	Bloomington, Ind	Dec. 6, 1859	26, 361
Blind, Map-type for the	S. P. Ruggles	Boston, Mass	Oct. 22, 1872	132, 371
Blind, Musical notation for the	C. Mahony	New York, N. Y	Oct. 4, 1859	25, 657
Blind, Printing-apparatus for the	D. A. Johnston	Memphis, Tenn	Feb. 19, 1867	62, 206
Blind, Printing-instrument for the	E. A. Beach	Stratford, Conn	June 24, 1856	15, 164
Blind, Stitching-gage for the	W. H. Richardson	Fort Smith, Ark	July 8, 1873	140, 645
Blind, Type for the	S. P. Ruggles	Boston, Mass	Oct 22, 1872	132, 370
Blind, Type to print for the	H. Robyn	Saint Louis, Mo	Feb. 19, 1867	62, 156
Blind, Writing-apparatus for the	J. R. Cole	Paducah, Ky	Mar. 26, 1872	125, 024
Blind, Writing-apparatus for the	J. Synnott	San Francisco, Cal	Nov. 19, 1867	71, 084
Blind, Writing-apparatus for the	A. Von Briesen	New York, N. Y	Nov. 14, 1871	121, 026
Blind	W. E. Brock	New York, N. Y	Mar. 8, 1870	100, 593
Blind, Adjuster for window	A. A. Starr	New York, N. Y	June 26, 1855	13, 140
Blind and awning, Window and door	G. M. McMahan	Mount Sterling, Ky	Feb. 11, 1868	74, 399
Blind and curtain, Apparatus for raising and lowering window.	G. Allix	Saint Helier's, Island of Jersey.	Nov. 19, 1867	71, 114
Blind and curtain fixture, Window	J. H. Kinsman	United States Army	Apr. 5, 1864	42, 198
Blind and shutter fastener	S. Barker	New York, N. Y	May 11, 1852	8, 933
Blind and shutter fastener	W. Crighton	Fall River, Mass	May 31, 1864	42, 929
Blind and shutter fastener	C. H. Eddy	Auburn, N. Y	Mar. 19, 1867	62, 947
Blind and shutter fastener, Window	E. Jaquith	Brattleborough, Vt	Dec. 26, 1837	5[illegible]7
Blind and shutter fastener, Window	J. P. McKean	Washington, D. C	Apr. 24, 1841	2, 065
Blind and shutter fastening	W. B. Barnard	Waterbury, Conn	Oct. 7, 1862	36, 597
Blind and shutter fastening	F. Chase	South Sutton, N. H	Mar. 25, 1862	34, 759
Blind and shutter fastening	W. J. Decker	Nyack, N. Y	Mar. 9, 1869	87, 647
Blind and shutter fastening	J. Frick	Philadelphia, Pa	Jan. 5, 1864	41, 064
Blind and shutter fastening	D. E. True	Leominster, Mass	July 12, 1864	43, 533
Blind and shutter mover and fastener	W. Maguire	Cincinnati, Ohio	Jan. 1, 1850	6, 990
Blind and shutter opener and fastener	J. F. Lawrence and L. A. Farnsworth.	Claremont, N. H	Apr. 2, 1850	7, 246

Index of patents issued from the United States Patent Office from 1790 *to* 1873, *inclusive*—Continued.

Invention.	Inventor.	Residence.	Date.	No.
Blind and shutter operator	J. R. Creighton	Cincinnati, Ohio	Jan. 13, 1852	8,647
Blind and shutter operator	R. V. Jones	Birmingham, Pa	Nov. 16, 1852	9,405
Blind and shutter operator	N. W. Speers	Cincinnati, Ohio	Dec. 16, 1851	8,597
Blind and shutter supporter	T. C. Ball	Springfield, Vt	May 20, 1862	35,347
Blind and window fastening	G. L. Reynolds	Newburgh, N. Y	Mar. 20, 1866	53,339
Blind-boring machine	J. H. Gibbs	Grand Rapids, Mich	Feb. 6, 1866	52,409
Blind, Butt for	O. S. Garretson	Buffalo, N. Y	June 19, 1866	55,643
Blind-butt, Self-locking	W. R. Goodrich	Utica, N. Y	Mar. 5, 1872	124,263
Blind-catch	J. Currier	Portland, Me	Dec. 24, 1867	72,609
Blind-catch	W. F. Seavey	Portland, Me	Apr. 13, 1869	88,814
Blind, Construction of	G. W. Day	Haverhill, Mass	Oct. 15, 1872	132,142
Blind, Device for opening and closing window	E. Bascom	New York, N. Y	Feb. 9, 1869	86,630
Blind, Device for opening and closing window	S. W. Woodward	Buffalo, N. Y	Apr. 17, 1866	54,077
Blind, door, &c., Window	L. Stevens and S. B. Ellithorp	Elmira, N. Y	June 26, 1855	13,141
Blind, Enameled window	T. J. Olsaver and W. P. Elliott	Aurora, Ill	Dec. 5, 1865	51,345
Blind-fastener	O. M. Andrews	Hecla Works, N. Y	Nov. 29, 1859	26,319
Blind-fastener	F. and F. Babcock	Middletown, Conn	June 1, 1869	90,625
Blind-fastener	F. and F. Babcock	Middletown, Conn	Sept. 13, 1870	107,210
Blind-fastener	J. M. Barnaby	West Harwich, Mass	Feb. 9, 1869	86,628
Blind-fastener	A. G. Batchelder	Lowell, Mass	June 27, 1871	116,257
Blind-fastener	A. Bingham	Newtonville, Mass	June 25, 1867	65,993
Blind-fastener	E. R. Chandler	Cambridgeport, Mass	Sept. 10, 1861	33,236
Blind-fastener	H. M. Clark	Meriden, Conn	June 12, 1866	55,577
Blind-fastener	W. H. Davis	Taunton, Mass	Oct. 4, 1859	25,634
Blind-fastener	G. K. Dearborn	South Boston, Mass	Oct. 17, 1865	50,552
Blind-fastener	G. K. Dearborn	Smithfield, R. I	Sept. 26, 1871	119,266
Blind-fastener	J. Johnson and S. Ingersoll	Brooklyn, N. Y	Feb. 2, 1869	86,552
Blind-fastener	W. S. Kirkham	Brantford, Conn	Nov. 6, 1869	38,581
Blind-fastener	J. Murphy	Boston, Mass	Dec. 28, 1858	22,446
Blind-fastener	W. Phelps, jr	Salem, Mass	Nov. 3, 1868	83,789
Blind-fastener	D. B. Randall	Augusta, Me	Oct. 31, 1865	50,775
Blind-fastener	G. T. Smith and W. E. Sparks	New Haven, Conn	Dec. 18, 1866	60,584
Blind-fastener	S. F. Stanton	Manchester, N. H	Jan. 12, 1869	85,867
Blind-fastener	C. E. Struck	New York, N. Y	May 31, 1870	103,795
Blind-fastener	D. E. True	Lake Village, N. H	Dec. 4, 1855	13,890
Blind-fastener	F. Veazie	Worcester, Mass	Dec. 1, 1868	84,661
Blind fastener and operator	J. Aborn	Providence, R. I	May 22, 1866	54,996
Blind fastener, Gravitation window	J. A. Carver	Taunton, Mass	Feb. 27, 1850	....
Blind fastener, Window	W. Avery	Salisbury, N. Y	Oct. 29, 1861	33,563
Blind fastener, Window	J. R. Baker	Jersey City, N. J	July 23, 1867	67,015
Blind fastener, Window	J. L. Bassett	Bridgeport, Conn	Sept. 25, 1847	5,305
Blind fastener, Window	C. P. Bell	Nashua, N. H	May 14, 1867	64,740
Blind fastener, Window	J. M. Evarts	New Haven, Conn	Aug. 21, 1847	5,252
Blind fastener, Window	S. Fansher	Southbury, Conn	Apr. 10, 1841	2,042
Blind fastener, Window	A. T. Finch	Meriden, Conn	Oct. 16, 1860	30,3[illegible]7
Blind fastener, Window	C. B. Francis	Newark, N. J	Jan. 1, 1867	60,872
Blind fastener, Window	E. A. Holbrook, J. E. Dodge, and G. H. Marshall.	Watertown, N. Y	Nov. 19, 1867	71,009
Blind fastener, Window	M. M. Isbel	New Haven, Conn	June 29, 1839	1,210
Blind fastener, Window	D. B. and C. C. Mosher	Seneca Falls, N. Y	Apr. 14, 1868	76,799
Blind fastener, Window	G. Welsh	Washington, D. C	Feb. 29, 1848	5,463
Blind-fastening	E. B. Beecher, J. G. Davis, H. S. Frost, and A. G. Davis.	Westville and Watertown, Conn.	Apr. 16, 1867	63,835
Blind-fastening	E. A. Chavantre	Newark, N. J	Nov. 19, 1867	94,719
Blind-fastening	J. E. Cryer	Greenpoint, N. Y	Sept. 14, 1869	71,135
Blind-fastening	S. Hall	New York, N. Y	May 23, 1865	47,816
Blind-fastening	J. J. Henry	North White Creek, N. Y	Nov. 27, 1860	30,739
Blind-fastening	W. C. Hicks	Boston, Mass	May 21, 1861	32,365
Blind-fastening	W. Humiston	Meriden, Conn	Feb. 26, 1867	62,337
Blind-fastening	S. W. Huntington	Augusta, Me	May 28, 1867	65,086
Blind-fastening	A. S. Lesner	Milltown, Me	Aug. 1, 1871	117,649
Blind-fastening	G. Lightfoot	Elgin, Ill	Nov. 12, 1867	70,726
Blind-fastening	W. C. Marshall	New York, N. Y	Mar. 5, 1867	62,656
Blind-fastening	B. Mayo	Chatham, Mass	Nov. 19, 1867	71,031
Blind-fastening	C. A. Palmer	Newburgh, N. Y	Feb. 6, 1866	52,442
Blind-fastening	R. Porter	Washington, D. C	Feb. 22, 1859	23,043
Blind-fastening	S. V. Quimby and W. G. Marston	Boston, Mass., and West Fairlee, Vt.	Oct. 31, 1865	50,733
Blind-fastening	H. Vansands	Middletown, Conn	May 5, 1857	17,243
Blind-fastening, &c	W. Toepfer and H. Rugee	Milwaukee, Wis	Feb. 3, 1863	37,597
Blind fastening, Window	I. Amos	Bel Air, Md	Nov. 28, 1871	121,309
Blind fastening, Window	A. C. Arnold	Norwalk, Conn	Oct. 24, 1865	50,546
Blind fastening, Window	J. Bacon	Bedford, Mass	Apr. 28, 1836	....
Blind fastening, Window	W. B. Barnard	Waterbury, Conn	Oct. 7, 1862	36,596
Blind fastening, Window	S. Lichtenthaeler	Litiz, Pa	July 14, 1846	4,633
Blind fastening, Window	J. Luther and A. Marsh	Worcester, Mass	Dec. 4, 1866	60,210
Blind fastening, Window	J. Luther and A. Marsh	Worcester, Mass	Aug. 20, 1867	67,891
Blind fastening, Window	F. A. Makepeace	Worcester, Mass	Oct. 2, 1866	58,441
Blind fastening, Window	N. F. Mathewson	Barrington, R. I	July 9, 1867	66,510
Blind fastening, Window	G. B. Melcher	Salem, Mass	Feb. 4, 1868	73,987
Blind fastening, Window	D. Mills	Paterson, N. J	Jan. 6, 1863	37,300
Blind fastening, Window	H. Munroe	Fall River, Mass	Oct. 2, 1866	58,461
Blind fastening, Window	T. J. Sloan	New York, N. Y	Mar. 26, 1867	63,317
Blind fastening, Window	J. Stewart	Utica, N. Y	Apr. 24, 1847	5,078
Blind fastening, Window	T. Stover	Cambridgeport, Mass	July 23, 1867	67,146
Blind fastening, Window	L. M. Townsley	Sedalia, Mo	Apr. 30, 1867	64,264
Blind fastening, Window	A. Warner	Brooklyn, N. Y	Apr. 9, 1867	63,768
Blind fastening, Window	A. J. Warner	Brooklyn, N. Y	Feb. 5, 1867	61,779
Blind fastening, Window	J. W. Whittier	Cambridge, Mass	Nov. 26, 1861	33,806
Blind fixture, Window	A. G. Batchelder	Lowell, Mass	Jan. 19, 1858	19,170
Blind, Folding	M. Blake	Sutton, N. H	Mar. 14, 1854	10,648
Blind, Folding window	S. S. Clark	Manchester, N. H	Apr. 7, 1857	16,966
Blind, Folding window	F. R. Osgood	Grand Rapids, Mich	Nov. 1, 1870	108,819
Blind for doors and windows, Metallic	W. E. Worthen	New York, N. Y	July 17, 1855	13,279
Blind for houses, Inside	J. Wright and T. Thompson	Elizabeth, N. J	May 21, 1872	127,006
Blind holder, Window	E. W. Bullard	Hardwick, Mass	Aug. 29, 1854	11,597
Blind-hook blanks, Cutting and forming	G. Orr	Needham, Mass	May 12, 1868	77,905
Blind, Inside	D. Y. Kilgore	Philadelphia, Pa	June 17, 1873	139,899

Index of patents issued from the United States Patent Office from 1790 *to* 1873, *inclusive*—Continued.

Invention.	Inventor.	Residence.	Date.	No.
Blind, Inside	E. Metcalf	Rome, N. Y	July 29, 1873	141, 286
Blind, Inside	W. Potter, jr	Andover, N. Y	May 13, 1873	138, 761
Blind, Inside window	S. W. Shorey	Galesburgh, Ill	Dec. 17, 1867	72, 332
Blind, Iron window	H. Blakely	New York, N. Y	Jan. 23, 1855	12, 292
Blind machinery, Window	D. H. Thompson	Springfield, Mass	May 4, 1852	8, 931
Blind-making machine	J. Milne	Philadelphia, Pa	June 18, 1872	128, 057
Blind, Metal-clad wooden	W. E. Brock	New York, N. Y	June 11, 1872	127, 736
Blind, Metallic	J. M. Jomain	Paris, France	July 23, 1867	66, 967
Blind, Metallic window	G. A. Lathrop	East Saginaw, Mich	Dec. 13, 1859	26, 438
Blind, Metallic window	C. Neer	Troy, N. Y	June 15, 1858	20, 576
Blind, Metallic window, &c	C. Neer	Albany, N. Y	Jan. 14, 1862	34, 162
Blind-mortising machine	M. Buck	Lebanon, N. H	Nov. 23, 1869	97, 040
Blind-mortising machine	B. T. Norris	Lynn, Mass	Apr. 10, 1855	12, 691
Blind, Movable window	N. Poulson	Washington, D. C	July 21, 1868	80, 215
Blind opener and shutter, Curvilinear	R. B. Rollf	Cincinnati, Ohio	Apr. 17, 1849	6, 347
Blind, Opening and closing outside	J. E. Clokey	Washington, D. C	Mar. 30, 1858	19, 751
Blind, Opening and shutting window	E. Keith	Bridgewater, Mass	Jan. 25, 1833	....
Blind opener and slat regulator, Combined	A. Ball	Milford, Mass	Jan. 21, 1873	135, 063
Blind opener and slat regulator, Combined	L. Gathmann	Chicago, Ill	Feb. 27, 1872	124, 050
Blind, Operating and fastening window	W. Allen, jr	Meriden, Conn	Apr. 4, 1848	5, 497
Blind-operating device	O. Williams	Governeur, N. Y	Apr. 26, 1864	42, 523
Blind, Operating window	T. Christian	New York, N. Y	Mar. 2, 1858	19, 488
Blind, Operating window	T. Christian	New York, N. Y	Sept. 7, 1858	21, 408
Blind, Operating window	A. Ferber	Elizabeth City, N. J	July 27, 1858	20, 996
Blind-operator	J. A. Dorman and J. E. Stearns	Worcester, Mass	Sept. 28, 1858	21, 638
Blind-operator	L. N. Fay and W. Mason	West Warren, Mass	Nov. 30, 1858	22, 172
Blind-operator	L. N. Fay and W. Mason	Warren, Mass	Feb. 14, 1860	27, 119
Blind-operator	J. Johnson	Genesco, N. Y	Feb. 28, 1860	27, 295
Blind operator and fastener	J. R. Creighton	Cincinnati, Ohio	Aug. 31, 1852	9, 231
Blind operator, Window	G. Jennison and M. F. Otis	Westborough, Mass	Apr. 4, 1871	113, 301
Blind or shutter fastener	W. Race	Seneca Falls, N. Y	Sept. 23, 1851	8, 387
Blind or shutter, Opening and closing iron	W. H. Brown	Worcester, Mass	Feb. 23, 1864	41, 676
Blind-rack	C. E. Smith	Goffstown, N. H	Nov. 16, 1869	96, 980
Blind, Railway-car	D. M. Hall	Bridgeport, Conn	Dec. 6, 1859	26, 351
Blind, "Retaining" window	N. Palmer	New York, N. Y	June 13, 1831	....
Blind rods and slats, Machine for wiring	G. Meyer	Cleveland, Ohio	Dec. 7, 1869	97, 541
Blind-rods, Hand-machine for wiring	B. C. Davis	Binghamton, N. Y	Oct. 11, 1859	25, 726
Blind-rods, Machine for trimming	B. C. Davis	Binghamton, N. Y	June 7, 1870	103, 848
Blind-rods, Machine for wiring	B. Boardman	Norwich, Conn	Sept. 1, 1857	18, 080
Blind-rods, Machine for wiring	T. R. Crosby	Newark, N. J	Dec. 13, 1859	26, 417
Blind-rods, Machine for wiring	F. H. Moore	Ithaca, N. Y	June 15, 1852	9, 032
Blind-rods, Machine for wiring	T. F. St. John	Le Roy, N. Y	Dec. 16, 1856	16, 252
Blind rods, Machine for wiring window	D. Kelly	Grand Rapids, Mich	Sept. 12, 1865	49, 888
Blind rods, Window	J. G. Baker	Washington, D. C	Oct. 18, 1859	25, 864
Blind-rods, Wiring	J. Coover	Chambersburgh, Pa	Aug. 7, 1860	29, 467
Blind-rod-wiring machine	J. Holzberger	Newark, N. J	Oct. 12, 1869	95, 800
Blind, Rolling window	S. W. Bidwell	Hartford, Conn	Oct. 5, 1858	21, 648
Blind-screen for shutter	B. J. Williams	Philadelphia, Pa	May 10, 1870	102, 900
Blind, Securing window	W. H. Mackrell	Bushwick, N. Y	June 13, 1831	....
Blind, Self-adjusting spring for window	H. Seely	Unadilla, N. Y	July 14, 1828	....
Blind, Sheet-iron	W. E. Ward	Port Chester, N. Y	Jan. 2, 1855	12, 145
Blind, Shifting	B. C. Howell, A. B. Thompson, and E. D. Snyder.	Ithaca and Owego, N. Y	Dec. 20, 1864	45, 499
Blind-shutter fastening	O. Paddock	Watertown, N. Y	Oct. 13, 1868	82, 980
Blind-slat adjuster	O. L. Houghton	Holden, Mo	Oct. 29, 1872	132, 581
Blind-slat adjuster	W. B. Sloan	Hamburgh, Iowa	May 28, 1872	127, 376
Blind-slat adjuster	W. B. Sloan	Hamburgh, Iowa	Jan. 21, 1873	135, 166
Blind-slat adjuster, Window	R. C. Beach and G. A. Berry	Tidioute, Pa	Dec. 16, 1873	145, 481
Blind-slat boring and mortising machine	T. Flesher	Dunkirk, N. Y	Nov. 21, 1871	121, 093
Blind-slat clasp and pivot, Metallic	G. R. Clarke	New York, N. Y	Mar. 5, 1867	62, 608
Blind-slat-crimping machine	M. Buck	Lebanon, N. H	Aug. 15, 1871	118, 102
Blind-slat-cutting machine	J. W. Helder	Shannon, Ill	Aug. 23, 1870	106, 694
Blind-slat fastener	G. W. Brooks	Bloomington, Ill	Sept. 9, 1873	142, 674
Blind-slat fastener	A. F. Champlin	Westerly, R. I	Oct. 28, 1873	144, 062
Blind-slat fastener	W. Sellers	New York, N. Y	Apr. 27, 1869	89, 439
Blind-slat fastener	T. G. Springer	New York, N. Y	Sept. 2, 1873	142, 526
Blind-slat fastening	J. D. Burdick	Ashway, R. I	Sept. 6, 1864	44, 072
Blind-slat fastening	J. M. Peirce	Mokena, Ill	May 19, 1868	78, 004
Blind-slat fastening	W. F. Redding	Utica, N. Y	June 16, 1863	38, 913
Blind-slat fastening	T. F. Rockwell	Yorkville, N. Y	Apr. 28, 1868	77, 218
Blind-slat fastening	T. R. Smith	Bennington, Vt	May 7, 1867	64, 588
Blind-slat holder, Venetian	J. Hampson	New Orleans, La	Aug. 21, 1841	2, 223
Blind-slat holder, Window	J. Boyd	Mamaroneck, N. Y	Dec. 1, 1868	84, 530
Blind-slat holder, Window	W. S. Mayo	New York, N. Y	Aug. 4, 1857	17, 937
Blind-slat machine	S. Jackson	Ossipee, N. H	June 19, 1860	28, 809
Blind-slat machine	W. F. Johnson and J. Doyle	Wetumpka, Ala	July 31, 1860	29, 380
Blind-slat machine	K. Kendal and L. H. Stark	Goffstown, N. H	Aug. 15, 1871	118, 023
Blind-slat machine	F. Leclere	Watertown, N. Y	Feb. 1, 1870	99, 327
Blind-slat machine	H. B. Smith	Lowell, Mass	Oct. 16, 1860	30, 429
Blind-slat machine	G. F. Woolston	Washington, D. C	Mar. 14, 1871	112, 666
Blind-slat machine, Window	E. R. Benson	Warsaw, N. Y	Oct. 4, 1853	10, 063
Blind-slat machine, Window	H. W. Farmer	Poultney, Vt	Apr. 24, 1860	27, 976
Blind-slat-mortising machine	C. W. Strout	Calais, Me	July 2, 1861	32, 727
Blind-slat operator	H. B. Lum	Sandusky, Ohio	Oct. 3, 1871	119, 625
Blind-slat operator	O. Paddock	Watertown, N. Y	Nov. 16, 1869	96, 950
Blind-slat operator	L. W. Swafford, E. Butler, and J. R. Hess.	Muscatine, Iowa	Oct. 27, 1868	83, 421
Blind-slat operator	J. B. Smith, S. A. Greely, and A. Campaigne.	Chicago, Ill	Sept. 20, 1870	107, 557
Blind-slat operator	D. R. Williams	Prospect, Conn	Mar. 19, 1850	7, 203
Blind-slat operator	Q. M. Youngs	Utica, N. Y	Aug. 29, 1871	118, 573
Blind-slat operator, Window	E. C. Byam	Fort Dodge, Iowa	Dec. 23, 1873	145, 842
Blind-slat-planing machine	C. Carlisle and L. Worcester	Woodstock, Vt	Mar. 16, 1858	19, 619
Blind-slat-planing machinery	G. Bonwill	Kent County, Del	Mar. 5, 1850	7, 133
Blind-slat-planing machinery	A. Woodworth, 3d	Worcester, Mass	Aug. 26, 1846	4, 721
Blind-slat regulator	J. T. O'Donohue and A. Leavitt.	New York, N. Y	Feb. 14, 1871	111, 770
Blind-slat staple	B. Boardman	Norwich, Conn	Mar. 30, 1858	19, 747

Index of patents issued from the United States Patent Office from 1790 to 1873, inclusive.—Continued.

Invention.	Inventor.	Residence.	Date.	No.
Blind-slat staple	C. H. Palmer	New York, N. Y	June 3, 1873	139, 516
Blind-slat stiles, Machine for mortising	D. T. Drake	Leominster, Mass	Apr. 28, 1857	17, 141
Blind-slat tenon	W. McFarland	New York, N. Y	Apr. 7, 1868	76, 491
Blind-slat-tenoning machine	H. Bickford	Cincinnati, Ohio	Apr. 27, 1869	89, 277
Blind-slat-tenoning machine	T. J. Bowdle, S. R. Lawder, and F. E. Johnston.	Piqua, Ohio	Oct. 6, 1868	82, 792
Blind-slat-tenoning machine	J. J. and T. Clark	Elgin, Ill	July 16, 1867	66, 678
Blind-slat-tenoning machine	J. J. Clark and T. Clark	Elgin, Ill	Oct. 6, 1868	82, 801
Blind-slat-tenoning machine	M. W. Clark	Worcester, Mass	July 28, 1868	80, 392
Blind-slat-tenoning machine	F. Douglas	Norwich, Conn	Sept. 27, 1870	107, 671
Blind-slat-tenoning machine	J. Kindleberger and W. A. Arnold.	San Francisco, Cal	Oct. 12, 1869	95, 810
Blind-slat-tenoning machine	J. M. Seymour	Newark, N. J	Apr. 24, 1866	54, 222
Blind-slat-tenoning machine	T. G. Stagg	Jersey City, N. J	Mar. 28, 1854	10, 710
Blind-slat-tenoning machine	L. F. Stevens	Elmira, N. Y	Aug. 9, 1859	25, 056
Blind slat, Window	A. Kohler	Williamsburgh, N. Y	May 7, 1872	126, 464
Blind-slat-wiring machine	P. Barry	Newark, N. J	May 21, 1867	64, 935
Blind-slat-wiring machine	B. C. Davis	Binghamton, N. Y	Oct. 15, 1872	132, 141
Blind-slat-wiring machine	E. F. Dunaway	Indianapolis, Ind	Jan. 1, 1867	60, 839
Blind-slat-wiring machine	G. V. Orton and W. H. Doane	Cincinnati, Ohio	Aug. 18, 1868	81, 103
Blind-slat-wiring machine	G. Pancake	Harrisburgh, Pa	May 12, 1868	77, 908
Blind-slats	M. W. Clark	Worcester, Mass	Feb. 22, 1870	100, 118
Blind-slats	D. Kelly	Muskegon, Mich	May 14, 1872	126, 713
Blind-slats and boring the stiles, Machine for tenoning.	H. Smith and T. J. Lumis	Norwich, Conn	Jan. 1, 1867	60, 800
Blind slats, Apparatus for operating window	S. Avery	Phœnix, N. Y	Apr. 15, 1851	8, 045
Blind-slats, Clamp for entering	J. Church	Saint Louis, Mo	July 25, 1871	117, 383
Blind-slats, Cutter-head for tenoning	M. W. Clark	Worcester, Mass	Mar. 31, 1868	76, 052
Blind-slats, Device for fastening	W. Palmer	New York, N. Y	Dec. 18, 1866	60, 545
Blind-slats, Device for forming round tenons on	T. C. Ball	Keene, N. H	Nov. 10, 1857	18, 569
Blind-slats, Device for holding	J. A. McCreary	Brooklyn, N. Y	Nov. 18, 1862	36, 960
Blind-slats, Device for moving	L. Gathmann	Chicago, Ill	Jan. 10, 1872	122, 595
Blind-slats, Machine for compressing the ends of	L. T. Smart	Manchester, N. H	May 19, 1857	17, 341
Blind-slats, Machine for cutting shoulder on	P. Clark	Nashville, Tenn	Feb. 13, 1872	123, 677
Blind-slats, Machine for cutting tenons on	S. C. Ellis	Albany, N. Y	Feb. 3, 1857	16, 534
Blind-slats, Machine for cutting tenons on	E. W. Roff	Newark, N. J	Nov. 7, 1854	11, 907
Blind-slats, Machine for entering	J. Church	Saint Louis, Mo	May 20, 1873	139, 043
Blind-slats, Machine for making	P. Schumacher	San Francisco, Cal	July 25, 1871	117, 471
Blind-slats, Machine for making	F. W. White	Norwich, Conn	Oct. 29, 1867	70, 382
Blind slats, Machine for making window	I. W. Gere	South Granby, N. Y	Nov. 30, 1858	22, 177
Blind-slats, Machine for setting staples in	J. Wyman	Schaghticoke, N. Y	Aug. 24, 1858	21, 292
Blind-slats, Machine for tenoning	L. Stevens	Elmira, N. Y	Apr. 28, 1857	17, 175
Blind-slats, &c., Machine for wiring	P. Barry	Newark, N. J	Nov. 2, 1869	96, 381
Blind-slats, Machine for wiring	E. F. Dunaway	Indianapolis, Ind	Jan. 30, 1866	52, 276
Blind-slats, Machine for wiring	J. M. Seymour and D. Whitlock	Newark, N. J	June 1, 1869	90, 789
Blind slats, Mode of adjusting window	B. C. English	Hartford, Conn	Sept. 23, 1856	15, 758
Blind-slats, Mold for making glass	E. B. Hungerford	Corning, N. Y	Mar. 18, 1873	136, 835
Blind slats, Operating window	J. D. Burdick	New Berne, N. C	Mar. 20, 1860	27, 520
Blind-slats, Spring for fastening	G. H. Dimond	Bridgeport, Conn	Sept. 17, 1867	68, 967
Blind-slats to receive the staples, Device for piercing.	J. Carpenter	Stonington, Conn	Aug. 25, 1857	18, 037
Blind slats, Window	F. Little	Saint Louis, Mo	Feb. 26, 1867	62, 348
Blind-splint machine	J. A. Welsh	Xenia, Ohio	Feb. 6, 1866	52, 473
Blind, Spring-holder for slat	W. L. Gallaudet	New York, N. Y	Nov. 11, 1856	16, 053
Blind-staple	J. B. Sargent	New Haven, Conn	Dec. 1, 1868	84, 585
Blind-staples, Machine for making and setting	J. Keith	Charlton, Mass	Mar. 14, 1871	112, 719
Blind-staples, Method of boxing	B. C. Davis	Binghamton, N. Y	May 23, 1871	115, 175
Blind-staples, Process of making	J. Keith	Providence, R. I	Aug. 27, 1872	130, 809
Blind-stile-boring machine	A. B. Carlin	Camden, N. J	Aug. 5, 1873	141, 545
Blind-stile-boring machine	S. E. Ellis	Jersey City, N. J	Oct. 29, 1872	132, 646
Blind-stile-boring machine	L. G. Kirkham	Derby, Conn	Apr. 15, 1873	137, 932
Blind-stile-boring machine	E. H. Smith	Whitestown, N. Y	Oct. 31, 1871	120, 465
Blind-stile-boring machine	J. F. Tudor	Camden, N. J	July 16, 1872	129, 439
Blind-stile-boring machine	A. M. Winn, J. Kindleberger, and W. A. Arnold.	San Francisco, Cal	Dec. 28, 1869	98, 455
Blind-stile boring and mortising machine	E. R. Longhead	Cincinnati, Ohio	May 19, 1863	38, 590
Blind-stile-mortising machine	L. M. Collins	Lebanon, N. H	May 16, 1871	114, 765
Blind-stiles, Machine for boring or mortising	L. Worcester	Lebanon, N. H	July 5, 1859	24, 688
Blind-stiles, Machine for mortising	M. W. Collins	Enfield, N. H	Aug. 6, 1872	130, 194
Blind-stiles, Machine for mortising	C. A. and E. P. Fenn and I. Cook	Saint Louis, Mo	Aug. 3, 1869	93, 291
Blind-stiles, Machine for spacing and boring	D. Dunham	Pawtucket, R. I	June 14, 1859	24, 427
Blind stop	P. A. Burgess	Butler, Mo	Dec. 26, 1871	122, 154
Blind-stop	W. A. Caswell	Providence, R. I	May 4, 1869	89, 557
Blind-stop	J. H. Cranston	Norwich, Conn	Oct. 28, 1873	144, 019
Blind-stop	J. Weber	New York, N. Y	Sept. 23, 1873	143, 207
Blind, Sun	J. Jeffreys	Upper Norwood, England	Apr. 19, 1864	42, 438
Blind, Suspending Venetian	J. Bohrer	Philadelphia, Pa	June 4, 1850	7, 408
Blind, Venetian	H. H. Andresen and H. Asbahr	Davenport, Iowa	May 19, 1868	78, 040
Blind, Venetian	G. F. Smith	Philadelphia, Pa	July 23, 1867	66, 995
Blind, Venetian	G. H. Woodworth	Brooklyn, N. Y	July 26, 1859	24, 900
Blind, Venetian window	C. D. Blinn	Port Huron, Mich	Nov. 28, 1865	51, 131
Blind, Venetian window	C. Rose	Allentown, Pa	Apr. 10, 1855	12, 695
Blind, Ventilating roller window	A. Cooper	Twickenham, England	May 2, 1871	114, 412
Blind, Ventilating window	H. Berdan and J. Bantly	Wayne, Mich	Nov. 30, 1869	97, 269
Blind, Window	W. Bellairs and H. Demott	Atkinson, Ill	May 26, 1868	78, 359
Blind, Window	W. H. Bixler	Easton, Pa	July 17, 1855	13, 251
Blind, Window	J. P. Boyd	La Porte, Ind	Oct. 25, 1870	108, 557
Blind, Window	W. E. Brock	New York, N. Y	July 4, 1871	116, 679
Blind, Window	E. Cate	Boston, Mass	May 1, 1847	5, 097
Blind, Window	E. Cate	Boston, Mass	May 8, 1847	5, 108
Blind, Window	F. Chase	South Sutton, N. H	July 24, 1855	13, 300
Blind, Window	L. W. Chase	Galion, Ohio	Mar. 27, 1866	53, 412
Blind, Window	A. M. Cochran	New York, N. Y	Feb. 3, 1857	16, 527
Blind, Window	T. Donato	New York, N. Y	June 7, 1870	103, 854
Blind, Window	D. D. Douglass	Springfield, Mass	June 11, 1861	32, 512
Blind, Window	S. Eich	East Toledo, Ohio	June 28, 1870	104, 717
Blind, Window	G. M. Fowler	Seymour, Conn	Apr. 23, 1872	125, 887
Blind, Window	A. S. Grenville and T. J. Lewis.	Cambridge and Boston, Mass.	Aug. 9, 1839	1, 279

Index of patents issued from the United States Patent Office from 1790 *to* 1873, *inclusive*—Continued.

Invention.	Inventor.	Residence.	Date.	No.
Blind, Window	J. Harding	Galesburgh, Ill	Jan. 12, 1869	85, 818
Blind, Window	S. Hebron	Buffalo, N. Y	Sept. 7, 1869	94, 599
Blind, Window	A. Herder	New York, N. Y	Sept. 7, 1858	21, 417
Blind, Window	I. H. Hobbs	Philadelphia, Pa	Aug. 29, 1871	118, 454
Blind, Window, &c	H. Hoffman	New York, N. Y	Dec. 1, 1863	40, 795
Blind, Window	W. P. Hoffman	San Francisco, Cal	Aug. 27, 1867	68, 076
Blind, Window	E. B. Hungerford	Elmira, N. Y	Feb. 27, 1866	52, 854
Blind, Window	A. A. Jaqua	New York, N. Y	Dec. 7, 1869	97, 514
Blind, Window	W. Johnston	Cincinnati, Ohio	Oct. 20, 1868	83, 286
Blind, Window	D. Kelly and W. Livingston	Grand Rapids, Mich	Feb. 10, 1857	16, 632
Blind, Window	C. K. Marshall	Vicksburgh, Miss	Sept. 24, 1867	69, 231
Blind, Window	C. G. Matchett	Greenville, Ohio	Mar. 12, 1867	62, 765
Blind, Window	S. W. Merrill	Assabet, Mass	May 1, 1866	54, 385
Blind, Window	G. Munger	Cambridge, Md	Mar. 20, 1817	....
Blind, Window	L. Park	Brady, Pa	Dec. 28, 1869	98, 403
Blind, Window	L. Park	Brady, Pa	Mar. 18, 1873	136, 858
Blind, Window	J. Parkerson	Boston, Mass	Sept. 11, 1828	....
Blind, Window	A. and M. Pirz	New York, N. Y	Oct. 5, 1869	95, 511
Blind, Window	S. Pocock	Woodstock, (Ontario,) Canada.	Oct. 11, 1870	108, 182
Blind, Window	W. F. Redding	Saratoga Springs, N. Y	July 10, 1866	56, 267
Blind, Window	J. C. Reed	Stamford, Conn	Nov. 28, 1865	51, 268
Blind, Window	S. M. Sherman	Fort Dodge, Iowa	Oct. 12, 1869	95, 737
Blind, Window	S. M. Sherman	Fort Dodge, Iowa	July 11, 1871	117, 001
Blind, Window	A. P. Smith	Sterling, Ill	July 10, 1866	56, 282
Blind, Window	C. W. Smith	Evans, N. Y	June 26, 1860	28, 908
Blind, Window	H. Smith and T. J. Lumis	Norwich, Conn	July 30, 1867	67, 363
Blind, Window and door	S. Steere	Gloucester, R. I	Mar. 25, 1835	....
Blind, Window	T. J. Stratton	Cleveland, Ohio	July 16, 1872	129, 435
Blind, Window	A. Van Wagenen	Boston, Mass	June 6, 1865	48, 116
Blind, Window	C. H. Warner	Pittsfield, Mass	Apr. 14, 1868	76, 855
Blind, Window	M. C. Weld	Closter, N. J	Aug. 12, 1873	141, 841
Blind, Window	G. Wilkinson	White Creek, N. Y	Jan. 8, 1842	2, 414
Blind, Window	L. H. Wooden	Hampstead, Md	July 9, 1872	128, 937
Blind-wiring machine, Window	B. C. Davis	Binghamton, N. Y	Mar. 22, 1870	101, 107
Blind-wiring machine	W. F. Dodge	Newark, N. J	Mar. 23, 1869	88, 145
Blind-wiring machine	E. F. Dunaway	Cincinnati, Ohio	Mar. 21, 1871	112, 791
Blind-wiring machine	J. Kindleberger and W. A. Arnold.	San Francisco, Cal	Sept. 28, 1869	95, 355
Blind-wiring machine	C. McGill	New Haven, Conn	Oct. 7, 1873	143, 521
Blind-wiring machine	J. H. Nelson	Little Falls, N. Y	Oct. 31, 1871	120, 454
Blinds	R. Hutton	Williamsburgh, N. Y	Jan. 1, 1867	60, 736
Blinds and slats, Apparatus for operating window	J. Jones	Clyde, N. Y	Dec. 24, 1850	7, 856
Blinds, Apparatus for opening and closing	C. Reed and E. Howe, jr	Cambridgeport, Mass	Sept. 25, 1849	6, 748
Blinds, &c., Apparatus for painting window	S. T. Field	Worcester, Mass	Apr. 18, 1854	10, 789
Blinds, Cast and wrought metal	R. White	Washington, D. C	Jan. 20, 1852	8, 679
Blinds, Corner-support for	G. W. Day	Haverhill, Mass	June 24, 1873	140, 120
Blinds, Device for operating slats of window	L. N. Fay and W. Mason	Warren, Mass	Aug. 4, 1857	17, 923
Blinds, Device for operating window	J. McMackin	New York, N. Y	Aug. 4, 1857	17, 938
Blinds, Hanging Venetian	H. W. Safford	Philadelphia, Pa	June 30, 1863	39, 069
Blinds, Horizontal spring catch for window	W. Phelps	Salem, Mass	July 7, 1839	....
Blinds, Locking and stopping window	J. Wetzel	Mott Haven, N. Y	May 30, 1865	48, 003
Blinds, Machine for boring window	L. S. Colburn	Oberlin, Ohio	Oct. 6, 1868	82, 803
Blinds, &c., Machine for cleaning	G. W. La Baw	Jersey City, N. J	Apr. 18, 1854	10, 792
Blinds, Machine for cutting rolls of window	L. H. Dwelley	Dorchester, Mass	Mar. 12, 1867	62, 829
Blinds, Machine for cutting slats for window	G. H. Denison	Suspension Bridge, N. Y	Jan. 26, 1864	41, 367
Blinds, Machine for making metallic slats for	J. S. Sanson and W. P. Farrand	Philadelphia, Pa	Dec. 16, 1856	16, 250
Blinds, Machine for making window	M. C. Stiles and T. S. Lewis	Hollis, Me	Jan. 24, 1854	10, 462
Blinds, Machine for mortising window	J. A. Peabody	Lowell, Mass	July 17, 1855	13, 271
Blinds, Machine for tenoning window	J. H. Palmer	Elmira, N. Y	Feb. 19, 1856	14, 289
Blinds, Machinery for boring window	J. Wiley	New Orleans, La	Dec. 25, 1849	6, 979
Blinds, Machinery for mortising frames of window	D. M. Cummings	North Enfield, N. H	Jan. 10, 1854	10, 403
Blinds, Means for holding window	H. A. Frost	Worcester, Mass	Jan. 23, 1855	12, 275
Blinds, Metallic frame for window	C. Neer	Albany, N. Y	May 17, 1859	24, 048
Blinds, Method of adjusting window	W. H. Babcock	Homer, N. Y	Oct. 12, 1858	21, 752
Blinds, Method of moving and fastening window	C. Reed	Cambridge, Mass	May 15, 1849	6, 455
Blinds, Method of opening, shutting, and fastening	W. Chase	Buffalo, N. Y	May 22, 1849	6, 466
Blinds, Mode of constructing slats for	W. E. Worthen and J. J. Althouse.	New York, N.Y	Jan. 11, 1859	22, 600
Blinds, Mode of manufacturing iron slats for window	W. E. Ward	Port Chester, N. Y	July 11, 1854	11, 311
Blinds, Mode of opening and closing window	G. Butterfield	Hopkinton, N. H	Sept. 4, 1840	1, 766
Blinds, Mode of opening and closing window	L. N. Fay and W. Mason	Warren, Mass	Aug. 4, 1857	17, 922
Blinds, Mode of operating window	J. Clark	Williamsburgh, N. Y	Jan. 18, 1859	22, 625
Blinds, Mode of raising and lowering Venetian	J. Weir	New York, N. Y	Oct. 8, 1840	1, 807
Blinds, Mortising and boring stiles for door and window.	D. Hathaway	Troy, N. Y	Feb. 5, 1833	....
Blinds, Opening and closing device for window	W. Wright	Cincinnati, Ohio	Apr. 10, 1847	5, 062
Blinds, Operating window	C. G. Bloomer	North Kingston, R. I	Oct. 18, 1859	25, 801
Blinds to windows, &c., Mode of adjusting	C. E. Parker and J. Sauger	Boston & Watertown, Mass	Aug. 7, 1855	13, 398
Blinds, Turn-buckle for window	J. L. Chapman	Philadelphia, Pa	Dec. 28, 1858	22, 470

Block:

See Alphabet-block.
Anvil-block.
Asphalt-block.
Basket-braiding block.
Bolster block.
Boot-crimping block.
Brake-block.
Bridge-block.
Brush-block.
Building block.
Butchers' block.
Cam and spring block.
Carriage-step block.
Carriage top-prop block.
Color-printing block.
Composition block.
Concrete-block.

Index of patents issued from the United States Patent Office from 1790 *to* 1873, *inclusive*—Continued.

Invention.	Inventor.	Residence.	Date.	No.
Block—Continued.				
See Conveyer-block.				
Cutting-block.				
Detaching-block.				
Flue-block.				
Gaff-block.				
Griping-block.				
Harness-pad block.				
Hat-block.				
Head-block.				
Hoisting-block.				
Horse-collar block.				
Keel-block.				
Last-block.				
Lead-block.				
Lettering-block.				
Meat-block.				
Muff-block.				
Muff-forming block.				
Music-note block.				
Oyster-block.				
Pavement-block.				
Paving-block.				
Pounding-block.				
Presser-block.				
Pulley-block.				
Pulling-block.				
Punch-block.				
Railway-brake block.				
Ribbon-block.				
Rubber-block.				
Sash-guide block.				
Saw-mill head-block.				
Shackle-block.				
Sheave-block.				
Ship's block.				
Snatch-block.				
Spelling-block.				
Stereotype-block.				
Stone-block.				
Strapping-block.				
Tackle-block.				
Toy-block.				
Toy building-block.				
T-rail block.				
Type-block.				
Waist-block.				
Wood-block.				
Block and tackle check	D. C. Guttridge and W. F. Rogers.	Canton, Ohio	Aug. 21, 1866	57, 316
Block-disengaging hook	S. Brown	San Francisco, Cal	Feb. 13, 1866	52, 636
Block-fitting machine	E. H. Woodsum	South Boston, Mass	Nov. 11, 1873	144, 427
Block press, Furnace	A. Hall	Perth Amboy, N. J	Mar. 18, 1873	136, 913
Block-sheave	C. Alger	Boston, Mass	July 1, 1836	....
Block-sheave	L. Aspinwall	Albany, N. Y	Apr. 22, 1835	....
Block-sheave	C. Curtis and T. C. Smith	Boston, Mass	Apr. 20, 1831	....
Block-sheave	N. H. Lewis	New York, N. Y	Aug. 26, 1816	....
Block-sheave, Bush for	J. Rudder	Norfolk, Va	Feb. 6, 1819	....
Blocks, hubs of wheels, &c., Bushing for	T. and D. Curtis	Washington, D. C	Jan. 23, 1826	....
Blocks, Manner of strapping	A. E. Wolf	Mystic River, Conn	Nov. 6, 1866	59, 496
Blocks, tackle, and pulleys of metal	J. Barron	Philadelphia, Pa	Oct. 20, 1834	....
Blood, Equalizing	S. R. Terrell	Burton, Miss	Feb. 5, 1836	......
Bloom-rolling machine	G. W. Billings	Chicago, Ill	May 27, 1873	139, 358
Blooming-furnace	B. B. Howell	Philadelphia, Pa	Nov. 6, 1828	....
Blotter	R. G. Allerton	New York, N. Y	June 9, 1857	17, 477
Blotter	S. H. Merrill	Washington, D. C	July 2, 1872	128, 556
Blotter	C. C. Moore	New York, N. Y	Dec. 5, 1865	51, 337
Blotter	C. C. Moore	New York, N. Y	Apr. 2, 1867	63, 417
Blotter	D. Walker	Newark, N. J	May 12, 1868	77, 783
Blotter, Automatic	J. E. Billings	Belmont, Mass	Oct. 8, 1867	69, 616
Blotter-holder	N. M. Shafer	New York, N. Y	Sept. 24, 1867	69, 131
Blotter, paper-weight, rule, cutter, and square, Combined.	A. H. Trego	Trenton, N. J	Oct. 10, 1865	50, 404
Blotter, Roll	P. B. Sheldon	Prattsburgh, N. Y	Feb. 19, 1861	31, 483
Blotter, Rotary	F. W. Frost and S. L. Hayward.	Somerville, Mass	Apr. 12, 1870	101, 852
Blotting-pad	R. Boeklen	Brooklyn, N. Y	May 14, 1867	64, 623
Blotting-pad	A. Q. Collins	Cambridge, Mass	Mar. 21, 1871	112, 787
Blotting-pad	J. F. French	Boston, Mass	July 19, 1870	105, 563
Blotting-pad	C. A. Gale	Demopolis, Ala	Dec. 14, 1869	97, 900
Blotting-pad	P. Gorsline	Elizabeth, N. J	Apr. 20, 1869	89, 142
Blotting-pad	G. C. Hinman	Boston, Mass	Aug. 23, 1870	106, 696
Blotting-pad	J. M. Keep	New York, N. Y	Apr. 5, 1870	101, 627
Blotting-pad	A. B. Kellogg	Buffalo, N. Y	Dec. 20, 1870	110, 245
Blotting-pad	D. Walker	Newark, N. J	Nov. 20, 1866	59, 933
Blower	W. H. Bailey	Mahanoy City, Pa	Nov. 14, 1871	120, 929
Blower	G. W. Bigelow	New Haven, Conn	Feb. 12, 1867	61, 919
Blower	H. B. Bigelow and G. Murray	New Haven, Conn., and Cambridgeport, Mass.	July 10, 1866	56, 165
Blower	E. Carleton	Cape Elizabeth, Me	June 27, 1871	116, 265
Blower	W. S. Colwell	Pittsburgh, Pa	Sept. 27, 1870	107, 665
Blower	F. Engel	Camden, N. J	Mar. 5, 1867	62, 620
Blower	J. A. Evarts	Meriden, Conn	Dec. 11, 1866	60, 350
Blower	J. N. Gilchrist	Connersville, Ind	May 31, 1870	103, 733
Blower	D. D. Hardy and E. E. Wood	Cincinnati, Ohio	June 21, 1870	104, 585
Blower	S. H. Hartman	Allegheny, Pa	Aug. 8, 1871	117, 776
Blower	B. Hotchkiss	New Haven, Conn	Nov. 3, 1863	40, 482
Blower	R. Lapham	New York, N. Y	June 19, 1860	28, 758
Blower	W. A. Parmele	New Haven, Conn	July 30, 1867	67, 345

Index of patents issued from the United States Patent Office from 1790 *to* 1873, *inclusive*—Continued.

Invention.	Inventor.	Residence.	Date.	No.
Blower	T. C. Richards	Milwaukee, Wis	Jan. 17, 1860	26, 863
Blower	T. Rogers	Fredericktown, Ohio	Oct. 24, 1871	120, 328
Blower	P. H. Roots	Connersville, Ind	Sept. 25, 1860	30, 157
Blower	B. F. Sturtevant	Boston, Mass	Feb. 2, 1869	86, 469
Blower	B. F. Sturtevant	West Roxbury, Mass	Apr. 19, 1870	102, 062
Blower	E. Suckon and E. Habel	Oldham, England	Jan. 6, 1863	37, 325
Blower	J. A. Svedberg	Washington, D. C	Jan. 30, 1872	123, 304
Blower	H. Thirion	Miricourt, France	Oct. 29, 1861	33, 613
Blower	W. W. Webb	Indianapolis, Ind	Mar. 28, 1871	113, 229
Blower	J. M. Williams	Connersville, Ind	Jan. 29, 1867	61, 592
Blower	T. H. Willson	Harrisburgh, Pa	Mar. 26, 1861	31, 844
Blower, Air	J. W. Newcomb	New York, N. Y	Jan. 23, 1872	122, 959
Blower and exhauster, Steam	J. Howarth	Salem, Mass	Mar. 1, 1870	100, 294
Blower and rotary-engine combined	H. P. Tenant	East Germantown, Ind	May 2, 1871	114, 489
Blower, Blast	J. Braugh	Aurora, Ill	June 30, 1857	17, 664
Blower-case	P. H. Roots	Connersville, Ind	Nov. 1, 1864	44, 892
Blower-case	B. F. Sturtevant	Boston, Mass	Mar. 2, 1869	87, 523
Blower, Coal-grate	R. Fuller and T. Thomas	New York, N. Y	May 22, 1827	......
Blower, Compound	A. K. Rider	New York, N. Y	Apr. 5, 1870	101, 510
Blower, Compound	T. Shaw	Philadelphia, Pa	July 8, 1873	140, 597
Blower cross-head	P. H. and F. M. Roots	Connersville, Ind	July 24, 1866	56, 614
Blower, Fan	H. B. Adams	New York, N. Y	Jan. 31, 1860	26, 962
Blower, Fan	S. Barnhart	Chillicothe, Ohio	July 31, 1855	13, 346
Blower, Fan	J. B. Charles	Ashland, Ohio,	Feb. 14, 1860	27, 108
Blower, Fan	P. Clark	Rahway, N. J	Oct. 23, 1866	58, 985
Blower, Fan	P. Clark	Rahway, N. J	Dec. 22, 1868	85, 213
Blower, Fan	R. Cook	Saratoga Springs, N. Y	Nov. 12, 1861	33, 694
Blower, Fan	F. P. Dimpfel	New York, N. Y	Dec. 28, 1839	1, 448
Blower, Fan	J. Ericsson	New York, N. Y	Aug. 16, 1870	106, 348
Blower, Fan	W. Farmer	New York, N. Y	Oct. 18, 1864	44, 715
Blower, Fan	J. C. Gartley and J. Fox	Philadelphia, Pa	July 17, 1855	13, 260
Blower, Fan	W. Kendrick	New York, N. Y	Dec. 5, 1865	51, 321
Blower, Fan	J. F. Lietch	Greene, N. Y	Dec. 24, 1861	34, 028
Blower, Fan	C. P. Marshall	Worcester County, Mass	Feb. 3, 1857	16, 547
Blower, Fan	W. P. Miller	San Francisco, Cal	Nov. 12, 1867	70, 736
Blower, Fan	M. V. Nobles	Saint Anthony, Minn	Dec. 15, 1863	40, 982
Blower, Fan	F. Ortlieb	Williamsburgh, N. Y	Mar. 13, 1866	53, 174
Blower, Fan	N. Parrish	Kalamazoo, Mich	Dec. 17, 1867	72, 416
Blower, Fan	D. and J. R. Pollock	Lancaster, Pa	June 19, 1855	13, 100
Blower, Fan	R. Porter	Malden, Mass	Jan. 3, 1865	45, 749
Blower, Fan	T. T. Prosser	Chicago, Ill	Dec. 23, 1873	145, 753
Blower, Fan	S. W. Ruggles	Fitchburgh, Mass	Aug. 8, 1854	11, 511
Blower, Fan	C. G. Sargent	Graniteville, Mass	July 4, 1865	48, 593
Blower, Fan	I. P. Smith	Orangetown, N. Y	Mar. 14, 1846	4, 424
Blower, Fan	B. F. Sturtevant	West Roxbury, Mass	Apr. 19, 1870	102, 063
Blower, Fan	H. Sweetapple	Napa, Cal	July 31, 1860	29, 417
Blower, Fan	L. D. Wheeler	Fitchburgh, Mass	Nov. 1, 1870	108, 949
Blower, Fan	W. Winter	Plainfield, N. J	Dec. 15, 1863	40, 974
Blower, Fan-wheel	A. Westcott	Syracuse, N. Y	Mar. 26, 1867	63, 343
Blower, Fire	A. J. Redway	Cincinnati, Ohio	Jan. 19, 1869	86, 635
Blower for blacksmith's forge	J. G. Tscheulin	Baltimore, Md	May 3, 1870	102, 626
Blower for furnace, Hydraulic	R. Cook	Saratoga Springs, N. Y	Apr. 16, 1850	7, 283
Blower for furnace of steam-boiler, &c., Hydro-carbon.	H. Gerner	New York, N. Y	July 18, 1865	48, 806
Blower for furnace, Steam	J. A. Bassett	Salem, Mass	Sept. 5, 1865	49, 823
Blower for smith's forge, Fan	L. Duskin and B. Sledge	Thomasville, N. C	Sept. 6, 1870	107, 167
Blower for steam-generator	D. M. Nichols	New York, N. Y	Oct. 3, 1865	50, 265
Blower, Forge	C. West and B. K. Price	Pittsburgh, Pa	Oct. 22, 1867	70, 140
Blower, Franklin-stove	D. Stuart	Philadelphia, Pa	Aug. 27, 1850	7, 608
Blower, Furnace	M. Alden	Ralston, Pa	Apr. 18, 1848	5, 513
Blower, Furnace	B. L. Johnson	Cassawago, Pa	Apr. 4, 1848	5, 498
Blower, Gas-engine	J. H. Bean	Cincinnati, Ohio	July 1, 1873	140, 397
Blower-holder	J. B. F. Davidge	New York, N. Y	Feb. 18, 1868	74, 514
Blower, Hopper	T. S. Barnum	Sharon, Conn	Jan. 18, 1810	......
Blower, Hot-air	B. F. Sturtevant	Jamaica Plain, Mass	Feb. 22, 1870	100, 238
Blower, Hydraulic	J. Darling	Cincinnati, Ohio	Dec. 24, 1850	7, 853
Blower, Locomotive steam-engine	R. Winans	Baltimore, Md	July 29, 1837	307
Blower, Pressure	W. C. Grimes	Philadelphia, Pa	Nov. 11, 1868	83, 846
Blower, Pressure	J. Perrault	Troy, N. Y	May 10, 1870	102, 964
Blower, Pressure	B. F. Sturtevant	Boston, Mass	July 13, 1869	92, 489
Blower, Pressure	B. F. Sturtevant	Jamaica Plain, Mass	Feb. 22, 1870	100, 239
Blower, Rotary	W. B. Barnard and E. Jordan	Waterbury, Conn	Sept. 27, 1859	25, 554
Blower, Rotary	F. Hainsworth	Chicago, Ill	Apr. 3, 1866	53, 609
Blower, Rotary	W. G. Hyndman	Cincinnati, Ohio	Aug. 9, 1870	106, 165
Blower, Rotary	W. G. Hyndman	Cincinnati, Ohio	Dec. 26, 1871	122, 118
Blower, Rotary	C. W. Isbell	New York, N. Y	Mar. 17, 1868	75, 635
Blower, Rotary	R. F. Knox	San Francisco, Cal	July 1, 1873	140, 509
Blower, Rotary	T. Leffel	Springfield, Ohio	May 14, 1872	126, 639
Blower, Rotary	H. C. McIlwain and A. Brumfiel	Connersville, Ind	May 24, 1870	103, 482
Blower, Rotary	H. C. McIlwain and A. Brumfiel	Connersville, Ind	Jan. 10, 1871	110, 929
Blower, Rotary	J. Mitchell	Philadelphia, Pa	Oct. 6, 1868	82, 736
Blower, Rotary	P. H. Roots	Connersville, Ind	Oct. 9, 1866	58, 745
Blower, Rotary	P. H. and F. M. Roots	Connersville, Ind	Jan. 21, 1868	73, 654
Blower, Rotary	P. H. and F. M. Roots	Connersville, Ind	Aug. 11, 1868	81, 009
Blower, Rotary	A. Smith	New York, N. Y	Feb. 4, 1862	34, 318
Blower, Rotary	B. F. Sturtevant	Boston, Mass	Feb. 2, 1869	86, 470
Blower, Rotary	J. A. Svedberg	Washington, D. C	Apr. 29, 1873	138, 448
Blower, Spiral cone	B. Brundred	Oldham, N. J	Sept. 26, 1835	......
Blower-stand	P. Bradford	New Haven, Conn	Oct. 3, 1871	119, 500
Blower, Steam	J. A. Bassett and O. C. Smith	Salem, Mass	Dec. 3, 1867	71, 569
Blower, Steam	G. W. Bright	Philadelphia, Pa	Jan. 22, 1867	61, 391
Blower, Steam	M. Foreman and J. R. Mathewson.	Philadelphia, Pa	May 7, 1867	64, 414
Blower, Steam	J. Hainsworth	Chicago, Ill	Mar. 3, 1868	75, 011
Blower, Steam	J. T. Hancock	Jamaica Plain, Mass	Aug. 3, 1869	93, 197
Blower, Steam	J. H. Johnson	Paducah, Ky	Sept. 25, 1866	58, 264
Blower, Steam	J. Simmonds	Brooklyn, N. Y	Mar. 6, 1866	53, 087
Blower, Steam	L. F. Smith	Philadelphia, Pa	Dec. 17, 1867	72, 426

Index of patents issued from the United States Patent Office from 1790 *to* 1873, *inclusive*—Continued.

Invention.	Inventor.	Residence.	Date.	No.
Blower, Steam	S. R. Wilmot	Bridgeport, Conn	Apr. 2, 1867	63, 595
Blower, Steam-generator	W. H. Squires	New York, N. Y	Sept. 24, 1867	69, 268
Blowers to furnaces of locomotives, Application of.	F. B. Blanchard	Brooklyn, N. Y	June 25, 1861	32, 614
Blowers to furnaces of locomotives, Application of.	F. B. Blanchard	New York, N. Y	Sept. 22, 1863	40, 014
Blower, Turbine fan	M. Smith	New Haven, Conn	July 25, 1865	48, 986
Blower-wheel	B. F. Sturtevant	West Roxbury, Mass	Oct. 29, 1867	70, 286
Blower-wheel, Pressure	B. F. Sturtevant	Jamaica Plain, Mass	Feb. 22, 1870	100, 236
Blower-wheel, Pressure	B. F. Sturtevant	Jamaica Plain, Mass	Feb. 22, 1870	100, 237
Blowing-apparatus	J. M. Bailey	Pittsburgh, Pa	Nov. 12, 1872	132, 891
Blowing-apparatus	D. Cumming	Sorrel Horse, Pa	Apr. 27, 1858	20, 045
Blowing-apparatus	R. H. Gilbert	Washington, D. C	Feb. 15, 1870	99, 876
Blowing-apparatus	P. W. McKenzie	Jersey City, N. J	Oct. 25, 1864	44, 809
Blowing-engine	J. Fritz and J. Moore	Bethlehem and Philadelphia, Pa.	Aug. 2, 1864	43, 678
Blowing-engine	A. C. Kirk	Glasgow, Great Britain	Nov. 24, 1868	84, 428
Blowing-engine	L. J. Knowles	Worcester, Mass	Sept. 12, 1871	118, 949
Blowing-engine, Means for repairing	T. Critchlow	Swatara Township, Pa	Jan. 5, 1869	85, 510
Blowing-machine	J. G. Baker	Philadelphia, Pa	Dec. 9, 1873	145, 382
Blowing-machine	J. Dougherty	Philadelphia, Pa	July 12, 1870	105, 318
Blowing-machine	M. Reichenbach and S. Golay	Paris, France	Jan. 26, 1869	86, 320
Blowing-machine	J. M. Williams	Connersville, Ind	May 23, 1871	115, 259
Blow-off for steam-boiler, Surface	J. S. Griffith	Saint Louis, Mo	May 9, 1871	114, 551
Blow-off pipe for boiler, Surface	J. Perkins	Baltimore, Md	Apr. 4, 1871	113, 716
Blow-off pipe for steam-boiler	J. S. Griffith	Saint Louis, Mo	June 20, 1871	116, 179
Blow-pipe	J. Cook	New York, N. Y	May 28, 1872	127, 151
Blow-pipe	W. T. Gillinder	Philadelphia, Pa	Dec. 5, 1865	51, 386
Blow-pipe	J. Hollely	New York, N. Y	Mar. 16, 1858	19, 636
Blow-pipe	J. S. Hull	Cincinnati, Ohio	Aug. 4, 1863	39, 398
Blow-pipe	J. B. Hyde	New York, N. Y	Sept. 13, 1870	107, 263
Blow-pipe	J. Kendy	San Francisco, Cal	May 16, 1865	47, 721
Blow-pipe	N. W. Kingsley	New York, N. Y	Apr. 3, 1866	53, 629
Blow-pipe	M. H. Knapp	Fulton, N. Y	July 16, 1872	129, 569
Blow-pipe	O. L. Lawson	Crestline, Ohio	May 13, 1856	14, 875
Blow-pipe	J. E. McClure and D. H. Ainsworth.	San Francisco and Salinas, Cal.	Nov. 4, 1873	144, 345
Blow-pipe	J. McFarland	Clinton, Ill	Sept. 18, 1866	58, 118
Blow-pipe	O. A. Moses	Charleston, S C	Aug. 21, 1866	57, 362
Blow-pipe	S. B. Palmer	Tully, N. Y	Sept. 23, 1856	15, 774
Blow-pipe	F. Shaller	Hudson, N. Y	Nov. 27, 1866	60, 070
Blow-pipe	J. R. Street	Washington, D. C	June 7, 1870	104, 078
Blow-pipe	L. B. Wilson	Cambridge, Ohio	Apr. 5, 1870	101, 692
Blow-pipe, Alcohol	E. Conway	Dayton, Ohio	July 7, 1857	17, 727
Blow-pipe, Construction of compound	J. B. Hyde	Newark, N. J	Oct. 18, 1859	25, 832
Blow-pipe for blast-furnace	J. Barker	Baltimore, Md	Mar. 3, 1837	134
Blow-pipe for enlarging blasting cavities	A. Stickney	Norwich, Vt	Sept. 20, 1853	10, 039
Blow-pipe for enlarging blasting cavities, Compound.	A. Stickney	Norwich, Vt	Sept. 20, 1853	10, 040
Blow-pipe, Furnace	J. Barker	Baltimore, Md	Feb. 12, 1836	....
Blow-pipe, Hydro-oxygen	R. Hare	Philadelphia, Pa	July 25, 1845	4, 104
Blow-pipe mechanisms	W. S. Burgess	Norristown, Pa	July 2, 1872	128, 587
Blow-pipe operations, Composition for supports in	J. B. Hyde	Newark, N. J	Nov. 20, 1860	30, 680
Blow-pipe, Self-acting	M. Pinner	New York, N. Y	Mar. 13, 1866	53, 181
Blow-pipe, Spirit	H. N. Macomber	Lynn, Mass	Mar. 11, 1856	14, 403
Blow-pipe, Steam	J. S. Anderson	Flintville, Wis	Jan. 21, 1873	135, 058
Blow-pipe, Table	R. Somerby	Louisville, Ky	Nov. 15, 1843	3, 336
Blubber, Knife for cutting up	W. Ball	New York, N. Y	Apr. 25, 1822	....
Blubber-mincing machine	G. and J. J. Kilburn	Fall River, Mass	Nov. 16, 1841	2, 368
Blubber mincing-machine, Whale	B. Taber	Fairhaven, Mass	Aug. 11, 1821	....
Blue for use in laundry and bleaching, Lump	J. H. Dilks	New York, N. Y	Dec. 31, 1867	72, 818
Blue, Manufacture of Prussian	J. M. Merrymon	Indianapolis, Ind	Jan. 10, 1865	45, 846
Bluing, Article of	E. L. Molineux	New York, N. Y	May 26, 1868	78, 313
Bluing-box	G. A. Moss	New York, N. Y	May 21, 1867	64, 897
Bluing-box	A. F. Pickens	New York, N. Y	Aug. 16, 1870	106, 402
Bluing cotton fiber	F. Wilkinson	Manchester, England	June 25, 1872	128, 267
Bluing for use in laundry and bleaching, Process of making soluble.	J. H. Dilks	New York, N. Y	Dec. 31, 1867	72, 817
Bluing, Method of preparing laundry	E. L. Molineux	New York, N. Y	Apr. 21, 1868	76, 935
Bluing-paper for laundry purposes	T. Dreidel	Cincinnati, Ohio	Nov. 12, 1867	70, 703
Bluing-paste	R. G. Vassar	Poughkeepsie, N. Y	Jan. 31, 1865	46, 160

Board:

See Alley board.
Arm or grain board.
Backgammon-board.
Billiard-board.
Biscuit-board.
Black-board.
Bread-board.
Bulletin-board.
Card and cribbage board.
Carriage dash-board.
Center-board.
Cheese-board.
Chess-board.
Chess and checker board.
Clapboard.
Comber-board.
Croquet-board.
Cutting-board.
Cutting or lap board.
Dash-board.
Dough-board.
Drawing-board.
End-board.
Game-board.
Guide-board.
Ironing-board.
Key-board.
Kneading-board.

Index of patents issued from the United States Patent Office from 1790 *to* 1873, *inclusive*—Continued.

Invention.	Inventor.	Residence.	Date.	No.
Board—Continued:				
See Knife-cleaning board.				
Knife-scouring board.				
Lap-board.				
Lea-board.				
Leather-board.				
Letter-board.				
Mold-board.				
Molders' match-board.				
Molding-board.				
Music black-board.				
Musical demonstrating-board.				
Organ-reed board.				
Paper board.				
Pasteboard.				
Pitch-board.				
Plow mold-board.				
Portable billiard-board.				
Press-board.				
Shearing-board.				
Shooting-board.				
Sign-board.				
Skirt-board.				
Sounding-board.				
Stove-board.				
Straw-board.				
Tally-board.				
Telegraph-switch board.				
Transposing-board.				
Tray or show board.				
Wash-board.				
Weather-board.				
Board edging and slitting machine	C. I. Hays and M. Newman	Unadilla, N. Y	Aug. 12, 1862	36, 150
Board-edging machine	J. K. Sanborn	Sandy Hill, N. Y	Oct. 24, 1871	120, 170
Board, &c., for use, Seasoning, drying, and fitting	A. Plumb	Buffalo, N. Y	Apr. 6, 1832	....
Board jointing and matching machine	D. Gleason and H. Frisbee	Bethany, N. Y	Apr. 8, 1826	....
Board-jointing apparatus	D. Foster	Whitestown, N. Y	May 28, 1850	7, 395
Board-jointing machine	E. B. Clark	Damascus, Pa	Jan. 31, 1827	....
Board raising and lowering mechanism	C. and A. Kilburn	Philadelphia, Pa	Dec. 21, 1869	98, 167
Board-slitting machine	A. T. Nichols	Norfolk, Va	Nov. 5, 1872	132, 854
Board-slitting machinery	J. R. Remington and R. Beal	Lowndes County, Ala., and Washington, D. C.	Jan. 15, 1847	4, 929
Boards and planks for making boxes, &c., Machine for mitering and dovetailing.	R. Urann	Boston, Mass	Oct. 26, 1839	1, 380
Boards, Device for tonguing and grooving tapering	J. Absterdam and W. B. Merrill.	Boston, Mass	Mar. 28, 1854	10, 703
Boards, &c., Machine for mitering and dovetailing the ends of.	A. Davis	Princeton, Mass	Aug. 21, 1839	1, 297
Boards, Machine for planing and reducing	J. Cumberland	Mobile, Ala	Mar. 6, 1847	4, 997
Boards, Machine for planing, matching, and grooving.	C. Taylor	Angola, N. Y	Feb. 7, 1829	....
Boards, Machine for squaring ends of	E. H. Rollins	Bangor, Me	June 18, 1872	127, 990
Boards, Machine for thinning	S. Case	Lumpkin, Ga	Sept. 4, 1860	29, 861
Boards, Machine for tonguing, grooving, and beading.	F. Fredly	Sugar Valley, Pa	Sept. 15, 1838	921
Boards, planks, &c., Machine for slitting	E. Olds	Brookfield, Mass	June 29, 1808	....
Boards, Shearing	S. Willard	Cincinnati, Ohio	May 9, 1832	....
Boards, Side-cutter head for jointing, tonguing, and grooving.	W. M. Hutton	Troy, N. Y	Oct. 26, 1838	988
Boards to uniform thickness, Machine for reducing and smoothing.	T. D. Knight	Charleston, Tenn	Mar. 3, 1857	16, 777
Boarding-machine	J. E. Wiggin	Stoneham, Mass	Feb. 26, 1867	62, 514
Boat:				
See Army-boat.				
Bed-boat.				
Bilge-boat.				
Buggy-boat.				
Canal-boat.				
Chain-boat.				
Collapsible boat.				
Cylinder boat.				
Dredging-boat.				
Duck-shooting boat.				
Ferry-boat.				
Folding boat.				
Gutta-percha boat.				
Ice-boat.				
Ice-breaking boat.				
Insubmersible boat.				
Life-boat.				
Log-boat.				
Metallic boat.				
Mud-boat.				
Night-soil boat.				
Oyster-boat.				
Paper boat.				
Portable boat.				
Rapid-boat.				
River-boat.				
Row-boat.				
Sectional boat.				
Shallow boat.				
Ship's boat.				
Submarine boat.				
Surf and life boat.				
Torpedo-boat.				
Tow-boat.				
Toy-boat.				

Index of patents issued from the United States Patent Office from 1790 *to* 1873, *inclusive*—Continued.

Index of patents issued from the United States Patent Office from 1790 *to* 1873, *inclusive*—Continued.

Invention.	Inventor.	Residence.	Date.	No.
Boat detaching tackle	J. R. Taylor	New York, N. Y	Jan. 15, 1867	61, 281
Boat-framer	J. Beetle	New Bedford, Mass	May 20, 1856	14, 903
Boat from its tackle, Detaching	S. F. Blunt	Baltimore, Md	Mar. 25, 1856	14, 489
Boat-hoisting apparatus	A. F. Crosman	Steamer Ossipee, United States Navy.	Nov. 12, 1867	70, 813
Boat hoisting, lowering, and detaching apparatus	J. Humphries	Washington, D. C	Oct. 17, 1871	119, 984
Boat-hook, Detaching	W. H. Mills	Philadelphia, Pa	Apr. 23, 1872	125, 900
Boat-hook handle	F. F. Bibber	Boston, Mass	May 17, 1870	103, 007
Boat knee, Dory	E. J. Matthews	Booth Bay, Me	Apr. 7, 1868	76, 487
Boat lowering and detaching apparatus	M. Joyce	Washington, D. C	Sept. 24, 1867	69, 220
Boat-lowering apparatus	R. Creuzbaur	New York, N. Y	Dec. 17, 1867	72, 170
Boat-lowering apparatus	R. Creuzbaur	New York, N. Y	Dec. 17, 1867	72, 171
Boat-lowering apparatus	A. F. Crosman	Steamer Ossipee, United States Navy.	Dec. 17, 1867	72, 268
Boat-lowering apparatus	W. Flowers and Z. S. Patton	Bangor, Me	July 24, 1860	29, 264
Boat-lowering apparatus	G. W. Mallory	Mystic Bridge, Conn	Mar. 21, 1871	112, 939
Boat-lowering device	H. Goulding	Dedham, Mass	Oct. 16, 1866	58, 810
Boat or scow	A. R. Tewksbury	Boston, Mass	Aug. 16, 1853	9, 949
Boat-raising machine	E. Turner	Rochester, N. Y	Dec. 31, 1825	....
Boat row-lock	C. C. Burrows	Mystic River, Conn	Oct. 15, 1867	69, 899
Boat-tackle hook, Self-relieving	H. G. Guyon	Brooklyn, N. Y	Jan. 19, 1864	41, 339
Boat-timbers, Mold for	J. Wallace	Rochester, N. Y	Aug. 9, 1831	....
Boat to be worked by animal power	D. Porter	Washington, D. C	Feb. 8, 1816	....
Boat-towing mechanism	G. S. Olin	Deer Lodge, Mont	Dec. 23, 1873	145, 813
Boats against injury from snags and sawyers, Fender to protect.	I. W. Kirk	Philadelphia, Pa	Feb. 24, 1843	2, 972
Boats and other vessels, Constructing	A. Dorman	Norfolk, Va	Oct. 25, 1832	....
Boats and other vessels of sheet-iron or other metal, Making.	J. Francis	New York, N. Y	Mar. 26, 1845	3, 974
Boats and rafts, Passing	B. Sanborn	Lyman, N. H	Apr. 11, 1836	....
Boats and sea-vessels, Mode of building	W. Annesley	New York, N. Y	Sept. 12, 1816	....
Boats and vessels, Constructing	F. Rotch	New Bedford, Mass	Nov. 29, 1811	....
Boats and vessels, Machine for raising	A. Warner	Rochester, N. Y	Nov. 16, 1826	....
Boats, Arrangement of device for lowering and detaching.	H. D. Veuve	Galveston, Tex	Mar. 16, 1858	19, 666
Boats, Attachments of trains of	W. Ingalls	Sanbornton, N. H	Jan. 3, 1865	45, 720
Boats, Building	G. W. Eddy	Waterford, N. Y	Feb. 28, 1834	....
Boats, Building	W. Hopkins		May 13, 1803	....
Boats, Collapsible float for	J. MacDonough	New York, N. Y	Mar. 27, 1866	53, 461
Boats, Construction of	P. Davis	Providence, R. I	Jan. 3, 1860	26, 657
Boats, Construction of	T. Thorpe	Washington, D. C	Aug. 31, 1827	....
Boats, Detachable hook for suspending	C. L. Williams	Quincy, Fla	June 5, 1860	28, 623
Boats, Device for pitching	W. H. Richardson	Stillwater, Minn	Feb. 4, 1873	135, 490
Boats, Engine for unloading and removing weights from.	T. Potter, sr	Bowling Green, Ky	Dec. 17, 1834	....
Boats, Flexible vertically-extensible attachment for	J. R. Adams	Oakland, Cal	Sept. 23, 1873	143, 052
Boats, Float for	A. T. Boon	Galesburgh, Ill	Apr. 10, 1866	53, 775
Boats from canals, &c., Machine for raising	E. Turner	Rochester, N. Y	Nov. 18, 1825	....
Boats from davits, Apparatus for disengaging	E. Oliver and G. Myers	Rotherham, Great Britain	Mar. 27, 1866	53, 550
Boats from davits, Means for detaching	T. Huntington	New Rochelle, N. Y	June 5, 1866	55, 303
Boats from one level to another, Taking	R. P. Bell	New York, N. Y	July 13, 1827	....
Boats from their davits, Hook for attaching and detaching.	H. Davidson	United States Army	Apr. 9, 1861	32, 036
Boats, &c., Manner of constructing and propelling	B. D. Beecher	Prospect, Conn	Dec. 31, 1839	1, 459
Boats, Manufacture of	W. H. Ferguson	Forest, Ill	Oct. 14, 1873	143, 687
Boats, Means for checking and securing	F. M. Howes	Somerville, Mass	Dec. 23, 1873	145, 875
Boats, Means for detaching	T. Shaw	Philadelphia, Pa	Apr. 1, 1873	137, 325
Boats, &c., Method of building	J. Francis	New York, N. Y	Oct. 11, 1841	2, 293
Boats, Mode of bracing and staying	F. Mertens	Cumberland, Md	May 28, 1867	65, 255
Boats, Molding-frame for the construction of	N. Thompson, jr	Brooklyn, E. D., N. Y	May 18, 1858	20, 308
Boats over dams, Passing	S. Underwood	Bath, N. H	Mar. 19, 1836	....
Boats, Protector for stems of	W. P. Davis and S. Elwell, jr	Gloucester, Mass	Sept. 21, 1869	94, 948
Boats, &c., Rowing and propelling	W. Shaw	Otsego County, N. Y	Feb. 19, 1812	....
Boats, Suspending	C. H. Hasker	Portsmouth, Va	May 29, 1860	28, 478
Boats to and from tackle, Means for attaching and detaching.	J. M. Brooke	United States Army	Aug. 5, 1856	15, 473
Boats to facilitate discharge of cargo, Fittings for	W. H. Bryan	Georgetown, D. C	July 29, 1851	8, 266
Boats, vessels, &c., Constructing	F. Rotch	Philadelphia, Pa	Aug. 3, 1812	......
Boats, Weigh-lock for	J. Brainerd	Rome, N. Y	July 17, 1839	1, 249
Bobbin	M. Bliss	Ionia, Mich	May 17, 1870	103, 009
Bobbin	H. Clarke	Dedham, Mass	June 28, 1853	9, 814
Bobbin	A. I. Earle	Valley Falls, R. I	June 3, 1873	139, 558
Bobbin	C. H. Fisk	Lowell, Mass	Nov. 26, 1867	71, 371
Bobbin	A. P. Holmes	Great Falls, N. H	Jan. 7, 1868	73, 185
Bobbin	H. J. Hubbard	Chicopee, Mass	Nov. 3, 1868	83, 635
Bobbin	D. Hussey	Nashua, N. H	Oct. 28, 1862	36, 782
Bobbin	T. G. McLaughlin	Glen Riddle, Pa	Aug. 5, 1873	141, 575
Bobbin	W. H. Ramsdell	Lowell, Mass	July 7, 1868	79, 687
Bobbin	C. H. Reynolds	North Kingston, R. I	Aug. 30, 1864	44, 016
Bobbin	G. Richardson	Lowell, Mass	July 23, 1872	129, 682
Bobbin	C. A. Shaw	Biddeford, Me	Dec. 15, 1863	40, 9[illegible]
Bobbin	J. N. Stearns	New York, N. Y	June 20, 1871	116, 108
Bobbin, Cotton-spool	N. Rider	Millbury, Mass	Dec. 31, 1833	....
Bobbin for roving and slubbing	I. Hayden	Lawrence, Mass	Aug. 4, 1857	17, 929
Bobbin for spinning, &c	L. Ferguson	Lowell, Mass	May 1, 1866	54, 465
Bobbin for spinning, &c	B. Wilbour	Scituate, R. I	Jan. 2, 1866	51, 887
Bobbin-holder	J. Salisbury	Scituate, R. I	Jan. 25, 1870	99, 111
Bobbin-holder for spinning	J. Goulding	Worcester, Mass	Oct. 3, 1865	50, 240
Bobbin-holder for spinning	J. Goulding	Worcester, Mass	Oct. 3, 1865	50, 241
Bobbin-holder for spinning	E. Wright	Worcester, Mass	Oct. 3, 1865	50, 311
Bobbin, Metallic	W. B. Rice	Utica, N. Y	Apr. 16, 1867	63, 813
Bobbin, Metallic	C. T. Smith	Utica, N. Y	Apr. 23, 1867	64, 158
Bobbin or spool	B. Saunders	Nashua, N. H	Aug. 25, 1863	39, 681
Bobbin or spool for factories, Trussel	T. Van Riper	Paterson, N. J	Aug. 16, 1826	....
Bobbin, Spinning	J. Davis and S. W. Foster	Lowell, Mass	Mar. 26, 1867	63, 225
Bobbin, Weft	W. E. Bass	Lawrence, Mass	Jan. 29, 1867	61, 598
Bobbin, Weft	O. Pearl	Lawrence, Mass	Apr. 3, 1866	53, 665
Bobbin-winder	J. S. Demarest	Elmira, N. Y	May 28, 1872	127, 155

Index of patents issued from the United States Patent Office from 1790 *to* 1873, *inclusive*—Continued.

Invention.	Inventor.	Residence.	Date.	No.
Bobbin-winder	H. A. House	Bridgeport, Conn	Mar. 7, 1871	112, 345
Bobbin-winder	D. F. Mellen	Manchester, N. H	Sept. 15, 1863	39, 997
Bobbin-winder	E. Wilder	Springfield, Mass	Apr. 16, 1872	125, 869
Bobbin-winder, Socket	J. Thorp and S. Shepard	Taunton, Mass	Oct 14, 1816	....
Bobbin-winders, Thread guiding and cutting device for.	T. M. Day and H. Shook	Washington, Ohio	Mar. 19, 1872	124, 667
Bobbin-winding machine	J. Adams and W. A. Tolman	Richmond, Ind	May 30, 1871	115, 264
Bobbin-winding machine	W. Atkinson	Philadelphia, Pa	Aug. 26, 1873	142, 188
Bobbin-winding machine	W. V. Gee	Philadelphia, Pa	Apr. 9, 1872	125, 564
Bobbin-winding machine	J. Goodyear	Yonkers, N. Y	Aug. 5, 1873	141, 434
Bobbin-winding machine	F. H. Morrill	Philadelphia, Pa	Sept. 21, 1869	95, 034
Bobbin-winding machine	F. H. Morrill	Philadelphia, Pa	Apr. 4, 1871	113, 325
Bobbin-winding machine, Cup of	J. W. Vaughn	New York, N. Y	May 30, 1871	115, 393
Bobbin-winding machine, Thread guide and holder for.	W. W. Altemus	Philadelphia, Pa	Dec. 27, 1870	110, 535
Bobbin-winding, Reverse motion for	G. Richardson	Lowell, Mass	Dec. 8, 1868	84, 764
Bobbins, &c., Cutting out cylinders for	L. Brown	Epsom, N. H	Apr. 24, 1849	6, 391
Bobbins, Driving	A. M. Eastman	Boston, Mass	Apr. 17, 1849	6, 344
Bobbins, Friction-brake for	T. Estes	North Bennington, Vt	Nov. 27, 1860	30, 725
Bobbins in machinery for spinning fibrous substances, Method of operating.	F. McCulley, jr	Paterson, N. J	Oct. 19, 1844	3, 801
Bobbins in shuttles for weaving, Securing	D. Leavitt	Cabotville, Mass	Aug. 18, 1842	2, 755
Bobbins in shuttles, Mode of securing	S. C. Mendenhall	Richmond, Ind	Aug. 29, 1865	49, 643
Bobbins, Machine for automatically winding	D. M. Church	Holyoke, Mass	July 16, 1872	129, 394
Bobbins, Machine for boring	V. D. Beach	Battle Creek, Mich	Dec. 3, 1867	71, 683
Bobbins, Machine for pointing the journals of	D. M. Church	Holyoke, Mass	May 13, 1873	138, 789
Bobbins, Machine for turning heads of	C. M. Spencer	Hartford, Conn	Apr. 8, 1873	137, 631
Bobbins, Machine for winding conical	G. S. Bradford	Bennington, Vt	Aug. 22, 1865	49, 582
Bobbins, Machinery for boring	C. E. Norris	Peacham, Vt	Apr. 24, 1849	6, 374
Bobbins, Machinery for winding conical	H. Marcellus and S. Ward	Amsterdam, N. Y	May 24, 1864	42, 861
Bobbins, Machinery for winding conical	C. Tompkins and J. Johnson	Troy, N. Y., and Roxbury, Mass.	Apr. 21, 1857	17, 120
Bobbins or spools, Method of strengthening	A. Hallowell	Lowell, Mass	Mar. 15, 1870	100, 754
Bobbins, Skewer for speeder	C. Harris	River Point, R. I	July 6, 1869	92, 189
Bobbins upon spindles, Driving	O. Pearl	Essex County, Mass	Jan. 29, 1850	7, 058
Bobbins, Winding yarn on weavers' or shuttle	J. Thorp	Providence, R. I	Mar. 20, 1829	....
Bodkin for inserting grooved ring into cloth	J. S. Turner	Middletown, Conn	Apr. 25, 1837	181
Bodkin for passing enlarged shank of button through cloth.	P. W. Gengembre	Boston, Mass	Sept. 27, 1864	44, 416
Body-brace	E. P. Banning	New York, N. Y	Nov. 1, 1864	44, 914
Body-brace	G. S. Browne	Hartford, Conn	Nov. 22, 1853	10, 248
Body-brace	H. Mellish	Walpole, N. H	Jan. 9, 1849	6, 023
Body brace and supporter, Child's	L. Spigelmyer	Hartleton, Pa	Apr. 12, 1870	101, 934
Body-conformator	S. O. Brigham	San Francisco, Cal	Aug. 7, 1866	56, 892
Body-protector	J. W. Torrey	Milford, Mass	Mar. 17, 1868	75, 710
Bog and bush, Machine for cutting	T. Spring	Granby, Conn	Apr. 27, 1833	....
Bog-cutter	R. Cummings	Lima, Ind	Nov. 20, 1847	5, 376
Bog-cutter	J. D. Filkins	Lima, Ind	Jan. 9, 1849	6, 018
Bog-cutter	C. E. Steller	Chicago, Ill	July 31, 1866	56, 822
Bog-cutter and drag	J. W. Newton	Geneva, Wis	Nov. 3, 1868	83, 784
Bog-cutter and drag	J. W. Newton	Geneva, Wis	Mar. 16, 1869	88, 801
Bog-cutting machine	A. Follet	Windham, Conn	Oct. 16, 1849	6, 802
Bog-cutting machine	C. Hoisington	Seward, Ill	June 30, 1863	39, 048
Bogging-machine	S. Collins	Hillsdale, N. Y	Feb. 22, 1827	....
Bogging-machine	J. A. Post	Orange County, N. Y	Apr. 23, 1828	....
Boiler:				
See Agricultural boiler.				
Back-log boiler.				
Base-burning boiler.				
Base-burning steam-boiler.				
Box boiler.				
Circular boiler.				
Clothes-boiler.				
Coffee-boiler.				
Collender-boiler.				
Cooking and washing boiler.				
Culinary boiler.				
Domestic boiler.				
Egg-boiler.				
Farmers' boiler.				
Feeder-boiler.				
Fire-extinguisher boiler.				
Heater-boiler.				
Heating-boiler.				
Hot-water boiler.				
Iron boiler.				
Kitchen-boiler.				
Lard-boiler.				
Locomotive-boiler.				
Marine steam-boiler.				
Milk-boiler.				
Paper-pulp boiler.				
Portable boiler.				
Portable-furnace boiler.				
Range-boiler.				
Revolving boiler.				
Roofing-boiler.				
Sheet-metal boiler.				
Steam-boiler.				
Steam-generating boiler.				
Steam-heater boiler.				
Stone-boiler.				
Stove-boiler.				
Sugar-boiler.				
Tubular boiler.				
Wash-boiler.				
Water-heating boiler.				
Water-tube steam-boiler.				
Boiler	H. Adler	Yellow Springs, Ohio	Oct. 15, 1867	69, 896

Index of patents issued from the United States Patent Office from 1790 *to* 1873, *inclusive*—Continued.

Index of patents issued from the United States Patent Office from 1790 *to* 1873, *inclusive*—Continued.

Invention.	Inventor.	Residence.	Date.	No.
Boiler-feeder, Automatic	J. Holtz	Baltimore, Md	Mar. 23, 1869	88, 168
Boiler-feeder, Automatic	J. Hoover	Lewisburgh, Ohio	Aug. 6, 1861	32, 995
Boiler-feeder, Automatic	S. B Hunt	New York, N. Y	May 13, 1862	35, 237
Boiler-feeder, Automatic	T. Loveridge and J. Grindrod	Philadelphia, Pa	Aug. 17, 1869	93, 826
Boiler-feeder, Automatic	P. N. J. Macabies	Paris, France	May 11, 1869	90, 047
Boiler-feeder, Automatic	H. McGann	Cleveland, Ohio	Dec. 1, 1868	84, 642
Boiler-feeder, Automatic	W. Moore	Kokoma, Ind	June 5, 1866	55, 338
Boiler-feeder, Automatic	S. J. Parker	Williamsport, Pa	Apr. 30, 1867	64, 356
Boiler-feeder, Automatic	J. N. Poage	Cincinnati, Ohio	Nov. 12, 1872	133, 052
Boiler-feeder, Automatic	E. Quinn	Washington, D. C	Jan. 30, 1866	52, 376
Boiler-feeder, Automatic	E. Quinn	Washington, D. C	Mar. 6, 1866	53, 042
Boiler-feeder, Automatic	R. Rafael	New York, N. Y	Sept. 12, 1865	49, 919
Boiler-feeder, Automatic	G. A. Riedel	Philadelphia, Pa	Sept. 19, 1865	50, 034
Boiler-feeder, Automatic	G. A. Riedel	Philadelphia, Pa	Sept. 19, 1865	50, 035
Boiler-feeder, Automatic	G. A. Riedel	Philadelphia, Pa	July 3, 1866	56, 096
Boiler feeder, Automatic	G. A. Riedel	Philadelphia, Pa	July 23, 1867	66, 993
Boiler-feeder, Automatic	E. Sheppard	Philadelphia, Pa	Sept. 22, 1868	82, 357
Boiler-feeder, Automatic	T. J. Sloan	New York, N. Y	Feb. 27, 1866	52, 898
Boiler-feeder, Automatic	H. E. Stager	Milwaukee, Wis	Aug. 10, 1869	93, 564
Boiler-feeder, Automatic	D. Vaughan	Cincinnati, Ohio	Mar. 26, 1872	124, 921
Boiler-feeder, Automatic	T. B. Webster	Sekaukus, N. J	Mar. 23, 1869	88, 246
Boiler-feeder, Automatic	J. R. Widgeon	Bucyrus, Ohio	Mar. 13, 1866	53, 238
Boiler-feeder, Automatic	J. R. Widgeon and F. E. Frey	Bucyrus, Ohio	Oct. 13, 1868	802, 13
Boiler feeder, Automatic steam	J. Wheelock	Worcester, Mass	Mar. 26, 1872	125, 106
Boiler-feeder, Balance	W. D. Allen	Durhamville, N. Y	Dec. 10, 1850	7, 817
Boiler-feeder for steam-engines	E. A. Woods	Utica, N. Y	July 3, 1860	29, 028
Boiler-feeder, Self-acting	F. D. Boyle	Evansville, Ind	Aug. 4, 1863	39, 378
Boiler feeder, Steam	S. J. Parker	Rochester, N. Y	May 28, 1872	127, 362
Boiler feeder, Steam	J. M. Case	Worthington, Ohio	Mar. 29, 1870	101, 225
Boiler feeder, Steam	W. J. Sanderson and S. Stanton	Syracuse, N. Y	May 15, 1860	28, 307
Boiler-flanges, Machine for turning	E. Paye	New York, N. Y	May 29, 1866	55, 209
Boiler-float	H. McGann	Cleveland, Ohio	Dec. 1, 1868	84, 502
Boiler-flue cleaner	J. Armbruster	Petroleum Centre, Pa	Oct. 28, 1873	144, 046
Boiler-flue cleaner	W. C. Baker	New York, N. Y	Nov. 17, 1868	84, 079
Boiler-flue cleaner	G. R. Dobbins	Lowell, Mass	Aug. 25, 1868	81, 351
Boiler-flue cleaner	J. Fairclough	Saint Joseph, Mo	Nov. 30, 1869	97, 372
Boiler-flue cleaner	M. and C. H. Morse	Franklin, Mass	Mar. 30, 1869	88, 405
Boiler-flue cleaner	B. Schaefer	Chicago, Ill	Jan. 1, 1867	60, 795
Boiler-flue cleaner	G. V. Sloat	Morrisania, N. Y	Dec. 1, 1868	84, 587
Boiler-flue cleaner	J. M. Spiegle	Philadelphia, Pa	Dec. 5, 1865	51, 362
Boiler-flue-cleaning apparatus	T. H. Donohue	Washington, D. C	Sept. 16, 1873	142, 775
Boiler-flue plug	W. M. Sinclair	Baltimore, Md	July 28, 1868	80, 313
Boiler-flues by steam jet, Cleaning	C. Dasenbrock	Cincinnati, Ohio	Oct. 3, 1871	119, 581
Boiler-flues, Machine for repairing	J. Hughes	Bloomington, Ill	Aug. 23, 1870	106, 589
Boiler-flues, Method of increasing the effective length and cleansing.	A. Chapman	Fairfax, Vt	July 17, 1849	6, 595
Boiler-flues, Steam-jet head for cleaning	J. M. Wheeler	Oxford, Conn	Mar. 31, 1868	76, 125
Boiler-flues, Thimble for protecting	J. C. Farmer	Providence, R. I	May 20, 1873	138, 998
Boiler for heating-purposes	J. Bradley	Baltimore, Md	May 5, 1868	77, 576
Boiler for using anthracite coal	J. Barken	Baltimore, Md	Feb. 7, 1827	......
Boiler for vaporizing volatile fluids	J. F. Haskins	Fitchburgh, Mass	Dec. 2, 1873	145, 175
Boiler-form	J. S. Jennings	Medina, N. Y	Mar. 12, 1867	62, 852
Boiler-forming apparatus	W. W. Hornberger	Chicago, Ill	Jan. 8, 1867	61, 068
Boiler-furnace	H. F. Baker	Boston, Mass	May 30, 1846	4, 546
Boiler-furnace	T. H. Clark	Saint Louis, Mo	May 9, 1865	47, 619
Boiler-furnace	J. Cole	Cincinnati, Ohio	Aug. 22, 1848	5, 720
Boiler-furnace	T. B. Davis	Boston, Mass	Sept. 20, 1864	44, 366
Boiler-furnace	A. de Pindray	Paris, France	Mar. 24, 1868	75, 739
Boiler-furnace	W. Ennis	Philadelphia, Pa	Mar. 16, 1869	87, 917
Boiler-furnace	S. A. Ford	Chicago, Ill	Aug. 19, 1873	141, 870
Boiler-furnace	A. Friedmann and F. E. d'Erlanger.	Paris, France	Aug. 25, 1863	39, 640
Boiler-furnace	M. L. Horton	Windsor, Vt	Nov. 30, 1869	97, 296
Boiler-furnace	S. Hungerford	Slaterville, N. Y	Aug. 15, 1848	5, 712
Boiler-furnace	H. R. Ives	New Haven, Conn	May 21, 1872	126, 965
Boiler-furnace	E. L. Miller	Brooklyn, N. Y	July 7, 1846	4, 626
Boiler-furnace	J. A. Miller	New York, N. Y	Apr. 4, 1865	47, 118
Boiler-furnace	G. H. Nott	Boston, Mass	Oct. 5, 1869	95, 601
Boiler-furnace	J. A. F. Overend	San Francisco, Cal	May 3, 1870	102, 581
Boiler-furnace	J. B. Root	New York, N. Y	Aug. 5, 1873	141, 594
Boiler-furnace	E. Skelly	Plaquemine, La	Dec. 21, 1858	22, 382
Boiler-furnace	L. Skinner	Chittenango, N. Y	Feb. 7, 1871	111, 580
Boiler-furnace	A. B. Smith	Geneva, N. Y	June 3, 1873	139, 522
Boiler-furnace	B. F. Smith	New Orleans, La	Apr. 2, 1872	125, 148
Boiler-furnace	C. D. Smith	Chicago, Ill	Sept. 30, 1873	143, 305
Boiler-furnace	P. Smith	New York, N. Y	Aug. 29, 1865	49, 662
Boiler-furnace	W. C. Smith	New Brunswick, N. J	Feb. 6, 1872	123, 427
Boiler-furnace	J. A. Streight	Albion, N. Y	Aug. 17, 1869	93, 922
Boiler-furnace	E. C. Strange and G. R. Huntley	Taunton, Mass	Mar. 7, 1865	46, 725
Boiler-furnace	U. B. Stribling	Madison, Ind	Mar. 28, 1871	113, 110
Boiler-furnace	T. Vicars, sr., T. Vicars, jr., and J. Smith.	Liverpool, England	Dec. 20, 1870	110, 313
Boiler-furnace	C. D. Williams	Saint Paul, Minn	Feb. 11, 1873	135, 869
Boiler-furnace	T. B. Wilson and W. R. Shaw	Meadville, Pa	June 6, 1865	48, 125
Boiler furnace and flue	W. H. Burns	Unionville, Mo	Feb. 15, 1870	99, 879
Boiler-furnace caloric-regulator	J. G. and E. W. H. Cooper	Hartford, Conn	Mar. 12, 1867	62, 821
Boiler-furnace crown, Steam	L. H. Waugh, J. A. Haughlin, and J Graham.	Wyandotte, Kans	July 16, 1872	129, 634
Boiler-furnace fire-plate	E. Boileau	Saint Louis, Mo	Oct. 3, 1871	119, 562
Boiler-furnace, Oil-burning	F. Hungerford	Rochester, N. Y	Sept. 2, 1873	142, 468
Boiler-furnace, Portable	D. R. Prindle	East Bethany, N. Y	Apr. 16, 1867	63, 811
Boiler-furnace, Return-flue	C. J. Harris	Bloomington, Ill	May 2, 1871	114, 437
Boiler furnace, Steam	H. W. Adams	Philadelphia, Pa	Oct. 15, 1872	132, 192
Boiler furnace, Steam	S. P. Bartley	Columbus, Ohio	Apr. 14, 1868	76, 58[illegible]
Boiler furnace, Steam	A. J. Bell and J. B. Friend	Ashland, Ky	Dec. 24, 1872	134, 243
Boiler furnace, Steam	A. W. Cram	Litchfield, Ill	Dec. 31, 1872	134, 465
Boiler furnace, Steam	G. H. Diehl	Chicago, Ill	Dec. 19, 1871	121, 993
Boiler furnace, Steam	R. S. Dillon	Detroit, Mich	Dec. 28, 1869	98, 238

Index of patents issued from the United States Patent Office from 1790 *to* 1873, *inclusive*—Continued.

Invention.	Inventor.	Residence.	Date.	No.
Boiler furnace, Steam	P. Estes	Leavenworth, Kans	Sept. 17, 1872	131, 431
Boiler furnace, Steam	M. A. Foster	Saint Louis, Mo	May 21, 1872	126, 946
Boiler furnace, Steam	M. A. Foster	Saint Louis, Mo	Oct. 15, 1872	132, 151
Boiler furnace, Steam	M. A. Foster	Saint Louis, Mo	Mar. 4, 1873	136, 497
Boiler furnace, Steam	M. A. Foster	Saint Louis, Mo	May 13, 1873	138, 875
Boiler furnace, Steam	C. H. Fox	New Orleans, La	Oct. 1, 1872	131, 871
Boiler furnace, Steam	C. H. Fox	New Orleans, La	Jan. 21, 1873	135, 105
Boiler furnace, Steam	C. H. Fox	New Orleans, La	Jan. 21, 1873	135, 106
Boiler furnace, Steam	J. B. Gardner and C. H. Swain	New York, N. Y	Aug. 11, 1868	80, 821
Boiler furnace, Steam	E. F. Griffin	Chicago, Ill	Dec. 24, 1872	134, 270
Boiler furnace, Steam	C. J. Hazstreem	Chicago, Ill	May 24, 1870	103, 324
Boiler furnace, Steam	J. Howes	Worcester, Mass	Oct. 22, 1872	132, 466
Boiler furnace, Steam	F. A. Huntington	San Francisco, Cal	Oct. 15, 1872	132, 209
Boiler furnace, Steam	S. Keyes	Bennington, Vt	Nov. 11, 1873	144, 393
Boiler furnace, Steam	T. F. Morrison	Bryan, Ohio	Apr. 25, 1871	114, 0[illegible]4
Boiler furnace, Steam	A. C. Rand	Aurora, Ill	May 6, 1873	138, 694
Boiler furnace, Steam	C. D. Smith	Chicago, Ill	Aug. 6, 1872	130, 249
Boiler furnace, Steam	C. D. Smith	Chicago, Ill	May 6, 1873	138, 588
Boiler furnace, Steam	A. Steinway	New York, N. Y	Aug. 6, 1872	130, 326
Boiler furnace, Steam	U. B. Stribling	Madison, Ind	Nov. 4, 1873	144, 296
Boiler furnace, Steam	M. K. Taylor	United States Army	Jan. 24, 1871	111, 154
Boiler furnace, Steam	R. L. Walker	Globe Village, Mass	Mar. 24, 1868	75, 817
Boiler furnace, &c., Steam	J. Westerman	Sharon, Pa	Mar. 18, 1873	136, 948
Boiler furnace, Steam	J. D. Whelpley and J. J. Storer	Boston, Mass	Mar. 31, 1868	76, 280
Boiler furnace, Tubular steam	H. W. Adams	Philadelphia, Pa	Aug. 6, 1872	132, 268
Boiler-furnaces, Apparatus for consuming smoke and gas and increasing draft in.	D. E. Somes	Washington, D. C	Apr. 28, 1868	77, 226
Boiler furnaces, Blast for steam	R. Gigodot	Lyons, France	Nov. 18, 1873	144, 757
Boiler-furnaces, Bridge-wall of	W. G. Hamilton	New York, N. Y	Jan. 4, 1859	22, 530
Boiler furnaces, Mouth-piece for steam	C. Stewart	Worcester, Mass	Oct. 28, 1873	144, 002
Boiler-gage	C. L. Frink	Rockville, Conn	June 9, 1866	55, 638
Boiler guard-plate	A. O'Neill	Portsmouth, O io	Feb. 20, 1866	52, 806
Boiler-head bolt-fastening	E. Clark	New York, N. Y	Apr. 24, 1866	54, 113
Boiler-head-flanging forge and furnace	J. Nixon	Altoona, Pa	June 30, 1868	79, 382
Boiler-head-flanging machine	S. Lowen	Temperanceville, Pa	July 18, 1871	117, 091
Boiler-heads, Bending flanges upon	W. W. Martin	Allegheny City, Pa	June 19, 1866	55, 687
Boiler-heads, Machine for bending flanges on	D. Howell	Louisville, Ky	Oct. 20, 1857	18, 452
Boiler-heads, Machine for bending the flanges of	J. T. G. Piedboeuf	Liege, Belgium	Oct. 22, 1872	132, 989
Boiler-heads, Machine for cutting oval holes in	J. McBride	Allegheny Ci y, Pa	Aug. 28, 1866	57, 533
Boiler-heads, Machine for cutting oval holes in	J. McBride	Allegheny City, Pa	Aug. 28, 1866	57, 534
Boiler-heads, Machinery for forming flanges upon	J. F. Keeler	Pittsburgh, Pa	May 22, 1866	54, 920
Boiler-heads, Method of flanging	W. B. Scaife	Pittsburgh, Pa	Jan. 31, 1871	111, 478
Boiler-heads, Securing removable	J. Booth and W. Heiser	Buffalo, N. Y	June 25, 1872	128, 207
Boiler-heater	P. Colvin	Pecatonica, Ill	Oct. 8, 1872	132, 056
Boiler heater and feeder	G. C. Williams	Catskill, N. Y	Nov. 25, 1873	144, 937
Boiler heater and filter	J. J. Doughty	Lake City, Minn	Sept. 29, 1868	82, 609
Boiler heater, Steam	D. Coughlin	Fall River, Mass	Dec. 2, 1873	145, 095
Boiler or steam generator	L. M. Richards	Cazenovia, N. Y	Mar. 30, 1815	....
Boiler or steam generator	L. M. Richards	Chagrin River, Ohio	Aug. 21, 1828	....
Boiler or stew-pan	W. B. Watkins	Jersey City, N. J	Sept. 7, 1869	94, 679
Boiler-plates, Machine for punching	R. Griffin	Syracuse, N. Y	Dec. 24, 1861	33, 989
Boiler-plates, Method of riveting	J. B. Henry	New York, N. Y	Jan. 17, 1860	26, 846
Boiler-plates, Mode of preparing and screwing in	J. Goulding	Boston, Mass	June 19, 1835	....
Boiler-rivet machine	C. B. Allen	Philadelphia, Pa	July 18, 1871	117, 137
Boiler-riveting machine	S. Bennett	New Orleans, La	June 30, 1857	17, 661
Boile safe y-gage	R. H. Jackson	Sandusky, Ohio	July 9, 1867	66, 593
Boiler safety-gage	J. Marshall	Greenwich, England	Dec. 22, 1868	85, 179
Boiler-scraper	E. L. Pratt	Beverly, Mass	May 11, 1869	89, 941
Boiler-stand	J. L. Mott	Mott Haven, N. Y	Jan. 25, 1870	99, 222
Boiler stand and heater	C. F. Hitchings	New York, N. Y	Apr. 1, 1873	137, 448
Boiler-supply chamber	J. L. Sullivan	Boston, Mass	Feb. 28, 1818	....
Boiler-thimble	G. W. Duvall	Norfolk, Va	May 15, 1866	54, 703
Boiler-tube	B. Fitts	Newark, N. J	May 1, 1866	54, 318
Boiler-tube cleaner	J. B. Christoffel	New York, N. Y	Mar. 12, 1867	62, 816
Boiler-tube cleaner	P. H. Coyle	Newark, N. J	Nov. 9, 1869	96, 552
Boiler-tube cleaner	P. H. Coyle	Newark, N. J	Apr. 26, 1870	102, 374
Boiler-tube cleaner	J. Green	Boston, Mass	July 12, 1870	105, 194
Boiler-tube cleaner	W. P. Heffron	Chicago, Ill	July 23, 1867	67, 112
Boiler tube cleaner	J. E. Regan	Chicago, Ill	Nov. 9, 1869	96, 617
Boiler-tube cleaner	H. Waterman	Brooklyn, N. Y	Mar. 13, 1866	53, 203
Boiler-tube cleaner, steam-jet	R. C. Hussey	Milford, Mass	Dec. 13, 1870	110, 044
Boiler-tube cutter	W. B. Smith	Charleston, S. C	Dec. 31, 1867	72, 927
Boiler-tube-cutting tool	F. Ramsey and J. Miller	New York, N. Y	Oct. 16, 1866	58, 886
Boiler-tube ferrule	J. U. Adams	Richfield, Mich	Feb. 4, 1868	74, 028
Boiler-tube ferrule	R. A. Copeland	Brooklyn, N. Y	Apr. 6, 1869	88, 611
Boiler-tube plug	I. La I Jane	Philadelphia, Pa	Feb. 7, 1871	111, 552
Boiler-tube plug	R. L. Neill	Paterson, N. J	June 28, 1870	104, 759
Boiler-tube-scaling tool	J. Weiner, jr	Prairie du Lac, Wis	Aug. 8, 1865	49, 327
Boiler-tube scraper	J. B. Christoffel	Williamsburgh, N. Y	Apr. 15, 1873	137, 826
Boiler-tube-scraping device	E. Green	Wakefield, England	Aug. 17, 1869	93, 874
Boiler-tubes, Apparatus for expanding and fastening.	R. Dudgeon	New York, N. Y	Feb. 5, 1867	61, 815
Boiler-tubes, Cleaning	J. J. Illingworth	Brooklyn, N. Y	July 25, 1865	48, 948
Boiler-tubes, Cleaning	D. McDowell	Kingston, West Indies	Mar. 6, 1866	53, 091
Boiler-tubes, Device for leaky	R. A. Copeland	Baltimore, Md	Jan. 21, 1868	73, 439
Boiler-tubes, Device for repairing	E. Clark	New York, N. Y	Sept. 1, 1863	39, 717
Boiler-tubes, Device for stopping leaks in	R. Lavery and S. Stuart	South Boston, Mass	Dec. 27, 1864	45, 615
Boiler-tubes, Drawing	S. J. Perry	Columbia, S. C	Aug. 21, 1860	29, 715
Boiler-tubes, Ferrule for	G. W. Durall	Norfolk, Va	Sept. 19, 1865	49, 987
Boiler-tubes, Ferrule for stopping leaks in	P. Quinn	South New Market, N. H	June 11, 1867	65, 603
Boiler-tubes in sea-going vessels, Mode of preventing corrosion of	G. Hauxhurst	Somerville, Cal	Dec. 1, 1868	84, 489
Boiler tubes in tube-sheets, Securing steam	W. Moorhouse	Philadelphia, Pa	Apr. 2, 1872	125, 321
Boiler-tubes, Method of fastening	J. Bowden	New York, N. Y	Jan. 1, 1867	60, 853
Boiler-tubes, Plug for leaky	J. M. Spiegle	Philadelphia, Pa	Apr. 16, 1872	125, 764
Boiler-tubes Ring for stopping leaks in	R. Lavery and S. Stuart	South Boston, Mass	Dec. 27, 1864	45, 61[illegible]
Boiler-tubes, Spring-expanding swage for	J. McCarty	Reading, Pa	July 29, 1851	8, 256
Boiler-tubes, Steam-jet for cleaning	J. M. Wheeler	Oxford, Conn	Dec. 17, 1867	72, 348

Index of patents issued from the United States Patent Office from 1790 to 1873, inclusive—Continued.

Invention.	Inventor.	Residence.	Date.	No.
Boiler-tubes, Swaging-tool for	I. S. Hamilton	Hamilton, Ohio	Dec. 5, 1871	121, 512
Boiler-tubes, Tool for attaching	T. Prosser	New York, N. Y	Apr. 17, 1849	6, 360
Boiler-tubes, Tool for cleaning	S. Van Auken	Binghamton, N. Y	Dec. 18, 1866	60, 653
Boiler-tubes, Tool for cutting off	R. H. Burke	Greenpoint, N. Y	Jan. 22, 1867	61, 392
Boiler-tubes, Tool for cutting off	D. A. Dacey	New York, N. Y	June 6, 1865	48, 054
Boiler-tubes, Tool for cutting off	P. Hoffman	Jersey City, N. J	Mar. 26, 1867	63, 250
Boiler-tubes, Tool for cutting off	R. Lavery	South Boston, Mass	Mar. 12, 1867	62, 859
Boiler-tubes, Tool for cutting off	D. M. Nichols	New York, N. Y	Mar. 20, 1866	53, 325
Boiler-tubes, Tool for cutting off	W. P. Slensby	Chicago, Ill	May 7, 1867	64, 454
Boiler-tubes, Tool for cutting off	N. Thomas	Chicago, Ill	June 5, 1866	55, 391
Boiler-tubes, Tool for cutting off	N. Wright	Jersey City, N. J	Jan. 22, 1867	61, 499
Boiler-tubes, Tool for expanding	R. McKenzie	New Orleans, La	Oct. 26, 1869	96, 133
Boiler-tubes, Tool for expanding and cutting off	I. S. Hamilton	Hamilton, Ohio	Dec. 5, 1871	121, 513
Boiler-tubes, Tool for fastening	A. Van Guysling	North Greenbush, N. Y	Dec. 15, 1863	40, 967
Boiler-tubes, Tool for plugging leaky	J. Ritchie	Detroit, Mich	Sept. 12, 1871	118, 818
Boiler-tubes, Tool for removing scale in	P. C. Rowe	Boston, Mass	May 22, 1866	54, 962
Boiler-tubes, Tool for sealing	J. Daley and J. H. Marvill	Philadelphia, Pa	Feb. 14, 1865	46, 339
Boiler, Tubular	C. Hawthorn	Pittsburgh, Pa	Dec. 20, 1864	45, 494
Boilers and other vessels, Mode of attaching handles to.	J. H. Brown	New York, N. Y	Dec. 11, 1866	60, 337
Boilers, Apparatus for packing straw into	H. B. Meech	Fort Edward, N. Y	Sept. 11, 1866	57, 947
Boilers, Arrangement of steam-cylinders in	J. S. Shapter	New York, N. Y	Aug. 19, 1856	15, 579
Boilers, Blow-off for	E. F. Husted	Harrisburgh, Tex	Sept. 10, 1872	131, 219
Boilers, Composition for preventing and removing incrustation from.	A. Temple	Bridgeport, Conn	Aug. 22, 1865	49, 569
Boilers, Composition for preventing incrustation in	G. R. Spannagel	Saint Louis, Mo	Sept. 12, 1865	49, 931
Boilers, Composition for removing incrustation from.	J. G. Gansz and J. J. Lavo	Saint Louis, Mo	Oct. 3, 1865	50, 237
Boilers, Composition for removing incrustation from.	N. S. Thomas	Painted Post, N. Y	Aug. 14, 1866	57, 219
Boilers, Composition for removing scale from	J. Buzby	Philadelphia, Pa	Apr. 11, 1865	47, 188
Boilers, Compound for removing scale from	A. B. Auer	Babcock's Grove, Ill	May 30, 1865	47, 914
Boilers, Device for forming	G. S. Pierce	Wilkesbarre, Pa	Dec. 7, 1869	97, 549
Boilers, Device for preventing incrustations in	T. Barfield	Athens, Ill	May 4, 1869	89, 725
Boilers, Device for removing incrustations of	W. E. Everett and M. M. Thompson	New York, N. Y	Feb. 12, 1856	14, 230
Boilers, Electrical protection for	A. T. Hay	Burlington, Iowa	June 24, 1873	140, 196
Boilers, Feeding	Hunsicker & Krauss	Northampton, Pa	Aug. 20, 1835	....
Boilers, Fusible plug for	J. Smith	Wentworth Road, Great Britain.	Mar. 28, 1865	47, 076
Boilers, Hand-hole joint for	G. White	Harlem, N. Y	Jan. 21, 1868	73, 557
Boilers, ice-houses, &c., to impede the passage of heat, Non-conducting composition for covering.	J. A. Jones	Middlesborough-on-Tees, Great Britain.	Mar. 26, 1867	63, 255
Boilers, Machine for forming	E. S. Sackett	Monroe, Wis	May 7, 1867	64, 577
Boilers, Man-hole lid for	R. Tippett	Harrisburgh, Pa	Apr. 15, 1873	137, 806
Boilers, Method of applying fusible metal to	E. H. Ashcroft	Boston, Mass	Mar. 19, 1850	7, 179
Boilers, Method of bracing the water-spaces of	B. O'Neill	Reading, Pa	Mar. 4, 1851	7, 962
Boilers, Method of removing incrustation from	D. Embree	Dayton, Ohio	Jan. 17, 1865	45, 914
Boilers, &c., Mode of riveting metallic plates for	R. Smith	Great Britain	Sept. 3, 1839	1, 312
Boilers, Mode of setting	E. Jenks	Portland, Me	June 1, 1805	....
Boilers, Safety-plug for	T. G. Eiswald	Providence, R. I	Jan. 14, 1868	73, 311
Boilers, Setting	C. Neames	New Orleans, La	Nov. 8, 1870	109, 039
Boilers, Smoke-extinguisher for	W. H. Nobles	Saint Paul, Minn	Dec. 31, 1867	72, 886
Boilers, steam-cylinders, fittings, &c., Manufacture of.	G. W. Bollman	Pittsburgh, Pa	Oct. 24, 1871	120, 235
Boilers, steam-pipes, &c., Non-conducting casing for.	F. Y. Arnold	Philadelphia, Pa	Aug. 9, 1870	106, 105
Boilers, steam-pipes, &c., Non-conducting covering for.	W. Harris	Philadelphia, Pa	Jan. 18, 1870	98, 865
	R. McConnel	Jacksonville, Ill	Aug. 8, 1865	49, 287
Boilers, Tool for fastening tubes in				
Boilers, Water-feed for	H. C. Bristol	East China, Mich	July 1, 1873	140, 462
Boilers with water, Mode of supplying	J. Fox	Lowell, Mass	Mar. 14, 1832	....
Boilers with water, Self-acting apparatus for supplying.	V. F Clenet	Paris, France	Aug. 4, 1863	39, 379
Boiling	C. Shepard	Cincinnatus, N. Y	Oct. 4, 1817	....
Boiling and condensing apparatus	G. S. G. Spence	Boston, Mass	July 31, 1860	29, 414
Boiling and distilling apparatus	W. Hoffmire	San Francisco, Cal	July 31, 1860	29, 376
Boiling and puddling furnace	J. I. Williams	Etna, Pa	May 12, 1868	77, 790
Boiling and puddling furnace	J. Zimmer	Pittsburgh, Pa	May 19, 1868	78, 172
Boiling and puddling furnaces, Chill-bosh for	T. Coates	Ironton, Ohio	June 7, 1870	103, 983
Boiling and puddling furnaces, Door and bit for	W. Sims	Pittsburgh, Pa	June 11, 1867	65, 773
Boiling and puddling furnaces, Fix for	J. D. Williams	Allegheny, Pa	Jan. 4, 1870	98, 534
Boiling-apparatus	J. McCormick	Madison, Ind	June 25, 1861	32, 636
Boiling liquids	R. M. Beach	Franklin, N. Y	Apr. 7, 1831	....
Bolster, Adjustable	G. Couch	Saint Louis, Mo	Oct. 31, 1871	120, 498
Bolster and pillow	T. S. Sperry	Chicago, Ill	Jan. 24, 1871	111, 270
Bolster for mattress, Adjustable	P. Kraher	Cincinnati, Ohio	Aug. 6, 1867	67, 436
Bolster, pillow, &c	C. P. Cooper	New York, N. Y	Oct. 7, 1873	143, 502
Bolster-plate	T. Morgan	Marquette, Mich	June 21, 1870	104, 628
Bolster-plates, Manufacture of	W. J. Lewis	Pittsburgh, Pa	July 29, 1873	141, 227
Bolster-plate, Manufacturing	W. J. Lewis and H. W. Oliver, jr	Pittsburgh, Pa	June 23, 1868	79, 237
Bolster, Spindle	I. P. Richards	Whitinsville, Mass	July 13, 1869	92, 647
Bolt:				
See Barn-door bolt.				
Barrel-bolt.				
Car-bolt.				
Carriage-bolt.				
Catch-bolt.				
Clover-bolt.				
Copper bolt.				
Cupboard-bolt.				
Door-bolt.				
Door and gate bolt.				
Draw-bolt.				
Expansion-bolt.				
Eye-bolt.				
Flour-bolt.				

Index of patents issued from the United States Patent Office from 1790 *to* 1873, *inclusive*—Continued.

Invention.	Inventor.	Residence.	Date.	No.
Bolt—Continued. *See* Flush-bolt. Guard-bolt. Insulating-bolt. Interlocked conical bolt. Key-bolt. King-bolt. Knob-bolt. Lathe-bilt. Lock-bolt. Locking-bolt. Middlings-bolt. Mill-bolt. Prison-door bolt. Rack-bolt. Rail-bolt. Safe-bolt. Safe-door bolt. Sash-bolt. Saw-frame bolt. Screw-bolt. Seal-bolt. Seal-locking bolt. Self-heading bolt. Self-locking bolt. Shingle-bolt. Ship-bolt. Shutter-bolt. Shutter-lock bolt. Slide-bolt. Spring-bolt. Spring-catch bolt. Square-necked bolt. Strap-bolt. T-bolt. Transient bolt. Tray bolt. Trunk-tray bolt. Wagon-box strap-bolt.				
Bolt	J. F. Carlin	Alexandria, Va	June 10, 1873	139, 767
Bolt	W. J. Clark	Southington, Conn	Oct. 20, 1863	40, 327
Bolt	W. C. Coles	Williamsburgh, N. Y	Apr. 4, 1871	113, 264
Bolt	T. A. Davies	New York, N. Y	Dec. 24, 1872	134, 262
Bolt	M. Harbster	Reading, Pa	July 26, 1870	105, 675
Bolt	G. Havell	Newark, N. J	Feb. 13, 1866	52, 570
Bolt	C. H. Hopkins	Lyndonville, Vt	Apr. 13, 1869	88, 959
Bolt	O. D. Hunter	Terrysville, Conn	Aug. 6, 1867	67, 549
Bolt	E. M. Judd	New Haven, Conn	Feb. 4, 1873	135, 560
Bolt	M. D. Kinkade	Brooklyn, N. Y	Mar. 12, 1872	124, 442
Bolt	P. Lecloux	Dijon, France	May 7, 1872	126, 404
Bolt	B. F. Lotridge	New York, N. Y	July 28, 1868	80, 295
Bolt	F. G. McClelland	Attica, Ohio	Nov. 29, 1870	109, 640
Bolt	J. H. Meissner	Jersey City, N. J	July 29, 1862	36, 014
Bolt	W. R. Miller	Baltimore, Md	Dec. 31, 1872	134, 391
Bolt	E. L. Roberts	Brooklyn, N. Y	July 27, 1869	93, 006
Bolt and bolt-head	J. Crompton	Little Falls, N. J	Apr. 9, 1867	63, 706
Bolt and latch	H. Baker	Lancaster, Pa	Jan. 21, 1868	73, 491
Bolt and nut machine, Combined	J. N. Smith	New Haven, Conn	Jan. 2, 1872	122, 411
Bolt and nut threading machine	F. S. Allen and C. F. Ritchel	New York, N. Y	Dec. 12, 1871	121, 743
Bolt and nut threading machine	J. Killefer	West Richfield, Ohio	June 15, 1869	91, 348
Bolt and rivet cutter	D. D. Cone and P. Polder	Panama, N. Y	July 1, 1873	140, 405
Bolt and rivet cutter	J. S. Henry and A. H. Reist	Manheim, Pa	Feb. 4, 1868	74, 087
Bolt and rivet cutter	C. B. Shaw	Victory, Wis	July 16, 1872	129, 370
Bolt and rivet heading machine	J. Van Brocklin	Middleport, N. Y	Aug. 20, 1850	7, 586
Bolt and rivet machine	N. Beauregard	San Francisco, Cal	Aug. 26, 1873	142, 193
Bolt and rivet machine	J. Morgan, jr	Wheeling, W. Va	Apr. 16, 1867	63, 927
Bolt and rivet machine	J. Morgan, jr	Wheeling, W. Va	May 21, 1867	64, 896
Bolt and rivet machine	J. Morgan, jr	Wheeling, W. Va	Apr. 26, 1870	102, 418
Bolt and rivet machine	J. C. Reed	Cincinnati, Ohio	Mar. 5, 1867	62, 565
Bolt and rivet machine	A. Reese	Pittsburgh, Pa	May 21, 1861	32, 381
Bolt and rivet machine	J. Wakefield	Birmingham, England	Dec. 10, 1867	72, 135
Bolt and rivet machine	W. E. Ward	Port Chester, N. Y	July 30, 1850	7, 538
Bolt and rivet machine	G. Worstenholm	Newark, N. J	Apr. 14, 1868	76, 873
Bolt and rivet making machine	J. R. Bassett	Cincinnati, Ohio	June 30, 1857	17, 660
Bolt and rivet making machine	J. Griffiths	Wheeling, W. Va	Feb. 6, 1872	123, 341
Bolt and rivet making machine	J. Paton, T. Campbell, and R. Paton.	Newburgh, Ohio	Nov. 29, 1864	45, 269
Bolt and rivet trimmer	M. D. Budd	Roscoe, Ill	June 4, 1867	65, 338
Bolt and rivet trimmer	M. Theisen	Waukon, Iowa	June 21, 1870	104, 509
Bolt and rod cutter	S. H. Preston	Worth, Pa	Apr. 15, 1873	137, 956
Bolt and rod cutter	H. Schmidt	Chicago, Ill	Sept. 2, 1873	142, 354
Bolt and rod cutter	L. H. Smith	Stryker, Ohio	Oct. 14, 1873	143, 645
Bolt and screw threading machine	R. Boeklen	New York, N. Y	June 17, 1873	139, 861
Bolt and spike drawing machine	J. C. Chapman	Charlestown, Mass	Jan. 6, 1863	37, 332
Bolt and spike drawing machine	H. E. Towle	Exeter, N. H	Sept. 3, 1861	33, 218
Bolt and spike heading machine	R. Boeklen	Brooklyn, N. Y	Mar. 7, 1871	112, 410
Bolt and spike making machine	J. S. Hall	Pittsburgh, Pa	July 28, 1868	80, 478
Bolt-blank	J. B. Clark	Plantsville, Conn	Nov. 2, 1869	96, 308
Bolt-blank-heating furnace	A. Alexander	Pittsburgh, Pa	Mar. 3, 1868	74, 970
Bolt-blanks, Apparatus for heating	J. B. Clark	Plantsville, Conn	June 20, 1871	116, 158
Bolt-blanks, Automatic feeder for	W. F. Parker	Meriden, Conn	June 4, 1867	65, 423
Bolt-blanks, Machine for upsetting	J. B. Clark	Plantsville, Conn	Jan. 16, 1872	122, 706
Bolt-clamp	C. E. Phillips	Deerfield, Mass	Dec. 21, 1869	98, 105
Bolt-cutter	A. S. Bailey	Knoxville, Ill	June 25, 1867	65, 989
Bolt-cutter	W. Britton	Abingdon, Ill	May 28, 1867	65, 161
Bolt-cutter	J. R. Brown	Cambridgeport, Mass	Sept. 20, 1870	107, 438
Bolt-cutter	J. R. Brown	Cambridgeport, Mass	July 4, 1871	116, 547
Bolt-cutter	J. R. Brown	Cambridgeport, Mass	Oct. 24, 1871	120, 149

Index of patents issued from the United States Patent Office from 1790 *to* 1873, *inclusive*—Continued.

Invention.	Inventor.	Residence.	Date.	No.
Bolt-cutter	J. R. Brown	Cambridgeport, Mass	Sept. 17, 1872	131, 423
Bolt-cutter	O. E. Butler and S. P. Dunham	Marshalltown, Iowa	Dec. 14, 1869	97, 874
Bolt-cutter	A. Carbnow	Potsdam, N. Y	May 19, 1868	78, 055
Bolt-cutter	L. J. Chapman	Vallejo, Cal	Feb. 18, 1873	135, 887
Bolt-cutter	C. Dreher	Detroit, Mich	Dec. 5, 1865	51, 300
Bolt-cutter	E. W. and R. Fawcett and W. E. Sefton.	Salem, Ohio	July 29, 1873	141, 265
Bolt-cutter	H. M. Handy	Niles, Mich	Apr. 9, 1867	63, 721
Bolt-cutter	W. W. Hill	Fulton, N. Y	Mar. 25, 1873	137, 076
Bolt-cutter	H. L. Howard	Mendon, Mich	Apr. 19, 1870	102, 006
Bolt-cutter	H. Howe	Oneonta, N. Y	July 28, 1868	80, 351
Bolt-cutter	J. Johnson	West Fallowfield Township, Pa.	June 4, 1867	65, 391
Bolt-cutter	J. Johnson	West Fallowfield Township, Pa.	Mar. 31, 1868	76, 197
Bolt-cutter	J. Johnson	Cochransville, Pa	Sept. 26, 1871	119, 231
Bolt-cutter	W. Mendham	Philadelphia, Pa	Apr. 19, 1870	102, 026
Bolt-cutter	F. Miller	Indianola, Ill	May 5, 1868	77, 637
Bolt-cutter	T. W. Moore	Richmond, Ind	Feb. 18, 1868	74, 575
Bolt-cutter	T. W. Moore	Richmond, Ind	Oct. 27, 1868	83, 525
Bolt-cutter	L. J. Newlan	Barton, N. Y	July 23, 1867	66, 986
Bolt-cutter	A. W. Owen and M. E. Lilley	East Canton, Pa	June 27, 1871	116, 478
Bolt-cutter	G. A. Ries	Belvidere, N. J	Oct. 17, 1865	50, 497
Bolt-cutter	J. S. Ryder	Sing Sing, N. Y	May 13, 1873	138, 940
Bolt-cutter	E. Schlenker	Buffalo, N. Y	July 4, 1865	48, 594
Bolt-cutter	R. Sischo	Tuscola, Ill	Oct. 10, 1865	50, 395
Bolt-cutter	E. A. Sloat	Theresa, N. Y	Jan. 7, 1868	73, 205
Bolt-cutter	O. J. Smith	Wauwatosa, Wis	Nov. 13, 1866	59, 673
Bolt-cutter	J. Strayer and T. Hazelhurst	South Bend, Ind	June 25, 1867	66, 107
Bolt-cutter	W. F. Strong	Charleston, S. C	Aug. 27, 1872	130, 880
Bolt-cutter	J. K. Taylor	Bridgeport, Conn	Dec. 11, 1860	30, 895
Bolt-cutter	J. Tomlinson	Onslow, Iowa	Feb. 4, 1873	135, 497
Bolt-cutter	J. Whittaker	Sandusky, N. Y	July 25, 1871	117, 495
Bolt-cutter	W. W. Worden	Waukesha, Wis	Dec. 31, 1867	72, 954
Bolt-cutter	W. W. Wright and J. Boody	Ellsworth, N. Y	June 4, 1867	65, 523
Bolt-cutter	W. E. Yeager	Lawrence, Kans	May 2, 1871	114, 383
Bolt cutting and shearing, Compound tool for	T. Smith	California, Mo	Sept. 1, 1868	81, 697
Bolt-cutting device	G. Adair and J. F. Pool	Monroe, Wis	Apr. 27, 1869	89, 267
Bolt-cutting device	L. Daniels	Oak Hill, N. Y	May 17, 1870	103, 152
Bolt-cutting machine	M. D. Budd	Roscoe, Ill	Dec. 24, 1861	33, 982
Bolt-cutting machine	J. A. Merriman	Chicago, Ill	Oct. 18, 1864	44, 773
Bolt-cutting shears	J. Guthrie	Wilmington, Del	Sept. 4, 1866	57, 705
Bolt-cutting shears	D. H. Hickok	Rockford, Ill	Feb. 20, 1866	52, 714
Bolt-cutting shears	G. W. Hyatt	Auburn, N. Y	May 23, 1865	47, 832
Bolt-cutting shears	S. W. Wright	Ellsworth, N. Y	Feb. 26, 1867	62, 462
Bolt cutting tool	J. E. Heath	Niles, Mich	Nov. 5, 1867	70, 563
Bolt die, Square-head	W. Shields	Philadelphia, Pa	Feb. 18, 1868	74, 616
Bolt die, Square-head	W. Shields	Philadelphia, Pa	Aug. 25, 1868	81, 419
Bolt die, T-head	W. J. Lewis	Pittsburgh, Pa	May 1, 1866	54, 377
Bolt-drawing machine	C. L. Stevenson	Charlestown, Mass	Oct. 26, 1858	21, 910
Bolt-drawing machine	S. Wilmarth	Charlestown, Mass	Nov. 29, 1859	26, 315
Bolt-fastening	J. M. Hopkins	New York, N. Y	May 1, 1866	54, 348
Bolt-fastening	V. Lapham	El Paso, Ill	Nov. 12, 1867	70, 866
Bolt-fastening	P. Peterson	Abingdon, Ill	Sept. 6, 1870	107, 096
Bolt-fastening	E. E. Stubbs	West Elkton, Ohio	Mar. 10, 1868	75, 488
Bolt-feeder	J. Cornwell	Kalamazoo, Mich	Mar. 23, 1869	88, 137
Bolt-feeder	O. Van Tassell	Naperville, Ill	Sept. 28, 1869	95, 289
Bolt feeder and cooler	W. Pickens	Chicago, Ill	Feb. 4, 1868	74, 125
Bolt-feeder for mills	B. A. Wing	Galesburgh, Mich	Feb. 22, 1870	100, 094
Bolt-forging machine, Die for	J. T. Willmarth	Northbridge, Mass	Apr. 17, 1855	12, 735
Bolt-head	F. S. Miles	Philadelphia, Pa	Oct. 13, 1868	82, 973
Bolt-head die, Square	J. Gribben	Allegheny, Pa	July 31, 1866	56, 745
Bolt-head-swaging die	A. Eames	Bridgeport, Conn	Aug. 9, 1859	25, 001
Bolt-head-trimming machine	M. Rugg	Southington, Conn	Aug. 31, 1842	2, 766
Bolt-head-trimming tool	A. P. Plant	Plantsville, Conn	June 8, 1869	91, 040
Bolt-head-turning machine	W. F. Swathel	Mount Carmel, Conn	Sept. 20, 1870	107, 561
Bolt-heading device	W. M. Thoroughgood	Salisbury, Md	May 13, 1873	138, 958
Bolt-heading device	J. M. Woods	Washington, Mo	Mar. 9, 1869	87, 747
Bolt-heading die	F. Bruso	Buffalo, N. Y	Sept. 6, 1870	107, 160
Bolt-heading die	J. B. Clark	Plantsville, Conn	Jan. 30, 1872	123, 084
Bolt-heading die	P. Eley	New York, N. Y	Apr. 4, 1871	113, 280
Bolt-heading die	C. Kane	Pittsburgh, Pa	May 15, 1866	54, 738
Bolt-heading die	C. Kane	Pittsburgh, Pa	Jan. 28, 1868	73, 728
Bolt-heading die	J. Kaylor	Pittsburgh, Pa	Mar. 16, 1869	87, 780
Bolt-heading die	W. J. Lewis	Pittsburgh, Pa	Mar. 31, 1868	76, 210
Bolt-heading machine	J. R. Abbe	Providence, R. I	Jan. 19, 1869	85, 983
Bolt-heading machine	J. R. Abbe	Providence, R. I	June 6, 1871	115, 555
Bolt-heading machine	H. E. Anthony	Providence, R. I	June 19, 1866	55, 597
Bolt-heading machine	O. C. Burdict	New Haven, Conn	Sept. 3, 1867	68, 555
Bolt-heading machine	O. C. Burdict	Providence, R. I	Nov. 30, 1869	97, 351
Bolt-heading machine	G. Chapman	Rockford, Ill	June 6, 1871	115, 702
Bolt-heading machine	H. M. Clark	New Britain, Conn	Jan. 15, 1856	14, 086
Bolt-heading machine	L. L. Davis	Laconia, N. H	Feb. 6, 1866	52, 393
Bolt-heading machine	P. Eley	New York, N. Y	Aug. 1, 1871	117, 527
Bolt-heading machine	A. B. Glover	Derby, Conn	June 19, 1866	55, 646
Bolt-heading machine	A. B. Glover	Birmingham, Conn	Mar. 17, 1868	75, 675
Bolt-heading machine	S. W. Goodyear and W. F. Parker.	Meriden, Conn	June 11, 1867	65, 561
Bolt-heading machine	R. Gracey	Pittsburgh, Pa	Dec. 17, 1867	72, 288
Bolt-heading machine	R. Gracey	Pittsburgh, Pa	Oct. 27, 1868	83, 376
Bolt-heading machine	W. Grant	Boston, Mass	Dec. 26, 1848	5, 986
Bolt-heading machine	J. Greenwood	Fitchburgh, Mass	Feb. 20, 1872	123, 822
Bolt-heading machine	C. Hall	New York, N. Y	Aug. 12, 1873	141, 711
Bolt-heading machine	C. Hall and E. Hubner	New York, N. Y	Sept. 18, 1866	58, 096
Bolt-heading machine	T. Hull and N. Thomas	Chicago, Ill	Feb. 28, 1871	112, 248
Bolt-heading machine	C. E. Hunter	Hinsdale, N. H	Jan. 2, 1872	122, 385
Bolt-heading machine	J. O. Jones	Brooklyn, N. Y	July 22, 1873	141, 059
Bolt-heading machine	C. and J. Kane	Pittsburgh, Pa	Apr. 10, 1866	53, 831

Index of patents issued from the United States Patent Office from 1790 *to* 1873, *inclusive*—Continued.

Invention.	Inventor.	Residence.	Date.	No.
Bolt-heading machine	E. Kaylor	Pittsburgh, Pa	Oct. 24, 1865	50, 599
Bolt-heading machine	E. Kaylor	Pittsburgh, Pa	June 12, 1866	55, 501
Bolt-heading machine	L. Kirkup	Brooklyn, N. Y	Feb. 6, 1866	52, 494
Bolt-heading machine	W. J. Lewis	Pittsburgh, Pa	Mar. 15, 1864	41, 929
Bolt-heading machine	M. D. Marcy	Worcester, Mass	Feb. 20, 1866	52, 727
Bolt-heading machine	J. W. McDermott	New York, N. Y	Feb. 6, 1866	52, 433
Bolt-heading machine	W. Melvell	Paterson, N. J	July 21, 1868	80, 198
Bolt-heading machine	J. Minter	Worcester, Mass	July 12, 1864	43, 521
Bolt-heading machine	J. Minter	Lowell, Mass	July 10, 1866	56, 247
Bolt-heading machine	D. G. Morrill	Catasauqua, Pa	Aug. 24, 1869	94, 021
Bolt-heading machine	F. B. Prindle	Southington, Conn	Dec. 31, 1867	72, 899
Bolt heading machine	F. B. Prindle	Southington, Conn	Jan. 11, 1870	98, 798
Bolt-heading machine	T. T. Prosser	Chicago, Ill	Apr. 13, 1869	88, 981
Bolt-heading machine	J. Root	New Haven, Conn	Oct. 29, 1867	70, 363
Bolt-heading machine	J. Root	New Haven, Conn	Mar. 3, 1868	75, 198
Bolt-heading machine	J. Root	New Haven, Conn	Mar. 23, 1869	88, 214
Bolt-heading machine	J. Root	New Haven, Conn	Mar. 15, 1870	100, 928
Bolt-heading machine	F. Schweizer	New York, N. Y	Nov. 7, 1865	50, 848
Bolt-heading machine	F. Schweizer	New York, N. Y	Mar. 20, 1866	53, 351
Bolt-heading machine	F. Schweizer	Green Point, N. Y	June 8, 1869	91, 171
Bolt-heading machine	N. Starks	Albany, N. Y	Dec. 23, 1851	8, 616
Bolt-heading machine	W. Swathel	Southington, Conn	Nov. 19, 1867	71, 243
Bolt-heading machine	H. Thompson	Worcester, Mass	Mar. 3, 1868	75, 221
Bolt-heading machine	P. P. Trayser	Baltimore, Md	Feb. 5, 1867	61, 896
Bolt-heading machine	A. Tucker	Gilford, N. H	Feb. 27, 1866	52, 912
Bolt-heading machine	B. C. Vanduzen	Cincinnati, Ohio	Mar. 22, 1859	23, 328
Bolt-heading machine	B. Walker	Birmingham, Conn	Oct. 23, 1866	59, 100
Bolt-heading machine	F. Watkins	Birmingham, England	Feb. 14, 1865	46, 434
Bolt-heading machine	C. D. Wiley and M. S. Norton	Junction, Minn	June 18, 1872	128, 083
Bolt-heading-machine die	J. Gribben	Allegheny, Pa	Aug. 21, 1866	57, 313
Bolt-heading-machine die	J. W. Tibbet	Cincinnati, Ohio	Sept. 4, 1866	57, 781
Bolt heads, Machine for making	C. H. and J. F. Emerson	New York, N. Y	Apr. 20, 1869	89, 211
Bolt-heads, Machine for making	M. D. Marcy	Worcester, Mass	Aug. 24, 1869	94, 122
Bolt-holder	S. R. Butterfield	Rome, N. Y	June 14, 1870	104, 264
Bolt-holder	B. Perry and A. Cornish	Lee, N. Y	May 21, 1867	64, 904
Bolt-holder	G. W. Phelps	Conneaut, Ohio	Aug. 11, 1868	80, 998
Bolt-keeper	J. M. Mitchell	Cincinnati, Ohio	May 16, 1871	114, 841
Bolt-keeper	G. M. Wood	Decatur, Ill	Oct. 16, 1866	58, 929
Bolt-keys, Machine for making	N. Adams	Altoona, Pa	Oct. 15, 1867	69, 740
Bolt-locking device	A. McKenny	Maumee City, Ohio	Aug. 1, 1871	117, 657
Bolt-machine	J. R. Abbe	Providence, R. I	Mar. 8, 1870	100, 581
Bolt-machine	A. Alexander	Pittsburgh, Pa	Aug. 15, 1865	49, 484
Bolt-machine	A. R. Bailey and W. W. Knowles.	New Haven and Plantsville, Conn.	Nov. 19, 1867	70, 939
Bolt-machine	H. Carter	Pittsburgh, Pa	Mar. 2, 1858	19, 485
Bolt-machine	D. S. Coe	Pine Meadow, Conn	June 27, 1871	116, 270
Bolt-machine	J. L. Hall	Abington, Mass	June 1, 1869	90, 661
Bolt-machine	M. Hardaway	Saint Louis, Mo	Apr. 13, 1869	88, 783
Bolt-machine	W. W. Hubbard	Philadelphia, Pa	Nov. 19, 1867	71, 012
Bolt-machine	J. O. Jones	Brooklyn, N. Y	Apr. 8, 1873	137, 688
Bolt-machine	C. and J. Kane	Pittsburgh, Pa	Apr. 10, 1866	53, 832
Bolt-machine	E. Kaylor	Pittsburgh, Pa	Aug. 22, 1865	49, 532
Bolt-machine	A. Marcellus	Rockford, Ill	Aug. 29, 1865	49, 638
Bolt-machine	H. M. Phillips	Indianapolis, Ind	Sept. 19, 1865	50, 028
Bolt-machine	E. Simkins	Allegheny, Pa	Aug. 24, 1858	21, 279
Bolt-machine	T. F. Taft	Fitchburgh, Mass	Feb. 12, 1856	14, 258
Bolt-machine	A. A. Wilder	Detroit, Mich	Nov. 19, 1872	133, 135
Bolt-machine	S. B. Wilkins and A. Marcellus	Rockford, Ill	June 17, 1873	140, 103
Bolt-machine, Method of constructing and operating the header in.	D. L. Weatherhead	Providence, R. I	May 8, 1849	6, 438
Bolt-making	D. E. Adams	Allegheny City, Pa	Sept. 18, 1866	58, 040
Bolt-making die	J. T. Willmarth	Northbridge, Mass	Jan. 16, 1855	12, 262
Bolt making machine	A. Alexander	Pittsburgh, Pa	Dec. 17, 1867	72, 152
Bolt-making machine	A. Alexander	Pittsburgh, Pa	Dec. 17, 1867	72, 153
Bolt-making machine	A. Charbono	Worcester, Mass	July 9, 1872	128, 853
Bolt-making machine	R. H. Cole	Saint Louis, Mo	Nov. 3, 1857	18, 534
Bolt-making machine	R. Crichton	Buchanan, Pa	May 8, 1855	12, 815
Bolt-making machine	C. Hall and E. Hubner	New York, N. Y	Mar. 27, 1866	53, 531
Bolt-making machine	M. Hardaway	Saint Louis, Mo	Oct. 11, 1864	44, 623
Bolt-making machine	W. Klemm and R. Dittrich	Pittsburgh, Pa	Feb. 25, 1868	74, 834
Bolt-making machine	E. B. Locke	Exeter, N. H	Mar. 30, 1869	88, 493
Bolt-making machine	C. Lusted	New York, N. Y	Sept. 12, 1865	49, 902
Bolt-making machine	W. E. Ward	Port Chester, N. Y	July 10, 1855	13, 241
Bolt-making machine	W. E. Ward	Port Chester, N. Y	May 12, 1863	38, 518
Belt making machine	F. Watkins	Birmingham, England	Dec. 8, 1868	84, 782
Bolt-making-machine die	R. Gracey	Pittsburgh, Pa	Oct. 27, 1868	83, 377
Bolt-reel	B. C. White	Des Moines, Iowa	Jan. 31, 1871	111, 501
Bolt-screwing and nut-tapping machine	W. W. Hubbard	Philadelphia, Pa	Feb. 6, 1866	52, 415
Bolt-screwing machine	A. Babbett	Auburn, N. Y	Dec. 19, 1865	51, 538
Bolt-straightening machine	C. E. Hunter	Hinsdale, N. H	Feb. 21, 1871	111, 941
Bolt-tapping machine	F. Watkins	Birmingham, England	Dec. 13, 1864	45, 452
Bolt-thread-cutting machine	J. J. Grant	Northampton, Mass	Nov. 16, 1869	96, 910
Bolt-threader	G. W. Mingus	Pomeroy, Ohio	May 31, 1870	103, 642
Bolt-threading die	A. Belaieff	St. Petersburg, Russia	July 13, 1869	92, 567
Bolt-threading die	J. E. Weaver	Temperanceville, Pa	June 14, 1870	104, 234
Bolt-threading machine	B. D. Beecher	Plantsville, Conn	May 12, 1868	77, 710
Bolt-threading machine	W. B. Bement	Philadelphia, Pa	Mar. 10, 1868	75, 239
Bolt-threading machine	O. P. and L. W. Briggs	Chicago, Ill	May 16, 1871	115, 009
Bolt-threading machine	O. C. Burton	Unionville, Conn	Jan. 16, 1872	122, 702
Bolt-threading machine	C. E. DeValin	Baltimore, Md	Nov. 2, 1869	96, 403
Bolt-threading machine	G. Emig	Cincinnati, Ohio	Dec. 3, 1872	133, 574
Bolt-threading machine	G. W. Frosst	Richmond, Va	May 14, 1872	126, 689
Bolt-threading machine	J. J. Grant	Greenfield, Mass	May 14, 1872	126, 602
Bolt-threading machine	M. Hamlin	Catawissa, Pa	July 19, 1870	105, 568
Bolt-threading machine	M. Hamlin	Catawissa, Pa	July 19, 1870	105, 569
Bolt-threading machine	M. Hine	New Haven, Conn	Mar. 29, 1870	101, 366
Bolt-threading machine	M. Hine	New Haven, Conn	Sept. 23, 1873	143, 154
Bolt-threading machine	W. Johnson	Lambertville, N. J	Aug. 24, 1869	93, 998

Index of patents issued from the United States Patent Office from 1790 *to* 1873, *inclusive*—Continued.

Invention.	Inventor.	Residence.	Date.	No.
Bolt-threading machine	M. Love	Corry, Pa	Nov. 22, 1870	109, 433
Bolt-threading machine	H. Martin	Louisville, Ky	Mar. 14, 1871	112, 612
Bolt-threading machine	H. Martin	Louisville, Ky	Mar. 28, 1871	113, 072
Bolt-threading machine	S. W. Putnam, jr	Fitchburgh, Mass	Jan. 24, 1871	111, 248
Bolt-threading machine	J. F. Rodgers	South Bend, Ind	Dec. 5, 1865	51, 355
Bolt-threading machine	C. Schneider	Newark, N. J	Nov. 14, 1871	120, 903
Bolt-threading machine	J. Schuessler and J. Kennedy	La Fayette, Ind	Sept. 15, 1868	82, 252
Bolt-threading machine	F. Schweizer	New York, N. Y	Mar. 5, 1867	62, 693
Bolt-threading machine	W. Sellers	Philadelphia, Pa	Dec. 1, 1857	18, 775
Bolt-threading machine	N. Thomas	Chicago, Ill	Jan. 25, 1870	99, 259
Bolt-threading machine	J. B. Wiggenhorn	Saint Louis, Mo	Nov. 2, 1869	96, 372
Bolt-threading machine	A. Wood	Worcester, Mass	July 7, 1868	79, 714
Bolt-threading machine	S. H. Wright	Lowell, Mass	Oct. 3, 1871	119, 681
Bolt-threading machine	S. H. Wright	Lowell, Mass	Apr. 30, 1872	126, 170
Bolt-threading, Lubricating-device for	W. Armstrong	Kent, Ohio	Oct. 25, 1870	108, 673
Bolt-trimmer	J. Blackinton	Roscoe, Ill	Oct. 22, 1867	69, 962
Bolt-trimmer	W. Dunlop	Fullerton, Canada	Dec. 17, 1872	133, 972
Bolt-trimmer	H. Howe	Oneonta, N. Y	June 18, 1867	65, 913
Bolt-trimmer	G. W. Lewis	Dansville, N. Y	Dec. 8, 1868	84, 701
Bolt-trimmer	A. B. White	Mendon, Mich	Apr. 14, 1868	76, 863
Bolt-trimming machine	A. Ford	Harmonsburgh, Pa	Sept. 10, 1872	131, 159
Bolt-trimming machine	W. Hannah	Middlefield, N. Y	Dec. 23, 1856	16, 301
Bolt-turning tool	L. Burns	Port Chester, Pa	Feb. 26, 1867	62, 390
Bolt-upsetting machine	B. and J. A. Briscoe	Detroit, Mich	Mar. 21, 1871	112, 775
Bolt-washer	D. Cumming, jr	Brooklyn, N. Y	Nov. 5, 1872	132, 807
Bolt-washer	G. G. Hickman	Coatesville, Pa	Aug. 14, 1866	57, 132
Bolt-washer	G. G. Hickman	Coatesville, Pa	Sept. 10, 1867	68, 742
Bolts and nuts, Machine for making	G. R. Postlethwaite	Birmingham, Great Britain	Jan. 17, 1871	111, 082
Bolts and rivets, Apparatus for clipping	Z. B. Cotant	Greenwich Station, Ohio	May 19, 1863	38, 564
Bolts and rivets, Machine for making	J. Howden	Glasgow, Scotland	May 10, 1864	42, 731
Bolts and rivets, Making	J. R. Bassett	Cincinnati, Ohio	Mar. 1, 1859	23, 138
Bolts and rivets, Manufacture of	W. Livingstone	Brooklyn, N. Y	Mar. 18, 1873	137, 009
Bolts and spikes, Drawing	R. Haynes	Portsmouth, Va	July 2, 1836	......
Bolts by hydraulic pressure, Machine for drawing	S. Wilmarth	Boston, Mass	Jan. 3, 1865	45, 785
Bolts, Cutter-head for pointing the ends of	O. C. Burdict	Buffalo, N. Y	Feb. 4, 1873	135, 520
Bolts, Device for cutting off	T. J. Emery	Charlestown, Mass	May 7, 1872	126, 384
Bolts, Device for rounding the ends of	J. I. Schermerhorn	Schenectady, N. Y	Nov. 11, 1873	144, 569
Bolts, Die for making	W. J. Clark	Southington, Conn	Oct. 18, 1864	44, 706
Bolts, Heading	E. and P. Coleman	Philadelphia, Pa	Sept. 16, 1856	15, 729
Bolts, Heading	J. Weathers	Greensburgh, Ind	June 11, 1861	32, 545
Bolts, Heading	G. Woodward	Brunswick, Me	Mar. 4, 1856	14, 381
Bolts, Machine for cutting off	H. M. Powers	Lancaster, Pa	Jan. 30, 1872	123, 124
Bolts, Machine for cutting off the ends of	J. Rewey	Berkshire, N. Y	May 8, 1811	
Bolts, Machine for cutting threads on	W. W. Hubbard	Philadelphia, Pa	Aug. 22, 1865	49, 524
Bolts, &c., Machinery for heading	E. Page	Albany, N. Y	Dec. 28, 1852	9, 506
Bolts, &c., Machinery for securing	J. Caswell	Syracuse, N. Y	Nov. 30, 1852	9, 428
Bolts, Manufacture of	W. J. Lewis	Pittsburgh, Pa	Apr. 4, 1865	47, 113
Bolts, Manufacture of	A. Nailer	Buffalo, N. Y	May 3, 1870	102, 566
Bolts, Method of making	W. J. Clark	Southington, Conn	Aug. 2, 1864	43, 669
Bolts, nuts, &c., Mode of squaring and finishing the heads of.	J. Bellemere	Philadelphia, Pa	Sept. 25, 1839	1, 342
Bolts or rivets, Machine for pointing	J. Stackler	West Winsted, Conn	May 25, 1869	90, 602
Bolts, rivets, and nails, Mode of attaching the heads of.	G. B. Brayton	Providence, R. I	May 26, 1863	38, 652
Bolts, rods, &c., Tool for cutting off	H. Peters	Davenport, Iowa	June 7, 1870	104, 061
Bolts, Socket for	H. W. Collender	New York, N. Y	Sept. 15, 1857	18, 193
Bolts, Threading	H. Abbott	Wakeman, Ohio	Apr. 17, 1860	27, 943
Bolts, Trimming or cutting	H. Beckwith	Grass Lake, Mich	Mar. 24, 1863	37, 943
Bolting-chest	J. Bell	Belleville, Ill	Apr. 9, 1861	31, 947
Bolting-chest	M. C. Cogswell and J. McKiernan	Buffalo, N. Y	June 12, 1860	28, 654
Bolting-cloth to reel, Mode of attaching	J. Woodville	Chillicothe, Ohio	Apr. 21, 1857	17, 126
Bolting-cloth to reel, Securing	G. M. Elliott	Hagerstown, Md	Mar. 19, 1834	
Bolting, dusting, and separating the ground material, Machinery for.	J. Woodward	Philadelphia, Pa	Apr. 6, 1858	19, 892
Bolting-machine	H. Cabanes	Bordeaux, France	Nov. 18, 1873	144, 739
Bolting-machine	J. H. Jones	Dayton, Ohio	Sept. 10, 1872	131, 278
Bolting-mill	E. H. Vittecoq	Beaumontel, France	Jan. 3, 1865	45, 802
Bolting-reel	J. T. Agner	Lexington, Va	May 11, 1869	89, 963
Bolting-reel	S. Corsett and O. D. Lowe	Middleville, Mich	July 4, 1871	116, 685
Bolting-reel	F. B. Lewis	Tiffin, Ohio	Sept. 20, 1870	107, 512
Bomb for killing whales	N. Schofield and W. W. Wright	Norwich, Conn	Mar. 10, 1857	16, 819
Bomb-lance	P. B. Comins	San Francisco, Cal	May 3, 1859	23, 827
Bomb-lance for killing whales	S. Barker	Hartford, Conn	Feb. 21, 1865	46, 437
Bomb or mine, Subterrene	J. MacGregor, jr	Wilton, N. Y	Mar. 23, 1842	2, 502
Bomb, shell, or grenade	E. T. Miller	Boston, Mass	Nov. 7, 1854	11, 901
Bombs, lances, and other projectiles, Guide for	I. Goodspeed and C. Crawley	Norwich, Conn	July 16, 1861	32, 830
Bonds, &c., Filing and recording	F. Munson	Chicago, Ill	Apr. 2, 1867	63, 419
Bonds, Mode of preventing the stealing of	J. Myers, jr	Brooklyn, E. D., N. Y	Mar. 15, 1870	100, 788
Bonds, &c., Preventing alteration in numbers on	G. W. Casilear	Washington, D. C	Nov. 24, 1868	84, 341
Bone and plaster mill	S. W. Powell	Brookville, Md	Dec. 17, 1867	72, 418
Bone-black. *See* Charcoal, Animal.				
Bone-black, Apparatus and process for revivifying.	A. Lonsky	Hoboken, N. J	Jan. 7, 1873	134, 686
Bone-black, Apparatus for cooling and purifying	D. H. Turner	New York, N. Y	May 12, 1868	77, 935
Bone-black, Apparatus for revivifying	C. N. Brock	Philadelphia, Pa	July 2, 1861	32, 679
Bone-black, Apparatus for revivifying	G. Finken	New York, N. Y	Aug. 25, 1863	39, 637
Bone-black, Artificial	H. Endemann	New York, N. Y	Mar. 9, 1869	87, 653
Bone-black cleaning and purifying machine	R. Ficken and F. L. Williams	Philadelphia, Pa	Mar. 5, 1867	62, 537
Bone-black-cooling apparatus	C. H. Senff	New York, N. Y	June 27, 1871	116, 361
Bone-black drier	P. Farley	New York, N. Y	Apr. 18, 1871	113, 754
Bone-black equalizer	D. Brasill and D. A. Mullane	New Orleans, La	Aug. 17, 1869	93, 668
Bone-black for filtering, Artificial	W. H. Kelsey	Cleveland, Ohio	Jan. 9, 1872	122, 526
Bone-black furnace, Apparatus for emptying the cooling-tubes of.	E. Langen	Cologne, Prussia	Aug. 3, 1869	93, 208
Bone-black, Furnace for reburning	G. Thulemeyer	New York, N. Y	Oct. 20, 1863	40, 371
Bone-black kiln	J. O. Donner	Jersey City, N. J	Nov. 16, 1869	96, 899

Index of patents issued from the United States Patent Office from 1790 to 1873, inclusive—Continued.

Invention.	Inventor.	Residence.	Date.	No.
Bone-black kiln	E. P. Eastwick	Baltimore, Md	Dec. 18, 1866	60, 492
Bone-black kiln	E. P. Eastwick	Baltimore, Md	Apr. 6, 1869	88, 700
Bone-black kiln	E. P. Eastwick	Baltimore, Md	Apr. 6, 1869	88, 701
Bone-black kiln	E. P. Eastwick	Baltimore, Md	Apr. 6, 1869	88, 702
Bone-black, Kiln for reburning	E. P. Eastwick	Baltimore, Md	May 16, 1871	114, 780
Bone-black kiln, Reburning and purifying	A. Weber	New York, N. Y	June 4, 1867	65, 457
Bone-black, Manufacture of	C. Y. Beach	Brooklyn, N. Y	Sept. 19, 1871	119, 005
Bone-black, Oven for reburning	W. Moller	New York, N. Y	Aug. 19, 1862	36, 230
Bone-black, Purifying	T. H. Quick	New York, N. Y	May 15, 1866	54, 771
Bone-black, Purifying	T. H. Quick	New York, N. Y	Nov. 26, 1867	71, 536
Bone-black purifying, screening, and cooling apparatus, Reburnt.	M. Hanford	Boston, Mass	May 18, 1869	90, 097
Bone-black reburning and ore-reducing furnace	A. Weber	New York, N. Y	July 26, 1870	105, 747
Bone-black, Revivification of	H. Kattenhorn	New York, N. Y	Jan. 25, 1859	22, 734
Bone-black revivifying	W. Bellows	Cincinnati, Ohio	Dec. 13, 1859	26, 457
Bone-black, Revivifying	J. Forrest	New York, N. Y	Aug. 25, 1863	39, 638
Bone-black-revivifying apparatus	W. Mitchell	New York, N. Y	Mar. 13, 1860	27, 462
Bone-black, Treating and revivifying	J. Rogers and L. Reid	Brooklyn, N. Y	July 20, 1869	92, 751
Bone-black-washing apparatus	C. Kinzler	New York, N. Y	July 10, 1860	29, 128
Bone burning or charring pot, Construction of	C. W. Pierce	Albany, N. Y	June 11, 1867	65, 597
Bone-charcoal, Retort for revivifying	G. A. Jasper	Charlestown, Mass	June 4, 1867	65, 389
Bone handle for canes, &c	J. Harvey	Philadelphia, Pa	July 9, 1867	66, 586
Bone-mill	E. P. Baugh	Philadelphia, Pa	Mar. 7, 1865	46, 627
Bone, &c., Mill for pulverizing	A. Newell	Red Wing, Minn	Sept. 8, 1868	81, 933
Bone setting apparatus	J. H. Willard	Brown Elm, Ohio	June 11, 1836	
Bones for manure, &c., Mode of grinding	J. Wister	Greencastle, Pa	May 8, 1866	54, 635
Bones, refuse meat, &c., Apparatus for boiling	R. W. Thing	Winchester, Mass	June 18, 1872	127, 995
Bonnet	S. A. Blake	New York, N. Y	Dec. 24, 1861	33, 978
Bonnet	A. Henri	Louisville, Ky	May 1, 1860	28, 082
Bonnet	F. Howard	Somerville, Mass	June 7, 1864	43, 028
Bonnet	S. H. Lyon and W. E. Doubleday	Brooklyn, N. Y	Mar. 19, 1861	31, 724
Bonnet and bonnet-frame pressing machine	W. Osborn	Louisville, Ky	Aug. 19, 1856	15, 570
Bonnet and hat pressing machine	E. Copleston	Wrentham, Mass	Aug. 15, 1865	49, 384
Bonnet and hat pressing machine	C. Merritt	Baltimore, Md	Mar. 13, 1844	3, 477
Bonnet-binding, Making	J. L. Weaver	Orange, Mass	Jan. 31, 1865	46, 163
Bonnet-box	C. A. Taylor	Chicago, Ill	June 26, 1860	28, 916
Bonnet-forming machine	C. O. Parmenter	Amherst, Mass	Mar. 25, 1862	34, 771
Bonnet-frame	G. O. Cooper and C. Southworth	Stoughton, Mass	Mar. 20, 1866	53, 274
Bonnet-frame	G. H. Hawkins	New York, N. Y	July 22, 1862	35, 934
Bonnet-frame	W. E. Kidd	New York, N. Y	Apr. 13, 1858	19, 932
Bonnet-frame clamp	H. A. Reynolds	New York, N. Y	May 1, 1860	28, 131
Bonnet-frames, Machine for forming	S. H. Bowker	Worcester, Mass	Feb. 2, 1858	19, 231
Bonnet-frames, Machine for stiffening netting for	P. C. Ritchie	New York, N. Y	Feb. 11, 1873	135, 730
Bonnet-frames, Manufacture of	R. T. Wilde	New York, N. Y	Apr. 24, 1860	28, 028
Bonnet-frames, Mode of constructing wire	H. Weed	Philadelphia, Pa	June 27, 1854	11, 186
Bonnet-frames, Mold for pressing	N. Spence	New York, N. Y	Nov. 28, 1854	12, 004
Bonnet-front former	G. A. Cox	Brooklyn, N. Y	Jan. 17, 1860	26, 836
Bonnet-fronts, Mold for pressing	W. E. Kidd	New York, N. Y	Nov. 28, 1854	11, 996
Bonnet, Portable	T. Hammond	New York, N. Y	Oct. 30, 1844	3, 809
Bonnet-pressing machine	G. M. Richardson	Barre, Mass	Oct. 2, 1866	58, 555
Bonnet-pressing machine	C. W. Russell	Philadelphia, Pa	Aug. 16, 1859	25, 219
Bonnet-pressing machine	S. and H. Squire	Monson, Mass	Nov. 12, 1867	70, 912
Bonnet-pressing machine	H. E. West	Attleborough, Mass	Jan. 29, 1861	31, 274
Bonnet-pressing machinery	R. Murdoch	Baltimore, Md	Oct. 12, 1842	2, 817
Bonnet-stands, Branch-holder for	J. R. Palmenbery	New York, N. Y	Aug. 2, 1859	24, 950
Bonnet-tips, Apparatus for pressing	T. Kendall	New York, N. Y	Sept. 3, 1844	3, 728
Bonnets and cap-fronts, &c , Machine for manufacturing.	W. H. Morrison	Nottingham, England	Oct. 18, 1859	25, 847
Bonnets and hats and other manufactures of straw, Manner of pressing and finishing	W. Chaplin	New York, N. Y	Sept. 10, 1840	1, 785
Bonnets and hats, Manufacturing grass	G. and S. Wells	Wethersfield, Conn	Dec. 29, 1821	
Bonnets and hats, Pressing straw	O. Plimpton	Foxborough, Mass	Dec. 28, 1832	
Bonnets and other articles of varying thickness, Machine for pressing straw.	H. E. West	Norton, Mass	July 6, 1858	20, 837
Bonnets, Machine for trimming straw-plait for	E. Smith	Franklin, Mass	Mar. 30, 1808	
Bonnets, Manufacturing	T. Bracher	New York, N. Y	Dec. 3, 1861	33, 872
Bonnets, Method of shaping	C. W. Russell	Philadelphia, Pa	Aug. 16, 1859	25, 218
Bonnets, Pressing	C. C. Dow	Windham, Conn	July 10, 1849	6, 585
Bonnets, &c., Pressing straw	S. Pittee	Foxborough, Mass	Sept. 14, 1825	
Book and manuscript holder	J. E. D. Comstock	New York, N. Y	July 10, 1866	56, 184
Book and method of binding, Copy	W. Davison	Baltimore, Md	Oct. 9, 1841	2, 286
Book and paper clamp	J. P. McLean	Brooklyn, N. Y	Sept. 23, 1873	143, 088
Book and paper trimming machine	G. Utley	Chapel Hill, N. C	Aug. 7, 1860	29, 532
Book and slate, Combined	F. Shepherd	New Haven, Conn	Nov. 2, 1858	21, 984
Book-backs, Machine for molding	J. K. Max	Springfield, Mass	Mar. 12, 1867	62, 767
Book-backs, Machine for shaping and finishing	G. H. Sanborn and J. E. Coffin	Boston, Mass., and Portland, Me.	Sept. 20, 1859	25, 548
Book-binder, Schoolboy's	T. Goodrum	Providence, R. I	Oct. 16, 1866	58, 940
Book-binders and others, Material for paste for	I. L. Plumer	Chelsea, Mass	Aug. 23, 1870	106, 617
Book-binder's beveling-machine	W. P. Chase	Boston Mass	May 19, 1868	77, 958
Book-binder's beveling-machine	H. L. Tumy	Cincinnati, Ohio	Dec. 17, 1867	72, 243
Book-binder's board, Drying	J. H. Longbotham	Brooklyn, N. Y	Jan. 3, 1854	10, 375
Book-binder's boards, Machinery for cutting	G. S. Schofield	Philadelphia, Pa	June 16, 1846	4, 575
Book-binder's clamp	G. F. Holland	Boston, Mass	June 11, 1872	127, 882
Book-binder's cloth-cutting table	C. Lemon	Washington, D C	Dec. 27, 1864	45, 620
Book-binder's cutting-press	C. Stimpson, jr	Boston, Mass	Oct. 17, 1831	
Book-binder's cutting press	J. J. Wells	Hartford, Conn	Mar. 23, 1824	
Book-binder's head-band	J. Schlichting	New York, N. Y	Apr. 6, 1869	88, 587
Book-binders, Ornamenting rolls and stamps for	D. H. Mason	Philadelphia, Pa	Jan. 26, 1826	
Book-binder's prepared paste	J. Woodward	Springfield, Mass	Feb. 20, 1866	52, 779
Book-binder's roll	J. Feely	New York, N. Y	Mar. 31, 1868	76, 065
Book-binder's sewing-table	M. T. Lincoln	Washington, D. C	Oct. 30, 1866	59, 240
Book-binder's standing press	M. K. Pelletreau	New York, N. Y	Oct. 2, 1860	30, 243
Book-binders, Supplemental table for	G. P. Goff	Washington, D. C	July 5, 1864	43, 456
Book-binder's use, Manufacture of gold-leaf for	R. E. Hastings	Philadelphia, Pa	Dec. 30, 1873	146, 001
Book-binding	W. I. Blackman	Columbus, Miss	May 4, 1869	89, 622
Book-binding	W Daniels	Brooklyn, N. Y	Dec. 17, 1867	72, 373
Book-binding	R. De Silver	Philadelphia, Pa	Sept. 14, 1812	

Index of patents issued from the United States Patent Office from 1790 *to* 1873, *inclusive*—Continued.

Invention.	Inventor.	Residence.	Date.	No.
Book-binding	W. Hancock	Great Britain	Oct. 28, 1837	444
Book-binding	A. Holbrook, jr	Lynn, Mass	June 23, 1868	79, 123
Book-binding	A. H. Jocelyn	New York, N. Y	Dec. 29, 1868	85, 450
Book-binding	J. S. Lever	Philadelphia, Pa	Nov. 10, 1868	83, 980
Book-binding	L. G. Matthews	New Albany, Ind	Dec. 1, 1868	84, 564
Book-binding	J. Meer	Philadelphia, Pa	Aug. 26, 1818	....
Book-binding	G. H. Reynolds	New York, N. Y	Feb. 22, 1870	100, 069
Book-binding	I. Reynolds	Dayton, Ohio	Dec. 21, 1869	98, 191
Book-binding	I. Reynolds	Dayton, Ohio	Jan. 23, 1872	122, 965
Book-binding	J. L. Rile	New York, N. Y	June 13, 1871	115, 896
Book-binding	A. H. Rowand	Allegheny, Pa	May 12, 1857	17, 299
Book-binding	D. Shive	Philadelphia, Pa	Dec. 21, 1869	98, 200
Book-binding	H. M. Shute	Waukegan, Ill	Feb. 4, 1868	74, 014
Book-binding	G. Smith	Bridgeport, Conn	Feb. 20, 1872	123, 947
Book-binding	W. Smith	New York, N. Y	June 23, 1868	79, 269
Book-binding	D. M. Smyth	Orange, N. J	Oct. 10, 1871	119, 894
Book-binding	J. T. Sullivan	Philadelphia, Pa	July 27, 1812	....
Book-binding	J. C. Terry	Springfield, Conn	Aug. 9, 1870	106, 234
Book-binding	J. Torrey, jr	Germantown, Pa	Aug. 8, 1829	....
Book-binding	T. Towndrow	New York, N. Y	May 29, 1860	28, 521
Book-binding apparatus	I. Reynolds	Dayton, Ohio	July 4, 1871	116, 757
Book-binding machine	J. Glass	Green Point, N. Y	May 2, 1871	114, 286
Book-binding machine	R. G. Lowrey	Brooklyn, N. Y	June 6, 1871	115, 621
Book, Blank	J. C. Bonnell	Burlington, Iowa	Feb. 11, 1873	135, 760
Book, Blank	H. Fischer	Chicago, Ill	Dec. 15, 1868	84, 869
Book, Blank account	C. Hopkins	New York, N. Y	Nov. 27, 1849	6, 905
Book-brace	W. Ives	Buffalo, N. Y	Jan. 23, 1855	12, 279
Book-case	A. Lamb	Cambridge, Mass	Apr. 16, 1861	32, 069
Book-case, Folding	E. Haskell	Dover, N. H	Apr. 22, 1873	138, 022
Book-case for schools, &c	P. T. Vannice	Kewanee, Ill	Jan. 10, 1871	110, 941
Book-case, Portable	E. Haskell	Canton, Mass	Feb. 24, 1863	37, 752
Book-case, Revolving	L. B. Pert	Tecumseh, Mich	Apr. 29, 1873	138, 279
Book-clamp	J. W. Jones	Harrisburgh, Pa	Oct. 24, 1865	50, 597
Book-clamp	W. A. Miller	Paterson, N. J	Dec. 16, 1873	145, 582
Book-clamp, Portable	C. W. Holbrook and E. F. Butler	Windsor Locks, Conn	Nov. 15, 1870	109, 213
Book-clamp, Portable	C. W. Sherwood	Chicago, Ill	Mar. 17, 1868	75, 588
Book-clamp, Portable	W. C. Watson	Paterson, N. J	Mar. 17, 1868	75, 660
Book clamp, School	W. C. Watson	Paterson, N. J	Sept. 24, 1867	69, 285
Book-clasp	C. Folsom	Cambridge, Mass	July 3, 1855	13, 166
Book clip, Check	A. B. Auer	Chicago, Ill	June 15, 1869	91, 198
Book, Copy	N. P. Beers	New York, N. Y	June 7, 1870	103, 965
Book, Copy	B. G. Howes	Worcester, Mass	Dec. 10, 1867	71, 882
Book, Copy	P. F. Van Everen	Brooklyn, N. Y	May 3, 1870	102, 732
Book, Copy	J. D. Williams	New York, N. Y	Apr. 19, 1870	102, 189
Book-cover	G. F. Barden	South Adams, Mass	Aug. 8, 1865	49, 213
Book-cover	W. L. Burlock	Philadelphia, Pa	Dec. 24, 1872	134, 249
Book-cover	A. H. Jocelyn	New York, N. Y	June 24, 1873	140, 275
Book-cover	W. C. Wendell	Albany, N. Y	Apr. 6, 1869	88, 684
Book-cover and stand	W. Milliken	Cambridge, Mass	Mar. 3, 1868	75, 040
Book-cover protector	C. L. Alexander and V. A. Osborn.	Washington, D. C	Sept. 24, 1867	69, 062
Book-cover protector	J. N. Larned	Buffalo, N. Y	Sept. 17, 1872	131, 356
Book-cover protector	A. L. Sewell	Chicago, Ill	June 22, 1869	91, 570
Book-cover protector	M. Thompson	New York, N. Y	Aug. 1, 1871	117, 697
Book-cover protector	P. F. Van Everen	Brooklyn, N. Y	May 3, 1870	102, 733
Book-cover protector	A. Van Patten	Weyauwega, Wis	Nov. 24, 1868	84, 397
Book-covers, Machine for making	L. Danforth	Buffalo, N. Y	May 23, 1854	10, 961
Book-covers, Machine for making	J. W. Harrison	Washington, D. C	Feb. 14, 1865	46, 353
Book-covers, Machine for making	M. and R. H. Rumrell	Brooklyn, N. Y	Apr. 23, 1867	64, 038
Book-covers, Ornamenting	W. McAdams	Albany, N. Y	Oct. 9, 1847	5, 327
Book-curb	M. A. H. Saurman	Philadelphia, Pa	May 11, 1869	90, 052
Book-cutting machine	F. J. Austin	New York, N. Y	Jan. 19, 1864	41, 337
Book for book-keeping	J. H. Gleim	Saint Louis, Mo	Dec. 24, 1867	72, 629
Book hand-rest	W. F. West	Haverstraw, N. Y	Dec. 17, 1872	134, 116
Book, Herbal and scrap	A. M. Safford	Springfield, Mass	June 14, 1864	43, 135
Book-holder	D. F. Dimon and G. H. Carsnell	Fishkill Landing, N. Y	July 19, 1864	43, 575
Book-holder	F. Emmons	Danvers, Mass	Mar. 23, 1869	88, 022
Book-holder	W. D. Gridley	New Britain, Conn	Apr. 27, 1869	89, 307
Book-holder	G. P. Johnson	Webster's Grove, Mo	Nov. 9, 1869	96, 702
Book holder	D. Moritz and R. White	Carmansville and Mott Haven, N. Y.	Oct. 15, 1872	132, 311
Book-holder	O. B. Parker	Woodville, Mass	June 26, 1866	55, 897
Book-holder	C. Phelps	Clayton, N. Y	May 21, 1872	126, 901
Book-holder	T. E. Platt	New Haven, Conn	Mar. 12, 1867	62, 774
Book-holder	W. S. Poulson	Cadiz, Ohio	June 1, 1869	90, 870
Book-holder	E. Propst and J. F. Avis	Tipton, Ind	Aug. 9, 1870	106, 285
Book-holder	H. Sherman	Waverly, Pa	Dec. 7, 1869	97, 110
Book-holder	C. W. Simpson	Bangor, Me	July 13, 1869	92, 482
Book-holder	D. I. Stagg	New York, N. Y	June 26, 1866	55, 924
Book-holder	W. J. Thorn	Westbrook, Me	Sept. 13, 1870	107, 310
Book-holder and leaf-turner	A. McFall	Yonkers, N. Y	Aug. 1, 1871	117, 654
Book-holder for pews	N. A. Wright	Prairie du Chien, Wis	Apr. 9, 1867	63, 776
Book-holder, Portable	C. C. Moore	New York, N. Y	Feb. 28, 1871	112, 165
Book-holder, Portable	H. A. Oesterle	Philadelphia, Pa	Nov. 21, 1871	121, 191
Book-holder, Portable	C. W. Sherwood	Chicago, Ill	Feb. 7, 1871	111, 577
Book-holding press	L. Heitkamp	New York, N. Y	Oct. 7, 1873	143, 410
Book-holding stand	J. S. Brown	Washington, D. C	Feb. 2, 1864	41, 420
Book, Hymn and tune	E. Curtice	Yonkers, N. Y	Feb. 12, 1867	61, 927
Book, Ivory-covered	J. H. Pratt	New York, N. Y	Apr. 26, 1864	42, 507
Book-leaf turner	C. C. Clapp	Hartford, Conn	Jan. 2, 1866	51, 804
Book-leaf-turning device	C. C. Clapp	Hartford, Conn	Oct. 15, 1867	69, 770
Book-leaves, Machine for turning	J. H. Schomacker and M. Kuemerle.	Philadelphia, Pa	Sept. 4, 1849	6, 697
Book, Manifold writing	A. S. Solomons	Washington, D. C	Dec. 6, 1864	45, 354
Book-mark	H. M. Ward and G. E. Dolton	Monee, Ill	June 17, 1873	139, 936
Book-mark holder	P. Tomppert, jr	Louisville, Ky	Dec. 4, 1866	60, 285
Book-marker	E. Cottle	Randolph, Mass	Aug. 30, 1870	106, 785
Book, Memorandum	J. H. Guest and E. Fawcett	New Albany, Ind	May 11, 1869	89, 928

Index of patents issued from the United States Patent Office from 1790 *to* 1873, *inclusive*—Continued.

Invention.	Inventor.	Residence.	Date.	No.
Book, Memorandum	H. M. Hinsdill	Grand Rapids, Mich	Jan. 7, 1873	134, 546
Book, Memorandum	I. N. Swasey	Yonkers, N. Y	July 11, 1871	116, 884
Book or music leaf turning apparatus	J. Grant	Hampstead, England	Apr. 20, 1869	89, 214
Book-paging apparatus	G. Leverich	Wellsburgh, N. Y	May 29, 1855	12, 954
Book-paging machine	W. C. Demain	Boston, Mass	Aug. 21, 1855	13, 477
Book-paging machine	R. L. Hawes	Worcester, Mass	Dec. 9, 1856	16, 207
Book-paging machine	H. Hochstrasser	Philadelphia, Pa	Sept. 26, 1854	11, 728
Book-paging machine	J. McAdams	Brooklyn, N. Y	Mar. 9, 1869	87, 693
Book-paging machine	S. E. Parrish	New York, N. Y	Mar. 23, 1852	8, 830
Book-paging machine	H. S. Taylor	Springfield, Mass	May 16, 1854	10, 933
Book-paging machine	E. Town	Jersey City, N. J	Jan. 31, 1854	10, 485
Book paging machinery, Blank	J. L. Burdick	New York, N. Y	Feb. 14, 1854	10, 533
Book-rack	D. Lewis	Boston, Mass	Dec. 9, 1862	37, 102
Book-rack	J. K. Otis	East Cambridge, Mass	July 25, 1871	117, 321
Book-rack	J. P. Tibbits	New York, N. Y	Nov. 16, 1869	97, 003
Book rack and stand	G. Gardener	Clarksville, N. J	Apr. 26, 1870	102, 248
Book, Record	H. Arden	Brooklyn, N. Y	July 25, 1871	117, 240
Book-repository	R. L. Dodge	Gallatin, Mo	June 7, 1870	103, 853
Book-rest	C. Sulivan	Boston, Mass	May 31, 1870	103, 682
Book-rest	L. Tarring	Washington, D. C	May 27, 1873	139, 341
Book, Scrap	S. L. Clemens	Hartford, Conn	June 24, 1873	140, 245
Book, Slated	H. B. Barnes	New York, N. Y	Aug. 6, 1872	130, 179
Book-stand	J. B. Annin	Rochester, N. Y	June 24, 1873	140, 107
Book-stand	H. M. Sweeney	Boston, Mass	Apr. 9, 1872	125, 500
Book stand or holder	W. W. Marston	New York, N. Y	Aug. 29, 1865	49, 639
Book-support	J. Densmore	Holley, N. Y	Mar. 12, 1872	124, 423
Book-support	R. B. Hindle	Saint Louis, Mo	July 1, 1873	140, 369
Book-support	J., A., and W. J. A. McCausland.	Providence, R. I	Feb. 14, 1871	111, 858
Book-support	D. E. Morgan	Cincinnati, Ohio	Jan. 23, 1872	122, 957
Book-support	C. J. North	Auburn, N. Y	June 13, 1871	115, 886
Book-support	S. M. Thomson	Providence, R. I	Mar. 21, 1871	112, 984
Book-supporter	L. Willson	Indianapolis, Ind	July 9, 1872	128, 835
Book, Tablet index	J. B. Lake, jr	Baltimore, Md	July 25, 1871	117, 433
Book-trimming machine	M. Riehl	Cincinnati, Ohio	Aug. 28, 1855	13, 501
Book-trimming machinery	L. F. Markham	Cambridgeport, Mass	Apr. 18, 1848	5, 523
Books, Adhesive compound for binding	D. Felt	New York, N. Y	Aug. 1, 1838	867
Books and music, Apparatus to hold and turn the leaves of.	C. B. Thayer	Boston, Mass	June 21, 1859	24, 504
Books, Apparatus for turning leaves of	H. C. Bridgham and J. M. Stewart.	New London and Norwich, Conn.	Sept. 12, 1854	11, 660
Books, Apparatus for turning leaves of	C. Desbeaux	Paris, France	Jan. 3, 1854	10, 381
Books, Binding invoice	J. L. Rile	New York, N. Y	Oct. 3, 1871	4, 577
Books, Binding mathematical	F. B. Wells	Fishkill, on the Hudson, N. Y.	Oct. 20, 1868	83, 345
Books, Binding mercantile	J. H. Gleim	Saint Louis, Mo	Oct. 20, 1868	83, 276
Books, Case for record	W. H. Somers	Urbana, Ill	Aug. 11, 1863	39, 503
Books, Clamp-strap for school	J. W. McKee	Brooklyn, N. Y	Sept. 24, 1867	69, 234
Books, Clamp-strap for school	L. F. Van De Weile	Brooklyn, N. Y	Nov. 26, 1867	71, 554
Books, &c., Clasp-lock for	L. Lall	New York, N. Y	Nov. 27, 1866	60, 017
Books, Composition for making copy-writing and drawing.	R. Wall	Philadelphia, Pa	Apr. 28, 1817	....
Books, Curving the backs of	J. A. Elder	Westbrook, Me	July 26, 1853	9, 886
Books, Embossed cover for	W. T. Anderson	Brooklyn, N. Y	July 5, 1864	43, 450
Books, Guide and blotter for writing	P. Martin	Medford, Mass	Sept. 3, 1872	131, 106
Books, Indexing	J. S. Hicks	Roslyn, N. Y	Sept. 23, 1873	143, 075
Books in the round, Machine for cutting	G. Trinks and L. Heitkamp	New York and Brooklyn, N. Y.	June 17, 1862	35, 639
Books, Machine for backing	W. Laighton	Portsmouth, N. H	Jan. 10, 1845	3, 880
Books, Machine for curving the backs of	J. E. Coffin	Portland, Me	June 12, 1866	55, 468
Books, Machine for cutting	A. O. Douglass	Philadelphia, Pa	Jan. 6, 1832	....
Books, Machine for cutting index to blank	G. Hodgkinson and T. F. Randolph.	Cincinnati, Ohio	Apr. 28, 1857	17, 149
Books, Machine for cutting the front of	I. Jones	Camden, N. J	Oct. 30, 1866	59, 229
Books, Machine for finishing the backs of	C. Starr	New York, N. Y	June 24, 1851	8, 179
Books, Machine for numbering the pages of	E. and C. E. Town	Jersey City, N. J	Oct. 5, 1858	21, 708
Books, Machine for numbering the pages of account.	J. McAdams	Boston, Mass	Aug. 12, 1851	8, 291
Books, Machine for rounding and backing	T. Bergner	Philadelphia, Pa	June 9, 1857	17, 480
Books, Machine for rounding and backing	J. E. Coffin	Westbrook, Me	July 8, 1856	15, 282
Books, Machine for rounding and backing	R. F. Foster, T. S. Baylie, and J. Harbin.	Washington, D. C	Mar. 25, 1873	137, 192
Books, Machine for rounding backs of	L. F. Markham	Cambridgeport, Mass	Dec. 5, 1854	12, 026
Books, Machine for shaping the backs of	J. E. Coffin	Portland, Me	June 14, 1859	24, 425
Books, Machine for trimming	A. C. Semple	New York, N. Y	Mar. 16, 1858	19, 654
Books, Machine for turning the leaves of	F. Suter	Brooklyn, N. Y	Dec. 22, 1857	18, 935
Books, Mode of making spring-backs for	L. Francis	New York, N. Y	Apr. 9, 1867	63, 626
Books, Paging	R. M. Leslie	Philadelphia, Pa	Feb. 15, 1853	9, 586
Books, Paging bound	J. McAdams	Boston, Mass	Mar. 29, 1853	9, 638
Books, Protecting bound	J. C. G. Kennedy	Washington, D. C	May 17, 1864	42, 779
Books, Register for account	A. F. Jones	Douglass, Mass	Sept. 29, 1863	40, 106
Books, Tool for embossing backs of	C. Starr	New York, N. Y	Jan. 21, 1851	7, 911
Boom and gaff joint	J. W. Norcross	Middletown, Conn	Dec. 27, 1864	45, 625
Boom-connection for masts	B. McGrath	Gloucester, Mass	June 12, 1866	55, 515
Boom for vessels	E. G. Gaillac	Cutler, Me	Feb. 15, 1870	99, 874
Boom-gear	C. R. Webb	Philadelphia, Pa	Apr. 14, 1868	76, 857
Boom-gudgeon	C. Sayward	Gloucester, Mass	July 14, 1868	79, 864
Boom jack or elevator	R. B. Condon	Belfast, Me	Oct. 1, 1872	131, 742
Boom-jaws, Elastic lining for	O. P. Rowland	Jamesport, N. Y	June 5, 1860	28, 608
Boom-jaws, Guide for	M. Gray	Newton, Mass	May 22, 1866	55, 001
Boom, Jib	W. E. Beman	Portland, Me	Apr. 28, 1868	77, 348
Boom-saddle and chafing-band for mast	W. T. Griffenberg	Wilmington, Del	Nov. 26, 1872	133, 439
Boom saddle and jaw	J. Davis, jr	Gloucester, Mass	Dec. 31, 1845	4, 345
Boom sling, Spritsail	G. Dowling	Fair Haven, Conn	Apr. 7, 1868	76, 309
Booms and gaffs, Band for	D. Dryburgh	Philadelphia, Pa	Oct. 5, 1869	95, 442
Booms and gaffs of vessels, Jaw for	A. Manning	Fair Haven, Conn	May 1, 1866	54, 379
Booms, Device for sheering	L. W. Pond	Eau Claire, Wis	Aug. 4, 1868	80, 663
Booms, Elastic anti-friction attachment for vessel's	H. Gregory, jr	Rockland, Me	Nov. 25, 1873	144, 975

Index of patents issued from the United States Patent Office from 1790 to 1873, inclusive—Continued.

Invention.	Inventor.	Residence.	Date.	No.
Booms, Outhaul-band for	G. Nevenger	Philadelphia, Pa	Dec. 12, 1871	121, 890
Booms, Outhaul for	G. W. Leighton and C. O. Cole	Portland, Me	Sept. 15, 1868	82, 133
Booms, Outhaul for	T. O'Neill	New York, N. Y	July 13, 1869	92, 539
Booms to masts, Connection of	A. Gill	Holmes' Hole, Mass	Apr. 25, 1871	114, 128
Booms to masts, Device for attaching	E. Rogers	Waterford, Conn	May 23, 1871	115, 241
Booms to masts, Means of attaching	M. McClain	Pemaquid, Me	Oct. 13, 1863	40, 273
Booms to masts, Truss for connecting	J. E. Tibbetts	Trenton, N. J	Aug. 17, 1869	93, 770
Boot	J. H. Agnew	Dobb's Ferry, N. Y	Apr. 28, 1863	38, 272
Boot	M. F. Chandler	Boston, Mass	Mar. 23, 1869	88, 131
Boot, &c	F. Closs	New Haven, Conn	Nov. 22, 1864	45, 138
Boot	E. D. Coffee	Holliston, Mass	Sept. 5, 1865	49, 723
Boot	L. Duvall	Big Spring, Ky	Sept. 6, 1859	25, 325
Boot	L. H. Farnsworth	Hudson, Mass	Sept. 23, 1873	143, 001
Boot	A. A. Felton and F. C. Floyd	Marblehead and Boston, Mass.	Dec. 10, 1872	133, 767
Boot	C. H. Fitch	Worcester, Mass	Nov. 8, 1870	109, 123
Boot	I. Hall	Boston, Mass	May 27, 1873	139, 385
Boot	J. Holland	Conshohocken, Pa	Jan. 7, 1868	73, 010
Boot	J. P. Jamison	New York, N. Y	Sept. 22, 1868	82, 417
Boot	P. Keffer	Reading, Pa	Dec. 13, 1859	26, 436
Boot	G. S. Lee	Worcester, Mass	Apr. 15, 1873	137, 781
Boot	J. S. Lewis	Baltimore, Md	Feb. 21, 1871	112, 056
Boot	J. H. Livingston	Providence, R. I	Mar. 23, 1869	88, 050
Boot	L. O. Makepeace	Lynn, Mass	Jan. 5, 1869	85, 681
Boot	G. C. Parker	Worcester, Mass	Dec. 16, 1873	145, 589
Boot	J. H. Walker	Worcester, Mass	Nov. 1, 1870	108, 948
Boot	P. West	Worcester, Mass	Jan. 30, 1872	123, 316
Boot	P. West and G. S. Lee	Worcester, Mass	Sept. 2, 1873	142, 424
Boot	W. W. Whitcomb	Boston, Mass	Sept. 3, 1872	131, 041
Boot	W. H. Willard	Cleveland, Ohio	Sept. 2, 1862	36, 381
Boot and gaiter	J. P. Herron	Washington, D. C	Aug. 18, 1863	39, 614
Boot and gaiter strap	W. J. Turner	Utica, N. Y	May 21, 1867	65, 027
Boot and pantaloon jack	I. S. Clough and S. S. Day	Brooklyn and New York, N. Y.	Apr. 30, 1861	32, 181
Boot and shoe	J. C. Adams	New London, N. H	Mar. 5, 1867	62, 587
Boot and shoe	J. M. Allen	Fredericktown, Ohio	Sept. 18, 1860	30, 034
Boot and shoe	R. Andrews	Milwaukee, Wis	Aug. 25, 1868	81, 457
Boot and shoe	D. M. Ayer	Lewiston, Me	Jan. 8, 1867	60, 987
Boot and shoe	S. Babbitt	Brazil, Ind	Feb. 1, 1870	99, 281
Boot and shoe	C. W. Bailey	Boston, Mass	Jan. 29, 1867	61, 502
Boot and shoe	F. D. Ballou	Abington, Mass	July 4, 1865	48, 614
Boot and shoe	L. R. Blake	Abington, Mass	Aug. 14, 1860	29, 562
Boot and shoe	L. R. Blake	Quincy, Mass	Sept. 27, 1864	44, 388
Boot and shoe	P. Boisset	Paris, France	Apr. 22, 1862	35, 057
Boot and shoe	A. O. Bourn	Providence, R. I	May 30, 1871	115, 422
Boot and shoe	J. S. Bowler	Lynn, Mass	Nov. 21, 1842	2, 859
Boot and shoe	M. Bray	Newton Centre, Mass	Dec. 19, 1871	121, 927
Boot and shoe	E. Brown	South Reading, Mass	Jan. 7, 1862	34, 086
Boot and shoe	E. Brown	Burlington, Vt	Oct. 26, 1869	96, 195
Boot and shoe	T. W. Brown	Malden, Mass	Apr. 16, 1872	125, 717
Boot and shoe	F. J. Burcham	Racine, Wis	Jan. 17, 1871	111, 039
Boot and shoe	A. Burke	New York, N. Y	Aug. 2, 1870	106, 030
Boot and shoe	D. H. Campbell and E. Woodward.	Sunderland, Scotland, and Charlestown, Mass.	June 6, 1871	115, 566
Boot and shoe	S. Chamberlain	Boston, Mass	Nov. 21, 1808	....
Boot and shoe	E. Chesterman	Roxbury, Mass	June 27, 1865	48, 368
Boot and shoe	E. Chesterman	Boston, Mass	May 12, 1868	77, 717
Boot and shoe	G. P. Clark	Brooklyn, N. Y	May 2, 1865	47, 521
Boot and shoe	D. N. P. Coffin, jr	Woburn, Mass	May 5, 1863	38, 373
Boot and shoe	N. Colver	Detroit, Mich	Sept. 12, 1854	11, 662
Boot and shoe	A. O. Crane	Hoboken, N. J	Apr. 23, 1861	32, 122
Boot and shoe	G. W. Day	Charlestown, Mass	June 28, 1864	43, 295
Boot and shoe	S. F. Dexter	Paris, N. Y	Oct. 16, 1860	30, 391
Boot and shoe	J. Dick	Philadelphia, Pa	Nov. 4, 1842	2, 840
Boot and shoe	T. H. Dodge	Worcester, Mass	July 30, 1872	130, 026
Boot and shoe	C. S. Dunbrack	Swampscott, Mass	Sept. 28, 1869	95, 210
Boot and shoe	T. G. Eiswald	St. Louis, Mo	Aug. 13, 1861	33, 032
Boot and shoe	H. Eldridge	Lynn, Mass	Mar. 10, 1868	75, 398
Boot and shoe	A. B. Ely	Newton, Mass	Dec. 31, 1867	72, 727
Boot and shoe	M. R. Ethridge	Locke's Mills, Me	July 17, 1866	56, 391
Boot and shoe	M. R. Ethridge	Locke's Mills, Me	Jan. 21, 1868	73, 589
Boot and shoe	M. Evans	Russiaville, Ind	Jan. 1, 1867	60, 707
Boot and shoe	A. T. Evory and A. Heston	La Porte, Ind	Nov. 6, 1866	59, 375
Boot and shoe	J. B. Field	Boston, Mass	Jan. 9, 1872	122, 519
Boot and shoe	S. T. Fowler	Brooklyn, N. Y	Aug. 7, 1866	56, 921
Boot and shoe	W. Francis	Boston, Mass	June 23, 1812	....
Boot and shoe	B. D. Godfrey	Milford, Mass	Mar. 28, 1865	47, 010
Boot and shoe	H. V. Gould	Dover, N. H	July 18, 1871	117, 168
Boot and shoe	T. Grason	Manchester, England	Sept. 6, 1864	44, 146
Boot and shoe	T. T. Hartford	Boston, Mass	Mar. 26, 1872	125, 047
Boot and shoe	D. E. Haywood	Melrose, Mass	Oct. 27, 1863	40, 408
Boot and shoe	E. Heaton and J. L. Joyce	New Haven, Conn	Oct. 8, 1861	33, 433
Boot and shoe	J. M. Hunter	New York, N. Y	Jan. 23, 1872	122, 948
Boot and shoe	W. F. Jobbins	New York, N. Y	May 25, 1869	90, 551
Boot and shoe	C. G. Johnson	London, England	July 23, 1861	32, 875
Boot and shoe	I. T. Jones	Sandwich, Mass	Aug. 1, 1865	49, 118
Boot and shoe	J. Kimball	Boston, Mass	June 19, 1866	55, 671
Boot and shoe	O. Lafreniere	New York, N. Y	Dec. 23, 1862	37, 233
Boot and shoe	O. Lafreniere	New York, N. Y	Jan. 19, 1864	41, 305
Boot and shoe	O. Lafreniere	New York, N. Y	Nov. 28, 1865	51, 195
Boot and shoe	W. Leathe	Woburn, Mass	June 22, 1869	91, 547
Boot and shoe	D. Lenain	New York, N. Y	May 14, 1861	32, 300
Boot and shoe	N. C. Lewis, jr	Boston, Mass	July 24, 1860	29, 344
Boot and shoe	G. W. Ludlow	Elizabeth, N. J	July 7, 1863	39, 156
Boot and shoe	M. Lumsden	San Francisco, Cal	May 26, 1868	78, 385
Boot and shoe	J. Macintosh and W. Boggett	London, Great Britain	July 27, 1869	93, 103
Boot and shoe	J. C. Mack	Philadelphia, Pa	Nov. 27, 1866	60, 024
Boot and shoe	G. A. Mansfield	Boston, Mass	Oct. 1, 1861	33, 396

Index of patents issued from the United States Patent Office from 1790 *to* 1873, *inclusive*—Continued.

Invention.	Inventor.	Residence.	Date.	No.
Boot and shoe	H. B. Marshall	Waldoborough, Me	Apr. 21, 1868	77, 063
Boot and shoe	C. Mayer	New York, N. Y	Aug. 9, 1864	43, 784
Boot and shoe	E. Mayer	Philadelphia, Pa	May 14, 1867	64, 780
Boot and shoe	G. McKay	Boston, Mass	Apr. 29, 1862	35, 105
Boot and shoe	C. Meyer	New Brunswick, N. J	June 18, 1861	32, 575
Boot and shoe	C. Meyer	New Brunswick, N. J	Mar. 18, 1862	34, 689
Boot and shoe	R. A. Miller	Boston, Mass	Apr. 26, 1870	102, 297
Boot and shoe	C. Mole	London, England	Dec. 10, 1867	71, 898
Boot and shoe	J. A. E. Moroney	Pontiac, Mich	Jan. 9, 1872	122, 632
Boot and shoe	W. Murray	Chicago, Ill	July 13, 1869	92, 634
Boot and shoe	S. Neiswender and G. King	Mexico, Ind	July 16, 1872	129, 580
Boot and shoe	J. L. Newton	Boston, Mass	Oct. 17, 1865	50, 487
Boot and shoe	O. Pacalin	New York, N. Y	June 19, 1866	55, 698
Boot and shoe	M. M. Pettes	West Concord, Vt	Oct. 22, 1861	33, 540
Boot and shoe	J. C. Plumer	Portland, Me	June 4, 1861	32, 487
Boot and shoe	J. C. Plumer	Boston, Mass	Jan. 9, 1866	51, 968
Boot and shoe	H. Port	New York, N. Y	Aug. 13, 1861	33, 051
Boot and shoe	H. Port and E Surgi	New Orleans, La	Oct. 16, 1860	30, 419
Boot and shoe	W. F. Prusha and E. L. Wales	Marlborough, Mass	May 2, 1871	114, 340
Boot and shoe	T. K. Reed	North Bridgewater, Mass.	May 23, 1865	47, 859
Boot and shoe	E. P. Richardson	Lawrence, Mass	May 28, 1867	65, 120
Boot and shoe	E. P. Richardson	Lawrence, Mass	Sept. 7, 1869	94, 648
Boot and shoe	E. T. Rogers	San Francisco, Cal	Feb. 18, 1868	74, 599
Boot and shoe	H. Rogers and L. Felton	Sudbury and Marlborough, Mass.	Feb. 4, 1873	135, 591
Boot and shoe	S. Rosenheimer	New York, N. Y	June 17, 1862	35, 629
Boot and shoe	G. F. Seaver	Ashland, Mass	July 30, 1872	129, 989
Boot and shoe	F. Senn	Forestville, N. Y	July 11, 1871	116, 872
Boot and shoe	P. Shaw	Boston, Mass	June 2, 1863	38, 766
Boot and shoe	G. and G. Smith	New York, N. Y	Feb. 25, 1868	74, 858
Boot and shoe	T. B. Smith	Boston, Mass	Apr. 2, 1867	63, 568
Boot and shoe	T. B. Smith	Boston, Mass	Apr. 2, 1867	63, 569
Boot and shoe	W. Smith	Bridesburgh, Pa	July 28, 1868	80, 366
Boot and shoe	R. Sommerville	Sandusky, Ohio	Dec. 24, 1872	134, 225
Boot and shoe	V. H. Spear	Lynn, Mass	July 16, 1872	128, 984
Boot and shoe	H. P. Stewart	Oak's Corners, N. Y	Dec. 18, 1866	60, 587
Boot and shoe	O. Stoddard	Jackson, Mich	Oct. 30, 1866	59, 288
Boot and shoe	B. F. Sturtevant	Boston, Mass	June 21, 1864	43, 235
Boot and shoe	G. W. Tash	Dover, N. H	Jan. 16, 1872	122, 778
Boot and shoe	E. Thayer	New York, N. Y	Jan. 8, 1867	61, 119
Boot and shoe	G. W. Tolhurst	New York, N. Y	Mar. 12, 1867	62, 907
Boot and shoe	W. H. Towers	Boston, Mass	Apr. 13, 1869	88, 824
Boot and shoe	C. H. Trask and J. B. Johnson.	Lynn, Mass	Feb. 20, 1866	52, 798
Boot and shoe	R. Vollschwitz	New York, N. Y	Jan. 22, 1867	61, 487
Boot and shoe	G. Wagner	Washington, D. C	Jan. 15, 1867	61, 287
Boot and shoe	G. W. Walker	Lowell, Mass	Aug. 17, 1869	93, 846
Boot and shoe	J. H. Walker	Worcester, Mass	Dec. 3, 1872	133, 687
Boot and shoe	P. Ware, jr	Boston, Mass	Dec. 19, 1871	122, 085
Boot and shoe	W. P. Ware	New York, N. Y	June 7, 1864	43, 052
Boot and shoe	L. H. Whitney	Washington, D. C	June 7, 1870	103, 950
Boot and shoe	W. Wickersham	Boston, Mass	Aug. 2, 1870	106, 013
Boot and shoe	H. Wight	East Cambridge, Mass	May 29, 1866	55, 188
Boot and shoe	B. C. Young	Boston, Mass	Oct. 1, 1867	69, 528
Boot and shoe and clog for the feet	G W. Martin	Boston, Mass	Aug. 4, 1868	80, 555
Boot and shoe blacking apparatus	I. Bickhart	Harlan, Ind	Jan. 27, 1863	37, 487
Boot and shoe blacking machine	J. M. and J. Connel	Newark, Ohio	Jan. 12, 1858	19, 075
Boot and shoe blacking machine	N. Eisenmann	New York, N. Y	Nov. 28, 1871	121, 343
Boot and shoe bottomings	C. Hay	Stoneham, Mass	Oct. 13, 1868	82, 946
Boot and shoe bottoms, Machine for molding	S. W. Baldwin	Yonkers, N. Y	May 27, 1873	139, 354
Boot and shoe buffing machine	G. C. Hawkins	Boston, Mass	Dec. 16, 1873	145, 501
Boot and shoe burnisher	L. I. Bumpus	Auburn, Me	Nov. 26, 1872	133, 301
Boot and shoe burnisher	R. Chauncey	Syracuse, N. Y	Mar. 14, 1871	112, 548
Boot and shoe burnishing machine	J. H. Howard	Stoneham, Mass	Feb. 13, 1872	123, 566
Boot and shoe burnishing machine	J. H. Howard	Stoneham, Mass	June 11, 1872	127, 772
Boot and shoe buttons, Machine for facing	N. B. Jenett and E. Everson	Haverhill, Mass	June 19, 1866	55, 664
Boot and shoe calk	J. L. Wager and A. L. Scudder	Sanford, N. Y	Aug. 23, 1870	106, 747
Boot and shoe channeling instrument	J. Cole	East Bloomfield, N. Y	Nov. 26, 1830	....
Boot and shoe channeling machine	A. E. Chickering and H. B. Tuttle	Albany, N. Y	Aug. 12, 1873	141, 693
Boot and shoe channeling machine	C. S. Dunbrack	Swampscott, Mass	Oct. 14, 1873	143, 561
Boot and shoe channeling machine	B. H. Hadley	Brooklyn, N. Y	Sept. 30, 1873	143, 237
Boot and shoe channeling machine	S. D. Tripp	Lynn, Mass	Nov. 8, 1870	109, 077
Boot and shoe channeling machine	H. S. Vrooman	Boston, Mass	June 13, 1871	115, 994
Boot and shoe cleaner	J. Chesley	Concord, N. H	June 19, 1860	28, 736
Boot and shoe cleaner	J. Malarkey	New York, N. Y	Sept. 24, 1872	131, 620
Boot and shoe cleaner	L. M. Newbury	Sparta, Wis	July 10, 1866	56, 252
Boot and shoe cleaner	W. H. Smith	Newport, R. I	Dec. 7, 1869	97, 716
Boot and shoe cleaning and polishing apparatus	S Horsley and E. H. Jones	Liverpool, England	Sept. 9, 1862	36, 408
Boot and shoe cleaning machine	T. C. Andrews	Leverington, Pa	July 18, 1865	48, 864
Boot and shoe cleaning machine	P. O. Ferheun and J. I. Ackerman	Hohokus, N. J	Aug. 27, 1872	130, 829
Boot and shoe coasting-guard	J. Fenning	Danbury, Conn	Aug. 5, 1862	36, 123
Boot and shoe conformator	L. Brooks	New York, N. Y	Apr. 28, 1868	77, 166
Boot and shoe counter	J. Brackett	Lynn, Mass	May 14, 1872	126, 778
Boot and shoe counter	G. W. Day	Haverhill, Mass	Nov. 5, 1872	132, 813
Boot and shoe counter and shank	M. E. Savoy	Corinth, N. Y	Sept. 1, 1868	81, 690
Boot and shoe counters, Cutting	S. C. Phinney	Stoughton, Mass	Nov. 14, 1871	120, 998
Boot and shoe counters, Machine for skiving	L. Hill	Stoneham, Mass	June 5, 1855	13, 003
Boot and shoe counters, Machine for skiving	H. S. Vrooman	Boston, Mass	Feb. 27, 1872	124, 098
Boot and shoe crimper	C. Glantz	Baltimore, Md	Apr. 8, 1873	137, 543
Boot and shoe crimping device	J. W. Maxfield	Potsdam, N. Y	July 16, 1867	66, 864
Boot and shoe crimping machine	L. O. Makepeace	Worcester, Mass	Sept. 10, 1872	131, 288
Boot and shoe, Elastic	P. Azam	Baltimore, Md	Sept. 24, 1816	....
Boot and shoe fastening	F. D. Ford	New Bedford, Mass	Feb. 7, 1871	111, 625
Boot and shoe fastening	G. H. Ward	Middletown, Conn	Feb. 18, 1873	136, 111
Boot and shoe feather-edging and channeling machine.	L. R. Blake	Fort Wayne, Ind	June 27, 1871	116, 402
Boot and shoe fender and sheath	J. Dillingham	Turner, Me	Feb. 18, 1862	34, 461
Boot and shoe gores, Elastic material for	C. Winslow	Boston, Mass	Feb. 18, 1873	136, 119
Boot and shoe hand-burnisher	J. G. Ross	Philadelphia, Pa	June 27, 1871	116, 491

Index of patents issued from the United States Patent Office from 1790 *to* 1873, *inclusive*—Continued.

Invention.	Inventor.	Residence.	Date.	No.
Boot and shoe holder	J. Ellison	Boston, Mass	July 18, 1865	48, 801
Boot and shoe, India-rubber	E. M. Chaffee	Roxbury, Mass	May 17, 1834	....
Boot and shoe, India-rubber	L. Elliott, jr	New Haven, Conn	Nov. 12, 1872	133, 020
Boot and shoe, India-rubber	B. D. Godfrey	Milford, Mass	Mar. 18, 1862	34, 682
Boot and shoe instep stretcher	M. Belding	Hartford, Conn	July 5, 1870	104, 923
Boot and shoe iron	J. Knox	Auburn, N. Y	Dec. 4, 1866	60, 198
Boot and shoe lacing	P. S. Foster	Richmond, Me	Mar. 9, 1869	87, 655
Boot and shoe lacing	C. Goodyear, jr	New York, N. Y	June 26, 1866	55, 852
Boot and shoe lacing	C. Goodyear, jr	New York, N. Y	June 26, 1866	55, 853
Boot and shoe lacing	L. A. Sprague	New York, N. Y	June 26, 1866	55, 923
Boot and shoe lining	T. Lucey and J. E. Murphy	Salem, Mass	Mar. 31, 1868	76, 216
Boot and shoe machine	J. E. Wiggin	Stoneham, Mass	Sept. 14, 1869	94, 801
Boot and shoe metal-tip	M. Pettengill	Le Roy, Minn	May 31, 1870	103, 772
Boot and shoe, Miner's	G. Latham and J. Burton	Jeddo, Pa	Mar. 12, 1872	124, 498
Boot and shoe, Moccasin	F. A. and F. G. Bishop	Bangor, Me	June 18, 1872	128, 101
Boot and shoe, Moccasin	T. Hersey	Bangor, Me	Sept. 6, 1870	107, 045
Boot and shoe, Moccasin	P. Kelleher and J. C. Randlett	Bangor, Me	Dec. 19, 1871	122, 030
Boot and shoe nail	B. D. Godfrey	Milford, Mass	Feb. 9, 1869	86, 832
Boot and shoe nail	B. Morahan	Brooklyn, N. Y	Sept. 13, 1864	44, 212
Boot and shoe nailing machine	L. R. Blake and A. S. Libbey	Fort Wayne, Ind., and Lawrence, Mass.	Jan. 23, 1872	122, 985
Boot and shoe nailing machine	W. N. Linnell	Cambridge, Mass	June 11, 1872	127, 779
Boot and shoe nailing machines, Device for preparing patterns for.	A. A. Reed	North Bridgewater, Mass.	Oct. 22, 1872	132, 492
Boot and shoe nailing machines, Driver for	A. S. Libbey	Lawrence, Mass	Oct. 14, 1873	143, 699
Boot and shoe patterns, Graduating	N. Silvester	Boston, Mass	Sept. 19, 1865	50, 043
Boot and shoe peg-attachment	D. H. Campbell and E. Woodward.	Sunderland, Scotland, and Charlestown, Mass.	June 6, 1871	115, 567
Boot and shoe pegging machine	J. H. Brown	Boston, Mass	Oct. 13, 1863	40, 306
Boot and shoe piping	C. Stone	Stoughton, Mass	Apr. 3, 1866	53, 699
Boot and shoe rivet	P. West	Worcester, Mass	Jan. 21, 1873	135, 051
Boot and shoe seam	S. A. Brackett and W. H. Whitcomb.	Boston, Mass	Dec. 10, 1872	133, 826
Boot and shoe seam	L. H. Farnsworth	Hudson, Mass	May 7, 1872	126, 537
Boot and shoe seam	C. F. Langford	Brooklyn, N. Y	July 30, 1872	129, 970
Boot and shoe shank	A. Bertram	New Albany, Ind	July 14, 1868	79, 941
Boot and shoe shank	G. Goodyear	New York, N. Y	Sept. 12, 1871	118, 851
Boot and shoe shank	G. Goodyear	New York, N. Y	Mar. 18, 1873	136, 991
Boot and shoe shank	T. H. Gordon and E. N. Dow	Hudson, N. Y	Nov. 5, 1872	132, 719
Boot and shoe shank	A. J. and A. J. Rice	Salem, Mass	Sept. 10, 1867	68, 652
Boot and shoe shank and toe laster	C. L. Graves	Osage, Iowa	Aug. 29, 1871	118, 527
Boot and shoe shank-bending machine	H. Barnes	Brookfield, Mass	May 7, 1872	126, 434
Boot and shoe shank-piece	J. M. Watson	Sharon, Mass	Jan. 17, 1871	111, 022
Boot and shoe shanks, Machines for burnishing	A. C. Carey	Malden, Mass	Sept. 23, 1873	142, 990
Boot and shoe shave	A. B. Clark	North Oxford, Mass	Mar. 15, 1870	100, 724
Boot and shoe shave	L. H. Farnsworth	Hudson, Mass	Dec. 22, 1868	85, 077
Boot and shoe shave	D. Harrington	Southbridge, Mass	Apr. 29, 1873	138, 328
Boot and shoe shave	A. E. Johnson	Oxford, Mass	July 30, 1867	67, 313
Boot and shoe shave	S. Packard	Grafton, Mass	Feb. 1, 1870	99, 466
Boot and shoe shave	B. A. Stockwell	Sutton, Mass	Mar. 12, 1872	124, 638
Boot and shoe shave	W. Wilber	New Salem, Mass	Feb. 16, 1869	86, 958
Boot and shoe shield	J. P. Bradley	Lawrence, Mass	Oct. 29, 1867	70, 157
Boot and shoe shield	O. Collier	Sacramento, Cal	Aug. 22, 1871	118, 201
Boot and shoe shield, Metallic	J. Platt and M. D. Brooks	Akron, Ohio	May 24, 1859	24, 150
Boot and shoe spring-shank	W. J. Neill	Lawrence, Kans	Dec. 30, 1873	145, 963
Boot and shoe stay or brace	T. K. Reed	East Bridgewater, Mass	June 18, 1867	65, 839
Boot and shoe stiffener	N. J. Simonds	Woburn, Mass	July 19, 1870	105, 501
Boot and shoe stiffening, Machine for crimping	N. J. Simonds	Woburn, Mass	Nov. 19, 1872	133, 262
Boot and shoe straightener	G. W. Wilford	Dayton, Ohio	Feb. 23, 1869	87, 129
Boot and shoe stretcher	E. R. Bardin	Newburgh, N. Y	June 13, 1871	115, 808
Boot and shoe stretcher	J. L. Devol	Parkersburgh, W. Va	June 29, 1869	91, 920
Boot and shoe stretcher	W. Frederick	Ashland, Pa	June 19, 1866	55, 637
Boot and shoe stretcher	W. Frederick	Pottsville, Pa	Apr. 7, 1868	76, 431
Boot and shoe stretcher	W. Holden	Philadelphia, Pa	May 1, 1855	12, 793
Boot and shoe stretcher	J. Lyons	Chippewa, Canada	Sept. 9, 1873	142, 710
Boot and shoe stretcher	T. C. Maris	Marietta, Ohio	July 9, 1872	128, 740
Boot and shoe stretcher	P. Veitch	San Francisco, Cal	Feb. 2, 1869	86, 475
Boot and shoe stretcher	J. G. Young, jr	Auburn, Me	Oct. 28, 1862	36, 818
Boot and shoe stretching instrument	G. Munro	Philadelphia, Pa	July 14, 1868	79, 850
Boot and shoe stud	H. S. Walcott	Boston, Mass	Apr. 28, 1868	77, 421
Boot and shoe tacking machine	D. M. Smyth	Lynn, Mass	Sept. 30, 1873	143, 388
Boot and shoe tap	J. C. Hancock and J. C. and E. P. Richardson.	Charlestown and Somerville, Mass.	June 27, 1871	116, 439
Boot and shoe tip	A. B. Ely	Newton, Mass	Sept. 24, 1867	69, 082
Boot and shoe tip	T. J. Mayall	Roxbury, Mass	Oct. 8, 1861	33, 440
Boot and shoe tip	G. A. Mitchell	Turner, Me	Mar. 12, 1861	31, 673
Boot and shoe tip	F. W. Rhinelander	New York, N. Y	Dec. 16, 1873	145, 590
Boot and shoe tip	N. Silverthorn	Prescott, Wis	Nov. 29, 1859	26, 329
Boot and shoe tip, Detachable	M. R. Hanley	Providence, R. I	May 20, 1873	139, 060
Boot and shoe toe plate	G. Beatty	Cleveland, Ohio	Aug. 31, 1869	94, 382
Boot and shoe top	J. Honecker	Columbus, Ohio	June 1, 1869	90, 753
Boot and shoe tree	T. R. Evans	Philadelphia, Pa	Sept. 19, 1871	119, 131
Boot and shoe tree and stretcher	T. R. Evans	Philadelphia, Pa	Aug. 5, 1873	141, 550
Boot and shoe trimming jack	J. Webb, jr	Portland, Me	Aug. 1, 1871	117, 582
Boot and shoe uppers, Corrugation of	W. Lee	New Haven, Conn	Mar. 8, 1870	100, 535
Boot and shoe uppers, Machine for cutting	P. Jackson	Saugus, Mass	Oct. 10, 1865	50, 360
Boot and shoe uppers, Machine for cutting	J. P. Molliere	Lyons, France	Nov. 13, 1855	13, 796
Boot and shoe uppers, Machinery for crimping	A. Knowlton	Boston, Mass	Sept. 2, 1873	142, 402
Boot and shoe uppers, soles, &c., from sheets of India-rubber, Machine for cutting.	J. and E. Arthur	New Brunswick, N. J	July 24, 1855	13, 296
Boot and shoe ventilator	A. Stocker	Watertown, N. Y	Nov. 12, 1867	70, 915
Boot and shoe, Water-proof	D. Clarkson	New York, N. Y	Dec. 2, 1835	....
Boot and shoe, Water-proof	A. Dana	Boston, Mass	Dec. 31, 1821	....
Boot and shoe, Water-proof	S. Eells, 2d	Middletown, Conn	Apr. 23, 1830	....
Boot and shoe, Water-proof	E. L. Simpson	Bridgeport, Conn	Sept. 8, 1863	39, 865
Boot and shoe, Water-proof	L. C. Tower	Rochester, N. Y	Feb. 23, 1869	87, 310
Boot and shoe welt and rand	H. F. Packard	North Bridgewater, Mass	July 4, 1871	116, 744
Boot and shoe welt trimmer	J. H. Allen	Wadsworth, Nev	July 18, 1871	117, 138

Index of patents issued from the United States Patent Office from 1790 *to* 1873, *inclusive*—Continued.

Invention.	Inventor.	Residence.	Date.	No.
Boot and shoe welts, Machine for cutting	S. D. Tripp	Stoneham, Mass	Jan. 14, 1862	34, 172
Boot and shoe wiper	J. K. Staman	Mifflin, Ohio	June 5, 1860	28, 614
Boot and shoe, Wooden-soled	J. Fulton	Zanesville, Ohio	Oct. 3, 1865	50, 236
Boot and shoe work trimmer	A. V. Hill	Limestone, N. Y	Feb. 25, 1868	74, 757
Boot, Balmoral	H. Hayward	Fitchburgh, Mass	Jan. 9, 1866	51, 944
Boot, Balmoral or laced	L. R. Stockbridge	Haverhill, Mass.	May 9, 1871	114, 724
Boot-blacking	A. Boudrou	Philadelphia, Pa	June 11, 1867	65, 535
Boot blacking and polishing machine	S. W. Huntington	Augusta, Me	Nov. 5, 1867	70, 571
Boot-blacking apparatus	H. Churchman	Horsham, England	June 29, 1869	91, 825
Boot-blacking apparatus	J. M Connel	Newark, Ohio	Jan. 18, 1859	22, 628
Boot-blacking case	F. G. Harding	Boston, Mass	July 25, 1865	48, 931
Boot-blacking kit	S. Van Gilder	Knoxville, Tenn	July 1, 1873	140, 447
Boot-blacking machine	M. Burnell	Arundel, England	May 4, 1869	89, 552
Boot-blacking machine	N. Eisenmann	New York, N. Y	Jan. 30, 1872	123, 160
Boot-blacking machine	A. E. White	Rockford, Ill	May 10, 1864	42, 707
Boot-blacking ottoman	D. B. Boynton	Boston, Mass	Feb. 6, 1866	52, 381
Boot-blacking stand	D. Keyser	Philadelphia, Pa	May 13, 1862	35, 240
Boot, bootee, &c., Iron-bound	E. Twombly	Norway, Mass	Aug. 28, 1812	....
Boot-brushing apparatus	M. Beck and C. Schmeidt	Philadelphia, Pa	July 29, 1873	141, 196
Boot, Button	J. L. Joyce	New Haven, Conn	Aug. 25, 1868	81, 378
Boot, Button	E. P. Taylor	New Bedford, Mass	July 28, 1868	80, 430
Boot-calk	H. Myer	Derby, Conn	Feb. 9, 1869	86, 857
Boot-clamp for base-ball players	E. S. Ellis	Trenton, N. J	Jan. 9, 1872	122, 587
Boot-clamp, Horizontal	E. G. Pomeroy	Newark, Ohio	Oct. 4, 1836	38
Boot-cleaning machine, Cylindrical	I. Pinkney	New York, N. Y	Apr. 16, 1817	....
Boot, Cloth	M. Crane	East Somerville, Mass	Oct. 22, 1872	132, 387
Boot-conformator	S. W. Shorey	Galesburgh, Ill	Dec. 7, 1869	97, 558
Boot, Congress	H. S. Holmes	Lynn, Mass	June 19, 1860	28, 754
Boot, Cork-sole	W. L. McCauley	Baltimore, Md	June 5, 1844	3, 615
Boot-counter machine	J. Brooks and C. F. Sylvester	North Bridgewater, Mass	July 11, 1865	48, 651
Boot-counters, Machine for cutting and skiving	V. Snell	North Bridgewater, Mass	Apr. 25, 1854	10, 835
Boot-counters, Machine for skiving	W. Butterfield and B. Stetson	Boston and Uxbridge, Mass	June 16, 1857	17, 603
Boot-counters, Machine for skiving	S. J. and C. H. Trofatter	Salem, Mass	Nov. 29, 1853	10, 288
Boot-cramp	H. L. Pierce	Saint Johnsbury, Vt	June 25, 1836	....
Boot-crimp	L. Barrett	Gainesville, N. Y	Oct. 26, 1852	9, 352
Boot-crimp	A. and G. W. Caywood	Ithaca, Ohio	Nov. 14, 1865	50, 904
Boot-crimp	J. Copeland	Weymouth, Mass	Jan. 20, 1844	3, 410
Boot-crimp	T. Daugherty	Erie, Pa	May 8, 1853	12, 816
Boot-crimp	H. S. Davis	Westernville, N. Y	June 27, 1846	4, 603
Boot-crimp	N. Dawes and H. Harrison	Little York, N. J	May 27, 1851	8, 127
Boot-crimp	N. Day	Ithaca, Ohio	Feb. 6, 1866	52, 394
Boot-crimp	E. P. Drake	Troy, N. Y	Nov. 15, 1843	3, 340
Boot-crimp	R. and S. Fairchild	Trumbull, Conn	May 10, 1845	4, 038
Boot-crimp	H. Ferre	Springfield, Mass	Sept. 25, 1839	1, 338
Boot-crimp	G. Fetter	Philadelphia, Pa	Mar. 4, 1856	14, 353
Boot-crimp	B. C. Finfrock	Stephenson's Depot, Va	Mar. 2, 1869	87, 333
Boot-crimp	E. K. Horner and W. Holland	Fayetteville, Pa	Oct. 2, 1849	6, 770
Boot-crimp	F. Kali and S. Andrews	Rochester, N. Y	Nov. 5, 1867	70, 440
Boot-crimp	F. L. Kathan and E. D. Rummer	Roscoe, Ill	June 30, 1868	79, 357
Boot-crimp	B. Livermore	Hartland, Vt	Oct. 16, 1849	6, 794
Boot-crimp	C. Lomax	Paoli, Ind	June 22, 1869	91, 756
Boot-crimp	G. W. Loy	Winchester, Va	Sept. 24, 1872	131, 552
Boot-crimp	E. Mann and A. J. F. Howard	Milford, Mass	Aug. 18, 1868	81, 096
Boot-crimp	A. Overholt	Gardenville, Pa	May 11, 1869	90, 016
Boot-crimp	S. Pasco and E. Perry	Cato, N. Y	Apr. 3, 1849	6, 260
Boot-crimp	B. Rowe	Maryland, N. Y	Dec. 17, 1842	2, 885
Boot-crimp	P. Sanders	Middletown, Pa	Nov. 26, 1872	133, 339
Boot-crimp	J. Sanderson	Cincinnati, Ohio	June 7, 1839	1, 167
Boot-crimp	C. Snow and T. N. Sadler	Spencer, Mass	May 21, 1845	4, 057
Boot-crimp	H. Stanley	Wilmington, Vt	Aug. 19, 1851	8, 305
Boot-crimp	P. Stevens, jr	Canton, Mass	July 15, 1844	3, 666
Boot-crimp	W. Taylor	Berlin, N. Y	Oct. 3, 1846	4, 793
Boot-crimp	J. Tipton and J. Carl	Malaga, Ohio	Jan. 21, 1868	73, 554
Boot-crimp	J. E. Tucker	Boston, Mass	Aug. 22, 1848	5, 723
Boot-crimp	O. J. Warren	Chicago, Ill	Mar. 15, 1864	41, 952
Boot-crimp	C White	Galway, N. Y	Feb. 12, 1845	3, 909
Boot-crimp	C. White	Galway, N. Y	Jan. 12, 1848	5, 412
Boot-crimp	J. G. Whittier	Attica, Ind	Apr. 2, 1861	31, 922
Boot-crimp	W. W. Willmott	Boston, Mass	Aug. 25, 1857	18, 074
Boot-crimp	H. Wright	Saco, Me	Jan. 21, 1868	73, 483
Boot-crimp	J. Young	West Galway, N. Y	Aug. 26, 1845	4, 165
Boot-crimper	O. M. Adams	Milford, Mass	Nov. 24, 1868	84, 402
Boot-crimper	J. B. Aikin	Somerton, Ohio	May 25, 1869	90, 477
Boot-crimper	J. Brewster	Worthington, Mass	Mar. 23, 1830	....
Boot-crimper	A. Dunbar	Sharon, Mass	Feb. 19, 1830	....
Boot-crimper	W. B. Gleason	Conneautville, Pa	Dec. 8, 1868	84, 743
Boot-crimper	H. Henley	Shoals, Ind	Apr. 4, 1871	113, 430
Boot-crimper	A. J. F. Howard	Milford, Mass	Mar. 31, 1868	76, 079
Boot-crimper	A. J. F. Howard	Milford, Mass	Aug. 18, 1868	81, 087
Boot-crimper	F. C. Jackson	Peru, Ind	Dec. 1, 1868	84, 629
Boot-crimper	S. W. Jamison	Newark, N. J	June 21, 1870	104, 596
Boot-crimper	F. P. Marcy	Keokuk, Iowa	Dec. 14, 1869	97, 944
Boot-crimper	D. C. Mowrey	Milford, Mass	June 25, 1867	66, 035
Boot-crimper	W. Polsgrove	Saint Thomas, Pa	Jan. 24, 1871	111, 245
Boot-crimper	E. Powell	New London, Ind	July 4, 1871	116, 750
Boot-crimper	E. Powell	New London, Ind	Feb. 27, 1872	124, 157
Boot-crimper	J. M. Read	Boston, Mass	July 7, 1868	79, 777
Boot-crimper	J. M Read	Boston, Mass	June 8, 1869	91, 162
Boot crimper	P. Richmond and A. McFarland.	Aberdeen and Allensville, Ind.	May 19, 1868	78, 131
Boot-crimper's rub-stick	A. J. F. Howard	Milford, Mass	July 25, 1871	117, 288
Boot-crimping	O. J. Warren	New York, N. Y	Mar. 27, 1866	53, 508
Boot-crimping apparatus	M. R. Marcell	Dansville, N. Y	Nov. 25, 1873	144, 995
Boot-crimping block	H. Bordner and D. Sullivan	Virginia City, Nev	Sept. 2, 1873	142, 369
Boot-crimping device	T. Madgett	Buffalo, N. Y	Nov. 17, 1863	40, 634
Boot-crimping device	W. C. Shipherd	Saratoga Springs, N. Y	June 10, 1862	35, 547
Boot-crimping machine	J. G. Baker, jr	Philadelphia, Pa	Feb. 17, 1857	16, 670
Boot-crimping machine	J. D. Batchelor	Upton, Mass	Nov. 7, 1865	50, 788

Index of patents issued from the United States Patent Office from 1790 *to* 1873, *inclusive*—Continued.

Invention.	Inventor.	Residence.	Date.	No.
Boot-crimping machine	J. D. Black	Boston, Mass	May 10, 1859	23, 977
Boot-crimping machine	H. Conklin	Kirkwood, N. Y	July 9, 1867	66, 566
Boot-crimping machine	R. H. Dorn	Port Henry, N. Y	June 2, 1868	78, 438
Boot-crimping machine	R. H. Dorn	Port Henry, N. Y	Jan. 30, 1872	123, 158
Boot-crimping machine	W. R. Dunn	Alton, Ind	May 4, 1869	89, 640
Boot-crimping machine	J. A. Eldridge	Milford, Mass	June 1, 1869	90, 828
Boot-crimping machine	B. Esch	Sandusky, Ohio	June 1, 1869	90, 648
Boot-crimping machine	H. Faus	Hayesville, Ohio	Mar. 5, 1867	62, 621
Boot-crimping machine	L. W. Hayden	Wilkesbarre, Pa	Mar. 12, 1861	31, 664
Boot-crimping machine	H. B. Horton	Northville, Mich	May 1, 1855	12, 794
Boot-crimping machine	T. Howe	Worcester, Mass	June 11, 1829	....
Boot-crimping machine	S. W. Jamison	New York, N. Y	May 7, 1867	64, 538
Boot-crimping machine	J. S. Landes	Lancaster, Pa	Feb. 14, 1865	46, 427
Boot-crimping machine	C. Lomax and H. Lindley	Paoli, Ind	Feb. 6, 1872	123, 492
Boot-crimping machine	S. Morehouse	Eastport, Me	June 19, 1827	....
Boot-crimping machine	J. A. Nesbit	Charlottesville, Ind	Mar. 3, 1868	75, 186
Boot-crimping machine	J. S. Nolen and C. C. Hinchman	Paulsborough, N. J	Mar. 20, 1860	27, 561
Boot-crimping machine	C. Pratt	Pratt's Hollow, N. Y	Dec. 23, 1862	37, 242
Boot-crimping machine	J. Rausch	Huntington, Ind	Dec. 20, 1870	110, 285
Boot-crimping machine	C. H. Rice	Port Henry, N. Y	Feb. 25, 1868	74, 848
Boot-crimping machine	P. Shaw	Abington, Mass	Oct. 23, 1860	30, 502
Boot-crimping machine	G. Utley	Chapel Hill, N. C	Dec. 19, 1854	12, 109
Boot-crimping machine	R. Warren	Jefferson, Ohio	Mar. 20, 1860	27, 586
Boot-crimping machine	H. Wing	Buffalo, N. Y	Apr. 12, 1864	42, 324
Boot-crimping machine	S. Witherby	Essex, Vt	May 12, 1832	....
Boot-crimping machine	G. W. Zeigler	Tiffin, Ohio	June 5, 1855	13, 023
Boot-crimping screw	B. S. Norris	Ripley, Ohio	Mar. 24, 1868	75, 784
Boot-fastening	A. A. Abbot	Boston, Mass	July 14, 1868	79, 800
Boot fastening, Gaiter	H. M. Whitmarsh	Abington, Mass	Sept. 16, 1862	36, 497
Boot-form	J. Chilcott and R. Snell	Brooklyn, N. Y	Apr. 10, 1855	12, 670
Boot-form	J. Howe	Milford, Mass	May 5, 1868	77, 489
Boot-form	L. N. Leland	Grafton, Mass	July 21, 1863	39, 293
Boot-forms, Machine for beveling	E. Holmes	Stoughton, Mass	Aug. 12, 1840	1, 716
Boot-forms, Machine for dressing	J. Burgess	Leicester, Mass	July 22, 1851	8, 246
Boot-fronts, Crimping	J. H. Punchard	Boston, Mass	May 8, 1830	....
Boot-fronts, Method of cutting	J. Dick	New York, N. Y	July 27, 1858	20, 992
Boot, Gaiter	S. Babbit	Kokomo, Ind	Mar. 7, 1865	46, 622
Boot, Gaiter	W. H. H. Babbitt	New Corner, Ind	Oct. 13, 1868	83, 017
Boot, Gaiter	C. K. Bradford	Lynn, Mass	Oct. 2, 1860	30, 197
Boot, Gaiter	J. C. Breed and C. K. Bradford	Lynn, Mass	Aug. 18, 1863	39, 544
Boot, Gaiter	C. Hersome	Boston, Mass	Nov. 19, 1872	133, 225
Boot, Gaiter	C. Hersome	Boston, Mass	Dec. 23, 1873	145, 801
Boot, Gaiter	R. B. Jacobs	Quincy, Ill	Nov. 6, 1866	59, 399
Boot, Gaiter	E. Mongaret	Newark, N. J	Mar. 16, 1869	87, 869
Boot, Gaiter	T. Powell	Richland, Ind	Sept. 19, 1865	50, [illegible]30
Boot, Gaiter	J. Schroeder	Cincinnati, Ohio	July 16, 1872	129, 178
Boot, Half	L. U. Williams	La Fayette, Ind	Aug. 26, 18 3	142, 512
Boot-jack	F. Ahl	West Meriden, Conn	Dec. 28, 1858	22, 404
Boot-jack	T. Anthony	Providence, R. I	Feb. 20, 1872	123, 759
Boot-jack	H. Arnot	Barclay, Pa	June 24, 1873	140, 179
Boot-jack	S. P. Babcock	Adrian, Mich	Dec. 28, 1869	98, 219
Boot-jack	H. D. Boss	Williamsburgh, N. Y	Apr. 16, 1867	63, 844
Boot-jack	W. Bearn	Geneva, N. Y	Nov. 4, 1862	36, 831
Boot-jack	C. Brown	Charlottesville, Va	Feb. 1, 1870	99, 517
Boot-jack	E. L. Brown	Chicago, Ill	May 18, 1869	90, 076
Boot-jack	W. W. Cansler	Baltimore, Md	Jan. 25, 1859	22, 700
Boot-jack	W. Case	Russia, N. Y	Dec. 7, 1869	97, 478
Boot-jack	C. Clay	Scranton, Pa	June 11, 1867	65, 543
Boot-jack	E. Coleman	San Francisco, Cal	Feb. 7, 1871	111, 613
Boot-jack	J. Crabtree	Cincinnati, Ohio	Jan. 3, 1871	110, 743
Boot-jack	H. Crocker	Brighton, Mass	May 21, 1872	126, 876
Boot-jack	P. Cullen	Bridgeport, Conn	May 4, 1869	89, 633
Boot-jack	J. Darden	Washington, D. C	Dec. 15, 1868	84, 862
Boot-jack	H. N. Degraw	Green Island, N. Y	Feb. 22, 1859	23, 015
Boot-jack	H. N. Degraw	Green Island, N. Y	Feb. 12, 1861	31, 374
Boot-jack	H. N. Degraw	Newburgh, N. Y	Nov. 13, 1866	59, 712
Boot-jack	F. Dorsett, sr	Chicago, Ill	Oct. 7, 1873	143, 408
Boot-jack	J. Durham	Cherry Grove, Ohio	Dec. 18, 1860	30, 913
Boot-jack	F. J. French	Whitingham, Vt	June 5, 1855	13, 002
Boot-jack	J. A. McKinstry	Springfield, Mass	Dec. 17, 1872	134, 084
Boot-jack	J. G. Moulton	Boston, Mass	Oct. 29, 1867	70, 246
Boot-jack	W. S. Peffer	Carlisle, Pa	Mar. 26, 1867	63, 292
Boot-jack	A. Pierpont	New Haven, Conn	May 22, 1866	54, 948
Boot-jack	M. A. Richardson	Sherman, N. Y	July 19, 1864	43, 626
Boot-jack	M. A. Richardson	Sh.rman, N. Y	May 16, 1871	114, 970
Boot-jack	M. T. Ridout	Milwaukee, Wis	Oct. 22, 1861	33, 543
Boot-jack	J. Roward	San Francisco, Cal	Mar. 14, 1871	112, 638
Boot-jack	A. P. Seymour	Hecla Works, N. Y	Oct. 29, 1867	70, 275
Boot-jack	O. S. Sikes	Saffield, Conn	May 18, 1858	20, 307
Boot-jack	S. B. Sumner	Grantville, Mass	Sept. 13, 1853	10, 016
Boot-jack	S. Thomson	Hartsville, Mass	Apr. 6, 1852	8, 865
Boot-jack	W. H. Towers	New York, N. Y	Jan. 4, 1861	32, 490
Boot-jack	J. Walker	Cincinnati, Ohio	Mar. 19, 1867	63, 121
Boot-jack	G. Wheeler	New York, N. Y	June 26, 1868	28, 927
Boot-jack	J. Wheeler	Athol, Mass	June 6, 1865	48, 122
Boot-jack	L. J. Wicks	Racine, Wis	Feb. 8, 1859	22, 923
Boot-jack	W. D. Young	Baltimore, Md	Jan. 25, 1859	22, 766
Boot-jack, Adjustable	G. Couch	Saint Louis, Mo	July 30, 1872	129, 936
Boot-jack and blacking-brush	H. J. Miller	Nashua, N. H	Sept. 24, 1867	69, 112
Boot-jack and blacking-brush	H. J. Miller	Nashua, N. H	Mar. 3, 1868	75, 181
Boot-jack and blacking-cabinet	L. P. Keach	Baltimore, Md	Jan. 26, 1869	86, 165
Boot-jack and blacking-case	B. Douglas	New York, N. Y	Sept. 25, 1866	58, 230
Boot-jack and brush	S. Kennedy	Rochester, Pa	Apr. 19, 1870	102, 014
Boot-jack and burglar-alarm combined	F. C. Goffin	Newark, N. J	Apr. 6, 1858	19, 844
Boot-jack and door-buffer	W. S. Chatham	Williamsport, Pa	Dec. 27, 1870	110, 433
Boot-jack and spur	T. Gunn	Hamilton County, Ind	July 26, 1870	105, 671
Boot-j.ck, nut-cracker, tack-hammer, and tack-puller.	G. R. Osborn and J. Crandell.	Il.on, N. Y	Apr. 17, 1866	54, 608

Index of patents issued from the United States Patent Office from 1790 *to* 1873, *inclusive*—Continued.

Invention.	Inventor.	Residence.	Date.	No.
Boot-jack, wrench, and nail-pull	O. Shepard	Alton, Ill	July 9, 1867	66 643
Boot-lacing	W. Banister	Boston, Mass	Feb. 2, 1869	86, 494
Boot-lacing device	A. McKenney and S. Carpenter.	Portland and Patten, Me.	June 25, 1867	66, 099
Boot-lacing, Mode of	R. Newton	Philadelphia, Pa	July 7, 1863	39, 163
Boot, Lady's	E. F. Doty	Ravenna, Ohio	Sept. 13, 1870	107, 231
Boot, Lady's	H. Libby	Evansville, Wis	June 13, 1865	48, 188
Boot, Lady's	W. Love	McConnellsville, Ohio	Dec. 28, 1869	98, 391
Boot, Lady's	D. H. Murphy	Lynn, Mass	Apr. 16, 1872	125, 834
Boot-leg	D. A. Haviland	Fort Dodge, Iowa	Sept. 3, 1861	33, 195
Boot-leg	C. H. Leffingwell	Providence, R. I	May 14, 1861	32, 335
Boot-leg	A. P. Nash	Weymouth, Mass	May 16, 1865	47, 743
Boot-leg stiffener	N. Gear	Indianapolis, Ind	Apr. 26, 1864	42, 544
Boot-leg straps, Method of securing	L. J. Worden	Utica, N Y	Jan. 26, 1858	19, 227
Boot-leg straps, Mode of attaching	J. A. Pickering	Milford, Mass	Apr. 5, 1859	23, 532
Boot-legs, Cramping Suwarrow	E. Lundy	New York, N. Y	Aug. 14, 1810	....
Boot-legs, Cramping Suwarrow	J. Sibley	New York, N. Y	Apr. 25, 1811	....
Boot-legs, Crimping	W. Gerrish	Poland, Me	Feb. 10, 1836	....
Boot-legs, Cutting and manufacturing	J. Vernon	Baltimore, Md	Oct. 21, 1811	....
Boot-legs, Machine for cramping	N. L. Moore	Smithfield, N. Y	Feb. 4, 1812	....
Boot-legs, Machine for crimping leather for	J. Van Winkle	Rochester, N. Y	Apr. 17, 1837	164
Boot-legs, Machine for turning	D. Bissell	Detroit, Mich	Dec. 3, 1861	33, 818
Boot-legs, Machine for turning	M. C. Chamberlin and W. Filkins.	Sheldon, N. Y	Nov. 25, 1856	16, 123
Boot-legs, Machine for turning	C. Collins	Warren, Ind	June 22, 1869	91, 606
Boot-legs, Machine for turning	A. Ransom	Manheim, N. Y	Jan. 29, 1861	31, 281
Boot-legs, Machine for turning	T. N. Saddler	Spencer, Mass	Nov. 8, 1836	73
Boot-legs, Machine for turning	J. Shearman	Fayetteville, Pa	Aug. 18, 1868	81, 301
Boot-legs, Mode of closing up	P. Ware and C. R. Tilton	Newton and Tisbury, Mass	Jan. 7, 1868	73, 062
Boot legs, Mode of siding	G. C. Parker	Worcester, Mass	July 8, 1873	147, 726
Boot-legs, Turning	J. H. Santord	Hopewell, N. Y	June 22, 1842	2, 686
Boot-lining	H. White	La Fayette, Ind	Aug. 26, 1873	142, 307
Boot, Mathematical	W. G. Crease and J. Morgan	Philadelphia, Pa	July 20, 1812	....
Boot, Moccasin	E. A. Buck	Bangor, Me	May 27, 1873	139, 234
Boot, Open-backed spring-box	W. Atchison	New York, N. Y	May 23, 1815	....
Boot or bootee	T. P. Mitchell	Haverhill, Mass	Dec. 2, 1873	145, 117
Boot or harness clamp	A. J. Curtis	Winterport, Me	Oct. 31, 1865	50, 766
Boot or shoe, Nailed	L. R. Blake	Boston, Mass	Aug. 8, 1865	49, 219
Boot or shoe, Pegged	S. Preston	Danvers, Mass	Mar. 8, 1833	....
Boot-packs, Method of cutting	W. G. Slater	Hart, Mich	Nov. 8, 1870	109, 065
Boot-pattern	J. F. Daniels	Greencastle, Ind	Sept. 10, 1872	131, 254
Boot-pattern	A. Forrist and C. A. Wheeler	Mount Vernon, Iowa	Sept. 24, 1861	33, 342
Boot-pattern	J. Rider	Wooster, Ohio	June 2, 1845	4, 068
Boot-pattern	S. C. Shive	Bloom Township, Pa	Aug. 14, 1847	5, 244
Boot-pattern	E. Shopbell	Ashland, Ohio	Feb. 8, 1870	99, 604
Boot-pattern	E. Shopbell	Ashland Ohio	Oct. 3, 1871	119, 538
Boot-pattern	W. Swarts	Pent Water, Mich	Oct. 19, 1869	95, 951
Boot, Plow	C. H. Ricker	Dover, N. H	Apr. 22, 1873	138, 196
Boot, Plowman's	A. G. Walker and S. Brown	Worcester, Mass	Aug. 19, 1873	142, 061
Boot-protector	J. U. Johnson	Springfield, Mass	Aug. 4, 1868	80, 549
Boot protector, Gaiter	F. N. Blodgett	Boston, Mass	Dec. 15, 1863	40, 901
Boot, Riding	B. C. Young	Boston, Mass	July 23, 1872	129, 776
Boot, Rubber	L. Elliott, jr	New Haven, Conn	Feb. 9, 1869	86, 827
Boot, Rubber	C. S. Foster and O. Taylor	Ashland and Philadelphia, Pa.	Aug. 29, 1871	118, 444
Boot, Rubber	C. E. Lins	Ashland, Pa	Aug. 15, 1871	118, 158
Boot-shank, Elastic	I. Gale	Natchez, Miss	July 11, 1844	3, 657
Boot-shank machine	L. Schije	Chicago, Ill	Dec. 22, 1868	85, 138
Boot-shank, Steel	H. and E. Briner	Manhattanville, N. Y	July 7, 1868	79, 631
Boot, shoe, or sandal, Metallic	G. W. Griswold	Abington, Pa	Apr. 5, 1864	42, 187
Boot, Skating	J. W. Pearson and H. O. Peabody.	Winchester, Mass	Jan. 1, 1861	31, 057
Boot-strap	F. H. Moore	Boston, Mass	Jan. 5, 1864	41, 087
Boot-strap fastener	S. Walker	Boston, Mass	Dec. 20, 1859	26, 552
Boot-strap guard	J. E. Curtis	Marlborough, Mass	Apr. 2, 1872	125, 274
Boot-strap, Metallic	D. Forrest	Eastport, Me	Mar. 30, 1869	88, 380
Boot-straps, Machine for making and wrapping webbing.	J. W. Richardson	South Braintree, Mass	Oct. 5, 1869	95, 516
Boot-stretcher	D. Harris	Litchfield, Ill	June 10, 1873	139, 671
Boot-stretcher	J. Harwood	Albany, N. Y	Jan. 25, 1870	99, 084
Boot-stretcher	J. Hoffman	Belvidere, N. J	Aug. 8, 1871	117, 777
Boot-stretcher	I. W. Myers	San Francisco, Cal	Jan. 24, 1871	111, 137
Boot-tops, &c., Revolving support for printing	A. P. Nash	Weymouth, Mass	June 11, 1872	127, 702
Boot-tops, Turning the edge of circular	P. C. Clapp	Stoughton, Mass	Apr. 13, 1858	19, 912
Boot-tree	J. Ayars	Brookfield, N. Y	Nov. 27, 1828	....
Boot-tree	W. H. Betts and I. H. Parker	Kokomo, Ind	July 19, 1859	24, 787
Boot-tree	T. Branigan	Beloit, Wis	Nov. 4, 1873	144, 312
Boot-tree	W. C. Clark	Baltimore, Md	June 30, 1863	39, 034
Boot tree	P. De Vries	Adrian, Mich	Nov. 19, 1867	70, 975
Boot-tree	C. T. Eames	Milford, Mass	May 27, 1856	14, 951
Boot-tree	O. V. Elliott	Mansfield, Pa	July 1, 1873	140, 490
Boot-tree	W. B. Fay and R. W. Collier	Upton, Mass	Apr. 5, 1859	23, 457
Boot-tree	D. Hastings	Deerfield, Mass	Dec. 15, 1837	514
Boot-tree	D. R. Hendrix	Pottstown, Pa	Oct. 28, 1851	8, 467
Boot-tree	J. Howe	Worcester, Mass	Oct. 24, 1848	5, 876
Boot-tree	W. and A. G. Kelsey	Delavan, Wis	Nov. 20, 1866	59, 842
Boot-tree	R. L. Lewis	Milford, Mass	Mar. 2, 1858	19, 508
Boot-tree	R. L. Lewis	Worcester, Mass	Mar. 5, 1867	62, 649
Boot-tree	M. Matthews	Wayne County, Ohio	Feb. 25, 1836	....
Boot-tree	H. B. Miller	Mayville, N. Y	Aug. 25, 1828	....
Boot-tree	O. P. Richardson	Worcester, Mass	June 23, 1863	38, 986
Boot tree	J. Russell	Philadelphia, Pa	July 7, 1846	4, 623
Boot-tree	D. Sadleir	McWilliamstown, Pa	Nov. 23, 1852	9, 425
Boot-tree	J. H. Sampson	Grafton, Mass	Dec. 4, 1855	13, 886
Boot-tree	W. Upfield	Lancaster, Ohio	June 25, 1850	7. 466
Boot-tree	W. Upfield	Lancaster, Ohio	Aug. 4, 1857	17, 947
Boot-tree	W. W. Willmott	Boston, Mass	Apr. 14, 1857	17, 067
Boot-tree	W. W. Willmott	Boston, Mass	May 4, 1858	20, 185

Index of patents issued from the United States Patent Office from 1790 *to* 1873, *inclusive*—Continued.

Invention.	Inventor.	Residence.	Date.	No.
Boot-tree	F. S. Wilt	Allentown, Pa	Dec. 17, 1867	72, 351
Boot-tree	A. J. Wisner	Homer, N. Y	July 13, 1858	20, 914
Boot-tree	H. Wright	Newcastle, Me	Jan. 16, 1849	6, 031
Boot-tree and stretcher	J. Bechtel	Roxbury, Pa	Aug. 25, 1868	81, 463
Boot-tree, Screw	G. Nichol	Madison, Va	Sept. 8, 1826	....
Boot-treeing machine	E. Hall, jr	Spencer, Mass	May 29, 1841	2, 110
Boot-trimming tool	L. C. Rogers	Danvers, Mass	Oct. 16, 1860	30, 427
Boot-tucking machine	S. C. Blodget	Rowley, Mass	June 11, 1836	....
Boot-vamps, Mode of cutting	E. L. Vertrees	Howe's Valley, Ky	Feb. 14, 1860	27, 173
Boot, Ventilated rubber	H. C. Cottrell	Norwich, Conn	Apr. 26, 1870	102, 228
Boot, Ventilated rubber	R. W. Perkins	Colchester, Conn	Apr. 26, 1870	102, 314
Boot, Ventilating	S. Perry	New York, N. Y	Aug. 21, 1866	57, 371
Boot, Water-proof	A. Cushman	Auburn, Me	Mar. 5, 1872	124, 257
Boots, &c., Adjusting pattern for	F. E. Augustine	Dubuque, Iowa	July 26, 1864	43, 631
Boots and gaiters, Machine for fitting fronts of	T. Lincoln	Saint Louis, Mo	Nov. 19, 1872	133, 106
Boots and other leather stock, Punching	C. H. Helms	Poughkeepsie, N. Y	Jan. 5, 1869	85, 661
Boots and shoes, Apparatus for crimping the stiffening of.	J. W. Hatch	Rochester, N. Y	Aug. 1, 1871	117, 027
Boots and shoes, Apparatus for holding and supporting.	E. Lemercier	Paris, France	Mar. 10, 1863	37, 886
Boots and shoes, Apparatus for molding box-toes for.	D. H. Packard	North Bridgewater, Mass	Oct. 21, 1873	143, 926
Boots and shoes, belts for ladies' dresses, &c., Clasp for.	E. W. Prussia	Marlborough, Mass	Aug. 11, 1868	80, 834
Boots and shoes, Black-ball for	G. A. Knowlton	Natick, Mass	Feb. 15, 1870	99, 915
Boots and shoes, Box-toe for	H. W. George	Danvers, Mass	Oct. 19, 1869	95, 894
Boots and shoes by rule, Cutting	S. Hart	Monkton, Vt	Mar. 3, 1821	....
Boots and shoes by substituting a metallic shank on outsole, Manner of manufacturing.	A. Thayer	Braintree, Mass	Apr. 24, 1841	2, 062
Boots and shoes, Cap for	B. F. Sage	Beverly, N. J	Jan. 23, 1872	122, 969
Boots and shoes, Channel for	R. Ashe	Boston, Mass	June 21, 1870	104, 534
Boots and shoes, Composition for printing designs on.	D. McKellar	Lowell, Mass	Mar. 2, 1869	87, 350
Boots and shoes, Compound rubber-enameled cloth for.	E. M. Stevens	Chelsea, Mass	Mar. 31, 1868	76, 265
Boots and shoes, Constructing	L. R. Blake	Boston, Mass	May 16, 1865	47, 696
Boots and shoes, Construction of	M. M. Wheeler	Galena, Ill	Feb. 25, 1873	136, 293
Boots and shoes, Cover for	W. E. Prall	Washington, D. C	Sept. 20, 1870	107, 538
Boots and shoes, Crimping	E. G. Pomeroy	Lancaster, Ohio	July 27, 1824	....
Boots and shoes, Cutting	J. Chilcott and R. Snell	Brooklyn, N. Y	Sept. 13, 1853	10, 099
Boots and shoes, Cutting and forming	J. Hall	Frederick Town, Md	Dec. 15, 1815	....
Boots and shoes, Device for holding	H. T. Dillon	Big Lick, Va	Jan. 14, 1868	73, 304
Boots and shoes, Device for tapping	G. Conkling	Conklinsville, N. Y	Aug. 9, 1864	43, 814
Boots and shoes, Die for making metallic shank for.	H. F. Whidden	South Abington, Mass	Aug. 29, 1871	118, 660
Boots and shoes, Edge-protecting welt for	J. Green	Brooklyn, N. Y	Oct. 14, 1873	143, 623
Boots and shoes, Elastic calk for	G. H. Clemens	New York, N. Y	Nov. 10, 1868	83, 930
Boots and shoes, Elastic goring for	J. Haskins	Boston, Mass	Oct. 13, 1868	82, 944
Boots and shoes, Elastic goring for	C. Winslow	Boston, Mass	Mar. 12, 1872	124, 527
Boots and shoes, Fastening	B. F. Allen and J. R. Ryerson	Saint Albans, Me	July 21, 1868	80, 109
Boots and shoes, Graduating pattern for	M. Meade	Boston, Mass	May 18, 1869	90, 115
Boots and shoes, Hand nail-driver for	E. Hale	Boston, Mass	July 28, 1868	80, 477
Boots and shoes, Hand-nailer for lasting	W. E. Fischer	Boston, Mass	June 1, 1869	90, 650
Boots and shoes, Head-block for holding	I. E. Allen	Windham, Me	Feb. 20, 1866	52, 657
Boots and shoes heels made of vulcanized wood, Method of attaching to the soles of.	F. H. Morgan	Beverly, Mass	May 11, 1869	90, 049
Boots and shoes, &c., Instrument for trimming welts of.	L. Clark	South Royalston, Mass	June 13, 1854	11, 078
Boots and shoes, Jack for nailing, &c	J. G. Ross	Philadelphia, Pa	Oct. 21, 1873	143, 786
Boots and shoes, Jack for the manufacture of	C. M. Gustin	Saccarappa, Me	Dec. 18, 1866	60, 507
Boots and shoes, Jointed tip for	G. A. Mitchell	Turner, Me	May 22, 1860	28, 395
Boots and shoes, Lasting	W. Wickersham	Boston, Mass	Aug. 22, 1871	118, 319
Boots and shoes lengthwise, Instrument for stretching.	W. Jones	Norfolk, Va	Nov. 20, 1866	59, 912
Boots and shoes, Lining for	J. Adams	Kokomo, Ind	Sept. 12, 1865	49, 946
Boots and shoes, Machine for burnishing shanks of	J. K. Blanchard, F. S. Hunt, and A. C. Carey.	Lynn and Malden, Mass	June 11, 1872	127, 838
Boots and shoes, Machine for crimping leather for	S. W. Jamison	Newark, N. J	June 10, 1873	139, 717
Boots and shoes, Machine for cutting out the uppers and soles of.	W. G. Greeley	Hingham, Mass	Feb. 14, 1860	27, 123
Boots and shoes, Machine for cutting pegs out of	T. Corey	Marlborough, Mass	May 15, 1866	54, 692
Boots and shoes, Machine for cutting rands for	J. H. Walker	Worcester, Mass	Dec. 3, 1872	133, 686
Boots and shoes, Machine for distributing nails for the manufacture of.	H. P. Fairfield	Boston, Mass	June 18, 1872	128, 134
Boots and shoes, Machine for feeding and inserting rivets in.	G. V. Sheffield	Boston, Mass	Apr. 30, 1872	126, 159
Boots and shoes, Machine for holding the uppers of	E. M. Dickinson	Fitchburgh, Mass	Apr. 11, 1865	47, 191
Boots and shoes, Machine for inserting screw-pegs in.	A. Cavalli	San Francisco, Cal	Apr. 1, 1873	137, 288
Boots and shoes, Machine for lasting the uppers of	M. R. Ethridge	Bethel, Me	Mar. 17, 1863	37, 907
Boots and shoes, Machine for making	E. Barnum	Massachusetts	Jan. 9, 1808	....
Boots and shoes, Machine for making	C. H. Southall and R. Heap	Staleybridge, England	Feb. 20, 1866	52, 802
Boots and shoes, Machine for making	E. Thayer	Leicester, Mass	Mar. 14, 1812	....
Boots and shoes, Machine for making	E. Thayer	Leicester, Mass	June 9, 1826	....
Boots and shoes, Machine for making shank-pieces for.	C. H., D. D., and F. M. Blake	Worcester, Mass	Jan. 7, 1873	134, 584
Boots and shoes, Machine for nailing and pegging	J. F. Sargent	Melrose, Mass	Sept. 7, 1869	94, 654
Boots and shoes, Machine for paring the edges of	H. Hodges	Lynn, Mass	Oct. 11, 1864	44, 688
Boots and shoes, Machine for pressing seams and cutting welts of.	E. Reed	Kingston, Mass	Feb. 23, 1869	87, 200
Boots and shoes, Machine for pressing seams and cutting welts for.	E. Reed	Kingston, Mass	July 26, 1870	105, 846
Boots and shoes, Machine for skiving counters for	W. A. Bacon	Campello, Mass	May 29, 1860	28, 531
Boots and shoes, Machine for trimming and burnishing the edges of.	C. J. Addy	Boston, Mass	Sept. 16, 1873	142, 756
Boots and shoes, Machine for turning channel-flaps for.	W. E. Fischer	Boston, Mass	July 2, 1872	128, 610
Boots and shoes, Machine for wrinkling the instep of.	C. Heisterman	Brownsville, Pa	Oct. 30, 1866	59, 219

Index of patents issued from the United States Patent Office from 1790 *to* 1873, *inclusive*—Continued.

Invention.	Inventor.	Residence.	Date.	No.
Boots and shoes, Machinery for burnishing the shanks of.	J. K. Blanchard, F. S. Hunt, and A. C. Carey.	Lynn and Malden, Mass	Mar. 12, 1872	124, 479
Boots and shoes, Machinery for crimping uppers for.	C. Glantz	Baltimore, Md	Dec. 30, 1873	145, 940
Boots and shoes, Machinery for lasting	A. C. Carey	Malden, Mass	Dec. 30, 1873	146, 043
Boots and shoes, Machinery for making wood shanks for.	W. N. Sprague	Keene, N. H	Nov. 25, 1873	145, 024
Boots and shoes, Making	J. Bedford	Philadelphia, Pa	July 16, 1806	....
Boots and shoes, Making	J. Frask	Hatfield, Mass	Apr. 5, 1826	....
Boots and shoes, Making	S. B. Hitchcock and J. Bement.	Homer, N. Y	July 30, 1811	....
Boots and shoes, Making	E. Martin	Salem, N. J	Jan. 12, 1824	....
Boots and shoes, Making	W. Montgomery	Philadelphia, Pa	Feb. 11, 1807	....
Boots and shoes, &c., Making furred	S. Eells	Connecticut	Feb. 24, 1816	....
Boots and shoes, Manufacture of	E. Alexander	Providence, R. I	Aug. 4, 1863	39, 370
Boots and shoes, Manufacture of	F. D. Ballou	Abington, Mass	Jan. 10, 1860	26, 808
Boots and shoes, Manufacture of	L. R. Blake	Abington, Mass	Aug. 14, 1860	29, 561
Boots and shoes, Manufacture of	L. R. Blake	Boston, Mass	May 18, 1869	90, 225
Boots and shoes, Manufacture of	L. R. Blake	Boston, Mass	Apr. 26, 1870	102, 362
Boots and shoes, Manufacture of	J. Boyle	New York, N. Y	July 29, 1873	141, 257
Boots and shoes, Manufacture of	W. N. Brookhouse	West Danvers, Mass	Oct. 4, 1870	107, 864
Boots and shoes, Manufacture of	M. F. Chandler and P. Ware	Boston, Mass	Dec. 24, 1872	134, 252
Boots and shoes, Manufacture of	W. Duchemin and A. Jeffries	Lynn, Mass	Aug. 27, 1867	68, 330
Boots and shoes, Manufacture of	C. Hawkes	Lynn, Mass	June 26, 1866	55, 858
Boots and shoes, Manufacture of	G. Hawkes	Lynn, Mass	June 29, 1869	91, 844
Boots and shoes, Manufacture of	L. and S. B. Holden	Woburn, Mass	Apr. 2, 1861	31, 929
Boots and shoes, Manufacture of	D. Howard		Apr. 10, 1800	....
Boots and shoes, Manufacture of	J. L. Joyce	New Haven, Conn	July 29, 1873	141, 357
Boots and shoes, Manufacture of	W. and J. Keats	Street, England	Dec. 10, 1867	72, 048
Boots and shoes, Manufacture of	W. and J. Keats	Leek, England	Feb. 11, 1868	74, 229
Boots and shoes, Manufacture of	C. A. Keith	Danvers, Mass	Aug. 12, 1873	141, 797
Boots and shoes, Manufacture of	D. Peck	New York, N. Y	Aug. 14, 1821	....
Boots and shoes, Manufacture of	H. Port	New York, N. Y	Aug. 4, 1863	39, 421
Boots and shoes, Manufacture of	D. Read	New York, N. Y	Sept. 26, 1865	50, 163
Boots and shoes, Manufacture of	E. P. Richardson	Lawrence, Mass	Apr. 27, 1869	89, 504
Boots and shoes, Manufacture of	S. J. Shaw	Marlborough, Mass	Feb. 13, 1872	123, 736
Boots and shoes, Manufacture of	E. W. Southworth	Ashland, Mass	Aug. 6, 1872	130, 162
Boots and shoes, Manufacture of	H. P. Stewart	Oak's Corners, N. Y	Dec. 18, 1866	60, 588
Boots and shoes, Manufacture of	H. G. Tyer and J. Helm	New Brunswick, N. J	Mar. 27, 1855	12, 607
Boots and shoes, Manufacture of	P. Ware, jr	Boston, Mass	Sept. 2, 1873	142, 538
Boots and shoes, Manufacture of	S. H. Whorf	Roxbury, Mass	Jan. 8, 1856	14, 080
Boots and shoes, Manufacture of	W. Wickersham	Boston, Mass	Aug. 2, 1870	106, 012
Boots and shoes, Manufacture of India-rubber	S. C. Smith	New York, N. Y	Dec. 7, 1837	503
Boots and shoes, Manufacture of vulcanized rubber	J. A. Greene	Brooklyn, N. Y	Apr. 6, 1869	88, 706
Boots and shoes, Manufacturing	A. Destony	New York, N. Y	Nov. 17, 1868	84, 245
Boots and shoes, Manufacturing	C. A. Ore	Philadelphia, Pa	May 5, 1831	....
Boots and shoes, Manufacturing	M. Pennock	East Marlborough, Pa	Dec. 14, 1830	....
Boots and shoes, Manufacturing counters for	S. C. Phinney	Stoughton, Mass	Feb. 9, 1869	86, 779
Boots and shoes, Mechanism for making counters for.	E. Andrews	Welchville, Me	July 8, 1873	140, 569
Boots and shoes, Metal tips for toes of	G. A. Mitchell	Turner, Me	Jan. 5, 1858	19, 040
Boots and shoes, Metallic counters for	A. R. Spaulding	Clinton, Me	Feb. 27, 1872	124, 094
Boots and shoes, Metallic shank for	E. Heaton	New Haven, Conn	Feb. 33, 1864	41, 701
Boots and shoes, Method of constructing	J. McComber	Rockford, Ill	Nov. 22, 1870	109, 408
Boots and shoes, Method of stretching	G. W. Griswold	Carbondale, Pa	Aug. 31, 1858	21, 334
Boots and shoes, Mock buttons and button-holes for the ornamentation of.	W. Butterfield	Boston, Mass	July 23, 1872	129, 785
Boots and shoes, Mode of cutting	J. B. Keen	Bridgeton, N. J	June 21, 1839	1, 178
Boots and shoes, Mode of cutting channels in	L. R. Blake	Boston, Mass	Jan. 21, 1868	73, 570
Boots and shoes, Mode of cutting out	S. Marshall	Philadelphia, Pa	June 23, 1829	....
Boots and shoes, Mode of lacing	W. Banister and A. H. Rowell	Lawrence, Mass	Mar. 31, 1868	76, 038
Boots and shoes, Mode of lining	B. S. Bryant	Hanson, Mass	Feb. 13, 1872	123, 674
Boots and shoes, Mode of securing taps on	T. H. Lindley	Providence, R. I	Oct. 22, 1872	132, 474
Boots and shoes, Mode of securing tips to	J. H. Jennings	New Bedford, Mass	Mar. 13, 1866	53, 150
Boots and shoes, Nail-presenting mechanism for	A. Knowlton and H. P. Fairfield.	Boston, Mass	July 23, 1872	129, 834
Boots and shoes, Nailing	L. R. Blake and A. S. Libby	Brooklyn, N. Y., and Lawrence, Mass.	July 1, 1873	140, 400
Boots and shoes, Pattern for cutting out the uppers of.	W. W. Merriam	Oswego, N. Y	Nov. 10, 1857	18, 594
Boots and shoes, Polished water-proof	J. Rynex, J. Haskins, and S. Knower.	Boston, Mass	Sept. 23, 1829	....
Boots and shoes, Process for preparing wood for	R. T. Havens	Wilmington, Ohio	May 1, 1866	54, 339
Boots and shoes, Process of ornamenting	E. J. Scott	Glasgow, Great Britain	May 18, 1869	90, 312
Boots and shoes, Rotary edge-key for polishing	S. H. Hodges	Lynn, Mass	Feb. 6, 1872	123, 477
Boots and shoes, Scale for cutting	S. F. Burdett and H. Still	Keokuk, Iowa, and Leavenworth City, Kans.	Nov. 1, 1859	25, 947
Boots and shoes, Screw-fastening for	J. Chilcott and R. Snell	Brooklyn, N. Y	Sept. 13, 1853	10, 021
Boots and shoes, Shank-piece for	J. V. Sheffield	Northbridge, Mass	May 3, 1870	102, 721
Boots and shoes, Shank-spring for	E. Heaton	New Haven, Conn	Nov. 19, 1867	71, 003
Boots and shoes, Shipping and show-case for	M. Buhler	Lamoille, Ill	June 17, 1873	140, 007
Boots and shoes, Siding	H. T. Daggett	South Braintree, Mass	July 7, 1868	79, 733
Boots and shoes, Spring bottom for	C. S. Hale and O. C. Hubbell	Cleveland, Ohio	Mar. 24, 1868	75, 900
Boots and shoes, Spring-shanks for	J. McGinley	Philadelphia, Pa	Mar. 13, 1849	6, 173
Boots and shoes, Ventilating	E. Thomas	Philadelphia, Pa	July 28, 1868	80, 518
Boots and shoes, Ventilating	A. Stocker	Watertown, N. Y	Sept. 27, 1864	44, 407
Boots and shoes, Ventilating rubber	B. H. Webb	North Cambridge, N. Y	Mar. 8, 1864	41, 879
Boots and shoes water-proof, Composition for making.	P. G. Nagle	Philadelphia, Pa	Feb. 10, 1837	125
Boots and shoes, Water-proof-composition shanks for.	W. H. Towers	Boston, Mass	Jan. 23, 1872	122, 925
Boots and shoes water-proof, Making	A. Buffum	Smithfield, R. I	Dec. 28, 1822	....
Boots and shoes water-proof, Making	P. G. Nagle	Philadelphia, Pa	Dec. 14, 1825	....
Boots and shoes, Wear-plate for	S. Minges	Rochester, N. Y	June 30, 1868	79, 492
Boots and shoes while applying the soles, Mechanism for protecting the uppers of.	J. Jenkins	Lynn, Mass	Aug. 23, 1859	25, 202
Boots and shoes whilst pegging, Mode of holding	S. Nourse	Danvers, Mass	Dec. 8, 1827	
Boots and shoes, Wire-driving machine for	W. Wickersham	Boston, Mass	Aug. 2, 1870	106, 011
Boots and shoes with nails and pegs, Manufacturing	N. Mills	New York, N. Y	Mar. 21, 1831	....

Index of patents issued from the United States Patent Office from 1790 *to* 1873, *inclusive*—Continued.

Invention.	Inventor.	Residence.	Date.	No.
Boots and shoes with wooden pegs, screws, notches, or creases, Manufacturing.	R. U. Richards	Norfolk, Conn	May 23, 1812	....
Boots and shoes without seams, Manufacture of the uppers of.	S. Middleton	England	Sept. 29, 1857	18, 291
Boots, Apparatus for drawing on	J. Russell	Saint Louis, Mo	July 16, 1872	129, 175
Boots, bootees, &c., Cutting uppers of	J. T. Buck	New Canaan, Conn	Oct. 27, 1835	....
Boots by hinges or boot-cramps, Manufacturing	N. Ayer	Saint Johnsbury, Vt	June 19, 1835	....
Boots, &c., Channel-opener for	F. Guscetti	New York, N. Y	May 13, 1873	138, 883
Boots, Clamp for crimping	E. G. Pomeroy	Newark, Ohio	Oct. 4, 18[illegible]6	....
Boots, Clamp for crimping leather for	J. M. Read	Boston, Mass	Mar. 16, 1841	2, 006
Boots, Construction of	L. R. Blake	Boston, Mass	Jan. 19, 1869	85, 989
Boots, Cramping	L. Lucas	Barre, Vt	July 25, 1832	....
Boots, Crimping	D. B. Barnum	New Fairfield, Conn	Aug. 5, 1833	....
Boots, Cutting	J. Adams	Kokomo, Ind	June 26, 1866	55, 799
Boots, Cutting	G. A. Brown	Milford, Mass	Mar. 15, 1864	41, 904
Boots, Cutting	T. Cranage	Warren, Ohio	Mar. 13, 1844	3, 481
Boo s, Cutting	S S. Drew	Dixon, Ill	Oct. 13, 1863	40, 308
Boots, Cutting	A. F. and J. A. Jones	Lexington, Ky	Mar. 14, 1848	5, 467
Boots, Cutting	D. Lynahon	Buffalo, N. Y	Oct. 18, 1853	10, 134
Boots, Cutting	A. J. Moore, S. Bleistein, and S. S. Shirk.	Lebanon, Pa	July 7, 1868	79, 676
Boots. Cutting gaiter	A. D. Drew	Dixon, Ill	Jan. 30, 1866	52, 274
Boots, Cutting leather for	J. Morgan	Philadelphia, Pa	Apr. 10, 1811	....
Boots, Cutting uppers of	J. S. Lewis	Athol, Mass	Nov. 27, 1855	13, 852
Boots, Cutting uppers of	O. Thibaudeau	Montreal, Canada	Aug. 20, 1872	130, 602
Boots, Cutting uppers of balmoral	H. Hayward	Fitchburgh, Mass	Jan. 9, 1866	51, 943
Boots, Device for pulling on	F. H. Moore	Boston, Mass	May 23, 1865	47, 847
Boots, Fastening for gaiter	P. S. Boothby	Biddeford, Me	Sept. 2, 1862	36, 383
Boots, Fastening straps to	P. H. Baker	Virginia City, Nev	Nov. 17, 1868	84, 157
Boots, Foxing and soling	A. G. Smith	Marathon, N. Y	May 12, 1868	77, 927
Boots, Lacing	F. Borchardt	Washington, D. C	Mar. 6, 1866	52, 954
Boots, Machine for blacking and cleaning	J. Folsom	Hallowell, Me	Apr. 14, 1835	....
Boots, Machine for crimping and forming the front of.	C. Day	Mineral Point, Wis	Dec. 14, 1869	97, 765
Boots, Machine for crimping leather for	M. S. Woodward	Marshallton, Pa	July 31, 1837	338
Boots, Machine for cutting gaiter	W. Snell	Easton, Pa	Apr. 10, 1849	6, 300
Boots, Machine for cutting out	B. Millett	Woburn, Mass	June 4, 1872	127, 630
Boots, Machine for drawing	L. H. Dole and N. Pickard	Rowley, Mass	July 12, 1834	....
Boots, Machine for manufacture of screwed	G. Galli	San Francisco, Cal	Sept. 1, 1868	81, 620
Boots, &c., Machine for piercing side-seams of	W. May	Binghamton, N. Y	May 30, 1871	115, 493
Boots, Machine for rubbing and rolling seams of	A. Thompson	Boston, Mass	May 6, 1873	138, 713
Boots, Machine for turning	H. Blodget and H. Boynton	Rowley, Mass	Sept. 26, 1835	....
Boots, Making	H. Thayer	Monson, Mass	May 17, 1870	103, 104
Boots, Making	J. Tumbull	Philadelphia, Pa	June 24, 1843	3, 143
Boots, Manufacture of	J. J. Christian	Yonkers, N. Y	Aug. 21, 1866	57, 289
Boots, Manufacture of	J. Scrimgeour	Brooklyn, N. Y	June 9, 1857	17, 524
Boots, Manufacturing	A. Burdick	Carroll, N. Y	Oct. 31, 1829	....
Boots, Manufacturing	P. Gordon	....	Aug. 10, 1791	....
Boots or shoes from skins with the hair on, Manufacturing.	S. H. and E. Brown and H. Whitman.	Norfolk, Conn	Apr. 16, 1833	....
Boots or shoes, Manufacturing	S. Gerhard and J. Vanneman	Camden, N. J	July 26, 1833	....
Boots, Pattern for cutting	A. D. Drew	Dixon, Ill	May 9, 1865	47, 623
Boots, Pattern for cutting	E. Shopbell	Ashland, Ohio	Jan. 27, 1863	37, 526
Boots, &c., Shank for	F. P. Buren	Trenton Mo	May 13, 1873	138, 851
Boots, shoes, &c., of gutta-percha combined with other fabrics, Making.	C. Keene	Sussex Place, England	May 23, 1848	5, 593
Boots, shoes, socks, &c., Water-proof	W. Atkinson	Tewkesbury, Mass	Mar. 7, 1834	....
Boots, Tap for rubber	F. Flynn	Smithfield, R. I	May 31, 1870	103, 594
Boots, Turning	P. Stevens	Stoughton, Mass	Mar. 4, 1836	....
Boots with gum-elastic gores, Gaiter	J. H. Dupont and T. Hyatt	New York, N. Y	Oct. 30, 1840	1, 841
Bootees and other articles, Eyes for lacing	L. Hoffmeister	Philadelphia, Pa	Jan. 5, 1864	41, 069
Bootees, Manufacture of	A. H. Silvester	Boston, Mass	Jan. 28, 1862	34, 273
Borax from native borate of lime, Manufacture of	T. Bell and H. Scholefield	South Shields, England	Oct. 9, 1855	13, 633
Borax from solutions used in treating wood, Process of recovering and reworking.	S. Beer	New York, N. Y	Dec. 1, 1868	84, 471
Borer, Compound slide and groove	Z. Holt	Chelmsford, Mass	May 27, 1833	....
Borer, Post-hole	A. F. Summers	Peoria, Ill	Aug. 25, 1868	81, 555
Boring and drilling machine	J. Goodin	Centralia, Ill	July 28, 1868	80, 475
Boring and drilling machine	J. J. Sheridan	New York, N. Y	Sept. 2, 1873	142, 416
Boring and drilling tool	L. Dow	Piermont, N. Y	Jan. 23, 1866	52, 148
Boring and grinding apparatus	S. Cary	Centreville, La	July 31, 1866	56, 705
Boring and marking machine	G. M Nickason	Ellenville, N. Y	Sept. 6, 1870	107, 091
Boring and mortising machine	H. Allen	Norwich, Conn	Apr. 11, 1854	10, 768
Boring and mortising machine	S. W. Bidwell	Hartford, Conn	Jan. 11, 1861	32, 509
Boring and mortising machine	C. Carter	Manchester, Mich	May 22, 1849	6, 458
Boring and mortising machine	J. J. Earley	Fairfield, Ohio	Sept. 15, 1868	82, 096
Boring and mortising machine	J. Humphrey	Ravenna, Ohio	Dec. 28, 1869	98, 265
Boring and mortising machine	A. O. Neal	Hyde Park, Mass	Jan. 26, 1869	86, 176
Boring and mortising machine	R. L. Nelson	Orange Court House, Va	Apr. 25, 1871	114, 183
Boring and mortising machine	J. Peters	Lebanon, Pa	Jan. 31, 1871	111, 472
Boring and mortising machine	C. G. Pollock	Cincinnati, Ohio	Sept. 20, 1859	25, 523
Boring and mortising machine	J. H. Power	Norwalk, Ohio	Jan. 31, 1837	115
Boring and mortising machine	R. D. Roys and N. French	Detroit, Mich	Jan. 23, 1845	3, 891
Boring and mortising machine	G. H. Stevens	Lowell, Wis	Nov. 18, 1856	16, 101
Boring and mortising machine	A. Swingle	Galveston, Tex	July 11, 1848	5, 661
Boring and mortising machine	S. W. Wright	Athens, Ohio	July 26, 1870	105, 760
Boring and mortising machine, Feed-motion for	J. M. Kendall	South Hardwick, Vt	Feb. 14, 1860	27, 134
Boring and mortising machinery	J. Wilkinson	Pennfield, N. Y	May 28, 1825	....
Boring and sawing machine	B. F. Goodspeed and D. H. Wiswell.	New York, N. Y	Apr. 16, 1834	....
Boring and tenoning machine	T. Place	Alfred Centre, N. Y	Mar. 12, 1867	62, 883
Boring and tenoning machine	A. Warren	Saugerties, N. Y	Apr. 17, 1826	....
Boring and tenoning machine, Wheelwright's	C. Cowdry and O. and C. C. Tolls.	Ithaca, N. Y	May 1, 1855	12, 776
Boring and tenoning machinery	D. Sperry	Colchester, Conn	Apr. 18, 1827	....
Boring and turning machine, Wood	A. and F. Brown	New York, N. Y	July 3, 1855	13, 158
Boring and turning machine, Wood	F. and A. Brown	New York, N. Y	Feb. 12, 1856	14, 223
Boring angular holes, Machine for	B. Merritt, jr	Newton, Mass	May 24, 1864	42, 863

Index of patents issued from the United States Patent Office from 1790 *to* 1873, *inclusive*—Continued.

Invention.	Inventor.	Residence.	Date.	No.
Boring-apparatus	S. Cary	Centreville, La	Aug. 7, 1866	57, 058
Boring-apparatus	S. R. and W. S. Hunter	Cortland, N. Y	May 16, 1865	47, 727
Boring-apparatus	J. Wheelock	Worcester, Mass	Oct. 11, 1870	108, 310
Boring-bar for boring and screw-cutting	E. S. Chapell	Milton, Mass	Sept. 3, 1867	68, 488
Boring-bit	S. Hipkins, jr	South Wheeling, W. Va	July 1, 1873	140, 370
Boring-bit	M. Jincks	Danville, N. Y	Apr. 2, 1867	63, 392
Boring-bit	D. Kelly	Muskegon, Mich	May 10, 1870	102, 829
Boring-bit	D. Kelly	Muskegon, Mich	July 11, 1871	116, 837
Boring-bit brace	H. S. Bartholomew	Bristol, Conn	May 28, 1867	65, 046
Boring-bit brace	J. B. Fellows	Concord, N. H	Sept. 24, 1867	69, 086
Boring-bit, Extension-shank for	W. S. Pattin	Portsmouth, Ohio	June 20, 1871	116, 090
Boring bit for boring gun-barrels, Nut	J. Green	Harper's Ferry, Va	Oct. 3, 1817	....
Boring bit, Hole	C. F. Kimball and A. Parsons	Portland, Me	Jan. 23, 1866	52, 174
Boring bit, Mineral	D. Shoemaker	Kittaning Township, Pa	Sept. 16, 1873	142, 949
Boring bit, Variable	W. Tucker	Glocester, R. I	Aug. 10, 1858	21, 160
Boring bit, Wood	C. Boernicke	Philadelphia, Pa	Apr. 16, 1867	63, 842
Boring bit, Wood	R. Cook	Saratoga Springs, N. Y	Aug. 18, 1868	81, 069
Boring-brace	J. A. and H. A. House	Bridgeport, Conn	Sept. 5, 1865	49, 758
Boring-brace attachment	J. S. Fray	Bridgeport, Conn	May 11, 1869	89, 925
Boring-drill	D. R. Erdmann	Philadelphia, Pa	Mar. 28, 1865	47, 001
Boring drill, Polygonal-hole	J. C. Broadley	Franklin, N. J	Dec. 14, 1869	97, 868
Boring-engine, Portable	T. Goodrum	Providence, R. I	Oct. 9, 1855	13, 646
Boring framing-timber, Machine for	J. Badger	Brooklyn, Conn	Jan. 20, 1838	572
Boring holes in posts, Machine for	T. T. Strode	Coatesville, Pa	Dec. 2, 1851	8, 509
Boring holes, Tool for	A. Eliaers	Boston, Mass	Dec. 20, 1864	45, 483
Boring-implements, Making	R. Cooke	Shelburne Falls, Mass	Nov. 13, 1855	13, 780
Boring-instrument, Guide-attachment for	A. Amory	New York, N. Y	July 27, 1869	92, 927
Boring-jar	J. Slusser	Cincinnati, Ohio	May 30, 1865	47, 993
Boring-machine	J. H. Aldrich	Portsmouth, N. H	Nov. 27, 1849	6, 909
Boring-machine	F. S. Allen and C. F. Ritchel	New York, N. Y	Nov. 21, 1871	121, 074
Boring-machine	R. Allison	Port Carbon, Pa	Oct. 9, 1866	58, 568
Boring-machine	C. N. Baldwin	Willington, Conn	Oct. 25, 1870	108, 552
Boring-machine	E. C. Barton	Bloomsburgh, Pa	Dec. 21, 1869	98, 014
Boring-machine	J. Bosenbury	Cherryville, N. J	Apr. 14, 1857	17, 017
Boring-machine	W. W. Carey and G. W. Harris	Lowell, Mass	Aug. 9, 1870	106, 120
Boring-machine	G. F. Cluff	Petersburgh, Ill	Nov. 7, 1871	120, 716
Boring-machine	J. B. Coffin	Mohicanville, Ohio	June 20, 1845	4, 085
Boring-machine	E. C. Cole	Pawling, N. Y	Aug. 6, 1872	130, 193
Boring-machine	A. M. Connett	Madison, Ind	July 21, 1868	80, 059
Boring-machine	G. S. Corwin	Riverhead, N. Y	Nov. 3, 1863	40, 459
Boring-machine	I. Cory	Dalton, Ind	Feb. 11, 1873	135, 693
Boring-machine	W. H. Deatrick	Heidlersburgh, Pa	Nov. 1, 1870	108, 890
Boring-machine	E. C. Dodge	Edgecomb, Me	Nov. 30, 1869	97, 280
Boring-machine	L. A. Dole	Salem, Ohio	July 6, 1858	20, 779
Boring-machine	A. Dool and P. B. White	Dowagiac, Mich	Mar. 31, 1868	76, 171
Boring-machine	E. P. Drake	Greenbush, N. Y	Apr. 23, 1861	32, 125
Boring-machine	J. Edgecomb	Worcester, Mass	Jan. 14, 1862	34, 137
Boring-machine	J. Edgecomb	Worcester, Mass	June 28, 1864	43, 364
Boring-machine	S. L. Fitts	Ashburnham, Mass	June 11, 1861	32, 55[illegible]
Boring-machine	J. W. Frazee	Peoria, Ill	July 12, 1870	105, 188
Boring-machine	W. C. Freeman	Louisiana, Mo	Oct. 22, 1872	132, 393
Boring-machine	J. Gardner	Bigler, Pa	Apr. 16, 1872	125, 802
Boring-machine	F. M. Gibson	Chelsea, Mass	Dec. 7, 1869	97, 499
Boring-machine	N. Gillet and J. Smith	Cazenovia, N. Y	Apr. 8, 1812	....
Boring-machine	E. A. Goodes	Philadelphia, Pa	Jan. 25, 1859	22, 724
Boring machine	J. Hampson	Newburgh, N. Y	Dec. 7, 1869	97, 506
Boring-machine	H. Hays	New York, N. Y	July 5, 1859	24, 633
Boring-machine	J. Isenberg	McConnellstown, Pa	Feb. 26, 1867	62, 491
Boring-machine	J. Johnson	Mifflinsburgh, Pa	Mar. 13, 1847	5, 011
Boring-machine	J. Jones	Camden, N. J	Sept. 26, 1848	5, 809
Boring-machine	F. L. King	Worcester, Mass	Nov. 23, 1869	97, 202
Boring-machine	S. U. King	Windsor, Vt	May 24, 1864	42, 914
Boring-machine	S. Klahr	Reamstown, Pa	Dec. 16, 1856	16, 241
Boring-machine	C. B. Knapp	Waterloo, Wis	Apr. 2, 1867	63, 532
Boring-machine	A. Leonard	Sullivan, Ohio	Sept. 17, 1861	33, 324
Boring-machine	R. Little	Freeport, Ill	May 16, 1871	114, 953
Boring-machine	C. R. Long	Louisville, Ky	Sept. 1, 1868	81, 655
Boring-machine	H. Longwell	Mansfield, Pa	June 17, 1873	139, 901
Boring-machine	J. Longyear	Grass Lake, Mich	Feb. 18, 1862	34, 436
Boring-machine	N. R. Merchant	Guilford, N. Y	May 28, 1861	32, 449
Boring-machine	J. L. Metcalfe	Quincy, Pa	Apr. 16, 1872	125, 828
Boring-machine	J. Meyer	Brooklyn, N. Y	June 16, 1863	38, 908
Boring-machine	R. O. Moorhouse and S. L. Wiegand.	Philadelphia, Pa	Aug. 12, 1873	141, 657
Boring-machine	W. Morstatt	New York, N. Y	June 14, 1870	104, 337
Boring-machine	J. H. Pardieck	Acton, Ind	Mar. 7, 1871	112, 372
Boring-machine	Z. C. Phillips	Allegheny City, Pa	Jan. 2, 1872	122, 402
Boring-machine	C. E. Pierce	Westminster, Md	May 21, 1872	126, 902
Boring-machine	H. Pitcher	Fond du Lac, Wis	May 13, 1873	138, 927
Boring-machine	W. P. Powers	North La Crosse, Wis	Aug. 1, 1871	117, 567
Boring-machine	E. Quinn	Trenton, N. J	Aug. 25, 1857	18, 057
Boring-machine	E. Quinn	Washington, D. C	Mar. 27, 1866	53, 485
Boring-machine	B. F. Rea. M. Pyke, and D. M. Rennoe.	South Bend, Ind	Oct. 28, 1873	144, 139
Boring-machine	J. Ribon	New York, N. Y	Jan. 4, 1870	98, 633
Boring-machine	G. F. Rice	Worcester, Mass	Dec. 21, 1858	22, 379
Boring-machine	W. Samuels and G. L. Stansbury.	Jackson Township, Ind	June 3, 1856	15, 02[illegible]
Boring-machine	S. T. Sanford	Fall River, Mass	July 12, 1853	9, 845
Boring-machine	J. W. Shaw	Wenona, Mich	Dec. 17, 1872	134, 059
Boring-machine	J. Simpson	Meadville, Pa	Feb. 27, 1872	124, 091
Boring-machine	D. Stanley and G. Johnson	Cincinnati, Ohio	Sept. 12, 1865	49, 933
Boring-machine	L. Stevens	Elmira, N. Y	Dec. 15, 1857	18, 872
Boring-machine	J. Strickler	Columbiana, Ohio	Aug. 26, 1873	142, 296
Boring-machine	M. Sweet	Troy, N. Y	Apr. 13, 1869	88, 821
Boring-machine	B. F. Taft	South Groton, Mass	Dec. 12, 1854	12, 078
Boring-machine	O. F. Teed	Guilford, N. Y	Oct. 15, 1872	132, 187
Boring-machine	J. Temple	Birmingham, Pa	Feb. 26, 1856	14, 327

Index of patents issued from the United States Patent Office from 1790 *to* 1873, *inclusive*—Continued.

Invention.	Inventor.	Residence.	Date.	No.
Boring-machine	A. J. Truxell	Lynchburgh, Va	Nov. 8, 1870	109, 078
Boring-machine	W. Tucker	Fiskedale, Mass	Jan. 28, 1870	104, 797
Boring-machine	J. Van Dyke	Grimsby, Canada	July 25, 1865	49, 060
Boring-machine	J. Waugh	Elmira, N. Y	May 31, 1859	24, 252
Boring-machine	J. Webster	Great Barrington, Mass	May 1, 1810	....
Boring-machine	A. Weikart	Green Village, Ohio	Nov. 1, 1845	4, 251
Boring-machine	A. Weikart	Greenford, Ohio	Jan. 15, 1850	7, 031
Boring-machine	W. H. Willcox	Tarrytown, N. Y	May 29, 1849	6, 484
Boring-machine	E. J. Worcester	Worcester, Mass	Dec. 27, 1870	110, 530
Boring-machine	A. Wyckoff and E. R. Morrison	Elmira, N. Y	Sept. 25, 1855	13, 606
Boring-machine	E. F. Young	Charlestown, Mass	June 26, 1866	55, 945
Boring machine, Cylinder	M. S. Otis	Rochester, N. Y	June 19, 1855	13, 117
Boring machine, Perpendicular	R. Selden		July 7, 1806	....
Boring machine, Rock	G. C. Doherty	Cumberland County, Ky	Aug. 29, 1838	897
Boring machine, Timber	R. Hubbell	Hudson, Ohio	Oct. 26, 1839	1, 382
Boring machine, Timber	R. Smith	Towanda, Pa	Feb. 10, 1843	2, 948
Boring machine, Wood	G. Dryden	Worcester, Mass	July 7, 1868	79, 640
Boring machine, Wood	H. Fleming	Vienna, N. J	Mar. 24, 1868	75, 891
Boring machine, Wood	B. F. Mohr	Mifflinburgh, Pa	Apr. 20, 1869	89, 163
Boring machine, Wood	A. Roff	Southport, Conn	Mar. 31, 1868	76, 103
Boring machine, Wood	L. Stevens	Elmira, N. Y	Oct. 6, 1857	18, 370
Boring machine, Wood	J. B. Thorp	Warrensville, Ohio	Mar. 24, 1868	75, 813
Boring-machines, Adjustment in	I. W. Ward	Birmingham, Pa	Mar. 18, 1856	14, 479
Boring-machines, Device for feeding and limiting the depth of hole in.	L. B Lloyd	Warwick Township, Pa	June 23, 1857	17, 630
Boring machines, Device for feeding the cutters intermittently in mortise.	H. E. Paine	Troy, N. Y	July 14, 1857	17, 799
Boring-machines, Method of adjusting cylinder in	W. B. Emery	Albany, N. Y	Feb. 27, 1855	12, 437
Boring-machines to objects, Method of securing	P. Baylor	Salem, Ohio	July 1, 1844	3, 645
Boring-machines, Variable crank for	G. C. Taft	Worcester, Mass	Dec. 10, 1867	72, 114
Boring-mill	F. E. Hahn	Philadelphia, Pa	Sept. 9, 1873	142, 694
Boring mill	W. Sellers	Philadelphia, Pa	June 23, 1857	17, 641
Boring-mill	J. Wheelock	Worcester, Mass	Mar. 12, 1872	124, 647
Boring-mill for metal	W. Sellers	Philadelphia, Pa	Aug. 5, 1862	36, 112
Boring, planing, and slotting metals, Machine for	N. Aylsworth	Rochester, N. Y	Jan. 2, 1855	12, 117
Boring post-holes in the earth, Machine for	J. S. Wertz	Middletown, Iowa	July 5, 1859	24, 682
Boring, reaming out, &c., Machine for	E. Johnson	Lexington Heights, N. Y	Nov. 7, 1826	....
Boring timber for mortising	B. Knight	Cranston, R. I	Oct. 23, 1834	....
Boring-tool	A. Allan	New York, N. Y	Oct. 12, 1869	95, 627
Boring-tool	F. S. Allen	New York, N. Y	May 28, 1872	127, 209
Boring-tool	W. Brodhead	Rondout, N. Y	Aug. 8, 1865	49, 336
Boring-tool	J. C. Chapman	Cambridgeport, Mass	Apr. 23, 1867	63, 992
Boring-tool	A. G. Hotchkiss	Wolcottville, Conn	July 5, 1870	104, 958
Boring-tool	W. J. Johnson and G. Tainter	Newton and Watertown, Mass.	Oct. 5, 1869	95, 483
Boring-tool	M. Joy	West Greenville, Pa	Aug. 8, 1865	49, 277
Boring-tool	W. P. Lathrop	West Winsted, Conn	Oct. 18, 1870	108, 367
Boring-tool	J. Miller	New York, N. Y	Jan. 29, 1867	61, 629
Boring-tool	G. W. Moore	Harrisburgh, Pa	Feb. 20, 1872	123, 786
Boring-tool	A. Steinbok	New York, N. Y	July 28, 1868	80, 515
Boring-tool	T. E. Stanley	Hazelhurst, Miss	July 12, 1870	105, 271
Boring-tool	C. C. Strong	Defiance, Ohio	July 6, 1869	92, 395
Boring-tool	N. Thompson	Saint John's Wood, England	Jan. 8, 1867	61, 121
Boring-tool	G. I. Washburn	Worcester, Mass	July 26, 1859	24, 894
Boring-tool	A. F. Whitin	Whitinsville, Mass	Apr. 23, 1872	126, 120
Boring-tool	E. F. Whitney and R. Jones	Union Mills, Pa	May 17, 1870	103, 265
Boring-tool	A. Wippo	Chicago, Ill	Dec. 17, 1867	72, 436
Boring-tool, Expanding	J. K. Kacerovsky	Bridgeport, Conn	Mar. 11, 1873	136, 736
Boring-tools, Coupling for shafts of	J. Esler	Brooklyn, N. Y	July 11, 1865	48, 667
Boring-tools, Coupling for shafts of	J. B. Stockton	Oil City, Pa	Oct. 3, 1865	50, 287
Boring-tools, Coupling for shafts of	J. Watson	Philadelphia, Pa	Sept. 26, 1865	50, 190
Boring-tools, Coupling shafts of	J. N. Bolles	Baltimore, Md	May 9, 1865	47, 613
Boring-tools, Coupling shafts of	D. G. Coppin	Cincinnati, Ohio	July 18, 1865	48, 793
Boring-tools, Coupling shafts of	S. Fawcett	Rochester, N. Y	Mar. 13, 1866	53, 219
Boring-tools, Coupling shafts of	E. Kaylor	Pittsburgh, Pa	Sept. 26, 1865	50, 138
Boring tools, Coupling shafts of	R. H. Lecky	Allegheny City, Pa	May 2, 1865	47, 554
Boring-tools, Coupling shafts of	R. H. Lecky	Allegheny City, Pa	May 2, 1865	47, 556
Boring-tools, Coupling shafts of	A. A. Wilson	Green Point, N. Y	May 23, 1865	47, 907
Boring wood	J. B. Pell	New York, N. Y	Mar. 2, 1836	....
Bosom and collar, Combined over	I. T. Dyer	Canton, Mo	Nov. 4, 1873	144, 267
Bosom, collar, and similar articles of apparel	A. Johnson	Brooklyn, N. Y	Feb. 25, 1873	136, 247
Bosom-expander	D. M. Church and C. A. Ellsworth.	Birmingham, Conn	May 8, 1860	28, 155
Bosom-holder, Elastic	G. W. Wright	Salem, Ohio	July 16, 1872	128, 994
Bosom-pad	B. Carter	Middletown, Conn	Jan. 8, 1869	90, 923
Bosom-pad	J. C. Cook	Buffalo, N. Y	Apr. 21, 1868	76, 894
Bosom-pad	E. W. Glover	Medford, Mass	Oct. 22, 1867	69, 988
Bosom-pad	A. H. Johnson	Hartford, Conn	May 5, 1868	77, 493
Bosom-pad	H. W. Libbey	Cleveland, Ohio	Mar. 3, 1868	75, 030
Bosom-pad	H. W. Libbey	Cleveland, Ohio	Mar. 3, 1868	75, 031
Bosom-pad	H. M. Millar	Louisville, Ky	Oct. 21, 1873	143, 921
Bosom-pad	C. A. Phillips	Chicago, Ill	Feb. 18, 1873	135, 936
Bosom-pad	J. Waterman	New York, N. Y	Mar. 1, 1870	100, 472
Bosom-pin	J. P. Derby	South Reading, Mass	Feb. 17, 1857	16, 640
Bottle	J. N. Bodine	Bridgeton, N. J	Aug. 14, 1860	29, 563
Bottle	R. Boeklen and H. T. Brown	Jersey City, N. J., and Brooklyn, N. Y.	July 25, 1854	11, 353
Bottle	C. W. Cahoon	Portland, Me	Nov. 28, 1865	51, 141
Bottle	C. W. Cahoon	Portland, Me	Nov. 28, 1865	51, 142
Bottle	H. S. Carley	Cambridgeport, Mass	Sept. 24, 1867	69, 177
Bottle	W. Clark	New York, N. Y	July 25, 1854	11, 357
Bottle	H. Codd	Camberwell, England	July 23, 1872	129, 652
Bottle	G. G. Hickman	Coatesville, Pa	Mar. 3, 1868	75, 014
Bottle	V. H. Lyon	Indianapolis, Ind	June 17, 1873	139, 905
Bottle	J. Maurer	New York, N. Y	Aug. 14, 1860	29, 611
Bottle	B. C. Odell	Kingston, N. Y	Oct. 8, 1872	132, 020
Bottle and bottle-stopper	H. Naylor	Oil City, Pa	Mar. 4, 1873	136, 534
Bottle and box opener	G. J. Hill	Buffalo, N. Y	Aug. 29, 1871	118, 453
Bottle and case, Combined	G. W. Banker and G. W. Peck	New York, N. Y	July 16, 1872	128, 940

Index of patents issued from the United States Patent Office from 1790 to 1873, inclusive—Continued.

Invention.	Inventor.	Residence.	Date.	No.
Bottle and glass case	J. Mathieu	Paris, France	Sept. 6, 1870	107, 189
Bottle and jug stopper	J. B. Alexander	Washington, D. C	June 18, 1867	65, 857
Bottle and transportation case	C. Burnham and I. G. Taite	Philadelphia, Pa	June 18, 1872	128, 109
Bottle, barrel, &c., stopper	S. Marsh	Detroit, Mich	Mar. 5, 1872	124, 277
Bottle box, Porter	G. W. Righter	Philadelphia, Pa	June 5, 1860	28, 606
Bottle-cap	M. V. Oiry	Philadelphia, Pa	Sept. 25, 1866	58, 281
Bottle cap and spoon, Mustard	H. J. White	Boston, Mass	Aug. 12, 1873	141, 844
Bottle cap or cover	J. G. Chillingworth	London, England	July 1, 1873	140, 346
Bottle cap or top	W. Burnet	New York, N. Y	July 2, 1867	66, 212
Bottle-capping machine	A. C. Jordan	New York, N. Y	May 14, 1872	126, 711
Bottle-capping machine	W. H. Sperling	Washington, N. J	June 20, 1871	116, 107
Bottle, Capsuling	J. Paterson	Edinburgh, North Britain	Nov. 28, 1871	121, 407
Bottle-casing	J. Dugan	New York, N. Y	Sept 9, 1873	142, 685
Bottle, Cast-iron mercury	X. Wrangle	New York, N. Y	Dec. 28, 1858	22, 476
Bottle, Caster	B. Beach	West Meriden, Conn	July 17, 1866	56, 486
Bottle, Caster	C. Casper	West Meriden, Conn	June 11, 1872	127, 740
Bottle, Caster	C. P. Crossman	West Warren, Mass	Sept. 15, 1863	39, 889
Bottle, Caster	A. Weber	Newark, N. J	July 1, 1873	140, 564
Bottle, Caster	A. Weber	Newark, N. J	Dec. 2, 1873	145, 138
Bottle-closing device	C. Herman	Baltimore, Md	June 25, 1867	66, 023
Bottle cork	I. B. Sampson	Albany, N. Y	May 13, 1873	138, 820
Bottle-cork fastener	D. Miller	Marietta, Ohio	May 14, 1861	32, 306
Bottle-cork fastening	J. Conner	Brooklyn, N. Y	June 11, 1872	127, 851
Bottle-corks, Labeling	F. W. Copcutt	New York, N. Y	Dec. 24, 1867	72, 606
Bottle-corks, Machine for making	J. Barron	Hampton, Va	Jan. 12, 1819	....
Bottle-corking	C. H. Porter	Albany, N. Y	July 30, 1867	67, 346
Bottle-corking apparatus	T. W. Gillett	New Haven, Conn	July 11, 1854	11, 281
Bottle-corking apparatus	A. C. Jordan	New York, N. Y	Aug. 26, 1873	142, 240
Bottle-corking apparatus	G. Migliavacca	Napa, Cal	Mar. 30, 1869	88, 404
Bottle-corking apparatus	H. Redlich	Chicago, Ill	May 20, 1862	35, 325
Bottle-corking apparatus	H. Unger	Logansport, Ind	Mar. 9, 1869	87, 732
Bottle-corking machine	J. Armstrong	San Francisco, Cal	Oct. 14, 1873	143, 606
Bottle-corking machine	L. S. Chichester	New York, N. Y	Feb. 22, 1859	23, 058
Bottle-corking machine	H. N. De Graw	Piermont, N. Y	Mar. 18, 1856	14, 446
Bottle-corking machine	D. Mueller	New York, N. Y	Apr. 4, 1871	113, 326
Bottle-corking machine	J. Wolff and W. N. Numsen	New York, N. Y., and Baltimore, Md.	Sept. 20, 1870	107, 582
Bottle, Cosmetic	M. H. Huntington	Watertown, N. Y	Oct. 14, 1873	143, 627
Bottle-cover	W. Bourguignon	Providence, R. I	Dec. 16, 1873	145, 484
Bottle-envelope	J. Seithen	Coblenz, Prussia	Feb. 12, 1856	14, 255
Bottle-fastener	G. Otto and G. W. Bauer	Washington, D. C	July 4, 1871	116, 742
Bottle-fastener	I. Winslow	Philadelphia, Pa	Dec. 18, 1849	6, 963
Bottle-fasteners, Key and cork-screw for	H. W. Putnam	Cleveland, Ohio	Sept. 23, 1862	36, 528
Bottle-fastening	J. Allender	New London, Conn	July 24, 1855	13, 338
Bottle-fastening	B. Bates	Baltimore, Md	Dec. 27, 1870	110, 421
Bottle-fastening	W. S. M. Beal	Baltimore, Md	Oct. 31, 1871	120, 363
Bottle-fastening	J. Jeannotat	Paterson, N. J	July 17, 1855	13, 266
Bottle-fastening	J. Spratt	Cincinnati, Ohio	Sept. 6, 1853	9, 995
Bottle-fastening	E. D. Weatherbee	Worcester, Mass	Apr. 4, 1871	113, 603
Bottle-fastening	H. and J. Wilson	Paterson, N. J., and New York, N. Y.	July 24, 1866	56, 653
Bottle-fastening, Cork-saving	C. L. Knecht	Clair Township, Pa	May 31, 1870	103, 624
Bottle-fastening, Register	J. Smylie	Philadelphia, Pa	Oct. 9, 1855	13, 659
Bottle-fastenings, Band for securing	E. D. Weatherbee	Shrewsbury, Mass	Apr. 16, 1872	125, 866
Bottle-fastenings, Ring and gudgeon for	J. C. Day	Hackettstown, N. J	Nov. 13, 1855	13, 782
Bottle-filler	T. Cochen	Williamsburgh, N. Y	June 5, 1866	55, 242
Bottle-filler	E. Jeanjaquet	New York, N. Y	May 4, 1869	89, 664
Bottle-filler	J. H. Parkhurst	Milwaukee, Wis	Sept. 17, 1872	131, 457
Bottle-filler	F. Schlich and A. Feyh	New York, N. Y	May 6, 1873	138, 534
Bottle filler and corker	T. W. Cowey	Cannonsburgh, Pa	Feb. 9, 1869	86, 816
Bottle-filling apparatus	A. Albertson	New York, N. Y	Oct. 11, 1864	44, 685
Bottle-filling apparatus	G. B. Bachmann	Brooklyn, N. Y	Nov. 10, 1868	83, 904
Bottle-filling apparatus	C. A. Gregory	Poughkeepsie, N. Y	Aug. 28, 1860	29, 781
Bottle-filling apparatus	C. A. Gregory	Poughkeepsie, N. Y	July 12, 1870	105, 328
Bottle-filling apparatus	C. A. Gregory	Quebec, Canada	Nov. 19, 1872	133, 094
Bottle-filling apparatus	J. Matthews, jr	New York, N. Y	Nov. 7, 1865	50, 832
Bottle-filling apparatus	J. Matthews, jr	New York, N. Y	Dec. 8, 1868	84, 836
Bottle-filling apparatus	J. Matthews	New York, N. Y	Apr. 29, 1873	138, 421
Bottle-filling apparatus	H. W. Putnam	Cleveland, Ohio	Oct. 29, 1861	33, 602
Bottle-filling apparatus	P. M. Sherwood	New York, N. Y	Nov. 24, 1868	84, 384
Bottle-filling apparatus	T. Simmons and D. H. Lowe	Brooklyn, N. Y	Dec. 27, 1870	110, 504
Bottle-filling machine	J. Alcorn	Charlestown, Mass	Feb. 9, 1869	86, 721
Bottle-filling machine	W. F. Davidson	Cincinnati, Ohio	Feb. 16, 1864	41, 608
Bottle filling machine	C. A. Gregory	Quebec, Canada	Aug. 6, 1872	130, 126
Bottle-filling machine	W. M. Tate	Zanesville, Ohio	Nov. 3, 1863	40, 516
Bottle, Filtering and pouring	V. M. Griswold	Peekskill, N. Y	Dec. 22, 1868	85, 088
Bottle for aërated liquids	J. D. Lynde	Philadelphia, Pa	Apr. 8, 1862	34, 894
Bottle for aërated liquids	T. Warker	New York, N. Y	Mar. 18, 1862	34, 709
Bottle for containing mercury	I. G. Johnson	Spuyten Duyvil, N. Y	Oct. 19, 1858	21, 835
Bottle for gaseous liquids	J. F. Kubly and C. F. Crailsheim.	New York, N. Y., and Paris, France.	Apr. 12, 1870	101, 889
Bottle for holding hydrofluoric acid	D. P. Webster	New York, N. Y	Apr. 14, 1868	76, 678
Bottle for infants and invalids, Cap for feeding	J. Thompson and J. G. Ingram	London, England	May 25, 1869	90, 606
Bottle for oil	C. W. Cahoon	Portland, Me	Feb. 7, 1865	46, 214
Bottle for tooth-powder, Toilet	W. A. Spalding	Waterbury, Conn	Aug. 15, 1871	118, 163
Bottle, Glass	J. Borden and J. L. Trimble	Medford, N. J	Nov. 25, 1873	144, 885
Bottle, Glass	J. McGann	Kensington, Pa	Nov. 26, 1830	....
Bottle, Graduated	G. W. Stoeckel	Pittsburgh, Pa	Feb. 6, 1866	52, 461
Bottle-handle	G. Ireland	Birmingham, England	Jan. 30, 1866	52, 373
Bottle-holder	W. O. Pond	Mobile, Ala	May 28, 1872	127, 268
Bottle holder and ice-box, Combined	S. R. Briggs	Owego, N. Y	July 16, 1872	129, 094
Bottle holder, Caster	A. E. Young	Dorchester, Mass	Sept. 5, 1865	49, 840
Bottle holder, Caster	A. E. Young	Dorchester, Mass	Sept. 5, 1865	49, 841
Bottle holding and transporting box	J. Matthews, jr	New York, N. Y	Mar. 5, 1867	62, 658
Bottle holding and transporting box	J. Matthews	New York, N. Y	June 10, 1873	139, 722
Bottle-lock	J. Dugan	New York, N. Y	Aug. 17, 1869	93, 866
Bottle-lock	L. Lehman	Harrisburgh, Pa	June 16, 1868	78, 976
Bottle lock	W. A. Ludden	Brooklyn, N. Y	Dec. 22, 1868	85, 111

Index of patents issued from the United States Patent Office from 1790 *to* 1873, *inclusive*—Continued.

Invention.	Inventor.	Residence.	Date.	No.
Bottle-making tool	J. Wilson	New York, N. Y	June 14, 1870	104, 390
Bottle, Medicine	W. H. Flinn	Nashua, N. H	Mar. 24, 1868	75, 744
Bottle, Medicine	W. H. Flinn	Nashua, N. H	Mar. 24, 1868	75, 745
Bottle-mold	J. L. Mason	New York, N. Y	Nov. 23, 1858	22, 129
Bottle-mold	L. Thomas	Philadelphia, Pa	June 23, 1868	79, 162
Bottle mold, Glass	J. J. Christie	Baltimore, Md	Dec. 17, 1867	72, 368
Bottle mold, Glass	J. J. Christie	Camden, N. J	Nov. 12, 1872	132, 897
Bottle mold, Glass	C. D. Fox	Philadelphia, Pa	Apr. 29, 1873	138, 323
Bottle mold, Glass	S. S. Shinn	Lancaster, N. Y	Nov. 16, 1858	22, 091
Bottle, Nursing	M. S. Burr	Boston, Mass	Aug. 27, 1867	68, 285
Bottle, Nursing	W. Hobson	Sandwich, Mass	June 17, 1873	139, 958
Bottle, Nursing	A. M. Knapp	Racine, Wis	Feb. 9, 1869	86, 762
Bottle, Nursing	F. J. La Forme	Boston, Mass	Nov. 29, 1859	26, 327
Bottle, Nursing	H. W. Libbey	Cleveland, Ohio	June 16, 1868	78, 881
Bottle, Nursing	E. J. Mallet, jr., and W. S. Ward	New York, N. Y	Apr. 26, 1870	102, 289
Bottle, Nursing	J. L. Mason	New York, N. Y	Apr. 26, 1870	102, 417
Bottle, Nursing	T. J. Mayall	Boston, Mass	July 1, 1873	140, 518
Bottle, Nursing	P. J. McElroy	East Cambridge, Mass	June 16, 1868	78, 987
Bottle, Nursing	W. B. Potter	Boston, Mass	Jan. 11, 1859	22, 579
Bottle, Nursing	E. Pratt	New York, N. Y	Aug. 9, 1845	4, 138
Bottle, Nursing	G. R. White	Boston, Mass	Apr. 22, 1873	138, 219
Bottle, Nursing	S. Zeno	New York, N. Y	Apr. 19, 1864	42, 427
Bottle-opener	C. R. Trimble	New York, N. Y	Oct. 10, 1871	119, 802
Bottle-opening instrument	J. Woolaver	Suisun, Cal	Nov. 7, 1865	50, 868
Bottle or caster, Salt	G. B. Richardson	Boston, Mass	Dec. 3, 1867	71, 643
Bottle-packer	R. T. Penick	Saint Joseph, Mo	Nov. 19, 1872	133, 173
Bottle-packing case	R. Carpenter	Roxbury, Mass	Aug. 4, 1863	39, 377
Bottle, Pepper	J. W. Gay	Brooklyn, N. Y	Jan. 26, 1864	41, 372
Bottle, Pepper caster	E. Wattis, sr	Philadelphia, Pa	Feb. 25, 1868	74, 869
Bottle-protector	O. Fitzgerald	Dexter, Me	Oct. 28, 1873	144, 082
Bottle-rack	W. Burrow	Great Malvern, Great Britain.	Dec. 22, 1868	85, 208
Bottle-rinser	J. Rone	Saint John's, Canada	Oct. 29, 1872	132, 603
Bottle, Sample	S. H. Gilman	New Orleans, La	Oct. 21, 1873	143, 753
Bottle, Screw-neck	J. L. Mason	New York, N. Y	Nov. 30, 1858	22, 186
Bottle, Show	H. Whitney	East Cambridge, Mass	Mar. 23, 1869	88, 105
Bottle, Siphon	J. B. Alexander	Washington, D. C	May 18, 1869	90, 215
Bottle, Siphon	C. J. Converse	Boston, Mass	Apr. 6, 1869	88, 610
Bottle, Siphon	G. W. Doty	Ravenna, Ohio	May 16, 1865	47, 705
Bottle, Siphon	C. Glover	New York, N. Y	Sept. 19, 1871	119, 028
Bottle, Siphon	J. E. Milliman	Jersey City, N. J	July 23, 1872	129, 852
Bottle, Siphon	T. Pimer	New London, Conn	Jan. 2, 1872	122, 403
Bottle, Spice	J. L. Likins	Vallejo, Cal	Mar. 19, 1872	124, 836
Bottle stand, Wire	G. D. Dudley	Lowell, Mass	Dec. 9, 1873	145, 284
Bottle-stopper	A. Albertson	New York, N. Y	Aug. 26, 1862	36, 266
Bottle-stopper	A. Albertson	New York, N. Y	Nov. 1, 1864	44, 912
Bottle-stopper	J. B. Alexander	Washington, D. C	July 7, 1868	79, 536
Bottle-stopper	N. Ames	Saugus Centre, Mass	Jan. 21, 1862	34, 227
Bottle-stopper	A. Barbarin	New Orleans, La	July 24, 1866	56, 516
Bottle-stopper	J. B. Basaloux	Saint Louis, Mo	Dec. 17, 1872	133, 915
Bottle-stopper	C. F. Baxter	Boston, Mass	July 14, 1863	39, 208
Bottle-stopper	J. Beard and M. Fairbanks	Boston, Mass	July 17, 1866	56, 349
Bottle-stopper	R. F. Bocemsdes	Wallingford, Conn	July 2, 1867	66, 290
Bottle-stopper	H. S. Carley	Cambridgeport, Mass	May 21, 1867	64, 838
Bottle-stopper	H. S. Carley	Cambridgeport, Mass	Sept. 3, 1867	68, 484
Bottle-stopper	H. S. Carley	Cambridgeport, Mass	Sept. 3, 1867	68, 485
Bottle-stopper	S. and S. C. Cary	New York, N. Y	Apr. 21, 1868	76, 994
Bottle-stopper	F. Catlin	New York, N. Y	Apr. 17, 1866	53, 948
Bottle-stopper	R. S. Connelly	Johnsonville, N. Y	Jan. 30, 1866	52, 269
Bottle-stopper	C. J. Converse	Boston, Mass	Dec. 22, 1868	85, 214
Bottle-stopper	J. T. Cree	Worcester, Mass	Aug. 23, 1870	106, 557
Bottle-stopper	M. C. Cronk	Auburn, N. Y	July 6, 1858	20, 778
Bottle-stopper	M. C. Cronk	Auburn, N. Y	Mar. 19, 1861	31, 703
Bottle-stopper	D. M. Cumings	Newburyport, Mass	Jan. 28, 1873	135, 267
Bottle-stopper	A. De Mestre	Bordeaux, France	Feb. 18, 1873	136, 045
Bottle-stopper	L. Dovell	Newark, N. J	Apr. 18, 1871	113, 751
Bottle-stopper	W. Ely	New York, N. Y	May 3, 1870	102, 669
Bottle-stopper	J. Ewing	New York, N. Y	July 6, 1858	20, 843
Bottle-stopper	H. B. Fox	Oxton, England	June 5, 1866	55, 438
Bottle-stopper	H. B. Fox and J. T. Hall	Oxton and Liverpool, England.	Nov. 19, 1867	70, 986
Bottle-stopper	H. Frank	Pittsburgh, Pa	Aug. 6, 1872	130, 208
Bottle-stopper	W. H. Gibbs	Cincinnati, Ohio	July 13, 1869	92, 601
Bottle-stopper	W. H. Gibbs	Cincinnati, Ohio	Aug. 3, 1869	93, 296
Bottle-stopper	W. H. Gibbs	Cincinnati, Ohio	July 26, 1870	105, 797
Bottle-stopper	C. Glover	New York, N. Y	June 27, 1871	116, 433
Bottle-stopper	C. Goldthwait	South Weymouth, Mass	Sept. 19, 1865	49, 996
Bottle-stopper	J. H. Gould	Newburyport, Mass	July 30, 1867	67, 292
Bottle-stopper	W. Graff	Philadelphia, Pa	Oct. 27, 1868	83, 485
Bottle-stopper	W. H. Hall	New York, N. Y	Sept. 13, 1864	44, 184
Bottle-stopper	J. T. Haviland	San Francisco, Cal	Jan. 5, 1869	85, 588
Bottle-stopper	P. R. Higley	Oshawa, Canada	Nov. 8, 1864	45, 005
Bottle-stopper	P. R. Higley	Oshawa, Canada	Feb. 20, 1872	123, 898
Bottle-stopper	W. L. Hoefer	Jeffersonville, N. Y	Nov. 15, 1870	109, 212
Bottle-stopper	H. Holl	Philadelphia, Pa	Feb. 26, 1867	62, 333
Bottle-stopper	W. Hunt	New York, N. Y	Jan. 4, 1853	9, 527
Bottle-stopper	T. Kendall	San Francisco, Cal	Nov. 7, 1854	11, 895
Bottle-stopper	E. and D. Kinsey	Cincinnati, Ohio	Nov. 16, 1852	9, 407
Bottle-stopper	J. Klee	Dayton, Ohio	Sept. 15, 1868	82, 230
Bottle-stopper	W. Kloenne	New York, N. Y	June 20, 1865	48, 341
Bottle-stopper	F. Kutscher	New Haven, Conn	June 15, 1869	91, 349
Bottle-stopper	F. Kutscher	New Haven, Conn	Feb. 25, 1873	136, 326
Bottle-stopper	G. W. Ladd and F. W. Copcutt	New York, N. Y	May 3, 1870	102, 685
Bottle-stopper	H. S. Lesher	New York, N. Y	Nov. 18, 1873	144, 777
Bottle-stopper	T. Lewis	Malden, Mass	Dec. 21, 1858	22, 370
Bottle-stopper	G. C. Lowe	New York, N. Y	Nov. 14, 1871	120, 821
Bottle-stopper	J. D. Lynde	Philadelphia, Pa	Mar. 25, 1862	34, 759

Index of patents issued from the United States Patent Office from 1790 *to* 1873, *inclusive*—Continued.

Invention.	Inventor.	Residence.	Date.	No.
Bottle-stopper	P. E. Malmström and P. E. Dummer.	New York, N. Y	Feb. 20, 1872	123, 920
Bottle-stopper	J. Mathews, jr	New York, N. Y	Aug. 13, 1867	67, 781
Bottle-stopper	T. J. Mayall	Boston, Mass	July 1, 1873	140, 517
Bottle-stopper	F. Miller	Newark, N. J	Aug. 21, 1866	57, 356
Bottle-stopper	T. W. Mirick	Boston, Mass	July 3, 1866	56, 079
Bottle-stopper	W. Morgenstern	New York, N. Y	Oct. 18, 1870	108, 506
Bottle-stopper	W. Morgenstern	New York, N. Y	Sept. 3, 1872	131, 111
Bottle-stopper	E. Morris, jr	New Haven, Conn	Feb. 20, 1866	52, 791
Bottle-stopper	E. D. Moyer	Philadelphia, Pa	June 20, 1865	48, 300
Bottle-stopper	J. Mulchahey	Springfield, Mass	Sept. 18, 1866	58, 174
Bottle-stopper	L. B. Myers	Elmore, Ohio	Apr. 3, 1866	53, 655
Bottle-stopper	J. Nathan	Washington, D. C	May 28, 1867	65, 259
Bottle-stopper	R. T. Osgood	Orland, Me	Aug. 1, 1865	49, 144
Bottle-stopper	J. Park	Philadelphia, Pa	June 27, 1871	116, 347
Bottle-stopper	J. H. Parkhurst	Saint Louis, Mo	Dec. 10, 1872	133, 883
Bottle-stopper	R. G. Pike	Middletown, Conn	Apr. 24, 1866	54, 201
Bottle-stopper	T. Pimer	New London, Conn	June 12, 1866	55, 589
Bottle-stopper	H. C. Pratt	Boston, Mass	June 28, 1870	104, 766
Bottle-stopper	J. A. Preston	Boston, Mass	Jan. 25, 1861	32, 647
Bottle-stopper	J. A. Preston	Boston, Mass	Aug. 5, 1862	36, 126
Bottle-stopper	H. F. Reiner	Blairsville, Pa	Feb. 18, 1873	136, 095
Bottle-stopper	L. Rhoades	Providence, R. I	Aug. 19, 1873	141, 950
Bottle-stopper	D. T. Robinson	Boston, Mass	Dec. 11, 1866	60, 424
Bottle-stopper	R. Robinson	Brooklyn, N. Y	Apr. 16, 1867	63, 942
Bottle-stopper	G. W. Rogers	New York, N. Y	Aug. 21, 1866	57, 382
Bottle-stopper	A. Scharlett	Newark, N. J	Feb. 20, 1866	52, 755
Bottle-stopper	F. Schlich	New York, N. Y	Sept. 5, 1865	49, 793
Bottle-stopper	F. Schlich	New York, N. Y	Feb. 28, 1871	112, 185
Bottle-stopper	W. A. Shaw	Boston, Mass	Dec. 17, 1861	33, 964
Bottle-stopper	N. Thompson	London, England	Dec. 4, 1866	60, 283
Bottle-stopper	N. Thompson	Brooklyn, N. Y	June 28, 1870	104, 794
Bottle-stopper	S. H. Simmons	La Fayette, Ind	Sept. 18, 1866	58, 153
Bottle-stopper	W. Vom Hofe	New York, N. Y	Nov. 5, 1867	70, 654
Bottle-stopper	T. B. Way	Bennington, Vt	Nov. 7, 1865	50, 864
Bottle-stopper	T. A. Weber	New York, N. Y	July 2, 1867	66, 270
Bottle-stopper	E. R. Wilbur	New York, N. Y	Apr. 25, 1865	47, 483
Bottle-stopper	J. B. Williams	New York, N. Y	Feb. 9, 1858	19, 323
Bottle-stopper	G. R. Willmot	Minden, Conn	Aug. 29, 1865	49, 671
Bottle-stopper	W. and D. Wilson	New York, N. Y	Apr. 26, 1870	102, 349
Bottle-stopper	I. A. and G. E. Woodbury	East Cambridge, Mass	Sept. 19, 1865	50, 063
Bottle-stopper	J. Woolaver	Suisun, Cal	Nov. 7, 1865	50, 867
Bottle-stopper	W. Wright	Phœnicia, N. Y	Nov. 14, 1871	120, 923
Bottle-stopper	I. Zamboni	Saint Louis, Mo	Mar. 3, 1868	75, 233
Bottle-stopper and coupling	W. D. Brown	Milwaukee, Wis	June 11, 1867	65, 537
Bottle-stopper and medicine-gage	S. H. Timmons	La Fayette, Ind	Nov. 20, 1866	59, 875
Bottle-stopper device	J. Hanley	New York, N. Y	Jan. 9, 1855	12, 202
Bottle-stopper fastener	D. T. Robinson	Boston, Mass	Mar. 20, 1866	53, 342
Bottle-stopper fastening	T. A. Ashburner	Philadelphia, Pa	Mar. 13, 1855	12, 501
Bottle-stopper fastening	H. T. Dewey	Brooklyn, N. Y	Jan. 9, 1872	122, 579
Bottle-stopper fastening	H. W. Putnam	Cleveland, Ohio	Mar. 15, 1859	23, 263
Bottle-stopper fastening	R. S. Stubbs	Dover, N. H	Dec. 31, 1867	72, 761
Bottle-stopper fastening, Machine for forming wire	H. W. Putnam	Bennington, Vt	May 30, 1871	115, 354
Bottle stopper, Glass	S. A. Whitney	Glassborough, N. Y	Jan. 1, 1861	31, 046
Bottle stopper, Ink	M. Ames	New Ipswich, N. H	Mar. 27, 1866	53, 390
Bottle stopper or cap	J. Quinn and G. W. Putnam	Boston, Mass	Feb. 2, 1869	86, 446
Bottle-stopper, Self-acting	D. A. Draper	East Cambridge, Mass	Oct. 13, 1863	40, 251
Bottle stopper, Smelling	E. F. Marble and R. W. Glidden	Attleborough, Mass	Apr. 15, 1873	137, 938
Bottle-stopper, Undetachable swinging	A. H. Forbes	New York, N. Y	Apr. 10, 1849	6, 297
Bottle-stopper, Valvular	C. Patterson	Philadelphia, Pa	Dec. 30, 1873	146, 018
Bottle stopper, Volatile salts	A. Hebbard	New York, N. Y	Jan. 7, 1873	134, 600
Bottle-stoppers, caster-wheels, syringe-pistons, &c., Manufacture of.	R. B. Hugunin	Cleveland, Ohio	Mar. 6, 1866	53, 002
Bottle-stoppers, Device for cutting wire or cord from	J. A. Traut	New Britain, Conn	Sept. 6, 1870	107, 125
Bottle, &c., stoppers, Device for securing	W. H. Richards	Auburndale, Mass	Jan. 7, 1868	73, 043
Bottle-stoppers, Machine for bending wire-fastening for.	H. W. Putnam	Bennington, Vt	May 23, 1871	115, 102
Bottle, Tooth-powder	J. B. Da Camara, jr	Newark, N. J	Nov. 19, 1867	71, 142
Bottle-uncorking device	A. Mannel	Reims, France	Jan. 29, 1867	61, 624
Bottle-washer	H. B. Davison	San Francisco, Cal	Nov 19, 1867	70, 973
Bottle-washer	W. Dick	New York, N. Y	Mar. 4, 1873	136, 423
Bottle-washing apparatus	F. Schlick and A. Feyh	New York, N. Y	Apr. 22, 1873	138, 046
Bottle-washing machine	H. N. Degraw	Watervliet, N. Y	Sept. 1, 1857	18, 086
Bottle-washing machine	C. Euler	Evansville, Ind	Sept. 12, 1871	118, 917
Bottle-washing machine	J. Matthews, jr	New York, N. Y	Aug. 22, 1865	49, 538
Bottle-washing machine	A. H. Rauch	Bethlehem, Pa	June 6, 1854	11, 000
Bottle-washing machine	N. H. Sirrelle	Baltimore, Md	June 29, 1869	92, 112
Bottle-washing machine	C. L. Werk and N. Verdin	Cincinnati, Ohio, and Yorkville, Ind.	Aug. 13, 1872	130, 552
Bottle-washing machine	W. B. White and J. A. Whiteford.	Saratoga Springs, N. Y	Apr. 27, 1859	20, 113
Bottle-wrapper	A. E. Francis	Ravenna, Ohio	May 27, 1873	139, 308
Bottle-wrapper	W. A. Hinman	New York, N. Y	Dec. 12, 1871	121, 718
Bottles, &c., air-tight, Closing	R. Arthur	Washington, D. C	Aug. 15, 1854	11, 513
Bottles and jars, Revolving plug for manufacturing	J. F. Bodine	Williamstown, N. J	Apr. 12, 1859	23, 640
Bottles and jars, Tool for forming lugs in the mouths of.	A. Stone	Philadelphia, Pa	Apr. 12, 1859	23, 623
Bottles and other vessels, Device for closing	J. Mathews	New York, N. Y	Apr. 15, 1873	137, 941
Bottles and other vessels, Machine for cutting cork stoppers for.	J. Power and A. J. Bailey	Boston and Charlestown, Mass.	May 20, 1862	35, 351
Bottles and pipes, Device for closing	D. L. and R. Bollerman	New York, N. Y	July 20, 1869	92, 782
Bottles and similar articles, Forming screw-threads, &c., in the necks of glass.	A. Stone	Philadelphia, Pa	Aug. 7, 1855	13, 402
Bottles, Apparatus for changing siphon	W. P. Clark	Medford, Mass	July 16, 1872	129, 002
Bottles, Apparatus for cutting the strings that secure corks in.	G. Blanchard	New York, N. Y	June 10, 1856	15, 098
Bottles, Apparatus for filling siphon	W. Gee	New York, N. Y	Jan. 21, 1868	73, 594
Bottles, Apparatus for inserting stoppers in	A. Stone	Philadelphia, Pa	June 18, 1861	32, 590

Index of patents issued from the United States Patent Office from 1790 to 1873, inclusive—Continued.

Invention.	Inventor.	Residence.	Date.	No.
Bottles, Attaching cork-retaining bails to	L. B. Flanders	Philadelphia, Pa	June 17, 1873	139, 886
Bottles, Attaching stoppers to	J. J. Eshleman	Philadelphia, Pa	Mar. 5, 1867	62, 536
Bottles, cans, &c., Device for sealing	M. B. Espy	Philadelphia, Pa	July 14, 1857	17, 783
Bottles, Case for indelible-ink	E. Daniels	Northampton, Mass	Aug. 7, 1860	29, 469
Bottles, Cleansing	M. C. Cronk	Auburn, N. Y	Aug. 7, 1849	6, 631
Bottles, Closing	T. S. Bowman	Saint Louis, Mo	Aug. 27, 1867	68, 162
Bottles, Closing	E. Hamilton	Chicago, Ill	Jan. 5, 1864	41, 067
Bottles, Closing	J. Matthews, jr	New York, N. Y	July 18, 1865	48, 822
Bottles, Closing	N. Prescott	Dorchester, Mass	Sept. 3, 1867	68, 456
Bottles, Closing	R. Robinson	New York, N. Y	Mar. 14, 1865	46, 864
Bottles, &c., Closing	N. Thompson	Saint John's Wood, England.	Oct. 13, 1863	40, 293
Bottles, Closing or stopping	E. Hamilton	Chicago, Ill	Apr. 5, 1864	42, 188
Bottles, Construction of glass	F. N. Bullard	Worcester, Mass	Oct. 30, 1866	59, 333
Bottles, Construction of nursing	E. Dupuy	New York, N. Y	Oct. 7, 1844	3, 780
Bottles, Cork-receptacle for	A. Honrath	New York, N. Y	July 30, 1867	67, 303
Bottles, Device for packing	G. C. Furber	Yreka, Cal	Aug. 9, 1870	106, 149
Bottles, Device for securing corks in	S. L. Gonverneur	Frederick City, Md	Feb. 7, 1871	111, 657
Bottles, Device for stopping	A. Andre	Chicago, Ill	May 5, 1863	38, 367
Bottles, &c., Device for stopping	N. Thompson	Saint John's Wood, England.	Oct. 13, 1863	40, 292
Bottles, Drip-cup for	W. R. Miller	Baltimore, Md	Dec. 24, 1872	134, 302
Bottles, Ejecting-apparatus for	W. S. Ward	New York, N. Y	Jan. 14, 1873	134, 953
Bottles, Fastening metallic collars to	E. Wattis, jr	Philadelphia, Pa	Jan. 21, 1868	73, 680
Bottles, &c., for transportation, Packing	T. M. Perot	Philadelphia, Pa	Sept. 15, 1863	39, 950
Bottles, Frame for making straw envelopes for	W. F. Tillinghast	Burlington, N. J	Mar. 4, 1873	136, 394
Bottles, Frame for securing liquor and other	F. J. Miller	Brooklyn, N. Y	Mar. 27, 1866	53, 540
Bottles, Hermetically sealing	M. B. Espy	Philadelphia, Pa	Sept. 30, 1856	15, 802
Bottles, Implement for grooving the mouths of glass.	E. Bennett	Philadelphia, Pa	July 3, 1866	55, 988
Bottles, Instrument for opening	J. Matthews, jr	New York, N. Y	June 27, 1865	48, 422
Bottles, Instrument for removing effervescing fluids from.	W. W. Meglone	Nashville, Tenn	Aug. 14, 1866	57, 256
Bottles, Instrument for removing twine and wire from.	J. T. Haviland	San Francisco, Cal	June 21, 1870	104, 453
Bottles, Instrument for removing wire from	J. S. Hazard	Newport, R. I	Oct. 16, 1866	58, 820
Bottles, jars, &c., Fastening for covers or stoppers of.	F. Klee	Brooklyn, N. Y	Jan. 19, 1869	86, 082
Bottles, jars, &c., Metallic cap for	W. J. Stevenson	New York, N. Y	June 8, 1858	20, 520
Bottles, jars, &c., Mode of closing the mouths of	N. Thompson	Saint John's Wood, England.	Sept. 24, 1867	69, 143
Bottles, Locking-cap for	L. M. Ballard	New York, N. Y	May 18, 1869	90, 221
Bottles, Locking-cap for	J. S. Hough	New York, N. Y	Sept. 27, 1870	107, 778
Bottles, Machine for coloring capsules for	H. Stiassny	New York, N. Y	Apr. 23, 1872	125, 912
Bottles, Manufacture of cruet	W. Pountney	Brooklyn, N. Y	July 10, 1866	56, 263
Bottles, Manufacture of stopples for	L. Bishop	Paris, France	June 11, 1867	65, 533
Bottles, Means of holding glass	J. Wood	Brooklyn, N. Y	May 22, 1866	54, 991
Bottles, Metallic capsule for	W. Betts	Wharf Road, England	Nov. 19, 1867	71, 124
Bottles, Method of drawing fluids from	I. W. Fox	Durhamville, N. Y	May 27, 1856	14, 982
Bottles, Nipple for nursing	H. D. Lockwood	Charlestown, Mass	May 28, 1872	127, 357
Bottles of clay, Apparatus for making	E. H. and H. E. Merrill	Akron, Ohio	June 9, 1868	78, 676
Bottles of clay, Making	E. H. and C. J. Merrill	Akron, Ohio	July 31, 1847	5, 206
Bottles or other vessels made from plastic substances, Tool for forming groove around the orifice of.	A. Stone	Philadelphia, Pa	Sept. 23, 1856	15, 788
Bottles, steam-pipes, &c., Covering for	J. B Crane	Dalton, Mass	Feb. 26, 1867	62, 318
Bottles, Stopping	A. Albertson	New York, N. Y	Oct. 11, 1864	44, 684
Bottles, Stopping	A. Albertson	New York, N. Y	Nov. 15, 1864	45, 112
Bottles, Stopping	A. Wiegand	Philadelphia, Pa	Sept. 29, 1863	40, 136
Bottles, Stopping mineral-water	A. Quantin	Philadelphia, Pa	July 25, 1854	11, 385
Bottles, Tool for forming lips on necks of	T. Barrett	Charlestown, Mass	July 27, 1869	93, 039
Bottles, &c., Tool for forming mouths of	H. Frank	Pittsburgh, Pa	Aug. 6, 1872	130, 207
Bottles, Tool for forming necks and orifices of glass	R. MacLardy	Pittsburgh, Pa	Feb. 28, 1860	27, 333
Bottles, Tool for forming necks of	L. F. Smith	Stonington, Conn	Dec. 9, 1862	37, 142
Bottles, Tool for forming screw-threads in the necks of glass.	G. M. Keefer	East Birmingham, Pa	Apr. 16, 1872	125, 739
Bottles, Tool for holding glass	E. McArdle	Cambridge, Mass	May 8, 1866	54, 572
Bottles, Tool for holding glass	T. B. Hewitt	Williamstown, N. J	Dec. 30, 1873	145, 945
Bottles, Valve-gage for	A. Quantin	Philadelphia, Pa	Oct. 25, 1853	10, 158
Bottles, Washing, filling, and corking	S. A. Bille	New York, N. Y	Nov. 8, 1828	....
Bottling-apparatus	J. Buser	New York, N. Y	Feb. 11, 1862	34, 347
Bottling-apparatus	H. B. Goodyear	New Haven, Conn	Mar. 7, 1865	46, 658
Bottling-apparatus	A. S. Taylor	San Francisco, Cal	Nov. 12, 1872	133, 068
Bottling fluids under gaseous pressure, Method of	A. Quantin	Philadelphia, Pa	Mar. 4, 1856	14, 368
Bottling gas-charged liquids, Machine for	E. D. Taylor	Hornellsville, N. Y	Aug. 15, 1871	118, 069
Bottling liquids	J. Klee	Dayton, Ohio	July 29, 1873	141, 360
Bottling liquids, Apparatus for	J. Matthews, jr	New York, N. Y	Mar. 6, 1866	53, 019
Bottling liquids under pressure	J. Matthews, jr	New York, N. Y	Jan. 5, 1864	41, 082
Bottling-machine	J. Armstrong and S. Marks	San Francisco, Cal	Nov. 12, 1872	133, 003
Bottling-machine	H. Carse	Pittsburgh, Pa	Dec. 8, 1868	84, 795
Bottling-machine	J. Matthews, jr	New York, N. Y	Feb. 2, 1864	41, 440
Bottling-machine	J. Matthews, jr	New York, N. Y	Jan. 29, 1867	61, 627
Bottling-machine for liquids	J. V. Mathivet	Cleveland, Ohio	Aug. 15, 1871	118, 036
Bottling-machines, Siruping-device for	W. Tollast	New York, N. Y	Apr. 23, 1872	126, 103
Bottling mineral-water, Method of	C. H. Thomas	Philadelphia, Pa	June 18, 1867	65, 842
Bottling soda, &c., Sirup-gage for	J. Schrink	Toledo, Ohio	June 28, 1864	43, 344
Bottling still liquids	J. Beard and M. Fairbanks	Boston, Mass	Dec. 6, 1864	45, 373
Bougie for stricture	R. J. Dodd	Philadelphia, Pa	Oct. 6, 1843	3, 297
Bouquet-holder	E. Dithridge	Pittsburgh, Pa	Mar. 20, 1866	53, 279
Bouquet-holder	A. D. Frye, jr	New York, N. Y	May 28, 1867	65, 204
Bouquet-holder	A. F. Ransom	Glen's Falls, N. Y	June 3, 1873	139, 477
Bouquet-holder	J. C. Reed	Boston, Mass	Aug. 29, 1871	118, 486
Bouquet-holder	E. Wilder	Springfield, Mass	July 16, 1872	129, 444
Bow-drill stock	D. F. Hartford	Boston, Mass	Aug. 27, 1867	68, 071
Bow-drill stock, Stringing	D. F. Hartford	Boston, Mass	Dec. 24, 1867	72, 632
Bow for archery	E. S Morton	Plymouth, Mass	May 14, 1872	126, 734
Bowl, Water	B. Brower	New York, N. Y	Aug. 5, 1873	141, 421
Bowl, Water	S. Hawson and T. Sweeney	Jersey City, N. J., and Brooklyn, N. Y.	May 7, 1872	126, 457

Index of patents issued from the United States Patent Office from 1790 *to* 1873, *inclusive*—Continued.

Invention.	Inventor.	Residence.	Date.	No.
Bowls, &c., Detachable nose for	G. Raymond	Fitchburgh, Mass	May 12, 1868	77,914
Bowls, Machine for making wooden	R. Simonds and G. N. Goodspeed.	Ludlow, Vt., and Winchendon, Mass.	July 31, 1860	29,411
Bowls, Machinery for turning	P. Hutchins, jr	Worthington, Mass	Sept. 25, 1847	5,306
Bowls, Method of making footed glass	E. G. Cate	Wheeling, W. Va	Oct. 28, 1873	144,061
Bowling-alley	A. T. Peirce	Fair Haven, Conn	July 13, 1869	92,467
Bowling-alley pin, Substitute for	J. M. Currier	Newburyport, Mass	Nov. 12, 1861	33,695
Box:				
See Adjustable box.				
Advertising-box.				
Alkali-box.				
Ammunition-box.				
Annealing-box.				
Anti-friction box.				
Ash-box.				
Axle-box.				
Bacon and ham box.				
Ballot-box.				
Berry-box.				
Blacking-box.				
Bluing-box.				
Camera-box.				
Candle-mold box.				
Cap-box.				
Car-spring box.				
Carriage-wheel box.				
Cartouch-box.				
Cartridge box.				
Centering-box.				
Chalk-line box.				
Change-box.				
Check-box.				
Cheese-box.				
Cigar-box.				
Cigar-fuse box.				
Coal-box.				
Collar-box.				
Collection-box.				
Conductor's change-box.				
Core-box.				
Coupling-box.				
Cracker-box.				
Cylindrical box.				
Dice-box.				
Die-box.				
Dredge-box.				
Elevator-box.				
Fare-box.				
Feed-box.				
File-box.				
Filler-box.				
Fire-box.				
Fire-alarm box.				
Free-box.				
Freezing-box.				
Fruit-box.				
Fur-box.				
Game-box.				
Garbage-box.				
Grape-box.				
Hat-box.				
Honey-box.				
Hop-box.				
Hub-box.				
Jewel-box.				
Jewelry-box.				
Journal-box.				
Laundry-box.				
Letter-box.				
Lubricating-box.				
Lunch-box.				
Mail-box.				
Market-box.				
Match-box.				
Metallic box.				
Miter-box.				
Money-box.				
Moth-proof box.				
Muff-box.				
Music-box.				
Musical box.				
Nut-box.				
Oil and paint box.				
Oil-stone box.				
Packing-box.				
Paper box.				
Pasteboard box.				
Passing-box.				
Peach-box.				
Peg-box.				
Pepper-box.				
Photographic-camera box.				
Photographic-paper box.				
Pill-box.				
Pitman-box.				
Polishing-box.				
Porter's box.				
Post-office box.				

Index of patents issued from the United States Patent Office from 1790 *to* 1873, *inclusive*—Continued.

Invention.	Inventor.	Residence.	Date.	No.
Box—Continued.				
See Powder-box.				
Preserving-box.				
Preserving and packing box.				
Propagating-box.				
Pump-box.				
Resin-box.				
Retaining-box.				
Round box.				
Safe-deposit box.				
Sample box.				
Sand-box.				
Scouring-box.				
Seidlitz-powder box.				
Setting-box.				
Settling-box.				
Sheep-tagging box.				
Sheet-metal box.				
Sheet-metal-can box.				
Shingle-gaging box.				
Shoe-box.				
Shovel-drop box.				
Show-box.				
Shuttle-box.				
Shuttle-drop box.				
Signal-box.				
Silver-ware box.				
Sluice-box.				
Spice-box.				
Spindle-step box.				
Spool-box.				
Step-box.				
Stop-cock box.				
Stove-blacking box.				
Strawberry-box.				
Stuffing-box.				
Tape-box.				
Telegraph-signal box.				
Thimble-box.				
Ticket-box.				
Tin box.				
Tobacco-box.				
Tobacco-cutting box.				
Tool-box.				
Toy money-box.				
Tree-box.				
Trunk-box.				
Tumbling-box.				
Turpentine-box.				
Twine-box.				
Wagon-box.				
Wagon and sleigh box.				
Water-closet box.				
Wheel-box.				
Wood-box.				
Wooden box.				
Wool-box.				
Work-box.				
Box	J. Cohn	New York, N. Y	Nov. 21, 1871	121, 156
Box	R. B. Davis	New York, N. Y	Mar. 26, 1872	125, 028
Box	R. B. Davis	New York, N. Y	Apr. 30, 1872	126, 272
Box	W. B. Guernsey	New York, N. Y	June 23, 1868	79, 113
Box	H. R. Heyl	Philadelphia, Pa	Oct. 8, 1872	132, 074
Box	H. R. Heyl	Philadelphia, Pa	Oct. 8, 1872	132, 075
Box	J. S. Lash	Philadelphia, Pa	Dec. 16, 1873	145, 663
Box	J. J. Leighton	Boston, Mass	Nov. 17, 1868	84, 200
Box	H. Manneck	New York, N. Y	Jan. 31, 1871	111, 463
Box	J. Nelson	Rockford, Ill	Aug. 16, 1870	106, 393
Box	E. C. Patterson	Rochester, N. Y	Apr. 1, 1873	137, 385
Box	W. M. Pierce	Sandusky, Ohio	June 18, 1872	128, 170
Box	H. S. Shepardson	Shelburne Falls, Mass	Jan. 23, 1872	122, 919
Box	C. J. Siercks	Chicago, Ill	Aug. 9, 1870	106, 221
Box	J. W. Wilcox	New York, N. Y	Nov. 3, 1868	83, 812
Box and bottle cap	W. L. Troxell	Brooklyn, N. Y	July 30, 1872	130, 086
Box and hub and hanging coach-body	D. Watson	Fayette, Mass	May 29, 1832	....
Box, axle, journal, &c	D. Cumming	Sorrel Horse, Pa	Nov. 25, 1856	16, 113
Box-boiler	J. Morris	New Haven, Conn	Oct. 3, 1812	....
Box-fastening	J. J. Greenough	Syracuse, N. Y	Oct. 24, 1871	120, 192
Box for case-hardening	J. Greene	Providence, R. I	Nov. 3, 1863	40, 477
Box-former	G. W. Swan	San Francisco, Cal	Sept. 23, 1873	143, 103
Box for transporting small fruit and berries	E. Secor	Lawrence, Mich	Jan. 1, 1867	60, 796
Box-heads, &c., Removable	S. Macferren	Philadelphia, Pa	Nov. 24, 1868	84, 366
Box-hook	C. Bruso	Worcester, Mass	Apr. 19, 1870	102, 087
Box-joints, Machine for making	J. Stimpson	Baldwinsville, Mass	Nov. 8, 1859	26, 060
Box lifter	B. H. Smith	Ipswich, Mass	May 20, 1873	139, 029
Box-machine	E. G. Alden	Cambridge, Mass	Apr. 4, 1871	113, 238
Box-machine	A. Davis	Washington, D. C	Apr. 18, 1854	10, 788
Box-machine	T. Kingsford	Oswego, N. Y	Sept. 3, 1872	131, 009
Box-machine	G. P. Roberts	Saint Louis, Mo	Mar. 3, 1863	37, 827
Box-making machine	B. E. Dexter	Gowanda, N. Y	Dec. 17, 1872	134, 039
Box-making machine	S. L. Hill	Williamsburgh, N. Y	Nov. 3, 1863	40, 480
Box-making machine	E. James	Tyngsborough, Mass	Nov. 24, 1868	84, 422
Box-making machine	T. C. Luther	Lee, Mass	Oct. 11, 1864	44, 690
Box-making machine	G. W. Swan	San Francisco, Cal	Aug. 26, 1873	142, 297
Box-making machine	H. Thayer	Brooklyn, N. Y	June 21, 1864	43, 239
Box-making machinery	W. M. Davis	Gardiner, Me	Jan. 16, 1849	6, 038
Box-nailing machine	C. Bauer and W. C. Munder	Newark, N. J	Nov. 8, 1864	44, 929
Box-nailing machine	E. Beard	Ottawa, Ill	July 9, 1872	128, 698

Index of patents issued from the United States Patent Office from 1790 *to* 1873, *inclusive*—Continued.

Invention.	Inventor.	Residence.	Date.	No.
Box-nailing machine	G. Wicke	New York, N. Y	June 16, 1863	38, 924
Box-opener	A. Barbarin	New Orleans, La	Oct. 13, 1868	83, 022
Box-opener	R. Blake	Scranton, Pa	Apr. 20, 1869	89, 013
Box-opener	R. H. Chinn, G. Hall, and J. J. Fitch.	Washington, D. C., and Morgantown, W. Va.	Dec. 26, 1871	122, 106
Box-opener	J. C. Gaston	Cincinnati, Ohio	Feb. 27, 1872	124, 049
Box-opener	W. Gould	Minneapolis, Minn	Feb. 27, 1872	124, 129
Box-opener	H. H. Hall	Tioga, Pa	Aug. 25, 1868	81, 497
Box-opener	J. W. Hankenson	Minneapolis, Minn	May 28, 1872	127, 342
Box-opener	T. B. Henkle	Knightstown, Ind	Jan. 24, 1871	111, 207
Box-opener	A. Heusser	Ellington, Conn	May 24, 1870	103, 330
Box-opener	M. J. Hinden	Detroit, Mich	Nov. 11, 1873	144, 454
Box-opener	L. Holtzscheiter	Philadelphia, Pa	Oct. 27, 1868	83, 499
Box-opener	A. F. Jackson	Minneapolis, Minn	July 16, 1872	129, 412
Box-opener	M. D. Lawrence	Springfield, Mass	Oct. 3, 1865	50, 30[illegible]
Box-opener	S. Mills	Jersey City, N. J	Apr. 22, 1873	138, 177
Box-opener	N. Purdey	Providence, Pa	Oct. 11, 1870	108, 293
Box opener	P. Stone	Charlestown, Mass	Feb. 4, 1868	74, 167
Box-opener	G. C. Taft	Worcester, Mass	Oct. 21, 1851	8, 457
Box-opener	H. C. Van Gieson	Paterson, N. J	Oct. 19, 1869	95, 957
Box-opener	C. P. S. Wardwell	Lake Village, N. H	Apr. 29, 1856	14, 783
Box-opener	J. Willard	Norwich, Conn	Sept. 1, 1868	81, 855
Box-opening apparatus	C. M. O'Hara	New York, N. Y	Aug. 3, 1869	93, 335
Box-opening instrument	G. C. Taft	Worcester, Mass	Apr. 13, 1852	8, 878
Box-opening tool	E. Hambujer	New York, N. Y	Nov. 7, 1865	50, 820
Box-opening tool	L. D. Howard	Saint Johnsbury, Vt	Nov. 9, 1869	96, 700
Box-opening tool	W. M. Keague	Brooklyn, N. Y	Mar. 15, 1864	41, 925
Box-opening tool	E. C. C. Kellogg	Hartford, Conn	May 23, 1865	47, 899
Box-stamping die, Wooden	W. Weeks	Albany, N. Y	Sept. 1, 1868	81, 852
Box-stuff, Machine for cutting	C. W. Royse	Rindge, N. H	May 6, 1873	138, 584
Box-trap for animals	B. B. and J. R. Hill	Worcester, Mass	Feb. 14, 1865	46, 356
Box-trap for animals	J. Stroop and J. Esteale	Allegheny, Pa	Nov. 6, 1843	3, 326
Box with anti-friction roller	W. Edwards	Baltimore, Md	Sept. 11, 1817	....
Boxes and axles, Packing	W. H. Hovey	Hartford, Conn	Aug. 13, 1850	7, 563
Boxes and cases, Method of making	H. Thayer	Brooklyn, N. Y	June 21, 1864	43, 240
Boxes and packages, Implement for handling	C. Hoffmann	New York, N. Y	Dec. 12, 1871	121, 873
Boxes, cartridge-cases, &c., Manufacture of	C. S. Wells	Springfield, Mass	Oct. 18, 1870	108, 542
Boxes, cases, &c., End or head for	H. Thayer	Warsaw, N. Y	Dec. 20, 1864	45, 538
Boxes, Casting	W. Butler and E. B. Rice	Worcester, Mass	May 31, 1833	....
Boxes, Device for joining	W. Duryea	New York, N. Y	Sept. 11, 1860	29, 957
Boxes, &c., Eccentric fastening for	W. Youngblood	Brooklyn, N. Y	Feb. 11, 1873	135, 873
Boxes from paper-pulp, Manufacture of	S. Wheeler and E. Jerome	Albany, N. Y	Feb. 12, 1867	61, 969
Boxes, Implement for straining band about	S. Marden	Newton, Mass	Oct. 15, 1867	69, 826
Boxes, Making	H. Thayer	Brooklyn, N. Y	June 21, 1864	43, 241
Boxes, Making	J. C. Walker	Concord, N H	Aug. 26, 1843	3, 231
Boxes, Manufacture of	A. N. Allen	Chicago, Ill	Mar. 26, 1872	124, 997
Boxes, Manufacture of	F. W. Fliedner	New York, N. Y	Jan. 31, 1865	46, 097
Boxes, Manufacture of	W. T. Slocum	Philadelphia, Pa	May 30, 1865	48, 031
Boxes, Manufacture of	C. Storer	Montreal, Canada	Nov. 26, 1872	133, 496
Boxes, Manufacture of	J. Trottier	Hennebon, France	June 11, 1872	127, 811
Boxes, Manufacturing	J. Sperry	New York, N. Y	Nov. 3, 1863	40, 507
Boxes, &c, Material for making	W. Painter	Baltimore, Md	Jan. 17, 1865	45, 950
Boxes, Method of bending wood for	S. Patterson	Berlin Heights, Ohio	Sept. 26, 1871	119, 340
Boxes, &c., Method of joining	J. Stimson	Baldwinsville, Mass	Feb. 3, 1857	16, 557
Boxes, &c., Method of joining corners of	J. Bell	Harlem, Mass	Jan. 25, 1853	9, 552
Boxes, Metallic corner-shield for	G. F. Sargent	Manchester, N. H	June 17, 1873	140, 080
Boxes, Mode of fitting heads in	C. Williams	Fallsburgh, Va	July 25, 1854	11, 397
Boxes, packages, &c., Manufacture of	H. Everett	Philadelphia, Pa	May 2, 1865	47, 532
Boxes, picture-frames, &c., Material for the manufacture of.	J. M. Merrick, jr	Boston, Mass	Dec. 15, 1868	85, 018
Boxes, Prop for holding up the lids of	A. Davis and T. Parsons	Boston, Mass	Aug. 29, 1871	118, 588
Boxes, &c., Sealing	R. M. Bartlett	Cincinnati, Ohio	Mar. 27, 1866	53, 517
Brace:				
See Ankle-brace.				
Ball-brace.				
Bit-brace.				
Body-brace.				
Boring-bit brace.				
Bracket-brace.				
Buggy-brace.				
Carriage-spring brace.				
Carriage-top brace.				
Chair-brace.				
Counter-brace.				
Crank-brace.				
Garment-brace.				
Gum-elastic brace.				
Knee-brace.				
Ratchet-brace.				
Sanitary-brace.				
Shoulder-brace.				
Spinal brace.				
Spring-brace.				
Spring and body brace.				
Suspending-brace.				
Thorough-brace.				
Trunk and piano-cover brace.				
Vehicle-spring brace.				
Wagon-brace.				
Wagon-spring brace.				
Brace	D. N. Baird	Warrenville, Ohio	Aug. 26, 1856	15, 632
Brace	A. W. Streeter	Shelburne Falls, Mass	Nov. 17, 1863	40, 652
Brace and lacing-device	S. J. Shaw and W. E. C. Worcester.	Marlborough, Mass	Oct. 16, 1866	58, 955
Brace and skirt-supporter combined	R. A. N. A. Ward	Philadelphia, Pa	Oct. 6, 1868	82, 901
Brace and suspender combined	E. L. Demorest and W. G. Cook	New York, N. Y	Mar. 9, 1869	87, 648
Brace, Attaching bit to	J. H. Nellis	Richmondville, N. Y	Feb. 12, 1867	62, 057
Brace, Attaching bit to	L. J. Parsons	New Haven, Conn	May 7, 1867	64, 444

Index of patents issued from the United States Patent Office from 1790 *to* 1873, *inclusive*—Continued.

Invention.	Inventor.	Residence.	Date.	No.
Brace, Bit	W. A. Ives	New Haven, Conn	May 7, 1872	126, 395
Brace-bit holder	J. P. Gordon	West Garland, Me	Jan. 16, 1866	52, 042
Brace-bit holder	M. V. Nobles	Rochester, N. Y	Dec. 19, 1865	51, 660
Brace-bit in socket, Mode of securing	E. W. Nichols	Worcester, Mass	May 15, 1855	12, 868
Brace-bit, Mode of securing	C. B. Rose	Sunderland, Mass	Oct. 25, 1864	44, 822
Brace-bit, Mode of securing	C. B. Rose	Sunderland, Mass	Oct. 25, 1864	44, 823
Brace-bit, Securing	J. Mix	West Cheshire, Conn	June 17, 1862	35, 618
Brace-bit stock	J. Comstock	New London, Conn	Dec. 13, 1853	10, 307
Brace-coupling, Adjustable	C. M. Hall	Yates City, Ill	Apr. 8, 1873	137, 669
Brace-drill	G. Gibbs	Canton, Ohio	Mar. 18, 1873	136, 830
Brace, &c., fastener	E. L. Parker	Birmingham, England	Jan. 3, 1871	110, 783
Brace or bit stock	D. P. Foster	Shelburne Falls, Mass	June 28, 1864	43, 302
Brace-stock, Catch for holding the bit in	C. M. Daboll	New London, Conn	May 16, 1854	10, 924
Braces or suspenders	M. Harris	New York, N. Y	Nov. 7, 1871	120, 583
Bracelet	A. O. Baker	Providence, R. I	Nov. 26, 1872	133, 291
Bracelet	W. H. Ball and T. Barnard	Newark, N. J	Sept. 13, 1870	107, 325
Bracelet	J. Barclay	Bergen, N. J	Sept. 20, 1870	107, 588
Bracelet	J. Barclay	Bergen, N. J	Apr. 9, 1872	125, 516
Bracelet	G. Burch	Newark, N. J	June 8, 1869	91, 081
Bracelet	H. Carlisle, jr	Philadelphia, Pa	Oct. 25, 1870	108, 683
Bracelet	D. D. Codding	North Attleborough, Mass.	Mar. 8, 1870	100, 504
Bracelet	T. L. Cornell	Derby, Conn	Jan. 14, 1873	134, 735
Bracelet	W. Edge	Newark, N. J	Nov. 19, 1872	133, 146
Bracelet	A. Forbes	Attleborough, Mass	Dec. 2, 1873	145, 164
Bracelet	J. W. Grant and C. H. Cook	Providence, R. I	May 27, 1873	139, 311
Bracelet	S. W. Grant	Providence, R. I	June 17, 1873	139, 888
Bracelet	C. M. Kinsel	Columbus, Ohio	Apr. 7, 1868	76, 470
Bracelet	H. Kipling	New York, N. Y	Apr. 2, 1861	31, 931
Bracelet	W. W. Knapp	Mansfield, Mass	Dec. 17, 1872	133, 943
Bracelet	M. H. Mason	Attleborough, Mass	Apr. 9, 1872	125, 402
Bracelet	J. H. Sprague	Providence, R. I	Oct. 3, 1871	119, 540
Bracelet	G. D. Stevens	New York, N. Y	Feb. 13, 1872	123, 740
Bracelet	F. M. Sweet	Syracuse, N. Y	Aug. 31, 1858	21, 381
Bracelet	J. Wilkinson	West Mount Vernon, N. Y.	July 30, 1872	130, 096
Bracelet	H. A. Williams	Mansfield, Mass	Sept. 23, 1873	143, 109
Bracelet-clasp	J. Mansure	Philadelphia, Pa	May 23, 1854	10, 973
Bracelet, &c., Constructing	J. S. Palmer	Providence, R. I	Mar. 19, 1861	31, 735
Bracelet, Constructing flat chains for	J. Christie	Newark, N. J	Jan. 5, 1864	41, 175
Bracelet-fastening	J. Bissinger	New York, N. Y	Feb. 28, 1860	27, 264
Bracelet-fastening	S. Cottle	New York, N. Y	Dec. 23, 1873	145, 788
Bracelet-fastening	R. S. Hamilton	Providence, R. I	Mar. 19, 1872	124, 815
Bracelet-fastening	F. Kursh	Philadelphia, Pa	Jan. 7, 1873	134, 681
Bracelet-fastening	B. Ranger	Brattleborough, Vt	Oct. 31, 1871	120, 535
Bracelet-fastening	B. Ranger and J. B. Smiley	Brattleborough, Vt	Sept. 30, 1873	143, 382
Bracelet-fastening	G. H. Soule	Jersey City, N. J	Aug. 4, 1868	80, 679
Bracelet-fastening	G. H. Soule	Jersey City, N. J	July 16, 1872	128, 983
Bracelet-fastening	G. O. Yeiser	Lexington, Ky	June 25, 1872	128, 447
Bracelet guard-chain	G. D. Stevens	New York, N. Y	Jan. 31, 1871	111, 489
Bracelet-joints, Manufacture of	J. B. Black	Providence, R. I	May 27, 1873	139, 361
Bracelet manufacture	G. Sanford	Providence, R. I	Oct. 2, 1860	30, 250
Bracelet, Manufacture of enameled	A. Codding, jr	North Attleborough, Mass.	June 22, 1869	91, 604
Bracelet, Manufacture of plated metal	J. Barclay	Attleborough, Mass	Aug. 24, 1869	94, 064
Bracelet, &c., Safety-clasp for	I. Hermann	New York, N. Y	Sept. 22, 1857	18, 245
Bracelet safety-latchet	G. H. Soule	Jersey City, N. J	Apr. 9, 1872	125, 495
Bracelet-snap	G. S. Grant	Providence, R. I	Apr. 20, 1869	89, 037
Bracelet stock or blank	I. B. Staples	Attleborough, Mass	Aug. 23, 1870	106, 740
Bracelet, Voltaic	T. Hall	Boston, Mass	Apr. 23, 1867	64, 098
Bracing for cylindrical structures	G. H. Johnson	Buffalo, N. Y	Mar. 9, 1869	87, 569
Bracket:				
See Adjustable bracket.				
Bird-cage bracket.				
Bucket-bracket.				
Bureau-bracket.				
Cornice-bracket.				
Creel-bracket.				
Desk-bracket.				
Eave-trough bracket.				
Extension-bracket.				
Fence-bar bracket.				
Flower-pot bracket.				
Gas-bracket.				
Hanging bracket.				
Hat and cap bracket.				
Horse-bracket.				
Iron-bracket.				
Lamp-bracket.				
Leader-bracket.				
Looking-glass bracket.				
Metallic bracket.				
Pointed bracket.				
Pump-bracket.				
Pump-handle bracket.				
Roofing-bracket.				
Scaffold-bracket.				
Scaffolding-bracket.				
Shelf-bracket.				
Shelving-bracket.				
Shingling-bracket.				
Shingling and slating bracket.				
Slating-bracket.				
Stair-rail bracket.				
Stove-door bracket.				
Toilet-bracket.				
Tongue-bracket.				
Wagon-tongue bracket.				
Warp-creel bracket.				
Wire-bracket.				
Bracket	L. Benecke	Brunswick, Mo	Apr. 29, 1873	138, 367

Index of patents issued from the United States Patent Office from 1790 *to* 1873, *inclusive*—Continued.

Invention.	Inventor.	Residence.	Date.	No.
Bracket	J. E. Chesley	Boston, Mass	Aug. 29, 1871	118, 433
Bracket	M. H. Matsinger	Philadelphia, Pa	June 27, 1865	48, 420
Bracket	G. W. Peirce	Boston, Mass	July 11, 1871	116, 862
Bracket	J. M. Whiting	Providence, R. I	May 30, 1871	115, 550
Bracket and rack	W. A. Middleton	Harrisburgh, Pa	Oct. 20, 1868	83, 195
Bracket and towel-rack combined	G. W. Peirce	Boston, Mass	Nov. 7, 1871	120, 665
Bracket-brace for stair-rails	E. Betts	Boston, Mass	Sept. 15, 1863	39, 875
Bracket-clamp	G. W. Spaulding and G. R. Smith.	Syracuse, N. Y	June 22, 1869	91, 683
Bracket-hanger	C. E. Bliven	Toledo, Ohio	Mar. 29, 1870	101, 219
Bracket-seat	J. J. Wilson	New York, N. Y	Apr. 4, 1871	113, 607
Bracket-sheave	C. H. Straffin	Boston, Mass	Apr. 9, 1872	125, 419
Bracket-shelf	I. H. Frost	Bristol, Conn	Sept. 13, 1870	107, 245
Bracket shelf and drawer	L. Gibbs	Canton, Ohio	Apr. 7, 1868	76, 434
Bracket, shelf, &c., Construction of	N. G. Burleigh	Boston, Mass	Sept. 19, 1871	119, 116
Bracket to glass, Means of attaching	L. J. Lavater	Paris, France	Dec. 31, 1867	72, 867
Brad and nail cutting machine	J. Berry and O. P. Rand	New Market, N. H	Mar. 30, 1837	155
Brad and sprig, Machine for cutting	G. Jenkins	Plymouth County, Mass	May 16, 1817	......
Brad-cutter, Revolving	A. B. Woods and E. Talbot, jr	Windsor, Conn	Feb. 13, 1835	......
Brad-cutting machine	S. Boyden, jr	Boston, Mass	June 27, 1815	......
Brad-cutting machine	W. J. Miller	Cold Spring, N. Y	June 27, 1854	11, 172
Brad-cutting machine	H. Waterman	New York, N. Y	Jan. 10, 1840	1, 465
Brad-setter	M. D. Converse	London, Ohio	Mar. 8, 1870	100, 665
Brad-setter	C. E. Smith	Columbus, Ohio	Sept. 7, 1869	94, 520
Brad-setter for glaziers' use	M. Kleeman	Columbus, Ohio	June 1, 1869	90, 668
Brad, sprig, and nail machine, Cylindrical	R. Turner	Boston, Mass	Feb 21, 1814	......
Brads, Finishing	H. Stanton	Syracuse, N. Y	Nov. 5, 1867	70, 642
Brads from iron plates, Cutting and manufacturing	E. Gammond	Gorham, Me	Oct. 20, 1830	......
Brads, Machine for cutting	J. Ellis	....	Feb. 10, 1807	......
Brads, nails, and spikes, Cutting	S. Belknap	Washington, D. C	Apr. 8, 1814	......
Braid	J. H. Smith and W. and A. Shedlock.	Norwich, Conn., and New York, N. Y.	Sept. 1, 1868	81, 834
Braid and embroidery die, Machine for making	J. J. and E. D. Parker	Marietta, Ohio	Oct. 2, 1866	58, 470
Braid-holder	A. F. Jennings	Fredonia, N. Y	Nov. 23, 1869	97, 198
Braid, Lapping	W. R. Arnold	Providence, R. I	June 18, 1867	65, 859
Braid-making	J. Fletcher	Providence, R. I	Aug. 11, 1868	80, 818
Braid-making machine	G. Rehfuss	Philadelphia, Pa	Jan. 28, 1868	73, 930
Braid, Manufacture of	J. W. Bowers	Newton, Mass	July 27, 1869	92, 933
Braid, Manufacture of	A. H. Boyd	Medway, Mass	Jan. 27, 1863	37, 541
Braid-pressing machinery, Trimmed	H. H. Robbins	Middleborough, Mass	Apr. 10, 1841	2, 044
Braid sizing and polishing machine	J. S. Fenner	Warren, R. I	Sept. 8, 1868	81, 886
Braid, trimming, &c., Manufacture of imitation	H. Loewenburg	New York, N. Y	Aug. 2, 1870	106, 068
Braid, trimming, &c., Process of making imitation	H. Loewenburg	New York, N. Y	Aug. 13, 1872	130, 510
Braid-winding machine	W. and A. Shedlock	New York, N. Y	Feb. 23, 1869	87, 117
Braiding-machine	J. A. Bazin	Canton, Mass	Aug. 8, 1854	11, 512
Braiding-machine	J. D. Butler	Lancaster, Mass	Feb. 9, 1869	86, 642
Braiding-machine	J. D. Butler	Lancaster, Mass	July 20, 1869	92, 938
Braiding-machine	J. D. Butler	Lancaster, Mass	Mar. 26, 1872	124, 882
Braiding-machine	H. W. Cady, J. M. Carpenter, and G. K. Winchester.	Pawtucket and Providence, R. I.	Oct. 29, 1861	33, 569
Braiding-machine	A. B. Clemons	Derby, Conn	Nov. 16, 1858	22, 100
Braiding-machine	W. Darker	West Philadelphia, Pa	Aug. 21, 1866	57, 435
Braiding-machine	E. B. Day	Boston, Mass	Feb. 7, 1860	27, 039
Braiding-machine	H. Fletcher	Providence, R. I	July 7, 1863	39, 137
Braiding-machine	J. Fletcher	Providence, R. I	July 7, 1863	39, 138
Braiding-machine	L. Hull	Charlestown, Mass	Aug. 7, 1855	13, 391
Braiding-machine	L. Hull	Charlestown, Mass	Oct. 16, 1866	58, 830
Braiding-machine	O. M. Inman	Providence, R. I	Feb. 13, 1866	52, 573
Braiding-machine	I. W. Lamb	West Novi, Mich	June 28, 1859	24, 565
Braiding-machine	G. Mason	Providence, R. I	Apr. 6, 1869	88, 576
Braiding-machine	J. McCahey and S. B. Salisbury	Providence, R. I	Mar. 21, 1871	112, 946
Braiding-machine	D. D. Sacket	Westfield, Mass	Jan. 22, 1840	1, 476
Braiding-machine	S. B. Salisbury and J. McCahey	Providence, R. I	Aug. 6, 1872	130, 319
Braiding-machine	S. Scholfield	Providence, R. I	June 29, 1869	91, 970
Braiding-machine	E. T. and E. Sizer and A. Halladay.	Westfield, Mass	Mar. 28, 1854	10, 718
Braiding-machine	T. J. Sloan	New York, N. Y	Aug. 14, 1866	57, 201
Braiding-machine	J. Thorp	Providence, R. I	Aug. 10, 1821	......
Braiding-machine	J. Thorp	Providence, R. I	July 10, 1826	......
Braiding-machine	W. Tunstill	Paterson, N. J	Aug. 19, 1862	36, 249
Braiding-machine	W. Tunstill	Paterson, N. J	May 28, 1867	65, 309
Braiding-machine	W. Tunstill	Paterson, N. J	Aug. 11, 1868	81, 038
Braiding-machine	F. L. Verkamp and C. F. Leopold.	Philadelphia, Pa	July 24, 1866	56, 643
Braiding-machine	G. R. Winchester	Providence, R. I	Jan. 1, 1861	31, 061
Braiding-machine	J. B. Wood	Providence, R. I	Dec. 22, 1863	41, 045
Braiding-machine carrier	D. Avery	Westfield, Mass	June 2, 1868	78, 411
Braiding-machine carrier	O. E. Drown	Pawtucket, R. I	June 12, 1866	55, 580
Braiding-machine carrier	S. Scholfield	Providence, R. I	Oct. 29, 1867	70, 273
Braiding-machine for covering skirt and other wire	O. R. Burnham	New York, N. Y	Apr. 25, 1865	47, 487
Braiding-machine for making three-strand braid	J. Taggart	Roxbury, Mass	Feb. 27, 1866	52, 936
Braiding-machine stop-motion	E. W. Dean	Norwich, Conn	Aug. 23, 1870	106, 672
Braiding machine stop-motion	H. B. Howe and W. J. Mackrell	New York, N. Y	Aug. 21, 1866	57, 326
Braiding-machines, Expansion-pulley for	J. Fewkes	Newton, Mass	Jan. 7, 1868	72, 991
Braiding-machines, Let-off mechanism for	J. M. Carpenter	Providence, R. I	Aug. 14, 1866	57, 084
Braiding-machines, Let-off mechanism for carrier for.	T. Greenhalgh	Raritan, N. J	Apr. 13, 1869	88, 956
Braiding-machines, Let-off and tension-device for spool of.	J. D. Butler	Lancaster, Mass	Mar. 8, 1870	100, 596
Braiding-machines, Spool let-off and tension-device.	W. J. Horstmann	Philadelphia, Pa	Sept. 21, 1869	95, 112
Braiding-machines, Take-up for	G. K. Winchester	Providence, R. I	Mar. 26, 1867	63, 194
Braiding-machines, &c., Thread-tension and delivery mechanism for.	L. Hull	Charlestown, Mass	May 10, 1864	42, 663
Braiding-machines, Thread-tension and thread-delivery in.	L. Hull	Charlestown, Mass	June 14, 1864	43, 115
Braiding-machines, Yarn-delivery apparatus for	G. F. Chambers and S. Robinson	Worcester, Mass	June 5, 1866	55, 239

Index of patents issued from the United States Patent Office from 1790 *to* 1873, *inclusive*—Continued.

Invention.	Inventor.	Residence.	Date.	No.
Braiding-machinery	L. Hull	Charlestown, Mass	Oct. 30, 1855	13,719
Brake:				
See Air-brake.				
Automatic brake.				
Car-brake.				
Carriage-brake.				
Cart-brake.				
Collision-brake.				
Cotton-lapper brake.				
Crimping-brake.				
Elevator-brake.				
Flax-brake.				
Flax-boll brake.				
Friction-brake.				
Frictional brake.				
Hemp-brake.				
Horse-power brake.				
Inclined-plane brake.				
Inclined-plane and hoist brake.				
Land-conveyance brake.				
Machinery-brake.				
Omnibus-brake.				
Pneumatic brake.				
Pulley-brake.				
Railway-brake.				
Railway-train brake.				
Self-adjusting brake.				
Sewing-machine brake.				
Shoe-brake.				
Sled-brake.				
Sleigh-brake.				
Spinning-mule brake.				
Steam-brake.				
Steam and air brake.				
Steam-power air-brake.				
Vehicle-brake.				
Wagon-brake.				
Brake and starter combined	J. A. Cody	New York, N. Y	Apr. 2, 1872	125,119
Brake-block holder	A. W. Dorr	Lake Valley, Cal	Jan. 19, 1869	86,007
Brake by signal-cord, Operating	W. G. Creamer	New Haven County, Conn.	Dec. 20, 1853	10,321
Brake coupling, Steam-power	G. Westinghouse, jr	Pittsburgh, Pa	Mar. 4, 1873	136,396
Brake coupling, Steam-power	G. Westinghouse, jr	Pittsburgh, Pa	Mar. 11, 1873	136,631
Brake-mechanism	O. Grüninger	New York, N. Y	July 8, 1873	140,700
Brake-mechanism for light machinery	J. M. Cayce	Franklin, Tenn	June 25, 1872	128,283
Brake reaction movement	H. B. Martin	San Francisco, Cal	June 17, 1873	140,057
Brake-rubbers, Mode of hanging	T. C. Ball	Keene, N. H	Aug. 2, 1859	24,918
Brake-shoe	J. Christy	Philadelphia, Pa	Sept. 12, 1865	49,948
Brake-shoe	H. R. McAlister	Harrisburgh, Pa	Aug. 20, 1872	130,734
Brake-shoe	J. W. Moffitt	Harrisburgh, Pa	May 6, 1873	138,514
Brake-shoe	J. S. Whitworth	Norfolk, Va	Feb. 13, 1872	123,655
Brake shoe, Car	J. Brahn	Jersey City, N. J	Feb. 25, 1868	74,792
Brake-shoe for railway-car, Composition-metal	W. McConway	Pittsburgh, Pa	Feb. 27, 1872	124,190
Brake-shoe, Malleable-iron	J. J. Torley	Pittsburgh, Pa	June 18, 1872	127,996
Bran-duster	E. R. Benton	Milwaukee, Wis	May 7, 1850	7,336
Bran-duster	E. R. Benton	Cleveland, Ohio	July 26, 1853	9,881
Bran-duster	J. M. Carr and J Hughes	Cambridge City, Ind	Apr. 1, 1851	8,014
Bran-duster	G. Clark and P. T. Elting	Sandusky, Ohio	Feb. 12, 1861	31,371
Bran-duster	J. Cook	Saint Louis, Mo	Mar. 12, 1867	62,733
Bran-duster	J. Damp	Ashland, Ohio	Aug. 15, 1871	117,999
Bran-duster	R. M. Dempsey	Indianapolis, Ind	Dec. 18, 1849	6,952
Bran-duster	P. T. Elting	Buffalo, N. Y	May 19, 1868	77,965
Bran-duster	L. Fagin	Cincinnati, Ohio	Feb. 17, 1852	8,738
Bran-duster	W. Hall	Saint Louis, Mo	Nov. 1, 1859	25,965
Bran-duster	A. Hildreth	Newark, Ohio	Feb. 17, 1852	8,739
Bran-duster	J. W. Houghtelin	Du Quoin, Ill	June 26, 1860	28,863
Bran-duster	S. Hughes	Hamilton, Ohio	Apr. 13, 1869	88,875
Bran duster	W. W. Huntley and A. Babcock.	Silver Creek, N. Y	May 12, 1863	38,484
Bran-duster	J. Johnston	Wilmington, Del	Oct. 24, 1854	11,832
Bran-duster and flour-bolt	J. H. Jones	Yellow Springs, Ohio	Oct. 24, 1871	120,198
Bran-duster	S. W. Kirk	Coatesville, Pa	July 22, 1851	8,248
Bran-duster	S. B. Manning	Allegheny, Pa	July 27, 1858	21,009
Bran-duster	W. A. McFarlan and T. C. Carpenter.	Wilmington, Del	May 27, 1851	8,124
Bran-duster	L. S. Reynolds	Indianapolis, Ind	June 28, 1853	9,819
Bran-duster	J. T. McNally	Brooklyn, N. Y	Mar. 25, 1873	137,228
Bran-duster	G. H. Reynolds	Peoria, Ill	Nov. 20, 1866	59,862
Bran-duster	J. Richmond	Lockport, N. Y	Feb. 27, 1866	52,886
Bran-duster	M. Smith	Rochester, N. Y	June 23, 1863	39,021
Bran-duster, Feeding-screen for	G. S. Cooper	Baraboo, Wis	Jan. 21, 1873	135,085
Branch pipe through the ground without excavating, Inserting.	J. Ridgway	New York, N. Y	July 16, 1842	2,722
Brand for barrel	S. Huse	Newburyport, Mass	June 28, 1832	....
Brand for branding flour-barrel, &c	W. Ross	New Orleans, La	Dec. 2, 1825	....
Brand for marking animals	F. H. Richards	Troy, N. Y	Nov. 19, 1867	71,217
Branding and stamping iron	C. T. Holloway	Baltimore, Md	Feb. 4, 1862	34,301
Branding-apparatus	J. W. Dodge	Malden, Mass	May 4, 1869	89,829
Branding-instrument	N. J. and J. P. Wemmer	Philadelphia, Pa	Feb. 11, 1868	74,263
Branding-iron	F. L. Penny	Boston, Mass	Mar. 9, 1869	87,588
Branding-iron	C Rundquist	Mankato, Minn	Nov. 19, 1867	71,068
Branding-iron	L. Stark	Chelsea, Mass	Mar. 9, 1869	87,720
Branding-stamp	W. C. Garretson and E. Draper	Oskaloosa, Iowa	Oct. 6, 1868	82,823
Branding, stamping, marking, &c., Apparatus for.	E. Barns, G. Hill, and J. B. Hawkins.	Ashtabula, Ohio	Feb. 25, 1835	....
Branding-tool	L. Stark	Chicopee, Mass	Jan. 1, 1850	6,993
Branding-tool	J. P. Worrall	Philadelphia, Pa	Jan. 23, 1866	52,238
Brandy and whisky by redistillation and filtration, Mode of purifying and rectifying.	R. Wanck	Gallipolis, Ohio	Dec. 7, 1829	....

Index of patents issued from the United States Patent Office from 1790 *to* 1873, *inclusive*—Continued.

Invention.	Inventor.	Residence.	Date.	No.
Brandy from grain or fruit, Making	C. J. Hütter		Feb. 11, 1803	....
Brandy manufacture	D. J. Browne and S. T. Bacon	Cambridge and Boston, Mass.	Jan. 22, 1867	61, 313
Brandy of domestic materials, Imitating	H. Moore	Aurora, N. Y	July 2, 1814	....
Brass, copper, and composition nails, Manufacturing.	G. W. Robinson	Attleborough, Mass	Mar. 17, 1813	....
Brass, &c., Furnace for melting	I. D. Bush	Detroit, Mich	Feb. 18, 1873	135, 967
Brass-polishing composition	W. H. Trissler	Cleveland, Ohio	Sept. 8, 1863	39, 848
Brazier	R. B. Wakefield	Springfield, Mass	Sept. 28, 1869	95, 291
Bread and cake receptacle	C. C. Savery	Philadelphia, Pa	Nov. 2, 1869	96, 487
Bread and candy cutter	F. Quinn	Keokuk, Iowa	Oct. 1, 1872	131, 781
Bread and cracker machine	W. R. Nevins and J. J. Yates	New York, N. Y	Sept. 28, 1858	21, 619
Bread and meat cutter	W. Budd and J. L. Husband	Philadelphia, Pa	Aug. 8, 1865	49, 225
Bread and meat cutter	S. Kepner	Pottstown, Pa	Apr. 10, 1866	53, 835
Bread and pastry board	J. McNamee	Easton, Pa	Jan. 1, 1861	31, 066
Bread and vegetable cutter	H. A. Titus	Gloversville, N. Y	Feb. 25, 1868	74, 864
Bread, Apparatus for making aërated	R. L. Howard and J. Danglish	London and Reading, England.	Jan. 23, 1866	52, 252
Bread, Apparatus for making aërated	A. Scratchard	Mile End, England	Apr. 26, 1870	102, 325
Bread-baking device	A. I. Quackenbush and G. Hawn.	Fort Plain, N. Y	Jan. 25, 1870	99, 109
Bread-board	W. H. Lewis	New York, N. Y	Jan. 7, 1868	73, 104
Bread-board and dough-tray	B. Fulton	Pulaski, Iowa	Oct. 17, 1871	119, 926
Bread-cutter	H. Berdan	New York, N. Y	Apr. 12, 1859	23, 548
Bread-cutter	J. Buckett	New York, N. Y	June 6, 1865	48, 127
Bread-cutter	I. S. Bunnell	Carbondale, Pa	Oct. 3, 1871	119, 569
Bread-cutter	M. Chapman	Greenfield, Mass	Feb. 2, 1858	19, 238
Bread-cutter	A. M. Dexter	Philadelphia, Pa	July 23, 1867	67, 032
Bread-cutter	G. D. Goodsell and N. E. Babcock.	Rockford, Ill	May 31, 1870	103, 601
Bread-cutter	W. S. Gray	Worcester, Mass	July 30, 1867	67, 191
Bread-cutter	C. Hansen and P. Andersen	Racine, Wis	May 14, 1872	126, 807
Bread-cutter	F. Hüllhorst	Freeport, Ill	Jan. 24, 1865	46, 003
Bread-cutter	G. L. Jones	Chicopee, Mass	Apr. 28, 1868	77, 383
Bread-cutter	A. E. and D. Lazell	Chicopee Falls, Mass	July 1, 1851	8, 193
Bread-cutter	C. Lemke	Cincinnati, Ohio	Oct 10, 1871	119, 861
Bread-cutter	J. Madden	Cleveland, Ohio	Apr. 2, 1867	63, 406
Bread-cutter	J. Madden	Cleveland, Ohio	July 30, 1867	67, 325
Bread-cutter	J. Madden and J. G. Haserot	Cleveland, Ohio	Jan. 7, 1868	73, 017
Bread-cutter	S. H. Martin and J. S. Williams	Mount Vernon, N. Y	May 7, 1872	126, 468
Bread-cutter	J. Oxley	Sheffield, England	May 10, 1864	42, 715
Bread-cutter	J. F. Plass	New York, N. Y	Apr. 25, 1865	47, 450
Bread-cutter	S. D. Simmons	San Francisco, Cal	July 25, 1865	48, 985
Bread-cutter	S. D. Simmons	Brooklyn, E. D., N. Y	June 4, 1867	65, 441
Bread-cutter	J. D. Soles	Lynn Township, Ill	Aug. 25, 1868	81, 427
Bread-cutter	G. D. Williams	Chicopee, Mass	Dec. 24, 1867	72, 709
Bread-cutting machine	R. P. March	Morristown, Pa	July 21, 1863	39, 298
Bread-cutting machine	J. Naughten	Cincinnati, Ohio	Nov. 10, 1857	18, 597
Bread, Device for raising and kneading	A. G. Good	Reading, Pa	June 15, 1869	91, 432
Bread-dough	N. Wyeth	Hingham, Mass	May 12, 1834	....
Bread-finisher	E. Treadwell	Philadelphia, Pa	Jan. 10, 1820	....
Bread-knife	J. Carrier	Marlborough, Conn	May 24, 1859	24, 099
Bread-knife	J. Frisch	Albany, N. Y	June 2, 1868	71, 586
Bread-knife	F. Roys	Berlin, Conn	Oct. 9, 1844	3, 783
Bread-machine	J. E. Hawkins	Lansingburgh, N. Y	Nov. 16, 1869	96, 804
Bread-machine	J. E. Hawkins	Lansingburgh, N. Y	Apr. 5, 1870	101, 615
Bread-machine	L. P. Jenks	Boston, Mass	May 10, 1870	102, 943
Bread, Machine for gaging size of loaf of	E. L. Moeschler	Rochester, N. Y	Feb. 26, 1867	62, 354
Bread, Machine for making ship and other	J. Starr	Middletown, Conn	Jan. 8, 1813	....
Bread machine, Loaf	J. D'Arcy	San Francisco, Cal	Nov. 19, 1867	70, 971
Bread, Machinery for manufacturing aërated	J. Danglish	Reading, England	July 4, 1865	48, 534
Bread, Making	W. Banks		Dec. 14, 1798	....
Bread-making	J. Perry	Brooklyn, N. Y	Nov. 24, 1863	40, 707
Bread-making apparatus	J. A. H. Le Gantvoort	Waupun, Wis	June 21, 1870	104, 662
Bread-making chest and table	B. Gonzales	Goodland, Ind	Oct. 28, 1862	36, 777
Bread-making machine	W. Carr	Bath, Me	July 22, 1843	3, 192
Bread-making machine	W. O. Drew	Georgetown, D. C	Mar. 31, 1863	38, 037
Bread-making machine	M. A. Jones	Frankfort, Ky	Mar. 24, 1868	75, 922
Bread-making machine	G. Richards	Manlius, N. Y	Feb. 8, 1813	....
Bread-making table	W. K. Wyckoff	Ripon, Wis	Mar. 15, 1859	23, 283
Bread, Manufacture of	B. Garvey	New York, N. Y	July 17, 1860	29, 158
Bread, Manufacture of	J. G. Moxey	Philadelphia, Pa	Dec. 19, 1865	51, 659
Bread, Manufacture of aërated	S. F. Ambler	Brooklyn, N. Y	Aug. 12, 1862	36, 134
Bread, Manufacture of light	W. J. Walker	Baltimore, Md	Apr. 9, 1867	63, 676
Bread-manufacture, Treating grain for	A. Sézille	Paris, France	Dec. 31, 1872	134, 443
Bread, meat, and vegetable cutter	G. Stackhouse	Mount Washington, Pa	May 19, 1868	78, 149
Bread, meat, &c., cutter for	D. Campbell	Elizabeth, N. J	May 30, 1865	48, 014
Bread-pan	W. A. Daggett	South Vineland, N. J	Nov. 22, 1870	109, 497
Bread-pan	W. A. Daggett	South Vineland, N. J	Dec. 6, 1870	109, 871
Bread-pan, Machine for forming	M. L. Best	Canton, Ohio	June 30, 1868	79, 438
Bread, Preparation of portable soup	G. Borden, jr	Galveston, Tex	Feb. 5, 1850	7, 066
Bread, Process for making	C. Crum	Hudson, N. Y	Mar. 6, 1855	12, 479
Bread, Raising	A. Conant	Lowell, Mass	Oct. 12, 1842	2, 816
Bread-raising apparatus	E. Buss	Springfield, Ohio	July 3, 1866	56, 002
Bread-raising apparatus	J. Sutton	New York, N. Y	Apr. 15, 1873	137, 974
Bread-raising preparation	R. P. Leonard	Keene, N. H	Apr. 27, 1869	89, 320
Bread-slicer	J. W. Currier	Springfield, Mass	May 16, 1871	114, 930
Bread-slicing machine	A. Iske and J. O Steinheiser	Lancaster, Pa	May 28, 1872	127, 242
Bread, soap, and black lead, Machine for cutting	W. B. Vincent	Boston, Mass	Feb. 13, 1866	52, 627
Bread-toaster	H. P. Brooks	Waterbury, Conn	Aug. 16, 1870	106, 462
Bread-toaster	A. Brown	Rochester, N. Y	Aug. 23, 1870	106, 654
Bread-toaster	D. Miller	Marietta, Ohio	Mar. 12, 1872	124, 605
Bread-toaster, Revolving	J. C. Paine	Dubuque, Iowa	Feb. 19, 1867	62, 218
Bread-worker	J. H. Balderston	Colora, Md	Feb. 18, 1873	135, 959
Breaker and leveler, Combined	D. Witt	Hubbardston, Mass	Feb. 9, 1869	86, 893
Breaker-roller	E. Dowden	Dykens, Pa	Mar. 1, 1870	100, 273
Breakfast and dining table	P. Barker	Worthington, Ohio	Aug. 6, 1828	....

Index of patents issued from the United States Patent Office from 1790 *to* 1873, *inclusive*—Continued.

Invention.	Inventor.	Residence.	Date.	No.
Breaking and grinding mill	W. Beal, jr	Lowell, Mass	Nov. 14, 1848	5, 916
Breaking-machine	J. D. Whelpley	Boston, Mass	June 28, 1870	104, 910
Breakwater	D. H. Armour	Columbia, Tex	June 7, 1859	24, 271
Breakwater	L. Gutekunst	Philadelphia, Pa	Jan. 18, 1870	98, 953
Breakwater, Construction of	D. Cunningham	Dundee, Scotland	Apr. 8, 1873	137, 659
Breast-cup	A. M. Knapp	Lowell, Mass	July 22, 1873	141, 005
Breast-cup	E. Waters	Troy, N. Y	Aug. 29, 1854	11, 623
Breast-developer, Pneumatic	J. M. Clark	Lancaster, Pa	Nov. 26, 1867	71, 459
Breast-pad	R. Collins	Chicopee, Mass	Dec. 31, 1867	72, 802
Breast-pad	A. S. and J. P. McLean	Brooklyn, N. Y	Jan. 1, 1867	60, 767
Breast-pad	D. K. Wertman	Centralia, Pa	Mar. 31, 1868	76, 124
Breast-pad and perspiration shield	H. S. Lesher	Brooklyn, N. Y	May 17, 1859	24, 033
Breast-pad, Lady's	J. A. Mason	Brooklyn, N. Y	Jan. 10, 1865	45, 843
Breast-pin	T. C. Eiswald	Providence, R. I	June 28, 1870	104, 840
Breast-pin	C. A. Pease	Boston, Mass	July 30, 1872	129, 902
Breast-pin	L. Sauter	Jersey City, N. J	Oct. 16, 1866	58, 894
Breast-pin	A. Weiller	New York, N. Y	Nov. 28, 1871	121, 440
Breast-pin, ear-ring, &c., Catch-fastening for	J. N. B. Jaquith	Boston, Mass	Nov. 15, 1864	45, 044
Breast-pin fastening	S. Ayres	Danville, Ky	Aug. 31, 1869	94, 270
Breast-pin fastening	G. Buhler	Newark, N. J	Feb. 23, 1864	41, 678
Breast-pin fastening	C. G. Cahoone and B. E. Brown	Providence, R. I	Mar. 30, 1869	88, 273
Breast-pin fastening	B. F. Grinnell	New York, N. Y	Jan. 18, 1859	22, 645
Breast-pin fastening	C. F. Kolb	Philadelphia, Pa	July 28, 1857	17, 881
Breast-pin fastening	J. A. Lehman	Philadelphia, Pa	Oct. 10, 1871	119, 860
Breast-pin fastening	T. W. F. Smitten	Brooklyn, N. Y	Sept. 1, 1868	81, 835
Breast-pin fastening	A. K. P. Walter	Richmond, Me	Sept. 17, 1867	69, 052
Breast-pin guard	J. M. Ross	Springfield, Mass	Mar. 10, 1857	16, 808
Breast-pin joint	D. O. Stanley	South Attleborough, Mass	Nov. 7, 1871	120, 601
Breast-pin safety-attachment	F. Catlin	New York, N. Y	July 6, 1869	92, 163
Breast-pin safety-attachment	C. F. Pierce	Providence, R. I	June 15, 1869	91, 261
Breast-pin, Shield to protect	J. H. Phillips	Washington, D. C	June 24, 1856	15, 212
Breast-pin, Spiral catch for	J. F. Mascher	Philadelphia, Pa	July 14, 1857	17, 800
Breast-pin, &c., Tongue for	S. Davidson	New York, N. Y	July 23, 1867	67, 029
Breast-pin, Tongue for	L. H. Sondheim	New York, N. Y	Mar. 25, 1873	137, 154
Breast-pins, &c., Safe-catch for	E. C. Benyaurd	Philadelphia, Pa	Mar. 6, 1855	12, 477
Breast-pipe	T. Lewis	Malden, Mass	Nov. 16, 1858	22, 080
Breast-protector	J. Stadermann and H. Sauerbier	New York, N. Y., and Newark, N. J.	Dec. 11, 1866	60, 436
Breast-protector	J. Stadermann and H. Sauerbier	New York, N. Y	Mar. 26, 1867	63, 323
Breast-protector, Mammiform	E. M. Marshall	Hillsdale, N. Y	June 28, 1864	43, 321
Breast-strap	A. L. Hill	Decatur, Ill	July 14, 1868	79, 977
Breast-strap for horses	C. P. Holmes	Gouverneur, N. Y	Dec. 24, 1872	134, 283
Breast-strap hook	H. Foulkes	Utica, N. Y	Aug. 28, 1866	57, 629
Breast-strap, Roller-attachment for	F. Jones	Prescott, Wis	Sept. 22, 1863	40, 045
Breast-strap shield	H. F. Willson	Elyria, Ohio	Apr. 25, 1865	47, 485
Breast-strap shield	H. F. Willson	Fort Wayne, Ind	Aug. 20, 1867	67, 934
Breast-strap slide	A. Buckham	Newark, N. J	May 3, 1864	42, 554
Breast-strap slide	J. H. Martin	Columbus, Ohio	Mar. 23, 1869	88, 192
Breast-strap slide	O. B. North	New Haven, Conn	Dec. 10, 1867	71, 901
Breast-strap slide	I. Roraback	South Bend, Ind	Aug. 13, 1867	67, 867
Breast-strap slide	S. Selleck	Rosendale, N. Y	Feb. 2, 1864	41, 450
Breast-strap slide	C. H. Stevens and W. Garrison	Syracuse, N. Y	Aug. 25, 1868	81, 553
Breasts, Lacteal or artificial method of constructing	C. M. Windship	Roxbury, Mass	Feb. 18, 1841	1, 985
Breathing-tube	J. S. Rose	Philadelphia, Pa	May 8, 1843	3, 079
Breech-loader	B. Burton	Brooklyn, N. Y	June 29, 1869	92, 013
Breech-loader	L. T. Delassize	New Orleans, La	July 20, 1869	92, 799
Breech-loader	Z. R. Von Wessely	New York, N. Y	July 13, 1869	92, 673
Breech-loader	W. G. Ward	New York, N. Y	June 29, 1869	92, 129
Breech-pin and self-capping gun, Sliding	C. Sharps	Cincinnati, Ohio	Sept. 12, 1848	5, 763
Breeching-hook	J. H. Littlefield	Cambridge Mass	June 27, 1865	48, 415
Breeching-hook	G. W. Miller	Springfield, Mass	Nov. 27, 1866	60, 033
Breeching-hook for vehicle	E. Brown	Leominster, Mass	July 4, 1865	48, 513
Breeching-loop	S. Ward	Princeton, Ind	July 9, 1872	128, 932
Breeching-strap fastening	A. W. Olds	Green Oak, Mich	Aug. 1, 1865	49, 143
Brewers and distillers, Apparatus for preparing mash for.	A. S. Swartz	Buffalo, N. Y	Mar. 26, 1867	63, 331
Brewers and distillers, Testing-instrument for	M. Augenstein	Brooklyn, N. Y	Nov. 15, 1870	109, 168
Brewer's boiler, Apparatus for heating	D. S. Blair	Albany, N. Y	Dec. 22, 1863	40, 990
Brewer's boiler, Coil for	J. Frageser and J. G. Schreiber	New York, N. Y	June 19, 1866	55, 747
Brewer's cooler	A. Wood	Pittsburgh, Pa	Sept. 15, 1857	18, 220
Brewer's mash-tun	B. G. Martin	Philadelphia, Pa	Dec. 12, 1865	51, 518
Brewer's mash-tun	J. Walker	Cincinnati, Ohio,	Feb. 12, 1867	62, 101
Breweries and bar, Collecting waste spirits from	A. Maginnis and W. McCormick.	Philadelphia, Pa	Mar. 1, 1870	100, 428
Breweries, Apparatus for mashing and cooling in	G. S. Yingling and S. F. Poorman.	Tiffin, Ohio	May 14, 1867	64, 824
Breweries, cellars, and beer-vaults, Apparatus for cooling.	L. Schulze	Philadelphia, Pa	June 4, 1872	127, 647
Breweries, Cooler for	A. Hammer	Reading, Pa	Sept. 15, 1857	18, 201
Breweries, Cooler for	A. Hammer	New York, N. Y	Apr. 18, 1865	47, 298
Breweries, Cooler for	C. R. M. Wall	Brooklyn, N. Y	Aug. 22, 1865	49, 573
Breweries, &c., Machine for washing	L. Beatty		May 17, 1816	
Breweries, Machine for washing shavings in	F. Hinckel	Albany, N. Y	Jan. 5, 1869	85, 526
Brewing	E. Beanes	Cordwallis, Great Britain	Mar. 23, 1869	88, 001
Brewing	W. H. Elliot	New York, N. Y	Jan. 7, 1868	72, 989
Brewing and distilling cooler	L. Reich	New York, N. Y	Apr. 3, 1866	53, 677
Brewing and distilling, Cooling and condensing apparatus for.	D. E. Somes	Washington, D. C	Feb. 28, 1865	46, 594
Brewing and preserving alcoholic drinks	J. Hopkins	Brownsville, Pa	May 8, 1849	6, 430
Brewing ale, beer, &c	J. McCormick	Boston, Mass	Nov. 16, 1869	96, 939
Brewing ale, porter, &c	F. M. Ruschaupt and G. Burbenne.	New York and Williamsburgh, N. Y.	Aug. 18, 1868	81, 214
Brewing-apparatus	R. L. Lloyd and A. Partenheimer.	Philadelphia, Pa	Jan. 27, 1824	
Brewing beer and ale	T. Behm	Norwich, N. Y	Aug. 1, 1838	868
Brewing beer and ale	L. Pasteur	Paris, France	Jan. 28, 1873	135, 245
Brewing beer and other malt-liquors	W. H. Elliot	New York, N. Y	Mar. 31, 1868	76, 177

Index of patents issued from the United States Patent Office from 1790 *to* 1873, *inclusive*—Continued.

Invention.	Inventor.	Residence.	Date.	No.
Brewing beer, &c., Process of using unmashed Indian corn in.	N. Baumann	Kalamazoo, Mich.	May 18, 1869	90,066
Brewing by steam	H. Hackley	New York, N. Y	Apr. 21, 1820	....
Brewing, malting, &c., Apparatus for	A. B. Walker	Warrington, England	Apr. 14, 1868	76,653
Brewing malt-liquor, Apparatus for	P. Conday	Philadelphia, Pa	Sept. 15, 1868	82,208
Brewing malt-liquor, Process of	C. R. M. Wall	Brooklyn, N. Y	Dec. 20, 1864	45,543
Brewing, Preparing mash for	S. C. Granger	Chicago, Ill	Nov. 26, 1861	33,779
Brewing, Process for	A. Hammer	New York, N. Y	Mar. 28, 1865	47,014
Brewing with Indian corn	A. Anderson		Jan. 26, 1801	....
Brewing with Indian corn	L. Haecker	Altenburg, Hungary	July 1, 1862	35,752
Brewing with maize	L. Haecker	Altenburg, Hungary	Dec. 8, 1863	40,836
Brick	D. L. Bartlett and G. H. Johnson.	Baltimore, Md	Aug. 28, 1866	57,461
Brick	J. Dennen	Chicago, Ill	Aug. 26, 1873	142,087
Brick	J. Grimm	Cuyahoga Falls, Ohio	Feb. 9, 1869	86,664
Brick	S. McLaughlin	Philadelphia, Pa	May 21, 1867	64,994
Brick	L. Till	Sandusky, Ohio	June 19, 1855	13,110
Brick	N. Towson	Washington, D. C	May 16, 1848	5,570
Brick and artificial stone, Machine for making	J. Fensom	Toronto, Canada	Jan. 16, 1872	122,714
Brick and concrete press	G. A. Trear	Chicago, Ill	Dec. 1, 1868	84,485
Brick and draining pipe	J. C. Bryant	Philadelphia, Pa	May 31, 1864	42,926
Brick and lime kiln, Controlling draft in	J. Leeds	Philadelphia, Pa	July 4, 1854	11,230
Brick and mortar elevator	W. Boswell	Pontiac, Mich	Sept. 12, 1871	118,783
Brick and mortar elevator	J. McNamara	Buffalo, N. Y	Oct. 4, 1864	44,544
Brick and mortar elevator	A. Pohl	Detroit, Mich	Feb. 18, 1868	74,590
Brick and mortar hod	E. B. Black, J. Hinkle, jr., and T. S. White.	Columbia, Pa	Mar. 30, 1869	88,361
Brick and mortar lift, Alternate	B. Dearborn	Boston, Mass	June 20, 1816	....
Brick and mortar machine	A. Parker	Sweden, Me	Mar. 5, 1830	....
Brick and other molds	H. Martin	Brooklyn, N. Y	Apr. 4, 1871	113,540
Brick and pantiles, Manufacturing	S. Brouwer		Aug. 17, 1793	....
Brick and pottery-ware kiln	J. N. Stanley	Brooklyn, N. Y	May 9, 1865	47,665
Brick and sand drier	S. D. Rader	Williamsport, Pa	June 8, 1869	91,041
Brick and stove-lining, Fire	D. Perry	West Mansfield, Mass	Jan. 23, 1872	122,908
Brick and tempering clay, Molding	J. C. Porter	Powhatan County, Va	Dec. 29, 1830	....
Brick and tile	B. P. Coston	Stirling, Pa	Oct. 22, 1835	....
Brick and tile after molding, Machine for pressing and finishing.	J. B. Wilson and A. B. Crossman.	Malden, Mass., and Huntington, N. Y.	Sept. 30, 1841	2,271
Brick and tile kiln	H. Aiken, H. McAllister, jr., and H. G. Morris.	Pittsburgh and Philadelphia, Pa.	Mar. 2, 1869	87,455
Brick and tile kiln	S. H. Clapp	Malden, Mass	June 8, 1869	90,929
Brick and tile kiln	J. Duff	Washington, D. C	Oct. 31, 1825	....
Brick and tile kiln	A. Morand	Brooklyn, N. Y	Apr. 16, 1872	125,832
Brick and tile machine	G. Baldwin	Monroe, Mich	Mar. 4, 1873	136,481
Brick and tile machine	I. C. Bryant	Washington, D. C	Apr. 18, 1871	113,847
Brick and tile machine	H. Clayton	Dorset Square, England	June 26, 1855	13,123
Brick and tile machine	E. Fisk and B. Hinkley	Fayette, Me	Sept. 8, 1827	....
Brick and tile machine	D. French	New York, N. Y	Aug. 22, 1810	....
Brick and tile machine	G. Hadfield		May 15, 1800	......
Brick and tile machine	J. Hotchkiss and E. Buss	Springfield, Ohio	Sept. 17, 1867	68,986
Brick and tile machine	W. Hutchinson	Salford, Great Britain	Apr. 4, 1871	113,300
Brick and tile machine	N. and P. W. Miller		Jan. 5, 1804	....
Brick and tile machine	G. Scott	Philadelphia, Pa	Apr. 5, 1870	101,525
Brick and tile machine	B. F. St. John and H. Horst	Shelbyville, Ind	Oct. 17, 1865	50,5[illegible]8
Brick and tile machine	Z. Street	Salem, Ohio	July 8, 1862	35,843
Brick and tile machine, Die for	C. Chambers, jr	Philadelphia, Pa	Sept. 15, 1863	39,884
Brick and tile machine, Die for	J. Hotchkiss and E. Buss	Springfield, Ohio	Apr. 30, 1867	64,223
Brick and tile making	W. L. Drake	Evanston, Ill	July 16, 1872	129,113
Brick and tile making	J. E. Stubbs and J. Bonner	Cincinnati, Ohio	May 10, 1822	....
Brick and tile making	J. Wood	Rockland County, N. Y	Dec. 2, 1836	97
Brick and tile press	B. Porter	Salem, Mass	May 18, 1814	....
Brick and tile pressing	S. Lane	Hallowell, Me	Sept. 30, 1825	....
Brick and tile pressing machine	J. Parker	Gardiner, Me	Nov. 29, 1828	....
Brick and tile, Pressing unburnt	E. Mayo	Hallowell, Me	Dec. 9, 1828	....
Brick and tiles, Machine for heating untempered clay for.	I. Gregg	Pittsburgh, Pa	May 19, 1863	38,580
Brick-burner	W. H. Towers	Boston, Mass	Feb. 12, 1867	62,089
Brick-burner, Perpetual	Z. Shaw	Ypsilanti, Mich	Dec. 28, 1869	98,306
Brick, Burning	N. Adams and A. Noyes	Cornwall and Newburgh, N. Y.	Dec. 28, 1829	....
Brick, Burning	J. W. Andrews	Norristown, Pa	Mar. 21, 1843	3,016
Brick, Burning	T. Billesbach	Kearney Junction, Nebr	Nov. 18, 1873	144,652
Brick, Burning	D. and G. M. Blocher	Cumberland, Md	June 5, 1855	12,991
Brick, Burning	R. Crutchfield	Botetourt County, Va	Feb. 7, 1824	....
Brick, Burning	A. J. Mullen and R. Hall	Greensborough, Ala	Feb. 9, 1858	19,309
Brick by pressing, Making	S. Briggs	Salem, Mass	Jan. 11, 1823	....
Brick by pressure, Making	D. Flagg, jr	Gardiner, Me	Dec. 17, 1824	....
Brick-clay, Machine for making	D. Phillips and J. Drummond	Whitestown, N. Y	May 15, 1832	....
Brick-clay, Machine for mixing	J. Chapman	Mad River Township, Ohio.	June 2, 1832	....
Brick-cleaning machine	T. M. Schleier	Knoxville, Tenn	Dec. 10, 1872	133,893
Brick, Coloring	W. Boies	Troy, N. Y	June 4, 1872	127,551
Brick, Coloring	C. B. Doty	Cortland, N. Y	Feb. 6, 1849	6,1[illegible]2
Brick, Composition for fire	D. Cannon and H. S. Lucas	Chester, Mass	July 24, 1847	5,198
Brick, Composition for fire	C. W. Fenton	Bennington, Vt	Sept. 22, 1837	393
Brick, Composition for fire	E. F. Rogers	Chelsea, Mass	Oct. 10, 1871	119,723
Brick, Composition for making	N. J. Wyeth	Cambridge, Mass	Mar. 28, 1844	3,517
Brick, &c., Compressing and smoothing unburnt	T. Norcross and G. Pollard	Hallowell, Me	Oct. 1, 1825	....
Brick-drier	J. K. Caldwell	Allegheny City, Pa	Jan. 21, 1868	73,433
Brick-drier	I. C. Hatch	Camden, N. J	June 9, 1868	78,802
Brick-drier	J. J. Johnston	Allegheny City, Pa	Sept. 24, 1867	69,217
Brick-drier	W. O. Leslie	Philadelphia, Pa	Aug. 18, 1868	81,094
Brick-drier	J. McDonald	Saratoga Springs, N. Y	Aug. 13, 1867	67,783
Brick-drier	J. M. Moyer	Pittsburgh, Pa	June 23, 1868	79,247
Brick-drier	S. M. Parish	Baldwinsville, N. Y	Aug. 16, 1864	43,861
Brick-drying	J. R. Bowers	Concord, N. H	July 2, 1867	66,206
Brick-drying	I. Gregg	Philadelphia, Pa	July 9, 1867	66,486
Brick-drying house	G. C. Bovey	Cincinnati, Ohio	Mar. 26, 1872	125,013

Index of patents issued from the United States Patent Office from 1790 *to* 1873, *inclusive*—Continued.

Invention.	Inventor.	Residence.	Date.	No.
Brick-drying kiln	E. W. Bingham	Williamsport, Pa	June 23, 1868	79,192
Brick-drying kiln	E. C. Dean, H. Hamilton, G. P. Tenney, and A. T. Putnam.	Detroit, Mich	Aug. 31, 1869	94,188
Brick-drying press	J. T. Shryock	Zanesville, Ohio	June 5, 1866	55,376
Brick-elevator	T. Mann	San Francisco, Cal	Feb. 16, 1869	86,932
Brick-elevator	J. H. Sears and B. Merritt	Boston and Chelsea, Mass	Mar. 19, 1861	31,726
Brick, &c., Enamel composition for	D. W. Clark	Bennington, Vt	June 7, 1859	24,282
Brick-finishing machine	W. S. Mayo	New York, N. Y	June 7, 1859	24,320
Brick, Fire	E. Seavey	Boston, Mass	June 12, 1860	28,692
Brick, Fire	R. W. Smith	Baltimore, Md	Sept. 27, 1825	....
Brick, Fire	S. K. Wellman	Nashua, N. H	Feb. 12, 1867	61,966
Brick for building-purposes	W. Smith	Saint Louis, Mo	Apr. 7, 1868	76,540
Brick for ceilings	M. Abord	Paris, France	Aug. 21, 1866	57,450
Brick for constructing metallurgic furnaces	H. Frank	Pittsburgh, Pa	Dec. 31, 1872	134,374
Brick for curved masonry-work	E. Hennessey	Washington County, D. C	Dec. 31, 1867	72,734
Brick for pavement, &c	R. Wright	Philadelphia, Pa	Dec. 17, 1867	72,352
Brick, Forming	C. H. Preston	New York, N. Y	June 19, 1847	5,170
Brick from dry clay, Machine for pressing	B. H. Brown	Washington, D. C	Dec. 8, 1838	1,026
Brick-hacking machine	D. Woodbury	Minneapolis, Minn	Nov. 5, 1867	70,669
Brick handling or piling machine	J. Sangster	Buffalo, N. Y	Jan. 7, 1868	73,123
Brick-hoisting machine	T. F. Christman	Wilson, N. C	June 28, 1859	24,540
Brick, Hollow	G. H. Johnson	New York, N. Y	Jan. 3, 1871	110,764
Brick, Implements for picking up and carrying	R. Bryden	Medford, Mass	Nov. 26, 1872	133,299
Brick-kiln	H. W. Adams	Philadelphia, Pa	July 21, 1868	80,046
Brick-kiln	H. W. Adams	Philadelphia, Pa	July 20, 1869	92,770
Brick-kiln	J. Blaisius	Washington, D. C	Dec. 24, 1872	134,124
Brick-kiln	O. Bennett	Boston, Mass	Apr. 5, 1870	101,416
Brick-kiln	D. Blocher	Baltimore, Md	July 1, 1873	140,343
Brick-kiln	F. F. Boudrye	San Francisco, Cal	Mar. 12, 1872	124,538
Brick-kiln	G. C. Bovey	Cincinnati, Ohio	Jan. 15, 1867	61,149
Brick-kiln	S. C. Brewer	Water Valley, Miss	June 20, 1871	116,016
Brick-kiln	W. V. Cecil	Monmouth, Ill	July 20, 1869	92,702
Brick-kiln	P. Clark	Brooklyn, N. Y	Feb. 2, 1869	86,363
Brick-kiln	S. H. Clapp	Malden, Mass	Mar. 24, 1868	75,730
Brick-kiln	C. B. Corey and C. M. Turner	Cleveland, Ohio	July 9, 1867	66,464
Brick-kiln	R. D. Cox	Philadelphia, Pa	Feb. 15, 1870	99,852
Brick-kiln	J. W. Crary	New Orleans, La	May 4, 1858	20,146
Brick-kiln	J. Eisele	Ann Arbor, Mich	Apr. 23, 1872	126,040
Brick-kiln	W. Ennis	Philadelphia, Pa	Jan. 25, 1870	99,174
Brick-kiln	W. Gilbert	Detroit, Mich	Sept. 29, 1868	82,511
Brick-kiln	J. H. Good	Pequa Township, Pa	Mar. 16, 1869	87,838
Brick-kiln	W. S. Hall	New York, N. Y	Apr. 12, 1870	101,870
Brick-kiln	W. Hallam	Cheltenham, Mo	Sept. 28, 1869	95,339
Brick-kiln	S. M. Hamilton	Baltimore, Md	Feb 15, 1870	99,886
Brick-kiln	S. M. Hamilton	Baltimore, Md	Feb. 15, 1870	99,887
Brick-kiln	S. M. Hamilton	Baltimore, Md	Mar. 22, 1870	101,124
Brick-kiln	S. M. Hamilton	Baltimore, Md	May 21, 1872	127,050
Brick-kiln	E. Haueisen, A. Wagner, and A. Nulsen.	Cincinnati, Ohio	Oct. 16, 1866	58,941
Brick-kiln	B. R. Hawley	Normal, Ill	Aug 22, 1871	118,364
Brick-kiln	B. R. Hawley	Normal, Ill	Apr. 2, 1872	125,292
Brick-kiln	B. R. Hawley	Normal, Ill	July 16, 1872	129,558
Brick-kiln	F. E. Hoffmann	Berlin, Prussia	June 6, 1871	115,734
Brick-kiln	G. Howland	Brunswick, N. Y	July 30, 1872	129,959
Brick-kiln	T. Lindsley	New York, N. Y	Oct. 24, 1871	120,202
Brick-kiln	T. Lindsley	New York, N. Y	Nov. 21, 1871	121,179
Brick-kiln	T. Lindsley	New York, N. Y	Jan. 9, 1872	122,528
Brick-kiln	W. Linton	Baltimore, Md	Jan. 20, 1852	8,678
Brick-kiln	A. W. M. Maass	Chicago, Ill	May 13, 1873	138,905
Brick-kiln	W. T. Mathews	Negaunee, Mich	Apr. 19, 1870	102,141
Brick-kiln	A. S. McBride	Saint Louis, Mo	July 9, 1867	66,604
Brick-kiln	J. M. McCarthy	Canal Dover, Ohio	Mar. 30, 1869	88,316
Brick-kiln	J. M. McCarthy	Canal Dover, Ohio	Mar. 28, 1871	113,185
Brick-kiln	J. McDonald	Saratoga Springs, N. Y	Nov. 27, 1866	60,029
Brick-kiln	J. McDonald	New York, N. Y	Oct. 27, 1868	83,394
Brick-kiln	L. R. Norman and W. F. Dieterichs, jr.	Saint Louis, Mo	Jan. 22, 1867	61,448
Brick-kiln	L. R. Norman and W. F. Dieterichs, jr.	Saint Louis, Mo	Jan. 22, 1867	61,449
Brick-kiln	J. Ogle	Baltimore, Md	May 9, 1848	5,551
Brick-kiln	C. D. Page	Grand Rapids, Mich	Mar. 29, 1864	42,106
Brick-kiln	C. A. Parker	New Orleans, La	July 12, 1870	105,241
Brick-kiln	N. F. Potter	Providence, R. I	May 24, 1870	103,500
Brick-kiln	F. Power	Saint Louis, Mo	July 7, 1868	79,595
Brick-kiln	S. D. Rader	Williamsport, Pa	June 18, 1867	65,943
Brick-kiln	S. D. Rader	Williamsport, Pa	Sept. 15, 1868	82,248
Brick-kiln	H. Read	Kensington, Pa	June 17, 1840	1,638
Brick-kiln	J. V. B. Remsen	New York, N. Y	Sept. 7, 1869	94,513
Brick-kiln	R. Robson	Buffalo, N. Y	Apr. 21, 1868	76,946
Brick-kiln	J. Russell	Elkton, Ky	Mar. 13, 1855	12,521
Brick-kiln	R. E. Schroeder	Rochester, N. Y	Sept. 28, 1852	9,285
Brick-kiln	W. A. Shepard	New York, N. Y	June 11, 1867	65,772
Brick-kiln	F. H. Smith	Baltimore, Md	Sept. 18, 1866	58,146
Brick-kiln	R. A. Smith	Newburyport, Mass	Nov. 19, 1872	133,127
Brick-kiln	J. S. Speights	Baltimore, Md	July 4, 1854	11,234
Brick-kiln	E. C. Sterling	Saint Louis, Mo	Nov. 8, 1870	109,150
Brick-kiln	F. Streyer	Clinton, Iowa	Aug. 6, 1872	130,254
Brick-kiln	H. Tugby	Woodville, England	July 29, 1873	141,404
Brick-kiln	B. Wallis	Baltimore, Md	June 6, 1871	115,793
Brick-kiln	P. J. Walsh and W. J. Taylor	Oil City, Pa	Mar. 4, 1873	136,568
Brick-kiln	H. D. Whittemore	New York, N. Y	Mar. 3, 1868	75,096
Brick-kiln, &c	E. V. Wingard	Williamsport, Pa	Dec. 21, 1869	98,134
Brick-kiln	A. J. Works	Fair Haven, Conn	July 20, 1869	92,923
Brick-kiln, Circular	F. E. Hoffmann	Berlin, Prussia	June 13, 1865	48,244
Brick-kiln, Covering or platting	S. R. Bakewell	Wellsburgh, Va	May 10, 1826	....
Brick-kiln, Perpetual	W. Gilbert	Detroit, Mich	Dec. 6, 1870	109,815
Brick knife	J. Garity	Brower, Mo	Aug. 22, 1871	118,230
Brick-lifter	K. J. Rugg	Cincinnati, Ohio	Apr. 18, 1871	113,799

Index of patents issued from the United States Patent Office from 1790 *to* 1873, *inclusive*—Continued.

Invention.	Inventor.	Residence.	Date.	No.
Brick, lime, &c., kiln	W. P. Hall	Piqua, Ohio	Nov. 14, 1871	120, 965
Brick-machine	N. Adams	Cornwall, N. Y	June 22, 1830	....
Brick-machine	N. Adams	Cornwall, N. Y	Oct. 14, 1834	....
Brick-machine	N. Adams	Newburgh, N. Y	Apr. 13, 1836	....
Brick-machine	H. Aiken	Pittsburgh, Pa	Dec. 22, 1868	85, 197
Brick-machine	F. Allen	Boston, Mass	June 22, 1858	20, 612
Brick-machine	F. Alsip	North McGregor, Iowa	Aug. 29, 1871	118, 504
Brick-machine	A. Anderson	Peekskill, N. Y	Sept. 12, 1871	118 777
Brick-machine	E. F. Andrews	Glasgow, Mo	Jan. 28, 1868	73, 863
Brick-machine	J. Armstrong	Saint Louis, Mo	Feb. 4, 1868	74, 030
Brick-machine	J. M. Austin	Georgetown, Mo	Dec. 13, 1870	109, 997
Brick-machine	C. B. Baker	Troy, N. Y	Sept. 25, 1866	58, 200
Brick-machine	J. H. Ballard and E. P. Bond	New Antioch, Ohio	Dec. 8, 1868	84, 724
Brick-machine	G. Bancker	New York, N. Y	June 15, 1858	20, 536
Brick-machine	G. Bancker	New York, N. Y	Jan. 25, 1859	22, 694
Brick-machine	H. C. Bankerd	Morgantown, W. Va	Apr. 2, 1872	125, 255
Brick-machine	J. M. Bannister	Phelps, N. Y	June 19, 1835	....
Brick-machine	T. Barker	Mexico, N. Y	Aug. 11, 1868	80, 850
Brick-machine	W. Barker and G. Martin	Schenectady, N. Y	Aug. 23, 1864	43, 893
Brick-machine	R. D. Bartlett	Baugor, Me	Aug. 8, 1854	11, 465
Brick-machine	W. C. Bartol	Huntingdon, Pa	Dec. 11, 1866	60, 323
Brick-machine	R. T. Barton	New Haven, Conn	Mar. 25, 1873	137, 122
Brick-machine	W. Beach and E. Lukens	Baltimore, Md	May 22, 1841	2, 101
Brick-machine	F. Beaujen	Parish of New Orleans, La.	Dec. 26, 1871	122, 214
Brick-machine	H. T. Beggs and J. Allen	Liberty and Lynchburgh, Va.	May 10, 1859	23, 892
Brick-machine	S. Belknap	Newburgh, N. Y	May 17, 1821	....
Brick-machine	S. W. Bennett, jr	Monroe, La	July 20, 1869	92, 778
Brick-machine	T. Bishop and D. Agnew	Vincennes, Ind	Jan. 4, 1870	98, 547
Brick-machine	E. S. Bituer	Lock Haven, Pa	Dec. 8, 1868	84, 727
Brick-machine	P. E. Bland	Saint Louis, Mo	Oct. 1, 1867	69, 308
Brick-machine	T. E. Bonner	Elkhart, Ind	Nov. 22, 1870	109, 376
Brick-machine	J. Booth	Mobile, Ala	Sept. 21, 1858	21, 545
Brick-machine	G. C. Bovey	Cincinnati, Ohio	Feb. 19, 1867	62, 249
Brick-machine	G. C. Bovey	Cincinnati, Ohio	Oct. 20, 1868	83, 244
Brick-machine	G. C. Bovey	Cincinnati, Ohio	Mar. 8, 1870	100, 590
Brick-machine	G. C. Bovey	Cincinnati, Ohio	Mar. 26, 1872	125, 012
Brick-machine	G. C. Bovey	Chillicothe, Ohio	May 13, 1873	138, 731
Brick-machine	H. Brad	Greencastle, Ind	Sept. 30, 1856	15, 798
Brick-machine	E. Braman and R. Peterson	Greencastle, Ind	July 8, 1856	15, 276
Brick-machine	J. Bretz, W. Sangster, and J. F. Bretz	Springfield, Ill	Dec. 22, 1868	85, 061
Brick-machine	A. H. Brown	Washington, D. C	Nov. 6, 1855	13, 747
Brick-machine	C. G. Brown	Caldwell N. Y	Oct. 11, 1841	2, 312
Brick-machine	L. Brown	Canandaigua, N. Y	Aug. 5, 1851	8, 269
Brick-machine	S. B. Brusstar	Kensington, Pa	Apr. 14, 1838	693
Brick-machine	M. and J. H. Bruck and F. A. Cushman.	Lebanon, N. H	May 27, 1836	14, 947
Brick-machine	A. H. and J. H. Buckwalter	Kimberton, Pa	June 17, 1862	35, 585
Brick-machine	H. C. Bull	Louisville, Ky	Feb. 20, 1866	52, 674
Brick-machine	H. Bulmer and C. Sheppard	Montreal, Canada	July 9, 1872	128, 787
Brick-machine	J. W. Burns	Henry, Ill	Apr. 23, 1867	64, 069
Brick-machine	J. D. Bush	Elyton, Ala	Oct. 21, 1873	143, 806
Brick-machine	R. and A. P. Campbell	Hillsdale, Mich	July 7, 1868	79, 633
Brick-machine	E. P. H. Capron	Springfield, Ohio	Aug. 15, 1865	49, 376
Brick-machine	E. P. H. Capron	Springfield, Ohio	May 8, 1866	54, 500
Brick-machine	E. P. H. Capron	Springfield, Ohio	July 31, 1866	56, 703
Brick-machine	E. P. H. Capron and J. F. Winchell.	Springfield, Ohio	July 31, 1866	56, 847
Brick-machine	E. P. H. Capron	Springfield, Ohio	Apr. 21, 1868	76, 888
Brick-machine	J. T. Carman	Springfield, Ill	Jan. 8, 1867	61, 048
Brick-machine	C. Carnell	Philadelphia, Pa	Feb. 2, 1858	19, 236
Brick-machine	F. L. Carnell	Philadelphia, Pa	July 16, 1872	129, 097
Brick-machine	D. Carpenter	Cortland, N. Y	July 26, 1839	1, 263
Brick-machine	J. Caswell	Syracuse, N. Y	Apr. 16, 1861	32, 046
Brick-machine	J. Caswell	Syracuse, N. Y	Apr. 16, 1861	32, 047
Brick-machine	C. Chambers, jr	Philadelphia, Pa	Oct. 6, 1863	40, 221
Brick-machine	C. Chambers, jr	Philadelphia, Pa	Nov. 1, 1870	108, 880
Brick-machine	C. Chambers, jr	Philadelphia, Pa	Dec. 6, 1870	109, 803
Brick-machine	J. L. Chapman	Philadelphia, Pa	June 14, 1870	104, 268
Brick-machine	C. Clark	Connellsville, Pa	Apr. 2, 1872	125, 272
Brick-machine	F. L. Clarke	Oakland, Ill	Apr. 5, 1870	101, 432
Brick-machine	P. Clark	Brooklyn, N. Y	Sept. 29, 1868	82, 492
Brick-machine	P. Clark	Brooklyn, N. Y	Feb. 9, 1869	86, 732
Brick-machine	W. Cole	Milan, Tenn	Aug. 19, 1873	141, 855
Brick-machine	J. B. Collen	Philadelphia, Pa	Nov. 17, 1857	18, 629
Brick-machine	A. E. Cooke	Philadelphia, Pa	July 6, 1869	92, 270
Brick-machine	J. Cooke	Muncy, Pa	July 6, 1869	92, 169
Brick-machine	J. Cooke	Muncy, Pa	Dec. 5, 1871	121, 450
Brick-machine	F. F. Cornell, jr	New York, N. Y	July 16, 1867	66, 800
Brick-machine	J. W. Crary	New Orleans, La	Aug. 17, 1858	21, 186
Brick-machine	J. W. Crary	Pensacola, Fla	Aug. 13, 1867	67, 728
Brick-machine	W. Crighton and H. Roesler	Fort Wayne, Ind	Apr. 7, 1868	76, 405
Brick-machine	L. B. Crittenden	Pittsburgh, Pa	July 9, 1867	66, 468
Brick-machine	J. C. Culver	Saint Louis, Mo	May 7, 1872	126, 618
Brick-machine	J. B. Curtis	Hillsdale, Mich	June 4, 1867	65, 351
Brick-machine	R. Cutler and G. C. Swallow	Saint Louis and Columbia, Mo.	Mar. 17, 1868	75, 668
Brick-machine	J. Dane, D. Healy, and G. Cummings.	Derby, Vt.	Aug. 5, 1851	8, 271
Brick-machine	J. C. Dean	Chicago, Ill	Dec. 15, 1868	84, 863
Brick-machine	P. K. Dederick	Albany, N. Y	Sept. 2, 1873	142, 375
Brick-machine	W. H. Degges	Washington, D. C	June 5, 1855	12, 998
Brick-machine	L. T. Delassize	New Orleans, La	Jan. 29, 1856	14, 155
Brick-machine	P. S. Devlan	Reading, Pa	Oct. 3, 1854	11, 745
Brick-machine	P. S. Devlan	Reading, Pa	Apr. 22, 1856	14, 713
Brick-machine	P. S. Devlan	Reading, Pa	Aug. 25, 1857	18, 040
Brick-machine	L. Dietrich	Sandwich, Ill	Apr. 7, 1868	76, 415

Index of patents issued from the United States Patent Office from 1790 *to* 1873, *inclusive*—Continued.

Invention.	Inventor.	Residence.	Date.	No.
Brick-machine	T. Dixcee	Woodfield Road, England	May 7, 1867	64, 504
Brick-machine	D. P. Dobbins, J. S. Richards, and J. Sangster.	Erie, Pa., and Buffalo, N. Y	Feb. 11, 1868	74, 207
Brick-machine	D. P. Dobbins and J. Sangster	Buffalo, N. Y	Oct. 4, 1870	108, 012
Brick-machine	J. A. Dorr, I. Hersey, and E. J. Oldfield.	New York, N. Y	Mar. 31, 1857	16, 907
Brick-machine	R. A. Douglas	Chicago, Ill	Sept. 4, 1866	57, 689
Brick-machine	H. Dueberg	New York, N. Y	Nov. 26, 1867	71, 466
Brick-machine	F. Durand	Paris, France	May 26, 1868	78, 268
Brick-machine	J. S. Elliott	East Boston, Mass	June 26, 1866	55, 841
Brick-machine	J. S. Elliott	Boston, Mass	Sept. 6, 1870	107, 017
Brick-machine	A. Elliot and J. O. Woodward	Taunton, Mass	Oct. 28, 1873	143, 972
Brick-machine	T. and W. A. Ellis	Philadelphia, Pa	Feb. 8, 1870	99, 658
Brick-machine	T. S. Emery	Philadelphia, Pa	May 10, 1870	102, 929
Brick-machine	J. A. Falconer and R. Graham	Jersey City, N. J	Sept. 22, 1868	82, 396
Brick-machine	E. Faron	New York, N. Y	Nov. 3, 1868	83, 769
Brick-machine	A. Ferguson, D. Ralston, and G. Hildreth.	Troy, N. Y	July 11, 1871	116, 942
Brick-machine	C. W. Ferguson	Jackson, Tenn	May 10, 1870	102, 794
Brick-machine	H. J. Ferguson	New York, N. Y	Aug. 28, 1866	57, 628
Brick-machine	G. B. Fisher	Chicago, Ill	Apr. 14, 1868	76, 617
Brick-machine	T. Forbes	Kansas City, Mo	Oct. 26, 1858	21, 876
Brick-machine	F. E. Frey	Bucyrus, Ohio	Aug. 11, 1868	80, 862
Brick-machine	W. C. Gaither	La Fayette, Ind	Nov. 26, 1872	133, 429
Brick-machine	R. M. Gano	Allegheny City, Pa	Jan. 21, 1868	73, 522
Brick-machine	R. M. Gano and R. S. Miller	Pittsburgh, Pa	July 28, 1868	80, 470
Brick-machine	A. Gans	Lincoln, Ill	July 16, 1867	66, 700
Brick-machine	B. M. Gard	Champaign County, Ohio	June 5, 1866	55, 274
Brick-machine	B. M. and E. R. Gard	Urbana, Ohio, and Chicago, Ill.	Feb. 22, 1870	100, 136
Brick-machine	B. M. and E. R. Gard	Urbana, Ohio, and Chicago, Ill.	Feb. 7, 1871	111, 629
Brick-machine	E. R. Gard	Chicago, Ill	Jan. 23, 1866	52, 156
Brick-machine	E. R. Gard	Chicago, Ill	Nov. 20, 1866	59, 831
Brick-machine	E. R. Gard	Chicago, Ill	May 28, 1867	65, 069
Brick-machine	I. M. Gattman	Cincinnati, Ohio	July 3, 1860	29, 036
Brick-machine	E. Geary	Harrisburgh, Pa	Dec. 8, 1868	84, 816
Brick-machine	G. W. B. Gedney	New York, N. Y	Sept. 18, 1855	13, 572
Brick-machine	J. George	Jackson, Mich	Mar. 14, 1865	46, 845
Brick-machine	J. George and H. Hague	Jackson, Mich	Apr. 3, 1866	53, 600
Brick-machine	G. W. Gilbert	Pittsburgh, Pa	Aug. 15, 1835	......
Brick-machine	T. M. Gisborne	Lymington, England	Feb. 20, 1866	52, 801
Brick-machine	S. Gissinger	Allegheny City, Pa	Oct. 21, 1862	36, 706
Brick-machine	S. Gissinger	Allegheny City, Pa	Dec. 10, 1867	72, 015
Brick-machine	D. W. Glendinning	Detroit, Mich	Oct. 14, 1873	143, 569
Brick-machine	D. Goldthorp and T. Hield	Hartford, Conn	Dec. 2, 1873	145, 169
Brick-machine	D. W. Gould	Independence, Iowa	Mar. 31, 1863	38, 041
Brick-machine	J. F. Gould	......	Mar. 1, 1806	......
Brick-machine	G. Graezzle	Hamilton, Ohio	Dec. 4, 1866	60, 175
Brick-machine	W. A. Graham	Carlisle, Pa	Mar. 17, 1868	75, 542
Brick-machine	J. Grant	Providence, R. I	Jan. 23, 1866	52, 245
Brick-machine	H. H. Gray	Haverstraw, N. Y	Dec. 1, 1868	84, 624
Brick-machine	E. R. Green and H. D. Phillips, jr.	Trenton, N. J	Feb. 4, 1868	74, 079
Brick-machine	I. Gregg	Pittsburgh, Pa	Aug. 5, 1851	8, 284
Brick-machine	I. Gregg	Philadelphia, Pa	Sept. 19, 1865	50, 070
Brick-machine	I. Gregg	Philadelphia, Pa	Oct. 30, 1866	59, 212
Brick-machine	I. Gregg and C. Green	Philadelphia, Pa	June 12, 1866	55, 583
Brick-machine	I. Gregg and H. Moser	Philadelphia and Pittsburgh, Pa.	May 19, 1863	38, 629
Brick-machine	M. Gregg	Philadelphia, Pa	June 17, 1851	8, 158
Brick-machine	J. B. Gridley	Albany, N. Y	Oct. 23, 1866	59, 006
Brick-machine	F. L. Hall	Oneida, N. Y	July 4, 1871	116, 587
Brick-machine	F. L. Hall	Oneida, N. Y	Apr. 30, 1872	126, 291
Brick-machine	E. Hallett	Hillsdale, Mich	Aug. 14, 1866	57, 128
Brick-machine	E. Hallett	Hillsdale, Mich	Apr. 4, 1871	113, 514
Brick-machine	G. Halloway	Montgomery County, Pa	Apr. 21, 1836	......
Brick-machine	J. A. Hamer	Reading, Pa	July 8, 1856	15, 293
Brick-machine	J. A. Hamer	Reading, Pa	Sept. 13, 1859	25, 467
Brick-machine	J. S. Hanna	Mercer, Pa	Nov. 23, 1829	......
Brick-machine	G. W. Harlam	Cincinnati, Ohio	Apr. 19, 1870	102, 115
Brick-machine	I. Harman	Tamaqua, Pa	Aug. 12, 1856	15, 546
Brick-machine	G. V. Harper	Franklinville, N. Y	Oct. 23, 1837	439
Brick-machine	P. Hayden	Pittsburgh, Pa	Aug. 6, 1867	67, 541
Brick-machine	P. Hayden	Pittsburgh, Pa	Sept. 8, 1868	81, 901
Brick-machine	B. S. Heath and T. W. Gardner	La Cygne, Kans., and Huntington, Ind.	July 16, 1872	129, 225
Brick machine	C. V. Hemenway	New London, Ohio	Sept. 21, 1869	95, 108
Brick machine	C. V. Hemenway	New London, Ohio	Apr. 5, 1870	101, 616
Brick-machine	D. Hess	Des Moines, Iowa	July 30, 1872	130, 046
Brick-machine	D. Hess	Blandville, Ky	Sept. 15, 1868	82, 116
Brick-machine	D. Hess	Des Moines, Iowa	Dec. 12, 1871	121, 871
Brick machine	J. A. Hill	Greencastle, Ind	Sept. 30, 1856	15, 808
Brick-machine	J. S. Hobbs and L. R. Elder	West Falmouth, Me	Jan. 4, 1870	98, 495
Brick-machine	J. Hockman	Mexico, Ind	Jan. 13, 1857	16, 385
Brick-machine	J. Hodge	Fair Play, S. C	Mar. 6, 1840	6, 509
Brick-machine	J. Hodges	Fair Play, S. C	June 3, 1837	220
Brick-machine	W. A. Horrall	Washington, Ind	Jan. 31, 1865	46, 188
Brick-machine	J. Hotchkiss	Yellow Springs, Ohio	July 17, 1860	29, 171
Brick-machine	J. Hotchkiss	Springfield, Ohio	Mar. 13, 1866	53, 223
Brick-machine	J. Hotchkiss and E. Buss	Springfield, Ohio	Nov. 21, 1865	51, 050
Brick-machine	J. Hotchkiss and E. Buss	Springfield, Ohio	Apr. 17, 1866	53, 980
Brick-machine	J. Hotchkiss and E. Buss	Springfield, Ohio	June 4, 1867	65, 383
Brick-machine	J. Hotchkiss and W. H. Schofield.	Yellow Springs, Ohio	May 5, 1857	17, 248
Brick-machine	J. Hotchkiss and P. W. Woliston.	Springfield, Ohio	Apr. 29, 1873	138, 251
Brick-machine	G. O. Houck and H. Gore	Springfield, Ohio	Feb. 16, 1858	19, 366

Index of patents issued from the United States Patent Office from 1790 *to* 1873, *inclusive*—Continued.

Invention.	Inventor.	Residence.	Date.	No.
Brick-machine	G. O. Houck and C. E. Sawyer	Springfield, Ohio	June 17, 1873	139, 894
Brick-machine	A. V. Hough	Greencastle, Ind	June 26, 1855	13, 129
Brick-machine	A. V. Hough and R. W. Jones	Greencastle, Ind	Mar. 17, 1857	16, 839
Brick-machine	G. H. Houghton	Marlin, Tex	July 16, 1872	129, 563
Brick-machine	W. H. Hovey	Springfield, Mass	Feb. 27, 1866	52, 852
Brick-machine	W. H. Hovey	Springfield, Mass	Aug. 6, 1867	67, 548
Brick-machine	W. H. Hovey	Springfield, Mass	Aug. 25, 1868	81, 506
Brick-machine	W. H. Hovey	Springfield, Mass	July 16, 1872	129, 411
Brick-machine	E. C. Hubbard	Green Bay, Wis	Jan. 24, 1871	111, 210
Brick-machine	E. R. Hubbard	New York, N. Y	Jan. 7, 1873	134, 672
Brick-machine	H. Hughes	Pekin, Ill	May 6, 1873	138, 651
Brick-machine	D. J. Hunter	Exeter, N. H	Nov. 16, 1869	96, 920
Brick-machine	D. J. Hunter	Somerville, Mass	Apr. 25, 1871	114, 011
Brick-machine	D. J. Hunter	Boston, Mass	Aug. 12, 1873	141, 646
Brick-machine	W. G. Hyndman	Cincinnati, Ohio	Aug. 20, 1867	67, 879
Brick-machine	G. W. Ives	North Haven, Conn	Sept. 17, 1867	68, 882
Brick-machine	D. J. Irwin	Noble, Ill	Mar. 4, 1873	136, 520
Brick-machine	D. J. Irwin and H. S. Langdon	Noble, Ill	Aug. 5, 1873	141, 560
Brick-machine	F. Jacobie	Albany, N. Y	July 12, 1864	43, 505
Brick-machine	J. W. Jayne	Sandusky, Ohio	May 5, 1857	17, 220
Brick-machine	J. J. Johnston	Allegheny City, Pa	Feb. 19, 1867	62, 207
Brick-machine	H. Jones	Fort Madison, Iowa	Feb. 6, 1872	123, 400
Brick-machine	J. Jones	Baltimore, Md	Sept. 11, 1866	57, 919
Brick-machine	R. W. Jones	Greencastle, Ind	Jan. 15, 1856	14, 100
Brick-machine	W. A. Jordan	Thibodeaux, La	Sept. 23, 1856	15, 766
Brick-machine	J. Keller	Paducah, Ky	May 25, 1869	90, 555
Brick-machine	J. Keller	Paducah, Ky	Aug. 16, 1870	106, 490
Brick-machine	P. H. Kells	Adrian, Mich	Mar. 19, 1867	63, 057
Brick-machine	P. H. Kells	Adrian, Mich	July 2, 1867	66, 355
Brick-machine	P. H. Kells	Adrian, Mich	Aug. 25, 1868	81, 511
Brick-machine	P. H. Kells	Adrian, Mich	Mar. 12, 1872	124, 590
Brick-machine	E. Kingsland	New York, N. Y	May 13, 1856	14, 873
Brick-machine	L. Kirk	Reading, Pa	Jan. 31, 1860	26, 997
Brick-machine	L. Kirk	Reading, Pa	Mar. 4, 1862	34, 580
Brick-machine	J. Klinkhardt	Saint Louis, Mo	June 29, 1869	92, 059
Brick-machine	J. Klinkhardt and W. Kiburz	Saint Louis, Mo	Nov. 24, 1868	84, 284
Brick-machine	J. L. Kucker	Philadelphia, Pa	May 23, 1871	115, 218
Brick-machine	J. Kutts	Philadelphia, Pa	Oct. 26, 1858	21, 888
Brick-machine	J. A. Lafler	Albion, N. Y	Jan. 6, 1863	37, 348
Brick-machine	J. A. Lafler	Albion, N. Y	Aug. 11, 1868	80, 976
Brick-machine	A. La Tourette and S. H. Smith	Venice and Waterloo, N. Y	Oct. 8, 1867	69, 683
Brick-machine	J. G. Lehr and H. D. Thorp	Harlan, Ind	Feb. 2, 1869	86, 423
Brick-machine	W. O. Leslie	Philadelphia, Pa	Aug. 6, 1867	67, 439
Brick-machine	W. O. Leslie	Philadelphia, Pa	May 12, 1868	77, 894
Brick-machine	W. O. Leslie	Philadelphia, Pa	June 30, 1868	79, 362
Brick-machine	W. O. Leslie	Philadelphia, Pa	Feb. 2, 1869	86, 557
Brick-machine	S. Lewis	Louisiana	Feb. 11, 1824	....
Brick-machine	D. Locke	Lexington, Mo	Apr. 19, 1859	23, 691
Brick-machine	R. Lockwood and C. C. Schmitt	New York, N. Y	Mar. 2, 1869	87, 416
Brick-machine	D. Lombard	Boston, Mass	Feb. 23, 1858	19, 470
Brick-machine	R. Long	Columbus, Ohio	Aug. 19, 1851	8, 301
Brick-machine	S. W. Long	Louisville, Ky	Nov. 5, 1867	70, 585
Brick-machine	W. H. Lotz and F. Baumann	Chicago, Ill	July 23, 1867	66, 979
Brick-machine	Z. Ludington	Uniontown, Pa	July 9, 1872	128, 738
Brick-machine	W. H. and H P. L. Machen, jr	Toledo, Ohio	Aug. 1, 1871	117, 551
Brick-machine	J. F. Mallinckrodt	Saint Louis, Mo	July 13, 1869	92, 625
Brick-machine	H. Manthé	New York, N. Y	June 14, 1870	104, 330
Brick-machine	J. Marshall	Fond du Lac, Wis	May 14, 1867	64, 778
Brick-machine	G. Martin	Milwaukee, Wis	July 16, 1867	66, 723
Brick-machine	H. Martin	Springfield, Mass	June 27, 1865	48, 419
Brick-machine	H. Martin	Keyport, N. J	Oct. 20, 1868	83, 297
Brick-machine	H. Martin	Cincinnati, Ohio	Sept. 17, 1872	131, 363
Brick-machine	H. Martin	Chicopee, Mass	May 13, 1873	138, 754
Brick-machine	I. Martin	Newark, N. J	Apr. 7, 1868	76, 337
Brick-machine	J. Martin	Jersey City, N. J	Oct. 20, 1868	83, 191
Brick-machine	S. Martin	Knobnoster, Mo	Apr. 1, 1873	137, 460
Brick-machine	P. Marvin	Warsaw, Ind	Mar. 12, 1867	62, 764
Brick-machine	B. J. McAfee	Delphi, Ind	May 26, 1868	78, 221
Brick-machine	G. W. McCann	Springfield, Ohio	Feb. 2, 1869	86, 567
Brick-machine	C. C. and J. McDermid	Cambria Mills, Mich	July 9, 1867	66, 605
Brick-machine	J. McDonald	New York, N. Y	Apr. 1, 1812	....
Brick-machine	J. McDonald	New York, N. Y	Aug. 6, 1867	67, 561
Brick-machine	J. C. McKenzie	Adrian, Mich	Mar. 10, 1868	75, 287
Brick-machine	J. N. McLean and J. Bennor	Philadelphia, Pa	May 14, 1872	126, 728
Brick-machine	J. N. McLean and J. Bennor	Philadelphia, Pa	Aug. 26, 1873	142, 114
Brick-machine	J. McManus	Pittsburgh, Pa	Feb. 9, 1869	86, 853
Brick-machine	J. McMurtry	Lexington, Ky	Aug. 8, 1854	11, 487
Brick-machine	A. R. McNair	New York, N. Y	May 15, 1866	54, 752
Brick-machine	J. Melling	Bolton, England	Oct. 22, 1861	33, 535
Brick-machine	W. Mendham and C. Chambers, jr.	Philadelphia, Pa	Nov. 8, 1870	109, 034
Brick-machine	J. Menefee	Saint Landry Parish, La	Aug. 7, 1823	....
Brick-machine	G. Metcalf	Leland, Ill	Jan. 28, 1868	73, 741
Brick-machine	J. W. Metz	Stout's Post-Office, Ohio	Jan. 28, 1873	135, 353
Brick-machine	E. Miller	....	July 17, 1802	....
Brick-machine	J. C. Miller	Bushnell, Ill	Sept. 8, 1868	81, 928
Brick-machine	J. Mills	Des Moines, Iowa	June 18, 1867	65, 931
Brick-machine	A. F. Mitchell	Valparaiso, Ind	July 18, 1871	117, 097
Brick-machine	J. M. Mitchell	Dunlap, Iowa	Dec. 9, 1873	145, 358
Brick-machine	J. Moffat	Buffalo, N. Y	Mar. 8, 1836	....
Brick-machine	L. Montgomery	Tunnel, Md	July 8, 1843	3, 167
Brick-machine	A. Morand	Leeds, England	June 27, 1871	116, 341
Brick-machine	A. Morand	Brooklyn, N. Y	Sept. 3, 1872	131, 021
Brick-machine	A. Morgan	Cedar Bayou, Tex	May 4, 1869	89, 680
Brick-machine	I. Morley	Allegheny City, Pa	Aug. 15, 1865	49, 420
Brick-machine	I. Morley	Pittsburgh, Pa	May 29, 1866	55, 146
Brick-machine	I. Morley	Pittsburgh, Pa	Feb. 19, 1867	62, 149
Brick-machine	J. M. Moyer	Pittsburgh, Pa	Sept. 17, 1867	68, 894

Index of patents issued from the United States Patent Office from 1790 *to* 1873, *inclusive*—Continued.

Invention.	Inventor.	Residence.	Date.	No.
Brick-machine	C. H. Murray	Southwark, England	June 24, 1873	140, 296
Brick-machine	D. Murtha	Philadelphia, Pa	May 10, 1864	42, 680
Brick-machine	C. Murtha	Philadelphia, Pa	May 29, 1866	55, 148
Brick-machine	B. F. Nave	Roanoke, Ind	Jan. 20, 1857	16, 449
Brick-machine	J. N. Newell	Des Moines, Iowa	June 30, 1863	39, 061
Brick-machine	A. N. Newton	Richmond, Ind	Dec. 4, 1866	68, 231
Brick-machine	C. Nolan	Niles, Mich	Apr. 7, 1868	76, 504
Brick-machine	J. North	New York, N. Y	Dec. 17, 1867	72, 220
Brick-machine	A. Nulson, E. Haneisen, and A. Wagner.	Cincinnati, Ohio	Jan. 15, 1867	61, 238
Brick-machine	A. Nulsen, E. Haneisen, and A. Wagner.	Cincinnati, Ohio	Aug. 18, 1868	81, 284
Brick-machine	M. Nye and A. J. Kniseley	Chicago, Ill	Feb. 25, 1868	74, 765
Brick-machine	W. Olds	Albany, Ill	July 13, 1869	92, 636
Brick-machine	W. F. O'Reilly	Starkville, Miss	Aug. 6, 1872	130, 236
Brick-machine	J. Ormerod	Peekskill, N. Y	Jan. 9, 1872	122, 642
Brick-machine	J. W. Osgood	Columbus, Ohio	Apr. 7, 1868	76, 341
Brick-machine	D. Packard	Saint Joseph, Mo	Jan. 19, 1869	86, 032
Brick-machine	W. H. Paige	Springfield, Mass	Dec. 6, 1864	45, 377
Brick-machine	S. J. Parker	Ithaca, N. Y	Jan. 14, 1868	73, 258
Brick-machine	S. Parks	San Francisco, Cal	May 26, 1857	17, 390
Brick-machine	J. Parsons	Cleveland, Ohio	Oct. 30, 1860	30, 541
Brick-machine	L. Patterson	Parker City, Pa	Dec. 9, 1873	145, 444
Brick-machine	Z. M. Paul	Alexandria, La	Oct. 3, 1854	11, 760
Brick-machine	J. W. Pease	Belmont, N. Y	Nov. 27, 1866	60, 050
Brick-machine	J. W. Pease	Belmont, N. Y	Dec. 15, 1868	84, 901
Brick-machine	J. W. Penfield	Willoughby, Ohio	Jan. 16, 1872	122, 851
Brick-machine	H. D. Phillips, jr., and C. H. Williams.	Trenton, N. J., and Matteawan, N. Y.	Mar. 26, 1872	126, 075
Brick-machine	Z. Phillips	Ossco, Mich	Oct. 18, 1870	108, 511
Brick-machine	J. F. M. Pollock	Manchester, England	Aug. 31, 1869	94, 337
Brick-machine	J. F. M. Pollock	Leeds, Great Britain	June 27, 1871	116, 484
Brick-machine	H. B. Ramsay	Indianapolis, Ind	Aug. 26, 1856	15, 618
Brick-machine	H. B. Ramsey	Rockville, Ind	Nov. 19, 1872	133, 175
Brick-machine	J. L. Ransom	Charleston, S. C	Mar. 30, 1858	19, 792
Brick-machine	L. E. Ransom	Trenton, Mich	Feb. 4, 1868	74, 000
Brick-machine	J. Reeder	Cincinnati, Ohio	Feb. 15, 1838	601
Brick-machine	D. B. Rich and C. D. Hubbard	Cambridge, Mass	Mar. 19, 1872	124, 761
Brick-machine	J. J. Riddle	Covington, Ky	July 22, 1851	8, 231
Brick-machine	S. Rigby, 3d	Newcastle, Pa	June 14, 1870	104, 354
Brick-machine	S. C. Ripley	New York, N. Y	Mar. 7, 1854	10, 612
Brick-machine	D. Rising	Atchester, Vt	Mar. 21, 1827	....
Brick-machine	D. Rising	Colchester, N. Y	Jan. 29, 1828	....
Brick-machine	T. H. Rodgers	Chicago, Ill	Apr. 10, 1866	53, 879
Brick-machine	A. Sabbaton	Reading, Pa	May 16, 1848	5, 586
Brick-machine	S. C. Salisbury	Milwaukee, Wis	July 27, 1858	21, 025
Brick-machine	A. H. Sampson	New Orleans, La	June 14, 1853	9, 785
Brick-machine	J. Samuels	Allentown, Pa	Apr. 20, 1852	8, 892
Brick-machine	H. Sands and G. Cummings	Cambridge, Mass., and West Derby, Vt.	Sept. 6, 1853	10, 005
Brick-machine	J. Sangster	Buffalo, N. Y	Oct. 23, 1866	59, 080
Brick-machine	J. Sangster	Buffalo, N. Y	Mar. 12, 1867	62, 781
Brick-machine	J. Sangster, D. P. Dobbins, and J. S. Richards.	Buffalo, N. Y., and Erie, Pa.	Jan. 7, 1868	73, 201
Brick-machine	W. Sangster	Joliet, Ill	Dec. 17, 1867	72, 421
Brick-machine	J. F. Schuffenecker	Keokuk, Iowa	Mar. 22, 1859	23, 315
Brick-machine	J. F. Schuffenecker	Saint Louis, Mo	Feb. 7, 1865	46, 273
Brick-machine	T. E. Seay	Columbia, Va	Apr. 11, 1854	10, 759
Brick-machine	D. W. Seeley and F. Jacobie	Albany, N. Y	May 8, 1866	54, 610
Brick-machine	H. C. Sergeant	Columbus, Ohio	June 11, 1867	65, 612
Brick-machine	H. C. Sergeant	Columbus, Ohio	June 11, 1867	65, 613
Brick-machine	H. C. Sergeant	Columbus, Ohio	Sept. 17, 1867	68, 907
Brick-machine	W. F. Shanks	Louisville, Ky	Dec. 17, 1867	72, 330
Brick-machine	W. A. Shepard	New York, N. Y	Jan. 8, 1867	61, 108
Brick-machine	S. Shreffler	Joliet, Ill	Aug. 22, 1865	49, 562
Brick-machine	S. Shreffler	Joliet, Ill	Oct. 8, 1867	69, 592
Brick-machine	J. Simpson	Decatur, Ga	Apr. 25, 1846	4, 481
Brick-machine	J. Simpson	Saint Louis, Mo	Jan. 28, 1868	73, 843
Brick-machine	D. Smith	Newburyport, Mass	June 9, 1868	78, 765
Brick-machine	F. H. Smith	Baltimore, Md	Oct. 3, 1854	11, 753
Brick-machine	F. H. Smith	Baltimore, Md	July 21, 1868	80, 231
Brick-machine	J. H. Smith and C. H. Florence	Richview, Ill	Apr. 21, 1868	77, 118
Brick-machine	J. N. Smith	Jersey City, N. J	Mar. 12, 1867	62, 782
Brick-machine	J. T. Smith	Springfield, Ill	Feb. 14, 1865	46, 399
Brick-machine	P. J. Smith	Philadelphia, Pa	Apr. 28, 1868	77, 224
Brick-machine	P. J. Smith	Philadelphia, Pa	Nov. 16, 1869	96, 985
Brick-machine	R. A. Smith	Newburyport, Mass	July 9, 1872	128, 822
Brick-machine	G. L. Smull	Meadville, Pa	June 15, 1858	20, 594
Brick-machine	T. Smurfit	Davisville, Mich	Dec. 21, 1869	98, 115
Brick-machine	S. L. Speissegger	Savannah, Ga	Mar. 2, 1852	8, 780
Brick-machine	A. J. Sprague	Toledo, Ohio	July 2, 1867	66, 408
Brick-machine	E. Sprague	Allegheny City, Pa	Dec. 22, 1868	85, 142
Brick-machine	A. Stewart	Baltimore, Md	Apr. 8, 1819	....
Brick-machine	H. W. Stillman	Port Washington, Wis	Aug. 2, 1859	24, 962
Brick-machine	T. Stone	Plainfield, Ind	Dec. 3, 1867	71, 813
Brick-machine	H. H. Strawbridge and D. Tyson.	New Orleans and Covington, La.	Nov. 9, 1852	9, 394
Brick-machine	S. Strong	Washington, D. C	May 26, 1863	38, 716
Brick-machine	R. Stuckwisch	Terre Haute, Ind	Nov. 16, 1869	96, 995
Brick-machine	P. L. Sword	Adrian, Mich	Mar. 26, 1867	63, 333
Brick-machine	P. L. Sword and G. S. Tiffany	Adrian, Mich	June 14, 1864	43, 162
Brick-machine	L. Sylvester	Philadelphia, Pa	Sept. 3, 1867	68, 396
Brick-machine	J. Taggart	Roxbury, Mass	Mar. 17, 1868	75, 596
Brick-machine	S. Talbott	Richmond, Va	Apr. 8, 1840	1, 539
Brick-machine	S. H. Taylor	Jacksonville, Ill	Nov. 29, 1870	109, 777
Brick-machine	J. S. Thomas	Saint Louis, Mo	July 8, 1873	140, 742
Brick-machine	H. D. Thorp and J. G. Lehr	Harlan, Ind	Feb. 1, 1870	99, 371
Brick-machine	S. Till	Sandusky, Ohio	Aug. 28, 1855	13, 502

Index of patents issued from the United States Patent Office from 1790 *to* 1873, *inclusive*—Continued.

Invention.	Inventor.	Residence.	Date.	No.
Brick-machine	J. V. Tompkins	Canandaigua, Mich	May 16, 1871	114, 884
Brick-machine	J. Treadway	Haverstraw, N. Y	Dec. 12, 1871	121, 855
Brick-machine	S. Ustick	Philadelphia, Pa	Apr. 18, 1854	10, 777
Brick-machine	S. Ustick	Philadelphia, Pa	July 7, 1857	17, 759
Brick-machine	S. Ustick	Philadelphia, Pa	Sept. 8, 1857	18, 166
Brick-machine	S. Ustick	Philadelphia, Pa	Apr. 27, 1859	20, 107
Brick-machine	J. Van Riswick	Washington, D. C	Mar. 8, 1859	23, 204
Brick-machine	L. M. Van Sickle	Woodbridge, N. J	May 26, 1868	78, 343
Brick-machine	B. Van Vranken	Schenectady, N. Y	Feb. 25, 1868	74, 956
Brick-machine	R. A. Ver Valen	Haverstraw, N. Y	June 29, 1852	9, 082
Brick-machine	J. A. Victor	Montgomery County, Ky	Sept. 4, 1855	13, 533
Brick machine	I. Z. A. Wagner	Philadelphia, Pa	Apr. 27, 1859	20, 109
Brick-machine	R. L. Walker	Globe Village, Mass	Aug. 21, 1866	57, 415
Brick-machine	W. S. Wallace	Americus, Ga	Aug. 28, 1860	29, 834
Brick-machine	P. and J. Walbrath	Chittenango, N. Y	Oct. 13, 1868	83, 010
Brick-machine	T. and J. Walsh and D. Evans	Brownsville, Pa	May 14, 1867	64, 726
Brick-machine	J. Ward	Boston, Mass	Oct. 14, 1862	36, 690
Brick-machine	J. Ward	Boston, Mass	Jan. 24, 1865	46, 055
Brick-machine	G. I. Washburn	Worcester, Mass	Sept. 15, 1857	18, 226
Brick-machine	G. I. Washburn and E. H. Bellows.	Worcester, Mass	Oct. 7, 1856	15, 863
Brick-machine	G. I. Washburn and E. H. Bellows.	Worcester, Mass	Apr. 21, 1857	17, 131
Brick-machine	C. Waterman	Bath, Me	July 2, 1836	....
Brick-machine	J. Watson	Buffalo, N. Y	June 5, 1866	55, 432
Brick-machine	J. Watson	Buffalo, N. Y	Mar. 12, 1867	62, 790
Brick-machine	W. S. Watson	Madison, Ind	June 7, 1859	24, 343
Brick-machine	W. S. Watson	Madison, Ind	Apr. 2, 1861	31, 918
Brick-machine	J. A. Welch	Xenia, Ohio	July 23, 1867	67, 007
Brick-machine	D. Wellington	Boston, Mass	Aug. 18, 1868	81, 813
Brick machine	P. V. Westfall	Kalamazoo, Mich	Dec. 10, 1867	72, 137
Brick-machine	F. Whitcomb	Chicago, Ill	May 31, 1870	103, 805
Brick-machine	H. White	Cleveland, Ohio	Sept. 7, 1858	21, 458
Brick-machine	W. G. White	Bedford, Ohio	Aug. 8, 1871	117, 842
Brick-machine	J. Whiteford	Pond City, Kans	Oct. 19, 1869	95, 962
Brick-machine	R. Wildman	Danbury, Conn	Apr. 12, 1859	23, 634
Brick-machine	J. Willerd	Baltimore, Md	Jan. 29, 1840	1, 484
Brick-machine	C. H. Williams	Rhinebeck, N. Y	Apr. 5, 1870	101, 690
Brick-machine	J. R. Williams	Taunton, Mass	Nov. 8, 1870	109, 089
Brick-machine	M. D. Williams	Dakota, Iowa	Nov. 1, 1870	108, 864
Brick-machine	R. Wilson	Houston, Tex	May 30, 1848	5, 6[illegible]5
Brick-machine	C. A. Winn	Lockhaven, Pa	June 2, 1868	78, 632
Brick-machine	R. Wolff	New York, N. Y	Jan. 15, 1867	61, 298
Brick-machine	R. Wolff	New York, N. Y	May 10, 1870	102, 9[illegible]3
Brick-machine	P. N. Woliston	Springfield, Ohio	June 5, 1866	55, 400
Brick-machine	P. N. Woliston	Springfield, Ohio	Aug. 11, 1868	80, 890
Brick-machine	J. S. Wood	Hartford, Conn	May 26, 1868	78, 348
Brick-machine	W. Wood	Hartford, Conn	Feb. 3, 1857	16, 561
Brick-machine	W. Wood	Hartford, Conn	Mar. 22, 1859	23, 331
Brick-machine	W. Wood	Hartford, Conn	Aug. 14, 1860	29, 645
Brick-machine	A. Woodworth, 3d, and S. Mower.	Boston, Mass	Aug. 31, 1852	9, 238
Brick-machine	C. D. Wrightington	Boston, Mass	Apr. 5, 1870	101, 696
Brick-machine	C. D. Wrightington and B. P. Rider.	Fairhaven and Chelsea, Mass.	June 2, 1868	78, 634
Brick machine, Concrete	B. Bisbee	Ames, Iowa	Mar. 2, 1869	87, 326
Brick machine, Concrete	W. Emmons	Sandwich, Ill	Apr. 14, 1868	76, 726
Brick machine, Concrete	M. S. Harsha	Batavia, Ill	Nov. 19, 1867	70, 999
Brick machine, Concrete	F. Hawkins	Chicago, Ill	May 26, 1868	78, 284
Brick machine, Concrete	I. Pardee	Vineland, N. J	Feb. 25, 1868	74, 769
Brick machine, Concrete	J. Stewart and D. Windsor	Sandwich, Ill	May 21, 1867	65, 024
Brick-machine, Cut-off for	C. Chambers, jr	Philadelphia, Pa	Nov. 30, 1869	97, 356
Brick-machine duster	C. Chambers, jr	Philadelphia, Pa	Jan. 24, 1865	45, 974
Brick, Machine for cleaning	J. Lyon	Norfolk, Va	Apr. 20, 1869	89, 263
Brick, Machine for dressing	J. McNamara	Buffalo, N. Y	May 26, 1868	78, 388
Brick, Machine for mixing clay, mortar, &c., for making.	A. Teel	Waterloo, N. Y	Mar. 12, 1839	1, 098
Brick, Machine for mixing earth for	B. K. Hill	Richmond County, Ga	Feb. 17, 1827	....
Brick, Machine for molding and drying	C. Vassar	Poughkeepsie, N. Y	Nov. 1, 1830	....
Brick, Machine for preparing clay for making	H. Whipple	Port Richmond, N. Y	Mar. 25, 1851	8, 001
Brick, Machine for preparing mortar for the manufacture of.	O. W. Seely	Sodus, N. Y	Mar. 5, 1839	1, 095
Brick, Machine for pressing and delivering	U. Ward	Washington, D. C	Dec. 15, 1835	....
Brick, Machine for striking unburnt	M. P. Crapo	Humboldt County, Cal	July 15, 1856	15, 329
Brick, Machine for tempering clay for	R. Stillman and J. Taylor	Kensington and Spring Garden, Pa.	Apr. 21, 1842	2, 571
Brick, Machine for turning or edging	C. O. Farrington	Brewer, Me	Feb. 1, 1859	22, 790
Brick-machine, Off-bearing apparatus for	C. Chambers, jr	Philadelphia, Pa	June 28, 1870	104, 705
Brick-machine, Preparing clay for	C. M. Ferris and N. Swan	New Milford, Conn., and Patterson, N. Y.	Apr. 16, 1850	7, 286
Brick machine, Press	W. C. Grimes	York, Pa	Dec. 2, 1834	....
Brick-machine, Rotary	G. Crangle	Philadelphia, Pa	June 3, 1856	15, 005
Brick-machine, Rotary	G. Crangle	Philadelphia, Pa	Jan. 27, 1857	16, 468
Brick-machine, Rotary	G. Crangle	Philadelphia, Pa	May 5, 1857	17, 203
Brick-machine, Rotary	M. C. Motch	Covington, Ky	Dec. 31, 1867	72, 883
Brick-machine, Soak-pit of	W. H. Degges	Washington, D. C	June 5, 1855	12, 997
Brick-machine, Die or mouth for	C. H. Murray	Southwark, England	June 24, 1873	140, 297
Brick, Machinery for the manufacture of	B. D. Berry	Edwardsville, Ill	Feb. 9, 1869	86, 633
Brick, Making	A. Frost	Cazenovia, N. Y	Sept. 21, 1808	....
Brick, Making	I. H. Garretson	Richland, Iowa	July 31, 1866	56, 742
Brick, Making	A. Kinsley	....	Feb. 1, 1793	....
Brick, Making	F. Lambert	Los Angeles, Cal	Jan. 17, 1871	111, 066
Brick making	S. Lowery	Philadelphia, Pa	Apr. 18, 1846	4, 457
Brick, Making	W. Mitchell	Henrico, Va	June 24, 1816	....
Brick-making	T. C. Prosser	Bay City, Mich	July 24, 1866	56, 608
Brick, Making	D. Ridgeway	....	Mar. 7, 1792	....
Brick-making	J. C. Salomon, jr	Washington, D. C	Apr. 25, 1854	10, 831
Brick-making and clay-grinding machine	W. Mitchell	Richmond, Va	Mar. 26, 1817	....

Index of patents issued from the United States Patent Office from 1790 *to* 1873, *inclusive*—Continued.

Invention.	Inventor.	Residence.	Date.	No.
Brick-making, Machine for preparing clay for	W. N. Graves	Saint Louis, Mo	June 29, 1869	92, 040
Brick, Making fire	E. Jenks	Canaan, Conn	Apr. 17, 1807	....
Brick, Making fire-proof	T. Caldwell	Philadelphia, Pa	July 21, 1823	....
Brick, Manner of forming and pressing	J. Miller	Olean, N. Y	Mar. 2, 1869	87, 354
Brick manufacture	S. D. Arnold	Pittsfield, Mass	Aug. 24, 1869	93, 944
Brick manufacture	S. H. Bowman	Halfmoon Bay, Cal	Apr. 28, 1868	77, 163
Brick manufacture	G. S. Hewitt	Boston, Mass	Mar. 15, 1870	100, 892
Brick manufacture	T. James	Canton, Md	June 1, 1858	20, 433
Brick manufacture	F. Jones	Boston, Mass	June 19, 1866	55, 667
Brick manufacture	T. C. Kier	Pittsburgh, Pa	June 4. 1872	127, 419
Brick manufacture	N. Parmeter	Gardner, Mass	May 17, 1859	24, 050
Brick manufacture	L. E. Ransom	Havana, Ohio	Mar. 20, 1855	12, 5[illegible]8
Brick manufacture	S. B. Spaulding	Brandon, Vt	July 2, 1867	66, 407
Brick, Manufacture of fire	B. Kreischer	New York, N. Y	May 2, 1871	114, 449
Brick, Manufacture of fire	G. Nimmo	Jersey City, N. J.	Apr. 30, 1867	64, 352
Brick, Manufacture of fire	J. Ostrander and J. S. Heartt	Troy, N. Y	Oct. 12, 1858	21, 774
Brick, Manufacture of fire	W. Peters	Baltimore, Md	Aug. 12, 1862	36, 195
Brick, Manufacture of fire	S. K. Wellman	Nashua, N. H	Apr. 30, 1867	64, 389
Brick, Manufacture of machine	S. W. Wood	Washington, D. C	May 6, 1856	14, 846
Brick, Manufacturing	C. Colles	....	Jan. 26, 1793	....
Brick, Manufacturing	E. W. Crittenden	Pittsburgh, Pa	Nov. 19, 1867	70, 969
Brick, Manufacturing	I. Gregg	Philadelphia, Pa	Oct. 22, 1872	132, 463
Brick, Manufacturing	J. Gregg	New Hampshire, Ohio	May 7, 1811	....
Brick, Manufacturing	R. Mansfield	....	Oct. 24, 1800	....
Brick, Manufacturing	R. Robberts	Berlin Township, Ohio	Mar. 2, 1833	....
Brick-mold	J. W. Andrews	Norristown, Pa	Mar. 1, 1859	23, 067
Brick-mold	J. A. Buckwater	Kimberton, Pa	Oct. 4, 1859	25, 626
Brick-mold	G. Carnell	Philadelphia, Pa	Dec. 5, 1871	121, 449
Brick-mold	M. Elder	Lansing, Mich	Sept, 11, 1860	29, 9[illegible]8
Brick-mold	T. and W. A. Ellis	Philadelphia, Pa	Mar. 16, 1869	87, 8[illegible]0
Brick-mold	J. Evans	Davenport, Iowa	Sept. 17, 1867	68, 862
Brick-mold	J. M. Ferrell	Philadelphia, Pa	Aug. 7, 1866	57, 041
Brick-mold	F. M. Franklin, O. K. McIntire, and W. Whitely.	Springfield, Ohio	Oct. 15, 1867	69, 909
Brick-mold	M. T. Glinsdal	Rockford, Ill	Apr. 5, 1870	101, 608
Brick-mold	G. Graessle	Hamilton, Ohio	Nov. 15, 1870	109, 313
Brick-mold	J. A. Hamer	Reading, Pa	Nov. 23, 1858	22, 119
Brick-mold	J. A. Hamer	Reading, Pa	Aug. 2, 1859	24, 972
Brick-mold	J. A. Hamer	Reading, Pa	Jan. 3, 1860	26, 736
Brick-mold	J. A. Hamer	West Vincent, Pa	Jan. 28, 1862	34, 282
Brick-mold	J. A. Hamer and T. Lippincott	Philadelphia, Pa	Aug. 1, 1865	49, 105
Brick-mold	S. Inman	Rockford, Ill	Nov. 30, 1869	97, 297
Brick-mold	S. Inman	Rockford, Ill	Dec. 7, 1869	97, 642
Brick-mold	T. James	Baltimore, Md	May 15, 1866	54, 734
Brick-mold	W. Langster and J. Bretz	Springfield, Ill	Sept. 8, 1868	82, 037
Brick-mold	A. McAlpin	Savannah, Ga	Apr. 12, 1870	101, 896
Brick-mold	M. Newlove	Burlington, Iowa	Dec. 21, 1869	98, 181
Brick-mold	J. F. Schuffenecker	Keokuk, Iowa	Mar. 27, 1860	27, 652
Brick-mold	J. F. Schuffenecker	Saint Louis, Mo	Feb. 7, 1865	46, 272
Brick-mold	S. Shreffer	Joliet, Ill	Mar. 13, 1866	53, 191
Brick-mold	R. Stuckwisch	Terre Haute, Ind	Oct. 3, 1871	119, 667
Brick-mold	S. H. Taylor	Jacksonville, Ill	Nov. 29, 1870	109, 778
Brick-mold and bottom-board	A. T. Putnam	Detroit, Mich	May 10, 1870	102, 862
Brick-mold for brick-pressing machine	B. H. Brown	Alexandria, D. C	Oct. 23, 1837	436
Brick-mold, Hand	C. Alvord	Syracuse, N. Y	Nov. 21, 1854	11, 959
Brick-mold piston	L. Sylvester	Philadelphia, Pa	Aug. 13, 1867	67, 684
Brick-mold safety-guard	B. Porter	Jackson, Mich	Aug. 25, 1868	81, 405
Brick-mold-sanding machine	R. Lent	Glasco, N. Y	Apr. 23, 1872	126, 063
Brick, Molding	D. Fox	Ashtabula, Ohio	Aug. 15, 1831	....
Brick, Molding	N. Johnson	Noolesville, Ind	June 20, 1854	11, 127
Brick, Molding	O. W. Seely	Syracuse, N. Y	May 19, 1863	38, 607
Brick, Molding	I. Town	New Haven, Conn	Sept. 27, 1844	3, 762
Brick-molding	T. Tufts	Somerville, Mass	May 14, 1867	64, 812
Brick molding and making machine	J. Lee and J. Ring	Ogden, N. Y	June 11, 1825	....
Brick molding and pressing	D. Flagg, jr	Gardiner, Me	Mar. 19, 1828	....
Brick molding and pressing	J. McDonald and R. McQueen	New York, N. Y	Nov. 19, 1828	....
Brick molding and pressing	J. Treadway	Haverstraw, N. Y	Mar. 21, 1865	46, 956
Brick molding and pressing machine	N. Adams	Cornwall, N. Y	Sept. 8, 1837	376
Brick molding and pressing machine	J. J. Alvord	Tecumseh, Mich	May 20, 1862	35, 287
Brick molding and pressing machine	D. Barnford	Deerfield, N. Y	Apr. 28, 1832	....
Brick molding and pressing machine	C. Chaney	Prospect, Me	Sept. 11, 1834	....
Brick molding and pressing machine	D. Philips	Natchez, Miss	June 23, 1832	....
Brick molding and pressing machine	H. Waterman	Bath, Me	Nov. 4, 1837	456
Brick molding and pressing machine	S. Waterman and C. Learned	Charleston, S. C	Apr. 14, 1838	694
Brick pressing and molding machinery	J. McDonald	New York, N. Y	Apr. 24, 1827	....
Brick-molding machine	J. Bolton	Saratoga Springs, N. Y	Aug. 23, 1838	891
Brick-molding machine	J. Booth and W. H. Stevenson	Columbus, Miss	Jan. 6, 1844	3, 399
Brick-molding machine	J. Butler	Buffalo, N. Y	Dec. 13, 1853	10, 319
Brick-molding machine	J. Coppuck	Louisville, Ky	July 1, 1836	....
Brick-molding machine	J. Drummond	Whitestown, N. Y	Mar. 6, 1832	....
Brick-molding machine	E. Fish	Fayette, Me	June 9, 1826	....
Brick-molding machine	J. W. Frost	Croton, N. Y	Nov. 20, 1849	6, 882
Brick-molding machine	W. C. Grimes	York, Pa	Dec. 2, 1834	....
Brick-molding machine	J. J. Hutchison and J. D. Brandbery.	Cape Girardeau, Mo	Oct. 16, 1860	30, 406
Brick-molding machine	T. P. Kneeland	Ogden, N. Y	June 21, 1825	....
Brick-molding machine	H. Mane	Point Coupee, La	Nov. 23, 1822	....
Brick-molding machine	I. P. Owen	Upper Alton, Ill	Apr. 10, 1843	3, 041
Brick-molding machine	R. Rankin	Frankfort, Me	Dec, 24, 1834	....
Brick-molding machine	L. E. Ransom	Mill Port, N. Y	Jan. 9, 1838	548
Brick-molding machine	S. Ustick	Philadelphia, Pa	July 10, 1847	5, 187
Brick-molding machine	J. & A. Wagner	Philadelphia, Pa	Aug. 11, 1857	17, 999
Brick-molding machine	D. Watson	Fayetteville, Me	May 6, 1826	....
Brick-molding machine	D. Wolfe	Mount Vernon, Ohio	Dec. [illegible], 1834	....
Brick, mortar, &c., Extension-machine for raising	J. Cox	Ebensburgh, Pa	June 5, 1849	6, 491
Brick-mortar, Machine for mixing and hoisting	J. Rinehart	Danville, Ill	June 6, 1835	....
Brick or artificial stone without burning, Making	J. B. Harris	Philadelphia, Pa	Aug. 21, 1810	....
Brick or building-block, Machine for pressing hollow.	M. and J. H. Buck and F. A. Cushman.	Lebanon, N. H	Dec. 9, 1856	16, 174

Index of patents issued from the United States Patent Office from 1790 to 1873, inclusive—Continued.

Invention.	Inventor.	Residence.	Date.	No.
Brick or building-blocks, Manufacture of	H. W. Angell	Waukesha, Wis	Dec. 11, 1866	60,320
Brick or hollow block, Building	G. H. Johnson and G. Milson	Buffalo, N. Y	Feb. 16, 1869	86,929
Brick or tiles, Steam-boiler	W. Dillon	Wheeling, W. Va	June 4, 1872	127,467
Brick, Paving	D. Moffet and J. Thomson	Philadelphia, Pa	Apr. 19, 1870	102,144
Brick, Paving	J. Overmyer	Indianapolis, Ind	Aug. 20, 1872	130,589
Brick-pottery kiln	J. B. De Palm	New York, N. Y	June 6, 1854	11,002
Brick-press	N. Adams	Canterbury, N. Y	Apr. 17, 1849	6,361
Brick-press	J. J. Alvord	Tecumseh, Mich	Sept. 26, 1865	50,088
Brick-press	C. B. Baker	Troy, N. Y	June 6, 1848	5,617
Brick-press	C. B. Baker	Troy, N. Y	Mar. 26, 1850	7,206
Brick-press	C. B. Baker	Troy, N. Y	Aug. 1, 1854	11,408
Brick-press	C. B. Baker and E. Gifford	Troy, N. Y	Sept. 7, 1844	3,731
Brick-press	P. Ball	Mount Vernon, Ohio	Mar. 2, 1836	....
Brick-press	W. Barker and G. Martin	Schenectady, N. Y	May 1, 1866	54,460
Brick-press	C. Becker	Flint, Mich	June 11, 1867	65,035
Brick-press	E. H. Bellows	Worcester, Mass	Oct. 6, 1857	18,318
Brick-press	J. Booth	Mobile, Ala	June 20, 1848	5,640
Brick-press	J. Boynton	East Hartford, Conn	Aug. 5, 1856	15,471
Brick-press	A. H. Brown	Georgetown, D. C	Sept. 5, 1854	11,658
Brick-press	B. H. Brown	Philadelphia, Pa	Oct. 3, 1844	3,770
Brick-press	J. T. Brown and M. Fuller	Midville, Ga	Dec. 11, 1849	6,933
Brick-press	R. Brunson	Chicago, Ill	Apr. 23, 1867	63,990
Brick-press	T. J. Burke	Sandwich, Ill	May 25, 1869	90,339
Brick-press	J. Butler	Buffalo, N. Y	Jan. 29, 1850	7,048
Brick-press	A. Carbonel	Philadelphia, Pa	May 12, 1842	2,619
Brick-press	C. Carnell	Kensington, Pa	Jan. 15, 1850	7,017
Brick-press	J. Chase, jr	Pegnonock, Conn	May 22, 1855	12,898
Brick-press	J. F. Clark	Morenci, Mich	Dec. 13, 1870	110,113
Brick-press	J. B. Collen	Reading, Pa	Jan. 1, 1856	14,012
Brick-press	T. Conklin	Woodbridge, Miss	Jan. 23, 1841	1,947
Brick-press	D. M. Crellis	Sandwich, N. H	Aug. 11, 1832	....
Brick-press	T. Culbertson	Cincinnati, Ohio	May 16, 1846	4,521
Brick-press	T. Culbertson and G. Scott	Philadelphia, Pa	June 25, 1850	7,453
Brick-press	J. Dane	West Derby, Vt	Oct. 24, 1848	5,878
Brick-press	W. L. Drake	Sturgis, Mich	Sept. 3, 1867	68,494
Brick-press	J. S. Elliott	West Needham, Mass	Feb. 14, 1860	27,117
Brick-press	J. M. Enos	Saint Joseph, Mo	Apr. 14, 1868	76,613
Brick-press	A. K. Fahnestock	Harrisburgh, Pa	Apr. 16, 1842	2,560
Brick-press	J. Finegan	Haverstraw, N. Y	Sept. 15, 1863	39,906
Brick-press	J. Grant	Providence, R. I	May 13, 1851	8,093
Brick-press	I. Gregg	Pittsburgh, Pa	June 6, 1848	5,618
Brick-press	I. Gregg	Pittsburgh, Pa	Aug. 1, 1854	11,422
Brick-press	A. Hall	Coxsackie, N. Y	May 22, 1847	5,128
Brick-press	R. R. Harbour	Oskaloosa, Iowa	June 9, 1857	17,546
Brick-press	T. Hartley	Pittsburgh, Pa	Apr. 11, 1846	4,451
Brick-press	J. W. Hope	New York, N. Y	June 4, 1850	7,414
Brick-press	H. J. Hughes	Davenport, Iowa	Feb. 5, 1856	14,195
Brick-press	J. Johnson	Fort Smith, Ark	Aug. 8, 1854	11,482
Brick-press	L. Kirk	Reading, Pa	June 17, 1856	15,135
Brick-press	A. J. Knisely	Chicago, Ill	Sept. 17, 1872	131,353
Brick-press	W. O. Leslie	Philadelphia, Pa	Aug. 11, 1868	80,977
Brick-press	S. Lillie, jr	Fort Wayne, Ind	Feb. 17, 1857	16,649
Brick-press	G. A. Metcalf	Malden, Mass	May 18, 1869	90,285
Brick-press	J. A. Millholland	Mount Savage Md	Jan. 17, 1871	111,076
Brick-press	J. P. Owen	Cincinnati, Ohio	July 26, 1845	4,123
Brick-press	C. D. Page	Rochester, N. Y	Sept. 17, 1867	68,896
Brick-press	J. L. Ransom	Mill Port, N. Y	Apr. 4, 1846	4,448
Brick-press	N. Read	Belfast, Me	Aug. 20, 1835	....
Brick-press	J. J. Riddle	Covington, Ky	Apr. 1, 1851	8,021
Brick-press	V. Roth	Evansville, Ind	Feb. 20, 1849	6,127
Brick-press	W. Sanford	Cambridge, Mass	Sept. 9, 1845	4,183
Brick-press	N. Sawyer	Baltimore, Md	Sept. 27, 1844	3,768
Brick-press	N. Sawyer	Baltimore, Md	Dec. 4, 1847	5,386
Brick-press	N. Sawyer	Baltimore, Md	Apr. 23, 1850	7,309
Brick-press	J. Scheitlin	Louisville, Ky	Jan. 21, 1851	7,908
Brick-press	D. M. Seeley	Albany, N. Y	May 22, 1866	54,967
Brick-press	J. Smedley	Columbia, Pa	Aug. 28, 1844	3,720
Brick-press	J. N. Smith	Jersey City, N. J	May 24, 1870	103,381
Brick-press	T. W. Smith	Alexandria, D. C	Jan. 30, 1841	1,959
Brick-press	A. A. Torpey	Chicago, Ill	Aug. 25, 1868	81,560
Brick-press	M. Twitchell	Gray, Me	Sept. 24, 1825	....
Brick-press	M. Twitchell	Gray, Me	June 10, 1844	3,622
Brick-press	S. Ustick	Philadelphia, Pa	Dec. 28, 1838	1,045
Brick-press	S. Ustick	Philadelphia, Pa	July 10, 1855	13,239
Brick-press	W. Wadsworth	Hartford, Conn	June 26, 1835	....
Brick-press	J. Z. A. Wagner	Philadelphia, Pa	Apr. 8, 1851	8,024
Brick-press	J. Waite	Leicester, Mass	Mar. 12, 1845	3,942
Brick-press	W. Wakely	Taunton, Mass	Apr. 9, 1872	125,636
Brick-press	W. B. Waldran and G. Hargitt	Shelby County, Tenn	July 10, 1849	6,582
Brick-press	J. W. Ward	Cambridge, Mass	May 30, 1848	5,610
Brick-press	H. Waterman	Bath, Me	Nov. 20, 1837	469
Brick-press	S. Whitman	New Albany, Ind	Apr. 23, 1850	7,313
Brick-press	E. D. Williams and T. Tyrell	Wilmington, Del., and York, Pa.	Oct. 17, 1854	11,817
Brick-press	A. Witmer	Henry, Ill	Sept. 6, 1864	44,133
Brick-press	J. Woodson	Rockbridge County, Va	Sept. 10, 1829	....
Brick-press	A. Woodworth	Worcester, Mass	May 8, 1843	3,074
Brick-press	A. Woodworth, 3d, and S. Mower.	Worcester, Mass., and Philadelphia, Pa.	Nov. 27, 1849	6,899
Brick-press	F. Zisemann	Saint Louis, Mo	Nov. 13, 1849	6,876
Brick-press bridle	J. G. Talcott	Glastenbury, Conn	Oct. 1, 1830	....
Brick-press bridle	J. Willard	Baltimore, Md	June 10, 1830	....
Brick press, Concrete	T. J. Burke	Chicago, Ill	Jan. 21, 1868	73,576
Brick press, Concrete	J. H. Wirt	Delphi, Ind	Apr. 21, 1868	77,153
Brick-press, Construction of	A. Hall	Cleveland, Ohio	Sept. 3, 1842	2,768
Brick-press, Finishing	L. B. Crittenden	Pittsburgh, Pa	June 2, 1868	78,434
Brick-press for pressing brick from dry clay	N. Sawyer and T. W. Smith	Washington, D. C	Aug. 13, 1838	881
Brick-press, Hydraulic	E. Rogers	Cleveland, Ohio	Sept. 23, 1856	15,778
Brick-press mold or box	J. McKenna	Cambria, Pa	Aug. 19, 1873	141,942

Index of patents issued from the United States Patent Office from 1790 *to* 1873, *inclusive*—Continued.

Invention.	Inventor.	Residence.	Date.	No.
Brick-press, Self-feeding	J. Winslow	Portland, Me	Dec. 8, 1826	
Brick-press, Spiral-molding	J. Parker	Gardiner, Me	Mar. 28, 1826	
Brick press, Unburnt	E. Mayo	Hallowell, Me	June 24, 1826	
Brick, Pressing	H. Crofoot	Oak Park, Ill	May 14, 1867	64,637
Brick, Pressing	J. Moore	Gardiner, Me	Aug. 24, 1825	
Brick, Pressing	O. W. Seely	Buffalo, N. Y	Aug. 27, 1867	68,244
Brick, Pressing	W. G. White	Bedford, Ohio	Mar. 30, 1869	88,353
Brick, Pressing and finishing	C. Hinkle	Allentown, Pa	June 1, 1833	
Brick pressing and molding machine	S. Costill	Philadelphia, Pa	Sept. 4, 1840	1,769
Brick-pressing machine	C. Berrian	Clinton City, Iowa	Sept. 1, 1868	81,738
Brick-pressing machine	M. Chittenden	Danbury, Conn	Oct. 10, 1865	50,333
Brick-pressing machine	W. H. Combs	Fort Wayne, Ind	Jan. 7, 1868	73,079
Brick-pressing machine	G. V. Harper	Batavia, N. Y	Apr. 25, 1838	711
Brick-pressing machine	J. Hotchkiss	Springfield, Ohio	Dec. 20, 1864	45,563
Brick-pressing machine	J. Howe	Alna, Me	May 18, 1827	
Brick pressing machine	T. A. Irick	Harrisonburgh, Va	July 27, 1831	
Brick-pressing machine	J. K. Lemon	Allegheny City, Pa	Apr. 11, 1865	47,209
Brick-pressing machine	A. McClung	Fairfield, Va	Mar. 26, 1831	
Brick-pressing machine	A. F. Mervine	Saint Louis, Mo	Sept. 12, 1837	382
Brick-pressing machine	B. R. Reed	Danvers, Mass	May 29, 1823	
Brick-pressing machine	B. Rolfe	Deering, N. H	Apr. 30, 1822	
Brick-pressing machine	N. Sawyer	Mount Vernon, Ohio	Apr. 8, 1835	
Brick-pressing machine	J. Sites	Harrisonburgh, Va	Mar. 29, 1831	
Brick-pressing machine	W. H. Walrath	Chittenango, N. Y	Oct. 9, 1866	58,700
Brick-pressing machine	J. Willerd	Baltimore, Md	May 2, 1826	
Brick-pressing machinery	A. B. Crossman	Huntington, N. Y	Feb. 9, 1827	
Brick-pressing machinery	C. Heath and J. Wilson	Malden and Boston, Mass	June 17, 1862	35,650
Brick, Pressing unburnt	T. Norcross	Hallowell, Me	Dec. 31, 1825	
Brick-re-pressing machine	J. K. Caldwell	Philadelphia, Pa	May 20, 1873	139,113
Brick-re-pressing machine	H. Maurer	New York, N. Y	June 29, 1869	91,856
Brick-re-pressing machine	A. J. Sprague	Toledo, Ohio	July 12, 1870	105,270
Brick, Reversible curb	E. Linson	Shoemakertown, Pa	Jan. 21, 1873	134,994
Brick, Scouring	J. Valentine	Woodbridge, N. J	Nov. 7, 1865	50,862
Brick, stock, tile, &c	D. Flagg, jr., and A. Parker	Sweden, N. Y	Dec. 28, 1832	
Brick, stone, and mortar, Elevating	C. G. Fairman	Lewiston, N. Y	Sept. 16, 1833	
Brick, stone, &c., Method of moving	S. Brown	New York, N. Y	July 31, 1827	
Brick, stove-linings, &c., Composition for fire	E. H. Richter	Taunton, Mass	Dec. 9, 1873	145,448
Brick-striker	P. Sweet	Ashtabula, Ohio	Feb. 20, 1835	
Brick, Striking	A. W. Duty	Sangerfield, N. Y	Mar. 7, 1833	
Brick-striking machine	E. and D. W. Duty	Painesville, Ohio	June 7, 1828	
Brick, tiles, and clay-ware, Making	J. Wood	Rockland County, N. Y	Mar. 3, 1829	
Brick, tiles, &c., Forming	J. Hawkins		July 11, 1797	
Brick, tiles, &c., from slag, Making	F. Fabre	Marseilles, France	May 31, 1870	103,591
Brick, tiles, &c., Making	J. F. Gould	Newburyport, Mass	Oct. 17, 1809	
Brick, tiles, &c., Making	E. G. Oldfield	Bordentown, N. J	Jan. 15, 1861	31,126
Brick, tiles, &c., Making	J. M. Reid	Pittsburgh, Pa	Apr. 2, 1872	125,144
Brick, tiles, &c., Making	D. Thackara	Woodbury, N. J	Dec. 14, 1869	97,992
Brick, Treadle-machine for	B. R. Reed	Danvers, Mass	May 29, 1823	
Brick, Treating clay and drying	J. Fisher	Reading, Pa	Aug. 10, 1869	93,526
Brick wall, Composition for cleaning and renovating.	W. B. Walters	Lock Haven, Pa	Aug. 18, 1868	81,233
Brick, Water and fire proof	T. H. Sherman	Scriba, N. Y	Dec. 30, 1833	
Brick-work, Joint groover for	A. M. Zabriskie	Bergen Point, N. J	Feb. 26, 1867	62,463
Brick-yard shed	R. O. Smith	Newburyport, Mass	Aug. 5, 1873	141,520
Bricks, Arching	W. F. Quinby	Wilmington, Del	Aug. 9, 1870	106,203
Bricks, Cutting clay into	J. Plumbe	San Francisco, Cal	June 12, 1855	13,042
Bricks, Form of building	E. Conkling	Cincinnati, Ohio	Jan. 8, 1856	14,052
Bricks, retorts, muffles, crucibles, &c., Manufacture of.	E. L. Seymour	New York, N. Y	Nov. 19, 1867	71,229
Bricklayer's pointer	J. S. Merriken	Baltimore, Md	May 13, 1873	138,911
Bridge	J. J. Alises	New York, N. Y	Oct. 4, 1864	44,498
Bridge	C. Baker	Saint Joseph, Mo	Aug. 31, 1869	94,272
Bridge	J. Boles, jr	Boston, Mass	May 20, 1865	47,920
Bridge	J. Boles, jr	Boston, Mass	May 30, 1865	48,013
Bridge	T. C. Boutel	Paris, France	May 2, 1871	114,401
Bridge	J. Bragg	Montreal, Canada	Jan. 4, 1820	
Bridge	J. C. Briggs	Concord, N. H	May 26, 1863	38,653
Bridge	G. H. Bruce	Lancaster, N. Y	Jan. 7, 1862	34,102
Bridge	T. Burr		Feb. 14, 1806	
Bridge	A. M. Campbell	Newark, N. J	Dec. 27, 1870	110,546
Bridge	S. and T. Champion	Washington, D. C	July 18, 1854	11,322
Bridge	L. K. Cole and H. Soule, jr	Syracuse, N. Y	Feb. 13, 1866	52,5[illegible]6
Bridge	G. W. Corey	Port Jervis, N. Y	July 16, 1867	66,799
Bridge	A. Cottrell	Newport, R. I	Jan. 19, 1864	43,099
Bridge	B. F. Davis	Hearne, Tex	Sept. 23, 1873	143,125
Bridge	E. Denmead and W. Bollman	Marietta, Ga., and Baltimore, Md.	May 19, 1868	78,073
Bridge	F. Dieckman	Cincinnati, Ohio	Mar. 28, 1871	113,030
Bridge	J. H. Diedrichs	Richmond, Va	Apr. 2, 1872	125,182
Bridge	T. Durden	Montgomery, Ala	June 1, 1858	20,414
Bridge	J. R. Durfee	Oshkosh, Wis	Sept. 16, 1873	142,776
Bridge	J. B. Eads	Saint Louis, Mo	Nov. 10, 1868	83,942
Bridge	J. B. Eads	Saint Louis, Mo	May 4, 1869	89,745
Bridge	J. B. Eads	Saint Louis, Mo	Sept. 2, 1873	142,378
Bridge	J. B. Eads	Saint Louis, Mo	Nov. 11, 1873	144,519
Bridge	C. H. Earle	Green Bay, Wis	Sept. 15, 1857	18,196
Bridge	S. Ensign	New Franklin, Ohio	Nov. 9, 1869	96,569
Bridge	A. Fink	Baltimore, Md	May 9, 1854	10,887
Bridge	A. Fink	Louisville, Ky	Apr. 9, 1867	63,714
Bridge	H. Flad	Saint Louis, Mo	Oct. 15, 1872	132,271
Bridge	J. Fowler		Feb. 24, 1797	
Bridge	S. F. Gassaway	Marietta, Ga	Sept. 18, 1847	5,297
Bridge	J. Gates	Saint Louis, Mo	Feb. 11, 1873	135,705
Bridge	L. Gay	Chili, N. Y	Nov. 4, 1846	4,837
Bridge	J. H. Gilbert	Roxbury, Mass	Sept. 18, 1866	58,094
Bridge	J. Glass, G. P. Schneider, and W. B. Rezner.	Cleveland, Ohio	Dec. 10, 1867	71,868
Bridge	F. Good	New London, Pa	Nov. 4, 1837	450

Index of patents issued from the United States Patent Office from 1790 *to* 1873, *inclusive*—Continued.

Invention.	Inventor.	Residence.	Date.	No.
Bridge	J. M. Goodwin	New York, N. Y	Sept. 16, 1873	142, 785
Bridge	T. B. Gregory	Champaign, Ill	July 12, 1870	105, 195
Bridge	R. Grotz	Chicago, Ill	Apr. 2, 1867	63, 507
Bridge	E. Hamilton	Chicago, Ill	May 26, 1868	78, 202
Bridge	D. Hammond	Canton, Ohio	July 3, 1866	56, 043
Bridge	D. Hammond, M. Adler, and J. Abbott.	Canton, Ohio	Feb. 11, 1873	135, 802
Bridge	F. Harbach	Pittsfield, Mass	Aug. 12, 1846	4, 694
Bridge	G. E. Harding	New York, N. Y	Oct. 22, 1872	132, 398
Bridge	S. P. Hastings	Tonawanda, N. Y	Oct. 15, 1872	132, 284
Bridge	P. Hendricks	Floris, Iowa	Nov. 26, 1867	71, 483
Bridge	J. G. Henszey	Philadelphia, Pa	June 22, 1869	91, 745
Bridge	G. P. Herthel, jr	Saint Louis, Mo	Jan. 18, 1870	98, 866
Bridge	H. L. Hervey and R. E. Osborne.	Quincy, Ill., and Springfield, Ohio.	Aug. 21, 1855	13, 461
Bridge	G. W. O. Hüygens	Saint Louis, Mo	Apr. 1, 1856	14, 584
Bridge	W. James	Richmond, Va	Apr. 16, 1867	63, 901
Bridge	J. Johnson	Mott Haven, N. Y	July 16, 1872	129, 479
Bridge	J. E. Kanser	New York, N. Y	Nov. 7, 1865	50, 827
Bridge	J. J. Kelley	Slippery Rock, Pa	Mar. 23, 1869	88, 181
Bridge	Z. King	Cleveland, Ohio	Sept. 25, 1866	58, 266
Bridge	L. Kirkup	Brooklyn, N. Y	Oct. 24, 1871	120, 282
Bridge	M. Kremser	Cleveland, Ohio	Feb. 27, 1866	52, 860
Bridge	J. Laird	Canton, Ohio	Aug. 31, 1869	94, 321
Bridge	J. and G. F. Laird	Canton, Ohio	Aug. 31, 1869	94, 322
Bridge	G. T. Lape	Summit, N. Y	May 12, 1868	77, 741
Bridge	O. G. Leopold	Cincinnati, Ohio	Dec. 4, 1866	60, 205
Bridge	J. H. Linville	Philadelphia, Pa	Nov. 24, 1868	84, 288
Bridge	L. Liscom	Boston, Mass	Mar. 31, 1868	76, 212
Bridge	R. Lockwood	Brooklyn, N. Y	Dec. 5, 1865	51, 328
Bridge	S. H. Long	United States Engineers	Nov. 13, 1847	5, 366
Bridge	S. H. Long	United States Army	Aug. 17, 1858	21, 203
Bridge	D. C. McCallum	Owego, N. Y	Jan. 20, 1857	16, 446
Bridge	D. McCurdy	Ottawa, Ohio	June 28, 1870	104, 867
Bridge	D. McCurdy	Ottawa, Ohio	June 28, 1870	104, 868
Bridge	D. McCurdy	Ottawa, Ohio	June 28, 1870	104, 869
Bridge	H. S. McDowell	Columbus, Tex	Jan. 11, 1870	98, 699
Bridge	J. A. McKay	Auburn, Ind	June 1, 1869	90, 767
Bridge	R. S. Merrill	Boston, Mass	May 19, 1868	78, 000
Bridge	D. A. Mitchell	Chicago, Ill	July 31, 1866	56, 777
Bridge	F. Monroe	Bruce, Mich	Apr. 17, 1866	54, 004
Bridge	R. and M. J. Montgomery	New York, N. Y	Sept. 1, 1868	81, 666
Bridge	G. C. Morgan	Chicago, Ill	Aug. 22, 1871	118, 258
Bridge	T. W. H. Moseley	Covington, Ky	Feb. 3, 1857	16, 572
Bridge	T. W. H. Moseley	Boston, Mass	Oct. 23, 1866	59, 054
Bridge	T. W. H. Moseley	Boston, Mass	Aug. 30, 1870	106, 855
Bridge	A. Oudry	Paris, France	May 13, 1863	35, 251
Bridge	T. Palmer		Dec. 17, 1797	
Bridge	C. H. Parker	Boston, Mass	Aug. 10, 1869	93, 638
Bridge	C. H. Parker	Boston, Mass	Jan. 4, 1870	98, 620
Bridge	C. H. Parker	Boston, Mass	Feb. 22, 1870	100, 185
Bridge	C. H. Parker	Boston, Mass	May 17, 1870	103, 233
Bridge	R. L. Partridge	Marysville, Ohio	June 11, 1872	127, 791
Bridge	C. W. Peale		Jan. 21, 1797	
Bridge	O. H. Perry and W. H. Allen	Beloit, Wis	Oct. 24, 1871	120, 319
Bridge	H. Pettit	Philadelphia, Pa	Feb. 25, 1873	136, 177
Bridge	C. Pfeifer	Saint Louis, Mo	Dec. 12, 1871	121, 894
Bridge	A. J. Post	Hudson City, N. J	Aug. 25, 1868	81, 406
Bridge	A. J. Post	Hudson City, N. J	Sept. 1, 1868	81, 817
Bridge	A. Reiling	Bellevue, Iowa	Dec. 16, 1873	145, 685
Bridge	N. Rider	Worcester, Mass	Nov. 26, 1845	4, 287
Bridge	I. Rogers	Cincinnati, Ohio	Sept. 30, 1856	15, 823
Bridge	I. Rogers	Washington, D. C	Feb. 10, 1863	37, 642
Bridge	R. W. Rogers	Pittsburgh, Pa	Dec. 29, 1868	85, 332
Bridge	H. G. Russell	Lincoln, Ill	Nov. 5, 1872	132, 800
Bridge	H. A. Rust and L. Hermann	Chicago, Ill	Sept. 8, 1868	81, 950
Bridge	J. Sanderson	Fredericksburgh, Ohio	Apr. 21, 1868	77, 103
Bridge	J. Seebold	Kantz, Pa	July 19, 1870	105, 497
Bridge	J. Seebold	Kantz, Pa	Sept. 6, 1870	107, 106
Bridge	J. Seebold	Kantz, Pa	May 2, 1871	114, 497
Bridge	C. S. Smith, C. H. Latrobe, and F. H. Smith.	Baltimore, Md	Jan. 18, 1870	99, 017
Bridge	F. H. Smith	Baltimore, Md	Dec. 11, 1866	60, 434
Bridge	F. H. Smith	Baltimore, Md	Apr. 27, 1869	89, 442
Bridge	F. H. Smith	Baltimore, Md	Mar. 10, 1868	75, 477
Bridge	F. H. Smith	Baltimore, Md	May 11, 1869	89, 948
Bridge	F. H. Smith	Baltimore, Md	Oct. 26, 1869	96, 278
Bridge	F. H. Smith	Baltimore, Md	June 25, 1872	128, 449
Bridge	R. W. Smith	Tippecanoe, Ohio	July 16, 1867	66, 900
Bridge	R. W. Smith	Toledo, Ohio	Dec. 7, 1869	97, 714
Bridge	C. B. Sreeves	Atchison, Kans	May 2, 1871	114, 363
Bridge	J. D. Steele	Pottstown, Pa	Apr. 9, 1867	63, 666
Bridge	J. Stickney		June 3, 1797	
Bridge	J. Tellweger	Louisville, Ky	Apr. 2, 1872	125, 244
Bridge	J. Templeman	Georgetown, D. C	Mar. 6, 1810	
Bridge	W. E. Thomas	Queenstown, Md	July 16, 1872	129, 374
Bridge	J. K. Thompson	Chicago, Ill	Sept. 8, 1868	81, 960
Bridge	I. Town	Fayetteville, N. C	Jan. 28, 1820	
Bridge	I. Town	New York, N. Y	Apr. 3, 1835	
Bridge	J. B. Tracy	Lincoln, Del	Dec. 5, 1871	121, 576
Bridge	W. P. Trowbridge	Newtown, N. Y	Sept. 7, 1869	94, 529
Bridge	L. E. Truesdell	Warren, Mass	Aug. 31, 1858	21, 388
Bridge	L. E. Truesdell	Chicago, Ill	Apr. 7, 1868	76, 558
Bridge	E. Trumbull	Little Falls, N. Y	July 10, 1841	2, 164
Bridge	M. Turley	Council Bluffs, Iowa	Dec. 13, 1870	110, 173
Bridge	J. Valleley	Canton, Ohio	Dec. 30, 1873	145, 034
Bridge	J. B. Valliquette	Chicago, Ill	Apr. 7, 1868	76, 560
Bridge	D. H. Van Duzer	Sugar Loaf, N. Y	Sept. 20, 1859	25, 537

Index of patents issued from the United States Patent Office from 1790 *to* 1873, *inclusive*—Continued.

Invention.	Inventor.	Residence.	Date.	No.
Bridge	L. Wernwag	Jefferson County, Va	Dec. 22, 1829	....
Bridge	I. H. Wheeler	Sciotoville, Ohio	Sept. 20, 1870	107, 576
Bridge	A. White	Boston, Mass	Feb. 3, 1852	8, 713
Bridge	T. B. White	New Brighton, Pa	Mar. 10, 1868	75, 502
Bridge, &c	R. T. L. Witty	Lowell, Mass	Oct. 14, 1835	....
Bridge	W. Woodmansee	Kingston, N. Y	Mar. 6, 1827	....
Bridge	J. S. Yerk and G. H. Heming	Tiffin, Ohio	Dec. 24, 1861	34, 023
Bridge	E. W. Young	Spring Gardens, Great Britain.	Sept. 28, 1869	95, 402
Bridge, Anchoring suspension-chain for	J. A. Roebling	Pittsburgh, Pa	Aug. 26, 1846	4, 710
Bridge and ferry stairs	D. Dunham	New York, N. Y	June 28, 1814	....
Bridge and other structure	A. Bonzano	Phœnixville, Pa	May 21, 1872	127, 017
Bridge and roof trusses, Bolster-block and pier or abutment-plate for.	J. M. Wilson	Philadelphia, Pa	Mar. 21, 1871	112, 878
Bridge and switch telegraph, Railway draw	W. C. McRea	Philadelphia, Pa	Oct. 3, 1854	11, 763
Bridge-arch	D. Forargue	Cleveland, Ohio	Apr. 2, 1872	125, 128
Bridge, Arched	J. Davenport	Massillon, Ohio	Sept. 22, 1868	82, 388
Bridge, Arched	J. B. Eads and A. Flad	Saint Louis, Mo	Oct. 12, 1869	95, 784
Bridge, Arched	W. B. Rezner	Cleveland, Ohio	July 2, 1872	128, 509
Bridge, Arched	J. Zellweger	Louisville, Ky	June 25, 1872	128, 349
Bridge, Arched trussed	H. L. Hervey	Quincy, Ill	Feb. 26, 1856	14, 314
Bridge, Automatic canal	D. Berry	Huntington, Ind	Nov. 22, 1859	26, 156
Bridge, Balance	J. Jessop	York Town, Pa	July 1, 1811	....
Bridge-block	J. R. Smith	Springfield, Mass	July 14, 1868	79, 869
Bridge, Boat and ferry	W. W. Virdin	Baltimore, Md	July 16, 1861	32, 846
Bridge-braces, Mode of connecting iron	A. D. Briggs	Springfield, Mass	June 18, 1861	32, 555
Bridge, Canal	B. G. Anderson	Chillicothe, Ohio	Oct. 14, 1856	15, 873
Bridge, Chain	J. Finley	Fayette County, Pa	June 17, 1808	....
Bridge, Chain	J. Templeman	Allegany County, Md	Aug. 16, 1808	....
Bridge, Chain suspension	E. W. and E. W. Serrell, jr	New York, N. Y	Oct. 21, 1873	143, 788
Bridge-clamp	N. Chapin	Chicago, Ill	Sept. 27, 1864	44, 397
Bridge-clamp	E. L. Truesdell	Chicago, Ill	July 26, 1870	105, 868
Bridge-column	J. Zellweger	Louisville, Ky	Dec. 16, 1873	145, 545
Bridge connections	T. C. Clarke and A. Bonzano	Philadelphia, Pa	Aug. 13, 1872	130, 479
Bridge, Corrugated-iron	R. Montgomery	New York, N. Y	Aug. 23, 1859	25, 210
Bridge counter-braces, Means for adjusting the effective length of.	D. C. McCallum	Owego, N. Y	July 15, 1851	8, 224
Bridge, Draw	G. W. R. Bayley and T. W. Nelson.	Brashear, La	Jan. 29, 1861	31, 222
Bridge, Draw	H. W. Cass	Lodi, Wis	Nov. 23, 1869	97, 044
Bridge, Draw	C. K. Marshall	New Orleans, La	July 7, 1868	79, 768
Bridge, Draw	J. L. Piper	Pittsburgh, Pa	Oct. 22, 1872	132, 410
Bridge, Draw	T. W. Pratt	Boston, Mass	Feb. 22, 1870	100, 065
Bridge, Draw	T. L. Speakman	Camden, N. J	Apr. 7, 1868	76, 542
Bridge, Draw	H. Whitney	East Cambridge, Mass	July 16, 1872	129, 638
Bridge, Drop	J. D. Woodruff and J. H. Butterworth.	Newark and Dover, N. J	Feb. 14, 1854	10, 527
Bridge, Ferry	W. J. Alsop	Camden, N. J	June 4, 1872	127, 542
Bridge, Ferry	C. J. Atkins	Louisiana, Mo	Aug. 19, 1873	141, 911
Bridge, Ferry	J. S. Bradford	New York, N. Y	Aug. 11, 1868	80, 902
Bridge, Ferry	J. A. Clarke	New York, N. Y	July 28, 1868	80, 391
Bridge, Ferry	A. C. Willson	Green Point, N. Y	Apr. 14, 1868	76, 867
Bridge, Floating	T. Schofield	Grass Valley, Cal	Mar. 20, 1860	27, 571
Bridge, Floating draw	N. B. Proctor	Burlington, Vt	May 20, 1856	14, 928
Bridge, Floating swing	J. N. Vrooman	Danube, N. Y	Apr. 15, 1840	1, 551
Bridge, Flood	T. A. Bryan	Baltimore, Md	Sept. 6, 1870	106, 995
Bridge for canal, Automatic draw	G. C. Bovey	Chillicothe, Ohio	May 8, 1860	28, 148
Bridge for playing pool	O. A. Hill	Westbrook, Me	Mar. 9, 1869	87, 566
Bridge for railway-car, Safety	A. J. Elder	Kansas City, Mo	Dec. 8, 1868	84, 808
Bridge foundation, Iron	J. B. Eads	Saint Louis, Mo	Sept. 2, 1873	142, 382
Bridge, Frame	G. W. Long	Fort Jackson, La	Mar. 10, 1830	....
Bridge, Frame	G. Tabb	Martinsburgh, Va	Feb. 23, 1816	....
Bridge-gate	E. R. Coyne	Chicago, Ill	May 2, 1871	114, 414
Bridge-gate	M. Kirsch	Chicago, Ill	Nov. 22, 1870	109, 520
Bridge-gate	J. D. Sturges	Chicago, Ill	Sept. 6, 1870	107, 119
Bridge-gate	A. Weide	Chicago, Ill	Sept. 7, 1869	94, 534
Bridge-gate	A. Wermerskirchen	Chicago, Ill	June 7, 1870	104, 086
Bridge-gate	J. Wilcke and M. Ellenbogen	Chicago, Ill	Mar. 1, 1870	100, 480
Bridge gate, Draw	G. A. May	Chicago, Ill	Oct. 12, 1869	95, 821
Bridge gate, Draw	F. Pairan	Dayton, Ohio	Apr. 18, 1871	113, 916
Bridge gate, Ferry	L. P. Decker	Brooklyn, N. Y	June 19, 1866	55, 628
Bridge gate, Swing	A. D. Northway	Kenosha, Wis	Dec. 12, 1871	121, 892
Bridge gates, Turning	R. Laderwig and A. Rosenberg	Berlin, Prussia	Feb. 27, 1872	124, 072
Bridge-girder	J. Davenport	Massillon, Ohio	Dec. 24, 1867	72, 611
Bridge-girder	J. W. Evans	New York, N. Y	Nov. 18, 1873	144, 751
Bridge-girder	P. C. Guion	Cincinnati, Ohio	Feb. 26, 1856	14, 313
Bridge-girder	D. Hammond and W. R. Reeves	Canton, Ohio	June 21, 1864	43, 202
Bridge-girder	D. Hammond and W. R. Reeves	Canton, Ohio	Feb. 2, 1869	86, 538
Bridge-girders, Compressive chords for	M. Adler	Canton, Ohio	June 25, 1872	128, 350
Bridge-guard, Ferry	J. A. Clarke	New York, N. Y	Mar. 17, 1868	75, 526
Bridge guard or barrier	J. Lehmann	Crown Point, Ind	Aug. 25, 1868	81, 383
Bridge, Iron	J. J. Beard	Columbus, Ohio	Feb. 16, 1864	41, 794
Bridge, Iron	C. Bender, C. H. Latrobe, and C. S. Smith.	New York, N. Y., Baltimore, Md., and Saint Louis, Mo.	July 29, 1873	141, 310
Bridge, Iron	H. C. Brundage	Buffalo, N. Y	Mar. 1, 1870	100, 254
Bridge, Iron	F. E. Canda	Chicago, Ill	Mar. 30, 1869	88, 446
Bridge, Iron	W. B. Cooper	Albany, N. Y	Feb. 18, 1873	135, 970
Bridge, Iron	J. B. Eads	Saint Louis, Mo	Sept. 2, 1873	142, 379
Bridge, Iron	J. B. Eads	Saint Louis, Mo	Sept. 2, 1873	142, 380
Bridge, Iron	J. B. Eads	Saint Louis, Mo	Sept. 2, 1873	142, 381
Bridge, Iron	L. Eikenberry	Easton, Pa	Jan. 25, 1859	22, 715
Bridge, Iron	L. Eikenberry	Easton, Pa	Jan. 22, 1861	31, 157
Bridge, Iron	J. P. Fisher	Rochester, N. Y	June 26, 1860	28, 845
Bridge, Iron	P. Johnson	Springfield, Mass	Nov. 18, 1873	144, 766
Bridge, Iron	M. Miller	Cleveland, Ohio	June 7, 1870	103, 911
Bridge, Iron	D. H. Morrison	Dayton, Ohio	Oct. 29, 1867	70, 245
Bridge, Iron	J. D. Pierce	Columbia, Mo	Aug. 5, 1873	141, 478
Bridge, Iron	S. S. Post	Jersey City, N. J	June 16, 1863	38, 910

Index of patents issued from the United States Patent Office from 1790 *to* 1873, *inclusive*—Continued.

Invention.	Inventor.	Residence.	Date.	No.
Bridge, Iron	W. Sellers	Philadelphia, Pa	Mar. 4, 1873	136, 389
Bridge, Iron	L. E. Truesdell	Warren, Mass	June 28, 1870	104, 902
Bridge, Iron	T. B. White	New Brighton, Pa	July 2, 1867	66, 433
Bridge, Iron	T. B. White	New Brighton, Pa	Mar. 9, 1869	87, 741
Bridge, Iron	J. Yandell and J. H. Johnson	Saint Louis, Mo	Oct. 17, 1854	11, 818
Bridge, Iron-arch	L. Kittenger	Massillon, Ohio	Oct. 3, 1871	119, 466
Bridge, Iron-truss	T. C. Clarke	Philadelphia, Pa	Nov. 5, 1872	132, 803
Bridge, Iron-truss	G. Halstead	Buffalo, N. Y	June 8, 1869	91, 124
Bridge, Iron-truss	J. H. Linville	Altoona, Pa	Jan. 14, 1862	34, 183
Bridge, Lattice	H. Haupt	York, Pa	Dec. 27, 1839	1, 445
Bridge, Lattice	L. E. Truesdell	Warren, Mass	June 3, 1856	15, 048
Bridge, Lattice and truss	G. B. Manley	Cogan Station, Pa	Apr. 30, 1867	64, 340
Bridge, Lift-draw	S. Whipple	Albany, N. Y	Dec. 24, 1872	134, 338
Bridge, Lifting	S. Swartz	Buffalo, N. Y	Feb. 25, 1873	136, 278
Bridge-pier	C. H. Lilienthal	Yonkers, N. Y	Nov. 29, 1870	109, 637
Bridge-pier	E. W. Smith	New York, N. Y	June 20, 1865	48, 317
Bridge, Pier for suspension	J. Gray	Cincinnati, Ohio	Dec. 24, 1872	134, 269
Bridge-pier, Iron	E. M. Grant	Macon, Ga	Dec. 22, 1868	85, 171
Bridge, Pivot	T. C. Clarke, A. Bonzano, and J. Griffen.	Philadelphia and Phœnixville, Pa.	June 18, 1872	128, 115
Bridge, Pivot	T. C. Clarke, A. Bonzano, and J. Griffen.	Philadelphia and Phœnixville, Pa.	Feb. 11, 1873	135, 776
Bridge-railing, Baluster for iron	S. Sellers and M. M. Manly	Philadelphia, Pa	Apr. 22, 1873	138, 049
Bridge, Rolling draw	R. Crosbie	Newark, N. J	Feb. 17, 1812	....
Bridge, Safety ferry	H. Lawrence	New York, N. Y	Mar. 13, 1855	12, 523
Bridge, Safety railway draw	J. K. and W. P. Gamble	Philadelphia, Pa	July 17, 1855	13, 258
Bridge safety-switch and signal, Draw	E. H. Tobey	Saint Louis, Mo	June 24, 1873	140, 319
Bridge, Self-acting draw	A. Koch	Rocktown, Pa	July 1, 1862	35, 765
Bridge, Self-acting draw	L. Schneider and J. A. Montgomery.	Williamsport, Pa	Sept. 4, 1860	29, 917
Bridge, Self-adjusting counter-brace of truss	J. Gray	Nashville, Tenn	Dec. 27, 1859	26, 583
Bridge, Self-adjusting platform for ferry	G. Sickels	Brooklyn, N. Y	June 7, 1853	9, 772
Bridge, Self-opening canal	J. Selser	Williamsport, Pa	Oct. 29, 1861	33, 606
Bridge signal-apparatus, Railway	T. S. Hall	New Haven, Conn	Apr. 4, 1871	113, 425
Bridge signal, Draw	L. B. Edgecomb	Troy, N. Y	July 17, 1866	56, 491
Bridge signal, Railway	A. Burnham	Taunton, Mass	July 6, 1858	20, 841
Bridge signal, Railway draw	A. F. Smith	Norwich, Conn	Oct. 2, 1866	58, 492
Bridge, Spiral-braced cylinder	I. Rogers	New York, N. Y	Nov. 10, 1841	2, 347
Bridge, Suspension	C. Bender	New York, N. Y	Dec. 10, 1867	71, 955
Bridge, Suspension	E. M. Carpenter	Middletown, N. Y	May 12, 1868	77, 800
Bridge, Suspension	A. S. Hallidie	San Francisco, Cal	July 2, 1867	66, 327
Bridge, Suspension	J. Royal	White Rock, Ill	Feb. 8, 1870	99, 597
Bridge, Suspension	J. Tomlinson	Putnam, Iowa	May 28, 1861	32, 440
Bridge, Swing	J. N. King	Murray, N. Y	May 29, 1855	12, 952
Bridge, Swing	A. R. Ring	Parma, N. Y	Nov. 9, 1838	1, 004
Bridge, Swing	J. Ross	Ipswich, Mass	Jan. 2, 1849	5, 997
Bridge, Swing	G. R. Winkler	Williamsport, Pa	Jan. 19, 1869	86, 117
Bridge, Traveling	F. Field	Adrian, Mich	Apr. 25, 1854	10, 817
Bridge, Trestle	A. Derrom	Paterson, N. J	July 4, 1865	48, 530
Bridge, Truss	J. S. Adams	Elgin, Ill	Aug. 30, 1870	106, 760
Bridge, Truss	J. Anderson	Gouverneur, N. Y	Mar. 18, 1873	136, 951
Bridge, Truss	J. P. Avery	Norwich, Conn	Nov. 5, 1861	33, 629
Bridge, Truss	A. Bannister	Alameda, Cal	July 22, 1873	141, 026
Bridge, Truss	W. Batchelder	Newburyport, Mass	July 11, 1865	48, 643
Bridge, Truss	G. O. Bishop	Hannibal, Mo	Apr. 24, 1860	27, 963
Bridge, Truss	J. Bole, 2d	Boston, Mass	May 19, 1863	38, 552
Bridge, Truss	W. F. Bonnell	Portland, Me	Aug. 20, 1872	130, 561
Bridge, Truss	D. C. Bower	Troy, Ohio	June 24, 1873	140, 181
Bridge, Truss	J. C. Briggs	Concord, N. H	Nov. 23, 1858	22, 106
Bridge, Truss	J. Brown, jr	Buffalo, N. Y	July 7, 1857	17, 722
Bridge, Truss	M. S. and H. B. Cartter	Saint Louis, Mo	June 14, 1870	104, 110
Bridge, Truss	M. S. and H. B. Cartter	Saint Louis, Mo	June 4, 1872	127, 564
Bridge, Truss	H. Childs	Henniker, N. H	Aug. 12, 1846	4, 693
Bridge, Truss	T. C. Clarke, A. Bonzano, and J. Griffen.	Philadelphia and Phœnixville, Pa.	July 1, 1873	140, 471
Bridge, Truss	A. Fink	Parkersburgh, Va	Mar. 3, 1857	16, 728
Bridge, Truss	A. Fink	Louisville, Ky	July 4, 1871	116, 787
Bridge, Truss	J. Foreman	Pottstown, Pa	June 9, 1868	78, 797
Bridge, Truss	J. Foreman	Pottstown, Pa	June 14, 1870	104, 295
Bridge, Truss	T. Hassard	New York, N. Y	Jan. 15, 1846	4, 359
Bridge, Truss	G. P. Herthel, jr	Saint Louis, Mo	Nov. 20, 1866	59, 769
Bridge, Truss	G. P. Herthel, jr	Saint Louis, Mo	Nov. 26, 1867	71, 484
Bridge, Truss	G. P. Herthel, jr	Saint Louis, Mo	May 18, 1869	90, 263
Bridge, Truss	W. Howe	Springfield, Mass	Aug. 28, 1846	4, 726
Bridge, Truss	W. Johnston	Lambertville, N. J	Nov. 29, 1870	109, 6[illegible]8
Bridge, Truss	J. L. Jones	Saint Louis, Mo	Nov. 6, 1860	30, 577
Bridge, Truss	J. L. Jones	Saint Louis, Mo	Aug. 4, 1863	39, 447
Bridge, Truss	J. H. Junkins	Upper Sandusky, Ohio	June 4, 1861	32, 480
Bridge, Truss	C. Kellogg	Athens, Pa	June 7, 1870	104, 036
Bridge, Truss	A. McGuffie	Rochester, N. Y	Mar. 25, 1862	34, 765
Bridge, Truss	A. McGuffie	Rochester, N. Y	May 27, 1862	35, 381
Bridge, Truss	J. A. McKay	Auburn, Ind	Feb. 7, 1871	111, 662
Bridge, Truss	T. W. Pratt	Boston, Mass	Apr. 25, 1871	114, 039
Bridge, Truss	F. Schwatka	United States Army	July 29, 1873	141, 293
Bridge, Truss	E. J. Story	Getzville, N. Y	Feb. 12, 1861	31, 415
Bridge, Truss	A. S. Swartz	Buffalo, N. Y	Sept. 22, 1857	18, 253
Bridge, Truss-frame	F. C. Lowthorp	Trenton, N. J	Feb. 19, 1867	62, 278
Bridge-trusses, Arrangement of arches in	C. M. Pennington	Rome, Ga	Jan. 7, 1851	7, 890
Bridge-trusses, Bearing-block for	J. L. Piper	Altoona, Pa	Oct. 22, 1861	33, 542
Bridge, Tubular	E. A. Baldwin	Elmira, N. Y	Aug. 8, 1854	11, 467
Bridge, Tubular	G. H. White	New York, N. Y	Oct. 25, 1870	108, 663
Bridge, Tubular arched	W. S. Levake	Cleveland, Ohio	July 5, 1870	104, 969
Bridge, Tubular arch	T. W. H. Moseley	Boston, Mass	May 31, 1870	103, 765
Bridge, Turn	J. Ingersoll	Grafton, Ohio	June 23, 1863	38, 966
Bridge, Turn	G. R. Winkler	Williamsport, Pa	Oct. 8, 1872	132, 038
Bridge, Wire-truss	C. Bender	Hesse-Darmstadt, Germany	Mar. 31, 1868	76, 041
Bridge, Wooden	S. K. Long	United States Engineers	Jan. 23, 1836	....

Index of patents issued from the United States Patent Office from 1790 *to* 1873, *inclusive*—Continued.

Invention.	Inventor.	Residence.	Date.	No.
Bridge, Wooden	G. W. Thayer	Springfield, Mass	Apr. 22, 1845	4, 004
Bridge, Wooden-framed brace	S. H. Long	United States Army	Nov. 7, 1839	1, 398
Bridge, Wooden-framed suspension	S. H. Long	United States Army	Nov. 7, 1839	1, 397
Bridge, Wooden or frame	S. H. Long	Baltimore, Md	Mar. 6, 1830	....
Bridge, Wooden truss	J. Burke	Saginaw, Mich	July 18, 1871	117, 042
Bridge, Wooden truss	T. W. Pratt	Boston, Mass	Apr. 1, 1873	137, 482
Bridge, Wrought-iron	A. P. Boller	Orange, N. J	Apr. 2, 1872	125, 117
Bridge, Wrought-iron	G. Heath	Little Falls, N. Y	May 27, 1862	35, 374
Bridge, Wrought-iron	J. H. Linville and J. L. Piper	Pittsburgh and Altoona, Pa	Oct. 31, 1865	50, 723
Bridges, Arched truss for	H. Lanergan	Boston, Mass	Apr. 23, 1850	7, 305
Bridges, Arched truss for	P. L. Weimer	Lebanon, Pa	Aug. 29, 1871	118, 566
Bridges across rivers, &c., Apparatus for passing suspension-wires for.	J. A. Roebling	Pittsburgh, Pa	Jan. 26, 1847	4, 945
Bridges, Bearing-block for truss	A. D. Briggs	Springfield, Mass	July 27, 1858	20, 987
Bridges, Building	T. Burr	Burr Haven, Pa	Apr. 3, 1817	....
Bridges, Building	J. Snyder	Union County, Pa	Feb. 3, 1834	....
Bridges, buildings, &c., Composition for covering wooden.	J. Heckel and M. Eichinger	Decatur, Ill	Apr. 7, 1868	76, 443
Bridges, buildings, &c., Method of preventing decay in the timbers of.	A. Allen	Cass County, Mich	Aug. 23, 1870	106, 647
Bridges, Cable-shackle for	T. G. Hulett	Niagara, N. Y	Dec. 8, 1868	84, 827
Bridges, &c., Cast-iron arch for	G. F. Lape	Summit, N. Y	Dec. 4, 1866	60, 199
Bridges, Cast-iron chord-connection for	C. Kellogg	Philadelphia, Pa	Feb. 23, 1869	87, 174
Bridges, Chord for	C. S. Smith	Baltimore, Md	Aug. 17, 1869	93, 917
Bridges, Connecting iron girders of	J. T. Ham	Covington, Ky	June 21, 1859	24, 460
Bridges, Connecting together the braces of truss	L. E. Truesdell	Warren, Mass	May 17, 1859	24, 068
Bridges, Connection for iron and steel	T. C. Clarke and A. Bonzano	Philadelphia, Pa	July 18, 1871	117, 047
Bridges, Connection for iron and steel	T. C. Clarke and A. Bonzano	Philadelphia, Pa	July 18, 1871	117, 048
Bridges, Connection for iron and steel	T. C. Clarke and A. Bonzano	Philadelphia, Pa	July 18, 1871	117, 049
Bridges, Connection for iron and steel	T. C. Clarke and A. Bonzano	Philadelphia, Pa	July 18, 1871	117, 050
Bridges, Connection for iron and steel	T. C. Clarke and A. Bonzano	Philadelphia, Pa	Dec. 12, 1871	121, 848
Bridges, Constructing	A. Canfield	Paterson, N. J	June 29, 1833	....
Bridges, Constructing	T. C. Clarke	Philadelphia, Pa	July 15, 1873	140, 888
Bridges, Constructing	G. Law	Easton, Pa	June 12, 1835	....
Bridges, &c., Constructing frame of	W. McKibbin	San Francisco, Cal	Mar. 9, 1858	19, 573
Bridges, Construction of	J. P. Bakewell	Pittsburgh, Pa	May 15, 1827	....
Bridges, Construction of	W. Bollman	Baltimore, Md	Jan. 6, 1852	8, 624
Bridges, Construction of	A. Bradway and E. Valentine	Monson, Mass	July 6, 1852	9, 090
Bridges, Construction of	B. Conner	Portsmouth, N. H	Apr. 23, 1812	....
Bridges, Construction of	J. J. Dyster	Philadelphia, Pa	Feb. 23, 1810	....
Bridges, Construction of	J. B. Gridley	Brooklyn, N. Y	July 6, 1852	9, 093
Bridges, Construction of	Z. King	Cleveland, Ohio	Nov. 15, 1864	45, 051
Bridges, Construction of	A. McGuffie	Rochester, N. Y	Dec. 17, 1861	33, 954
Bridges, Construction of	S. B. B. Nowlan	New York, N. Y	Mar. 18, 1873	136, 935
Bridges, Construction of	T. Pope	New York, N. Y	Apr. 18, 1807	....
Bridges, Construction of	C. S. Smith, C. H. Latrobe, and F. H. Smith.	Baltimore, Md	Dec. 14, 1869	97, 975
Bridges, Construction of	E. Stanley	Bennington, N. Y	Sept. 2, 1851	8, 337
Bridges, Construction of	C. W. Warner	Essex, Vt	Aug. 27, 1872	130, 959
Bridges, Construction of	H. Wilton	Wrightsville, Pa	June 24, 1839	1, 192
Bridges, Construction of iron-truss	S. Whipple	Utica, N. Y	Apr. 24, 1841	2, 064
Bridges, Driving piles for	J. Stone		Mar. 10, 1791	....
Bridges, Elliptical or oval truss-frame for	J. Barnes	Springtie'd, Mass	Mar. 27, 1849	6, 230
Bridges, &c., Fastening and combining the truss-frames of.	J. Price and J. T. Phillips	Golden, Md	Feb. 23, 1841	1, 994
Bridges, Gate of swinging	L. Anderson	Chicago, Ill	Dec. 14, 1869	97, 855
Bridges, Girder and chord for iron	T. B. Mills and B. M. Smith	Iola, Kan	Nov. 12, 1872	132, 975
Bridges, Hydraulic spindle and turning-apparatus for draw.	P. L. Fox and G. P. Herthel, jr.	Saint Louis, Mo	June 26, 1866	55, 844
Bridges, Iron abutment for	J. S. Goshorn	Fort Wayne, Ind	Feb. 7, 1871	111, 636
Bridges, Iron truss-frame for	F. C. Lowthorp	Trenton, N. J	June 30, 1857	17, 684
Bridges, &c., Iron truss-frame for	F. C. Lowthorp	Trenton, N. J	Oct. 3, 1857	18, 548
Bridges, Key or packing block for	N. Chapin	Chicago, Ill	Sept. 27, 1864	44, 398
Bridges, Lock bar for	L. E. Truesdell	Chicago, Ill	May 26, 1868	78, 403
Bridges, Manner of crossing rivers, &c., by moving platforms suspended to.	H. Leach	Philadelphia, Pa	Mar. 4, 1842	2, 478
Bridges, Manufacture of tension eye-bar for	F. H. Smith	Baltimore, Md	June 18, 1872	128, 184
Bridges, Metallic abutment for	A. Wheelock	Fort Wayne, Ind	Feb. 15, 1870	99, 989
Bridges, Metallic beam and girder for	J. Gill	Cincinnati, Ohio	Apr. 27, 1869	89, 400
Bridges, Metallic column for	A. B. Ives	Bloomington, Ill	Dec. 31, 1867	72, 859
Bridges, Metallic shoe for truss	D. H. Morrison	Dayton, Ohio	Apr. 27, 1858	20, 082
Bridges, Method of attaching the arch to the truss-frame in.	I. D. Steele	Pottstown, Pa	Feb. 20, 1849	6, 126
Bridges, Method of building	A. Cottrell	Newport, R. I	Nov. 10, 1841	2, 334
Bridges, &c., Method of increasing strength of beams or rafters of.	J. R. Remington	Lowndes County, Ala	May 19, 1843	3, 095
Bridges, Method of turning	W. N. Berkeley	Cedar Rapids, Iowa	June 5, 1866	55, 230
Bridges, Method of turning	W. N. Berkeley	Cedar Rapids, Iowa	June 5, 1866	55, 231
Bridges, Mode of adjustment of truss-frames of	J. W. Murphy	Philadelphia, Pa	Apr. 30, 1861	32, 199
Bridges, Mode of constructing, setting, and removing.	J. Du Bois	Williamsport, Pa	Oct. 7, 1862	36, 606
Bridges, Plate for securing chord, brace, &c., of truss.	F. C. Lowthorp	Trenton, N. J	Mar. 13, 1860	27, 457
Bridges, &c., Segmental truss for	G. S. Avery	Lewisborough, N. Y	July 28, 1857	17, 864
Bridges, Shoe for truss	M. Lass g	Chicago, Ill	Nov. 19, 1872	133, 252
Bridges, Timber-splice for	J. J. Hooker	Owego, N. Y	Oct. 15, 1872	132, 287
Bridges, Transporting	T. and S. Champion	Washington, D. C	Nov. 22, 1853	10, 250
Bridges, &c., Truss-beam for	P. M. Frees and Z. King	Cincinnati and Milan, Ohio	Oct. 1, 1861	33, 384
Bridges, Truss-frame for	W. Howe	Warren, Mass	July 10, 1840	1, 685
Bridges, Truss-frame for	W. Howe	Warren, Mass	Aug. 3, 1840	1, 711
Bridges, Truss-frame for	E. Jacobs	Cincinnati, Ohio	Jan. 3, 1860	26, 680
Bridges, Truss-frame for	J. H. Linville	Philadelphia, Pa	Dec. 2, 1873	145, 114
Bridges, Truss-frame for	T. W. and C. Pratt	Norwich, Conn., and Boston, Mass.	Apr. 4, 1844	3, 523
Bridges, Truss-girder for	S. D. Kendall	Brooklyn, N. Y	Jan. 21, 1862	34, 209
Bridges, Truss-girder for	A. McGuffie	Rochester, N. Y	Feb. 4, 1862	34, 311
Bridges, Tubular connection for	J. W. Sprague	Roches er, N. Y	Oct. 18, 1859	25, 852
Bridges, Turn-table for pivot	A. Bonzano	Phoenixville, Pa	May 21, 1872	127, 018

Index of patents issued from the United States Patent Office from 1790 *to* 1873, *inclusive*—Continued.

Invention.	Inventor.	Residence.	Date.	No.
Bridges, Turn-table for swing	T. C. Clarke and A. Bonzano	Philadelphia and Phœnixville, Pa.	Oct. 15, 1872	132, 254
Bridges, Turn-table for swing	G. Walter	Phœnixville, Pa	Mar. 5, 1872	124, 400
Bridges with draws, Method of building wooden	G. Wilkinson	White Creek, N. Y	May 15, 1827	....
Bridges, Wrought-iron pier for	T. B. Mills	Iola, Kans	Oct. 15, 1872	132, 307
Bridging navigable streams	B. F. Lee	New York, N. Y	Mar. 2, 1852	8, 781
Bridle	G. A. Albright and W. R. Burns	Lancaster, Pa	Nov. 27, 1866	59, 937
Bridle	A. Bauerschmitt	Rochester, N. Y	July 7, 1868	79, 628
Bridle	W. R. Beans	Brownsburgh, Pa	Oct. 15, 1867	69, 893
Bridle	M. H. Buchanan	Washington County, Va	Feb. 15, 1870	99, 834
Bridle	W. F. Clark	Hagaman's Mills, N. Y	Nov. 17, 1868	84, 170
Bridle	M. Haberbush and E. Kreckel	Lancaster, Pa	Nov. 27, 1866	59, 996
Bridle	J. C. Haines	Lewistown, Pa	July 10, 1866	56, 213
Bridle	J. Harris	Kansas, Ill	Apr. 16, 1867	63, 886
Bridle	S. B. Hartman	Millersville, Pa	June 28, 1864	43, 308
Bridle	S. B. Hartman	Millersville, Pa	Nov. 7, 1865	50, 822
Bridle	S. B. Hartman	Millersville, Pa	Nov. 13, 1866	59, 596
Bridle	P. Laporte	Richmond, Va	Aug. 15, 1822	....
Bridle	A. H. Langholz	Chicago, Ill	Feb. 3, 1863	37, 583
Bridle	J. F. Mason	Benton's Port, Iowa	May 28, 1867	65, 101
Bridle	J. McKibben	Lima, Ohio	Dec. 8, 1868	84, 838
Bridle	R. B. Norvell	Huntsville, Ala	May 10, 1859	23, 939
Bridle	J. A. Putt	Marlborough, Ohio	Nov. 26, 1867	71, 324
Bridle	A. H. Rockwell	Harpersville, N. Y	Dec. 4, 1866	60, 254
Bridle	E. R. Terry	New Haven, Conn	June 30, 1868	79, 334
Bridle	H. Seitz	Marietta, Pa	Sept. 26, 1848	5, 804
Bridle	R. Smether	Orange County, Va	Dec. 10, 1812	....
Bridle	J. H. Wilson	Brentwood, Tenn	Dec. 10, 1872	133, 817
Bridle and bit connection	C. B. Hogg	Boston, Mass	Mar. 8, 1864	41, 845
Bridle and bit, Horse	F. L. Haskell	Leominster, Mass	Sept. 3, 1872	130, 994
Bridle and halter, Combined	J. McKibben	Lima, Ohio	Mar. 5, 1867	62, 662
Bridle-attachment, Safety	R. Finck	Lancaster, Pa	Dec. 31, 1867	72, 720
Bridle-bit	S. D. Arnold	New Britain, Conn	Aug. 7, 1866	56, 872
Bridle-bit	J. B. Baker	Syracuse, N. Y	June 7, 1859	24, 275
Bridle-bit	D. S. Balch	Bradford, Vt	Aug. 23, 1839	1, 299
Bridle-bit	A. P. Baldwin	Newark, N. J	Dec. 1, 1868	84, 469
Bridle-bit	G. W. Barnes	Mount Vernon, N. Y	Mar. 19, 1872	124, 789
Bridle-bit	S. C. Boughton	Waterford, N. Y	Sept. 12, 1871	118, 900
Bridle-bit	J. Burns	East Topham, Vt	July 2, 1872	128, 532
Bridle-bit	D. H. Carpenter	Hartford, Conn	June 17, 1873	140, 010
Bridle-bit	H. Crane	New York, N. Y	June 5, 1860	28, 563
Bridle-bit	J. M. Crawford	Philadelphia, Pa	July 2, 1867	66, 221
Bridle-bit	O. Crook	Dayton, Ohio	Aug. 6, 1867	67, 509
Bridle-bit	B. I. Day	Gibson County, Ind	May 13, 1856	14, 856
Bridle-bit	E. Day	West Springfield, Mass	Nov. 28, 1865	51, 151
Bridle-bit	G. W. Eddy	Waterford, N. Y	Oct. 15, 1872	132, 149
Bridle-bit	A. B. Ely	Newton, Mass	Mar. 23, 1869	88, 021
Bridle-bit	J. M. Fabré	Bordeaux, France	June 17, 1873	140, 023
Bridle-bit	M. J. Firey	Mansfield, Ohio	June 14, 1870	104, 133
Bridle-bit	M. J. Firey	Mansfield, Ohio	June 14, 1870	104, 134
Bridle-bit	W. S. Ford	Clinton, Ill	May 12, 1868	77, 810
Bridle-bit	M. Foreacre	New Harrisburgh, Ohio	Aug. 2, 1870	106, 044
Bridle-bit	F. N. Frost	New Britain, Conn	Aug. 7, 1866	56, 923
Bridle-bit	J. P. Gates	Lincoln, Ill	Oct. 15, 1867	69, 910
Bridle-bit	A. Gilliam	Pittsburgh, Pa	July 11, 1871	116, 945
Bridle-bit	C. L. Ginkinger	Sterling, Ill	Apr. 15, 1873	137, 913
Bridle-bit	W. B. Hayden	Columbus, Ohio	Mar. 26, 1867	63, 156
Bridle-bit	N. Hayward	Roanoke, Ind	Jan. 2, 1872	122, 383
Bridle-bit	C. M. Huckins	East Topsham, Vt	Oct. 12, 1869	95, 801
Bridle-bit	W. F. and W. R. Johnson	Wetumpka, Ala	July 24, 1860	29, 284
Bridle-bit	F. B. Kalkbrenner	Clinton, Mo	Nov. 1, 1870	108, 795
Bridle-bit	S. M. King	Lancaster, Ohio	July 31, 1866	56, 762
Bridle-bit	A. H. Langholz	Chicago, Ill	Aug. 30, 1864	44, 002
Bridle-bit	J. Letchworth	Buffalo, N. Y	June 1, 1869	90, 857
Bridle-bit	J. Letchworth	Buffalo, N. Y	Jan. 7, 1873	134, 684
Bridle-bit	W. P. Letchworth	Buffalo, N. Y	May 10, 1870	102, 838
Bridle-bit	J. Lowbridge	Pittsburgh, Pa	Sept. 24, 1872	131, 691
Bridle-bit	A. P. Mason	Gowanda, N. Y	June 15, 1869	91, 463
Bridle-bit	P. S. McGuiness	New York, N. Y	June 2, 1868	78, 466
Bridle-bit	C. H. Miller	Buffalo, N. Y	Aug. 25, 1868	81, 395
Bridle-bit	J. H. Minnich	Tuscarawas, Ohio	Mar. 16, 1869	87, 864
Bridle-bit	A. Niel	Brooklyn, N. Y	Jan. 11, 1859	22, 571
Bridle-bit	D. M. Nixon	Danville, Ill	Feb. 23, 1869	87, 281
Bridle-bit	J. K. Norton	Flushing, Ohio	Feb. 4, 1868	74, 122
Bridle-bit	J. H. J. O'Neill	New Haven, Conn	July 7, 1863	39, 165
Bridle-bit	H. Pierce	Sharon, Conn	Mar. 15, 1834	....
Bridle-bit	E. N. Price	Salem, Mass	June 13, 1854	11, 083
Bridle-bit	J. C. Price	New Philadelphia, Ohio	Mar. 26, 1867	63, 297
Bridle-bit	W. S. Robbins	New Bedford, Mass	Dec. 8, 1868	84, 843
Bridle-bit	J. M. Roberds	Washington, D. C	Feb. 26, 1861	31, 557
Bridle-bit	A. H. Rockwell	Harpersville, N. Y	Nov. 12, 1867	70, 745
Bridle-bit	H. T. Romertze	Philadelphia, Pa	May 12, 1863	38, 541
Bridle-bit	B. L. Rowley	New Britain, Conn	Mar. 11, 1873	136, 767
Bridle-bit	P. Schoonmaker	New Britain, Conn	July 28, 1868	80, 510
Bridle-bit	J. Spoonhour and S. R. Boyd	Green Township and Chambersburgh, Pa.	Dec. 3, 1867	71, 806
Bridle-bit	C. E. Stockder	West Meriden, Conn	Sept. 8, 1863	39, 843
Bridle-bit	J. A. Swan	North Anson, Me	May 17, 1870	103, 103
Bridle-bit	H. C. Thompson	Mount Sterling, Ky	June 28, 1870	104, 793
Bridle-bit	W. D. Titus and R. W. Fenwick	Brooklyn, N. Y	Feb. 13, 1855	12, 397
Bridle-bit	A. Vanauken	Ludlowville, N. Y	Nov. 14, 1871	120, 913
Bridle-bit	Vicenzo, Count de Tergolina	London, England	July 29, 1873	141, 334
Bridle-bit	A. Viridet	Glasgow, Ky	May 25, 1869	90, 612
Bridle-bit	G. Webb	Lewiston, Me	Jan. 28, 1868	73, 853
Bridle-bit	A. S. Weymouth	Boston, Mass	July 30, 1861	32, 933
Bridle-bit	B. F. Wheeler	Calais, Vt	July 12, 1870	105, 282
Bridle-bit	R. P. Whelan	Leavenworth, Kans	Dec. 31, 1867	72, 950

Index of patents issued from the United States Patent Office from 1790 *to* 1873, *inclusive*—Continued.

Invention.	Inventor.	Residence.	Date.	No.
Bridle-bit	W. F. M. Williams	Augusta, Ga	Jan. 10, 1860	26, 804
Bridle-bit	L. D. Woodmansee	Mad River Township, Ohio	Jan. 1, 1867	60, 980
Bridle-bit attachment	C. M. Alexander	Washington, D. C	Feb. 11, 1862	34, 343
Bridle-bit attachment	J. D. Tracy	Springfield, Mass	Oct. 23, 1860	30, 510
Bridle-bit, Check-piece for	W. P. Wolfington	Louisville, Ky	Feb. 27, 1872	124, 187
Bridle-bit, Combination-lever	H. M. Cornell	Brighton, Ill	Nov. 14, 1871	120, 860
Bridle-bit, Flexible	B. L. Rowley	New Brighton, Conn	Apr. 14, 1868	76, 821
Bridle-bit, Method of connecting the check-piece to the mouth-piece of.	K. Frazer	Syracuse, N. Y	May 12, 1857	17, 268
Bridle-bit mouth-piece	A. P. Baldwin	Newark, N. J	Nov. 23, 1869	97, 022
Bridle-bit, Safety	S. S. Petersheim	Upper Leacock Township, Pa.	Apr. 30, 1872	126, 231
Bridle-bit slide-bar	A. P. Mason	Franklinville, N. Y	June 6, 1871	115, 753
Bridle-blind	J. Patterson, jr	Bangor, Me	Dec. 2, 1873	145, 233
Bridle blind, Harness	J. L. Brown	Connellsville, Pa	Oct. 18, 1870	108, 440
Bridle blind, Horse	J. B. Low	Homerville, Ohio	Dec. 5, 1871	121, 528
Bridle blind, Horse	J. G. Tibbets	New York, N. Y	Oct. 9, 1841	2, 285
Bridle-blind, Operating	A. Simis	Brooklyn, N. Y	Dec. 29, 1868	85, 406
Bridle, Breaking and training	W. O. Bartlett	New York, N. Y	June 5, 1866	55, 226
Bridle brow-band	F. Meinberg	New York, N. Y	Dec. 24, 1872	134, 213
Bridle check and brace	W. F. Pendleton	King and Queen County, Va	Feb. 20, 1833	....
Bridle, Driving	A. Rice and L. Leach	Fresno, Cal	Jan. 7, 1868	73, 042
Bridle for preventing horses from kicking	D. V. Grace and J. S. Elliott	Coshocton, Ohio	Feb. 9, 1869	86, 662
Bridle-front	W. T. Mersereau	Orange, N. Y	Aug. 6, 1872	130, 144
Bridle-front, Machine for forming	I. Manning	Philadelphia, Pa	Dec. 18, 1866	60, 531
Bridle, Gag-runner connection for	J. C. Covert	Farmer Village, N. Y	Dec. 10, 1872	133, 834
Bridle-halter	G. W. Griswold	Logansport, Ind	July 22, 1862	35, 932
Bridle, Harness	G. Horter	New Orleans, La	July 5, 1870	105, 081
Bridle, Horse	J. Muller	Philadelphia, Pa	Dec. 23, 1873	145, 892
Bridle, Horse	M. A. Penn	Sumter, S. C	Apr. 30, 1872	126, 326
Bridle, Horse	J. C. Smith	Brookhaven, N. Y	Mar. 23, 1842	2, 510
Bridle, Nerving	J. V. Reardon	Elkton, Md	Mar. 23, 1869	88, 210
Bridle pulley-bit	W. Brower	Baltimore, Md	July 23, 1867	66, 941
Bridle-rein spring-snap	M. X. Tschus	Bloomington, Ill	July 5, 1859	24, 677
Bridle, Riding	J. C. Smith	Brookhaven, N. Y	Sept. 17, 1842	2, 780
Bridle-rosette	W. F. Niles	Leominster, Mass	Oct. 29, 1867	70, 251
Bridle-rosette	J. O'Brien	Geneseo, Ill	May 3, 1870	102, 579
Bridle-rosette	J. O'Brien	Cedar Rapids, Iowa	Oct. 25, 1870	108, 725
Bridle, Safety	G. W. Barnes	Mount Vernon, N. Y	Aug. 11, 1868	80, 897
Bridle, Safety	A. B. Christ and H. H. Stehman	Manor Township, Pa	Jan. 23, 1866	52, 139
Bridle, Safety	D. M. Donehoo	Beaver, Pa	Jan. 29, 1867	61, 522
Bridle, Safety	D. M. Donehoo	Beaver, Pa	July 2, 1867	66, 312
Bridle, Safety	B. R. Du Val	Portsmouth, Va	Aug. 27, 1872	130, 794
Bridle, Safety	J. M. Elder and P. A. Bishop	Elyria, Ohio	May 13, 1873	138, 872
Bridle, Safety	E. R. Ferry	New Haven, Conn	Oct. 13, 1868	83, 055
Bridle, Safety	F. A. Hannaford	New York, N. Y	Oct. 22, 1867	70, 089
Bridle, Safety	S. B. Hartman	Millersville, Pa	May 28, 1867	65, 216
Bridle, Safety	E. W. Lindeman	Manor Township, Pa	Sept. 24, 1867	69, 106
Bridle, Safety	J. McKillop	Brooklyn, N. Y	June 2, 1868	78, 533
Bridle, Safety	J. Weatherhead	San José, Cal	Mar. 7, 1871	112, 398
Bridle, Safety	S. V. R. York	Antwerp, N. Y	Dec. 22, 1868	85, 158
Bridle safety-strap	H. H. Rockwell	New London, Conn	Dec. 3, 1867	71, 648
Bridle to prevent horses from kicking or running away.	J. M. Lanier	Eufaula, Ala	Oct. 26, 1858	21, 889
Bridle-winker	W. and W. F. Boyd	Watertown, Mass	June 26, 1855	13, 119
Bridle winker, Harness	W. Boyd	Mansfield, Mass	July 19, 1870	105, 544
Bridle-winker, Metallic	M. O. Stanley	South Danvers, Mass	Sept. 6, 1864	44, 121
Bridle winkers, Manufacture of harness	E. Ward	Newark, N. J	May 24, 1870	103, 530
Bridles, Machine for punching, splitting, and creasing.	J. B Gathright	Louisville, Ky	Dec. 9, 1873	145, 292
Bridles, Manufacture of	D. A. Read	New York, N. Y	Oct. 24, 1826	....
Bridles, Metallic check-piece for	J. C. Baxter	Washington, D. C	Oct. 29, 1867	70, 315
Brine and other liquid evaporator	L. R. Cornell	Syracuse, N. Y	July 18, 1871	117, 052
Brine and other liquid evaporator	S. Platt	Goderich, Canada	Feb. 2, 1869	86, 443
Brine and other liquids, Process and apparatus for purifying.	G. Clark	Buffalo, N. Y	June 6, 1871	115, 573
Brine and salted meat to remove the salt, Treating	A. Whitelaw	Glasgow, Scotland	May 31, 1864	42, 988
Brine-evaporator	C. W. Atkeson	Henderson, Ky	June 16, 1857	17, 548
Brine-evaporator	D. Brigham	New York, N. Y	Apr. 27, 1858	20, 034
Brine-evaporator	J. Buchanan	Detroit, Mich	Dec. 6, 1870	109, 802
Brine-evaporator	S. D. Gilson	Syracuse, N. Y	Sept. 19, 1871	119, 136
Brine-evaporator	M. P. Hayes	Seaforth, Canada	Sept. 5, 1871	118, 718
Brine-evaporator	J. Heim	New York, N. Y	Mar. 8, 1870	100, 528
Brine-evaporator	R. G. Leckie	Acton Vale, Canada	Jan. 30, 1872	123, 182
Brine-evaporator	R. G. Leckie	Montreal, Canada	Jan. 30, 1872	123, 181
B ine-evaporator	J. McGrew	Ravenswood, W. Va	Nov. 19, 1872	133, 239
Brine, &c., evaporator and concentrator	R. G. Leckie	Acton Vale, Canada	May 16, 1871	114, 831
Brine evaporator, Salt	C. E. Tripler	Philadelphia, Pa	Sept. 24, 1872	131, 721
Bristle-assorting machinery	N. H. Spafford	Providence, R. I	Mar. 17, 1863	37, 927
Bristle-bundling machine	N. H. Spafford	Baltimore, Md	Apr. 17, 1866	54, 033
Bristle cleaning and assorting machine	G. E. Burt	Westford, Mass	Feb. 7, 1854	10, 498
Bristle-cleaning apparatus	H. W. Mosher and J. A. Conboie	New York, N. Y	Mar. 29, 1859	23, 385
Bristle-combing machine	L. F. Lannay and W. F. Parks	Indianapolis, Ind., and Baltimore, Md.	May 8, 1866	54, 564
Bristle-combing machine	N. H. Spafford	Baltimore, Md	Apr. 17, 1866	54, 034
Bristle-separator	A. Randel	New York, N. Y	Aug. 19, 1856	15, 573
Bristle washing and combing machine combined	L. F. Lannay and W. F. Parks.	Indianapolis, Ind., and Baltimore, Md.	Dec. 1, 1868	84, 561
Bristles, felt, fur, wool, &c., Cutter and trimmer for	S. F. Harlow	Boston, Mass	June 30, 1868	79, 468
Bristles, Machine for assorting	N. H. Spafford	Baltimore, Md	Oct. 30, 1866	59, 286
Bristles, Machine for combing and assorting	N. H. Spafford	Baltimore, Md	Jan. 22, 1867	61, 480
Bristles, Machine for separating	N. H. Spafford	Baltimore, Md	Feb. 20, 1866	52, 763
Bristles, &c., Machine for washing	L. F. Lannay	Indianapolis, Ind	May 19, 1868	78, 102
Broaching-machine	A. P. Stephens	Brooklyn, N. Y	July 22, 1873	141, 091
Brogan	C. E. Tyler	Georgetown, Mass	Apr. 9, 1872	125, 505
Broiler	S. Bowers	Penn Yan, N. Y	July 21, 1868	80, 125
Broiler	W. F. Browne	New York, N. Y	June 29, 1869	92, 008
Broiler	G. Chilson	Boston, Mass	May 27, 1862	35, 361

Index of patents issued from the United States Patent Office from 1790 *to* 1873, *inclusive*—Continued.

Invention.	Inventor.	Residence.	Date.	No.
Broiler	L. H. Colborne and D. H. Lowe	New York, N. Y	Feb. 7, 1871	111, 516
Broiler	D. W. Denman and W. K. Tillotson.	Detroit, Mich	Mar. 29, 1870	101, 236
Broiler	A. Dick	Buffalo, N. Y	Nov. 1, 1870	108, 768
Broiler	J. M. Dick	Buffalo, N. Y	Mar. 24, 1863	38, 018
Broiler	B. G. Fitzhugh	Frederick, Md	Oct. 17, 1871	119, 974
Broiler	A. G. Gibson	Cincinnati, Ohio	Mar. 17, 1868	75, 673
Broiler	A. L. H. Graham	Chester, Pa	Mar. 29, 1870	101, 361
Broiler	J. Grossius and D. J. Mullaney.	Cincinnati, Ohio	Sept. 3, 1872	131, 057
Broiler	W. T. Howard	Baltimore, Md	Apr. 18, 1871	113, 886
Broiler	A. C. Hull	Saint Louis, Mo	Mar. 1, 1870	100, 410
Broiler	M. T. Hynes	Boston, Mass	Jan. 3, 1871	110, 763
Broiler	H. H. Johnson	New Haven, Conn	Aug. 6, 1867	67, 435
Broiler	W. J. Johnson and H. A. Hildreth.	Newton and Lowell, Mass	Oct. 19, 1869	96, 909
Broiler	G. H. Link and C. D. Curtis	Syracuse, N. Y	Nov. 16, 1869	96, 930
Broiler	J. Mallory	Penn Yan, N. Y	Nov. 3, 1868	83, 649
Broiler	B. Marshall	Marietta, Ohio	June 21, 1870	104, 611
Broiler	B. and S. N. Marshall	Marietta, Ohio	Oct. 15, 1872	132, 167
Broiler	J. C. Nobles	Ilion, N. Y	Nov. 7, 1871	120, 768
Broiler	J. T. Page	Rochester, N. Y	Aug. 9, 1870	106, 280
Broiler	J. T. Page	Rochester, N. Y	July 16, 1872	129, 362
Broiler	E. B. Phelps and J. P. McLean.	Brookyln, N. Y	Mar. 21, 1871	112, 846
Broiler	D. E. Roe	Elmira, N. Y	June 13, 1871	115, 984
Broiler	D. E. Roe	Elmira, N. Y	Aug. 9, 1870	106, 210
Broiler	G. S. Saxton	Saint Louis, Mo	Nov. 16, 1869	96, 973
Broiler	O. J. Smith	Wauwatosa, Wis	Oct. 10, 1871	119, 892
Broiler	O. J. Smith	Wauwatosa, Wis	Oct. 1, 1872	131, 910
Broiler	R. P. Smith	New York, N. Y	Mar. 5, 1872	124, 296
Broiler	W. S. Stiver and J. S. Williams.	Brooklyn, N. Y	June 7, 1870	104, 075
Broiler	C. Walsh	Newark, N. J	Dec. 12, 1871	121, 917
Broiler	J. Willging	Bubuque, Iowa	Dec. 31, 1872	134, 410
Broiler and furnace, Combined	J. S. Runyan	Columbus, Ohio	Aug. 9, 1870	106, 288
Broiler and toaster	W. F. Collier and J. H. Bigelow	Worcester, Mass	Mar. 24, 1868	76, 032
Broiler and toaster	T. C. Law	Green Island, N. Y	Nov. 21, 1865	51, 064
Broiler and toaster	J. M. Read and J. M. Smith	Boston, Mass	Dec. 27, 1870	110, 589
Broiler and toaster	M. H. Wiley	Boston, Mass	Mar. 5, 1872	124, 306
Broiler and toaster, Wire	H. A. Hildreth and W. J. Johnson.	Lowell and Newton, Mass.	Apr. 18, 1865	47, 302
Broiler and toaster, Wire	C. L. Prouty	Worcester, Mass	June 22, 1869	91, 664
Broiler, Meat	L. Holms	Keene, N. H	Mar. 24, 1868	75, 914
Broiler, Meat	G. T. Teel	Hoboken, N. J	Aug. 30, 1864	44, 026
Broiler, Meat	H. Willard	Grand Rapids, Mich	Apr. 26, 1870	102, 348
Broiler, Reversible	S. Smith	Brooklyn, N. Y	May 7, 1872	126, 585
Broiler, Steak	D. C. Teller	Terre Haute, Ind	July 16, 1867	66, 911
Broiler, Steak	G. W. Walker	Boston, Mass	Feb. 4, 1862	34, 339
Broiling-apparatus	M. E. A. W. Evard	Leesburgh, Va	Apr. 7, 1868	76, 314
Broiling-apparatus	O. F. Morrill	Boston, Mass	Dec. 6, 1859	26, 368
Broiling-furnace and cooking-range, Combined	W. Resor	Cincinnati, Ohio	Aug. 3, 1858	21, 085
Broiling, toasting, &c., Apparatus for	H. W. Harkness and W. A. Terry.	Bristol, Conn	Aug. 24, 1858	21, 297
Bromine and iodine, Apparatus for the manufacture of.	D Alter	Freeport, Pa	Feb. 26, 1867	62, 464
Bromine. Apparatus for making	H. Lerner	Pomeroy, Ohio	July 27, 1869	93, 099
Bromine, Apparatus for the manufacture of	H. Lerner and E. C. Harpold	Mason City and Hartford City, W. Va.	Oct. 15, 1872	132, 296
Bromine, Apparatus for the manufacture of	D. C. Turner	Clifton, W. Va	Apr. 1, 1873	137, 512
Bromine, Apparatus for the production of	H. Stieren and W. A. Nisbet	Mason, W. Va., and Natrona, Pa.	May 17, 1870	103, 253
Bromine from bittern, &c., Apparatus for producing	G. Leyer and J. A. Winter	Pomeroy, Ohio	Mar. 25, 1873	137, 222
Bromine from bittern, Manufacture of	G. A. Hagemann	Natrona, Pa	Sept. 22, 1868	82, 309
Bromine, Manufacture of	D. Alter and E. Gillespie	Freeport, Pa	July 5, 1848	5, 658
Bromine, Manufacture of	J. J. Jühler	Natrona, Pa	Jan. 3, 1871	110, 662
Brooch, ear-ring, &c	H. Oliver	Philadelphia, Pa	Feb. 22, 1859	23, 042
Brooch-fastening	W. Sackermann	New York, N. Y	Oct. 18, 1870	108, 520
Bronze and other matters, Process of removing earthy matters from.	M. Smith	Somerville, Mass	Dec. 13, 1870	110, 081
Bronze or metallic powder, Surfacing fabrics with	J. B. Batchelder	Boston, Mass	Apr. 27, 1869	89, 274
Bronze-powder manufacture	L. Brandeis	Brooklyn, N. Y	Apr. 3, 1866	53, 563
Bronze-powder, Process of making	L. Brandeis	New York, N. Y	Sept. 16, 1851	8, 365
Bronzing and gilding	J. L. Duffee	Washington, D. C	Apr. 19, 1870	102, 198
Bronzing columns, pillars, monuments, &c	L. Brandeis	Brooklyn, N. Y	July 16, 1872	129, 207
Bronzing-compound	A. Towne	Philadelphia, Pa	Nov. 12, 1872	132, 993
Bronzing-liquid	H. Hoffman	New York, N. Y	Oct. 6, 1857	18, 338
Bronzing-machine	G. H. Babcock	Westerly, R. I	Oct. 25, 1859	25, 874
Bronzing-machine	E. F. Benton	Buffalo, N. Y	July 11, 1871	116, 918
Bronzing-machine	E. F. Benton	Buffalo, N. Y	Oct. 3, 1871	119, 498
Bronzing-machine	E. F. Benton	Buffalo, N. Y	Dec. 26, 1871	122, 216
Bronzing-machine	L. G. Chaput	New York, N. Y	Aug. 13, 1872	130, 475
Bronzing-machine	L. G. Chaput and W. and J. Braidwood.	New York, N. Y	Nov. 18, 1873	144, 741
Bronzing-machine	S. Crump	Brooklyn, N. Y	Aug. 23, 1870	106, 667
Bronzing-machine	J. K. Lowe	Cleveland, Ohio	Aug. 28, 1866	57, 527
Bronzing-machine	J. K. Lowe	Cleveland, Ohio	Feb. 12, 1867	61, 044
Bronzing-machine	G. L. Mayes	Buffalo, N. Y	Jan. 29, 1867	61, 550
Bronzing machine	J. H. Nevins	Williamsburgh, N. Y	Oct. 3, 1871	119, 637
Bronzing-machine	I. L. G. Rice	Cambridge, Mass	Feb. 21, 1871	111, 973
Bronzing-machine	C. Shoop	Buffalo, N. Y	Apr. 23, 1872	126, 097
Bronzing-machine	H. Skidmore	Mount Vernon, N. Y	Feb. 9, 1869	86, 875
Bronzing-machine	J. F. Tapley	Springfield, Mass	Dec. 22, 1863	41, 029
Bronzing-machine	J. F. Tapley	Springfield, Mass	Nov. 19, 1867	71, 085
Bronzing-machine, Bronze-collecting attachment to	S. Crump	New York, N. Y	Apr. 12, 1870	101, 830
Bronzing or coloring iron, Process of	H. Tucker	Newton, Mass	Dec. 15, 1863	40, 964
Bronzing-pad	L. G. Chaput	New York, N. Y	Oct. 21, 1873	143, 880
Bronzing printed work	B. G. George	London, England	May 25, 1869	90, 521
Bronzing wall-paper, Machine for	W. G. Mackay	New York, N. Y	June 25, 1861	32, 667
Broom	E. A. Anderson	Danville, Tex	Aug. 15, 1871	117, 959
Broom, &c	J. H. Anderson	Terre Haute, Ind	Aug. 2, 1870	106, 021

Index of patents issued from the United States Patent Office from 1790 to 1873, inclusive—Continued.

Invention.	Inventor.	Residence.	Date.	No.
Broom	J. and G. Bacon	Medina, Wis	Nov. 28, 1865	51, 127
Broom	N. E. Badgley	New York, N. Y	Jan. 28, 1868	73, 769
Broom	W. N. Bates	Cedar Rapids, Iowa	Sept. 15, 1863	39, 874
Broom	J. D. Bell	Wattsborough, Va	June 24, 1873	140, 180
Broom	S. Bennett	Hartford, Conn	Jan. 2, 1866	51, 791
Broom	J. D. Blood	Amsterdam, N. Y	July 16, 1872	129, 089
Broom	C. Boeckh	Toronto, Canada	Mar. 11, 1873	136, 694
Broom	T. E. C. Brinley	Louisville, Ky	Apr. 18, 1871	113, 845
Broom	E. D. Bronson and M. W. Dillingham.	Amsterdam, N. Y	July 30, 1872	129, 926
Broom	J. Buercky	Overpeck's Station, Ohio	Apr. 14, 1868	76, 710
Broom	M. Burnett	Boston, Mass	June 29, 1869	91, 907
Broom	S. Carpenter	Cedar Rapids, Iowa	Mar. 22, 1864	41, 973
Broom	J. M. Clark	Dayton, Ohio	May 23, 1865	47, 799
Broom	E. P. Cooley	New York, N. Y	July 31, 1866	56, 717
Broom	R. E. Copson	Hamburgh, Iowa	Aug. 15, 1871	117, 986
Broom	E. M. Crandal	Marshalltown, Iowa	June 28, 1870	104, 834
Broom	E. M. Crandal	Chicago, Ill	Oct. 1, 1872	131, 854
Broom	R. F. Dobson	Darlington, Wis	Feb. 27, 1872	124, 040
Broom	R. F. Dobson	Goderich, Canada	Aug. 4, 1868	80, 613
Broom	R. W. English	Buffalo, N. Y	July 2, 1872	128, 609
Broom	T. R. Evans	Blacksburgh, Va	Dec. 5, 1871	121, 501
Broom	D. P. Farnham	Rock County, Wis	Apr. 24, 1866	54, 249
Broom	W. S. Hancock	Chicago, Ill	May 10, 1870	102, 936
Broom	A. C. Hoag	Clinton, Ill	Apr. 22, 1862	35, 023
Broom	H. C. Ingersoll	Bangor, Me	July 1, 1862	35, 759
Broom	D. Kaufman	Boiling Spring, Pa	Feb. 19, 1861	31, 463
Broom	O. W. Kellogg	Ripon, Wis	Mar. 7, 1865	46, 678
Broom	T. Langdon and H. C. Kellogg	Quasqueton, Iowa	May 14, 1861	32, 299
Broom	T. Langdon and C. Weitman	Hazleton, Iowa	July 17, 1860	29, 179
Broom	H. Lumbard	Chicago, Ill	Jan. 7, 1868	73, 107
Broom	W. A. Middleton	Harrisburgh, Pa	July 18, 1871	117, 192
Broom	C. T. Moore	Concord, N. H	July 27, 1852	9, 160
Broom	H. E. Newton	Manchester, N. H	Jan. 22, 1867	61, 446
Broom	D. J. Owen	Springville Lynn, Pa	May 31, 1859	24, 231
Broom	J. H. Parsons	Jonesville, Mich	Apr. 26, 1870	102, 310
Broom	F. Reese	Calera, Ala	Apr. 8, 1873	137, 721
Broom	C. L. Reid	Louisville, Ky	Mar. 21, 1871	112, 960
Broom	S. M. Sherman	Fort Dodge, Iowa	Aug. 6, 1861	33, 010
Broom	A. Sinclair	West Waterville, Me	July 13, 1869	92, 483
Broom	W. C. Spellman	Hartford, Conn	Mar. 1, 1870	100, 336
Broom	W. C. Spellman	Hartford, Conn	Nov. 7, 1871	120, 791
Broom	G. Stackpole	Elizabeth, N. J	Apr. 5, 1870	101, 675
Broom	S. Standish	Eureka, Nev	Feb. 25, 1873	136, 273
Broom	W. H. Towers	New York, N. Y	Sept. 4, 1860	29, 926
Broom	W. H. Towers	New York, N. Y	Nov. 5, 1861	33, 686
Broom	T. Walter	Philadelphia, Pa	Mar. 1, 1870	100, 343
Broom	C. Weitman	Independence, Iowa	May 14, 1861	32, 322
Broom	W. E. S. Whitmore	Augusta, Me	June 20, 1871	116, 126
Broom	A. Willis	Chicago, Ill	Aug. 8, 1871	117, 844
Broom	J. Wisner	Aurora, N. Y	June 5, 1866	55, 409
Broom	T. Wright	New York, N. Y	Nov. 13, 1866	59, 733
Broom	D. Young	Burlington, Ill	Nov. 28, 1865	51, 253
Broom and brush	R. Kinsley	Cabotville, Mass	May 17, 1836	......
Broom and brush	T. H. Powers	Wyocena, Wis	May 13, 1856	14, 883
Broom and brush handle fastening	E. F. Dunaway	Cincinnati, Ohio	May 23, 1871	115, 040
Broom and brush handle holder	F. S. Pinkham	Boston, Mass	Jan. 19, 1869	85, 956
Broom and brush head	G. T. Reed	Philadelphia, Pa	Aug. 21, 1866	57, 378
Broom and brush head	G. T. Reed	Philadelphia, Pa	Mar. 5, 1867	62, 686
Broom and brush holder	G. B. Cunningham	Northampton, Mass	June 11, 1872	127, 743
Broom and brush holder	B. D. Wallace	Boston, Mass	Nov. 2, 1869	96, 516
Broom and brush holding clamp	A. B. Thompson	Owego, N. Y	Mar. 22, 1870	101, 062
Broom and brush, Tying	J. H. Anderson	Terre Haute, Ind	Mar. 21, 1871	113, 069
Broom and mop head	E. J. Green	Valparaiso, Ind	Oct. 10, 1865	50, 352
Broom and mop holder	H. L. Franklin and E. Clark	Nashua, N. H	Jan. 11, 1870	98, 756
Broom and mop holder	G. B. Isham	Burlington, Vt	Nov. 14, 1871	120, 818
Broom and scraper	D. Elliot	New York, N. Y	Sept. 14, 1869	94, 728
Broom and whisk	E. P. Cooley	New York, N. Y	June 14, 1870	104, 118
Broom-bag	E. D. Bronson	Amsterdam, N. Y	Feb. 18, 1873	136, 026
Broom-band	F. G. Harding	Boston, Mass	Sept. 10, 1872	131, 270
Broom-brace	F. O. Willey	Wilmette, Ill	Feb. 22, 1870	100, 238
Broom-bridle	J. F. Blondel	Thomaston, Me	Dec. 31, 1872	134, 459
Broom-bridle	J. H. Subers and J. H. Troup	Philadelphia, Pa	Oct. 17, 1871	120, 122
Broom-clamp	W. L. Babcock	Erie, Pa	June 25, 1872	128, 204
Broom-clamp	T. F. Boyer	Harrisburgh, Pa	Apr. 10, 1866	53, 776
Broom-clamp	J. Day	Murray, N. Y	Nov. 27, 1866	59, 977
Broom-clamp	J. Day	Holley, N. Y	Oct. 15, 1867	69, 780
Broom-clamp	A. L. Harwood	Malone, N. Y	May 22, 1866	54, 897
Broom-clamp	H. B. Lyon and G. M. Hopkins	Albion, N. Y	Mar. 5, 1867	62, 548
Broom-clamp	S. Mason	Indian Springs, Md	Mar. 24, 1857	16, 877
Broom-clamp	W. D. Merick	Rochester, N. Y	Apr. 9, 1872	125, 603
Broom-clasp	N. Homes	Laona, N. Y	May 14, 1861	32, 292
Broom-clasp	P. H. Miles	Boston, Mass	June 5, 1866	55, 345
Broom-clasp	S. Parr	Boston, Mass	Dec. 19, 1865	51, 614
Broom-clasp	P. B. Sheldon	Prattsburgh, N. Y	June 28, 1859	24, 582
Broom-clasp	H. Tilden	Boston, Mass	June 5, 1866	55, 394
Broom, Corn	C. L. W. Baker	Hartford, Conn	June 11, 1861	32, 504
Broom-corn and sorghum stripper	K. W. Doudna	Millwood Township, Ohio	Mar. 13, 1866	53, 126
Broom corn-breaking machine	C. Campbell	Yellow Head, Ill	May 13, 1862	35, 214
Broom-corn cutting and assorting machine	M. D. Bradley	Ballston Spa, N. Y	July 28, 1868	80, 443
Broom-corn duster	J. L. Stranahan	Chicago, Ill	Apr. 15, 1873	137, 805
Broom-corn, Machine for assorting	L. D. Grosvenor	Harvard, Mass	Jan. 1, 1851	7, 872
Broom-corn, Machine for combing seed off	G. E. Burt	Harvard, Mass	Apr. 8, 1856	14, 593
Broom-corn, Machine for cutting and separating	A. Walrath and J. Snell	Fort Plain, N. Y	Sept. 3, 1872	131, 108
Broom-corn, Machine for removing the seed from	J. D. Brown	Preble County, Ohio	Sept. 3, 1867	68, 346
Broom-corn, Machine for sizing	O. M. Truair	Mount Morris, N. Y	Dec. 17, 1861	33, 968
Broom-corn, Machine for stripping seed from	L. D. Grosvenor	South Groton, Mass	Sept. 23, 1851	8, 375
Broom corn-scraping machine	B. J. and J. S. Billings	Gorham, N. Y	Oct. 15, 1831	......

Index of patents issued from the United States Patent Office from 1790 *to* 1873, *inclusive*—Continued.

Invention.	Inventor.	Residence.	Date.	No.
Broom-corn-seed stripper	G. E. Burt and E. A. Hildreth	Harvard, Mass	Sept. 20, 1870	107, 445
Broom-corn-stripping machine	J. B. Stine	Rohrersville, Md	Sept. 24, 1872	131, 718
Broom-corn to stripper, Machine for feeding	S. C. Kenaga	Kankakee, Ill	Oct. 15, 1872	132, 158
Broom-crotch supporter	H. Hopkins	Wellfleet, Mass	Aug. 30, 1870	106, 822
Broom, Detachable	G. H. Pierce	Richmond, Canada	Aug. 20, 1872	130, 594
Broom-envelope	E. M. Crandal	Chicago, Ill	Oct. 1, 1872	131, 855
Broom-handle	J. Strong	College Hill, Ohio	Sept. 20, 1870	107, 559
Broom-handle	W. H. Towers	New York, N. Y	Oct. 15, 1861	33, 502
Broom-handle socket	H. Achew	Cincinnati, Ohio	Dec. 20, 1870	110, 325
Broom-handles, Clamp for splicing	C. L. W. Baker	Camden, N. J	Dec. 30, 1873	145, 041
Broom-handles, Machine for sawing sticks for	T. J. Alexander	Westerville, Ohio	Sept. 20, 1853	10, 023
Broom-handles, Machine for turning	G. M. Morrow	Clarksville, Ohio	Oct. 13, 1868	83, 082
Broom-handles, moldings, &c., Apparatus for painting or coating.	S. A. Shepard	Pittsburgh, Pa	May 13, 1873	138, 767
Broom-hanger	M. A. Clifford	Boston, Mass	Sept. 23, 1873	143, 063
Broom-hanger	C. F. Lewis	Wakeman, Ohio	Oct. 8, 1872	132, 089
Broom-hanger	J. L. Patterson	Wheeler Station, Ind	Jan. 1, 1867	60, 779
Broom-head	A. Alden	East Cambridge, Mass	Apr. 14, 1868	76, 688
Broom-head	E. A. Alexander and H. C. Kellogg.	Buchanan County, Iowa	Oct. 1, 1867	69, 300
Broom-head	L. Allen	Berkeley Springs, W. Va	July 9, 1867	66, 441
Broom-head	J. M. Allison	Salina, Pa	July 27, 1869	93, 033
Broom-head	J. D. M. Armbrust	Apolloborough, Pa	June 26, 1866	55, 948
Broom-head	F. G. Bakes	Vevay, Ind	July 10, 1866	56, 162
Broom-head	H. Barker	Aurora, Ind	Apr. 23, 1867	63, 983
Broom-head	E. M. Bayne	Uniontown, Pa	Nov. 6, 1866	59, 343
Broom-head	C. Blom, jr., and J. Aling	Holland, Mich	Dec. 5, 1871	121, 578
Broom-head	F. C. Blender	Lima, Ohio	June 13, 1865	48, 232
Broom-head	W. P. Brooks	Fairmont, Minn	Dec. 18, 1866	60, 615
Broom-head	D. J. Brougher	Harrisburgh, Pa	Dec. 26, 1865	51, 689
Broom-head	J. D. Browne	Cincinnati, Ohio	Oct. 24, 1865	50, 554
Broom-head	J. Buchanan	Aurora, Ind	Nov. 21, 1865	51, 013
Broom-head	J. Buchanan	Aurora, Ind	Apr. 24, 1866	54, 104
Broom-head	H. Buck	Harrisburgh, Pa	Jan. 30, 1866	52, 263
Broom-head	H. Buck	Harrisburgh, Pa	May 8, 1866	54, 498
Broom-head	J. T. Carpenter	Harrisburgh, Pa	Feb. 26, 1867	62, 471
Broom-head	F. B. Carroll	Noblesville, Ind	Jan. 1, 1867	60, 688
Broom-head	O. L. Castle	Upper Alton, Ill	Mar. 26, 1867	63, 211
Broom-head	J. O. Clay	Hudson, Wis	Apr. 3, 1866	53, 576
Broom-head	B. C. Cook	Richmond, Va	Feb. 4, 1873	135, 525
Broom-head	N. B. Cooper	Gratis Ohio	Feb. 27, 1866	52, 823
Broom-head	J. Danner	Canton, Ohio	Apr. 10, 1866	53, 791
Broom-head	B. F. Early	Palmyra, Pa	Nov. 6, 1866	59, 372
Broom-head	J. S. Elkins	Marquette, Wis	Apr. 17, 1866	53, 962
Broom-head	S. S. Evans	El Paso, Ill	June 26, 1866	55, 843
Broom-head	D. P. Farnham	Janesville, Wis	July 30, 1867	67, 180
Broom-head	J. U. Fiester	Winchester, Ohio	Jan. 2, 1866	51, 819
Broom-head	C. Fiscus	Washington, D. C	Apr. 25, 1871	114, 120
Broom-head	G. W. Golay	Vevay, Ind	June 19, 1866	55, 769
Broom-head	S. B. Guernsey	Chicago, Ill	May 1, 1866	54, 332
Broom-head	N. Hail	New Market, Md	Mar. 20, 1866	53, 296
Broom-head	C. C. Hand	Cincinnati, Ohio	June 27, 1865	48, 392
Broom-head	M. Haneline	Clear Creek, Ind	June 26, 1866	55, 856
Broom-head	J. Harris	Marquette, Wis	May 1, 1866	54, 338
Broom-head	J. Harris	Marquette, Wis	Oct. 23, 1866	59, 011
Broom-head	A. Harroun, jr	Onondaga, N. Y	Aug. 21, 1866	57, 320
Broom-head	G. W. Hoffman	Harrisburgh, Pa	Dec. 5, 1865	51, 318
Broom-head	J. M. Hotaling	Waterport, N. Y	Jan. 29, 1867	61, 621
Broom-head	J. S. Hugg	Philadelphia, Pa	Feb. 19, 1867	62, 202
Broom head	W. G. Hughes	Hebron, Ind	May 21, 1867	64, 979
Broom-head	B. Hunt	Farmland, Ind	Apr. 16, 1867	63, 899
Broom-head	J. E. Hunter	Mechanicsburgh, Ohio	Apr. 3, 1866	53, 624
Broom-head	J. W. Keene and W. E. Snediker	Utica, N. Y	Aug. 7, 1866	56, 953
Broom head	E. Kelley	Locust Grove, Ohio	July 16, 1867	66, 715
Broom-head	J. Kiefer	Hamilton, Ohio	May 22, 1866	54, 921
Broom-head	M. C. Kilgore	Washington, Iowa	May 8, 1866	54, 559
Broom-head	A. B. King	Seven Mile, Ohio	Mar. 27, 1866	53, 452
Broom-head	I. Kohn	Edgerton, Ohio	Aug. 27, 1867	68, 209
Broom-head	J. Liget	Posey Township, Ind	June 5, 1866	55, 316
Broom-head	J. H. Lightner	Shirleysburgh, Pa	July 3, 1866	56, 067
Broom-head	J. C. McLelland and J. Graham	Pittsburgh, Pa	Nov. 27, 1866	60, 030
Broom-head	C. Messenger	Chicago, Ill	June 12, 1866	55, 519
Broom head	C. Messenger	Chicago, Ill	Dec. 4, 1866	60, 221
Broom-head	W. A. Middleton	Harrisburgh, Pa	July 31, 1866	56, 859
Broom-head	W. A. Middleton	Harrisburgh, Pa	Apr. 12, 1870	101, 901
Broom-head	C. E. Miller	Amelia, Ohio	Oct. 18, 1864	44, 736
Broom-head	C. E. Miller	Cincinnati, Ohio	June 13, 1865	48, 195
Broom-head	C. E. Miller	Cincinnati, Ohio	Dec. 19, 1865	51, 658
Broom-head	H. B. Miller and M. P. Weston.	Grand Rapids, Mich	Mar. 12, 1867	62, 768
Broom-head	J. A. Miller	Somerville, Ohio	Oct. 24, 1865	50, 610
Broom-head	T. Moore	Bloomington, Ill	Nov. 27, 1866	60, 038
Broom-head	W. B. Moore	Philadelphia, Pa	July 17, 1866	56, 434
Broom-head	J. H. Mumma	Harrisburgh, Pa	Apr. 3, 1866	53, 654
Broom-head	D. P. Myers	Salem, Ill	Mar. 20, 1866	53, 323
Broom-head	G. R. Nebinger	Lewisberry, Pa	May 1, 1866	54, 391
Broom-head	M. V. Nobles and J. Holcomb	Elmira, N. Y., and Towanda, Pa.	Aug. 13, 1867	67, 793
Broom-head	D. J. Owen and J. G. Brydges	Springville, Pa	Feb. 11, 1873	135, 661
Broom-head	T. G. Packer	Mexico, N. Y	Aug. 6, 1867	67, 573
Broom-head	W. Paine and R. E. Caviness	Fairfield, Iowa	July 17, 1866	56, 461
Broom-head	G. W. Parsons	Harrisburgh, Pa	Apr. 24, 1866	54, 200
Broom-head	G. W. Parsons	Harrisburgh, Pa	Jan. 9, 1867	51, 964
Broom-head	D. Peters	Eaton, Ohio	May 15, 1866	54, 765
Broom-head	T. H. Powers	Milwaukee, Wis	June 27, 1865	48, 434
Broom-head	M. Quinby and J. E. Sturdevant.	Skinner's Eddy, Pa	July 17, 1866	56, 446
Broom-head	J. W. Sanford	Bath, N. Y	Aug. 20, 1867	67, 916
Broom-head	S. S. and J. G. Sherman	McHenry, Ill	Apr. 10, 1866	53, 893

Index of patents issued from the United States Patent Office from 1790 *to* 1873, *inclusive*—Continued.

Invention.	Inventor.	Residence.	Date.	No.
Broom-head	J. E. Short	New Richmond, Ohio	Jan. 30, 1866	52, 330
Broom-head	A. Silvers	Collinsville, Ohio	Dec. 19, 1865	51, 663
Broom-head	J. A. Sinclair	Woodsfield, Ohio	July 23, 1867	67, 075
Broom-head	G. Smith	Woodstown, N. J	Aug. 29, 1871	118, 493
Broom-head	L. S. Smith	Gorsuch's Mills, Md	Nov. 19, 1867	71, 238
Broom-head	G. T. Spaulding	Brodhead, Wis	Apr. 17, 1866	54, 035
Broom-head	W. C. Spellman	Baltimore, Md	Apr. 13, 1869	88, 922
Broom-head	W. C. Spellman	Providence, R. I	May 31, 1870	103, 791
Broom-head	W. D. Stroud	Oshkosh, Wis	July 3, 1866	56, 119
Broom-head	W. D. Stroud	Oshkosh, Wis	Feb. 5, 1867	61, 774
Broom-head	J. Taylor and R. M. Lafferty	Three Rivers, Mich	Sept. 11, 1866	57, 998
Broom-head	S. D. Thurston	Somerville, Ohio	Dec. 19, 1865	51, 631
Broom-head	H. Trumbull	Central College, Ohio	July 24, 1866	56, 640
Broom-head	H. H. B. Vincent	Oshkosh, Wis	Dec. 4, 1866	60, 291
Broom-head	J. Wasson	Fairwater, Wis	June 26, 1866	55, 936
Broom-head	J. Wisner and T. Rose	Aurora and Cortlandville, N. Y.	Oct. 15, 1867	69, 884
Broom head and clamp	M. W. Owens	Waterford, Pa	Aug. 21, 1866	57, 369
Broom-head, Metallic	O. L. Castle	Upper Alton, Ill	Oct. 4, 1864	44, 515
Broom-head stock	A. D. Forbes	Rockford, Ill	June 5, 1866	55, 269
Broom-holder	F. B. Batchelder	Prairie du Chien, Wis	May 26, 1868	78, 252
Broom-holder	C. T. Beardsley	Hamden, Conn	June 20, 1871	116, 140
Broom-holder	W. H. Bixler	Easton, Pa	Nov. 22, 1870	109, 375
Broom-holder	Z. Howe	Lowell, Mich	Jan. 10, 1871	110, 917
Broom-holder	H. B. McCool	Pottsville, Pa	Mar. 12, 1872	124, 445
Broom-holder	J. G. Powell and W. A. Morse	Philadelphia, Pa	Oct. 8, 1867	69, 586
Broom-holder	C. P. Snow	Freeport, Ill	June 28, 1870	104, 787
Broom-holder	L. W. Turner	Yalesville, Conn	May 25, 1869	90, 411
Broom-holder	H. W. Warner	Watertown, Conn	July 2, 1867	66, 431
Broom-jaw	I. Webster	Bucksport, Me	June 15, 1869	91, 290
Broom machine, Splint	J. Crum and A. Larwill	Ramapo, N. Y	Mar. 27, 1849	6, 233
Broom-making	T. Floyd	Chambersburgh, Va	Jan. 26, 1858	19, 190
Broom-needle	C. M. Cowardin	Gardiner Station, Tenn	Oct. 10, 1871	119, 745
Broom or brush	M. L. Byrn	New York, N. Y	Dec. 12, 1865	51, 423
Broom or brush	J. H. Power	Middletown, Iowa	July 10, 1860	29, 099
Broom or brush head	J. E. Phillips	Philadelphia, Pa	July 4, 1865	48, 587
Broom or brush holder	A. G. Davis	Watertown, Conn	Jan. 7, 1868	73, 169
Broom or mop clamp	E. Chapman	Lacon, Ill	Sept. 13, 1870	107, 336
Broom or mop clamp	E. Chapman	Salisbury, Mo	Jan. 30, 1872	123, 083
Broom or mop holder	H. L. Franklin and E. Clark	Nashua, N. H	Sept. 14, 1869	94, 734
Broom or whisk, Clothes	B. Morahan	Brooklyn, N. Y	July 9, 1867	66, 611
Broom-protector	G. Hunt	New York, N. Y	Apr. 15, 1873	137, 774
Broom, Shear	C. Randall, J. F. Moore, and J. Randall.	West Eau Claire, Wis	Feb. 2, 1869	86, 588
Broom, Splint	J. W. Wheeler	Cleveland, Ohio	May 24, 1859	24, 181
Broom, Stable	E. J. Richmond and T. Wright	New York, N. Y	Apr. 16, 1861	32, 083
Broom, Stable, &c	T. Wright	New York, N. Y	Feb. 1, 1870	99, 512
Broom-stand	E. A. Harris	Chicago, Ill	Aug. 29, 1871	118, 451
Broom-straw, Coloring and toughening	S. Greger	Cleveland, Ohio	Nov. 12, 1872	132, 961
Broom-tying machine	J. W. Congdon	Marietta, Ohio	Sept. 12, 1871	118, 845
Broom, Whisk	E. P. Cooley	New York, N. Y	May 9, 1871	114, 646
Broom, Whisk	H. A. Lee	New York, N. Y	Mar. 5, 1872	124, 365
Broom, Whisk	R. Y. Martin	New York, N. Y	May 9, 1871	114, 697
Broom, Whisk	G. Stackpole	Elizabeth, N. J	Mar. 21, 1871	112, 976
Broom, Whisk	G. Stackpole	Elizabeth, N. J	Apr. 4, 1871	113, 358
Brooms, Attachment for	J. H. Mumma	Harrisburgh, Pa	Nov. 21, 1865	51, 074
Brooms, billiard-cues, &c., Rack for	E. Richmond	Brooklyn, N. Y	Sept. 17, 1867	69, 026
Brooms, brushes, mops, &c., Machine for making	J. M. Spooner	Belchertown, Mass	Apr. 28, 1838	718
Brooms, Construction of	A. Mitchell	Eaton, Pa	Jan. 5, 1858	19, 039
Brooms, Device for the construction of	S. M. Sherman	Fort Dodge, Iowa	Apr. 28, 1863	38, 341
Brooms, Flanged collar for	H. A. Lee	New York, N. Y	Oct. 10, 1871	119, 775
Brooms, Gudgeon for	N. Robbins, jr	Rockport, Mass	July 9, 1867	66, 633
Brooms, &c., Machine for cutting splints for manufacture of.	L. Gleason	Le Roy, N. Y	Oct. 9, 1841	2, 289
Brooms, Machine for making	J. H. Hinton	Lancaster, Pa	Mar. 13, 1844	3, 483
Brooms, Machine for making	S. Rowe	Baltimore, Md	Dec. 1, 1857	18, 770
Brooms, Machine for making	J. Thomas	West Chester, Pa	Sept. 18, 1849	6, 717
Brooms, Machine for making	S. H. Weed	Poughkeepsie, N. Y	Feb. 3, 1819	....
Brooms, Machine for manufacturing splints for	J. W. Wheeler	Cleveland, Ohio	Apr. 13, 1858	19, 971
Brooms, Machine for winding wire or twine on	W. Beaman	Salem, N. J	Aug. 17, 1843	3, 219
Brooms, Machinery for making	H. Warner	Hamilton County, Ohio	Feb. 15, 1848	5, 444
Brooms, Manufacture of	E. P. Marble	Sutton Centre, Mass	Jan. 31, 1871	111, 464
Brooms, Manufacture of	W. B. Walker	Bennington, N. H	Aug. 1, 1854	11, 451
Brooms, Metallic clasp or head for	I. Cheney	Leyden, Mass	June 25, 1839	1, 198
Brooms, Metallic head for	H. G. Smith	Muscatine, Iowa	Apr. 3, 1860	27, 746
Brooms, Metallic tip for suspending	M. C. Hawkins	Edenborough, Pa	Oct. 8, 1867	69, 664
Brooms or brushes, Manufacturing	D. Wooster	China, N. Y	Feb. 16, 1829	....
Brooms, Preparing wisps for	J. E. Phillips	Philadelphia, Pa	May 8, 1866	54, 591
Brooms, Screw-ferrule for	M. W. Dillingham	Amsterdam, N. Y	Nov. 5, 1872	132, 817
Brooms, &c., Shape and formation of hickory	A. Sclater	Oxford Township, Pa	Feb. 15, 1826	....
Brooms, Sprinkling-attachment for	P. Louis	New York, N. Y	Dec. 18, 1866	60, 637
Brush	L. Abbott	Lewiston, Me	Nov. 26, 1872	133, 347
Brush	A. Alden	New York, N. Y	May 23, 1865	47, 781
Brush	J. B. Alden	Worcester, Mass	Mar. 19, 1867	62, 987
Brush	J. Ames	Lansingburgh, N. Y	Mar. 7, 1871	112, 404
Brush	J. Ames, jr	Lansingburgh, N. Y	Aug. 13, 1872	130, 402
Brush	C. L. W. Baker	Camden, N. J	Nov. 11, 1873	144, 496
Brush	J. A. Bell	Tyrone, Pa	July 16, 1872	129, 205
Brush	C. Boeckh	Buffalo, N. Y	Sept. 21, 1869	94, 940
Brush	J. Boggs	Harrisburgh, Pa	May 1, 1866	54, 284
Brush	S. Brillinger	Clarence Centre, N. Y	Sept. 21, 1869	94, 941
Brush	A. W. Brown	Lansingburgh, N. Y	Nov. 17, 1868	84, 166
Brush	J. Buercky	Overpeck's Station, Ohio	Oct. 29, 1867	70, 161
Brush	W. W. Clark	New York, N. Y	Feb. 4, 1868	74, 048
Brush	R. J. Combs	Bergen, N. J	Oct. 11, 1870	108, 108
Brush	I. Cross	New London, Ohio	July 5, 1853	9, 827
Brush	J. F. W. Dorman	Baltimore, Md	June 9, 1868	78, 727
Brush	A. C. Estabrook	Florence, Mass	June 19, 1866	55, 764

Index of patents issued from the United States Patent Office from 1790 *to* 1873, *inclusive*—Continued.

Invention.	Inventor.	Residence.	Date.	No.
Brush	J. A. Fanshawe and J. A. Jaques.	Tottenham, England	Jan. 7, 1862	34, 109
Brush	L. P. Faught	Foxborough, Mass	May 1, 1866	54, 464
Brush	D. Fleming	Brooklyn, N. Y	Mar. 5, 1861	31, 593
Brush	W. H. Forker	Meadville, Pa	Aug. 13, 1867	67, 745
Brush	J. A. Grant	Ottawa, Canada	Nov. 14, 1871	120, 964
Brush	H. A. Harvey	Orange, N. J	Nov. 21, 1871	121, 050
Brush	J. Hayman	Poole, England	Dec. 24, 1872	134, 278
Brush	D. L. Keller	Norwalk, Ohio	Mar. 14, 1871	112, 718
Brush	L. Kissling	East Cambridge, Mass	July 16, 1872	129, 143
Brush	D. W. Lapham	Baltimore, Md	Oct. 31, 1871	120, 523
Brush	J. C. Lawrence	Brooklyn, N. Y	Apr. 24, 1866	54, 179
Brush	T. J. Mayall	Roxbury, Mass	Mar. 5, 1861	31, 613
Brush	D. A. McDonel and P. Z. Klock	Ashland, Pa	Oct. 22, 1872	132, 479
Brush	F. McLaughlin	Boston, Mass	Sept. 17, 1867	69, 008
Brush	F. McLaughlin	Boston, Mass	Jan. 11, 1870	98, 787
Brush	J. Michales, jr., and R. J. Combs	Bergen, N. J	Dec. 26, 1871	122, 186
Brush	J. Minetree	Petersburgh, Va	Sept. 12, 1871	118, 871
Brush	S. Morris	Charlestown, Mass	Aug. 4, 1863	39, 417
Brush	F. Murrow	Williamsburgh, N. Y	Apr. 27, 1852	8, 911
Brush	W. M. Newton	Baltimore, Md	Aug. 18, 1868	81, 101
Brush	C. W. Palmer	Cleveland, Ohio	June 3, 1873	139, 474
Brush	J. and F. Pirrung	Chicago, Ill	Dec. 12, 1871	121, 811
Brush	C. F. Russet	Brooklyn, N. Y	July 5, 1870	105, 130
Brush	K. Shaler	Madison, Conn	Dec. 21, 1858	22, 381
Brush	J. H. Tatum	New York, N. Y	May 11, 1858	20, 226
Brush	W. Tusch	Brooklyn, N. Y	May 22, 1860	28, 422
Brush	C. Twyford	Red Bank, N. J	Mar. 29, 1864	42, 131
Brush	A. Van Dusen	Chicago, Ill	Aug. 15, 1865	49, 457
Brush	P. Wagner	New York, N. Y	Apr. 17, 1873	138, 213
Brush	A. M. White	Port Chester, N. Y	Apr. 4, 1865	47, 157
Brush	A. M. White	New York, N. Y	May 21, 1867	65, 029
Brush	J. S. White	Portland, Me	Jan. 21, 1873	135, 053
Brush	J. L. Whiting	Portland, Me	Aug. 4, 1863	39, 439
Brush	J. L. Whiting	Boston, Mass	Sept. 8, 1868	81, 966
Brush	J. L. Whiting	Boston, Mass	Mar. 29, 1870	101, 332
Brush	J. L. Whiting	Boston, Mass	Aug. 30, 1870	106, 902
Brush	J. L. Whiting	Boston, Mass	Sept. 27, 1870	107, 742
Brush	J. L. Whiting	Boston, Mass	Nov. 8, 1870	109, 084
Brush	J. L. Whiting	Boston, Mass	June 27, 1871	116, 382
Brush	J. L. Whiting	Boston, Mass	Aug. 29, 1871	118, 661
Brush	O. D. Woodbury	New York, N. Y	Apr. 26, 1870	102, 460
Brush	E. J. Worcester	Worcester, Mass	June 18, 1867	65, 982
Brush	A. A. Young	Boston, Mass	July 16, 1867	66, 762
Brush and boot-jack, Blacking	S. Gissinger	Allegheny City, Pa	Feb. 20, 1866	52, 787
Brush and box, Combined blacking	F. Hatch	La Crosse, Wis	Dec. 18, 1866	60, 511
Brush and box, Combined blacking	H. S Kerr	Philadelphia, Pa	Sept. 12, 1871	118, 805
Brush and box, Combined blacking	W. H. H. Saunders	Troy, N. Y	Nov. 6, 1866	59, 461
Brush and box, Portable shoe	E. A. Pierce	New York, N. Y	Apr. 26, 1870	102, 430
Brush and broom, Dust	A. Dietz	New York, N. Y	July 3, 1866	56, 018
Brush and broom handle	L. F. Cavanaugh	Newfield, N. Y	July 1, 1851	8, 200
Brush and broom handle	E. Turk	Harrisburgh, Pa	May 18, 1832	....
Brush and broom holder	S. G. Groff	Vogansville, Pa	Dec. 5, 1871	121, 458
Brush and card handle	D. Witt and A. Wait	Hubbardston, Mass	Nov. 16, 1869	97, 012
Brush and case, Blacking	J. Schwab	Bridgeport, Conn	June 14, 1870	104, 361
Brush and case combined, Shoe	C. Hamilton	New York, N. Y	Jan. 1, 1867	60, 886
Brush and comb combined	A. A. Young	Boston, Mass	July 7, 1868	79, 621
Brush and fan, Automatic fly	E. J. Clark	Kalamazoo, Mich	Apr. 21, 1868	76, 996
Brush and fan, Automatic fly	C. C. Short	Osgood, Ind	Jan. 15, 1867	61, 269
Brush and handle attachment, Whitewash	W. B. Burtnett and J. P. McIntosh.	New York and Brooklyn, N. Y.	May 30, 1865	47, 927
Brush and holder, Blacking	D. Bowker	Boston, Mass	Jan. 26, 1864	41, 359
Brush and mixer for stove-blacking	G. S. Goodspeed	Providence, R. I	Jan. 30, 1872	123, 099
Brush and mop head	T. T. Prosser	Chicago, Ill	Dec. 24, 1867	72, 677
Brush and mop holder	P. O'Brian and C. L. W. Baker	New York, N. Y., and Hartford, Conn.	Aug. 27, 1872	130, 8?9
Brush and mop holder	I. Smith	Rochester, N. Y	May 13, 1873	138, 946
Brush and mop, Scrubbing	J. F. Mason	Brooklyn, N. Y	Nov. 17, 1868	84, 129
Brush and mop-wringer, Scrubbing	E. Rees	Stoddertsville, Pa	May 10, 1870	102, 865
Brush and rubber, Combination for	A. S. Miles	Brooklyn, N. Y	Aug. 13, 1867	67, 787
Brush and scraper, Boot and shoe	W. A. Morrison	Morrisania, N. Y	Oct. 11, 1859	25, 755
Brush and scraper for sink	J. H. Osgood	Boston, Mass	Oct 17, 1871	120, 090
Brush attachment	S. Pearson	Cincinnati, Ohio	Mar. 29, 1870	101, 307
Brush, Automatic fan and fly	W. Carpenter	Metamora, Ill	July 30, 1861	32, 970
Brush, Automatic fly	H. C. Chandler	Peru, Ind	Dec. 12, 1871	121, 750
Brush, Automatic fly	W. H. Chipley	Libertytown, Md	Nov. 28, 1871	121, 335
Brush, Automatic fly	B. F. Day	East Freedom, Pa	Aug. 25, 1868	81, 349
Brush-back	W. U. Dudley	Port Richmond, N. Y	June 15, 1869	91, 314
Brush, Barber's	J. A. Wiedershelm	Philadelphia, Pa	Apr. 2, 1867	63, 448
Brush, Bathing	J. Marshall	New York, N. Y	June 1, 1869	90, 763
Brush, Bathing	J. Marshall	Brooklyn, N. Y	Feb. 21, 1871	111, 955
Brush, Blacking	R. Adams	Cincinnati, Ohio	Oct. 8, 1867	69, 603
Brush, Blacking	R. Adams	Cincinnati, Ohio	Mar. 9, 1869	87, 614
Brush, Blacking	B. F. Averill	Dunkirk, N. Y	July 11, 1871	116, 794
Brush, Blacking	C. L. W. Baker	Hartford, Conn	Apr. 27, 1869	89, 459
Brush, Blacking	C. Britzinghoffer	Philadelphia, Pa	Oct. 10, 1871	119, 815
Brush, Blacking	G. R. Burdon	Waltham, Mass	Nov. 5, 1867	70, 515
Brush, Blacking	C. D. Day	Chatham, Conn	Aug. 25, 1868	81, 431
Brush, Blacking	J. H. Doughty	New York, N. Y	Feb. 18, 1868	74, 674
Brush, Blacking	N. Eisenmann	New York, N. Y	Feb. 20, 1872	123, 815
Brush, Blacking	W. S. Fickett	Rochester, N. Y	Aug. 12, 1873	141, 638
Brush, Blacking	W. A. Green	Troy, N. Y	May 10, 1864	42, 655
Brush, Blacking	J. R. Howard	Boston, Mass	Aug. 15, 1871	118, 015
Brush, Blacking	H. S. Kerr	Philadelphia, Pa	Apr. 2, 1872	125, 200
Brush, Blacking	G. W. Lishawa	Cincinnati, Ohio	Jan. 25, 1870	99, 095
Brush, Blacking	C. W. Maguire	Brooklyn, N. Y	Apr. 1, 1873	137, 376
Brush, Blacking	W. C. McGill	Cincinnati, Ohio	May 5, 1868	77, 506
Brush, Blacking	C. Mulchahey	Springfield, Mass	Dec. 4, 1866	60, 226

Index of patents issued from the United States Patent Office from 1790 *to* 1873, *inclusive*—Continued.

Invention.	Inventor.	Residence.	Date.	No.
Brush, Blacking	H. E. Newton	Manchester, N. H	Jan. 28, 1868	73, 746
Brush, Blacking	G. R. Owen	Utica, N. Y	Nov. 7, 1871	120, 663
Brush, Blacking	C. A. Paret	Nashville, Tenn	Nov. 12, 1867	70, 889
Brush, Blacking	A. N. Thompson	Holyoke, Mass	Oct. 26, 1869	96, 165
Brush, Blacking	F. W. C. Von Kessler and A. F. Medenwald.	Chicago, Ill	Apr. 29, 1873	138, 353
Brush, Blacking	N. G. Whitmore	Mansfield, Mass	May 1, 1866	54, 472
Brush-block	W. B. Burtnett	New York, N. Y	Apr. 30, 1867	64, 195
Brush block, Whitewash	C. Williams	Philadelphia, Pa	Feb. 23, 1858	19, 459
Brush-blocks, Machine for boring	T. Mitchell	Lansingburgh, N. Y	Jan. 10, 1860	26, 778
Brush-blocks, Machine for boring	T. Mitchell	Lansingburgh, N. Y	Feb. 19, 1861	31, 471
Brush-blocks, Machine for making	S. Costill	Philadelphia, Pa	Feb. 25, 1824	....
Brush blocks, Machine for shaping hair	A. G. Mitchell	Lansingburgh, N. Y	Jan. 31, 1860	27, 005
Brush-blocks, Machinery for boring	S. Taylor and A. R. Davis	East Cambridge, Mass	Dec. 19, 1848	5, 974
Brush-blocks with bristles, Machine for filling	S. Taylor and A. R. Davis	Cambridge and Boston, Mass.	May 1, 1845	4, 027
Brush, Boiler-flue	C. H. Bush	Fall River, Mass	June 26, 1866	55, 815
Brush, Boiler-flue	P. H. Coyle	Newark, N. J	Nov. 3, 1868	83, 607
Brush, Boiler-flue	R. King	Brooklyn, N. Y	Nov. 27, 1866	60, 013
Brush, Boiler-flue	G. P. Leonard and W. Lanster	Fall River, Mass	Mar. 29, 1864	42, 092
Brush, Boiler-flue	P. H. Ryan	Cincinnati, Ohio	July 6, 1869	92, 211
Brush, Boiler-flue	B. M. Spencer	Newark, N. J	Mar. 14, 1871	112, 645
Brush, box, and holder, Combined blacking	E. W. Woodruff	Washington, D. C	Aug. 13, 1872	130, 460
Brush-bridle	G. Hergesheimer	Philadelphia, Pa	Feb. 11, 1868	74, 224
Brush, Broom	A. S. Goodman	Duval County, Fla	May 8, 1849	6, 423
Brush, broom, and mop holder	C. L. W. Baker	Hartford, Conn	Apr. 4, 1871	113, 244
Brush, broom, &c., handles, Attachment for, (canceled.)	A. Eddowes	Frankford, Pa	Jan. 29, 1867	61, 658
Brush case, Shoe	C. D. Thum	Philadelphia, Pa	Aug. 3, 1858	21, 092
Brush, Circular	M. Robbins and C. Heery	Cincinnati, Ohio	May 3, 1864	42, 625
Brush-clamp	A. Huston	Bristol, Me	Oct. 8, 1867	69, 674
Brush clamp, Scrubbing	C. B. Clark	Buffalo, N. Y	Mar. 10, 1868	75, 369
Brush clamp, Paint	G. R. Gardiner	Westerly, R. I	July 30, 1867	67, 286
Brush clasp, Paint	G. W. Hupp	Elwood, Ind	July 12, 1870	105, 212
Brush, Cloth and hat	J. Marshall	New York, N. Y	Sept. 28, 1869	95, 244
Brush, Cloth or hair	H. Aiken	Dracut, Mass	May 24, 1830	....
Brush, Clothes	A. J. Walker	Flatbush, N. Y	Feb. 27, 1872	124, 023
Brush, Coiled-wire	J. B. Christoffel	Williamsburgh, N. Y	Apr. 29, 1873	138, 317
Brush, &c., Combined scrubbing	E. K. Wood	De Witt, Iowa	Aug. 23, 1870	106, 644
Brush, Damping	J. K. Park	Marlborough, N. Y	Jan. 1, 1867	60, 931
Brush, Device for attaching handle to whitewash	W. P. Burtnett and J. P. McIntosh.	New York and Highland Mills, N. Y.	Oct. 17, 1865	50, 449
Brush, Device for trimming cylindrical	A. G. Risley	Utica, N. Y	Dec. 13, 1870	110, 073
Brush, Dust	W. M. Conger	Newark, N. J	May 14, 1872	126, 677
Brush, Dust	G. G. Finn	Cleveland, Ohio	May 21, 1872	126, 945
Brush, Dust	A. Schelling	Erie, Pa	Mar. 12, 1872	124, 634
Brush, Dust	S. Taylor	Boston, Mass	Aug. 6, 1867	67, 461
Brush, Dust	E. Thayer	Worcester, Mass	Aug. 27, 1867	68, 259
Brush, Dusting	R. H. Aldrich	Northampton, Mass	Mar. 12, 1867	62, 724
Brush, Dusting	A. S. Hadley	Boston, Mass	Mar. 12, 1867	62, 742
Brush, Dusting	C. M. Moody	Greenfield, Mass	Apr. 18, 1865	47, 318
Brush, Dusting	T. G. Porter	Louisville, Ky	July 25, 1871	117, 456
Brush, Dusting	L. R. Witherell and A. B. Crandall.	Galesburgh, Ill	June 7, 1870	104, 092
Brush, Ear	G. W. Wood	New York, N. Y	Apr. 26, 1870	102, 351
Brush, Flexible	R. N. Eagle	Washington, D. C	Feb. 27, 1866	52, 833
Brush, Flexible-back	J. J. Adams	New York, N. Y	June 18, 1861	32, 552
Brush, Flue	J. D. Kunkel	Cincinnati, Ohio	Aug. 17, 1869	93, 723
Brush, Fly	B. F. Brown	Cotlin, Ind	Mar. 5, 1872	124, 324
Brush, Fly	W. M. Cline	Sillard's Mills, Tenn	Apr. 23, 1872	126, 022
Brush, Fly	J. E. Darnall	Washington, D. C	Nov. 29, 1870	109, 720
Brush, Fly	H. Fisher	Canton, Ohio	Nov. 14, 1865	50, 926
Brush, Fly	J. A. Lyle	Bridgeport, Ohio	Nov. 18, 1873	144, 779
Brush, Fly	H. R. Robbins	Baltimore, Md	Sept. 21, 1869	95, 141
Brush, Fly	J. M. Runyon	Pemberton, Ohio	June 25, 1872	128, 253
Brush, Fly	D. Shankland and E. B. Hopkinson.	Nevada City, Cal	Apr. 4, 1871	113, 581
Brush, Fly	S. R. Wilmot	La Fayette, Ind	Nov. 5, 1850	7, 763
Brush, Folding	P. Henrichs	Erie, Pa	June 20, 1871	116, 184
Brush, Folding hair	C. Crossman	Tompkinsville, N. Y	May 15, 1866	54, 695
Brush, Foot	J. W. Osborne	Brooklyn, N. Y	May 16, 1871	114, 847
Brush for cannon	P. Birchmeyer	Syracuse, N. Y	Feb. 21, 1865	46, 441
Brush for cleaning metallic plates	E. A. Harvey	Wilmington, Del	Sept. 5, 1865	49, 755
Brush for cleaning teeth, Finger	G. M. Allerton	Dover Plains, N. Y	June 18, 1872	128, 093
Brush for cleaning travelers	H. S. Houghton	Blackstone, Mass	June 17, 1856	15, 131
Brush for cleaning tumblers	A. Fischer	New York, N. Y	Aug. 16, 1870	106, 476
Brush for cleaning tumblers	A. Fischer	New York, N. Y	Aug. 1, 1871	117, 614
Brush for dressing warps	S. Taylor	Lowell, Mass	May 28, 1842	2, 651
Brush for dressing warps	S. Taylor	Cambridge, Mass	July 8, 1856	15, 308
Brush for finger-nails	W. Thomson	Buffalo, N. Y	Dec. 27, 1859	26, 629
Brush for foundry use, Steel-wire	P. Farley	Philadelphia, Pa	Oct. 29, 1872	132, 528
Brush for mucilage-bottle	W. Burnet	New York, N. Y	Feb. 2, 1864	41, 422
Brush for mucilage, painting, gluing, &c	J. W. McGill	Washington, D. C	July 9, 1867	66, 606
Brush for ordnance, Cleaning	J. T. Greenfield	Dover, England	Oct. 5, 1869	95, 468
Brush for washing windows	P. C. Rowe	Boston, Mass	June 21, 1859	24, 491
Brush, Fountain	D. H. Chamberlain and J. Hartshorn.	Boston, Mass	Jan. 30, 1855	12, 309
Brush, Fountain	J. Davis	McLean, N. Y	Oct. 15, 1867	69, 901
Brush, Fountain	L. B. Hoit	New York, N. Y	Feb. 22, 1859	23, 028
Brush, Fountain	R. Lapham	New York, N. Y	Dec. 9, 1873	145, 301
Brush, Fountain	Z. Poitras	Chicago, Ill	Apr. 18, 1871	113, 923
Brush, Fountain	J. B. Warren	South Danvers, Mass	Nov. 19, 1867	71, 094
Brush, Fountain blacking	J. R. Howard	Worcester, Mass	May 20, 1862	35, 316
Brush, Fountain blacking	A. D. Pentz	New York, N. Y	Feb. 7, 1871	111, 566
Brush, Fountain paint	D. J. Kellogg	Toledo, Ohio	Jan. 17, 1871	110, 978
Brush, Fountain paint	D. J. Kellogg	Toledo, Ohio	Apr. 4, 1871	113, 305
Brush from cotton-fields, Machine for cutting	E. Peck	Canton, Ill	Feb. 9, 1858	19, 311
Brush, Galvanic metal friction	L. A. Hoffman	Berlin, Prussia	June 25, 1861	32, 625

Index of patents issued from the United States Patent Office from 1790 *to* 1873, *inclusive*—Continued.

Invention.	Inventor.	Residence.	Date.	No.
Brush, Hair	J. B. Burgess	New York, N. Y	Apr. 14, 1835	....
Brush, Hair	S. M. Firey	Clear Spring, Md	Aug. 23, 1870	106, 680
Brush, Hair	J. N. George and J. R. Sanborn	Boston and Waltham, Mass	Oct. 29, 1867	70, 194
Brush, Hair	J. R. Ingersoll	New York, N. Y	May 22, 1860	28, 375
Brush, Hair	J. Mayer	Philadelphia, Pa	June 20, 1865	48, 295
Brush, Hair	J. F. McClure	Boston, Mass	Mar. 19, 1861	31, 727
Brush, Hair-dyeing	W. B. Coates	Philadelphia, Pa	June 8, 1869	91, 089
Brush-handle	A. Alden	New York, N. Y	Sept. 4, 1866	57, 656
Brush-handle	C. Alvord	Westford, Wis	Mar. 12, 1867	62, 801
Brush-handle	C. Brintzinghoffer and G. Eckert.	Philadelphia, Pa	Oct. 31, 1871	120, 466
Brush-handle	R. S. Craig	Cincinnati, Ohio	Jan. 21, 1873	135, 090
Brush-handle	S. D. Foster	Portland, Me	Apr. 2, 1872	125, 279
Brush-handle	C. L. Larder	Brooklyn, N. Y	Mar. 9, 1869	87, 684
Brush-handle	F. Rudolph and W. Kasefaug	Jersey City, N. J	Nov. 29, 1864	45, 276
Brush-handle attachment	R. Wyatt	Brooklyn, N. Y	Mar. 29, 1870	101, 400
Brush handle, Lather	W. H. Miles, jr	Brooklyn, N. Y	Nov. 11, 1873	144, 553
Brush handle, Mucilage	T. N. Hickcox	Brooklyn, N. Y	Apr. 20, 1869	89, 222
Brush handle, Tooth and nail	G. A. Scott	New York, N. Y	Dec. 3, 1872	133, 600
Brush handles, Machine for driving	J. Ames, jr	Lansingburgh, N. Y	Aug. 26, 1873	142, 137
Brush handles, Machine for driving	P. Peartree	Lansingburgh, N. Y	Apr. 29, 1873	138, 344
Brush handles, Machine for driving	P. Peartree	Lansingburgh, N. Y	July 23, 1872	129, 748
Brush handles, Machine for finishing	T. Mitchell	Lansingburgh, N. Y	June 23, 1857	17, 631
Brush handles, Machine for finishing hair	T. Mitchell	Lansingburgh, N. Y	June 28, 1859	24, 571
Brush-handles, Screw-socket for	W. H. Johnson	Philadelphia, Pa	Oct. 20, 1868	83, 173
Brush, Hat	C. F. Phelps	Boston, Mass	May 19, 1863	38, 632
Brush, Hat	R. D. Radcliffe	Palmyra, N. Y	Mar. 7, 1871	112, 492
Brush, Hat	W. B. Shedd	East Boston, Mass	Aug. 19, 1862	36, 239
Brush-head	C. J. Moore and L. S. Gambold	Coatesville, Ind	June 22, 1869	91, 556
Brush, Helical-wire	F. F. Field	Stapleton, N. Y	Oct. 10, 1871	119, 752
Brush-holder	C. L. W. Baker	Camden, N. J	Dec. 16, 1873	145, 479
Brush-holder	C. B. Clark	Buffalo, N. Y	July 28, 1868	80, 453
Brush-holder	J. Messinger	Springfield, Vt	Nov. 19, 1867	71, 037
Brush-holder	B. Morahan	Brooklyn, N. Y	July 9, 1867	66, 612
Brush-holder	A. H. Trego	Philadelphia, Pa	Mar. 19, 1872	124, 865
Brush-holder and mop-head	H. P. Gregg	Cincinnati, Ohio	Sept. 1, 1868	81, 626
Brush-holder, Dust-pan	W. M. Couger	Newark, N. J	May 21, 1872	126, 931
Brush, Holder for hat	J. M. Osgood	Chelsea, Mass	Apr. 21, 1863	38, 240
Brush holder, Fountain	W. A. Shepard	Chicago, Ill	July 5, 1870	105, 135
Brush holder, Painter's	J. Lemoine	Winchendon, Mass	Apr. 30, 1872	126, 219
Brush holder, Whitewash	A. Iske	Lancaster, Pa	Sept. 24, 1867	69, 097
Brush, Horse	R. Dickson	Lansingburgh, N. Y	Apr. 8, 1873	137, 536
Brush, Horse	J. Hayworth	Manchester, England	Jan. 16, 1866	52, 118
Brush, Hydraulic	T. Wellham	Washington, D. C	Jan. 31, 1865	46, 167
Brush, India-rubber tooth	S. W. Francis	New York, N. Y	July 6, 1869	92, 298
Brush, Lather	W. H. Miles, jr	New York, N. Y	Oct. 31, 1871	120, 390
Brush, Leather-backed horse	O. Jones	South Englewood, N. J	Sept. 3, 1867	68, 513
Brush-machine	E. F. Bradley	New Haven, Conn	Apr. 1, 1873	137, 411
Brush-machine	M. Dillon	Albany, N. Y	Feb. 11, 1873	135, 634
Brush-machine	E. A. Hill	Cambridge, Mass	Sept. 16, 1873	142, 913
Brush-machine	J. Ruegg	Saint Louis, Mo	Oct. 9, 1860	30, 353
Brush-machine	E. D. Van Horn and C. N. Farr	Philadelphia, Pa	May 6, 1873	138, 545
Brush-making	W. Steel	New York, N. Y	Aug. 17, 1835	....
Brush-making	W. Steel	New York, N. Y	Aug. 17, 1835	....
Brush-making machine	E. F. Bradley	London, England	Dec. 10, 1872	133, 827
Brush-making machine	J. Pickering	Philadelphia, Pa	Oct. 24, 1871	120, 164
Brush-making machine	J. Ruegg	Saint Louis, Mo	Nov. 20, 1868	30, 693
Brush-making machine	L. A. Tripp	New York, N. Y	Oct. 27, 1857	18, 528
Brush-making machine	A. M. White	Thompsonville, Conn	Dec. 22, 1868	85, 193
Brush-making machine	A. M. White	Thompsonville, Conn	June 1, 1869	90, 903
Brush-making machinery	C. D. Rogers, M. P. Wilkins, and H. A. Hawey.	Utica, N. Y., Jersey City and Orange, N. J.	June 25, 1872	128, 251
Brush manufacture	R. Ashworth	Fall River, Mass	Aug. 6, 1872	130, 270
Brush manufacture	S. Barnes	New Haven, Conn	Sept. 7, 1858	21, 464
Brush manufacture	A. R. Davis	East Cambridge, Mass	Aug. 19, 1851	8, 299
Brush manufacture	A. R. Davis	East Cambridge, Mass	May 11, 1852	8, 938
Brush manufacture	A. C. Estabrook	Florence, Mass	Feb. 4, 1873	135, 415
Brush manufacture	A. H. Kidney and R. J. Simpson.	New York, N. Y	Feb. 27, 1872	124, 141
Brush manufacture	C. F. Ruset	Brooklyn, N. Y	July 12, 1870	105, 373
Brush manufacture	M. Stewart	Philadelphia, Pa	Dec. 5, 1854	12, 037
Brush manufacture	W. H. Van Kleeck	Lansingburgh, N. Y	Jan. 23, 1872	123, 064
Brush manufacture	M. P. Wilkins and C. D. Rogers	Jersey City, N. J	Feb. 26, 1867	62, 460
Brush-manufacturing device	C. F. Russet	Brooklyn, N. Y	July 5, 1870	105, 131
Brush, Marking	E. P. Clark	Northampton, Mass	Sept. 29, 1863	40, 089
Brush, Marking	T. Fowler	Richmond Valley, N. Y	Dec. 24, 1861	33, 986
Brush, Marking	F. W. Wentworth	Boston, Mass	June 24, 1873	140, 2[illegible]8
Brush, Means of attaching handle to whitewash	W. B. Burtnett	New York, N. Y	May 7, 1867	64, 406
Brush, Mechanical fly	H. E. Aughinbaugh	Harrisburgh, Pa	June 6, 1871	11[illegible], 560
Brush, mop, and wringer, Combined scrubbing	J. D. Smith	Sacramento, Cal	July 8, 1873	140, 655
Brush, mop, and wringer, Scrubbing	L. Frey and J. Hahn	Chicago, Ill	Oct. 31, 1865	50, 701
Brush, Mucilage	W. W. Beach	New York, N. Y	July 9, 1867	66, 446
Brush, Mucilage	D. Bly	Macon, Ga	Mar. 30, 1869	88, 265
Brush, Mucilage	M. W. House	Cleveland, Ohio	Mar. 16, 1869	87, 776
Brush, Mucilage and marking	W. R. Anderson	New York, N. Y	Feb. 19, 1867	62, 108
Brush, Mucilage and marking	E. H. Boswell	Philadelphia, Pa	Aug. 1, 1865	49, 072
Brush, Nail	W. Thomson	Buffalo, N. Y	July 31, 1860	29, 419
Brush of saw cotton-gin	E. Keith	Bridgewater, Mass	Apr. 28, 1857	17, 155
Brush or card, Curry	J. Voak	Penn Yan, N. Y	Feb. 21, 1865	46, 510
Brush or comb, Hair	T. Divine	Charleston, S. C	June 14, 1870	104, 125
Brush or fan, Fly	M. Laveen	Moorefield, Va	Apr. 10, 1860	27, 844
Brush, Paint	J. Ames, jr	Lansingburgh, N. Y	Apr. 25, 1871	114, 086
Brush, Paint	C. S. Benjamin and E. Story	Washington, Ill	Feb. 22, 1870	100, 108
Brush, Paint	J. D. Bonney	Pembroke, Mass	July 2, 1867	66, 291
Brush, Paint	W. B. Burtnett	New York, N. Y	Aug. 23, 1870	106, 544
Brush, Paint	W. B. Burtnett	New York, N. Y	Jan. 3, 1871	110, 628
Brush, Paint	G. H. Crinnock	Brooklyn, N. Y	May 13, 1873	138, 787
Brush, Paint	W. Cover	Jenner's Cross Roads, Pa	Jan. 8, 1867	61, 053

Index of patents issued from the United States Patent Office from 1790 to 1873, inclusive—Continued.

Invention.	Inventor.	Residence.	Date.	No.
Brush, Paint	A. Cutter	Chelsea, Mass	Feb. 25, 1868	74, 752
Brush, Paint	M. Diilon	Albany, N. Y	Feb. 11, 1873	135, 635
Brush, Paint	B. A. Drayton	Utica, N. Y	July 9, 1867	66, 475
Brush, Paint	J. M. Estabrook	Milford, Mass	Oct. 29, 1867	70, 182
Brush, Paint	L. P. Faught	Foxborough, Mass	Sept. 19, 1865	50, 067
Brush, Paint	W. H. Forker	Meadville, Pa	Nov. 5, 1867	70, 542
Brush, Paint	W. H. Forker	Meadville, Pa	May 5, 1868	77, 475
Brush, Paint	F. P. Furnald, jr., R. W. Champion, and I. N. Davies.	New York and Brooklyn, N. Y., and Bergen City, N. J.	May 4, 1869	89, 649
Brush, Paint	F. P. Furnald, jr., R. W. Champion, and I. N. Davies.	New York, N. Y.	Dec. 21, 1869	98, 158
Brush, Paint	H. B. Gillman and H. S. Beamish.	Milford, Mass	Aug. 27, 1867	68, 066
Brush, Paint	J. J. Gorman	Cincinnati, Ohio	Jan. 14, 1873	134, 745
Brush, Paint	J. J. Gorman	Cincinnati, Ohio	June 17, 1873	139, 887
Brush, Paint	W. Hicks	Steubenville, Ohio	Jan. 2, 1855	12, 182
Brush, Paint	E. Hiss	Delaware, Ohio	July 31, 1866	56, 750
Brush, Paint	L. A. Lightenhome	Chicago. Ill	Dec. 17, 1872	133, 996
Brush, Paint	J. Marchbank	Lansingburgh, N. Y	Nov. 20, 1866	59, 850
Brush, Paint	J. S. Martin	Boston, Mass	June 20, 1854	11, 129
Brush, Paint	A. McDonald	Washington, Ill	Nov. 1, 1870	108, 923
Brush, Paint	A. McDonald and J. M. White.	Washington, Ill	Aug. 16, 1870	106, 384
Brush, Paint	W. H. Miles, jr	Brooklyn, N. Y	Nov. 18, 1862	36, 962
Brush, Paint	J. W. Moore	Cambridgeport, Mass	Mar. 31, 1868	76, 230
Brush, Paint	G. G. Morris	Boston, Mass	Feb. 1, 1870	99, 338
Brush, Paint	J. Rayls	Washington. Ill	Jan. 25, 1870	99, 276
Brush, Paint	H. Rosenthal	New York, N. Y	Apr. 30, 1867	64, 369
Brush, Paint	H. Rosenthal	New York, N. Y	Aug. 6, 1867	67, 588
Brush, Paint	F. S. Shearer	Washington, Ill	Mar. 7, 1871	112, 387
Brush, Paint	G. L. Shuttleworth	Sharon, Vt	Sept. 6, 1870	107, 200
Brush, Paint	S. Standish	Eureka, Nev	June 24, 1873	140, 314
Brush, Paint	A. S. Thompson	Little Falls, Minn	Aug. 5, 1873	141, 522
Brush, Paint	G. K. Thompson	Greene, N. Y	Jan. 25, 1870	99, 260
Brush, Paint	P. Wagner	New York, N. Y	Feb. 25, 1873	136, 288
Brush, Paint	D. White	Portland, Me	Nov. 24, 1868	84, 327
Brush, Paint	J. S. White	Boston, Mass	May 7, 1867	64, 607
Brush, Paint	J. L. Whiting	Boston, Mass	Oct. 18, 1870	108, 420
Brush, Paint	J. N. Woodward	Aurora, Ill	May 14, 1867	64, 731
Brush, Paint and varnish	J. McKittrick	Brooklyn, N. Y	Feb. 18, 1868	74, 566
Brush, Paint and varnish	A. Randal	Pittsburgh, Pa	Jan. 30, 1872	123, 293
Brush, Paint and varnish	E. Thayer	Worcester, Mass	May 7, 1867	64, 596
Brush, Paint and varnish	G. A. White	Boston, Mass	Jan. 15, 1867	61, 292
Brush, Painters' stripping	P. Feeck	Seneca Falls, N. Y	Nov. 19, 1872	133, 088
Brush, Paper-hangers'	J. M McComb	Lancaster, Ohio	Nov. 25, 1873	144, 999
Brush, &c., Pocket	P. Henrichs	Erie, Pa	June 2[illegible], 1871	116, 185
Brush, Pocket	T. F. Stumpf	New York, N. Y	Dec. 27, 1870	110, 603
Brush-rack	E. F. Ames	Lansingburgh, N. Y	Aug. 13, 1872	130, 401
Brush-rack	J. Ames and N. H. Horton	Lansingburgh and New York, N. Y.	July 30, 1867	67, 247
Brush, Reservoir damping	W. Shriver	New York, N. Y	May 28, 1867	65, 290
Brush, Revolving hair	J. Bayston	Chicago, Ill	Feb. 25, 1868	74, 743
Brush, Rotary	G. Carlisle	Attleborough, Mass	Oct. 14, 1873	143, 666
Brush, Rotary	S. Stuart	Sterling, Mass	May 29, 1866	55, 176
Brush, Rotary hair	E. G. Camp	Bristol, England	Mar. 8, 1864	41, 985
Brush, Rotary horse	W. W. McKay	Ossian, Iowa	Dec. 8, 1868	84, 837
Brush, Sash	J. B. Word	Lansingburgh, N. Y	Aug. 20, 1867	68, 022
Brush, Scrubbing	R. M. Bicknell and C. J. Abel.	Philadelphia, Pa	Sept. 4, 1847	5, 267
Brush, Scrubbing	A. S. Brinser	Falmouth, Pa	Oct. 8, 1872	132, 049
Brush, Scrubbing	R. M. Brooks	Griffin, Ga	July 21, 1868	80, 128
Brush, Scrubbing	G. W. Brown	Providence, R. I	July 6, 1869	92, 154
Brush, Scrubbing	G. Carver	Chambersburgh, Pa	Aug. 1, 1844	3, 689
Brush, Scrubbing	W. C. Cleveland	Cambridge, Mass	May 8, 1866	54, 505
Brush, Scrubbing	A. E. Colman	New York, N. Y	Nov. 10, 1868	83, 932
Brush, Scrubbing	W. Devines	Williamsburgh, N. Y	June 20, 1871	116, 030
Brush, Scrubbing	A. J. Doolittle	Hamden, Conn	July 16, 1867	66, 812
Brush, Scrubbing	B. Figer	Cleveland, Ohio	July 3, 1866	56, 025
Brush, Scrubbing	B. G. Fitzhugh	Frederick, Md	Sept. 24, 1872	131, 674
Brush, Scrubbing	S. Gibson	Safe Harbor, Pa	Oct. 6, 1868	82, 705
Brush, Scrubbing	S. Gibson	Safe Harbor, Pa	Oct. 26, 1869	96, 219
Brush, Scrubbing	S. A. Gibson and J. B. De Haas	Clearfield. Pa	July 18, 1871	117, 167
Brush, Scrubbing	C. F. Gillett	Sparta, Wis	July 30, 1872	129, 944
Brush, Scrubbing	R. P. Gillett	Sparta, Wis	July 3, 1866	56, 035
Brush, Scrubbing	W. L. Haller	Philadelphia, Pa	Apr. 30, 1861	32, 224
Brush, Scrubbing	D. E. Hayward	Malden, Mass	Mar. 10, 1868	75, 421
Brush, Scrubbing	C. Herald	Pittsburgh, Pa	Oct. 14, 1873	143, 695
Brush, Scrubbing	B. F. Kaller	Shrewsbury, Pa	Apr. 5, 1870	101, 630
Brush, Scrubbing	D. Minderle	Saint Louis, Mo	Sept. 13, 1870	107, 397
Brush, Scrubbing	P. O'Brian	New York, N. Y	June 27, 1871	116, 346
Brush, Scrubbing	J. Odell	Petroleum Centre, Pa	Aug. 9, 1870	106, 196
Brush, Scrubbing	R. Rockwell and Z. B. Custer.	Petroleum Centre, Pa	Dec. 6, 1870	109, 946
Brush, Scrubbing	S. C. Rundlett and R. Dodge.	Portland, Me	Mar. 26, 1867	63, 181
Brush, Scrubbing	A. Schweizer and G. Jansen	Cleveland, Ohio	Aug. 26, 1862	36, 309
Brush, Scrubbing	J. See	Philadelphia, Pa	Mar. 15, 1870	100, 932
Brush, Scrubbing	J. N. Valley and J. A. Stetson, jr.	North East, Pa	Oct. 24, 1871	120, 350
Brush, Scrubbing	R. Wyatt	Brooklyn, N. Y	Feb. 5, 1867	61, 910
Brush, Self-feeding blacking	G. Hamilton and J. Post	New York, N. Y	Feb. 23, 1864	41, 700
Brush, Self-supplying mucilage	C. Hamilton	New York, N. Y	Aug. 13, 1867	67, 648
Brush, Shaving	W. S. Jewett	New York, N. Y	Apr. 10, 1849	6, 293
Brush, Shaving	W. T. Wylie	Newcastle, Pa	May 14, 1867	64, 732
Brush-shears	C. Brombacher	New York, N. Y	Mar 26, 1867	63, 205
Brush, Shoe	J. J. Adams	Boston, Mass	Feb. 10, 1852	8, 714
Brush, Shoe	C. L. W. Baker and L S. Hills	Hartford, Conn	May 14, 1867	64, 736
Brush, Shoe	F. D. Holland	Lewiston, Me	May 3, 1870	102, 540
Brush, Shoe	C. F. J. Moller and C. Sholes	Milwaukee, Wis	Aug. 14, 1866	57, 168
Brush, Shoe	J. E. Nolin	Chicago, Ill	June 9, 1868	78, 683

Index of patents issued from the United States Patent Office from 1790 *to* 1873, *inclusive*—Continued.

Invention.	Inventor.	Residence.	Date.	No.
Brush, Shoe	G. R. Owen	Rome, N. Y	Aug. 29, 1871	118, 638
Brush, Shoe	E. A. G. Roulstone	Roxbury, Mass	Nov. 27, 1866	60, 063
Brush, Shoe	H. E. Scotchmer	Chicago, Ill	Apr. 3, 1866	53, 689
Brush, Shoe	G. Wale	Hoboken, N. J	Feb. 25, 1873	136, 289
Brush, Shoe	R. M. Whipple	Cambridge, Mass	Jan. 6, 1863	37, 315
Brush, Shoe and stove	F. M. Carnes	New York, N. Y	Nov. 13, 1866	59, 709
Brush-sleeve	J. S. Tilton	Philadelphia, Pa	Feb. 11, 1868	74, 258
Brush-socket	P. Wagner	New York, N. Y	Apr. 1, 1873	137, 515
Brush, Steam-generator-flue	P. H. Coyle	Newark, N. J	June 22, 1869	91, 523
Brush, Stencil	W. R. Allen	Saint Louis, Mo	May 17, 1859	23, 997
Brush, Stencil	J. S. Costello	Saint Louis, Mo	Aug. 13, 1867	67, 726
Brush, Stencil	D. K. Herr	Locust Valley, Pa	Apr. 10, 1866	53, 923
Brush stock and handle	A. A. Young	Boston, Mass	Feb. 4, 1868	74, 026
Brush stock and handle	A. A. Young	Boston, Mass	Feb. 4, 1868	74, 027
Brush-stock, Method of holding bristles in	C. D. Rogers and M. P. Wilkins	Utica, N. Y., and Jersey City, N. J.	Oct. 29, 1867	70, 270
Brush, Stove	W. Small	Brooklyn, N. Y	July 9, 1872	128, 917
Brush, Stove-polishing	L. C. Crowell	West Dennis, Mass	Sept. 7, 1869	94, 477
Brush to hat, Device for attaching	A. A. Voer	Delaware, Ohio	Apr. 9, 1872	125, 422
Brush, Toilet	S. Wilder	Hingham, Mass	Mar. 5, 1872	124, 409
Brush, Tooth	G. M. Allerton	Dover Plains, N. Y	July 9, 1872	128, 840
Brush, Tooth	P. Blake	New Haven, Conn	Mar. 8, 1830	......
Brush, Tooth	E. F. Burrows	Mystic River, Conn	May 18, 1869	90, 235
Brush, Tooth	R. K. Chandler	Ruther Glen, Va	Jan. 25, 1870	99, 161
Brush, Tooth	T. Maitland	Williamsport, Pa	June 2, 1868	78, 599
Brush, Tooth	T. F. Maury	Washington, D. C	Feb. 18, 1868	74, 560
Brush, Tooth	R. Nelson	Albany, N. Y	July 19, 1864	43, 597
Brush, Tooth	J. D. and W. O'Donoghue	New York, N. Y	July 1, 1873	140, 429
Brush, Tooth	C. Roberts	Newark, N. J	Feb. 16, 1869	87, 070
Brush, Tooth	C. Rosefield	Washington, D. C	May 8, 1866	54, 604
Brush, Tooth	T. H. Spencer	Providence, R. I	May 7, 1867	64, 455
Brush, Tooth	H. N. Wadsworth	Washington, D. C	Nov. 17, 1857	18, 653
Brush, Tooth	H. N. Wadsworth	Washington, D. C	June 19, 1860	28, 794
Brush, Tooth	W. B. Watkins	Jersey City, N. J	Apr. 13, 1869	88, 825
Brush, Tooth and nail	G. A. Scott	New York, N. Y	Dec. 3, 1872	133, 599
Brush trimmer, Tooth	J. Stone	Waterford, N. Y	Oct. 8, 1872	132, 031
Brush trimmer, Tooth	J. Stone	Waterford, N. Y	Oct. 8, 1872	132, 032
Brush, Tumbler	H. Lumbard	Chicago, Ill	Mar. 24, 1868	75, 940
Brush, Tumbler	G. Wiesler	Chicago, Ill	Sept. 1, 1868	81, 718
Brush, Warp	S. Taylor	East Cambridge, Mass	May 12, 1863	38, 516
Brush, wash-board, and roller	I. Hussey	Ironton, Ohio	Sept. 16, 1873	142, 853
Brush-wheel	P. Felker	Providence, R. I	May 10, 1870	102, 932
Brush, Whisk	H. S. Blunt	New York, N. Y	Mar. 26, 1872	125, 010
Brush, Whisk	M. L. Dickinson	West Troy, N. Y	Sept. 30, 1862	36, 560
Brush, Whitewash	W. B. Burtnett and J. P. McIntosh.	New York and Brooklyn, N. Y.	Jan. 17, 1865	45, 907
Brush, Whitewash	E. S. Curtis	Charlestown, Mass	June 2, 1820	......
Brush, Whitewash	A. Foss	Wayne County, Ohio	July 16, 1867	66, 822
Brush, Whitewash	J. Loughridge	Pittsburgh, Pa	Mar. 31, 1863	38, 051
Brush, Whitewash	D. W. Shaw and W. A. Megraw	Baltimore, Md	June 1, 1858	20, 447
Brush, Whitewash and paste	J. S. White	Portland, Me	Jan. 2, 1872	122, 421
Brush, Window	J. Stofer	Cleveland, Ohio	Nov. 20, 1866	59, 932
Brush, Window	J. S. White	Boston, Mass	Apr. 30, 1867	64, 266
Brushes, Binder for paint	J. F. Canning	Boston, Mass	Dec. 17, 1867	72, 364
Brushes, brooms, &c., Grasses for making	S. H. Weed	New York, N. Y	Feb. 28, 1825	......
Brushes, Construction of	J. Marchbank	Lansingburgh, N. Y	Aug. 30, 1870	106, 845
Brushes, Drip-guard for	W. Buck	Portsmouth, Mich	Jan. 16, 1872	122, 701
Brushes, Ferrule for paint	W. B. Burtnett	New York, N. Y	Aug. 23, 1870	106, 545
Brushes for blending colors, Manufacturing	G. M. Morris	Philadelphia, Pa	Mar. 6, 1835	......
Brushes for whitewashing, &c., Manner of attaching bristles to the stock of.	R. B. Lewis	Hallowell, Me	Feb. 23, 1841	1, 992
Brushes from broom-corn, Making	B. Crossdale	Byberry Pa	Dec. 21, 1819	......
Brushes, Girdle for paint	A. M. Piper and O. Allen	Springfield, Mass	Feb. 2, 1869	86, 586
Brushes, Guard for paint	E. C. Haserick	Lake Village, N. H	Mar. 1, 1864	41, 772
Brushes, Machine for making	O. D. Woodbury	New York, N. Y	Dec. 27, 1870	110, 529
Brushes, Machine for manufacturing	W. A. Foskett and H. B. Tyler	New Haven, Conn	July 6, 1869	92, 181
Brushes, Machine for manufacturing the wooden part of.	T. Mitchell	Lansingburgh, N. Y	Sept. 9, 1856	15, 702
Brushes, Machine for trimming bristles of	S. Taylor	East Cambridge, Mass	May 17, 1844	3, 593
Brushes, Machinery for manufacturing	G. Willett	Saint Albans, Vt	Sept. 26, 1871	119, 439
Brushes, Machinery for manufacturing	G. Willett	Saint Albans, Vt	Sept. 26, 1871	119, 440
Brushes, Machinery for trimming	B. Babbit	New York, N. Y	Oct. 14, 1846	4, 814
Brushes, Manufacture of paint	J. T. Steer	New York, N. Y	Mar. 31, 1857	16, 950
Brushes, Manufacturing	J. J. Adams	Boston, Mass	Mar. 12, 1842	2, 490
Brushes, Preparation of bristles for	C. Williams	Philadelphia, Pa	July 19, 1853	9, 869
Brushes, Socket for paint and other	J. W. Davis	Washington, D. C	Jan. 5, 1864	41, 060
Brush-wood, Machine for shaping	J. Ames, jr	Lansingburgh, N. Y	Dec. 16, 1873	145, 546
Brushing and polishing apparatus, Hand	W. H. Willson	New York, N. Y	Sept. 22, 1868	82, 465
Buck-board spring	T. H. Brown	Chicago, Ill	May 10, 1870	102, 762
Bucket	R. T. Brown	Newport, Ky	Oct. 28, 1873	143, 959
Bucket	J. V. Denell	Brooklyn, N. Y	Feb. 25, 1873	136, 140
Bucket	J. H. Tomlinson	Chicago, Ill	June 1, 1869	90, 798
Bucket and measure	J. Hageman	Williamsburgh, Ohio	Oct. 7, 1862	36, 613
Bucket and strainer, Milk	D. N. West	Smithsburgh, Md	Sept. 3, 1867	68, 400
Bucket, Army feed and water	R. B. Fitts	Philadelphia, Pa	Nov. 19, 1861	33, 737
Bucket bracket, Sap	J. J. Pollett	Oconomowoc, Wis	Aug. 27, 1872	130, 863
Bucket, Butter	J. H. Stimpson	Baltimore, Md	Aug. 17, 1858	21, 220
Bucket, Chamber	W. W. Knight	Philadelphia, Pa	Apr. 3, 1866	53, 632
Bucket, Chamber	C. G. Schneider	Washington, D. C	July 8, 1862	35, 841
Bucket, Coal	L. Hayner	Clifton Park, N. Y	June 22, 1869	91, 743
Bucket, Collapsible	C. W. Curtiss	New Haven, Conn	Oct. 23, 1860	30, 465
Bucket cover, Sap	R. Marshall	Hobart, N. Y	Oct. 10, 1871	119, 779
Bucket cover, Sap	D. and E. Smith	Gilsum and Keene, N. H	Oct. 17, 1871	119, 952
Bucket, Covered	F. D. Kellogg and G. N. Ives	New Haven, Conn	Nov. 28, 1871	121, 288
Bucket, Dinner	J. Haines	West Middleburgh, Ohio	Mar. 12, 1867	62, 842
Bucket, Dinner	F. E. Heinig	Louisville, Ky	Sept. 30, 1873	143, 241
Bucket, Dumping	F. B. Colton	Philadelphia, Pa	Dec. 26, 1871	122, 227
Bucket-ear	H. Callahan	Dayton, Ohio	May 7, 1867	64, 484

Index of patents issued from the United States Patent Office from 1790 *to* 1873, *inclusive*—Continued.

Invention.	Inventor.	Residence.	Date.	No.
Bucket-ear	L. Rowland	Philadelphia, Pa	May 2, 1865	47, 573
Bucket, Elevator	O. W. Clark	Appleton, Wis	Aug. 4, 1868	80, 602
Bucket, Feed	R. C. Sturges	Barnstable, Mass	Dec. 31, 1867	72, 935
Bucket, Field	G. Wood	Strasburgh, Pa	May 14, 1861	32, 328
Bucket, Folding	H. W. Wilcox	Columbus, Pa	Jan. 31, 1865	46, 168
Bucket for preserving butter, fruit, &c	E. G. Hofman	Saint Louis, Mo	Oct. 11, 1864	44, 626
Bucket for raising water, Endless-chain	J. Dutton	Aston Township, Delaware County, Pa.	Oct. 9, 1841	2, 290
Bucket for removing coal, &c	J. S. Lloyd	Salem, N. J	Apr. 24, 1860	27, 993
Bucket for the manufacture of maple-sugar, Sap	J. H. Fairchild	Highgate, Vt	June 10, 1862	35, 561
Bucket for wells, Self-tilting	A. J. Cook	North Branford, Conn	May 29, 1866	55, 062
Bucket, Hanging well	S. F. Dexter	Paris, N. Y	Mar. 15, 1859	23, 233
Bucket, Hoisting	E. J. Hulbert and A. N. N. Aubin.	Portland, Conn	Oct. 31, 1871	120, 522
Bucket holder, Sap	A. Franklin	Galena, Ohio	Sept. 19, 1871	119, 024
Bucket hoop, Sap	J. Bullock	Readsborough, Vt	June 19, 1866	55, 611
Bucket, Sap	J. W. Currier	Newbury, Vt	Mar. 31, 1868	76, 168
Bucket, Sap	C. C. Post	Hinesburgh, Vt	Sept. 13, 1870	107, 407
Bucket, Sap	J. Purdy	Cherburne, N. Y	Oct. 4, 1817	
Bucket, Self-dumping coal	J. Wüst	Philadelphia, Pa	July 13, 1858	20, 912
Bucket, Sheet-metal	W. Austin	Philadelphia, Pa	Aug. 12, 1873	141, 748
Bucket, Water	C. Ballinger	Buchanan, Pa	Apr. 30, 1872	126, 249
Bucket, Weighing	D. D. Stelle	New Brunswick, N. J	Jan. 10, 1865	45, 873
Bucket, Well	A. J. Clemmons	Aberdeen, Miss	Aug. 16, 1870	106, 326
Bucket, Well	D. P. Farnham	Johnstown Centre, Wis	Apr. 3, 1860	27, 708
Bucket, Well	C. F. Stites	Cincinnati, Ohio	July 1, 1873	140, 439
Bucket, Wood	S. S. Vail	Keokuk, Iowa	Sept. 20, 1870	107, 568
Buckets and tubs, Tool for finishing	J. W. Bartlett and A. Morris	Harmar and Marietta, Ohio	July 28, 1863	39, 334
Buckets, Apparatus for raising and tilting water	H. W. Sabin and L. B. Benton	Reed's Corner and Penn Yan, N. Y.	Mar. 13, 1849	6, 190
Buckets, Brake and ratchet for elevating and lowering.	I. T. Smith	Richmond, Va	Feb. 22, 1870	100, 201
Buckets, Construction of sheet-metal	J. Fallows	Philadelphia, Pa	Nov. 5, 1867	70, 427
Buckets, Device for holding sap	J. Bevins	Unadilla Forks, N. Y	Nov. 5, 1867	70, 394
Buckets, Ear of wooden	L. A. Fleming	New York, N. Y	Nov. 9, 1869	96, 571
Buckets in raising water from wells, Self-operating device for tilting.	D. P. Farnham	Milton, Wis	Feb. 3, 1857	16, 535
Buckets, Metallic guard for water	J. B. Hyzer	Janesville, Wis	Dec. 13, 1864	45, 412
Buckets, Mode of emptying well	E. Willard	Egremont, Mass	June 15, 1826	
Buckets, pails, tubs, &c., Machine for making	N. Rider	Sturbridge, Mass	Apr. 1, 1829	
Buckets, Raising tilting	I. I. Vedder and H. Vine	Schenectady, N. Y	Feb. 1, 1848	5, 425
Buckets, Stud for attaching bail to	W. Brown and C. Stevens	Saint Louis, Mo	July 2, 1872	128, 585
Buckets, Wire ear for metal	J. M. Shank	Dayton, Ohio	Aug. 3, 1869	93, 355
Buckle	J. J. Adair	Portland, Ind	Apr. 19, 1870	102, 076
Buckle	M. Adams	Chilmark, Mass	Mar. 22, 1870	100, 963
Buckle	J. K. Andrews	Antrim, Ohio	Nov. 19, 1867	71, 116
Buckle	H. Aschenbach	Washington, D. C	Oct. 31, 1865	50, 673
Buckle	W. Babin	New York, N. Y	Mar. 21, 1868	75, 722
Buckle	G. L. Bailey	Portland, Me	Apr. 8, 1862	34, 868
Buckle	T. Bailey and H. H. Young	Fairfax County, Va., and Washington, D. C.	Aug. 17, 1869	93, 792
Buckle	T. G. Bailey	Wassaic, N. Y	July 4, 1865	48, 503
Buckle	I. Banister	Newark, N. J	Mar. 15, 1864	41, 900
Buckle	I. Banister	Newark, N. J	Nov. 8, 1864	44, 927
Buckle	I. Banister	Newark, N. J	Feb. 14, 1865	46, 324
Buckle	I. Banister	Newark, N. J	July 7, 1868	79, 626
Buckle	J. Barron	Mobile, Ala	Apr. 30, 1867	64, 273
Buckle	J. Bavier	Newark, N. J	Feb. 14, 1865	46, 326
Buckle	H. Bernheimer and H. Newman	New York, N. Y	Aug. 17, 1869	93, 665
Buckle	E. C. Blakeslee	Waterbury, Conn	Nov. 19, 1867	70, 944
Buckle	J. M. Borchardt	New York, N. Y	Aug. 26, 1873	142, 076
Buckle	G. A. Brown	Kalamazoo, Mich	Feb. 2, 1869	86, 501
Buckle	J. Buche	Apple River, Ill	Nov. 28, 1871	121, 325
Buckle	I. W. Burch	Fayette, Miss	Dec. 14, 1869	97, 891
Buckle	S. P. Burdick	New York, N. Y	May 19, 1868	77, 955
Buckle	F. Busch	New York, N. Y	Oct. 8, 1872	132, 051
Buckle	W. C. Bussey	San Francisco, Cal	Aug. 20, 1872	130, 565
Buckle	D. S. Butler	Otterville, Mo	Oct. 26, 1868	96, 083
Buckle	C. A. Button	Pontiac, Mich	Dec. 4, 1866	60, 135
Buckle	C. S. Cissna	Burlington, Iowa	May 8, 1866	54, 504
Buckle	J. G. Clifton	Northfield, Ind	July 28, 1868	80, 454
Buckle	A. H. Cole	Sylvania, Ohio	Oct. 10, 1865	50, 337
Buckle	E. Cole	Fairfield, Mich	Sept. 24, 1867	69, 181
Buckle	E. Cole	Fairfield, Mich	Sept. 24, 1867	69, 182
Buckle	E. P. Corwin	Washington, Ill	Dec. 13, 1870	110, 115
Buckle	J. Cory	Wayne, Mich	Sept. 15, 1868	82, 091
Buckle	L. D. Cowles	Romeo, Mich	Aug. 4, 1868	80, 605
Buckle	L. D. Cowles	Romeo, Mich	Dec. 6, 1870	109, 871
Buckle	S. P. Crafts	New Haven, Conn	Jan. 16, 1866	52, 112
Buckle	J. Cumberland and J. R. McClintock.	Mobile, Ala., and New York, N. Y.	Dec. 21, 1858	22, 352
Buckle	T. B. DeForest	Birmingham, Conn	Nov. 20, 1866	59, 896
Buckle	T. B. DeForest	Birmingham, Conn	Mar. 5, 1867	62, 533
Buckle	N. Dice	Xenia, Ind	Jan. 4, 1870	98, 572
Buckle	S. H. Doughty	Nyack, N. Y	May 6, 1873	138, 487
Buckle	F. Douglas	Norwich, Conn	July 14, 1863	39, 217
Buckle	E. F. Driggs	Brooklyn, N. Y	Oct. 24, 1871	120, 187
Buckle	T. Duncan	Brookville, Md	June 21, 1870	104, 564
Buckle	E. F. Eaton	Northford, Conn	Sept. 28, 1869	95, 332
Buckle	A. R. Egbert	Philadelphia, Pa	May 1, 1866	54, 313
Buckle	L. Elsberg	New York, N. Y	Jan. 7, 1868	73, 176
Buckle	H. Fautz	Newark, N. J	July 30, 1872	130, 032
Buckle	O. A. Field	Minneapolis, Minn	Aug. 6, 1872	130, 119
Buckle	L. Fogg	Boston, Mass	June 2, 1863	38, 793
Buckle	M. Fowler	Wolcottville, Conn	Mar. 12, 1867	62, 832
Buckle	M. Fowler	Wolcottville, Conn	Oct. 6, 1868	82, 821
Buckle	N. D. Fowler	Valley Ford, Cal	Jan. 3, 1872	122, 315
Buckle	R. E. Frye	Manchester, N. H	Jan. 23, 1863	52, 154

Index of patents issued from the United States Patent Office from 1790 *to* 1873, *inclusive*—Continued.

Invention.	Inventor.	Residence.	Date.	No.
Buckle	J. N. Gaston	Lyons City, Iowa	Oct. 15, 1866	[illegible],793
Buckle	G. L. Gerard	New Haven, Conn	Aug. 6, 1867	67,428
Buckle	G. L. Gerard	New Haven, Conn	Jan. 14, 1868	73,242
Buckle	F. F. Greenwood	Hornsey, England	Dec. 14, 1869	97,969
Buckle	H. C. Griggs	Waterbury, Conn	Aug. 28, 1866	57,632
Buckle	H. C. Griggs	Waterbury, Conn	July 2, 1867	66,524
Buckle	H. C. Griggs	Waterbury, Conn	Apr. 21, 1868	77,033
Buckle	J. F. J. Gunning and I. T. Myer	New York, N. Y	June 26, 1866	55,854
Buckle	A. Hagny	Keokuk, Iowa	May 29, 1866	55,088
Buckle	J. C. Hall	Fayette, Miss	Apr. 3, 1860	27,714
Buckle	W. S. Hall	Quincy, Mass	Aug. 8, 1865	49,261
Buckle	E. Hambujer	Detroit, Mich	Mar. 19, 1867	63,040
Buckle	M. Haneline	Huntington, Ind	Mar. 9, 1869	87,563
Buckle	J. B. R. Hardeman	Tehuacana, Tex	June 18, 1872	128,037
Buckle	S. S. Hartshorn	Orange, Conn	July 10, 1855	13,218
Buckle	S. S. Hartshorn	Orange, Conn	Dec. 11, 1855	13,907
Buckle	S. S. Hartshorn	New Haven, Conn	July 24, 1860	29,270
Buckle	S. S. Hartshorn	New Haven, Conn	Feb. 13, 1866	52,568
Buckle	S. S. Hartshorn	New Haven, Conn	Feb. 26, 1867	62,485
Buckle	J. W. Hatch	Manlius, N. Y	Feb. 20, 1844	3,440
Buckle	C. B. Hatfield	Boston, Mass	June 13, 1865	48,236
Buckle	C. B. Hatfield	Boston, Mass	Oct. 31, 1865	50,706
Buckle	G. Havell	Newark, N. J	Aug. 23, 1864	43,945
Buckle	G. Havell	Newark, N. J	Aug. 8, 1871	117,882
Buckle	J. B. Hawley	New Haven, Conn	Jan. 15, 1867	61,192
Buckle	P. P. R. Hayden	New York, N. Y	Jan. 11, 1853	9,534
Buckle	H. Herbert	Jersey City, N. J	Oct. 27, 1868	83,381
Buckle	J. W. Hinman	Omro, Wis	Dec. 3, 1861	33,840
Buckle	J. P. Hisley	Syracuse, N. Y	Aug. 10, 1869	93,440
Buckle	A. H. Hopkins	Goshen, Ind	Oct. 8, 1867	69,669
Buckle	O. L. Hopson and H. P. Brooks	Waterbury, Conn	May 12, 1863	38,482
Buckle	O. L. Hopson and H. P. Brooks	Waterbury and Wolcottville, Conn.	Oct. 9, 1866	58,725
Buckle	G. C. Huntress	Elkhorn, Wis	June 11, 1867	65,749
Buckle	A. Hurd	Yonkers, N. Y	Feb. 11, 1868	74,367
Buckle	J. C. Hyde	West Haven, Conn	Nov. 15, 1870	109,321
Buckle	J. H. James	Warren, R. I	May 12, 1868	77,885
Buckle	W. B. Johnson	Bowling Green, Ky	Aug. 27, 1867	68,204
Buckle	W. V. Kay	Chicago, Ill	June 1, 1869	90,849
Buckle	G. R. Kelsey	Middletown, Conn	Jan. 15, 1850	7,025
Buckle	G. R. Kelsey	West Haven, Conn	Aug. 30, 1864	43,997
Buckle	G. R. Kelsey	West Haven, Conn	May 29, 1866	55,113
Buckle	G. R. Kelsey	West Haven, Conn	June 5, 1866	55,311
Buckle	H. Laurence	Manlius, N. Y	July 13, 1844	3,662
Buckle	B. S. Lawson	New York, N. Y	July 4, 1865	48,569
Buckle	H. Lowenberg	New York, N. Y	May 22, 1866	54,928
Buckle	W. Maclean and J. H. Harris	Vermont, Ill	June 1, 1869	90,859
Buckle	F. W. Maes	Ise lohn, Prussia	Jan. 28, 1868	73,734
Buckle	C. A. Mallory	Cambridge, Mass	Mar. 6, 1866	53,017
Buckle	T. P. Marshall	Trenton, N. J	July 5, 1859	24,649
Buckle	C. W. Martin	Mount Pleasant, Iowa	Jan. 21, 1868	73,620
Buckle	J. F. Martin	Harrisburgh, Oreg	May 9, 1871	114,580
Buckle	J. H. Martin	Columbus, Ohio	Apr. 18, 1871	113,902
Buckle	J. A. Mashmeyer	Beardstown, Ill	Apr. 21, 1868	77,064
Buckle	C. Maxwell and J. G. Lindner	Syracuse, N. Y	Apr. 2, 1872	125,315
Buckle	J. McLellen	Chambersburgh, Pa	July 24, 1866	56,590
Buckle	D. McMillan and A. Rowan	Webster City, Iowa	Mar. 21, 1871	112,947
Buckle	G. O. Monroe	New York, N. Y	Dec. 26, 1865	51,740
Buckle	C. F. Moore	Waveland, Ind	Oct. 22, 1872	132,482
Buckle	O. W. Morley	Ellisburgh, N. Y	Dec. 9, 1862	37,105
Buckle	J. H. Morris	Paxton, Ill	May 2, 1871	114,461
Buckle	M. Murphy	Washington, D. C	July 31, 1866	56,785
Buckle	H. Neumann	New York, N. Y	Feb. 12, 1867	62,059
Buckle	H. Neumann	New York, N. Y	Jan. 21, 1868	73,633
Buckle	T. L. Ogier	West Chester, Pa	May 14, 1867	64,693
Buckle	W. Parsons	Palmyra, N. Y	Sept. 9, 1873	142,721
Buckle	J. Peabody	Dixmont Centre, Me	Nov. 28, 1865	51,210
Buckle	J. Peckham	New Haven, Conn	Sept. 4, 1866	57,758
Buckle	J. Peckham	New Haven, Conn	May 30, 1871	115,513
Buckle	L. W. Perkins	Beloit, Wis	Apr. 10, 1866	53,866
Buckle	E. A. Pierce	Brighton, Mass	Apr. 22, 1862	35,038
Buckle	I. N. Plotts	New York, N. Y	Feb. 13, 1866	52,597
Buckle	I. N. Plotts	New York, N. Y	June 12, 1866	55,533
Buckle	N. Post	East Cleveland, Ohio	Oct. 10, 1865	50,286
Buckle	T. O. Potter and J. W. Smith	Boston, Mass	Jan. 9, 1872	122,533
Buckle	F. Puetz	Buffalo, N. Y	Dec. 6, 1870	109,941
Buckle	L. Rhoades	Newport, R. I	Oct. 22, 1867	70,019
Buckle	F. C. Richer	Gilmer, Tex	May 4, 1869	89,689
Buckle	E. G. Rockwood	Hillsdale, Mich	May 10, 1864	42,689
Buckle	W. Roemer	Newark, N. J	Sept. 3, 1872	131,028
Buckle	A. Roesler	Warsaw, Ill	May 24, 1859	24,145
Buckle	G. W. Roland	Salem, Oregon	May 11, 1869	90,026
Buckle	I. Roraback	South Bend, Ind	Aug. 13, 1867	67,808
Buckle	F. A. Ress and S. De La Mater	Terre Haute, Ind	June 13, 1871	115,985
Buckle	L. W. Russell	Galesburgh, Mich	June 19, 1866	55,717
Buckle	R. F. Russell	Hazelton, Pa	Mar. 12, 1872	124,514
Buckle	C. W. Saladee	Putnam, Ohio	Aug. 8, 1865	49,309
Buckle	H. Sanders	Utica, N. Y	Apr. 2, 1872	125,335
Buckle	A. V. Sargent	Syracuse, N. Y	June 1, 1869	90,878
Buckle	C. Sears and F. Townsend	Monmouth County, N. J., and Kings County, N. Y.	Mar. 21, 1865	46,948
Buckle	A. B. Shaw	Medford, Mass	Aug. 12, 1873	141,729
Buckle	J. Shepard	New Britain, Conn	Nov. 15, 1864	45,088
Buckle	W. Shove	Elizabethport, N. J	June 13, 1854	11,090
Buckle	D. L. Smith	Waterbury, Conn	June 13, 1865	48,241
Buckle	E. A. Smith	Waterbury, Conn	Jan. 22, 1867	61,477
Buckle	E. A. and D. L. Smith	Waterbury, Conn	July 31, 1866	56,811

Index of patents issued from the United States Patent Office from 1790 *to* 1873, *inclusive*—Continued.

Invention.	Inventor.	Residence.	Date.	No.
Buckle	E. A. and D. L. Smith	Waterbury, Conn	Apr. 25, 1871	114, 214
Buckle	E. A. and D. L. Smith	Waterbury, Conn	May 30, 1871	115, 535
Buckle	J. E. Smith	Waterbury, Conn	Apr. 23, 1861	32, 152
Buckle	J. E. Smith	Waterbury, Conn	June 6, 1865	48, 135
Buckle	P. W. Smith	Abington, Ill	Oct. 13, 1868	83, 102
Buckle	W. W. Smith	Marshall, Mich	July 18, 1854	11, 336
Buckle	L. A. Sprague	Brooklyn, N. Y	May 27, 1862	35, 401
Buckle	J. Stanbrough	Newark, N. J	Nov. 7, 1865	50, 852
Buckle	C. S. Stearns and T. Corey	Marlborough, Mass	Nov. 14, 1865	50, 992
Buckle	G. E. Stedman	Boston, Mass	Dec. 6, 1870	109, 849
Buckle	G. F. Stephens	Portland, Oreg	June 6, 1871	115, 654
Buckle	J. Stevens	New York, N. Y	Jan. 12, 1864	41, 267
Buckle	S. G. Sturges	Newark, N. J	July 16, 1872	129, 257
Buckle	H. R. Swan	Norwalk, Conn	Nov. 23, 1869	97, 133
Buckle	S. A. Tenny	Muskego, Wis	Oct. 6, 1868	82, 768
Buckle	D. S. Thompson	West Haven, Conn	June 26, 1866	55, 933
Buckle	W. McK. Thornton	Clinton, Wis	Sept. 3, 1867	68, 468
Buckle	W. McK. Thornton	Clinton, Wis	May 4, 1869	89, 836
Buckle	J. Tiebout	Brooklyn, N. Y	July 24, 1860	29, 332
Buckle	I. B. Verplank	Mentz, N. Y	Mar. 9, 1844	3, 471
Buckle	J. Waterman	New York, N. Y	Feb. 13, 1866	52, 652
Buckle	D. Webber	Houlton, Me	June 20, 1871	116, 124
Buckle	W. Welsh	McHenry, Ill	Dec. 4, 1866	60, 302
Buckle	P. White	Dixmont Centre, Me	July 4, 1865	48, 610
Buckle	H. S. Wilkin	Brooklyn, N. Y	May 9, 1871	114, 631
Buckle	J. J. Wilkins	Virdey, Ill	May 15, 1866	54, 803
Buckle	H. C. Wissel	Indiana, Pa	Aug. 18, 1868	81, 318
Buckle	C. E. Woodman	Boston, Mass	Apr. 20, 1869	89, 110
Buckle	C. E. Woodman and C. B. Hatfield.	Boston, Mass	Apr. 4, 1865	47, 159
Buckle	G. P. Woodruff	Watertown, Conn	Jan. 6, 1857	16, 347
Buckle	H. S. Woodruff	Janesville, Wis	Feb. 12, 1867	61, 979
Buckle	H. S. Woodruff	Janesville, Wis	Jan. 9, 1872	122, 545
Buckle	E. L. Woods	Alliance, Ohio	Dec. 17, 1867	72, 255
Buckle	H. B. Worcester	Chicago, Ill	Apr. 23, 1872	126, 003
Buckle	W. Yost	Butterville, Ohio	July 18, 1871	117, 232
Buckle and clasp	W. Church	Birmingham, England	Feb. 18, 1840	1, 490
Buckle and loop	S. C. Talcott	Ashtabula, Ohio	July 25, 1871	117, 347
Buckle and loop, Attaching	L. C. Chase	Boston, Mass	June 14, 1864	43, 093
Buckle and ring	R. C. Dunham	New Britain, Conn	Oct. 9, 1866	58, 619
Buckle and ring, Halter	L. E. Jones and T. M. Barber	Syracuse, N. Y	Feb. 21, 1871	112, 048
Buckle and snap, Combined	S. G. and W. E. Sturges	Newark, N. J.	June 22, 1869	91, 685
Buckle-attachment	W. E. Barton	East Hampton, Conn	June 6, 1865	48, 039
Buckle-attachment	R. T. Moss	Cambridge, Ohio	Oct. 22, 1867	70, 105
Buckle, Belt	I. Alexander	San Francisco, Cal	June 28, 1870	104, 683
Buckle, Belt	F. Clausen	San Francisco, Cal	Sept. 22, 1868	82, 291
Buckle, Belt	F. Clausen	San Francisco, Cal	May 25, 1869	90, 501
Buckle, Belt	W. Cummings	Sacramento, Cal	Aug. 11, 1868	80, 924
Buckle, Belt	P. M. Haas	Youngstown, Ohio	May 21, 1872	127, 048
Buckle, Belt	G. R. Kelsey	West Haven, Conn	Oct. 2, 1866	58, 430
Buckle, Belt	F. and C. Lemme	San Francisco, Cal	May 2, 1865	47, 556
Buckle, Breeching-loop	J. H. McGarrah	Princeton, Ind	Jan. 28, 1873	135, 238
Buckle, Bridle	D. S. Butler	Brownsville, Mo	Feb. 20, 1872	123, 866
Buckle-chape and strap-loop	G. Crouch	Westport, Conn	July 9, 1872	128, 714
Buckle-clasp	E. D. Ballou	Abington, Mass	May 29, 1866	55, 197
Buckle-closing die	M. Fowler	Wolcottville, Conn	Feb. 11, 1868	74, 335
Buckle, Double	E. W. Clark	Tallahassee, Fla	July 21, 1868	80, 139
Buckle-fastening	F. H. Gladding	Providence, R. I	Feb. 25, 1873	136, 151
Buckle-fastening	C. Goodyear, jr., and L. A. Sprague.	New York, N. Y	May 10, 1864	42, 726
Buckle-fastening	R. Meyer	Buffalo, N. Y	Jan. 29, 1867	61, 628
Buckle-fastening	W. Wiley, jr	Kokomo, Ind	Sept. 26, 1865	50, 195
Buckle for clothing	E. A. Smith	Waterbury, Conn	Nov. 16, 1869	96, 981
Buckle for grain-bands, bag-ties, &c	L. Kniffen	Rochester, Pa	Mar. 2, 1869	87, 500
Buckle for gaging reciprocating saws	H. W. Brown	Warren, Pa	May 27, 1873	139, 363
Buckle for harness	K. Thrashure	Manlius, N. Y	Jan. 16, 1845	3, 883
Buckle for harness	J. W. Ropp and R. C. Kibby	Elyria, Ohio	Mar. 11, 1873	136, 766
Buckle for harness, Trace	W. R. Knowles	Columbiana, Ohio	Feb. 15, 1870	99, 914
Buckle for harness-tug	R. Tattershall	Beloit, Wis	Oct. 11, 1864	44, 693
Buckle for harness, Wedge	K. Frasier	Syracuse, N. Y	Sept. 8, 1868	81, 993
Buckle for skirt-hoop	J. Stevens and J. Hanley	New York, N. Y	Dec. 21, 1858	22, 385
Buckle for waist-belt	W. U. Bohm	San Francisco, Cal	Jan. 27, 1863	37, 489
Buckle for wearing-apparel	E. Parker	Plymouth, Conn	Sept. 2, 1856	15, 666
Buckle for wearing-apparel	W. Slade	Gum Creek, Ga	Sept. 2, 1856	15, 671
Buckle gag-runner	J. McMartin	Janesville, Wis	Nov. 17, 1863	40, 636
Buckle, Girth	L. C. Chase	Boston, Mass	Nov. 8, 1859	26, 013
Buckle, Halter	F. Ditton	Auburn, N. Y	June 2, 1868	78, 516
Buckle, Halter	A. McGaffey	Burlington, Vt	Dec. 3, 1872	133, 657
Buckle, Halter	P. A. Snyder	Butterville, Ohio	July 18, 1871	117, 214
Buckle, Hames-tug	L. Wetzell	Washington, D. C	Jan. 7, 1868	73, 148
Buckle, Harness	J. Allbee	Squaw Grove, Ill	Dec. 9, 1873	145, 270
Buckle, Harness	J. Ammidon	Springfield, Mass	Jan. 7, 1862	34, 085
Buckle, Harness	A. E. Bailey and H. Nichols	Middleville, N. Y	Nov. 19, 1867	70, 940
Buckle, Harness	A. Bedford	Coldwater, Mich	June 2, 1868	78, 568
Buckle, Harness	A. Bedford	Coldwater, Mich	May 17, 1870	103, 128
Buckle, Harness	S. Bingham, jr	Poestenkill, N. Y	Dec. 10, 1850	7, 818
Buckle, Harness	O. Brown	Albia, Iowa	Oct. 31, 1871	120, 413
Buckle, Harness	A. B. Buell	Westmoreland, N. Y	June 19, 1847	5, 166
Buckle, Harness	O. S. Burges	Columbus, Ohio	Oct. 10, 1848	5, 838
Buckle, Harness	G. S. Caldwell	Syracuse, N. Y	Apr. 16, 1867	63, 782
Buckle, Harness	W. H. Cocks	Richmond, Ind	Sept. 17, 1867	68, 846
Buckle, Harness	J. W. Covel	Bangor, Me	July 31, 1860	29, 361
Buckle, Harness	L. D. Cowles	Armada, Mich	Oct. 25, 1864	44, 786
Buckle, &c., Harness	L. D Cowles	Armada, Mich	Oct. 25, 1864	44, 787
Buckle, Harness	T. Crakes	Mishawaka, Ind	June 20, 1871	116, 028
Buckle, Harness	P. S. Crawford	Rockford, Ill	May 26, 1868	78, 364
Buckle, Harness	E. S. Dawson	Syracuse, N. Y	Jan. 12, 1869	85, 798
Buckle, Harness	F. W. Dean	Tremont, Ill	May 25, 1869	90, 430

Index of patents issued from the United States Patent Office from 1790 *to* 1873, *inclusive*—Continued.

Invention.	Inventor.	Residence.	Date.	No.
Buckle, Harness	J. S. Embich	Green Village, Pa	May 21, 1850	7, 377
Buckle, Harness	K. Frazer	Fayetteville, N. Y	Mar. 26, 1845	3, 970
Buckle, Harness	K. Frazer	Syracuse, N. Y	Sept. 16, 1873	142, 907
Buckle, Harness	W. D. Hillis	Cuyahoga, Ohio	Jan. 26, 1847	4, 943
Buckle, Harness	R. A. Holmes	New York, N. Y	Sept. 19, 1848	5, 790
Buckle, Harness	J. Howey	New Pittsburgh, Ohio	Mar. 8, 1848	5, 465
Buckle, Harness	J. Ives	Mount Carmel, Conn	July 27, 1869	92, 973
Buckle, Harness	C. C. Lee	Falls Church, Va	May 27, 1873	139, 253
Buckle, Harness	A. C. Luther	Canton, Ohio	Apr. 20, 1869	89, 057
Buckle, Harness	J. H. Morris	Normal, Ill	Jan. 30, 1872	123, 281
Buckle, Harness	D. M. Nixon	Danville, Ill	May 17, 1864	42, 787
Buckle, Harness	O. B. North	New Haven, Conn	Sept. 23, 1873	143, 180
Buckle, Harness	C. B. Payne	Bloomington, Ill	May 19, 1868	78, 124
Buckle, Harness	M. W. Pond	Elyria, Ohio	Aug. 19, 1862	36, 235
Buckle, Harness	N. Post	East Cleveland, Ohio	Mar. 18, 1856	14, 469
Buckle, Harness	J. Prendergast	Boston, Mass	Nov. 10, 1857	18, 601
Buckle, Harness	J. Purplee	Wellington, Ohio	Oct. 4, 1864	44, 554
Buckle, Harness	G. Reyer	Indianapolis, Ind	Apr. 19, 1870	102, 040
Buckle, Harness	C. W. Saladee	Putnam, Ohio	May 2, 1865	47, 574
Buckle, Harness	S. S. Sargeant	Newark, N. J	May 14, 1872	126, 649
Buckle, Harness	J. L. Selleck	Baldwinsville, N. Y	Apr. 29, 1873	138, 291
Buckle, Harness	O. B. Smith	Monticello, N. Y	Dec. 21, 1858	22, 383
Buckle, Harness	M. M. Stewart	Mayfield, Ky	July 9, 1872	128, 824
Buckle, Harness	S. P. Taylor	Oxford, Ohio	June 30, 1868	79, 519
Buckle, Harness	W. H. Taylor	Baldwinsville, N. Y	July 14, 1868	79, 874
Buckle, Harness	E. Todd	Columbus, Ohio	May 22, 1846	6, 477
Buckle, Harness	S. E. Tyler and R. Tattershall	Beloit, Wis	Dec. 5, 1865	51, 367
Buckle, Harness	D. Vogt	Trenton, Mich	May 10, 1870	102, 889
Buckle, Harness	A. Walker	New Haven, Conn	Dec. 10, 1872	133, 904
Buckle, Harness and trace	H. Hise	Ottawa, Ill	Aug. 25, 1863	39, 651
Buckle, Harness-trace	P. Burns	Syracuse, N. Y	Sept. 24, 1872	131, 658
Buckle, Harness-trace	H. H. Hartzell	Holden, Mo	Sept. 30, 1873	143, 284
Buckle, Harness-tug	C. S. Abeel	Marshalltown, Iowa	Aug. 22, 1871	118, 326
Buckle, Harness-tug	G. H. Buckins	Canton, Ohio	June 29, 1869	92, 011
Buckle, Harness-tug	J. H. Feraw	Hinsdale, N. Y	July 27, 1858	20, 997
Buckle, Harness-tug	F. Seifert	Knoxville, Iowa	Feb. 4, 1873	135, 601
Buckle, Harness-tug	W. Straw and R. H. Armstrong	Hudson, Mich	May 11, 1858	20, 222
Buckle, Hat	J. N. Burton	Senoria, Ga	Mar. 10, 1868	75, 359
Buckle, Hitching-strap	P. J. Stoll	Marshallville, Ohio	Dec. 22, 1868	85, 186
Buckle, Lever	L. A. Sprague	New York, N. Y	Mar. 7, 1865	46, 719
Buckle, Lever	H. W. Warner	Greenfield, Mass	June 6, 1865	48, 121
Buckle-making machine	M. Fowler	Wolcottville, Conn	Aug. 20, 1867	67, 865
Buckle-making machine	J. Robbins	Auburn, N. Y	Dec. 7, 1869	97, 700
Buckle-making tool	R. Durning	Lawrenceville, Pa	Feb. 16, 1864	41, 610
Buckle manufacture	S. S. Hartshorn	Orange, Conn	Nov. 7, 1854	11, 892
Buckle, Mechanical spring	J. Green	New York, N. Y	May 25, 1807	
Buckle-polishing machine	R. G. Pine	Sing Sing, N. Y	Apr. 5, 1856	14, 633
Buckle, ring, &c	K. Frazer	Syracuse, N. Y	May 6, 1862	35, 150
Buckle, Safety harness	J. Chestnut, jr	Hustontown, Pa	Dec. 21, 1869	98, 147
Buckle, Self-fastening	W. W. Spencer	Pittsburgh, Pa	June 2, 1868	78, 491
Buckle, Self-tightening	M. Marvin	Salem, Oreg	Apr. 5, 1870	101, 482
Buckle, Shoe	J. Elleman	Providence, R. I	Oct. 10, 1865	50, 345
Buckle, Spring	J. F. Morsell	Stamford, Conn	Nov. 19, 1867	71, 041
Buckle, Suspender	C. Benedict	Waterbury, Conn	Oct. 22, 1850	7, 726
Buckle, Suspender	J. Bingham	Philadelphia, Pa	Feb. 4, 1843	2, 940
Buckle, Suspender	P. Blake	New Haven, Conn	Mar. 29, 1864	42, 067
Buckle, Suspender	H. Dubosq	Philadelphia, Pa	Apr. 25, 1844	3, 559
Buckle, Suspender	S. Hamm	Philadelphia, Pa	Sept. 23, 1873	143, 144
Buckle, Suspender	S. S. Hartzhorn	Naugatuck, Conn	Sept. 25, 1849	6, 736
Buckle, Suspender	A. Pototsky	New York, N. Y	July 14, 1868	79, 918
Buckle, Suspender	W. Scarlett	Newark, N. J	May 14, 1850	7, 370
Buckle, Suspender	A. Shenfield	New York, N. Y	Mar. 21, 1871	112, 857
Buckle, Suspender	E. Steele	Waterbury, Conn	Dec. 3, 1850	7, 814
Buckle, Suspender	O. Webb	New York, N. Y	July 5, 1817	
Buckle tab-plate	E. L. Parker	Birmingham, England	Feb. 13, 1872	123, 640
Buckle-tongue, Detachable	A. Worster	Hannibal, N. Y	Dec. 4, 1849	6, 931
Buckle-tongues, Tool for cutting holes in cloth or leather for.	A. Bedford	Coldwater, Mich	Aug. 25, 1868	81, 464
Buckle, Trace	R. J. Algeo	Kalamazoo, Mich	July 31, 1866	56, 689
Buckle, Trace	R. J. Baker	Madison, Wis	Aug. 27, 1867	68, 147
Buckle, Trace	E. K. Brayton and J. Baugh	Eau Claire, Wis	July 22, 1873	141, 108
Buckle, Trace	L. Brooks	Mount Pleasant, Iowa	Nov. 22, 1870	109, 378
Buckle, Trace	T. Brownlee	Fairbury, Ill	July 1, 1873	140, 463
Buckle, Trace	J. H. H. Buell	Oriskany, N. Y	Aug. 24, 1869	94, 070
Buckle, Trace	W. D. Bunker	Portage, Wis	Sept. 29, 1868	82, 489
Buckle, Trace	I. Clark	Dryden, Mich	Aug. 8, 1871	117, 742
Buckle, Trace	A. H. Cole	Adrian, Mich	May 9, 1871	114, 530
Buckle, Trace	E. A. Crownhart	Bridgeport, Conn	June 1, 1869	90, 641
Buckle, Trace	E. S. Dawson	Syracuse, N. Y	Feb. 9, 1869	86, 822
Buckle, Trace	M. H. Densmore	Shickshinny, Pa	Apr. 4, 1871	113, 406
Buckle, Trace	M. B. De Silva and G. T. Benjamin.	Cleveland, Ohio	Jan. 21, 1873	135, 093
Buckle, Trace	J. W. Denton	Paris, Ill	Aug. 14, 1866	57, 098
Buckle, Trace	C. Fillmore	Romeo, Mich	Dec. 31, 1867	72, 832
Buckle, Trace	O. Finch	Owego, N. Y	Sept. 17, 1867	68, 864
Buckle, Trace	K. Frazer	Syracuse, N. Y	Apr. 13, 1869	88, 952
Buckle, Trace	M. Gayhart	Young America, Wis	June 23, 1868	79, 064
Buckle, Trace	W. W. Gordon and D. Pettengill.	Delhi, N. Y	Oct. 6, 1868	82, 709
Buckle, Trace	W. B. Hayden	Columbus, Ohio	Oct. 8, 1867	69, 563
Buckle, Trace	H. Hise	Chicago, Ill	July 14, 1868	79, 978
Buckle, Trace	A. H. Hopson	Taylorville, Ill	Aug. 2, 1870	105, 941
Buckle, Trace	J. Kennedy	Osage Mission, Kans	Aug. 5, 1873	141, 565
Buckle, Trace	E. M. Kinne	Cuba, N. Y	Mar. 30, 1869	88, 489
Buckle, Trace	W. W. Kittleman	Bloomfield, Iowa	Dec. 27, 1870	110, 572
Buckle, Trace	W. W. Kittleman	Bloomfield, Iowa	Sept. 5, 1871	118, 724
Buckle, Trace	E. F. Lacy	Danville, Ill	Sept. 3, 1867	68, 756
Buckle, Trace	J. Lindsey	Litchfield, Ill	Mar. 26, 1872	125, 060

Index of patents issued from the United States Patent Office from 1790 *to* 1873, *inclusive*—Continued.

Invention.	Inventor.	Residence.	Date.	No.
Buckle, Trace	J. Lindsey	Litchfield, Ill	Nov. 26, 1872	133, 458
Buckle, Trace	D. F. Maine	Mansfield, Ohio	Sept. 19, 1865	50, 017
Buckle, Trace	J. H. Martin	Columbus, Ohio	Aug. 31, 1869	93, 229
Buckle, Trace	T. C. Martin and J. Offineer	Perrysville, Ohio	May 10, 1870	102, 843
Buckle, Trace	C. H. Miller	Buffalo, N. Y	Aug. 25, 1868	81, 394
Buckle, Trace	G. Oldham, jr	Cuba, N. Y	Apr. 25, 1871	114, 184
Buckle, Trace	C. B. Payne	Bloomington, Ill	Aug. 6, 1867	67, 448
Buckle, Trace	D. K. Peacock	Little Valley, N. Y	Aug. 8, 1871	117, 923
Buckle, Trace	W. G. Riley	Sullivan, Ind	Apr. 25, 1871	114, 201
Buckle, Trace	W. A. Robinson	Grand Rapids, Mich	Dec. 7, 1869	97, 704
Buckle, Trace	S. S. Sargeant	Newark, N. J	Nov. 26, 1872	133, 340
Buckle, Trace	C. Schwaner	Keokuk, Iowa	Sept. 10, 1867	68, 796
Buckle, Trace	C. H. Stevens	Fayetteville, N. Y	July 19, 1870	105, 509
Buckle, Trace	W. S. Thayer	Smithsborough, N. Y	Apr. 9, 1872	125, 631
Buckle, Trace	J. Thornton and C. F. Demmen	Wellsville, N. Y	Apr. 26, 1870	102, 333
Buckle, Trace	W. M. Thornton	Clinton, Wis	July 24, 1866	56, 638
Buckle, Trace	J. Welker	Attica, N. Y	June 15, 1869	91, 390
Buckle, Trace	H. S. Woodruff	Janesville, Wis	Nov. 14, 1865	50, 979
Buckle, Trace	A. Worster	Hannibal, N. Y	June 22, 1869	91, 807
Buckle, Trace	A. Worster	Syracuse, N. Y	June 22, 1869	91, 808
Buckle, Trace	A. Worster	Syracuse, N. Y	Oct. 31, 1871	120, 561
Buckle, Trace	W. Wyckoff	Chagrin Falls, Ohio	Aug. 22, 1865	49, 580
Buckle, Tug	C. W. Adams	Wheeling, W. Va	Feb. 11, 1873	135, 744
Buckle, Tug	J. C. Barrows	Centreville, Iowa	May 21, 1872	126, 920
Buckle, Tug	D. S. Butler	Otterville, Mo	June 1, 1869	90, 725
Buckle, Tug	G. P. Cole	Hudson, Mich	Mar. 31, 1868	76, 162
Buckle, Tug	H. Hise	Ottawa, Ill	Aug. 28, 1866	57, 507
Buckle, Tug	N. H. Howard	Beloit, Wis	Sept. 1, 1863	39, 734
Buckle, Tug	C. D. W. Ries	Edwards, N. Y	May 2, 1865	47, 570
Buckle, Turn	T. Gaillard	Brooklyn, N. Y	Mar. 18, 1873	136, 910
Buckle, Turn	M. White	Brooklyn, N. Y	Apr. 23, 1872	125, 999
Buckle, Wedge	M. W. Pond, jr., and A. T. Ballantine.	Titusville, Pa	Feb. 11, 1868	74, 243
Buckle with button-hole attachment	B. J. Greely	Boston, Mass	Aug. 16, 1870	106, 356
Buckles and straps, Metallic fastening for	H. H. Mansfield	South Canton, Mass	Oct. 9, 1866	58, 657
Buckles, Attachment for	C. H. Pratt	Boston, Mass	May 24, 1870	103, 395
Buckles, Clip for attaching	S. G. and W. E. Sturges	Newark, N. J	Aug. 24, 1869	94, 042
Buckles, Cutting and finishing harness	J. Carman	Hudson, N. Y	Oct. 12, 1814	....
Buckles, Machine for making suspender	C. A. Lent	Newark, N. J	Jan. 30, 1849	6, 074
Buckles, Machine for making suspender	W. Scarlett	Newark, N. J	Apr. 10, 1849	6, 311
Buckles, Machinery for making	L. P. Mitchell	Waterbury, Conn	Dec. 19, 1865	51, 606
Buckles, Machinery for making four-sided	A. and O. B. North and S. Frink.	New Britain, Conn	May 28, 1850	7, 398
Buckles, Making	G. B. McDonald	New Albany, Ind	May 14, 1867	64, 782
Buckles, Manufacture of	G. R. Kelsey	West Haven, Conn	Feb. 18, 1862	34, 429
Buckles, &c., Method of attaching loops to	L. C. Chase	Boston, Mass	June 13, 1865	48, 153
Buckles, Mode of fastening on	L. Hilbright	Newark, N. J	Oct. 4, 1864	44, 530
Buckles to straps, Mode of attaching	N. H. Furness	New York, N. Y	July 16, 1872	129, 022
Buckles to suspenders, &c., Attaching	J. Abernethy	Woodbury, Conn	July 3, 1849	6, 575
Buckwheat and barley huller	T. Register	West Township, Ohio	Apr. 5, 1832	....
Buckwheat-cleaning machine	D. Pease, jr	Floyd, N. Y	July 14, 1846	4, 628
Buckwheat-cleaning machine	J. H. Reed	Penn Township, Pa	Sept. 4, 1860	29, 940
Buckwheat-huller	C. B. Horton	Elmira, N. Y	May 22, 1855	12, 908
Buckwheat-huller	C. B. Horton	Elmira, N. Y	Aug. 13, 1861	33, 040
Buckwheat-huller	T. Nelson	Troy, N. Y	Mar. 15, 1870	100, 790
Buckwheat-huller, Cellular	A. Crawford	Wilkesbarre, Pa	Feb. 23, 1869	87, 093
Buckwheat, Hulling	W. Ager	Rohrsburgh, Pa	June 29, 1852	9, 064
Buckwheat-hulling machine	J. Baysore	Freeport, Ill	Jan. 7, 1868	73, 156
Buckwheat, Machine for scouring and hulling	J. N. Treadwell	Redding, Conn	Sept. 27, 1859	25, 593
Buckwheat-refiner	D. D. Brewster	West Laurens, N. Y	Apr. 25, 1871	114, 103
Buckwheat-size, Manufacture of	W. A. Comstock	Providence, R. I	Nov. 14, 1848	5, 915
Budding-knife	E. D. and R. Gird	Cedar Lake, N. Y., and Healdsburgh, Cal.	Feb. 4, 1862	34, 328
Buds from blossoming, Delaying	R. Moore	Rowan County, N. C	Mar. 16, 1822	....
Buffet-table	W. H. Tufts	Lynn, Mass	Nov. 11, 1873	144, 424
Buffing-knives, Implement for turning the edge of shoemakers'.	B. B. Webster	East Haverhill, Mass	May 10, 1870	102, 984
Buffing-machine	W. W. Messer, jr	Boston, Mass	Apr. 1, 1873	137, 465
Buffing wheel	E. and W. Dixon	Newark, N. J	Dec. 16, 1873	145, 492
Bug-destroying machine, Steam	J. Howlet	Greenborough, N. C	July 10, 1834	....
Bug or roach trap	J. M. Keep	New York, N. Y	May 23, 1871	115, 215
Bugs, perfuming houses, and cleaning furniture, Destroying.	J. H. Clark	Connersville, Ind	May 31, 1834	....
Buggy	J. H. Bye	Sterling, Ill	Dec. 8, 1863	40, 817
Buggy	J. R. Gilman	South Bend, Ind	Apr. 25, 1871	114, 000
Buggy	J. S. McClelland	Jefferson, Ind	Aug. 8, 1854	11, 486
Buggy	C. T. Stoddard	Colebrook, N. H	Apr. 8, 1873	137, 577
Buggy and wagon top	G. Fuchs	Milwaukee, Wis	Apr. 13, 1869	88, 954
Buggy-boats, Wheel of	P. Davis	Providence, R. I	July 12, 1859	24, 725
Buggy-body	C. P. Kimball	Portland, Me	Apr. 16, 1872	125, 817
Buggy-brake	I. L. Myers	Ferguson Township, Pa	Mar. 28, 1871	113, 193
Buggy-brake, Automatic	L. T. Conant	New Lisbon, Ohio	Aug. 23, 1870	106, 555
Buggy-coupling	L. G. Peel	Preston, Ga	Apr. 27, 1869	89, 336
Buggy-gear, Elastic	I. N. Topliff	Elyria, Ohio	June 4, 1872	127, 441
Buggy-gearing	J. B. Augur	Poughkeepsie, N. Y	May 10, 1870	102, 905
Buggy hanging-top	C. Smith	Stockbridge, Mich	Oct. 22, 1867	70, 128
Buggy, Joint-bodied	E. J. Green	Cedarville, N. Y	June 6, 1854	11, 042
Buggy, Joint-bodied	E. J. Green	Valparaiso, Ind	Apr. 12, 1859	23, 567
Buggy, Joint-bodied	E. J. Green and M. H. Wheeler	Cedarville, N. Y	Apr. 29, 1856	14, 766
Buggy pole and shaft, Combined	G. Steiner	Decdsville, Ind	July 16, 1872	129, 066
Buggy-reach	J. C. Hilsabeck	Montovallo, Mo	Nov. 7, 1871	120, 644
Buggy-reach	J. W. Reeder	West Manchester, Ohio	Oct. 15, 1872	132, 320
Buggy running-gear	E. P. Carter	Arcade, N. Y	Oct. 10, 1871	119, 819
Buggy-seat	C. Haas	Chicago, Ill	June 21, 1870	104, 583
Buggy-seat	E. T. Mithoff and J. W. Dann	Columbus, Ohio	Jan. 24, 1871	111, 232
Buggy-seat, Adjustable	D. and N. Kroninger	Eagle Point, Pa	Oct. 31, 1871	120, 444
Buggy-seat, Folding	T. H. Wood	New York, N. Y	July 26, 1870	105, 758
Buggy-seat rail	J. Carlisle	Mount Gilead, Ohio	Sept. 3, 1867	68, 486

Index of patents issued from the United States Patent Office from 1790 to 1873, inclusive—Continued.

Invention.	Inventor.	Residence.	Date.	No.
Buggy-seat shifting-rail	C. Disser	West Union, Ohio	Sept. 10, 1867	68, 717
Buggy-seats, Machine for boring	G. W. Lemley	Pavilion, N. Y	Apr. 29, 1862	35, 059
Buggy-shifting rail	H. French and R. Meyer	Buffalo, N. Y	Dec. 21, 1869	98, 048
Buggy-spring	H. H. Hill	Pontiac, Ill	July 18, 1871	117, 171
Buggy-spring	W. Humphreys	Brooklyn, N. Y	Oct. 29, 1867	70, 219
Buggy-spring	G. W. Kenan	Upper Sandusky, Ohio	Sept. 13, 1870	107, 386
Buggy-spring and attachment	G. A. Brown	Reading, Mich	Oct. 3, 1871	119, 564
Buggy-spring clip	R. A. Clark	Unadilla, N. Y	Mar. 14, 1871	112, 549
Buggy-tap	W. S. Johnson	Henderson, Ky	Jan. 21, 1868	73, 530
Buggy-top	R. Bower	Lima, Ohio	Feb. 13, 1872	123, 611
Buggy-top	A. M. Cory	New Providence, N. J	Dec. 7, 1869	97, 479
Buggy-top	L. H. Gano	Ripon, Wis	June 18, 1861	32, 558
Buggy-top	H. Hibbard	Henrietta, N. Y	July 15, 1851	8, 222
Buggy-top	J. C. McCully	Atchison, Kans	July 9, 1872	128, 895
Buggy-top	W. Tanner and W. Shimanaur	Findley, Ohio	June 11, 1872	127, 715
Buggy-top	J. S. Wayne	Quincy, Ill	Aug. 24, 1869	94, 049
Buggy-top bed	A. M. Corey	New Providence, N. J	June 7, 1870	103, 846
Buggy-top-bow setter	O. Smith	Bloomington, Ill	June 8, 1869	90, 965
Buggy-top, Detachable	A. M. Plimpton	Hornellsville, N. Y	Sept. 3, 1867	68, 455
Buggy-top fastening	D. S. Early	Hummelstown, Pa	Oct. 20, 1868	83, 269
Buggy-top, Fastening	H. F. Holt	Fredonia, N. Y	Nov. 26, 1867	71, 304
Buggy-top frame	J. H. Havens	Troy, Ohio	June 4, 1861	32, 477
Buggy-top joint and fastening	H. M. Curtis	Ypsilanti, Mich	Aug. 6, 1867	67, 418
Buggy-top prop	A. Huff and A. J. Mitchell	Louisville, Ky	Jan. 16, 1872	122, 833
Buggy-top roller	J. Palmer	Mechanicsburgh, Pa	Feb. 11, 1868	74, 414
Buggy-top, Shifting	B. L. Benson	Fairview, Ind	July 4, 1871	116, 540
Buggy-top, Shifting	R. C. Diehl	Scott Township, Columbia County, Pa.	July 1, 1873	140, 351
Buggy-top, Shifting	D. Eldridge	Salem, Ohio	Feb. 15, 1870	99, 865
Buggy-top, Shifting	T. Lodge	New Lisbon, Ohio	Oct. 20, 1868	83, 183
Buggy-top, Shifting	S. S. Meily	Lebanon, Pa	June 19, 1866	55, 690
Buggy-top, Shifting	G. Stricker	Catawissa, Pa	Aug. 9, 1870	106, 292
Buggy-tops, Device for shifting	W. B. Slutter	Warsaw, Ind	Aug. 17, 1869	93, 759
Buggy-tops, Machine for setting	J. B. Weller	Bellbrook, Ohio	Oct. 10, 1871	119, 728
Buggy-tops, Shifting-rail for	J. F. Regan	Chicago, Ill	Oct. 17, 1871	119, 951
Buggy-tops, Supporting top for folding	A. Dorm	Mount Healthy, Ohio	Nov. 8, 1870	109, 116
Buggies, Shifting-rail for	I. Bronson	Lockport, N. Y	Apr. 19, 1870	101, 980
Buggies, Shifting top-rail for	J. H. Harter	Nevada, Ohio	June 25, 1872	128, 305
Bugle, horn, cornet, &c	H. G. Lehnert	Boston, Mass	Feb. 13, 1866	52, 580
Bugle, Kent	R. Willis	West Point, N. Y	Nov. 10, 1827	....
Bugles, Manufacture of keyed	G. W. Shaw	Thompson, Conn	Aug. 4, 1845	4, 132
Buhr, Metallic	A. T. Boon	Galesburgh, Ill	Nov. 10, 1863	40, 549
Buhr-mill	S. G. Rollins	Boston, Mass	Dec. 6, 1870	109, 841
Buhr-stone mill	G. Sanford	Poughkeepsie, N. Y	Feb. 1, 1859	22, 829
Builder's jack	J. F. Darley	Nebraska City, Nebr	May 28, 1872	127, 314
Building	W. Damerel	Brooklyn, N. Y	Dec. 3, 1867	71, 587
Building	W. J. Fryer, jr	New York, N. Y	Apr. 13, 1869	88, 953
Building	J. Johnson and E. D. Davis	Brooklyn, N. Y	Sept. 17, 1867	68, 884
Building	J. Potts	Harrisburgh, Pa	Aug. 3, 1869	93, 227
Building	J. Touaillon	San Francisco, Cal	Feb. 15, 1870	99, 973
Building and roof, Iron	C. H. Parker	Boston, Mass	Apr. 30, 1872	126, 323
Building-block	N. Boch	New York, N. Y	June 6, 1871	115, 685
Building-block	J. L. Boone	San Francisco, Cal	June 4, 1872	127, 554
Building-block	F. W. Colby	Streater, Ill	Oct. 21, 1873	143, 809
Building-block	G. DeWitt and J. Fairman	Belleville, N. J., and New York, N. Y.	June 24, 1873	140, 122
Building-block	A. Foster and J. A. Messinger	Milwaukee, Wis	Jan. 16, 1855	12, 264
Building-block	S. T. Fowler	Brooklyn, N. Y	June 3, 1873	139, 462
Building-block	F. J. Huber	West Cleveland, Ohio	Aug. 12, 1862	36, 155
Building-block	C. S. Hutchinson	Burlington, N. J	Mar. 6, 1866	53, 004
Building-block	T. Hyatt	New York, N. Y	Sept. 2, 1873	142, 475
Building-block	R. M. Seldis	New York, N. Y	Oct. 28, 1873	144, 149
Building-block	J. S. Stewart	Homer, N. Y	Dec. 24, 1867	72, 557
Building-block and artificial stone	J. Leffler	Rochester, N. Y	Dec. 22, 1868	85, 231
Building-block and method of forming same	A. Derrom	Paterson, N. J	Jan. 30, 1872	123, 156
Building-block, Artificial	G. E. Van Derburgh	New York, N. Y	July 11, 1865	48, 744
Building-block, Child's	C. M. Crandall	Montrose, Pa	Feb. 5, 1867	61, 721
Building-block, Compound	A. Derrom	Paterson, N. J	Feb. 6, 1872	123, 385
Building-block, Hollow	M. R. Pierce	New York, N. Y	Nov. 21, 1871	121, 193
Building-block machinery	A. L. Finch	Sing Sing, N. Y	June 4, 1867	65, 365
Building-block mould	T. J. Lowry	Conneautville, Pa	July 28, 1868	80, 358
Building-block, Silicated	G. E. Van Derburgh	New York, N. Y	July 11, 1865	48, 745
Building-blocks, Casting	J. D. Wise	German Township, Ohio	Feb. 16, 1869	86, 961
Building-blocks, Compound for forming	G. Heim	Naperville, Ill	Apr. 27, 1869	89, 311
Building-blocks, Fire-proof	W. T. Van Zandt and L. A. Tartière.	New York, N. Y	Mar. 11, 1873	136, 684
Building-blocks from clay, Machine for molding and pressing.	A. Foster and G. M. Foster	New York, N. Y., and Fairhaven, Conn.	July 22, 1856	15, 374
Building-blocks from slag, Manufacture of	C. Diebold	Lebanon, Pa	Apr. 12, 1870	101, 835
Building-blocks, Mold for forming	A. Derrom	Paterson, N. J.	May 20, 1873	139, 050
Building-blocks, pavements, &c., Composition for forming.	S. E. Carr	Danville, Pa	Oct. 13, 1868	83, 037
Building, Corrugated metallic	R. Montgomery	New York, N. Y	Apr. 27, 1869	89, 540
Building-elevator	J. S. Baldwin	Newark, N. J	Oct. 20, 1868	83, 237
Building-elevator	D. H. Chamberlain	West Roxbury, Mass	Oct. 27, 1868	83, 461
Building-elevator	E. Keech	Poughkeepsie, N. Y	June 17, 1873	139, 896
Building-elevator	G. Müllar	New York, N. Y	Nov. 4, 1873	144, 350
Building-elevator	I. S. Schuyler and S. I. Thursby	Brooklyn, N. Y	June 17, 1873	140, 082
Building-elevator	D. B. Thompson	Brooklyn, N. Y	Mar. 3, 1868	75, 220
Building-facing	M. B. Dyott	Philadelphia, Pa	Aug. 16, 1853	9, 937
Building-facing	T. A. Hunter and J. Blewitt	New York, N. Y	Nov. 16, 1869	96, 921
Building, Fire-proof	J. J. Bartlett	New York, N. Y	Apr. 2, 1872	125, 163
Building, Fire-proof	R. M. Hoe	New York, N. Y	May 25, 1869	90, 361
Building, Fire-proof	A. K. Holte	Chicago, Ill	Mar. 4, 1873	136, 515
Building, Fire-proof	G. H. Johnson	New York, N. Y	Sept. 30, 1873	143, 351
Building, Fire-proof	J. H. Johnson and E. R. Hall	Chicago, Ill	Nov. 26, 1872	133, 448
Building, Fire-proof	E. May	Indianapolis, Ind	Jan. 26, 1869	86, 312
Building, Fire-proof	E. May	Indianapolis, Ind	May 4, 1869	89, 782

Index of patents issued from the United States Patent Office from 1790 *to* 1873, *inclusive*—Continued.

Invention.	Inventor.	Residence.	Dato.	No.
Building, Fire-proof	S. W. Sisson and W. C. Wetmore	Pulaski, Mich	Mar. 12, 1872	124, 453
Building, Firé-proof	L. A. Tartière	New York, N. Y	Sept. 23, 1873	143, 196
Building, Fire-proof	J. E. Mulford	New York, N. Y	May 27, 1873	139, 415
Building, Fire-proof	L. A. Tartière	New York, N. Y	Sept, 23, 1873	143, 197
Building, Fire proof	E. Vacher	New York, N. Y	Dec. 16, 1873	145, 700
Building, Fire-proof	J. H. Walker	Worcester, Mass	Sept. 2, 1873	142, 422
Building, Fire-proof	A. Wanner	New York, N. Y	Mar. 22, 1870	101, 191
Building, Fire-proof iron	E. Harmon	Washington, D. C	Jan. 2, 1855	12, 161
Building for preserving milk, fruit, &c	N. W. Clark	Detroit, Mich	Aug. 29, 1865	49, 604
Building for school-rooms, academies, &c	S. W. Taylor and J. W. Martin	Lowville, N. Y	Apr. 16, 1825	....
Building, Frame	L. H. Russell	Hyde Park, Mass	Oct. 22, 1872	132, 415
Building-fronts, Mode of constructing	I. S. Miller	New York, N. Y	Apr. 6, 1869	88, 578
Building-heater	J. A. Lawson	Troy, N. Y	Feb. 7, 1865	46, 250
Building-heater	G. S. G. Spence	Boston, Mass	June 28, 1859	24, 593
Building, Horticultural	F. Ludlow	Lake View, Ill	June 1, 1869	90, 760
Building, Iron	S. Colwell	Philadelphia, Pa	Apr. 11, 1854	10, 756
Building, Iron	J. M. Cornell	New York, N. Y	Jan. 16, 1872	122, 709
Building, Iron	B. J. La Mothe	New York, N. Y	Oct. 17, 1854	11, 809
Building, Iron	T. W. H. Mosely	Boston, Mass	Aug. 30, 1870	106, 854
Building-material elevator	J. C. Bennett and D. N. Green	Coldwater, Mich	May 24 1870	103, 414
Building-material elevator	J. H. Coe	Brighton, Mich	June 24, 1873	140, 116
Building-material elevator	J. King	Quincy, Ill	Sept. 3, 1872	131, 608
Building-materials, Composition for	S. Bissell	Hartford, Conn	Mar. 5, 1857	62, 521
Building-materials, Composition used as	N. C. Raymond	Austin, Tex	Oct. 12, 1858	21, 778
Building-materials, Machine for elevating	J. King	Quincy, Ill	May 20, 1873	139, 161
Building-materials, Raising	C. Samson	Brattleborough, Vt	Mar. 27, 1834	....
Building or room for the preservation of food, and for other purposes.	D. E. Somes	Washington, D. C	Feb. 7, 1865	46, 276
Building-pieces, Cast-iron	R. Wood	Philadelphia, Pa	Dec. 15, 1863	40, 975
Building, Portable	F. M. Bain	Delaware, Ohio	Aug. 8, 1871	117, 721
Building, Portable	D. S. Whittenball	Saint Louis, Mo	Mar. 24, 1868	76, 019
Building-purposes, Compound for	G. Heim	Naperville, Ill	Sept. 28, 1869	95, 226
Building-purposes, Staging for	E. D. Walker	Millbury, Mass	July 25, 1865	49, 617
Building-staging	W. Arronquier	Worcester Mass	Apr. 10, 1866	53, 768
Building-ventilator	G. R. Barker	Philadelphia, Pa	Oct. 21, 1873	143, 868
Building-ventilator	T. Boyd	Cambridgeport, Mass	Dec. 10, 1867	71, 964
Building-ventilator	J. Leeds	Philadelphia, Pa	Sept. 15, 1863	39, 937
Building-ventilator	G. W. Muir	Manchester, England	July 29, 1862	36, 059
Building-ventilator	S. O'Neil	New York, N. Y	July 2, 1872	128, 502
Building, Wooden	J. Busser	Troy, Ohio	Nov. 19, 1867	71, 130
Building-yard	A. W. Thompson	New York, N. Y	Apr. 30, 1872	126, 240
Buildings against fire, Securing	E. Mix	Batavia, N. Y	Nov. 22, 1832	....
Buildings, Apparatus for elevating and carrying material for.	M. F. Lyons	Brooklyn, N. Y	May 21, 1872	126, 890
Buildings, Apparatus for heating	S. F. Gold	Cornwall, Conn	June 21, 1859	24, 456
Buildings, Apparatus for heating	L. W. Leeds	New York, N. Y	Mar. 1, 1859	23, 096
Buildings, Apparatus for heating	G. Marlow	Cincinnati, Ohio	Sept. 11, 1860	29, 983
Buildings, Apparatus for heating	O. Packard	Roxbury, Mass	Mar. 9, 1842	2, 483
Buildings, Apparatus for heating	H. Richardson	Janesville, Wis	May 2, 1865	47, 569
Buildings, Apparatus for heating and ventilating	W. H. Churchman	Janesville, Wis	Nov. 23, 1858	22, 109
Buildings, Apparatus for heating and ventilating	M. W. Lester and M. Hjortsberg	Chicago, Ill	Jan. 3, 1860	26, 686
Buildings, Apparatus for heating and ventilating	J. Sawyer	Fitchburgh, Mass	Apr. 8, 1856	14, 642
Buildings, Apparatus for heating and ventilating	J. Stover	Richmond, Ind	Oct. 11, 1870	108, 202
Buildings, Apparatus for moving	E. H. Avery	Belvidere, Ill	Oct. 23, 1866	58, 970
Buildings, Apparatus for moving	W. N. Hemenway	Pecatonica, Ill	June 11, 1872	127, 766
Buildings, Apparatus for moving	M. N. Gordon	Foster's Crossing, Ohio	Sept. 13, 1870	107, 249
Buildings, Apparatus for moving	J. S. McIntire	Chicago, Ill	Aug. 15, 1865	49, 427
Buildings, Apparatus for moving	J. S. McIntire	Chicago, Ill	Oct. 10, 1865	50, 375
Buildings, Apparatus for moving	J. H. Moore	Binghamton, N. Y	Nov. 5, 1867	70, 596
Buildings, Apparatus for warming	B. Blaney	Boston, Mass	Sept. 7, 1844	3, 730
Buildings, Boiler for warming	C. F. Hitchings	New York, N. Y	Dec. 16, 1873	145, 654
Buildings, Brick cornice for	T. K. Beale	Alexandria, D. C	May 28. 1814	....
Buildings, Clamp for raising	N. Pickard	Rowley, Mass	May 12, 1863	38, 501
Buildings, Composition for coating the outside of	J. Müller	Newark, N. J	Sept. 19, 1871	119, 167
Buildings, Compounds for sanitary and decorative articles used in.	J. Rust	Vauxhall, England	Sept. 23, 1873	143, 096
Buildings, Connection for the beams and columns of iron.	J. Banks	New York, N. Y	Feb. 25, 1851	7, 951
Buildings, Constructing	A. Derrom	Paterson, N. J	Jan. 23, 1872	122, 937
Buildings, Constructing	L. Knapp	New York, N. Y	June 28, 1836	....
Buildings, Construction and ventilation of the walls of.	B. F. Farrar	Springfield, Mass	May 7, 1867	64, 512
Buildings, Construction of	W. Beschke	Philadelphia, Pa	Mar. 4, 1873	136, 407
Buildings, Construction of	H. H. Bryant	Boston, Mass	June 3, 1873	139, 451
Buildings, Construction of	B. J. La Mothe	New York, N. Y	Nov. 19, 1867	71, 185
Buildings, Construction of	W. McGiniss	Canandaigua, N. Y	June 4, 1872	127, 497
Buildings, Construction of	A. McPherson	Santa Cruz, Cal	Dec. 14, 1869	97, 948
Buildings, Construction of	W. J. Morden	Indianapolis, Ind	Jan. 21, 1873	135, 044
Buildings, Construction of	T. W. H. Moseley	Hydo Park, Mass	Aug. 22, 1871	118, 382
Buildings, Construction of	J. Tall	Southwark, England	May 6, 1873	138, 710
Buildings, Construction of frame, roof, and floor of iron.	J. Bogardus	New York, N. Y	May 7, 1850	7, 337
Buildings, Construction of metallic	S. Willard	Cincinnati, Ohio	Mar. 18, 1851	7, 993
Buildings, Construction of walls of	S. A. Clemens	Rockford, Ill	Feb. 4, 1862	34, 890
Buildings, Construction of wooden	O. C. Dodge	Brooklyn, N. Y	Mar. 5, 1872	124, 344
Buildings, Cooling	T. Krausch	New York, N. Y	Oct. 25, 1870	108, 707
Buildings, Cornice for	C. C. Hare	Louisville, Ky	May 19, 1868	78, 083
Buildings, Covering for steps of	A. A. Tremeschin	New York, N. Y	May 7, 1872	126, 428
Buildings, Device for moving	S. Inman	Rockford, Ill	Sept. 20, 1870	107, 617
Buildings, Foundation for	A. F. Cooper	San Francisco, Cal	Mar. 1, 1870	100, 262
Buildings from fire, Protecting	W. D. Baker	East Abington, Mass	Jan. 2, 1872	122, 350
Buildings, Furnace for heating	W. D. Bartlett	Amesbury, Mass	July 30, 1861	32, 955
Buildings, Furnace for heating	W. H. Churchman	Janesville, Wis	Aug. 14, 1860	29, 571
Buildings, Furnace for warming	G. A. G. Spence	Boston, Mass	June 5, 1855	13, 015
Buildings, Hatchway for	I. Amies	Philadelphia, Pa	June 8, 1869	91, 063
Buildings, Heating	T. Boyd	Allegheny City, Pa	June 16, 1868	78, 859
Buildings, Heating	R. Mitchell	Portland, Me	Apr. 11, 1842	2, 530
Buildings, Iron front for	J. Alexander and N. J. Burchell	Green Point and New York, N. Y.	May 25, 1869	90, 478

Index of patents issued from the United States Patent Office from 1790 *to* 1873, *inclusive*—Continued.

Invention.	Inventor.	Residence.	Date.	No.
Buildings, Iron front for	P. H. Jackson	New York, N. Y	Nov. 16, 1869	96, 922
Buildings, Machine for moving	S. Wells	Elmore, Ohio	May 22, 1860	28, 445
Buildings, Machine for removal of	E. Bowen	Ledyard, N. Y	Apr. 9, 1829	....
Buildings, &c., Machine for removing	L. Pullman	Portland, N. Y	Aug. 21, 1841	2, 225
Buildings, Means of ventilating	S. M. Stone	New Haven, Conn	Dec. 18, 1860	30, 938
Buildings, Method of moving	J. H. Moore	Binghamton, N. Y	May 7, 1867	64, 439
Buildings, Method of moving	J. H. Moore	Binghamton, N. Y	Apr. 21, 1868	77, 074
Buildings, Method of raising beats in	J. Van Gaasbeek	Mount Vernon, N. Y	Apr. 2, 1867	63, 583
Buildings, Method of removing	T. W. Prather	Iowa City, Iowa	Apr. 23, 1867	64, 032
Buildings, Mode of constructing	C. M. Amsden	Wooster, Ohio	May 28, 1872	127, 289
Buildings, Mode of constructing	F. O. Rogers	Niles, Mich	Dec. 11, 1866	60, 425
Buildings, Mode of constructing	A. Tanner	Hoboken, N. J	Nov. 13, 1866	59, 730
Buildings, Mode of constructing cast-iron	W. D. Terry	Boston, Mass	Feb. 5, 1856	14, 208
Buildings, Mode of constructing iron	A. J. Saxton	New York, N. Y	Aug. 8, 1854	11, 509
Buildings, Mode of constructing iron	S. J. Seely	Brooklyn, N. Y	May 7, 1861	32, 256
Buildings, Mode of covering	H. Knowles	Colchester, Conn	Oct. 11, 1828	....
Buildings, Mode of facing the walls of	T. S. Lambert	Peekskill, N. Y	Dec. 8, 1863	40, 844
Buildings. Mode of strengthening and improving sheet-iron.	S. J. Seely	Brooklyn, N. Y	Mar. 1, 1864	41, 787
Buildings of concrete, &c., Sectional mold for putting up.	J. R. Richards	Mount Joy, Pa	June 18, 1867	65, 945
Buildings, Safety-hatch for	G. N. Creamer	Trenton, N. J	Mar. 1, 1870	100, 264
Buildings, Seat for public	A. H. Allen	Boston, Mass	Dec. 5, 1854	12, 017
Buildings, Seat for public	A. Eliaers	Boston, Mass	Nov. 28, 1854	11, 991
Buildings, Service-pipe for	E. Hagan	New York, N. Y	Sept. 8, 1868	81, 895
Buildings, Sheathing-board for	W. E. Hale	Chicago, Ill	Feb. 1, 1870	99, 432
Buildings, Siding for	C. Avery	San Francisco, Cal	Sept. 13, 1870	107, 323
Buildings, Staging for	W. Arronquier	Worcester, Mass	Apr. 11, 1865	47, 179
Buildings, Stationary fire-pipe for	H. Palmieri	Philadelphia, Pa	Mar. 4, 1873	136, 537
Buildings, Steam device for washing	C. Nivert	Paris, France	Nov. 17, 1868	84, 132
Buildings, Underpinning for	I. S. Hill and A. Burnham	Boston and North Chelsea, Mass.	May 11, 1869	89, 995
Buildings, Ventilating	R. Mayo and R. Mills	Washington, D. C	Oct. 24, 1836	....
Buildings, Ventilating	L. B. Valk	Brooklyn, N. Y	Sept. 9, 1873	142, 598
Buildings, Wall for	J. Weathers	Greensburgh, Ind	Aug. 23, 1870	106, 749
Buildings, &c., Warming and ventilating	H. Ruttan	Coburg, Canada	Dec. 5, 1848	5, 958
Buildings water-proof, Mode of making	J. W. Kingman	North Bridgewater, Mass	June 10, 1862	35, 526
Bullet	J. Reim and J. Stock	New York, N. Y	Oct. 7, 1873	143, 419
Bullet-casting apparatus	E. May	Indianapolis, Ind	May 20, 1862	35, 320
Bullet-casting machine	R. Chadwick and N. Allen	Hartford, Conn	May 13, 1862	35, 275
Bullet-casting machine	J. P. Driver	Marengo, Iowa	Jan. 13, 1863	37, 389
Bullet, Elongated	E. D. Williams	Philadelphia, Pa	Dec. 9, 1862	37, 145
Bullet, Expanding	E. D. Williams	New York, N. Y	July 19, 1864	43, 615
Bullet, Explosive	S. H. Mead, jr	New York, N. Y	Dec. 10, 1872	133, 714
Bullet for fire-arms	G. W. Billings	New York, N. Y	Oct. 6, 1863	40, 153
Bullet for fire-arms	E. D. Williams	New York, N. Y	Sept. 27, 1864	44, 492
Bullet for rifled fire-arms	W. Rorbo	New York, N. Y	Sept. 5, 1865	49, 792
Bullet for small-arms	E. G. Allen	Boston, Mass	Dec. 6, 1864	45, 306
Bullet for small-arms	J. G. DeCoursey	Philadelphia, Pa	Apr. 3, 1866	53, 582
Bullet for small-arms, Compound	I. W. Shaler and R. Shaler	Brooklyn, N. Y., and Mattison, Conn.	Aug. 12, 1862	36, 197
Bullet-machine	J. D. Custer	Norristown, Pa	June 14, 1864	43, 102
Bullet-machine	J. A. Knight	Saint Louis, Mo	Sept. 14, 1858	21, 505
Bullet-machine	C. H. Remington	Dubuque, Iowa	Oct. 1, 1867	69, 481
Bullet-machine	W. Spillman	Marion Station, Miss	Nov. 19, 1867	71, 075
Bullet-machine	W. H. Ward	Auburn, N. Y	Nov. 10, 1857	18, 616
Bullet machine	C. Young	Auburn, N. Y	Sept. 7, 1858	21, 463
Bullet-making machine	R. Gornall	Baltimore, Md	Apr. 30, 1861	30, 232
Bullet-making machine	J. E. Granniss	New York, N. Y	Aug. 10, 1869	93, 613
Bullet-making machine	E. Nugent	Brooklyn, N. Y	Feb. 15, 1859	22, 974
Bullet-making machine	G. R. Stetson	New Haven, Conn	Nov. 12, 1872	133, 066
Bullet-making machinery	J. Drummond	New York, N. Y	May 9, 1848	5, 563
Bullet-mold	W. Ashton	Middletown, Conn	May 1, 1855	12, 774
Bullet-mold	T. Campbell and H. B. Poorman	Saint Louis, Mo	Jan. 6, 1857	16, 327
Bullet-mold	W. A. Clark	Bethany, Conn	Apr. 15, 1862	34, 944
Bullet-mold	H. L. DeZeng	Geneva, N. Y	Mar. 31, 1857	16, 910
Bullet-mold	J. S. Keith and J. Brooks	Canton, Mass	Feb. 20, 1855	12, 411
Bullet-mold	W. M. Storm	New York, N. Y	Apr. 25, 1854	10, 834
Bullet-mold, Revolving	J. Bradford	Chicago, Ill	Jan. 28, 1873	135, 197
Bullet-patch	A. C. Hobbs	Bridgeport, Conn	Apr. 4, 1871	113, 431
Bullet-pressing die	E. Brown	Brooklyn, N. Y	Apr. 9, 1872	125, 376
Bullets, Machine for lubricating	A. Ball	Worcester, Mass	May 23, 1865	47, 784
Bullets, Machine for making elongated	E. C. Hussey	Brooklyn, N. Y	June 17, 1862	35, 651
Bullets, Machine for making hollow	R. Gornall	Baltimore, Md	Dec. 14, 1858	22, 286
Bullets, Machine for molding	L. Hebard and W. S. Brown	Lexington, Cal	Mar. 6, 1866	52, 996
Bullets, Machine for patching	S. W. Wood	Cornwall, N. Y	Feb. 25, 1873	136, 352
Bullets, &c., Manufacture of	G. W. Campbell	Belleville, N. J	Nov. 20, 1847	5, 371
Bullets, Mode of patching	F. D. Newbury	Albany, N. Y	Feb. 10, 1857	16, 629
Bullets or pills, Machine for spherifying	J. F. Ostrander	New York, N. Y	Apr. 3, 1849	6, 265
Bullets, Patching Minie	O. D. Lull	Watkins, N. Y	Dec. 1, 1863	40, 761
Bulletin-board	A. M. Ernsberger	Danville, Ill	Nov. 28, 1871	121, 347
Bullion, Process for refining	J. Reynolds	San Francisco, Cal	Mar. 20, 1866	53, 340
Bullion, Process of reducing gold	R. S. McCulloh	Princeton, N. J	Sept. 24, 1850	7, 670
Bumper-spring	L. J. Frazee	Louisville, Ky	Dec. 31, 1872	134, 471
Bumper-spring	R. Levington	Monroe, Mich	Jan. 17, 1865	45, 927
Bundling-machine	E. J. Reddy	Bayville, N. Y	Aug. 4, 1868	80, 665
Bundling-press	C. R. Taylor	Ionia, Mich	Sept. 12, 1871	118, 829
Bung	J. F. Applegate	New Albany, Ind	June 14, 1870	104, 244
Bung	J. F. Applegate	New Albany, Ind	Aug. 2, 1870	106, 023
Bung	J. F. Applegate and C. Feiock	New Albany, Ind	Mar. 22, 1870	101, 078
Bung	T. Burke	New York, N. Y	June 18, 1872	128, 014
Bung	O. R. Burnham	New York, N. Y	Dec. 12, 1865	51, 422
Bung	W. Calhoun	West Troy, N. Y	Jan. 19, 1869	85, 903
Bung	N. L. Chappell and C. H. Pettit	New York, N. Y., and Jersey City, N. J.	Mar. 10, 1868	75, 367
Bung	W. F. Class	Cleveland, Ohio	Mar. 4, 1873	136, 415
Bung	D. M. Cumings	Newburyport, Mass	July 5, 1870	104, 035
Bung	V. Fountain, jr	West New Brighton, N. Y	Sept. 20, 1870	107, 473

Index of patents issued from the United States Patent Office from 1790 *to* 1873, *inclusive*—Continued.

Invention.	Inventor.	Residence.	Date.	No.
Bung	V. Fountain, jr	West New Brighton, N. Y	Dec. 5, 1871	121, 607
Bung	H. K. Hazlett	Saint Louis, Mo	Oct. 14, 1873	143, 573
Bung	V. A. Houdaille	Paris, France	Oct. 26, 1869	96, 116
Bung	H. Hufendick and E. Spangenberg.	Saint Louis, Mo	Nov. 27, 1866	60, 011
Bung	J. Kirby	Cincinnati, Ohio	Jan. 31, 1871	111, 352
Bung	J. B. Lefferson	New York, N. Y	Feb. 18, 1868	74, 702
Bung	D. Lightenstadt and R. Pentlarge.	Brooklyn and New York, N. Y.	Apr. 26, 1870	102, 285
Bung	J. G. Marriott and J. Ruegg	Saint Louis, Mo	July 9, 1872	128, 742
Bung	D. B. Rickey	San Francisco, Cal	Feb. 6, 1872	123, 421
Bung	C. C. Stremme	Austin, Tex	Apr. 14, 1868	76, 670
Bung	A. Warth	Stapleton, N. Y	July 19, 1870	105, 613
Bung	A. Warth	Stapleton, N. Y	Aug. 2, 1870	106, 100
Bung	E. White and W. Shilock	New York, N. Y	Jan. 28, 1868	73, 856
Bung and bung-inserter	D. B. Rickey	San Francisco, Cal	Sept. 19, 1871	119, 094
Bung and bush	J. Ruegg	Saint Louis, Mo	Oct. 22, 1867	70, 024
Bung and bushing	A. D. Behan	Syracuse, N. Y	Dec. 24, 1872	134, 242
Bung-attachment to barrels	A. Wieners	Williamsburgh, N. Y	Dec. 12, 1871	121, 834
Bung, Barrel	M. S. Drake	Newark, N. J	Jan. 22, 1867	61, 328
Bung, Beer-barrel	E. Kraff	Tyrone, Pa	Dec. 23, 1873	145, 878
Bung, Beer-cask	M. Hoy	Philadelphia, Pa	May 22, 1866	54, 904
Bung-borer	J. G. Baker and H. Asbury	Philadelphia, Pa	Sept. 22, 1868	82, 374
Bung-borer	W. A. Ives	New Haven, Conn	Aug. 9, 1870	106, 168
Bung-borer	W. A. Ives	New Haven, Conn	May 23, 1871	115, 211
Bung-bush	O. P. and L. W. Briggs	Chicago, Ill	Mar. 11, 1873	136, 696
Bung-bush	W. Kenyon and A. Menzies	New York, N. Y	June 9, 1863	38, 830
Bung-bush inserter	L. Littlejohn	New York, N. Y	May 6, 1873	138, 568
Bung-bush inserter	L. Littlejohn	New York, N. Y	Dec. 23, 1873	145, 867
Bung-bushes, Apparatus for molding	J. More	New York, N. Y	Dec. 3, 1872	133, 592
Bung-bushes, Tool for seating	L. Littlejohn	New York, N. Y	Aug. 5, 1873	141, 511
Bung-cutter	J. Christiansen	Milwaukee, Wis	July 28, 1863	39, 339
Bung-cutter	B. and F. Geyler	Cincinnati, Ohio	Mar. 23, 1869	88, 030
Bung-cutter	A. J. Gibson	Cincinnati, Ohio	June 15, 1869	91, 225
Bung-cutter	A. Goetzinger	Cincinnati, Ohio	July 13, 1869	92, 439
Bung-cutter	C. W. Harris	Pittsburgh, Pa	July 21, 1863	39, 288
Bung-cutter	J. Kirby	Cincinnati, Ohio	June 7, 1859	24, 310
Bung-cutter	J. Kirby	Cincinnati, Ohio	Dec. 24, 1867	72, 505
Bung-cutter	J. I. Munroe	Woburn, Mass	Apr. 12, 1870	101, 903
Bung-cutter	J. I. Munroe	Woburn, Mass	July 9, 1872	128, 745
Bung-cutter	A. W. C. Sternberg	Davenport, Iowa	May 23, 1871	115, 253
Bung-cutter	N. J. Templeton	Cincinnati, Ohio	July 19, 1870	105, 606
Bung-cutter	J. Tiebout	Brooklyn, N. Y	June 5, 1860	28, 640
Bung-cutter	C. Van Derzee	Albany, N. Y	June 24, 1862	35, 741
Bung-cutting machine	A. Donaldson	Salem, Mass	Jan. 15, 1818	....
Bung-cutting machine	A. J. Gibson	Cincinnati, Ohio	Jan. 5, 1869	85, 579
Bung-cutting machine	J. Kirby	Cincinnati, Ohio	Sept. 12, 1848	5, 759
Bung-cutting machine	J. Kirby	Cincinnati, Ohio	Sept. 29, 1857	18, 287
Bung-cutting machine	J. Lyon and G. H. Brady	New York, N. Y	Nov. 16, 1858	22, 101
Bung-cutting machine	J. H. Murrill	Baltimore, Md	Apr. 21, 1868	76, 936
Bung-cutting machine	J. G. Schmidt	Rochester, N. Y	May 7, 1867	64, 581
Bung-cutting machine	J. E. Smith	Buffalo, N. Y	Dec. 4, 1866	60, 272
Bung-cutting machine	W. L. Standish	Pittsburgh, Pa	July 23, 1867	67, 079
Bung-cutting machine	F. Zünkeler	Cincinnati, Ohio	Sept. 13, 1864	44, 267
Bung-cutting machinery	J. P. Gaume	Cincinnati, Ohio	June 6, 1848	5, 613
Bung-elevator	D. F. Fetter	New York, N. Y	Dec. 13, 1870	110, 127
Bung-extractor	J. Kirby	Cincinnati, Ohio	Jan. 31, 1871	111, 351
Bung-extractor	F. Miller and H. Pernot	New York, N. Y	Nov. 26, 1867	71, 402
Bung, Fermentation	W. W. Woodruff	New Britain, Conn	Apr. 21, 1868	77, 154
Bung for barrels	C. A. Neuhaus	New York, N. Y	June 27, 1865	48, 427
Bung for barrels and other vessels	A. G. Day	Seymour, Conn	June 27, 1865	48, 377
Bung for beer-barrels	J. E. McBeth	New Orleans, La	Jan. 22, 1867	61, 348
Bung for casks	M. Hickey	Boston, Mass	Aug. 15, 1865	49, 473
Bung for casks	A. A. Stimson	Boston, Mass	June 30, 1868	79, 407
Bung for casks, barrels, &c	J. Miller	Buffalo, N. Y	Mar. 19, 1867	63, 076
Bung for casks or barrels	M. C. Cronk	Auburn, N. Y	Sept. 3, 1867	68, 417
Bung for coal-oil barrels, &c	J. S. Loomis and A. Thompson	Brooklyn, N. Y	Feb. 17, 1863	37, 722
Bung for oil-casks	A. Walton	Philadelphia, Pa	Sept. 16, 1862	36, 490
Bung-hole borer and reamer	J. Kirby	Cincinnati, Ohio	Sept. 20, 1859	25, 512
Bung-holes, Tool for facing	T. T. Prosser and G. W. Gillette	Chicago, Ill	Feb. 11, 1873	135, 843
Bung-inserter	J. Gillies	Glasgow, Great Britain	Dec. 19, 1871	122, 006
Bung-lock	H. Fisc	Lanesville, Ind	Nov. 1, 1870	108, 897
Bung-making	W. Long and J. Garand	West Troy and Troy, N. Y.	Aug. 10, 1869	93, 457
Bung-making machine	J. Batchelder	Canaan, N. H	Sept. 13, 1864	44, 251
Bung, Metallic	W. Boynton	Auburn, N. Y	Feb. 12, 1867	61, 993
Bung, Metallic	T. B. Smith	Marietta, Ohio	July 19, 1859	24, 827
Bung of cask	J. Keane	New York, N. Y	Sept. 27, 1859	25, 606
Bung, Self-venting	C. F. Spencer	Cleveland, Ohio	Aug. 19, 1873	142, 051
Bung socket and plug for barrels	S. J. Geoghegan and W. Ulmer	New York, N. Y	Feb. 24, 1863	37, 747
Bung-spout	J. Marvin and W. T. Hulse	Port Jefferson, N. Y	Aug. 29, 1871	118, 545
Bung-stave for barrels	F. Acker	San Francisco, Cal	Dec. 20, 1864	45, 553
Bung-tap for casks	G. W. Banker	Saint Louis, Mo	Feb. 16, 1869	87, 021
Bung, Valve	F. Dahis	Williamsburgh, N. Y	Feb. 8, 1859	22, 857
Bung, Vent	B. R. Cole	Buffalo, N. Y	July 11, 1871	116, 809
Bung, Vent	C. H. Miller and W. Ascough	Buffalo, N. Y	Sept. 12, 1871	118, 811
Bung with automatic vent, Metallic	A. Ruoff	Detroit, Mich	Aug. 10, 1869	93, 481
Bungs, Combined bush and wrench for	J. Lacey and G. B. Cornell	Chicago, Ill	Aug. 29, 1871	118, 617
Bungs for barrels, Machine for cutting	J. G. Schmidt	Rochester, N. Y	Dec. 11, 1866	60, 430
Bungs for casks, Machines for making	W. Donaldson	Cincinnati, Ohio	June 16, 1868	78, 938
Bungs for casks, Making	R. Pentlarge	Brooklyn, N. Y	Dec. 23, 1873	145, 897
Bungs for casks, &c., Ventilating	J. B. Melvin	Lowell, Mass	Apr. 16, 1867	63, 920
Bungs from barrels, Extracting	H. Meyers and A. Webb	Hyde Park and Scranton, Pa.	July 17, 1866	56, 431
Bungs impervious to liquids and gases, Mode of rendering wooden.	P. Geier	Cincinnati, Ohio	Feb. 23, 1869	87, 163
Bungs, Machine for cutting	R. Barlow	Philadelphia, Pa	June 29, 1833	....
Bungs, Machine for cutting	G. D. Yates	Hartford, Conn	May 2, 1835	....
Bungs, Machine for making	C. Abel	Morrisania, N. Y	Nov. 12, 1872	132, 943
Bungs, Machine for making	R. Boeklen	Brooklyn, N. Y	Jan. 28, 1873	135, 196

Index of patents issued from the United States Patent Office from 1790 *to* 1873, *inclusive*—Continued.

Invention.	Inventor.	Residence.	Date.	No.
Bungs, Manufacture of	L. Gray	Pittsburgh, Pa	Aug. 25, 1863	39, 644
Bungs. Manufacture of	B. D. Sanders	Wellsburgh, W. Va	June 1, 1869	90, 690
Bungs, Manufacturing	R. Barlow	Philadelphia, Pa	Dec. 1, 1832	....
Bungs or corks, Machine for cutting	P. Hayden	Pittsburgh, Pa	Feb. 9, 1864	41, 506
Bungs out of barrels, Instrument for wrenching	A. Herdo	Baltimore, Md	Oct. 8, 1867	69, 563
Bungs, plugs, &c., Mold for casting	A. H. Rowand	Allegheny, Pa	Mar. 1, 1864	41, 786
Bunter-shape swaging and forming die	A. E. Barnard	Akron, Ohio	Dec. 3, 1867	71, 567
Buoy	W. M. Ellis	Washington, D. C	Oct. 7, 1856	15, 845
Buoy, Channel	W. W. Goff	Eagle Harbor, Mich	July 7, 1868	79, 750
Buoy-light	L. Stevens	Washington, D. C	Mar. 26, 1872	125, 096
Buoy, Tidal-alarm	J. Taggart	Roxbury, Mass	June 24, 1856	15, 200
Buoys and other floating bodies, Method of obtaining foundations and of mooring ships to.	A. Mitchell	Belfast, Ireland	Apr. 1, 1845	3, 986
Buoying vessels, Apparatus for	E. Goulard	New York, N. Y	Apr. 2, 1861	31, 885
Bureau	J. H. Better	New York, N. Y	Jan. 24, 1860	26, 881
Bureau	G. S. Graf	Pittsburgh, Pa	May 10, 1870	102, 809
Bureau	C. Kilburn	Philadelphia, Pa	Aug. 30, 1870	106, 941
Bureau	H. Rocke	New York, N. Y	Feb. 6, 1872	123, 422
Bureau and bath-tub, Combined dressing	J. E. Gilman	Hartford, Conn	Sept. 20, 1870	107, 479
Bureau and bedstead	J. Stock	El Paso, Ill	Aug. 13, 1867	67, 816
Bureau and clothes-drier, Combined	W. Hathaway	Northbridge, Mass	June 18, 1872	128, 038
Bureau and commode	G. W. Koch	New York, N. Y	Sept. 5, 1865	49, 766
Bureau and ironing-table combined	W. W. Adams	Rockford, Ill	May 20, 1873	139, 101
Bureau and trunk, Combination of	A. V. Ryder	New York, N. Y	Aug. 25, 1863	39, 679
Bureau and wardrobe, Combined	H. H. Stangaard	Chicago, Ill	Dec. 9, 1873	145, 312
Bureau and washstand, Combined	J. Schneemann	New York, N. Y	Apr. 23, 1872	125, 991
Bureau boot-blacking attachment	W. E. Phelps	Elmwood, Ill	May 24, 1870	103, 365
Bureau, Bracket	O. Andrews	Lanesville, Mass	July 23, 1872	129, 704
Bureau cabinet. Dressing	W. E. Beames	New York, N. Y	June 15, 1869	91, 409
Bureau-drawer fastening	A. J. Grant	Williamstown, N. Y	July 22, 1873	141, 001
Bureau-drawer fastening	G. Wode	Elizabethport, N. J	July 30, 1850	7, 541
Bureau dressing-table	N. Perry	Boston, Mass	Oct. 13, 1809	....
Bureau, Folding	J. E. Lawrence and J. S. Young.	Philadelphia, Pa	Dec. 26, 1871	122, 179
Bureau or wardrobe bedstead	C. May	Cincinnati, Ohio	Mar. 4, 1873	136, 443
Bureau, Portable	L. Heywood, J. L. Ross, and J. K. Otis.	Boston, Mass	Aug. 22, 1854	11, 551
Bureau, Sectional	E. Gill	New York, N. Y	Jan. 12, 1869	85, 811
Bureau toilet-attachment	H. W. Eastman	Baltimore, Md	Apr. 28, 1868	77, 263
Bureau, Wardrobe	J. H. F. Lehmann	New York, N. Y	June 11, 1872	127, 778
Bureau, wash-stand, and commode, Combined	L. Aling	Zeeland, Mich	Mar. 19, 1872	124, 653
Bureau, wash-stand, and wardrobe, Combined	T. W. Moore	New York, N. Y	Apr. 1, 1873	137, 380
Bureaus and wash-stands, Construction of	J. D. Burton	Boston, Mass	Jan. 12, 1858	19, 069
Bureaus, &c., Device for holding together the different parts of.	D. A. Mullane and J. O. L. Murray.	New Orleans, La	Feb. 1, 1870	99, 460
Bureaus, &c., Device for holding together the different parts of.	J. O. L. Murray and D. A. Mullane.	New Orleans, La	Oct. 5, 1869	95, 504
Burglar-alarm	G. S. Acker	Kalamazoo. Mich	Oct. 15, 1867	69, 888
Burglar-alarm	H. P. Beardsley and G. Wilcox.	Corunna, Mich	Sept. 22, 1868	82, 275
Burglar-alarm	H. Behn	New York. N. Y	Mar. 19, 1867	62, 998
Burglar-alarm	H. Bergstein	San Francisco, Cal	June 1, 1869	90, 809
Burglar-alarm	G. W. Bigelow	New Haven, Conn	Apr. 10, 1860	27, 772
Burglar-alarm	A. Bingham	Boston, Mass	Aug. 21, 1855	13, 478
Burglar-alarm	C. A. Blake	Philadelphia, Pa	Nov. 27, 1866	59, 949
Burglar-alarm	F. W. Blakemore	Philadelphia, Pa	Dec. 23, 1873	145, 836
Burglar-alarm	L. W. Blakeslee and A. D. Smith.	Cincinnati, Ohio	Dec. 31, 1867	72, 786
Burglar-alarm	J. G. Bolen	New York, N. Y	Oct. 21, 1851	8, 439
Burglar-alarm	O. M. Brooks and R. W. Soper.	Janesville, Wis	July 9, 1867	66, 457
Burglar-alarm	H. L. Brower	New York, N. Y	Feb. 25, 1873	136, 210
Burglar-alarm	E. Brown	Rindge, N. H	Oct. 4, 1853	10, 077
Burglar-alarm	E. Brown	Lowell, Mass	Oct. 31, 1854	11, 856
Burglar-alarm	E. Brown	Lowell, Mass	July 3, 1855	13, 157
Burglar-alarm	H. L. Brown	Middletown, Conn	Dec. 9, 1873	145, 332
Burglar-alarm	G. Bruce, sr	Sing Sing, N. Y	May 21, 1861	32, 349
Burglar-alarm	I. N. Buck	Elgin, Ill	Dec. 22, 1868	85, 066
Burglar-alarm	I. N. Buck	Elgin, Ill	Apr. 27, 1869	89, 286
Burglar-alarm	R. Bunker	Hudson, Wis	Mar. 5, 1867	62, 604
Burglar-alarm	R. M. Campbell	East Cambridge, Mass	Mar. 8, 1859	23, 215
Burglar-alarm	H. D. Chance	Allentown, Pa	June 1, 1869	90, 636
Burglar-alarm	J. G. Clark	Augusta, Ga	May 24, 1859	24, 177
Burglar-alarm	E. F. Clegg	North Harpersfield, N. Y	Nov. 29, 1870	109, 588
Burglar-alarm	G. A. Colton	Adrian, Mich	Jan. 1, 1867	60, 695
Burglar-alarm	D. Coon	Ithaca, N. Y	May 26, 1857	17, 406
Burglar-alarm	S. Coon	Ithaca, N. Y	Sept. 22, 1857	18, 236
Burglar-alarm	J. F. Coppock	West Newton, Ind	Apr. 8, 1873	137, 532
Burglar-alarm	T. P. Coulston	Philadelphia, Pa	Aug. 22, 1871	118, 345
Burglar-alarm	C. J. Crum and W. Irwin	Circleville, Ohio	Dec. 31, 1867	72, 723
Burglar-alarm	B. F. and J. F. Cunningham	Flora, Ill	Dec. 24, 1867	72, 459
Burglar-alarm	A. W. Decrow	Bangor, Me	Sept. 14, 1858	21, 555
Burglar-alarm	A. W. Decrow	Bangor, Me	Dec. 12, 1865	51, 511
Burglar-alarm	L. E. Denison	Saybrook, Conn	Oct. 22, 1840	1, 835
Burglar-alarm	C. A. Eaton	Minneapolis, Minn	Sept. 17, 1867	68, 857
Burglar-alarm	D. E. Eaton	Boston. Mass	Oct. 30, 1855	13, 738
Burglar-alarm	W. H. Emmons and F. Kissam.	New York, N. Y., and Newark. N. J.	Oct. 26, 1869	96, 094
Burglar-alarm	A. H. Enholm	Saint Louis, Mo	July 3, 1860	28, 977
Burglar-alarm	W. Farnham	Janesville, Wis	Dec. 4, 1866	60, 162
Burglar-alarm	J. Foster	Green Point, N. Y	Oct. 31, 1854	11, 859
Burglar-alarm	R. G. Fowler	Olney, Ill	Jan. 1, 1867	60, 711
Burglar-alarm	W. F. Gardiner	Bethany, Canada	Dec. 12, 1871	121, 862
Burglar-alarm	M. A. Genung	Granville, Ohio	Nov. 3, 1863	40, 469
Burglar-alarm	H. Green	Norwalk, Conn	Jan. 4, 1870	98, 489
Burglar-alarm	D. Haldeman	Morgantown, Va	Feb. 6, 1855	12, 351
Burglar-alarm	S. Hamilton, jr	Tolland, Mass	Dec. 4, 1855	13, 874
Burglar-alarm	A. F. Hammond	Houston, Ohio	May 8, 1866	54, 531
Burglar-alarm	G. R. Harding	Manchester, Va	Feb. 23, 1869	87, 256
Burglar-alarm	E. H. Hendrickson	Brooklyn, N. Y	June 24, 1873	140, 134
Burglar-alarm	M. C. Heptinstall	Enfield, N. C	Mar. 13, 1866	53, 144

Index of patents issued from the United States Patent Office from 1790 *to* 1873, *inclusive*—Continued.

Invention.	Inventor.	Residence.	Date.	No.
Burglar-alarm	H. Hersch, B. Bauman, and H. C. Locher.	Lancaster, Pa	Apr. 13, 1858	19, 973
Burglar-alarm	H. L. Hervey	Quincy, Ill	Dec. 4, 1855	13, 870
Burglar-alarm	I. and A. Herzberg	Philadelphia, Pa	Apr. 2, 1872	125, 293
Burglar-alarm	I. and A. Herzberg	Philadelphia, Pa	July 16, 1872	129, 344
Burglar-alarm	W. O. Hills	Nottingham, N. Y	Mar. 6, 1866	52, 999
Burglar-alarm	H. Holcroft	Media, Pa	Mar. 5, 1872	124, 356
Burglar-alarm	S. B. Holden	Woburn, Mass	Oct. 11, 1859	25, 788
Burglar-alarm	M. A. Holland	Passaic, N. J	Sept. 12, 1871	118, 939
Burglar-alarm	H. P. Hood	Indianapolis, Ind	Sept. 9, 1873	142, 630
Burglar-alarm	E. Hoole	New York, N. Y	May 1, 1866	54, 353
Burglar-alarm	T. N. Howell	Circleville, Ohio	Apr. 2, 1872	125, 296
Burglar-alarm	M. J. Hunt	Rising Sun, Md	Dec. 13, 1870	110, 043
Burglar-alarm	J. C. Huntly	Philadelphia, Pa	June 12, 1860	28, 671
Burglar-alarm	A. G. Hutchinson	Stoneycroft, near Liverpool, England.	July 13, 1869	92, 610
Burglar-alarm	J. J. Jackson	Curwinsville, Pa	Sept. 7, 1869	94, 604
Burglar-alarm	N. Jensen	Washington, D. C	Nov. 9, 1858	22, 024
Burglar-alarm	J. J. Kane	Brooklyn, N. Y	Dec. 30, 1873	146, 006
Burglar-alarm	P. Kane and W. Floyd	South Perry, Ohio	Dec. 3, 1861	33, 842
Burglar-alarm	A. Kazenmayer and L. Valois	Newark, N. J	Feb. 11, 1868	74, 375
Burglar-alarm	E. C. C. Kellogg	Hartford, Conn	Nov. 19, 1867	71, 180
Burglar-alarm	C. Knisely	Chicago, Ill	Mar. 24, 1868	75, 771
Burglar-alarm	N. P. Larsen	Chicago, Ill	Sept. 8, 1868	81, 913
Burglar-alarm	R. Lee	Cincinnati, Ohio	Mar. 7, 1871	112, 359
Burglar-alarm	G. A. Lilliendahl	New York, N. Y	Feb. 15, 1859	22, 959
Burglar-alarm	A. J. Loomis	Madrid, N. Y	May 23, 1865	47, 841
Burglar-alarm	G. W. Lore	Owasso, Mich	June 4, 1872	127, 421
Burglar-alarm	M. Lunt	Cambridgeport, Mass	Dec. 21, 1869	98, 078
Burglar-alarm	E. F. Mallory	West Springfield, Pa	Sept. 3, 1867	68, 520
Burglar-alarm	D. E. McDougall	Springfield, Mass	June 20, 1854	11, 131
Burglar-alarm	J. McDowell	Washington, Pa	Feb. 21, 1871	111, 959
Burglar-alarm	W. McLachlan	New York, N. Y	Nov. 4, 1856	16, 017
Burglar alarm	W. H. McPherson	Nashville, Tenn	Mar. 18, 1873	137, 016
Burglar-alarm	E. M. and I. E. Mix	Ithaca, N. Y	Sept. 29, 1857	18, 292
Burglar-alarm	J. Morgan, jr	Wheeling, W. Va	July 25, 1871	117, 444
Burglar-alarm	M. P. Murphy	New York, N. Y	Mar. 6, 1866	53, 030
Burglar-alarm	J. T. Mygatt and J. Downing	Binghamton, N. Y	Mar. 28, 1871	113, 082
Burglar-alarm	R. W. Newbery	New York, N. Y	Oct. 24, 1871	120, 313
Burglar-alarm	M. R. Perkins	Portsmouth, N. H	July 29, 1873	141, 291
Burglar-alarm	C. E. Pierce	New York, N. Y	June 25, 1867	66, 040
Burglar-alarm	M. Pierson and M. D. Manville	Adams, N. Y	Jan. 12, 1869	85, 848
Burglar-alarm	H. H. Potter	Carthage, N. Y	July 10, 1866	56, 262
Burglar-alarm	M. L. Powell	Newcastle, Ind	July 23, 1861	32, 891
Burglar-alarm	W. Reynolds	Manchester, N. H	July 12, 1870	105, 369
Burglar-alarm	W. Reynolds	Manchester, N. H	Jan. 17, 1871	111, 003
Burglar-alarm	H. R. Robbins	Baltimore, Md	Oct. 19, 1858	21, 849
Burglar-alarm	H. R. Robbins	Baltimore, Md	June 18, 1867	65, 949
Burglar-alarm	A. J. Ross	Rochester, N. Y	May 29, 1866	55, 165
Burglar-alarm	A. Q. Ross	Cincinnati, Ohio	Sept. 27, 1859	25, 586
Burglar-alarm	A. Q. Ross	Cincinnati, Ohio	Oct. 31, 1871	120, 399
Burglar-alarm	T. Royer	Lancaster, Pa	Nov. 26, 1867	71, 537
Burglar-alarm	R. Shaler	Madison, Conn	Mar. 15, 1870	100, 933
Burglar-alarm	I. Silvernail	Byron, Mich	Oct. 26, 1869	96, 277
Burglar-alarm	G. Simpson	Waterbury, Vt	June 5, 1866	55, 378
Burglar-alarm	D. B. Skelly	Lockport, N. Y	Nov. 19, 1867	71, 073
Burglar-alarm	S. Stewart	Philadelphia, Pa	Aug. 9, 1859	25, 057
Burglar-alarm	B. L. Stone	San Francisco, Cal	Feb. 14, 1865	46, 402
Burglar-alarm	B. L. Stone	New York, N. Y	Dec. 12, 1865	51, 489
Burglar-alarm	C. H. Stone and C. W. Livingston.	South Groton, Mass	Apr. 7, 1863	38, 136
Burglar-alarm	J. H. Thorp	New York, N. Y	Dec. 6, 1870	109, 970
Burglar-alarm	J. G. Trout	Philadelphia, Pa	Apr. 2, 1867	63, 582
Burglar-alarm	C. Waterman	New York, N. Y	Mar. 19, 1867	63, 124
Burglar-alarm	R. M. Webb	New York, N. Y	July 17, 1866	56, 471
Burglar-alarm	D. Wells	Philadelphia, Pa	Jan. 2, 1855	12, 177
Burglar-alarm	I. M. Wells	Jeffersonville, Ohio	June 11, 1867	65, 710
Burglar-alarm	I. M. Wells	Jeffersonville, Ohio	Feb. 25, 1868	74, 779
Burglar-alarm	J. N. Wells	Brooklyn, N. Y	Sept. 14, 1869	94, 929
Burglar-alarm	S. Whitaker	Macon, Ill	Aug. 6, 1867	67, 619
Burglar-alarm	H. Wickham, jr	Chicago, Ill	June 19, 1866	55, 754
Burglar-alarm	J. P. Wilson and J. F. Thomas	Frankfort and Ilion, N. Y	Feb. 8, 1859	22, 911
Burglar-alarm	H. J. Wolters	Chester, Mass	Nov. 17, 1868	84, 153
Burglar-alarm	L. J. Worden and E. H. Space	Clinton, N. Y	Jan. 27, 1852	8, 699
Burglar-alarm	W. D. Wright	Baltimore, Md	Mar. 2, 1858	19, 527
Burglar-alarm	H. Yerty	Sidney, Ohio	Oct. 30, 1866	59, 307
Burglar-alarm and lock	E. Warne	Broadway, N. J	Sept. 12, 1865	49, 940
Burglar-alarm and animal-trap, Combined	G. Smith	New York, N. Y	June 11, 1861	32, 539
Burglar-alarm and door-fastener	F. Oakley	London, England	Aug. 28, 1866	57, 654
Burglar-alarm and door-fastener, Combined	W. W. Marston	New York, N. Y	May 7, 1872	126, 558
Burglar-alarm and hotel-room indicator	L. C. Gosson	Trenton, N. J	Apr. 35, 1871	114, 001
Burglar-alarm and lock-apparatus	C. E. Pierce	New York, N. Y	Dec. 3, 1867	71, 637
Burglar alarm and signal, Circuit-closer for electrical.	E. Holmes and H. C. Roome	Brooklyn, N. Y., and Jersey City, N. J.	Nov. 7, 1871	120, 744
Burglar-alarm and table-bell	A. Iske	Lancaster, Pa	Dec. 8, 1868	84, 696
Burglar-alarm apparatus for portable safes, &c	S. J. Hoffman	Mobile, Ala	May 28, 1872	127, 165
Burglar-alarm drawer	J. Murphy	Boston, Mass	Mar. 14, 1871	112, 619
Burglar-alarm, Electrical	H. E. Walter	Richfield Springs, N. Y	May 13, 1873	138, 965
Burglar-alarm, Electro-magnetic	J. Haller	Ann Arbor, Mich	Sept. 25, 1860	30, 141
Burglar-alarm, Electro-magnetic	W. J. Biggar, J. C. Blood, and D. M. Griswold.	Conneaut, Ohio	July 14, 1868	79, 895
Burglar-alarm, Electro-magnetic	J. G. Butler	Glen's Falls, N. Y	May 2, 1871	114, 406
Burglar-alarm, Electro-magnetic	E. C. Clay	Malden, Mass	Nov. 1, 1859	25, 950
Burglar-alarm, Electro-magnetic	G. E. Cook and J. H. Guest	New York, N. Y	Aug. 22, 1871	118, 199
Burglar-alarm, Electro-magnetic	J. M. Dillo	Cooperstown, Pa	Nov. 29, 1870	109, 723
Burglar-alarm, Electro-magnetic	W. B Guernsey	Jersey City, N. J	Oct. 11, 1870	108, 257
Burglar-alarm, Electro-magnetic	W. B. Guernsey	Jersey City, N. J	Mar. 14, 1871	112, 704
Burglar-alarm, Electro-magnetic	W. B. Guernsey	Jersey City, N. J	Mar. 14, 1871	112, 705

Index of patents issued from the United States Patent Office from 1790 *to* 1873, *inclusive*—Continued.

Invention.	Inventor.	Residence.	Date.	No.
Burglar-alarm, Electro-magnetic	W. B. Guernsey	Jersey City, N. J	Mar. 14, 1871	112, 706
Burglar-alarm, Electro-magnetic	W. B. Guernsey	Jersey City, N. J	Apr. 30, 1872	126, 288
Burglar-alarm, Electro-magnetic	G. F. Milliken	Somerville, Mass	Oct. 11, 1859	25, 753
Burglar-alarm, Electro-magnetic	J. P. Snyder	Brooklyn, N. Y	Apr. 4, 1871	113, 589
Burglar-alarm, Electro-magnetic	W. E. Tracer	Philadelphia, Pa	Mar. 28, 1871	113, 036
Burglar-alarm for door spring	G. W. R. Pollock	Boston, Mass	May 25, 1869	90, 575
Burglar-alarm for window	M. A. Holland	Passaic, N. J	Sept. 12, 1871	118, 940
Burglar-alarm for window	W. H. Winans	Coxsackie, N. Y	Mar. 13, 1866	53, 239
Burglar-alarm lock	A. Corey	Casstown, Ohio	May 25, 1858	20, 333
Burglar-alarm lock	A. L. Gennerat	Paris, France	May 28, 1867	65, 207
Burglar-alarm, Portable	J. Pennepacker	Philadelphia, Pa	Sept. 30, 1873	143, 379
Burglar-alarm, Portable	J. H. Thorp	Saint Louis, Mo	May 27, 1873	139, 440
Burglar-alarm, Portable	J. N. Webster and D. Fey	Peoria, Ill	July 23, 1872	129, 698
Burglar and fire alarm	J. Holmes and C. W. Nickerson.	Pittsburgh, Pa	Feb. 12, 1867	61, 033
Burglar and fire alarm combined	L. Giebrich	Ottumwa, Iowa	Oct. 24, 1871	120, 261
Burglar and fire alarm, Electro-magnetic	E. Blunt, jr	Bay Ridge, N. Y	June 30, 1868	79, 440
Burglar and fire alarm, Electro-magnetic	J. H. Guest	Brooklyn, N. Y	July 14, 1868	79, 973
Burglar and safety alarm, Electro-magnetic	A. O. Willcox	Philadelphia, Pa	July 2, 1872	128, 691
Burglar-trap	W. Carr	Yellow Springs, Ohio	May 5, 1868	77, 582
Burial-apparatus	W. H. McGavran	Connotton, Ohio	Nov. 7, 1871	120, 657
Burial-case	A. C. Barstow	Providence, R. I	Apr. 19, 1859	23, 652
Burial-case	E. H. Borton	Saint Louis, Mo	June 9, 1863	38, 857
Burial-case	J. B. Cox	San Francisco, Cal	Oct. 7, 1873	143, 438
Burial-case	A. Crosby	Westfield, N. Y	June 22, 1869	91, 611
Burial-case	J. A. Dandridge	Buffalo, N. Y	Sept. 28, 1869	95, 202
Burial-case	P. H. Griffin	Albany, N. Y	Jan. 24, 1871	111, 117
Burial-case	J. Hackett	Louisville, Ky	Dec. 5, 1871	121, 616
Burial-case	J. R. Hathaway	Westfield, N. Y	Feb. 18, 1868	74, 531
Burial-case	J. R. Hathaway	Westfield, N. Y	Feb. 2, 1869	86, 396
Burial-case	R. F. Hill	Philadelphia, Pa	Dec. 17, 1867	72, 295
Burial-case	R. J. Howdon	Cincinnati, Ohio	Mar. 19, 1872	124, 747
Burial-case	R. Hunt	Milford, N. J	June 28, 1870	104, 737
Burial-case	I. Lorde	Moline, Ill	Jan. 17, 1871	110, 984
Burial-case	J. L. Lovett, J. Wippich, and J. Wood.	Salem, Mass	Feb. 27, 1866	52, 865
Burial-case	W. K. Miller	Canton, Ohio	Aug. 28, 1866	57, 545
Burial-case	C. C. W. Morgan	Holly Springs, Miss	Nov. 19, 1872	133, 166
Burial-case	G. W. Nash	Columbus, Ohio	Aug. 6, 1872	130, 235
Burial-case	A. S. Patterson	Westfield, N. Y	Aug. 17, 1869	93, 832
Burial-case	J. Peak and F. T. Pinkham	Boston, Mass	Mar. 22, 1864	42, 018
Burial-case	G. W. Scollay	Saint Louis, Mo	Mar. 18, 1862	34, 700
Burial-case	G. W. Scollay	Washington, D. C	Feb. 20, 1866	52, 756
Burial-case	F. B. Shearer	Columbus, Ohio	Jan. 24, 1871	111, 263
Burial-case	G. Shilling	Baltimore, Md	Sept. 20, 1870	107, 552
Burial-case	I. C. Shuler	Amsterdam, N. Y	May 23, 1871	115, 116
Burial-case	E. A. Skeele	Saint Louis, Mo	Sept. 1, 1863	39, 758
Burial-case	S. Stein	Rochester, N. Y	Mar. 19, 1872	124, 769
Burial-case	J. H. Van Houten	New York, N. Y	Oct. 8, 1867	69, 596
Burial-case	F. Vester	Newark, N. J	Aug. 25, 1868	81, 437
Burial-case	J. H. Weaver	Baltimore, Md	May 7, 1861	32, 261
Burial-case	J. Weidenmann	Hartford, Conn	Feb. 13, 1872	123, 599
Burial-case, Air-tight	C. Timmerman	Amsterdam, N. Y	June 12, 1866	55, 555
Burial-case, Composition	F. W. Brown	Albany, N. Y	Mar. 28, 1871	113, 138
Burial-case, Metallic	A. C. Barstow	Providence, R. I	Jan. 27, 1863	37, 484
Burial-case, Metallic	M. H. Crane	Cincinnati, Ohio	May 5, 1863	38, 443
Burial case, Metallic	M. H. Crane	Cincinnati, Ohio	May 7, 1867	64, 496
Burial-case, Mold for cement	P. B. Viele	Rochester, N. Y	Dec. 3, 1872	133, 684
Burial-case, Self-sealing	P. F. Lawshe	Rochester, Minn	May 5, 1868	77, 627
Burial-case, Wooden	J. Gawler	Washington, D. C	May 11, 1869	89, 982
Burial-cases, Composition for the manufacture of	J. R. Hathaway	Westfield, N. Y	Oct. 27, 1868	83, 495
Burial-cases, Device for making ends of	E. T. Smith and J. S. Winston	New York, N. Y	May 30, 1871	115, 536
Burial-cases, Vent for	W. W. Woodward	Cincinnati, Ohio	Sept. 3, 1872	131, 073
Burial-casket	J. A. Fogg	Salem, Mass	May 1, 1866	54, 321
Burial-casket	H. Henika and M. F. Carder	Kalamazoo, Mich	June 3, 1873	139, 465
Burial-casket	C. S. Hurlbut	Springfield, Mass	Apr. 20, 1869	89, 148
Burial-casket	J. O. Moore	Albany, N. Y	Aug. 8, 1871	117, 800
Burial-casket	J. Scott	Philadelphia, Pa	Oct. 24, 1871	120, 171
Burial-casket	E. T. Smith and J. S. Winston	New York, N. Y	Jan. 31, 1871	111, 393
Burial-casket	S. Stein	Rochester, N. Y	Oct. 29, 1872	132, 605
Burial-casket	S. Stein	Rochester, N. Y	Jan. 7, 1873	134, 570
Burial-casket, Composition	A. N. Atwood	Philadelphia, Pa	Mar. 4, 1873	136, 404
Burial-casket fastening	E. S Earley	Philadelphia, Pa	Nov. 26, 1867	71, 468
Burial-casket handle	A G. Chapman	East Hampton, Conn	Apr. 1, 1873	137, 289
Burial-casket handle	C. Strong	Winsted, Conn	Jan. 24, 1871	111, 271
Burial caskets, Composition for	W. H. Ross	Brooklyn, N. Y	July 29, 1873	141, 238
Burial caskets, Lid-fastening for	W. Hamilton	Allegheny City, Pa	Sept. 13, 1870	107, 253
Burner	S. C. Pruden	Harmony, Ohio	Jan. 28, 1868	73, 834
Burner, Aëro-gas	W. Jones	Chelsea, Mass	Jan. 5, 1869	85, 671
Burner, Aëro-gas	W. Jones and M. H. Collins	Chelsea, Mass	Aug. 7, 1866	56, 949
Burner, Aëro-vapor	W. Bryent	Boston, Mass	Nov. 21, 1865	51, 011
Burner, Aëro-vapor	O. F. Morrill	Chelsea, Mass	Oct. 20, 1863	40, 353
Burner, Air and vapor	O. F. Morrill	Boston, Mass	Oct. 20, 1857	18, 465
Burner and lamp-post, Combined vapor	B. D. Evans	Columbus, Ohio	June 1, 1869	90, 8[illegible]0
Burner and reflector, Gas	H. Berg and A. Blessing	Springfield, Mass	Jan. 1, 1867	60, 674
Burner and stop-cock, Gas	E. Jones	Boston, Mass	Oct. 3, 1865	50, 302
Burner and wick-tube of vapor-lamp	M. Safford	Boston, Mass	July 20, 1858	20, 977
Burner, Argand	C. E. Ball	Philadelphia, Pa	June 24, 1873	140, 108
Burner, Argand	E. P. Gleason	New York, N. Y	Dec. 17, 1867	72, 187
Burner, Argand	E. R. Walker	New York, N. Y	Dec. 17, 1867	72, 241
Burner, Argand gas	W. W. Batchelder	New York, N. Y	June 15, 1858	20, 604
Burner, Argand gas	T. Clough	New York, N. Y	May 13, 1873	138, 858
Burner, Argand gas	G. Darricott and J. Nason	Boston, Mass	July 26, 1839	1, 261
Burner, Argand gas	J. B. Fuller	Norwich, Conn	July 26, 1870	105, 795
Burner, Argand gas	G. W. Hatch	Brooklyn, N. Y	June 25, 1872	128, 307
Burner, Argand gas	H. W. Hayden	Waterbury, Conn	Jan. 2, 1872	122, 382
Burner, Argand gas	C. H. Johnson	Boston, Mass	Nov. 13, 1855	13, 789
Burner, Argand gas	C. H. Johnson	Boston, Mass	Apr. 21, 1857	17, 1[illegible]2

Index of patents issued from the United States Patent Office from 1790 *to* 1873, *inclusive*—Continued.

Invention.	Inventor.	Residence.	Date.	No.
Burner, Argand gas	C. H. Johnson	Boston, Mass	June 20, 1865	48, 340
Burner, Argand gas	H. Monier	Paris, France	Aug. 23, 1859	25, 209
Burner, Argand gas	R. Murray and G. Oakes	Boston, Mass	Apr. 24, 1866	54, 193
Burner, Argand gas	J E. Stanwood	Malden, Mass	Aug. 3, 1858	21, 090
Burner, Argand gas	J. G. Webb	Williamsburgh, N. Y	Oct. 14, 1851	8, 437
Burner, Argand lamp	J. B. Fuller	Norwich, Conn	Sept. 10, 1872	131, 265
Burner, Argand lamp	H. W. Haydon	Waterbury, Conn	June 13, 1871	115, 955
Burner, Argand lamp	T. H. Mott	New York, N. Y	July 11, 1871	116, 984
Burner, Argand lamp	J. Ravoux	New York, N. Y	June 25, 1872	128, 325
Burner, Argand oil	G. K. Osborn	New York, N. Y	June 21, 1870	104, 635
Burner attachment, Gas	J. Kopp	Hoboken, N. J	Sept. 15, 1868	82 231
Burner attachment, Gas	J. Scholl	Soho, England	Aug. 4, 1868	80, 568
Burner attachment, Gas	F. Shaller	Hudson, N. Y	Nov. 10, 1868	83, 886
Burner, Base	W. B. Treadwell	Albany, N. Y	Aug. 3, 1869	93, 248
Burner, Candle	J. A. Pease	Catskill, N. Y	Oct. 10, 1871	119, 785
Burner, Chandelier gas	R. Nutting	Randolph, Vt	Feb. 28, 1871	112, 172
Burner check, Gas	J. H. Jennings	New Bedford, Mass	Mar. 8, 1870	100, 634
Burner chimney, Gas	J. Stratton	Brooklyn, N. Y	July 25, 1865	49, 010
Burner, Coal-oil	W. W. Batchelder	New York, N. Y	Apr. 25, 1865	47, 381
Burner, Coal-oil	M. B. Dyott	Philadelphia, Pa	Jan. 6, 1863	37, 281
Burner, Coal-oil	S. Fredrick	New York, N. Y	Apr. 21, 1863	38, 223
Burner, Coal-oil	W. Fulton	Cranberry, N. J	May 27, 1862	35, 370
Burner, Coal-oil	J. G. Leffingwell	Newark, N. J	Dec. 6, 1864	45, 375
Burner, Coal-oil	W. O. B. Merrill	Philadelphia, Pa	June 10, 1862	35, 533
Burner, Coal-oil	E. Trittin	Philadelphia, Pa	Mar. 31, 1863	38, 070
Burner, Coal-oil	T. Wood	Westport, Conn	July 24, 1866	56, 655
Burner, Conical arch charcoal	E. B. Gilbert	Euphrata, N. Y	Nov. 7, 1835	....
Burner, Fluid	Y. Bailey	West Chester, Pa	Feb. 20, 1855	12, 409
Burner for Argand lamps	A. Olcott	Rochester, N. Y	Mar. 16, 1852	8, 805
Burner for carburcted air	J. A. Bassett	Salem, Mass	Mar. 14, 1865	46, 770
Burner for coal-oil lamps	J. S. Bradford	Baltimore, Md	July 1, 1862	35, 801
Burner for coal-oil lamps	J. Donning	Paterson, N. J	July 22, 1862	35, 925
Burner for coal-oil lamps	A. J. Gibson	Worcester, Mass	Apr. 1, 1862	34, 831
Burner for coal-oil lamps	A. Taplin	Providence, R. I	June 10, 1862	35, 552
Burner for coal-oil lamps	A. C. Wilhelm	Philadelphia, Pa	Sept. 8, 1863	39, 836
Burner for cooking and heating, Hydrocarbon	H. W. Dopp	Buffalo, N. Y	June 27, 1865	48, 379
Burner for cooking or heating, Vapor	H. S. Saroni	Baltimore, Md	Mar. 15, 1870	100, 807
Burner for cooking, &c., Petroleum	J. P. Hayes	Philadelphia, Pa	Sept. 26, 1865	50, 121
Burner for cooking-purposes, Gas	A. Geiss	Buffalo, N. Y	Nov. 28, 1865	51, 170
Burner for cooking-purposes, Petroleum	W. H. Smith	New York, N. Y	Jan. 2, 1866	51, 876
Burner for gas-lamps, Argand	J. G. Webb	Williamsburgh, N. Y	Aug. 7, 1849	6, 625
Burner for gas-stoves	T. H. Brymer	New York, N. Y	Mar. 27, 1866	53, 404
Burner for gas-stoves	I. R. Clark and S. T. Savage	New York and Albany, N. Y	Apr. 24, 1866	54, 114
Burner for gas-stoves	T. J. Kelly	New York, N. Y	Nov. 14, 1865	50, 938
Burner for gas-stoves	E. Osmond	Cincinnati, Ohio	Mar. 14, 1865	46, 861
Burner for heating and cooking, Wick	H. W. Dopp	Buffalo, N. Y	Sept. 11, 1866	57, 880
Burner for heating &c., Gas	E. P. Gleason	New York, N. Y	Dec. 17, 1867	72, 188
Burner for heating, Gas	J. Van	Cincinnati, Ohio	Sept. 2, 1873	142, 360
Burner for heating-purposes, Gas	H. Y. Lazear	New York, N. Y	May 7, 1867	64, 544
Burner for heating-purposes, Hydrocarbon	J. Youmans and J. Reed	Davenport, Iowa	Dec. 11, 1866	60, 455
Burner for heating-purposes, Petroleum-gas	D. L. Holden	New Orleans, La	June 25, 1867	66, 025
Burner for heating, Vapor	S. Child, jr., and R. A. Copeland	Baltimore, Md	Aug. 27, 1867	68, 045
Burner for heating, Vapor	C. W. Duncan	Baltimore, Md	July 30, 1867	67, 277
Burner for heating, &c., Vapor	R. R. Lewis	New York, N. Y	Feb. 19, 1861	31, 466
Burner for hot-air, steam, and hydrocarbon fluid, Annular petroleum.	G. L. Moody	New York, N. Y	Jan. 29, 1867	61, 632
Burner for hydrocarbon fluid	R. S. Merrill	Boston, Mass	Dec. 17, 1867	72, 414
Burner for kerosene-lamp	T. Raymond	Brooklyn, N. Y	May 12, 1863	38, 537
Burner for lamps, Aëro-vapor	O. F. Morrill	Boston, Mass	May 18, 1858	20, 289
Burner for lamps and lanterns	J. H. Irwin	Chicago, Ill	Feb. 14, 1865	46, 363
Burner for lamps, Coal-oil	J. Dodin	Brooklyn, N. Y	Dec. 23, 1862	37, 220
Burner for lamps, Coal-oil	J. T. Van Kirk	Philadelphia, Pa	Mar. 17, 1863	37, 930
Burner for locomotive head-lights	A. C. Vaughan	Philadelphia, Pa	Nov. 26, 1867	71, 410
Burner for locomotive head-lights, Lamp	D. T. Briggs	Albany, N. Y	Feb. 16, 1869	87, 024
Burner for oil-lamp	J. G. Leffingwell	Newark, N. J	Apr. 5, 1864	42, 204
Burner for pine-knots, &c	J. Price	Nashville, Tenn	Dec. 18, 1839	1, 434
Burner for purifying gas	J. Danks	Troy, N. Y	Apr. 23, 1861	32, 124
Burner for spirit-gas lamps	R. W. Sargent	Philadelphia, Pa	Oct. 12, 1852	9, 334
Burner for stills, engines, &c., Hydrocarbon	I. Helme	Philadelphia, Pa	Nov. 6, 1866	59, 393
Burner for stoves, Vapor-generating	D. E. Ryan	Saint Louis, Mo	Sept. 27, 1870	107, 816
Burner for vapor-lamps	C. F. Allen	Indianapolis, Ind	Feb. 1, 1859	22, 774
Burner for vapor-lamps	J. L. Butler, W. S. Hosford, and D. W. Smith.	Brooklyn, N. Y	Mar. 6, 1860	27, 346
Burner for vapor-lamps	T. Connelly	Philadelphia, Pa	Jan. 24, 1860	26, 888
Burner for vapor-lamps	H. W. Dopp and W. S. Mead	Buffalo, N. Y	Feb. 21, 1860	27, 211
Burner for vapor-lamps	A. Geiger	Dayton, Ohio	Jan. 31, 1860	26, 983
Burner for vapor-lamps	F. Heidrick	Philadelphia, Pa	Aug. 10, 1858	21, 166
Burner for vapor-lamps	J. S. Hull	Cincinnati, Ohio	Feb. 2, 1864	41, 434
Burner for vapor-lamps	J. S. Hull	Cincinnati, Ohio	Sept. 25, 1866	58, 261
Burner for vapor-lamps	H. Johnson	Washington, D. C	Apr. 12, 1859	23, 583
Burner for vapor-lamps	C. B. Loveless	Syracuse, N. Y	June 8, 1858	20, 498
Burner for vapor-lamps	J. K. O'Neil	Kingston, N. Y	May 18, 1858	20, 296
Burner for vapor-lamps	W. H. Racey	New York, N. Y	Sept. 20, 1859	25, 525
Burner for vapor-lamps	R. Ramsey	Philadelphia, Pa	May 24, 1859	24, 147
Burner for vapor-lamps	G. W. Randall	Boston, Mass	July 27, 1858	21, 053
Burner for vapor-lamps	E. D. Rosencrantz and W. H. Smith.	New York, N. Y	Jan. 4, 1859	22, 536
Burner for vapor-lamps	E. Trittin	Philadelphia, Pa	May 15, 1860	28, 333
Burner for vapor-lamps	T. Varney	San Francisco, Cal	May 11, 1858	20, 232
Burner for vapor-lamps	S. Wales	Boston, Mass	Dec. 28, 1858	22, 465
Burner for vapor-lamps	E. M. Williams	Philadelphia, Pa	Dec. 7, 1858	22, 270
Burner for vapor-stoves	R. L. Howell	Baltimore, Md	Jan. 22, 1867	61, 432
Burner, Gas	B. Andreas	Frankfort-on-the-Main, Germany.	May 27, 1873	139, 352
Burner, Gas	A. Arnoux	New York, N. Y	June 4, 1838	764
Burner, Gas	J. W. Averill	Newmarket, N. H	Aug. 5, 1873	141, 415
Burner, Gas	Y. Baily	Philadelphia, Pa	Oct. 12, 1858	21, 733
Burner, Gas	A. Barbarin	New Orleans, La	Sept. 1, 1868	81, 733

Index of patents issued from the United States Patent Office from 1790 to 1873, inclusive—Continued.

Invention.	Inventor.	Residence.	Date.	No.
Burner, Gas	J. F. Barker	Springfield, Mass	July 26, 1870	105, 768
Burner, Gas	J. A. Bassett	Salem, Mass	May 23, 1865	47, 786
Burner, Gas	W. W. Batchelder	New York, N. Y	Sept. 22, 1857	18, 230
Burner, Gas	J. Battin	Philadelphia, Pa	June 6, 1846	4, 563
Burner, Gas	H. Berg	Union Hill, N. J	May 23, 1865	47, 787
Burner, Gas	H. Berg and A. Blessing	Springfield, Mass	Oct. 16, 1866	58, 764
Burner, Gas	W. Blake	Boston, Mass	Aug. 9, 1845	4, 141
Burner, Gas	W. Blake	Boston, Mass	Apr. 5, 1859	23, 441
Burner, Gas	W. J. Brassington	Brooklyn, N. Y	Aug. 18, 1868	81, 063
Burner, Gas	S. R. Brick	Philadelphia, Pa	May 24, 1853	9, 742
Burner, Gas	J. S. Bridgman and E. G. Wellman.	Brockport, N. Y	July 7, 1868	79, 545
Burner, Gas	J. Brönner	Frankfort-on-the-Main, Prussia.	Dec. 8, 1868	84, 675
Burner, Gas	A. Buckhom	Delhi, N. Y	Feb. 6, 1872	123, 327
Burner, Gas	T. Clough	Dobbs's Ferry, N. Y	June 14, 1870	104, 271
Burner, Gas	T. Clough	New York, N. Y	Nov. 7, 1871	120, 715
Burner, Gas	S. L. Cole	Burlington, Vt	Nov. 29, 1859	26, 255
Burner, Gas	S. L. Cole	Brooklyn, N. Y	June 2, 1868	78, 578
Burner, Gas	J. B. Coolidge	Boston, Mass	Oct. 9, 1866	58, 606
Burner, Gas	R. Cornelius	Philadelphia, Pa	June 22, 1858	20, 626
Burner, Gas	J. Cornell and B. McDougall	Brooklyn and New York, N. Y.	Dec. 9, 1856	16, 176
Burner, Gas	J. W. Cremin	New York, N. Y	Sept. 7, 1869	94, 476
Burner, Gas	J. W. Cremin	New York, N. Y	Jan. 11, 1870	98, 744
Burner, Gas	C. A. Cummings and C. Douglass.	New London, Conn	Jan. 15, 1856	14, 091
Burner, Gas	H. H. Dodge	Georgetown, D. C	Oct. 23, 1860	30, 470
Burner, Gas	V. Dubourg	Paris, France	Oct. 10, 1865	50, 429
Burner, Gas	A. E. Dupas	New Orleans, La	Sept. 13, 1870	107, 234
Burner, Gas	A. E. Dupas	New Orleans, La	Feb. 14, 1871	111, 825
Burner, Gas	W. S. Dyer	Portland, Me	Mar. 22, 1864	41, 981
Burner, Gas	E. M. Echalleus	Switzerland	Dec. 28, 1846	4, 913
Burner, Gas	J. S. Fancher	Newark, N. J	Sept. 1, 1863	39, 725
Burner, Gas	F. A. Fisher	Crawford, N. J	May 28, 1872	127, 329
Burner, Gas	I. R. Fisher	Reading, Pa	Aug. 3, 1869	93, 189
Burner, Gas	T. B. Fogarty	New York, N. Y	Feb. 18, 1873	135, 978
Burner, Gas	T. B. Fogarty	New York, N. Y	Feb. 18, 1873	135, 979
Burner, Gas	E. Foote	Yonkers, N. Y	Apr. 15, 1873	137, 905
Burner, Gas	C. S. Ford	Philadelphia, Pa	Mar. 31, 1868	76, 069
Burner, Gas	C. S. Ford	Philadelphia, Pa	June 28, 1870	104, 723
Burner, Gas	C. S. Ford	Philadelphia, Pa	Oct. 25, 1870	108, 579
Burner, Gas	J. S. Ford	Philadelphia, Pa	Oct. 8, 1867	69, 556
Burner, Gas	C. Franz	Cincinnati, Ohio	Mar. 16, 1869	87, 922
Burner, Gas	A. Fulton	Albany, N. Y	Nov. 22, 1870	109, 404
Burner, Gas	S. Gardner, jr	New York, N. Y	June 16, 1868	78, 871
Burner, Gas	S. Gardner	New York, N. Y	Mar. 26, 1872	125, 042
Burner, Gas	A. D. Gates	Binghamton, N. Y	June 30, 1857	17, 674
Burner, Gas	J. Gilfillan	Hartford, Conn	Aug. 2, 1859	24, 932
Burner, Gas	R. Gill	New York, N. Y	Aug. 24, 1869	94, 103
Burner, Gas	E. P. Gleason	Providence, R. I	Apr. 14, 1857	17, 035
Burner, Gas	A. G. Hamaker	Peoria, Ill	Aug. 7, 1860	29, 486
Burner, Gas	G. W. Hatch	Brooklyn, N. Y	Apr. 1, 1873	137, 303
Burner, Gas	L. E. Hicks	New York, N. Y	Sept. 14, 1858	21, 497
Burner, Gas	C. H. Johnson	Boston, Mass	June 26, 1855	13, 130
Burner, Gas	W. L. Jukes	New York, N. Y	Aug. 3, 1869	93, 310
Burner, Gas	W. L. Jukes	New York, N. Y	Nov. 2, 1869	96, 441
Burner, Gas	W. L. Jukes	New York, N. Y	Dec. 7, 1869	97, 517
Burner, Gas	F. C. Krause	New York, N. Y	Aug. 3, 1858	21, 076
Burner, Gas	F. Küp	Frankfort-on-the-Main, Germany.	Oct. 10, 1865	50, 431
Burner, Gas	A. M. Laevelson	Quincy, Ill	Dec. 7, 1869	97, 652
Burner, Gas	J. G. Leffingwell and G. W. Thompson.	Newark, N. J., and New York, N. Y.	Apr. 2, 1861	31, 893
Burner, Gas	W. H. Lindsay	Brooklyn, N. Y	Sept. 29, 1857	18, 289
Burner, Gas	R. B. Locke	New York, N. Y	Apr. 7, 1868	76, 333
Burner, Gas	R. B. Locke and W. B. Ulrich	New Orleans and Concordia Parish, La.	Apr. 16, 1867	63, 802
Burner Gas	F. Lunkenheimer	Cincinnati, Ohio	Sept. 8, 1863	39, 820
Burner, Gas	W. Mallord	Brooklyn, N. Y	June 27, 1854	11, 168
Burner, Gas	H. L. McAvoy	Baltimore, Md	Sept. 19, 1865	50, 075
Burner, Gas	J. McGlensey	Philadelphia, Pa	June 19, 1860	28, 761
Burner, Gas	C. P. Miller	Philadelphia, Pa	Sept. 10, 1861	33, 258
Burner, Gas	H. Monier	Paris, France	May 12, 1868	77, 749
Burner Gas	C. Monson and S. Moore	New Haven Conn	Feb. 19, 1861	31, 472
Burner, Gas	G. Mooney	Providence, R. I	Dec. 17, 1867	72, 415
Burner, Gas	G. Mooney	Providence, R. I	Aug. 25, 1868	81, 524
Burner, Gas	H. B. Myer	Philadelphia, Pa	Nov. 10, 1868	83, 876
Burner, Gas	H. B. Myer	Philadelphia, Pa	May 30, 1871	115, 506
Burner, Gas	J. Neal	Boston, Mass	May 6, 1856	14, 822
Burner, Gas	A. Ostrander	New York, N. Y	Jan. 11, 1859	22, 574
Burner, Gas	S. W. Pingree	Lawrence, Mass	Apr. 2, 1872	125, 327
Burner, Gas	J. Poole	New York, N. Y	July 2, 1861	32, 738
Burner, Gas	A. C. Rand	New York, N. Y	June 23, 1868	79, 081
Burner, Gas	A. H. Ray	Boston, Mass	June 15, 1858	20, 584
Burner, Gas	P. Reitmeier	Chicago, Ill	Jan. 23, 1872	123, 047
Burner, Gas	J. and T. D. Richardson	New York, N. Y	June 24, 1873	140, 164
Burner, Gas	J. Rigby	Cincinnati, Ohio	June 17, 1873	139, 919
Burner, Gas	C. Ritter	Reading, Pa	Oct. 24, 1865	50, 628
Burner, Gas	W. H. Rodgers	Brooklyn, N. Y	May 12, 1868	77, 917
Burner, Gas	M. Rosenwax	New York, N. Y	Mar. 14, 1871	112, 637
Burner, Gas	G. C. Roundey	New York, N. Y	May 5, 1863	38, 417
Burner, Gas	E. P. Russell	Manlius, N. Y	Dec. 8, 18 8	84, 768
Burner, Gas	D. E. Ryan	Cincinnati, Ohio	June 3, 1873	139, 481
Burner, Gas	J. Scholl	London, England	Dec. 24, 1867	72, 545
Burner, Gas	I. W. Shaler	Brooklyn, N. Y	Apr. 15, 1873	137, 964
Burner, Gas	W. F. Shaw	Boston, Mass	Apr. 22, 1856	14, 737
Burner, Gas	I. Simmons	Baltimore, Md	June 10, 1873	139, 828

Index of patents issued from the United States Patent Office from 1790 *to* 1873, *inclusive*—Continued.

Invention.	Inventor.	Residence.	Date.	No.
Burner, Gas	J. L. Smith	Louisville, Ky	May 22, 1866	54, 971
Burner, Gas	D. H. Solliday	Philadelphia, Pa	Mar. 20, 1849	6, 212
Burner, Gas	D. H. Solliday	Philadelphia, Pa	Sept. 6, 1859	25, 372
Burner, Gas	R. N. Stewart	Philadelphia, Pa	Feb. 18, 1862	34, 450
Burner, Gas	W. B. Stofer	Memphis, Tenn	Oct. 3, 1871	119, 480
Burner, Gas	J. Stratton	Philadelphia, Pa	Nov. 21, 1865	51, 121
Burner, Gas	D. Sullivan and M. McIntyre	Cincinnati, Ohio	Mar. 23, 1858	19, 720
Burner, Gas	W. Tallman	Cincinnati, Ohio	Apr. 13, 1858	19, 959
Burner, Gas	G. W. Thompson	New York, N. Y	May 1, 1860	28, 113
Burner, Gas	J. F. Tozer	Binghamton, N. Y	Oct. 5, 1858	21, 728
Burner, Gas	J. and J. Wadsworth	Marple and Salford, England.	Apr. 19, 1864	42, 421
Burner, Gas	J. C. Walsh	Lockport, N. Y	June 9, 1857	17, 530
Burner, Gas	T. Ward	Columbus, Ohio	Mar. 19, 1872	124, 866
Burner, Gas	J. Webster and O. Spencer	Cleveland, Ohio	Feb. 14, 1854	10, 529
Burner, Gas	A. H. Wood	Boston, Mass	Nov. 9, 1852	9, 396
Burner, Gas	A. H. Wood	Boston, Mass	Sept. 21, 1858	21, 586
Burner, Gas	S. E. Woodworth and J. S. Wethered.	San Francisco, Cal	June 12, 1860	28, 708
Burner, Gas	W. Wright	Saint Louis, Mo	Aug. 17, 1858	21, 229
Burner, Gas	W. Wright	New York, N. Y	Jan. 11, 1859	22, 609
Burner, Gas	W. Wright	New York, N. Y	June 12, 1860	28, 709
Burner, Gas and lamp	J. Horton	New York, N. Y	June 8, 1869	91, 020
Burner, Gas or vapor	G. P. Ganster	New York, N. Y	Aug. 20, 1872	130, 632
Burner, Globe-holder and cooler combined for vapor	J. J. and F. G. Palmer	Pittsburgh, Pa	Mar. 14, 1871	112, 624
Burner, Hollow wick lamp	J. W. Emerson	Millbury, Mass	Oct. 25, 1870	108, 694
Burner, Hydrocarbon	M. L. Callender	New York, N. Y	Nov. 20, 1860	30, 703
Burner, Hydrocarbon	M. L. Callender	New York, N. Y	Feb. 18, 1862	34, 402
Burner, Hydrocarbon	M. L. Callender	New York, N. Y	Mar. 31, 1863	38, 031
Burner, Hydrocarbon	C. Carpenter, jr	Astoria, N. Y	Feb. 11, 1868	74, 136
Burner, Hydrocarbon	F. Cook	New York, N. Y	Jan. 21, 1868	73, 506
Burner, Hydrocarbon	A. W. Cook and R. Dempster	Buffalo, N. Y	June 9, 1868	78, 788
Burner, Hydrocarbon	S. E. Crow	Stratford, England	Oct. 13, 1868	82, 925
Burner, Hydrocarbon	A. De Landsee	Paris, France	Mar. 1, 1870	100, 268
Burner, Hydrocarbon	H. Everett	New York, N. Y	July 7, 1868	79, 563
Burner, Hydrocarbon	J. Gray	San Francisco, Cal	Nov. 17, 1868	84, 110
Burner, Hydrocarbon	A. J. Griffin	Lowell, Mass	Apr. 16, 1867	63, 881
Burner, Hydrocarbon	M. Herzog and D. Cohn	Vienna, Austria, and London, England.	July 3, 1866	56, 155
Burner, Hydrocarbon	S. A. Hill	Oil City, Pa	Jan. 5, 1869	85, 663
Burner, Hydrocarbon	J. S. Hull	Cincinnati, Ohio	Mar. 3, 1868	75, 165
Burner, Hydrocarbon	W. L. Imlay	Philadelphia, Pa	Jan. 14, 1868	73, 335
Burner, Hydrocarbon	S. P. Legg	Springfield, Mass	July 28, 1868	80, 413
Burner, Hydrocarbon	D. H. Lowe	Boston, Mass	Aug. 11, 1868	80, 980
Burner, Hydrocarbon	N. May and H. F. Stivers	San Francisco, Cal	Jan. 19, 1869	86, 024
Burner, Hydrocarbon	E. P. McCarthy	San Francisco, Cal	July 27, 1869	93, 105
Burner, Hydrocarbon	H. A. V. Post and J. Garrard	Cincinnati, Ohio	Oct. 22, 1867	70, 117
Burner, Hydrocarbon	C. Sauvage	Paris, France	Feb. 9, 1869	86, 871
Burner, Hydrocarbon	J. Stratton	Philadelphia, Pa	Mar. 20, 1866	53, 383
Burner, Hydrocarbon	J. Stratton	Philadelphia, Pa	Mar. 31, 1868	76, 115
Burner, Hydrocarbon	E. W. Taylor	Norristown, Pa	Nov. 17, 1868	84, 148
Burner, Hydrocarbon	F. W. Thayer	Boston, Mass	Apr. 7, 1868	76, 552
Burner, Hydrocarbon	L. Verstraet	Paris, France	Nov. 17, 1868	84, 234
Burner, Hydrocarbon	L. Verstraet	Paris, France	Jan. 12, 1869	85, 877
Burner, Hydrocarbon	J. H. White	San Francisco, Cal	Jan. 21, 1868	73, 682
Burner, Hydrocarbon	H. W. Yerington	Jersey City, N. J	Oct. 20, 1868	83, 352
Burner, Hydrocarbon-vapor	H. W. Dopp and M. J. Stark	Buffalo, N. Y	Mar. 12, 1872	124, 425
Burner, Hydrocarbon-vapor	A. M. Mace	Springfield, Mass	Oct. 26, 1858	21, 893
Burner, Illuminating incense	E. W. Hastings	Boston, Mass	Aug. 15, 1871	118, 126
Burner, Incense	E. W. Hastings	Boston, Mass	July 25, 1871	117, 281
Burner, Kerosene	G. Neilson	Boston, Mass	Sept. 27, 1864	44, 441
Burner, Kerosene	L. C. White	Waterbury, Conn	July 3, 1866	56, 131
Burner, Kerosene	S. R. Wilmot	Brooklyn, N. Y	July 18, 1865	48, 800
Burner, Kerosene-lamp	H. F. Adams and W. Berry	Syracuse, N. Y	June 24, 1862	35, 660
Burner, Kerosene-lamp	A. B. Hendryx	Derby, Conn	Aug. 29, 1865	49, 680
Burner, Kerosene-oil	P. D. Cummings	Portland, Me	Apr. 8, 1862	34, 880
Burner, Kerosene-oil	H. and J. Sangster	Buffalo, N. Y	June 27, 1865	48, 450
Burner, Lamp	J. R. Ackerman, E. B. Campbell, and N. O. Golden.	Dobb's Ferry, N. Y	Apr. 21, 1868	76, 966
Burner, Lamp	B. F. Adams	Boston, Mass	Aug. 16, 1870	106, 302
Burner, Lamp	B. F. Adams	Boston, Mass	Aug. 16, 1870	106, 303
Burner, Lamp	T. Adams	Hudson City, N. J	Sept. 15, 1868	82, 059
Burner, Lamp	T. Adams	Hudson City, N. J	July 20, 1869	92, 771
Burner, Lamp	B. R. Alden	New York, N. Y	Oct. 21, 1862	36, 694
Burner, Lamp	J. B. Alexander	Washington, D. C	Apr. 23, 1867	64, 056
Burner, Lamp	J. B. Alexander	Washington, D. C	Mar. 16, 1869	87, 808
Burner, Lamp	J. B. Alexander	Washington, D. C	Dec. 14, 1869	97, 854
Burner, Lamp	J. Allen	New York, N. Y	Aug. 25, 1868	81, 321
Burner, Lamp	J. K. Andrews	Antrim, Ohio	Nov. 13, 1866	59, 704
Burner, Lamp	N. L. Archer and C. Deavs	New York, N. Y	Feb. 19, 1867	62, 244
Burner, Lamp	L. J. Atwood	Waterbury, Conn	June 9, 1868	78, 637
Burner, Lamp	L. J. Atwood	Waterbury, Conn	Jan. 18, 1870	98, 836
Burner, Lamp	L. J. Atwood	Waterbury, Conn	Apr. 18, 1871	113, 833
Burner, Lamp	L. J. Atwood	Waterbury, Conn	Nov. 26, 1872	133, 397
Burner, Lamp	L. J. Atwood	Waterbury, Conn	May 6, 1873	138, 601
Burner, Lamp	J. R. Baker	Kendallville, Ind	Jan. 5, 1864	41, 048
Burner, Lamp	P. Baker	Chicago, Ill	July 2, 1867	66, 203
Burner, Lamp	P. Baker	Chicago, Ill	Aug. 18, 1868	81, 128
Burner, Lamp	P. Baker	Chicago, Ill	Apr. 26, 1870	102, 355
Burner, Lamp	P. Baker	Ansonia, Conn	Feb. 6, 1872	123, 376
Burner, Lamp	G. E. Baldwin	West Meriden, Conn	Dec. 10, 1867	71, 949
Burner, Lamp	G. A. Beidler	Philadelphia, Pa	Apr. 21, 1868	76, 979
Burner, Lamp	H. M. Beidler	Philadelphia, Pa	Oct. 19, 1869	95, 870
Burner, Lamp	G. Berkstresser	Bedford, Pa	June 7, 1870	103, 967
Burner, Lamp	E. Blackman	Norwalk, Conn	July 20, 1869	92, 695
Burner, Lamp	E. C. Blakeslee	Waterbury, Conn	Sept. 29, 1868	82, 480
Burner, Lamp	A. Bliss	New York, N. Y	Nov. 24, 1868	84, 406
Burner, Lamp	J. O. Blythe	Philadelphia, Pa	Mar. 24, 1863	37, 945

Index of patents issued from the United States Patent Office from 1790 *to* 1873, *inclusive*—Continued.

Invention.	Inventor.	Residence.	Date.	No.
Burner, Lamp	J. W. Brimblecom	Lynn, Mass	Apr. 14, 1868	76, 592
Burner, Lamp	C. Britain	Saint Joseph, Mich	Sept. 27, 1864	44, 393
Burner, Lamp	C. P. Brockett	New Haven, Conn	Apr. 22, 1862	35, 010
Burner, Lamp	H. Brown	New York, N. Y	Feb. 10, 1863	37, 606
Burner, Lamp	A. W. Browne	Brooklyn, N. Y	Feb. 25, 1868	74, 793
Burner, Lamp	A. W. Browne	Brooklyn, N. Y	June 15, 1869	91, 208
Burner, Lamp	G. E. Brush	Danbury, Conn	Aug. 22, 1871	118, 193
Burner, Lamp	C. W. Cahoon	Portland, Me	Dec. 15, 1868	84, 993
Burner, Lamp	G. J. Capewell	West Cheshire, Conn	Sept. 25, 1866	58, 213
Burner, Lamp	G. J. Capewell	West Cheshire, Conn	Nov. 13, 1866	59, 554
Burner, Lamp	G. J. Capewell	West Cheshire, Conn	Mar. 10, 1868	75, 363
Burner, Lamp	W. Carleton	Boston, Mass	Aug. 11, 1868	80, 909
Burner, Lamp	B. F. Chappell	Hartford, Conn	Mar. 11, 1873	136, 586
Burner, Lamp	G. Chinnock	New York, N. Y	Apr. 28, 1868	77, 254
Burner, Lamp	G. H. Chinnock	New York, N. Y	Oct. 26, 1869	96, 200
Burner, Lamp	P. J. Clark	West Meriden, Conn	June 16, 1863	38, 926
Burner, Lamp	J. R. Cole	Demopolis, Ala	Sept. 14, 1869	94, 811
Burner, Lamp	M. H. Collins	Chelsea, Mass	Mar. 1, 1870	100, 260
Burner, Lamp	H. Coulter	Philadelphia, Pa	Apr. 14, 1868	76, 716
Burner, Lamp	W. R. Cranna	San Francisco, Cal	Sept. 29, 1868	82, 495
Burner, Lamp	P. Crans, jr	Philadelphia, Pa	Apr. 17, 1866	53, 953
Burner, Lamp	R. R. Crosby	Boston, Mass	June 28, 1870	104, 709
Burner, Lamp	J. D. Custer	Norristown, Pa	Mar. 25, 1862	34, 742
Burner, Lamp	J. Dodin	Brooklyn, N. Y	Aug. 11, 1863	39, 524
Burner, Lamp	J. H. Doolittle	Ansonia, Conn	July 8, 1873	140, 687
Burner, Lamp	M. B. Dyott	Philadelphia, Pa	Dec. 7, 1858	22, 230
Burner, Lamp	R. N. Eagle	Washington, D. C	Mar. 2, 1869	87, 480
Burner, Lamp	J. P. Egan	Zanesville, Ohio	May 9, 1865	47, 625
Burner, Lamp	L. Erving	Brooklyn, N. Y	Apr. 7, 1868	76, 426
Burner, Lamp	H Fairbanks	Boston, Mass	Apr. 12, 1864	42, 281
Burner, Lamp	S. W. Fowler	Brooklyn, N. Y	May 3, 1870	102, 674
Burner, Lamp	S. W. Fowler	Brooklyn, N. Y	June 27, 1871	116, 292
Burner, Lamp	S. W. Fowler	Brooklyn, N. Y	Apr. 16, 1872	125, 672
Burner, Lamp	J. A. Frey	Washington, D. C	Dec. 18, 1866	60, 499
Burner, Lamp	J. A. Frey	New York, N. Y	May 21, 1867	64, 965
Burner, Lamp	F. H. Fuller	South Boston, Mass	July 14, 1868	79, 969
Burner, Lamp	G. P. Fuller	Humphrey, N. Y	Jan. 10, 1871	110, 846
Burner, Lamp	J. B. Fuller	Norwich, Conn	Nov. 23, 1869	97, 069
Burner, Lamp	J. B. Fuller	Norwich, Conn	May 31, 1870	103, 598
Burner, Lamp	E. A. Galbraith	Boston, Mass	June 23, 1868	79, 221
Burner, Lamp	T. W. Gardner	Terre Haute, Ind	Jan. 7, 1873	134, 657
Burner, Lamp	E. L. Gilman	Somerville, Mass	Oct. 5, 1869	95, 460
Burner, Lamp	R. Gorsline	Rochester, N. Y	July 28, 1868	80, 281
Burner, Lamp	J. Gracie and R. H. Boyd	Pittsburgh, Pa	May 5, 1868	77, 481
Burner, Lamp	J. B Gray	Hudson, Wis	June 23, 1863	38, 960
Burner, Lamp	W. H. Gray	Saint Louis, Mo	Apr. 18, 1871	113, 876
Burner, Lamp	W. H. Gray and S. Ross	Saint Louis, Mo., and Washington, D. C.	June 13, 1871	115, 953
Burner, Lamp	E. J. Hale	Foxcroft, Me	May 16, 1871	114, 805
Burner, Lamp	T. Hall	Bergen, N. J	Sept. 18, 1866	58, 097
Burner, Lamp	T. F. Halley and J. F. Livingston.	Washington, D. C	July 25, 1871	117, 412
Burner, Lamp	J. O. Harris	Reading, Pa	May 17, 1864	42, 765
Burner, Lamp	J. O. Harris	Reading, Pa	Dec. 20, 1864	45, 493
Burner, Lamp	J. O. Harris	Reading, Pa	Mar. 21, 1865	46, 301
Burner, Lamp	H. W. Hayden	Waterbury, Conn	Aug. 16, 1870	106, 363
Burner, Lamp	H. W. Hayden	Waterbury, Conn	May 30, 1871	115, 315
Burner, Lamp	H. W. Hayden	Waterbury, Conn	May 30, 1871	115, 466
Burner, Lamp	E. K. Haynes	Boston, Mass	Jan. 26, 1869	86, 301
Burner, Lamp	E. K. Haynes	Boston, Mass	June 6, 1871	115, 608
Burner, Lamp	A. N. Henderson	Buffalo, N. Y	June 2, 1863	38, 742
Burner, Lamp	G. Hillegass	Philadelphia, Pa	Apr. 10, 1866	53, 824
Burner, Lamp	G. Hillegass	Philadelphia, Pa	July 27, 1869	93, 087
Burner, Lamp	T. Hipwell	Camden, N. J	Oct. 31, 1871	120, 383
Burner, Lamp	R. Hoadley and H. A. Shipman	Ansonia, Conn	Apr. 7, 1868	76, 450
Burner, Lamp	E. Hobbis and A. McNair	Newark and Bloomfield, N. J.	Mar. 1, 1864	41, 774
Burner, Lamp	W. W. Horton	Providence, R. I	May 5, 1868	77, 614
Burner, Lamp	J. Hubbard	Dayton, Ohio	Aug. 10, 1869	93, 442
Burner, Lamp	J. S. Hull	Cincinnati, Ohio	Aug. 4, 1863	39, 399
Burner, Lamp	J. S. Hull	Cincinnati, Ohio	Aug 4, 1863	39, 400
Burner, Lamp	H. C. Hunt	Ottumwa, Iowa	Feb. 3, 1863	37, 600
Burner, Lamp	J. G. Hunt	Cincinnati, Ohio	Apr. 3, 1866	53, 623
Burner, Lamp	H. C. Hutchinson	Cayuga, N. Y	May 6, 1862	35, 157
Burner, Lamp	H. C. Hutchinson	Cayuga, N. Y	Mar. 8, 1864	41, 846
Burner, Lamp	J. H. Irwin	Philadelphia, Pa	Feb. 1, 1870	99, 443
Burner, Lamp	W. P. Jenney and G. W. Taylor	Fairhaven, Mass	Dec. 20, 1870	110, 241
Burner, Lamp	M. Jincks	Dansville, N. Y	May 5, 1868	77, 620
Burner, Lamp	M. Jincks	Wallace, N. Y	Nov. 30, 1869	97, 298
Burner, Lamp	J. Johnson and F. Bailey	New York, N. Y	Dec. 7, 1858	22, 253
Burner, Lamp	J. H. Johnson	Newark, N. J	May 3, 1870	102, 552
Burner, Lamp	A. Judson	Brooklyn, N. Y	Nov. 20, 1866	59, 772
Burner, Lamp	A. C. Ketcham	New York, N. Y	Oct. 21, 1862	36, 717
Burner, Lamp	A. H. Knapp	Medford, Mass	Apr. 7, 1857	16, 981
Burner, Lamp and lantern	C. W. T. Krausch	Chicago, Ill	Mar. 10, 1863	37, 868
Burner, Lamp	C. H. Kupfer	Hoboken, N. J	Sept. 22, 1863	40, 050
Burner, Lamp	G. Lavere	Bridgeport, Conn	May 12, 1868	77, 821
Burner, Lamp	J. C. Love	Philadelphia, Pa	Sept. 17, 1867	68, 889
Burner, Lamp	J. C. Love	Philadelphia, Pa	Dec. 17, 1867	72, 209
Burner, Lamp	J. C. Love	Philadelphia, Pa	June 8, 1869	91, 141
Burner, Lamp	J. C. Love	Philadelphia, Pa	Aug. 31, 1869	94, 421
Burner, Lamp	W. D. Ludlow	New York, N. Y	May 17, 1870	103, 213
Burner, Lamp	G. Lumpton	Indianapolis, Ind	Dec. 13, 1870	110, 055
Burner, Lamp	G. R. Lyon	Waterbury Conn	July 5, 1870	104, 971
Burner, Lamp	J. Magee	Chelsea, Mass	Mar. 31, 1868	76, 089
Burner, Lamp	J. Magoun	East Cambridge, Mass	Jan. 5, 1864	41, 179
Burner, Lamp	C. B. Mann	Baltimore, Md	Mar. 28, 1871	113, 183
Burner, Lamp	J. J. Marcy	Meriden, Conn	Dec. 2, 1862	37, 047
Burner, Lamp	J. J. Marcy	Meriden, Conn	July 21, 1863	39, 320

Index of patents issued from the United States Patent Office from 1790 *to* 1873, *inclusive*—Continued.

Invention.	Inventor.	Residence.	Date.	No.
Burner, Lamp	J. J. Marcy	West Meriden, Conn	Dec. 4, 1866	60, 215
Burner, Lamp	J. J. Marcy	West Meriden, Conn.	Apr. 7, 1868	76, 482
Burner, Lamp	L. J. Marcy	Newport, R. I	Aug. 11, 1868	80, 984
Burner, Lamp	G. A. Mason	Chelsea, Mass	June 30, 1868	79, 369
Burner, Lamp	C. B. Matthews	Oquawka, Ill	Sept. 9, 1862	36, 417
Burner, Lamp	W. McCaine	Groton, Mass	Dec. 24, 1867	72, 659
Burner, Lamp	J. P. McGee	Trenton, Tenn	Sept. 22, 1868	82, 334
Burner, Lamp	W. C. McGill	Cincinnati, Ohio	Apr. 14, 1868	76, 645
Burner, Lamp	W. C. McGill	Cincinnati, Ohio	Feb. 21, 1871	111, 960
Burner, Lamp	J. McHenry	Cincinnati, Ohio	Aug. 4, 1863	39, 413
Burner, Lamp	R. S. Merrill	Boston, Mass	July 18, 1865	48, 824
Burner, Lamp	R. S. Merrill	Boston, Mass	July 10, 1866	56, 245
Burner, Lamp	R. S. Merrill	Boston, Mass	June 30, 1868	79, 488
Burner, Lamp	R. S. Merrill and W. Carlton	Boston, Mass	June 1, 1869	90, 863
Burner, Lamp	R. S. Merrill	Cambridge, Mass	Mar. 8, 1870	100, 633
Burner, Lamp	R. S. Merrill	Hyde Park, Mass	June 21, 1870	104, 624
Burner, Lamp	R. S. Merrill	Hyde Park, Mass	June 21, 1870	104, 625
Burner, Lamp	R. S. Merrill	Boston, Mass	Jan. 17, 1871	111, 074
Burner, Lamp	R. S. Merrill	Boston, Mass	Nov. 28, 1871	121, 394
Burner, Lamp	R. S. Merrill	Hyde Park, Mass	Dec. 9, 1873	145, 458
Burner, Lamp	C. M. Mills and G. W. Remsen	Lincoln, Del	May 5, 1868	77, 514
Burner, Lamp	J. Minifie	Baltimore, Md	July 28, 1868	80, 494
Burner, Lamp	H. K. Needham	Titusville, Pa	Mar. 24, 1868	75, 959
Burner, Lamp	G. Neilson	Boston, Mass	June 18, 1867	65, 933
Burner, Lamp	G. Neilson	Boston, Mass	Mar. 17, 1868	75, 565
Burner, Lamp	G. Neilson	Boston, Mass	Mar. 17, 1868	75, 566
Burner, Lamp	G. Neilson	Boston, Mass	Mar. 24, 1868	75, 960
Burner, Lamp	G. Neilson	Boston, Mass	Dec. 8, 1868	84, 752
Burner, Lamp	G. K. Osborn	Brooklyn, N. Y	Oct. 29, 1867	70, 252
Burner, Lamp	G. K. Osborn	Brooklyn, N. Y	Apr. 14, 1868	76, 653
Burner, Lamp	W. Painter	Fallston, Md	June 30, 1863	39, 102
Burner, Lamp	R. W. Park	Philadelphia, Pa	Mar. 17, 1868	75, 697
Burner, Lamp	A. Parsons	Portland, Me	Feb. 26, 1867	62, 438
Burner, Lamp	J. M. Perkins	Cleveland, Ohio	July 27, 1869	93, 117
Burner, Lamp	A. H. Platt	Yellow Springs, Ohio	Jan. 31, 1865	46, 138
Burner, Lamp	A. H. Platt	Philadelphia, Pa	June 2, 1868	78, 607
Burner, Lamp	S. B. Platt	Derby, Conn	June 13, 1871	115, 890
Burner, Lamp	P. Prettymann	ParadiseSpring Farm, Oreg	Aug. 17, 1869	93, 744
Burner, Lamp	H. Read	Providence, R. I	Dec. 10, 1867	71, 913
Burner, Lamp	F. J. Rebbeck and E. M. Davies	Pittsburgh, Pa	Sept. 2, 1862	36, 367
Burner, Lamp	E. B. Requa	Jersey City, N. J	July 15, 1862	35, 893
Burner, Lamp	E. B Requa	South Bergen, N. J	Mar. 24, 1868	75, 978
Burner, Lamp	W. F. Rippon and G. A. Johnson.	Providence, R. I	Sept. 14, 1869	94, 776
Burner, Lamp	F. S. Robinson	Boston, Mass	Apr. 21, 1868	76, 945
Burner, Lamp	F. S. Robinson	Boston, Mass	Dec. 5, 1871	121, 550
Burner, Lamp	W. Robinson	Funkville, Pa	July 9, 1867	66, 635
Burner, Lamp	W. Robinson	Brooklyn, N. Y	June 2, 1868	78, 539
Burner, Lamp	S. Ross	Washington, D. C	Oct. 24, 1871	120, 214
Burner, Lamp	W. J. Ross	Worcester, Mass	May 12, 1868	77, 844
Burner, Lamp	T. Rowatt, jr	London, England	Jan. 29, 1867	61, 634
Burner, Lamp	D. E. Rugg	Sing Sing, N. Y	Feb. 9, 1869	86, 694
Burner, Lamp	S. Russell	Waterbury, Conn	July 16, 1872	129, 598
Burner, Lamp	J. F. Sanford	Keokuk, Iowa	Oct. 16, 1866	58, 893
Burner, Lamp	J. F. Sanford	Keokuk, Iowa	Dec. 4, 1866	60, 263
Burner, Lamp	J. F. Sanford	Keokuk, Iowa	Jan. 5, 1869	85, 697
Burner, Lamp	J. F. Sanford	Keokuk, Iowa	Feb. 9, 1869	86, 809
Burner, Lamp	O. I. Savage and G. P. Hawley	Ithaca, N. Y	May 5, 1863	38, 422
Burner, Lamp	J. W. Schreiber	New York, N. Y	June 16, 1868	79, 014
Burner, Lamp	F. Shaller	Hudson, N. Y	June 22, 1869	91, 778
Burner, Lamp	A. J. Simpson and J. B. Currier	Lowell, Mass	Sept. 2, 1862	36, 374
Burner, Lamp	A. G. Smith	Jersey City, N. J	Dec. 8, 1868	84, 775
Burner, Lamp	G. Smith	Providence, R. I	May 14, 1867	64, 804
Burner, Lamp	G. Smith	Providence, R. I	Dec. 31, 1867	72, 925
Burner, Lamp	G. L. Smith	Bridgeport, Conn	June 14, 1870	104, 366
Burner, Lamp	G. L. Smith	Bridgeport, Conn	Mar. 28, 1871	113, 104
Burner, Lamp	R. L. Smith	West Meriden, N. Y	Mar. 15, 1864	41, 965
Burner, Lamp	W. H. Smith	New York, N. Y	Mar. 29, 1864	42, 122
Burner, Lamp	W. H. Smith	New York, N. Y	June 12, 1866	55, 546
Burner, Lamp	C. St. John	Boston, Mass	Dec. 13, 1864	45, 443
Burner, Lamp	C. St. John	Charlestown, Mass	Mar. 10, 1868	75, 483
Burner, Lamp	F. A. Taber	New Bedford, Mass	Jan. 31, 1871	111, 400
Burner, Lamp	A. Taplin	Somerville, Mass	Mar. 16, 1869	87, 988
Burner, Lamp	A. Taplin	Somerville, Mass	Apr. 26, 1870	102, 449
Burner, Lamp	A. Taplin	Forrestville, Conn	May 3, 1870	102, 728
Burner, Lamp	A. Taplin	Forrestville, Conn	Jan. 24, 1871	111, 274
Burner, Lamp	A. Taplin	Forrestville, Conn	Sept. 19, 1871	119, 061
Burner, Lamp	A. Taplin and H. D. Bradley	Forrestville, Conn	Aug. 31, 1869	94, 451
Burner, Lamp	A. Thirault	Brooklyn, N. Y	Mar. 9, 1869	87, 601
Burner, Lamp	E. J. Toof	Madison, Iowa	Aug. 11, 1868	80, 843
Burner, Lamp	J. Trent	Millerton, N. Y	Apr. 4, 1871	113, 472
Burner, Lamp	E. Trittin	Philadelphia, Pa	Aug. 19, 1862	36, 262
Burner, Lamp	A. C. Vaughn	Philadelphia, Pa	Nov. 6, 1866	59, 518
Burner, Lamp	S. W. Warren	Boston, Mass	Sept. 14, 1869	94, 796
Burner, Lamp	C. C. Warwick	Philadelphia, Pa	Oct. 27, 1863	40, 439
Burner, Lamp	J. H. Weeden	Waterbury, Conn	Sept. 7, 1869	94, 533
Burner, Lamp	W. N. Weeden	Waterbury, Conn	Feb. 18, 1873	136, 113
Burner, Lamp	M. J. Wellman	New York, N. Y	Jan. 7, 1873	134, 718
Burner, Lamp	W. Westlake	Chicago, Ill	Nov. 9, 1869	96, 645
Burner, Lamp	W. Westlake	Chicago, Ill	Mar. 22, 1870	101, 066
Burner, Lamp	J. S. Wetherby	New York, N. Y	Apr. 26, 1870	102, 342
Burner, Lamp	H. J. White	Boston, Mass	May 10, 1870	102, 897
Burner, Lamp	A. Whitlock	Danbury, Conn	June 4, 1867	65, 459
Burner, Lamp	S. W. Wilcox	Mendon, Mass	Oct. 2, 1866	58, 524
Burner, Lamp	N. W. Williams	Frankford, Pa	July 8, 1862	35, 860
Burner, Lamp	J. D. Willoughby	Shippensburgh, Pa	Apr. 26, 1870	102, 457
Burner, Lamp	S. R. Wilmot	Bridgeport, Conn	Oct. 4, 1870	108, 078
Burner, Lamp	S. R. Wilmot	Bridgeport, Conn	Oct. 25, 1870	108, 667
Burner, Lamp	J. Wolstenholme	Providence, R. I	Feb. 3, 1863	37, 599

Index of patents issued from the United States Patent Office from 1790 *to* 1873, *inclusive*—Continued.

Invention.	Inventor.	Residence.	Date.	No.
Burner, Lamp	J. Wood	Nottingham, England	June 6, 1865	48, 142
Burner, Lamp	J. B. Wortham	Huntsville, Ala	May 28, 1867	65, 322
Burner, Lamp	D. P. Wright and C. Butler	Birmingham, England	Mar. 22, 1870	101, 073
Burner, Lamp	H. Wright	Pittsburgh, Pa	Jan. 27, 1863	37, 540
Burner, Lamp	M. B. Wright	West Meriden, Conn	June 23, 1863	38, 999
Burner, Lamp	M. B. Wright	West Meriden, Conn	Jan. 5, 1864	41, 172
Burner, Lamp	M. B. Wright	Meriden, Conn	June 18, 1867	65, 851
Burner, Lamp	H. M. Wyatt	Somerville, Mass	June 16, 1868	78, 978
Burner, Lamp	J. N. Wyatt	Baltimore, Md	Mar. 25, 1873	137, 276
Burner, Lamp	J. H. Wygant and C. W. Vanderbeck.	Hackensack, N. Y	Aug. 16, 1864	43, 879
Burner, Lamp gas	R. Nutting	Randolph, Vt	June 7, 1870	103, 917
Burner, Light-house lamp	I. Dunham	Bristol, Me	June 20, 1836	....
Burner, Naphtha	L. A. Gouch	Yonkers, N. Y	Dec. 17, 1867	72, 191
Burner, Night	W. P. Newhall	Peekskill, N. Y	Dec. 20, 1864	45, 513
Burner of burning-fluid lamp	C. A. Greene	Philadelphia, Pa	Apr. 21, 1857	17, 086
Burner of burning-fluid lamp	R. W. Sargent	Philadelphia, Pa	Mar. 17, 1857	16, 852
Burner, Oxyhydrocarbon-gas	J. D. Averell	New York, N. Y	Oct. 14, 1873	143, 555
Burner, Oxyhydrogen	A. W. Wilkinson	New York, N. Y	Feb. 6, 1872	123, 536
Burner, Oxyhydrogen	A. W. Wilkinson	New York, N. Y	Feb. 6, 1872	123, 537
Burner, Oxyhydrogen-gas	A. W. Wilkinson	New York, N. Y	Mar. 19, 1872	124, 869
Burner, Petroleum-gas	G. A. Hyver	New Orleans, La	Dec. 10, 1867	71, 883
Burner, Petroleum-stove	W. E. Jervey	New Orleans, La	Feb. 26, 1867	62, 338
Burner, Petroleum-stove	W. E. Jervey	New Orleans, La	Feb. 26, 1867	62, 339
Burner, Porcelain gas	T. G. Arnold and B. Irving	New York, N. Y	Mar. 12, 1867	62, 725
Burner, Reflecting gas	T. Grist	Philadelphia, Pa	June 2, 1868	78, 451
Burner, Reflecting lamp	C. H. Tessy	Utica, N. Y	June 4, 1872	127, 660
Burner, Refuse	W. Glue	Muskegon, Mich	Dec. 23, 1873	145, 861
Burner regulator, Gas	J. S. Bromhead	Peckham, England	June 29, 1869	92, 007
Burner regulator, Gas	W. Clark	Boston, Mass	Aug. 14, 1866	57, 087
Burner regulator, Gas	R. Gill	New York, N. Y	Dec. 7, 1869	97, 627
Burner regulator, Gas	W. Jones	Chelsea, Mass	Nov. 14, 1871	120, 882
Burner regulator, Gas	E. Lawler	Hartford, Conn	July 25, 1871	117, 305
Burner regulator, Gas	W. Mallerd	Brooklyn, N. Y	June 27, 1854	11, 167
Burner regulator, Gas	W. Mallerd	Bridgeport, Conn	Dec. 18, 1860	30, 977
Burner regulator, Gas	A. Mayer	Philadelphia, Pa	Sept. 12, 1854	11, 674
Burner regulator, Gas	H. Shultz	Milwaukee, Wis	Apr. 12, 1870	101, 771
Burner regulator, Gas	A. H. Wood	Boston, Mass	Feb. 19, 1861	31, 506
Burner, Revolving gas	F. McLewel	New York, N. Y	Apr. 18, 1871	113, 906
Burner, Self-closing gas	G. E. Smith	New York, N. Y	Oct. 3, 1871	119, 478
Burner, Self-generating vapor	J. S. Gray	New York, N. Y	Sept. 9, 1862	36, 404
Burner, Self-lighting gas	A. Barbarin	New Orleans, La	Sept. 1, 1868	81, 734
Burner, Self-regulating gas	G. W. Thompson	New York, N. Y	May 27, 1862	35, 402
Burner, Smoke and steam	J. W. Kingman and A. Eurgens	Laramie City, Wyo	July 29, 1873	141, 277
Burner socket, Gas	J. Todd	Madison, Ind	May 3, 1864	42, 609
Burner, Spirit-gas	C. Miller	Saint Louis, Mo	June 7, 1859	24, 355
Burner, Tar or petroleum	J. Law	London, Canada	Feb. 11, 1873	135, 649
Burner tips made from soapstone, &c., Mode of hardening gas.	H. J. Smith	Boston, Mass	Sept. 22, 1868	82, 445
Burner to burn spirits of turpentine, Argand oil	C. Carr	Philadelphia, Pa	June 20, 1840	1, 644
Burner, Tubular-wick	H. W. Dopp	Buffalo, N. Y	Nov. 20, 1866	59, 898
Burner, Vapor	J. E. Ambrose	Lombard, Ill	Aug. 17, 1869	93, 661
Burner, Vapor	E. H. Anderson	Easton, Md	Apr. 3, 1860	27, 676
Burner, Vapor	W. Aurich	Chicago, Ill	Aug. 31, 1869	94, 269
Burner, Vapor	W. Aurich	Chicago, Ill	Mar. 22, 1870	101, 079
Burner, Vapor	J. W. Baker	Columbus, Ohio	May 10, 1870	102, 749
Burner, Vapor	S. D. Baldwin	Chicago, Ill	Apr. 27, 1869	89, 271
Burner, Vapor	S. D. Baldwin	Chicago, Ill	Apr. 5, 1870	101, 413
Burner, Vapor	S. D. Baldwin	Chicago, Ill	Nov. 7, 1871	120, 613
Burner, Vapor	W. E. Bartlett	Newburgh, N. Y	May 23, 1871	115, 015
Burner, Vapor	W. W. Batchelder	New York, N. Y	Aug. 21, 1866	57, 276
Burner, Vapor	J. Benson and A. H. Watkins	Boston, Mass	Feb. 18, 1873	136, 021
Burner, Vapor	J. Benson and A. H. Watkins	Boston, Mass	Feb. 18, 1873	136, 022
Burner, Vapor	D. Berkey	Huntington, Ind	Mar. 29, 1870	101, 215
Burner, Vapor	W. Bliesner	Saint Louis, Mo	Jan. 18, 1870	98, 842
Burner, Vapor	C. B. Brown	Placerville, Cal	Aug. 22, 1871	118, 192
Burner, Vapor	W. N. Brown	Camden, N. J	May 15, 1860	28, 250
Burner, Vapor	J. Burns	Keokuk, Iowa	July 9, 1872	128, 703
Burner, Vapor	M. L. Callender	New York, N. Y	Sept. 16, 1862	36, 452
Burner, Vapor	D. H. Carpenter	Wallingford, Conn	Aug. 4, 1857	17, 916
Burner, Vapor	L. Chandor	St. Petersburg, Russia	Aug. 17, 1869	93, 674
Burner, Vapor	L. Chandor	St. Petersburg, Russia	Dec. 28, 1869	98, 228
Burner, Vapor	J. Cook	Saint Louis, Mo	Sept. 14, 1869	94, 716
Burner, Vapor	J. Cook	New York, N. Y	Nov. 7, 1871	120, 627
Burner, Vapor	W. E. Darrah	Baltimore, Md	Aug. 11, 1868	80, 926
Burner, Vapor	J. R. De Mahy	New Orleans, La	Sept. 14, 1869	94, 722
Burner, Vapor	J. R. De Mahy and J. P. Cross	New Orleans, La	Apr. 13, 1869	88, 854
Burner, Vapor	H. C. De Witt	Waukegan, Ill	Mar. 1, 1870	100, 270
Burner, Vapor	T. P. Doane	New York, N. Y	Dec. 5, 1875	121, 497
Burner, Vapor	M. B. Dyott	Philadelphia, Pa	July 4, 1871	116, 573
Burner, Vapor	M. B. Dyott	Philadelphia, Pa	Sept. 3, 1872	131, 086
Burner, Vapor	H. Fairbanks	South Brookfield, Mass	June 23, 1857	17, 622
Burner, Vapor	H. Fayette	Brooklyn, N. Y	Feb. 20, 1872	123, 879
Burner, Vapor	J. E. Findley	Memphis, Tenn	Jan. 11, 1870	98, 680
Burner, Vapor	D. R. Fletcher	Covington, Ky	June 7, 1870	104, 009
Burner, Vapor	L. Fischer	Brooklyn, N. Y	Mar. 30, 1869	88, 287
Burner, Vapor	L. Fischer	Brooklyn, N. Y	June 22, 1869	91, 533
Burner, Vapor	M. F. Gale	New York, N. Y	June 17, 1873	140, 029
Burner, Vapor	M. F. Gale	New York, N. Y	June 17, 1873	140, 030
Burner, Vapor	T. S. Gates and A. H. Fritchey	Franklin County, Ohio	June 1, 1869	90, 659
Burner, Vapor	T. S. Gates and A. H. Fritchey	Columbus, Ohio	Aug. 17, 1869	93, 698
Burner, Vapor	T. S. Gates and A. H. Fritchey	Columbus, Ohio	May 23, 1871	115, 189
Burner, Vapor	T. S. Gates and A. H. Fritchey	Columbus, Ohio	Oct. 10, 1871	119, 839
Burner, Vapor	E. Gillert	Saint Louis, Mo	Aug. 23, 1870	106, 574
Burner, Vapor	L. A. Gouch	Yonkers, N. Y	July 26, 1870	105, 669
Burner, Vapor	F. Gould	Paterson, N. J	Apr. 26, 1870	102, 251
Burner, Vapor	J. S. Gray	New York, N. Y	Dec. 27, 1864	45, 600
Burner, Vapor	B. D. Greene	Sturgis, Mich	Feb. 15, 1870	99, 878

Index of patents issued from the United States Patent Office from 1790 to 1873, inclusive—Continued.

Index of patents issued from the United States Patent Office from 1790 to 1873, inclusive—Continued.

Invention.	Inventor.	Residence.	Date.	No.
Burners, Automatic attachment to gas	A. R. Marshall	Stratford, Conn	Aug. 26, 1856	15, 614
Burners, Automatic cut-off for gas	J. B. Smith	Pittston, Pa	Feb. 11, 1868	74, 440
Burners, Automatic lighting-attachment for lamps and taper.	W. H. Weeks	New York, N. Y	Jan. 25, 1870	99, 123
Burners, Carbureting-attachment for gas	J. H. Steiner	Reading, Pa	Nov. 1, 1870	108, 844
Burners, Chimney-holder for gas	E. P. Gleason	New York, N. Y	Nov. 13, 1866	59, 588
Burners, Chimney-holder for gas	G. Mooney	Providence, R. I	July 16, 1872	129, 158
Burners, Clock-attachment to gas	P. C. Bensel	New York, N. Y	May 14, 1872	126, 620
Burners, Clutch for supporting water bowls under gas.	S. Gardner	New York, N. Y	June 4, 1872	127, 590
Burners, Construction of gas	J. McHenry	Cincinnati, Ohio	Mar. 17, 1857	16, 848
Burners, Construction of gas	J. Stevens and J. Johnson	New York, N. Y	Sept. 27, 1859	25, 591
Burners, Construction of gas	H. K. Symmes	Newton, Mass	Oct. 4, 1859	25, 686
Burners, Construction of lamp	W. N. Weeden	Waterbury, Conn	Oct. 1, 1872	131, 917
Burners, Construction of vapor	W. W. Batchelder	New York, N. Y	Oct. 4, 1859	25, 621
Burners, Construction of vapor	W. H. Hunt	Brooklyn, N. Y	Oct. 18, 1859	25, 830
Burners, Construction of vapor-lamp	W. W. Batchelder	New York, N. Y	Oct. 18, 1859	25, 799
Burners, Device for drawing wick through	F. A. Blaetterlein	West Meriden, Conn	Dec. 31, 1867	72, 785
Burners, Device for regulating by electricity the issue of gas from.	C. W. Smith	Evans, N. Y	May 18, 1858	20, 305
Burners, Electric lighting-attachment for gas	H. C. Appleby	Conneaut, Ohio	June 25, 1872	128, 201
Burners for holding vessels or shades over the flame, Attachment to lamp or gas.	W. L. Fish	Newark, N. J	Nov. 17, 1863	40, 617
Burners for lamps, Mode of suspending	A. Moore and J. A. Cole	Northville, N. Y	Mar. 7, 1865	46, 691
Burners for vapor-lamps, Construction of	R. Steel	Philadelphia, Pa	Nov. 1, 1859	25, 986
Burners, Globe and holder for gas	G. M. Ramsay	New York, N. Y	June 17, 1873	140, 075
Burners, Lamp for lighting gas	R. Thompson	Lowell, Mass	Dec. 17, 1850	7, 848
Burners, Light-intensifying attachment for gas	S. T. Bacon	Boston, Mass	June 11, 1872	127, 829
Burners, Manufacture of Argand	E. S. Archer	New York, N. Y	Jan. 31, 1865	46, 063
Burners, Manufacture of Argand gas	G. Mooney	Providence, R. I	Jan. 14, 1868	73, 367
Burners or lamps, Shade-holder for gas	G. Wedekind	Philadelphia, Pa	May 20, 1862	35, 341
Burners, Perforation in lamp	W. H. Smith	New York, N. Y	Mar. 3, 1863	37, 845
Burners, Protector for gas or vapor	R. Nutting	Randolph, Vt	May 2, 1871	114, 329
Burners, Regulating-attachment for gas	W. Mallerd	Bridgeport, Conn	May 8, 1866	54, 569
Burners, Regulating gas	H. B. Myer	Philadelphia, Pa	Nov. 10, 1868	83, 990
Burners, Regulator for gas	W. Mallerd	Bridgeport, Conn	Apr. 18, 1865	47, 362
Burners, Rest for supporting glass bowls underneath horizontal gas.	S. Gardner	New York, N. Y	Apr. 30, 1872	126, 140
Burners, Revolving attachment for gas	J. O. Belknap	Mobile, Ala	Apr. 1, 1873	137, 406
Burners, Self-lighting attachment for gas	S. Gardiner, jr	New York, N. Y	Feb. 16, 1869	87, 039
Burners, Shade for lamp and gas	M. H. Collins	Chelsea, Mass	Nov. 8, 1870	108, 972
Burners, Shade-ring for lamp	H. W. Hayden	Waterbury, Conn	Dec. 14, 1869	97, 772
Burners, Shield for gas	I. W. Shaler	Brooklyn, N. Y	Sept. 27, 1870	107, 824
Burners, Shield for gas	H. J. Wattles	Rockford, Ill	June 21, 1870	104, 516
Burners, Shield for naphtha-gas	H. H. Edgerton	Fort Wayne, Ind	July 25, 1871	117, 396
Burners, Stop-cock and regulator for gas	A. E. Deloueste	Buffalo, N. Y	Feb. 18, 1873	135, 895
Burners to lamps, Attaching	W. P. Miller	San Francisco, Cal	July 31, 1866	56, 775
Burners to lamps, Attaching	H. Weston	Towanda, Pa	May 21, 1867	64, 925
Burners to lamps, Device for attaching	J. B. Alexander	Washington, D. C	Nov. 26, 1867	71, 261
Burners, Tip for gas	R. Lanstrom	Cincinnati, Ohio	Dec. 31, 1867	72, 741
Burners, Valve for gas	A. Mayer	Philadelphia, Pa	Mar. 13, 1855	12, 515
Burners, Ventilating-fan for gas	H. Seher	Saint Louis, Mo	Dec. 18, 1866	60, 566
Burners, Wick-adjuster for Argand lamp	W. B. Curtiss	Bridgeport, Conn	June 7, 1870	103, 993
Burners, Wick-tube for lamp	C. L. Daboll	New London, Conn	May 19, 1863	38, 567
Burning-fluid	B. H. Chadbourn	Saint Louis, Mo	Oct. 30, 1866	59, 182
Burning-fluid	J. P. Cross	Watertown, N. Y	Aug. 14, 1866	57, 095
Burning-fluid	H. H. Etter	Washington, D. C	Mar. 19, 1867	63, 027
Burning-fluid	G. L. Fattie	Buffalo, N. Y	Nov. 20, 1866	59, 797
Burning-fluid	G. W. Flowers and J. C. and D. W. Happersett.	Urbana, Ohio	Feb. 25, 1868	74, 756
Burning fluid	A. Gesner	Williamsburgh, N. Y	May 23, 1855	12, 936
Burning-fluid	J. Griffin	Stanford, N. Y	Mar. 8, 1859	23, 167
Burning-fluid	J. G. Hester	Raleigh, N. C	Sept. 24, 1867	69, 210
Burning-fluid	W. W. Jacobs	Hagerstown, Md	Mar. 19, 1867	63, 054
Burning-fluid	J. Jann	New Windsor, Md	Feb. 13, 1866	52, 574
Burning-fluid	J. Jann	New Windsor, Md	Sept. 4, 1866	57 727
Burning-fluid	J. J. Kamm	Fort Wayne, Ind	Apr. 9, 1867	63, 727
Burning fluid	J. T. Leete	New York, N. Y	Apr. 30, 1867	64, 232
Burning-fluid	W. R. Loomis, N. Wells, H. Hitchcock, and S. G. Stryker.	Elmira, N. Y	July 2, 1867	66, 364
Burning-fluid	D. Mansfield	Oshkosh, Wis	June 26, 1866	55, 880
Burning-fluid	T. Martin and J. G. Evans	Muscatine, Iowa	Dec. 3, 1867	71, 629
Burning-fluid	G. McLean	Brooklyn, N. Y	Oct. 29, 1867	70, 346
Burning-fluid	G. H. Melten and J. C. Hazleton.	Washington, D. C	Sept. 4, 1866	57, 749
Burning-fluid	C. W. Pinkham	Fond du Lac, Wis	Mar. 25, 1862	34, 772
Burning-fluid	W. B. Rogers	Chicago, Ill	Dec. 18, 1866	60, 559
Burning-fluid	J. B. Scott	Hyattsville, Md	Sept. 18, 1866	58, 180
Burning-fluid	E. D. Seely	Brookline, Mass	Aug. 21, 1866	57, 390
Burning-fluid	G. W. Spangle	Clifton Springs, N. Y	Oct. 16, 1866	58, 905
Burning-fluid	M. L. Stoddard	Corning, N. Y	July 30, 1867	67, 373
Burning-fluid	A. C. Vaughan	Rainsburgh, Pa	Apr. 3, 1866	53, 709
Burning-fluid	I. B. Wiggin	Washington, D. C	Apr. 9, 1867	63, 777
Burning-fluid	W. Wilber	New York, N. Y	Mar. 8, 1859	23, 210
Burning-fluid composition	B. F. Hebard	Neponset, Mass	Feb. 19, 1861	31, 457
Burning-fluid compound	A. Gesner	Williamsburgh, N. Y	May 29, 1855	12, 987
Burning-fluid for illumination, Compound	H. B. Brace and W. T. Swart	Canandaigua, N. Y	May 8, 1866	54, 495
Burning-fluid, Illuminating	L. D. Ferguson	Corning, N. Y	Apr. 2, 1867	63, 376
Burning-fluids, Composition for	C. N. Tyler	Buffalo, N. Y	Mar. 24, 1863	38, 015
Burning fluids, Composition for treating	H. B. Wellman	Indianapolis, Ind	Oct. 22, 1867	70, 054
Burning-fluids, Manufacture of	W. Corfield	Philadelphia, Pa	Apr. 17, 1866	54, 060
Burning-fluids, Manufacture of	W. Corfield	Philadelphia, Pa	Apr. 17, 1866	54, 061
Burning-fluids, Manufacture of	L. L. Hill	Greenport, N. Y	June 15, 1858	20, 558
Burning-fluids, Mode of preparing	R. E. Campbell	New York, N. Y	Oct. 30, 1866	59, 177
Burning fluids, Testing	P. Millspaugh	Kent, Conn	May 28, 1872	127, 259
Burning hydrocarbons and bagasse	E. S. Roman	Cantrelle, La	Apr. 23, 1872	125, 989
Burning-kiln	J. Green	Saint Louis, Mo	Jan. 12, 1869	85, 813
Burning-kiln	B. Kreischer	New York, N. Y	Sept. 1, 1868	81, 793

Index of patents issued from the United States Patent Office from 1790 to 1873, inclusive—Continued.

Invention.	Inventor.	Residence.	Date.	No.
Burning-kiln	B. Kreischer	New York, N. Y	Aug. 17, 1869	93, 891
Burning-kiln	G. A. Wedekind and H. Dueberg.	New York, N. Y	Dec. 15, 1868	85, 042
Burning liquid-fuel and generating steam, Apparatus for.	W. T. Scheide	Tidioute, Pa	June 24, 1873	140, 220
Burning liquids lighter than water, Apparatus for.	A. T. Schmidt	Pittsburgh, Pa	Nov. 11, 1862	36, 917
Burning ornamental figures upon wood	H. Wood	New York, N. Y	Feb. 19, 1850	7, 111
Burnisher	C. Frampton	Brooklyn, N. Y	Apr. 20, 1858	19, 988
Burnishing-machine	C. H. Helms	Poughkeepsie, N. Y	Nov. 28, 1865	51, 180
Burnishing-machine	D. F. Randall	Hartford, Conn	Oct. 22, 1861	33, 558
Burnishing-machine	N. C. Stow	Stoneham, Mass	Jan. 30, 1866	52, 336
Burnishing-machine	A. M. White	Hartford, Conn	Nov. 20, 1860	30, 707
Burnishing-machine	L. S. White	Hartford, Conn	Aug. 24, 1858	21, 304
Burnishing-machine	L. S. White	Waterbury, Conn	Apr. 5, 1859	23, 520
Burnishing-machine	L. S. White	Waterbury, Conn	Oct. 11, 1859	25, 783
Burnishing machine, Metal	J. Stever	Bristol, Conn	May 1, 1855	12, 799
Burnishing metal, Process for	E. Satterlee	Albany, N. Y	Mar. 20, 1849	6, 200
Burr-cylinder	J. Bidwell	New York, N. Y	Nov. 15, 1859	26, 081
Burr, Locking	J. J. Steward	Big Prairie, Ohio	June 1, 1869	90, 699
Burring-cylinder	C. G. Sargent	Lowell, Mass	Oct. 9, 1849	6, 778
Burring-machine	A. Crane	Lowell, Mass	Oct. 11, 1845	4, 231
Burring-machine	Z. Parkhurst	New York, N. Y	Sept. 11, 1847	5, 282
Burring-machine	O. W. Stow	Southington, Conn	Dec. 28, 1858	22, 459
Burring-machine	T. S. Washburn	Lowell, Mass	Oct. 11, 1845	4, 230
Burring-machine burr-box	Z. Parkhurst	Milford, Mass	July 10, 1866	56, 257
Burring-machines, Guard-cylinder for	F. A. Calvert	Lowell, Mass	Aug. 14, 1847	5, 240
Burring-machines, Guard or stripper for	A. Wright	Lowell, Mass	Jan. 23, 1849	6, 057
Burring-machines, &c., Stripping and feed roll for.	J. K. Proctor	Philadelphia, Pa	Nov. 26, 1872	133, 482
Bush, Lubricating	S. H. Everett	Milton, Ohio	Sept. 4, 1866	57, 695
Bush-spindle	S. Merchant	Ohio County, Va	July 22, 1834	....
Bushing, Anti-frictional	F. S. Burr	Brooklyn, N. Y	Apr. 1, 1872	137, 415
Bushing for wheels	T. Blake	Stockton, Cal	Oct. 6, 1868	82, 790
Bustle	J. I. Barnum	Brooklyn, N. Y	June 11, 1872	127, 832
Bustle	M. H. Beckworth	Camden, N. Y	Aug. 24, 1869	93, 950
Bustle	I. W. Birdseye	Birmingham, Conn	Nov. 7, 1871	120, 616
Bustle	M. K. Bortree	Jackson, Mich	Feb. 25, 1873	136, 127
Bustle	M. Boupart	Fordham, N. Y	Sept. 16, 1873	142, 764
Bustle	J. Broughton	Brooklyn, N. Y	Nov. 1, 1870	108, 872
Bustle	J. Broughton	Brooklyn, N. Y	Nov. 1, 1870	108, 873
Bustle	G. P. Bryant	Boston, Mass	July 30, 1872	129, 883
Bustle	B. Davis	Brooklyn, N. Y	Oct. 18, 1859	25, 865
Bustle	A. Douglas	New York, N. Y	Apr. 21, 1857	17, 082
Bustle	T. A. Earl	North Attleborough, Mass.	Oct. 11, 1859	25, 786
Bustle	T. F. Fessenden	Providence, R. I	May 28, 1872	127, 327
Bustle	I. W., jr., and A. H. Hakes	Norwich, Conn	Apr. 19, 1850	23, 681
Bustle	J. H. Hall	Ansonia, Conn	Feb. 11, 1873	135, 801
Bustle	J. B. Loomis	Chelsea, Mass	Aug. 18, 1868	81, 281
Bustle	H. H. May	Birmingham, Conn	June 25, 1872	128, 412
Bustle	D. McInroy	Brooklyn, E. D., N. Y	Oct. 4, 1870	108, 039
Bustle	C. B. Pollock	Norwich, Conn	July 9, 1872	128, 813
Bustle	C. A. Postley	Jersey City, N. J	Dec. 7, 1858	22, 242
Bustle	D. G. Rollin	New York, N. Y	Sept. 14, 1869	94, 915
Bustle	D. Smith	Litchfield Corner, Me	Nov. 12, 1872	133, 062
Bustle	S. Smith	Boston, Mass	Dec. 17, 1872	134, 010
Bustle	S. and D. L. Smith	Skowhegan, Me	Aug. 13, 1872	130, 446
Bustle	T. S. Sperry	New York, N. Y	Jan. 28, 1873	135, 379
Bustle	T. Stockman	New York, N. Y	Feb. 11, 1873	135, 858
Bustle	G. R. Taber	Boston, Mass	Apr. 30, 1872	126, 164
Bustle	A. W. Thomas	Philadelphia, Pa	June 25, 1872	128, 337
Bustle	A. W. Thomas	Philadelphia, Pa	July 15, 1873	140, 966
Bustle	A. J. Thompson	Malden, Mass	Oct. 18, 1859	25, 854
Bustle	J. Wehl	New York, N. Y	Aug. 6, 1872	130, 345
Bustle	G. W. Yerby	New York, N. Y	Oct. 18, 1859	25, 861
Bustle and skirt	H. N. Daggett	Attleborough, Mass	July 13, 1858	20, 865
Bustle, Extension	G. V. Pierce	Jersey City, N. J	May 23, 1871	115, 235
Bustle for lady's dress	G. V. and E. A. Pierce	New York, N. Y	Nov. 23, 1858	22, 133
Bustle hoops, Clasp for the ends of	F. S. Otis	Brooklyn, N. Y	Jan. 17, 1860	26, 876
Bustle, Lady's	J. W. Bradley	New York, N. Y	Nov. 22, 1859	26, 159
Bustle, Lady's	B. F. Moore	New York, N. Y	Aug. 23, 1859	25, 211
Bustles, Fastening hoop-ends in tabs of	L. De Forest	Birmingham, Conn	Sept. 23, 1862	36, 510
Butcher's cleaver	C. Hart	Unionville, Conn	Oct. 1, 1872	131, 754
Butcher's knife	P. Houseman and C. C. Campbell.	Rural Retreat, Va	Oct. 11, 1870	108, 141
Butcher's spreader	F. B. Guthrie	Crawfordsville, Ind	Sept. 3, 1872	131, 096
Butt	T. W. Brown	Reading, Pa	Jan. 19, 1869	85, 902
Butt	J. A. Frary	New Britain, Conn	Feb. 2, 1869	86, 524
Butt-blanks, Machine for trimming	C. Kenney	West Troy, N. Y	July 26, 1844	3, 682
Butt-centering machine	E. Parker	New Britain, Conn	July 19, 1870	105, 488
Butt-machine	T. Tracy	New Britain, Conn	Mar. 19, 1867	62, 981
Butt, Post	J. Holland	Conshohocken, Pa	May 15, 1860	28, 275
Butt, Reversible	G. W. Field	Lowell, Mass	Nov. 29, 1870	109, 604
Butt, Reversible	J. Kindleberger and W. A. Arnold	San Francisco, Cal	Sept. 14, 1869	94, 756
Butt, Spring	T. Fredericks	Newark, N. J	Feb. 16, 1869	86, 978
Butt, Spring	L. Preston	Elizabethport, N. J	June 1, 1869	9[illegible], 686
Butt, Spring	W. Wells	Ashtabula, Ohio	Nov. 17, 1868	84, 240
Butts or hinges for hanging and fastening window blinds and shutters, Method of constructing.	A. C. Palmer	Utica, N. Y	Jan. 27, 1843	2, 936
Butts, Process of finishing sheet metal	E. C. Blakeslee	Waterbury, Conn	Dec. 17, 1872	134, 029
Butter and cheese, Preparing milk for	C. Ainsworth	Littleton, N. Y	Nov. 19, 1833	....
Butter and cutting curd, Machine for working	J. Buck	Chatham, Conn	Dec. 5, 1825	....
Butter and lard package	J. L. Cone	Waterloo, N. Y	July 4, 1871	116, 684
Butter and lard tub, Covered	S. E. Southland	Jamestown, N. Y	Sept. 11, 1866	57, 989
Butter and other articles, Vessel for packing	W. Pratt	New York, N. Y	June 14, 1870	104, 198
Butter, Apparatus for making	A. Denison	Woodville, Ohio	Sept. 21, 1869	95, 096
Butter-box	W. B. Guernsey	Norwich, N. Y	Feb. 26, 1867	62, 410
Butter, &c., Box and bag for packing	J. D. Smedley	Chicago, Ill	Mar. 31, 1868	76, 110
Butter, Box or tub for putting up	J. Parce	Fairport, N. Y	Oct. 4, 1864	44, 551

Index of patents issued from the United States Patent Office from 1790 *to* 1873, *inclusive*—Continued.

Invention.	Inventor.	Residence.	Date.	No.
Butter-bucket	J. T. Dumont	Kansas City, Mo	Mar. 11, 1873	136, 713
Butter-bucket	J. Gilberds and M. Harris	Jamestown, N. Y	Sept. 2, 1873	142, 456
Butter bucket or package	N. C. Burnap	Argusville, N. Y	Dec. 3, 1872	133, 628
Butter by machinery, Mode of making	E. Waterhouse	Gardiner, Me	Sept. 29, 1825	....
Butter-carrier	J. B. Crozier	Cumberland, Ohio	Jan. 16, 1872	122, 758
Butter-carrier	B. Yaw	New Concord, Ohio	Nov. 12, 1872	132, 998
Butter, Case for packing	S. H. Matthews	Nottingham, Pa	Sept. 3, 1872	131, 015
Butter-coloring compound	G. Bogart, W. H. Cramer, and W. L. Lewis.	Laporte City, Iowa	Sept. 16, 1873	142, 891
Butter-cooler	E. Kaufman and A. Weber	Philadelphia, Pa	Sept. 8, 1868	82, 005
Butter-cooler	G. W. Smith	Hartford, Conn	July 5, 1859	24, 636
Butter-cooler	J. H. Stimpson	Baltimore, Md	May 15, 1855	12, 876
Butter-cooler	J. H. Stimpson	Baltimore, Md	July 13, 1858	20, 902
Butter, Curing and preserving	J. F. Saiger	Shelby, Ohio	Dec. 28, 1869	98, 421
Butter-cutter	A. N. Merritt	Gardner, Mass	Oct. 8, 1867	69, 690
Butter cutter and lifter, Gaged	T. E. Colbrunn	Cleveland, Ohio	Aug. 26, 1873	142, 207
Butter cutter and stamp, Combined	N. Clough	Lowell, Mass	Nov. 23, 1869	97, 049
Butter, Device for purifying	G. W. Putnam	Smithfield, N. Y	Mar. 4, 1862	34, 592
Butter-dish	W. E. Hawkins	Wallingford, Conn	Feb. 11, 1868	74, 221
Butter-dish	N. Lawrence	Taunton, Mass	Dec. 10, 1867	71, 889
Butter-dish	W. W. Lyman	West Meriden, Conn	July 28, 1868	80, 297
Butter-dish	I. A. Richards	Brookfield, Mass	Feb. 18, 1868	74, 722
Butter-dish drainer	F. C. Booth	Meriden, Conn	Apr. 23, 1872	125, 876
Butter-excavator	N. J. Eaton	Montana, Iowa	Jan. 18, 1870	98, 938
Butter-extractor	T. Curtis	Holly, Mich	June 14, 1870	104, 120
Butter-firkin clamp	D. M. Lockridge	Otto, N. Y	Nov. 2, 1869	96, 451
Butter from cheese, whey, &c., Making	H. C. Markham	West Turin, N. Y	Dec. 11, 1866	60, 399
Butter from cream, Apparatus for reducing	S. D. Warner and O. W. Thomas	Richmond, Ill	Feb. 22, 1870	100, 224
Butter from firkins, Implement for cutting	N. Woodbury	Salem, Mass	May 11, 1852	8, 947
Butter from milk, Producing	N. Orcutt	Binghamton, N. Y	May 17, 1864	42, 821
Butter from whey, Manufacture of	J. Suggett	Cortlandville, N. Y	Dec. 18, 1866	60, 656
Butter from whey, Manufacturing	I. Page	Adams, N. Y	June 23, 1868	79, 078
Butter-jar	J. Smith	East Liverpool, Ohio	Sept. 21, 1869	95, 156
Butter-kettle	J. Liming	Philadelphia, Pa	July 11, 1871	116, 844
Butter-knife holder	H. Benton	Guilford, Conn	Apr. 19, 1864	42, 339
Butter-knife rest	B. D. Reed	Westfield, Mass	July 13, 1869	92, 468
Butter-knife rest	B. D. Reed	Westfield, Mass	Jan. 21, 1873	135, 156
Butter-machine	D. Rogers	Mount Gilead, Ohio	Aug. 24, 1869	94, 0[illegible]3
Butter, Machine for manufacturing	A. Curtiss	Paris, N. Y	Apr. 20, 1830	....
Butter, Machine for weighing and printing	W. S. Reinert	Spring Garden, Pa	May 9, 1854	10, 896
Butter, Making	B. G. and G. Burtis	New York, N. Y	Feb. 27, 1807	....
Butter, Making	D. H. McGregory	Detroit, Mich	Sept. 10, 1867	68, 639
Butter-making	A. Mot	Washington, D. C	July 19, 1870	105, 479
Butter-making apparatus	F. P. Deuel	Tecumseh, Mich	Mar. 23, 1869	88, 016
Butter-making mold	G. Matthewman and A. Leininger.	Brooklyn, N. Y	June 6, 1865	48, 082
Butter, Manufacture of	J. P. Crampton	Madison County, Ind	Nov. 5, 1867	70, 417
Butter, Manufacture of	Z. Phinney	Greene County, N. Y	Mar. 4, 1814	....
Butter, Method of preparing coloring-matter for	D. W. Dake	Brooklyn, N. Y	Nov. 27, 1866	59, 975
Butter, milk, and other articles, Cooler for preserving.	W. Garrard	Fallston, Pa	Nov. 27, 1866	59, 993
Butter, Mode of churning	J. Strobeck	Parishville, N. Y	Nov. 19, 1867	71, 082
Butter, Mode of purifying rancid	C. Peck	Marshall, Ill	Nov. 2, 1869	96, 477
Butter, Mode of putting up and preserving	J. Wilcox	Springfield, Mass	July 30, 1867	67, 391
Butter, Mode of restoring rancid	J. W. Prentiss	Pultney, N. Y	Oct. 4, 1859	25, 672
Butter, Mode of working and pressing	T. D. Gail	Eden, N. Y	Oct. 10, 1840	1, 815
Butter-mold	O. Allen	San Francisco, Cal	Feb. 14, 1865	46, 319
Butter-mold	J. S. Bullar	Chagrin Falls, Ohio	Apr. 17, 1866	54, 054
Butter-mold	A. J. Derrick	Sheridan, Nev	Dec. 5, 1871	121, 496
Butter-mold	H. W. Hopkins	Milford, N. H	Jan. 1, 1867	60, 894
Butter-mold	M. T. Ridout	Milwaukee, Wis	May 27, 1862	35, 393
Butter-mold	D. G. Williams	Quincy, Mich	Apr. 9, 1872	125, 644
Butler mold and print	J. S. Cerya	Dupont, Ind	Nov. 23, 1869	97, 053
Butter-molds, Tool for boring	J. S. Bullard	Chagrin Falls, Ohio	June 14, 1864	43, 092
Butter molding and working machine	J. C. Hervey	Cincinnati, Ohio	Apr. 27, 1869	89, 480
Butter-molding machine	A. Nudd	Wampum, Wis	June 6, 1865	48, 088
Butter-package	H. P. Adams	Cleveland, Ohio	Oct. 29, 1872	132, 555
Butter-package	J. Andrews	Cleveland, Ohio	Apr. 15, 1873	137, 752
Butter-package	T. W. Ryding	Tully, N. Y	Oct. 19, 1869	95, 937
Butter-package	J. Thayer	Palmyra, Wis	Nov. 2, 1869	96, 506
Butter, Package for preserving and transporting	E. H. Benners	Brooklyn, N. Y	Oct. 8, 1872	131, 930
Butter, Packing and preserving	W. B. Guernsey	Norwich, N. Y	Feb. 26, 1867	62, 411
Butter-paddle	D. L. Grover	Groton, N. Y	May 13, 1873	138, 800
Butter-pail	S. D. King	Middletown, N. Y	June 4, 1872	127, 612
Butter-pail	A. Robertson	East Rupert, Vt	May 9, 1871	114, 714
Butter-print press	L. Coates and J. T. Criswell	Collamer, Pa	Sept. 16, 1873	142, 838
Butter-printer	W. C. Stern and J. W. Robinson.	London Grove, Pa	Nov. 8, 1870	109, 070
Butter-printer	B. Yaw	New Concord, Ohio	Nov. 12, 1872	132, 999
Butter-printing machine	D. E. Dutrow	Washington, D. C	Jan 28, 1873	135, 323
Butter-printing machine	A. F. Hines	Washington, D. C	July 8, 1873	140, 704
Butter-printing machine	J. S. Miller and S. L. Wiegand	Philadelphia, Pa	May 22, 1860	28, 394
Butter, Process of purifying	L. S. Robbins	New York, N. Y	July 28, 1868	80, [illegible]06
Butter, Refining	G. W. Kirchhöffer	Chicago, Ill	June 10, 1873	139, 796
Butter-rolls, Forming and gaging	C. H. Fancher	San Francisco, Cal	Mar. 25, 1873	137, 064
Butter-safe	T. Pyle	Oxford, Pa	Feb. 27, 1872	124, 158
Butter-stamp	T. Mabbett, jr	Vineland, N. J	May 14, 1872	126, 641
Butter-tray, Portable	L. Beemer	Libertyville, N. J	May 9, 1871	114, 546
Butter-trier	W. H. Sloan	Saint Louis, Mo	Oct. 1, 1867	69, 498
Butter-tub	A. R. Bailey	Elmore, Vt	Aug. 25, 1868	81, 459
Butter-tub	G. S. Batcheller	Saratoga Springs, N. Y	Mar. 2, 1869	87, 323
Butter-tub	A. J. Drake	Middletown, N. Y	Sept. 16, 1873	14[illegible], 843
Butter-tub	J. Gilberds	Jamestown, N. Y	Dec. 26, 1871	122, 166
Butter-tub	D. A. Gilbert	Morristown, Vt	Apr. 21, 1868	77, 030
Butter-tub	D. A. Gilbert	Morristown, Vt	June 16, 1868	78, 955
Butter-tub	E. Guyer	Wolcott, Vt	Oct. 13, 1868	82, 939
Butter-tub	J. M. Hale	Georgia Plains, Vt	Nov. 9, 1869	96, 584
Butter-tub	A. B. Harris	Morrisville, Vt	June 16, 1868	78, 963

Index of patents issued from the United States Patent Office from 1790 to 1873, inclusive—Continued.

Invention.	Inventor.	Residence.	Date.	No.
Butter-tub	H. Holt	Brooklyn, N. Y	Nov. 19, 1872	133, 226
Butter-tub	D. Lown	Poughkeepsie, N. Y	July 20, 1869	92, 734
Butter-tub, &c	W. Marsh	Waterford, Pa	Feb. 14, 1871	111, 758
Butter-tub	A. T. Peck	Scott, N. Y	Sept. 2, 1862	36, 361
Butter-tub	A. C. Sawyer	Canton, N. Y	Sept. 14, 1869	94, 917
Butter-tub	G. Smith	Castile, N. Y	Oct. 22, 1872	132, 495
Butter-tub	C. H. White	Emmett Township, Mich	Mar. 28, 1871	113, 122
Butter tub and cooler	A. J. Connelly and T. Benjamin	Philadelphia, Pa	June 11, 1872	127, 742
Butter-tub, &c., Hasp for	H. C. Carter	New York, N. Y	Nov. 25, 1873	144, 889
Butter-worker	J. P. Adams	Whitney's Point, N. Y	Sept. 12, 1865	51, 408
Butter-worker	J. P. Adams	Whitney's Point, N. Y	May 1, 1866	54, 272
Butter-worker	J. P. Adams and J. P. Corbin	Whitney's Point, N. Y	Aug. 9, 1870	106, 104
Butter-worker	J. A. Allen	Deerfield, Mass	Feb. 12, 1861	31, 364
Butter-worker	N. W. Bancroft	Burlington, Vt	Aug. 3, 1858	21, 106
Butter-worker	J. H. Bennett	Bennington, Vt	Mar. 25, 1856	14, 530
Butter-worker	N. Bennett	Sherman, N. Y	Sept. 17, 1861	33, 290
Butter-worker	C. A. Boynton	Hyde Park, Vt	July 17, 1860	29, 135
Butter-worker	J. M. Brush	Eyota, Minn	Nov. 22, 1870	109, 381
Butter-worker	S. H. Bush	Boistfort, Wash	Dec. 16, 1873	145, 624
Butter-worker	E. Butler and G. M. Peck	Pompey, N. Y., and Abington, Pa.	Oct. 27, 1857	18, 497
Butter-worker	J. L. Colburn	West Burke, Vt	Apr. 7, 1868	76, 304
Butter-worker	G. S. Coleman	Alexandria, Va	Oct. 3, 1871	119, 575
Butter-worker	W. Cunningham	Oxford, N. Y	Jan. 21, 1868	73, 582
Butter-worker	D. W. Dake	Chicago, Ill	Jan. 14, 1873	134, 788
Butter-worker	D. W. Dake	Beloit, Wis	Nov. 18, 1873	144, 662
Butter-worker	D. W. Dake	Beloit, Wis	Dec. 9, 1873	145, 338
Butter-worker	E. J. Dickey	Hopewell Cotton Works, Pa.	July 12, 1853	9, 838
Butter-worker	O. L. Dow	Hancock, N. H	Apr. 5, 1870	101, 444
Butter-worker	R. R. Eastman	Granby, Mass	Nov. 27, 1866	59, 985
Butter-worker	E. Farnum	Blackstone, Mass	Feb. 5, 1867	61, 822
Butter-worker	C. W. Gage	Homer, N. Y	June 16, 1857	17, 564
Butter-worker	H. Garrett	Richmond, Mo	Feb. 4, 1868	74, 076
Butter-worker	C. L. Gilpatrick	Lewiston, Me	Sept. 8, 1863	39, 808
Butter-worker	W. N. Golden	Coldwater, Mich	June 3, 1873	139, 571
Butter-worker	E. Gore	Bennington, Vt	July 25, 1854	11, 370
Butter-worker	W. H. Hart	Medfield, Mass	June 26, 1866	55, 857
Butter-worker	L. S. Ingraham	Grafton, Ohio	Aug. 7, 1860	29, 492
Butter-worker	N. Johnson	Guilford, N. Y	Jan. 12, 1864	41, 223
Butter-worker	J. Jones	Philadelphia, Pa	July 5, 1859	24, 698
Butter-worker	S. Keen	East Bridgewater, Mass	Feb. 18, 1868	74, 546
Butter-worker	L. L. Kellogg	Leon, N. Y	July 25, 1871	117, 428
Butter-worker	R. Lapham	New York, N. Y	May 14, 1872	126, 638
Butter-worker	J. B. Lyons	Milton, Conn	Nov. 24, 1863	40, 697
Butter-worker	J. McBride	Ithaca, N. Y	June 10, 1873	139, 723
Butter-worker	P. P. Meredith	Stevensville, Mont	Sept. 26, 1871	119, 385
Butter-worker	S. E. Morse	Montgomery, Vt	Mar. 8, 1864	41, 853
Butter-worker	W. C. Möser	East Nantmeal Township, Pa.	Nov. 26, 1867	71, 318
Butter-worker	B. D. Pease	Madison, Pa	Nov. 26, 1861	33, 794
Butter-worker	G. M. Rhoades	Hamilton, N. Y	July 2, 1861	32, 717
Butter-worker	E. Ring	Mecklenburgh, N. Y	July 25, 1854	11, 387
Butter-worker	J. Robinson	Calais, Vt	June 19, 1866	55, 714
Butter-worker	J. Romans	Homeville, Pa	May 28, 1872	127, 271
Butter-worker	G. Ruston	Freeport, Ill	June 4, 1872	127, 520
Butter-worker	E. E. Scott	Beloit, Wis	Sept. 30, 1873	143, 260
Butter-worker	W. S. and E. H. Shoemaker	Towsontown, Md., and Columbus, Ohio.	Apr. 19, 1870	102, 055
Butter-worker	W. E. Skinner	Milford, Mich	May 14, 1867	64, 803
Butter-worker	W. E. Skinner	Milford, Mich	Aug. 6, 1872	130, 159
Butter-worker	C. F. Smith	Litchfield, Conn	Mar. 13, 1866	53, 192
Butter-worker	I. L. Smith and C. C. Colburn	Burlington, Vt., and Massena, N. Y.	Nov. 17, 1857	18, 649
Butter-worker	J. M. Smith	Lyme, Conn	Jan. 12, 1858	19, 103
Butter-worker	L. A. Smith	Pineville, Pa	Aug. 23, 1853	9, 959
Butter-worker	O. Snow	Burlington, Vt	Sept. 21, 1869	95, 158
Butter-worker	H. Soggs	Columbus, Pa	Aug. 16, 1859	25, 145
Butter-worker	P. M. Stackhouse	Pineville, Pa	July 8, 1873	140, 739
Butter-worker	L. S. Starrett	Newburyport, Mass	Mar. 21, 1865	46, 953
Butter-worker	L. W. Stites	Brooklyn, Ohio	May 15, 1860	28, 312
Butter-worker	M. Sweet	Sidney, N. Y	Feb. 19, 1863	37, 664
Butter-worker	A. Swift	East Elmore, Vt	Apr. 5, 1864	42, 238
Butter-worker	S. H. Wade	Montgomery Centre, Vt	May 28, 1867	65, 315
Butter-worker	E. L. Walker	Twin Grove, Wis	Dec. 5, 1871	121, 559
Butter-worker	E. P. Walker	Belchertown, Mass	Apr. 21, 1868	77, 135
Butter-worker	W. Weaver	Phœnixville, Pa	July 11, 1871	117, 042
Butter-worker, &c	J. T. Whipple	Chicago, Ill	Jan. 5, 1869	85, 551
Butter-worker	W. H. Wiley	Lockport, N. Y	June 12, 1860	28, 706
Butter-worker	A. Willard	Vergennes, Vt	June 2, 1868	78, 502
Butter-worker	I. M. Williams	Blanchester, Ohio	Feb. 6, 1855	12, 366
Butter-worker	Z. Williams	Ithaca, N. Y	Sept. 7, 1858	21, 460
Butter-worker	P. G. Woodard	Waterford, Pa	Mar. 19, 1861	31, 758
Butter-worker	P. G. Woodard	Waterford, Pa	May 23, 1871	115, 144
Butter worker and mold	T. D. Smith	Independence, Ohio	July 3, 1866	56, 112
Butter worker and packer	C. F. Barager	Candor, N. Y	Oct. 23, 1866	58, 971
Butter, Working	J. Seymour	Coventry, N. Y	Dec. 20, 1859	26, 527
Butter worker and printing machine	A. S. and S. B. McDowell	Philadelphia and Montgomery County, Pa.	Oct. 15, 1867	69, 923
Butter-working machine	S. Bishop	Redding, Conn	Jan. 8, 1842	2, 419
Butter-working machine	G. Hotchkiss	Windsor, N. Y	June 7, 1859	24, 305
Butter-working machine	E. H. Merryman	Springfield, Ill	Nov. 27, 1849	6, 898
Butter-working machine	M. A. Richardson	Sherman, N. Y	June 10, 1862	35, 543
Butter-working machine	E. Wilson and M. Lee	Redding, Conn	Feb. 7, 1842	2, 447
Butteris	S. Davis	New Trenton, Ind	July 4, 1871	116, 692
Butteris	D. I. Foust	Crestline, Ohio	Mar. 19, 1872	124, 804
Butteris, Blacksmiths'	R. Kilmer and J. W. Williams	Newtown, Pa	Apr. 21, 1857	17, 128
Butteris, Blacksmiths'	J. H. Rinamy	Findley, Ohio	June 11, 1872	127, 708

Index of patents issued from the United States Patent Office from 1790 *to* 1873, *inclusive*—Continued.

Invention.	Inventor.	Residence.	Date.	No.
Button	J. N. Allen	Providence, R. I	June 17, 1873	139, 991
Button	H. Ansley	Washington, D. C	Aug. 4, 1868	80, 699
Button	J. F. Bapterosses	Paris, France	Jan. 19, 1858	19, 120
Button	E. T. Barnum	Waterbury, Conn	Sept. 12, 1865	49, 846
Button	C. Beeker and M. Wise	New York, N. Y	Dec. 28, 1869	98, 338
Button	P. H. Benedict	Syracuse, N. Y	Mar. 14, 1865	46, 772
Button	E. Bredt	New York, N. Y	May 5, 1868	77, 443
Button	A. W. Browne	Brooklyn, N. Y	Sept. 25, 1866	58, 332
Button	A. W. Browne	Brooklyn, N. Y	May 14, 1867	64, 742
Button	F. M. Bugbee	Kingsville, Ohio	Jan. 28, 1868	73, 871
Button	L. L. Burdon	Providence, R. I	June 29, 1869	91, 906
Button	G. J. Capewell	Cheshire, Conn	July 16, 1872	128, 948
Button	G. J. Capewell	Cheshire, Conn	July 16, 1872	128, 949
Button	H. Carlos	New York, N. Y	Jan. 8, 1867	60, 997
Button	M. P. Carpenter	New York, N. Y	Apr. 15, 1873	137, 824
Button	V. Charlet	Hoboken, N. J	July 30, 1867	67, 267
Button	E. A. Cobb	Philadelphia, Pa	July 18, 1871	117, 150
Button	I. Cole	New York, N. Y	Mar. 30, 1869	88, 451
Button	J. F. Collins and A. Neill	New York, N. Y	May 31, 1870	103, 571
Button	G. Cooke	Winchester, Mass	Dec. 10, 1867	71, 988
Button	A. P. Critchlow	Northampton, Mass	Nov. 30, 1869	97, 363
Button	P. Davey	Ironton, Ohio	Nov. 29, 1859	26, 258
Button	F. Douglas	Norwich, Conn	Apr. 10, 1866	53, 796
Button	J. Durand	New York, N. Y	Sept. 9, 1873	142, 686
Button	R. N. Eagle and C. D. Smith	Washington, D. C	Aug. 14, 1866	57, 101
Button	A. A. Feldtrappe and R. Dutfoy	Paris, France	Oct. 13, 1863	40, 254
Button	C. A. French, 2d	Boston, Mass	May 1, 1866	54, 324
Button	P. W. Gengembre	Boston, Mass	Jan. 19, 1864	41, 292
Button	P. W. Gengembre	Boston, Mass	Dec. 13, 1864	45, 400
Button	P. W. Gengembre	Boston, Mass	Dec. 13, 1864	45, 401
Button	P. W. Gengembre	Boston, Mass	Dec. 13, 1864	45, 402
Button	H. Gerner	New York, N. Y	Nov. 14, 1865	50, 927
Button	R. H. Guilford	West Cheshire, Conn	Sept. 3, 1867	68, 562
Button	R. H. Guilford	West Cheshire, Conn	May 24, 1870	103, 451
Button	J. Hatch	Attleborough, Mass	Feb. 20, 1845	3, 915
Button	C. L. Horack	Willimantic, Conn	Nov. 16, 1869	96, 808
Button	D. Howarth	Portland, Me	May 8, 1866	54, 549
Button	L. A. Jefferson	Bridgeport, Conn	Feb. 23, 1869	87, 262
Button	J. Jenk	Washington, D. C	Apr. 9, 1867	63, 642
Button	J. M. Johnson	Mamaroneck, N. Y	Apr. 17, 1866	53, 986
Button	J. M. Johnson	New York, N. Y	May 15, 1866	54, 736
Button	J. Kenmuir	Leavenworth, Kans	Dec. 28, 1869	98, 271
Button	M. R. Kenyon	Providence, R. I	Mar. 16, 1869	87, 854
Button	J. Koberle	Saint Louis, Mo	Dec. 1, 1868	84, 555
Button	S. Krom	New York, N. Y	June 5, 1860	28, 587
Button	S. B. Lane	Waterbury, Conn	Nov. 19, 1872	133, 160
Button	H. Link	Little Falls, N. Y	Aug. 17, 1869	93, 726
Button	C. M. Loomis	Hartford, Conn	June 6, 1865	48, 079
Button	F. Loos	Germantown, Pa	Jan. 29, 1867	61, 547
Button	P. F. Manras	New York, N. Y	Dec. 4, 1866	60, 217
Button	E. Maynard	Washington, D. C	May 23, 1865	47, 843
Button	G. W. McGill	Washington, D. C	May 28, 1867	65, 250
Button	G. A. Meacham	New York, N. Y	Jan. 10, 1860	26, 776
Button	G. A. Meacham	New York, N. Y	July 2, 1861	32, 703
Button	G. A. Meacham	New York, N. Y	Aug. 13, 1861	33, 046
Button	G. A. Meacham	New York, N. Y	Apr. 8, 1862	34, 897
Button	R. J. Monks	Boston, Mass	May 28, 1872	127, 183
Button	M. D. Moore	Brooklyn, N. Y	May 19, 1868	78, 116
Button	C. Mudler	Cleveland, Ohio	June 2, 1868	78, 535
Button	C. N. Nickerson	Gloucester, Mass	Oct. 27, 1868	83, 403
Button	O. Paddock	Watertown, N. Y	May 18, 1869	90, 119
Button	F. I. Palmer	Springfield, Mass	Mar. 27, 1866	53, 471
Button	F. J. Peabody	Medford, Mass	Aug. 4, 1868	80, 563
Button	F. J. Perkins	Salem, Mass	Apr. 28, 1868	77, 313
Button	G. W. Phillips	Fresh Pond, N. Y	Aug. 1, 1871	117, 564
Button	C. M. Platt	Waterbury, Conn	July 10, 1866	56, 261
Button	C. M. Platt	Waterbury, Conn	Nov. 14, 1871	121, 000
Button	H. Prouhet	Saint Louis, Mo	Dec. 3, 1867	71, 641
Button	J. N. Prugger	New York, N. Y	June 4, 1867	65, 503
Button	W. H. Reed	Philadelphia, Pa	June 6, 1865	48, 095
Button	W. H. Reed	New York, N. Y	Feb. 19, 1867	62, 153
Button	J. L. Remlinger	Providence, R. I	Aug. 17, 1869	93, 748
Button	P. E. Richardière	Paris, France	Feb. 24, 1863	37, 774
Button	C. E. Richards	Attleborough, Mass	Feb. 13, 1866	52, 608
Button	E. A. Robinson	Waterbury, Conn	Aug. 14, 1866	57, 260
Button	C. Robitaille	Brooklyn, N. Y	Apr. 17, 1866	54, 071
Button	A. H. Savage	Ashtabula, Ohio	Sept. 3, 1872	131, 067
Button	G. A. Schultz	Louisville, Ky	Apr. 4, 1871	113, 577
Button	A. Selkirk	Albany, N. Y	Mar. 6, 1866	53, 086
Button	A. M. Smith	Brooklyn, N. Y	Sept. 25, 1866	58, 310
Button	D. M. Somers	Brooklyn, N. Y	Oct. 22, 1867	70, 039
Button	D. M. Somers and W. S. Atwood	Brooklyn, N. Y., and Newark, N. J.	Dec. 31, 1867	72, 929
Button	C. F. Spencer	Rochester, N. Y	Oct. 23, 1866	59, 090
Button	J. A. Spooner and J. Ellerby	Brooklyn, N. Y	Feb. 1, 1870	99, 365
Button	J. R. Spooner	Lowell, Ohio	June 25, 1867	66, 053
Button	A. E. Thurber	Providence, R. I	Mar. 18, 1873	136, 882
Button	W. W. Wade	Medford, Mass	Mar. 23, 1869	88, 099
Button	F. Washbourne	Brooklyn, N. Y	Apr. 22, 1873	138, 107
Button	B. B. Whaley	Brooklyn, E. D., N. Y	Oct. 18, 1864	44, 759
Button	E. S. Wheeler	Westport, Conn	Jan. 3, 1865	45, 781
Button	E. S. Wheeler	Westport, Conn	Mar. 24, 1868	76, 016
Button	W. B. White	North Attleborough, Mass.	Aug. 22, 1865	49, 595
Button	J. F. Wild	New York, N. Y	Mar. 14, 1865	46, 840
Button	F. Wittram	San Francisco, Cal	Oct. 6, 1868	82, 7[illegible]8
Button and lacing hooks. Machine for setting	H. C. Bradford	Providence, R. I	Feb. 11, 1873	135, 763
Button and locket. Combined sleeve	W. C. Almy	Providence, R. I	May 7, 1872	126, 368
Button and stud attachment	H. Freeman	Petroleum Centre, Pa	May 13, 1873	138, 745

Index of patents issued from the United States Patent Office from 1790 *to* 1873, *inclusive*—Continued.

Invention.	Inventor.	Residence.	Date.	No.
Button and stud, Shirt	J. T. Thornton	Providence, R. I	May 6, 1873	138, 595
Button and stud, Sleeve	B. Clayton	Philadelphia, Pa	Feb. 12, 1867	62, 098
Button-attachment for apparel	I. Lewine	New York, N. Y	June 19, 1866	55, 798
Button-backs, Machine for forming	J. C. Cooke	Waterbury, Conn	July 27, 1852	9, 146
Button blanks, Machine for grinding pearl	J. D. Hall	Philadelphia, Pa	Jan. 25, 1870	99, 183
Button, Clasp	A. Flatley	Brooklyn, N. Y	Mar. 11, 1873	136, 648
Button, Covered	P. Kirkham	Birmingham, England	Aug. 14, 1849	6, 651
Button, Covered	N. C. Newell	Springfield, Mass	Aug. 28, 1866	57, 555
Button, Cuff	F. McCarthy	Chicago, Ill	June 14, 1873	140, 211
Button, Cuff and collar	H. W. Little	Muncie, Ind	Jan. 23, 1872	122, 899
Button, Dead-eyed wood	D. G. Fowler	New Branford, Conn	May 8, 1833	....
Button, Detachable metal	T. Kirk	Waterbury, Conn	Nov. 8, 1864	44, 958
Button-dies, Machine for grinding steel	W. Robinson	Attleborough, Mass	Mar. 3, 1829	....
Button-fastener	J. C. Gaston	Cincinnati, Ohio	May 24, 1870	103, 443
Button-fastener	R. B. Griffin, jr	Baltimore, Md	Nov. 26, 1867	71, 382
Button-fastener	H. W. Hewett	New York, N. Y	Dec. 10, 1840	1, 889
Button-fastener	J. Lafvendahl	East Boston, Mass	Apr. 16, 1861	32, 105
Button-fastener	G. A. Meacham	New York, N. Y	Apr. 8, 1862	34, 895
Button-fastener	A. M. Richmond	New York, N. Y	Apr. 25, 1871	114, 200
Button-fastener	E. Ripley	Troy, N. Y	July 21, 1868	80, 224
Button-fastener	R. Weaver	Washington, D. C	June 16, 1868	78, 903
Button-fastening	J. F. Blood	Providence, R. I	June 1, 1869	90, 631
Button-fastening	E. Brady	Philadelphia, Pa	Nov. 9, 1869	96, 544
Button-fastening	A. Brookmann	Chicago, Ill	May 6, 1873	138, 608
Button-fastening	D. Cannata	Jersey City, N. J	June 17, 1873	140, 008
Button-fastening	G. J. Capewell	West Cheshire, Conn	Feb. 12, 1867	62, 001
Button-fastening	G. D. Clark	Plainville, Conn	Aug. 4, 1868	80, 710
Button-fastening	F. Dahis	Brooklyn, N. Y	Nov. 14, 1865	50, 988
Button-fastening	I. F. Eaton	Brooklyn, N. Y	Oct. 21, 1873	143, 892
Button-fastening	B. Geiger and H. Wocher	Philadelphia, Pa	Nov. 9, 1869	96, 689
Button-fastening	L. Goodwin	New York, N. Y	June 29, 1858	20, 707
Button-fastening	W. Holloway	Buffalo, N. Y	July 8, 1873	140, 627
Button-fastening	H. Humphrey	Adrian, Mich	Oct. 29, 1867	70, 218
Button-fastening	J. Johnson	New York, N. Y	May 8, 1866	54, 556
Button-fastening	J. M. Johnson	New York, N. Y	Dec. 4, 1866	60, 194
Button-fastening	W. Kuhlenschmidt	New York, N. Y	Apr. 23, 1861	32, 136
Button-fastening	F. M. La Boiteaux	Cottage Hill, Ohio	Nov. 8, 1870	109, 024
Button-fastening	E. F. Lee	New York, N. Y	Nov. 8, 1870	109, 134
Button-fastening	H. S. Magrane	Hoboken, N. J	Jan. 28, 1868	73, 735
Button-fastening	M. Ormsbee	Brooklyn, N. Y	June 10, 1873	139, 808
Button-fastening	C. H. Reid	Danbury, Conn	Aug. 19, 1873	142, 043
Button-fastening	A. Rix	San Francisco, Cal	Sept. 22, 1868	82, 440
Button fastening	M. Rosenthal	Philadelphia, Pa	Mar. 17, 1868	75, 650
Button-fastening	J. B. Rumsey	Tiffin, Ohio	Apr. 17, 1866	54, 022
Button-fastening	W. B. Smith	New York, N. Y	Mar. 4, 1873	136, 556
Button-fastening	E. J. F. Stolpe	Washington, D. C	May 6, 1873	138, 708
Button-fastening	J. R. Underhill	Brooklyn, N. Y	June 11, 1867	65, 708
Button-fastening	E. S. Wheeler	Westport, Conn	Aug. 12, 1873	141, 743
Button-fastening	M. Wise	New York, N. Y	Apr. 19, 1870	102, 190
Button for fastening cupboard and other doors, Plate turn.	P., E. W., and J. A. Blake	New Haven, Conn	Mar. 21, 1843	3, 017
Button-forming machine	S. G. Pitts	Leominster, Mass	Sept. 15, 1868	82, 243
Button, Garment	A. C. Wilhelm	Philadelphia, Pa	Feb. 11, 1873	135, 739
Button, Glass	A. W. Demuth	New York, N. Y	May 31, 1864	42, 931
Button, Glass	A. M. Smith	Brooklyn, N. Y	Jan. 28, 1873	135, 375
Button, Glass	A. W. Welton	Cheshire, Conn	Oct. 12, 1852	9, 337
Button grinding and polishing machine	G. J. Capewell	West Cheshire, Conn	Aug. 28, 1866	57, 471
Button-holder	M. J. Cooper	New York, N. Y	Dec. 16, 1873	145, 536
Button-hole	E. F. Dieterichs	Philadelphia, Pa	July 10, 1866	56, 190
Button-hole	H. B. Fairman	New York, N. Y	June 27, 1865	48, 484
Button-hole	C. D. Smith	Washington, D. C	Aug. 14, 1866	57, 202
Button-hole and buckle	L. A. Kettle	Philadelphia, Pa	Aug. 24, 1869	94, 002
Button-hole clamp and guide	L. Reding	Norwalk, Ohio	Mar. 28, 1871	113, 093
Button-hole cutter	P. Bauer	Newark, N. J	July 16, 1872	129, 309
Button-hole cutter	C. E. Bean	Oswego, N. Y	June 11, 1872	127, 835
Button-hole cutter	T. W. Brown	Boston, Mass	May 23, 1854	10, 972
Button-hole cutter	T. C. Bush	New Haven, Conn	Sept. 13, 1870	107, 332
Button-hole cutter	D. G. Chase	Boston, Mass	Dec. 28, 1869	98, 349
Button-hole cutter	W. Chicken	Boston, Mass	July 7, 1857	17, 725
Button-hole cutter	J. S. Crane	Lake Village, N. H	Feb. 11, 1868	74, 315
Button-hole cutter	D. H. Cunningham	Waltham, Mass	Sept. 6, 1870	107, 009
Button-hole cutter	C. N. Cutter	Worcester, Mass	Jan. 1, 1867	60, 700
Button hole cutter	A. Day	Detroit, Mich	Feb. 18, 1873	135, 893
Button hole cutter	T. B. Doolittle	Bridgeport, Conn	Sept. 3, 1872	131, 085
Button-hole cutter	W. W. Egnew	Detroit, Mich	Jan. 30, 1872	123, 250
Button hole cutter	J. V. D. Eldredge	Detroit, Mich	Dec. 31, 1872	134, 366
Button-hole cutter	I. J. Fearing	South Weymouth, Mass	May 14, 1861	32, 281
Button-hole cutter	W. Fitzgerald	Boston, Mass	Apr. 30, 1867	64, 300
Button-hole cutter	H. Hempel	New York, N. Y	June 11, 1867	65, 671
Button-hole cutter	J. A. and H. A. House	Bridgeport, Conn	Apr. 3, 1866	53, 619
Button-hole cutter	A. Humann	New York, N. Y	Feb. 25, 1868	74, 827
Button-hole cutter	C. M. Johnson	Hartford, Conn	Dec. 10, 1872	133, 708
Button-hole cutter	F. C. Leypoldt	Philadelphia, Pa	Dec. 11, 1860	30, 925
Button-hole cutter	F. C. Leypoldt	Philadelphia, Pa	July 25, 1865	48, 962
Button-hole cutter	W. Lieber	New York, N. Y	Aug. 21, 1866	57, 342
Button-hole cutter	A. J. Lytle	West Union, Ohio	Oct. 20, 1868	83, 293
Button-hole cutter	W. C. McGill	Cincinnati, Ohio	June 3, 1873	139, 472
Button-hole cutter	W. A. Morse	Philadelphia, Pa	July 18, 1871	117, 100
Button-hole cutter	H. H. Pinkham	New Market, N. H	July 9, 1872	128, 802
Button-hole cutter	W. S. Porter	Boston, Mass	Dec. 15, 1868	84, 902
Button hole cutter	J. C. Powell	Philadelphia, Pa	May 9, 1871	114, 598
Button-hole cutter	F. G. Sanborn	Boston, Mass	Jan. 24, 1865	46, 028
Button-hole cutter	G. H. Seymour and W. B. Barnard.	Waterbury, Conn	Aug. 28, 1866	57, 584
Button-hole cutter	M. M. Shellaberger	Rudolph County, Ind	Feb. 23, 1864	41, 725
Button-hole cutter	E. Stern and J. S. Newell	Dorchester and Newton, Mass.	Dec. 9, 1862	37, 115
Button-hole cutter	C. F. Tebbets and G. Nutting	Fitchburgh, Mass	May 27, 1873	139, 437

Index of patents issued from the United States Patent Office from 1790 *to* 1873, *inclusive*—Continued.

Invention.	Inventor.	Residence.	Date.	No.
Button-hole cutter	C. Van Hoosen	New York, N. Y	June 17, 1873	139, 983
Button-hole cutter	F. H. Walker	Boston, Mass	June 30, 1868	79, 418
Button-hole cutter	F. H. Walker	Boston, Mass	Dec. 14, 1869	97, 996
Button-hole cutter and punch	A. L. Whitney	Fitchburgh, Mass	Apr. 8, 1873	137, 745
Button-hole cutter, eyelet-puncher, and scissors-sharpener, Combined.	W. C. McGill	Cincinnati, Ohio	June 11, 1872	127, 783
Button-hole-cutter gage	G. Stackpole	Elizabeth, N. J	Apr. 16, 1872	125, 702
Button-hole-cutting machine	G. Rehfuss	Philadelphia, Pa	Aug. 2, 1864	43, 707
Button-hole guide-plate	A. W. Webster	Ansonia, Conn	June 27, 1871	116, 378
Button-hole clasp, Metallic	J. R. Little	Jamaica Plains, N. Y	Sept. 21, 1869	94, 965
Button-hole stitch	D. W. G. Humphrey	Chelsea, Mass	Oct. 7, 1862	36, 616
Button-hole stitch	W. Weitling	New York, N. Y	Feb. 18, 1862	34, 454
Button-hole-stitching machine	D. W. G. Humphrey	Chelsea, Mass	June 13, 1871	115, 857
Button-hole-stitching machine	D. W. G. Humphrey	Chelsea, Mass	Feb. 6, 1872	123, 348
Button-hole-stitching machine	R. H. Peabody	Chelsea, Mass	June 9, 1868	78, 821
Button-hole twist, Preparing	R. Morrison	Yonkers, N. Y	Mar. 8, 1870	100, 548
Button-holes, Apparatus for making	F. Lindner	Dayton, Ohio	Oct. 9, 1866	58, 654
Button-holes, Apparatus for piercing cloth for	D. W. Whitney	New York, N. Y	Sept. 30, 1862	36, 594
Button-holes, Cutting	C. Currier	Providence, R. I	June 22, 1858	20, 632
Button-holes, Edge-finish for	D. W. G. Humphrey	Chelsea, Mass	Apr. 9, 1872	125, 393
Button-holes, Guide for working	O. Avery	Bethany, Pa	Oct. 14, 1856	15, 872
Button-holes in fabrics, Mode of weaving	L. J. Knowles	Warren, Mass	Mar. 7, 1865	46, 679
Button-holes, Machine for cutting and re-enforcing	J. T. Bruen and G. M. Jacobs.	New York, N. Y	Nov. 27, 1866	59, 957
Button-holes, Mode of making	H. Loewenberg	Boston, Mass	May 6, 1862	35, 163
Button-holes, Mode of securing	J. Walters	New York, N. Y	Dec. 3, 1872	133, 554
Button-hook and handkerchief-holder combined	G. D. Stevens	New York, N. Y	Oct. 4, 1870	108, 063
Button-hook, Lacing	D. Heaton	Providence, R. I	Nov. 26, 1872	133, 312
Button-hooks, Device for setting	J. S. Palmer	Providence, R. I	May 25, 1869	90, 382
Button-hooks, Instrument for setting	J. S. Palmer	Providence, R. I	Sept. 28, 1869	95, 257
Button-hooks, Machine for making	J. S. Palmer	Providence, R. I	June 1, 1869	90, 681
Button-hooks, Machine for making	L. Towne	Providence, R. I	Feb. 2, 1869	86, 473
Button-hooks, Machine for setting	P. Esser and F. A. Steere	North Providence, R. I	May 19, 1868	78, 077
Button, Imitation	S. G. Jones	North Bridgewater, Mass	Feb. 27, 1872	124, 139
Button, Imitation	W. H. Shurtleff	Providence, R. I	Jan. 30, 1872	123, 209
Button-key	J. Lawrence	New Haven, Conn	Oct. 18, 1864	44, 771
Button key	H. St. John	New Haven, Conn	Nov. 24, 1863	40, 714
Button, Lacing	D. Heaton	Providence, R. I	July 16, 1872	129, 474
Button, Lacing	D. Heaton	Providence, R. I	Nov. 19, 1872	133, 223
Button, Lacing	D. Heaton	Providence, R. I	Dec. 10, 1872	133, 857
Button-lacing hook	W. H. Shurtleff	Providence, R. I	June 11, 1867	65, 615
Button-machine	C. Volkert	New York, N. Y	Sept. 20, 1870	107, 570
Button-machinery	L. E. Hicks	Middletown, Conn	Apr. 24, 1847	5, 079
Button-making die	A. C. Sweetland	North Attleborough, Mass.	Sept. 26, 1865	50, 185
Button-making machine	J. F. Bapterosses	Paris, France	Aug. 12, 1873	141, 749
Button-making machine	H. Bock	New York, N. Y	Feb. 14, 1865	46, 330
Button-making machine	W. Kraemer	Cincinnati, Ohio	Oct. 30, 1866	59, 234
Button-making machine	L. D. Phillips	New York, N. Y	Nov. 27, 1866	60, 053
Button-manufacture	L. Moses	New York, N. Y	Feb. 25, 1868	74, 764
Button-manufacture	T. Prosser	Paterson, N. J	July 29, 1841	2, 199
Button-manufacture, Machine for forming collets, washers, &c., for.	M. Ferre	Williamsburgh, Mass	July 28, 1842	2, 740
Button mold for casting wire-eyed buttons, Old single-jointed pewter.	J. B. Collins	Meriden, Conn	Apr. 12, 1815	....
Button-molds, Manufacture of	J. Hayden and R. Hyde	Williamsburgh and Chesterfield, Mass.	Aug. 7, 1849	6, 635
Button-molds, Manufacturing and polishing wooden	J. Norton	Southington, Conn	June 13, 1816	....
Button-molds of wood, Manufacturing	A. Mathews	Southington, Conn	Apr. 26, 1815	....
Button-molds, Tool for making	J. T. Hawkins	Salisbury, Vt	Sept. 23, 1873	143, 073
Button-molding die	W. M. Welling	New York, N. Y	Oct. 25, 1870	108, 660
Button needle and fastener	J. A. Ostburg	Boston, Mass	June 20, 1871	116, 087
Button or fastener, Sleeve	S. J. Shaw	Marlborough, Mass	Dec. 27, 1864	45, 646
Button or garment-fastener	R. Bocklen and W. Stoehlen	Brooklyn, N. Y	Aug. 13, 1861	33, 025
Button or lacing hooks, Machine for setting	H. C. Bradford	Providence, R. I	June 14, 1870	104, 257
Button or lacing hooks, Machine for setting	H. C. Bradford	Providence, R. I	Feb. 27, 1872	124, 029
Button or stud	J. B. Carter	Hartsville, Ind	Aug. 31, 1869	94, 183
Button or stud	C. A. Newton	Providence, R. I	Aug. 8, 1871	117, 916
Button or stud	D. R. Rae and T. F. Lewis	Providence, R. I	Feb. 27, 1872	124, 010
Button or stud, Collar	J. I. Waddell	Annapolis, Md	Apr. 15, 1873	137, 807
Button or stud, Shirt	G. R. Burdon	Providence, R. I	July 16, 1872	128, 946
Button or stud, Shirt	L. W. Fifield	Worcester, Mass	Jan. 17, 1871	111, 049
Button or stud, Shirt	T. J. Holmes	Malden, Mass	Dec. 30, 1873	145, 948
Button-ornamenting machine	J. Tunnicliff and P. Cahill	Northampton, Mass	Nov. 26, 1867	71, 429
Button, Picture	R. E. Hitchcock	Waterbury, Conn	Aug. 13, 1861	33, 038
Button-planing machine	J. G. Vallentine	Naugatuck, Conn	Mar. 7, 1865	46, 763
Button-rings, Machine for making	S. B. Lane	Waterbury, Conn	Sept. 3, 1867	68, 516
Button-riveting machine	J. J. Mervesp	New York, N. Y	Jan. 4, 1870	98, 512
Button-shank gage	J. F. Russell	Washington, D. C	Apr. 26, 1870	102, 436
Button shanks, Method of forming sleeve	W. H. Blake	Waterbury, Conn	Nov. 23, 1869	97, 156
Button, Silk-covered	H. Heinemann	New York, N. Y	July 8, 1851	8, 205
Button, Sleeve	S. Bogart	New York, N. Y	Jan. 12, 1864	41, 191
Button, Sleeve	J. Caldwell and H. B. Winslow	Providence, R. I	July 30, 1872	130, 015
Button, Sleeve	J. P. Derby	Boston, Mass	Mar. 31, 1857	16, 909
Button, Sleeve	J. C. Harrington and D. S. Cooke.	Providence, R. I	Nov. 5, 1872	132, 761
Button, Sleeve	W. H. Wilson	Providence, R. I	Feb. 24, 1863	37, 784
Button, Spring-catch	T. K. Reed and H. F. Packard	East Bridgewater and North Bridgewater, Mass.	Aug. 23, 1864	43, 928
Button, stud, &c	D. Rait	New York, N. Y	Apr. 6, 1852	8, 860
Button, stud, &c	T. S. Sedgwick	Onargo, Ill	Aug. 18, 1868	81, 300
Button, Suspender	E. Smith	Naugatuck, Conn	Apr. 16, 1861	32, 087
Button, Swivel	E. H. Porter	New Britain, Conn	Mar. 20, 1866	53, 333
Button, Window	E. K. Breckenridge	West Meriden, Conn	Nov. 30, 1869	97, 348
Buttons, American wire-eyed	F. Hayden	Waterbury, Conn	Oct. 1, 1830	....
Buttons, Apparatus for centering shanks or eyes on.	W. H. Blake	Waterbury, Conn	Feb. 1, 1870	99, 394
Buttons, Attaching the shanks to mineral and composition.	C. L. Potter	Providence, R. I	Dec. 13, 1870	110, 070
Buttons, &c., Attachment of	N. Ames	Saugus Centre, Mass	Mar. 22, 1864	41, 969

Index of patents issued from the United States Patent Office from 1790 *to* 1873, *inclusive*—Continued.

Invention.	Inventor.	Residence.	Date.	No.
Buttons cast in mold, Construction of an eye for metal.	I. Ives	Bristol, Conn	Aug. 7, 1815	....
Buttons, Composition for	E. S. Wheeler	Westport, Conn	Nov. 14, 1865	50, 974
Buttons, Composition for making wire-eyed	S. H. Woodruff and A. Matthews.	Connecticut	Mar. 1, 1816	....
Buttons, Detachable covering for	F. H. Gould	Newark, N. J	Apr. 14, 1868	76, 746
Buttons, Die for forming sleeve	H. Ansley	Washington, D. C	Apr. 5, 1870	101, 565
Buttons, Fastener for sleeve	H. Cogswell	Providence, R. I	May 11, 1858	20, 194
Buttons, Finishing wired-neck metal	H. Mathews	Southington, Conn	Sept. 12, 1815	....
Buttons from straw boards, Manufacture of	E. M. Pomeroy	Wallingford, Conn	Aug. 21, 1849	6, 654
Buttons, handles for knives, and for other purposes, Material for the manufacture of.	L. E. Chittenden	Washington, D. C	Jan. 24, 1865	45, 977
Buttons, Holding shanks of molds for glass	G. Matthewman	Williamsburgh, N. Y	Oct. 10, 1865	50, 374
Buttons in the mold, Setting the eyes of metal	I. Ives	Bristol, Conn	Aug. 7, 1815	....
Buttons, Machine for attaching	W. S. Platt and G. J. Capewell	Cheshire, Conn	Sept. 5, 1871	118, 743
Buttons, Machine for making covered	W. W. Wade	Medford, Mass	Apr. 27, 1869	89, 450
Buttons, Machine for making wire-necked metal	H. Mathews	Southington, Conn	Sept. 12, 1815	....
Buttons, Machine for molding glass	C. Vigneron	Providence, R. I	Apr. 19, 1870	102, 070
Buttons, Machine for pressing glass	T. Guilford	Cheshire, Conn	Apr. 10, 1866	53, 816
Buttons, Making paper	E. M. Pomeroy	Wallingford, Conn	Sept. 23, 1843	3, 281
Buttons, Manufacture of	P. Kirkham	Waterbury, Conn	Dec. 18, 1849	6, 953
Buttons, Manufacture of	C. M. Platt	Waterbury, Conn	May 6, 1873	138, 525
Buttons, Manufacture of wooden	L. L. and A. L. Platt	Newtown, Conn	June 27, 1854	11, 176
Buttons, Manufacturing	C. Goodyear	Philadelphia, Pa	Jan. 12, 1831	....
Buttons, Manufacturing coat and waistcoat	G. W. Robinson	....	Mar. 24, 1804	....
Buttons, Manufacturing cord	N. Perkins	Wawarsing, N. Y	Aug. 17, 1852	9, 210
Buttons, Manufacturing dead-eyed wood	D. Fowler	Branford, Conn	June 13, 1831	....
Buttons, Manufacturing metallic	J. O. M. Ingersoll	Ithaca, N. Y	Aug. 18, 1857	18, 014
Buttons, Manufacturing metallic flexible-shank	J. Hayden, jr	Williamsburgh, Mass	Feb. 17, 1831	....
Buttons, Means for fastening	I. F. Eaton	Brooklyn, N. Y	Oct. 21, 1873	143, 891
Buttons, Mode of fastening	W. A. and F. V. Johnson and H. S. Worth.	Oxford, Pa	Oct. 7, 1873	143, 512
Buttons, Mode of finishing glass	S. Richards	Attleborough, Mass	Aug. 19, 1822	....
Buttons, Mold for casting metallic	G. W. Robinson	New Haven, Conn	May 14, 1812	....
Buttons, Mold for fancy	F. Maass	Newark, N. J	Oct. 21, 1873	143, 916
Buttons on cloth, Machine for riveting	W. J. Gordon and E. D. Gilbert	Philadelphia, Pa	Mar. 7, 1865	46, 660
Buttons on heads, &c., of whips, Forming worked	R. S. Brown	Philadelphia, Pa	Feb. 21, 1842	2, 462
Buttons, Ornamenting metallic	H. W. Hayden	Waterbury, Conn	July 11, 1854	11, 263
Buttons, Preparing wood for the manufacture of	R. H. Isbell	New Milford, Conn	Dec. 24, 1872	134, 286
Buttons, Process of varnishing	E. M. Pomeroy	Wallingford, Conn	Feb. 19, 1850	7, 102
Buttons, Punching-machine for manufacture of covered.	A. C. Arnold	Norwalk, Conn	Apr. 23, 1842	2, 580
Buttons, Smoothing and rounding the edges of metallic.	I. Ives	Bristol, Conn	Aug. 7, 1815	....
Buttons to cards, Securing	E. S. Boynton	New York, N. Y	Aug. 29, 1865	49, 674
Buttons to cloth, Method of attaching	H. S. Poole	Boston, Mass	Aug. 11, 1841	2, 219
Buttons to cloth, Method of making and attaching metallic.	F. Hayden	Waterbury, Conn	July 10, 1840	1, 682
Buttons to fabrics, Apparatus for securing	G. Rehfuss	Philadelphia, Pa	Feb. 27, 1866	52, 885
Buttons to fabrics, Apparatus for securing	G. Rehfuss	Philadelphia, Pa	Feb. 27, 1866	52, 884
Buttons to fabrics, Device for securing	D. M. Somers	Brooklyn, N. Y	Oct. 12, 1869	95, 847
Buttons to fabrics, Fastening	W. H. Reed	Philadelphia, Pa	Nov. 15, 1864	45, 077
Buttons to fabrics, Instrument for attaching	H. Mauch	Providence, R. I	Oct. 20, 1868	83, 193
Buttons to fabrics, Instrument for attaching	D. M. Somers and W. S. Atwood	Brooklyn, N. Y	Nov. 3, 1868	83, 669
Buttons to fabrics, Machine for attaching	G. J. Capewell	West Cheshire, Conn	Apr. 14, 1868	76, 600
Buttons to fabrics, Machine for riveting	W. J. Gordon	Philadelphia, Pa	Jan. 22, 1867	61, 334
Buttons to fabrics, Machine for riveting	J. J. Mervesp	Brooklyn, N. Y	Oct. 29, 1872	132, 537
Buttons, &c., to fabrics, Mode of attaching	H. B. Walbridge	Brooklyn, N. Y	Nov. 19, 1872	133, 273
Buttons to fabrics, Securing	G. J. Capewell	West Cheshire, Conn	June 8, 1869	91, 083
Buttons to garments, Device for attaching	G. J. Capewell	Cheshire, Conn	July 16, 1872	128, 950
Buttons to garments, Securing	J. W. Roberts	New Monmouth, N. J	July 24, 1866	56, 612
Buttons to garments, Securing	C. F. Spencer	Rochester, N. Y	Mar. 12, 1867	62, 784
Buttons, Tool for setting hook	H. C. Bradford	Providence, R. I	Nov. 7, 1871	120, 703
Buttons, &c., Treating wood for the manufacture of sleeve.	O. Knipler	Bridgeport, Conn	May 14, 1872	126, 816
Buttons, Turning	D. French	Bridgeport, Pa	Apr. 23, 1816	....
Buttons while polishing, Hold-fast for	I. Ives	New Haven, Conn	June 18, 1814	....
C.				
Cab	J. Pol	New York, N. Y	Jan. 29, 1867	61, 675
Cab and Cradle	G. H. Henkel	Hartford City, Ind	Aug. 10, 1869	93, 437
Cab, Brakeman's	H. C. Glasgow	Chicago, Ill	Apr. 1, 1862	34, 829
Cabbage-cutter	H. Aeuer	Muscatine, Iowa	Jan. 22, 1867	61, 304
Cabbage-cutter	H. Carver	Edinburgh, Va	Aug. 26, 1851	8, 310
Cabbage-cutter	A. Fischer	Dayton, Ohio	Apr. 27, 1858	20, 054
Cabbage-cutter	J. D. Schaub	Birmingham, Pa	Apr. 5, 1870	101, 520
Cabbage-cutter	F. S. Vogel and J. R. Albright	Lancaster, Pa	Mar. 30, 1869	88, 349
Cabbage-cutter	J. C. Wilkins	Fox Chase, Pa	Jan. 3, 1860	26, 725
Cabbage-cutting machine	F. Berkeymeyer and J. Dengler	Greenwich, Pa	Nov. 14, 1826	....
Cabbage-cutting machine	G. G. Elias	Lancaster, Pa	Nov. 22, 1859	26, 173
Cabin-chair	W. Thomas	Hingham, Mass	Apr. 10, 1855	12, 703
Cabin, Floating safety	M. I. Butler	Nashville, Tenn	Oct. 25, 1859	25, 881
Cabin for steam and other vessels, Floating	W. R. Jackson	Baltimore, Md	June 5, 1855	13, 006
Cabin-table	H. J. Nichols	Searsport, Me	Aug. 23, 1870	106, 608
Cabinet	R. Bacon	Boston, Mass	Feb. 15, 1870	99, 746
Cabinet and bed	R. F. Clayton	Boston, Mass	Jan. 30, 1872	123, 085
Cabinet, Blacking	L. P. Keach	Baltimore, Md	July 20, 1869	92, 838
Cabinet-chair	S. Pearson	Boston, Mass	Oct. 18, 1859	25, 849
Cabinet-chair and secretary combined	C. S. Trevitt	Washington, D. C	Apr. 8, 1873	137, 738
Cabinet, College	W. W. Lovering	San Francisco, Cal	Dec. 18, 1866	60, 529
Cabinet for ladies	A. J. Forbes	San Francisco, Cal	Nov. 16, 1869	96, 788
Cabinet-hook	J. B. Sargent	New Haven, Conn	June 15, 1869	91, 369
Cabinet-maker's tool	R. W. Tanner	Albany, N. Y	Dec. 14, 1869	97, 833
Cabinet-purposes, Combination of wood and paper for.	A. C. Spencer	Bridgeport, Conn	June 30, 1868	79, 511
Cabinet-ventilator	S. Harndon	Reading, Mass	Apr. 20, 1869	89, 219
Cabinet-work, Machine for polishing	J. B. Morris	Ansonia, Conn	July 24, 1860	29, 293

Index of patents issued from the United States Patent Office from 1790 *to* 1873, *inclusive*—Continued.

Invention.	Inventor.	Residence.	Date.	No.
Cable-chain	I. Jennings	New York, N. Y	Oct. 29, 1821	....
Cable, Electric	J. L. Arman	Bordeaux, France	Jan. 21, 1868	73, 487
Cable for railway-guide, Propelling	C. T. Harvey	Tarrytown, N. Y	July 2, 1867	66, 330
Cable hook, Chain	E. Applegate	Wilmington, Del	Apr. 29, 1856	14, 758
Cable-link-bending machine	R. M. Green	Baltimore, Md	Mar. 12, 1867	62, 839
Cable meter, Drill	L. C. Bristol	Victor, N. Y	Apr. 3, 1866	53, 564
Cable-stopper	W. H. Bridge	Boston, Mass	Feb. 23, 1858	19, 403
Cable-stopper	E. R. Cheney and J. J. Emery	Boston, Mass., and Owl's Head, Me.	June 21, 1870	104, 425
Cable-stopper	E. R. Cheney and J. J. Emery	Boston, Mass., and Owl's Head, Me.	Aug. 2, 1870	166, 031
Cable-stopper	P. H. Jackson	New York, N. Y	Aug. 10, 1858	21, 135
Cable-stopper	J. M. Kilner	Chester, England	June 24, 1873	140, 202
Cable-stopper	P. Murray	Wilwaukee, Wis	June 5, 1866	55, 343
Cable-stopper	G. S. Perkins	Essex, Mass	Jan. 12, 1864	41, 235
Cable-stopper	J. Reed	Marshfield, Mass	Jan. 30, 1855	12, 325
Cable-stopper	J. Robinson	Barnegat, N. J	Dec. 9, 1862	37, 109
Cable-stopper	J. Stitt	San Francisco, Cal	July 19, 1870	105, 510
Cable stopper, Chain	E. R. Cheney	Boston, Mass	Jan. 30, 1872	123, 152
Cable stopper, Chain	J. E. Crane	Lowell, Mass	Apr. 5, 1853	9, 645
Cable stopper, Chain	J. E. Crane	Lowell, Mass	Jan. 19, 1858	19, 131
Cable stopper, Chain	M. P. Mix	New York, N. Y	Nov. 3, 1838	998
Cable stopper, Chain	O. Nichols	Lowell, Mass	Apr. 4, 1854	10, 724
Cable stopper, Chain	O. Nichols	Lowell, Mass	Apr. 4, 1854	10, 725
Cable stopper, Chain	C. Perley	New York, N. Y	June 13, 1854	11, 080
Cable stopper, Chain	C. Perley	New York, N. Y	Nov. 29, 1859	26, 292
Cable stopper, Chain	J. Tucker	Washington, D. C	Jan. 3, 1860	26, 722
Cable, Submarine	P. S. Devlan	Jersey City, N. J	Sept. 15, 1863	39, 896
Cable surge-reliever	J. J. Emery	Owl's Head, Me	Sept. 21, 1869	94, 950
Cables and spin ropes of any size, Machine to lay	W. Schultz	Baltimore, Md	June 24, 1809	....
Cables, Apparatus for improving the quality of	N. Cutting	Washington, D. C	Aug. 14, 1806	....
Cables, Apparatus for working and stoppering chain.	W. H. Harfield	London, England	Aug. 5, 1862	36, 085
Cables, Apparatus for working and stoppering chain.	W. H. Harfield	London, England	Aug. 5, 1862	36, 086
Cables, Arrangement of means for working and stoppering chain.	T. Brown	London, England	July 25, 1854	11, 404
Cables, Elastic chain or surge-spring for ships'	A. H. Wright	Philadelphia, Pa	Mar. 13, 1860	27, 505
Cables from sudden strain, Apparatus for relieving ships'.	L. Bissell	Brooklyn, N. Y	Feb. 28, 1845	3, 932
Cables, Link-shackle of chain	W. J. Hotchkiss	Derby, Conn	Jan. 1, 1861	31, 021
Cables, Insulating submarine	G. B. Simpson	Washington, D. C	May 21, 1867	65, 019
Cables, Machine for adjusting chain	C. Hall	New York, N. Y	Aug. 14, 1866	57, 127
Cables, Machine for laying bridge	J. Gray	Cincinnati, Ohio	Dec. 26, 1871	122, 247
Cables, &c., Machine for proving	J. Judge	Washington, D. C	Nov. 29, 1828	....
Cables, Machine for wrapping wire	J. Gray	Cincinnati, Ohio	Dec. 26, 1871	122, 246
Cables, Making chain	E. Bartholomew	Boston, Mass	May 17, 1826	....
Cables, Pressure-stopper for chain	J. Emerson	Worcester, Mass	Sept. 25, 1855	131, 593
Cables, Surge-reliever for	J. Bingham	Philadelphia, Pa	July 24, 1860	29, 338
Caboose	J. Youle	....	May 25, 1795	....
Caboose	G. Youle	New York, N. Y	Mar. 21, 1806	....
Caboose	G. Youle	New York, N. Y	July 27, 1809	....
Caboose, Construction of iron	W. Ashbridge	....	June 28, 1803	....
Caboose, Ship's	J. Wilson	New York, N. Y	Aug. 17, 1843	3, 224
Cage. Eccentric	T. E. Rollins	Corning, N. Y	Dec. 27, 1864	45, 639
Cage, Wire	M. Grebner	New York, N. Y	June 10, 1873	139, 784
Caisson	A. G. Wolfgram	Apex, N. C	Nov. 25, 1873	145, 039
Caisson, Cast-iron	J. P. Duffey	Philadelphia, Pa	July 13, 1852	9, 113
Caisson for sinking pier	J. B. Eads	Saint Louis, Mo	Aug. 15, 1871	118, 118
Caissons, Dumb waiter for	H. Flad	Saint Louis, Mo	Nov. 22, 1870	109, 505
Caissons for founding piers of bridges and for laying pipes under water, Constructing	G. Daniels	Philadelphia, Pa	Feb. 28, 1834	....
Cake and bread, Box for preserving	A. R. Ledoux	Cornwall Landing, N. Y	Feb. 4, 1873	135, 433
Cake and fruit basket	C. H. Latham	Lowell, Mass	Aug. 15, 1871	118, 027
Cake baker, Griddle	J. Mull	Troy, N. Y	Apr. 3, 1866	53, 744
Cake-closet	G. A. Higgins	New York, N. Y	Apr. 5, 1870	101, 618
Cake-cutter	G. R. Peckham	Worcester, Mass	Nov. 17, 1857	18, 647
Cake-cutter	G. O. Sanderson	Boston, Mass	May 19, 1868	78, 137
Cake-cutter	J. Webster	Charlestown, Mass	May 20, 1873	139, 217
Cake-cutter and rolling-pin	I. N. Pyle	Decatur, Ind	Oct. 31, 1865	50, 732
Cake-cutting machine	D. J. Little	Albany, N. Y	Oct. 8, 1872	132, 034
Cake-machine	J. Repetti	Philadelphia, Pa	May 25, 1869	90, 577
Cake-mixer	T. Holmes	Williamsburgh, N. Y	Aug. 22, 1871	118, 243
Cake-mixer	J. Lafetra	New York, N. Y	Oct. 13, 1868	83, 069
Cake-pan	W. C. Butler	Louisville, Ky	Aug. 27, 1872	130, 843
Cake-pan	J. B. Firth	Brooklyn, N. Y	July 8, 1873	140, 619
Cake-pan	J. H. Smith	Brooklyn, N. Y	Aug. 2, 1870	105, 991
Cake-pan	J. H. Smith	Brooklyn, N. Y	Aug. 2, 1870	105, 992
Cake-stirrer	S. M. Clark	Beaver Dam, Wis	Nov. 28, 1871	121, 336
Cakes, Cutting and panning	J. H. Shrote	Baltimore, Md	Oct. 11, 1859	25, 767
Calcimines	E. B. Benedict	Susquehanna Depot, Pa	July 23, 1872	129, 645
Calcium-light, Method of producing	C. L. Coombs and J. A. Basset	Washington, D. C., and Salem, Mass.	Aug. 3, 1869	93, 178
Calcium-magnesium-light, Producing	C. A. Dresser	New York, N. Y	Dec. 10, 1867	71, 860
Calculating and registering machine	T. T. Strode	Mortonville, Pa	Feb. 4, 1868	74, 170
Calculating-apparatus	A. Johnson	Springfield, Mass	Dec. 22, 1868	85, 229
Calculating-balance	B. W. Ogburn	Whittles' Mills, Va	July 14, 1868	80, 003
Calculating device, Price	A. Sinclair	West Waterville, Me	Dec. 14, 1869	97, 974
Calculating interest, Machine for	J. Hatfield	Glen's Falls, N. Y	May 6, 1844	3, 574
Calculating-machine	J. B. Alexander	Baltimore, Md	Mar. 15, 1864	41, 898
Calculating-machine	E. D. Barbour	Boston, Mass	Aug. 13, 1872	130, 404
Calculating-machine	E. D. Barbour	Boston, Mass	Nov. 19, 1872	133, 188
Calculating-machine	J. J. Bavanowski	Poland	Sept. 5, 1848	5, 746
Calculating-machine	G. W. Edelman	Philadelphia, Pa	Dec. 22, 1846	4, 902
Calculating-machine	T. Esersky	St. Petersburg, Russia	Nov. 11, 1873	144, 523
Calculating-machine	G. B. Grant	Cambridge, Mass	July 16, 1872	129, 335
Calculating-machine	G. B. Grant	Cambridge, Mass	Apr. 29, 1873	138, 245
Calculating-machine	W. M. Haines	Rochester, N. Y	May 1, 1849	6, 403

Index of patents issued from the United States Patent Office from 1790 to 1873, inclusive—Continued.

Invention.	Inventor.	Residence.	Date.	No.
Calculating-machine	L. Keiler	Catawissa, Pa	Jan. 21, 1868	73, 449
Calculating-machine	J. A. Loomis and A. Johnson	Springfield, Mass	Jan. 28, 1868	73, 732
Calculating-machine	A. Mendenhall	Cerro Gordo, Ind	Aug. 13, 1867	67, 786
Calculating-machine	J. W. Nystrom	Philadelphia, Pa	Mar. 4, 1851	7, 961
Calculating-machine	D. D. Parmelee	New Paltz, N. Y	Feb. 5, 1850	7, 074
Calculating-machine	A. C. Pierson	Rahway, N. J	Mar. 12, 1867	62, 882
Calculating-machine	A. C. Pierson	Rahway, N. J	Feb. 4, 1868	73, 995
Calculating-machine	J. H. R. Reffelt	Hoboken, N. J	Sept. 14, 1869	94, 772
Calculating-machine	W. Robjohn	New York, N. Y	Aug. 6, 1872	130, 244
Calculating-machine	N. Rowland	Hilltown, Pa	Jan. 9, 1866	51, 972
Calculating-machine	R. Teasdale	Alberton, Ga	Dec. 5, 1871	121, 687
Calculating-machine	S. S. Young	Eaton, Ohio	July 24, 1849	6, 602
Calculator	A. Brody	Union, Mich	Apr. 26, 1870	102, 216
Calculator, Arithmetical	J. P. Miller	Boston, Mass	Sept. 1, 1863	39, 740
Calculator, Interest	B. C. Coldwell	Lockhaven, Pa	July 16, 1872	129, 531
Calculator, Tax	C. D. Crane	Fort Wayne, Ind	May 5, 1863	38, 374
Calculator, Tax	I. S. Hyatt	Rockford, Ill	May 12, 1868	77, 736
Calculi, Apparatus for removing	W. A. Dudley	Petersburgh, Va	Oct. 23, 1860	30, 471
Caldron	H. Newsham	Baltimore, Md	Feb. 12, 1856	14, 271
Caldron, Agricultural	E. E. Sill and A. H. Bennett	Rochester, N. Y	Nov. 29, 1870	109, 659
Caldron and furnace for agriculturists and others, Combined.	J. L. Mott	New York, N. Y	Dec. 1, 1840	1, 873
Caldron, steam-boiler, and furnace, Combined	L. E. Hopkins	New York, N. Y	Oct. 11, 1841	2, 306
Calendar	C. W. Bryan	Springfield, Mass	Feb. 26, 1867	62, 313
Calendar	G. L. Coburn	Hartford, Conn	Oct. 12, 1869	95, 655
Calendar	J. L. Dagg	Philadelphia, Pa	May 4, 1830	....
Calendar	Vve. A. Maurin and G. Toiray	Paris, France	May 17, 1870	103, 216
Calendar	W. McAdams	Newton, Mass	Sept. 26, 1871	119, 381
Calendar	J. M. Patton	Indianapolis, Ind	Jan. 26, 1864	41, 391
Calendar	J. F. Tannatt	Springfield, Mass	Mar. 1, 1870	100, 338
Calendar	A. S. Vose	Randolph, Vt	Mar. 17, 1868	75, 659
Calendar	W. P. Ware	New York, N. Y	July 17, 1866	56, 470
Calendar, Advertising	R. C. Ogden	New York, N. Y	May 7, 1872	126, 481
Calendar-catch	R. C. Ogden	New York, N. Y	June 24, 1873	140, 360
Calendar, Counting-house	J. Bryner	Peoria, Ill	Feb. 28, 1860	27, 267
Calendar for almanacs	J. H. Mead	New York, N. Y	Nov. 15, 1864	45, 064
Calendar, Hand-setting	C. H. Wight	Baltimore, Md	Mar. 29, 1870	101, 333
Calendar, Perpetual	S. L. Barinds	Saint Joseph, Mo	May 26, 1868	78, 356
Calendar, Perpetual	H. Harris	Newark, N. J	Aug. 7, 1866	56, 935
Calendar, Perpetual	H. W. Holly	Norwich, Conn	Jan. 3, 1865	45, 795
Calendar, Perpetual	C. T. Pooler	Deansville, N. Y	May 12, 1868	77, 837
Calendar, Pocket	D. E. Crosby	Brooklyn, N. Y	Feb. 16, 1864	41, 605
Calendar, Pocket	H. C. Foote	McGaheysville, Va	July 17, 1860	29, 156
Calendar, Portable	J. N. Dudley	Mitchell, Iowa	May 6, 1862	35, 153
Calendar, Writing-desk	S. J. Tucker	Philadelphia, Pa	June 22, 1869	91, 690
Calender-roll	G. G. Clark	Providence, R. I	Mar. 16, 1858	19, 623
Calender-rolls, Device for starting and stopping	W. T. Porter	Wilmington, Del	June 23, 1868	79, 080
Calender-rolls, Feed-regulator for	M. Lawler	Holyoke, Mass	Jan. 14, 1873	134, 810
Calender-rolls, Manufacturing	J. Worsley	Providence, R. I	Dec. 23, 1856	16, 319
Calendering-machine	H. E. Rogers	South Manchester, Conn	Oct. 5, 1869	95, 606
Calendering-machine	D. Scofield	Gloucester, N. J	Sept. 16, 1873	142, 872
Calf-weaner	T. A. R. Keech	Bladensburgh, Md	Dec. 26, 1871	122, 119
Calf-weaning device	J. J. Welling	Cedar Falls, Iowa	Dec. 10, 1861	33, 912
Calico, Machine for printing	J. Green	Lowell, Mass	Nov. 21, 1865	51, 039
Calico, Machine for rinsing	G. I. Prentiss	Tiverton, R. I	Apr. 4, 1846	4, 445
Calico, Roller for printing	J. Hope	Providence, R. I	Oct. 5, 1858	21, 723
Calipers	J. Atkins	Washington, D. C	Mar. 24, 1868	75, 827
Calipers	H. A. Boardman	New Haven, Conn	Feb. 5, 1867	61, 799
Calipers	C. E. Brown	Florence, Mass	June 20, 1865	48, 257
Calipers	J. H. Call	Springfield, Mass	May 28, 1861	32, 410
Calipers	J. H. Culver	San Francisco, Cal	Apr. 30, 1867	64, 203
Calipers	C. A. Fairfield	Springfield, Mass	July 21, 1863	39, 281
Calipers	T. Goodrum	Providence, R. I	Sept. 29, 1868	82, 514
Calipers	F. Gould	Huntington, N. Y	Apr. 12, 1859	23, 564
Calipers	W. P. Hopkins	Lawrence, Mass	Jan. 3, 1871	110, 657
Calipers	C. Jillson	Worcester, Mass	Aug. 16, 1864	43, 854
Calipers	B. G. Martin	Philadelphia, Pa	Dec. 12, 1865	51, 517
Calipers	G. L. McKnight	Worcester, Mass	May 28, 1867	65, 253
Calipers	W. H. Miner	Boston, Mass	Oct. 14, 1873	143, 584
Calipers	W. A. Morse	Boston, Mass	Jan. 26, 1864	41, 387
Calipers	T. C. Page and G. W. Hadley	Chicopee, Mass	Feb. 8, 1870	99, 698
Calipers	H. K. Porter	Boston, Mass	June 7, 1870	103, 926
Calipers	S. Sawyer	Fitchburgh, Mass	July 7, 1868	79, 603
Calipers	P. Seaver	Oxford, Mass	June 27, 1854	11, 180
Calipers	W. A. Sharpe	Syracuse, N. Y	Oct. 25, 1870	108, 640
Calipers	W. Siar	Franklin, Pa	Feb. 15, 1870	99, 961
Calipers	R. D. O. Smith	Washington, D. C	Dec. 20, 1864	45, 529
Calipers	P. Soper	Buffalo, N. Y	Aug. 28, 1866	57, 588
Calipers	C. D. Sutton	Kensico, N. Y	Jan. 3, 1860	26, 716
Calipers	D. C. Talbot	Worcester, Mass	Jan. 27, 1863	37, 531
Calipers	F. C. Washburn	Millville, Mass	Jan. 10, 1865	45, 894
Calipers	A. V. D. Westervelt	New Brunswick, N. J	Feb. 5, 1867	61, 902
Calipers	S. Whalen	Burnt Mills, N. Y	Dec. 26, 1865	51, 767
Calipers	A. E. Whitmore	Boston, Mass	July 5, 1870	105, 153
Calipers and dividers	M. G. Imbach	Hartford, Conn	Nov. 19, 1867	71, 178
Calipers and dividers	J. D. Moon	Chelsea, Mass	Sept. 7, 1858	21, 435
Calipers and dividers	L. Shelters	Manchester, N. H	July 30, 1867	67, 360
Calipers and dividers	E. Wright	Worcester, Mass	Sept. 24, 1867	69, 292
Calipers and dividers, Process of making	J. B. Gooding	Waltham, Mass	July 10, 1866	56, 323
Calipers and poising-tool, Jewelers' combined	F. E. Allen	Keene, N. H	Feb. 28, 1871	112, 203
Calipers and T-square	J. Bennor	Philadelphia, Pa	Dec. 10, 1867	71, 843
Calipers die, Spring	N. C. Smith	Berlin, Conn	Sept. 14, 1869	94, 920
Calipers for measuring irregular forms	E. T. Miller	Charlestown, Mass	May 27, 1856	14, 984
Calipers for taper surfaces	E. C. C. Kellogg	Hartford, Conn	July 16, 1872	129, 349
Calipers gage, Fixed	J. Richards	Cincinnati, Ohio	Oct. 15, 1867	69, 953
Calipers, rule, and wire-gage combined	F. A. Adams	Shelburne Falls, Mass	Jan. 5, 1869	85, 553
Calipers, Sliding	A. E. Whitmore	Boston, Mass	July 27, 1869	93, 026
Calipers, Sliding	A. E. Whitmore	Somerville, Mass	Apr. 5, 1870	101, 649
Calipers, Spring	W. W. Smith	Boston, Mass	Oct. 1, 1850	7, 689

Index of patents issued from the United States Patent Office from 1790 *to* 1873, *inclusive*—Continued.

Invention.	Inventor.	Residence.	Date.	No.
Calipers, Stem	W. C. Cross	Boston, Mass	July 16, 1872	129, [illegible]36
Calipers, Transverse	W. J. Van Ness	Baltimore, Md	Oct. 30, 1849	6, 841
Calk bar, Toe	R. B. Caswell	Springfield, Mass	Mar. 7, 1871	112, 321
Calk-sharpener	H. Kline	Marshalltown, Iowa	Dec. 1, 1868	84, 5[illegible]3
Calk-sharpening machine	G. W. Lane	Chichester, N. H	May 23, 1871	115, 068
Calks and blanks for the same, Manufacture of toe	T. Dooley	South Boston, Mass	June 2, 1868	78, 581
Calks, Blank or bar for toe	P. F. Burke	Worcester, Mass	Feb. 2, 1869	86, 503
Calking ships, &c., Composition for	H. Le Grand	Havre, France	Oct. 22, 1872	132, 365
Calligraph	C. Thurber	Worcester, Mass	June 23, 1857	17, 647
Calligraph	C. Thurber	Brooklyn, N. Y	Nov. 27, 1860	30, 777
Caloric-engine	W. T. Hallefas	New York, N. Y	Apr. 18, 1871	113, 764
Caloric-engine	A. A. Henderson	Portsmouth, N. H	Oct. 9, 1860	30, 315
Caloric-engine	H. Messer	Roxbury, Mass	Oct. 6, 1863	40, 178
Caloric-engine	N. A. Otto	Deutz, Germany	Dec. 2, 1873	145, 123
Caloric engine	T. Schwartz	New York, N. Y	Dec. 20, 1864	45, 526
Caloric-engine	H. D. Wallen, jr	Fort Columbus, N. Y	Oct. 13, 1868	83, 114
Caloriferes	S. Whitmarsh	Northampton, Mass	Aug. 17, 1852	9, 206
Cam, Adjustable	C. F. Annan	Boston, Mass	Dec. 27, 1870	110, 537
Cam-groove-cutting machine	J. S. George and W. Houghtaling.	Bridgeport, Conn	Apr. 1, 1873	137, 358
Cam-groove, Machine for dressing	G. M. Pratt and V. A. King	Middletown, Conn	Feb. 4, 1873	135, 584
Cam-lever	S. Whitman	Londonderry, Vt	Feb. 15, 1870	99, 991
Cam-press	T. R. Hopkins	Petersburgh, Va	Aug. 23, 1859	25, 232
Cam-press	E. Thomas	Beverly, Va	Dec. 21, 1858	22, 387
Cam, Sectional adjustable slotted	F. D. Elderfield	Saint Louis, Mo	Aug. 5, 1873	141, 548
Cam, Variable	W. H. Andrews	New Haven, Conn	Nov. 26, 1861	33, 771
Cams for pressing and raising weights, &c., Combination of.	A. S. Greenville	Cambridgeport, Mass	Dec. 30, 1835	....
Caboose	J. Bouis	Baltimore, Md	Dec. 31, 1812	....
Camera:				
See Multiplying-camera.				
Photographic camera.				
Solar-camera.				
Stereoscopic camera.				
Camera and developing-box, Combined	E. C. Ratzell	Philadelphia, Pa	Mar. 7, 1871	112, 380
Camera-box support	O. Ackerman	Carthage, N. Y	Apr. 25, 1871	114, 082
Camera-boxes, Guide-slide for	O. Loehr	New York, N. Y	Apr. 2, 1872	125, 202
Camera focusing-attachment	A. St. Clair	Cedar Rapids, Iowa	Dec. 31, 1872	134, 402
Camera-obscura	G. F. Kolb	Philadelphia, Pa	Apr. 15, 1862	34, 970
Camera-screen	F. Peabody	Louisville, Ky	Feb. 1, 1870	99, 343
Camera-stand	N. S. Bowdish	Richfield Springs, N. Y	July 29, 1873	141, 256
Camera-stand	E. M. Corbett	New York, N. Y	June 24, 1862	35, 671
Camera-stand	A. R. Cribfield	Lincoln, Ill	Apr. 4, 1871	113, 267
Camera-stand	W. W. Dames	San José, Cal	Apr. 19, 1870	101, 985
Camera-stand	R. B. Douglas	Cleveland, Ohio	Apr. 12, 1864	42, 279
Camera-stand	J. W. Harper	Cleveland, Ohio	Dec. 5, 1865	51, 311
Camera-stand	B. Holler	Brooklyn, N. Y	Mar. 18, 1873	136, 997
Camera-stand	H. J. Lewis	Brooklyn, N. Y	Mar. 29, 1859	23, 428
Camera-stand	T. H. McBride and D. Baldwin	East Birmingham, Pa	Sept. 27, 1864	44, 438
Camera-stand	C. H. Snively	Millersburgh, Pa	Nov. 7, 1871	120, 790
Camera-stand	E. P. Spahn	Newark, N. J	May 7, 1872	126, 586
Camera-stand	I. H. Stoddard	Amenia, N. Y	Aug. 17, 1869	93, 763
Camera-stand	A. E. Turnbull	Upper Sandusky, Ohio	Sept. 7, 1869	94, 672
Camera-stand	J. A. Whipple	Boston, Mass	Aug. 18, 1863	39, 602
Camp-baker, Folding	F. Lehnen	Marquette, Mich	Sept. 30, 1873	143, 288
Camp chair	P. J. Hardy	New York, N. Y	Aug. 20, 1861	33, 082
Camp-chest	A. S. Carner	Brooklyn, N. Y	Nov. 19, 1861	33, 734
Camp-chest	F. Graves	Avoca, N. Y	Oct. 4, 1864	44, 578
Camp-chest	C. W. Irwin	Saint Louis, Mo	Dec. 17, 1861	33, 946
Camp-chest	G. C. Lane	Buffalo, N. Y	Oct. 22, 1861	33, 529
Camp-chest	G. Parr	Buffalo, N. Y	June 25, 1861	32, 643
Camp chest and table combined	W. Chase	Buffalo, N. Y	Oct. 29, 1861	33, 570
Camp-kit	J. Walkey	Monroe, Wis	Dec. 20, 1864	45, 542
Camp pan and baker	C. Bush	New York, N. Y	Oct. 22, 1861	33, 514
Camp-stool	A. Ashald	Garrettsville, Ohio	Sept. 17, 1861	33, 286
Camp table or stool	J. Cram	Boston, Mass	May 12, 1863	38, 470
Camphor for preserving furs, &c., Preparing crude	W. F. Simes	Philadelphia, Pa	June 11, 1872	127, 807
Camphor, Preparing	W. F. Simes	Philadelphia, Pa	Mar. 11, 1873	136, 623
Camphor, Refining	H. Mead	New Haven, Conn	Feb. 12, 1810	....
Camphor, Refining and making	J. Green	Charlestown, Mass	Apr. 27, 1812	....
Camphor-wash mixture	C. W. Crozier	Knoxville, Tenn	July 11, 1854	11, 247
Can:				
See Alkali-can.				
Armored can.				
Butter-can.				
Confectioner's can.				
Cotton-can.				
Cotton or woolen can.				
Cotton-sliver can.				
Dairy-can.				
Dinner-can.				
Dredging-can.				
Fruit-can.				
Grocer's can.				
Hydrocarbon-liquid can.				
Lard-can.				
Lard and packing can.				
Liquid-can.				
Marking-can.				
Measuring-can.				
Metal can.				
Metallic can.				
Milk-can.				
Nitro-glycerine can.				
Oil-can.				
Oil-dripping can.				
Organ-can.				
Oyster-can.				
Oyster-packing can.				
Packing-can.				

Index of patents issued from the United States Patent Office from 1790 *to* 1873, *inclusive*—Continued.

Invention.	Inventor.	Residence.	Date.	No.
Can—Continued.				
See Packing and atomizing can.				
Paint-can.				
Preserving-can.				
Rectangular can.				
Roofing-can.				
Roving-can.				
Safety-can.				
Sealed can.				
Sealing-can.				
Seamless can.				
Sheet-metal can.				
Shipping-can.				
Sirup-can.				
Spice-can.				
Sprinkling-can.				
Tea-can.				
Tin can.				
White-lead can.				
Wood-incased can.				
Wooden-cased can.				
Can	A. D. Armstrong	Pittsburgh, Pa	Sept. 24, 1867	69, 154
Can	C. A. Murdock	Milwaukee, Wis	May 20, 1873	139, 181
Can and bottle, Sealing	J. D. Willoughby	Carlisle, Pa	Jan. 4, 1859	22, 535
Can and jar, Sealing	J. Bellerjeau	Philadelphia, Pa	Mar. 31, 1868	76, 149
Can-cap, Uncut	J. I. Livingston	Pittsburgh, Pa	Mar. 2, 1869	87, 415
Can-cover lock	H. W. Shepard	New York, N. Y	Apr. 9, 1872	125, 622
Can-cover lock	H. W. Shepard	New York, N. Y	Apr. 9, 1872	125, 623
Can-filler	R. Newton	Millville, N. J	May 6, 1873	138, 574
Can filling and soldering apparatus	L. C. Straub	Pittsburgh, Pa	June 20, 1871	116, 114
Can-handle	L. A. Sunderland	Madison, Ohio	Nov. 30, 1869	97, 326
Can-hook	G. Webber	Portland, Me	Sept. 11, 1849	6, 702
Can-making die	J. L. Gray	Baltimore, Md	Apr. 2, 1867	63, 503
Can-manufacture	J. T. Ackley and J. K. Trux	Philadelphia, Pa	Apr. 10, 1866	53, 765
Can-opener	H. C. Alexander	New York, N. Y	Nov. 16, 1869	96, 761
Can-opener	H. C. Alexander	New York, N. Y	Jan. 25, 1870	99, 046
Can-opener	R. H. Atwell	Baltimore, Md	Feb. 9, 1869	86, 626
Can-opener	A. Barker	Wyoming, Pa	May 17, 1870	103, 125
Can-opener	F. G. Beach	Hartford, Conn	Apr. 6, 1869	88, 536
Can-opener	W. M. Bleakley	Verplank, N. Y	June 29, 1869	91, 902
Can-opener	W. M. Bleakley	Verplank, N. Y	Oct. 19, 1869	95, 873
Can-opener	S. O. Church	West Meriden, Conn	Jan. 15, 1867	61, 161
Can-opener	M. C. Davis	Folsom, Cal	July 13, 1869	92, 520
Can-opener	E. F. Dewey	San Francisco, Cal	Sept. 28, 1869	95, 205
Can-opener	E. M. Dewey	San Francisco, Cal	Aug. 29, 1871	118, 593
Can-opener	W. L. Hubbell	Brooklyn, N. Y	Oct. 22, 1867	69, 996
Can-opener	G. C. Humphreys	Washington, D. C	Nov. 17, 1868	84, 122
Can-opener	G. G. Joyce	Baltimore, Md	Aug. 10, 1869	93, 541
Can-opener	J. Kaufman	New York, N. Y	Sept. 6, 1870	107, 061
Can-opener	O. J. Livermore	Worcester, Mass	June 26, 1866	55, 878
Can-opener	W. W. Lyman	Meriden, Conn	July 12, 1870	105, 346
Can-opener	W. W. Lyman	West Meriden, Conn	July 19, 1870	105, 583
Can-opener	T. A. McFarland	Meadville, Pa	May 21, 1867	64, 891
Can-opener	C. J. C. Petersen	Port Chester, N. Y	June 17, 1873	140, 072
Can-opener	A. C. Platt	Sandusky, Ohio	Aug. 23, 1870	106, 723
Can-opener	J. J. Reed	Lyons, Iowa	Mar. 25, 1873	137, 149
Can-opener	C. F. Ritchel	Chicago, Ill	May 12, 1868	77, 916
Can-opener	L. B. Smith	West Meriden, Conn	June 17, 1873	140, 088
Can-opener	N. F. Stone	Chicago, Ill	Apr. 14, 1868	76, 669
Can-opener	W. Thomas	Geneseo, Ill	Nov. 26, 1872	133, 500
Can-opener	S. E. Totten	Brooklyn, N. Y	Jan. 22, 1867	61, 484
Can-opener	E. J. Warner	Waterbury, Conn	Jan. 5, 1858	19, 063
Can-opener	J. A. Wells	Holly Springs, Miss	Aug. 10, 1869	93, 505
Can-opener	J. Wood	New York, N. Y	July 8, 1873	140, 604
Can-opener	F. S. Wyman	Chicago, Ill	July 28, 1868	80, 326
Can-opener and knife or fork, Combined	T. Kenderdine	Lisbon, Iowa	Aug. 26, 1873	142, 109
Can-opener and pipe-cutter	D. A. Barnes	Chicago, Ill	Oct. 28, 1873	144, 051
Can-opening machine	W. H. Forker	Meadville, Pa	Oct. 29, 1867	70, 188
Can-opening tool	G. A. Dickson	Woodcock Township, Pa	Dec. 24, 1867	72, 464
Can-opening tool	M. T. McCormick	Meadville, Pa	Apr. 7, 1868	76, 490
Can-opening tool	E. T. Orne	Chicago, Ill	Nov. 6, 1866	59, 513
Can or bottle stopper	J. Drenton	Philadelphia, Pa	Dec. 23, 1862	37, 221
Can or canister top	A. Bliss	Newark, N. J	Oct. 21, 1851	8, 440
Can or flask	J. Dunton	Philadelphia, Pa	Mar. 3, 1863	37, 843
Can screw-tap	L. R. Boyd	New York, N. Y	June 13, 1871	115, 927
Can-sealing apparatus	H. Y. Wildey	Philadelphia, Pa	Oct. 16, 1860	30, 410
Can-top	L. F. Betts	Chicago, Ill	Sept. 1, 1868	81, 585
Can-top	C. E. Dayton	Meriden, Conn	May 16, 1871	114, 941
Cans and bottles, Elastic cap for sealing	R. Davis	Brookhaven, N. Y	Feb. 24, 1857	16, 684
Cans and boxes, Manufacturing	J. W. Millett	Batchellerville, N. Y	Oct. 18, 1864	44, 737
Can and kettle bails, Construction of ears for	T. Evans	Newark, N. J	Apr. 14, 1868	76, 728
Cans and vessels, Apparatus for exhausting air from and hermetically sealing.	A. M. Purnell	Washington, D. C	Nov. 25, 1856	16, 126
Cans, Apparatus for sealing	J. Green	Cincinnati, Ohio	July 11, 1854	11, 297
Cans, barrels, &c., Apparatus for testing	W. D. Brooks	Baltimore, Md	Dec. 5, 1871	121, 581
Cans, Construction of	H. W. Millar	Utica, N. Y	Sept. 19, 1865	50, 022
Cans for transportation, Packing	J. F. Drummond	New York, N. Y	Feb. 25, 1862	34, 547
Cans, &c., Handle for	N. Bray	Boston, Mass	Feb. 2, 1869	86, 500
Cans, &c., Lid or cover for	J. Bryant	Brooklyn, N. Y	Nov. 10, 1863	40, 552
Cans, &c., Machine for applying screw mouth-pieces to.	H. O. Lothrop	Milford, Mass	Aug. 28, 1866	57, 524
Cans, Machine for fastening bottoms to	R. Brady	New York, N. Y	Sept. 28, 1869	95, 190
Cans, Machine for heading	E. Norton and A. H. Fancher	Chicago, Ill	Oct. 29, 1872	132, 595
Cans, Machine for holding and soldering	J. Redheffer	Kansas City, Mo	Feb. 25, 1873	136, 265
Cans, Machine for making sheet-metal screw-necks and screw-caps for.	J. H. Stone	Hamilton, Canada West	Nov. 28, 1871	121, 435
Cans, &c., Machinery for laying roving in	J. W. Strange	Taunton, Mass	Oct. 23, 1847	5, 337
Cans, Method of hermetically sealing	W. Borrman	Cincinnati, Ohio	Aug. 25, 1857	18, 035

Index of patents issued from the United States Patent Office from 1790 *to* 1873, *inclusive*—Continued.

Invention.	Inventor.	Residence.	Date.	No.
Cans, Mode of laying roving in	J. Tatham and D. Cheetham	Rochdale, England	Nov. 18, 1845	4, 277
Cans, Safety-cap for	H. C. Alexander	New York, N. Y	June 21, 1870	104, 402
Cans, Safety-cap for	H. C. Alexander	New York, N. Y	July 12, 1870	105, 157
Cans, Screw-cap for	A. N. Lapierre	New York, N. Y	Nov. 2, 1869	96, 447
Cans, Seam for	A. L. Webster	Cleveland, Ohio	July 5, 1870	105, 152
Cans, Self-locking lid for	J. W. Weimel and W. Domer	Pittsburgh, Pa	Oct. 22, 1872	132, 507
Cans while being soldered, Device for holding	T. Kerr and J. C. Kelly	Edinburgh, Ind	Apr. 7, 1868	76, 330
Cans with tomatoes, &c., Apparatus for filling	C. S. Bucklin	Red Bank, N. J	Oct. 14, 1873	143, 613
Canning and preserving meat, &c., Process and apparatus for.	N. H. Shipley	Baltimore, Md	Feb. 6, 1872	123, 366
Canal	W. H. Doane	Cincinnati, Ohio	Sept. 5, 1871	118, 699
Canal	H. Hill	Cabin Creek, W. Va	Apr. 22, 1873	138, 156
Canal and navigation thereof	H. H. Day	New York, N. Y	Mar. 12, 1867	62, 736
Canal and other boats, Machine for ascertaining the weight of cargoes in.	A. Amsden	Rochester, N. Y	June 27, 1838	810
Canal and river boat	S. Doolittle	Utica, N. Y	Nov. 19, 1833	....
Canal and river boat	A. Plantou	Philadelphia, Pa	Mar. 18, 1835	....
Canal and river lock	J. Davies	Schuylkill Haven, Pa	Nov. 6, 1860	30, 564
Canal-boat	B. T. Babbitt	New York, N. Y	June 11, 1872	127, 826
Canal-boat	T. W. Bakewell	Cincinnati, Ohio	Aug. 25, 1829	....
Canal-boat	E. C. Bancroft	Syracuse, N. Y	Jan. 2, 1872	122, 351
Canal-boat	J. Bromwell	Cincinnati, Ohio	June 23, 1829	....
Canal-boat	J. C. Cook	New Haven, Conn	July 9, 1872	128, 713
Canal-boat	J. M. Dodge	Newark, N. J	Aug. 6, 1872	130, 110
Canal-boat	J. English	Syracuse, N. Y	Nov. 28, 1871	121, 346
Canal-boat	J. E. Gibson	Port Carbon, Pa	July 20, 1858	20, 944
Canal-boat	H. J. Hatch	Chicago, Ill	Apr. 30, 1872	126, 204
Canal-boat	C. W. Hermance	Schuylersville, N. Y	Jan. 2, 1872	122, 463
Canal-boat	D. Hinchy	Santiago, Chili	Feb. 27, 1872	124, 060
Canal-boat	R. Hooper	Baltimore, Md	July 25, 1871	117, 419
Canal-boat	J. Huges	New Berne, N. C	Feb. 27, 1872	124, 136
Canal-boat	W. A. Leggo	Montreal, Canada	May 6, 1873	138, 664
Canal-boat	J. McCausland	Kingston, N. Y	June 14, 1834	....
Canal-boat	J., J., and J. McCausland	Kingston and Esopus, N. Y	Sept. 21, 1858	21, 572
Canal-boat	N. H. Murray	Louisville, Ky	June 4, 1872	127, 424
Canal-boat	W. H. Newell	Jersey City, N. J	Jan. 23, 1872	123, 039
Canal-boat	I. M. Perry	Slate Cut, Ind	Mar. 12, 1872	124, 622
Canal-boat	B. Phillips	Philadelphia, Pa	Apr. 21, 1828	....
Canal-boat	E. Randolph	Salt Creek, Ohio	Jan. 9, 1838	560
Canal-boat	E. Reed	Pottstown, Pa	Apr. 6, 1833	....
Canal-boat	H. Wickham, jr	Chicago, Ill	Jan. 16, 1872	122, 874
Canal-boat and other vessels for the transportation of grain.	D. E. Somes	Washington, D. C	Oct. 6, 1868	82, 887
Canal-boat fender	J. Rowland	Hancock, Md	June 5, 1847	5, 147
Canal-boat for transshipment of merchandise	J. O. Conner	Philadelphia, Pa	Oct. 14, 1835	....
Canal-boat stanchion	C. Van Name	Binghamton, N. Y	June 11, 1861	32, 544
Canal-boat, Steam	D. W. Crocker	Philadelphia, Pa	May 3, 1834	....
Canal-boat, Steam	J. Elgar	Baltimore, Md	Nov. 7, 1835	....
Canal-boat, Steam	R. Hugunin	Albany, N. Y	Mar. 24, 1823	....
Canal-boat, Steam	E. Lynch	Georgetown, D. C	Oct. 15, 1872	132, 300
Canal-boat, Steam	G. Parker	Worcester, Mass	Mar. 27, 1849	6, 239
Canal-boat, Steam	J. F. Wright	Erie, Pa	Feb. 14, 1828	....
Canal-boats and other vessels, Method of unloading.	W. Loughridge	Weverton, Md	May 9, 1854	10, 891
Canal-boats, Arrangement of lever and catch for tow-line of.	J. W. Caldwell	Rochester, N. Y	Nov. 14, 1854	11, 957
Canal-boats, Attaching paddle-wheels to	R. Jane	Otego, N. Y	Nov. 24, 1857	18, 694
Canal-boats, Attachment of the tow-line of	C. W. Gage	Homer, N. Y	Apr. 21, 1863	38, 224
Canal-boats, Attachment of whiffletree to the tow-line of.	A. Clow	Port Byron, N. Y	May 20, 1862	35, 300
Canal-boats, barges, &c., Constructing and applying locomotive-engines to.	C. Bonycastle	Charlottesville, Va	Jan. 21, 1834	....
Canal-boats, Construction of	A. Judson	Unadilla, N. Y	Aug. 17, 1858	21, 201
Canal-boats, Construction of	G. B. Martin	New York, N. Y	Jan. 7, 1873	134, 555
Canal-boats, Construction of	A. Van Order	Ithaca, N. Y	Sept. 10, 1861	33, 272
Canal-boats, Construction of	B. Williams	Mendon, N. Y	Mar. 3, 1829	....
Canal-boats, Deck for	A. A. Bissell	Lockport, N. Y	Oct. 30, 1866	59, 171
Canal-boats for carrying horses by which they are towed, Construction of.	J. H. Long	Lewistown, Pa	Apr. 5, 1838	676
Canal-boats for repairing, Machine for raising	N. R. Penrose and S. F. Palmer	Beaver Meadow, Pa	May 11, 1839	1, 143
Canal-boats from water, Arrangement of means for freeing.	W. Loughridge	Weverton, Md	July 11, 1854	11, 293
Canal-boats in sections and manner of uniting them, Constructing.	R. Frazer	Waynesburgh, Pa	Sept. 10, 1840	1, 776
Canal-boats, &c., Lessening friction in	P. Freeman	Morris County, N. J	June 1, 1825	....
Canal-boats, Machine for moving	W. R. King	Washington, D. C	Feb. 1, 1870	99, 323
Canal-boats, Machinery for towing	O. Dehesuil and M. Eyth	Brussels, Belgium, and Stuttgart, Wurtemberg.	May 31, 1870	103, 724
Canal-boats, Machinery for weighing	B. Bull	New York, N. Y	June 20, 1826	....
Canal-boats, Means of snubbing	T. W. Edgar	Espy, Pa	Mar. 18, 1873	136, 982
Canal-boats, Method of discharging cargo from	A. Young	Georgetown, D. C	May 2, 1854	10, 843
Canal-boats, Mode of unloading	T. Sharp	Chicago, Ill	Aug. 25, 1863	39, 683
Canal-boats on inclined planes, Raising and lowering.	W. Knight	Morristown, N. J	Aug. 5, 1828	....
Canal-boats or sections thereof, Revolving cradle for unloading.	J. Elgar and B. Hallowell	Baltimore, Md., and Alexandria, Va.	Apr. 10, 1849	6, 303
Canal-boats out of the water for repair, Machine for lifting.	S. C. Jones	Rochester, N. Y	June 16, 1826	....
Canal-boats, Raising and lowering	W. Wiard	Avon, N. Y	May 1, 1828	....
Canal-boats, Sheet-iron twin for	L. Parmelee	Poughkeepsie, N. Y	Nov. 26, 1835	....
Canal-boats, ships, &c., Raising	W. W. Smith	Rochester, N. Y	Feb. 23, 1830	....
Canal-boats, Singletree safety-hook for towing	T. Jackson	Reading, Pa	June 25, 1839	1, 196
Canal-boats to be repaired, Machine for raising	S. Doolittle	Rochester, N. Y	Oct. 25, 1825	....
Canal-boats, Tow-line attachment for	C. Bentz	Mindenville, N. Y	Sept. 13, 1864	44, 154
Canal-boats, Tow-line for	J. Sanford	Weston, Conn	Feb. 16, 1829	....
Canal-boats, Towing	P. Cooper	New York, N. Y	Jan. 24, 1820	....
Canal-boats, Towing	C. T. Harvey	Tarrytown, N. Y	Feb. 2, 1869	86, 395
Canal-boats, Towing	J. L. Simms and W. T. Duvall	Georgetown, D. C	July 30, 1872	130, 080

Index of patents issued from the United States Patent Office from 1790 *to* 1873, *inclusive*—Continued.

Invention.	Inventor.	Residence.	Date.	No.
Canal-boats, Towing	I. P. Tice	New York, N. Y	Feb. 25, 1873	136, 343
Canal-boats, Towing-apparatus for	W. O. Buchanan	Montreal, Canada	Mar. 5, 1872	124, 326
Canal-boats, Towing-apparatus for	A. H. Emery and G. Leverich	New York, N. Y	June 21, 1870	104, 4[illegible]9
Canal-boats, Towing-apparatus for	S. F. Palmer	New York, N. Y	Apr. 26, 1853	9, 687
Canal-boats, Towing-apparatus for	S. W. and J. F. Palmer	Auburn, N. Y	Nov. 8, 1870	109, 045
Canal-boats, Towing-hook for	J. and A. H. Doty	West Falls, N. Y	May 24, 1870	103, 310
Canal-digging machine	J. Humes	Richmond, Va	Nov. 10, 1821	
Canal-gates, Mode of closing wickets in	D. N. Kownover	Danville, Pa	June 13, 1854	11, 077
Canal-lock	G. Bender	New York, N. Y	Aug. 26, 1822	
Canal-lock	M. Bishop	Putnam, Ohio	Sept. 17, 1867	68, 833
Canal-lock	J. Burt	Detroit, Mich	May 28, 1867	65, 054
Canal-lock	H. H. Day	New York, N. Y	Oct. 8, 1867	69, 6[illegible]9
Canal-lock	J. W. Gentry and G. W. Barcus.	Peytona, W. Va	July 4, 1871	116, 583
Canal-lock	G. Heath	Little Falls, N. Y	June 25, 1867	66, 151
Canal-lock	G. Heath	Annapolis, Md	Dec. 6, 1870	109, 899
Canal-lock	D. Rodgers	Little Falls Town, N. Y	Jan. 4, 1828	
Canal-lock	S. J. Seely	Brooklyn, N. Y	Dec. 23, 1862	37, 265
Canal-lock	I. Townsend	Capeville, Va	May 28, 1872	127, 389
Canal-lock	W. W. Virdin	Havre de Grace, Md	Jan. 20, 1852	8, 668
Canal-lock	J. White	Philadelphia, Pa	Oct. 19, 1819	
Canal-lock	D. Wilkinson	Cohoes, N. Y	May 14, 1836	
Canal-lock	C. W. Williams	Port Jervis, N. Y	Nov. 29, 1859	26, 314
Canal-lock gate	V. Brown	Clifton Park, N. Y	May 14, 1836	
Canal-lock gate	R. English	Legro, Ind	July 1, 1841	2, 154
Canal-lock gate	F. Livingston	Waterford, N. Y	Apr. 13, 1838	687
Canal-lock gate	C. Neer	Troy, N. Y	Mar. 9, 1852	8, 789
Canal-lock gate	S. J. Seely	New York, N. Y	Nov. 3, 1857	18, 555
Canal-lock gate	S. S. Seely	Albany, N. Y	May 8, 1860	28, 201
Canal-lock gate	R. Taylor	New York, N. Y	Mar. 26, 1861	31, 836
Canal-lock gate	D. Wilkinson	Cohoes, N. Y	Aug. 17, 1835	
Canal-lock gate	C. W. Williams	Port Jervis, N. Y	Apr. 12, 1859	23, 635
Canal-lock gate	G. W. Wood and L. O. Webster	Utica, N. Y	June 13, 1854	11, 103
Canal-lock-gate step	H. Rexford	Sandy Hill, N. Y	Apr. 28, 1868	77, 405
Canal-lock gates, Device for raising	W. Thomas	Ottawa, Ill	Apr. 4, 1865	47, 139
Canal-lock gates, Operating	K. T. Hurlburt and H. Thompson.	Port Byron, N. Y	Oct. 9, 1860	30, 323
Canal-lock gates, Valve or wicket for	G. Heath	Little Falls, N. Y	July 1, 1862	35, 756
Canal-lock gates, Wicket for	A. H. Griggs	Newark, N. J	May 17, 1864	42, 761
Canal-lock indicator	V. Brown	Clifton Park, N. Y	May 14, 1836	
Canal-lock mechanism	G. Heath	Annapolis, Md	Dec. 27, 1870	110, 459
Canal-lock paddle-gate	J. F. King	Waterford, N. Y	Nov. 29, 1828	
Canal-locks, Making paddle-gates for	D. Rodgers	Little Falls, N. Y	Feb. 17, 1826	
Canal-locks, Preserving wooden	S. Guilford	Lebanon, Pa	July 10, 1826	
Canal-locks, Saving water in	J. P. Fairlamb	Wilmington, Del	Nov. 27, 1823	
Canal-locks, Saving water in passing boats through	J. Dewees	Pottsville, Pa	Dec. 31, 1832	
Canal-locks, &c., Sliding valve for	W. Lake	Richmond, Va	June 7, 1839	1, 163
Canal-locks, Sluice-gate for	G. W. Hildreth	Lockport, N. Y	Mar. 19, 1840	1, 517
Canal-locks, Wicket-gate for	W. L. Potter	Clifton Park, N. Y	Aug. 31, 1839	1, 310
Canal-navigation by boats	S. D. Ingham	New Hope, Pa	Apr. 19, 1831	
Canal stop-dam	I. Knapp	Medina, N. Y	May 13, 1862	35, 242
Canal waste-way and sluice-gate	A. J. Whitney	Harrisburgh, Pa	Dec. 6, 1870	109, 984
Canal-wicket	J. D. Marshbank	Lancaster, Pa	Feb. 2, 1864	41, 463
Canals and railways, Transportation on	J. Elgar	Baltimore, Md	Nov. 7, 1835	
Canals and removing earth, Digging	J. Brainard	Rome, N. Y	Feb. 10, 1826	
Canals, Balance-lock for	J. White	Philadelphia, Pa	May 17, 1839	1, 155
Canals, Constructing	J. Dougherty	Philadelphia, Pa	Feb. 24, 1843	2, 973
Canals, Discharging water from floating dry-docks for.	S. F. Palmer	New York, N. Y	Feb. 1, 1859	22, 818
Canals, Double-inclined plane for	A. Tanner	Warren, Pa	Apr. 15, 1825	
Canals, Feed-regulator for	C. Ross	West Buddick, Ohio	May 21, 1850	7, 384
Canals, Feeding	J. G. Brewer	Lone Tree, Nebr	Nov. 26, 1872	133, 353
Canals, &c., from being closed by ice, Mode of preventing.	R. A. Chesebrough	New York, N. Y	June 1, 1869	90, 727
Canals, Machine for ditching and excavating ground for.	G. Henricks	Urbana, Ohio	Aug. 5, 1829	
Canals, Machine for raising or lowering boats on	E. Morris	Bloomfield, Pa	Oct. 13, 1829	
Canals, &c., Means of keeping open the navigation of	J. Mullaly	New York, N. Y	Oct. 21, 1873	143, 833
Canals, Mode of hauling earth from	O. Phelps	Lansing, N. Y	July 16, 1827	
Canals, Mode of raising boats up and down elevations in.	R. Graves	Brooklyn, N. Y	July 26, 1827	
Canals, Safety-gate for	J. Van Dorn	Glen, N. Y	May 14, 1827	
Canceling-apparatus	T. S. Hudson	East Cambridge, Mass	Oct. 30, 1866	59, 225
Cancer, Method of drawing and curing	J. Ware	Philadelphia, Pa	Sept. 20, 1815	
Candle	J. L. Field	Kensington, Great Britain	May 12, 1868	77, 725
Candle	H. Ryder	New Bedford, Mass	Oct. 17, 1871	12[illegible], 105
Candle and lamp wick, Treating	T. S. Williams and F. A. Taber	Boston, Mass	May 24, 1870	10[illegible], 534
Candle and ornament holder for Christmas-trees	G. Anton	Philadelphia, Pa	Apr. 27, 1869	89, 270
Candle apparatus, Mold	G. Kendall	Providence, R. I	May 3, 1853	9, 696
Candle-cap	J. H. Foote	Pittsfield, Mass	Nov. 17, 1868	84, 103
Candle-cutting apparatus	J. Jones	Brooklyn, N. Y	Apr. 15, 1856	14, 662
Candle-dipping machine	J. Aborn	Burlington County, N. J	Mar. 20, 1821	
Candle-dipping machine	J. A. and A. F Jones	Lexington, Ky	May 16, 1848	5, 576
Candle-dipping machine	C. A. McPhetridge	Saint Louis, Mo	Dec. 9, 1856	16, 211
Candle-dipping machine	V. Squarza	New York, N. Y	Mar. 4, 1856	14, 376
Candle-guard	B. Morgan	San Francisco, Cal	July 22, 1873	141, 066
Candle-holder	E. Daire	Amiens, France	July 19, 1864	43, 628
Candle holder	C. Kirchof	Newark, N. J	Dec. 24, 1867	72, 506
Candle-holder	M. Schall	New York, N. Y	Sept. 24, 1867	69, 254
Candle-holder	J. Verch	Albany, N. Y	July 10, 1866	56, 293
Candle-holder, Economical	P. Ward and B. Allison	Philadelphia, Pa	July 20, 1812	
Candle machine, Mold	W. C. Childs	Boston, Mass	Oct. 28, 1856	15, 968
Candle machine, Mold	B. D. Sanders	Holliday's Cove, Va	Mar. 3, 1857	16, 754
Candle machines, Construction of	M. Massey	Cleveland, Ohio	Apr. 24, 1860	27, 995
Candle-making	F. Fuller	New York, N. Y	Sept. 29, 1821	
Candle-making	B. F. Shelabarger	Mifflintown, Pa	June 5, 1847	5, 139
Candle-making apparatus	W. Humiston	Troy, N. Y	Dec. 23, 1851	8, 607
Candle-making machine	E. Cowles	Hounslow, England	Jan. 19, 1869	86, 059

Index of patents issued from the United States Patent Office from 1790 *to* 1873, *inclusive*—Continued.

Invention.	Inventor.	Residence.	Date.	No.
Candle-making machine	J. Jones	Baltimore, Md	Oct. 26, 1858	21,882
Candle-making machine	J. Sainthorp	Buffalo, N. Y	Mar. 6, 1855	12,492
Candle-making, Preparing fats for	M. W. Brown	Buffalo, N. Y	Oct. 13, 1857	18,381
Candle-manufacture	J. G. Davis	Buffalo, N. Y	Aug. 13, 1850	7,559
Candle-manufacturing machine	H. Grambo	Philadelphia, Pa	Jan. 1, 1867	60,718
Candle, Many-wicked	B. D. Sanders	Holliday's Cove, Va	Sept. 30, 1856	15,821
Candle, Miner's	P. R. Gottstein	Houghton, Mich	Apr. 12, 1870	101,857
Candle, Mold	J. Dunlap	New Holland, Pa	Mar. 8, 1836	....
Candle, Mold	H. Halvorson	Cambridge, Mass	Dec. 13, 1859	26,429
Candle, Mold and dipped	J. Zwisler	New York, N. Y	July 1, 1814	....
Candle-mold apparatus	L. C. Ashley	Troy, N. Y	Dec. 25, 1855	13,973
Candle-mold apparatus	H. Camp	Dunkirk, N. Y	Jan. 22, 1850	7,033
Candle-mold apparatus	W. Humiston	Troy, N. Y	Apr. 4, 1854	10,730
Candle-mold apparatus	W. Humiston	Troy, N. Y	July 24, 1855	13,334
Candle-mold box	G. A. Stanley	Cleveland, Ohio	May 8, 1860	28,210
Candle-mold machine	L. C. Ashley	Troy, N. Y	Jan. 9, 1855	12,193
Candle-mold machine	D. E. and M. Battershall	Troy, N. Y	Dec. 20, 1853	10,331
Candle-mold machine	A. Hengstenberg	Muscatine, Iowa	Nov. 11, 1856	16,056
Candle-mold tip	I. Cole	Brooklyn, N. Y	Apr. 29, 1873	138,380
Candle-molds, Machine for making	M. Burlingame	Garrattsville, N. Y	Dec. 7, 1869	97,749
Candle-molds, Tubular plunger for	H. Ryder	New Bedford, Mass	Nov. 6, 1866	59,460
Candle-molding	J. Drummond	New York, N. Y	Feb. 20, 1846	4,389
Candle-molding apparatus	J. Gamble and J. S. Hill	Cincinnati, Ohio	Dec. 30, 1841	2,405
Candle-molding apparatus	G. A. Stanley	Cleveland, Ohio	May 8, 1860	28,209
Candle-molding apparatus	G. A. Stanley	Cleveland, Ohio	July 31, 1860	29,416
Candle-molding machine	T. King	Troy, N. Y	Nov. 6, 1860	30,605
Candle-molding machine	J. Robingson	New Brighton, Pa	Sept. 2, 1856	15,668
Candle-molding machine	G. Roth	Cincinnati, Ohio	Oct. 28, 1862	36,798
Candle-molding machine	J. Wales	New York, N. Y	Mar. 28, 1871	113,117
Candle-molding machinery	J. H. Tuck	Nantucket, Mass	July 11, 1837	265
Candle or taper holder, Wax	J. Fritsch	Carlstadt, N. J	Aug. 8, 1871	117,763
Candle-snuffers	O. W. Stow and A. Barnes	Southington, Conn	Nov. 24, 1857	18,713
Candle, Tubular	F. Taber	Boston, Mass	May 24, 1870	103,388
Candle-wick	J. H. Tatum	New York, N. Y	Aug. 21, 1860	29,729
Candle-wick	C. A. Wortendyke	Godwinville, N. J	Mar. 30, 1852	8,849
Candle-wick	C. A. Wortendyke	Godwinville, N. J	Jan. 1, 1861	31,049
Candle-wick, Cotton-yarn	G. Dickinson	New York, N. Y	Feb. 21, 1828	....
Candle-wick, Preparation of	S. K. Weeden	Providence, R. I	Aug. 23, 1859	25,227
Candle-wicks, Dipping and cutting	W. Morey	Worcester, Mass	Aug. 15, 1835	....
Candles, Apparatus for making dipped	P. R. Gottstein	Houghton, Mich	Dec. 10, 1867	72,019
Candles, Apparatus for making mold	A. L. Brown	New Haven, Conn	Oct. 2, 1849	6,759
Candles, Apparatus for molding	H. Leonard and H. Ryder	New Bedford, Mass	Dec. 13, 1859	26,440
Candles, Apparatus for molding	A. Meucci	Clifton, N. Y	Sept. 25, 1860	30,180
Candles by machinery, Dipping	W. Day	Gardiner, Me	Mar. 11, 1826	....
Candles by machinery, Making	J. M. Tard	Trenton, N. J	Dec. 4, 1821	....
Candles, Casting or molding spermaceti	W. W. Swain	New Bedford, Mass	Jan. 14, 1820	....
Candles, Composition for	J. L. Klein	New York, N. Y	Nov. 22, 1864	45,160
Candles, Composition for and mode of making	P. Farrell	New York, N. Y	Dec. 16, 1833	....
Candles, Composition for coating	C. Morfit	New York, N. Y	Jan. 10, 1860	26,780
Candles, Drip-cup for	D. M. Ayer	Lawrence, Mass	July 15, 1873	140,755
Candles from paraffine, Manufacture of	C. Havard	New York, N. Y	Sept. 19, 1865	50,000
Candles, Machine for dipping	J. Aborn	Trenton, N. J	May 19, 1832	....
Candles, Machine for dipping	S. Blydenburg		Mar. 22, 1798	....
Candles, Machine for dipping	S. Stansbury	New York, N. Y	Jan. 6, 1809	....
Candles, Machine for making mold	A. Black	New York, N. Y	May 27, 1862	35,359
Candles, Machine for manufacturing dip	W. Miller	New York, N. Y	Jan. 6, 1809	....
Candles, Machine for molding	W. Thomas	New York, N. Y	Apr. 3, 1860	27,763
Candles, Machinery for molding	F. Meyrose	Saint Louis, Mo	Aug. 7, 1860	29,506
Candles, Machinery for molding	G. A. Stanley	Cleveland, Ohio	Aug. 2, 1859	24,960
Candles, Machinery for molding	G. A. Stanley	Cleveland, Ohio	Jan. 10, 1860	26,797
Candles, Machinery for molding	G. A. Stanley	Cleveland, Ohio	Jan. 10, 1860	26,798
Candles, Making	J. S. Sampson		June 26, 1797	....
Candles, Making mold	D. M. Randolph	Richmond, Va	Aug. 1, 1815	....
Candles, Making tallow and wax	J. Zwisler	Baltimore, Md	Apr. 2, 1812	....
Candles, Manufacture of	H. Halvorson	Cambridge, Mass	Jan. 10, 1860	26,763
Candles, Manufacture of	C. Harvard	New York, N. Y	May 2, 1871	114,438
Candles, Manufacture of	E. Marsh	Alton, Ill	Apr. 30, 1842	2,600
Candles, Manufacture of	A. Meucci	Clifton, N. Y	Jan. 25, 1859	22,739
Candles, Manufacture of	J. H. Tatum	New York, N. Y	Oct. 5, 1858	21,706
Candles, Manufacture of	J. H. Tatum	New York, N. Y	Jan. 11, 1859	22,592
Candles, Manufacture of	J. K. Truax	Pittsburgh, Pa	Apr. 9, 1872	125,632
Candles, Manufacture of molded	J. L. Field	Lambeth, Great Britain	Jan. 31, 1865	46,197
Candles, Manufacture of paraffine	J. L. Klein	New York, N. Y	Nov. 22, 1864	45,161
Candles, Manufacture of paraffine	E. C. Leonard	New Bedford, Mass	Nov. 22, 1859	26,193
Candles, Manufacture of paraffine	H. Ryder	New Bedford, Mass	Nov. 20, 1866	59,749
Candles, Manufacturing	R. Robotham		June 2, 1794	....
Candles, Manufacturing	J. S. Sampson		Aug. 6, 1790	....
Candles, Manufacturing dipped	T. M. Scott	Falls Township, Pa	Apr. 1, 1830	....
Candles, Manufacturing mold	T. Hewitt, jr	Philadelphia, Pa	May 4, 1831	....
Candles, Manufacturing mold	T. Hewitt, jr	Philadelphia, Pa	June 13, 1831	....
Candles, Mode of ornamenting	A. Field and W. B. Nation	Lambeth and Surrey County, England.	Apr. 13, 1869	88,779
Candles, Mold for making	T. J. Dyer and A. T. Richmond.	New Bedford, Mass	July 20, 1831	....
Candles, Molding	J. Mower and S. P. Bower	Strasburgh, Pa	Mar. 3, 1837	136
Candles, Molding paraffine	H. Leonard	New Bedford, Mass	Feb. 8, 1859	22,921
Candles, Preparation of tallow for making	F. Garcin	Philadelphia, Pa	Mar. 11, 1856	14,397
Candles, Preparing tallow for the manufacture of	J. Kirkman	New York, N. Y	Oct. 31, 1840	1,844
Candles, Process of treating fatty bodies for the manufacture of.	H. Mége	Paris, France	May 24, 1864	42,901
Candles, Treating fatty matter for the manufacture of.	A. R. St. Cyr	Lyons, France	Apr. 12, 1870	101,935
Candlestick	C. W. Blakeslee	Northfield, Conn	Aug. 21, 1855	13,450
Candlestick	W. Church	England	Mar. 28, 1840	1,528
Candlestick	F. C. Cone	San Francisco, Cal	Oct. 11, 1870	108,109
Candlestick	B. Dearborn		Oct. 29, 1804	....
Candlestick	C. H. Doughty	Newburgh, N. Y	Feb. 25, 1873	136,223
Candlestick	S. Gardiner, jr	New York, N. Y	Feb. 15, 1870	99,875

Index of patents issued from the United States Patent Office from 1790 *to* 1873, *inclusive*—Continued.

Invention.	Inventor.	Residence.	Date.	No.
Candlestick	S. D. Hill.	Downieville, Cal	Aug. 26, 1873	142, 162
Candlestick	W. H. H. Hinds	Groton, Mass	Oct. 31, 1865	50, 708
Candlestick	W. H. H. Hinds	Groton, Mass	Sept. 8, 1868	82, 600
Candlestick	W. H. H. Hinds	Ayer, Mass	Dec. 16, 1873	145, 502
Candlestick	A. E. Lyman	Williamsburgh, Mass	Mar. 25, 1862	34, 758
Candlestick	J. Manning	Middletown, Conn	Jan. 1, 1851	7, 875
Candlestick	S. L. Marsden and S. R. Burrell	Westville, Conn., and New York, N. Y.	Nov. 26, 1861	33, 788
Candlestick	H. Ogborn	Richmond, Ind	Dec. 3, 1867	71, 782
Candlestick	Z. I. Pratt	Chicago, Ill	Mar. 18, 1873	136, 864
Candlestick	A. Rix	San Francisco, Cal	Sept. 25, 1866	58, 296
Candlestick	F. A. Rockwell	Ridgefield, Conn	Dec. 16, 1851	8, 594
Candlestick	A. E. Rogers	La Grande, Oreg	Mar. 18, 1873	137, 029
Candlestick	H. E. Rogers	South Manchester, Conn	July 24, 1860	29, 314
Candlestick	A. E. Rogers and G. W. Webb	La Grande, Oreg	June 18, 1872	127, 989
Candlestick	T. Rose	Cortlandville, N. Y	June 23, 1857	17, 640
Candlestick	H. Ryder	New Bedford, Mass	July 12, 1870	105, 257
Candlestick, &c	S. Slocomb	Cambridge, Mass	Nov. 2, 1858	21, 987
Candlestick	J. Spratt	Cincinnati, Ohio	Nov. 10, 1857	18, 606
Candlestick	F. A. Taber	Baltimore, Md	May 4, 1869	89, 811
Candlestick	A. Whiteley	Springfield, Ohio	Jan. 8, 1856	14, 074
Candlestick	J. Williams	San Mateo, Cal	May 14, 1872	126, 765
Candlestick	H Zahn	San Francisco, Cal	Dec. 14, 1869	97, 848
Candlestick	H. Zahn	San Francisco, Cal	July 26, 1870	105, 875
Candlestick, Camp	C. Alexander	Washington, D. C	Jan. 7, 1862	34, 045
Candlestick for ships, Swinging	J. J. Walton and E. A. Barrett	New York, N. Y	Feb. 25, 1873	136, 290
Candlestick for tents, shops, &c., Adjustable	A. E. Lyman	Williamsburgh, Mass	Jan. 12, 1864	41, 226
Candlestick, Miner's safety	T. A. Washburn	Gold Hill, Nev	Dec. 17, 1872	134, 113
Candle stick or holder	S. J. Rockwood	Elsah, Ill	Jan. 21, 1868	73, 652
Candlestick, Pewter	J. Witherie	Boston, Mass	Oct. 24, 1817	....
Candlestick, Portable	C. P. Gorely	Boston, Mass	Nov. 19, 1867	71, 161
Candlestick, Press-mold	S. T. Barnes	Columbus, Ohio	July 19, 1853	9, 852
Candlestick, Sheet-metal	J. W. Smith	Poultney, Vt	July 25, 1854	11, 389
Candlesticks, Construction of iron	W. P. Merriam, N. C. Harris, W. Wheeler, and E. N. Merriam.	Poultney, Vt	Apr. 26, 1853	9, 685
Candy-box	G. Ruger	La Fayette City, Ind	June 4, 1872	127, 431
Candy-cigar machine	H. Geilhausen	New York, N. Y	Aug. 22, 1865	49, 515
Candy-cutter	J. W. Kaskel	Paducah, Ky	Dec. 30, 1873	146, 076
Candy-cutter	F. Quinn	Keokuk, Iowa	Oct. 14, 1873	143, 590
Candy cutter, Corn	D. Davenport	Albany, N. Y	Aug. 20, 1867	67, 848
Candy-cutting machine	C. Wentz, A. Green, and O. P. Conner.	Trenton, N. J	Feb. 7, 1871	111, 592
Candy-jar	W. C. King	Pittsburgh, Pa	Dec. 17, 1872	134, 072
Candy-jar lid	W. C. King	Pittsburgh, Pa	May 6, 1873	138, 503
Candy-machine	J. S. Batchelder	Fort Wayne, Ind	June 7, 1870	103, 962
Candy-machine	G. K. Farrington and S. Brown, jr	Xenia, Ohio	May 11, 1858	20, 240
Candy, Machine for making sugar	B. O'Brien	Rochester, N. Y	Jan. 13, 1852	8, 657
Candy-making machine	T. and G. M. Mills	Philadelphia, Pa	Feb. 14, 1871	111, 765
Candy-manufacture	H. C. Wilkins	Albany, N. Y	Apr. 10, 1866	53, 913
Candy, Manufacture of	W. J. Burns	Georgetown, Ky	Jan. 30, 1872	123, 149
Candy, Medical compound or phosphated	C. S. Allen	New York, N. Y	Apr. 16, 1872	125, 714
Candy-molding machine	E. K. Powers	Grand Rapids, Mich	Sept. 22, 1868	82, 347
Candy-rolling machine	R. M. Marshall	Dayton, Ohio	July 23, 1861	32, 882
Candy-slicing machine	J. P. Anderson	Philadelphia, Pa	Aug. 1, 1871	117, 589
Candy, Sugar	H. and G. Garrison	Newburgh, N. Y	Apr. 10, 1844	3, 534
Candy-tongs, &c., Machine for making	T. and G. M. Mills	Philadelphia, Pa	Sept. 1, 1868	81, 665
Candy-twisting machine	J. Gardner	Philadelphia, Pa	Nov. 3, 1857	18, 541
Candy ware, Manufacturing sugar	L. Astolfi	Philadelphia, Pa	Nov. 20, 1812	....
Candying-machine	F. W. C. Spiess	New York, N. Y	Feb. 11, 1873	135, 672
Cane	F. Eckstein	New York, N. Y	Dec. 30, 1873	146, 054
Cane	M. Osborn	Albion, Mich	May 20, 1873	139, 020
Cane and billiard-cue, Combined walking	C. A. Bogert	Bay City, Mich	Dec. 26, 1871	122, 218
Cane and lamp, Combined	T. Crossley	Bridgeport, Conn	Nov. 26, 1867	71, 460
Cane and maize cutter	J. W. Cormack	Quincy, Ill	Nov. 1, 1853	10, 178
Cane and seat combined	C. H. Dascomb	Cleveland, Ohio	Aug. 20, 1861	33, 073
Cane and sorghum stripper	J. A. Campbell	Stow, Ohio	May 21, 1867	64, 836
Cane and sorghum stripper	C. P. Hale	Calhoun, Ky	Feb. 26, 1867	62, 413
Cane and stool, Convertible	J. Wade	Richmond, Ind	Jan. 7, 1862	34, 096
Cane and stubble shaver	P. G. Kleinpeter	Plaquemine, La	Aug. 10, 1869	93, 453
Cane and telescope combined	G. W. Wilson	Concord, N. H	July 28, 1868	80, 324
Cane and thermometer, Combined	J. L. Reber	Philadelphia, Pa	Dec. 24, 1867	72, 559
Cane and umbrella combined	H. Beebe	Hudson City, N. J	Nov. 5, 1867	70, 506
Cane and umbrella combined	G. Bockstaller	New York, N. Y	Jan. 7, 1868	73, 074
Cane and umbrella handle	A. Wanner	Hoboken, N. J	Oct. 11, 1870	108, 218
Cane and whip, Combined	C. L. Bushnell	Jefferson, Ohio	Jan. 11, 1870	98, 664
Cane and whip, Combined	C. L. Bushnell	Cherry Valley, Ohio	Nov. 15, 1870	109, 297
Cane and willow stripper	A. F. Ward and J. H. Bean	Marietta, Ohio	Nov. 24, 1868	84, 324
Cane-cleaner	S. Bean	Syracuse, Ohio	Mar. 3, 1868	74, 976
Cane, Compartment	L. C. Heylin	Philadelphia, Pa	Oct. 13, 1868	82, 949
Cane-coverer	J. Allison	Saint Martinsville, La	Mar. 6, 1860	27, 339
Cane-coverer	E. H. Angamer	New Orleans, La	Aug. 28, 1860	29, 842
Cane-coverer	J. P. Bryan	Princeton, Ky	June 24, 1843	3, 151
Cane-crusher, Hydraulic	C. A. Dickinson	Rosedale, La	Apr. 1, 1873	137, 349
Cane-crushing mill	H. C. Emery	Lincoln, Ohio	July 5, 1859	24, 621
Cane-cutter	J. P. Bryan	Princeton, Ky	July 8, 1843	3, 158
Cane-cutter	E. Owen	Byron, Ind	May 30, 1846	4, 551
Cane fiber for paper and other purposes, Treating	B. A. Lavender and H. Lowe	Baltimore, Md	Apr. 4, 1854	10, 722
Cane for paying omnibus-fare	S. W. Francis	New York, N. Y	Mar. 30, 1858	19, 765
Cane, Physician's	S. T. Trowbridge	Decatur, Ill	Jan. 3, 1860	26, 721
Cane-handle	J. Harvey and E. Ford	Philadelphia, Pa	Oct. 2, 1860	30, 225
Cane-handle	H. Nitzsche	Philadelphia, Pa	Aug. 21, 1866	57, 367
Cane-juice, Apparatus for applying sulphurous acid gas in purification of.	J. Communy	New Orleans, La	Dec. 11, 1860	30, 870
Cane-juice, Apparatus for bleaching and defecating	J. C. Marsh	Alexandria, La	Dec. 28, 1869	98, 285
Cane-juice, Apparatus for clarifying	W. A. Jordan	New Orleans, La	July 12, 1864	43, 509
Cane-juice, Apparatus for defecating	H. B. Bond	Terre Browne Parish, La	Oct. 6, 1868	82, 682
Cane-juice, Apparatus for defecating	C. K. Marshall	New Orleans, La	Mar. 29, 1870	101, 288

Index of patents issued from the United States Patent Office from 1790 to 1873, inclusive—Continued.

Invention.	Inventor.	Residence.	Date.	No.
Cane-juice, Apparatus for defecating	E. H. Wheeler	New Orleans, La	May 8, 1860	28, 225
Cane-juice, Apparatus for extracting	D. Moffat	New Orleans, La	Sept. 23, 1873	143, 089
Cane-juice, Apparatus for separating gum from	H. Gortner	Deavertown, Ohio	Sept. 18, 1866	58, 095
Cane-juice, Apparatus f r treating	W. L. Shaffer and J. F. Wood	Chacahoula Station, La	Oct. 22, 1872	132, 417
Cane-juice, Apparatus for treating	G. R. Taylor	Thibodeaux, La	July 1, 1873	140, 443
Cane-juice boxes, Construction of	L. Tregre	Parish Saint John the Baptist, La.	Sept. 6, 1850	25, 354
Cane-juice by means of sulphurous-acid gas, Apparatus for clarifying	A. Labauve	Convent, La	Aug. 24, 1869	94, 008
Cane-juice, Clarific tion of	J. Spangenberg	Jefferson Parish, La	Mar. 27, 1849	6, 219
Cane-juice, Clarifying	F. Domenech	Ponce, Island of Puerto Rico.	Dec. 27, 1859	26, 573
Cane-juice, Clarifying	W. J. McIntosh	Georgia	Mar. 7, 1828	....
Cane-juice-clarifying apparatus	P. Marceline and E. Eude	New Orleans, La	May 22, 1860	28, 385
Cane-juice concentrated by steam	D. Strobel, jr	Washington, D. C.	May 9, 1831	....
Cane-juice, Defecating	D. F. Boyd	Mansfield, Ohio	Feb. 7, 1860	27, 033
Cane-juice, Defecating	A. B. Sharp	Paincourtville, La	Jan. 7, 1868	73, 054
Cane-juice, Defecating	L. Wray	London, England	June 30, 1857	17, 713
Cane-juice, Defecating and bleaching	M. Landry	Iberville Parish, La	Aug. 8, 1871	117, 787
Cane-juice defecating and bleaching machine	P. Paille	Saint James Parish, La	Jan. 19, 1869	85, 955
Cane-juice, Defecating and clarifying	R. A. Stewart	Parish of Saint Bernard, La	Jan. 11, 1859	22, 590
Cane-juice, Evaporating	S. A. Poché	Saint James Parish, La	June 21, 1870	104, 491
Cane-juice evaporation	R. Wright	London, England	Oct. 16, 1860	30, 401
Cane-juice evaporator	H. Bessemer	Baxter House, England	Mar. 8, 1853	9, 607
Cane-juice evaporator	J. S. Blymyer	Mansfield, Ohio	Dec. 20, 1870	110, 192
Cane-juice evaporator	T. Boutté	New Iberia, La	Apr. 7, 1868	76, 392
Cane-juice evaporator	M. S. Bringier	Ascension Parish, La	Sept. 21, 1869	94, 942
Cane-juice evaporator	M. S. Bringier	Ascension Parish, La	Oct. 26, 1869	96, 081
Cane-juice evaporator	W. Edgerton	Spiceland, Ind	Aug. 15, 1865	49, 392
Cane-juice evaporator	F. C. Fulghum	Arba, Ind	Sept. 13, 1864	44, 177
Cane-juice evaporator	F. Groves	New Oxford, Pa	Mar. 21, 1865	46, 969
Cane-juice evaporator	L. S. Hereford	West Baton Rouge Parish, La.	Sept. 21, 1869	94, 959
Cane-juice evaporator	S. A. Poché	Saint James Parish, La	Nov. 17, 1868	84, 134
Cane-juice, &c., evaporator	E. Sperry	Chicago, Ill	Apr. 4, 1871	113, 590
Cane-juice, &c., evaporat r and concentrator	A. Fryer	Manchester, England	May 28, 1867	65, 205
Cane-juice evaporator, Setting kettles for	F. M. Brignac	Saint James Parish, La	Oct. 3, 1871	119, 501
Cane-juice, Machine for bleaching	E. Skelly	Plaquemine, La	Oct. 26, 1869	96, 155
Cane juice, Machine for expressing	H. Bessemer	Middlesex County, England	June 3, 1851	8, 137
Cane-juice, Mode of applying sulphurous-acid gas in the defecation of.	R. B. Brashear	Pattersonville, La	Dec. 6, 1859	26, 401
Cane-juice, Mode of defecating	L. Reid and E. H. Swift	New York, N. Y., and Middlefield, Conn.	Dec. 4, 1866	60, 242
Cane-juice, Mode of defecating	L. Reid and E. H. Swift	New York, N. Y., and Middlefield, Conn.	Dec. 4, 1866	60, 243
Cane-juice, Mode of defeca ing	L. Reid and E. H. Swift	New York, N. Y., and Middlefield, Conn.	Dec. 4, 1866	60, 244
Cane-juice, Mode of defecating	L. Reid and E. H. Swift	New York, N. Y., and Middlefield, Conn.	Dec. 4, 1866	60, 245
Cane-juice, Mode of defecating	L. Reid and E. H. Swift	New York, N. Y., and Middlefield, Conn.	Dec. 4, 1866	60, 246
Cane-juice, Mode of treating	J. E. Pattison	Houma, La	Sept. 11, 1866	57, 958
Cane-juice with sulphur fumes, Apparatus for treating.	W. G. Billiu	Thibodeaux, La	Aug. 19, 1873	141, 914
Cane-juice with sulphurous acid, Apparatus for treating.	J. E. Pattison	Thibodeaux, La	Jan. 21, 1868	73, 640
Cane-juice, &c., with sulphurous-acid gas, Apparatus for impregnating.	E. Skelly	Plaquemine, La	Sept. 15, 1868	82, 164
Cane-juice with sulphurous-acid gas, Apparatus for treating.	J. W. Austin	Plaquemine, La	Nov. 29, 1870	109, 571
Cane-juice with sulphurous-acid gas, Apparatus for treating.	J. Dymond	New York, N. Y	Jan. 7, 1873	134, 655
Cane-juice with sulphurous-acid gas, Apparatus for treating.	G. A. Huwald	Knoxville, Tenn	Aug. 20, 1861	33, 086
Cane-juice with suphurous-acid gas, Apparatus for treating.	T. Morillon and U. Naquin	La Fourche Parish, La	July 2, 1867	66, 377
Cane-juice, &c., with sulphurous acids, Bleaching	B. R. Hawley	Normal, Ill	July 16, 1872	129, 341
Cane-mill	L. Biddle	Knoxville, Iowa	Jan. 21, 1870	104, 544
Cane-mill	W. Briggs	Greencastle, Iowa	Nov. 20, 1866	59, 889
Cane-mill	B. F. Cauffman	Millerstown, Pa	Jan. 28, 1868	73, 779
Cane-mill	D. M. Cook	Mansfield, Ohio	Aug. 11, 1863	39, 467
Cane-mill	J. W. Richardson, D. L. Davis, and W. C. Howell.	Sligo, Ohio	May 22, 1866	54, 960
Cane mill	H. B. Stephens and D. J. Powers	Madison, Wis	Oct. 26, 1869	96, 283
Cane-mill	O. E. Woodbury	Madison, Wis	Nov. 14, 1865	50, 978
Cane-mill and steam-engine	J. Moore	Madison, Ind	Feb. 18, 1868	74, 574
Cane, &c., Mill for grindi g	I. A. Hedges	Cincinnati, Ohio	Feb. 1, 1859	22, 802
Cane-press	E. Powell	Conneautville, Pa	Apr. 10, 1860	27, 830
Cane, Rifle	A. Crow	Middlefield, Mass	May 8, 1860	28, 160
Cane-scraper	L. A. Bringier and N. B. Trist	Ascension Parish and New Orleans, La.	July 13, 1869	92, 420
Cane seat	G. W. Martin	Boston, Mass	July 28, 1868	80, 300
Cane-seat chairs, Construction of	C. M. Rohr	Portland, Oreg	June 14, 1870	104, 207
Cane seat for chairs	W. F. Howe	Galveston, Tex	Sept. 3, 1872	131, 069
Cane seat for chairs	J. B. Sawyer	Templeton, Mass	June 11, 1861	32, 535
Cane-stripper	J. H. Barloy	Sedalia, Mo	Sept. 24, 1867	69, 161
Cane-stripper	W. N. Barr	Richmond, Ind	Sept. 18, 1866	58, 049
Cane-stripper	J. C. Brown	Crawfordsville, Ind	Oct. 1, 1867	69, 310
Cane-stripper	W. Gladden and R. F. Bishop	Chrome Hill, Md	Oct. 10, 1865	50, 350
Cane-stripper	J. A. Hall	Memphis Tenn	Aug 8, 1865	49, 260
Cane-stripper	J. A. Hall	Columbus, Ohio	Apr. 10, 1866	53, 818
Cane-stripper	C. A. Hego	Friedberg, N. C	Oct. 11, 1870	108, 135
Cane-stripper	R. C. James	Denison, Tex	July 22, 1873	141, 057
Cane-stripper	M. Mellinger	Dayton, Ohio	Jan. 1, 1867	60, 768
Cane-stripper	I. E. and J. A. Overpeck	Overpeck Station, Ohio	Mar. 12, 1867	62, 876
Cane-stripper	H. Rockwell	Roanoke, Ind	Dec. 12, 1865	51, 482
Cane-stripper	G. E. Sellers	Seller's Landing, Ill	Jan. 24, 1865	46, 031

Index of patents issued from the United States Patent Office from 1790 *to* 1873, *inclusive*—Continued.

Invention.	Inventor.	Residence.	Date.	No.
Cane-stripper	W. Todd	Barnesville, Ohio	Apr. 5, 1864	42, 241
Cane stripper and knife combined	R. Conarroe	Camden, Ohio	July 3, 1866	56, 009
Cane-stripping device	T. W. Peirce	Minneapolis, Minn	Sept. 5, 1865	49, 785
Cane-stripping machine	D. C. Flint	Bushnell, Ill	May 22, 1866	54, 880
Cane-stubble shaver	F. F. Patout	Jeanerett, La	May 23, 1871	115, 094
Cane, Sword	S. A. Hudson	Worcester, Mass	Sept. 9, 1851	8, 346
Cane, umbrella, pistol, dagger, and camp-stool combined.	D. Morrison	Portland, Me	Apr. 2, 1867	63, 552
Cane, Walking	A. Cain	Holyoke, Mass	July 12, 1859	24, 718
Cane, Walking	C. K. Peney	Worcester, Mass	Sept. 30, 1873	143, 248
Canes, crutches, &c., Mode of constructing the bottom ends of ferrules for.	J. Ball	Buffalo, N. Y	Oct. 11, 1841	2, 297
Canister: *See* Grocer's canister. Paint-canister. Powder-canister. Tea-canister.				
Canister	E. Mather	Chicago, Ill	July 23, 1872	129, 842
Canisters, Measuring-stopple for	W. M. Smith	Washington, D. C	Sept. 25, 1866	58, 311
Cannon	J. Adams	Cleveland, Ohio	Oct. 25, 1859	25, 929
Cannon	J. W. Cochran	Lowell, Mass	Mar. 23, 1836	....
Cannon	A. Krupp	Essen, Prussia	Nov. 27, 1855	13, 851
Cannon	J. A. Terrell	Bloomfield, Ky	Dec. 29, 1868	85, 491
Cannon and fire-arms, Construction of	N. A. Patterson	Kingston, Tenn	Nov. 3, 1863	40, 498
Cannon and other fire-arms, Manufacture of	C. W. Lancaster	London, England	July 5, 1853	9, 830
Cannon, Apparatus for planing the chambers of	A. Alexander	Pittsburgh, Pa	Oct. 13, 1863	40, 225
Cannon, Automatic	C. E. Barnes	Lowell, Mass	July 8, 1836	15, 315
Cannon, &c., Automatic finger for closing the vents of	A. Le Mat	New Orleans, La	June 7, 1859	24, 313
Cannon-balls, Flask for casting packings around	L. Evans	Morgantown, Va	Oct. 30, 1860	30, 533
Cannon-ball, &c., from malleable iron, lead, &c., Machine for manufacturing.	L. Grandy and T. Osgood	Troy, N. Y	Feb. 3, 1841	1, 965
Cannon-balls, &c., Mode of forming molds for casting.	A. Elliot	Philadelphia, Pa	Oct. 6, 1843	3, 295
Cannon, Bolt and disk sectional	J. Fitzgerald	New York, N. Y	Feb. 6, 1849	6, 090
Cannon, Boring	L. A. B. Walbach	United States Army	Aug. 23, 1853	9, 961
Cannon boring and rifling apparatus	P. Foy	New York, N. Y	Mar. 11, 1862	34, 661
Cannon, Breech-loading	H. J. Allen	Arkadelphia, Ark	Apr. 25, 1871	113, 963
Cannon, Breech-loading	J. W. Hollensbury	Alexandria, Va	Dec. 28, 1858	22, 427
Cannon, Breech-loading	E. Marshall	New York, N. Y	Dec. 14, 1858	22, 299
Cannon, Breech-loading	J. H. Merrill	Baltimore, Md	Mar. 22, 1859	23, 306
Cannon, Breech-loading	J. H. Murrill	Baltimore, Md	June 15, 1858	20, 608
Cannon, Breech-loading	W. E. Osborn	Milton, N. Y	Sept. 12, 1854	11, 678
Cannon, Breech-loading	J. B. Prescott	Waterford, N. Y	Jan. 28, 1862	34, 263
Cannon, Breech-loading	E. S. Wright and T. P. Gould	Buffalo, N. Y	Dec. 14, 1858	22, 325
Cannon by electricity, Firing	G. W. Beardslee	College Point, N. Y	Aug. 18, 1863	39, 543
Cannon, Casting	A. H. Emery	New York, N. Y	Oct. 4, 1864	44, 521
Cannon, Casting	J. B. Tarr	Fairhaven, Mass	Jan. 18, 1870	98, 894
Cannon, Constructing	C. Perley	New York, N. Y	May 5, 1863	38, 4[illegible]9
Cannon, Device for firing	D. Treadwell	Cambridge, Mass	Nov. 25, 1862	37, 017
Cannon, Discharging	H. Whitcomb	Adams, N. Y	Oct. 25, 1826	....
Cannon-elevating apparatus	G. M. Ransom	United States Navy	Nov. 15, 1859	26, 124
Cannon for chain-shot	E. Gordon	Hingham, Mass	Feb. 17, 1836	....
Cannon for chain-shot	A. Lemmer	Newark, N. J	Nov. 18, 1851	8, 528
Cannon for chain-shot, Double	W. M. Jeffers	Elmira, N. Y	June 21, 1859	24, 518
Cannon, Forging	A. Hitchcock	New York, N. Y	Aug. 8, 1865	49, 266
Cannon, Friction-primer for	W. Ball	Chicopee, Mass	Mar. 23, 1852	8, 820
Cannon-hoops, Manufacture of	D. Treadwell	Cambridge, Mass	May 10, 1864	42, 701
Cannon-lock	E. Hidden and S. Sawyer	New York, N. Y	Apr. 29, 1842	2, 594
Cannon-lock, Compression	J. Shaw	Philadelphia, Pa	Dec. 3, 1832	....
Cannon-lock, Portable	J. Shaw	Philadelphia, Pa	Dec. 3, 1832	....
Cannon, Machine for boring the chambers of	W. McClery	Pittsburgh, Pa	Apr. 12, 1864	42, 332
Cannon, Machine for turning rimbase of	E. Kaylor	Pittsburgh, Pa	Oct. 24, 1865	50, 598
Cannon, Machinery for welding and forming wrought-iron.	D. Treadwell	Cambridge, Mass	June 20, 1846	4, 589
Cannon, Malleable-iron	G. W. Chapman	New York, N. Y	June 16, 1836	....
Cannon, Manufacture of	T. N. Hornsby	Simpsonville, Ky	Sept. 3, 1867	68, 509
Cannon, Manufacture of	D. Treadwell	London, England	Dec. 11, 1855	13, 927
Cannon, Manufacture of wrought	H. Ames	Falls Village, Conn	Aug. 16, 1864	43, 825
Cannon, Manufacture of wrought-iron	J. Griffen	Safe Harbor, Pa	Dec. 25, 1855	13, 984
Cannon, Manufacture of wrought-iron and steel	R. Cook	Saratoga, N. Y	Feb. 1, 1842	2, 443
Cannon, Manufacturing cast-iron	C. Alger	Boston, Mass	May 30, 1837	208
Cannon, Many-barrelled	G. Natcher	Sidney, Ohio	Dec. 27, 1864	45, 623
Cannon, Many-chambered breech-loading	C. C. Terrel	Shullsburgh, Wis	Feb. 5, 1856	14, 215
Cannon, Method of making wrought-iron	S. Hunt	Torrington, Conn	Nov. 24, 1843	3, 358
Cannon, Mode of charging	J. Dodge	Dummerston, Vt	July 15, 1856	15, 357
Cannon, Mode of discharging	J. Dodge	Dummerston, Vt	Aug. 4, 1857	17, 920
Cannon, Mode of loading rifled	L. Houghton	Philadelphia, Pa	Apr. 3, 1855	12, 629
Cannon, Mounting and manœuvering	O. Hopkins	New York, N. Y	Dec. 17, 1861	3[illegible], 944
Cannon of wrought iron or wrought iron and steel, Method of making.	D. Treadwell	Cambridge, Mass	Feb. 12, 1845	3, 906
Cannon, Pendulum-sight for	R. Smith	Brooklyn, N. Y	Oct. 13, 1863	40, 288
Cannon, Percussion-lock and vent for	W. H. Bell	Norfolk, Va	Oct. 1, 1830	....
Cannon, Percussion-lock for	R. Beale	Washington, D. C	Jan. 43, 1835	....
Cannon, Percussion-lock for	E. Hidden	New York	Jan. 14, 1831	....
Cannon, Percussion-lock for	E. Hidden	New York	Dec. 16, 1831	....
Cannon, Percussion-lock for	E. Hidden	New York	Aug. 20, 1834	....
Cannon, Percussion-lock for	J. Shaw	Philadelphia, Pa	Oct. 24, 1828	....
Cannon, Percussion-primer for	L. and W. H. Bell	Fortress Monroe, Va	Dec. 8, 1829	....
Cannon, Pointing	J. Black	Northumberland, Pa	Jan. 17, 1818	....
Cannon-pointing apparatus	J. Hobday	Portsmouth, Va	May 30, 1837	207
Cannon, Primer and percussion for	J. Shaw	Philadelphia, Pa	Dec. 3, 1832	....
Cannon-rammer	M. C. Borgia	Philadelphia, Pa	Oct. 22, 1861	33, 513
Cannon, Repeating	J. H. Headrick	Wythe County, Va	Dec. 20, 1870	110, 233
Cannon, Repeating	S. Huffman	Charlestown, Ill	Jan. 23, 1855	12, 295
Cannon, Repeating	T. Tufts	Somerville, Mass	Mar. 7, 1865	46, 762
Cannon, Revolving	E. Brehm	Jersey City, N. J	Dec. 2[illegible], 1870	110, 194
Cannon, Revolving	A. Schausten	Michigan City, Ind	Feb. 4, 1868	74, 152

Index of patents issued from the United States Patent Office from 1790 to 1873, inclusive—Continued.

Invention.	Inventor.	Residence.	Date.	No.
Cannon, Rifled	A. C. Stimers	Castleton, N. Y	July 26, 1870	105, 736
Cannon-rifling machine	A. Bonzano	Detroit, Mich	Mar. 17, 1863	37, 898
Cannon, Rotary cylinder	J. W. Cochran	Lowell, Mass	Oct. 22, 1834	....
Cannon-sight	P. Maltby	Cleveland, Ohio	June 28, 1864	43, 319
Cannon sight	J. A. Wagener	Charleston, S. C	Mar. 8, 1853	9, 615
Cannon traverse-board	W. H. Bell	Washington, D. C	May 14, 1836	....
Cannon-vent	J. W. Cochran	Lowell, Mass	Mar. 23, 1836	....
Cannon, Wrought-iron	A. Eames	Chicopee Falls, Mass	Feb. 5, 1847	4, 960
Cannons by attached fusee, Firing	E. Gomez	New York, N. Y	Jan. 7, 1862	34, 056
Canopy	J. Ellisdon	Liverpool, England	Oct. 10, 1871	119, 698
Canopy for tents and bed-netting	J. B. Holmes	Cincinnati, Ohio	Feb. 18, 1868	74, 535
Canopy holder, Musquito	L. M. Bates	Wooster, Ohio	July 25, 1871	117, 370
Canopy, Lawn	F. H. and W. H. Vick	Rochester, N. Y	Dec. 5, 1871	121, 693
Canopy, Musquito	M. L. Thompson	Brooklyn, N. Y	Feb. 23, 1864	47, 730
Canopied chair	T. Elkinton	Philadelphia, Pa	Nov. 11, 1873	144, 521
Canopies, curtains, &c., Support for	J. B. Holmes	Philadelphia, Pa	June 18, 1872	128, 041
Cant-hook	E. Broad	Saint Anthony's Falls, Minn.	Jan. 7, 1868	73, 075
Cant-hook	W. S. Colburn	Loami, Ill	June 11, 1867	65, 727
Cant-hook	J. E. Emerson	Trenton, N. J	Feb. 9, 1869	86, 828
Cant-hook	O. P. Frantz and E. Broad	Saint Anthony, Minn	Aug. 24, 1869	93, 981
Cant-hook	J. W. Gerrish	Bethel, Me	Oct. 8, 1867	69, 560
Cant-hook	W. Q. Greely	Saint Anthony, Minn	Jan. 4, 1870	98, 584
Cant-hook	G. W. Herring	Bangor, Me	Mar. 3, 1868	75, 162
Cant-hook	P. Hinds	Cedar Run, Pa	Jan. 3, 1860	26, 737
Cant-hook	T. Hopkins	Cincinnati, Ohio	Feb. 26, 1867	62, 489
Cant-hook	J. A. Howe	Bangor, Me	Sept. 17, 1867	68, 878
Cant-hook	E. Jewett	Rindge, N. H	Sept. 17, 1867	68, 883
Cant-hook	A. Kennard	Clearfield, Pa	Jan. 31, 1871	111, 460
Cant-hook	W. P. Kilgore	Hampden, Me	June 29, 1869	91, 853
Cant-hook	E. Mansfield	Orono, Me	Aug. 19, 1873	142, 032
Cant-hook	J. McDonald	Oshkosh, Wis	Aug. 18, 1868	81, 098
Cant-hook	A. B. Reeves	Knightstown, Ind	Apr. 18, 1871	113, 796
Cant-hook	P. Shults	Rockwood, N. Y	Aug. 24, 1869	94, 038
Cant-hook	W. Tetro	Northampton, Mass	Dec. 20, 1870	110, 309
Cant-hook	R. Whittier	Oshkosh, Wis	Aug. 19, 1873	141, 906
Cant-hook for moving logs, Adjustable	M. Allcutt	Hancock, N. H	Dec. 16, 1856	16, 222
Canteen	C. Bartholomae	New York, N. Y	July 9, 1861	32, 744
Canteen	B. Beers	New Fairfield, Conn	Jan. 11, 1859	22, 541
Canteen	L. F. Bronnum	Brooklyn, N. Y	Jan. 6, 1863	37, 273
Canteen	L. Cantel	New York, N. Y	Oct. 14, 1862	36, 641
Canteen	J. Case	Philadelphia, Pa	July 9, 1861	32, 752
Canteen	F. Gardner	Roxbury, Mass	Nov. 4, 1862	36, 835
Canteen	S. Herbert	New York, N. Y	Oct. 29, 1861	33, 586
Canteen	R. Kelley	Red Bank, Cal	Feb. 4, 1873	135, 432
Canteen	J. A. Montgomery	Williamsport, Pa	Sept. 24, 1861	33, 360
Canteen	S. G. Morrison	Williamsport, Pa	Dec. 24, 1861	34, 004
Canteen	J. M. Trowbridge	United States Army	Nov. 17, 1863	40, 655
Canteen and lunch-box	K. Thoman	Cleveland, Ohio	Feb. 6, 1866	52, 468
Canteen-filler	S. H. Russell	Boston, Mass	Aug. 20, 1861	33, 105
Canteen, Hospital	H. Beck	Detroit, Mich	Mar. 18, 1873	136, 808
Canteen, plate, cup, and funnel	C. O. Farciot	Philadelphia, Pa	Jan. 31, 1865	46, 095
Canvas and cordage, Solution for preserving	C. Nelson	Gloucester, Mass	Jan. 7, 1873	134, 559
Canvas, Frame for stretching	H. Bryant	Hartford, Conn	Sept. 25, 1849	6, 731
Canvas, &c., Machine for cutting	H. H. Pember	New York, N. Y	Jan. 29, 1867	61, 683
Canvas, Preventing mildew in	T. Bathy	Smith's Creek, Mich	Nov. 21, 1871	121, 038
Canvas-stretcher	C. Dowd	New Haven, Conn	June 12, 1866	55, 579
Canvas-stretcher	J. B. Flagg and G. Storer	New Haven and New Britain, Conn.	Oct. 9, 1866	58, 627
Canvas-stretcher	H. W. Holly	Brooklyn, N. Y	Aug. 26, 1873	142, 232
Canvas stretching and protecting frame	A. Dickerman	Boston, Mass	Aug. 5, 1873	141, 547
Canvas to form tarpaulins, Coating	C. Cobb	Charlestown, Mass	Aug. 12, 1873	141, 764
Caoutchouc and allied gums, Compounds of	G. A. Engelhard and R. F. H. Havemann.	New York, N. Y., and New Brunswick, N. J.	Nov. 22, 1859	26, 175
Caoutchouc and allied gums, Roller for working	T. Sault	Seymour, Conn	Feb. 14, 1860	27, 160
Caoutchouc and other gums, Material produced by treating.	J. B. Newbrough and E. Fagan.	New York, N. Y	Jan. 28, 1868	73, 917
Caoutchouc and other gums, Treating	J. B. Newbrough and E. Fagan.	New York, N. Y	Jan. 21, 1868	73, 545
Caoutchouc and other vulcanizable gums, Treating	L. O. P. Meyer	Newtown, Conn	Apr. 4, 1854	10, 741
Caoutchouc, Apparatus for curing	W. R. Bagnall	Chelsea, Mass	May 5, 1863	38, 369
Caoutchouc, Artificial	A. G. Day	New York, N. Y	Oct. 9, 1866	58, 615
Caoutchouc cement for cloth, leather, &c	E. M. Chaffee	United States	Aug. 31, 1836	16
Caoutchouc, Composition formed of	A. Willmann	New York, N. Y	Feb. 21, 1860	27, 251
Caoutchouc, Composition of	R. F. Havemann	New Brunswick, N. J	Jan. 29, 1861	31, 240
Caoutchouc, Composition of	R. F. Havemann	New Brunswick, N. J	Jan. 29, 1861	31, 241
Caoutchouc, Curing and treating	E. E. Marcy	New York, N. Y	Aug. 30, 1859	25, 271
Caoutchouc, Curing and treating	E. E. Marcy	New York, N. Y	Aug. 30, 1859	25, 272
Caoutchouc, Curing and treating	E. E. Marcy	New York, N. Y	Aug. 30, 1859	25, 273
Caoutchouc, Dissolving	P. Mackie	New York, N. Y	Mar. 23, 1836	....
Caoutchouc dressing and bleaching	C. Goodyear	New York, N. Y	June 17, 1837	240
Caoutchouc, &c., Fabric manufactured from	O. Falke and P. Shrag	New York, N. Y	Apr. 26, 1864	42, 533
Caoutchouc fluid to render articles water-proof	G. H. Richards	Washington, D. C	Apr. 11, 1831	....
Caoutchouc, gutta-percha, and similar gums, Mode of treating.	J. B. Newbrough and E. Fagan.	New York, N. Y	Oct. 29, 1867	70, 250
Caoutchouc hose-tubing	T. J. Mayall	Roxbury, Mass	Feb. 26, 1861	31, 552
Caoutchouc in single-chamber apparatus, Vulcanizing.	B. W. Franklin	New York, N. Y	Sept. 10, 1861	33, 246
Caoutchouc into shreds, Cutting	W. Atkinson	New York, N. Y	Oct. 6, 1835	....
Caoutchouc into strips and threads, Machine for cutting.	L. Hull	Charlestown, Mass	Jan. 20, 1863	37, 446
Caoutchouc or India-rubber	L. Hull	Charlestown, Mass	Mar. 10, 1863	37, 866
Caoutchouc or India-rubber balls, Method of manufacturing.	E. M. Chaffee	Cambridgeport, Mass	Jan. 21, 1841	1, 939
Caoutchouc previous to grinding, Preparing	J. W. Harman	New York, N. Y	Jan. 15, 1846	4, 357
Caoutchouc, &c., Process for changing, curing, or treating.	H. A. Ayling	Boston, Mass	May 10, 1864	42, 633
Caoutchouc, &c., Product from	H. A. Ayling	Boston, Mass	May 10, 1864	42, 632
Caoutchouc spring	F. M. Ray	New York, N. Y	Mar. 27, 1849	6, 231

Index of patents issued from the United States Patent Office from 1790 *to* 1873, *inclusive*—Continued.

Invention.	Inventor.	Residence.	Date.	No.
Caoutchouc to cloths, &c., Application of	E. M. Chaffee	Roxbury, Mass	Aug. 31, 1836	....
Caoutchouc to cloth, &c., Method of applying	C. Meyer	New Brunswick, N. J	Mar. 19, 1861	31, 729
Caoutchouc, Tool for manufacturing goods of	D. D. Parmelee	New York, N. Y	Oct. 5, 1858	21, 697
Caoutchouc, Treating	L. Hull	Charlestown, Mass	Dec. 23, 1862	37, 231
Caoutchouc, Treatment of	A. G. Day	Seymour, Conn	Aug. 10, 1858	21, 122
Caoutchouc, Treatment of	M. Mattson	Boston, Mass	Mar. 1, 1859	23, 103
Caoutchouc, Vulcanizing	B. W. Franklin	New York, N. Y	Oct. 8, 1861	33, 464
Caoutchouc-vulcanizing apparatus	G. E. Hayes	Buffalo, N. Y	Mar. 5, 1861	31, 599
Caoutchouc with sulphur, Mode of preparing	N. Hayward	Woburn, Mass	Feb. 24, 1839	1, 090
Cap	J. W. Bryant	Welaka, Fla	Sept. 23, 1862	36, 549
Cap	I. K. Gittens, jr	Green Point, N. Y	Oct. 1, 1861	33, 386
Cap	S. Goldstone	Philadelphia, Pa	Sept. 4, 1866	57, 702
Cap	M. N. Myers	Boston, Mass	May 6, 1873	138, 681
Cap	B. Scharl	Boston, Mass	Mar. 18, 1873	137, 032
Cap	C. and F. Stattmann	Chicago, Ill	Oct. 23, 1866	59, 092
Cap and nozzle, Metallic	E. S. Covell	Brooklyn, N. Y	June 7, 1870	103, 988
Cap, Army and Navy	W. F. Warburton	Philadelphia, Pa	Aug. 26, 1862	36, 315
Cap-box	A. F. Gove	Lincoln, Vt	May 14, 1872	126, 692
Cap, Fireman's	P. Ackerman	Bangor, Me	July 2, 1872	128, 451
Cap-fronts, Machine for cutting	G. Burgess	New York, N. Y	Feb. 26, 1850	7, 114
Cap-fronts, Mode of binding	L. Londinsky	New York, N. Y	June 26, 1860	28, 878
Cap, Military	S. Mossman	Cleveland, Ohio	Aug. 25, 1863	39, 667
Cap, Military	J. S. Smith	New York, N. Y	Aug. 21, 1860	29, 724
Cap, Military	J. F. Whipple	New York, N. Y	July 16, 1861	32, 849
Cap, Military fatigue	C. Kollinky, J. Ehrlich, and J. De Zeyk.	Washington, D. C	Nov. 5, 1861	33, 651
Cap setting and extracting device	E. S. Holmes	Grand Rapids, Mich	June 10, 1873	139, 674
Cap-shearing block	R. Cook and T. Hanford	New Hartford, N. Y	Oct. 3, 1871	119, 449
Cap, Traveling	J. F. Sargent	Tunbridge, Vt	Mar. 29, 1870	101, 383
Cap, Water-proof and elastic	L. L. Macomber	Gardiner, Me	Oct. 11, 1831	....
Caps, Former for forming seamless felt	J. L. Bridge and W. B. Lodge	Vernon, N. Y	May 8, 1860	28, 149
Caps, Machine for cutting leather visors for	J. Hawkins	Roxbury, Mass	Feb. 30, 1832	....
Caps, Mode of preventing corrosion in metallic	L. R. Boyd	New York, N. Y	Mar. 30, 1869	88, 439
Capped nails	C. Walsh	Newark, N. J	Sept. 30, 1873	143, 393
Capstan	J. S. Brown	Schenectady, N. Y	July 4, 1871	116, 548
Capstan	E. Buel	Silver Creek, N. Y	Apr. 19, 1870	102, 088
Capstan	D. N. B. Coffin, jr	Boston, Mass	July 2, 1867	66, 299
Capstan	D. N. B. Coffin, jr	Newton Centre, Mass	Mar. 15, 1870	100, 859
Capstan	Z. E. Coffin	Newton Centre, Mass	June 24, 1862	35, 730
Capstan	H. Davies	Portsmouth, Ohio	Apr. 26, 1864	42, 465
Capstan	J. Edson	Boston, Mass	Aug. 21, 1866	57, 302
Capstan	J. Edson	Boston, Mass	Nov. 12, 1867	70, 820
Capstan	J. Edson	Boston, Mass	Nov. 9, 1869	96, 568
Capstan	J. Ericsson	New York, N. Y	Jan. 18, 1870	98, 940
Capstan	J. Gardner	New York, N. Y	Aug. 3, 1869	93, 295
Capstan	W. D. Grimshaw	New York N. Y	Nov. 28, 1865	51, 174
Capstan	W. D. Grimshaw	Newark, N. J	Dec. 18, 1866	60, 505
Capstan	A. Morse	Boston, Mass	Mar. 12, 1836	....
Capstan	J. Reed	Marshfield, Mass	Apr. 5, 1859	23, 499
Capstan	J. W. Riggs	Wade, Ohio	Sept. 6, 1870	107, 104
Capstan	P. Roberts	New York, N. Y	Feb. 17, 1852	8, 746
Capstan	W. W. Vanderbilt	New York, N. Y	Dec. 1, 1868	84, 660
Capstan	C. L. Willis	Washington, D. C	Apr. 6, 1869	88 761
Capstan and crab, Portable	A. Elmen	Shabbona Grove, Ill	Aug. 9, 1859	25 079
Capstan and windlass	D. N. B. Coffin, jr	Boston, Mass	Nov. 27, 1866	59, 969
Capstan and windlass	I. G. Morgan	Ithaca, N. Y	Oct. 20, 1863	40, 352
Capstan and windlass and cable-stopper, Ship's	J. Grylls	Portsea, England	Dec. 12, 1842	2, 876
Capstan and windlass, Arrangement of ship's	J. Reed	Marshfield, Mass	June 20, 1854	11, 139
Capstan and windlass, Combined	J. S. Getchell	Machias, Me	May 14, 1861	32, 284
Capstan and windlass, Ship's	J. Emerson	Worcester, Mass	June 17, 1856	15, 123
Capstan for ships, Compound	C. Perley	New York, N. Y	Aug. 4, 1857	17, 940
Capstan for ships, Rail	W. H. Willard	Cleveland, Ohio	Aug. 11, 1863	39, 518
Capstan, Portable	E. G. Ament	Oswego, Ill	Sept. 13, 1864	44, 268
Capstan, Portable	G. Cook	Bristol Station, Ill	May 28, 1861	32, 414
Capstan, Power	D. N. B. Coffin, jr	Boston, Mass	Nov. 21, 1865	51, 107
Capstan, Reversible	J. A. H. Ellis and A. Gordon	Rochester, N. Y	June 27, 1854	11, 156
Capstan, Ship's	R. Dunbar and J. F. Robertson	Buffalo, N. Y	June 30, 1857	17, 715
Capstan, Ship's	S. Gaty	Saint Louis, Mo	May 27, 1856	14, 983
Capstan, Ship's	I. F. Holloway	Saline Mines, Ill	June 28, 1859	24, 558
Capstan, Ship's	J. B. Holmes	New York, N. Y	July 17, 1855	13, 262
Capstan, Ship's	J. B. Holmes	New York, N. Y	Mar. 3, 1857	16, 774
Capstan, Ship's	S. Huse	New York, N. Y	Aug. 11, 1857	17, 969
Capstan, Ship's	D. Knowlton	Camden, Me	Aug. 11, 1857	17, 971
Capstan, Ship's	D. Knowlton	Camden, Me	June 21, 1859	24, 467
Capstan, Ship's	C. E. Marwick	Portland, Me	Aug. 25, 1857	18, 053
Capstan, Ship's	C. Oaks	Rochester, N. Y	May 16, 1835	....
Capstan, Ship's	C. Perley	New York, N. Y	Oct. 21, 1856	15, 933
Capstan, Ship's	C. Perley	New York, N. Y	Mar. 5, 1861	31, 619
Capstan, Ship's	D. and G. Tallcot	Oswego, N. Y	Mar. 4, 1856	14, 377
Capstan, Ship's	D. and G. Tallcot	Oswego, N. Y	May 27, 1856	14, 986
Capstan, Ship's	J. R. Taylor	New York, N. Y	Apr. 27, 1858	20, 131
Capstan, Ship's	I. Wilson and F. D. Beckwith	New London, Conn	June 15, 1837	238
Capstan, Steamboat	J. Schaffer	Manchester, Pa	Oct. 21, 1856	15, 954
Capstan, Steamboat	J. Schaffer	West Manchester, Pa	Mar. 31, 1857	16, 935
Caps an, Steam-working	J. S. McMillin	Pittsburgh, Pa	Feb. 20, 1866	52, 739
Capstan, Variable	J. E. Andrews	Boston, Mass	Apr. 24, 1849	6, 396
Capstan, Winch	D. Knowlton	Camden, Me	June 19, 1866	55, 673
Capstans of vessels, Application of steam-power to	J. S. McMillin	Pittsburgh, Pa	Apr. 16, 1867	63, 917
Capstans, Purchase for	J. Edgecomb	Gardiner, Me	Mar. 28, 1871	113, 032
Capsules, Machine for making plated	J. J. Baranowski	London, England	Apr. 1, 1873	137, 403
Capsules, Manufacture of	D. Dick	New York, N. Y	Aug. 8, 1865	49, 242
Capsules, Metallic	W. Betts	City Road, England	Sept. 3, 1861	33, 179
Capsules of copaiba, Making	P. Cauhaupe	New Lebanon, N. Y	Dec. 24, 1861	33, 983
Car, Aërial	W. Morrow	San Francisco, Cal	Mar. 30, 1869	88, 324
Car, Aërial steam	F. Marriott	San Francisco, Cal	Nov. 23, 1869	97, 100
Car and cable coupling	W. S. Nearing	Morris Run, Pa	Dec. 31, 1872	134, 437
Car and carriage axles and boxes, Railway	D. C. Force and F. Davis	Baltimore, Md	Nov. 6, 1834	....
Car and carriage wheels, Chilling	P. Davis	Baltimore, Md	July 29, 1834	....

Index of patents issued from the United States Patent Office from 1790 *to* 1873, *inclusive*—Continued.

Invention.	Inventor.	Residence.	Date.	No.
Car and driving-wheel, Railway	N. C. Lombard	Cambridge, Mass	Sept. 4, 1869	95, 122
Car and dwelling ventilator	J. Bradley	New York, N. Y	Apr. 25, 1871	114, 1[illegible]2
Car and engine wheels, Constructing railway	J. Stimpson	Baltimore, Md	Oct. 23, 1834	....
Car and locomotive axles, Mode of strengthening railway.	Z. Durkee	Philadelphia, Pa	Jan. 9, 1838	549
Car and locomotive-engine wheel	R. Winans	Baltimore, Md	Nov. 19, 1833	....
Car and mail-bag receiver, Mail	W. G. Sanford	Union City, N. Y	May 26, 1868	78, 331
Car and school seat	W. H. Joeckel	New York, N. Y	Dec. 10, 1861	33, 887
Car and switch, Railway	I. N. Stanley	Philadelphia, Pa	Mar. 12, 1840	1, 512
Car and tender loading apparatus	J. Williams	Bell's Depot, Tenn	Dec. 26, 1871	122, 207
Car and track, Coal	G. Martz	Pottsville, Pa	Nov. 23, 1869	97, 207
Car and track for elevating on inclined plane	J. W. Pearce	Suisun, Cal	Sept. 1, 1868	81, 677
Car and truck connection	J. J. Sherman	Albany, N. Y	Apr. 14, 1863	38, 182
Car and truck, Railway	W. Youmans	Lansingburgh, N. Y	Nov. 12, 1872	133, 001
Car and truck-wheel, Coal	J. Patterson	Pittsburgh, Pa	Mar. 15, 1870	100, 795
Car and vehicle spring	W. R. Nichols and C. W. Pickering.	Philadelphia, Pa	Apr. 26, 1870	102, 422
Car and window washer	P. S. Devlan	Jersey City, N. J	Feb. 25, 1873	136, 310
Car apron or duster and bridge, Railway	W. H. Ward	Auburn, N. Y	Nov. 26, 1867	71, 558
Car-axle	B. Ahrens and D. Gerhard	Reading, Pa	Sept. 16, 1873	142, 757
Car-axle	J. Anthony	Greenbush, N. Y	Dec. 24, 1867	72, 584
Car-axle	F. A. Braymer and M. W. Lyman.	Chicago, Ill	Dec. 24, 1872	134, 247
Car-axle	W. A. Brickill	New York, N. Y	July 9, 1867	66, 556
Car-axle	L. Brown and J. and J. Leland	Worcester, Mass	Apr. 24, 1860	27, 966
Car-axle	S. S. Burt	Marquette, Mich	Nov. 12, 1867	70, 799
Car-axle	J. W. Clark	Manchester, Wis	Nov. 7, 1865	50, 796
Car-axle	R. Cromelien	Washington, D. C	July 7, 1868	79, 555
Car-axle	W. B. Fahnestock	Lancaster, Pa	May 19, 1868	77, 968
Car-axle	M. P. Hadley	Bluffton, Wis	June 11, 1872	127, 868
Car-axle	J. W. Herd	Decorah, Iowa	Mar. 28, 1865	47, 015
Car-axle	J. W. Hard	Decorah, Iowa	Mar. 26, 1872	125, 046
Car-axle	B. J. La Mothe	New York, N. Y	Sept. 27, 1864	44, 434
Car-axle	G. W. Miltimore	Janesville, Wis	Dec. 10, 1872	133, 790
Car-axle	G. W. Miltimore	Janesville, Wis	Nov. 4, 1873	144, 347
Car-axle	H. Mooers	Toledo, Ohio	Feb. 16, 1869	86, 937
Car-axle	W. Phelps	Sycamore, Ill	July 3, 1860	29, 001
Car-axle	T. R. Timby	Tarrytown, N. Y	Mar. 11, 1873	136, 791
Car-axle	C. D. Tisdale	East Boston, Mass	Aug. 11, 1863	39, 533
Car-axle	E. H. Williamson	Philadelphia, Pa	June 18, 1872	128, 084
Car-axle adjustment	R. Eaton	Eaton Lodge, England	Feb. 1, 1870	9 , 418
Car-axle and axle-box	G. H. Perry and C. B. Hawley	Salt Lake City, Utah	Oct. 8, 1872	132, 100
Car-axle and wheel	J. Montgomery	Croton, N. Y	June 2, 1868	78, 467
Car-axle bearing	L. Brauer	Washington, D. C	Oct. 12, 1869	95, 867
Car-axle bearing, Railway	E. D. Murfey	New York, N. Y	June 27, 1871	116, 475
Car-axle cap	W. Werts	Pana, Ill	June 9, 1868	78, 776
Car-axle, Divided	S. S. Hickok	Methuen, Mass	July 30, 1872	130, 047
Car-axle, Divided	D. B. Hunt	San Francisco, Cal	May 4, 1869	89, 767
Car-axle, Divided	J. K. Nelson	Green Point, N. Y	Nov. 10, 1868	83, 991
Car-axle, Divided	R. Vose	New York, N. Y	Apr. 22, 1856	14, 747
Car-axle, Divided railway	W. S. Loughborough	Victor, N. Y	June 22, 1852	9, 056
Car-axle, Hollow	W. A. Lewis	Chicago, Ill	Oct. 10, 1871	119, 866
Car axle, Railway	R. N. Allen	Pittsford, Vt	May 27, 1873	139, 226
Car axle, Railway	J. Armstrong	New Orleans, La	Mar. 16, 1869	87, 818
Car axle, Railway	H. D. Burghardt	Pittsfield, Mass	Aug. 17, 1869	93, 671
Car axle, Railway	C. Cole	Troy, N. Y	Mar. 15, 1870	100, 860
Car axle, Railway	D. M. Cummings	Enfield, N. H	June 15, 1869	91, 424
Car axle, Railway	J. H. Dinsmore	Boston, Mass	June 11, 1872	127, 857
Car axle, Railway	E. Doty and G. W. Miltimore	Janesville, Wis	Oct. 10, 1871	119, 831
Car axle, Railway	S. H. Dubois	Buffalo, N. Y	Jan. 6, 1863	37, 280
Car axle, Railway	R. Dutch	Jersey City, N. J	July 13, 1869	92, 592
Car axle, Railway	A. E. Elmer	Greenfield, Mass	Jan. 15, 1867	61, 180
Car axle, Railway	P. G. Gardiner	New York, N. Y	Feb. 12, 1856	14, 232
Car axle, Railway	C. P. Hewett	Kingston, Wis	May 16, 1865	47, 723
Car axle, Railway	F. Hudner	New York, N. Y	Jan. 25, 1870	99, 195
Car axle, Railway	E. T. Ligon	Demopolis, Ala	Mar. 9, 1869	87, 687
Car axle, Railway	E. J. Mallett	New York, N. Y	Nov. 22, 1859	26, 194
Car axle, Railway	J. E. McConnell	Wolverton, England	Oct. 31, 1854	11, 869
Car axle, Railway	N. Miller and E. Bancroft	Franklin, Mass., and Providence, R. I.	Dec. 15, 1843	3, 377
Car axle, Railway	J. Montgomery	Baltimore, Md	Apr. 24, 1860	28, 004
Car axle, Railway	J. C. Nye	Cincinnati, Ohio	Mar. 29, 1864	42, 105
Car axle, Railway	A. E. Smith	Bronxville, N. Y	Jan. 8, 1861	31, 092
Car axle, Railway	F. Sturneyk	Saint Paul, Minn	Aug. 23, 1870	106, 635
Car axle, Railway	T. C. Theaker	New York, N. Y	Apr. 15, 1873	137, 977
Car axle, Railway	L. E. Truesdell	Chicago, Ill	Mar. 22, 1870	101, 187
Car axle, Railway	J. Van Slooten	New Orleans, La	May 18, 1869	90, 321
Car-axle-straightening apparatus	B. S. Shoter	Whistler, Ala	Jan. 18, 1870	99, 014
Car-axles and bearings, Mode of oiling	B. D. Stevens	Lawrence, Mass	June 23, 1863	39, 017
Car-axles and shafts, Construction of	J. Montgomery	Croton Landing, N. Y	Feb. 14, 1871	111, 862
Car axles, Automatic lubricator for railway	W. Baker	Utica, N. Y	Aug. 11, 1857	17, 957
Car axles, Automatic lubricator for railway	A. B. Latta	Cincinnati, Ohio	Aug. 11, 1857	17, 972
Car axles, Box and journal for railway	I. P. Wendell	Philadelphia, Pa	Mar. 2, 1858	19, 530
Car axles, Box-case and lubricator for railway	G. W. and J. C. Geisendorff	Cincinnati, Ohio	Apr. 6, 1858	19, 840
Car-axles, Machine for determining the load of	J. H. Erhardt	Dresden, Saxony	Feb. 13, 1866	52, 653
Car-axles, Machine for rolling	T. Cooper	Cincinnati, Ohio	Oct. 17, 1865	50, 458
Car-axles, Oil-box for	J. F. Sharp	Wilmington, Del	Mar. 16, 1869	87, 880
Car axles, Oil-box for	T. B. Stewart	Hartford, Conn	May 31, 1870	103, 676
Car-axles or shaftings, Bearing for	C. Williams	Adrian, Mich	Feb. 9, 1864	41, 563
Car-axles, Preventing consequences of breaking	J. S. Kite	Philadelphia, Pa	July 14, 1834	....
Car-axles, Ribbed metal plates to construct hollow	W. A. Lewis	Chicago, Ill	Mar. 19, 1872	124, 834
Car-axles with boxes, Device for connecting	T. Pritchard	Philadelphia, Pa	June 24, 1873	140, 303
Car, Barrel	W. A. Plantz	Iowa Falls, Iowa	May 23, 1871	115, 097
Car-basket racks, Mode of attaching	M. Tower	Boston, Mass	July 11, 1871	116, 891
Car basket, Railway	J. F. Hudson	East Cambridge, Mass	July 1, 1873	140, 534
Car basket, Railway	M. Tower	Boston, Mass	Nov. 14, 1871	121, 024
Car-bodies and trucks, Connecting and disconnecting.	C. D. Tisdale	Boston, Mass	June 10, 1873	139, 835

Index of patents issued from the United States Patent Office from 1790 to 1873, inclusive—Continued.

Invention.	Inventor.	Residence.	Date.	No.
Car-bodies, Hanging	L. B. Thyng	Lowell, Mass	Nov. 18, 1845	4,276
Car bodies, Mode of supporting railway	R. Imlay	Philadelphia, Pa	Sept. 21, 1837	389
Car-bodies with trucks, Mode of connecting	C. S. Moore	Alexandria, Va	July 3, 1860	28,995
Car-body elevator, Railway	R. Wells	Jeffersonville, Ind	Sept. 7, 1869	94,680
Car body frame	S. Merrick	New Brighton, Pa	Apr. 2, 1867	63,548
Car-body, Iron	T. E. Warren	Troy, N. Y	Oct. 18, 1853	10,142
Car body, Railway	G. S. Hacker	Charleston, S. C	Jan. 21, 1841	1,937
Car body, Railway	R. L. Omensetter	Philadelphia, Pa	May 28, 1872	127,186
Car boiler and engine, Street	W. Baxter	Newark, N. J	Nov. 14, 1871	120,930
Car bolster, Railway	J. Marquis and J. W. Kimmel	Crestline, Ohio	May 28, 1867	65,098
Car bolt, Freight	C. E. Shanahan	South Bend, Ind	Nov. 5, 1872	132,739
Car box case and pedestal, Railway	J. C. Geisendorff	Cincinnati, Ohio	July 13, 1858	20,871
Car box, Railway	G. F. Lynch	Milwaukee, Wis	Jan. 23, 1866	52,181
Car box, Railway	D. Matthew	Philadelphia, Pa	Jan. 12, 1858	19,095
Car box, Railway	I. P. Wendell	Philadelphia, Pa	Oct. 16, 1866	58,927
Car-brake	A. M. Allen	New York, N. Y	Jan. 11, 1870	98,731
Car-brake	A. I. Ambler	Chicago, Ill	Sept. 22, 1863	40,005
Car-brake	A. I. Ambler	Chicago, Ill	Aug. 30, 1864	44,036
Car-brake	W. W. Babcock	Harmar, Ohio	Oct. 27, 1868	83,442
Car-brake	W. Ball	Oregon, Mo	June 25, 1872	128,277
Car-brake	J. L. Barnes	Etna Green, Ind	Oct. 15, 1867	69,892
Car-brake	W. T. Batty	Canton, Ohio	Apr. 28, 1868	77,159
Car-brake	J. H. Beatty	Franklin, Pa	Jan. 19, 1869	85,987
Car-brake	C. Bemis	Mishawaka, Ind	Jan. 1, 1867	60,850
Car-brake	W. P. Blades	Baltimore, Md	July 14, 1868	79,805
Car-brake	V. W. Blanchard	Bridport, Vt	Mar. 13, 1866	53,106
Car-brake	A. A. Bliven	Jersey City, N. J	Mar. 30, 1869	88,438
Car-brake	G. W. Bridgman	Somerville, Mass	June 11, 1861	32,549
Car-brake	J. F. Brode	Memphis, Tenn	Nov. 21, 1871	121,150
Car-brake	J. M. Brown	Cincinnati, Ohio	July 22, 1862	35,967
Car-brake	W. H. Browne and W. M. Pegram.	Baltimore, Md	Mar. 11, 1873	136,581
Car-brake	J. N. Brush	Olmstead County, Minn	Apr. 22, 1873	138,126
Car-brake	W. H. Burke	Brighton, Mass	Mar. 17, 1868	75,518
Car-brake	G. E. Burt	Harvard, Mass	Nov. 6, 1866	59,355
Car-brake	W. L. Burt	Boston, Mass	Aug. 1, 1865	49,082
Car-brake	J. A. Campbell	South Boston, Mass	Feb. 4, 1868	73,950
Car-brake	F. A. Canfield	Dover, N. J	Jan. 9, 1872	122,564
Car-brake	F. M. Chapman	New York, N. Y	Dec. 3, 1872	133,629
Car-brake	L. Clark	Pine Island, Minn	June 23, 1868	79,206
Car-brake	J. Cockshoot, jr., and H. Weatherill.	Manchester, Great Britain	Oct. 13, 1868	83,042
Car-brake	J. M. Collins	New Bedford, Mass	Mar. 7, 1865	46,642
Car-brake	G. W. Combs	Canandaigua, N. Y	Apr. 14, 1868	76,715
Car-brake	T. B. Comins, jr	Lowell, Mass	Sept. 10, 1867	68,700
Car-brake	T. B. Comins, jr	Lowell, Mass	Sept. 10, 1867	68,701
Car-brake	W. G. Creamer	Brooklyn, N. Y	Jan. 21, 1868	73,509
Car-brake	D. S. Cross	Cincinnati, Ohio	Feb. 3, 1863	37,568
Car-brake	J. Davis	Allegheny City, Pa	May 29, 1866	55,067
Car-brake	J. Davis	Allegheny City, Pa	Aug. 20, 1867	67,962
Car-brake	S. Davis	Dartmouth, Mass	Dec. 10, 1867	71,856
Car-brake	F. Dengler	North Vernon, Ind	Jan. 7, 1868	72,984
Car-brake	P. S. Devlan	Elizabethport, N. J	July 9, 1861	32,758
Car-brake	J. D'homergue	New York, N. Y	Dec. 20, 1853	10,336
Car-brake	D. Dick and O. W. Preston, jr	Corning, N. Y	Jan. 7, 1868	72,985
Car-brake	S. R. Dimmock	Syracuse, N. Y	Aug. 8, 1865	49,243
Car-brake	S. F. Dimock	Spencer, Ohio	May 7, 1867	64,409
Car-brake	D. H. Dotterer	Philadelphia, Pa	Dec. 22, 1868	85,374
Car-brake	W. H. Dunham and J. Widney	Allegheny City, Pa	Dec. 3, 1867	71,591
Car-brake	E. H. Dunn	Paris, France	Dec. 3, 1867	71,720
Car-brake	W. Ebbitt	New York, N. Y	Jan. 23, 1872	123,003
Car-brake	W. Ebbitt	New York, N. Y	June 24, 1873	140,260
Car-brake	J. B. Ellinwood	Hillsborough, N. H	Sept. 26, 1848	5,807
Car-brake	E. Farnsworth	Tipton, Pa	Apr. 22, 1873	138,141
Car-brake	A. W. Filer and L. T. Hatfield	Danby, Ill	Aug. 29, 1871	118,443
Car-brake	N. B. Forrest	Auburn, N. Y	July 3, 1866	56,030
Car-brake	W. S. Foster	Foster's Crossing, Ohio	Dec. 10, 1872	133,844
Car-brake	J. W. Gibbs	New Haven, Conn	Apr. 17, 1866	53,971
Car-brake	J. C. Gibson	Sacramento, Cal	Sept. 24, 1872	131,678
Car-brake	H. A. Goodman	Omaha, Neb	Aug. 2, 1870	106,052
Car-brake	W. D. Goodnow	Albany, N. Y	Oct. 18, 1864	44,718
Car-brake	M. W. Griswold	New York, N. Y	Aug. 9, 1870	106,152
Car-brake	S. Guilbert	New York, N. Y	May 1, 1866	54,333
Car-brake	C. H. Gustin	Worcester, Mass	July 18, 1865	48,810
Car-brake	O. J. Hardgrove	Canton, Ohio	Feb. 27, 1866	52,848
Car-brake	E. P. Harrington	Volusia, N. Y	Nov. 11, 1873	144,537
Car-brake	S. E. Harrison	New Haven, Conn	May 28, 1872	127,233
Car-brake	G. H. Henkel	Middletown, Ohio	Apr. 24, 1866	54,152
Car-brake	A. C. Herron	West Farms, N. Y	Feb. 12, 1861	31,387
Car-brake	A. Higley	South Bend, Ind	Dec. 18, 1866	60,515
Car-brake	A. Higley	South Bend, Ind	Feb. 19, 1867	62,198
Car-brake	A. Higley	South Bend, Ind	Feb. 19, 1867	62,199
Car-brake	A. Higley	South Bend, Ind	Mar. 12, 1867	62,847
Car-brake	J. Hirst	Jamaica, N. Y	Dec. 1, 1868	84,490
Car-brake	J. Hough and J. Moore	Buckingham and Bart, Pa	Dec. 14, 1858	22,291
Car-brake	R. Hurd	Morrison, Ill	June 28, 1870	104,738
Car-brake	J. W. Jacobs	Jeffersonville, Ind	Mar. 12, 1872	124,581
Car-brake	E. F. Jewett	Plainville, Ohio	May 1, 1860	28,087
Car-brake	G. N. Jones	Oshkosh, Wis	Sept. 22, 1868	82,324
Car-brake	M. Karg	Albany, N. Y	Nov. 18, 1873	144,681
Car-brake	J. Katzenberg	New York, N. Y	Dec. 31, 1867	72,861
Car-brake	W. R. and H. E. Kay	Westerly, R. I	June 25, 1861	32,665
Car-brake	P. Kefler	Reading, Pa	Dec. 18, 1860	30,946
Car-brake	P. Keffer	Reading, Pa	Oct. 27, 1868	83,508
Car-brake	T. A. Kelley	Cleveland, Ohio	Nov. 26, 1867	71,391
Car-brake	W. H. Kilburn	Kennedy, N. Y	June 19, 1866	55,670
Car-brake	W. Kimball	Woburn, Mass	June 18, 1872	127,979
Car-brake	J. L. Knowlton	Sharon Hill, Pa	Mar. 25, 1873	137,079

Index of patents issued from the United States Patent Office from 1790 *to* 1873, *inclusive*—Continued.

Invention.	Inventor.	Residence.	Date.	No.
Car-brake	A. Langellier	Concord, N. H	Sept. 23, 1873	143, 083
Car-brake	C. B. Lashar	New York, N. Y	Dec. 24, 1861	34, 000
Car-brake	J. W. Latcher and W. J. Powell	Amsterdam, N. Y	Dec. 27, 1864	45, 617
Car-brake	S. M. Lee	New London, Iowa	Apr. 16, 1867	63, 909
Car-brake	S. M. Lee	New London, Iowa	July 28, 1868	80, 290
Car-brake	A. Z. Long	Scranton, Pa	Oct. 29, 1867	70, 235
Car-brake	G. F. Lynch	Milwaukee, Wis	Jan. 16, 1866	52, 063
Car-brake	G. F. Lynch	Milwaukee, Wis	Aug. 14, 1866	57, 161
Car-brake	S. Marden	Newton, Mass	Feb. 11, 1868	74, 235
Car-brake	J. McCabe	Rondout, N. Y	Jan. 23, 1872	123, 033
Car-brake	S. McCambridge	Philadelphia, Pa	Nov. 28, 1865	51, 204
Car-brake	S. McCambridge	Philadelphia, Pa	May 8, 1866	54, 573
Car-brake	S. McCambridge	Philadelphia, Pa	Feb. 5, 1867	61, 844
Car-brake	S. McCambridge	Philadelphia, Pa	July 28, 1868	80, 419
Car-brake	S. McCambridge and E. G. Martin.	Philadelphia, Pa	Sept. 18, 1866	58, 115
Car-brake	S. McCambridge and E. G. Martin.	Philadelphia, Pa	July 28, 1868	80, 420
Car-brake	H. A. Mears	Pecatonica, Ill	May 1, 1860	28, 098
Car-brake	G. L. Miller	De Witt, N. Y	Aug. 18, 1868	81, 192
Car-brake	G. S. Miller, E. B. Peck, and W. Olmsted.	Thompsonville, Bridgeport, and Thompsonville, Conn.	Feb. 23, 1864	41, 744
Car-brake	J. Mitchell	La Porte, Ind	Dec. 10, 1867	72, 069
Car-brake	J. H. Moore and J. E. Gary	Chicago, Ill	Feb. 11, 1868	74, 240
Car-brake	J. H. Moore and J. E. Gary	Chicago, Ill	Dec. 29, 1868	85, 326
Car-brake	W. E. Moore	Crawfordsville, Ind	Mar. 15, 1859	23, 259
Car-brake	B. Morahan	New York, N. Y	June 28, 1864	43, 370
Car-brake	W. T. Morrow	Chicago, Ill	Dec. 22, 1863	41, 042
Car-brake	D. Myers	Chicago, Ill	Jan. 30, 1866	52, 310
Car-brake	D. Myers	Chicago, Ill	Jan. 30, 1866	52, 311
Car-brake	D. Myers	Chicago, Ill	Jan. 30, 1866	52, 312
Car-brake	D. Myers	Chicago, Ill	Oct. 16, 1866	58, 877
Car-brake	D. Myers	Chicago, Ill	Dec. 4, 1866	60, 228
Car-brake	D. Myers	Chicago, Ill	June 30, 1868	79, 379
Car-brake	W. Naylor	Mildmay Park, England	Nov. 4, 1873	144, 351
Car-brake	W. Nelson	Flatbush, N. Y	Dec. 10, 1872	133, 879
Car-brake	H. W. Norvill	Livingston, Ala	Aug. 21, 1860	29, 712
Car-brake	G. F. Outten	Norfolk, Va	Oct. 25, 1859	25, 911
Car-brake	P. Pardee	New Haven, Conn	Jan. 1, 1867	60, 930
Car-brake	W. T. Parsons	Thomasville, Ga	June 9, 1868	78, 759
Car-brake	J. B. Pelton	Mount Pleasant, Md	Dec. 31, 1872	134, 484
Car-brake	J. B. Pelton	Mount Pleasant, Md	Nov. 18, 1873	144, 787
Car-brake	J. Pettingill, jr	Jackson, N. H	July 16, 1861	32, 841
Car-brake	G. Quick and J. N. Wallis	Fleming, N. Y	Nov. 26, 1867	71, 325
Car-brake	J. W. Reid	New York, N. Y	Sept. 18, 1866	58, 136
Car-brake	G. H. Reynolds	Parsons, Kans	Feb. 20, 1872	123, 840
Car-brake	J. W. Rice	Springfield, Mass	Apr. 23, 1867	64, 036
Car-brake	E. O. Richard	Quebec, Canada	Sept. 23, 1873	143, 187
Car-brake	D. T. Robinson	Boston, Mass	Mar. 27, 1866	53, 544
Car-brake	F. Root	Boston, Mass	Aug. 25, 1868	81, 411
Car-brake	A. M. Rouse	Saint Louis, Mo	Jan. 14, 1873	134, 934
Car-brake	J. B. Rumsey	Tiffin, Ohio	Mar. 13, 1866	53, 235
Car-brake	L. D. Rundell	South Westerlo, N. Y	Oct. 30, 1866	59, 273
Car-brake	W. H. M. Sanger	Bay Side, N. Y	Jan. 21, 1873	135, 161
Car-brake	A. H. Sassaman	Lebanon, Pa	June 23, 1868	79, 149
Car-brake	S. W. Y. Shimonsky	Cheyenne, Dak	Aug. 25, 1868	81, 414
Car-brake	G. H. Seymour	Newark, Ohio	Apr. 5, 1870	101, 667
Car-brake	J. Shannon	Cohoes, N. Y	May 6, 1873	138, 535
Car-brake	J. Sheward and G. A. Stanbery.	Dunkirk, N. Y	Apr. 23, 1867	64, 040
Car-brake	W. S. Shotwell	Paterson, N. J	Sept. 24, 1867	69, 262
Car-brake	T. E. Sickels	Kennett's Square, Pa	July 12, 1870	105, 264
Car-brake	C. W. Singer	Anderson Store, Va	Oct. 16, 1866	58, 956
Car-brake	L. S. Sisson	West Edmeston, N. Y	Dec. 15, 1868	85, 034
Car-brake	C. A. Smith	Jersey City, N. J	May 16, 1871	114, 983
Car-brake	J. L. Smith	Tuscola, Ill	Sept. 3, 1867	68, 519
Car-brake	J. W. W. Smith	Canton, Mo	Feb. 23, 1869	87, 214
Car-brake	W. H. Smith and J. Steger	New York, N. Y	Feb. 25, 1868	74, 860
Car-brake	C. Spofford	Boston, Mass	Nov. 12, 1867	70, 911
Car-brake	J. Steger	New York, N. Y	Oct. 27, 1868	83, 418
Car-brake	J. Steger	New York, N. Y	June 28, 1870	104, 897
Car-brake	E. Stiles	New York, N. Y	Apr. 14, 1868	76, 843
Car-brake	W. Stinehart and J. Taggart	Charlestown, Mass	Feb. 27, 1849	6, 150
Car-brake	B. Tatham and J. Steger	New York, N. Y	Oct. 27, 1868	83, 422
Car-brake	J. Temple	Selin's Grove, Pa	June 26, 1866	55, 964
Car-brake	J. Temple	Bellefonte, Pa	Jan. 30, 1872	123, 133
Car-brake	J. Temple	Mooresburgh, Pa	Aug. 5, 1873	141, 608
Car-brake	E. Thayer	Chatham, N. Y	Aug. 12, 1846	4, 690
Car-brake	S. H. Timmons	La Fayette, Ind	Dec. 4, 1866	60, 284
Car-brake	W. W. Todd and J. Vandercar	Brooklyn, N. Y	Sept. 19, 1865	50, 051
Car-brake	H. H. Trenor	New York, N. Y	Oct. 17, 1865	50, 517
Car-brake	H. H. Trenor	New York, N. Y	Aug. 7, 1866	57, 015
Car-brake	L. A. Velu and E. F. and L. E. A. Fosse.	Paris, France	Nov. 27, 1866	60, 094
Car-brake	I. H. Voorhies	Ypsilanti, Mich	Mar. 25, 1873	137, 264
Car-brake	J. N. Ward	Brooklyn, N. Y	Nov. 2, 1858	21, 996
Car-brake	W. Warinner	Creelsborough, Ky	Sept. 9, 1873	142, 658
Car-brake	W. Warner	Philadelphia, Pa	Mar. 20, 1866	53, 365
Car-brake	W. Warwick and H. C. Duggan	Pittsburgh, Pa	Nov. 4, 1873	144, 240
Car-brake	A. A. Weidemeyer	Williamsburgh, N. Y	Jan. 2, 1872	122, 419
Car-brake	J. White and T. Lingle	South Amboy, N. J	Mar. 10, 1868	75, 501
Car-brake	E. Whitehead	Cincinnati, Ohio	July 10, 1866	56, 302
Car-brake	T. J. Whitney	Whitpain Township, Pa	May 19, 1868	78, 166
Car-brake	J. G. Wiggin	Moultonville, N. H	Dec. 9, 1873	145, 470
Car-brake	W. E. Wilcox	Cleveland, Ohio	Feb. 6, 1866	52, 501
Car-brake	J. W. Williams	Somerville, N. J	Mar. 12, 1867	62, 912
Car-brake	J. F. Wood, 2d	Cohocton, N. Y	Oct. 22, 1867	70, 145

Index of patents issued from the United States Patent Office from 1790 *to* 1873, *inclusive*—Continued.

Invention.	Inventor.	Residence.	Date.	No.
Car-brake	T. C. Woods	Marion County, Ky	Aug. 25, 1868	81, 568
Car-brake	J. E. Worthman	Mobile, Ala	Dec. 10, 1872	133, 913
Car-brake	W. C. Wright	New York, N. Y	Jan. 15, 1861	31, 137
Car brake and starter	E. Bonneval	Boston, Mass	Mar. 14, 1871	112, 534
Car brake and starter	J. A. Cody	Cleveland, Ohio	May 9, 1871	114, 529
Car brake and starter	J. A. Cole	Adams, N. Y	July 27, 1869	93, 059
Car brake and starter	M. Henderson	Detroit, Mich	May 26, 1868	78, 371
Car brake and starter	R. Heneage	Buffalo, N. Y	Sept. 17, 1867	68, 875
Car brake and starter	C. M. Hinckley	Boston, Mass	Mar. 26, 1872	125, 049
Car brake and starter	C. L. Irving	Indianapolis, Ind	Apr. 27, 1869	89, 410
Car brake and starter	R. R. James	Rising Sun, Ind	July 2, 1872	128, 491
Car brake and starter	W. J. Johnson	New Orleans, La	Aug. 11, 1868	80, 964
Car brake and starter	E. P. Jones	Shell Mound, Miss	Mar. 15, 1870	100, 960
Car brake and starter	J. M. McMaster	Rochester, N. Y	July 6, 1869	92, 335
Car brake and starter	J. M. McMaster	Rochester, N. Y	Jan. 11, 1870	98, 788
Car brake and starter	C. D. Moody	Saint Louis, Mo	May 12, 1868	77, 903
Car brake and starter	D. M. Moore	Windsor, Vt	July 20, 1869	92, 869
Car brake and starter	J. Paradis	Brooklyn, N. Y	Mar. 21, 1871	112, 954
Car brake and starter	I. Rider	Indianapolis, Ind	Feb. 16, 1869	87, 068
Car brake and starter	L. J. Smith and D. S. Knight	Hamilton, Ohio, and New York, N. Y.	Apr. 28, 1868	77, 223
Car brake and starter	W. M. Starr	Washington, D. C	Oct. 24, 1871	120, 341
Car brake and starter	A. B. Vandemark	Phelps, N. Y	Feb. 9, 1869	86, 885
Car brake and starter	J. Wiley, 2d	South Reading, Mass	Nov. 19, 1867	71, 102
Car brake and starter	J. W. Wilson	New York, N. Y	Feb. 1, 1870	99, 509
Car brake and starter	J. S. Wood	Lansing, Mich	Aug. 4, 1868	80, 695
Car brake and starter, Combined	C. B. Broadwell	New Orleans, La	July 23, 1872	129, 782
Car brake and starter combined, Street	C. L. Irving	Indianapolis, Ind	Oct. 21, 1873	143, 909
Car brake and starter, Railway	R. R. Carpenter	Tippecanoe, Ohio	Mar. 30, 1869	88, 447
Car brake and starting apparatus	T. W. Murray	New York, N. Y	Sept. 3, 1867	68, 452
Car-brake apparatus, Steam-power	G. Westinghouse, jr	Pittsburgh, Pa	June 6, 1871	115, 667
Car-brake, Atmospheric	W. L. Chambers	Pleasant Unity, Pa	July 6, 1869	92, 265
Car-brake, Atmospheric	S. Marsh	Littleton, N. H	Apr. 12, 1870	101, 895
Car-brake attachment	J. Kirkley	Chicago, Ill	Sept. 22, 1868	82, 329
Car-brake, Automatic	J. R. Crabill	La Crosse, Ill	July 11, 1871	116, 814
Car-brake, Automatic	J. Hartman, jr	Philadelphia, Pa	Dec. 26, 1865	51, 715
Car-brake, Automatic	M. Wilkin and J. Clark	London, England	Mar. 15, 1870	100, 958
Car brake, Automatic railway	G. En-Earl	Boston, Mass	June 3, 1873	139, 557
Car brake, Automatic railway	P. R. Higley	Oshawa, Canada	Mar. 8, 1864	41, 890
Car brake, Automatic railway	W. R. Jackson	Baltimore, Md	Sept. 8, 1857	18, 150
Car-brake beam	D. Wellington	Virginia City, Nev	Dec. 16, 1873	145, 605
Car-brake block	B. De Vout	Harrisburgh, Pa	Dec. 5, 1865	51, 298
Car brake, Bumper railway	L. Brauer	Sommerville, Tenn	May 12, 1857	17, 257
Car-brake, Coal	D. Wetsel	Morris, Pa	May 20, 1873	139, 097
Car-brake, Eccentric	E. Morris	Bloomfield, N. J	Sept. 19, 1838	928
Car-brake, Electro-magnetic	F. F. A. Achard	Paris, France	Nov. 20, 1866	59, 805
Car-brake, Electro-magnetic	H. S. Daggett	La Fayette, Ind	July 11, 1871	116, 818
Car-brake, Electro-magnetic	J. Olmsted	Galesburgh, Ill	Apr. 27, 1869	89, 495
Car-brake, Electro-magnetic	J. Olmsted	Knoxville, Ill	Jan. 18, 1870	98, 880
Car-brake for city-railways	R. W. Jenks, jr., and F. A. Steere.	Providence, R. I	Apr. 17, 1860	27, 910
Car-brake for horse-railways	J. Stephenson	New York N. Y	Feb. 23, 1869	87, 122
Car brake, Hand	J. McGinn	Norwalk, Ohio	Dec. 10, 1872	133, 872
Car brake, Horse	G. R. Barker	Germantown, Pa	Sept. 17, 1861	33, 287
Car brake, Horse	J. Stephenson	New York, N. Y	Dec. 27, 1859	26, 626
Car brake, Hydraulic	J. F. Taylor	Charleston, S. C	Nov. 11, 1873	144, 578
Car-brake, Hydraulic or air	W. M. Henderson	Philadelphia, Pa	Oct. 28, 1873	143, 980
Car brake, Hydraulic railway	W. M. Henderson	Philadelphia, Pa	Aug. 12, 1873	141, 790
Car-brake, Iron	S. Morse	Springfield, Mass	Sept. 6, 1853	10, 004
Car-brake, Magnetic	J. Olmstead	Knoxville, Ill	Jan. 8, 1867	61, 089
Car-brake pipe, Atmospheric	G. Westinghouse, jr	Pittsburgh, Pa	Nov. 29, 1870	109, 695
Car-brake, Pneumatic	D. Myers and A. B. Pullman	Chicago, Ill	Nov. 1, 1870	108, 932
Car-brake, Propelling	R. Heneage	Buffalo, N. Y	Feb. 26, 1867	62, 419
Car brake, Railway	L. Adams	Mattoon, Ill	Oct. 28, 1873	144, 013
Car brake, Railway	A. M. Allen	New York, N. Y	June 15, 1869	91, 404
Car brake, Railway	A. I. Ambler	Milwaukee, Wis	Apr. 1, 1862	34, 855
Car brake, Railway	A. I. Ambler	Milwaukee, Wis	May 27, 1862	35, 408
Car brake, Railway	A. I. Ambler	Milwaukee, Wis	June 17, 1862	35, 647
Car brake, Railway	A. I. Ambler	Milwaukee, Wis	June 24, 1862	35, 727
Car brake, Railway	A. I. Ambler	Chicago, Ill	Sept. 22, 1863	40, 007
Car brake, Railway	J. S. Anderson	Flintville, Wis	June 3, 1873	139, 527
Car brake, Railway	F. Armstrong	New Orleans, La	Aug. 9, 1859	24, 981
Car brake, Railway	D. Arndt and D. C. Washington	Cleveland, Ohio	Sept. 19, 1871	119, 103
Car brake, Railway	S. and W. W. Balkwill	Cleveland, Ohio	July 30, 1872	129, 860
Car brake, Railway	V. Barnes	Washington, D. C	Mar. 11, 1856	14, 385
Car brake, Railway	L. B. Batcheller	Arlington, Vt	Jan. 24, 1854	10, 440
Car brake, Railway	F. G. Bates	Springfield, Mass	Feb. 18, 1873	136, 019
Car brake, Railway	A. Bean	Dedham, Mass	Mar. 6, 1860	27, 344
Car brake, Railway	N. Berkeley	Aldie, Va	Aug. 3, 1869	93, 166
Car brake, Railway	J. T. Blois	Jonesville, Mich	Apr. 20, 1869	89, 014
Car brake, Railway	M. S. Borthwick	Montana, Iowa	Nov. 9, 1869	96, 542
Car brake, Railway	J. L., I., and D. W. Branch	Charleston, S. C	Jan. 5, 1858	19, 012
Car brake, Railway	F. E. Canda	Chicago, Ill	May 16, 1865	47, 700
Car brake, Railway	J. H. Champlin	Essex, Conn	Jan. 24, 1865	45, 975
Car brake, Railway	H. E. Chapman	Albany, N. Y	Dec. 7, 1858	22, 229
Car brake, Railway	S. F. Clonser	Salt Lake City, Utah	July 23, 1872	129, 789
Car brake, Railway	H. M. Collier	Binghamton, N. Y	June 29, 1858	20, 769
Car brake, Railway	M. P. Coons	Brooklyn, N. Y	Aug. 15, 1854	11, 517
Car brake, Railway	W. E. Cooper	Dunkirk, N. Y	Apr. 12, 1859	23, 663
Car brake, Railway	W. G. Creamer	New York, N. Y	Nov. 4, 1856	16, 004
Car brake, Railway	J. M. Crosby	Marathon, N. Y	Aug. 24, 1869	94, 083
Car brake, Railway	J. M. Crosby and W. Ballard	Caroline, N. Y	Feb. 8, 1870	99, 539
Car brake, Railway	D. S. Cross	Cincinnati, Ohio	Apr. 4, 1865	47, 091
Car brake, Railway	G. W. Crowe	Cincinnati, Ohio	July 1, 1873	140, 349
Car brake, Railway	C. D. Culver	Mauch Chunk, Pa	Dec. 29, 1868	85, 369
Car brake, Railway	G. W. Cummings	Philadelphia, Pa	June 1, 1858	20, 468
Car brake, Railway	J. Darling	Whistler, Ala	Apr. 16, 1872	125, 665
Car brake, Railway	M. F. Daugherty	Portsmouth, Va	Oct. 3, 1871	119, 582

Index of patents issued from the United States Patent Office from 1790 *to* 1873, *inclusive*—Continued.

Invention.	Inventor.	Residence.	Date.	No.
Car brake, Railway	H. Davis	Baltimore, Md	Sept. 13, 1859	25, 392
Car brake, Railway	J. Davis	Allegheny City, Pa	Oct. 20, 1863	40, 332
Car brake, Railway	J. Davis	Allegheny City, Pa	June 7, 1864	43, 010
Car brake, Railway	D. Derr	Bellefonte, Pa	Feb. 26, 1861	31, 583
Car brake, Railway	S. R. Dimock	Pittsfield, Mass	Dec. 9, 1862	37, 088
Car brake, Railway	G. Dorsch	Schenectady, N. Y	Apr. 13, 1858	19, 917
Car brake, Railway	C. B. Eaton	Grafton, Ill	June 20, 1871	116, 169
Car brake, Railway	C. H. Eisenbrandt	Baltimore, Md	May 25, 1858	20, 339
Car brake, Railway	D. M. Elder	Monmouth, Ill	Feb. 8, 1870	99, 545
Car brake, Railway	J. F. Elder	Blairsville, Pa	Jan. 28, 1873	135, 212
Car brake, Railway	R. M. Evans	Laconia, N. H	Apr. 8, 1856	14, 640
Car brake, Railway	K. Exeter, sr	Munich, Bavaria	July 30, 1872	130, 029
Car brake, Railway	K. Exeter, sr	Munich, Bavaria	July 30, 1872	130, 030
Car brake, Railway	D. H. Fegor	Cincinnati, Ohio	Mar. 23, 1858	19, 734
Car brake, Railway	F. M. Finnell	Covington, Ky	Nov. 29, 1870	109, 727
Car brake, Railway	W. G. Foster	Apalachin, N. Y	Feb. 1, 1870	99, 424
Car brake, Railway	E. D. B. Freer	Lima Centre, Mich	Oct. 26, 1869	96, 098
Car brake, Railway	M. S. Frost	Detroit, Mich	June 3, 1856	15, 038
Car brake, Railway	J. C. Gove	Cleveland, Ohio	Apr. 4, 1871	113, 290
Car brake, Railway	S. Gumaer	Chicago, Ill	Jan. 26, 1858	19, 192
Car brake, Railway	J. T. Guthrie	Pittsburgh, Pa	Dec. 29, 1868	85, 302
Car brake, Railway	W. Hall	North Adams, Mass	July 20, 1852	9, 135
Car brake, Railway	D. Harrigan	Winchester, Mass	Nov. 4, 1856	16, 011
Car brake, Railway	O. J. Harrington	Manchester, Pa	Mar. 15, 1864	41, 917
Car brake, Railway	O. J. Harrington	Manchester, Pa	Apr. 5, 1864	42, 189
Car brake, Railway	A. Higley	South Bend, Ind	Aug. 14, 1866	57, 133
Car brake, Railway	A. Higley	Cleveland, Ohio	Apr. 12, 1870	101, 874
Car brake, Railway	L. Hill and S. D. Tripp	Stoneham and Lynn, Mass	Mar. 7, 1871	112, 456
Car brake, Railway	R. W. Hix	New York, N. Y	Dec. 11, 1860	30, 921
Car brake, Railway	B. Holly	Seneca Falls, N. Y	Feb. 10, 1852	8, 730
Car brake, Railway	T. Hopper	Newark, N. J	June 1, 1858	20, 429
Car brake, Railway	T. and H. Hopper and C. C. Coats.	Newark, N. J	June 7, 1870	103, 886
Car brake, Railway	J. C. Hosmer	Boston, Mass	Apr. 30, 1872	126, 208
Car brake, Railway	G. Hotchkiss	Windsor, N. Y	Mar. 20, 1855	12, 552
Car brake, Railway	J. Hough	Buckingham, Pa	Apr. 14, 1863	38, 166
Car brake, Railway	J. Houston and E. Ross	Manchester, N. H	July 20, 1852	9, 141
Car brake, Railway	E. N. Huntsman	Allegheny, Pa	Feb. 8, 1870	99, 678
Car brake, Railway	M. Ingersoll	Grafton, Ohio	Mar. 6, 1866	53, 006
Car brake, Railway	E. P. Jones	Shell Mound, Miss	Mar. 15, 1870	100, 900
Car brake, Railway	J. Jones	Utica, N. Y	July 29, 1862	36, 007
Car brake, Railway	J. Jones	West Albany, N. Y	Sept. 12, 1865	49, 885
Car brake, Railway	E. M. Judd	New Britain, Conn	Dec. 9, 1862	37, 098
Car brake, Railway	L. Kirk	Reading, Pa	May 10, 1859	23, 923
Car brake, Railway	J. J. Kiser	Middletown, Ind	Oct. 26, 1869	96, 240
Car brake, Railway	J. and W. Kitchen and S. Samuels.	Accrington, England	Nov. 26, 1867	71, 392
Car brake, Railway	B. Kraft	Reading, Pa	Apr. 20, 1852	8, 899
Car brake, Railway	J. S. Lamar	Augusta, Ga	July 30, 1872	129, 968
Car brake, Railway	J. W. Latcher	Northville, N. Y	Feb. 14, 1865	46, 366
Car brake, Railway	C. H. Lathrop	Jersey City, N. J	Dec. 26, 1871	122, 264
Car brake, Railway	D. P. Léfebre and L. P. Dorre	France	Mar. 29, 1870	101, 280
Car brake, Railway	A. H. Lighthall	Albany, N. Y	May 10, 1870	102, 840
Car brake, Railway	H. A. Lincoln and H. T. Douglass.	New Haven, Conn	Aug. 2, 1859	24, 943
Car brake, Railway	J. P. Martin	Philadelphia, Pa	July 13, 1852	9, 116
Car brake, Railway	W. S. Martin	Waukegan, Ill	Dec. 22, 1863	41, 013
Car brake, Railway	A. F. McClone	Ellicott's Mills, Md	Apr. 25, 1865	47, 440
Car brake, Railway	J. W. McGlashan	Montreal, Canada	July 18, 1871	117, 190
Car brake, Railway	T. G. McLaughlin	Kensington, Pa	May 4, 1852	8, 924
Car brake, Railway	T. G. McLaughlin	Philadelphia, Pa	Aug. 15, 1854	11, 527
Car brake, Railway	T. J. Mead	Port Byron, N. Y	Sept. 6, 1859	25, 345
Car brake, Railway	G. H. Merriam	Portland, Me	Feb. 13, 1872	123, 718
Car brake, Railway	J. Mitchell	Osceola, Iowa	Aug. 18, 1857	18, 018
Car brake, Railway	W. Montgomery	Roxbury, Mass	July 6, 1852	9, 098
Car brake, Railway	G. W. Morris	Pittsburgh, Pa	May 6, 1873	138, 678
Car brake, Railway	J. Mulvey and C. Ohlemacher	Aurora, Ill	Sept. 3, 1861	33, 210
Car brake, Railway	D. Myers	South Bend, Ind	Dec. 23, 1862	37, 238
Car brake, Railway	D. Myers	South Bend, Ind	July 21, 1863	39, 306
Car brake, Railway	W. Naylor	Mildmay Park, England	July 23, 1872	129, 855
Car brake, Railway	M. P. Norton	Tinmouth, Vt	Nov. 7, 1854	11, 904
Car brake, Railway	S. Nunamaker	Osceola Mills, Pa	Aug. 13, 1872	130, 526
Car brake, Railway	M. Obermiller	Tiffin, Ohio	Jan. 3, 1860	26, 702
Car brake, Railway	J. Paradis	Brooklyn, N. Y	Oct. 24, 1871	120, 316
Car brake, Railway	L. Parker	Manchester Station, Conn	July 9, 1861	32, 783
Car brake, Railway	D. J. Parmele	San Francisco, Cal	Dec. 15, 1868	84, 963
Car brake, Railway	T. Payne	Detroit, Mich	Dec. 14, 1869	97, 800
Car brake, Railway	O. L. Pease and L. E. Skinner	Xenia and Cincinnati, Ohio	Jan. 4, 1870	98, 621
Car brake, Railway	W. Perkins	Plympton, Mass	July 19, 1859	24, 818
Car brake, Railway	W. D. Pope	Gadsden, Ala	Sept. 9, 1873	142, 649
Car brake, Railway	W. Portlock and J. R. Dodds	New London, Iowa	Nov. 3, 1868	83, 661
Car brake, Railway	N. Potter	Hillsdale, Mich	Feb. 2, 1858	19, 260
Car brake, Railway	I. N. Pyle	Decatur, Ind	Aug. 11, 1863	39, 495
Car brake, Railway	S. Randall	Centreville, R. I	Nov. 3, 1868	83, 728
Car brake, Railway	B. F. Reimer	Philadelphia, Pa	June 20, 1854	11, 138
Car brake, Railway	E. E. Rice	Hallowell, Me	June 26, 1855	13, 139
Car brake, Railway	J. L. G. Rice	Cambridge, Mass	Nov. 1, 1870	108, 830
Car brake, Railway	J. W. Rice	Springfield, Mass	Aug. 3, 1858	21, 086
Car brake, Railway	J. W. Rice	Springfield, Mass	Dec. 28, 1858	22, 455
Car brake, Railway	J. W. Rice	Springfield, Mass	June 29, 1869	92, 097
Car brake, Railway	H. T. Robbins	Lowell, Mass	Sept. 4, 1849	6, 689
Car brake, Railway	M. H. Rumpf	Paris, France	Oct. 20, 1868	83, 321
Car brake, Railway	L. A. Russell	Shrewsbury, Vt	Mar. 8, 1871	112, 499
Car brake, Railway	E. W. Sandford	Brooklyn, N. Y	Aug. 16, 1870	106, 412
Car brake, Railway	J. Schoenberr	Reading, Pa	Aug. 10, 1852	9, 189
Car brake, Railway	E. S. Scripture and J. H. Darrah.	Brooklyn, N. Y., and Aurora, Ill.	June 29, 1869	92, 104
Car brake, Railway	M. Shimer	Union Township, Pa	Dec. 5, 1854	12, 033

Index of patents issued from the United States Patent Office from 1790 *to* 1873, *inclusive*—Continued.

Invention.	Inventor.	Residence.	Date.	No.
Car brake, Railway	H. C. Sides	Baltimore, Md	July 12, 1843	3, 171
Car brake, Railway	E. Slater	Girard, Pa	Jan. 11, 1870	98, 716
Car brake, Railway	R. L. Smith	Philadelphia, Pa	Apr. 14, 1857	17, 058
Car brake, Railway	T. W. Smith	Alexandria, Va	Jan. 19, 1858	19, 157
Car brake, Railway	W. F. H. Smith	Milwaukee, Wis	Nov. 14, 1871	121, 013
Car brake, Railway	G. A. Somerby and C. W. Fogg.	Waltham, Mass	Aug. 14, 1855	13, 440
Car brake, Railway	W. Somerville, jr	Mitchell Station, Va	Aug. 21, 1860	29, 725
Car brake, Railway	L. Stebbins	Hinsdale, N. Y	Jan. 21, 1873	135, 017
Car brake, Railway	J. Steger	New York, N. Y	Jan. 25, 1870	99, 257
Car brake, Railway	F. A. Stevens	Burlington, Vt	Nov. 25, 1851	8, 552
Car brake, Railway	W. F. Stewart	Patuxent Forge, Md	Oct. 4, 1859	25, 708
Car brake, Railway	S. R. Stinard	Paterson, N. J	Oct. 19, 1869	96, 051
Car brake, Railway	J. W. Swales	San Francisco, Cal	Sept. 7, 1869	94, 525
Car brake, Railway	B. Tatham and J. Steger	New York, N. Y	June 8, 1869	91, 181
Car brake, Railway	A. Tatzel, sr., and F. Kinn	New York, N. Y	Mar. 26, 1872	124, 985
Car brake, Railway	B. O. Thompson	Chicago, Ill	Nov. 3, 1868	83, 674
Car brake, Railway	L. F. Thompson and A. G. Bachelder.	Charlestown and Lowell, Mass.	July 6, 1852	9, 109
Car brake, Railway	C. W. Tierney	Altoona, Pa	Feb. 7, 1871	111, 584
Car brake, Railway	A. F. Toulmir	Ellicott's Mills, Md	Nov. 29, 1859	26, 307
Car brake, Railway	F. Townsend	Albany, N. Y	July 6, 1869	92, 230
Car brake, Railway	I. Townsend	Capeville, Va	Nov. 21, 1871	121, 140
Car brake, Railway	L. W. Tracy	New York, N. Y	Mar. 21, 1871	112, 865
Car brake, Railway	L. Treadwell	New York, N. Y	Apr. 3, 1849	6, 273
Car brake, Railway	G. Trinks	Jersey City, N. J	Apr. 5, 1853	9, 655
Car brake, Railway	E. B. Turner	Providence, R. I	Mar. 13, 1860	27, 486
Car brake, Railway	A. P. Tutton	Reading, Pa	Apr. 19, 1859	23, 727
Car brake, Railway	J. B. Van Dyne	Nashville, Tenn	Dec. 7, 1869	97, 730
Car brake, Railway	E. P. Vinning	Grand Rapids, Mich	Apr. 12, 1870	101, 791
Car brake, Railway	R. M. Wade	Wadesville, Va	Apr. 7, 1857	17, 004
Car brake, Railway	W. B. Wait	Portsmouth, N. H	July 27, 1858	21, 058
Car brake, Railway	T. Walber	New York, N. Y	Mar. 16, 1852	8, 812
Car brake, Railway	I. Walker	Lynn, Mass	Sept. 7, 1869	94, 530
Car brake, Railway	J. N. Walker	Cincinnati, Ohio	Sept. 16, 1862	36, 489
Car brake, Railway	L. Watson	South Plymouth, Mich	Dec. 20, 1861	45, 545
Car brake, Railway	J. E. Weaver	Lancaster, Pa	Feb. 7, 1871	111, 591
Car brake, Railway	A. Wellshmidt	Albany, N. Y	Nov. 7, 1871	120, 603
Car brake, Railway	G. Westinghouse, jr	Pittsburgh, Pa	Sept. 9, 1873	142, 600
Car brake, Railway	A. L. Whipple	Elmira, N. Y	Nov. 30, 1858	22, 213
Car brake, Railway	S. M. Whipple	North Adams, Mass	Mar. 9, 1858	19, 599
Car brake, Railway	T. J. Whitney	Broad Axe, Pa	Aug. 4, 1863	39, 440
Car brake, Railway	A. Whittemore	Cambridgeport, Mass	Oct. 15, 1872	132, 225
Car brake, Railway	G. W. Windsor	Allegheny, Pa	Jan. 26, 1858	19, 222
Car brake, Railway	G. W. B. Yocom and E. Cowan	Arcata, Cal	Nov. 2, 1869	96, 375
Car brake, Railway	G. W. Zeigler	Tiffin, Ohio	May 11, 1858	20, 237
Car-brake, Re-action	J. Hall	Granville, Ohio	Apr. 22, 1862	35, 020
Car-brake, Safety	A. S. Martin	Washington, D. C	Aug. 30, 1870	106, 847
Car brake, Self-acting coal	J. D. Leonard	Cleveland, Ohio	Sept. 9, 1873	142, 572
Car-brake, Self-acting safety	G. S. Griggs	Roxbury, Mass	Dec. 31, 1839	1, 452
Car-brake shoe	J. Bing	Philadelphia, Pa	Oct. 6, 1863	40, 156
Car-brake shoe	J. Bing	Philadelphia, Pa	Sept. 25, 1866	58, 207
Car-brake shoe	E. L. Countiss	Philadelphia, Pa	Mar. 19, 1867	62, 940
Car-brake shoe	S. D. Danfield	Philadelphia, Pa	Oct. 24, 1865	50, 656
Car-brake shoe	G. Drake	Farmington, Me	Mar. 3, 1868	75, 001
Car-brake shoe	C. H. Sollers and J. Rhoads	Harrisburgh, Pa	Nov. 21, 1865	51, 093
Car-brake shoe	I. P. Wendell	Philadelphia, Pa	Oct. 1, 1867	69, 377
Car-brake shoe	H. Werntz	Pine Grove, Pa	Mar. 20, 1866	53, 369
Car-brake shoe	J. Wood	Red Bank, N. J	Jan. 5, 1864	41, 114
Car-brake shoe	J. Wood	Red Bank, N. J	Nov. 15, 1864	45, 106
Car-brake shoe, Railway	S. B. Gardner	Freeport, Ill	Oct. 12, 1869	95, 677
Car-brake, Steam	V. C. Buckner	Boonville, Mo	Jan. 2, 1866	51, 797
Car-brake, Steam	T. and H. Hopper	Newark, N. J	Oct. 1, 1867	69, 437
Car-brake, Steam-actuated	J. T. Bassett	Galesburgh, Ill	Oct. 17, 1871	119, 913
Car-brake, Steam and air	J. W Gardner	Cleveland, Ohio	Jan. 23, 1872	122, 884
Car-brake, Steam and air	J. Y. Smith	Pittsburgh, Pa	July 23, 1872	129, 868
Car brake, Steam railway	H. Miller	New York, N. Y	Jan. 2, 1855	12, 166
Car brake, Street	J. Stephenson	New York, N. Y	June 4, 1872	127, 525
Car-brake to prevent accidents in descending inclined planes on railways.	M. W. King	New York, N. Y	May 8, 1840	1, 587
Car-brake, Vacuum	R. J. Wilson	Pittsburgh, Pa	Nov. 14, 1871	120, 922
Car-brake wheel, Railway	C. A. Waterbury	New York, N. Y	May 13, 1873	138, 968
Car-brakes, Arrangement of bumper for self-acting.	J. J. McComb	New Orleans, La	June 12, 1855	13, 038
Car-brakes, Brake-block for	J. P. Levan	Altoona, Pa	Apr. 26, 1864	42, 493
Car-brakes, Connecting a series of	P. Moody	Camden, N. J	Sept. 26, 1854	11, 732
Car-brakes, Graduating the tension of	W. Loughridge	Weverton, Md	Apr. 10, 1855	12, 685
Car brakes, Lever of railway	L. Paige	Cavendish, Vt	Mar. 25, 1856	14, 515
Car-brakes, Machinery for operating	J. Marks	Dunkirk, N. Y	Mar. 28, 1854	10, 701
Car-brakes, Machinery for operating	J. Marks and J. Howarth	Boston and Salem, Mass	Mar. 28, 1854	10, 702
Car brakes, Machinery for operating railway	J. R. Grant	Utica, N. Y	Aug. 25, 1842	2, 760
Car brakes, Mechanism for operating railway	E. R. Roe	Bloomington, Ill	Aug. 11, 1857	17, 983
Car brakes, Method of applying railway	I. J. Webber	Salem, Mass	July 7, 1857	17, 763
Car-brakes, Method of applying steam-power to	W. Loughridge	Weverton, Md	Apr. 19, 1864	42, 385
Car-brakes, Method of engaging and disengaging self acting.	G. F. Leach	Boston, Mass	Nov. 14, 1854	11, 937
Car-brakes, Operating	N. Hodge	North Adams, Mass	Oct. 2, 1849	6, 762
Car-brakes, Operating	W. Loughridge	Weverton, Md	Apr. 12, 1864	42, 301
Car-brakes, Operating	G. W. Mitchell	Jackson, Tenn	Dec. 6, 1859	26, 365
Car-brakes, Operating	J. Y. Smith	Pittsburgh, Pa	Aug. 6, 1872	130, 323
Car-brakes, Operating	L. Stebbins	Hartford, Conn	Apr. 18, 1848	5, 510
Car brakes, Operating railway	S. N. Goodale	Saint Louis, Mo	Oct. 31, 1871	120, 429
Car brakes, Operating railway	M. McGee	Jackson, Mich	Mar. 9, 1858	19, 574
Car brakes, Operating railway	D. Mumma, jr	Harrisburgh, Pa	Nov. 15, 1859	26, 117
Car brakes, Operating railway	A. G. Safford	Boston, Mass	Dec. 23, 1862	37, 246
Car brakes, Operating railway	C. B. Turner	Buffalo, N. Y	Nov. 14, 1848	5, 918
Car-brakes, Radial arm for	T. G. McLaughlin	Philadelphia, Pa	June 20, 1854	11, 130
Car brakes, Rubber of railway	H. M. Collier	Binghamton, N. Y	Oct. 20, 1857	18, 435
Car, Brick	J. K. Caldwell	Pittsburgh, Pa	Aug. 13, 1867	67, 632

Index of patents issued from the United States Patent Office from 1790 *to* 1873, *inclusive*—Continued.

Invention.	Inventor.	Residence.	Date.	No.
r, Brick-carrying	J. K. Caldwell	Pittsburgh, Pa	Mar. 10, 1868	75, 243
r-bridge, Safety	E. Sturgeon	Columbiana, Ohio	Sept. 8, 1868	81, 938
r buffer and draw-bar, Railway	E. L. Camm	Patterson, Pa	Dec. 3, 1867	71, 580
r buffer, Railway	P. Allen and B. Valiquette	Rutland, Vt	Apr. 6, 1869	88, 600
r-buffer spring, Railway	J. Haldeman	West Point, Va	Apr. 2, 1872	125, 191
r-buffer s ring, Railway	C. W. Saladee	Saint Catharine's, Canada	Jan. 28, 1873	135, 369
r bumper and draw-head, Railway	A. Ross and J. Arthur	Freeport, Ill	Nov. 15, 1870	109, 347
r-bumper and draw-head spring	C. F. Allen	Paw Paw, Mich	May 6, 1862	35, 196
r bumper and draw-head spring, Railway	J. C. Jackson	Rochester, N. Y	Jan. 20, 1863	37, 448
r-bumper attachment	J. P. Laird	Altoona, Pa	Feb. 7, 1865	46, 248
r-bumper brake, Railway	F. Armstrong	New Orleans, La	Nov. 11, 1856	16, 042
r bumper, Railway	J. Taney and J. H. Brown	Bangor, Me	Oct. 13, 1868	83, 066
r, carriage, truck, &c., for railways	J. Harrison, jr	Philadelphia, Pa	Apr. 24, 1838	706
r, Cattle	J. H. Aldrich	Nashua, N. H	Apr. 9, 1867	63, 686
r, Cattle	E. Fontaine	Fort Wayne, Ind	Mar. 31, 1868	76, 067
r, Cattle	M. T. Kehoo	Amsterdam, N. Y	Jan. 1, 1867	60, 906
r, Cattle	Z. Street	Salem, Ohio	Nov. 2, 1869	96, 500
r, Cattle	L. Swearingen	Valley River Falls, Va	May 29, 1860	28, 517
r, Cattle	A. Welch	Southall, England	June 4, 1872	127, 443
r chair, Railway	W. Palmer	New York, N. Y	May 30, 1871	115, 510
r-chock for railway-rail	W. O. Stephenson	Marion County, Ind	Mar. 11, 1873	136, 625
r, Circular	J. Crane	Schenectady, N. Y	Oct. 1, 1830	....
r, City-railway	W. C. Allison	Philadelphia, Pa	Jan. 3, 1860	26, 730
r, City-railway	W. C. Allison	Philadelphia, Pa	May 29, 1860	28, 530
r, City-railway	J. Grice and R. H. Long	New York, N. Y., and Philadelphia, Pa.	Dec. 11, 1860	30, 918
r, City-railway	J. Harris, jr	Roxbury, Mass	Sept. 4, 1860	29, 882
r, City-railway	J. Ruth	Philadelphia, Pa	Apr. 14, 1863	38, 181
r, Coal	T. McCrory	Fayette City, Pa	June 14, 1870	104, 332
r, Compartment	W. D. Mann	Mobile, Ala	Jan. 9, 1872	122, 622
r-conductors, Check on	P. F. Milligan	Washington, D. C	Apr. 9, 1867	63, 649
r connection, Railway	W. P. Anderson	New York, N. Y	May 18, 1869	90, 216
r, Convertible freight	T. Fogg	Saint Mary's, Canada	Apr. 22, 1873	138, 142
r, Convertible freight	W. Worsley	Little Falls, N. J	Apr. 15, 1873	137, 871
r couch, Railway	W. A. Brown	Philadelphia, Pa	July 17, 1860	29, 137
r couch, Railway	J. B. Creighton	Tiffin, Ohio	Sept. 28, 1858	21, 600
r couch, Railway	E. C. Knight	Philadelphia, Pa	Feb. 28, 1860	27, 297
r couch, Railway	F. R. Myers and F. H. Furniss	Cleveland, Ohio	Sept. 7, 1858	21, 436
r couch, Railway	G. W. Williamson	Goldsborough, Pa	Apr. 6, 1869	88, 685
r couch, Railway	J. Hartman, jr	Philadelphia, Pa	Sept. 7, 1858	21, 469
r-coupler	S. K. Christy	Noblesville, Ind	Nov. 3, 1868	83, 761
r-coupler	T. Ray	Pelham, Canada	May 23, 1871	115, 104
r-coupler	C. E. Stevens	New York, N. Y	Mar. 22, 1859	23, 321
r-coupler	W. D. Tisdale	Cortland, N. Y	Mar. 11, 1873	136, 627
r-coupler	P. Weatherbee	Port Washington, Ohio	June 21, 1870	104, 670
r-coupler	J. B. Atwater	Berlin, Wis	Mar. 8, 1859	23, 145
r coupler and buffer	E. Miller	Janesville, Wis	Jan. 31, 1865	46, 1[illegible]6
r coupler and buffer, Railway	P. G. Gardiner	New York, N. Y	Oct. 25, 1870	108, 698
r-couplers, Buffer-head for	W. Rickards, jr	Franklin, Pa	July 19, 1870	105, 491
r-coupling	G. S. Acker	Kalamazoo, Mich	Oct. 20, 1868	83, 124
r-coupling	J. W. Adams	Spring Creek, Wis	May 26, 1868	78, 173
r-coupling	L. Adams	Blanchester, Ohio	Dec. 13, 1859	26, 403
r-coupling	M. K. Adams	Mountain Eagle, Pa	Dec. 3, 1867	71, 673
r-coupling	H. Adkins	Plymouth, Ill	Sept. 18, 1866	58, 041
r-coupling	J. H. Akin	Wyandotte City, Kans	Mar. 5, 1872	124, 310
r-coupling	O. Albrecht	Philadelphia, Pa	June 17, 1873	139, 850
r-coupling	H. Allen and A. H. Baldwin	Houston, Tex	Sept. 24, 1872	131, 587
r-coupling	J. W. Allen and E. C. Boyles	Mount Pleasant, Iowa	Jan. 2, 1872	122, 304
r-coupling	R. N. Allen	Pittsford, Vt	July 19, 1870	105, 437
r-coupling	J. D. Alvord	Springfield, Mass	Sept. 18, 1849	6, 728
r-coupling	A. I. Ambler	Milwaukee, Wis	Sept. 2, 1862	36, 382
r-coupling	A. A. Ames	Minneapolis, Minn	Oct. 8, 1872	132, 042
r-coupling	J. D. Anderson	Corry, Pa	May 28, 1867	65, 151
r-coupling	W. S. Anderson	Shelbyville, Tenn	Aug. 4, 1868	80, 584
r-coupling	T. Andress	Auroraville, Wis	Nov. 11, 1873	144, 428
r-coupling	J. N. Anthoine	Biddeford, Me	Oct. 29, 1872	132, 618
r-coupling	J. D. M. Armbrust	Apolloborough, Pa	Dec. 1, 1868	84, 465
r-coupling	R. S. Arnall	Wright City, Mo	Mar. 12, 1867	62, 803
r-coupling	R. S. Arnall	Wright City, Mo	Aug. 13, 1867	67, 703
r-coupling	T. Arndt	Mount Joy, Pa	Dec. 19, 1865	51, 535
r-coupling	T. Arndt	Mount Joy, Pa	Aug. 25, 1868	81, 323
r-coupling	T. H. Arnold	Arlington, Ill	June 9, 1863	38, 801
r-coupling	B. Atkinson	Indianapolis, Ind	July 8, 1873	140, 667
r-coupling	A. A. Atwater	Smith Valley, N. Y	Nov. 11, 1873	144, 494
r-coupling	J. B. Atwater	Berlin, Wis	Feb. 1, 1859	22, 776
r-coupling	G. Aulick	Winchester, Va	Apr. 18, 1854	10, 787
r-coupling	C. P. Bachelder	Franklin, N. H	Dec. 24, 1867	72, 441
r-coupling	J. Bailor	Cannon City, Minn	Sept. 4, 1866	57, 658
r-coupling	P. Baker	Oakland, Md	Nov. 12, 1867	70, 776
r-coupling	W. R. Baker	Trempealeau, Wis	June 14, 1870	104, 098
r-coupling	A. C. Baker and J. Van Dyne	Hyde Park, N. Y	Sept. 2, 1862	36, 331
r-coupling	C. W. Baldwin	Boston, Mass	Aug. 28, 1866	57, 618
r-coupling	H. Baldwin	Nashville, Tenn	Apr. 16, 1850	7, 280
r-coupling	H. Bale	Petersburgh, Ill	Oct. 22, 1872	132, 429
r-coupling	D. H. Ball	Sinnamahoning, Pa	Jan. 31, 1871	111, 419
r-coupling	D. H. Ball	Sinnamahoning, Pa	July 4, 1871	116, 663
r-coupling	T. A. Banta	Bloomington, Ind	Oct. 29, 1872	132, 619
r-coupling	E. W. Barker	Portland, Me	Dec. 17, 1872	133, 963
r-coupling	E. W. Barker	Portland, Me	July 15, 1873	140, 805
r coupling	E. T. Barlow	San Francisco, Cal	Aug. 4, 1863	39, 373
r-coupling	E. T. Barlow	San Francisco, Cal	Nov. 12, 1872	133, 006
r-coupling	P. C. Barlow	Beverly, W. Va	July 25, 1871	117, 368
r coupling	W. F. Barlow	Monmouth, Ill	Dec. 10, 1867	71, 951
r-coupling	J. D. Barnard	Frostburgh, Md	Sept. 12, 1871	118, 836
r-coupling	W. B. Barnes	Plymouth, Mass	July 29, 1873	141, 258
r-coupling	H. W. Barnum	Omaha, Nebr	June 4, 1872	127, 450
r-coupling	J. W. Barrett	Calhoun, Ga	June 27, 1871	116, 307

Index of patents issued from the United States Patent Office from 1790 *to* 1873, *inclusive*—Continued.

Invention.	Inventor.	Residence.	Date.	No.
Car-coupling	R. M. Barthelmess and C. C. Millar.	Savannah, Ga	Nov. 3, 1868	83, 591
Car-coupling	J. Bassler	Galesburgh, Ill	Mar. 19, 1872	124, 780
Car-coupling	J. W. Bates	Minneapolis, Minn	Jan. 7, 1873	134, 629
Car-coupling	R. F. Baughn	Lexington, Miss	July 6, 1869	92, 249
Car-coupling	D. S. Beals	Adrian, Mich	July 21, 1868	80, 117
Car-coupling	G. M Beardsley	Fenton, Mich	Nov. 5, 1867	70, 505
Car-coupling	T. Beddow and A. T. Jackson	New Albany, Ind	July 22, 1873	141, 103
Car-coupling	J. B. Behrens	Pearl, Ill	June 4, 1867	65, 331
Car-coupling	J. S. Bell	Hackettstown, N. J	June 21, 1864	43, 175
Car-coupling	W. G. Bell	Pittsburgh, Pa	Dec. 15, 1868	84, 933
Car-coupling	W. W. Bell	Chicago, Ill	Feb. 15, 1870	99, 817
Car-coupling	W. E. Beman	Portland, Me	Mar. 18, 1873	136, 958
Car-coupling	L. D. Bennett	Willimantic, Conn	Aug. 26, 1873	142, 142
Car-coupling	C. W. Benson	Frederick City, Md	Feb. 15, 1870	99, 818
Car-coupling	W. Bergmann	Philadelphia, Pa	July 3, 1866	55, 989
Car-coupling	J. Bestwick, jr., and A. Alden	Dedham, Mass	Mar. 20, 1860	27, 516
Car-coupling	A. and S. Beucus	Waupun, Wis	June 21, 1870	104, 543
Car coupling	B. Bevelander	Boston, Mass	Mar. 9, 1869	87, 622
Car-coupling	W. C. Bibb	Morgan County, Ga	Aug. 22, 1871	118, 184
Car-coupling	E. Bickell	Milton, Pa	July 29, 1873	141, 312
Car-coupling	E. R. Bigelow	Salem, Mass	Dec. 31, 1867	72, 717
Car-coupling	C. S. Bigler	Harrisburgh, Pa	Feb. 11, 1873	135, 686
Car-coupling	T. L. Birch and J. C. Noble	Washington, Pa	Feb. 4, 1862	34, 289
Car-coupling	G. S. Bishop	Washington, D. C	Oct. 12, 1858	21, 737
Car-coupling	G. S. Bishop	Washington, D. C	Mar. 3, 1863	37, 805
Car-coupling	W. J. Blackman	Columbus Miss	Feb. 23, 1869	87, 135
Car-coupling	H. Blackmore	Pittsburgh, Pa	Mar. 22, 1864	42, 041
Car-coupling	T. B. Blackstone	Chicago, Ill	Nov. 10, 1868	83, 907
Car-coupling	H. I. Blakeslee	Concord, Pa	June 23, 1863	38, 939
Car-coupling	H. Blanchard, jr	Boston, Mass	Dec. 6, 1870	109, 797
Car-coupling	A. W. Bohaker	Granvi le, Nova Scotia	Oct. 7, 1873	143, 491
Car-coupling	H. W. Boifeuillet	Savannah, Ga	Dec. 29, 1868	85, 359
Car-coupling	C. C. Bole	Conemaugh, Pa	Dec. 10, 1872	133, 824
Car-coupling	E. Bolman and G. S. W. Clarke	Halifax, Nova Scotia	May 16, 1871	114, 755
Car-coupling	T. H. Bomar	Atlanta, Ga	Sept. 1, 1868	81, 741
Car-coupling	A. T. Boon and D. M. Osborn	Galesburgh, Ill	Apr. 9, 1867	63, 696
Car-coupling	J. Boothroyd	Michigan City, Ind	Jan. 24, 1871	111, 170
Car-coupling	L. J. Bosworth	Monmouth, Ill	Apr. 18, 1871	113, 730
Car-coupling	J. W. Boughton	Appleton, Wis	July 18, 1865	48, 787
Car-coupling	J. W. Boughton	Appleton, Wis	Apr. 3, 1866	53, 560
Car-coupling	L. Boyd and P. Kriegbaum	Springfield, Ohio	Nov. 12, 1867	70, 689
Car-coupling	W. A. Boyden	Harrisburgh, Pa	Sept. 23, 1873	143, 055
Car-coupling	W. L. Braddock	Boston, Mass	Mar. 30, 1869	88, 440
Car-coupling	D. Bradford	Hamilton, Canada	Jan. 28, 1873	135, 316
Car-coupling	A. J. Braley	Berlin, Vt	Jan. 26, 1869	86, 129
Car-coupling	A. Branshaw	Fond du Lac, Wis	May 11, 1869	89, 913
Car-coupling	G. Brenner and G. T. Polk	Poughkeepsie, N. Y	Mar. 14, 1871	112, 536
Car-coupling	J. Broadley	Bradford, England	Aug. 13, 1872	130, 408
Car-coupling	W. C. Brooks	Stoneham, Pa	Oct. 28, 1873	144, 015
Car-coupling	P. Brown	Louisvilie, Ky	Oct. 15, 1872	132, 238
Car-coupling	P. Brown	Louisville, Ky	Nov. 26, 1872	133, 406
Car-coupling	H. A. Buck	Meadville, Pa	Apr. 19, 1864	42, 343
Car-coupling	R. B. Buckner	Gilroy, Cal	Aug. 12, 1873	141, 756
Car-coupling	J. H. Bull	Hereford, Md	July 11, 1871	116, 801
Car-coupling	C. T. Burchardt	New York, N. Y	July 28, 1868	80, 271
Car-coupling	C. C. Burns	Greensburgh, Ind	Mar. 6, 1866	52, 962
Car-coupling	W. E. Bush	Damascus, Pa	Oct. 20, 1868	83, 252
Car-coupling	W. C. Bussey	Rockgrove, Ill	July 17, 1847	5, 194
Car-coupling	W. C. Bussey	Jackson, Cal	Aug. 30, 1864	43, 969
Car-coupling	R. Butt	Harrisburgh, Pa	Nov. 11, 1873	144, 439
Car-coupling	C. C. Cady	West Union, Iowa	Jan. 8, 1867	61, 047
Car-coupling	T. Caldwell and L. C. Wilcox	Buffalo, N. Y	Feb. 23, 1869	87, 142
Car-coupling	W. Callow, jr	Baltimore, Md	May 30, 1871	115, 433
Car-coupling	D. C. Camerer	Martinsburgh, Pa	Aug. 19, 1873	141, 991
Car-coupling	E. Campbell	Medusa, N. Y	June 13, 1871	115, 819
Car-coupling	G. G. Campbell	Janesville, Wis	Oct. 24, 1865	50, 559
Car-coupling	S. O. Campbell	Tipton, Mo	Dec. 14, 1869	97, 876
Car-coupling	R. Campion and J. W. Thompson, jr.	Camden, N. J	Mar. 23, 1869	88, 130
Car-coupling	M. H. Card and J. W. Stewart	Fulton, Ill., and Lyons, Iowa.	May 15, 1866	54, 683
Car-coupling	M. H. Card and T. Tripp	Chicago, Ill	July 19, 1864	43, 569
Car-coupling	S. P. Carll and A. Shute	Richmond, Ind	June 28, 1870	104, 704
Car-coupling	J. W. Carrier	Springfield, Mass	Mar. 29, 1859	23, 423
Car-coupling	E. Cary	Burlington, Iowa	Aug. 2, 1864	43, 734
Car-coupling	E. Cary	Burlington, Iowa	Mar. 13, 1866	53, 215
Car-coupling	E. W. Chadwick	Edgertown, Mass	Aug. 18, 1868	81, 067
Car-coupling	J. H. Chadwick	Bristol, R. I	Nov. 17, 1868	84, 049
Car-coupling	S. E. Chaney	Hillsborough, Ohio	July 11, 1865	48, 656
Car-coupling	A. F. Chandler	Fall River, Mass	Nov. 25, 1873	144, 954
Car-coupling	W. J. Chaplin	Kalamazoo, Mich	Feb. 11, 1873	135, 775
Car-coupling	J. A. J. Chapman	Kansas City, Mo	Jan. 30, 1872	123, 150
Car-coupling	A. P. Chatham	Canoga, N. Y	Nov. 1, 1853	10, 176
Car-coupling	A. H. Clark	Fond du Lac, Wis	July 16, 1867	66, 677
Car-coupling	A. H. Clark	Otisville, Mich	Oct. 12, 1869	95, 652
Car-coupling	W. C. Clark	Portland, Me	July 4, 1865	48, 617
Car-coupling	W. H. H. Clark	Burlington, Iowa	July 27, 1869	93, 055
Car-coupling	G. E. Clarke	Racine, Wis	Dec. 26, 1865	51, 695
Car-coupling	T. P. Clines	Louisville, Ky	Dec. 3, 1872	133, 505
Car-coupling	C. Clinton	Blooming Grove, N. Y	Feb. 14, 1865	46, 336
Car-coupling	C. D. Clinton	Peoria, Ill	July 17, 1866	56, 371
Car-coupling	W. B. Coates	Philadelphia, Pa	Jan. 22, 1867	61, 399
Car-coupling	J. T. L. Cochran	Columbia, Tenn	Nov. 25, 1873	144, 956
Car-coupling	S. M. Cochran	Baltimore, Md	Jan. 1, 1851	7, 866
Car-coupling	W. A. Cochran	Flat Rock, Ind	Nov. 18, 1873	144, 658
Car-coupling	F. Coffin	Claremont, N. H	Oct. 27, 1868	83, 464
Car-coupling	G. W. Coffin	Pittsburgh, Pa	Feb. 18, 1873	136, 053

Index of patents issued from the United States Patent Office from 1790 *to* 1873, *inclusive*—Continued.

Invention.	Inventor.	Residence.	Date.	No.
Car-coupling	C. M. Colby	Corinth, Vt	Aug. 29, 1871	118, 436
Car-coupling	V. and E. Cole	Detroit, Mich	Dec. 18, 1866	60, 479
Car-coupling	J. Coleman	Lynchburgh, Va	May 3, 1870	102, 500
Car-coupling	W. T. Collins	Winchester, Ill	Feb. 18, 1873	135, 890
Car-coupling	G. Collyer	Philadelphia, Pa	Feb. 10, 1863	37, 612
Car-coupling	T. F. Conner	Odin, Ill	Oct. 22, 1867	69, 972
Car-coupling	C. C. Converse	Erie, Pa	Nov. 11, 1873	144, 386
Car-coupling	J. M. Cook	Washington, D. C	Sept. 8, 1868	81, 985
Car-coupling	W. Cook	Belvidere, Ill	Feb 26, 1867	62, 475
Car-coupling	J. G. W. Coolidge	Portland, Me	Aug. 29, 1865	49, 676
Car-coupling	W. R. Coovert	London, Pa	Nov. 4, 1873	144, 257
Car-coupling	S. A. Corser	Holyoke, Mass	Nov. 7, 1865	50, 797
Car-coupling	C. B. Cotler	Harrisburgh, Pa	June 22, 1858	20, 627
Car-coupling	J. Couch	Harrison, Me	Aug. 15, 1865	49, 385
Car-coupling	R. A. Cowell	Cleveland, Ohio	Mar. 5, 1867	62, 613
Car-coupling	S. H. Cowles	Oakville, Conn	Mar. 24, 1868	75, 866
Car-coupling	E. S. Cram	New Hampton, N. H	Apr. 20, 1869	89, 202
Car-coupling	J. Crist	Tiffin, Ohio	Aug. 26, 1873	142, 209
Car-coupling	T. H. Cross	East Boston, Mass	Sept. 23, 1873	142, 993
Car-coupling	G. D. Crosthwait	Murfreesborough, Tenn	Feb. 18, 1873	136, 039
Car-coupling	W. W. Culpepper	Augusta, Ga	June 12, 1860	28, 660
Car-coupling	G. E. Cuming	La Fayette, Ind	June 18, 1867	65, 882
Car-coupling	J. W. Currier	Springfield, Mass	June 1, 1869	90, 730
Car-coupling	S. Daggett, jr	Charleston, S. C	Mar. 20, 1860	27, 531
Car-coupling	R. Daily	Canal Township, Pa	Mar. 24, 1868	75, 738
Car-coupling	G. E. Darling and M. Heus	Marytown, Wis	July 4, 1871	116, 566
Car-coupling	A. H. S. Davis	Farmington, Me	Jan. 2, 1872	122, 368
Car-coupling	P. W. Davis	Portland, Oreg	Aug. 15, 1871	117, 992
Car-coupling	W. A. Dean	New Lexington, Ohio	Nov. 26, 1872	133, 421
Car-coupling	J. C. Dearborn	Candia, N. H	Dec. 20, 1870	110, 214
Car-coupling	P. H. Decker and N. Lee	Chicago, Ill	Aug. 12, 1873	141, 635
Car-coupling	T. W. Defrees	South Bend, Ind	June 7, 1870	103, 850
Car-coupling	C. R. Densmore and J. A. Vrooman.	Oil City, Pa	Oct. 5, 1869	95, 570
Car-coupling	J. Depeu	Peekskill, N. Y	July 9, 1867	66, 571
Car-coupling	J. Depeu and J. D. Hall	Peekskill, N. Y	July 2, 1867	66, 309
Car-coupling	J. Dinsmore	Dinsmore Station, Pa	Apr. 30, 1872	126, 136
Car-coupling	M. Disney	San Francisco, Cal	Dec. 3, 1867	71, 717
Car-coupling	M. Disney	Oakland, Cal	Nov. 19, 1872	133, 085
Car-coupling	M. Disney	Oakland, Cal	June 24, 1873	140, 124
Car-coupling	W. J. Dodge	Kasoag, N. Y	July 29, 1862	35, 994
Car-coupling	M. C. Doubleday	Sharon, Vt	Feb. 25, 1873	136, 222
Car-coupling	R. H. Dowling	Newark, Ohio	Sept. 9, 1873	142, 682
Car-coupling	R. H. Dowling and E. S. Perry	Fenton, Mich., and Clay Lick, Ohio.	Nov. 7, 1871	120, 746
Car-coupling	J. L. Duncan	Fremont, Ohio	Sept. 23, 1873	142, 998
Car-coupling	J. Dunott	Philadelphia, Pa	Dec. 7, 1869	97, 620
Car-coupling	H. W. Earl	Baltimore, Md	July 4, 1871	116, 696
Car-coupling	C. Eastin	Louisville, Ky	Jan. 9, 1872	122, 586
Car-coupling	J. Ebee	Hummelstown, Pa	Oct. 29, 1867	70, 326
Car-coupling	G. Edmonds	New Orleans, La	Oct. 14, 1873	143, 680
Car-coupling	J. Elbertson	Kirksville, Mo	Nov. 10, 1868	83, 945
Car-coupling	A. J. Elder	Kansas City, Mo	Oct. 13, 1868	83, 052
Car-coupling	J. Enos	Chicago, Ill	Oct. 21, 1873	143, 894
Car-coupling	J. M. Enos	Saint Joseph, Mich	Aug. 26, 1873	142, 219
Car-coupling	J. M. and J. Enos	Saint Joseph, Mich	Nov. 21, 1871	121, 047
Car-coupling	L. A. Evans	Chester, Pa	Oct. 11, 1870	108, 124
Car-coupling	J. M. Everhart	Pittston, Pa	July 7, 1868	79, 643
Car-coupling	R. F. Fairlie	London, England	Feb. 23, 1869	87, 158
Car-coupling	H. Fake	Chicago, Ill	Sept. 6, 1864	44, 085
Car-coupling	M. G. Farnam	Clifton, Canada	Jan. 2, 1872	122, 375
Car-coupling	M. Ferren	Freedom, N. H	Sept. 30, 1873	143, 231
Car-coupling	T. Firth and J. W. Hollis	Cincinnati, Ohio	Sept. 24, 1872	131, 673
Car-coupling	F. A. Fleming	Curwensville, Pa	Oct. 21, 1873	143, 752
Car-coupling	H. H. Fleming	Kokomo, Ind	Nov. 7, 1865	50, 811
Car-coupling	C. S. Flower and C. F. Graves	Kickapoo City, Kans., and Hickory, Iowa.	Nov. 26, 1872	133, 364
Car-coupling	E. L. Foreman	Rantoul, Ill	Apr. 25, 1871	114, 124
Car coupling	W. H. Forker	Meadville, Pa	Sept. 27, 1864	44, 484
Car-coupling	J. J. Fort	Oshkosh, Wis	Mar. 17, 1863	37, 908
Car-coupling	J. Fortier	Fairport, N. Y	Feb. 4, 1868	73, 964
Car-coupling	C. Foster	Oshkosh, Wis	Mar. 8, 1864	41, 837
Car-coupling	R. G. Fowler	Olney, Ill	Sept. 18, 1866	58, 090
Car-coupling	F. Fox and F. A. Howarth	Providence, R. I	Feb. 4, 1873	135, 537
Car-coupling	J. J. Fraikin	Fort Howard, Wis	Aug. 5, 1873	141, 432
Car-coupling	E. J. Frazier	Peoria, Ill	June 5, 1866	55, 271
Car-coupling	A. M. Freeman and A. M. Stoner.	Springfield, Ohio	Jan. 8, 1867	61, 003
Car-coupling	J. P. Freeman	Dalton, Ga	Oct. 20, 1868	83, 272
Car-coupling	G. B. French	Dunbarton, N. H	Jan. 29, 1867	61, 616
Car-coupling	J. H. Froman	Plattsburgh, Mo	Aug. 30, 1870	106, 807
Car-coupling	J. A. Gale	West Medway, Mass	June 24, 1873	140, 131
Car-coupling	C. Gallagher	Taunton, Mass	Dec. 24, 1872	134, 199
Car-coupling	M. Gally	Marion, N. Y	Mar. 5, 1867	62, 625
Car-coupling	P. G. Gardiner	New York, N. Y	Apr. 9, 1872	125, 561
Car-coupling	P. G. Gardiner	New York, N. Y	Apr. 9, 1872	125, 562
Car-coupling	M. C. Gardner	Rochester, N. Y	Dec. 8, 1863	40, 833
Car-coupling	C. H. Gerhart	Farmer City, Ill	Mar. 25, 1873	137, 067
Car-coupling	E. M. George	Three Rivers, Mich	May 16, 1871	114, 797
Car-coupling	J. B. German	Walnut Hills, Ohio	Mar. 26, 1867	63, 239
Car-coupling	M. F. Gibbs	Livonia, N. Y	June 4, 1867	65, 373
Car-coupling	E. N. Gifford	Cleveland, Ohio	Aug. 26, 1873	142, 226
Car coupling	F. M. Gifford	Brant, N. Y	Mar. 7, 1865	46, 656
Car-coupling	J. W. Gillam	Newton, N. J	July 18, 1871	117, 067
Car-coupling	J. W. and J. W. Gillam, jr	Newton, N. J	Feb. 18, 1873	135, 984
Car-coupling	H. C. Gilliland	Wellsville, Mo	June 27, 1871	116, 431
Car-coupling	S. Gissinger	Lawrenceville, Pa	Nov. 12, 1867	70, 8[illegible]9
Car-coupling	H. C. Glasgow	Chicago, Ill	June 9, 1863	38, 819

Index of patents issued from the United States Patent Office from 1790 to 1873, inclusive—Continued.

Invention.	Inventor.	Residence.	Date.	No.
Car-coupling	H. C. Glasgow	Chicago, Ill	Mar. 1, 1864	41, 767
Car-coupling	H. C. Glasgow	Cleveland, Ohio	Oct. 6, 1868	82, 707
Car-coupling	H. C. Glasgow	Cleveland, Ohio	Oct. 6, 1868	82, 708
Car-coupling	J. L. D. Good	Jefferson, Pa	Jan. 7, 1873	134, 648
Car-coupling	M. Goolaren	Taunton, Mass	May 13, 1873	138, 748
Car-coupling	R. Goole	Abingdon, Ill	Dec. 24, 1867	72, 482
Car-coupling	J. M. Gow	Rock Island, Ill	Feb. 9, 1864	41, 502
Car-coupling	J. M. Gow	Rock Island, Ill	July 5, 1864	43, 399
Car-coupling	W. F. Grassler	Muncy, Pa	Oct. 11, 1870	108, 254
Car-coupling	W. F. Grassler	Muncy, Pa	Nov. 26, 1872	133, 437
Car-coupling	W. F. Grassler and A. J. Cutter	Lewisburgh, Pa	Aug. 26, 1862	36, 293
Car-coupling	W. F. Grassler	Muncy, Pa	Oct. 31, 1871	120, 430
Car-coupling	R. W. Green	Bradford, Pa	Feb. 12, 1867	61, 028
Car-coupling	S. Gregory	Jonesville, Mich	Mar. 28, 1871	113, 160
Car-coupling	J. Griffith and W. F. Miller	Adamsburgh, Pa	Sept. 30, 1873	143, 281
Car-coupling	P. I. Gross	Manheim Centre, N. Y	Feb. 21, 1865	46, 465
Car-coupling	J. Growdon	New Enterprise, Pa	Feb. 25, 1873	136, 237
Car-coupling	J. Gum	Marseilles, Ill	Oct. 21, 1873	143, 756
Car-coupling	D. C. Guttridge	Canton, Ohio	Oct. 9, 1866	58, 723
Car-coupling	F. B. Hall	Hartford, Conn	Apr. 30, 1861	32, 223
Car-coupling	A. S. and H. H. Hallett	East Abington, Mass	Dec. 5, 1871	121, 617
Car-coupling	E. C. Hamlin	Pavilion, N. Y	Jan. 14, 1862	34, 143
Car-coupling	J. B. Hards and W. Hodnett	Chicago, Ill	Aug. 2, 1870	106, 057
Car-coupling	C. R. Hardy	Lexington, Ind	Aug. 4, 1868	80, 730
Car-coupling	D. Harger	Des Moines, Iowa	Jan. 28, 1868	73, 889
Car-coupling	J. B. Harper	Saint John, Mo	June 13, 1871	115, 845
Car-coupling	J. Harris	Green Lake, Wis	Feb. 6, 1866	52, 410
Car-coupling	J. H. Harris	Virginia, Ill	Apr. 2, 1867	63, 514
Car-coupling	A. Hartman	Canton, Ohio	Aug. 28, 1866	57, 504
Car-coupling	A. Hartman	Canton, Ohio	May 28, 1867	65, 079
Car-coupling	E. W. Harvey	Springfield, Mass	June 4, 1872	127, 601
Car-coupling	N. Haskins	Hillsborough County, N. H.	Oct. 29, 1850	7, 741
Car-coupling	W. D. Hatch	Worcester, Mass	Oct. 2, 1849	6, 754
Car-coupling	W. W. Haver	Schuyler, N. Y	Sept. 16, 1873	142, 849
Car-coupling	H. Hawley	Lynchburgh, Va	Mar. 12, 1872	124, 490
Car-coupling	G. W. Haynie	Olney, Ill	Mar. 10, 1868	75, 420
Car-coupling	J. C. Heaton	Fitchburgh, Mich	Feb. 18, 1868	74, 532
Car-coupling	A. Hebbard	Galesburgh, Ill	Apr. 13, 1858	19, 925
Car-coupling	R. Hemming	Boston, Mass	Nov. 6, 1847	5, 354
Car-coupling	G. H. Henfield	San Francisco, Cal	Sept. 3, 1867	68, 439
Car-coupling	T. R. Herd	Allegheny, Pa	Dec. 28, 1869	98, 377
Car-coupling	J. W. Hess	Montandon, Pa	Dec. 16, 1873	145, 652
Car-coupling	T. Hess	West Penn, Pa	Feb. 22, 1870	100, 147
Car-coupling	J. B. Heverling	Greenville, Ohio	Nov. 21, 1871	121, 051
Car-coupling	O. Howes	Kankakee, Ill	Aug. 4, 1868	80, 735
Car-coupling	J. Hiers	West Manayunk, Pa	Aug. 26, 1873	142, 230
Car-coupling	A. Hillman	Devonshire, England	Dec. 17, 1867	72, 200
Car-coupling	J. H. Hills	Burlington, Vt	Apr. 21, 1863	38, 225
Car-coupling	W. W. Hinman and W. W. Nevill.	Jacksonville, Ill	May 29, 1866	55, 104
Car-coupling	J. E. Hitt	Bement, Ill	Feb. 4, 1873	135, 552
Car-coupling	C. M. Hoag	Nassau, N. Y	Aug. 30, 1870	106, 936
Car-coupling	A. I. Hobbs	Kokomo, Ind	Sept. 12, 1865	49, 879
Car-coupling	H. Holden	Hartford, Conn	Mar. 19, 1867	63, 049
Car-coupling	J. F. L. Holman	Hamilton, Canada	Sept. 23, 1873	143, 071
Car-coupling	C. Holtz	Chicago, Ill	Oct. 2, 1866	58, 418
Car-coupling	J. Hood	Milwaukee, Wis	Jan. 31, 1860	26, 990
Car-coupling	W. H. Hoover	North Benton, Ohio	Mar. 10, 1868	75, 270
Car-coupling	C. L. Horack	Hastings, Minn	Sept. 26, 1871	119, 359
Car-coupling	C. L. Horack	Hastings, Minn	May 14, 1872	126, 702
Car-coupling	C. F. Hornbeck	Slatersville, N. Y	Jan. 11, 1870	98, 770
Car-coupling	F. E. Howard	Geneseo, N. Y	Sept. 2, 1873	142, 395
Car-coupling	H. R. Howe	Hartwick, N. Y	July 28, 1868	80, 486
Car-coupling	H. R. Howe	Hartwick, N. Y	Feb. 9, 1869	86, 673
Car-coupling	H. R. Howe	Hartwick, N. Y	July 4, 1871	116, 595
Car-coupling	E. P. Howland	Worcester, Mass	Sept. 15, 1863	39, 927
Car-coupling	E. P. Howland	Worcester, Mass	Apr. 4, 1865	47, 108
Car-coupling	E. C. Hubbard	Green Bay, Wis	Nov. 26, 1872	133, 369
Car-coupling	H. Hughes	Sarona, N. Y	June 26, 1866	55, 870
Car-coupling	T. G. Hughes, A. Nutting, and L. Aldrich.	Horton, Iowa	Jan. 9, 1872	122, 610
Car-coupling	F. A. Hull	Belvidere, Ill	July 14, 1868	79, 982
Car-coupling	F. M. Hunt	Marshallville, Ga	Apr. 2, 1872	125, 298
Car-coupling	H. C. Hunt	Amboy, Ill	Dec. 3, 1861	33, 841
Car-coupling	O. Z. Hurd and J. W. Ardinger.	Mount Pulaski, Ill	Jan. 26, 1869	86, 161
Car-coupling	R. H. Huston	Keokuk, Iowa	May 28, 1867	65, 2[illegible]8
Car-coupling	F. A. Illingworth	Waltham, Mass	Dec. 26, 1871	122, 175
Car-coupling	W. M. Inge and E. P. Wheeler	Corinth, Miss	May 7, 1872	126, 460
Car-coupling	M. Ingersoll	Grafton, Ohio	May 22, 1866	54, 913
Car-coupling	J. S. Ingram	Louisville, Ky	Nov. 5, 1872	132, 835
Car-coupling	W. M. Ingstrum	Hornellsville, N. Y	Mar. 22, 1870	101, 018
Car-coupling	G. W. Irish	Memphis, N. Y	Oct. 25, 1870	108, 598
Car-coupling	O. P. Ives	Syracuse, N. Y	May 31, 1870	103, 748
Car-coupling	W. R. Jamison	Taylorstown, Pa	July 30, 1867	67, 311
Car-coupling	E. H. Janney	Alexandria, Va	Apr. 21, 1868	77, 046
Car-coupling	E. A. Janney	Alexandria, Va	Apr. 29, 1873	138, 405
Car-coupling	E. V. Jeinsen	New York, N. Y	Feb. 19, 1867	62, 203
Car-coupling	J. B. Johnson	Laurel, Ind	Jan. 28, 1868	73, 902
Car-coupling	J. T. Johnson and N. T. Smith	Grand Rapids, Mich	Mar. 15, 1864	41, 924
Car-coupling	W. J. Johnson	New Orleans, La	June 21, 1870	104, 462
Car-coupling	W. Johnston	Decatur, Mich	May 9, 1871	114, 566
Car-coupling	G. H. Jones and L. D. Boyce	Rochester, N. Y	Apr. 26, 1870	102, 271
Car-coupling	J. H. Jones	Williamsport, Pa	Aug. 13, 1867	67, 767
Car-coupling	J. W. Jones	Hereford, Md	Apr. 25, 1871	114, 015
Car-coupling	J. W. Jones	Hereford, Md	Mar. 19, 1872	124, 684
Car-coupling	J. W. Jones	Towsontown, Md	Mar. 4, 1873	136, 523
Car-coupling	A. J. Jouroe	Houston, Tex	June 18, 1872	128, 047
Car-coupling	J. H. Kavanagh	Joliet, Ill	Nov. 27, 1866	60, 012

Index of patents issued from the United States Patent Office from 1790 *to* 1873, *inclusive*—Continued.

Invention.	Inventor.	Residence.	Date.	No.
Car-coupling	J. Keck	Dwight, Ill	Dec. 9, 1873	145,428
Car-coupling	E. L. Keeler	Pittsburgh, Pa	Aug. 2, 1859	24,938
Car-coupling	E. B. Keith	Galesburgh, Mich	Jan. 11, 1870	98,775
Car-coupling	E. H. Keith	Peoria, Ill	Dec. 11, 1866	60,384
Car-coupling	J. Kelly	Woodberry, Md	Jan. 1, 1867	60,741
Car-coupling	C. H. Kendall	McConnellsburgh, Pa	Jan. 7, 1873	134,676
Car-coupling	J. E. Kendall	Cairo, Ill	June 25, 1872	128,314
Car-coupling	P. Kendrick	Trenton, N. J	Sept. 9, 1873	142,634
Car-coupling	P. Kennedy, jr, and A. B. Diss	Watertown, N. Y	Feb. 11, 1873	135,714
Car-coupling	J. H. Kenworthey	West Point, Ind	Oct. 24, 1871	120,199
Car-coupling	L. Kenworthy	Adel, Iowa	Dec. 24, 1872	134,148
Car-coupling	W. Kenyon	Crawfordsville, Ind	May 7, 1872	126,554
Car-coupling	J. Kingsbury	Ravenna, Ohio	Sept. 4, 1866	57,732
Car-coupling	F. S. Kirkbride	Wyandotte, Kans	June 11, 1872	127,894
Car-coupling	G. L Kitson	Philadelphia, Pa	Dec. 12, 1865	51,461
Car-coupling	A. K. Kline	Readington, N. J	Mar. 5, 1872	124,274
Car-coupling	A. K. Kline	Readington, N. J	Mar. 11, 1873	136,655
Car-coupling	P. Knobbeck	Wyandotte, Kans	June 30, 1868	79,481
Car-coupling	C. B. Knowles	Nashville, Tenn	July 23, 1872	129,668
Car-coupling	C. H. Knowlton	Rockland, Me	Nov. 26, 1872	133,456
Car-coupling	C. H. Knowlton	Rockland, Me	Apr. 1, 1873	137,455
Car-coupling	G. E. Knox	Ballston Spa, N. Y	Sept. 23, 1873	143,165
Car-coupling	G. Koeb	Springfield, Ohio	July 29, 1873	141,278
Car-coupling	C. Köhler	Galena, Ill	Dec. 8, 1868	84,700
Car-coupling	X. Krapf and J. F. Boerckel	Allentown, Pa	Dec. 9, 1873	145,353
Car-coupling	C. F. Kuhnle and A. Row	Philadelphia, Pa	Mar. 19, 1872	124,750
Car-coupling	J. Lacey and G. Watkins	Bristol, Wis	Sept. 19, 1865	50,010
Car-coupling	J. J. Lahaye	Reading, Pa	Oct. 29, 1872	132,672
Car-coupling	N. E. Laman	Dayton, Ohio	May 17, 1870	103,207
Car-coupling	T. R. Land	Grass Valley, Cal	Dec. 30, 1873	146,0[illegible]8
Car-coupling	J. K. Landis	Palmyra, Pa	Nov. 3, 1868	83,715
Car-coupling	E. Lane	Old Town, Me	May 7, 1872	126,401
Car-coupling	A. Langellier	Concord, N. H	Aug. 12, 1873	141,648
Car-coupling	A. Langellier	Concord, N. H	Nov. 18, 1873	144,624
Car-coupling	T. Lanstone	Washington D. C	June 13, 1871	115,964
Car-coupling	G. C. Lawton	Syracuse, N. Y	June 6, 1865	48,076
Car-coupling	W. Layland	Mixersville, Ind	Jan. 18, 1859	22,657
Car-coupling	C. Layton	Matawan, N. J	June 8, 1869	91,028
Car-coupling	C. Layton	Matawan, N. J	May 28, 1872	127,251
Car-coupling	L. J. Lecocq	Argenteuil, France	July 7, 1868	79,664
Car-coupling	S. D. Lecompte	Leavenworth County, Kans.	Feb. 4, 1868	73,984
Car-coupling	W. Leib and G. B. Hornbeek	Winchester, Ill	Feb. 26, 1867	62,345
Car-coupling	H. L. B. Lewis	New York, N. Y	Sept. 18, 1849	6,730
Car-coupling	I. B. Lewis	Albion, Mich	Aug. 5, 1873	141,445
Car-coupling	J. E. Lewis	Boston, Mass	July 30, 1872	129,896
Car-coupling	E. Lindsley	Neenah, Wis	May 7, 1867	64,547
Car-coupling	D. Lippy	Mansfield, Ohio	Sept. 11, 1866	57,931
Car-coupling	R. Lloyd	Cleveland, Ohio	Oct. 21, 1873	143,828
Car-coupling	J. B. Lochbaum	Chambersburgh, Pa	Aug. 20, 1872	130,585
Car-coupling	S. D. Locke	Janesville, Wis	Aug. 8, 1865	49,348
Car-coupling	S. L. Loomis	Byron, N. Y	Nov. 12, 1867	70,729
Car-coupling	A. Z. Long	Scranton, Pa	June 8, 1869	91,140
Car-coupling	J. Long	Mechanicsburgh, Pa	Dec. 21, 1869	98,076
Car-coupling	J. T. Lowrey	La Fayette, Ind	Jan. 19, 1864	41,308
Car-coupling	H. C. Lowrie	Fort Wayne, Ind	Sept. 2, 1873	142,487
Car-coupling	G. W. Loyd	Markleysburgh, Pa	Apr. 23, 1872	125,967
Car-coupling	A. A. Lusk and S. A. Wells	Wooster, Ohio	Apr. 3, 1866	53,639
Car-coupling	I. V. and W. J. Lynn	Pittsburgh, Pa	Mar. 23, 1869	88,189
Car-coupling	S. Madden	Eureka South, Cal	Oct. 13, 1868	82,966
Car-coupling	S. Mahurin	Liberty, Ill	Dec. 6, 1870	109,830
Car-coupling	M. B. Malott	Richmond, Ind	July 26, 1870	105,706
Car-coupling	J. C. Maloy	Johnstown, Pa	Dec. 2, 1873	145,067
Car-coupling	J. A. Manning	Ashtabula, Ohio	July 28, 1868	80,493
Car-coupling	H. E. Marchand	Louisville, Ky	May 21, 1872	126,973
Car-coupling	H. E. Marchand	Pittsburgh, Pa	Mar. 25, 1873	137,225
Car-coupling	J. L. Mareness	Constantine, Mich	May 14, 1872	126,724
Car-coupling	A. S. Markham	Bushnell, Ill	Dec. 5, 1865	51,330
Car-coupling	C. Markley	New York, N. Y	July 19, 1870	105,470
Car-coupling	B. F. Marsden	Galena, Ill	Dec. 20, 1864	45,509
Car-coupling	L. Marshall	Mount Sterling, Ill	Feb. 6, 1872	123,496
Car-coupling	F. W. Marston and O. Jones	Philadelphia, Pa	Mar. 18, 1873	137,014
Car-coupling	J. A. Mason	Keokuk, Iowa	June 28, 1870	104,750
Car-coupling	C. Maus	Danville, Pa	Nov. 23, 1869	97,208
Car-coupling	J. Mayben	Milroy, Pa	Jan. 24, 1871	111,224
Car-coupling	W. H. Mayo	Hillsburgh, Nova Scotia	May 21, 1867	64,890
Car-coupling	A. McCarter	Lancaster, Pa	Mar. 26, 1867	63,277
Car-coupling	D. McComas	Calhoun, Mo	Sept. 12, 1871	118,957
Car-coupling	G. W. McEwen	Lock Haven, Pa	Dec. 3, 1872	133,539
Car-coupling	C. McInturff	Greeneville, Tenn	Dec. 8, 1868	84,747
Car-coupling	E. T. McKean	Hammonton, N. J	Feb. 22, 1870	100,173
Car-coupling	H. McKee	Chandlerville, Ill	June 21, 1864	43,219
Car-coupling	J. McLaughlin	Duncannon, Pa	Jan. 1, 1867	60,920
Car-coupling	A. McLean	Boston, Mass	Apr. 20, 1869	89,061
Car-coupling	J. S. McMurray	Toronto, Canada	Mar. 3, 1868	75,178
Car-coupling	W. H. Meadows	McMinnville, Tenn	Dec. 27, 1870	110,580
Car-coupling	J. H. Mears and G. Cameron	Oshkosh, Wis	Oct. 18, 1859	25,844
Car coupling	T. and J. W. Meiklo	Louisville, Ky	Sept. 9, 1873	142,713
Car-coupling	J. W. Melcher	Oshkosh, Wis	Apr. 7, 1868	76,494
Car-coupling	A. Melot and J. T. Fry	Reading, Pa	Sept. 26, 1865	50,148
Car coupling	J. P. Mendenhall	Farmington, Ill	July 31, 1860	29,395
Car-coupling	G. H. Merriam	Portland, Me	Aug. 20, 1872	130,651
Car-coupling	J. A. Merrill and D. W. Kempton.	Denver, Colo	Oct. 7, 1873	143,524
Car coupling	F. H. Meyers	Wilmington, Del	Jan. 1, 1867	60,923
Car-coupling	A. Middleton, jr	Philadelphia, Pa	Sept. 2, 1873	142,492
Car-coupling	J. T. Middleton	Harveysburgh, Ohio	Nov. 23, 1869	97,212
Car-coupling	W. J. Millar	McKeesport, Pa	Dec. 24, 1867	72,664

Index of patents issued from the United States Patent Office from 1790 to 1873, inclusive—Continued.

Invention.	Inventor.	Residence.	Date.	No.
Car-coupling	H. Millard	Philadelphia, Pa	May 13, 1873	138, 912
Car-coupling	C. L. Miller	Cuba, N. Y	Sept. 9, 1873	142, 715
Car-coupling	D. M. Miller	South Bend, Ind	Sept. 30, 1873	143, 368
Car-coupling	D. W. Miller and M. Brestle, jr.	Middletown, Pa	Oct. 1, 1867	69, 464
Car-coupling	E. Miller	Janesville, Wis	Mar. 31, 1863	38, 057
Car-coupling	J. Miller	Cuba, N. Y	Jan. 29, 1867	61, 553
Car-coupling	J. Miller	Carrollton, Ohio	Oct. 15, 1867	69, 927
Car-coupling	J. Miller	Carrollton, Ohio	Oct. 22, 1867	70, 103
Car-coupling	S. Miller	Holley, N. Y	July 8, 1873	140, 720
Car-coupling	J. D. Mills	Alexandria, Va	Sept. 30, 1873	143, 369
Car-coupling	S. Mills	Madison, Wis	Dec. 24, 1867	72, 665
Car-coupling	S. Mills	Madison, Wis	Apr. 21, 1868	77, 071
Car-coupling	S. Milne	Perthshire, Scotland	Oct. 8, 1867	69, 574
Car-coupling	T. S. Minniss	Meadville, Pa	Nov. 20, 1866	59, 858
Car-coupling	T. S. Minniss	Meadville, Pa	May 14, 1867	64, 689
Car-coupling	I. N. Mitchell	Arcanum, Ohio	July 20, 1869	92, 866
Car-coupling	W. B. Mitchell	Chicago, Ill	Dec. 16, 1873	145, 584
Car-coupling	G. W. Moffitt	Washington, D. C	Dec. 17, 1861	33, 958
Car-coupling	B. Monroe	Bristol, R. I	June 23, 1868	79, 245
Car-coupling	L. Monzert	New York, N. Y	Aug. 25, 1868	81, 397
Car-coupling	B. D. Moody	Darksville, Mo	May 20, 1873	139, 016
Car-coupling	H. T. Moody	Newburyport, Mass	Mar. 9, 1869	87, 582
Car-coupling	L. Moody	Malden, Mass	Jan. 3, 1865	45, 733
Car-coupling	L. Moody	Malden, Mass	Sept. 26, 1865	50, 152
Car-coupling	L. Moody	Malden, Mass	Dec. 19, 1865	51, 608
Car-coupling	B. Moore	Seaford, Del	Jan. 7, 1873	134, 695
Car-coupling	F. Moore and J. A. Baker	Carrollton, Ohio	Oct. 8, 1867	69, 693
Car-coupling	G. R. Moore	Lyons, Iowa	Nov. 19, 1867	71, 202
Car-coupling	G. R. Moore	Lyons, Iowa	Nov. 19, 1867	71, 203
Car-coupling	G. R. Moore	Philadelphia, Pa	Dec. 23, 1873	145, 746
Car-coupling	S. C. Moore	Last Chance, Iowa	June 25, 1872	128, 237
Car-coupling	T. M. Moore	Newton, N. J	Apr. 28, 1868	77, 398
Car-coupling	H. H. Morgan and A. Gerry	San Francisco, Cal	Nov. 28, 1871	121, 252
Car-coupling	T. Morgan	Marquette, Mich	July 4, 1871	116, 738
Car-coupling	D. C Morris	New Sharon, Iowa	Apr. 8, 1873	137, 617
Car-coupling	J. C. Morris	Greeneville, Tenn	Dec. 20, 1870	110, 269
Car-coupling	J. P. Morris	Bloomington, Ill	July 23, 1867	67, 064
Car-coupling	R. B. Morris	Harrisonville, Mo	Jan. 2, 1872	122, 480
Car-coupling	W. C. Morse	Boston, Mass	Aug. 8, 1865	49, 292
Car-coupling	J. Morton	Cincinnati, Ohio	Dec. 31, 1872	134, 393
Car-coupling	J. Moulton	Moultonville, N. H	Mar. 11, 1873	136, 610
Car-coupling	J. Mount	Monroe Township, N. J	Jan. 3, 1871	110, 770
Car-coupling	H. Mulhollen	Fostoria, Pa	Apr. 1, 1873	137, 470
Car-coupling	J. F. Mullowny, J. Cope, and S. R. Brooks.	Pittsburgh, Connellsville, and Pittsburgh, Pa.	Dec. 2, 1873	145, 228
Car-coupling	W. Musgrove and J. S. Sharp	Studholm Parish and Sussex Parish, Canada.	Aug. 27, 1872	130, 934
Car-coupling	J. W. Musser and R. Carkhuff.	Lewisburgh, Pa	Feb. 14, 1871	111, 767
Car-coupling	J. F. Nagel	Ligonier, Pa	May 18, 1869	90, 290
Car-coupling	F. Nalley	Battle Ground, Ind	Dec. 26, 1871	122, 189
Car-coupling	D. S. Neal	Lynn, Mass	Sept. 3, 1850	7, 620
Car-coupling	R. Neisch and C. G. Hirner	Allentown, Pa	Nov. 5, 1872	132, 852
Car-coupling	W. L. Newell and J. S. Simmerman.	Millville, N. J	Feb. 20, 1866	52, 736
Car-coupling	W. Nichols	Centralia, Ill	May 30, 1871	115, 507
Car-coupling	J. A. Niman	Mansfield, Ohio	July 3, 1866	56, 085
Car-coupling	A. T. Norgan	Pottsville, Pa	Aug. 2, 1870	105, 970
Car-coupling	N. W. Northrup	Greene, N. Y	Oct. 21, 1862	36, 758
Car-coupling	S. G. Northrop	Wilmington, N. C	June 11, 1872	127, 790
Car-coupling	G. W. Noyes	Norwich, Conn	Aug. 27, 1867	68, 105
Car-coupling	S. O'Blenis	Greensburgh, Pa	July 30, 1867	67, 209
Car-coupling	H. L. Ogden	Atkinson, Ill	Nov. 20, 1866	59, 860
Car-coupling	J. H. Oliver	Baltimore, Md	Aug. 29, 1871	118, 476
Car-coupling	J. H. J. O'Neill	New Haven, Conn	May 21, 1867	64, 898
Car-coupling	A. Oot	Minetto, N. Y	Oct. 23, 1860	30, 496
Car-coupling	A. V. B. Orr	Steeleville, Pa	July 16, 1867	66, 733
Car-coupling	J. H. Osgood, jr	Boston, Mass	Apr. 14, 1863	38, 178
Car-coupling	J. Osman and J. F. Potter	Linden Hall, Pa	Nov. 17, 1868	84, 066
Car-coupling	S. A. Otis	Boston, Mass	Oct. 7, 1873	143, 479
Car-coupling	C. Ottinger	Philadelphia, Pa	July 9, 1872	128, 900
Car-coupling	E. E. Packer, jr., and J. Daley	Philadelphia, Pa	Dec. 18, 1866	60, 544
Car-coupling	S. K. Paden	Pulaski, Pa	July 16, 1872	129, 163
Car-coupling	A. G. Page	Augusta, Me	Nov. 28, 1865	51, 209
Car-coupling	J. R. Palmer	Mariposa, Cal	Dec. 6, 1870	109, 932
Car-coupling	J. H. Parsons	Quincy, Mich	Feb. 13, 1866	52, 592
Car-coupling	J. H. Parsons	Quincy, Mich	Mar. 12, 1867	62, 772
Car-coupling	W. B. Parsons	Short Tract, N. Y	May 25, 1869	90, 573
Car-coupling	W. B. Parsons	Short Tract, N. Y	Apr. 19, 1870	102, 149
Car-coupling	W. R. Patton	Des Moines, Iowa	Aug. 16, 1870	106, 399
Car-coupling	D. H. Payne and G. Boxley	Troy, N. Y	Mar. 6, 1866	53, 037
Car-coupling	J. H. Payne	Roseville, Minn	Oct. 14, 1873	143, 636
Car-coupling	H. C. Payson	Haydenville, Mass	Sept. 24, 1867	69, 123
Car-coupling	G. L. Peabody	Buxton, Me	Aug. 6, 1872	130, 238
Car-coupling	J. Pearson	Sacramento, Cal	Oct. 1, 1872	131, 826
Car-coupling	E. W. Peloubet	Newark, N. J	July 29, 1873	141, 290
Car-coupling	D. O. Pender	Palmyra, Mich	Apr. 15, 1873	137, 860
Car-coupling	T. N. Pengelly	Detroit, Mich	Feb. 25, 1873	136, 176
Car-coupling	A. Perrin	Cleveland, Ohio	June 23, 1868	79, 254
Car-coupling	W. V. Perry	Beaver Dam, Wis	July 25, 1871	117, 453
Car-coupling	J. Pettengill, jr	Lisbon, N. H	July 2, 1867	66, 385
Car-coupling	J. M. Phelps	Cogan Station, Pa	Mar. 11, 1873	136, 758
Car-coupling	A. Pierce	Olmsted, Ohio	Sept. 11, 1866	57, 962
Car-coupling	H. W. Pike	Middleport, N. Y	Apr. 23, 1872	125, 985
Car-coupling	W. W. Pitman	Freehold, N. J	May 28, 1872	127, 188
Car-coupling	E. F. Plant	Burr Oak, Mich	Mar. 11, 1873	136, 759
Car-coupling	H. Plumb	Philadelphia, Pa	May 23, 1871	115, 236
Car-coupling	W. D. Pope	Gadsden, Ala	Oct. 14, 1873	143, 638

Index of patents issued from the United States Patent Office from 1790 *to* 1873, *inclusive*—Continued.

Invention.	Inventor.	Residence.	Date.	No.
Car coupling	A. Porter	Irving, Ill	May 30, 1871	115, 517
Car-coupling	C. Porter	Nunda, N. Y	Mar. 4, 1873	136, 540
Car-coupling	H. H. Potter	Sterlingville, N. Y	Dec. 9, 1873	145, 446
Car-coupling	R. S. Potter	Chicago, Ill	Aug. 28, 1860	29, 815
Car-coupling	T. K. Power	Arsenal Post-office, Pa	Mar. 2, 1869	87, 366
Car-coupling	T. D. Powers	Rochester, Wis	Oct. 16, 1866	58, 883
Car-coupling	D. R. Pratt	Worcester, Mass	Dec. 12, 1848	5, 961
Car-coupling	A. J. Prescott	Catawissa, Pa	Sept. 6, 1870	107, 196
Car-coupling	A. Pritz	Dayton, Ohio	Mar. 25, 1873	137, 238
Car-coupling	S. Puffer	Oxford, N. Y	June 11, 1867	65, 602
Car-coupling	H. Purlier, J. Harlan, and E. C. Cheek.	Cincinnati, Ohio	Apr. 19, 1859	23, 705
Car-coupling	A. Pursell	Williamsport, Pa	Apr. 8, 1873	137, 719
Car-coupling	G. W. Putnam	South Glen's Falls, N. Y	Dec. 5, 1871	121, 660
Car-coupling	G. W. Putnam	Moreau, N. Y	June 4, 1872	127, 644
Car-coupling	G. W. Putnam	South Glen's Falls, N. Y	Oct. 14, 1873	143, 716
Car-coupling	S. S. Quest	Wellsburgh, W. Va	Aug. 28, 1866	57, 566
Car-coupling	G. Quick and J. N. Wallis	Fleming, N. Y	May 22, 1866	54, 955
Car-coupling	C. M. Radcliff	Piermont, N. Y	Apr. 19, 1864	42, 400
Car-coupling	J. W. Radebaugh	Lancaster, Ohio	Nov. 19, 1872	133, 252
Car-coupling	J. C. Ransier	Lyons, N. Y	Apr. 5, 1859	23, 498
Car-coupling	R. Rawson	Quincy, Mich	Apr. 3, 1860	27, 737
Car-coupling	A. Ray	Granville, Mo	Apr. 6, 1869	88, 736
Car-coupling	J. H. Reed	New Haven, Conn	Apr. 25, 1865	47, 455
Car-coupling	J. H. Reed	New Haven, Conn	Sept. 4, 1866	57, 767
Car-coupling	J. V. Reed	New Albany, Ind	Sept. 16, 1873	142, 943
Car-coupling	S. Reed	Liberty, Pa	Nov. 11, 1873	144, 476
Car-coupling	S. H. and G. A. Reed	Fredericktown, Ohio	Feb. 21, 1871	111, 972
Car-coupling	N. Reeves	Du Quoin, Ill	Apr. 16, 1867	63, 940
Car-coupling	S. B. Reploglo	Roaring Springs, Pa	Mar. 4, 1873	136, 547
Car-coupling	S. B. Replogle	Roaring Springs, Pa	Sept. 16, 1873	142, 815
Car-coupling	H. Resley	Cumberland, Md	Jan. 14, 1868	73, 385
Car-coupling	W. A. and J. M. Rex, jr	Butler, Ind	Aug. 9, 1870	106, 204
Car-coupling	C. M. Reynolds	Champaign, Ill	Apr. 9, 1867	63, 750
Car-coupling	W. Richards, jr	Franklin, Pa	May 30, 1871	115, 522
Car-coupling	R. Rickkon	Rochester, N. Y	May 24, 1859	24, 146
Car-coupling	L. P. Rider	Pittsburgh, Pa	Nov. 11, 1873	144, 412
Car-coupling	J. Ridings and J. O. Roberts	New Castle, Del	Aug. 13, 1867	67, 677
Car-coupling	J. D. Riggs	Buckley, Ill	Feb. 6, 1872	123, 510
Car-coupling	M. Rinehart	Monroe, Mich	Jan. 17, 1865	45, 939
Car-coupling	A. G. Ritz	Elizabethtown, Ind	Jan. 12, 1869	85, 767
Car-coupling	H. R. Robbins	Baltimore, Md	Sept. 26, 1871	119, 409
Car-coupling	J. N. Robbins	Goshen, Ohio	Nov. 9, 1869	96, 732
Car-coupling	N. Robbins, jr	Rockport, Mass	June 12, 1866	55, 537
Car-coupling	C. F. Rodrick	Lynn, Mass	May 7, 1867	64, 574
Car-coupling	S. Rogers	London, England	July 1, 1873	140, 545
Car-coupling	S. O. Rogers, jr	Stamfordville, N. Y	Mar. 3, 1868	75, 055
Car-coupling	W. B. Rogerson and H. Beyea	Paterson, N. J	Apr. 18, 1871	113, 932
Car-coupling	H. S. Root	Muncy, Pa	Feb. 22, 1870	100, 192
Car-coupling	B. R. Rose	Kansas City, Mo	Sept. 27, 1870	107, 814
Car-coupling	J. Royal, M. A. Lentz, and J. M. Deibert.	La Fayette, Ind	May 23, 1871	115, 242
Car-coupling	J. Royal, M. A. Lentz, and J. M. Deibert.	La Fayette, Ind	Feb. 11, 1873	135, 849
Car-coupling	L. Ruel	Saint Johnsbury, Vt	Oct. 28, 1873	144, 034
Car-coupling	H. M. Rulon	Monmouth, Ill	May 30, 1865	47, 985
Car-coupling	J. B. Rumsey	Washington, D. C	Aug. 21, 1866	57, 385
Car-coupling	J. C. Rupp and S. Ott	Newark, Del	June 6, 1871	115, 643
Car-coupling	E. Russell	Waynesburgh, Pa	Dec. 1, 1868	84, 648
Car-coupling	H. G. Russell	Lincoln, Ill	Nov. 11, 1873	144, 479
Car-coupling	T. W. and T. D. Ryan	Maumee City, Ohio	Oct. 21, 1873	143, 932
Car-coupling	J. S. Sammons	New York, N. Y	June 5, 1860	28, 609
Car-coupling	A. Sanders	Penn Yan, N. Y	Sept. 1, 1868	81, 689
Car-coupling	S. S. Sartwell	Camden, N. Y	May 2, 1871	114, 343
Car-coupling	A. Shorg and B. Van Valkenburgh.	Cobleskill, N. Y	Sept. 23, 1873	143, 099
Car-coupling	L. O. Schultz	Mattoon, Ill	Nov. 5, 1867	70, 625
Car-coupling	P. H. Schuyler	Lyme, Ohio	Aug. 27, 1867	68, 120
Car-coupling	E. R. Scott	Noblesville, Ind	Oct. 14, 1873	143, 720
Car-coupling	L. Scott and P. Trimner	Burgettstown, Pa	July 28, 1868	80, 426
Car-coupling	J. Scislove	Tiffin, Ohio	Oct. 14, 1873	143, 593
Car-coupling	W. F. Senior	Ripley, Ohio	Sept. 16, 1873	142, 873
Car-coupling	C. S. Servoss	Wilmington, N. C	May 7, 1872	126, 494
Car-coupling	F. J. Seybold	Chicago, Ill	Aug. 19, 1873	141, 895
Car-coupling	J. B. Shelly	Richland Township, Pa	Apr. 16, 1872	125, 698
Car-coupling	H. J. Shepardson	Shelburne Falls, Mass	Nov. 7, 1865	50, 882
Car-coupling	J. Shepler	Lambertville, N. J	May 9, 1871	114, 612
Car-coupling	G. W. Shingleton	Auburn, N. Y	June 4, 1867	65, 513
Car-coupling	L. H. Shuler	Crawfordsville, Ind	Aug. 7, 1860	29, 526
Car-coupling	W. P. Siddens	Danville, Ill	June 18, 1872	128, 182
Car-coupling	W. P. Siddens	State Line City, Ind	July 15, 1873	140, 957
Car-coupling	J. E. Simpson	Malden Bridge, N. Y	July 13, 1869	92, 547
Car-coupling	J. P. Sinclair	Little Prairie Ronde, Mich	Aug. 19, 1862	36, 241
Car-coupling	W. H. Skidmore	Secor, Ill	Dec. 19, 1871	122, 070
Car-coupling	S. Slack	Oxford, Pa	May 10, 1864	42, 696
Car-coupling	D. V. B. Smart	Troy, N. Y	Apr. 14, 1868	76, 833
Car-coupling	H. A. Smead and C. H. Huntly	Pavilion, N. Y	May 27, 1862	35, 399
Car-coupling	E. D. Smith	Sutton Township, Canada	Oct. 14, 1873	143, 728
Car-coupling	J. Smith and J. F. Irvin	La Porte, Ind	May 21, 1867	64, 918
Car-coupling	J. E. Smith	Jackson, Pa	Sept. 16, 1873	142, 818
Car-coupling	J. L. Smith	Penn Township, Pa	Oct. 29, 1867	70, 279
Car-coupling	J. W. and J. P. Smith	Elder's Ridge, Pa	Jan. 28, 1868	73, 935
Car-coupling	L. J. Smith	New York, N. Y	Oct. 4, 1870	107, 971
Car-coupling	O. L. Smith and J. F. Utton	Providence, R. I	Sept. 12, 1871	118, [illegible]
Car-coupling	S. H. Smith	Venice Centre, N. Y	Sept. 24, 1867	69, 266
Car-coupling	T. Smith	Waterford, N. Y	July 22, 1873	141, 177
Car-coupling	T. B. Smith and A. Hinchman	Pleasant Hill, Mo	Mar. 16, 1869	87, [illegible]
Car-coupling	W. B. Snedaker	Phœnix, N. Y	Oct. 18, 1870	108, 464

Index of patents issued from the United States Patent Office from 1790 *to* 1873, *inclusive*—Continued.

Invention.	Inventor.	Residence.	Date.	No.
Car-coupling	W. B. Snedaker	Syracuse, N. Y	Nov. 4, 1873	144, 293
Car-coupling	P. H. Snelling	Wartrace, Tenn	July 30, 1867	67, 367
Car-coupling	D. B. Snyder	Millville, N. J	Aug. 21, 1866	57, 397
Car-coupling	H. Soggs	Columbus, Pa	Feb. 5, 1867	61, 771
Car-coupling	H. Soggs	Columbus, Pa	Mar. 30, 1869	88, 342
Car-coupling	J. P. Spangle	Hopewell Centre, N. Y	Aug. 14, 1866	57, 206
Car-coupling	J. P. Spangle	Hopewell Centre, N. Y	Apr. 9, 1867	63, 662
Car-coupling	T. W. Sparks	Rochester, N. Y	July 25, 1871	117, 475
Car-coupling	J. F. Spaulding	Rutland, Vt	Apr. 20, 1869	89, 089
Car-coupling	C. Spear	Chapinsville, N. Y	Nov. 6, 1866	59, 517
Car-coupling	G. D. Spooner and J. F. F. Hale	Rutland, Vt	Aug. 14, 1866	57, 208
Car-coupling	G. C. Sprangler	Allegheny City, Pa	Apr. 4, 1871	113, 462
Car-coupling	E. Staples and W. W. Gould	Skowhegan, Me	Mar. 5, 1867	62, 700
Car-coupling	L. S. Starrett	Athol, Mass	Feb. 7, 1871	111, 695
Car-coupling	A. B. Steele	Winsted, Conn	Aug. 25, 1868	81, 551
Car-coupling	T. Steinhauer	Syracuse, N. Y	Mar. 31, 1868	76, 112
Car-coupling	D. M. Steward	Dayton, Ohio	July 14, 1868	80, 026
Car-coupling	O. S. St. John	Willoughby, Ohio	Dec. 8, 1868	84, 716
Car-coupling	O. S. St. John	Willoughby, Ohio	Dec. 29, 1868	85, 489
Car-coupling	J. T. Stoakes	New Church Parish, England.	Dec. 31, 1867	72, 933
Car-coupling	G. F. Stone	Baltimore, Md	Apr. 30, 1872	126, 344
Car-coupling	T. B. Stout	Keyport, N. J	Aug. 8, 1854	11, 498
Car-coupling	W. A. Stowell	Mooretown, Vt	May 21, 1867	64, 921
Car-coupling	X. St. Pierre	Ophir City, Utah	Oct. 28, 1873	144, 038
Car-coupling	A. Strain	Greenfield, Ohio	Dec. 9, 1873	145, 371
Car-coupling	A. F. Street	Zanesville, Ohio	Dec. 13, 1870	110, 088
Car-coupling	A. Stroh	Port Jervis, N. Y	June 11, 1861	32, 549
Car-coupling	I. W. Stuart, jr	Charlottesville, Ind	Mar. 19, 1867	62, 978
Car-coupling	F. D. Sturges and W. M. Young	Mount Vernon, Ohio	Apr. 27, 1869	89, 355
Car-coupling	J. R. Sueeop	Birmingham, Pa	Feb. 18, 1873	136, 011
Car-coupling	A. W. Sullenberger	Laurel, Ind	Mar. 10, 1868	75, 489
Car-coupling	D. Sutherland	Milo, Ill	Nov. 19, 1872	133, 268
Car-coupling	J. M. Sutton	Sutton's Corners, Pa	Mar. 18, 1873	136, 879
Car-coupling	H. C. Swan	Washington, D. C	Jan. 30, 1872	123, 207
Car-coupling	J. Swan	Baltimore, Md	Oct. 22, 1867	70, 131
Car-coupling	B. F. Sweet	Fond du Lac, Wis	Oct. 29, 1861	33, 612
Car-coupling	N. Swigart	West Richfield, Ohio	July 16, 1872	129, 300
Car-coupling	P. Swineford	Middleburgh, Pa	Oct. 21, 1873	143, 791
Car-coupling	A. B. and F. S. Taft	Montreal, Canada	Apr. 3, 1866	53, 764
Car-coupling	F. F. Taylor and G. Withington	San Francisco and Ione City, Cal.	Sept. 16, 1873	142, 962
Car-coupling	O. Taylor	Grand Rapids, Wis	Oct. 14, 1873	143, 646
Car-coupling	J. Temple	Bellefonte, Pa	Apr. 5, 1870	101, 543
Car-coupling	J. Temple	Bellefonte, Pa	Sept. 19, 1871	119, 196
Car-coupling	J. Temple	Bellefonte, Pa	Jan. 30, 1872	123, 134
Car-coupling	J. Temple	Danville, Pa	Feb. 18, 1873	135, 948
Car-coupling	J. Temple	Mooresburgh, Pa	Aug. 19, 1873	142, 059
Car-coupling	G. B. Terry and W. G. Hawley	Pittsford and Gorham, N. Y	Sept. 27, 1870	107, 837
Car-coupling	E. D. Thompson	Lawrence, Kans	July 12, 1870	105, 278
Car-coupling	J. A. Thompson	Readington, N. J	Dec. 24, 1872	134, 329
Car-coupling	P. M. Thompson	Toronto, Canada	Sept. 16, 1873	142, 965
Car-coupling	W. M. Thompson	Carlisle, Pa	Oct. 22, 1872	132, 501
Car-coupling	S. Thorp	Turner, Me	Aug. 19, 1862	36, 247
Car-coupling	S. and W. Thorpe	Turner, Me	Feb. 18, 1868	74, 631
Car-coupling	A. C. Tichnor	Council Bluffs, Iowa	Sept. 8, 1868	81, 961
Car-coupling	W. E. Tickler and E. T. and D. M. Marshall.	Pierceton, Ind	July 31, 1866	56, 866
Car-coupling	J. Timms and W. P. Brown	Malta, Ohio	Sept. 19, 1871	119, 097
Car-coupling	C. D. Tisdale	East Boston, Mass	June 2, 1863	38, 792
Car-coupling	D. J. Tittle	Albany, N. Y	Nov. 27, 1866	60, 092
Car-coupling	D. J. Tittle	Albany, N. Y	July 2, 1867	66, 418
Car-coupling	W. Todd	Portland, Me	Jan. 28, 1873	135, 387
Car-coupling	J. B. Tracy	Lincoln, Del	Dec. 12, 1871	121, 823
Car-coupling	J. B. Tracy	Lincoln, Del	Oct. 7, 1873	143, 429
Car-coupling	H. Trefry	Winfield, Mich	June 20, 1871	116, 238
Car-coupling	A. H. Trego	Lambertville, N. J	June 11, 1861	32, 543
Car-coupling	T. B. Tremper	Rockland Lake, N. Y	Dec. 5, 1871	121, 690
Car-coupling	H. H. Trenor	New York, N. Y	Aug. 7, 1866	57, 014
Car-coupling	J. Trent	Millertown, N. Y	Oct. 1, 1867	69, 511
Car-coupling	T. Tripp	Chicago, Ill	Mar. 21, 1865	46, 958
Car-coupling	A. Truxell and F. J. Williams	Toledo, Ohio	Feb. 11, 1873	135, 866
Car-coupling	N. A. Tucker	Burlington, Vt	Feb. 10, 1863	37, 649
Car-coupling	E. A. Turner	New York, N. Y	May 28, 1867	65, 310
Car-coupling	R. D. Turner	New York, N. Y	July 8, 1862	35, 849
Car-coupling	W. E. Twining	Morrison, Ill	Mar. 24, 1868	76, 006
Car-coupling	J. N. and S. T. Vandergrit, S. D. French, and E. S. Stone.	Wabash, Ind	Jan. 7, 1868	73, 140
Car-coupling	J. B. Van Deusen	New York, N. Y	Mar. 4, 1862	34, 604
Car-coupling	J. Van Dyne	Crum Elbow, N. Y	Dec. 15, 1863	40, 966
Car-coupling	I. W. Van Houten	Philadelphia, Pa	July 3, 1860	29, 022
Car-coupling	I. L. Vansant	Glasgow, Del	Mar. 30, 1869	88, 424
Car-coupling	M. Van Slyke and D. W. Wood	Rome, N. Y	Nov. 2, 1869	96, 514
Car-coupling	J. Vansteenberg	Chicago, Ill	May 17, 1870	103, 108
Car-coupling	W. Van Valkinburgh	Smithville, N. Y	July 31, 1866	56, 837
Car-coupling	J. J. Vaughan	Alexandria, Va	May 22, 1860	28, 444
Car-coupling	J. B. Vedder	Gloversville, N. Y	May 30, 1871	115, 394
Car-coupling	H. B. Verrie and D. G. Wightman.	North Kingston, R. I	Nov. 23, 1869	97, 250
Car-coupling	L. and W. H. Waddell	Staunton, Va	June 5, 1860	28, 620
Car-coupling	W. H. and L. Waddell and J. A. Lutz.	Churchville, Va	Sept. 16, 1873	142, 970
Car-coupling	J. Waite	Yarmouth, Me	Sept. 9, 1873	142, 750
Car-coupling	W. Walker	Woodside, Cal	Sept. 20, 1870	107, 571
Car-coupling	S. J. Wallace	Carthage, Ill	Oct. 23, 1866	59, 101
Car-coupling	W. K. Wallace and E. C. Rutledge.	Crawfordsville and Shannondale, Ind.	May 9, 1871	114, 752
Car-coupling	W. V. Wallace	New York, N. Y	Apr. 27, 1869	89, 525

Index of patents issued from the United States Patent Office from 1790 *to* 1873, *inclusive*—Continued.

Invention.	Inventor.	Residence.	Date.	No.
Car-coupling	D. Walter	Evansport, Ohio	Nov. 19, 1872	133, 181
Car-coupling	W. E. Warner and M. J. Palmer	Newark and Syracuse, N. Y	Aug. 6, 1867	67, 468
Car-coupling	W. Y. Warner	Wilmington, Del	Mar. 19, 1867	62, 984
Car-coupling	W. Y. Warner	Wilmington, Del	Nov. 26, 1867	71, 559
Car-coupling	M. Waterbury	Polo, Ill	Feb. 11, 1862	34, 384
Car-coupling	C. Weaver	Easton, Pa	Dec. 4, 1866	60, 299
Car-coupling	G. C. E. Weber	Cleveland, Ohio	Jan. 9, 1872	122, 690
Car-coupling	H. Webster	Elgin, Ill	Aug. 4, 1863	39, 436
Car-coupling	H. Webster	Elgin, Ill	Jan. 16, 1866	52, 097
Car-coupling	G. H. Weeks	Allegan, Mich	Jan. 10, 1871	110, 880
Car-coupling	W. Weiler	Washington, N. J	Jan. 21, 1868	73, 681
Car-coupling	E. F. Wells	New York, N. Y	Nov. 29, 1864	45, 288
Car-coupling	J. M. Wells	Painesville, Ohio	Nov. 4, 1873	144, 298
Car-coupling	C. O. Wheeler	Matteson, Ill	Apr. 24, 1866	54, 237
Car-coupling	E. P. Wheeler	Corinth, Miss	Aug. 6, 1872	130, 262
Car-coupling	J. M. Wheeler	Afton, Iowa	Sept. 17, 1872	131, 416
Car-coupling	J. M. Wheeler and C. W. Chase	Batavia, Iowa	Oct. 19, 1869	96, 065
Car-coupling	J. P. Whipple	Whitewater, Wis	Apr. 8, 1873	137, 642
Car-coupling	J. White	Harrison, Ohio	Aug. 4, 1868	80, 688
Car-coupling	N. S. White	Port Chester, N. Y	Oct. 4, 1864	44, 571
Car-coupling	J. Whiteford	Pond City, Kans	Feb. 22, 1870	100, 092
Car-coupling	D. G. Whitmore	Bridgewater, Va	Nov. 9, 1869	96, 749
Car-coupling	E. R. Whitney	Plattsburgh, N. Y	Apr. 7, 1868	76, 368
Car-coupling	E. R. Whitney	Plattsburgh, N. Y	June 23, 1868	79, 283
Car-coupling	O. J. Whitney	Clifton Springs, N. Y	July 16, 1867	66, 922
Car-coupling	N. Whitten	Etna, Me	May 5, 1868	77, 558
Car-coupling	C. Whitus	Philadelphia, Pa	Apr. 23, 1872	126, 000
Car-coupling	W. F. Wickersham and E. Roush.	Springfield, Ill	Apr. 21, 1868	77, 150
Car-coupling	J. Widney	Allegheny City, Pa	July 5, 1864	43, 447
Car-coupling	J. Widney	Carlisle, Pa	Apr. 24, 1866	54, 238
Car-coupling	J. Wilcox	Canton, Pa	Aug. 12, 1873	141, 846
Car-coupling	E. Wiley	Philadelphia, Pa	May 20, 1873	139, 221
Car-coupling	W. Williams	Harrisonburgh, Va	Jan. 2, 1872	122, 424
Car-coupling	C. C. Wilson	Kewanee, Ill	June 30, 1863	39, 087
Car-coupling	E. W. Wilson and J. E. Erwin	Springfield, Mass	Nov. 14, 1865	50, 994
Car-coupling	G. W. Wilson	Abingdon, Ill	Sept. 4, 1866	57, 807
Car-coupling	J. F. Wilson	Pittsburgh, Pa	Jan. 19, 1869	85, 979
Car-coupling	L. B. Wilson	Caldwell, Ohio	Nov. 26, 1872	133, 512
Car-coupling	L. B. Wilson	Caldwell, Ohio	Feb. 11, 1873	135, 871
Car-coupling	J. T. Wilson and T. J. Louis	East Liberty and Port Perry, Pa.	Jan. 15, 1867	61, 296
Car-coupling	W. Winer	Union City, Ind	Apr. 5, 1870	101, 694
Car-coupling	W. M. Wiswell	Portland, Me	Oct. 28, 1873	144, 008
Car-coupling	J. B. Witherle	Upton, Mass	July 15, 1856	15, 355
Car-coupling	G. Withington and F. F. Taylor.	Ione City and San Francisco, Cal.	Mar. 18, 1873	136, 889
Car-coupling	H. E. Wolcott	Elbridge, N. Y	Mar. 12, 1872	124, 648
Car-coupling	R. T. Wolcott	Claremont, N. H	June 21, 1870	104, 678
Car-coupling	G. E. Wood	Providence, R. I	May 10, 1864	42, 710
Car-coupling	M. R. Wood	Chicago, Ill	Nov. 11, 1873	144, 490
Car-coupling	B. A Worden	Scranton, Pa	Apr. 23, 1872	126, 122
Car-coupling	G. Worden	Pittston, Pa	Jan. 2, 1872	122, 509
Car-coupling	G. Worden	Pittston, Pa	Dec. 31, 1872	134, 503
Car-coupling	J. F. Wotring	Willey, W. Va	June 25, 1867	66, 061
Car-coupling	J. C. Wrenshall	Baltimore, Md	June 21, 1870	104, 679
Car-coupling	D. D. Wright	Oakville, Canada	Apr. 27, 1869	89, 544
Car-coupling	D. D. Wright	Oakville, Canada	Aug. 20, 1872	130, 779
Car-coupling	E. M. Wright	Wyandotte, Kans	May 24, 1864	42, 897
Car-coupling	G. Yates	West Dresden, N. Y	June 14, 1859	24, 422
Car-coupling	J. C. Young	Bloomington, Ind	June 8, 1869	91, 194
Car-coupling	J. J. Zabriskie, jr., and C. M. Powers.	Ridgewood, N. J	Dec. 31, 1872	134, 414
Car-coupling	A. Zeigler	Cumberland, Md	Sept. 23, 1873	143, 215
Car-coupling	S. H. Zink	Knobnoster, Mo	Jan. 28, 1873	135, 255
Car-coupling	E. Zorger	Greensburgh, Ind	Jan. 1, 1867	60, 815
Car coupling and buffer	A. Stevens	Portland, Me	May 14, 1872	126, 849
Car-coupling apparatus	R. F. Randolph, jr	East Palestine, Ohio	Sept. 20, 1870	107, 623
Car-coupling attachment	W. G. Brown and J. W. Jedkins.	Monmouth, Me	Jan. 28, 1873	135, 262
Car-coupling, Automatic	W. Bragg	Connersville, Ind	Oct. 27, 1868	83, 358
Car-coupling, Automatic	D. P. Cory	Cranford, N. J	Jan. 3, 1871	110, 741
Car-coupling, Automatic	W. W. Jeffery and C. Snyder	Greenview and Middleton, Ill.	Nov. 10, 1868	83, 857
Car-coupling, Automatic	P. Laflin	Warren, Mass	Oct. 27, 1868	83, 512
Car-coupling, Automatic	J. McLain and J. Kelsey	Saint Mary's, Ohio	May 25, 1869	90, 569
Car-coupling, Automatic	H. T. Romertye	Philadelphia, Pa	Jan. 28, 1862	34, 284
Car-coupling, Automatic	H. Tarbox	Warwick, R. I	Nov. 3, 1868	83, 673
Car-coupling, City-railway	G. Collyer and A. H Patterson	Philadelphia, Pa	July 17, 1860	29, 142
Car-coupling, Device for	L. L. Bond	Chicago, Ill	Mar. 11, 1873	136, 640
Car coupling-hook, Coal	F. Bush	Boonton, N. J	Sept. 19, 1871	119, 117
Car coupling, Horse-railway	B. E. Sampson	Boston, Mass	July 27, 1858	21, 026
Car coupling-link, Railway	G. Ryer	Bridgeport, Conn	July 16, 1872	129, 368
Car-coupling-link supporter	J. U. Fiester	Winchester, Ohio	Sept. 3, 1872	130, 986
Car-coupling pins, Die for making	C. H. Williams	Cleveland, Ohio	July 15, 1873	140, 980
Car-coupling pins, Die for manufacturing	C. H. Williams	Cleveland, Ohio	July 15, 1873	140, 981
Car-coupling pins, Machine for rolling	F. W. Davidson	Cleveland, Ohio	Nov. 16, 1869	96, 782
Car-coupling pins, Machine for rolling	W. Davis and J. White	Cleveland, Ohio	Feb. 22, 1870	100, 125
Car coupling, Railway	S. J. Anderson	Cazenovia, N. Y	Mar. 15, 1870	100, 837
Car coupling, Railway	R. K. Andrews	South Valley, N. Y	Aug. 17, 1869	93, 850
Car coupling, Railway	A. A. Atwater	Trumansburgh, N. Y	Nov. 7, 1871	120, 610
Car coupling, Railway	H. A. Barnes	Milwaukee, Wis	Nov. 1, 1859	25, 938
Car coupling, Railway	R. W. Baylor	Norfolk, Va	Sept. 7, 1869	94, 547
Car coupling, Railway	G. S Bishop	Washington, D. C	July 27, 1858	20, 983
Car coupling, Railway	J. Blakeney	Springfield, Ohio	May 17, 1870	103, 130
Car coupling, Railway	E. A Bohne	Brookhaven, Wis	Aug. 31, 1869	94, 386
Car coupling, Railway	H. F. Breneman	Rapho Township, Pa	Aug. 10, 1869	93, 407
Car coupling, Railway	W. H. Burridge and N. L. Post	Cleveland, Ohio	May 4, 1858	20, 139

Index of patents issued from the United States Patent Office from 1790 *to* 1873, *inclusive*—Continued.

Invention.	Inventor.	Residence.	Date.	No.
Car coupling, Railway	L. F. Buschmann	New York, N. Y	Feb. 8, 1870	99, 632
Car coupling, Railway	J. Campbell, V. B. Lighthizer, and P. Shannon.	Steubenville, Ohio	Aug. 24, 1858	21, 244
Car coupling, Railway	P. Campbell	Carrolltown, Pa	May 16, 1871	114, 758
Car coupling, Railway	S. O. Campbell	Centretown, Mo	Aug. 9, 1870	106, 119
Car coupling, Railway	R. Carkhuff	Lewisburgh, Pa	May 24, 1864	42, 835
Car coupling, Railway	R. D. Chatterton	Bath, Great Britain	June 28, 1864	43, 375
Car coupling, Railway	T. J. Christy	Noblesville, Ind	Apr. 3, 1866	53, 574
Car coupling, Railway	W. C. Clark	Portland, Me	Dec. 8, 1863	40, 820
Car coupling, Railway	J. M. Connel	Newark, Ohio	Jan. 5, 1858	19, 021
Car coupling, Railway	M. Connelly	Baltimore, Md	Oct. 5, 1869	95, 431
Car coupling, Railway	J. W. Corey	Crawfordsville, Ind	Sept. 14, 1858	21, 486
Car coupling, Railway	W. Cottrell	Bordentown, N. J	Oct. 5, 1869	95, 434
Car coupling, Railway	R. A. Cowell	Cleveland, Ohio	Oct. 6, 1868	82, 807
Car coupling, Railway	R. A. Cowell	Cleveland, Ohio	Sept. 6, 1870	107, 008
Car coupling, Railway	J. A. Cutting and G. Butterfield	Boston, Mass	Oct. 7, 1846	4, 802
Car coupling, Railway	J. Davis	Allegheny City, Pa	Oct. 20, 1863	40, 331
Car coupling, Railway	T. J. Delany	London County, Va	May 17, 1870	103, 156
Car coupling, Railway	J. L. Devol and A. L. Peadro	Parkersburgh, W. Va	Aug. 16, 1870	106, 471
Car coupling, Railway	L. M. Doddridge	Portland, Ind	Mar. 9, 1869	87, 649
Car coupling, Railway	G. W. Doolittle	Richfield Springs, N. Y	Jan. 26, 1858	19, 186
Car coupling, Railway	T. B. Dora	Mattoon, Ill	Sept. 7, 1869	94, 579
Car coupling, Railway	J. W. H. Doubler	Chicago, Ill	Mar. 1, 1870	100, 272
Car coupling, Railway	H. Dübs and S. G. Goodall-Copestake.	Glasgow, Great Britain	Mar. 7, 1871	112, 431
Car coupling, Railway	C. H. Eisenbrandt	Baltimore, Md	May 24, 1859	24, 109
Car coupling, Railway	J. Elbertson	Kirksville, Mo	July 6, 1869	92, 293
Car coupling, Railway	J. T. England	Baltimore, Md	Dec. 4, 1855	13, 869
Car coupling, Railway	W. J. Evans	Homer, Iowa	Mar. 8, 1870	100, 515
Car coupling, Railway	A. C. Fell	Caledonia, Ohio	Mar. 12, 1872	124, 430
Car coupling, Railway	H. L. Fidler	Congress, Ohio	Dec. 24, 1872	134, 135
Car coupling, Railway	J. C. Fischer and W. E. Kittredge.	Milwaukee, Wis	July 26, 1870	105, 791
Car coupling, Railway	C. Flanders	Charlestown, Mass	Dec. 16, 1856	16, 230
Car coupling, Railway	A. Geiss	Buffalo, N. Y	Mar. 22, 1870	100, 999
Car coupling, Railway	F. E. Gleason	Columbus, Ohio	May 18, 1858	20, 264
Car coupling, Railway	J. G. Goshon	Shippensburgh, Pa	Dec. 27, 1859	26, 568
Car coupling, Railway	W. F. Grassler	Muncy, Pa	May 17, 1870	103, 172
Car coupling, Railway	R. Green	Boonton, N. J	Feb. 8, 1870	99, 562
Car coupling, Railway	W. H. Hall	Malone, N. Y	Jan. 19, 1869	86, 011
Car coupling, Railway	G. Harris	Ipswich, Mass	Apr. 20, 1869	89, 145
Car coupling, Railway	A. S. Hart	San Francisco, Cal	Dec. 21, 1869	98, 058
Car coupling, Railway	D. Hart	Romulus, N. Y	June 7, 1870	104, 024
Car coupling, Railway	A. Hebert	Malone, N. Y	June 14, 1870	104, 306
Car coupling, Railway	A. G. Heckrotte	New York, N. Y	July 17, 1855	13, 264
Car coupling, Railway	S. R. Herd	Allegheny City, Pa	Feb. 22, 1870	100, 146
Car coupling, Railway	J. W. Hess	Montandon, Pa	Aug. 9, 1870	106, 159
Car coupling, Railway	J. R. Hill	Millville, N. J	Nov. 7, 1865	50, 824
Car coupling, Railway	N. Hill	Leavenworth City, Kans	Dec. 14, 1869	97, 918
Car coupling, Railway	O. Hood, jr	Turner, Me	July 17, 1860	29, 219
Car coupling, Railway	D. A. Hopkins	Elmira, N. Y	Aug. 1, 1854	11, 428
Car coupling, Railway	D. D. Howe	Beaver Dam, Wis	Nov. 10, 1868	83, 966
Car coupling, Railway	L. and J. K. Huddle	Tiffin, Ohio	Jan. 24, 1871	111, 123
Car coupling, Railway	G. C. Hugg	Berlin, N. J	May 31, 1870	103, 618
Car coupling, Railway	R. M. Hughes	Pleasant Grove, Pa	Mar. 5, 1861	31, 603
Car coupling, Railway	L. Ibeck	Kickapoo, Ill	Nov. 7, 1871	120, 746
Car coupling, Railway	J. H. Johnson	Dresden, Mo	Aug. 16, 1870	106, 367
Car coupling, Railway	W. C. Johnson	Fort Madison, Iowa	Nov. 30, 1869	97, 410
Car coupling, Railway	J. H. Jones	Scio, N. Y	Apr. 10, 1855	12, 680
Car coupling, Railway	O. Kelsey	Commerce, Mich	July 20, 1869	92, 839
Car coupling, Railway	C. P. Kenyon	Wilson, N. C	Sept. 14, 1858	21, 562
Car coupling, Railway	J. D. Kerrison	New York, N. Y	Nov. 16, 1869	96, 813
Car coupling, Railway	L. Laley	Goshen, Ind	Nov. 16, 1869	96, 816
Car coupling, Railway	J. Larimore and J. M. Williams	Connersville, Ind	Sept. 28, 1869	95, 360
Car coupling, Railway	G. Lavally, jr	Champlain, N. Y	June 26, 1860	28, 872
Car coupling, Railway	A. Lhapham and D. H. Burns	Brooklyn, N. Y	May 25, 1858	20, 392
Car coupling, Railway	L. D. Livermore	Hartland, Vt	Nov. 11, 1851	8, 514
Car coupling, Railway	H. E. Loane	Baltimore, Md	Mar. 23, 1858	19, 705
Car coupling, Railway	H. L. Lockwood	Denmark, Iowa	Nov. 30, 1869	97, 303
Car coupling, Railway	F. B. Lord	Cincinnati, Ohio	Nov. 16, 1869	96, 932
Car coupling, Railway	D. Lynahon and C. J. Wing	Buffalo, N. Y	Oct. 28, 1856	15, 997
Car coupling, Railway	J. Marston	Saratoga Springs, N. Y	Oct. 26, 1869	96, 130
Car coupling, Railway	G. W. McEuen and C. Eves	Millville, Pa	Oct. 31, 1871	120, 526
Car coupling, Railway	J. McKinney	Lansing, Mich	Sept. 4, 1860	29, 900
Car coupling, Railway	E. D. Meier	Saint Louis, Mo	June 6, 1871	115, 627
Car coupling, Railway	G. H. Merriam	Portland, Me	Aug. 8, 1871	117, 909
Car coupling, Railway	J. S. Merriken	Baltimore, Md	Oct. 19, 1869	96, 070
Car coupling, Railway	J. Miller	Olean, N. Y	Nov. 14, 1854	11, 940
Car coupling, Railway	W. H. H. Miller	Williamsport, Pa	Aug. 28, 1860	29, 806
Car coupling, Railway	R. L. Mills and P. Carpenter	Lancaster, Ohio	July 5, 1859	24, 651
Car coupling, Railway	J. A. Morrison	Brady's Bend, Pa	Oct. 12, 1869	95, 711
Car coupling, Railway	C. Norpel	Newark, Ohio	Dec. 27, 1859	26, 608
Car coupling, Railway	N. Norris	Buchanan, Mich	Oct. 4, 1870	107, 950
Car coupling, Railway	J. M. Osgood, jr., and F. B. Shaw	Boston, Mass	Jan. 15, 1861	31, 127
Car coupling, Railway	G. W. Parshall	Middlefield, N. Y	Apr. 19, 1859	23, 698
Car coupling, Railway	J. Pearson	Sterling, Iowa	Jan. 26, 1858	19, 204
Car coupling, Railway	P. Perry	Troy, N. Y	Oct. 26, 1858	21, 901
Car coupling, Railway	S. D. Pratt	Penn Yan, N. Y	Oct. 3, 1871	119, 475
Car coupling, Railway	W. Prosser	Kendall, N. Y	July 21, 1857	17, 845
Car coupling, Railway	W. V. Pulliam	Kansas City, Mo	Oct. 12, 1869	95, 835
Car coupling, Railway	J. H. Quackenbush	Owasso, Mich	July 6, 1858	20, 817
Car coupling, Railway	M. Quinn	Wataga, Ill	Oct. 26, 1869	96, 146
Car coupling, Railway	J. F. Rague	Dubuque, Iowa	Dec. 29, 1857	18, 990
Car coupling, Railway	E. Rice	Canandaigua, N. Y	Mar. 6, 1855	12, 490
Car coupling, Railway	J. W. Rice	Springfield, Mass	Mar. 30, 1858	19, 794
Car coupling, Railway	J. Riley	Chicago, Ill	July 6, 1869	92, 365
Car coupling, Railway	A. Roll	South Amboy, N. J	Nov. 28, 1865	51, 223
Car coupling, Railway	A. H. Rowand	Allegheny, Pa	Jan. 1, 1861	31, 036
Car coupling, Railway	J. Ryan	Wilmington, Del	July 17, 1855	13, 274

Index of patents issued from the United States Patent Office from 1790 *to* 1873, *inclusive*—Continued.

Invention.	Inventor.	Residence.	Date.	No.
Car coupling, Railway	J. Schneider	Chicago, Ill	Jan. 5, 1858	19, 049
Car coupling, Railway	G. Shatswell	Waukegan, Ill	Nov. 16, 1869	96, 976
Car coupling, Railway	G. C. Sherman	Chicago, Ill	Sept. 26, 1871	119, 416
Car coupling, Railway	J. C. Smith	Stoughstown, Pa	July 6, 1869	92, 383
Car coupling, Railway	M. B. Smith	Mattoon, Ill	Feb. 21, 1871	111, 985
Car coupling, Railway	O. L. Smith	Providence, R. I	Mar. 30, 1869	88, 337
Car coupling, Railway	E. F. Sneider	West Penn, Pa	Feb. 22, 1870	100, 204
Car coupling, Railway	D. G. W. Snyder	Williamsport, Md	July 6, 1869	92, 386
Car coupling, Railway	A. L. Spear	Flint, Mich	Nov. 23, 1869	97, 242
Car coupling, Railway	W. T. Spies	Baltimore, Md	May 20, 1862	35, 333
Car coupling, Railway	J. R. Swift	New Orleans, La	Nov. 29, 1859	26, 303
Car coupling, Railway	A. B. Thompson	Oswego, N. Y	Dec. 22, 1868	85, 147
Car coupling, Railway	S. Thorp and W. D. Shurtleff	Turner, Me	July 17, 1860	29, 205
Car coupling, Railway	W. C. Tilton	Spring Place, Ga	July 20, 1869	92, 902
Car coupling, Railway	J. B. Tracy	Lincoln, Del	Oct. 10, 1871	119, 897
Car coupling, Railway	J. Turnbull	Edinburgh, Scotland	June 29, 1869	92, 126
Car coupling, Railway	J. Turner	East Nassau, N. Y	July 20, 1852	9, 144
Car coupling, Railway	E. M. Van Hoesen and N. H. Brown.	Syracuse, N. Y	Sept. 26, 1871	119, 431
Car coupling, Railway	J. B. Vedder	Gloversville, N. Y	Jan. 11, 1870	98, 723
Car coupling, Railway	W. V. Wallace	New York, N. Y	Aug. 3, 1869	93, 375
Car coupling, Railway	W. V. Wallace	New York, N. Y	Oct. 19, 1869	96, 059
Car coupling, Railway	J. C. Ward	Charleston, S. C	Oct. 14, 1856	15, 909
Car coupling, Railway	D. Warren	Gettysburgh, Pa	Jan. 14, 1859	24, 420
Car coupling, Railway	R. Wells	Bloomington, Ill	Aug. 3, 1869	93, 378
Car coupling, Railway	A. Wellshmidt	Albany, N. Y	Jan. 23, 1872	122, 928
Car coupling, Railway	N. H. Wentworth and M. L. Ames.	Somersworth, N. H	Mar. 15, 1859	23, 282
Car coupling, Railway	G. W. Wheat	Philipsburgh, Pa	Oct. 4, 1870	107, 988
Car coupling, Railway	O. M. Whitman	North Haverhill, N. H	Aug. 3, 1869	93, 381
Car coupling, Railway	J. C. Wilson	Appleton, Wis	Oct. 5, 1869	95, 546
Car coupling, Railway	G. Winters	Portsmouth, Pa	Sept. 16, 1851	8, 359
Car coupling, Railway	S. W. Wood	Washington, D. C	Feb. 12, 1856	14, 265
Car coupling, Railway	O. D. Woodruff	Southington, Conn	June 8, 1869	90, 977
Car coupling, Reversible railway	J. Boothroyd	Michigan City, Ind	Sept. 8, 1857	18, 132
Car-coupling, Self-acting	A. G. Safford	Boston, Mass	Dec. 11, 1849	6, 947
Car coupling, Self-disengaging railway	J. C. Price	New Philadelphia, Ohio	Feb. 17, 1857	16, 654
Car coupling, Spring	F. Steinhart	Dansville, N. Y	Apr. 26, 1859	23, 793
Car coupling, Street	J. Stephenson	New York, N. Y	Jan. 7, 1873	134, 616
Car-couplings, Automatic attachment for	G. H. Merriam	Portland, Me	Dec. 16, 1873	145, 673
Car-couplings, Link-guide for	G. Stillson	Binghamton, N. Y	Dec. 24, 1872	134, 173
Car-couplings, Link-guide for	W. Warinner and W. L. D. Johnson.	Creelsborough, Ky	Nov. 4, 1873	144, 297
Car crank, Hand	P. Greel	Meadville, Pa	Feb. 9, 1864	41, 574
Car-door	J. H. Robertson	New York, N. Y	Apr. 18, 1871	113, 931
Car door, Baggage	H. L. Clarke	La Porte, Ind	Sept. 5, 1854	11, 656
Car-door fastening	J. K. Smith	Port Clinton, Pa	Feb. 12, 1836	....
Car-door fastening, Railway	H. D. Bird	Petersburgh, Va	Jan. 29, 1867	61, 652
Car door, Grain	J. Bassler	Galesburgh, Ill	Mar. 12, 1872	124, 535
Car door, Grain	T. A. Bissell and R. Miller	Aurora, Ill	Oct. 15, 1872	132, 237
Car door, Grain	S. E. Bright	Elkhorn, Wis	Sept. 10, 1867	68, 694
Car door, Grain	S. E. Knott	Chicago, Ill	May 25, 1869	90, 560
Car-door holder	G. Crandell	Washington, D. C	Apr. 19, 1864	42, 452
Car-door, &c., lock	G. B. F. Cooper	New Albany, Ind	May 14, 1867	64, 635
Car-door lock	A. V. Hartwell	Chicago, Ill	Oct. 26, 1869	96, 230
Car-door lock	J. L. Howard	Hartford, Conn	Jan. 18, 1870	98, 967
Car door, Railway	T. R. Leighton	Cameron, Mo	Mar. 9, 1869	87, 685
Car door, Railway	B. Martin	Prairie du Chien, Wis	Apr. 30, 1867	64, 236
Car door, Railway	C. Barker	Knox County, Ill	May 17, 1870	103, 126
Car door, Railway freight	H. L. Clark	Rahway, N. J	Aug. 29, 1871	118, 514
Car door, Street	D. R. Hart	Saint Louis, Mo	Aug. 16, 1870	106, 362
Car doors, Lock for freight	W. S. Brewster	Chicago, Ill	Feb. 4, 1873	135, 402
Car doors, Opening railway	T. Castor	Philadelphia, Pa	July 2, 1861	32, 681
Car-doors, Operating	J. G. and G. M. Brill	Philadelphia, Pa	Dec. 23, 1873	145, 839
Car-doors, Operating	J. A. O'Haire	West Troy, N. Y	Sept. 16, 1873	142, 810
Car-doors, &c., Seal for	D. W. Long	Baltimore, Md	July 14, 1857	17, 796
Car, Dumping	O. M. Avery	Pensacola, Fla	Apr. 29, 1873	138, 361
Car, Dumping	C. P. Bailey	Zanesville, Ohio	Jan. 24, 1854	10, 441
Car, Dumping	A. J. Ballard	Cohoes, N. Y	Oct. 18, 1870	108, 313
Car, Dumping	J. W. Bancroft	Philadelphia, Pa	Jan. 8, 1867	61, 038
Car, Dumping	C. Barrett	Boston, Mass	Dec. 19, 1871	121, 981
Car, Dumping	C. Barrett	Boston, Mass	Feb. 20, 1872	123, 762
Car, Dumping	C. Barrett	Boston, Mass	July 16, 1872	129, 515
Car, Dumping	T. Bootsmann	Tompkinsville, N. Y	June 14, 1870	104, 254
Car, Dumping	T. Bootsmann	New Brighton, N. Y	May 27, 1873	139, 362
Car, Dumping	L. C. Brady	Chambersville, Pa	Nov. 18, 1873	144, 654
Car, Dumping	J. Braidwood	Wilmington, Ill	July 24, 1866	56, 518
Car, Dumping	D. J. Brimmer	North Petersburgh, N. Y	Mar. 28, 1871	113, 013
Car, Dumping	N. W., C. W., and N. H. Camp	Saratoga Springs, N. Y., and Wilkesbarre, Pa.	Aug. 8, 1871	117, 739
Car, Dumping	W. Chisholm	Cleveland, Ohio	June 30, 1868	79, 445
Car, Dumping	F. B. Colton	Philadelphia, Pa	Dec. 26, 1871	122, 226
Car, Dumping	J. G. Conlon	New Orleans, La	July 13, 1869	92, 426
Car, Dumping	D. S. Cook	Wrightsville, Pa	Apr. 23, 1872	126, 029
Car, Dumping	P. Daniels	Jackson, Mich	July 28, 1868	80, 339
Car, Dumping	P. K. Dederick	Albany, N. Y	Nov. 15, 1870	109, 188
Car, Dumping	J. Disterdick	Kelley's Mills, Ohio	Apr. 23, 1872	126, 036
Car, Dumping	J. R. Dubois	Virginia City, Nev	Nov. 5, 1872	132, 818
Car, Dumping	J. Elliott, J. P. Harrington, and W. R. Davenport.	Erie, Pa	Nov. 25, 1873	144, 966
Car, Dumping	C. Gates	Burlington, Ind	Aug. 17, 1869	93, 872
Car, Dumping	D. Glover	Cass Township, Pa	July 12, 1859	24, 732
Car, Dumping	G. B. Goodwin and S. McCord	Milwaukee, Wis	Dec. 22, 1868	85, 086
Car, Dumping	J. M. Goodwin	Cleveland, Ohio	Aug. 13, 1872	130, 424
Car, Dumping	J. M. Hanford and J. Wood	Middletown, N. Y	June 3, 1873	139, 575
Car, Dumping	W. H. Harding and G. F. Morse	Portland, Me	Apr. 4, 1871	113, 655
Car, Dumping	G. W. Hart	Aurora, Ind	Dec. 1, 1857	18, 743
Car, Dumping	E. C. Hegeler	La Salle, Ill	Sept. 27, 1870	107, 683

Index of patents issued from the United States Patent Office from 1790 *to* 1873, *inclusive*—Continued.

Invention.	Inventor.	Residence.	Date.	No.
Car, Dumping	J. Hughes	New Berne, N. C	July 15, 1873	140, 779
Car, Dumping	J. Hughes	New Berne, N. C	Aug. 19, 1873	142, 021
Car, Dumping	E. H. Jackson	Boston, Mass	July 31, 1866	56, 756
Car, Dumping	I Keith	West Sandwich, Mass	July 13, 1869	92, 457
Car, Dumping	J. Kimbel	Zanesville, Ohio	Oct. 3, 1854	11, 750
Car, Dumping	S. D. King	Middletown, N. Y	Nov. 8, 1870	109, 029
Car, Dumping	S. D. King	Middletown, N. Y	Feb. 21, 1871	112, 052
Car, Dumping	S. D. King	Middletown, N. Y	Oct. 10, 1871	119, 856
Car, Dumping	S. D. King	Middletown, N. Y	Apr. 2, 1872	125, 397
Car, Dumping	W. R. Maffit	Wilkesbarre, Pa	Oct. 4, 1864	44, 539
Car, Dumping	C. W. McLean and W. M. Elton	New Berne, N. C., and Brooklyn, N. Y.	July 9, 1872	128, 744
Car, Dumping	T. McVay	Braddock's Field, Pa	Sept. 12, 1871	118, 959
Car, Dumping	W. Merrington and N. Kirkwood.	McKeesport, Pa	Nov. 1, 1870	108, 810
Car, Dumping	A. Nettleton	Springfield, Mass	Jan. 30, 1849	6, 065
Car, Dumping	J. G. Payson	Foxborough, Mass	July 1, 1873	140, 534
Car, Dumping	A. Peteler	New Brighton, N. Y	Mar. 16, 1869	87, 966
Car, Dumping	A. Peteler	New Brighton, N. Y	May 30, 1871	115, 514
Car, Dumping	A. H. Petsch	Charleston, S. C	Aug. 1, 1854	11, 441
Car, Dumping	W. Riley, jr	Terre Haute, Ind	Oct. 25, 1870	108, 632
Car, Dumping	W. Robinson	Bellfontaine, Ohio	Dec. 31, 1872	134, 488
Car, Dumping	S. Rousculp and I. B. Shambaugh.	Thornville and Scio, Ohio	Aug. 29, 1871	118, 557
Car, Dumping	C. H. Sage	Fulton, N. Y	Aug. 31, 1869	94, 445
Car, Dumping	W. A. Sharp	Tama City, Iowa	Apr. 18, 1871	113, 804
Car, Dumping	E. C. Smeed	Lawrence, Kans	Oct. 18, 1870	108, 400
Car, Dumping	O. L. Smith	Providence, R. I	Mar. 22, 1870	101, 057
Car, Dumping	E. Thompson	Hokah, Minn	Nov. 26, 1867	71, 552
Car, Dumping	J. M. Thompson	Quincy, Cal	Aug. 6, 1872	130, 334
Car, Dumping	J. M. Thompson	Quincy, Cal	Aug. 6, 1872	130, 335
Car, Dumping	J. C. and F. A. Wiswell	Lennoxville, Canada, and Beebe Plain, Vt.	June 20, 1871	116, 127
Car, Dumping	J. C. and F. A. Wiswell	Lennoxville, Canada, and Beebe Plain, Vt.	May 14, 1872	126, 859
Car-dumping apparatus	E. Cockill	Llewellyn, Pa	Sept. 19, 1871	119, 122
Car, Dumping railway	A. B. Cooley	Philadelphia, Pa	July 3, 1860	28, 969
Car duster and ventilator, Railway	J. P. Curry	New York, N. Y	Aug. 30, 1870	106, 786
Car duster, Railway	L. M. Platt	Chicago, Ill	June 15, 1869	91, 366
Car draw-bar, Street	J. C. Gove	Cleveland, Ohio	Mar. 2, 1869	87, 486
Car draw-head, Railway	H. C. Lowrie	Fort Wayne, Ind	Dec. 23, 1873	145, 881
Car, Drying	J. K. Caldwell	Allegheny City, Pa	Nov. 16, 1869	96, 882
Car, Earth	R. H. Emerson	Chicago, Ill	Apr. 11, 1854	10, 775
Car elevating and transferring apparatus, Railway	W. T. Beekman	Petersburgh, Ill	Dec. 16, 1873	145, 611
Car-elevator	H. Arden	Cincinnati Ohio	May 5, 1868	77, 706
Car elevator, Coal	P. H. Lamey	Wiconisco, Pa	Feb. 4, 1873	135, 565
Car elevator, Coal	P. H. Lamey	Wiconisco, Pa	July 22, 1873	141, 148
Car, Extension railway	J. S. Brown	Lowell, Mass	Jan. 15, 1856	14, 083
Car, Fire-proof railway	G. C. Bestor	Peoria, Ill	Aug. 30, 1870	106, 771
Car-floor slat-matting	S. Lewis	Williamsburgh, N. Y	Sept. 12, 1871	118, 952
Car, Foot	N. Hodge	North Adams, Mass	June 22, 1852	9, 054
Car for carrying petroleum	J. Clark	Canandaigua, N. Y	Nov. 3, 1863	40, 458
Car for carrying petroleum	J. Clark	Pontiac, Mich	Mar. 18, 1873	136, 813
Car for carrying petroleum, &c	J. Scott	Lawrenceville, Pa	Jan. 20, 1863	37, 461
Car for carrying petroleum, &c	S. J. Seely	Brooklyn, N. Y	June 2, 1863	38, 765
Car for coal-mines, Dumping	M. G. Smith and W. P. Stephens	Kingston, Pa	Oct. 9, 1866	58, 736
Car for day and night service, Railway	J. B. Creighton	Tiffin, Ohio	May 18, 1858	20, 254
Car for dumping earth, &c	M. Berney	Syracuse, N. Y	Sept. 11, 1849	6, 712
Car for elevated railways	J. B. Newbrough	New York, N. Y	Dec. 5, 1871	121, 539
Car for grading, Dumping	W. Price	Cincinnati, Ohio	Nov. 2, 1869	96, 481
Car for inclined planes, Safety	J. Tittle	Johnstown, Pa	Feb. 10, 1846	4, 381
Car for mines, Ore and timber	G. Williams	Sterling, Colo	July 17, 1866	56, 480
Car for plank-roads, wooden rails, &c	G. Morgan	Calhoun, Tenn	June 11, 1850	7, 427
Car for preventing accidents, Railway	F. W. Jenkins	Brooklyn, N. Y	June 19, 1866	55, 663
Car for rail and other roads	J. A. Whitford	Saratoga Springs, N. Y	Jan. 29, 1841	1, 931
Car for railways and locomotive-engine wheel	M. W. Baldwin	Philadelphia, Pa	June 29, 18[illegible]3	....
Car for railways, Hand	A. Welsch	Chicago, Ill	Dec. 13, 1859	26, 453
Car for railways, Metallic	B. J. La Mothe	New York, N. Y	Sept. 24, 1861	33, 350
Car for railways, Sleeping	C. L. Harrington	Buffalo, N. Y	Aug. 3, 1858	21, 070
Car for railways, Sleeping	E. Wheeler	Elmira, N. Y	Aug. 3, 1858	21, 099
Car for removing gravel and earth on railways	G. Palmer	Greenbush, N. Y	Jan. 16, 1843	2, 909
Car for transportation of coal	L. Myers	Philadelphia, Pa	June 24, 1851	8, 177
Car for transportation of coal, &c	R. Winans	Baltimore, Md	June 26, 1847	5, 175
Car for transporting and drying peat	D. E. Teal	Norwich, N. Y	Feb. 11, 1868	74, 255
Car for transporting petroleum	J. and A. Densemore	Meadville, Pa	Apr. 10, 1866	53, 794
Car for turning curves, Railway	J. H. Quail	Philadelphia, Pa	Feb. 28, 1844	3, 457
Car-frame	R. M. C. Parker	Memphis, Tenn	Jan. 7, 1873	134, 701
Car frame, Railway	H. Bachman	Lancaster, Pa	May 2, 1835	....
Car frames with metallic joints, Constructing railway.	T. L. Nickols	Alexandria, Va	Dec. 4, 1860	30, 833
Car, Freight	J. D. Billings	Rutland, Vt	May 31, 1859	24, 189
Car, Freight	S. W. Downey	Piedmont, W. Va	Jan. 14, 1868	73, 308
Car, Freight	C. R. Foote and J. Orton	Williamstown, Mass	Jan. 12, 1864	41, 212
Car, Freight	L. Myers	Philadelphia, Pa	July 1[illegible], 1865	48, 830
Car, Freight	T. R. Timby	Tarrytown, N. Y	Oct. 31, 1871	120, 552
Car, Grain	A. E. Gordon	New Brunswick, N. J	Dec. 5, 1871	121, 612
Car, Grain	W. H. Long and J. E. Lavey	Plymouth, Ind	May 26, 1868	78, 383
Car, Grain	S. W. Wood	Cornwall, N. Y	Dec. 24, 1872	134, 181
Car, Grain-drying	C. S. Dole	Chicago, Ill	May 9, 1871	114, 534
Car, Grain-dumping	L. Bammerlin	Massillon, Ohio	Jan. 3, 1871	110, 724
Car, Gravel	T. C. Hendry	Conyers, Ga	Dec. 13, 1859	26, 460
Car, Hand	W. T. Beekman	Petersburgh, Ill	Feb. 21, 1871	112, 008
Car, Hand	L. J. Cathell	Salisbury, Md	Jan. 30, 1872	123, 322
Car, Hand	J. Collins	Fairview, Ohio	Jan. 16, 1872	122, 814
Car, Hand	M. E. Hastings	Salisbury, Md	June 27, 1871	116, 527
Car, Hand	J. D. Hinckley	Adrian, Mich	June 17, 1873	140, 039
Car, Hand	D. M. Hunt	Southampton Mills, Pa	Mar. 11, 1873	136, 652
Car, Hand	D. Johnston	Eddyville, Iowa	June 20, 1871	116, 062

Index of patents issued from the United States Patent Office from 1790 *to* 1873, *inclusive*—Continued.

Invention.	Inventor.	Residence.	Date.	No.
Car, Hand	L. H. Kenyon	East Greenwich, R. I.	Oct. 7, 1873	143, 513
Car hanger, Railway	T. S. Hudson	Cambridge, Mass	Apr. 30, 1872	126, 299
Car-heater	J. C. Eckert	Dayton, Ohio	Oct. 20, 1868	83, 142
Car-heater	A. H. Lighthall and C. F. North	Cohoes, N. Y	Mar. 3, 1868	75, 172
Car-heater	W. S. McNeil and O. S. Cadwell, jr.	Springfield, Mass	Aug. 25, 1868	81, 392
Car-heater	T. Smith and J. O. Reilly	Baltimore, Md	Oct. 6, 1868	82, 885
Car heater and ventilator	E. Himrod	Dunmore, Pa	Mar. 16, 1869	87, 846
Car heater and ventilator	W. S. McNeil	Springfield, Mass	June 8, 1869	91, 148
Car heater and ventilator, Railway	S. Darling	Bangor, Me	June 30, 1868	79, 449
Car heater and ventilator, Railway	S. W. Francis	Newport, R. I	Apr. 28, 1868	77, 270
Car heater and ventilator, Railway	T. H. Mott	New York, N. Y	July 29, 1873	141, 372
Car heater and ventilator, Railway	E. L. Roberts	New York, N. Y	Aug. 18, 1868	81, 211
Car heater and ventilator, Railway	T. F. Strong	Fond du Lac, Wis	July 2, 1861	32, 726
Car heater and ventilator, Railway	A. Weeks	Minneapolis, Minn	Apr. 27, 1869	89, 529
Car heater and ventilator, Railway	C. F. Whorf	Saint Louis, Mo	Apr. 22, 1873	138, 062
Car heater, Passenger	G. K. Dearborn	Abington, Mass	Jan. 28, 1862	34, 280
Car heater, Railway	J. G. Allen	Philadelphia, Pa	Sept. 6, 1870	107, 149
Car heater, Railway	J. G. Allen	Philadelphia, Pa	July 11, 1871	116, 914
Car heater, Railway	I. R. Amsdam	Buffalo, N. Y	Aug. 25, 1868	81, 322
Car heater, Railway	T. B. Atterbury	Pittsburgh, Pa	June 18, 1872	127, 945
Car heater, Railway	W. C. Baker	New York, N. Y	Mar. 10, 1868	75, 345
Car heater, Railway	W. H. Beal	Philadelphia, Pa	Mar. 9, 1869	87, 532
Car heater, Railway	B. Berghausen and A. L. Kiesling.	Cologne, Germany	Nov. 4, 1873	144, 183
Car heater, Railway	E. Bradley and J. G. Fulghum	Nashville, Tenn	June 18, 1872	128, 103
Car heater, Railway	H. M. Britton	Cincinnati, Ohio	Sept. 8, 1868	81, 873
Car heater, Railway	C. Carpenter	Buffalo, N. Y	Aug. 18, 1868	81, 137
Car heater, Railway	D. C. Chipman	Noblesville, Ind	June 29, 1869	91, 824
Car heater, Railway	A. C. Crary	Utica, N. Y	Mar. 2, 1869	87, 472
Car heater, Railway	A. Davidsohn	Saint Louis, Mo	Dec 8, 1868	84, 735
Car heater, Railway	I. Dripps	Fort Wayne, Ind	Oct. 6, 1868	82, 810
Car heater, Railway	W. B. Farwell	New York, N. Y	Sept. 15, 1868	82, 210
Car heater, Railway	J. Gibson, jr	Albany, N. Y	Dec. 28, 1869	98, 248
Car heater, Railway	P. Grandjean	Paris, France	Oct. 25, 1870	108, 702
Car heater, Railway	W. G. Kendrick	Wilmington, Del	Aug. 13, 1867	67, 770
Car heater, Railway	J. E. Kline	Wheeling, W. Va	Sept. 21, 1869	95, 026
Car heater, Railway	G. S. Koontz, E. Potts, and M. D. Lewis.	Washington, D. C., and Baltimore, Md.	Mar. 23, 1869	88, 183
Car heater, Railway	F. McManus	Ellenburgh Centre, N. Y	Mar. 23, 1869	88, 155
Car heater, Railway	F. M. Meddock	Mainsville, Ohio	Oct. 13, 1868	83, 076
Car heater, Railway	W. Meller	McKeesport, Pa	Mar. 8, 1870	100, 543
Car heater, Railway	J. P. Michaels and L. W. Broadwell.	Vienna, Austria	Jan. 28, 1873	135, 239
Car heater, Railway	A. C. Miner	Philadelphia, Pa	June 16, 1868	78, 990
Car heater. Railway	W. Pauli	Alexandria, Va	Nov. 27, 1860	30, 753
Car heater, Railway	C. F. Pike	Providence, R. I	Mar. 26, 1872	124, 973
Car heater, Railway	J. Pino	New York, N. Y	Oct. 9, 1860	30, 347
Car heater, Railway	J. Rice	Bloomington, Ind	July 28, 1868	80, 505
Car heater, Railway	H. R. Robbins	Baltimore, Md	May 2, 1871	114, 349
Car heater, Railway	A. M. Rodgers	Brooklyn, N. Y	Apr. 4, 1871	113, 348
Car heater, Railway	C. Sanborn	Chichester, N. H	July 20, 1869	92, 753
Car heater, Railway	E. S. Scripture and W. Stockman.	Brooklyn, N. Y	Sept. 9, 1873	142, 737
Car heater, Railway	J. Shackleton	Rahway, N. J	May 30, 1871	115, 533
Car heater, Railway	F. Shaller	Hudson, N. Y	Mar. 1, 1870	100, 333
Car heater, Railway	C. Smith	Hermon, Me	Jan. 26, 1869	86, 255
Car heater, Railway	E. Spencer	Elizabeth, N. J	Dec. 15, 1868	84, 969
Car heater, Railway	F. J. Steinhauser and H. M. Shreiner.	Lancaster, Pa	Nov. 2, 1869	96, 498
Car heater, Railway	G. F. Stone	Baltimore, Md	Apr. 30, 1872	126, 343
Car heater, Railway	B. D. Thompson	New York, N. Y	Sept. 26, 1871	119, 249
Car heater, Railway	A. Weeks	Minneapolis, Minn	Jan. 5, 1869	85, 712
Car heater, Railway	J. H. Weibel	Geneva, Switzerland	Nov. 11, 1873	144, 425
Car heater, Railway	W. Westlake	Milwaukee, Wis	July 29, 1862	36, 044
Car heater, Steam	G. B. Riggins	New York, N. Y	June 18, 1872	128, 174
Car heater, Steam railway	A. C. Crary	Utica, N. Y	June 22, 1869	91, 524
Car heater, Street	J. Gibson, jr	Albany, N. Y.	Jan. 1, 1867	60, 714
Car heaters, Coupling for steam	W. N. McDuffey and B. F. Jacques.	Petersburgh, Va	Jan. 21, 1873	135, 137
Car heaters, Pipe connection in railway	M. S. Bolt	Elmira, N. Y	Jan. 5, 1869	85, 559
Car-hooks, Machine for bending	D. G. Morris	Catasauqua, Pa	Aug. 10, 1869	93, 467
Car-hooks, Machine for bending and punching	D. G. Morris	Catasauqua, Pa	Aug. 9, 1870	106, 188
Car, Horse-railway	D. T. Robinson	Boston, Mass	Jan. 8, 1867	61, 021
Car, Ice	F. L. Kidder	Brooklyn, N. Y	Mar. 18, 1862	34, 718
Car indicator, Railway	C. H. Coffin	Boston, Mass	June 10, 1873	139, 771
Car indicator, Street-railway	J. Knight	Philadelphia, Pa	June 30, 1868	79, 480
Car, Iron	R. Montgomery	New York, N. Y	Aug. 7, 1860	29, 510
Car, Iron railway	J. Davenport	Massillon, Ohio	Mar. 22, 1859	23, 333
Car, Iron railway	H. Merrill	New York, N. Y	Mar. 31, 1863	38, 082
Car, Iron railway	J. Miner and S. Merrick	New Brighton, Pa	Jan. 10, 1860	26, 777
Car jack, Railway	E. C. Patterson	Rochester, N. Y	June 16, 1868	78, 994
Car-jumper	C. C. Dow	Philadelphia, Pa	Mar. 2, 1869	87, 399
Car-light	R. Cathcart	Baltimore, Md	Oct. 9, 1860	30, 297
Car-links, Manufacture of	G. H. Sellers	Phœnixville, Pa	Mar. 29, 1864	42, 147
Car-loading machine	S. J. Bingham	Garlandsville, Miss	Jan. 30, 1872	123, 146
Car-lock	H. Ritchie	Newark, N. J	Apr. 7, 1857	17, 013
Car lock, Freight	O. F. Burton	New York, N. Y	July 16, 1872	129, 524
Car lock, Freight	H. C. Jones	Newark, N. J	Dec. 11, 1855	13, 911
Car lock, Freight	J. F. Keeler	Cleveland, Ohio	Oct. 2, 1860	30, 229
Car lock, Freight	T. Slaight	Newark, N. J	Sept. 23, 1856	15, 783
Car lock, Railway	C. T. Gibson	Baltimore, Md	Aug. 8, 1871	117, 764
Car, Locomotive	W. Romans	Columbus, Ohio	Jan. 28, 1862	34, 270
Car, Locomotive	H. F. Shaw	West Roxbury, Mass	Oct. 3, 1865	50, 282
Car, Locomotive and railway	J. P. Fairlamb and L. C. Judson.	Philadelphia, Pa	Jan. 9, 1838	558
Car, Marine	A. Bloomquist and C. Crook	New York, and Yonkers, N. Y.	July 17, 1866	56, 351
Car, Marine	G. H. Young	Charlestown, Mass	July 24, 1866	56, 660

Index of patents issued from the United States Patent Office from 1790 *to* 1873, *inclusive*—Continued.

Invention.	Inventor.	Residence.	Date.	No.
Car-mat	J. O'Neill	Brooklyn, N. Y	Dec. 16, 1873	145, 558
Car, Metallic railway	B. J. La Mothe	New York, N. Y	July 26, 1870	105, 699
Car, Metallic railway	J. A. Roebling	Trenton, N. J	Oct. 16, 1860	30, 426
Car-mover	F. L. Bailey	Freeport, Ind	Dec. 8, 1868	84, 789
Car-mover	S. Becker and P. Loucks	York, Pa	Apr. 26, 1870	102, 357
Car-mover	R. A. Cowell	Cleveland, Ohio	July 29, 1873	141, 327
Car-mover	J. Douglass	McConnellstown, Pa	Apr. 7, 1868	76, 421
Car-mover	H. B. Morrison	Le Roy, N. Y	Mar. 10, 1868	75, 447
Car-mover	E. Springer	Davis, Ill	Apr. 12, 1870	101, 780
Car mover, Railway	E. Spinger	Davis, Ill	Nov. 10, 1868	84, 012
Car-moving device	J. Foreman	Pottstown, Pa	Apr. 26, 1870	102, 388
Car, Oil-tank	G. W. Ilgenfritz and M. Schall	York, Pa	July 7, 1868	79, 573
Car or carriage spring, Railway	G. Douglass	Scranton, Pa	Dec. 29, 1857	18, 961
Car, Passenger-railway	T. Castor	Philadelphia, Pa	Feb. 21, 1860	27, 203
Car, Passenger-railway	E. Y. Robbins	Cincinnati, Ohio	Nov. 3, 1868	83, 731
Car, Peat	T. J. Wells	Saint Anthony, Minn	Jan. 29, 1867	61, 493
Car, Pendulous railway	S. T. Jones	Philadelphia, Pa	Feb. 22, 1830	....
Car, Petroleum	J. Densmore and G. W. N. Yost.	Meadville and Corry, Pa	June 26, 1866	55, 830
Car, Petroleum	J. Densmore and G. W. N. Yost.	Meadville and Corry, Pa	June 26, 1866	55, 831
Car, Petroleum	J. and A. Densmore and W. N. Yost.	Meadville and Corry, Pa	June 26, 1866	55, 832
Car-platform	H. S. Wilcox	West Meriden, Conn	Aug. 27, 1867	68, 327
Car-platform bridge	B. G. Fitzhugh	Ellicott City, Md	July 7, 1868	79, 646
Car-platform bridge	A. Rank	Salem, Ohio	Apr. 28, 1868	77, 321
Car platform, Railway	R. A. Cowell	Cleveland, Ohio	Jan. 10, 1871	110, 901
Car platform, Railway	J. Gilmer	Monticello, Fla	Oct. 5, 1869	95, 579
Car platform, Railway	H. Holcroft and C. S. Smith	Chester Valley, Pa	June 2, 1863	38, 743
Car platform, Safety	C. R. Abbot	Elmira, N. Y	Sept. 3, 1867	68, 543
Car-platform stakeholder	C. H. Bryan	Racine, Wis	July 25, 1865	48, 899
Car, Pneumatic	L. Ransom	Lansingburgh, N. Y	Dec. 10, 1867	72, 082
Car, Pneumatic railway	H. G. Yates	Kalamazoo, Mich	Sept. 9, 1873	142, 605
Car, Pneumatic street	D. Myers	Chicago, Ill	Oct. 18, 1870	108, 380
Car, Pneumatic street	C. W. Wailey	New Orleans, La	Nov. 24, 1868	84, 447
Car propelled by horse-power, Railway	D. W. Crocker	Philadelphia, Pa	Oct. 30, 1834	....
Car-propeller	J. Day	Holley, N. Y	Sept. 2, 1873	142, 443
Car-propeller	G. W. Earl	New York, N. Y	Oct. 28, 1873	144, 076
Car-propeller	P. W. Phillips	Bristol, England	Dec. 13, 1864	45, 450
Car-propeller	R. Steel and S. Austin	Philadelphia, Pa	Nov. 4, 1873	144, 235
Car-propelling apparatus	C. T. Harvey	Tarrytown, N. Y	Apr. 16, 1867	63, 887
Car-propelling apparatus	J. Roy	New Orleans, La	Dec. 27, 1870	110, 501
Car propulsion	R. De Leidi	Brooklyn, N. Y	Feb. 18, 1873	135, 972
Car-pusher	A. S. Bailey	Paxton, Ill	June 3, 1873	139, 529
Car-pusher	R. Lane	Freeport, Ill	Oct. 4, 1870	107, 926
Car-pushing device	R. Odenath	Philadelphia, Pa	June 18, 1872	128, 165
Car pushing-jack, Railway	R. A. Cowell	Cleveland, Ohio	Dec. 7, 1869	97, 480
Car pushing-jack, Railway	E. Hutson	Brockport, N. Y	Jan. 7, 1868	73, 101
Car-rack	A. Bridges	New York, N. Y	May 3, 1870	102, 482
Car-rack	T. S. Hudson	Cambridge, Mass	Apr. 30, 1872	126, 298
Car, Railway	E. H. Ashcroft	Lynn, Mass	May 15, 1866	54, 662
Car, Railway	A. E. Beach	Stratford, Conn	Sept. 5, 1865	49, 695
Car, Railway	W. Bell	Perth Amboy, N. J	Feb. 13, 1872	123, 610
Car, Railway	G. and G. T. Benjamin and H. S. Weston.	Millersburgh, Ohio	Dec. 18, 1866	60, 465
Car, Railway	H. Buck	Polo, Ill	Mar. 4, 1873	136, 359
Car, Railway	I. Bullock	New York, N. Y	Oct. 11, 1841	2, 316
Car, Railway	J. Busser	Troy, Ohio	Dec. 28, 1869	98, 227
Car, Railway	T. Castor	Philadelphia, Pa	Dec. 6, 1864	45, 316
Car, Railway	G. W. Cook	Rock Island, Ill	Dec. 26, 1865	51, 698
Car, Railway	E. Crane	Dorchester, Mass	Nov. 22, 1859	26, 166
Car, Railway	W. D. Crane	New York, N. Y	Dec. 7, 1869	97, 608
Car, Railway	L. B. Crittenden	Pittsburgh, Pa	July 9, 1867	66, 467
Car, Railway	M. M. Crooker	Rutland, Vt	May 26, 1868	78, 188
Car, Railway	J. Davis and W. Ashdown	Baltimore, Md	Mar. 4, 1836	....
Car, Railway	E. H. Derby and T. West	Boston and Roxbury, Mass	Aug. 22, 1865	49, 508
Car, Railway	G. W. Eddy	Waterford, N. Y	Feb. 11, 1868	74, 325
Car, Railway	J. Elgar	Baltimore, Md	Oct. 1, 1830	....
Car, Railway	J. S. Fairfax	Wheeling, W. Va	Jan. 1, 1867	60, 868
Car, Railway	J. P. Fairlamb	Philadelphia, Pa	Jan. 19, 1833	....
Car, Railway	D. Fitzgerald	New York, N. Y	May 11, 1869	90, 060
Car, Railway	J. Foreman	Pottstown, Pa	Sept. 10, 1867	67, 619
Car, Railway	W. C. Fuller	England	Oct. 23, 1846	4, 827
Car, Railway	E. D. Gird	Syracuse, N. Y	Mar. 19, 1872	124, 734
Car, Railway	A. Gregg	Forest City, Cal	Feb. 19, 1867	62, 127
Car, Railway	J. W. Griffiths	East Boston, Mass	May 9, 1871	114, 675
Car, Railway	G. S. Hacker	Charleston, S. C	Mar. 5, 1850	7, 140
Car, Railway	W. S. Hall	Quincy, Mass	July 4, 1865	48, 553
Car, Railway	C. T. Harvey	Tarrytown, N. Y	July 7, 1868	79, 756
Car, Railway	S. C. Hawkins	Patchogue, N. Y	Oct. 17, 1865	50, 472
Car, Railway	J. H. Kaufman	Lisburn, Pa	Mar. 20, 1860	27, 547
Car, Railway	I. Knight	Baltimore, Md	Apr. 28, 1836	....
Car, Railway	B. J. La Mothe	New York, N. Y	Apr. 4, 1854	10, 721
Car, Railway	M. C. Lawless	Montana, Iowa	Oct. 12, 1869	95, 697
Car, Railway	E. T. Ligon	Demopolis, Ala	Nov. 3, 1868	83, 717
Car, Railway	I. G. Macfarlane	Wilkinsburgh, Pa	Apr. 23, 1872	125, 969
Car, Railway	I. G. Macfarlane	Wilkinsburgh, Pa	Sept. 17, 1872	131, 360
Car, Railway	I. G. Macfarlane	Wilkinsburgh, Pa	June 10, 1873	139, 680
Car, Railway	F. Marin	Geneva, Switzerland	Sept. 30, 1873	143, 363
Car, Railway	C. McWayne	Sacramento, Cal	Oct. 22, 1861	33, 534
Car, Railway	E. Miller	Brooklyn, N. Y	July 24, 1866	56, 594
Car, Railway	W. Miller and H. E. Towle	Boston, Mass., and New York, N. Y.	May 3, 1864	42, 590
Car, Railway	J. Miner and S. Merrick	New Brighton, Pa	Nov. 29, 1859	26, 282
Car, Railway	W. Partridge	Philadelphia, Pa	Aug. 29, 1865	49, 648
Car, Railway	S. Pennock	Kennett Square, Pa	Dec. 31, 1867	72, 891
Car, Railway	A. Planton	Philadelphia, Pa	June 3, 1837	218
Car, Railway	B. P. Power and J. Coyne	Baltimore, Md	Feb. 16, 1869	87, 002

Index of patents issued from the United States Patent Office from 1790 *to* 1873, *inclusive*—Continued.

Invention.	Inventor.	Residence.	Date.	No.
Car, Railway	J. R. Reader	New York, N. Y	Nov. 13, 1866	59, 652
Car, Railway	A. V. Rider	New York, N. Y	May 14, 1872	126, 837
Car, Railway	D. T. Robinson	Boston, Mass	Oct. 29, 1867	70, 269
Car, Railway	J. F. Rodgers	Troy, N. Y	Sept. 26, 1848	5, 815
Car, Railway	C. W. Saladee	Pittsburgh, Pa	Dec. 9, 1873	145, 365
Car, Railway	C. W. Saladee	Pittsburgh, Pa	Dec. 9, 1873	145, 366
Car, Railway	S. J. Seely	Buffalo, N. Y	Apr. 24, 1860	28, 041
Car, Railway	S. Skillman	Jersey City, N. J	Jan. 10, 1865	45, 871
Car, Railway	S. Snyder	Lancaster, Pa	Nov. 10, 1832	....
Car, Railway	S. Vallo	Philadelphia, Pa	Apr. 4, 1865	47, 156
Car, Railway	J. C. Wands	Nashville, Tenn	Aug. 19, 1873	142, 062
Car, Railway	C. Waterbury	Bridgeport, Conn	June 29, 1852	9, 084
Car, Railway	P. H. Watson	Ashtabula, Ohio	Jan. 5, 1869	85, 720
Car, Railway	R. T. M. Wells	Franklin Centre, Vt	Jan. 3, 1865	45, 778
Car, Railway	R. T. M. Wells	Roxbury, Mass	July 10, 1866	56, 301
Car, Railway	R. Winans	Baltimore, Md	Oct. 1, 1834	....
Car, Railway	J. Withers	Bart Township, Pa	Mar. 25, 1835	....
Car, Railway	J. Withycombe and C. Reiblein.	Cleveland, Ohio	Jan. 26, 1864	41, 409
Car, Railway	J. Wright	Columbia, Pa	Sept. 10, 1829	....
Car, Railway and dumping	A. Welsch	Chicago, Ill	Sept. 29, 1863	40, 134
Car, Railway bathing	L. Bagger	Washington, D. C	Nov. 26, 1872	133, 398
Car, Railway cattle	E. Payne and J. D. Cleghorn	Chicago, Ill	Nov. 9, 1869	96, 722
Car, Railway cattle	C. F. Piko	Providence, R. I	Feb. 1, 1870	99, 471
Car, Railway cattle	J. B. Shafer	Grafton, Va	July 31, 1860	29, 409
Car, Railway cattle	J. W. Street	Marshalltown, Iowa	Nov. 2, 1869	96, 362
Car, Railway dining	G. M. Pullman	Chicago, Ill	Apr. 27, 1869	89, 537
Car, Railway dumping	T. A. McFarland	Meadville, Pa	May 24, 1864	42, 862
Car, Railway freight	J. H. Aldrich	Nashua, N. H	Nov. 5, 1867	70, 384
Car, Railway freight	R. Eaton	Montreal, Canada	Jan. 1, 1867	60, 865
Car, Railway freight	W. A. Goodwin	Newton, Mass	Feb. 23, 1869	87, 098
Car, Railway freight	R. H. Gordon, sr	Cleveland, Ohio	May 27, 1873	139, 243
Car, Railway freight	B. P. Lamason	Milton, Pa	Feb. 11, 1873	135, 717
Car, Railway freight	L. Savage	Ashtabula, Ohio	Mar. 17, 1868	75, 581
Car, Railway freight	J. P. Woodbury	Boston, Mass	Aug. 31, 1869	94, 461
Car, Railway hand	H. L. Brown	Adrian, Mich	Sept. 7, 1869	94, 469
Car, Railway hand	H. Fisher	Alliance, Ohio	Nov. 29, 1859	26, 263
Car, Railway hand	J. C. Hearne	Pleasant Hill, Mich	June 6, 1871	115, 609
Car, Railway hotel	G. M. Pullman	Chicago, Ill	Apr. 27, 1869	89, 538
Car, Railway passenger	J. Stephenson	New York, N. Y	Apr. 22, 1833	....
Car, Railway passenger	J. T. Worley	Cleveland, Ohio	Dec. 26, 1871	122, 208
Car, Railway sleeping	J. S. Du Bois	Saint Louis, Mo	Nov. 8, 1870	109, 119
Car, Railway sleeping	G. W. Hunt	Hopkinton, Mass	Dec. 10, 1867	72, 045
Car, Railway sleeping	T. Luce and J. H. Morrison	Detroit, Mich	Jan. 4, 1859	22, 506
Car, Railway stock	G. R. Blanchard	Baltimore, Md	Aug. 25, 1868	81, 468
Car, Railway stock	J. S. Kendall	Northfield, Minn	May 25, 1869	90, 557
Car, Railway stock	J. S. Kendall	Northfield, Minn	June 1, 1869	90, 851
Car, Railway stock	H. Lee	Beloit, Wis	June 1, 1869	90, 856
Car, Railway stock	W. M. Lyon	Salem, Ohio	May 23, 1871	115, 074
Car, Railway stock	A. Rank	Salem, Ohio	Mar. 12, 1872	124, 625
Car, Railway stock	A. Rank	Salem, Ohio	Mar. 12, 1872	124, 626
Car, Railway stock	A. Rank, H. King, and J. Sharp	Salem, Ohio	Feb. 14, 1871	111, 873
Car, Railway stock	S. W. Remer	Taunton, Mass	Mar. 5, 1872	124, 387
Car, Railway stock	W. Stark, J. G. Fisher, and S. Fitch.	White Pigeon, Mich., and Toledo, Ohio.	Nov. 21, 1871	121, 212
Car, Railway stock	W. Stark, J. G. Fisher, and S. Fitch.	White Pigeon, Mich., and Toledo, Ohio.	Nov. 21, 1871	121, 213
Car, Railway street	S. H. Lettle	Rosemond, Ill	June 17, 1873	140, 052
Car, Refrigerating	A. Booth	Chicago, Ill	Sept. 13, 1870	107, 217
Car, Refrigerator	L. Kniffen	Worcester, Mass	Sept. 24, 1867	69, 223
Car, Refrigerator railway	J. D. Potts and B. P. Lamason	Philadelphia and Milton, Pa.	June 28, 1870	104, 765
Car-register	L. H. French	Philadelphia, Pa	Aug. 28, 1860	29, 778
Car-register	J. and C. Gschwind	New York, N. Y	Nov. 6, 1866	59, 387
Car register, Railway	S. F. Covington	Indianapolis, Ind	Dec. 27, 1859	26, 565
Car register, Railway	P. S. Gerhardt	Philadelphia, Pa	June 30, 1868	79, 339
Car-replacer	C. C. Ash	Manor Hill, Pa	May 16, 1871	114, 745
Car-replacer	F. L. Bailey	Freeport, Ind	Aug. 14, 1855	13, 417
Car-replacer	D. H. Ball and J. Brooks	Sinnamahoning, Pa	Jan. 3, 1871	110, 723
Car-replacer	J. T. Baxter	Finksburgh, Md	Sept. 17, 1872	131, 384
Car-replacer	J. T. Baxter	Finksburgh, Md	Apr. 29, 1873	138, 311
Car-replacer	A. G. Black	Wooster, Ohio	Oct. 22, 1867	70, 069
Car-replacer	J. G. Burkhardt	Brooklyn, N. Y	Nov. 4, 1873	144, 188
Car-replacer	P. Cartwright	New York, N. Y	Mar. 5, 1872	124, 251
Car-replacer	G. Chambers	Ithaca, N. Y	Dec. 4, 1866	60, 137
Car-replacer	R. Davis	Utica, N. Y	June 30, 1868	79, 325
Car-replacer	N. H. Edgerton	Pottsville, Pa	June 18, 1867	65, 799
Car-replacer	D. Edwards	New York, N. Y	Apr. 7, 1868	76, 424
Car-replacer	B. W. Felton	Roxbury, Mass	Dec. 3, 1867	71, 596
Car-replacer	D. Fisher and W. Cumming	Oil City, Pa	Jan. 28, 1868	73, 789
Car-replacer	G. Fowler	Macon, Ill	Dec. 20, 1864	45, 485
Car-replacer	C. Hurst	New York, N. Y	Mar. 3, 1868	75, 029
Car-replacer	S. S. Jamison, jr	Saltsburgh, Pa	Apr. 14, 1868	76, 768
Car-replacer	C. King	Morristown, N. J	July 2, 1867	66, 359
Car-replacer	B. S. Lawson	New York, N. Y	Nov. 23, 1869	97, 204
Car-replacer	J. Mabie	New York, N. Y	Nov. 29, 1864	45, 254
Car-replacer	N. Pullman	New Oregon, Iowa	Apr. 7, 1868	76, 520
Car-replacer	H. Schreiner	Philadelphia, Pa	Dec. 22, 1868	85, 137
Car-replacer	L. Straus	Louisville, Ky	Oct. 29, 1867	70, 375
Car-replacer	A. N. Towne	Chicago, Ill	Jan. 28, 1868	73, 940
Car-replacer	H. Voth	Saint Louis, Mo	Mar. 25, 1873	137, 265
Car-replacer	A. Whittemore	Cambridgeport, Mass	Aug. 26, 1873	142, 135
Car-replacer or guide-rail	J. P. Lipps	Newark, N. J	July 21, 1868	80, 191
Car replacer, Railway	R. Harper	Chelsea, Mass	Dec. 15, 1863	40, 928
Car replacer, Railway	H. H. Holmes	Elmira, N. Y	Feb. 1, 1870	99, 318
Car replacer, Railway	E. Snyder	Providence, Pa	July 6, 1869	92, 387
Car-replacing jack	D. Moritz	Buffalo, N. Y	Sept. 12, 1871	118, 965
Car, Reversible street	W. T. Jenks	Toledo, Ohio	May 20, 1873	139, 063

Index of patents issued from the United States Patent Office from 1790 to 1873, inclusive—Continued.

Invention.	Inventor.	Residence.	Date.	No.
Car, Revolving	D. Lott	Lottsville, Pa	Aug. 1, 1865	49, 126
Car-roof	J. L. Burnham	Nashville, Tenn	Apr. 2, 1872	125, 266
Car-roof	N. C. Day	Nashua, N. H	July 16, 1872	129, 215
Car-roof	J. Garry	Cleveland, Ohio	Oct. 11, 1870	108, 130
Car-roof	J. B. Slichter	Chicago, Ill	Aug. 26, 1873	142, 129
Car-roof	J. C. Wands	Nashville, Tenn	Mar. 4, 1873	136, 569
Car roof, Railway	C. Dummeldinger	Cleveland, Ohio	June 18, 1867	65, 888
Car roof, Railway	W. H. Myers	Norwich, Conn	Aug. 14, 1866	57, 173
Car roof, Railway	J. Palmer	Cleveland, Ohio	June 21, 1864	43, 223
Car roof, Railway	J. Palmer	Cleveland, Ohio	July 2, 1867	66, 379
Car roof, Railway	B. F. Pickett	Nashville, Tenn	Apr. 26, 1870	102, 316
Car roof, Railway	O. V. Scaife	Pittsburgh, Pa	Apr. 5, 1864	42, 229
Car roof, Railway	J. Stephenson	New York, N. Y	Jan. 22, 1867	61, 482
Car roof, Railway	A. P. Winslow	Cleveland, Ohio	Aug. 9, 1859	25, 071
Car, Rotating dumping	W. A. Hawkes	Corinth, N. Y	June 7, 1859	24, 301
Car safety-apparatus, Railway	K. E. Holmes	Cambridgeport, Mass	Oct. 10, 1871	119, 766
Car, Safety railway	W. Kinkead	Elkton, Md	Dec. 29, 1837	535
Car safety-shoe, Railway	S. W. Emery and E. P. Doyen	Portland, Me	Mar. 12, 1872	124, 560
Car-seal	J. Dewe	Toronto, Canada	Nov. 22, 1870	109, 394
Car-seat	W. L. Bass	Cambridge, Mass	July 20, 1852	9, 128
Car-seat	S. G. Blackman	Waterbury, Conn	Aug. 4, 1868	80, 703
Car-seat	A. C. Blondyn	Saint Joseph, Mo	Oct. 26, 1858	21, 870
Car-seat	E. Booth and E. Ripley	Troy, N. Y	Nov. 11, 1851	8, 508
Car-seat	J. Briggs	Boston, Mass	July 6, 1852	9, 091
Car-seat	J. Casseday	Philadelphia, Pa	Feb. 22, 1870	100, 116
Car-seat	J. R. Chiles	Richmond, Va	July 30, 1867	67, 165
Car-seat	W. G. Creamer	Brooklyn, N. Y	Jan. 21, 1868	73, 510
Car-seat	J. S. Diack	Aurora, Ill	May 11, 1869	89, 976
Car-seat	A. S. Dotter	Philadelphia, Pa	July 2, 1867	66, 228
Car-seat	F. Farrel	Cincinnati, Ohio	June 3, 1873	139, 561
Car-seat	W. M. Henderson	Baltimore, Md	Aug. 16, 1859	25, 116
Car-seat	S. B. Holden	Sedalia, Mo	Apr. 7, 1868	76, 325
Car-seat	J. F. C. Hollings	Detroit, Mich	Nov. 19, 1872	133, 102
Car-seat	P. P. Joseff	Philadelphia, Pa	Nov. 2, 1858	21, 967
Car-seat	C. P. Kimball	Portland, Me	July 14, 1868	79, 837
Car-seat	E. Lockwood and G. W. Pitman	Bordentown, N. J	June 13, 1865	48, 191
Car-seat	E. Lockwood and G. W. Pitman	Bordentown, N. J	Apr. 10, 1866	53, 842
Car-seat	S. McGregor	Logansport, Ind	Mar. 27, 1860	27, 645
Car-seat	P. W. Nolan	New York, N. Y	Dec. 2, 1873	145, 229
Car-seat	W. Painter	Wilmington, Del	Aug. 31, 1858	21, 356
Car-seat	F. I. Palmer	Knoxville, Tenn	Mar. 13, 1860	27, 469
Car-seat	W. G. Philips and N. Coleman	Newport, Del	May 7, 1872	126, 485
Car-seat	T. Rainey	New York, N. Y	July 23, 1861	32, 892
Car-seat	E. Ripley and E. L. Brundage	Troy, N. Y	Dec. 9, 1851	8, 583
Car-seat	C. Rowland	Washington, D. C	Mar. 24, 1868	75, 982
Car-seat	J. W. Sibbet	Cincinnati, Ohio	Nov. 2, 1858	21, 985
Car-seat	R. Stilwell and E. L. Brundage	New York and Troy, N. Y	Apr. 22, 1851	8, 059
Car-seat	A. D. Tate	Peekskill, N. Y	Nov. 2, 1869	96, 504
Car-seat	F. F. Wagner	Harrisburgh, Pa	Sept. 1, 1868	81, 712
Car-seat	W. Wells	Salem, Mass	Aug. 9, 1870	106, 297
Car-seat	J. S. Wheat	South Wheeling, W. Va	May 28, 1867	65, 318
Car-seat	N. S. Whipple	Detroit, Mich	Apr. 2, 1872	125, 364
Car-seat, Adjustable	C. A. Buck and J. Lovett	Saint Louis, Mo	Aug. 1, 1871	117, 599
Car-seat, Adjustable	C. Stevenbank and J. Quinn	Wilmington, Del	May 30, 1871	115, 539
Car seat, Adjustable railway	W. N. Bragg	Richmond, Va	Oct. 9, 1866	58, 713
Car seat and berth, Railway	S. C. Case	Detroit, Mich	June 22, 1858	20, 622
Car seat and berth, Railway	Z. Cobb	Chicago, Ill	July 6, 1858	20, 777
Car seat and chair	W. N. Bragg	Richmond, Va	June 2, 1868	78, 570
Car seat and couch	H. L. Arnold	Elk Horn, Wis	Dec. 21, 1858	22, 338
Car seat and couch	W. M. Baker	Walpole, Ind	Jan. 25, 1859	22, 693
Car seat and couch	G. W. Fairchild	Holyoke, Mass	Dec. 14, 1858	22, 283
Car seat and couch	I. N. Forrester	Fairfax Court-House, Va	Aug. 24, 1858	21, 251
Car seat and couch	R. E. Fowler	Clayton, N. Y	Sept. 7, 1858	21, 412
Car seat and couch	K. Freeman	Fond du Lac, Wis	Aug. 31, 1858	21, 331
Car seat and couch	A. M. Holmes	Eaton, N. Y	Sept. 14, 1858	21, 536
Car seat and couch	I. W. Lamb	Salem, Mich	Sept. 3, 1867	68, 368
Car seat and couch	D. Pennoyer	North East, N. Y	Aug. 28, 1860	29, 813
Car seat and couch	T. Sharp	Carlisle, Pa	Aug. 14, 1866	57, 198
Car seat and couch	T. C. Theaker	Bridgeport, Ohio	Apr. 27, 1869	89, 542
Car seat and couch, Railway	H. Allen	New York, N. Y	June 12, 1866	55, 448
Car seat and couch, Railway	E. Burke	Philadelphia, Pa	Oct. 23, 1860	30, 517
Car seat and couch, Railway	J. H. Fisher	Placerville, Cal	Oct. 23, 1860	30, 472
Car seat and couch, Railway	J. Good	Philadelphia, Pa	Feb. 22, 1859	23, 061
Car seat and couch, Railway	J. L. Hamilton	Saint Joseph, Mo	Aug. 6, 1872	130, 219
Car seat and couch, Railway	W. R. Jackson	Baltimore, Md	Apr. 12, 1859	23, 581
Car seat and couch, Railway	T. E. McNeill	Philadelphia, Pa	May 31, 1859	24, 225
Car seat and couch, Railway	E. D. Sargent	Indianapolis, Ind	Aug. 9, 1859	25, 049
Car seat and couch, Railway	N. Thompson, jr	Brooklyn, N. Y	Dec. 28, 1858	22, 462
Car seat and couch, Railway	T. T. Woodruff	Alton, Ill	Dec. 2, 1856	16, 159
Car seat and couch, Railway	T. T. Woodruff	Alton, Ill	Dec. 2, 1856	16, 160
Car seat and couch, Railway	T. T. Woodruff	Philadelphia, Pa	May 31, 1859	24, 257
Car seat and couch, Railway	T. T. Woodruff	Philadelphia, Pa	Jan. 24, 1860	26, 942
Car seat and couch, Sleeping	T. E. McNeill	Philadelphia, Pa	May 24, 1859	24, 136
Car seat and desk combined, Railway	W. C. Huffman	Toledo, Ohio	Feb. 4, 1873	135, 557
Car seat and sleeping-couch, Railway	P. G. Green	Chicago, Ill	Dec. 21, 1858	22, 364
Car-seat arm	A. L. Babcock	New Haven, Conn	Feb. 12, 1867	61, 914
Car-seat arm, Railway	A. Prier	Milwaukee, Wis	Nov. 28, 1871	121, 235
Car-seat back	T. E. Warren	Troy, N. Y	July 30, 1850	7, 539
Car-seat back, Removable	P. F. Duchemin	Somerville, Mass	Jan. 24, 1871	111, 184
Car-seat backs, Support for	G. Higginson	Newark, N. J	Aug. 4, 1868	80, 736
Car-seat bolt	C. A. McEvoy	Richmond, Va	May 8, 1860	28, 190
Car-seat cushions, Redyeing	T. Brown	Albany, N. Y	July 31, 1866	56, 697
Car-seat frame	G. Buntin	Boston, Mass	Dec. 5, 1871	121, 486
Car-seat frames, Arm-rest for	T. S. Hudson	Cambridge, Mass	June 18, 1872	128, 044
Car seat, Horse	M. T. Glynn and J. L. Goodman	Boston, Mass	Sept. 26, 1871	119, 344
Car-seat indicator	F. H. Carney	Boston, Mass	Oct. 16, 1866	58, 771

Index of patents issued from the United States Patent Office from 1790 *to* 1873, *inclusive*—Continued.

Invention.	Inventor.	Residence.	Date.	No.
Car-seat link-joint	R. Hitchcock	Springfield, Mass	Feb. 11, 1868	74, 359
Car-seat lock	G. W. R. Bayley and J. McCluskey.	Algiers, La	Jan. 7, 1868	73, 155
Car-seat lock	S. B. Bowles	Brooklyn, N. Y	Feb. 26, 1867	62, 311
Car-seat lock	A. Duncan and J. M. Ziegler	Aurora, Ill	Feb. 21, 1865	46, 456
Car-seat lock	M. P. Ford	Columbus, Ohio	July 9, 1867	66, 479
Car-seat lock	E. Hambuger	Detroit, Mich	Sept. 3, 1867	68, 436
Car-seat lock	A. Loeffelholz and A. Prier	Milwaukee, Wis	Dec. 20, 1870	110, 254
Car-seat lock	G. McGregor	Cincinnati, Ohio	Sept. 29, 1863	40, 113
Car-seat lock	E. Miller	New York, N. Y	Aug. 2, 1870	105, 965
Car-seat lock	R. B. More	Cincinnati, Ohio	July 21, 1863	39, 303
Car seat, Railway	J. M. Allen	Washington, D. C	Nov. 21, 1871	121, 145
Car seat, Railway	A. S. Babbit	Keesville, N. Y	Sept. 27, 1864	44, 379
Car seat, Railway	C. P. Bailey	Zanesville, Ohio	Aug. 3, 1852	9, 161
Car seat, Railway	C. P. Bailey	Muskingum, Ohio	July 12, 1853	9, 851
Car seat, Railway	C. P. Bailey	Zanesville, Ohio	Oct. 10, 1854	11, 772
Car seat, Railway	C. P. Bailey	Zanesville, Ohio	Oct. 13, 1857	18, 375
Car seat, Railway	J. M. Baird	Wheeling, Va	Aug. 17, 1858	21, 178
Car seat, Railway	A. Barbarin	New Orleans, La	July 13, 1869	92, 418
Car seat, Railway	A. Barney	Wilmington, Del	Jan. 7, 1873	134, 627
Car seat, Railway	H. S. Blood	Jefferson, La	Sept. 29, 1868	82, 482
Car seat, Railway	J. Briggs	Boston, Mass	Feb. 15, 1853	9, 583
Car seat, Railway	J. A. Brown	Bath, Me	Sept. 3, 1867	68, 347
Car seat, Railway	A. B. Buell	Westmoreland, N. Y	May 11, 1852	8, 935
Car seat, Railway	D. Buzzell	Charlestown, Mass	Apr. 13, 1858	19, 910
Car seat, Railway	D. H. Chamberlain	West Roxbury, Mass	June 20, 1871	116, 154
Car seat, Railway	W. L. Childs	Piermont, N. Y	Feb. 1, 1859	22, 782
Car seat, Railway	J. H. Cocke	Bremo, Va	June 19, 1855	13, 079
Car seat, Railway	W. Crandell	Westfield, N. Y	Jan. 3, 1871	110, 746
Car seat, Railway	J. S. Denman	Brooklyn, N. Y	Jan. 12, 1858	19, 079
Car seat, Railway	J. C. De Witt	West Bloomfield, N. J	Aug. 31, 1858	21, 326
Car seat, Railway	A. B. Dinsmore	Springfield, Mass	Sept. 26, 1871	119, 331
Car seat, Railway	G. L. Dulaney	Mount Jackson, Va	Dec. 28, 1858	22, 471
Car seat, Railway	I. Fay	Cambridgeport, Mass	Sept. 2[illegible], 1853	10, 029
Car seat, Railway	W. Graham and L. McLaren	Philadelphia, Pa	Sept. 26, 1854	11, 724
Car seat, Railway	J. T. Hammitt	Philadelphia, Pa	Dec. 5, 1854	12, 023
Car seat, Railway	S. Hickok	Buffalo, N. Y	Aug. 9, 1853	9, 919
Car seat, Railway	S. B. Holden	Meadville, Pa	Aug. 25, 1863	39, 632
Car seat, Railway	E. Jeffers	Dorchester, Mass	Aug. 21, 1855	13, 464
Car seat, Railway	B. J. La Mothe	New York, N. Y	July 14, 1857	17, 794
Car seat, Railway	B. J. La Mothe	Detroit, Mich	May 13, 1873	138, 899
Car seat, Railway	C. B. Lasher	New York, N. Y	Oct. 4, 1864	44, 536
Car seat, Railway	C. M. Mann	Detroit, Mich	Aug. 31, 1858	21, [illegible]52
Car seat, Railway	F. Martin	Aurora, Ind	Feb. 12, 1867	62, 047
Car seat, Railway	M. M. Martin	Cochran, Ind	May 26, 1868	78, 304
Car seat, Railway	M. M. Martin	Cochran, Ind	Aug. 1, 1871	117, 553
Car seat, Railway	M. M. and F. Martin	Aurora, Ind	Aug. 21, 1866	57, 351
Car seat, Railway	G. T. McLauthlin	Boston, Mass	Mar. 4, 1856	14, 364
Car seat, Railway	J. McMurtry	Fayette County, Ky	July 27, 1858	21, 052
Car seat, Railway	T. E. McNeill	Philadelphia, Pa	Jan. 11, 1859	22, 568
Car seat, Railway	J. Millar	Paterson, N. J	June 22, 1858	20, 654
Car seat, Railway	E. Miller	New York, N. Y	Apr. 12, 1870	101, 755
Car seat, Railway	W. E. Milligan	New York, N. Y	Apr. 25, 1854	10, 818
Car seat, Railway	E. H. Olmstead	Savannah, Ga	Aug. 6, 1867	67, 572
Car seat, Railway	J. M. O'Neill	Clinton, Iowa	Aug. 30, 1870	106, 953
Car seat, Railway	J. I. Pease	Stockbridge, Mass	Aug. 23, 1870	106, 615
Car seat, Railway	G. W. Perry and J. D. Billings	Wilmington, Del	Dec. 8, 1868	84, 755
Car seat, Railway	G. W. Perry and J. D. Billings	Wilmington, Del	May 18, 1869	90, 297
Car seat, Railway	S. M. Perry	New York, N. Y	July 27, 1852	9, 155
Car seat, Railway	S. H. Rhoades and W. Carroll	Clyde, Ohio	Oct. 15, 1867	69, 938
Car seat, Railway	G. W. Sayre	Pisgah, Ohio	Apr. 18, 1865	47, 342
Car seat, Railway	P. I. Schopp	Louisville, Ky	June 25, 1872	128, 428
Car seat, Railway	E. F. Shornberger	Philadelphia, Pa	Jan. 3, 1865	45, 759
Car seat, Railway	A. D. Smith	Meredith, N. Y	Apr. 3, 1855	12, 644
Car seat, Railway	A. M. Smith	Rochester, N. Y	Aug. 21, 1855	13, 471
Car seat, Railway	C. A. Smith	Piermont, N. Y	Sept. 13, 1859	25, 448
Car seat, Railway	A. W. Snow	Norwich, Conn	June 26, 1849	6, 552
Car seat, Railway	W. H. Soper	Baltimore, Md	Aug. 23, 1870	106, 739
Car seat, Railway	D. Stone	Milwaukee, Wis	Oct. 5, 1858	21, 727
Car seat, Railway	J. B. Sutherland	Detroit, Mich	Sept. 28, 1869	95, 283
Car seat, Railway	J. H. Swan	New York, N. Y	Sept. 22, 1857	18, 252
Car seat, Railway	T. C. Theaker	Bridgeport, Ohio	Aug. 10, 1869	93, 660
Car seat, Railway	W. B. Thomas and S. Hickok	Buffalo, N. Y	Apr. 25, 1854	10, 837
Car seat, Railway	F. F. Wagner	Harrisburgh, Pa	Oct. 6, 1868	82, 899
Car seat, Railway	F. F. Wagner and P. P. Dickinson.	Harrisburgh, Pa	June 21, 1859	24, 511
Car seat, Railway	W. M. Warren	Watertown, Conn	July 26, 1853	9, 880
Car seat, Railway	W. M. Warren	Watertown, Conn	Aug. 23, 1853	9, 960
Car seat, Railway	E. Wheeler	Elmira, N. Y	Sept. 20, 1859	25, 499
Car seat, Railway	A. M. White	Thompsonville, Conn	July 14, 1868	80, 041
Car seat, Railway	G. Willard	Boston, Mass	May 6, 1856	14, 841
Car seat, Railway	D. H. Wiswell	Buffalo, N. Y	Nov. 16, 1852	9, 413
Car seat, Reversible	T. J. Close	Philadelphia, Pa	May 3, 1870	102, 498
Car seat, Reversible	P. F. Duchemin	Somerville, Mass	Mar. 18, 1873	136, 822
Car-seat, Revolving and reclining	A. Rapp	Elmira, N. Y	Dec. 10, 1872	133, 721
Car seat, Sleeping	R. Dirks	Philadelphia, Pa	Aug. 9, 1859	24, 998
Car seat, Street	C. H. Foster	San Francisco, Cal	Mar. 2, 1869	87, 335
Car-seats, Head-rest for	J. C. Giffing	New York, N. Y	Dec. 26, 1871	122, 165
Car-seats, Head-rest for	E. M. Judd	New Haven, Conn	Dec. 6, 1870	109, 823
Car-seats, Head-rest for	H. W. Safford	New York, N. Y	Dec. 28, 1869	98, 420
Car-seats, Head-rest for	G. Sanford	New York, N. Y	Apr. 29, 1862	35, 112
Car seats, Head-rest for railway	N. Gates	Middletown, Ohio	June 20, 1865	48, 270
Car seats, Head-rest for railway	W. M. McCauley	Washington, D. C	Sept. 1, 1857	18, 122
Car seats, Head-rest for railway	W. R. Phelps	New York, N. Y	July 4, 1865	48, 586
Car-seats, Hinged joint for	G. W. Perry	Wilmington, Del	Feb. 6, 1872	123, 417
Car seats, Lock for railway	A. H. Churchill	Boston, Mass	Sept. 17, 1872	131, 331
Car-seats, Metallic band for trimming	D. F. Randall	Chicopee, Mass	Jan. 28, 1868	73, 927
Car-seats, Mode of locking	D. H. Baker	Jersey City, N. J	Aug. 9, 1864	43, 753
Car seats, Pocket for railway	S. Simonson	Bridgeport, Conn	Aug. 31, 1869	94, 428

Index of patents issued from the United States Patent Office from 1790 *to* 1873, *inclusive*—Continued.

Index of patents issued from the United States Patent Office from 1790 *to* 1873, *inclusive*—Continued.

Invention.	Inventor.	Residence.	Date.	No.
Car-spring	E. J. Horner	Wilmington, Del	May 11, 1869	89,999
Car spring	C. R. Hurlburt	Seymour, Conn	Dec. 14, 1858	22,292
Car-spring	C. F. Jeffries	Philadelphia, Pa	Dec. 7, 1869	97,645
Car-spring	A. H. King	Rahway, N. J	Feb. 27, 1872	123,999
Car-spring	A. H. King	Rahway, N. J	July 9, 1872	128,7[illegible]3
Car-spring	W. Kingsley	New York, N. Y	May 8, 1860	28,237
Car-spring	J. Leland	Springfield, Mass	Jan. 24, 1871	111,127
Car-spring	G. H. Lewis	Providence, R. I	June 28, 1864	43,316
Car-spring	W. J. F. Liddell	Erie, Pa	Mar. 6, 1860	27,411
Car-spring	W. J. F. Liddell	Erie, Pa	Mar. 20, 1866	53,376
Car-spring	W. Marshall	New York, N. Y	June 14, 1864	43,121
Car-spring	J. R. Mathews	New London, Conn	Oct. 5, 1869	95,497
Car-spring	J. J. McCormick and J. E. Jerrold.	Paterson, N. J	July 17, 1860	29,222
Car-spring	G. W. McMinn	Cincinnati, Ohio	Nov. 26, 1867	71,317
Car-spring	A. Middleton, jr	Philadelphia, Pa	Apr. 23, 1872	126,073
Car-spring	A. Middleton, jr	Philadelphia, Pa	May 6, 1873	138,675
Car-spring	J. S. Miller	Springfield, Mass	Aug. 20, 1867	67,897
Car-spring	A. W. Moses	Philadelphia, Pa	Sept. 23, 1873	143,175
Car-spring	J. Murray	New York, N. Y	June 6, 1865	48,084
Car-spring	D. Myers	Chicago, Ill	Dec. 4, 1866	60,227
Car-spring	E. Myers	Jersey City, N. J	May 13, 1873	138,920
Car-spring	W. Newbauer	Philadelphia, Pa	Aug. 1, 1865	49,137
Car-spring	W. R. Nichols	Philadelphia, Pa	July 3, 1866	56,084
Car-spring	W. R. Nichols	Philadelphia, Pa	May 19, 1868	78,120
Car-spring	F. E. Oliver	New York, N. Y	May 10, 1864	42,682
Car-spring	J. G. Pugsley	New York, N. Y	Aug. 4, 1863	39,422
Car-spring	J. B. Quirk	Philadelphia, Pa	Dec. 17, 1872	133,952
Car-spring	J. B. Quirk	Philadelphia, Pa	Apr. 29, 1873	138,433
Car-spring	W. F. Ray	Fort Wayne, Ind	Dec. 10, 1867	71,912
Car-spring	F. W. Rhinelander	New York, N. Y	May 31, 1870	103,778
Car-spring	G. A. Riedel	Philadelphia, Pa	Apr. 19, 1864	42,402
Car-spring	G. A. Riedel	Philadelphia, Pa	Aug. 2, 1864	43,708
Car-spring	G. A. Riedel	Philadelphia, Pa	Apr. 18, 1865	47,373
Car-spring	H. E. Roeder	New York, N. Y	Sept. 24, 1861	33,366
Car-spring	A. H. Rowand	Allegheny, Pa	Oct. 9, 1866	58,677
Car-spring	T. Shaw	Philadelphia, Pa	Aug. 22, 1865	49,560
Car-spring	J. J. C. Smith	Philadelphia, Pa	Nov. 7, 1865	50,849
Car-spring	J. J. C. Smith	Philadelphia, Pa	Nov. 7, 1865	50,850
Car-spring	J. B. Smyth	Philadelphia, Pa	Apr. 24, 1866	54,227
Car-spring	W. Tosbach	New York, N. Y	Jan. 1, 1867	60,805
Car-spring	G. L. Turner	New York, N. Y	June 18, 1861	32,591
Car-spring	U. P. Vidal	Philadelphia, Pa	Apr. 26, 1864	42,519
Car-spring	R. Vose	New York, N. Y	Jan. 3, 1860	26,723
Car-spring	R. Vose	New York, N. Y	June 5, 1860	28,619
Car-spring	R. Vose	New York, N. Y	June 12, 1860	28,703
Car-spring	R. Vose	New York, N. Y	Mar. 11, 1862	34,657
Car-spring	R. Vose	New York, N. Y	Oct. 28, 1862	36,813
Car-spring	R. Vose	New York, N. Y	May 19, 1863	38,642
Car-spring	R. Vose	New York, N. Y	Oct. 6, 1863	40,218
Car-spring	R. Vose	New York, N. Y	Dec. 5, 1865	51,368
Car-spring	R. Vose	New York, N. Y	Aug. 27, 1867	68,133
Car-spring	R. Vose	New York, N. Y	Aug. 27, 1867	68,134
Car-spring	R. Vose	New York, N. Y	Dec. 10, 1867	71,926
Car-spring	R. Vose	New York, N. Y	Dec. 31, 1867	72,941
Car-spring	R. Vose	New York, N. Y	July 19, 1870	105,514
Car-spring	R. Vose and C. D. Gibson	New York, N. Y	June 2, 1863	38,777
Car-spring	L. Vote	Pittsburgh, Pa	Nov. 5, 1872	132,879
Car-spring	C. Wheeler, jr	Auburn, N. Y	Dec. 14, 1869	97,842
Car-spring box	J. W. Evans	New York, N. Y	Jan. 5, 1869	85,518
Car spring, Conical plate railway	J. J. Speed, jr., and J. A. Bailey	Detroit, Mich	Sept. 11, 1855	13,552
Car-spring, Corrugated spiral	C. French	Seymour, Conn	Apr. 15, 1862	34,952
Car-spring fastener	J. W. Wood	Philadelphia, Pa	Aug. 30, 1864	44,033
Car-spring, India-rubber	S. Peatfield	Ipswich, Mass	Sept. 28, 1858	21,624
Car-spring, India-rubber	R. Vose	New York, N. Y	Aug. 28, 1866	57,600
Car spring, India-rubber railway	T. F. Allen	Dyersville, Iowa	Oct. 23, 1860	30,450
Car-spring, Metallic	A. Egan	Pesth, Hungary	Sept. 10, 1872	131,154
Car-spring, Metallic	D. Johnson	Chicago, Ill	Sept. 9, 1856	15,698
Car-spring, Nest-spiral	R. Vose	New York, N. Y	Sept. 26, 1871	119,253
Car-spring, Nest-spiral	R. Vose	New York, N. Y	Sept. 26, 1871	119,254
Car-spring, Pneumatic	J. Merlett	Bound Brook, N. J	Jan. 9, 1867	51,956
Car spring, Railway	T. F. Allen	Dyersville, Iowa	Jan. 15, 1861	31,102
Car spring, Railway	T. F. Allyn	Nyack, N. Y	Jan. 11, 1870	98,732
Car spring, R[illegible]way	T. F. Allyn	Nyack, N. Y	July 16, 1872	129,448
Car spring, R[illegible]way	T. F. Allyn	Nyack, N. Y	Nov. 19, 1872	133,674
Car spring, Railway	J. F. Babcock	Boston, Mass	Mar. 22, 1870	101,080
Car spring, Railway	W. Barry and G. Franklin	Philadelphia, Pa	Dec. 21, 1869	98,140
Car spring, Railway	J. C. Blair	Pittsburgh, Pa	Dec. 29, 1857	18,950
Car spring, Railway	A. Bridges	New York, N. Y	July 29, 1862	36,050
Car spring, Railway	E. Cliff	Oswego, N. Y	May 9, 1871	114,645
Car spring, Railway	J. W. Cochran	New York, N. Y	July 6, 1869	92,267
Car spring, Railway	J. W. Cochran	New York, N. Y	Oct. 10, 1871	119,823
Car spring, Railway	W. F. Converse	Harrison, Ohio	Nov. 8, 1859	26,019
Car spring, Railway	W. F. Converse	Harrison, Ohio	Aug. 1, 1865	49,086
Car spring, Railway	J. W. Culmer	Pittsburgh, Pa	Jan. 7, 1873	134,645
Car spring, Railway	D. G. Daniels	Chicago, Ill	Jan. 11, 1870	98,672
Car spring, Railway	A. B. Davis	Philadelphia, Pa	Feb. 15, 1859	22,941
Car spring, Railway	A. M. De Hart	Reading, Pa	May 4, 1858	20,148
Car spring, Railway	R. Dudley and B. Hershey	Erie, Pa	Feb. 28, 1871	112,229
Car spring, Railway	G. Elliot	Saint Louis, Mo	Sept. 19, 1871	119,129
Car spring, Railway	J. W. Evans	New York, N. Y	Mar. 26, 1861	31,792
Car spring, Railway	J. W. Evans	New York, N. Y	Jan. 6, 1863	37,283
Car spring, Railway	J. W. Evans	New York, N. Y	June 25, 1872	128,292
Car spring, Railway	J. J. Fields	Brooklyn, N. Y	July 27, 1858	20,998
Car spring, Railway	H. Gardiner	New York, N. Y	June 1, 1858	20,418
Car spring, Railway	H. Gardiner	New York, N. Y	Apr. 7, 1863	38,105
Car spring, Railway	H. Gardiner	New York, N. Y	Nov. 15, 1870	109,312
Car spring, Railway	P. G. Gardiner	New York, N. Y	Dec. 11, 1855	13,905

Index of patents issued from the United States Patent Office from 1790 *to* 1873, *inclusive*—Continued.

Invention.	Inventor.	Residence.	Date.	No.
Car spring, Railway	P. G. Gardiner	New York, N. Y	Mar. 10, 1863	37, 862
Car spring, Railway	P. G. Gardiner	New York, N. Y	July 6, 1869	92, 182
Car spring, Railway	P. G. Gardiner	New York, N. Y	July 6, 1869	92, 183
Car spring, Railway	P. G. Gardiner	New York, N. Y	Aug. 24, 1869	93, 983
Car spring, Railway	P. G. Gardiner	New York, N. Y	Aug. 24, 1869	93, 984
Car spring, Railway	P. G. Gardiner	New York, N. Y	Aug. 24, 1869	94, 101
Car spring, Railway	P. G. Gardiner	New York, N. Y	Oct. 29, 1872	132, 570
Car spring, Railway	G. F. Godley	New York, N. Y	June 24, 1873	140, 192
Car spring, Railway	A. Hay	Philadelphia, Pa	Aug. 30, 1859	25, 264
Car spring, Railway	H. Jeffrey and H. Fisher	Aurora Station, Ind	Apr. 23, 1872	125, 959
Car spring, Railway	D. Johnson	Chicago, Ill	Jan. 24, 1860	26, 905
Car spring, Railway	A. H. King	Rahway, N. J	Nov. 5, 1872	132, 765
Car spring, Railway	A. Middleton, jr	Philadelphia, Pa	July 16, 1872	129, 155
Car spring, Railway	J. Millholland	Baltimore, Md	Sept. 23, 1843	3, 278
Car spring, Railway	J. Mitchell	Sheffield, England	July 19, 1870	105, 478
Car spring, Railway	S. Morse	Springfield, Mass	Feb. 23, 1858	19, 435
Car spring, Railway	J. Murphy	New York, N. Y	Aug. 21, 1866	57, 365
Car spring, Railway	H. M. Paine	Worcester, Mass	Oct. 27, 1857	18, 515
Car spring, Railway	A. Potts	Philadelphia, Pa	Dec. 27, 1870	110, 497
Car spring, Railway	F. M. Ray	Catskill, N. Y	Nov. 3, 1838	1, 000
Car spring, Railway	F. W. Rhinelander	New York, N. Y	Feb. 1, 1870	99, 475
Car spring, Railway	P. Riley	Shamokin, Pa	June 21, 1839	1, 180
Car spring, Railway	D. B. Rogers	Pittsburgh, Pa	Feb. 23, 1858	19, 448
Car spring, Railway	D. B. Rogers and J. A. Wood	Pittsburgh, Pa	July 26, 1859	24, 888
Car spring, Railway	C. Russell	Massillon, Ohio	July 21, 1863	39, 310
Car spring, Railway	W. Slicer	Baltimore, Md	June 17, 1873	140, 084
Car spring, Railway	W. Tosbach	New York, N. Y	Aug. 30, 1864	44, 027
Car spring, Railway	G. L. Turner	New York, N. Y	Aug. 21, 1860	29, 732
Car spring, Railway	R. Vose	New York, N. Y	July 21, 1863	39, 314
Car spring, Railway	R. Vose	New York, N. Y	June 28, 1870	104, 907
Car spring, Railway	H. Waterman	Hudson, N. Y	Jan. 26, 1858	19, 219
Car spring, Railway	A. T. Watson	Castleton, N. Y	Mar. 20, 1860	27, 587
Car spring, Railway	A. T. Watson	New York, N. Y	Apr. 24, 1866	54, 234
Car spring, Railway	R. Winans	Baltimore, Md	June 14, 1834	....
Car spring, Railway	J. E. Wootten	Philadelphia, Pa	Apr. 21, 1863	38, 255
Car spring, Railway	S. Yerkes, jr	Philadelphia, Pa	May 9, 1871	114, 741
Car-spring, Spiral	F. W. Rhinelander	New York, N. Y	Mar. 15, 1870	100, 926
Car-spring, Vulcanized India-rubber	H. A. Alden	Matteawan, N. Y	Jan. 4, 1870	98, 540
Car-spring, Vulcanized rubber	H. W. Beins	New York, N. Y	July 5, 1859	24, 693
Car-springs, End-fastener for	G. Elliot	Saint Louis, Mo	June 28, 1870	104, 718
Car-springs from mandrels, Machine for disengaging	P. G. Gardiner	New York, N. Y	Mar. 31, 1857	16, 916
Car springs, Hanging or arranging railway	W. E. Cooper	Dunkirk, N. Y	Nov. 8, 1859	26, 068
Car springs, Machine for creasing plates for railway	P. G. Gardiner	New York, N. Y	Mar. 31, 1857	16, 915
Car-springs, Machine for making	A. Hebbard	Springfield, Mass	Mar. 1, 1870	100, 400
Car-springs, Machine for testing and measuring the strength of.	P. G. Gardiner	New York, N. Y	Mar. 30, 1858	19, 767
Car-springs, Manufacture of	N. and A. Middleton, jr	Philadelphia, Pa	Feb. 18, 1873	135, 929
Car springs, Packer for railway	P. G. Gardiner	New York, N. Y	Nov. 30, 1869	97, 385
Car-springs, Tempering steel	P. G. Gardiner	New York, N. Y	Sept. 28, 1858	21, 603
Car-springs, Wrought-iron mold for vulcanizing rubber.	C. H. Franklin	Jersey City, N. J	Sept. 14, 1869	94, 815
Car-stake holder	G. A. Brown	Kalamazoo, Mich	Apr. 14, 1868	76, 596
Car-stake holder	O. R. Parmele	Aurora, Ill	Dec. 17, 1867	72, 226
Car-stake holder	W. P. Wentworth	Detroit, Mich	May 26, 1868	78, 405
Car-stake holder, Platform	W. J. Willits	Detroit, Mich	May 12, 1868	77, 943
Car-stake holder, Railway	A. R. Burdick	Racine, Wis	Jan. 10, 1865	45, 891
Car-stake supporter	W. H. Masterman and W. T. Hooper.	Stockton, Cal	Feb. 4, 1873	135, 436
Car-standard	R. Clarke	Mount Vernon, Ohio	June 30, 1868	79, 315
Car-standard, Folding	S. Little	Loretto, Pa	June 28, 1864	43, 317
Car standard, Railway	S. S. Beeman	Saint Albans, Vt	July 18, 1871	117, 146
Car-starter	P. Bates, jr	Pittsburgh, Pa	Jan. 28, 1873	135, 193
Car-starter	L. D. Benner	Boston, Mass	Jan. 14, 1873	134, 840
Car-starter	J. Bevan	Hudson, N. Y	Sept. 13, 1870	107, 330
Car-starter	I. N. Bevans	Thomaston, Conn	June 30, 1868	79, 529
Car-starter	R. Bogardus	New York, N. Y	June 21, 1870	104, 411
Car-starter	R. Bogardus	New York, N. Y	July 2, 1872	128, 527
Car-starter	J. Boswell and J. W. Brindle	Wilmington, Ohio	Feb. 23, 1869	87, 136
Car-starter	S. R. and A. C. Bradley	Brooklyn, N. Y	May 13, 1873	138, 848
Car-starter	C. B. Broadwell	New Orleans, La	Mar. 19, 1872	124, 662
Car-starter	W. H. Butler and R. G. Hatfield.	New York, N. Y	June 12, 1866	55, 464
Car-starter	T. Cooper	Philadelphia, Pa	Apr. 29, 1873	138, 233
Car-starter	J. Corbeil	Lind, Wis	July 29, 1873	141, 326
Car-starter	A. H. Crozier	New York, N. Y	Nov. 4, 1873	144, 260
Car-starter	A. B. Davis	Catahoula Parish, La	Aug. 3, 1869	93, 283
Car-starter	G. W. Davis and A. E. Smith	Providence, R. I	May 4, 1869	89, 636
Car-starter	D. A. Dickinson	Baltimore, Md	Oct. 18, 1870	108, 460
Car-starter	G. Fetter	Philadelphia, Pa	May 20, 1873	139, 134
Car-starter	G. W. Field and J. Steger	New York, N. Y	June 3, 1873	139, 563
Car-starter	D. W. Garst	Washington, D. C	Nov. 19, 1872	133, 218
Car-starter	J. W. Houghtelin	Detroit, Mich	Apr. 30, 1867	64, 224
Car-starter	T. W. Johnston	Chicago, Ill	July 15, 1873	140, 781
Car-starter	J. B. Jones	Philadelphia, Pa	Feb. 18, 1873	135, 920
Car-starter	W. A. Jordan	New Orleans, La	Nov. 11, 1873	144, 546
Car-starter	W. Keeler	Towanda, Pa	Sept. 24, 1872	131, 689
Car-starter	S. H. Kenny	Dwight, Ill	Nov. 19, 1872	133, 157
Car-starter	G. B. Kirkham	New York, N. Y	Jan. 31, 1871	111, 353
Car-starter	W. W. Lamberton and D. R. Lemman.	New Orleans, La	Feb. 4, 1873	135, 564
Car-starter	C. P. Leavitt	New York, N. Y	Dec. 5, 1871	121, 635
Car-starter	G. Lowden	Brooklyn, N. Y	June 10, 1873	139, 721
Car-starter	C. J. Moore	Joliet, Ill	July 22, 1873	141, 159
Car-starter	W. H. Newton	Newport, R. I	Jan. 3, 1871	110, 760
Car-starter	J. North	New York, N. Y	Dec. 5, 1871	121, 540
Car-starter	B. F. Oakes	Milford, Me.	Oct. 21, 1873	143, 837
Car-starter	L. Rodenhausen	Philadelphia, Pa	Mar. 24, 1868	75, 981
Car-starter	L. C. Rodier and F. G. Bates	Springfield, Mass	Apr. 29, 1873	138, 440

Index of patents issued from the United States Patent Office from 1790 *to* 1873, *inclusive*—Continued.

Invention.	Inventor.	Residence.	Date.	No.
Car-starter	W. E. Snediker	Charlotteburgh, N. J	Nov. 19, 1872	133, 265
Car-starter	J. Steger	New York, N. Y	Dec. 29, 1868	85, 407
Car-starter	J. F. Stokes	Philadelphia, Pa	Apr. 6, 1869	88, 675
Car-starter	J. F. Stokes	Philadelphia, Pa	June 27, 1871	116, 508
Car-starter	W. M. and W. E. Stratton	West Troy, N. Y	May 21, 1872	126, 993
Car-starter	R. R. Taylor	Reading, Pa	Mar. 2, 1869	87, 524
Car-starter	J. G. Thompson	Stockton, N. Y	Dec. 16, 1873	145, 600
Car-starter	I. C. Wallace and J. W. Andrews.	Detroit, Mich	Dec. 30, 1873	146, 112
Car-starter	M. N. Ward	Bangor, Me	Oct. 26, 1869	96, 172
Car-starter	W. M. Watson	Tonica, Ill	June 4, 1872	127, 531
Car-starter	J. J. Wheeler	Grinnell, Iowa	Jan. 21, 1873	135, 187
Car-starter	A. Whittimore	Cambridgeport, Mass	June 24, 1873	140, 229
Car-starter	A. Whittimore	Cambridgeport, Mass	Oct. 21, 1873	143, 948
Car-starter	A. Whittimore	Cambridgeport, Mass	Dec. 9, 1873	145, 468
Car-starter	G. A. Wilbur	Skowhegan, Me	July 13, 1869	92, 499
Car-starter	N. J. Wilkinson	Kalamazoo, Mich	Mar. 4, 1873	136, 398
Car-starter	V. Wirick	Chicago, Ill	Dec. 2, 1873	145, 076
Car-starter	F. J. Wright and L. W. Wandell.	New York, N. Y	Jan. 24, 1871	111, 294
Car starter and brake	T. R. Sinclaire	New York, N. Y	July 31, 1866	56, 810
Car starter and brake	J. Wiley, 2d	South Reading, Mass	Mar. 12, 1867	62, 911
Car-starter, Electrical	J. and W. H. Clark	Philadelphia, Pa	Nov. 26, 1867	71, 458
Car-starter for street-railways	M. Toulmin	New Orleans, La	Aug. 5, 1873	141, 474
Car starter, Horse	H. Schreiner	Philadelphia, Pa	Mar. 14, 1871	112, 640
Car starter, Railway	A. Amory	New York, N. Y	May 30, 1871	115, 266
Car starter, Railway	C. B. Broadwell	New Orleans, La	July 26, 1870	105, 635
Car starter, Railway	C. B. Broadwell	New Orleans, La	Aug. 6, 1872	130, 275
Car starter, Railway	D. Cumming	Sorrel Horse, Pa	Apr. 26, 1859	23, 777
Car starter, Railway	A. A. Wilder	Detroit, Mich	Feb. 19, 1867	62, 302
Car starter, Street	A. B. Davis	Catahoula Parish, La	Aug. 3, 1869	93, 282
Car starter, Street	T. S. E. Dixon	Janesville, Wis	Nov. 9, 1869	96, 557
Car starter, Street	G. P. Frick	Baltimore, Md	Oct. 11, 1870	108, 127
Car starter, Street	B. Lepper	Saint Louis, Mo	June 7, 1870	103, 897
Car starter, Street	H. Welch	Schuylersville, N. Y	June 21, 1870	104, 673
Car starter, Street-railway	J. D. S. Newell	New Orleans, La	Oct. 1, 1872	131, 772
Car starting and stopping apparatus	J. B. Waring	New York, N. Y	Mar. 24, 1868	75, 818
Car-starting apparatus	J. Steger	New York, N. Y	July 9, 1867	66, 648
Car-starting apparatus	J. Steger	New York, N. Y	Jan. 28, 1868	73, 764
Car starting-apparatus, City-railway	S. N. Sanford	Cleveland, Ohio	Apr. 3, 1860	27, 742
Car, Steam	H. F. Knapp	New York, N. Y	July 23, 1872	129, 833
Car, Steam street	T. C. Robinson and G. P. Clark	Boston, Mass	Dec. 29, 1868	85, 331
Car-step, Adjustable	W. Neumann	Saint Louis, Mo	Aug. 18, 1868	81, 194
Car, Stock	G. A. Egan	Covington, Ky	Feb. 4, 1873	135, 532
Car, Stock	G. W. Fox	Laramie, Wyo	May 16, 1871	114, 795
Car, Stock	T. E. Knauss	Zaleski, Ohio	Dec. 26, 1871	122, 120
Car, Stock	H. Lee	Beloit, Wis	Oct. 8, 1872	132, 088
Car, Stock	T. J. McCarty	Salem, Ohio	Oct. 7, 1873	143, 414
Car, Stock	A. Rank	Salem, Ohio	Feb. 14, 1871	111, 872
Car, Stock	A. Rank	Salem, Ohio	July 11, 1871	116, 866
Car, Stock	O. Severance	Middlebury, Vt	Nov. 18, 1873	144, 798
Car, Stock	W. Stark	Bronson, Mich	Aug. 2, 1864	43, 720
Car, Stock	Z. Street	Salem, Ohio	Aug. 30, 1870	106, 887
Car, Stock	Z. Street	Salem, Ohio	Aug. 30, 1870	106, 888
Car, Stock	Z. Street	Salem, Ohio	Mar. 26, 1872	125, 097
Car, Stock	A. Welch	Southall, England	Dec. 24, 1872	134, 335
Car, Stock and freight	J. B. Calkins	Pacific, Mo	July 11, 1871	116, 804
Car, Stock and freight	J. B. Calkins	Pacific, Mo	Dec. 26, 1871	122, 104
Car-strap	H. S. Vrooman	Boston, Mass	Jan. 2, 1872	122, 417
Car strap, Street	M. Warne	Philadelphia, Pa	Apr. 1, 1873	137, 397
Car, Street	C. B. Broadwell	New Orleans, La	Feb. 28, 1871	112, 215
Car, Street	M. De Graff	Chicago, Ill	Aug. 24, 1869	94, 086
Car, Street	Z. Eastman	Chicago, Ill	June 8, 1869	91, 105
Car, Street	J. I. Herrick	Milwaukee, Wis	May 5, 1868	77, 485
Car, Street	W. T. Jenks	Toledo, Ohio	Jan. 28, 1873	135, 277
Car, Street	J. F. Madison and H. McLaughlin.	Saint Louis, Mo	Aug. 3, 1869	93, 322
Car, Street	J. A. Miller	New York, N. Y	Jan. 26, 1864	41, 386
Car, Street	J. E. Ridgeway	Philadelphia, Pa	Apr. 26, 1870	102, 435
Car, Street	P. Shaw	Boston, Mass	Apr. 20, 1869	89, 086
Car, Street	J. Stephenson	New York, N. Y	Jan. 22, 1867	61, 481
Car, Street	J. Stephenson	New York, N. Y	Feb. 23, 1869	87, 120
Car, Street	J. Stephenson	New York, N. Y	May 14, 1872	126, 756
Car, Street	J. Stephenson	New York, N. Y	May 14, 1872	126, 757
Car, Street	J. Stephenson	New York, N. Y	June 4, 1872	127, 526
Car, Street	M. P. Turner	Des Moines, Iowa	Feb. 8, 1870	99, 732
Car, Street-railway	E. L. Dorsey	Washington, D. C	May 7, 1872	126, 449
Car, Street-railway	J. J. Gutierrez	Jefferson Parish, La	June 7, 1870	103, 874
Car, Street-railway	W. H. T. Hughes	Brooklyn, N. Y	Dec. 17, 1872	134, 060
Car, Street-railway	S. T. Jones	Philadelphia, Pa	Feb. 22, 1830	....
Car, Street-railway	J. Stephenson	New York, N. Y	Nov. 29, 1864	45, 281
Car, Street-railway	J. Stephenson	New York, N. Y	Feb. 23, 1869	87, 121
Car, Street steam-railway	J. P. Woodbury	Boston, Mass	Jan. 24, 1865	46, 043
Car, Street steam-railway	J. P. Woodbury	Boston, Mass	May 30, 1865	48, 008
Car-tank cover	L. C. Cattell	Cleveland, Ohio	Dec. 14, 1869	97, 879
Car, track, and operating apparatus for mines	W. B. Frue	Houghton, Mich	Mar. 22, 1870	101, 115
Car, Track-laying	J. S. Lake	Smith's Landing, N. J	Jan. 22, 1867	61, 344
Car unloader, Grain	M. W. Bosworth	Binghamton, N. Y	Dec. 23, 1873	145, 780
Car-ventilator	B. T. Babbitt	New York, N. Y	Jan. 30, 1855	12, 306
Car-ventilator	J. B. Bausman	Rochester, Pa	Apr. 9, 1861	31, 943
Car-ventilator	W. C. Betts	Brooklyn, N. Y	Jan. 17, 1871	110, 950
Car-ventilator	J. A. Caldwell	Springfield, Mass	Aug. 28, 1866	57, 470
Car-ventilator	J. J. Crowley	Whistler, Ala	Feb. 18, 1873	135, 971
Car-ventilator	J. M. Dexter	Elmira, N. Y	Jan. 10, 1871	110, 906
Car-ventilator	C. C. Gerhardt	Wyandotte, Kans	Mar. 4, 1873	136, 502
Car-ventilator	G. Hardy	Lawrence, Mass	May 29, 1866	55, 694
Car-ventilator	M. T. Hitchcock	Springfield, Mass	Feb. 18, 1868	74, 534
Car-ventilator	M. T. Hitchcock	Springfield, Mass	Dec. 23, 1873	145, 871

Index of patents issued from the United States Patent Office from 1790 *to* 1873, *inclusive*—Continued.

Invention.	Inventor.	Residence.	Date.	No.
Car-ventilator	R. Hitchcock	Springfield, Mass	Aug. 20, 1867	67, 877
Car-ventilator	R. Hitchcock	Springfield, Mass	Mar. 24, 1868	75, 910
Car-ventilator	R. Hitchcock	Springfield, Mass	Sept. 7, 1869	94, 494
Car-ventilator	W. H. Hunt	Bolton, Conn	Aug. 30, 1870	106, 940
Car-ventilator	S. C. Maine	Boston, Mass	Sept. 16, 1873	142, 799
Car-ventilator	A. J. Morrison	Troy, N. Y	Sept. 16, 1873	142, 807
Car-ventilator	D. C. Richardson	Lawrence, Mass	Feb. 25, 1868	74, 849
Car-ventilator	W. M. Russell and D. E. Holmes.	Cincinnati, Ohio	Aug. 18, 1868	81, 297
Car-ventilator	A. B. Spencer	Rochester, N. Y	Apr. 5, 1864	42, 234
Car-ventilator	C. Wadsworth	New York, N. Y	May 6, 1862	35, 190
Car-ventilator and dust-screen, Pocket	J. B. Timberlake	Salem, Ohio	May 27, 1873	139, 278
Car-ventilator and refrigerator	W. E. Phelps	Elmwood, Ill	Sept. 27, 1870	107, 716
Car-ventilator, Automatic	I. Buckingham	Seymour, Conn	May 12, 1868	77, 867
Car-ventilator, Eduction	M. T. Hitchcock	Springfield, Mass	Sept. 28, 1869	95, 346
Car ventilator, Railway	M. C. Andrews	Lawrence, Mass	May 26, 1868	78, 174
Car ventilator, Railway	G. B. Armstrong and G. F. McLellan.	Chicago, Ill., and Washington, D. C.	Dec. 27, 1870	110, 416
Car ventilator, Railway	G. W. R. Bayley and J. McCluskey.	Algiers, La	July 7, 1868	79, 541
Car ventilator, Railway	L. C. Beardsley	Cleveland, Ohio	Oct. 29, 1861	33, 565
Car ventilator, Railway	J. Bevan	Jersey City, N. J	June 13, 1854	11, 101
Car ventilator, Railway	I. Bonnell, jr	Chicago, Ill	Mar. 8, 1870	100, 589
Car ventilator, Railway	W. A. Brown	Philadelphia, Pa	Dec. 24, 1861	33, 979
Car ventilator, Railway	J. H. Bruce	Wyandotte, Kans	June 4, 1872	127, 559
Car ventilator, Railway	W. Conard	Burlington, N. J	July 5, 1870	105, 046
Car ventilator, Railway	W. G. Creamer	Brooklyn, N. Y	Aug. 20, 1861	33, 071
Car ventilator, Railway	W. G. Creamer	Brooklyn, N. Y	Nov. 12, 1867	70, 812
Car ventilator, Railway	W. G. Creamer	Brooklyn, N. Y	May 11, 1869	89, 974
Car ventilator, Railway	W. G. Creamer	Brooklyn, N. Y	Feb. 20, 1872	123, 770
Car ventilator, Railway	H. A. Custis	Richmond, Va	May 31, 1870	103, 722
Car ventilator, Railway	S. Darling	Providence, R. I	Mar. 15, 1870	100, 870
Car ventilator, Railway	I. Dripps	Fort Wayne, Ind	Mar. 24, 1868	75, 878
Car ventilator, Railway	W. B. Dunning	Geneva, N. Y	Dec. 17, 1867	72, 274
Car ventilator, Railway	E. B. Forbush	Buffalo, N. Y	Feb. 21, 1860	27, 212
Car ventilator, Railway	D. H. Fox and J. Fink	Reading, Pa	May 8, 1855	12, 818
Car ventilator, Railway	T. W. Freeborn	Newport, R. I	May 14, 1872	126, 797
Car ventilator, Railway	F. H. Furniss	Cleveland, Ohio	Sept. 17, 1861	33, 302
Car ventilator, Railway	R. C. Graves	Barnesville, Ohio	Apr. 16, 1867	63, 880
Car ventilator, Railway	G. B. Hall and J. Shaffer	Kansas City, Mo	Sept. 26, 1871	119, 349
Car ventilator, Railway	A. Hapgood	Worcester, Mass	May 22, 1860	28, 365
Car ventilator, Railway	C. H. Haskins	Saint Louis, Mo	Nov. 26, 1867	71, 385
Car ventilator, Railway	R. Heneage and F. W. Breed	Buffalo, N. Y	May 26, 1868	78, 206
Car ventilator, Railway	G. A. Hines	Brattleborough, Vt	Oct. 17, 1871	119, 982
Car ventilator, Railway	M. T. Hitchcock	Springfield, Mass	July 28, 1868	80, 411
Car ventilator, Railway	M. T. Hitchcock	Springfield, Mass	Jan. 18, 1870	98, 965
Car ventilator, Railway	R. Hitchcock	Springfield, Mass	Oct. 26, 1869	96, 114
Car ventilator, Railway	J. L. Howard	Hartford, Conn	Sept. 15, 1863	39, 925
Car ventilator, Railway	J. L. Howard	Hartford, Conn	Oct. 29, 1867	70, 216
Car ventilator, Railway	J. L. Howard	Hartford, Conn	July 18, 1871	117, 076
Car ventilator, Railway	J. L. Howard	Hartford, Conn	July 25, 1871	117, 289
Car ventilator, Railway	M. G. Imbach	Hartford, Conn	Dec. 17, 1867	72, 203
Car ventilator, Railway	N. Jones	Buffalo, N. Y	June 27, 1871	116, 319
Car ventilator, Railway	D. C. Justison	Wilmington, Del	Nov. 14, 1871	120, 980
Car ventilator, Railway	S. E. Kirkpatrick	Saint Albans, Vt	Apr. 9, 1872	125, 461
Car ventilator, Railway	J. Lesperance	Saint Louis, Mo	Feb. 9, 1869	86, 766
Car ventilator, Railway	S. C. Maine	Boston, Mass	Apr. 9, 1872	125, 401
Car ventilator, Railway	T. J. Mell	Macon, Ga	May 18, 1869	90, 181
Car ventilator, Railway	S. Merrick	New Brighton, Pa	May 26, 1863	38, 691
Car ventilator, Railway	D. Merrill	Worcester, Mass	Apr. 8, 1862	34, 898
Car ventilator, Railway	J. Miller and W. Ketting	Jersey City, N. J	Sept. 10, 1861	33, 259
Car ventilator, Railway	J. H. Moore	Chicago, Ill	Jan. 29, 1867	61, 555
Car ventilator, Railway	J. H. Moore	Chicago, Ill	Oct. 1, 1867	69, 357
Car ventilator, Railway	C. Newcomb	New York, N. Y	Oct. 9, 1860	30, 340
Car ventilator, Railway	E. Norton	Brooklyn, N. Y	Dec. 21, 1869	98, 695
Car ventilator, Railway	D. W. Noyes	Bennington, Vt	Mar. 11, 1873	136, 756
Car ventilator, Railway	R. L. Omensetter	Philadelphia, Pa	Mar. 12, 1872	124, 613
Car ventilator, Railway	R. Reniff and W. W. Buttolph	Bloomington, Ill	Feb. 19, 1867	62, 225
Car ventilator, Railway	W. M. Russell and D. E. Holmes.	Cincinnati, Ohio	Feb. 9, 1869	86, 780
Car ventilator, Railway	H. J. Ruttan	Coburg, Canada	Feb. 6, 1872	123, 513
Car ventilator, Railway	A. G. Safford	Boston, Mass	Oct. 19, 1869	95, 938
Car ventilator, Railway	T. H. B. Sanders	Pittsburgh, Pa	Nov. 14, 1865	50, 960
Car ventilator, Railway	W. Schairath	Bielefeld, Prussia	Nov. 10, 1868	84, 004
Car ventilator, Railway	J. D. Simmons	Quincy, Ill	Dec. 23, 1873	145, 760
Car ventilator, Railway	O. Slaglo	London, Ohio	Dec. 21, 1869	98, 201
Car ventilator, Railway	A. B. Spencer	Rochester, N. Y	Oct. 6, 1863	40, 199
Car ventilator, Railway	G. Spencer	Utica, N. Y	Nov. 8, 1853	10, 216
Car ventilator, Railway	W. C. Stickney	Steubenville, Ohio	Apr. 16, 1872	125, 855
Car ventilator, Railway	O. J. Styner and J. Egan	La Fayette, Ind	Nov. 2, 1869	96, 501
Car ventilator, Railway	A. B. Sweetland	Fitchburgh, Mass	July 4, 1871	116, 774
Car ventilator, Railway	A. B. Sweetland	Fitchburgh, Mass	Jan. 23, 1872	123, 059
Car ventilator, Railway	O. W. Swift	New Haven, Conn	Aug. 8, 1871	117, 941
Car ventilator, Railway	J. B. Talmadge	Winsted, Conn	Mar. 14, 1865	46, 831
Car ventilator, Railway	J. A. Thompson	Cayuga, N. Y	Oct. 29, 1861	33, 614
Car ventilator, Railway	C. P. Tillinghast	Providence, R. I	Jan. 3, 1871	110, 803
Car ventilator, Railway	J. G. Treadwell	Albany, N. Y	Oct. 11, 1859	25, 776
Car ventilator, Railway	A. P. Vining	Scranton, Pa	Oct. 17, 1865	50, 522
Car ventilator, Railway	W. Westlake	Milwaukee, Wis	July 29, 1862	36, 063
Car ventilator, Railway	J. S. Williamson and B. J. Bicknell.	Memphis, Tenn	Aug. 27, 1872	130, 965
Car ventilator, Railway	E. H. Winchell	New York, N. Y	Oct. 10, 1871	119, 809
Car ventilator, Railway	J. Wright	Richmond, Va	July 16, 1872	129, 201
Car ventilator, Railway	R. B. Wright	Norfolk, Va	Oct. 23, 1860	30, 515
Car-ventilators, Device for operating	G. W. Perry	Wilmington, Del	Apr. 30, 1872	126, 327
Car ventilators, Device to open railway	W. C. Stickney and J. McGee	Steubenville, Ohio	Dec. 22, 1868	85, 143
Car ventilating and warming apparatus, Railway	J. J. Watson, W. Hardiker, and T. Toye.	Buffalo, N. Y	Dec. 18, 1860	30, 996

Index of patents issued from the United States Patent Office from 1790 *to* 1873, *inclusive*—Continued.

Invention.	Inventor.	Residence.	Date.	No.
Car ventilating-attachment, Railway	J. Shaw	Bridgeport, Conn	Oct. 15, 1867	69, 847
Car, wagon, and other vehicles	T. Stone	Plainfield, Ind	June 30, 1868	79, 410
Car-washer	E. W. Leavens	Boston, Mass	Dec. 24, 1872	134, 295
Car, Weighing	J. H. Zinn	Kingston, Tenn	June 30, 1866	55, 946
Car-wheel	R. N. Allen and L. W. Kimball	Pittsford, Vt	May 11, 1869	89, 908
Car-wheel	A. Atwood	New York, N. Y	July 28, 1868	80, 380
Car-wheel	A. Atwood	Brooklyn, N. Y	July 1, 1873	140, 339
Car-wheel	J. E. Atwood	Pittsburgh, Pa	Nov. 11, 1873	144, 495
Car-wheel	J. Baker	Boston, Mass	Oct. 4, 1853	10, 062
Car-wheel	J. Baldwin	Lynn, Mass	Nov. 1, 1870	108, 825
Car-wheel	G. S. Bosworth	Troy, N. Y	Oct. 23, 1860	30, 458
Car-wheel	S. B. Chapman	New York, N. Y	Mar. 17, 1868	75, 521
Car-wheel	J. L. Constable	New York, N. Y	Feb. 20, 1866	52, 683
Car-wheel	J. M. Cook	Taunton, Mass	Dec. 5, 1848	5, 953
Car-wheel	A. F. Cooper	Cambridge, Mass	Oct. 14, 1873	143, 560
Car-wheel	W. Dickinson	Brooklyn, N. Y	Oct. 16, 1866	58, 786
Car-wheel	J. V. Dinsmore	Milford, Mass	May 14, 1867	64, 642
Car-wheel	G. Dock	Wiconisco, Pa	Mar. 3, 1868	74, 999
Car-wheel	G. W. Eddy	Waterford, N. Y	Dec. 26, 1845	4, 330
Car-wheel	G. W. Eddy	Waterford, N. Y	Jan. 8, 1850	6, 999
Car-wheel	G. Elmslie	Toronto, Canada	Nov. 4, 1873	144, 195
Car-wheel	W. B. Fahnestock	Lancaster, Pa	Mar. 30, 1858	19, 763
Car-wheel	D. P. Fales	West Poultney, Vt	Sept. 27, 1853	10, 057
Car-wheel	J. Farnsworth, jr	Madison, Ind	Nov. 1, 1853	10, 184
Car-wheel	H. B. Fernald	Dedham, Mass	June 29, 1869	91, 926
Car-wheel	A. C. Fletcher	New York, N. Y	Apr. 30, 1872	126, 280
Car-wheel	A. C. Fletcher	New York, N. Y	Dec. 23, 1873	145, 856
Car-wheel	F. A. Touts	Bloomington, Ill	May 13, 1873	138, 798
Car-wheel	D. Forrest	Eastport, Mo	July 23, 1867	67, 036
Car-wheel	T. Glasco	Wilmington, Del	Apr. 4, 1846	4, 447
Car-wheel	W. Goodman	Boston, Mass	Dec. 27, 1870	110, 503
Car-wheel	F. Harbach	Pittsfield, Mass	Nov. 6, 1847	5, 360
Car-wheel	F. Harbach	Pittsfield, Mass	Nov. 6, 1847	5, 361
Car-wheel	J. Harris	Marquette, Wis	Oct. 24, 1865	50, 579
Car-wheel	J. Harris	Marquette, Wis	Nov. 5, 1867	70, 560
Car-wheel	C. Hart	Bridgeport, Conn	Dec. 13, 1853	10, 309
Car-wheel	C. T. Harvey	Tarrytown, N. Y	July 7, 1868	79, 757
Car-wheel	R. B. Huguoin	Cleveland, Ohio	Mar. 2, 1869	87, 496
Car-wheel	L. B. Hunt	New York, N. Y	July 11, 1871	116, 961
Car-wheel	G. K. Kane	York, Pa	Mar. 6, 1847	5, 002
Car-wheel	J. W. Kern	Portland, Oreg	Feb. 18, 1873	136, 068
Car-wheel	J. S. Kingsland	Stryker, Ohio	Feb. 27, 1866	52, 859
Car-wheel	C. E. Kleinschmidt	Cleveland, Ohio	Nov. 19, 1867	71, 021
Car-wheel	W. A. Lewis	Chicago, Ill	Oct. 10, 1871	119, 867
Car-wheel	H. C. Lockwood	Baltimore, Md	Nov. 26, 1872	133, 461
Car-wheel	Z. H. Mann	Newport, Ky	Oct. 4, 1853	10, 073
Car-wheel	R. C. Mansell	Ashford, England	Oct. 9, 1866	58, 741
Car-wheel	W. V. Many	Albany, N. Y	Feb. 1, 1848	5, 424
Car-wheel	G. B. Massey	New York, N. Y	June 18, 1867	65, 925
Car-wheel	H. Merrill	Brooklyn, N. Y	Apr. 22, 1873	138, 036
Car-wheel	H. W. Moore	Jersey City, N. J	June 22, 1869	91, 762
Car-wheel	H. W. Moore	Jersey City, N. J	June 7, 1870	104, 053
Car-wheel	G. Natorp	New York, N. Y	Nov. 3, 1868	83, 722
Car-wheel	D. P. Nickerson	Cleveland, Ohio	May 28, 1867	65, 109
Car-wheel	W. H. Nobles	Saint Paul, Minn	Oct. 13, 1868	82, 978
Car-wheel	J. Pugh	Franklin, Tenn	June 15, 1858	20, 583
Car-wheel	P. Putnam	Laconia, N. H	June 28, 1864	43, 337
Car-wheel	J. Raddin	Lynn, Mass	May 14, 1867	64, 796
Car-wheel	J. Raddin	Lynn, Mass	Feb. 25, 1868	74, 959
Car-wheel	J. Raddin	Lynn, Mass	Apr. 14, 1868	76, 811
Car-wheel	R. Ramsay	Irwin's Station, Pa	Jan. 14, 1873	134, 929
Car-wheel	F. M. Ray	New York, N. Y	Dec. 17, 1846	4, 894
Car-wheel	E. S. Robinson	New York, N. Y	Sept. 25, 1866	58, 298
Car-wheel	J. C. Rupp and S. Ott	Newark, Del	Jan. 9, 1872	122, 661
Car-wheel	E. Sampson	Lansingburgh, N. Y	May 7, 1867	64, 579
Car-wheel	J. K. Sax and G. W. Kear	Pittston and Kingston, Pa	Sept. 9, 1873	142, 587
Car-wheel	S. J. Seely	New York, N. Y	Jan. 31, 1865	46, 145
Car-wheel	T. Sharp	Chicago, Ill	Sept. 29, 1863	40, 123
Car-wheel	G. W. and H. Sizer	Springfield, Mass	Apr. 17, 1847	5, 076
Car-wheel	A. Small	York, Pa	Dec. 10, 1846	4, 882
Car-wheel	J. Y. Smith	Pittsburgh, Pa	Feb. 9, 1869	86, 878
Car-wheel	S. P. Smith	Troy, N. Y	May 29, 1860	28, 512
Car-wheel	W. W. Snow	Jersey City, N. J	Feb. 19, 1861	31, 488
Car-wheel	G. W. and L. W. Snyder	Port Carbon and Lykens, Pa.	Mar. 4, 1873	136, 392
Car-wheel	W. R. Thomas	Catasauqua, Pa	June 16, 1868	79, 029
Car-wheel	W. R. Thomas	Catasauqua, Pa	Aug. 17, 1869	93, 769
Car-wheel	J. and N. Tiranoff and A. Kousakoff	St. Petersburg, Russia	Sept. 16, 1873	142, 968
Car-wheel	F. W. Townrow	United States Army	Jan. 2, 1872	122, 340
Car-wheel	S. A. Traugh	Cincinnati, Ohio	Nov. 19, 1867	71, 247
Car-wheel	N. K. Wade and J. Kaye	Pittsburgh, Pa	Sept. 4, 1860	29, 927
Car-wheel	A. B. Wakefield and B. A. Berryman	Saint Louis, Mo	Mar. 25, 1873	137, 266
Car-wheel	P. H. Watson	Ashtabula, Ohio	May 9, 1871	114, 628
Car-wheel	J. W. Weston	New York, N. Y	Apr. 5, 1870	101, 686
Car-wheel	W. Willoughby	Markwell, Miss	June 15, 1858	20, 610
Car-wheel	W. Wilmington	Toledo, Ohio	July 28, 1868	80, 323
Car-wheel	W. Wilmington	Toledo, Ohio	Sept. 22, 1868	82, 466
Car-wheel	W. Wilmington	Toledo, Ohio	Feb. 11, 1873	135, 870
Car-wheel	C. Wilson and J. H. McNall	Clinton, Pa	Feb. 5, 1867	61, 786
Car-wheel, Adjustable	G. G. Sobdell	Wilmington, Del	Feb. 20, 1872	123, 919
Car-wheel, Adjustable-gage	W. B. Snow	Brooklyn, N. Y	Aug. 15, 1871	118, 065
Car wheel and axle	D. Babson, 2d	Rockport, Mass	Mar. 6, 1866	52, 949
Car wheel and axle	F. Hudner	New York, N. Y	Aug. 31, 1869	94, 414
Car wheel and axle	J. S. Upton	Battle Creek, Mich	June 4, 1872	127, 661
Car wheel and axle	J. A. Woodbury	Boston, Mass	Mar. 9, 1869	87, 746
Car wheel and axle, Changeable-gage	P. Putnam	Laconia, N. H	Aug. 29, 1871	118, 642

Index of patents issued from the United States Patent Office from 1790 *to* 1873, *inclusive*—Continued.

Invention.	Inventor.	Residence.	Date.	No.
Car wheel and axle, Changeable-gage	C. D. Tisdale	Boston, Mass	Aug. 15, 1871	118, 170
Car wheel and axle, Railway	T. C. Hargrave	Boston, Mass	Aug. 18, 1868	81, 083
Car wheel and axle, Railway	W. Hudgin	Athens, Ga	Feb. 7, 1871	111, 543
Car wheel and axle, Railway	P. Putnam	Laconia, N. H	Dec. 7, 1869	97, 552
Car wheel and axle, Railway	C. D. Tisdale	Boston, Mass	May 25, 1869	90, 410
Car-wheel and car-axle, Combined	N. W. Northrup	Greene, N. Y	Oct. 28, 1862	36, 790
Car wheel and frog	W. H. Childe	Gainesville, Ala	Sept. 15, 1868	82, 086
Car-wheel, Anti-friction	G. C. Beecher	Livonia, N. Y	Jan. 6, 1863	37, 269
Car-wheel brake	W. McCammon	Albany, N. Y	Dec. 12, 1846	4, 886
Car-wheel, Cast-iron	A. Atwood	Troy, N. Y	May 15, 1847	5, 112
Car-wheel, Cast-iron	E. B. Baker	Charleston District, S. C	Jan. 9, 1849	6, 024
Car-wheel, Cast-iron	J. Boon	Lancaster, Pa	Apr. 16, 1850	7, 282
Car-wheel, Cast-iron	T. S. Bourshett	Little Falls, N. Y	Nov. 13, 1849	6, 863
Car-wheel, Cast-iron	A. G. Bristol and J. C. Jackson	Rochester, N. Y	Feb. 24, 1852	8, 751
Car-wheel, Cast-iron	A. T. Converse and W. S. Cooley.	Norwich, Conn	Jan. 9, 1849	6, 026
Car-wheel, Cast-iron	J. M. Cook	Taunton, Mass	Jan. 9, 1849	6, 022
Car-wheel, Cast-iron	L. Dean and A. Higham	Utica, N. Y	Jan. 9, 1849	6, 019
Car-wheel, Cast-iron	P. Dorsch	Schenectady, N. Y	June 15, 1852	9, 017
Car-wheel, Cast-iron	T. J. Eddy	Waterford, N. Y	July 29, 1851	8, 255
Car-wheel, Cast-iron	A. Fuller	Boston, Mass	Aug. 27, 1850	7, 599
Car-wheel, Cast-iron	P. G. Gardiner	New York, N. Y	Mar. 11, 1851	7, 967
Car-wheel, Cast-iron	G. W. Glass	Allegheny City, Pa	Apr. 25, 1854	10, 816
Car-wheel, Cast-iron	C. Hart	New York, N. Y	Dec. 25, 1849	6, 971
Car-wheel, Cast-iron	C. Hart and N. Washburn	Rochester, N. Y	Apr. 3, 1849	6, 269
Car-wheel, Cast-iron	A. Hebbard	Worcester, Mass	May 20, 1851	8, 106
Car-wheel, Cast-iron	A. Hebbard	Worcester, Mass	June 29, 1852	9, 071
Car-wheel, Cast-iron	J. Henry	Lynchburgh, Va	June 20, 1854	11, 124
Car-wheel, Cast-iron	L. Kinsley	Norfolk County, Mass	Mar. 12, 1850	7, 169
Car-wheel, Cast-iron	L. Kinsley	Norfolk County, Mass	Mar. 12, 1850	7, 170
Car-wheel, Cast-iron	G. G. Lobdell	Wilmington, Del	July 14, 1868	79, 842
Car-wheel, Cast-iron	G. G. Lobdell	Wilmington, Del	Jan. 12, 1869	85, 745
Car-wheel, Cast-iron	W. V. Many	Albany, N. Y	May 1, 1847	5, 095
Car-wheel, Cast-iron	G. R. McFarlane	Hollidaysburgh, Pa	Jan. 14, 1851	7, 903
Car-wheel, Cast-iron	H. W. Moore	Bridgeport, Conn	Mar. 2, 1852	8, 777
Car-wheel, Cast-iron	H. W. Moore	Jersey City, N. J	Sept. 20, 1858	21, 614
Car-wheel, Cast-iron	O. Moulton	Blackstone, Mass	Mar. 2, 1852	8, 772
Car-wheel, Cast-iron	A. L. Mowry	Cincinnati, Ohio	June 2, 1857	17, 442
Car-wheel, Cast-iron	G. Peacock	Selma, Ala	Nov. 26, 1867	71, 408
Car-wheel, Cast-iron	T. Perkins and W. McMahon	Baltimore, Md	Apr. 10, 1843	3, 037
Car-wheel, Cast-iron	D. Prew	Taunton, Mass	June 13, 1854	11, 056
Car-wheel, Cast-iron	D. R. Rall	Rochester, N. Y	June 1, 1852	8, 985
Car-wheel, Cast-iron	H. H. Scoville	Chicago, Ill	July 13, 1852	9, 121
Car-wheel, Cast-iron	B. Severson	Schenectady, N. Y	Oct. 21, 1851	8, 455
Car-wheel, Cast-iron	B. Severson	Philadelphia, Pa	July 4, 1854	11, 233
Car-wheel, Cast-iron	J. B. Tarr	Fairhaven, Mass	July 7, 1868	79, 611
Car-wheel, Cast-iron	S. Thurston	Scranton, Pa	May 25, 1852	8, 975
Car-wheel, Cast-iron	W. B. Treadwell	Albany, N. Y	Jan. 9, 1849	6, 021
Car-wheel, Cast-iron	S. Truscott	Columbia, Pa	Jan. 16, 1849	6, 030
Car-wheel, Cast-iron	I. Van Kuran	Rochester, N. Y	May 1, 1849	6, 415
Car-wheel, Cast-iron	I. Van Kuran	Boston, Mass	May 20, 1851	8, 108
Car-wheel, Cast-iron	N. Washburn	Worcester, Mass	Oct. 8, 1850	7, 710
Car-wheel, Cast-iron	A. Whitney	Philadelphia, Pa	May 22, 1847	5, 126
Car-wheel, Cast-iron	A. Whitney	Philadelphia, Pa	May 22, 1847	5, 127
Car-wheel, Cast-iron	A. Whitney	Philadelphia, Pa	Mar. 19, 1850	7, 202
Car-wheel, Cast-iron	W. Wilmington	Toledo, Ohio	Aug. 9, 1870	106, 243
Car-wheel, Cast-iron	H. H. Wiser	Rochester, N. Y	Dec. 4, 1849	6, 939
Car-wheel, Cast-iron	H. W. Woodruff	Watertown, N. Y	Jan. 6, 1852	8, 644
Car-wheel, Cast-iron plate	H. Felton, P. D. Cummings, and H. Hinckley.	Portland, Me	Jan. 23, 1849	6, 041
Car wheel, Cast-iron railway	W. W. Bergstresser	Harrisburgh, Pa	Jan. 11, 1840	1, 470
Car wheel, Cast-iron railway	J. M. Ross	Springfield, Mass	Mar. 17, 1857	16, 851
Car wheel, Cast-iron railway	B. Severson	Schenectady, N. Y	Sept. 17, 1850	7, 658
Car wheel, Cast-iron railway	J. M. Sigourney	Watertown, N. Y	Oct. 21, 1856	15, 935
Car-wheel, Cast-metal	G. G. Lobdell	Wilmington, Del	Apr. 15, 1862	34, 972
Car-wheel, Cast-steel	C. W. Stafford	Saybrook, Conn	Sept. 6, 1864	44, 120
Car-wheel, Cast-steel	J. B. Tarr	Chicago, Ill	July 30, 1867	67, 227
Car-wheel, Changeable-gage	J. Hamilton and G. F. Morse	Portland Me	Oct. 18, 1870	108, 475
Car-wheel, Elastic	J. J. Sherman	Albany, N. Y	Apr. 23, 1872	126, 096
Car-wheel, Elastic	J. M. Whiting	Providence, R. I	Nov. 14, 1871	121, 032
Car-wheel, Elastic	J. A. Woodbury	Boston, Mass	July 25, 1871	117, 498
Car wheel for curved roads, Railway	A. Look	Waterford, N. Y	Dec. 31, 1833	....
Car-wheel for lubricating purposes	J. W. Latcher	Albany, N. Y	May 22, 1866	54, 925
Car-wheel gears, Self-adjusting	G. Sewell	Brooklyn, N. Y	May 16, 1871	114, 979
Car wheel, Locomotive	J. B. Tarr	Fairhaven, Mass	Jan. 18, 1870	98, 895
Car-wheel lubricator	W. A. Bullard	Kalamazoo, Mich	Dec. 9, 1873	145, 395
Car-wheel lubricator	W. W. Crane	Auburn, N. Y	Nov. 26, 1872	133, 418
Car-wheel lubricator	W. W. Martin	Allegheny City, Pa	Jan. 21, 1868	73, 621
Car-wheel lubricator	J. H. Murray	Hollidaysburgh, Pa	Sept. 30, 1873	143, 370
Car-wheel lubricator	J. M. Porter	Frostburgh, Md	May 2, 1871	114, 473
Car-wheel lubricator	C. Smith	Irwin Station, Pa	Oct. 24, 1871	120, 337
Car-wheel mold	J. K. Sax	Pittston, Pa	June 28, 1870	104, 777
Car-wheel mold	W. E. Worth	San Francisco, Cal	Jan. 3, 1871	110, 717
Car-wheel-molding flask	J. O'Brian	Louisville, Ky	Sept. 3, 1872	131, 115
Car wheel, Railway	R. N. Allen	Pittsford, Vt	July 16, 1872	128, 939
Car wheel, Railway	J. Baker	Lancaster, Pa	Mar. 20, 1835	......
Car wheel, Railway	T. C. Ball	Keene, N. H	Nov. 9, 1858	22, 049
Car wheel, Railway	A. G. Barrett	Barrett, Kans	Nov. 21, 1871	121, 075
Car wheel, Railway	C. K. Bradford	Lynnfield, Mass	May 10, 1870	102, 908
Car wheel, Railway	G. B. Bryant	Pottsville, Pa	Oct. 31, 1871	120, 489
Car wheel, Railway	H. C. Bulkley	Springfield, Mass	Mar. 30, 1858	19, 810
Car wheel, Railway	D. Cockley	Lancaster, Pa	Oct. 21, 1839	1, 377
Car wheel, Railway	E. Crane	Dorchester, Mass	Nov. 8, 1859	26, 022
Car wheel, Railway	T. C. Craven	Albany, N. Y	July 23, 1872	129, 655
Car wheel, Railway	T. Curtis	New Hudson, Mich	Sept. 6, 1864	44, 078
Car wheel, Railway	C. Delafield and F. G. Johnson	Castleton and Northfield, N. Y.	Aug. 31, 1869	94, 293
Car wheel, Railway	T. J. Eddy	Waterford, N. Y	Aug. 2, 1853	9, 897

Index of patents issued from the United States Patent Office from 1790 *to* 1873, *inclusive*—Continued.

Invention.	Inventor.	Residence.	Date.	No.
Car wheel, Railway	J. N. Farrar	Pepperell, Mass	Feb. 8, 1870	99, 547
Car wheel, Railway	J. N. Farrar	Pepperell, Mass	Nov. 15, 1870	109, 310
Car wheel, Railway	A. C. Fletcher	New York, N. Y	Mar. 23, 1869	88, 154
Car wheel, Railway	A. C. Fletcher	New York, N. Y	May 4, 1869	89, 752
Car wheel, Railway	W. J. Fryer, jr., and W. Freeborn.	New York, N. Y	Mar. 6, 1866	52, 986
Car wheel, Railway	A. Fuller	Providence, R. I	Oct. 14, 1840	1, 824
Car wheel, Railway	P. G. Gardiner	New York, N. Y	May 1, 1847	5, 098
Car wheel, Railway	J. D. Green	Troy, N. Y	Mar. 29, 1870	101, 259
Car wheel, Railway	J. B. Handyside	Glasgow, Great Britain	Oct. 31, 1871	120, 432
Car wheel, Railway	N. Hodge	Adams, Mass	Nov. 18, 1851	8, 526
Car wheel, Railway	N. Hodge	North Adams, Mass	June 1, 1852	8, 979
Car wheel, Railway	W. W. Hubbell and R. H. Hubbell.	Philadelphia and Delaware County, Pa.	Mar. 30, 1858	19, 776
Car wheel, Railway	L. B. Hunt	Leverett, Mass	Nov. 30, 1869	97, 407
Car wheel, Railway	L. B. Hunt	New York, N. Y	Nov. 15, 1870	109, 320
Car wheel, Railway	L. B. Hunt	New York, N. Y	Jan. 24, 1871	111, 211
Car wheel, Railway	A. C. Ketchum	New York, N. Y	July 15, 1856	15, 339
Car wheel, Railway	A. Komp	New York, N. Y	Jan. 25, 1870	99, 210
Car wheel, Railway	A. B. Latta	Cincinnati, Ohio	Dec. 1, 1857	18, 752
Car wheel, Railway	E. A. Lester	Boston, Mass	Aug. 9, 1859	25, 020
Car wheel, Railway	G. G. Lobdell	Wilmington, Del	Feb. 19, 1861	31, 467
Car wheel, Railway	H. C. Lockwood	Baltimore, Md	Nov. 14, 1871	120, 985
Car wheel, Railway	W. H. Mason	Boston, Mass	Feb. 23, 1869	87, 180
Car wheel, Railway	J. L. Mott	New York, N. Y	Mar. 21, 1854	10, 672
Car wheel, Railway	J. T. Owen	Philadelphia, Pa	Nov. 30, 1869	97, 433
Car wheel, Railway	J. T. Owen	Philadelphia, Pa	Dec. 21, 1869	98, 099
Car wheel, Railway	W. H. Paige	Springfield, Mass	July 22, 1873	141, 011
Car wheel, Railway	S. E. Parish	Nashville, Tenn	Feb. 16, 1858	19, 380
Car wheel, Railway	M. Phelan	Beaver County, Pa	Dec. 1, 1857	18, 767
Car wheel, Railway	D. Prew	Providence, R. I	Nov. 26, 1872	133, 336
Car wheel, Railway	J. Raddin	Lynn, Mass	Jan. 5, 1869	85, 693
Car wheel, Railway	F. M. Ray, sr	New York, N. Y	Apr. 23, 1872	126, 085
Car wheel, Railway	J. Rogers	Cincinnati, Ohio	July 27, 1869	93, 123
Car wheel, Railway	S. Rogers	Pittsburgh, Pa	Feb. 23, 1858	19, 445
Car wheel, Railway	J. K. Sax and G. W. Kear	Kingston, Pa	Apr. 6, 1869	88, 743
Car wheel, Railway	W. Smith	Pittsburgh, Pa	Jan. 10, 1860	26, 821
Car wheel, Railway	W. W. Spafford	Peterborough, N. H	Feb. 14, 1860	27, 163
Car wheel, Railway	J. H. Steiner	Philadelphia, Pa	June 19, 1860	28, 816
Car wheel, Railway	E. Stiles	New York, N. Y	Apr. 14, 1868	76, 844
Car wheel, Railway	A. W. Straub	Philadelphia, Pa	Jan. 16, 1866	52, 089
Car wheel, Railway	T. R. Timby	Saratoga, N. Y	Mar. 2, 1869	87, 445
Car wheel, Railway	F. H. Trevithick, jr	New York, N. Y	Aug. 2, 1870	106, 001
Car wheel, Railway	O. O. Van Orman	Harrisville, Ohio	Sept. 10, 1861	33, 273
Car wheel, Railway	Z. Washburn	Hopedale, Mass	Nov. 30, 1869	97, 329
Car wheel, Railway	R. A. Wilder	Schuylkill Haven, Pa	Mar. 28, 1854	10, 714
Car wheel, Railway	J. A. Woodbury	Boston, Mass	Apr. 9, 1872	125, 649
Car wheel, Railway	G. W. N. Yost	Corry, Pa	Aug. 3, 1869	93, 386
Car-wheel, Self-oiling	W. Owen	Hubbard, Ohio	June 29, 1869	91, 863
Car-wheel, Steel	J. B. Tarr	Fairhaven, Mass	June 28, 1870	104, 792
Car wheel to prevent friction, Railway	S. Krauser	Reading, Pa	Nov. 2, 1831	....
Car-wheel with independent flange and tread	W. S. McLean	Pittsburgh, Pa	Aug. 1, 1854	11, 438
Car-wheel, Wrought-iron	H. Aiken	Franklin, N. H	Oct. 1, 1850	7, 676
Car wheel, Wrought-iron-plate railway	G. W. Alden	New York, N. Y	May 12, 1857	17, 250
Car wheels and axles by incasing, Protecting	A. L. Finch	New Britain, Conn	Apr. 20, 1852	8, 886
Car-wheels, Annealing and cooling cast-iron	A. Whitney	Philadelphia, Pa	Apr. 25, 1848	5, 531
Car-wheels, Annealing-pit for annealing	W. J. Cochran	Baltimore, Md	Nov. 3, 1868	83, 605
Car-wheels, Apparatus for casting	S. H. Whitaker	Covington, Ky	Nov. 5, 1867	70, 486
Car-wheels, Apparatus for regulating the contraction of.	S. Truscott	Columbia, Pa	July 16, 1850	7, 515
Car-wheels, Casting	L. H. Allen	Tamaqua, Pa	June 10, 1856	15, 109
Car-wheels, Casting	J. W. Ells	Pittsburgh, Pa	July 25, 1871	117, 397
Car-wheels, Casting	D. Finley	Champlain, N. Y	May 4, 1858	20, 151
Car-wheels, Casting	J. K. and N. B. Morange	Pittsburgh, Pa	May 16, 1871	114, 958
Car-wheels, Casting	A. W. Moses and J. H. Springer	Philadelphia, Pa	Nov. 8, 1859	26, 045
Car-wheels, Casting	A. A. Needham	Rockford, Ill	Dec. 22, 1857	18, 924
Car-wheels, Casting	C. Needham	Worcester, Mass	Jan. 3, 1871	110, 779
Car-wheels, Casting	R. Poole	Baltimore, Md	Apr. 20, 1858	20, 022
Car-wheels, Casting	J. K. Sax	Pittston, Pa	Jan. 9, 1872	122, 538
Car-wheels, Casting	J. Segmüller	Pittsburgh, Pa	Mar. 5, 1872	124, 223
Car-wheels, Casting	N. Washburn	Worcester, Mass	Apr. 23, 1872	125, 917
Car wheels, Casting railway	N. Aylsworth	Rochester, N. Y	Mar. 24, 1857	16, 868
Car-wheels, Center-chill for	J. W. Latcher	Albany, N. Y	Aug. 7, 1866	56, 958
Car-wheels, Chill for casting	T. Sharp	Chicago, Ill	Oct. 6, 1863	40, 190
Car-wheels, Chill for casting	W. Wilmington	Toledo, Ohio	Dec. 15, 1868	85, 046
Car-wheels, Clamp to be used in the manufacture of wrought-iron.	H. Aiken	Franklin, N. H	Apr. 2, 1850	7, 229
Car-wheels, Constructing	W. M. Arnold	New York, N. Y	June 4, 1872	127, 544
Car-wheels, Constructing	J. K. and N. B. Morange	Pittsburgh, Pa	Sept. 6, 1870	107, 083
Car wheels, Constructing railway	W. R. Thomson	Cleveland, Ohio	June 10, 1856	15, 092
Car wheels, Constructing railway	A. Tiers	Kensington, Pa	Dec. 2, 1835	....
Car-wheels, Cooling	R. Poole	Baltimore, Md	July 13, 1858	20, 924
Car-wheels, Cooling cast-iron	J. M. Sigourney	Watertown, N. Y	Sept. 18, 1855	13, 585
Car-wheels, Cope for casting	A. Alling	Chicago, Ill	Dec. 27, 1870	110, 534
Car-wheels, Core-box for	T. Maher	Cleveland, Ohio.	Oct. 19, 1869	95, 919
Car-wheels, Device for annealing	H. W. Moore	Bridgeport, Conn	Dec. 5, 1865	51, 338
Car-wheels, Drilling and boring	D. Walker	Gunpowder, Md	Dec. 28, 1832	....
Car-wheels, Fastening the disk and rim of	A. Breaer	Saugatuck, Conn	May 30, 1854	10, 983
Car-wheels, Flask for casting	W. R. Thomas	Catasauqua, Pa	Oct. 29, 1867	70, 290
Car-wheels, Machine for forging	W. M. Lee	New York, N. Y	Jan. 2, 1855	12, 135
Car-wheels, Machine for making cast-steel	J. B. Terr	Chicago, Ill	July 23, 1867	67, 000
Car-wheels, Machine for making wrought-iron	N. Starks	Albany, N. Y	Oct. 29, 1850	7, 746
Car-wheels, Machine for making wrought-iron	J. C. Vaughn	Greenbush, N. Y	June 24, 1851	8, 173
Car-wheels, Making	S. Vanstone	Providence, R. I	June 4, 1867	65, 454
Car-wheels, Making locomotive-engine and railway	H. R. Dunham	New York, N. Y	Feb. 15, 1838	611
Car-wheels, Making wrought-iron	G. B. Hartson	New York, N. Y	July 11, 1854	11, 243
Car-wheels, Manner of constructing railway	W. Creed	Boston, Mass	Feb. 24, 1843	2, 979
Car-wheels, Manufacture of	E. Finch	Liverpool, England	Aug. 21, 1849	6, 657

Index of patents issued from the United States Patent Office from 1790 *to* 1873, *inclusive*—Continued.

Invention.	Inventor.	Residence.	Date.	No.
Car-wheels, Manufacture of	J. Scoville	Buffalo, N. Y	June 26, 1866	55, 916
Car wheels, Manufacture of railway	J. D. Murphy	Pottsville, Pa	May 16, 1865	47, 780
Car-wheels, Manufacturing cast-iron	G. S. Bosworth	Troy, N. Y	Oct. 19, 1858	21, 863
Car-wheels, Metal for and mode of manufacturing	W. G. Hamilton	New York, N. Y	Dec. 22, 1868	85, 089
Car-wheels, Method of attaching and lubricating	W. R. Reece	Tremont, Pa	Feb. 13, 1866	52, 603
Car-wheels, Method of constructing	C. Kingsland	McKeesport, Pa	Dec. 17, 1867	72, 405
Car wheels, Method of making cast-iron railway	E. A. Lester	Boston, Mass	Aug. 10, 1844	3, 700
Car-wheels, Method of regulating the contraction of.	J. Murphy	Kensington, Pa	Aug. 7, 1849	6, 633
Car-wheels, Mode of cutting the seats, slots, or grooves for the reception of keys in the hubs and axles of.	T. J. Butler	Johnstown, Pa	Dec. 31, 1839	1, 458
Car-wheels, Mode of lubricating	W. Youmans	Lansingburgh, N. Y	June 13, 1865	48, 230
Car-wheels, Mode of making cast-iron	J. Bonny, C. Bush, and G. C. Lobdell.	Wilmington, Del	Mar. 17, 1838	637
Car-wheels, Mode of making cast-iron	H. Mooers	Beaver Meadows, Pa	Mar. 10, 1838	634
Car-wheels, Mode of making cast-iron	S. Truscott, G. Wolf, and J. Dougherty.	Columbia, Pa	Mar. 17, 1838	640
Car wheels, Mode of making cast-iron railway	W. W. Pennell	Lancaster, Pa	Feb. 8, 1839	1, 076
Car-wheels, Mold for casting	J. B. Tarr	Chicago, Ill	Nov. 5, 1867	70, 482
Car-wheels, Mold for casting	J. B. Tarr	Fairhaven, Mass	Sept. 16, 1873	142, 821
Car-wheels, Mold for casting	N. Washburn	Worcester, Mass	June 20, 1871	116, 246
Car-wheels, Mounting and securing	W. A. Lewis	Chicago, Ill	Mar. 19, 1872	124, 835
Car-wheels, Tempering the tread of	J. A. Woodbury	Boston, Mass	Apr. 9, 1872	125, 651
Car-wheels to axles, Applying	H. Gartside	Baltimore, Md	Aug. 6, 1872	130, 124
Car-wheels to axles, Mechanism for adjusting and securing.	G. G. Lobdell	Wilmington, Del	May 2, 1871	114, 452
Car-wheels to axles, Mode of attaching	G. M. Palmer	Clinton, Mass	Jan. 7, 1862	34, 070
Car-wheels to axles, Mode of attaching	G. Sewell	Brooklyn, N. Y	Jan. 30, 1866	52, 328
Car-wheels to axles, Mode of attaching	R. S. Tarrey	Bangor, Me	July 5, 1864	43, 440
Car-wheels to axles, Securing	A. M. Lood and G. G. Lobdell	Wilmington, Del	May 24, 1870	103, 484
Car-wheels to different gages, Means for adjusting	W. B. Snow	New York, N. Y	Aug. 23, 1870	106, 737
Car-wheels, Treating cast iron for the manufacture of.	H. M. Woodward	Saint Louis, Mo	Nov. 10, 1868	84, 041
Car-wheels upon axles, Adjusting	J. Kaiser	Wilmington, Del	Feb. 20, 1872	123, 913
Car-wheels upon axles, Mode of adjusting	H. Helm	Allegheny City, Pa	Nov. 7, 1865	50, 823
Car-wheels upon axles, Securing	J. L. Mott	New York, N. Y	June 6, 1854	11, 041
Car, Wheelbarrow dumping	H. J. Peters	Quebec, Canada	Apr. 15, 1873	137, 862
Car-window	J. Beetle	New Bedford, Mass	May 27, 1856	14, 945
Car-window	G. S. Knapp	Winona, Minn	Jan. 18, 1870	98, 981
Car-window	W. McCaull	Philadelphia, Pa	Feb. 20, 1872	123, 833
Car-window	G. W. Perry	Wilmington, Del	Sept. 21, 1869	95, 134
Car-window deflector	W. Conard	Burlington, N. J	Sept. 6, 1870	107, 163
Car window fixture, Railway	J. D. Hall	Philadelphia, Pa	Oct. 18, 1864	44, 770
Car-window protector	H. G. Carr	Lewistown, Pa	June 4, 1867	65, 342
Car window, Railway	J. K. Andrews	Antrim, Ohio	Oct. 9, 1866	58, 710
Car window, Railway	T. W. Emery	Buffalo, N. Y	Mar. 15, 1864	41, 911
Car window, Railway	G. Mann, jr	Ottawa, Ill	Jan. 5, 1864	41, 079
Car window, Railway	E. A. Schoeller	Connellsville, Pa	Mar. 14, 1871	112, 639
Car window, Railway	G. Spencer	Utica, N. Y	Aug. 15, 1854	11, 535
Car-window screen, Railway	J. E. Earle	New Haven, Conn	Dec. 30, 1873	146, 053
Car-window screen, Railway	F. U. Stokes	Cincinnati, Ohio	Jan. 22, 1867	61, 367
Car-window shield	H. S. Hale	Philadelphia, Pa	Dec. 30, 1873	146, 066
Car-window stop, Adjustable	C. Page	Meriden, Conn	July 22, 1873	141, 165
Car-window, Ventilating	C. B. Knevals	New York, N. Y	Dec. 23, 1873	145, 805
Car-window, Ventilating	G. Mann, jr	Ottawa, Ill	Nov. 7, 1865	50, 831
Car-window ventilator and cinder and dust guard	O. C. Rife	North Manchester, Ind	July 1, 1873	140, 541
Car-windows, Dust-guard for	O. C. Rife	North Manchester, Ind	Jan. 28, 1873	135, 365
Car windows, Opening and shutting device for railway.	J. F. Lash	Toronto, Canada	Nov. 15, 1870	109, 326
Car-windows, Portable deflector for	J. C. Stoddard	Worcester, Mass	May 1, 1866	54, 436
Car-windows, Spring-attachment to	G. Cornwall	Brooklyn, N. Y	Jan. 21, 1873	135, 086
Car, Wrecking	G. Herrick	Nashville, Tenn	Aug. 21, 1866	57, 323
Cars, Adjustable canopy for railway	I. E. Jones	Cincinnati, Ohio	May 17, 1859	24, 030
Cars, Adjustable draw-head for railway	D. P. Corey and J. Crane, jr	Crawford, N. J	May 30, 1871	115, 439
Cars, Adjusting coupling-links of railway	T. Andrews	North Easton, Mass	Feb. 5, 1861	31, 289
Cars, Air-spring for railway	G. M. Alsop	Philadelphia, Pa	May 31, 1859	24, 184
Cars and applying brakes, Disconnecting railway	J. Buck	Fitchburgh, Mass	Sept. 30, 1856	15, 833
Cars and canal-boats up and down inclined planes, Conveying railway.	G. Brown	New York, N. Y	Oct. 6, 1837	299
Cars and carriages by horse-power, Propelling	H. G. Vanderwerken	Greenbush, N. Y	Dec. 1, 1857	18, 781
Cars and carriages, Spring for railway	P. G. Gardiner	New York, N. Y	Apr. 26, 1859	23, 766
Cars and locomotives, Mode of preventing jarring and jolting of railway.	R. A. Riley	Greenfield, Ind	Feb. 25, 1862	34, 525
Cars and locomotives, Self-separating link for connecting railway.	C. H. Hunt and W. Browne	Fredericksburgh, Va	Dec. 26, 1837	538
Cars and locomotives when without steam, Windlass for moving.	C. Page	West Meriden, Conn	Oct. 5, 1858	21, 696
Cars and other vehicles, Apparatus for heating	C. C. Converse	Brooklyn, N. Y	Feb. 19, 1867	62, 254
Cars, Apparatus for bending and punching frames of draw-heads for railway.	P. L. Weimer	Lebanon, Pa	Oct. 31, 1865	50, 755
Cars, Apparatus for city-railway	S. Green	Lambertville, N. J	July 12, 1859	24, 776
Cars, Apparatus for feeding and watering stock in	W. Stark, J. G. Fisher, and S. Fitch.	White Pigeon, Mich., and Toledo, Ohio.	Nov. 21, 1871	121, 214
Cars, Apparatus for forming bumper-carriers for railway.	W. C. Allison	Philadelphia, Pa	June 25, 1867	65, 987
Cars, Apparatus for receiving and delivering mail on railway.	A. Jordan	Washington, D. C	Oct. 10, 1865	50, 435
Cars, Apparatus for supplying pneumatic springs to railway.	S. G. Randall	New York, N. Y	Nov. 8, 1864	44, 972
Cars, Applying fly-wheels to hand	C. T. Kipp and J. Lawrenson	New York, N. Y	July 14, 1857	17, 793
Cars, Applying steam-power to street	L. W. Langdon	Northampton, Mass	Nov. 30, 1869	97, 300
Cars, Arranging couches in railway	E. C. Knight	Philadelphia, Pa	June 28, 1859	24, 563
Cars, Attaching railway	L. Reckering and J. Lightner	Boston, Mass	June 28, 1836	......
Cars, Automatic stop for mining	J. Tamblin	Virginia City, Nev	Dec. 8, 1868	84, 778
Cars, Basket-back for railway	W. G. Creamer	Brooklyn, N. Y	July 6, 1869	92, 174
Cars, Bearing for railway	D. R. Pratt	Worcester, Mass	Oct. 30, 1860	30, 547
Cars, Boat for transporting railway	J. Wheelock	Lancaster, N. Y	Jan. 25, 1859	22, 759

Index of patents issued from the United States Patent Office from 1790 *to* 1873, *inclusive*—Continued.

Invention.	Inventor.	Residence.	Date.	No.
Cars, boats, &c., by condensed air, Propelling	A. McGrew	Cincinnati, Ohio	Oct. 27, 1835	....
Cars, Body-bolster for railway	A. Ward	Altoona, Pa	June 21, 1859	24, 512
Cars, Bolster for railway	J. Christy	Philadelphia, Pa	Feb. 5, 1867	61, 713
Cars, Bow-spring for railway	T. F. Allyn	Nyack, N. Y	Sept. 8, 1868	81, 969
Cars, Box for railway	R. Levington	Monroe, Mich	Apr. 17, 1849	6, 348
Cars, Brake-block for railway	L. Paige	Cavendish, Vt	Jan. 16, 1855	12, 245
Cars, Brake-block for railway	W. Wilmore	Scranton, Pa	Feb. 2, 1869	86, 613
Cars, Brake for checking and starting	R. Grant	New York, N. Y	Oct. 10, 1854	11, 785
Cars, Brake for stopping and starting	G. E. Burt and E. A. Hildreth	Harvard, Mass	Sept. 10, 1867	68, 601
Cars, Brake-head for railway	N. P. Stevens	Keene, N. H	Apr. 19, 1859	23, 722
Cars, Breakage-signal for railway	S. Jackson	Philadelphia, Pa	Jan. 2, 1872	122, 386
Cars, Brick-drier for	C. Chambers, jr	Philadelphia, Pa	Mar. 30, 1869	88, 274
Cars, Buffer for railway	R. D. Chatterton	Bath, England	Feb. 9, 1864	41, 483
Cars, Buffer-head and draw-bar for	J. T. Wilson	Pittsburgh, Pa	Apr. 4, 1871	113, 608
Cars, Buffer-spring for railway	A. H. Rowand	Allegheny City, Pa	Sept. 29, 1863	40, 122
Cars, Bumper arrangement for uncoupling railway	W. O. George	Richmond, Va	Oct. 7, 1856	15, 839
Cars by compressed air, Apparatus for propelling street.	W. H. H. Bowers	Franklin, Ky	Sept. 2, 1873	142, 433
Cars by "safety-box," Strengthening axles of railway.	P. and W. C. Allison	Philadelphia, Pa	Nov. 3, 1841	2, 322
Cars by stationary power, Propelling	A. R. Cribfield	Lincoln, Ill	Mar. 12, 1872	124, 557
Cars, Cattle feeding and watering device for railway	W. Reid	Granton, North Britain	Mar. 17, 1868	75, 701
Cars, Center-plate for railway	G. W. Bennett	White Haven, Pa	Mar. 3, 1868	75, 115
Cars, Change-gate for railway	J. B. Slawson	New York, N. Y	Jan. 4, 1868	73, 396
Cars, Coiled spring for railway	C. French	Seymour, Conn	Oct. 7, 1856	15, 869
Cars, Collision-apparatus for railway	J. Knlirski	Charleston, S. C	Sept. 9, 1856	15, 699
Cars, Combined brake and propelling mechanism for	J. W. Hill	Jefferson, Iowa	July 29, 1873	141, 272
Cars, Connecting-link for railway	R. Hemming	Boston, Mass	Oct. 11, 1845	4, 233
Cars, Connection for railway	J. R. Crabill	La Crosse, Ill	Apr. 4, 1871	113, 633
Cars, Connection of brakes with	J. Kimball and H. Rice	Concord, N. H	Jan. 1, 1850	6, 988
Cars, Constructing	S. J. Seely	Brooklyn, N. Y	May 12, 1863	38, 507
Cars, Constructing and applying bumpers and draft-springs on railway.	F. M. Ray	Catskill, N. Y	July 29, 1841	2, 201
Cars, Constructing and connecting railway	R. Grant	Philadelphia, Pa	July 22, 1837	294
Cars, Constructing railway	L. I. Germain	Catskill, N. Y	May 7, 1839	1, 145
Cars, Construction of	J. E. Leeper	Godfrey, Ill	June 20, 1871	116, 069
Cars, Construction of iron railway	S. Merrick	New Brighton, Pa	Oct. 2, 1866	58, 448
Cars, Construction of peat	J. Bundy	West Liberty, Iowa	May 19, 1868	78, 051
Cars, Construction of railway	C. M. Atkins	Pottsville, Pa	Oct. 28, 1862	36, 762
Cars, Construction of railway	W. A. Davis	Baltimore, Md	Oct. 5, 1838	963
Cars, Construction of railway	D. H. Dotterer	Philadelphia, Pa	Feb. 14, 1865	46, 341
Cars, Construction of railway	K. Thompson and S. D. Beerbrower.	Oxford, Pa	Dec. 2, 1873	145, 255
Cars, Construction of railway	W. G. Von Straden	Strathroy, Canada	Sept. 24, 1872	131, 725
Cars, Contrivance for protecting passengers in railway.	S. F. Holbrook	Boston, Mass	Feb. 21, 1854	10, 547
Cars, Coupling and uncoupling	W. A. Herrick	Leeds, Me	June 19, 1860	28, 751
Cars, Coupling-head for railway	R. M. Hughes	Oxford, Pa	Feb. 24, 1863	37, 787
Cars, Deck-sash or ventilator-opener for railway	J. E. Cross	Adrian, Mich	July 22, 1873	141, 037
Cars, Deflector for railway	J. A. Rockwood	Normal, Ill	Jan. 9, 1872	122, 655
Cars, Detective register for doors of railway	W. C. Smith	Georgetown, D. C	Apr. 26, 1859	23, 791
Cars, Device for applying steam-power to street-railway.	W. W. Crane	Auburn, N. Y	May 13, 1873	138, 793
Cars, Device for changing the gage of railway	D. Todd	Detroit, Mich	Jan. 30, 1872	123, 308
Cars, Device for discharging grain from railway	S. W. Hawes	Jersey City, N. J	Oct. 17, 1871	120, 065
Cars, Device for partially excluding dust from railway.	V. P. Corbett	New York, N. Y	Nov. 13, 1855	13, 779
Cars, Device for propelling street	S. Jones and B. Terfloth	New Orleans, La	July 5, 1870	105, 088
Cars, Device for turning street	B. I. Day	Vanderburgh County, Ind	Jan. 12, 1869	85, 732
Cars, Door-catch for railway	C. Graham	Kingston, Pa	Apr. 16, 1872	125, 808
Cars, Double and single tree attachment for street	J. F. Lowe	Louisville, Ky	Nov. 8, 1870	109, 029
Cars, Draft-bar for horse	J. Trent	Millerton, N. Y	Feb. 8, 1870	99, 730
Cars, Draft-bar for railway	H. J. Lombaert	Philadelphia, Pa	Mar. 12, 1861	31, 670
Cars, Draft-pole for horse	S. A. Otis	Boston, Mass	Dec. 5, 1871	121, 656
Cars, Draw-bar iron for buffers of railway	J. T. Wilson	Pittsburgh, Pa	June 11, 1872	127, 819
Cars, Draw-head and bumper for railway	D. Shaaber	Reading, Pa	June 13, 1871	115, 986
Cars, Draw-head for railway	W. S. Shotwell	Paterson, N. J	July 30, 1867	67, 368
Cars, Draw-spring for railway	R. A. Wilder	Cressona, Pa	May 19, 1863	38, 618
Cars, Driving-gear for hand	J. D. Hinckley	Adrian, Mich	Apr. 15, 1873	137, 922
Cars, Dumping-platform for railway	J. W. Harrison	Niles, Mich	Oct. 21, 1873	143, 758
Cars, Dust-arrester for railway	W. M. K. Thornton	Rolla, Mo	Apr. 12, 1870	101, 787
Cars, Dust-deflector for railway	J. P. O. Lownsdale	Portland, Oreg	June 29, 1869	91, 947
Cars, Dust-deflector for windows of railway	J. M. Cook	Taunton, Mass	Oct. 16, 1855	13, 676
Cars, Dust-shield for railway	W. M. K. Thornton	Saint Louis, Mo	Oct. 3, 1871	119, 545
Cars, Easing shocks in stopping railway	C. Davenport	Cambridge, Mass	Sept. 9, 1835	....
Cars, Electro-motor for	S. Jones	New Orleans, La	Jan. 31, 1871	111, 348
Cars, Elevator for loading	R. D. Chatterton	Bath, England	Feb. 9, 1864	41, 482
Cars, Elliptic cushion for railway	S. R. Jones	York, Pa	Apr. 27, 1858	20, 070
Cars, Equalizing beam and lever in railway	J. H. Dennis	Louisville, Ky	Nov. 26, 1861	33, 776
Cars, Excluding dust from railway	J. M. Cook	Taunton, Mass	Apr. 19, 1853	9, 671
Cars, Excluding dust from railway	E. Hamilton	Bridgeport, Conn	May 27, 1851	8, 121
Cars, Excluding dust from railway	O. Newton and J. A. Crever	Pittsburgh, Pa	Mar. 14, 1854	10, 626
Cars, Excluding dust from railway	E. C. Salisbury	New York, N. Y	July 31, 1855	13, 364
Cars, Excluding dust from railway	J. Wood	Jersey City, N. J	Feb. 26, 1856	14, 331
Cars, Extension holding-strap for street	T. Cogswell	Boston, Mass	Mar. 13, 1866	53, 116
Cars, Folding-seat for street-railway	K. Egan	New York, N. Y	Apr. 29, 1873	138, 321
Cars for preserving and transporting meat, fish, and vegetables, Construction of railway.	C. F. Pike	Providence, R. I	Dec. 31, 1867	72, 895
Cars, Framing railway	T. M. Mullen	Philadelphia, Pa	Apr. 3, 1860	27, 734
Cars from being thrown from the track, Machine for preventing engines and railway.	A. L. Johnson	Baltimore, Md	Nov. 1, 1859	25, 970
Cars from one track to another, Method of transferring.	J. Denhard	Reading, Pa	June 25, 1867	66, 132
Cars from one track to another, Mode of switching off railway.	M. Semple	Philadelphia, Pa	June 7, 1859	24, 336
Cars from one track to another, Transferring	W. Wharton, jr	Philadelphia, Pa	Sept. 18, 1860	30, 100
Cars from one track to another, Transferring railway.	J. Ashenfelder	Philadelphia, Pa	Oct. 9, 1860	30, 284

Index of patents issued from the United States Patent Office from 1790 to 1873, inclusive—Continued.

Invention.	Inventor.	Residence.	Date.	No.
Cars from running off the track, Preventing	L. Ball	Auburn, N. Y	June 22, 1858	20, 614
Cars from the track, Device for removing	D. R. Erdmann	Philadelphia, Pa	Sept. 5, 1865	49, 737
Cars, Furnace for railway	H. M. Hutchinson	Baltimore, Md	Mar. 13, 1860	27, 449
Cars, Grain-door for	L. F. Frazee	Jersey City, N. J	May 9, 1871	114, 661
Cars, Grain-door for	H. Stahlnecker	Allentown, Pa	Jan. 23, 1872	123, 055
Cars, Grain-door for	H. Stahlnecker	Allentown, Pa	Jan. 23, 1872	123, 056
Cars, Grain-door for railway	M. H. Card and L. Safford	Freeport and Chicago, Ill	Aug. 22, 1871	118, 339
Cars, Grain-door for railway	G. B. Rich	La Fayette, Ind	Mar. 19, 1867	62, 972
Cars, Guard for railway	F. M. Daunoy	New Orleans, La	Mar. 14, 1867	64, 639
Cars, Guide-wheel for railway	J. B. Wickersham	New York, N. Y	Mar. 3, 1857	16, 762
Cars, Head-rest for railway	R. Hamilton	Franklin, Ind	Feb. 26, 1867	62, 484
Cars, Head-rest for railway	P. A. La France and J. D. Dinsmore.	Elmira, N. Y	Sept. 11, 1866	57, 926
Cars, Head-rest for railway	W. B. Slaughter	Chicago, Ill	Aug. 19, 1856	15, 581
Cars, Head-supporter for railway	J. N. Williams	Dubuque, Iowa	Feb. 13, 1855	12, 400
Cars, Heating and ventilating apparatus for railway.	C. F. Allen and L. W. Campbell.	Aurora, Ill	Nov. 5, 1867	70, 495
Cars, Heating and ventilating railway	D. H. Dotterer	Philadelphia, Pa	Feb. 25, 1868	74, 899
Cars, Heating and ventilating railway	S. Lloyd	Washington, D. C	Feb. 11, 1868	74, 386
Cars, Heating and ventilating railway	T. H. B. Sanders	Philadelphia, Pa	May 29, 1866	55, 168
Cars, Heating railway	R. A. Chesebrough	New York, N. Y	Jan. 28, 1868	73, 780
Cars, Heating railway	A. C. Crary	Utica, N. Y	May 12, 1868	77, 871
Cars, Hoisting and dumping coal	G. Martz	Pottsville, Pa	Apr. 3, 1855	12, 633
Cars, &c., Implement for sealing railway	F. W. A. Krause	Baltimore, Md	Oct. 13, 1857	18, 400
Cars, &c., India-rubber spring for	T. B. De Forest	New York, N. Y	Aug. 16, 1859	25, 100
Cars, Instrument for coupling railway	A. McOmber and M. Ward	Schenectady, N. Y	Mar. 8, 1870	100, 542
Cars, Jaw for dump and coal	J. M. Foss	Saint Albans, N. Y	June 25, 1872	128, 219
Cars, Lavatory attachment for railway	J. G. Murdock	Cincinnati, Ohio	Oct. 26, 1869	96, 259
Cars, Lever for railway	J. Noble	Rochester, N. Y	Nov. 19, 1867	71, 046
Cars, Lifting-jack for moving rail	N. B. Carpenter and J. Powers.	New York, N. Y	Feb. 6, 1855	12, 345
Cars, Lighting railway	A. Longstreet	Chicago, Ill	Apr. 27, 1869	89, 539
Cars, Link for coupling railway	G. W. Putnam	South Glen's Falls, N. Y	Oct. 1, 1872	131, 905
Cars, Link-guide for coupling	N. L. Post	East Cleveland, Ohio	Feb. 20, 1872	123, 930
Cars, Loading and unloading baggage and freight from.	O. C. Brown	Iberia, Ohio	May 6, 1873	138, 557
Cars, Loading cattle upon	L. O. Cottle	Cedar Rapids, Iowa	June 18, 1872	127, 961
Cars, Loading railway flat	G. W. Penniston	North Vernon, Ind	May 6, 1873	138, 577
Cars, Lock for doors of baggage	T. Slaight	Newark, N. J	Sept. 11, 1866	57, 986
Cars, Lock for railway	T. Slaight	Newark, N. J	Feb. 5, 1861	31, 332
Cars, Locking-door for railway	E. W. Morse	Chicago, Ill	Nov. 22, 1864	45, 165
Cars, locomotives, &c., Spring for railway	W. Duff	Baltimore, Md	Jan. 9, 1841	1, 928
Cars, Machine for bending truck-sides for railway	J. H. Helm	Pittsburgh, Pa	Sept. 23, 1873	143, 010
Cars, Machine for moving railway	C. W. T. Krausch	Chicago, Ill	Mar. 3, 1863	37, 818
Cars, Machine for replacing railway	H. N. Degraw	Piermont, N. Y	Jan. 29, 1856	14, 154
Cars, Machine for unloading railway	J. Dable	Chicago, Ill	July 28, 1868	80, 276
Cars, Machine for propelling	G. T. Beauregard	New Orleans, La	Nov. 30, 1869	97, 343
Cars, Machinery for propelling railway	J. Busser and J. B. Harmer	Philadelphia, Pa	May 8, 1860	28, 153
Cars, Machine for unloading flat	G. S. Caldwell	Auburn, N. Y	May 6, 1873	138, 476
Cars, Machinery for unloading railway	J. Dable	Chicago, Ill	Aug. 7, 1866	56, 906
Cars, Metallic safety-seat for railway	H. Martin	Chicago, Ill	Jan. 15, 1867	61, 222
Cars, Method of preventing dust, &c., from entering the windows of railway.	P. M. Pyfer	Baltimore, Md	Mar. 10, 1857	16, 806
Cars, Method of self-ventilation for railway	V. P. Corbett	Corbettsville, N. Y	Mar. 20, 1855	12, 541
Cars, Mode of applying steam as a motor to city-railway.	W. Darker, jr	Philadelphia, Pa	Nov. 22, 1859	26, 230
Cars, Mode of arranging couches in railway	E. C. Knight	Philadelphia, Pa	Sept. 27, 1859	25, 570
Cars, Mode of attaching stakes to railway	J. Fortun	Cienfuegos, Island of Cuba	Nov. 28, 1865	51, 278
Cars, Mode of collecting letters on street-railway	J. B. Murray	New York, N. Y	May 20, 1862	35, 323
Cars, Mode of confining the driver's seat in city-railway.	W. C. Allison	Philadelphia, Pa	Nov. 8, 1859	26, 066
Cars, Mode of constructing the heating and lighting apparatus on railway.	A. J. Gibson	Cincinnati, Ohio	Dec. 8, 1868	84, 740
Cars, Mode of coupling and uncoupling	S. H. Hamilton	Bushnell, Ill	Sept. 5, 1865	49, 754
Cars, Mode of dumping railway	W. Pearce and J. Lowrie	Piedmont, Va	Apr. 21, 1857	17, 114
Cars, Mode of fastening and unfastening drop-doors in coal.	W. Burt	Marquette, Mich	Dec. 11, 1866	60, 340
Cars, Mode of loading dirt	C. Phillips	Detroit, Mich	Jan. 8, 1856	14, 066
Cars, Mode of operating and dumping earth	R. Ray	Louisport, Ky	Sept. 4, 1855	13, 528
Cars, Mode of operating railway	C. E. Willis	New York, N. Y	Oct. 4, 1864	44, 574
Cars, Mode of switching street	J. S. Reid	Muncie, Ind	July 25, 1865	48, 978
Cars, Mode of watering cattle on railway	W. Robinson	Rochester, N. Y	Oct. 29, 1861	33, 605
Cars off the track, Rail for switching	J. C. Mather	New York, N. Y	Aug. 24, 1858	21, 266
Cars, Oil-box for railway	E. F. Hurlbut and R. S. Potter	Chicago, Ill	May 10, 1864	42, 732
Cars on rails, Apparatus for retaining	W. Payne	New York, N. Y	Mar. 5, 1850	7, 146
Cars on railways, Machinery for moving	A. Foster and H. Brown	New York, N. Y	Jan. 18, 1859	22, 638
Cars on railways, Mode of propelling	C. T. Harvey	Tarrytown, N. Y	May 8, 1866	54, 537
Cars on railways, Propelling	J. A. Bennet	Kings County, N. Y	Oct. 9, 1860	30, 287
Cars on the track, Adjustable rail for replacing	C. Perley	New York, N. Y	June 13, 1854	11, 079
Cars on the track, Adjustable rail for replacing	J. A. Stephan	La Fayette, Ind	Oct. 11, 1859	25, 771
Cars on the track, Device for moving	J. W. Pettengill	Rockford, Ill	Sept. 25, 1866	58, 285
Cars on track, Machine for replacing railway	J. White	Boston, Mass	June 22, 1858	20, 675
Cars, Operating dumping	A. C. Johnson	Meadville, Pa	Apr. 18, 1854	10, 805
Cars, Operating dumping	R. Ray	Louisport, Ky	Sept. 4, 1855	13, 529
Cars over elevations, Taking	S. Cram	New York, N. Y	June 11, 1836	....
Cars over obstructions, Conveying city-railway	P. I. Biderman	Philadelphia, Pa	Oct. 9, 1860	30, 289
Cars, Passenger-support for city	J. Hanley	New York, N. Y	Dec. 13, 1864	45, 467
Cars, Pedestal for railway	D. H. Feger	New York, N. Y	Aug. 4, 1857	17, 953
Cars, Pedestal for railway	I. P. Wendell and S. Ustick	Philadelphia, Pa	Oct. 10, 1865	50, 427
Cars, Pedestal for street-railway	D. B. Hart	Saint Louis, Mo	Apr. 23, 1872	126, 054
Cars, Pipe-coupling for heating	H. R. Robbins	Baltimore, Md	Jan. 18, 1870	99, 003
Cars, Pipe-coupling for heating and ventilating railway.	F. R. Hunt	Leavenworth, Kans	Mar. 15, 1870	100, 896
Cars, Platform between railway	J. Newman	Baltimore, Md	July 26, 1859	24, 885
Cars, Plow for unloading	J. McMullin	Casey, Iowa	Jan. 28, 1873	135, 351
Cars, Pole-adjuster for horse	A. G. Safford	Boston, Mass	Apr. 25, 1871	114, 205
Cars, Pole for horse	T. Pendergast	Saint Louis, Mo	Dec. 29, 1868	85, 473
Cars, Pole for horse-railway	D. F. Robinson	Boston, Mass	Dec. 4, 1866	60, 250
Cars, Portable seat for drivers upon	J. F. Campbell and C. Tinney	Williamsburgh, N. Y	May 21, 1867	64, 837

Index of patents issued from the United States Patent Office from 1790 *to* 1873, *inclusive*—Continued.

Invention.	Inventor.	Residence.	Date.	No.
Cars, Preventing dust from entering railway	D. S. Darling	Brooklyn, N. Y	Jan. 10, 1854	10, 402
Cars, Propelling	I. Avery	Tunkhannock, Pa	Sept. 25, 1847	5, 308
Cars, Propelling	C. T. Harvey	Tarrytown, N. Y	Apr. 16, 1867	63, 888
Cars, Propelling	C. T. Harvey	Tarrytown, N. Y	May 21, 1867	64, 862
Cars, Propelling	W. J. Sage	Steubenville, Ohio	Jan. 28, 1862	34, 269
Cars, Propelling railway	S. G. Randall	New York, N. Y	May 23, 1865	47, 858
Cars, Propelling street	H. C. Bull and B. Bloomfield	New Orleans, La	Mar. 5, 1872	124, 327
Cars, Propelling street	J. W. Conway	Madison, Ind	Aug. 28, 1866	57, 623
Cars, Propelling street	G. S. Petry	Troy Grove, Ill	Apr. 9, 1867	63, 652
Cars, Propelling street	J. L. Simms and W. T. Duvall	Georgetown, D. C	Apr. 2, 1872	125, 224
Cars, Propulsion of street	C. M. Mann	Detroit, Mich	June 6, 1865	48, 081
Cars, Pull-iron for horse	A. S. Jimmerson	New York, N. Y	Jan. 5, 1869	85, 670
Cars, Register for horse	C. B. Angell	Coventry, R. I	May 12, 1863	38, 456
Cars, Register for street	J. B. Greenhut	Chicago, Ill	Dec. 12, 1865	51, 453
Cars, Retracker for railway	J. D. Potts	Pittsburgh, Pa	Nov. 26, 1861	33, 795
Cars, Rolling shoes for replacing	W. L. Gilroy	Philadelphia, Pa	May 26, 1863	38, 671
Cars, Running-gear for city-railway	J. Grice and R. H. Long	New York, N. Y., and Philadelphia, Pa.	Feb. 21, 1860	27, 217
Cars, Running-gear for railway	S. B. Childs	Syracuse, N. Y	Sept. 25, 1866	58, 216
Cars, Running-gear for railway	T. A. Davies	New York, N. Y	Dec. 9, 1851	8, 576
Cars, Running-gear for railway	J. H. Dennis	Louisville, Ky	Jan. 14, 1862	34, 134
Cars, Running-gear for railway	S. B. Driggs	New York, N. Y	Mar. 14, 1865	46, 784
Cars, Running-gear for railway	R. Hornbrook	Cincinnati, Ohio	Apr. 24, 1860	27, 982
Cars, Running-gear for railway	S. Howard	Elyria, Ohio	May 28, 1861	32, 423
Cars, Running-gear for railway	J. Ingersoll	Grafton, Ohio	Aug. 24, 1858	21, 259
Cars, Running-gear for railway	I. Knight	Baltimore, Md	Mar. 28, 1848	5, 493
Cars, Running-gear for railway	J. S. Lester	Atlanta, Ga	Oct. 7, 1873	143, 516
Cars, Running-gear for railway	W. Nebinger	Sharpsburgh, Md	Oct. 21, 1851	8, 451
Cars, Running-gear for railway	J. R., D. W., and J. Perry	Wilkesbarre, Pa	Feb. 9, 1869	86, 685
Cars, Running-gear for railway	D. G. Smith	Carbondale, Pa	Dec. 5, 1854	12, 036
Cars, Running-gear for railway	J. Stephenson	New York, N. Y	July 25, 1865	49, 004
Cars, Running-gear for railway	J. Stimpson	Baltimore, Md	Oct. 23, 1834	....
Cars, Running-gear for railway	H. D. Taylor	Newark, N. J	Feb. 3, 1852	8, 710
Cars, Running-gear for railway	H. H. Tronor	New York, N. Y	Oct. 17, 1865	50, 518
Cars, Running-gear for railway	T. Wilson	Silver Creek, Ill	Feb. 25, 1862	34, 544
Cars, Running-gear for street	Z. Eastman	Chicago, Ill	May 25, 1869	90, 513
Cars, Running-gear for street-railway	A. McNair	Newark, N. J	May 13, 1862	35, 244
Cars, Safety-attachment for railway	H. A. Newhall	Newton, Mass	May 18, 1858	20, 293
Cars, Safety-attachment for street-railway	J. Fogarty	Brooklyn, N. Y	Sept. 7, 1869	94, 587
Cars, Safety-attachment for railway	G. W. Brady	New York, N. Y	Mar. 3, 1868	74, 980
Cars, Safety-attachment for railway	C. Mahon	Washington, D. C	Oct. 23, 1855	13, 705
Cars, Safety-brake for railway	F. Wolf	Philadelphia, Pa	Sept. 20, 1864	44, 361
Cars, Safety bridge and gate for railway	A. H. Allen	Hartford, Conn	Aug. 13, 1867	67, 701
Cars, Safety-bridge for railway	L. Hempstead and L. S. Hills	Hartford, Conn	Aug. 21, 1866	57, 453
Cars, Safety-bridge for railway	E. Sturgeon	Columbiana, Ohio	Aug. 15, 1871	118, 167
Cars, Safety-bridge for railway	L. Traxler	Butler, Ohio	July 2, 1867	66, 419
Cars, Safety-coupling for railway	E. H. Anderson	Milford, Del	Feb. 3, 1857	16, 520
Cars, Safety-guard for railway	J. G. Crocker	Utica, N. Y	Jan. 1, 1856	14, 014
Cars, Safety-guard for railway	T. Gillen	Philadelphia, Pa	June 23, 1863	39, 011
Cars, Safety-guard for railway	S. Males	Cincinnati, Ohio	June 11, 1867	65, 582
Cars, Safety-guard for railway	W. Siefert	New York, N. Y	Jan. 29, 1867	61, 637
Cars, Safety-guard for railway	T. Walter	Philadelphia, Pa	Feb. 23, 1869	87, 126
Cars, Safety-guard for railway	J. A. Wilkinson	Wilson, N. Y	July 26, 1870	105, 753
Cars, Safety-hatch for railway	R. Liston	Albany, N. Y	Feb. 18, 1873	135, 923
Cars, Safety-padlock for railway	G. W. Stevens	Albany, N. Y	Jan. 7, 1868	73, 133
Cars, Safety-platform between railway	J., jr., and S. V. Kline	Chicago, Ill	Apr. 15, 1856	14, 665
Cars, Safety-platform for	H. E. Marchand	Pittsburgh, Pa	May 6, 1873	138, 669
Cars, Safety-platform for railway	R. Strode	Coatesville, Pa	Nov. 18, 1873	144, 804
Cars, Safety-step for railway	B. F. Beckwith, J. H. Rynerson, and A. N. Clark.	Clayton, Ind	Mar. 5, 1872	124, 318
Cars, Safety-top for railway	A. Potts	Philadelphia, Pa	Aug. 11, 1857	17, 982
Cars, Sand-distributer for railway	C. M. Bromwick	South Boston, Mass	Dec. 19, 1865	51, 646
Cars, Scraper-attachment to	E. B. Wells	Northampton, Mass	Jan. 7, 1868	73, 212
Cars, Seal-bolt for railway	P. H. Mann and G. P. Terry	Albany, N. Y	Dec. 15, 1868	84, 891
Cars, Seal-bolt for railway	J. P. Moore	Boston, Mass	Dec. 1, 1868	84, 503
Cars, &c., Seal for railway freight	H. D. Mears and W. Houlton, jr	Baltimore, Md	July 14, 1857	17, 801
Cars, &c., Seal for railway freight	H. D. Mears and W. Houlton, jr	Baltimore, Md	July 14, 1857	17, 802
Cars, Seat for driver and conductor of street	T. G. Hambly	San Francisco, Cal	Nov. 7, 1865	50, 819
Cars, Settee for railway-passenger	J. B. Easland	Bridgeport, Conn	Sept. 2, 1862	36, 343
Cars, Shackle for railway	H. A. Barns	Milwaukee, Wis	May 13, 1862	35, 2[illegible]7
Cars, Singletree for horse	J. Wills	Rock Island, Ill	Apr. 15, 1873	137, 980
Cars, Sleeping-chair for railway	J. Danner	Canton, Ohio	Dec. 27, 1859	26, 571
Cars, Sliding door for railway box	J. Bassler	Galesburgh, Ill	Aug. 2, 1870	105, 888
Cars, Sliding door for railway	A. G. Safford	Boston, Mass	Aug. 8, 1865	49, 308
Cars, Spiral spring for railway	J. Murray	New York, N. Y	Oct. 15, 1872	132, 213
Cars, Spiral spring for railway	F. M. Ray	New York, N. Y	Apr. 18, 1854	10, 784
Cars, Spring craft and bumper for railway	P. Alberson	New Haven, Conn	Sept. 8, 1838	908
Cars, Spring-platform for railway	C. H. Lewis	Malden, Mass	Mar. 25, 1856	14, 508
Cars, Spring-seat for railway	T. J. Gifford	Salem, Mass	Nov. 1, 1870	108, 777
Cars, Sprinkling-attachment for railway	H. Mitchell	Cincinnati, Ohio	June 19, 1860	28, 764
Cars, Stake-holder for platform	E. A. Eddy	Racine, Wis	July 18, 1865	48, 799
Cars, Stake-holder for platform	E. A. Eddy	Racine, Wis	July 18, 1865	48, 800
Cars, Stake-holder for railway	T. A. Slack	Peoria County, Ill	Dec. 10, 1867	72, 097
Cars, Standard for lumber	H. Jacob	Loretto, Pa	Apr. 5, 1864	42, 194
Cars, Starting	H. H. Covert	Detroit, Mich	Aug. 28, 1866	57, 624
Cars, Starting	A. F. French	Franklin, Vt	Aug. 1, 1865	49, 195
Cars, Starting	J. McMurtry	Lexington, Ky	Feb. 25, 1868	74, 927
Cars, Starting and stopping	A. G. Crossman	Huntington, N. Y	Nov. 12, 1867	70, 814
Cars, Starting and stopping	J. Phillips, D. W. Southwick, and D. A. Arnold.	Pawtucket, R. I	Oct. 22, 1867	70, 114
Cars, Starting and stopping	P. Rhoads	Carlisle, Pa	Mar. 8, 1871	112, 494
Cars, Starting and stopping city-railway	J. H. Wygant	Hackensack, N. J	Aug. 7, 1860	29, 536
Cars, Starting and stopping street	E. M. Scott	Auburn, N. Y	Apr. 30, 1867	64, 373
Cars, Starting-apparatus for horse	A. Cary	Worcester, Mass	Jan. 21 1862	34, 199
Cars, Starting-apparatus for railway	E. Woodward and J. S. Millett	Charlestown, Mass	Sept. 29, 1868	82, 671
Cars, Starting-apparatus for street	T. B. Jordan	Gloucester, N. J	Apr. 9, 1867	63, 726
Cars, Starting city-railway	G. P. Frick	Baltimore, Md	June 7, 1859	24, 293
Cars, Starting city-railway	G. Hamel	Abington, Pa	Nov. 15, 1859	26, 161
Cars, Starting horse-railway	W. Henderson and J. W. Fowle	Boston, Mass	May 16, 1865	47, 722

Index of patents issued from the United States Patent Office from 1790 *to* 1873, *inclusive*—Continued.

Invention.	Inventor.	Residence.	Date.	No.
Cars, Starting railway	W. Lawton	New York, N. Y	Sept. 5, 1865	49, 770
Cars Starting railway	W. Palmer	New York, N. Y	Oct. 3, 1854	11, 759
Cars, Starting railway	T. R. Sinclaire	New York, N. Y	Dec. 19, 1865	51, 626
Cars, Starting street	J. Adams	Newark, Del	Feb. 5, 1867	61, 699
Cars, Starting street	A. S. Armstrong	Saint Bernard Parish, La	Feb. 26, 1867	62, 304
Cars, Starting street	J. S. Briggs	South Bend, Ind	Feb. 25, 1862	34, 477
Cars, Starting street	T. F. Kums and W. W Burson	Rockford, Ill	Sept. 11, 1866	57, 925
Cars, State-room for railway	W. Brown	Duncannon, Pa	Feb. 4, 1868	73, 949
Cars, Steam-brake for railway	S. N. Goodale	Cleveland, Ohio	May 30, 1865	47, 943
Cars, Steam-brake for railway	N. Nilson	Minneapolis, Minn	Nov. 11, 1873	144, 410
Cars, Steam-coupling for railway	S. A. Appold	Baltimore, Md	Aug. 23, 1870	106, 648
Cars, Steam-heater for railway	C. A. Mabie, T. H. Whitcomb, and J. T. Brown.	Albion, N. Y	Jan. 2, 1872	122, 326
Cars, Steam-pipe coupling for railway	J. Conner	Philadelphia, Pa	Dec. 13, 1870	110, 114
Cars, steamers, &c., Apparatus for illuminating railway.	W. Foster, jr., and G. P. Ganster.	New York, N. Y	Dec. 8, 1868	84, 814
Cars, Step for street	A. A. Duly	New York, N. Y	Jan. 11, 1870	98, 750
Cars, Stopping and starting	T. S. Bigelow	Lake Mills, Wis	June 30, 1863	39, 091
Cars, Stopping and starting	E. T. Colburn	Boston, Mass	Nov. 5, 1867	70, 528
Cars, Stopping and starting	J. Higgin	Manchester, England	Jan. 8, 1861	31, 080
Cars, Stopping and starting	C. S. Hunt	Terre Bonne Parish, La	Mar. 10, 1868	75, 426
Cars, Stopping and starting	J. E. Kelsey	Providence, R. I	May 1, 1866	54, 363
Cars, Stopping and starting city-railway	E. S. Ritchie	Brookline, Mass	July 3, 1860	29, 107
Cars, Stopping and starting railway	J. A. Emerick	Philadelphia, Pa	Apr. 23, 1861	32, 127
Cars, Stopping and starting railway	F. C. Kutt	Hackensack, N. J	Aug. 21, 1860	29, 700
Cars, Stopping and starting railway	P. Louis	New York, N. Y	Jan. 15, 1861	31, 140
Cars, Stopping and starting railway	B. Morohan	Brooklyn, N. Y	Jan. 15, 1861	31, 124
Cars, Stopping and starting railway	J. Steger	New York, N. Y	Sept. 15, 1863	39, 999
Cars, Stopping and starting street	J. M. Starr	Richmond, Ind	Nov. 11, 1873	144, 484
Cars, Street-indicator for city	W. Brown	Duncannon, Pa	Sept. 20, 1870	107, 440
Cars, Support and advertising medium for street	M. Warne	Philadelphia, Pa	Oct. 31, 1871	120, 471
Cars, Support for passengers in	H. S. Vrooman	Boston, Mass	Apr. 28, 1868	77, 328
Cars, Suspending upper berths in sleeping	E. H. Paine	Louisville, Ky	Jan. 11, 1870	98, 792
Cars, Swing-jack for railway	J. H. Clark	Westbrook, Me	Dec. 26, 1865	51, 696
Cars, Switch for changing gage of	T. Fogg	St. Mary's, Canada	Apr. 25, 1871	114, 123
Cars, Switching-apparatus for street-railway	P. S. Dusouchet	New Orleans, La	Aug. 11, 1868	80, 932
Cars through tunnel, Method of transporting	J. H. Crane	Charlestown, Mass	May 14, 1867	64, 636
Cars to railway-tracks of different gages, Mode of applying.	C. D. Tisdale	East Boston, Mass	Mar. 10, 1863	37, 889
Cars to turn short curves, Railway track or rail for	H. M. Naglee	Philadelphia, Pa	Aug. 22, 1840	1, 726
Cars, Tongue-support for railway street	J. M. Tiernan	Pittsburgh, Pa	Dec. 17, 1867	72, 430
Cars, Trussed-spring bolster for railway	J. Anderson	Wilmington, N. C	Aug. 12, 1873	141, 618
Cars, Turning railway	A. Shermer	Philadelphia, Pa	Sept. 9, 1835	....
Cars, Unloading	J. Dable	Chicago, Ill	Nov. 16, 1869	96, 781
Cars, Unloading coal and other	A. Patrick	Alleghany County, Md	Aug. 15, 1854	11, 530
Cars, Unloading grain	D. J. Whittemore	Milwaukee, Wis	Oct. 16, 1866	58, 928
Cars, Unloading grain from	E. M. Clark	Detroit, Mich	Nov. 8, 1864	44, 937
Cars, Unloading railway	F. Haase and W. Rost	Oak Park, Ill	June 11, 1867	65, 743
Cars upon railway-track, Replacing	L. B. Flanders	Dunkirk, N. Y	Dec. 6, 1853	10, 301
Cars upon springs, Mode of suspending	A. Bridges	Newton, Mass	June 12, 1866	55, 457
Cars upon the track, Apparatus for replacing railway.	S. P. Coon	Milwaukee, Wis	June 19, 1855	13, 080
Cars upon the track, Manner of replacing railway	S. H. Bean	Philadelphia, Pa	Oct. 11, 1845	4, 232
Cars upon the track, Mechanism for retaining	G. P. Ketcham	Bedford, Ind	Feb. 6, 1855	12, 371
Cars upon the track, Spiral wheel for replacing railway.	R. F. R. Lewis	Annapolis, Md	Apr. 10, 1855	12, 684
Cars upon the track, Switch for replacing	N. Pullman	New Oregon, Iowa	May 1, 1866	54, 478
Cars, Ventilating and excluding dust from railway	R. Cook	Saratoga Springs, N. Y	Aug. 19, 1851	8, 298
Cars, Ventilating and excluding dust from railway	A. B. Spencer	Rochester, N. Y	May 4, 1858	20, 176
Cars, Ventilating and warming railway	A. J. Marshall	Warrenton, Va	Aug. 20, 1867	67, 894
Cars, Ventilating grain	W. S. Sampson	New York, N. Y	Oct. 17, 1871	120, 109
Cars, Ventilating railway	J. G. Allen	Philadelphia, Pa	Aug. 12, 1873	141, 617
Cars, Ventilating railway	C. Atwood	Birmingham, Conn	July 10, 1855	13, 204
Cars, Ventilating railway	N. S. Barnum and L. Whitney	New Haven, Conn	Jan. 6, 1852	8, 622
Cars, Ventilating railway	H. Bradford and E. Morris	New York, N. Y	June 4, 1850	7, 409
Cars, Ventilating railway	S. A. Clemens	Springfield, Mass	Nov. 22, 1853	10, 251
Cars, Ventilating railway	J. Cunningham	Reading, Pa	Mar. 12, 1850	7, 158
Cars, Ventilating railway	G. F. Foote	Buffalo, N. Y	July 11, 1854	11, 268
Cars, Ventilating railway	C. D. Gibson	New York, N. Y	July 7, 1863	39, 140
Cars, Ventilating railway	T. S. Lambert	Peekskill, N. Y	Dec. 8, 1863	40, 843
Cars, Ventilating railway	H. L. B. Lewis	Philadelphia, Pa	Oct. 30, 1855	13, 725
Cars, Ventilating railway	W. H. Medcalfe	Baltimore, Md	Jan. 22, 1856	14, 139
Cars, Ventilating railway	G. Neilson	Boston, Mass	Jan. 24, 1854	10, 449
Cars, Ventilating railway	W. Pauli	Alexandria, Va	May 8, 1855	12, 827
Cars, Ventilating railway	C. Pepper	Albany, N. Y	Apr. 20, 1858	20, 021
Cars, Ventilating railway	C. Reed and B. K. Mould	Chicago, Ill	Aug. 8, 1854	11, 494
Cars, Ventilating railway	H. J. Ruttan	Coburg, Canada West	Jan. 9, 1866	52, 009
Cars, Ventilating railway	A. F. Smith and W. Wagner	Norwich, Conn., and Palatine Bridge, N. Y.	Sept. 23, 1862	36, 536
Cars, Ventilating railway	J. K. Taylor	Binghamton, N. Y	Oct. 30, 1855	13, 732
Cars, Ventilating railway	R. R. Taylor	Reading, Pa	Feb. 22, 1859	23, 049
Cars, Ventilating-window for railway	S. Darling	Providence, R. I	Aug. 23, 1870	106, 558
Cars, Ventilating-window for railway	R. Monroe, E. Stone, and E. St. John.	Elmira, N. Y	Dec. 19, 1865	51, 607
Cars, Ventilating-window for railway	M. C. Murphy	Boston, Mass	June 21, 1870	104, 486
Cars, Ventilating-window for railway	G. Neilson	Boston, Mass	May 30, 1854	10, 960
Cars, Ventilating-window for railway	H. M. Paine	Worcester, Mass	Jan. 6, 1852	8, 645
Cars, Warming passenger	J. B. Johnson	Lynn, Mass	June 17, 1862	35, 612
Cars, Warming railway	A. C. Crary	Utica, N. Y	Apr. 13, 1869	88, 8[illegible]2
Cars, Warming railway	G. W. Eddy	Waterford, N. Y	Mar. 31, 1868	76, 175
Cars, Warming railway	T. N. Morse	Fairhaven, Mass	Nov. 16, 1869	96, 945
Cars, Warming railway	T. Townsend	Albany, N. Y	July 24, 1846	4, 654
Cars, Water-can for railway	L. T. Richer	New York, N. Y	Apr. 3, 1866	53, 748
Cars, Water-tank for railway stock	J. B. Calkins	Pacific, Mo	Feb. 25, 1873	136, 132
Cars with steam, Apparatus for heating railway	G. W. Samson	Washington, D. C	July 16, 1861	32, 843
Cars, Wooden mat for	W. Groat	Green Island, N. Y	June 12, 1866	55, 489
Caramels, Manufacture of dry	T. Hyatt	Philadelphia, Pa	Mar. 13, 1866	53, 249
Carbine-socket	J. S. P. Taylor	Oxford, Ohio	June 27, 1865	48, 462

Index of patents issued from the United States Patent Office from 1790 *to* 1873, *inclusive*—Continued.

Invention.	Inventor.	Residence.	Date.	No.
Carbon and other oils, Vessel for transporting	R. C. Glyde	Pittsburgh, Pa	Feb. 11, 1862	34, 359
Carbon, Apparatus for manufacturing sulphuret of.	E. Deiss	Paris, France	Apr. 27, 1858	20, 047
Carbon-battery connection	A. S. Ogden	Newark, N. J	June 26, 1866	55, 892
Carbon-battery connector	C. T. Chester	Hackensack Township, N. J	Nov. 28, 1865	51, 144
Carbon, Black pigment for mineral	P. O'Reilly	Hartford, Conn	June 8, 1869	91, 038
Carbon for use in the arts, Preparation for mineral	J. Dickinson	Bay Ridge, N. Y	June 1, 1869	90, 824
Carbon, Mode of baking articles composed of	D. G. B. Fowler	New York, N. Y	Nov. 23, 1858	22, 115
Carbon-tool	H. and J. L. Young	Middletown, Conn., and New York, N. Y.	Oct. 12, 1869	95, 866
Carbonating and dispensing artificial mineral-waters, Mode of.	D. and T. Kolb	Washington, D. C	Feb. 23, 1869	87, 177
Carbonic-acid engine	N. H. Barbour	Auburn, N. Y	Mar. 14, 1865	46, 769
Carbonic-acid-gas engine	J. C. Salomon, jr	Cincinnati, Ohio	Dec. 9, 1851	8, 577
Carbonic-acid-gas generator	O. Zwietusch	Milwaukee, Wis	Dec. 23, 1873	145, 774
Carbonic oxide for treating metals, Generating and applying.	T. Shaw	Philadelphia, Pa	Nov. 17, 1868	84, 220
Carboys and bottles, Machine for forming rings on.	T. Barrett	Charlestown, Mass	June 30, 1868	79, 434
Carboys, Machine for finishing	L. Hyde	Ellenville, N. Y	Feb. 22, 1859	23, 063
Carboys, Tilting-stand for	A. W. Caverly	New York, N. Y	Nov. 11, 1873	144, 442
Carbureter	H. C. Appleby	Conneaut, Ohio	June 23, 1868	79, 048
Carbureter	J. D. Averell	New York, N. Y	July 30, 1872	130, 004
Carbureter	J. D. Averell	New York, N. Y	Dec. 24, 1872	134, 240
Carbureter	W. W. Bierce	Cleveland, Ohio	Jan. 7, 1868	73, 073
Carbureter	A. F. H. Braun	San Francisco, Cal	June 25, 1872	128, 356
Carbureter	M. P. Coons	Brooklyn, N. Y	Aug. 11, 1868	80, 918
Carbureter	W. H. Covel	New York, N. Y	June 15, 1869	91, 213
Carbureter	J. R. Cross	New York, N. Y	Apr. 30, 1872	126, 189
Carbureter	O. P. Drake	Boston, Mass	Oct. 1, 1872	131, 814
Carbureter	C. F. Dunderdale	New York, N. Y	May 25, 1869	90, 436
Carbureter	C. F. Dunderdale	New York, N. Y	Mar. 1, 1870	100, 274
Carbureter	G. Edmonds	New Orleans, La	May 23, 1871	115, 182
Carbureter	W. H. Elston	Marshall, Mich	Feb. 25, 1873	136, 228
Carbureter	J. B. Fish	Providence, Pa	May 21, 1872	127, 039
Carbureter	F. A. Fisher	Crawford, N. J	June 4, 1872	127, 409
Carbureter	F. A. Fisher	Elizabeth, N. J	July 22, 1873	140, 998
Carbureter	T. B. Fogarty	New York, N. Y	Feb. 18, 1873	135, 981
Carbureter	T. B. Fogarty	Warren, Mass	Feb. 18, 1873	135, 982
Carbureter	E. J. Fraser	Erie, Pa	Aug. 20, 1867	67, 971
Carbureter	C. N. Gilbert, J. F. Barker, and E. N. Ives.	Springfield, Mass	Jan. 8, 1867	61, 004
Carbureter	T. Holmes	Brooklyn, N. Y	Feb. 11, 1873	135, 806
Carbureter	H. Holton	Saint Louis, Mo	Apr. 2, 1872	125, 194
Carbureter	E. S. Hutchinson and H. L. McAvoy.	Baltimore, Md	Jan. 9, 1866	51, 946
Carbureter	J. B. Hyde	New York, N. Y	July 16, 1872	129, 566
Carbureter	M. W. Kidder	Lowell, Mass	Sept. 13, 1870	107, 268
Carbureter	J. F. G. Kromschroeder	London, England	Apr. 1, 1873	137, 307
Carbureter	J. F. and G. E. Lockwood	Taylorsville, Ill	Sept. 2, 1873	142, 545
Carbureter	J. B. Lyman	Rockford, Ill	Dec. 30, 1873	146, 082
Carbureter	W. T. McMillen	Cincinnati, Ohio	Oct. 7, 1873	143, 523
Carbureter	J. Millward	Fayetteville, N. Y	Aug. 16, 1870	106, 389
Carbureter	E. L. Mix	Rochester, N. Y	May 11, 1869	90, 012
Carbureter	J. Musgrave	Cincinnati, Ohio	Nov. 25, 1873	144, 858
Carbureter	T. W. Ofeldt	Newark, N. J	Sept. 17, 1872	131, 369
Carbureter	G. H. Peacock	Fairport, N. Y	Aug. 27, 1867	68, 231
Carbureter	F. S. Pease	Buffalo, N. Y	Nov. 6, 1866	59, 446
Carbureter	C. H. Pierson	Plainfield, N. J	May 28, 1872	127, 366
Carbureter	F. Ransom	Buffalo, N. Y	July 30, 1867	67, 216
Carbureter	J. F. M. Rigod	Paris, France	Oct. 8, 1872	132, 025
Carbureter	I. W. Shaler	Brooklyn, N. Y	Oct. 7, 1873	143, 534
Carbureter	I. Simmons	Baltimore, Md	Dec. 2, 1873	145, 248
Carbureter	H. Slatter	Covington, Ky	Sept. 22, 1868	82, 359
Carbureter	J. B. Terry	Brooklyn, N. Y	Dec. 17, 1872	133, 957
Carbureter	W. Thompson and J. E. Hall	Cleveland, Ohio	Dec. 3, 1867	71, 665
Carbureter	A. W. Wilkinson	New York, N. Y	Feb. 6, 1872	123, 539
Carbureter	A. W. Wilkinson	New York, N. Y	June 17, 1873	140, 105
Carbureter	C. B. Willoughby	Uhricksville, Ohio	June 23, 1868	79, 290
Carbureter	H. Woodward	London, England	Aug. 18, 1868	81, 238
Carbureter, Air	E. S. Archer	New York, N. Y	Sept. 6, 1864	44, 060
Carbureter, Air	J. F. Barker	Springfield, Mass	Apr. 21, 1868	76, 880
Carbureter, Air	J. F. Barker	Springfield, Mass	June 6, 1871	115, 562
Carbureter, Air	J. F. Barker and C. N. Gilbert	Springfield, Mass., and New York, N. Y.	Aug. 3, 1869	93, 267
Carbureter, Air	J. F. Barker and C. N. Gilbert	Springfield, Mass., and New York, N. Y.	Aug. 3, 1869	93, 268
Carbureter, Air	J. F. Barker and C. N. Gilbert	Springfield, Mass., and New York, N. Y.	Aug. 17, 1869	93, 795
Carbureter, Air	J. A. Bassett	Salem, Mass	Mar. 14, 1865	46, 771
Carbureter, Air	J. A. Bassett	Salem, Mass	Apr. 18, 1865	47, 272
Carbureter, Air	J. A. Bassett	Salem, Mass	Oct. 31, 1865	50, 675
Carbureter, Air	C. C. Beers	Boston, Mass	Apr. 25, 1871	113, 968
Carbureter, Air	A. D. Bell	San Francisco, Cal	Feb. 28, 1871	112, 111
Carbureter, Air	D. Bickford	Boston, Mass	Nov. 28, 1865	51, 128
Carbureter, Air	J. F. Birchard	Milwaukee, Wis	July 11, 1865	48, 706
Carbureter, Air	F. H. Brown	Chicago, Ill	June 26, 1866	55, 949
Carbureter, Air	F. H. Brown	Chicago, Ill	June 26, 1866	55, 950
Carbureter, Air	W. H. Burkland	London, England	Feb. 14, 1865	46, 432
Carbureter, Air	H. A. Chapin	New York, N. Y	Jan. 24, 1871	111, 175
Carbureter, Air	J. Chase	Windsor Locks, Conn	Nov. 14, 1865	50, 905
Carbureter, Air	J. Chase	Windsor Locks, Conn	Nov. 14, 1865	50, 987
Carbureter, Air	W. H. Clarke	Saint Anthony's Falls, Minn.	Mar. 26, 1867	63, 215
Carbureter, Air	W. F. Cozzens and J. H. Jones	Saint Louis, Mo	Nov. 12, 1867	70, 809
Carbureter, Air	H. G. Dayton	Maysville, Ky	May 21, 1872	127, 031
Carbureter, Air	S. R. Divine	New York, N. Y	Sept. 4, 1866	57, 686
Carbureter, Air	B. Douglas and W. H. Walton	New York and Brooklyn, N. Y.	Jan. 29, 1867	61, 656

Index of patents issued from the United States Patent Office from 1790 *to* 1873, *inclusive*—Continued.

Invention.	Inventor.	Residence.	Date.	No.
Carburetor, Air	O. P. Drake	Boston, Mass	May 6, 1862	35, 144
Carbureter, Air	O. P. Drake	Boston, Mass	Apr. 24, 1866	54, 132
Carbureter, Air	C. M. Drennan	Boston, Mass	Sept. 26, 1865	50, 103
Carbureter, Air	C. F. Dunderdale	New York, N. Y	Nov. 30, 1869	97, 283
Carbureter, Air	E. Dunscomb	Boston, Mass	May 9, 1865	47, 679
Carbureter, Air	H. F. Eberts and J. Fanning	Detroit, Mich	Nov. 30, 1869	97, 285
Carbureter, Air	H. Fairbanks	Boston, Mass	Apr. 10, 1866	53, 798
Carbureter, Air	R. B. Fitts	Philadelphia, Pa	May 16, 1871	114, 787
Carbureter, Air	T. F. Frank	Buffalo, N. Y	Nov. 27, 1866	59, 991
Carbureter, Air	F. Hainsworth	Chicago, Ill	June 27, 1865	48, 391
Carbureter, Air	D. Hurd	Chicago, Ill	May 2, 1865	47, 550
Carbureter, Air	E. S. Hutchinson and H. L. McAvoy.	Baltimore, Md	Feb. 5, 1867	61, 739
Carbureter, Air	J. H. Irwin	Chicago, Ill	Apr. 11, 1865	47, 256
Carbureter, Air	J. H. Irwin	Chicago, Ill	Aug. 22, 1865	49, 526
Carbureter, Air	J. H. Irwin	Chicago, Ill	Oct. 3, 1865	50, 250
Carbureter, Air	J. H. Irwin	Chicago, Ill	Oct. 3, 1865	50, 251
Carbureter, Air	J. H. Irwin	Chicago, Ill	June 25, 1867	66, 153
Carbureter, Air	J. H. Irwin and I. Simmons	Chicago, Ill	Apr. 11, 1865	47, 258
Carbureter, Air	T. Judd and E. Doty	Janesville, Wis	Apr. 29, 1873	138, 409
Carbureter, Air	C. B. Loveless	Syracuse, N. Y	Jan. 2, 1866	51, 841
Carbureter, Air	C. B. Loveless	Syracuse, N. Y	Apr. 10, 1866	53, 843
Carbureter, Air	W. M. Marshall	Philadelphia, Pa	July 7, 1868	79, 667
Carbureter, Air	H. L. McAvoy	Baltimore, Md	Aug. 23, 1864	43, 948
Carbureter, Air	H. L. McAvoy	Baltimore, Md	Nov. 22, 1864	45, 206
Carbureter, Air	H. L. McAvoy	Baltimore, Md	Dec. 13, 1864	45, 456
Carbureter, Air	H. L. McAvoy	Baltimore, Md	Feb. 7, 1865	46, 302
Carbureter, Air	H. L. McAvoy	Baltimore, Md	Sept. 19, 1865	50, 076
Carbureter, Air	H. L. McAvoy	Baltimore, Md	Aug. 14, 1866	57, 164
Carbureter, Air	H. L. McAvoy	Baltimore, Md	Sept. 11, 1866	57, 940
Carbureter, Air	D. McDonald	Albany, N. Y	Aug. 21, 1866	57, 442
Carbureter, Air	S. T. McDougall	New York, N. Y	June 5, 1866	55, 324
Carbureter, Air	J. McGeary	Salem, Mass	Oct. 16, 1866	58, 861
Carbureter, Air	P. Mihan	Boston, Mass	July 11, 1865	48, 772
Carbureter, Air	P. Mihan	Boston, Mass	Aug. 28, 1866	57, 543
Carbureter, Air	M. J. A. Mille	Paris, France	Aug. 22, 1865	49, 596
Carbureter, Air	G. Odiorne	Boston, Mass	Nov. 1, 1864	44, 883
Carbureter, Air	H. Oertel	Memphis, Tenn	Sept. 13, 1870	107, 403
Carbureter, Air	A. Patterson	Birmingham, Pa	Oct. 2, 1866	58, 471
Carbureter, Air	F. S. Pease	Buffalo, N. Y	Aug. 6, 1867	67, 576
Carbureter, Air	R. H. Plass	New York, N. Y	June 21, 1870	104, 642
Carbureter, Air	J. T. and R. H. Plass	New York, N. Y	Sept. 15, 1868	82, 244
Carbureter, Air	E. A. Pond	Rutland, Vt	Oct. 17, 1865	50, 491
Carbureter, Air	E. A. Pond and M. S. Richardson.	Rutland, Vt	Sept. 19, 1865	50, 029
Carbureter, Air	E. A. Pond and M. S. Richardson.	Rutland, Vt	Mar. 27, 1866	53, 481
Carbureter, Air	A. W. Porter	New York, N. Y	Sept. 3, 1872	131, 025
Carbureter, Air	A. C. Rand	Union Mills, Pa	Feb. 26, 1867	62, 364
Carbureter, Air	G. Rex	Philadelphia, Pa	May 9, 1871	114, 709
Carbureter, Air	G. Reznor	Mercer, Pa	Mar. 26, 1872	125, 085
Carbureter, Air	J. Richard	New York, N. Y	Nov. 3, 1868	83, 730
Carbureter, Air	J. F. Rowley, W. M. Sloane, and J. E. Woodruff.	Buffalo, N. Y	Aug. 28, 1866	57, 639
Carbureter, Air	J. Sangster	Buffalo, N. Y	Mar. 10, 1868	75, 468
Carbureter, Air	J. Sangster	Buffalo, N. Y	Mar. 10, 1868	75, 469
Carbureter, Air	I. W. Shaler	Brooklyn, N. Y	Nov. 16, 1869	96, 942
Carbureter, Air	W. A. Simonds	Boston, Mass	Mar. 21, 1865	46, 976
Carbureter, Air	W. A. Simonds	Boston, Mass	Aug. 15, 1865	49, 448
Carbureter, Air	B. Sloper	Saint Louis, Mo	June 13, 1871	115, 988
Carbureter, Air	J. F. Spence	Brooklyn, N. Y	Jan. 16, 1866	52, 087
Carbureter, Air	J. F. Spence	Williamsburgh, N. Y	Sept. 4, 1866	57, 788
Carbureter, Air	J. F. Spence	Brooklyn, N. Y	Aug. 2, 1870	105, 994
Carbureter, Air	J. F. Spence and L. D. Tousley	Newark, N. J	Jan. 25, 1870	99, 274
Carbureter, Air	J. H. Springer and J. C. McDonald.	Philadelphia, Pa	July 16, 1867	66, 749
Carbureter, Air	L. Stevens	Fitchburgh, Mass	Oct. 2, 1866	58, 559
Carbureter, Air	L. Stevens	Fitchburgh, Mass	Nov. 6, 1866	59, 473
Carbureter, Air	L. Stevens	Fitchburgh, Mass	Nov. 6, 1866	59, 474
Carbureter, Air	L. Stevens	Fitchburgh, Mass	May 28, 1867	65, 296
Carbureter, Air	J. Stratton	Philadelphia, Pa	Mar. 31, 1868	76, 114
Carbureter, Air	J. B. Terry	Auburndale, Mass	Feb. 7, 1865	46, 280
Carbureter, Air	J. B. Terry	Auburndale, Mass	Sept. 12, 1865	49, 934
Carbureter, Air	J. B. Terry	Auburndale, Mass	June 19, 1866	55, 741
Carbureter, Air	W. Thompson	Cleveland, Ohio	Mar. 27, 1866	53, 504
Carbureter, Air	E. F. Van Houten	Newark, N. J	Aug. 19, 1873	141, 968
Carbureter, Air	J. H. Van Houten	Newark, N. J	Nov. 22, 1870	109, 562
Carbureter, Air	J. S. Wood	Philadelphia, Pa	Nov. 24, 1868	84, 332
Carburetor, Air and gas	A. Barbarin	New Orleans, La	Oct. 5, 1869	95, 412
Carburetor, Air and gas	J. F. Barker and C. N. Gilbert	Springfield, Mass	July 16, 1867	66, 777
Carbureter, Air and gas	A. Bartholf	New York, N. Y	Oct. 18, 1870	108, 432
Carbureter, Air and gas	H. A. Chapin	New York, N. Y	Oct. 4, 1870	108, 005
Carbureter, Air and gas	H. G. Dayton	Maysville, Ky	Oct. 8, 1872	131, 943
Carbureter, Air and gas	O. P. Drake	Boston, Mass	Oct. 1, 1872	131, 815
Carbureter, Air and gas	J. Jonson	Toledo, Ohio	May 4, 1869	89, 665
Carbureter, Air and gas	F. H. Lutkewitte	Saint Louis, Mo	Apr. 4, 1871	113, 317
Carbureter, Air and gas	L. Marks	San Francisco, Cal	May 2, 1871	114, 316
Carbureter, Air and gas	W. J. Nichols	Buffalo, N. Y	July 13, 1869	92, 635
Carbureter, Air and gas	O. Tirrill	Brooklyn, N. Y	Aug. 22, 1871	118, 302
Carbureter, Air and gas	S. Whitney	Flushing, N. Y	June 6, 1871	115, 798
Carbureter, Air, gas, &c	A. C. Messenger	Syracuse, N. Y	June 19, 1866	55, 778
Carbureter and generator, Gas	F. A. Fisher	Westfield Township, N. J	Feb. 21, 1871	112, 026
Carbureter and regulator, Gas	J. A. Bassett	Salem, Mass	June 25, 1867	66, 067
Carbureter-burner	I. W. Shaler	Brooklyn, N. Y	Sept. 30, 1873	143, 385
Carbureter, Coal-gas	W. A. Earseman and R. W. Gray	Pittsburgh, Pa	Dec. 31, 1867	72, 825
Carbureter-feeder	E. M. Smith	New York, N. Y	Oct. 23, 1866	59, 142
Carbureter for locomotive head-lights	F. S. Pease	Buffalo, N. Y	Oct. 22, 1867	70, 014
Carbureter, Gas	J. L. Bartlett	Stockton, Cal	Oct. 4, 1870	107, 853

Index of patents issued from the United States Patent Office from 1790 *to* 1873, *inclusive*—Continued.

Invention.	Inventor.	Residence.	Date.	No.
Carbureter, Gas	J. A. Bassett	Salem, Mass	Mar. 4, 1862	34, 557
Carbureter, Gas	J. A. Bassett	Salem, Mass	July 29, 1862	35, 984
Carbureter, Gas	J. A. Bassett	Salem, Mass	Aug. 18, 1863	39, 541
Carbureter, Gas	J. A. Bassett	Salem, Mass	June 25, 1867	66, 066
Carbureter, Gas	W. W. Bierce	Cleveland, Ohio	Feb. 12, 1867	61, 918
Carbureter, Gas	W. W. Bierce	Cleveland, Ohio	July 23, 1867	66, 937
Carbureter, Gas	J. F. Boynton	Syracuse, N. Y	Sept. 25, 1866	58, 209
Carbureter, Gas	G. W. Coleman	Kalamazoo, Mich	Apr. 23, 1872	126, 024
Carbureter, Gas	G. B. Dyer	New York, N. Y	Aug. 3, 1869	93, 288
Carbureter, Gas	S. Gwynn	New York, N. Y	Apr. 28, 1863	38, 357
Carbureter, Gas	P. Hogan	Albany, N. Y	Apr. 17, 1866	53, 979
Carbureter, Gas	A. K. Johnston	New York, N. Y	Sept. 4, 1866	57, 729
Carbureter, Gas	J. Kidd	New York, N. Y	Oct. 20, 1868	83, 289
Carbureter, Gas	J. Kidd	New York, N. Y	Mar. 9, 1869	87, 682
Carbureter, Gas	W. H. Laubach	Philadelphia, Pa	May 14, 1867	64, 776
Carbureter, Gas	S. T. McDougall	New York, N. Y	Jan. 3, 1865	45, 729
Carbureter, Gas	A. W. Porter	New York, N. Y	Nov. 25, 1873	144, 863
Carbureter, Gas	W. A. Simonds	Boston, Mass	Apr. 23, 1867	64, 156
Carbureter, Gas	T. D. Worrall	New York, N. Y	Sept. 4, 1866	57, 812
Carbureter, Gas	W. M. Wright	Baltimore, Md	July 17, 1866	56, 503
Carbureter, Gas and air	A. T. Boon and A. D. Perry	Galesburgh, Ill	July 28, 1868	80, 268
Carbureter, Gas and air	J. F. Boynton	Syracuse, N. Y	Jan. 22, 1867	61, 309
Carbureter, Gas and air	M. P. Coons	Brooklyn, N. Y	July 4, 1871	116, 563
Carbureter, Gas and air	D. Hall	New York, N. Y	Apr. 2, 1867	63, 511
Carbureter, Gas and air	J. Kidd	London, England	Mar. 12, 1867	62, 855
Carbureter, Gas and air	G. W. Porter	Boston, Mass	Apr. 30, 1867	64, 361
Carbureter, Gas and air	J. S. Stephenson	Cleveland, Ohio	Mar. 26, 1867	63, 326
Carbureter, Hydrogen-gas	J. Ambuhl	Morristown, N. J	May 16, 1871	114, 744
Carbureter, Hydrogen-gas	R. V. De Guinon	Jersey City, N. J	Dec. 3, 1872	133, 569
Carbureters, Air-supplying machine for	P. Kelly	Dayton, Ohio	Nov. 9, 1869	96, 704
Carbureters, Automatic feed for	E. S. Hutchinson	Baltimore, Md	Oct. 2, 1866	58, 422
Carbureters, Blast-apparatus for	F. S. Pease	Buffalo, N. Y	June 11, 1867	65, 594
Carbureters, Blast-apparatus for	F. S. Pease	Buffalo, N. Y	June 11, 1867	65, 595
Carbureters, Capillary material for filling gas and air.	J. A. Bassett	Salem, Mass	Jan. 1, 1867	60, 670
Carbureters in railway-cars, Apparatus for forcing air into.	C. F. Dunderdale	New York, N. Y	Mar. 15, 1870	100, 737
Carbureters in railway-cars, &c., Automatic blast for.	E. S. Hutchinson	Baltimore, Md	Oct. 30, 1866	59, 226
Carbureters, &c., Machine for producing blast in gas.	E. A. Pond and M. S. Richardson.	Rutland, Vt	June 18, 1867	65, 939
Carbureters, Rotary air-wheel for gas	J. F. Spence and L. D. Towsley.	Brooklyn, N. Y., and Newark, N. J.	Sept. 20, 1870	107, 635
Carbureters, Siphon-can for	R. S. Osborn	Belleville, N. J	Feb. 20, 1872	123, 926
Carbureting air	C. Lawrence	Cincinnati, Ohio	Mar. 8, 1870	100, 534
Carbureting air	J. C. Pedrick	Washington, D. C	July 9, 1867	66, 622
Carbureting air and applying the same, Apparatus for.	A. Brin	Paris, France	Sept. 1, 1868	81, 590
Carbureting air and gas, Apparatus for	J. B. Hyde	New York, N. Y	Sept. 13, 1870	107, 262
Carbureting air and gas, Apparatus for	O. Terrill	Boston, Mass	Aug. 31, 1869	94, 360
Carbureting air and regulating its flow, Apparatus for	J. S. Wood	Philadelphia, Pa	July 9, 1867	66, 545
Carbureting air, Apparatus for	A. Barbarin and A. E. Dupas	New Orleans, La., and Paris, France.	Oct. 26, 1869	96, 074
Carbureting air, Apparatus for	A. E. Dupas and A. Barbarin	Paris, France, and New Orleans, La.	June 28, 1870	104, 716
Carbureting air, Apparatus for	J. F. Lafroque	Paris, France	Sept. 14, 1869	94, 898
Carbureting air, Apparatus for	J. D. Spang	Dayton, Ohio	Nov. 8, 1870	109, 148
Carbureting air, Combination apparatus for	L. Stevens	Fitchburgh, Mass	Sept. 10, 1867	68, 666
Carbureting air, Process of	J. H. Irwin	Chicago, Ill	Apr. 11, 1865	47, 257
Carbureting air to produce inflammable gas, Machine for.	L. Stevens	Fitchburgh, Mass	Apr. 9, 1867	63, 667
Carbureting and applying air for lighting and heating, Apparatus for.	J. Tiffany	Albany, N. Y	Nov. 2, 1869	96, 364
Carbureting air and enriching gas and for illuminating and heating, Liquids for.	J. F. Boynton	Syracuse, N. Y	Sept. 18, 1866	58, 054
Carbureting-apparatus	T. Judd and C. H. Pierson	Philadelphia, Pa	July 8, 1873	140, 711
Carbureting-apparatus	W. A. Simonds	Boston, Mass	July 12, 1870	105, 378
Carbureting apparatus, Gas	J. Gair	New York, N. Y	Feb. 15, 1870	99, 769
Carbureting-attachment for gas-burner	J. H. Butler, jr	Park Ridge, Ill	Sept. 10, 1872	131, 210
Carbureting gas	J. A. Bassett	Salem, Mass	June 25, 1867	66, 068
Carbureting gas and air	J. F. Boynton	Syracuse, N. Y	Nov. 5, 1867	70, 512
Carbureting gas and air, Liquid for	L. E. Holden	Cleveland, Ohio	Jan. 29, 1867	61, 662
Carbureting gas and oil for the same	J. Kidd	New York, N. Y	Mar. 9, 1869	87, 681
Carbureting gas for heating and illuminating, Mode of.	J. A. Bassett	Salem, Mass	June 25, 1867	66, 069
Carbureting gas from steam and hydrocarbons	W. H. Gwynne	White Plains, N. Y	July 28, 1863	39, 342
Carbureting gas, Hydrocarbon-fluid for	J. A. Bassett	Salem, Mass	June 18, 1867	65, 866
Carbureting gas-lamp	C. E. Ball	New York, N. Y	Oct. 15, 1872	132, 132
Carbureting gas, Liquid for	J. A. Bassett	Salem, Mass	May 21, 1867	64, 831
Carbureting gas, Method of	C. M. Williams	New York, N. Y	Jan. 8, 1867	61, 033
Carbureting gas, Process and material for	J. A. Bassett	Salem, Mass	Sept. 1, 1868	81, 736
Carbureting hydrogen-gas	C. B. Loveless	Syracuse, N. Y	June 13, 1871	115, 873
Carbureting illuminating-gas	W. H. Burridge	Cleveland, Ohio	Jan. 29, 1867	61, 606
Carbureting illuminating-gas	T. M. Fell	Brooklyn, N. Y	Sept. 10, 1872	131, 157
Carbureting-lamp	A. W. Porter and J. S. Gray	New York, N. Y	Feb. 20, 1872	123, 929
Carbureting lamp	J. W. Post	New York, N. Y	Nov. 19, 1872	133, 118
Carbureting-machine	A. E. Dupas and A. Barbarin.	New Orleans, La	Mar. 28, 1870	113, 147
Carbureting machine, Air	A. Barbarin	New Orleans, La	Oct. 26, 1869	96, 073
Carbureting machine, Air	T. F. Frank	Buffalo, N. Y	Oct. 20, 1868	83, 147
Carbureting machine, Air	J. H. Van Houten	Newark, N. J	Jan. 21, 1873	135, 020
Carbureting-machine, Apparatus for forcing air into.	J. F. Birchard	Milwaukee, Wis	May 8, 1866	54, 491
Carbureting wheel, Air	J. H. Van Houten	Newark, N. J	Nov. 22, 1870	109, 561
Card and brush, Combined	W. H. Prouty	Hanson, Mass	July 7, 1868	79, 596
Card and cribbage board	R. S. Jennings	Philadelphia, Pa	Jan. 14, 1868	73, 337
Card and other cylinders, Device for traversing	F. Herboth	Newark, N. J	June 3, 1873	139, 466
Card and other wire, Drawing	R. Prouty	Spencer, Mass	Jan. 19, 1822	....

Index of patents issued from the United States Patent Office from 1790 *to* 1873, *inclusive*—Continued.

Invention.	Inventor.	Residence.	Date.	No.
Card and pin-cushion, Business	D. C. Beamer	Philadelphia, Pa	Sept. 3, 1867	68, 339
Card-board and scab-board, Machine for planing	W. Kimball and S. Willard, jr	Mount Vernon, N. H	Oct. 23, 1813	....
Card-board cutter	L. Knickerbocker	Philadelphia, Pa	June 2, 1863	38, 750
Card-board drier	E. F. Bailey	Holderness, N. H	Aug. 27, 1867	68, 146
Card-board drier	E. F. Bailey	Ashland, N. H	July 2, 1872	128, 455
Card board, Playing	R. S. Jennings	Philadelphia, Pa	Aug. 27, 1867	68, 302
Card-board, Smoothing	D. Stearns	Brattleborough, Vt	Mar. 10, 1814	....
Card-boards for the handles and finishing them, Preparing.	H. Whittemore	Newton, N. Y	Apr. 27, 1832	....
Card-cabinet	A. T. Woodward	New York, N. Y	June 14, 1870	104, 391
Card-case	G. H. and J. James	London, England	July 20, 1869	92, 832
Card-case	F. A. Lamontagne	Montreal, Canada	Sept. 25, 1866	58, 357
Card-case	G. V. Metzel	Baltimore, Md	July 27, 1869	92, 986
Card-case	H. H. Miller and T. Bennett	Saint Louis, Mo	June 3, 1873	139, 513
Card-clothing	A. F. Bishop, J. H. Aiken, J. M. Pendleton, and A. W. Gates.	Norwalk, Conn., and New York, N. Y.	July 6, 1869	92, 149
Card-clothing	A. W. Gates	New York, N. Y	June 21, 1870	104, 445
Card-clothing	R. Kitson	Lowell, Mass	Oct. 5, 1858	21, 685
Card-clothing clamp	J. O. Lewis	Worcester, Mass	Jan. 4, 1870	98, 507
Card clothing, Manufacture of	E. S. Lawrence	Worcester, Mass	Oct. 20, 1868	83, 179
Card-clothing, Trimming	E. B. Howe	Lowell, Mass	Dec. 23, 1856	16, 275
Card clothing upon carding-cylinders, Clamps for stretching.	J. O. Lewis	Worcester, Mass	Apr. 11, 1865	47, 210
Card cutting and assorting machine, Playing	V. E. Mauger	New York, N. Y	Nov. 21, 1871	121, 117
Card-cutting machine	E. J. Hunt	Concord, N. H	Feb. 4, 1868	74, 095
Card-cutting machinery	E. Cowles	Cleveland, Ohio	June 8, 1869	90, 931
Card-cylinder	J. M. Stone	North Andover, Mass	July 14, 1868	79, 872
Card-cylinder cleaner	J. H. Smith and E. Squires	Raritan, N. J	Sept. 10, 1872	131, 185
Card-cylinders, Grinding and cleaning	W. B. Ingram	Manchester, Conn	Apr. 6, 1869	88, 635
Card-cylinders, Machinery for grinding	J. Parker	Biddeford, Me	Mar. 3, 1857	16, 744
Card-exhibiting apparatus	I. M. Miller	Huntsville, Ala	Oct. 24, 1871	120, 309
Card-exhibitor	W. Duryea	New York, N. Y	Apr. 10, 1855	12, 674
Card, Flexible hand	G. F. Ells	Douglas, N. Y	Aug. 8, 1871	117, 755
Card for carding fibrous substances, Self stripping	H. Barbour and J. Gleason	Lowell, Mass	Dec. 4, 1844	3, 843
Card for carding wool, cotton, &c	E. Faber	Pittsburgh, Pa	Jan. 24, 1832	....
Card for hooks and eyes, Paper	D. Fowler, jr	Northford, Conn	Apr. 21, 1863	38, 259
Card for liquids, Sample	H. Mustedt	New York, N. Y	Nov. 16, 1869	96, 930
Card for social games	P. West and G. S. Lee	Worcester, Mass	Sept. 2, 1873	142, 423
Card-globe, Folding	D. Townsend	Fiddletown, Cal	Feb. 16, 1869	87, 082
Card-globe, Folding	D. Townsend	Felchville, Vt	Mar. 22, 1870	101, 185
Card-grinder	R. Kitson	Lowell, Mass	Nov. 11, 1851	8, 512
Card-grinder	B. S. Roy	Lowell, Mass	Aug. 18, 1868	81, 213
Card-grinding cylinder	J. O. Lewis	Worcester, Mass	Dec. 24, 1867	72, 509
Card-grinding machine	T. C. Kirkham	Ancaster, Canada	July 1, 1873	140, 376
Card-grinding machine	S. G. Ladd and G. W. Crown	Lowell, Mass	Mar. 26, 1867	63, 165
Card-grinding machine	J. Robb	Lawrence, Mass	Feb. 2, 1869	86, 452
Card, Hand	G. F. Ells	Troy, N. Y	Apr. 23, 1867	64, 004
Card, Hand	E. S. Ells and G. F. Ells	Fair Haven, Vt., and Troy, N. Y.	Oct. 25, 1864	44, 791
Card, Hand	R. H. Waite	Hubbardston, Mass	Feb. 11, 1868	74, 261
Card-handles, Machine for finishing	I. S. Waite	Hubbardston, Mass	Mar. 3, 1868	75, 082
Card-holder	W. I. Adams	New York, N. Y	Mar. 17, 1868	75, 507
Card-holder	S. E. Adamson	Philadelphia, Pa	Dec. 28, 1869	98, 327
Card-holder	B. Brower	New York, N. Y	Apr. 30, 1872	126, 259
Card-holder	J. Dean	Worcester, Mass	Aug. 26, 1862	36, 283
Card-holder	C. R. Doane	Brooklyn, N. Y	Dec. 21, 1869	98, 154
Card-holder	P. B. Groat	Hannibal, Mo	Dec. 17, 1872	134, 051
Card-holder	S. L. Hill	Brooklyn, N. Y	Dec. 10, 1867	71, 878
Card-holder	A. A. Marks	New York, N. Y	Sept. 25, 1866	58, 270
Card-holder	W. R. Oatley	Rochester, N. Y	Aug. 24, 1869	94, 127
Card-holder	H. H. Pember	New York, N. Y	May 21, 1867	64, 902
Card-holder	L. A. Roberts	Boston, Mass	Apr. 5, 1864	42, 260
Card-holder	W. H. Ryninger	Baltimore, Md	Oct. 15, 1872	132, 325
Card-holder	E. Stewart	Fort Madison, Iowa	July 18, 1871	117, 120
Card-mount	J. H. Caterson	Philadelphia, Pa	Oct. 21, 1873	143, 878
Card or label holder	E. F. Stephens	Towanda, Pa	May 28, 1867	65, 131
Card or ticket case	C. C. Blakemore	Washington, D. C	June 23, 1868	79, 194
Card, Postal	W. I. Lindlon	Cleveland, Ohio	Dec. 19, 1871	122, 041
Card-press, Cameo	J. R. Smith	Rockville, Canada	Oct. 15, 1872	132, 330
Card-rack	E. D. Averell	New York, N. Y	Nov. 5, 1867	70, 500
Card-rack	J. F. Curtis	Chicago, Ill	Nov. 1, 1870	108, 887
Card-rack	D. A. Danforth and F. M. Winchester.	Elkhart, Ind	May 27, 1873	139, 298
Card-rack	J. J. Gray	Boston, Mass	Jan. 28, 1873	135, 272
Card-rack	J. M. Keep	New York, N. Y	Oct. 2, 1866	58, 428
Card-rack	M. Lepp	Albany, N. Y	July 28, 1868	80, 415
Card-rack	E. R. McKean	Washington, D. C	Nov. 26, 1872	133, 378
Card-rack	G. A. Nelson	Chicago, Ill	Oct. 22, 1867	70, 107
Card-rack	L. H. Olmstead	Brooklyn, N. Y	Mar. 8, 1870	100, 656
Card-rack	L. C. Raindle	Chicago, Ill	Oct. 17, 1871	119, 995
Card-rack	E. Safford	Boston, Mass	Sept. 4, 1866	57, 776
Card-rack	H. R. Van Eps	Peoria, Ill	Apr. 29, 1873	138, 454
Card-rack	C. A. Wall	Grand Rapids, Mich	Oct 17, 1871	120, 134
Card-rack	W. Wendell	Milwaukee, Wis	Sept. 20, 1870	107, 574
Card-rack	C. F. Wilson	Brooklyn, N. Y	Jan. 11, 1870	98, 831
Card, Reading	H. F. Bond	Waltham, Mass	Feb. 28, 1860	27, 266
Card, Reading	B. Snyder	Trenton, N. J	Aug. 19, 1862	36, 242
Card-safe	C. S. Crane	Selma, Alabama	Feb. 18, 1868	74, 509
Card-setting machine	J. Russell	Springfield, Mass	Oct. 8, 1867	69, 769
Card-setting machine	J. Russell	Springfield, Mass	Feb. 25, 1868	74, 853
Card-setting-machine cutter	D. McFarland	Worcester, Mass	Dec. 7, 1869	97, 667
Card-setting machinery	T. A. Dickinson	Worcester, Mass	Mar. 10, 1868	75, 388
Card strapper and grinder	W. H. Chandler	North Scituate, R. I	Mar. 17, 1868	75, 624
Card-stripping machinery	J. F. Foss	Lowell, Mass	May 7, 1872	126, 387
Card-stripping machines, Cam for	S. L. Crockett and B. T. Mills	Lowell, Mass	Apr. 21, 1868	76, 895
Card-stripping mechanism	G. E. Taft	Northbridge, Mass	Apr. 9, 1872	125, 501
Card-stripping mechanism, Traversing cams for	G. E. Taft	Whitinsville, Mass	July 8, 1873	140, 740

Index of patents issued from the United States Patent Office from 1790 to 1873, inclusive—Continued.

Invention.	Inventor.	Residence.	Date.	No.
Card-teeth, Bracing and supporting	C. Speer	New York, N. Y	Nov. 16, 1852	9, 411
Card-teeth-cutting machine	J. Lamb	Leicester, Mass	Aug. 1, 1827	....
Card-teeth for machine-case	J. L. Tuttle	New York, N. Y	Oct. 14, 1856	15, 905
Card-teeth, Machine	W. Montgomery	Roxbury, Mass	June 13, 1854	11, 070
Card-teeth, Machine for grinding	G. Emerson	North Providence, R. I	Dec. 5, 1848	5, 948
Card-teeth, Machine for setting	D. McFarland	Worcester, Mass	June 25, 1867	66, 098
Card-teeth, Machine for sticking	G. W. Coats and J. Russell	Springfield, Mass	Aug. 1, 1854	11, 434
Card-teeth, Process of making and using elastic steel.	E. Jenks	Colebrook, Conn	Nov. 13, 1813	....
Cards and drawing can-hoops, Bending iron	J. Butterworth	Philadelphia County, Pa	July 20, 1831	....
Cards, Apparatus for shuffling and dealing	H. E. Piquet	Sartrouville, France	Oct. 27, 1868	83, 540
Cards, Box for supplying business	W. and W. H. Lewis	New York, N. Y	Nov. 22, 1853	10, 255
Cards, Cleaning machine	G. Wellman	Lowell, Mass	Dec. 6, 1853	10, 298
Cards, Composition for preparing cotton and wool machine.	J. M. Gates	Warren, Mass	Sept. 14, 1815	....
Cards, &c., Cylinder for carrying and supporting	S. R. Parkhurst	West Bloomfield, N. J	Jan. 23, 1849	6, 043
Cards, filleting or cut, prick, and set machine	R. Meriam	Leicester, Mass	May 2, 1831	....
Cards for carding cotton, wool, &c., Manufacture of	G. Taber	Canton, Ohio	Aug. 1, 1838	863
Cards, labels, &c., Method of manufacturing show	A. J. Connell	New York, N. Y	Nov. 3, 1868	83, 763
Cards, Machine for cleaning machine	H. Woodman	Biddeford, Me	Mar. 13, 1860	27, 495
Cards, Machine for grinding and facing	G. Drake	Windsor, Conn	Feb. 28, 1817	....
Cards, Machine for grinding cotton	N. Smith and A. Crandall	North Kingston, R. I	Mar. 14, 1854	10, 643
Cards, Machine for removing wire teeth from	J. A. Baham, R. C. Wilson, and S. French.	Auburn, N. Y	Aug. 4, 1868	80, 586
Cards, Making hand and other	E. L. Sprague	Leicester, Mass	Mar. 30, 1868	76, 111
Cards, Manufacturing machine and animal	W. Wheeler	West Poultney, Vt	July 5, 1859	24, 684
Cards, Manufacturing wool	A. Whittemore		June 5, 1797	....
Cards, Mode of ornamenting show	F. B. Scott	Buffalo, N. Y	Aug. 15, 1865	49, 444
Cards, Playing	H. Billings	Boston, Mass	Aug. 26, 1873	142, 075
Cards, Playing	J. J. Levy	New York, N. Y	Sept. 15, 1868	82, 134
Cards, Playing	J. Stevens	Mount Vernon, N. Y	Sept. 21, 1869	95, 160
Cards, Rub-rolls for condenser	W. Ferguson	Amsterdam, N. Y	Dec. 3, 1872	133, 638
Cards, Scientific playing	C. Goodwin	Chicago, Ill	Feb. 8, 1870	99, 561
Cards, Sliding slate for computation	G. N. Jackson	Chicago, Ill	Aug. 7, 1866	56, 943
Cards, Straining and grinding	J. Boynton	Windham County, Conn	Mar. 30, 1811	....
Cards, Writing and drawing	H. A. Clark and H. J. Griswold	Boston, Mass., and Norwich, Conn.	Aug. 7, 1866	56, 903
Carding and drawing engines, Wool	C. Jackson and J. Movi	Cazenovia, N. Y	Feb. 5, 1850	7, 072
Carding and mixing wool and cotton	S. H. Adams and J. A. Wood	Cohoes, N. Y	June 11, 1850	7, 421
Carding and other machines, Apparatus for feeding wool to.	J. S. Bolette	Gaffontaine Cornesse, Belgium.	Aug. 23, 1864	43, 959
Carding and other machines, Construction of cylinders for.	J. M. Stone	North Andover, Mass	Feb. 21, 1871	111, 988
Carding and other preparing machines, Feeding device for.	E. Pettitt	Manchester, England	Feb. 7, 1871	111, 674
Carding and picking machines, Roller feed for	J. Dempster	Naugatuck, Conn	June 26, 1866	55, 828
Carding and spinning machine, Yarn	M. Chase	Baltimore, Md	Mar. 23, 1842	2, 511
Carding and spinning wool	P. C. Curtis	Paris, N. Y	Oct. 15, 1823	....
Carding and spinning wool by one continued operation, Machine for.	A. Holmes	Pomfret, N. Y	Jan. 8, 1810	....
Carding by which variegated slivers are produced	J. Holmes and E. French	Lee, Mass	May 18, 1852	8, 948
Carding, Composition to be applied before	Z. Parkhurst	Grafton, Mass	Aug. 19, 1826	....
Carding-cylinders, Clothing for	C. G. Sargent and F. A. Calvert	Lowell, Mass	Mar. 9, 1858	19, 585
Carding-cylinders, Machine for cleaning	A. A. Hawley	Methuen, Mass	Aug. 29, 1865	49, 679
Carding-cylinders, Machinery for grinding card-teeth of.	C. Hardy	Biddeford, Me	Feb. 5, 1861	31, 315
Carding-cylinders, Stripper for	F. M. Abbott and E. F. Fields	Boston, Mass., and Lewiston, Me.	Feb. 25, 1868	74, 874
Carding-engine	S. R. and G. W. Ballard	Coldwater, Mich	Mar. 19, 1867	62, 921
Carding-engine	J. Boyd	Philadelphia, Pa	May 24, 1859	24, 092
Carding-engine	J. Boynton	South Coventry, Conn	July 12, 1843	3, 174
Carding-engine	G. Bradley	Paterson, N. J	Nov. 19, 1861	33, 762
Carding-engine	J. and J. Butterworth	Trenton, N. J	Nov. 9, 1869	96, 671
Carding-engine	F. A. Calvert	Lowell, Mass	Sept. 22, 1863	40, 018
Carding-engine	E. C. Cleveland and J. M. Bassett.	Worcester, Mass	Jan. 26, 1869	86, 211
Carding-engine	J. Davis	East Wilton, N. H	Dec. 17, 1861	33, 972
Carding-engine	J. Dyson	Fulton, S. C	Feb. 20, 1849	6, 135
Carding-engine	J. Dyson	Fulton, S. C	Dec. 6, 1859	26, 347
Carding-engine	J. Dyson	Philadelphia, Pa	Sept. 15, 1863	39, 902
Carding-engine	O. F. Fitch	Morristown, Ind	Mar. 12, 1867	62, 830
Carding-engine	J. Fitton	Cavendish, Vt	Dec. 11, 1860	30, 875
Carding-engine	J. Fitton	Cavendish, Vt	Jan. 14, 1862	34, 138
Carding-engine	D. T. Gage	Philadelphia, Pa	Feb. 2, 1864	41, 462
Carding-engine	H. N. Gambril and S. F. Burgee	Woodbury, Md	Sept. 1, 1857	18, 124
Carding-engine	B. H. Jenks	Bridesburgh, Pa	Mar. 2, 1869	87, 342
Carding-engine	D. S. Kimball	Lowell, Mass	Nov. 19, 1861	33, 744
Carding-engine	E. Leigh	Manchester, England	Sept. 26, 1865	50, 211
Carding-engine	H. Marsden and T. H. Blamires	Huddersfield, England	Dec. 5, 1865	51, 333
Carding-engine	T. McQuirk and O. Cole	Millville, Mass	Nov. 20, 1866	59, 919
Carding-engine	H. L. Moulton	Camden, N. J	Oct. 10, 1865	50, 377
Carding-engine	W. K. Platt	Philadelphia, Pa	Sept. 1, 1863	39, 776
Carding-engine	R. Plews	Smithfield, R. I	July 28, 1863	39, 355
Carding-engine	C. Pooley	Charlton-upon-Medlock, England.	Aug. 22, 1846	4, 706
Carding-engine	A. D. Shattuck	Grafton, Mass	Sept. 23, 1856	15, 781
Carding-engine	A. D. Shattuck	Grafton, Mass	Sept. 23, 1856	15, 784
Carding-engine	H. Storms	Ann Arbor, Mich	Nov. 11, 1862	36, 923
Carding-engine	W. H. Walton and G. H. Phinney.	Brooklyn and New York, N. Y.	Sept. 22, 1857	18, 257
Carding-engine	S. Wethered	Baltimore, Md	Aug. 16, 1859	25, 153
Carding-engine	J. C. Whitin	Strothbridge, Mass	July 7, 1863	39, 187
Carding-engine, Condensing	I. Stead	Philadelphia, Pa	Apr. 29, 1862	35, 114
Carding engine, Cotton	W. B. Leonard	Fishkill, N. Y	Sept. 16, 1833	....
Carding-engine doffer	B. D. Wheat	Mount Carmel, Ill	Jan. 19, 1869	85, 975
Carding-engine doffer	R. Lord and L. Hutton	Rittenhouse, Pa	Jan. 31, 1865	46, 120
Carding-engine feeding-attachment	J. Lawton	Glenham, N. Y	Sept. 28, 1869	95, 237

Index of patents issued from the United States Patent Office from 1790 *to* 1873, *inclusive*—Continued.

Invention.	Inventor.	Residence.	Date.	No.
Carding-engine feeding-device	G. Bruce	Corydon, Ind	Dec. 11, 1866	60, 338
Carding-engine feeding-mechanism	A. A. Dow	Glenham, N. Y	Sept. 28, 1869	95, 208
Carding-engine feeding-mechanism	T. Sampson	Wanskuck, R. I	Mar. 24, 1868	75, 798
Carding-engine guide	J. Bachelder	Norwich, Conn	Jan. 28, 1868	73, 866
Carding-engine rack	L. Monroe	Lowell, Mass	Mar. 10, 1868	75, 290
Carding-engine sliver-guide	H. Kent	Lewiston, Me	Feb. 25, 1862	34, 508
Carding-engine winding-frame	W. and J. Leach	New Harmony, Ind	Aug. 25, 1868	81, 514
Carding-engines, Adjusting feed-roller for	L. Holmes	Newton, Mass	Apr. 13, 1869	88, 874
Carding-engines, Apparatus for spinning direct from doffers of.	T. Welham	Philadelphia, Pa	Oct. 23, 1866	59, 106
Carding-engines, Arrangement of the feeding or delivering roller of.	H. Barbour	Lowell, Mass	May 19, 1843	3, 094
Carding-engines, Attaching card-clothing to cylinders of.	D. H. Rowe	Pana, Ill	Dec. 22, 1868	85, 133
Carding-engines, Cleaning cards of	S. Greene	Woonsocket, R. I	Nov. 21, 1854	11, 964
Carding-engines, Cleaning top-flats of	W. H. Walton	New York, N. Y	Dec. 9, 1856	16, 196
Carding-engines, Lifting-flats in self-stripping	B. Dobson and W. Slater	Bolton, England	Aug. 24, 1869	94, 089
Carding-engines, Lubricating the traversing-guide in machines for feeding.	B. S. Roy	Olneyville, R. I	Mar. 8, 1870	100, 671
Carding-engines, Machine for oiling wool for	J. H. Aiken	Norwalk, Ohio	Oct. 30, 1866	59, 308
Carding-engines, Machine for preparing cotton for	R. Pilson	Laurel, Md	Oct. 30, 1866	59, 259
Carding-engines, Machine for spooling wool from the breaker of.	Z. Allen	Providence, R. I	Sept. 10, 1859	1, 316
Carding-engines, Machine for stripping top-flat of	S. L. Crockett and B. T. Mills	Lowell, Mass	Oct. 23, 1866	58, 989
Carding-engines, Machinery for cleaning top-flats of	H. Woodman	Biddeford, Me	July 8, 1856	15, 313
Carding-engines, Machinery for feeding	S. R. Parkhurst	New York, N. Y	Jan. 6, 1863	37, 304
Carding-engines, Machinery for stripping top-flats of.	G. Wellman	Lowell, Mass	Jan. 27, 1857	16, 504
Carding-engines, Means of operating doffer-combs of	A. A. Bennett	Norwalk, Conn	May 29, 1866	55, 046
Carding-engines, Mode of treating wood for manufacture of.	B. H. Jenks	Bridesburgh, Pa	May 29, 1866	55, 111
Carding-engines or preparing cotton, wool, &c., for spinning, Machinery or apparatus for making laps for feeding.	J. Mason	Rochdale, Great Britain	Feb. 10, 1843	2, 947
Carding-engines, Stop-motion for feeding-mechanism of.	W. E. Ainsworth and A. D. Wright.	Lowell, Mass	Mar. 19, 1867	62, 917
Carding-engines, Waste-saver for	C. F. Morrison	Rifton Glen, N. Y	Oct. 27, 1868	83, 526
Carding-engines, Waste-saving attachment to	A. A. Bennett	Norwalk, Conn	Apr. 18, 1865	47, 274
Carding-engines, Wool-oiling apparatus for	P. C. Kirk and M. Pendergast	Lawrence, Mass	Dec. 11, 1866	60, 386
Carding-engines, &c., Wool-oiling machinery for	W. H. Salisbury	Providence, R. I	Oct. 2, 1866	58, 576
Carding fibrous substances, Machine for	H. Wightman	Pittsburgh, Pa	Feb. 12, 1845	3, 904
Carding hair of neat-cattle	W. Shotwell and A. Kinder	New York, N. Y	Nov. 4, 1813	....
Carding-machine	E. Atkinson	Brookline, Mass	June 25, 1872	128, 202
Carding-machine	R. Bartlett	Ripley, Ohio	Oct. 25, 1832	....
Carding-machine	A. A. Bennett and G. Vine	Norwalk, Conn	Jan. 5, 1869	85, 556
Carding-machine	C. Bishop	Newtown, Conn	Sept. 26, 1846	4, 778
Carding-machine	T. G. Boone	Brooklyn, N. Y	Mar. 20, 1849	6, 197
Carding-machine	F. T. Chase and J. H. Platt	Dudley, Mass	June 4, 1872	127, 566
Carding-machine	L. Colburn	Fairfield, Vt	Nov. 20, 1832	....
Carding-machine	J. Davis	East Milton, N. H	Oct. 13, 1857	18, 423
Carding-machine	J. Davis	East Milton, N. H	Feb. 12, 1861	31, 425
Carding-machine	J. Dempster and H. Holcroft	Media, Pa	Nov. 9, 1869	96, 556
Carding-machine	E. French	North Adams, Mass	Apr. 9, 1872	125, 447
Carding-machine	H. N. Gambrill and S. F. Burgee	Woodbury Mills, Md	Feb. 27, 1855	12, 469
Carding-machine	C. S. Goodwin	Springfield, Mass	Mar. 5, 1872	124, 351
Carding-machine	P. S. Haines	Newburgh, N. Y	June 6, 1865	48, 059
Carding-machine	D. W. Hayden	Windham, Conn	Oct. 2, 1849	6, 758
Carding-machine	J. Haythorn and J. Martin	Thompsonville, Conn	Mar. 24, 1868	75, 906
Carding-machine	H. Houghton	Somers, Conn	Apr. 21, 1857	17, 094
Carding-machine	G. Jaquith	Concord, Mass	June 7, 1870	103, 889
Carding-machine	C. Jones	Yonkers, N. Y	May 14, 1872	126, 813
Carding-machine	P. L. King and E. Blasdell	Sparta and Lawrenceburgh Township, Ind.	Oct. 14, 1830	....
Carding-machine	J. McCarty	Somerset, Pa	June 19, 1849	6, 539
Carding-machine	J. McDonald	Detroit, Mich	June 26, 1866	55, 881
Carding-machine	M. W. Obenchain	Springfield, Ohio	July 20, 1846	4, 642
Carding-machine	L. O'Brien	Indianapolis, Ind	Oct. 6, 1863	40, 181
Carding-machine	H. Palmerler	Shoreham, Vt	May 25, 1811	....
Carding-machine	S. H. Parkhurst	Providence, R. I	Oct. 10, 1835	....
Carding-machine	S. R. Parkhurst	West Bloomfield, N. J	June 20, 1848	5, 643
Carding-machine	S. R. Parkhurst	New York, N. Y	May 21, 1861	32, 380
Carding-machine	D. Pheteplace	Lewiston, Me	June 18, 1872	127, 985
Carding-machine	C. E. Price and J. Haythorn	Thompsonville, Conn	Aug. 31, 1858	21, 364
Carding-machine	L. St. George	North Bellingham, Mass	May 28, 1872	127, 199
Carding-machine	D. Tainter	Worcester, Mass	Apr. 18, 1865	47, 345
Carding-machine	D. Tainter	Worcester, Mass	May 9, 1865	47, 668
Carding-machine	E. Thompson	Lowell, Mass	June 9, 1826	....
Carding-machine	G. Thresh	Oxford, Me	Sept. 6, 1870	107, 204
Carding-machine	S. Tillon	Newtown, Conn	Sept. 8, 1827	....
Carding-machine	U. G. Warner	Ripley, Ohio	Oct. 1, 1830	....
Carding-machine	J. Woodard	Portage County, Ohio	May 2, 1821	....
Carding-machine alarm	J. Haythorn and C. E. Price	Thompsonville, Conn	Aug. 18, 1868	81, 084
Carding-machine by gleaning-savers	J. Hugus	Greenbush, Pa	Sept. 15, 1815	....
Carding-machine card	W. Turner, S. Shore, and W. Halliwell.	Rochdale, England	Apr. 24, 1866	54, 270
Carding-machine card	E. Waite	Franklin City, Mass	May 1, 1866	54, 450
Carding-machine cleaner and grinder	L. W. Boynton	Hartford, Conn	Dec. 13, 1870	110, 004
Carding machine, Cloth	J. Jessup	Orange County, N. Y	Feb. 6, 1813	....
Carding-machine condenser, Woolen	L. L. Gowdy	Montgomery, N. Y	Oct. 11, 1841	2, 311
Carding-machine, Condensing	J. C. Shaw	Manayunk, Pa	Jan. 28, 1868	73, 760
Carding machine, Cotton or wool	E. and A. Crane	Lowell, Mass	Jan. 30, 1841	1, 962
Carding machine, Cotton or wool	J. Munroe	Palmer, Mass	Oct. 11, 1841	2, 314
Carding-machine cylinders, Means for securing the clothing on.	H. Bennett	Waterbury, Conn	Nov. 7, 1871	120, 615
Carding-machine doffer	C. Atwood	Middletown, Conn	Nov. 1, 1830	....
Carding-machine doffer-combs, Mechanism for operating.	J. K. Proctor	Philadelphia, Pa	June 24, 1873	140, 304
Carding-machine doffer-stripper	A. M. Comstock	Holden, Mass	Dec. 10, 1872	133, 832

Index of patents issued from the United States Patent Office from 1790 *to* 1873, *inclusive*—Continued.

Invention.	Inventor.	Residence.	Date.	No.
Carding-machine feed-mechanism	W. A. Lawton	Providence, R. I	Nov. 29, 1870	109, 634
Carding-machine feed-roller	H. G. Elsworth	Enfield, Conn	Sept. 4, 1847	5, 272
Carding-machine feeder	G. S. Harwood	Boston, Mass	Nov. 19, 1867	71, 001
Carding-machine feeder, Weighing-attachment for	P. C. Evans and H. J. H. King	Brimscombe, England, and Glasgow, Scotland.	Oct. 4, 1870	107, 890
Carding-machine feeding-apparatus	J. W. Barbour	Winooski Falls, Vt	July 9, 1872	128, 697
Carding-machine feeding-apparatus	D. Tainter	Worcester, Mass	July 30, 1867	67, 226
Carding-machine feeding-device	J. W. Barbour	Winooski Falls, Vt	Sept. 27, 1870	107, 751
Carding-machine feeding-mechanism	W. Clissold	Stroud, England	Apr. 23, 1867	64, 077
Carding-machine feeding-mechanism	B. W. Taugee	Woodville, R. I	Feb. 16, 1869	86, 953
Carding-machine feeding-mechanism	B. W. Taugee	Dorrville, R. I	Feb. 16, 1869	86, 954
Carding-machine for preparing bats for felting	S. G. Blackman	Norwalk, Conn	Feb. 5, 1850	7, 065
Carding-machine grinding-attachment	A. J. Burke	Mansfield, Conn	June 14, 1870	104, 262
Carding-machine guide	F. W. and E. Albertine	Hanover, Conn	June 25, 1867	66, 112
Carding-machine roll	E. S. Worcester	Worcester, Mass	Feb. 20, 1872	123, 968
Carding-machine stripper	L. M. Capron	Worcester, Mass	Nov. 16, 1869	96, 884
Carding-machine teeth	C. Hindle, J. C. Milton, and O. Arnold.	Worcester, Mass	July 23, 1872	129, 662
Carding-machine teeth	W. H Whiting	Wellington, Conn	Sept. 27, 1870	107, 842
Carding-machine to form bats for wool hats	A. Guild	Dedham, Mass	Mar. 31, 1806	....
Carding machine, Wool	J. H. Arnold	Belmont, Ohio	Sept. 25, 1826	....
Carding machine, Wool	C. Atwood	Middletown, Conn	Apr. 18, 1829	....
Carding machine, Wool	D. M. Bacon	Huntingdon, Pa	Sept. 10, 1828	....
Carding machine, Wool	G. Booth	Poughkeepsie, N. Y	Oct. 13, 1812	....
Carding machine, Wool	J. Davis	Wilton, N. H	Aug. 4, 1863	39, 381
Carding machine, Wool	N. Freeman	Lowell, Mass	Dec. 31, 1839	1, 462
Carding machine, Wool	E. Hale, jr., and S. and J. Hale.	Haverhill, Mass	Feb. 18, 1825	....
Carding machine, Wool	F. Nowell	Lowell, Mass	June 3, 1856	15, 016
Carding machine, Wool	S. C. Philbrick	Rockville, Conn	Dec. 3, 1867	71, 784
Carding machine, Wool	J. W. Shankland	Summerfield, Ohio	May 5, 1829	....
Carding machine, Wool	H. A. Shannon	Columbia County, N. Y	Apr. 5, 1828	....
Carding machine, Wool	D. Smith	Philadelphia, Pa	June 14, 1809	....
Carding machine, Wool	D. Tainter	Worcester, Mass	Sept. 29, 1863	40, 131
Carding machines, Apparatus for stripping top-flats of.	E. C. Pfaff	Chemnitz, Saxony	Apr. 4, 1871	113, 339
Carding-machines, Cleaning top-cards of	H. Woodman	Biddeford, Me	Aug. 1, 1854	11, 448
Carding-machines, Composition coating for drawing-rollers for.	B. Borden, G. Townsend, and E. A. Green.	Pawtucket and Lincoln, R. I.	Aug. 20, 1872	130, 694
Carding-machines, Condensing-tube for	W. Germain	Rockbottom, Mass	Sept. 24, 1867	69, 205
Carding-machines, &c., Condensing-tube for	A. W. Skinner	Providence, R. I	Jan. 21, 1873	135, 015
Carding-machines, Construction of	N. Rider	Sturbridge, Mass	Mar. 12, 1825	....
Carding-machines, Dividing-apparatus for condensing.	E. Bede	Verviers, Belgium	May 7, 1872	126, 439
Carding-machines, Machine for drawing and spinning wool, &c., from.	J. Goulding	Worcester, Mass	Oct. 5, 1869	95, 580
Carding-machines, &c., Machine for feeding wool, &c., to.	W. Clissold	Stroud, England	July 20, 1869	92, 705
Carding-machines, Machine for grinding top-cards and the workers, strippers, and licker-in cylinders of.	C. Hardy	Biddeford, Me	Apr. 16, 1867	63, 884
Carding-machines, Machinery for cleaning top-cards of.	H. Woodman	Biddeford, Me	Dec. 1, 1857	18, 787
Carding-machines, Machinery for oiling wool in	J. Eccles	Philadelphia, Pa	May 16, 1865	47, 767
Carding-machines, Machinery for oiling wool in	G. S. Harwood	Boston, Mass	Jan. 31, 1865	46, 104
Carding-machines, Machinery for oiling wool in	J. W. Hussey	Boston, Mass	Jan. 31, 1865	46, 189
Carding-machines, Machinery for oiling wool in	C. Jones	Boston, Mass	July 31, 1866	56, 758
Carding-machines, Machinery for oiling wool in	J. Shinn	Philadelphia, Pa	Jan. 31, 1865	46, 194
Carding-machines, Mechanism for adjusting roller of.	E. Lord	Todmorden, England	Aug. 15, 1871	118, 029
Carding-machines, Mechanism for stripping top-flats of.	F. Morf	Wetzikon, Switzerland	May 10, 1870	102, 851
Carding-machines, Operating condensing-roller in.	E. Stafford	Philadelphia, Pa	Sept. 3, 1867	68, 464
Carding-machines, Self-feed for	R. W. Lewis	Beacon Falls, Conn	Jan. 15, 1867	61, 219
Carding-machines, Stop-mechanism for	C. W. Anderson	Grosvenor Dale, Conn	Mar. 1, 1870	100, 247
Carding-machines, Stripper-carrying frame for	J. F. Foss	Lowell, Mass	May 23, 1871	115, 185
Carding-machines, Stripping top-flats of	G. Wellman	Lowell, Mass	Mar. 18, 1856	14, 481
Carding-machines, Waste-removing device for	G. W. Craner	Darby, Pa	July 15, 1873	140, 814
Carding, Machinery for cutting and preparing flax, &c., for.	J. and C. Beach, T. Beach, and W. G. R. Mowry.	Connecticut, Massachusetts, and Rhode Island.	Aug. 29, 1848	5, 734
Carding, spinning, and roping machine	T. Norton and G. Biddis	Milford, Pa	Apr. 15, 1813	....
Carding wool	J. Boynton	South Coventry, Conn	Apr. 11, 1829	....
Carding wool	J. Boynton	South Coventry, Conn	Mar. 11, 1833	....
Carding wool	L. French	New Haven, Conn	May 18, 1814	....
Carding wool and other fibrous material	C. Wing	Gardiner, Me	Oct. 21, 1830	....
Carding wool, cotton, &c	D. Adams	Richmond, Va	July 27, 1833	....
Cargoes of vessels, Apparatus for removing	J. Manderson and S. Favinger	Philadelphia, Pa	Jan. 9, 1866	52, 001
Carmine, Method of manufacturing	G. A. Siegle	Brooklyn, N. Y	July 16, 1867	66, 897
Carpentering	J. Bailey	Philadelphia, Pa	Apr. 7, 1827	....
Carpenter's bench	J. Jones	Newark, N. J	Jan. 28, 1873	135, 342
Carpenter's bench	R. C. Love	Augusta, Me	Feb. 7, 1871	111, 553
Carpenter's bench	J. W. Mahan	Lexington, Ill	Sept. 16, 1856	15, 739
Carpenter's bench	A. B. Marshall	Medford, Mass	Apr. 9, 1867	63, 645
Carpenter's bench	R. McConnell	Lawrenceville, Pa	Oct. 16, 1866	58, 858
Carpenter's bench	F. Starke	Dayton, Ohio	Sept. 12, 1871	118, 980
Carpenter's bench-clamp	J. E. A. Gibbs	Mill Point, Va	Feb. 17, 1857	16, 642
Carpenter's bench-dog	E. B. McCoy	Winsted, Conn	May 19, 1868	77, 998
Carpenter's bench-gage	F. A. Traut	New Britain, Conn	Nov. 18, 1862	36, 973
Carpenter's bench-hook	S. Swan	New York, N. Y	June 2, 1868	78, 620
Carpenter's bench-hook	C. H. Weston	Lowell, Mass	Feb. 4, 1868	74, 182
Carpenter's bench, Stop for	L. Augur and J. L. Lord	Chester, Conn	May 29, 1849	6, 485
Carpenter's brace and bit fastener	H. Perkins	North Bridgewater, Mass	Nov. 1, 1853	10, 189
Carpenter's bracket, &c., Holding-bolt for	J. W. Kennedy	Plainfield, Conn	Mar. 23, 1858	19, 700
Carpenter's clamp	J. Cadwell	Cincinnati, Ohio	Apr. 24, 1860	27, 968
Carpenter's clamp	B. H. Green	Princeton, N. J	Aug. 9, 1853	9, 917
Carpenter's clamp	C. L. Jones	Richmond, Va	Nov. 27, 1860	30, 705
Carpenter's gage	T. E. Barrow	Mansfield, Ohio	Apr. 13, 1869	88, 833
Carpenter's gage	A. H. Blaisdell	Newton Corners, Mass	June 23, 1868	79, 052
Carpenter's gage	W. Brodhead	Meadville, Pa	Apr. 21, 1868	76, 884

Index of patents issued from the United States Patent Office from 1790 to 1873, inclusive—Continued.

Invention.	Inventor.	Residence.	Date.	No.
Carpenter's gage	O. Brown and T. F. Berry	Capron, Ill	July 7, 1868	79, 632
Carpenter's gage	J. Bryant	Brooklyn, N. Y	Aug. 19, 1856	15, 556
Carpenter's gage	F. W. Coy	Boston, Mass	May 19, 1868	78, 065
Carpenter's gage	B. T. Currier	Boston, Mass	July 11, 1865	48, 663
Carpenter's gage	M. Horton	Brooklyn, N. Y	May 23, 1865	47, 824
Carpenter's gage	G. T. Lape	New York, N. Y	Feb. 5, 1867	61, 840
Carpenter's gage	P. Lawyer	Richmondville, N. Y	Mar. 19, 1867	63, 062
Carpenter's gage	J. McCrum	Locust Grove, Ohio	July 11, 1865	48, 703
Carpenter's gage	G. Miller	Washington, D. C	Jan. 17, 1865	45, 932
Carpenter's gage	G. Miller	Washington, D. C	Oct. 17, 1865	50, 484
Carpenter's gage	R. Phillips	Gardiner, Me	Jan. 15, 1867	61, 248
Carpenter's gage	M. C. Robichau	Marblehead, Mass	July 22, 1873	141, 014
Carpenter's gage	E. Sahm	Greenville, Pa	Nov. 4, 1873	144, 359
Carpenter's gage	D. W. Simmons	Lynn, Mass	May 30, 1871	115, 368
Carpenter's gage	H. P. Sisson	Rutland, Vt	Dec. 27, 1870	110, 596
Carpenter's gage	H. Skinner and W. Greenhalgh	West Farms, N. Y	Aug. 22, 1854	11, 572
Carpenter's gage	J. A. Traut	New Britain, Conn	Oct. 22, 1872	132, 421
Carpenter's gage	J. A. Traut	New Britain, Conn	Aug. 5, 1873	141, 475
Carpenter's implement	E. Gray	Oldtown, Me	Sept. 7, 1869	94, 688
Carpenter's shooting-board	J. Jones	Newark, N. J	Jan. 3, 1871	110, 765
Carpet	J. Cochran, jr	Malden, Mass	Mar. 1, 1870	100, 377
Carpet	G. Crompton	Worcester, Mass	Jan. 31, 1871	111, 325
Carpet	G. Crompton	Worcester, Mass	June 18, 1872	128, 023
Carpet	T. Crossley	Roxbury, Mass	Mar. 16, 1852	8, 798
Carpet	T. Crossley	Bridgeport, Conn	Oct. 12, 1869	95, 775
Carpet	J. Dornan	Philadelphia, Pa	Sept. 9, 1873	142, 681
Carpet	D. Hirschberg	Baltimore, Md	Nov. 16, 1869	96, 915
Carpet	G. Iskiyan	New York, N. Y	Dec. 23, 1873	145, 803
Carpet	R. Scott	Philadelphia, Pa	Sept. 16, 1873	142, 947
Carpet-bag	C. F. Blakslee	Brooklyn, N. Y	Mar. 19, 1867	63, 002
Carpet-bag	N. Groel	Newark, N. J	Nov. 7, 1865	50, 815
Carpet-bag	J. M. Matthews	New York, N. Y	Apr. 12, 1859	23, 596
Carpet-bag	A. J. Robrecht	Newark, N. J	Sept. 22, 1868	82, 352
Carpet-bag	E. A. G. Roulstone	Roxbury, Mass	Oct. 30, 1866	59, 270
Carpet-bag	E. A. G. Roulstone	Roxbury, Mass	Mar. 26, 1867	63, 178
Carpet-bag	E. A. G. Roulstone	Roxbury, Mass	Mar. 26, 1867	63, 179
Carpet-bag	A. Sonnekalb and J. W. Lieb	Newark, N. J	Feb. 27, 1866	52, 902
Carpet-bag	F. J. Thring	New York, N. Y	Jan. 31, 1854	10, 484
Carpet-bag	J. Zepfel	New York, N. Y	June 9, 1857	17, 545
Carpet-bag button and pin	W. Roemer	Newark, N. J	Dec. 28, 1869	98, 300
Carpet-bag catch	G. Crouch	New York, N. Y	Mar. 9, 1869	87, 549
Carpet-bag clasp	J. Sellers and A. L. Pennock	Philadelphia, Pa	May 25, 1840	1, 620
Carpet-bag frame	P. Born	New York, N. Y	July 10, 1866	56, 168
Carpet-bag frame	G. Havell	Newark, N. J	June 5, 1866	55, 290
Carpet-bag frame	F. Herman	Newark, N. J	Feb. 2, 1869	86, 542
Carpet-bag frame	S. Lagowitz	Newark, N. J	July 7, 1863	39, 152
Carpet-bag frame	S. Lagowitz	Newark, N. J	Sept. 13, 1864	44, 202
Carpet-bag frame	A. Sonnekalb and J. W. Lieb	Newark, N. J	Aug. 21, 1866	57, 399
Carpet-bag frame	C. and Z. Walsh	Newark, N. J	Aug. 14, 1866	57, 262
Carpet-bag-frame-bending machine	H. Havell	Newark, N. J	Nov. 10, 1868	83, 852
Carpet-bag frames, &c., Machinery for bending	E. L. Gaylord	Newark, N. J	Dec. 7, 1852	9, 445
Carpet-bag lock	Z. Walsh	Newark, N. J	Jan. 24, 1860	26, 959
Carpet-beater	W. H. Hankinson	New York, N. Y	Oct. 25, 1870	108, 589
Carpet-beater	W. H. Hankinson	New York, N. Y	May 20, 1873	139, 145
Carpet-beater	J. Hothersall	New York, N. Y	Apr. 16, 1872	125, 815
Carpet-beater	J. Hothersall	New York, N. Y	Dec. 17, 1872	134, 059
Carpet-beater	J. Hothersall	New York, N. Y	Sept. 23, 1873	143, 155
Carpet-beater	J. Hothersall and J. Banks	New York, N. Y	July 11, 1871	116, 958
Carpet-beater	S. Jordan	Brooklyn, N. Y	Aug. 17, 1869	93, 718
Carpet-beater	W. G. Mowry and C. Pulis	New York, N. Y	July 1, 1873	140, 525
Carpet-beater	J. W. and W. A. Wheeler	Cleveland, Ohio	Dec. 26, 1871	122, 297
Carpet beater and cleaner	A. Cutler and E. S. Wright	New York, N. Y	Apr. 10, 1860	27, 780
Carpet beater and cleaner	W. H. Hankinson	New York, N. Y	Feb. 12, 1867	61, 029
Carpet beater and cleaner	G. P. Mitchell	Philadelphia, Pa	Sept. 13, 1864	44, 210
Carpet beater and cleaner	A. Stevenson	New York, N. Y	Dec. 14, 1869	97, 824
Carpet beating and brushing machine	W. Peters	Charlestown, Mass	July 31, 1849	6, 618
Carpet-beating machine	J. Harris, jr., and D. Holmes	Roxbury and Chelsea, Mass	Feb. 23, 1858	19, 465
Carpet-beating machine	T. and W. H. Jordan	Brooklyn and New York, N. Y.	Aug. 1, 1871	117, 543
Carpet-beating machine	L. Miner	San Francisco, Cal	Nov. 2, 1869	96, 461
Carpet-binding, Metal	R. P. Johnston	Steubenville, Ohio	Aug. 15, 1871	118, 019
Carpet-cleaner	H. W. Bates	Allston, Mass	July 22, 1873	140, 990
Carpet-cleaner	A. M. George and J. W. Carter	Nashua, N. H., and Brooklyn, N. Y.	June 4, 1861	32, 473
Carpet-cleaner	H. H. Lindhorst	Saint Louis, Mo	Jan. 31, 1871	111, 355
Carpet-cleaner	T. Lüke	Saint Louis, Mo	June 11, 1867	65, 683
Carpet-cleaner	H. L. Nichols	New York, N. Y	May 22, 1860	28, 398
Carpet-cleaner	A. W. Noney	Bridgeport, Conn	Aug. 17, 1858	21, 211
Carpet-cleaner	J. Spaulding	San Francisco, Cal	July 29, 1873	141, 243
Carpet-cleaner	R. Terry and F. W. Hafkemeyer	Chicago, Ill	Oct. 25, 1870	108, 651
Carpet-cleaner	G. W. Young	San Francisco, Cal	Sept. 24, 1867	69, 152
Carpet cleaning and finishing machine	J. Wilkinson, jr	Leeds, England	Apr. 2, 1872	125, 240
Carpet-cleaning machine	G. W. Bishop	Stamford, Conn	May 26, 1868	78, 178
Carpet-cleaning machine	J. C. Craft	Baltimore, Md	Mar. 7, 1871	112, 421
Carpet-cleaning machine	D. A. Drew	Philadelphia, Pa	Jan. 25, 1870	99, 073
Carpet-cleaning machine	W. H. Jordan	New York, N. Y	Apr. 5, 1864	42, 254
Carpet-cleaning machine	H. H. Lindhorst	Saint Louis, Mo	June 14, 1870	104, 171
Carpet-cleaning machine	T. Lüke	Saint Louis, Mo	Mar. 23, 1869	88, 188
Carpet-cleaning machine	W. McArthur	Philadelphia, Pa	Aug. 28, 1866	57, 532
Carpet-cleaning machine	W. McArthur	Philadelphia, Pa	Mar. 16, 1869	87, 952
Carpet-cleaning machine	E. S. Poucher	New York, N. Y	May 25, 1869	90, 390
Carpet-cleaning machine	G. C. Smith and C. T. Story	Boston, Mass	Nov. 12, 1872	132, 927
Carpet-cleaning machine	J. Wentworth	Palatine, N. Y	Nov. 6, 1849	6, 855
Carpet, Device for slitting and looping rags for	L. C. Palmer	Howard, Pa	Nov. 21, 1871	121, 124
Carpet-duster	T. Ferry	Wilmington, Del	Aug. 23, 1870	106, 679
Carpet-duster	J. Rolls	New York, N. Y	Nov. 6, 1860	30, 590
Carpet-fabric, &c	T. Cressley	Bridgeport, Conn	Feb. 27, 1866	52, 825
Carpet-fabric	S. Hunter and W. Kerr	Philadelphia, Pa	July 23, 1872	129, 829

Index of patents issued from the United States Patent Office from 1790 *to* 1873, *inclusive*—Continued.

Invention.	Inventor.	Residence.	Date.	No.
Carpet-fabric	W. Wallace	Philadelphia, Pa	June 14, 1870	104, 232
Carpet fabric, Felted	T. Crossley	Bridgeport, Conn	Oct. 12, 1869	95, 776
Carpet-fastener	W. B. Blaisdell and J. E. Atwood.	Lynn, Mass	Sept. 12, 1865	49, 850
Carpet-fastener	C. B. Browne	Geneseo, Ill	Feb. 18, 1873	135, 884
Carpet-fastener	F. O. Clark	Des Moines, Iowa	Aug. 13, 1872	130, 369
Carpet-fastener	J. C. Craft	Baltimore, Md	Dec. 3, 1872	133, 568
Carpet-fastener	S. Culver	Newark, N. J	Nov. 17, 1857	18, 631
Carpet-fastener	R. De Charms	Philadelphia, Pa	Dec. 21, 1858	22, 354
Carpet-fastener	M. Dewey and I. Phillips	Clarendon, N. Y	Aug. 31, 1858	21, 325
Carpet-fastener	W. Filkins	Lancaster, N. Y	May 25, 1858	20, 341
Carpet-fastener	S. N. French	Fitchburgh, Mass	June 8, 1869	91, 111
Carpet-fastener	J. H. Friederich	Rochester, N. Y	Mar. 6, 1866	52, 985
Carpet-fastener	R. A. Gawler	Concord, N. H	Oct. 23, 1866	59, 002
Carpet-fastener	A. Givandan	Washington, D. C	Apr. 18, 1871	113, 874
Carpet-fastener	M. Gramiss	Waterbury, Conn	Apr. 12, 1859	23, 566
Carpet-fastener	C. Gullmann	Poughkeepsie, N. Y	Sept. 11, 1866	57, 895
Carpet-fastener	C. Gullmann	Poughkeepsie, N. Y	Apr. 9, 1867	63, 718
Carpet-fastener	I. W. Hart and O. Norton	New Britain, Conn	Feb. 11, 1868	74, 352
Carpet-fastener	C. Harting	Washington, D. C	May 7, 1872	126, 456
Carpet-fastener	C. Harting	Washington, D. C	Sept. 30, 1873	143, 238
Carpet-fastener	L. S. Hicks	Omro, Wis	July 9, 1867	66, 588
Carpet-fastener	J. O. Jones	Boston, Mass	June 27, 1865	48, 410
Carpet-fastener	B. D. Kested	Glen, N. Y	Oct. 21, 1873	143, 784
Carpet-fastener	G. G. Noyes	Worcester, Mass	Sept. 20, 1859	25, 519
Carpet-fastener	J. Reynolds	New Britain, Conn	Aug. 31, 1858	21, 365
Carpet-fastener	J. W. Saumenig	Baltimore, Md	Apr. 30, 1872	126, 334
Carpet-fastener	A. M. Smith	New York, N. Y	May 31, 1859	24, 242
Carpet-fastener	J. V. C. Smith	New York, N. Y	June 22, 1869	91, 573
Carpet-fastener	M. D. and S. A. Snyder	Clarendon, N. Y	June 28, 1859	24, 586
Carpet-fastener	M. D. and S. A. Snyder	Clarendon, N. Y	Apr. 16, 1861	32, 089
Carpet-fastener	C. F. Spencer	Rochester, N. Y	Mar. 22, 1859	23, 319
Carpet fastener	J. H. Stanton	Franklin, Ohio	Oct. 11, 1870	108, 200
Carpet-fastener	J. A. Taylor	Cowlesville, N. Y	Apr. 26, 1859	23, 797
Carpet-fastener	T. H. Tyndale	Springfield, Ill	Mar. 16, 1869	87, 991
Carpet-fastener	C. A. Wakefield	Dalton, Mass	Jan. 19, 1858	19, 164
Carpet-fastener	R. W. Walker	Washington, D. C	Apr. 19, 1870	102, 185
Carpet-fastener	W. Weaver	Salem, Ohio	Oct. 30, 1866	59, 298
Carpet-fastener	G. E. West and W. R. Cunningham.	La Fayette, Ind	Oct. 22, 1867	70, 055
Carpet-fastener	A. J. Williams	Seneca Falls, N. Y	Mar. 25, 1873	137, 118
Carpet fastener and protector, Stair	J. Connor, jr	Chicago, Ill	May 26, 1868	78, 263
Carpet fastener, Stair	C. Rice	New York, N. Y	Dec. 27, 1859	26, 617
Carpet-fastening	G. W. Andrews and J. P. Burnham.	Chicago, Ill	Aug. 29, 1865	49, 600
Carpet-fastening	W. Barnan	Deerfield, Mass	Sept. 27, 1864	44, 384
Carpet-fastening	D. N. B. Coffin, jr	Newton, Mass	June 9, 1857	17, 488
Carpet-fastening	S. R. C. Denison	Rochester, N. Y	Aug. 5, 1856	15, 478
Carpet-fastening	G. Gregory	New Haven, Conn	Oct. 15, 1872	132, 282
Carpet-fastening	E. Jackman and E. G. Dunham	Portland, Conn	July 10, 1855	13, 220
Carpet-fastening	W. S. Loughborough	Rochester, N. Y	June 5, 1855	13, 009
Carpet-fastening	J. J. Märki	Chicago, Ill	June 28, 1870	104, 864
Carpet-fastening	J. Matson	Bridgeport, Conn	July 23, 1867	66, 981
Carpet-fastening	F. Miller	New York, N. Y	June 19, 1855	13, 094
Carpet-fastening	W. H. Penrose	Philadelphia, Pa	July 28, 1857	17, 890
Carpet-fastening	J. A. Robbins	Medford, Mass	Mar. 14, 1871	112, 633
Carpet-fastening	R. E. Schroeder	Rochester, N. Y	July 28, 1857	17, 897
Carpet-holder	E. Shopbell	Ashland, Ohio	May 29, 1866	55, 170
Carpet-holder	F. Smith	Alexandersville, Ohio	Feb. 4, 1868	74, 160
Carpet-holder	H. Thayer	Warsaw, N. Y	Apr. 6, 1858	19, 882
Carpet-lining	G. W. Chipman	Melrose, Mass	Dec. 18, 1866	60, 476
Carpet-lining	G. W. Chipman	Boston, Mass	Aug. 11, 1868	80, 913
Carpet-lining	J. F. Fales	Walpole, Mass	Feb. 27, 1866	52, 845
Carpet-lining	W. Fuzzard	Chelsea, Mass	Apr. 23, 1867	64, 092
Carpet-lining	J. R. Harrington	New York, N. Y	Apr. 23, 1861	32, 134
Carpet-lining	J. R. Harrington	Brooklyn, N. Y	Sept. 27, 1870	107, 682
Carpet-lining	J. R. Harrington	Brooklyn, N. Y	Apr. 18, 1871	113, 765
Carpet-lining machine	J. R. Harrington	Brooklyn, N. Y	July 29, 1873	141, 270
Carpet lining	M. A. Johnson	Lowell, Mass	June 18, 1867	65, 814
Carpet-lining	J. C. Mayall	Boston, Mass	Jan. 31, 1871	111, 465
Carpet-lining	M. Mayall	Roxbury, Mass	Sept. 15, 1868	82, 236
Carpet-linings, &c., Fabric for	J. L. Kendall and R. H. Trested	Foxborough, Mass., and New York, N. Y.	May 17, 1870	103, 198
Carpet-linings, Machine for folding	J. C. Mayall	Boston, Mass	June 27, 1871	116, 467
Carpet-linings, Machine for making	J. Foster, jr., and F. J. Dill	Camden, N. J., and Foxborough, Mass.	Feb. 9, 1869	86, 830
Carpet-linings, Machine for making	J. R. Harrington	Dayton, Ohio	Apr. 1, 1856	14, 585
Carpet-linings, Machine for making	J. R. Harrington	New York, N. Y	Sept. 11, 1860	29, 970
Carpet-linings, Machine for making	J. R. Harrington	Brooklyn, N. Y	Jan. 2, 1872	122, 381
Carpet-linings, Machine for manufacture of paper	C. A. Pease	Astoria, N. Y	Jan. 17, 1871	111, 081
Carpet-linings, Machine for manufacturing	E. H. Bailey	Brooklyn, N. Y	Sept. 23, 1873	143, 053
Carpet-linings, Manufacture of	S. M. Allen	Boston, Mass	Feb. 24, 1863	37, 728
Carpet-linings, Manufacture of	J. R. Harrington	Brooklyn, N. Y	July 23, 1867	67, 018
Carpet-linings, Manufacture of	W. A. Mauran	Providence, R. I	Aug. 2, 1870	105, 960
Carpet matting or lining	P. Sweeny	New York, N. Y	Oct. 15, 1872	131, 333
Carpet nails or tacks	W. P. Patton	Harrisburgh, Pa	May 19, 1863	38, 598
Carpet pad, Stair	G. W. Chipman	Melrose, Mass	Apr. 3, 1866	53, 573
Carpet, Printed	T. Crossley	Roxbury, Mass	Aug. 16, 1853	9, 935
Carpet, Printed piled	T. Crossley	Bridgeport, Conn	June 10, 1873	139, 706
Carpet-printing block	T. Crossley	Bridgeport, Conn	Aug. 16, 1870	106, 468
Carpet-printing machine	T. Crossley	Bridgeport, Conn	Oct. 12, 1869	95, 777
Carpet-protector	H. W. Eskildson	Boston, Mass	July 11, 1871	116, 822
Carpet-rag cutter	W. Eberhard	Akron, Ohio	Sept. 13, 1870	107, 236
Carpet-rag cutter and looper, Combined	S. P. Converse	Greenville, Ohio	July 9, 1872	128, 857
Carpet-rag looper	G. W. Ansley	Marengo Township, Mich	July 9, 1872	128, 774
Carpet-rag looper	W. Bollinger	Millerstown, Pa	Sept. 17, 1872	131, 420
Carpet-rag looper	W. Clayton, jr	Bristol, Conn	July 15, 1873	140, 869
Carpet-rag looper	J. F. Cooper	Frankton, Ind	Dec. 2, 1873	145, 094

Index of patents issued from the United States Patent Office from 1790 to 1873, inclusive—Continued.

Invention.	Inventor.	Residence.	Date.	No.
Carpet-rag looper	F. J. Egger	Springfield, Ohio	Sept. 16, 1873	142, 778
Carpet-rag looper	G. L. Price	Clifton Springs, N. Y	Feb. 2, 1869	86, 445
Carpet-rag looper and button-hole cutter, Combined.	G. W. Morris and W. Lenhart.	Corry, Pa	Nov. 11, 1873	144, 472
Carpet-rag looper, button-hole cutter, and press-board combined.	S. M. Whitten	Algansee, Mich	Mar. 11, 1873	136, 633
Carpet-rod	H. Thry	New York, N. Y	Feb. 9, 1869	86, 714
Carpet-sack	A. Rose	Bath, N. Y	Jan. 22, 1867	61, 467
Carpet, Stamped paper	F. Guy	Baltimore, Md	Feb. 23, 1819	....
Carpet-stretcher	H. Blan	Washington, D. C	Feb. 2, 1858	19, 230
Carpet-stretcher	W. A. Boles	Shelbyville, Ind	Aug. 5, 1873	141, 418
Carpet-stretcher	J. H. Bosworth	Bath, Me	Dec. 18, 1866	60, 469
Carpet-stretcher	J. Boyd	Lowell, Mass	Dec. 19, 1865	51, 545
Carpet-stretcher	I. W. Bragg	Cincinnati, Ohio	Feb 15, 1859	22, 930
Carpet-stretcher	W. Brown	New York, N. Y	Feb. 9, 1869	86, 728
Carpet-stretcher	E. W. Bullard	Barre, Mass	May 28, 1872	127, 303
Carpet-stretcher	W. P. D. Claybrook	Palmyra, Mo	Jan. 30, 1872	123, 239
Carpet-stretcher	F. J. Collier	Cannonsburgh, Pa	Mar. 21, 1865	46, 882
Carpet-stretcher	W. C. Conant	New York, N. Y	Oct. 5, 1858	21, 654
Carpet-stretcher	S. G. Dare	New York, N. Y	Aug. 11, 1868	80, 925
Carpet-stretcher	J. H. De Poe	Boonton, N. J	Aug. 22, 1871	118, 214
Carpet-stretcher	A. L. Dunbar	Sheldon, Ill	Jan. 14, 1868	73, 310
Carpet-stretcher	G. O. Dunlap	Chicopee, Mass	Feb. 12, 1867	61, 928
Carpet-stretcher	S. Elliott	Sonora, Cal	Aug. 1, 1871	117, 528
Carpet-stretcher	A. C. Ellis	Birmingham, Mich	July 23, 1872	129, 802
Carpet-stretcher	L. Frankhauser	Columbus, Ohio	Jan. 14, 1873	134, 873
Carpet-stretcher	C. E. Gale	Aurelius, N. Y	Jan. 31, 1871	111, 337
Carpet-stretcher	J. B. Greenalgh	Providence, R. I	Jan. 19, 1869	85, 925
Carpet-stretcher	J. S. Green and T. D. Bradt	Watertown, N. Y	May 6, 1873	138, 560
Carpet-stretcher	G. S. Greenleaf and C. Buckland.	Springfield, Mass	Feb. 12, 1861	31, 383
Carpet-stretcher	H. M. Hartshorn	Malden, Mass	June 26, 1860	28, 858
Carpet-stretcher	N. Hill	Caton, N. Y	Feb. 14, 1865	46, 357
Carpet-stretcher	H. Hungerford	New York, N. Y	Oct. 16, 1866	58, 831
Carpet-stretcher	H. Hungerford	New York, N. Y	Jan. 29, 1867	61, 663
Carpet-stretcher	W. J. Johnson	Newton, Mass	Feb. 19, 1867	62, 138
Carpet-stretcher	J. Kally	Canton, Ohio	Oct. 23, 1866	59, 129
Carpet-stretcher	P. Kelly	New York, N. Y	Apr. 29, 1873	138, 333
Carpet-stretcher	C. A. Lindner	Cincinnati, Ohio	Oct. 9, 1866	58, 653
Carpet-stretcher	J. Lindsay	New York, N. Y	May 14, 1872	126, 818
Carpet-stretcher	J. Lindsay	New York, N. Y	Aug. 5, 1873	141, 446
Carpet-stretcher	J. Luther	Buchanan, Mich	Nov. 11, 1873	144, 464
Carpet-stretcher	J. B. Martindale	Newcastle, Ind	Dec. 4, 1866	60, 216
Carpet-stretcher	C. S. McRobert	Plymouth, Mich	Feb. 4, 1868	73, 986
Carpet-stretcher	H. A. Mead	Cuba, N. Y	July 25, 1865	48, 968
Carpet-stretcher	A. F. Michael and H. N. Duncan.	Lockport, N. Y	July 1, 1873	140, 522
Carpet-stretcher	W. Minster	Washington, D. C	July 28, 1868	80, 495
Carpet-stretcher	G. Mosman	Chicopee, Mass	Jan. 2, 1866	51, 853
Carpet-stretcher	G. Mosman	Chicopee, Mass	May 14, 1867	64, 788
Carpet-stretcher	G. G. Mudge	Pittsburgh, Ind	July 18, 1865	48, 829
Carpet-stretcher	S. Pennock	Geneva, Ill	Jan. 5, 1869	85, 690
Carpet-stretcher	H. Powelson	New Brunswick, N. J	Sept. 23, 1873	143, 032
Carpet-stretcher	D. Pray	Boston, Mass	June 4, 1872	127, 515
Carpet-stretcher	A. S. Richards	Montgomery County, Md	Nov. 1, 1870	108, 938
Carpet-stretcher	H. Ridley	Hartford, Conn	Aug. 24, 1858	21, 303
Carpet-stretcher	W. A. Robinson	Grand Rapids, Mich	Oct. 22, 1867	70, 023
Carpet-stretcher	C. Rückert	New York, N. Y	Jan. 26, 1869	86, 253
Carpet-stretcher	E. P. Shaffer	Rochester, N. Y	Apr. 25, 1871	114, 053
Carpet-stretcher	N. K. Shelton	Wabash, Ind	Feb. 25, 1873	136, 339
Carpet-stretcher	L. B. Southworth	Deep River, Conn	Apr. 7, 1868	76, 355
Carpet-stretcher	S. Stevenson	Dansville, N. Y	Nov. 3, 1868	83, 741
Carpet-stretcher	G. W. Story	Kansas City, Mo	Apr. 5, 1870	101, 677
Carpet-stretcher	T. B. Stout	Keyport, N. J	June 8, 1869	91, 179
Carpet-stretcher	W. W. Taylor	Newark, N. J	July 9, 1867	66, 649
Carpet-stretcher	C. Terry	Saint Louis, Mo	Apr. 29, 1873	138, 470
Carpet-stretcher	H. N. Tucker	Stoughton, Mass	Dec. 3, 1872	133, 552
Carpet-stretcher	E. W. Twing	Springfield, Mass	June 26, 1866	55, 935
Carpet-stretcher	O. Vanorman	Fon du Lac, Wis	Sept. 10, 1872	131, 196
Carpet-stretcher	O. Vanorman	Fon du Lac, Wis	Apr. 8, 1873	137, 739
Carpet-stretcher	I. P. Warner	Marengo, Ill	Aug. 13, 1867	67, 690
Carpet-stretcher	J. Warner	New Britain, Conn	Mar. 9, 1858	19, 596
Carpet-stretcher	J. W. Weatherby	Kingsville, Ohio	Oct. 18, 1853	10, 143
Carpet-stretcher	W. Weaver	Salem, Ohio	Apr. 30, 1867	64, 387
Carpet-stretcher	W. Wheeler	West Poultney, Vt	Oct. 18, 1859	25, 858
Carpet-stretcher	D. White	Normal, Ill	Apr. 1, 1873	137, 522
Carpet-stretcher	T. Wilson and J. W. Appleyard	Chicago, Ill	Apr. 20, 1869	89, 107
Carpet-stretcher	E. Wood	Monson, Mass	Aug. 12, 1862	36, 187
Carpet stretcher and hammer	F. M. Osborn	Dover Plains, N. Y	May 29, 1866	55, 154
Carpet stretcher and holder	J. S. Munger	Olean, N. Y	June 11, 1867	65, 686
Carpet stretcher and nailer	E. S. Wheeler	Westport, Conn	June 15, 1869	91, 392
Carpet-stretcher and tack-driver	W. Brown	Springfield, Mass	Feb. 5, 1867	61, 803
Carpet-stretcher and tack-driver	W. Brown	New York, N. Y	July 30, 1867	67, 159
Carpet-stretcher and tack-hammer, Combined	W. Brown	New York, N. Y	Aug. 8, 1871	117, 735
Carpet-stretcher and tack-holder	F. Ashley	New York, N. Y	Oct. 16, 1866	58, 751
Carpet-stretcher and tack-holder	F. W. Judd	New Britain, Conn	Dec. 14, 1869	97, 929
Carpet-stretcher and tack-holder	R. M. Mansur	Augusta, Me	June 23, 1868	79, 242
Carpet stretcher and tacker	J. K. Bancroft and R. C. Bache.	Philadelphia, Pa	May 24, 1870	103, 410
Carpet stretcher and tacker	Z. A. Ward	Pittsfield, Mass	Dec. 16, 1873	145, 604
Carpet-stretcher, tack driver and puller combined.	L. Colby and J. D. Gilman	Morrissville, Vt., and Boston, Mass.	Jan. 19, 1869	85, 908
Carpet-stretcher, tack-holder, and nail-puller, Combined.	H. C. Velie	Poughkeepsie, N. Y	Aug. 20, 1872	130, 774
Carpet-sweeper	J. B. Baker	Syracuse, N. Y	July 27, 1869	92, 929
Carpet-sweeper	W. G. Budlong	Hartford, Conn	May 24, 1859	24, 176
Carpet-sweeper	A. C. Carey	Ipswich, Mass	Oct. 19, 1858	21, 815
Carpet-sweeper	J. H. Crane	Charlestown, Mass	Aug. 16, 1859	25, 099
Carpet-sweeper	H. Davis	Bethlehem, Conn	May 24, 1859	24, 103

Index of patents issued from the United States Patent Office from 1790 *to* 1873, *inclusive*—Continued.

Invention.	Inventor.	Residence.	Date.	No.
Carpet-sweeper	J. Edson	Boston, Mass	Oct. 5, 1858	21, 660
Carpet-sweeper	J. Edson	Boston, Mass	Apr. 5, 1859	23, 526
Carpet-sweeper	J. Edson	Boston, Mass	Aug. 16, 1859	25, 104
Carpet-sweeper	D. C. Hall	Hannibal, Mo	July 11, 1871	116, 833
Carpet-sweeper	D. Harris	Boston, Mass	Oct. 5, 1858	21, 673
Carpet-sweeper	H. H. Herrick	East Boston, Mass	Aug. 17, 1858	21, 233
Carpet-sweeper	H. H. Herrick	East Boston, Mass	Sept. 6, 1859	25, 332
Carpet-sweeper	D. Hess	West Union, Iowa	July 10, 1860	29, 077
Carpet-sweeper	R. C. Higgins	Boston, Mass	May 9, 1871	114, 680
Carpet-sweeper	R. C. Higgins and A. Fuller	Boston, Mass	Nov. 16, 1869	96, 807
Carpet-sweeper	W. Miller	Boston, Mass	June 24, 1873	140, 293
Carpet-sweeper	H. A. Palmer and A. H. Spencer.	Hingham and Boston, Mass	Dec. 30, 1873	146, 016
Carpet-sweeper	N. B. Pratt	Deep River, Conn	Feb. 8, 1859	22, 890
Carpet-sweeper	N. B. Pratt	Deep River, Conn	Feb. 15, 1859	22, 975
Carpet-sweeper	S. F. Pratt	Roxbury, Mass	Jan. 18, 1859	22, 671
Carpet-sweeper	G. Purrington, jr., and J. H. Purrington.	New York, N. Y., and Mattapoisett, Mass.	Jan. 1, 1867	60, 785
Carpet-sweeper	S. P. Rowell	Reading, Mass	Oct. 5, 1858	21, 701
Carpet-sweeper	R. Shaler	Madison, Conn	Sept. 7, 1858	21, 451
Carpet-sweeper	G. F. Taylor	New York, N. Y	July 6, 1869	92, 226
Carpet-sweeper	O. H. Weed	Boston, Mass	May 18, 1869	90, 211
Carpet-sweeper	O. H. Weed	Boston, Mass	May 30, 1871	115, 399
Carpet-sweeper	F. O. Willey and D. B. McEnery.	La Fayette, Ind	Apr. 2, 1872	125, 369
Carpet-sweeper, Fan	A. C. Carey	Lynn, Mass	Jan. 4, 1859	22, 488
Carpet-sweeper guard	A. J. Knight	New York, N. Y	May 24, 1870	103, 344
Carpet-sweepers, Driving-gear wheel for	A. J. Knight	Brooklyn, N. Y	July 12, 1870	105, 223
Carpet-sweeping machines, Guard for	G. F. Taylor	New York, N. Y	Sept. 29, 1868	82, 566
Carpet-sweeping machines, Gear for	G. F. Taylor	New York, N. Y	June 7, 1870	103, 939
Carpet-sweeping machines, Gear for	G. F. Taylor	New York, N. Y	Aug. 16, 1870	106, 429
Carpet-tacks	T. A. Mitchell	Washington, D. C	Mar. 29, 1870	101, 374
Carpet-tacking machine	F. H. Staffer	Philadelphia, Pa	Apr. 26, 1870	102, 331
Carpet to floor, Securing	E. Jackman	Portland, Conn	Dec. 12, 1854	12, 061
Carpet-underlie	N. Edwards	Jericho, Vt	July 26, 1870	105, 661
Carpet-wadding	T. H. Dunham	Boston, Mass	May 1, 1866	54, 312
Carpet-wadding	T. H. Dunham	Boston, Mass	Apr. 23, 1867	64, 084
Carpet-wadding	E. Waite	Franklin, Mass	July 9, 1867	66, 539
Carpet, washing, scouring, and fulling cloth and working hat-bodies, Machine for making wool or fur.	H. Stayton	Lockport, N. Y	Nov. 25, 1829	....
Carpet, Woolen	W. Harrington	Harrison, N. Y	June 11, 1829	....
Carpets and other fabrics from jute, flax, &c., Manufacture of.	T. Crossley	Bridgeport, Conn	Jan. 21, 1868	73, 512
Carpets and rugs, Manufacture of double-pile	J. Goulding	Worcester, Mass	Jan. 20, 1857	16, 437
Carpets and rugs, Manufacturing	J. G. McNair	West Farms, N. Y	Oct. 24, 1854	11, 834
Carpets, chests, drawers, wardrobes, &c., Aromatic lining for.	J. M. Perkins	Plainfield, N. J	Apr. 7, 1868	76, 342
Carpets, Compound for cleaning	L. Marks	Cincinnati, Ohio	Dec. 27, 1870	110, 481
Carpets, coverlids, diapers, &c., Weaving	E. Meily, jr., and J. and S. Mellinger.	Lebanon, Pa	Mar. 1, 1834	....
Carpets, Fabric for underlaying	W. S. Pratt	Brooklyn, N. Y	Nov. 14, 1856	16, 036
Carpets, Finishing	S. Fay	Lowell, Mass	Oct. 23, 1855	13, 702
Carpets, Flooring or dust-rack for	G. J. Colby	Waterbury, Vt	July 25, 1865	48, 907
Carpets, Implement for slitting and joining rags for	J. Beal	Port Gibson, N. Y	Aug. 10, 1869	93, 514
Carpets, Implement for slitting and joining rags for	M. Green	Coldwater, Mich	Apr. 25, 1871	114, 001
Carpets, Implement for slitting and looping rags for	D. A. Russell	Windham, Ohio	Feb. 21, 1871	111, 977
Carpets, Machine for sizing backs of	H. G. Thompson	New York, N. Y	Oct. 21, 1862	36, 738
Carpets, Making ingrain	J. and N. Haight	New York, N. Y	Aug. 12, 1820	....
Carpets, Making ingrain	D. B. Kerr	New York, N. Y	Sept. 23, 1856	15, 767
Carpets, Making ingrain	W. A. Prince	New York, N. Y	Feb. 12, 1823	....
Carpets, Making woolen	W. Harrington	Harrison, N. Y	Mar. 3, 1829	....
Carpets, Manufacture of	H. A. Clark	Boston, Mass	Sept. 2, 1873	142, 439
Carpets, Manufacturing	J. G. McNair	West Farms, N. Y	Aug. 7, 1855	13, 395
Carpets, Manufacturing two-ply	T. Crossley	Boston, Mass	Aug. 22, 1854	11, 564
Carpets, Manufacturing two and three ply	A. Smith	West Farms, N. Y	Dec. 10, 1850	7, 825
Carpets, Slitting and joining rags for	B. F. Cady	Chittenango, N. Y	Jan. 25, 1870	99, 154
Carpets, Taking figures of ingrain	W. Sherwood	Somersworth, N. H	Apr. 20, 1830	....
Carpets, Tool for laying and stretching	F. Cist, W. Kossak, and W. H. Godfrey.	Saint Louis, Mo	June 12, 1860	28, 650
Carpets, Weaving Brussels and other pile	J. B. Buzzell	Clinton, Mass	Aug. 22, 1871	118, 338
Carpeting and embossed matting, India-rubber	J. H. Cheever	New York, N. Y	Apr. 12, 1870	101, 823
Carpeting and rugs, Manufacture of	J. Humphries	New York, N. Y	Dec. 10, 1838	1, 028
Carpeting, Felt for	A. Byington	Herkimer, N. Y	May 6, 1829	....
Carriage	B. F. Adams	Bangor, Me	Aug. 17, 1869	93, 791
Carriage	R. W. Benedict	Brant, N. Y	June 10, 1856	15, 097
Carriage	C. Brown	Adrian, Mich	Nov. 10, 1868	83, 917
Carriage	S. C. Brown and L. J. Hicks	Macedon, N. Y	July 17, 1837	279
Carriage	C. T. Bush	Rensselaerville, N. Y	Apr. 3, 1866	53, 563
Carriage	J. S. Cisco	Xenia, Ohio	Aug. 28, 1855	13, 487
Carriage	I. A. Clippinger	Newton, Iowa	Nov. 16, 1869	96, 887
Carriage	L. W. Coe	Auburn, Me	Feb. 20, 1872	123, 869
Carriage	G. R. Comstock	Manheim, N. Y	Jan. 23, 1855	12, 272
Carriage	C. Conderman	Hornellsville, N. Y	June 18, 1867	65, 876
Carriage	L. D. Cowles	Armada, Mich	Jan. 21, 1862	34, 197
Carriage	J. W. Crannell	Olivet, Mich	Jan. 6, 1857	16, 353
Carriage	J. Curtis	Cincinnati, Ohio	Mar. 26, 1867	63, 223
Carriage	J. Curtis	Cincinnati, Ohio	Oct. 3, 1871	119, 579
Carriage	H. E. Delessert	Paris, France	Aug. 12, 1873	141, 704
Carriage	C. N. Dennett	Amesbury, Mass	Nov. 15, 1870	109, 189
Carriage	J. L. Dolson	Charlotte, Mich	May 25, 1869	90, 351
Carriage	G. B. Durkee	Alden, N. Y	May 27, 1851	8, 118
Carriage	G. W. Ether and S. A. Sperry	Ann Arbor, Mich	Sept. 4, 1860	29, 866
Carriage	E. and C. Everett, jr	Washington, D. C	Dec. 17, 1850	7, 835
Carriage	T. A. and A. F. Fisher	Beardstown, Ill	Apr. 30, 1867	64, 299
Carriage	A. W. Forwood	Scott County, Ky	Mar. 27, 1847	5, 034

Index of patents issued from the United States Patent Office from 1790 *to* 1873, *inclusive*—Continued.

Invention.	Inventor.	Residence.	Date.	No.
Carriage	J. Fox	Manchester, N. J	Aug. 10, 1852	9, 183
Carriage	E. Frauer	Cobleskill, N. Y	Mar. 1, 1864	41, 765
Carriage	D. Freeman	Burford, Canada	Oct. 21, 1856	15, 923
Carriage	J. Gale, M. B. Ames, and F. Blaisdale.	Lawrence, Mass	Oct. 8, 1867	69, 559
Carriage	L. Glesenkamp	Pittsburgh, Pa	Apr. 15, 1873	137, 914
Carriage	S. P. Graham	Columbus, Ohio	Sept. 13, 1870	107, 360
Carriage	A. S. Grant	Waupun, Wis	May 17, 1864	42, 760
Carriage	C. H. Guard	Toronto, Canada	Feb. 21, 1871	111, 928
Carriage	B. Hale	Newburyport, Mass	Oct. 4, 1817	....
Carriage	G. W. Ham	Parsonfield, Me	Sept. 13, 1870	107, 252
Carriage	J. C. Ham	New York, N. Y	July 27, 1869	92, 964
Carriage	N. L. Hatch	Cape Elizabeth, Me	Dec. 22, 1868	85, 093
Carriage	J. Hatfield	Cleveland, Ohio	June 18, 1867	65, 910
Carriage	G. L. Haussknecht	New Haven, Conn	Dec. 16, 1851	8, 588
Carriage	J. R. Hiller	Woodland, Cal	Aug. 30, 1870	106, 817
Carriage	E. Hitt	Katonah, N. Y	Feb. 18, 1868	74, 689
Carriage	M. G. Hubbard	New York, N. Y	July 24, 1855	13, 311
Carriage	S. Jackson	Newark, N. J	Apr. 6, 1869	88, 637
Carriage	J. Jones	Clyde, N. Y	Jan. 14, 1851	7, 906
Carriage	C. P. Kimball	Portland, Me	Nov. 15, 1864	45, 050
Carriage	J. T. Kimball	Kennebunk, Me	July 22, 1845	4, 121
Carriage	L. King	Madison, N. Y	Dec. 23, 1851	8, 609
Carriage	T. Knox	Snickersville, Va	Mar. 15, 1828	....
Carriage	L. Kutscher	New York, N. Y	Nov. 27, 1866	60, 016
Carriage	L. W. Mason	Shelburne Falls, Mass	Apr. 11, 1865	47, 211
Carriage	J. R. McAlister	Heuvelton, N. Y	July 13, 1869	92, 536
Carriage	H. Moon	Red Creek, N. H	Mar. 3, 1868	75, 183
Carriage	J. H. Moore	Warren, Mass	Apr. 9, 1867	63, 739
Carriage	G. H. and E. Morgan	Edgware Road, England	Nov. 6, 1866	59, 525
Carriage	G. H. and E. Morgan	Edgware Road, England	Nov. 6, 1866	59, 526
Carriage	J. J. Morris	New Bedford, N. J	Aug. 28, 1866	57, 548
Carriage	E. C. Newton	Batavia, Ill	Nov. 28, 1871	121, 295
Carriage	W. Ottmann	New York, N. Y	Nov. 26, 1872	133, 475
Carriage	T. B. Patten	West Amesbury, Mass	Jan. 28, 1873	135, 287
Carriage	J. Patterson	Franklinsville, N. Y	Apr. 16, 1850	7, 290
Carriage	B. Peck	Philadelphia, Pa	July 5, 1814	....
Carriage	T. W. and H. K. Porter	Boston, Mass	Mar. 24, 1868	75, 973
Carriage	U. Reynolds	New York, N. Y	May 1, 1866	54, 410
Carriage	E. Robbins	Worcester, Mass	Apr. 18, 1865	47, 334
Carriage	E. Robbins	Worcester, Mass	June 20, 1865	48, 310
Carriage	J. Rock	Hastings, England	Sept. 17, 1867	68, 904
Carriage	W. Ross	New York, N. Y	Jan. 14, 1809	....
Carriage	J. L. Rowley	Steuben County, Ind	June 13, 1854	11, 085
Carriage	J. S. Royce	Leicester, N. Y	May 8, 1847	5, 107
Carriage	C. W. Saladee	Saint Catharine's, Canada	Oct. 17, 1871	120, 106
Carriage	B. E. Sampson	Boston, Mass	Oct. 25, 1864	44, 826
Carriage	A. Searls	San Francisco, Cal	Dec. 10, 1867	72, 191
Carriage	I. M. Singer	New York, N. Y	Oct. 25, 1859	25, 920
Carriage	E. Soper	New York, N. Y	Dec. 3, 1867	71, 805
Carriage	J. C. Spencer	Phelps, N. Y	May 27, 1851	8, 120
Carriage	L. Theobald	Bremen, Ind	Dec. 28, 1869	98, 443
Carriage	C. Thomas	Boston, Mass	Dec. 27, 1870	110, 606
Carriage	C. Thomas	Boston, Mass	Apr. 4, 1871	113, 705
Carriage	L. H. Thomas	Waterbury, Vt	May 10, 1864	42, 700
Carriage	G. K. Tichenor	Wayland, N. Y	Sept. 2, 1873	142, 531
Carriage	S. Titcomb	Amesbury, Mass	Aug. 18, 1868	81, 227
Carriage	J. D. Van Hoevenbergh	Kingston, N. Y	Nov. 27, 1866	60, 093
Carriage	J. D. Van Hoevenbergh	Kingston, N. Y	May 26, 1868	78, 340
Carriage	M. S. Watkins	Somerville, Tenn	June 25, 1850	7, 467
Carriage	F. M. Watson	Columbia, Tenn	July 22, 1873	141, 190
Carriage	J. Whitehead	Ames Station, Iowa	July 28, 1868	80, 377
Carriage	E. S. Wicklin and J. D. Weaver	Carlinville, Ill	Sept. 4, 1860	29, 931
Carriage	J. B. Withey	Chicago, Ill	Sept. 24, 1872	131, 728
Carriage	C. B. Wood	New York, N. Y	May 14, 1861	32, 327
Carriage, Ambulance	T. Wilkins	Greenville, Ill	Nov. 22, 1864	45, 200
Carriage and buggy top bow-irons	G. and A. Woeber	Davenport, Iowa	Oct. 15, 1867	69, 885
Carriage and car axle	S. Coleman	Mount Pleasant, Va	Mar. 2, 1836	....
Carriage and car axles, Oiling	W. Kenworthy and J. H. Pollitt	Buchanan, Pa	Dec. 7, 1869	97, 651
Carriage and car wheel	A. F. Cooper	San Francisco, Cal	May 31, 1870	103 573
Carriage and car wheel and axle-box	J. A. Maynard	Newtonville, Mass	July 12, 1870	105, 228
Carriage and cart boxes, Casting	C. Darby	Worcester, Mass	Jan. 22, 1825	....
Carriage and cradle, Child's	C. W. Higgins	Waukesha, Wis	Nov. 5, 1867	70, 566
Carriage and gig springs, Connecting	A. Davis	Easton, Md	Mar. 18, 1835	....
Carriage and harness, Wheel	G. Barnard	United States	May 25, 1838	748
Carriage and machinery when wheel is used	Williams and Wing	Hartford, Conn	May 16, 1835	....
Carriage and other vehicle wheel	A. F. Cooper	San Francisco, Cal	Feb. 15, 1870	99, 851
Carriage and perambulator handle, Child's	W. E. Crandall	New York, N. Y	Aug. 2, 1870	106, 033
Carriage and railway-car spring	H. Gardiner	New York, N. Y	Jan. 3, 1860	26, 668
Carriage and sleigh combined	J. S. Drake	New York, N. Y	Aug. 3, 1869	93, 184
Carriage and sleigh top	D. K. Hickok	Morrisville, Wis	Mar. 24, 1868	75, 908
Carriage and velocipede, Baby	J. Scheen	New Haven, Conn	Apr. 2, 1867	63, 433
Carriage and velocipede combined, Child's	J. C. Cline	Philadelphia, Pa	Nov. 2, 1869	96, 396
Carriage and wagon brake	J. G. Bicknell	Cambridge, Mass	Mar. 1, 1870	100, 357
Carriage and wagon jack	W. N. Rowe	Sharpsburgh, Md	Aug. 16, 1859	25, 141
Carriage and wagon seat	C. K. Lehmann	Savannah, Ohio	Oct. 7, 1873	143, 515
Carriage and wagon spring	P. Hill	Veteran, N. Y	Nov. 25, 1837	489
Carriage and wagon spring	G. W. La Baw	Jersey City N. J	Feb. 25, 1862	34, 549
Carriage and wheel, Railway	R. Grant	Baltimore, Md	Nov. 3, 1838	999
Carriage attachment	G. J. Capewell	West Cheshire, Conn	Sept. 17, 1867	68, 951
Carriage-axle	S. Adams	New York, N. Y	Feb. 1, 1848	5, 426
Carriage-axle	S. Barker	Hartford, Conn	Oct. 30, 1866	59, 162
Carriage-axle	W. D. Bollinger	Cedar Rapids, Iowa	Sept. 29, 1868	82, 483
Carriage-axle	W. A. Clark	Woodbridge, Conn	Mar. 22, 1870	101, 097
Carriage-axle	S. S. Cook	Woonsocket, R. I	Dec. 9, 1873	145, 280
Carriage axle	A. B. Crandall	Sumner, Ill	May 28, 1872	127, 222
Carriage axle	D. Dalzell	South Egremont, Mass	Jan. 4, 1870	98, 473
Carriage-axle	T. H. Elder	Chicago, Ill	Mar. 30, 1869	88, 376

Index of patents issued from the United States Patent Office from 1790 *to* 1873, *inclusive*—Continued.

Invention.	Inventor.	Residence.	Date.	No.
Carriage-axle	T. Falvey	Racine, Wis	Feb. 5, 1867	61,821
Carriage-axle	J. J. Flack	Joliet, Ill	Sept. 4, 1849	6,688
Carriage-axle	S. Forrester	Allegheny, Pa	Dec. 7, 1869	97,622
Carriage-axle	S. Forrester	Allegheny, Pa	Dec. 7, 1869	97,623
Carriage-axle	M. R. Freeman	Macon, Ga	July 26, 1870	105,793
Carriage-axle	K. Goddard	Philadelphia, Pa	June 15, 1852	9,023
Carriage-axle	J. Grabach	Clyde, Ohio	Aug. 17, 1869	93,707
Carriage-axle	E. H. Green	Baltimore, Md	June 13, 1854	11,063
Carriage-axle	W. N. Hall	Springfield, Tex	July 26, 1870	105,801
Carriage-axle	W. T. Harrington	Roxbury, Mass	May 24, 1864	42,911
Carriage-axle	E. W. Ives	Hamden, Conn	Apr. 25, 1871	114,147
Carriage-axle	H. Killam	New Haven, Conn	Sept. 27, 1870	107,783
Carriage-axle	H. Killam	New Haven, Conn	Jan. 3, 1871	110,766
Carriage-axle	W. A. Lewis	Joliet, Ill	Mar. 8, 1870	100,646
Carriage-axle	L. Littlejohn	New York, N. Y	June 7, 1870	103,900
Carriage-axle	G. A. Lloyd	San Francisco, Cal	Mar. 29, 1870	101,370
Carriage-axle	J. H. Moffett	Reading, Mich	June 29, 1869	92,081
Carriage-axle	D. W. Phillips and W. Maher	Covington, N. Y	Apr. 23, 1828	....
Carriage-axle	J. A. C. Ruffner	Hillsdale, Pa	Feb. 9, 1869	86,693
Carriage-axle	W. H. Saunders	Hastings, N. Y	June 27, 1854	11,179
Carriage-axle	F. Scheib	New York, N. Y	Apr. 5, 1870	101,521
Carriage-axle	I. Slack	Avondale, Pa	Oct. 10, 1846	4,809
Carriage-axle	A. E. Smith	Bronxville, N. Y	Oct. 19, 1869	96,043
Carriage-axle	A. E. Smith	Bronxville, N. Y	Dec. 28, 1869	98,436
Carriage-axle	A. E. Smith	Bronxville, N. Y	July 12, 1870	105,266
Carriage-axle	A. E. Smith	Bronxville, N. Y	Sept. 6, 1870	107,112
Carriage-axle	A. E. Smith	Bronxville, N. Y	Nov. 29, 1870	109,681
Carriage-axle	T. Spurrier	Sharon, Pa	June 8, 1869	90,968
Carriage-axle	G. H. Thomas	New York, N. Y	June 6, 1865	48,111
Carriage-axle	O. Tracy	Fitchburgh, Mass	Dec. 12, 1846	4,889
Carriage-axle	F. Volkmann and A. Miller	Philadelphia, Pa	Mar. 23, 1869	88,240
Carriage-axle	E. F. Wagner	Houston, Tex	June 13, 1871	115,913
Carriage-axle	E. Wells	New Haven, Conn	Mar. 14, 1871	112,757
Carriage-axle	J. F. Wilbur and T. Tuttle	Pownal, Me	Feb. 16, 1869	86,959
Carriage-axle	J. B. Wilson	Philadelphia, Pa	Sept. 14, 1869	94,932
Carriage-axle	J. T. Wilson	Pittsburgh, Pa	Mar. 9, 1869	87,609
Carriage-axle adjuster	J. Childs	West Troy, N. Y	Mar. 5, 1867	62,607
Carriage-axle and axle box	B. A. Berryman	Saint Louis, Mo	Jan. 21, 1873	135,068
Carriage axle and box	C. Beach	Newark, N. J	June 26, 1807	....
Carriage axle and box	F. Davis	Baltimore, Md	Nov. 24, 1834	....
Carriage axle and boxing	J. W. and A. W. Beer	Rural Valley, Pa	Aug. 8, 1871	117,730
Carriage-axle and carriage-yoke	S. Rowell	Amesbury, Mass	Dec. 6, 1870	109,842
Carriage axle and hub	L. Blair	Painesville, Ohio	Sept. 10, 1867	68,596
Carriage axle and journal	L. Dorman	Worcester, Mass	Aug. 14, 1866	57,100
Carriage-axle, Anti-friction	A. Allcott	Haverhill, Mass	Mar. 29, 1870	101,205
Carriage-axle, Anti-friction	E. C. Otis	Voluntown, Conn	July 24, 1866	56,601
Carriage-axle arm	A. J. Bell	Greenupsburgh, Ky	Mar. 20, 1860	27,517
Carriage-axle connection	J. W. Kingsbury	New Bedford, Mass	Oct. 5, 1869	95,488
Carriage-axle die	W. W. Simmons	Birmingham, Conn	Dec. 8, 1868	84,845
Carriage-axle gage	H. Harper	Berlin, Wis	Nov. 18, 1862	36,951
Carriage-axle gage	M. Merk	Rochester, N. Y	Sept. 14, 1869	94,834
Carriage-axle iron	S. J. Dennis	Boston, Mass	May 13, 1873	138,795
Carriage-axle lubricator	N. B. Brown	Antwerp, N. Y	Apr. 24, 1866	54,246
Carriage-axle lubricator	J. E. Emerson	San Francisco, Cal	Apr. 10, 1860	27,785
Carriage-axle lubricator	J. Killefer	West Richfield, Ohio	Apr. 26, 1870	102,408
Carriage-axle lubricator	E. Thomas	Kickapoo, Ill	Nov. 5, 1867	70,650
Carriage-axle lubricator	A. A. Vedder	Lysander, N. Y	Oct. 6, 1857	18,364
Carriage axle, Reversible	J. R. Renkin	Hillsdale, Pa	Oct. 12, 1869	95,726
Carriage axle shield	B. F. Robbins	Harwich, Mass	Sept. 26, 1871	119,281
Carriage-axles, Device for oiling	J. Vanderpool	Hackensack, N. J	Mar. 1, 1870	100,342
Carriage-axles, Gage for setting	L. Taylor	Marlborough, Mass	May 21, 1872	126,995
Carriage-axles, Machine for making	B. W. Foster	Auburn, N. Y	Mar. 24, 1868	75,893
Carriage-axles, Machine for making	C. Young	Auburn, N. Y	May 8, 1866	54,638
Carriage-axles, Machine for making	C. Young	Auburn, N. Y	May 8, 1866	54,639
Carriage-axles, Machine for rolling	T. H. Miller	Lancaster, Pa	Aug. 27, 1861	33,155
Carriage-axles, Machine for rolling	J. C. Richardson	New Haven, Conn	Mar. 11, 1873	136,620
Carriage-axles, Machine for rolling	J. C. Richardson	Philadelphia, Pa	Dec. 16, 1873	145,526
Carriage-axles, Machine for turning	J. G. Aram	Cordova, Ill	May 28, 1872	127,211
Carriage-axles, Machine for turning	H. E. Forrest	Boston, Mass	Apr. 15, 1873	137,769
Carriage-axles, Machine for turning	W. Jones	Brooklyn, N. Y	Nov. 25, 1873	144,908
Carriage-axles, Machine for upsetting	Z. Doolittle	Perry, Ga	July 6, 1858	20,780
Carriage-axles, Manufacture of	J. C. and J. Lones, C. Vernon, and E. Holden.	Southwick, England	Dec. 16, 1873	145,510
Carriage-axles, Manufacture of	A. and J. Schirck and J. Smith	Rochester, N. Y	Mar. 4, 1873	136,460
Carriage-axles, Manufacture of	A. E. Smith	Bronxville, N. Y	Aug. 2, 1870	106,086
Carriage-axles, Method of forming	J. Le Ferre	Charlestown, Mass	May 26, 1868	78,213
Carriage-axles, Oil-cup for	L. Gregory	Battle Creek, Mich	June 21, 1864	43,197
Carriage-axles, Pipe box or skein for	J. Jones	Galway, N. Y	Apr. 1, 1845	3,984
Carriage-axles, Sand-box for	J. S. Steele	Rockingham, Vt	Feb. 19, 1867	62,231
Carriage-axles, Securing nuts to	K. Goddard	Philadelphia, Pa	May 27, 1856	14,953
Carriage-axles, Wrench for nuts of	C. N. Morgan	Granby, Mass	Aug. 7, 1866	56,980
Carriage-axle-tree	A. Johnson	Newark, N. J	Feb. 9, 1833	....
Carriage axle-tree, Railway and other wheeled	R. Winans	Baltimore, Md	July 20, 1831	....
Carriage-axle-trees, Gage for setting	L. D. Cross	Phelps, N. Y	Mar. 18, 1873	136,819
Carriage-axle-trees, Lessening the friction in	R. Kilborn	Great Barrington, Mass	Apr. 12, 1808	....
Carriage-axle-trees, Method of turning	J. Hennon	Brighton, Pa	July 1, 1856	15,233
Carriage-axle-trees, Mode of greasing	F. Biemler	New York	Aug. 22, 1816	....
Carriage, Baby	C. H. Amidon	Miller's Falls, Mass	Jan. 7, 1873	134,623
Carriage, Baby	J. Higgins	Salem Crossing, Ind	June 7, 1870	103,882
Carriage, Baby	S. McIntire	Brooklyn, N. Y	Mar. 11, 1873	136,607
Carriage Baby	S. S. Woodruff	Brooklyn, N. Y	May 14, 1867	64,822
Carriage, Ball	A. D. Bishop	New York, N. Y	Mar. 29, 1864	42,066
Carriage-bodies, &c., Compound or rough stuff to be applied to.	E. Scharnikow	Margarettville, N. Y	Aug. 30, 1870	106,875
Carriage-bodies, Construction of	S. P. Graham	Richland Centre, Ind	Sept. 17, 1867	68,980
Carriage-bodies, Device for adjusting and hanging	J. D. Cole	Phelps, N. Y	Apr. 13, 1869	88,944
Carriage-bodies, Hanging	D. B. Barnum	New Fairfield, Conn	Oct. 16, 1839	1,369
Carriage-bodies, Hanging	G. A. Blair and A. S. Gladding	Johnsonburgh, N. Y	Jan. 21, 1868	73,492

Index of patents issued from the United States Patent Office from 1790 *to* 1873, *inclusive*—Continued.

Invention.	Inventor.	Residence.	Date.	No.
Carriage-bodies, Hanging	I. W. Brittan	Medina, Ohio	Oct. 26, 1839	1,381
Carriage-bodies, Hanging	B. F. Brown	Dorchester, Mass	Dec. 12, 1854	12,051
Carriage-bodies, Hanging	J. M. De Ruyter	New York, N. Y	Mar. 6, 1847	4,998
Carriage-bodies, Hanging	W. Doulin	Youngstown, Ohio	Nov. 1, 1859	25,958
Carriage-bodies, Hanging	S. Fairchild	Trumbull, Conn	Jan. 18, 1848	5,413
Carriage-bodies, Hanging	A. Hosmer	Bath, Ohio	June 2, 1845	4,065
Carriage-bodies, Hanging	M. G. Hubbard	Hume, N. Y	Feb. 12, 1850	7,085
Carriage-bodies, Hanging	M. G. Hubbard	Geneva, N. Y	Nov. 26, 1850	7,796
Carriage-bodies, Hanging	I. Jackson	West Grove, Pa	Mar. 20, 1849	6,213
Carriage-bodies, Hanging	J. Jones	Clyde, N. Y	July 22, 1851	8,234
Carriage-bodies, Hanging	J. Jones	Clyde, N. Y	July 22, 1851	8,236
Carriage-bodies, Hanging	E. Lane	Philadelphia, Pa	June 2, 1863	38,751
Carriage-bodies, Hanging	L. C. Miner	Hartford, Conn	June 14, 1859	24,398
Carriage-bodies, Hanging	A. W. Porter	Little Falls, N. Y	Nov. 13, 1855	13,797
Carriage-bodies, Hanging	J. Reynolds	Newberry, Pa	July 9, 1844	3,653
Carriage-bodies, Hanging	H. Scharch	New York, N. Y	Oct. 23, 1866	59,081
Carriage-bodies, Hanging	J. Speed	Crawfordsville, Ind	Feb. 27, 1847	4,989
Carriage-bodies, Hanging	C. C. Stringfellow and D. W. Surles.	Lumpkin, Ga	Jan. 15, 1861	31,134
Carriage-bodies, Hanging	A. Vallerchamp	McDowellsville, Pa	Oct. 12, 1839	1,362
Carriage-bodies, Hanging	C. J. Woolson	Cleveland, Ohio	Sept. 11, 1847	5,281
Carriage bodies, Making	J. Reeder	Lebanon, Ohio	Mar. 4, 1828	
Carriage-bodies, Mode of suspending	H. W. Libbey	Cleveland, Ohio	Jan. 28, 1868	73,821
Carriage-body	H. Dunlap	Georgetown, D. C	Aug. 27, 1812	
Carriage-body	W. C. and J. Dunn	New York, N. Y	June 11, 1861	32,513
Carriage-body	E. Kirsch	New Haven, Conn	July 31, 1860	29,386
Carriage-body	C. Thomas	Boston, Mass	Jan. 31, 1871	111,491
Carriage-body	E. M. Williams	Columbus, Ohio	Jan. 30, 1872	123,213
Carriage-body brace	J. H. Ormsby	Dixon, Ill	Oct. 12, 1869	95,828
Carriage-body brace	J. Taylor	Beloit, Ohio	Oct. 12, 1869	95,851
Carriage-body loop	F. A. Cowles	Plantsville, Conn	Mar. 15, 1870	100,864
Carriage-body loop	C. H. Guard	Troy, N. Y	Aug. 25, 1863	39,699
Carriage-body loop	W. W. Knowles	Plantsville, Conn	July 18, 1871	117,179
Carriage body, Standing-roof landau	E. Gibson	New York	May 10, 1811	
Carriage-body-supporting irons, Elastic bearing for	J. D. Sarven	Columbia, Tenn	Feb. 4, 1868	74,011
Carriage-body-supporting irons, Elastic bearing for	J. D. Sarven	Columbia, Tenn	Feb. 4, 1868	74,012
Carriage-body top	U. Reynolds	New York, N. Y	Sept. 25, 1866	58,292
Carriage-bolt	O. C. Burdict	New Haven, Conn	Sept. 3, 1867	68,554
Carriage-bolt	O. C. Burdict	New Haven, Conn	Sept. 26, 1871	119,309
Carriage-bolt	I. Newton	Cleveland, Ohio	Aug. 12, 1873	141,661
Carriage-bolt	A. Pond	Hamden, Conn	Apr. 11, 1865	47,245
Carriage-bolt	J. Strawn	Plymouth, Mich	Apr. 7, 1868	76,546
Carriage-bolts, Die for making	E. H. Plant	Plantsville, Conn	Mar. 18, 1873	137,023
Carriage-bolts, Machine for making	W. Keplin	Newcastle, Pa	Mar. 19, 1867	62,963
Carriage-bolts, Machine for making	J. T. Wood and E. C. Smith	Allegheny County, Pa	Dec. 6, 1864	45,367
Carriage-bolts, Method of Making	S. Frisbie and A. S. Upson	Farmington, Conn	Oct. 1, 1867	69,333
Carriage-boot	P. T. Gates	Plattsburgh, N. Y	Jan. 15, 1867	61,188
Carriage-bow	I. N. Topliff	Adrian, Mich	Dec. 27, 1870	110,513
Carriage-bow cover and slat-iron, Combined	I. N. Topliff	Elyria, Ohio	May 16, 1871	114,885
Carriage-bow iron	H. M. Bidwell	New Haven, Conn	Jan. 16, 1866	52,016
Carriage-bow iron	A. W. Clark and G. W. Marble	Charlestown, N. H	Nov. 3, 1868	83,693
Carriage-bow iron	G. W. Slater	New Haven, Conn	Apr. 9, 1867	63,660
Carriage-bow setter	H. C. Hoover	Greencastle, Pa	Mar. 24, 1868	75,916
Carriage-bows, Attaching props to	L. Sawyer	South Amesbury, Mass	May 15, 1866	54,782
Carriage-bows, Attaching the props of	D. B. Wright and L. Sawyer	South Amesbury, Mass	Aug. 31, 1858	21,391
Carriage-box	T. B. Whitlock		Feb. 23, 1802	
Carriage box and axle	J. A. Smith	New Haven, Conn	Mar. 23, 1838	651
Carriage box, Wheel	J. Nicholson	Herkimer, N. Y	Apr. 28, 1810	
Carriage boxes and seats, Corner-support for	W. Fisher	Marathon, N. Y	Sept. 6, 1870	107,025
Carriage boxes and seats, Metallic corner-support for.	O. H. Smith and W. Fisher	Marathon, N. Y	Mar. 22, 1870	101,172
Carriage-brace	J. Howe	Mount Pleasant, Iowa	Oct. 6, 1868	82,839
Carriage-brace	J. B. Pelton	Sandusky, N. Y	Jan. 15, 1867	61,246
Carriage-brace	M. Powe	Belvidere, N. J	Feb. 4, 1868	74,139
Carriage-brace joint	F. B. Morse	New Haven, Conn	June 11, 1867	65,761
Carriage-brake	W. Ballard	Lapeer, N. Y	June 23, 1868	79,186
Carriage-brake	E. Behr	New York, N. Y	Aug. 7, 1860	29,453
Carriage-brake	A. S. Boyer	Bernville, Pa	Dec. 21, 1869	98,018
Carriage-brake	J. E. Briggs	Watertown, N. Y	Apr. 2, 1861	31,867
Carriage-brake	L. R. Carpenter	Lancaster, Ohio	Dec. 3, 1861	33,865
Carriage-brake	E. Chapman	Akron, Ohio	Sept. 26, 1846	4,775
Carriage-brake	W. Clayton	Marshallton, Pa	Aug. 18, 1846	4,701
Carriage-brake	H. B. S. Davis	Farmington, Me	Sept. 20, 1870	107,462
Carriage-brake	G. L. Dickson	Carbondale, Pa	June 1, 1858	20,412
Carriage-brake	W. Ellmaker and C. Hurst	Earl Township, Pa	Apr. 22, 1862	35,016
Carriage-brake	D. D. Gibson and W. Cobbs	Damascoville, Ohio	Feb. 12, 1845	3,907
Carriage-brake	G. Griest	Adams County, Pa	June 5, 1849	6,489
Carriage-brake	G. Hauck	Mechanicsburgh, Pa	June 9, 1857	17,506
Carriage-brake	S. D. Kimble	Allegheny City, Pa	Oct. 20, 1868	83,174
Carriage-brake	B. F. Leet	Dayton, Nev	Dec. 28, 1869	98,277
Carriage-brake	M. K. Lewis	Iowa City, Iowa	Apr. 8, 1862	34,892
Carriage-brake	M. K. Lewis	Iowa City, Iowa	June 2, 1863	38,752
Carriage-brake	M. S. Marshall and J. G. Bicknell.	Somerville and Cambridge, Mass.	Feb. 9, 1869	86,770
Carriage brake	A. B. McFarlan	Downingtown, Pa	Apr. 17, 1849	6,355
Carriage-brake	W. D. Sheldon	Wolcott, N. Y	June 7, 1864	43,044
Carriage-brake	J. Sollenberger	Higginsport, Ohio	Mar. 7, 1854	10,604
Carriage-brake	W. T. Welch, jr	Churchville, Md	Mar. 12, 1850	7,177
Carriage-brake	A. Wnuck	Cincinnati, Ohio	Mar. 14, 1871	112,665
Carriage-brake	M. S. Woodward	Marshallton, Pa	Dec. 4, 1843	3,361
Carriage-brake, Adjustable	J. A. Letts	Trumansburgh, N. Y	Jan. 29, 1861	31,249
Carriage-brake mechanism	L. Wilber	Putney, Vt	Jan. 20, 1863	37,468
Carriage brake, Railway	P. J. O. Conway	Philadelphia, Pa	Sept. 10, 1840	1,777
Carriage-brake, Self-acting	S. Cope	Salem, Ohio	Dec. 22, 1846	4,900
Carriage-brake, Self-acting	J. Du Bois, jr	Cascade, Pa	June 13, 1846	4,571
Carriage-brake, Self-acting	W. Ellmaker	New Holland, Pa	Oct. 22, 1861	33,522
Carriage brake, Self-acting	A. Larrowe	Cohocton, N. Y	Mar. 27, 1860	27,639
Carriage-brake, Self-acting	Z. C. Robbins	Washington, D. C	June 13, 1846	4,569

Index of patents issued from the United States Patent Office from 1790 *to* 1873, *inclusive*—Continued.

Invention.	Inventor.	Residence.	Date.	No.
Carriage-brakes, Apparatus for operating	C. Stoner	Gettysburgh, Pa	Aug. 28, 1847	5, 264
Carriage-brakes, Means of operating	W. Gearley and I. Krebs	Winchester, Va	Jan. 4, 1859	22, 498
Carriage-brakes, Means of operating	I. Krebs	Winchester, Va	Jan. 4, 1859	22, 504
Carriage, &c., Buoyant	H. Stanton	Washington, D. C	Feb. 27, 1847	4, 984
Carriage-button	W. P. Bateman	Barrington, R. I	Oct. 1, 1867	69, 506
Carriage-button	C. H. Field	Providence, R. I	Dec. 27, 1870	110, 358
Carriage-button, Elastic	T. E. King	Painesville, Ohio	May 28, 1867	65, 691
Carriage, chair, and cradle, Combined	G. W. Hawk	Chicago, Ill	June 21, 1864	43, 206
Carriage check brace	I. D. Johnson	Kennett Square, Pa	Apr. 28, 1868	77, 196
Carriage, Child's	A. F. R. Arndt	Detroit, Mich	Oct. 21, 1873	143, 603
Carriage, Child's	C. Askam	Philadelphia, Pa	May 14, 1861	32, 271
Carriage, Child's	G. L. Atwater	New Haven, Conn	June 4, 1872	127, 404
Carriage, Child's	J. A. Bechler	Philadelphia, Pa	Jan. 7, 1873	134, 630
Carriage, Child's	J. Bein and W. Ulrich	Newark, N. J	Feb. 11, 1868	74, 284
Carriage, Child's	F. Boylston	New York, N. Y	Oct. 6, 1868	82, 683
Carriage, Child's	F. Boylston	New York, N. Y	Apr. 9, 1872	125, 533
Carriage, Child's	R. G. Britton	Springfield, Vt	Jan. 24, 1871	111, 103
Carriage, Child's	R. G. Britton	Springfield, Vt	Feb. 11, 1873	135, 764
Carriage, Child's	A. Christian	New York, N. Y	Apr. 24, 1866	54, 111
Carriage, Child's	I. Cole	Newark, N. J	Jan. 30, 1872	123, 241
Carriage, Child's	B. P. Crandall	New York, N. Y	Dec. 28, 1869	98, 351
Carriage, Child's	J. A. Crandall	Brooklyn, N. Y	Jan. 11, 1870	98, 670
Carriage, Child's	J. A. Crandall	Brooklyn, N. Y	Jan. 14, 1873	134, 856
Carriage, Child's	J. C. Crandall	New York, N. Y	Jan. 3, 1871	110, 744
Carriage, Child's	W. E. Crandall	New York, N. Y	Feb. 22, 1870	100, 121
Carriage, Child's	W. E. Crandall	New York, N. Y	Jan. 3, 1871	110, 745
Carriage, Child's	R. P. Crandall and J. A. Conover.	New York, N. Y	Apr. 2, 1867	31, 872
Carriage, Child's	C. W. F. Dare	New York, N. Y	Jan. 23, 1872	122, 998
Carriage, Child's	A. Dick	Buffalo, N. Y	Apr. 23, 1867	64, 088
Carriage, Child's	R. G. Elder	New York, N. Y	May 10, 1870	102, 927
Carriage, Child's	R. G. Elder	New York, N. Y	Mar. 14, 1871	112, 696
Carriage, Child's	J. A. H. Ellis	Springfield, Vt	June 22, 1869	91, 615
Carriage, Child's	I. N. Forrester	Bridgeport, Conn	Dec. 27, 1870	110, 561
Carriage, Child's	I. N. Forrester	Bridgeport, Conn	Nov. 8, 1870	108, 993
Carriage, Child's	A. D. Fowler	Newark, N. J	Dec. 31, 1867	72, 833
Carriage, Child's	T. Galt	Rock Island, Ill	May 13, 1873	138, 746
Carriage, Child's	T. Galt	Rock Island, Ill	Oct. 21, 1873	143, 818
Carriage, Child's	L. Havasy	Hoboken, N. J	Oct. 14, 1873	143, 624
Carriage, Child's	J. N. Hazelip	Baltimore, Md	Dec. 9, 1873	145, 298
Carriage, Child's	C. Holt	Jersey City, N. J	Nov. 7, 1871	120, 645
Carriage, Child's	J. G. Kamphaus	Pittsburgh, Pa	Oct. 14, 1873	143, 628
Carriage, Child's	J. G. Krieger	Washington, D. C	Oct. 3, 1871	119, 523
Carriage, Child's	H. Lutz	New York, N. Y	Sept. 19, 1871	119, 162
Carriage, Child's	C. G. Macht	New York, N. Y	Feb. 6, 1872	123, 408
Carriage, Child's	T. A. Madison	Terre Haute, Ind	Apr. 2, 1867	63, 541
Carriage, Child's	G. Martienssen	Brooklyn, N. Y	June 6, 1871	115, 623
Carriage, Child's	O. Mather	Newport, Ky	July 18, 1865	48, 821
Carriage, Child's	G. Maynard	Greenfield, Mass	Dec. 14, 1858	22, 300
Carriage, Child's	W. P. McKinstry	New York, N. Y	Aug. 31, 1858	21, 353
Carriage, Child's	G. H. Mellen	New York, N. Y	Mar. 29, 1870	101, 295
Carriage, Child's	H. H. and J. W. Prindle	Sandusky, Ohio	Nov. 19, 1867	71, 061
Carriage, Child's	H. M. Richardson	Boston, Mass	Oct. 7, 1873	143, 421
Carriage, Child's	G. F. C. Rosenthal	Philadelphia, Pa	Aug. 9, 1870	106, 286
Carriage, Child's	G. L. Shepard	Albany, N. Y	July 8, 1873	140, 598
Carriage, Child's	L. Snow and J. Haseltine	Boston, Mass	Dec. 16, 1873	145, 692
Carriage, Child's	F. Snyder	New York, N. Y	June 17, 1873	139, 978
Carriage, Child's	C. Spring and A. Spring	Dorchester and Weston, Mass.	Mar. 19, 1867	62, 976
Carriage, Child's	E. Talkingham	San Francisco, Cal	Dec. 5, 1871	121, 453
Carriage, Child's	W. H. Towers	Boston, Mass	Oct. 28, 1873	144, 106
Carriage, Child's	D. Troxell	Newark, N. J	July 16, 1872	129, 072
Carriage, Child's	H. W. Warner	Greenfield, Mass	Aug. 29, 1871	118, 656
Carriage, Child's	F. H. Way	Brooklyn, N. Y	Nov. 19, 1872	133, 130
Carriage, Child's	H. Weed	New Haven, Conn	Sept. 10, 1872	131, 317
Carriage, Child's	W. B. Whitney	Leominster, Mass	Mar. 14, 1871	112, 662
Carriage, Child's	J. B. Wightman	Brooklyn, N. Y	June 13, 1871	115, 920
Carriage, Child's	J. B. Wightman	Brooklyn, N. Y	Jan. 7, 1873	134, 576
Carriage, Child's folding	T. G. Stagg	East New York, N. Y	July 19, 1870	105, 505
Carriage, Child's folding	H. Lutz	New York, N. Y	Nov. 7, 1871	120, 757
Carriage, Child's three-wheeled	J. H. Gould	New York, N. Y	June 10, 1856	15, 071
Carriage-circle	J. R. McGuire	Warren, Ohio	Sept. 24, 1867	69, 233
Carriage-circle	E. Wilson	Plattsburgh, N. Y	June 11, 1872	127, 818
Carriage-circle-bending machine	S. S. Daniels	Kendallville, Ind	Mar. 31, 1868	76, 059
Carriage-circle coupling	G. G. Larkin	West Amesbury, Mass	Apr. 5, 1864	42, 199
Carriage-clip	L. J. M. Baker	Enon, Ohio	Dec. 31, 1867	72, 779
Carriage-clip	A. Bixby	Lansing, Mich	Oct. 12, 1869	95, 761
Carriage-clip	W. Bound	Hackensack, N. J	Jan. 29, 1867	61, 601
Carriage-clip	E. Hoxie	Montezuma, N. Y	Mar. 26, 1867	63, 252
Carriage-clip	L. A. Johnson	Candor, N. Y	Apr. 5, 1870	101, 467
Carriage-clip	T. McCreary	Matteawan, N. Y	July 28, 1868	80, 360
Carriage-clip	F. B. Morse	Milwaukee, Wis	Feb. 6, 1866	52, 440
Carriage-clip	F. B. Morse	Plantsville, Conn	Oct. 26, 1869	96, 252
Carriage-clip	F. B. Morse	Plantsville, Conn	Oct. 25, 1870	108, 720
Carriage-clip	F. B. Morse	Plantsville, Conn	Dec. 27, 1870	110, 581
Carriage-clip	G. B. Salmon	Saint Paul, Minn	May 14, 1867	64, 711
Carriage-clip	M. Seward	New Haven, Conn	Mar. 14, 1871	112, 743
Carriage-clip bar	F. B. Morse	Plantsville, Conn	Dec. 20, 1870	110, 386
Carriage-clip blank and die for making	H. M. Beecher	Plantsville, Conn	Sept. 12, 1871	118, 780
Carriage-clip die	W. Noble	Derby, Conn	June 27, 1871	116, 345
Carriage-clip-forging die	M. Seward	New Haven, Conn	Apr. 25, 1871	114, 051
Carriage-clip-forming die	W. W. Knowles	Plantsville, Conn	June 27, 1871	116, 455
Carriage-clip-forming die	W. W. Knowles and L. S. White.	Plantsville, Conn	June 27, 1871	116, 456
Carriage-clip-forming machine	W. S. Ward	Plantsville, Conn	Apr. 1, 1873	137, 517
Carriage-clip-swaging die	F. B. Morse	Plantsville, Conn	Oct. 11, 1870	108, 283
Carriage clips, Apparatus for compressing and inserting rubber blocks into.	T. H. Brown and C. E. Gilman	Chicago, Ill	Apr. 4, 1871	113, 624

Index of patents issued from the United States Patent Office from 1790 *to* 1873, *inclusive*—Continued.

Index of patents issued from the United States Patent Office from 1790 *to* 1873, *inclusive*—Continued.

Invention.	Inventor.	Residence.	Date.	No.
Carriage-dash rail	B. B. Noyes and O. G. Stratton	Greenfield, Mass	July 12, 1870	105, 362
Carriage-dash rail	B. B. Noyes and O. G. Stratton	Greenfield, Mass	Feb. 11, 1873	135, 834
Carriage, Dash-rail for child's	M. Hine	New Haven, Conn	Apr. 1, 1873	137, 446
Carriage-door	J. Carson	Buffalo, N. Y	Nov. 11, 1873	144, 440
Carriage-door	J. Cunningham	Rochester, N. Y	Apr. 22, 1873	138, 008
Carriage-door	P. Devilliard and A. Postweiler	Paris France	Oct. 8, 1867	69, 641
Carriage-door	P. Leck	Hartford, Conn	Dec. 22, 1868	85, 108
Carriage-door	A. Wright	Wilmington, Del	Dec. 12, 1871	121, 922
Carriage-door and window-sash support	J. C. Ham	New York, N. Y	May 2, 1871	114, 436
Carriage-door handle	E. Wells	New Haven, Conn	Aug. 15, 1871	118, 083
Carriage door, Landau	H. Killam	New Haven, Conn	May 14, 1872	126, 715
Carriage door, Landau	E. Wells	New Haven, Conn	Mar. 15, 1870	100, 956
Carriage door, Landau	F. Wood	Bridgeport, Conn	Mar. 6, 1866	53, 075
Carriage-door lock	J. Ives	Hampden, Conn	July 20, 1846	4, 646
Carriage draft-poles, Device for sustaining	S. B. Whitney	Coxsackie, N. Y	Feb. 4, 1868	74, 184
Carriage, Dumping	J. R. True	Richmond, Me	Aug. 15, 1871	118, 072
Carriage-evener	C. L. Ames	Bangor, Me	Nov. 26, 1867	71, 262
Carriage, Extension	J. A. Naylor	Rahway, N. J	Sept. 4, 1860	29, 902
Carriage extension-seat	F. J. Flowers	Rahway, N. J	Dec. 27, 1859	26, 578
Carriage, Folding	T. G. Stagg	East New York, N. Y	Dec. 24, 1872	134, 226
Carriage folding-step	G. Gregory	New Haven, Conn	May 9, 1871	114, 673
Carriage folding-step	G. H. Vollhardt	New Haven, Conn	June 6, 1871	115, 664
Carriage folding-step	E. Wells	New Haven, Conn	June 6, 1871	115, 665
Carriage folding-top	W. G. Foglesong	Xenia, Ohio	Apr. 17, 1855	12, 751
Carriage foot-rail	T. W. and H. K. Porter	Boston, Mass	Sept. 23, 1873	143, 031
Carriage for common roads, Steam	F. Alger	Boston, Mass	June 13, 1871	115, 802
Carriage for railways, Steam	J. H. Moore and W. P. Parrott	Boston, Mass	Dec. 2, 1851	8, 561
Carriage for tram-ways, Steam	J. Grantham	London, England	Sept. 2, 1873	142, 459
Carriage forward-gear	J. J. D. Meincke	Milwaukee, Wis	Apr. 28, 1868	77, 395
Carriage, Four-wheel	T. Brooks and D. W. Eames	Rutland, N. Y	Dec. 6, 1827	....
Carriage, Four-wheel	J. B. Swan	Albany, N. Y	July 24, 1823	....
Carriage front, Landaulet	E. Wells	New Haven, Conn	Dec. 10, 1872	133, 910
Carriage-front, Removable	C. F. Albright and L. Burkhard.	Pottsville, Pa	Sept. 24, 1861	33, 326
Carriage-gate	J. Ellis	Detroit, Mich	Jan. 28, 1862	34, 247
Carriage-gearing	C. Custer	Norristown, Pa	Sept. 27, 1870	107, 668
Carriage gearing	C. Custer	Norristown, Pa	Mar. 21, 1871	112, 905
Carriage gearing	J. R. McAlister	Richville, N. Y	Sept. 4, 1866	57, 745
Carriage-gearing	C. W. Saladee	Circleville, Ohio	Feb. 9, 1869	86, 866
Carriage-guard	F. B. Shaw	Boston, Mass	Mar. 5, 1867	62, 569
Carriage-guard	I. M. Singer	Paris, France	Feb. 5, 1867	61, 883
Carriage, Hand	W. Allen and J. W. Bond	Saint Paul, Minn	June 6, 1871	115, 674
Carriage, Hand	D. S Shanabrook	Greencastle, Pa	June 29, 1869	92, 106
Carriage, Hand-motive	J. Allgaier	Philadelphia, Pa	Feb. 22, 1870	100, 097
Carriage, Hand-propelling	R. Kind	New York, N. Y	Feb. 13, 1872	123, 707
Carriage handle, Child's	R. G. Elder	New York, N. Y	Feb. 1, 1870	99, 420
Carriage handle, Child's	J. H. White	Newark, N. J	Feb. 20, 1872	123, 960
Carriage head-block	J. C. Bates	Warrensburgh, Mo	Aug. 3, 1869	93, 163
Carriage head-block	T. M. Cluxton	Rising Sun, Ind	Oct. 20, 1868	83, 256
Carriage head-block	D. Hinman	Southington, Conn	May 9, 1871	114, 681
Carriage head-block	F. Van Patten	Auburn, N. Y	July 23, 1872	129, 768
Carriage head-block-plate-forming die	W. Terrell	Ansonia, Conn	Sept. 26, 1871	119, 286
Carriage hold-back	W. R. Baker	Wellington Square, Canada	May 16, 1871	114, 746
Carriage hold-back	J. Davis	Elmira, N. Y	Oct. 22, 1861	33, 555
Carriage hold-back	T. F. Griffiths	Dansville, N. Y	Sept. 2, 1862	36, 347
Carriage hold-back	H. A. Harris	Battle Creek, Mich	Dec. 23, 1862	37, 227
Carriage hold-back	J. Hunlock	Wyoming Valley, Pa	Jan. 25, 1870	99, 196
Carriage hold-back	T. F. Kiff	Havana, N. Y	Sept. 21, 1869	94, 962
Carriage hold-back	J. A. Lannert	Cleveland, Ohio	Sept. 26, 1871	119, 370
Carriage hold-back	J. A. Mackinnon	Cleveland, Ohio	Oct. 20, 1868	83, 294
Carriage hold-back	R. Nutting	Randolph, Vt	May 19, 1863	38, 597
Carriage hold-back	R. Rolph	Coventry, N. Y	Sept. 15, 1863	39, 958
Carriage hold-back	D. Terry	Wakeman, Ohio	Sept. 23, 1873	143, 199
Carriage hold-back	A. Webster	Montpelier, Vt	Sept. 25, 1855	13, 604
Carriage hold-back	E. Wilson	Northbridge, Mass	Nov. 6, 1866	59, 494
Carriage hook, Landau	O. S. Osborn	New Haven, Conn	June 3, 1873	139, 515
Carriage, Hose	I. S. Schuyler and L. A. Rockwell.	New York, N. Y	Sept. 7, 1858	21, 449
Carriage-hound	J. Maddock	Dubuque, Iowa	Sept. 24, 1861	33, 355
Carriage-iron	H. K. Porter	Boston, Mass	Dec. 30, 1873	146, 093
Carriage-jack	M. Andriot	Mount Washington, Ohio	July 24, 1866	56, 510
Carriage-jack	M. Andriot	Mount Washington, Ohio	Sept. 25, 1866	58, 198
Carriage-jack	D. Bull	Amboy, Ill	Nov. 16, 1869	96, 880
Carriage-jack	J. O. Burch	Buffalo, N. Y	July 6, 1869	92, 157
Carriage-jack	J. Card	Cleveland, Ohio	Sept. 25, 1860	30, 180
Carriage-jack	O. Churchill	Canton, Pa	Feb. 25, 1868	74, 894
Carriage-jack	T. G. Clinton and G. H. and E. H. Knight.	Cincinnati, Ohio	Mar. 5, 1850	7, 135
Carriage-jack	G. L. Cummings	New York, N. Y	Mar. 17, 1863	37, 902
Carriage-jack	G. L. Cummings	New York, N. Y	Aug. 1, 1865	49, 090
Carriage-jack	W. S. Douglass	Richmond, Vt	Dec. 7, 1869	97, 618
Carriage-jack	D. Elliott and E. Seely	New York, N. Y	Aug. 3, 1869	93, 289
Carriage-jack	J. F. Emmert	Quincy, Pa	Sept. 17, 1867	68, 970
Carriage-jack	A. W. Field	Vergennes, Vt	Apr. 25, 1865	47, 408
Carriage-jack	R. Fink	Batavia, Ill	May 9, 1865	47, 628
Carriage-jack	A. R. Giles	Adams, N. Y	Aug. 2, 1870	106, 050
Carriage-jack	T. L. Goble	Orange, N. Y	Apr. 30, 1867	64, 302
Carriage-jack	J. H. Hadley	Boston, Mass	Mar. 16, 1869	87, 927
Carriage-jack	H. L. Hammond	Providence, R. I	Nov. 3, 1868	83, 773
Carriage-jack	J. F. Hammond	Providence, R. I	Oct. 23, 1866	59, 008
Carriage-jack	D. Hiestand	Pughtown, Pa	May 16, 1871	114, 816
Carriage-jack	D. Hiestand	Pughtown, Pa	Mar. 25, 1873	137, 202
Carriage-jack	A. Higley	South Bend, Ind	Oct. 31, 1865	50, 707
Carriage-jack	F. Hovey	New York, N. Y	Dec. 28, 1869	98, 379
Carriage-jack	T. W. Johnston	Richmond, Me	Jan. 25, 1870	99, 090
Carriage-jack	A. W. Keeler and J. Eckert	La Fayette, N. Y	Apr. 13, 1869	88, 789
Carriage-jack	D. Marshall	Northville, Mich	Aug. 16, 1870	106, 379
Carriage-jack	J. P. Moore	Boston, Mass	Sept. 3, 1867	68, 451
Carriage-jack	A. Myers	Van Wert, Ohio	Feb. 18, 1868	74, 576

Index of patents issued from the United States Patent Office from 1790 *to* 1873, *inclusive*—Continued.

Invention.	Inventor.	Residence.	Date.	No.
Carriage-jack	C. H. Paine	Providence, R. I	Sept. 30, 1862	36, 587
Carriage-jack	C. H. Paine	Providence, R. I	Mar. 22, 1864	42, 050
Carriage-jack	C. H. Paine	Providence, R. I	Feb. 4, 1868	73, 992
Carriage-jack	C. H. Paine	Providence, R. I	Mar. 2, 1869	87, 358
Carriage-jack	C. J. Philleo	Kenyonville, N. Y	Aug. 3, 1869	93, 343
Carriage-jack	J. J. Pike	Chelsea, Mass	Oct. 9, 1860	30, 346
Carriage-jack	J. C. Plumer	Boston, Mass	Jan. 2, 1866	51, 861
Carriage-jack	P. C. Porter	Augusta, Me	Sept. 3, 1867	68, 572
Carriage-jack	O. T. Potter	Scott, N. Y	Jan. 22, 1867	61, 455
Carriage-jack	H. L. Riouff	Pleasant Ridge, Ohio	July 18, 1871	117, 114
Carriage-jack	J. F. Seaman	Cortlandville, N. Y	Aug. 10, 1869	93, 484
Carriage-jack	H. S. Shepardson	Shelburne Falls, Mass	Jan. 1, 1867	60, 945
Carriage-jack	J. B. Small	Boston, Mass	Nov. 12, 1867	70, 908
Carriage-jack	J. Stener	Albany, N. Y	July 20, 1869	92, 899
Carriage-jack	O. B. Sutton	Kensico, N. Y	Sept. 3, 1867	68, 395
Carriage-jack	J. N. Thatcher	Martinsburgh, W. Va	May 25, 1869	90, 473
Carriage-jack	I. Varney	Kennebunk, Me	Nov. 12, 1867	70, 763
Carriage-jack	A. H. Wellbrock	Boston, Mass	May 23, 1871	115, 140
Carriage-jack	J. B. White	Detroit, Mich	Nov. 1, 1868	84, 665
Carriage-jack	D. R. Wight	Southbridge, Mass	Dec. 23, 1873	145, 922
Carriage-jack	J. E. Woll	Allegheny City, Pa	Aug. 17, 1869	93, 786
Carriage-jack, bag-holder, and weighing-scale combined.	N. Berkeley	Aldie, Va	Sept. 5, 1871	118, 678
Carriage-joint	R. Nickson	Akron, Ohio	Sept. 10, 1867	68, 780
Carriage, Joint-bodied	A. H. Niles	Georgetown, N. Y	May 15, 1855	12, 869
Carriage jump-seat	C. P. Kimball	Portland, Me	Sept. 24, 1867	69, 102
Carriage-knob	R. P. Cowles	New Haven, Conn	June 27, 1865	48, 373
Carriage-knob	E. S. Wheeler	Westport, Conn	Jan. 19, 1869	85, 976
Carriage-clamp support	T. P. White	Bridgeport, Conn	June 27, 1871	116, 381
Carriage, Land	R. C. Parvin	Philadelphia, Pa	Jan. 16, 1872	122, 850
Carriage, Land and steam	S. Fairman	Nassau, N. Y	Mar. 27, 1830	....
Carriage, Landau	H. Killam	New Haven, Conn	Dec. 10, 1872	133, 862
Carriage, Landau	E. Wells	New Haven, Conn	Mar. 14, 1871	112, 758
Carriage, Landaulet	E. Wells	New Haven, Conn	Dec. 6, 1870	109, 981
Carriage-lock	J. A. Bower	Middlefield, Ohio	Apr. 28, 1868	77, 162
Carriage lock or brake, Spring	W. Clayton	Marshallton, Pa	June 18, 1842	2, 676
Carriage-lock-plate blanks, Machine for cutting	T. Insall and J. F. Dovey	Philadelphia, Pa	Sept. 16, 1873	142, 854
Carriage, Locomotive	R. Winans	Baltimore, Md	July 28, 1846	4, 665
Carriage, Locomotive	R. Winans	Baltimore, Md	Oct. 14, 1846	4, 812
Carriage, Locomotive and other railway	A. C. Jones	Philadelphia, Pa	Oct. 10, 1840	1, 812
Carriage loop and billet cover	N. Jenny, jr	Pittsburgh, Pa	Dec. 8, 1868	84, 829
Carriage-makers' tools	G. Atkinson	San Francisco, Cal	Mar. 7, 1871	112, 311
Carriage, Mechanism for connecting a horse with a	A. Colburn and E. G. Stanley	Lynn and Fitchburgh, Mass.	Dec. 17, 1867	72, 167
Carriage-motor	D. Morrison	Portland, Me	Dec. 31, 1867	72, 881
Carriage moved by hand	D. Nino, jr	Reading, Pa	May 4, 1813	....
Carriage neck-yoke leathers	H. Sanders	Utica, N. Y	Dec. 13, 1870	110, 074
Carriage-nut	J. P. Skinner	Plantsville, Conn	Oct. 17, 1871	120, 004
Carriage or buggy seat, Shifting	S. W. Beach	South Bend, Ind	June 14, 1870	104, 248
Carriage or perambulator, Child's	B. P. Crandall, jr	Williamsburgh, N. Y	Apr. 4, 1871	113, 402
Carriage panels and veneers off circular logs, Machine for cutting.	J. White and P. Quimby	Belfast, Me	Sept. 12, 1829	....
Carriage-perch	I. P. Bacon	Bedford, Mass	Mar. 14, 1871	112, 528
Carriage-perch	W. H. Cooper and G. Gregory	New Haven, Conn	Jan. 21, 1868	73, 438
Carriage-perch	L. E. Stilwill	Franklinville, N. Y	Dec. 2, 1851	8, 568
Carriage perch connection	D. A. Mathews	Geneva, N. Y	Mar. 17, 1868	75, 688
Carriage-perch coupling	W. S. Lord	Pulaski, Tenn	Oct. 28, 1856	15, 979
Carriage-pole	B. Foltz	Rockford, Ill	Jan. 5, 1869	85, 519
Carriage-pole	C. K. Mellinger	Millersville, Pa	Oct. 1, 1867	69, 356
Carriage-pole	V. N. Mitchell	Concord, N. H	Apr. 7, 1868	76, 496
Carriage-pole	H. W. Painter	New Haven, Conn	Aug. 14, 1866	57, 179
Carriage-pole	G. N. Shaw	Muir, Mich	Feb. 2, 1869	86, 459
Carriage-pole, Adjustable	M. A. Koon	Catskill, N. Y	Sept. 15, 1868	82, 127
Carriage-pole, Adjustable	L. C. Miner	Hartford, Conn	Aug. 4, 1863	39, 415
Carriage pole and shaft combined	A. Moore and J. Aylwerd	Mission San José, Cal	Aug. 10, 1869	93, 466
Carriage pole and thill	J. G. Perry	Kingston, R. I	Mar. 27, 1866	53, 478
Carriage-pole attachment	H. F. Edwards	Worcester, Mass	Mar. 23, 1869	88, 149
Carriage-pole, Convertible	F. Fowler	West Haven, Conn	Apr. 21, 1868	76, 906
Carriage-pole coupling	C. A. Moore	Akron, Ohio	Sept. 6, 1870	107, 082
Carriage-pole support	H. B. Hurd	Aurora, Ill	Apr. 28, 1868	77, 382
Carriage-pole supporter	S. E. Bolles	Mattapoisett, Mass	Nov. 26, 1861	33, 811
Carriage-pole tip	A. Benedict	Albany, N. Y	May 12, 1868	77, 796
Carriage-pole tip	S. Mason	Hamden, Conn	Dec. 23, 1873	145, 885
Carriage-poles, Hook for supporting	S. S. Bent	Portchester, N. Y	Apr. 20, 1869	89, 118
Carriage-prop	W. Finn	Poughkeepsie, N. Y	Aug. 20, 1867	67, 968
Carriage-prop	L. Sawyer	South Amesbury, Mass	Apr. 5, 1870	101, 518
Carriage-prop	C. Thomas	West Newbury, Mass	Sept. 22, 1857	18, 254
Carriage-prop block	C. H. Davis	Syracuse, N. Y	Dec. 10, 1872	133, 764
Carriage-prop joint	A. Searls	Newark, N. J	Sept. 24, 1872	131, 568
Carriage-prop joint	E. W. Waite	New Haven, Conn	Aug. 11, 1868	80, 845
Carriage-prop joint, Adjustable	A. Searls	San Francisco, Cal	Nov. 5, 1867	70, 628
Carriage, Propeller	G. T. Palmer	Brooklyn, N. Y	May 21, 1872	126, 900
Carriage-protector	G. B. Brown	Newburgh, N. Y	May 27, 1873	139, 364
Carriage-rail, Shifting	W. H. Keeney	Waupun, Wis	July 16, 1872	129, 140
Carriage-raising machine	E. Huson	Ithaca, N. Y	Feb. 18, 1862	34, 427
Carriage, Riding	W. and J. Jessup	Guilford, N. C	June 1, 1827	....
Carriage-rocker	A. S. Wells	Hopkinton, R. I	Apr. 23, 1872	125, 998
Carriage rocker, Child's	A. D. Juelson	Wooster, Ohio	Mar. 10, 1868	75, 278
Carriage, Rocking	A. Armando	New York, N. Y	Sept. 21, 1869	94, 990
Carriage, Rocking	A. C. Griswold and W. R. Griswold.	Hartford and Durham, Conn.	June 7, 1859	24, 299
Carriage, Rolling lever	H. Chapman	Corinth, N. Y	Mar. 24, 1831	....
Carriage-runner attachment	J. W. Moore	Watseka, Ill	Jan. 18, 1870	98, 990
Carriage running-gear	N. Adams	Cornwall, N. Y	Feb. 11, 1862	34, 342
Carriage running-gear	J. C. Anderson and A. W. Benson.	Saginaw, Mich	Aug. 15, 1871	118, 093
Carriage running gear	J. Calef	Buffalo, N. Y	Aug. 16, 1859	25, 091
Carriage running-gear	F. Crick	Beamesville, Ohio	Aug. 14, 1866	57, 094

Index of patents issued from the United States Patent Office from 1790 *to* 1873, *inclusive*—Continued.

Invention.	Inventor.	Residence.	Date.	No.
Carriage running-gear	G. L. Hausskuecht	New Haven, Conn	Jan. 13, 1852	8, 648
Carriage running-gear	W. Hemme	Michigan Valley, Kans	June 11, 1872	127, 767
Carriage running-gear	W. Hemme	Michigan Valley, Kans	July 30, 1872	129, 954
Carriage running-gear	R. Kline and R. M. Jack	Pottstown, Pa	May 20, 1873	139, 164
Carriage running gear	W. A. Lewis	Chicago, Ill	July 23, 1872	129, 838
Carriage running-gear	R. Murdoch	Baltimore, Md	June 24, 1856	15, 189
Carriage running-gear	R. Murdoch	Baltimore, Md	May 19, 1857	17, 337
Carriage running-gear	T. O'Brion	Quincy, Mich	June 21, 1870	104, 634
Carriage running-gear	J. Pine	New York, N. Y	Nov. 5, 1850	7, 758
Carriage running-gear	J. Rancevan	Carthage, Ohio	Mar. 28, 1871	113, 092
Carriage running-gear	C. F. Verleger	Baltimore, Md	Feb. 3, 1852	8, 711
Carriage running-gear	J. L. Ware	Mantorville, Minn	Mar. 4, 1873	136, 570
Carriage running-gear	E. Wiglo	Bay City, Mich	Apr. 25, 1871	114, 072
Carriage running-gear	E. Wiglo	Bay City, Mich	Feb. 27, 1872	124, 026
Carriage running-gear	J. B. Withey	Lexington, Mich	Jan. 28, 1868	73, 941
Carriage running-gear	J. B. Withey	Detroit, Mich	Dec. 27, 1870	110, 528
Carriage running-gear, Land	J. Blocher	Buffalo, N. Y	Apr. 2, 1867	63, 358
Carriage, Safety	R. Beale	Washington, D. C	May 12, 1832	....
Carriage safety-attachment	C. Ducrux	New York, N. Y	Jan. 1, 1867	60, 705
Carriage-sash fastener and supporter	W. Stewart	Hartford, Conn	May 4, 1869	89, 604
Carriage sash-strap roller	J. H. Bloodgood	Bridgeport, Conn	May 17, 1870	103, 131
Carriage-seat	J. H. Adams	Portland, Me	June 2, 1868	78, 563
Carriage-seat	D. Aspinwall	South Bend, Ind	Feb. 13, 1872	123, 547
Carriage-seat	E. Chamberlin	Lansingburgh, N. Y	Dec. 24, 1867	72, 602
Carriage-seat	G. R. Comstock	Manheim, N. Y	Jan. 23, 1855	12, 273
Carriage-seat	C. D. Flynt	Collinsville, Ill	May 28, 1867	65, 201
Carriage seat	H. H. Forbes and H. C. Sears	New Bedford, Mass	Apr. 21, 1868	77, 023
Carriage-seat	J. Gale and M. B. Ames	Lawrence, Mass	June 29, 1869	92, 036
Carriage-seat	S. P. Graham	Columbus, Ohio	Oct. 5, 1869	95, 466
Carriage-seat	S. P. Graham	London, Canada	June 13, 1871	115, 842
Carriage seat	S. P. Graham	London, Canada	Mar. 12, 1872	124, 433
Carriage-seat	E. H. Harris	Palmetto, Ga	Nov. 8, 1859	26, 032
Carriage-seat	G. L. Hudson	Romeo, Mich	Nov. 2, 1869	96, 434
Carriage-seat	I. Kinney	Woodstock, Canada	Aug. 17, 1869	93, 825
Carriage-seat	C. K. Mellinger	Lebanon, Pa	Jan. 7, 1873	134, 692
Carriage-seat	J. N. Miller	Bellefontaine, Ohio	July 22, 1873	141, 065
Carriage-seat	F. B. Morse	Milwaukee, Wis	May 15, 1866	54, 755
Carriage-seat	A. J. Ritter	Rahway, N. J	Aug. 25, 1863	39, 677
Carriage-seat	G. Feichert	New Haven, Conn	Sept. 15, 1863	39, 971
Carriage-seat	H. Timkin	Saint Louis, Mo	Aug. 13, 1872	130, 546
Carriage-seat	S. Toomey	Wilmot, Ohio	Jan. 11, 1870	98, 721
Carriage-seat	R. Walker	Batavia, N. Y	Jan. 23, 1866	52, 229
Carriage-seat	L. J. Woodruff	Mohawk, N. Y	Sept. 11, 1866	58, 016
Carriage-seat, Adjustable	D. Aspinwall	South Bend, Ind	Dec. 31, 1872	134, 452
Carriage-seat, Adjustable	S. W. Beach	Ypsilanti, Mich	Apr. 4, 1871	113, 387
Carriage-seat, Adjustable	S. W. Beach	Ypsilanti, Mich	May 23, 1871	115, 152
Carriage-seat, Adjustable	G. and D. Cook	New Haven, Conn	Feb. 3, 1857	16, 528
Carriage-seat, Adjustable	D. N. Flanders	South Royalton, Vt	Feb. 12, 1856	14, 231
Carriage-seat, Adjustable	J. Fleming	Philadelphia, Pa	Apr. 7, 1868	76, 428
Carriage-seat, Adjustable	W. H. Gregg and W. Bowe	Wilmington, Del	Aug. 24, 1869	93, 987
Carriage-seat, Adjustable	J. A. Naylor	Rahway, N. J	June 26, 1860	28, 892
Carriage-seat, Adjustable	H. H. Potter	Carthage, N. Y	Dec. 14, 1858	22, 304
Carriage-seat, Adjustable	I. L. Vansant	Red Lion, Del	June 19, 1860	28, 792
Carriage-seat, Adjustable	A. Wright	Wilmington, Del	Apr. 12, 1870	101, 959
Carriage seat and top	L. Z. Dodds	South Bend, Ind	Apr. 4, 1871	113, 504
Carriage seat and top	E. L. Yancey	Batavia, N. Y	Sept. 24, 1872	131, 585
Carriage seat and top, Combined	F. Jackson	Sparta, Ohio	Jan. 1, 1867	60, 737
Carriage-seat back	J. Burt	Sturgis, Mich	Nov. 5, 1867	70, 517
Carriage-seat back, Adjustable	E. A. Rice	Wilmington, Vt	June 18, 1872	128, 171
Carriage-seat backs, Manufacture of	B. Hurlburt	Fort Wayne, Ind	June 27, 1871	116, 449
Carriage-seat clamp	H. J. Northrup	Lansingburgh, N. Y	Jan. 24, 1871	111, 140
Carriage-seat, Elastic or spring	J. Nichols	Providence, R. I	Oct. 2, 1822	....
Carriage-seat fastener	L. D. Belnap	Jonesville, Mich	Aug. 27, 1872	130, 785
Carriage seat fastener	M. Brockway, jr	Angola, Ind	July 8, 1873	140, 572
Carriage seat fastening	W. Beers	Milan, Ohio	Apr. 27, 1869	89, 276
Carriage-seat fastening	J. H. Fellows	Alba, Pa	July 26, 1870	105, 789
Carriage-seat fastening	M. C. Remington	Auburn, N. Y	May 28, 1867	65, 118
Carriage-seat joint	J. A. Hanna	Bel Air, Md	Nov. 28, 1871	121, 362
Carriage-seat lock	W. Conway	Rushville, N. Y	Oct. 20, 1868	83, 258
Carriage-seat, Self-adjusting	J. C. Kimball	New Haven, Conn	Jan. 1, 1861	31, 023
Carriage-seat shifting-rail	F. Baumgarten	Brooklyn, N. Y	Apr. 23, 1867	64, 008
Carriage-seat shifting-rail	C. Disser	West Union, Ohio	Apr. 19, 1870	101, 986
Carriage-seat shifting-rail	H. Dressel	Springfield, Vt	July 29, 1873	141, 335
Carriage-seat shifting-rail	J. Fellows	Chicago, Ill	Oct. 2, 1866	58, 542
Carriage-seat shifting-rail	S. Toomey	Wilmot, Ohio	Apr. 21, 1868	76, 959
Carriage-seat shifting-rail	J. Zahn	Fredonia, N. Y	Mar. 5, 1867	62, 719
Carriage-seat, Sliding	S. N. Beecher	Milford, Conn	Mar. 24, 1868	75, 841
Carriage-seat, Sliding	W. A. Bird	Newark, N. J	Apr. 17, 1860	27, 881
Carriage-seat, Sliding	R. T. Briggs	Amesbury, Mass	Nov. 22, 1870	109, 377
Carriage-seat spring	W. Scott	Plymouth, Mich	Nov. 5, 1867	70, 475
Carriage-seat, Spring-back	N. Cowles and A. Hulbert	Edgefield, S. C	Oct. 11, 1859	25, 725
Carriage seats, Attaching the rails of	C. Schofield	Trumbull, Conn	Apr. 19, 1859	23, 712
Carriage-seats, Clamp for movable	S. W. Beach	Ypsilanti, Mich	Nov. 8, 1870	109, 102
Carriage-seats, Construction of	B. Hurlburt	Milford, Conn	Nov. 6, 1866	59, 508
Carriage-seats, Corner-post for	S. S. Stanley	Sandusky, Ohio	Jan. 30, 1872	123, 302
Carriage seats, Head-rest for railway	E. Hambujer	Detroit, Mich	Mar. 29, 1864	42, 084
Carriage-seats, Mode of attaching	C. Krebs	West Springfield, Mass	Dec. 7, 1869	97, 524
Carriage-shackle	J. Brennan	New Haven, Conn	May 14, 1867	64, 626
Carriage-shackle	W. F. Gilbert	Derby, Conn	Sept. 1, 1868	81, 768
Carriage-shackle	W. W. Knowles	Southington, Conn	Apr. 24, 1866	54, 253
Carriage-shackle	G. G. Larkin	West Amesbury, Mass	Sept. 22, 1868	82, 420
Carriage-shackle	L. M. Lawless	Genesco, Ill	Sept. 5, 1871	118, 729
Carriage-shackle	J. Low	New Britain, Conn	Feb. 9, 1869	86, 847
Carriage-shackle	F. B. Morse	New Haven, Conn	June 30, 1868	79, 494
Carriage-shackle	F. B. Morse	Plantsville, Conn	Oct. 26, 1869	96, 256
Carriage-shackle	J. H. J. O'Neill	New Haven, Conn	Oct. 2, 1866	58, 465
Carriage-shackle	G. T. Pearsall	Apalachin, N. Y	Apr. 31, 1867	64, 249
Carriage-shackle	J. E. Prudden	Birmingham, Conn	Oct. 29, 1876	70, 358

Index of patents issued from the United States Patent Office from 1790 to 1873, inclusive—Continued.

Invention.	Inventor.	Residence.	Date.	No.
Carriage-shackle	T. S. Smith	New Haven, Conn	Nov. 13, 1866	59, 728
Carriage-shackle	F. M. Weller	Evanston, Ill	May 28, 1867	65, 317
Carriage-shackle	L. Wilkinson	New Haven, Conn	Sept. 17, 1867	68, 924
Carriage-shackle-blank die	W. B. Smith	Plantsville, Conn	Aug. 9, 1870	106, 225
Carriage-shackle die	R. R. Miller	Plantsville, Conn	Jan. 4, 1870	98, 610
Carriage-shackle die	L. S. White	Plantsville, Conn	Apr. 12, 1870	101, 952
Carriage-shackle-eyes, Die for forging	H. M. Beecher	Plantsville, Conn	Apr. 30, 1872	126, 252
Carriage-shackle-forming die	H. M. Beecher	Plantsville, Conn	June 20, 1871	116, 012
Carriage-shackles, Machine for drilling	J. B. Clark	Plantsville, Conn	Oct. 4, 1870	107, 875
Carriage-shackles, Process of forging	F. B. Morse	Plantsville, Conn	Aug. 9, 1870	106, 190
Carriage-shaft connection	C. Tholl	Boston, Mass	Oct. 29, 1867	70, 289
Carriage-shaft-holding attachment	A. C. Maxfield	Biddeford, Me	Oct. 14, 1873	143, 582
Carriage-shaft iron	W. W. Knowles	Plantsville, Conn	May 13, 1873	138, 753
Carriage shaft or pole coupling	C. G. Dudley and J. Gulden	Key Port, N. J	May 3, 1870	102, 515
Carriage-shaft-shackle die	H. M. Beecher	Plantsville, Conn	Aug. 24, 1869	93, 951
Carriage shifting-seat	C. R. Mellinger	Manor Township, Pa	Nov. 20, 1866	59, 920
Carriage shifting-top	A. Soursin	Saint Louis, Mo	July 16, 1867	66, 746
Carriage slat-iron	F. B. Morse	Plantsville, Conn	Oct. 26, 1869	96, 253
Carriage-spring	D. S. Abbott	Ischua, N. Y	Dec. 13, 1870	199, 993
Carriage-spring	J. B. Ashley	New Bedford, Mass	Nov. 11, 1867	71, 118
Carriage-spring	J. Bacon	Bedford, Mass	Mar. 9, 1842	2, 484
Carriage-spring	J. Balbach	San José, Cal	Feb. 2, 1869	86, 348
Carriage-spring, &c	M. L. Ballard	Canton, Ohio	Apr. 3, 1866	53, 556
Carriage-spring	B. M. Beckwith	Plattsburgh, N. Y	July 3, 1866	55, 985
Carriage-spring	L. Bissell	New York, N. Y	May 20, 1851	8, 105
Carriage-spring	L. Bissell	New York, N. Y	Nov. 4, 1851	8, 498
Carriage-spring	P. E. Bomboy	Espy, Pa	Dec. 3, 1867	71, 574
Carriage-spring	M. H. Bonwill	Canterbury, Del	Nov. 17, 1818	....
Carriage-spring	P. Broadbooks	Batavia, N. Y	July 25, 1871	117, 253
Carriage-spring	R. B. Brown	Essex, Vt	Dec. 14, 1841	2, 385
Carriage-spring	J. Bullock	Windsor, N. Y	Dec. 9, 1873	145, 333
Carriage spring	C. H. Butterfield	Sturbridge, Mass	Jan. 1, 1867	60, 831
Carriage-spring	A. Buzzell	West Fairlee, Vt	Sept. 15 1868	82, 082
Carriage-spring	H. S. Clark	Wyalusing, Pa	Aug. 30, 1859	25, 246
Carriage-spring	J. Cone	Reading, Conn	Aug. 26, 1808	....
Carriage-spring	J. Curtis	Cincinnati, Ohio	Nov. 11, 1873	144, 514
Carriage-spring	T. De Witt	Detroit, Mich	Sept. 17 1867	68, 966
Carriage-spring	G. Douglass	Bridgeport, Conn	June 2, 1868	78, 439
Carriage-spring	W. H. English	Macon, Ga	Sept. 24, 1867	69, 197
Carriage-spring	J. U. Fiester	Winchester, Ohio	June 17, 1856	15, 126
Carriage-spring	J. M. Forrest	Norfolk, Va	Jan. 31, 1860	26, 981
Carriage-spring	J. S. Foster	Salem, Mass	June 14, 1870	104, 135
Carriage-spring	C. B. Galentine	Brooklyn Centre, Ohio	July 14, 1863	39, 224
Carriage-spring	P. G. Gardiner	New York, N. Y	Apr. 2, 1861	31, 881
Carriage-spring	E. L. Gaylord	Terryville, Conn	Sept. 29, 1868	82, 510
Carriage-spring	J. W. Gilmer and W. H. De Valin.	Sacramento, Cal	Aug. 17, 1869	93, 703
Carriage-spring	D. R. Gould and W. S. Wickham.	Chestertown, N. Y	Sept. 6, 1870	107, 173
Carriage-spring	A. B. Greenwalt	Baltimore, Md	Aug. 21, 1866	57, 312
Carriage-spring	C. S. S. Griffing	Salem, Ohio	Mar. 25, 1873	137, 197
Carriage-spring	G. R. Groot	Cincinnati, Ohio	July 13, 1869	92, 525
Carriage-spring	C. H. Guard	Brownville, N. Y	June 10, 1851	8, 152
Carriage-spring	C. F. Hall	Rockford, Ill	Apr. 29, 1873	138, 247
Carriage-spring	E. Hall	Oxford, N. Y	July 4, 1871	116, 705
Carriage-spring	G. W. Harlan	Cincinnati, Ohio	Sept. 9, 1873	142, 627
Carriage-spring	G. L. Hausknecht	New Haven, Conn	July 15, 1851	8, 221
Carriage-spring	B. T. Henry	New Haven, Conn	May 21, 1867	64, 866
Carriage-spring	B. T. Henry	New Haven, Conn	Mar. 8, 1870	100, 626
Carriage-spring	W. B. Higgins	San Francisco, Cal	May 12, 1868	77, 880
Carriage-spring	E. C. Hodge and D. H. Mann	Oneonta and Delhi, N. Y	June 22, 1869	91, 538
Carriage-spring	B. R. Hood	Clinton, N. C	Oct. 20, 1857	18, 451
Carriage-spring	G. Hopson	Bridgeport, Conn	Oct. 14, 1873	143, 576
Carriage-spring	M. C. Hubbard	Rochester, N. Y	July 22, 1851	8, 244
Carriage-spring	M. G. Hubbard	New York, N. Y	May 15, 1855	12, 890
Carriage-spring	M. G. Hubbard	New York, N. Y	May 22, 1855	12, 910
Carriage-spring	R. and I. C. Humphries	Cantwell's Bridge, Del	Apr. 22, 1814	....
Carriage-spring	N. Hungerford	Ithaca, N. Y	Mar. 31, 1836	....
Carriage-spring	F. A. Huntington	San Francisco, Cal	Dec. 15, 1868	85, 008
Carriage-spring	H. T. Hyde	Troy, N. Y	Apr. 3, 1840	6, 276
Carriage-spring	J. M. and E. Ingold	Allegheny, Pa	Mar. 5, 1867	62, 543
Carriage-spring	E. Ives and J. Hill	New Haven, Conn	June 3, 1808	....
Carriage-spring	J. Jackson	Owego, N. Y	Oct. 20, 1868	83, 170
Carriage-spring	G. W. La Baw and P. F. Campbell.	Jersey City, N. J	Aug. 19, 1862	36, 220
Carriage-spring	D. M. Lane	West Philadelphia, Pa	June 8, 1858	20, 497
Carriage-spring	G. H. Laub	Newark, Mo	Aug. 14, 1860	29, 605
Carriage-spring	A. A. Livingston	Wilmington, Ill	Dec. 3, 1872	133, 651
Carriage-spring	J. R. Locke	San Francisco, Cal	Oct. 6, 1868	82, 726
Carriage-spring	J. R. Locke	San Francisco, Cal	Oct. 6, 1868	82, 727
Carriage-spring	G. S. Manning	Springfield, Ill	June 5, 1866	55, 319
Carriage-spring	E. Maynard	Brooklyn, N. Y	Mar. 1, 1859	23, 102
Carriage-spring	E. Maynard	Brooklyn, N. Y	Apr. 3, 1860	27, 731
Carriage-spring	A. R. Miller	Attica, N. Y	Nov. 26, 1861	33, 789
Carriage-spring	J. M. Miller	Cincinnati, Ohio	Dec. 29, 1868	85, 323
Carriage-spring	R. Montgomery	New York, N. Y	Feb. 5, 1856	14, 197
Carriage-spring	F. B. Morse	Plantsville, Conn	Nov. 1, 1870	108, 929
Carriage-spring	T. Murgatroyd, jr	Smithville, Canada	Apr. 24, 1855	12, 764
Carriage-spring	T. Murgatroyd	Hiawatha, Kans	May 27, 1873	139, 325
Carriage-spring	H. H. Olds	New Haven, Conn	Aug. 22, 1865	49, 545
Carriage-spring	H. Pace, sr	Cincinnati, Ohio	Oct. 14, 1835	....
Carriage-spring	R. W. Parker	Woburn, Mass	Nov. 29, 1864	45, 265
Carriage-spring	L. H. Parsons	Stockbridge, Mass	June 23, 1824	....
Carriage-spring	W. Patton	Towanda, Pa	Jan. 9, 1838	569
Carriage-spring	S. B. Peet	New York, N. Y	Sept. 13, 1859	25, 439
Carriage-spring	C. P. Phillips	Syracuse, N. Y	Nov. 22, 1864	45, 173
Carriage-spring	J. W. Post	Lansing, Mich	Jan. 7, 1873	134, 703

Index of patents issued from the United States Patent Office from 1790 to 1873, inclusive—Continued.

Invention.	Inventor.	Residence.	Date.	No.
Carriage-spring	B. F. Power	Morgan County, Ohio	June 29, 1869	92, 093
Carriage-spring	D. R. Pratt	Worcester, Mass	Mar. 20, 1849	6, 215
Carriage-spring	J. B. Pressey and D. Sheets	Suisun City, Cal	Oct. 16, 1860	30, 422
Carriage-spring	T. H. Prusbaw	Fredonia, N. Y	Nov. 22, 1870	109, 544
Carriage-spring	J. G. Reiff	Farmersville, Pa	Oct. 8, 1867	69, 568
Carriage-spring	G. N. Reynolds	Charleston, S. C	Apr. 30, 1819	......
Carriage-spring	J. D. Richardson	Houston, Tex	Apr. 29, 1873	138, 438
Carriage-spring	A. J. Ritter	Rahway, N. J	June 27, 1865	48, 444
Carriage-spring	B. H. Roberts	Fall River, Mass	Nov. 24, 1868	84, 378
Carriage-spring	J. D. Sarven	Columbia, Tenn	Feb. 4, 1868	74, 009
Carriage-spring	J. D. Sarven	Columbia, Tenn	Feb. 4, 1868	74, 010
Carriage-spring	A. Selkirk	Albany, N. Y	Sept. 26, 1865	50, 209
Carriage-spring	W. Sharp	Burdett, N. Y	Apr. 7, 1838	682
Carriage-spring	T. J. Shears	Ypsilanti, Mich	Oct. 20, 1868	83, 217
Carriage-spring	C. Sheldon	Middleburgh, N. Y	Jan. 25, 1870	99, 249
Carriage-spring	D. Shockey	Waynesborough, Pa	Dec. 28, 1869	98, 433
Carriage spring	A. E. Smith	Bronxville, N. Y	Sept. 21, 1869	94, 981
Carriage-spring	W. Smith	Shrewsbury, Pa	Oct. 11, 1864	44, 668
Carriage-spring	E. T. Sprout	Springville, Pa	July 18, 1848	5, 674
Carriage-spring	S. Steward	Trenton, N. J	Oct. 25, 1870	108, 649
Carriage-spring	A. C. Stowe	San José, Cal	Nov. 24, 1868	84, 316
Carriage-spring	A. C. Stowe	San José, Cal	Dec. 22, 1868	85, 144
Carriage-spring	W. W. Sutliff	Town Line, Pa	Mar. 24, 1868	75, 999
Carriage-spring	W. Taylor	East Zora, Canada	Nov. 7, 1865	50, 886
Carriage-spring	G. W. Tew	Kansas City, Mo	Dec. 21, 1869	98, 207
Carriage-spring	W. S. Thomas	Norwich, N. Y	Oct. 30, 1849	6, 839
Carriage-spring	W. F. Vernier	Philadelphia, Pa	Nov. 24, 1868	84, 446
Carriage-spring	R. Walker	Harrisville, Ohio	Dec. 9, 1873	145, 374
Carriage-spring	R. E. Walker	Dresden, Mo	Aug. 2, 1870	106, 005
Carriage-spring	W. Wharton	Birmingham, England	Feb. 10, 1863	37, 653
Carriage-spring	J. B. Whitcomb	Beloit, Wis	Feb. 18, 1873	136, 116
Carriage-spring	W. F. Whitney	Milton, N. Y	Nov. 3, 1868	83, 810
Carriage-spring	D. D. Wisell	Zanesville, Ind	Oct. 10, 1871	119, 907
Carriage-spring	G. Woeber	Davenport, Iowa	Dec. 1, 1863	40, 787
Carriage-spring	A. E. Wolcott	Chicago, Ill	May 18, 1869	90, 144
Carriage-spring	A. E. Wolcott	Chicago, Ill	May 18, 1869	90, 145
Carriage-spring	A. E. Wolcott	Chicago, Ill	May 18, 1869	90, 146
Carriage-spring	T. H. Wood	New York, N. Y	May 27, 1873	139, 348
Carriage-spring	E. G. Woodside	Augusta, Me	May 4, 1838	725
Carriage-spring	E. M. Wright	Wyandotte, Kans	Nov. 1, 1864	44, 908
Carriage-spring, Adjustable	I. Carter	Champlain, N. Y	Feb. 7, 1860	27, 036
Carriage-spring, Adjustable	R. S. Morse	Dixfield, Me	Nov. 1, 1853	10, 188
Carriage-spring, Adjustable	G. Palmer	Littlestown, Pa	July 24, 1860	29, 306
Carriage-spring, and attaching carriage-bodies thereto.	J. Ives and J. Walters	Brooklyn, N. Y	Oct. 6, 1830	......
Carriage spring and coupling	F. De Witt	Detroit, Mich	May 7, 1867	64, 501
Carriage-spring and mode of attachment	C. W. Saladee	St. Catharine's, Canada	Feb. 20, 1872	123, 937
Carriage-spring attachment	O. E. Bonnett	Cannonsville, N. Y	Oct. 3, 1871	119, 560
Carriage-spring bars, Metallic scroll-ends for	A. L. Warburton and H. Bendir	Fort Wayne, Ind	Feb. 4, 1868	74, 178
Carriage, Spring-body	A. Moffit	Brownsville, Pa	Aug. 8, 1854	11, 490
Carriage-spring brace	J. H. Chadwick	Wheaton, Ill	Feb. 18, 1868	74, 499
Carriage-spring brace	T. Dutton	Washington, D. C	Oct. 14, 1856	15, 914
Carriage-spring brace	W. Evans	Eureka, Wis	Feb. 15, 1870	99, 867
Carriage-spring brace	C. C. Gleason	Wauconda, Ill	Sept. 26, 1865	50, 114
Carriage-spring brace	L. C. Miller	Humphrey, N. Y	Apr. 28, 1868	77, 306
Carriage-spring brace	L. C. Miller	Humphrey, N. Y	Jan. 24, 1871	111, 229
Carriage-spring brace	D. W. Norris	Paxton, Ill	Apr. 18, 1871	113, 915
Carriage-spring brace	E. T. Sprouth	Dimock, Pa	Sept. 7, 1844	3, 729
Carriage-spring brace and clip	E. J. Green	Valparaiso, Ind	June 7, 1864	43, 019
Carriage-spring clip	D. W. Baird	Geneva, N. Y	June 10, 1873	139, 648
Carriage-spring clip and brace	J. H. Deal	Hornellsville, N. Y	July 23, 1867	66, 953
Carriage-spring clip and plate	H. M. Beecher	Plantsville, Conn	Jan. 2, 1872	122, 428
Carriage-spring-clip plate	N. C. Dean	Union Springs, N. Y	Jan. 14, 1873	134, 859
Carriage-spring clips, Manufacture of	H. M. Beecher	Plantsville, Conn	Jan. 30, 1872	123, 079
Carriage-spring coupling	U. S. Hall	Watkins, N. Y	Dec. 10, 1872	133, 705
Carriage-spring, Elastic	T. Long	Vandalia, Ill	Nov. 5, 1867	70, 446
Carriage-spring, Elliptic	H. R. Hawkins	Akron, Ohio	Dec. 10, 1867	72, 035
Carriage-spring for light vehicles	R. Burns, jr	New York, N. Y	July 18, 1854	11, 345
Carriage-spring guard	O. H. Wheeler	Hamlin, Mich	June 14, 1870	104, 239
Carriage-spring guard	T. Winans	Baltimore, Md	Feb. 16, 1858	19, 396
Carriage-spring-head ears, Die for forging	J. Evans	New Haven, Conn	June 14, 1870	104, 292
Carriage-spring-head ears, Die for forging	J. Evans	New Haven, Conn	June 21, 1870	104, 440
Carriage-spring-head-forging die	J. H. Mason	New Haven, Conn	June 20, 1871	116, 206
Carriage-spring heads, Machine for filing	C. B. and G. Gilbert	Philadelphia, Pa	Nov. 26, 1872	133, 432
Carriage-spring heads, Machine for heading	J. Evans	New Haven, Conn	Oct. 29, 1861	33, 580
Carriage-spring heads, Machine for milling	W. Evans	New Haven, Conn	Oct. 4, 1870	108, 013
Carriage-spring heads, Manufacturing	W. R. Petrie	Westville, Conn	June 14, 1870	104, 194
Carriage-spring jack	R. R. Miller	Plantsville, Conn	Feb. 22, 1870	100, 176
Carriage-spring perch	E. R. Ferry	New Haven, Conn	Oct. 26, 1869	96, 216
Carriage spring-seat	F. M. Hubbard	Ripon, Wis	July 31, 1866	56, 753
Carriage-spring supporter	D. H. Brown	Utica, Mo	Feb. 14, 1871	111, 809
Carriage-spring supporter	N. A. Newton	Schoolcraft, Mich	May 21, 1872	127, 096
Carriage-spring, Thorough-brace	J. Mix	New Haven, Conn	June 17, 1808	....
Carriage spring Wheel	W. Wing and H. Salisbury	Hartford, Conn	Aug. 29, 1805	....
Carriage-spring, Wooden	L. Birckhead	Philadelphia, Pa	Dec. 30, 1814	....
Carriage-spring, Wooden	J. Greenwood	New Castle, Del	Apr. 28, 1818	....
Carriage-spring, Wooden	L. H. Thrall	Troy, N. Y	Nov. 10, 1813	....
Carriage-springs, Adjustable shackle for	J. Bullard	North Hyde Park, Vt	Dec. 13, 1870	110, 006
Carriage-springs, Adjustable shackle for tightening	F. P. Hutchinson	Manchester, N. H	June 25, 1872	128, 399
Carriage-springs, Arrangement of	R. P. March	Jeffersonville, Pa	Apr. 7, 1857	16, 986
Carriage-springs, Arrangement of	C. A. McElroy	Delaware, Ohio	Mar. 10, 1857	16, 802
Carriage-springs, Arrangement of	T. Phillips	Ann Arbor, Mich	Mar. 25, 1861	31, 823
Carriage-springs, Arrangement of	E. Roughton	Frostburgh, Md	Feb. 26, 1861	31, 569
Carriage-springs, Attaching	U. S. Hall	Chemung, N. Y	May 9, 1871	114, 676
Carriage-springs, Attaching	D. A. Morton	Groton, N. Y	Jan. 9, 1838	551
Carriage-springs, Attaching	L. O. Rice	Berlin, Canada	July 6, 1858	20, 820
Carriage-springs, Connecting	J. A. Topliff and G. H. Ely	Elyria, Ohio	Dec. 19, 1871	122, 079
Carriage-springs, Device for holding	R. Rowell and F. H. Briggs	Boston, Mass	Feb. 27, 1866	52, 889

Index of patents issued from the United States Patent Office from 1790 *to* 1873, *inclusive*—Continued.

Invention.	Inventor.	Residence.	Date.	No.
Carriage-springs, Equalizing	D. G. Rollin	New York, N. Y	Jan. 12, 1858	19, 102
Carriage-springs, Forming heads of	S. H. Hartman	Pittsburgh, Pa	May 18, 1858	20, 268
Carriage-springs, Goose-neck for hanging	S. M. Wier	New Haven, Conn	May 10, 1870	102, 999
Carriage-springs, Machine for forming	W. Harty	Bridgeport, Conn	Mar. 28, 1871	113, 164
Carriage-springs, Machine for grinding	H. M. Wentworth	Gardiner, Me	Mar. 21, 1871	112, 873
Carriage-springs, Machine for shaping light	L. H. Richardson	Westfield, Mass	June 18, 1872	128, 173
Carriage-springs, Manner of applying	J. S. Tough	Baltimore, Md	June 9, 1843	3, 126
Carriage-springs, Manufacturing steel	L. Gleason	Stafford, N. Y	Dec. 24, 1834	....
Carriage-springs, Method of forming heads of	B. T. Henry	New Haven, Conn	Dec. 28, 1869	98, 376
Carriage-springs, Method of manufacturing leaves of steel.	M. Seabury	Waterville, N. Y	Apr. 29, 1839	1, 137
Carriage-springs, Mill for rolling steel	J. Stondinger	Newark, N. J	July 17, 1830	....
Carriage-springs, Mode of adjusting	M. G. Hubbard	Penn Yan, N. Y	July 1, 1856	15, 234
Carriage-springs, Mode of applying	I. Jones, A. M. Eels, and H. Griswold.	Delaware County, N. Y	July 16, 1838	842
Carriage-springs, Mode of equalizing the action of.	C. W. Saladee	Saint Catharine's, Canada.	Apr. 9, 1872	125, 413
Carriage-stay	G. G. Larkin	Portland, Me	Aug. 23, 1870	106, 593
Carriage, Steam	G. W. Barnett	Urbana, Ohio	Nov. 22, 1864	45, 130
Carriage. Steam	L. Bigelow	Petersham, Mass	Aug. 29, 1823	....
Carriage, Steam	Z. P. Dederick and I. Grass	Newark, N. J	Mar. 24, 1868	75, 874
Carriage, Steam	M. Fletcher	Louisville, Ky	Sept. 4, 1866	57, 696
Carriage, Steam	J. S. Hall	Pittsburgh, Pa	Mar. 31, 1857	16, 919
Carriage, Steam	J. V. Merrick	Philadelphia, Pa	Apr. 17, 1860	27, 920
Carriage, Steam land	C. H. Baker	Red Wing, Minn	July 3, 1860	28, 955
Carriage, Steam land	J. B. McKinley	Spencer County, Ky	Feb. 14, 1871	111, 761
Carriage-step	F. Baker	New York, N. Y	Apr. 2, 1867	63, 458
Carriage-step	H. T. Betts	Springfield, Mass	June 4, 1861	32, 460
Carriage-step	C. H. Gould	Boston, Mass	Apr. 8, 1873	137, 547
Carriage-step	G. A. Keene	Lynn, Mass	Dec. 24, 1872	134, 291
Carriage-step	G. A. Keene	Lynn, Mass	Feb. 11, 1873	135, 815
Carriage-step	W. H. Knowles	Plantsville, Conn	July 26, 1870	105, 876
Carriage-step	D. and E. Z. Little	Gettysburgh, Pa	Oct. 7, 1846	4, 795
Carriage-step	F. B. Morse	Plantsville, Conn	Mar. 22, 1870	101, 150
Carriage-step	F. B. Morse	Plantsville, Conn	Apr. 4, 1871	113, 551
Carriage-step	F. B. Morse	Plantsville, Conn	Aug. 29, 1871	118, 632
Carriage-step	G. Panchot	Hastings, Minn	Oct. 20, 1868	83, 305
Carriage-step	C. Parker and W. Volger	Canterbury, N. H	Oct. 1, 1867	69, 364
Carriage-step	J. Pendergast	New Haven, Conn	May 19, 1872	124, 697
Carriage-step	G. M. Plympton	New York, N. Y	Feb. 18, 1868	74, 589
Carriage-step	E. Wells	New Haven, Conn	Apr. 2, 1872	125, 235
Carriage-step	J. H. Yager	Trenton, Ohio	Apr. 2, 1867	63, 601
Carriage step and wheel fender	J. W. Gosling	Cincinnati, Ohio	May 4, 1869	89, 759
Carriage-step block	P. F. Hulbert	Chatham, N. Y	Mar. 20, 1866	53, 302
Carriage step cover and wheel fender	J. Curtis	Cincinnati, Ohio	Dec. 8, 1868	84, 802
Carriage step cover and wheel fender	J. Roberts	Cincinnati, Ohio	May 25, 1869	90, 584
Carriage-step die	F. B. Morse	Plantsville, Conn	Dec. 12, 1871	121, 803
Carriage-step-forming die	L. Burns	Port Chester, N. Y	May 24, 1870	103, 296
Carriage-step guard	R. H. Goodwin, G. L. Gamage, and R. J. P. Goodwin.	Boston and Lynn, Mass., and Manchester, N. H.	Jan. 4, 1870	98, 488
Carriage-step screen	A. L. Ross	Cleves, Ohio	May 5, 1868	77, 531
Carriage-step shield	C. H. Gould	Boston, Mass	Sept. 20, 1870	107, 482
Carriage-steps, India-rubber tread for	G. A. Keene	Newburyport, Mass	June 11, 1867	65, 754
Carriage-steps, Method of forming	W. N. Knowles	Plantsville, Conn	June 7, 1870	104, 040
Carriage-steps, Method of making	F. B. Morse	Plantsville, Conn	Apr. 25, 1871	114, 025
Carriage, Street	G. S. McHenry	Kansas City, Mo	Aug. 22, 1871	118, 255
Carriage. Street-railway	W. L. Burt	Cambridge, Mass	Aug. 12, 1862	36, 137
Carriage stump-joint	F. B. Morse	New Haven, Conn	July 21, 1868	80, 202
Carriage stump-joint	F. B. Morse	New Haven, Conn	Aug. 18, 1868	81, 193
Carriage stump-joint	F. B. Morse	Plantsville, Conn	Oct. 19, 1869	96, 024
Carriage stump-joint	F. B. Morse	Plantsville, Conn	Oct. 19, 1869	96, 025
Carriage, Swing	W. Hewett	Trenton, N. J	Apr. 14, 1868	76, 629
Carriage, Three-wheeled	C. H. Barrows	Willimantic, Conn	June 21, 1870	104, 409
Carriage, Three-wheeled	J. Gehr	Mercersburgh, Pa	Oct. 1, 1867	69, 335
Carriage, Three-wheeled pleasure	C. W. Saladee	Columbus, Ohio	July 15, 1856	15, 345
Carriage-thill	J. P. Tyson	Philadelphia, Pa	Mar. 17, 1868	75, 711
Carriage-thill hold-back	P. S. Van Wagner	Saltfleet Township, Canada	Nov. 16, 1869	96, 851
Carriage to be moved by manual labor, Four-wheeled.	L. Cook	Whitestown, N. Y	Mar. 28, 1811	....
Carriage to be propelled by mechanical powers	J. J. Staples	....	Apr. 25, 1794	....
Carriage to overcome obstructions in roads	H. Knowles	Colchester, Conn	Aug. 29, 1833	....
Carriage-tongue, Child's	E. A. Morse	Rutland, Vt	Feb. 7, 1871	111, 558
Carriage-tongue shackle	F. R. Pollard	Canaan, N. H	July 24, 1866	56, 606
Carriage-top	W. Bauder	Circleville, Ohio	May 16, 1871	114, 751
Carriage-top	N. Benedict	Aurelius, N. Y	Jan. 12, 1858	19, 065
Carriage-top	G. Bockstaller	Chicago, Ill	June 3, 1873	139, 450
Carriage-top	P. Boyden	Sandy Creek, N. Y	Mar. 29, 1859	23, 347
Carriage-top	N. G. Burr	Homer, N. Y	Aug. 18, 1868	81, 135
Carriage-top	R. M. Colton	Southbridge, Mass	Apr. 30, 1872	126, 130
Carriage-top	C. A. Dearborn	New Bedford, Mass	Oct. 28, 1873	144, 069
Carriage top	L. Z Dodds and R. Walsh	Three Rivers, Mich	Aug. 29, 1865	49, 611
Carriage-top	D. B. Dorsey	Chillicothe, Mo	Dec. 23, 1873	145, 730
Carriage-top	S. Emmons and E. S. Simpson	Geneva, N. Y	Nov. 19, 1867	71, 151
Carriage-top	J. Enders	Boston, Mass	June 27, 1865	48, 386
Carriage-top	J. M. Freeman	Belleville, N. Y	Feb. 14, 1860	27, 121
Carriage-top	J. N. Gill	Oshkosh, Wis	Nov. 18, 1873	144, 612
Carriage-top	A. J. Hall and R. Patten	Morristown, Vt	Nov. 22, 1859	26, 183
Carriage-top	H. Hayes	Quincy, Ill	Mar. 11, 1856	14, 400
Carriage-top	S. T. Huntington	Syracuse, N. Y	June 20, 1854	11, 126
Carriage-top	K. T. Hurlburt	Lyons, N. Y	July 11, 1865	48, 688
Carriage top	M. T. Jackson	Montrose, Pa	Mar. 1, 1870	100, 295
Carriage-top	R. S. Jennings	Waterbury, Conn	Mar. 31, 1857	16, 925
Carriage-top	R. S. Jennings	Waterbury, Conn	June 30, 1857	17, 680
Carriage-top	A. McKenzie	Westminster, England	Sept. 19, 1871	119, 166
Carriage-top	R. Miller	Middlefield, Ohio	Apr. 4, 1854	10, 723
Carriage-top	P. Owens	Chicago, Ill	Sept. 24, 1867	69, 119
Carriage-top	W. I. Peck	Carthage, N. Y	July 29, 1873	141, 377
Carriage-top	L. Righter	Salem, Ohio	Jan. 12, 1869	85, 853
Carriage-top	W. F. Rundell	Genoa, N. Y	Nov. 27, 1866	60, 066

Index of patents issued from the United States Patent Office from 1790 *to* 1873, *inclusive*—Continued.

Invention.	Inventor.	Residence.	Date.	No.
Carriage-top	J. F. Sargent	North Tunbridge, Vt	Aug. 4, 1868	80, 670
Carriage-top	H. Sayler	Saint Paris, Ohio	Nov. 18, 1873	144, 704
Carriage-top	F. C. Schaffer	Brooklyn, N. Y	Sept. 13, 1859	25, 445
Carriage-top	W. Schoch	Plumsteadville, Pa	Feb. 8, 1870	99, 601
Carriage-top	E. S. Scripture	Brooklyn, N. Y	June 9, 1868	78, 836
Carriage-top	W. Smith and E. M. Pike	McDonough, N. Y	Jan. 28, 1868	73, 763
Carriage-top	J. H. Snyder	Rockford, Ill	Aug. 19, 1873	142, 050
Carriage-top	R. H. Wright	New Bloomfield, Pa	Apr. 6, 1869	88, 597
Carriage-top	G. H. Young	New York, N. Y	May 20, 1873	139, 225
Carriage top and back, Shifting	R. M. Stivers and G. W. V. Smith.	New York, N. Y	Sept. 23, 1862	36, 539
Carriage-top bow	J. F. Fowler	Alliance, Ohio	June 28, 1870	104, 724
Carriage-top bows, Machine for adjusting	A. Soursin	Saint Louis, Mo	July 16, 1867	66, 747
Carriage-top brace	J. L. Allen	New Haven, Conn	Oct. 15, 1850	7, 715
Carriage-top brace, Concealed jointed	D. W. Baird	Geneva, N. Y	Sept. 30, 1873	143, 316
Carriage-top-brace joint	G. Gregory and F. B. Morse	New Haven, Conn	Apr. 16, 1867	63, 792
Carriage-top-brace joint	F. B. Morse	New Haven, Conn	Apr. 23, 1867	64, 024
Carriage-top brace, Stump-joint for	F. Van Patten and E. D. Clapp.	Auburn, N. Y	Nov. 29, 1870	109, 782
Carriage-top button-hole	S. A. Budd	Cleveland, Ohio	Nov. 12, 1867	70, 797
Carriage top, Calash	G. and D. Cook	New Haven, Conn	Jan. 27, 1857	16, 467
Carriage-top fixture	N. B. Richardson	Somerville, N. J	Nov. 1, 1870	108, 831
Carriage-top, Folding	T. H. Wood	New York, N. Y	July 12, 1870	105, 287
Carriage-top frame	J. H. Flagg	Perkinsville, Vt	Feb. 25, 1868	74, 809
Carriage-top joint	W. H. Busser	Sidney, Ohio	Jan. 26, 1869	86, 278
Carriage-top joint	J. H. Combs	Stamford, Conn	Oct. 14, 1873	143, 669
Carriage-top joint	A. C. Shelton and B. Tuttle	Plymouth, Conn	Dec. 29, 1857	18, 992
Carriage-top joint	W. B. C. Stirling and J. W. Pohlman.	Batavia, Ohio	Dec. 2, 1873	145, 135
Carriage-top joint	R. W. Stone	Solsville, N. Y	Nov. 3, 1857	18, 558
Carriage-top joint	J. A. Topliff and G. H. Ely	Elyria, Ohio	Oct. 15, 1872	132, 188
Carriage-top, Molded	G. L. Swett and J. P. Lockey	Leominster, Mass	Nov. 15, 1870	109, 272
Carriage-top, Moving	O. E. Mallory	Batavia, N. Y	June 28, 1870	104, 863
Carriage-top prop	C. R. Abbot	Elmira, N. Y	May 28, 1867	65, 150
Carriage-top prop	J. Bauer	Cincinnati, Ohio	Dec. 3, 1872	133, 619
Carriage-top prop	L. W. Blessing	Wilmington, Del	Sept. 16, 1873	142, 889
Carriage-top prop	F. A. Bradley	New Haven, Conn	Sept. 15, 1868	82, 203
Carriage-top prop	F. A. Bradley	New Haven, Conn	May 16, 1871	114, 909
Carriage-top prop	G. Cook and H. I. Kimball	New Haven, Conn	Dec. 27, 1859	26, 564
Carriage-top prop	W. P. Elam	Petersburgh, Ill	Dec. 30, 1873	145, 935
Carriage-top prop	R. S. Grummon	Newark, N. J	Apr. 23, 1867	64, 010
Carriage-top prop	F. B. Morse	Plantsville, Conn	Oct. 26, 1869	96, 254
Carriage-top prop	J. F. Mullen	New York, N. Y	Jan. 21, 1868	73, 632
Carriage-top prop	W. B. Pardee	New Haven, Conn	Dec. 1, 1868	84, 573
Carriage-top prop	A. Searls	San Francisco, Cal	Nov. 19, 1867	71, 228
Carriage-top prop	A. Searls	Newark, N. J	Aug. 2, 1870	105, 985
Carriage-top prop	A. Searls	Newark, N. J	Mar. 5, 1872	124, 291
Carriage-top prop	A. Searls	Newark, N. J	Sept. 24, 1872	131, 569
Carriage-top prop	D. M. Valentine	New York, N. Y	Apr. 16, 1872	125, 772
Carriage-top-prop block	W. N. Barnett	Urbana, Ohio	Jan. 23, 1866	52, 126
Carriage-top-prop block	W. H. Stickel	Knightstown, Ind	July 30, 1867	67, 371
Carriage-top-prop-block washer	A. D. Westbrook	Astoria, N. Y	Dec. 26, 1871	122, 205
Carriage-top-prop joint	C. W. Saladee	Saint Catharine's, Canada	Oct. 17, 1871	120, 107
Carriage-top-prop joint	E. W. Waite	New Haven, Conn	Sept. 22, 1868	82, 456
Carriage-top-prop rest	H. W. Libbey	Cleveland, Ohio	June 4, 1867	65, 403
Carriage-top protector	R. Nickson	Akron, Ohio	Oct. 23, 1866	59, 056
Carriage-top rest	C. C. Lawrence and J. Lewis	Marengo, Mich	Nov. 30, 1869	97, 301
Carriage-top rest	J. Lewis	Marengo, Mich	July 5, 1870	105, 097
Carriage-top rest	W. O. Snyder	Philadelphia, Pa	Jan. 19, 1869	86, 107
Carriage-top setter	J. Poffenbarger	Farmersville, Ohio	Sept. 23, 1873	143, 183
Carriage-top, Shifting	A. V. Heyden	Milwaukee, Wis	Oct. 23, 1866	59, 014
Carriage-top, Shifting	G. R. Lucas	Mannsville, N. Y	Jan. 5, 1869	85, 680
Carriage-top, Shifting	O. E. Mallory	Batavia, N. Y	Aug. 30, 1870	106, 947
Carriage-top, Shifting	O. E. Mallory	Batavia, N. Y	Nov. 22, 1870	109, 528
Carriage-top, Shifting	O. E. Mallory	Batavia, N. Y	Apr. 30, 1872	126, 313
Carriage-top support	H. J. Lingenfelter	Glen, N. Y	Nov. 5, 1872	132, 766
Carriage-tops, Apparatus for raising and lowering	A. Quigley	Sheldrake, N. Y	Apr. 22, 1856	14, 735
Carriage-tops, Apparatus for setting bows for	E. Hayes and M. Hayes	Wheeling, Va., and Washington, Pa.	July 3, 1855	13, 171
Carriage-tops, Attaching movable	J. S. Belcher	Albany, N. Y	July 10, 1860	29, 049
Carriage-tops, Box-loop for	C. H. Davis	Syracuse, N. Y	Sept. 21, 1869	95, 004
Carriage-tops, Elevating and lowering	J. L. Allen	Syracuse, N. Y	Feb. 19, 1850	7, 097
Carriage-tops, Lowering, raising, and fastening	Z. S. Ogden	Glen's Falls, N. Y	Jan. 3, 1854	10, 373
Carriage-tops, Machine for making braces for	B. F. Hooper	Birmingham, Conn	Apr. 9, 1861	32, 028
Carriage-tops, Mode of adjusting	C. W. Saladee	Columbus, Ohio	Sept. 9, 1856	15, 725
Carriage-tops, Mode of adjusting	C. W. Saladee	Columbus, Ohio	Sept. 1, 1857	18, 106
Carriage-tops, Mode of attaching	W. Harrocks	Poughkeepsie, N. Y	July 21, 1868	80, 180
Carriage-tops, Raising	J. L. Allen	New Haven, Conn	Jan. 14, 1851	7, 897
Carriage-tops, Raising and lowering	S. Goddard and H. Warfield	Truxton, N. Y	Feb. 19, 1850	7, 100
Carriage-tops, Raising and lowering	G. Stover	Centre Hill, Pa	Oct. 30, 1866	59, 289
Carriage-tops, Raising and lowering	J. R. Winchester	Medina, N. Y	June 20, 1854	11, 144
Carriage-tops, Shifting rail for	P. G. Clancy	Augusta, Me	Sept. 17, 1867	68, 843
Carriage-tops, Shifting-rail for	S. Johns	Waupun, Wis	Apr. 24, 1866	54, 169
Carriage-tops, Shifting-rail for	W. Reynolds	New York, N. Y	May 28, 1867	65, 119
Carriage-tops, Shifting-rail for	J. J. Waldron	East Durham, N. Y	Mar. 2, 1869	87, 527
Carriage-tops, Slat-iron for	J. W. Sheppard	Plantsville, Conn	Feb. 20, 1872	123, 942
Carriage-tops, Slat-iron for	G. W. Traphagen	Glen's Falls, N. Y	Oct. 30, 1866	59, 322
Carriage transom or king-bolt and rocker-plate	J. A. Judd	Newton, Mass	Oct. 3, 1871	119, 463
Carriage, Traveling	G. H. Richards	New London, Conn	July 8, 1821	......
Carriage-trimming	C. Bried	Newark, N. J	May 21, 1867	64, 942
Carriage-trimmings, Manufacture of rubber-coated	J. W. Munson	Bridgeport, Conn	June 7, 1870	104, 056
Carriage, Two-wheeled	J. Page	New York	Sept. 14, 1840	1, 789
Carriage, wagon, &c	E. Lane	Philadelphia, Pa	Nov. 28, 1865	51, 196
Carriage-washer, Wooden	T. M. Hart	New Bedford, Mass	Dec. 1, 1868	84, 488
Carriage-washing machine	O. P. Weston	Shattuckville, Mass	Aug. 15, 1871	118, 085
Carriage, Water-proof mail	B. B. Pleasants	Brookville, Md	Dec. 7, 1837	5[illegible]9
Carriage-wheel	G. L. Ackerman	Troy, N. Y	Apr. 16, 1845	4, 001
Carriage wheel	L. Adams	Amherst, Mass	Mar. 31, 1868	76, 033
Carriage-wheel	C. Anderegg	Lawrenceburgh, Ind	July 16, 1892	129, 449

Index of patents issued from the United States Patent Office from 1790 to 1873, inclusive—Continued.

Invention.	Inventor.	Residence.	Date.	No.
Carriage-wheel	C. H. Appel	Allentown, Pa	Feb. 6, 1872	123,375
Carriage-wheel	S. Atha	West Liberty, Ohio	Nov. 9, 1869	96,656
Carriage-wheel	C. C. Ayer	Chelsea, Mass	Feb. 5, 1867	61,793
Carriage-wheel	C. C. Ayer	Chelsea, Mass	Nov. 12, 1867	70,681
Carriage-wheel	J. R. Baird	Vincennes, Ind	Mar. 8, 1870	100,584
Carriage-wheel	J. C. Baker	Adams Centre, N. Y	July 9, 1861	32,742
Carriage-wheel	A. Beale	Stamford, Conn	Sept. 10, 1867	68,594
Carriage-wheel	N. S. Bean	Manchester, N. H	Feb. 5, 1867	61,703
Carriage-wheel	H. Beebe	Haverstraw, N. Y	Mar. 12, 1834	.....
Carriage-wheel	I. E. Bower	Bainbridge, Ga	Nov. 14, 1871	120,847
Carriage-wheel	R. Brooks, jr	Rockport, Mass	Oct. 15, 1867	69,757
Carriage-wheel	T. Brownfield	Georges Township, Pa	Aug. 19, 1856	15,554
Carriage-wheel	S. R. Bryant	Waterford, Pa	Aug. 20, 1872	130,621
Carriage-wheel	S. B. Buck	Elyria, Ohio	July 19, 1870	105,546
Carriage-wheel	G. G. W. Burnham	Baltimore County, Md	Apr. 18, 1871	113,851
Carriage-wheel	J. G. Buzzell	Lynn, Mass	Oct. 1, 1867	69,403
Carriage-wheel	J. G. Buzzell	Lynn, Mass	Oct. 6, 1868	82,690
Carriage-wheel	J. G. Buzzell	Lynn, Mass	Jan. 18, 1870	98,920
Carriage-wheel	C. F. Carman	Hamburgh, Iowa	June 8, 1869	90,993
Carriage-wheel	D. W. Clark and S. H. Gray	Bridgeport, Conn	May 22, 1855	12,897
Carriage-wheel	C. Clarke	Coral, Ill	Aug. 18, 1868	81,141
Carriage-wheel	J. Coney	South Boston, Mass	Mar. 16, 1869	87,823
Carriage-wheel	S. D. Cook	West Liberty, Ohio	June 25, 1872	128,212
Carriage-wheel	J. M. Coombs	Boston, Mass	Apr. 9, 1867	63,705
Carriage-wheel	W. Cooper	Columbia, S. C	Mar. 3, 1825	.....
Carriage-wheel	S. D. Craft	New York, N. Y	Nov. 7, 1871	120,720
Carriage-wheel	C. Cummings	Providence, R. I	Mar. 16, 1869	87,913
Carriage-wheel	A. J. Curtis	Winterport, Me	Jan. 2, 1866	51,808
Carriage-wheel	D. P. Davis	New York, N. Y	July 27, 1869	93,067
Carriage-wheel	W. H. De Valin	Sacramento, Cal	Sept. 1, 1868	81,758
Carriage-wheel	H. E. Dodson	West Liberty, Ohio	Oct. 3, 1871	119,511
Carriage-wheel	F. N. Draper and A. Danison	West Liberty, Ohio	Sept. 19, 1871	119,082
Carriage-wheel	H. C. and J. W. Drew	Waterloo, Mich	Feb. 27, 1866	52,832
Carriage-wheel	J. Eastman and G. C. Rix	Bath, N. H	Dec. 23, 1830	.....
Carriage-wheel	W. P. Elam	Petersburgh, Ill	Sept. 21, 1869	95,098
Carriage-wheel	C. W. Fillmore	Marengo, Ill	Feb. 6, 1872	123,468
Carriage-wheel	J. P. Fisher	Rochester, N. Y	Dec. 18, 1860	30,915
Carriage-wheel	H. K. Flinchbaugh	Conestoga Centre, Pa	Aug. 18, 1863	39,561
Carriage-wheel	W. K. Foster	Bangor, Me	Nov. 22, 1864	45,150
Carriage-wheel	W. K. Foster	Bangor, Me	Oct. 8, 1867	69,557
Carriage-wheel	C. M. Foulke	Philadelphia, Pa	Apr. 6, 1869	88,705
Carriage-wheel	G. W. Gilbert	Radnor, Pa	May 26, 1863	38,669
Carriage-wheel	J. Goodman	Blackfriars Road, England	Feb. 21, 1865	46,524
Carriage-wheel	J. S. Graves	Lima, N. Y	Oct. 10, 1871	119,841
Carriage-wheel	D. Grim	Pittsburgh, Pa	Mar. 16, 1869	87,926
Carriage-wheel	J. W. Guider	Saint Joseph, Mo	Apr. 12, 1870	101,860
Carriage-wheel	H. Gwynn	Baltimore, Md	Dec. 16, 1873	145,646
Carriage-wheel	G. G. Hickman	Coatesville, Pa	Apr. 24, 1866	54,155
Carriage-wheel	S. B. Hindman	Richmond, Ind	Oct. 1, 1872	131,757
Carriage-wheel	I. Holmes	Moscow, N. Y	Jan. 1, 1847	4,918
Carriage-wheel	D. A. Johnson and F. M. Gibson	Chelsea, Mass	Oct. 23, 1860	30,479
Carriage-wheel	M. Johnson	Three Rivers, Mich	Mar. 26, 1872	125,053
Carriage-wheel	J. A. Johnston	Topeka, Kans	May 21, 1872	127,063
Carriage-wheel	J. A. Johnston	Topeka, Kans	May 21, 1872	127,064
Carriage-wheel	J. B. Jones	Sparta, Ill	Sept. 29, 1868	82,530
Carriage-wheel	T. M. Jones and C. W. Fillmore	Chicago, Ill	Nov. 1, 1870	108,794
Carriage-wheel	G. Kenny	Nashua, N. H	Aug. 18, 1868	81,175
Carriage-wheel	H. Keyes	Terre Haute, Ind	Dec. 28, 1869	98,273
Carriage-wheel	A. H. Leach	Marathon, N. Y	Apr. 26, 1870	102,280
Carriage-wheel	C. Leavitt	Cleveland, Ohio	Jan. 14, 1862	34,149
Carriage-wheel	O. Look	Bridgeport, Conn	Aug. 31, 1869	94,325
Carriage-wheel	J. H. Loughridge	Key West, Fla	Aug. 8, 1871	117,902
Carriage-wheel	W. H. Marshall	Sutton, N. H	Nov. 19, 1867	71,193
Carriage-wheel	W. S. Mayo	New York, N. Y	Feb. 9, 1869	86,772
Carriage-wheel	R. W. McClelland	Springfield, Ill	June 29, 1869	91,859
Carriage-wheel	R. W. McClelland	Springfield, Ill	Feb. 8, 1870	99,691
Carriage-wheel	J. McCreery	Springfield, Ill	May 30, 1871	115,497
Carriage-wheel	C. A. Miller	Urbana, Ohio	Apr. 2, 1872	125,206
Carriage-wheel	W. F. Moody	Auburn, N. Y	Sept. 28, 1869	95,370
Carriage-wheel	W. F. Morton	New Haven, Conn	May 28, 1867	65,257
Carriage-wheel	W. F. Morton	New Haven, Conn	Feb. 4, 1868	74,117
Carriage-wheel	J. and T. Nevison, jr	Morgan, Ohio	June 30, 1868	79,495
Carriage-wheel	T., jr., and J. Nevison	Morgan, Ohio	Feb. 18, 1868	74,579
Carriage-wheel	A. M. Oe[illegible]bock	Toledo, Ohio	Feb. 20, 1872	123,836
Carriage-wheel	J. O'Connor	Jackson, Mo	Apr. 16, 1872	125,840
Carriage-wheel	C. Palmer	Hamilton, Nev	Jan. 9, 1872	122,646
Carriage-wheel	A. Prentiss	Prentiss Vale, Pa	May 14, 1867	64,794
Carriage-wheel	A. Prentiss	Otto, Pa	May 14, 1867	64,795
Carriage-wheel	V. Price	New York, N. Y	May 4, 1869	89,835
Carriage-wheel	W. Race and B. Holly	Seneca Falls, N. Y	Jan. 30, 1855	12,317
Carriage-wheel	J. Raddin	Lynn, Mass	June 13, 1865	48,207
Carriage-wheel	J. Raddin	Lynn, Mass	Dec. 24, 1867	72,538
Carriage-wheel	J. A. Reed	New Market, N. J	Sept. 14, 1869	94,839
Carriage-wheel	J. Ridge	Wayne County, Ind	Sept. 20, 1870	107,543
Carriage-wheel	J. Ridge	Richmond, Ind	July 30, 1872	130,074
Carriage-wheel	J. Rowe	Cincinnati, Ohio	Jan. 26, 1847	4,946
Carriage-wheel	J. D. Sarven	Columbia, Tenn	June 9, 1857	17,520
Carriage-wheel	J. Scott	Ocala, Fla	Dec. 26, 1865	51,756
Carriage-wheel	G. W. Seymour	Whitney's Point, N. Y	Sept. 1, 1868	81,828
Carriage-wheel	S. S. Sherman and S. D. Piper	West Eau Claire, Wis	Aug. 3, 1869	93,357
Carriage-wheel	J. T. Shimer	Easton, Pa	Aug. 25, 1868	81,545
Carriage-wheel	S. E. Shute and W. C. Starr	Richmond, Ind	July 23, 1872	129,686
Carriage-wheel	J. Y. Sitton	Due West, S. C	Apr. 25, 1871	114,058
Carriage-wheel	J. Skelley	Brooklyn, N. Y	Jan. 30, 1855	12,330
Carriage-wheel	A. B. Smith	Plattsmouth, Nebr	May 19, 1868	78,143
Carriage-wheel	T. R. Smith	San Francisco, Cal	Sept. 7, 1869	94,521
Carriage-wheel	H. G. Spafford	Albany, N. Y	Nov. 25, 1814	.....
Carriage-wheel	J. C. Sparks	Philadelphia, Pa	Mar. 3, 1868	75,213

Index of patents issued from the United States Patent Office from 1790 *to* 1873, *inclusive*—Continued.

Invention.	Inventor.	Residence.	Date.	No.
Carriage-wheel	C. S. Stearns	Marlborough, Mass	Feb. 9, 1869	86, 709
Carriage-wheel	C. S. Stearns	Marlborough, Mass	Apr. 6, 1869	88, 748
Carriage-wheel	R. W. Thomson	England	May 8, 1847	5, 104
Carriage-wheel	E. Tolles	Hartford, Conn	Dec. 27, 1839	1, 440
Carriage-wheel	I. Van Gorder	Warren, Ohio	Jan. 7, 1833	....
Carriage-wheel	S. Vreeland	Cuba, N. Y	July 20, 1869	92, 915
Carriage-wheel	R. Walker	Batavia, N. Y	Sept. 11, 1866	58, 030
Carriage-wheel	I. B. Ward	Camden, N. J	Dec. 25, 1849	6, 977
Carriage-wheel	S. M. H. Ward	New York, N. Y	Dec. 22, 1868	85, 259
Carriage-wheel	H. G. Weibling	Denver City, Colo	Jan. 20, 1863	37, 480
Carriage-wheel	E. S. Winchester	Boston, Mass	Nov. 28, 1865	51, 251
Carriage-wheel	M. Wonser	Norwalk, Ohio	May 17, 1870	103, 114
Carriage-wheel	G. B. Woodard and A. B. Woodard.	Bolivar and Alfred Centre, N. Y.	July 26, 1864	43, 651
Carriage-wheel	J. Woodburn	Saint Louis, Mo	July 24, 1866	56, 681
Carriage-wheel	J. Woodburn	Saint Louis, Mo	Mar. 12, 1872	124, 468
Carriage-wheel	E. G. Woodside	San Francisco, Cal	June 1, 1869	90, 714
Carriage, Wheel	S. W. Dana	Rutland, Vt	Aug. 30, 1808	....
Carriage, Wheel	D. F. Goodhue and E. H. Carey.	Cincinnati, Ohio	May 14, 1861	32, 285
Carriage, Wheel	W. H. Lewis	Greenwood, Mass	Aug. 23, 1864	43, 919
Carriage, Wheel	B. J. Malfeson	Burlington, N. J	Apr. 6, 1824	....
Carriage, Wheel	A. K. Stone	Oronoco, Minn	Apr. 9, 1867	63, 668
Carriage, Wheel	A. K. Stone	Oronoco, Minn	Apr. 9, 1867	63, 669
Carriage wheel and axle	J. H. Lewis	Duxbury, Mass	Oct. 22, 1867	70, 098
Carriage wheel and axle, Railway	C. D. Tisdale	Boston, Mass	Dec. 14, 1869	97, 994
Carriage-wheel and dress-guard	W. R. Bush	Albany, N. Y	Mar. 13, 1860	27, 427
Carriage-wheel axle	G. W. Ray	Rankin's Depot, Tenn	May 14, 1872	126, 742
Carriage-wheel axle and box	A. R. Reynolds	Skaneateles, N. Y	Dec. 5, 1840	1, 883
Carriage-wheel axle and hub	H. F. Phillips	Skaneateles, N. Y	Sept. 18, 1841	2, 260
Carriage-wheel bearings, Lubricator for	W. P. White	Orland, Me	Nov. 19, 1867	71, 101
Carriage-wheel box	L. Brown	Berkshire, Mass	May 30, 1806	....
Carriage-wheel box	W. A. Clark	Westville, Conn	Dec. 12, 1871	121, 706
Carriage-wheel box	J. Gridley	Boston, Mass	May 23, 1806	....
Carriage-wheel box	C. H. Holdredge	Westerly, R. I	Dec. 1, 1868	84, 548
Carriage-wheel box	R. W. McClelland	Pekin, Ill	Oct. 12, 1858	21, 766
Carriage-wheel box	W. Sharp	Millport, N. Y	Feb. 28, 1860	27, 314
Carriage-wheel box	A. Woodruff	Hartford, Conn	Aug. 6, 1872	130, 172
Carriage-wheel box, Self-fastening	T. Massey	New London, Conn	June 11, 1829	....
Carriage-wheel brake	C. Walker	Lewisburgh, Va	July 8, 1839	1, 222
Carriage-wheel brakes, Mode of operating	W. Dunning	Dunningsville, Pa	Nov. 1, 1845	4, 254
Carriage-wheel dress-protector	P. G. Hubert and J. W. Pitney.	New York, N. Y	Apr. 27, 1869	89, 315
Carriage-wheel, Elastic	E. S. Pratt and J. B. Thompson.	Boston, Mass	Mar. 15, 1864	41, 910
Carriage-wheel, Elastic	S. D. Woodbury	Lynn, Mass	Nov. 26, 1861	33, 809
Carriage-wheel fender	S. R. Ramsdell	Providence, R. I	Sept. 4, 1866	57, 765
Carriage-wheel for preventing horses from running away.	R. Jarvis	Boston, Mass	Mar. 29, 1834	....
Carriage-wheel gear	A. Baxter	Howard, N. Y	Apr. 19 1870	102, 079
Carriage-wheel, Iron	R. Crane, jr	Woodbury, Conn	May 4, 1805	....
Carriage-wheel, Iron	J. D. Murphey	Baltimore, Md	Apr. 19, 1859	23, 695
Carriage-wheel jack	H. Hooton and J. G. Bicknell	Boston and Cambridge, Mass.	May 31, 1859	24, 213
Carriage-wheel lubricator	S. S. Vollum and W. H. Green	New York, N. Y	Dec. 6, 1870	109, 977
Carriage-wheel, Metallic	W. Beach	Baltimore, Md	Mar. 2, 1858	19, 478
Carriage-wheel, Metallic	A. P. Ware	Camden County, N. J	Feb. 12, 1867	61, 962
Carriage-wheel-painting machine	S. B. Fuller	Worthington, Mass	Sept. 23, 1856	15, 759
Carriage wheel, Railway	J. P. Allen	Manchester, Mass	Apr. 20, 1869	89, 003
Carriage wheel, Railway	J. Elgar	Philadelphia, Pa	Nov. 19, 1833	....
Carriage wheel, Railway	A. R. Morrill	Northfield, Vt	Feb. 15, 1859	22, 972
Carriage-wheel, Self-moving	R. W. Thomson	Edinburgh, Great Britain	Nov. 9, 1869	96, 635
Carriage-wheel-spoke socket	A. J. Carleton	Springfield, Mass	Apr. 12, 1870	101, 821
Carriage-wheel-spoking pit	J. Collins	Crawfordsville, Ind	Aug. 8, 1871	117, 745
Carriage-wheel, Spring	J. Lamb and C. H. Root	McDonough, N. Y	Jan. 1, 1851	7, 874
Carriage-wheel, Spring	B. Ruggles	Warsaw, N. Y	Sept. 8, 1834	....
Carriage-wheel, Steam	R. W. Thomson	Edinburgh, Great Britain	Dec. 21, 1869	98, 126
Carriage-wheel-tenon-cutting machine	J. Reynolds	Dutchess, N. Y	June 24, 1815	....
Carriage-wheel-washing device	W. T. Sweet	Fayette, N. Y	Apr. 16, 1867	63, 960
Carriage-wheel wrench	L. B. Fisk	Lockport, N. Y	Apr. 21, 1868	76, 900
Carriage-wheel, Wrought-iron	J. McCollum	Wilsonville, Ala	May 10, 1844	3, 578
Carriage-wheels after tiring, Machine for immersing	J. Morris	Bloomfield, N. J	Sept. 23, 1843	3, 276
Carriage-wheels, Anti-friction box for	J. B. Blanchard	Sacramento, Cal	Sept. 17, 1861	33, 292
Carriage-wheels, Box-setter for	W. Witbeck	Troy, N. Y	Nov. 6, 1866	59, 495
Carriage-wheels, Confining	C. Force	Baltimore, Md	Apr. 28, 1836	....
Carriage-wheels, Facilitating the making of	B. L. Greenough	Lebanon, N. H	Sept. 12, 1815	....
Carriage-wheels, Fastening	B. Berndt and F. Barsch	Williamsport, Pa	Dec. 12, 1871	121, 841
Carriage-wheels, Fastening	W. Elder	Mill Hall, Pa	Dec. 27, 1870	110, 557
Carriage-wheels, Hooping or tiring	R. Hunt, 2d	Litchfield County, Conn	Mar. 20, 1821	....
Carriage-wheels, Lubricating axle-boxes of	W. Diller	Lancaster, Pa	Mar. 9, 1858	19, 551
Carriage-wheels, Machine for compressing	G. Cook	New Haven, Conn	July 21, 1863	39, 275
Carriage-wheels, Machine for compressing	H. Killam	New Haven, Conn	Oct. 15, 1867	69, 818
Carriage-wheels, Machine for finishing the exterior of rims of.	R. Fretz	Montville, Ohio	July 5, 1859	24, 623
Carriage-wheels, Machine for making	C. H. Guard	Brownville, N. Y	Sept. 7, 1852	9, 242
Carriage-wheels, Machine for making	C. H. Guard	Troy, N. Y	Feb. 4, 1862	34, 300
Carriage-wheels, Machine for making	G. W. Hatch	Parkman, Ohio	Dec. 22, 1863	41, 004
Carriage-wheels, Making	J. Whitaker	Dingman's Ferry, Pa	June 24, 1822	....
Carriage-wheels, Method of attaching	J. H. Riemkasten	Franklin Grove, Ill	Oct. 27, 1863	40, 431
Carriage-wheels, Method of boxing	C. Schmidt	Union, Me	Mar. 11, 1856	14, 434
Carriage-wheels, Method of constructing	E. S. Scripture	Syracuse, N. Y	Apr. 1, 1845	3, 979
Carriage-wheels, Method of constructing	S. Toomey	Wilmot, Ohio	May 5, 1868	77, 680
Carriage-wheels, Mode of applying anti-friction rollers and balls to the axles and boxes of.	J. G. Tibbets	New York, N. Y	July 22, 1839	1, 254
Carriage-wheels, Mold for casting boxes for	L. Farwell	Lancaster, Mass	Mar. 5, 1810	....
Carriage-wheels, Mold for casting boxes for	S. Smith, 2d	Amherst, Mass	July 6, 1810	....
Carriage-wheels, Removable runner for	G. A. Keene	Newburyport, Mass	Sept. 6, 1864	44, 141
Carriage-wheels to axles, Securing	I. Bicknell	Cincinnati, Ohio	July 12, 1870	105, 298
Carriage-wheels to axles, Securing	H. S. Fischer and D. Bruhn	Xenia, Ohio, and Eckenforde, Prussia.	Jan. 28, 1873	135, 327
Carriage-wheels to axles, Securing	E. P. Hoyt	New York, N. Y	Sept. 10, 1861	33, 251

Index of patents issued from the United States Patent Office from 1790 *to* 1873, *inclusive*—Continued.

Invention.	Inventor.	Residence.	Date.	No.
Carriage-whip holder	E. W. Scott	Wauregan, Conn	Dec. 27, 1870	110, 503
Carriage-window	J. F. Dohan	Binghamton, N. Y	Dec. 27, 1870	110, 444
Carriage-window	J. Henogen and E. Kruger	Saint Louis, Mo	Aug. 26, 1873	142, 229
Carriage-window	C. M. Oblenis	New York, N. Y	May 9, 1871	114, 592
Carriage-window	J. Ogden and D. R. Hart	Troy, N. Y	Mar. 21, 1846	4, 433
Carriage-window	J. T. Ogden	Boston, Mass	Feb. 20, 1855	12, 430
Carriage-window frame	F. Baker	New York, N. Y	May 21, 1867	64, 829
Carriage-window holder	J. H. Moore and W. Johnston	New Haven, Conn	Apr. 28, 1868	77, 397
Carriage window, Railway	E. T. Colburn	Boston, Mass	Jan. 1, 1867	60, 694
Carriage-window-sash holder	S. E. Totten, jr	New York, N. Y	Mar. 11, 1873	136, 793
Carriage with calash top	G. Holloway	Baltimore, Md	Sept. 9, 1825	....
Carriage with shifting seat	G. Simon	Reading, Pa	Dec. 20, 1853	10, 342
Carriage-work, Collar for ornamental	M. Seward	New Haven, Conn	Feb. 5, 1861	31, 330
Carriage-wrench	E. T. Ford	Stillwater, N. Y	July 13, 1869	92, 438
Carriages, Adjustable pole for	S. H. Bishop	Orange, Conn	May 5, 1857	17, 191
Carriages, Adjustable pole for	J. E. Prudden	Birmingham, Conn	Apr. 2, 1867	63, 423
Carriages and placing steps by the sides, Hanging	J. I. Wells	Hartford, Conn	Jan. 24, 1815	....
Carriages, Anti-rattler for	D. C. Gately	Newtown, Conn	Feb. 2, 1869	86, 387
Carriages, Apparatus for propelling	T. A. Háres	New York, N. Y	July 6, 1869	92, 306
Carriages, Apparatus for propelling	D. Swank	Newton, Iowa	July 13, 1869	92, 668
Carriages, Axle and thorough-box for	W. Slicer	Baltimore, Md	July 5, 1837	255
Carriages, Block for top-prop joint for	J. J. Wilson	New York, N. Y	Apr. 4, 1871	113, 477
Carriages, boats, &c., Machine for propelling	B. Langdon	Whitehall, N. Y	Feb. 22, 1817	....
Carriages, boats, mills, &c., by weights, Machine for propelling.	M. F. Colburn	Baltimore, Md	Apr. 7, 1829	....
Carriages, Body-loop for	H. A. Luttgens	Paterson, N. J	Oct. 17, 1871	120, 079
Carriages, Body-loop-head for	D. Wilcox	Ansonia, Conn	May 18, 1869	90, 326
Carriages, Boot-attachment to	M. M. Follett	Westborough Post-Office, Mass.	Feb. 4, 1868	74, 071
Carriages, &c., Box for receiving money in	J. Rodgers	New York, N. Y	Feb. 23, 1858	19, 446
Carriages, Button-hole for	S. C. Talcott	Ashtabula, Ohio	July 2, 1867	66, 413
Carriages by steam, Propelling	E. Clarke	New York, N. Y	Sept. 9, 1825	....
Carriages by steam, Propelling	C. Reynolds	East Windsor, Conn	Aug. 21, 1811	....
Carriages, Calash or folding top for	I. Cogswell, jr	Eastville, Ill	Feb. 24, 1863	37, 734
Carriages, Central-draft joint of	L. O. Rice	Caistorville, Canada	June 23, 1857	17, 638
Carriages, Changing the speed of steam	J. Griffin	Louisville, Ky	Feb. 19, 1861	31, 455
Carriages, Combined safety attachment and brake for.	C. Ducreux	New York, N. Y	Jan. 12, 1869	85, 883
Carriages, Combined step-cover and wheel-fender for.	J. W. Gosling	Cincinnati, Ohio	Feb. 26, 1867	62, 406
Carriages, Constructing	R. Nutting	Randolph, Vt	July 14, 1857	17, 805
Carriages, Constructing	E. W. Seymour	Lisle, N. Y	May 6, 1862	35, 204
Carriages, Constructing	J. C. Stroebel	....	Sept. 19, 1803	....
Carriages, Constructing	J. B. Swan	Albany, N. Y	Sept. 29, 1818	....
Carriages, &c., Construction and application of wheels to.	G. D. Bridgeman	New Haven, Conn	July 16, 1829	....
Carriages, Construction of	F. Biemler	New York, N. Y	Jan. 21, 1812	....
Carriages, Construction of	D. Neal	Milford, Del	Feb. 26, 1812	....
Carriages, Coupling four-wheeled	A. Osgood	Charlestown, Ohio	Jan. 27, 1843	2, 932
Carriages, Device for propelling	T. U. and H. H. Hamilton	Panama, N. Y	July 13, 1869	92, 607
Carriages, Die for forging offsets or stay-ends for	D. Wilcox	Birmingham, Conn	Nov. 4, 1873	144, 375
Carriages, Die for forging, trimming, and shaping spring-clips for.	F. B. Morse	Plantsville, Conn	Feb. 7, 1871	111, 668
Carriages, Double perch and fifth-wheel for	D. C. Doran	Mount Healthy, Ohio	Aug. 15, 1871	118, 115
Carriages, Draft-clip tie for	P. Blake	New Haven, Conn	May 26, 1863	38, 650
Carriages, Dress-guard for	G. W. Raitt	Cincinnati, Ohio	Oct. 16, 1866	58, 885
Carriages, Elastic running-gear for	G. E. Garretson	Russellville, Ky	Nov. 29, 1870	109, 608
Carriages, Elliptical spring for	F. Hatch and J. W. Terry	South Cortland, N. Y	July 10, 1839	1, 230
Carriages, Elliptical spring for	S King	Suffield, Conn	Oct. 31, 1839	1, 387
Carriages, Extension-pole and hold-back for	W. W. Rexford	Lock Sheldrake, N. Y	Nov. 24, 1868	84, 376
Carriages, Extension-reach for	E. Wilson	Prattsburgh, N. Y	Oct. 16, 1855	13, 690
Carriages, Extension-seat for	J. A. Naylor	Rahway, N. J	Aug. 21, 1860	29, 709
Carriages, Fan-attachment to child's	J. Reimsch	New York, N. Y	Sept. 24, 1867	69, 127
Carriages, Flap-fastener for the dasher of	R. Clingen	Boston, Mass	May 17, 1870	103, 142
Carriages, Folding double-step for	J. Pendergast	New Haven, Conn	June 11, 1872	127, 707
Carriages for children, Hanging	G. Maynard	Greenfield, Mass	July 27, 1858	21, 012
Carriages, Front gear for	C. L. Leonard	Wells' Bridge, N. Y	May 14, 1872	126, 720
Carriages, Front platform for	J. Heiden	New York, N. Y	Feb. 2, 1869	86, 397
Carriages, Hanging	S. Fairchild	Trumbull, Conn	Mar. 14, 1846	4, 414
Carriages, Hanging bodies of two-wheeled	I. Woodcock	Worcester, Mass	Apr. 18, 1848	5, 514
Carriages, &c., Heating	A. McWilliams	Washington, D. C	Nov. 29, 1832	....
Carriages, Horizontal wooden spring for	L. Sommer	Downington, Pa	July 22, 1811	....
Carriages, Horse-holder attachment to	G. W. Goodwyn	Petersburgh, Va	Feb. 21, 1871	111, 924
Carriages into sleighs, Converting wheel	O. B. Hale	Chicopee, Mass	Jan. 1, 1867	60, 884
Carriages, Leading-bar of four-horse	L. W. Stockton	Uniontown, Pa	Sept. 29, 1825	....
Carriages, Machinery for propelling steam	E. Ware	Bayonne, N. J	Aug. 20, 1867	68, 015
Carriages, Main bolt or goose-neck stay on	A. B. Shaeffer	Ephratah, Pa	May 26, 1868	78, 240
Carriages, Main spring for	J. Mix	New Haven, Conn	Apr. 18, 1807	....
Carriages, Manufacture of rub-irons for	H. W. Oliver, jr	Pittsburgh, Pa	Mar. 18, 1873	136, 857
Carriages, Measuring distances traveled by	Fuller and Richardson	Brunswick, Me	May 29, 1835	....
Carriages, Metal-plated shoe for	J. Du Bois	Williamsport, Pa	May 19, 1863	38, 571
Carriages, Method of attaching top to seat of	L. Jacobs and E. C. Landon	Castile, N. Y	Nov. 20, 1855	13, 821
Carriages, Method of forming body-loops for	R. R. Miller	Plantsville, Conn	Jan. 3, 1871	110, 773
Carriages, Mode of attaching animals to	H. B. Hale and T. Flagler	Grass Lake, Mich	Mar. 10, 1868	75, 262
Carriages, Mode of attaching sleigh-runners to wheel.	H. G. Guyon	New York, N. Y	Sept. 13, 1838	916
Carriages, Mode of connecting and disconnecting railway.	J. Stimpson	Baltimore, Md	Dec. 10, 1840	1, 885
Carriages, Mode of connecting springs to children's	J. H. Flagg	New York, N. Y	Oct. 15, 1872	132, 150
Carriages, Mode of making the skeins of axle-arms for.	G. Schreyer	Columbus, Ohio	May 7, 1861	32, 255
Carriages, Mode of regulating the speed of	T. Blanchard	Springfield, Mass	Dec. 28, 1825	....
Carriages, Mode of suspending or hanging pleasure	J. Henderson	Guilford, Conn	Dec. 26, 1808	....
Carriages, Motive-mechanism for	G. Kilner and F. H. Simmons	Sullivan, Ill	June 7, 1870	103, 895
Carriages, Motive-power for	S. L. Langdon	New Orleans, La	Mar. 8, 1870	100, 643
Carriages, Movable top for	J. C. Kimball	New Haven, Conn	Sept. 13, 1859	25, 420
Carriages on inclined plane, Transporting	M. Robinson	Henrico County, Va	Apr. 9, 1828	....
Carriages, Pole-iron socket for	U. Reynolds	New York, N. Y	Aug. 21, 1866	57, 379

Index of patents issued from the United States Patent Office from 1790 *to* 1873, *inclusive*—Continued.

Invention.	Inventor.	Residence.	Date.	No.
Carriages, Preventing rattling in	W. S. Chapman	Cincinnati, Ohio	Aug. 8, 1854	11, 471
Carriages, Propelling	C. K. Bradford	Lynn, Mass	Mar. 13, 1866	53, 214
Carriages, Propelling	W. Faris		Apr. 29, 1797	....
Carriages, Propelling wheeled	D. S. Fisher	Cedar Spring, Ind	May 28, 1867	65, 199
Carriages, Rub-iron for	F. B. Morse	Milwaukee, Wis	June 19, 1866	55, 692
Carriages, Runner-attachment for	C. F. Brigham	Worcester, Mass	Dec. 22, 1868	85, 2[illegible]4
Carriages, Saddle-clip for	F. Seward	New Haven, Conn	May 28, 1872	127, 275
Carriages, Sand-cap for	A. O. Colburn and H. T. Stanard.	Wayne, Mich	Apr. 14, 1868	76, 605
Carriages, &c., Securing the wheels of	A. Bruns	Davenport, Iowa	Mar. 23, 1858	19, 676
Carriages, Shifting-rail for	A. E. Bailey	Middleville, N. Y	Apr. 2, 1867	63, 457
Carriages, Shifting-rail for	H. F. Holt	Fredonia, N. Y	July 2, 1867	66, 343
Carriages, Shifting-top rail for	C. H. Ayres	Hightstown, N. J	Oct. 8, 1872	131, 928
Carriages so as to ease the lateral motion of the bodies thereof, Constructing railway.	A. Bridges and C. Davenport	Cambridgeport, Mass	May 4, 1841	2, 071
Carriages, Spiral spring for	W. Croasdale	Hartsville, Pa	Feb. 3, 1837	116
Carriages, Spring and oscillating axle for children's	J. Longbridge	Pittsburgh, Pa	Apr. 23, 1872	126, 066
Carriages, Spring-perch for	S. Tomlinson	Bridgeport, Conn	May 16, 1842	2, 624
Carriages, Spring-power for propelling	W. K. Chase	Charlestown, Mass	Apr. 3, 1866	53, 572
Carriages, Steering-apparatus for steam	E. C. Jones	Pittsburgh, Pa	Aug. 11, 1857	17, 970
Carriages, Sustaining weights and applying power to wheeled.	S. Chapman, jr	Windsor, Mass	Mar. 2, 1835	....
Carriages, Third seat for	A. E. Thayer	Plymouth, Conn	Sept 24, 1867	69, 270
Carriages, Thorough-brace for	F. A. Jewett	Abington, Mass	Aug. 19, 1856	15, 567
Carriages, Top iron and prop for	C. W. Saladee and W. Bauder	Circleville, Ohio	Feb. 9, 1869	86, 696
Carriages, Top iron and prop for	C. W. Saladee and W. Bauder	Circleville, Ohio	Feb. 9, 1869	86, 697
Carriages, Top-prop nut for	J. Ives	Mount Carmel, Conn	July 9, 1867	66, 496
Carriages, Turning-circle for	G. Kenny	Milford, N. H	Nov. 25, 1856	16, 122
Carriages, Turning-plate for	T. A. Edmison	Lake Port, Mich	Sept. 24, 1867	69, 194
Carriages, Umbrella-support for	A. Clarke	Sheboygan Falls, Wis	Feb. 6, 1872	123, 380
Carriages, Wear-iron for	I. G. Lefler	Philadelphia, Pa	Sept. 8, 1857	18, 153
Carriages when descending hills, Impeding	G. Bunker	Truxton, N. Y	July 5, 1833	....
Carriages when descending hills, Mode of retarding	E. Slifer	Boonsborough, Md	Jan. 16, 1826	....
Carriages with the perch by means of springs, Connecting the body of.	G. Nichols	Trumbull, Conn	Apr. 10, 1844	3, 527
Carriages with the reach and head-block or rocker, Coupling the forward axle-tree of four-wheeled.	A. H. Hart	Chagrin Falls, Ohio	Sept. 23, 1843	3, 274
Carriages, Wooden C-spring for	W. Robinson	Wilmington, Del	Nov. 27, 1810	....
Carrier:				
See Butter-carrier.				
Egg-carrier.				
Grain-carrier.				
Hay-carrier.				
Hod-carrier.				
Ice-carrier.				
Lathe-carrier.				
Sod-carrier.				
Spur-carrier.				
Straw-carrier.				
Trace-carrier.				
Water-carrier.				
Carronade, Elevating screw-box and cap of	E. Hidden	New York, N. Y	Apr. 26, 1826	....
Carrousel	W. Schneider	Davenport, Iowa	July 25, 1871	117, 336
Carryall	F. Shelton	Jackson, N. C	Dec. 2, 1834	....
Cart	N. R. Baldwin	Afton, N. Y	Feb. 5, 1861	31, 293
Cart	Z. Butt	Ocala, Fla	Mar. 6, 1866	52, 963
Cart	J. W. Cahoon	Philadelphia, Pa	Dec. 31, 1867	72, 795
Cart	H. Holcroft and C. S. Smith	Media, Pa	Aug. 30, 1864	43, [illegible]91
Cart	B. Ricketson and A. B. Smith	New Bedford, Mass., and Clinton, Pa.	July 12, 1864	43, 549
Cart and brake, Self-adjusting	I. Showalter	Chester County, Pa	July 18, 1871	117, 213
Cart and carriage wheel	W. Woodbridge	Kennebec, Me	May 17, 1836	....
Cart and railway for leveling hills, &c., Chain	J. H. Morison	Boscawen, N. H	Sept. 28, 1812	....
Cart and wagon, Dumping	I. B. Conklin	Pemberton, N. J	Feb. 16, 1864	41, 604
Cart and wagon, Dumping	W. W. Rogers	Hampden Corner, Me	Aug. 4, 1868	80, 669
Cart, Ash	R. A. Smith	Philadelphia, Pa	Jan. 3, 1865	45, 761
Cart-bodies, Mode of operating	T. Mussey	New London, Conn	Nov. 1, 1845	4, 250
Cart-body	W. Bradley	Vienna, Me	June 2, 1868	78, 419
Cart-body catch	C. F. Chew	Swedesborough, N. J	Apr. 23, 1872	125, 935
Cart-body fastening	E. Spalding	Plainfield, N. H	July 4, 1871	116, 641
Cart-body fastening, Tip	J. E. Seavey	Kennebunkport, Me	May 21, 1867	64, 913
Cart-boxes, Mold for running	S. Smith, 2d	Amherst, Mass	Oct. 17, 1809	....
Cart-brake	H. Holcroft and C. S. Smith	Media, Pa	Oct. 3, 1865	50, 248
Cart-brake	S. Y. Ives	Meriden, Conn	Feb. 5, 1867	61, 740
Cart, Brick	J. Evans	Philadelphia, Pa	May 31, 1870	103, 589
Cart, Coal	R. Heckscher	New York, N. Y	Feb. 7, 1860	27, 049
Cart, Dumping	J. H. C. Applegate	Bridgeton, N. J	Dec. 29, 1868	85, 353
Cart, Dumping	O. Benson and J. G. Falk	Chicago, Ill	Oct. 3, 1871	119, 444
Cart, Dumping	T. Blodgett	Belchertown, Mass	Sept. 6, 1864	44, 068
Cart, Dumping	C. A. Carpenter	Glen Cove, N. Y	May 17, 1864	42, 746
Cart, Dumping	G. L. Collins	Trenton, N. J	Nov. 21, 1871	121, 0[illegible]6
Cart, Dumping	F. Dengler	North Vernon, Ind	July 27, 1869	93, 069
Cart, Dumping	S. Doubleday	Baltimore, Md	June 4, 1872	127, 407
Cart, Dumping	B. G. Fitzhugh	Frederick, Md	Oct. 17, 1871	119, 976
Cart, Dumping	B. G. Fitzhugh	Frederick, Md	Apr. 22, 1873	138, 013
Cart, Dumping	B. G. Fitzhugh	Frederick, Md	June 17, 1873	140, 025
Cart, Dumping	N. W. Godfrey	Locust Valley, N. Y	Sept. 17, 1867	68, 977
Cart, Dumping	R. Ham and J. Durgin	Bangor, Me	Aug. 11, 1868	80, 823
Cart, Dumping	W. Hand	Plainfield, N. J	Apr. 4, 1871	113, 293
Cart, Dumping	A. A. Jennings	Webster, N. Y	Jan. 28, 1868	73, 725
Cart, Dumping	J. S. Lash	Carlisle, Pa	Sept. 13, 1859	25, 424
Cart, Dumping	G. E. Newell	Pawtucket, R. I	Jan. 28, 1868	73, 918
Cart, Dumping	R. A. Smith	Philadelphia, Pa	Nov. 8, 1864	44, 983
Cart, Dumping	M. F. Wickersham	Springfield, Ill	Sept. 7, 1869	94, 681
Cart, Dumping	M. F. Wickersham	Springfield, Ill	Sept. 21, 1869	95, 176
Cart, Dumping	F. H. Williams	Washington, D. C	Sept. 21, 1869	94, 988
Cart, Dumping	G. Zoanny	Napa, Cal	Dec. 3, 1872	133, 615
Cart, Excavating	W. Harles	Washington, Mo	Feb. 4, 1873	135, 546

Index of patents issued from the United States Patent Office from 1790 to 1873, inclusive—Continued.

Invention.	Inventor.	Residence.	Date.	No.
Cart for removing earth	J. Price	Lockport, N. Y	May 18, 1827	....
Cart, Hand	W. B. Glover	Boston, Mass	Sept. 3, 1872	131, 095
Cart, Hand-dumping	W. Farmer	New York, N. Y	Mar. 16, 1869	87, 831
Cart, Hay-rack for	H. R. Hawkins	Akron, Ohio	July 10, 1860	29, 075
Cart, Hemp	Z. Feagan	Palmyra, Mo	Mar. 26, 1861	31, 795
Cart-loading apparatus	B. G. Fitzhugh	Frederick, Md	Apr. 15, 1873	137, 768
Cart, Log	A. Kirkwood	Jackson County, Miss	Aug. 29, 1871	118, 460
Cart, Log	J. Stitt	Saint John's, Mich	Nov. 17, 1868	84, 145
Cart, Manure	T. L. Cotten	Madison County, Miss	Aug. 9, 1870	106, 125
Cart, Manure	J. K. Holland	Beaufort County, N. C	July 9, 1850	7, 491
Cart, Manure	D. Reid	Washington, N. C	May 3, 1853	9, 697
Cart, Manure	B. Teague	Moscow, Tenn	Aug. 22, 1871	118, 298
Cart, Milk	J. Harris	New York, N. Y	June 6, 1871	115, 606
Cart, Night	J. H. Lynch	Baltimore, Md	Aug. 20, 1867	67, 892
Cart or wagon, Weighing	N. E. Doane	Hannibal, Mo	Jan. 22, 1861	31, 155
Cart, Ox	M. S. Woodbury	Bethel, Vt	Feb. 2, 1869	86, 619
Cart, Self-balanced hand	G. Coolidge	Watertown, Mass	June 13, 1831	....
Cart, Self-loading	L. A. Beardsley	Fredericksburgh, Va	Dec. 22, 1868	85, 200
Cart, Self-loading	J. S. Brown	Washington, D. C	June 9, 1857	17, 486
Cart, Self-loading	Z. Butt	Lincolntown, N. C	Mar. 13, 1855	12, 504
Cart, Self-loading	R. B. Cantrell	Tenafly, N. J	May 13, 1873	138, 854
Cart, Self-loading	J. A. Sprague and B. O'Connor	Dayton, Ohio	Mar. 20, 1855	12, 562
Cart, Self-loading	G. W. Whitson	Asneville, N. C	July 21, 1868	80, 259
Cart, Self loading and dumping	W. H. Herbert	New Albany, Ind	Feb. 13, 1872	123, 565
Cart, Self loading and dumping	J. B. Hulbert	Hermon, N. Y	May 3 , 1871	115, 321
Cart, Self loading and dumping	C. C. McKinley	Champaign, Ill	July 16, 1872	129, 154
Cart, Self loading and dumping	S. Stone	Kirkersville, Ohio	Aug. 1, 1854	11, 442
Cart, Self loading and dumping	B. T. Stowell	Waddam's Grove, Ill	Apr. 27, 1852	8, 913
Cart, Self loading and unloading	J. Wilkinson	Hopewell Cotton-Works Post-Office, Pa.	May 1, 1855	12, 804
Cart, Self-loading hay	E. Holt	Wheaton, Ill	Jan. 3, 1865	45, 715
Cart, S lf-loading hay	I. M. Williams	Blanchester, Ohio	Nov. 3, 1868	83, 749
Cart, Self-weighing	E. Blackman	Danbury, Conn	Oct. 7, 1862	36, 631
Cart, Street-sprinkling	L. Rodenhausen	Philadelphia, Pa	Aug. 13, 1867	67, 805
Cart, Water	H. Austin	East Liberty, Ohio	Nov. 27, 1860	30, 710
Cart, wagon, &c., Box and axle-tree for	W. Batchelor	New York, N. Y	May 2, 1816	....
Cart, Weighing	G. M. Barth	Philadelphia, Pa	Feb. 14, 1860	27, 184
Cart, Weighing	N. B. Livingston	Portland, Ind	Sept. 30, 1851	8, 391
Cart, Weighing	J. W. Martin	Burlington, N. J	May 20, 1856	14, 939
Cart, Weighing	J. W. Martin	Philadelphia, Pa	Nov. 2, 1858	21, 999
Cart, wheelbarrow, and turnip-drill, Combined	A. M. Newland	Olivet, Mich	July 5, 1870	10[illegible], 983
Carts, &c., Apparatus for unloading	C. Downer	Philadelphia, Pa	July 24, 1849	6, 609
Carts, &c., Combination of springs with the back-chains of.	T. S. Speakman	Philadelphia, Pa	July 18, 1848	5, 673
Carte de visite exhibitor	P. G. Hubert	New York, N. Y	Mar. 19, 1867	62, 959
Cartouch-box	R. Dingee	New York, N. Y	Aug. 15, 1835	....
Cartouch-box	J. Mix	New York, N. Y	June 3, 1813	....
Cartouch-box, brush, &c., Machine for boring blocks for.	V. Bogenreiff	Georgetown, D. C	July 10, 1810	....
Cartridge	J. Abraham and T. R. Bayliss	Birmingham, England	Oct. 27, 1868	83, 434
Cartridge	C. R. Alsop	Middletown, Conn	Jan. 27, 1863	37, 481
Cartridge	C. F. Brown	Warren, R. I	May 29, 1855	12, 942
Cartridge	S. Crispin	New York, N. Y	Apr. 12, 1864	42, 329
Cartridge	G. H. Daw	London, England	May 4, 1869	89, 563
Cartridge	J. H. Ferguson	Baltimore, Md	June 28, 1859	24, 548
Cartridge	E. Gonez	New York, N. Y	Jan. 25, 1870	99, 078
Cartridge	E. Gonez	New York, N. Y	Jan. 25, 1870	99, 079
Cartridge	B. B. Hotchkiss	Sharon, Conn	July 10, 1860	29, 080
Cartridge	W. W. Hubbell	Philadelphia, Pa	Apr. 23, 1872	126, 058
Cartridge	S. Jackson	Philadelphia, Pa	Jan. 10, 1865	45, 830
Cartridge	E. Lindner	New York, N. Y	May 12, 1857	17, 287
Cartridge	J. Logan and G. E. Hart	Newark, N. J	Sept. 16, 1873	142, 924
Cartridge	J. C. Mayberry	White Rock, Ill	June 24, 1862	35, 699
Cartridge	E. Maynard	Washington, D. C	June 17, 1856	15, 141
Cartridge	E. Maynard	Washington, D. C	Sept. 29, 1863	40, 111
Cartridge	I. M. Milbank	Greenfield Hill, Conn	May 30, 1871	115, 498
Cartridge	R. R. Moffatt	Brooklyn, N. Y	Dec. 20, 1870	110, 264
Cartridge	G. W. Morse	Baton Rouge, La	Oct. 28, 1856	15, 996
Cartridge	G. W. Morse	Baton Rouge, La	June 29, 1858	20, 727
Cartridge	A. N. Newton	Richmond, Ind	Mar. 20, 1855	12, 556
Cartridge	W. F. Parker	Meriden, Conn	Mar. 23, 1869	88, 202
Cartridge	W. R. Pomery	Millersburgh, Ohio	Aug. 5, 1862	36, 108
Cartridge	E. O. Potter	New York, N. Y	July 22, 1862	35, 949
Cartridge	J. Riedel	Pleasant Hill, Ky	Sept. 9, 1856	15, 707
Cartridge	T. P. Shaffner	Louisville, Ky	Dec. 19, 1865	51, 672
Cartridge	G. Smith	Buttermilk Falls, N. Y	June 30, 1857	17, 702
Cartridge	W. H. Smith	Charlestown, Mass	Feb. 8, 1870	99, 721
Cartridge	D. Smith and J. W. Storrs	Springfield, Mass	Apr. 20, 1869	89, 088
Cartridge	H. Smith and D. B. Wesson	Norwich, Conn	Aug. 8, 1854	11, 496
Cartridge	J. R. Van Vechten	New York, N. Y	Mar. 9, 1869	87, 735
Cartridge	C. S. Wells	Springfield, Mass	May 30, 1871	115, 548
Cartridge	C. S. Wells	Springfield, Mass	Jan. 2, 1872	122, 504
Cartridge	R. White	Davenport, Iowa	Nov. 26, 1861	33, 805
Cartridge	R. White	Lowell, Mass	Feb. 28, 1871	112, 305
Cartridge	N. G. Whitmore	Mansfield, Mass	June 28, 1870	104, 912
Cartridge	N. G. Whitmore	Mansfield, Mass	Aug. 20, 1872	130, 679
Cartridge	D. E. Williams	Davenport, Iowa	Oct. 18, 1870	108, 543
Cartridge	F. Wohlgemuth	New York, N. Y	Nov. 2, 1869	96, 373
Cartridge and percussion-cap box, Combined	J. T. Warren and R. A. Chesebrough.	Stafford and New York, N. Y.	Nov. 8, 1864	44, 999
Cartridge-belt	A. Mills	United States Army	Aug. 20, 1867	67, 898
Cartridge, Blasting	H. S. Lucas	Chester, Mass	Oct. 9, 1866	58, 656
Cartridge, Blasting	T. P. Shaffner	Louisville, Ky	Dec. 19, 1865	51, 673
Cartridge-box	A. A. Bennett	Cincinnati, Ohio	Jan. 27, 1863	37, 485
Cartridge-box	E. Blakeslee	Plymouth, Conn	Dec. 20, 1864	45, 469
Cartridge-box	T. F. Brabson	Brooklyn, N. Y	May 13, 1873	138, 847
Cartridge-box	R. L. Bryan and J. A. Bigelow	Franklin, Mich	Jan. 30, 1866	52, 357

Index of patents issued from the United States Patent Office from 1790 *to* 1873, *inclusive*—Continued.

Invention.	Inventor.	Residence.	Date.	No.
Cartridge-box	F. Bush	Boston, Mass	Dec. 23, 1862	37, 216
Cartridge-box	F. Bush	Boston, Mass	Feb. 10, 1863	37, 607
Cartridge-box	F. Chillingworth	Springfield, Mass	June 15, 1869	91, 419
Cartridge-box	S. Crispin	New York, N. Y	Dec. 1, 1-68	84, 616
Cartridge-box	S. A. Day	Bowling Green, Ohio	Jan. 11, 1870	98, 748
Cartridge-box	A. Domis	New York, N. Y	Apr. 1, 1862	34, 820
Cartridge-box	J. Elbertson	Kirksville, Mo	Apr. 21, 1868	77, 016
Cartridge-box	W. H. Elliott	Ilion, N. Y	June 17, 1873	139, 885
Cartridge-box	J. W. Frazier	Newark, N. J	Feb. 20, 1872	123, 883
Cartridge-box	J. W. Frazier	Newark, N. J	Feb. 20, 1872	123, 884
Cartridge-box	W. Freeborn	Tivoli, N. Y	Dec. 10, 1867	72, 011
Cartridge-box	C. Howlett	New York, N. Y	May 28, 1867	65, 225
Cartridge-box	G. Jassath	New York, N. Y	Sept. 17, 1861	33, 306
Cartridge-box	J. R. King	Washington, D. C	Nov. 15, 1870	109, 365
Cartridge-box	A. D. Laidley	Philadelphia, Pa	Aug. 15, 1865	49, 420
Cartridge-box	M. C. Leonard	Washington, D. C	Jan. 22, 1867	61, 345
Cartridge-box	J. C. Ludlum	Brooklyn, N. Y	Dec. 20, 1870	110, 379
Cartridge-box	J. C. McGinness	Washington, D. C	June 15, 1869	91, 249
Cartridge-box	S. McKeever	United States Army	June 10, 1873	139, 846
Cartridge-box	S. McKeever	United States Army	June 10, 1873	139, 847
Cartridge-box	J. Miller	United States Army	Mar. 26, 1872	125, 069
Cartridge-box	W. H. Morris	Cold Spring, N. Y	July 23, 1867	67, 065
Cartridge-box	A. C. Newcomb and B. Lyon	Springfield, Mass	Dec. 3, 1867	71, 633
Cartridge-box	H. E. Paine	Troy, N. Y	Dec. 22, 1868	85, 241
Cartridge-box	J. Pease	Boston, Mass	Oct. 31, 1865	50, 730
Cartridge-box	J. I. Pittman	New York, N. Y	Jan. 12, 1869	85, 849
Cartridge-box	W. Rossiter	Newark, N. J	Aug. 8, 1865	49, 304
Cartridge-box	P. F. Schneider	Hartford, Conn	Jan. 21, 1868	73, 549
Cartridge-box	J. S. Smith	Brooklyn, N. Y	Mar. 12, 1861	31, 680
Cartridge-box	P. S. and F. M. Thomson	Hudson City, N. J	Nov. 12, 1872	132, 992
Cartridge-box	J. T. Warren	Stafford, N. Y	June 28, 1864	43, 373
Cartridge-box	H. S. Weston	Akron, Ohio	July 12, 1864	43, 539
Cartridge-box	M. V. B. White	Troy, N. Y	Feb. 14, 1865	46, 411
Cartridge-box fastening	W. Z. W. Chapman	New York, N. Y	Mar. 4, 1862	34, 563
Cartridge box fastening	J. M. Willson	Washington, D. C	Dec. 6, 1859	26, 4.2
Cartridge-box, Revolving	C. Howlett	Manchester, Conn	Aug. 22, 1865	49, 523
Cartridge-box, Revolving	P. F. Schneider	Hartford, Conn	July 31, 1866	56, 804
Cartridge-bullet	W. H. Dibble	Middletown, Conn	Sept. 29, 1863	40, 092
Cartridge-cap extractor	J. Logan and D. W. Eldridge	Boston, Mass	Dec. 13, 1870	110, 052
Cartridge-cap extractor	W. C. Pickersgill	Providence, R. I	Dec. 14, 1869	97, 805
Cartridge capping and uncapping device	G. S. Green, jr	Mott Haven, N. Y	Mar. 25, 1873	137, 071
Cartridge capping and uncapping device	G. V. McGraw	Mankato, Minn	July 8, 1873	140, 718
Cartridge capping and uncapping device	J. F. Nettleton	Branford, Conn	Apr. 22, 1873	138, 180
Cartridge capping device	E. A. Kelsey	West Meriden, Conn	Aug. 20, 1872	130, 723
Cartridge-capping machine	E. A. Kelsey	West Meriden, Conn	Aug. 20, 1872	130, 724
Cartridge-capping tool	J. L. Raub	Meriden, Conn	Apr. 8, 1873	137, 720
Cartridge-case	S. A. Day	Bowling Green, Ohio	Apr. 26, 1870	102, 375
Cartridge-case	B. C. English	Hartford, Conn	Oct. 8, 1861	32, 429
Cartridge-case	G. P. Foster	Providence, R. I	Apr. 10, 1860	27, 791
Cartridge-case	J. P. Lindsay	New York, N. Y	July 24, 1860	29, 287
Cartridge-case	G. W. Merse	Baton Rouge, La	May 11, 1858	20, 214
Cartridge-case	T. J. Powers	New York, N. Y	May 17, 1870	103, 079
Cartridge case	O. Shevenell	Marion, Ala	Apr. 19, 1870	102, 051
Cartridge-case	S. W. Wood	Cornwall, N. Y	Oct. 15, 1872	132, 227
Cartridge-case cleaner	F. H. Aiken	Franklin, N. H	June 8, 1869	91, 058
Cartridge-case for revolving fire-arms	J. H. Vickers	Worcester, Mass	Sept. 8, 1863	39, 869
Cartridge-case holder, Metallic	S. C. Greene	Vicksburgh, Miss	Mar. 22, 1870	101, 121
Cartridge-case, Metallic	W. C. Dodge	Washington, D. C	July 4, 1865	48, 536
Cartridge-case, Metallic	E. C. Dunning	Bridgeport, Conn	Mar. 18, 1862	34, 713
Cartridge-case, Metallic	E. Maynard	Washington, D. C	Jan. 11, 1859	22, 565
Cartridge-case, Metallic	W. Tibbals	Hartford, Conn	Feb. 23, 1869	87, 125
Cartridge-case, Metallic	S. W. Wood	Cornwall, N. Y	Oct. 28, 1873	144, 012
Cartridge-case, Applying percussion priming to	A. K. Johnston and L. Dow	New York, N. Y	May 10, 1864	42, 666
Cartridge-cases, Forming	C. Sharps	Philadelphia, Pa	Nov. 13, 1860	30, 647
Cartridge-cases, Machine for heading	T. I. Powers	New York, N. Y	June 18, 1867	65, 940
Cartridge-cases, Machine for loading metallic	C. H. Davis	Philadelphia, Pa	Aug. 9, 1864	43, 780
Cartridge-cases, Machine for making	T. J. Powers	New York, N. Y	Apr. 24, 1866	54, 255
Cartridge-cases, Machine for making percussion	E. Allen	Worcester, Mass	Feb. 14, 1860	27, 094
Cartridge cases, Machine for necking	B. Payne	South Coventry, Conn	Oct. 17, 1865	50, 489
Cartridge-cases, Manufacture of metallic	D. Williamson	New York, N. Y	June 29, 1869	92, 136
Cartridge-cases, Material for	A. B. Ely	Newton, Mass	Apr. 13, 1869	88, 948
Cartridge-charger	A. C. Hobbs	Bridgeport, Conn	June 15, 1869	91, 442
Cartridge-charger	P. Powell	Cincinnati, Ohio	Dec. 22, 1868	85, 189
Cartridge-cutter, Fire-arm-muzzle	C. H. Bradley	West Chester, Pa	Jan. 28, 1862	34, 235
Cartridge-ejector	J. M. Marlin	Hartford, Conn	Apr. 5, 1870	101, 637
Cartridge ejector for breech-loading fire-arms	C. H. Ballard	Worcester, Mass	Apr. 9, 1867	63, 605
Cartridge-ejector for breech-loading fire-arms	H. Hammond	Hartford, Conn	Dec. 31, 1867	72, 849
Cartridge-ejector for breech-loading fire-arms	W. H. and G. W. Miller	West Meriden, Conn	Aug. 27, 1867	68, 099
Cartridge-ejector for revolving fire-arms	J. T. and G. M. Smith and J. J. Sweeney.	Springfield, Mass	Mar. 18, 1873	136, 871
Cartridge-ejector for revolving fire-arms	C. S. Wells	New Haven, Conn	Dec. 10, 1872	133, 732
Cartridge, Electrical gun	T. P. Mott and S. Gardner, jr	New York, N. Y	May 6, 1873	138, 679
Cartridge-envelope	A. K. Johnston and L. Dow	Middletown, Conn., and Topeka, Kans.	Oct. 1, 1861	33, 393
Cartridge, Explosive	W. Schnitz	Philadelphia, Pa	Dec. 29, 1868	85, 482
Cartridge-extractor	H. Lord	Hartford, Conn	Jan. 14, 1868	73, 351
Cartridge-extractor for fire-arms	H. Reynolds	Springfield, Mass	Nov. 22, 1864	45, 176
Cartridge extractor, Ordnance	N. Thompson	Brooklyn, N. Y	Nov. 19, 1872	133, 271
Cartridge-feeder for gun-hammers	T. Shaw	Philadelphia, Pa	Dec. 21, 1869	98, 198
Cartridge-filling machine	W. C. Dodge and R. D. O. Smith	Washington, D. C	July 17, 1866	56, 489
Cartridge-filling machine	T. J. Powers	New York, N. Y	Jan. 22, 1867	61, 456
Cartridge-filling machine	J. G. Stowe and E. F. Allen	Providence, R. I	July 12, 1864	43, 550
Cartridge, Fixed	G. Buckel and E. Dorsch	Monroe, Mich	July 22, 1856	15, 369
Cartridge for artillery and blasting	T. P. Shaffner	Louisville, Ky	Sept 14, 1869	94, 847
Cartridge for atmospheric fire-arms	P. Giffard	Paris, France	Dec. 17, 1872	134, 048
Cartridge for breech-loading fire-arms	J. D. Greene	Cambridge, Mass	Sept. 8, 1859	18, 143
Cartridge for breech-loading fire-arms	B. King	Providence, R. I	Mar. 4, 1862	34, 579
Cartridge for breech-loading fire-arms	I. M. Milbank	Greenfield Hill, Conn	Feb. 6, 1872	123, 352

Index of patents issued from the United States Patent Office from 1790 *to* 1873, *inclusive*—Continued.

Invention.	Inventor.	Residence.	Date.	No.
Cartridge for breech-loading fire-arms	D. Moore	Williamsburgh, N. Y	Oct. 31, 1854	11, 870
Cartridge for breech-loading fire-arms, Nippled	T E. Sturtevant	Boston, Mass	June 12, 1866	55, 552
Cartridge for breech-loading fire-arms, Shot	C. E. Sneider	Baltimore, Md	July 4, 1871	116, 640
Cartridge for breech-loading guns	W. W. Marston and F. Goodell	New York, N. Y	May 18, 1852	8, 956
Cartridge for breech-loading rifled fire-arms	H. Berdan	New York, N. Y	Feb. 7, 1865	46, 292
Cartridge for cannon, Metal	W. E. Moore	Crawfordsville, Ind	Apr. 28, 1863	38, 322
Cartridge for fire-arms	J. W. Cochran	New York, N. Y	Mar. 13, 1860	27, 428
Cartridge for fire-arms	E. Gomez and W. Mills	New York, N. Y	Aug. 24, 1858	21, 253
Cartridge for fire-arms	T. T. S. Laidley	Watertown, Mass	June 24, 1873	140, 144
Cartridge for fire-arms	I. M. Milbank	Greenfield Hill, Conn	Sept. 3, 1872	131, 016
Cartridge for fire-arms	I. M. Milbank	Greenfield Hill, Conn	Sept. 3, 1872	131, 017
Cartridge for fire-arms	I. M. Milbank	Greenfield Hill, Conn	Sept. 3, 1872	131, 018
Cartridge for fire-arms	J. Rupertus	Philadelphia, Pa	Oct. 8, 1867	69, 707
Cartridge for fire-arms	A. Shannon	New York, N. Y	Mar. 4, 1862	34, 615
Cartridge for fire-arms	J. W. Smith	Iowa Point, Kans	Jan. 30, 1866	52, 370
Cartridge for fire-arms	S. W. Wood	Cornwall, N. Y	Oct. 28, 1873	144, 011
Cartridge for fire-arms, Envelope of	A. K. Johnston and L. Dow	Middletown, Conn., and Topeka Kans.	Jan. 7, 1862	34, 061
Cartridge for loose ammunition, Metallic	W. H. Risley	Berlin, Conn	Mar. 27, 1866	53, 490
Cartridge for ordnance	T. Yates	Milwaukee, Wis	Dec. 27, 1864	45, 666
Cartridge for revolving fire-arms	J. M. Cooper	Pittsburgh, Pa	Dec. 6, 1864	45, 319
Cartridge for revolving fire-arms	D. Williamson	Brooklyn, N. Y	Jan. 5, 1864	41, 183
Cartridge for small-arms	T. Cullen	San Francisco, Cal	Jan. 7, 1868	72, 982
Cartridge for small-arms	D. M. Mefford	Cincinnati, Ohio	Apr. 18, 1865	47, 317
Cartridge heads, Method of re-enforcing metallic	S. W. Wood	Cornwall, N. Y	May 7, 1872	126, 613
Cartridge-holder	L. J. Gaines	West Meriden, Conn	Mar. 18, 1873	136, 987
Cartridge-holder	J. S. Smith	Brooklyn, N. Y	Dec. 1, 1868	84, 651
Cartridge-loader	G. H. Ferriss	Utica, N. Y	Sept. 12, 1871	118, 849
Cartridge-loader	E. Maynard	Washington, D. C	Apr. 2, 1861	31, 898
Cartridge-loader	J. M. Taylor	Lexington, Ky	July 13, 1869	92, 669
Cartridge-loader	J. S. Warner	Ogdensburgh, N. Y	Dec. 3, 1872	133, 607
Cartridge loader, Pocket	G. F. Dutch	New York, N. Y	Aug. 13, 1872	130, 414
Cartridge-loading apparatus	F. A. Thuer	East Hartford, Conn	Jan. 4, 1870	98, 529
Cartridge-loading device	T. L. Sturtevant	Framingham, Mass	July 22, 1873	141, 185
Cartridge-loading machine	M. V. B. Hill	Bridgeport, Conn	Sept. 28, 1869	95, 345
Cartridge-loading machine	A. C. Hobbs	Bridgeport, Conn	Feb. 18, 1873	135, 913
Cartridge-loading machine	T. L. Sturtevant	Framingham, Mass	Apr. 29, 1873	138, 294
Cartridge-machine	J. H. Gill	Philadelphia, Pa	Dec. 14, 1869	97, 904
Cartridge-machine	D. Smith	Springfield, Mass	Nov. 27, 1866	60, 074
Cartridge-magazine	W. H. Elliot	New York, N. Y	Sept. 12, 1871	118, 916
Cartridge-making machine	W. H. Horstman and H. J. Behrens.	New York, N. Y	Sept. 15, 1863	39, 923
Cartridge-making machine	B. S. Roberts	United States Army	Mar. 9, 1869	87, 593
Cartridge, Metallic	E. Allen	Worcester, Mass	Sept. 25, 1860	30, 109
Cartridge, Metallic	E. Allen	Worcester, Mass	May 16, 1865	47, 688
Cartridge, Metallic	E. G. Allen	Boston, Mass	Feb. 16, 1864	41, 590
Cartridge, Metallic	W. Bakewell	Pittsburgh, Pa	July 7, 1863	39, 109
Cartridge, Metallic	H. Berdan	New York, N. Y	Feb. 27, 1866	52, 818
Cartridge, Metallic	H. Berdan	New York, N. Y	Sept. 29, 1868	82, 587
Cartridge, Metallic	A. J. Bergen	Brooklyn, N. Y	Feb. 26, 1867	62, 466
Cartridge, Metallic	C. J. Bergen	Brooklyn, N. Y	May 17, 1864	42, 815
Cartridge, Metallic	A. S. Blake	Waterbury, Conn	June 5, 1866	55, 233
Cartridge. Metallic	E. M. Boxer	Woolwich, England	June 29, 1869	91, 818
Cartridge, Metallic	F. E. Boyd	Boston, Mass	Feb. 8, 1870	99, 528
Cartridge, Metallic	B. Burton	Brooklyn, N. Y	Feb. 25, 1873	136, 130
Cartridge, Metallic	J. J. Chaudun	Paris, France	July 20, 1869	92, 795
Cartridge, Metallic	J. W. Cochran	New York, N. Y	Nov. 7, 1871	120, 625
Cartridge, Metallic	J. W. Cochran	New York, N. Y	May 28, 1872	127, 308
Cartridge, Metallic	J. S. Crary	Salem, N. Y	July 25, 1871	117, 388
Cartridge, Metallic	S. Crispin	New York, N. Y	Apr. 4, 1871	113, 634
Cartridge, Metallic	C. F. and J. E. De Dartein	Strasburg, France	Nov. 7, 1871	120, 630
Cartridge, Metallic	A. C. Depew and J. Slatcher	Bridgeport, Conn	Dec. 7, 1869	97, 615
Cartridge, Metallic	D. C. Farrington	Lowell, Mass	Dec. 31, 1872	134, 368
Cartridge, Metallic	S. Foreband and H. C. Wadsworth.	Worcester, Mass	Dec. 5, 1871	121, 606
Cartridge, Metallic	A. N. C. Garard	Paris, France	Apr. 19, 1870	102, 109
Cartridge, Metallic	R. J. Gatling	Hartford, Conn	May 3, 1870	102, 675
Cartridge, Metallic	I. P. Gillespie	New Albany, Ind	Oct. 15, 1861	33, 481
Cartridge, Metallic	E. Gomez	New York, N. Y	Feb. 8, 1870	99, 666
Cartridge, Metallic	A. Hall	Danville, Iowa	Sept. 15, 1863	39, 915
Cartridge, Metallic	A. C. Hobbs	Bridgeport, Conn	July 18, 1871	117, 173
Cartridge, Metallic	B. B. Hotchkiss	New York, N. Y	Aug. 31, 1869	94, 210
Cartridge, Metallic	J. C. Howe	Worcester, Mass	Aug. 16, 1864	43, 851
Cartridge, Metallic	H. Kellogg	New Haven, Conn	July 15, 1862	35, 878
Cartridge, Metallic	C. D. Leet and B. B. Hotchkiss	Vienna, Austria, and New York, N. Y.	Dec. 28, 1869	98, 278
Cartridge, Metallic	J. Logan and D. W. Eldredge	Boston, Mass	Dec. 7, 1869	97, 537
Cartridge, Metallic	E. Martin	Springfield, Mass	Mar. 23, 1869	88, 191
Cartridge, Metallic	E. Martin	Springfield, Mass	July 12, 1870	105, 348
Cartridge, Metallic	E. Martin	Springfield, Mass	Feb. 14, 1871	111, 856
Cartridge, Metallic	E. Maynard	Washington, D. C	Sept. 8, 1863	39, 823
Cartridge, Metallic	E. Maynard	Washington, D. C	Sept. 29, 1863	40, 112
Cartridge, Metallic	J. V. Meigs	Washington, D. C	Mar. 2, 1869	87, 352
Cartridge, Metallic	J. V. Meigs	Washington, D. C	June 8, 1869	90, 951
Cartridge, Metallic	H. Metcalfe	New York, N. Y	Nov. 14, 1871	120, 9[illegible]0
Cartridge, Metallic	I. M. Milbank	Greenfield Hill, Conn	Aug. 10, 1869	93, 545
Cartridge, Metallic	I. M. Milbank	Greenfield Hill, Conn	Aug. 10, 1869	93, 546
Cartridge, Metallic	I. M. Milbank	Greenfield Hill, Conn	Jan. 2, 1872	122, [illegible]99
Cartridge, Metallic	I. M. Milbank	Greenfield Hill, Conn	Feb. 6, 1872	123, 351
Cartridge, Metallic	I. M. Milbank	Greenfield Hill, Conn	Apr. 16, 1872	125, 830
Cartridge, Metallic	I. M. Milbank	Greenfield Hill, Conn	Feb. 25, 1873	136, 168
Cartridge, Metallic	R. R. Moffatt	Brooklyn, N. Y	Dec. 20, 1870	110, 265
Cartridge, Metallic	S. Newhouse	Oneida, N. Y	Jan. 18, 1870	98, 995
Cartridge, Metallic	W. I. Page	East Boston, Mass	Dec. 6, 1870	109, 931
Cartridge, Metallic	A. Payne	Bridgeport, Conn	Oct. 31, 1871	120, 529
Cartridge, Metallic	A. Payne	Bridgeport, Conn	Dec. 12, 1871	121, 808
Cartridge, Metallic	G. R. Pierce	Grand Rapids, Mich	Oct. 24, 1871	120, 323
Cartridge, Metallic	T. J. Powers	New York, N. Y	Oct. 17, 1865	50, 536

Index of patents issued from the United States Patent Office from 1790 to 1873, inclusive—Continued.

Invention.	Inventor.	Residence.	Date.	No.
Cartridge, Metallic	T. J. Powers	New York, N. Y	June 13, 1871	115, 892
Cartridge, Metallic	T. J. Powers	New York, N. Y	June 20, 1871	116, 094
Cartridge, Metallic	B. S. Roberts	United States Army	Feb. 23, 1869	87, 297
Cartridge, Metallic	T. J. Rodman and S. Crispin	Watertown, Mass., and New York, N. Y.	Dec. 15, 1863	40, 988
Cartridge, Metallic	C. Sharps	Philadelphia, Pa	Apr. 15, 1862	34, 987
Cartridge, Metallic	D. Smith	Springfield, Mass	June 15, 1869	91, 278
Cartridge, Metallic	W. H. Smith	Charlestown, Mass	Dec. 28, 1869	98, 439
Cartridge, Metallic	W. S. Smoot	Ilion, N. Y	June 20, 1871	116, 105
Cartridge, Metallic	W. S. Smoot	Ilion, N. Y	Oct. 24, 1871	120, 338
Cartridge, Metallic	H. C. Spaulding	Brooklyn, N. Y	Jan. 24, 1865	46, 034
Cartridge, Metallic	G. R. Stetson	New Haven, Conn	Oct. 31, 1871	120, 403
Cartridge, Metallic	W. Tibbals	South Coventry, Conn	May 25, 1869	90, 607
Cartridge, Metallic	R. White	Lowell, Mass	Dec. 14, 1869	97, 843
Cartridge, Metallic	R. White	Lowell, Mass	Jan. 10, 1871	110, 881
Cartridge, Metallic	W. H. Wills	Boston, Mass	Nov. 29, 1864	45, 292
Cartridge, Metallic	O. F. Winchester	New Haven, Conn	Jan. 1, 1867	60, 814
Cartridge-opener	J. S. Butterfield and S. Marshall.	Philadelphia, Pa	May 13, 1856	14, 850
Cartridge packing-case	J. W. Frazier	New York, N. Y	July 16, 1872	129, 545
Cartridge, Patched	W. H. Elliott	Plattsburgh, N. Y	July 15, 1862	35, 872
Cartridge percussion-primer	R. R. Moffatt	Brooklyn, N. Y	Dec. 20, 1870	110, 266
Cartridge-pouch	H. Hammond	Hartford, Conn	Feb. 26, 1867	62, 415
Cartridge, Primed metallic	S. Crispin	New York, N. Y	Dec. 15, 1863	40, 978
Cartridge, Primed metallic	W. W. Marston	New York, N. Y	Nov. 3, 1863	40, 490
Cartridge, Primed metallic	E. K. Root	Hartford, Conn	Oct. 11, 1864	44, 660
Cartridge-primer	I. C. Farrington	Lowell, Mass	Dec. 17, 1872	133, 929
Cartridge-primer	A. C. Hobbs and J. Orcutt	Bridgeport, Conn	Oct. 24, 1871	120, 196
Cartridge-primer	B. B. Hotchkiss	New York N. Y	Feb. 15, 1870	99, 899
Cartridge-primer	I. M. Milbank	Greenfield Hill, Conn	May 31, 1870	103, 641
Cartridge primer, Fire-arm	H. Smith and D. B. Wesson	Norwich and New Haven, Conn.	Jan. 22, 1856	14, 147
Cartridge-retractor for breech-loading fire-arms	E. Allen	Worcester, Mass	Mar. 7, 1865	46, 617
Cartridge-retractor for breech-loading fire-arms	A. Ball	Windsor, Vt	Jan. 1, 1867	60, 664
Cartridge-retractor for breech-loading fire-arms	F. Beals	New Haven, Conn	Feb. 7, 1865	46, 207
Cartridge-retractor for breech-loading fire-arms	J. W. Cochran	New York, N. Y	Feb. 20, 1866	52, 679
Cartridge-retractor for breech-loading fire-arms	G. P. and G. F. Foster	Mohawk, N. Y	Sept. 19, 1865	49, 991
Cartridge-retractor for breech-loading fire-arms	J. Gray	Medford, Mass	June 20, 1865	48, 337
Cartridge-retractor for breech-loading fire-arms	E. Maynard	Washington, D. C	July 25, 1865	48, 966
Cartridge-retractor for breech-loading fire-arms	E. S. Piper	Springfield, Mass	Dec. 5, 1865	51, 391
Cartridge-retractor for breech-loading fire-arms	W. S. Smoot	Washington, D. C	Aug. 27, 1867	68, 250
Cartridge-retractor for breech-loading fire-arms	C. M. Spencer	South Manchester, Conn	July 29, 1862	36, 062
Cartridge-retractor for breech-loading fire-arms	T. L. Sturtevant	Boston, Mass	Nov. 7, 1865	50, 854
Cartridge-retractor for breech-loading fire-arms	F. Truelender	Salem, N. J	May 10, 1864	42, 702
Cartridge-retractor for breech-loading fire-arms	H. H. Wolcott	Yonkers, N. Y	June 13, 1865	48, 227
Cartridge-retractor for magazine fire-arms	E. Stabler	Montgomery County, Md	Dec. 6, 1864	45, 356
Cartridge-retractor for many-chambered fire-arms	W. C. Dodge	Washington, D. C	Jan. 17, 1865	45, 912
Cartridge-retractor for revolving fire-arms	W. Clows	Ilion, N. Y	Feb. 25, 1873	136, 134
Cartridge-retractor for revolving fire-arms	H. Hammond	Bridgeport, Conn	Jan. 23, 1866	52, 165
Cartridge-retractor for revolving fire-arms	R. D. O. Smith	Washington, D. C	July 12, 1864	43, 529
Cartridge-retractor for revolving fire-arms	S. W. Wood	Cornwall, N. Y	Jan. 16, 1866	52, 105
Cartridge-shell	C. H. Todd	Montgomery, Ala	Mar. 16, 1869	87, 990
Cartridge-shell ejector for revolving fire-arms	G. H. Harrington	Worcester, Mass	Feb 7, 1871	111, 534
Cartridge-shell extractor	J. M. Martin	Hartford, Conn	Feb. 8, 1870	99, 690
Cartridge-shell for drill-purposes	A. C. Hobbs	Bridgeport, Conn	Sept. 26, 1871	119, 357
Cartridge-shell for magazine fire-arms	G. H. Dupee	New Haven, Conn	Feb. 13, 1872	123, 622
Cartridge-shell-forming machine	A. C. Hobbs and T. V. Boyden.	Bridgeport, Conn	Sept. 14, 1869	94, 745
Cartridge-shells, Construction of	J. F. Cranston	Springfield, Mass	Aug. 25, 1868	81, 478
Cartridge-shells, Device for manufacturing metallic.	E. A. Worthen	Springfield, Mass	Nov. 29, 1870	109, 791
Cartridge-shells, Die for making	J. Gardner	New Haven, Conn	May 21, 1872	126, 949
Cartridge-shells, Machine far drawing	A. S. Warner	Springfield, Mass	July 10, 1866	56, 332
Cartridge-shells, Machine for forming external recesses in the heads of.	A. C. Hobbs	Bridgeport, Conn	Sept. 14, 1869	94, 744
Cartridge-shells, Machine for heading	T. V. Boyden	Bridgeport, Conn	May 9, 1871	114, 639
Cartridge-shells, Machine for making	W. A. McIntire	Springfield, Mass	Apr. 16, 1867	63, 915
Cartridge-shells, Machine for re-enforcing	C. S. Wells	Bridgeport, Conn	Apr. 9, 1872	125, 508
Cartridge-shells, Machine for tapering	S. W. Wood	Cornwall, N. Y	May 7, 1872	126, 609
Cartridge-shells, Machine for tapering	S. W. Wood	Cornwall, N. Y	May 7, 1872	126, 610
Cartridge-shells, Machine for tapering	S. W. Wood	Cornwall, N. Y	May 7, 1872	126, 611
Cartridge-shells, Machine for tapering	S. W. Wood	Cornwall, N. Y	May 7, 1872	126, 612
Cartridge-shells, Manufacture of	D. Smith	Springfield, Mass	Dec. 7, 1869	97, 561
Cartridge-shells with bullets, Machine for interlocking.	A. C. Hobbs	Bridgeport, Conn	Oct. 28, 1873	143, 981
Cartridge, Shot	L. B. Bruen	Brooklyn, N. Y	Jan. 27, 1863	37, 491
Cartridge, Shot	B. L. Budd	New York, N. Y	Mar. 25, 1862	34, 806
Cartridge, Shot	A. R. Davis	East Cambridge, N. Y	Mar. 20, 1855	12, 545
Cartridge, Shot	W. O. Howard	New York, N. Y	Mar. 3, 1868	75, 019
Cartridge, Shot	W. B. Johns	United States Army	July 14, 1857	17, 792
Cartridge, Shot	C. W. Lancaster	London, England	Dec. 7, 1869	97, 653
Cartridge, Shot	A. D. Laws	Bridgeport, Conn	Sept. 3, 1872	131, 104
Cartridge, Shot	C. W. Lovett, jr	Boston, Mass	Apr. 4, 1871	113, 677
Cartridge, Shot	R. R. Moffatt	Brooklyn, N. Y	Dec. 20, 1870	110, 383
Cartridge, Shot	S. W. Paine	Williamsport, Pa	Jan. 31, 1871	111, 377
Cartridge, Shot	S. W. Paine	Rochester, N. Y	Feb. 25, 1873	136, 336
Cartridge, Shot	C. E. Sneider	Baltimore, Md	May 10, 1870	102, 984
Cartridge, Shot	C. E. Sneider	Baltimore, Md	Sept. 10, 1872	131, 189
Cartridge, Shot metallic	E. K. Root	Hartford, Conn	May 5, 1863	38, 414
Cartridge, Skin	J. Hotchkiss	Middletown, Conn	Feb. 11, 1862	34, 367
Cartridge, Skin	W. M. Storm	New York, N. Y	Oct. 29, 1861	33, 611
Cartridge, Solid	R. Bartholow	United States Army	Aug. 5, 1862	36, 066
Cartridge-tearer for muskets	D. Kelly	Grand Rapids, Mich	Dec. 16, 1862	37, 171
Cartridge tube and conveyer forming a fire-arm	C. W. Büchel	New York, N. Y	Feb. 20, 1849	6, 136
Cartridge-tube, &c., for fire-arms, Detached metallic	D. Minesinger	Beaver, Pa	Feb. 27, 1849	6, 159
Cartridge, Water-proof	R. Bartholow	United States Army	May 21, 1861	32, 345
Cartridges and setting and ejecting caps, Implement for loading.	H. B. Hooker	Rochester, N. Y	May 21, 1872	126, 962

Index of patents issued from the United States Patent Office from 1790 *to* 1873, *inclusive*—Continued.

Invention.	Inventor.	Residence.	Date.	No.
Cartridges, Apparatus for setting bullets in	W. C. Pickersgill	Providence, R. I	Dec. 14, 1869	97, 806
Cartridges, Apparatus for setting caps in metallic	W. C. Pickersgill	Providence, R. I	Dec. 14, 1869	97, 804
Cartridges, Applying fire-extinguishing	W. M. Storm	New York, N. Y	Oct. 9, 1855	13, 660
Cartridges, Applying percussion priming to	A. K. Johnston and L. Dow	New York, N. Y	May 10, 1864	42, 667
Cartridges around bullets, Implement for compressing.	J. S. Adams	Taunton, Mass	May 30, 1865	48, 010
Cartridges, Ball	R. O. Doremus and B. L. Budd.	New York, N. Y	Mar. 18, 1862	34, 725
Cartridges, Ball	L. Wells	Astoria, N. Y	Sept. 15, 1857	18, 217
Cartridges, caps, &c., Forming metallic cases for	S. W. Wood	Cornwall, N. Y	Oct. 28, 1873	144, 010
Cartridges, Device for crimping	C. E. Sneider	Baltimore, Md	Sept. 10, 1872	131, 188
Cartridges, Fabric for envelope for	A. K. Johnston and L. Dow	New York, N. Y	May 10, 1864	42, 668
Cartridges, Filling metallic	H. Smith and D. B. Wesson	Springfield, Mass	Apr. 17, 1860	27, 933
Cartridges for ordnance, &c., Graduating accelerating.	J. M. Crockett	Newbern, Va	Sept. 10, 1867	68, 609
Cartridges from breech-loading fire-arms, Nipple for discharging or withdrawing.	W. C. Hicks	New Haven, Conn	Mar. 10, 1857	16, 797
Cartridges, Implement for capping	H. M. Bronson	Sandusky, Ohio	Nov. 11, 1873	144, 435
Cartridges, Implement for uncapping, capping, and charging.	W. M. Fowler	Brooklyn, N. Y	Aug. 26, 1873	142, 157
Cartridges, Instrument for extracting caps from	W. Clews	Ilion, N. Y	Oct. 3, 1871	119, 506
Cartridges, Machine for attaching bails to	D. Ellis and G. R. Stetson	New Haven, Conn	June 6, 1865	48, 056
Cartridges, Machine for cupping metallic	T. J. Powers	New York, N. Y	Apr. 11, 1865	47, 246
Cartridges, Machine for manufacture of metallic	E. Allen	Worcester, Mass	Mar. 19, 1861	31, 695
Cartridges, Machine for priming metallic	T. J. Powers	New York, N. Y	Aug. 14, 1866	57, 258
Cartridges, Machine for tapering metallic	S. W. Wood	Cornwall, N. Y	May 7, 1872	126, 608
Cartridges made of fusible metals, &c	W. H. Tooth	Broxton, England	Mar. 4, 1873	136, 468
Cartridges, Means for uncapping	C. A. King	Springfield, Mass	Oct. 17, 1871	120, 075
Cartridges, Metallic wad for	E. Maynard	Washington, D. C	Apr. 19, 1864	42, 388
Cartridges, Method of attaching balls to wooden	W. Hunt	New York, N. Y	Aug. 10, 1848	5, 699
Cartridges, Packing	S. Colt	Hartford, Conn	Mar. 15, 1859	23, 230
Cartridges, Packing	E. K. Root	Hartford, Conn	Jan. 18, 1859	22, 675
Cartridges, Packing	C. Sharps	Philadelphia, Pa	July 10, 1860	29, 108
Cartridges, Priming	G. A. Fitch	Kalamazoo, Mich	Oct. 16, 1866	58, 800
Cartridges, Priming	A. Moffatt	Washington, D. C	Mar. 13, 1865	53, 168
Cartridges, Priming	C. E. Sneider	Baltimore, Md	Oct. 11, 1864	44, 692
Cartridges, Priming	T. L. Sturtevant	Boston, Mass	Mar. 27, 1866	53, 501
Cartridges, Priming metallic	H. Berdan	New York, N. Y	Mar. 20, 1866	53, 388
Cartridges, Priming metallic	A. J. Bergen	Brooklyn, N. Y	Feb. 26, 1867	62, 467
Cartridges, Priming metallic	B. Burton	Brooklyn, N. Y	Aug. 11, 1868	81, 058
Cartridges, Priming metallic	J. F. Cranston	Springfield, Mass	Sept. 17, 1867	68, 960
Cartridges, Priming metallic	J. F. Cranston	Springfield, Mass	Jan. 28, 1868	73, 877
Cartridges, Priming metallic	S. Crispin	New York, N. Y	Aug. 8, 1865	49, 237
Cartridges, Priming metallic	R. J. Gathing	Indianapolis, Ind	June 16, 1868	78, 953
Cartridges, Priming metallic	C. Jackson and J. G. Pusey	Providence, R. I	Oct. 24, 1865	50, 592
Cartridges, Priming metallic	T. T. S. Laidley	Springfield, Mass	Dec. 5, 1865	51, 324
Cartridges, Priming metallic	T. T. S. Laidley	Springfield, Mass	June 19, 1866	55, 676
Cartridges, Priming metallic	E. Martin	Springfield, Mass	July 18, 1865	48, 820
Cartridges, Priming metallic	E. Maynard	Washington, D. C	Dec. 13, 1864	45, 420
Cartridges, Priming metallic	E. Maynard	Tarrytown, N. Y	Oct. 23, 1866	59, 044
Cartridges, Priming metallic	E. Maynard	Tarrytown, N. Y	Jan. 15, 1867	61, 225
Cartridges, Priming metallic	H. Meigs, jr	Bergen Point, N. J	Jan. 28, 1868	73, 739
Cartridges, Priming metallic	I. M. Milbank	Greenfield Hill, Conn	Feb. 19, 1867	62, 283
Cartridges, Priming metallic	T. J. Powers	New York, N. Y	Apr. 24, 1866	54, 254
Cartridges, Priming metallic	T. J. Powers	New York, N. Y	June 1, 1869	90, 871
Cartridges, Priming metallic	J. Rider	Newark, Ohio	Nov. 5, 1867	70, 612
Cartridges, Priming metallic	E. K. Root	Hartford, Conn	Nov. 15, 1864	45, 079
Cartridges, Priming metallic	C. Sharps	Philadelphia, Pa	Dec. 1, 1863	40, 772
Cartridges, Priming metallic	D. Smith	Springfield, Mass	June 11, 1867	65, 774
Cartridges, Priming metallic	C. E. Sneider	Baltimore, Md	Nov. 22, 1864	45, 210
Cartridges, Priming metallic	T. L. Sturtevant	Boston, Mass	Apr. 17, 1866	54, 038
Cartridges, Priming metallic	W. Tibbals	South Coventry, Conn	May 26, 1868	78, 337
Cartridges, Scraping disk or wad for ordnance	J. M. Connel	Newark, Ohio	Nov. 29, 1864	45, 227
Cartridges water-proof, Rendering	A. K. Johnston and L. Dow	New York, N. Y	June 24, 1862	35, 687
Cartridges, Water-proof	R. O. Doremus and B. L. Budd	New York, N. Y	Mar. 25, 1862	34, 744
Cartridges, Winged metallic	A. D. Perry	New York, N. Y	Mar. 5, 1850	7, 147
Carving and engraving, Hand-tool for	G. B. Soley	Philadelphia, Pa	Mar. 21, 1871	112, 860
Carving and molding machine, Wood	M. T. Boult	Battle Creek, Mich	July 4, 1871	116, 543
Carving and ornamenting machine, Wood	M. T. Boult	Battle Creek, Mich	June 15, 1869	91, 410
Carving device, Wood	N. Ruger	West Farms, N. Y	July 29, 1856	15, 441
Carving-fork	H. Garbanati	Brooklyn, N. Y	Dec. 27, 1859	26, 579
Carving-fork and knife-sharpener combined	E. S. Scofield	Rochester, N. Y	July 21, 1868	80, 226
Carving in wood, Imitation of open	W. H. May	Bridgeport, Conn	Jan. 29, 1867	61, 549
Carving-knife	C. W. Sykes	New York, N. Y	Nov. 8, 1859	26, 061
Carving-knife	O. W. Taft	New York, N. Y	May 3, 1870	102, 617
Carving knife and fork holder	A. T. Foster	Albany, N. Y	Dec. 10, 1867	72, 009
Carving-machine	H. Augur	New Haven, Conn	Dec. 23, 1846	4, 906
Carving-machine	H. Augur	New Haven, Conn	Jan. 23, 1849	6, 058
Carving-machine	C. E. Bacon	Buffalo, N. Y	Sept. 21, 1852	9, 269
Carving-machine	V. W. Blanchard	Bridport, Vt	May 11, 1869	89, 911
Carving-machine	J. W. Campbell	New York, N. Y	Aug. 15, 1871	117, 978
Carving-machine	L. S. Chichester	Williamsburgh, N. Y	June 3, 1851	8, 141
Carving-machine	H. Cottrell	Newark, N. J	Nov. 18, 1873	144, 745
Carving-machine	H. Grubenbecher	New York, N. Y	Apr. 15, 1873	137, 837
Carving-machine	A. Henkel	New York, N. Y	Apr. 13, 1869	88, 869
Carving-machine	A. McCreight	Tranquility, Ohio	Mar. 31, 1868	76, 093
Carving-machine	G. Merrill	Newburyport, Mass	Sept. 15, 1868	82, 145
Carving-machine	G. Merrill	Newburyport, Mass	Sept. 22, 1868	82, 430
Carving-machine	B. J. Tayman	Philadelphia, Pa	May 21, 1872	126, 994
Carving-machine	H. Thomas	Brooklyn, N. Y	June 17, 1873	139, 980
Carving-machine bit	C. F. Bauersfeld	Cincinnati, Ohio	Aug. 1, 1854	11, 407
Carving machine, Wood	H. H. Adams	Newburyport, Mass	Sept. 1, 1868	81, 722
Carving machine, Wood	A. Bisse	Quincy, Ill	Dec. 3, 1867	71, 568
Carving machine, Wood	I. Lindsley	Providence, R. I	Dec. 22, 1857	18, 917
Carving machine, Wood	I. M. Singer	New York, N. Y	Dec. 11, 1855	13, 921
Carving machine, Wood	J. Westworth	Chicago, Ill	June 6, 1871	115, 669
Carving, polishing, &c., Machine for	R. T. Smith	Nashua, N. H	Nov. 12, 1872	132, 928
Carving-table	R. E. Deane	New York, N. Y	Oct. 2, 1866	58, 387
Carving-table	W. Howard	Watertown, N. Y	July 16, 1872	129, 565
Carving-tables, Heating	S. Patrick	Galesburgh, Ill	Feb. 21, 1865	46, 491
Carving-tool	M. T. Boult	Battle Creek, Mich	Mar. 14, 1871	112, 680

Index of patents issued from the United States Patent Office from 1790 *to* 1873, *inclusive*—Continued.

Invention.	Inventor.	Residence.	Date.	No.
Carving wood	M. T. Boult	Battle Creek, Mich	Mar. 15, 1870	100,848
Carving wood or metal, Machine for	I. M. Singer	Pittsburgh, Pa	Apr. 10, 1849	6,310
Case:				
See Album-case.				
Bacon and ham case.				
Blacking-case.				
Bolt-case.				
Book-case.				
Bottle-case.				
Bottle and glass case.				
Bottle and transportation case.				
Burial-case.				
Card-case.				
Cartridge-case.				
Cast-metal case.				
Clock-case.				
Condenser-case.				
Corn-sheller case.				
Corpse preserving case.				
Daguerreotype-case.				
Document-case.				
Drawing-case.				
Dressing-case.				
Fan-case.				
Filing-case.				
Fire-kindler case.				
Flower-case.				
Folding case.				
Glass case.				
Governor-case.				
Gridiron-case.				
Jewel-case.				
Jewelry and silver-ware case.				
Kneeling-case.				
Lace and ribbon case.				
Lamp-case.				
Lamp-ratchet-wheel case.				
Latch-case.				
Lock-case.				
Match-case.				
Medicine-case.				
Melodeon-case.				
Metal case.				
Miniature-case.				
Moth-proof case.				
Needle-case.				
Odometer-case.				
Oil-case.				
Organ-case.				
Packing-case.				
Pen and pencil case.				
Pencil-case.				
Photographic-card case.				
Piano-forte case.				
Picture-case.				
Pie-case.				
Pin-case.				
Pin-package case.				
Post-office letter-case.				
Postage-stamp case.				
Postal-card case.				
Preserving-case.				
Printer's type-case.				
Pulley-case.				
Pump-case.				
Razor-case.				
Reading-case.				
Record-book case.				
Ribbon-case.				
Ribbon and velvet case.				
Salinometer-case.				
Sample-case.				
Scissors-case.				
Sewing-case.				
Sewing-machine case.				
Sheet-metal case.				
Shipping-case.				
Show-case.				
Skirt-case.				
Spectacle-case.				
Spool-case.				
Spool-exhibiting case.				
Spool-silk case.				
Spool-thread case.				
Steam-gage case.				
Stereoscope-case.				
Tape-measure case.				
Ticket-case.				
Tobacco-case.				
Tobacco-pipe case.				
Toilet-case.				
Transportation-case.				
Turbine-case.				
Turbine water-wheel case.				
Type-case.				
Valve-case.				
Watch-case.				
Water-wheel case.				
Wood-case.				
Work-case.				

Index of patents issued from the United States Patent Office from 1790 *to* 1873, *inclusive*—Continued.

Invention.	Inventor.	Residence.	Date.	No.
Case-stand	A. F. De Puy	New York, N. Y	Aug. 30, 1870	106, 921
Cash-box, Alarm	J. D. Perkins	New York, N. Y	May 18, 1869	90, 187
Casing for reverberatory and other furnaces	W. F. Durfee	Bridgeport, Conn	Feb. 23, 1869	87, 152
Cask	J. Connolly	Boston, Mass	July 21, 1863	39, 274
Cask and barrel	M. Hickey	Boston, Mass	Oct. 16, 1866	58, 821
Cask and barrel	J. Marshall	Brooklyn, N. Y	Mar. 12, 1872	124, 601
Cask and barrel for oil	A. Thompson	Brooklyn, N. Y	Jan. 20, 1863	37, 477
Cask and barrel headings	H. Andrews	Canaan, Conn	Mar. 2, 1836	....
Cask and box identifying mark	E. A. Locke	Boston, Mass	Oct. 16, 1866	58, 847
Cask, barrel, &c	J. Merrill	Boston, Mass	Oct. 2, 1866	58, 449
Cask, barrel, &c	J. Merrill	Boston, Mass	Oct. 2, 1866	58, 450
Cask, barrel, &c	J. Merrill	Boston, Mass	Nov. 13, 1866	59, 622
Cask, barrel, and keg	J. Merrill	Boston, Mass	Oct. 2, 1866	58, 451
Cask, Beer	M. Seitz	Williamsburgh, N. Y	May 27, 1873	139, 334
Cask, Brewers'	J. Wiley	Allegheny City, Pa	June 18, 1872	128, 003
Cask, Brewers' stocking	J. Jakel	Detroit, Mich	July 29, 1873	141, 354
Cask-filler	D. Cope	Liverpool, England	June 7, 1870	103, 845
Cask for containing fermentable beverages	J. Hamilton and R. Paterson	Glasgow, Great Britain	Feb. 22, 1870	100, 029
Cask for fermenting wine	J. Glenert	Washington, Mo	July 16, 1867	66, 701
Cask for holding oil, quicksilver, &c	A. D. Campbell and E. Perce	New York, N. Y	Jan. 7, 1862	34, 051
Cask for lager-beer	J. J. Schillinger	New York, N. Y	May 3, 1870	102, 716
Cask for paste	H. Braunhold	New York, N. Y	Apr. 4, 1871	113, 622
Cask for preserving beer, &c	J. Haege	Shiloh, Ill	Jan. 24, 1865	45, 994
Cask-handle	J. L. Jones	Utica, N. Y	Feb. 9, 1869	86, 759
Cask-heads, Machine for holding	J. D. Leach	Penobscot, Me	Aug. 28, 1866	57, 522
Cask-heater	S. Burgess	Wayne, Pa	Apr. 21, 1857	17, 076
Cask-hoops, Machine for shaving	J. G. Morgan	Colton, N. Y	Sept. 4, 1866	57, 753
Cask-hoops, Machine for shaving	S. Wagner	Monroe, Wis	Oct. 4, 1864	44, 567
Cask-machine	S. King	Suffield, Conn	Mar. 23, 1836	....
Cask, Metallic	W. B. Scaife	Pittsburgh, Pa	Apr. 24, 1860	28, 014
Cask, Oil-proof	G. E. Van Derburgh	Mamaroneck, N. Y	Mar. 18, 1862	34, 707
Cask or barrel	J. Marshall	Brooklyn, N. Y	July 18, 1871	117, 185
Cask, Sheet-metal	S. J. Seely	Brooklyn, N. Y	Aug. 12, 1862	36, 175
Cask-stopper faucet-attachment	C. Raggio	Memphis, Tenn	Nov. 9, 1869	96, 726
Cask-washing machine	W. Johnson	Milwaukee, Wis	May 25, 1869	90, 550
Cask-washing machine	W. Robinson	Bridgewater, England	Dec. 1, 1863	40, 797
Cask, Water-tight	D. C. Rand and M. Wadhams	Perinton, N. Y	Aug. 12, 1862	36, 168
Casks and barrels, Device for raising	R. Smith	Brooklyn, N. Y	Jan. 14, 1868	73, 398
Casks and barrels, Machine for pitching	A. Warth	Stapleton, N. Y	May 16, 1871	114, 999
Casks and barrels, Machinery for making	J. Hale	Oakum, Mass	June 21, 1828	....
Casks and barrels, Method of repairing	C. A. Baldwin	Boston, Mass	Oct. 11, 1864	44, 591
Casks, Apparatus for applying liquids to	J. O. Woodruff	Albany, N. Y	July 17, 1866	56, 483
Casks, Apparatus for pitching	F. Brenner	Cincinnati, Ohio	Mar. 25, 1873	137, 173
Casks, Apparatus for steaming lard and oil	C. J. Yergason	Brooklyn, N. Y	May 17, 1870	103, 116
Casks, Apparatus for transferring liquids from	D. Sexton	San Gabriel, Cal	Nov. 22, 1864	45, 183
Casks, barrels, and kegs, Manufacture of	J. Merrill	Boston, Mass	May 29, 1866	55, 137
Casks, barrels, &c., Apparatus for pitching	G. Meyer and J. Dick	Quincy, Ill	Aug. 5, 1873	141, 449
Casks, barrels, hogsheads, &c., Application of hot water or steam in making.	J. Thompson	Philadelphia, Pa	Dec. 30, 1829	....
Casks, &c., Composition for coating ale	C. P. Matthews	Grantham, England	Sept. 5, 1871	118, 738
Casks, Composition for lining ale and beer	J. Werner	Mannheim, Baden	Jan. 25, 1870	99, 124
Casks, Construction of metallic	J. I. Bard	New Orleans, La	Apr. 8, 1873	137, 590
Casks containing liquids, Ventilation of	L. Whilhelm	Buffalo, N. Y	June 19, 1860	28, 799
Casks, Device for closing the mouths of	J. F. C. Rider	South New Market, N. H	Apr. 2, 1872	125, 220
Casks from saturated timber, Machine for cutting headings for.	L. Wells	Hartsville, N. Y	Jan. 27, 1838	582
Casks, &c., from solid pieces, Method of turning	J. P. Osborn	Staunton, N. J	June 20, 1854	11, 136
Casks, Gage for	J. W. Cochran	New York, N. Y	Apr. 28, 1857	17, 185
Casks, &c., Gage for contents of	J. K. Barney	Warren, R. I	Oct. 19, 1858	21, 809
Casks, Gaging and ullaging	W. W. Cooper	Washington, D. C	Oct. 31, 1865	50, 689
Casks, Hoop-lock for	T. Hanvey	Elma, N. Y	July 12, 1864	43, 494
Casks, Hooping	D. and E. Perry	Pawtucket, R. I	Mar. 19, 1867	63, 088
Casks, Instrument for gaging	J. K. Barney	Warren, R. I	June 21, 1859	24, 438
Casks, Instrument for gaging	E. R. McKean	Nashville, Tenn	July 12, 1870	105, 352
Casks, Instrument for measuring liquid in	W. C. McCarthy	Pittsburgh, Pa	Nov. 21, 1865	51, 069
Casks, Joint of metallic	M. Wappich	Sacramento, Cal	July 9, 1867	66, 540
Casks, Lining for coal-oil	S. G. Morrison	Williamsport, Pa	Sept. 16, 1862	36, 474
Casks, Machine for making heads of	E. P. Spaulding	Saint Louis, Mo	Mar. 7, 1865	46, 717
Casks, Machine for pitching lager-beer and other	H. A. Ratterman	Cincinnati, Ohio	June 7, 1870	104, 062
Casks, Machine for chamfering, crozing, and howeling.	P. Estes	Adrian, Mich	Dec. 3, 1846	4, 869
Casks, Machinery for making	J. Hamilton	New York, N. Y	Apr. 13, 1852	8, 873
Casks, Making	U. Emmons	Green County, N. Y	Jan. 8, 1823	....
Casks, Making	J. Little	Hillsborough, N. H	July 25, 1818	....
Casks, Manufacturing	W. Reid	West Hebron, N. Y	Apr. 19, 1864	42, 445
Casks, Metal lock for wooden hoops for	H. W. Catlin	Burlington, Vt	July 19, 1864	43, 621
Casks, &c., Method of cooling and drawing fluid from.	F. Espenschade	Williamsport, Pa	June 24, 1856	15, 177
Casks, Method of securing heads in seamless	D. Phillips and W. Reid	Shaftsbury and West Arlington, Vt.	Apr. 16, 1867	63, 810
Casks, Mode of cleaning musty beer and other	D. Willard, jr	Pittsford, N. Y	Aug. 31, 1869	94, 460
Casks oil-proof, Rendering	S. Gardner	New York, N. Y	Oct. 3, 1865	50, 238
Casks or barrels, Machine for driving hoops on	J. A. Loomis	Fond du Lac, Wis	Aug. 15, 1865	49, 425
Casks or barrels, Rolling	E. L. Collins	Wellfleet, Mass	Jan. 5, 1864	41, 139
Casket-handle	D. Leonard	Winsted, Conn	Jan. 4, 1870	98, 506
Casket-handle	A. McGuire	Winchester, Conn	Aug. 16, 1870	106, 496
Casket-handle	W. M. Smith	West Meriden, Conn	Nov. 12, 1867	70, 759
Casket-handle	C. Strong	Winsted, Conn	May 7, 1872	126, 500
Casket-handle	H. C. Wilcox	West Meriden, Conn	Aug. 10, 1869	93, 508
Casket, Jewel	J. Mathiew	Paris, France	Jan. 11, 1870	98, 785
Caskets, Manufacture of	T. Hegarty	Saint Louis, Mo	Jan. 15, 1861	31, 119
Cast-iron chair	J. L. Mott	New York, N. Y	Oct. 2, 1847	5, 317
Cast-metal case for spring-balances	J. Chatillon	New York, N. Y	Dec. 10, 1867	71, 980
Cast-metal dies, Manufacture of	L. Chapman	Collinsville, Conn	Nov. 23, 1869	97, 046
Cast metal, Pressing	J. B. Tarr	Fairhaven, Mass	Oct. 31, 1871	120, 467
Cast metal, Surfacing articles of	H. Tucker	Newton, Mass	June 1, 1869	90, 892
Casts and fancy articles, Composition for forming	M. Schall	New York, N. Y	Mar. 3, 1868	75, 058
Casts, Composition for making anatomical	J. Hurford	Salem, Ohio	Mar. 13, 1866	53, 225

Index of patents issued from the United States Patent Office from 1790 to 1873, inclusive—Continued.

Invention.	Inventor.	Residence.	Date.	No.
Casts, fancy articles, toys, &c., Composition for	M. Schall	New York, N. Y	June 30, 1863	39, 070
Casts for fancy articles, Compound for making	H. Hirsch	New York, N. Y	Mar. 5, 1872	124, 355
Casts for pads, Apparatus for taking	F. Kesmodel	San Francisco, Cal	July 9, 1861	32, 773
Casts from the faces of living persons, Mode of taking.	C. Mills	Washington, D. C	Apr. 4, 1865	47, 121
Casts, Mode of preparing plaster	T. Taylor	Washington, D. C	Oct. 6, 1868	82, 891
Castanets	G. F. Fessenden	Arlington, Mass	June 1, 1869	90, 832
Caster	J. T. Barnes	Hudson City, N. J	June 25, 1867	66, 116
Caster	T. Beach	Freeport, Pa	Aug. 7, 1866	57, 036
Caster	J. Bradbury	Berlin, Conn	Nov. 7, 1871	120, 568
Caster	M. S. Brownell	Adrian, Mich	May 4, 1869	89, 628
Caster	S. Curtis	New York, N. Y	Sept. 30, 1873	143, 334
Caster	J. N. Dinsmore	Kendall Mills, Me	June 18, 1872	128, 129
Caster	W. P. Elliott	Cincinnati, Ohio	Apr. 6, 1869	88, 558
Caster	F. G. Ford	New York, N. Y	Aug. 3, 1869	93, 292
Caster	F. A. Gardner	Danbury, Conn	Jan. 24, 1871	111, 193
Caster	E. G. Gory	Cincinnati, Ohio	June 11, 1872	127, 862
Caster	G. E. Grosse	Massillon, Ohio	Apr. 26, 1870	102, 253
Caster	J. Kintz	West Meriden, Conn	Sept. 20, 1870	107, 507
Caster	J. Kintz	West Meriden, Conn	June 6, 1871	115, 619
Caster	C. Knisely	Chicago, Ill	Apr. 19, 1864	42, 381
Caster	C. Knisely	Chicago, Ill	Apr. 19, 1864	42, 382
Caster	C. Lewando	Boston, Mass	Nov. 17, 1868	84, 126
Caster	W. C. McGill	Cincinnati, Ohio	Apr. 27, 1869	89, 418
Caster	J. Miller	Olean, N. Y	Feb. 16, 1869	86, 997
Caster	G. B. Munn	New Brunswick, N. J	July 16, 1872	128, 972
Caster	J. W. Pugh	Grand Rapids, Mich	June 9, 1868	78, 690
Caster	J. M. Riley	Newark, N. J	Sept. 11, 1866	57, 971
Caster	T. L. Rivers	Saint Louis, Mo	June 29, 1869	91, 873
Caster	J. Toler	Newark, N. J	May 20, 1873	139, 212
Caster	A. C. Twining	New Haven, Conn	Feb. 4, 1868	74, 019
Caster	G. W. Waitt	Philadelphia, Pa	Dec. 23, 1873	145, 769
Caster	J. White	Providence, R. I	Dec. 24, 1867	72, 575
Caster Adjustable	W. C. Dodge	Washington, D. C	May 17, 1864	42, 754
Caster and cake-basket	J. W. Larimore	Chicago, Ill	Feb. 16, 1869	87, 054
Caster and fan, Automatic	E. A. H. Nordyke	Richmond, Ind	Oct. 20, 1857	18, 466
Caster and fruit and cake dish	J. W. Larimore	Chicago, Ill	Feb. 2, 1869	86, 422
Caster and spoon-holder, Combined	L. Evans	Pittsburgh, Pa	Nov. 29, 1870	109, 602
Caster attachment for furniture	J. H. Travis	Charlestown, Mass	June 17, 1873	140, 097
Caster' Ball	A. F. Ahrens	Philadelphia, Pa	May 8, 1847	5, 102
Caster, Ball	S. S. Hickok and D. B. Clement	Boston, Mass	Apr. 14, 1868	76, 630
Caster, Ball	F. S. Smith	New Haven, Conn	Nov. 26, 1867	71, 546
Caster, Ball	L. Wilkinson	Boston, Mass	June 9, 1868	78, 850
Caster, Ball furniture	J. Holmes	Boston, Mass	Apr. 1, 1862	34, 833
Caster, Ball furniture	J. C. Pedrick	Washington, D. C	Aug. 16, 1859	25, 138
Caster, Ball furniture	B. A. Russell	Deep River, Conn	Jan. 25, 1859	22, 751
Caster, Bottle	E. Gleason	Dorchester, Mass	Oct. 21, 1856	15, 946
Caster, Chair	T. Fry	Brooklyn, N. Y	Apr. 10, 1860	27, 792
Caster for bedsteads, Trap	D. Henderson	Boston, Mass	Mar. 15, 1864	41, 919
Caster for billiard-tables and furniture	W. Reagan	New York, N. Y	June 14, 1870	104, 201
Caster for trunks and furniture, Ball	J. Knight	Newark, N. J	Aug. 26, 1856	15, 611
Caster-frame	F. J. Miller	Brooklyn, N. Y	Feb. 12, 1867	61, 947
Caster, Furniture	A. T. Adams	Indianapolis, Ind	Oct. 6, 1868	82, 783
Caster, Furniture	A. C. Arnold and O. G. Hanschildt.	Norwalk, Conn	May 7, 1872	126, 433
Caster, Furniture	M. L. Babb	Cape Elizabeth, Me	June 13, 1865	48, 146
Caster, Furniture	G. L. Bailey	Portland, Me	Mar. 20, 1855	12, 578
Caster, Furniture	D. S. Barnes	New York, N. Y	July 5, 1859	24, 607
Caster, Furniture	J. T. Barnes	Hudson City, N. J	Oct. 30, 1866	59, 163
Caster, Furniture	R. J. Beardsley	Brooklyn, N. Y	Feb. 14, 1865	46, 331
Caster, Furniture	L. Bertsche	Allegheny, Pa	Jan. 18, 1870	98, 912
Caster, Furniture	W. I. Blackman	Columbus, Miss	Jan. 30, 1872	123, 147
Caster, Furniture	H. D. Blake	New Hartford Centre, Conn	Apr. 27, 1858	20, 031
Caster, Furniture	J. H. Bloomfield	Chicago, Ill	Nov. 11, 1862	36, 890
Caster, Furniture	S. A. Bracket	Boston, Mass	Dec. 31, 1872	134, 350
Caster, Furniture	J. D. Bradley	Washington, D. C	Aug. 16, 1864	43, 830
Caster, Furniture	J. Brown	Utica, N. Y	Apr. 21, 1868	76, 885
Caster, Furniture	J. D. Browne	Madisonville, Ohio	June 18, 1872	128, 107
Caster, Furniture	T. P. Burger	Oyster Bay, N. Y	Dec. 15, 1857	18, 839
Caster, Furniture	L. F. Cerf	New York, N. Y	Nov. 26, 1867	71, 363
Caster, Furniture	S. Chandler	New York, N. Y	June 8, 1869	91, 086
Caster, Furniture	S. Chandler	New York, N. Y	Nov. 2, 1869	96, 393
Caster, Furniture	F. G. Ford	Washington, D. C	Mar. 28, 1865	47, 007
Caster, Furniture	F. G. Ford	New York, N. Y	Oct. 23, 1866	58, 999
Caster, Furniture	F. G. Ford	New York, N. Y	May 17, 1870	103, 165
Caster, Furniture	F. G. Ford	Bridgeton, N. J	Oct. 8, 1872	132, 066
Caster, Furniture	E. E. Furney	Chicopee, Mass	June 9, 1868	78, 798
Caster, Furniture	G. H. Glad	Boston Higulands, Mass	Nov. 11, 1873	144, 530
Caster, Furniture	C. R. Gorgas and W. H. Smith	Wooster, Ohio	July 9, 1861	32, 766
Caster, Furniture	E. Hambujer	Detroit, Mich	Mar. 19, 1867	62, 954
Caster, Furniture	J. W. Hewitt and G. R. Lynch	Allegheny City, Pa	July 7, 1868	79, 571
Caster, Furniture	S. S. Hickock	Methuen, Mass	Dec. 19, 1871	122, 016
Caster, Furniture	P. B. Holmes	New York, N. Y	Oct. 3, 1865	50, 249
Caster, Furniture	J. S. and J. W. Hyatt	Albany, N. Y	July 9, 1872	128, 884
Caster, Furniture	J. Johnson	Brooklyn, N. Y	Mar. 4, 1873	136, 522
Caster, Furniture	W. Johnson	Milwaukee, Wis	June 19, 1866	55, 665
Caster, Furniture	T. M. Kane and C. Brown	Goshen, N. Y	Feb. 6, 1866	52, 420
Caster, Furniture	J. Kinzer	Pittsburgh, Pa	Feb. 16, 1858	19, 369
Caster, Furniture	A. H. Lightall	Albany, N. Y	Dec. 3, 1872	133, 650
Caster, Furniture	E. Lindner	New York, N. Y	Feb. 26, 1861	31, 548
Caster, Furniture	S. N. Long	South Chatham, Mass	May 12, 1868	77, 743
Caster, Furniture	W. T. Mersereau	Newark, N. J	Apr. 4, 1865	47, 117
Caster, Furniture	H. Munroe	Fall River, Mass	Mar. 17, 1868	75, 564
Caster, Furniture	H. Munroe	Fall River, Mass	Aug. 11, 1868	80, 990
Caster, Furniture	H. Naylor	Pekin, Ill	Oct. 16, 1866	58, 879
Caster, Furniture	P. B. O'Brien and W. E. Sparks	New Haven, Conn	Dec. 10, 1867	71, 904
Caster, Furniture	J. Parry	Manchester, Great Britain	Jan. 28, 1873	135, 286
Caster, Furniture	J. C. Plumer	Boston, Mass	June 5, 1866	55, 358

Index of patents issued from the United States Patent Office from 1790 *to* 1873, *inclusive*—Continued.

Invention.	Inventor.	Residence.	Date.	No.
Caster, Furniture	S. C. Pratt	Boston, Mass	Aug. 11, 1868	81, 001
Caster, Furniture	J. M. Riley	Newark, N. J	Nov. 25, 1862	37, 008
Caster, Furniture	J. B. Sargent	New Haven, Conn	July 12, 1870	105, 374
Caster, Furniture	C. B. Sheldon	New York, N. Y	Dec. 24, 1872	134, 223
Caster, Furniture	C. B. Sheldon	New York, N. Y	Mar. 25, 1873	137, 249
Caster, Furniture	C. B. Sheldon	New York, N. Y	Mar. 25, 1873	137, 250
Caster, Furniture	C. B. Sheldon	New York, N. Y	Mar. 25, 1873	137, 251
Caster, Furniture	C. B. Sheldon	New York, N. Y	Apr. 8, 1873	137, 728
Caster, Furniture	C. B. Sheldon	New York, N. Y	June 3, 1873	139, 619
Caster, Furniture	F. Smith	Boston, Mass	Jan. 1, 1867	60, 799
Caster, Furniture	I. A. Stafford	Essex, N. Y	Oct. 23, 1860	30, 505
Caster, Furniture	A. G. Stevens	Manchester, N. H	Apr. 25, 1871	114, 061
Caster, Furniture	S. B. Ulmann	New York, N. Y	Feb. 12, 1850	7, 093
Caster, Furniture	W. W. Wade	Springfield, Mass	May 17, 1853	9, 733
Caster, Furniture	A. Walker	New Haven, Conn	Jan. 3, 1865	45, 773
Caster, Furniture	L. S. White	Chicopee, Mass	Jan. 31, 1854	10, 488
Caster, Furniture	L. S. White	Chicopee, Mass	Aug. 8, 1854	11, 506
Caster, Furniture	J. A. Wiedersheim	Philadelphia, Pa	Oct. 2, 1866	58, 523
Caster, Furniture	J. H. Wilhelm and F. G. Ensign	Chicago, Ill	Dec. 26, 1865	51, 770
Caster, Furniture	C. G. Wilson	Brooklyn, N. Y	Sept. 7, 1869	94, 682
Caster, Glass table	A. E. Young	Dorchester, Mass	July 1, 1862	35, 799
Caster, Globe	W. Hunt	New York, N. Y	Apr. 22, 1833	....
Caster or bottle-holder	C. H. Latham	Lowell, Mass	Oct. 1, 1872	131, 822
Caster, Pepper	L. Soehlmann	Jersey City, N. J	Sept. 25, 1866	58, 312
Caster, Pepper	F. Wolf	South Boston, Mass	Aug. 17, 1869	93, 785
Caster, Pickle	H. C. Wilcox	West Meriden, Conn	Feb. 20, 1872	123, 961
Caster, Revolving	C. H. Latham and J. S. Lugg	Lowell, Mass	July 4, 1871	116, 722
Caster, Revolving bottle	E. Gleason	Dorchester, Mass	Dec. 1, 1857	18, 740
Caster, Salt and pepper	J. Bird	Philadelphia, Pa	Sept. 9, 1873	142, 670
Caster, Sewing-machine	L. O. Allen	Gardiner, Me	Aug. 25, 1868	81, 454
Caster, Sewing-machine	T. T. Bishop and H. J. Merret.	Evansville, Ind	Mar. 28, 1871	1 3, 135
Caster, Sewing-machine	D. J. Clark	Evansville, Ind	June 4, 1872	127, 571
Caster, Sewing-machine	E. R. Clark	Marshfield, Ind	Sept. 9, 1873	142, 615
Caster, Sewing-machine	F. H. Duncan	Evansville, Ind	Aug. 15, 1871	118, 117
Caster, Sewing-machine	W. P. Elliot	New Haven, Conn	Apr. 12, 1870	101, 843
Caster, Sewing-machine	W. P. Elliot	New Haven, Conn	Apr. 12, 1870	101, 844
Caster, Sewing-machine	W. D. Hatch	Antrim, N. H	Oct. 3, 1871	119, 606
Caster, Sewing-machine	R. Hathaway	Chicopee, Mass	Mar. 24, 1868	75, 755
Caster, Sewing-machine	H. Jones	Richmond, Ind	May 23, 1871	115, 060
Caster, Sewing-machine	J. B. Lincoln	Providence, R. I	Mar. 25, 1873	137, 141
Caster, Sewing-machine	S. McAfferty	North Shenango, Pa	July 16, 1872	129, 354
Caster, Sewing-machine	J. H. Plank	Bloomfield, Iowa	June 3, 1873	139, 606
Caster, Sewing-machine	G. K. Proctor	Salem, Mass	Oct. 17, 1871	120, 098
Caster, Sewing-machine	G. K. Proctor	Salem, Mass	June 3, 1873	139, 608
Caster, Sewing-machine	J. K. Proctor	Malden, Mass	Nov. 25, 1873	145, 011
Caster, Sewing-machine	J. Robertson	Northampton, Mass	July 29, 1873	141, 236
Caster, Sewing-machine	B. F. Ryder	New York, N. Y	Apr. 12, 1870	101, 924
Caster, Sewing-machine	B. F Ryder	New York, N. Y	Mar. 14, 1871	112, 740
Caster, Sewing-machine	J. B. Sargent	New Haven, Conn	May 31, 1870	103, 782
Caster, Sewing-machine	H. A. Skinner	Worcester, Mass	Nov. 7, 1871	120, 783
Caster, Sewing-machine	J. E. Smith	Sharpsburgh, Ky	Sept. 30, 1873	143, 387
Caster, Sewing-machine	C. F. Stafford and L. Stansberry	Evansville, Ind	June 6, 1871	115, 779
Caster, Sewing-machine	N. D. Stoops	Newark, N. J	Oct. 10, 1865	50, 402
Caster, Sewing-machine	J. M. Veasey	Denver, Colo	Mar. 29, 1870	101, 328
Caster, Sewing-machine	J. M. Veasey	Denver, Colo	July 16, 1872	129, 629
Caster, Sewing-machine	J. N. Wilkins	Chicago, Ill	June 12, 1866	55, 567
Caster, Sewing-machine	W. W. Wright	Lynn, Mass	Feb. 27, 1872	124, 106
Caster-socket	A. C. Twining	New Haven, Conn	Mar. 3, 1868	75, 080
Caster, Spring	E. J. Hall	Highgate, Vt	Dec. 17, 1861	33, 974
Caster, Spring	E. J. Hall	Highgate, Vt	Feb. 18, 1862	34, 463
Caster-stand	G. D. Dudley	Lowell, Mass	Jan. 14, 1873	134, 738
Caster-stand	C. Reistle	Brooklyn, N. Y	Dec. 31, 1867	72, 758
Caster, Stove-leg	E. H. Harding	Philadelphia, Pa	July 16, 1872	129, 550
Caster, Stove-leg, &c	H. A. Humphrey	Milwaukee, Wis	May 30, 1871	115, 322
Caster, Sirup	E. Bigelow	Springfield, Mass	Apr. 6, 1858	19, 824
Caster, Table	H. A. Dickes	New York, N. Y	Oct. 5, 1869	95, 572
Caster, Table	H. Fachs	New York, N. Y	Sept. 16, 1873	142, 905
Caster, Table	J. Gibson, jr	Albany, N. Y	Aug. 8, 1871	117, 765
Caster, Table	R. Gleason, jr	Dorchester, Mass	Mar. 8, 1859	23, 218
Caster, Table	H. A. Hiestand	Hellam, Pa	Oct. 15, 1872	132, 285
Caster, Table	C. H. Latham	Lowell, Mass	June 28, 1870	104, 743
Caster, Table	E. B. Manning	Middletown, Conn	Oct. 15, 1872	132, 301
Caster, Table	A. B. Searles	Providence, R. I	Apr. 13, 1869	88, 911
Caster, Table	A. B. Searles	Providence, R. I	Apr. 13, 1869	88, 912
Caster, Table	T. Shaw	Providence, R. I	Mar. 25, 1873	137, 248
Caster, Table	C. B. Sheldon	New York, N. Y	July 29, 1873	141, 390
Caster, Table	D. Sherwood	Lowell, Mass	Feb. 25, 1868	74, 945
Caster, Table	D. Sherwood	Lowell, Mass	Feb. 2, 1869	86, 463
Caster, Table	D. Sherwood	Lowell, Mass	Dec. 28, 1869	98, 432
Caster, Table	D. Sherwood	Lowell, Mass	Mar. 22, 1870	101, 169
Caster, Table	D. Sherwood	Lowell, Mass	Nov. 1, 1870	108, 838
Caster, Table	D. Sherwood and G. D. Dudley	Lowell, Mass	July 26, 1870	105, 732
Caster, Table	D. Sherwood E. P. Woods, and G. D. Dudley.	Lowell, Mass	July 26, 1870	105, 731
Caster, Table	W. M. Smith	Augusta, Ga	Feb. 15, 1870	99, 965
Caster, Table	G. D. Woodworth	Cincinnati, Ohio	July 16, 1872	129, 507
Caster, Table-car or	E. L. Crandall	Williamstown, N. Y	Apr. 27, 1869	89, 294
Caster, Trunk	J. W. C. and J. E. Haskell	Chicago, Ill	Sept. 22, 1868	82, 310
Caster, Trunk	G. Havell	Newark, N. J	Dec. 10, 1872	133, 856
Caster, Trunk	W. O. Headley	Newark, N. J	July 25, 1865	48, 937
Caster, Trunk	L. Horton and J. E. McGaw	Manchester, N. H	Mar. 3, 1868	75, 017
Caster, Trunk	H. T. Lee	Jersey City, N. J	Oct. 11, 1864	44, 669
Caster, Trunk	T. L. Rivers	Newark, N. J	Nov. 7, 1871	120, 670
Caster, Trunk	T. L. Rivers	Newark, N. J	July 2, 1872	128, 659
Caster, Trunk	M. Schwerin	Newark, N. J	Oct. 11, 1870	108, 193
Caster, Trunk	A. J. Sessions	Bristol, Conn	Oct. 11, 1870	108, 300
Caster, Trunk	W. H. and L. Young	Boston, Mass	Dec. 31, 1867	72, 956
Caster, Trunk	W. H. and L. Young	Boston, Mass	July 7, 1868	79, 798

Index of patents issued from the United States Patent Office from 1790 *to* 1873, *inclusive*—Continued.

Invention.	Inventor.	Residence.	Date.	No.
Caster, Wall or bracket	A. J. Forbes and W. G. Fletcher	Boston, Mass	June 29, 1869	91, 835
Caster-wheel	T. Beach	New York, N. Y	Apr. 19, 1864	43, 338
Caster wheel, Furniture	C. B. Sheldon	New York, N. Y	June 24, 1873	140, 310
Caster wheel, Furniture	C. B. Sheldon	New York, N. Y	June 24, 1873	140, 311
Caster-wheel, Glass	J. B. Capewell	Gloucester, N. J	Nov. 7, 1865	50, 795
Casters and applying them to bedsteads, Mode of constructing.	P., E. W., and J. A. Blake	New Haven, Conn	June 30, 1838	821
Casters, Construction of cruet	W. E. Hawkins	New York, N. Y	Oct. 29, 1867	70, 209
Casters, Detachable fixture for	A. C. Twining	New Haven, Conn	May 18, 1869	90, 137
Casters, Device for supporting furniture	H. E. Richards	Newark, N. J	Dec. 7, 1858	22, 243
Casters, Finishing furniture	P. B. Tyler	Springfield, Mass	Oct. 14, 1856	15, 902
Casters for stove-legs, Adjustable stop for	W. Coughlin	Clarksville, Ohio	Sept. 27, 1870	107, 762
Casters from vulcanizable compounds, Manufacture of.	C. Goodyear, jr	New York, N. Y	May 13, 1862	35, 231
Casters, Manufacture of ball	R. Hinton	Roxbury, Mass	Dec. 14, 1852	9, 464
Casters, Roller of furniture	P. B. Tyler and B. Lathrop	Springfield, Mass	Aug. 8, 1854	11, 502
Casters to furniture, Mode of attaching	W. B. Bartram	Norwalk, Conn	Jan. 30, 1866	52, 257
Casters to trunks, Attaching	I. H. Gilling	New York, N. Y	Apr. 12, 1850	23, 672
Casters to trunks, Attaching	L. S. Maring	Fall River, Mass	Nov. 27, 1855	13, 853
Casters, Tool for boring recesses for	B. F. Graves	Boston, Mass	Aug. 22, 1854	11, 587
Casting and annealing articles made of scoria	W. H. Smith	Philadelphia, Pa	Mar. 22, 1859	23, 317
Casting-apparatus	J. P. Broadmeadow	Bridgeport, Conn	Apr. 4, 1871	113, 249
Casting, Apparatus for attaching pieces of metal to each other by.	H. B. Osgood	Thompsonville, Conn	Jan. 13, 1852	8, 658
Casting chilled plates	R. Poole	Baltimore, Md	Aug. 2, 1859	24, 976
Casting chilled rolls, Method of giving rotary motion to metal in.	J. C. Parry	Pittsburgh, Pa	Feb. 26, 1850	7, 125
Casting-composition	G. Nimmo	Jersey City, N. J	July 25, 1865	48, 973
Casting copper cylinders	F. Adams	Somerville, Mass	Apr. 30, 1861	32, 169
Casting-flask	G. P. Sisson	Florence, Mass	Oct. 1, 1867	69, 372
Casting for steam-pipes, boilers, &c	W. T. Kosinski	Philadelphia, Pa	Sept. 13, 1870	107, 387
Casting hollow articles	J. Brunner	New York, N. Y	Oct. 12, 1869	95, 645
Casting hollow ware	J. Ziegler	Dayton, Ohio	Nov. 3, 1868	83, 751
Casting hollow ware, &c., Method of making patterns for.	E. Ripley	Troy, N. Y	Aug. 31, 1844	3, 724
Casting lugs and dovetails, Device for	G. W. Herrick	Stuyvesant, N. Y	Oct. 6, 1868	82, 715
Casting metal	E. Ripley	Troy, N. Y	Jan. 15, 1856	14, 115
Casting metal	R. Ross	Middlebury, Vt	Mar. 22, 1870	101, 046
Casting metal, Apparatus for forming molds for	A. H. Lowell	Manchester, N. H	June 18, 1867	65, 922
Casting metal, Method of	J. Rives	Paris, France	Sept. 29, 1868	82, 642
Casting, Metal or second patterns for	F. N. Still	New York, N. Y	Jan. 28, 1851	7, 915
Casting metals under pressure, Method of	J. J. C. Smith	Philadelphia, Pa	May 18, 1869	90, 318
Casting, Method of supporting chills in	W. H. Wiley	Fredonia, N. Y	July 28, 1868	80, 321
Casting-mold	S. A. Corser	Northampton, Mass	July 10, 1860	29, 123
Casting-mold	J. R. Davies	Racine, Wis	Sept. 10, 1872	131, 214
Casting-mold	J. R. Davis	Racine, Wis	Mar. 10, 1863	37, 857
Casting-mold	W. Murdock	Jersey City, N. J	May 13, 1863	35, 248
Casting-mold	M. Nelson	New York, N. Y	Apr. 21, 1857	17, 109
Casting-mold	W. B. Robinson	Detroit, Mich	Dec. 10, 1872	133, 801
Casting-mold	N. Thompson	Brooklyn, N. Y	Dec. 12, 1871	121, 736
Casting mold, Metal	E. N. Cleaves	Boston, Mass	Feb. 23, 1869	87, 071
Casting mold, Metal	J. Farrar and W. Groves	Providence, R. I	July 30, 1867	67, 181
Casting molds and cores, Composition for metal	C. Grauer	Philadelphia, Pa	May 18, 1869	90, 257
Casting-molds, Device for forming	W. T. Horrobin	Biddeford, Me	Feb. 28, 1865	46, 564
Casting-molds for metal trundle-heads, Method of making.	E. Lester	Little Falls, N. Y	Feb. 12, 1807	....
Casting molds, Lining for metal	J. Farrar and L. F. Whiting	Providence, R. I., and Boston, Mass.	Jan. 26, 1869	86, 145
Casting-molds, Making	R. Jobson	Wordsley, England	Mar. 29, 1859	23, 375
Casting-molds, Making	F. N. Still	Buffalo, N. Y	Oct. 7, 1846	4, 803
Casting-molds, Manufacture of dry	J. P. Townsend	New York, N. Y	Aug. 16, 1864	43, 885
Casting-molds, Method of constructing metallic	W. Hainsworth	Sharpsville, Pa	Mar. 9, 1869	87, 663
Casting-molds, Method of making	J. G. Holt	Chicago, Ill	June 5, 1866	55, 294
Casting or smut machine	D. Tomlinson	Brookfield, Conn	May 20, 1812	....
Casting ornamental borders	J. L. Lewis	....	Oct. 8, 1824	....
Casting-pattern	A. L. Finch	Sing Sing, N. Y	Apr. 26, 1870	102, 384
Casting-pattern	J. L. Jackson	New York, N. Y	June 7, 1870	103, 888
Casting-pattern	L. H. Mans	Danville, Pa	Feb. 5, 1836	....
Casting pipe	A. Brady	New York, N. Y	Sept. 18, 1860	30, 044
Casting pipe	T. J. Lovegrove	Philadelphia, Pa	May 23, 1865	47, 901
Casting pipe	G. Rogers	Philadelphia, Pa	Mar. 5, 1867	62, 688
Casting pot-hole covers, Pattern for	W. J. Fryer	West Troy, N. Y	July 2, 1867	66, 317
Casting-press for metal	J. B. Tarr	Fairhaven, Mass	Aug. 31, 1869	94, 253
Casting refractory metals, Apparatus for	M. Smith	Philadelphia, Pa	Oct. 22, 1867	70, 038
Casting rolls, Method of giving rotary motion to fluid iron in.	J. C. Parry	Pittsburgh, Pa	May 21, 1850	7, 383
Casting under pressure, Mold for	J. B. Tarr	Fairhaven, Mass	Dec. 20, 1870	110, 307
Castings and preparing cast-iron patterns, Process of reducing iron.	C. R. Ely	Sheldon, Vt	Apr. 2, 1861	31, 880
Castings, Apparatus for making molds for metal	A. Weaber	Philadelphia, Pa	July 13, 1869	92, 677
Castings, Apparatus for molding	P. W. Lamb	Albany, N. Y	June 12, 1866	55, 504
Castings, Apparatus for producing refined iron and steel.	J. W. Middleton	Philadelphia, Pa	July 30, 1872	129, 899
Castings, Apparatus for treating malleable-iron	A. F. Andrews	New Haven, Conn	Jan. 30, 1872	123, 073
Castings, Blackwashing mold for	W. and D. Ferguson	New York, N. Y	Mar. 13, 1860	27, 438
Castings, Cleaning	A. Ralston	West Middletown, Pa	Mar. 8, 1859	23, 193
Castings, Composition for making chilled	J. Reichenbach	Allegheny, Pa	Apr. 20, 1869	89, 076
Castings direct from the blast-furnace, Producing	J. W. Middleton	Philadelphia, Pa	Oct. 18, 1870	108, 375
Castings, Furnace for tempering	W. M. Watson	Tonica, Ill	Oct. 7, 1873	143, 548
Castings, Grinder for cleaning	G. Miller	Providence, R. I	July 26, 1870	105, 711
Castings, Grinder or rattler for cleaning	G. Miller	Johnston, R. I	Feb. 22, 1870	100, 175
Castings, Machine for making cast-steel	J. B. Tarr	Chicago, Ill	Aug. 28, 1866	57, 644
Castings, Machine for molding for metal	D. Brown	Baltimore, Md	June 27, 1854	11, 191
Castings, Machine for smoothing oxide and sand on	B. Seymour	Utica, N. Y	Dec. 2, 1835	....
Castings, Machine for trimming	A. S. Gear	Boston, Mass	Apr. 23, 1872	125, 948
Castings, Making chilled	G. W. Bolman and W. Neemes	Pittsburgh, Pa	Oct. 31, 1865	50, 680
Castings, Making chilled	W. Butler	Little Falls, N. Y	Mar. 18, 1856	14, 442

Index of patents issued from the United States Patent Office from 1790 to 1873, inclusive—Continued.

Invention.	Inventor.	Residence.	Date.	No.
Castings, Malleable-iron	A. F. Andrews	New Haven, Conn	Jan. 30, 1872	123, 072
Castings, Metal for	G. Whitney	Philadelphia, Pa	July 16, 1872	129, 261
Castings, Metallic pin for cooling the interior of	W. H. Saunders	Greensburgh, N. Y	Nov. 26, 1835	....
Castings, Mill for cleaning	H. R. Remsen	Albany, N. Y	Apr. 7, 1857	17, 012
Castings, Mode of making cast-steel	T. J. Chubb	Williamsburgh, N. Y	June 8, 1869	90, 925
Castings, Mold for making	S. A. Carser	Northampton, Mass	Apr. 5, 1864	42, 251
Castings, Mold for steel	P. G. Gardiner	New York, N. Y	Apr. 12, 1859	23, 670
Castings, Molding for metal	J. P. Broadmeadow	Bridgeport, Conn	Nov. 29, 1859	26, 321
Castings, Preparing metallic patterns for	T. G. Bucklin	West Troy, N. Y	May 8, 1849	6, 440
Castings, Process of making thin iron	H. and W. E. Bleecker and S. D. Vose.	Albany, N. Y	Dec. 25, 1849	6, 969
Castings, Process of chilling	J. L. Mott	New York, N. Y	June 13, 1848	5, 636
Castings, Split	J. Yocom, jr	Philadelphia, Pa	June 20, 1871	116, 134
Castings, Tempering steel	C. Parking and S. Trethewey	Pittsburgh, Pa	July 20, 1869	92, 747
Castings, Tumbling-barrel for cleaning	F. N. Bixby	West Meriden, Conn	Apr. 1, 1873	137, 409
Cat-ball	T. H. Joyce	New York, N. Y	Nov. 7, 1871	120, 650
Cat-head and shank-painter stopper	C. Perley	New York, N. Y	Apr. 2, 1850	7, 249
Cat hook and stopper	D. H. Cousins	Surry, Me	Aug. 6, 1872	130, 198
Catamenial and urinal bandage and receptacle	M. Vedder	New York, N. Y	May 20, 1862	35, 338
Catamenial bandage	C. E. Clark	Boston, Mass	Feb. 22, 1859	23, 059
Catamenial bandage	F. Dahis and F. Doermer	Brooklyn, N. Y	July 31, 1860	29, 362
Catamenial bandage	D. F. Robertson	Middletown, N. Y	Dec. 20, 1864	45, 523
Catamenial guard and supporter	J. A. Belvin, jr	Baltimore, Md	Sept. 10, 1867	68, 688
Catamenial sack	A. F. Baum	New York, N. Y	June 2, 1868	78, 414
Catamenial sack	J. C. Bewzinger	Catonsville, Md	Sept. 4, 1866	57, 665
Catamenial sack	G. E. Brinckerhoff	Brooklyn, N. Y	Nov. 17, 1868	84, 083
Catamenial sack	W. A. Dinsmore	South Boston, Mass	July 26, 1870	105, 785
Catamenial sack	H. W. Libbey	Cleveland, Ohio	Mar. 10, 1868	75, 434
Catamenial sack	C. Manheim	New York, N. Y	Mar. 3, 1868	75, 036
Catamenial sack	E. L. Perry	New York, N. Y	Sept. 12, 1865	49, 915
Catamenial supporter	A. A. Starr	New York, N. Y	Aug. 22, 1854	11, 574
Cataract-instrument	T. R. Williams	Philadelphia, Pa	June 14, 1826	....
Cataract by tubes and cannular points, Removing	F. B. Shaw	Philadelphia, Pa	July 27, 1815	....
Catch-bolt	W. Salisbury	Wheeling, Va	Nov. 29, 1859	26, 296
Catch for clasps	J. Bingham	Philadelphia, Pa	Sept. 11, 1847	5, 285
Catch for hanging drapery	A. and C. A. Warner	Bristol, Conn	Jan. 4, 1859	22, 521
Catch, Hand	J. P. R. James	Pepin, Minn	Aug. 27, 1867	68, 082
Caterpillar-destroying compound	G. F. Whisenant	Chapel Hill, Tex	Jan. 14, 1873	134, 959
Caterpillar-nests, Instrument for destroying	J. S. Needham	South Danvers, Mass	Dec. 13, 1864	45, 428
Caterpillars, Instrument for destroying embryo	A. Casebeer	Sipesville, Pa	Dec. 4, 1866	60, 136
Catheter and syringe, Combined	N. B. Sornborger	Northampton, Mass	Jan. 14, 1868	73, 402
Catheter, Metallic flexible	I. Balch and M. Carter	Salisbury, Mass	Oct. 26, 1816	....
Cattle, Apparatus for breachy	J. P. Leddy and W. Rogers	Mount Carroll, Ill	May 15, 1860	28, 286
Cattle, Apparatus for watering	S. W. Wood	Rochester, N. Y	Oct. 28, 1851	8, 479
Cattle-blinder	M. Backmayer	Lyons, N. Y	Apr. 29, 1873	138, 224
Cattle-card	W. M. Warren	Watertown, Conn	Mar. 26, 1872	124, 991
Cattle, Compound for destroying vermin in	F. Kalteyer	San Antonio, Tex	Aug. 10, 1869	93, 622
Cattle, Device for removing obstacles from the throats of.	C. Schule	North East, Pa	Apr. 2, 1872	125, 337
Cattle, Device for watering	O. Wheedon	Medina, N. Y	Mar. 13, 1866	53, 207
Cattle during transportation, Device for feeding	W. Reid	Granton, Scotland	Mar. 16, 1869	87, 970
Cattle-fastening	K. Gibbs	Berwick, Me	Nov. 26, 1861	33, 780
Cattle-fastening device	S. E. Southland	Jamestown, N. Y	May 20, 1862	35, 331
Cattle from jumping, Device for preventing	C. Bettinger	South Danville, N. Y	Sept. 21, 1869	95, 072
Cattle-gag	W. Kegg	Lasellsville, N. Y	Oct. 23, 1866	59, 035
Cattle-gate, Railway	J. Bowman and J. B. Overmyer	Reading, Ohio	Oct. 26, 1869	96, 193
Cattle-gate, Railway	M. Hall, jr	Osborn, Ohio	July 12, 1859	24, 778
Cattle-guard gate	A. Freeman	Lowell, Mich	Nov. 5, 1867	70, 429
Cattle-guard gate, Railway	J. H. Mallory	La Porte, Ind	Mar. 7, 1871	112, 473
Cattle guard, Railway	C. Brenneman	Orrville, Ohio	Nov. 26, 1867	71, 272
Cattle-guard, Railway	C. Caton	Boyd's Mills, Ohio	Aug. 1, 1871	117, 609
Cattle-guard, Railway	J. Forrest	Manchester, N. Y	Aug. 13, 1861	33, 035
Cattle-guard, Railway	P. Mougey	Marshallsville, Ohio	May 5, 1868	77, 642
Cattle-guard, Railway	J. L. Rowley	Angola, Ind	Mar. 29, 1859	23, 398
Cattle-guard, Railway	S. Strack	Dover Township, Pa	Oct. 24, 1871	120, 343
Cattle-guard, Railway	H. Tagart	Jacksontown, Ohio	May 5, 1868	77, 677
Cattle-guard, Railway	R. M. Yorks	Schoolcraft, Mich	Apr. 29, 1873	138, 308
Cattle, Herding and securing	J. Wilkinson	Urbana, Ill	June 2, 1868	78, 631
Cattle-hitch	C. H. Sawyer	Hollis, Me	Aug. 7, 1866	57, 049
Cattle-horn tip	J. C. Thompson	Charlestown, Mass	Feb. 9, 1869	86, 882
Cattle, Instrument for relieving choke and bloat in	N. Q. Munger and G. B. Pomeroy.	Casco and South Haven, Mich.	June 29, 1869	92, 085
Cattle-leading clasp	J. Welton	Waterbury, Conn	Oct. 9, 1855	13, 672
Cattle, Machine for watering	M. Smith		Mar. 16, 1804	....
Cattle-mill	La Paype, sr	Baltimore, Md	Nov. 4, 1805	....
Cattle, Mode of watering	A. Allen	Troy, Pa	July 10, 1824	....
Cattle-pricker	R. A. Carson and W. T. Peter	Briensburgh, Ky	Feb. 25, 1868	74, 795
Cattle, Remedy for murrain in	H. Jacobs	Fayetteville, Tenn	Aug. 17, 1869	93, 717
Cattle, Salt-trough for	T. Gladding	East Berlin, Conn	Jan. 19, 1869	86, 066
Cattle, Shears for marking	S. D. Baldwin	Chicago, Ill	May 23, 1865	47, 785
Cattle, Skinning	H. S. Lewis	Communipaw, N. J	Apr. 16, 1867	63, 910
Cattle-stanchion	E. S. Alvord	Harmony, N. Y	May 10, 1870	102, 904
Cattle-stanchion	N. W. Boody	Westbrook, Me	Jan. 4, 1870	98, 467
Cattle-stanchion	J. B. Crowell	Newport, N. H	Oct. 30, 1866	59, 180
Cattle-stanchion	W. C. Gifford	Jamestown, N. Y	May 10, 1870	102, 804
Cattle-stanchion	G. W. Hatch	Parkman, Ohio	July 30, 1850	7, 524
Cattle-stanchion	G. A. Keene	Newburyport, Mass	Mar. 15, 1864	41, 926
Cattle-stanchion	J. Manley	Hope, Me	Apr. 23, 1867	64, 017
Cattle-stanchion	C. H. Mann	Fairlee, Vt	Sept. 3, 1867	68, 372
Cattle-stanchion	H. Maycock	Verona, N. Y	Jan. 3, 1865	45, 728
Cattle-stanchion	J. A. Rosback	Hermon, N. Y	Jan. 24, 1871	111, 275
Cattle-stanchion	L. S. Safford	Hope, Me	Oct. 13, 1868	82, 995
Cattle-stanchion	C. W. Sawdey	Poolville, N. Y	Nov. 4, 1873	144, 360
Cattle-stanchion	J. D. Scott	Alviso, Cal	Aug. 30, 1870	106, 876
Cattle-tie	W. Allport	New Britain, Conn	Jan. 26, 1869	86, 119
Cattle-tie	E. P. Banks	Portland, Me	May 14, 1867	64, 621
Cattle-tie	G. Hull	Port Crane, N. Y	Aug. 28, 1860	29, 790
Cattle-tie	S. T. Hutchins	North Anson, Me	Mar. 21, 1871	112, 922

Index of patents issued from the United States Patent Office from 1790 *to* 1873, *inclusive*—Continued.

Invention.	Inventor.	Residence.	Date.	No.
Cattle-tie	J. Ives	Mount Carmel, Conn	Aug. 29, 1865	49, 630
Cattle tie	A. F. Migeon	Wolcottville, Conn	Mar. 30, 1869	88, 403
Cattle-tie	C. S. Rundlett	Portland, Me	Mar. 12, 1867	62, 780
Cattle-tie	H. C. Small	Portland, Me	June 19, 1866	55, 727
Cattle-tie	J. Wiard	New Britain, Conn	June 9, 1868	78, 849
Cattle-tie for stalls	C. M. Baker	Bingham, Me	Jan. 15, 1867	61, 138
Cattle-tie, Safety	C. P. Winslow	Westborough, Me	Mar. 2, 1869	87, 454
Cavil	J. A. Wood	Pittsburgh, Pa	Jan. 9, 1872	122, 692
Caviar, Manufacture of	R. G. Westacott	Worcester, Mass	Jan. 7, 1851	7, 895
Ceiling and floor, Fire-proof	J. W. Bassett	New York, N. Y	Apr. 22, 1873	138, 118
Ceiling and roof, Fire-proof	J. Gilbert	Philadelphia, Pa	May 14, 1867	64, 659
Ceiling and wall for building	C. N. Poole	Sandwich, Ill	Apr. 18, 1871	113, 793
Ceiling and wall ventilator	O. S. Trexler	Naperville, Ill	Sept. 10, 1867	68, 807
Ceiling, Fire-proof	F. Baumann and G. F. Letz	Chicago, Ill	June 7, 1870	103, 963
Ceiling, Fire-proof	J. B. Cornell	New York, N. Y	Mar. 23, 1858	19, 682
Ceiling, Fire-proof	B. J. Harris	Richmond, Va	May 17, 1814	....
Ceiling, Fire-proof	S. P. Snead	Louisville, Ky	June 15, 1869	91, 375
Ceiling-ornament	E. T. Bussell	Indianapolis, Ind	Dec. 12, 1871	121, 845
Celery-collar	J. Simpson	York, England	July 23, 1872	129, 758
Cell-lock	E. Kershaw	Boston, Mass	Jan. 29, 1856	14, 178
Cellar, Artificial	V. Haeffner	Dobb's Ferry, N. Y	Dec. 9, 1862	37, 095
Cellar, vault, &c	H. Hallark	New York, N. Y	Oct. 24, 1826	....
Cellar, Water-proof	T. New	Brooklyn, N. Y	Apr. 4, 1871	113, 328
Cellars, Apparatus for draining	A. F. Erich	Baltimore, Md	Apr. 3, 1866	53, 594
Cellars, Mode of constructing walls and floors of	A. R. Moen	New York, N. Y	Feb. 26, 1856	14, 323
Cellars, vaults, magazines, &c., Construction of	E. Ludlow	New York, N. Y	Dec. 14, 1824	....
Cellars, water-closets, &c., Apparatus for emptying	R. Boeklen	Brooklyn, N. Y	Aug. 26, 1873	142, 200
Cement	D. Arndt	Cleveland, Ohio	Aug. 30, 1870	106, 911
Cement	H. Billings	Beardstown, Ill	May 1, 1860	28, 055
Cement	C. Fricke	Mobile, Ala	May 1, 1860	28, 070
Cement	C. Fricke	Mobile, Ala	May 29, 1860	28, 464
Cement	A. S. Jourdan	Nashville, Tenn	Nov. 20, 1866	59, 771
Cement	P. A. Letourneur	New Orleans, La	Sept. 11, 1860	29, 979
Cement	E. V. Machette, jr., and E. M. Crary.	Philadelphia, Pa	Dec. 1, 1868	84, 638
Cement	W. McKay	Ottawa, Canada	Nov. 12, 1872	132, 973
Cement	N. Parmeter	Gardner, Mass	May 3, 1859	23, 856
Cement	C. Saffray	New York, N. Y	May 5, 1868	77, 537
Cement	J. Stansfield	Brooklyn, N. Y	Sept. 26, 1865	50, 185
Cement	D. B. Tooly	Albion, N. Y	Sept. 10, 1867	68, 671
Cement	G. W. Upham	Amherst, N. H	Sept. 22, 1868	82, 454
Cement	B. S. Welch	Brooklyn, N. Y	May 18, 1852	8, 962
Cement	L. Woolworth	Albion, Wis	Apr. 2, 1867	63, 449
Cement and appliances for preparing and using the same.	J. McKenzie and J. M. Stebbins.	Philadelphia, Pa	Nov. 21, 1871	121, 118
Cement and artificial stone, Manufacture of	G. S. Dean	San Francisco, Cal	Jan. 23, 1872	122, 880
Cement and as a plastic material for molding various articles, Composition to be used as a.	S. Sorel	Paris, France	Mar. 6, 1866	53, 092
Cement and metallic pipe, Combination	H. Knight	Jersey City, N. J	Aug. 27, 1861	33, 152
Cement and metallic pipe, Combination	H. Knight	Brooklyn, N. Y	Apr. 7, 1863	38, 112
Cement, Apparatus for spreading	J. H. Pulte	Cincinnati, Ohio	Sept. 4, 1866	57, 764
Cement, Artificial stone or marble	O. Parker	New York, N. Y	Sept. 9, 1835	....
Cement, Asphaltic	C. G. Reinhold	Milton, Pa	Mar. 21, 1865	46, 975
Cement, Asphaltic	A. Straub	Milton, Pa	Nov. 17, 1863	40, 649
Cement, Bituminous compound for	C. Poullalier	New York, N. Y	Mar. 3, 1838	620
Cement, Chemical water-proof	C. Fletcher	Boston, Mass	Nov. 23, 1831	....
Cement-compound	J. Fairchild	Eagleville, Ohio	Sept. 10, 1867	68, 720
Cement-compound	J. R. Remington	Macon County, Ala	July 4, 1854	11, 237
Cement, Compound hydraulic	A. Pfund	New York, N. Y	Feb. 4, 1873	135, 582
Cement-felt for covering steam boilers, pipes, &c	W. T. Kosinski	Brooklyn, N. Y	Jan. 29, 1867	61, 648
Cement, Fire and water	J. Coburn	Middlesex County, Mass	Sept. 3, 1828	....
Cement, Fire and water proof	S. R. Scharf	Baltimore, Md	Apr. 6, 1869	88, 745
Cement, Fire and water proof	W. Yates and D. Dolan	Manchester, England	Mar. 14, 1846	4, 420
Cement for architectural purposes, Artificial-stone	O. Parker	New York, N. Y	Sept. 9, 1835	....
Cement for artificial stone	J. A. Henshaw	Cambridge, Mass	Apr. 9, 1872	125, 390
Cement for blocks, pillars, &c	C. Clinton	Minisink, N. Y	Oct. 28, 1835	....
Cement for calking ships, &c	E. Heylin	Rochester, N. Y	June 22, 1869	91, 537
Cement for cisterns	Carson and Roberts	York, N. Y	Oct. 17, 1835	....
Cement for coating and protecting wood	H. M. Westman	East Boston, Mass	Oct. 25, 1870	108, 661
Cement for coating wood, &c	A. Pelletier	Washington, D. C	Apr. 14, 1868	76, 806
Cement for covering buildings, &c	J. Bump	Kirtland, Ohio	Sept. 3, 1840	1, 765
Cement for fastening door-knobs, &c	N. B. Hall and H. Jones	Branford, Conn	June 2, 1868	78, 592
Cement for fixing door-knobs, &c	P. Kennedy	New York, N. Y	June 11, 1867	65, 680
Cement for forming artificial stone	J. D. Greenwood and R. W. Keen.	England	Oct. 9, 1839	1, 361
Cement for grinding cylinders	J. Stephan	Boston, Mass	Oct. 28, 1851	8, 474
Cement for leather	A. Leach	Lynn, Mass	Nov. 20, 1866	59, 774
Cement for leather and other substances	S. F. Hilton	Providence, R. I	Aug. 13, 1861	33, 065
Cement for leather, &c., Water-proof	R. Hinshelwood and C. A. A. During.	New York, N. Y	May 12, 1863	38, 480
Cement for lining oil-barrels	S. H. Jones	Sandy Spring, Md	Aug. 20, 1867	67, 880
Cement for making water-tight joints in coping, roofing, &c.	J. Judge	New York, N. Y	Jan. 19, 1869	86, 018
Cement for manufacture of cement-pipes, Preparation of.	J. W. Stockwell	Portland, Me	July 19, 1870	105, 511
Cement for mending china, glass, &c	R. W. Patten	New York, N. Y	Mar. 12, 1872	124, 617
Cement for pavements, &c., Composition	A. M. Shaw	Lebanon, N. H	Mar. 10, 1868	75, 473
Cement for pavements, drain-pipes, &c., Asphalt	E. J. De Smedt	New York, N. Y	Feb. 7, 1871	111, 520
Cement for pavements, walks, roofs, &c	G. H. Smith	New York, N. Y	May 17, 1870	103, 095
Cement for paving and building	J. E. Hover	Philadelphia, Pa	Oct. 4, 1870	107, 910
Cement for preparing masts, spars, &c	A. Jeffery	Great Britain	Apr. 6, 1843	3, 027
Cement for roofs or walls of buildings	C. Clinton	New York, N. Y	July 13, 1827	....
Cement for sealing preserve-cans	J. B. Wilson	Fisherville, N. J	Mar. 1, 1864	41, 823
Cement for setting slates, making gutters, &c., Composition for.	J. Fullagar and M. Byrne	New York, N. Y	June 15, 1869	91, 223
Cement for steam-joints	J. G. Kilgour	Brooklyn, N. Y	Nov. 2, 1865	51, 060
Cement for stone	H. Schneider	Cleveland, Ohio	Jan. 2, 1866	51, 867

Index of patents issued from the United States Patent Office from 1790 *to* 1873, *inclusive*—Continued.

Invention.	Inventor.	Residence.	Date.	No.
Cement for walks, floors, pavements, &c	J. S. Baldwin, W. H. Jones, and E. N. Gibbs.	Elmira, Rochester, and Elmira, N. Y.	Feb. 12, 1867	61, 984
Cement for walls, &c	A. Scott	New Berne, N. C	Aug. 15, 1814	....
Cement for wood, brick, stone, or iron work	R. Walsh	Boston, Mass	Jan. 5, 1832	....
Cement from basanite, Hydraulic	E. C. Warner	Albany, N. Y	Oct. 6, 1837	371
Cement from slag, Preparing	J. J. Bodmer	Newport, Great Britain	Nov. 5, 1867	70, 510
Cement, Gum-elastic	C. Goodyear	New Haven, Conn	Sept. 9, 1835	....
Cement, Hydraulic	L. Kidder	New York, N. Y	Jan. 15, 1836	....
Cement, Hydraulic	O. Parker	New York, N. Y	Sept. 9, 1835	....
Cement, Hydraulic	Parker, Clowes, and Garfield	New York, N. Y	Aug. 27, 1835	....
Cement, Hydraulic	J. White	Syracuse, N. Y	Jan. 23, 1836	....
Cement impervious to moisture, Hardening and rendering.	S. Goodwin	New York, N. Y	Apr. 16, 1841	2, 048
Cement in making cistern-reservoir, &c., Mode of applying.	T. Coyle	Baltimore, Md	Aug. 16, 1837	358
Cement-kiln	J. E. Park	Rutherford County, Tenn	Dec. 3, 1872	133, 664
Cement-lined pipe	M. Stephens	Brooklyn, N. Y	Apr. 15, 1873	137, 970
Cement-lined pipe	M. Stephens	Brooklyn, N. Y	Sept. 2, 1873	142, 528
Cement, Making	W. H. Smith	Georgetown, D. C	June 10, 1844	3, 621
Cement, Manufacture of	J. E. Park	La Vergne, Tenn	May 13, 1873	138, 924
Cement, Manufacture of	D. O. Saylor	Allentown, Pa	Sept. 26, 1871	119, 413
Cement, Manufacture of hydraulic	D. O. Saylor	Allentown, Pa	May 21, 1872	126, 989
Cement, Marble	G. G. Goriboldi	Buffalo, N. Y	Aug. 20, 1867	67, 868
Cement, Mastic	W. H. Chase	United States Engineers	Apr. 16, 1845	3, 999
Cement, mastic, and japan from grahamite, Manufacture of.	H. Wurtz	New York, N. Y	Aug. 13, 1867	67, 696
Cement, Mode of incorporating bituminous liquids with wet earths for.	W. H. Johnson	Springfield, Ill	Dec. 9, 1856	16, 208
Cement of boiled coal-tar and earth	H. P. Gengembre	Allegheny City, Pa	July 11, 1854	11, 269
Cement or earthen tubes, Mold for	B. S. and C. M. Pierce	New Bedford, Mass	Aug. 1, 1854	11, 440
Cement or hydraulic lime, Water-proof	R. Leckie	Washington, D. C	Mar. 31, 1829	....
Cement or mortar, Composition	W. Bleser	New York, N. Y	Nov. 22, 1859	26, 158
Cement or mortar, Water-proof	S. Gilford	Washington, D. C	Jan. 16, 1827	....
Cement or pigments, Water-proof	E. Deutsch	Havre, France	May 25, 1844	3, 598
Cement, paint, &c., Flexible water and air proof	J. T. Howe	New York, N. Y	Jan. 31, 1829	....
Cement pipe	H. Knight	Brooklyn, N. Y	Nov. 27, 1866	60, 014
Cement pipe, Branch	E. Lockhart, F. Roberts, and H. Knight.	Louisville, Ky., and Brooklyn, N. Y.	July 28, 1868	80, 357
Cement-pipe joint	M. Stephens	Brooklyn, N. Y	Aug. 24, 1869	94, 146
Cement-pipe machine	E. T. Jewett	Saint Albans Bay, Vt	June 28, 1864	43, 310
Cement-pipe mold	D. Copeland, jr	Rochester, N. Y	May 23, 1871	115, 029
Cement-pipe mold	H. Knight	Jersey City, N. J	Apr. 8, 1862	34, 890
Cement-pipe mold	H. Knight	Jersey City, N. J	May 13, 1862	35, 243
Cement-pipe mold	F. I. Sage	Springfield, Mass	July 29, 1873	141, 388
Cement pipes, Apparatus for coating	E. Dayton	Meriden, Conn	Nov. 2, 1869	96, 313
Cement pipes, Branch coupling for	M. Stephens	Brooklyn, N. Y	Apr. 2, 1872	125, 345
Cement pipes, Composition for	J. A. Middleton	New York, N. Y	Dec. 10, 1872	133, 874
Cement pipes, Device for lining	M. Stephens	Brooklyn, N. Y	Apr. 23, 1872	126, 100
Cement pipes, Forming hydraulic	J. B. and W. F. Poague	Fancy Hill, Va	Nov. 29, 1853	10, 286
Cement pipes, Machine for making	J. E. Earle	New Haven, Conn	Sept. 5, 1865	49, 827
Cement pipes, Machine for making	H. Holden	New Haven, Conn	Sept. 20, 1864	44, 369
Cement pipes, Machine for making	J. Howarth	Salem, Mass	July 14, 1863	39, 233
Cement pipes, Machine for molding	H. Knight	Jersey City, N. J	June 24, 1862	35, 692
Cement pipes, Machinery for making	W. Goodwin	New Haven, Conn	Sept. 5, 1865	49, 828
Cement pipes, Manufacture of	J. A. Middleton	New York, N. Y	Dec. 10, 1872	133, 875
Cement pipes, Manufacture of	A. P. Stephens	Brooklyn, N. Y	June 4, 1872	127, 438
Cement pipes, Manufacture of hydraulic	H. Knight	Jersey City, N. J	May 14, 1861	32, 298
Cement pipes, Manufacture of water-proof	A. F. Jaloureau	Paris, France	May 24, 1859	24, 125
Cement pipes, &c., Means for making	D. S. Ogden	New York, N. Y	May 26, 1863	38, 695
Cement pipes, Mold for molding	H. Knight	Jersey City, N. J	May 8, 1860	28, 184
Cement, Plaster called the threefold	E. Godfrey	New York, N. Y	Sept. 9, 1825	....
Cement, Plastic	G. E. Hopkins	Harwich, Mass	Sept. 7, 1869	94, 495
Cement, Rubber	H. J. Ball	Oswego, N. Y	Nov. 29, 1870	109, 570
Cement, Silicated	G. E. Vanderburgh	Mamaroneck, N. Y	May 29, 1860	28, 541
Cement tiles, pipes, pavements, &c., Composition for forming.	I. Marsh, jr., and G. Marsh	Milton and Lewisburgh, Pa.	June 9, 1863	38, 833
Cement to be used in sewers and drains and for constructing flues and other parts of buildings.	J. Kleckner	Mottville, Mich	Mar. 8, 1870	100, 706
Cement to be used under water	J. Grant	Saratoga, N. Y	Nov. 11, 1817	....
Cement, Treating argillaceous limestone to obtain hydraulic.	F. Coignet	Paris, France	Feb. 8, 1870	99, 637
Cement walk, pavement, and road	C. Burgess	Rochester, N. Y	Sept. 27, 1870	107, 750
Cement, Water	S. Guilford	Lebanon, Pa	Jan. 11, 1826	....
Cement, Water	T. F. Purcell and A. B. McFarlin.	Williamsport, Pa	Dec. 30, 1833	....
Cement, Water	D. M. Randolph	Richmond, Va	Sept. 26, 1821	....
Cement, Water-proof	A. Brower	New York, N. Y	July 27, 1858	20, 985
Cement, Water-proof	G. W. Caton	Canandaigua, N. Y	Feb. 26, 1867	62, 393
Cement, Water-proof	T. S. Clark	Charlestown, Mass	July 26, 1870	105, 648
Cement, Water-proof	W. Y. Singleton	Springfield, Ill	Dec. 26, 1845	4, 333
Cementation of rails, axles, &c., Method of effecting the.	T. W. Dodds	Rotherham, England	July 2, 1867	66, 310
Center and lathe dog, Combined	A. J. Truxell	Lynchburgh, Va	Nov. 8, 1870	109, 079
Center-bit	W. H. McMillar and S. Devoe	New York, N. Y	Aug. 13, 1867	67, 785
Center-bit	W. H. Richards	Deerfield Corners, N. Y	Apr. 16, 1872	125, 759
Center-bit, Fastening	A. W. Streeter	Shelburne Falls, Mass	Jan. 23, 1855	12, 289
Center-board	A. G. Crossman	Huntington, N. Y	May 23, 1871	115, 173
Center-board	F. Dominy	Penataquit, N. Y	Nov. 19, 1867	70, 977
Center-board	G. M. Fay	Eureka, Cal	Aug. 22, 1865	49, 514
Center-board	B. Kennon	New Orleans, La	May 11, 1869	90, 046
Center-board	J. G. Saunders	Narragansett, R. I	Oct. 1, 1867	69, 492
Center board and box for vessels	D. P. Nickerson	Cleveland, Ohio	Jan. 22, 1867	61, 351
Center-board, Folding	J. M. Hoffman	Buffalo, N. Y	Apr. 10, 1849	6, 299
Center-board for sailing-vessels	W. F. Davis	Boston, Mass	Mar. 5, 1867	62, 614
Center-board for vessels	J. Call	Richmond, Me	Sept. 9, 1873	142, 677
Center-board for vessels	R. Chambers	Detroit, Mich	Jan. 8, 1867	61, 049
Center-board for vessels	A. G. Crossman	Huntington, N. Y	Apr. 25, 1871	113, 984
Center board for vessels	J. Dean	Detroit, Mich	Oct. 22, 1872	132, 380

Index of patents issued from the United States Patent Office from 1790 *to* 1873, *inclusive*—Continued.

Invention.	Inventor.	Residence.	Date.	No.
Center-board for vessels	J. Dillon	New York, N. Y	July 27, 1869	93, 070
Center-board for vessels	J. Espalla	Mobile, Ala	Nov. 25, 1873	144, 968
Center-board for vessels	D. G. Gerard	Patchogue, N. Y	July 3, 1860	28, 979
Center-board for vessels	F. J. Macfarlan	San Francisco, Cal	Dec. 10, 1867	72, 058
Center-board for vessels	J. J. Moule	Huntington, N. Y	June 20, 1871	116, 079
Center-board for vessels	J. F. Potts	Apalachicola, Fla	Nov. 16, 1858	22, 088
Center-board for vessels	N. Pratt	Nicholson, Pa	Mar. 1, 1859	23, 114
Center-board for vessels	D. Robertson	Detroit, Mich	Feb. 4, 1868	74, 003
Center-board, Jointed	T. Maskell	Franklin, La	Oct. 9, 1849	6, 774
Center-board of navigable vessels	B. Joline	Westfield, N. Y	Apr. 2?, 1858	19, 996
Center-board vessels, Construction of	C. E. Ketchum and W. L. Hunt	Port Jefferson, N. Y	July 10, 1860	29, 035
Center-board winch	H. V. Corbett	Buffalo, N. Y	Nov. 26, 1867	71, 283
Center-board winch	E. C. Hammond	Oswego, N. Y	Nov. 24, 1868	84, 275
Center-boards and rudders for shoal-water vessels, Arrangement of.	G. Chase	Prudence Island, R. I	Feb. 8, 1853	9, 574
Center-boards, Device for operating	J. N. Buell	Middletown, Conn	Nov. 15, 1864	45, 018
Center-boards for vessels, Attachment for	G. Storer and G. W. Storer	New Britain and Portland, Conn.	Jan. 8, 1867	61, 029
Center-boards for vessels, Method of hanging	W. W. Bates	Chicago, Ill	May 14, 1867	64, 739
Center-boards of vessels, Hanging	J. F. Hall	Westerly, R. I	Feb. 20, 1866	52, 708
Center-boards to vessels, Attaching	G. S. Burrows	Mystic River, Conn	Nov. 18, 1856	16, 084
Center-table	E. Lampman	Catskill, N. Y	Dec. 18, 1866	60, 525
Center-turning tool	H. D. Richardson	East Hampton, Mass	May 4, 1869	89, 657
Centering and squaring device	C. O. Gardiner	Springfield, Ohio	Dec. 4, 1866	60, 169
Centering bar of iron	N. F. Newell	Northbridge, Mass	Jan. 29, 1861	31, 257
Centering box or bearing, Self	M. S. Bullock	Pottsville, Pa	Apr. 18, 1871	113, 739
Centering-device	E. E. Lazell	Philadelphia, Pa	Sept. 15, 1868	82, 131
Centering-device	N. L. Revere	Worcester, Mass	Mar. 2, 1869	87, 451
Centering-implement	F. Deluce	Boston, Mass	Feb. 18, 1862	34, 412
Centering-machine	E. McNiel	Groton, N. Y	May 30, 1871	115, 337
Centering-machine	E. F. Whiton	West Stafford, Conn	July 14, 1857	17, 814
Centering-tool	W. I. Alvord	Bridgeport, Conn	Nov. 9, 1869	96, 653
Centering-tool	R. Hayworth	South New Market, N. H	Sept. 3, 1867	68, 504
Centrifugal battery	A. Potts	Philadelphia, Pa	May 19, 1857	17, 339
Centrifugal crushing-mill	C. H. Griffin	Chelsea, Mass	Nov. 22, 1864	45, 213
Centrifugal disk revolving in air and water	T. W. Rammell	London, England	May 10, 1864	42, 716
Centrifugal drawing-machine	H. N. Glass and H. W. Bartol	Philadelphia, Pa	May 16, 1865	47, 714
Centrifugal machine	R. J. Barr	Philadelphia, Pa	Aug. 4, 1868	80, 702
Centrifugal machine	E. J. M. Becker	New York, N. Y	May 20, 1873	139, 108
Centrifugal machine	J. F. Brinjes	White Chapel, England	Nov. 2, 1869	96, 304
Centrifugal machine	J. D. Browne	Cincinnati, Ohio	June 12, 1866	55, 461
Centrifugal machine	C. T. Burchardt	New York, N. Y	Mar. 4, 1873	136, 485
Centrifugal machine	A. Chenu	Paris, France	Sept. 3, 1872	131, 681
Centrifugal machine	J. Cottle	Boston, Mass	July 16, 1872	129, 322
Centrifugal machine	G. B. Hartson and E. J. Woolsey	New York, N. Y	Feb. 13, 1866	52, 569
Centrifugal machine	S. S. Hepworth	Boston, Mass	Sept. 22, 1868	82, 314
Centrifugal machine	S. S. Hepworth	Cold Spring, N. Y	June 14, 1870	104, 149
Centrifugal machine	H. Hunt	Oskaloosa, Iowa	Mar. 27, 1866	53, 448
Centrifugal machine	J. O. Joyce	Dayton, Ohio	Aug. 28, 1866	57, 517
Centrifugal machine	A. Mackey and E. Müller	New York and Williamsburgh, N. Y.	Mar. 27, 1866	53, 463
Centrifugal machine	J. Sparrow	Portland, Me	May 6, 1873	138, 705
Centrifugal machine for filtering liquids	H. N. Fryatt	Belleville, N. J	June 3, 1862	35, 441
Centrifugal machine or hydro-extractor	E. C. Cleveland	Worcester, Mass	Aug. 20, 1867	67, 953
Centrifugal machine, Self-balancing	D. M. Weston	Boston, Mass	Sept. 8, 1868	82, 049
Centrifugal machines, Apparatus for liquoring sugar in.	F. Seiberlich	Charlestown, Mass	Aug. 8, 1865	49, 310
Centrifugal machines, Apparatus for supplying liquor to.	W. R. Meins	Boston, Mass	Oct. 16, 1866	58, 864
Centrifugal machines, Discharger for	H. Merrill	Brooklyn, N. Y	Apr. 23, 1867	64, 182
Centrifugal machines, Feeder for	H. Merrill	Brooklyn, N. Y	Apr. 23, 1867	64, 183
Centrifugal machines, Mode of liquoring sugar in	R. T. Sprague	Boston, Mass	Aug. 20, 1867	67, 924
Centrifugal power-regulator, Pneumatic	C. A. Sullivan	Starkville, Miss	Dec. 28, 1869	98, 314
Centrifugal sugar-machine	H. W. Bartol	Philadelphia, Pa	Oct. 26, 1869	96, 186
Centrifugal sugar-machine	J. R. Brown	Winchester, Ind	Nov. 27, 1866	59, 956
Centrifugal sugar-machine	J. Corby	Gravesend, England	Mar. 12, 1872	124, 484
Centrifugal sugar-machine	J. Cottle	Boston, Mass	Apr. 16, 1872	125, 724
Centrifugal sugar-machine	P. Cramer	Jersey City, N. J	Nov. 4, 1873	144, 319
Centrifugal sugar-machine	W. Elmenhorst and F. O. Mathiessen.	Jersey City, N. J	Apr. 21, 1868	77, 017
Centrifugal sugar-machine	G. E. Evans	Boston, Mass	Sept. 3, 1867	68, 356
Centrifugal sugar-machine	G. E. Evans	Boston, Mass	Oct. 1, 1867	69, 328
Centrifugal sugar-machine	A. Fesca	Berlin, Prussia	Mar. 26, 1872	125, 036
Centrifugal sugar-machine	C. Fischer	Gloucester, N. J	Nov. 18, 1873	144, 752
Centrifugal sugar-machine	B. Hasket and W. B. Cox	West Milton, Ohio	Nov. 13, 1866	59, 598
Centrifugal sugar-machine	J. B. Hill	Allegheny City, Pa	Dec. 10, 1867	71, 877
Centrifugal sugar-machine	D. King	Brooklyn, N. Y	Nov. 25, 1851	8, 545
Centrifugal sugar-machine	H. W. and R. Lafferty	Gloucester City, N. J	Mar. 23, 1869	88, 184
Centrifugal sugar-machine	H. W. and R. Lafferty	Gloucester City, N. J	Mar. 23, 1869	88, 185
Centrifugal sugar-machine	H. W. and R. Lafferty	Gloucester City, N. J	Aug. 16, 1870	106, 491
Centrifugal sugar-machine	A. Mackey	New York, N. Y	June 18, 1867	65, 923
Centrifugal sugar-machine	A. Mackey	New York, N. Y	Mar. 17, 1868	75, 687
Centrifugal sugar-machine	H. Priew	Magdeburg, Prussia	Feb. 11, 1873	135, 727
Centrifugal sugar-machine	P. Tully	San Francisco, Cal	July 19, 1870	105, 5?0
Centrifugal sugar-machine	W. Van Anden	Poughkeepsie, N. Y	June 10, 1851	8, 156
Centrifugal sugar-machine	L. Weinrich	Berlin, Prussia	Apr. 2, 1872	125, 358
Centrifugal sugar-machine	C. O. West and J. Carey	Martinsville, Ohio	May 1, 1866	54, 456
Centrifugal sugar-machine	D. M. Weston	Boston, Mass	Apr. 9, 1867	63, 770
Centrifugal sugar-machine	H. A. Wilder	Millville, N. Y	Nov. 9, 1869	96, 752
Centrifugal sugar-machines, Device for feeding	A. Kusenberg	Philadelphia, Pa	Jan. 5, 1869	85, 528
Centrifugal ventilator	A. P. Blake	Milton, Mass	Jan. 31, 1865	46, 067
Centripetal press	J. E. Serrell and D. Smith	New York, N. Y	July 3, 1849	6, 563
Centrolinead	W. J. von Kammerhueber	Washington, D. C	July 15, 1856	15, 359
Cerasine or wax, Treating bituminous materials for the manufacture of.	H. Ujhely and C. Beurle	Vienna, Austria	Sept. 3 1872	131, 137
Cereals, Apparatus for decorticating and cleaning	W. W. Gibson	Edinburgh, North Britain	July 14, 1868	79, 970
Cerotypography, Feed-motion for	J. McElheran	Brooklyn, N. Y	Aug. 17, 1858	21, 208
Cess-pool	G. T. Bohen	San Francisco, Cal	Dec. 27, 1864	45, 577

Index of patents issued from the United States Patent Office from 1790 *to* 1873, *inclusive*—Continued.

Invention.	Inventor.	Residence.	Date.	No.
Cess-pools, &c., Apparatus for cleaning	W. C. McCarthy	Pittsburgh, Pa	Apr. 22, 1873	138, 034
Cess-pools, sinks, &c., Apparatus for cleaning	J. P. F. Datichy	Brooklyn, N. Y	Sept. 16, 1873	142, 840
Cess-pools, vaults, privies, &c., Apparatus for cleaning.	W. C. McCarthy	Pittsburgh, Pa	June 28, 1870	104, 866
Chafe-iron	E. Hackett	Concord, N. H	July 21, 1868	80, 166
Chafe-iron for wheeled-vehicle	E. P. Roche	Bath, Me	June 4, 1872	127, 645
Chaffing mill, Grain	G. Wilcox	Neenah, Wis	June 16, 1868	78, 907
Chain	J. Blocher	Williamsville, N. Y	Dec. 4, 1860	30, 797
Chain	J. F. Brewer	Plantsville, Conn	Apr. 27, 1869	89, 282
Chain	P. D. Cummings	Portland, Me	June 5, 1860	28, 630
Chain	J. Good	Brooklyn, N. Y	Oct. 18, 1870	108, 473
Chain	J. G. Jung	Newark, N. J	Apr. 6, 1869	88, 643
Chain	W. Wallace	Ansonia, Conn	Feb. 5, 1867	61, 777
Chain, Adjustable runner to be attached to	A. Adamson	Washington, D. C	Mar. 5, 1867	62, 589
Chain, Adjusting-slide for	R. J. Pond	Morrisania, N. Y	Apr. 5, 1870	101, 503
Chain and rope on canal and railway, Using	J. M. Palisse and S. S. Durfee	Hudson, N. Y	Feb. 25, 1835	....
Chain-blocking device	P. Kendrick	Trenton, N. J	Sept. 15, 1868	82, 124
Chain-boats for inland navigation	G. F. Saltonstall	Society Hill, S. C	July 12, 1834	....
Chain, Box-slide for ornamental	O. J. Valentine	Newark, N. J	Mar. 18, 1873	136, 946
Chain, Braced	J. H. Edwards	Lanark, Ill	Feb. 27, 1872	124, 042
Chain-bucket wheel, Construction of the buckets in the.	S. Dutton, jr	Aston, Pa	Feb. 26, 1840	1, 499
Chain-cable, Machine for manufacturing	W. D. Grimshaw	Newark, N. J	Aug. 13, 1867	67, 751
Chain, Casting	C. C. Van Alstine	New Haven, Conn	Aug. 25, 1868	81, 563
Chain, Chain-pump	J. M. Connel	Newark, Ohio	June 21, 1864	43, 256
Chain, Cog	T. Shaw	Philadelphia, Pa	Nov. 12, 1867	70, 752
Chain-connecting link	S. Vanstone	Providence, R. I	Oct. 29, 1867	70, 380
Chain-coupling	M. Osborn	Cleveland, Ohio	Jan. 9, 1872	122, 644
Chain-coupling link	S. T. Lamb	New Albany, Ind	Nov. 21, 1871	121, 225
Chain, Elastic	C. E. Richards	North Attleborough, Mass	May 1, 1866	54, 411
Chain elevator and bucket	J. A. Ball	Grass Valley, Cal	Nov. 16, 1869	96, 866
Chain, Flat	C. King and S. P. Johnson	Cleveland, Ohio	Sept. 14, 1869	94, 757
Chain for hauling down ships, Safety	J. Fales and T. D. Brown	Bedford, Mass	Mar. 9, 1833	....
Chain for ornament	L. Towne	Providence, R. I	Nov. 1, 1864	44, 899
Chain for power-press	N. Chapman	Mystic River, Conn	Jan. 1, 1856	14, 009
Chain for water-elevator	P. Anderson	East Avon, N. Y	May 2, 1865	47, 595
Chain, Frame	D. Leslie	New York, N. Y	Nov. 19, 1827	....
Chain from sheet-metal, Making	L. Towne	Providence, R. I	Jan. 10, 1860	26, 801
Chain, &c., from slipping, Wheel to prevent	J. Cooper	Augusta County, Va	June 17, 1823	....
Chain-holder	S. Gladding	Providence, R. I	July 11, 1865	48, 675
Chain-hook	M. Colgan	Port Jervis, N. Y	Apr. 11, 1865	47, 241
Chain-hook	G. H. Draper	North Attleborough, Mass.	May 12, 1863	38, 532
Chain-hook	W. Straw	Dalton, N. H	July 11, 1854	11, 306
Chain-hook	J. R. Thorne	Waldoborough, Me	June 27, 1871	116, 511
Chain-hook	J. Weed	Lyons, Iowa	Oct. 15, 1872	132, 224
Chain, Hook for vest	A. Wallach	New York, N. Y	June 7, 1859	24, 362
Chain-hook or cable-stopper	E. Davidson	Providence, R. I	Feb. 6, 1866	52, 392
Chain hook, Ox	F. G. Johnson	Brooklyn, N. Y	May 12, 1863	38, 490
Chain, Horse	H. W. Knowlton	Saratoga Springs, N. Y	July 25, 1865	48, 957
Chain inclinometer	H. Schüssler	San Francisco, Cal	Jan. 14, 1868	73, 391
Chain lanyard	R. Rogers	Dover, N. H	Feb. 6, 1823	....
Chain-link	J. P. Kirk	Austin, Tex	Nov. 13, 1860	30, 632
Chain-link	J. Packer	New York, N. Y	July 14, 1863	39, 239
Chain-link	W. C. Short	Providence, R. I	July 5, 1870	105, 004
Chain-link	S. Vanstone	Providence, R. I	Apr. 7, 1868	76, 562
Chain-link	G. W. N. Yost	Yellow Springs, Ohio	Sept. 11, 1860	30, 019
Chain link and bar	D. A. Peloubet	Hudson City, N. J	Oct. 25, 1870	108, 621
Chain-link-bending machine	H. Boyd	East Bridgewater, Mass	Oct. 24, 1871	120, 148
Chain-link, Elastic	E. Myers	Creagerstown, Md	July 11, 1871	116, 986
Chain-link flattening and bending machine	P. Kendrick	Trenton, N. J	July 28, 1868	80, 354
Chain-link rods, Machine for preparing	G. Homfray	Halesowen Parish, England	Feb. 26, 1867	62, 335
Chain-link-trimming machine	F. Van Patten	Ilion, N. Y	Nov. 21, 1865	51, 102
Chain-links, Apparatus for bending	P. L. Weimer	Lebanon, Pa	Oct. 31, 1865	50, 758
Chain-links, Apparatus for welding	H. Reynolds	Aurora, N. Y	Aug. 31, 1869	94, 441
Chain-links, Apparatus for welding	E. Tangye	Brussels, Belgium	May 14, 1867	64, 722
Chain-links, Device for swaging	V. Draper	North Attleborough, Mass.	Sept. 26, 1865	50, 200
Chain-links, Machine for attaching ornaments to	V. Draper	Attleborough, Mass	July 5, 1870	105, 054
Chain-links, Machine for bending	E. L. Keeler	Allegheny, Pa	Aug. 7, 1866	57, 0[illegible]3
Chain-links, Machine for bending	C. B. Long	Worcester, Mass	Dec. 16, 1873	145, 511
Chain-links, Machine for bending	D. Roy	Mill Creek Township, Pa	Dec. 2, 1873	145, 072
Chain-links, Machine for cutting coiled bars for	G. Homfray	Halesowen Parish, England	Feb. 26, 1867	62, 488
Chain-links, Machine for making	A. M. George	Nashua, N. H	Feb. 27, 1855	12, 439
Chain-links, Machine for making	H. Reynolds	Aurora, N. Y	May 3, 1870	102, 711
Chain-links, Machine for making	J. H. Snyder	Troy, N. Y	Aug. 16, 1870	106, 419
Chain links, Machine for making ornamental	E. I. Levavasseur	Paris, France	Apr. 29, 1873	138, 413
Chain-links, Machine for stamping	P. S. Bishop	Attleborough, Mass	Apr. 24, 1866	54, 101
Chain-links, Machine for welding	W. B. Hayden	Columbus, Ohio	Sept. 20, 1870	107, 613
Chain links, Ornamental	J. J. Freeman	Attleborough, Mass	Mar. 11, 1873	136, 594
Chain-lock	L. F. Cahn	New York, N. Y	Nov. 7, 1871	120, 619
Chain-locker pipe	C. Perley	New York, N. Y	Nov. 6, 1855	13, 760
Chain, Loop for bearing	J. Bird	New York, N. Y	Aug. 6, 1867	67, 486
Chain-machine	G. W. Binnix	Sunbury, Pa	Apr. 1, 1873	137, 408
Chain-machine	A. J. Clemmons	Aberdeen, Mass	Dec. 12, 1871	121, 849
Chain-machine	J. Daykin and W. B. Case	Cleveland, Ohio	Oct. 28, 1873	143, 968
Chain-machine	L. Fitzpatrick and J. Schinneller.	Temperanceville, Pa	Jan. 21, 1868	73, 518
Chain-machine	B. Hershey	Erie, Pa	May 20, 1873	139, 151
Chain-machine	F. Leonard	Cleveland, Ohio	July 8, 1873	140, 583
Chain-machine	F. Leonard	Cleveland, Ohio	Dec. 2, 1873	145, 063
Chain-machine	L. Towne	Providence, R. I	Oct. 20, 1857	18, 490
Chain machinery, Arrangement of jack	H. Marshall and S. S. Cook	Stamford, Conn	Mar. 16, 1852	8, 815
Chain-making	C. Sleppy	Newport, Pa	Sept. 27, 1853	10, 050
Chain-making machine	J. Copley, jr	Allegheny City, Pa	Sept. 10, 1867	68, 709
Chain-making machine	W. Dennison	Cambridge, Mass	Nov. 23, 1869	97, 173
Chain-making machine	L. King	East Cleveland, Ohio	Aug. 9, 1864	43, 778
Chain-making machine	W. J. Lewis	Pittsburgh, Pa	Jan. 12, 1858	19, 094
Chain-making machine	E. H. Perry	Providence, R. I	Aug. 31, 1858	21, 362
Chain-making machine	L. Souther	Springfield, Ill	Aug. 12, 1873	141, 734

Index of patents issued from the United States Patent Office from 1790 *to* 1873, *inclusive*—Continued.

Invention.	Inventor.	Residence.	Date.	No.
Chain-making machine	E. Weissenborn	New York, N. Y	Dec. 11, 1855	13, 929
Chain, Neck	G. D. Stevens	New York, N. Y	Aug. 22, 1871	118, 294
Chain or band	J. H. Doerr	Philadelphia, Pa	Feb. 1, 1870	99, 298
Chain or belt, Driving	W. Clissold	Dudbridge, England	Dec. 15, 1863	40, 910
Chain, Ornamental	W. F. Davis	North Attleborough, Mass	Sept. 16, 1873	142, 841
Chain, Ornamental, &c	E. S. Richards	Attleborough, Mass	June 9, 1863	38, 842
Chain-plate attachment	T. W. Porter, J. D. Leach, and S. Hutchings.	Boston, Mass., and Penobscot, Me.	Apr. 27, 1869	89, 339
Chain power, Endless	W. McCreery	Pittsburgh, Pa	Jan. 7, 1868	73, 191
Chain, Runner for	W. H. Stroup	Pittsburgh, Pa	Mar. 26, 1867	63, 329
Chain-shackle	E. Bangs	Provincetown, Mass	Feb. 8, 1870	99, 623
Chain-shackle	J. Snelling	East Boston, Mass	Apr. 13, 1858	19, 955
Chain, Sheet-metal	J. Lancelott	Cranston, R. I	May 4. 1858	20, 183
Chain shot battery	C. B. Thayer	Boston, Mass	July 24, 1860	29, 331
Chain, Spring	H. Turner	Boston, Mass	Mar. 24, 1868	75, 814
Chain-stopper	W. D. Baker	East Abington, Mass	Aug. 17, 1869	93, 793
Chain-stopper	W. H. Gray	Dover, N. H	Aug. 24, 1858	21, 296
Chain-stretching machine	C. Hall	New York, N. Y	Aug. 30, 1864	43, 987
Chain, Surveyor's	J. M. Grumman	Brooklyn, N. Y	Apr. 19, 1859	23, 680
Chain toggle, Rafting	E. Evans	North Tonawanda, N. Y	Aug. 13, 1872	130, 363
Chain-wheel	J. Hines and E. D. McCord	Sandy Hill, N. Y	Nov. 20, 1829	....
Chain-wheel and paddle for boat	R. R. Livingston	Clermont, N. Y	June 13, 1812	....
Chain-wheels, Right and left	R. Bulkley	New York, N. Y	Oct. 8, 1821	....
Chains, bracelets, &c., Method of forming the parts, links, &c., of.	P. M. C. Béziel	Paris, France	Feb. 19, 1867	62, 178
Chains, Construction of ornamental	I. Lindsley	Pawtucket, R. I	Mar. 19, 1872	124, 837
Chains, Machine for making	J. C. Brown	Providence, R. I	Nov. 29, 1859	26, 247
Chains, Machine for making	W. Malick	Erie, Pa	Aug. 3, 1869	93, 213
Chains, Machine for making	E. H. Perry	Providence, R. I	July 20, 1858	20, 955
Chains, Machine for making ball	D. T. Munger	Waterbury, Conn	Nov. 19, 1867	71, 042
Chains, Machine for making jack	C. Atwood and G. Kellogg	Birmingham, Conn	Nov. 12, 1850	7, 768
Chains, Machine for making links of cable and other	A. Homfray	Witley Lodge, England	Nov. 12, 1867	70, 845
Chains, Machine for making links of jack	A. Wyckoff	Wellsburgh, N. Y	Feb. 14, 1854	10, 528
Chains, Machine for making ornamental	W. Bancroft and J. Wood	Birmingham, England	Nov. 12, 1872	132, 947
Chains, Machine for making ornamental	J. A. Field	Providence, R. I	Nov. 26, 1872	133, 427
Chains, Machine for twisting curb	L. Towne	Providence, R. I	Aug. 18, 1857	18, 027
Chains, Machine used in the manufacture of	W. C. Edge	Newark, N. J	Apr. 23, 1872	125, 940
Chains, Machinery for making	J. M. Crawford	Newcastle, Pa	Feb. 17, 1852	8, 737
Chains, Making gold	I. Lindsley	Providence, R. I	Aug. 7, 1860	29, 503
Chains, Making ornamental	J. Lancelott	Cranston, R. I	Mar. 22, 1859	23, 303
Chains, Making ornamental	J. Lancelott	South Providence, R. I	Oct. 18, 1859	25, 837
Chains, Manufacture of	W. B. Wadsworth	Cleveland, Ohio	Mar. 23, 1869	88, 100
Chains, Manufacture of flat ornamental chains	J. J. Freeman	Attleborough, Mass	Jan. 16, 1872	122, 824
Chains, Manufacture of ornamental	E. N. Foote	Northampton, Mass	June 25, 1872	128, 381
Chains, Method of constructing	J. G. Jung	Newark, N. J	Nov. 24, 1868	84, 359
Chains, Method of fastening blocks in triple	P. Kendrick	Trenton, N. J	Aug. 26, 1873	142, 110
Chains, Method of making iron	E. Weissenborn	New York, N. Y	Aug. 6, 1861	33, 014
Chains, Safety-attachment for watch	M. Pollak	New York, N. Y	Aug. 3, 1869	93, 344
Chains, Tool for making jack	W. Todd	Stamford, Conn	Apr. 8, 1851	8, 029

Chair:

See Accoucheur's chair.
Adjustable chair.
Arm-chair.
Baby's chair.
Barber's chair.
Boat-chair.
Cabinet-chair.
Cane-seat chair.
Canopied chair.
Card-board chair.
Child's chair.
Cottage-chair.
Cradle-chair.
Crib-chair.
Dentist's chair.
Dining-chair.
Eagle-chair.
Easy-chair.
Electric chair.
Enema-chair.
Excursion-chair.
Exercising-chair.
Extension-chair.
Fan-chair.
Folding-chair.
Garden-chair.
Harness-maker's chair.
High-chair.
Invalid-chair.
Knock-down chair.
Lounging-chair.
Metallic chair.
Night-chair.
Nursery-chair.
Obstetric chair.
Obstetrical chair.
Opera-chair.
Operating-chair.
Oscillating chair.
Photograph-chair.
Photographer's posing-chair.
Posing-chair.
Rail-chair.
Railway-chair.
Railway-coupling chair
Reception-chair.

Index of patents issued from the United States Patent Office from 1790 to 1873, inclusive—Continued.

Invention.	Inventor.	Residence.	Date.	No.
Chair—Continued. See Reclining-chair. Recumbent chair. Revolving chair. Rocking-chair. School-chair. Sea sitting-chair. Sewing-machine chair. Sheep-shearing chair. Spittoon-chair. Split-bottom chair. Spring-chair. Spring-back chair. Step-chair. Step-ladder chair. Swinging chair. Switch-chair. Swiveled chair. Tilting chair. Tip-chair. Tipping chair. Toilet-chair. Wall-wainscot chair.				
Chair	D. L. Akers	Evansville, Ind	Dec. 3, 1872	133, 555
Chair, &c	L. H. Baker	Washington, D. C	June 25, 1872	128, 272
Chair	L. H. Baker	Washington, D. C	Jan. 14, 1873	134, 834
Chair	J. Baughman and B. R. Chalk	Mount Washington, Md	Mar. 18, 1873	136, 956
Chair	E. F. Benjamin	Utica, N. Y	Aug. 17, 1835	....
Chair	M. Brennan	Cambridgeport, Mass	July 2, 1872	128, 459
Chair	P. Buckley	Vienna, N. J	July 13, 1869	92, 576
Chair	J. Chase	Orange, Mass	Nov. 9, 1869	96, 548
Chair	F. J. Coates	Cincinnati, Ohio	Aug. 20, 1867	67, 956
Chair	D. C. Colby	Washington, D. C	Sept. 29, 1868	82, 602
Chair	H. Cole	Cincinnati, Ohio	Nov. 12, 1867	70, 698
Chair	M. C. Cronk	Auburn, N. Y	May 22, 1866	54, 869
Chair	J. Daley	Baltimore, Md	Feb. 9, 1827	....
Chair	J. Defoe	Detroit, Mich	Aug. 27, 1872	130, 903
Chair	G. O. Donnell	New Lebanon, N. Y	Mar. 2, 1852	8, 771
Chair	W. T. Doremus	New York, N. Y	June 17, 1873	139, 948
Chair	G. Feldkamp	Cincinnati, Ohio	Oct. 28, 1873	144, 080
Chair	J. Fernald	Boston, Mass	July 22, 1856	15, 405
Chair	L. W. Ferris	Owego, N. Y	Mar. 27, 1855	12, 587
Chair	G. Gardner	Glen Gardner, N. J	Apr. 4, 1871	113, 287
Chair	W. Gardner	Glen Gardner, N. J	June 3, 1873	139, 568
Chair	J. Habermehl	Wheeling, W. Va	June 20, 1865	48, 272
Chair	J. Habermehl	Wheeling, W. Va	July 24, 1866	56, 554
Chair	H. S. Hale	Philadelphia, Pa	Dec. 30, 1873	146, 065
Chair	J. T. Hammitt	Philadelphia, Pa	Dec. 7, 1852	9, 449
Chair	W. W. Haupt	Mountain City, Tex	Oct. 17, 1871	120, 064
Chair	W. W. Haupt	Mountain City, Tex	Nov. 5, 1872	132, 762
Chair	D. B. Hedden	Newark, N. J	Nov. 17, 1868	84, 118
Chair	L. Heywood	Gardner, Mass	Jan. 7, 1873	134, 545
Chair	G. H. Hoagland	Port Jervis, N. Y	Oct. 1, 1861	69, 435
Chair	J. A. and H. A. House	Bridgeport, Conn	June 13, 1865	48, 177
Chair	C. B. Howard	Atlanta, Ga	May 14, 1872	126, 703
Chair	G. Hunzinger	New York, N. Y	Mar. 30, 1869	88, 297
Chair	W. H. Jockel	New York, N. Y	Jan. 18, 1870	98, 973
Chair	M. W. King	New York, N. Y	Aug. 25, 1840	1, 737
Chair	A. Lapham	Paterson, N. J	Oct. 5, 1869	95, 491
Chair	J. Leo	New York, N. Y	July 27, 1869	92, 977
Chair	J. Lewis	New York, N. Y	Nov. 19, 1872	133, 233
Chair	L. Lindquest	Pittsburgh, Pa	July 13, 1869	92, 620
Chair	C. R. Long	Louisville, Ky	Jan. 11, 1870	98, 783
Chair	C. R. Long	Louisville, Ky	Dec. 13, 1870	110, 053
Chair	C. O. Lundberg	Chicago, Ill	Oct. 6, 1863	40, 175
Chair	R. S. Mains	New York, N. Y	July 9, 1872	128, 804
Chair	J. Morrison	Indianapolis, Ind	Aug. 8, 1871	117, 915
Chair	J. Morrison and H. M. Hutchinson.	Philadelphia, Pa	Nov. 4, 1873	144, 349
Chair	G. W. Morstatt	New York, N. Y	Mar. 5, 1872	124, 281
Chair	C. M. O'Hara	Hillsborough, Ohio	Apr. 30, 1872	126, 342
Chair	C. M. O'Hara	Hillsborough, Ohio	Oct. 1, 1872	131, 892
Chair	V. P. Parkhurst	Templeton, Mass	May 15, 1866	54, 762
Chair	J. K. Rowley	Chicago, Ill	May 13, 1873	138, 939
Chair	J. F. Sargent	South Strafford, Vt	Apr. 24, 1866	54, 217
Chair	C. C. Schmitt	New York, N. Y	Oct. 9, 1866	58, 682
Chair	P. M., O., and A. S. Snell	Williamsburgh, Ohio	Nov. 14, 1871	120, 833
Chair	A. Taylor	Brooklyn, N. Y	Jan. 30, 1872	123, 131
Chair	D. E. Teal	Norwich, N. Y	May 5, 1863	38, 428
Chair	J. H. Travis	Charlestown, Mass	June 6, 1871	115, 787
Chair	C. Tucker	Terre Haute, Ind	Jan. 31, 1871	111, 494
Chair	J. Ungerer	Brooklyn, N. Y	Oct. 16, 1866	58, 917
Chair	H. Willard	Grand Rapids, Mich	Apr. 12, 1870	101, 957
Chair	G. C. Winchester	Ashburnham, Mass	July 18, 1871	117, 132
Chair	G. C. Winchester and M. V. B. Howe.	Ashburnham, Mass	Jan. 1, 1867	60, 978
Chair	J. C. Zimmerman	Thomaston, Ga	Dec. 20, 1870	110, 413
Chair, Adjustable	G. Wilson	Chicago, Ill	Sept. 20, 1870	107, 581
Chair and bed, Combined	J. H. Green	Louisville, Ky	Nov. 5, 1872	132, 826
Chair and bed, Combined	G. D. Heatwole	Bridgewater, Va	Apr. 4, 1871	113, 662
Chair and bed, Combined	J. E. Pitcher	Louisville, Ky	Aug. 1, 1871	117, 565
Chair and bedstead	J. H. Greenleaf	New Haven, Conn	May 28, 1867	65, 072
Chair and cane, Combined	D. O. Parker	Liverpool, Nova Scotia	Aug. 8, 1871	117, 810
Chair and car seat	B. M. Darling	Woonsocket, R. I	Jan. 26, 1869	86, 141
Chair and car spring seat	W. T. Doremus	New York, N. Y	Dec. 17, 1872	133, 970
Chair and cradle	G. W. Hawk	Chicago, Ill	May 2, 1865	47, 542
Chair and cradle, Combined	A. Abrahams	Syracuse, N. Y	Sept. 19, 1871	119, 071
Chair and cradle, Combined	E. Stoney	Walkerton, Canada	Apr. 18, 1871	113, 812

Index of patents issued from the United States Patent Office from 1790 *to* 1873, *inclusive*—Continued.

Invention.	Inventor.	Residence.	Date.	No.
Chair and cradle rocker	C. Wetterhan	Fond du Lac, Wis	June 8, 1869	91, 187
Chair and crib, Combined	S. Ray and M. R. Shalters	Alliance, Ohio	Feb. 7, 1860	27, 069
Chair and crib for children, Combined	W. B. Carpenter	New York, N. Y	Feb. 6, 1855	12, 357
Chair and couch	J. E. Jonett	New York, N. Y	Aug. 6, 1867	67, 556
Chair and desk	C. B. Sherman	Troy, N. Y	Sept. 10, 1867	68, 659
Chair and desk, Combined	W. A. Ehlman	Milwaukee, Wis	July 24, 1866	56, 540
Chair and desk, Combined	E. J. Smith	Washington, D. C	June 25, 1872	128, 432
Chair and fan	A. Dyson	Saint Louis, Mo	Nov. 23, 1869	97, 063
Chair and fan, Combined	F. Handschuh	Allentown, Pa	July 10, 1866	56, 214
Chair and furniture tip	F. H. Holton	Brooklyn, N. Y	Sept. 27, 1870	107, 685
Chair and ladder	W. Bergmann	Philadelphia, Pa	Aug. 15, 1871	118, 096
Chair and lounge	E. Hagan	New York, N. Y	Nov. 15, 1870	109, 202
Chair and lounge	P. J. Hardy	New York, N. Y	Aug. 13, 1867	67, 758
Chair and lounge	M. P. Harley	Philadelphia, Pa	July 26, 1870	105, 677
Chair and lounge	G. Knell	Moorestown, N. J	Mar. 31, 1868	76, 202
Chair and lounge	T. Winter	Boston, Mass	May 5, 1868	77, 697
Chair and lounge, Combined	G. W. Cropcup	Philadelphia, Pa	July 16, 1872	129, 537
Chair and lounge, Combined	F. J. Gardner	Washington, N. C	Jan. 25, 1859	22, 722
Chair and lounge combined, Invalid	G. G. Boardman	Albia, Iowa	Mar. 18, 1873	136, 962
Chair and other seat, Spring-bottom for	P. Gallagher	Pleasant Unity, Pa	Dec. 28, 1858	22, 419
Chair and secretary, Combined	G. C. Taylor	Thibodeaux, La	Sept. 2, 1873	142, 418
Chairs and settees into their frames, Machine for pressing the seats and backs of.	G. A. Watkins	Cavendish, Vt	July 13, 1869	92, 496
Chair and sofa	A. H. Hoffmeier	Lancaster, Pa	Oct. 1, 1872	131, 758
Chair and sofa bottom	J. Sutter	New York, N. Y	May 3, 1864	42, 602
Chair and sofa seat	F. Wittram	San Francisco, Cal	Dec. 7, 1869	97, 579
Chair and step-ladder	A. Madson	Paterson, N. J	Jan. 12, 1869	85, 835
Chair and step-ladder combined	B. F. Green	Syracuse, N. Y	July 1, 1873	140, 363
Chair and step-ladder combined	I. Jörgenson and R. Olson	Racine, Wis	Apr. 4, 1871	113, 304
Chair and step-ladder, Combined	A. Liesche	Syracuse, N. Y	Aug. 2, 1870	106, 067
Chair and step-ladder combined	A. Liesche	Syracuse, N. Y	Jan. 30, 1872	123, 183
Chair and step-ladder combined	A. Liesche	Syracuse, N. Y	June 18, 1872	127, 980
Chair and step-ladder combined	C. B. Rawson	Worcester, Mass	Dec. 3, 1872	133, 594
Chair and stool irons	H. Ocorr	Sheboygan, Wis	June 13, 1871	115, 979
Chair and stool seat	F. W. Dickerman	New York, N. Y	Nov. 7, 1871	120, 632
Chair-back-scraping machine	E. S. French	Westminster, Mass	Oct. 4, 1870	108, 015
Chair-backs and cradle-ends	T. W. Moore	New York, N. Y	May 21, 1872	126, 978
Chair-backs, Bows for	C. Kilburn	Philadelphia, Pa	Jan. 14, 1873	134, 896
Chair-backs, Machine for cutting	J. A. Dyer	Newburgh, Ohio	May 21, 1861	32, 398
Chair-backs, Machine for cutting	E. Edwards and J. Cowee, jr	Keene, N. H	Mar. 18, 1862	34, 675
Chair-backs, Machine for dressing	S. L. Fitts	Ashburnham, Mass	July 14, 1863	39, 220
Chair-backs, Machine for manufacturing	S. E. Foster	Fitchburgh, Mass	July 13, 1858	20, 918
Chair-backs, Machine for molding	J. Lemman	Cincinnati, Ohio	Aug. 17, 1869	93, 893
Chair-backs, Machine for molding	J. Lemman	Cincinnati, Ohio	Apr. 18, 1871	113, 898
Chair-backs, Machinery for sawing arabesque	J. H. Better	New York, N. Y	July 31, 1847	5, 208
Chair bedstead and crib	W. McGregor	Chicago, Ill	May 17, 1870	103, 066
Chair-bottom	Z. B. Bellows	Cortlandville, N. Y	Mar. 15, 1859	23, 225
Chair-bottom	J. Elliot, jr	Philadelphia, Pa	May 26, 1812	....
Chair-bottom	A. Ellis	Dedham, Mass	June 12, 1811	....
Chair-bottom	P. C. Ingersoll	Green Point, N. Y	Feb. 1, 1870	99, 441
Chair-bottom	C. W. Royse	Peterborough, N. H	Nov. 19, 1867	71, 067
Chair-bottom	C. Russell	Wilmington, Ohio	Sept. 26, 1865	50, 166
Chair bottom and back	W. Bramhill	New York, N. Y	Nov. 28, 1865	51, 132
Chair-bottoms, Machine for molding	J. Lemman	Cincinnati, Ohio	Jan. 17, 1871	110, 981
Chair-brace	G. F. Ells	Deposit, N. Y	Mar. 18, 1873	136, 824
Chair-cane	R. Porter	Washington, D. C	July 11, 1854	11, 271
Chair, Cane-seat	J. R. Cannon	New Albany, Ind	Sept. 7, 1858	21, 409
Chair, couch, &c	C. Adams	Boston, Mass	Apr. 18, 1831	....
Chair, couch, and stretcher	J. E. Jouett	Brooklyn, N. Y	Nov. 6, 1866	59, 403
Chair-coupling clamp	J. P. Brooks	Newark, N. J	Feb. 13, 1872	123, 549
Chair, cradle, cot, &c	J. T. Wightman	Charleston, S. C	Oct. 5, 1869	95, 544
Chair, Desk or table attachment for	S. L. Bligh	Pit Hole City, Pa	Oct. 24, 1871	120, 234
Chair fan-attachment	B. L. Jordan	Mercersburgh, Pa	June 17, 1873	140, 047
Chair foot-rest	G. L. Badlam and C. W. Lang	Brandon, Vt	May 4, 1869	89, 827
Chair foot-rest	E. Collins	New York, N. Y	Jan. 14, 1873	134, 733
Chair-frame	G. Gardner	Glen Gardner, N. J	Sept. 9, 1873	142, 625
Chair-frame	M. E. Halsey	New York, N. Y	Sept. 26, 1854	11, 725
Chair frame	L. Heywood and E. E. Horton	Gardner, Mass	Jan. 7, 1873	134, 544
Chair-frame	W. M. Smith	Columbus, Ohio	Dec. 28, 1869	98, 440
Chair-frame	W. M. Smith	Columbus, Ohio	Dec. 27, 1870	110, 598
Chair head-rest	C. A. Mills	Dubuque, Iowa	Oct. 21, 1856	15, 931
Chair-legs, Tip for	E. Coogan and H. Miller	Washington, D. C	Nov. 10, 1868	83, 933
Chair-legs, Tip for	E. S. Winchester	Boston, Mass	Nov. 5, 1867	70, 490
Chair, lounge, and step-ladder	J. Gerdom, jr	West Albany, N. Y	Sept. 17, 1867	68, 973
Chair-manufacturing machine	I. Lewis	Irville, Ohio	May 25, 1830	....
Chair or stool support	H. Wadsworth	Duxbury, Mass	May 7, 1872	126, 429
Chair-posts, Manufacturing	E. Farrington	New York, N. Y	Oct. 26, 1816	....
Chair rail, Continuous	C. A. Stancliff and J. Mingis	Williamsport, Pa	July 6, 1858	20, 828
Chair-rims, &c., Method of bending	S. M. Barrett	Cincinnati, Ohio	July 6, 1869	92, 145
Chair-rocker	M. Wilcox and C. Depledge	Cassadaga, N. Y	Nov. 25, 1873	145, 036
Chair-rocker	L. B. Yale	Bainbridge, N. Y	Mar. 17, 1868	75, 617
Chair-rocker	W. J. Zakrzewska	Berlin, Prussia	Apr. 12, 1870	101, 802
Chair-rocker and lounge	W. H. Whiterow	New Albany, Ind	Mar. 5, 1872	124, 238
Chair-rocker and lounge combined	H. Haidt	New York, N. Y	Oct. 22, 1872	132, 397
Chair-rocker, Detachable	W. Pinkerman	Bridgeport, Conn	Feb. 20, 1866	52, 741
Chair-rocker, Elastic	J. Barron	Cincinnati, Ohio	Nov. 26, 1867	71, 357
Chair-seat	L. B. Batcheller	Rochester, N. Y	Sept. 11, 1860	30, 022
Chair-seat	A. Bingham	Sherry, N. H	June 19, 1866	55, 605
Chair-seat	A. Bingham	Surry, N. H	Aug. 6, 1867	67, 485
Chair-seat	O. A. Bingham	Gardner, Mass	Sept. 7, 1869	94, 553
Chair-seat	O. A. Bingham	Cavendish, Vt	Mar. 22, 1870	101, 090
Chair-seat	H. Bjorkman and C. J. Lagergren.	Glen Gardner, N. J	Oct. 22, 1872	132, 431
Chair-seat	H. Bjorkman and C. J. Lagergren.	Glen Gardner, N. J	Dec. 3, 1872	133, 622
Chair-seat	H. Buchter	Louisville, Ky	Oct. 20, 1868	83, 250
Chair-seat	G. Buckle	Detroit, Mich	Dec. 29, 1868	85, 363
Chair-seat	E. L. Buckingham	Jefferson, Wis	Sept. 15, 1868	82, 081

Index of patents issued from the United States Patent Office from 1790 to 1873, inclusive—Continued.

Index of patents issued from the United States Patent Office from 1790 *to* 1873, *inclusive*—Continued.

Invention.	Inventor.	Residence.	Date.	No.
Chalk-line winder	J. H. Rose	Mount Sterling, Ill	Oct. 30, 1866	59, 268
Chalking lines, Method of	S. B. Knight	North Providence, R. I	Mar. 27, 1855	12, 599
Chamber and other vessels, Cover for	J. S. Davidson and N. Lorton	Cranberry, N. J	Aug. 18, 1868	81, 261
Chamber-closet, Portable	W. J. Lyman	East Hampton, Mass	Feb. 18, 1868	74, 558
Chamber-closet, Portable	W. J. Lyman	East Hampton, Mass	July 14, 1868	79, 994
Chamber-pot	F. Imhorst	New York, N. Y	Mar. 19, 1872	124, 824
Chamber-pot	A. Rankin	New York, N. Y	Jan. 30, 1866	52, 320
Chamber-vessel	C. H. Berry	East Somerville, Mass	Apr. 5, 1870	101, 419
Chamber-vessel	A. Rankin	New York, N. Y	June 5, 1866	55, 361
Chamber-vessel	V. Rhodes	Memphis, Tenn	Dec. 20, 1870	110, 286
Chamber-vessel	C. Robinson	Boston, Mass	Apr. 14, 1868	76, 817
Chamber-vessel cover	W. Stockton	New York, N. Y	May 10, 1870	102, 877
Chamber-vessel seat	I. Freed	Harrisburgh, Pa	Oct. 29, 1867	70, 191
Chamber-utensil	J. C. Stoddard	Worcester, Mass	Sept. 27, 1859	25, 592
Chameleon whirligig	L. O. Franke	Baltimore, Md	July 26, 1870	105, 792
Chameleotrope	S. W. Anderson	New York, N. Y	Mar. 1, 1870	100, 248
Chamfering and crozing machine	H. Wilde	Newark, N. J	Aug. 12, 1862	36, 186
Chamfering-machine	B. F. Mattox and S. Corson	West Ridge, Ill	Mar. 23, 1869	88, 153
Chamfering-machine	J. Stufflebeen	Milwaukee, Wis	May 24, 1864	42, 886
Chamfering-tool	W. Johnson, 2d	Hampstead, N. H	June 21, 1859	24, 465
Chandelier	W. L. Bradley	West Meriden, Conn	Jan. 7, 1873	134, 585
Chandelier	T. Buckley	New York, N. Y	Jan. 4, 1870	98, 469
Chandelier	T. Buckley	New York, N. Y	Nov. 7, 1871	120, 707
Chandelier	J. A. Evarts	West Meriden, Conn	May 26, 1868	78, 365
Chandelier	I. P. Frink	New York, N. Y	Apr. 9, 1872	125, 560
Chandelier	C. F. Jacobsen	New York, N. Y	June 8, 1869	91, 135
Chandelier	C. F. Jacobsen	New York, N. Y	Mar. 7, 1871	112, 351
Chandelier	J. Kintz	West Meriden, Conn	May 20, 1873	139, 066
Chandelier	P. Loth	New York, N. Y	Apr. 18, 1865	47, 312
Chandelier	R. J. Skinner	Chicago, Ill	May 14, 1867	64, 719
Chandelier	R. J. Skinner	Chicago, Ill	Mar. 3, 1868	75, 064
Chandelier	E. M. Smith	New York, N. Y	Oct. 17, 1871	120, 114
Chandelier	J. F. Travis	New York, N. Y	Dec. 15, 1868	84, 975
Chandelier and lamp, Apparatus for raising and lowering.	H. S. Hall	Boston, Mass	Dec. 28, 1869	98, 255
Chandelier attachment, Gas	A. Bliss	New York, N. Y	Nov. 5, 1867	70, 298
Chandelier center	J. Kintz	West Meriden, Conn	Oct. 10, 1871	119, 773
Chandelier center	J. Kintz	West Meriden, Conn	Aug. 26, 1873	142, 165
Chandelier center	J. Meah	Meriden, Conn	Oct. 10, 1871	119, 780
Chandelier center-light fixture	R. F. White	Hoboken, N. J	July 18, 1871	117, 131
Chandelier drop-light	C. E. Cornelius	Philadelphia, Pa	Dec. 2, 1873	145, 053
Chandelier, Drop-light	W. C. Vosburg	Brooklyn, N. Y	Apr. 7, 1868	76, 360
Chandelier, Extension	L. Hull	Charlestown, Mass	Aug. 26, 1873	142, 107
Chandelier, Extension	H. Tucker	Newton, Mass	Aug. 17, 1869	93, 927
Chandelier extension-fixtures	J. A. Evarts	West Meriden, Conn	Apr. 21, 1868	77, 019
Chandelier extension-tube	E. Russell	Waterbury, Conn	Apr. 9, 1872	125, 619
Chandelier-hook	W. Hubbard	West Meriden, Conn	Sept. 3, 1872	131, 100
Chandelier or hanging lamp	W. Lawrence	Meriden, Conn	Mar. 23, 1831	....
Chandelier or hanging lamp	W. Lawrence	Meriden, Conn	Mar. 10, 1834	....
Chandelier, Reflecting	C. F. Jacobsen	New York, N. Y	Mar. 12, 1872	124, 582
Chandelier, Sliding	G. F. Blaisse	Philadelphia, Pa	June 17, 1873	140, 003
Chandelier, Sliding or extension	J. Braunen	Philadelphia, Pa	July 1, 1873	140, 459
Chandelier, Vapor	C. E. Smith and H. J. Rice	Columbus, Ohio	Aug. 23, 1870	106, 629
Chandeliers from the crystallization of salts, Manufacturing.	F. Ransom	Buffalo, N. Y	Nov. 3, 1829	....
Chandeliers, lamps, &c., in imitation of glass, Manufacture from the crystallization of salts.	F. B. Merrill	Buffalo, N. Y	June 13, 1829	....
Change-box	J. B. Eustis	New Orleans, La	June 11, 1867	65, 555
Change-box, Railway-conductor's	J. B. Slawson	New York, N. Y	Aug. 20, 1872	130, 756
Change-gate	A. W. Wood	Saint Louis, Mo	July 15, 1873	140, 926
Channeling and beveling machine	I. Manning	Philadelphia, Pa	Aug. 27, 1867	68, 094
Channeling and edging tools	L. Bauer	San Francisco, Cal	Apr. 1, 1873	137, 404
Channeling-machine	G. McKay	Boston, Mass	Apr. 5, 1864	42, 211
Channeling-machine	G. McKay and L. B. Blake	Boston and Quincy, Mass	Aug. 23, 1864	43, 923
Channeling-machine	C. Stoddard	North Brookfield, Mass	Apr. 5, 1864	42, 237
Channeling-machine	H. S. Vrooman	Hoboken, N. J	Jan. 1, 1867	60, 807
Channeling-tool	A. Bottum	Bridgeport, Conn	Dec. 8, 1863	40, 814
Channeling-tool	F. E. Droll	Saint Charles, Mo	Feb. 25, 1868	74, 806
Channeling-tool	G. D. Edmands	Saugus, Mass	Mar. 30, 1869	88, 283
Channeling-tool	J. B. Johnson	Lynn, Mass	July 28, 1863	39, 366
Channeling-tool	G. W. Pruyne	Mexico, N. Y	May 5, 1868	77, 653
Channeling-tool for harness-maker	E. D. Gould	Lockport, N. Y	Feb. 18, 1862	34, 421
Charcoal, Animal: *See* Bone-black.				
Charcoal, Apparatus for cooling and saving	G. A. Jasper	Charlestown, Mass	Mar. 22, 1870	101, 019
Charcoal, Apparatus for the manufacture of	L. S. Goodrich	Waverly, Tenn	July 23, 1873	129, 814
Charcoal, Burning	A. Grimes	Lancaster, N. Y	Dec. 23, 1856	16, 304
Charcoal, Charring wood for	I. Doolittle	Bennington, Vt	Dec. 14, 1829	....
Charcoal, Cleansing and revivifying	G. A. Jasper	Charlestown, Mass	Apr. 18, 1865	47, 308
Charcoal, Cleansing animal	G. A. Jasper	Charlestown, Mass	Mar. 27, 1866	53, 534
Charcoal, Cooling and purifying animal	D. H. Turner	New York, N. Y	Sept. 17, 1867	68, 915
Charcoal for rectifying spirits, Retort for preparing	J. McCann	Saint Louis, Mo	Apr. 27, 1869	89, 492
Charcoal for refining sugar, Revivifying animal	A. H. Leplay and J. F. J. Cruisinier.	Paris, France	May 6, 1862	35, 160
Charcoal from peats, Making	C. Fales	Worcester, Mass	Feb. 11, 1807	....
Charcoal-furnace	C. W. Briggs	Springfield, Mass	Sept. 1, 1868	81, 742
Charcoal-furnace	W. T. Downs	Saint Louis, Mo	Dec. 28, 1869	98, 239
Charcoal-furnace	J. McNeill	New York, N. Y	Mar. 27, 1855	12, 602
Charcoal-furnace	A. J. Redway	Cincinnati, Ohio	July 16, 1867	66, 738
Charcoal-furnace	W. S. Wright	Saint Louis, Mo	Oct. 6, 1863	40, 207
Charcoal-kiln	C. T. Harvey	Chicago, Ill	Aug. 5, 1862	36, 090
Charcoal-kiln, Mode of forming	M. Carroll	Pellico Plains, Tenn	Apr. 28, 1838	720
Charcoal-making apparatus	K. S. Chaffee	Cambridge, Mass	July 24, 1866	56, 528
Charcoal manufacture	W. P. McConnell	Washington, D. C	Nov. 4, 1851	8, 492
Charcoal, Manufacturing	A. Kurtz	Philadelphia, Pa	June 28, 1816	....
Charcoal, Mode of treating animal	E. Beanes	London, England	Aug. 2, 1864	43, 748
Charcoal, Process and apparatus for the manufacture of.	L. S. Goodrich	Waverly, Tenn	July 23, 1872	129, 815

Index of patents issued from the United States Patent Office from 1790 *to* 1873, *inclusive*—Continued.

Invention.	Inventor.	Residence.	Date.	No.
Charcoal, Process of screening	J. S. Evans	Irondale, Mo	Dec. 15, 1868	84, 866
Charcoal, Purification of animal	C. F. L. Wandel	Bernburg, Germany	May 25, 1869	90, 617
Charcoal, Purifying animal	H. Eissfeldt and C. Thumb	Sollingen, Duchy of Brunswick, and Magdeburg, Prussia.	Apr. 4, 1871	113, 279
Charcoal, Treating animal	E. Beanes	London, England	Apr. 5, 1864	42, 156
Charcoal used in rectifying spirits, Revivifying	C. L. Fleischmann	Washington, D. C	Feb. 25, 1873	136, 147
Charcoal used in rectifying spirits, Revivifying	A. Ernst	Baltimore, Md	Feb. 25, 1873	136, 229
Charring wood	S. S. Perry	Charles City County, Va	Apr. 8, 1856	14, 619
Chart-holder	D. Shryock	Hannibal, Mo	Sept. 19, 1871	119, 054
Chart-roller	E. L. Hagar	Empire City, Colo	May 12, 1868	77, 813
Charts, landscapes, &c., Machine for copying	C. Thompson	Bristol, R. I	Feb. 5, 1806	....
Charts, Method of finding courses and bearings on marine.	E. R. Knorr	Washington, D. C	May 1, 1860	28, 089
Chartæ lusoriæ, Fair dealer of the	R. Bailey	Washington, D. C	May 15, 1812	....
Chasing-mill	W. M. Force	Newark, N. J	Sept. 20, 1864	44, 298
Chasing-mill	C. Moore	Trenton, N. J	May 18, 1858	20, 290
Check and driving line	C. M. Alexander	Washington, D. C	July 14, 1868	79, 932
Check, Baggage	G. Bailey	Buffalo, N. Y	June 3, 1862	35, 431
Check, Baggage	E. Hoole	Mount Vernon, N. Y	Oct. 5, 1858	21, 677
Check, Baggage	J. Murdock, jr., and W. W. Spencer.	Cincinnati, Ohio	Aug. 22, 1865	49, 543
Check-box, Conductors'	J. F. Gaunt	Newark, N. J	June 10, 1873	139, 780
Check-box, Conductors'	T. W. Knox	New York, N. Y	May 9, 1865	47, 646
Check-box, Railway-conductors'	E. Keith	Buffalo, N. Y	June 4, 1872	127, 487
Check-box, Railway-conductors' registering	J. S. Stridiron	Detroit, Mich	May 28, 1872	127, 200
Check-holder	A. A. Baker	Camden, N. J	Mar. 28, 1871	113, 131
Check-hook	C. A. Ball	New York, N. Y	Apr. 3, 1866	53, 726
Check-hook	A. Bedford	Cold Water, Mich	Nov. 3, 1868	83, 594
Check-hook	H. W. Burress	New Brighton, Pa	Jan. 21, 1873	135, 075
Check-hook	H. A. Collins	Springfield, Mass	Aug. 16, 1864	43, 834
Check-hook	E. Deming	Middletown, Conn	Sept. 3, 1867	68, 559
Check-hook	N. Dieterich	Sandwich, Ill	July 9, 1867	66, 473
Check-hook	J. H. Jones	Williamsport, Pa	Sept. 17, 1867	68, 890
Check-hook	C. B. Payne	Clinton, Ill	July 20, 1869	92, 879
Check-hook	A. V. M. Sprague	Rochester, N. Y	July 1, 1873	140, 555
Check-hook	G. Theobalt	Springfield, Mass	Dec. 7, 1869	97, 569
Check hook and terret fastening	A. L. Hill	Decatur, Ill	June 23, 1868	79, 227
Check hook and terret fastening	A. L. Hill	Decatur, Ill	Oct. 20, 1868	83, 157
Check-protector	J. Adair	Pittsburgh, Pa	Mar. 5, 1872	124, 309
Check-rein	T. Heaton	Cornwall, N. Y	Apr. 9, 1867	63, 635
Check-rein holder	D. Reynolds	Rockford, Ill	Nov. 30, 1869	97, 413
Check-runner	J. Haggerty	Corry, Pa	Aug. 26, 1873	142, 166
Checks, drafts, &c., Fluid for writing on	C. L. Lawrence	New York, N. Y	June 6, 1871	115, 744
Checks, drafts, &c., from fraud, Mode of securing	J. Hester	Knoxville, Ill	Mar. 24, 1868	75, 758
Checks, drafts, &c., Manufacturing blanks for	J. Atwater	New Haven, Conn	Jan. 21, 1829	....
Checks, drafts, &c., Manufacturing blanks for	J. Atwater	New Haven, Conn	Aug. 18, 1829	....
Checks, drafts, &c., Manufacturing blanks for	J. Atwater and N. and S. S. Jocelyn.	New Haven, Conn	June 11, 1829	....
Checks for preventing forgeries	J. D. Pope	Baltimore, Md	Mar. 8, 1834	....
Checker-men	J. W. Hyatt, jr	Albany, N. Y	June 15, 1869	91, 233
Checkers, Construction of	J. V. H. Nott	New York, N. Y	Dec. 24, 1867	72, 670
Cheese and butter cutting machine	J. H. Thomas	Lynn, Mass	Feb. 14, 1871	111, 788
Cheese and cider press	L. Caswell	Harrison, Me	Dec. 18, 1826	....
Cheese, Apparatus for manufacturing	P. W. Strong	Evans' Mills, N. Y	Nov. 23, 1869	97, 131
Cheese-bandage	T. Hamer and G. W. Robinson.	Boylston and Sandy Creek, N. Y.	June 4, 1872	127, 600
Cheese-bandage	H. N. Kimball	Watertown, N. Y	Aug. 6, 1867	67, 557
Cheese, Bandaging and boxing	J. Blood	Watertown, N. Y	May 10, 1870	102, 755
Cheese-box	F. Bleeka	Elgin, Ill	Nov. 2, 1869	96, 302
Cheese-box	D. M. Cole	Elgin, Ill	Feb. 25, 1868	74, 797
Cheese-box	J. J. Hecox	Lyons, N. Y	Nov. 7, 1871	120, 741
Cheese-box	V. P. Kimball	Watertown, N. Y	May 18, 1869	90, 107
Cheese-box	N. and F. Lewis	Adams, N. Y	Mar. 26, 1867	63, 267
Cheese-box	C. Stoll	Mokena, Ill	May 1, 1866	54, 437
Cheese-box and butter-tub	F. H. Wilson	Weathersfield, N. Y	Jan. 7, 1868	73, 151
Cheese-box detector	J. P. Conkling	Batchellerville, N. Y	May 22, 1866	54, 866
Cheese-box, Machine for making	T. Hanvey	Elma, N. Y	Mar. 12, 1867	62, 844
Cheese, Boxing, bandaging, and preparing	A. M. Utley, H. N. Kimball, and W. Reynolds.	Watertown, N. Y	Oct. 6, 1868	82, 895
Cheese, butter, and bread cutter	B. F. Adams	Bangor, Me	Nov. 11, 1851	8, 501
Cheese, cider, &c., Machine to press	I. Nichols	Otsego County, N. Y	Oct. 12, 1809	....
Cheese, cider, &c., Pressing	D. Holmes	Paris, Me	Feb. 6, 1832	....
Cheese, Compound for preserving	F. Raymond and A. Miller	Cleveland, Ohio	Oct. 27, 1868	83, 408
Cheese-cover	E. L. Pratt	Philadelphia, Pa	June 21, 1859	2, 452
Cheese-curd cutter	W. A. Bemis	Spencer, Mass	Aug. 27, 1867	68, 279
Cheese-curd cutter	H. A. Blakeman	Cuyler, N. Y	Jan. 19, 1864	41, 271
Cheese-curd cutter	I. Hunter, jr	New Braintree, Mass	Dec. 23, 1834	....
Cheese-curd cutter	H. Keeney	Potter Centre, N. Y	Aug. 29, 1865	49, 631
Cheese-curd from whey, Mode of separating	S. Greene	Rome, N. Y	May 28, 1867	65, 211
Cheese-curd, Machine for cutting	A. Morris	Sackett's Harbor, N. Y	May 2, 1829	....
Cheese-curd rake	E. A. Palmer	Clayville, N. Y	June 23, 1868	79, 250
Cheese-curd sink	H. C. Markham	Collinsville, N. Y	Mar. 7, 1871	112, 364
Cheese, Curing	A. Holdredge	West Burlington, N. Y	Dec. 28, 1869	98, 262
Cheese-cutter	S. R. Bailey	Bath, Me	Mar. 30, 1869	88, 357
Cheese-cutter	J. G. Barker	Watertown, Mass	Aug. 14, 1860	29, 559
Cheese-cutter	G. W. Cushman	Aiken, S. C	Jan. 25, 1870	99, 168
Cheese-cutter	J. G. Dreher	Pine Grove, Pa	Dec. 1, 1868	84, 539
Cheese-cutter	J. Haines	Middleburgh, Ohio	July 10, 1866	56, 212
Cheese-cutter	G. C. and P. B. Jones	Alna, Me	Feb. 16, 1869	87, 049
Cheese-cutter	J. Locke	Lewisburgh, Pa	May 13, 1873	138, 905
Cheese-cutter	W. A. McDonald	Alna, Me	Mar. 30, 1869	88, 509
Cheese-cutter	M. Morse and P. W. Sawyer	Gray, Me	May 26, 1868	78, 228
Cheese-cutter	T. H. Pollock and D. Bliven	Greenville, Conn	Apr. 5, 1859	23, 492
Cheese-cutter	J. W. [illegible]	Lewisburgh, Pa	Oct. 1, 1872	131, 784
Cheese-cutter	D. Stevens	Newark, N. J	June 7, 1870	94, 339
Cheese-cutter and box	S. S. Brown	Woonsocket, R. I	Oct. 6, [illegible]	[illegible] 795
Cheese-cutting machine	J. G. Baker	Philadelphia, Pa	Nov. [illegible], 1871	1[illegible]2, 311

Index of patents issued from the United States Patent Office from 1790 *to* 1873, *inclusive*—Continued.

Invention.	Inventor.	Residence.	Date.	No.
Cheese-cutting machine	W. K. Foster	Bangor, Me	Aug. 24, 1852	9, 214
Cheese-cutting machine	W. Rhoads, jr., and T. Gerhard.	Reading, Pa	Oct. 22, 1867	70, 020
Cheese for market, Preparing	L. J. Randoll	Chardon, Ohio	Mar. 6, 1866	53, 043
Cheese-frame	A. C. Ainger and S. W. Webster	Stockholm, N. Y	Dec. 9, 1862	37, 140
Cheese-frame	T. M. Brintnall	Medina, Ohio	Aug. 15, 1871	117, 974
Cheese, fruit, &c., Press for	B. G. Martin	New York, N. Y	Jan. 14, 1873	134, 910
Cheese, Gear-press for	H. Erwin	Boston, Mass	Dec. 28, 1808	....
Cheese-hoop	J. Beach	De Ruyter, N. Y	May 23, 1854	10, 956
Cheese-hoop	J. Beach	De Ruyter, N. Y	Oct. 18, 1859	25, 809
Cheese-hoop	A. F. Bent	Antwerp, N. Y	Dec. 22, 1868	85, 201
Cheese-hoop	G. B. Boomer	Syracuse, N. Y	Feb. 4, 1873	135, 514
Cheese-hoop	L. Chapin	Antwerp, N. Y	June 9, 1868	78, 643
Cheese-hoop	M. B. Fraser	Rome, N. Y	Jan. 9, 1872	122, 520
Cheese-hoop	E. Hodgkins	Carthage, N. Y	Jan. 2, 1872	122, 464
Cheese-hoop	A. Holdredge and B. F. and H. H. Harrington.	West Burlington and New Berlin, N. Y.	Mar. 14, 1871	112, 597
Cheese-hoop	O. A. King	Bedford, Ohio	Aug. 13, 1867	67, 658
Cheese-hoop	H. W. Millar	Utica, N. Y	May 29, 1866	55, 140
Cheese-hoop	H. W. Millar	Utica, N. Y	Nov. 16, 1869	96, 942
Cheese-hoop	E. A. Palmer	Clayville, N. Y	Nov. 13, 1866	59, 636
Cheese-hoop	H. A. Roe	Madison, Ohio	Aug. 28, 1860	29, 824
Cheese-hoop	J. L. Sprague	Hermon, N. Y	Sept. 7, 1869	94, 661
Cheese-hoop	W. Sternberg	Bridgeport, N. Y	Mar. 21, 1871	112, 977
Cheese-hoop	W. Sternberg	Bridgeport, N. Y	Apr. 18, 1871	113, 809
Cheese-hoop	S. Purdy	Whitestown, N. Y	Apr. 7, 1868	76, 345
Cheese-hoop	C. P. S. Wardwell	Lake Village, N. H	June 9, 1857	17, 536
Cheese-hoop	S. Wilson	Watertown, N. Y	Sept. 13, 1870	107, 315
Cheese-hoop, Adjustable	W. P. Thomson	Watertown, N. Y	Mar. 22, 1870	101, 184
Cheese-hoop flange	A. Chandler	Rome, N. Y	May 2, 1871	114, 263
Cheese-hoop follower	H. Cooper	Watertown, N. Y	May 4, 1869	89, 560
Cheese, Hoop for curing and packing	W. B. Nickelson	Lowville, N. Y	Nov. 13, 1866	59, 630
Cheese-hoop making	H. M. Viets	Carlisle, Ohio	June 23, 1868	79, 164
Cheese-hoops, Casting metallic	T. Brown	Georgetown, N. Y	Mar. 23, 1858	19, 677
Cheese-hoops, Expanding	R. Van Horn	Northfield, Ohio	Aug. 28, 1866	57, 599
Cheese-hoops, &c., Machine for cutting and slitting	P. Bryant	Chesterfield, Mass	May 15, 1849	6, 447
Cheese, Machine for cutting the curd of	S. Thomson	Monterey, Mass	Mar. 7, 1865	46, 735
Cheese, Machine for turning and curing	H. Webber	East Richfield, N. Y	Apr. 22, 1835	....
Cheese, Machine for turning and curing	H. Webber	East Richfield, N. Y	Apr. 22, 1835	....
Cheese-making apparatus	E. L. Yancy and C. E. Dorman	Batavia and Pembroke, N. Y.	Nov. 1, 1870	108, 866
Cheese-making machine	B. Armstrong	Huntsburgh, Ohio	Jan. 14, 1868	73, 281
Cheese manufacture	J. W. Andrews and N. J. Ogden	Dryden, N. Y	Apr. 13, 1869	88, 830
Cheese manufacture	J. Budlong	Chardon, Ohio	Apr. 10, 1866	53, 777
Cheese manufacture	W. S. Cornell	New York, N. Y	Mar. 31, 1868	76, 167
Cheese manufacture	W. McAllister	Gerry, N. Y	Nov. 13, 1860	30, 638
Cheese manufacture	F. A. Redington and G. McCluer.	Fredonia, N. Y	Feb. 8, 1859	22, 891
Cheese, Mode of applying nets to pine-apple	L. M. Norton	Litchfield, Conn	June 4, 1827	....
Cheese, Mode of covering	U. Bushnell	Gustavus, Ohio	Jan. 6, 1852	8, 625
Cheese, Mode of preparing rennet for use in making	L. B. Arnold	Lansing, N. Y	June 15, 1869	91, 298
Cheese, Netting for forming pine-apple	W. Starr	Norway, N. Y	Dec. 27, 1831	....
Cheese-press	J. Aiken	Warner, N. H	Jan. 6, 1863	37, 327
Cheese-press	P. Allen	Burlington, N. Y	May 13, 1809	....
Cheese-press	R. Allen	Cleveland, Ohio	Dec. 13, 1870	110, 105
Cheese-press	J. Arnold	Pawlings, N. Y	Oct. 26, 1807	....
Cheese-press	J. Arnold	Harmony, N. Y	Apr. 2, 1841	2, 036
Cheese-press	B. Atwell	Burlington, N. Y	July 18, 1809	....
Cheese-press	C. Auborn	Watertown, N. Y	Apr. 9, 1861	31, 940
Cheese-press	A. G. Bagg	Holland Patent, N. Y	Jan. 25, 1870	99, 132
Cheese-press	E. Barnes	North Brookfield, Mass	Sept. 5, 1834	....
Cheese-press	S. Bartlett	Hocking County, Ohio	Feb. 28, 1842	2, 469
Cheese-press	J. Bigelow	Montpelier, Vt	Jan. 25, 1816	....
Cheese-press	G. B. Boomer, T. G. Morse, and R. E. Boschert.	Phœnix, N. Y	Nov. 1, 1870	108, 753
Cheese-press	J. Card	Fairport, Ohio	Oct. 22, 1850	7, 728
Cheese-press	D. A. Church	Friendship, N. Y	May 4, 1841	2, 072
Cheese-press	C. A. Codding	Augusta, Mich	July 16, 1861	32, 820
Cheese press	C. A. Codding	Augusta, Mich	Jan. 28, 1862	34, 241
Cheese-press	G. R. Comstock	Manheim, N. Y	July 24, 1855	13, 337
Cheese-press	S. Cope	Enterprise, Ill	Mar. 29, 1859	23, 352
Cheese-press	E. J. Crane	La Porte, Ind	Nov. 12, 1867	70, 810
Cheese-press	H. Dickerman	Great Barrington, Mass	Dec. 27, 1808	....
Cheese-press	A. H. Emery	Mexico, N. Y	June 21, 1859	24, 449
Cheese-press	J. Erdle	South Bristol, N. Y	Sept. 1, 1868	81, 614
Cheese-press	J. A. Fletcher	Irasburgh, Vt	June 20, 1840	1, 650
Cheese-press	M. B. Fraser	Steuben, N. Y	July 21, 1868	80, 158
Cheese-press	A. Gaunt	Springfield, N. J	July 6, 1839	1, 218
Cheese-press	J. Goulding	Worcester, Mass	May 27, 1814	....
Cheese-press	W. H. Guy	Jonesville, Mich	Sept. 10, 1861	33, 248
Cheese-press	M. A. Hackley	Belleville, N. Y	Mar. 22, 1853	9, 625
Cheese-press	C. L. Haines	North Newburgh, Me	Apr. 18, 1871	113, 763
Cheese-press	L. Hale	Hollis, N. H	June 30, 1838	818
Cheese-press	B. F. Harriman	Warner, N. H	July 8, 1862	35, 820
Cheese-press	J. Hibbard	Weathersfield, N. Y	May 25, 1858	20, 346
Cheese-press	B. Hinkley	Fayette, Me	Oct. 15, 1832	....
Cheese-press	S. Y. Ives	Meriden, Conn	Aug. 25, 1868	81, 509
Cheese-press	L. Kellogg	Ravenna, Ohio	Feb. 6, 1849	6, 101
Cheese-press	H. Kendall	East Dorset, Vt	Oct. 26, 1858	21, 883
Cheese-press	S. Kibbe	Schoharie, N. Y	July 18, 1834	....
Cheese-press	L. Martin	Granville, N. Y	Dec. 19, 1808	....
Cheese-press	S. B. McCullough and J. R. West.	Rock Springs, Md., and Lancaster County, Pa.	July 6, 1869	92, 201
Cheese-press	C. C. Musselman	Somerset, Pa	May 21, 1867	64, 998
Cheese-press	N. Norcross	Livermore, Me	Apr. 19, 1864	42, 393
Cheese-press	M. Owen	Potsdam, N. Y	Jan. 5, 1864	41, 169
Cheese-press	W. C. Pancost	Geneva Township, Ohio	Jan. 8, 1856	14, 065
Cheese-press	J. Paterson	Indianapolis, Ind	Apr. 23, 1861	32, 142
Cheese-press	D. Phelps	Bangor, Me	June 12, 1835	....

Index of patents issued from the United States Patent Office from 1790 *to* 1873, *inclusive*—Continued.

Invention.	Inventor.	Residence.	Date.	No.
Cheese-press	R. Porter	Billerica, Mass	Apr. 15, 1840	1, 554
Cheese-press	J. Pride	Potsdam, N. Y	Dec. 9, 1824	....
Cheese-press	W. H. Ragan	Fillmore, Ind	June 4, 1867	65, 431
Cheese-press	E. Raymond	Sherburn, N. Y	Feb. 21, 1810	....
Cheese-press	C. H. Robertson	Middleport, N. Y	Dec. 15, 1857	18, 862
Cheese-press	A. N. Severance	Cherry Valley, Ohio	Mar. 26, 1850	7, 225
Cheese-press	W. H. Stevens	Winona, Minn	Nov. 6, 1866	59, 475
Cheese-press	J. D. Stratton and T. Wilson	Mackinaw, Ill	Sept. 15, 1868	82, 174
Cheese-press	M. C. Taft	Potsdam, N. Y	Apr. 10, 1860	27, 845
Cheese-press	L. C. Tanney	Olmstead, Ohio	Dec. 13, 1864	45, 444
Cheese-press	C. Taylor	Little Falls, N. Y	Mar. 22, 1859	23, 323
Cheese-press	W. Thomas and W. Rhoades	Mukwonago, Wis	Dec. 11, 1866	60, 438
Cheese-press	W. W. Townsend	Addison County, Vt	June 13, 1812	....
Cheese-press	W. W. Townsend	Shoreham, Vt	Dec. 18, 1839	1, 433
Cheese-press	J. L. Treat	New York, N. Y	Sept. 29, 1863	40, 150
Cheese-press	A. Tyrrill	Fowler, Ohio	Dec. 31, 1833	....
Cheese-press	E. Warner	Waterbury, Conn	Apr. 12, 1808	....
Cheese-press	R. Webb and J. Cox	Madison, Conn	Feb. 27, 1830	....
Cheese-press	S. White	Bridgewater, Vt	Aug. 15, 1837	355
Cheese-press	P. Wilbor	Milan, Ohio	Aug. 22, 1854	11, 580
Cheese-press	P. Wilson	Newport, Me	June 23, 1868	79, 286
Cheese-press	L. C. Winslow	Canton, N. Y	Jan. 5, 1864	41, 113
Cheese press and hoop	D. P. Nickerson	Cleveland, Ohio	Aug. 27, 1861	33, 157
Cheese, &c., press, Combined	C. C. Musselman	Somerset, Pa	Jan. 11, 1870	98, 702
Cheese-press, "Lever and eccentric-wheel"	J. S. and E. Pulsifer	Ipswich, Mass	Feb. 14, 1831	....
Cheese-press, Self acting	I. Carter	Plattsburgh, N. Y	Aug. 14, 1849	6, 641
Cheese-press, Self-acting	B. Gillett and L. Allis	Hartford, Conn	Aug. 26, 1851	8, 311
Cheese-press, Self-acting	E. Hall	Persia, N. Y	Dec. 4, 1847	5, 381
Cheese-press, Self-acting	D. Hitchcock and C. Stone	New York	July 24, 1828	....
Cheese-press, Self-acting	C. B. and J. Kingsbury	Utica, N. Y	Dec. 18, 1847	5, 397
Cheese-press, Self-acting	W. Leach	Clarkson, N. Y	Feb. 8, 1859	22, 920
Cheese-press, Self-acting	S. Mann	Alstead, N. H	Sept. 25, 1849	6, 742
Cheese-press, Self-acting	J. Martin, jr.	Azatalan, Wister	Nov. 26, 1844	3, 840
Cheese-press, Self-acting	B. H. Otis	Cleveland, Ohio	Mar. 27, 1849	6, 225
Cheese-press, Self-acting	S. W. Ruggles	Fitchburgh, Mass	July 4, 1854	11, 241
Cheese-press, Self-acting	C. Stone	Rootstown, Ohio	Aug. 7, 1847	5, 220
Cheese-press, Self-acting	C. Stone and F. K. and G. S. Collins.	Rootstown and Ravenna, Ohio.	July 28, 1842	2, 739
Cheese-press, Self acting	C. Stone and F. K. and G. S. Collins.	Rootstown and Ravenna, Ohio.	Aug. 6, 1842	2, 747
Cheese-press, Self-acting	C. Stone and G. S. Collins	Rootstown and Ravenna, Ohio.	May 29, 1845	4, 063
Cheese-press, Self-acting	J. Underwood	Montpelier, Vt	June 25, 1850	7, 465
Cheese-press, Self-adjusting	R. Porter	Billerica, Mass	Feb. 6, 1835	....
Cheese-press, Self-propelling hanging-lever	J. S. Cram	Hanover, N. H	Dec. 27, 1831	....
Cheese-presses, Construction of	H. Kendall	Danby, Vt	July 15, 1843	3, 178
Cheese, Pressing	W. McAllister	Gerry, N. Y	Sept. 4, 1860	29, 899
Cheese, Pressing	H. A. Stone	Battle Creek, Mich	Mar. 26, 1861	31, 834
Cheese-pressing machine	L. Caswell	Harrison, Me	Dec. 9, 1825	....
Cheese-pressing machine	M. Norton	Goshen, Conn	Oct. 13, 1830	....
Cheese, Process for making	H. O. Freeman	Sherburne, N. Y	Feb. 18, 1873	136, 051
Cheese, Process for manufacturing	M. A. Sheaffer	Elizabethtown, Pa	Dec. 7, 1869	97, 709
Cheese, Process of manufacturing German hand	F. C. and T. F. Mende	Philadelphia, Pa	Oct. 5, 1869	95, 500
Cheese safe, gage, and cutter	E. G. Bulgin	Vienna, N. J	July 7, 1868	79, 546
Cheese-shelf	A. N. Severance	Cherry Valley, Ohio	May 1, 1847	5, 093
Cheese, Shelving for curing and storing	J. H. Phillips	Colebrook, Ohio	Nov. 24, 1857	18, 702
Cheese-skipper extractor	C. Green	Osseo, Mich	Feb. 4, 1873	135, 542
Cheese-table	E. L. Yancy	Batavia, N. Y	Dec. 15, 1868	84, 980
Cheese-table, shelving, &c	A. M. Utley	Watertown, N. Y	May 4, 1869	89, 814
Cheese, Turning	R. Scott	Watertown, N. Y	Mar. 6, 1866	53, 048
Cheese-turning apparatus	J. Q. Black	Richland Centre, Wis	Feb. 28, 1871	112, 112
Cheese-turning apparatus	A. Mears	Brashear, N. Y	Oct. 6, 1863	40, 214
Cheese-turning cover	Q. C. Culley	Ashtabula, Ohio	Apr. 21, 1868	77, 004
Cheese-vat	A. B. Armstrong	Dorset, Vt	Aug. 29, 1871	118, 507
Cheese-vat	G. Austin	Denmark, N. Y	Mar. 19, 1867	62, 991
Cheese-vat	A. G. Bagg	Holland Patent, N. Y	Nov. 27, 1866	59, 941
Cheese-vat	D. F. Barclay	Elgin, Ill	July 8, 1873	140, 670
Cheese-vat	H. H. Bent	Antwerp, N. Y	Mar. 17, 1868	75, 515
Cheese-vat	J. A. Carlisle and G. A. Bowers	Elgin, Ill	July 10, 1866	56, 176
Cheese-vat	P. Calvin	Pecatonica, Ill	July 28, 1868	80, 335
Cheese-vat	J. H. Crumb and L. Sears	De Ruyter, N. Y	June 18, 1867	65, 881
Cheese-vat	F. E. Day	Kennedy, N. Y	Dec. 26, 1871	122, 232
Cheese-vat	L. C. Hains	Bedford, Ohio	June 19, 1866	55, 649
Cheese-vat	L. C. Hains	Bedford, Ohio	Apr. 9, 1867	63, 630
Cheese-vat	W. Howard	Watertown, N. Y	May 12, 1868	77, 734
Cheese-vat	J. Jones, C. D. Faulkner, F. L. Jones, and H. K. Faulkner.	Utica, N. Y	Jan. 30, 1872	123, 107
Cheese-vat	R. M. Livingston	Manteno, Ill	Apr. 20, 1869	89, 157
Cheese-vat	F. X. Manahan	Utica, N. Y	Feb. 25, 1862	34, 511
Cheese-vat	D. W. Maples	Homer, N. Y	Apr. 30, 1861	32, 198
Cheese-vat	H. W. Millar	Brooklyn, N. Y	Nov. 8, 1870	109, 139
Cheese-vat	W. H. Obitts	Elyria, Ohio	Nov. 22, 1870	109, 541
Cheese-vat	W. H. Obitts	Elyria, Ohio	Apr. 30, 1872	126, 321
Cheese-vat	W. Ralph	Holland Patent, N. Y	Sept. 25, 1860	30, 156
Cheese-vat	W. Ralph	Utica, N. Y	Nov. 15, 1864	45, 076
Cheese-vat	H. A. Roe	West Andover, Ohio	Dec. 12, 1854	12, 070
Cheese-vat	H. A. Roe	West Andover, Ohio	June 22, 1858	20, 663
Cheese-vat	H. A. Roe	Madison, Ohio	Jan. 27, 1863	37, 524
Cheese-vat	O. Sage	Wellington, Ohio	Oct. 4, 1859	25, 576
Cheese-vat	O. Sage	Wellington, Ohio	May 20, 1862	35, 327
Cheese-vat	O. Sage	Wellington, Ohio	Mar. 5, 1867	62, 690
Cheese-vat	E. G. Seeger, jr	Ilion, N. Y	Nov. 5, 1872	132, 864
Cheese-vat	A. Slaughter	Middletown, N. Y	Feb. 12, 1867	61, 959
Cheese-vat	E. H. and W. A. Stuart	Cedarville, N. Y	Feb. 21, 1871	112, 090
Cheese-vat	A. Westcott	Syracuse, N. Y	Jan. 22, 1867	61, 372
Cheese-vat	C. M. Wilkins	Madison, Ohio	Nov. 22, 1859	26, 222
Cheese vat, Apparatus for agitation of milk in	J. C. House	Lowville, N. Y	Aug. 27, 1867	68, 198
Cheese-vat fastener	S. P. Halleck	Oriskany, N. Y	July 25, 1871	117, 411

Index of patents issued from the United States Patent Office from 1790 *to* 1873, *inclusive*—Continued.

Invention.	Inventor.	Residence.	Date.	No.
Cheese-vat for forming pine-apple cheese	L. M. Norton	Goshen, Conn	Apr. 17, 1810	....
Cheese-vat heater	H. Cooper	Watertown, N. Y	Feb. 12, 1861	31, 373
Cheese-vat heater	H. W. Miller	Utica, N. Y	June 18, 1867	65, 823
Cheese-vat heater	H. H. Roe	Madison, Ohio	Sept. 10, 1872	131, 302
Cheese-vat operator	C. M. Wilkins	West Andover, Ohio	Apr. 2, 1861	31, 925
Cheese, Vat or press-box for	A. N. Severance	Cherry Valley, Ohio	Apr. 30, 1850	7, 328
Cheese-vat, Steam	J. A. Davis	Watertown, N. Y	Oct. 12, 1869	95, 662
Chemical catholicon	I. W. Smith	Lockport, N. Y	May 28, 1830	....
Chemise, Lady's	R. L. Jones	Sacramento, Cal	Aug. 3, 1869	93, 390
Chemise, Nursing	H. Wolf	New York, N. Y	Oct. 29, 1872	132, 613
Chemistry, Method of teaching the rudiments of	S. M. Gaines	Glasgow, Ky	Dec. 29, 1868	85, 299
Chenille	W. Canter	New York, N. Y	Oct. 29, 1867	70, 163
Chenille, Machine for making	J. Thomas	New York, N. Y	Aug. 30 1864	44, 050
Chenille, Machine for manufacturing	W. Canter	New York, N. Y	July 21, 1868	80, 134
Chenille, Machine for manufacturing	G. Comings and L. Mensing	New York, N. Y	Jan. 13, 1863	37, 385
Chenille, Machinery for manufacturing	W. Canter	New York, N. Y	July 22, 1862	35, 969
Chenille, Machinery for manufacturing	W. Canter	New York, N. Y	Jan. 13, 1863	37, 415
Cherry-pitter	W. C. Barr	Macon City, Mo	Feb. 2, 1869	86, 349
Cherry-seeder	L. P. Evans	Springville, Pa	May 14, 1867	64, 651
Cherry-stoner	E. Buck and E. W. Kirk	Cincinnati, Ohio	Nov. 25, 1873	144, 887
Cherry-stoner	H. Buckwalter	Kimberton, Pa	Nov. 17, 1863	40, 604
Cherry-stoner	A. M. Comstock	Galesburgh, Ill	Dec. 5, 1871	121, 592
Cherry-stoner	F. G. and E. A. Floyd	Macomb, Ill	Jan. 22, 1867	61, 331
Cherry-stoner	G. Geer	Galesburgh, Ill	Apr. 9, 1867	63, 716
Cherry-stoner	G. Geer	Galesburgh, Ill	July 7, 1868	79, 748
Cherry-stoner	J. S. Lash	Philadelphia, Pa	Aug. 12, 1873	141, 649
Cherry stoner	J. Marchant	Farmington, Ill	Apr. 19, 1870	102, 021
Cherry-stoner	A. Rakestraw	Peoria, Ill	June 23, 1868	79, 257
Cherry-stoner	O. L. Robinson	Owasso, Mich	July 16, 1867	66, 889
Cherry-stoner	E. Smith	Farmington, Ill	Aug. 6, 1867	67, 000
Cherry-stoner	J. W. Thompson	Salem, Ohio	Oct. 30, 1866	59, 321
Cherry-stoner	T. Van Kannel	Chester, Ill	May 5, 1863	38, 434
Cherry-stoner	D. E. Warner	Chicago, Ill	Jan. 21, 1873	135, 050
Cherry stoner	W. Weaver	Phœnixville, Pa	May 15, 1866	54, 797
Cherry stoner	J. N. Webster	Peoria, Ill	May 31, 1870	103, 802
Cherry-stoner	C. E. Wright	Auburn, N. Y	Oct. 2, 1866	58, 531
Cherry-stoner	R. Wright	Brooklyn, N. Y	Feb. 4, 1868	74, 187
Cherry-stoner	R. Wright	Brooklyn, N. Y	May 5, 1868	77, 561
Cherry-stoning machine	J. Baker	Washington, D. C	Mar. 2, 1858	19, 476
Cherry-stoning machine	E. C. Custer	Evansburgh, Pa	July 26, 1859	24, 856
Cherry-stoning machine	T. Van Kannel	Chester, Ill	Oct. 14, 1862	36, 683
Cherry-stoning machine	T. Van Kannel	Cincinnati, Ohio	June 6, 1865	48, 137
Chess and checker board	S. L. Fleishman	Pittsburgh, Pa	Nov. 12, 1872	132, 905
Chess-board	F. C. Schaefer	Dubuque, Iowa	Feb. 27, 1866	52, 891
Chest:				
See Bolting-chest.				
Camp-chest.				
Fire-proof chest.				
Flour-chest.				
Meal-chest.				
Medicine chest.				
Steam-chest.				
Chest and box fastening	J. H. Marvil	Laurel, Del	May 14, 1872	126, 819
Chest and table	G. W. Ziegler	Saint Louis, Mo	Sept. 5, 1865	49, 821
Chest, Butter	F. S. Sears	Charlestown, Mass	June 22, 1869	91, 776
Chest-expander	S. M. Barnett	New Orleans, La	Feb. 5, 1867	61, 702
Chest-expander	S. M. Barnett	New York, N. Y	Apr. 4, 1871	113, 384
Chest of drawers	C. H. Walker	Warren, Mass	May 20, 1862	35, 340
Chest-protector	P. Lear	Boston, Mass	Feb. 28, 1871	112, 258
Chest-protector	E. F. Wilder	West Roxbury, Mass	Mar. 25, 1873	137, 275
Chest-protector and shirt-bosom support, Combined	J. A. Aston and C. C. McMurphy.	Leavenworth, Kans	Sept. 2, 1873	142, 366
Chevron	F. S. Johnston	Philadelphia, Pa	Jan. 21, 1873	135, 124
Chignon	M. M. Cohen	Boston, Mass	Aug. 2, 1870	105, 914
Chignon	E. Ulman	New York, N. Y	Mar. 5, 1872	124, 299
Child's chair	J. H. Apel	Boston, Mass	Dec. 22, 1868	85, 050
Child's chair	R. Ardrey	Philadelphia, Pa	Dec. 23, 1873	145, 829
Child's chair	J. F. Downing	Erie, Pa	May 6, 1873	138, 6[illegible]0
Child's chair	J. F. Downing	Erie, Pa	July 15, 1873	140, 900
Child's chair	J. F. Harris and E. D. Childs	Charlestown, Mass	Apr. 8, 1873	137, 610
Child's chair	A. H. Wehser	San Francisco, Cal	June 21, 1870	104, 517
Child's chair and carriage	J. Lee	New York, N. Y	June 15, 1869	91, 350
Child's chair and wagon	J. Knowles	Lowell, Mass	July 28, 1846	4, 666
Child's chair and walker	C. Holtz	Chicago, Ill	May 8, 1866	54, 546
Chill for casting chilled rolls	R. Tolmie	Wilmington, Del	Feb. 20, 1872	123, 953
Chill for mold-boards and other castings	W. Rall	South Bend, Ind	Dec. 31, 1872	134, 439
Chill-molds, Method of taking air off	G. R. H. Leffler	Baltimore, Md	Apr. 17, 1866	53, [illegible]93
Chill plate and flask	D. Long and S. A. Miller	Louisville, Ky	Aug. 27, 1872	130, 926
Chilled rollers, Mold for casting	A. Hammond	Jacksonville, Ill	Oct. 6, 1863	40, 167
Chilled rolls, Casting	G. G. Lobdell	Wilmington, Del	June 10, 1873	139, 798
Chilled rolls, Casting	J. R. Pond	New Hartford, Conn	Aug. 6, 1872	130, 151
Chilled wheels, Manufacture of cast	G. Whiting	Philadelphia, Pa	July 16, 1872	129, 382
China, glass, and other articles, Mode of protecting	A. C. Rand	Union Mills, Pa	Apr. 9, 1867	63, 653
China, glass, &c., Composition for mending	H. Bascom	Weston, Mass	June 10, 1811	....
China, glass, &c., Solution for gilding	L. P. Augenard	New York, N. Y	June 14, 1864	43, 180
Chimney	R. M. Bassett and G. Mallory	Birmingham and Watertown, Conn.	Dec. 1, 1863	40, 730
Chimney	J. Browell	San Francisco, Cal	Apr. 1, 1873	137, 412
Chimney	C. H. Brown	Atlantic, Iowa	Oct. 17, 1871	120, 031
Chimney	D. Cooley, jr., and G. N. Philips	....	Aug. 25, 1800	....
Chimney	A. B. Ewing	Lewisburgh, Tenn	Mar. 28, 1870	113, 156
Chimney	G. Gridley	Newburyport, Mass	Mar. 13, 1808	....
[illegible]	[illegible]	Temperanceville, Ohio	July 2, 1867	66, 339
[illegible]	S. [illegible]	Mount Pleasant, Ind	Oct. 20, 1868	83, 282
Chimney	S. Hopkins	Napoleon, Ohio	June 13, 1871	115, 961
Chimney	L. Lecesne	Philadelphia, Pa	June 26, 1809	....
Chimney	J. Leeds	Philadelphia, Pa	Mar. 8, 1859	23, 179
Chimney	B. F. Mann	Oakland, Cal	Oct. 12, 1869	95, 702

Index of patents issued from the United States Patent Office from 1790 *to* 1873, *inclusive*—Continued.

Invention.	Inventor.	Residence.	Date.	No.
Chimney	S. M. McCord	Springfield, Ohio	Aug. 1, 1871	117, 555
Chimney	W. Musbach and C. R. Smith	Middletown, N. Y	July 6, 1869	92, 341
Chimney	S. Oakman	Boston, Mass	July 20, 1871	117, 320
Chimney	C. C. Phelps	Janesville, Wis	Apr. 25, 1865	47, 448
Chimney	E. S. Phelps, jr	Wyanet, Ill	Dec. 10, 1867	72, 151
Chimney	P. Portois	San Francisco, Cal	Sept. 21, 1869	94, 972
Chimney	W. G. Reed	Chelsea, Mass	Apr. 20, 1869	89, 075
Chimney	F. Richardson	Hebron, Ill	Apr. 19, 1870	102, 042
Chimney	C. W. Saladee and T. R. Eddy	Newark, Ohio	Oct. 16, 1866	58, 892
Chimney	C. F. Smith and J. Speth	Aurora, Ill	Apr. 2, 1867	63, 436
Chimney	A. J. Sprague	Springfield, Mo	Sept. 13, 1870	107, 421
Chimney	R. Stuart		Feb. 24, 1797	
Chimney	B. W. Taber	Quaker Street, N. Y	July 24, 1860	29, 330
Chimney	A. G. D. Tuthill	Utica, N. Y	June 8, 1826	
Chimney	A. S. Whittemore	Willimantic, Conn	Nov. 12, 1867	70, 927
Chimney	A. Wilhelms	St. Petersburg, Russia	Dec. 1, 1868	84, 600
Chimney, Air-back for	J. Root	Southington, Conn	Feb. 13, 1812	
Chimney and fire-place	J. Briggs	Toronto, Canada	July 9, 1872	128, 847
Chimney and fire-place	J. Briggs	Toronto, Canada	May 20, 1873	139, 111
Chimney and fire-place	M. Perin	Connersville, Ind	Sept. 26, 1835	
Chimney and fire-place	A. Sphon	Conrio, Pa	Sept. 22, 1814	
Chimney-attachment	A. H. Lanphear	Atchison, Kans	Sept. 27, 1870	107, 694
Chimney-attachment to increase the draft and prevent smoking.	J. Hurd, jr	Stoneham, Mass	Apr. 24, 1841	2, 063
Chimney-cap	M. Anderson	Brooklyn, N. Y	Aug. 6, 1867	67, 477
Chimney-cap	T. D. Bailey	Lowell, Mass	Mar. 14, 1871	112, 529
Chimney-cap	L. F. Betts	Albion, Mich	Jan. 6, 1863	37, 270
Chimney-cap	T. Boyd	Cambridgeport, Mass	July 22, 1873	141, 107
Chimney-cap	W. Brownell	Newport, R. I	Sept. 16, 1856	15, 726
Chimney-cap	W. S. Burch	Washington, D. C	July 14, 1846	4, 631
Chimney-cap	W. Chappell	Buffalo, N. Y	Oct. 6, 1868	82, 692
Chimney-cap	M. Chase	Boston, Mass	Mar. 7, 1846	4, 392
Chimney-cap	J. Clark	Washington, D. C	Sept. 5, 1854	11, 640
Chimney-cap	M. H. Collins	Boston, Mass	Apr. 2, 1850	7, 232
Chimney-cap	W. Creutzfeldt	Washington, D. C	Nov. 6, 1847	5, 356
Chimney-cap	J. W. Davies	Richmond, Va	Nov. 6, 1855	13, 772
Chimney-cap	G. W. Demond	Boston, Mass	May 2, 1865	47, 525
Chimney-cap	C. Douglas	Cleveland, Ohio	Nov. 23, 1858	22, 112
Chimney-cap	C. Douglas	Hebron, Conn	May 24, 1859	24, 107
Chimney-cap	T. Ewbank	New York, N. Y	Dec. 17, 1842	2, 888
Chimney-cap	F. A. Finn	New York, N. Y	Dec. 12, 1848	5, 962
Chimney-cap	T. J. Fitzpatrick	New Orleans, La	July 24, 1860	29, 262
Chimney-cap	A. Hamann	Washington, D. C	July 22, 1845	4, 117
Chimney-cap	J. Hammond	Adams Centre, N. Y	Oct. 8, 1867	69, 660
Chimney-cap	J. P. Hayes	Boston, Mass	Oct. 10, 1848	5, 839
Chimney-cap	E. Hinkley and G. W. Crowell	Cleveland, Ohio	Sept. 19, 1865	50, 086
Chimney-cap	W. H. Horton	Jersey City, N. J	Sept. 19, 1865	50, 002
Chimney-cap	W. H. Horton	Jersey City, N. J	Mar. 20, 1866	53, 301
Chimney-cap	A. B. Johnson	Washington, Ind	Dec. 19, 1871	122, 022
Chimney-cap	B. Kihlholz	Saint Louis, Mo	Oct. 26, 1858	21, 884
Chimney-cap	J. H. Kirkwood	Cleveland, Ohio	Sept. 12, 1865	49, 890
Chimney-cap	T. A. Mann	West Greenville, Pa	Apr. 26, 1864	42, 476
Chimney-cap	I. Mayhew	Albion, Mich	Sept. 1, 1857	18, 100
Chimney-cap	B. F. and J. G. Miller	New York, N. Y	Sept. 13, 1870	107, 282
Chimney-cap	I. L. Mott	New York, N. Y	Dec. 17, 1842	2, 887
Chimney-cap	E. Myrick	Harvard, Mass	May 25, 1869	90, 380
Chimney-cap	W. J. Pettingell	Lowell, Mass	July 11, 1871	116, 864
Chimney-cap	H. Reynolds	New York, N. Y	Jan. 30, 1866	52, 322
Chimney-cap	A. M. Rice	Boston, Mass	Apr. 9, 1850	7, 275
Chimney-cap	C. W. Russell	Washington, D. C	Dec. 16, 1851	8, 595
Chimney-cap	C. K. Scudder	Brooklyn, N. Y	May 15, 1849	6, 449
Chimney-cap	J. H. Shedd and B. Worcester	Waltham, Mass	July 3, 1866	56, 109
Chimney-cap	A. L. Sweet	Norwich, Conn	Feb. 16, 1864	41, 649
Chimney-cap	J. Tomlinson	Racine, Wis	Sept. 8, 1863	39, 846
Chimney-cap	H. J. Weed	Cazenovia, N. Y	Apr. 14, 1868	76, 859
Chimney-cap	E. Whiteley	Boston, Mass	Mar. 5, 1850	7, 152
Chimney-cap, Adjustable	P. H. Carlin	Brooklyn, N. Y	Oct. 15, 1872	132, 249
Chimney-cap, Cast-metal	W. Green	Snyder Township, Pa	Oct. 12, 1869	95, 795
Chimney-cap for increasing draft in furnace, &c	J. P. Espy	Philadelphia, Pa	June 29, 1833	
Chimney-cap for preventing the emission of sparks	E. A. G. Young	New Castle, Del	July 22, 1833	
Chimney-cap or conical ventilator	P. Lear	Medford, Mass	Jan. 23, 1866	52, 177
Chimney cap or cowl	C. G. Miller	Cincinnati, Ohio	Nov. 12, 1867	70, 734
Chimney-cap plates, Fastening for	W. Griffiths	Philadelphia, Pa	Sept. 13, 1864	44, 182
Chimney-caps, Mode of constructing	B. Kenney	Northfield, Mass	July 22, 1839	1, 257
Chimney, Cast-iron	D. June	Fremont, Ohio	Jan. 22, 1867	61, 342
Chimney, Cast-iron	A. W. McMillen	Chicago, Ill	Mar. 31, 1868	76, 094
Chimney-clasp	C. F. Espick	Plymouth, Ind	June 2, 1868	78, 584
Chimney-cleaner	T. H. Donohue	Washington, D. C	May 5, 1868	77, 466
Chimney-cleaner	G. S. Knapp	Winona, Minn	Jan. 18, 1870	98, 980
Chimney-cleaner and fire-safe, Combined	C. F. Eckstein and L. Jurgens	Prescott, Wis	June 25, 1872	128, 376
Chimney-cleaning machine	J. Bruff	Baltimore, Md	Dec. 16, 1814	
Chimney-cleaning machine	S. Dow	Elizabeth Borough, N. J	June 11, 1829	
Chimney-collar	J. H. Congdon	Coventry, R. I	May 23, 1871	115, 108
Chimney-collar	J. Stokely	Hiram, Ohio	Jan. 29, 1867	61, 639
Chimney-cowl	W. N. Abbott	New York, N. Y	Apr. 25, 1871	113, 961
Chimney-cowl	S. M. Allen	Boston, Mass	Apr. 21, 1842	2, 568
Chimney-cowl	C. W. Bache	Philadelphia, Pa	July 26, 1870	105, 624
Chimney-cowl	C. B. Barlow	Portsmouth, N. H	Apr. 26, 1870	102, 208
Chimney-cowl	D. C. Battey and C. L. Svensson.	Topeka, Kan	Aug. 10, 1869	93, 400
Chimney-cowl	A. Bedlow	Newport, R. I	June 7, 1859	24, 276
Chimney-cowl	J. Burgy	Powhatan Point, Ohio	Aug. 5, 1873	141, 541
Chimney-cowl	E. P. H. Capron	Springfield, Ohio	Mar. 1, 1870	100, 372
Chimney-cowl	L. N. Chapin	New Lisbon Township, N. Y	Jan. 25, 1870	99, 162
Chimney-cowl	T. W. Chatfield	Utica, N. Y	Oct. 14, 1856	15, 916
Chimney-cowl	A. E. Clement	Wapakonetta, Ohio	June 30, 1863	79, 457
Chimney-cowl	J. J. Currier	Gloucester, Mass	Sept. 29, 1868	82, 497
Chimney-cowl	H. S. Decker	New York, N. Y	Sept. 1, 1868	81, 609

Index of patents issued from the United States Patent Office from 1790 *to* 1873, *inclusive*—Continued.

Invention.	Inventor.	Residence.	Date.	No.
Chimney-cowl	N. Douglas	Goshen, Ind	Apr. 5, 1870	101, 443
Chimney-cowl	W. C. Frailey	Ironton, Ohio	Aug. 4, 1868	80, 618
Chimney-cowl	G. H. Garderwine	Nokomis, Ill	Sept. 16, 1873	142, 909
Chimney-cowl	B. J. Goodsell	Pent Water, Mich	Nov. 19, 1867	70, 993
Chimney-cowl	D. Hahn	Reserve, Ind	Mar. 22, 1870	101, 123
Chimney-cowl	M. H. Halo and S. Horton	Newburyport, Mass	Feb. 17, 1857	16, 644
Chimney-cowl	E. Hewett	Saint Leonard's, England	Nov. 2, 1869	96, 430
Chimney-cowl	B. Irrgang	Philadelphia, Pa	Oct. 20, 1868	83, 166
Chimney-cowl	D. F. Jauss	Harrisburgh, Pa	Apr. 21, 1868	77, 047
Chimney-cowl	M. Lockhart	Douglas, Isle of Man	Mar. 1, 1870	100, 422
Chimney-cowl	P. Mihan	Boston, Mass	Dec. 16, 1856	16, 246
Chimney-cowl	G. Millerd	Waterbury, Conn	May 15, 1860	28, 291
Chimney-cowl	F. W. Mulvany	New York, N. Y	July 16, 1872	129, 160
Chimney-cowl	W. H. Myers	Philadelphia, Pa	Apr. 8, 1873	137, 561
Chimney-cowl	E. T. Noualhier	Paris, France	Sept. 29, 1868	82, 632
Chimney-cowl	J. F. Pond	Cleveland, Ohio	June 1, 1869	90, 684
Chimney-cowl	J. H. Richardson	Philadelphia, Pa	May 20, 1873	139, 080
Chimney-cowl	J. G. Roth	New York, N. Y	Oct. 10, 1871	119, 885
Chimney-cowl	T. S. Speakman	Camden, N. J	May 25, 1869	90, 600
Chimney-cowl	P. Sumner	New York, N. Y	Feb. 20, 1843	2, 964
Chimney-cowl	G. W. Thatcher	Philadelphia, Pa	Aug. 12, 1856	15, 536
Chimney-cowl	C. F. Thomas	Taunton, Mass	Jan. 29, 1856	14, 171
Chimney-cowl	G. G. Thomas	Saint Louis, Mo	July 11, 1871	116, 887
Chimney-cowl	C. Turner	Southampton, England	July 2, 1872	128, 514
Chimney-cowl	F. Villard	Mount Eaton, Ohio	Feb. 15, 1870	99, 983
Chimney-cowl	J. A. Wagoner	Kilgore, Ohio	June 18, 1867	65, 969
Chimney-cowl	J. Walker	Boston, Mass	July 18, 1871	117, 129
Chimney-cowl	J. W. Whiting and C. E. Whittemore.	Bay City, Mich	Feb. 9, 1869	86, 891
Chimney-cowl, Self-clearing	C. H. Watkins	New York, N. Y	Aug. 19, 1856	15, 584
Chimney-fastener	R. W. Hawkins	Pittsburgh, Pa	May 5, 1863	38, 388
Chimney, fire-place, air-flue, and ventilator	J. C. Brush	Washington, D. C	Jan. 28, 1814	....
Chimney-flue	W. J. Fryer, jr	Albany, N. Y	Feb. 9, 1864	41, 498
Chimney-flue	C. T. Harvey	Chicago, Ill	Mar. 22, 1864	41, 993
Chimney-flue base	C. F. Rothe	Baltimore, Md	Aug. 13, 1872	130, 539
Chimney-furnace	L. White	Waterbury, Conn	Oct. 14, 1873	143, 739
Chimney-heater	T. M. Aspinall and S. H. Whitleck.	Piqua, Ohio	Apr. 10, 1866	53, 770
Chimney holder and fastening	R. H. Dewey	Pittsfield, Mass	Feb. 6, 1866	52, 399
Chimney-jack, Ship	J. Kingsborough	Cleveland, Ohio	Apr. 30, 1867	64, 229
Chimney-joint	M. H. Kelsey	Red Bank, N. J	May 7, 1867	64, 428
Chimney-lining	C. Schivers and S. Ustick	Philadelphia, Pa	Oct. 15, 1861	33, 498
Chimney or flue attachment	J. E. Starns	Worthington, Ind	Oct. 7, 1873	143, 540
Chimney or globe holder	R. Wright and J. H. Race	Brooklyn, N. Y	Aug. 5, 1873	141, 478
Chimney-safe	G. B. Clarke	Leonardsville, N. Y	Feb. 20, 1855	12, 404
Chimney scraping and sweeping machine	J. Hunt	Baltimore, Md	July 12, 1817	....
Chimney-scraping machine	M. Benson	Cincinnati, Ohio	May 15, 1823	....
Chimney, Smoke preventer	L. Silliman	Albany, N. Y	July 20, 1831	....
Chimney smoking, Apparatus to prevent	U. B. A. Lange	Philadelphia, Pa	Oct. 14, 1834	....
Chimney-stack	B. F. Miller	New York, N. Y	Oct. 2, 1855	13, 620
Chimney-stack blower	N. L. Blanchard	Spuyten Duyvil, N. Y	July 25, 1871	117, 252
Chimney stack or cap	M. M. Camp	New Haven, Conn	Sept. 4, 1855	13, 520
Chimney, Steamboat	W. J. Hamilton	Cairo, Ill	Feb. 20, 1872	123, 825
Chimney-stop	C. H. Earle	De Pere, Wis	Aug. 29, 1871	118, 521
Chimney, Stove	C. Varle	Fredericktown, Md	July 1, 1814	....
Chimney-sweeping	W. Hall	New York, N. Y	Dec. 19, 1815	....
Chimney-sweeping machine	S. S. Edmonston	New York, N. Y	Nov. 8, 1820	....
Chimney-sweeping machine	A. Lane	New York, N. Y	Sept. 22, 1818	....
Chimney-sweeping machine	J. W. Moore	Washington, D. C	Aug. 8, 1821	....
Chimney-top	T. Boyd	Cambridge, Mass	Sept. 14, 1869	94, 864
Chimney-top	J. C. H. Brown	Jersey City, N. J	Dec. 16, 1873	145, 621
Chimney-top	G. Elbreg	Cincinnati, Ohio	Feb. 17, 1863	37, 683
Chimney-top	G. Elbreg	Cincinnati, Ohio	Feb. 2, 1864	41, 427
Chimney-top	H. English	Wilmington, Del	Sept. 15, 1868	82, 098
Chimney-top	A. L. Geserick	Saint Louis, Mo	Dec. 13, 1864	45, 403
Chimney-top	J. Gorton	New York, N. Y	Feb 25, 1873	136, 234
Chimney-top	R. W. Griffith	Georgetown, D. C	Feb. 14, 1871	111, 839
Chimney-top	N. Hackett	Albany, N. Y	Jan. 1, 1861	31, 015
Chimney-top	B. A. Henriksen	San Francisco, Cal	Oct. 10, 1865	50, 356
Chimney-top	M. S. Kavanagh	Detroit, Mich	Apr. 4, 1871	113, 527
Chimney-top	J. D. Kennard	Barnesville, Ohio	July 2, 1872	128, 633
Chimney-top	T. Ketchen	New York, N. Y	Dec. 5, 1871	121, 633
Chimney-top	H. Markthaler	Elizabeth, N. J	June 29, 1869	91, 950
Chimney-top	M. E. Mead	Darien, Conn	Nov. 29, 1870	109, 642
Chimney-top	H. Palmer	Barnesville, Ohio	Jan. 7, 1873	134, 700
Chimney-top	C. M. Reynolds	Mifflin, Wis	Jan. 11, 1870	98, 800
Chimney-top	W. Richards	London, England	May 2, 1871	114, 342
Chimney-top	D. S. Robinson	Pittsburgh, Pa	Mar. 29, 1870	101, 313
Chimney-top	J. Snively	Williamsburgh, Pa	Aug. 27, 1867	68, 126
Chimney-top	G. Wingate	Boston, Mass	Nov. 11, 1873	144, 586
Chimney-top, Iron	J. Pettingell	Lowell, Mass	Oct. 9, 1860	30, 345
Chimney-top, Revolving	C. L. Garfield	Albany, N. Y	Aug. 26, 1873	142, 225
Chimney-top, Revolving	F. Villard	Mount Eaton, Ohio	Mar. 5, 1867	62, 578
Chimney-tops, Self-regulating draft for	J. A. Royce	Lee, Mass	Sept. 23, 1856	15, 779
Chimney, Ventiduct-topping	J. Ennis	Brooklyn, N. Y	Oct. 1, 1830	....
Chimney-ventilator	M. Collins	Boston, Mass	Apr. 25, 1846	4, 487
Chimney-ventilator	J. J. Pemberton	Oakland, Ill	July 27, 1869	92, 999
Chimneys and fire-places, Construction of	L. Kingsbury	Livonia, N. Y	Feb. 9, 1825	....
Chimneys and flues, Construction of	J. Kleckner	Mottville, Mich	Mar. 8, 1870	100, 705
Chimneys and railway-car, Cowl for	S. Lutz	Philadelphia, Pa	Jan. 9, 1872	122, 619
Chimneys, Apparatus for increasing draft of	A. Niel	Brooklyn, N. Y	Jan. 11, 1859	22, 570
Chimneys, Building	J. Gilbert	Stark County, Ohio	Nov. 13, 1844	3, 826
Chimneys by means of steam, Method of creating draft in.	W. H. Martin	Brooklyn, N. Y	Mar. 31, 1868	76, 219
Chimneys, Cap for regulating the draft of	J. Hurd	Stoneham, Mass	Dec. 12, 1844	3, 854
Chimneys, Carbon-arrester for	H. Chase	Lynn, Mass	Sept. 2, 1856	15, 645
Chimneys, Cleaning	T. Hinkley	Hallowell, Me	Oct. 7, 1831	....
Chimneys, Constructing	H. Autes	Harrisburgh, Pa	Oct. 24, 1831	....
Chimneys, Construction of	J. B. Kelsey	Newburyport, Mass	Sept. 11, 1847	5, 287

Index of patents issued from the United States Patent Office from 1790 *to* 1873, *inclusive*—Continued.

Invention.	Inventor.	Residence.	Date.	No.
Chimneys, Construction of factory	S. Rodman	New Bedford, Mass	July 11, 1848	5, 664
Chimneys, Curing smoky	D. Bain	Baltimore, Md	Feb. 5, 1833	....
Chimneys, Curing smoky	S. Chase	Williamsport, Pa	July 26, 1824	....
Chimneys, Curing smoky	J. Plant	Washington, D. C	Nov. 21, 1845	4, 279
Chimneys, Curing smoky back and hearth of	H. Pollock	Baltimore, Md	Mar. 11, 1834	....
Chimneys, Device for lowering and raising steam-boat.	C. and R. Hawthorn	Allegheny, Pa	Feb. 20, 1872	123, 896
Chimneys, Device for lowering and raising steam-boat.	W. Weaver	New Albany, Ind	Jan. 30, 1872	123, 314
Chimneys, Device for preventing leakage about	A. Lang	Buffalo, N. Y	Dec. 21, 1869	98, 074
Chimneys, Draft in	E. Skinner	Sandwich, N. H	Apr. 3, 1834	....
Chimneys, Fire-frame for	J. Correja	Brooklyn, N. Y	Dec. 3, 1867	71, 708
Chimneys, fire-guards &c., Cast-iron copings for	C. Neer	Waterford, N. Y	Sept. 11, 1829	....
Chimneys, fire-places, &c., Construction of	E. Rand	Hudson, N. Y	Mar. 27, 1816	....
Chimneys, Guard for preventing leakage around	J. F. Schuyler	Fostoria, Ohio	Dec. 2, 1873	145, 245
Chimneys, Machine for cleaning	J. Slaughter	Strasburgh, Pa	Nov. 4, 1846	4, 835
Chimneys, Mode of constructing the draft of	G. H. Crosley	New Haven, Ohio	Jan. 28, 1840	1, 479
Chimneys, Preventing smoke and extinguishing fire in.	J. Sullivan	Washington, D. C	Apr. 27, 1832	....
Chimneys, Preventive for smoking	F. Crey	Baltimore, Md	Oct. 8, 1821	....
Chimneys, Rain-excluder for	J. J. Thomas	....	Oct. 2, 1804	....
Chimneys, Regulating draft in steamboat and other	J. B. Campbell	Cincinnati, Ohio	Mar. 19, 1867	62, 937
Chimneys, stoves, and fire-places, Construction of	L. D. Detroismonts	New York, N. Y	Apr. 5, 1817	....
Chimneys to prevent smoking, Building	A. H. Read	Montrose, Pa	Apr. 3, 1829	....
Chimneys to prevent smoking, Constructing	O. Richardson	Medway, Mass	Apr. 18, 1810	....
Chimneys, Wind-guard for	F. M. Butler	New York, N. Y	Aug. 10, 1858	21, 115
Chisel	R. and S. Fairchild	Trumbull, Conn	Feb. 27, 1847	4, 990
Chisel	C. E. L. Jelliffe	Bayonne, N. J	Oct. 7, 1873	143, 413
Chisel, Cutting and clearing	G. Page	Keene, N. H	Aug. 14, 1833	....
Chisel, Dovetailing	N. H. Robinson	Owasso, Mich	May 31, 1870	103, 659
Chisel for cutting gains	H. Bigelow	Skowhegan, Me	Aug. 16, 1870	106, 310
Chisel for opening boxes	D. N. Dunzack	Salem, Mass	June 26, 1860	28, 848
Chisel for pointing pickets	A. Damitio	Detroit, Mich	Jan. 30, 1872	123, 243
Chisel, Grooving	H. G. Terwilliger	Scranton, Pa	Mar. 8, 1870	100, 690
Chisel-handle	R. V. Hilton, J. G. Webster, and H. E. Wheeler.	Lowell, Mass	May 12, 1868	77, 881
Chisel-holder	J. Russell	Sing Sing, N. Y	Apr. 10, 1866	53, 884
Chisel-holder for file-cutting machine	W. J. Birdsall	Newark, N. J	Nov. 23, 1869	97, 030
Chisel in mortising-machine, Device for reversing	C. B. Rogers	Norwich, Conn	Oct. 27, 1857	18, 521
Chisel in mortising-machine, Method of reversing.	D. M. Cummings and P. C. Cambridge, jr.	North Enfield, N. H	Nov. 3, 1857	18, 535
Chisel, Mortising	O. Adams and J. Hatch	San Francisco, Cal	Sept. 15, 1868	82, 058
Chisel, Mortising	M. Feigel	New Utrecht, N. Y	June 22, 1869	91, 531
Chisel, Mortising	J. B. Fisher	Beaver Dam, Wis	Feb. 8, 1859	22, 863
Chisel, Mortising	C. J. Heistand	Rapho, Pa	July 28, 1857	17, 878
Chisel, Mortising	C. Hinz	San Francisco, Cal	Aug. 10, 1869	93, 534
Chisel, Mortising	G. P. Ketcham	Bedford, Ind	May 12, 1857	17, 285
Chisel, Mortising	I. W. McGaffey	Philadelphia, Pa	Jan. 10, 1854	10, 421
Chisel, Mortising	G. Page	Keene, N. H	July 7, 1835	....
Chisel, Mortising	C. Rhinehart	Marietta, Pa	Apr. 8, 1835	....
Chisel, Mortising	J. A. Scroggs	Burlington, Vt	Sept. 8, 1857	18, 161
Chisel, Mortising	L. S. Shuler and J. Carpenter	Jeffersonville, Ind	Aug. 27, 1872	130, 874
Chisel, Mortising	J. M. Smith	Warren, N. J	July 28, 1868	80, 428
Chisel, Mortising-machine	E. McConnell	Sharon Pa	Mar. 28, 1871	113, 075
Chisel, Stone-cutter's	W. C. Peckham	Troy, Ohio	Oct. 29, 1872	132, 541
Chisel, Turning	R. P. Buttles and S. Sweet	Mansfield, Pa	Apr. 19, 1870	101, 981
Chisels, Socket-handle for	L. F. Richardson	Worcester, Mass	June 19, 1855	13, 101
Chisels to mandrels, Joint for uniting mortising	J. R. Perry	Port Clinton, Pa	Nov. 4, 1856	16, 020
Chloride of calcium engine	E. Lamm	New Orleans, La	Mar. 12, 1872	124, 594
Chlorine, Apparatus for manufacture of	H. Deacon	Widnes, England	Aug. 22 1871	118, 209
Chlorine, Apparatus for producing	H. Deacon	Widnes, England	Aug. 22, 1871	118, 211
Chlorine, bleaching-powder, carbonate of soda, and other products, Process of preparing.	T. Macfarlane	Acton Vale, Canada	Aug. 22, 1865	49, 597
Chlorine, Compound for neutralizing	E. N. Horsford	Cambridge, Mass	Oct. 10, 1854	11, 786
Chlorine, Manufacture of	H. Deacon	Appleton, England	Dec. 29, 1868	85, 370
Chlorine, Manufacture of	H. Deacon	Lancaster County, England	July 29, 1873	141, 333
Chlorine, Producing	L. E. Aubertin	Paris, France	Dec. 24, 1872	134, 190
Chocolate-drops and other confections, Apparatus for manufacture of.	W. C. Murdock and E. K. Haynes.	Boston, Mass	Jan. 4, 1870	98, 615
Chocolate-drops and other confections, Apparatus for manufacture of.	S. A. Parker	Cambridge, Mass	Oct. 17, 1871	119, 946
Chocolate, Grinding	G. W. Waite	Baltimore, Md	June 25, 1836	....
Chocolate ingredients, Heating	G. W. Waite	Baltimore, Md	June 25, 1836	....
Chocolate, Manufacture of	J. M. O. Tamin	New York, N. Y	Aug. 12, 1873	141, 832
Chocolate, Molding	G. W. Waite	Baltimore, Md	June 25, 1836	....
Chocolate-paste	L. F. Leger	New York, N. Y	Oct. 5, 1869	95, 492
Chocolate, Soluble	J. Corell	New York, N. Y	Apr. 22, 1873	138, 007
Cholera, Method of treating	A. C. Campbell	Mount Morris, N. Y	Mar. 27, 1866	53, 407
Chopper: *See* Beefsteak-chopper. Cornstalk-chopper. Cotton-chopper. Grain-chopper. Meat-chopper. Sausage-chopper. Stalk-chopper. Vegetable-chopper.				
Chopping-knife, Hand	F. M. Untiedt	East Orange, N. J	June 22, 1869	91, 795
Chopping-machine	J. A. Eberly	Reamstown, Pa	Jan. 23, 1872	123, 004
Chopping-machine	E. Newcomer	Columbia, Pa	May 9, 1871	114, 589
Chord-bar die	W. Forshaw	Chicago, Ill	Nov. 22, 1870	109, 506
Chord-bar-head die	F. J. Smith	Chicago, Ill	Apr. 5, 1870	101, 529
Chromates, Process for obtaining	J. C. Booth	Philadelphia, Pa	July 19, 1853	9, 853
Chrome compound	A. K. Eaton	New York, N. Y	Apr. 28, 1863	38, 297
Chrome vermillion, Process of preparing	J. Huber	New York, N. Y	Sept. 20, 1864	44, 370
Chromic yellow, Making	R. A. Tilghman	Philadelphia, Pa	Jan. 16, 1843	2, 910
Chromium, Manufacture of the salts of	B. Marqulies	Trieste, Austria	Aug. 29, 1865	49, 682
Chronograph, Electro-ballistic	P. Le Boulengé	Antwerp, Belgium	Jan. 2, 1866	51, 905

Index of patents issued from the United States Patent Office from 1790 to 1873, inclusive—Continued.

Invention.	Inventor.	Residence.	Date.	No.
Chronometer	P. Bantel	New York, N. Y	July 21, 1868	80, 051
Chronometer escapement	R. Barclay	Buffalo, N. Y	Oct. 14, 1862	36, 637
Chronometer escapement	C. Fasoldt	Albany, N. Y	Mar. 7, 1865	46, 652
Chronometer escapement	J. Fulton	Louisville, Ky	Mar. 3, 1857	16, 727
Chronometer escapement	V. Giroud	New York, N. Y	Dec. 12, 1848	5, 963
Chronometer escapement	W. H. Hammond	New York, N. Y	Aug. 30, 1859	25, 261
Chronometer escapement	P. Humbert	Boston, Mass	Feb. 26, 1861	31, 543
Chronometer escapement	J. Karr	Washington, D. C	Sept. 20, 1864	44, 317
Chronometer escapement	J. Karr	Washington, D. C	Nov. 28, 1865	51, 191
Chronometer escapement	T. Morison	New York, N. Y	Oct. 19, 1858	21, 865
Chronometer escapement	T. Morrison	Kingston, N. Y	June 12, 1860	28, 719
Chronometer escapement	A. H. Potter	Williamsburgh, N. Y	Jan. 21, 1868	73, 646
Chronometer escapement	G. P. Reed	Boston, Mass	Apr. 7, 1868	76, 346
Chronometer escapement	G. P. Reed	Boston, Mass	Mar. 9, 1869	87, 707
Chronometer escapement	H. Rothfelder	New York, N. Y	July 11, 1865	48, 726
Chronometer escapement	O. W. Waste	Pittsford, N. Y	Sept. 24, 1844	3, 759
Chronometer for longitude	J. Sheldon	Millville, N. Y	Nov. 20, 1849	6, 877
Chronometer, Solar	L. Mifflin	Germantown, Pa	May 21, 1867	64, 892
Chronometric lock	W. L. Bass	Boston Mass	Dec. 23, 1851	8, 603
Chronometric lock	A. Holbrook	Milford, Mass	Apr. 13, 1858	19, 927
Chronometric lock	A. Holbrook and H. D. Fish	Milford and Hardwick, Mass.	Apr. 28, 1857	17, 150
Chronometric lock	J. Y. Savage	New York, N. Y	Oct. 9, 1847	5, 321
Chuck	T. R. Almond	Fitchburgh, Mass	Aug. 19, 1873	141, 978
Chuck	T. G. Arnold	New York, N. Y	Dec. 4, 1866	60, 116
Chuck	W. F. Bacon	Skowhegan, Me	Aug. 31, 1869	94, 376
Chuck	S. H. Bellows	Middletown, Conn	Aug. 6, 1872	130, 103
Chuck	G. E. Brettell	Rochester, N. Y	May 25, 1869	90, 338
Chuck	J. C. Chapman	Cambridgeport, Mass	Dec. 4, 1866	60, 138
Chuck	W. T. Cole	New York, N. Y	Sept. 24, 1867	69, 184
Chuck	S. G. Dare	New York, N. Y	Dec. 22, 1868	85, 073
Chuck	G. B. Fairman	Rochester, N. Y	Mar. 30, 1869	88, 377
Chuck	C. F. Hadley	Chicopee, Mass	Nov. 17, 1868	84, 057
Chuck	G. W. Harris and W. H. Haight	New York, N. Y	June 25, 1867	66, 081
Chuck	B. Haviland	Hudson, N. Y	Aug. 25, 1868	81, 500
Chuck	E. Horton	Windsor Locks, Conn	Aug. 26, 1873	142, 163
Chuck	M. Love	Corry, Pa	Nov. 22, 1870	109, 434
Chuck	J. W. Martin and E. Parry	Northern Liberties, Pa	Aug. 28, 1849	6, 681
Chuck	R. W. Morse	East Berlin, Conn	Aug. 7, 1866	56, 981
Chuck	L. H. Olmsted	Stamford, Conn	May 15, 1866	54, 760
Chuck	L. Parmelee	New Haven, Conn	Oct. 28, 1873	144, 128
Chuck	B. W. Peirce	New Bedford, Mass	Oct. 22, 1867	70, 112
Chuck	R. and T. Ross	Middlebury, Vt	Aug. 21, 1866	57, 383
Chuck	I. Smith	New York, N. Y	July 10, 1866	56, 329
Chuck	I. Smith	New York, N. Y	July 10, 1866	56, 330
Chuck	J. M. Smith	Seymour, Conn	Sept. 3, 1867	68, 537
Chuck	W. Staub	Philadelphia, Pa	Oct. 31, 1865	50, 747
Chuck	S. P. M. Tasker	Philadelphia, Pa	July 26, 1870	105, 860
Chuck	J. F. Thomas	Ilion, N. Y	Oct. 18, 1870	108, 535
Chuck	R. H. Thorn	Syracuse, N. Y	Sept. 18, 1866	58, 152
Chuck	A. B. Underhill	Meadville, Pa	Dec. 6, 1864	45, 364
Chuck	J. H. Westcott	Oneida, N. Y	Feb. 25, 1873	136, 349
Chuck	D. E. Whitton	West Stafford, Conn	Oct. 9, 1866	58, 704
Chuck	E. S. Williams	Cambridge, Mass	Sept. 28, 1869	95, 297
Chuck and countersink, Combined	D. Argerbright	Gratis, Ohio	Aug. 21, 1860	29, 657
Chuck, Arrangement for lathe	L. A. Dole	Salem, Ohio	July 25, 1854	11, 364
Chuck, Automatic friction dog-lathe	L. Coes	Worcester, Mass	May 17, 1870	103, 015
Chuck, Auxilliary jaw for planer	C. H. Riggs	Windsor Locks, Conn	June 1, 1869	90, 783
Chuck, Centering	G. H. Miller	Binghamton, N. Y	Sept. 9, 1873	142, 642
Chuck, Centering and squaring	G. R. Parker	Worcester, Mass	June 4, 1867	65, 422
Chuck, Dredge	D. Keller	Baltimore, Md	Jan. 19, 1869	85, 936
Chuck, Drill	E. H. Babcock	Canandaigua, N. Y	June 16, 1868	78, 916
Chuck, Drill	Q. S. Backus	Winchendon, Mass	Sept. 29, 1868	82, 583
Chuck, Drill	J. Fox	Philadelphia, Pa	Feb. 7, 1860	27, 044
Chuck, Drill	F. G. Johnson	Brooklyn, N. Y	July 3, 1866	56, 059
Chuck, Drill	G. W. Miller	Woonsocket, R. I	July 27, 1869	93, 108
Chuck, Drill	L. Parmelee	New Haven, Conn	Sept. 30, 1873	143, 377
Chuck, Drill	P. Philippi	Beardstown, Ill	Sept. 19, 1871	119, 173
Chuck, Drill	C. S. Wells and L. H. Mayot	Springfield, Mass	Mar. 20, 1866	53, 368
Chuck, Expanding	W. Webb	Waterbury, Conn	Mar. 23, 1869	88, 245
Chuck for boring and mortising machine	E. K. Wisell	Warren, Ohio	Jan. 22, 1850	7, 045
Chuck for boring fire-arm cylinders	C. H. Alsop	Middletown, Conn	July 2, 1861	32, 675
Chuck for centering, &c	D. N. Smith	Boston, Mass	Aug. 3, 1858	21, 088
Chuck for cutting barrel-heads	F. Fruit	Jefferson City, Mo	Nov. 15, 1853	10, 228
Chuck for cutting disks of paper, &c	M. Kaefer	New York, N. Y	Apr. 10, 1860	27, 810
Chuck for grinding crystal	J. S. Warner	Ogdensburgh, N. Y	Jan. 11, 1870	98, 820
Chuck for holding bodies of different shapes, Planer	R. Henderson	Thomaston, Conn	June 22, 1869	91, 625
Chuck for holding buttons	E. Russell	Naugatuck, Conn	Dec. 4, 1866	60, 258
Chuck for holding drills	A. F. Cushman	Hartford, Conn	Dec. 24, 1872	134, 259
Chuck for holding drills	W. X. Stevens	East Brookfield, Mass	May 21, 1872	126, 910
Chuck for holding pipe-fittings	M. Walty	Buffalo, N. Y	Aug. 5, 1873	141, 612
Chuck for holding valve-cock to be dressed	J. L. Hayden	Haydensville, Mass	Oct. 3, 1871	119, 516
Chuck for iron-planing	M. C. Gardner	Rochester, N. Y	June 25, 1867	66, 014
Chuck for lathe, Centering	S. Keagy	Mineral Point, Pa	Mar. 20, 1860	27, 598
Chuck for lathe, Self-centering	G. O. Buckley	New Bedford, Mass	Feb. 28, 1871	112, 119
Chuck for lathe, Self-centering	G. O. Buckley	New Bedford, Mass	Feb. 20, 1872	123, 863
Chuck for lathe, Slide	C. F. Stackpole	Woburn, Mass	Aug. 16, 1870	106, 420
Chuck for lathes and planes, Magnetic	J. A. Jaques, J. T. Oakley, and L. Sterne.	Tottenham, Bermondsey, and Westminster, England.	Apr. 15, 1873	137, 875
Chuck for metal-turning lathe	A. F. Cushman	Hartford, Conn	Dec. 5, 1871	121, 494
Chuck for planing-machine	J. S. Hoar	West Acton, Mass	Feb. 11, 1868	74, 360
Chuck for screw-cutting	C. Deavs	New York, N. Y	Nov. 28, 1871	121, 340
Chuck for screw-cutting	R. Nuttall and J. Kirkpatrick	Allegheny, Pa	May 4, 1858	20, 168
Chuck for screw-cutting	R. Nuttall and J. Kirkpatrick	Allegheny, Pa	May 24, 1859	24, 152
Chuck for screw-cutting lathe	E. C. Plimpton and S. Taylor	Bridgeport, Conn	Jan. 30, 1872	123, 197
Chuck for sleigh-bells, Lathe	W. E. Barton	East Hampton, Conn	Dec. 9, 1873	145, 383
Chuck for turning eccentrics	J. W. Russell	Springfield, Mass	June 19, 1855	13, 104
Chuck for turning elliptical cylinders	P. S. Cahoon and S. F. Ross	La Grange, Mo	Jan. 2, 1855	12, 180

Index of patents issued from the United States Patent Office from 1790 *to* 1873, *inclusive*—Continued.

Invention.	Inventor.	Residence.	Date.	No.
Chuck for turning staves	F. Robbins	Acton, Mass	July 7, 1863	39, 173
Chuck, Gripe	D. Peeler	Boston, Mass	Mar. 31, 1836	.. ....
Chuck, Jeweler's	L. S. Hill	Grand Rapids, Mich	Jan. 25, 1870	99, 191
Chuck, Lathe	C. E. Albro	Fulton, N. Y	Oct. 17, 1871	120, 015
Chuck, Lathe	C. Archer	Nelsonville, Ohio	July 23, 1872	129, 705
Chuck, Lathe	W. Bellows	Cincinnati, Ohio	May 25, 1869	90, 487
Chuck, Lathe	J. A. Bunce	East Berlin, Conn	Mar 27, 1866	53, 405
Chuck, Lathe	S B. Burritt	New York, N. Y	June 20, 1865	48, 259
Chuck, Lathe	J. Christman and W. Gilfillan	Syracuse, N. Y	Apr. 14, 1863	38, 148
Chuck, Lathe	S. J. Cone	Middletown, Conn	July 4, 1865	48, 521
Chuck, Lathe	A. F. Cushman	Hartford, Conn	Jan. 10, 1871	110, 903
Chuck, Lathe	H. M. Darling	Bridgeport, Conn	Oct. 26, 1869	96, 207
Chuck, Lathe	F. Davison	Richmond, Va	Mar. 24, 1868	75, 872
Chuck, Lathe	J. S. Detrick	San Francisco, Cal	Aug. 11, 1868	80, 928
Chuck, Lathe	S. Goodfellow	Troy, N. Y	Aug. 17, 1858	21, 232
Chuck, Lathe	S. C. Goodsell	Westville, Conn	Apr. 8, 1873	137, 674
Chuck, Lathe	W. Grant	Boston, Mass	Jan. 23, 1849	6, 046
Chuck, Lathe	E. Horton	Windsor Locks, Conn	Nov. 13, 1855	13, 787
Chuck, Lathe	J. Hyde	Troy, N. Y	Dec. 9, 1851	8, 580
Chuck, Lathe	W. Johnson	Lambertville, N. J	Apr. 5, 1859	23, 472
Chuck, Lathe	W. Johnson	Lambertville, N. J	July 29, 1873	141, 276
Chuck, Lathe	A. Judson	Brooklyn, N. Y	Dec. 8, 1868	84, 698
Chuck, Lathe	W. H. King	Newark, N. J	Nov. 22, 1870	109, 423
Chuck, Lathe	J. L. Mason	New York, N. Y	Mar. 30, 1858	19, 786
Chuck, Lathe	J. S. Moody	Saco, Me	Aug. 25, 1868	81, 523
Chuck, Lathe	M. Neckermann	Pittsburgh, Pa	Apr. 8, 1856	14, 632
Chuck, Lathe	J. O'Connor	Buffalo, N. Y	Oct. 8, 1867	69, 577
Chuck, Lathe	C. H. Reid	Danbury, Conn	Aug. 12, 1873	141, 817
Chuck, Lathe	W. A. Reilly	Cincinnati, Ohio	May 30, 1865	47, 981
Chuck, Lathe	J. Rich	Painesville, Ohio	Aug. 31, 1869	93, 239
Chuck, Lathe	J. Rich	Painesville, Ohio	Nov. 9, 1869	96, 730
Chuck, Lathe	J. Rich	Painesville, Ohio	June 7, 1870	104, 063
Chuck, Lathe	J. Rich	Painesville, Ohio	Sept. 13, 1870	107, 291
Chuck, Lathe	J. Rich	Painesville, Ohio	Mar. 28, 1871	113, 095
Chuck, Lathe	E. A. L. Roberts	New York, N. Y	Oct. 4, 1859	25, 574
Chuck, Lathe	R. Rothwell	Dover, N. H	Apr. 3, 1866	53, 683
Chuck, Lathe	T. Shrewsbury	Camden, N. J	Oct. 8, 1872	132, 109
Chuck, Lathe	J. Sutter	New York, N. Y	Dec. 6, 1864	45, 359
Chuck, Lathe	F. Tully	Philadelphia, Pa	Nov. 19, 1872	133, 272
Chuck, Lathe	S. G. Twambly	Saco, Me	Aug. 13, 1861	33, 056
Chuck, Lathe	L. Von Gunten	Cincinnati, Ohio	Dec. 4, 1866	60, 292
Chuck, Lathe	A. H. Wagner	Prairie City, Ill	July 4, 1871	116, 649
Chuck, Lathe	J. R. Washburn	West Stafford, Conn	Sept. 29, 1868	82, 571
Chuck, Lathe	D. E. Whiton	West Stafford, Conn	Oct. 20, 1868	83, 349
Chuck, Machinists' lathe	A F Cushman	Hartford, Conn	Nov. 14, 1871	120, 863
Chuck, Nut-squaring	H. F. Wheeler	Boston, Mass	Aug. 4, 1868	80, 792
Chuck or holder, Self-centering	T. H. Worrall	Lawrence, Mass	July 4, 1865	48, 612
Chuck, Planer	R. N. Bruce	Springfield, Mass	Mar. 3, 1868	74, 982
Chuck, Planer	C. H. Riggs	Windsor Locks, Conn	May 19, 1868	78, 132
Chuck, Planer	W. H. Warren	Worcester, Mass	Mar. 10, 1868	75, 498
Chuck, Planing	A. Newell and W. Pim	Chicago, Ill	May 3, 1870	102, 577
Chuck, Screw-cutting	F. H. Higgins	Bordentown, N. J	Jan. 23, 1866	52, 247
Chuck, Screw-cutting	T. Kennedy	Mount Carmel, Conn	Jan. 30, 1866	52, 294
Chuck, Scroll	A. F. Cushman	Hartford, Conn	Dec. 5, 1865	51, 384
Chuck, Self-centering	E. B. Beach	West Meriden, Conn	Sept. 6, 1864	44, 067
Chuck, Self-centering	T. Brooks	Middletown, Conn	Oct. 10, 1865	50, 329
Chuck, Self-centering	S. T. Jackson	Sheboygan Falls, Wis	Oct. 24, 1865	50, 593
Chuck, Self-centering	T. H. Worrall	Manchester, N. H	Mar. 7, 1865	46, 747
Chuck, Self-centering	J. W. Bartlett and A. Morris	Harmar and Marietta, Ohio	Sept. 8, 1863	39, 789
Chuck, Universal	M. Alden	Philadelphia, Pa	Aug. 11, 1863	39, 457
Chuck, Universal	S. S. Hogle	Rockville, N. Y	Nov. 16, 1841	2, 366
Chuck, Universal	W. H. King	Troy, N. Y	Apr. 25, 1865	47, 428
Chuck, Warping	J. T. Haskins	Rockport, Mass	June 16, 1868	78, 964
Chuck, Watch-makers'	H. H. Heskett	Le Roy, Ill	July 4, 1871	116, 591
Chuck, Watch-makers'	J. Mansir	Richmond, Me	Nov. 14, 1871	120, 988
Chuck, Watch-makers'	A. K. P. Walker	Richmond, Me	Aug. 1, 1871	117, 703
Chuck, Watch-makers' lathe	W. Kerr	Boston, Mass	May 30, 1871	115, 524
Chuck, Watch-makers' lathe	S. S. Lavey	Plymouth, Ind	Sept. 17, 1867	68, 998
Chuck, Watch-makers' lathe	J. Stark	Waltham, Mass	Aug. 12, 1873	141, 824
Chuck, Watch-makers' lathe	W. Stephens	Richmond, Ind	Mar. 10, 1857	16, 811
Chuck, Watch-makers' lathe	G. H. Waldin	Burlington, Iowa	Feb. 22, 1859	23, 050
Chuck, Wood-lathe	R. H. Dowling	Fenton, Mich	May 23, 1871	115, 179
Chucks, Device for holding and carrying pipe-fittings.	A. J. Peavey and F. B. Cotton	Boston, Mass	Dec. 23, 1873	145, 896
Chucks, Jaw for lathe	M. C. Johnson	New Bedford, Mass	Aug. 26, 1873	142, 239
Church and school seat	C. Perley	New York, N. Y	May 24, 1859	24, 151
Church-pew head rest	J. H. Weeden	Waterbury, Conn	June 15, 1869	91, 389
Church-seat	C. O. Mealia	Brooklyn, N. Y	Jan. 16, 1872	122, 730
Churn	H. Abbott	North Huron, N. Y	June 19, 1860	28, 723
Churn	H. W. Adams	Milton, Pa	Jan. 7, 1868	72, 959
Churn	L. Adams	Redding, Conn	Apr. 16, 1842	2, 559
Churn	J. Aiken	Warner, N. H	Mar. 7, 1865	46, 749
Churn	D. C. Aldrich	Anamosa, Iowa	Feb. 7, 1865	46, 202
Churn	J. Alexander	Gallipolis, Ohio	Feb. 2, 1869	86, 343
Churn	W. Alexander	Union Valley, N. Y	May 14, 1867	64, 618
Churn	H. Allen, jr	Wallingford, Conn	Mar. 14, 1865	46, 766
Churn	L. O. Allen	Gardiner, Me	Apr. 10, 1866	53, 706
Churn	S. S. Allen	Belvidere, N. Y	May 4, 1869	89, 616
Churn	C. T. Anderson	Hyattstown, Md	June 18, 1861	32, 553
Churn	C. T. Anderson	Clarksburgh, Md	May 2, 1865	47, 507
Churn	C. T. Anderson	Clarksburgh, Md	Apr. 26, 1870	102, 354
Churn	J. Andrews	Woburn, Mass	Apr. 23, 1850	7, 298
Churn	C. Angerine	New York, N. Y	Aug. 17, 1835	....
Churn	O. A. Anthony	Mayfield, N. Y	Sept. 3, 1872	131, 076
Churn	J. S. Appleton	White River Junction, Vt	Aug. 17, 1858	21, 176
Churn	W. F. Armstrong and M. Payne.	Cardington, Ohio	July 16, 1861	32, 814
Churn	R. S. Arnall	Wright City, Mo	July 23, 1867	67, 095

Index of patents issued from the United States Patent Office from 1790 *to* 1873, *inclusive*—Continued.

Invention.	Inventor.	Residence.	Date.	No.
Churn	E. Archer	Davisville, W. Va	Aug. 5, 1873	141, 480
Churn	M. B. Atkinson	Georgetown, D. C	Apr. 12, 1870	101, 810
Churn	A. Austin	Altona, Ill	Sept. 27, 1859	25, 553
Churn	S. S. Ayers	Plainfield, N. J	Mar. 12, 1867	62, 804
Churn	L. Bacon	Charlotte, Mich	July 26, 1864	43, 632
Churn	S. L. Bagley	Hillsdale, N. Y	Mar. 24, 1827	....
Churn	C. Baker	Charlton, N. Y	June 13, 1831	....
Churn	D. D. Baker	West Alexandria, Ohio	Apr. 21, 1868	76, 879
Churn	H. D. Baker	Pittstown Corners, N. Y	Feb. 16, 1858	19, 334
Churn	H. F. Baker	Centreville, Ind	Apr. 10, 1849	6, 298
Churn	T. Baker	Saint John's, Mich	Mar. 15, 1870	100, 711
Churn	A. Bailey	Poultney, Vt	Oct. 6, 1831	....
Churn	T. K. Bailey	Lockport, N. Y	Apr. 24, 1866	54, 092
Churn	A. Baird	Schoharie, N. Y	Mar. 25, 1825	....
Churn	S. Ballard, sr	Sullivan, Ind	May 7, 1867	64, 471
Churn	J. A. Balzart	Piqua, Ohio	Sept. 18, 1866	58, 047
Churn	H. B. Barber	Scott, N. Y	Dec. 24, 1867	72, 588
Churn	H. Barr	Independence, Iowa	Nov. 18, 1862	36, 935
Churn	W. E. Barr	Ripley's, W. Va	Aug. 27, 1872	130, 836
Churn	J. C. Barrett	Collins, N. Y	Oct. 19, 1829	....
Churn	D. Bartholomew and D. C. Dinsmore.	Kirkville, Iowa	May 19, 1868	78, 042
Churn	N. S. Barton	Mannsville, N. Y	Aug. 31, 1869	94, 381
Churn	M. L. Bauder	Elyria, Ohio	Jan. 19, 1858	19, 117
Churn	C. F. Baylor	Clinton, N. J	Apr. 25, 1865	47, 383
Churn	J. Beach	Northfield, Mass	Jan. 24, 1811	....
Churn	S. and M. Bear	Versailles, Ohio	Sept. 24, 1867	69, 065
Churn	W. Beaton	Grinnell, Iowa	Oct. 4, 1864	44, 505
Churn	J. Beckley	Stiles, Iowa	May 6, 1873	138, 604
Churn	E. H. Beckwith	Westernville, N. Y	Nov. 20, 1866	59, 811
Churn	L. W. Beecher	Avon, N. Y	Nov. 24, 1857	18, 671
Churn	C. H. and E. G. Beeman	North Fairfax, Vt	July 13, 1869	92, 566
Churn	B. Beers	New Fairfield, Conn	Dec. 8, 1857	18, 797
Churn	G. Beisner	Chicago, Ill	Nov. 3, 1868	83, 595
Churn	H. C. Bell	Heyworth, Ill	Mar. 24, 1868	75, 842
Churn	H. C. Bell	Edina, Mo	July 30, 1872	129, 918
Churn	E. O. Bennett	Mount Pleasant, Iowa	Oct. 1, 1867	69, 391
Churn	J. Bennett	Brutus, N. Y	July 25, 1832	....
Churn	H. Bentley	Ballston, N. Y	Apr. 20, 1844	3, 556
Churn	E. L. Bergstresser	Berrysburgh, Pa	Feb. 21, 1865	46, 440
Churn	G. Berkstresser	Bedford, Pa	Aug. 31, 1869	94, 176
Churn	S. Besser	Dorchester, Ill	July 7, 1868	79, 542
Churn	W. T. Best	Scranton, Pa	Apr. 28, 1868	77, 160
Churn	H. H. Bigard, E. H. Kellogg, and N. A. Prentiss.	Fowler, N. Y	Feb. 15, 1870	99, 819
Churn	A. Bills	Baltimore, Md	July 29, 1816	....
Churn	A. G. Binns	Goshen Township, Ohio	Aug. 26, 1862	36, 269
Churn	T. Bisbing	Buckstown, Pa	Dec. 10, 1867	71, 958
Churn	C. G. Bishop	Poughkeepsie, N. Y	July 18, 1865	48, 786
Churn	L. Bissell	North Bergen, N. Y	July 10, 1860	29, 052
Churn	D. O. Blair	Abingdon, Ill	Feb. 19, 1867	62, 179
Churn	F. Blecka	Elgin, Ill	June 25, 1867	66, 122
Churn	J. C. Bodine	Camden, N. J	Nov. 20, 1866	59, 759
Churn	T. H. Body	White Creek, Wis	Jan. 26, 1869	86, 274
Churn	T. Bogan	Lacon, Ill	Aug. 27, 1867	68, 034
Churn	L. Bogner	Rochester, Ind	Aug. 6, 1872	130, 104
Churn	J. Bolton	Philadelphia, Pa	Aug. 2, 1808	....
Churn	C. A. Boone	Shickshinny, Pa	May 3, 1870	102, 481
Churn	J. Borst	East Cobbleskill, N. Y	Jan. 22, 1867	61, 389
Churn	J. P. Bortle	Claverack, N. Y	Apr. 19, 1825	....
Churn	J. Borton and W. H. Hartly	Quaker City, Ohio	Feb. 11, 1873	135, 761
Churn	C. L. Bottum	Dansville, N. Y	Feb. 24, 1863	37, 730
Churn	C. Boyer	Marshall, Mich	Oct. 8, 1867	69, 620
Churn	J. Boyers	Granville, Va	Aug. 14, 1855	13, 421
Churn	J. Boyers	Orrville, Ohio	July 3, 1866	55, 996
Churn	W. Boynton, jr	Auburn, N. Y	Apr. 15, 1862	34, 936
Churn	W. Boynton	Auburn, N. Y	Feb. 20, 1866	52, 664
Churn	C. H. Bradley	Coatesville, Pa	Apr. 28, 1868	77, 252
Churn	R. Bradley	Williston, Vt	July 21, 1835	....
Churn	J. W. Bradly and G. H. Jordon.	Rocheport, Mo	June 23, 1868	79, 197
Churn	A. H. Brainerd	Rome, N. Y	Apr. 23, 1867	63, 989
Churn	V. M. R. Branch	Richmond, Va	Sept. 1, 1868	81, 589
Churn	M. Bratt	Maysville, Ky	Oct. 23, 1866	58, 976
Churn	C. W. Brewer	Racine, Wis	Dec. 29, 1868	85, 272
Churn	I. Brewster	Blenheim, N. Y	May 28, 1830	....
Churn	I. Brewster	Blenheim, N. Y	Dec. 31, 1833	....
Churn	I. Brewster	Schoharie County, N. Y	Jan. 7, 1835	....
Churn	J. C. Bridgman	London, Ohio	May 22, 1866	54, 846
Churn	W. W. Brigg	Home, Tenn	July 20, 1869	92, 788
Churn	G. N. Brigham	Montpelier, Vt	July 24, 1866	56, 520
Churn	J. Brinkerhoff	Auburn, N. Y	Dec. 23, 1862	37, 214
Churn	J. L. and T. R. Britt	Raleigh, N. C	Oct. 14, 1873	143, 612
Churn	A. Broadway	Monson, Mass	Nov. 25, 1816	....
Churn	A. H. Brown	Springfield, Vt	Oct. 8, 1867	69, 623
Churn	D. C. Brown	New York, N. Y	Jan. 24, 1860	26, 880
Churn	G. C. Brown	Atlanta, Ga	Mar. 22, 1870	101, 091
Churn	H. Brown	New York, N. Y	Apr. 6, 1858	19, 828
Churn	J. Brown	Hallowell, Me	June 18, 1834	....
Churn	J. F. Brown	New London, Conn	July 2, 1867	66, 295
Churn	M. M. Brown	Pimento, Ind	Oct. 8, 1867	69, 624
Churn	W. Brown	Duncannon, Pa	May 11, 1858	20, 189
Churn	L. A. Brown and H. Bigelow	Hartford, Conn	Oct. 5, 1852	9, 311
Churn	E. Brown and A. Keith	Winfield, N. Y	June 19, 1822	....
Churn	E. T. Brownfield	Smithfield, Pa	Mar. 17, 1868	75, 621
Churn	G. N. Broughton	Bellefontaine, Ohio	Aug. 13, 1872	130, 473
Churn	S. W. Bruce	Laguardo, Tenn	Jan. 18, 1870	98, 918
Churn	J. H. Bruner	McKean, Ohio	Feb. 9, 1832	....

Index of patents issued from the United States Patent Office from 1790 *to* 1873, *inclusive*—Continued.

Invention.	Inventor.	Residence.	Date.	No.
Churn	A. P. Bryson	Prospect, Pa	Dec. 1, 1868	84, 532
Churn	G. G. Buchanan	Cotton Plant, Miss	Nov. 11, 1873	144, 437
Churn	R. Buck	Baltimore, Md	June 23, 1807	
Churn	T. W. Buck	Fawn River, Mich	Oct. 8, 1867	69, 538
Churn	W. E. Budd	Chatham, N. J	Apr. 4, 1871	113, 251
Churn	E. Buel	Sheridan, N. Y	Oct. 11, 1864	44, 595
Churn	J. M. Buell	Zanesville, Ohio	Aug. 7, 1860	29, 460
Churn	J. H. Bump	Morris, N. Y	Oct 26, 1858	21, 871
Churn	F. and L. Burdick	South East, N. Y., and Lockhaven, Pa.	Oct. 5, 1869	95, 560
Churn	T. I. Burhyte	Fond du Lac, Wis	Feb. 26, 1867	62, 470
Churn	T. J. Burke and S. B. Gassette	Chicago, Ill	Oct. 31, 1865	50, 684
Churn	W. H. Burnham and B. Hibbard.	Cortland Village, N. Y	July 29, 1856	15, 412
Churn	W. and D. C. Burson	Salineville, Ohio	Sept. 18, 1866	58, 059
Churn	E. Burt	Princeton, N. J	Nov. 20, 1809	
Churn	S. Bushnell, 2d	Saybrook, Conn	Dec. 20, 1830	
Churn	M. Byard	Milan, Ind	Oct. 13, 1857	18, 384
Churn	P. Byrns and G. Stannard	Mindora, Wis	Nov. 5, 1867	70, 406
Churn	M. P. Callender	Astoria, Oreg	Sept. 3, 1872	130, 976
Churn	M. Calvert	Marshall, Ohio	June 23, 1868	79, 103
Churn	J. D. Campbell and J. Elliott	Jamestown, Ind	Sept. 24, 1872	131, 660
Churn	S. N. Campbell	Elgin, Ill	Oct. 18, 1859	25, 804
Churn	W. Campbell	Waterloo, Pa	Sept. 13, 1859	25, 383
Churn	A. Carbnow	Potsdam, N. Y	Dec. 18, 1866	60, 473
Churn	W. L. Card	Gardner, Ill	Feb. 12, 1867	61, 9[illegible]5
Churn	J. Carlton	Walla Walla, Wash	Dec. 15, 1868	84, 858
Churn	R. Carmack	Marongo, Ill	Apr. 16, 1872	125, 660
Churn	D. H. Carpenter and H. L. Slaghs.	Hector and Lodi, N. Y	Feb. 18, 1868	74, 498
Churn	A. C. Carrell	Granville, Ohio	Oct. 25, 1832	
Churn	J. S. Carson	Brookhaven, Miss	Aug. 25, 1868	81, 341
Churn	C. H. Carver	Taunton, Mass	Feb. 25, 1868	74, 796
Churn	S. S. Case	Marion, N. Y	Nov. 3, 1868	83, 815
Churn	S. S. Case	Marion, N. Y	May 16, 1871	114, 922
Churn	J. E. Casey	Cortland Village, N. Y	Mar. 27, 1866	53, 521
Churn	H. Caslow	York, Pa	June 14, 1870	104, 267
Churn	C. J. Chalfant	Unionville, Pa	July 30, 1867	67, 266
Churn	W. C. Chamberlain	Dubuque, Iowa	Jan. 29, 1867	61, 515
Churn	W. C. Chamberlain	Dubuque, Iowa	Aug. 3, 1869	93, 174
Churn	N. P. Chaney	Potsdam, N. Y	Sept. 1, 1868	81, 599
Churn	F. B. Chapman	Salisbury, Mo	Feb. 21, 1871	111, 907
Churn	J. W. Chapman	Madison, Ind	Sept. 5, 1871	118, 687
Churn	N. Chapman	Milford, Mass	Jan. 30, 1866	52, 268
Churn	N. Chapman	Milford, Mass	Apr. 13, 1869	88, 847
Churn	J. Chapple	Jasper, N. Y	Jan. 18, 1870	98, 924
Churn	J. I. Cheatham	Athens, Ga	July 6, 1869	92, 164
Churn	E. Chipman	New York, N. Y,	Jan. 12, 1864	41, 193
Churn	E. Chipman	New York, N. Y	Mar. 21, 1865	46, 880
Churn	J. B. Christian and J. P. Beach	Hamburgh, Iowa	Aug. 13, 1872	130, 477
Churn	J. M. Chritton	Joliet, Ill	Jan. 15, 1867	61, 160
Churn	N. B. Clabaugh	Frederick, Md	July 2, 1867	66, 219
Churn	J. Clark	Brush Valley, Pa	Jan. 10, 1871	110, 897
Churn	S. Clark	Morris County, N. J	Oct. 4, 1822	
Churn	G. B. Clarke	Leonardsville, N. Y	Sept. 23, 1851	8, 373
Churn.	U. L. Clark	Manor Township, Pa	Dec. 31, 1833	
Churn	G. Clayton and C. B. Allen	Willoughby, Ohio	Jan. 21, 1868	73, 503
Churn	E. B. Clement	Barnet, Vt	Jan. 20, 1852	8, 671
Churn	E. B. Clement	Barnet, Vt	Feb. 13, 1855	12, 377
Churn	E. B. Clement	Barnet, Vt	Feb. 21, 1860	27, 205
Churn	D. Cleveland	Sheffield, Mass	July 7, 1808	
Churn	D. Cleveland	Sheffield, Mass	July 11, 1808	
Churn	L. Cleveland	Holliston, Mass	Feb. 7, 1811	
Churn	A. Clift, jr	Mystic River, Conn	May 22, 1866	54, 861
Churn	H. Clift	Mystic River, Conn	Sept. 25, 1866	58, 337
Churn	M. Clifton	Peoria, Ill	Feb. 16, 1869	87, 027
Churn	J. Closs	Decatur, Ind	May 31, 1859	24, 197
Churn	D. Clough	Auburn, N. Y	Feb. 5, 1867	61, 716
Churn	P. L. Clow	Cohoes, N. Y	Nov. 15, 1859	26, 092
Churn	J. C. Clymer	Galion, Ohio	Mar. 26, 1867	63, 216
Churn	J. Cochran, jr	Auburn, Mo	Dec. 12, 1871	121, 755
Churn	J. T. Coe	Chambersburgh, Pa	Feb. 18, 1868	74, 505
Churn	T. Coffield and B. Egli	Natrona, Pa	Nov. 8, 1870	108, 969
Churn	J. B. Coffman	New Richmond, Ohio	Jan. 19, 1869	86, 002
Churn	L. S. Colburn	Oberlin, Ohio	June 30, 1863	39, 035
Churn	C. Colby	San Francisco, Cal	Nov. 19, 1867	70, 959
Churn	E. Coleman	Woburn, Mass	Mar. 9, 1869	87, 639
Churn	T. Conely	Grafton, Ill	June 25, 1872	128, 364
Churn	A. J. Conner	Louisville, Ky	Apr. 14, 1868	76, 606
Churn	A. L. Converse	Springfield, Ill	May 5, 1868	77, 460
Churn	G. W. Cook	Saint Louis, Mo	Feb. 28, 1844	3, 460
Churn	L. M. Cook	Owatonna, Minn	July 23, 1867	66, 949
Churn	W. M. Cook	Lyons, Iowa	Nov. 13, 1866	59, 560
Churn	D. C. Cooley	Wilkesbarre, Pa	Feb. 23, 1869	87, 147
Churn	J. Cooper	Dublin, Ind	July 10, 1866	56, 340
Churn	N. B. Cooper	Gratis. Ohio	July 3, 1860	28, 970
Churn	G. W. Corbit, J. M. Orput, and G. M. Case.	Malta, Ill	Apr. 28, 1868	77, 172
Churn	A. B. Corby	Binghamton, N. Y	May 5, 1868	77, 462
Churn	A. and H. K. Cornell	Cambridge, N. Y	Jan. 15, 1816	
Churn	J. Copeland and G. P. Martin	Quasqueton. Iowa	June 17, 1862	35, 588
Churn	G. W. Cottingham and J. H. Binkley.	Columbus, Tex	Oct. 8, 1872	131, 939
Churn	F. Cotton	New York, N. Y	Jan. 9, 1835	
Churn	E. P. and J. A. Cowles	Oakfield, N. Y	Mar. 3, 1857	16, 717
Churn	A. J. Cox	Indianapolis, Ind	Mar. 26, 1872	124, 883
Churn	J. A. Cozad	Mercer, Pa	July 27, 1869	93, 061
Churn	J. Crail	Warren, Ohio	May 5, 1831	

Index of patents issued from the United States Patent Office from 1790 *to* 1873, *inclusive*—Continued.

Invention.	Inventor.	Residence.	Date.	No.
Churn	J. Cram	Chicago, Ill	July 16, 1867	66, 681
Churn	J. Cram	Chicago, Ill	Jan. 10, 1871	110, 902
Churn	G. Cramton	Marshall, Mich	Apr. 12, 1864	42, 275
Churn	A. G. Crane	Ottumwa, Iowa	June 11, 1872	127, 852
Churn	F. J. Crissey	Leesburgh, Va	June 26, 1866	55, 825
Churn	M. C. Crank	Auburn, N. Y	Aug. 13, 1861	33, 030
Churn	J. E. Cryer	Green Point, N. Y	July 23, 1867	67, 105
Churn	A. W. Cunningham	West Middletown, Pa	Feb. 28, 1860	27, 276
Churn	W. H. Curtin and W. Lammers	Clement and Breeze, Ill	July 26, 1870	105, 652
Churn	S. T. Curtis	El Paso, Ill	June 9, 1868	78, 791
Churn	G. A. Dabney	San José, Cal	Feb. 2, 1869	86, 371
Churn	C. H. Dana	West Lebanon, N. H	July 14, 1857	17, 781
Churn	R. Daniels	Woodstock, Vt	May 21, 1872	127, 030
Churn	F. Danzenbaker	Bridgeton, N. J	Sept. 18, 1866	58, 228
Churn	J. Darrow	Warren, Ohio	June 2, 1832	....
Churn	J. J. Davelin	Philadelphia, Pa	Mar. 19, 1867	63, 023
Churn	J. B. Davidson	Oberlin, Ohio	Apr. 19, 1864	42, 354
Churn	W. C. T. Davidson and W. H. Durrett.	Hannibal, Mo	June 4, 1872	127, 406
Churn	J. Davies	Mazomania, Wis	July 9, 1867	66, 469
Churn	J. Davis, 2d	Lake Village, N. H	Mar. 13, 1866	53, 123
Churn	J. Davis, jr	Lake Village, N. H	Nov. 20, 1866	59, 790
Churn	R. W. Davis	Rodgersville, N. Y	Apr. 2, 1850	7, 233
Churn	R. W. Davis	Rodgersville, N. Y	Feb. 28, 1854	10, 566
Churn	W. Davis	Arrow Rock, Mo	Oct. 1, 1867	69, 324
Churn	J. Davison	Plymouth, Mich	July 2, 1867	66, 306
Churn	J. T. Dawson	Frostburgh, Md	Apr. 9, 1867	63, 708
Churn	L. Day	Buffalo, N. Y	Jan. 31, 1860	26, 970
Churn	A. B. Dean	Louisville, Ky	Aug. 3, 1869	93, 285
Churn	H. Decker	Lebanon, Ohio	Feb. 26, 1867	62, 329
Churn	G. Deckman	Malvern, Ohio	Apr. 2, 1867	63, 485
Churn	L. Dederick	New York, N. Y	Sept. 20, 1870	107, 464
Churn	D. Deshon, 2d	Somerset, Pa	Apr. 3, 1860	27, 701
Churn	P. S. Devlan	Reading, Pa	June 14, 1859	24, 382
Churn	J. L. Devol	Parkersburgh, W. Va	May 3, 1870	102, 509
Churn	H. Dickerman	Great Barrington, Mass	May 9, 1809	....
Churn	S. Dickerman and S. M. Parsons.	Meriden, Conn	Oct. 1, 1830	....
Churn	I. L. Dickinson	Richmond, Ind	Jan. 31, 1854	10, 487
Churn	J. Dodder	Washington, Iowa	Jan. 30, 1866	52, 272
Churn	H. Doolittle	Alton, Ill	June 23, 1863	38, 951
Churn	H. Doolittle	Aurora, Ind	Oct. 11, 1864	44, 614
Churn	E. L. Dorsey	Greenwood, Ind	Apr. 12, 1859	23, 556
Churn	Z. S. Doty	Groton, N. Y	Mar. 17, 1829	....
Churn	Z. S. Doty	Massillon, Ohio	Aug. 31, 1831	....
Churn	J. H. Doughty	Adamsville, Ohio	Oct. 8, 1861	33, 469
Churn	J. H. Doughty	Adamsville, Ohio	Feb. 18, 1862	34, 416
Churn	W. C. Douthett	Rochelle, Ill	May 12, 1868	77, 873
Churn	W. C. Douthett	Rochelle, Ill	Oct. 13, 1868	83, 050
Churn	G. H. Dow	Freeport, Ill	July 7, 1868	79, 739
Churn	N. Drew	Howell, Mich	July 16, 1867	66, 687
Churn	S. G. Dugdale	Richmond, Ind	July 15, 1851	8, 219
Churn	J. G. Dungan	Steubenville, Ohio	Oct. 9, 1855	13, 638
Churn	S. P. Dunham and A. Hipple	Killbourne, Ohio	Apr. 17, 1860	27, 894
Churn	D. Dunton	Brooklyn, N. Y	Apr. 3, 1866	53, 591
Churn	P. Dunwald	Corning, N. Y	Feb. 19, 1861	31, 447
Churn	D. Dutcher	Springfield, N. Y	June 10, 1851	8, 143
Churn	W. T. Eastes	Madison County, Ind	Nov. 26, 1867	71, 469
Churn	B. R. Eaton	Clifton, Wis	Feb. 19, 1867	62, 121
Churn	A. G. Eddy	Ashfield, Mass	Dec. 9, 1862	37, 090
Churn	S. D. Edgar	Dayton, Ohio	Mar. 23, 1869	88, 148
Churn	J. B. Edgell, E. A. Alexander, and H. C. Kellogg.	Quasqueton, Iowa	Jan. 20, 1863	37, 437
Churn	W. Edmister and S. Johnson	Mount Vernon, Ohio	July 11, 1865	48, 666
Churn	J. P. Edmonds	Rochelle, Ill	July 9, 1867	66, 478
Churn	J. J. Edwards	Columbus, Wis	Sept. 27, 1864	44, 410
Churn	C. L. Eggert	Lawrence, Kans	Aug. 20, 1867	67, 964
Churn	R. and W. J. Elarton	Hillsborough, Iowa	Sept. 28, 1869	95, 212
Churn	S. S. Elder	Springfield, Ill	Dec. 1, 1868	84, 619
Churn	A. H. Elliott	Albion, Mich	May 3, 1870	102, 518
Churn	C. H. Elliott	York, Pa	Apr. 28, 1868	77, 431
Churn	A. N. Elzy	Placerville, Cal	Nov. 26, 1867	71, 289
Churn	P. Embree	West Chester, Pa	Mar. 20, 1860	27, 536
Churn	E. R. Embry	Richmond, Ky	Nov. 23, 1869	97, 179
Churn	G. W. Emerson	Peru, Ill	Apr. 30, 1867	64, 210
Churn	S. F. Emerson	Seville, Ohio	Dec. 22, 1863	40, 997
Churn	S. F. Emerson	Seville, Ohio	June 16, 1863	38, 891
Churn	F. M. English	Evansville, Ind	July 11, 1871	116, 940
Churn	W. Estabrook	Salem, Ohio	Nov. 19, 1833	....
Churn	J. W. Evans	Forsyth, Ga	May 29, 1860	28, 462
Churn	T. R. Evans	Blacksburgh, Va	Apr. 5, 1870	101, 599
Churn	J. J. Everst	Cumberland, Md	Nov. 26, 1867	71, 472
Churn	J. Ewing	Worcester, Mass	Jan. 29, 1830	....
Churn	B. Fairbanks	Worcester, Mass	Mar. 5, 1810	....
Churn	F. T. Fairchild	Sheboygan, Wis	May 3, 1870	102, 523
Churn	G. K. Farrington	Xenia, Ohio	Sept. 28, 1858	21, 637
Churn	J. Fassauer	Wheeling, Iowa	Sept. 1, 1868	81, 615
Churn	W. S. Ferrier	Indiana, Pa	Aug. 7, 1866	56, 918
Churn	T. T. Ffirth	Camden, N. J	Dec. 23, 1862	37, 254
Churn	J. U. Fiester	Winchester, Ohio	Feb 26, 1856	14, 309
Churn	J. U. Fiester	Winchester, Ohio	Feb. 15, 1859	22, 945
Churn	J. E. Finley	Memphis, Tenn	Mar. 12, 1867	62, 740
Churn	J. E. Finley	Memphis, Tenn	Sept. 3, 1867	68, 560
Churn	J. E. Finley	Memphis, Tenn	May 5, 1868	77, 601
Churn	J. E. Finley	Memphis, Tenn	May 4, 1869	89, 645
Churn	J. E. Finley	Memphis, Tenn	May 16, 1871	114, 785
Churn	D. Fisher	College Corner, Ohio	Jan. 1, 1851	7, 870
Churn	M. Fisk	Adrian, Mich	Dec. 5, 1871	121, 604

Index of patents issued from the United States Patent Office from 1790 *to* 1873, *inclusive*—Continued.

Invention.	Inventor.	Residence.	Date.	No.
Churn	D. A. Fiske	Delavan, Wis	Mar. 27, 1866	53, 432
Churn	D. A. Fiske	Delavan, Wis	Aug. 4, 1868	80, 616
Churn	G. C. Fitch	Randolph, N. Y	Mar. 17, 1868	75, 530
Churn	J. P. Fitch	New York, N. Y	Jan. 17, 1860	26, 841
Churn	J. H. Fleming	Groton, Ohio	May 26, 1868	78, 199
Churn	B. S. Fletcher	Cornish, N. H	May 22, 1866	54, 878
Churn	O. V. Flora and J. S. Bogle	Madison, Ind., and Springfield, Ohio.	Apr. 2, 1867	63, 493
Churn	N. C. Folger	New Orleans, La	Oct. 13, 1868	83, 057
Churn	J. W. Forsyth	Leesburgh, Va	Oct. 9, 1866	58, 628
Churn	C. Foss	Perry, Ohio	June 11, 1829	....
Churn	A. W. Foster	Millbridge, Me	Apr. 5, 1870	101, 453
Churn	G. W. Fowler	Jenner's Cross Roads, Pa	Aug. 27, 1867	68, 060
Churn	J. Fowler and W. L. Walter	Homer, N. Y	July 30, 1861	32, 939
Churn	D. Frankfoder	Wakarusa, Ind	Mar. 21, 1871	112, 796
Churn	S. D. Frazier	Tekonsha, Mich	Feb. 23, 1864	41, 693
Churn	T. Freeman	Westfield, Ill	Mar. 7, 1871	112, 332
Churn	D. Frey and D. Sanders	Homer, N. Y	Aug. 16, 1864	43, 844
Churn	J. P. Friest	Chillicothe, Mo	Nov. 18, 1873	144, 755
Churn	W. Fritts	Flanders, N. J	Dec. 19, 1871	122, 004
Churn	I. N. Frost	Peoria, Ill	May 26, 1868	78, 368
Churn	A. Fuqua	Sandford, Ind	Aug. 12, 1873	141, 709
Churn	W. Furbish	Hallowell, Me	Mar. 6, 1833	....
Churn	N. Gabel	Gratis, Ohio	Aug. 20, 1861	33, 080
Churn	C. W. Gage	Homer, N. Y	Nov. 15, 1864	45, 033
Churn	A. S. Galliher	Bristol, Tenn	Mar. 9, 1869	87, 657
Churn	A. O. Gallup and E. A. Hewitt	Salem and New London, Conn.	Apr. 18, 1865	47, 292
Churn	A. O. Gallup and E. A. Hewitt	Salem and Groton, Conn	May 18, 1869	90, 255
Churn	M. Gascon	Malvern, Ohio	Aug. 30, 1870	106, 929
Churn	H. Gardiner	New York, N. Y	Dec. 23, 1862	37, 224
Churn	H. Gardiner	New York, N. Y	Feb. 22, 1870	100, 025
Churn	J. C. Gaston	Cincinnati, Ohio	Apr. 16, 1867	63, 791
Churn	J. C. Gaston	Cincinnati, Ohio	June 25, 1867	66, 015
Churn	J. C. Gaston	Cincinnati, Ohio	Dec. 24, 1867	72, 475
Churn	D. Gates	Captina Post-Office, Ohio	May 14, 1867	64, 758
Churn	J. W. Gault	Pleasant Township, Ohio	Sept. 24, 1867	69, 088
Churn	J. Geiger	Peoria County, Ill	Mar. 30, 1869	88, 289
Churn	C. George	Ligonier, Pa	June 18, 1867	65, 899
Churn	J. B. Ghormley	Bellefontaine, Ohio	Oct. 10, 1865	50, 349
Churn	J. Glattner	Suspension Bridge, N. Y	Mar. 9, 1869	87, 659
Churn	A. J. Gibson	Worcester, Mass	Sept. 13, 1864	44, 179
Churn	A. and Z. A. Gifford	Somerset, N. Y	Jan. 17, 1871	110, 968
Churn	G. W. Gilbert	Bettsville, Ohio	Jan. 7, 1862	34, 110
Churn	J. C. Gilbert	Galesburgh, Ill	July 14, 1868	79, 821
Churn	G. E. Gill and J. B. Tillinghast	Chillicothe, Ohio	June 19, 1849	6, 538
Churn	A. E. Gillilan	Marion, Iowa	June 2, 1868	78, 589
Churn	T. Gillmor	Saint Louis, Mo	July 3, 1866	56, 036
Churn	E. L. Gilman	Somerville, Mass	Oct. 8, 1867	69, 653
Churn	C. L. Gilpatrick	Saco, Me	Sept. 13, 1859	25, 405
Churn	S. Gissinger	Allegheny, Pa	Sept. 20, 1859	25, 502
Churn	S. Gissinger	Allegheny City, Pa	July 14, 1863	39, 225
Churn	S. Gissinger	Manchester, Pa	Feb. 2, 1864	41, 429
Churn	J. Gire	Louden City, Ill	Oct. 10, 1871	119, 840
Churn	D. H. Gobin	Springfield, Ill	July 16, 1872	129, 471
Churn	G. Goewey	New York, N. Y	Dec. 17, 1861	33, 973
Churn	S. M. Golden	Marcelline, Ill	Jan. 22, 1867	61, 415
Churn	J. L. Good	Elizabethtown, Pa	Mar. 9, 1869	87, 660
Churn	R. Goodwin	North Bergen, N. Y	May 4, 1842	2, 603
Churn	W. F. Goodwin	Metuchen, N. J	Apr. 12, 1870	101, 856
Churn	G. W. Goodwyn	Petersburgh, Va	May 19, 1868	78, 081
Churn	W. B. Gordnier	Cowdersport, Pa	May 8, 1860	28, 170
Churn	M. C. Gordon	Knightstown, Ind	Oct. 15, 1867	69, 795
Churn	W. L. Gordon	Dalton, Ga	Aug. 17, 1869	93, 818
Churn	E. Gore	Bennington, Vt	Jan. 2, 1855	12, 127
Churn	C. R. Gorgas	Wooster, Ohio	May 31, 1864	42, 939
Churn	B. Graham	Lyons, Iowa	June 5, 1866	55, 281
Churn	M. Granger	Syracuse, N. Y	July 14, 1830	....
Churn	A. W. Gray	Bennington, Ohio	May 21, 1867	64, 971
Churn	S. Gray	Genesee, N. Y	Aug. 17, 1810	....
Churn	G. H. Gregory	North Wilton, Conn	Dec. 21, 1869	98, 161
Churn	T. F. Griffiths	Dansville, N. Y	Oct. 27, 1863	40, 404
Churn	E. Groat	Napa, Cal	Sept. 5, 1871	118, 712
Churn	E. Groat	Napa, Cal	Sept. 5, 1871	118, 713
Churn	G. Groom	Brockville, Canada	July 18, 1871	117, 070
Churn	H. H. Grover	Auburn, N. Y	Nov. 30, 1829	....
Churn	D. L. Grover and L. S. Wright	Groton, N. Y	Aug. 12, 1862	36, 147
Churn	J. J. Gruver and A. D. Wiggins	New Market, Ohio	Nov. 5, 1867	70, 431
Churn	H. S. Gurney and H. Merrill	Memphis, Mich	Mar. 21, 1871	112, 806
Churn	J. Gustine	New Petersburgh, Ohio	May 14, 1834	....
Churn	A. Guthrie	Chicago, Ill	July 26, 1859	24, 907
Churn	B. Haden, jr	Trenton, N. J	June 15, 1822	....
Churn	H. Hagans	Brandonville, Va	July 23, 1861	32, 868
Churn	T. Haigh	Harrisburgh, Pa	Sept. 8, 1868	81, 896
Churn	J. Hale	Hillsborough, N. H	Dec. 15, 1819	....
Churn	A. Hall	Loysville, Ohio	Oct. 9, 1849	6, 777
Churn	A. W. Hall	New York, N. Y	Jan. 31, 1865	46, 185
Churn	A. W. Hall	New York, N. Y	June 5, 1866	55, 287
Churn	A. W. Hall	New York, N. Y	June 12, 1866	55, 491
Churn	S. Z. Hall	Camden, N. J	Aug. 2, 1864	43, 686
Churn	S. Z. Hall	Camden, N. J	Nov. 22, 1864	45, 155
Churn	W. S. Hall	Quincy, Mass	Aug. 2, 1859	24, 934
Churn	J. A. Ham and W. Carpenter, jr	Barry, Mo	Aug. 31, 1869	94, 311
Churn	F. Hamblin	Madrid Springs, N. Y	Feb. 1, 1870	99, 312
Churn	W. Hamilton	Saint Catharine, Mo	Mar. 19, 1861	31, 715
Churn	A. Hamlin	Schoharie, N. Y	Mar. 13, 1866	53, 141
Churn	B. Handforth	Chicago, Ill	Feb. 19, 1867	62, 129
Churn	J. A. Hanger	Staunton, Va	Aug. 31, 1869	94, 312

Index of patents issued from the United States Patent Office from 1790 *to* 1873, *inclusive*—Continued.

Invention.	Inventor.	Residence.	Date.	No.
Churn	J. O. and G. C. Hanger	Churchville, Va	Jan. 18, 1870	98, 958
Churn	A. Hanson	Windham, Me	Mar. 2, 1836	....
Churn	J. W. Hardie	New York, N. Y	Mar. 13, 1860	27, 446
Churn	E. T. Harlan	Star City, Ind	Mar. 31, 1868	76, 185
Churn	J. Harper	Hillsborough, Iowa	Mar. 30, 1869	88, 474
Churn	S. Harper	Lawrence, Kans	Aug. 17, 1869	93, 879
Churn	T. B. Harper	Xenia, Ohio	Apr. 27, 1858	20, 062
Churn	B. N. Harris	Talbotton, Ga	July 6, 1869	92, 308
Churn	F. M. Harris	Winnamac, Ind	June 14, 1870	104, 304
Churn	J. D. Harrison	Middletown, Ohio	Apr. 23, 1872	126, 052
Churn	R. H. Harrison	Washington, D. C	Mar. 28, 1854	10, 690
Churn	M. S. Harsha	Sycamore, Ill	Dec. 13, 1859	26, 459
Churn	A. H. Hart	Stockbridge, Wis	Aug. 25, 1863	39, 650
Churn	G. Hart	Atwater, Ohio	June 20, 1865	48, 277
Churn	G. B. Hart	Buffalo Township, Iowa	Oct. 1, 1872	131, 877
Churn	C. Harvey	Cairo, N. Y	June 25, 1872	128, 306
Churn	M. B. Hassler	Columbia City, Ind	Sept. 13, 1859	25, 410
Churn	J. Hatfield and H. M. Goldsmith	Falmouth, Ind., and Burlington, Iowa.	July 13, 1858	20, 878
Churn	J. Hathaway	Canandaigua, N. Y	Aug. 22, 1828	....
Churn	G. W. Hawk	Chicago, Ill	Apr. 2, 1867	63, 515
Churn	O. Hawley and J. W. Ward	Wheeling, W. Va	July 2, 1867	66, 235
Churn	S. Hays	Poultney, N. Y	Mar. 8, 1808	....
Churn	N. S. Hazen	La Fayette, Ind	May 31, 1870	103, 612
Churn	A. J. Heavner	Time, Ill	Jan. 14, 1868	73, 327
Churn	W. H. Henderson	West Point, Ill	July 21, 1868	80, 174
Churn	J. Henry	Steubenville, Ohio	Oct. 2, 1866	58, 415
Churn	H. Hensel	Moon Township, Pa	Aug. 1, 1871	117, 629
Churn	W. A. Herrick	Greene, Me	July 21, 1835	....
Churn	H. L. Hervey	Philadelphia, Pa	Aug. 8, 1865	49, 345
Churn	C. Hess	Lyons City, Iowa	May 26, 1868	78, 286
Churn	C. Hess	Lyons, Iowa	Apr. 6, 1869	88, 568
Churn	A. E. Hewett	Homer, N. Y	Apr. 26, 1864	42, 481
Churn	S. Hewit	Seneca Falls, N. Y	July 14, 1857	17, 790
Churn	S. Hewit	Seneca Falls, N. Y	May 1, 1866	54, 343
Churn	S. Hewit	Seneca Falls, N. Y	Nov. 10, 1868	83, 853
Churn	J. Hewitt	Carmichael, Pa	Aug. 12, 1862	36, 151
Churn	P. Hill	Millport, N. Y	Feb. 4, 1868	74, 088
Churn	T. M. Hill	Eaton, Ohio	Dec. 5, 1865	51, 320
Churn	H. A. Hincheer	Hustonville, Ky	Apr. 1, 1873	137, 369
Churn	F. M. Hindman and N. Hiatt	Sidney, Iowa	Aug. 23, 1870	106, 695
Churn	E. Hinman	Syracuse, N. Y	Aug. 11, 1863	39, 529
Churn	E. Hitchcock	Sturbridge, Mass	June 8, 1869	91, 016
Churn	D. F. Hitt	Galena, Ill	Oct. 7, 1842	2, 800
Churn	A. D. Hoffman	Minneapolis, Minn	May 19, 1868	78, 091
Churn	W. H. Holdam	Crab Orchard, Ky	Apr. 22, 1873	138, 089
Churn	S. B. Holden	Woburn, Mass	Apr. 20, 1869	89, 046
Churn	E. F. Holloway	Knightstown, Ind	June 20, 1865	48, 278
Churn	R. G. Holmes	Worcester, Mass	May 8, 1860	28, 177
Churn	C. P. Holmes and A. L. Howell	Gouverneur and Mohawk, N. Y.	Mar. 1, 1870	100, 292
Churn	G. P. Hopkins	Cabot, Vt	Mar. 29, 1859	23, 374
Churn	W. B. Hopkins	Oakfield, N. Y	Mar. 26, 1861	31, 806
Churn	W. Hosier	Washington Township, Ind	May 30, 1865	47, 952
Churn	N. Hospers	Pella, Iowa	Aug. 13, 1872	130, 428
Churn	M. B. Hough	Dover, Ohio	Jan. 21, 1839	1, 072
Churn	J. W. F. How	Douglas County, Oreg	Dec. 17, 1872	133, 940
Churn	S. B. Howd	Arcadia, N. Y	Dec. 12, 1846	4, 887
Churn	N. Howe	Windham, Conn	Apr. 25, 1808	....
Churn	H. W. Howland	Calhoun, Ill	Sept. 24, 1867	69, 213
Churn	J. Houston	Lake Village, N. H	Nov. 17, 1863	40, 623
Churn	E. Hoyt	Stamford, Conn	July 3, 1866	56, 050
Churn	S. Huff	New Vienna, Ohio	Apr. 24, 1849	6, 389
Churn	J. S. Huffman	Brownsburgh, Va	May 25, 1869	90, 544
Churn	A. Humphrey	Gray, Me	May 9, 1825	....
Churn	W. Humphrey	Ohio	Jan. 5, 1814	....
Churn	G. W. Hurst	Chestertown, Md	Apr. 9, 1867	63, 639
Churn	S. Hutchings and J. D. Leach	Penobscot, Me	Aug. 14, 1860	29, 597
Churn	C. Hutchins	Baldwin City, Kans	Oct. 1, 1872	131, 821
Churn	P. Hutchinson	Boston, Mass	Nov. 26, 1867	71, 489
Churn	T. H. Hutchinson	Gorham, N. H	Jan. 19, 1869	85, 933
Churn	H. Hutchison	Three Rivers, Mich	July 18, 1865	48, 815
Churn	A. Huyck	Our Town, Wis	June 18, 1867	65, 915
Churn	D. Hyde	Bridgeport, N. Y	Oct. 22, 1867	69, 998
Churn	B. Illingworth	Freeport, Ill	Sept. 11, 1866	57, 913
Churn	B. Illingworth	Freeport, Ill	Jan. 28, 1868	73, 895
Churn	W. L. Imlay	Philadelphia, Pa	Sept. 26, 1865	50, 129
Churn	J. Irving	Boston, Mass	Apr. 30, 1816	....
Churn	J. Jackson	Coopersville, Mich	June 20, 1871	116, 194
Churn	W. Jackson and J. Clarke	Syracuse, N. Y	May 7, 1861	32, 250
Churn	J. N. Jacobs	Crittenden, Ky	Mar. 1, 1870	100, 412
Churn	H. E. James	West Alexandria, Pa	May 11, 1869	90, 002
Churn	J. C. Jay and J. Younce	Wabash, Ind	June 4, 1867	65, 488
Churn	T. A. Jebb	Buffalo, N. Y	Nov. 15, 1859	26, 109
Churn	T. A. Jebb	Buffalo, N. Y	July 2, 1861	32, 697
Churn	F. A. Jewett	Shrewsbury, Mass	June 16, 1868	78, 877
Churn	D. Johnson	New York, N. Y	Sept. 14, 1858	21, 501
Churn	J. C. Johnson	Uniontown, Pa	July 9, 1872	128, 730
Churn	J. B. Johnston	Saint Matthews, Ky	Jan. 25, 1870	99, 206
Churn	G. Jones	Grand Rapids, Mich	June 1, 1869	90, 665
Churn	L. Jones	Canton, Conn	Dec. 10, 1808	
Churn	J. A. Jordan	Shelbyville, Tenn	Mar. 30, 1858	19, 782
Churn	J. A. Jordan	Shelbyville, Tenn	Dec. 19, 1871	122, 026
Churn	J. W. Jordan	Lexington, Va	Dec. 13, 1870	110, 047
Churn	R. Justis	Dublin, Ind	Jan. 21, 1862	34, 208
Churn	R. Keeso	Cardington, Ohio	June 13, 1865	48, 182
Churn	R. Keese	Bennington, Ohio	Apr. 9, 1867	63, 728
Churn	J. W. Kelberg	Pittsburgh, Pa	Oct. 16, 1860	30, 409

Index of patents issued from the United States Patent Office from 1790 to 1873, inclusive—Continued.

Invention.	Inventor.	Residence.	Date.	No.
Churn	J. D. Kellogg, jr	Northampton, Mass	Sept. 4, 1866	57, 730
Churn	W. Kelly	Hastings, Mich	May 24, 1859	24, 127
Churn	W. C. Kemp	Palmyra, Mo	Sept. 14, 1869	94, 753
Churn	E. Kenney	Livermore, Me	Sept. 19, 1865	50, 009
Churn	J. Kepler	Crawfordsville, Ind	June 2, 1868	78, 526
Churn	S. A. Kerr	Arbor Hill, Va	June 19, 1860	28, 757
Churn	J. J. Kimball	Naperville, Ill	May 2, 1871	114, 306
Churn	M. W. Kilgore	Baltimore, Md	Nov. 19, 1867	71, 182
Churn	P. Killin	Mount Healthy, Ohio	July 12, 1864	43, 513
Churn	P. Killin	Mount Healthy, Ohio	Aug. 30, 1864	43, 999
Churn	A. Kindermann	Cleveland, Ohio	July 13, 1869	92, 458
Churn	W. E. Kinert	Bluffton, Ind	Dec. 29, 1868	85, 452
Churn	J. King	Suckasunny, N. J	Jan. 5, 1869	85, 594
Churn	J. King	Suckasunny, N. J	Sept. 14, 1869	94, 830
Churn	S. P. Kingsley	Springfield, Wis	May 28, 1867	65, 234
Churn	N. S. Kinyon	Chenango Forks, N. Y	Jan. 22, 1867	61, 436
Churn	L. Kittinger and L. Ruch	Canal Fulton, Ohio	July 2, 1872	128, 549
Churn	J. Klingensmith	Warren, Ohio	Nov. 30, 1869	97, 413
Churn	C. B. Knowles	Fayette, Me	Aug. 2, 1832	....
Churn	A. Köhler and M. W. Wilson	Noblesville, Ind	Jan. 19, 1869	86, 083
Churn	H. Kuhlmann	Cincinnati, Ohio	Aug. 30, 1870	106, 836
Churn	A. Ladd	Saint Lawrence, N. Y	Oct. 4, 1870	108, 035
Churn	H. R. Ladd	Orwell, Ohio	May 19, 1863	38, 587
Churn	L. Lake	Middlebury, Pa	July 19, 1859	24, 845
Churn	L. Lamb	Berlin, Conn	Sept. 2, 1856	15, 661
Churn	W. Lamb	Rochelle, Ill	Mar. 24, 1868	75, 772
Churn	J. Lane	Homer, N. Y	May 15, 1815	....
Churn	S. S. Langdon	Cleveland, Ohio	Aug. 16, 1859	25, 126
Churn	W. W. Lapham	Decatur, Ill	Oct. 18, 1864	44, 732
Churn	R. Lapham and R. P. Wilson	New York, N. Y	Feb. 8, 1859	22, 879
Churn	B. U Lapish	Durham, N. H	Aug. 15, 1809	....
Churn	P. C. Lamb	Allentown, Pa	Mar. 31, 1868	76, 206
Churn	S. Leach	Wilbraham, Mass	June 1, 1869	90, 758
Churn	L. Leavenworth	Trumansburgh, N. Y	Mar. 18, 1856	14, 458
Churn	H. Leber	Bellfair Mills, Va	Sept. 15, 1868	82, 235
Churn	C. H. Lee	Oskaloosa, Iowa	Nov. 12, 1867	70, 725
Churn	J. Lees	Racine, Wis	Oct. 28, 1862	36, 787
Churn	S. F. Lefler	Racine, Wis	Jan. 5, 1858	19, 034
Churn	J. J. Lehaye	Reading, Pa	Aug. 16, 1859	25, 162
Churn	G. H. Lenher	Richmond, Va	Dec. 11, 1866	60, 391
Churn	E. C. Leonard	Binghamton, N. Y	June 12, 1866	55, 508
Churn	J. S. Lewis	Elkport, Iowa	June 7, 1870	103, 898
Churn	P. F. Lewis	Columbus, Pa	Apr. 20, 1869	89, 155
Churn	J. Liebhaber	Bless, Bavaria	Apr. 21, 1868	76, 928
Churn	G. Lightfoot	Elgin, Ill	Dec. 9, 1856	16, 210
Churn	F. A. Lindal	Stockton, N. Y	Dec. 14, 1869	97, 937
Churn	N. H. Lindley	Redding, Conn	Aug. 25, 1842	2, 758
Churn	N. H. Lindley and W. Perry	Redding and Bridgeport, Conn.	Mar. 10, 1843	2, 993
Churn	W. H. Link	Shanesville, Ohio	Oct. 10, 1871	119, 870
Churn	T. Ling	Portland, Me	Aug. 21, 1844	3, 714
Churn	N. B. Livingston	Portland, Ind	July 6, 1852	9, 097
Churn	A. Lloyd	Millersburgh, Ill	Sept. 7, 1869	94, 619
Churn	J. A. Lloyd	Saint Paul, Minn	June 30, 1863	39, 055
Churn	M. Lockwood	Cuba, N. Y	Nov. 26, 1872	133, 462
Churn	T. E. Lockwood	Cincinnati, Ohio	July 17, 1866	56, 425
Churn	M. C. Longacre	Cleveland, Ohio	Feb. 5, 1861	31, 355
Churn	W. Loomis	Ashford, Conn	June 7, 1832	....
Churn	A. D. Lord	Bethany, N. Y	Aug. 20, 1872	130, 730
Churn	P. S. Lowell	Farmington, Me	May 29, 1835	....
Churn	D. Lown	Poughkeepsie, N. Y	Nov. 3, 1868	83, 779
Churn	S. D. Lucas	Winterpock, Va	Sept. 21, 1869	95, 029
Churn	J. Luccock and J. M. Gowdy	Peoria, Ill	Apr. 29, 1862	35, 101
Churn	E. Lynch	Buffalo, N. Y	Apr. 10, 1860	27, 864
Churn	H. N. Mackey	Morgantown, Va	Apr. 28, 1857	17, 159
Churn	H. H. Macklin	New Springfield, Ohio	Oct. 22, 1867	70, 009
Churn	J. O. Maclaskey	Perth Amboy, N. J	Dec. 27, 1870	110, 616
Churn	J. Macnish	Berlin, Wis	Apr. 20, 1858	20, 025
Churn	J. Macnish	Berlin, Wis	July 6, 1858	20, 803
Churn	J. Macnish	Berlin, Wis	July 6, 1858	20, 804
Churn	R. Mahr	New York, N. Y	Nov. 19, 1867	71, 029
Churn	D. L. Main	Brooklyn, Mich	Aug. 25, 1868	81, 518
Churn	C. A. Maltby	Roland, Ill	July 5, 1870	104, 972
Churn	P. J. Manning	Troy, Ill	Sept. 21, 1869	95, 124
Churn	G. W. Manson	Buxton, Me	Feb. 12, 1867	62, 046
Churn	J. A. Marden	Boston, Mass	Oct. 29, 1872	132, 591
Churn	M. R. Marcell	Dansville, N. Y	July 27, 1858	21, 010
Churn	J. A. Marine	Mooresville, Ind	Mar. 19, 1872	124, 841
Churn	T. R. Markillie	Winchester, Ill	Aug. 27, 1861	33, 154
Churn	J. L Marsh	Centreville, Ind	Mar. 9, 1869	87, 691
Churn	D. Marshall	Genoa, N. Y	June 5, 1866	55, 320
Churn	J. Masten	Lee, Ohio	Oct. 21, 1873	143, 919
Churn	C. Matheney	Greensburgh, Ind	Dec. 6, 1870	109, 919
Churn	W. D. Matthews	Columbia, Tenn	Nov. 6, 1866	59, 428
Churn	J. Mayes	Oxford, N. Y	May 14, 1872	126, 725
Churn	J. Mayhew	West Tisbury, Mass	July 19, 1870	105, 471
Churn	J. Maxey	Kewanna, Ind	Dec. 17, 1867	72, 310
Churn	R. Maxwell	Lewis County, Va	Aug. 24, 1852	9, 218
Churn	M. A. McAfee	Talbotton, Ga	Mar. 30, 1869	88, 399
Churn	J. McBride	Ithaca, N. Y	Feb. 7, 1871	111, 555
Churn	W. H. McClintock	Frankfort, Ohio	May 31, 1859	24, 223
Churn	J. McCoord	Washington, N. Y	June 13, 1809	....
Churn	R. B. McCormick	Bloomington, Ill	Apr. 9, 1872	125, 601
Churn	R. T. McCormick	Greencastle Junction, Ind	Aug. 23, 1870	106, 599
Churn	W. R. McCutcheon	Washington, Iowa	Sept. 11, 1866	57, 942
Churn	W. R. McCutcheon	Washington, Iowa	June 4, 1867	65, 496
Churn	J. McElroy	Allegheny City, Pa	Aug. 10, 1869	93, 462
Churn	W. D. McFadden	Senatobia, Miss	Feb. 23, 1869	87, 185

Index of patents issued from the United States Patent Office from 1790 *to* 1873, *inclusive*—Continued.

Invention.	Inventor.	Residence.	Date.	No.
Churn	H. B. McFall	Mount Solon, Va	June 7, 1870	103, 908
Churn	G. H. McGlothlen	Chariton, Iowa	Aug. 30, 1870	106, 848
Churn	W. McKeever	Staunton, Va	May 7, 1872	126, 560
Churn	J. McKenzie	Portland, Me	Aug. 27, 1867	68, 097
Churn	J. J. McLane	Sagetown, Ill	June 9, 1868	78, 809
Churn	J. McLaughlin	Goshen, Ohio	July 13, 1852	9, 117
Churn	W. S. McManus and R. S. Merryman.	Brunswick, Me	June 1, 1869	90, 674
Churn	E. McMillan, jr	Wilmington, Ohio	Nov. 20, 1866	59, 802
Churn	D. C. McNeil	De Witt, Iowa	Sept. 3, 1867	68, 523
Churn	A. H. McWaine	Shickshinny, Pa	Dec. 28, 1869	98, 288
Churn	G. McWilliams	Fostoria, Ohio	Jan. 7, 1868	73, 023
Churn	J. Megown	New London, Mo	Mar. 19, 1867	63, 074
Churn	J. H. Mendenhall	Cerro Gordo, Ind	Sept. 4, 1866	57, 750
Churn	J. P. Meranda	Springfield, Ohio	July 19, 1870	105, 475
Churn	S. H. Merridith	Oxford, Ohio	Feb. 9, 1864	41, 525
Churn	D. C. Merrill	South Paris, Me	Mar. 26, 1867	63, 282
Churn	J. O. Merrill	Chichester, N. H	May 10, 1859	23, 986
Churn	C. Merriman, jr	Middletown, Conn	Apr. 21, 1836	....
Churn	C. Messenger	Cleveland, Ohio	Mar. 23, 1869	88, 156
Churn	W. P. and H. T. Messick	Clarkesville, Tex	Sept. 24, 1872	131, 623
Churn	J. Mewhinney	Liberty Township, Ohio	July 30, 1831	....
Churn	J. R. Mickey	Waterford, Pa	Feb. 26, 1861	31, 554
Churn	J. R. Mickey	Chicago Ill	Sept. 18, 1866	58, 192
Churn	J. L. Middleton	Zanesville, Ohio	Sept. 1, 1868	81, 810
Churn	C. J. Miller, jr	Richmond, Ky	Nov. 9, 1869	96, 604
Churn	F. Miller	Frostburgh, Md	Nov. 23, 1869	97, 103
Churn	M. B. Miller	Peoria County, Ill	Mar. 30, 1869	88, 320
Churn	I. Millington	Warren, N. Y	Mar. 2, 1809	....
Churn	A. J. Mills	Scott, N. Y	Feb. 5, 1867	61, 850
Churn	M. B. Mills	East Mendon, N. Y	Aug. 27, 1867	68, 100
Churn	S. Mills	Clinton, Ill	June 9, 1868	78, 812
Churn	J. Mitchell	Gasport, N. Y	Mar. 8, 1859	23, 186
Churn	J. Mitchell	Aleppo Township, Pa	Apr. 17, 1860	27, 927
Churn	J. E. Mitchell	Paris, Canada	Dec. 10, 1872	133, 717
Churn	J. H. Monce	Hopkinsville, Ohio	June 23, 1868	79, 244
Churn	O. F. Montfort	Dearborn, Mich	July 11, 1871	116, 855
Churn	H. H. Montgomery	Greensburgh, Ind	Sept. 26, 1871	119, 387
Churn	A. Moe	Plainfield, N. J	Aug. 17, 1869	93, 827
Churn	S. Moon, jr	Downingtown, Pa	Oct. 24, 1808	....
Churn	L. Mooney	Allegheny City, Pa	Nov. 27, 1866	60, 035
Churn	M. Moses	Malone, N. Y	Dec. 10, 1872	133, 878
Churn	J. Moran	Millport, Pa	Oct. 8, 1872	132, 096
Churn	C. R. Morehouse	Cardington, Ohio	Nov. 21, 1865	51, 073
Churn	E. Morgan	French Creek, N. Y	Dec. 7, 1869	97, 674
Churn	W. Morgan	Middlebrook, Va	Mar. 20, 1860	27, 559
Churn	T. and L. Morrison	Groton, N. Y	Oct. 16, 1829	....
Churn	M. Morse and P. W. Sawyer	Gray, Me	Apr. 14, 1868	76, 649
Churn	G. W. Moster and E. C. Packer.	Alliance, Ohio	Jan. 19, 1869	86, 094
Churn	H. Mott	Bellevue, Mich	May 8, 1866	54, 583
Churn	J. Moyers	Hillsborough, Ohio	Sept. 13, 1870	107, 284
Churn	A. P. Moyers, I. Searles, and G. W. Spencer.	Prattsville, N. Y	June 17, 1862	35, 620
Churn	S. W. Mudge	Rome, N. Y	Sept. 10, 1861	33, 262
Churn	S. W. Mudge	Rome, N. Y	Nov. 5, 1861	36, 659
Churn	H. Mumford	Ulster County, N. Y	Mar. 28, 1811	....
Churn	C. Murdock	Baltimore, Md	Feb. 20, 1849	6, 133
Churn	R. Murphy	Jasper, N. Y	July 5, 1864	43, 423
Churn	R. Murphy	Jasper, N. Y	Feb. 16, 1869	86, 999
Churn	J. W. Myers	Lyons, Iowa	Apr. 30, 1867	64, 348
Churn	J. Neal	Sheboygan, Wis	June 4, 1867	65, 417
Churn	M. Neal	Kalamazoo, Mich	Oct. 25, 1864	44, 836
Churn	M. Neal	Kalamazoo, Mich	Jan. 30, 1866	52, 313
Churn	J. L. Nelson	Lewisburgh, W. Va	Aug. 10, 1869	93, 550
Churn	W. Newberry	Clarksville, Mo	Oct. 29, 1867	70, 249
Churn	A. Newbrough	Madisonville, Ky	Aug. 1, 1865	49, 138
Churn	D. Newbrough	Clarksburgh, Ind	Mar. 6, 1860	27, 377
Churn	W. Newbrough	Mohican, Ohio	Apr. 15, 1856	14, 677
Churn	A. A. Newman	Sparta, Ill	Aug. 29, 1865	49, 646
Churn	E. P. Newman	New Albany, Ind	May 12, 1868	77, 753
Churn	J. L. Nettleton	West Cheshire, Conn	June 15, 1869	91, 360
Churn	H. A. Nevers and C. Ross	Claremont, N. H	Nov. 20, 1860	30, 686
Churn	J. P. Nichols	New Richmond, Ohio	Jan. 11, 1870	98, 703
Churn	H. C. Nicholson	Mount Washington, Ohio	June 2, 1857	17, 444
Churn	T. Nicholson	Nelson County, Ky	Aug. 10, 1809	....
Churn	T. Nicholson	New Market, Va	Mar. 31, 1836	....
Churn	A. S. Norcross	Hallowell, Me	Sept. 19, 1834	....
Churn	T. S. Nutter	Harrisburgh, Ohio	Aug. 3, 1869	93, 219
Churn	S. J. O'Brien	New York	Dec. 22, 1829	....
Churn	J. O'Donald	Clinton, Ill	Jan. 16, 1866	52, 066
Churn	J. Oothoudt	Lebanon, N. Y	Nov. 10, 1829	....
Churn	J. Oothoudt	Minneapolis, Minn	Aug. 4, 1868	80, 658
Churn	J. H. Ormsby and R. S. Harton	Holden, Mo	June 14, 1870	104, 191
Churn	D. Osborn	Berkshire County, Mass	Jan. 8, 1810	....
Churn	D. Osgood, jr	Blue Hill, Me	July 9, 1838	831
Churn	J. E. Overaker	Redwood, N. Y	Apr. 6, 1869	88, 662
Churn	S. R. Owen	Stewartsville, Mo	Dec. 15, 1868	85, 026
Churn	R. D. Ozburn	Lena, Ill	Sept. 7, 1869	94, 506
Churn	J. Paff	Eden, N. Y	July 17, 1860	29, 189
Churn	E. Page	Streetsborough, Ohio	Feb. 9, 1858	19, 310
Churn	G. N. Palmer	Greene, N. Y	Aug. 31, 1869	94, 435
Churn	G. N. Palmer	Greene, N. Y	Apr. 26, 1870	102, 425
Churn	J. T. Palmer	Greencastle, Ind	Sept. 13, 1864	44, 216
Churn	S. M. Palmer	Greene, N. Y	Jan. 30, 1872	123, 289
Churn	V. Palmer	Castalia, Ohio	Dec. 11, 1866	60, 414
Churn	J. Park	Joliet, Ill	July 31, 1860	29, 397
Churn	T. B. Parke	Near Downieville, Cal	June 27, 1871	116, 348
Churn	J. Parker	Biddeford, Me	June 10, 1862	35, 540

Index of patents issued from the United States Patent Office from 1790 *to* 1873, *inclusive*—Continued.

Invention.	Inventor.	Residence.	Date.	No.
Churn	J. R. Parker	Sing Sing, N. Y	May 31, 1859	24, 233
Churn	R. Parker	North Cohocton, N. Y	Sept. 3, 1861	33, 214
Churn	W. Parks	Meadville, Pa	Feb. 7, 1871	111, 562
Churn	J. D. Parrot	Morristown, N. J	Nov. 13, 1866	59, 637
Churn	A. Patterson	Birmingham, Pa	Mar. 1, 1859	23, 111
Churn	M. Payne	Cardington, Ohio	Dec. 9, 1862	37, 106
Churn	T. Payne	Grand Rapids, Mich	Dec. 24, 1867	72, 535
Churn	A. Pease	Weston, Vt	Sept. 16, 1856	15, 741
Churn	J. N. Pease	Panama, N. Y	Mar. 7, 1865	46, 695
Churn	L. P. Pease	Mount Carmel, Ill	Oct. 16, 1855	13, 686
Churn	R. H. Peck	Wolcott, Vt	Nov. 26, 1861	33, 815
Churn	W. C. Peck	Wheeling, W. Va	Oct. 1, 1867	69, 475
Churn	J. Pelsor	Brooklyn, Ill	Dec. 24, 1867	72, 673
Churn	P. Penington	Union City, Ind	July 7, 1868	79, 773
Churn	W. H. Pennock	Mermaid, Del	May 24, 1870	103, 364
Churn	G. S. Perfater	Camp Point, Ill	Mar. 28, 1871	113, 089
Churn	H. Phelps	Williston, Vt	July 21, 1835	....
Churn	E. J. Phillips	Prescott, Wis	Apr. 11, 1865	47, 219
Churn	E. H. Philo	Half Moon, N. Y	June 9, 1863	38, 865
Churn	H. C. Pierce	Homer, N. Y	Apr. 29, 1862	35, 110
Churn	T. Pierce	Hartwick, N. Y	Nov. 10, 1841	2, 343
Churn	D. Pierpont	New Haven, Conn	Apr. 22, 1808	....
Churn	J. Pike	Syracuse, N. Y	Dec. 18, 1860	30, 930
Churn	J. G. Pike	Lisbon, N. Y	Apr. 28, 1838	719
Churn	A. J. Pope	Strongsville, Ohio	Dec. 4, 1866	60, 240
Churn	E. Porter	Tallmadge, Ohio	June 7, 1864	43, 040
Churn	E. Porter	Tallmadge, Ohio	Oct. 15, 1867	69, 934
Churn	R. Porter	Bellerica, Mass	May 10, 1838	735
Churn	S. T. W. Potter	Scott, N. Y	June 5, 1866	55, 360
Churn	A. M. Powell	Collinsville, Ill	June 22, 1869	91, 562
Churn	S. Power	Lawrenceville, Pa	June 23, 1832	....
Churn	E. L. Pratt	Philadelphia, Pa	Aug. 30, 1859	25, 306
Churn	D. K. Price	Ossian, N. Y	Jan. 19, 1864	41, 322
Churn	I. T. Price	Leesville, Ohio	Sept. 25, 1866	58, 288
Churn	J. F. Quimby	Stetson, Me	Apr. 17, 1866	54, 013
Churn	A. Ralston	West Middletown, Pa	Sept. 21, 1858	21, 575
Churn	B. Randall	North Pownal, Me	Mar. 11, 1835	....
Churn	D. B. Randall	West Glover, Vt	Mar. 27, 1866	53, 487
Churn	J. Rankin	New York, N. Y	Apr. 4, 1865	47, 129
Churn	J. Rankin	New York, N. Y	Jan. 16, 1866	52, 075
Churn	J. Rankin	New York, N. Y	Mar. 20, 1866	53, 335
Churn	J. Rankin and J. N. McIntire	New York, N. Y	June 21, 1864	43, 227
Churn	F. Ransom	Buffalo, N. Y	Aug. 30, 1864	44, 015
Churn	G. S. Rarey	Columbus, Ohio	Apr. 27, 1858	20, 089
Churn	J. B. Raynor	Mazo Manie, Wis	Feb. 25, 1868	74, 941
Churn	A. Reed	Columbia County, N. Y	Apr. 25, 1808	....
Churn	J. H. Reed	La Fayette, Ind	Jan. 3, 1871	110, 678
Churn	C. C. Reese	Attica, Ind	June 16, 1868	79, 002
Churn	W. W. Reid	Rochester, N. Y	Oct. 16, 1860	30, 424
Churn	J. K. Reiner	Line Lexington, Pa	Nov. 27, 1866	60, 058
Churn	J. Rengel	Lancaster, N. Y	Dec. 17, 1872	134, 100
Churn	J. L. Ressler	Ramsburgh, Pa	Sept. 7, 1869	94, 645
Churn	T. Rettew	West Vincent Township, Pa.	Nov. 5, 1867	70, 470
Churn	E. Reynolds	Omro, Wis	Sept. 7, 1869	94, 646
Churn	A. Rhoades	Pontiac, Mich	June 6, 1865	48, 096
Churn	C. Rhodes	Morrow, Ohio	May 18, 1852	8, 959
Churn	H. Rice	Youngstown, Ohio	Sept. 13, 1864	44, 219
Churn	T. Rich	Kingston, N. Y	Apr. 14, 1868	76, 815
Churn	I. S. Richardson	Boston, Mass	June 10, 1851	8, 146
Churn	J. C. Richardson and L. Taylor	Prairie du Chien and Jordan, Wis.	Oct. 25, 1870	108, 631
Churn	J. Ricker	Bangor, Me	Aug. 9, 1834	....
Churn	J. Rickey	Centre Township, Ohio	Oct. 25, 1832	....
Churn	J. Risher	Delaware, Ohio	Dec. 24, 1867	72, 682
Churn	S. Risler	Locktown, N. J	Dec. 14, 1869	97, 815
Churn	S. Risler	Locktown, N. J	Nov. 29, 1870	109, 759
Churn	J. L. Riter and R. C. Swann	Brownsville, Ind	Apr. 30, 1867	64, 367
Churn	F. W. Robbins	Solon, Ohio	Dec. 3, 1867	71, 645
Churn	Z. C. Robbins	Saint Louis, Mo	June 26, 1849	6, 556
Churn	Z. C. Robbins	Saint Louis, Mo	Jan. 8, 1850	7, 066
Churn	C. H. L. Roberts	Morrison, Ill	Apr. 23, 1867	64, 149
Churn	F. L. Roberts	Jacksonville, Ill	Nov. 16, 1869	96, 967
Churn	H. Roberts	Seneca Falls, N. Y	Feb. 5, 1836	....
Churn	H. and R. V. Robie	Eaton, N. Y	Nov. 16, 1858	22, 090
Churn	D. Robinson	Franklin, N. Y	May 3, 1811	....
Churn	F. J. Robinson	Laconia, N. H	Apr. 10, 1866	53, 876
Churn	J. J. Robinson	Clinton, Ill	Dec. 5, 1865	51, 354
Churn	W. Robinson	Bellefontaine, Ohio	Dec. 23, 1862	37, 244
Churn	W. Robinson	Bellefontaine, Ohio	Oct. 24, 1865	50, 631
Churn	W. C. Robinson	Saltsburgh, Pa	Feb. 25, 1868	74, 943
Churn	H. Rohrer	Strasburgh Township, Lancaster County, Pa.	Dec. 6, 1859	26, 377
Churn	A. Rose	Penn Yan, N. Y	June 29, 1858	20, 730
Churn	A. A. Rose	Binghamton, N. Y	Feb. 26, 1867	62, 502
Churn	T. Rose	Cortlandville, N. Y	June 17, 1862	35, 628
Churn	T. Rose	Cortlandville, N. Y	Apr. 7, 1868	76, 350
Churn	L. Rosenkrans	Urbana, N. Y	May 19, 1827	....
Churn	A. A. Ross	Horicon, N. Y	July 28, 1868	80, 507
Churn	N. D. Ross	Braintrim, Pa	June 5, 1860	28, 607
Churn	R. F. Ross	Marshall County, Miss	Feb. 22, 1870	100, 076
Churn	T. Ross	Pickaway, Ohio	Jan. 26, 1831	....
Churn	J. H. Roundey	Old Town, Me	June 25, 1867	66, 042
Churn	J. H. Rowe	Fort Wayne, Ind	June 16, 1868	79, 008
Churn	J. H. Rowley	Vanceburgh, Ky	Dec. 10, 1867	72, 087
Churn	M. V. B. Rowley	Worcester, N. Y	Sept. 17, 1867	69, 029
Churn	W. M. Rumrill	Roanoke, Ind	Mar. 23, 1869	88, 078
Churn	H. D. Rumsey	Homer, N. Y	Sept. 10, 1867	68, 655
Churn	J. B. Rumsey	Port Huron, Mich	Jan. 28, 1868	73, 932

Index of patents issued from the United States Patent Office from 1790 *to* 1873, *inclusive*—Continued.

Invention.	Inventor.	Residence.	Date.	No.
Churn	L. Runyon	Newark, N. Y	Oct. 17, 1871	120, 103
Churn	E. P. Russell	Manlius, N. Y	Nov. 3, 1868	83, 664
Churn	E. W. Russell	Ashley, Mo	Oct. 15, 1867	69, 843
Churn	J. L. Rust	Oquaka Junction, Ill	July 3, 1866	56, 103
Churn	J. L. Rust	Keithburgh, Ill	July 11, 1871	116, 871
Churn	I. F. Ryerson	Pierceton, Ind	Feb. 27, 1866	52, 890
Churn	H. Saggan	Newark, N. J	Oct. 11, 1870	108, 297
Churn	C. W. Saladee	Newark, Ohio	Jan. 19, 1869	85, 967
Churn	G. H. Sanborn	Boston, Mass	Aug. 28, 1866	57, 573
Churn	J. F. Sanborn	Hardwick, Vt	June 27, 1865	48, 449
Churn	W. W. Sanborn	Lyons City, Iowa	May 21, 1867	65, 014
Churn	J. Sangster	Buffalo, N. Y	Mar. 20, 1860	27, 570
Churn	J. R. Sapp	Danville, Ohio	Aug. 2, 1870	106, 079
Churn	S. E. Saul	New York, N. Y	Apr. 4, 1865	47, 134
Churn	H. Saxton	Paris, N. Y	Nov. 6, 1829	....
Churn	G. W. Sayre	Pisgah, Ohio	Aug. 9, 1864	43, 797
Churn	J. B. Schermerhorn	New York, N. Y	June 5, 1844	3, 616
Churn	C. Schifferly	Bourbon, Ind	Jan. 7, 1868	73, 125
Churn	A. Schlingman, D. Glander, and J. Campbell.	West Alexandria, Ohio	Nov. 3, 1868	83, 732
Churn	J. B. Schuette	Lockington, Ohio	Apr. 5, 1870	101, 666
Churn	H. Schültdrees	Brookville, Ind	Apr. 25, 1871	114, 050
Churn	L. Scott	Burgettstown, Pa	May 19, 1868	78, 139
Churn	J. C. Scribner	Holderness, N. H	Mar. 20, 1866	53, 352
Churn	J. F. Seaman	Cortlandville, N. Y	May 29, 1866	55, 169
Churn	A. G. Searls	Cleveland, Ohio	Mar. 25, 1862	34, 784
Churn	D. W. Seeley	Albany, N. Y	Aug. 27, 1861	33, 164
Churn	O. Seely	Syracuse, N. Y	Nov. 22, 1864	45, 182
Churn	O. W. Seely	Buffalo, N. Y	Aug. 28, 1866	57, 582
Churn	J. W. Sefton	Gettysburgh, Pa	Mar. 20, 1866	53, 380
Churn	J. S. Severance	Homer, N. Y	Feb. 20, 1866	52, 767
Churn	A. M. Seymour, jr	Madison, Wis	Dec. 3, 1867	71, 652
Churn	L. W. Shaeffer	West Milton, Ohio	Sept. 10, 1867	68, 798
Churn	A. Shaffer	Vandalia, Mich	Apr. 4, 1871	113, 580
Churn	S. G. Shanks	Richmond, Ky	July 12, 1870	105, 262
Churn	Z. B. Shannon	Port Washington, Ohio	Oct. 30, 1866	59, 282
Churn	J. Shappell	Lynnville, Pa	Dec. 20, 1870	110, 296
Churn	J. Shaver	Lawrence, Ill	Aug. 8, 1871	117, 821
Churn	B. W. Shaw and G. A. Simmons	Morristown, Vt	Mar. 3, 1868	75, 205
Churn	C. A. Shaw	Biddeford, Me	Dec. 9, 1856	16, 193
Churn	E. F. Shaw	Wyoming, Mich	July 14, 1868	80, 021
Churn	J. and W. A. Shaw	Hinkley, Ohio	Sept. 22, 1868	82, 356
Churn	T. D. Shaw	Westfield, Ohio	Jan. 15, 1867	61, 268
Churn	A. Sheble	Philadelphia, Pa	Nov. 27, 1811	....
Churn	D. Shelden	Pultney, N. Y	Sept. 13, 1827	
Churn	N. Shelton	Odessa, N. Y	Feb. 15, 1870	99, 960
Churn	J. H. Shepard	Canaan, Mass	Oct. 1, 1811	....
Churn	N. H. Sherburne	Campton, Ill	July 13, 1858	20, 898
Churn	D. Sherman and R. W. Fenwick.	Uniontown, Md., and Washington, D. C.	July 31, 1860	29, 445
Churn	H. Shively and R. S. McEwen	Fredericksburgh, Ohio	Mar. 6, 1830	....
Churn	R. W. Shriner	Woodland, Mich	Jan. 1, 1867	60, 946
Churn	A. Shuffert and G. Cooper	Wyandotte, Mich	May 26, 1868	78, 398
Churn	F. Shurr and J. Palmer	Milwaukee, Wis	Jan. 2, 1866	51, 873
Churn	R. L. Shute	Philadelphia, Pa	Nov. 14, 1865	50, 963
Churn	H. Sidle	Dillsburgh, Pa	Nov. 26, 1861	33, 802
Churn	H. Sidle	Minneapolis, Minn	June 25, 1867	66, 178
Churn	I. J. Siler	Arcanum, Ohio	Jan. 21, 1868	73, 659
Churn	J. Simpson	Libertyville, Ill	June 1, 1869	90, 882
Churn	H. Skinner	Attica, N. Y	Dec. 16, 1851	8, 596
Churn	J. C. Slaughter	Crumpton, Md	May 12, 1868	77, 926
Churn	W. Slaughter	Westerville, Ohio	Jan. 19, 1864	41, 328
Churn	A. Smith	Tyngsborough, Mass	Apr. 11, 1810	....
Churn	B. J. Smith	Osage Mission, Kans	Nov. 22, 1870	109, 556
Churn	D. Smith	Emmetsburgh, Md	Apr. 21, 1831	....
Churn	H. E. Smith	New York, N. Y	Aug. 6, 1872	130, 322
Churn	J. W. X. Smith	Independence, Iowa	Feb. 8, 1870	99, 720
Churn	S. Smith	Yohoghany, Pa	Dec. 14, 1869	97, 820
Churn	S. Smith	Clarksburgh, N. Y	Dec. 14, 1869	97, 976
Churn	T. K. Smith	Oskaloosa, Iowa	Nov. 27, 1866	60, 077
Churn	W. C. Smith	Yantic, Conn	July 9, 1867	66, 646
Churn	W. C. Smith	Yantic, Conn	Sept. 22, 1868	82, 446
Churn	J. F. Smith and W. Brown	Galena and Rose, N. Y	Aug. 31, 1858	21, 374
Churn	T. C. Smith and N. L. Francis	Oquawka, Ill	Sept. 19, 1871	119, 193
Churn	H. Soggs	Columbus, Pa	Nov. 29, 1864	45, 277
Churn	H. Soggs	Columbus, Pa	July 25, 1865	48, 987
Churn	G. Sowle and P. Brewer	Blenheim, N. Y	Mar. 22, 1830	....
Churn	E. Spain	Mount Holly, N. J	Apr. 23, 1828	....
Churn	E. Spain	Philadelphia, Pa	May 16, 1848	5, 585
Churn	E. Spain	Philadelphia, Pa	Sept. 29, 1868	82, 652
Churn	M. H. Spaulding	Morrisville, Vt	July 16, 1867	66, 901
Churn	G. Spayd	Alma, Mich	Sept. 12, 1871	118, 826
Churn	I. H. Spelman	Bazetta, Ohio	Oct. 15, 1867	69, 855
Churn	A. L. Sperry	Auburn, Ind	Aug. 30, 1859	25, 285
Churn	G. Sperry	Potter's Corners, Pa	Jan. 1, 1867	60, 952
Churn	J. Springer	Clinton, Wis	July 2, 1872	128, 512
Churn	E. N. Sprinkle	Marion, Va	Nov. 1, 1859	25, 985
Churn	S. Stackhouse	Cazenovia, N. Y	Mar. 11, 1808	....
Churn	J. Stadler and G. M. Streng	Detroit and Plymouth, Mich.	Aug. 11, 1868	80, 882
Churn	C. W. Stafford	Burlington, Iowa	Nov. 16, 1858	22, 093
Churn	O. W. Stanford	Cincinnati, Ohio	June 12, 1860	28, 696
Churn	O. W. Stanford	Lebanon, Ohio	July 3, 1866	56, 115
Churn	R. Stanley	Chariton, Ohio	Jan. 29, 1867	61, 691
Churn	C. B. Stanton	Scott, N. Y	Mar. 12, 1867	62, 899
Churn	C. C. Stearns	Bucksport, Me	Aug. 17, 1835	....
Churn	B. H. Steele	Barnesville, Ohio	May 16, 1871	114, 873
Churn	M. V. B. Stinemetz	Annville, Pa	Feb. 5, 1867	61, 7[illegible]2

Index of patents issued from the United States Patent Office from 1790 *to* 1873, *inclusive*—Continued.

Invention.	Inventor.	Residence.	Date.	No.
Churn	A. Stephens	Washington, Iowa	Nov. 29, 1864	45, 280
Churn	J. H. Stephens	Orange Court-House, Va	Mar. 23, 1869	88, 095
Churn	T. B. Stephens	Washington, Iowa	Apr. 12, 1870	101, 936
Churn	D. H. Stevens	Enosburgh Falls, Vt	Sept. 10, 1872	131, 231
Churn	G. R. Stevens	Chicago, Ill	July 7, 1868	79, 702
Churn	I. V. Stevens	Pomeroy, Ohio	Feb. 5, 1861	31, 338
Churn	J. Stilwell	Griffin, Ga	May 21, 1861	32, 388
Churn	W. W Stilwell	Oxford, Wis	Jan. 31, 1871	111, 490
Churn	V. Stirewalt	Albany, Ga	Feb. 12, 1861	31, 413
Churn	O. Stoddard	Busti, N. Y	Feb. 15, 1859	22, 989
Churn	H. C. Stoll	Mokena, Ill	Sept. 4, 1866	57, 794
Churn	S. S. Stokes	Westborough, Ohio	June 30, 1868	79, 409
Churn	W. H. Stonaker	Cooperstown, Pa	Aug. 15, 1865	49, 450
Churn	J. Stubbs	Dublin, Ind	July 5, 1859	24, 673
Churn	T. Stumm	Ada, Ohio	June 18, 1872	128, 080
Churn	A. Stump	Bodega, Cal	June 23, 1868	79, 156
Churn	C. Sweeney	East Bloomfield, N. Y	Dec. 22, 1868	85, 187
Churn	S. Sweet, jr	Readfield, Mass	June 13, 1831	....
Churn	J. B. Sweetland	Pontiac, Mich	Oct. 18, 1864	44, 755
Churn	J. B. Sweetland	Pontiac, Mich	Feb. 5, 1867	61, 892
Churn	J. G. Talbot	Sloansville, N. Y	Sept. 13, 1870	107, 306
Churn	W. H. Tambling	Mazo Manie, Wis	Mar. 12, 1867	62, 785
Churn	W. H. Tambling	Berlin, Wis	June 29, 1858	20, 740
Churn	J. Taylor	Rushville, Ill	Sept. 13, 1859	25, 453
Churn	J. G. Taylor	East Bethlehem, Pa	Sept. 10, 1867	68, 805
Churn	D. E. Teal	Norwich, N. Y	Feb. 6, 1866	52, 467
Churn	C. M. Terrell and N. W. Hussey	Oskaloosa, Iowa	Dec. 17, 1867	72, 338
Churn	J. E. Thomas	Winchester, Ohio	Feb. 12, 1836	....
Churn	J. Thompson	Vevay, Ind	Oct. 28, 1862	36, 811
Churn	J. Thompson	Vevay, Ind	Mar. 22, 1864	42, 029
Churn	J. Thompson	Vevay, Ind	Oct. 24, 1865	50, 645
Churn	J. W. Thompson	Bureau Junction, Ill	Sept. 1, 1868	81, 842
Churn	J. S. Thomson	Wyalusing, Pa	July 27, 1839	1, 265
Churn	L. Thomson	Sturbridge, Mass	June 24, 1809	....
Churn	A. E. Thorn	Fletcher, Ohio	Apr. 2, 1867	63, 580
Churn	T. J. Thorn	Skaneateles, N. Y	Jan. 30, 1866	52, 340
Churn	T. Thorne	Clinton, N. Y	Apr. 12, 1833	....
Churn	F. Thorpe	Shelbyville, Ill	Sept. 23, 1856	15, 787
Churn	W. Tibbits	La Fayette, N. Y	May 24, 1864	42, 887
Churn	J. A. Tice	Windsor, Ill	Mar. 30, 1869	88, 529
Churn	N. C. Tiffany and E. Robison	Caroline, N. Y	Dec. 14, 1830	....
Churn	W. H. Tillou and S. Shumway	Le Roy, N. Y	June 26, 1866	55, 934
Churn	J. Tingley	Waterford, N. J	Aug. 11, 1863	39, 507
Churn	J. Tingley	Philadelphia, Pa	Feb. 25, 1868	74, 954
Churn	J. Toll	Locust Grove, Ohio	Feb. 25, 1868	74, 955
Churn	E. Townsend	Canaan, N. Y	July 12, 1808	....
Churn	W. W. Townsend	Sandy Hill, N. Y	Mar. 22, 1808	....
Churn	A. Traver and P. Nichols	Troy, N. Y	Oct. 10, 1871	119, 898
Churn	D. E. True	Lake Village, N. H	Sept. 8, 1857	18, 165
Churn	W. H. Truesdell	Elgin, Ill	Dec. 22, 1857	18, 936
Churn	W. B. Tucker	Hillsborough, Ohio	Mar. 12, 1867	62, 786
Churn	W. B. Tucker	Columbus, Ohio	Dec. 1, 1868	84, 658
Churn	J. Turner	Poland, Me	Aug. 15, 1835	....
Churn	C. R. Tuttle	New Brighton, Pa	Nov. 25, 1862	37, 016
Churn	W. Twining	Philadelphia, Pa	Feb. 27, 1872	124, 176
Churn	S. Tyler	New Gloucester, Me	June 25, 1836	....
Churn	S. S. Ulrey	North Manchester, Ind	Sept. 21, 1869	95, 167
Churn	C. M. Vail	Susquehanna Depot, Pa	Feb. 16, 1858	19, 389
Churn	C. D. Van Allen	Syracuse, N. Y	July 23, 1861	32, 907
Churn	C. D. Van Allen	Syracuse, N. Y	June 17, 1862	35, 638
Churn	J. Van Aukin, 2d	Knox, N. Y	Sept. 28, 1831	....
Churn	J. Vanatter	Stratford, Canada	Jan. 16, 1872	122, 870
Churn	A. J. Vannatta	Vanatta, Ohio	Dec. 4, 1866	60, 289
Churn	J. Vandolah and E. Curry	Dillsborough, Ind	Dec. 22, 1857	18, 937
Churn	I. Van Gorder	Warren, Ohio	June 27, 1832	....
Churn	C. A. Van Horn	Chenango, N. Y	Aug. 6, 1867	67, 615
Churn	S. Van Meter	Henderson, Ill	June 28, 1870	104, 800
Churn	G. H. Van Vleck	Buffalo, N. Y	May 8, 1860	28, 219
Churn	D. Variel	Minot, Me	July 1, 1836	....
Churn	W. A. Vertrees	Winchester, Mo	Dec. 9, 1856	16, 203
Churn	J. Vincent and S. Leslie	Quasqueton, Iowa	Feb. 11, 1862	34, 383
Churn	C. Vogt and X. Krapf	Allentown, Pa	July 23, 1867	67, 085
Churn	A. Votaw	New Garden, Ohio	June 11, 1867	65, 620
Churn	G. Votee	Berlin, Conn	May 10, 1809	....
Churn	W. H. and L. Waddell	Churchville, Va	June 16, 1868	79, 035
Churn	A. C. Wade	Paris, Ill	Aug. 7, 1866	57, 051
Churn	I. M. Wade	Clinton, Mich	June 26, 1855	13, 133
Churn	A. Walker	Claremont, N. H	June 23, 1863	39, 023
Churn	M. D. Wallace	White Creek, N. Y	May 7, 1867	64, 463
Churn	G. B. Waller	Franklin, Ill	Nov. 27, 1866	60, 097
Churn, &c	M. Walton	Marlborough, Ohio	Oct. 8, 1867	69, 598
Churn	D. T. Ward	Mansfield, Ohio	Dec. 18, 1860	30, 941
Churn	D. T. Ward	Cardington, Ohio	Nov. 28, 1865	51, 246
Churn	D. T. Ward	Cardington, Ohio	Jan. 21, 1868	73, 479
Churn	E. Ward	New York, N. Y	Feb. 14, 1860	27, 175
Churn	J. S. Ward	Plattsburgh, Mo	Dec. 5, 1871	121, 560
Churn	C. Warner	Louisville, Ky	June 12, 1849	6, 527
Churn	C. D. Warner	Syracuse, N. Y	June 11, 1867	65, 623
Churn	G. W. Warren	Alma, N. Y	Apr. 20, 1869	89, 098
Churn	T. A. Warner	Gettysburgh, Pa	Apr. 16, 1867	63, 969
Churn	C. H. Warren and A. C. Baldwin.	Tiffin, Ohio	Dec. 20, 1864	45, 544
Churn	P. H. Watson	Rockford, Ill	May 16, 1848	5, 573
Churn	J. Watts	Brazil, Ind	Sept. 1, 1868	81, 716
Churn	J. H. Weaver and D. M. Mefford	Chillicothe, Ohio, and Jeffersonville, Ind.	May 19, 1863	38, 635
Churn	B. Webb	Tolland, Conn	Aug. 22, 1816	....
Churn	C. Webb	Wallingford, Conn	Nov. 26, 1840	1, 860

Index of patents issued from the United States Patent Office from 1790 *to* 1873, *inclusive*—Continued.

Invention.	Inventor.	Residence.	Date.	No.
Churn	E. Webber	Gardiner, Me	Dec. 5, 1854	12,043
Churn	H. Webster	Ogdensburgh, N. Y	Feb. 6, 1855	12,370
Churn	W. Weddington	Winterset, Iowa	July 23, 1867	67,090
Churn	F. Wegner and C. Schleeter	West Troy, N. Y	Feb. 15, 1870	99,985
Churn	M. D. Wells	Morgantown, Va	July 17, 1855	13,281
Churn	R. P. Wells	Dayton, Ohio	Feb. 8, 1870	99,612
Churn	I. M. West	Wilmington, Ohio	June 27, 1865	48,469
Churn	I. M. West	Wilmington, Del	Aug. 28, 1866	57,606
Churn	L. Westbrook	New York, N. Y	May 10, 1859	23,968
Churn	A. Westcott	Syracuse, N. Y	Jan. 7, 1862	34,082
Churn	A. Westcott	Syracuse, N. Y	Apr. 29, 1862	35,120
Churn	A. Westcott	Syracuse, N. Y	Mar. 15, 1864	41,954
Churn	A. Westcott	Syracuse, N. Y	Mar. 7, 1865	46,739
Churn	A. Westcott	Syracuse, N. Y	Feb. 27, 1866	52,919
Churn	A. Westcott	Syracuse, N. Y	June 12, 1866	55,566
Churn	A. Westcott	Syracuse, N. Y	Apr. 21, 1868	77,144
Churn	A. Westcott	Syracuse, N. Y	Dec. 8, 1868	84,784
Churn	H. P. Westcott	Seneca Falls, N. Y	Apr. 4, 1865	47,145
Churn	H. P. Westcott	Seneca Falls, N. Y	Nov. 13, 1866	59,691
Churn	I. E. Weston and A. Streeter	Winchendon, Mass	May 31, 1870	103,803
Churn	A. Wharff	New Gloucester, Me	June 16, 1836	....
Churn	S. A. Wheelock	Charlton, Mass	Sept. 2, 1862	36,379
Churn	S. J. Whipple	Orville, Cal	Jan. 21, 1868	73,556
Churn	H. Whisler	New Market, Ohio	June 5, 1866	55,407
Churn	M. Whisler	New Market, Ohio	Jan. 29, 1867	61,645
Churn	E. P. Whitcomb	Coldwater, Mich	Apr. 10, 1866	53,912
Churn	C. N. White	Batesville, Miss	Aug. 25, 1868	81,445
Churn	H. W. White	Olney, Ill	May 8, 1866	54,632
Churn	J. White	Cleveland, Ohio	Mar. 27, 1866	53,512
Churn	N. Whitney	Augusta, Me	June 7, 1827	....
Churn	R. W. Whitney	South Berwick, Me	July 7, 1863	39,205
Churn	L. Whittier	Vienna, Me	Feb. 10, 1836	....
Churn	F. Whitton	South Carrollton, Ky	Dec. 1, 1868	84,668
Churn	L. Wiard and W. H. Nelson	Spring Township, Pa	Dec. 24, 1867	72,576
Churn	L. J. Wicks	Racine, Wis	Mar. 8, 1859	23,208
Churn	L. J. Wicks	Racine, Wis	July 5, 1859	24,686
Churn	D. Wedmayer	Lansing, Mich	July 6, 1869	92,411
Churn	A. Wieting	Fort Plain, N. Y	Mar. 5, 1872	124,304
Churn	M. J. Wikoff	Stout's Post-Office, Ohio	July 26, 1870	105,751
Churn	E. Wilcox	Hamburgh, Iowa	Aug. 22, 1871	118,320
Churn	J. H. Wildasin and J. A. Peck	Saint Charles, Iowa	Sept. 14, 1869	94,802
Churn	A. G. Wilkins, G. N. Grodle, and F. L. Niner.	Cooperstown, Pa	May 25, 1869	90,414
Churn	S. B. Willard	Bloomfield, N. Y	May 18, 1808	....
Churn	D. A. Willbanks	Harmony Grove, Ga	Feb. 13, 1872	123,656
Churn	E. Willemin	Salem Township, Ohio	Oct. 25, 1832	....
Churn	C. B. Williams	Bourbon, Ind	Feb. 11, 1868	74,467
Churn	J. B. Williams	Glastenbury, Conn	May 30, 1871	115,552
Churn	R. Williams	Yonkers, N. Y	Oct. 8, 1872	132,037
Churn	A. Willson	Colden, N. Y	Feb. 14, 1860	27,181
Churn	G. W. Wilson	Freeport, Ill	Apr. 2, 1867	63,596
Churn	R. Wilson	Rees Corners, Md	Aug. 3, 1869	93,264
Churn	S. C. Wilson	Olney, Ill	Aug. 27, 1867	68,273
Churn	T. J. Wilson	New Lisbon, Ind	Jan. 23, 1872	122,978
Churn	W. E. Wilson	Central Station, W. Va	May 8, 1866	54,634
Churn	A. Wing	Washington, N. Y	May 26, 1806	....
Churn	B. L. Winner	Belvidere, Ill	Aug. 15, 1865	49,464
Churn	D. H. Wiswell	Buffalo, N. Y	Mar. 13, 1860	27,504
Churn	M. Witmer	Cedar Rapids, Iowa	Mar. 9, 1869	87,743
Churn	J. Witmore	Litchfield, Conn	Dec. 8, 1809	....
Churn	G. L. Witsil	Philadelphia, Pa	Oct. 27, 1863	40,450
Churn	G. L. Witsil	Philadelphia, Pa	Sept. 27, 1864	44,480
Churn	G. L. Witsil	Philadelphia, Pa	July 3, 1866	56,153
Churn	G. L. Witsil	Philadelphia, Pa	Apr. 30, 1867	64,393
Churn	G. Wolf	Williamsport, Md	Jan. 16, 1866	52,103
Churn	I. Wood	Fayette County, Ind	June 26, 1835	....
Churn	M. Wood	Babe's Corners, Mich	June 9, 1868	78,706
Churn	J. K. Wood and D. R. Speer	Allegheny City and Pittsburgh, Pa.	Dec. 1, 1868	84,524
Churn	D. M. Woodin	Brandon, Wis	May 29, 1860	28,528
Churn	C. Wright and W. Phelps	Sycamore, Ill	June 19, 1860	28,802
Churn	O. Wyman	Dedham, Mass	July 17, 1835	....
Churn	J. M. Yeager	Lanesville, Ind	Aug. 29, 1871	118,664
Churn	J. Young	Adrian, Ohio	July 24, 1866	56,661
Churn	C. S. Young, H. Wissinger, and T. T. Williams.	Minta, Pa	Sept. 19, 1871	119,068
Churn	C. E. Zimmerman	Cincinnati, Ohio	Aug. 11, 1868	81,056
Churn and butter-worker	O. R. Fyler	Brattleborough, Vt	July 27, 1852	9,148
Churn and butter-worker	S. L. Hall	West Salem, Mass	Aug. 4, 1868	80,624
Churn and butter-worker	A. Hawver and W. C. Hanyen	Galva, Ill	Jan. 14, 1862	34,144
Churn and butter-worker	A. Willard	Boston, Mass	Sept. 23, 1851	8,382
Churn and butter-worker combined	J. Randall	Grand Rapids, Mich	Aug. 22, 1865	49,550
Churn and butter-worker, Combined	S. H. Scribner	Stowe, Vt	Aug. 6, 1867	67,594
Churn and butter-worker combined	C. H. Smith	Boston, Mass	Jan. 19, 1869	85,970
Churn and egg-beater combined	G. C. Westover	Paducah, Ky	Jan. 22, 1867	61,494
Churn and ice-cream freezer	C. Higley	Port Byron, N. Y	June 30, 1868	79,349
Churn and ice-cream freezer	T. W. Pomeroy	East Hampton, Mass	June 26, 1866	55,960
Churn and ice-cream freezer combined	G. C. Westover	Paducah, Ky	Jan. 28, 1868	73,766
Churn and pump power	F. Danzenbaker	Bridgeton, N. J	May 21, 1867	64,950
Churn and washing-machine	J. Devotie	Vernon, N. Y	Dec. 5, 1808	....
Churn and washing-machine	H. Kingsberry	Hebron, Conn	June 26, 1830	....
Churn and washing-machine	T. Ling	Winthrop, Me	Sept. 9, 1835	....
Churn and washing machine	C. Otis	Finksburgh, Md	June 12, 1835	....
Churn and washing-machine	I. Parke	Delhi, N. Y	Jan. 16, 1835	....
Churn and washing-machine	J. M. Peirce	Mokena, Ill	Nov. 6, 1866	59,447
Churn and washing-machine	D. Read	Slaterville, N. Y	June 16, 1828	....
Churn, Apparatus for operating	P. L. Jordan	Lexington, Miss	May 4, 1871	113,435
Churn, Atmospheric	S. Ballard	Meig's Creek, Ohio	May 16, 1848	5,567

Index of patents issued from the United States Patent Office from 1790 *to* 1873, *inclusive*—Continued.

Invention.	Inventor.	Residence.	Date.	No.
Churn, Atmospheric	N. Chapin	Cortlandville, N. Y	May 9, 1848	5, 560
Churn, Atmospheric	J. C. Coult and A. B. Davis	Philadelphia, Pa	May 15, 1849	6, 457
Churn, Atmospheric	P. F. Ellicott	Philadelphia, Pa	June 25, 1850	7, 454
Churn, Atmospheric	S. F. Emerson	Canaan, Ohio	Apr. 2, 1850	7, 236
Churn, Atmospheric	S. P. Francisco	Reading, Pa	June 19, 1849	6, 544
Churn, Atmospheric	D. C. Hall	Hannibal, Mo	Apr. 14, 1868	76, 753
Churn, Atmospheric	W. H. Johnson and P. Lewis	Springfield, Ill	May 9, 1848	5, 561
Churn, Atmospheric	R. McCutcheon	Towanda, Pa	June 2, 1857	17, 439
Churn, Atmospheric	J. O'Neil	Xenia, Ohio	July 30, 1850	7, 531
Churn, Atmospheric	W. D. Prindle and C. M. York	Tiffin, Ohio	Jan. 29, 1867	61, 567
Churn, Atmospheric	J. Young	West Galway, N. Y	Jan. 22, 1850	7, 046
Churn, Atmospheric-air	E. V. Coe	Warwick, N. Y	Apr. 7, 1831	....
Churn-attachment	W. M. Pyle	Greensburgh, Ind	Mar. 27, 1866	53, 484
Churn, Balanced lever	C. Angerine	New York, N. Y	Apr. 19, 1832	....
Churn, Barrel	L. H. Muzzey	Springfield, Ohio	Mar. 22, 1864	42, 013
Churn, Barrel	S. H. Swasey	Morristown, Vt	Jan. 7, 1868	73, 134
Churn, Barrel	P. Thompson	Springfield, Ohio	Mar. 22, 1864	42, 030
Churn, beer-cooler, &c	S. S. Elder	Springfield, Ill	Dec. 18, 1866	60, 493
Churn-body	J. C. Hills	Willoughby, Ohio	May 24, 1864	42, 851
Churn, Cradle	J. Barber	Caroline, N. Y	Jan. 28, 1830	....
Churn-dasher	E. J. Ashton	Utica, Ind	Nov. 14, 1871	120, 928
Churn-dasher	A. A. Avery	Cardiff, N. Y	Mar. 19, 1867	62, 992
Churn-dasher	C. J. Baldwin	Norwalk, Ohio	Jan. 26, 1869	86, 269
Churn-dasher	A. E. Banks	Detroit, Mich	Dec. 17, 1867	72, 154
Churn-dasher	G. W. Barker	Saint John's, Mich	Dec. 9, 1873	145, 272
Churn-dasher	H. F. Bartlett	La Grange, Mo	Aug. 16, 1870	106, 453
Churn-dasher	J. W. Barton	Clifton Springs, N. Y	Feb. 18, 1868	74, 485
Churn-dasher	S. E. Bauder	Birmingham, Ohio	Oct. 11, 1870	108, 232
Churn-dasher	S. E. Bauder	Birmingham, Ohio	Mar. 12, 1872	124, 536
Churn-dasher	A. Belt	Newton, Iowa	Dec. 14, 1869	97, 859
Churn-dasher	A. T. Bleyley	Conception, Mo	Sept. 1, 1868	81, 586
Churn-dasher	F. Bosom	Saint Louis, Mich	Dec. 28, 1869	98, 221
Churn-dasher	T. Bosom	Jonesville, Mich	May 10, 1870	102, 758
Churn-dasher	D. Boyd	Vevay, Ind	Dec. 30, 1873	145, 985
Churn-dasher	A. H. Brainerd	Rome, N. Y	June 2, 1868	78, 511
Churn-dasher	I. Brewbaker	Fincastle, Va	Apr. 19, 1870	102, 084
Churn-dasher	J. A. Brooks	Madison County, Tenn	Dec. 3, 1872	133, 626
Churn-dasher	A. C. Brown	Sycamore, Ill	Apr. 14, 1863	38, 145
Churn-dasher	R. Brown	Columbus, Miss	Dec. 27, 1870	110, 429
Churn-dasher	W. C. Broyhill and W. D. Sperry	Tremont, Ill	Nov. 14, 1871	120, 849
Churn-dasher	J. M. Buchanan	Lawrenceville, Ill	May 4, 1869	89, 629
Churn-dasher	I. N. Buck	Elgin, Ill	Oct. 13, 1857	18, 382
Churn-dasher	G. Bunting	Liberty, Ind	Nov. 22, 1859	26, 226
Churn-dasher	J. Carl	Grenada, Miss	Apr. 20, 1869	89, 125
Churn-dasher	J. S. Carson	Brookhaven, Miss	Aug. 25, 1868	81, 340
Churn-dasher	J. W. Cheney and B. Ingalls	Shelbyville, Ill	June 22, 1869	91, 715
Churn-dasher	C. L. Cole	Bushnell, Ill	Mar. 9, 1869	87, 638
Churn-dasher	W. M. Combs	Auburn, N. Y	Feb. 18, 1873	136, 035
Churn dasher	I. B. Compton	Seward, Nebr	Oct. 14, 1873	143, 559
Churn-dasher	E. G. Connelly	Jasper, Ind	July 17, 1866	56, 374
Churn-dasher	N. B. Cooper	Gratis, Ohio	Nov. 8, 1859	26, 020
Churn-dasher	A. W. Cramer	Bethany, Pa	Nov. 15, 1864	45, 026
Churn-dasher	H. A. Crance	Lewisburgh, Pa	Aug. 11, 1868	80, 921
Churn dasher	R. Crawford	Mercer, Pa	Mar. 3, 1868	74, 995
Churn-dasher	T. Crutcher	Edgefield, Tenn	Dec. 21, 1869	98, 152
Churn-dasher	J. J. Cumming	Independence, Mo	Aug. 27, 1867	68, 049
Churn-dasher	M. O. Davis	Warrensburgh, N. Y	Jan. 21, 1868	73, 583
Churn-dasher	G. Deckman	Malvern, Ohio	July 31, 1866	56, 728
Churn-dasher	S. F. Dolloff	Bloomington, Ill	May 23, 1871	115, 177
Churn-dasher	G. H. Dow	Freeport, Ill	Sept. 3, 1867	68, 354
Churn-dasher	P. Edgerton	Rutland, Vt	June 14, 1870	104, 127
Churn-dasher	M. Fish	Adrian, Mich	Sept. 7, 1869	94, 586
Churn-dasher	J. M. Fletcher	Sidney, Ohio	Nov. 16, 1869	96, 906
Churn-dasher	G. R. Forsyth	Pemberton, Ohio	Feb. 19, 1867	62, 124
Churn-dasher	D. K. France	Congress, Ohio	Sept. 13, 1859	25, 494
Churn-dasher	E. H. Funk	Newark, Ohio	Sept. 15, 1868	82, 216
Churn-dasher	J. D. Garlick	Lyons, N. Y	Feb. 26, 1850	7, 118
Churn-dasher	J. Gelston	Cincinnati, Ohio	May 22, 1866	54, 891
Churn-dasher	A. J. Gibson	Cincinnati, Ohio	June 12, 1866	55, 484
Churn-dasher	W. H. H. Gorham and B. H. Williams.	Greenwich, Ohio	Aug. 23, 1870	106, 575
Churn-dasher	H. Grass	Olney, Ill	Aug. 27, 1867	68, 067
Churn-dasher	J. A. Gridley	Southampton, Mass	May 1, 1849	6, 411
Churn-dasher	D. L. Grover	Groton, N. Y	Oct. 17, 1871	119, 980
Churn-dasher	W. J. Hale	Ashley, Ill	Apr. 13, 1869	88, 957
Churn-dasher	A. W. Hall	New York, N. Y	Dec. 11, 1866	60, 363
Churn-dasher	M. A. Hamilton	Detroit, Mich	Nov. 9, 1869	96, 693
Churn-dasher	J. Harris	Palestine, Ill	Aug. 30, 1870	106, 935
Churn-dasher	M. R. Heliker	Norwalk, Ohio	Dec. 29, 1868	85, 445
Churn-dasher	G. Heliker and A. Burlen	Greenwich, Ohio	July 5, 1870	105, 074
Churn-dasher	M. Heliker and O. A. White	Norwalk, Ohio	Oct. 13, 1868	82, 947
Churn-dasher	J. M. Hill	Fairfield, Ill	July 12, 1870	105, 332
Churn-dasher	J. Hobbs	North Sandford, N. Y	Sept. 26, 1865	50, 122
Churn-dasher	A. J. Hudson	Camden, Tenn	Dec. 2, 1873	145, 107
Churn-dasher	M. B. Hudson	Canandaigua, N. Y	Apr. 9, 1867	63, 723
Churn-dasher	A. B. Hurd	Watkins, N. Y	July 23, 1867	67, 118
Churn-dasher	A. B. Hutchins	Patchogue, N. Y	Mar. 5, 1867	62, 633
Churn-dasher	S. Jackson	Jay, Me	June 11, 1836	....
Churn-dasher	M. Jincks	Steuben County, N. Y	June 30, 1863	39, 050
Churn-dasher	D. Johnson	Chicago, Ill	Apr. 11, 1865	47, 259
Churn-dasher	C. Johnston	Clarksville, Mo	Mar. 28, 1871	113, 172
Churn-dasher	W. F. Jones	Easton, Kans	Apr. 25, 1871	114, 016
Churn-dasher	W. F. Jones	Easton, Kans	May 30, 1871	115, 323
Churn-dasher	W. Kegg	Lasellsville, N. Y	Aug. 3, 1869	93, 207
Churn-dasher	J. D. Kellogg, jr	Northampton, Mass	June 9, 1868	78, 749
Churn-dasher	C. King	Scipio, N. Y	Apr. 4, 1846	4, 449
Churn-dasher	A. Kirlin	Rock Island, Ill	June 5, 1866	55, 313
Churn-dasher	G. Lange	East Saginaw, Mich	June 15, 1869	91, 454

Index of patents issued from the United States Patent Office from 1790 *to* 1873, *inclusive*— Continued.

Invention.	Inventor.	Residence.	Date.	No.
Churn-dasher	J. Leaken	Clinton, Ill	Oct. 29, 1867	70, 229
Churn-dasher	E. H. Lord and W. Thomson	Homer, N. Y	Dec. 15, 1868	84, 953
Churn dasher	M. E. J. Marr	Jefferson, La	Apr. 7, 1868	76, 484
Churn-dasher	J. Marsh	Petersburgh, Ill	July 30, 1850	7, 527
Churn-dasher	J. L. Marsh	Richmond, Ind	Feb. 11, 1868	74, 396
Churn-dasher	D. W. Mauriee	Springfield, Ohio	May 22, 1866	54, 930
Churn-dasher	A. W. McClure	Richmond, Ind	Nov. 5, 1872	132, 767
Churn-dasher	J. W. McClure	Jefferson City, Mo	May 17, 1870	103, 219
Churn-dasher	J. W. McClure	Saint Louis, Mo	May 30, 1871	115, 496
Churn-dasher	G. W. McCormick	Saint Francis County, Ark	May 27, 1873	139, 406
Churn-dasher	D. McCurdy	Ottawa, Ohio	Mar. 14, 1865	46, 810
Churn-dasher	H. McDonough	New York, N. Y	Mar. 10, 1868	75, 286
Churn-dasher	S. McGuffin	Rising Sun, Ind	Apr. 30, 1867	64, 238
Churn-dasher	F. McTarnahan	Santa Clara County, Cal	July 30, 1867	67, 205
Churn-dasher	J. B. Mellor	New Hope, Mo	Dec. 27, 1870	110, 487
Churn-dasher	D. S. Miller	West Alexandria, Ohio	June 30, 1868	79, 491
Churn-dasher	H. Mulholland	Union Mills, Pa	July 25, 1871	117, 446
Churn-dasher	L. T. Newell	Geneva, Ohio	June 14, 1870	104, 189
Churn-dasher	M. A. Ober	Chazy, N. Y	Oct. 1, 1867	69, 363
Churn-dasher	F. Ogden	Fisherville, Ky	Nov. 29, 1870	109, 654
Churn-dasher	D. K. Overhiser	Williamsport, Pa	Aug. 10, 1869	93, 471
Churn dasher	W. S. Owen	Council Bluffs, Iowa	Apr. 27, 1869	89, 497
Churn-dasher	M. J. Palmer	Homer, N. Y	Mar. 25, 1862	34, 770
Churn-dasher	M. J. Palmer and H. R. Ingalls	Homer and Groton, N. Y	Jan. 6, 1863	37, 357
Churn-dasher	B. M. Parks	Saint Louis, Mo	Mar. 24, 1868	75, 963
Churn-dasher	J. W. Pettengill	Rockford, Ill	Aug. 20, 1867	68, 000
Churn-dasher	G. H. Pool	New York, N. Y	May 15, 1866	54, 769
Churn-dasher	H. S. Potter	Hawley, Pa	Oct. 17, 1871	120, 097
Churn-dasher	G. Radbruch	Hoboken, N. J	Oct. 5, 1869	95, 514
Churn-dasher	F. Ransom	Buffalo, N. Y	Sept. 24, 1867	69, 248
Churn-dasher	G. Ridler	Rickardsville, Iowa	Nov. 4, 1873	144, 290
Churn-dasher	J. T. Rittenhouse	Urbana, Ill	Nov. 20, 1866	59, 781
Churn-dasher	H. B. Robinson	Birmingham, Ala	Dec. 16, 1873	145, 592
Churn-dasher	R. W. Robinson	Clinton, Ill	Nov. 19, 1867	71, 065
Churn-dasher	A. Rose	Penn Yan, N. Y	Oct. 25, 1859	25, 914
Churn-dasher	N. Routzahn	Middletown, Md	Mar. 19, 1850	7, 199
Churn-dasher	L. Scott	Burgettstown, Pa	Nov. 8, 1870	109, 061
Churn-dasher	J. M. See	Griffin, Ga	May 2, 1871	114, 478
Churn-dasher	R. S. Sherman	Napanock, N. Y	Aug. 6, 1850	7, 550
Churn-dasher	J. Smith	Kansas, Ill	Oct. 8, 1867	69, 718
Churn-dasher	M. J. Smith	Dansville, N. Y	Nov. 7, 1865	50, 851
Churn-dasher	N. H. Spencer	Canandaigua, N. Y	Oct. 23, 1866	59, 031
Churn-dasher	A. Sperry	Tremont, Ill	Dec. 21, 1869	98, 117
Churn-dasher	O. Sperry and J. W. Hopson	Hartfield, N. Y	Mar. 23, 1869	88, 226
Churn-dasher	H. Stanton	Richfield, N. Y	Dec. 18, 1849	6, 961
Churn-dasher	N. Starbuck	Wilmington, Ohio	Mar. 21, 1865	46, 952
Churn-dasher	H. N. Stearns	Chardon, Ohio	Mar. 11, 1862	34, 652
Churn-dasher	A. T. Still	Baldwin City, Kans	Dec. 19, 1871	122, 075
Churn-dasher	B. F. Stoler and I. W. Warner	Ladoga and Crawfordsville, Ind.	July 25, 1871	117, 479
Churn-dasher	S. Stout	Tremont, Ill	Apr. 4, 1871	113, 361
Churn-dasher	H. Tilden	Philadelphia, Pa	Nov. 22, 1864	45, 194
Churn-dasher	J. Thomas	Huntingdon, Pa	May 7, 1867	64, 460
Churn-dasher	M. H. Thomas	Dansville, N. Y	Oct. 6, 1868	82, 892
Churn-dasher	T. W. Tyler	Corry, Pa	Aug. 4, 1868	80, 685
Churn-dasher	P. Van Antwerp	Coeymans, N. Y	Feb. 16, 1843	2, 957
Churn-dasher	A. C. Vaughn	Johnstown, Pa	Mar. 6, 1860	27, 396
Churn-dasher	R. A. Vick	Holly Springs, Miss	Aug. 13, 1872	130, 395
Churn-dasher	W. and M. C. Walker	Lancaster, Pa	Aug. 6, 1850	7, 554
Churn-dasher	D. F. Wallace and D. T. Cockerill.	Ripley, Ohio	Aug. 6, 1867	67, 617
Churn-dasher	J. J. Watson	Buffalo, N. Y	Oct. 16, 1860	30, 438
Churn-dasher	F. H. Weaver	Marietta, Ga	Sept. 6, 1870	107, 138
Churn-dasher	H. L. Wells	Chillicothe, Mo	May 9, 1871	114, 736
Churn-dasher	M. D. Wells	Morgantown, Va	Mar. 19, 1861	31, 756
Churn-dasher	E. B. West	Saint Anthony, Minn	May 12, 1868	77, 939
Churn-dasher	H. P. Westcott	Seneca Falls, N. Y	Aug. 18, 1863	39, 600
Churn-dasher	O. A. White	Norwalk, Ohio	May 25, 1869	90, 413
Churn-dasher	J. E. Williams and M. Lemon	Binghamton, N. Y	May 12, 1868	77, 789
Churn-dasher	P. Wineman	Loyds ille, Ohio	July 26, 1859	24, 898
Churn-dasher	T. H. Withers and J. Dolfinger	Louisville, Ky	Apr. 6, 1869	88, 688
Churn-dasher	B. Wright	Cardiff, N. Y	May 31, 1864	42, 984
Churn-dasher	E. M. Wright	Wilmington, Ohio	May 16, 1865	47, 763
Churn-dasher	S. Yates	Marshall, Mo	Oct. 13, 1868	83, 015
Churn dasher	T. P. York	Terre Haute, Ind	Sept. 28, 1869	95, 401
Churn-dasher, Adjustable	T. G. Clinton and G. H. and E. H. Knight.	Cincinnati, Ohio	Oct. 2, 1849	6, 764
Churn dasher and lid	S. P. Hopkins	Port Deposit, Md	Aug. 25, 1868	81, 372
Churn dasher, Atmospheric	S. Case and A. W. Pratt	Pultneyville, N. Y	June 19, 1866	55, 622
Churn dasher, Atmospheric	J. C. Gaston	Cincinnati, Ohio	May 21, 1867	64, 969
Churn dasher, Atmospheric	W. M. Wright	Pittsburgh, Pa	Sept. 11, 1849	6, 711
Churn-dasher-crank fixture	C. Blush and M. Harbster	Lucas, Ohio, and Reading, Pa.	Mar. 22, 1870	100, 969
Churn-dasher head	B. F. and A. H. Stover	Ladoga, Ind	May 19, 1868	78, 025
Churn-dasher, Metallic	O. Updike	Grass Lake, Mich	May 10, 1870	102, 887
Churn-dasher, Reciprocating	T. Earle	Valley Falls, R. I	Aug. 19, 1873	142, 007
Churn-dasher rod	M. G. Decrow	Newark, Ohio,	Oct. 17, 1871	120, 046
Churn-dasher, Rotary	L. W. Colver	Saint Louis, Mo	Sept. 18, 1849	6, 726
Churn-dasher, Rotary	D. N. Egbert	Hudson, Ohio	Sept. 18, 1849	6, 727
Churn-dasher, Rotary	H. S. Wells	Oquawka, Ill	Jan. 2, 1872	122, 505
Churn-dasher, Spiral	C. R. and J. Hight	Geneva, Ill	July 9, 1850	7, 490
Churn-dasher staff	D. L. Grover	Groton, N. Y	Apr. 9, 1872	125, 453
Churn-dashers, Device for moving	A. W. Hall	New York, N. Y	Mar 21, 1865	46, 970
Churn-dashers, Fastening blade of	S. T. Lamb	New Washington, Ind	Oct. 16, 1860	30, 411
Churn-dashers, Operating	W. Kegg	Lasellsville, N. Y	Sept. 21, 1869	95, 023
Churn-dashers, Working rotary and vertical	W. R. Nash	Bridgeport, Conn	May 7, 1850	7, 348
Churn, Dog	F. Traxler	Scottsburgh, N. Y	June 12, 1866	55, 556
Churn, Double-dasher	E. Mitchell	Pittston, Me	May 22, 1841	2, 102

Index of patents issued from the United States Patent Office from 1790 *to* 1873, *inclusive*—Continued.

Invention.	Inventor.	Residence.	Date.	No.
Churn, Double revolving	L. Barney and A. A. Beach	Groton, N. Y	Feb. 5, 1830	
Churn, Floating-wheel	E. Dewey	Butternuts, N. Y	Oct. 1, 1830	
Churn-gearing	A. C. Mason	Springfield, Vt	July 31, 1866	56, 771
Churn, Geneva double dasher	W. Sutton	Geneva, N. Y	Oct. 1, 1830	
Churn, Horizontal	J. Davidson	Cheshire, N. H	Apr. 3, 1812	
Churn, Horizontal-vibrating	T. Pratt	Cheshire County, N. H	Sept. 12, 1811	
Churn, Labor-saving	A. Bristol	Hillsdale, N. Y	Apr. 28, 1830	
Churn, Lever	W. Cook	Southport, N. Y	Dec. 7, 1829	
Churn, Lever	P. H. Kemball	Salem, Mass	June 13, 1831	
Churn, Lever	J. Ladd	Holderness, N. H	June 22, 1832	
Churn-lid screen	E. Reynolds	Winneconne, Wis	Apr. 13, 1869	88, 983
Churn-machine	P. Cornell	Brutus, N. Y	Oct. 1, 1830	
Churn-motion	D. Morris	Bartlett, Ohio	July 14, 1868	80, 001
Churn-motor	J. B. Sweetland	Pontiac, Mich	May 20, 1873	139, 208
Churn-operating apparatus	G. A. Dabney	San José, Cal	Mar. 4, 1862	34, 567
Churn-operating apparatus	D. W. Ketcham	Owasso, Mich	Mar. 26, 1872	124, 900
Churn-operating apparatus	H. J. Klingenberg and J. J. Mau.	Davenport, Iowa	June 29, 1869	91, 942
Churn-operating device	E. R. Hall and W. H. Town	Syracuse, N. Y	Mar. 15, 1870	100, 753
Churn-operating device	A., J., and C. Lamb	Jeffersonville, N. Y	Jan. 27, 1863	37, 511
Churn-operating device	O. W. Seely	Syracuse, N. Y	Mar. 24, 1863	38, 013
Churn-operating machinery	C. S. Williamson	Covert, N. Y	Dec. 28, 1869	98, 454
Churn, Oscillating	E. W. Bullard	Barre, Mass	Nov. 7, 1871	120, 708
Churn, Oscillating	N. E. Wilson	Wilsonburgh, W. Va	July 19, 1870	105, 533
Churn, Oval	J. Oothoudt	Lebanon, N. Y	Mar. 10, 1830	
Churn, Pendulum	C. Augevine	New York, N. Y	Feb. 28, 1831	
Churn, Pendulum	S. Hitchcock	Vernon, N. Y	Aug. 7, 1813	
Churn, Pneumatic	A. P. Smith	Litchfield, Conn	May 2, 1865	47, 607
Churn-power	J. Budd	Pittsford, N. Y	June 4, 1867	65, 337
Churn-power	J. Christley	Slippery Rock, Pa	May 7, 1867	64, 490
Churn-power	B. F. Frampton	Punxatawney, Pa	July 18, 1871	117, 166
Churn-power	A. Fuller and W. H. Howe	Amsterdam and Port Jackson, N. Y.	Oct. 4, 1864	44, 523
Churn-power	I. S. Goolman	Monrovia, Ind	Apr. 6, 1869	88, 629
Churn-power	L. A. Haight	Cairo, N. Y	Aug. 29, 1871	118, 529
Churn-power	J. V. Hartman	Marathon, Ohio	Apr. 9, 1867	63, 632
Churn-power	E. Hoag	Rensselaerville, N. Y	Dec. 1, 1863	40, 751
Churn-power	D. J. Knapp	Fallsburgh, N. Y	May 29, 1866	55, 120
Churn-power	G. Lewis	Panama, N. Y	June 7, 1864	43, 076
Churn-power	W. A. Lewis	Springfield, Vt	Mar. 18, 1873	136, 925
Churn-power	D. McCurdy	Ottawa, Ohio	June 15, 1869	91, 467
Churn-power	G. T. Montague	Keokuk, Iowa	June 21, 1870	104, 627
Churn-power	J. D. Parrot	Morristown, N. J	Sept. 8, 1863	39, 827
Churn-power	R. N. Smith	New York, N. Y	Apr. 19, 1870	102, 171
Churn-power	H. Swarthout	Altay, N. Y	Mar. 12, 1867	62, 905
Churn-power	J. B. Sweetland	Fostoria, Ohio	Jan. 5, 1864	41, 107
Churn-power, Endless platform for	A. B. Smith	Rochester, Pa	Sept. 1, 1868	81, 833
Churn propelled by weights	A. Bacon	Windsor, N. Y	Oct. 10, 1835	
Churn, Reciprocating	E. Barrett and G. W. Fenimore.	Franklin, Tenn	July 15, 1873	140, 871
Churn, Reciprocating	L. I. Bodenhamer	Kernersville, N. C	July 15, 1873	140, 880
Churn, Reciprocating	G. P. Coan	Wyandotte, Mich	June 10, 1873	139, 658
Churn, Reciprocating	H. Hatch	Jefferson, Me	Aug. 26, 1873	142, 102
Churn, Reciprocating	G. M. Heim	Brownsville, Ind	May 13, 1873	138, 888
Churn, Reciprocating	A. D. Huntley	Smyrna Mills, Me	Oct. 21, 1873	143, 906
Churn, Reciprocating	L. B. Keeler	Westerville, Ohio	June 24, 1873	140, 280
Churn, Reciprocating	M. Litty	Williamsville, Nebr	Apr. 22, 1873	138, 168
Churn, Reciprocating	M. W. Staples	Richmond, Va	July 15, 1873	140, 796
Churn, Reciprocating	W. M. Thompson and J. L. Mahurin.	Rockfield, Ind	July 1, 1873	140, 445
Churn, Reciprocating	E. T. Wheeler	Cannelton, Ind	Oct. 21, 1873	143, 800
Churn, Revolving	N. King	Washington, D. C	Mar. 10, 1808	
Churn, Revolving-dasher	H. Branch	New York, N. Y	Apr. 18, 1832	
Churn, Rocking	W. Keeler and J. Waring		June 23, 1803	
Churn, Rocking	D. Parmele	Dutchess County, N. Y	Sept. 8, 1808	
Churn, Rocking	J. G. Philip	Kinderhook, N. Y	Feb. 15, 1827	
Churn, Rocking	A. C. Stiles	South Bloomfield, Ohio	Sept. 27, 1844	3, 764
Churn, Rocking	E. Thomas	Harrisonburgh, Va	May 30, 1838	753
Churn, Rotary	J. W. Arnold	Fairport, N. Y	Oct. 8, 1872	131, 990
Churn, Rotary	W. Brand and G. Puder	Evansville, Ind	June 24, 1873	140, 112
Churn, Rotary	W. H. Bunch	Windsor, N. C	Aug. 12, 1873	141, 692
Churn, Rotary	F. E. Clarkson	Highland, Kans	Apr. 29, 1873	138, 229
Churn, Rotary	A. L. Cornell	New York, N. Y	Nov. 15, 1859	26, 093
Churn, Rotary	B. Eason	Easonville, Ala	Feb. 25, 1873	136, 226
Churn, Rotary	H. H. Grover	North Cohocton, N. Y	Nov. 15, 1853	10, 245
Churn, Rotary	J. Harwood	Cobleskill, N. Y	Sept. 24, 1867	69, 093
Churn, Rotary	E. A. Hewitt	Groton, Conn	July 29, 1873	141, 348
Churn, Rotary	O. B. Loomis	Windsor, Conn	Apr. 2, 1850	7, 247
Churn, Rotary	W. McClure	Sinking Spring, Ohio	Jan. 28, 1873	135, 281
Churn, Rotary	G. Walker	Whitley's Point, Ill	May 27, 1873	139, 345
Churn, Spiral-spring	L. Hinkson	Hallowell, Me	Jan. 7, 1835	
Churn, Swinging	W. F. and N. Davis	Castleton, Vt	Nov. 23, 1852	9, 416
Churn, Thermometer	J. K. Pilkay	Carlisle, Pa	Feb. 16, 1869	87, 064
Churn-thermometer	J. H. Smiley	Caroline, N. Y	Oct. 31, 1871	120, 464
Churn, Tin	T. E. Warner	Harford County, Md	Feb. 11, 1834	
Churn-top	E. Cox	Point Pleasant, Ohio	Apr. 17, 1866	53, 952
Churn, Valve-piston	B. Cushwa	Clear Spring, Md	Jan. 24, 1829	
Churn, Ventilating portable	E. P. Williams	Yorkville, S. C	May 26, 1868	78, 249
Churns and washing-machines, Operating	J. T. Bever	Springville, Ill	Jan. 6, 1863	37, 330
Churns, Construction of	A. and W. A. Crowell	Salisbury, Conn	June 20, 1840	1, 648
Churns, Cutting floats of	R. Ryerson	Jay, Me	July 17, 1835	
Churns, Device for operating	H. E. Addis	Springfield, Ill	July 7, 1863	39, 107
Churns, Device for operating	O. Edson	Franklinville, N. Y	May 26, 1863	38, 663
Churns, Device for operating	G. C. Ferris	Sharon, Wis	Apr. 14, 1863	38, 158
Churns, Device for operating	H. Soggs	Columbus, Pa	Dec. 1, 1863	40, 775
Churns, Machine attached to the top of	L. Stevens		May 8, 1804	
Churns, &c., Machine for operating	I. Morse	West Franklin, Pa	Apr. 21, 1868	77, 077
Churns, Machinery for operating	J. J. Taylor	Attica, Ind	Aug. 11, 1863	39, 532

Index of patents issued from the United States Patent Office from 1790 *to* 1873, *inclusive*—Continued.

Invention.	Inventor.	Residence.	Date.	No.
Churns, Machinery for working	P. B. Pratt	Kent, Conn	July 22, 1833	....
Churns, Manner of working	J. H. Monce	Hopkinsville, Ohio	Feb. 4, 1868	74, 114
Churns, &c., Mechanical movement for operating	J. P. Nichols	New Richmond, Ohio	Dec. 4, 1866	60, 232
Churns, Mechanism for operating	G. True	Funchal Island, Madeira	Mar. 29, 1864	42, 129
Churns, Mode of constructing and operating	S. P. W. Douglass	Lansingburgh, N. Y	Jan. 9, 1838	554
Churns, Mode of operating	J. Redding	New Castle, Ind	June 6, 1865	48, 094
Churns, Mode of operating	I. M. Williams	Blanchester, Ohio	Oct. 1, 1861	33, 422
Churns, Operating	A. G. Brush	Great Bend, Pa	June 15, 1858	20, 545
Churns, Operating	J. Forsyth	Wheeling, Va	Nov. 9, 1858	22, (22
Churns, &c., Operating	M. Swan	Potter Hill, N. Y	Aug. 17, 1858	21, 221
Churning and working butter	W. D. Baughn	Milford, Mich	July 9, 1867	66, 445
Churning-apparatus	J. P. Curtis	Wytheville, Va	June 28, 1870	104, 710
Churning-apparatus	J. Letort	Wytheville, Va	July 5, 1870	104, 968
Churning-apparatus	E. J. Moore	Westfield, N. Y	Apr. 7, 1868	76, 497
Churning-apparatus	E. J. Moore	Westfield, N. Y	Oct. 13, 1868	83, 080
Churning-apparatus	J. Thompson	Hartville, Ohio	July 2, 1867	66, 416
Churning, Apparatus for tempering cream preparatory to.	E. T. Brownfield	Smithfield, Pa	Mar. 17, 1868	75, 622
Churning, Art of	I. F. Waring	Columbia Township, Ohio	Apr. 10, 1830	....
Churning butter, Mode of	I. Herrick	Merrimack, N. H	Apr. 21, 1868	76, 913
Churning, Inclined wheel applied to	G. F. Reeve and J. Ketcham	Orange County, N. Y	Aug. 10, 1821	....
Churning-machine	B. Atwell and I. Nichols	Otsego County, N. Y	Oct. 14, 1809	....
Churning-machine	E. Bacon	Hancock County, Mass	July 26, 1810	....
Churning-machine	I. Baker	....	Feb. 20, 1802	....
Churning-machine	S. H. Baker	Wells Township, Bradford County, Pa.	Jan. 10, 1828	....
Churning-machine	S. Clarke	Parkman, Me	Apr. 22, 1835	....
Churning-machine	G. Crandell	Rhinebeck, N. Y	Aug. 20, 1867	67, 960
Churning-machine	B. Cutler	Washington, N. Y	Oct. 3, 1807	....
Churning-machine	N. Harrington	Whitestown, N. Y	Oct. 11, 1809	....
Churning-machine	E. G. Jones	Otsego, N. Y	Apr. 21, 1809	....
Churning-machine	M. Knight	Pownal, Me	May 9, 1835	....
Churning-machine	A. Murray	Athens, N. Y	June 27, 1829	....
Churning-machine	J. Pierce	....	Apr. 10, 1802	....
Churning-machine	W. A. Rhoades	Lincolnville, Pa	July 6, 1869	92, 360
Churning-machine	G. Sanford	Ellenville, N. Y	May 4, 1852	8, 927
Churning-machine	J. Scripture	Alford, Mass	Dec. 15, 1807	....
Churning-machine	D. G. Taylor	Campbellsville, Ky	Dec. 7, 1869	97, 565
Churning, Machine for saving cream while	M. Love	Corry, Pa	July 21, 1868	80, 078
Churning, Power for	A. A. Drake	Flanders, N. J	July 8, 1862	35, 813
Chute and fish-way	J. D. Brewer	Muncy, Pa	Apr. 30, 1872	126, 257
Chute and water-wheel	H. Van Dewater	Philadelphia, Pa	Sept. 19, 1848	5, 785
Chute for dams	A. Addis	Washington Township, Pa.	Oct. 4, 1834	....
Chute for delivering timber	J. W. Haines	Genoa, Nev	Sept. 20, 1870	107, 611
Chute for horizontal water-wheels	I. Mallery	Etna, N. Y	Aug. 30, 1859	25, 270
Chute for river or canal navigation	A. Livermore	Tremont, Pa	Nov. 27, 1860	30, 739
Chute for water-wheels	C. B. Whitney	Ithaca, N. Y	Jan. 12, 1858	19, 115
Chute-gate	J. M. Thompson	Quincy, Cal	Sept. 17, 1872	131, 477
Chute, Lumber	W. Van Name and J. A. Wakefield.	Chippewa Falls, Wis	Jan. 28, 1873	135, 302
Cider, ale, &c., Compound for refining	W. M. Davis	Cleveland, Ohio	May 28, 1867	65, 063
Cider and bark mill	I. Quintard	Stanfield, Conn	Apr. 5, 1806	....
Cider and cheese press	E. Benedict	New Marlborough, Mass	Mar. 21, 1808	....
Cider and cheese press	E. Benedict	New Marlborough, Mass	June 18, 1808	....
Cider and vinegar from the offals of a distillery, Making.	W. Richardson	Kingston, N. Y	Sept. 26, 1816	....
Cider and wine mill	T. F. Deniston, G. C. Presser, and J. J. Deniston.	Torrey, N. Y	Aug. 17, 1869	93, 861
Cider and wine mill	W. B. Farrar	Greensborough, N. C	Apr. 4, 1871	113, 283
Cider and wine mill	J. R. Gates	Louisville, Ky	Oct. 29, 1861	33, 581
Cider and wine mill	A. McCreight and R. W. Glasgow.	Tranquility, Ohio	Mar. 18, 1873	136, 847
Cider and wine mill	J. Walton	Sunfish, Ohio	June 2, 1868	78, 558
Cider and wine press	C. Beach	Penn Yan, N. Y	Aug. 21, 1866	57, 277
Cider and wine press	O. Kromer	Sandusky, Ohio	July 23, 1872	129, 836
Cider, &c., Concentrating and preserving	G. Borden, jr	Amenia, N. Y	July 22, 1862	35, 919
Cider, Furnace for clarifying	C. Cory	Lima, Ind	Sept. 13, 1864	44, 162
Cider into wine, Converting	H. Seabolt	Scipio, N. Y	Nov. 11, 1812	....
Cider, Machine for making	M. B. Bliss	Pittston, Me	Apr. 21, 1829	....
Cider, Machine for preparing apples for the manufacture of.	G. B. Hamlin	Willimantic, Conn	Aug. 16, 1870	106, 359
Cider-making	G. B. Hamlin	Willimantic, Conn	Feb. 21, 1871	111, 930
Cider-making machine	W. Lucas	Rushville, Ill	Dec. 31, 1867	72, 872
Cider-mill	H. Abbott	Huron, N. Y	Dec. 23, 1856	16, 261
Cider-mill	W. Aikin and W. W. Drummond.	Louisville, Ky	Apr. 30, 1872	126, 244
Cider-mill	T. Appelget	Princeton, N. J	Nov. 20, 1866	59, 807
Cider-mill	R. C. Archibald	La Fayette, Ind	Aug. 27, 1867	68, 145
Cider-mill	W. Barr	Ypsilanti, Mich	July 11, 1871	116, 798
Cider-mill	J. Bauman	Shepherdstown, Pa	June 27, 1854	11, 151
Cider-mill	P. J. Berlin	Blairsville, Pa	Dec. 16, 1862	37, 147
Cider-mill	N. Booth	Cheshire, Conn	July 12, 1834	....
Cider-mill	J. Bowen	Yellow Bud, Ohio	Oct. 13, 1863	40, 237
Cider-mill	J. Bowen and A. T. Foster	Clarksburgh, Ohio	Apr. 18, 1871	113, 731
Cider-mill	E. W. Branch	East Henrietta, N. Y	Jan. 8, 1867	60, 992
Cider-mill	E. W. Branch	East Henrietta, N. Y	July 2, 1867	66, 207
Cider-mill	S. and R. W. Caldwell	Chillicothe, Ohio	Apr. 16, 1861	32, 044
Cider-mill	C. L. Carter	Union City, Ind	June 15, 1869	91, 210
Cider-mill	J. Case	Selma, Ohio	Aug. 10, 1852	9, 178
Cider-mill	N. Chapin	Cortlandville, N. Y	Nov. 21, 1848	5, 936
Cider-mill	N. Cha-in	Syracuse, N. Y	Sept. 2, 1851	8, 339
Cider-mill	O. Clarke	Rockford, Ill	June 14, 1864	43, (95
Cider-mill	W. and L. Clayton	West Philadelphia, Pa	July 11, 1865	48, 657
Cider-mill	G. R. Cluxton	Ripley, Ohio	Aug. 6, 1872	130, 192
Cider-mill	J. A. Crever and F. H. Keeney	Cincinnati, Ohio	Aug. 1, 1865	49, 088
Cider-mill	G. W. D. Culp	Allenville, Ind	Nov. 14, 1846	4, 852
Cider-mill	R. M. Curtice	North Adams, Mich	Jan. 10, 1860	26, 752
Cider-mill	P. Dickson	Erie, Pa	Sept. 27, 1864	44, 408

Index of patents issued from the United States Patent Office from 1790 *to* 1873, *inclusive*—Continued.

Invention.	Inventor.	Residence.	Date.	No.
Cider-mill	J. Diehl and W. Wilson	Brooklyn, N. Y	Aug. 6, 1861	32, 988
Cider-mill	N. Eaton	Woburn, Mass	Dec. 10, 1872	133, 840
Cider-mill	J. Eiberneiser	Cincinnati, Ohio	Oct. 26, 1858	21, 874
Cider-mill	O. S. Garretson	Buffalo, N. Y	Jan. 11, 1870	98, 757
Cider-mill	L. Gebhart	Orangeville, Ohio	Jan. 21, 1868	73, 523
Cider-mill	S. A. Hebard	North Stamford, Conn	Sept. 1, 1863	39, 731
Cider-mill	M. W. Hilton	Bloomington, Ind	Feb. 23, 1858	19, 421
Cider-mill	A. D. Hoffman	Belleville, Mich	Nov. 8, 1859	26, 037
Cider-mill	S. J. Homan	Walden, N. Y	June 5, 1866	55, 297
Cider-mill	H. Hurd	Spring Hill, Ill	May 24, 1864	42, 912
Cider-mill	S. G. Hurlbut	Cleveland, Ohio	Sept. 6, 1864	44, 096
Cider-mill	S. Jackson	Hamilton, Ohio	Jan. 15, 1850	7, 022
Cider-mill	E. Jenkins	Harmony, Pa	May 17, 1836	....
Cider-mill	T. J. Kindleberger	Springfield, Ohio	May 29, 1855	12, 953
Cider-mill	T. J. Kindleberger	Springfield, Ohio	Feb. 9, 1864	41, 514
Cider-mill	J. Krauser	Reading, Pa	Aug. 30, 1853	9, 972
Cider-mill	H. Lightner	Neffs Mills, Pa	Aug. 8, 1871	117, 898
Cider-mill	J. Lytch	Laurinburgh, N. C	Nov. 22, 1870	109, 527
Cider-mill	B. Mackerley	New Petersburgh, Ohio	Nov. 14, 1856	16, 040
Cider-mill	S. Males	Cincinnati, Ohio	Sept. 6, 1870	107, 187
Cider-mill	S. Males	Cincinnati, Ohio	Feb. 13, 1866	52, 583
Cider-mill	W. M. McDowell and C. E. Baechtel.	Hagerstown, Md	Aug. 29, 1865	49, 641
Cider-mill	J. McGrew	Ravenswood, W. Va	Sept. 17, 1872	131, 453
Cider-mill	N. E. Miller	Canaan Centre, Ohio	Aug. 5, 1873	141, 582
Cider-mill	W. S. Oborn	Marion, Ohio	July 7, 1868	79, 771
Cider-mill	H. E. Paine and S. H. Russel	Leroy, Ohio	Mar. 5, 1827	....
Cider-mill	H. K. Parsons	Harrisburgh, Pa	Oct. 11, 1864	44, 651
Cider-mill	N. A. Patterson	Knoxville, Tenn	Oct. 3, 1871	119, 472
Cider-mill	D. F. Phillips	Republic, Ohio	Nov. 25, 1851	8, 549
Cider-mill	E. H. Philo	Half Moon, N. Y	Mar. 27, 1860	27, 650
Cider-mill	C. Pool and M. Eddy	Blissfield, Mich	Sept. 26, 1865	50, 158
Cider-mill	E. S. Purdy	Croton, N. Y	Mar. 12, 1867	62, 884
Cider-mill	J. Redlein	Brooklyn, N. Y	Jan. 23, 1866	52, 203
Cider-mill	C. Rice	Barre, Mass	Nov. 11, 1830	....
Cider-mill	W. Rice	Fitchburgh, Masss	June 3, 1873	139, 615
Cider-mill	L. O. Rockwood	Ottawa, Ill	June 17, 1873	139, 975
Cider-mill	J. Rosenkrans	Avoca, N. Y	May 3, 1859	23, 862
Cider-mill	G. R. Ruland and W. W. Green, jr.	Byron Centre, N. Y	June 21, 1864	43, 229
Cider-mill	J. E. Saugi	Washington, D. C	Jan. 28, 1873	135, 370
Cider-mill	M. P. Schenck	Fulton, N. Y	May 6, 1873	138, 533
Cider-mill	D. Scully	Baltimore, Md	July 5, 1864	43, 434
Cider-mill	G. Seger	Humberstone, Canada	May 23, 1871	115, 112
Cider-mill	H. Sells	Vienna, Canada	Sept. 4, 1866	57, 833
Cider-mill	T. Sharp	Louisville, Ky	Nov. 24, 1863	40, 711
Cider-mill	W. Shaw	New Gordon, Ohio	Nov. 20, 1866	59, 864
Cider-mill	C. Sheaffer	Lebanon, Pa	Mar. 19, 1836	....
Cider-mill	H. O. Sheidley	Republic, Ohio	Dec. 29, 1857	18, 993
Cider-mill	T. A. Shinn	Baden, Pa	Aug. 27, 1867	68, 246
Cider-mill	T. Showerman	Covington, N. Y	July 20, 1825	....
Cider-mill	J. K. P. Smith	Jeffersonville, Ind	Oct. 25, 1870	108, 645
Cider-mill	A. Spencer	Grampian Hills, Pa	July 1, 1862	35, 787
Cider-mill	M. Stevens	Lucas, Ohio	May 11, 1858	20, 220
Cider-mill	L. R. Taylor	Clark Township, Ind	Sept. 13, 1870	107, 424
Cider-mill	J. H. Thomas and P. P. Mast	Springfield, Ohio	Nov. 21, 1865	51, 101
Cider-mill	T. Van Kannel	Cincinnati, Ohio	July 2, 1867	66, 427
Cider-mill	H. T. Watkins	Anderson, Ind	Feb. 5, 1861	31, 344
Cider-mill	J. I. White	Zanesville, Ohio	Dec. 3, 1872	133, 609
Cider-mill	W. N. Whitely, J. Fassler, and O. S. Kelly.	Springfield, Ohio	Jan. 14, 1868	73, 417
Cider-mill	H. L. Whitman	Saint Louis, Mo	Nov. 19, 1872	133, 133
Cider-mill	J. H. Williams	Sandusky, Ohio	Nov. 13, 1866	59, 700
Cider-mill	J. D. Willoughby	Shippensburgh, Pa	Mar. 3, 1868	75, 101
Cider-mill	D. T. Willson	Harrisburgh, Pa	Jan. 2, 1872	122, 508
Cider-mill	C. Wilson	Clinton, Pa	Sept. 15, 1868	82, 261
Cider-mill	L. Wilson	Springfield, Ohio	Mar. 5, 1867	62, 585
Cider-mill	L. Wilson	Springfield, Ohio	Dec. 7, 1869	97, 743
Cider-mill	D. Zeigler	Lewistown, Pa	July 25, 1854	11, 401
Cider mill and fruit-press	L. A. Warner	Freeport, Ill	Oct. 2, 1866	58, 514
Cider mill and press	U. Emmons	New York, N. Y	Jan. 31, 1829	....
Cider mill and press	F. and G. F. Hovey	New York, N. Y	June 1, 1869	90, 843
Cider mill and press	M. Jones	East Saginaw, Mich	Oct. 29, 1872	132, 536
Cider mill and press	H. and H. S. Paul	Kittery, Me., and Cambridge, Mass.	Nov. 26, 1872	133, 476
Cider mill and press	O. Pettibone	Hartford, Conn	Mar. 1, 1815	....
Cider mill and press	E. Wangaman	Blairsville, Pa	July 21, 1868	80, 253
Cider mill and press	M. Winger	Ephratah, Pa	Dec. 10, 1867	71, 935
Cider mill and press, Combined	O. M. Brock	Monrocton, Pa	July 18, 1871	117, 041
Cider mill and press combined	D. H. Krauser	Pottsville, Pa	Apr. 18, 1871	113, 778
Cider mill and press, Portable	F. Fredley	Sugar Valley, Pa	Aug. 3, 1838	875
Cider-mill, Cast-iron	P. Pryer	Genesee County, N. Y	May 29, 1835	....
Cider-mill, Convertible	S. Males	Cincinnati, Ohio	Mar. 17, 1857	16, 847
Cider-mill, corn-sheller, and fodder-cutter, Mode of combining.	J. P. Adams	Chester, Ill	Aug. 25, 1863	39, 620
Cider-mill press	M. Stevens	Smithville, Ohio	July 31, 1866	56, 824
Cider-mill, Rotary-cylinder	S. Freeman, jr	New Marlborough, Mass	Mar. 14, 1828	....
Cider or wine mill	S. Krauser	Reading, Pa	Oct. 30, 1855	13, 741
Cider-press	A. Brooks	Tolland, Conn	Oct. 5, 1869	95, 558
Cider-press	O. Clark	Rockford, Ill	Apr. 26, 1864	42, 528
Cider-press	J. H. Harper	Pittsburgh, Pa	Nov. 19, 1867	71, 165
Cider-press	J. Holbrook	Sherburne, Mass	July 18, 1871	117, 075
Cider-press	F. Hovey	New York, N. Y	Apr. 26, 1870	102, 402
Cider press	J. Maerhoffer	Boonville, Mo	June 1, 1869	90, 672
Cider-press	D. Pride	Potsdam, N. Y	June 11, 1829	....
Cider-press	E. Primm	Petersburgh, Ill	Nov. 26, 1867	71, 533
Cider-press	D. Reed	Easton, Mass	Mar. 3, 1829	....
Cider-press	C. Ritter	Reading, Pa	June 21, 1859	24, 490

Index of patents issued from the United States Patent Office from 1790 *to* 1873, *inclusive*—Continued.

Invention.	Inventor.	Residence.	Date.	No.
Cider-press	J. Schaffer and E. Stoner	Westminster, Md	Oct. 5, 1869	95, 608
Cider-press	A. W. Shidler	South Bend, Ind	Mar. 17, 1868	75, 589
Cider-press	A. D. Strong	Ashtabula, Ohio	July 2, 1867	66, 262
Cider-press	C. H. Thomas	Milton, N. Y	Oct. 24, 1865	50, 665
Cider-press, Lever	H. Peters	Penn Township, Pa	Apr. 29, 1873	138, 280
Cider-press, Screw	S. Sanderson	Shelby, N. Y	Oct. 1, 1872	131, 785
Cider, Putting up and preserving	M. Halsted and J. L. Wheeler	Brooklyn, N. Y	Mar. 18, 1873	136, 914
Cider, wine, &c., with sulphurous acid, Apparatus for treating.	D. M. Mefford	Huron County, Ohio	Dec. 31, 1872	134, 389
Cigar	T. Blanchard	Boston, Mass	Mar. 30, 1858	19, 746
Cigar	S. Davis	Montreal, Canada	Oct. 11, 1864	44, 695
Cigar	D. Davison	New York, N. Y	July 4, 1865	48, 527
Cigar	F. L. Hilbright	Newark, N. J	July 28, 1868	80, 284
Cigar	W. C. Kneeland	Brooklyn, N. Y	Dec. 10, 1861	33, 889
Cigar	T. W. Kreitz	Quincy, Ill	May 28, 1872	127, 172
Cigar	I. Lindsley	Providence, R. I	July 31, 1860	29, 436
Cigar	E. B. Mead	Pittsfield, Mass	June 24, 1873	140, 153
Cigar	C. Quartley	Baltimore, Md	Feb. 11, 1868	74, 246
Cigar	W. P. Surgey	Hackney, Great Britain	Dec. 9, 1856	16, 200
Cigar	M. Turley and J. M. Innes	Council Bluffs, Iowa	June 11, 1872	127, 939
Cigar	C. Van Dyeck	Nashville, Tenn	Nov. 6, 1866	59, 485
Cigar	C. Walton	Washington, D. C	June 6, 1865	48, 119
Cigar and cigarette	T. Griffin	Roxbury, Mass	Mar. 23, 1869	88, 033
Cigar and cigarette making machine	J. and A. Marengo	Burlington, Vt	June 16, 1868	78, 985
Cigar and cigarette manufacture	L. Morgenthan	Manheim, Baden	Mar. 14, 1865	46, 855
Cigar and match case	P. J. Clark	West Meriden, Conn	Apr. 3, 1860	27, 693
Cigar and pipe mouth-piece	B. S. Stokes	Manchester, N. H	June 3, 1862	35, 491
Cigar-ash holder, &c	A. Philipp	Manchester, Great Britain	Mar. 30, 1869	88, 408
Cigar binders, fillers, and wrappers, Forming	R. W. Heywood	Baltimore, Md	May 28, 1872	127, 235
Cigar-box	H. Fowler	Detroit, Mich	Dec. 9, 1873	145, 290
Cigar-box	P. Greenwald	Syracuse, N. Y	June 4, 1872	127, 597
Cigar-box	W. B. Hale, jr	Milford, Mass	Aug. 20, 1872	130, 713
Cigar-box	E. Henkle	North Scituate, R. I	July 26, 1870	105, 681
Cigar-box	C. Jerome	New Haven, Conn	Mar. 1, 1870	100, 296
Cigar-box	E. C. Patterson	Rochester, N. Y	Oct. 28, 1873	144, 129
Cigar-box	W. R Rhoades	Auburn, N. Y	Jan. 16, 1872	122, 854
Cigar-box	M. Richardson	Brooklyn, N. Y	Mar. 29, 1870	101, 381
Cigar-box	H Schmeer	Syracuse, N. Y	Apr. 23, 1872	125, 910
Cigar-box	T. A. Wiley	Lancaster, Pa	July 4, 1871	116, 782
Cigar-box, Perforated	R. S. Jennings	New York, N. Y	Jan. 25, 1870	99, 204
Cigar-box, Water-proof	J. L. Thomson	Syracuse, N. Y	June 27, 1871	116, 373
Cigar-boxes from redwood, Manufacture of	C. A. Hooper	San Francisco, Cal	Dec. 23, 1873	145, 735
Cigar-bunch pressing and molding machine	W. D. Brewer	Charlestown, Mass	Jan. 21, 1873	135, 030
Cigar-bunch-shaping mold	A. Pearl	Brooklyn, N. Y	July 18, 1871	117, 200
Cigar-bunches, Machine for making	S. Scholfield	Providence, R. I	Dec. 10, 1872	133, 725
Cigar-bunches, Machine for making	S. Scholfield	Providence, R. I	July 15, 1873	140, 848
Cigar-bunches, Machine for making	W. Weis	Saint Paul, Minn	Nov. 15, 1870	109, 280
Cigar-bunches, Machine for making	D. A. Wightman	East Greenwich, R. I	July 15, 1873	140, 860
Cigar-bunches, Machine for making	D. A. Wightman	East Greenwich, R. I	July 15, 1873	140, 861
Cigar-bunches, Machine for pressing	G. Pierce	Boston, Mass	Jan. 14, 1873	134, 768
Cigar-bunches, Machine for pressing and molding	W. D. Brewer	Charlestown, Mass	July 25, 1871	117, 377
Cigar-bunches, Manufacture of	A. Pearl	New York, N. Y	May 17, 1870	103, 236
Cigar-bunches, Manufacture of	S. Scholfield	Providence, R. I	July 16, 1872	129, 599
Cigar-bunches, Mold for shaping and drying	A. Pearl	New York, N. Y	Oct. 11, 1870	108, 290
Cigar-bunches, Retainer for holding pressed and molded.	W. D. Brewer	Charlestown, Mass	Aug. 29, 1871	118, 428
Cigar-bunches, Retainer for pressed and molded	W. D. Brewer	Charlestown, Mass	Jan. 21, 1873	135, 031
Cigar-bunching machine	H. B. Bunster	New York, N. Y	Mar. 4, 1873	136, 411
Cigar-bunching machine	S. T. Hennaman	Baltimore, Md	Aug. 13, 1872	130, 496
Cigar-bundling apparatus	C. A. Siecke	Philadelphia, Pa	May 19, 1868	78, 142
Cigar-bundling machine	F. A. Henckell	New York, N. Y	Mar. 2, 1869	87, 493
Cigar-case	C. A. Perry	Elkhorn, Wis	Nov. 21, 1865	51, 080
Cigar-case	S. N. Risley	Brooklyn, N. Y	Dec. 15, 1868	84, 906
Cigar-clamp	N. A. Buhl	New York, N. Y	Oct. 24, 1871	120, 240
Cigar-cutter	F. Funke	Detroit, Mich	July 2, 1872	128, 481
Cigar-cutter	R. A. Stendell	New York, N. Y	July 16, 1872	129, 182
Cigar-cutter	L. S. Stimson	Lowell, Mass	Nov. 8, 1870	109, 153
Cigar cutter and holder combined	J. Brady	Brooklyn, N. Y	Dec. 17, 1872	134, 030
Cigar cutting and perforating machine	J., T., and A. Levy	New York, N. Y	Apr. 15, 1873	137, 850
Cigar-drier	O. Vallandingham	Saint Louis, Mo	Mar. 23, 1869	88, 237
Cigar-drying mold	N. W. Palmer	New York, N. Y	June 3, 1873	139, 517
Cigar-ends, Machine for cutting off	F. W. Hoffmann	Morrisania, N. Y	Sept. 3, 1867	68, 441
Cigar-fillers, Apparatus for arranging	S. Scholfield	Providence, R. I	July 15, 1873	140, 850
Cigar-fillers, Machine for bunching and binding	H Schmidt	New York, N. Y	Sept. 24, 1872	131, 709
Cigar-fillers, Machine for making	G. A. Reniger	Stuttgart, Wurtemberg	May 1, 1866	54, 476
Cigar-fillers, Machine for preparing	J. Maffet	Lancaster, Pa	May 16, 1832	....
Cigar-fillers, Machine for pressing and shaping	C. H. Palmer	New York, N. Y	Jan. 28, 1873	135, 243
Cigar-filling	S. Scholfield	Providence, R. I	Jan. 17, 1871	111, 089
Cigar-fillings, Mold for drying	S. B. Jerome	New Haven, Conn	Sept. 13, 1870	107, 266
Cigar-fuse box	H. Reimann	Brooklyn, N. Y	Apr. 3, 1866	53, 678
Cigar-gage and butt-cutter	H. Peterson	Chicago, Ill	Sept. 10, 1867	68, 785
Cigar-header	G. Moebs	Detroit, Mich	May 26, 1858	78, 312
Cigar-heading socket	T. Thorp	New York, N. Y	Mar. 13, 1860	27, 484
Cigar-holder	C. Appel	Hoboken, N. J	May 21, 1867	64, 826
Cigar-holder	L. Auguste	New York, N. Y	Nov. 29, 1864	45, 215
Cigar-holder	J. K. Chase	New York, N. Y	Mar. 12, 1872	124, 545
Cigar-holder	M. Johnston	South Boston, Mass	Mar. 26, 1861	31, 808
Cigar-holder	T. J. Lewis	Chicago, Ill	Apr. 22, 1873	138, 032
Cigar-holder	J. D. W. Olney	Providence, R. I	Oct. 29, 1872	132, 685
Cigar-holder	W. K. Vanderslice, jr	San Francisco, Cal	Jan. 21, 1868	73, 478
Cigar-holder	M. V. B. Young	New York, N. Y	July 28, 1868	80, 527
Cigar-holder and hat-hook	C. Gschwind and J. Grether	Union Hill, N. J	Aug. 14, 1866	57, 126
Cigar holder and perforator	R. J. Sheehy	Boston, Mass	June 4, 1872	127, 649
Cigar-holding case	S. R. Wilmot	Bridgeport, Conn	Feb. 23, 1869	87. 314
Cigar-knife	J. H. Abbott	Frederick City, Md	Aug. 16, 1864	43, 823
Cigar labeling device	R. H. Andrews	Washington, D. C	Feb. 14, 1871	111, 804
Cigar-light	W. Belcher	New Haven, Conn	Oct. 2, 1866	58, 537
Cigar-lighter	M. F. Gale	New York, N. Y	Nov. 21, 1871	121, 049

Index of patents issued from the United States Patent Office from 1790 *to* 1873, *inclusive*—Continued.

Invention.	Inventor.	Residence.	Date.	No.
Cigar-lighter	E. P. Gleason	New York, N. Y	Nov. 13, 1866	59, 587
Cigar-lighter	J. B. Miller	Rondout, N. Y	Oct. 31, 1871	120, 453
Cigar-lighter, Gas	J. W. Tracy	Saint Louis, Mo	Nov. 26, 1867	71, 428
Cigar-lighter, Gas jet	G. B. Snow and T. G. Lewis	Buffalo, N. Y	Feb. 6, 1866	52, 457
Cigar-lighter, Suspended gas	D. F. Brandon	Chicago, Ill	Jan. 5, 1869	85, 636
Cigar-lighters, Machine for making	H. Reimann	Hartford, Conn	Nov. 24, 1857	18, 706
Cigar-lighters, Manufacture of friction-match	W. Porter	Saint Stephen, Canada	Sept. 27, 1870	107, 810
Cigar-lighters, Match for	W. Porter	Saint Stephens' Parish, Canada.	Nov. 29, 1870	109, 660
Cigar-lighters, Plane for cutting	W. H. Drips	Cincinnati, Ohio	Aug. 26, 1873	142, 216
Cigar-lighting cinder	H. Reimann	Hartford, Conn	Mar. 23, 1858	19, 717
Cigar-lighting cinders, Apparatus for containing and igniting.	H. Reimann	Hartford, Conn	Mar. 9, 1858	19, 580
Cigar-machine	J. Allen and J. Fanning	Brooklyn, N. Y	July 26, 1870	105, 620
Cigar-machine	W. G. Ayres and S. L. Cole	Brooklyn, N. Y	Feb. 15, 1870	99, 745
Cigar-machine	I. S. Barber	New York, N. Y	June 24, 1862	35, 728
Cigar-machine	R. A. Bright, jr	Providence, R. I	Oct. 20, 1868	83, 247
Cigar-machine	C. G. A. Brinckmann	New York, N. Y	Sept. 6, 1864	44, 070
Cigar-machine	G. Buckle	Monroe, Mich	Sept. 5, 1865	49, 709
Cigar-machine	G. B. Clarke	New York, N. Y	Apr. 20, 1869	89, 200
Cigar-machine	R. M. Cole	Burlington, Vt	Apr. 13, 1869	88, 850
Cigar-machine	S. L. Cole	Brooklyn, N. Y	June 20, 1871	116, 026
Cigar-machine	W. Dawson	Huntington, Conn	Apr. 29, 1856	14, 763
Cigar-machine	J. de Bary	Offenbach, Germany	May 28, 1861	32, 405
Cigar-machine	C. J. Delbridge	Rochester, N. Y	July 15, 1873	140, 896
Cigar-machine	H. Erfurth	Leipsic, Germany	June 18, 1872	128, 133
Cigar-machine	T. Ernst	Fort Madison, Iowa	July 15, 1873	140, 906
Cigar-machine	E. J. Fisk	South Byron, N. Y	Dec. 19, 1865	51, 578
Cigar-machine	I. A. Heald	Carlisle, Mass	May 31, 1864	42, 946
Cigar-machine	I. A. Heald	Washington, D. C	Feb. 2, 1869	86, 541
Cigar-machine	I. A. Heald	Lowell, Mass	Apr. 18, 1871	113, 880
Cigar-machine	J. T. Hennaman	Baltimore, Md	July 1, 1873	140, 501
Cigar-machine	R. W. Heywood	Baltimore, Md	May 21, 1872	126, 960
Cigar-machine	J. C. Hintz	Cincinnati, Ohio	Oct. 5, 1869	95, 478
Cigar-machine	W. W. Huse	Brooklyn, N. Y	Feb. 12, 1861	31, 390
Cigar-machine	J. Lauritzen	Newark, N. J	Oct. 4, 1870	107, 927
Cigar-machine	F. Meyer and H. Schild	New York, N. Y	Jan. 18, 1870	98, 877
Cigar-machine	F. C. Miller	Cincinnati, Ohio	Jan. 23, 1872	122, 955
Cigar-machine	C. Müller	Albany, N. Y	July 21, 1868	80, 204
Cigar-machine	C. Müller	Albany, N. Y	Oct. 26, 1860	96, 257
Cigar-machine	H. Müller and C. Major	New York, N. Y	Feb. 19, 1861	31, 518
Cigar-machine	R. Neisch	Allentown, Pa	Dec. 20, 1870	110, 270
Cigar-machine	R. Neisch	Allentown, Pa	July 16, 1872	129, 489
Cigar-machine	J. Ochs	Litiz, Pa	Sept. 10, 1872	131, 177
Cigar-machine	J. O'Reilly	Baltimore, Md	Oct. 25, 1870	108, 629
Cigar-machine	W. H. Pease	Fulton, Wis	July 2, 1872	128, 560
Cigar-machine	J. Prentice	New York, N. Y	Sept. 6, 1864	44, 114
Cigar-machine	J. Prentice and W. F. Wuterich.	New York, N. Y	Nov. 26, 1867	71, 532
Cigar-machine	G. A. Reiniger	Stuttgart, Wurtemberg	May 29, 1866	55, 217
Cigar-machine	R. B. Robbins	Adrian, Mich	Mar. 12, 1872	124, 629
Cigar-machine	H. Shild and G. J. Prentice	New York, N. Y	Jan. 18, 1870	98, 890
Cigar-machine	S. Scholfield	Providence, R. I	Aug. 9, 1870	106, 214
Cigar-machine	S. Scholfield	Providence, R. I	Nov. 28, 1871	121, 298
Cigar-machine	S. Scholfield	Providence, R. I	Sept. 24, 1872	131, 567
Cigar-machine	S. Scholfield	Providence, R. I	July 15, 1873	140, 845
Cigar-machine	S. Scholfield	Providence, R. I	July 15, 1873	140, 846
Cigar-machine	G. W. Tanner	Providence, R. I	July 25, 1871	117, 482
Cigar-machine	G. W. Tanner	Providence, R. I	Sept. 17, 1872	131, 474
Cigar-machine	G. W. Tanner and F. D. Bliss	Providence, R. I	July 26, 1870	105, 859
Cigar-machine	I. Ten Eyck and J. O. Reilley	New York, N. Y	Sept. 13, 1870	107, 307
Cigar-machine	J. Thompson	New York, N. Y	Feb. 14, 1865	46, 404
Cigar-machine	H. E. Tylander	Keokuk, Iowa	May 27, 1873	139, 280
Cigar-machine	J. L. Weatherhead	Philadelphia, Pa	Apr. 16, 1872	125, 709
Cigar-machine	J. Wettstein	Baltimore, Md	Nov. 23, 1869	97, 255
Cigar-machine roll	D. A. Wightman	East Greenwich, R. I	July 15, 1873	140, 859
Cigar-machinery	W. Kramer and J. Wise	Milwaukee, Wis., and New York, N. Y.	Aug. 20, 1867	67, 887
Cigar-maker's filler-box	G. Barry	Chicago, Ill	Dec. 26, 1871	122, 211
Cigar-maker's mold	J. Prentice	New York, N. Y	Jan. 12, 1869	85, 764
Cigar-making apparatus	J. F. Shepard	Hampton Falls, N. H	May 12, 1868	77, 846
Cigar-making machine	L. Beauché	Paris, France	Feb. 16, 1858	19, 341
Cigar-making machine	J. Hafer and J. A. Henderson	Bedford, Pa	June 18, 1867	65, 805
Cigar-making machine	H. J. Hall	Brookline, Mass	Jan. 23, 1872	123, 014
Cigar-making machine	I. A. Heald	Carlisle, Mass	May 22, 1866	54, 900
Cigar-making machine	J. A. Heald	Springfield, Mass	Aug. 6, 1861	32, 993
Cigar-making machine	W. W. Huse	Brooklyn, N. Y	Dec. 6, 1864	45, 326
Cigar-making machine	J. McKee and T. W. Fletcher	New York, N. Y	Mar. 16, 1869	87, 955
Cigar-making machine	M. V. McKinney	Louisville, Ky	Sept. 19, 1871	119, 040
Cigar-making machine	H. Pierce	Winchester, N. H	Dec. 10, 1846	4, 885
Cigar-making machine	T. Thorp	New York, N. Y	Dec. 6, 1859	26, 382
Cigar-making machine	T. Thorp	New York, N. Y	May 1, 1860	28, 115
Cigar-making machine	A. Weeks	Syracuse, N. Y	June 30, 1868	79, 423
Cigar-making machine	J. Wettstein	Baltimore, Md	May 16, 1871	115, 002
Cigar-making machine	F. Wuterich	New York, N. Y	Dec. 18, 1860	31, 002
Cigar-making machine	F. Wuterich	New York, N. Y	Nov. 5, 1861	33, 687
Cigar-manufacture	W. C. Kneeland	Brooklyn, N. Y	July 28, 1868	80, 287
Cigar-mold	G. Barry	Chicago, Ill	Feb. 6, 1872	123, 323
Cigar-mold	J. Baxter	Detroit, Mich	Mar. 26, 1872	125, 005
Cigar-mold	N. H. Borgfeldt	New York, N. Y	Nov. 22, 1870	109, 490
Cigar-mold	N. H. Borgfeldt	New York, N. Y	Jan. 3, 1871	110, 732
Cigar-mold	N. H. Borgfeldt	New York, N. Y	Oct. 29, 1872	132, 622
Cigar-mold	N. Dubrul	Joliet, Ill	May 9, 1871	114, 655
Cigar-mold	N. Dubrul	Joliet, Ill	May 16, 1871	114, 932
Cigar-mold	N. Du Brul	Chicago, Ill	Sept. 9, 1873	142, 683
Cigar-mold	I. Guthman	Morrison, Ill	June 25, 1872	128, 386
Cigar-mold	B. Hawkins	Trenton, N. J	June 11, 1872	127, 764
Cigar-mold	J. J. Lahaye and J. M. Lyons	Reading, Pa	Dec. 19, 1871	122, 034
Cigar-mold	T. D. McGuire	Brooklyn, N. Y	May 6, 1873	138, 672

Index of patents issued from the United States Patent Office from 1790 *to* 1873, *inclusive*—Continued.

Invention.	Inventor.	Residence.	Date.	No.
Cigar-mold	F. C. Miller	Cincinnati, Ohio	Feb. 4, 1873	135, 572
Cigar-mold	C. H. Palmer	New York, N. Y	Mar. 11, 1873	136, 615
Cigar-mold	J. Prentice	New York, N. Y	May 23, 1871	115, 101
Cigar-mold	S. G. Rice	Albany, N. Y	July 2, 1872	128, 510
Cigar-mold	S. G. Rice	Albany, N. Y	Dec. 31, 1872	134, 398
Cigar mold and press	J. Ryan	Detroit, Mich	Oct. 3, 1871	119, 653
Cigar-mold clamp	S. Wilmot	Detroit, Mich	Mar. 4, 1873	136, 399
Cigar-mold press	G. Barry	Chicago, Ill	Feb. 27, 1872	123, 972
Cigar-mold press	F. Brown	New York, N. Y	Oct. 22, 1872	132, 351
Cigar-mold press	F. Brown	New York, N. Y	Oct. 22, 1872	132, 352
Cigar-molds, Machine for filling	F. C. Miller	Cincinnati, Ohio	July 23, 1872	129, 674
Cigar-molds, Machine for making	M. H. Eeimerdinger	New York, N. Y	May 21, 1872	126, 957
Cigar-molds, Tool for boring	H. F. Moeller and H. P. Brandt	Davenport, Iowa	Nov. 21, 1871	121, 059
Cigar-molding apparatus	J. Charter	Sterling, Ill	Apr. 23, 1872	126, 018
Cigar-molding device	T. J. Winship	Montreal, Canada	Apr. 8, 1873	137, 749
Cigar, money, &c., box	N. Thompson	Brooklyn, E. D., N. Y	Dec. 1, 1868	84, 655
Cigar mouth-piece	J. Ball	Elmira, N. Y	Mar. 28, 1865	46, 986
Cigar mouth-piece	I. S. Barber	New York, N. Y	Nov. 13, 1866	59, 544
Cigar, Medicated	J. Barrett	Chicago, Ill	Mar. 2, 1869	87, 320
Cigar, Medicated	L. Walther	New York, N. Y	Oct. 12, 1869	95, 858
Cigar perforator	E. A. Konter	Brooklyn, N. Y	Dec. 10, 1872	133, 864
Cigar-piercer	H. N. Foster	East Greenwich, R. I	Mar. 15, 1870	100, 744
Cigar-pipe	H. E. Doster	Bethlehem, Pa	Sept. 1, 1868	81, 610
Cigar-pipe	A. A. Pathi	Paris, France	Oct. 6, 1868	82, 743
Cigar-pipe	E. Schlichting	New York, N. Y	Dec. 31, 1867	72, 912
Cigar-point splitter	A. Sickenberger	Chicago, Ill	Nov. 11, 1873	144, 570
Cigar-press	J. Campbell	Lancaster, Pa	Oct. 2, 1866	58, 538
Cigar-press	G. Heiss	Lancaster, Pa	Nov. 20, 1866	59, 911
Cigar-press	A. Iske	Lancaster, Pa	July 3, 1866	56, 055
Cigar-press	M. Leippe	Lancaster, Pa	July 24, 1866	56, 578
Cigar-press	G. Studer	Richmond, Ind	Dec. 29, 1868	85, 344
Cigar-pressing machine	J. Campbell	Lancaster, Pa	June 19, 1866	55, 619
Cigar-punch	S. J. Bestor	Hartford, Conn	June 14, 1870	104, 250
Cigar-rack for hats	F. I. Miller	Brooklyn, N. Y	June 19, 1860	28, 763
Cigar-sample box	J. C. W. Frishmuth	Philadelphia, Pa	May 23, 1871	115, 188
Cigar-shaped pipe	S. N. Buynitzky	Washington, D. C	Mar. 4, 1873	136, 487
Cigar-shaped smoker	D. D. Foley	Washington, D. C	Aug. 23, 1864	43, 906
Cigar-shield	G. E. Brinkerhoff	New York, N. Y	Mar. 15, 1870	100, 850
Cigar-tip	J. Clark	Lowell, Mass	July 13, 1869	92, 423
Cigar-tip	W. M. Herron	Allegheny, Pa	Mar. 4, 1873	136, 514
Cigar-tip cutter	F. Timm and T. Fantini	Stapleton, N. Y	Feb. 25, 1873	136, 285
Cigar-tip machine	W. W. Huse	Brooklyn, N. Y	Dec. 6, 1864	45, 325
Cigar-tips, Composition for covering	J. H. Harris	Pittsfield, Mass	May 14, 1872	126, 698
Cigar-tips, Forming	S. L. Cole	Brooklyn, N. Y	Oct. 18, 1870	108, 331
Cigar-tips, Instrument for cutting	C. Froehlich	Philadelphia, Pa	Dec. 3, 1867	71, 600
Cigar-trimmer	J. H. Christman	Syracuse, N. Y	July 16, 1872	129, 101
Cigar-trimmer	A. Cramer	Detroit, Mich	June 24, 1873	140, 117
Cigar-trimmer	A. Hettinger	Philadelphia, Pa	May 20, 1873	139, 152
Cigar-trimmer	S. Scholfield	Providence, R. I	July 15, 1873	140, 847
Cigar-tuck cutter	S. Scholfield	Providence, R. I	Dec. 24, 1872	134, 222
Cigar-wrapper	H. Durell	Morrisania, N. Y	Sept. 14, 1858	21, 558
Cigar-wrapper	C. E. Raffee	Barrington, R. I	Sept. 19, 1865	50, 038
Cigar-wrapper	J. S. Suter and G. M. Palmer	Baltimore, Md	Oct. 5, 1858	21, 704
Cigar-wrappers, Apparatus for cutting	R. Appleby	Beverly, N. J	Apr. 8, 1873	137, 524
Cigar-wrappers, Cutting	S. Scholfield	Providence, R. I	Oct. 15, 1872	132, 183
Cigar-wrappers, Manufacture of	F. Dixon	Lynn, Mass	Sept. 27, 1859	25, 604
Cigar-wrapping machine	S. Scholfield	Providence, R. I	July 15, 1873	140, 849
Cigar-wrapping machine	G. W. Tanner and F. D. Bliss	Providence, R. I	July 5, 1870	105, 140
Cigars and plug-tobacco, Machine for forming	W. Hall and E. J. Bennett	Boston, Mass	Nov. 30, 1869	97, 292
Cigars, Apparatus for cutting the ends of	M. J. Hinden	Detroit, Mich	Mar. 21, 1871	112, 808
Cigars, Bunch-mold machine for	J. Wettstein	Highland, Ill	Dec. 31, 1872	134, 502
Cigars, &c., Compound for lighting	C. J. M. Sohet and H. C. T. Molvant.	New York, N. Y	Nov. 20, 1866	59, 868
Cigars, Device for perforating	J. Houghton and G. Wingfield	New York and Brooklyn, N. Y.	May 21, 1867	64, 978
Cigars, Forming bunches for mold	C. M. Mann	Detroit, Mich	Sept. 17, 1872	131, 362
Cigars for tying, Clamp for holding	M. Ali	Philadelphia, Pa	May 15, 1866	54, 811
Cigars, &c., Friction-match for lighting	H. Reiman	Brooklyn, N. Y	Nov. 7, 1865	50, 843
Cigars, Implement for cutting, perforating, and lighting.	C. F. Smith	Springfield, Mass	Apr. 7, 1868	76, 537
Cigars, Instrument for perforating	O. Guinand	Vicksburgh, Miss	July 2, 1867	66, 325
Cigars, Lighting	W. B. Dondes	Canton, Ohio	July 30, 1867	67, 276
Cigars, Machine for compressing and cutting the filling for.	W. W. Huse	Brooklyn, N. Y	July 16, 1867	66, 845
Cigars, Machine for cutting off	C. and F. W. Hoffman	Morrisania, N. Y	June 13, 1865	48, 174
Cigars, Machine for cutting off	F. W. Hoffman	Morrisania, N. Y	Nov. 13, 1866	59, 606
Cigars, Machine for cutting off	P. Zern and W. Warwick	Pittsburgh, Pa	May 28, 1867	65, 325
Cigars, Machine for cutting off the ends of	J. G. Maier and C. W. Schaeffer	Baltimore, Md	Nov. 9, 1869	96, 714
Cigars, Machine for examining and replacing	J. Levy	Wolcottville, Conn	Aug. 29, 1871	118, 541
Cigars, Machine for making	W. Dawson	Huntington, Conn	June 15, 1852	9, 016
Cigars, Machine for making the bodies of	G. A. Reiniger	Stuttgart, Wurtemburg	Oct. 29, 1861	33, 603
Cigars, Machine for manufacturing	J. Ball	Elmira, N. Y	Jan. 10, 1865	45, 808
Cigars, Machine for putting on the wrappers of	G. A. Reiniger	Stuttgart, Wurtemburg	Oct. 29, 1861	33, 604
Cigars, Machine for trimming the ends of	P. A. La France	Elmira, N. Y	Feb. 9, 1869	86, 764
Cigars, Machinery for making	G. Barker	New York, N. Y	July 9, 1861	32, 743
Cigars, Machinery for making	S. E. Hartwell and W. M. and D. Fowler.	New York, N. Y., and Waterbury, Conn.	May 8, 1847	5, 110
Cigars, Making	J. Ball	Buffalo, N. Y	Oct. 12, 1842	2, 809
Cigars, Method and apparatus for making	E. A. Metz	Cincinnati, Ohio	Sept. 5, 1871	118, 739
Cigars, Molding	J. Charter	Sterling, Ill	July 11, 1871	116, 930
Cigars, &c., Mouth-piece for	W. Thompson	Dublin, Ireland	Mar. 31, 1868	76, 119
Cigars, &c., Powder for lighting	C. W. Roseling	Cleveland, Ohio	Apr. 18, 1865	47, 335
Cigars, Process of treating and drying	J. Cuddy	Pittsburgh, Pa	Mar. 4, 1873	136, 480
Cigars, Self-igniting	J. Marck	New York, N. Y	Apr. 16, 1834	......
Cigars, snuff, &c., Process of preparing plants to be used in.	P. V. Rumel	Paris, France	Dec. 14, 1869	97, 962

Index of patents issued from the United States Patent Office from 1790 *to* 1873, *inclusive*—Continued.

Index of patents issued from the United States Patent Office from 1790 *to* 1873, *inclusive*—Continued.

Invention.	Inventor.	Residence.	Date.	No.
Clamp—Continued.				
See Flask-clamp.				
Floor-clamp.				
Flooring-clamp.				
Fruit-jar clamp.				
Furnacemen's clamp.				
Furnace-mold clamp.				
Gas-fitter's clamp.				
Glass-blower's clamp.				
Hand-clamp.				
Harness-clamp.				
Harness-pad clamp.				
Hawser-clamp.				
Hitching-clamp.				
Hog-holding clamp.				
Hub-clamp.				
Iron-structure clamp.				
Joiner's clamp.				
Line-clamp.				
Molder's clamp.				
Mop-clamp.				
Music-stand clamp.				
Newspaper-clamp.				
Paper-clamp.				
Picket-holding clamp.				
Picture-frame clamp.				
Pin-clamp.				
Pipe and faucet clamp.				
Planking clamp.				
Pole-clamp.				
Portable clamp.				
Rail-clamp.				
Regulating-clamp.				
Rigging-clamp.				
Rigging-setting clamp.				
Rope-clamp.				
Rope or wire clamp.				
Saddler's clamp.				
Safety-clamp.				
Sash and door clamp.				
Saw-clamp.				
Saw-filing clamp.				
Scaffold-pole clamp.				
Screw-clamp.				
Sewing-clamp.				
Sheet-piling clamp.				
Ship-planking clamp.				
Shoemaker's clamp.				
Slate-frame clamp.				
Stage-clamp.				
Stay-log clamp.				
Stitching-clamp.				
Strap-clamp.				
Suspending-clamp.				
Tassel-clamp.				
Thill-coupling clamp.				
Timber-holding clamp.				
Trunk-clamp.				
Tube and rod clamp.				
Tubing-clamp.				
Watchmaker's chain-clamp.				
Whip-making clamp.				
Whip-socket clamp.				
Clamp	G. F. Almy	Toledo, Ohio	Mar. 19, 1872	124, 776
Clamp	A. Anderson	Madison, Wis.	Aug. 11, 1868	80, 894
Clamp	C. S. Bonney	Philadelphia, Pa	Feb. 18, 1873	135, 882
Clamp	S. C. Bradley	New Haven, Conn	Feb. 15, 1870	99, 826
Clamp	M. V. Brigham	Mannsville, N. Y	Sept. 7, 1869	94, 557
Clamp	M. G. Burkhardt	Cincinnati, Ohio	Dec. 14, 1869	97, 872
Clamp	C. B. Canfield	Oriskany, N. Y	May 3, 1870	102, 487
Clamp	G. H. Coe and G. H. Snow	New Haven, Conn	Dec. 10, 1867	71, 983
Clamp	T. O. Cornish	Woonsocket, R. I	Dec. 12, 1871	121, 851
Clamp	J. J. Dominic	Gallupville, N. Y	Jan. 17, 1871	110, 961
Clamp	L. Feely	Rochester, N. Y	Aug. 19, 1873	142, 010
Clamp	F. Glasser	Mystic Bridge, Conn	Sept. 13, 1870	107, 247
Clamp	G. W. Goulden	Waverly, N. Y	Sept. 28, 1869	95, 337
Clamp	E. B. Hayes	Vergennes, Vt	Mar. 22, 1870	101, 126
Clamp	F. M. Holmes	Boston, Mass	Sept. 9, 1873	142, 697
Clamp	N. J. Holt and J. Leach	Howell and Detroit, Mich	June 24, 1873	140, 136
Clamp	P. F. Hulbert	Chatham, N. Y	June 5, 1866	55, 302
Clamp	J. S. Ladow	Mechanicsville, N. Y	Jan. 25, 1870	99, 212
Clamp	G. D. Lambert	New Haven, Conn	Mar. 8, 1870	100, 642
Clamp	J. J. Lebeau	Cincinnati, Ohio	June 21, 1870	104, 606
Clamp	J. F. Metz	Baltimore, Md	May 21, 1872	126, 895
Clamp	S. A. Morse	New Bedford, Mass	Apr. 16, 1867	63, 929
Clamp	W. F. Otis	New London, Ohio	Oct. 29, 1872	132, 538
Clamp	O. L. Payne	Batavia, Ill	July 13, 1869	92, 642
Clamp	W. H. Payne and H. Imhof	Lockport, N. Y	Sept. 16, 1873	142, 938
Clamp	J. H. Phillips	Troy, N. Y	June 18, 1872	128, 064
Clamp	E. K. Purdy	Schoolcraft, Mich	Oct. 13, 1868	82, 985
Clamp	W. Sailer	Philadelphia, Pa	Aug. 18, 1868	81, 298
Clamp	W. Sailer	Philadelphia, Pa	Nov. 16, 1869	96, 971
Clamp	J. E. Sinclair	Worcester, Mass	July 15, 1873	140, 852
Clamp	W. Strevell	Jersey City, N. J	Jan. 1, 1867	60, 959
Clamp	J. A. Traut	New Britain, Conn	Sept. 10, 1872	131, 195
Clamp	L. Wharton	Salem, Ohio	Aug. 30, 1870	106, 900
Clamp and wrench, Combined	E. Maguire	Princeton, Ill	Nov. 26, 1872	133, 325
Clamp-mill for turning metals	W. H. Brainard	Branford, Conn	July 16, 1872	129, 092

Index of patents issued from the United States Patent Office from 1790 *to* 1873, *inclusive*—Continued.

Invention.	Inventor.	Residence.	Date.	No.
Clamp-milling machine	A. B. Lawther	Stonington, Conn	Apr. 5, 1864	42, 201
Clamping-device	E. King	Fredonia, N. Y	Sept. 17, 1867	68, 886
Clamping-device	E. Simmons	South Providence, R. I	Sept. 26, 1865	50, 175
Clamping-device	C. Stout	Waverly Heights, Pa	June 17, 1873	139, 931
Clamping-machine	J. H. Humes	East Saginaw, Mich	June 14, 1870	104, 315
Clamping-machine	E. Wheeler	Marlborough, Mass	Jan. 27, 1857	16, 506
Clamping-machine, Carpenter's	W. R. Axe	Beloit, Wis	Jan. 22, 1861	31, 145
Clamping-pontil	F. H. James and N. B. Gatchell	Lancaster, N. Y	Nov. 21, 1865	51, 058
Clapboard	H. Osgood	Hartland, Me	Nov. 7, 1865	50, 8[illegible]9
Clapboard	A. A. Wilder	Detroit, Mich	Jan. 10, 1860	26, 803
Clapboard and lath cutting machine	E. Day	Grand Detour, Ill	June 18, 1842	2, 674
Clapboard and shingle sawing machine	J. Jaquith	Sherburn, Mass	June 26, 1817	....
Clapboard-gage	W. E. Babcock	East Pembroke, N. Y	June 27, 1871	116, 256
Clapboard-gage	J. C. Biddlecom	Macedon, N. Y	May 3, 1870	102, 649
Clapboard-gage	A. Carson	Memphis, Tenn	July 2, 1867	66, 216
Clapboard-gage	A. Deys	Rockford, Ill	Oct. 4, 1870	108, 010
Clapboard-gage	G. Hall	Middletown, Ohio	June 4, 1867	65, 378
Clapboard-gage	E. Horton	Dundee, N. Y	July 12, 1870	105, 210
Clapboard-gage	S. Inman	Rockford, Ill	Sept. 3, 1861	33, 199
Clapboard-gage	G. Smith	Omaha, Nebr	Nov. 30, 1869	97, 452
Clapboard-gage	H. Van Deusen	Phelps, N. Y	Dec. 6, 1859	26, 386
Clapboard-joint	W. Baker	Utica, N. Y	May 16, 1854	10, 903
Clapboard-machine	B. Corser	Mount Morris, N. Y	Jan. 16, 1849	6, 033
Clapboard-machine	C. S. Davis	Orono, Me	Dec. 7, 1869	97, 484
Clapboard-machine	O. R. and L. C. Kendall	Groton, N. H	Mar. 30, 1869	88, 306
Clapboard-machine	D. Newton	Dalton, N. H	Jan. 31, 1833	....
Clapboard-machine	A. A. Wilder	Detroit, Mich	Oct. 30, 1855	13, 734
Clapboard or siding gage	J. W. Arnold	Fairport, N. Y	July 9, 1872	128, 696
Clapboard sawing and planing machine	E. Parker	Rock Island, Ill	Dec. 20, 1853	10, 341
Clapboard-sawing machine	D. Bartholomew	Wolcott, Vt	July 8, 1843	3, 165
Clapboard-sawing machine	S. Goss	Milford, N. H	June 3, 1837	226
Clapboard-sawing machine	A. A. Holmes	Epsom, N. H	Sept. 2, 1873	142, 339
Clapboard-sawing machine	D. F. Mellen	Wentworth, N. H	Aug. 22, 1854	11, 568
Clapboard-sawing machine	O. and D. Parker	Hubbardstown, Mass	Dec. 24, 1834	....
Clapboard-sawing machine	C. Tyler	Milford, N. H	Aug. 30, 1838	900
Clapboard-sawing machinery	E. Pray, E. Benjamin, and J. S. Stone.	Maine	Dec. 28, 1824	....
Clapboard, tipping, &c., Sawing	E. Carleton and S. Whiting, jr.	Bath, N. H	Mar. 25, 1830	....
Clapboards from round logs, Making	H. Whittemore	Worcester, Mass	Aug. 26, 1831	....
Clapboards, Gage for holding	W. H. Cummings and I. Babcock.	Boonsborough, Iowa	May 28, 1867	65, 178
Clapboards, Machine for beveling the ends of	S. W. Curtis	Stoughton, Mass	May 26, 1843	3, 104
Clapboards, Machine for planing	J. Atkins	Augusta, Me	Feb. 25, 1873	136, 201
Clapboards, Machine for sapping logs for	E. Webber	Gardiner, Me	June 27, 1871	116, 377
Clapboarding	F. Buscher	Dunkirk, N. Y	Jan. 9, 1872	122, 562
Clapboarding-clamp	W. P. Wentworth	Detroit, Mich	Mar. 12, 1867	62, 792
Clapboarding-gage	H. D. Vandercook	Marshall, Mich	July 17, 1860	29, 2[illegible]6
Clarifying and condensing the juice of fruit	C. Cory	Lima, Ind	May 24, 1864	42, 841
Clarinet	A. Fritsche	New York, N. Y	Jan. 10, 1871	110, 845
Clarinet	J. Rebhun	New York, N. Y	July 27, 1869	93, 005

Clasp:

See Bag-clasp.
Band-clasp.
Bank-bill clasp.
Bed-clothes clasp.
Belt-clasp.
Broom-clasp.
Buckle-clasp.
Cattle-leading clasp.
Colter-clasp.
Compression-clasp.
Corset-clasp.
Corset-busk clasp.
Curtain-clasp.
Dress-looping clasp.
Elastic-tube clasp.
Glove-clasp.
Halter-clasp.
Harness-clasp.
Harness-maker's clasp.
Harness-tug clasp.
Hoop-skirt clasp.
Lamp-shade clasp.
Leather-strap clasp.
Lever-clasp.
Lightning-rod clasp.
Limb-clasp.
Mail-bag clasp.
Metallic clasp.
Necktie clasp.
Paint-brush clasp.
Pocket-book clasp.
Regulating-clasp.
Rope clasp.
Safety-clasp.
Scarf-clasp.
Seat-clasp.
Shoe-clasp.
Side-arm clasp.
Skirt-hoop clasp.
Spring-clasp.
Stay-log clasp.
Stocking-supporter clasp.
Suspender-clasp.
Traveling-bag clasp.
Trunk-clasp.
Tug-clasp.
Wearing-apparel clasp.
Whip-socket clasp.

Index of patents issued from the United States Patent Office from 1790 *to* 1873, *inclusive*—Continued.

Invention.	Inventor.	Residence.	Date.	No.
Clasp	J. H. Eastman	Boston, Mass	Dec. 2, 1873	145, 097
Clasp	C. T. P. Ware	New York, N. Y	Jan. 17, 1854	10, 436
Clasp-hook	D. Hayes	Cambridge, Mass	June 30, 1868	79, 347
Clasp-ring	L. A. Sanford	Wolcott, Conn	Sept. 29, 1868	82, 643
Clasps, Machine for making	J. Cutler	Chicopee, Mass	Dec. 13, 1859	26, 419
Clavicle-adjuster	A. M. Day	Bennington, Vt	July 5, 1853	9, 828
Claw-bar	G. H. Beard	Cincinnati, Ohio	June 12, 1860	28, 645
Claw-bar	G. Brownell	Mitchell, Ind	Nov. 14, 1865	50, 899
Claw-bar	D. Christie	Chillicothe, Ohio	July 18, 1871	117, 046
Claw-bar	M. Cornelius	Cincinnati, Ohio	Oct. 4, 1864	44, 576
Claw-bar	M. Hennasy	Cranford, N. J	July 21, 1868	80, 072
Claw-bar	H. Jeffrey	Vincennes, Ind	Oct. 10, 1865	50, 361
Claw-bar	I. Lamplugh	Peoria, Ill	Dec. 16, 1862	37, 172
Claw-bar	W. S. Terhune	Ridgewood, N. J	Apr. 1, 1873	137, 333
Claw-bar	C. Winter	Chillicothe, Ohio	Mar. 7, 1871	112, 401
Clay and cement pipe mold	P. McIntyre	Hartford, Conn	Oct. 15, 1872	132, 168
Clay and cement pipe mold	J. Sharpe	Paterson, N. J	July 8, 1873	140, 734
Clay and peat press	B. Van Vrauken	Schenectady, N. Y	June 19, 1866	55, 748
Clay, Apparatus for treating	I. Gregg	Philadelphia, Pa	July 9, 1867	66, 488
Clay articles, Mold for forming	C. A. Fischer	Baltimore, Md	July 15, 1873	140, 910
Clay-cleaning apparatus	L. P. Norton	Bennington, Vt	Jan. 28, 1868	73, 941
Clay-crusher	A. Hall	Perth Amboy, N. J	Jan. 11, 1870	98, 764
Clay for potters' use, Machine for condensing pap or slops of.	J. Muir	New York, N. Y	Jan. 3, 1865	45, 736
Clay for potters' use, Process of preparing	J. Muir	New York, N. Y	Jan. 3, 1865	45, 737
Clay grinding and separating mill, Combined	F. B. Norton and F. Hancock	Worcester, Mass	Apr. 7, 1868	76, 505
Clay, &c., grinding machine	A. Alexander	Pittsburgh, Pa	Apr. 2, 1872	125, 159
Clay-grinding machine	B. Porter	Jackson, Mich	Apr. 10, 1866	53, 868
Clay-grinding machine	W. H. Thomas	Chicago, Ill	July 9, 1867	66, 536
Clay-heating apparatus	I. Gregg	Philadelphia, Pa	July 9, 1867	66, 487
Clay-kneading machine	H. H. Thayer	Sandwich, Mass	June 5, 1855	13, 017
Clay, Machine for breaking	N. Boynton	Danville, Vt	Feb. 27, 1833	....
Clay, Machine for pulverizing	J. O'Neil	Kingston, N. Y	July 10, 1855	13, 224
Clay, Machine for tempering and preparing	N. Adams	Cornwall, N. Y	Dec. 16, 1833	....
Clay, Machine for working	H. Leguay	Saint Louis, Mo	Sept. 14, 1858	21, 506
Clay-machinery	G. D. Goodrich	Chicago, Ill	Jan. 26, 1869	86, 148
Clay-mill	L. Moore	Baraboo, Wis	Aug. 4, 1868	80, 652
Clay-mill	N. F. Potter	Providence, R. I	July 14, 1868	80, 008
Clay-mill	J. A. Vaughn, H. B. Camp, H. E. Merrill and C. J. Merrill.	Cuyahoga Falls and Akron, Ohio, and Alton, Ill.	Dec. 9, 1873	145, 373
Clay-mill	C. Webster, W. Camp, and S. L. Stall.	Akron, Ohio	Mar. 22, 1864	42, 055
Clay-mixer	A. J. Knisely	Chicago, Ill	Oct. 29, 1872	132, 670
Clay-mixing machine	A. Parkhurst	Scriba, N. Y	Apr. 11, 1831	....
Clay, Mode of dressing damp	J. Steele	Buffalo, N. Y	May 9, 1865	47, 684
Clay mold for casting metal	J. J. C. Smith	Philadelphia, Pa	Dec. 29, 1868	85, 340
Clay-molding machine	S. Hambleton and G. P. Herthel, jr.	Saint Louis, Mo	Feb. 16, 1869	87, 043
Clay-molding machine	R. Hill	Saint Louis, Mo	Mar. 23, 1869	88, 166
Clay-molding machine	T. Hoadley	Cleveland, Ohio	Sept. 7, 1858	21, 419
Clay pipe	T. Wickersham	Newbury, Pa	May 13, 1828	....
Clay-pipe die	G. D. and H. A. Goodrich	Joliet, Ill	Oct. 16, 1866	58, 851
Clay pipe for conduits	S. Bartlett	Hartford, Conn	Oct. 1, 1805	....
Clay-pipe machine	G. D. Goodrich	Joliet, Ill	Feb. 5, 1867	61, 732
Clay-pipe machine	C. Stotz and G. Smith	Perth Amboy, N. J	Dec. 29, 1868	85, 490
Clay-pipe machine	S. Ustick	Philadelphia, Pa	Mar. 20, 1860	27, 602
Clay-pipe manufacture	G. D. and H. A. Goodrich	Joliet, Ill	July 2, 1867	66, 319
Clay-pipe manufacture	H. A. Goodrich	Joliet, Ill	July 2, 1867	66, 320
Clay-pipe manufacture	J. Putnam	Salem, Mass	Sept. 30, 1851	8, 403
Clay-pipe-pressing machine	T. Shaw	Philadelphia, Pa	Dec. 28, 1869	98, 430
Clay pipes, Apparatus for turning heavy	W. Wassall	Wellsville, Ohio	Aug. 31, 1869	94, 364
Clay pipes, Machine for forming	C. P. Wardwell	Lake Village, N. H	Apr. 21, 1857	17, 125
Clay pipes, Machine for making	H. Augood and S. Ustick	Mansfield Township, N. J., and Philadelphia, Pa.	May 24, 1859	24, 174
Clay pipes, Machine for making	J. Jones	Baltimore, Md	Jan. 25, 1859	22, 730
Clay pipes, Machine for making	W. Linton	Baltimore, Md	Aug. 23, 1859	25, 233
Clay pipes, Making	J. Bower	East Bethlehem, Pa	Dec. 1, 1826	....
Clay pipes, Manufacture of	G. D. Goodrich	Joliet, Ill	Jan. 7, 1868	72, 997
Clay pipes, Manufacture of	H. A. Goodrich and J. Amos	Joliet, Ill	Feb. 4, 1868	74, 078
Clay-pulverizer and stone-separator	F. H. Smith	Baltimore, Md	Mar. 9, 1869	87, 716
Clay pulverizing and cleaning machine	G. F. Blake	Medford, Mass	Nov. 26, 1861	33, 810
Clay-pulverizing machine	G. C. Bovey	Chillicothe, Ohio	May 20, 1873	139, 110
Clay retorts, Decarbonizing	G. W. Edge	Jersey City, N. J	Sept. 19, 1865	49, 989
Clay, Tempering	S. Miller and G. Roller	Manchester Post-Office, Md	July 31, 1846	4, 676
Clay, Tempering	J. W. Ward	Cambridge, Mass	June 6, 1848	5, 615
Clay-tempering apparatus	L. E. Ransom	Trenton, Mich	May 4, 1869	89, 685
Clay-tempering machine	S. Barnes	Rochester, Pa	June 25, 1872	128, 278
Clay-tempering machine	J. D. Custer	Norristown, Pa	June 7, 1859	24, 350
Clay-tempering machine	G. E. Noyes	Washington, D. C	Sept. 28, 1869	95, 374
Clay-tempering mill	G. Carnell, S. Williams, and W. Ellis.	Philadelphia, Pa	Oct. 27, 1868	83, 361
Clay-tempering wheel	F. L. Carnell	Philadelphia, Pa	May 16, 1871	114, 919
Clay tubes, Machine for making	J. H. Rowell and H. Wise	Fredericktown, Pa	May 10, 1827	....
Clay-washing and stone-separating machine	E. Wilzinski	Chicago, Ill	Feb. 25, 1868	74, 967
Clay-working machine	D. and G. Duchemin	Cincinnati, Ohio	Dec. 2, 1851	8, 565
Cleaner:				
See Boiler-flue cleaner.				
Boot and shoe cleaner.				
Cane-cleaner.				
Card-cylinder cleaner.				
Carpet-cleaner.				
Cartridge-case cleaner.				
Chimney-cleaner.				
Clothes-cleaner.				
Coffee-cleaner.				
Coffee and grain cleaner.				
Comb-cleaner.				

Index of patents issued from the United States Patent Office from 1790 *to* 1873, *inclusive*—Continued.

Invention.	Inventor.	Residence.	Date.	No.
Cleaner—Continued.				
See Cotton-cleaner.				
Cotton-seed cleaner.				
Dish-cleaner.				
Flax and hemp cleaner.				
Floor-cleaner.				
Flue-cleaner.				
Fork-cleaner.				
Garden-walk cleaner.				
Grain-cleaner.				
Grain and malt cleaner.				
Gun-cleaner.				
Harvester-track cleaner				
Hop-pole cleaner.				
Knife-cleaner.				
Knife and fork cleaner.				
Lamp-chimney cleaner.				
Ore-cleaner.				
Plow-cleaner.				
Rag-cleaner.				
Railway-track cleaner.				
Rice-cleaner.				
Sadiron-cleaner.				
Sewer-cleaner.				
Shoe-cleaner.				
Silk-cleaner.				
Slate cleaner.				
Stable-cleaner.				
Steam-boiler-flue cleaner.				
Steam-jet boiler-tube cleaner.				
Stove-pipe cleaner.				
Street-cleaner.				
Track-cleaner.				
Tube-cleaner.				
Watch-cleaner.				
Well-cleaner.				
Wheat-cleaner.				
Window-cleaner.				
Cleaning and boring device	J. B. Jordan	Aurora, Wis	June 30, 1868	79, 356
Cleaning and polishing attachment to sheet-metal rolls.	J. B. Hastings	Ironton, Ohio	July 6, 1869	92, 309
Cleansing-liquid	E. J. Balcear	Martinez, Cal	May 18, 1869	90, 064
Cleat and capstan, Combined	D. Snedeker	Lockport, N. Y	June 29, 1869	92, 116
Cleat and chock, Iron	F. B. Stevens and W. Brown	Weehawken and Hoboken, N. J.	Apr. 27, 1869	89, 514
Cleat chock	A. Lake	Smith's Landing, N. J	Nov. 5, 1867	70, 580
Cleat for sail-boats, Automatic	L. Hill	Alexandria, Va	Dec. 3, 1867	71, 615
Cleat or ring-bolt, Shifting	J. E. Murray	Provincetown, Mass	June 8, 1869	90, 952
Cleaver	C. Hammond	Philadelphia, Pa	Aug. 10, 1869	93, 614
Clevis	W. W. Atteberry	Chesterfield, Ill	Aug. 10, 1869	93, 396
Clevis	D. M. Castle	Constantine, Mich	Dec. 20, 1870	110, 200
Clevis	E. Evans	Montgomery, Ala	June 1, 1869	90, 736
Clevis	I. Evans	Lebanon, Ohio	May 16, 1848	5, 581
Clevis	G. W. Holton	Berlin, Ky	Apr. 27, 1869	89, 407
Clevis	E. R. Kagarice	New Enterprise, Pa	Nov. 5, 1872	132, 724
Clevis	E. A. Palmer	Clayville, N. Y	Sept. 16, 1856	15, 743
Clevis	S. W. Pope	Louisville, Ky	Aug. 15, 1871	118, 050
Clevis	E. M. Potter	Kalamazoo, Mich	Jan. 7, 1868	73, 197
Clevis	J. H. Shaw	Inlet, Ill	May 23, 1871	115, 113
Clevis	F. Sigrist	Napa County, Cal	Nov. 27, 1860	30, 766
Clevis	Z. B. Sims	Bonham, Tex	Aug. 31, 1869	94, 348
Clevis	R. C. Whitehouse	Booth Bay, Me	Apr. 28, 1868	77, 426
Clevis and plow-shares, Apparatus for rolling	F. Murray	Pittsburgh, Pa	Apr. 23, 1867	64, 131
Clevis and stirrup bending machine	W. C. Kaiser	Louisville, Ky	Aug. 9, 1870	106, 172
Clevis bar and hook	R. Gibbs	Spring Hill, Mo	May 27, 1873	139, 381
Clevis-blank die	J. Kritch	Cleveland, Ohio	Aug. 25, 1868	81, 380
Clevis-blanks, Apparatus for bending	T. Meikle	Louisville, Ky	July 27, 1869	93, 106
Clevis-blank, Machine for rolling	M. Loughran	Pittsburgh, Pa	Dec. 24, 1867	72, 512
Clevis, Clamp for making	V. M. Chafee	Xenia, Ill	Jan. 31, 1860	26, 968
Clevis, Elastic link for	L. Fliedner	Cleveland, Ohio	Apr. 6, 1869	88, 619
Clevis-iron	T. P. Warren	Norfolk, Va	June 9, 1868	78, 775
Clevis-making machine	J. S. Hall	Pittsburgh, Pa	Oct. 4, 1870	107, 901
Clevis, Substitute for	J. and W. D. Howell and J. Sipe.	Clark County, Ohio	Jan. 15, 1850	7, 021
Clevis, Three-horse	J. Fowler	Allegan, Mich	June 30, 1868	79, 463
Clevis, Three-horse	S. H. Frederick	Matteson, Mich	July 27, 1869	92, 953
Clew-blocks to clews, Means of attaching	E. A. Sawyer	Portland, Me	Jan. 5, 1864	41, 096
Clew-thimble	T. Carroll	Middletown, Conn	May 17, 1864	42, 817
Clew-thimble	W. W. Wilcox	Middletown, Conn	Apr. 14, 1863	38, 192
Climbing poles, Machine for	H. D. Chapman	Baltimore, Md	Mar. 11, 1851	7, 966
Climozonator	W. Elmer	New York, N. Y	Feb. 23, 1869	87, 155
Clinch-ring die	S. Vanstone	Providence, R. I	Mar. 15, 1870	100, 823
Clinch-rings, Machine for making	J. A. Coleman	Providence, R. I.	June 13, 1865	48, 157
Clinching and nipping tool	E. Warren	Marshall, Mich	Nov. 3, 1863	40, 522
Clinching and nipping tool	D. A. Wilson	Cambridge, Vt	Oct. 17, 1865	50, 539
Clinching-iron	D. H. Williams	Antwerp, N. Y	May 29, 1866	55, 189
Clinometer and level	J. L. L. Knox	Pittsburgh, Pa	Dec. 31, 1867	72, 740
Clip:				
See Album-clip.				
Axle-clip.				
Carriage-clip.				
Carriage and saddle clip.				
Carriage-saddle clip.				
Carriage-spring clip.				
Crinoline-clip.				
Curtain-tassel clip.				
Harness-clip.				
Letter-clip.				

Index of patents issued from the United States Patent Office from 1790 *to* 1873, *inclusive*—Continued.

Invention.	Inventor.	Residence.	Date.	No.
Clip—Continued. *See* Paper-clip. Ribbon-roll clip. Shaft-clip. Spring-clip. Suspension-clip. Tassel-clip. Ticket-clip. Trace-clip. Tug-clip. Wagon-clip. Wagon-axle-skein clip. Whiffletree-clip.				
Clip-circle	I. N. Topliff	Adrian, Mich	Oct. 15, 1867	69, 866
Clipping apparatus, Animal	A. D. Kenshaw	London, England	Apr. 21, 1868	77, 093
Clipping-machine	J. W. Moyer	Cooperstown, N. Y	Apr. 2, 1872	125, 209
Clipping machine, Horse	P. Adie	Strand, England	June 30, 1868	79, 293
Clipping-shears	G. F. Evans	Norway, Me	Sept. 19, 1871	119, 019
Clipping-shears	C. F. Harlow	Boston, Mass	Aug. 8, 1871	117, 774
Clipping-shears	G. H. Pratt	Boston, Mass	June 20, 1871	116, 216
Clipping-shears	J. K. Priest and R. T. Smith	Nashua, N. H	Jan. 16, 1872	122, 852
Clipping-shears	R. T. Smith and J. K. Priest	Nashua, N. H	Apr. 23, 1872	125, 911
Clipping-shears	J. C. Wilson, A. Walker, and J. Foster.	New York, N. Y	Dec. 15, 1868	84, 926
Clipping-shears	J. C. Wilson, A. Walker, and J. Foster.	New York, N. Y	Sept. 14, 1869	94, 803
Clipping-shears	R. Wyatt	New York, N. Y	Aug. 22, 1871	118, 417
Clipping shears, Horse	S. H. Folsom	East Cambridge, Mass	May 19, 1863	38, 576
Cloak and coat suspender	J. D. Leach and E. S. Wardwell	Penobscot and Bucksport, Me.	July 7, 1868	79, 580
Cloak and tent, Convertible	W. B. Johns	Georgetown, D. C	Oct. 22, 1861	33, 528
Cloak, bed, tent, &c., Combined	T. C. Brecht and S. B. Sigismond.	United States Navy and Washington, D. C.	Oct. 14, 1862	36, 685
Cloak, Military	F. W. Weiss	Mount Vernon, N. Y	Dec. 10, 1861	33, 910
Cloak stand, Lady's	J. R. Palmenberg	New York, N. Y	July 25, 1865	48, 989
Cloaks, Cutting	A. S. Thompson	Albion, Pa	Dec. 11, 1855	13, 926
Clock	R. T. Andrews	Plymouth Hollow, Conn	May 19, 1863	38, 543
Clock	W. B. Barnes	Forestville, Conn	Nov. 6, 1860	30, 558
Clock	S. Blydenburgh and W. Beebe.	New York, N. Y	Apr. 26, 1833	....
Clock	C. Boardman and J. A. Wells	Hartford, Conn	Jan. 1, 1847	4, 914
Clock	J. Bogardus	New York, N. Y	Mar. 2, 1830	....
Clock	L. F. and W. W. Carter	Bristol, Conn	Feb. 19, 1867	62, 112
Clock	A. D. Crane	Caldwell, N. J	Mar. 18, 1829	....
Clock	A. D. Crane	Newark, N. J	Feb. 10, 1841	1, 973
Clock	R. P. Cunningham	Eastford, Conn	Dec. 22, 1857	18, 890
Clock	J. D. Custer	Norristown, Pa	Nov. 24, 1830	....
Clock	T. A. Davies	New York, N. Y	Jan. 15, 1846	4, 334
Clock	T. A. Davies	New York, N. Y	Aug. 12, 1846	4, 687
Clock	H. G. Dyar	New York, N. Y	Nov. 6, 1827	....
Clock	A. Gould	Henrietta, N. Y	Oct. 1, 1830	....
Clock	J. Henry	Maysville, Ky	Sept. 13, 1820	....
Clock	J. Ives	Bristol, Conn	July 1, 1836	....
Clock	C. Kirk	Bristol, Conn	Aug. 26, 1843	3, 233
Clock	C. Kirk	Bristol, Conn	Apr. 3, 1847	5, 045
Clock	W. Lindon	New Haven, Conn	Nov. 26, 1867	71, 519
Clock	J. B. Mayer	Niagara Falls, N. Y	Sept. 15, 1868	82, 266
Clock	J. M. Schrock and J. G. Fisher.	Millersburgh, Ohio, and Quincy, Ill.	Oct. 3, 1846	4, 791
Clock	C. Schwippl	New York, N. Y	June 21, 1864	43, 230
Clock	J. S. Segor	New York, N. Y	May 22, 1833	....
Clock	C. and M. Stevens	Boston, Mass	Mar. 4, 1862	34, 599
Clock	E. Terry	Plymouth, Conn	Mar. 4, 1826	....
Clock	S. B. Terry	Waterbury, Conn	Mar. 31, 1868	76, 117
Clock	S. B. Terry	Waterbury, Conn	Dec. 1, 1868	84, 517
Clock	T. Thompson	Washington, D. C	Jan. 25, 1870	99, 261
Clock, &c	H. Twiss	Meriden, Conn	May 13, 1834	....
Clock	S. Willard	Boston, Mass	Dec. 8, 1819	....
Clock	R. Woolworth	New Haven, Conn	Apr. 7, 1868	76, 370
Clock, Alarm	J. E. Buerk	Boston, Mass	Sept. 18, 1866	58, 058
Clock, Alarm	D. M. Charters	Xenia, Ohio	Oct. 21, 1873	143, 881
Clock-alarm	J. Decker	Sparta, N. J	Mar. 5, 1867	62, 531
Clock, Alarm	J. F. Mascher	Philadelphia, Pa	Feb. 8, 1859	22, 883
Clock, Alarm	W. A. Terry	Bristol, Conn	Oct. 29, 1867	70, 376
Clock-alarm	J. S. Turner	New Haven, Conn	July 13, 1852	9, 123
Clock, Alarm	C. H. Warner	New Haven, Conn	Apr. 7, 1868	76, 567
Clock-alarm attachment	J. H. Davis	Chillicothe, Mo	Dec. 13, 1870	110, 016
Clock-alarm, Self-acting	O. N. Angell	Johnston, R. I	June 20, 1834	....
Clock and advertiser combined	G. M. Levette	Indianapolis, Ind	Feb. 18, 1868	74, 704
Clock and burgular alarm, Combined	G. K. Proctor	Beverly, Mass	Aug. 7, 1860	29, 520
Clock and fly-trap, Combined	C. Kallmann	Newbury, N. Y	Apr. 6, 1869	88, 718
Clock and watch escapement	D. J. Mozart, L. Beach, and L. Hubbell.	New York, N. Y., and Farmington and Bristol, Conn.	Dec. 8, 1863	40, 851
Clock and watch key	P. J. Hoffliger	Philadelphia, Pa	Sept. 30, 1873	143, 285
Clock and watch movement	D. J. Mozart	New York, N. Y	Aug. 5, 1862	36, 103
Clock, Astronomical	H. Miller	East Hanover, Pa	May 5, 1825	....
Clock-bell	L. C. Butch	Lancaster, Ohio	May 31, 1870	103, 559
Clock, Burglar-alarm	J. Mathewman	New Haven, Conn	July 6, 1858	20, 810
Clock, Burglar-alarm	G. D. Sargent	Boston, Mass	July 6, 1858	20, 852
Clock, Calendar	W. A. Atkins and J. C. Burritt	Ithaca, N. Y	Sept. 19, 1854	11, 711
Clock, Calendar	W. H. Akins and J. C. Burritt.	Berkshire and Ithaca, N. Y	Nov. 17, 1857	18, 665
Clock, Calendar	E. Allen	Glastenbury, Conn	Apr. 15, 1856	14, 645
Clock, Calendar	E. Allen	Glastenbury, Conn	Sept. 2, 1865	15, 637
Clock-calendar	A. Boardman	Forestville, Conn	July 2, 1867	66, 289
Clock, Calendar	W. W. Carter	Bristol, Conn	Sept. 15, 1863	39, 883
Clock, Calendar	W. K. Chase	Charlestown, Mass	Oct. 19, 1865	51, 556
Clock, Calendar	C. M. Clinton and L. Mood	Ithaca, N. Y	June 25, 1867	66, 003
Clock, Calendar	C. M. Clinton and L. Mood	Ithaca, N. Y	July 30, 1867	67, 166
Clock, Calendar	C. M. Clinton and L. Mood	Ithaca, N. Y	July 9, 1872	128, 854

Index of patents issued from the United States Patent Office from 1790 *to* 1873, *inclusive*—Continued.

Invention.	Inventor.	Residence.	Date.	No.
Clock, Calendar	C. M. Clinton and L. Mood	Ithaca, N. Y	Nov. 11, 1873	144, 384
Clock-calendar	A. Frankfeld	New York, N. Y	Oct. 14, 1873	143, 618
Clock, Calendar	D. J. Gale	Sheboygan Falls, Wis	Nov. 16, 1869	96, [illegible]92
Clock, Calendar	J. H. H. Hawes	Ithaca, N. Y	May 17, 1853	9, 727
Clock, Calendar	H. B. Horton	Ithaca, N. Y	Apr. 18, 1865	47, 306
Clock, Calendar	H. B. Horton	Ithaca, N. Y	Aug. 28, 1866	57, 510
Clock, Calendar	H. B. Horton and M. L. Wood.	Ithaca, N. Y	June 11, 1867	65, 748
Clock, Calendar	S. P. La Due	Rockford, Iowa	Sept. 13, 1859	25, 468
Clock, Calendar	B. B. Lewis	Bristol, Conn	Feb. 4, 1862	34, 341
Clock, Calendar	B. B. Lewis	Hartford, Conn	June 21, 1864	41, 214
Clock, Calendar	B. B. Lewis	Bristol, Conn	Dec. 29, 1868	85, 456
Clock, Calendar	G. Maranville	Hampton Corners, N. Y	Mar. 5, 1861	31, 612
Clock, Calendar	E. M. and J. E. Mix	Ithaca, N. Y	Jan. 31, 1860	27, 023
Clock, Calendar	E. M. and J. E. Mix	Ithaca, N. Y	Mar. 4, 1862	34, 613
Clock, Calendar	E. P. Monroe	Albany, N. Y	Feb. 10, 1857	16, 628
Clock, Calendar	D. J. Mozart	New York, N. Y	Feb. 28, 1865	46, 577
Clock, Calendar	D. J. Mozart, L. Beach, and L. Hubbell.	New York, N. Y., and Farmington and Bristol, Conn.	Jan. 5, 1864	41, 122
Clock, Calendar	G. B. Owen	New York, N. Y	Apr. 24, 1866	54, 198
Clock, Calendar	E. Prichard	Waterbury, Conn	June 5, 1860	28, 603
Clock-calendar	J. K. Seem	Canton, Pa	Jan. 7, 1868	73, 127
Clock-calendar	J. K. Seem	Macomb, Ill	Dec. 24, 1872	134, 319
Clock, Calendar	H. Skinner	Huron, Ohio	Mar. 2, 1858	19, 519
Clock, Calendar	T. T. Strode	Mortonville, Pa	Sept. 25, 1860	30, 166
Clock, Calander	T. T. Strode	Mortonville, Pa	Aug. 1, 1865	49, 169
Clock, Calendar	W. A. Terry	Bristol, Conn	June 16, 1868	79, 026
Clock-calendar	W. A. Terry	Bristol, Conn	Jan. 25, 1870	99, 258
Clock, Calendar	M. J. Whitmore	Potsdam, N. Y	Jan. 13, 1857	16, 418
Clock, Calendar	J. Williams	Hartford, Conn	Sept. 19, 1854	11, 713
Clock, Calendar	J. Williams	Hartford, Conn	July 24, 1855	13, 341
Clock-calendar	N. T. Worthley	Brunswick, Me	Sept. 16, 1873	142, 975
Clock-calendar movement	G. R. Williams	Ithaca, N. Y	Sept. 16, 1873	142, 829
Clock-case	H. B. Horton	Ithaca, N. Y	Aug. 28, 1866	57, 511
Clock-case	D. Monnin	Paris, France	Dec. 3, 1867	71, 631
Clock-case	G. B. Owen	New York, N. Y	Aug. 5, 1862	36, 105
Clock-case	C. W. Roberts	Chicago, Ill	Dec. 24, 1872	134, 168
Clock-case, Composition	S. B. H. Vance and E. M. Smith	New York, N. Y	June 30, 1868	79, 521
Clock-case, Glass	C. A. Moore	Westbrook, Conn	Oct. 17, 1871	119, 990
Clock case making	J. Ives	Bristol, Vt	Mar. 21, 1822	....
Clock cases, Adjustable foot for	O. R. Luther	Waterbury, Conn	Apr. 26, 1870	102, 413
Clock collet die	H. C. Thompson	Bristol, Conn	Apr. 21, 1868	76, 958
Clock, Cuckoo	C. K. Giles	Chicago, Ill	Oct. 8, 1867	69, 561
Clock-dial	S. E. Root	Bristol, Conn	May 10, 1859	23, 950
Clock-dial, Composition	S. Barnes	New Haven, Conn	Oct. 6, 1868	82, 788
Clock-dial sash	G. Hills	Plainville, Conn	Dec. 20, 1864	45, 497
Clock-dials, Enamel for	T. G. Leibnaw and A. G. Heaney	Plainville, Conn	Apr. 12, 1870	101, 891
Clock-dials, Setting	G. Hills	Plainville, Conn	July 5, 1870	105, 077
Clock, Electric	L. Bradley	Jersey City, N. J	Sept. 28, 1869	95, 316
Clock, Electric	W. M. Davis	Cincinnati, Ohio	Oct. 24, 1871	120, 185
Clock, Electric	A. Hall	Loydsville, Ohio	Sept. 26, 1854	11, 723
Clock, Electric	V. Himmer	New York, N. Y	Jan. 4, 1870	98, 593
Clock, Electric	V. Himmer	New York, N. Y	Jan. 4, 1870	98, 594
Clock, Electric	V. Himmer	New York, N. Y	June 4, 1872	127, 483
Clock, Electric	M. Hipp	Neufchatel, Switzerland	June 1, 1869	90, 841
Clock, Electric	S. A. Kennedy	Attleborough, Pa	Feb. 1, 1870	99, 321
Clock, Electric	S. A. Kennedy, S. W. Holt, and J. Gerlach.	Attleborough and Philadelphia, Pa.	Dec. 3, 1867	71, 624
Clock, Electric	F. J. Ritchie	Edinburgh, Scotland	Oct. 21, 1873	143, 847
Clock, Electric	E. Wilson	New York, N. Y	Feb. 1, 1870	99, 386
Clock, Electric	E. Wilson	Elizabeth, N. J	Feb. 27, 1872	124, 104
Clock, Electric-circuit-breaking	E. Holmes	New York, N. Y	Mar. 26, 1867	63, 158
Clock, Electro-magnetic watch	J. M. Batchelder	Cambridge, Mass	Sept. 3, 1872	130, 971
Clock-escapement	C. J. Addy	Roxbury, Mass	Nov. 22, 1859	26, 150
Clock-escapement	B. Bacon	Morrison, Ill	May 1, 1866	54, 277
Clock-escapement	C. Fasoldt	Albany, N. Y	Apr. 8, 1873	137, 603
Clock-escapement	E. Groux	Rome, N. Y	Aug. 21, 1866	57, 315
Clock-escapement	W. Hart	Mayville, Wis	Dec. 24, 1861	33, 990
Clock-escapement	W. Hart	Mayville, Wis	Aug. 4, 1863	39, 395
Clock-escapement	H. T. Hewitt	Scotch Plains, N. J	Nov. 21, 1865	51, 044
Clock-escapement	W. C. Kellum	San Francisco, Cal	Nov. 3, 1868	83, 775
Clock-escapement	W. C. Kellum	San Francisco, Cal	Nov. 3, 1868	83, 776
Clock-escapement	B. B. Lewis	Bristol, Conn	Aug. 30, 1870	106, 843
Clock-escapement	J. C. Pitel	West Meriden, Conn	Apr. 23, 1861	32, 144
Clock-escapement	A. Platt	New York, N. Y	Nov. 4, 1873	144, 287
Clock-escapement	C. Reinhart	New Haven, Conn	June 16, 1868	79, 003
Clock-escapement	E. K. Reynolds	New York, N. Y	Oct. 2, 1855	13, 623
Clock-escapement	M. Tromly	Cincinnati, Ohio	Aug. 24, 1869	94, 148
Clock-escapement	W. J. Weaver and J. M. Sandifer.	Somerset, Ky	Aug. 8, 1865	49, 323
Clock for steam-boilers, Detective	H. Pieper	New York, N. Y	June 4, 1872	127, 641
Clock-fronts, Hinging	A. Allen	New Haven, Conn	Nov. 26, 1867	71, 438
Clock, Galvanic	M. G. Farmer	Salem, Mass	Sept. 21, 1852	9, 279
Clock, Globe	S. E. G. Rawson	Saratoga Springs, N. Y	Jan. 22, 1867	61, 459
Clock, Globe	T. R. Timby	Saratoga Springs, N. Y	May 2, 1865	47, 585
Clock, Hydraulic	O. Abbruzzo	St. Margherita, Italy	Nov. 26, 1867	71, 437
Clock, Illuminated	J. Glenn	New York, N. Y	Dec. 6, 1853	10, 302
Clock, Illuminated	E. Wade	Elizabeth, N. J	June 10, 1873	139, 839
Clock-key, Safety	P. Laflin	Warren, Mass	Feb. 9, 1869	86, 845
Clock, Machine	G. Richardson	Lowell, Mass	Mar. 3, 1868	75, 196
Clock-machinery	W. Dean	Pleasant Valley, N. Y	Dec. 31, 1821	....
Clock, Marine	V. Giroud	New York, N. Y	Nov. 3, 1863	40, 474
Clock, Marine	L. Hubbell	Bristol, Conn	Nov. 28, 1865	51, 184
Clock-movement	B. B. Lewis	Bristol, Conn	Apr. 18, 1871	113, 781
Clock-movement	M. Tromly	Mount Vernon, Ill	Nov. 3, 1868	83, 802
Clock-movements, Equalizing spring for	H. Smith	Boston, Mass	Nov. 13, 1866	59, 668
Clock-movements, Machine for turning pillars for.	W. H. Nettleton, C. Raymond, and A. Hatch.	Bristol, Conn	Nov. 17, 1857	18, 661

Index of patents issued from the United States Patent Office from 1790 to 1873, inclusive—Continued.

Invention.	Inventor.	Residence.	Date.	No.
Clock, Musical	T. A. Kohn	New York, N. Y	Apr. 24, 1866	54, 175
Clock or time-piece	W. Pardee	Albany, N. Y	May 22, 1835	....
Clock-pendulum	F. Kesselmeier	Wooster, Ohio	Apr. 10, 1844	3, 531
Clock-pendulum	R. Leslie	....	Jan. 30, 1793	....
Clock, Pendulum	G. M. Phelps	Troy, N. Y	July 10, 1860	29, 097
Clock-pendulum	W. D. Whalen	Northville, Mich	Dec. 4, 1866	60, 303
Clock-pendulum rod	R. W. Norton	New Haven, Conn	Feb. 7, 1871	111, 672
Clock-pillar	W. H. Nettleton	Bristol, Conn	Mar. 29, 1864	42, 104
Clock-plates, Mode of boring	J. Curtis	Cairo, N. Y	Aug. 22, 1814	....
Clock, Programme	S. F. Estell	Richmond, Ind	Jan. 11, 1870	98, 678
Clock, Programme	S. F. Estell	Chicago, Ill	Oct. 10, 1871	119, 833
Clock, Programme	S. F. Estell	Chicago, Ill	Sept. 30, 1873	143, 230
Clock, Public	A. D. Crane	Boston, Mass	Feb. 16, 1858	19, 351
Clock-registering attachment	S. Foumier	New Orleans, La	July 6, 1858	20, 786
Clock regulator, Marine	A. I. Goodrich	Waterbury, Conn	Dec. 3, 1867	71, 738
Clock, Repeating	C. W. Roberts	Austin, Ill	Dec. 8, 1868	84, 709
Clock, Self-winding	E. Casselberry	Saint Louis, Mo	Aug. 2, 1842	2, 745
Clock, Self-winding	R. Hitchcock	Watertown, N. Y	Sept. 10, 1861	33, 250
Clock-spring	J. S. Ives	Bristol, Conn	May 23, 1836	....
Clock-springs by currents of air, Means of winding	C. B. Hoard	Watertown, N. Y	Apr. 3, 1860	27, 721
Clock-springs, Method of tempering	W. Barnes	Bristol, Conn	Nov. 27, 1866	59, 943
Clock-springs, Mode of applying	J. S. Ives	New York, N. Y	May 4, 1838	723
Clock, Striking	L. Myers	Philadelphia, Pa	Sept. 10, 1872	131, 175
Clock-striking attachment	N. E. Mulford	Madison, N. J	Apr. 21, 1868	77, 080
Clock-striking mechanism	G. A. Jones and H. H. Warner	New York, N. Y., and Bristol, Conn.	May 30, 1871	115, 481
Clock striking mechanism	J. B. Mayer	Niagara Falls, N. Y	Sept. 15, 1868	82, 267
Clock-striking mechanism	C. W. Roberts	Chicago, Ill	Dec. 12, 1871	121, 780
Clock-striking movement	J. H. La Bau	Brooklyn, N. Y	June 22, 1869	91, 753
Clock, Swinging	G. Herrmann	Newport, R. I	July 25, 1871	117, 284
Clock, Telegraph	J. Chandler	Syracuse, N. Y	Nov. 5, 1867	70, 410
Clock, Thirty-hour brass and wooden	E. Terry	Litchfield County, Conn	June 12, 1816	....
Clock, Thirty-hour wooden	E. Terry	Plymouth, Conn	Mar. 4, 1826	....
Clock, Thirty-hour wooden-wheeled	E. Terry	Plymouth, Conn	May 18, 1825	....
Clock, Thirty-hour wooden-wheeled	E. Terry	Plymouth, Conn	July 5, 1826	....
Clock, Thirty-hour wooden-wheeled	E. Terry	Plymouth, Conn	Sept. 9, 1825	....
Clock, Time and striking parts of a	I. Ives	Bristol, Conn	June 24, 1809	....
Clock, time-keeper, and watch	E. Terry	....	Nov. 17, 1797	....
Clock, Tower	M. G. Crane	Roxbury, Mass	Oct. 8, 1861	33, 462
Clock, Turret	C. F. Johnson	Owego, N. Y	July 28, 1846	4, 662
Clock, Watch	J. Hamblet, jr	Boston, Mass	July 1, 1862	35, 755
Clock, Watchman's	W. Winter	Plainfield, N. J	July 19, 1864	43, 616
Clock, Watchman's time-checking	I. G. Blake	Worcester, Mass	Apr. 25, 1871	113, 970
Clock-weights, Construction of	R. F. Bond	Cambridge, Mass	Apr. 3, 1860	27, 684
Clock-wheels, Casting	L. J. Kilborn	Pennsylvania	Oct. 13, 1809	....
Clock, Winding	R. Hitchcock	Watertown, N. Y	Jan. 29, 1861	31, 242
Clock, Wooden-wheeled	E. Terry	Plymouth, Conn	May 26, 1823	....
Clock-work-turning gage	H. F. Henderson and J. E. Ladd	Bristol, Conn	Dec. 27, 1870	110, 460
Clocks and dial-indicators, Escapement for electrical.	B. F. Edmands and J. Hamblet, jr.	Boston and Charlestown, Mass.	Nov. 26 1867	71, 470
Clocks and other time-pieces, Manner of applying alarms to.	B. Knight	Slatersville, R. I	Sept. 10, 1840	1, 780
Clocks, Attachment for alarm	E. T. Quimby	New Ipswich, N. H	June 14, 1859	24, 433
Clocks, Attachment for pendulum	O. P. McDonald	Carbondale, Ill	May 5, 1868	77, 504
Clocks, Balance-pendulum for	R. R. Ramsdell and G. A. Whitcomb.	Marlborough Depot, N. H.	Oct. 18, 1870	108, 390
Clocks by currents of air, Winding	R. Hitchcock	Watertown, N. Y	Jan. 13, 1863	37, 397
Clocks, Compensating-pendulum for	W. L. Coffinberry	Grand Rapids, Mich	Dec. 28, 1858	22, 413
Clocks, Dead-beat verge for	N. Pomeroy	Hartford, Conn	July 13, 1869	92, 644
Clocks, Engine for cutting and pointing the teeth of wheels and pinions for.	J. Curtis and D. Bradley	Cairo, N. Y., and Connecticut.	Aug. 22, 1814	....
Clocks, Escapement of	O. R. Tyler	Bradford, Vt	Sept. 6, 1833	....
Clocks, Glass wheel for	J. P. Bakewell	Pittsburgh, Pa	Oct. 1, 1830	....
Clocks, Illuminating public	T. I. Bailey	Nashville, Tenn	Sept. 12, 1865	51, 411
Clocks, Lighting-attachment for alarm	H. X. Wright	Memphis, Tenn	Mar. 28, 1871	113, 236
Clocks, &c., Machine for cutting wheels for wooden	A. Hopkins	Litchfield, Conn	Aug. 22, 1814	....
Clocks, &c., Machine for pointing wire for	A. Sperry	Waterbury, Conn	Aug. 22, 1814	....
Clocks, &c., Machine for winding up	J. B. Powell	Philadelphia, Pa	Aug. 2, 1859	24, 977
Clocks, Manufacturing wooden	O. R. Tyler	Chelsea, Vt	June 13, 1831	....
Clocks, Mode of applying the vibratory springs of balance.	S. B. Terry	Plymouth, Conn	Nov. 29, 1853	10, 277
Clocks, Multiple time-dial for	J. F. Niehaus	Saint Louis, Mo	Mar. 26, 1872	125, 073
Clocks or time-pieces by atmospheric condensed air, Machine for propelling.	A. Morse, jr	Bloomfield, Me	Sept. 18, 1835	....
Clocks or time-pieces, Escapement of	J. Fulton	Shelby County, Ky	Dec. 30, 1835	....
Clocks or watches, Alarm-bell to be fixed to	B. F. Freymuth	Philadelphia, Pa	Dec. 22, 1814	....
Clocks, Pinion of	I. Ives	Bristol, Conn	Feb. 24, 1812	....
Clocks, Pinion-rolling and pinion-wheel for	J. Ives	Hartford County, Conn	Apr. 12, 1833	....
Clocks, Propelling-power for	J. Ives	Bristol, Conn	Feb. 24, 1845	3, 928
Clocks, Spring, combined spiral, applied to	S. B. Terry	Plymouth, Conn	Nov. 9, 1830	....
Clocks, Striking-attachment to	A. Johnson	West Newton, Ind	Apr. 30, 1867	64, 328
Clocks, Striking-movement of	F. Kienast	Ansonia, Conn	Oct. 18, 1870	108, 362
Clocks, Striking-part of	J. Bogardus	New York	May 18, 1832	....
Clocks, Striking-part of	J. Ives	Hartford County, Conn	Apr. 12, 1833	....
Clocks, Striking-part of	N. Jerome	Bristol, Conn	June 27, 1839	1, 200
Clocks, Striking-part of	L. J. Kilborn	Pennsylvania	Oct. 12, 1809	....
Clocks, Striking-part of	G. Parker	Utica, N. Y	Apr. 7, 1832	....
Clocks, Striking-part of	R. Porter	Billerica, Mass	June 22, 1832	....
Clocks, Striking-part of	J. S. Seger	New York	Nov. 27, 1832	....
Clocks, Striking-part of steeple	G. Denble	Canton, Ohio	July 25, 1854	11, 362
Clocks, Striking-works for	B. Bacon	Morrison, Ill	Sept. 11, 1866	57, 843
Clocks, Striking-works of	G. H. Leeds and C. N. Thorpe	Philadelphia, Pa	May 20, 1873	139, 166
Clocks, Suspending pendulum of	G. Heninger	Lena, Ill	Feb. 26, 1867	62, 330
Clocks, Suspending the balance-wheel of	E. Terry	Plymouth, Conn	Aug. 9, 1845	4, 159
Clocks, Time-part of common wooden	J. Harrison	Boston, Mass	Aug. 22, 1814	....
Clocks to indicate the comparative time in all longitudes, Panoramic attachment for.	G. M. Stone	Fredericksburgh, Va	June 21, 1859	24, 501
Clocks, Tubular shaft for	G. H. Blakesley	Bristol, Conn	Apr. 12, 1870	101, 815

Index of patents issued from the United States Patent Office from 1790 *to* 1873, *inclusive*—Continued.

Invention.	Inventor.	Residence.	Date.	No.
Clocks, Turning and slitting pinions for wooden	H. Bronson and J. Curtis	Waterbury, Conn., and Cairo, N. Y.	Aug. 22, 1814	....
Clocks vertically, Device for adjusting	J. F. Keeler	Cleveland, Ohio	May 1, 1860	28, 088
Clocks, Winding-machine for	R. Ward	Waterbury, Conn	Nov. 5, 1829	....
Clocks, Winding-stop for weight	O. H. Woodworth	Columbia City, Ind	May 19, 1868	78, 170
Clocks, Wire bell for	H. C. Thompson	Bristol, Conn	Nov. 5, 1867	70, 484
Clod and corn-stalk fender	G. H. Jackson	College Corner, Ind	Feb. 15, 1870	99, 905
Clod breaker and pulverizer	J. B. Turner	Jacksonville, Ill	July 6, 1869	92, 233
Clod breaking and pulverizing machine	H. H. Hull	Bergen, N. Y	Sept. 26, 1871	119, 361
Clod-crusher	T. H. Ashton	Defiance, Ohio	Oct. 6, 1868	82, 784
Clod-crusher	J. G. Ernst	York, Pa	Aug. 4, 1863	39, 389
Clod-crusher	W. Fenstermacher	Shippensburgh, Pa	Jan. 3, 1865	45, 705
Clod-crusher	S. Hewit	Seneca Falls, N. Y	Apr. 7, 1863	38, 109
Clod-crusher	C. Mahan, sr	Jamestown, Ohio	Oct. 29, 1861	33, 624
Clod-crusher	J. B. Okey	Indianapolis, Ind	Feb. 21, 1871	112, 071
Clod-crusher	J. Schlosser	Piqua, Ohio	Sept. 5, 1871	118, 749
Clod-crusher	E. B. Way	Jerseyville, Ill	Mar. 29, 1859	23, 415
Clod-crusher and harrow	G. W. Dubuisson	Jerusalem, N. Y	July 7, 1863	39, 132
Clod-crusher and harrow combined	W. Young and J. Wortham	Shelbyville, Tenn	Sept. 9, 1873	142, 755
Clod crusher and pulverizer	J. W. Pollock	Bryan, Ohio	Aug. 1, 1871	117, 680
Clod crusher and pulverizer	C. R. Ramsey	Farmers' Centre, Ohio	June 14, 1870	104, 353
Clod-fender	D. Applegate	Noblesville, Ind	Aug. 31, 1869	94, 268
Clod-fender	F. L. Bailey	Freeport, Ind	Mar. 7, 1871	112, 405
Clod-fender	J. C. and W. F. Curryer	Thorntown, Ind	Apr. 27, 1869	89, 470
Clod-fender	A. L. Dirst	Seward, Ill	Feb. 18, 1873	135, 896
Clod-fender	W. L. Dearth and G. P. Bondebush.	Jefferson, Ind	Dec. 21, 1869	98, 041
Clod-fender	F. M. Gardner	Brown Township, Ohio	Oct. 12, 1869	95, 676
Clod-fender	R. T. Gillespie	Millport, Ohio	Feb. 7, 1871	111, 631
Clod-fender	R. T. Gillespie	Millport, Ohio	Apr. 16, 1872	125, 732
Clod-fender	R. Harpster	West Cairo, Ohio	Nov. 22, 1870	109, 511
Clod-fender	J. W. Loveless	Clark's Hill, Ind	July 20, 1869	92, 852
Clod-fender	F. M. and J. D. Lowden	Lawrence, Ind	Dec. 14, 1869	97, 785
Clod-fender	J. Lowe	Lebanon, Ind	Oct. 1, 1867	69, 352
Clod-fender	D. O. Moore and F. Reid	Everton, Ind	Jan. 18, 1870	98, 989
Clod-fender	G. L. Perry	Berlin, Wis	Aug. 22, 1871	118, 267
Clod-fender	G. Seeger, J. W. Loveless, and J. W. Thorp.	Clark's Hill, Ind	June 22, 1869	91, 777
Clod-fender	J. W. Tull	Zionsville, Ind	Dec. 21, 1869	98, 128
Clod-fender and cultivator combined	B. F. Neely	Daleville, Ind	May 10, 1870	102, 959
Clod-fender for growing plants	L. H. Shular	Crawfordsville, Ind	Sept. 14, 1869	94, 784
Clod-fender, Rotary	L. M. Doddridge	New Mount Pleasant, Ind.	Sept. 14, 1869	94, 875
Clod-fender, Rotary	J. F. Woolley	Pleasant Ridge, Ohio	Sept. 7, 1869	94, 684
Clods in the field, Implement for dividing	J. N. Davis	Martinsville, Ohio	Sept. 27, 1864	44, 404
Clog	J. A. Davis	Watertown, N. Y	Nov. 24, 1868	84, 267
Clog or patten	C. W. Stearns	Springfield, Mass	Apr. 22, 1851	8, 053
Closet: *See* Cake-closet. Chamber-closet. Earth-closet. Hot-closet. Water-closet.				
Closet and bed	W. Kelley	Bath, Me	Apr. 19, 1870	102, 012
Closet for milk	E. H. Nash	Westford, Conn	July 27, 1858	21, 016
Cloth and blankets from sheep's wool, Making	A. Barnes, S. Gray, and J. Clark	Windham, Conn	Feb. 3, 1813	....
Cloth and clothes pin	R. Hathaway	Chicopee, Mass	June 2, 1868	78, 523
Cloth and fabric, Manufacture of rubber and other coated.	J. W. Cobb and E. A. Hill	Melrose and Quincy, Mass.	Aug. 11, 1868	80, 809
Cloth and hat-bodies, Machine for shrinking bodies in the manufacture of felt.	H. A. Wells	New York, N. Y	Sept. 11, 1841	2, 245
Cloth and other fabrics, Compound for cleaning	F. T. Huntoon	Fulton City, Ill	May 31, 1870	103, 747
Cloth and paper fabrics, Manufacture of combined	J. H. Newton	Holyoke, Mass	Mar. 1, 1870	100, 436
Cloth and similar fabrics and slabs for pavements, Manufacture of floor.	F. Walton	Linoleum Works, Staines, England.	Feb. 23, 1869	87, 227
Cloth, Apparatus for coating and flocking	E. M. Chaffee	Providence, R. I	Sept. 20, 1864	44, 281
Cloth, Apparatus for felting	J. Andrews	Belleville, N. J	Jan. 31, 1845	3, 900
Cloth, Apparatus for frizzling	S. M. Moschcowitz	New York, N. Y	Feb. 15, 1870	99, 782
Cloth, Apparatus for singeing cotton	J. A. Miller	New York, N. Y	Jan. 14, 1868	73, 362
Cloth, Apparatus for sponging	E. Utley	Appleton, Wis	Mar. 12, 1872	124, 461
Cloth, Bolting	R. Dawson	....	May 12, 1796	....
Cloth brushing and winding machine	R. C. Varnel	West Somers, N. Y	Mar. 13, 1844	3, 487
Cloth-bushes in holes, Mode of securing	C. Bollermann	New York, N. Y	May 17, 1864	42, 740
Cloth by felting, Machine for making	O. Barrett, jr	Troy, N. Y	Dec. 8, 1812	....
Cloth by machinery, Mode of making	H. Raymond	New York, N. Y	June 27, 1829	....
Cloth by thrashing, Raising nap on woolen	T. Hurd and J. Fox	Lowell, Mass	June 23, 1830	....
Cloth by water, Machine for shearing woolen or other.	F. B. Kellogg	Marlborough, Mass	Nov. 22, 1805	....
Cloth, Calendering	Z. Bliss	Johnston, R. I	Oct. 17, 1835	....
Cloth, Carding and raising a nap on woolen	J. A. Christie	Elizabethtown, N. J	Jan. 24, 1816	....
Cloth, Cement for edges of	R. Brackett	Boston, Mass	Mar. 14, 1833	....
Cloth, Circular tenter-bar for drying	S. R. Parkhurst	Meriden, R. I	Dec. 2, 1834	....
Cloth, Composition for coating marine	J. G. Colcord	Boston, Mass	Aug. 6, 1872	130, 279
Cloth, Composition for stiffening felt	P. O'Rork	Norwalk, Conn	May 29, 1866	55, 153
Cloth, card, and paper cutter combined	I. B. Millner	Watkins, N. Y	Apr. 2, 1872	125, 319
Cloth-creaser	W. J. Crane	Carbondale, Pa	Mar. 10, 1868	75, 378
Cloth-creasing frame	A. W. Todd	Chicago, Ill	Feb. 18, 1868	74, 636
Cloth, Cross-cut eclipse shearing-machine for shearing woolen.	R. Daniels	Woodstock, Vt	Apr. 7, 1838	681
Cloth, &c., Crossing the fibers in forming the bats for felt.	A. C. Arnold	Norwalk, Conn	June 10, 1851	8, 147
Cloth-cutter	B. Hansell, J. McCann, and S. McCambridge.	Philadelphia, Pa	Sept. 8, 1863	39, 862
Cloth-cutting machine	V. H. Buschman	Baltimore, Md	May 15, 1866	54, 681
Cloth-cutting machine	S. M. Eisman	New York, N. Y	July 30, 1872	129, 939
Cloth-cutting machine	I. Fenno	Boston, Mass	Jan. 14, 1873	134, 793
Cloth-cutting machine	I. Fenno and P. Howe	Boston, Mass	July 16, 1872	129, 327
Cloth-cutting machine	I. Fenno and P. Howe	Boston, Mass	Aug. 27, 1872	130, 910
Cloth-cutting machine	N. C. Fluck	Gloucester, England	Oct. 28, 1873	144, 023

Index of patents issued from the United States Patent Office from 1790 to 1873, inclusive—Continued.

Invention.	Inventor.	Residence.	Date.	No.
Cloth-cutting machine	A. Heller	New York, N. Y	Apr. 30, 1872	126, 207
Cloth-cutting machine	J. Kent	New York, N. Y	Mar. 11, 1873	136, 602
Cloth-cutting machine	F. Koch and R. Brass	Williamsburgh, N. Y	July 16, 1872	129, 285
Cloth-cutting machine	W. Raenchle	Philadelphia, Pa	Apr. 18, 1871	113, 927
Cloth-cutting machine	A. Warth	Stapleton, N. Y	Apr. 9, 1872	125, 638
Cloth-cutting machine	A. Warth	Stapleton, N. Y	Aug. 6, 1872	130, 343
Cloth-cutting machine	A. Warth	Stapleton, N. Y	Aug. 6, 1872	130, 344
Cloth-cutting machine	E. B. Wells	New York, N. Y	July 25, 1871	117, 352
Cloth-cutting machine	G. Westerhauser	Brooklyn, N. Y	June 18, 1872	128, 194
Cloth-damping machine	W. Hebdon	New York, N. Y	Mar. 16, 1869	87, 930
Cloth-deseaming machine	T. E. Chase	Boston, Mass	Apr. 30, 1872	126, 264
Cloth, Device for turning down the edges of elastic	G. H. Chesbro	Stafford, Conn	Apr. 27, 1858	20, 037
Cloth, &c., Die for taking impressions from	J. J. C. Smith	Somerville, Mass	Apr. 4, 1871	113, 699
Cloth-dotter	S. S. Gould	Worcester, Mass	May 30, 1865	47, 944
Cloth doubling and folding machine	J. W. Farwell	Lewiston, Me	Feb. 27, 1872	124, 044
Cloth, Dressing	C. W. Cook	Lowell, Mass	Jan. 23, 1834	....
Cloth-dressing apparatus	J. Johnston and J. D. Snyder	Saltsburgh, Pa	Mar. 13, 1849	6, 188
Cloth-dressing machine	I. Sanford	....	Mar. 27, 1799	....
Cloth-dressing machinery	J. C. Carlisle	Armagh, Pa	Oct. 21, 1846	4, 821
Cloth, Dressing woolen	S. R. Parkhurst	Mendon, Mass	Dec. 23, 1833	....
Cloth, Dressing woolen and cotton	C. W. Cook	Lowell, Mass	May 30, 1833	....
Cloth, Dressing woolen or mixed	C. W. Cook	Lowell, Mass	Apr. 23, 1831	....
Cloth, Drying	D. W. Kennedy	Staunton, Va	June 27, 1854	11, 163
Cloth, Drying	R. Preston	North Pownal, Vt	Feb. 14, 1854	10, 522
Cloth-drying, &c., Circular revolving tenter-bar for	S. R. Parkhurst	Worcester, Mass	Oct. 28, 1835	....
Cloth-drying machine	N. P. Akin	Philmont, N. Y	Sept. 24, 1872	131, 586
Cloth-drying machine	C. F. Bennett	Philadelphia, Pa	Sept. 12, 1865	49, 947
Cloth-drying machine	L. W. Boynton	Hartford, Conn	Apr. 2, 1867	63, 461
Cloth-drying machine	A. Chambers	Providence, R. I	Nov. 3, 1868	83, 690
Cloth-drying machine	J. Hurd, jr	Boston, Mass	Jan. 23, 1830	....
Cloth-drying machinery	C. F. Bennett	Warehouse Point, Conn	Nov. 15, 1859	26, 141
Cloth-drying machinery	B. Sexton	East Windsor, Conn	May 8, 1860	28, 202
Cloth, Elastic	H. H. Day	New York, N. Y	Aug. 30, 1859	25, 249
Cloth, Elastic gore	C. Winslow	Lynn, Mass	Aug. 4, 1857	17, 950
Cloth, Evaporating and condensing machinery for	J. Goulding and R. Bracket	Lynn, Mass	Aug. 15, 1835	....
Cloth, Feathered	A. A. Condit	Muncie, Ind	Jan. 8, 1867	61, 000
Cloth, felt, &c., Water-proof coating for	J. Ditto	New York, N. Y	Apr. 15, 1862	34, 947
Cloth, Felting	J. Weight	Lawrence, Mass	Jan. 6, 1852	8, 636
Cloth-felting machinery	G. G. Bishop	Norwalk, Conn	Mar. 23, 1852	8, 821
Cloth-finishing machine	J. Earnshaw	East Greenwich, R. I	Dec. 1, 1868	84, 483
Cloth-finishing machine	G. C. Howard	Philadelphia, Pa	Aug. 18, 1868	81, 170
Cloth-finishing machine	D. Hussey	Nashua, N. H	Apr. 20, 1869	89, 048
Cloth-finishing machines, Tray for	A. Woolson	Springfield, Vt	July 22, 1873	141, 192
Cloth-finishing machinery	H. James	Norwalk, Conn	Feb. 9, 1864	41, 581
Cloth-finishing press	C. Heubach	Chicago, Ill	May 23, 1871	115, 203
Cloth-finishing, Steam-cylinder for	A. Webster	Seneca Falls, N. Y	Nov. 5, 1867	70, 658
Cloth, Finishing woolen	Z. Allen	Providence, R. I	Feb. 23, 1830	....
Cloth, Folding and measuring	W. C. Wright	Boston, Mass	June 20, 1854	11, 145
Cloth folding and measuring machine	A. M. Cheney	Charlotte, Mich	Mar. 18, 1873	136, 967
Cloth folding and measuring machine	J. Spalding	Morristown, Vt	Aug. 28, 1841	2, 230
Cloth folding and measuring machinery	J. Baxendale	Providence, R. I	Dec. 11, 1855	13, 900
Cloth folding and measuring machinery	S. C. Durgin	North Chelmsford, Mass	Mar. 9, 1844	3, 469
Cloth, Folding and uniting guide for the edges of two pieces of.	I. M. Rose	New York, N. Y	Feb. 20, 1866	52, 749
Cloth-folding instrument	H. Moschcowitz	New York, N. Y	Mar. 26, 1872	124, 968
Cloth-folding machine	D. R. Ambrose and O. L. Reynolds.	Portsmouth and Dover, N. H.	July 22, 1851	8, 240
Cloth-folding machine	H. Dunphy	New York, N. Y	Nov. 12, 1867	70, 706
Cloth-folding machine	J. D. Elliot	Grafton, Mass	July 9, 1861	32, 761
Cloth-folding machine	J. D. Elliot	Grafton, Mass	Apr. 30, 1867	64, 208
Cloth-folding machine	W. F. Heywood	Cumberland, R. I	July 3, 1866	56, 048
Cloth-folding machine	A. Simpson	Woonsocket, R. I	Dec. 28, 1869	98, 308
Cloth-folding machine	W. Wheeler, jr	North Providence, R. I	May 7, 1867	64, 466
Cloth-folding machinery	A. C. Cary and D. C. Bagley	Amesbury, Mass	Feb. 12, 1850	7, 079
Cloth for cutting, Gage for marking	E. E. Emery	Boston, Mass	Oct. 14, 1873	143, 681
Cloth for felting hat-bodies, &c	W. Fuzzard	Charlestown, Mass	Apr. 1, 1856	14, 559
Cloth, Forming bats for felt	M. D. Whipple	Charlestown, Mass	Oct. 26, 1858	21, 930
Cloth, Forming, heating, &c., metal plates in pressing woolen.	V. Vedder	Amsterdam, N. Y	Feb. 6, 1811	....
Cloth, Forming nap on woolen	Z. Allen	Providence, R. I	Feb. 2, 1830	....
Cloth from wool and silk, Manufacture of	R. Daniels	Woodstock, Vt	Oct. 8, 1840	1, 809
Cloth from wool and silk, Manufacture of	R. Daniels	Woodstock, Vt	Oct. 10, 1840	1, 813
Cloth, Fulling	M. W. Northrup and R. R. Dillon.	Newton, N. J	Dec. 4, 1823	....
Cloth, Fulling	R. Winans	Warwick, N. Y	June 26, 1821	....
Cloth fulling and milling machine, Felt	H. A. Wells	New York	Sept. 18, 1841	2, 255
Cloth-fulling machine	R. Hunt	Orange, Mass	July 5, 1870	105, 082
Cloth-fulling machinery	J. H. Jennings and T. Brierly	Clayville, N. Y	Jan. 24, 1854	10, 453
Cloth, Gage for cutting bias pieces of	S. T. Taylor	New York, N. Y	Aug. 23, 1870	106, 741
Cloth, &c., Gas-proof	W. B. S. Taylor	New York, N. Y	May 14, 1872	126, 851
Cloth, Gig-mill for dressing	A. Woolson	Springfield, Vt	Apr. 19, 1853	9, 678
Cloth, Gig-mill for napping	E. Gessner	Awe, Saxony	Feb. 24, 1857	16, 685
Cloth-guiding apparatus	E. O. Potter	North Providence, R. I	Apr. 16, 1867	63, 939
Cloth-hardening machine, Felt	H. A. Wells	New York	Sept. 18, 1841	2, 256
Cloth-holder for washing crockery, &c	C. F. Greeley	East Kingston, N. H	Aug. 2, 1859	24, 933
Cloth-holder in needle-work	N. Daniels	Milford, Mass	Dec. 27, 1859	26, 570
Cloth, Hurd's patent metallic napper for	J. M. Pratt	Dudley, Mass	Oct. 3, 1838	957
Cloth, Implement for cutting	G. W. Griswold	Carbondale, Pa	Oct. 18, 1853	10, 132
Cloth, Instrument for ripping sutures in	T. B. Converse	New York, N. Y	July 11, 1865	48, 662
Cloth in the piece, Machinery for fulling	M. D. Whipple	Charlestown, Mass	Oct. 26, 1858	21, 931
Cloth in the process of fulling, Machine for stretching.	B. D. Whitney and G. W. Lawton.	Winchendon, Mass	Mar. 25, 1840	1, 522
Cloth, Machine called "The wheel of knives," for shearing and raising the nap on.	S. G. Dorr	....	Oct. 20, 1792	....
Cloth-machine, Cross-napping	J. Taylor and J. Smith	New Lebanon, N. Y	May 4, 1842	2, 605
Cloth, Machine for brushing and finishing	S. Hart	Hempstead, N. Y	July 27, 1812	....
Cloth, Machine for cutting out	J. Harraday	New York, N. Y	May 30, 1854	10, 986
Cloth, Machine for dressing and drying woolen	D. Henderson	Merrimack, N. H	July 8, 1862	35, 823

Index of patents issued from the United States Patent Office from 1790 *to* 1873, *inclusive*—Continued.

Invention.	Inventor.	Residence.	Date.	No.
Cloth, Machine for finishing woolen	E. Birkenshaw	Ashuelot, N. H	Nov. 12, 1867	70, 688
Cloth, Machine for folding and measuring	H. Boot	New Bedford, Mass	Apr. 1, 1851	8, 005
Cloth, Machine for folding and plaiting	E. D. Gird	Syracuse, N. Y	July 9, 1872	128, 722
Cloth, Machine for fulling and felting	J. D. Lounsbury, J. Arnold, J. A. McLean, and G. G. Bishop.	Norwalk, Conn	July 15, 1829	....
Cloth, Machine for fulling and finishing felted	M. D. Whipple	Cambridge, Mass	Jan. 2, 1866	51, 884
Cloth, &c., Machine for ironing and polishing	H. Hamill	New York, N. Y	Apr. 2, 1872	125, 289
Cloth, Machine for manufacturing felt	T. B. Butler	Norwalk, Conn	July 21, 1857	17, 828
Cloth, Machine for napping and brushing up	J. Bryan and S. D. Fuller	Mendam County, N. J	Apr. 14, 1820	....
Cloth, Machine for napping, teazling, shearing, or bushing.	J. Taylor	Waltham, Mass	Oct. 28, 1815	....
Cloth, Machine for napping woolen	B. N. Bursons	New York, N. Y	Apr. 16, 1817	....
Cloth Machine for plaiting	W. M. Storm	New York, N. Y	Dec. 26, 1871	122, 137
Cloth, Machine for raising nap on	A. Houget	Verviers, Belgium	Apr. 16, 1867	63, 895
Cloth, Machine for raising nap on	E. T. Marble	Worcester, Mass	Jan. 12, 1864	41, 227
Cloth, Machine for raising nap on	S. Mulliken		Mar. 11, 1791	....
Cloth, Machine for raising nap on	E. Starr and N. Couch	Sullivan Township, N. Y	Mar. 20, 1817	....
Cloth, Machine for raising nap on	A. Zechille	Grossenhain, Saxony	Jan. 22, 1867	61, 376
Cloth, Machine for rubbing and polishing painted	D. Cushing	Wheeling, Va	June 10, 1856	15, 066
Cloth, Machine for shearing	B. Swift	Washington, N. Y	May 25, 1806	....
Cloth, Machine for shearing nap from woolen	M. Hurd	Augusta County, N. Y	Dec. 7, 1829	....
Cloth, Machine for shearing woolen	S. Parsons	Hoosick Falls, N. Y	Nov. 25, 1838	1, 015
Cloth, Machine for shearing woolen and other	L. Stanley		June 25, 1803	....
Cloth, Machine for singeing	A. Robeson	New Bedford, Mass	Sept. 8, 1826	....
Cloth, Machine for sizing, stretching, and drying	W. Bailey	Oswego, N. Y	June 11, 1872	127, 731
Cloth, Machine for trimming, smoothing, and folding cotton.	J. and H. H. Higgins	East Greenwich, R. I	Mar. 10, 1849	6, 152
Cloth, Machine for turning selvages in	J. T. Boyd	Charlestown, Mass	June 29, 1858	20, 695
Cloth, Machine for turning the edges of	J. P. Marston	Charlestown, Mass	May 5, 1857	17, 224
Cloth, Machine for winding up	J. Goulding and R. Bracket	Boston, Mass	Nov. 30, 1835	....
Cloth, Machinery for crossing the fibers of wool in making felt.	T. B. Butter	Norwalk, Conn	Apr. 14, 1857	17, 020
Cloth, Machinery for double-folding wide	Z. Allen	Providence, R. I	July 16, 1850	7, 502
Cloth, Machinery for finishing the nap of woolen	J. Dobson	Philadelphia, Pa	Nov. 25, 1873	144, 859
Cloth, Machinery for folding and measuring	J. D. Elliot	Leicester, Mass	Sept. 11, 1855	13, 543
Cloth, Machinery for forming vats for felt	T. B. Butler	Norwalk, Conn	Oct. 8, 1861	33, 426
Cloth, Machinery for fulling	C. A. Read and T. Cotter	New Hartford, N. Y	Sept. 24, 1850	7, 673
Cloth, Machinery for making felt	G. G. Bishop	Norwalk, Conn	June 25, 1861	32, 611
Cloth, Machinery for manufacturing felt	T. B. Butler	Norwalk, Conn	June 9, 1857	17, 487
Cloth, Machinery for measuring and folding	A. R. Austin	Providence, R. I	Mar. 6, 1847	4, 994
Cloth, Machinery for measuring and folding	E. G. Woodman	North Chelmsford, Mass	Mar. 6, 1847	4, 993
Cloth, Machinery for napping	J. C. Millar and C. N. Tyler	Starrucca, Pa., and Washington, D. C.	May 5, 1857	17, 227
Cloth, Machinery for raising the nap of woolen	Z. Allen	Providence, R. I	Aug. 10, 1829	....
Cloth, Machinery for templing	P. C. Curtis	Paris, N. Y	June 16, 1825	....
Cloth, Making ribbon of strips of	A. M. Eastman	New York, N. Y	Sept. 5, 1854	11, 643
Cloth-mangle machine	T. Rundle	Boston, Mass	Nov. 11, 1830	....
Cloth manufacture	J. P. and R. G. Hazard	Providence, R. I	Dec. 6, 1828	....
Cloth, Manufacture of	F. Wolcott	Stow, Mass	July 21, 1835	....
Cloth, Manufacture of elastic	H. H. Day	New York, N. Y	May 29, 1860	28, 456
Cloth, Manufacture of elastic	J. W. Newell	New Brunswick, N. J	Sept. 24, 1861	33, 361
Cloth, Manufacture of elastic	R. Solis	New York, N. Y	Nov. 7, 1848	5, 908
Cloth, Manufacture of enameled	W. H. Haines	Newark, N. J	Jan. 9, 1866	51, 997
Cloth, Manufacture of enameled	E. M. Stevens	Chelsea, Mass	Mar. 24, 1868	75, 807
Cloth, Manufacture of felt	G. G. Bishop	Norwalk, Conn	Mar. 10, 1857	16, 783
Cloth, Manufacture of felt	J. E. Pollard	Norfolk, Mass	Oct. 7, 1873	143, 528
Cloth, Manufacture of felted	C. T. Young	Lawrence, Mass	July 11, 1865	48, 757
Cloth, Manufacture of leather	T. Storey and W. V. Wilson	Lancaster and East London, England.	Nov. 6, 1866	59, 530
Cloth, Manufacture of ornamental felt	O. B. Tomlinson	Athens, Pa	June 5, 1855	13, 018
Cloth, Manufacture of ribbed elastic	H. H. Day	New York, N. Y	Aug. 23, 1859	25, 180
Cloth, Manufacture of vellnted	C. H. Brand	Williamsburgh, N. Y	Apr. 25, 1848	5, 534
Cloth, Manufacturing flying shears for shearing woolen.	S. Parsons	Hoosick Falls, N. Y	June 7, 1838	774
Cloth, Machine indicator for manufacturing	W. H. Brown	Lowell, Mass	June 29, 1869	91, 822
Cloth, Manufacturing of flax and wire	P. Laporte	Augusta County, Va	July 12, 1830	....
Cloth-marker	A. Thomas	Hoboken, N. J	Nov. 29, 1870	109, 686
Cloth-marker	A. Thomas	Hoboken, N. J	Nov. 29, 1870	109, 687
Cloth-measuring instrument	E. F. Whiton	West Stafford, Conn	Apr. 23, 1850	7, 314
Cloth-measuring machine	I. Mills	Hamilton, Canada	July 25, 1871	117, 443
Cloth, Method of cutting	E. J. Lake	Washington, D. C	Dec. 26, 1871	122, 260
Cloth, Method of drying napped	W. Chapin	Staffordsville, Conn	Feb. 20, 1872	123, 768
Cloth, Method of producing diagonal	R. C. Helm	New Brunswick, N. J	Apr. 15, 1862	34, 960
Cloth, &c., Method of shearing diamond figures of	C. P. Barber	Watervliet, N. Y	Mar. 10, 1843	2, 996
Cloth, Mode of adding nap to and making waterproof.	W. K. Phipps	Framington, Mass	Aug. 31, 1839	1, 308
Cloth, Mode of bucking	A. Robeson, jr	Newport, R. I	Sept. 13, 1853	10, 014
Cloth, Mode of cutting out	E. Campbell	Philadelphia, Pa	Nov. 6, 1823	....
Cloth, Mode of forming the bat for making felt	T. B. Butler	Norwalk, Conn	Feb. 2, 1858	19, 235
Cloth, Mode of printing and embossing	L. Murr	Philadelphia, Pa	Mar. 24, 1868	75, 957
Cloth, Mode of shearing satinets and other woolen.	J. Pitts	Smithfield, R. I	Oct. 17, 1842	2, 822
Cloth, Napping	E. Benham	Roxbury, Mass	Jan. 22, 1833	....
Cloth, Napping	D. Merwin, jr., and H. Killogg.	Hudson, N. Y	Oct. 28, 1814	....
Cloth, Napping and steaming	S. R. Parkhurst	Providence, R. I	June 24, 1834	....
Cloth-napping machine	T. S. Barnum and E. Smith	Litchfield, Conn	Apr. 4, 1815	....
Cloth-napping machine	J. J. Bryent	Andover, N. H	Sept. 2, 1818	....
Cloth-napping machine	S. Marsh	Fairfax, Vt	July 20, 1825	....
Cloth-napping machine	M. R. Norris and L. Phillips	Covington, N. Y	Mar. 21, 1829	....
Cloth-napping machinery	J. Weight	Lawrence, Conn	June 13, 1854	11, 105
Cloth of wool, hair, &c., without spinning or weaving, Machine for forming webs for.	J. Arnold	Norwalk, Conn	July 15, 1829	....
Cloth of wool, &c., without spinning or weaving, Machine for forming webs of.	J. Arnold and G. G. Bishop	Norwalk, Conn	Oct. 20, 1836	66
Cloth, Ornamenting	J. C. Wood	Philadelphia, Pa	Dec. 14, 1821	....
Cloth, paper, &c., Composition for flocking	A. Erhard	New York, N. Y	Nov. 8, 1864	44, 944
Cloth-plaiting machine	H. Dunphy	New York, N. Y	May 27, 1862	35, 367
Cloth-plaiting machine	J. F. Sachse	Philadelphia, Pa	Dec. 24, 1867	72, 685

Index of patents issued from the United States Patent Office from 1790 to 1873, inclusive—Continued.

Invention.	Inventor.	Residence.	Date.	No.
Cloth-plaiting machine	J. A. Sawer	Worcester, Mass	Feb. 6, 1872	123, 425
Cloth-press	C. H. Weston and J. Dennis	Lowell, Mass	Jan. 26, 1869	86, 334
Cloth-press	C. H. Weston and J. Dennis	Lowell, Mass	May 17, 1870	103, 262
Cloth-press	C. H. Weston and J. Dennis	Lowell, Mass	May 17, 1870	103, 263
Cloth-press, Steam	J. J. Crawford	Glasgow, Scotland	Nov. 16, 1869	96, 893
Cloth-press, Steam	J. Dennis and C. H. Weston	Lowell, Mass	Aug. 19, 1873	142, 006
Cloth-pressing machine	P. Howe	Boston, Mass	June 20, 1871	116, 057
Cloth-pressing machine	P. Howe	Boston, Mass	Oct. 10, 1871	119, 708
Cloth-pressing machine	P. Howe	Boston, Mass	Dec. 12, 1871	121, 720
Cloth-pressing, Steam device for	C. H. Weston	Lowell, Mass	Mar. 16, 1869	87, 994
Cloth, Process of manufacturing	A. Ruzé	Gaillon, France	June 27, 1871	116, 497
Cloth, Process of milling, fulling, &c	M. Lee	Otsego, N. Y	Nov. 6, 1817	......
Cloth-rack	H. C. Smith, D. A. Kelly, and J. E. Murdock, jr.	Clarksville, Ohio	Feb. 11, 1868	74, 439
Cloth-rack	A. W. Voegtly	Hannibal, Ohio	Sept. 10, 1872	131, 235
Cloth, Raising nap on	W. Burt	......	July 23, 1797	......
Cloth, Raising nap on	W. Duncan and J. Davidson	Acworth, N. H	May 29, 1815	......
Cloth, Raising nap on	J. Mathes	Barre, Vt	May 27, 1813	......
Cloth, Raising nap on	J. Wilkinson	New York, N. Y	May 12, 1825	......
Cloth scouring and fulling machine	H. Hickox	Rutland, N. Y	Mar. 26, 1825	......
Cloth, Shears for shearing	W. Stillman	Westerly, R. I	Apr. 28, 1815	......
Cloth, Shears for shearing woolen	W. Stillman	Westerly, R. I	June 11, 1811	......
Cloth-shears, Revolving	J. Collins	Anson, Me	June 10, 1817	......
Cloth, Shearing	G. Booth	Poughkeepsie, N. Y	Oct. 13, 1812	......
Cloth, Shearing	B. Cummings	Palmer, Mass	Mar. 2, 1811	......
Cloth, Shearing	R. Daniels	Woodstock, Vt	May 13, 1834	......
Cloth, Shearing	R. Daniels	Woodstock, Vt	Aug. 22, 1834	......
Cloth, Shearing	D. Dewey	Poultney, Vt	June 27, 1809	......
Cloth, Shearing	W. Kennedy	Frankford, Ky	June 12, 1812	......
Cloth, Shearing	H. Mathews	Delaware	May 15, 1810	......
Cloth, Shearing	J. Molleneux	Hempstead, N. Y	Apr. 30, 1811	......
Cloth, Shearing	H. Osborn and W. L. Fraser	......	Apr. 25, 1816	......
Cloth, Shearing	J. D. Smith	Fredericktown, Md	May 24, 1816	......
Cloth, Shearing	E. Sprague	Danbury, Conn	May 9, 1810	......
Cloth, Shearing	S. Stewart, E. Hovey, and J. Henderson.	Pittstown, N. Y	June 21, 1808	......
Cloth, Shearing	B. Swift	New York, N. Y	May 24, 1810	......
Cloth, Shearing	E. Willmarth	Rumney, Mass	Feb. 28, 1811	......
Cloth, Shearing and laying the nap of	L. Dickerman	Schaghticoke, N. Y	July 18, 1812	......
Cloth, Shearing broad	J. Davidson	Springfield, Vt	May 29, 1834	......
Cloth-shearing machine	G. Bostwick	Brookfield, Conn	Sept. 28, 1812	......
Cloth-shearing machine	E. Burt	Princeton, N. J	June 23, 1807	......
Cloth-shearing machine	Z. Cary	Oxford County, Me	Feb. 20, 1821	......
Cloth-shearing machine	J. Collins	Anson, Me	Mar. 6, 1827	......
Cloth-shearing machine	M. Craven	Dedham, Mass	Dec. 12, 1871	121, 760
Cloth-shearing machine	D. Dewy	Rutland County, Va	Mar. 16, 1818	......
Cloth-shearing machine	R. Dorr	Kenderhook, N. Y	Mar. 8, 1807	......
Cloth-shearing machine	E. Heald	Norridgewock, Me	Dec. 4, 1822	......
Cloth-shearing machine	W. Hovey	Worcester, Mass	Dec. 17, 1824	......
Cloth-shearing machine	S. Hills	Hudson, N. Y	Oct. 22, 1813	......
Cloth-shearing machine	E. Hotchkiss and A. Jaque	Brattleborough, Vt	Dec. 15, 1819	......
Cloth-shearing machine	G. C. Kellogg	New Hartford, Conn	Mar. 4, 1811	......
Cloth-shearing machine	I. and G. C. Kellogg	New Hartford, Conn	Apr. 7, 1828	......
Cloth-shearing machine	C. H. Orth and F. Strohn	Steubenville, Ohio	Oct. 11, 1814	......
Cloth-shearing machine	S. Parsons	Hoosick, N. Y	Mar. 2, 1819	......
Cloth-shearing machine	E. Remington	Frankfort, N. Y	Aug. 13, 1817	......
Cloth-shearing machine	I. Sanford	Providence, R. I	Mar. 26, 1814	......
Cloth-shearing machine	W. Stillman	Westerly, R. I	Jan. 17, 1818	......
Cloth-shearing machine	B. Swift	Washington, N. Y	July 1, 1814	......
Cloth-shearing machine	B. Swift	Washington, N. Y	Feb. 7, 1824	......
Cloth-shearing machine	J. A. Thurston	Providence, R. I	Oct. 24, 1871	120, 219
Cloth-shearing machine	M. D. Whipple	Charlestown, Mass	Dec. 1, 1857	18, 796
Cloth-shearing machine	A. Woolson	Springfield, Vt	May 28, 1850	7, 407
Cloth-shearing machine	A. Woolson	Springfield, Vt	Aug. 16, 1864	43, 878
Cloth-shearing-machine rest	A. Woolson	Springfield, Vt	Oct. 29, 1872	132, 706
Cloth-shearing machine, Shears for	S. A. Britt	Cazenovia, N. Y	Aug. 10, 1829	......
Cloth-shearing machine, Woolen	E. Stowell	Worcester, Mass	Apr. 26, 1808	......
Cloth-shearing machines, Guiding-apparatus for	L. M. Collins	Lebanon, N. H	Apr. 16, 1872	125, 722
Cloth, Shearing woolen and other	S. Kellogg	......	Jan. 31, 1795	......
Cloth, Shuttle for weaving	J. Baldwin	Nashua, N. H	Jan. 31, 1840	1, 485
Cloth, silk, paper, &c., Compound to remove grease from.	M. B. Kimm	Grand Rapids, Mich	Feb. 22, 1870	100, 043
Cloth sizing and dressing machine	P. Moody	Waltham, Mass	Jan. 17, 1818	......
Cloth-smoothing device	C. L. Frink	Rockville, Conn	Dec. 3, 1867	71, 599
Cloth-sponging apparatus	I. A. Davis	Philadelphia, Pa	July 12, 1870	105, 182
Cloth-sponging apparatus	J. R. Paul	Philadelphia, Pa	Nov. 26, 1867	71, 529
Cloth-sponging apparatus	L. Rothschild	New Haven, Conn	Apr. 19, 1864	42, 466
Cloth-sponging machine	G. Dayspring and E. Fitzki	Washington, D. C	Sept. 14, 1869	94, 720
Cloth, Spreading and drying India-rubber upon	W. Atkinson	New York	Aug. 15, 1835	......
Cloth, Spreading-roller for stretching	J. I. Hillard	Fall River, Mass	Apr. 15, 1856	14, 659
Cloth, Steam cylinder for finishing	A. Brown	Springfield, Vt	Mar. 12, 1872	124, 481
Cloth steaming and shrinking machine	W. Hebdon	New York, N. Y	Oct. 5, 1869	95, 584
Cloth-steaming apparatus	L. M. Heery	Hinsdale, Mass	May 23, 1871	115, 200
Cloth-steaming machine	H. S. Green	Sherbrooke, Canada	Feb. 4, 1873	135, 543
Cloth-steaming machine	C. H. Weston	Lowell, Mass	Jan. 14, 1873	134, 956
Cloth stretcher and drier	E. B. Bigelow	Boston, Mass	Sept. 5, 1848	5, 754
Cloth stretcher and smoother	J. Butcher	Lowell, Mass	Nov. 5, 1850	7, 764
Cloth, Stretching and drying	P. Hild	New York, N. Y	June 11, 1872	127, 691
Cloth, Stretching and drying	D. and H. Stearns	Pittsfield, Mass	Feb. 21, 1854	10, 545
Cloth stretching and drying machine	W. Bailey	Brooklyn, N. Y	May 20, 1873	139, 038
Cloth stretching and drying machine	T. Barrows	Dedham, Mass	Dec. 2, 1851	8, 563
Cloth stretching and drying machinery	B. J. Tayman	Philadelphia, Pa	Nov. 14, 1854	11, 952
Cloth-stretching machine	S. H. Austin	Providence, R. I	Apr. 12, 1870	101, 811
Cloth-stretching machine	E. C. Cleveland	Worcester, Mass	Dec. 4, 1860	30, 801
Cloth-stretching machine	A. C. Cerpe	Stafford, Conn	Dec. 10, 1867	71, 990
Cloth-stretching machine	H. P. Roche	Utica, N. Y	Dec. 3, 1867	71, 647
Cloth-stretching roller	N. Simmons	Providence, R. I	Dec. 4, 1855	13, 888
Cloth-strip bristles	A. P. Peyroux	New Orleans, La	Oct. 24, 1871	120, 320

Index of patents issued from the United States Patent Office from 1790 *to* 1873, *inclusive*—Continued.

Invention.	Inventor.	Residence.	Date.	No.
Cloth, Substitute for teasel and card for raising the nap of.	I. Sanford	Providence, R. I	Mar. 26, 1814	....
Cloth-tearing engine	J. Biddis	....	May 6, 1800	....
Cloth, Teazling	J. Beckwith	Lyme, Conn	May 16, 1817	....
Cloth, Teazling	J. Olney	Westmoreland, N. Y	Mar. 29, 1817	....
Cloth teazling and napping machine	A. Foster	Whitestown, N. Y	Aug. 24, 1821	....
Cloth teazling or napping machine	B. Swasey	Mount Vernon, Me	Aug. 8, 1837	350
Cloth, Tenter-bar for shaping articles of	S. L. Fiske	Philadelphia, Pa	Mar. 3, 1868	75, 143
Cloth, Tentering	W. Shaw and P. G. Green	Wales, Mass	June 20, 1854	11, 141
Cloth tentering and drying machine	A. Avery	Worcester, Mass	Aug. 24, 1869	94, 166
Cloth tentering and drying machine	J. S. Winsor	Providence, R. I	Apr. 9, 1861	32, 021
Cloth-tentering machine	G. S. Rogers	Thetford, Vt	Dec. 26, 1871	122, 283
Cloth, the weft of which is made of hair, grass, &c.	J. Downie	Paterson, N. J	Dec. 12, 1865	51, 436
Cloth upon loom, Apparatus for measuring and marking.	F. W. Howe	North Chelmsford, Mass	June 6, 1846	4, 556
Cloth used by bank-note engravers, Cleaning	H. M. Baker	New York, N. Y	Feb. 25, 1868	74, 878
Cloth, Varnish for enameling	W. H. Haines	Newark, N. J	Jan. 9, 1866	51, 998
Cloth-varnishing machine	S. B. B. Nowlan	New York, N. Y	Sept. 11, 1866	57, 955
Cloth, Vibrating machine for napping	S. Duncan	Northampton, N. Y	Jan. 21, 1828	....
Cloth washing and fulling machine	S. Arnold	Philmont, N. Y	Oct. 17, 1871	119, 958
Cloth washing, rinsing, and squeezing machine	J. Lee, jr	Charlestown, Mass	Dec. 24, 1867	72, 647
Cloth washing, scouring, fulling, and cleaning machine.	D. S. Dean	....	Feb. 29, 1804	....
Cloth, Weaving double	S. Fay	Lowell, Mass	June 20, 1854	11, 120
Cloth while fulling, &c., Machine for overhauling or taking wrinkles out of.	J. Tillou	New Haven, Conn	Dec. 14, 1840	1, 902
Cloth-whipping machine	E. Eaton	Norwalk, Conn	Mar. 2, 1869	87, 330
Cloth winding and folding machine	T. P. Forsyth	Dalton, Ind	Apr. 18, 1854	10, 782
Cloth-winding machine	G. F. Hargis	Decatur, Ill	Mar. 23, 1869	88, 257
Cloth with India rubber, &c., Machine for coating	G. S. Dwight	New York, N. Y	Feb. 16, 1869	87, 087
Cloth without spinning and weaving, Machine for manufacturing felt.	T. R. Williams	United States	Dec. 14, 1840	1, 897
Cloth without spinning or weaving, Mode of manufacturing.	N. Peck and D. Taylor	Fairfield County, Conn	June 29, 1829	....
Cloth, Woven	A. Ruzé	Gaillon, France	June 27, 1871	116, 498
Clothes and flower sprinkler	D. Bickford	Boston, Mass	Jan. 15, 1867	61, 146
Clothes and hat hook	G. B. Fowler	New York, N. Y	Dec. 15, 1863	40, 923
Clothes and hat hook	R. W. Randall	Biddeford, Me	Feb. 14, 1871	111, 777
Clothes and hat rack	C. Bradfield	Newark, N. J	Mar. 7, 1865	46, 751
Clothes and hat rack	H. E. Fickett	Brooklyn, N. Y	Aug. 23, 1864	43, 905
Clothes and hat rack combined	O. F. Burgess	Decorah, Iowa	May 21, 1872	127, 022
Clothes and mop wringer	C. E. Gage	Fond du Lac, Wis	Jan. 1, 1867	60, 761
Clothes and mop wringer	L. Hannum	Cortland, N. Y	May 12, 1867	62, 843
Clothes and picture hanger	F. M. Everingham	Collingwood, N. Y	Sept. 10, 1867	68, 616
Clothes, Apparatus for ironing	C. R. Hoyt	New York, N. Y	Dec. 3, 1867	71, 758
Clothes-bar	H. Willard	Vergennes, Vt	Feb. 18, 1862	34, 456
Clothes-beater	A. Jameson	Boston, Mass	Apr. 16, 1872	125, 738
Clothes-boiler	D. Kellogg	Ypsilanti, Mich	Dec. 8, 1868	84, 832
Clothes-boiler	J. H. Rickett	West Dover, Vt	June 29, 1869	91, 967
Clothes-boiler	L. H. Whitney	Washington, D. C	Sept. 14, 1869	94, 931
Clothes boiler, drainer, &c., Combined	F. Browning	Watchel, England	Dec. 19, 1865	51, 670
Clothes-basket	J. Stimpson	Baldwinsville, Mass	July 25, 1865	49, 007
Clothes-brushing machine	W. M. Blume	New York, N. Y	May 28, 1872	127, 301
Clothes-clamp	L. H. Cushman	Monmouth, Me	Nov. 17, 1857	18, 6 2
Clothes-clamp	E. Hedge and T. H. Fleming	Liverpool and Canton, Ill	June 27, 1871	116, 307
Clothes-clamp	C. L. Poorman	Bellaire, Ohio	May 23, 1871	115, 099
Clothes-clamp	J. Sedgebury	Philadelphia, Pa	Nov. 6, 1855	13, 765
Clothes-clamp	W. H. Towers	Philadelphia, Pa	Nov. 21, 1854	11, 977
Clothes-clamp	W. H. Towers	Philadelphia, Pa	Feb. 12, 1856	14, 262
Clothes-clamp	W. Tunstill	Brooklyn, N. Y	July 8, 1873	140, 659
Clothes-clamp	C. Warner	New York, N. Y	Oct. 4, 1859	25, 695
Clothes-cleaner	J. Braun	Rochester, N. Y	Dec. 22, 1868	85, 060
Clothes-cleansing pestle	E. Pollard	Albany, N. Y	Dec. 28, 1858	22, 451
Clothes, Compound for extracting oil, paint, grease, &c., from.	C. B. Skiff	Jersey City, N. J	June 22, 1869	91, 680
Clothes, Compound for imparting a gloss to	W. D. Beaumont	Baltimore, Md	Oct. 8, 1850	7, 695
Clothes, Device to aid in ironing	C. S. Whipple	Waterford, Conn	Oct. 15, 1872	131, 340
Clothes, Dry-scouring	T. L. Jennings	New York	Mar. 3, 1821	....
Clothes-drier	W. H. Acker	Tarrytown, N. Y	Dec. 15, 1868	84, 928
Clothes-drier	L. J. Adams	Hoosick Falls, N. Y	Oct. 26, 1869	96, 181
Clothes-drier	G. W. Ainsworth	Waterbury, Vt	Apr. 16, 1872	125, 713
Clothes-drier	O. P. Allen	Rindge, N. H	Sept. 11, 1860	29, 943
Clothes-drier	C. R. Anderson	Saint Louis, Mo	Dec. 6, 1870	109, 860
Clothes-drier	I. B. Arnold	Providence, R. I	Oct. 1, 1867	69, 302
Clothes-drier	W. Arronquier	Worcester, Mass	May 26, 1868	78, 351
Clothes-drier	C. Bange	Saint Louis, Mo	May 5, 1868	77, 440
Clothes-drier	J. Barnett	Dayton, Ohio	Mar. 20, 1866	53, 257
Clothes-drier	J. R. Bassett	Cincinnati, Ohio	June 18, 1872	127, 948
Clothes-drier	C. B. Bennett	Amboy, Ill	Dec. 31, 1867	72, 782
Clothes-drier	H. S. Black	Buchanan, Mich	May 9, 1871	114, 519
Clothes-drier	J. M. Blake	Buffalo, N. Y	Sept. 14, 1869	94, 703
Clothes-drier	H. S. Blood	New Orleans, La	Apr. 5, 1864	42, 160
Clothes-drier	J. B. Blood	Lynn, Mass	Sept. 22, 1868	82, 280
Clothes-drier	H. C. Boardman	Morrisville, Vt	Dec. 11, 1860	30, 868
Clothes drier	A. Bosworth	Champlain, N. Y	May 17, 1870	103, 133
Clothes-drier	R. H. Boughner	East Germantown, Ind	Mar. 23, 1869	88, 123
Clothes-drier	J. Briggs	Peterborough, N. H	May 31, 1870	103, 712
Clothes-drier	J. L. Brigham	Saint Paul, Minn	Jan. 17, 1871	110, 952
Clothes-drier	B. Britton	Galena, Ill	Mar. 5, 1867	62, 600
Clothes-drier	B. S. Brown	Chicago, Ill	Feb. 22, 1870	100, 114
Clothes-drier	B. S. Brown	New York, N. Y	Mar. 5, 1872	124, 218
Clothes-drier	H. Brown	New York, N. Y	Aug. 20, 1867	67, 959
Clothes-drier	O. C. Brown	Iberia, Ohio	July 17, 1866	56, 300
Clothes-drier	W. L. Brown	Shortsville, N. Y	May 24, 1870	103, 424
Clothes-drier	D. M. Buckley	Athens, Ohio	Apr. 21, 1868	76, 900
Clothes-drier	E. Bucklin, jr	Pawtucket, R. I	May 16, 1865	47, 698
Clothes-drier	W. H. Buell	Union City, Mich	June 21, 1870	104, 652
Clothes-drier	J. Burch and B. Webb	Warren, N. Y	Nov. 25, 1873	144, 951

Index of patents issued from the United States Patent Office from 1790 to 1873, inclusive—Continued.

Invention.	Inventor.	Residence.	Date.	No.
Clothes-drier	M. C. Burr	Owatanna, Minn	Aug. 19, 1862	36, 204
Clothes-drier	E. Buss	Yellow Springs, Ohio	Apr. 2, 1861	31, 868
Clothes-drier	F. R. Butler	Rocky Hill, Conn	Aug. 31, 1869	94, 182
Clothes-drier	J. M. Butters	Lovell, Me	Aug. 22, 1865	49, 498
Clothes-drier	J. M. Butters	North Fryeburgh, Me	June 2, 1868	78, 575
Clothes-drier	J. Caffrey	Covington, Ky	Mar. 12, 1872	124, 543
Clothes-drier	J. Caffrey	Covington, Ky	Oct. 15, 1872	132, 196
Clothes-drier	L. S. Calkins	El Paso, Ill	July 23, 1867	67, 102
Clothes-drier	M. T. Campbell	Lima, Pa	Aug. 18, 1868	81, 249
Clothes-drier	C. Carrier	Oswego, N. Y	July 20, 1869	92, 794
Clothes-drier	E. Carter	Rensselaer, N. Y	Sept. 7, 1869	94, 562
Clothes-drier	R. D. Chandler	Fair Haven, N. J	Oct. 29, 1867	70, 165
Clothes-drier	A. J. Chase	Boston, Mass	Jan. 5, 1869	85, 562
Clothes-drier	T. H. Chubb and W. G. Marston	Post Mills, Vt	May 9, 1871	114, 527
Clothes-drier	E. P. Clark	Millbury, Mass	July 20, 1869	92, 797
Clothes-drier	H. H. Clark	Cincinnati, Ohio	Mar. 5, 1872	124, [illegible]
Clothes-drier	J. V. Clark	Camden, N. J	Apr. 12, 1870	101, 712
Clothes-drier	S. Cole	Pawtucket, R. I	July 25, 1865	48, 910
Clothes-drier	T. C. Collins	Little Hocking, Ohio	Sept. 7, 1869	94, 567
Clothes-drier	I. C. Conner	Dover, N. H	Sept. 4, 1866	57, 6[illegible]
Clothes-drier	I. A. Coons	Middletown, Ohio	July 30, 1867	67, 270
Clothes-drier	E. B. Corby	Bloomfield, N. J	Dec. 27, 1870	110, 551
Clothes-drier	G. F. Couty	Paris, France	Nov. 7, 1871	120, 719
Clothes-drier	F. Crandall	Erie, Pa	July 9, 1867	66, 466
Clothes-drier	M. C. Cronk	Auburn, N. Y	Nov. 8, 1859	26, 023
Clothes-drier	D. E. Crosby and S. E. Strickland.	South Vineland, N. J	Aug. 24, 1869	93, 970
Clothes-drier	H. P. Crouse	Hartland, Mich	Apr. 7, 1868	76, 305
Clothes-drier	E. Culver	Shelburne, Mass	Feb. 21, 1865	46, 452
Clothes-drier	L. Cutting	San Francisco, Cal	Sept. 27, 1870	107, 763
Clothes-drier	W. A. Daggett	Landis Township, N. J	Oct. 4, 1870	108, 008
Clothes-drier	J. D. Davenport	North Providence, R. I	May 19, 1868	78, 069
Clothes-drier	A. Day	Skowhegan, Me	Feb. 7, 1871	111, 519
Clothes-drier	I. N. Deal	Brooklyn, N. Y	Feb. 11, 1868	74, 318
Clothes-drier	J. K. Derby	Jamestown, N. Y	June 13, 1871	115, 829
Clothes-drier	D. M. Devoe	New York, N. Y	Feb. 24, 1863	37, 739
Clothes-drier	E. Dickerman	Richmond, Vt	Oct. 30, 1860	30, 530
Clothes-drier	O. R. Dinsmoor	Auburn, N. H	July 13, 1858	20, 868
Clothes-drier	J. P. Dorman	Galesburgh, Ill	July 4, 1865	48, 537
Clothes-drier	J. H. Doughty	New York, N. Y	Mar. 28, 1865	46, 999
Clothes-drier	J. H. Doughty	New York, N. Y	Aug. 27, 1867	68, 054
Clothes-drier	H. Du Bois	Marlborough, N. Y	Mar. 10, 1868	75, 251
Clothes-drier	J. H. Durand	Niles, Mich	Jan. 1, 1861	31, 013
Clothes-drier	J. T. Elliott	Grand Rapids, Mich	Feb. 5, 1867	61, 817
Clothes-drier	J. T. Elliott	Grand Rapids, Mich	Dec. 20, 1870	110, 347
Clothes-drier	J. Emmert	Dunleith, Ill	Oct. 25, 1870	108, 575
Clothes-drier	J. W. Epperson and T. W. Farrell.	Woodhull, Ill	Apr. 10, 1866	53, 797
Clothes-drier	J. B. Fellows	Augusta, Me	Nov. 28, 1871	121, 349
Clothes-drier	H. E. Fickett	Glen's Falls, N. Y	Sept. 4, 1860	29, 870
Clothes-drier	M. Flanders	Kendall, N. Y	May 16, 1871	114, 934
Clothes-drier	E. S. French	Westminster, Mass	Jan. 21, 1873	136, 107
Clothes-drier	W. Galaway	Sheboygan Falls, Wis	May 22, 1866	54, 886
Clothes-drier	C. A. Gale	Boston, Mass	Nov. 1, 1859	26, 004
Clothes-drier	S. L. George	Decatur, Mich	Aug. 7, 1866	56, 926
Clothes-drier	E. G. Gibson	Owego, N. Y	Sept. 28, 1858	21, 639
Clothes-drier	R. Gilbert	Morrisville, Vt	Aug. 28, 1860	29, 780
Clothes-drier	E. B. Gildersleeve	Wading River, N. Y	Mar. 18, 1873	136, 831
Clothes-drier	J. and W. Gunn	Louisville, Ky	Nov. 15, 1870	109, 200
Clothes-drier	C. Goldthwait	South Weymouth, Mass	Feb. 25, 1862	34, 487
Clothes-drier	C. Goldthwait	South Weymouth, Mass	Feb. 17, 1863	37, 686
Clothes-drier	F. W. Goodale and J. J. Brennan.	Danbury, Conn	May 30, 1871	115, 461
Clothes-drier	H. Gransden	Dubuque, Iowa	July 9, 1867	66, 582
Clothes-drier	A. Graves	Roscoe, Ill	June 24, 1873	140, 193
Clothes-drier	W. S. Graves and A. S. Capron	Kansas City, Mo., and Grass Lake, Mich.	Aug. 17, 1869	93, 708
Clothes-drier	J. S. Gray	Boston, Mass	Jan. 2, 1872	122, 378
Clothes-drier	J. Greenhalgh, jr	Glendale, R. I	July 10, 1867	68, 735
Clothes-drier	A. W. Griffith	Boston, Mass	June 9, 1868	78, 661
Clothes-drier	A. M. Gurley	Waterville, N. Y	Feb. 9, 1869	86, 665
Clothes-drier	W. J. Hadden	Clinton, Ill	Dec. 3, 1872	133, 530
Clothes-drier	J. C. Haines	West Philadelphia, Pa	Apr. 19, 1870	101, 999
Clothes-drier	E. R. Hall	Utica, N. Y	Apr. 7, 1868	76, 441
Clothes-drier	R. Hamblin	Mishawaka, Ind	June 18, 1867	65, 905
Clothes-drier	J. J. Hamilton	Newcastle, Ind	Mar. 30, 1858	19, 772
Clothes-drier	G. H. Hammond	Davenport, N. Y	Aug. 4, 1868	80, 729
Clothes-drier	H. J. Hancock	New York, N. Y	Apr. 14, 1868	76, 756
Clothes-drier	A. Harbison	Newcastle, Pa	Sept. 7, 1869	94, 595
Clothes-drier	O. H. Harding and D. G. Williams.	Quincy, Mich	July 25, 1871	117, 414
Clothes-drier	O. H. Harding and J. Willis	Quincy, Mich	June 4, 1872	127, 481
Clothes-drier	T. G. Harold	Brooklyn, N. Y	Jan. 14, 1864	43, 113
Clothes-drier	E. Hause	Tecumseh, Mich	Apr. 6, 1869	88, 566
Clothes-drier	A. P. Hawse and G. R. Shippy	Wolcott, Vt	Apr. 6, 1869	88, 631
Clothes-drier	B. B. Hawse	Morrisville, Vt	Jan. 3, 1860	26, 674
Clothes-drier	M. R. Heliker	Norwalk, Ohio	Sept. 14, 1869	94, 822
Clothes-drier	D. K. Hickok	Morrisville, Vt	Dec. 20, 1859	26, 496
Clothes-drier	D. K. Hickok	Morrisville, Vt	Aug. 21, 1860	29, 694
Clothes-drier	A. H. Hill	Saint Johnsbury, Vt	Aug. 29, 1871	118, 612
Clothes-drier	J. O. Hill	Carbondale, Ill	June 11, 1872	127, 881
Clothes-drier	I. Hogeland	Indianapolis, Ind	Dec. 13, 1870	110, 137
Clothes-drier	A. S. Hopson	Plain View, Minn	Sept. 22, 1868	82, 408
Clothes-drier	L. Horn	Wolfborough, N. H	Dec. 15, 1863	40, 936
Clothes-drier	M. D. Hotchkiss	Sheboygan Falls, Wis	May 15, 1866	54, 727
Clothes-drier	H. A. Houghton	Lyme, N. H	May 27, 1862	35, 375
Clothes-drier	L. D. Howard	Saint Johnsbury, Vt	Feb. 14, 1871	111, 747
Clothes-drier	D. Hull	Newburgh, N. Y	Apr. 9, 1861	31, 980

Index of patents issued from the United States Patent Office from 1790 *to* 1873, *inclusive*—Continued.

Invention.	Inventor.	Residence.	Date.	No.
Clothes-drier	C. A. Hunt	Urbana, Ill	June 24, 1862	35, 684
Clothes-drier	C. R. Hurlbut	Yorkshire, N. Y	May 24, 1859	24, 123
Clothes-drier	L. T. Ilgen	Cedarville, Ill	Aug. 14, 1866	57, 144
Clothes-drier	C. H. Jackson	Saint Louis, Mo	Nov. 21, 1865	51, 057
Clothes-drier	D. Johnson	Chicago, Ill	Aug. 2, 1859	24, 974
Clothes-drier	J. Johnson	New York, N. Y	Aug. 14, 1860	29, 599
Clothes-drier	J. Johnson	New York, N. Y	Oct. 30, 1860	30, 551
Clothes-drier	J. Johnson	Perry, Ill	June 13, 1871	115, 866
Clothes-drier	L. N. Johnson and B. Selloway	Montpelier, Vt	Aug. 24, 1869	93, 999
Clothes-drier	W. Johnston	Appleton, Wis	June 30, 1868	79, 474
Clothes-drier	J. Kaspar	Pomeroy, Ohio	Nov. 15, 1870	109, 219
Clothes-drier	G. A. Keene	Lynn, Mass	Dec. 12, 1871	121, 722
Clothes-drier	D. J. Kellogg	Rochester, N. Y	June 13, 1865	48, 183
Clothes-drier	H. H. Kendrick	Fulton, N. Y	May 10, 1870	102, 831
Clothes-drier	J. W. Kenning	Quincy, Mich	Dec. 13, 1870	110, 145
Clothes-drier	G. King	Eminence, Ky	May 11, 1869	89, 870
Clothes-drier	H. N. King and A. Z. Mason	Adrian, Mich	Oct. 1, 1867	69, 349
Clothes-drier	H. Knight	Westminster, Mass	Oct. 31, 1871	120, 443
Clothes-drier	A. Krotzer	Woodville, Ohio	Mar. 11, 1862	34, 637
Clothes-drier	C. H. L'Amoureux	New York, N. Y	Apr. 23, 1872	126, 062
Clothes-drier	J. Lee	Galesburgh, Ill	Sept. 24, 1861	33, 353
Clothes-drier	L. Ling	Pulaski, N. Y	Nov. 8, 1864	44, 964
Clothes-drier	C. F. Linscott	Chicago, Ill	July 4, 1871	116, 606
Clothes-drier	H. J. Lockwood	Wayne, Pa	Nov. 7, 1871	120, 756
Clothes-drier	J. C. Longshore	Mansfield, Ohio	Oct. 19, 1869	95, 917
Clothes-drier	I. Lyndo	Marathon, N. Y	Mar. 3, 1863	37, 819
Clothes-drier	H. G. Mack	Oswego, N. Y	July 27, 1869	92, 982
Clothes-drier	N. F. Mathewson	Bloomington, Ill	Sept. 24, 1872	131, 696
Clothes-drier	W. C. Maynard	Marathon, N. Y	Dec. 19, 1871	122, 043
Clothes-drier	G. McNeil	Chestnut Hill, Pa	Feb. 11, 1862	34, 372
Clothes-drier	R. Merrill	Elmira, N. Y	Feb. 21, 1860	27, 231
Clothes-drier	A. S. Miller	Nottingham, Ind	Sept. 9, 1873	142, 714
Clothes-drier	C. G. Miller	Brattleborough, Vt	Nov. 3, 1863	40, 493
Clothes-drier	D. Miller	Marietta, Ohio	Oct. 31, 1871	120, 452
Clothes-drier	R. M. Miller	Port Andrew, Wis	Dec. 28, 1869	98, 398
Clothes-drier	A. J. Mills and E. M. Hewett	Scott, N. Y	Apr. 23, 1867	64, 129
Clothes-drier	W. N. and A. K. Moore	Neenah, Wis	Nov. 29, 1870	109, 647
Clothes-drier	R. M. Morriell	Plymouth, Ind	Sept. 3, 1867	68, 526
Clothes-drier	S. Morrill	Andover, N. H	Nov. 11, 1856	16, 065
Clothes drier	D. Morris	Cutler, Ohio	May 24, 1870	103, 486
Clothes-drier	J. F. Mullowny	Pittsburgh, Pa	June 20, 1871	116, 081
Clothes-drier	J. Mumma	Middletown, Ohio	Jan. 19, 1869	86, 095
Clothes-drier	F. S. Nettleton and E. J. Fuller	Leominster, Mass	Mar. 22, 1870	101, 153
Clothes-drier	G. W. Nowell	Lawrence, Mass	Feb. 17, 1863	37, 724
Clothes-drier	J. J. Newman	Middletown, Ohio	Aug. 6, 1867	67, 567
Clothes-drier	R. L. Normando	Higginsville, N. Y	Nov. 28, 1872	121, 404
Clothes-drier	W. B. Noyes	Dorchester, N. H	Feb. 18, 1868	74, 715
Clothes-drier	T. Oakley	Booneville, N. Y	Aug. 10, 1869	93, 551
Clothes-drier	R. H. Oates	Toronto, Canada	Nov. 6, 1866	59, 527
Clothes-drier	A. O'Dell	Napanee, Canada	Nov. 1, 1870	108, 818
Clothes-drier	G. Oldham	Westfield, N. Y	Aug. 24, 1869	94, 023
Clothes-drier	W. W. S. Orberton	Haverhill, Mass	May 29, 1866	55, 208
Clothes-drier	J. P. Packer	Flemington, Pa	Dec. 10, 1872	133, 882
Clothes-drier	G. W. Page	Henrietta, Ohio	Nov. 12, 1872	132, 920
Clothes-drier	E. L. Parker	Painesville, Ohio	Feb. 21, 1871	112, 072
Clothes-drier	S. Parker	Forest Grove, N. J	Mar. 27, 1866	53, 541
Clothes drier	A. H. Patch	Hamilton, Mass	June 28, 1870	104, 761
Clothes-drier	A. H. Patch	Hamilton, Mass	Feb. 7, 1871	111, 563
Clothes-drier	W. P. Patton	Harrisburgh, Pa	May 19, 1863	38, 631
Clothes-drier	J. A. Pease	New York, N. Y	Oct. 21, 1862	36, 726
Clothes-drier	A. W. Phillips	Fairfield, N. Y	June 25, 1872	128, 323
Clothes-drier	R. Phillips	Boston, Mass	Mar. 8, 1870	100, 662
Clothes-drier	E. N. Porter and I. J. Currier	Wolcott, Vt	Mar. 28, 1871	113, 204
Clothes-drier	E. T. Porter	Washington, D. C	Sept. 28, 1858	21, 626
Clothes-drier	Z. B. Putnam and H. H. McDonald.	Belfast, Me	Dec. 26, 1871	122, 280
Clothes-drier	G. Race	Norwich, N. Y	June 28, 1859	24, 575
Clothes-drier	D. B. Randall and A. A. Williams.	Glover, Vt	Sept. 17, 1867	69, 023
Clothes-drier	W. F. Redding	Saratoga Springs, N. Y	July 9, 1867	66, 520
Clothes-drier	J. W. Reed and H. A. Jones	Pittsburgh, Pa	Aug. 22, 1871	118, 272
Clothes-drier	G. W. Richardson	Taunton, Mass	Sept. 6, 1870	107, 199
Clothes-drier	C. Robinson	Cambridgeport, Mass	Oct. 2, 1860	30, 249
Clothes-drier	C. Robinson	Cambridgeport, Mass	Apr. 23, 1861	32, 147
Clothes-drier	C. B. Rogers	Plainfield, N. J	Feb. 26, 1867	62, 443
Clothes-drier	E. D. Sanford	Baltimore, Md	June 25, 1867	66, 045
Clothes-drier	C. G. Sargent	Chelsea, Mass	Jan. 29, 1861	31, 260
Clothes-drier	A. F. Saunders	Chelsea, Mass	Aug. 25, 1863	39, 706
Clothes-drier	A. Scheff	Raymondville, N. Y	Sept. 13, 1870	107, 295
Clothes-drier	H. Schryver	Kingston, N. Y	May 3, 1870	102, 717
Clothes-drier	J. Seeman and S. P. Catrow	Middletown, Ohio	Jan. 22, 1867	61, 473
Clothes-drier	C. C. Sheldon	Randolph, N. Y	Jan. 23, 1872	123, 051
Clothes-drier	E. Sims	Antwerp, N. Y	Jan. 31, 1865	46, 151
Clothes-drier	G. P. Sisson	Florence, Mass	Aug. 27, 1867	68, 317
Clothes-drier	W. A. Sloppy	Berwick, Pa	Dec 19, 1871	122, 071
Clothes-drier	D. C. Smart	Cambridgeport, Mass	July 4, 1871	116, 639
Clothes-drier	C. F. Smith and A. Heather	Chicago, Ill	Sept. 19, 1871	119, 191
Clothes-drier	G. C. Smith	Hamilton, Ohio	Oct. 3, 1871	119, 539
Clothes-drier	G. C. Smith and C. H. Dietrich	Middleville, Mich	Nov. 7, 1871	120, 785
Clothes-drier	O. S. Smith and C. R. Hopkins	Middletown, Conn	Nov. 21, 1871	121, 208
Clothes-drier	T. F. Snover	Menasha, Wis	Aug. 14, 1866	57, 204
Clothes-drier	L. A. Stare	Oconomowoc, Wis	Apr. 19, 1870	102, 059
Clothes-drier	A. Stechschult	Glendorf, Ohio	Mar. 28, 1871	113, 106
Clothes-drier	E. E. Stedman	Randolph, Ohio	Aug. 1, 1871	117, 095
Clothes-drier	H. M. Stevenson	South Peacham, Vt	Jan. 3, 1871	110, 691
Clothes-drier	R. B. Stillman	Almond, N. Y	June 16, 1868	78, 902
Clothes-drier	A. C. Stowe	San José, Cal	Apr. 2, 1872	125, 227
Clothes-drier	A. J. Stowell	Dunlap, Iowa	June 4, 1872	127, 527

Index of patents issued from the United States Patent Office from 1790 *to* 1873, *inclusive*—Continued.

Invention.	Inventor.	Residence.	Date.	No.
Clothes-drier	L. M. Streetor	Oshkosh, Wis	June 14, 1870	104, 227
Clothes-drier	H. D. Struse	Brooklyn, N. Y	Sept. 29, 1868	82, 657
Clothes-drier	T. A. Summers	Rochester, N. Y	Sept. 27, 1864	44, 469
Clothes-drier	H. Swan	Woodstock, Vt	Jan. 17, 1871	111, 011
Clothes-drier	A. L. Taylor	Springfield, Vt	Sept. 7, 1869	94, 527
Clothes-drier	E. B. Taylor	Natick, Mass	Mar. 7, 1865	46, 731
Clothes-drier	S. H. Tift	Morrisville, Vt	July 20, 1858	20, 964
Clothes-drier	S. H. Tift	Morrisville, Vt	July 27, 1858	21, 035
Clothes-drier	G. F. Tilton	Salem, Mass	Nov. 14, 1865	50, 969
Clothes-drier	S. H. Titus	Pennington, N. J	May 28, 1867	65, 305
Clothes-drier	L. A. Towne	La Crosse, Wis	July 20, 1869	92, 905
Clothes-drier	S. I. Trask	Guilford, N. Y	Apr. 3, 1866	53, 705
Clothes-drier	W. Tredenick	Providence, R. I	Dec. 27, 1870	110, 607
Clothes-drier	J. N. Valley	Detroit, Mich	May 17, 1870	103, 257
Clothes-drier	H. J. and D. D. Van Valkenburgh.	Rabbit River, Mich	Sept. 17, 1872	131, 483
Clothes-drier	J. K. Wagner	Potsdam, N. Y	Feb. 14 1871	111, 888
Clothes-drier	J. Walker	Kansas City, Mo	Dec. 17, 1867	72, 341
Clothes-drier	L. B. Waterman	Chicago, Ill	July 28, 1868	80, 316
Clothes-drier	O. H. Waters	Baltimore, Md	Sept. 13, 1859	25, 474
Clothes-drier	J. R. Watkins	Maine Prairie, Minn	June 30, 1868	79, 524
Clothes-drier	D. R. Watson	Moawequa, Ill	Jan. 14, 1873	134, 828
Clothes-drier	S. Way	La Porte, Ind	Feb. 23, 1869	87, 312
Clothes-drier	M. B. Wheaton	New York, N. Y	Apr. 14, 1868	76, 862
Clothes-drier	J. B. White	Detroit, Mich	Dec. 8, 1868	84, 849
Clothes-drier	L. M. Whitman	Sterling, Ill	May 9, 1871	114, 630
Clothes-drier	H. Willard	Vergennes, Vt	June 18, 1867	65, 979
Clothes-drier	E. B. Winship	Racine, Wis	July 16, 1872	129, 385
Clothes-drier	L. Winterhalder and D. Wilson	New York, N. Y	Apr. 13, 1869	88, 937
Clothes-drier	D. Witt	Hubbardston, Mass	Dec. 29, 1868	85, 469
Clothes-drier	M. H. Wood	Carlisle, Ohio	Aug. 8, 1871	117, 847
Clothes-drier	G. L. Woods	Manchester, N. H	May 28, 1872	127, 206
Clothes-drier	S. Woodward	Sutton, N. H	Nov. 21, 1854	11, 985
Clothes-drier	L. Woodworth	Morrison, Ill	Jan. 22, 1867	61, 498
Clothes-drier	L. C. Wright	Lockport, N. Y	Nov. 20, 1866	59, 935
Clothes-drier, Adjustable	H. S. Boynton	Cortland, Vt	Apr. 14, 1868	76, 589
Clothes-drier and awning combined	C. E. Hyde	Oswego, N. Y	Nov. 28, 1871	121, 371
Clothes-drier and ironing-board	M. Power	Chicago, Ill	Nov. 21, 1871	121, 127
Clothes-drier and ironing-table	W. Reichenback	Chicago, Ill	Apr. 6, 1869	88, 739
Clothes-drier and pendant seat combined	J. Hirons	Buchanan, Mich	Nov. 7, 1871	120, 585
Clothes-drier and stand	W. H. Earnest	Parkersburgh, W. Va	Sept. 3, 1867	68, 355
Clothes-drier and stand combined	G. Favinger	Pittsford, Mich	June 11, 1867	65, 735
Clothes-drier and stove-pipe shelf	G. E. Hoyt	Hebron, N. H	Dec. 7, 1869	97, 511
Clothes-drier attachment for stove-pipes	A. P. Anthony	Morrison, Ill	May 28, 1867	65, 152
Clothes-drier, Detachable stove-pipe	H. Whitney	Chicago, Ill	June 22, 1869	91, 803
Clothes, Drier for scoured	J. Braun	Bridgewater, Pa	Sept. 24, 1867	69, 171
Clothes-drier for stove-pipes	J. B. Waterman	Chicago, Ill	Dec. 7, 1869	97, 736
Clothes-drier, Revolving	K. H. Elliott and J. Brown	Morrisville, Vt	Nov. 12, 1861	33, 697
Clothes-drier, Revolving	J. McCaskey, jr	Orville, Ohio	June 1, 1869	90, 764
Clothes-drier, Rotating	W. Boyers	Mount Carroll, Ill	Mar. 25, 1862	34, 802
Clothes-drier, Stove-pipe	C. M. Herreman	Mankato, Minn	Aug. 22, 1871	118, 241
Clothes-drier, Wardrobe	B. S Brown	New York, N. Y	Mar. 5, 1872	124, 247
Clothes-drier, Window	W. Powers	Preston, N. Y	Jan. 6, 1863	37, 359
Clothes-drier, Window	J. R. and J. E. Shepard	Waukegan, Ill	July 15, 1862	35, 898
Clothes-drying frame	C. Stone	Ravenna, Ohio	June 22, 1858	20, 669
Clothes-drying machine	J. O. Luther and P. Staab	Grafton, Wis	June 27, 1871	116, 333
Clothes-drying machine	W. Price	Cincinnati, Ohio	Dec. 20, 1864	45, 521
Clothes-fastener	P. Frost	Springfield, Vt	Mar. 8, 1864	41, 838
Clothes-fastener	L. Leavenworth	Trumansburgh, N. Y	Mar. 8, 1859	23, 178
Clothes-frame	E. R. Bigelow	Salem, Mass	Sept. 10, 1861	33, 232
Clothes-frame	C. A. Boynton	Hyde Park, Vt	July 3, 1860	28, 961
Clothes-frame	H. Buell	Mount Morris, N. Y	June 7, 1864	43, 069
Clothes-frame	J. Burr	Baltimore, Md	July 26, 1859	24, 904
Clothes-frame	P. Cody	Hamilton, N. Y	Sept. 25, 1860	30, 124
Clothes-frame	D. C. Colby	Keene, N. H	Jan. 25, 1859	22, 767
Clothes-frame	W. A. Daggett	South Vineland, N. J	Apr. 20, 1869	89, 131
Clothes-frame	J. Danner	Canton, Ohio	July 28, 1863	39, 340
Clothes-frame	J. Danner	Canton, Ohio	Jan. 26, 1869	86, 140
Clothes-frame	E. Dickerman	Middlefield, Conn	Aug. 20 1861	33, 075
Clothes-frame	J. E. Earle	New Haven, Conn	Nov. 25, 1862	36, 994
Clothes-frame	C. J. Ferguson	New York, N. Y	July 17, 1860	29, 151
Clothes-frame	H. T. Field and D. Harrington	Worcester, Mass	Nov. 5, 1872	132, 717
Clothes-frame	H. M. Fletcher	Newport, N. H	Apr. 5, 1859	23, 460
Clothes frame	J. Fraser	Rochester, N. Y	May 15, 1860	28, 266
Clothes-frame	L. F. Frazee	Tottenville, N. Y	Feb. 26, 1861	31, 538
Clothes-frame	J. Gasser	Toledo, Ohio	July 12, 1859	24, 731
Clothes-frame	J. Greek	Evansville, Ind	Feb. 23, 1864	41, 698
Clothes-frame	A. Greenwood	Toulon, Ill	July 17, 1860	29, 163
Clothes-frame	W. Hathaway	Worcester, Mass	Dec. 21, 1858	22, 398
Clothes-frame	W. Hathaway	Providence, R. I	July 3, 1860	28, 983
Clothes-frame	D. Henshaw	Fitchburgh, Mass	Feb. 1, 1859	22, 804
Clothes-frame	D. E. Holmes	Halifax, Mass	Oct. 11, 1859	25, 737
Clothes-frame	H. J. Holmes	Warren, Mass	July 12, 1859	24, 739
Clothes-frame	H. Hempton	Fairhaven, Mass	Feb. 26, 1850	7, 120
Clothes-frame	L. L. Knight	Barre, Mass	Apr. 16, 1861	32, 104
Clothes-frame	M. J. Knox	Knox Corners, N. Y	June 18, 1861	32, 569
Clothes-frame	M. J. Knox	Knox Corners, N. Y	Apr. 22, 1862	35, 027
Clothes-frame	S. T. Lamb	New Washington, Ind	Sept. 18, 1860	30, 069
Clothes-frame	H. Littlejohn	Troy, N. Y	Jan. 7, 1862	34, 113
Clothes-frame	J. P. Mayhugh	Leitersburgh, Md	Feb. 24, 1863	37, 762
Clothes-frame	J. C. Miller	Rockport, Ind	Dec. 30, 1873	146, 087
Clothes-frame	H. A. Nutting	South Amherst, Ind	May 10, 1859	23, 941
Clothes-frame	E. Page	Streetsborough, Ohio	June 15, 1858	20, 579
Clothes-frame	S. W. and J. F. Palmer	Auburn, N. Y	Oct. 18, 1859	25, 868
Clothes-frame	H. Parkhurst	De Kalb, Ill	Aug. 9, 1859	25, 039
Clothes-frame	R. Ramsey	New Wilmington, Pa	Apr. 12, 1859	23, 607
Clothes-frame	D. Read	Hamilton, N. Y	Mar. 29, 1859	23, 392

Index of patents issued from the United States Patent Office from 1790 *to* 1873, *inclusive*—Continued.

Invention.	Inventor.	Residence.	Date.	No.
Clothes-frame	T. S. Scoville	New York, N. Y	Jan. 3, 1860	26, 710
Clothes-frame	L. B. Waterman	Chicago, Ill	Feb. 15, 1859	22, 993
Clothes, Hand-rubber for washing	G. F. J. Colburn	Newark, N. J	Mar. 8, 1870	100, 603
Clothes-hanger	J. O. Montignani	Albany, N. Y	Oct. 14, 1862	36, 666
Clothes hanger	A. J. Walker	New York, N. Y	June 14, 1864	43, 144
Clothes-holder	W. Z. Brown	Decatur, Ill	Nov. 7, 1871	120, 570
Clothes-holder for clothes-lines	M. V. Bulla	South Bend, Ind	Nov. 22, 1870	109, 382
Clothes-hook	G. M. Hubbard	New Haven, Conn	Feb. 13, 1872	123, 699
Clothes-hook	O. A. North	New Britain, Conn	Jan. 12, 1869	85, 756
Clothes-hook	S. S. Putnam	Dorchester, Mass	Sept. 17, 1867	69, 021
Clothes-hook	S. S. Putnam	Dorchester, Mass	Oct. 8, 1867	69, 587
Clothes-hook	H. M. Whitmarsh and S. S. Putnam.	Abington and Dorchester, Mass.	Jan. 29, 1867	61, 590
Clothes hook and line holder combined	T. Weaver	Harrisburgh, Pa	Aug. 18, 1868	81, 312
Clothes-horse	E. Culver, jr	Shelburne Falls, Mass	Aug. 17, 1858	21, 231
Clothes-horse	T. S. Lewis	Kendall's Mills, Me	Dec. 28, 1858	22, 435
Clothes-horse, &c., Combined	H. L. Stillson	Plattsburgh, N. Y	Sept. 15, 1868	82, 256
Clothes-horse frames, Connecting	H. Luther	Providence, R. I	May 19, 1841	2, 098
Clothes-ironing apparatus	C. Alden	Cassadaga, N. Y	Nov. 8, 1859	26, 005
Clothes-ironing machine	J. Shaefer	Lancaster, Pa	Sept. 7, 1858	21, 450
Clothes, Knuckle-protector for washing	G. W. Doty	Wooster, Ohio	Dec. 5, 1871	121, 498
Clothes-line	J. W. Bliss	Hartford, Conn	Apr. 23, 1867	64, 063
Clothes-line	P. C. Johnson	Central City, Colo	Nov. 30, 1869	97, 409
Clothes-line adjuster	R. White	Newport, Pa	Oct. 6, 1868	82, 911
Clothes line and clamp	A. D. Rust	Vernon, Mich	Feb. 5, 1867	61, 875
Clothes-line clamp	C. C. Fellows	Centre Sandwich, N. H	Oct. 22, 1867	69, 977
Clothes-line clamp	C. W. Howard	Philadelphia, Pa	Oct. 2, 1866	58, 419
Clothes-line clamp	G. R. Nebinger	Lewisberry, Pa	Feb. 18, 1868	74, 713
Clothes-line clamp	T. W. Owens	Granville, Ohio	July 19, 1870	105, 483
Clothes-line clamp	W. S. and E. H. Shoemaker	Towsontown, Md., and Lancaster, Ohio.	May 11, 1869	90, 055
Clothes-line clamp	A. T. Thayer and J. B. Le Maire.	New York, N.Y., and Hudson City, N. J.	Oct. 1, 1872	131, 912
Clothes-line clamp	G. W. Wilbar	Taunton, Mass	Feb. 1, 1870	99, 385
Clothes-line clamp	W. Winter	Philadelphia, Pa	Aug. 14, 1866	57, 263
Clothes-line clip	J. S. Rowley	Chateaugay, N. Y	July 16, 1867	66, 892
Clothes-line conductor	D. Reed and A. Shaeffer	Medway, Ohio	Apr. 4, 1871	113, 563
Clothes-line fastener	J. G. and P. A. Ames	Baltimore, Md	June 24, 1873	140, 234
Clothes-line fastener	F. Clymer	Galion, Ohio	Mar. 9, 1869	87, 636
Clothes-line fastener	E. K. Elliott and N. J. Baxter	Cuyahoga Falls, Ohio, and Washington, D. C.	Aug. 2, 1870	105, 927
Clothes-line fastener	H. J. Hendey	Wolcottsville, Conn	Feb. 14, 1871	111, 843
Clothes-line fastener	B. B. Herrick	Decatur, Mich	Nov. 29, 1870	109, 733
Clothes-line fastener	J. Johnson, S. J. Smith, and S. Ingersoll.	Brooklyn, N. Y	Mar. 23, 1869	88, 175
Clothes-line fastener	M. H. Lineback	Greenfield, Ind	Sept. 21, 1869	95, 120
Clothes-line fastener	M. McManus	East Saginaw, Mich	Jan. 2, 1872	122, 476
Clothes-line fastener	H. Ogborn	Richmond, Ind	Mar. 1, 1870	100, 438
Clothes-line fastening	S. A. Barr	Pittsburgh, Pa	July 30, 1867	67, 156
Clothes-line holder	H. Browne	Des Moines, Iowa	May 31, 1870	103, 714
Clothes-line holder	D. Bull	Amboy, Ill	Sept. 28, 1869	95, 316
Clothes-line holder	A. Comey	Cuyahoga Falls, Ohio	Feb. 25, 1868	74, 798
Clothes-line holder	W. Cooke	New York, N. Y	Aug. 19, 1873	141, 921
Clothes-line holder	A. Cooper	Harrisburgh, Pa	Oct. 19, 1869	95, 881
Clothes-line holder	J. Davis	Harrisburgh, Pa	May 17, 1870	103, 155
Clothes-line holder	E. Dingman	Liverpool, N. Y	June 20, 1871	116, 034
Clothes-line holder	J. W. Gladding	Normal, Ill	Apr. 28, 1868	77, 274
Clothes-line holder	J. B. Hubecker	Newport, Pa	Nov. 21, 1871	121, 167
Clothes-line holder	A. L. Hurtt	Monticello, Ind	May 3, 1870	102, 548
Clothes-line holder	C. A. Kalck	Philadelphia, Pa	June 21, 1870	104, 597
Clothes-line holder	H. Morgan	Springfield, Mass	May 12, 1868	77, 750
Clothes-line holder	H. Ogborn	Richmond, Ind	July 6, 1869	92, 206
Clothes-line holder	O. S. Perkins and J. R. Richards	Mount Joy, Pa	July 7, 1868	79, 593
Clothes-line holder	J. C. Rankin	Mount Vernon, N. Y	Mar. 15, 1870	100, 803
Clothes-line holder	P. Riordan	Washington, D. C	Dec. 31, 1867	72, 908
Clothes-line holder	J. Robbins	Centralia, Ill	Sept. 14, 1869	94, 914
Clothes-line holder	A. J. Simpson	Washington, D. C	July 2, 1867	66, 403
Clothes-line holder	E. W. Talbott	Napoleon, Ohio	Jan. 3, 1871	110, 802
Clothes-line holder	C. L. Topliff	Brooklyn, N. Y	May 9, 1871	114, 728
Clothes-line holder	J. L. Wilcox	Preble, N. Y	Nov. 5, 1867	70, 665
Clothes line holder and stretcher	N. E. Buffington	North Providence, R. I	Jan. 21, 1870	104, 419
Clothes-line hook	J. Garvey and M. H. Kimball	San Francisco, Cal	Nov. 1, 1870	108, 776
Clothes-line hook	E. H. Gray	Winchester, Ill	May 5, 1868	77, 605
Clothes-line hook	J. L. Howard	New York, N. Y	July 30, 1867	67, 196
Clothes-line-hook block	J. W. Norcross	East Boston, Mass	July 30, 1867	67, 341
Clothes-line housing	A. Trumbull	New Britain, Conn	May 30, 1871	115, 544
Clothes-line operator	C. Barron	La Fayette, Ind	Oct. 18, 1870	108, 431
Clothes-line pole	C. B. Brown	New Rochelle, N. Y	Mar. 11, 1873	136, 641
Clothes-line post	B. Chesnut	Philadelphia, Pa	Oct. 19, 1858	21, 818
Clothes-line protector and stretcher	W. J. Ripley	Cincinnati, Ohio	May 2, 1871	114, 345
Clothes-line reel	J. Brizee	Alvarado, Cal	May 13, 1873	138, 785
Clothes-line reel	G. F. Corliss	Mansfield, Ohio	Nov. 11, 1873	144, 3[illegible]7
Clothes-line reel	S. and J. Drake	Canton, Ill	July 2, 1872	128, 539
Clothes-line reel	G. B. Griffin	Madison, Wis	Aug. 20, 1867	67, 872
Clothes-line reel	G. Holman	Waterville, N. Y	Nov. 15, 1870	109, 318
Clothes-line reel	I. E. Loughborough	Pittsford, N. Y	Jan. 29, 1867	61, 672
Clothes-line reel	H. W. Prouty and A. Thompson	Boston, Mass	Mar. 19, 1872	124, 698
Clothes-line reel	D. D. Pugh	Brooklyn, N. Y	June 21, 1870	104, 495
Clothes-line reel	C. Rosenthal	Philadelphia, Pa	July 22, 1873	141, 015
Clothes-line reel	J. D. S'arritt	Chicago, Ill	Aug. 6, 1867	67, 459
Clothes-line reel	C. H. Straffin	Boston, Mass	Nov. 21, 1871	121, 135
Clothes-line reel	J. Valentine and H. B. Stevens	Buffalo, N. Y	Dec. 15, 1868	84, 919
Clothes line reel and house	M. H. Card and A. Saylee	Fulton, Ill	Feb. 12, 1867	61, 924
Clothes-line reel, Automatic	W. Farrah	Des Moines, Iowa	Aug. 9, 1870	106, 146
Clothes-line sliding-support	M. Bubser	Jersey City, N. J	Jan. 14, 1873	134, 849
Clothes-line spring-clamp	E. S. Haskins	Boston, Mass	Mar. 14, 1854	10, 635
Clothes-line stretcher	S. Crowell	Philadelphia, Pa	Jan. 26, 1869	86, 139
Clothes-line support	J. E. Roache	New York, N. Y	Aug. 26, 1873	142, 278

Index of patents issued from the United States Patent Office from 1790 *to* 1873, *inclusive*—Continued.

Invention.	Inventor.	Residence.	Date.	No.
Clothes-line supporter	J. Andrews	New Bedford, Mass	Oct. 26, 1869	96, 183
Clothes-line supporter	T. Riley	Williamsburgh, N. Y	July 4, 1871	116, 632
Clothes-line supporter	F. W. Tilton and M. C. Swift	New Bedford, Mass	Aug. 18, 1868	81, 310
Clothes-lines, &c., Device for fastening	A. E. Schartz	New York, N. Y	Mar. 11, 1873	136, 768
Clothes-lines, Machinery for straining and preserving.	E. Allyn and C. B. Hildreth	Boston, Mass	Nov. 26, 1840	1, 863
Clothes-lines, Spring-clamp for	F. S. Hotchkiss and C. W. Blakeslee.	Northfield, Conn	Dec. 13, 1853	10, 311
Clothes-lines, Spring-clamp for	D. M. Smith	Springfield, Vt	Oct. 25, 1853	10, 163
Clothes, Machine for washing and pressing	J. Read	New York, N. Y	Apr. 10, 1839	1, 116
Clothes-mangle	D. Arndt	Toledo, Ohio	Mar. 2, 1869	87, 457
Clothes-mangle	F. A. Desloge	Saint Louis, Mo	June 8, 1869	91, 095
Clothes-mangle	S. Short	Cincinnati, Ohio	Dec. 23, 1873	145, 910
Clothes-mangle	H. E. Smith	New York, N. Y	Nov. 2, 1869	96, 359
Clothes-mangle	H. E. Smith	New York, N. Y	Nov. 2, 1869	96, 360
Clothes-mangle	E. D. Taylor and D. Cohn	Hornellsville, N. Y	Nov. 23, 1869	97, 245
Clothes, Mode of marking and cutting out	A. Ward	Huntsville, Ala	June 16, 1821	....
Clothes, Mode of scouring and washing	J. Goulding	Dedham, Mass	Aug. 24, 1827	....
Clothes or towel rack	F. A. Balch	Hingham, Wis	July 9, 1867	66, 442
Clothes-pin	S. Aldrich	Springfield, Vt	Sept. 14, 1852	9, 257
Clothes-pin	T. C. Ball	Bellows Falls, Vt	Apr. 2, 1872	125, 253
Clothes-pin	O. A. Bishop	Chicago, Ill	Mar. 7, 1871	112, 315
Clothes-pin	H. T. Boutell	Springfield, Vt	Aug. 27, 1867	68, 161
Clothes-pin	G. Bradley and N A. Walker	Rockford, Ill	Nov. 29, 1870	109, 580
Clothes-pin	A. W. Brinkerhoff	Upper Sandusky, Ohio	July 23, 1867	67, 100
Clothes-pin	R. G. Britton	Springfield, Vt	Oct. 1, 1867	69, 398
Clothes-pin	L. Bullock	Bellows Falls, Vt	Oct. 29, 1872	132, 627
Clothes-pin	B. Burling	Whitehall, N. Y	Sept. 26, 1871	119, 311
Clothes-pin	W. E. Burlingame	Willet, N. Y	Aug. 17, 1869	93, 672
Clothes-pin	E. A. Cone	Milford, Mich	Sept. 9, 1862	36, 394
Clothes-pin	N. B. Cooper	Liberty, Ind	Nov. 26, 1867	71, 457
Clothes-pin	J. O. Couch	Middlefield, Conn	June 9, 1868	78, 651
Clothes-pin	W. M. Doty	New York, N. Y	Mar. 26, 1867	63, 231
Clothes-pin	W. M. Doty	New York, N. Y	Dec. 31, 1867	72, 823
Clothes-pin	W. M. Doty	New York, N. Y	May 5, 1868	77, 598
Clothes-pin	R. Emerson	Rockford, Ill	June 11, 1872	127, 751
Clothes-pin	G. K. Farrington	Alcatraz Island, Cal	June 28, 1870	104, 720
Clothes-pin	P. Finley	Memphis, Tenn	Apr. 28, 1868	77, 268
Clothes-pin	T. L. Goble	Orange, N. Y	Dec. 18, 1866	60, 627
Clothes-pin	K. H. Goss	Cedar Springs, Mich	Apr. 4, 1871	113, 289
Clothes-pin	J. Greenwood	Fitchburgh, Mass	Nov. 15, 1864	45, 119
Clothes-pin	J. Haigney and F. M. Hedman	East Boston, Mass	Sept. 15, 1868	82, 114
Clothes-pin	H. D. Haraden	Hartford, Vt	Apr. 21, 1868	77, 037
Clothes-pin	D. C. Harlow	Hannibal, Mo	July 30, 1872	129, 950
Clothes-pin	G. A. Harris	Buchanan, Mich	Jan. 3, 1871	110, 649
Clothes-pin	D. K. Hickok	Morrisville, Vt	Mar. 10, 1868	75, 422
Clothes-pin	R. W. Huston	Washington, D. C	Mar. 26, 1872	124, 955
Clothes-pin	J. P. R. James	Read's Landing, Minn	Sept. 3, 1867	68, 510
Clothes-pin	C C. Johnson	Springfield, Vt	Apr. 2, 1867	63, 393
Clothes-pin	P. Johnson	Wauconda, Ill	Mar. 30, 1869	88, 390
Clothes-pin	D. D. Jones	Scranton, Pa	Jan. 21, 1868	73, 609
Clothes-pin	J. E. Lines	Bryan, Ohio	Aug. 10, 1869	93, 456
Clothes-pin	A. B. Lipsey	West Hoboken, N. J	Apr. 4, 1871	113, 313
Clothes-pin	A. B. Lipsey	West Hoboken, N. J	Feb. 27, 1872	124, 071
Clothes-pin	S. B. Lucas	Hinsdale, N. Y	Apr. 2, 1872	125, 311
Clothes-pin	L. Matthews	Antrim, Ohio	Sept. 29, 1868	82, 624
Clothes-pin	H. Mellish	Walpole, N. H	Oct. 17, 1871	119, 938
Clothes-pin	H. Mellish	Walpole, N. H	Sept. 23, 1873	143, 024
Clothes-pin	W. Miller	Boston, Mass	Dec. 20, 1870	110, 263
Clothes-pin	W. Patterson	Lowell, Mass	May 14, 1867	64, 698
Clothes-pin	D. Pierce	Sunapee, N. H	May 25, 1858	20, 364
Clothes-pin	S. Prior	Salem, N. J	Mar. 22, 1832	....
Clothes-pin	J. A. Rand	Morrisville, Vt	Sept. 8, 1868	81, 945
Clothes-pin	J. G. Roth	New York, N. Y	June 30, 1868	79, 502
Clothes-pin	R. S. Sanborn	Ripon, Wis	Sept. 11, 1866	57, 977
Clothes-pin	H. W. Sargeant, jr	Boston, Mass	Dec. 13, 1864	45, 458
Clothes-pin	H. W. Sargeant, jr	Boston, Mass	Apr. 11, 1865	47, 223
Clothes-pin	I. W. Searles	Tiffin, Ohio	June 21, 1870	104, 654
Clothes-pin	E. Seaver	Boston, Mass	July 9, 1867	66, 523
Clothes-pin	E. Seaver	Boston, Mass	May 5, 1868	77, 540
Clothes-pin	L. T. Simon	New York, N. Y	June 1, 1869	90, 881
Clothes-pin	D. M. Smith	Springfield, Vt	Apr. 9, 1867	63, 759
Clothes-pin	L. and C. H Sprague	Henderson, N. Y	Dec. 26, 1871	122, 199
Clothes-pin	D. M. Strain, jr	Des Moines, Iowa	July 13, 1869	92, 488
Clothes-pin	A. L. Taylor	Springfield, Vt	Apr. 7, 1868	76, 547
Clothes-pin	W. H. Towers	New York, N. Y	June 21, 1859	24, 503
Clothes-pin	C. N. Tyler	New York, N. Y	Mar. 23, 1869	88, 097
Clothes-pin	V. D. Urso and B. Charles	Evansville, Ind	Aug. 12, 1873	141, 740
Clothes-pin	F. Walker	New Orleans, La	Feb. 9, 1869	86, 888
Clothes-pin	W. G. Ward	Savona, N. Y	Sept. 11, 1866	58, 007
Clothes-pin	W. G. Ward	Savona, N. Y	Feb. 19, 1867	62, 240
Clothes-pin	H. J. Wattles	Rockford, Ill	Feb. 28, 1871	112, 303
Clothes-pin	H. J. Wattles	Rockford, Ill	Nov. 28, 1871	121, 303
Clothes-pin	W. Wellington	Rockford, Ill	Mar. 1, 1870	100, 345
Clothes-pin	W. Wellington	Rockford, Ill	Feb. 4, 1873	135, 501
Clothes-pin	H. Wells	Cambridge, Mass	July 9, 1872	128, 934
Clothes-pin	W. H. Wells and J. Hawse	Newport Centre, Vt	Sept. 24, 1867	69, 2[illegible]8
Clothes pin holder	V. Reifsnider	Chicago, Ill	Aug. 17, 1869	93, 905
Clothes-pin joints, Machine for wiring	A. C. Mason	Springfield, Vt	Sept. 6, 1859	25, 344
Clothes-pin machine	H. and M. Blake	Hartland, Vt	May 1, 1855	12, 775
Clothes-pin machine	S. Inman	Rockford, Ill	Feb. 27, 1872	124, 137
Clothes-pin-making machine	A. J. Ockington	Stratford Hollow, N. H	Sept. 14, 1869	94, 838
Clothes pin or clamp	G. F. Barden	Dover, N. H	Nov. 13, 1866	59, 545
Clothes pin or clamp	P. Gardner	Gloucestershire, England	July 20, 1869	92, 715
Clothes pin or clasp	A. L. Keeports and W. Yount	Littlestown, Pa	Mar. 7, 1871	112, 466
Clothes-pin-slitting machine	O. P. Allen	Rindge, N. H	May 14, 1850	7, 355
Clothes-pins, Arbor for turning	B. B. and A. J. Ockington	Stratford, N. H	July 5, 1870	104, 988
Clothes-pins, Machine for cutting slots in	J. Humphrey	Keene, N. H	Mar. 31, 1857	16, 923

Index of patents issued from the United States Patent Office from 1790 *to* 1873, *inclusive*—Continued.

Invention.	Inventor.	Residence.	Date.	No.
Clothes-pins, Machine for making	B. B. and A. J. Ockington	Stratford Hollow, N. H	Dec. 16, 1873	145, 587
Clothes-pins, Machine for making	E. Parker	Burlington, Iowa	Jan. 15, 1856	14, 110
Clothes-pins, Machine for making	G. W. Parker	Fitzwilliam, N. H	Mar. 18, 1856	14, 466
Clothes-pins, Machine for making	J. B. Smith	Sunapee, N. H	Dec. 29, 1868	85, 338
Clothes-pins, Machine for slitting	J. B. Smith	Sunapee, N. H	Feb. 21, 1854	10, 553
Clothes-pins, Machinery for making	R. Emerson	Rockford, Ill	July 16, 1872	129, 118
Clothes-pins, Machinery for making	J. B. Smith	Sunapee, N. H	Oct. 28, 1873	144, 152
Clothes-pins, Machinery for turning	A. Greenwood	Marlborough, N. H	Dec. 11, 1849	6, 935
Clothes-pins, Tool for slotting	J. Humphrey	Keene, N. H	Dec. 28, 1858	22, 430
Clothes-pinchers	H. Kewley	Port Hudson, Mich	May 31, 1864	42, 951
Clothes-pole	W. W. Armington	New Haven County, Conn	Oct. 2, 1866	58, 535
Clothes-pole	F. W. Tilton	New Bedford, Mass	June 19, 1866	55, 744
Clothes-pole, Extension	J. and W. Denton	Amsterdam, N. Y	Sept. 5, 1871	118, 698
Clothes-post	C. P. Jadwin	Carbondale, Pa	July 30, 1867	67, 310
Clothes-post, Extension	G. Dittenhaver	Napoleon, Ohio	Jan. 7, 1868	73, 171
Clothes-pounder	A. W. Bunnell	Linesville Station, Pa	July 2, 1872	128, 531
Clothes-pounder	A. W. Hall	New York, N. Y	Oct. 1, 1872	131, 752
Clothes-pounder	S. F. Hawley	Sandy Hill, N. Y	Oct. 21, 1873	143, 901
Clothes-pounder	S. Hinkel	Goodville, Pa	Apr. 22, 1873	138, 024
Clothes-pounder	S. T. McDougal	Brooklyn, N. Y	July 7, 1868	79, 671
Clothes-pounder	B. S. Morgan	Delhi, Iowa	Mar. 17, 1868	75, 562
Clothes-pounder	M. K. Morris	Louisville, Ky	Aug. 13, 1872	130, 523
Clothes-pounder	J. W. Norton	Pioneer, Pa	Nov. 15, 1870	109, 240
Clothes-pounder	D. W. Rawson	Croydon, N. H	Apr. 22, 1873	138, 044
Clothes-pounder	E. S. Saxton	Greenfield, Ill	July 22, 1873	141, 082
Clothes-pounder	O. J. Stickles	Canton, N. Y	Sept. 21, 1869	94, 983
Clothes-pounder	S. Thomson	West Otis, Mass	May 5, 1857	17, 240
Clothes-press	J. S. Nicholson	Anamosa, Iowa	Sept. 22, 1868	82, 341
Clothes-presser and water-expeller	T. Fowler	Seymour, Conn	Jan. 26, 1869	86, 146
Clothes-pressing machine	J. Sage	Berlin, Conn	Apr. 14, 1810	....
Clothes-pressing machine	H. E. Smith	Fitchburgh, Mass	May 20, 1873	139, 201
Clothes, Pressing water from	C. Angerine	New York, N. Y	Feb. 25, 1836	....
Clothes-rack	J. Alcorn	Charlestown, Mass	June 8, 1869	90, 979
Clothes-rack	H. M. Andrews and J. H. Cleveland.	North Bay, N. Y	Mar. 28, 1871	113, 129
Clothes-rack	H. Bauman and U. Mueller	Canton, Ohio	Oct. 4, 1870	107, 996
Clothes-rack	T. D. Berry	Lowell, Mass	Aug. 16, 1859	25, 086
Clothes-rack	C. K. Breneman	Newport, Pa	Sept. 22, 1868	82, 378
Clothes-rack	C. B. Crosby	Cortlandville, N. Y	Nov. 28, 1865	51, 149
Clothes-rack	W. S. Foster	Marilla, N. Y	Feb. 22, 1859	23, 020
Clothes-rack	G. W. and E. J. Godfrey	Leslie, Mich	May 28, 1872	127, 232
Clothes-rack	O. C. Green	Dublin, Ind	Oct. 18, 1859	25, 820
Clothes-rack	A. A. Harris	Ravenna, Ohio	Aug. 10, 1858	21, 131
Clothes-rack	J. Hatfield	Sparta, Wis	Oct. 26, 1869	96, 107
Clothes-rack	V. M. Heath	Morristown, Vt	Sept. 7, 1869	94, 598
Clothes-rack	I. Hogeland	Indianapolis, Ind	Dec. 8, 1868	84, 694
Clothes-rack	J. Johnson	New York, N. Y	July 5, 1870	105, 086
Clothes-rack	E. F. Lyman	Indianapolis, Ind	Dec. 10, 1867	72, 057
Clothes-rack	D. Miller	Marietta, Ohio	Dec. 19, 1871	121, 953
Clothes-rack	J. O. Montignani	Albany, N. Y	Sept. 5, 1865	49, 779
Clothes-rack	J. O. Montignani	Albany, N. Y	Oct. 23, 1866	59, 133
Clothes-rack	H. W. Ross	Brooklyn, N. Y	Nov. 12, 1872	133, 058
Clothes-rack	S. I. Russell	Chicago, Ill	Dec. 22, 1857	18, 930
Clothes-rack	C. J. and G. W. Schaefer	Yonkers, N. Y	Sept. 3, 1872	131, 068
Clothes-rack	A. G. Schmidt	New York, N. Y	Nov. 7, 1871	120, 671
Clothes-rack	C. Stone	Ravenna, Ohio	Jan. 12, 1858	19, 107
Clothes-rack	H. Thomas and R. Wallace	New York, N. Y	July 6, 1869	92, 400
Clothes-rack	E. Werden	Pittsfield, Mass	July 27, 1869	93, 025
Clothes-rack	C. H. Wolcott	Jamestown, N. Y	Aug. 2, 1870	106, 102
Clothes-rack	C. H. Wolcott	Jamestown, N. Y	Aug. 22, 1871	118, 416
Clothes-rack	G. Young, jr	Saratoga Springs, N. Y	July 20, 1858	20, 974
Clothes-rack, Adjustable	J. Brainerd and W. H. Burridge.	Cleveland, Ohio	Jan. 5, 1864	41, 134
Clothes rack and drier	A. Hornor	Ross, Ind	Aug. 10, 1869	93, 620
Clothes rack and stand	W. B. Kimball	Peterborough, N. H	Aug. 10, 1869	93, 626
Clothes-receptacle, ironing-board, and drier, Combined.	S. T. McDougall	Brooklyn, N. Y	Mar. 14, 1871	112, 614
Clothes-reel	D. L. Huff	Bay City, Mich	Sept. 9, 1873	142, 631
Clothes-reel	J. McMahon	Ann Arbor, Mich	July 22, 1873	141, 064
Clothes, Roller for expressing water from	J. Allender	New London, Conn	Jan. 11, 1859	22, 539
Clothes, &c., Rotary pounder for washing	C. Aunock	Elbridge, N. Y	Mar. 10, 1838	626
Clothes-rubber	S. Foster	Lansing, Mich	Feb. 28, 1871	112, 235
Clothes, Rubber for washing	J. Charlton	Allegheny City, Pa	Apr. 14, 1868	76, 603
Clothes-scourer	D. Dickinson	Chatham, Conn	Oct. 1, 1830	....
Clothes-sprinkler	F. Ashley	New York, N. Y	Oct. 30, 1866	59, 158
Clothes-sprinkler	E. T. Colburn	Boston, Mass	Dec. 12, 1865	51, 509
Clothes-sprinkler	S. N. Davies	Muskegon, Mich	Nov. 6, 1860	30, 565
Clothes-sprinkler	S. G. Dugdale	Richmond, Ind	Nov. 30, 1869	97, 369
Clothes-sprinkler	W. P. Gannett	Boston, Mass	May 22, 1866	55, 008
Clothes-sprinkler	J. L. Kendall	New York, N. Y	June 26, 1866	55, 956
Clothes-sprinkler	E. H. Kirkham	Boston, Mass	Mar. 3, 1868	75, 168
Clothes-sprinkler	M. Moriarty	Bangor, Me	May 15, 1866	54, 819
Clothes-sprinkler	H. A. Morse	Canton, Mass	July 3, 1866	56, 082
Clothes-sprinkler	T. Payne	Ridgefield, Conn	Jan. 18, 1859	22, 669
Clothes-sprinkler	E. Schnurr	Monroe, Mich	Sept. 5, 1865	49, 794
Clothes-sprinkler	I. W. Shaler	Brooklyn, N. Y	Mar. 19, 1867	63, 107
Clothes-sprinkler	T. R. Smith and J. Mitchell	Jacksonville, Ill	Jan. 18, 1870	99, 021
Clothes-sprinkler	W. E. Staniford	Bucksport, Me	Feb. 27, 1866	52, 935
Clothes-sprinkler	E. B. Taylor	South Sudbury, Mass	May 28, 1867	65, 299
Clothes-sprinkler	J. W. Walters	Tiffin, Ohio	June 30, 1868	79, 531
Clothes-sprinkler	W. V. Wilson	Philadelphia, Pa	Apr. 14, 1868	76, 870
Clothes-squeezer	F. Arnold	Middle Haddam, Conn	Oct. 23, 1860	30, 451
Clothes-squeezer	G. D. Trumpore	Newark, N. J	Nov. 6, 1860	30, 596
Clothes-stick	C. Kuder	Rochester, N. Y	Apr. 2, 1867	63, 397
Clothes-washer	W. R. Brooks	Phelps, N. Y	June 3, 1873	139, 494
Clothes-washer	H. D. Crooker	Chester, Pa	Feb. 18, 1873	136, 038
Clothes-washer	J. K. Dugdale	White Water, Ind	Jan. 18, 1870	98, 855
Clothes-washer	J. K. Dugdale	White Water, Ind	Jan. 18, 1870	98, 856

Index of patents issued from the United States Patent Office from 1790 *to* 1873, *inclusive*—Continued.

Invention.	Inventor.	Residence.	Date.	No.
Clothes-washer	F. Ernst	San Francisco, Cal	Aug. 20, 1867	67, 858
Clothes-washer	W. I. Miller and B. O. Irons	Linesville, Pa	Mar. 19, 1872	124, 844
Clothes-washer	W. H. Nice	Wadsworth, Ohio	Dec. 17, 1872	134, 000
Clothes-washer	H. J. Noyes	Ashtabula, Ohio	July 2, 1872	128, 501
Clothes-washer	H. W. Pell	Rome, N. Y	Sept. 26, 1871	119, 399
Clothes-washer	P. Read	Hinesburgh, Vt	Nov. 26, 1872	133, 485
Clothes-washer	D. P. Sulouff	Milton, Pa	Nov. 21, 1871	121, 216
Clothes-washer	D. P. Sulouff	Milton, Pa	Nov. 21, 1871	121, 217
Clothes-washer	G. J. Terrel	North Blanford, Mass	June 17, 1873	139, 979
Clothes-washer	T. Weaver	Harrisburgh, Pa	Aug. 6, 1872	130, 168
Clothes washer and drier	E. Rees	Stoddartsville, Pa	Feb. 8, 1870	99, 594
Clothes washer and wringer	A. Clark	Plymouth, Ohio	Nov. 2[illegible], 1870	109, 385
Clothes washer and wringer	J. Cram	Boston, Mass	Sept. 15, 1863	39, 990
Clothes washer and wringer	R. G. Holmes	Worcester, Mass	Nov. 26, 1861	33, 812
Clothes-washer, Hand	P. Falardo and G. H. Snow	Newark, N. J., and New Haven, Conn.	Feb. 15, 1870	99, 870
Clothes-washer, Steam	M. S. Lamb	Davenport, Iowa	Feb. 22, 1870	100, 156
Clothes-washer, Vacuum	M. Johnstone	Spartanburgh, S. C	July 30, 1872	129, 961
Clothes, Washing	N. Briggs		Mar. 28, 1797	
Clothes, Washing	E. Weld		June 26, 1799	
Clothes washing and cleansing machine	W. Price	Cincinnati, Ohio	Mar. 7, 1865	46, 701
Clothes-washing and cloth-fulling machine	O. D. Wade	China, N. Y	Sept. 9, 1835	
Clothes-washing and corn-shelling machine	B. Rice	Denmark, N. Y	Nov. 23, 1827	
Clothes washing and drying machine	T. Pearce	Hartwick, N. Y	Dec. 29, 1832	
Clothes washing and wringing machine, Lavater	E. Weld		Sept. 17, 1800	
Clothes-washing machine	W. E. Arnold	Haddam, Conn	Aug. 3, 1829	
Clothes-washing machine	S. Benson	Waterville, Me	May 25, 1840	1, 616
Clothes-washing machine	W. H. Blood	San Francisco, Cal	Jan. 12, 1864	41, 190
Clothes-washing machine	R. Brainard	Haddam, Conn	Nov. 23, 1829	
Clothes-washing machine	S. Hinds	Montrose, Pa	Apr. 25, 1829	
Clothes-washing machine	I. Leavitt, A. Gilmore, and W. Sturtevant.	Turner, Me	Aug. 9, 1839	1, 282
Clothes-washing machine	M. Mellinger	Dayton, Ohio	Aug. 12, 1862	36, 162
Clothes-washing machine	R. W. Oliphant	North Granville, N. Y	June 7, 1838	769
Clothes-washing machine	L. Procter	New York, N. Y	Nov. 16, 1841	2, 369
Clothes-washing machine	S. Swett, jr	Portsmouth, N. H	July 12, 1839	1, 236
Clothes-washing machine	H. N. Walter	Norwich, N. Y	June 22, 1841	2, 137
Clothes-washing machine	G. Waterman	Johnston, R. I	May 11, 1841	2, 084
Clothes, Washing, pressing, ironing, crimping, and drying.	J. Newhall	Dayton, Ohio	June 13, 1831	
Clothes washing, rinsing, and wringing machine	W. J. Fulsom and J. Hayden	Hallowell, D. M	Dec. 17, 1805	
Clothes-washing rubber	H. Burk	Mineral Point, Ohio	July 24, 1866	56, 523
Clothes-whisk and hat-brush combined	A. M. Richmond	New York, N. Y	Apr. 23, 1872	126, 090
Clothes-wringer	A. Albrecht	Philadelphia, Pa	Mar. 14, 1871	112, 669
Clothes-wringer	C. H. Amidon	Greenfield, Mass	May 21, 1867	64, 932
Clothes-wringer	A. M. Bailey	Middlefield, Conn	Mar. 21, 1871	112, 884
Clothes-wringer	A. M. Bailey and J. O. Couch	Middlefield, Conn	Jan. 14, 1862	34, 178
Clothes-wringer	S. A. Bailey	Waterford, Mass	Mar. 13, 1866	53, 098
Clothes-wringer	C. E. Bancroft	Waterbury, Vt	May 20, 1862	35, 290
Clothes-wringer	C. H. Bangs	Farmington, Me	June 11, 1872	127, 831
Clothes-wringer	O. D. Barrett	Fulton, N. Y	Oct. 1, 1861	33, 411
Clothes-wringer	E. G. W. Bartlett	Providence, R. I	May 24, 1870	103, 282
Clothes-wringer	E. G. W. Bartlett	Providence, R. I	May 23, 1871	115, 150
Clothes-wringer	E. G. W. Bartlett	Providence, R. I	July 4, 1871	116, 665
Clothes-wringer	E. G. W. Bartlett	Providence, R. I	Apr. 30, 1872	126, 173
Clothes wringer	C. W. Bassett	Newton, Mass	May 14, 1872	126, 774
Clothes-wringer	E. Blakeman and J. R. Gill	Charleston, Ill	Oct. 25, 1864	44, 779
Clothes-wringer	T. O. Bogert	Cincinnati, Ohio	Jan. 7, 1873	134, 633
Clothes-wringer	J. Brinkerhoff	Auburn, N. Y	Dec. 26, 1871	122, 220
Clothes-wringer	W. P. Brooks and J. D. Hartzell	Ozawkie, Kans	July 1, 1837	140, 314
Clothes-wringer	H. J. Burr	Bloomfield, Conn	Sept. 30, 1873	143, 220
Clothes-wringer	E. P. H. Capron	Hudson, N. Y	Aug. 29, 1871	118, 431
Clothes-wringer	C. E. Carter	Martinsville, Ohio	May 23, 1871	115, 161
Clothes-wringer	R. S. Cathcart	Cincinnati, Ohio	Sept. 17, 1872	131, 392
Clothes-wringer	R. S. Cathcart	Cincinnati, Ohio	Dec. 31, 1872	134, 461
Clothes-wringer	R. S. Cathcart	Cincinnati, Ohio	Jan. 7, 1873	134, 641
Clothes-wringer	D. B. Clement	Milton, Mass	Apr. 8, 1862	34, 920
Clothes-wringer	D. B. Clement	Milton, Mass	Jan. 20, 1863	37, 472
Clothes-wringer	J. D. Cochran	Milford, N. H	June 24, 1862	35, 670
Clothes-wringer	G. J. Colby	Waterbury, Vt	Dec. 4, 1860	30, 802
Clothes-wringer	D. M. Cole	Elgin, Ill	June 18, 1872	128, 119
Clothes-wringer	D. M. Cole	Elgin, Ill	June 3, 1873	139, 545
Clothes-wringer	W. Cooper	Independence, Iowa	Jan. 4, 1870	98, 566
Clothes-wringer	W. Cooper	Ypsilanti, Mich	June 4, 1872	127, 577
Clothes-wringer	E. A. Corbin and H. Albrecht	Philadelphia, Pa	June 24, 1873	140, 249
Clothes-wringer	E. H. Covel	New York, N. Y	Nov. 12, 1867	70, 808
Clothes-wringer	E. H. Covel	New York, N. Y	Feb. 11, 1868	74, 201
Clothes-wringer	P. Cramer	Providence, R. I	July 28, 1868	80, 336
Clothes-wringer	P. Cramer	Barrington, R. I	Aug. 24, 1869	94, 082
Clothes-wringer	R. R. Crosby and J. Harris	Boston, Mass	Oct. 29, 1861	33, 575
Clothes-wringer	C. A. Cummings and F. M. Swallow.	Worcester, Mass	Feb. 11, 1862	34, 395
Clothes-wringer	J. E. Daniels and G. S. Kendall	Boston, Mass	July 8, 1862	35, 810
Clothes-wringer	C. H. De Knight	Pittsburgh, Pa	Aug. 9, 1870	106, 136
Clothes-wringer	E. Dickerman	Richmond, Vt	Apr. 10, 1860	27, 781
Clothes wringer	J. C. Dickey	Saratoga Springs, N. Y	Aug. 28, 1866	57, 485
Clothes-wringer	W. S. Douglas	Richmond, Vt	Jan. 21, 1868	73, 584
Clothes-wringer	S. F. Emerson	Seville, Ohio	May 5, 1863	38, 380
Clothes-wringer	T. B. Emerson	Seville, Ohio	Oct. 29, 1867	70, 181
Clothes-wringer	P. Falardo	Danbury, Conn	Aug. 3, 1869	93, 188
Clothes-wringer	R. E. Ferguson	Chicago, Ill	Oct. 4, 1870	107, 893
Clothes-wringer	R. E. Ferguson	Chicago, Ill	Mar. 26, 1872	124, 942
Clothes-wringer	T. J. U. Fisk	Macon City, Mo	June 25, 1872	128, 294
Clothes-wringer	H. G. Folger	Wadsworth, Ohio	July 4, 1865	48, 545
Clothes-wringer	M. M. Follet	Lake City, Minn	Dec. 14, 1869	97, 899
Clothes-wringer	J. Fox	Farmersville, Iowa	Dec. 26, 1871	122, 164
Clothes-wringer	A. C. Gallahue	New York, N. Y	Oct. 30, 1866	59, 208
Clothes-wringer	G. E. Gault and A. W. Winall	Cincinnati, Ohio	Jan. 7, 1873	134, 658

Index of patents issued from the United States Patent Office from 1790 *to* 1873, *inclusive*—Continued.

Invention.	Inventor.	Residence.	Date.	No.
Clothes-wringer	W. Gibbs and R. J. Bell	Carlisle, Pa	Apr. 1, 1862	34,827
Clothes-wringer	R. Gipson	Shelby, Ohio	Oct. 25, 1864	44,796
Clothes-wringer	R. Gipson	Shelby, Ohio	June 12, 1866	55,486
Clothes-wringer	D. D. Gitt	Arendtsville, Pa	May 24, 1864	42,908
Clothes-wringer	F. A. Gleason	Brooklyn, N. Y	Sept. 10, 1867	68,732
Clothes-wringer	A. H. Goss	Auburn, N. Y	Apr. 2, 1872	125,129
Clothes-wringer	C. Graham	Cincinnati, Ohio	Dec. 31, 1872	134,472
Clothes-wringer	G. B. Griffin	Madison, Wis	June 4, 1861	32,475
Clothes-wringer	L. Hale	Hollis, N. H	Oct. 31, 1871	120,512
Clothes-wringer	J. W. Hampton	Mount Pleasant, Iowa	Nov. 14, 1871	120,968
Clothes-wringer	D. M. Harris and S. S. Burnet	Salem, Mass	May 13, 1862	35,234
Clothes-wringer	J. Harrison and G. W. Harris	Brooklyn and New York, N. Y.	July 16, 1867	66,835
Clothes-wringer	J. Harrison and G. W. Harris	Brooklyn and New York, N. Y.	July 16, 1867	66,836
Clothes-wringer	C. E. Haynes	Boston, Mass	May 13, 1873	138,803
Clothes-wringer	S. S. Hemenway	Boston, Mass	May 30, 1865	47,951
Clothes-wringer	C. W. Higgins and A. S. Willard	Somerville and Charlestown, Mass.	June 19, 1860	28,752
Clothes-wringer	R. G. Holmes	Worcester, Mass	Sept. 8, 1863	39,813
Clothes-wringer	C. H. Hudson	New York, N. Y	July 25, 1871	117,291
Clothes-wringer	R. B. Hugunin	Cleveland, Ohio	Mar. 10, 1868	75,425
Clothes-wringer	J. Johnson	New York, N. Y	Jan. 28, 1862	34,281
Clothes-wringer	J. Johnson	New York, N. Y	June 28, 1864	43,368
Clothes-wringer	G. H. Kidney	Cleveland, Ohio	July 22, 1862	35,940
Clothes-wringer	A. King	Philadelphia, Pa	Mar. 21, 1871	112,815
Clothes-wringer	E. King	Dunkirk, N. Y	Jan. 9, 1872	122,527
Clothes-wringer	C. H. Knox	Mount Pleasant, Iowa	July 2, 1867	66,362
Clothes-wringer	J. H. Kooser	Pekin, Ill	Oct. 15, 1872	132,294
Clothes-wringer	A. Lapham and F. E. Pratt	New York and Mott Haven, N. Y.	Apr. 28, 1868	77,386
Clothes-wringer	J. S. Lash	Philadelphia, Pa	Oct. 23, 1866	59,041
Clothes-wringer	J. Lee	Galesburgh, Ill	Feb. 6, 1866	52,423
Clothes-wringer	D. Lyman	Middlefield, Conn	Oct. 17, 1865	50,482
Clothes-wringer	D. Lyman	Middlefield, Conn	Feb. 27, 1866	52,867
Clothes-wringer	D. Lyman	Middlefield, Conn	Mar. 26, 1867	63,272
Clothes-wringer	D. Lyman	Middlefield, Conn	Mar. 26, 1867	63,273
Clothes-wringer	D. Lyman	Middlefield, Conn	Dec. 17, 1867	72,407
Clothes-wringer	A. Magowan	Trenton, N. J	Apr. 12, 1870	101,749
Clothes-wringer	J. Makechney	Trenton, N. J	Feb 6, 1872	123,495
Clothes-wringer	M. Mallon	Rahway, N. J	July 16, 1872	129,043
Clothes-wringer	J. S. Maughlin and W. C. Marr	Onawa, Ind	Feb. 27, 1872	124,073
Clothes-wringer	T. E. McDonald	Trenton, N. J	Mar. 5, 1872	124,367
Clothes-wringer	T. F. McDonald	Trenton, N. J	Jan. 28, 1873	135,237
Clothes-wringer	T. E McDonald	New Brunswick, N. J	Nov. 18, 1873	144,627
Clothes-wringer	J. McLaughlin	Steubenville, Ohio	Oct. 16, 1855	13,684
Clothes-wringer	J. McLaughlin	Steubenville, Ohio	Sept. 20, 1870	107,518
Clothes-wringer	J. M. McMaster	Rochester, N. Y	Sept. 17, 1867	68,893
Clothes-wringer	W. T. McMillen and E. P. Conrick	Cincinnati, Ohio, and Delavan, Wis.	July 24, 1866	56,591
Clothes-wringer	C. V. Mead	Trenton, N. J	Sept. 26, 1871	119,384
Clothes-wringer	R. O. Meldrum and A. B. Paxson	Griffin's Mills and East Hamburgh, N. Y.	Jan. 24, 1860	26,914
Clothes-wringer	A. B Mercier	Providence, R. I	July 31, 1866	56,773
Clothes-wringer	C. Messenger	Warren, Ohio	Mar. 11, 1862	34,639
Clothes-wringer	B. D. Morrell	Lisbon, N. H	Aug. 25, 1863	39,666
Clothes-wringer	H. Nash	Cincinnati, Ohio	Oct. 9, 1866	58,669
Clothes-wringer	A. O'Dell	Napanee, Canada	Oct. 25, 1870	108,620
Clothes-wringer	J. O'Donald	Clinton, Ill	Dec. 26, 1865	51,743
Clothes-wringer	C. H. Packard	North Bridgewater, Mass	Feb. 18, 1862	34,445
Clothes-wringer	C. H. Packard	North Bridgewater, Mass	Sept. 8, 1863	39,864
Clothes-wringer	A. H. Page	South Boston, Mass	Jan. 29, 1867	61,680
Clothes-wringer	G. Palmer	Littlestown, Pa	Jan. 22, 1867	61,353
Clothes-wringer	S. W. and J. F. Palmer	Auburn, N. Y	May 18, 1869	90,185
Clothes-wringer	S. W. and J. F. Palmer	Auburn, N. Y	Dec. 5, 1871	121,657
Clothes-wringer	J. A. Park	Lansing, Mich	Oct. 29, 1872	132,687
Clothes-wringer	J. N. Pease	Panama, N. Y	May 16, 1865	47,774
Clothes-wringer	J. N. Pease	Panama, N. Y	May 15, 1866	54,764
Clothes-wringer	J. N. Pease and G. Lewis	Panama, N. Y	July 24, 1866	56,676
Clothes-wringer	M. Pierce	Winona, Minn	Apr. 28, 1868	77,315
Clothes-wringer	J. N. Poage	Cincinnati, Ohio	Dec. 31, 1872	134,485
Clothes-wringer	J. F. Pond	Cleveland, Ohio	Jan. 2, 1866	51,862
Clothes-wringer	T. Pool	Brunswick, Ohio	June 24, 1862	35,705
Clothes-wringer	G. S. Prindle	Washington, D. C	Feb. 4, 1873	135,585
Clothes-wringer	H. W. Putnam	Cleveland, Ohio	Dec. 17, 1861	33,969
Clothes-wringer	H. W. Putnam	Cleveland, Ohio	Sept. 16, 1862	36,480
Clothes-wringer	B. Reed	Allegheny, Pa	Apr. 14, 1868	76,659
Clothes-wringer	O. Reeves	Greenport, N. Y	July 17, 1866	56,449
Clothes-wringer	N. A. Rhoads	Waterbury, Vt	Mar. 11, 1862	34,646
Clothes-wringer	N. A. Rhoads	Waterbury, Vt	Jan. 27, 1863	37,521
Clothes-wringer	W. B. Rhoads	South Dedham, Mass	Jan. 25, 1861	32,659
Clothes-wringer	H. Robbins	Cincinnati, Ohio	July 31, 1866	56,865
Clothes-wringer	C. Robinson	Boston, Mass	July 8, 1873	140,592
Clothes-wringer	J. G. Roth	New York, N. Y	Apr. 12, 1870	101,922
Clothes-wringer	S. P. Rowell	Melrose, Mass	July 15, 1862	35,910
Clothes-wringer	W. Rowell	New York, N. Y	Sept. 3, 1867	68,576
Clothes-wringer	E. P. Russell	Manlius, N. Y	Dec. 14, 1869	97,965
Clothes-wringer	E. P. Russell	Manlius, N. Y	Feb. 20, 1872	123,794
Clothes-wringer	A. F. Saunders	Chelsea, Mass	June 17, 1862	35,631
Clothes-wringer	J. Seaman	Groton, N. Y	Nov. 18, 1873	144,705
Clothes-wringer	I. A. Sergeant	Springfield, Ohio	July 27, 1858	21,029
Clothes-wringer	L. Shmetzer	Chicago, Ill	July 12, 1870	105,375
Clothes-wringer	M. E. Smilie and W. Cooley	Waterbury, Vt	May 7, 1872	126,584
Clothes-wringer	G. Smith	Highland Falls, N. Y	Aug. 10, 1869	93,488
Clothes-wringer	H. E. Smith	New York, N. Y	Mar. 3, 1868	75,066
Clothes-wringer	H. E. Smith	New York, N. Y	May 30, 1870	115,372
Clothes-wringer	H. E. Smith	New York, N. Y	June 4, 1872	127,521
Clothes-wringer	H. E. Smith	New York, N. Y	Sept. 24, 1872	131,714

Index of patents issued from the United States Patent Office from 1790 *to* 1873, *inclusive*—Continued.

Invention.	Inventor.	Residence.	Date.	No.
Clothes-wringer	H. E. Smith	New York, N. Y	Sept. 24, 1872	131, 715
Clothes-wringer	H. E. Smith	Fitchburgh, Mass	May 20, 1873	139, 200
Clothes-wringer	R. Smith	Towanda, Pa	Dec. 1, 1857	18, 777
Clothes-wringer	C. F. Spaulding	Saint Johnsbury, Vt	May 3, 1864	42, 607
Clothes-wringer	E. Spaulding	Morrisville, Vt	Apr. 16, 1861	32, 090
Clothes-wringer	A. H. Spencer	Providence, R. I	Feb. 1, 1870	99, 364
Clothes-wringer	J. H. Stedman	Randolph, Vt	Sept. 10, 1861	33, 271
Clothes-wringer	E. M. Stevens	Boston, Mass	Apr. 29, 1862	35, 115
Clothes-wringer	W. M. Storm	New York, N. Y	Mar. 17, 1868	75, 707
Clothes-wringer	L. H. Thomas	Waterbury, Vt	Mar. 25, 1862	34, 795
Clothes-wringer	A. Tower	New York, N. Y	Nov. 2, 1869	96, 511
Clothes-wringer	W. H. Towers	Boston, Mass	Apr. 25, 1871	114, 231
Clothes-wringer	G. P. Towle	Boston, Mass	July 15, 1862	35, 911
Clothes-wringer	N. Van Auken	Amsterdam, N. Y	May 20, 1862	35, 335
Clothes-wringer	R. Vose and J. W. Evans	New York, N. Y	Nov. 5, 1872	132, 782
Clothes-wringer	S. Walker	Boston, Mass	June 17, 1862	35, 643
Clothes-wringer	J. Webb	Spartauburgh, Pa	Sept. 15, 1868	82, 259
Clothes-wringer	H. Weble	Hoboken, N. J	May 8, 1866	54, 631
Clothes-wringer	N. B. White	South Dedham, Mass	Mar. 4, 1862	34, 618
Clothes-wringer	W. Whitney	Baldwinsville, Mass	Dec. 3, 1861	33, 861
Clothes-wringer	D. F. Williams	Cumberland, R. I	Jan. 2, 1866	51, 888
Clothes-wringer	R. P. Wilson	New York, N. Y	June 24, 1862	35, 726
Clothes-wringer	G. L. Witsil	Philadelphia, Pa	May 28, 1867	65, 148
Clothes-wringer	G. L. Witsil	Philadelphia, Pa	Mar. 3, 1868	75, 231
Clothes-wringer	J. Young	Amsterdam, N. Y	Apr. 23, 1867	64, 180
Clothes-wringer	J. Young	Amsterdam, N. Y	Mar. 23, 1869	88, 110
Clothes wringer and mangle	S. W. and J. F. Palmer	Auburn, N. Y	Nov. 15, 1864	45, 071
Clothes wringer and mangle, Combined	B. O. Thompson	Chicago, Ill	June 22, 1869	91, 794
Clothes wringer and mangle combined	J. D. Tift	Cuyahoga Falls, Ohio	June 24, 1862	35, 716
Clothes wringer and washer roller	R. B. Hugunin	New York, N. Y	July 17, 1866	56, 418
Clothes-wringer attachment	C. L. Carter	Union City, Ind	Aug. 27, 1867	68, 043
Clothes-wringer bench	S. A. Bailey	Waterford, Mass	Mar. 13, 1866	53, 099
Clothes-wringer, Centrifugal	H. Rosamyer, jr	Rochester, Pa	Aug. 19, 1873	142, 045
Clothes-wringer clamp	J. D. Burdick	Ashway, R. I	June 28, 1864	43, 286
Clothes-wringer roll	H. E. Smith	Cincinnati, Ohio	Feb. 13, 1866	52, 615
Clothes-wringer rolls, Spindle for	T. E. McDonald	Trenton, N. J	Sept. 26, 1871	119, 235
Clothes-wringer roller	E. P. H. Capron	Hudson, N. Y	Aug. 5, 1873	141, 424
Clothes-wringer roller	J. Critcherson	Boston, Mass	Feb. 11, 1862	34, 394
Clothes-wringer roller	J. B. Forsyth	Roxbury, Mass	Nov. 20, 1866	59, 798
Clothes-wringer roller	E. King	Dunkirk, N. Y	Aug. 20, 1872	130, 582
Clothes-wringer roller	J. Murphy	New York, N. Y	Oct. 16, 1866	58, 874
Clothes-wringers, Roller for	J. F. Holt	Providence, R. I	July 25, 1865	49, 030
Clothes-wringer roller and fastening	R. B. Hugunin	Cleveland, Ohio	Mar. 6, 1866	53, 001
Clothes-wringers, Composition-roll for	W. H. Towers	Boston, Mass	June 21, 1870	104 514
Clothes-wringers, Gearing for	G. C. Wright	Leroy, Ohio	May 17, 1870	103, 269
Clothes-wringers, Preparing wood for the bearings in	J. Brinkerhoff	Auburn, N. Y	Oct. 15, 1872	132, 194
Clothes-wringers to tubs, Mode of attaching	D. Lyman	Middlefield, Conn	Apr. 2, 1861	31, 895
Clothes, Wringing	J. H. Clark	Westbrook, Me	May 8, 1860	28, 156
Clothes-wringing	J. R. Gill, W. E. Palmer, and W. W. Webb.	Alton, Ill	Mar. 4, 1862	34, 610
Clothes-wringing hook	J. H. Pratt	Lynn, Mass	Feb. 21, 1871	112, 074
Clothes-wringing machine	S. A. Bailey	New London, Conn	Apr. 5, 1859	23, 436
Clothes-wringing machine	R. P. Bradley	Cuyahoga Falls, Ohio	Aug. 12, 1856	15, 543
Clothes-wringing machine	E. Dickerman	Middlefield, Conn	Feb. 18, 1862	34, 459
Clothes-wringing machine	K. H. Elliott	Eden, Vt	Apr. 8, 1862	34, 885
Clothes-wringing machine	S. F. Emerson	Seville, Ohio	Sept. 16, 1862	36, 458
Clothes-wringing machine	E. L. Hagar	Frankfort, N. Y	June 1, 1858	20, 470
Clothes-wringing machine	R. G. Holmes	Worcester, Mass	Sept. 8, 1863	39, 814
Clothes-wringing machine	R. B. Hugunin	Cleveland, Ohio	Sept. 20, 1864	44, 313
Clothes-wringing machine	W. Joslin	Cleveland, Ohio	Aug. 19, 1862	36, 218
Clothes-wringing machine	D. Lyman	Middlefield, Conn	Feb. 17, 1863	37, 699
Clothes-wringing machine	J. P. Martin	Philadelphia, Pa	Oct. 5, 1852	9, 302
Clothes-wringing machine	T. H. Peavey	Montville, Me	Apr. 12, 1859	23, 646
Clothes-wringing machine	N. W. Peebles	Brunswick, Ohio	Sept. 2, 1862	36, 362
Clothes-wringing machine	H. W. Putnam	Cleveland, Ohio	Oct. 21, 1862	36, 728
Clothes-wringing machine	I. D. Robinson	Waterbury, Vt	Oct. 28, 1862	36, 860
Clothes-wringing machine	S. Squires	Boston, Mass	Nov. 18, 1862	36, 983
Clothes-wringing machine	D. W. Swift	West Falmouth, Mass	Jan. 28, 1862	34, 276
Clothes-wringing machine	J. W. Wheeler and H. S. Bishop	Cleveland, Ohio	Feb. 10, 1863	37, 655
Clothes-wringing press	C. Robinson	Boston, Mass	Apr. 4, 1871	113, 347
Clothing-clasp	C. Seaver, jr	Boston, Mass	Apr. 4, 1865	47, 135
Clothing, Dummy for displaying	W. E. Brock	New York, N. Y	Apr. 7, 1868	76, 394
Clothing, Mode of fitting	R. Bisbee	Boston, Mass	Mar. 3, 1868	74, 978
Clothing, Stand for displaying	W. E. Brock	New York, N. Y	July 23, 1867	67, 021
Clothing, Submarine	C. S. Merriman	Afton, Iowa	Aug. 10, 1869	93, 544
Clover and other grass seeds, Machine for hulling	A. Keagy	Morrison's Cove, Pa	June 24, 1839	1, 190
Clover and other seeds, Cleaning	J. Roberts, jr		Feb. 13, 1796	
Clover and other seeds, Hulling	W. Jones and A. Miller	Hagerstown, Md	Sept. 27, 1864	44, 431
Clover and rice hulling machine	J. W. Matthews and M. S. Kahle	Lexington, Va	Jan. 17, 1834	
Clover and rice machine	Brayley and Walker	Phillips, Me	June 6, 1835	
Clover-bolt	E. K. Collins	Chili, N. Y	Aug. 16, 1859	25, 097
Clover chaff from straw, Bolt for separating	J. Bolton	Harrisburgh, Pa	July 28, 1831	
Clover, Cleaning	J. Goodyear, jr	South Middletown, Pa	June 2, 1836	
Clover-huller	J. Allen	Frease's Store, Ohio	Feb. 13, 1855	12, 372
Clover-huller	J. Birdsell	Hamorton, Pa	May 23, 1848	5, 599
Clover-huller	A. B. Crawford	Wooster, Ohio	Nov. 28, 1854	11, 990
Clover-huller	J. Hibbs	Tullytown, Pa	Jan. 30, 1855	12, 314
Clover-huller	M. H. Mansfield	Ashland, Ohio	June 21, 1864	43, 217
Clover-huller	J. R. Mitchell	Danville, Pa	July 20, 1843	3, 182
Clover-huller	A. Overocker	McHenry, Ill	July 5, 1859	24, 657
Clover-huller	C. Reif	Hartleton, Lewis Township, Pa.	May 31, 1859	24, 237
Clover-huller	C. Reif	Lewis Township, Pa	Apr. 21, 1863	38, 242
Clover-huller	R. Stadden	Milton, Pa	Sept. 10, 1850	7, 637
Clover huller and cleaner	T. Church	Lewisburgh, Pa	Jan. 9, 1872	122, 568
Clover-huller, Concave of	T. Carpenter	Manlius, N. Y	Mar. 21, 1854	10, 667
Clover hulling and thrashing machine	J. C. Birdsell	Rush, N. Y	May 18, 1858	20, 249
Clover-hulling cylinders, Fastening the teeth to	S. Karns	Bloody Run, Pa	Nov. 8, 1853	10, 208

Index of patents issued from the United States Patent Office from 1790 to 1873, inclusive—Continued.

Invention.	Inventor.	Residence.	Date.	No.
Clover-hulling machine	A. B. Crawford	Wooster, Ohio	Dec. 31, 1844	3,867
Clover-hulling machine	N. Eames	Hanover, Pa	June 21, 1859	24,447
Clover-hulling machine	J. D. Forrey	Lewistown, Pa	Dec. 18, 1860	30,962
Clover-hulling machine	H. Hozer	Wooster, Ohio	June 14, 1845	4,080
Clover-hulling machine	M. H. Mansfield	Mifflintown, Pa	June 6, 1846	4,558
Clover-hulling machine	S. W. Powell	Turbet, Pa	Aug. 16, 1845	4,146
Clover-machine	W. Loomis	Ashford, Conn	July 2, 1836	
Clover-machine	M. H. Mansfield	Ashland, Ohio	Mar. 25, 1862	34,764
Clover-machine	J. Ross	Boundbrook, N. J	Feb. 6, 1835	
Clover-machine	D. Whiting	Ashland. Ohio	May 31, 1870	103,806
Clover, Machine for rubbing out	N. Price	Frederick County, Md	Mar. 2, 1811	
Clover-picker	W. T. Mills	Galesburgh, Mich	Feb. 1, 1859	22,817
Clover-seed and cleaning grain, Screen for hulling	M. H. Mansfield	Ashland, Ohio	Aug. 1, 1854	11,459
Clover-seed and corn sheller, &c	R. Rittenhouse	Amwell Township, Pa	Mar. 19, 1833	
Clover-seed bolting and cleaning machine	J. C. Birdsell	West Henrietta, N. Y	Dec. 13, 1859	26,409
Clover-seed cleaner	G. Faber	Chambersburgh, Pa	Apr. 5, 1832	
Clover-seed cleaner, &c	H. Hoth	Wild, Me	Sept. 26, 1835	
Clover-seed, Cleaning	J. Manning	Lambertsville, N. Y	Jan. 6, 1836	
Clover-seed, Cleaning	W. Sampson and C. Curtis	New Haven, Vt	Jan. 6, 1809	
Clover-seed-cleaning machine	J. Botton	Warren, N. Y	Jan. 28, 1822	
Clover-seed-cleaning machine	J. Cottle		Mar. 21, 1803	
Clover-seed-cleaning machine	D. Rankin	Augusta County, Va	Mar. 18, 1834	
Clover-seed-cleaning machine	A. Spicer		Apr. 22, 1802	
Clover-seed-cleaning machine	H. Spickard	Fincastle, Va	Aug. 16, 1814	
Clover-seed from the "pod," Machine for separating	T. Kirk		July 28, 1803	
Clover-seed, Gathering	J. Smith	Fredericksburgh, Va	Apr. 28, 1815	
Clover-seed huller	J. Bolton	Warren, N. Y	Jan. 9, 1823	
Clover-seed huller	G. and E. Faber	Pittsburgh, Pa	Oct. 13, 1832	
Clover-seed huller	J. Gans	Fayette County, Pa	Mar. 12, 1833	
Clover-seed huller	T. Gollogher	Fairfield County, Ohio	Feb. 28, 1833	
Clover-seed huller	G. Monohon	Augusta Township, Ohio	Apr. 27, 1832	
Clover-seed huller	P. Reading	Trenton, N. J	July 31, 1832	
Clover-seed huller	C. Seabold, jr	New Berlin, Pa	Mar. 6, 1832	
Clover-seed huller	S. West	Harford County, Md	Jan. 16, 1835	
Clover-seed huller and cleaner	W. C. Grimes	York, Pa	Mar. 3, 1841	1,996
Clover-seed huller and grain-chopper	G. Wales	Centre Township, Pa	July 24, 1832	
Clover-seed, Hulling	S. M. Baily	Attleborough, Pa	Aug. 23, 1834	
Clover-seed, Hulling	C. B. Baldwin	Faircastle, Va	June 16, 1836	
Clover seed, Hulling	J. Hopper and A. Doughty	Moresborough, Pa	June 30, 1836	
Clover-seed, Hulling	E. Horn	Rochester County, Va	Jan. 30, 1834	
Clover-seed, Hulling	G. B. and W. F. Poague	Lexington, Va	Feb. 17, 1836	
Clover-seed, Hulling	J. Pollock	Richmond, Ind	Feb. 19, 1850	7,104
Clover-seed, Hulling	H. Robbins	Kennebec, Me	June 20, 1836	
Clover-seed, Hulling	W. Rowe	Phillips, Me	Apr. 25, 1834	
Clover-seed, Hulling and cleaning	M. H. Mansfield	Ashland, Ohio	Feb. 27, 1855	12,462
Clover-seed, Hulling and cleaning	B. Wood	Doylestown, Pa	Aug. 11, 1834	
Clover-seed hulling and cleaning machine	I. V. Blackwell	Ovid, N. Y	Mar. 30, 1858	19,745
Clover-seed hulling and cleaning machine	F. E. Cook	Guilford, Ohio	June 4, 1861	32,470
Clover-seed hulling and cleaning machine	J. Kuhn	Centreville, Pa	June 25, 1861	32,630
Clover-seed hulling and cleaning machine	A. Matthews	Island Creek, Ohio	Dec. 13, 1831	
Clover-seed hulling and cleaning machine	P. Reading	Trenton, N. J	Oct. 25, 1831	
Clover-seed hulling and cleaning machine	D. S. Wagener	Penn Yan, N. Y	Feb. 12, 1861	31,420
Clover-seed hulling and cleaning machine	S. White	Chambersburgh, Pa	Aug. 10, 1828	
Clover-seed hulling and cleaning machine	W. Williams	Buckingham Township, Pa	Aug. 12, 1831	
Clover-seed hulling and thrashing machine	H. Bangs	New York, N. Y	Apr. 29, 1834	
Clover-seed-hulling machine	W. M. Barton	Cheeks X Roads, Tenn	Dec. 20, 1837	525
Clover-seed-hulling machine	J. Flook	Middletown, Md	May 10, 1838	733
Clover-seed-hulling machine	G. Gardner	York Springs, Pa	May 16, 1848	5,580
Clover-seed-hulling machine	W. C. Grimes	York, Pa	Nov. 8, 1834	
Clover-seed-hulling machine	W. C. Grimes	York, Pa	Nov. 8, 1834	
Clover-seed-hulling machine	D. Hunsicker	Hartley, Pa	May 8, 1838	728
Clover-seed-hulling machine	W. E. Lukens	Cadiz, Ohio	Mar. 26, 1834	
Clover-seed-hulling machine	M. F. Noraconk and D. Hoats	Milton, Pa	Dec. 18, 1860	30,982
Clover-seed-hulling machine	J. Worrell		Feb. 27, 1804	
Clover-seed machine	I. Correll	New Philadelphia, Ohio	Dec. 31, 1833	
Clover-seed machine	L. Keck	Tyrone Township, Pa	Dec. 16, 1833	
Clover-seed machine	W. Kuhn, G. Hassinger, and W. Stiles.	Union County, Pa	Dec. 24, 1833	
Clover-seed machine	C. Landes	Mount Sidney, Va	Dec. 24, 1833	
Clover-seed machine	E. Rider	Lovingston, Va	Dec. 28, 1833	
Clover-seed machine	H. Robbins	Wilton, Me	Sept. 6, 1833	
Clover-seed shelling and hulling machine	M. Zorger	York Post-Office, Pa	May 10, 1805	
Clover-seed-shelling machine	J. Gorgas	Fredericksburgh, Pa	Jan. 15, 1830	
Clover-seed-shelling machine	M. Withers		Apr. 30, 1804	
Clover-seeds, &c., Machine for cleaning	S. Arnold	Botetourt, Va	Jan. 25, 1815	
Clover-seeds, Machine for cleaning	I. H. Haskins	Columbia, N. Y	May 6, 1824	
Clover-seeds, Machine for cleaning	M. Miller		July 19, 1802	
Clover-seeds, Machine for gathering	D. K. Wertman and W. H. Reinbold.	Centralia, Pa	Oct. 2, 1866	58,517
Clover-seeds, Machine for getting out	S. Condon	New Hartford, Conn	Mar. 3, 1809	
Clover-seeds, Machine for getting out	W. Loomis	Ashford, Conn	Apr. 27, 1822	
Clover-seeds, Machine for hulling and cleaning	B. Sutton	Romulus, N. Y	Feb. 10, 1825	
Clover-seeds, Machine for saving	M. S. Kahle	Lexington, Va	May 6, 1856	14,816
Clover-seeds, &c., Machine for separating	H. Hunsicker	Lewisburgh, Pa	Feb. 12, 1861	31,389
Clover-seeds, Machine far washing, churning, and getting out.	R. Patton	Columbia, Pa	June 13, 1808	
Clover-seeds, rice, and barley, Machine for hulling	W. Manning	Westfield Township, Pa	Nov. 24, 1830	
Clover-seeds, Separating chaff from	R. Ranger	Wilton, Me	Aug. 21, 1834	
Clover-seeds, Thrashing and cleaning	S. Raub, jr	Wilkesbarre, Pa	Mar. 10, 1834	
Clover-seeds, wheat, &c., from the husks, Separating.	D. Buckman		Dec. 21, 1803	
Clover-separator	C. L. Allen	Flat Rock, Mich	Mar. 18, 1873	136,805
Clover-separator	C. Reif	Hartleton, Pa	Aug. 8, 1854	11,493
Clover separator and huller	D. M. Heikes	Franklin Township, Pa	May 12, 1868	77,731
Clover-stripper and hay-rake, Combined	R. H. Blair and A W. Beatty	Saltsburgh, Pa	Oct. 22, 1861	33,512
Club-feet and crooked legs, Apparatus for straightening.	H. R. Allen	Charleston, Ill	Jan. 28, 1868	73,768
Club-feet apparatus	E. H. Chamberlin	Cincinnati, Ohio	Dec. 11, 1847	5,393

Index of patents issued from the United States Patent Office from 1790 *to* 1873, *inclusive*—Continued.

Invention.	Inventor.	Residence.	Date.	No.
Club-feet, Apparatus for the cure of	Z. Hussey	Chillicothe, Ohio	Dec. 14, 1852	9, 472
Club-feet, Apparatus for treating	G. B. Wood	Chicago, Ill	Aug. 30, 1870	106, 907
Club-feet, Apparatus for treatment of	J. B. Brown	Boston, Mass	Apr. 30, 1840	1, 572
Club-feet, Surgical instrument for treatment of	E. A. Grant	Louisville, Ky	May 9, 1871	114, 669
Clutch	J. Hartman, jr	Philadelphia, Pa	Apr. 26, 1864	42, 4[illegible]3
Clutch	A. Heth and G. Hall	Adams, N. Y	May 28, 1867	65, 220
Clutch	S. Ingersoll	Stamford, Conn	May 12, 1863	38, 486
Clutch	W. Knight and N. W. Lewis	Bridgeport, Conn	June 24, 1873	140, 142
Clutch	W. I. Risedorph	Albany, N. Y	Sept. 7, 1869	94, 649
Clutch	H. F. Shaw	West Roxbury, Mass	Aug. 10, 1869	93, 486
Clutch	J. W. Tuttle	Newton, Mass	Oct. 11, 1870	108, 303
Clutch, Anchor	H. Fleming	Chicago, Ill	Oct. 11, 1864	44, 621
Clutch and brake, Friction	D. Banks, jr	New York, N. Y	June 8, 1869	90, 982
Clutch and brake, Friction	D. Banks, jr	Middletown, Conn	Sept. 10, 1872	131, 207
Clutch applied to rudder-head, Spring	E. O. P. Andrews	Boston, Mass	Aug. 10, 1848	5, 700
Clutch, Centrifugal friction	R. Reynolds	Stockport, N. Y	Mar. 3, 1857	16, 748
Clutch, Chain	H. Pitcher	Fond du Lac, Wis	Dec. 13, 1870	110, 069
Clutch, Combined friction and ratchet	A. W. Hall	Northfield, Vt	Dec. 19, 1871	122, 009
Clutch, Elevating	C. C. Blodgett	Watertown, N. Y	Apr. 14, 1868	76, 588
Clutch for belt-pulley, Friction	J. H. Blessing	Albany, N. Y	Apr. 18, 1871	113, 841
Clutch for connecting and disconnecting machinery.	D. M. Smyth	New York, N. Y	Dec. 19, 1865	51, 665
Clutch for engaging and disengaging gearing, Friction.	G. D. Emerson	Calumet, Mich	Apr. 12, 1870	101, 846
Clutch for flour-packer	J. T. Noye	Buffalo, N. Y	June 17, 1856	15, 145
Clutch for hydraulic-wheel press	A. B. Couch	Worcester, Mass	Sept. 14, 1869	94, 717
Clutch for machinery, Spiral friction	J. Hanley	New York, N. Y	Dec. 18, 1866	60, 509
Clutch for power-press	N. C. Stiles	Meriden, Conn	Jan. 30, 1866	52, 335
Clutch for suspending hay-fork	W. Dixon and L. Heath	Adams, N. Y	Oct. 1, 1867	69, 326
Clutch for water-wheel, Self-releasing	G. W. Wesley	Meadville, Pa	Apr. 18, 1871	113, 826
Clutch, Friction	H. Aiken	Philadelphia, Pa	Mar. 12, 1872	124, 529
Clutch, Friction	S. B. Alger	Oswego, N. Y	Apr. 1, 1873	137, 335
Clutch, Friction	E. Allen	Norwich, Conn	May 20, 1873	138, 980
Clutch, Friction	D. Banks	New York, N. Y	May 25, 1869	90, 481
Clutch, Friction	N. Barlow	Saint Louis, Mo	Aug. 13, 1850	7, 557
Clutch, Friction	F. G. Bates	Springfield, Mass	Oct. 15, 1872	132, 234
Clutch, Friction	E. B. Bigelow	Boston, Mass	Aug. 17, 1869	93, 798
Clutch, Friction	J. S. Brown	Pawtucket, R. I	Apr. 26, 1864	42, 525
Clutch, Friction	W. H. Brown	Worcester, Mass	Nov. 28, 1865	51, 134
Clutch, Friction	W. C. Burch and G. D. Oatley	Gloucester, N. J	June 13, 1871	115, 818
Clutch, Friction	C. E. Burwell	Springfield, Mass	July 9, 1872	128, 705
Clutch, Friction	C. W. Cardot	Jamestown, N. Y	June 8, 1869	90, 992
Clutch, Friction	G. Clisbee	Marlborough, Mass	July 18, 1871	117, 234
Clutch, Friction	T. Coldwell	Newburgh, N. Y	Nov. 15, 1870	109, 299
Clutch, Friction	G. D. Emerson	Calumet, Mich	Aug. 10, 1869	93, 604
Clutch, Friction	P. Ferguson and F. G. Bates	New Haven, Conn., and Springfield, Mass.	Jan. 16, 1872	122, 822
Clutch, Friction	E. T. Ford	Stillwater, N. Y	Sept. 1, 1868	81, 617
Clutch, Friction	J. J. Grant	Greenfield, Mass	Aug. 26, 1873	142, 227
Clutch, Friction	J. J. Grant	Greenfield, Mass	Sept. 9, 1873	142, 564
Clutch, Friction	A. W. Hall	East Lebanon, N. H	Feb. 4, 1868	74, 080
Clutch, Friction	M. Hawkins	Birmingham, Conn	Nov. 16, 1869	96, 913
Clutch, Friction	G. W. Hedges	San Francisco, Cal	Oct. 31, 1871	120, 434
Clutch, Friction	S. Ingersoll	Brooklyn, N. Y	Jan. 25, 1870	99, 199
Clutch, Friction	W. W. Jerome, S. B. Alger, and C. H. Sage.	Norwich, N. Y	Nov. 29, 1870	109, 740
Clutch, Friction	J. B. Johnson and W. H. Birch	San Francisco, Cal	Apr. 7, 1868	76, 328
Clutch, Friction	O. Lull	Rochester, N. Y	May 31, 1870	103, 634
Clutch, Friction	L. H. Olmsted	Newark, N. J	Sept. 27, 1864	44, 448
Clutch, Friction	F. A. Pratt	Hartford, Conn	Feb. 22, 1870	100, 064
Clutch, Friction	G. S. Reynolds	Lebanon, N. H	Apr. 4, 1871	113, 566
Clutch, Friction	R. Reynolds	Stockport, N. Y	Dec. 24, 1861	34, 012
Clutch, Friction	G. Sickels	Brooklyn, N. Y	Mar. 2, 1852	8, 782
Clutch, Friction	H. K. Smith	Norwich, Conn	Dec. 5, 1865	51, 360
Clutch, Friction	T. Stebins	San Francisco, Cal	Oct. 1, 1872	131, 795
Clutch, Friction	T. A. Weston	Ridgewood, N. J	July 30, 1872	129, 914
Clutch, Friction	S. C. Wright	Fitchburgh, Mass	Apr. 16, 1867	63, 977
Clutch, Friction	W. Wright	New York, N. Y	June 15, 1852	9, 043
Clutch-gearing	L. S. Fithian	Brooklyn, N. Y	Aug. 8, 1871	117, 758
Clutch-gearing	E. Nicholson	Cleveland, Ohio	Nov. 1, 1870	108, 817
Clutch, Harvester	F. Bramer	Little Falls, N. Y	Aug. 22, 1871	118, 333
Clutch in machine for packing flour	S. Taggart	Indianapolis, Ind	Dec. 19, 1854	12, 107
Clutch, Lathe	R. Allen	Jersey City, N. J	Dec. 4, 1866	60, 113
Clutch, Machinery	F. G. Bates	Springfield, Mass	Mar. 12, 1872	124, 476
Clutch, Machinery	W. B. Duckworth	Hamden, Conn	Apr. 22, 1873	138, 139
Clutch, Machinery	T. F. Hammer	Branford, Conn	July 11, 1865	48, 769
Clutch, Machinery	W. E. Hawkins	Wallingford, Conn	Feb. 27, 1872	124, 058
Clutch, Machinery	J. E. Plummer and J. P. Noyes	Binghamton, N. Y	Nov. 22, 1870	109, 450
Clutch mechanism	D. M. Weston	Boston, Mass	Oct. 3, 1871	119, 677
Clutch mechanism, Friction	J. J. Coburn	Philadelphia, Pa	Apr. 22, 1873	138, 075
Clutch mechanism, Friction	M. G. Crane and A. M. Polsey	Newton and Boston, Mass.	Feb. 15, 1870	99, 761
Clutch mechanism, Friction pawl or	W. R. Close	Bangor, Me	June 27, 1871	116, 413
Clutch or pulley, Friction	H. S. Shepardson	Shelburne Falls, Mass	June 14, 1864	43, 138
Clutch or rope-holder	C. A. Emery	Springfield, Mass	Sept. 19, 1865	49, 990
Clutch, Sail	E. A. Sawyer	Portland, Me	June 6, 1865	48, 103
Clutch-shipper	F. J. Plummer	Worcester, Mass	Aug. 27, 1867	68, 108
Clutch, Slaughtering	R. Savage	Chicago, Ill	Mar. 23, 1869	88, 217
Clutch, Tubing	J. N. Angier	Titusville, Pa	Nov. 16, 1869	96, 766
Coach, &c	B. Hale	Newburyport, Mass	Jan. 17, 1818	....
Coach adapted to the prairies, Steam	J. Semple	Alton, Ill	May 1, 1845	4, 029
Coach-alarm	W. Hunt	New York, N. Y	July 30, 1827	....
Coach and other carriage	F. Bremler	New York, N. Y	Apr. 24, 1810	....
Coach, barouche, &c	R. Gedney	New York, N. Y	Apr. 7, 1832	....
Coach-door	J. Penfield and D. F. Woolsey	Bridgeport, Conn	Oct. 12, 1869	95, 832
Coach-doors, Stop for	H. Killam	New Haven, Conn	Dec. 10, 1861	33, 892
Coach-lace, Making	W. G. Barnet	Newark, N. J	Nov. 18, 1825	....
Coach, &c., Mail	S. Draper	Brookfield, Mass	Aug. 26, 1819	....
Coach or carriage	J. Allgaier	Philadelphia, Pa	June 10, 1873	139, 753

Index of patents issued from the United States Patent Office from 1790 *to* 1873, *inclusive*—Continued.

Invention.	Inventor.	Residence.	Date.	No.
Coach or carriage	J. Allgaier	Philadelphia, Pa	July 8, 1873	140, 666
Coach-pad	B. F. Hooper	Newark, N. J	Apr. 14, 1868	76, 762
Coach-panel	E. A. Lester	Boston, Mass	Mar. 18, 1835	
Coach, pleasure-carriage, railway-car, &c	T. Shriver	Cumberland, Md	Nov. 7, 1839	1, 399
Coach-step	G. Carter	Newark, N. J	Nov. 26, 1831	
Coach-step	C. M. King	Newark, N. J	Dec. 31, 1833	
Coach-tongues, Mode of supporting	Z. B. Wakeman	Beloit, Wis	Mar. 10, 1857	16, 813
Coaches, &c., Hanging curtains or blinds in	P. Harvey	Philadelphia, Pa	May 9, 1807	
Coaches, Making post and other	R. Ward	Schenectady, N. Y	June 2, 1825	
Coaches, Securing baggage on post	J. Stratton	Greenfield, Mass	June 29, 1830	
Coal and generating gas, Cooking	W. G. Valentin	London, England	Jan. 13, 1863	37, 412
Coal and grain boat elevator	S. K. Hoxsie	Philadelphia, Pa	May 18, 1869	90, 103
Coal and ore separator	H. Bradford	Reading, Pa	Sept. 30, 1873	143, 219
Coal and ore separators, Feeding-device for	H. Bradford	Reading, Pa	Sept. 30, 1873	143, 323
Coal and ores, Desulphurizing	J. I. Storer	Philadelphia, Pa	Apr. 9, 1861	32, 012
Coal and ores, Purification of	J. Burroughs	Ridgway, Pa	Apr. 3, 1860	27, 689
Coal and ores, Purification of	B. F. Penimen	New York, N. Y	Oct. 25, 1864	44, 817
Coal and other minerals, Machinery for moving	J. E. Wooten	Reading, Pa	June 7, 1870	104, 093
Coal and other minerals, Mode of cutting	T. Harrison	Tudhoe, England	May 3, 1864	42, 626
Coal and other substances, Machine for breaking.	R. A. Wilder	Cressona, Pa	Mar. 18, 1873	136, 887
Coal and rock cutting machine	H. F. Brown	Indianapolis, Ind	Sept. 16, 1873	142, 896
Coal and slate separator	H. Bradford	Reading, Pa	Oct. 29, 1872	132, 623
Coal and wood box	J. Mallin	Chicago, Ill	May 2, 1871	114, 312
Coal, &c., Apparatus for applying oil and water to assist the combustion of.	S. C. Salisbury	New York, N. Y	Apr. 24, 1866	54, 216
Coal, &c., Apparatus for burning fine	E. Thayer	Worcester, Mass	Sept. 13, 1864	44, 263
Coal, Apparatus for raising and dumping	E. Morris	Bergen, N. J	July 8, 1856	15, 300
Coal, Artificial lump	R. Covert	Brooklyn, N. Y	Nov. 8, 1864	44, 940
Coal, Artificial lump	R. Covert	Brooklyn, N. Y	June 27, 1865	48, 372
Coal-barge	L. F. Frazee	Jersey City, N. J	Dec. 13, 1870	110, 130
Coal-barge	R. Hartley	Pittsburgh, Pa	May 31, 1870	103, 607
Coal-barge	J. A. Preston	New Haven, Conn	Sept. 24, 1867	69, 245
Coal-barge	J. A. Preston	New Haven, Conn	May 24, 1870	103, 502
Coal, Bit for boring	S. Gissinger	Manchester, Pa	Dec. 17, 1867	72, 389
Coal, &c., Bit for boring	S. Hipkins, jr	Wheeling, W. Va	Jan. 14, 1873	134, 805
Coal-boring machine	S. Hipkins, jr	Wheeling, W. Va	Jan. 14, 1873	134, 804
Coal-boring machine	D. Shoemaker	Kittaning Township, Pa	Sept. 16, 1873	142, 950
Coal-box	T. L. Bozart, jr	Indianapolis, Ind	Jan. 24, 1871	111, 171
Coal-box	C. W. Coffin	Pittsburgh, Pa	Oct. 31, 1871	120, 494
Coal-box	B. R. Deacon	Montreal, Canada	Apr. 12, 1870	101, 833
Coal-box	C. Hoefinghoff	Cincinnati, Ohio	July 13, 1869	92, 447
Coal-box	S. A. Simison	Earlville, Ill	Jan. 14, 1868	73, 394
Coal-box and fire-iron holder, Combined	A. F. Tripp	Buffalo, N. Y	Dec. 24, 1872	134, 230
Coal-box and fire-iron standard	E. B. Jewett	Buffalo, N. Y	Dec. 10, 1872	133, 780
Coal-breaker	H. Bradford	Reading, Pa	Oct. 21, 1873	143, 745
Coal-breaker	W. De Haven and P. Umholtz	Minersville, Pa	Feb. 8, 1848	5, 440
Coal-breaker	J. A. Dickson	Scranton, Pa	July 4, 1865	48, 532
Coal-breaker	J. Fox	Philadelphia, Pa	Apr. 25, 1865	47, 409
Coal-breaker	B. Haywood	Pottsville, Pa	May 21, 1845	4, 058
Coal-breaker	T. Petherick	Pottsville, Pa	Apr. 22, 1856	14, 732
Coal-breaker	W. Richardson	Philadelphia, Pa	Sept. 2, 1845	4, 172
Coal-breaker	P. Umholtz	Tremont, Pa	Mar. 20, 1860	27, 581
Coal-breaker	P. Umholtz	Tremont, Pa	June 13, 1865	48, 224
Coal-breaker	R. A. Wilder	Cressona, Pa	Sept. 2, 1873	142, 426
Coal breaker and separator	L. P. Garner	Ashland, Pa	May 25, 1869	90, 439
Coal breaking and screening machine	J. Battin	Philadelphia, Pa	Oct. 6, 1843	3, 292
Coal-breaking machine	J. Battin	Philadelphia, Pa	Feb. 12, 1844	3, 438
Coal-breaking machine	A. Bolton	Port Carbon, Pa	Mar. 2, 1858	19, 481
Coal-breaking machine	J. R. Deihm and J. Snell	Pottsville, Pa	Oct. 27, 1857	18, 501
Coal-breaking machine	L. P. Garner	Ashland, Pa	Feb. 19, 1861	31, 451
Coal-breaking machine	J. Jones and S. P. Bidder, jr	Stratford and Mitcham, England.	Aug. 31, 1869	94, 216
Coal-breaking machine	C. W. Kennedy and R. T. Brown	Williamsburgh, N. Y	May 10, 1859	23, 922
Coal-breaking machine	R. A. Wilder	Cressona, Pa	Feb. 19, 1861	31, 502
Coal-breaking machine	R. A. Wilder	Cressona, Pa	Dec. 24, 1872	134, 233
Coal-breaking machines, Conveyer and separator for.	R. A. Wilder	Cressona, Pa	Dec. 24, 1872	134, 234
Coal-breaking machinery	G. E. Hoyt	Brooklyn, N. Y	Feb. 21, 1860	27, 220
Coal-breaking machinery	I. P. Lykens	Pottsville, Pa	Feb. 14, 1860	27, 191
Coal-breaking roll	W. R. Reece	Tremont, Pa	Sept. 8, 1863	39, 835
Coal burner, Anthracite	J. N. Olney	Providence, R. I	Dec. 26, 1833	
Coal-chute	E. Maguire	Kewanee, Ill	Aug. 20, 1867	67, 995
Coal-chute	H. Merriman	Bloomington, Ill	Dec. 8, 1868	84, 749
Coal-chute	W. E. Phelps	Elmwood, Ill	Nov. 28, 1871	121, 413
Coal-chute	L. D. and C. C. Roberts	Cleveland, Ohio	May 4, 1869	89, 793
Coal-chute	J. Rhodes	Dunkirk, N. Y	June 6, 1871	115, 640
Coal-chute	C. W. Williams	Port Jervis, N. Y	Nov. 5, 1872	132, 884
Coal-chute, Extension	J. Heatherington	Bellaire, Ohio	Feb. 18, 1868	74, 686
Coal, Composition for desulphurizing	J. H. Connelly	Wheeling, W. Va	Aug. 9, 1864	43, 760
Coal conveyer and and elevator	J. T. Hoole	Buffalo, N. Y	Sept. 24, 1872	131, 683
Coal conveying and dumping apparatus	H. C. Clark and R. B. Little	Providence, R. I	June 2, 1866	78, 430
Coal, Conveying, cleaning, and assorting	J. G. Brant	Cumberland, Md	Mar. 14, 1846	4, 415
Coal, Cooling animal	W. Moller	New York, N. Y	Feb. 5, 1867	61, 851
Coal-cracker	T. Poore	Carbondale, Pa	May 12, 1857	17, 294
Coal-crusher	H. C. Rogers	Scranton, Pa	June 14, 1864	43, 133
Coal-cutting machine	G. E. Donisthorpe	Leeds, England	Sept. 22, 1868	82, 391
Coal-cutting machine	G. E. Donisthorpe	Leeds, England	Sept. 29, 1868	82, 608
Coal-cutting machine	S. Firth	Leeds, England	Apr. 8, 1873	137, 669
Coal-delivering sack	W. S. Shackleton	Cleveland, Ohio	Apr. 4, 1871	113, 353
Coal-delivering sack	W. S. Shackleton	Cleveland, Ohio	Sept. 9, 1873	142, 741
Coal, Device for boring and excavating	A. Buchanan	Brooklyn, N. Y	June 20, 1865	48, 258
Coal-digger	W. Ward	Pittsburgh, Pa	Apr. 12, 1870	101, 793
Coal-discharging apparatus	E. F. Flood	Chicago, Ill	Mar. 30, 1869	88, 379
Coal-drilling machine	J. Grimm	Darlington Township, Pa	Nov. 23, 1869	97, 080
Coal, Drier for preparing waste	T. M. Mitchell	Philadelphia, Pa	July 20, 1869	92, 737
Coal-dumping apparatus	R. Jenkins and T. Woods	Allegheny County, Pa	June 6, 1871	115, 738
Coal-dumping apparatus	E. R. Kerr	Kewanee, Ill	Oct. 2, 1866	58, 549
Coal dust and cinders, Mode of utilizing	A. L. Fleury	Pittsburgh, Pa	Feb. 13, 1866	52, 554

Index of patents issued from the United States Patent Office from 1790 to 1873, inclusive—Continued.

Invention.	Inventor.	Residence.	Date.	No.
Coal-dust as fuel in furnaces, Process of using anthracite.	A. Berney	Jersey City, N. J	Apr. 15, 1873	137, 820
Coal-dust for fuel, Mode of preparing	A. D. Ditmars	Lancaster, Pa	Aug. 18, 1868	81, 149
Coal-dust, Furnace for burning	G. B. Deppen and E. Levengood.	Myerstown, Pa	Nov. 16, 1858	22, 067
Coal-dust, peat, &c., Method of consolidating	W. J. Cheyney and E. T. Dieterichs.	Wallingford and Philadelphia, Pa.	Mar. 14, 1865	46, 777
Coal-elevator	A. S. Bailey	Chicago, Ill	Feb. 22, 1870	100, 103
Coal elevator	L. S. Chichester	New York, N. Y	Aug. 17, 1869	93, 676
Coal-elevator	J. C. Clifford	Yonkers, N. Y	Oct. 3, 1871	119, 574
Coal elevator	J. P. Tucker	South Reading, Mass	June 12, 1866	55, 557
Coal elevator and distributor	H. C. Clark and R. B. Little	Providence, R. I	Oct. 1, 1867	69, 407
Coal elevator and weigher	L. S. Chichester	Brooklyn, N. Y	Aug. 17, 1869	93, 677
Coal elevator bucket	A. B. Nimbs	Buffalo, N. Y	Sept. 6, 1864	44, 108
Coal for metallurgic operations, Preparing	W. J. Lynd	Golden City, Colo	Jan. 4, 1870	98, 607
Coal for smelting ores, Preparing	W. J. Lynd	Golden City, Colo	Jan. 4, 1870	98, 606
Coal for welding iron, Method of desulphurizing	J. H. Elward	Polo, Ill	Feb. 20, 1866	52, 699
Coal from slate, Apparatus for separating	B. F. Day	Hazleton, Pa	July 9, 1872	128, 791
Coal furnace, Anthracite	M. B. Bulkley	Pottsville, Pa	Jan. 16, 1835	....
Coal furnace, Anthracite	W. Church	Boston, Mass	Nov. 20, 1826	....
Coal furnace, Anthracite	D. Olmsted	New Haven, Conn	Nov. 5, 1834	....
Coal furnace, Anthracite	J. L. Sullivan	New York, N. Y	Nov. 26, 1825	....
Coal furnace, Anthracite	O. Woodruff	New York, N. Y	Nov. 7, 1825	....
Coal, Furnace for burning fossil	D. Stansbury	Belleville, N. J	Apr. 15, 1825	....
Coal-hod	J. H. Brown	Lynn, Mass	Aug. 5, 1873	141, 485
Coal-hod	E. R. Hall	Buffalo, N. Y	July 17, 1866	56, 408
Coal-hod	L. W. Hemp	Saint Louis, Mo	Dec. 31, 1872	134, 379
Coal-hod	R. W. Huston	Calais, Me	Nov. 22, 1859	26, 188
Coal-hod	E. A. Jeffery	New Haven, Conn	Aug. 23, 1864	43, 916
Coal-hod	E. A. Jeffery	New Haven, Conn	Feb. 27, 1866	52, 856
Coal-hod	C. F. Kneeland	Buffalo, N. Y	Aug. 12, 1856	15, 519
Coal-hod	J. A. Lawson	Troy, N. Y	Aug. 27, 1867	68, 213
Coal-hod	W. N. Martin	Bristol, R. I	Nov. 7, 1854	11, 898
Coal-hod	J. R. Miller	Cincinnati, Ohio	May 3, 1864	42, 623
Coal-hod	F. G. and W. F. Needringhaus.	Saint Louis, Mo	Oct. 20, 1868	83, 301
Coal-hod	J. Pfitzinger	Buffalo, N. Y	Oct. 22, 1867	70, 015
Coal-hod	J. Pilbeam	Seneca Falls, N. Y	Sept. 22, 1863	40, 061
Coal-hod	J. H. Pocock	Chicago, Ill	Nov. 20, 1866	59, 925
Coal-hod	H. B. Safford	Lancaster, N. Y	Sept. 9, 1873	142, 734
Coal-hod	C. Smith	Brooklyn, N. Y	Oct. 24, 1871	120, 336
Coal-hod	J. G. Somes	Charlestown, Mass	Apr. 27, 1869	89, 444
Coal-hod	S. Thomson, G. Smith, and J. S. Jennings.	Brooklyn, N. Y	Mar. 20, 1866	53, 384
Coal-hod	W. Wilson	Boston, Mass	May 3, 1870	102, 639
Coal-hod	A. A. Yeatman and J. M. Mason.	Washington, D. C	Jan. 15, 1867	61, 301
Coal hod and screen	A. Porter	Charlestown, Mass	Feb. 25, 1868	74, 770
Coal hod and sifter, Combined	R. Bogle	Milton, Pa	Dec. 26, 1871	122, 147
Coal hod and sifter, Combined	B. F. Brown	Portland, Me	Nov. 27, 1866	59, 954
Coal-hod, ash-sifter, and slop-pail combined	C. Jones	Brooklyn, N. Y	May 30, 1867	48, 020
Coal-hod bottom	E. W. Kimball	Hudson, N. Y	Jan. 21, 1868	73, 535
Coal-hod, Screen	M. S. Nichols and R. Weaver	Central Village, Conn	Mar. 15, 1870	100, 791
Coal-hod stand	W. M. Conger	Newark, N. J	May 14, 1872	126, 676
Coal-hods, Construction of sheet-metal	M. G. Fagan	Troy, N. Y	July 7, 1868	79, 564
Coal-hods, Construction of sheet-metal	J. McCoy	Philadelphia, Pa	Nov. 19, 1867	71, 032
Coal hoister and conveyer	J. Green	New York, N. Y	Aug. 1, 1871	117, 534
Coal, Hoisting and dumping	G. Martz	Pottsville, Pa	Oct. 30, 1866	59, 243
Coal hoisting and dumping apparatus	W. B. Culver	Scranton, Pa	Jan. 4, 1859	22, 492
Coal hoisting and dumping machine	G. Martz	Pottsville, Pa	Apr. 13, 1858	19, 939
Coal-hole cover	J. Gault	Boston, Mass	July 23, 1861	32, 865
Coal-hole cover	L. A. Kimberly	New Haven, Conn	Nov. 22, 1870	109, 422
Coal-hole cover	F. H. Moore	Boston, Mass	Apr. 3, 1855	12, 637
Coal-hole cover, Safety	F. H. Moore	Boston, Mass	Jan. 15, 1856	14, 107
Coal-hole guard	J. C. Jenks	Boston, Mass	Mar. 4, 1865	14, 359
Coal-holes, Composition-cover for	J. F. Wood	Everett, Mass	Nov. 26, 1872	133, 513
Coal-holes, Safety-port for	S. W. Frost	Boston, Mass	Apr. 3, 1855	12, 623
Coal-hopper and platform-scales, Combined	F. E. and L. I. Howe	New York, N. Y., and Boston, Mass.	May 5, 1868	77, 488
Coal in cellars, Machine for depositing	W. Bell	Boston, Mass	Feb. 26, 1856	14, 301
Coal into blocks for fuel, Press for compacting the waste particles of.	T. M. Mitchell	Philadelphia, Pa	Nov. 30, 1869	97, 309
Coal into solid lumps, Method of converting fine	W. Easby	Washington, D. C	Aug. 29, 1848	5, 739
Coal, Kiln for charring	C. Kownslar	Mill Creek, Va	June 20, 1825	....
Coal-lifter	J. B. Creemer	Philadelphia, Pa	Oct. 23, 1855	13, 699
Coal-loading device	D. Risher, jr	Dravosburgh, Pa	Sept. 8, 1868	81, 946
Coal, Machine for breaking and screening	H. Thomas	Beaver Meadow, Pa	Dec. 5, 1843	3, 368
Coal, Machine for cracking anthracite	J. S. Hubbell	New York, N. Y	Aug. 17, 1835	....
Coal, Machine for cutting	J. Gillott and P. Copley	Barnsley, England	Nov. 11, 1873	144, 529
Coal, Machine for desulphurizing bituminous	D. Morgan	Hammondsville, Ohio	Jan. 1, 1869	90, 772
Coal, Machine for loading	C. Bushor	Philadelphia, Pa	July 2, 1861	32, 680
Coal, &c., Machine for loading	C. Bushor	Philadelphia, Pa	May 20, 1862	35, 297
Coal, Machine for separating slate and other foreign substances from.	E. Borda and D. Glover	Woodside, Pa	Oct. 13, 1857	18, 380
Coal, Machine for slating	T. Garretson	Pottsville, Pa	Mar. 30, 1858	19, 768
Coal, Machine for slating	J. Gass	Trevorton, Pa	Nov. 24, 1857	18, 687
Coal, Machine for undermining	G. D. Whitcomb	Chicago, Ill	Aug. 29, 1871	118, 501
Coal, Method of burning waste	J. D. Whelpley and J. J. Storer	Boston, Mass	Mar. 13, 1866	53, 208
Coal, minerals, &c., Method of mining	W. Locke, J. Warrington, W. E. Carrett, W. E. Marshall, and J. Telford.	Kippax, England	May 15, 1866	54, 833
Coal-mining apparatus	G. E. Donisthorpe	Leeds, England	Sept. 1, 1868	81, 759
Coal-mining apparatus	G. E. Donisthorpe	Leeds, England	Sept. 1, 1868	81, 760
Coal-mining machine	E. K. and J. M. Bruce	Liberty, Pa	Sept. 19, 1865	49, 972
Coal-mining machine	W. Case	Troy, Ill	June 3, 1873	139, 541
Coal-mining machine	C. A. Chamberlin	Allegheny City, Pa	Mar. 9, 1858	19, 543
Coal-mining machine	G. E. Donisthorpe	Leeds, England	Apr. 7, 1868	76, 417
Coal-mining machine	G. E. Donisthorpe	Leeds, England	Apr. 7, 1868	76, 418
Coal-mining machine	G. E. Donisthorpe	Leeds, England	Apr. 7, 1868	76, 419

Index of patents issued from the United States Patent Office from 1790 *to* 1873, *inclusive*—Continued.

Invention.	Inventor.	Residence.	Date.	No.
Coal-mining machine	G. E. Donisthorpe	Leeds, England	Sept. 22, 1868	82, 390
Coal-mining machine	C. L. Driesslein	Chicago, Ill	Mar. 11, 1873	136, 712
Coal-mining machine	G. Elbreg	Brazil, Ind	Jan. 14, 1873	134, 870
Coal-mining machine	J. S. Fisk and J. Westerman	Meadville and Sharon, Pa	Jan. 17, 1865	45, 917
Coal-mining machine	W. W. Grier and R. H. Boyd	Hulton, Pa	July 12, 1864	43, 493
Coal-mining machine	W. W. Grier and R. H. Boyd	Hulton, Pa	Oct. 24, 1865	50, 577
Coal-mining machine	F. M. W. Price	Danville, Ill	Sept. 9, 1873	142, 582
Coal-mining machine	E. Simkins	Allegheny, Pa	Oct. 26, 1858	21, 908
Coal-mining machine	H. Spear	Portland, Me	Dec. 10, 1872	133, 900
Coal-mining-machine drill-carriage	S. Gissinger	Allegheny City, Pa	Dec. 17, 1867	72, 390
Coal-mining machinery	J. Alexander	Gartsherrie, Scotland	Feb. 18, 1873	135, 874
Coal-mining machinery	J. G. Jones	Monmouthshire, Wales	Dec. 5, 1865	51, 405
Coal-mining tool	I. Lamplugh	Peoria, Ill	Dec. 19, 1871	122, 035
Coal, Mixing apparatus for preparing waste	T. M. Mitchell	Philadelphia, Pa	July 20, 1869	92, 738
Coal, &c., Mode of pulverizing and preparing for use.	J. E. Lundgren	Stockholm, Sweden	Apr. 5, 1864	42, 257
Coal-oil for heating purposes, Apparatus for burning.	H. W. Dopp	Buffalo, N. Y	Jan. 20, 1863	37, 436
Coal-oil furnace	T. Shaw	Philadelphia, Pa	May 29, 1860	28, 539
Coal-oil heater	H. W. Dopp	Buffalo, N. Y	July 7, 1863	39, 129
Coal or charcoal, Furnace for burning stone	J. Eslin	Philadelphia, Pa	June 19, 1830	....
Coal, ore, &c., washer	M. Evrard	St. Etienne, France	Aug. 26, 1873	142, 221
Coal, Preparing	H., jr., and E. Mayhew	Lancaster, Pa	Mar. 6, 1860	27, 373
Coal, Process and apparatus for utilizing waste	T. M. Mitchell	Philadelphia, Pa	July 20, 1869	92, 736
Coal, Producing combustion by applying high steam and hydrogen gas to anthracite.	P. Chase	New York, N. Y	Oct. 7, 1831	....
Coal products to obtain benzole, Treating	J. Rowley	Camberwell, England	Mar. 22, 1870	101, 048
Coal raising and dumping apparatus	J. Delaney	Ashland, Pa	June 8, 1869	91, 093
Coal raising and moving	A. Lawton	Philadelphia, Pa	Nov. 16, 1869	96, 927
Coal-raising apparatus	A. Lawton	Philadelphia, Pa	July 13, 1869	92, 461
Coal-screen	E. G. Belknap	Philadelphia, Pa	May 16, 1871	114, 753
Coal-screen	H. L. Cake	Pottsville, Pa	Jan. 24, 1860	26, 890
Coal-screen	J. R. Deihm and J. Snell	Pottsville, Pa	June 21, 1864	43, 185
Coal-screen	R. B. Douty	Shamokin, Pa	May 19, 1863	38, 569
Coal-screen	T. Farron	Lincoln Township, Pa	Jan. 10, 1872	122, 589
Coal-screen	J. P. Fennell	Philadelphia, Pa	June 19, 1855	13, 083
Coal-screen	B. L. Fetherolf	Tamaqua, Pa	Jan. 23, 1872	122, 882
Coal-screen	L. P. Garner	Ashland, Pa	May 11, 1869	89, 927
Coal-screen	G. E. Hoyt and F. Nishwitz	Brooklyn, N. Y	Jan. 19, 1858	19, 175
Coal-screen	J. Laubenstein	Minersville, Pa	Feb. 4, 1862	34, 306
Coal-screen	G. Martz	Pottsville, Pa	Mar. 6, 1855	12, 486
Coal-screen	A. M. Olds	Chicago, Ill	Jan. 24, 1865	46, 019
Coal-screen	J. A. Robinson	Pittston, Pa	Mar. 28, 1865	47, 041
Coal-screen	J. B. Smith	Dunmore, Pa	Aug. 7, 1866	57, 052
Coal-screen	J. Snell and J. R. Deihm	Pottsville, Pa	May 24, 1859	24, 155
Coal-screen	J. Snell and J. R. Deihm	Pottsville, Pa	Sept. 10, 1861	33, 268
Coal-screen	W. Sparks	New York, N. Y	Sept. 12, 1865	49, 932
Coal-screen	W. Sparks	New York, N. Y	Nov. 16, 1869	96, 991
Coal-screen	E. Thomas	Shickshinny, Pa	Dec. 6, 1870	109, 969
Coal-screen	G. Whittle	New York, N. Y	Oct. 29, 1867	70, 305
Coal-screen	S. W. Woodward	Buffalo, N. Y	Apr. 29, 1873	138, 355
Coal screen and chute	M. R. Roberts	San Francisco, Cal	June 17, 1873	140, 077
Coal-screen, Corrugated-iron revolving	E. W. Weston	Providence, Pa	Nov. 19, 1867	71, 099
Coal-screens, Wire cloth for	C. P. Leitzinger	Scranton, Pa	June 18, 1872	128, 177
Coal-screens, Wire-cloth for	J. W. Brock	Scranton, Pa	Nov. 12, 1872	132, 949
Coal screening or sifting machine	B. S. Hort	Kensington, Pa	Feb. 7, 1842	2, 451
Coal-scuttle	S. J. Anderson	Cazenovia, N. Y	Apr. 26, 1870	102, 202
Coal-scuttle	A. Bardell and S. Smith	New York, N. Y	Mar. 12, 1867	62, 807
Coal-scuttle	F. L. Blair	Allegheny, Pa	Jan. 11, 1870	98, 661
Coal-scuttle	J. A. Bragaw	Kingston, N. Y	Oct. 10, 1871	119, 738
Coal-scuttle	M. L. Byrn	New York, N. Y	Nov. 28, 1865	51, 139
Coal-scuttle	G. Chambers	Ithaca, N. Y	Dec. 13, 1864	45, 388
Coal-scuttle	H. C. Clark	Williamsburgh, N. Y	Dec. 24, 1872	134, 253
Coal-scuttle	J. W. Coombs	Mount Vernon, N. Y	June 3, 1862	35, 436
Coal-scuttle	B. F. Cowan	New York, N. Y	Jan. 8, 1867	61, 054
Coal-scuttle	J. L. Ellithorp and P. Sloan	Canajoharie, N. Y	May 25, 1869	90, 437
Coal-scuttle	E. Eltinge	Kingston, N. Y	Dec. 11, 1866	60, 349
Coal-scuttle	E. Eltinge	Kingston, N. Y	June 20, 1871	116, 036
Coal-scuttle	B. Fielding	Cincinnati, Ohio	July 4, 1871	116, 699
Coal-scuttle	G. H. and D. W. Hazelton	Philadelphia, Pa	Apr. 4, 1871	113, 429
Coal-scuttle	C. F. Henis	Cincinnati, Ohio	Nov. 27, 1866	60, 003
Coal-scuttle	C. Hodgetts	Williamsburgh, N. Y	May 31, 1870	103, 615
Coal-scuttle	W. Hoffmire	New York, N. Y	Aug. 13, 1872	130, 498
Coal-scuttle	J. Holden	Philadelphia, Pa	Aug. 14, 1866	57, 137
Coal-scuttle	G. Howland	Brunswick, N. Y	Feb. 4, 1873	135, 554
Coal-scuttle	J. W. Jarboe	Brooklyn, E. D., N. Y	May 4, 1869	89, 771
Coal-scuttle	T. T. Markland, jr	Philadelphia, Pa	Nov. 1, 1864	44, 875
Coal-scuttle	E. Mather	Chicago, Ill	Sept. 12, 1871	118, 807
Coal-scuttle	W. Miller	New York, N. Y	Mar. 10, 1863	37, 871
Coal-scuttle	O. Morse	Rochester, N. Y	July 21, 1868	80, 203
Coal-scuttle	J. Myers, jr	New York, N. Y	July 29, 1856	15, 434
Coal-scuttle	J. T. Page	Rochester, N. Y	Dec. 22, 1868	85, 240
Coal-scuttle	J. C. Parrish	Petersburgh, Va	May 2, 1871	114, 335
Coal-scuttle	J. Pfeifer	Philadelphia, Pa	Jan. 22, 1867	61, 356
Coal-scuttle	J. Pfeifer	Philadelphia, Pa	June 13, 1871	115, 888
Coal-scuttle	H. S. Pratt	Hartford, Conn	Nov. 14, 1865	50, 953
Coal-scuttle	H. S. Reynolds	New York, N. Y	June 28, 1870	104, 885
Coal-scuttle	M. Saulson	Troy, N. Y	July 13, 1869	92, 546
Coal-scuttle	T. and J. M. Scantlin	Evansville, Ind	July 7, 1868	79, 692
Coal-scuttle	S. B. Sexton	Baltimore, Md	Jan. 31, 1865	46, 148
Coal-scuttle	D. Smith	Albany, N. Y	Dec. 10, 1872	133, 806
Coal-scuttle	G. Smith	Brooklyn, N. Y	July 31, 1866	56, 812
Coal-scuttle	G. Smith	Williamsburgh, N. Y	Feb. 27, 1872	124, 093
Coal-scuttle	G. D. Smith	Washington, D. C	Apr. 16, 1867	63, 953
Coal-scuttle	T. Smith	Cincinnati, Ohio	Oct. 31, 1865	50, 744
Coal-scuttle	A. S. Thompson	Little Falls, Minn	Sept. 30, 1873	143, 311
Coal-scuttle	J. G. Treadwell	Albany, N. Y	Apr. 23, 1861	32, 158

Index of patents issued from the United States Patent Office from 1790 *to* 1873, *inclusive*—Continued.

Invention.	Inventor.	Residence.	Date.	No.
Coal-scuttle	W. B. Treadwell	Albany, N. Y	Apr. 14, 1863	38, 188
Coal-scuttle	W. B. Treadwell	Albany, N. Y	Jan. 12, 1864	41, 244
Coal-scuttle	J. J. White	Norfolk, Va	Sept. 23, 1873	143, 208
Coal-scuttle	D. Wight	New London, Conn	Jan. 15, 1867	61, 295
Coal-scuttle	D. Wright and W. A. Kirby	Auburn, N. Y	Mar. 12, 1867	62, 915
Coal-scuttle and ash-screen, Combined	A. T. Carling and L. Rockwell	Ellenville, N. Y	Oct. 31, 1865	50, 685
Coal-scuttle and ash-sifter combined	C. McCleaver	Newark, N. J	Dec. 17, 1872	134, 081
Coal-scuttle and ash-sifter, Combined	A. McNeill	Washington, D. C	Apr. 20, 1858	20, 000
Coal-scuttle and ash-sifter, Combined	T. Parker	Philadelphia, Pa	Sept. 20, 1864	44, 336
Coal scuttle and sifter	C. L. W. Baker	Hartford, Conn	Aug. 7, 1866	56, 874
Coal scuttle and sifter	W. Hazlet and W. H. Flanigan	Philadelphia, Pa	May 3, 1870	102, 679
Coal-scuttle cover	I. Chase, jr	Boston, Mass	Jan. 8, 1856	14, 050
Coal-scuttles, Construction of	J. and J. Scott and W. Miller	Brooklyn, N. Y	Nov. 19, 1867	71, 226
Coal-separator	J. B. Wilford	Reading, Pa	Sept. 30, 1873	143, 395
Coal-shafts, Safety-cage for	D. Glover	Cass Township, Schuylkill County, Pa.	June 7, 1859	24, 296
Coal-shovel	J. F. Brewer	Plantsville, Conn	Feb. 22, 1870	100, 008
Coal-shovel	M. G. Fagan	Troy, N. Y	Aug. 24, 1869	94, 094
Coal-shovel	J. H. Farmer	Detroit, Mich	Aug. 8, 1871	117, 756
Coal-shovel handle	J. Pfeifer	Philadelphia, Pa	Sept. 4, 1866	57, 759
Coal-sifter	S. Longmaid	Lawrence, Mass	July 16, 1867	66, 718
Coal-sifter	H. Wells	Hartford, Conn	Dec. 31, 1839	1, 450
Coal-splitting machine	J. H. Lyon	Baltimore, Md	Feb. 23, 1858	19, 429
Coal-tar, Composition made from	F. M. Hillstream	Lawrence, Kans	May 31, 1870	103, 614
Coal-tar in iron-furnaces, Use of	I. G. Johnson	Spuyten Duyvil, N. Y	July 14, 1857	17, 791
Coal-tar to manufacture roofing, Process of treating	A. H. Perkins	Janesville, Wis	Oct. 7, 1862	36, 632
Coal-tar, Utilization of	R. S. Child	Philadelphia, Pa	July 9, 1861	32, 753
Coal-trap, Safety	T. W. Pratt	Boston, Mass	Oct. 10, 1865	50, 387
Coal, Treating acid tars from	G. Chevrier	Paris, France	Aug. 30, 1870	106, 915
Coal, Tub for handling	P. K. Dederick	Albany, N. Y	Aug. 20, 1872	130, 571
Coal washer and separator	A. Komp	New York, N. Y	June 18, 1867	65, 818
Coal-washing machine	J. P. Evans	Borough of Hazleton, Pa	Sept. 14, 1858	21, 559
Coal-washing machine	G. Lander	New York, N. Y	May 30, 1871	115, 486
Coat	P. Cohen	Saint Joseph, Mo	Sept. 24, 1867	69, 180
Coat	H. Kuhlman	Boston, Mass	May 14, 1872	126, 718
Coat and hat hook	G. F. J. Colburn	Newark, N. J	Nov. 1, 1864	44, 853
Coat and hat hook	J. Danner	Canton, Ohio	Mar. 6, 1866	52, 974
Coat and hat hook	N. and H. L. Judd	New Haven, Conn., and Brooklyn, N. Y.	May 10, 1870	102, 945
Coat and hat hook	J. B. Sargent	New Haven, Conn	Nov. 12, 1867	70, 749
Coat and hat hook	W. Schmitt	New York, N. Y	Sept. 17, 1867	69, 032
Coat and hat rack	J. M. Keep	New York, N. Y	Nov. 8, 1870	109, 017
Coat and hat rack	S. Macferran and S. Ustick	Philadelphia, Pa	Feb. 21, 1865	46, 528
Coat and hat rack, Folding	J. H. Monce	New York, N. Y	Sept. 6, 1870	107, 080
Coat drying and pressing apparatus	J. Braun	Rochester, N. Y	Dec. 22, 1868	85, 058
Coat-form	W. B. Olds	Meriden, Conn	Apr. 6, 1852	8, 858
Coat-hook and line-holder	W. A. Middleton	Harrisburgh, Pa	Mar. 23, 1869	88, 157
Coat-pattern, Adjustable	G. P. Sweezy	Riverhead, N. Y	Nov. 8, 1870	109, 076
Coat-rack	J. B. Lumsey	Sturgis, Mich	June 23, 1868	79, 259
Coat-sleeves, Device for closing the ends of	H. F. Herkner	New York, N. Y	May 31, 1870	103, 816
Coat sling or carrier	D. F. Drake	Somerville, Mass	Nov. 25, 1862	37, 029
Coat support	R. C. Kelly	West Meriden, Conn	Dec. 1, 1868	84, 495
Coat with inner sleeve	J. W. Moyer	Cherry Valley, N. Y	Jan. 24, 1865	46, 016
Coats and vests, Taking the form and measure of gentlemen to cut.	T. Vandoren, sr	Washington, D. C	Dec. 17, 1867	72, 432
Coats, Block for stretching	S. M. Perkins	Springfield, Pa	July 27, 1852	9, 154
Coats, Drafting out fore part of	A. Ward	Moyamensing, Pa	Sept. 28, 1837	415
Coats in one piece, Mode of cutting bodies of	W. M. Wiswell	Portland, Me	Apr. 10, 1839	1, 119
Coats, Instrument for drafting	S. Corley	Lexington, S. C	Dec. 29, 1857	18, 958
Coats, &c., Lock for	C. B. Trimble	New York, N. Y	Dec. 12, 1865	51, 524
Coating iron, &c., Composition for	F. J. Seybold	Chicago, Ill	Feb. 11, 1873	135, 668
Coating metals	J. D. Grüneberg and S. H. Gilbert.	Spring Hill, N. J	Mar. 24, 1868	75, 898
Coating or electroplating iron, brass, copper, &c., with tin.	W. E. Tilley	Middlesex County, England	June 18, 1872	128, 081
Coating with tin and other metals, Apparatus for	E. H. Davies	Pittsburgh, Pa	July 9, 1872	128, 862
Coating wood and iron, Composition for	E. F. Prentiss	Philadelphia, Pa	Aug. 26, 1873	142, 117
Coating wood and other articles to render them acid-proof, Compound for.	R. Newell	Philadelphia, Pa	July 1, 1873	140, 530
Coating wood and other materials, Composition for	C. L. Robertson	Providence, R. I	Apr. 2, 1867	63, 428
Cob and feed mill	H. Ormsby and E. R. Sumner	Beloit, Wis	July 23, 1861	32, 914
Cob and grain mill	J. R. Marston	New York, N. Y	Apr. 19, 1859	23, 693
Cob and stalk cutter	T. B. Jones	Carlville, Ala	Oct. 11, 1853	10, 110
Cock	C. M. Alburger	Philadelphia, Pa	May 21, 1867	64, 851
Cock	A. S. Davendorf	Galesburgh, Ill	July 8, 1873	140, 685
Cock	J. W. Faxon	Boston, Mass	Oct. 14, 1873	143, 683
Cock	J. P. Gallagher	Saint Louis, Mo	July 11, 1865	48, 673
Cock	W. H. Hedges and M. E. Campfield.	Newark, N. J	Jan. 24, 1871	111, 205
Cock	E. Hubball	Baltimore, Md	Oct. 4, 1820	....
Cock	N. Jenkins	Boston, Mass	Apr. 18, 1865	47, 309
Cock	H. Jones	Philadelphia, Pa	Feb. 27, 1872	124, 096
Cock	J. J. Lowry	Pittsburgh, Pa	Jan. 5, 1864	41, 077
Cock	S. Norton	Stockport, Great Britain	May 23, 1871	115, 091
Cock	M. T. F. O'Donnell	Boston, Mass	Sept. 24, 1872	131, 556
Cock	B. Pickering	Dayton, Ohio	July 24, 1860	29, 309
Cock	J. Powell	Cincinnati, Ohio	Dec. 5, 1865	51, 349
Cock	T. Prosser	Brooklyn, E. D., N. Y	Feb. 27, 1872	124, 082
Cock	J. Regester	Baltimore, Md	July 11, 1865	48, 721
Cock	J. Regester	Baltimore, Md	July 18, 1871	117, 112
Cock	H. S. Ross	Chicago, Ill	Nov. 19, 1872	133, 120
Cock	H. S. Ross	Chicago, Ill	Aug. 26, 1873	142, 122
Cock	D. H. Stickney	Cincinnati, Ohio	Oct. 18, 1859	25, 853
Cock	H. Strater, jr	Boston, Mass	July 16, 1872	129, 616
Cock	T. H. Thayer	New Haven, Conn	Aug. 2, 1870	106, 093
Cock	J. W. Trafton	Springfield, Mass	Aug. 9, 1870	106, 237
Cock, Air-cushion stop	D. A. Robinson	Washington, D. C	Aug. 6, 1872	130, 243
Cock, Ale or beer	H. Getty	Hoboken, N. J	Mar. 14, 1871	112, 701

Index of patents issued from the United States Patent Office from 1790 *to* 1873, *inclusive*—Continued.

Invention.	Inventor.	Residence.	Date.	No.
Cock and alarm-whistle, Gage	A. Miller	Cleveland, Ohio	June 29, 1858	20,726
Cock and case for pipes leading from street-mains, Stop.	J. G. Weldon	Pittsburgh, Pa	June 7, 1864	43,056
Cock and check-valve, Combined stop	A. T. Waldron	Waterford, N. Y	May 13, 1873	138,963
Cock and faucet, Valve	A. Crossley	Philadelphia, Pa	Apr. 16, 1872	125,792
Cock and filter in combination, Stop	A. and H. Johnson	New York, N. Y	Nov. 27, 1849	6,910
Cock and fixed socket, Combined removable	C. Sullivan	Boston, Mass	Feb. 7, 1871	111,699
Cock and swinging joint, Gas	C. F. Thieme	Philadelphia, Pa	Nov. 25, 1856	16,129
Cock, Angle valve	J. H. Davis	Allegheny City, Pa	Feb. 8, 1870	99,650
Cock, Anti-concussion water	M. W. Bailey	Pottstown, Pa	Feb. 13, 1872	123,606
Cock, Automatic gas	C. MacRae	New York, N. Y	July 10, 1866	56,240
Cock, Automatic lubricating water and gas	E. F. Brooks	Baltimore, Md	Nov. 18, 1873	144,735
Cock, Barreling	A., J., and T. McKenna	Pittsburgh, Pa	Jan. 8, 1867	61,015
Cock, Basin	A. Crossley	Philadelphia, Pa	Sept. 24, 1872	131,601
Cock, Basin	A. D. Davis	Chicago, Ill	Aug. 20, 1872	130,570
Cock, Basin	C. Harrison	New York, N. Y	Apr. 8, 1856	14,628
Cock, Basin	R. Leitch	Baltimore, Md	Mar. 3, 1857	16,736
Cock, Basin	C. A. Newton	Providence, R. I	Dec. 20, 1870	110,387
Cock, Basin	G. W. Randall	Boston, Mass	May 10, 1859	23,989
Cock, Basin stop	H. Eling	New York, N. Y	Aug. 21, 1855	13,457
Cock, Bib	J. H. Davis	Allegheny City, Pa	Feb. 8, 1870	99,649
Cock, Block-tin stop	J. Morris	New Haven, Conn	Mar. 7, 1816	....
Cock, Boiler gage	J. French	Newport, Ky	Aug. 20, 1867	67,866
Cock, Boiler gage	W. T. Howard	Baltimore, Md	Oct. 2, 1866	58,546
Cock, Boiler gage	J. G. Raymond	Rondout, N. Y	Oct. 8, 1867	69,702
Cock, Bottle	L. A. Perrault	Natchez, Miss	Mar. 1, 1870	100,321
Cock box for water and gas mains, Stop	O. F. Woodford	Chicago, Ill	Aug. 10, 1869	93,657
Cock boxes, Top of gas and water stop	W. W. Pullis	Saint Louis, Mo	Nov. 8, 1870	109,049
Cock boxing, Stop	W. H. Graham	Saint Louis, Mo	Oct. 28, 1873	143,978
Cock case, Stop	J. G. Weldon	Pittsburgh, Pa	Nov. 1, 1864	44,904
Cock, Cast-iron valve	J. H. Davis	Allegheny City, Pa	Feb. 8, 1870	99,653
Cock, Check-valve	J. H. Davis	Allegheny City, Pa	Feb. 8, 1870	99,652
Cock, Compression	E. Allt	New York, N. Y	July 1, 1873	140,337
Cock, Compression	O. N. Ames	Haydenville, Mass	Aug. 29, 1871	118,505
Cock, Compression	H. J. Bailey and J. Porteous	Pittsburgh, Pa	Dec. 3, 1872	133,558
Cock, Compression	G. E. Boisselier	Saint Louis, Mo	Dec. 8, 1868	84,792
Cock, Compression	W. Dinnen	Detroit, Mich	Apr. 4, 1871	113,503
Cock, Compression	C. A. Howard	New Haven, Conn	June 9, 1868	78,804
Cock, Compression	J. Maclaren	Scranton, Pa	Mar. 19, 1872	124,840
Cock, Compression	A. Pearce	Cambridgeport, Mass	Dec. 17, 1872	134,095
Cock, Compression	C. Perkes	Philadelphia, Pa	Oct. 19, 1869	96,033
Cock, Confluent	J. H. G. Hawes	Newark, N. J	May 24, 1870	103,329
Cock, Conical stop	J. E. Jones	Tidioute, Pa	Mar. 26, 1872	124,959
Cock connection, Locked plug	J. B. Edson	Brooklyn, N. Y	Jan. 9, 1872	122,517
Cock, Cut-off stop	W. H. Pollard	Seneca Falls, N. Y	July 30, 1867	67,214
Cock, Cylinder	D. B. Dennison	Ottumwa, Iowa	Feb. 25, 1873	136,221
Cock, Cylinder	M. B. Mason and J. S. McCrum	Kansas City, Mo	Oct. 17, 1871	120,080
Cock, Cylinder	J. Porteous	Cincinnati, Ohio	June 27, 1871	116,485
Cock, Diaphragm stop	W. E. Banta	Springfield, Ohio	Oct. 4, 1870	107,852
Cock, Draft	W. H. Bate	East Somerville, Mass	Dec. 20, 1870	110,334
Cock, Draft	W. P. Clark	Medford, Mass	Dec. 12, 1871	121,754
Cock, Draft	A. J. Morse	Boston, Mass	June 22, 1869	91,763
Cock, Drop-handle urn	H. and E. L. Bailey	Brooklyn, N. Y., and Philadelphia, Pa.	Aug. 14, 1866	57,246
Cock, Electric gas-stop	J. A. Heyl	Boston, Mass	Oct. 16, 1866	58,943
Cock-eye	C. Boehmer, jr	Madison, Wis	Nov. 6, 1866	59,347
Cock-eye	J. Haggerty	East Springfield, Pa	Sept. 10, 1867	68,737
Cock, Filter stop	A. and H. Johnson	New York, N. Y	Nov. 14, 1848	5,926
Cock, Filtering	D. Bartlett, jr	Boston, Mass	Oct. 15, 1850	7,716
Cock, Filtering	L. P. Jenks and F. Draper	Boston and East Cambridge, Mass.	Nov. 2, 1858	21,964
Cock, Filtering	J. F. Ostrander	New York, N. Y	Apr. 4, 1846	4,440
Cock, Filtering	T. F. Wenman	New York, N. Y	Apr. 4, 1846	4,437
Cock, Filtering stop	S. H. Lewis	New York, N. Y	Jan. 26, 1847	4,939
Cock, Filtering stop	W. Read	New York, N. Y	Oct. 24, 1846	4,824
Cock for boilers, Gage	W. G. Thomas	Centralia, Pa	Jan. 21, 1868	73,672
Cock for carbureters, &c	S. Rust, jr	Cincinnati, Ohio	Nov. 29, 1870	109,671
Cock for controlling discharge through two pipes	J. and T. D. Richardson	New York, N. Y	Aug. 26, 1873	142,120
Cock for drawing beer	J. Moffet	New York, N. Y	Sept. 16, 1873	142,860
Cock for drawing liquids	E. Dickinson	Amherst, Mass	Dec. 17, 1823	....
Cock for drawing liquor	J. Bliss	New York, N. Y	Sept. 24, 1821	....
Cock for filling soda-bottles, Confluent	C. G. Ferron	New York, N. Y	July 16, 1872	129,016
Cock for filtering, Stop	R. E. House	New York, N. Y	June 27, 1846	4,593
Cock for flexible tubes, Compression	H. Fairbanks	Boston, Mass	Jan. 17, 1871	110,964
Cock for gas-burners	S. B. H. Vance	New York, N. Y	Mar. 31, 1868	76,277
Cock for gas-burners, Automatic stop	G. E. Smith	San Francisco, Cal	Dec. 15, 1868	84,914
Cock for hot water and steam, Stop	J. Sheriff	Pittsburgh, Pa	Jan. 16, 1849	6,032
Cock for hydrants, Stop	H. R. Dunham	New York, N. Y	Jan. 10, 1843	2,908
Cock for hydrants, Valve	S. Pfleger	Reading, Pa	May 31, 1870	103,773
Cock for hydrants, Valve	B. Stancliffe	Philadelphia, Pa	May 15, 1827	
Cock for hydraulic presses, Connecting stop	C. Wilson	New York, N. Y	Oct. 28, 1843	3,319
Cock for locomotives, &c., Cylinder	C. H. Hopkins	Lyndonville, Vt	Mar. 11, 1873	136,724
Cock for mains, Branch stop	R. A. Hill	Washington, D. C	May 25, 1869	90,541
Cock for pumps, Blow-off	T. Shaw	Philadelphia, Pa	Aug. 19, 1862	36,238
Cock for racking off beer	F. Wagner	Danville, Pa	Aug. 4, 1868	80,787
Cock for soda-water and other liquids, Draft	J. D. O'Donnell	Washington, D. C	Oct. 21, 1873	143,777
Cock for soda-water and sirup	W. Gee	New York, N. Y	Apr. 22, 1873	138,143
Cock for soda-water apparatus, Draft	W. P. Clark	Boston, Mass	July 31, 1866	56,709
Cock for soda-water apparatus, Draft	L. D. Hoyt and R. Murray	Medford and Boston, Mass	June 27, 1865	48,489
Cock for steam-heaters, Air	S. J. Gold	New Haven, Conn	Feb. 26, 1856	14,312
Cock for steam-radiators, Automatic air	J. R. Nichols	Boston, Mass	July 16, 1872	129,291
Cock for water-pipes	W. Johnson	Philadelphia, Pa	Dec. 29, 1868	85,309
Cock, Gage	H. J. Bailey	Pittsburgh, Pa	Aug. 5, 1873	141,416
Cock, Gage	P. Ball	Worcester, Mass	Apr. 3, 1866	53,555
Cock, Gage	J. F. Bellemore and F. R. Fleer	Reading, Pa	July 22, 1873	141,104
Cock, Gage	J. Broughton	New York, N. Y	Sept. 12, 1865	51,418
Cock, Gage	J. B. Christoffel	Williamsburgh, N. Y	Mar. 22, 1870	100,981
Cock, Gage	W. H. Downing	Shamburgh, Pa	June 4, 1872	127,468

Index of patents issued from the United States Patent Office from 1790 *to* 1873, *inclusive*—Continued.

Invention.	Inventor.	Residence.	Date.	No.
Cock, Gage	C. L. Frink	Rockville, Conn	June 19, 1866	55, 640
Cock, Gage	A. Fuller	Brooklyn, N. Y	July 9, 1867	66, 579
Cock, Gage	H. Hise	Ottawa, Ill	Jan. 6, 1863	37, 292
Cock, Gage	L. T. Hulbert	Painesville, Ohio	Jan. 16, 1872	122, 766
Cock, Gage	B. E. Lehnan and R. Ross	Bethlehem, Pa	June 6, 1871	115, 746
Cock, Gage	P. McGrath	Plattsburgh, N. Y	Aug. 8, 1871	117, 907
Cock, Gage	R. L. Mills	Lancaster, Pa	Nov. 30, 1858	22, 189
Cock, Gage	A. A. Murray	Baltimore, Md	Nov. 21, 1873	143, 923
Cock, Gage	N. Ray	Schenectady, N. Y	Dec. 17, 1872	134, 098
Cock, Gage	S. Shepherd	Nashua, N. H	Sept. 20, 1864	44, 347
Cock, Gage	L. F. Smith	Philadelphia, Pa	July 19, 1870	105, 503
Cock, Gage	F. Stebbins	Hinsdale, N. H	Aug. 11, 1868	81, 027
Cock, Gage	E. A. Walker	Nashville, Tenn	July 25, 1865	49, 016
Cock, Gage	G. L. Watson	Nesquehoning, Pa	Dec. 21, 1869	98, 132
Cock, Gage	C. T. Woodman	Boston, Mass	Nov. 28, 1865	51, 274
Cock, Gage	J. E. Wootten	Philadelphia, Pa	Mar. 1, 1859	23, 136
Cock, Gas	P. Keller	New York, N. Y	Jan. 21, 1868	73, 534
Cock, Gas	J. G. Leffingwell	Newark, N. J	Feb. 19, 1861	31, 465
Cock, Gas	C. B. Littlefield	Boston, Mass	Oct. 8, 1867	69, 566
Cock, Gas	E. M. Morris	Baltimore, Md	Dec. 9, 1873	145, 442
Cock, Gas	M. Stratton	Philadelphia, Pa	Mar. 2, 1869	87, 522
Cock, Gas	J. C. Wightman	Boston, Mass	July 9, 1861	32, 804
Cock, Gas stop	J. Humphrey	Boston, Mass	July 22, 1866	15, 376
Cock, Globe	J. Powell	Cincinnati, Ohio	May 2, 1865	47, 565
Cock, Globe	J. Worcester	Newport, Ky	June 19, 1866	55, 756
Cock, Globe-valve	J. H. Davis	Allegheny City, Pa	Feb. 8, 1870	99, 651
Cock, Globe-valve	F. Lunkenheimer	Cincinnati, Ohio	Mar. 7, 1865	46, 685
Cock, Grease	R. M. Wade	Wadesville, Va	June 8, 1852	9, 010
Cock handle, Boiler gage	E. H. Ashcroft	Lynn, Mass	Jan. 1, 1867	60, 817
Cock, Hopper	P. Regitz	Chicago, Ill	June 15, 1869	91, 483
Cock, Hydrant	E. Hubball	Baltimore, Md	May 11, 1841	2, 086
Cock, Hydrant stop	H. L. Frailey	Lancaster, Pa	Apr. 3, 1866	53, 736
Cock, Hydrant stop	L. Magers, F. Davis, and W. Dukehart.	Baltimore, Md	June 22, 1842	2, 683
Cock, Hydrant waste	G. W. Robertson	Philadelphia, Pa	Jan. 10, 1860	26, 785
Cock key, Hydrant	P. H. Griffin	Albany, N. Y	Oct. 6, 1868	82, 827
Cock, Lock	H. Essex	Meadville, Pa	Apr. 16, 1872	125, 799
Cock, Lock stop	J. E. Jones	Tidioute, Pa	Feb. 21, 1871	111, 943
Cock, Locked	H. Essex	Meadville, Pa	Mar. 21, 1871	112, 910
Cock, Locking stop	E. Davis and J. M. Stiles	Camden, N. J	Mar. 14, 1871	112, 693
Cock lubricator, Gas	C. H. Johnson	Boston, Mass	Mar. 10, 1857	16, 820
Cock, Making stop	G. Fenn	New York, N. Y	July 12, 1823	....
Cock, Metallic screw	J. Garey	Baltimore, Md	Apr. 23, 1822	....
Cock, Oil	J. Hare, jr	Paterson, N. J	Apr. 17, 1860	27, 902
Cock or faucet	C. Harrison	New York, N. Y	Sept. 8, 1868	91, 900
Cock or lock for the passage of fluids	J. Witherle	Boston, Mass	Jan. 16, 1811	....
Cock or outlet-valve, Waste	S. J. Olsson	Chicago, Ill	Oct. 28, 1873	143, 995
Cock, Pull	G. Leach	New York, N. Y	June 5, 1860	28, 588
Cock, Pull	H. Strater, jr	Boston, Mass	July 16, 1872	129, 069
Cock, Racking	A. Roos	New York, N. Y	Nov. 11, 1873	144, 565
Cock, Regulating	C. E. Seal	Winchester, Va	Sept. 2, 1873	142, 521
Cock, Rotating stop	D. Hurd	Chicago, Ill	May 2, 1865	47, 546
Cock, Safety	J. Stowell	Charlestown, Mass	Aug. 6, 1867	67, 460
Cock, Screen stem-valve	S. D. Fales	Smithfield, R. I	Apr. 4, 1865	47, 097
Cock, Self-acting basin	S. C. Wentworth	Haydenville, Mass	Nov. 19, 1872	133, 131
Cock, Self-boring stop	A. Weed	Boston, Mass	June 2, 1868	78, 499
Cock, Self-closing	J. E. Boyle	New York, N. Y	July 16, 1872	128, 998
Cock, Self-closing	M. S. Clark	New York, N. Y	Aug. 12, 1873	141, 630
Cock, Self-closing	W. Dalziel	New York, N. Y	Feb. 7, 1871	111, 518
Cock, Self-closing	N. Jenkins	Boston, Mass	June 27, 1865	48, 407
Cock, Self-closing	J. M. Meharg	Montreal, Canada	Aug. 8, 1871	117, 908
Cock, Self-closing auger stop	A. Weed	Boston, Mass	Mar. 8, 1870	100, 697
Cock, Self-closing stop	J. Pigot	Brooklyn, N. Y	May 6, 1873	138, 580
Cock, Self-lubricating stop	G. Parker	Boston Highlands, Mass	Sept. 3, 1872	131, 065
Cock, Spring valve	M. C. Hawkins, J. W. Goodwin, and J. Cummings.	Erie, Pa	Dec. 15, 1857	18, 847
Cock, Steam	A. Fuller	Cincinnati, Ohio	Aug. 31, 1858	21, 332
Cock, Steam	A. Hallowell	Lowell, Mass	May 28, 1867	65, 075
Cock, Steam	A. Hallowell and H. R. Barker	Lowell, Mass	Nov. 28, 1865	51, 177
Cock, Steam	W. Johnson and M. Silmser	Auburn, N. Y	July 19, 1859	24, 808
Cock, Steam	R. Ross and W. Holland	Philadelphia, Pa	Aug. 24, 1858	21, 276
Cock, Steam	T. Sanford	Claremont, N. H	May 14, 1861	32, 314
Cock, Steam	J. B. Sargent and F. W. Towne	Fitchburgh, Mass	June 27, 1865	48, 452
Cock, Steam	A. Swardkins	South Boston, Mass	Apr. 30, 1861	32, 212
Cock, Steam	A. Tyler and G. F. Kendall	Fitchburgh, Mass	Aug. 29, 1865	49, 666
Cock, Steam	J. L. Winslow	Westbrook, Me	Aug. 17, 1858	21, 237
Cock, Steam and liquid stop	J. Breeden	Birmingham, England	Apr. 19, 1870	101, 977
Cock, Steam-boiler alarm gage	H. Wilkins	Brownsville, Pa	Apr. 19, 1864	42, 425
Cock, Steam-boiler gage	F. W. Bacon	West Newton, Mass	July 5, 1859	24, 692
Cock, Steam-boiler gage	J. Holdcraft	Philadelphia, Pa	Mar. 6, 1866	53, 079
Cock, Steam-boiler gage	W. Painter	Baltimore, Md	Jan. 16, 1872	122, 847
Cock, Steam-boiler gage	J. H. Vreeland and C. H. Lathrop.	Rutherford Park and Jersey City, N. J.	Oct. 1, 1872	131, 799
Cock, Steam-boiler try	J. F. Cook	Baltimore, Md	Sept. 20, 1859	25, 544
Cock, Steam-boiler try	J. Cumming	Boston, Mass	Oct. 18, 1859	25, 810
Cock, Steam-gage	E. H. Ashcroft	Lynn, Mass	Aug. 6, 1867	67, 479
Cock, Steam-gage	A. Bisbee	Chelsea, Mass	Sept. 18, 1855	13, 563
Cock, Steam-gage	S. Blackman	Reading, Pa	Dec. 7, 1869	97, 595
Cock, Steam-gage	J. Broughton	New York, N. Y	Feb. 13, 1866	52, 521
Cock, Steam-gage	T. B. Dexter	Lynn, Mass	Oct. 15, 1867	69, 782
Cock, Steam-gage	V. Giroud	New York, N. Y	Aug. 29, 1865	49, 623
Cock, Steam-gage	F. Henke	Scranton, Pa	May 15, 1866	54, 722
Cock, Steam-gage	J. Sanders	East Boston, Mass	June 4, 1867	65, 511
Cock, Steam-gage	J. C. Schaefer	Philadelphia, Pa	Feb. 6, 1866	52, 452
Cock, Steam-gage	D. Williams and E. Joseph	Gallipolis, Ohio	June 7, 1870	104, 090
Cock, Steam, gas, and water stop	W. H. De Valin	Sacramento, Cal	Dec. 1, 1868	84, 617
Cock, Steam-generator gage	M. M. Robinson	Dongola, Ill	Mar. 20, 1866	53, 344
Cock, Steam-generator gage	T. Shaw	Philadelphia, Pa	May 21, 1867	65, 018
Cock, Steam-generator gage	J. Waters	Minneapolis, Minn	Mar. 16, 1869	87, 992

Index of patents issued from the United States Patent Office from 1790 *to* 1873, *inclusive*—Continued.

Invention.	Inventor.	Residence.	Date.	No.
Cock, Steam-generator try	J. Regester	Baltimore, Md	Mar. 20, 1866	53, 337
Cock, Steam-radiator	S. J. Gold	New Haven, Conn	Mar. 25, 1856	14, 500
Cock, Steam, water, &c	W. Thomas	New York, N. Y	Mar. 25, 1856	14, 526
Cock, Stop	H. Allen	New York, N. Y	Nov. 12, 1841	2, 351
Cock, Stop	G. C. Bailey	Pittsburgh, Pa	June 4, 1872	127, 547
Cock, Stop	J. W. Birkett	Brooklyn, N. Y	Sept. 16, 1873	142, 763
Cock, Stop	J. Breeden	Birmingham, England	Feb. 22, 1870	100, 113
Cock, Stop	H. A. Chapin	Springfield, Mass	Aug. 21, 1860	29, 744
Cock, Stop	J. C. Chapman	Cambridgeport, Mass	Sept. 7, 1869	94, 563
Cock, Stop	T. C. Clarke	Philadelphia, Pa	Mar. 14, 1846	4, 419
Cock, Stop	D. N. B. Coffin, jr	Lynn, Mass	Jan. 9, 1855	12, 195
Cock, Stop	Z. E. Coffin	Boston, Mass	Apr. 30, 1867	64, 198
Cock, Stop	W. S. Cooper	Philadelphia, Pa	June 24, 1873	140, 248
Cock, Stop	G. Cuppers	New York, N. Y	Sept. 13, 1864	44, 164
Cock, Stop	T. Daniels	Toledo, Ohio	Feb. 14, 1860	27, 112
Cock, Stop	A. Davis	Boston, Mass	Oct. 16, 1839	1, 371
Cock, Stop	W. H. De Valin	Sacramento, Cal	May 1, 1866	54, 305
Cock, Stop	J. Doering	Philadelphia, Pa	Jan. 7, 1868	72, 986
Cock, Stop	G. W. Eddy	Waterford, N. Y	June 3, 1873	139, 559
Cock, Stop	G. D. Hadley	Cincinnati, Ohio	July 2, 1867	66, 326
Cock, Stop	C. F. Johnson and J. J. Speed, jr	Oswego and Ithaca, N. Y	June 21, 1839	1, 181
Cock, Stop	M. C. Kilgore	Washington, Iowa	Apr. 3, 1866	53, 627
Cock, Stop	H. P. Kreiner	Berlin, Prussia	Jan. 19, 1869	86, 020
Cock, Stop	C. W. Laurie	Philadelphia, Pa	Sept. 23, 1873	143, 167
Cock, Stop	B. E. Lehman	Bethlehem, Pa	Oct. 16, 1866	58, 845
Cock, Stop	J. Maclaren	Scranton, Pa	Jan. 23, 1872	123, 031
Cock, Stop	P. E. Malmström and P. Dummer.	New York, N. Y	July 25, 1871	117, 438
Cock, Stop	J. P. Mern	New York, N. Y	Mar. 25, 1873	137, 144
Cock, Stop	F. J. Miller	New York, N. Y	Nov. 21, 1843	3, 344
Cock, Stop	H. C. Montgomery	Boston, Mass	Oct. 15, 1872	132, 308
Cock, Stop	J. Morris	New Haven, Conn	Mar. 1, 1815	....
Cock, Stop	J. Morris	New Haven, Conn	May 15, 1822	....
Cock, Stop	H. Müller	Vienna, Austria	Oct. 24, 1871	120, 311
Cock, Stop	R. Nicoll	New York, N. Y	June 5, 1860	28, 596
Cock, Stop	C. C. Parsons	Boston, Mass	June 19, 1866	55, 700
Cock, Stop	O. C. Phelps	Boston, Mass	Mar. 14, 1854	10, 640
Cock, Stop	J. Radston	San Francisco, Cal	Nov. 7, 1871	120, 668
Cock, Stop	J. Regester	Baltimore, Md	Sept. 15, 1868	82, 161
Cock, Stop	J. Regester and W. H. Bowen	Baltimore, Md	Sept. 2, 1873	142, 350
Cock, Stop	J. Ridgway	New York, N. Y	Apr. 16, 1842	2, 563
Cock, Stop	F. Roach	Boston, Mass	June 19, 1866	55, 784
Cock, Stop	J. Robertson	New York, N. Y	May 8, 1840	1, 583
Cock, Stop	L. C. Rodier and F. G. Bates	Springfield, Mass	Nov. 18, 1873	144, 700
Cock, Stop	C. Schultz and T. Warker	New York, N. Y	Mar. 31, 1868	76, 106
Cock, Stop	J. Seeberger	Troy, N. Y	Feb. 8, 1870	99, 714
Cock, Stop	D. Sharman	Warren, N. Y	July 5, 1814	....
Cock, Stop	E. F. Spaulding	Cambridgeport, Mass	Aug. 5, 1873	141, 471
Cock, Stop	E. Stebbins	Chicopee, Mass	Apr. 19, 1859	23, 721
Cock, Stop	J. Stevens	New York, N. Y	Aug. 27, 1872	130, 876
Cock, Stop	H. Stratter, jr	Roxbury, Mass	June 26, 1866	55, 931
Cock, Stop	T. Stubblefield	Columbus, Ga	Apr. 26, 1859	23, 796
Cock, Stop	I. C. Tate	New London, Conn	June 14, 1859	24, 416
Cock, Stop	P. Walker	....	Apr. 10, 1800	....
Cock, Stop	U. West and G. Dobbs	New York, N. Y	Apr. 30, 1842	2, 596
Cock, Stop	A. W. Wilkinson	New York, N. Y	Feb. 6, 1872	123, 534
Cock, Stop	E. Wright	Boston, Mass	Oct. 4, 1853	10, 082
Cock, Stop and waste	W. Z. Hatcher	Philadelphia, Pa	Aug. 22, 1854	11, 550
Cock, Supply	W. S. Carr	New York, N. Y	Jan. 5, 1858	19, 013
Cock, Supply and waste	W. S. Cooper	Philadelphia, Pa	Aug. 1, 1871	117, 606
Cock, Swing compression basin	W. Gordon	Philadelphia, Pa	May 28, 1872	127, 340
Cock, Tap	C. Renard, M. Perret, and J. C. Voituret.	Mâcon, France	Nov. 9, 1869	96, 618
Cock, Three-way	F. S. Pease	Buffalo, N. Y	June 27, 1865	48, 430
Cock to prevent water freezing in pent-stocks, &c	D. Lathrop, jr	Norwich, Conn	Dec. 5, 1832	....
Cock, Two-way	D. F. Dodge	Lowville, N. Y	Nov. 30, 1869	97, 366
Cock, Two-way stop	R. Leitch	Baltimore, Md	Aug. 19, 1862	36, 222
Cock, Valve	S. Adams	Boston, Mass	May 25, 1858	20, 314
Cock, Valve	R. Berryman	Boston, Mass	Dec. 6, 1870	109, 796
Cock, Valve	W. Chesley	Cincinnati, Ohio	Jan. 31, 1865	46, 077
Cock, Valve	J. Cluley and B. Stancliff	Philadelphia, Pa	Nov. 8, 1820	....
Cock, Valve	W. S. Cooper	Philadelphia, Pa	Mar. 10, 1868	75, 376
Cock, Valve	B. Eakins	Spring Garden, Pa	Apr. 4, 1854	10, 733
Cock, Valve	J. B. Gibson	Cincinnati, Ohio	July 21, 1868	80, 066
Cock, Valve	J. Griffiths	Philadelphia, Pa	Feb. 14, 1854	10, 516
Cock, Valve	N. Jenkins	Boston, Mass	Aug. 1, 1865	49, 116
Cock, Valve	J. C. Macdonald	Cincinnati, Ohio	Sept. 14, 1858	21, 510
Cock, Valve	J. C. Macdonald	Saint Louis, Mo	Sept. 27, 1870	107, 697
Cock, Valve	R. Nickerson and A. B. Cotton	Athens, Ga	May 8, 1860	28, 192
Cock, Valve	T. Ramsden and H. M. Davis	Allegheny City and Pittsburgh, Pa	July 20, 1869	92, 748
Cock, Valve	J. R. and H. S. Robinson	Clinton, Mass	Aug. 31, 1858	21, 366
Cock, Valve	R. P. Ross	Bethlehem, Pa	July 2, 1872	128, 663
Cock, Valve	P. C. Rowe	Boston, Mass	Mar. 26, 1872	125, 086
Cock, Valve	F. D. Sanno	Philadelphia, Pa	June 29, 1821	....
Cock, Valve	C. R. Vaillant	Whistler, Ala	Jan. 4, 1870	98, 646
Cock, Valve	J. Walsh	Philadelphia, Pa	Jan. 30, 1872	123, 311
Cock, Valve	J. Walsh	Philadelphia, Pa	Aug. 12, 1873	141, 839
Cock, Valve	J. Wilson	Philadelphia, Pa	Mar. 1, 1870	100, 481
Cock, Water	J. Gregg	Manchester, N. H	Apr. 20, 1869	89, 143
Cock, Water	P. A. Mayor	New York, N. Y	July 16, 1872	129, 485
Cock, Water	H. S. North and T. Thompson	Middletown, Conn	May 11, 1869	90, 015
Cock, Water	G. Youle	....	Aug. 25, 1803	....
Cock, Water and air	J. L. Chapman	Baltimore, Md	Oct. 14, 1841	2, 304
Cock, Water-basin	H. W. Smith	Hartford, Conn	Mar. 8, 1859	23, 198
Cock, Water-basin	H. W. Smith	Hartford, Conn	Apr. 12, 1859	23, 619
Cock, Water-closet	J. Broughton	New York, N. Y	Oct. 25, 1864	44, 783
Cock, Water-closet	H. H. Craigie	New York, N. Y	May 11, 1869	89, 856

Index of patents issued from the United States Patent Office from 1790 *to* 1873, *inclusive*—Continued.

Invention.	Inventor.	Residence.	Date.	No.
Cock, Water-closet	H. Jones	Philadelphia, Pa	Jan. 4, 1870	98, 599
Cock, Water-closet	B. P. Shear	Charlestown, Mass	Sept. 19, 1871	119, 058
Cock, Water-closet	D. Wellington	Boston, Mass	Nov. 15, 1859	26, 145
Cock, Water-closet self-closing	C. Harrison	New York, N. Y	July 6, 1869	92, 190
Cock, Way	S. P. Mervine, jr	Philadelphia, Pa	June 18, 1872	128, 160
Cock, Weighted gage	W. H. McMillan	Philadelphia, Pa	Mar. 5, 1872	124, 214
Cock, Weighted gage	S. P. M. Tasker and W. H. McMillan.	Philadelphia, Pa	Mar. 25, 1873	137, 259
Cocks, Apparatus for automatically operating gas	S. Gardiner, jr	New York, N. Y	Aug. 15, 1871	118, 808
Cocks, Box for street stop	H. A. Moore and E. O. and S. C. Frink.	Indianapolis, Ind	Feb. 18, 1868	74, 573
Cocks by electro-magnetism, Turning gas	S. Gardiner, jr	New York, N. Y	June 19, 1866	55, 642
Cocks, Case for water and gas	G. McIlwain	Philadelphia, Pa	Oct. 29, 1861	33, 592
Cocks for hydrants, Constructing	J. Martin	Baltimore, Md	Feb. 10, 1841	1, 972
Cocks in pipes under hydrostatic pressure, Machine for tapping and inserting stop.	H. Allen	New York, N. Y	Nov. 21, 1843	3, 348
Cocks, Locking-case for stop	V. T. Hall	Brooklyn, N. Y	May 11, 1869	89, 930
Cocks, Locking-device for stop	V. T. Hall	Brooklyn, N. Y	May 11, 1869	89, 929
Cocks, Machine for dressing metal	H. Essex	Meadville, Pa	Nov. 11, 1873	144, 524
Cocks, Machine for finishing plugs of stop	J. W. Lyon	Brooklyn, N. Y	Mar. 6, 1860	27, 370
Cocks, Machine for forming guard or gas	J. W. Lyon	Brooklyn, N. Y	Feb. 21, 1860	27, 228
Cocks, Manufacture of	C. A. Creasey	Philadelphia, Pa	Apr. 29, 1842	2, 589
Cocks, Manufacture of stop	J. L. Lowry	Pittsburgh, Pa	Sept. 20, 1864	44, 326
Cocks, Method of governing the action of valve	F. H. Bartholomew	New York, N. Y	June 20, 1854	11, 113
Cocks, Method of operating stop	D. N. Dunzack	Salem, Mass	Jan. 31, 1860	26, 975
Cocks for steam-cylinders, Device for operating	W. H. Woods	San Francisco, Cal	Aug. 10, 1869	93, 509
Cocks or valves of water and gas pipes, Stop-box for	J. Smith	Saint Louis, Mo	Aug. 4, 1868	80, 776
Cocks, Plug for arresting flow of stop	J. H. Rhodes	Brooklyn, N. Y	July 16, 1872	129, 168
Cocks, Tool for making plugs for gas and water	W. Tweedle	Providence, R. I	Apr. 20, 1869	89, 184
Cocks, Valvular arrangement for basin	E. G. Burnham	Springfield, Mass	June 9, 1857	17, 539
Cocks with pipes, Connecting	D. A. Webster	New York, N. Y	June 29, 1852	9, 085
Cocks with safety-plugs, Apparatus or	P. A. Chambeaux	Paris, France	Dec. 30, 1873	146, 045
Cockle and garlic separator	J. W. Neal	Big Lick, Va	July 16, 1867	66, 872
Cockle and garlic separator	J. W. Neal and A. J. Truxell	Big Lick, Va	Oct. 20, 1868	83, 198
Cockle, &c., from wheat, Machine for separating	G. H. Rich	Geneva, Ill	Aug. 26, 1873	142, 119
Cockle-separating machine	F. W. Mace	Waukaw, Wis	June 29, 1869	92, 073
Cockle-separator	S. W. Andrews and L. Godfrey	Greeneville, Tenn	July 13, 1869	92, 559
Cocoa, Preparation of	P. Pearson	Leeds, Great Britain	Mar. 16, 1869	87, 965
Cocoa-nut cutter	D. Fitzgerald	New York, N. Y	Dec. 22, 1831	....
Cocoa-nut cutter and grater	J. Gardner	Philadelphia, Pa	Aug. 6, 1867	67, 529
Cocoa-nut, Desiccated	G. B. Williams	New York, N. Y	Nov. 17, 1868	84, 241
Cocoa-nuts for pies, &c., Preparing	N. A. Classon	Windham, Conn	Dec. 23, 1873	145, 722
Cocoa-nuts, Manufacture of desiccated	G. W. Waitt	Philadelphia, Pa	July 7, 1868	79, 790
Cocoa-nuts, Machine for granulating	T. and G. M. Mills	Philadelphia, Pa	June 10, 1873	139, 804
Cocoons, Construction of lodgements in cocooneries for attachment of the.	S. M. Jenkins	Easton, Md	Sept. 28, 1839	1, 347
Cocoonery for removing filth &c., from the hurdles	B. Benson	Smyrna, Del	Jan. 10, 1840	1, 468
Coffee and grain cleaner and separator	R. Frisby	Cleveland, Ohio	Sept. 5, 1871	118, 710
Coffee and other substances, Apparatus for making extracts and decoctions from.	L. Brauer	Washington, D. C	Dec. 1, 1868	84, 609
Coffee and spice mill	A. Clark	Berlin, Conn	July 20, 1832	....
Coffee and spice mill	E. Parker and H. White	Meriden, Conn	June 22, 1832	....
Coffee and spice mill	H. Petrie	Chicago, Ill	Sept. 21, 1869	95, 135
Coffee and spice mill	C. W. Pierce	Oak Hill, N. Y	Jan. 6, 1863	37, 378
Coffee and spice mill	A. Sizer	Cheshire, Conn	Dec. 22, 1831	....
Coffee and spice mill handle	J. Kinzer	Pittsburgh, Pa	May 15, 1866	54, 740
Coffee and tea drawer	J. O. Shriner	Newcastle, Ind	Sept. 12, 1865	49, 929
Coffee and tea maker	A. Bencini	Milton, N. C	Sept. 27, 1838	952
Coffee and tea pot	G. Heiss and M. Schmidt	Houston, Tex	June 15, 1869	91, 333
Coffee and tea pot	J. M. Ingraham	New York, N. Y	Mar. 30, 1858	19, 760
Coffee and tea pot	E. A. Kelsey	Meriden, Conn	July 23, 1861	32, 876
Coffee and tea pot	S. McGuffin	Rising Sun, Ind	May 5, 1868	77, 507
Coffee and tea pot	M. Simons	Middletown, Conn	May 11, 1868	90, 030
Coffee and tea pot	T. B. and J. Stout	Keyport, N. J	June 22, 1869	91, 787
Coffee and tea pot	R. Strickland	Albany, N. Y	Nov. 10, 1868	84, 018
Coffee and tea pot handle	W. Westlake	Chicago, Ill	Mar. 16, 1869	87, 809
Coffee and tea pot strainer	N. Ames	Saugus Centre, Mass	Sept. 17, 1861	33, 316
Coffee and tea pot strainer	W. Case	Waterloo, Iowa	July 30, 1861	32, 969
Coffee and tea pot strainer	M. Simons	Middletown, Conn	Mar. 5, 1867	62, 697
Coffee and tea steamer	C. G. Murch	Chicago, Ill	Oct. 13, 1868	82, 976
Coffee and tea steeper	J. B. Wakeman and A. M. Bush	Hancock, N. Y	June 7, 1870	103, 946
Coffee and water cup for soldiers	C. L. Barritt	New York, N. Y	Sept. 22, 1863	40, 017
Coffee, Apparatus and process for roasting	O. H. Taylor	Brooklyn, N. Y	Nov. 10, 1868	83, 889
Coffee, Apparatus and process for treating	J. Ashcroft	Brooklyn, N. Y	Apr. 18, 1871	113, 832
Coffee, Apparatus for maturing raw or green	J. Ashcroft	Brooklyn, N. Y	Oct. 31, 1871	120, 410
Coffee-berries, Machine for breaking	I. Adams	Boston, Mass	Jan. 13, 1835	....
Coffee-berries, Machine for breaking outer husks of	T. Ditson	Boston, Mass	Jan. 13, 1835	....
Coffee-boiler	E. B. Manning	Middletown, Conn	July 12, 1870	105, 347
Coffee boiler	C. H. Scholle	Cincinnati, Ohio	June 8, 1869	91, 170
Coffee-boiler	W. H. Stewart and J. H. Tilley	Orion, Wis	June 29, 1869	91, 879
Coffee-boiler	N. Waterman	Boston, Mass	Sept. 8, 1863	39, 851
Coffee-boiler	E. F. Woodward	Brooklyn, N. Y	Mar. 25, 1862	34, 801
Coffee-boiler, Alarm	E. K. Sargeant	Boonton, N. J	Sept. 26, 1865	50, 169
Coffee can and crusher	D. C. Colby	Washington, D. C	June 4, 1867	65, 474
Coffee, &c., cleaner	J. Johnson	New York, N. Y	Apr. 18, 1871	113, 890
Coffee-cleaner	S. G. Taylor	Baltimore, Md	Mar. 22, 1870	101, 180
Coffee cleaner and polisher	J. W. Brady	Catonsville, Md	July 27, 1869	93, 045
Coffee cleaner and polisher	J. H. Brookmire	Saint Louis, Mo	Dec. 6, 1870	109, 865
Coffee cleaner and polisher	J. H. Brookmire	Saint Louis, Mo	Oct. 15, 1872	132, 136
Coffee cleaner and polisher	H. C. Lockwood	Baltimore, Md	Jan. 25, 1870	99, 215
Coffee cleaner and polisher	W. Newell	Philadelphia, Pa	July 13, 1858	20, 891
Coffee cleaner, drier, and polisher	W. Nowell	Philadelphia, Pa	Sept. 18, 1860	30, 083
Coffee-cleaning machine	J. W. Brady	Catonsville, Md	Mar. 8, 1870	100, 492
Coffee-cleaning machine	J. W. Brady	Baltimore, Md	Mar. 8, 1870	100, 493
Coffee-cleaning machine	W. H. Elton	Baltimore, Md	May 3, 1870	102, 519
Coffee-cleaning machine	J. M. Moore	New York, N. Y	July 16, 1872	129, 359
Coffee, Compound for coating roasted	J. T. Cooke	Brooklyn, N. Y	Oct. 1, 1872	131, 852
Coffee, &c., cooler	J. Burns	New York, N. Y	Jan. 22, 1867	61, 393

Index of patents issued from the United States Patent Office from 1790 *to* 1873, *inclusive*—Continued.

Invention.	Inventor.	Residence.	Date.	No.
Coffee-cooler	D. G. Harrison and J. Reynolds	Cincinnati, Ohio	June 30, 1863	39, 098
Coffee-crushing machine	A. Schacht	Chicago, Ill	July 30, 1872	130, 078
Coffee for transportation, Mode of preparing	T. H. Berry	Lynn, Mass	Apr. 23, 1867	63, 987
Coffee-generator	C. Fobes	Whitewater, Wis	July 30, 1867	67, 185
Coffee, grain, &c., Process for cleaning	G. W. Hungerford	Chicago, Ill	Sept. 19, 1871	119, 149
Coffee-grinder	C. Krutz	Adrian, Mich	May 28, 1872	127, 249
Coffee, Grinding	T. Bruff, sr		Jan. 8, 1798	....
Coffee-grinding mill	L. S. Chichester	New York, N. Y	Oct. 9, 1860	30, 298
Coffee-grinding mill	J. Fitzgerald	New York, N. Y	June 25, 1845	4, 089
Coffee-grinding mill	L. R. Livingston and C. Adams	Pittsburgh, Pa	Sept. 25, 1840	1, 795
Coffee-grinding mill	H. Twiss	Meriden, Conn	June 19, 1837	243
Coffee-grinding mill	C. W. Van Vliet	Fishkill Landing, N. Y	Nov. 20, 1855	13, 837
Coffee-huller	A. Angell	Newburgh, N. Y	Nov. 13, 1866	59, 538
Coffee-huller	D. Lombard	Boston, Mass	Jan. 28, 1868	73, 819
Coffee-huller	N. Read	Belfast, Me	Sept. 10, 1822	....
Coffee-huller	T. T. Woodruff	Philadelphia, Pa	Nov. 5, 1872	132, 887
Coffee huller and polisher	C. De St. Charles	Jalapa, Mexico	Nov. 3, 1868	83, 609
Coffee hulling and scouring machine	R. P. Walker	New York, N. Y	Dec. 20, 1853	10, 328
Coffee-hulling machine	R. Abbey	New York, N. Y	Jan. 1, 1825	....
Coffee-hulling machine	R. Anderson	Brooklyn, N. Y	June 26, 1866	55, 947
Coffee, Machine for cleaning	W. H. Elton	Baltimore, Md	Apr. 27, 1869	89, 298
Coffee, Machine for scouring and polishing	W. Newell	Philadelphia, Pa	July 19, 1859	24, 817
Coffee, Machine for washing and cleaning	S. Thompson	Baltimore, Md	Oct. 18, 1870	108, 407
Coffee-maker	J. Denley and T. H. Heberling	Warsaw, Ill	Aug. 3, 1858	21, 066
Coffee-maker	F. Liesche	East New York, N. Y	June 12, 1866	55, 509
Coffee-maker	J. V. Meigs	Washington, D. C	May 22, 1866	54, 933
Coffee-maker	J. Petsch and S. N. Buynitzky	Hanover, Prussia, and St. Petersburg, Russia.	Feb. 25, 1868	74, 937
Coffee-maker	J. W. Thyng	Salem, Mass	Dec. 17, 1867	72, 429
Coffee-maker	N. Waterman	Suffolk County, Mass	Feb. 26, 1850	7, 129
Coffee-maker	H. A. Zopff	Milwaukee, Wis	Oct. 10, 1865	50, 412
Coffee-making vessel	A. Berney	Jersey City, N. J	Mar. 16, 1869	87, 903
Coffee, Manufacture of roasted	E. E. Rinehart	Pittsburgh, Pa	June 29, 1869	91, 870
Coffee, Method of cleaning and polishing	W. Newell	Philadelphia, Pa	Oct. 3, 1857	18, 552
Coffee-mill	J. R. Adams	New York, N. Y	Dec. 17, 1867	72, 259
Coffee-mill	W. H. Barnes	New London, Conn	Sept. 8, 1868	81, 869
Coffee-mill	C. H. Beatty	Wheeling, Va	June 27, 1854	11, 152
Coffee-mill	T. W. Brown	Boston, Mass	July 19, 1870	105, 545
Coffee-mill	J. Carrington	Wallingford, Conn	Apr. 3, 1829	....
Coffee-mill	N. Chapman	Hopedale, Mass	Oct. 16, 1866	58, 772
Coffee-mill	A. Clark	Berlin, Conn	Aug. 14, 1833	....
Coffee-mill	I. F. Colby	Washington, D. C	June 9, 1868	78, 648
Coffee-mill	C. R. Edwards	Niagara City, N. Y	Mar. 13, 1866	53, 129
Coffee-mill	R. B. Fitts	Philadelphia, Pa	Mar. 22, 1859	23, 290
Coffee-mill	S. C. Jantzen	Philadelphia, Pa	June 17, 1873	139, 960
Coffee-mill	J. G. Lane	Washington, N. Y	Oct. 16, 1866	58, 946
Coffee-mill	W. J. Lane	Washington, N. Y	Jan. 14, 1868	73, 347
Coffee-mill	A. Lepage	Woodhaven, N. Y	Oct. 24, 1871	120, 287
Coffee-mill	J. Luther	Warren, R. I	Aug. 11, 1843	3, 215
Coffee mill	J. C. Milligan	Brooklyn, N. Y	Aug. 2, 1870	105, 966
Coffee mill, &c	E. Morse and C. Putnam	Knoxville, Tenn	Sept. 9, 1835	....
Coffee-mill	C. and E. Parker	Meriden, Conn	May 5, 1868	77, 649
Coffee mill	E. Parker	Meriden, Conn	Oct. 29, 1861	33, 599
Coffee-mill	J. and E. Parker	Meriden, Conn	Feb. 7, 1860	27, 065
Coffee-mill	C. W. Peckham	New Haven, Conn	Apr. 13, 1836	....
Coffee-mill	F. Raymond	Woodhaven, N. Y	Feb. 14, 1871	111, 778
Coffee-mill	F. C. Richer	Gilmer, Tex	Aug. 16, 1870	106, 407
Coffee-mill	J. Rittenhouse	Germantown, Pa	July 2, 1839	1, 215
Coffee-mill	L. Schulz	Cincinnati, Ohio	June 10, 1873	139, 824
Coffee-mill	B. Smith	Cincinnati, Ohio	June 9, 1818	....
Coffee-mill	E. Watrous	Mystic River, Conn	July 28, 1868	80, 317
Coffee-mill	J. Watrous, jr	Mystic River, Conn	Aug. 6, 1867	76, 618
Coffee-mill and apple-parer	D. C. Warner	Chicago, Ill	Jan. 31, 1871	111, 466
Coffee-mill, Double	T. H. Witherby and J. Torrey	Millbury, Mass	July 17, 1832	....
Coffee-mill fastener	J. Winkler	Hudson City, N. J	Feb. 2, 1869	86, 484
Coffee-mill, Portable	S. H. Witmer	Cincinnati, Ohio	June 28, 1864	43, 374
Coffee-mill, Steel	I. Wilson	New London, Conn	Mar. 6, 1818	....
Coffee, Mode of extracting the strength from	L. Martelley	New York, N. Y	Sept. 30, 1825	....
Coffee or tea pot	E. B. Manning	Middletown, Conn	July 19, 1870	105, 584
Coffee-package	H. C. Lockwood	Baltimore, Md	Aug. 26, 1873	142, 248
Coffee, pepper, &c	D. Richmond	McArthurstown, Ohio	Oct. 14, 1835	....
Coffee-percolator	J. H. Nason	Franklin, Mass	Dec. 26, 1865	51, 741
Coffee-polisher	E. J. Codd	Baltimore, Md	July 12, 1870	105, 175
Coffee-polisher	J. T. Randall	Baltimore, Md	May 3, 1870	102, 591
Coffee polisher and cleaner	W. Newell	Philadelphia, Pa	Oct. 12, 1869	95, 827
Coffee, Polishing	J. T. Randall	Baltimore, Md	Mar. 14, 1871	112, 738
Coffee polishing and cleaning	W. and S. Thompson	New York, N. Y., and Baltimore, Md.	Jan. 31, 1871	111, 403
Coffee-polishing machine	J. Guardiola	Chocolá, Central America	July 30, 1872	129, 947
Coffee-polishing machine	C. C. Warren and J. B. Baldy	Toledo, Ohio	Dec. 6, 1870	109, 978
Coffee-pot	N. Agnew	Delaware, Canada	Feb. 7, 1871	111, 505
Coffee-pot	N. Barlow	New York, N. Y	Oct. 19, 1858	21, 808
Coffee-pot	J. Beaumont	Hartford, Conn	Nov. 6, 1869	30, 559
Coffee-pot	E. S. Behringer	Brooklyn, N. Y	July 30, 1872	129, 882
Coffee-pot	J. Blackie	New York, N. Y	May 7, 1867	64, 476
Coffee-pot	W. S. Blaisdell and E. Estabrook	Factory Point, Vt	Aug. 26, 1873	142, 195
Coffee-pot	E. Blunt, jr	New York, N. Y	Nov. 3, 1868	83, 686
Coffee-pot	E. Blunt, jr	New York, N. Y	Aug. 10, 1869	93, 587
Coffee pot	B. Bordman	Malden, Mass	July 14, 1868	79, 943
Coffee-pot	R. Brown and E. A. Blaisdell	Goffstown, N. H	Nov. 14, 1871	120, 936
Coffee-pot	S. I. S. Cawthon and A. F. Tatom	Troy, Ala	Nov. 14, 1871	120, 938
Coffee-pot	W. Chesterman	Centralia, Iowa	July 19, 1859	24, 795
Coffee-pot	W. Chesterman	Centralia, Iowa	Jan. 24, 1860	26, 889
Coffee-pot	H. J. Childs	New York, N. Y	Jan. 7, 1873	134, 514
Coffee-pot	H. J. Childs	New York, N. Y	Jan. 7, 1873	134, 515
Coffee-pot	H. J. Childs	New York, N. Y	Mar. 11, 1873	136, 703
Coffee-pot	E. H. Covell	New York, N. Y	Feb. 8, 1859	22, 876
Coffee-pot	J. Cragg	Baltimore, Md	Oct. 31, 1871	120, 417

Index of patents issued from the United States Patent Office from 1790 *to* 1873, *inclusive*—Continued.

Invention.	Inventor.	Residence.	Date.	No.
Coffee-pot	S. Crowell, jr	Palmyra, N. Y	Sept. 13, 1859	25, 391
Coffee-pot	J. Denley	Warsaw, Ill	July 24, 1860	29, 253
Coffee-pot	J. Dodge	New Orleans, La	Nov. 9, 1869	96, 558
Coffee-pot	J. Dodge	New Orleans, La	July 5, 1870	105, 051
Coffee-pot	J. G. Dyer	Chicago, Ill	June 16, 1868	78, 943
Coffee-pot	O. T. Eddy	Philadelphia, Pa	Sept. 20, 1859	25, 495
Coffee-pot	W. Edson	Boston, Mass	Oct. 2, 1866	58, 396
Coffee-pot	W. H. Elliot	Plattsburgh, N. Y	Jan. 25, 1859	22, 716
Coffee-pot	W. C. C. Erskine	Nether Kinnedder, Dunfermline, Scotland.	May 18, 1869	90, 159
Coffee-pot	G. K. Farrington	Xenia, Ohio	Jan. 24, 1860	26, 945
Coffee-pot	H. B. Fay	New York, N. Y	Oct. 25, 1859	25, 890
Coffee-pot	W. Funk and G. W. Fort	Warrensburgh, Mo	Aug. 23, 1870	106, 572
Coffee-pot	J. F. Fitch, B. G. Devoe, and R. W. B. McLellan.	Vandalia, Ill	Mar. 15, 1870	100, 880
Coffee-pot	D. G. Fletcher	Racine, Wis	May 31, 1859	24, 261
Coffee-pot	J. H. Treeto	Wheaton, Ill	Feb. 22, 1859	23, 021
Coffee-pot	D. S. French	Montgomery, Ala	Mar. 28, 1871	113, 156
Coffee-pot	H. P. Gatchell	Ravenna, Ohio	Nov. 22, 1859	26, 229
Coffee-pot	C. D. Goodrich	Ann Arbor, Mich	Jan. 30, 1872	123, 258
Coffee-pot	J. C. Gove	Cleveland, Ohio	Mar. 13, 1866	53, 139
Coffee-pot	B. Grigsby and T. C. Braselton	Princeton, Ind	Feb. 4, 1873	135, 544
Coffee-pot	J. E. Hall	Cleveland, Ohio	Sept. 25, 1855	13, 595
Coffee pot	N. D. Hartley and M. S. Morehouse.	Quincy, Ill	Apr. 22, 1862	35, 021
Coffee-pot	J. Heberling	Mount Pleasant, Ohio	May 30, 1871	115, 467
Coffee-pot	J. W. Hedenberg	Saint Louis, Mo	Jan. 4, 1859	22, 501
Coffee-pot	L. Hildenbrand	Michigan City, Ind	Dec. 6, 1870	109, 901
Coffee-pot	M. Hofman	San Francisco, Cal	Dec. 3, 1872	133, 582
Coffee-pot	G. Hotte	New York, N. Y	Feb. 1, 1870	99, 438
Coffee-pot	N. Hotz	Greenpoint, N. Y	Aug. 18, 1868	81, 169
Coffee-pot	E. H. Huch	Brunswick, Germany	Jan. 7, 1873	134, 603
Coffee-pot	W. N. Hutchinson	Bideford, England	Mar. 12, 1872	124, 579
Coffee-pot	P. H. Inman and C. B. Withington.	Janesville, Wis	Apr. 25, 1871	114, 012
Coffee-pot	G. Jones	Saugerties, N. Y	Apr. 16, 1867	63, 903
Coffee-pot	R. H. Kuper	Lockport, N. Y	Apr. 4, 1871	113, 674
Coffee-pot	R. H. Kuper	New York, N. Y	May 7, 1872	126, 555
Coffee-pot	J. L. Labiaux	Newark, N. J	Feb. 23, 1869	87, 179
Coffee-pot	N. Lawrence	Taunton, Mass	June 22, 1869	91, 754
Coffee-pot	J. H. Lee	Charlestown, Mass	Nov. 28, 1865	51, 198
Coffee-pot	J. H. Lee	Charlestown, Mass	Dec. 4, 1866	60, 204
Coffee-pot	J. E. Lewis	Kittery, Me	Aug. 3, 1869	93, 317
Coffee-pot	L. H. Little	Copake, N. Y	Mar. 21, 1865	46, 917
Coffee-pot	J. MacGregor, jr	Troy, N. Y	Apr. 11, 1854	10, 752
Coffee-pot	J. Magee	Lawrence, Mass	Mar. 6, 1860	27, 371
Coffee-pot	J. T. McNamee	Baltimore, Md	May 23, 1871	115, 080
Coffee-pot	S. Mento	Alliance, Ohio	Mar. 8, 1870	100, 544
Coffee-pot	C. A. Merchant and G. L. Patterson.	Frankfort, Ky	Feb. 1, 1859	22, 816
Coffee-pot	W. J. Miller	Middletown, Conn	Feb. 14, 1871	111, 861
Coffee-pot	E. Moneuse and L. Duparquet	New York, N. Y	July 27, 1869	92, 987
Coffee-pot	E. Moneuse and L. Duparquet	New York, N. Y	Oct. 5, 1869	95, 599
Coffee-pot	E. Moneuse and L. Duparquet	New York, N. Y	Oct. 12, 1869	95, 710
Coffee-pot	H. W. Mosher	Warren, Ill	Apr. 23, 1861	32, 141
Coffee-pot	E. B. Mudge	Yonkers, N. Y	Oct. 8, 1872	131, 965
Coffee-pot	J. Nason	New York, N. Y	Mar. 3, 1868	75, 045
Coffee-pot	G. Neilson	Boston, Mass	Oct. 25, 1859	25, 909
Coffee-pot	G. Neilson	Boston, Mass	July 24, 1860	29, 302
Coffee-pot	J. B. Parish	Cleveland, Ohio	Apr. 12, 1859	23, 603
Coffee-pot	J. W. Patterson	New York, N. Y	Nov. 21, 1871	121, 126
Coffee-pot	J. W. Patterson and J. S. Hill	Cincinnati, Ohio	Apr. 7, 1868	76, 514
Coffee-pot	P. Perry	Charlestown, Mass	Sept. 17, 1867	69, 017
Coffee-pot	E. Pincus and D. B. Emerick	Philadelphia, Pa	Nov. 21, 1865	51, 083
Coffee-pot	J. R. Remington	Lowndes County, Ala	Dec. 22, 1846	4, 904
Coffee-pot	D. T. Robinson	Boston, Mass	Jan. 8, 1867	61, 022
Coffee-pot	D. Rowland	Washington, D. C	Sept. 17, 1844	3, 749
Coffee-pot	F. I. Sage	Cromwell, Conn	July 18, 1871	117, 210
Coffee-pot	S. T. Savage	Greenbush, N. Y	June 15, 1869	91, 274
Coffee-pot	S. T. Savage	Brooklyn, N. Y	Apr. 5, 1870	101, 517
Coffee-pot	D. M. Skinner	Sandwich Centre, N. H	Jan. 5, 1869	85, 540
Coffee-pot	J. B. Smith	Milwaukee, Wis	Nov. 19, 1867	71, 236
Coffee-pot	J. B. Smith	Milwaukee, Wis	Nov. 19, 1867	71, 237
Coffee-pot	J. B. Smith	Milwaukee, Wis	Dec. 29, 1868	85, 339
Coffee-pot	J. B. Smith	Milwaukee, Wis	Mar. 12, 1872	124, 454
Coffee-pot	O. F. Stedman	Westfield, N. Y	Sept. 14, 1869	94, 787
Coffee-pot	D. Stewart	Annapolis, Md	Apr. 9, 1861	32, 011
Coffee-pot	J. F. Still	West Farms, N. Y	Nov. 8, 1870	109, 152
Coffee-pot	M. J. Stubbings	Youngstown, Ohio	Sept. 23, 1873	143, 102
Coffee-pot	J. H. Swing	Cleveland, Ohio	Apr. 25, 1865	47, 406
Coffee-pot	F. I. Tarlton	Baltimore, Md	Dec. 3, 1872	133, 681
Coffee-pot	H. Thal and G. Schlottmann	New Haven, Conn	Nov. 10, 1868	84, 020
Coffee-pot	H. Tilden	Boston, Mass	Jan. 8, 1867	61, 122
Coffee-pot	O. M. Tinkham	Pomfret, Vt	May 23, 1871	115, 134
Coffee-pot	H. Von Holten	Hoboken, N. J	Sept. 21, 1869	95, 056
Coffee-pot	C. B. Waite and J. W. Senner	Fredericksburgh, Va	Apr. 22, 1856	14, 748
Coffee-pot	J. C. Walker	Waco Village, Tex	Aug. 20, 1867	67, 932
Coffee-pot	A. B. Walters	Philadelphia, Pa	June 1, 1869	90, 707
Coffee-pot	S. V. Warner	Buffalo, N. Y	Oct. 19, 1869	95, 959
Coffee-pot	J. M. Webb	Somerville, Tenn	Feb. 26, 1856	14, 334
Coffee-pot	J. E. Weber and P. Knutson	La Crosse, Wis	Nov. 25, 1873	144, 936
Coffee-pot	W. Westlake	Chicago, Ill	Oct. 2, 1866	58, 518
Coffee-pot	J. P. Williams	Mobile, Ala	Mar. 29, 1870	101, 336
Coffee-pot	W. M. Williams	Saint Louis, Mo	Nov. 24, 1868	84, 456
Coffee-pot	P. B. Willoughby and H. G. Phelps.	Judd, Wis	July 27, 1869	93, 153
Coffee-pot	E. F. Woodward	Brooklyn, N. Y	June 4, 1867	65, 461
Coffee-pot	T. Yates	Dubuque, Iowa	June 19, 1860	28, 803

Index of patents issued from the United States Patent Office from 1790 to 1873, inclusive—Continued.

Invention.	Inventor.	Residence.	Date.	No.
Coffee-pot	I. Yeamans	Brooklyn, N. Y	June 22, 1869	91, 696
Coffee pot	H. Young	New York, N. Y	Jan. 3, 1865	45, 787
Coffee-pot	J. Zimmerman	Royalton Centre, N. Y	Dec. 17, 1867	72, 353
Coffee-pot attachment	M. De Graff	Chicago, Ill	Jan. 25, 1870	99, 068
Coffee-pot, boiler, digester, oven, and lamp	J. Montgomery	New York, N. Y	June 1, 1869	90, 676
Coffee-pot digester	W. L. Gilroy	Philadelphia, Pa	Nov. 23, 1869	97, 077
Coffee-pot holder	J. T. Words and E. H. Leseman	Toledo, Ohio	Nov. 28, 1871	121, 444
Coffee-pot, pitcher, &c	J. Gibson, jr	Albany, N. Y	Dec. 28, 1869	98, 244
Coffee-pot stand	O. Ferris	Pawling, N. Y	Oct. 31, 1871	120, 425
Coffee-pot strainer	G. A. Barron	Pembroke, Me	Dec. 27, 1870	110, 420
Coffee-pot strainer	C. L Gilpatric	Hyde Park, Mass	Feb. 22, 1870	100, 137
Coffee, Prepared	B. B. Lewis	Bristol, Conn	Mar. 2, 1869	87, 346
Coffee, Preparation for clarifying	C. L. Tucker	Chicago, Ill	May 2, 1871	114, 492
Coffee, Preparation of	T. Hyatt	Philadelphia, Pa	Mar. 13, 1866	53, 250
Coffee, Process for cleaning and polishing	C. C. Warren and J. B. Baldy	Toledo, Ohio	June 14, 1870	104, 363
Coffee, Process for polishing	G. W. Hungerford	Chicago, Ill	Sept. 19, 1871	119, 148
Coffee, Process for preparing	L. D. Gale	Washington, D. C	June 20, 1865	48, 268
Coffee, Process of cleaning	W. H. Butler	Chicago, Ill	Jan. 2, 1872	122, 306
Coffee, Process of cleaning and renovating	W. H. Butler	Chicago, Ill	June 18, 1872	127, 955
Coffee, Process of treating	J. W. Gillies	New York, N.Y	June 27, 1871	116, 299
Coffee, rice, &c., Pestle for hulling	J. Guardiola	Chocolá, Central America	Apr. 30, 1872	126, 900
Coffee, Roasted	J. Arbuckle, jr	Allegheny City, Pa	Jan. 21, 1868	73, 486
Coffee-roaster	J. Ashcroft	Brooklyn, N. Y	Oct. 17, 1871	119, 959
Coffee-roaster	B. T. Babbitt	New York, N. Y	Mar. 24, 1868	75, 829
Coffee roaster	R. L. Bate and J. Caulkins	Adrian, Mich	Nov. 1, 1859	25, 941
Coffee-roaster	F. M. Bode	Vienna, Austria	July 28, 1868	80, 329
Coffee-roaster	A. Broman	Kewanee, Ill	Dec. 3, 1872	133, 625
Coffee-roaster	J. Brown	Southampton, Ill	Sept. 24, 1872	131, 597
Coffee-roaster	R. Brown	Ashtabula, Ohio	Apr. 6, 1858	19, 827
Coffee-roaster	J. Burns	New York, N. Y	Oct. 18, 1864	44, 704
Coffee-roaster	C. C. Butt	Duck Hill, Miss	Jan. 2, 1872	122, 357
Coffee-roaster	J. W. Carter	Boston, Mass	Nov. 12, 1846	4, 849
Coffee-roaster	A. Cohn	Louisville, Ky	Sept. 14, 1869	94, 810
Coffee-roaster	L. B. Crittenden	Pittsburgh, Pa	Apr. 6, 1869	88, 612
Coffee-roaster	B. F. Dailey and E. Dougherty, jr.	Mount Pleasant, Iowa	Dec. 3, 1872	133, 633
Coffee-roaster	W. L. Dalbey	Richmond, Ind	July 9, 1872	128, 715
Coffee-roaster	N. Davis	Boston, Mass	Dec. 13, 1870	110, 017
Coffee-roaster	G. W. Dodson	Mitchell, Ind	Apr. 23, 1872	126, 037
Coffee-roaster	G. W. Dodson	Mitchell, Ind	May 27, 1873	139, 377
Coffee-roaster	J. E. Edmundson	Bartlett, Ohio	Sept. 22, 1868	82, 393
Coffee-roaster	J. Galloway	Chetopah, Kans	Sept. 21, 1869	95, 015
Coffee-roaster	J. Galloway	Webster, Ill	May 30, 1871	115, 302
Coffee-roaster	H. M. Gilbert	Ada, Ohio	Sept. 27, 1870	107, 771
Coffee-roaster	W. L. Gilroy	Philadelphia, Pa	Apr. 12, 1859	23, 563
Coffee-roaster	T. J. Hall	Bryan, Tex	Nov. 23, 1869	97, 083
Coffee-roaster	J. Hart	Kekoskee, Wis	Apr. 15, 1873	137, 839
Coffee-roaster	T. Heermans	Mitchellville, Tenn	Sept. 7, 1858	21, 416
Coffee-roaster	T. Heermans	Mitchellville, Tenn	Jan. 18, 1859	22, 649
Coffee-roaster	T. Heermans	Pleasant Hill, Mo	June 30, 1868	79, 469
Coffee-roaster	T. Heermans	Mattoon, Ill	Aug. 12, 1873	141, 789
Coffee-roaster	J. C. Holston	Derry, N. H	Apr. 8, 1862	34, 923
Coffee-roaster	L. Houcke	Springfield, Ohio	Jan. 10, 1871	110, 916
Coffee-roaster	T. Hoyt	New York, N. Y	Sept. 22, 1863	40, 037
Coffee-roaster	F. Humphrey	Philadelphia, Pa	Mar. 13, 1866	53, 148
Coffee-roaster	E. J. Hyde	Philadelphia, Pa	July 1, 1862	35, 758
Coffee-roaster	E. J. Hyde	Philadelphia, Pa	Feb. 2, 1864	41, 436
Coffee-roaster	J. Jay	Jonesborough, Ind	Dec. 7, 1869	97, 644
Coffee-roaster	T. Joyce	Brooklyn, N. Y	Nov. 18, 1862	36, 958
Coffee-roaster	C. L. Kelling	Mechanicsburgh, Pa	Apr. 15, 1862	34, 968
Coffee-roaster	R. Landstrom	Boston, Mass	Mar. 13, 1860	27, 454
Coffee-roaster	W. J. Lane	Millbrook, N. Y	Dec. 16, 1873	145, 576
Coffee-roaster	A. Larson	Galesburgh, Ill	Apr. 9, 1872	125, 579
Coffee-roaster	N. Linden	Chicago, Ill	Nov. 15, 1870	109, 228
Coffee-roaster	R. Little	Middle Branch, Ohio	Aug. 28, 1860	29, 798
Coffee-roaster	H. C. Lockwood	Baltimore, Md	Dec. 23, 1873	145, 880
Coffee-roaster	I. Long	Terre Haute, Ind	May 11, 1869	89, 934
Coffee-roaster	C. Mackh	Elgin, Ill	June 22, 1869	91, 553
Coffee-roaster	B. K. Maltby	Cincinnati, Ohio	May 26, 1868	78, 386
Coffee-roaster	B. K. Maltby	Cincinnati, Ohio	Apr. 27, 1869	89, 490
Coffee-roaster	D. D. Martin	Cincinnati, Ohio	Nov. 28, 1871	121, 292
Coffee-roaster	H. B. Mas-er	Sunbury, Pa	Aug. 7, 1866	56, 964
Coffee-roaster	G. W. Merrick	Adrian, Mich	May 21, 1872	127, 086
Coffee roaster	C. A. Mills	Hazel Green, Wis	Apr. 28, 1863	38, 320
Coffee-roaster	C. A. Mills	Bristol, Conn	Nov. 7, 1865	50, 878
Coffee-roaster	R. L. Mills	Springfield, Ohio	May 23, 1871	115, 228
Coffee-roaster	S. Nowlan	New York, N. Y	June 23, 1863	38, 977
Coffee-roaster	A. Obst	Cambridgeport, Mass	May 2, 1871	114, 330
Coffee-roaster	C. T. Palmer	Norwich, Conn	Oct. 19, 1869	96, 030
Coffee-roaster	J. B. Peake and J. A. Lusby	Washington, D. C	June 29, 1869	92, 090
Coffee-roaster	H. W. Persing	Chicago, Ill	May 25, 1869	90, 386
Coffee-roaster	C. J. C. Petersen	Davinport, Iowa	Oct. 19, 1858	21, 845
Coffee-roaster	S. Pierce	Troy, N. Y	Aug. 14, 1855	13, 447
Coffee-roaster	P. Plant	Washington, D. C	July 31, 1866	56, 861
Coffee-roaster	A. Ransom	Hartford, Conn	Dec. 31, 1833	......
Coffee-roaster	J. R. Remington	Baltimore, Md	Jan. 7, 1847	4, 922
Coffee-roaster	H. E. Richard	Newark, N. J	Oct. 8, 1861	33, 453
Coffee-roaster	E. Schneider and A. Kolman	New Tripoli, Pa	Nov. 24, 1857	18, 710
Coffee-roaster	J. P. Simmons	Baldwinsville, N. Y	May 3, 1859	23, 867
Coffee-roaster	A. Stillman	Poland, N. Y	Dec. 28, 1849	1, 919
Coffee-roaster	N. S. Thompson	Richmond, Ind	Aug. 29, 1871	118, 497
Coffee-roaster	S. Tower	Grand Rapids, Mich	Aug. 31, 1858	21, 387
Coffee-roaster	S. and N. Van Dyk	Saint Louis, Mo	Aug. 20, 1861	33, 113
Coffee-roaster	W. H. Welch	Bloomington, Ill	June 17, 1873	139, 984
Coffee-roaster	A. W. Weyburn	Minneapolis, Minn	Feb. 25, 1873	136, 292
Coffee-roaster	E. Whiteley	Boston, Mass	Apr. 22, 1851	8, 057
Coffee-roaster	N. L. Whitney	Effingham, Ill	Feb. 5, 1867	61, 905
Coffee-roaster	B. I. Williams	Lansing, Mich	Apr. 2, 1872	125, 241

Index of patents issued from the United States Patent Office from 1790 *to* 1873, *inclusive*—Continued.

Invention.	Inventor.	Residence.	Date.	No.
Coffee-roaster	P. Williamson	Baltimore, Md	Mar. 20, 1820	....
Coffee-roaster	T. R. Wood	Cincinnati, Ohio	Apr. 17, 1849	6, 345
Coffee-roaster	F. W. Zochert	Watertown, Wis	Aug. 3, 1869	93, 389
Coffee-roaster and grain-drier	G. D. Jones	New York, N. Y	Feb. 7, 1865	46, 301
Coffee-roaster cover	L. J. Dyke	Hamilton, N. Y	Mar. 18, 1873	136, 980
Coffee-roaster operated by steam	I. C. Smith	New York, N. Y	June 4, 1872	127, 654
Coffee, Roasting	W. Johnston and J. D. Flansburg.	Philadelphia, Pa	Nov. 17, 1868	84, 193
Coffee, Roasting	W. H. Trissler and E. Brecht.	Fairview, Pa	Apr. 30, 1850	7, 329
Coffee-roasting machine	J. D. Harrington	Rochester, N. Y	May 17, 1859	24, 024
Coffee-roasting machine	P. Williamson	Baltimore, Md	June 18, 1825	....
Coffee-roasting process	J. W. Gillies	New York, N. Y	June 27, 1871	116, 298
Coffee-settler	W. F. Rossman	Hudson, N. Y	Apr. 25, 1865	47, 460
Coffee-settling composition	G. W. Carleton	Brunswick, Me	July 31, 1866	56, 704
Coffee, spice, &c., Box for	H. W. Hutchins	Livermore Falls, Me	Jan. 4, 1870	98, 502
Coffee-steeper	J. D. Adney	Chicago, Ill	June 10, 1873	139, 645
Coffee-steeper	R. S. Sanborn	Sycamore, Ill	Apr. 2, 1861	31, 910
Coffee substitute	E. Dugdale	Griffin, Ga	Oct. 21, 1873	143, 889
Coffee substitute	E. Dugdale	Griffin, Ga	Oct. 21, 1873	143, 890
Coffee, tea, and spice can	J. M. Earl	Springfield, Mass	Dec. 13, 1870	110, 125
Coffee, Treating damaged	F. Evans	New York, N. Y	Jan. 14, 1873	134, 791
Coffee, Treating damaged	F. Evans	New York, N. Y	Jan. 14, 1873	134, 792
Coffee-urn	C. Hitchcock	Milldale, Conn	Dec. 16, 1873	145, 653
Coffee-urn	G. Jones	New Haven, Conn	Dec. 8, 1868	84, 830
Coffee-urn	E. Martin	Waterbury, Conn	Apr. 19, 1870	102, 139
Coffee-washing machine	J. Guardiola	Chocolá, Central America	July 16, 1872	129, 278
Coffer-dam	E. Bell	Saint Paul, Minn	Jan. 21, 1868	73, 566
Coffer-dam	J. Braidwood	Wilmington, Ill	June 5, 1866	55, 235
Coffer-dam	W. Easby	Washington, D. C	Nov. 19, 1833	....
Coffer-dam	A. Folsom	New York, N. Y	Jan. 31, 1865	46, 098
Coffer-dam	A. Gilmore	Buffalo, N. Y	Apr. 10, 1866	53, 919
Coffer-dam	C. H. Sanborn	Roxbury, Mass	Feb. 26, 1867	62, 444
Coffer-dam	S. S. Walley	Charlestown, Pa	Sept. 15, 1846	4, 759
Coffer-dam	J. E. Walsh	New York, N. Y	Jan. 24, 1871	111, 156
Coffer-dam	J. E. Walsh	New York, N. Y	Jan. 24, 1871	111, 157
Coffer-dam	J. E. Walsh	New York, N. Y	Apr. 4, 1871	113, 374
Coffer-dam	J. E. Walsh	New York, N. Y	Oct. 24, 1871	120, 352
Coffer-dam and boat	W. H. Applegate	Le Claire, Iowa	May 21, 1867	64, 933
Coffer-dam, Portable and convertible	S. Lewis	Williamsburgh, N. Y	July 6, 1869	92, 324
Coffer-dam, Sectional	T. Bracher	Rahway, N. J	Oct. 19, 1869	95, 976
Coffin	W. G. Algeo	Allegheny, Pa	Jan. 11, 1870	98, 730
Coffin	S. Avery	Phœnix, N. Y	Oct. 17, 1871	120, 021
Coffin	S. Avery and L. Delill	Phœnix, N. Y	Apr. 7, 1868	76, 376
Coffin	J. D. Bayliss	Alexandria, Va	Jan. 5, 1869	85, 507
Coffin	W. Broomhall	Circleville, Ohio	May 25, 1869	90, 491
Coffin	J. Burns	Providence, R. I	July 17, 1866	56, 364
Coffin	C. L. Carter and E. Jones	New York, N. Y	May 29, 1860	28, 451
Coffin	D. Clarke	Ipswich, Mass	July 10, 1866	56, 182
Coffin	E. H. Covel	New York, N. Y	May 10, 1864	42, 641
Coffin	J. E. Cox	Cincinnati, Ohio	Sept. 6, 1870	107, 164
Coffin	E. Ellingen	Mineral Point, Wis	Sept. 8, 1868	81, 885
Coffin	T. B. Estep	Cincinnati, Ohio	Oct. 1, 1867	69, 419
Coffin	T. B. Estep and W. C. Heffer-man.	Cincinnati, Ohio	Oct. 1, 1867	69, 420
Coffin	J. E. Evarts	Madison, Conn	Aug. 11, 1868	80, 816
Coffin	L. Fay	Cincinnati, Ohio	May 31, 1864	42, 936
Coffin	A. D. Fisk	New York, N. Y	Nov. 14, 1848	5, 920
Coffin	J. A. Fogg	Salem, Mass	Feb. 6, 1866	52, 405
Coffin	J. A. Fogg	Stockport, England	Sept. 4, 1866	57, 829
Coffin	J. Good	Philadelphia, Pa	Dec. 12, 1854	12, 058
Coffin	T. Graham	Philadelphia, Pa	Apr. 25, 1865	47, 414
Coffin	A. W. Hendrick	Batavia, Ill	Sept. 21, 1869	95, 109
Coffin	M. M. Hersman	Delavan, Ill	Dec. 19, 1871	121, 943
Coffin	F. H. Hill	Chicago, Ill	Nov. 10, 1868	83, 964
Coffin	T. Holmes	Washington, D. C	May 10, 1864	42, 659
Coffin	D. and S. E. Hooker	West Poultney, Vt	Mar. 2, 1858	19, 503
Coffin	J. M. Lyeth	Baltimore, Md	June 27, 1854	11, 166
Coffin	W. J. Lyman and A. E. Lyman	East Hampton and Williamsburgh, Mass.	Apr. 29, 1862	35, 102
Coffin	M. R. Margerum	Trenton, N. J	Sept. 22, 1868	82, 333
Coffin	H. Marshall	Cincinnati, Ohio	Oct. 4, 1859	25, 659
Coffin	S. Merrick	New Brighton, Pa	Nov. 17, 1868	84, 130
Coffin	J. D. Nietscke	Somerset, Ohio	Sept. 24, 1867	69, 238
Coffin	P. E. Ober	Beverly, Mass	Jan. 21, 1873	135, 006
Coffin	C. Potter and E. Jones	Pawlet, Vt., and Middle Granville, N. Y.	Apr. 7, 1868	76, 344
Coffin	C. E. H. Richardson	Philadelphia, Pa	Jan. 4, 1859	22, 537
Coffin	D. Sholl	Cincinnati, Ohio	Mar. 27, 1855	12, 605
Coffin	I. C. Shuler	Amsterdam, N. Y	Mar. 29, 1859	23, 401
Coffin	I. C. Shuler	Amsterdam, N. Y	July 12, 1870	105, 377
Coffin	B. Smith	Cincinnati, Ohio	July 14, 1868	79, 921
Coffin	H. Smith, jr	Summit, N. Y	Apr. 23, 1867	64, 159
Coffin	H. D. Sprague	Portland, Me	July 10, 1866	56, 287
Coffin	T. M. Taylor	New York, N. Y	Mar. 22, 1870	101, 181
Coffin	F. Tighe	Rockland, Me	Sept. 23, 1873	143, 204
Coffin	P. Washburn, H. G. O. White, and G. A. Copeland.	Taunton, Mass	June 27, 1854	11, 185
Coffin	J. C. Williams	Newton, N. J	Jan. 28, 1868	73, 857
Coffin	S. H. Young	Saint Louis, Mo	Sept. 29, 1863	40, 137
Coffin, Artificial stone or marble	J. White	New York	July 18, 1835	....
Coffin-bier	P. Joyce	Rochester, N. Y	Mar. 9, 1869	87, 570
Coffin, Corpse-preserving	J. Y. Black	Cleveland, Ohio	Dec. 20, 1870	110, 337
Coffin, Deodorizing	A. E. Lyman	New York, N. Y	Apr. 18, 1865	47, 313
Coffin-fastening	W. S. Crane	Rome, Ga	Oct. 21, 1873	143, 748
Coffin-fastening	W. Hamilton	Allegheny City, Pa	June 28, 1870	104, 730
Coffin for use in case of doubtful death	C. H. Eisenbrandt	Baltimore, Md	Nov. 15, 1843	3, 335
Coffin from paper or other pulp	F. Keenan	Brownville, N. Y	Feb. 20, 1872	123, 781
Coffin, Glass	G. B. Field	Saint Louis, Mo	Dec. 11, 1860	30, 874

Index of patents issued from the United States Patent Office from 1790 *to* 1873, *inclusive*—Continued.

Invention.	Inventor.	Residence.	Date.	No.
Coffin, Glass	G. W. Scollay	Saint Louis, Mo	Oct. 2, 1860	30, 252
Coffin, Glass	J. N. and T. Wallis	Fleming, N. Y	May 20, 1873	139, 095
Coffin-handle	I. Almy	Farmer, N. Y	Apr. 25, 1865	47, 375
Coffin-handle	A. B. Bailey	Cobalt, Conn	Sept. 13, 1870	107, 212
Coffin-handle	A. Clark	Amsterdam, N. Y	Dec. 26, 1865	51, 693
Coffin-handle	N. Hayden	Essex, Conn	Oct. 22, 1872	132, 399
Coffin-handle	J. S. Ray	East Haddam, Conn	Mar. 1, 1870	100, 445
Coffin-handle	J. S. Ray	East Haddam, Conn	Apr. 15, 1873	137, 958
Coffin-handle	H. Rogers, jr	West Meriden, Conn	May 6, 1873	138, 696
Coffin-handle	C. Strong	Winsted, Conn	Dec. 14, 1869	97, 827
Coffin-handle	C. Strong	Winsted, Conn	May 13, 1873	138, 768
Coffin-handle	B. W. Wooster	Albany, N. Y	Feb. 11, 1862	34, 387
Coffin-handles, Casting	D. W. Sexton	East Hampton, Conn	June 13, 1865	48, 215
Coffin-head brace	J. Gawler	Washington, D. C	Nov. 9, 1869	96, 581
Coffin-lid	J. S. Merrill	Poland, Me	May 26, 1863	38, 713
Coffin-lids, Hinging	J. C. Seelye	Cambridge, Mass	July 18, 1865	48, 842
Coffin, Metallic	J. A. Gray	Richmond, Va	June 11, 1836	....
Coffin, Metallic	G. Nearstheimer	Cincinnati, Ohio	Apr. 6, 1869	88, 728
Coffin, Metallic	J. H. Renshaw	Knoxville, Tenn	Feb. 12, 1861	31, 401
Coffin, Metallic	I. C. Shuler	Amsterdam, N. Y	Apr. 12, 1859	23, 616
Coffin-nail cap	S. A. Barker	Providence, R. I	Jan. 11, 1870	98, 733
Coffin nails and screw heads, Machine for finishing	A. A. Randall	New Haven, Conn	June 19, 1866	55, 783
Coffin-plate	G. Brabrook	Taunton, Mass	July 1, 1873	140, 457
Coffin-plate	W. H. Green	Meriden, Conn	Apr. 19, 1864	42, 367
Coffin-plate	G. B. Ransom	Chester, Conn	Jan. 21, 1873	135, 155
Coffin-receptacle	J. H. Shields	Louisville, Ky	Nov. 21, 1871	121, 206
Coffin, Refrigerator	J. S. Cox	Delaware, Ohio	Mar. 10, 1868	75, 377
Coffin, Sheet-metal	J. D. Farrington, jr., and T. P. Austin.	New York, N. Y., and Portland, Conn.	Nov. 18, 1873	144, 604
Coffin, Sheet-metal	I. C. Shuler	Amsterdam, N. Y	Dec. 6, 1859	26, 379
Coffin, Sheet-metal	W. S. Wood	New York, N. Y	Dec. 24, 1872	134, 182
Coffin-sides, Apparatus for bending	J. P. Albin	Cincinnati, Ohio	Dec. 23, 1873	145, 827
Coffin-tops, Press for making	A. W. Hendrick	Batavia, Ill	Oct. 5, 1869	95, 475
Coffin, Ventilating	A. E. Lyman	Williamsburgh, Mass	Oct. 14, 1862	36, 660
Coffin, Wooden	F. Brübach	Lancaster, Pa	Oct. 9, 1860	30, 292
Coffin, Wooden	M. R. Margerum	Trenton, N. J	Sept. 26, 1865	50, 144
Coffins and other articles from asphaltic composition, Manufacture of.	D. W. Denton	Ithaca, N. Y	Jan. 19, 1864	41, 284
Coffins, Apparatus for supporting and lowering	C. A. Thompson and J. O. Coleman.	Hopkinsville, Ky	Dec. 5, 1871	121, 688
Coffins, &c., Cement for coating and sealing	I. Charles	Allegheny City, Pa	May 16, 1871	114, 761
Coffins, Compound for covering	J. W. Bower	Greencastle, Ind	June 6, 1871	115, 687
Coffins, Constructing	I. C. Shuler	Amsterdam, N. Y	Apr. 27, 1858	20, 095
Coffins, Constructing sheet-metal	I. C. Shuler	Amsterdam, N. Y	June 14, 1859	24, 409
Coffins, Construction of	F. Skiff	New York, N. Y	Apr. 20, 1847	5, 084
Coffins, Construction of glass	J. R. Cannon	New Albany, Ind	Oct. 25, 1859	25, 883
Coffins, Construction of sheet-metal	I. C. Shuler	Amsterdam, N. Y	July 5, 1859	24, 635
Coffins, Construction of sheet-metal	I. C. Shuler	Amsterdam, N. Y	Sept. 6, 1859	25, 350
Coffins, Covering	L. Snider	Indianapolis, Ind	Oct. 4, 1859	25, 682
Coffins from hydraulic cement, Constructing	Dayton, Hoyt, and White	Salina, N. Y	June 6, 1835	....
Coffins from hydraulic cement, Constructing	J. White	New York, N. Y	July 18, 1835	....
Coffins, Fastening-key for	J. Homrighouse	Royalton, Ohio	Mar. 19, 1872	124, 745
Coffins, Head-rest for	J. P. Waugh	South Scriba, N. Y	Aug. 29, 1871	118, 565
Coffins, Life-detector for	T. A. Schroeder and H. Wuest	Hoboken, N. J	Dec. 5, 1871	121, 666
Coffins, &c., Lifting-handle for	T. M. Taylor	New York, N. Y	June 28, 1870	104, 899
Coffins, Manufacturing cement	M. Leonard	Syracuse, N. Y	July 2, 1839	1, 214
Coffins, Measuring-scale for	J. W. Hyde	Lewiston, Ill	Sept. 25, 1866	58, 262
Coffins, Mode of disinfecting	S. H. Young	Saint Louis, Mo	May 7, 1867	64, 467
Coffins, &c., Molding for	G. S. Eaton	Williamsburgh, N. Y	June 18, 1872	127, 966
Coffins, &c., Name-plate for	G. Brabrook	Taunton, Mass	Mar. 24, 1868	75, 726
Coffins, Preserving the wood of	J. M. Dufournet and L. Clemendot.	Paris, France	May 12, 1868	77, 8[illegible]6
Cog-gearing spring	J. L. Rees	Peoria, Ill	June 4, 1867	65, 506
Cog-wheel	F. A. Morley	Sodus Point, N. Y	Feb. 10, 1863	37, 634
Cog-wheel coupling, Universal	E. Smith	Adams County, Ill	Jan. 10, 1871	110, 938
Cog-wheel-cutting machinery	J. P. Gaume	Cincinnati, Ohio	June 6, 1848	5, 614
Cog-wheel for gearing	H. I. Crandall	New Bedford, Mass	Oct. 27, 1868	83, 469
Cog-wheels, Connection of	A. Skaats, jr	New Haven, Conn	May 3, 1864	42, 605
Cog-wheels, &c., Machine for making patterns for	W. Obenchain	Logansport, Ind	Apr. 5, 1859	23, 484
Cog-wheels, Machinery to supersede the use of	J. Cooper	Staunton, Va	Feb. 22, 1826	....
Coil, Electro-magnetic induction	J. S. Camacho	Havana, Cuba,	Apr. 29, 1873	138, 316
Coil, Induction	J. Kidder	New York, N. Y	Jan. 16, 1866	52, 054
Coil-spring and its attachments	T. Rose and P. S. Buell	Cortland and Windsor, N. Y	Dec. 7, 1869	97, 705
Coil-springs, Mandrel for	R. Vose and J. Anderson	New York, N. Y	Jan. 5, 1869	85, 549
Coil-springs, Manufacture of	W. H. Ward	Auburn, N. Y	Mar. 4, 1873	136, 473
Coiled springs, Machine for making	J. Harrison, jr	New York, N. Y	Jan. 27, 1857	16, 483
Coiled springs, Machine for packing	J. W. Evans	New York, N. Y	Mar. 2, 1869	87, 332
Coin assorting and computing apparatus	E. Baltzley	New Philadelphia, Ohio	Feb. 13, 1872	123, 607
Coin-assorting apparatus	J. W. Meaker	Chicago, Ill	Apr. 7, 1868	76, 492
Coin-assorting apparatus	J. W. Meaker	Chicago, Ill	Apr. 7, 1868	76, 493
Coin-counting implement	A. Whittemore	Cambridgeport, Mass	Jan. 14, 1873	134, 962
Coin-counting machine	M. F. Bonzano	New Orleans, La	June 17, 1856	15, 117
Coin-counting machine	R. Tyler	New Orleans, La	Oct. 11, 1841	2, 320
Coin-detector	H. Maranville	Clinton, Ohio	Feb. 14, 1860	27, 140
Coin detector, Counterfeit	W. Painter	Fallston, Md	July 8, 1862	35, 834
Coin detector, Counterfeit	G. B. Smith	Baltimore, Md	Sept. 6, 1853	9, 997
Coin-holder	L. Landry	San Francisco, Cal	May 29, 1866	55, 121
Coke, Desulphurizing	G. Nock	Pittsburgh, Pa	May 29, 1860	28, 543
Coke from anthracite and other coal, Manufacturing	M. Isaacs	Philadelphia, Pa	Apr. 7, 1831	....
Coke from Colorado and other coal, Process of preparing.	W. J. Lynd	Golden City, Colo	Aug. 10, 1869	93, 629
Coke from lignites, Process of making	H. Engelmann	Salt Lake City, Utah	Mar. 11, 1873	136, 592
Coke-furnace	T. Price	Steubenville, Ohio	Dec. 6, 1870	109, 940
Coke, Manufacture of	W. McPheeters and C. Pearce	Harmony, Ind	Aug. 1, 1871	117, 714
Coking fossil-coal, Modes of	G. Lander	Irwin, Pa	Mar. 19, 1872	124, 688
Coking fossil-coal, Mode of	G. Lander	Irwin, Pa	Mar. 19, 1872	124, 689
Coking wood by waste-heat of iron-furnaces	A. H. Tait	Plattsburgh, N. Y	Aug. 22, 1848	5, 722
Colander boiler	B. F. Porter	Manchester, N. H	May 21, 1867	94, 905

Index of patents issued from the United States Patent Office from 1790 *to* 1873, *inclusive*—Continued.

Invention.	Inventor.	Residence.	Date.	No.
Collapsible boat	C. F. Lichtner	Chicago, Ill	Aug. 25, 1863	39, 661
Collapsible boat	N. Thompson, jr.	Williamsburgh, N. Y	Aug. 28, 1855	13, 510
Collapsible boat	N. Thompson, jr.	Brooklyn, N. Y	Feb. 19, 1858	19, 317
Collar	J. T. Bruen	Brooklyn, N. Y	Jan. 7, 1873	134, 638
Collar	H. G. Emery and M. C. Fuller	Boston, Mass	July 19, 1870	105, 442
Collar	A. Flatley	Brooklyn, N. Y	Apr. 1, 1873	137, 353
Collar	J. H. Parmelee	Chicopee, Ill	July 23, 1867	67, 134
Collar	G. F. Rice	Worcester, Mass	Mar. 25, 1873	137, 096
Collar	C. W. Saladee	Circleville, Ohio	Jan. 26, 1869	86, 180
Collar	C. W. Saladee	Circleville, Ohio	Feb. 23, 1869	87, 116
Collar and bosom combined	E. Hatch	Charlestown, Mass	Feb. 11, 1868	74, 355
Collar and bosom, Detached shirt	C. E. Richards	North Attleborough, Mass	Dec. 20, 1864	45, 566
Collar and bosom, Shirt	C. E. Richards	North Attleborough, Mass	July 25, 1865	49, 039
Collar and cravat combined	F. D. James	Tamworth, N. H	June 17, 1873	139, 959
Collar and cuff	J. Blakey and H. B. Fox	Liverpool and Oxton, England.	May 5, 1868	77, 573
Collar and cuff	E. P. Furlong	Springfield, Mass	Nov. 18, 1873	144, 611
Collar and cuff box, Combined	J. C. Bauer	New York, N. Y	Oct. 18, 1870	108, 315
Collar and cuff drier	D. W. De Forest	Petersburgh, Va	Nov. 25, 1873	144, 838
Collar and cuff, Lady's	W. E. Lockwood	Philadelphia, Pa	Apr. 26, 1859	23, 771
Collar and cuff, Water-proof	G. W. Ray	Springfield, Mass	June 13, 1865	48, 239
Collar and hame	W. O'Brien and H. Wentworth	Omaha, Nebr	Mar. 29, 1870	101, 303
Collar and hame	J. L. Wooden	Greensburgh, Ind	Mar. 8, 1870	100, 701
Collar and hame, Combined	F. Jones	Burlington, Iowa	July 13, 1869	92, 534
Collar and hame, Harness	J. H. Ferguson	Greenville, Ind	Feb. 22, 1870	100, 022
Collar and hame, Horse	O. Cann	Coldwater, Mich	Apr. 4, 1871	113, 253
Collar and hame, Horse	H. Connick	Albert Lea, Minn	Aug. 24, 1869	93, 968
Collar and hame, Horse	A. Dunbar	New York, N. Y	May 19, 1868	78, 075
Collar and hame, Horse	A. Dunbar	Woodstock, Canada	Oct. 3, 1871	119, 585
Collar and hame, Horse	M. Killacky	Philadelphia, Pa	Feb. 28, 1865	46, 606
Collar and hame, Horse	S. B. Stewart	Centre Township, Pa	June 30, 1863	39, 076
Collar and hame, Horse	E. Wilder	South Hingham, Mass	Aug. 3, 1869	93, 262
Collar and harness, Combined horse	G. W. N. Yost	Cincinnati, Ohio	Jan. 19, 1858	19, 169
Collar and muff combined	M. Wannagat	New York, N. Y	Apr. 16, 1872	125, 862
Collar and neck-tie	W. Hunter	Berkeley Springs, W. Va.	Apr. 24, 1866	54, 168
Collar and neck-tie attachment	C. W. Powell	Milford, Conn	Nov. 13, 1866	59, 646
Collar and neck-tie combined	G. F. Perkins	New York, N. Y	Mar. 3, 1868	75, 047
Collar and neck-tie fastener	E. Raw	New York, N. Y	Oct. 20, 1868	83, 318
Collar and spreader for double harness, Breast	J. M. Myers	Louisville, Ky	Aug. 6, 1867	67, 566
Collar and tag cutting machine	S. S. Gray	Boston, Mass	Dec. 30, 1873	145, 941
Collar attachment, Shirt	J. Proud	New York, N. Y	July 24, 1866	56, 610
Collar, Axle	E. S. Scripture	New York, N. Y	June 4, 1861	32, 499
Collar, Belvidere shirt	W. J. Cantelo and R. M. Kerrison.	Philadelphia, Pa	Nov. 19, 1833	......
Collar-blank	G. K. Snow	Watertown, Mass	Oct. 29, 1872	132, 545
Collar block	J. Jacobs	Oneida, Ill	Feb. 4, 1868	73, 977
Collar block, Horse	A. Benham	Belvidere, Ill	Mar. 8, 1848	5, 464
Collar block, Horse	E. L. Brazenor	Birmingham, Great Britain	Apr. 12, 1870	101, 819
Collar block, Horse	W. H. Bustin	Watertown, Mass	Dec. 19, 1848	5, 975
Collar block, Horse	E. D. Gould	Darien, N. Y	Apr. 6, 1858	19, 846
Collar block, Horse	B. W. McClure	Wyoming, Iowa	Oct. 11, 1864	44, 642
Collar block, Horse	B. W. McClure and G. Marsh	Pike Hollow, N. Y	Aug. 24, 1858	21, 307
Collar block, Horse	P. Moodey	Indianapolis, Ind	June 26, 1855	13, 132
Collar block, Horse	O. Morgan	Henry, Ill	July 2, 1861	32, 708
Collar block, Horse	T. J. Van Benschoten	Poughkeepsie, N. Y	July 3, 1855	13, 189
Collar, Breast	G. W. Blaksley	Rockford, Ill	Apr. 13, 1869	88, 838
Collar, Breast	S. E. Stowell	Charlestown, Mass	Jan. 16, 1866	52, 088
Collar, Caoutchouc shirt	J. A. Pease	New York, N. Y	Apr. 7, 1863	38, 122
Collar cap, Harness	A. P. Mason	Franklinville, N. Y	June 27, 1871	116, 465
Collar cap, Horse	R. J. Algeo	Kalamazoo, Mich	Oct. 29, 1872	132, 515
Collar cap, Horse	R. J. Algeo	Kalamazoo, Mich	Mar. 18, 1873	136, 804
Collar cap, Horse	D. Curtis	Chicago, Ill	Aug. 2, 1870	105, 917
Collar cap, Horse	D. Curtis	Sun Prairie, Wis	May 14, 1872	126, 681
Collar cap, Horse	A. P. Mason	Franklinville, N. Y	Mar. 12, 1872	124, 444
Collar cap, Horse	J. Sellors	Bellevue, Mich	Apr. 19, 1870	102, 052
Collar cap, Horse	J. F. Walsh	Hazel Green, Wis	Oct. 4, 1870	108, 071
Collar-clasp	V. Fogerty	Boston, Mass	June 21, 1864	43, 190
Collar, Coach	W. Hottensteen	......	Apr. 10, 1800	......
Collar, Dog	P. Daly and J. Barry	Boston, Mass	Apr. 30, 1872	126, 135
Collar-edge protector	C. W. Saladee	Newark, Ohio	Oct. 22, 1867	70, 025
Collar-fastening	M. C. Battey	Washington, D. C	May 11, 1869	89, 967
Collar-fastening	C. H. L. Roberts and W. C. Dudley.	Morrison, Ill	Oct. 6, 1868	82, 879
Collar fastening, Horse	A. Bratnober	Webster County, Iowa	Oct. 25, 1870	108, 559
Collar fastening, Horse	H. H. Fleming	Kokomo, Ind	Nov. 21, 1865	51, 033
Collar fastening, Horse	J. P. and J. E. Force	Constantine, Mich	Dec. 8, 1868	84, 687
Collar fastening, Horse	E. B. Gould	Liberty, Ind	Jan. 26, 1869	86, 298
Collar fastening, Horse	B. H. Hobart and D. C. Lampman.	Troy, Pa	Oct. 6, 1868	82, 836
Collar fastening, Horse	M. F. McIntyre	Girard, Pa	May 25, 1869	90, 374
Collar fastening, Horse	W. A. Robinson	Grand Rapids, Mich	Apr. 27, 1869	89, 346
Collar fastening, Horse	W. A. Sharp and J. A. Shannon	Tama City, Iowa	Aug. 25, 1868	81, 416
Collar fastening, Horse	E. H. Sprague	Mount Vernon, Ohio	Mar. 25, 1873	137, 105
Collar fastening, Horse	A. Van Fleet	Ashton, Ill	July 21, 1868	80, 246
Collar fastening, Horse	E. L. Welbourn	Union City, Ind	Oct. 18, 1870	108, 418
Collar fastening, Horse	D. C. Westfall	Mifflin, Pa	Oct. 1, 1867	69, 520
Collar fastening, Horse	C. Wheeler	Warsaw, Ohio	Oct. 24, 1871	120, 356
Collar fastening, Shirt	G. W. Brientnall	Lancaster, Pa	Aug. 5, 1873	141, 484
Collar fastening, Shirt	F. Hess	Baltimore, Md	May 21, 1867	64, 867
Collar fastening, Shirt	C. E. Palmer	Newburyport, Mass	July 28, 1868	80, 424
Collar fastening, Shirt	G. Straszer	Manchester, Mo	Dec. 30, 1873	145, 974
Collar fastening, Shirt	A. Wood	East Henrietta, N. Y	Jan. 15, 1867	61, 300
Collar for attaching cow-bells	T. H. Body	Kilbourn City, Wis	May 10, 1870	102, 756
Collar for dress-coats, &c	H. Clark	Brooklyn, Conn	Nov. 7, 1828	......
Collar for drill-rod	V. T. Priest	Decatur, Ill	July 24, 1866	56, 607
Collar for harness	J. W. Briggs	Cleveland, Ohio	June 3, 1851	8, 133
Collar for ladies and gentlemen	F. Field	Troy, N. Y	Aug. 4, 1863	39, 390
Collar, Fur	W. King	New York, N. Y	Mar. 24, 1868	75, 928

Index of patents issued from the United States Patent Office from 1790 *to* 1873, *inclusive*—Continued.

Invention.	Inventor.	Residence.	Date.	No.
Collar Fur	J. H. Kappelhoff and S. Rauh	New York, N. Y	July 12, 1870	105, 340
Collar, Fur	R. M. Seldis	New York, N. Y	June 15, 1869	91, 371
Collar gage, Horse	J. M. Everitt	Hackettstown, N. J	June 17, 1873	139, 949
Collar, Horse	C. Alvord	Westford, Wis	Aug. 28, 1866	57, 457
Collar, Horse	W. M. Baker	Greenwich Station, Ohio	Dec. 7, 1869	97, 587
Collar, Horse	E. Batwell	Ypsilanti, Mich	Apr. 15, 1873	137, 879
Collar, Horse	A. Beckwith	New Orleans, La	Dec. 7, 1869	97, 592
Collar, Horse	E. W. Briding and F. G. Maxwell.	Baltimore, Md	Nov. 27, 1860	30, 715
Collar, Horse	J. Bullock	Baltimore, Md	Jan. 10, 1860	26, 748
Collar, Horse	H. C. Call	Sterling, Conn	Nov. 14, 1835	....
Collar, Horse	S. G. Cheever and J. Forgie	Boston, Mass	Oct. 8, 1867	69, 627
Collar, Horse	J. Cogan	Cambridge, Mass	Feb. 9, 1869	86, 812
Collar, Horse	C. C. Cotton	Buchanan, Mich	July 9, 1872	128, 858
Collar, Horse	A. J. Cronk	Peoria, Ill	Aug. 6, 1867	67, 508
Collar, Horse	C. K. Cuckler	Columbus, Ohio	Oct. 19, 1858	21, 821
Collar, Horse	F. C. Curtis	Columbia, S. C	Aug. 4, 1845	4, 136
Collar, Horse	A. Ducastel	New York, N. Y	Mar. 1, 1870	100, 381
Collar, Horse	C. R. Durfee	Rochester, N. Y	Oct. 9, 1866	58, 620
Collar, Horse	C. Durrant	Lyndonville, N. Y	June 16, 1863	38, 889
Collar, Horse	S. B. Edson	Kokomo, Ind	Mar. 28, 1865	47, 000
Collar, Horse	E. P. Edstrom	Somerville, Mass	Apr. 30, 1867	64, 296
Collar, Horse	E. P. Edstrom	Somerville, Mass	Oct. 22, 1867	70, 079
Collar, Horse	J. Endo	Buffalo, N. Y	Dec. 18, 1860	30, 912
Collar, Horse	J. Englaender	Sedalia, Mo	June 7, 1870	104, 000
Collar, Horse	J. Englaender	Sedalia, Mo	July 19, 1870	105, 443
Collar, Horse	C. Fisher	Waukon, Iowa	Feb. 9, 1864	41, 497
Collar, Horse	C. J. Fisher	Waukon, Iowa	July 17, 1860	29, 154
Collar, Horse	C. J. Fisher	Waukon, Iowa	Sept. 5, 1865	49, 743
Collar, Horse	M. Gordon	Brighton, Iowa	Oct. 15, 1872	132, 206
Collar, Horse	W. H. Gray	New York, N. Y	Apr. 25, 1871	114, 131
Collar, Horse	W. Guilfoyle	New York, N. Y	Apr. 8, 1873	137, 608
Collar, Horse	L. Guinniss	Danville, Ill	Mar. 28, 1871	113, 161
Collar, Horse	I. H. Hall and J. Lowrey	Wheeling, Va	Sept. 21, 1852	9, 272
Collar, Horse	T. Harvey	Baltimore, Md	Apr. 12, 1859	23, 575
Collar, Horse	T. Harvey	Baltimore, Md	Apr. 12, 1859	23, 576
Collar, Horse	J. G. Haymaker	Salem Cross Roads, Pa	Oct. 1, 1867	69, 429
Collar, Horse	H. Holton	Rochester, N. Y	May 16, 1833	....
Collar, Horse	J. Hopkins	Warren County, Ohio	Jan. 23, 1836	....
Collar, Horse	G. Horter	New Orleans, La	Apr. 5, 1870	101, 619
Collar, Horse	P. B. Horton	San Francisco, Cal	Aug. 27, 1872	130, 919
Collar, Horse	I. Houghtling	Houghton, Mich	Apr. 7, 1868	76, 456
Collar, Horse	R. Humphrey	West Troy, N. Y	Apr. 5, 1870	101, 623
Collar, Horse	W. Kays	Boston, Mass	June 7, 1870	104, 035
Collar, Horse	L. B. Kenny	Charlotte, Mich	July 19, 1870	105, 580
Collar, Horse	O. Lafreniere	New York, N. Y	Jan. 11, 1859	22, 562
Collar, Horse	O. Lafreniere	Brooklyn, N. Y	July 8, 1873	140, 714
Collar, Horse	H. B. Latham	Huntington, N. Y	Apr. 6, 1852	8, 856
Collar, Horse	W. Leonard	Boston, Mass	Sept. 3, 1867	68, 369
Collar, Horse	D. Lincoln	Johnsonsburgh, N. Y	July 30, 1867	67, 201
Collar, Horse	J. R. Lindner	New York, N. Y	Sept. 6, 1853	9, 990
Collar, Horse	J. C. Mahaffey	Little York, Ill	Mar. 30, 1869	88, 312
Collar, Horse	C. K. Marshall	New Orleans, La	Jan. 12, 1869	85, 747
Collar, Horse	C. K. Marshall	New Orleans, La	July 26, 1870	105, 821
Collar, Horse	G. F. Marshall	Cleveland, Ohio	Nov. 15, 1864	45, 060
Collar, Horse	B. W. McClure	Wyoming, Iowa	Mar. 30, 1869	88, 400
Collar, Horse	J. Meyer	Williamsburgh, N. Y	July 20, 1869	92, 864
Collar, Horse	T. Moore	New York, N. Y	Jan. 14, 1868	73, 368
Collar, Horse	J. Nack	Hudson, N. Y	Aug. 27, 1872	130, 935
Collar, Horse	G. F. Parsons	Baltimore, Md	Nov. 29, 1864	45, 267
Collar, Horse	N. Post	Madrid, N. Y	July 22, 1843	3, 194
Collar, Horse	I. A. Powell	Morrison, Ill	Nov. 13, 1866	59, 647
Collar, Horse	R. Rickey	Rutland, Ohio	Nov. 11, 1851	8, 517
Collar, Horse	D. T. Bobinson	Boston, Mass	May 7, 1867	64, 448
Collar, Horse	H. Sanders	Utica, N. Y	Apr. 5, 1870	101, 515
Collar, Horse	J. N. Schmitz	Kilbourn City, Wis	June 10, 1873	139, 822
Collar, Horse	J. W. Schwaner	Egg Harbor City, N. J	Apr. 18, 1871	113, 802
Collar, Horse	S. Shattuc	Henrietta, Ohio	Dec. 18, 1855	13, 965
Collar, Horse	T. J. Shipley and W. A. Moody	Montezuma, Iowa	Oct. 8, 1867	69, 712
Collar, Horse	A. Snively	Terre Haute, Ind	Feb. 20, 1872	123, 948
Collar, Horse	J. H. Sperbeck	Warsaw, N. Y	Mar. 17, 1868	75, 590
Collar, Horse	A. A. Stannard	Ithaca, N. Y	Oct. 17, 1865	50, 505
Collar, Horse	J. A. Sutherland	Elmwood, Ill	Sept. 22, 1868	82, 361
Collar, Horse	S. P. Taylor	Oxford, Ohio	Aug. 4, 1860	80, 682
Collar, Horse	W. J. Thorn	New York, N. Y	Feb. 28, 1871	112, 196
Collar, Horse	W. M. Thornton	Bloomsburgh, Pa	June 21, 1853	9, 806
Collar, Horse	J. C. Tredway	Buffalo, N. Y	Feb. 19, 1867	62, 301
Collar, Horse	J. H. Van Sice	Buffalo, N. Y	Nov. 10, 1863	40, 582
Collar, Horse	J. L. Van Wert	Tolland, Mass	Jan. 11, 1870	98, 722
Collar, Horse	E. Webber	Portage, Mich	Apr. 14, 1868	76, 858
Collar, Horse	L. Wegmann and C. F. Diessel	Allegheny City, Pa	Dec. 31, 1867	72, 947
Collar, Horse	G. Werner and R. Robinson	Canajoharie, N. Y	June 22, 1836	....
Collar, Horse	E. Whitney	Chenango, N. Y	June 4, 1834	....
Collar, Horse	E. Whitney	Albany, N. Y	Oct. 27, 1863	40, 440
Collar, Horse	J. Whitney	Franklinville, N. Y	Feb. 27, 1872	124, 184
Collar, Horse	C. Wolf	Rantoul, Ill	Nov. 27, 1866	60, 107
Collar, Horse	C. Wolf	Danville, Ill	May 5, 1868	77, 698
Collar, Horse	J. J. Wright	Richmond, Va	Oct. 1, 1872	131, 925
Collar, Horse	W. Youngblood	New York, N. Y	May 5, 1868	77, 701
Collar, Horse breast	W. T. Albro	Ellisburgh, N. Y	July 2, 1872	128, 520
Collar, Horse breast	R. D. Kendall	Richville, N. Y	July 9, 1872	128, 890
Collar, Horse breast	W. E. Leonard	Boston, Mass	Dec. 20, 1870	110, 377
Collar, Horse breast	J. Nellis	Ypsilanti, Mich	May 30, 1871	115, 346
Collar, Horse breast	J. G. Taylor	Philadelphia, Pa	Nov. 27, 1860	30, 775
Collar, Horse breast	G. Van Wagenen	Pittsburgh, Pa	Apr. 2, 1872	125, 353
Collar, Lady's	C. O. Crosby	New Haven, Conn	Jan. 5, 1864	41, 140
Collar, Lady's imitation	C. Lang	New York, N. Y	Aug. 14, 1866	57, 154
Collar lining, Horse	D. Curtis	Sun Prairie, Wis	Apr. 29, 1873	138, 383

Index of patents issued from the United States Patent Office from 1790 to 1873, inclusive—Continued.

Invention.	Inventor.	Residence.	Date.	No.
Collar-machine	H. F. Knapp	New York, N. Y	Apr. 28, 1868	77, 294
Collar machine	J. F. Walker	Albany, N. Y	Nov. 3, 1868	83, 814
Collar machine, Horse	D. Cleavland	Owego, N. Y	Sept. 13, 1834	....
Collar-making die	G. K. Snow	Watertown, Mass	Oct. 29, 1872	132, 546
Collar, Man's	D. Mackay	United States Army	Mar. 27, 1866	53, 462
Collar, Metallic	L. Billon	Brooklyn, N. Y	Sept. 5, 1865	49, 702
Collar, Metallic horse	C. K. Marshall	New Orleans, La	June 23, 1868	79, 137
Collar, Metallic shirt	O. Ernst	New York, N. Y	Aug. 30, 1864	43, 981
Collar, Molded cloth and paper	S. S. Gray	Boston, Mass	Jan. 19, 1864	41, 294
Collar-molding apparatus	S. S. Gray	Boston, Mass	Nov. 19, 1867	70, 996
Collar-molding machine	G. H. Spaulding	Norwich, Conn	May 26, 1868	78, 242
Collar-pad	P. H. Beaver	Montandon, Pa	Mar. 25, 1873	137, 049
Collar-pad	G. P. Cole	Hudson, Mich	July 18, 1871	117, 151
Collar, Pad and lining for horse	S. W. Baker	Providence, R. I	Mar. 9, 1869	87, 619
Collar pad, Breast	R. E. Miles	Louisville, Ky	Feb. 16, 1869	86, 995
Collar pad, Horse	J. Frazer	Dowagiac, Mich	Nov. 8, 1870	108, 995
Collar pad, Horse	J. Frazer	Dowagiac, Mich	Mar. 21, 1871	112, 797
Collar pad, Horse	L. L. Hull	Oskaloosa, Iowa	Mar. 14, 1871	112, 713
Collar pad Horse	J. S. Huston	Mechanicsburgh, Pa	Apr. 26, 1870	102, 403
Collar pad, Horse	T. Newbold	Salisbury, Mo	Nov. 5, 1872	132, 769
Collar pad, Horse	J. F. Welsh	Hazel Green, Wis	Dec. 27, 1870	110, 518
Collar-pad press, Horse	J. Frazer	Dowagiac, Mich	Mar. 29, 1870	101, 252
Collar pads, Crimp for	J. S. Barkdull	Ballston, N. Y	July 13, 1844	3, 661
Collar, Reversible	C. W. Saladee	Circleville, Ohio	Jan. 26, 1869	86, 338
Collar, Rudder	S. Leach	Penobscot, Me	Mar. 1, 1870	100, 419
Collar shell-forming die, Horse	J. W. Schwaner	Egg Harbor City, N. J	Jan. 3, 1871	110, 685
Collar, Shirt	S. A. Bemis	Springfield, Mass	Feb. 13, 1866	52, 516
Collar, Shirt	O. P. Dorman	New York, N. Y	Apr. 8, 1873	137, 537
Collar, Shirt	A. A. Evans	Boston, Mass	July 18, 1865	48, 802
Collar, Shirt	S. S. Gray	Boston, Mass	June 23, 1863	38, 961
Collar, Shirt	W. Hunt	New York, N. Y	July 25, 1854	11, 376
Collar, Shirt	W. Hunt	New York, N. Y	Jan. 1, 1856	14, 019
Collar, Shirt	J. A. Pease	New York, N. Y	June 16, 1863	38, 909
Collar, Shirt	V. N. Taylor	Springfield, Mass	Mar. 26, 1872	124, 920
Collar, Sleeping	L. Doderick	New York, N. Y	May 17, 1870	103, 026
Collar-stay	S. Kaufman	Fairbury, Ill	Nov. 10, 1868	83, 973
Collar, Steel shirt	L. Billon	Brooklyn, N. Y	Apr. 19 1864	42, 429
Collar, Steel shirt	R. Woodward, J. Priest, and O. Ernst.	New York, N. Y	Aug. 30, 1864	44, 051
Collar stuffer, Horse	E. B. Miller	Greeneville, Tenn	Mar. 17, 1868	75, 641
Collar-stuffing machine, Horse	S. B. McCorkle	Greeneville, Tenn	July 14, 1868	79, 997
Collar-stuffing machine, Horse	L. P. Woods	Indiana, Pa	Jan. 30, 1872	123, 139
Collar top, Horse	I. Hicks	Hartford, Wis	Oct. 4, 1870	107, 905
Collar, Turn-over shirt	N. Evans, jr	Boston, Mass	Feb. 23, 1864	41, 692
Collar, Water-proof	H. C. Gibson	Camden, N. J	Apr. 10, 1866	53, 808
Collar, Wooden horse	Z. C. Robbins	Washington, D. C	Aug. 29, 1871	118, 555
Collars and neck-ties, Stand for displaying	S. S. Gray and C. E. Staniels	Boston, Mass	May 7, 1872	126, 541
Collars, Apparatus for forming	S. S. Gray	Boston, Mass	July 5, 1864	43, 401
Collars, Apparatus for stuffing horse	W. C. Habberton	Mount Carmel, Ill	Jan. 3, 1860	26, 671
Collars, Attachment for breast	R. E. Miles	Louisville, Ky	Sept. 10, 1867	68, 774
Collars, Block for horse	L. S. Davis	New Paris, Ohio	Feb. 7, 1854	10, 502
Collars, Blocking hame	N. Post	Norfolk, N. Y	July 24, 1834	....
Collars, Clasp for securing shirt	J. Barbier	Boston, Mass	May 28, 1867	65, 155
Collars, Compound fabric for the production of shirt.	W. Hunt	New York, N. Y	May 4, 1869	89, 768
Collars, cuffs, and other articles of wearing-apparel, Coating and water-proofing.	S. W. H. Ward	New York, N. Y	Nov. 10, 1868	83, 893
Collars, cuffs, bosoms, and other articles of wearing-apparel, Fabric for.	W. E. Lockwood	Philadelphia, Pa	July 20, 1869	92, 851
Collars, cuffs, &c., Fabric for the manufacture of	J. Restein	Philadelphia, Pa	Aug. 24, 1869	94, 030
Collars, cuffs, &c., Fabric for the manufacture of enameled.	H. C. Gibson	Camden, N. J	July 12, 1864	43, 489
Collars, cuffs, &c., Manufacture of	A. Taylor	Philadelphia, Pa	Oct. 17, 1865	50, 513
Collars, Cutting top of horse	T. Deming	East Hartford, Conn	Mar. 6, 1835	....
Collars, Device for fastening shirt	P. W. Smith	Chicopee Falls, Mass	Oct. 20, 1868	83, 332
Collars, Device for forming horse	I. T. Crum	Chicago, Ill	Feb. 12, 1867	62, 014
Collars, Expanding-block for horse	R. R. Gray	Crawfordsville, Ind	June 19, 1855	13, 087
Collars, Fabric for covering horse	E. Sullivan	New York, N. Y	June 16, 1868	79, 024
Collars, Fabric for shirt	C. F. Pidgin	Boston, Mass	Nov. 16, 1869	96, 954
Collars, Fastening and strengthening horse	E. Harbaugh	Washington, Iowa	Dec. 29, 1868	85, 382
Collars from sheets of paper, &c., Method of cutting	G. K. Snow	Watertown, Mass	Oct. 29, 1872	132, 547
Collars, Lining for horse	D. Curtis	Sun Prairie, Wis	May 14, 1872	126, 682
Collars, Locking-device for dog	A. R. Scott	Albany, N. Y	June 6, 1871	115, 647
Collars, Machine for applying re-enforcing patches to button-holes of.	H. F. Cary	Boston, Mass	Nov. 10, 1868	83, 927
Collars, Machine for applying strengthening-patch to button holes of.	E. F. Bradley	Derby, Conn	Jan. 19, 1869	85, 899
Collars, Machine for cutting out	G. K. Snow	Watertown, Mass	Oct. 29, 1872	132, 544
Collars, Machine for filling horse	A. Schrick and H. Hildenbrand.	Saint Louis, Mo	Nov. 13, 1866	59, 726
Collars, Machine for filling horse	A. Schrick and H. Hildenbrand.	Saint Louis, Mo	Dec. 17, 1867	72, 423
Collars, Machine for forming horse	F. Cunningham	Chicago, Ill	Feb. 27, 1866	52, 826
Collars, Machine for forming horse	I. Davis	Mechanicsburgh, Ohio	Nov. 4, 1851	8, 482
Collars, Machine for making horse	C. Angevine	New York, N. Y	Oct. 27, 1835	....
Collars, Machine for measuring horses for	W. H. Flynn	Somerville, Mass	Feb. 8, 1870	99, 660
Collars, Machine for pressing and stuffing horse	W. Guilfoyle	New York, N. Y	June 6, 1871	115, 727
Collars, Machine for stretching horse	H. Barton	West Carlisle, Ohio	July 9, 1838	827
Collars, Machine for stretching horse	A. Schrick and H. Hildenbrand.	Saint Louis, Mo	Nov. 13, 1866	59, 727
Collars, Machine for stretching or adjusting size of horse.	J. P. Osborn	Reddington, N. J	Jan. 30, 1841	1, 961
Collars, Machine for stuffing horse	J. Albright	Greeneville, Tenn	Nov. 25, 1856	16, 107
Collars, Machine for stuffing horse	W. Fauntleroy	New Harmony, Ind	Sept. 15, 1868	82, 100
Collars, Machine for stuffing horse	W. Haworth	New York, N. Y	June 26, 1847	5, 177
Collars, Machine for stuffing horse	W. H. Haworth	Philadelphia, Pa	Mar. 17, 1857	16, 834
Collars, Machine for stuffing horse	J. W. Howell	New Paris, Ohio	Feb. 14, 1854	10, 534
Collars, Machine for stuffing horse	S. B. McCorkle	Greeneville, Tenn	Dec. 18, 1855	13, 949

Index of patents issued from the United States Patent Office from 1790 *to* 1873, *inclusive*—Continued.

Invention.	Inventor.	Residence.	Date.	No.
Collars, Machine for stuffing horse	L. Plouk	Newton, N. C	July 6, 1858	20, 816
Collars, Machine for stuffing horse	H. G. Robertson	Greeneville, Tenn	June 10, 1856	15, 107
Collars, Machine for stuffing horse	J. C. Tobias	Lincoln, Ill	July 2, 1857	17, 902
Collars, Machine for stuffing horse	W. L. Whittaker	Cumberland, Md	Mar. 6, 1865	12, 494
Collars, Machine for stuffing horse	T. Wiles	Somerset, Ohio	Mar. 21, 1845	3, 964
Collars, M chine to manufacture horse	W. Criswell	Butler, Pa	Oct. 16, 1849	6, 804
Collars, Machinery for making shirt	O. W. Edson	Troy, N. Y	Feb. 26, 1856	14, 308
Collars, Making horse	T. W. Murphey	New Egypt, N. J	Dec. 5, 1865	51, 341
Collars, Manufacture of japanned or enameled horse.	G. and H. Duxon and H. Perry	Brooklyn, N. Y, and Newark, N. J.	Dec. 12, 1871	121, 859
Collars, Mode of cutting leather for horse	T. Parkinson	Sparta, N. Y	July 17, 1841	2, 183
Collars, Mold-press for horse	M. C. Chamberlin	Sheldon, N. Y	May 6, 1856	14, 803
Collars, Spring for horse	B. J. Barton and R. J. Stanley	Washington, Iowa	Dec. 7, 1869	97, 589
Collars, Stuffing and stretching horse	W. Haworth	Dayton, Ohio	May 7, 1845	4, 037
Collars, Stuffing horse	G. W. Hobart	Silverton, Oreg	May 18, 1869	90, 170
Collars, Sweat-shield for horse	C. B. Hogg	Boston, Mass	Feb. 23, 1869	87, 257
Collarette	C. O. Crosby	New Haven, Conn	Mar. 15, 1864	41, 907
Collection-box, Portable	T. J. Homer	Saint Louis, Mo	Dec. 6, 1859	26, 356
Collet	S. A. Morse	East Bridgewater, Mass	Mar. 3, 1864	42, 592
Collice	J. Flock	Newark, N. J	May 10, 1864	42, 652
Collimator	G. N. Fairchild and T. Joyce	New York, N. Y	Dec. 18, 1860	30, 914
Collision-brake	C. B. Guy	Lybrand, Iowa	Mar. 7, 1865	46, 662
Collodion and its compounds, Machine for treating.	J. A. McClelland	Louisville, Ky	June 1, 1869	90, 766
Collodion and its compounds, Mode of producing useful articles from.	J. A. McClelland	Louisville, Ky	Oct. 26, 1869	96, 132
Collodion and its compounds, Process of coating objects with.	J. A. McClelland	Louisville, Ky	July 26, 1870	105, 823
Collodion compound	J. A. McClelland	Louisville, Ky	Oct. 21, 1873	143, 772
Collodion, Method of making solid	J. W. and I. S. Hyatt	Albany, N. Y., and Rockford, Ill.	June 15, 1869	91, 341
Collodion, Preparing soluble cotton for the manufacture of.	H. T. Anthony	New York, N. Y	Oct. 21, 1873	143, 865
Collodion, Solidified	C. A. Seely	New York, N. Y	June 23, 1868	79, 261
Colors and dyes, Process of treating asphaltum to obtain.	J. Brönner and H. Gutzkow	Frankfort-on-the-Main, Prussia.	Dec. 7, 1869	97, 597
Colors and lakes, Apparatus for preparing	J. Lucas	Philadelphia, Pa	Oct. 25, 1870	108, 713
Colors and paints from ores, &c., Preparing	H. Alexander	Baltimore, Md	Jan. 14, 1813	....
Colors and painting, Mixing	L. Allwine	....	Feb. 24, 1797	....
Colors and pigments, Manufacture of	E. Harrsch	New York, N. Y	Mar. 30, 1869	88, 291
Colors and their application to fabrics, Manufacture of.	A. Paraf	New York, N. Y	Dec. 20, 1870	110, 277
Colors, Compressing and imprinting	L. J. B. Wells	Philadelphia, Pa	Jan. 24, 1817	....
Colors for calico, Making permanent	A. Boulu	Philadelphia, Pa	Dec. 24, 1814	....
Colors for painting, printing, &c., Making	F. Guy	....	Dec. 30, 1803	....
Colors for printing and dyeing, Manufacture and application of.	A. Paraf	New York, N. Y	Nov. 15, 1870	109, 341
Colors from analine, Method of preparing	X. Karcheski	Belleville, N. J	Mar. 14, 1865	46, 804
Colors in calico-printing, Material for transferring.	C. A. Broquette	France	Apr. 15, 1851	8, 035
Colors, Making yellow, nankeen, or buff	J. B. Nones	Philadelphia, Pa	Apr. 28, 1825	....
Colors, Manufacture of	E. Harrsch	New York, N. Y	May 25, 1869	90, 359
Colors, Manufacture of	A. Leykauf	Nürnberg, Bavaria	Feb. 23, 1869	87, 270
Colors, Mode of applying distemper	F. G. Spilsbury, F. Corbaux, and A. S. Byrne.	England	July 10, 1840	1, 676
Colors, Mode of forming yellow	T. Bedwell		Apr. 20, 1796	....
Colors, Press for printing different	S. Brown	Syracuse, N. Y	Jan. 2, 1855	12, 178
Colors, printers' ink, &c., Grinding painters'	J. Cist		Dec. 3, 1803	....
Colors to cloth, &c., Composition for restoring	J. Warncke	Buffalo, N. Y	Mar. 3, 1863	37, 838
Colors with lime, Preparing	J. Nichols, jr	Broadalbin, N. Y	Apr. 12, 1815	....
Colored woolens, &c., Mode of producing mixed	S. Vigoureux	Rheims, France	Mar. 8, 1864	41, 878
Coloring compound or Bremen blue	C. H. Petsch	Morrisania, N. Y	Sept. 10, 1872	131, 297
Coloring fabrics, Re	J. M. Wallace	New York, N. Y	Apr. 25, 1871	114, 069
Coloring-machine, Parti	S. Smith	Acton, Mass	Feb. 21, 1854	10, 560
Coloring material for dyeing and printing	C. Lauth	Paris, France	Oct. 26, 1869	96, 242
Coloring matter for dyers, Producing	J. Eberhardt	Philadelphia, Pa	Mar. 21, 1865	46, 888
Coloring matter or paint, Preparing green	Baron A. De Carrendeffez	New York, N. Y	Oct. 12, 1807	....
Coloring matter, Vegetable	C. Seidel	New York, N. Y	Mar. 31, 1868	76, 107
Coloring matters from anthracine, Manufacture of.	W. H. Perkin	Sudbury, England	June 4, 1872	127, 426
Coloring matters from vegetable substances, Producing.	L. M. F. Bretonniére	Laval, France	Sept. 16, 1873	142, 892
Coloring matters, Manufacturing	J. Holliday	Huddersfield, Great Britain	Dec. 5, 1865	51, 404
Coloring matters, Manufacturing	H. Stephens	Great Britain	Oct. 28, 1837	441
Coloring muslin, paper, &c., Process for	F. Beck	New York, N. Y	Nov. 9, 1869	96, 661
Coloring paper and other fabrics	F. Beck	New York, N. Y	Oct. 4, 1870	107, 997
Coloring the surface of metals, Process for	M. Edwards	Cambridge, Mass	Jan. 31, 1860	26, 978
Colortrope	O. Nicholson	New York, N. Y	Oct. 11, 1870	108, 170
Colter	R. Emerson	Rockford, Ill	Mar. 11, 1873	136, 647
Colter	H. M. Skinner	Rockford, Ill	Sept. 13, 1870	107, 298
Colter and gage-wheel combined, Revolving extension.	W. H. Willard	Cleveland, Ohio	Dec. 2, 1862	37, 065
Colter-clasp	C. H. Thomas	Cassville, N. Y	Aug. 12, 1873	141, 675
Colter-cleaner	A. B. Mattoon	Auburn, N. Y	June 15, 1869	91, 464
Colter-holder	J. Aughe	Dayton, Ohio	Mar. 10, 1868	75, 237
Colter, Revolving	R. L. Pitcher and R. Ellwood	Sycamore, Ill	Jan. 19, 1869	85, 957
Colter, Revolving	C. E. Steller	Chicago, Ill	Feb. 23, 1869	87, 220
Colter, Rotary	F. J. Underwood	Rock Island, Ill	Oct. 19, 1869	96, 057
Column, Building	J. L. Mott	New York, N. Y	June 11, 1836	....
Column, Fire-proof	W. A. Berkey	Grand Rapids, Mich.	Jan. 16, 1872	122, 797
Column, Fire-proof	T. Hyatt	New York, N. Y	Dec. 2, 1873	145, 180
Column, Iron	W. A. Gunn	Lexington, Ky	Jan 2, 1872	122, 379
Column, Metallic	C. Bender	Phœnixville, Pa	Nov. 28, 1871	121, 318
Column, Metallic	S. Brandeis	Philadelphia, Pa	Aug. 26, 1873	142, 201
Column, Metallic	J. B. Cornell	New York, N. Y	Feb. 11, 1868	74, 312
Column, Metallic	J. A. Kay	Saint Charles, Mo	Aug. 15, 1871	118, 021
Column, Metallic	R. Montgomery	New York, N. Y	Jan. 19, 1869	86, 028
Column, Metallic	J. L. Piper	Pittsburgh, Pa	May 13, 1873	138, 817
Column, Metallic	J. L. Piper	Pittsburgh, Pa	Aug. 12, 1873	141, 665
Column, Metallic	F. H. Smith	Baltimore, Md	Nov. 28, 1871	121, 432
Column, Metallic	F. H. Smith	Baltimore, Md	May 14, 1872	126, 841

Index of patents issued from the United States Patent Office from 1790 *to* 1873, *inclusive*—Continued.

Invention.	Inventor.	Residence.	Date.	No.
Column, Metallic	G. Walters and T. Shaffer	Phœnixville, Pa	Feb. 16, 1869	87, 016
Column or tube	F. H. Smith	Baltimore, Md	Nov. 2, 1869	96, 357
Column, Rolled iron or steel	F. H. Smith	Baltimore, Md	May 24, 1870	103, 380
Column, Wrought-iron	A. Bonzano	Phœnixville, Pa	May 21, 1872	127, 019
Column, Wrought-iron	T. C. Clarke	Philadelphia, Pa	Sept. 24, 1872	131, 502
Column, Wrought-iron	L. Herman	Detroit, Mich	Jan. 21, 1873	134, 987
Column, Wrought-iron	J. P. Kennedy	New York, N. Y	Sept. 12, 1871	118, 948
Column, Wrought-iron	J. W. Murphy	Philadelphia, Pa	Dec. 13, 1870	110, 154
Column, Wrought-iron	J. H. Linville	Philadelphia, Pa	Oct. 22, 1872	132, 475
Column, Wrought-iron	C. S. Smith	Baltimore, Md	Nov. 19, 1872	133, 263
Column, Wrought-iron	G. Walters and T. Shaffer	Phœnixville, Pa	Oct. 20, 1868	83, 226
Column, Wrought iron and steel	C. H. Parker	Boston, Mass	May 9, 1871	114, 705
Columns, Connection for compound tubular metallic.	J. A. Kay	Saint Charles, Mo	Aug. 20, 1872	130, 721
Columns, Flask for casting iron	H. Demmick	New York, N. Y	Aug. 21, 1860	29, 745
Columns from corrosion, Art of protecting metallic	J. H. Linville	Philadelphia, Pa	July 16, 1872	129, 241
Columns, Machine for facing ends of	D. Kennedy	Detroit, Mich	July 16, 1872	129, 568
Columns, &c., Machine for ornamenting	C. Durand	Springfield, N. J	Sept. 22, 1818	....
Columns, Manufacture of wrought-iron	D. Halstead	Buffalo, N. Y	June 8, 1869	91, 125
Columns, Method of constructing	G. Walters and T. Shaffer	Phœnixville, Pa	Sept. 29, 1868	82, 663
Columns, &c., Method of constructing	G. Walters and T. Shaffer	Phœnixville, Pa	Sept. 29, 1868	82, 664
Columns, Method of constructing wrought-iron	G. Walters and T. Shaffer	Phœnixville, Pa	Oct. 27, 1868	83, 425
Columns, Method of securing together the sides of cast-metal.	A. J. Bowers	Richmond, Va	Jan. 11, 1859	22, 542
Columns, shafts, braces, &c., Construction of	S. J. Reeves	Philadelphia, Pa	June 17, 1862	35, 582
Comb:				
See Band-comb.				
Carding-comb.				
Curry-comb.				
Dressing-comb.				
Enameled-metal comb.				
Fine-tooth comb.				
Fountain-comb.				
Hair-comb.				
Head-comb.				
Horn comb.				
Horn and tortoise-shell comb.				
Ivory comb.				
Lady's comb.				
Long comb.				
Metal comb.				
Metal-backed comb.				
Pocket-comb.				
Round comb.				
Shell-comb.				
Shell and horn comb.				
Side-comb.				
Toilet-comb.				
Ventilating-comb.				
Comb	J. H. Briggs	Brooklyn, N. Y	Oct. 15, 1867	69, 755
Comb	E. Brown	Wappinger's Falls, N. Y	Jan. 30, 1866	52, 262
Comb	H. Brown and S. N. Noyes	West Newbury, Mass	June 1, 1869	90, 816
Comb	T. L. Calkins	Hartford, Conn	Mar. 17, 1857	16, 859
Comb	F. A. L. Cassidey	Newnansville, Fla	Mar. 5, 1867	62, 606
Comb	G. F. J. Colburn	Newark, N. J	Jan. 17, 1865	45, 909
Comb	G. F. J. Colburn	Newark, N. J	Jan. 31, 1865	46, 082
Comb	J. S. Dickinson	Essex, Conn	Apr. 7, 1868	76, 414
Comb	J. Emerson	Lowell, Mass	Dec. 18, 1866	60, 494
Comb	C. Foster	Wappinger's Falls, N. Y	Jan. 28, 1868	73, 884
Comb	J. H. Hicks	Brooklyn, N. Y	Nov. 27, 1866	60, 004
Comb	O. Johnson	Grand Lodge, Mich	Jan. 30, 1872	123, 177
Comb	E. H. Knight	Washington, D. C	Dec. 4, 1866	60, 197
Comb	C. H. Noyes	Brooklyn, N. Y	Apr. 4, 1871	113, 330
Comb	E. M. Noyes	Newark, N. J	Apr. 24, 1860	28, 008
Comb	E. M. Noyes	Newark, N. J	June 7, 1864	43, 038
Comb	J. P. Noyes	Newark, N. J	June 5, 1866	55, 349
Comb	H. M. Paine	Newark, N. J	Apr. 6, 1869	88, 582
Comb	W. Pauly	College Point, N. Y	Dec. 17, 1867	72, 324
Comb	L. Picot	Hoboken, N. J	Nov. 13, 1866	59, 645
Comb	L. Picot	Hoboken, N. J	Aug. 11, 1868	80, 833
Comb	L. Picot	Hudson City, N. J	Apr. 4, 1871	113, 340
Comb	J. C. Reed	New York, N. Y	June 14, 1870	104, 202
Comb	I. Rice	New York, N. Y	Nov. 20, 1866	59, 926
Comb	C. L. Robertson	Providence, R. I	Apr. 13, 1869	88, 811
Comb	T. Schreiber	Wheeling, W. Va	Nov. 13, 1866	59, 664
Comb	J. Smith	Leominster, Mass	Sept. 29, 1868	82, 560
Comb	I. H. Southworth	Essex, Conn	Oct. 10, 1865	50, 400
Comb	E. Sperry	New Haven, Conn	Oct. 10, 1829	....
Comb and brush	T. Lanston	Washington, D. C	May 30, 1871	115, 488
Comb-attachment	G. Stackhouse	Mount Washington, Pa	June 29, 1869	91, 984
Comb-blanks, Device for softening	W. and H. W. Noyes	Newburyport, Mass	Apr. 30, 1872	126, 154
Comb-blanks, Machine for sizing	W. Fosket and B. S. Stedman	Meriden, Conn	Aug. 26, 1856	15, 634
Comb-cleaner	C. E. Gibbs	Boston, Mass	May 10, 1870	102, 803
Comb-cleaner	A. Sahlstrom	Chicago, Ill	June 27, 1871	116, 500
Comb-cleaner	E. J. Toof	Fort Madison, Iowa	Apr. 28, 1868	77, 416
Comb-cleaner	C. P. S. Wardwell	Lake Village, N. H	Dec. 18, 1860	30, 949
Comb-cutting machine	H. S. Cook	Leominster, Mass	June 3, 1851	8, 129
Comb-cutting machine	S. Curtis	Newtown, Conn	Nov. 18, 1851	8, 522
Comb-cutting machine	N. Toot	Philadelphia, Pa	Oct. 28, 1819	....
Comb-cutting machine	B. Haskell	Paris, France	Nov. 3, 1819	....
Comb-cutting machine	T. W. Hill	Leominster, Mass	June 10, 1851	8, 144
Comb-cutting machine	D. E. Noyes	Philadelphia, Pa	Oct. 14, 1819	....
Comb-dressing machinery	C. B. Rogers	Saybrook, Conn	Dec. 20, 1845	4, 321
Comb-dressing machinery	E. Wilson	Redding, Conn	Mar. 14, 1848	5, 472
Comb for combing wool, flax, cotton, &c	J. B. Siccardi and J. Hide	New York, N. Y	Feb. 14, 1865	46, 397
Comb-frame	W. Rasey	Remington, Ind	Sept. 30, 1873	143, 383
Comb-holder	E. E. Wheeler	South Norwalk, Conn	Nov. 4, 1873	144, 242
Comb machine, Twining	D. Carrington and I. Ives	Litchfield, Conn	Aug. 20, 1813	....

Index of patents issued from the United States Patent Office from 1790 *to* 1873, *inclusive*—Continued.

Invention.	Inventor.	Residence.	Date.	No.
Comb-making machine	J. Pitts, C. Houghton, and J. Rice, jr.	Lancaster, Mass	Oct. 1, 1830	....
Comb, Metal	A. Porter	Hartford, Conn	June 14, 1834	....
Comb or hair-pin, Ventilating	E. Clark	Louisville, Ky	Sept. 3, 1872	130, 978
Comb-presses, Fluting and bending	R. Munson	New York, N. Y	May 22, 1832	....
Comb-sawing machine	W. Booth	College Point, N. Y	Mar. 5, 1872	124, 243
Comb-sawing machine	G. F. H. Brown	Leominster, Mass	Aug. 11, 1868	80, 855
Comb-teeth, Cutting	L. Adams	Redding, Conn	May 2, 1835	....
Comb-teeth, Cutting	J. Brown	Springfield, Mass	Dec. 8, 1824	....
Comb-teeth, Cutting	M. J. Littleboy	Philadelphia, Pa	May 28, 1816	....
Comb-teeth, Cutting and pointing	I. Tryon	....	Feb. 22, 1798	....
Comb-teeth, Die for cutting metallic	C. Foster	Wappinger's Falls, N. Y	June 2, 1868	78, 585
Comb-teeth, Machine for sawing	P. Pratt	New York, N. Y	Apr. 20, 1825	....
Comb-teeth, Machinery for cutting	W. Noyes, jr	West Newbury, Mass	June 7, 1859	24, 358
Combs, Cutting	J. H. Derby	Leominster, Mass	Mar. 26, 1814	....
Combs, Cutting horn and tortoise-shell for	S. Allen	....	Apr. 1, 1815	....
Combs, Machine for cutting all kinds of	T. G. Thomas	Philadelphia, Pa	June 14, 1817	....
Combs, Machine for cutting the teeth of	J. S. Ives	Bristol, Conn	Oct. 8, 1840	1, 811
Combs, Machine for making	P. Pratt	....	Apr. 12, 1799	....
Combs, Machine for making	P. Pratt	Saybrook, Conn	Mar. 5, 1808	....
Combs, Machine for manufacturing	D. Pettibone	Philadelphia, Pa	Aug. 11, 1818	....
Combs, Machine for slitting tortoise-shell for making.	W. Redheffer	Penn Township, Pa	June 18, 1842	2, 679
Combs, Manufacturing	J. Brown	Providence, R. I	June 11, 1829	....
Combs, Manufacturing	A. B. Newton	Baltimore, Md	Mar. 31, 1834	....
Combs, Manufacturing	B. and W. Redheffer	Penn Township, Pa	May 26, 1834	....
Combs, Manufacturing	E. Sperry	New Haven, Conn	Mar. 27, 1816	....
Combs, Mode of forming and shaping	S. Lambert	Hanover County, Va	Jan. 9, 1829	....
Combs, Ornamenting and making	E. Mustin	Philadelphia, Pa	June 27, 1829	....
Combs, Press for molding	W. and H. W. Noyes	Newburyport, Mass	Sept. 24, 1872	131, 626
Combs, &c., Pressing and rendering transparent horse-hoofs, &c., for making.	E. M. Canviss	Southington, Conn	May 6, 1812	....
Combs, Rolling backs of	N. Bishop	Danbury, Conn	Nov. 17, 1827	....
Combs, Rubbing down and polishing	L. B. Prindle and D. Curtis	Newtown, Conn	Oct. 10, 1829	....
Combs, Steel plate for pressing horn for	U. Bailey	West Newbury, Mass	Feb. 2, 1828	....
Combs from cattle-hoofs, Mode of making	R. Gedney	New York	June 26, 1809	....
Comber-boards, Mechanism for operating	J. S. Templeton	Glasgow, Great Britain	Oct. 4, 1870	107, 979
Combing-machine	I., B., and H. Smith and C. Bradley.	Bradford, England	Apr. 1, 1873	137, 326
Combing-machine	E. Tavernier	Lille, France	Jan. 9, 1872	122, 678
Combing-machine comb	C. Weiler	Landenburgh, Pa	Apr. 18, 1871	113, 825
Combing-machines, Mechanism for operating the nippers of.	H. Daniels	Pawtucket, R. I	Aug. 17, 1869	93, 811
Combination and register padlock	H. S. Shepardson	Shelburne Falls, Mass	Sept. 13, 1870	107, 414
Combination, Bench	W. Weaver	Nashua, N. H	Nov. 5, 1867	70, 657
Combination-lock	M. Adams	Chilmark, Mass	Nov. 2, 1869	96, 376
Combination-lock	F. W. Alexander	Baltimore, Md	Apr. 30, 1861	32, 171
Combination-lock	S. Bentley and C. Mee	Detroit, Mich	Mar. 15, 1870	100, 714
Combination-lock	H. Clarke	Baltimore, Md	Feb. 4, 1873	135, 523
Combination-lock	S. Colton	Philadelphia, Pa	Jan. 6, 1844	3, 395
Combination-lock	J. W. H. Doubler	Darlington, Wis	May 23, 1871	115, 037
Combination-lock	H. Gross	Tiffin, Ohio	May 11, 1869	89, 989
Combination-lock	P. W. Hall	Calvert, Tex	July 1, 1873	140, 500
Combination-lock	W. N. Hall	Springfield, Tex	Sept. 12, 1871	118, 930
Combination-lock	A. D. Hoffman	Chicago, Ill	Aug. 19, 1873	141, 876
Combination-lock	F. B. Kalkbrenner	Clinton, Mo	Oct. 18, 1870	108, 360
Combination-lock	W. A. Kerr	Williamsport, Pa	July 16, 1872	129, 482
Combination-lock	I. W. Lamb	Salem, Mich	July 20, 1869	92, 844
Combination-lock	H. S. Leland	Mount Union, Ohio	Mar. 30, 1869	88, 490
Combination-lock	S. Loyd	New York, N. Y	Apr. 4, 1871	113, 316
Combination-lock	F. P. Marsden	Galena, Ill	Dec. 26, 1871	122, 124
Combination-lock	S. Miller	Gratis, Ohio	Aug. 8, 1871	117, 912
Combination-lock	J. Moffet	New York, N. Y	Apr. 9, 1872	125, 475
Combination-lock	J. H. Morse	Peoria, Ill	Dec. 4, 1860	30, 830
Combination-lock	G. H. Peacock	Webster, N. Y	Oct. 17, 1871	119, 948
Combination-lock	G. H. Peacock	Webster, N. Y	June 11, 1872	127, 706
Combination-lock	S. Perry	Newport, N. Y	June 22, 1858	20, 658
Combination-lock	G. M. Phelps	Williamsburgh, N. Y	Dec. 23, 1862	37, 241
Combination-lock	J. Pigot	Brooklyn, N. Y	July 16, 1872	129, 052
Combination-lock	O. E. Pillard	New Britain, Conn	June 1, 1869	90, 682
Combination-lock	N. Reed	Otisville, N. Y	Aug. 71, 1869	93, 747
Combination-lock	S. K. Seelye	Hudson, Mich	Nov. 22, 1870	109, 457
Combination-lock	J. T. Taylor	Newnan, Ga	Sept. 17, 1872	131, 475
Combination-lock	A. B. Vandemark	Phelps, N. Y	Dec. 1, 1868	84, 659
Combination-lock	E. Vorbe	San Francisco, Cal	May 4, 1869	89, 817
Combination-lock	J. B. White	Detroit, Mich	Dec. 1, 1868	84, 664
Combination-lock	J. B. White	Detroit, Mich	Aug. 27, 1872	130, 964
Combination-lock	J. P. White	Savannah, Ga	Sept. 21, 1869	95, 058
Combination lock and key	S. L. Chase	Lockport, N. Y	Nov. 6, 1847	5, 359
Combination-lock for doors	S. Andrews	Perth Amboy, N. J	Sept. 30, 1841	2, 276
Combination-lock for doors	W. C. Bussey	San Francisco, Cal	Apr. 7, 1868	76, 300
Combination-lock for doors, safes, &c	R. Newell	New York, N. Y	Sept. 17, 1844	3, 747
Combination-padlock	M. P. Thatcher	Pontiac, Mich	Dec. 7, 1869	97, 568
Combination-tool	C. A. Foster	Fitchburgh, Mass	Apr. 19, 1870	102, 105
Combined supporter	S. Dike	New York, N. Y	Aug. 24, 1869	94, 087
Combining or mixing two or more substances, Apparatus for.	G. W. Wilson	Chelsea, Mass	June 6, 1871	115, 799
Combustion-power	A. Day	Bordentown, N. J	Jan. 19, 1811	....
Combustion, System of supporting	J. A. Bassett and E. L. Norfolk	Salem, Mass	Mar. 7, 1865	46, 624
Comminuting various substances, Apparatus for	G. B. Canning	Brooklyn, N. Y	Mar. 11, 1873	136, 700
Commode	J. D. Averell	New York, N. Y	Oct. 7, 1873	143, 488
Commode	W. Prangley	Salisbury, England	Nov. 5, 1872	132, 775
Commode and wash-stand combined	S. P. Boone	Americus, Ga	Aug. 29, 1871	118, 510
Commode, Chamber	T. Elkins	Albany, N. Y	Jan. 9, 1872	122, 518
Commode, Chamber	E. S. Farson	Philadelphia, Pa	Sept. 15, 1868	82, 099
Commode, Disinfecting	H. J. Alvord	Detroit, Mich	July 31, 1866	56, 870
Commode, Earth	G. F. Stone	Baltimore, Md	Apr. 9, 1872	125, 627
Commode, Earth	E. Woodruff	Elizabeth, N. J	Nov. 1, 1870	108, 950
Commode, Folding	R. G. Elder	New York, N. Y	Nov. 28, 1871	121, 344

Index of patents issued from the United States Patent Office from 1790 to 1873, inclusive—Continued.

Invention.	Inventor.	Residence.	Date.	No.
Commutator, Electric	L. B. Firman	Chicago, Ill	Mar. 24, 1868	75, 743
Compass	P. Roessler	New Haven, Conn	Sept. 19, 1865	50, 037
Compass	H. Stewart	Clinton, Mass	Apr. 21, 1868	77, 123
Compass	O. Stoddard	Detroit, Mich	Aug. 27, 1872	130, 879
Compass and magnetic needle	J. Hanks	Troy, N. Y	July 22, 1833	....
Compass, Azimuth	E. S. Ritchie	Brookline, Mass	Aug. 1, 1865	49, 157
Compass, Beam	J. Lyman	Lenox, Mass	Feb. 21, 1871	111, 954
Compass, Beam	M. Toulmin	New Orleans, La	Sept. 16, 1873	142, 823
Compass, Correcting the deviation of the mariner's	L. F. A. Arson	Paris, France	May 31, 1870	103, 701
Compass for determining variations from local causes.	J. R. St. John	New York, N. Y	Mar. 2, 1852	8, 785
Compass for mining	J. Blomgren	New York, N. Y	Oct. 25, 1870	108, 555
Compass, Instrument for determining the variation of the.	E. S. Ritchie	Brookline, Mass	Jan. 3, 1865	45, 753
Compass-joint	T. Alteneder	Philadelphia, Pa	Feb. 14, 1871	111, 715
Compass-joint, Measuring	T. Alteneder	Philadelphia, Pa	July 16, 1850	7, 501
Compass, Liquid	J. and G. H. Bliss	Brooklyn, N. Y	Jan. 24, 1871	111, 169
Compass, Liquid	E. Blunt	Brooklyn, N. Y	Dec. 5, 1865	51, 290
Compass, Magnetic	H. W. Hunter	New York, N. Y	May 6, 1862	35, 156
Compass, Marine	S. Custer	Salem, Va	June 26, 1866	55, 827
Compass, Marine	E. S. Ritchie	Brookline, Mass	July 19, 1870	105, 492
Compass, Mariner's	J. Ball	Buffalo, N. Y	Mar. 6, 1835	....
Compass, Mariner's	J. and G. H. Bliss	Brooklyn, N. Y	May 24, 1870	103, 286
Compass, Mariner's	J. and G. H. Bliss	Brooklyn, N. Y	May 24, 1870	103, 287
Compass, Mariner's	H. Colby	Rochester, N. Y	May 1, 1847	5, 096
Compass, Mariner's	S. Custer	Salem, Va	July 16, 1867	66, 805
Compass, Mariner's	J. S. Pender	New York, N. Y	Sept. 27, 1864	44, 451
Compass, Mariner's	E. S. Ritchie	Brookline, Mass	Sept. 9, 1862	36, 422
Compass, Mariner's	E. S. Ritchie	Brookline, Mass	Apr. 7, 1863	38, 125
Compass, Mariner's	E. S. Ritchie	Brookline, Mass	Apr. 7, 1863	38, 126
Compass, Mariner's	E. S. Ritchie	Brookline, Mass	Apr. 10, 1866	53, 875
Compass, Mariner's and surveyor's	W. C. Poole	Lancaster, Pa	July 31, 1840	1, 707
Compass, Mariner's or surveyor's	W. Russell	New Bedford, Mass	Dec. 1, 1809	....
Compass, Mariner's time	R. Reeder	Cincinnati, Ohio	Feb. 9, 1847	4, 964
Compass-needle, Magnetizing	S. Custer	Salem, Va	July 16, 1867	66, 806
Compass needle, Marine and surveying	M. Smith	New York, N. Y	June 15, 1830	....
Compass or theodolite, Surveying	J. Eames	Newry, Me	Feb. 11, 1835	....
Compass-protractor	F. H. West	San Francisco, Cal	Sept. 25, 1860	30, 187
Compass, quadrant, and protractor	F. Whiteley	Stanardsville, Va	Dec. 6, 1836	99
Compass, Self-registering ship's	R. H. Peverly	Chelsea, Mass	June 3, 1856	15, 017
Compass, Ship's	James, Earl of Caithness	Middlesex County, England	Nov. 5, 1867	70, 520
Compass, Ship's	J. Prime	Washington, N. C	Feb. 12, 1856	14, 251
Compass, Ship's	G. W. Wood	Brooklyn, N. Y	Mar. 21, 1871	112, 999
Compass, Solar	H. O. Cook	New York, N. Y	Aug. 12, 1873	141, 766
Compass, Solar	B. S. Lyman	Philadelphia, Pa	July 18, 1871	117, 184
Compass, Surveying	G. W. Dickinson, jr	Breckenridge, Va	Feb. 21, 1860	27, 210
Compass, Surveying	W. J. Young	Philadelphia, Pa	Jan. 17, 1832	....
Compass, Surveying	W. J. Young	Philadelphia, Pa	Jan. 11, 1834	....
Compass, Surveyor's	N. Bassett	Wilmington, Del	June 28, 1836	....
Compass, Surveyor's	S. Kern	Strasburgh, Va	July 28, 1846	4, 675
Compass, Surveyor's	J. Locke	Cincinnati, Ohio	July 16, 1850	7, 510
Compass, Surveyor's	H. B. Martin	Santa Rosa, Cal	June 7, 1864	43, 036
Compass, Surveyor's	S. R. Miller	Front Royal, Va	Oct. 22, 1835	....
Compass, Universal	S. Dew	Romney, Va	Apr. 13, 1822	....
Compasses and calipers	J. E. Earle	Leicester, Mass	Aug. 1, 1854	11, 420
Compasses and calipers	F. P. Pfleghar and W. Schollhorn.	New Haven, Conn	Jan. 9, 1866	51, 967
Compasses and calipers, Combined beam	W. Burrows	New York, N. Y	Dec. 29, 1868	85, 430
Compasses, Card for liquid	E. S. Ritchie	Brookline, Mass	June 2, 1863	38, 762
Compasses, Binnacle for mariner's	G. W. Richey and H. E. Bixby	Saint Louis, Mo	July 4, 1871	116, 631
Compasses, Card for mariner's liquid	E. S. Ritchie	Brookline, Mass	Jan. 24, 1871	111, 254
Compasses, Construction of	T. Hagerty	Richmond, Va	July 30, 1872	130, 036
Compasses, Construction of	T. Hagerty	Richmond, Va	July 30, 1872	130, 037
Compasses, Construction of spring	T. Hagerty	Richmond, Va	July 30, 1872	130, 038
Compasses, Electro-magnetic attachment to ships'	A. Foucaut	Orleans, France	July 19, 1870	105, 562
Compasses insensible to local attraction, Rendering.	J. S. Gisbone and W. Simpson	Birkenhead and Liverpool, England.	Mar. 8, 1864	41, 839
Compasses, Local-attraction indicator for ships'	H. Glover	Brooklyn, N. Y	Sept. 17, 1872	131, 435
Compasses, Mode of fixing mariners'	L. Langley	Gosport, Va	June 23, 1828	....
Compasses, Pencil-attachment for	C. Schott	Nashville, Tenn	July 12, 1870	105, 376
Compasses, Pencil-attachment to	C. L. Tyler	Ithaca, N. Y	Nov. 2, 1869	96, 366
Compasses, Preventing the deviation of ships'	J. W. Girdlestone	Strand, England	Oct. 25, 1870	108, 585
Compasses used in calking seams	G. Dowling	Fair Haven, Conn	June 11, 1867	65, 654
Compensating or equilibrium spring	C. Shea	Newark, N. J	Oct. 12, 1869	95, 736
Composing-stick	L. Buschmann	Newark, N. J	Oct. 21, 1873	143, 875
Composing-stick	A. F. Cloudman and G. W. Coffin.	Brooklyn, N. Y., and Charlestown, Mass.	Oct. 18, 1870	108, 451
Composing-stick	J. M. Eaton	Charlestown, Mass	Aug. 10, 1869	93, 426
Composing-stick	F. W. Murray	Cincinnati, Ohio	Mar. 16, 1869	88, 800
Composing-stick	R. W. Thing	Boston, Mass	Jan. 26, 1869	86, 257
Composing-stick	W. T. Tillinghast	Dayton, Ohio	May 22, 1866	54, 979
Composing-stick	J. L. Wait	East Cambridge, Mass	May 19, 1868	78, 033
Composing-stick	J. Wilson	Boston, Mass	Aug. 6, 1872	130, 170
Composing-stick	R. C. Young	Middletown, Conn	Oct. 18, 1870	108, 549
Composing-stick, Printer's	S. W. Brown	Syracuse, N. Y	May 22, 1860	28, 436
Composing-stick, Printer's	A. Calhoun	Hartford, Conn	Aug. 31, 1858	21, 321
Composing-stick, Printer's	O. F. Grover	Middletown, Conn	July 15, 1856	15, 358
Composing-stick, Printer's	P. S. Hoe	New York, N. Y	Nov. 5, 1872	132, 722
Composing stick, Printer's	J. and W. Tidgewell	Middletown, Conn	June 2, 1857	17, 457
Composing-stick, Printer's	W. T. Tillinghast	Dayton, Ohio	Jan. 27, 1857	16, 500
Composing-stick, Printer's	D. Winder	Cincinnati, Ohio	Apr. 7, 1857	17, 007
Composite pipe	A. P. Stephens	Brooklyn, N. Y	May 26, 1868	78, 336
Composition-box	T. B. Gunning	New York, N. Y	Oct. 3, 1871	119, 603
Composition handle or pull	W. B. Gleason	Boston, Mass	Mar. 22, 1870	101, 119
Compositor's stand	F. Vallee	Philadelphia, Pa	Apr. 8, 1873	137, 639
Compost	E. Blanchard	Greenfield Mills, Md	Aug. 9, 1859	24, 988
Compost for soil	A. B. Martin	Baltimore, Md	June 2, 1819	....
Compound engine	A. Hartupee	Pittsburgh, Pa	Apr. 16, 1872	125, 812

Index of patents issued from the United States Patent Office from 1790 *to* 1873, *inclusive*—Continued.

Invention.	Inventor.	Residence.	Date.	No.
Compound engine	W. Wright	Newburgh, N. Y	Nov. 18, 1873	144, 817
Compound gage	A. Williams	Philadelphia, Pa	May 26, 1857	17, 403
Compound steam-engine	W. W. Crane	Auburn, N. Y	June 3, 1873	139, 549
Compound steam-engine	L. Huntoon	Natick, Mass	Jan. 28, 1873	135, 223
Compound tool	J. Dillon	New York, N. Y	Dec. 30, 1873	145, 992
Compress	C. W. Armstrong	Detroit, Mich	Nov. 30, 1869	97, 265
Compress, Double-acting	J. H. Fellows	Lewisport, Ky	Dec. 20, 1864	45, 559
Compress-table	H. A. Burr	Brooklyn, N. Y	July 21, 1868	80, 132
Compressed-air engine	E. H. Grant	Washington, D. C	Sept. 7, 1869	94, 594
Compressed-air motor	H. Bushnell	New Haven, Conn	Apr. 15, 1873	137, 889
Compressor, Spiral-curvilinear	W. Nelson	Batavia, N. Y	Nov. 13, 1828	....
Compressing and baling press	D. S. Gardner and N. A. Manning.	Greene, N. Y	Mar. 25, 1862	34, 750
Compressing and beater press	G. Ertel	Liberty, Ill	Mar. 31, 1868	76, 063
Compression-lock	J. Powell	Cincinnati, Ohio	Jan. 18, 1870	99, 001
Computing-apparatus	T. Wallworth	Newton Heath, Great Britain.	Feb. 18, 1868	74, 641
Computing-apparatus	E. Wright	Medford, Mass	Aug. 17, 1869	93, 849
Computing-machine	J. H. Chidester	Cleveland, Ohio	Dec. 18, 1866	60, 475
Computing-machine	A. W. Davies	Cleveland, Ohio	June 18, 1867	65, 883
Concave-cutting device	H. C. Rosin	Chicago, Ill	Aug. 29, 1871	118, 489
Concentrator	J. Hendy	San Francisco, Cal	Apr. 17, 1866	53, 976
Concentrator	J. Hendy	San Francisco, Cal	May 19, 1868	78, 089
Concentrator, Metallic	Z. Wheeler	San Francisco, Cal	Sept. 6, 1864	44, 130
Conception, Preventing	J. B. Beers	Rochester, N. Y	Aug. 28, 1846	4, 729
Concertina, Key-face for	L. A. Seward	New Orleans, La	Oct. 26, 1869	96, 150
Concrete, Apparatus for feeding and mixing gravel, &c., in forming.	A. D. Foote	Washington, D. C	July 16, 1872	129, 330
Concrete arches for buildings, Construction of	C. C. Dennett	Nottingham, England	Jan. 4, 1870	98, 571
Concrete block for buildings and other purposes	T. Heap	Saint Joseph, Mo	Dec. 28, 1869	98, 373
Concrete-block machine	L. Dodge and L. J. Magnusson	Chicago, Ill	Dec. 29, 1868	85, 291
Concrete-block-making machine	O. V. Evans	Ripley, Ohio	Sept. 22, 1868	82, 301
Concrete-block mold	J. P. Campbell	Dayton, Ohio	June 4, 1872	127, 562
Concrete-block press	L. S. Warner	Chicago, Ill	May 12, 1868	77, 854
Concrete building-block press	O. L. Jordan	Dowagiac, Mich	Jan. 21, 1868	73, 600
Concrete-composition for walks, flooring, &c	R. S. Lewis	Rockville, Conn	Nov. 22, 1870	109, 524
Concrete for pipes, bricks, &c	T. J. Barron	Brooklyn, N. Y	Feb. 14, 1871	111, 806
Concrete for pipes, tubes, buildings, &c	T. J. Barron	Brooklyn, E. D., N. Y	Jan. 24, 1871	111, 166
Concrete, &c., Machine for mixing	S. Putnam and T. Burt	Rockville, Conn	Jan. 17, 1871	111, 000
Concrete-pipes, Machine for making	G. L. Eagan	San Francisco, Cal	Apr. 9, 1872	125, 551
Condensation and refrigeration, Method of	N. W. Wheeler	Brooklyn, N. Y	July 3, 1866	56, 130
Condenser	E. H. Ashcroft	Lynn, Mass	Nov. 5, 1867	70, 389
Condenser	B. T. Babbitt	New York, N. Y	Sept. 1, 1863	39, 709
Condenser	A. C. Brown	Philadelphia, Pa	July 10, 1860	29, 054
Condenser	S. W. Brown	Lowell, Mass	Dec. 19, 1854	12, 089
Condenser	T. Callan	Philadelphia, Pa	Sept. 12, 1865	49, 855
Condenser	L. Cook	Whitestown, N. Y	Mar. 26, 1811	....
Condenser	J. H. Fairchild	Highgate, Vt	Mar. 27, 1866	53, 528
Condenser	A. C. Fletcher	New York, N. Y	July 11, 1865	48, 710
Condenser	A. Hartupee and H. P. Gengembre.	Pittsburgh, Pa	Dec. 13, 1864	45, 408
Condenser	J. Houpt	Springtown, Pa	Dec. 14, 1869	97, 923
Condenser	G. A. Jasper	Charlestown, Mass	July 5, 1864	43, 413
Condenser	W. Jeggle and L. A. Brooks	Chicago, Ill	Apr. 2, 1867	63, 391
Condenser	W. A. Lighthall	New York, N. Y	Feb. 7, 1865	46, 254
Condenser	W. A. Lighthall	New York, N. Y	Apr. 21, 1868	76, 929
Condenser	J. F. Llewellyn	Louisville, Ky	Sept. 11, 1866	57, 932
Condenser	P. Mihan and M. A. Lane	Boston and Charlestown, Mass.	Sept. 18, 1860	30, 078
Condenser	F. Ortlieb	Williamsburgh, N. Y	Sept. 3, 1867	68, 382
Condenser	W. Phelan	Peoria, Ill	Apr. 14, 1868	76, 655
Condenser	W. Phelan	Peoria, Ill	Oct. 20, 1868	83, 309
Condenser	F. Ransom	Buffalo, N. Y	Oct. 13, 1868	83, 092
Condenser	J. Root	Painesville, Ohio	May 26, 1834	....
Condenser	T. Shaw	Philadelphia, Pa	Sept. 28, 1869	95, 275
Condenser	J. F. Spence	Williamsburgh, N. Y	Mar. 27, 1866	53, 498
Condenser	J. M. Spiegle	Philadelphia, Pa	Jan. 17, 1865	45, 941
Condenser	G. Stump	New York, N. Y	Aug. 25, 1863	39, 688
Condenser	H. A. Towne	Hannibal, Mo	Aug. 19, 1873	142, 060
Condenser	G. R. Vanderbilt	Mount Vernon, N. Y	Mar. 15, 1864	41, 949
Condenser	G. I. Washburn	Worcester, Mass	Dec. 8, 1863	40, 872
Condenser	J. C. Wharton	Nashville, Tenn	Sept. 11, 1866	58, 0[illegible]9
Condenser	F. Wegmann	Naples, Italy	Aug. 30, 1870	106, 973
Condenser	N. W. Wheeler	Brooklyn, N. Y	July 9, 1867	66, 541
Condenser	W. L. and T. Winans	London, England, and Baltimore, Md.	Oct. 27, 1868	83, 430
Condenser, Air	O. Abruzzo	New York, N. Y	Nov. 19, 1867	70, 934
Condenser, Air-heating steam	P. J. Rice and D. A. Scott	Ashtabula and Cincinnati, Ohio.	Aug. 9, 1870	106, 206
Condenser and boiler, Steam-engine	B. Crawford	Allegheny City, Pa	Sept. 7, 1844	3, 732
Condenser and feed-water apparatus, Combined	J. S. Gibson	Martinsburgh, W. Va	Nov. 4, 1873	144, 331
Condenser and feed-water heater	W. Phelan	Peoria, Ill	May 10, 1870	102, 965
Condenser and feed-water heater, Steam-engine	J. Dilworth and J. C. Hodgins.	Toronto, Canada	Feb. 21, 1871	111, 916
Condenser and feeder, Steam-boiler	F. A. Fischer	Hartzburgh, Germany	May 20, 1873	139, 136
Condenser and lime-extracting heater	J. Huntington	Cleveland, Ohio	Mar. 15, 1870	100, 766
Condenser and refiner for spirituous liquors	W. Neil	San Francisco, Cal	May 6, 1873	138, 517
Condenser and stuffing-box, Vapor-engine	P. V. Du Trembley	Paris, France	Dec. 4, 1849	6, 929
Condenser and water-heater, Steam-engine	J. S. Hooton	New Carlisle, Ind	Mar. 5, 1861	31, 600
Condenser-case	W. A. Lighthall	New York, N. Y	Feb. 7, 1865	46, 253
Condenser, Coal-gas	A. Babbett and W. W. Binney.	Auburn, N. Y	June 7, 1870	103, 824
Condenser, Coal-oil	J. F. Bennett	Pittsburgh, Pa	May 22, 1860	28, 341
Condenser, Coal-oil	W. G. W. Jaeger	Baltimore, Md	June 28, 1859	24, 561
Condenser, Compound surface	W. A. Lighthall	New York, N. Y	July 4, 1871	116, 728
Condenser for alcohol-stills	E. Smeeth	Chicago, Ill.	Oct. 26, 1869	96, 157
Condenser for brewers' boilers	C. Clifford	Fulton, N. Y	Dec. 15, 1868	84, 995
Condenser for carbonic acid and for drawing off and applying the same for cooling and freezing.	T. S. C. Lowe	New York, N. Y	Apr. 2, 1867	63, 405
Condenser for carding-engines	G. R. Gardiner	Westerly, R. I	Nov. 5, 1867	70, 543

Index of patents issued from the United States Patent Office from 1790 *to* 1873, *inclusive*—Continued.

Invention.	Inventor.	Residence.	Date.	No.
Condenser for carding-machines	N. Lucas	Norwich, Conn	Sept. 23, 1873	143, 020
Condenser for coal-oil stills	C. W. Grannis	Gowanda, N. Y	Sept. 9, 1862	36, 403
Condenser for distillers, Refrigerating	F. Haeck	Brussels, Belgium	Nov. 8, 1864	45, 003
Condenser for distillation	T. O'Connor	New York	July 9, 1807	......
Condenser for fibrous material	W. H. Howard	Philadelphia, Pa	May 15, 1855	12, 863
Condenser for gas-works	P. Munzinger	Philadelphia, Pa	Nov. 8, 1870	109, 142
Condenser for heating mash in distilling	A. Anderson	....	Jan. 26, 1801	....
Condenser for illuminating-gas, Friction	W. H. St. John and S. O. Rockwell.	Brooklyn, N. Y., and Jersey City, N. J.	Apr. 4, 1871	113, 463
Condenser for lard-rendering kettles, Vapor	W. M. Bartram	Philadelphia, Pa	Sept. 15, 1868	82, 195
Condenser for list-speeders	W. Mattison	Northbridge, Mass	Sept. 1, 1857	18, 121
Condenser for making potable water	W. A. Lighthall	New York, N. Y	May 20, 1862	35, 319
Condenser for marine engines	J. Houpt	Springtown, Pa	July 19, 1870	105, 457
Condenser for marine engines, Surface	D. Carpenter	Brooklyn, N. Y	Sept. 12, 1854	11, 661
Condenser for oil-stills	J. Adair	Pittsburgh, Pa	June 10, 1862	35, 497
Condenser for oil-stills	H. W. Faucett and T. McGowan.	Titusville and Meredith, Pa.	Aug. 8, 1871	117, 873
Condenser for rectifying-apparatus	A. Feubert	Buffalo, N. Y	Aug. 29, 1871	118, 601
Condenser for spirits, steam, and other vapors	A. W. Cram	Saint Louis, Mo	Jan. 19, 1869	85, 910
Condenser for stills	T. J. Dean	Saint Louis, Mo	July 20, 1869	92, 941
Condenser for stills	J. Harrison and C. Low	Fawn Grove, Pa	May 24, 1870	103, 326
Condenser for stills	C. Moffit	Baltimore, Md	July 2, 1867	66, 243
Condenser for stills	H. C. Sherman	Buffalo, N. Y	Mar. 11, 1862	34, 648
Condenser for stills	C. E. Werner	New Castle, Ill	Dec. 6, 1853	10, 305
Condenser for stills	J. Yates and E. Deuell	Brooklyn, N. Y	Apr. 25, 1871	114, 245
Condenser for vacuum-pans, &c	C. W. Dyrant and J. Griffith	New York, N. Y	Oct. 15, 1872	132, 263
Condenser, Gas	I. N. Stanley	Brooklyn, N. Y	Apr. 18, 1871	113, 942
Condenser, Gas	E. Thompson	Madison, Wis	May 24, 1870	103, 392
Condenser, Hydro-atmospheric	J. P. F. Datichy	New York, N. Y	Aug. 30, 1864	43, 976
Condenser, Jet	J. P. F. Datichy	West Hoboken, N. J	Jan. 15, 1867	61, 167
Condenser, Marine	B. T. Babbitt	New York, N. Y	Sept. 9, 1873	142, 665
Condenser of steam-engines and apparatus for supplying boilers with water.	J. Echols	Columbus, Ga	Aug. 11, 1841	2, 212
Condenser, Oil-vapor	I. W. Wetmore	Erie, Pa	Sept. 15, 1863	39, 978
Condenser or cooler for alcoholic and other liquids	J. R. Neil	Brooklyn, N. Y	Oct. 17, 1871	119, 942
Condenser or refrigerator	W. A. Lighthall	New York, N. Y	Feb. 14, 1865	46, 368
Condenser, Potable water	W. A. Lighthall	New York, N. Y	Apr. 22, 1862	35, 029
Condenser-pump, Employment of an auxiliary engine in combination with the.	J. Ericsson	New York, N. Y	Apr. 3, 1849	6, 255
Condenser, Revolving	J. F. Spence	Williamsburgh, N. Y	May 1, 1866	54, 428
Condenser, Steam	J. L. Alberger	Buffalo, N. Y	May 20, 1873	139, 102
Condenser, Steam	J. L. Alberger	Buffalo, N. Y	June 24, 1873	140, 232
Condenser, Steam	B. C. Atkinson	Newburyport, Mass	June 22, 1869	91, 506
Condenser, Steam	A. Cail	Paris, France	Oct. 10, 1871	119, 817
Condenser, Steam	J. N. Dennisson	Newark, N. J	Feb. 8, 1859	22, 916
Condenser, Steam	J. K. Ferguson	Portland, Ky	July 31, 1866	56, 738
Condenser, Steam	J. Houpt	Springtown, Pa	Apr. 19, 1870	102, 005
Condenser, Steam	C. Hughes	Colon, Cuba	Nov. 30, 1869	97, 405
Condenser, Steam	T. L. Jones	Natchez, Miss	Apr. 26, 1870	102, 272
Condenser, Steam	A. Kennedy and J. H. Berkshire	Muscatine, Iowa	Feb. 27, 1872	124, 065
Condenser, Steam	J. T. King	New York, N. Y	Feb. 12, 1856	14, 244
Condenser, Steam	E. Korting	Vienna, Austria	Jan. 14, 1873	134, 900
Condenser, Steam	E. Korting	Vienna, Austria	July 29, 1873	141, 361
Condenser, Steam	W. A. Lighthall	New York, N. Y	Dec. 17, 1861	33, 952
Condenser, Steam	W. R. Pitts and G. K. Gluyas	San Francisco, Cal	Oct. 1, 1872	131, 779
Condenser, Steam	A. Van Orsdale	Jasper, N. Y	Sept. 8, 1868	81, 964
Condenser, Steam	W. Wright	New York, N. Y	July 11, 1871	116, 909
Condenser, Steam-engine	J. Absterdam	New York, N. Y	Oct. 2, 1866	58, 362
Condenser, Steam-engine	H. Anderson	Peoria County, Ill	Sept. 27, 1870	107, 748
Condenser, Steam-engine	E. Baldwin	Philadelphia, Pa	July 9, 1850	7, 486
Condenser, Steam-engine	L. Bollman	New York, N. Y	Apr. 3, 1855	12, 619
Condenser, Steam-engine	W. Craig and H. L. Brevoort	Brooklyn, N. Y	Mar. 28, 1871	113, 021
Condenser, Steam-engine	B. Crawford	Pittsburgh, Pa	Nov. 1, 1853	10, 179
Condenser, Steam-engine	J. T. Denniston	Lyons, N. Y	Aug. 26, 1856	15, 604
Condenser, Steam-engine	A. C. Fletcher	New York, N. Y	June 30, 1863	39, 040
Condenser, Steam-engine	S. A. Goodwin	Buffalo, N. Y	Feb. 18, 1873	135, 906
Condenser, Steam-engine	J. Houpt	Springtown, Pa	May 25, 1869	90, 542
Condenser, Steam-engine	B. F. Lemmon	New Albany, Ill	Aug. 7, 1860	29, 499
Condenser, Steam-engine	W. A. Lighthall	New York, N. Y	Dec. 17, 1861	33, 951
Condenser, Steam-engine	D. Matthew	Philadelphia, Pa	Sept. 2, 1856	15, 663
Condenser, Steam-engine	J. M. Miller	New York, N. Y	Dec. 4, 1866	60, 222
Condenser, Steam-engine	F. Ransom	Buffalo, N. Y	June 22, 1869	91, 770
Condenser, Steam-engine	J. Shirt and C. Briggs	Tamworth, Great Britain	Dec. 8, 1868	84, 773
Condenser, Steam-engine	T. E. Sickels	Kennett's Square, Pa	July 7, 1863	39, 176
Condenser, Steam-engine	T. Skidmore	New York, N. Y	Dec. 1, 1821	....
Condenser, Steam-engine	A. F. Smith	Norwich, Conn	Sept. 15, 1863	39, 965
Condenser, Steam-engine	F. G. Smith	Columbia, Tenn	July 11, 1854	11, 274
Condenser, Steam-engine	H. K. Stephens	Cincinnati, Ohio	Dec. 4, 1843	3, 366
Condenser, Steam-engine	F. B. Stevens	Weehawken, N. J	Dec. 3, 1861	33, 856
Condenser, Steam-engine	F. B. Stevens	Weehawken, N. J	Dec. 3, 1861	33, 857
Condenser, Steam-engine	F. B. Stevens	New York, N. Y	Aug. 4, 1863	39, 439
Condenser, Steam-engine	F. B. Stevens	New York, N. Y	Nov. 3, 1863	40, 510
Condenser, Steam-engine	A. C. Twining	New Haven, Conn	Aug. 12, 1862	36, 183
Condenser, Steam-engine	G. Wales	Brooklyn, N. Y	Jan. 21, 1873	135, 180
Condenser, Steam-engine	G. I. Washburn	Worcester, Mass	Oct. 6, 1863	40, 204
Condenser, Steam-engine	H. Waterman	Hudson, N. Y	Dec. 12, 1854	12, 079
Condenser, Steam-engine	W. Wright	New York, N. Y	Feb. 6, 1872	123, 541
Condenser, Steam-engine jet	G. W. Hall	Havana, N. Y	May 14, 1872	126, 696
Condenser, Steam-engine jet	J. Houpt	Springtown, Pa	Sept. 17, 1872	131, 351
Condenser, Steam-engine, &c., surface	J. Cragg and S. Archbold	Baltimore, Md., and Washington, D. C.	Feb. 19, 1861	31, 441
Condenser, Steam-engine surface	P. Hogg	New York, N. Y	Oct. 30, 1855	13, 721
Condenser, Steam-engine surface	J. M. Miller	New York, N. Y	May 20, 1856	14, 923
Condenser, Steam-engine surface	J. P. Pirsson	New York, N. Y	Apr. 2, 1850	7, 250
Condenser, Steam-engine surface	W. Sewell	New York, N. Y	Mar. 20, 1860	27, 573
Condenser, Steam-engine surface	A. Smith	Niagara Falls, N. Y	Dec. 20, 1859	26, 529
Condenser, Steam-engine surface	N. Thompson, jr	Williamsburgh, N. Y	May 20, 1856	14, 932
Condenser, Steam-pump	D. Stoddart	San Francisco, Cal	Dec. 16, 1873	145, 538
Condenser, Surface	D. Barnum	New York, N. Y	May 24, 1859	24, 037

Index of patents issued from the United States Patent Office from 1790 *to* 1873, *inclusive*—Continued.

Index of patents issued from the United States Patent Office from 1790 *to* 1873, *inclusive*—Continued.

Invention.	Inventor.	Residence.	Date.	No.
Confectionery, Applying sirup by steam to	R. L. and A. Stuart	New York, N. Y	Mar. 7, 1833	....
Confectionery-cutter	M. Laemmel	Bay Ridge, N. Y	Jan. 30, 1872	123, 265
Confectionery for druggists	A. Seitz	Hoboken, N. J	Nov. 29, 1870	109, 677
Confectionery-jar	J. S. Batchelder	Fort Wayne, Ind	Sept. 12, 1871	118, 898
Confectionery, Machine for making	S. S. Campbell and J. Goodwin	Philadelphia, Pa	Oct. 7, 1862	36, 601
Confectionery, Machine for mixing paste for	R. Duff	New York, N. Y	May 2, 1871	114, 423
Confectionery, Machine for making	J. Gardner	Philadelphia, Pa	Dec. 22, 1868	85, 083
Confectionery, Manufacture of	L. E. Chase	Charlestown, Mass	May 1, 1866	54, 296
Confectionery, Manufacture of	G. and C. B. Miller	Philadelphia, Pa	Oct. 18, 1870	108, 505
Confectionery or cocoa-nut candy	H. N. and T. J. Harbach	Philadelphia, Pa	Mar. 28, 1871	113, 047
Conformator	E. Roseen	New York, N. Y	Nov. 5, 1867	70, 621
Conic sections and the lines of the globe, Apparatus for illustrating.	F. Shepherd	New Haven, Conn	Dec. 22, 1857	18, 931
Conical-edged knife, Machinery for grinding	J. L. Plimpton	Westfield, Mass	May 4, 1852	8, 926
Connecting-rod	E. Brown	New York, N. Y	Sept. 22, 1868	82, 379
Connecting-rod	W. G. Freeman	Richmond, Va	Jan. 10, 1871	110, 842
Connecting-rod	J. F. Haskins	Fitchburgh, Mass	Dec. 24, 1872	134, 276
Connecting-rod	E. S. Pierce	Hartford, Conn	Mar. 3, 1868	75, 051
Connecting-rod	T. T. Prosser	Chicago, Ill	Dec. 23, 1873	145, 752
Connecting-rod	W. L. Switzer	Zanesville, Ohio	Dec. 23, 1873	145, 917
Connecting-rod	S. N. Wate, jr	Danville, Pa	July 9, 1872	128, 831
Connecting-rod	S. N. Wate, jr	Danville, Pa	Nov. 19, 1872	133, 182
Connecting-rod	B. F. Wilson	Salem, Ohio	July 22, 1873	141, 191
Connecting-rod	J. W. Zinn	Morrison's Mills, Fla	Dec. 19, 1871	122, 095
Connecting-rod adjustment	R. D. O. Smith	Washington, D. C	June 16, 1868	79, 019
Connecting-rod coupling	H. S. Dodge	Lockport, N. Y	Dec. 12, 1865	51, 512
Connecting-rod for locomotives	D. Pollock	Lancaster, Pa	Dec. 10, 1861	33, 902
Connecting-rod for machinery	T. Hall	Bergen, N. J	Mar. 19, 1867	63, 039
Connecting-rod joint	T. Shaw	Philadelphia, Pa	Feb. 8, 1866	52, 455
Connecting-rod, Steam-engine, &c	L. Bissell	New York, N. Y	May 14, 1850	7, 357
Connecting-rods, Adjusting the brasses of	J. R. Sees	New York, N. Y	Mar. 18, 1856	14, 473
Connecting-rods, Apparatus for adjusting eccentrics to.	G. Fowler	Philmont, N. Y	June 1, 1869	90, 655
Connecting-rods applied to cranks	R. Boeklen	Jersey City, N. J	Oct. 11, 1859	25, 716
Connecting-rods, &c., Method of securing keys in	G. H. Coney	Boston, Mass	Sept. 11, 1855	13, 541
Convalescent chair	J. Mead	Albany, N. Y	Mar. 13, 1817	....
Converters, Lining Bessemer	A. L. Holler	Brooklyn, N. Y	June 21, 1870	104, 592
Convertible fork and hook	L. Riggs	Lansing, Mich	Jan. 14, 1868	73, 390
Conveyor block	W. De Witt	Tallmadge, Mich	Apr. 26, 1870	102, 377
Conveyor, elevator, and hopper-boy	S. Walgemore	Washington County, D. C	Feb. 22, 1812	....
Conveyor-"flight"	J. M. Lemon	Polk City, Iowa	June 15, 1869	91, 351
Cook-fork	H. Smith	Des Moines, Iowa	Apr. 14, 1868	76, 835
Cooking and air-heating furnace	O. Packard	Roxbury, Mass	May 26, 1842	2, 642
Cooking and boiling, Conjurer for	T. Passmore		Dec. 23, 1796	....
Cooking and evaporating apparatus	T. J. Newby	Richmond, Ind	Oct. 11, 1870	108, 288
Cooking and heating apparatus, Petroleum	J. S. Hull	Cincinnati, Ohio	Sept. 25, 1866	58, 260
Cooking and steam-heating apparatus	E. Whiteley	Cambridge, Mass	Oct. 13, 1863	40, 300
Cooking and warming apartments, Apparatus for	D. Stephens	Kirtland, Ohio	Oct. 18, 1837	431
Cooking and warming apparatus	D. Willis	New York, N. Y	July 25, 1854	11, 399
Cooking and washing, Boiler attachment for	I. C. Schromm	Des Moines, Iowa	Oct. 1, 1872	131, 789
Cooking-apparatus	B. Antognini	New Orleans, La	Aug. 14, 1847	5, 239
Cooking-apparatus	E. E. Bennett	Kingsbury, N. Y	Feb. 15, 1828	....
Cooking-apparatus	J. Bennett	Brutus, N. Y	July 25, 1832	....
Cooking-apparatus	H. C. Berry	Wauseon, Ohio	Aug. 16, 1870	106, 457
Cooking-apparatus	S. D. and W. T. Day	Westfield, Mass	June 8, 1832	....
Cooking-apparatus	M. J. De Leon	Baltimore, Md	June 24, 1873	140, 253
Cooking apparatus	J. U. Fiester	Winchester, Ohio	June 10, 1862	35, 512
Cooking-apparatus	W. Fulton	Elizabeth City, N. J	Feb. 4, 1862	34, 297
Cooking-apparatus	W. Fulton	Elizabeth, N. J	Dec. 9, 1862	37, 092
Cooking-apparatus	J. M. Gale and I. M. Avery	New York, N. Y	June 2, 1868	78, 588
Cooking-apparatus	J. Gallagher	Cleveland, Ohio	Sept. 20, 1870	107, 477
Cooking-apparatus	N. Gergen	Buffalo, N. Y	Nov. 21, 1871	121, 164
Cooking-apparatus	J. Grime	Beekmantown, N. Y	Dec. 28, 1840	1, 918
Cooking-apparatus	R. W. Hill	Naugatuck, Conn	Aug. 23, 1859	25, 196
Cooking-apparatus	C. Hood	Seneca Falls, N. Y	Apr. 15, 1873	137, 843
Cooking-apparatus	J. Jennings	New York, N. Y	May 14, 1830	....
Cooking-apparatus	A. C. Kasson	Milwaukee, Wis	July 10, 1866	56, 232
Cooking-apparatus	J. Morris	New Haven, Conn	Oct. 3, 1812	....
Cooking-apparatus	W. W. Parrott	Boston, Mass	Mar. 11, 1837	142
Cooking-apparatus	G. Pierce	New York, N. Y	May 6, 1856	14, 828
Cooking-apparatus	J. Singer	Chicago, Ill	Dec. 1, 1863	40, 773
Cooking-apparatus	J. Smolinski	New York, N. Y	May 25, 1852	8, 974
Cooking apparatus	E. Sperry	Chicago, Ill	July 25, 1871	117, 476
Cooking-apparatus	D. Westerfield	New York, N. Y	Mar. 24, 1827	....
Cooking-apparatus	E. Whiteley	Cambridge, Mass	Aug. 18, 1863	39, 603
Cooking-apparatus	J. Zimmerman	Royalton, N. Y	May 9, 1865	47, 675
Cooking-apparatus, Alcohol	T. G. Clinton	Washington, D. C	Nov. 25, 1856	16, 112
Cooking-apparatus and house-warmer	R. Johnson	Baltimore, Md	Nov. 19, 1833	....
Cooking-apparatus and refrigerator	J. and I. Newburg	New York, N. Y	Nov. 6, 1866	59, 441
Cooking-apparatus, Camp	D. McKenzie	Brooklyn, N. Y	Sept. 24, 1861	33, 357
Cooking-apparatus, Gas	W. L. Fish	Newark, N. J	Feb. 24, 1863	37, 745
Cooking-apparatus, Gas	D. G. Haskins	Cambridge, Mass	Oct. 29, 1867	70, 207
Cooking apparatus, Gas and steam	J. S. Gallaher, jr	Washington, D. C	Feb. 12, 1856	14, 233
Cooking-apparatus, Lamp	J. G. Covey	Saint John, Canada	May 21, 1872	126, 874
Cooking-apparatus, Lamp for	S. Cooper	Washington, D. C	June 18, 1872	128, 022
Cooking-apparatus, Portable	G. B. Isham	Burlington, Vt	Jan. 19, 1869	85, 934
Cooking-apparatus, Portable	D. F. Jauss	Harrisburgh, Pa	Nov. 19, 1872	133, 155
Cooking-apparatus, Portable	J. and W. Toothill	Wallingford, Conn	Dec. 10, 1861	33, 909
Cooking-apparatus, Portable	G. Yinger	Harrisburgh, Pa	Feb. 11, 1873	135, 682
Cooking-apparatus, Portable lamp	A. M. Silver and F. White	London, England	Feb. 18, 1873	136, 104
Cooking apparatus, Steam	J. Bonis	Baltimore, Md	Jan. 6, 1812	....
Cooking apparatus, Steam	J. O. Clay	Hudson, Wis	Nov. 23, 1869	97, 048
Cooking apparatus, Steam	J. G. Covey	Saint John, Canada	May 30, 1871	115, 437
Cooking apparatus, Steam	H. W. Horton	Wheaton, Ill	May 24, 1859	24, 178
Cooking apparatus, Steam	J. A. Little	Cartersburgh, Ind	May 28, 1872	127, 253
Cooking apparatus, Steam	B. G. Martin	New York, N. Y	Apr. 19, 1864	42, 442
Cooking apparatus, Steam	F. Millikin	Boston, Mass	Apr. 21, 1863	38, 238
Cooking apparatus, Steam	A. F. W. Neynaber	Philadelphia, Pa	Nov. 28, 1865	51, 208

Index of patents issued from the United States Patent Office from 1790 *to* 1873, *inclusive*—Continued.

Invention.	Inventor.	Residence.	Date.	No.
Cooking apparatus, Steam	E. Savage	Chicago, Ill	Sept. 29, 1868	82, 557
Cooking apparatus, Steam	C. W. Sterick	Mechanicsburgh, Pa	July 16, 1872	129, 613
Cooking apparatus, Steam	L. K. Williams	Hudson, Mich	Apr. 2, 1872	125, 155
Cooking-apparatus, Water-heater surrounding fire-pot of.	E. Whiteley	Boston, Mass	June 17, 1856	15, 156
Cooking, Applying heat by means of iron castings and grates for.	P. E. Sanborn	Troy, N. Y	June 11, 1829	....
Cooking-boiler	L. S. De Bibory	Baltimore, Md	May 11, 1852	8, 939
Cooking by steam, Vessel for	L. S. Hall	Washington, D. C	Feb. 16, 1864	41, 618
Cooking-furnace	H. Engelmann	Salt Lake City, Utah	Aug. 12, 1873	141, 778
Cooking-furnace	H. Engelmann	Salt Lake City, Utah	Aug. 12, 1873	141, 779
Cooking-furnace	H. Gleason	Boston, Mass	Dec. 15, 1837	513
Cooking furnace and oven, Portable	S. B. Badger	Dover, N. H	Jan. 30, 1829	....
Cooking furnace, Charcoal	A. Madison	Cincinnati, Ohio	Dec. 28, 1869	98, 282
Cooking-furnace, Portable	A. Cross	Cazenovia, N. Y	May 12, 1830	....
Cooking-furnace, Portable	W. Haggerty, C. Lawrence, and T. Frazer.	New York, N. Y	May 22, 1830	....
Cooking-furnace, Portable	J. D. Kellogg, jr	Northampton, Mass	Aug. 10, 1869	93, 538
Cooking-furnace, Portable	R. H. Waldron	Portsmouth, N. H	Mar. 30, 1869	88, 352
Cooking furnace, Summer	R. O. Stevenson	Baltimore, Md	Apr. 5, 1870	101, 676
Cooking-machine	F. Butler	....	Aug. 22, 1800	....
Cooking-machine	J. Seger	New York, N. Y	Nov. 14, 1815	....
Cooking-machine, Portable	D. Asher	Philadelphia, Pa	Feb. 18, 1825	....
Cooking or boiling apparatus	T. K. Anderson	Boston, Mass	Mar. 22, 1833	....
Cooking-table	E. D. Dodge	Worcester, Mass	Sept. 6, 1870	107, 015
Cooking-utensil	B. W. Dunklee	Boston, Mass	Feb. 14, 1860	27, 115
Cooking-utensil	T. Godfrey	New York, N. Y	Jan. 19, 1864	41, 338
Cooking-utensil	J. Mansfield	Jefferson, Wis	Feb. 4, 1873	135, 483
Cooking-utensil	J. A. Morrison	Brady's Bend, Pa	Apr. 19, 1870	102, 031
Cooking-utensil	E. L. Packard	Stoughton, Mass	Oct. 18, 1870	108, 385
Cooking-utensil	J. Smith and I. E. Hall	Logan, Ohio	Aug. 11, 1868	80, 881
Cooking-utensil	S. Spoor	Phelps, N. Y	Jan. 19, 1869	86, 108
Cooking-utensil	E. J. Sprague	Youngstown, Ohio	May 27, 1873	139, 433
Cooking-utensil	F. P. Warren	East Court Gosham, Great Britain.	Apr. 23, 1872	126, 114
Cooking-utensil for boiling and steaming	J. Stevens	Middletown, Md	Oct. 31, 1848	5, 890
Cooking-utensil, Hollow cast-iron	A. V. Van Hoevenbergh	Southside, N. Y	Apr. 20, 1858	20, 009
Cooking-utensils, Cover for	L. B. Oviatt	Brooklyn Village, Ohio	Sept. 27, 1870	107, 803
Cooking-vessel	M. V. B. Johnson	Holden, Mo	May 24, 1870	103, 468
Cooking-vessel	W. Y. Thomson	Oyster Bay, N. Y	Mar. 4, 1873	136, 467
Cooking-vessel	W. W. Tice	California, Ohio	Sept. 17, 1872	131, 479
Cooking-vessel for frying, steaming, &c	R. Broome	Central Falls, R. I	Apr. 30, 1867	64, 278
Cooking vessel or boiler	W. Y. Thomson	Oyster Bay, N. Y	Oct. 15, 1872	132, 334
Cooking, washing, &c., Apparatus for	S. S. Fitch	New York, N. Y	Nov. 28, 1865	51, 164
Cooking with quick-lime, Apparatus for	W. W. Albro	Binghamton, N. Y	Mar. 4, 1856	14, 340
Cooler: *See* Ale, beer, and water cooler. Beer-cooler. Brewer's cooler. Brewing and distilling cooler. Butter-cooler. Butter-tub cooler. Coffee-cooler. Corpse-cooler. Dairy-cooler. Double cooler. Filter-cooler. Flour-cooler. Graduated cooler. Lard-cooler. Lining for cooler. Liquid-cooler. Liquor-cooler. Mash-cooler. Milk-cooler. Provision-cooler. Refrigerator water-cooler. Sirup-cooler. Soap-cooler. Soda-water cooler. Vapor-cooler. Water-cooler. Water and beer cooler. Wine-cooler.				
Cooler	G. D. Blocher	Indianapolis, Ind	Aug. 21, 1866	57, 281
Cooler	W. F. Messenger and H. Rehahn.	New York, N. Y	Sept. 22, 1857	18, 263
Cooler	C. F. Pike	Providence, R. I	Jan. 25, 1870	99, 107
Cooler, Air	P. Nézeraux	Paris, France	Mar. 11, 1873	136, 753
Cooler, Air, liquid, &c	D. E. Somes	Washington, D. C	Aug. 6, 1872	130, 250
Cooler and filter	H. W. Fisher	Philadelphia, Pa	Sept. 24, 1867	69, 200
Cooler and freezer	A. C. Twining	New Haven, Conn	Dec. 24, 1861	34, 018
Cooler and freezer	A. C. Twining	New Haven, Conn	Apr. 22, 1862	35, 051
Cooler and preserver	C. F. Pike	Providence, R. I	Nov. 7, 1871	120, 667
Cooler and preserver	D. E. Somes	Washington, D. C	Mar. 8, 1870	100, 683
Cooler and refrigerator	J. Agato	Pittsford, N. Y	Aug. 31, 1869	94, 373
Cooler and refrigerator	A. Koch	Baltimore, Md	May 5, 1868	77, 624
Cooler and refrigerator	P. H. Vander Weyde	New York, N. Y	July 19, 1870	105, 609
Cooler and ventilator	J. J. Schillinger	New York, N. Y	Aug. 17, 1869	93, 840
Cooler, Room	A. M. Lesley	New York, N. Y	June 3, 1873	139, 470
Coolers and condensers, Construction of tube-sheets for.	W. A. Lighthall	New York, N. Y	June 11, 1861	32, 522
Cooling air in buildings and chambers, Mode of	D. E. Somes	Washington, D. C	June 27, 1865	48, 456
Cooling air in buildings, Mode of	D. E. Somes	Washington, D. C	Oct. 11, 1864	44, 672
Cooling air, Mode of	D. E. Somes	Washington, D. C	Nov. 28, 1865	51, 237
Cooling and conveying up meal, &c	G. F. Sal onstall	....	Aug. 21, 1831	....
Cooling and disinfecting apparatus	S. C. Maine	Boston, Mass	Dec. 4, 1866	60, 212

Index of patents issued from the United States Patent Office from 1790 *to* 1873, *inclusive*—Continued.

Invention.	Inventor.	Residence.	Date.	No.
Cooling and preserving meats, fruits, vegetables, &c., Apparatus for.	C. F. Pike	Providence, R. I	Dec. 11, 1866	60, 552
Cooling and preserving milk and other liquids	D. E. and F. C. Somes	Washington, D. C	May 16, 1871	114, 985
Cooling and preserving perishable articles, Process and apparatus for.	D. E. Somes	Washington, D. C	Oct. 19, 1869	96, 048
Cooling and purifying air in breweries, packing-houses, &c.	L. Schulze	Philadelphia, Pa	Aug. 19, 1873	142, 046
Cooling and ventilating dwellings and other buildings.	D. E. Somes	Washington, D. C	Feb. 28, 1865	46, 596
Cooling and ventilating rooms, &c., Method of	A. S. Lyman	New York, N. Y	Mar. 25, 1856	14, 510
Cooling and ventilating ships and other vessels	D. E. Somes	Washington, D. C	Feb. 28, 1865	46, 593
Cooling and ventilating ships and other vessels, Mode of.	D. E. Somes	Washington, D. C	June 27, 1865	48, 457
Cooling buildings and making ice, Apparatus for	W. S. Mason	Raleigh, N. C	June 21, 1870	104, 614
Cooling, freezing, and heating apparatus	D. E. Somes	Washington, D. C	Oct. 15, 1867	69, 955
Cooling, freezing, and preserving solids, liquids, and gases.	D. E. Somes	Washington, D. C	Feb. 28, 1871	112, 294
Cooling parts of the body, Apparatus for	O. M. Fuller	Catasauqua, Pa	Aug. 2, 1864	43, 679
Cooling preserving-house, packing-house, refrigerator, &c.	D. E. Somes	Washington, D. C	Feb. 28, 1865	46, 595
Cooling rooms and buildings, Apparatus for	T. D. Kingan	Indianapolis, Ind	Apr. 29, 1873	138, 411
Cooling storage-rooms, Apparatus for	J. Ring	Saint Louis, Mo	July 15, 1873	140, 792
Cooling-tub for water and beer	A. Haustetter	Philadelphia, Pa	July 12, 1864	43, 498
Coop, Chicken	J. R. Achenbach	Saddle River, N. J	Nov. 15, 1870	109, 166
Coop, Chicken	S. S. Bent	Port Chester, N. Y	May 19, 1868	78, 044
Coop, Chicken	W. J. H. Kappe	Quincy, Ill	June 24, 1873	140, 277
Coop, Chicken	J. H. Mabbett	Jersey City, N. J	May 19, 1868	78, 109
Coop, Folding	E. P. Lawrence	Worcester, Mass	Dec. 9, 1873	145, 302
Coop, Folding chicken	G. E. Cleeton	New Haven, Conn	Dec. 7, 1869	97, 605
Coop, Folding chicken	E. J. Wilcox	Joy Mills, Pa	Nov. 14, 1871	120, 921
Coop, Fowl	J. B. Smith	North Haven, Conn	Aug. 29, 1871	118, 494
Coop, Poultry	S. S. Bent	Port Chester, N. Y	Mar. 23, 1869	88, 118
Coop, Poultry	J. Golder	Fort Recovery, Ohio	Dec. 22, 1868	85, 226
Coop, Poultry	M. Potter	Girard, Pa	Apr. 2, 1872	125, 142
Coop, Poultry	W. J. Sloan	Smith's Ferry, Pa	Mar. 16, 1869	87, 798
Cooper's croze	J. F. Brodhead	Kingston, N. Y	Oct. 8, 1838	967
Cooper's croze and howel	W. R. Davis	Union City, Pa	Sept. 23, 1873	142, 995
Cooper's hoops out of split timber, Machine for making.	J. McWhorter	Brookville, Ind	Nov. 6, 1843	3, 328
Cooper's howel, Adjustable	M. Moriarty	Bangor, Me	July 16, 1872	129, 419
Cooper's tool	J. Christy	Clyde, Ohio	Dec. 21, 1869	98, 029
Cooper's tool	J. P. Heacock	Marlborough, Ohio	Nov. 27, 1855	13, 846
Cooper's tool	M. Sutton	Penfield, N. Y	Sept. 9, 1835	....
Cooper's tool	J. P. Wood	Troy, Ohio	Apr. 17, 1860	27, 955
Cooper's ware, Machinery for dressing headings for.	E. Greenlee	Summer Hill, Pa	July 21, 1863	39, 268
Cooper's ware, Sawing round bodies for	S. Newton	Hamilton County, Ohio	June 29, 1833	....
Cooper's work, Machinery for	H. Wright	Onondaga, N. Y	Oct. 23, 1822	....
Cooper's work, Manufacture of	H. Waters	Watertown, N. Y	Apr. 3, 1828	....
Coopering-machine	O. Barber	Hartford, Conn	Jan. 8, 1810	....
Cop-tube	J. Eaton	Townsend Harbor, Mass	Apr. 13, 1858	19, 918
Cop-tube	J. Marland and E. Crockett	Lawrence, Mass	Apr. 28, 1857	17, 164
Cop-tube	N. Whitmore	Somerville, Mass	Jan. 6, 1857	16, 363
Cop-tube and machine for making	J. E. Coffin	Portland, Me	Jan. 2, 1872	122, 362
Cop-tube machines, Die for	J. Eaton	Townsend Harbor, Mass	Jan. 30, 1855	12, 311
Cop-tube-making machine	H. and J. Douglas	Glasgow, Scotland	Oct. 12, 1869	95, 670
Cop-tubes, Machine for making	R. Douglas	Lowell, Mass	Apr. 30, 1872	126, 192
Cop-tubes, Machinery for making	W. Whitmore	Lynn, Mass	June 12, 1847	5, 157
Cop-waste, Machine for picking	A. A. Wood	Jersey City, N. J	June 22, 1858	20, 677
Cop-winding machine	W. Chadwick and S. Lownds	Brooklyn, N. Y	Oct. 7, 1873	143, 497
Cop-winding machine	B. H. Jenks	Bridesburgh, Pa	Aug. 21, 1866	57, 330
Cops, Composition for pasting	J. Dunkerley and J. Knight	Paterson, N. J	Jan. 19, 1864	41, 286
Copper and brass goods, Process of utilizing the waste formed in cleaning.	F. Wilcox	Waterbury, Conn	Nov. 2, 1869	96, 525
Copper and cast-steel, Combining	J. Park, jr	Pittsburgh, Pa	Jan. 14, 1868	73, 375
Copper and in separating other metals therefrom, Manufacture of.	J. B. Elkington	Birmingham, England	Feb. 22, 1870	100, 131
Copper and other ores, Process for the reduction of	H. Stull	Ione City, Cal	Dec. 30, 1873	145, 031
Copper boiler	A. C. Brownell	Brooklyn, N. Y	Sept. 15, 1863	39, 881
Copper bolt for ship-building	Berg and Ivers	New York	Mar. 15, 1824	....
Copper bolts, Uniting	G. Morgan	Onancock, Va	May 2, 1843	3, 070
Copper, Coating metals with	O. Gauduin, J. B. J. Mignon, and S. H. Rouart.	Paris, France	July 22, 1873	141, 132
Copper for boilers, &c., Mode of preparing sheet	A. O'Neill	Portsmouth, Ohio	Apr. 6, 1869	88, 660
Copper from its ores, Extracting	N. Haskell	San Francisco, Cal	Mar. 22, 1870	101, 009
Copper from its ores, Extracting	T. S. Hunt and J. Douglass, jr	Montreal and Quebec, Canada.	Feb. 9, 1869	86, 754
Copper from ores, Extracting	F. W. Dähne	Swansea, Great Britain	June 10, 1862	35, 509
Copper, Manufacture of sheet	L. Powe	Pittsburgh, Pa	Oct. 28, 1862	36, 822
Copper, Melting	J. Kintz	West Meriden, Conn	Sept. 26, 1871	119, 365
Copper, nickel, and cobalt, Separating	A. Monnier	Philadelphia, Pa	Sept. 29, 1863	40, 116
Copper-ores, Process of reducing	J. Napier	Shacklewell, England	June 5, 1847	5, 140
Copper-ores, Reduction of	J. Napier	Shacklewell Lane, England	Feb. 29, 1848	5, 461
Copper-plates, Finishing	B. F. Dudley	Boston, Mass	Oct. 18, 1870	108, 337
Copper, Process for production of sulphate and oxides of.	H. Holland	Westfield, Mass	Dec. 27, 1859	26, 589
Copper pyrites, Treating	C. M. T. Du Motay	Paris, France	Oct. 18, 1870	108, 462
Copper-roasting furnaces, Purifying the waste gases from.	A. Bigelow and J. S. Baldwin	Newark, N. J	May 18, 1869	90, 067
Copper sheathing, Machinery for cutting and punching.	W. H. Danforth	Salem, Mass	June 13, 1848	5, 625
Copper sheathing-nails, &c., Mold for casting	T. McIlwham	Princeton, N. J	Oct. 6, 1807	....
Copper tubes, Casing	J. F. Guthrie	South Bridgewater, Mass	Mar. 26, 1872	125, 044
Copper tubes, Casting	J. F. Guthrie	Somerville, Mass	Nov. 16, 1869	96, 911
Copper tubes, Machinery for making	E. Hamilton	Bridgeport, Conn	May 28, 1850	7, 397
Copper vessels, Planishing	H. Kay and T. Avery, jr	Brooklyn and Morrisania, N. Y.	July 17, 1860	29, 177
Copper, Welding	E. Renaud	Washington, D. C	Dec. 16, 1873	145, 686

Index of patents issued from the United States Patent Office from 1790 to 1873, inclusive—Continued.

Invention.	Inventor.	Residence.	Date.	No.
Copper, Welding	C. L. Schurr and W. G. Rehbein	Baltimore, Md	Nov. 14, 1871	121, 009
Copperas, Manufacture of	R. D. Birch	Philadelphia, Pa	Jan. 31, 1871	111, 305
Copperas, Method of making	I. Tyson	Baltimore, Md	Feb. 15, 1827	....
Copy-holder	J. S. Butler	Silver City, Idaho	Nov. 2, 1869	96, 391
Copy-holder	W. R. Carter	Brooklyn, N. Y	Oct. 14, 1873	143, 616
Copy-holder	L. G. Davis	Salem, Ind	Dec. 17, 1872	134, 036
Copy-holder	H. B. Denny	Washington, D. C	July 13, 1869	92, 588
Copy-holder	S. French and R. D. Chase	Orange, Mass	May 13, 1873	138, 877
Copy-holder	A. B. Manard	Rockford, Ill	Nov. 28, 1871	121, 291
Copy-holder	C. B. Moseley and L. L. Wooley.	Medford, Mass	Jan. 22, 1867	61, 444
Copy-holder	H. A. Tremper	Hammonton, N. J	Dec. 24, 1867	72, 569
Copy-holder	A. Westcott	Syracuse, N. Y	Aug. 17, 1869	93, 931
Copy-holder	H. R. Williams	Buffalo, N. Y	Mar. 14, 1871	112, 664
Copy-holder, Compositor's	P. A. La France	Elmira, N. Y	Nov. 12, 1867	70, 865
Copy-holder, Printer's	H. W. Knight	Seneca Falls, N. Y	Nov. 2, 1869	96, 445
Copy-holder, Printer's	W. H. and C. J. Young	Cambridge, Mass	Sept. 14, 1869	94, 807
Copies from manuscript, Process of multiplying	A. C. F. N. De St. Victor	Paris, France	Jan. 21, 1868	73, 514
Copies of manuscript, &c., Mode of taking	M. B. Hardin	New York, N. Y	Feb. 5, 1867	61, 733
Copying	C. Willcox	New Haven, Conn	Oct. 24, 1871	120, 223
Copying and folding press	S. W. Odell	Saint Louis, Mo	Dec. 9, 1873	145, 306
Copying-apparatus	W. J. Purcell	New York, N. Y	June 27, 1871	116, 351
Copying-apparatus, Portable	W. Van Auden	Poughkeepsie, N. Y	Sept. 7, 1858	21, 456
Copying colored and defective drawings	I Rehn	Washington, D. C	May 16, 1871	114, 968
Copying designs, Apparatus for	T. Hall	Newton, Mass	Oct. 1, 1872	131, 819
Copying figures, &c., Machine for	F. C. Meyer	Philadelphia, Pa	Apr. 24, 1860	28, 040
Copying letters, Press for	G. Burnham	Philadelphia, Pa	Oct. 8, 1850	7, 696
Copying-machine	L. Carpenter	Oswego, N. Y	Dec. 31, 1842	2, 894
Copying manuscript	J. Jones	Clyde, N. Y	June 1, 1852	8, 980
Copying-press	C. Adams	Pittsburgh, Pa	Jan. 24, 1854	10, 438
Copying-press	J. H. Atwater	Providence, R. I	Jan. 13, 1863	37, 379
Copying-press	S. G. Cabell	Quincy, Ill	June 18, 1867	65, 873
Copying-press	C. Chambers, jr	Philadelphia, Pa	Oct. 2, 1860	30, 204
Copying-press	E. Clark	New York, N. Y	Dec. 18, 1860	30, 959
Copying-press	D. G. Coppin	Cincinnati, Ohio	July 16, 1872	129, 321
Copying-press	J. Fensom	Toronto, Canada	July 11, 1871	116, 824
Copying-press	J. Fowler	Saugatuck, Mich	June 29, 1869	92, 032
Copying-press	G. C. Gage	Waterford, N. Y	Apr. 20, 1869	89, 035
Copying-press	C. F. Grabo	Boston, Mass	Aug. 14, 1860	29, 585
Copying-press	W. H. Hawkins	Cleveland, Ohio	Mar. 29, 1870	101, 262
Copying-press	C. Y. Heckler	Philadelphia, Pa	May 21, 1861	32, 363
Copying-press	F. Hovey	New York, N. Y	Mar. 29, 1864	42, 141
Copying-press	T. P. How	Brooklyn, N. Y	Apr. 7, 1868	76, 457
Copying-press	J. M. Keep	New York, N. Y	Aug. 10, 1869	93, 536
Copying-press	C. Knauer	Pittsburgh, Pa	June 3, 1856	15, 011
Copying-press	P. Lawrence and G. Jefferys	New York, N. Y	May 30, 1867	48, 021
Copying-press	A. Le Clercq	New York, N. Y	Dec. 26, 1871	122, 265
Copying-press	E. and J. B. Platt	Clarke County, Ga	Oct. 26, 1858	21, 902
Copying-press	W. Shriver	New York, N. Y	June 13, 1865	48, 217
Copying-press	W. Shriver	New York, N. Y	Feb. 13, 1872	123, 584
Copying-press	E. H. Smith	New York, N. Y	June 14, 1853	9, 786
Copying-press	W. M. Smith	Washington, D. C	May 12, 1867	17, 307
Copying-press	W. M. Smith	Washington, D. C	Feb. 23, 1869	87, 304
Copying-press	J. D. Spaulding and D. N. B. Coffin, jr.	Boston, Mass	Jan. 16, 1866	52, 086
Copying-press	G. C. Tait	Worcester Mass	June 21, 1864	43, 266
Copying-press	G. Tangye	Birmingham, England	Oct. 26, 1869	96, 285
Copying-press	W. W. Underhill	Boston, Mass	Aug. 10, 1869	93, 567
Copying-press	A. Whitcomb	Worcester, Mass	Jan. 4, 1859	22, 524
Copying-press	A. Whitcomb	Worcester, Mass	July 4, 1871	116, 781
Copying-press	A. A. Wilder	Detroit, Mich	Mar. 11, 1851	7, 978
Copying-press bed	W. Shriver	New York, N. Y	Aug. 6, 1872	130, 320
Copying-press damper	A. Pearl	New York, N. Y	Oct. 13, 1868	83, 088
Copying press, Letter	G. C. Taft	Worcester, Mass	Apr. 24, 1860	28, 020
Copying-press, Portable	J. H. Atwater	Providence, R. I	Apr. 2, 1861	31, 860
Copying-press, Portable	H. M. Paine	Worcester, Mass	Oct. 2, 1849	6, 752
Copying-press table	B. Brower	New York, N. Y	Aug. 5, 1873	141, 422
Copying surface by electricity	A. Bain	London, England	Dec. 5, 1848	5, 957
Copying writing, maps, &c., Process of	J. Underwood	London, England	Mar. 31, 1863	38, 086
Cord and line reel	H. W. Chamberlain	Jersey City, N. J	Oct. 2, 1866	58, 378
Cord-catch	C. C. Moore	New York, N. Y	May 3, 1870	102, 575
Cord-clamp	S. W. Meredith	Greensburgh, Ind	Mar. 12, 1872	124, 604
Cord-clamp	S. W. Meredith	Greensburgh, Ind	Aug. 6, 1872	130, 143
Cord-coupling	L. I. Ware	Warren, R. I	May 2[illegible], 1851	8, 099
Cord-covering machine	J. Bachelder	Norwich, Conn	Sept. 1, 1868	81, 577
Cord-covering machine	J. Buser	New York, N. Y	Sept. 5, 1865	49, 825
Cord-covering machine	T. N. Dale, jr., and G. Kraink	Paterson, N. J	Sept. 6, 1870	107, 010
Cord-covering machine	J. E. Gillespie and T. Kohn	Hartford, Conn	Apr. 1, 1873	137, 360
Cord-covering machine	H. Heinemann and J. Buser	New York, N. Y	Dec. 18, 1860	30, 944
Cord-covering machine	R. Lewis	New York, N. Y	Apr. 4, 1871	113, 675
Cord-covering machine	W. H. Palmer, jr	Middletown, Conn	Dec. 1, 1868	84, 506
Cord-covering machine	J. Turner	Norwich, Conn	Sept. 1, 1868	81, 845
Cord folding and measuring machine	G. P. Farmer	Philadelphia, Pa	May 10, 1870	102, 931
Cord-holder	J. P. Gruger and C. Makinson	Lancaster, Pa	Apr. 21, 1868	77, 034
Cord-holder for picture-frames, &c	H. D. Heureuse	New York, N. Y	June 8, 1869	90, 998
Cord-hook for door-springs, Adjustable	W. B. Barnard	Bristol, Conn	Mar. 5, 1850	7, 132
Cord-making machine	H. Boardman	Lancaster, Pa	Feb. 2, 1869	86, 497
Cord-making machine	H. Boardman	Lancaster Township, Pa	Aug. 29, 1871	118, 426
Cord-making machine	W. Guest	London, England	July 27, 1869	92, 960
Cord-making machine	J. McIntire	Hopewell Cotton Works, Pa	Jan. 25, 1870	99, 099
Cord-making machine	E. Otis	New Haven, Conn	Dec. 23, 1873	145, 747
Cord-making machine	G. T. Wright	New Preston, Conn	Aug. 3, 1869	93, 265
Cord-making machinery	W. E. Nichols	East Haddam, Conn	Dec. 11, 1849	6, 942
Cord plaiting and twisting	W. H. Zahn	New York, N. Y	May 8, 1855	12, 845
Cord-stretcher	R. White	Decatur, Ill	Oct. 22, 1867	70, 057
Cord twisting and plaiting machine	J. T. Williams	Newark, N. J	May 3, 1864	42, 613
Cord-winder	C. Goodwin	New Brunswick, N. J	Apr. 15, 1862	34, 954
Cords, braids, &c., Machine for starching and glazing.	D. McInroy	New York, N. Y	Dec. 12, 1865	51, 471

Index of patents issued from the United States Patent Office from 1790 *to* 1873, *inclusive*—Continued.

Invention.	Inventor.	Residence.	Date.	No.
Cords, Guide for laying	W. Taylor	Berlin, N. Y	Feb. 19, 1861	31, 494
Cords into a series of united skeins, Machine for winding.	E. Brown	South Otselic, N. Y	Feb. 6, 1866	52, 382
Cords, Machine for dressing worsted	I. E. Palmer	Hackensack, N. J	Apr. 18, 1871	113, 917
Cords, &c., Machine for drying sized or dyed	D. McInroy	New York, N. Y	July 30, 1867	67, 328
Cords, Machine for making covered	J. Turner	Norwich, Conn	June 15, 1869	91, 498
Cords, Machine for weaving a covering for	J. Danby	New York, N. Y	Mar. 20, 1866	53, 372
Cords, Machinery for manufacturing plaited	C. Feickert	New York, N. Y	Mar. 9, 1858	19, 554
Cords, Machinery for weaving shade	T. Nelson	Troy, N. Y	Dec. 16, 1856	16, 248
Cords, Method of double-stretching strands of banding.	T. Unsworth	Manchester, England	Mar. 26, 1872	124, 988
Cords or bands, Machinery for making	T. Unsworth and E. Whalley	Preston, England	Aug. 22, 1871	118, 408
Cords or covering around cords, Machine for weaving.	F. Veerkamp and F. Leopold	Philadelphia, Pa	Aug. 23, 1864	43, 937
Cords, ropes, &c., Coupling-attachment for	J. L. Howard	Hartford, Conn	Apr. 17, 1860	27, 906
Cords, ropes, &c., Machine for making	J. O. Mathieu	Paris, France	Jan. 24, 1865	46, 057
Cords, ropes, &c., Machine for manufacturing	J. A. De Maniquet	Paris, France	July 5, 1864	43, 461
Cords, Stop-motion for machine for covering	R. Lewis	New York, N. Y	Apr. 9, 1872	125, 467
Cords, wires, &c., Covering	F. Beck	New York, N. Y	Dec. 1, 1863	40, 801
Cordage and improving its quality, Machine for manufacturing.	R. Fulton and N. Cutting	New York, N. Y., and Washington, D. C.	Mar. 4, 1808	....
Cordage by machinery, Mode of making	R. Graves	Brooklyn, N. Y	July 25, 1827	....
Cordage, Flexible	H. H. Matteson	Buffalo, N. Y	Jan. 10, 1854	10, 411
Cordage-laying machine	R. Greaves	Boston, Mass	Feb. 1, 1821	....
Cordage-machine	J. P. Arnold	Louisville, Ky	Mar. 24, 1857	16, 867
Cordage-machine	J. P. Arnold	Louisville, Ky	May 19, 1857	17, 310
Cordage-machine	C. Cobb	Plymouth, Mass	July 17, 1866	56, 372
Cordage-machine	A. Hathaway	Boston, Mass	July 9, 1839	1, 228
Cordage-machine	J. W. Peer	Schenectady, N. Y	July 6, 1852	9, 101
Cordage-machine	J. Pine	Hoosick Falls, N. Y	Feb. 24, 1857	16, 694
Cordage, Machine for making	A. Hill	Walpole, N. Y	June 30, 1812	....
Cordage, Machine for making	W. Joslin	Waterford, N. Y	Mar. 23, 1852	8, 825
Cordage, Machine for making	I. E. Palmer	Hackensack, N. J	Mar. 16, 1869	87, 964
Cordage, Machine for manufacturing	S. and J. A. Bazen	Canton, Mass	Oct. 17, 1817	....
Cordage, Machine for manufacturing long	W. E. Meginnis	Philadelphia, Pa	Nov. 9, 1839	1, 404
Cordage, Machine for pressing tar out of yarn for	T. Barnitt	Philadelphia, Pa	May 20, 1822	....
Cordage-machines, Laying top for	W. Robinson	Warsaw, N. Y	Jan. 20, 1857	16, 452
Cordage-machinery	H. T. Jennings, C. S. Collier, and T. P. How.	Bethany and Buffalo, N. Y.	Nov. 16, 1852	9, 414
Cordage-machinery	H. Pearce	Cincinnati, Ohio	May 22, 1855	12, 920
Cordage-machinery	G. Stephenson	Northfield, Ind	May 31, 1859	24, 244
Cordage-machinery	P. B. Tyler	Springfield, Mass	June 27, 1854	11, 202
Cordage, Machinery for braiding	J. A. Bazin	Canton, Mass	June 29, 1858	20, 690
Cordage, Machinery for making	B. F. Adams	New Bedford, Mass	June 13, 1846	4, 574
Cordage, Machinery for making	F. Kellsey	Middletown, Conn	Feb. 8, 1825	....
Cordage, Machinery for making	R. Porter	Washington, D. C	Feb. 21, 1854	10, 559
Cordage, Machinery for making cotton	F. Slaughter and D. Perry	Fredericksburgh, Va	Jan. 1, 1850	6, 992
Cordage, Machinery for making cotton	F. Slaughter and D. Perry	Fredericksburgh, Va	Jan. 8, 1850	7, 007
Cordage, Machinery for manufacturing	W. Joslin	Waterford, N. Y	Jan. 19, 1847	4, 931
Cordage, Making	E. Bartholomew	Boston, Mass	May 17, 1826	....
Cordage, Making	J. Drummond	Brooklyn, N. Y	July 22, 1833	....
Cordage, Making and laying	C. L. Sargent	Suffolk, Mass	Oct. 4, 1817	....
Cordage-making machine	J. Hall	Munroe Township, N. Y	June 11, 1867	65, 565
Cordage-making machine	W. B. Leonard	Fishkill, N. Y	Jan. 9, 1819	....
Cordage-making machine	D. Perry	Fredericksburgh, Va	June 15, 1852	9, 040
Cordage, Manufacturing	G. Parkinson	....	June 16, 1794	....
Cordage, Manufacturing	J. Pitman	....	May 25, 1795	....
Cordage, &c., Mode of laying	R. Graves	Boston, Mass	Nov. 22, 1820	....
Cordage, Top-sled for	R. Graves	Boston, Mass	Mar. 28, 1821	....
Cordage uninflammable, Process for rendering	J. H. Johnson	New Orleans, La	Nov. 26, 1850	7, 797
Cordage, webbing, &c., Manufacturing braided	J. A. Bazin	Canton, Mass	June 29, 1858	20, 691
Corded bindings for India-rubber and other fabrics, Machine for making.	C. A. Ensign	Naugatuck, Conn	July 17, 1866	56, 393
Cording, webbing, &c., Machine for making	J. A. Bazin	Canton, Mass	July 17, 1866	56, 485
Cordial, Anti-bilious stomach	S. Lozarus	....	Dec. 21, 1802	....
Core-bar	R. T. Crane	Chicago, Ill	Aug. 4, 1868	80, 607
Core-bar for casting pipes	J. Enright	Louisville, Ky	Oct. 13, 1868	82, 931
Core bar for casting pipes	J. Enright	Louisville, Ky	June 14, 1870	104, 397
Core-bar for castings	D. Gallagher	Cincinnati, Ohio	Sept. 23, 1873	143, 005
Core-bar for forming cores for casting pipes	G. Peacock	West Troy, N. Y	Feb. 8, 1853	9, 577
Core-bar for molds used in casting metal	F. Shickle	Saint Louis, Mo	June 29, 1869	92, 108
Core-bar for pipe-molding	J. Demarest	Mott Haven, N. Y	Apr. 8, 1856	14, 637
Core-barrel	J. E. Thomas	Pittsburgh, Pa	Oct. 4, 1864	44, 563
Core-barrel, Collapsing	R. Lye	Pittsburgh, Pa	May 28, 1872	127, 178
Core-barrel, Collapsing	W. Smith	Pittsburgh, Pa	Jan. 17, 1871	111, 091
Core-barrel for castings	J. B. Aston	Pittsburgh, Pa	Sept. 9, 1873	142, 662
Core-barrel for castings	W. Smith	Pittsburgh, Pa	Sept. 9, 1873	142, 746
Core-box	J. C. Chapman	Waltham, Mass	Feb. 6, 1872	123, 329
Core-box	J. S. Harper	Baltimore, Md	June 5, 1860	28, 574
Core-box	A. Van Horn	New York, N. Y	Jan. 27, 1857	16, 502
Core-carriage	S. Fulton	Conshohocken, Pa	Apr. 16, 1861	32, 060
Core, Collapsing	A. T. Brodie and R. R. Smith	Pittsburgh, Pa	Jan. 24, 1871	111, 173
Core, Dry-sand	W. Gage and R. B. Felthousen	Buffalo, N. Y	July 7, 1857	17, 732
Core, Dry-sand	W. Gage and R. B. Felthousen	Buffalo, N. Y	Dec. 29, 1857	18, 964
Core for casting	J. Herald	Unadilla, N. Y	Dec. 13, 1870	110, 038
Core for casting iron, glass, &c., Expansible	A. Balding	Wheeling, W. Va	Mar. 8, 1870	100, 585
Core for castings, Iron	A. C. Mott	Philadelphia, Pa	Jan. 4, 1870	98, 516
Core for dikes	W. A. Thompson	Brooklyn, N. Y	Jan. 30, 1872	123, 306
Core for molding plastic substances	J. Pilgrim	New Britain, Conn	Dec. 28, 1858	22, 450
Core-making machine	B. S. Benson	Baltimore, Md	July 7, 1868	79, 629
Core or form for making castings, Composition	A. Burt	Detroit, Mich	July 20, 1869	92, 699
Core-powder, Composition for	W. B. Lupton	Pittsburgh, Pa	Mar. 27, 1866	53, 460
Core, Sectional	W. A. Butler	New York, N. Y	May 13, 1873	138, 853
Core-spindle for casting	D. A. Webster and G. F. Burroughs.	New York, N. Y., and Lumberton, N. J.	Oct. 20, 1857	18, 481
Core-spindle joint	W. F. Perkins	Boston, Mass	Apr. 30, 1872	126, 230
Core, Supporting	E. B. Phillips	Cambridge, Mass	Feb. 14, 1871	111, 775

Index of patents issued from the United States Patent Office from 1790 to 1873, inclusive—Continued.

Invention.	Inventor.	Residence.	Date.	No.
Core, Venting	G. G. Cressey	Philadelphia, Pa	Oct. 20, 1868	83, 135
Cores, Apparatus for making solid	S. J. Peet	New York, N. Y	Mar. 1, 1870	100, 318
Cores Device for forming	H. Parker	Gananoque, Canada	Dec. 23, 1873	145, 748
Cores, Flask for forming	E. R. Austin	Norwalk, Conn	Dec. 24, 1867	72, 586
Cores for axle-skeins and hub-boxes, Making sand	J. G. Holt	Chicago, Ill	Nov. 20, 1866	59, 840
Cores for castings, Composition for making	E. Rees	Cincinnati, Ohio	Dec. 17, 1850	7, 843
Cores for castings, Machine for making and holding.	L. H. Crocker	Cincinnati, Ohio	Oct. 22, 1850	7, 729
Cores for castings, Making	I. Kellogg	New Hartford, Conn	Apr. 25, 1846	4, 483
Cores for castings, Mode of making and venting	J. Harrison, jr	Philadelphia, Pa	Aug. 8, 1865	49, 264
Cores for foundery purposes, Venting	H. Tucker	Newton, Mass	Nov. 13, 1866	59, 684
Cores for molding articles of lead and other metals, Method of making.	L. Brandeis	Brooklyn, N. Y	Dec. 22, 1868	85, 056
Cores for molding iron, Compound for forming	J. I. Vinton	Altoona, Pa	Apr. 20, 1869	89, 187
Cores for pipe-castings, Method of making	W. E. Bird	West Bridgewater, Mass	Aug. 27, 1867	68, 033
Cores for stench-traps and other metal castings, Manufacture of.	C. Lightbody, jr	Brooklyn, N. Y	Oct. 15, 1872	132, 299
Cores from hollow castings, Method of loosening metallic.	J. C. Parry	Pittsburgh, Pa	Dec. 24, 1850	7, 859
Cores in flasks, Implement for undercutting sand	W. L. McDowell	Philadelphia, Pa	Feb. 22, 1870	100, 172
Cores in molds, Anchor for securing	Z. Ellis	Philadelphia, Pa	Jan. 11, 1870	98, 676
Cores, Machine for making pipe	W. and G. Braid	New York, N. Y	Aug. 15, 1865	49, 368
Cores, Machine for producing	S. J. Peet	New York, N. Y	Mar. 1, 1870	100, 320
Cores, Manufacture of	S. Fulton	Conshohocken, Pa	June 8, 1869	91, 008
Cores, Molding	J. P. Davis	Middletown, Conn	May 30, 1865	47, 937
Cores, Molding and compressing	C. Warner	Louisville, Ky	Jan. 9, 1849	6, 013
Cores, Venting metallic	A. Shepard	New Britain, Conn	Nov. 17, 1868	84, 072
Corer and cutter, Apple	J. Bowsir	Basil, Ohio	Dec. 6, 1864	45, 312
Corer and cutter, Apple	A. Frost	Seymour, Ind	Aug. 11, 1868	80, 938
Corer and cutter, Apple	S. Mead	Fort Branch, Ind	Mar. 5, 1872	124, 368
Corer and cutter, Apple	J. M. Meschutt	Newark, N. J	July 16, 1872	129, 289
Corer and cutter, Apple	C. D. Read	Lowell, Mass	Feb. 16, 1869	87, 004
Corer and quarterer, Apple	J. M. Hussam	Mount Vernon, Me	Oct. 27, 1868	83, 494
Corer and quarterer, Apple	B. J. McFeely	Chestnut Springs, Pa	Sept. 27, 1870	107, 794
Corer and quarterer, Apple	J. S. Tripp	South Danby, N. Y	Sept. 13, 1864	44, 239
Corer and slicer, Apple	G. Custer	Norristown, Pa	July 23, 1867	66, 951
Corer and slicer, Apple	E. Dean and C. O. Potter	Jersey City, N. J	July 9, 1872	128, 865
Corer and slicer, Apple	R. J. Dodd	Orth, Ind	Apr. 12, 1870	101, 838
Corer and slicer, Apple	R. Onderdonk	New York, N. Y	Feb. 20, 1866	52, 740
Corer and slicer, Apple	D. R. Reed	Tekonsha, Mich	July 14, 1868	80, 010
Corer and slicer, Apple	I. Rogers	West Chehalem, Oreg	July 14, 1868	80, 014
Corer and slicer, Apple	S. Saucerman	Freeport, Ill	July 25, 1865	48, 981
Corer and slicer, Apple	H. W. Williams	Galesburgh, Ill	Feb. 6, 1872	123, 540
Corer and slicer, Apple	G. C. Wright	Le Roy, Ohio	Oct. 22, 1867	70, 062
Corer and slicer, Apple	M. B. Wright	West Meriden, Conn	Dec. 28, 1869	98, 457
Corer and slicer, Fruit	C. E. Thurston and J. H. Wilkinson.	South New Market, N. H	May 7, 1872	126, 426
Corer, Apple	A. N. Alcott	Gowanda, N. Y	Feb. 23, 1858	19, 402
Corer, Apple	S. C. Collins	Oregon, Mo	Nov. 14, 1871	120, 857
Corer, Apple	M. M. Hatch	Portland, Me	July 21, 1868	80, 172
Corer, Apple	M. P. Smith	Baltimore, Md	Sept. 3, 1872	131, 126
Corer, Apple	G. L. Swett and B. F. Drake	Leominster, Mass	Sept. 28, 1869	95, 286
Corer, Fruit	E. J. Marsters	Shaw's Flat, Cal	Aug. 23, 1870	106, 706
Coring and quartering apples	C. Gates	Rutland County, Vt	Dec. 15, 1810	....
Coring and quartering machine, Apple	C. Lounsberry	Nichols, N. Y	Aug. 10, 1858	21, 141
Coring and quartering machine, Apple	J. J. Vankersen	Kalamazoo, Mich	Mar. 6, 1866	53, 063
Coring and slicing machine, Apple	C. H. Gifford	Auburn, Mass	Jan. 5, 1864	41, 147
Coring, slicing, and stringing machine, Apple	N. Bennett	Sherman, N. Y	June 13, 1865	48, 149
Cork	W. H. Towers	New York, N. Y	Dec. 23, 1862	37, 249
Cork, Air-tight	J. S. Davison	Cranberry, N. J	Dec. 1, 1863	40, 742
Cork and bung cutting machinery	W. R. Crocker	Norwich, Conn	Jan. 27, 1863	37, 543
Cork, Artificial	L. Boch and A. F. Wheeler	Sheboygan, Wis	Aug. 8, 1865	49, 220
Cork, Artificial	E. L. Perry and E. D. Lazell	Brooklyn, N. Y	Sept. 12, 1865	49, 916
Cork, Bottle	W. H. Newton	Newport, R. I	Feb. 21, 1871	112, 070
Cork-composition, Water-proof	A. Stevens	New York, N. Y	Dec. 7, 1858	22, 246
Cork-cutter	E. F. Harrington	Boston, Mass	Apr. 12, 1870	101, 730
Cork-cutter	L. Hills	Boston	June 18, 1827	....
Cork-cutter	E. O. Schartau	Philadelphia, Pa	Dec. 13, 1870	110, 075
Cork-cutting machine	R. P. Abernethy	Cincinnati, Ohio	July 6, 1858	20, 770
Cork-cutting machine	R. P. Abernethy and M. M. Wombaugh.	Cincinnati, Ohio	July 6, 1858	20, 771
Cork-cutting machine	A. F. Allen	Providence, R. I	July 16 1872	129, 304
Cork-cutting machine	O. Arnold	Pawtucket, R. I	Oct. 26, 1869	96, 184
Cork-cutting machine	A. J. Bailey	Charlestown, Mass	May 29, 1866	55, 036
Cork-cutting machine	H. Boardman	Lancaster, Pa	July 15, 1862	35, 867
Cork-cutting machine	E. A. Brimson	New York, N. Y	Aug. 24, 1869	93, 958
Cork-cutting machine	E. Conroy	Boston, Mass	Nov. 2, 1858	21, 944
Cork-cutting machine	E. Conroy	Boston, Mass	Feb. 4, 1862	34, 291
Cork-cutting machine	T. S. Disston	Philadelphia, Pa	Jan. 21, 1873	134, 982
Cork-cutting machine	L. W. Felt	Keene, N. H	June 25, 1867	66, 141
Cork-cutting machine	L. W. Felt	Keene, N. H	Apr. 14, 1868	76, 615
Cork-cutting machine	I. Goodspeed	Norwich, Conn	Oct. 27, 1863	40, 444
Cork-cutting machine	G. Hammer	Philadelphia, Pa	Oct. 14, 1851	8, 422
Cork-cutting machine	G. Hammer	Philadelphia, Pa	Feb. 15, 1859	22, 949
Cork-cutting machine	G. Hammer	Philadelphia, Pa	May 22, 1866	54, 896
Cork-cutting machine	G. Hammer	Philadelphia, Pa	Nov. 11, 1868	83, 850
Cork cutting machine	P. Hayden	Pittsburgh, Pa	Dec. 19, 1865	51, 587
Cork-cutting machine	W. King	New York, N. Y	July 8, 1851	8, 208
Cork-cutting machine	G. Lloyd	Philadelphia, Pa	Sept. 29, 1863	40, 144
Cork-cutting machine	A. Mackie	Philadelphia, Pa	Jan. 9, 1866	52, 000
Cork-cutting machine	C. R. Macy	Hyde Park, N. Y	Oct. 31, 1840	1, 842
Cork-cutting machine	A. Millar	New York, N. Y	Jan. 29, 1861	31, 253
Cork-cutting machine	A. Millar	New York, N. Y	Apr. 9, 1861	31, 990
Cork-cutting machine	G. Purves	New York, N. Y	Aug. 22, 1871	118, 269
Cork-cutting machine	G. Rawlings	Philadelphia, Pa	Oct. 30, 1827	....
Cork-cutting machine	S. Sawyer	Boston, Mass	June 10, 1840	1, 623
Cork-cutting machinery	H. F. Cox and A. Millar	Jersey City, N. J., and New York, N. Y.	Aug. 20, 1861	33, 122
Cork-cutting tool	A. Brass	Newark, N. J	Nov. 15, 1859	26, 083

Index of patents issued from the United States Patent Office from 1790 *to* 1873, *inclusive*—Continued.

Invention.	Inventor.	Residence.	Date.	No.
Cork-drawer	C. Alexander	Washington, D. C	Aug. 7, 1860	29, 539
Cork-drawer	C. Chinnock	Brooklyn, N. Y	Apr. 14, 1863	38, 147
Cork-extractor	J. Autenrith	Philadelphia, Pa	Sept. 1, 1868	81, 728
Cork-extractor	E. A. Burgess	New Haven, Conn	May 21, 1861	32, 396
Cork-extractor	E. Button	Annapolis, Md	June 2, 1868	78, 513
Cork-extractor	G. L. Gibson, jr	Concord, N. C	Apr. 27, 1869	89, 477
Cork-extractor	C. Gooch	Cincinnati, Ohio	Jan. 25, 1870	99, 080
Cork-extractor	C. F. Hunt	Brooklyn, N. Y	July 8, 1873	140, 706
Cork-extractor	J. P. Miers and J. Groendyke	Lebanon, N. J	Jan. 26, 1864	41, 385
Cork-extractor	J. L. Morrill	New York, N. Y	May 17, 1864	42, 784
Cork-extractor	J. Morton	Philadelphia, Pa	Jan. 14, 1868	73, 370
Cork-extractor	C. Rosenberry	Chicago, Ill	Oct. 16, 1866	58, 889
Cork-extractor	J. Walker	Cincinnati, Ohio	Jan. 22, 1867	61, 488
Cork-extractor	W. G. Waterman	Middletown, Conn	Dec. 17, 1867	72, 247
Cork-extractor	C. G. Wilson	Brooklyn, N. Y	July 13, 1869	92, 552
Cork-fastener	E. D. Weatherbee	Worcester, Mass	May 11, 1869	90, 037
Cork for filling beds, mattresses, &c	S. Bates	Boston, Mass	Dec. 28, 1832	....
Cork-inserting apparatus	W. Rheiner and L. H. Wolff	Detroit, Mich	Jan. 15, 1867	61, 255
Cork into strips, Machinery for cutting	C. Gregor	New York, N. Y	Mar. 18, 1862	34, 716
Cork-machine	A. Albertson	New York, N. Y	May 3, 1859	23, 880
Cork-machine	H. Boardman	Lancaster, Pa	Sept. 19, 1865	49, 971
Cork-machine	E. Conroy	South Boston, Mass	June 16, 1857	17, 557
Cork-machine	I. Goodspeed	Norwich, Conn	June 4, 1861	32, 497
Cork-machine	H. Locke	South Boston, Mass	June 21, 1859	24, 471
Cork-machine	A. Millar	New York, N. Y	Apr. 16, 1861	32, 075
Cork-machine	J. Power	Boston, Mass	July 3, 1855	13, 200
Cork-machine	E. O. Schartau	Philadelphia, Pa	Dec. 13, 1870	110, 076
Cork, Metal-capped	E. Street	East Haven, Conn	Apr. 19, 1870	102, 181
Cork or stopper holder	G. H. Plummer	New York, N. Y	Dec. 2, 1873	145, 235
Cork-polishing machine	H. F. Cox and A. Millar	Jersey City, N. J., and New York, N. Y.	July 19, 1859	24, 841
Cork-press	C. L. Lochman	Carlisle, Pa	Aug. 27, 1867	68, 093
Cork-presser	J. Ewing	New York, N. Y	June 28, 1870	104, 841
Cork-pull	F. G. Bielefield and C. C. E. Schwartz.	Berlin, Prussia, and Hamburgh.	Apr. 4, 1865	47, 161
Cork-pull	S. E. Clapp	Cambridge, Mass	Jan. 21, 1868	73, 435
Cork-pull	C. Loffler	Hoboken, N. J	Oct. 30, 1866	59, 241
Cork-pull	G. W. Schermerhorn	East Limington, Me	Sept. 22, 1868	82, 355
Cork-pull	C. T. Simpers	Philadelphia, Pa	Nov. 14, 1871	120, 830
Cork-pull	J. D. Van Zandt	Brooklyn, N. Y	July 30, 1867	67, 234
Cork-pull	D. Williamson	New York, N. Y	Feb. 25, 1868	74, 966
Cork-pull	W. C. Wyckoff	Brooklyn, N. Y	May 21, 1861	32, 394
Cork-screw	J. Adt	Wolcottville, Conn	May 8, 1866	54, 640
Cork-screw	P. Blake	New Haven, Conn	Mar. 27, 1860	27, 665
Cork-screw	J. Bussey	Cincinnati, Ohio	Feb. 18, 1868	74, 495
Cork-screw	M. L. Byrn	New York, N. Y	Mar. 27, 1860	27, 615
Cork-screw	C. Chinnock	Brooklyn, N. Y	Nov. 24, 1863	40, 674
Cork-screw	S. E. Clapp	Cambridge, Mass	Feb. 11, 1868	74, 199
Cork-screw	J. L. Clark	Chester, Conn	Nov. 22, 1864	45, 137
Cork-screw	W. Dickson	Albany, N. Y	Aug. 2, 1870	106, 036
Cork-screw	J. E. Earle	New Haven, Conn	June 23, 1868	79, 216
Cork-screw	W. Fradgley	Greenbush, N. Y	June 10, 1862	35, 514
Cork-screw	S. McCown	Stamford, Conn	Nov. 26, 1867	71, 316
Cork-screw	W. C. McGill	Cincinnati, Ohio	Jan. 8, 1867	61, 080
Cork-screw	C. L. Ridgway	Boston, Mass	Aug. 18, 1868	81, 292
Cork-screw	A. T. Russel	New York, N. Y	Jan. 21, 1862	34, 216
Cork-screw	J. A. Smith	Brooklyn, N. Y	Dec. 6, 1870	109, [illegible]58
Cork-screw	G. Twigg	Birmingham, England	Jan. 21, 1868	73, 677
Cork-screw	W. H. Van Gieson	Passaic, N. J	Jan. 22, 1867	61, 485
Cork-screw attachment	W. Dickson	Albany, N. Y	June 6, 1871	115, 585
Cork-screw, cork-puller, and can-opener combined	J. Harrigan	Fort Wadsworth, N. Y	July 25, 1871	117, 278
Cork-screws, Holding-frame for	H. M. Creamer	Brooklyn, N. Y	Apr. 14, 1863	38, 155
Cork, Sirup	A. J. Morse	Boston, Mass	June 8, 1869	91, 152
Cork-slicing machine	J. Power	Boston, Mass	Aug. 8, 1865	49, 299
Cork-trimming machine	B. T. Roath	Norwich, Conn	Aug. 16, 1864	43, 867
Cork-wood, Machine for slicing	H. Boardman	Lancaster, Pa	Dec. 6, 1864	45, 310
Corks by steam, Mode of softening	B. Potter, jr	Charlestown, Mass	Nov. 18, 1856	16, 098
Corks for stoppers, Machine for cutting	J. D. Crocker	Norwich, Conn	Mar. 25, 1862	34, 741
Corks from bottles, Instrument for extracting	J. T. Ashley	Brooklyn, N. Y	Oct. 23, 1866	58, 969
Corks in bottles, &c., Method of fastening	G. Bousigues, (dit Bley)	Rheims, France	Mar. 6, 1866	53, 090
Corks in bottles, Mode of securing	R. M. Huston	Calais, Me	May 31, 1859	24, 215
Corks, Machine for manufacturing	W. R. Crocker	Norwich, Conn	Oct. 30, 1855	13, 714
Corks, Machinery for cutting	P. C. Traver	Newburgh, N. Y	Mar. 6, 1847	5, 003
Corks of oil-cans, Method of protecting	E. A. More	Saint Louis, Mo	July 25, 1865	48, 972
Corks, rubber, &c., Compound of	L. Bauhoefer	Philadelphia, Pa	Sept. 3, 1867	68, 408
Corn and cane cutter	J. Peck	Oakland, Tenn	Aug. 28, 1844	3, 721
Corn and clover shelling and thrashing machine, combined with a grist-mill.	D. Mullier	Wooster, Ohio	Jan. 24, 1832	....
Corn and cob breaking and grinding machine	J. and W. Murray	Baltimore, Md	Feb. 12, 1842	2, 459
Corn and cob crusher	A. Glover	Powhatan Point, Ohio	June 5, 1860	28, 571
Corn and cob crusher	J. S. Griffith	Huntingdon, Pa	Feb. 6, 1855	12, 348
Corn and cob crusher	J. L. McKnight	Buchanan, Va	Dec. 15, 1843	3, 373
Corn and cob crusher	J. M. Mowrer	Millheim, Pa	Feb. 15, 1870	99, 933
Corn and cob cutter	S. B. Shinn	Philadelphia, Pa	May 3, 1859	23, 865
Corn and cob grinding mill	S. A. Bantz and W. Andrew	Frederick, Md	July 22, 1851	8, 243
Corn and cob grinding mill	S. L. Herr	Mexico, Pa	Apr. 4, 1844	3, 524
Corn and cob mill	S. A. Briggs	Philadelphia, Pa	July 3, 1860	29, 033
Corn and cob mill	J. De Frain	Philadelphia, Pa	Feb. 15, 1859	22, 997
Corn and cob mill	A. Fisher	Tuscaloosa, Ala	Aug. 28, 1847	5, 266
Corn and cob mill	R. D. Granger	Philadelphia, Pa	Sept. 18, 1855	13, 569
Corn and cob mill	H. Hall	Mansfield, Ohio	Dec. 15, 1857	18, 844
Corn and cob mill	D. S. James	New Market, Va	Aug. 21, 1855	13, 476
Corn and cob mill	J. O. Joyce	Cincinnati, Ohio	Aug. 5, 1856	15, 488
Corn and cob mill	J. H. King	Martinsburgh, W. Va	Nov. 26, 1872	133, 455
Corn and cob mill	E. A. Knowlton	Columbia, S. C	Feb. 12, 1845	3, 908
Corn and cob mill	R. F. Maynard	Baltimore, Md	Apr. 7, 1857	16, 988
Corn and cob mill	J. M. Miller	Mobile, Ala	Jan. 20, 1843	2, 923
Corn and cob mill	G. Patten	Washington, D. C	Oct. 30, 1855	13, 730

Index of patents issued from the United States Patent Office from 1790 *to* 1873, *inclusive*—Continued.

Invention.	Inventor.	Residence.	Date.	No.
Corn and cob mill	C. Roberts	Belleville, Ill	July 1, 1856	15, 255
Corn and cob mill	J. P. Ross	Lewisburgh, Pa.	Nov. 1, 1845	4, 249
Corn and cob mill	W. Sailor	Philadelphia, Pa	May 17, 1850	24, 082
Corn and cob mill	T. B. Stout	Keyport, N. J	Dec. 25, 1855	14, 002
Corn and cob mill	T. Ucker and A. Hutchins	Amanda, Ohio	July 21, 1868	80, 244
Corn and cob mill	B. Winter	Buckingham Court-House, Va.	Apr. 27, 1858	20, 121
Corn and cob mills, Securing the legs of sectional	R. F. Maynard	Baltimore, Md	Apr. 7, 1857	16, 987
Corn and cob crushing machine	S. K. Ganntt	Greenville, Tenn	May 25, 1827	....
Corn and fertilizer dropper	A. Towberman and J. Keys	Washington, Ill	Nov. 2, 1869	96, 510
Corn and grain drying machine	B. Parry	Bucks County, Pa	July 7, 1810	....
Corn and grain ventilator and drier	D. A. Dickenson	Baltimore, Md	June 16, 1868	78, 935
Corn and grinding bark, Cracking	M. J. Whiton	Amsterdam, N. Y	Apr. 30, 1834	....
Corn and malt, Kiln drying	J. Hughson	Clinton County, N. Y	July 18, 1811	....
Corn and other grain, Process and apparatus for curing	H. H. Beach	Rome, N. Y	May 7, 1872	126, 511
Corn and for other purposes, Machine for shelling and cleaning.	L. Stevens	....	May 8, 1804	....
Corn and other seed planting machine	E. L. Miller	Brooklyn, N. Y	Apr. 10, 1841	2, 047
Corn and phosphate drill	J. W. Wood and G. Moore	New Leeds Corner and Fairview School-House, Md.	Jan. 31, 1871	111, 416
Corn and potato coverer	J. Swart	Hoffman's Ferry, N. Y.	Aug. 4, 1868	80, 680
Corn, Band-tightener for shocks of	J. C. Jay	Bear Creek Township, Ind.	Mar. 9, 1869	87, 678
Corn balls, Machine for molding parched	R. Arnold	Hartford, Conn	Nov. 20, 1860	30, 661
Corn-breaker	W. Furbish	Hallowell, Me	Dec. 26, 1833	....
Corn-breaking machine	W. Furbish	Hallowell, Me	Mar. 15, 1833	....
Corn-cake cutter	L. Folker	Tewksbury, Mass	Dec. 10, 1867	71, 864
Corn-cake machine	C. C. Harriman	Warner, N. H	Mar. 5, 1867	62, 628
Corn-cake machine	H. and C. Littlefield	Tewksbury, Mass	July 30, 1867	67, 202
Corn-cake machine	W. Manning	Chelmsford, Mass	July 10, 1866	56, 241
Corn-cake mold	B. Witherell	Charlestown, Mass	Dec. 3, 1867	71, 831
Corn-cakes, Machine for making	W. Manning	Chelmsford, Mass	Nov. 22, 1870	109, 529
Corn, cob, and husk mill	E. Mire	New Orleans, La	Aug. 7, 1860	29, 509
Corn-cob cutter	I. Straub	Cincinnati, Ohio	July 25, 1854	11, 390
Corn-coverer	A. J. Combs	Olney, Ill	Aug. 27, 1867	68, 329
Corn-coverer	J. D. Haynie	New Antioch, Ohio	June 9, 1868	78, 665
Corn-coverer	I. N. Monroe	Bridgeport, Ill	Oct. 25, 1870	108, 717
Corn-coverer	J. A. Moore	Salem, N. J	Nov. 25, 1873	144, 918
Corn-coverer	J. Tweedy	Vernon, Ind	Jan. 28, 1873	135, 301
Corn-coverer	D. Weygandt	Jeromesville, Ohio	June 4, 1872	127, 534
Corn-crib	C. B. Clark	Pleasant Grove, Iowa	Mar. 26, 1872	125, 021
Corn-crib	N. T. Fitch	Forsyth, Ill	Oct. 22, 1867	70, 080
Corn-crib	A. B. Furbee	Dresden, Ohio	Dec. 6, 1859	26, 348
Corn-crib	J. M. Hughes and A. J. Mapes.	Independence, Mo	Apr. 29, 1873	138, 332
Corn-crib and thrashing-floor, Combined	J. R. Jordan and J. Campbell.	West Alexandria, Ohio	Dec. 15, 1868	85, 011
Corn-crusher	W. Beal	Lowell, Mass.	May 30, 1854	10, 979
Corn-crusher	A. Bolander	Akron, Ohio	Aug. 22, 1871	118, 188
Corn-crusher	T. B. Coursey	Frederica, Del	May 31, 1859	24, 198
Corn-cutter	H. V. Corbett	Allendale, Mich,	Dec. 13, 1870	110, 014
Corn cutter, Green	V. Baker	Otisfield, Me	May 31, 1870	103, 543
Corn, Device for marking and planting	J. P. Zeller	South Bend, Ind	Sept. 7, 1869	94, 687
Corn, Disk for shelling	J. P. Smith	Hummelstown, Pa	Nov. 25, 1856	16, 127
Corn-drill	R. F. Patton	Quincy, Ohio	Sept. 21, 1869	95, 132
Corn-drill	B. W. and N. T. Remy	Brookville, Ind	Mar. 28, 1871	113, 205
Corn-dropper	R. M. and W. H. Boman	London, Ohio	Dec. 16, 1873	145, 552
Corn-dropper	M. R. W. Caldwell	Jackson, Ohio	Nov. 29, 1870	109, 584
Corn-dropper	L. M. Doddridge, H. Reitenour, and J. B. Swhier.	New Mount Pleasant, Ind.	May 4, 1869	89, 742
Corn-dropper	J. H. Gross	Niantic, Ill	Jan. 24, 1871	111, 200
Corn-dropper	J. H Junkins	Upper Sandusky, Ohio	July 30, 1872	129, 963
Corn-dropper	R. B. Killin	Canton, Ohio	June 11, 1867	65, 578
Corn-dropper	C. E. Lipe	Fort Plain, N. Y	Sept. 3, 1867	68, 760
Corn-dropper	J. Nevison	Morgan, Ohio	Dec. 1, 1868	84, 571
Corn-dropper	J. L. Smith	Pemberton, N. J	June 7, 1870	103, 936
Corn-dropper	L. Weaver	Canton, Ohio	Oct. 15, 1867	69, 876
Corn dropper and cultivator, Combined	P. P. Gardner	Stoneborough, Pa	July 6, 1869	92, 184
Corn-drier	S. Bernheisel	Tyrone Township, Pa	Feb. 5, 1856	14, 181
Corn, Edible preparation from Indian	J. W. Haskins	Charlestown, Mass	Feb. 12, 1867	61, 936
Corn-elevator	A. Erkenbrecher	Cincinnati, Ohio	Aug. 27, 1867	68, 293
Corn fodder, Cutting and grinding	B. and D. H. Harnish	Lancaster Pequea, Pa	Aug. 22, 1871	118, 234
Corn-fodder cutting and grinding machine	A. Goodhart	Newville, Pa	Aug. 20, 1867	67, 975
Corn for grinding, Process for preparing	W. Standing	Duquoin, Ill	June 10, 1873	139, 743
Corn fork, Green	W. L. Gilroy	Philadelphia, Pa	June 1, 1869	90, 836
Corn from the cob, Device for cutting	F. A. Morley	New York, N. Y	Aug. 21, 1866	57, 361
Corn from the cob, Device for cutting green	J. Burt and L. F. Dunn	Oneida, N. Y	June 19, 1866	55, 614
Corn from the cob for table use, Apparatus for stripping.	W. C. McGill	Cincinnati, Ohio	Apr. 10, 1866	53, 849
Corn from the cob, Implement for cutting green	W. L. Gilroy	Philadelphia, Pa	May 25, 1869	90, 522
Corn from the cob, Knife for cutting green	I. Winslow	Philadelphia, Pa	Dec. 5, 1865	51, 379
Corn from the cob, Knife for removing	J. W. Jones	Portland, Me	Apr. 24, 1866	54, 170
Corn from the cob, Machine for cutting green	W. B. Coates	Philadelphia, Pa	May 13, 1856	14, 855
Corn from the cob, Machine for removing green	T. S. Lewis	Portland, Me	Aug. 24, 1869	94, 013
Corn from the cob, Machine for separating green	H. Walsh	Philadelphia, Pa	Sept. 30, 1856	15, 835
Corn from the stalks, Machine for severing the ears of.	A. J. and J. A. French	Franklin, Vt	Oct. 27, 1857	18, 505
Corn, Gathering and husking	J. D Hill	Fort Scott, Kans	Sept. 3, 1867	68, 507
Corn grinder and crusher	W. D Wilson	Richmond, Ind	May 29, 1855	12, 977
Corn grinding and crushing machine	A. P. H. Jordon	Madisonville, Tenn	Oct. 28, 1835	....
Corn grinding and shelling machine	G. M. Weaver	Montgomery County, Pa	June 12, 1835	....
Corn ground, Machine for furrowing	W. H. Warwick	Dunlevy, Ohio	Oct. 16, 1866	58, 923
Corn, Hand implement for severing the butts and separating husks from ears of.	I. N. Whitaker	Pecatonica, Ill	June 2, 1857	17, 466
Corn holder, Hot	W. A. Morgan and T. B. Mosher	Brooklyn and New York, N. Y.	Aug. 31, 1869	94, 330
Corn-houses, Method of ventilating	N. Seitz	Mellmore, Ohio	June 14, 1859	24, 407
Corn huller, sheller, and feed-cutter	T. Thomasson	Calhoun, Mo	Nov. 8, 1870	109, 157
Corn, Hulling	W. Carpenter	Newcastle, Pa	Jan. 22, 18[illegible]6	....

Index of patents issued from the United States Patent Office from 1790 *to* 1873, *inclusive*—Continued.

Invention.	Inventor.	Residence.	Date.	No.
Corn-husks, Machine for hackling	W. A. Fullerton	Louisville, Ky	July 11, 1854	11, 277
Corn-husks, Machine for hackling	G. B. Stacy	Richmond, Va	Mar. 23, 1869	88, 092
Corn-husks, Machine for stemming	D. M. Mefford	Jeffersonville, Ind	Oct. 2, 1860	30, 239
Corn-husks, Slitting	A. Barrett	Baltimore, Md	Apr. 21, 1836	....
Corn-husker	L. A. Aspinwall	Albany, N. Y	Apr. 12, 1870	101, 809
Corn-husker	E. M. Bates	East Rochester, Ohio	June 18, 1867	65, 867
Corn-husker	D. Bedell	Seneca Falls, N. Y	Nov. 17, 1857	18, 625
Corn-husker	D. Bookwalter	Gardner, Ill	May 18, 1869	90, 230
Corn-husker	G. K. Brown	Moultenborough, N. H	Oct. 20, 1857	18, 433
Corn-husker	T. J. Brown	Clio, Ohio	Aug. 21, 1866	57, 283
Corn-husker	R. Bryson	Schenectady, N. Y	Oct. 13, 1857	18, 385
Corn-husker	I. S. Bunnell	Carbondale, Pa	May 19, 1868	78, 052
Corn-husker	T. J. Burgess	Rondout, N. Y	June 28, 1870	104, 693
Corn-husker	J. M. Carl sle	Sumter, S. C	Jan. 7, 1873	134, 590
Corn-husker	G. W. Carr	Philadelphia, Pa	Oct. 14, 1873	143, 667
Corn-husker	E. H. Carver and G. M. Baker	Humberstone, Canada, and Buffalo, N. Y.	Apr. 4, 1871	113, 495
Corn-husker	J. Cawthra	Rochester, N. Y	Nov. 10, 1857	18, 571
Corn-husker	J. Cawthra	Rochester, N. Y	May 18, 1858	20, 253
Corn-husker	J. C. Clapp	Seneca Falls, N. Y	June 7, 1859	24, 281
Corn-husker	H. A. Doster	Bethlehem, Pa	Nov. 17, 1857	18, 658
Corn-husker	A. R. Davis	East Cambridge, Mass	Feb. 9, 1858	19, 325
Corn-husker	A. R. Davis	East Cambridge, Mass	Jan. 25, 1859	22, 710
Corn-husker	H. A. Doster	Bethlehem, Pa	Mar. 22, 1859	23, 295
Corn-husker	J. M. Evarts	New Haven, Conn	Mar. 12, 1872	124, 486
Corn-husker	N. Evinger	Sandford, Ind	Mar. 15, 1870	100, 740
Corn-husker	J. and J. L. Fagan	San Antonio River, Tex	Mar. 9, 1858	19, 552
Corn-husker	E. Field	Geneseo, Ill	July 6, 1869	92, 295
Corn-husker	C. Ford	Forest City, Ill	Mar. 10, 1868	75, 403
Corn-husker	E. F. French	Franklin, Vt	May 12, 1857	17, 269
Corn-husker	E. F. French	New York, N. Y	May 16, 1865	47, 710
Corn-husker	J. H. Gano	Tremont, Ohio	Sept. 11, 1866	57, 888
Corn-husker	A. M. George	Nashua, N. H	Oct. 6, 1857	18, 331
Corn-husker	H. P. Gerrish	Sandoval, Ill	Oct. 6, 1857	18, 332
Corn-husker	J. W. Glass	Richland, Ind	Apr. 2, 1867	63, 501
Corn-husker	J. I. Gorton	Sing Sing, N. Y	Dec. 15, 1868	84, 876
Corn-husker	S. A. Gould	Seneca Falls, N. Y	Nov. 10, 1857	18, 584
Corn-husker	M. H. Gragg	South Boston, Mass	July 19, 1859	24, 843
Corn husker	S. N. Gragg	Shelburne Falls, Mass	July 5, 1859	24, 628
Corn-husker	A. Graham	Roxbury, Mass	Oct. 20, 1857	18, 447
Corn-husker	L. A. Grover	Roxbury, Mass	July 6, 1858	20, 849
Corn-husker	H. L. Hall	Woodbridge, Iowa	Apr. 6, 1869	88, 708
Corn-husker	J. M. Hartnett	Waukegan, Ill	Sept. 1, 1868	81, 631
Corn-husker	B. Hazen	Cincinnati, Ohio	June 22, 1858	20, 637
Corn-husker	J. D. Heaton and W. A. Clark	Dixon, Ill	Jan. 19, 1858	19, 142
Corn-husker	J. B. Heich	Cincinnati, Ohio	Oct. 13, 1857	18, 396
Corn-husker	H. N. Hill	Pontiac, Mich	July 30, 1867	67, 301
Corn-husker	J. Hindman	Olathe, Kans	Jan. 22, 1867	61, 428
Corn-husker	J. Hood	Milwaukee, Wis	Sept. 13, 1870	107, 259
Corn-husker	L. H. Johnson	Branford, Conn	Apr. 7, 1868	76, 464
Corn-husker	S. Johnston	West Shelby, N. Y	Mar. 27, 1860	27, 638
Corn-husker	W. D. Jones	Hagaman's Mills, N. Y	Jan. 5, 1869	85, 593
Corn-husker	W. D. Jones	Hagaman's Mills, N. Y	May 18, 1869	90, 175
Corn-husker	C. A. Lang	Palmyra, Me	June 3, 1873	139, 586
Corn-husker	L. Leavenworth	Trumansburgh, N. Y	June 15, 1858	20, 568
Corn-husker	C. N. Lewis	Seneca Falls, N. Y	Nov. 17, 1857	18, 644
Corn-husker	C. N. Lewis	Seneca Falls, N. Y	May 4, 1858	20, 163
Corn-husker	D. Lombard	Boston, Mass	Feb. 9, 1858	19, 326
Corn-husker	B. B. Meacham	Ridleysville, Fla	May 25, 1858	20, 360
Corn-husker	L. R. Mears	South Abington, Mass	June 22, 1858	20, 653
Corn-husker	D. M. Mefford	Perrysburgh, Ohio	Dec. 22, 1857	18, 922
Corn-husker	D. M. Mefford	Jeffersonville, Ind	June 26, 1860	28, 884
Corn-husker	A. Merwin	Saint Joseph, Mich	Jan. 3, 1871	110, 772
Corn-husker	T. Percival	Augusta, Me	May 26, 1868	78, 321
Corn-husker	O. S. Perkins and L. A. Crandall	New Haven, Conn	May 25, 1869	90, 574
Corn-husker	C. J. C. Peterson	Davenport, Iowa	Aug. 31, 1858	21, 363
Corn-husker	I. Philbrook	Shelby County, Ill	Mar. 13, 1866	53, 180
Corn-husker	P. Philip	Stockport, N. Y	Aug. 9, 1870	106, 276
Corn-husker	P. Philip	Stockport, N. Y	Feb. 11, 1873	135, 840
Corn-husker	P. Philip	Stockport, N. Y	Feb. 11, 1873	135, 841
Corn-husker	W. Pickett and A. Hills	Naugatuck, Conn	Mar. 2, 1858	19, 512
Corn-husker	O. M. Pond	Independence, Iowa	Feb. 19, 1867	62, 151
Corn-husker	W. N. Rowe	Sharpsburgh, Md	Feb. 8, 1859	22, 894
Corn-husker	J. Russell	Brooklyn, N. Y	May 18, 1869	90, 311
Corn-husker	D. Sager	New York, N. Y	July 2, 1867	66, 255
Corn-husker	D. Sager	New York, N. Y	Oct. 3, 1871	119, 654
Corn-husker	J. Sechrist	Connellsville, Pa	Sept. 24, 1867	69, 258
Corn-husker	G. F. Shaw	Woburn, Mass	July 12, 1859	24, 765
Corn-husker	S. A. Skinner	Lawrence, Mass	Nov. 17, 1857	18, 662
Corn-husker	D. C. Smith	Tecumseh, Mich	May 11, 1858	20, 223
Corn-husker	D. C. Smith	Tecumseh, Mich	Aug. 2, 1859	24, 958
Corn-husker	T. S. Smith	Cincinnati, Ohio	Mar. 15, 1870	100, 941
Corn-husker	W. H. Smith	Newport, R. I	Oct. 6, 1857	18, 358
Corn-husker	P. P. Snell	Manheim, N. Y	Feb. 6, 1872	123, 428
Corn-husker	N. T. Spear	Boston, Mass	Sept. 14, 1858	21, 522
Corn-husker	N. T. Spear	New York, N. Y	Apr. 10, 1860	27, 841
Corn-husker	J. Stengel and C. C. Davy	Croton and Big Prairie, Mich.	July 11, 1871	117, 011
Corn-husker	G. E. Stewart	East Saginaw, Mich	July 7, 1868	79, 703
Corn-husker	J. Ure	Saginaw, Mich	Oct. 21, 1873	143, 797
Corn-husker	F. M. Walker	Greensborough, N. C	Feb. 9, 1858	19, 320
Corn-husker	G. R. Walker	Washington, D. C	Mar. 5, 1861	31, 637
Corn-husker	L. F. Ward	Marathon, N. Y	Feb. 23, 1858	19, 458
Corn-husker	R. Warriner, J. H. Baker, and G. B. Slocum.	Saratoga Springs, N. Y	June 7, 1870	104, 085
Corn-husker	D. F. Welsh	Bucyrus, Ohio	Aug. 16, 1870	106, 436
Corn-husker	S. Wesson	Worcester, Mass	Sept. 22, 1868	82, [illegible]

Index of patents issued from the United States Patent Office from 1790 *to* 1873, *inclusive*—Continued.

Invention.	Inventor.	Residence.	Date.	No.
Corn-husker	A. Whitcomb	Worcester, Mass	Apr. 27, 1869	89, 533
Corn-husker	D. Williams	Saginaw City, Mich	Aug. 27, 1867	68, 272
Corn-husker	J. F. Winchell	Springfield, Ohio	Jan. 1, 1867	60, 977
Corn-husker	C. O. Yale	Rome, N. Y	June 16, 1868	78, 908
Corn husker and picker	S. H. Mitchell	Lacon, Ill	May 7, 1872	126, 565
Corn husker and sheller	M. Jones	Amelia County, Va	May 5, 1868	77, 494
Corn husker and sheller and grain thrasher and cleaner, Combined.	J. W. Huntoon	Washington, D. C	Sept. 13, 1870	107, 378
Corn husker and sheller, Hand	J. M. Gray	Louisville, Ky	Dec. 27, 1870	110, 565
Corn-husker and stalk-cutter	E. Briggs, sr	Fayette, Iowa	July 9, 1867	66, 455
Corn-husker, Field	J. H. Whitney and W. W. Marsh.	Rochester, Minn., and De Kalb, Ill.	Nov. 7, 1871	120, 689
Corn-husker, Hand	S. L. Bligh	Sandy Lake, Pa	Aug. 16, 1870	106, 311
Corn-husker, Hand	A. W. Brinkerhoff	Upper Sandusky, Ohio	Apr. 23, 1872	125, 931
Corn-husker, Hand	H. L. Hall	Woodbridge, Iowa	Feb. 25, 1873	136, 157
Corn-husker, Hand	J. G. Johnson	Carthage, Ill	July 25, 1871	117, 296
Corn-husker, Hand	S. H. Mitchell	Lacon, Ill	Dec. 3, 1872	133, 659
Corn-husker, Hand	C. M. O'Hara	Cincinnati, Ohio	Aug. 1, 1871	117, 670
Corn-husker roller	J. Russell	Brooklyn, N. Y	Feb. 13, 1872	123, 580
Corn husker, sheller, and cleaner	C. J. Legg	Penn Yan, N. Y	June 6, 1865	48, 077
Corn husker, sheller, and stripper	F. Hafelfinger and R. N. Eagle	Washington, D. C	Nov. 24, 1868	84, 419
Corn-husker, straw and stalk cutter	R. Warriner and J. H. Baker	Saratoga Springs, N. Y	June 23, 1868	79, 166
Corn husking and shelling machine	A. Lane	Moscow, Ky	Feb. 27, 1872	124, 068
Corn husking and shelling machine	J. Wind	Thomasville, Ga	Dec. 4, 1860	30, 860
Corn-husking bench	J. E. Draper	Northville, Mich	Feb. 28, 1871	112, 131
Corn-husking device	A. W. Brinkerhoff	Upper Sandusky, Ohio	Sept. 2, 1862	36, 333
Corn-husking glove	A. C. Meyn	Jerseyville, Ill	May 7, 1872	126, 474
Corn-husking implement	O. J. Warren	Des Moines, Iowa	Feb. 25, 1873	136, 194
Corn-husking instrument	H. Bushnell	Norwich, Conn	Nov. 14, 1826	......
Corn-husking machine	L. A. Aspinwall	Albany, N. Y	Nov. 18, 1873	144, 590
Corn-husking machine	G. W. Bachman	Clifton Springs, N. Y	July 7, 1857	17, 720
Corn-husking machine	D. Bookwalter	Gardner, Ill	Oct. 13, 1868	83, 033
Corn-husking machine	R. Bryson	Schenectady, N. Y	Dec. 9, 1856	16, 204
Corn-husking machine	E. H. Carver	Preble, N. Y	May 31, 1870	103, 561
Corn-husking machine	A. W. Case	South Manchester, Conn	Dec. 13, 1864	45, 387
Corn-husking machine	J. Cutler	Putney, Vt	July 31, 1837	324
Corn-husking machine	D. A. Dickinson	Baltimore, Md	Apr. 30, 1867	64, 206
Corn-husking machine	W. Emery, jr	Chester, Ill	July 7, 1857	17, 731
Corn-husking machine	H. P. Gerrish	Boscawen, N. H	Nov. 4, 1856	16, 008
Corn-husking machine	E. S. Holmes	Lockport, N. Y	Feb. 10, 1857	16, 633
Corn-husking machine	J. M. Hubbard	West Haven, Conn	Dec. 19, 1865	51, 589
Corn-husking machine	A. R. Hurst	New Cumberland, Pa	Mar 31, 1857	16, 924
Corn-husking machine	M. C. Jeffers	New York, N. Y	Oct. 18, 1870	108, 484
Corn-husking machine	H. W. Knowlton	Saratoga Springs, N. Y	Jan. 14, 1868	73, 251
Corn-husking machine	W. Lewis	Seneca Falls, N. Y	Mar. 3, 1857	16, 737
Corn husking machine	J. Massey	Buffalo, N. Y	Mar. 3, 1857	16, 740
Corn-husking machine	J. Naeber	North Orange, N. J	May 17, 1859	24, 047
Corn-husking machine	J. Perkins	West Killingley, Conn	Nov. 4, 1856	16, 023
Corn-husking machine	J. Russell	Brooklyn, N. Y	Mar. 21, 1871	112, 967
Corn-husking machine	J. Russell	New York, N. Y	June 11, 1872	127, 801
Corn-husking machine	D Sager	New York, N. Y	June 16, 1868	79, 011
Corn-husking machine	W. H. Smith	Newport, R. I	Oct. 28, 1856	15, 985
Corn-husking machine	M. W. Stevens and E. G. Kingsley.	Stoughton, Mass	Oct. 20, 1857	18, 473
Corn-husking machine	O. Stoddard	Busti, N. Y	June 3, 1856	15, 047
Corn-husking machine	H. Strait	Covington, Ky	Mar. 3, 1857	16, 758
Corn-husking machine	J. Taggart and L. A. Grover	Roxbury, Mass	Dec. 9, 1856	16, 201
Corn-husking roll	P. Philip	Stockport, N. Y	Mar. 14, 1871	112, 735
Corn-husking shield	A. C. Robinson	Louisiana, Mo	Apr. 16, 1867	63, 941
Corn-husking thimble	G. W. Gash and C. L. Owens	Clinton, Ill	Apr. 15, 1873	137, 771
Corn in the cob, Cutting and grinding	J. Urney	Wilmington, Del	Oct. 25, 1845	4, 244
Corn in the cob, Grinding	W. Mayo	Henrico, Va	May 15, 1812	......
Corn in the ear and other grain, Grinding	T. Briggs	East Bloomfield N. Y	Jan. 10, 1834	......
Corn into meal, Machine for grinding	T. Baker	Statesburgh, S. C	Jan. 21, 1829	......
Corn-knife	G. Stevens	Zionsville, Ind	Apr. 29, 1873	138, 447
Corn knife, Green	W. L. Gilroy	Philadelphia, Pa	Sept. 22, 1868	82, 306
Corn knife, Green	J. Harrington	New London, Conn	Sept. 22, 1868	82, 403
Corn, &c., Machine for covering	T. Williams	Pittsylvania, Va	Dec. 19, 1822	......
Corn, Machine for cutting the stalks of standing	W. B. Coates	Philadelphia, Pa	Dec. 9, 1856	16, 177
Corn, Machine for facilitating the husking of	G. Young, jr	Saratoga Springs, N. Y	Nov. 17, 1857	18, 656
Corn, Machine for grinding cobs and	S. Stukey	Sugar Grove, Ohio	Oct. 16, 1866	58, 912
Corn, &c., Machine for grinding shelled	J. Webster	Philadelphia, Pa	July 31, 1826	......
Corn, Machine for marking and covering	E. Barto	Tiffin, Ohio	Nov. 10, 1868	83, 905
Corn, &c., Machine for planting	E. Bunce	Westford, Mass	July 16, 1838	841
Corn, Machine for removing husks from	J. Young	Varick, N. Y	Dec. 24, 1861	34, 033
Corn, Machine for shelling and cleaning	J. S. Gardiner	Canandaigua, N. Y	June 11, 1829	......
Corn-meal for shipment, Preparing	L. S. Chichester	Brooklyn, N. Y	Feb. 25, 1873	136, 306
Corn-mill	C. Leavitt	Cleveland, Ohio	May 11, 1858	20, 208
Corn-mill	J. W. Taylor	Philadelphia, Pa	May 31, 1859	24, 249
Corn, Mill for grinding and crushing	J. C. and C. B. Baldwin	Virginia	June 26, 1839	1, 199
Corn, Mill for shelling and grinding	H. R. Miller	Louisville, Ky	Dec. 5, 1854	12, 030
Corn picker and husker, Field	G. and C. Meader	Prairie Centre, Ill	Dec. 13, 1870	110, 061
Corn picking and husking machine	S. R. Kenyon	Greenville, R. I	Aug. 27, 1867	68, 085
Corn picking and husking machine	S. R. Kenyon	Greenville, R. I	Mar. 28, 1871	113, 174
Corn picking and husking machine	S. R. Kenyon	Greenville, R. I	Nov. 28, 1871	121, 384
Corn-picking machine	S. W. May	Galesburgh, Ill	Dec. 28, 1858	22, 440
Corn-planter	H. Blair	Glenross, Md	Oct. 14, 1834	......
Corn-planter	T. V. Bush	Clark County, Ky	Dec. 17, 1834	......
Corn-planter, Hand	C. L. Green	Johnson's Creek, N. Y	Jan. 2, 1866	51, 825
Corn planting and working machine	W. Ross	Middle Baxton Township, Pa.	June 24, 1826	......
Corn-planting, Furrowing-device for	J. Plumb	Clarksville, N. J	Feb. 13, 1866	52, 598
Corn-planting machine	J. Blocher	Lancaster, Pa	Apr. 12, 1814	......
Corn-popper	J. H. Bigelow	Worcester, Mass	Aug. 3, 1869	93, 271
Corn-popper	W. F. Collier	Worcester, Mass	July 20, 1869	92, 939
Corn-popper	W. F. Collier	Worcester, Mass	Jan. 31, 1871	111, 319
Corn-popper	A. F. Curtis and O. N. Palmer	Delaware, Ohio	May 14, 1872	126, 080
Corn-popper	D. A. Denison	Troy, Mich	Dec. 17, 1867	72, 173

Index of patents issued from the United States Patent Office from 1790 *to* 1873, *inclusive*—Continued.

Invention.	Inventor.	Residence.	Date.	No.
Corn-popper	G. D. Dudley	Lowell, Mass	Aug. 13, 1867	67, 736
Corn-popper	B. B. and J. R. Hill	Worcester, Mass	July 27, 1869	92, 967
Corn-popper	J. W. Howe and J. K. Barton	Worcester, Mass	Dec. 10, 1867	71, 881
Corn-popper	W. J. Johnson	Newton, Mass	July 4, 1871	116, 600
Corn-popper	E. G. Kinsley	Stoughton, Mass	Nov. 12, 1867	70, 723
Corn-popper	W. W. S. Orbeton	Haverhill, Mass	Oct. 30, 1866	59, 253
Corn-popper	C. H. S. Schultz	Cincinnati, Ohio	Oct. 29, 1867	70, 368
Corn-popper	M. H. Wiley	Boston, Mass	Mar. 5, 1872	124, 305
Corn-popper and coffee-roaster	L. A. Warner	Freeport, Ill	Apr. 7, 1868	76, 362
Corn-popper and coffee roaster	L. A. Warner	Freeport, Ill	July 19, 1870	105, 5[illegible]0
Corn, Preparation from Indian	E. F. Prentiss and C. C. Parsons.	Philadelphia, Pa., and Boston, Mass.	Mar. 26, 1867	63, 175
Corn, Preparing seed	J. M. Petit	Monroe Township, Ohio	Mar. 21, 1871	112, 845
Corn preserved green, Indian	I. Winslow	Philadelphia, Pa	Apr. 8, 1862	34, 928
Corn, Process for treating Indian	E. F. Prentiss and C. C. Parsons.	Philadelphia, Pa., and Boston, Mass.	Mar. 26, 1867	63, 174
Corn-rows, &c., Laying of	P. Moseley	Benton, Miss	Dec. 12, 1842	2, 882
Corn-separator	E. McLane	Young America, Ill	May 4, 1869	89, 589
Corn-shaving machine	E. Watts	Keyport, N. J	Aug. 29, 1871	118, 564
Corn-sheller	A. Adams	Sandwich, Ill	Sept. 28, 1858	21, 594
Corn-sheller	A. Adams	Sandwich, Ill	Aug. 6, 1861	32, 971
Corn-sheller	A. Adams	Sandwich, Ill	May 15, 1866	54, 659
Corn-sheller	A. Adams	Sandwich, Ill	Feb. 20, 1872	123, 758
Corn-sheller	A. Adams	Sandwich, Ill	Jan. 28, 1873	135, 3[illegible]6
Corn-sheller	C. Adams	Oak Hill, N. Y	Aug. 12, 1856	15, 502
Corn-sheller	C. Adams	Pittsburgh, Pa	Aug. 17, 1858	21, 174
Corn-sheller	H. A. Adams	Sandwich, Ill	Oct. 15, 1872	132, 128
Corn-sheller	A. B. Allen	New York, N. Y	July 15, 1862	35, 864
Corn-sheller	J. M. C. Armsby	Worcester, Mass	Jan. 7, 1851	7, 881
Corn-sheller	D. Bacon	Brewersville, Ind	Aug. 25, 1868	81, 458
Corn-sheller	C. B. Baldwin	Cincinnati, Ohio	July 16, 1842	2, 718
Corn-sheller	I. C. Baldwin	Staunton, Va	Oct. 11, 1836	....
Corn-sheller	C. Beach	Penn Yan, N. Y	Jan. 1, 1867	60, 825
Corn-sheller	W. Beach	Baltimore, Md	Apr. 18, 1846	4, 460
Corn-sheller	W. Beach	Baltimore, Md	Dec. 26, 1848	5, 982
Corn-sheller	P. Bergen	New York, N. Y	Mar. 30, 1858	19, 809
Corn sheller	G. Bevitt	Madison, Wis	July 2, 1867	66, 205
Corn-sheller	C. Bishop	Norwalk, Ohio	Oct. 9, 1855	13, 634
Corn-sheller	T. W. Bishop	Austin, Ind	Nov. 5, 1867	70, 396
Corn-sheller	W. Black	Allegheny City, Pa	Oct. 21, 1856	15, 920
Corn-sheller	F. A. Bolles	Unadilla, N. Y	June 18, 1867	65, 868
Corn-sheller	M. Bomberger	Hummelstown, Pa	Jan. 4, 1859	22, 481
Corn-sheller	J. Bowles	Augusta, Ga	May 4, 1869	89, 550
Corn-sheller	C. H. Brady	Mount Joy, Pa	Sept. 17, 1867	68, 941
Corn-sheller	C. H. Brady	Mount Joy, Pa	Mar. 31, 1868	76, 154
Corn-sheller	B. Bridendolph	Clear Spring, Md	Dec. 20, 1859	26, 471
Corn-sheller	J. D. Briggs	Saratoga, N. Y	June 14, 1845	4, 079
Corn-sheller	J. Brinkerhoff	Auburn, N. Y	Apr. 12, 1864	42, 271
Corn-sheller	J. Brinkerhoff	Auburn, N. Y	Feb. 28, 1865	46, 540
Corn-sheller	J. Brinkerhoff	Auburn, N. Y	Aug. 13, 1867	67, 713
Corn-sheller	J. Brinkerhoff	Auburn, N. Y	Mar. 3, 1868	74, 981
Corn-sheller	F. C. Brown and J. R. Shangle.	Hightstown, N. J	Apr. 22, 1873	138, 125
Corn-sheller	L. S Bundy and L. F. Edgerton	Hyde Park, Vt	May 14, 1861	32, 273
Corn-sheller	W. R. Burns	Lancaster, Pa	Apr. 3, 1866	53, 567
Corn-sheller	N. Burr	Batavia, Ill	Nov. 8, 1859	26, 010
Corn-sheller	T. D. Burrall	Geneva, N. Y	Dec. 6, 1845	4, 300
Corn-sheller	T. D. Burrall	Geneva, N. Y	Mar. 24, 1863	38, 002
Corn-sheller	J. R. Cadwell	Onondaga, Mich	Feb. 13, 1872	123, 676
Corn-sheller	M. Carpenter	Lancaster, Pa	Oct. 25, 1832	....
Corn-sheller	M. Carpenter	Lancaster, Pa	Aug. 8, 1833	....
Corn-sheller	C. W. Carter	Westville, Ind	Mar. 29, 1859	23, 424
Corn-sheller	J. A. Cauldwell	Horseheads, N. Y	Dec. 1, 1868	84, 610
Corn-sheller	R. Chalfant	West Grove, Pa	Feb. 27, 1847	4, 979
Corn-sheller	P. C. Chipron	Highland, Ill	Feb. 11, 1868	74, 306
Corn-sheller	A. and C. N. Clow	Port Byron, N. Y	June 26, 1855	13, 122
Corn-sheller	D. Codd	Ottawa, Canada	Nov. 10, 1868	83, 832
Corn-sheller	S. S. Cole	Henryville, Ind	Mar. 30, 1869	88, 367
Corn-sheller, &c	G. S. Coleman	Alexandria, Va	Sept. 27, 1870	107, 761
Corn-sheller	W. Colwell	Chillicothe, Ill	Oct. 23, 1866	58, 986
Corn-sheller	E. Converse	Cincinnati, Ohio	Jan. 7, 1846	4, 348
Corn-sheller	A. M. Cook	Milford, Mass	Oct. 6, 1857	18, 325
Corn-sheller	H. W. Cornell	Owego, N. Y	Nov. 2, 1869	96, 306
Corn-sheller	H. W. Cornell	Owego, N. Y	Aug. 1, 1871	117, 607
Corn-sheller	H. W. Cornell	Owego, N. Y	June 18, 1872	128, 124
Corn-sheller	C. S. C. Crane	Taunton, Mass	May 27, 1856	14, 990
Corn-sheller	G. Danforth	Friendsville, Ill	Aug. 21, 1860	29, 673
Corn-sheller	A. B. Davis	Philadelphia, Pa	Apr. 13, 1858	19, 915
Corn-sheller	A. B. Davis and T. Crook, jr	Philadelphia, Pa	Feb. 18, 1862	34, 410
Corn-sheller	J. Davis	Oaks, Wis	Feb. 20, 1866	52, 690
Corn-sheller	L. H. Davis	Kennett s Square, Pa	Sept. 6, 1853	10, 002
Corn-sheller	M. Day	Baltimore, Md	July 14, 1868	79, 961
Corn-sheller	M. Day	Baltimore, Md	July 14, 1868	79, 962
Corn-sheller	L. Day	Baltimore, Md	June 13, 1871	115, 939
Corn sheller	J. H. Derby	Leominster, Mass	Nov. 10, 1841	2, 337
Corn-sheller	P. Dickinson	Amherst, Mass	Sept. 6, 1853	10, 003
Corn-sheller	A. Dillman	Plainfield, Ill	Sept. 8, 1859	18, 139
Corn-sheller	O. R. Dinsmore	West Chester, N. H	Feb. 24, 1839	1, 088
Corn-sheller	J. Dodson	Guilford, N. C	June 15, 1826	....
Corn-sheller	S. E. Donnell	Greensborough County, N. C.	Apr. 5, 1833	....
Corn-sheller	E. Dond	Oshkosh, Wis	Nov. 17, 1868	84, 173
Corn-sheller	N. Drake	Newton, N J	Apr. 3, 1860	27, 705
Corn-sheller	Dunbar and Powers	Portland, Me	June 26, 1835	....
Corn-sheller	B. Edwards	Laceyville, Pa	May 16, 1848	5, 578
Corn sheller	D. Eldridge	Philadelphia, Pa	Nov. 19, 1850	7, 781
Corn-sheller	D. Eldridge	Philadelphia, Pa	June 1, 1852	8, 978
Corn-sheller	F. Elliot	Greensborough, N. C	Nov. 19, 1833	....
Corn-sheller	S. Elliott	Wayne County, Ind	Oct. 9, 1855	13, 640

Index of patents issued from the United States Patent Office from 1790 *to* 1873, *inclusive*—Continued.

Invention.	Inventor.	Residence.	Date.	No.
Corn-sheller	F. Fanning	Atchison, Kans	June 8, 1869	91, 003
Corn-sheller	P. Ferrier	Ypsilanti, Mich	Mar. 16, 1869	87, 920
Corn-sheller	D. E. Field	Leaksville, N. C	Feb. 15, 1870	99, 768
Corn-sheller	S. Field	Oakham, Mass	Jan. 18, 1870	98, 944
Corn-sheller	G. W. Fitts	South Hampton, N. H	July 11, 1865	48, 670
Corn-sheller	S. Fletcher and J. P. Pike	Bloomfield, Me	Jan. 3, 1860	26, 662
Corn-sheller	J. S. Fowler	Peoria, Ill	May 13, 1862	35, 227
Corn-sheller	C. C. French	West Stockbridge, Mass	Jan. 15, 1861	31, 115
Corn-sheller	W. Gee	Prince George's County, Va	May 10, 1832	......
Corn-sheller	B. Gilbert	Pittsburgh, Pa	Jan. 3, 1854	10, 390
Corn-sheller	W. Gilman	Ottawa, Ill	June 12, 1866	55, 485
Corn-sheller	P. A. Gladwin	Chester, Conn	Apr. 24, 1840	1, 567
Corn-sheller	L. B. Glover	Easton, Conn	July 31, 1846	4, 677
Corn-sheller	G. Goewey	Philadelphia, Pa	Feb. 10, 1863	37, 662
Corn-sheller	G. Goewey	Philadelphia, Pa	Oct. 18, 1864	44, 768
Corn-sheller	G. Goewey	Philadelphia, Pa	Oct. 29, 1867	70, 195
Corn-sheller	N. Goldsborough	Easton, Md	Feb. 12, 1841	1, 975
Corn-sheller	J. W. Gordon	Jamestown, N. C	Oct. 7, 1846	4, 806
Corn-sheller	J. Gould	Grinnell, Iowa	Dec. 10, 1867	72, 020
Corn-sheller	H. A. Graeff	Birdsborough, Pa	July 9, 1867	66, 485
Corn-sheller	S. L. Graves	Springfield, Ill	Sept. 17, 1850	7, 653
Corn-sheller	A. W. Gray	Middletown, Vt	Mar. 31, 1836	....
Corn-sheller	D. G. Greene	North Bridgewater, Mass	Mar. 9, 1858	19, 603
Corn-sheller	R. Green	Cussawago, Pa	May 18, 1858	20, 266
Corn-sheller	S. Gumaer	Aurora, Ill	Nov. 7, 1854	11, 891
Corn-sheller	D. C. Guttridge	Pittsburgh, Pa	Aug. 29, 1871	118, 605
Corn-sheller	D. Hall	Strasburgh Township, Pa	Nov. 12, 1832	....
Corn-sheller	J. R. Hamilton	Portland, Oreg	Jan. 14, 1868	73, 323
Corn-sheller	J. R. Hamilton	Kingston, Minn	Nov. 15, 1870	109, 315
Corn-sheller	D. W. Harris and E. P. Carter	Yorkshire, N. Y	Nov. 6, 1849	6, 847
Corn-sheller	J. S. Harris	Poultney, Vt	Sept. 18, 1835	....
Corn-sheller	G. W. Hathaway	Tioga, Pa	Oct. 16, 1860	30, 403
Corn-sheller	M. Hausman	Huntington, Ind	Sept. 4, 1860	29, 886
Corn-sheller	J. M. Hawley	Holton, Ind	Jan. 5, 1869	85, 590
Corn-sheller	A. Higley	Warren, Ohio	Mar. 17, 1863	37, 912
Corn-sheller	F. Hollen and A. C. Holland	Marion, Ill	Apr. 15, 1873	137, 842
Corn-sheller	D. S. Hollister	Baltimore, Md	June 13, 1846	4, 572
Corn-sheller	W. W. Holt	Dunkirk, N. Y	Apr. 9, 1872	125, 392
Corn-sheller	M. and S. Housman	Huntington, Ind	Dec. 11, 1866	60, 375
Corn-sheller	M. and S. Housman	Huntington, Ind	Feb. 11, 1868	74, 364
Corn-sheller	W. H. Hovey	Springfield, Mass	Apr. 19, 1859	23, 686
Corn-sheller	R. Hoyt	Miamisburgh, Ohio	Oct. 31, 1834	....
Corn-sheller	L. T. Hulbert and A. P. Teachout.	Painesville and Madison, Ohio.	June 20, 1871	116, 192
Corn-sheller	D. Hutchinson	Fort Ancient, Ohio	Jan. 17, 1865	45, 924
Corn-sheller	E. L. Hutchinson	Auburn, N. Y	Aug. 5, 1873	141, 559
Corn-sheller	J. Hutchison	Three Rivers, Mich	Nov. 19, 1872	133, 228
Corn-sheller	W. Janes	Ashford, Conn	May 6, 1819	....
Corn-sheller	G. F. Johnson	Marshall, Iowa	Aug. 25, 1868	81, 375
Corn-sheller	J. B. Johnson	Alma, Ill	Aug. 12, 1873	141, 795
Corn-sheller	W. Johnson	Boscawen, N. H	Dec. 17, 1834	....
Corn-sheller	J. J. Johnston	Allegheny, Pa	Dec. 11, 1855	13, 912
Corn-sheller	J. J. Johnston	Allegheny, Pa	Sept. 23, 1856	15, 765
Corn-sheller	J. J. Johnston	Allegheny, Pa	Apr. 19, 1859	23, 687
Corn-sheller	A. H. Jones	Fallsington, Pa	Nov. 5, 1861	33, 648
Corn-sheller	E. Jordan	Pickens County, Ala	Oct. 4, 1870	107, 919
Corn-sheller	J. Jordan	Red Wing, Minn	June 29, 1869	92, 056
Corn-sheller	E. Kelley	Locust Grove, Ohio	Mar. 16, 1869	88, 790
Corn-sheller	I. Kepler	Milton, Pa	Apr. 24, 1849	6, 382
Corn-sheller	C. Ketchum	Penn Yan, N. Y	Feb. 7, 1865	46, 245
Corn-sheller	N. S. Ketchum	Marshalltown, Iowa	June 4, 1872	127, 610
Corn-sheller	M. C. Kilgore	Washington, Iowa	Mar. 12, 1867	62, 857
Corn-sheller	S. H. Kisinger	Williamsport, Md	Oct. 31, 1839	1, 385
Corn-sheller	W. D. Leavitt	New Orleans, La	Aug. 10, 1869	93, 455
Corn-sheller	C. J. Legg	Penn Yan, N. Y	Sept. 22, 1863	40, 052
Corn-sheller	A. F. Severance	Concord, N. H	Mar. 29, 1864	42, 114
Corn-sheller	J. R. Lindner	Cincinnati, Ohio	Feb. 2, 1858	19, 253
Corn-sheller	W. Linsley	Waddam Township, Ill	Mar. 9, 1852	8, 788
Corn-sheller	W. J. Ludlow	Cleveland, Ohio	Feb. 2, 1869	86, 562
Corn-sheller	W. H. Main	Liverpool, Ohio	June 22, 1858	20, 650
Corn-sheller	W. Manning	South Trenton, N. J	Aug. 4, 1843	3, 208
Corn-sheller	J. Marshall	Cordova, Ill	Dec. 9, 1873	145, 356
Corn-sheller	E. Mathers	Morgantown, Va	Apr. 29, 1856	14, 771
Corn-sheller	T. J. Mayall	Boston, Mass	Apr. 23, 1872	126, 067
Corn-sheller	W. M. Mayall	Gray, Me	Nov. 16, 1869	96, 938
Corn-sheller	G. Maynard	Greenfield, Mass	Sept. 12, 1854	11, 672
Corn-sheller	W. McAll	Talladega, Ala	Apr. 13, 1844	3, 540
Corn-sheller	T. U. McFarlan and L. H. Davis.	Salem, Ohio, and West Chester, Pa.	Apr. 6, 1858	19, 862
Corn-sheller	R. M. McGrath	La Fayette, Ind	Apr. 15, 1873	137, 942
Corn-sheller	J. H. McPheeters and P. P. Gross.	Palmyra, Mo	July 7, 1868	79, 675
Corn-sheller	S. McQuiston	Morris, Ill	Oct. 8, 1861	33, 442
Corn-sheller	J. A. Merriman	Chicago, Ill	Feb. 18, 1868	74, 569
Corn-sheller	W. Miller	Bloomington, Ind	Aug. 3, 1869	93, 328
Corn-sheller	J. Miller and N. Dubrul	Joliet, Ill	May 23, 1871	115, 227
Corn-sheller	E. L. Millis	Rochester Depot, Ohio	Aug. 9, 1853	9, 924
Corn-sheller	A. C. Mills	Oaktown, Ind	July 28, 1868	80, 362
Corn-sheller	E. Morrison	Franklin, N. H	June 10, 1856	15, 105
Corn-sheller	E. Morse	Knoxville, Tenn	Sept. 9, 1835	....
Corn-sheller	J. W. Morton	Brunswick, Ohio	Nov. 24, 1857	18, 700
Corn-sheller	J. Mumma	Middletown, Pa	June 12, 1849	6, 526
Corn-sheller	J. Murray	Baltimore, Md	Oct. 7, 1846	4, 805
Corn-sheller	F. Nelson	Wyandotte, Mich	Jan. 24, 1871	111, 139
Corn-sheller	L. T. Newell	Springville, N. Y	Mar. 5, 1867	62, 671
Corn-sheller	T. J. Newland	Wolcott, Vt	July 17, 1860	29, 188
Corn-sheller	G. and H. O'Conner	Mishawaka, Ind	July 11, 1871	116, 987
Corn-sheller	I. E. Overpeck	Overpeck Station, Ohio	Nov. 27, 1866	60, 046

Index of patents issued from the United States Patent Office from 1790 *to* 1873, *inclusive*—Continued.

Invention.	Inventor.	Residence.	Date.	No.
Corn-sheller	C. Page	Sanbornton, N. H	Mar. 13, 1834	....
Corn-sheller	E. Parker	Baltimore, Md	Apr. 20, 1858	20, 003
Corn-sheller	J. J. Parker	Marietta, Ohio	Sept. 29, 1857	18, 296
Corn-sheller	S. J. Parmele	Killingworth, Conn	Dec. 24, 1861	34, 008
Corn-sheller	A. H. Patch	Hamilton, Mass	July 4, 1871	116, 627
Corn-sheller	A. H. Patch	Hamilton, Mass	Apr. 2, 1872	125, 217
Corn-sheller	W. P. Patton and W. A. Middleton.	Harrisburgh, Pa	Jan. 25, 1870	99, 106
Corn-sheller	R. Pleifer	Linz, Austria	Jan. 18, 1870	98, 909
Corn-sheller	C. G. Pressey and J. B. Dudley	Andover, N. H	Mar. 30, 1843	3, 025
Corn-sheller	D. O. Prouty and E. Whitman	Philadelphia, Pa., and Baltimore, Md.	May 29, 1849	6, 421
Corn-sheller	I. G. Putnam	Tioga, Pa	May 22, 1860	28, 440
Corn-sheller	E. Rand and A. L. Norcross	Hallowell, Me	Feb. 13, 1835	....
Corn-sheller	J. B. Rand and W. A. N. Long	Fisherville, N. H	Aug. 13, 1861	33, 052
Corn-sheller	J. Rankin	Binghamton, N. Y	Jan. 28, 1873	135, 362
Corn-sheller	P. Reading	Trenton, N. J	Dec. 27, 1824	....
Corn-sheller	P. Reading	Batavia, Ohio	Sept. 25, 1841	2, 266
Corn-sheller	W. Reading	Washington, D. C	July 13, 1852	9, 120
Corn-sheller	D. K. Reeder	Elliottsburgh, Pa	June 5, 1866	55, 362
Corn-sheller	G. W. Reid	Evansville, Ind	May 3, 1853	9, 698
Corn-sheller	G. W. Reisinger	Harrisburgh, Pa	Sept. 13, 1870	107, 410
Corn-sheller	G. W. Reisinger	Harrisburgh, Pa	Dec. 6, 1870	109, 945
Corn-sheller	I. I. Richardson	New York, N. Y	Apr. 17, 1849	6, 320
Corn-sheller	S. Richardson	Rochester, N. Y	June 17, 1862	35, 625
Corn-sheller	J. W. Ricker	Boston, Mass	Mar. 25, 1862	34, 775
Corn-sheller	J. W. Ricker	Chelsea, Mass	May 3, 1870	102, 593
Corn-sheller	J. W. Ricker and T. S. Lewis	Chelsea, Mass	Aug. 8, 1865	49, 303
Corn-sheller	J. Robb	Lewistown, Pa	Dec. 25, 1855	13, 997
Corn-sheller	C. Robbins and R. P. Burlingame	Chicago, Ill	Apr. 1, 1862	34, 846
Corn-sheller	W. Roberts	Farnham, N. Y	June 16, 1868	79, 007
Corn-sheller	J. Ross	Roundbrook, N. J	Apr. 12, 1833	....
Corn-sheller	J. M. Ross	Linden Hall, Pa	June 29, 1869	92, 103
Corn-sheller	S. P. Ross and N. Haller	Pittsburgh and Allegheny City, Pa.	Aug. 31, 1869	94, 444
Corn-sheller	S. W. Ryckman	Pontiac, Mich	Feb. 7, 1860	27, 077
Corn-sheller	N. C. and E. A. Scofield	Norwich, Conn	Jan. 20, 1843	2, 924
Corn-sheller	S C. Scofield	Chicago, Ill	June 6, 1871	115, 646
Corn-sheller	F. H. Schroeder	Bushnell, Ill	May 30, 1865	47, 988
Corn-sheller	H. Sells	Vienna, Canada	Jan. 16, 1872	122, 740
Corn-sheller	J. H. Sharp	Wortsville, N. J	Apr. 28, 1868	77, 410
Corn-sheller	H. F. and G. F. Shaw	West Roxbury, Mass	Oct. 31, 1865	50, 740
Corn-sheller	W. E. Sheffield	New York	Apr. 15, 1823	....
Corn-sheller	E F. Sherman	Chicopee Falls, Mass	Aug. 21, 1866	57, 393
Corn-sheller	E. F. Sherman	Chicopee, Mass	Feb. 18, 1868	74, 726
Corn-sheller	J. Shipe	Upper Augusta, Pa	Aug. 2, 1864	43, 713
Corn-sheller	A. Siddall	Ransom, Mich	June 28, 1859	24, 583
Corn-sheller	I. B. Siddle	Caswell County, N. C	Mar. 19, 1867	63, 112
Corn-sheller	C. Sines	Village Green, Pa	Oct. 10, 1848	5, 848
Corn-sheller	J. Small	Bridgewater, Pa	Mar. 27, 1849	6, 228
Corn-sheller	J. P. Small	Gilmanton, N. H	July 21, 1835	....
Corn-sheller	E. A. Smead	Tioga, Pa	June 5, 1860	28, 612
Corn-sheller	A. B. Smith	Wellsburgh, W. Va	Nov. 14, 1871	120, 909
Corn-sheller	A. J. Smith	Piqua, Ohio	Aug. 29, 1854	11, 620
Corn-sheller	F. N. Smith	Kinderhook, N. Y	June 1, 1843	3, 114
Corn-sheller	H. E. Smith	Philadelphia, Pa	Dec. 9, 1856	16, 191
Corn-sheller	J. P. Smith	Hummelstown, Pa	Jan. 18, 1853	9, 549
Corn-sheller	J. P. Smith	Hummelstown, Pa	Nov. 7, 1854	11, 913
Corn-sheller	J. P. Smith	Hummelstown, Pa	Feb. 20, 1855	12, 454
Corn-sheller	J. P. Smith	Hummelstown, Pa	Dec. 11, 1855	13, 922
Corn-sheller	J. P. Smith	Hummelstown, Pa	Mar. 4, 1856	14, 374
Corn-sheller	J. P. Smith	Hummelstown, Pa	Jan. 19, 1858	19, 160
Corn-sheller	J. P. Smith	Hummelstown, Pa	Feb. 8, 1859	22, 898
Corn-sheller	J. P. Smith	Hummelstown, Pa	June 19, 1860	28, 784
Corn-sheller	J. P. Smith	Hummelstown, Pa	May 6, 1862	35, 185
Corn-sheller	J. P. Smith	Hummelstown, Pa	Dec. 15, 1868	85, 035
Corn-sheller	J. P. Smith	Hummelstown, Pa	June 22, 1869	91, 572
Corn-sheller	E. E. Stedman	Randolph, Ohio	May 21, 1867	64, 919
Corn-sheller	D. C. Sterry, 1st	Worcester, Mass	Sept. 3, 1872	131, 129
Corn-sheller	A. H. Stevens	Geneva, N. Y	May 16, 1848	5, 569
Corn-sheller	A. H. Stevens	Warsaw, N. Y	Apr. 22, 1856	14, 745
Corn-sheller	E. M. Stevens	Boston, Mass	Dec. 23, 1856	16, 291
Corn-sheller	A. Stickney	Concord, N. H	Oct. 6, 1857	18, 361
Corn-sheller	A. Stickney	Concord, N. H	Oct. 29, 1861	33, 627
Corn-sheller	W. D. Stroud	Oshkosh, Wis	Apr. 9, 1867	63, 671
Corn-sheller	P. Sweeney	New York, N. Y	Jan. 31, 1865	46, 155
Corn-sheller	A. Swift	Wolcott, Vt	Apr. 8, 1862	34, 912
Corn-sheller	P. P. Taft	Taftsville, Vt	July 6, 1858	20, 831
Corn-sheller	J. H. Taylor and A. J. Cowles	Westfield, N. Y	Feb. 11, 1835	....
Corn-sheller	S Terry	Boscawen, N. H	Nov. 26, 1867	71, 551
Corn-sheller	C. Thomas	Lancaster, Pa	Sept. 3, 1832	....
Corn-sheller	A. B. Thompson	Oswego, N. Y	June 7, 1870	103, 941
Corn-sheller	A. B. Thompson	Oswego, N. Y	Oct. 31, 1871	120, 549
Corn-sheller	G. W. Tolhurst	Liverpool, Ohio	Oct. 4, 1859	25, 688
Corn-sheller	M. Trimble	Princeton, Ill	Mar. 26, 1861	31, 839
Corn-sheller	G. Turner	Cambridge, Mass	Apr. 29, 1862	35, 119
Corn-sheller	J. Turner	Poland, Me	Aug. 15, 1835	....
Corn-sheller	A. B. Vant and A. M. Cook	Milford, Mass	Jan. 11, 1859	22, 595
Corn-sheller	J. Warren	Lodi, Ohio	Feb. 18, 1868	74, 643
Corn-sheller	J. Warren	Lodi, Ohio	Apr. 28, 1868	77, 227
Corn-sheller	J. R Warrington	Damascoville, Ohio	May 2, 1848	5, 548
Corn-sheller	W. F. Waters	Dunkirk, N. Y	Aug. 20, 1872	130, 777
Corn-sheller	H. P. Watts	Lynchburgh, Va	Nov. 16, 1869	97, 008
Corn-sheller	T. Weaver	Harrisburgh, Pa	July 6, 1869	92, 410
Corn-sheller	T. Weaver	Harrisburgh, Pa	Aug. 24, 1869	94, 050
Corn-sheller	D. G. Wells	Joliet, Ill	Jan. 16, 1872	122, 749
Corn-sheller	W. Wells	Boston, Mass	Jan 4, 1859	22, 523
Corn-sheller	F. C. Whiley	Lancaster, Ohio	May 21, 1872	127, 127

Index of patents issued from the United States Patent Office from 1790 to 1873, inclusive—Continued.

Invention.	Inventor.	Residence.	Date.	No.
Corn-sheller	W. H. Whiterow	New Albany, Ind	Aug. 18, 1868	81, 121
Corn-sheller	W. H. Whiterow and W. Detrick.	New Albany, Ind	Mar. 16, 1869	87, 811
Corn-sheller	J. A. Whitford	Saratoga Springs, N Y	Jan. 23, 1841	1, 946
Corn-sheller	J. R. Wilbur	Chicopee, Mass	Feb. 25, 1868	74, 965
Corn-sheller	C. Willis	Chelsea, Mass	Jan. 27, 1841	1, 952
Corn-sheller	J. B. Wolford	Lancaster, Ohio	July 26, 1870	105, 872
Corn-sheller	T. Wright	New Village, N. J	June 12, 1838	778
Corn-sheller	G. A. Xander	Hamburgh, Pa	Jan. 3, 1854	10, 376
Corn-sheller	J. C. Zimmerman	Eberly's Mill, Pa	June 9, 1868	78, 714
Corn-sheller and apple-grinder, Combined	M. H. Ripley and W. N. Temple	Minneapolis, Minn	Sept. 15, 1868	82, 250
Corn-sheller and bean-thrasher	B. P. Pendexter	Mechanics' Falls, Me	June 26, 1866	55, 899
Corn sheller and cleaner	R. Gray	Northfield, N. H	Jan. 16, 1835	....
Corn sheller and cleaner	J. Hubler and R. M. McGrath	La Fayette, Ind	July 1, 1862	35, 757
Corn sheller and cleaner	J. C. Richards	La Fayette, Ind	Sept. 25, 1860	30, 185
Corn sheller and cleaner	N. Shuck	Baltimore, Md	Sept. 8, 1868	82, 039
Corn sheller and cleaner	M. F. Williamson and J. J. Swigert.	Hyattsville, Ohio	July 23, 1861	32, 909
Corn-sheller and fanning-mill combined	J. P. Heagland and G. E. Moser	Centralia, Pa	Sept. 10, 1867	68, 744
Corn-sheller and grain-hulling machine	J. Mercer	Harrisville, Ohio	June 24, 1839	1, 187
Corn sheller and separator	B. and D. H. Harnish	Lancaster and Pequea, Pa.	May 21, 1872	127, 051
Corn sheller and separator	E. Knapp	Jamestown, N. Y	Sept. 27, 1864	44, 433
Corn sheller and separator feeder combined	J. Bernheisel, sr	Green Park, Pa	Dec. 31, 1867	72, 783
Corn-sheller and straw-cutter combined	J. P. Smith	Schuylkill Haven, Pa	Apr. 9, 1872	125, 415
Corn-sheller and vegetable-slicer combined	J. P. Smith	Hummelstown, Pa	May 3, 1870	102, 607
Corn-sheller and wheat-thrasher, &c	Z. Phinney	Cairo, N. Y	Feb. 16, 1815	....
Corn sheller case	A. Borneman	Lancaster, Ohio	Jan. 21, 1873	135, 029
Corn-sheller for table use	E. L. Tevis	Philadelphia, Pa	Jan. 16, 1866	52, 092
Corn sheller, Green	V. Barker	Otisfield, Me	Nov. 9, 1869	96, 658
Corn-sheller, Hand	G. C. Ballard	Cleveland, Ohio	Nov. 5, 1872	132, 708
Corn-sheller, Hand	O. A. Bryhn and W. T. Farre	Montreal, Canada	June 27, 1871	116, 262
Corn-sheller, Hand	C. Christian	Milwaukee, Wis	Mar. 10, 1868	75, 368
Corn-sheller, Hand	J. C. Cunyer	Thorntown, Ind	Apr. 13, 1869	89, 001
Corn-sheller, Hand	J. E. Finley	Memphis, Tenn	Oct. 11, 1870	108, 126
Corn-sheller, Hand	J. O. Fraizer	Worthington, Ind	Nov. 12, 1872	132, 958
Corn-sheller, Hand	J. M. Hawley	Alma, Ill	Feb. 11, 1873	135, 709
Corn-sheller, Hand	A. McLean and J. H. Ross	Carondelet, Mo	June 18, 1872	128, 056
Corn-sheller, Hand	W. A. Middleton	Harrisburgh, Pa	July 26, 1870	105, 825
Corn-sheller, Hand	C. M. O'Hara	Bolivar, Tenn	Nov. 23, 1869	97, 109
Corn-sheller, Hand	C. M. O'Hara	Cincinnati, Ohio	May 2, 1871	114, 331
Corn-sheller, Hand	C. M. O'Hara	Cincinnati, Ohio	July 18, 1871	117, 105
Corn-sheller, Hand	C. H. Pickering	Memphis, Tenn	May 24, 1870	103, 497
Corn-sheller, Hand	T. Weaver	Harrisburgh, Pa	Apr. 12, 1870	101, 949
Corn-sheller, Hand	T. Weaver	Harrisburgh, Pa	Nov. 26, 1872	133, 346
Corn-sheller, Hand	W. H. Wilson	Boston, Mass	Jan. 30, 1872	123, 319
Corn-sheller, Longitudinal	G. E. Waring	Poundridge, N. Y	Mar. 16, 1827	....
Corn-sheller, Phinney's	H. Gallagher	Pittsburgh, Pa	Oct. 29, 1818	....
Corn-sheller teeth	H. H. Reuter	New Hope, Mo	Jan. 23, 1872	122, 968
Corn-shellers, Cob-carrier for	H. H. Eby	Mendota, Ill	Jan. 14, 1873	134, 790
Corn-shellers, Concave for	L. J. Miller	Cincinnati, Ohio	Oct. 8, 1872	132, 017
Corn-shellers, Concave of	D. Hoats	Milton, Pa	Jan. 22, 1850	7, 036
Corn-shellers, Device for feeding corn to	H. C. Robison	Monmouth, Ill	Jan. 10, 1865	45, 862
Corn-shellers, Feeding-elevator for	P. Kaufman	Hudson, Ill	Aug. 12, 1873	141, 717
Corn-shellers separately or jointly with a fan or cutter, Arrangement of machinery for operating.	W. L. Potter	Clifton Park, N. Y	Apr. 5, 1859	23, 488
Corn, Shelling	I. A. Hedges	Elmira, N. Y	Feb. 3, 1836	....
Corn, Shelling	H. G. Neal	Poultney, Vt	Feb. 10, 1836	....
Corn, Shelling	I. Smith	Downington, Pa	Feb. 13, 1836	....
Corn shelling and cleaning machine	L. A. Beebe	Chicago, Ill	Oct. 21, 1862	36, 700
Corn shelling and cleaning machine	L. Kamp	Vanderburgh County, Ind.	Jan. 31, 1871	111, 350
Corn shelling and cleaning machine	J. Reed	Marshfield, Mass	Sept. 1, 1831	....
Corn shelling and cleaning machine	J. W. Webb	Mount Morris, N. Y	July 16, 1838	840
Corn-shelling and grain and plaster grinding mill	B. M. Kemp	Fort Plain, N. Y	Jan. 31, 1829	....
Corn shelling and grinding	S. Slater and S. Noblit	Philadelphia, Pa	May 12, 1834	....
Corn shelling and grinding machine	G. Seymour	Cedar Rapids, Iowa	July 25, 1861	32, 898
Corn shelling and grinding machinery	S. Fowks	Catskill, N. Y	May 4, 1825	....
Corn shelling and husking machine	S. S. Allen	Miamisburgh, Ohio	Jan. 15, 1840	1, 472
Corn shelling and winnowing machine	B. Clough	Natick, Mass	Feb. 17, 1863	37, 674
Corn-shelling machine	A. Bailey	Poultney, Vt	Nov. 1, 1825	....
Corn-shelling machine	J. C. Baldwin	Staunton, Va	Oct. 11, 1836	45
Corn-shelling machine	J. Barnes and N. T. Loomis	Cornwall, Conn	Apr. 13, 1831	....
Corn-shelling machine	J. Brown	Providence, R. I	Mar. 18, 1828	....
Corn-shelling machine	C. Bulkeley	Manchester, Vt	May 25, 1824	....
Corn-shelling machine	E. W. Coffin	Gilead, Me	Dec. 23, 1834	....
Corn-shelling machine	B. Crooker	New York, N. Y	Dec. 2, 1824	....
Corn-shelling machine	T. J. Dean	Virgil, N. Y	Dec. 8, 1828	....
Corn-shelling machine	L. E. Denison	Saybrook, Conn	Oct. 8, 1838	972
Corn-shelling machine	L. E. Denison	Saybrook, Conn	Aug. 12, 1839	1, 283
Corn-shelling machine	J. Fuller	Rockland, Va	Mar. 19, 1816	....
Corn-shelling machine	P. Grosjean	Louisville, Ky	July 29, 1828	....
Corn-shelling machine	W. C. Hawley	New York, N. Y	June 22, 1825	....
Corn-shelling machine	J. Heavin	Fredericktown, Md	May 8, 1810	....
Corn-shelling machine	D. Hitchcock	New York, N. Y	June 13, 1831	....
Corn-shelling machine, &c	C. Hoxie	Hudson, N. Y	Dec. 8, 1825	....
Corn-shelling machine	W. Hoyt	Vernon, Ind	Apr. 29, 1828	....
Corn-shelling machine	W. Hoyt	Vernon, Ind	Dec. 17, 1830	....
Corn-shelling machine	W. Hoyt	Vernon, Ind	June 13, 1831	....
Corn-shelling machine	S. Lane	Hallowell, Me	Sept. 9, 1825	....
Corn-shelling machine	N. Lindsay	Catskill, N. Y	Mar. 28, 1821	....
Corn-shelling machine	H. Lippold	Silver Creek, N. Y	Aug. 15, 1871	118, 139
Corn-shelling machine	A. Little	Columbia, Conn	Dec. 23, 1824	....
Corn-shelling machine	W. McIlroy and B. and W. Boon	Greenwich, N. J	Mar. 30, 1839	1, 112
Corn-shelling machine	J. Moon	Morrisville, Pa	June 27, 1825	....
Corn-shelling machine	T. Newman	Guilford County, N. C	Feb. 7, 1827	....
Corn-shelling machine	J. Parker and H. M. Smith	Richmond, Va	Apr. 9, 1831	....
Corn-shelling machine	W. R. Parker	Milton, Del	July 9, 1839	1, 227
Corn-shelling machine	L. Peck	Brookfield, Conn	Apr. 9, 1824	....
Corn-shelling machine	P. Pilsbury	....	Oct. 25, 1803	....

Index of patents issued from the United States Patent Office from 1790 *to* 1873, *inclusive*—Continued.

Invention.	Inventor.	Residence.	Date.	No.
Corn-shelling machine	R. Porter	Billerica, Mass	Sept. 12, 1838	912
Corn-shelling machine	F. Price	New York	May 4, 1825	....
Corn-shelling machine	J. S. Rackham	Waterport, N. Y	Oct. 20, 1868	83, 314
Corn-shelling machine	H. and E. J. Rosevelt	New York, N. Y	Jan. 26, 1821	....
Corn shelling machine	E. Russell	Greensborough, N. C	Oct. 24, 1826	....
Corn-shelling machine	S. Spooner	Petersham, Mass	Feb. 27, 1823	....
Corn-shelling machine	G. W. Tolhurst	Liverpool, Ohio	Nov. 30, 1858	22, 206
Corn-shelling machine	T. Wellman, jr	Brooklin, Vt	Oct. 9, 1834	....
Corn-shelling machine	L. Whitney	New York, N. Y	Nov. 13, 1824	....
Corn-shelling machine	L. J. Wicks	Racine, Wis	Aug. 24, 1858	21, 288
Corn-shelling machine and family mill	E. Bond	Mendon, N. Y	June 13, 1831	....
Corn-shield	B. Brandreth	Sing Sing, N. Y	June 4, 1872	127, 454
Corn-shock binder	J. E. Hunter	Mechanicsburgh, Ohio	May 25, 1869	90, 451
Corn-shock binder	C. Stowe	Braceville, Ohio	Apr. 24, 1860	28, 019
Corn-shocks, Device for loading and unloading	W. M. Mason	Polo, Ind	Mar. 22, 1864	42, 008
Corn-shocker	G. E. Johnson	Smith Valley, N. Y	Dec. 9, 1873	145, 423
Corn shucking and shelling machine	S. Kingsbery	Carrollton, Ga	Oct. 6, 1857	18, 342
Corn shucking and shelling machine	J. J. Rallow	Fredericksburgh, Va	July 3, 1855	13, 182
Corn-stacking horse	L. S. Barker	Pittsford, Mich	Dec. 19, 1865	51, 540
Corn-stalk chopper	J. Hollingsworth	Chicago, Ill	Oct. 29, 1872	132, 578
Corn-stalk cutter	R. H. Avery	Galesburgh, Ill	Aug. 6, 1872	130, 100
Corn-stalk cutter	S. Bryan	Jefferson, Wis	May 14, 1867	64, 743
Corn-stalk cutter	M. Clark	Oakley, Ill	June 15, 1869	91, 420
Corn-stalk cutter	G. W. Cole	Canton, Ill	July 14, 1863	39, 214
Corn-stalk cutter	J. W. Cornell	Lawn Ridge, Ill	Aug. 8, 1871	117, 746
Corn-stalk cutter	T. A. Galt and G. S. Tracy	Sterling, Ill	Nov. 28, 1871	131, 353
Corn-stalk cutter	A. Hunt	Macomb, Ill	Sept. 10, 1867	68, 749
Corn-stalk cutter	H. Jackson	Elmira, Ill	Mar. 9, 1869	87, 676
Corn-stalk cutter	J. R. Marshall	Marine, Ill	Aug. 21, 1860	29, 705
Corn-stalk cutter	H. Martin	Round Grove, Ill	June 4, 1872	127, 623
Corn-stalk cutter	G. D. McClure	Denver Station, Ill	Apr. 10, 1866	53, 848
Corn-stalk cutter	A. J. Nebergall	Cedar County, Iowa	Sept. 6, 1870	107, 090
Corn-stalk cutter	J. B. Sherlock	Port Byron, Ill	Oct. 19, 1869	96, 042
Corn-stalk cutter	S. Walters	Dallas City, Ill	Mar. 5, 1872	124, 401
Corn-stalk cutter	D. Wilde	Washington, Iowa	July 16, 1872	129, 384
Corn stalk cutter	J. Wood	Pella, Iowa	Feb. 7, 1871	111, 709
Corn-stalk cutter and corn-husker	J. Russell	Brooklyn, N. Y	Dec. 18, 1866	60, 643
Corn-stalk cutter and cultivator combined	M. Gordon	Washington, Iowa	Apr. 21, 1868	76, 909
Corn-stalk cutter and stripper	N. Gabel	Preble County, Ohio	Jan. 30, 1866	52, 282
Corn-stalk cutter preparatory to plowing	J. D. and J. H. Wilde	Washington, Iowa	Feb. 18, 1868	74, 652
Corn-stalk cutting and grinding machine	W. G. Huyett	Williamsburgh, Pa	Dec. 22, 1857	18, 905
Corn-stalk cutting and raking machine	T. M. Hill and S. D. Tuttle	Eaton, Ohio	Nov. 27, 1866	60, 098
Corn-stalk-cutting knife	G. D. Goodsell and N. E. Babcock	Rockford, Ill	Feb. 8, 1870	99, 560
Corn-stalk-cutting machine	A. Glendening	Butler County, Pa	Sept. 25, 1823	....
Corn-stalk-cutting machine	J. M. Goff	Ionia, Ill	Sept. 11, 1866	57, 893
Corn-stalk-cutting machine	H. Johnston	Collinsville, Ill	Apr. 12, 1859	23, 644
Corn-stalk knife	J. M. Brick	Marlton, N. J	Apr. 22, 1873	138, 069
Corn-stalk pith for use in the arts, Preparing	W. M. Bryant	Alexandria, Va	May 3, 1870	102, 484
Corn-stalks in the field, Machine for cutting	H. Bilharz	Seneca, Ill	July 2, 1867	66, 287
Corn-stalks in the field, Machine for cutting up	F. M. Green	Sullivan, Ill	Aug. 24, 1858	21, 254
Corn-stalks, Machine for cutting and crushing	H. and A. Hersh	Lancaster County, Pa	Mar. 9, 1858	19, 561
Corn-stalks, Machine for cutting and grinding	E. Potts	Tredyffrin Township, Pa	July 31, 1847	5, 207
Corn-stalks, Machine for cutting and pulverizing	W. M. Taylor	Newburgh, Ohio	Nov. 19, 1872	133, 270
Corn-stalks, Machine for cutting standing	F. J. Freeman	Heyworth, Ill	Apr. 2, 1861	31, 928
Corn-stalks, Machine for shocking	S. B. Lawrence	Hookstown, Pa	July 24, 1860	29, 286
Corn-stalks on the ground, Device for cutting	T. W. McDill	Perry, Ill	July 11, 1865	48, 704
Corn-stubbles preparatory to plowing, Machine for cutting.	J. Augspurger	Trenton, Ohio	Sept. 1, 1857	18, 076
Corn-weeder	S. March	Norfolk, Va	Apr. 16, 1867	63, 912
Corn with malt extract, Treating Indian	M. Cziner	New York, N. Y	Nov. 7, 1871	120, 721
Corns, bunions, &c., Composition for curing	A. J. Ferguson	Sharon, Pa	Aug. 25, 1868	81, 486
Corns, bunions, &c., Implements for removing	C. L. Roorback	Saint Clair, Pa	Dec. 13, 1870	110, 162
Corns, Composition for curing	G. Oakley	Quincy, Ill	July 27, 1869	92, 993
Corns, Eradicating and curing	W. Davis	Williamsburgh, Va	Sept. 9, 1835	....
Corns, Eradicator for	C. Wheat	Geneva, N. Y	Oct. 12, 1858	21, 790
Corns, Eradicator for	P. Williamson	New York, N. Y	May 17, 1838	742
Corns, Instrument for removing	J. C. Jacobsohn	New York, N. Y	Oct. 22, 1872	122, 468
Corns, Tincture for curing	E. Smith	New Brunswick, N. J	Jan. 20, 1826	....
Corner protector, Stair and room	H. C. Richards	Cincinnati, Ohio	July 31, 1866	56, 800
Corner-strip	G. Corbett	Pittsburgh, Pa	Sept. 24, 1872	131, 506
Cornet, &c	I. Fiske	Worcester, Mass	Oct. 30, 1866	59, 204
Cornet, &c	I. Fiske	Worcester, Mass	Feb. 11, 1868	74, 331
Cornet	L. Schreiber	New York, N. Y	Sept. 12, 1865	49, 925
Cornet, &c	L. Schreiber	New York, N. Y	May 7, 1867	64, 582
Cornet-bells, Machine for forming	L. W. Spencer	New York, N. Y	Apr. 9, 1867	63, 761
Cornets, Machine for cutting the wind-passages in the rotary valves of.	L. W. Spencer	New York, N. Y	Apr. 16, 1867	63, 819
Cornets, Machine for forming the branch-tubes of valve-cases for.	L. W. Spencer	New York, N. Y	Apr. 9, 1867	63, 760
Cornice and gutter, Metallic	J. B. Cornell	New York, N. Y	Nov. 4, 1873	144, 259
Cornice-bracket, Adjustable metallic	A. T. Perkins and N. Waterman	Toledo, Ohio	Mar. 5, 1872	124, 382
Cornice, Curtain	C. W. Hill	New York, N. Y	June 15, 1869	91, 441
Cornice, Drapery	H. R. Watson	Albany, N. Y	Nov. 12, 1872	132, 941
Cornice, Extension window	A. Pohl	Brooklyn, N. Y	May 28, 1872	127, 367
Cornice for window-curtains, Adjustable	O. L. Gardner	New York, N. Y	Apr. 20, 1869	89, 139
Cornice-mold	M. Meany, J. McGinnis, and W. Cunningham.	Brooklyn, N. Y	Mar. 29, 1870	101, 293
Cornice-moldings, Machine for making	C. L. Wood and C. A. Sheridan.	Cleveland, Ohio	Apr. 5, 1870	101, 556
Cornice, Ornamental	Y. J. McGeary	Newark, N. J	Feb. 15, 1870	99, 930
Cornice-plastering mold	C. P. Walter	Aston Township, Pa	Oct. 9, 1866	58, 701
Cornice, Running	A. Leverty	Bridgeport, Conn	May 26, 1868	78, 381
Cornice, Stucco	A. Derrom	Paterson, N. J	May 20, 1873	139, 049
Cornice-tool	J. P. Ballantine	Detroit, Mich	Dec. 10, 1872	133, 820
Cornice, Window	D. Coney and J. H. Norcross	Augusta, Me., and Melrose, Mass.	Mar. 12, 1872	124, 549
Cornice, Window	R. N. Hoffman	Chicago, Ill	Mar. 15, 1870	100, 763
Cornice, Window	A. J. Holmes	Saratoga Springs, N. Y	Apr. 16, 1867	63, 893
Cornice, Window	W. Lloyd	New York, N. Y	Sept. 24, 1872	131, 551

Index of patents issued from the United States Patent Office from 1790 to 1873, inclusive—Continued.

Invention.	Inventor.	Residence.	Date.	No.
Cornice, Window	W. Lloyd	New York, N. Y	Sept. 17, 1872	131, 358
Cornice, Window-curtain	C. W. Hill	New York, N. Y	June 22, 1869	91, 746
Cornice, Window-curtain	W. Lloyd	New York, N. Y	Dec. 19, 1871	122, 037
Cornices and moldings, Tool for forming plaster	S. Groesbeck	New York, N. Y	Sept. 17, 1850	7, 654
Cornices, Construction of metallic	J. M. Blackburn, C. L. Wood, B. K. Price, and C. A. Sheridan.	Cleveland, Ohio	Apr. 5, 1870	101, 572
Cornices, Machine for bending sheet-metal for	C. A. Buttles and D. Murphy	Milwaukee, Wis	Oct. 12, 1869	95, 650
Cornices, Machine for rolling	A. Johnson	Cairo, N. Y	Dec. 22, 1857	18, 906
Cornices of sheet-metal, Machine for forming	J. Lee	Bolivar, Ohio	June 12, 1860	28, 676
Cornices to windows, Mode of attaching	A. Peple	East Billerica, Mass	Mar. 22, 1870	101, 158
Cornish-engine	J. Storer	Peekskill, N. Y	Aug. 30, 1870	106, 886
Cornucopia, Transparent	W. Lohse	New York, N. Y	Dec. 12, 1871	121, 791
Corpse-cooler	S. H. Crump	Reading, Pa	July 29, 1873	141, 311
Corpse-cooler	E. S. Earley	Philadelphia, Pa	Jan. 28, 1873	135, 210
Corpse-cooler	J. Hoffman	Toledo, Ohio	Sept. 2, 1873	142, 393
Corpse-cooler	F. N. Troll	Baltimore, Md	Sept. 2, 1873	142, 533
Corpse-preserver	R. C. Andrus	Poughkeepsie, N. Y	Dec. 6, 1870	109, 861
Corpse-preserver	G. D. Blocher	Indianapolis, Ind	Feb. 26, 1867	62, 310
Corpse-preserver	L. D. Bunn	Morristown, N. J	Oct. 28, 1862	36, 765
Corpse-preserver	J. T. Carpenter	Downingtown, Pa	May 2, 1871	114, 407
Corpse-preserver	J. L. Clark	Providence, R. I	May 25, 1869	90, 426
Corpse-preserver	S. Cobb	Cincinnati, Ohio	Jan. 27, 1857	16, 466
Corpse-preserver	C. W. Compton	Newark, N. J	Nov. 5, 1867	70, 530
Corpse-preserver	J. E. Cox	Baltimore, Md	Aug. 22, 1871	118, 346
Corpse-preserver	H. M. Diggins	Cincinnati, Ohio	Apr. 18, 1871	113, 861
Corpse-preserver	H. V. Griffith	Altoona, Pa	Oct. 18, 1870	108, 350
Corpse-preserver	D. L. Holden	Covington, Ky	Feb. 13, 1872	123, 697
Corpse-preserver	J. Kunsman, sr	Reading, Pa	May 22, 1866	55, 013
Corpse-preserver	H. Kersten	Wheeling, W. Va	Sept. 16, 1873	142, 919
Corpse-preserver	H. Lee	Washington, D. C	May 17, 1870	103, 000
Corpse-preserver	E. F. Lenox and C. Eckhart	Trenton, N. J	June 21, 1870	104, 607
Corpse-preserver	M. R. Margerum	Trenton, N. J	May 2, 1871	114, 315
Corpse-preserver	M. E. Mott	Rouse's Point, N. Y	May 26, 1868	78, 314
Corpse-preserver	G. W. Nash	Columbus, Ohio	May 23, 1871	115, 229
Corpse-preserver	C. O. Peck	Pittsfield, Mass	Dec. 9, 1873	145, 307
Corpse-preserver	C. F. Pike	Providence, R. I	Dec. 31, 1867	72, 893
Corpse-preserver	A. G. Reed	Philadelphia, Pa	Mar. 30, 1869	88, 510
Corpse-preserver	J. J. Reicherts	Delaware, Ohio	Sept. 29, 1868	82, 552
Corpse-preserver	S. Stockton and J. Schepler	Lambertville, N. J	Sept. 27, 1870	107, 831
Corpse-preserver	P. Taltavull	Washington, D. C	Apr. 29, 1873	138, 449
Corpse-preserver	J. C. Taylor	Trenton, N. J	July 5, 1870	105, 013
Corpse-preserver	J. F. and E. G. Waters	Philadelphia, Pa	Mar. 5, 1872	124, 300
Corpse-preserver	B. Wilson	Morristown, N. J	Nov. 3, 1863	40, 529
Corpse-preserving	C. A. Seely and C. J. Eames	New York, N. Y	Feb. 18, 1868	74, 607
Corpse preserving and embalming	J. A. Mitchell	Maysville, Ky	Aug. 6, 1872	130, 232
Corpse-preserving box	P. Wendhiser	Rockville, Conn	Dec. 17, 1867	72, 346
Corpse-preserving case	J. Gravenstine	Philadelphia, Pa	July 25, 1871	117, 407
Corpse-preserving case	A. G. Reed	Philadelphia, Pa	July 12, 1870	105, 368
Corpse-preserving case	J. Searing	Morristown, N. J	Dec. 6, 1864	45, 349
Corpse-preserving case	J. S. Waterman	Roxbury, Mass	Apr. 23, 1867	64, 172
Corpse-preserving case	J. S. Waterman	Roxbury, Mass	Apr. 7, 1868	76, 568
Corpse-preserving casket	N. F. Curran	Baltimore, Md	Sept. 24, 1872	131, 668
Corpse-preserving casket	C. H. Kimball	Quincy, Mass	Jan. 28, 1868	73, 729
Corpse-preserving composition	J. M. Gallaher	Carthage, N. Y	Oct. 28, 1873	144, 085
Corpse-receptacle	T. Holmes	Washington, D. C	July 21, 1863	39, 291
Corpses, Device for handling	H. Huber	Crestline, Ohio	Nov. 26, 1872	133, 447
Corpses in place, Device for securing the features of	A. S. Chesebrough	Hartford, Conn	May 3, 1870	102, 480
Corpses, Refrigerator for	R. Fredrick and G. A. Trump	Baltimore, Md	May 9, 1846	4, 504
Corrugated boiler	R. Montgomery	New York, N. Y	Oct. 29, 1850	7, 742
Corrugated fabrics, Manufacturing	F. Baare and J. G. Garelly	New York, N. Y	July 5, 1859	24, 691
Corrugated knives, Machine for grinding	J. B. Wilson	New York, N. Y	Nov. 9, 1869	96, 756
Corrugated metals, Rolling	R. Montgomery	New York, N. Y	Dec. 27, 1859	26, 607
Corrugated plates, Manufacture of	S. J. Seely	Brooklyn, N. Y	Sept. 9, 1862	36, 424
Corrugated steel plates as an article of manufacture, Curved.	R. Montgomery	New York, N. Y	Mar. 19, 1867	63, 077
Corrugating and molding sheet-metals, Machine for	A. Johnson	Brooklyn, N. Y	Feb. 8, 1870	99, 684
Corrugating circular metal plates	R. B. Hugunin	Cleveland, Ohio	Apr. 19, 1864	42, 377
Corrugating-machine	J. G. Baker	Washington, D. C	Dec. 15, 1863	40, 897
Corrugating machine, Metal	S. J. Seely	Brooklyn, N. Y	Feb. 3, 1863	37, 593
Corrugating machine, Sheet-metal	W. Mann	Newcastle, Pa	Apr. 12, 1870	101, 750
Corrugating machine, Sheet-metal	G. R. Moore	Lyons, Iowa	Feb. 18, 1868	74, 572
Corrugating machine, Sheet-metal	F. Roys	East Berlin, Conn	June 3, 1873	139, 480
Corrugating metal plates	J. Francis	New York, N. Y	June 2, 1863	38, 799
Corrugating metal plates	R. Montgomery	New York, N. Y	Feb. 21, 1854	10, 549
Corrugating metal plates, Machine for	A. W. Gray	Middletown, Vt	Dec. 10, 1872	133, 773
Corrugating metal plates, Machine for	R. Montgomery	New York, N. Y	Apr. 12, 1859	23, 599
Corrugating metals, Apparatus for	J. Montgomery	New York, N. Y	May 10, 1870	102, 849
Corrugating metals, Machine for	J. Moffet	New York, N. Y	July 16, 1872	129, 290
Corrugating metals, Machine for	R. Montgomery	New York, N. Y	Dec. 22, 1868	85, 262
Corrugating metallic sheets	R. Montgomery	New York, N. Y	June 21, 1859	24, 480
Corrugating sheet-iron, Machine for	A. and J. Reese	Pittsburgh, Pa	Feb. 25, 1873	136, 267
Corrugating sheet-metal	T. W. H. Moseley	Boston, Mass	Aug. 4, 1863	39, 418
Corrugating sheet-metal	W. E. Worthen and H. B. Renwick.	New York, N. Y	July 5, 1859	24, 689
Corrugating sheet-metals, Machine for	S. G. Booth	New York, N. Y	Apr. 4, 1854	10, 732
Corrugating sheet-metals, Machine for	R. Montgomery	New York, N. Y	Apr. 26, 1859	23, 774
Corrugating sheet-metals, Machine for	F. Roys	East Berlin, Conn	Mar. 15, 1870	100, 929
Corrugating sheet-metals, Machine for	J. Wilson, C. Green, and W. Wilson, jr.	Wilmington, Del	Apr. 19, 1859	23, 736
Corrugating sheet-metals, Roller for	S. G. Booth	New York, N. Y	Jan. 23, 1855	12, 268
Corset	M. Adler	New Haven, Conn	July 16, 1872	129, 264
Corset	M. H. Beckworth	Camden, N. Y	June 11, 1867	65, 636
Corset	J. Bowers	New York, N. Y	June 6, 1865	48, 045
Corset	M. P. Bray	Birmingham, Conn	Apr. 4, 1871	113, 392
Corset	M. P. Bray	New Haven, Conn	Apr. 23, 1872	125, 877
Corset	A. J. Brooks	Philadelphia, Pa	Aug. 26, 1862	36, 272
Corset	M. Brush	New York, N. Y	July 21, 1815	....
Corset	W. J. Cantello	New York, N. Y	Dec. 31, 1821	....

Index of patents issued from the United States Patent Office from 1790 *to* 1873, *inclusive*—Continued.

Invention.	Inventor.	Residence.	Date.	No.
Corset	M. L. Changeur	Paris, France	July 16, 1867	66, 794
Corset	L. L. Chapman	Camden, N. J	Dec. 15, 1863	40, 907
Corset	M. Cohn	New York, N. Y	Apr. 15, 1873	137, 893
Corset	S. Collins	New Haven, Conn	Apr 26, 1864	42, 460
Corset	J. S. Crotty	New York, N. Y	Sept. 3, 1872	130, 983
Corset	C. Z. Cummings	Buffalo, N. Y	Jan. 14, 1868	73, 235
Corset	S. A. Dake	Eureka, Wis	Nov. 19, 1872	133, 209
Corset	H. H. Dayton	Worcester, Mass	July 7, 1863	39, 126
Corset	R. De Baun	Chicago, Ill	Oct. 3, 1871	119, 583
Corset	T. B. De Forest	Birmingham, Conn	July 28, 1868	80, 462
Corset	S. Dixon	Nottingham, England	Jan. 21, 1873	135, 097
Corset	E. Drucker	Paris, France	May 7, 1867	64, 530
Corset	D. H. Fanning	Worcester, Mass	May 25, 1869	90, 353
Corset	D. H. Fanning	Worcester, Mass	Mar. 1, 1870	100, 278
Corset	S. B. Fisler	Newark, N. J	Feb. 23, 1869	87, 160
Corset	H. S. Flood	San Francisco, Cal	Sept. 10, 1872	131, 262
Corset	L. H. Foy	Worcester, Mass	Sept. 15, 1863	39, 908
Corset	L. H. Foy	Worcester, Mass	Sept. 15, 1863	39, 909
Corset	L. H. Foy	Newton Centre, Mass	July 7, 1868	79, 647
Corset	T. S. Gilbert	Birmingham, Conn	Aug. 10, 1869	93, 528
Corset	T. S. Gilbert	Birmingham, Conn	Feb. 8, 1870	99, 664
Corset	T. S. Gilbert	Birmingham, Conn	Apr. 4, 1871	113, 419
Corset	T. S. Gilbert	Birmingham, Conn	Oct. 1, 1872	131, 873
Corset	T. S. Gilbert	Birmingham, Conn	July 22, 1873	141, 134
Corset	C. A. Griswold	Willimantic, Conn	Feb. 5, 1867	61, 825
Corset	C. A. Griswold	Willimantic, Conn	July 4, 1871	116, 585
Corset	E. Hambujer	Detroit, Mich	June 26, 1866	55, 972
Corset	T. F. Hamilton	New Haven, Conn	June 13, 1871	115, 954
Corset	T. F. Hamilton	New Haven, Conn	Feb. 25, 1873	136, 320
Corset	C. L. Hamlin	New York, N. Y	Nov. 14, 1871	120, 967
Corset	J. W. Lane	Bristol, England	Jan. 14, 1873	134, 902
Corset	L. H. and A. F. Loomer and L. M. Smith.	Birmingham, Conn	Dec. 16, 1873	145, 665
Corset	H. A. Lyman	London, England	Nov. 30, 1869	97, 418
Corset	H. E. Marchand	Louisville, Ky	Jan. 8, 1869	90, 950
Corset	A. S. McLean	Williamsburgh, N. Y	Dec. 28, 1858	22, 443
Corset	E. J. Meriman	New York, N. Y	Sept. 8, 1868	81, 926
Corset	E. J. Meriman	New York, N. Y	Feb. 2, 1869	86, 570
Corset	W. Miller	New York, N. Y	July 30, 1867	67, 333
Corset	W. W. Netterfield	Rochester, N. Y	Sept. 15, 1868	82, 147
Corset	S. Ottenheimer	New York, N. Y	Apr. 23, 1872	126, 079
Corset	L. A. Palmer	Boston, Mass	Nov. 16, 1869	96, 951
Corset	S. M. Perry	Plainfield, N. J	July 31, 1866	56, 794
Corset	C. Preston	Detroit, Mich	May 23, 1865	47, 856
Corset	M. Russell	Union Bridge, Md	Apr. 8, 1873	137, 724
Corset	C. D. Rutherford	Brooklyn, N. Y	Dec. 11, 1866	60, 428
Corset	M. Sebille	New York, N. Y	Sept. 15, 1863	39, 964
Corset	W. H. Stroup	Pittsburgh, Pa	Sept. 24, 1867	69, 140
Corset	J. Waterman	New York, N. Y	Oct. 7, 1873	143, 479
Corset	A. M. Weber	Oshkosh, Wis	Apr. 15, 1873	137, 985
Corset, Abdominal	J. P. McLean	New York, N. Y	Nov. 8, 1859	26, 039
Corset, Abdominal	C. Smith	Louisville, Ky	Apr. 27, 1869	89, 513
Corset, Abdominal and skirt-supporter	J. McNeven	New York, N. Y	Aug. 11, 1868	80, 988
Corset and bustle, Combined	L. H. Foy	Worcester, Mass	May 1, 1866	54, 323
Corset and skirt-supporter	E. Blakeslee	Plymouth, Conn	June 19, 1866	55, 608
Corset and skirt-supporter combined	W. Bacheller	West Newbury, Mass	Jan. 22, 1867	61, 380
Corset and skirt-supporter combined	L. Spigelmeyer	Easton, Pa	Nov. 21, 1871	121, 210
Corset and skirt-supporter, Combined	M. J. C. Vanorstrand	Pekin, Ill	Dec. 19, 1871	122, 081
Corset-busk	E. Heaton	New Haven, Conn	Feb. 16, 1869	86, 920
Corset-busk	T. Wallace, jr	Ansonia, Conn	Oct. 13, 1863	40, 298
Corset-busk clasp	W. Devines	Brooklyn, N. Y	Apr. 3, 1866	53, 734
Corset, Child's.	H. G. Emery and M. C. Fuller	Boston, Mass	Mar. 26, 1872	124, 891
Corset, Child's.	M. B. Solomon	Charlestown, Mass	Apr. 7, 1868	76, 354
Corset-clasp	M. E. Bulkley	Providence, R. I	May 28, 1867	65, 163
Corset-clasp	J. Burke	Boston, Mass	Oct. 7, 1873	143, 403
Corset-clasp	W. B. Cargill	New Haven, Conn	Mar. 24, 1868	75, 856
Corset-clasp	J. W. Carter	Greenville, N. J	Aug. 14, 1866	57, 085
Corset-clasp	C. O. Crosby	New Haven, Conn	Apr. 16, 1867	63, 863
Corset-clasp	L. Hill	North Brookfield, Mass	Mar. 12, 1867	62, 848
Corset-clasp	P. Lippmann	New York, N. Y	Sept. 30, 1873	143, 359
Corset-clasp	J. P. MacLean	Brooklyn, N. Y	Nov. 18, 1873	144, 689
Corset-clasp	T. A. Nelson	Birmingham, Conn	July 21, 1863	39, 322
Corset clasp and spring	P. H. Niles	Boston, Mass	Dec. 20, 1870	110, 273
Corset-clasp	J. B. Roby	Cambridge, Mass	Aug. 26, 1873	142, 279
Corset-clasp	F. Straus	New York, N. Y	Aug. 6, 1869	88, 752
Corset-clasp	R. Wallace and D. G. and H. E. Fowler.	Wallingford, Conn	Oct. 17, 1865	50, 524
Corset-fastening	J. Bowers	New York, N. Y	Mar. 19, 1867	63, 005
Corset-fastening	M. P. Bray	Ansonia, Conn	Mar. 22, 1870	100, 970
Corset-fastening	W. B. Cargill	New Haven, Conn	Jan. 28, 1868	73, 873
Corset-fastening	W. B. Cargill	New Haven, Conn	May 19, 1868	78, 056
Corset-fastening	W. B. Cargill	Waterbury, Conn	Feb. 8, 1870	99, 633
Corset-fastening	S. Chapman	New York, N. Y	June 14, 1864	43, 094
Corset-fastening	J. F. Dubber	Brooklyn, N. Y	May 7, 1867	64, 507
Corset-fastening	M. E. Frentz	New Albany, Ind	June 8, 1869	91, 112
Corset-fastening	L. Jarchow	New York, N. Y	Dec. 7, 1869	97, 643
Corset-fastening	J. P. Love	New York, N. Y	May 28, 1867	65, 246
Corset-fastening	F. W. Marston	Boston, Mass	Dec. 14, 1869	97, 788
Corset-fastening	P. H. Niles and F. W. Marston	Boston, Mass	Dec. 15, 1868	84, 899
Corset-fastening	C. Schieck	New York, N. Y	Dec. 27, 1870	110, 593
Corset-fastening	G. O. Schneller	Ansonia, Conn	May 27, 1873	139, 424
Corset-fastening	H. N. Sherman	Beloit, Wis	Jan. 26, 1869	86, 183
Corset-fastening	M. T. Smith	New York, N. Y	Aug. 10, 1869	93, 489
Corset-fastening	A. W. Webster	Ansonia, Conn	Nov. 19, 1867	71, 092
Corset-fastening, Supporting-busk for	M. E. Bulkley	Providence, R. I	Dec. 26, 1871	122, 152
Corset-pad	M. P. R. Tilton	Trenton, N. J	Dec. 20, 1870	110, 310
Corset-pad, Elastic	B. Bernstein	New York, N. Y	Aug. 6, 1872	130, 182
Corset-rings, &c., Groove in	C. Buckland	Middletown, Conn	June 2, 1836	....

Index of patents issued from the United States Patent Office from 1790 to 1873, inclusive—Continued.

Invention.	Inventor.	Residence.	Date.	No.
Corset, Skeleton	D. H. Fanning	Worcester, Mass	Feb. 15, 1870	99, 871
Corset, Skeleton	T. S. Gilbert	Birmingham, Conn	Apr. 4, 1871	113, 418
Corset skirt-supporter	J. W. Brooks	Boston, Mass	June 8, 1869	90, 920
Corset skirt-supporter	J. W. Brooks	Boston, Mass	Jan. 25, 1870	99, 146
Corset skirt-supporter	J. W. Brooks	Boston, Mass	May 31, 1870	103, 556
Corset skirt-supporter	L. H. Foy	Worcester, Mass	July 22, 1862	35, 930
Corset skirt-supporter	L. H. Foy	Worcester, Mass	Sept. 15, 1863	39, 910
Corset skirt-supporter	L. H. Foy	Worcester, Mass	Sept. 15, 1863	39, 911
Corset skirt-supporter	L. H. Foy	Worcester, Mass	Mar. 22, 1864	41, 987
Corset skirt-supporter	L. H. Foy	Worcester, Mass	Nov. 29, 1864	45, 296
Corset, Skirt-supporting	C. A. Griswold	Willimantic, Conn	July 10, 1866	56, 210
Corset, Skirt-supporting	L. S. Scofield	Boston, Mass	Aug. 23, 1864	43, 930
Corset, Skirt-supporting	S. Young	Elmira, N. Y	Nov. 7, 1871	120, 808
Corset, Spinal	A. Abbé	Boston, Mass	May 26, 1857	17, 356
Corset-spring	H. Bennett	New York, N. Y	Nov. 9, 1869	96, 665
Corset-spring	S. H. Brown and C. H. Willets	New York, N. Y	Apr. 14, 1868	76, 708
Corset-spring	T. B. De Forest and T. S. Gilbert.	Birmingham, Conn	Jan. 21, 1868	73, 440
Corset-spring	J. Hananer and N. Sartor	New York, N. Y	June 7, 1870	104, 022
Corset-spring	T. A. Hares	New York, N. Y	Aug. 30, 1870	106, 934
Corset-spring	F. W. Marston	Philadelphia, Pa	Aug. 16, 1870	106, 381
Corset-spring	G. O. Schneller	Ansonia, Conn	Feb. 20, 1872	123, 938
Corset-spring	G. O. Schneller	Ansonia, Conn	Sept. 10, 1872	131, 305
Corset-spring	G. O. Schneller	Ansonia, Conn	Dec. 31, 1872	134, 490
Corset-spring	G. O. Schneller	Ansonia, Conn	July 8, 1873	147, 733
Corset-spring, Extension	S. H. Barnes	New York, N. Y	July 17, 1866	56, 345
Corset-spring fastener	E. Kunze	Buchholz, Saxony	Apr. 30, 1872	126, 217
Corset-spring-punching machine	P. Brooks	Waterbury, Conn	Apr. 18, 1871	113, 737
Corset steel	M. Adler	New Haven, Conn	Sept. 3, 1872	130, 967
Corset steel	F. L. and S. H. Barnes	New York, N. Y	Aug. 10, 1869	93, 399
Corset steel	C. S. Chaffee	Birmingham, Conn	Jan. 21, 1873	135, 079
Corset steel	J. L. Fitzpatrick	Waterbury, Conn	Nov. 9, 1869	96, 685
Corset steels, &c., Japaning	C. H. Bassett	Derby, Conn	Apr. 26, 1864	42, 457
Corset-weaving	B. J. Goullioud	Paris, France	Jan. 27, 1863	37, 546
Corset, Woven	J. Ottenheimer	New York, N. Y	Nov. 25, 1873	144, 921
Corsets and abdominal supporters, Manufacturing	E. Adams	Boston, Mass	Jan. 21, 1841	1, 940
Corsets and bustles, Manufacturing	D. Lamoureux	New York, N. Y	Jan. 4, 1859	22, 532
Corsets, Bust or stay for	T. B. De Forest	Birmingham, Conn	Sept. 15, 1868	82, 209
Corsets, Device for attaching steels to	W. A. and H. E. Starrett	Lawrence, Kans	Oct. 4, 1870	107, 974
Corsets, Device for measuring, laying out, and forming.	M. Williams	Camden, Ohio	Mar. 29, 1870	101, 337
Corsets, Fastening for stays of	J. W. Brooks	Boston, Mass	Apr. 20, 1869	89, 018
Corsets, Machine for rounding whalebone for	J. A. Sevey	Boston, Mass	June 15, 1869	91, 370
Corsets, Skirt-supporting hook for	D. H. Fanning	Worcester, Mass	Nov. 15, 1870	109, 309
Corsets, Steam former for shaping and forming	C. Heptonstall	Providence, R. I	Aug. 2, 1870	106, 069
Corselets for medicinal and other purposes, Manufacturing.	A. Abbe	Worcester, Mass	Apr. 2, 1841	2, 035
Corundum-wheels, Mode of making	A. W. Calder	San Francisco, Cal	Aug. 10, 1869	93, 413
Corundum-wheels, Mold for making	E. H. Danforth	Jamestown, N. Y	June 13, 1865	48, 160
Cosmetic	I. M. Wilson	Sequin, Tex	Feb. 25, 1868	74, 871
Cosmetic compound	H. Z. Sill	Pittsburgh, Pa	Feb. 27, 1872	124, 018
Costumery	W. F. Munroe	Boston, Mass	July 2, 1872	128, 559
Cot and chair, Combined folding	T. C. Potter	Williston, Vt	June 25, 1872	128, 423
Cot and chest, Combined camp	T. J. Griffin	Brooklyn, N. Y	Jan. 28, 1862	34, 250
Cot and stretcher, Field-hospital	W. Dann	Cincinnati, Ohio	Dec. 20, 1864	45, 479
Cot-bath, Elastic	W. C. Palmer	New York, N. Y	Nov. 24, 1832	....
Cot, Camp	C. Mottam	New York, N. Y	July 23, 1861	32, 884
Cot, Camp and hospital	G. M. Powell, C. D. Lincoln, and G. Evans.	River Falls, Wis., Biddeford, Me., and Richburgh, N. Y.	Sept. 15, 1863	39, 954
Cot, chair, &c., Reclining valetudinary	J. Mead	Albany, N. Y	Mar. 18, 1816	....
Cot, Hammock	J. C. Day	Jersey City, N. J	Oct. 28, 1862	36, 768
Cot, lounge, and chair	G. B. Gourley and O. G. Brady.	New York, N. Y	Sept. 3, 1861	33, 192
Cot or bedstead	W. Wells	Harrisburgh, Pa	July 23, 1861	32, 919
Cot or cross-bedstead sofa	G. Sickels	Middletown, Conn	Sept. 25, 1840	1, 800
Cot, Soldier's	E. W. Pierce and W. J. Clark	Southington, Conn	Jan. 7, 1862	34, 089
Cot, Spring	T. J. Griffin	Brooklyn, N. Y	Apr. 8, 1873	137, 675
Cottage-chair	C. O. Collignon	Closter, N. Y	Mar. 10, 1868	75, 373
Cotton after ginning, Machine for cleaning and meating.	J. Simons and J. McJames	....	May 17, 1804	....
Cotton and corn-stalk cutter	G. S. Roudebrush	Natchez, Miss	Nov. 13, 1860	30, 645
Cotton and corn-stalk puller	W. Altick	Dayton, Ohio	July 24, 1866	56, 509
Cotton and corn-stalks, Machine for extracting	J. Bishop	Austin, Tex	Feb. 19, 1861	31, 437
Cotton and corn-stalks, Machine for pulling and cutting.	H. F. Hicks	Grand View, Ind	Nov. 8, 1859	26, 034
Cotton and feeding to gin, Cleaning seed	M. B. Clarke	Newnan, Ga	Dec. 19, 1854	12, 091
Cotton and hay press	B. B. Alfred	La Grange, Ga	Nov. 19, 1867	71, 113
Cotton and hay press	B. B. Alfred	La Grange, Ga	Nov. 26, 1867	71, 439
Cotton and hay press	G. H. Aylworth	Brighton, Ill	Nov. 7, 1871	120, 612
Cotton and hay press	S. T. Baker	Portland, Me	Dec. 17, 1834	....
Cotton and hay press	L. Balles, J. Prescott, and W. A. Bickford.	Memphis, Tenn	Feb. 13, 1841	1, 979
Cotton and hay press	W. Bullock	Jersey City, N. J	Sept. 28, 1843	3, 288
Cotton and hay press	N. Chapman	Mystic River, Conn	Jan. 10, 1860	26, 750
Cotton and hay press	N. Chapman	Milford, Mass	Jan. 15, 1867	61, 159
Cotton and hay press	A. W. Clarkson	Due West, S. C	Feb. 27, 1872	124, 035
Cotton and hay press	E. S. Collins	Trenton, Tenn	Dec. 5, 1871	121, 591
Cotton and hay press	E. S. Collins	Trenton, Tenn	Dec. 16, 1873	145, 629
Cotton and hay press	J. W. Conway	Franklin, Ind	Mar. 13, 1860	27, 429
Cotton and hay press	J. W. Conway	Madison, Ind	Apr. 2, 1867	63, 477
Cotton and hay press	J. G. Cummings	Columbus, Miss	July 5, 1870	104, 936
Cotton and hay press	J. K. Davis	Monticello, S. C	Sept. 28, 1869	95, 328
Cotton and hay press	W. Deering	Louisville, Ky	Sept. 10, 1867	68, 613
Cotton and hay press	J. S. Duffy	Battle Ground, Ind	Mar. 29, 1870	101, 239
Cotton and hay press	E. Eliason, jr	Fredericksburgh, Va	Jan. 21, 1835	....
Cotton and hay press	P. G. Gardiner	New York, N. Y	Apr. 16, 1842	2, 555
Cotton and hay press	S. C. Goodsell and D. Frisbie	New Haven, Conn	Sept. 25, 1866	58, 341
Cotton and hay press	R. Greene	Greenville, N. C	Dec. 7, 1869	97, 631

Index of patents issued from the United States Patent Office from 1790 *to* 1873, *inclusive*—Continued.

Invention.	Inventor.	Residence.	Date.	No.
Cotton and hay press	J. P. Herron	Atlanta, Ga	Sept. 13, 1870	107, 371
Cotton and hay press	H. F. Hicks	Grand View, Ind	July 24, 1860	29, 341
Cotton and hay press	J. J. Hines	Evergreen, Ala	Sept. 7, 1869	94, 602
Cotton and hay press	M. Jaques and H. Freeman	Woodbridge, N. J	Oct. 2, 1811	....
Cotton and hay press	J. E. Kelsey and J. A. Potter	Poughkeepsie, N. Y., and Providence, R. I.	Sept. 25, 1840	1, 798
Cotton and hay press	D. Knowles	Philadelphia, Pa	Nov. 22, 1870	109, 424
Cotton and hay press	C. K. Marshall	New Orleans, La	Apr. 18, 1871	113, 900
Cotton and hay press	J. Massey	Thomasville, Ga	Dec. 15, 1857	18, 854
Cotton and hay press	J. C. McCurry	Wall Hill, Miss	Jan. 30, 1872	123, 275
Cotton and hay press	A. McGowen	Houston, Tex	Aug. 8, 1871	117, 794
Cotton and hay press	J. L. Nelson	Greenville, N. C	Jan. 2, 1872	122, 483
Cotton and hay press	J. D. Nix	Noble, Ill	Nov. 21, 1871	121, 121
Cotton and hay press	G. W. Penniston	North Vernon, Ind	Dec. 1, 1857	18, 766
Cotton and hay press	L. Potter	Warren, Ohio	Apr. 24, 1847	5, 088
Cotton and hay press	D. Reynolds	Prospect, Md	Oct. 14, 1873	143, 641
Cotton and hay press	J. G. Rux	Raymond, Miss	May 21, 1867	64, 909
Cotton and hay press	W. Russell	Atlanta, Ga	Feb. 18, 1868	74, 603
Cotton and hay press	W. M. Smith	Augusta, Ga	Aug. 16, 1870	106, 417
Cotton and hay press	W. M. Smith	Augusta, Ga	May 23, 1871	115, 126
Cotton and hay press	R. Stallings	Louisburgh, N. C	Apr. 4, 1871	113, 700
Cotton and hay press	E. Stockbridge	Houston, Tex	July 5, 1859	24, 672
Cotton and hay press	C. W. Stopple	Houston, Tex	Aug. 9, 1870	106, 229
Cotton and hay press	R. Triplett	Davis County, Ky	May 19, 1834	....
Cotton and hay press	C. P. Wagner	New York, N. Y	May 14, 1867	64, 814
Cotton and hay press	G. P. Webster, jr	Cross Bridge, Tenn	July 25, 1871	117, 491
Cotton and hay press	T. D. Wilson	Corydon, Ind	June 6, 1827	....
Cotton and hay press	S. Wolff	Vicksburgh, Miss	May 31, 1859	24, 256
Cotton and hay press, Portable	A. G. Murray	Annapolis, Md	Jan. 9, 1835	....
Cotton and linen waste, Treating	E. N. Horsford	Cambridge, Mass	Sept. 15, 1857	18, 203
Cotton and other fabrics, Sizing	J. W. Speyer	Hamburg, Germany	May 24, 1870	103, 384
Cotton and other fibrous materials, Combing	J. Noble	Leeds, England	June 27, 1854	11, 199
Cotton and other fibrous materials for carding, Machine for preparing.	R. Kitson	Lowell, Mass	Sept. 22, 1863	40, 049
Cotton and other fibrous materials, Machine for preparing.	C. Whipple	Providence, R. I	Dec. 6, 1864	45, 371
Cotton and other fibrous materials, Machine for treating compressed.	W. Wanklyn	Albion Mills, Bury, England.	Feb. 23, 1864	47, 731
Cotton and other fibrous materials, Pressing	H. L. Conner	Natchez, Miss	July 5, 1833	....
Cotton and other fibrous substances, Cleaning	J. C. Hurd	Medway, Mass	Apr. 18, 1854	10, 803
Cotton and other fibrous substances, Cleaning	E. Lord	Todmorden, Great Britain	Jan. 9, 1866	52, 008
Cotton and other plants, Cultivation of	P. Poullain	Greensborough, Ga	May 26, 1868	78, 233
Cotton and other presses	P. G. Gardiner	New York, N. Y	Feb. 28, 1845	3, 930
Cotton and other presses, Self-adjusting platens for	J. C. Colt	New York, N. Y	Apr. 22, 1845	4, 006
Cotton and other seeds, Cleaning	T. Rowe	New York, N. Y	Mar. 16, 1869	87, 975
Cotton and other seeds, Hulling	L. D. Cavarly	Waterford, Conn	Feb. 12, 1834	....
Cotton and sugar-cane elevator	E. Price	Waterproof, La	May 20, 1856	14, 927
Cotton and tobacco press	N. Cheek	Chapel Hill, N. C	Apr. 12, 1870	101, 822
Cotton and tobacco press	B. R. Curtis	Richmond, Va	Jan. 29, 1827	....
Cotton and wool factories, Straightening and soldering drums or cylinders for.	L. N. Perry	Worcester, Mass	Jan. 23, 1829	....
Cotton and wool ginning machine	S. R. Parkhurst	New York, N. Y	May 1, 1845	4, 023
Cotton and wool picking and cleaning machine	S. R. Parkhurst	Bloomfield, N. J	July 24, 1866	56, 675
Cotton and wool, Roping and spinning	J. Brown	Providence, R. I	Aug. 8, 1812	....
Cotton and woolen rolls, Machine for splicing	G. Barton, jr	Shaftsburgh, Vt	Apr. 22, 1826	....
Cotton and woolen waste from oil, grease, &c., Process of cleaning.	H. M. Baker	Washington, D. C.	June 15, 1869	91, 407
Cotton, Apparatus for preparing	C. Lewandowski	Paris, France	Jan. 1, 1867	60, 754
Cotton-bagging, Machine for rolling and measuring.	T. H. Murphy	New Orleans, La	May 17, 1859	24, 046
Cotton-bagging, Manufacture of	T. Tebow	Lexington, Ky	May 30, 1871	115, 388
Cotton-bale fastening	M. Tildesley	Willenhall, England	Oct. 12, 1869	95, 854
Cotton-bale hoop	G. W. Penniston	North Vernon, Ind	Feb. 1, 1859	22, 823
Cotton-bale tie	J. Booth	Saint Louis, Mo	May 15, 1866	54, 675
Cotton-bales, Applying and securing metal bands on.	J. J. McComb	Liverpool, England	Oct. 23, 1866	59, 151
Cotton-bales, tobacco-hogsheads, &c., Packing-machine for.	T. Jennings	Stateburgh, S. C	Mar. 3, 1829	....
Cotton-band, Metallic	R. Lewis	Charleston, S. C	Apr. 5, 1859	23, 474
Cotton-band, Metallic	R. Lewis	Charleston, S. C	Apr. 5, 1859	23, 475
Cotton bats or laps, Method of making	J. C. Smith and G. C. Kellogg	New Hartford, Conn	Feb. 20, 1843	2, 969
Cotton-batting	H. B. and H. T. Lawton	Cohoes and Troy, N. Y	Mar. 13, 1849	6, 189
Cotton-batting	E. P. Rider	Brooklyn, N. Y	May 18, 1852	8, 958
Cotton-batting, Manufacture of	J. Essex	Bennington, Vt	Feb. 10, 1846	4, 372
Cotton-batting, Mode of glazing	D. Goff	Rehoboth, Mass	Jan. 15, 1846	4, 353
Cotton-batting, Sizing and drying	H. A. Stearns	Cincinnati, Ohio	Sept. 19, 1848	5, 773
Cotton-batting sizing and drying apparatus	E. P. Rider	New York, N. Y	July 30, 1850	7, 533
Cotton beating and picking machine	D. Harding	Lowell, Mass	June 25, 1867	66, 020
Cotton before ginning, Machine for cleaning	B. Seguine	Alexandria, La	July 3, 1843	3, 154
Cotton being carded, Mechanism for mixing soapstone with.	T. Welham	Philadelphia, Pa	Apr. 13, 1869	88, 997
Cotton, Bleaching damaged	J. B. Richards	Kilburn, England	Dec. 23, 1873	145, 816
Cotton, Bleaching stained	J. A. Meany	Brooklyn, N. Y	Apr. 3, 1866	53, 646
Cotton burring and ginning machine	J. Goulding	Worcester, Mass	May 31, 1864	42, 940
Cotton-can	R. R. Hulme	Providence, R. I	June 4, 1872	127, 486
Cotton, Carding, drawing, and roping	W. Tiffany and P. Allen	Otsego, N. Y	July 17, 1815	....
Cotton-check	S. W. Odell	Ouachita Parish, La	Aug. 31, 1869	94, 334
Cotton-chopper	C. Bailey and G. K. Bagby	Kinston, N. C	Apr. 29, 1873	138, 363
Cotton-chopper	J. Caston	Bowdon, Ga	Dec. 23, 1873	145, 849
Cotton-chopper	C. B. Douglas	Montgomery, Ala	Apr. 4, 1871	113, 640
Cotton-chopper	J. M. Garrett	Brenham, Tex	Dec. 30, 1873	146, 061
Cotton-chopper	R. C. Holt	Morehouse Parish, La	June 14, 1870	104, 154
Cotton-chopper	W. Holt	Dawson, Ga	May 3, 1870	102, 541
Cotton-chopper	J. R. Hood	Wedowee, Ala	Jan. 31, 1871	111, 346
Cotton-chopper	I. J. Kidd	Young's Settlement, Tex	Apr. 28, 1868	77, 293
Cotton-chopper	J. A. Lutz	Waynesborough, Va	Nov. 1, 1870	108, 918
Cotton-chopper	E. T. Matthews	Galveston, Tex	Oct. 8, 1872	132, 015
Cotton-chopper	A. G. Powell	Smithfield, N. C	Dec. 19, 1871	122, 057

Index of patents issued from the United States Patent Office from 1790 *to* 1873, *inclusive*—Continued.

Invention.	Inventor.	Residence.	Date.	No.
Cotton-chopper	W. Price	Mount Olive, N. C	Apr. 8, 1873	137, 715
Cotton-chopper	K. Puckett	Parish of Morehouse, La	Mar. 26, 1867	63, 176
Cotton-chopper	W. C. Tilton	Spring Place, Ga	May 6, 1873	138, 596
Cotton-chopper	E. B. Turnipseed	Columbia, S. C	May 16, 1871	114, 889
Cotton-chopper	D. F. Welsh	Nevada, Ohio	Jan. 17, 1871	111, 023
Cotton chopper and cultivator	J. D. Dunn	Griffin, Ga	Feb. 22, 1870	100, 128
Cotton chopper and cultivator	J. M. Harcrow	Marshall, Tex	Apr. 16, 1872	125, 811
Cotton chopper and cultivator	M. L. Nearn	Double Bridges, Tenn	Nov. 4, 1873	144, 281
Cotton chopper and cultivator, Combined	A. F. Roberts	Knoxville, Tenn	Oct. 28, 1873	143, 997
Cotton chopper and cultivator, Combined	J. B. Underwood	Fayetteville, N. C	July 8, 1873	140, 746
Cotton-chopper and grain-cultivator	D. Mosely	Ozark, Ark	Mar. 7, 1871	112, 481
Cotton chopper and scraper	H. B. Cage	Madison Station, Wis	Oct. 12, 1869	95, 651
Cotton chopper and scraper, Combined	W. C. Bibb	Madison, Ga	Feb. 28, 1871	112, 209
Cotton chopper and thinner	D. P. Lewis	Huntsville, Ala	Jan. 22, 1867	61, 438
Cotton chopper, cultivator, and drill	J. A. Hall	Keokuk, Iowa	Aug. 1, 1865	49, 104
Cotton chopper, scraper, and cultivator	F. A. Leonhard	Columbia, Tenn	Sept. 12, 1871	118, 951
Cotton-chopper, Self-adjusting rotary	S. A. Jefferson	Franklin, Tenn	Oct. 18, 1870	108, 358
Cotton-cleaner	S. C. Ames	Washington, Ark	Sept. 11, 1860	29, 945
Cotton-cleaner	J. L. Coker	Hartsville, S. C	Dec. 10, 1872	133, 761
Cotton-cleaner	A. S. Eastham	Wharton, Tex	Mar. 12, 1861	31, 661
Cotton-cleaner	J. Gilliam	Reedy Fork, S. C	Oct. 10, 1829	......
Cotton-cleaner	I. Hayden	Lawrence, Mass	Sept. 11, 1860	29, 971
Cotton-cleaner	E. A. Hearne	Lowndes County, Ala	Feb. 19, 1861	31, 456
Cotton-cleaner	J. Johnson	Hempstead County, Ark	Oct. 20, 1857	18, 454
Cotton-cleaner	W. H. Johnson	Richmond, Ark	Oct. 2, 1860	30, 227
Cotton-cleaner	J. H. Kinyon and J. Hollingsworth	Chicago, Ill	Apr. 22, 1856	14, 725
Cotton-cleaner	F. McCarthy	Demopolis, Ala	Feb. 12, 1845	3, 912
Cotton-cleaner	J. Ralston	Brenham, Tex	Feb. 4, 1873	135, 586
Cotton-cleaner	J. Ryder, W. Carpenter, and H. R. Jolley	Clinton, La	Dec. 18, 1860	30, 989
Cotton-cleaner	Z. B. Sims	Bonham, Tex	July 4, 1871	116, 764
Cotton-cleaner	C. Smith	Knoxville, Tex	Sept. 11, 1860	30, 003
Cotton-cleaner	C. S. Tarpley	Jackson, Miss	Jan. 1, 1861	31, 069
Cotton-cleaner	J. W. Thorn	Courtland, Ala	Oct. 16, 1860	30, 435
Cotton-cleaner	J. W. Thorn	Courtland, Ala	Feb. 25, 1868	74, 776
Cotton-cleaner	J. Wind	Thomasville, Ga	Nov. 13, 1847	5, 369
Cotton cleaner, Sea-island	J. Reed	Marshfield, Mass	Aug. 10, 1827	......
Cotton, Cleaning	T. Shapard	Haywood County, Tenn	Dec. 24, 1867	72, 691
Cotton cleaning and ginning machine	G. Macdonald	Aston, England	Jan. 8, 1867	61, 078
Cotton-cleaning machine	F. A. Calvert and C. G. Sargent	Lowell and Westford, Mass	Feb. 3, 1857	16, 526
Cotton-cleaning machine	L. S. Chichester	New York, N. Y	July 14, 1857	17, 819
Cotton-cleaning machine	R. J. Clay	Williamsburgh, N. Y	Jan. 1, 1867	60, 859
Cotton-cleaning machine	L. T. Clement	Smyrna, Tenn	Oct. 26, 1869	96, 202
Cotton-cleaning machine	J. Gilmore	New Orleans, La	May 22, 1860	28, 361
Cotton-cleaning machine	R. H. Hilton	New Berne, N. C	Feb. 25, 1868	74, 822
Cotton-cleaning machine	J. E. Hooper	Baltimore, Md	Jan. 30, 1866	52, 289
Cotton-cleaning machine	B. Jackman	Louisville, Ky	Dec. 11, 1860	30, 880
Cotton-cleaning machine	C. Leavitt	Quincy, Ill	Apr. 11, 1854	10, 762
Cotton-cleaning machine	T. Oliver	Yazoo City, Miss	May 18, 1858	20, 270
Cotton-cleaning machine	G. T. Sadler	Lawrence County, Ala	Mar. 10, 1823	......
Cotton-cleaning machinery	S. W. Brown	Lowell, Mass	Oct. 24, 1854	11, 826
Cotton-cleaning machinery	I. Hayden	Lawrence, Mass	Feb. 11, 1862	34, 363
Cotton-cleaning machinery	D. Hess	West Union, Iowa	Oct. 25, 1859	25, 897
Cotton, clover, and other seed huller	J. Whiteman	Philadelphia, Pa	June 26, 1835	......
Cotton-coated seeds, Process for separating the fibers from the husks in	T. Rose and R. E. Gibson	Earlestown, England	July 26, 1870	105, 729
Cotton, &c., combing machine	H. Conant	Providence County, R. I	Feb. 8, 1870	99, 641
Cotton-combing machine	I. Dimock	Florence, Mass	Sept. 12, 1865	49, 865
Cotton-combing machine	C. Whipple and R. J. Stafford	Providence and Smithfield, R. I.	Mar. 4, 1862	34, 606
Cotton-combing machine, Feeding-device for	C. F. Hadley and E. Johnson	Chicopee, Mass., and Wethersfield, Conn.	June 15, 1869	91, 229
Cotton-compress	E. L. Morse	Saint Louis, Mo	Nov. 3, 1868	83, 783
Cotton, &c., compress	E. L. Morse	Saint Louis, Mo	Apr. 16, 1867	63, 808
Cotton-compresser	H. Waterman	Bath, Me	May 10, 1838	731
Cotton, Condensing	A. Man	Smithfield, R. I	Apr. 28, 1836	......
Cotton-cultivator	C. T. Reams	Raleigh, N. C	Apr. 15, 1873	137, 959
Cotton, &c., Double-speeder for roping	P. Moody	Boston, Mass	Apr. 3, 1819	......
Cotton, Double-speeder for roving	A. Arnold	North Providence, R. I	Aug. 10, 1836	......
Cotton, &c., Drawing	C. Whipple	Providence, R. I	Feb. 16, 1858	19, 394
Cotton drawing and spinning machine	J. B. Fuller	Norwich, Conn	Aug. 25, 1868	81, 357
Cotton, &c., Drying	J. Philbrick	Cold Springs, Miss	Feb. 12, 1836	......
Cotton, Drying wet seed	G. G. Henry	Mobile, Ala	Dec. 6, 1859	26, 353
Cotton-duck, Dressing	H. N. Gambrill	Baltimore, Md	Oct. 21, 1851	8, 444
Cotton, &c., Dust-room connected with machines for picking	R. Kitson	Lowell, Mass	Aug. 19, 1862	36, 219
Cotton, Dust-room in cleaning	J. Whitehill	Newburgh, N. Y	July 16, 1867	66, 921
Cotton-elevator	W. Potter and E. Crane	Lowell, Mass	Sept. 3, 1867	68, 386
Cotton-flannel, Manufacturing	A. S. Carleton	Clinton, Mass	Mar. 24, 1857	16, 870
Cotton, flax, &c., Can for manufacturing	H. Moses	Paterson, N. J	Mar. 12, 1833	......
Cotton for molding purposes, Preparing plastic	J. M. Legaré	Aiken, S. C	Dec. 29, 1857	18, 980
Cotton, &c., for spinning, Machine for preparing	J. Taylor	Oldham, England	Mar. 29, 1864	42, 127
Cotton from the bolls in the field, Picking	S. S. Rembert and J. Prescott	Memphis, Tenn	Sept. 10, 1850	7, 631
Cotton from the seed, Cleaning	J. Reed	Marshfield, Mass	Feb. 3, 1826	......
Cotton-gin	F. T. Ackland, H. G. Mitchell, and M. Mustapha.	Zagazig, Egypt	Sept. 18, 1866	58, 187
Cotton-gin	C. N. Andrews	Saint Louis, Mo	Sept. 19, 1871	119, 001
Cotton-gin	W. P. Baker	Boston, Mass	Nov. 20, 1838	1, 013
Cotton-gin	B. G. Beadle	Memphis, Tenn	Nov. 1, 1869	25, 943
Cotton-gin	J. Beath	Boston, Mass	July 12, 1839	1, 233
Cotton-gin	W. Bell	......	Nov. 24, 1803	......
Cotton-gin	W. F. Bowen	Stark, Fla	July 11, 1871	116, 924
Cotton-gin	J. B. Brackett and W. Dearborn.	Boston, Mass	Mar. 26, 1867	63, 136
Cotton-gin	J. B. Brackett and W. Dearborn.	Boston, Mass	Mar. 9, 1869	87, 535
Cotton-gin	C. Brakell	Oldham, England	Dec. 5, 1865	51, 402

Index of patents issued from the United States Patent Office from 1790 *to* 1873, *inclusive*—Continued.

Invention.	Inventor.	Residence.	Date.	No.
Cotton-gin	R. M. Brooks	Woodbury, Ga	Apr. 14, 1868	76, 594
Cotton-gin	H. W. Brown	Millville, N. J	Mar. 23, 1858	19, 679
Cotton-gin	I. F. Brown	Columbus, Ga	Apr. 23, 1861	32, 116
Cotton-gin	I. F. Brown	New London, Conn	Sept. 1, 1863	39, 767
Cotton-gin	A. H. Burdine	Chulahoma, Miss	Aug. 28, 1860	29, 765
Cotton-gin	L. Campbell	Columbus, Miss	Jan. 10, 1854	10, 401
Cotton-gin	L. Campbell	Columbus, Miss	May 22, 1855	12, 894
Cotton-gin	E. Carver, jr	Bridgewater, Mass	June 13, 1823	....
Cotton-gin	J. E. Carver	Bridgewater, Mass	Jan. 2, 1866	51, 892
Cotton-gin	J. G. Case	New London, Conn	Feb. 20, 1872	123, 868
Cotton-gin	J. A. Chanfourier	Paris, France	June 11, 1867	65, 643
Cotton-gin	L. J. Chichester	New York, N. Y	Feb. 9, 1858	19, 324
Cotton-gin	L. S. Chichester	Brooklyn, N. Y	July 25, 1854	11, 355
Cotton-gin	L. S. Chichester	New York, N. Y	Nov. 20, 1855	13, 815
Cotton-gin	L. S Chichester	New York, N. Y	Feb. 3, 1857	16, 565
Cotton-gin	L. S. Chichester	New York, N. Y	Oct. 12, 1858	21, 795
Cotton-gin	L. S. Chichester	New York, N. Y	Jan. 10, 1860	26, 815
Cotton-gin	H. Clark	New London, Conn	Feb. 25, 1836	....
Cotton-gin	H. Clark	Eufaula, Ala	Aug. 29, 1848	5, 740
Cotton-gin	H. Clark	Newport, Fla	Feb. 13, 1855	12, 376
Cotton-gin	R. J. Clay	Green Point, N. Y	Mar. 9, 1869	87, 635
Cotton-gin	J. M. Clough	Ilion, N. Y	June 7, 1870	103, 981
Cotton-gin	J. M. Clough	Ilion, N. Y	Nov. 19, 1872	133, 080
Cotton-gin	P. E. Collins	Mobile, Ala	Oct. 4, 1859	25, 630
Cotton-gin	H. Conklin	Poughkeepsie, N. Y	June 7, 1839	1, 168
Cotton-gin	S. T. Conn	New York, N. Y	June 11, 1829	....
Cotton-gin	E. A. Cooper	Westminster, Great Britain	Apr. 3, 1866	53, 753
Cotton-gin	T. C. Craven	Greenbush, N. Y	Feb. 9, 1864	41, 487
Cotton-gin	O. Crawford	....	June 22, 1807	....
Cotton-gin	E. Cruse	Charleston, S. C	Nov. 18, 1816	....
Cotton-gin	B. Dobson and W. Slater	Bolton, England	Mar. 30, 1869	88, 374
Cotton-gin	J. Du Bois	Greensborough, Ala	Jan. 8, 1850	6, 998
Cotton-gin	J. Du Bois	Greensborough, Ala	Apr. 27, 1858	20, 051
Cotton-gin	J. Du Bois	Greensborough, Ala	July 18, 1871	117, 058
Cotton-gin	F. Durand	Paris, France	Feb. 24, 1863	37, 743
Cotton-gin	F. Durand	Paris, France	Sept. 19, 1865	50, 080
Cotton-gin	H. L. Emery	Albany, N. Y	Sept. 4, 1860	29, 867
Cotton-gin	H. L. Emery	Albany, N. Y	Mar. 30, 1869	88, 464
Cotton-gin	W. B. Emery	Albany, N. Y	May 9, 1865	47, 626
Cotton-gin	A. Fessenden	Beaufort, S. C	July 9, 1867	66, 577
Cotton-gin	C. L. Fleischmann	New York, N. Y	Jan. 16, 1866	52, 037
Cotton-gin	C. L. Fleischmann	Washington, D. C	May 4, 1869	89, 751
Cotton-gin	H. H. Fultz	Lexington, Miss	Oct. 9, 1855	13, 641
Cotton-gin	J. E. Furguson	Micanopy, Fla	Jan. 1, 1861	31, 062
Cotton-gin	N W. Gaddy	Nichols, S. C	Nov. 18, 1873	114, 668
Cotton-gin	T. C. Garlington	La Fayette, Ala	Feb. 23, 1858	19, 415
Cotton-gin	E. Gottheil	Galveston, Tex	Apr. 19, 1859	23, 679
Cotton-gin	J. Goulding	North Wilbraham, Mass	Aug. 28, 1860	29, 780
Cotton-gin	B. D. Gullett	Aberdeen, Miss	Jan. 10, 1854	10, 406
Cotton-gin	B. D. Gullett	Aberdeen, Miss	Feb. 23, 1858	19, 417
Cotton-gin	B. D. Gullett	Amite City, La	Sept. 7, 1869	94, 488
Cotton-gin	B. D. Gullett	Amite City, La	July 1, 1873	140, 365
Cotton-gin	R. R. Gwathmey	Philadelphia, Pa	Apr. 5, 1870	101, 610
Cotton-gin	S. Z. Hall	Sing Sing, N. Y	Mar. 16, 1869	87, 771
Cotton-gin	S. Z. Hall	Ossining, N. Y	July 5, 1870	105, 070
Cotton-gin	R. Hancock, sr., and E. W. Carr	Philadelphia, Pa	Feb. 6, 1811	....
Cotton-gin	B. Hempstead	Little Rock, Ark	Sept. 23, 1873	143, 074
Cotton-gin	W. L. Henderson	Comrawattee, West India	Nov. 28, 1871	121, 365
Cotton-gin	H. Holmes	....	May 12, 1796	....
Cotton-gin	W. W. Howell	Columbus, Miss	Feb. 28, 1860	27, 290
Cotton-gin	B. H. Jenks and W. A. Tuttle	Philadelphia, Pa	Jan. 3, 1860	26, 681
Cotton-gin	I. Jennings	New York, N. Y	Jan. 17, 1817	....
Cotton-gin	A. Jones	New Orleans, La	Apr. 25, 1837	180
Cotton-gin	E. Jones	London, England	Sept. 24, 1872	131, 546
Cotton-gin	A. P. Keith	Bridgewater, Mass	Jan. 2, 1855	12, 132
Cotton-gin	E. Keith	Bridgewater, Mass	Dec. 22, 1846	4, 901
Cotton-gin	E. Keith	Bridgewater, Mass	Jan. 27, 1857	16, 488
Cotton-gin	J. W. Kokemuller	Bluffton, S. C	Aug. 13, 1867	67, 773
Cotton-gin	T. J. Laws	Washington, Ark	Mar. 16, 1852	8, 803
Cotton-gin	W. T. Layton	Darlington, S. C	May 22, 1849	6, 463
Cotton-gin	C. Leavitt and W. H. Burridge	Cleveland, Ohio	Nov. 24, 1868	84, 287
Cotton-gin	J. Leavitt, C. Lane, and T. Leavitt.	Suffield, Conn	Mar. 24, 1825	....
Cotton-gin	W. B. Lindsay	New Orleans, La	May 27, 1856	14, 965
Cotton-gin	W. H. Livingston	New York, N. Y	Apr. 5, 1864	42, 206
Cotton-gin	J. Lynch	Tuscaloosa, Ala	July 22, 1833	....
Cotton-gin	O. W. Massey	Macon, Ga	July 4, 1871	116, 615
Cotton-gin	M. McAuley	Thomas County, Ga	Apr. 24, 1849	6, 378
Cotton-gin	F. McCarthy	Demopolis, Ala	July 3, 1840	1, 675
Cotton-gin	F. McCarthy	Orange Springs, Fla	July 30, 1867	67, 327
Cotton-gin	J. McCreight	Winnsborough, S. C	July 2, 1836	....
Cotton-gin	W. and J. McCreight	Winnsborough, S. C	Feb. 5, 1836	....
Cotton-gin	R. A. L. McCurdy	Sabine Parish, La	June 26, 1855	13, 131
Cotton-gin	R. McKenna	White's Station, Tenn	May 31, 1870	103, 638
Cotton-gin	R. McKenna	White's Station, Tenn	Oct. 18, 1870	108, 500
Cotton-gin	R. McKenna	White's Station, Tenn	Mar. 5, 1872	124, 278
Cotton-gin	R. McKenna	White's Station, Tenn	July 9, 1872	128, 743
Cotton-gin	F. M. McMeekin	Morrison's Mills, Fla	Dec. 11, 1866	60, 402
Cotton-gin	F. M. McMeekin	Morrison's Mills, Fla	May 23, 1871	115, 226
Cotton-gin	C. A. McPhetridge	Saint Louis, Mo	Nov. 18, 1856	16, 096
Cotton-gin	W. McLendon	Greenville, Ga	Dec. 27, 1859	26, 604
Cotton-gin	J. B. Mell	Riceborough, Ga	Apr. 3, 1855	12, 635
Cotton-gin	J. B. Mell	Riceborough, Ga	Oct. 21, 1856	15, 930
Cotton-gin	J. B. Miles	Chicot, Ark	July 22, 1856	15, 381
Cotton-gin	O. Murray	New Market, N. H	Feb. 4, 1873	135, 485
Cotton-gin	D. G. Olmstead	Vicksburgh, Miss	Jan. 12, 1858	19, 097
Cotton-gin	D. G. Olmstead	Vicksburgh, Miss	Dec. 20, 1859	26, 516
Cotton-gin	J. F. Orr	Orrville, Ala	Jan. 13, 1857	16, 394

Index of patents issued from the United States Patent Office from 1790 *to* 1873, *inclusive*—Continued.

Invention.	Inventor.	Residence.	Date.	No.
Cotton-gin	J. F. Orr	Orrville, Ala	Jan. 5, 1858	19, 041
Cotton-gin	E. Osgood	Boston, Mass	May 11, 1858	20, 216
Cotton-gin	E. Osgood	Boston, Mass	Oct. 18, 1859	25, 848
Cotton-gin	E. Osgood	New York, N. Y	Dec. 22, 1863	41, 046
Cotton-gin	E. Osgood	Boston, Mass	Aug. 13, 1872	130, 438
Cotton-gin	H. C. Parkhurst	New York, N. Y	Aug. 31, 1858	21, 357
Cotton-gin	S. R. Harkhurst	New York, N. Y	Sept. 11, 1849	6, 703
Cotton-gin	S. R. Parkhurst	New York, N. Y	Apr. 23, 1850	7, 307
Cotton-gin	S. R. Parkhurst	New York, N. Y	Apr. 27, 1858	20, 086
Cotton-gin	S. R. Parkhurst	Bloomfield, N. J	Jan. 9, 1867	51, 962
Cotton-gin	S. R. Parkhurst	Mont Clair, N. J	Jan. 11, 1870	98, 705
Cotton-gin	N. A. Patterson	Kingston, Tenn	Oct. 23, 1860	30, 497
Cotton-gin	S. Pennoyer	Cross River, N. Y	July 24, 1822	....
Cotton-gin	J. Perkins	Bridgewater, Mass	June 14, 1834	....
Cotton-gin	D. Philips	Jefferson County, Miss	Apr. 3, 1829	....
Cotton-gin	J. Platt and W. Richardson	Oldham, Great Britain	Oct. 28, 1862	36, 789
Cotton-gin	A. A. Porter	Griffin, Ga	Dec. 22, 1868	85, 128
Cotton-gin	D. Pratt	Prattville, Ala	July 14, 1857	17, 806
Cotton-gin	M. E. Pratt	Prattville, Ala	July 15, 1873	140, 791
Cotton-gin	W. F. Pratt	East Bridgewater, Mass	Aug. 30, 1859	25, 307
Cotton-gin	W. F. Pratt	East Bridgewater, Mass	July 6, 1869	92, 208
Cotton-gin	W. A. Purdom	Jackson, Miss	Nov. 4, 1856	16, 022
Cotton-gin	P. Reading	Trenton, N. J	Apr. 13, 1836	....
Cotton-gin	C. G. Sargent	Westford, Mass	Apr. 20, 1869	89, 083
Cotton-gin	C. G. Sargent	Westford, Mass	May 11, 1869	89, 890
Cotton-gin	C. G. Sargent and A. B. Ely	Westford and Newton, Mass.	May 11, 1869	89, 891
Cotton-gin	P. C. Sawyer	Macon, Ga	June 10, 1873	139, 820
Cotton-gin	H. V. Scattergood	Albany, N. Y	June 12, 1866	55, 542
Cotton-gin	H. V. Scattergood	Albany, N. Y	June 25, 1867	66, 202
Cotton-gin	J. Simpson	Lewisville, S. C	Aug. 14, 1855	13, 441
Cotton-gin	C. Spofford and C. H. Hersey	Boston, Mass	June 19, 1866	55, 787
Cotton-gin	C. Spofford and C. H. Hersey	Boston, Mass	Aug. 20, 1867	67, 923
Cotton-gin	J. Stevens	New York, N. Y	May 30, 1865	48, 032
Cotton-gin	R. A. Stough	Griffin, Ga	Apr. 13, 1869	88, 924
Cotton-gin	L. G. Sturdevant	Delaware, Ohio	July 23, 1841	2, 190
Cotton-gin	J. Tetlon	Taunton, Mass	July 13, 1858	20, 904
Cotton-gin	E. Town	Washington, D. C	May 8, 1866	54, 625
Cotton-gin	J. L. Tuttle	New York, N. Y	Oct. 14, 1856	15, 906
Cotton-gin	J. L. Tuttle	Bridesburgh, Pa	Sept. 21, 1858	21, 582
Cotton-gin	J. A. Ventress	Woodville, Miss	June 29, 1858	20, 747
Cotton-gin	P. Von Schmidt	Washington, D. C	Oct. 17, 1846	4, 817
Cotton-gin	J. Watrous, jr	Mystic River, Conn	Apr. 10, 1866	53, 910
Cotton-gin	J. W. Webb	Cotton Valley, Ala	May 18, 1869	90, 210
Cotton-gin	H. L. Weeks	Hannahatchie, Ga	Sept. 6, 1853	9, 998
Cotton-gin	E. Whiting	....	Jan. 22, 1801	....
Cotton-gin	W. Whittemore, jr	West Cambridge, Mass	May 25, 1839	1, 158
Cotton-gin	F. L. Wilkinson	Adams' Run, S. C	Mar. 9, 1858	19, 598
Cotton-gin	J. Wilson	Anderson Court-House, S. C	Sept. 27, 1859	25, 600
Cotton-gin	J. N. Wilson and G. W. Payne	Memphis, Tenn	Apr. 27, 1859	20, 120
Cotton-gin	A. Q. Withers	Byhalia, Miss	Oct. 5, 1858	21, 714
Cotton-gin	F. Wuterich and J. Koerber	New York, N. Y	Nov. 8, 1859	26, 065
Cotton gin and machine cards, Manufacturing cylinders for.	J. L. Tuttle	New York, N. Y	Oct. 14, 1856	15, 904
Cotton gin and picker	J. B. Brackett and W. Dearborn	Boston, Mass	Aug. 27, 1867	68, 035
Cotton gin and picker	E. Osgood	Boston, Mass	Jan. 15, 1867	61, 239
Cotton-gin attachment	H. P. Harrell	Roxobel, N. C	Sept. 19, 1871	119, 140
Cotton-gin bush	E. Keith	Bridgewater, Mass	Sept. 19, 1845	4, 196
Cotton-gin, Common foot	I. B. Barnes	Beaufort, S. C	Nov. 6, 1826	....
Cotton-gin feeder	S. Z. Hall	Seguin, Tex	Sept. 11, 1860	29, 968
Cotton-gin feeder	L. Z. Hall	Sing Sing, N. Y	Sept. 10, 1872	131, 163
Cotton-gin feeder	N. Hoggatt	Madison Parish, La	July 18, 1871	117, 074
Cotton-gin feeder	J. Prescott	Rockford, Ill	Oct. 13, 1857	18, 410
Cotton-gin feeder	J. Ralston	Brenham, Tex	Sept. 6, 1870	107, 102
Cotton-gin feeding-attachment	S. Z. Hall	Camden, N. J	Aug. 6, 1867	67, 533
Cotton-gin flue	J. W. Gaines	Clarksville, Tex	Aug. 13, 1872	130, 423
Cotton-gin flue	J. B. Peyton	Raymond, Miss	Feb. 5, 1861	31, 326
Cotton-gin, Foot	W. Gould	McIntosh County, Ga	Feb. 20, 1821	....
Cotton-gin for ginning long staple and other kinds of cotton, Roller.	E. Carver	Bridgewater, Mass	Sept. 27, 1838	949
Cotton, Gin for linting	G. W. Payne	Memphis, Tenn	Aug. 23, 1870	106, 613
Cotton-gin frame, Cast-iron	E. A. Lester	Boston, Mass	Jan. 8, 1831	....
Cotton-gin grate	E. Keith	Bridgewater, Mass	Mar. 4, 1836	....
Cotton-gin knife-roller	T. H. Rushton and W. Dobson	Bolton, England	June 24, 1873	140, 218
Cotton-gin, Long-stapled	C. Willey, jr	Chicago, Ill	Apr. 27, 1852	8, 907
Cotton-gin, Railway	D. Philips	Georgetown, Pa	May 22, 1841	2, 103
Cotton-gin rib	I. F. Brown	Columbus, Ga	July 18, 1854	11, 317
Cotton-gin rib	W. J Horton	Newburgh, Ala	July 20, 1869	92, 724
Cotton-gin rib	J. Robison	New York, N. Y	Oct. 15, 1872	132, 217
Cotton-gin ribs, Manufacturing	J. W. Webb	Cotton Valley, Ala	Feb. 24, 1857	16, 699
Cotton-gin, Roller	W. Bell and J. S. De Montmollin	....	Mar. 7, 1803	....
Cotton-gin, Roller	E. Carver	Bridgewater, Mass	Jan. 17, 1842	2, 429
Cotton-gin, Roller	T. Ely	New York, N. Y	Dec. 11, 1845	4, 302
Cotton-gin, Roller	R. Reynolds, jr	Beaufort, S. C	Feb. 2, 1844	3, 425
Cotton-gin, Roller	J. Schley	Columbus, Ga	Nov. 14, 1848	5, 921
Cotton-gin roller	W. Wanklyn	Albion Mills, Bury, Great Britain.	Nov. 15, 1864	45, 109
Cotton-gin roller, Metallic fluted	G. F. Saltonstall	....	Sept. 2, 1801	....
Cotton-gin saw	A. D. Brown	Columbus, Ga	Aug. 28, 1855	13, 484
Cotton-gin saw	E. Carver	Bridgewater, Mass	Jan. 4, 1845	3, 875
Cotton-gin saw	T. C. Craven	Philadelphia, Pa	May 30, 1871	115, 441
Cotton-gin saw	P. Gardner	Woodville, Mass	Apr. 22, 1830	....
Cotton-gin, Saw	T. J. James	Princeton, Miss	May 7, 1842	2, 608
Cotton-gin, Saw	H. H. Kelley	Port Gibson, Miss	May 19, 1843	3, 091
Cotton-gin, Saw	C. A. McPhetridge	Natchez, Miss	Apr. 24, 1841	2, 068
Cotton-gin, Saw	W. B. Stewart	Cincinnati, Ohio	May 19, 1843	3, 097
Cotton-gin saw	W. Sutton	Washington, D. C	Nov. 24, 1868	84, 392
Cotton-gin-saw teeth	T. B. Oglesby	Hempstead, Tex	May 6, 1873	138, 575

Index of patents issued from the United States Patent Office from 1790 *to* 1873, *inclusive*—Continued.

Invention.	Inventor.	Residence.	Date.	No.
Cotton-gin-saw teeth, Machine for punching and swaging.	J. M. Clough	Ilion, N. Y	Jan. 2, 1872	122, 307
Cotton-gin-saw teeth, Manufacture of	T. C. Craven	Northampton, Mass	May 21, 1872	126, 875
Cotton-gin saws, Filing	C. P. Pool	New Market, Ala	Aug. 9, 1859	25, 042
Cotton-gin saws, Machine for filing	J. T. Turner	Bridgewater, Mass	June 2, 1857	17, 458
Cotton-gin, Self-feeding	J. A. Chaufourier	Paris, France	Apr. 12, 1870	101, 709
Cotton-gin sharpener	A. H. Burdine	Chulahoma, Miss	July 19, 1859	24, 790
Cotton-gins and corn-mills, Running-gear for	B. Huckaby	Huntsville, Ala	Aug. 16, 1824	....
Cotton-gins, Boxing for	W. S. Cooley	Norwich, Conn	Jan. 7, 1835	....
Cotton gins, &c., Construction of horse-power for	J. M. Albertson	New London, Conn	June 7, 1870	103, 821
Cotton-gins, Construction of rubber rollers for	W. Dearborn	Boston, Mass	Aug. 27, 1867	68, 052
Cotton-gins, Constructing saw-cylinders for	A. Jones	New York, N. Y	July 20, 1842	2, 731
Cotton-gins, Electroplating with nickel the metallic parts of.	L. Watrous	Mystic River, Conn	Nov. 22, 1870	109, 475
Cotton-gins, Feeder for roller	L. J. Mallard and W. S. Baker	Riceborough, Ga	June 17, 1856	15, 138
Cotton-gins, Grate of saw	A. Washburn	Bridgewater, Mass	June 16, 1841	2, 133
Cotton-gins, Mechanism for driving	W. L. May	Linwood, Ala	Nov. 14, 1869	97, 945
Cotton-gins. Propelling	P. Knox	Augusta, Ga	Dec. 7, 1826	....
Cotton-gins, Roller for	I. F. Brown	New London, Conn	Jan. 3, 1865	45, 695
Cotton-gins, Saw and grate for	E. Carver, jr	Bridgewater, Mass	June 12, 1823	....
Cotton-gins, Saw-cylinder for	J. Idler	Philadelphia, Pa	Dec. 1, 1837	498
Cotton-gins, Tool for turning cylinder-rings for	J. Gibbons	West Troy, N. Y	June 16, 1868	78, 954
Cotton, Ginning	J. Murry	....	Dec. 23, 1796	....
Cotton, Ginning	R. Watkins	....	Dec. 23, 1796	....
Cotton, Ginning and cleaning	S. Sawyer	Boston, Mass	Mar. 30, 1833	....
Cotton, Ginning and cleaning	C. Speer	New York, N. Y	Oct. 10, 1854	11, 795
Cotton ginning and cleaning by a combination of rolls.	S. Sawyer	Boston, Mass	Mar. 30, 1833	....
Cotton ginning, carding, and spinning machine	J. M'Bride	Nashville, Tenn	Aug. 8, 1805	....
Cotton-ginning machine	W. Bell and S. De Montmollin	....	Apr. 7, 1802	....
Cotton-ginning machine	R. R. Gathmey	Middletown, Ky	Dec. 31, 1867	72, 846
Cotton-ginning machine	I. Jennings	New York, N. Y	Dec. 27, 1815	....
Cotton-ginning machine	L. H. Moseley	Poughkeepsie, N. Y	Nov. 25, 1837	486
Cotton-ginning machine	J. Stevens	Poughkeepsie, N. Y	Nov. 25, 1837	485
Cotton-ginning machine	E. Whitney	....	Mar. 14, 1794	....
Cotton-ginning machinery	J. Percy	Albany, N. Y	Apr. 29, 1862	35, 109
Cotton-glazing machine	S. Turner	Cranston, R. I	Oct. 6, 1835	....
Cotton goods, Machine for finishing	C. S. Davis	Harrisburgh, Pa	Jan. 24, 1860	26, 895
Cotton goods, Warping, dressing, &c	J. Morgan	Baltimore, Md	Apr. 5, 1821	....
Cotton, hay, and cheese press	E. and L. L. Macomber	Gardiner, Me	Aug. 15, 1835	....
Cotton, hay, and hemp press	W. H. Morris	Troy, Tenn	May 24, 1870	103, 356
Cotton, hay, &c., Apparatus for compressing	F. Weldon	Kilmorony, Ireland	Mar. 25, 1873	137, 160
Cotton, hay, &c., Machine for binding and securing	J. Simmons	Philadelphia, Pa	Nov. 7, 1809	....
Cotton-hiller	A. W. Washburn	Yazoo City, Miss	Mar. 25, 1856	14, 539
Cotton-hopper	G. F. Saltonstall	Fayetteville, N. C	Dec. 31, 1817	....
Cotton-inspecting machine	L. Viales	New Orleans, La	Oct. 29, 1818	....
Cotton in the field, Machine for picking	J. W. Thorn	Courtland, Ala	Oct. 6, 1857	18, 363
Cotton in the seed, Machine for separating trash from.	J. Idler	Philadelphia, Pa	Dec. 31, 1838	1, 050
Cotton into yarn, Manufacturing	L. Crane	Ware, Mass	Mar. 26, 1825	....
Cotton laps, Machine for making	T. C. Craven	Hudson, N. Y	Feb. 4, 1873	135, 528
Cotton-lapper brake	D. Hussey	Nashua, N. H	Oct. 16, 1866	58, 945
Cotton-lapper brake	R. Kitson	Lowell, Mass	Sept. 22, 1863	40, 048
Cotton-lapper brake	R. Kitson	Lowell, Mass	Mar. 3, 1868	75, 169
Cotton-lapping machines, Friction-brakes for	E. Van Winkle	Paterson, N. J	Aug. 10, 1869	93, 649
Cotton, linen, and other fabrics to prevent them from burning, Solution to be applied to.	J. McGill	Boston, Mass	May 1, 1866	54, 382
Cotton, linen, &c., Printing and dyeing	A. Paraf	Mulhouse, France	Nov. 7, 1865	50, 885
Cotton-lint room, Fire-proof	R. R. Warren	Raleigh, N. C	Aug. 19, 1873	142, 065
Cotton-lint room, Revolving	W. T. Crenshaw	Burton, Tex	May 13, 1873	138, 865
Cotton, Long trunks for cleaning	I. Hayden	Lawrence, Mass	Dec. 1, 1857	18, 742
Cotton, Machine for cleaning	J. Kershaw	Paterson, N. J	Aug. 11, 1868	80, 826
Cotton, Machine for cleaning	B. J. F. Owen	Memphis, Tenn	Dec. 15, 1868	85, 024
Cotton, &c., Machine for cleaning and opening	J. E. Van Winkle	Paterson, N. J	June 2, 1863	38, 794
Cotton, Machine for cleaning unginned	R. M. Livingstone	Mobile, Ala	July 20, 1843	3, 190
Cotton, Machine for forming rolls of	C. White, J. Goulding, and S. Lowder.	Dedham, Mass	June 25, 1824	....
Cotton, Machine for ginning and cleaning	L. T. Clement	Smyrna, Tenn	July 27, 1869	93, 057
Cotton, Machine for packing	O. Stith	Lawrenceville, Va	Aug. 25, 1829	....
Cotton, &c., Machine for preparing	W. and F. W. Crighton	Manchester, England	Jan. 22, 1867	61, 322
Cotton, &c., Machine for roping and spinning	W. Carmichall	Sand Lake, N. Y	June 10, 1826	....
Cotton, Machine for roping and spinning	P. Moody	Boston, Mass	Feb. 19, 1821	....
Cotton, Machine for separating seed from	J. Eve	....	Dec. 6, 1803	....
Cotton, Machine for topping	A. A. Dickson	Griffin, Ga	Oct. 4, 1853	10, 065
Cotton, Machine for whipping and cleaning	S. P. Mason	Killingly, Conn	July 8, 1834	....
Cotton, Machine for winding	D. Brown, jr	Warren, R. I	Feb. 5, 1807	....
Cotton, Machinery for cleaning	S. W. Brown	Lowell, Mass	Sept. 8, 1855	13, 564
Cotton, Machinery for cleaning	R. M. Livingston	Mobile, Ala	Mar. 6, 1847	4, 999
Cotton, Machinery for cleaning	R. Needham	Memphis, Tenn	Mar. 13, 1847	5, 008
Cotton, Machinery for combing	M. D. Whipple	Charlestown, Mass	Oct. 26, 1858	21, 932
Cotton, Machinery for ginning or picking	F. A. Calvert	Lowell, Mass	Sept. 17, 1850	7, 646
Cotton, &c., Machinery for picking	R. Kitson	Lowell, Mass	Oct. 31, 1854	11, 865
Cotton-machinery, Sizing-roll for	J. M. Dunlop	Manchester, Great Britain	Nov. 1, 1864	44, 911
Cotton, Manner of constructing and affixing the ribs of saw-gins for ginning.	A. Copeland	Bridgewater, Mass	Apr. 8, 1840	1, 547
Cotton, Manufacturing	E. Congdon	Norwich, Conn	Mar. 12, 1824	....
Cotton, Manufacturing	J. T. Sharrock	Winchester, Va	June 20, 1823	....
Cotton, Mode of making machine and hand cards for	W. Barker	Smithfield, R. I	Aug. 12, 1815	....
Cotton, Mode of packing	W. C. Thomas	Richmond, Va	Feb. 15, 1827	....
Cotton-opener	R. Kitson	Lowell, Mass	Oct. 4, 1870	107, 922
Cotton-opener	R. Kitson	Lowell, Mass	Nov. 11, 1873	144, 394
Cotton-openers, &c., Feed-mechanism for	W. Noton	Oldham, England	Feb. 25, 1873	136, 173
Cotton-openers, &c., Feed-regulator for	D. Harding	Lowell, Mass	Aug. 26, 1873	142, 101
Cotton-openers, Feed-regulator for	R. Kitson	Lowell, Mass	Dec. 9, 1873	145, 300
Cotton openers, &c., Feeding-mechanism for	W. E. Whitehead	Miles Platting, England	Dec. 20, 1870	110, 318
Cotton opening and cleaning machine	S. Fay	Lowell, Mass	Jan. 22, 1867	61, 411
Cotton opening and cleaning machine	R. Kitson	Lowell, Mass	Dec. 11, 1866	60, 387
Cotton-opening machine	W. C. Jillson and A. B. Palmer	Willimantic, Conn	Dec. 20, 1870	110, 368

Index of patents issued from the United States Patent Office from 1790 *to* 1873, *inclusive*—Continued.

Invention.	Inventor.	Residence.	Date.	No.
Cotton or hay press	J. S. Allums	Cuseta, Ga	Dec. 18, 1866	60, 457
Cotton or hay press	U. Page	Ringgold, La	July 5, 1870	104, 991
Cotton or hay press	J. Wentz	Girard, Ala	Apr. 14, 1868	76, 860
Cotton or other bale-goods, Machine for pressing	J. Idler		Sept. 24, 1802	....
Cotton or wool, Machinery for roving	W. Whitehead	Paterson, N. J	Apr. 11, 1825	....
Cotton or wool, Vibrating rolling-machine for	J. Hopkins	Strasburgh, Pa	Jan. 14, 1824	....
Cotton or woolen can	H. W. Shepard	New York, N. Y	Feb. 11, 1873	135, 853
Cotton or woolen can	H. W. Shepard	New York, N. Y	Feb. 11, 1873	135, 854
Cotton-packer	L. S. Chichester	New York, N. Y	Dec. 20, 1859	26, 546
Cotton, Packing	W. Hart	Petersburgh, Va	May 4, 1825	....
Cotton, Packing and pressing	J. Mead	Aurora, Ind	Aug. 14, 1847	5, 235
Cotton-packing machine	W. J. Cocke	Cabin Point, Va	Feb. 4, 1828	....
Cotton-packing machine	J. Cooke	Fayetteville, N. C	Oct. 12, 1821	....
Cotton-packing machine	L. Laysard	Halifax, N. C	Sept. 28, 1825	....
Cotton-picker	W. Apperly	Louisville, Ky	Aug. 2, 1870	106, 022
Cotton-picker	J. E. Carver	Bridgewater, Mass	May 14, 1867	64, 629
Cotton-picker	R. F. Cooke	Newark, N. J	May 26, 1868	78, 362
Cotton-picker	R. F. Cooke	Brooklyn, N. Y	Mar. 29, 1870	101, 231
Cotton-picker	B. I. Dreeson	Marion County, Tex	Oct. 18, 1870	108, 461
Cotton-picker	B. J. Dreeson and J. L. Buskett	Schleswig, Germany, and Saint Louis, Mo.	July 4, 1871	116, 694
Cotton-picker	W. Goodwin and S. D. G. Niles	Helena, Ark	Mar. 28, 1871	113, 159
Cotton-picker	J. Griffin	Louisville, Ky	July 3, 1860	28, 980
Cotton-picker	J. Griffin	Louisville, Ky	Jan. 22, 1861	31, 165
Cotton-picker	J. Griffin	Louisville, Ky	Mar. 5, 1861	31, 596
Cotton-picker	G. A. Howe	Brooklyn, N. Y	Mar. 13, 1866	53, 147
Cotton-picker	G. A. Howe	Brooklyn, N. Y	Mar. 27, 1866	53, 447
Cotton-picker	J. Hughes	New Berne, N. C	Mar. 28, 1871	113, 170
Cotton-picker	L. Jennings	Brooklyn, N. Y	July 31, 1860	29, 435
Cotton-picker	W. D. Ludlow	New York, N. Y	Jan. 30, 1866	52, 303
Cotton-picker	D. M. McRae	Webberville, Tex	Aug. 23, 1870	106, 601
Cotton-picker	J. G. Page	Memphis, Tenn	Dec. 4, 1866	60, 235
Cotton, &c., picker	G. F. Palmer	Rochester, N. H	Feb. 8, 1870	99, 699
Cotton-picker	C. Payne and B. Vandecar	Brandon, Vt., and Waterford, N. Y.	Feb. 11, 1868	74, 242
Cotton-picker	A. Pettingill	East Livermore, Me	Jan. 5, 1869	85, 532
Cotton-picker	N. F. Sandelin	New York, N. Y	Mar. 26, 1872	124, 978
Cotton-picker	I. S. Schuyler	New York, N. Y	July 30, 1861	32, 968
Cotton-picker	B. G. Shields	Marlin, Tex	Sept. 16, 1856	15, 746
Cotton-picker	Z. B. Sims	Bonham, Tex	Sept. 3, 1872	131, 124
Cotton-picker	H. Stevens	Memphis, Tenn	Oct. 25, 1864	44, 828
Cotton-picker	A. Tiensch	Memphis, Tenn	Apr. 10, 1866	53, 901
Cotton picker and cleaner	S. H. Gilman	Galveston, Tex	Sept. 1, 1868	81, 622
Cotton picker and cleaner	Z. B. Sims	Bonham, Tex	Aug. 31, 1869	94, 352
Cotton, Picker and lap machine for manufacturing	J. Whitehead	Godwinville, N. J	July 22, 1833	....
Cotton-picker cylinder	J. Pitts	Lancaster, Mass	Feb. 28, 1854	10, 578
Cotton-picker, Electrical	R. F. Cook	Brooklyn, N. Y	June 7, 1870	103, 986
Cotton-picker, Hand	W. B. Cargill	Waterbury, Conn	Mar. 6, 1860	27, 348
Cotton-picker, Hand	G. A. Howe	Worcester, Mass	Dec. 4, 1855	13, 877
Cotton-picker wallet	G. H. Peabody	Columbus, Ga	Nov. 29, 1859	26, 288
Cotton-pickers, Screen-cylinder for	R. Kitson	Lowell, Mass	Apr. 21, 1868	76, 926
Cotton-picking device	J. Griffin	Louisville, Ky	June 5, 1866	55, 283
Cotton-picking machine	J. Pinnell and H. Maxon	Barbourville, Va	Sept. 10, 1828	....
Cotton-picking machine	W. E. Prall	Knoxville, Tenn	Feb. 27, 1866	52, 880
Cotton-plant protector	A. L. Blanc	Louisiana, La	Mar. 22, 1870	101, 028
Cotton-plants, Apparatus for destroying worms on	M. Perl	Houston, Tex	June 15, 1869	91, 365
Cotton-plants, Destroying worms in	T. W. Mitchell	Richmond, Tex	Jan. 3, 1871	110, 774
Cotton-plants, Machine for cutting up	B. T. Currier	Bath, Me	Mar. 6, 1860	27, 352
Cotton-plants, Machine for destroying worms on	W. Ewing	Columbia, La	Oct. 19, 1869	95, 995
Cotton-plants, Machine for thinning	C. A. McCaughan	Moscow, Tenn	Feb. 5, 1867	61, 845
Cotton-plants, Machine for thinning	J. Weaver	Washington, D. C	July 5, 1837	253
Cotton-plants, Preventing rot &c., in	S. W. Pomeroy	Brighton, Mass	May 6, 1824	....
Cotton-press	E. H. Adams	Taladega, Ala	May 17, 1859	23, 995
Cotton-press	W. W. Anderson	Wartrace, Tenn	Jan. 16, 1872	122, 752
Cotton-press	J. B. Armstrong	Barnwell D., S. C	Dec. 20, 1853	10, 329
Cotton press	T. Ashcraft	Randolph County, Ala	Mar. 6, 1849	6, 158
Cotton-press	Z. Atkinson	Richmond, Ga	Feb. 1, 1859	22, 775
Cotton-press	A. Baldwin	New York, N. Y	Oct. 5, 1869	95, 411
Cotton-press	W. C. Banks	Como Depot, Miss	June 18, 1867	65, 865
Cotton-press	W. C Banks	Como Depot, Miss	Jan. 23, 1872	122, 983
Cotton-press	C. J. Beasley	Petersburgh, Va	Sept. 21, 1869	94, 993
Cotton press	C. J. Beasley	Petersburgh, Va	Feb. 22, 1870	100, 105
Cotton-press	C. J. Beasley	Petersburgh, Va	Nov. 28, 1871	121, 317
Cotton-press	W. I. Blackman	Columbus, Miss	June 14, 1870	104, 103
Cotton-press	J. P. Bolin	Orangeburgh County, S. C	June 20, 1871	116, 144
Cotton-press	S. Booton	Seguin, Tex	Oct. 18, 1870	108, 320
Cotton-press	T. J. Bottoms and J. A. Bullock	Thomas County, Ga	Aug. 31, 1858	21, 317
Cotton-press	M. W. Bradford	Greenwood, La	Mar. 5, 1872	124, 245
Cotton-press	W. Bradley	West Point, Ga	June 18, 1872	128, 104
Cotton-press	J. M. Brooks, jr	Griffin, Ga	Mar. 11, 1873	136, 697
Cotton-press	R. M. Brooks	Greenville, Ga	Oct. 2, 1860	30, 200
Cotton-press	R. M. Brooks	Woodbury, Ga	Apr. 14, 1868	76, 593
Cotton-press	R. M. Brooks	U. S., Ga	Mar. 7, 1871	112, 413
Cotton-press	A. D. Brown	Clinton, Ga	Jan. 22, 1850	7, 047
Cotton-press	W. Bullock	Jersey City, N. J	Jan. 4, 1845	3, 873
Cotton-press	C. A. Caldwell	Concord, N. C	Oct. 5, 1869	95, 563
Cotton-press	J. Carson	Raleigh, N. C	Nov. 4, 1830	....
Cotton-press	F. A. L. Cassidey	Newnansville, Fla	May 14, 1867	64, 630
Cotton-press	J. Chambers	Alexandria, La	May 19, 1843	3, 087
Cotton-press	N. Chapman	Mystic River, Conn	Aug. 8, 1854	11, 472
Cotton-press	N. Chapman	Mystic River, Conn	Jan. 12, 1858	19, 071
Cotton-press	N. Cheek	Chapel Hill, N. C	Dec. 27, 1870	110, 549
Cotton-press	C. C. Conner	Ripley, Tenn	Apr. 4, 1871	113, 265
Cotton-press	C. C. Conner	Ripley, Tenn	July 23, 1872	129, 792
Cotton-press	W. P. Craig	Newport, Ky	May 7, 1861	32, 240
Cotton-press	J. G. Cummings	Columbus, Miss	Aug. 20, 1867	67, 961
Cotton-press	G. C. Davies	Dayton, Ohio	Apr. 25, 1865	47, 490
Cotton-press	H. J. Davis	Wetumpka, Ala	May 2, 1871	114, 271

Index of patents issued from the United States Patent Office from 1790 *to* 1873, *inclusive*—Continued.

Invention.	Inventor.	Residence.	Date.	No.
Cotton-press	T. F. De Bruler	Rockport, Ind	Apr. 26, 1859	23, 759
Cotton-press	P. K. Dederick	Albany, N. Y	Jan. 7, 1873	134, 592
Cotton-press	J. P. Derden	Bastrop, La	Mar. 4, 1873	136, 422
Cotton-press	A. Devall	New Orleans, La	Apr. 17, 1847	5, 067
Cotton-press	S. Dike	Columbia, S. C	Oct. 16, 1860	30, 394
Cotton-press	J. A. Disbrow and J. E. Cronk	Poughkeepsie, N. Y	Feb. 2, 1858	19, 279
Cotton-press	E. Duchamp	Saint Martinsville, La	Feb. 23, 1858	19, 413
Cotton-press	J. C. Duvoll	Sardis, Miss	June 11, 1867	65, 655
Cotton-press	E. N. Elliott	Port Gibson, Miss	Nov. 22, 1859	26, 174
Cotton-press	J. T. Elliot	Carrollton, Miss	Oct. 22, 1850	7, 731
Cotton-press	G. Faulkner	Warrenton, N. C	Apr. 30, 1872	126, 194
Cotton-press	C. I. Fay	North Lincoln, Me	Jan. 31, 1854	10, 472
Cotton-press	W. Field	Providence, R. I	Apr. 6, 1858	19, 838
Cotton-press	G. Fitz	Clinton, Miss	June 3, 1837	224
Cotton-press	S. Fry	New York, N. Y	May 7, 1842	2, 611
Cotton-press	H. H. Fultz	Lexington, Mass	Aug. 14, 1855	13, 426
Cotton-press	C. Gardiner	Richmond, Ala	Oct. 16, 1847	5, 332
Cotton-press	P. G. Gardiner	New York, N. Y	Mar. 20, 1844	3, 503
Cotton-press	P. G. Gardiner	New York, N. Y	Sept. 4, 1860	29, 874
Cotton-press	P. G. Gardiner	New York, N. Y	Oct. 23, 1860	30, 473
Cotton-press	P. G. Gardiner	New York, N. Y	Mar. 26, 1861	31, 796
Cotton-press	F. Gilbert	Natchez, Miss	Apr. 9, 1861	31, 967
Cotton-press	G. Glenn	Louisburgh, N. C	Apr. 12, 1826	....
Cotton-press	A. M. Glover	Waterborough, S. C	July 3, 1855	13, 199
Cotton-press	G. W. Grader	Memphis, Tenn	Sept. 26, 1871	119, 346
Cotton-press	J. B. Gridley	Louisville, Ky	Feb. 14, 1871	111, 739
Cotton-press	I. Griffin	Milford, Ga	Jan. 8, 1861	31, 070
Cotton-press	J. H. Groves	Greenwood, Miss	Jan. 2, 1872	22, 458
Cotton-press	J. T. Ham	Sinatobia, Miss	Jan. 10, 1860	26, 764
Cotton-press	M. B. Hand	Handsborough, Miss	Aug. 16, 1859	25, 161
Cotton-press	R. J. Harrison	Raleigh, N. C	Feb. 14, 1871	111, 840
Cotton-press	J. Hawthorn	Thomas County, Ga	May 17, 1859	24, 026
Cotton-press	W. Haynie	Memphis, Tenn	Dec. 6, 1870	109, 897
Cotton-press	J. R. Hitchcock and W. F. Serrel.	New York, N. Y	Sept. 30, 1839	1, 349
Cotton-press	C. C. Howard	Lowndesborough, Ala	Mar. 11, 1873	136, 725
Cotton-press	H. Hughes	Port Gibson, Miss	May 12, 1857	17, 278
Cotton-press	C. S. Hunt	Bridgewater, Mass	Jan. 15, 1856	14, 098
Cotton-press	T. R. Jackson	Dallas, Tex	Sept. 30, 1873	143, 349
Cotton-press	R. Jernigan	Waynesborough, N. C	May 15, 1827	....
Cotton-press	W. J. Johnson	Mobile, Ala	Mar. 13, 1849	6, 175
Cotton-press	A. Jones	New Orleans, La	Oct. 26, 1838	992
Cotton-press	M. M. Jones	Morrisville, N. Y	May 15, 1860	28, 281
Cotton-press	J. B. Knight	New Orleans, La	Sept 26, 1871	119, 367
Cotton-press	W. W. Knowles	Bastrop, Tex	Aug. 30, 1870	106, 833
Cotton-press	S. Lamb	New York, N. Y	May 12, 1843	3, 086
Cotton-press	S. Lamb	New York, N. Y	Mar. 16, 1844	3, 489
Cotton-press	W. D. Leavitt	New Orleans, La	Aug. 20, 1872	130, 728
Cotton-press	T. D. Leonard	Waco, Tex	Nov. 18, 1873	144, 775
Cotton-press	L. Lewis	Vicksburgh, Miss	Mar. 2, 1852	8, 774
Cotton-press	L. Lewis	Vicksburgh, Miss	Aug. 17, 1852	9, 197
Cotton-press	L. Lewis	Vicksburgh, Miss	Oct. 17, 1871	119, 934
Cotton-press	R. Lewis	Charleston, S. C	Mar. 18, 1873	136, 841
Cotton-press	N. I. Lilly	Selma, Ala	Mar. 8, 1859	23, 180
Cotton-press	E. W. Long and I. N. Patten	Memphis, Tenn	Mar. 21, 1871	112, 822
Cotton-press	C. N. Lovejoy	Columbia, S. C	Oct. 25, 1859	25, 904
Cotton-press	J. Loving	Moscow, Tenn	Mar. 9, 1858	19, 571
Cotton-press	M. Lynch	Horn Lake, Miss	July 30, 1872	130, 060
Cotton-press	B. G. Martin	New York, N. Y	Mar. 18, 1873	136, 846
Cotton-press	C. Martratt	Waterford, N. Y	Oct. 26, 1858	21, 894
Cotton-press	H. Mason	Lancaster, Mass	July 24, 1860	29, 290
Cotton-press	R. Mauldin	Marietta, Miss	Aug. 15, 1871	118, 142
Cotton-press	A. Z. McBride	Hannahatchee, Ga	Feb. 5, 1861	31, 323
Cotton-press	T. H. McCray	Tellico, Tex	Mar. 13, 1860	27, 459
Cotton-press	E. McDonnell	Baltimore, Md	Mar. 19, 1867	62, 965
Cotton-press	A. B. McGennigil	Helena, Ark	July 4, 1871	116, 733
Cotton-press	J. W. McIntyre	Memphis, Tenn	Apr. 16, 1867	63, 916
Cotton-press	T. E. McNeill	Lynchburgh, Va	Nov. 20, 1866	59, 853
Cotton-press	J. W. Miller	Shannon, Miss	May 14, 1872	126, 731
Cotton-press	C. W. Millerd	Monticello, Ark	Mar. 23, 1869	88, 159
Cotton-press	G. Milliran	Byhalia, Miss	June 5, 1860	28, 592
Cotton-press	J. Mitchell	Rutherford, Tenn	Mar 12, 1836	....
Cotton-press	J. J. Morrison	Atlanta, Ga	Mar. 2, 1869	87, 505
Cotton-press	M. Murchison	Denmark, Tenn	Oct. 23, 1860	30, 493
Cotton-press	W. B. North	Jersey City, N. J	June 13, 1848	5, 632
Cotton-press	D. G. Olmstead	Vicksburgh, Miss	Jan. 26, 1858	19, 202
Cotton-press	W. T. Opie	Scarborough, Ga	Sept. 4, 1860	29, 904
Cotton-press	M. L. Parry	Galveston, Tex	Jan. 27, 1857	16, 494
Cotton-press	W. W. Patrick	Midway, S. C	June 17, 1873	139, 970
Cotton-press	I. N. Patten and E. W. Long	Shelby County, Tenn	Dec. 20, 1870	110, 278
Cotton-press	P. Payne	Claiborne County, Miss	Aug. 10, 1829	....
Cotton-press	P. Payne and J. Rundell	Port Gibson, Miss	July 20, 1831	....
Cotton-press	P. Payne and J. Rundell	Claiborne County, Miss	Jan. 25, 1833	....
Cotton-press	G. Peck	Fairfield, Conn	Mar. 9, 1844	3, 466
Cotton-press	W. Pendleton and H. M. Boardman.	Augusta, Ga	May 10, 1870	102, 963
Cotton-press	D. Philips	Natchez, Miss	Apr. 27, 1832	....
Cotton-press	P. W. Porter	Columbia, Tenn	Aug. 11, 1842	2, 752
Cotton-press	R. Powers	Charleston, Miss	Feb. 4, 1873	135, 486
Cotton-press	J. Prescott	Memphis, Tenn	Nov. 9, 1844	3, 815
Cotton-press	J. Price	Nashville, Tenn	Dec. 7, 1839	1, 426
Cotton-press	J. P. Pridgeon	Marion Court-House, S. C	July 15, 1873	140, 841
Cotton-press	W. F. Provost	Barnwell D., S. C	Sept. 14, 1844	3, 739
Cotton-press	W. F. and C. J. Provost	Barnwell D., S. C	Nov. 21, 1843	3, 347
Cotton-press	W. F. and C. J. Provost	Selma, Ala	Nov. 20, 1855	13, 826
Cotton-press	W. F. and C. J. Provost	Selma, Ala	Oct. 21, 1856	15, 936
Cotton-press	H. W. Randle	Burnsville, Ala	Feb. 16, 1858	19, 381
Cotton-press	H. W. Randle	Burnsville, Ala	May 3, 1859	23, 860

Index of patents issued from the United States Patent Office from 1790 *to* 1873, *inclusive*—Continued.

Invention.	Inventor.	Residence.	Date.	No.
Cotton-press	F. M. Ray	Catskill, N. Y	Aug. 25, 1840	1, 738
Cotton-press	S. S. Rembert	Memphis, Tenn	Aug. 22, 1871	118, 275
Cotton-press	J. R. Remington	Montgomery, Ala	Apr. 15, 1843	3, 051
Cotton-press	W. H. Reynolds	New Orleans, La	May 6, 1873	138, 583
Cotton-press	S. D. Roberts	Washington, La	July 2, 1867	66, 394
Cotton-press	H. Ross	Rockport, Ind	Mar. 23, 1858	19, 714
Cotton-press	I. G. Roux	Raymond, Miss	Mar. 29, 1859	23, 397
Cotton-press	T. H. Scarborough	Brownsville, Tenn	Oct. 16, 1834	....
Cotton-press	M. M. Scherer	Batesville, Ark	Sept. 2, 1873	142, 517
Cotton-press	J. Schley	Savannah, Ga	Aug. 15, 1871	118, 060
Cotton-press	R. Scott, jr	Madison, Ind	Oct. 9, 1860	30, 356
Cotton-press	J. C. Sellers	Woodville, Miss	Aug. 28, 1860	29, 827
Cotton-press	W. Sewell, jr	Macon, Ga	June 15, 1844	3, 631
Cotton-press	W. A. Shepard	New York, N. Y	Oct. 24, 1865	50, 635
Cotton-press	H. Shrader	Burnsville, Ala	Mar. 30, 1858	19, 821
Cotton press	F. Simmons	New Orleans, La	Apr. 25, 1871	114, 056
Cotton-press	T. D. Simpson and W. S. Lamkin.	Marshall, Tex	Dec. 26, 1871	122, 197
Cotton-press	J. Slocum	Syracuse, N. Y	Apr. 16, 1845	3, 997
Cotton-press	R. Smith	Towanda, Pa	May 29, 1847	5, 135
Cotton-press	R. Smith	Towanda, Pa	Dec. 29, 1857	18, 995
Cotton-press	T. S. Smith	Tooner's Station, Tenn	July 29, 1873	141, 393
Cotton-press	N. W. Speers	Memphis, Tenn	Dec. 20, 1870	110, 304
Cotton-press	W. T. Stewart	Moscow, Tenn	July 30, 1872	129, 9[illegible]8
Cotton-press	H. D. Stover and W. Hutchinson.	New York, N. Y	Oct. 8, 1867	69, 721
Cotton-press	E. Stuart	Shufordsville, Miss	July 23, 1867	67, 147
Cotton-press	U. T. Stuart and C. E. Stewart	Fayette County, Tenn	Mar. 8, 1859	23, 201
Cotton-press	W. H. Tappey, W. C. Lumsden, and A. Steel.	Petersburgh, Va	Sept. 15, 1868	82, 178
Cotton-press	J. Templeton	Florence, Ga	Sept. 5, 1871	118, 756
Cotton-press	D. R. Torbet	Columbus, Ga	July 30, 1867	67, 230
Cotton-press	P. B. Tyler	Philadelphia, Pa	Jan. 16, 1845	3, 885
Cotton-press	G. Utley	Chapel Hill, N. C	Feb. 21, 1871	112, 095
Cotton-press	W. C. Van Hoesen	Catskill, N. Y	Apr. 2, 1841	2, 026
Cotton-press	W. C. Van Hoesen	Catskill, N. Y	Feb. 1, 1842	2, 445
Cotton-press	I. J. Way	Memphis, Tenn	Nov. 14, 1865	50, 971
Cotton, &c., press	W. and D. K. West	Kentish Town, England	July 16, 1872	129, 636
Cotton-press	P. B. Wever	Scarborough, Ga	Aug. 21, 1860	29, 736
Cotton-press	O. Whitney	Augusta, Me	Mar. 17, 1843	3, 006
Cotton-press	D. Wilkinson	North Providence, R. I	Dec. 8, 1825	....
Cotton-press	J. T. Williams	Blakely, Ga	Dec. 17, 1872	134, 021
Cotton-press	P. Williams	Lodi, Miss	Dec. 27, 1859	27, 635
Cotton-press	P. Williams	Winona, Miss	Jan. 21, 1868	73, 683
Cotton-press	P. and R. A. Williams	Winona, Miss	Sept. 16, 1873	142, 882
Cotton-press	R. G. Williams	Hannahatchee, Ga	July 20, 1858	20, 973
Cotton-press	U. T. Wilson	Independence, Miss	July 11, 1871	117, 027
Cotton-press	J. G. Winger	Vicksburgh, Miss	July 13, 1852	9, 124
Cotton-press	F. W. Witting	Yorktown, Tex	Feb. 16, 1858	19, 399
Cotton-press	D. H. Wooldridge	Humboldt, Tenn	June 10, 1873	139, 845
Cotton-press	P. M. Wright	New York, N. Y	Nov. 26, 1844	3, 835
Cotton-press	Y. F. Wright	Green Hill, Ga	May 1, 1860	28, 124
Cotton-press	Y. F. Wright	Green Hill, Ga	July 30, 1867	67, 243
Cotton-press	R. N. Wyatt	Tehula, Miss	Mar. 5, 1872	124, 307
Cotton-press and feeder	H. Zellner	Columbia, Tenn	Oct. 15, 1867	69, 887
Cotton-press and horse-power combined	J. M. Albertson	New London, Conn	Oct. 10, 1871	119, 731
Cotton press and tramper	C. K. Marshall	New Orleans, La	Apr. 18, 1871	113, 901
Cotton press, gin, and horse-power combined	J. M. Shaw, sr	Water Valley, Miss	May 28, 1872	127, 276
Cotton-press, Horizontal rack and pinion	Z. Bronson	Jasper County, Ga	July 7, 1829	....
Cotton-press, Lever	C. Williams	Petersburgh, Va	June 3, 1826	....
Cotton-press, Self-acting	J. Grout	Hocking City, Ohio	June 12, 1855	13, 000
Cotton-press, Steam	A. Baldwin	New York, N. Y	May 17, 1870	103, 123
Cotton-press, Steam	T. J. De Yampert	Mobile, Ala	Oct. 27, 1857	18, 502
Cotton-press, Steam	C. Hurst	New Orleans, La	Aug. 22, 1848	5, 730
Cotton-press, Steam	J. Roy	New Orleans, La	Dec. 15, 1857	18, 864
Cotton-press, Water-power	J. Durden	Washington, Ala	June 23, 1825	....
Cotton-presses, Self-releasing door of	G. W. Penniston	North Vernon, Ind	Apr. 14, 1857	17, 053
Cotton-pressing and packing machine	J. H. McClelland	Fairfield District, S. C	Dec. 28, 1826	....
Cotton-pressing machine	J. Boatwright and J. Nathans	Richland, S. C	Nov. 21, 1826	....
Cotton-pressing machine	J. N. Gordon	Plymouth, N. C	Oct. 8, 1825	....
Cotton-pressing machine	F. Shaler	Georgetown, Ohio	May 5, 1824	....
Cotton-pressing machine	R. V. W. and J. Thorne	New York, N. Y	Feb. 22, 1810	....
Cotton-pressing machine	P. White	Chatham County, N. C	Feb. 19, 1827	....
Cotton, Process of treating raw	J. C. Hurd	Medway, Mass	May 12, 1857	17, 279
Cotton-railways, Drawing-head for	W. B. Leonard	Fishkill, N. Y	Sept. 16, 1833	....
Cotton-renovating machine	J. B. Lyons	Milton, Conn	Dec. 13, 1870	110, 149
Cotton-rolls, Process for utilizing immature	J. Hughes	New Berne, N. C	May 23, 1871	115, 209
Cotton roller-gin	W. Whittemore, jr	West Cambridge, Mass	Mar. 7, 1834	....
Cotton roller-gin	W. Whittemore, jr	West Cambridge, Mass	May 29, 1835	....
Cotton, Rolling-machine for cleaning	G. F. Saltonstall		May 14, 1803	....
Cotton, Rolling or twisting rovings of	W. Whitehead, jr	Paterson, N. J	June 14, 1826	....
Cotton, &c., Roping	L. Brewster	Poughkeepsie, N. Y	Dec. 17, 1834	....
Cotton, Roping	W. Fowler	Fishkill, N. Y	Mar. 23, 1836	....
Cotton roping, Machine for making	P. Moody	Boston, Mass	Jan. 19, 1821	....
Cotton roping, Machine for making	S. Shepard	Taunton, Mass	Mar. 23, 1821	....
Cotton, Roping, twisting, and winding	D. Grive	Providence, R. I	Sept. 18, 1818	....
Cotton-roping, Counter-twist speeder for	J. Whitehead	Manchester, Va	May 29, 1841	2, 108
Cotton roping, Machine for making	J. Whitehead	Manchester, Va	June 24, 1839	1, 186
Cotton roping, slack threads, &c., Making	S. Whiting	Franklin, Mass	Nov. 17, 1824	....
Cotton, Roving	J. A. Bradshaw	Foxborough, Mass	Dec. 8, 1832	....
Cotton-roving, Drawing-can for	M. Mead	Lowell, Mass	May 6, 1862	35, 169
Cotton-roving machine	A. Arnold	North Providence, R. I	Jan. 21, 1823	....
Cotton-roving machine	W. Bryant	Davidson County, Tenn	Apr. 29, 1816	....
Cotton roving, &c., Machine for condensing or preparing.	J. Graves	New Ipswich, N. H	Sept. 1, 1843	3, 250
Cotton-roving machines, Speeder for	W. Mason	Taunton, Mass	May 4, 1838	724
Cotton roving, Manufacturing	G. Brewster	Poughkeepsie, N. Y	Mar. 28, 1827	....
Cotton, Roving or roping	L. H. Mosely	Lisbon, Conn	Nov. 19, 1833	....

Index of patents issued from the United States Patent Office from 1790 *to* 1873, *inclusive*—Continued.

Invention.	Inventor.	Residence.	Date.	No.
Cotton roving, Speeder for making	S. P. Mason	Leesville, Conn	Dec. 29, 1830	....
Cotton-sampling borer	E. A. Clark	Jackson, Tenn	Aug. 19, 1873	141,998
Cotton, Saw-mill for cleaning	G. F. Saltonstall		Jan. 4, 1803	....
Cotton-scraper	C. H. Burbidge	Middletown, Conn	Nov. 27, 1860	30,718
Cotton-scraper	J. M. Cobb	Jackson, Tenn	June 26, 1860	28,835
Cotton-scraper	I. W. Collins and R. Y. Wilkinson.	Clinton, La	Nov. 27, 1860	30,721
Cotton-scraper	M. Earnhart	Cold Water, Miss	Nov. 15, 1859	26,096
Cotton-scraper	W. C. Finney	Fayette County, Tenn	Apr. 24, 1849	6,379
Cotton-scraper	T. T. Fleming	Memphis, Tenn	Aug. 27, 1867	68,296
Cotton-scraper	C. A. Gaines	Watson, Miss	Oct. 5, 1858	21,667
Cotton-scraper	J. Henderson	Bluff Springs, Miss	Mar. 8, 1859	23,171
Cotton-scraper	J. D. Houston	Pope's Depot, Miss	Jan. 15, 1861	31,122
Cotton-scraper	W. Jarrell	Humboldt, Tenn	July 29, 1873	141,355
Cotton scraper	I. J. Kidd	Young's Settlement, Tex	Apr. 28, 1868	77,292
Cotton-scraper	W. L. Millholen	Centre, Ala	Nov. 27, 1860	30,746
Cotton-scraper	J. H. Mitchell	Germantown, Tenn	Sept. 13, 1859	25,434
Cotton-scraper	P. Sharkey	Brownsville, Miss	Apr. 26, 1859	23,788
Cotton-scraper	J. S. Smith	Helena, Ark	Feb. 9, 1869	86,704
Cotton-scraper	H. Starke	Wilkinson County, Miss	Feb. 3, 1824	....
Cotton-scraper	A. W. Washburn	Yazoo City, Miss	Mar. 25, 1856	14,540
Cotton-scraper	J. G. Winger	Vicksburgh, Miss	Oct. 27, 1857	18,525
Cotton scraper and chopper	N. M. Hale	Cleborne, Tex	Nov. 8, 1870	109,124
Cotton scraper and cultivator, Combined	B. F. Bowling	Holly Springs, Miss	Dec. 28, 1869	98,341
Cotton, Screen for machine for treating	R. Kitson	Lowell, Mass	Aug. 11, 1868	80,975
Cotton-seed and corn grinding machine	J. Martin	Petersburgh, Va	May 16, 1835	....
Cotton-seed and guano distributer	J. T. Graves	Wilson, N. C	Oct. 18, 1870	108,349
Cotton seed and rice hulling	J. Kellogg	New Hanover County, N. C	Mar. 30, 1835	....
Cotton-seed cleaner	T. W. Brown	Cudworth, Barnsley, England.	Aug. 4, 1868	80,593
Cotton-seed cleaner	W. H. Delamere	Deptford, England	May 28, 1872	127,224
Cotton-seed cleaner	A. Wells	Morgantown, W. Va	Dec. 4, 1866	60,300
Cotton-seed-cleaning machine	A. I. Hardin	Shelby, N. C	Nov. 6, 1860	30,573
Cotton seed-cleaning process	J. G. Page	Rockford, Ill	Dec. 26, 1865	51,745
Cotton-seed heater	W. M. Force	Newark, N. J	Mar. 26, 1872	124,945
Cotton-seed huller	H. C. Bradford	Providence, R. I	Jan. 17, 1871	111,034
Cotton-seed huller	W. P. Callahan and D. R. De Bush.	Dayton, Ohio	Jan. 18, 1870	98,921
Cotton-seed huller	W. R. Fee	Cincinnati, Ohio	Sept. 13, 1870	107,349
Cotton-seed huller	W. R. Fee	Cincinnati, Ohio	Nov. 1, 1870	108,896
Cotton-seed huller	J. Harrington	New London, Conn	Dec. 13, 1870	110,134
Cotton-seed huller	L. Johnson	Madison, Ga	May 29, 1833	....
Cotton-seed huller	C. A. Lowber	Medina, N. Y	Dec. 6, 1859	26,372
Cotton-seed huller	P. Martin	New Orleans, La	July 31, 1860	29,393
Cotton-seed huller	G. H. Peabody	New York, N. Y	July 27, 1869	92,997
Cotton-seed huller	J. Perkins	Providence, R. I	June 19, 1866	55,701
Cotton-seed huller	P. Reading	Trenton, N. J	Apr. 13, 1836	....
Cotton-seed huller	E. C. Singer	New Orleans, La	July 5, 1870	105,136
Cotton-seed huller	J. D. Stillman	Memphis, Tenn	June 29, 1869	91,880
Cotton-seed huller	W. H. Trott, D. R. Torbett, and F. A. Pomeroy.	Columbus, Ga	Jan. 2, 1872	122,341
Cotton-seed huller	A. J. Vandegrift	Covington, Ky	June 28, 1870	104,799
Cotton-seed huller	F. A. Wells	Memphis, Tenn	Oct. 26, 1869	96,177
Cotton-seed huller	W. Wilber	New Orleans, La	Sept. 11, 1855	13,556
Cotton-seed, Hulling	H. Hubbard	Claremont, N. H	Apr. 19, 1834	....
Cotton-seed, Hulling	J. Walker	Dover, England	Mar. 27, 1855	12,610
Cotton-seed hulling and separating machine	W. Wilber	New York, N. Y	Jan. 27, 1857	16,509
Cotton-seed-hulling machine	W. R. Fee	Cincinnati, Ohio	Aug. 11, 1857	17,961
Cotton-seed-hulling machine	J. Lineback	Salem, N. C	Mar. 31, 1814	....
Cotton-seed-hulling machine	Miller and Lawes	Washington County, Miss	Oct. 27, 1835	....
Cotton-seed-hulling machine	J. B. Ruperts	Jersey City, N. J	Jan. 30, 1866	52,321
Cotton-seed-hulling machine	J. Smith	Petersburgh, Va	Mar. 15, 1845	3,951
Cotton-seed-hulling machine	J. Tiffany	Syracuse, N. Y	Sept. 18, 1860	30,096
Cotton-seed machine	F. A. E. G. De Massas	Hoxton, England	Jan. 16, 1866	52,116
Cotton-seed mill	I. F. Brown	New London, Conn	Jan. 23, 1872	122,877
Cotton-seed, rice, &c., machine	N. Mixon	Madison, Ga	Dec. 20, 1833	....
Cotton-seed separator and planter	S. W. Thompson	Otsego, Ohio	Oct. 19, 1869	96,054
Cotton seeds and motes, Machine for linting and relinting.	G. W. Grader	Memphis, Tenn	Aug. 31, 1869	94,304
Cotton-seeds and separating the hull from the kernel, Machine for hulling and husking.	F. Follet	Petersburgh, Va	Dec. 15, 1829	....
Cotton-seeds by roller gin, Separating	W. and W. Whittemore, jr	West Cambridge, Mass	Mar. 21, 1833	....
Cotton-seeds, Engine for separating fibers from the husks of.	T. Rose and R. E. Gibson	Earlestown, England	July 26, 1870	105,728
Cotton-seeds for extracting oil, Preparing	O. Reichenbach	Norristown Township, Pa.	Oct. 23, 1855	13,708
Cotton-seeds for planting, Machine for preparing	R. C. Wrenn	Covington, Ky	Dec. 4, 1855	13,894
Cotton seeds for planting, Method of preparing	W. Blessing	Jeffersonville, Ohio	July 3, 1866	56,140
Cotton-seeds for planting, Preparing	P. C. Ingersoll	Green Point, N. Y	June 25, 1867	66,089
Cotton-seeds for planting, Preparing	R. M. Lafferty	Three Rivers, Mich	July 7, 1868	79,765
Cotton-seeds, Hulling and breaking	C. Leck and W. Jenks	Columbia, S. C	Dec. 17, 1834	....
Cotton-seeds, Machine for detaching short fibers from.	L. P. Jenks	Boston, Mass	June 25, 1861	32,626
Cotton-seeds, Machine for hulling or husking	J. Smith	Petersburgh, Va	Dec. 28, 1829	....
Cotton-seeds, Machine for husking and separating the hulls from kernels of.	F. Follet	Petersburgh, Va	Jan. 21, 1829	....
Cotton-seeds, Machine for planting	N. E. Badgley	New York, N. Y	Oct. 16, 1866	58,752
Cotton-seeds, Machine for planting	I. W. McGaffey	Chicago, Ill	July 17, 1866	56,430
Cotton-seeds, Machine for removing lint from	W. F. Pratt	East Bridgewater, Mass	June 29, 1869	91,866
Cotton-seeds, Machinery for breaking	T. Rose and R. E. Gibson	Oxton and New Brighton, England.	July 27, 1869	93,124
Cotton-seeds, Process for hulling	D. W. Messer	Boston, Mass	July 24, 1855	13,317
Cotton-seeds, Process of cleaning	J. Kirkman	Peoria, Ill	Nov. 26, 1867	71,499
Cotton-seeds, Process of separating fibers from	J. Duval	New Orleans, La	Aug. 2, 1870	105,923
Cotton-seeds, Treating	J. J. Powers	Memphis, Tenn	Mar. 14, 1871	112,628
Cotton, silk, &c., Roving, spinning, and doubling	J. Jones	Manchester, England	May 16, 1835	....
Cotton-sliver can	W. Hamer	Little Lever, near Bolton, England.	Oct. 8, 1867	69,658
Cotton-speeder	S. Parmelee	Poughkeepsie, N. Y	Aug. 29, 1833	....

Index of patents issued from the United States Patent Office from 1790 *to* 1873, *inclusive*—Continued.

Invention.	Inventor.	Residence.	Date.	No.
Cotton-spindle	N. Rider	Dudley, Mass	Nov. 3, 1832	....
Cotton-spindles, Step and bolster for	C. H. Chapman	Shirley, Mass	Feb. 8, 1870	99, 534
Cotton spreader and picker	J. C. Whitin	Northbridge, Mass	July 20, 1832	....
Cotton-stalk cutter or pulverizer	G. Gorman	Lamar, Miss	Sept. 20, 1853	10, 043
Cotton-stalk knocker	M. M. Carruth	Helena, Ark	Apr. 15, 1873	137, 825
Cotton-stalks in the field, Machine for cutting	F. Bradshaw	Greene County, Ala	Feb. 12, 1850	7, 078
Cotton-stalks, Machine for cutting standing	J. W. Bocage	Cypress Mills, Ark	Sept. 11, 1855	13, 538
Cotton-stalks, Machine for cutting standing	S. Bowerman	Detroit, Mich	Aug. 28, 1855	13, 505
Cotton-stalks, Machine for gathering	R. Ray	Louisport, Ky	Aug. 14, 1855	13, 436
Cotton-stalks, Machine for pulling and cutting	S. Beers	Naugatuck, Conn	Jan. 17, 1860	26, 828
Cotton-sweep	T. E. C. Brinly	Louisville, Ky	Nov. 22, 1870	109, 491
Cotton, Teeth of machine for picking	B. M. Smith	Brooklyn, N. Y	May 8, 1866	54, 619
Cotton-thinner	J. Gatling	Murfreesborough, N. C	June 19, 1835	... .
Cotton-thinner	E. M. Harris and J. Cleghorn	Cass County, Ga	Aug. 21, 1847	5, 257
Cotton-thinning machine	I. W. Burch	Fayette, Miss	Oct 5, 1869	95, 422
Cotton-thinning machine	E. M. Greeson	Americus, Ga	Apr. 12, 1870	101, 962
Cotton-tie	E. B. Bishop	New Orleans, La	July 23, 1867	67, 098
Cotton-tie	W. F. Buckelew	Shreveport, La	Apr. 16, 1867	63, 849
Cotton-tie	W. I. Carroll	Natchez, Miss	Jan. 23, 1866	52, 137
Cotton-tie	J. H. Fraley	New Orleans, La	Dec. 10, 1867	71, 867
Cotton-tie	J. W. Hedenberg	Chicago, Ill	Dec. 4, 1866	60, 187
Cotton-tie	J. F. Milligan	Saint Louis, Mo	Nov. 6, 1866	59, 512
Cotton-tie	M. A. Tarlton	New Orleans, La	Oct. 30, 1866	59, 293
Cotton-tie	C. W. Wailey	New Orleans, La	Oct. 9, 1866	58, 698
Cotton-tie fastening	T. McIntire	Portsmouth, Ohio	Sept. 11, 1866	57, 945
Cotton-tie-forming die	C. W. Wailey	New Orleans, La	July 30, 1867	67, 236
Cotton-tie stretcher	S. Mather	New Braunfels, Tex	Aug. 22, 1871	118, 254
Cotton to gin, Machinery for opening and feeding	M. B. Clarke	Newnan, Ga	Dec. 4, 1855	13, 898
Cotton to market, Rafting baled	G. R. Griffith	Mobile, Ala	Sept. 25, 1841	2, 267
Cotton-ties, Fastening ends of	A. Barbarin	New Orleans, La	June 25, 1867	66, 065
Cotton, Utilizing the silky down of the wild	M. H. Simpson	Boston, Mass	Mar. 7, 1871	112, 391
Cotton wadding	C. L. Fleischman	Washington, D. C	June 19, 1847	5, 161
Cotton wadding, Apparatus for drying the sizing on	O. Tenny	Dorchester, Mass	Jan. 10, 1845	3, 881
Cotton-waste and other fibers from oil, &c., Process of cleaning.	H. M. Baker	Washington, D. C	Jan. 11, 1870	98, 658
Cotton-waste and other fibrous materials, Cleaning.	H. M. Baker	Brooklyn, N. Y	Nov. 7, 1871	120, 564
Cotton-waste, Cleaning	H. M. Baker	New York, N. Y	July 28, 1868	80, 381
Cotton-waste, Cleaning	G. Sagar	Chicago, Ill	June 17, 1873	139, 921
Cotton-waste for cleaning machinery, Preparing	A. Peple	Billerica, Mass	Nov. 1, 1870	108, 821
Cotton-waste for cleaning machinery, Preparing certain kinds of.	A. Peple	East Billerica, Mass	Feb. 15, 1870	99, 945
Cotton-waste, Machinery for picking and separating	D. Goff	Pawtucket, R. I	Aug. 4, 1868	80, 724
Cotton waste or rags previous to their being operated on by the cutting and dusting machinery, Machine for dressing.	E. Smith	North Sudbury, Mass	Sept. 10, 1840	1, 782
Cotton-waste, &c., Process of cleaning	G. W. Sylvester	Belleville, N. J	Jan. 3, 1871	110, 800
Cotton-waste-separating machine	F. S. Robinson	Boston, Mass	Oct. 7, 1862	36, 625
Cotton-whipper	W. Hopkins	Plainfield, Conn	Mar. 6, 1823	....
Cotton whipper and cleaner	H. G. Davis	Clarke County, Ala	May 16, 1845	4, 050
Cotton-whipper, Cylindrical grate	J. S. Simmons	Scituate, R. I	Oct. 1, 1830	....
Cotton-whipper, Oblique	L. Osgood	Abington Post-Office, Conn	Oct. 27, 1835	... .
Cotton-whipper, Revolving	E. Baker	Warwick, R. I	June 4, 1830	....
Cotton-winding, Double-speeder for	W. Hines	Coventry, R. I	Feb. 6, 1819	....
Cotton, Wire-screen for cleaning	J. E. Crane	Lowell, Mass	Jan. 24, 1860	26, 887
Cotton, wool, fur, and other fibrous materials, Machinery for cleaning and separating.	I. Hayden	Lawrence, Mass	Mar. 17, 1857	16, 833
Cotton-wool, Machine for cleaning and picking	E. Raymond	Norton, Mass	Jan. 18, 1812	....
Cotton-worm destroyer	J. Helm	Hochheim, Tex	May 20, 1873	139, 062
Cotton-worm destroyer	J. W. Johnson	Columbus, Tex	Dec. 16, 1873	145, 571
Cotton-worm destroyer	J. W. Johnson	Columbus, Tex	Dec. 16, 1873	145, 572
Cotton-worms, &c., Machine for exterminating	C. Steinmann	Napoleonville, La	Feb. 4, 1868	74, 165
Couch, Accommodation	J. Mead	Albany, N. Y	Mar. 14, 1817	....
Couch, Accouchement	E. L. Moore	San Francisco, Cal	Mar. 11, 1873	136, 663
Couch, Adjustable	G. Widmer	New York, N. Y	May 12, 1868	77, 856
Coach and car truss	G. F. Chalender	Burlington, Iowa	Oct. 7, 1873	143, 498
Couch, Folding	A. J. Bell	Cincinnati, Ohio	Mar. 31, 1868	76, 148
Couch, Hospital	J. Keck	Barrington, Ill	Dec. 24, 1872	134, 147
Couch, Invalid	C. L. Taillant	New York, N. Y	Dec. 20, 1859	26, 534
Couch, Nursing	J. H. Cogshall	Lexington, Mich	Feb. 12, 1867	62, 010
Couch or cradle	A. E. and J. B. Blood and F. W. Pope.	Lynn, Mass	Aug. 11, 1868	80, 801
Couch or cradle	R. Hale	Chicago, Ill	Jan. 28, 1868	73, 892
Couch, Variety	E. Carver	Bridgewater, Mass	June 12, 1838	775
Counter and desk seat	W. R. Pomeroy	Millersburgh, Ohio	May 28, 1867	65, 115
Counter and show-case	L. F. Vienot	New York, N. Y	Apr. 12, 1870	101, 790
Counter-brace, Metallic	J. L. Cooper	Preston, Conn	Oct. 13, 1868	82, 921
Counter-knife	J. Feed	Reading, Pa	Apr. 5, 1870	101, 542
Counter-seat	D. H. Krauser	Pottsville, Pa	May 10, 1870	102, 947
Counter-shears	N. Stow	Binghamton, N. Y	Mar. 4, 1873	136, 558
Counter, Show	A. Beardsley	Mount Zion, Iowa	Oct. 26, 1869	96, 188
Counter-supporter	J. Reising	Aurora, Ill	Oct. 23, 1866	59, 075
Counterfeits, Check to detect	J. Perkins	....	Mar. 19, 1799	....
Counterpane	Z. Allen	Providence, R. I	Aug. 23, 1853	9, 962
Countersink	S. L. Abbott	Deering, Me	July 25, 1871	117, 237
Countersink	A. G. Bachelder	Lowell, Mass	May 10, 1853	9, 705
Countersink	R. P. Buttles	Mansfield, Pa	July 6, 1869	92, 261
Countersink	W. H. Dodge	Mishawaka, Ind	Jan. 30, 1872	123, 246
Countersink	S. E. Holbrook, jr	Charlestown Mass	May 24, 1870	103, 461
Countersink	L. H. Hunt	Rockingham, Vt	Feb. 9, 1869	86, 674
Countersink	L. H. Hunt	Saxton's River, Vt	May 21, 1872	126, 963
Countersink	F. H. Palmer	Foxcroft, Me	Feb. 28, 1871	112, 176
Countersink	M. M. Petts	Worcester, Mass	Dec. 27, 1870	110, 494
Countersink	W. B. Shedd	East Boston, Mass	Nov. 1, 1870	108, 837
Countersink	H. S. Shepardson	Shelburne Falls, Mass	Mar. 8, 1864	41, 894
Countersink	D. F. Sutton	Toledo, Ohio	Nov. 8, 1870	109, 154
Countersink	A. Wheeler	Brattleborough, Vt	Apr. 12, 1870	101, 796
Countersink	P. A. Whitney	Woodstock, Vt	Oct. 20, 1868	83, 348
Countersink	A. Williams	Wellsville, Ohio	Feb. 20, 1866	52, 776

Index of patents issued from the United States Patent Office from 1790 *to* 1873, *inclusive*—Continued.

Invention.	Inventor.	Residence.	Date.	No.
Countersink and bit	W. A. Clark	Woodbridge, Conn	Aug. 17, 1869	93, 807
Countersink and plug borer	W. H. Dodge	Mishawaka, Ind	Feb. 6, 1872	123, 463
Countersink-bit	H. C. Lewis	Essex, Conn	Dec. 4, 1866	60, 207
Countersink-gage	A. Wheeler	Brattleborough, Vt	July 11, 1871	116, 901
Counting-machine	J. A. Bazin	Canton, Mass	Dec. 23, 1856	16, 323
Counting-machine	S. Comfort	Morrisville, Pa	Feb. 20, 1866	52, 681
Counting-machine	J. Dolbeer	San Francisco, Cal	Dec. 20, 1864	45, 482
Counting-machine	P. Stillman	New York, N. Y	Aug. 22, 1854	11, 577
Counting-machine	U. Turnar	Versailles, Ky	July 2, 1867	66, 269
Counting-machine	T. J. Young	Philadelphia, Pa	Mar. 11, 1862	34, 665
Counting-machine and machine for indicating motion.	W. Y. Sterling	Bridgeport, Conn	Sept. 19, 1854	11, 703
Counting-register	A. P. Atkinson	Vermont, Ill	Nov. 7, 1871	120, 609
Counting-register	H. Chandler	Buffalo, N. Y	July 30, 1872	130, 017
Counting-register	J. S. Detrick	San Francisco, Cal	Aug. 4, 1868	80, 612
Counting-register	R. P. Hinds	Chicago, Ill	Jan. 28, 1873	135, 336
Counting-register	W. H. McNary	Brooklyn, N. Y	May 17, 1870	103, 221
Counting-register	C. W. Pyle	Wilmington, Del	Apr. 18, 1871	113, 794
Counting-register	G. Sickels	Boston, Mass	Sept. 28, 1869	95, 389
Counting-register	G. H. Van Vleck	Buffalo, N. Y	Mar. 25, 1873	137, 262
Counting-register	A. M. White	Bridgeport, Conn	Apr. 30, 1872	126, 361
Counting-register, Locomotive	E. P. Curtis	Cleveland, Ohio	Apr. 2, 1872	125, 179
Coupling:				
See Aqueduct-coupling.				
Auger-shaft coupling.				
Axle-coupling.				
Barge-coupling.				
Belt-coupling.				
Brace-coupling.				
Brake-coupling.				
Car-coupling.				
Car-heater coupling.				
Carriage-felly coupling.				
Chain-coupling.				
Cord-coupling.				
Drill-rod coupling.				
Drop-light coupling.				
Elastic coupling.				
Felly-joint coupling.				
Fire-engine coupling.				
Flexible coupling.				
Friction coupling.				
Gas and water main coupling.				
Gas and water pipe coupling.				
Harvester-pitman coupling.				
Hollow-shaft coupling.				
Hose-coupling.				
Hose and pipe coupling.				
Leader-pipe coupling.				
Lightning-rod coupling.				
Locomotive-coupling.				
Melodeon-coupling.				
Mill-shaft coupling.				
Octave-coupling.				
Organ-coupling.				
Perch-coupling.				
Pipe-coupling.				
Pitman-coupling.				
Platform spring-coupling.				
Plow-coupling.				
Pulley-coupling.				
Pump-rod coupling.				
Rail-coupling.				
Railway-coupling.				
Railway-rail coupling.				
Rigging-coupling.				
Rod-coupling.				
Rope-band coupling.				
Safety-coupling.				
Seeding-machine coupling.				
Shaft-coupling.				
Shaft and pole coupling.				
Shafting-coupling.				
Spring-coupling.				
Steam-heater coupling.				
Steam or air brake coupling.				
Stove-pipe coupling.				
Strap-coupling.				
Sucker-rod coupling.				
Telegraph-wire coupling.				
Thill-coupling.				
Tongue-coupling.				
Train-boat coupling.				
Tumbling-shaft coupling.				
Union coupling.				
Universal coupling.				
Universal-joint coupling.				
Vehicle-coupling.				
Vehicle-spring coupling.				
Wagon-coupling.				
Wagon-reach coupling.				
Wheel-felly coupling.				
Whiffletree-coupling.				
Wire-rigging coupling.				
Coupling	J. Heuermann	Davenport, Iowa	Sept. 15, 1868	82, 117
Coupling	M. Newman, 2d, N. C. Whitcomb, and G. C. Cole.	Lanesborough, Pa., and Hartford, Conn.	June 13, 1854	11, 074
Coupling and brake	T. A. Weston	King's Norton, England	Mar. 3, 1868	75, 227

Index of patents issued from the United States Patent Office from 1790 *to* 1873, *inclusive*—Continued.

Invention.	Inventor.	Residence.	Date.	No.
Coupling and steering apparatus	J. McCreary	Middletown, Pa	July 23, 1872	129, 844
Coupling-bar for railway car, locomotive, &c	W. D. Chesnut	Wilmington, Del	Feb. 20, 1844	3, 445
Coupling-box for shafting	W. B. Dunning	Geneva, N. Y	June 22, 1858	20, 634
Coupling-iron for railway and other carriages	T. G. Owen	Baltimore, Md	July 1, 1840	1, 666
Coupling-jack	H. A. Brown and E. B. Keith	Galesburgh, Miss	Sept. 27, 1870	107, 656
Coupling-pins, Machine for making	C. H. Williams	Cleveland, Ohio	Dec. 13, 1870	110, 179
Coupling-pipe	W. Hudgin	Washington, D. C	Apr. 6, 1858	19, 852
Coupling-pipe, Wrought-iron	S. Vanstone	Providence, R. I	June 28, 1870	104, 9[illegible]5
Coupling-spring, Gum-elastic	S. M. Hoover	Carlisle, Pa	Apr. 18, 1865	47, 305
Coupon, Mode of numbering	S. M. Clark	Washington, D. C	July 9, 1867	66, 461
Court-plaster, Preparation of	L. C. Gale	Chicago, Ill	May 1, 1866	54, 326
Coverlet	C. K. Pevey	Worcester, Mass	July 15, 1873	140, 948
Coverlet	H. Wettstein	Philadelphia, Pa	Jan. 29, 1867	61, 588
Cover-lifter, hammer, &c., Combined	R. M. Lafferty	Three Rivers, Mich	June 4, 1867	65, 397
Cow and sheep rack	R. Lovett	Canton, Ohio	May 15, 1866	54, 745
Cow-catcher	C. Darling	Utica, N. Y	June 8, 1852	8, 996
Cow-catcher	T. B. Smith	Triune, Tenn	July 11, 1854	11, 273
Cow-catcher, Railway	W. J. Orr	Manorville, Pa	Dec. 31, 1867	72, 752
Cow-tail holder	N. Dutton	Janesville, Wis	Apr. 30, 1867	64, 207
Cow-tail holder	W. H. Gray	Ashfield, Mass	Mar. 14, 1871	112, 587
Cow-tail holder	J. Knight	Whitestown, N. Y	May 31, 1870	103, 753
Cow-tail holder	G. Tanner	Freetown, N. Y	June 21, 1870	104, 661
Cows and calves from sucking and for leading cattle, Device for preventing.	A. S. Haven	Barre, Mass	Feb. 4, 1868	74, 086
Cows from kicking, Device for preventing	T. Pyle	Nottingham, Pa	Aug. 27, 1872	130, 943
Cows from kicking, Device for preventing	H. J. Sadler and S. H. Spencer	Mecca, Ohio	July 8, 1873	140, 594
Cows while being milked, Device for confining	L. Brown	Evans, N. Y	Nov. 13, 1866	59, 550
Cowl: *See* Car-cowl. Chimney-cowl. Emery-wheel cowl. Ventilating-cowl.				
Cowl	C. W. Atkeson	Saint Louis, Mo	Mar. 3, 1868	75 109
Cowl	W. F. G. Beeuwkes	Holland, Mich	Jan. 22, 1867	61, 387
Crabs, Device for securing and feeding soft	C. Drexler	Washington, D. C	Dec. 17, 1867	72, 177
Cracker and biscuit cutting	J. Clark and H. Henderson	Baltimore, Md	June 13, 1831	....
Cracker and biscuit cutting	S. P. Clark	Baltimore, Md	Nov. 7, 1835	....
Cracker and biscuit cutting	J. P. Fairlamb and M. Dunot	Wilmington, Del	June 13, 1831	....
Cracker and biscuit cutting	T. and T. H. Havener	Washington, D. C	Oct. 17, 1835	....
Cracker and biscuit cutting	W. R. Nivens	New York, N. Y	Oct. 17, 1835	....
Cracker and biscuit cutting	J. S. Stiles	Baltimore, Md	Aug. 9, 1831	....
Cracker and biscuit machine	T. Bladen	Philadelphia, Pa	Mar. 16, 1830	....
Cracker, biscuit, &c	T Bladen	Philadelphia, Pa	Oct. 1, 1830	....
Cracker, biscuit, &c	D. Poole	Dauphin County, Pa	May 20, 1834	....
Cracker-box	C. F. Thurston	Cambridgeport, Mass	Mar. 12, 1872	124, 459
Cracker-crusher	A. Clarke and T. Reece	Philadelphia, Pa	Jan. 15, 1867	61, 163
Cracker cutter and stamping machine	C. Baldwin	Goffstown, N. H	Nov. 7, 1848	5, 906
Cracker-cutting machine	E. O. Brinkerhoff	New York, N. Y	Aug. 25, 1863	39, 628
Cracker-cutting machine	C. P. Forbes	Baltimore, Md	July 17, 1841	2, 180
Cracker-cutting machine	W. R. Nevins	New York, N. Y	Nov. 10, 1841	2, 344
Cracker-cutting machine	W. R. Nevins	New York, N. Y	Aug. 20, 1850	7, 580
Cracker-cutting machinery	W. Perkins	Boston, Mass	Apr. 2, 1841	2, 029
Cracker-dough, Rolling and cutting	W. R. Nevins	New York, N. Y	Mar. 2, 1836	....
Cracker-machine	W. Cairns	Jersey City, N. J	Nov. 12, 1872	133, 014
Cracker-machine	W. Cairns	Jersey City, N. J	Jan. 31, 1871	111, 315
Cracker-machine	P. Emmons	New York, N. Y	Feb. 13, 1855	12, 383
Cracker-machine	J. Fox	Lansingburgh, N. Y	Feb. 1, 1859	22, 793
Cracker-machine	J. Fox	Lansingburgh, N. Y	Oct. 14, 1873	143, 686
Cracker-machine	W. M. Garrison	New York, N. Y	June 5, 1866	55, 276
Cracker-machine	G. Y. Gray	Niles, Mich	May 11, 1869	89, 985
Cracker-machine	J. E. Hawkins	Lansingburgh, N. Y	June 25, 1867	66, 082
Cracker-machine	J. and J. C. Holyland	Rochester, N. Y	Sept. 28, 1858	21, 6[illegible]6
Cracker-machine	J. and J. C. Holyland	Rochester, N. Y	Nov. 27, 1860	30, 732
Cracker-machine	J. Johnson and O. Freeman	Boston, Mass	May 17, 1844	3, 585
Cracker-machine	G. J. Kingsbury	Rochester, N. Y	Oct. 14, 1873	143, 579
Cracker-machine	C. Marsh, 2d	Natchez, Miss	July 24, 1860	29, 295
Cracker-machine	C. Marsh, 2d	Natchez, Miss	Nov. 9, 1869	96, 715
Cracker-machine	J. McCollum	New York, N. Y	Mar. 23, 1852	8, [illegible]28
Cracker-machine	J. McCollum	New York, N. Y	Feb. 15, 1859	22, 966
Cracker-machine	C. Neer	Troy, N. Y	June 15, 1858	20, 577
Cracker-machine	L. A. Rockwell	Tremont, N. Y	June 17, 1873	139, 920
Cracker-machine	G. R. Skillman	Baltimore, Md	Apr. 4, 1871	113, 356
Cracker machine	T. Sloat	Brooklyn, N. Y	Apr. 20, 1869	89, 250
Cracker-making machine	R. Darling	East Greenwich, R. I	Sept. 30, 1841	2, 277
Cracker-making machine	D. Seward	Philadelphia, Pa	Nov. 26, 1867	71, 420
Cracker-making machine	H. Winslow	Swansey, Mass	Dec. 14, 1840	1, 896
Cracker-molding machine	P. Emmons	New York, N. Y	Aug. 1, 1854	11, 418
Cracker or meat biscuit	E. Greenfield	New York, N. Y	Feb. 15, 1870	99, 880
Cracker, Oyster	W. P. Lyon	Portchester, N. Y	May 8, 1866	54, 566
Cracker rolling and cutting machine	D. Pool	Philadelphia, Pa	Dec. 24, 1824	....
Crackers, biscuit, &c., Cutting	J. Clarke and H. Henderson	Philadelphia, Pa	Sept. 18, 1833	....
Crackers, biscuit, &c., Machine for cutting	J. Cooper	Philadelphia, Pa	Mar. 11, 1830	....
Crackers, biscuit, pilot-bread, &c., Machine for cutting.	J. Clark and H. Henderson	Baltimore, Md	Sept. 13, 1830	....
Crackers, Machine for cutting	G. M. Kendall	Catskill, N. Y	May 3, 1833	....
Crackers, Machine for cutting	L. Kirtland	New Haven, Conn	Sept. 4, 1834	....
Crackers, Manufacture of cream	D. M. Holmes	Brooklyn, N. Y	Oct. 9, 1866	58, 644
Crackers, Mode of making cylindrical strips of dough in the manufacture of.	F. C. Treadwell, jr., and H. McCollum.	New York, N. Y., and Windham, Conn.	Oct. 11, 1859	25, 775
Crackers, Molding	J. G. Driscoll	Auburn, N. Y	Nov. 19 1833	....
Crackers, ship-biscuit, &c	J. and C. Bruce	Kings County, N. Y	Mar. 13, 1832	....
Crackers, ship-bread, &c	N. Daskam and D. G. Wood	Geneva, N. Y	Aug. 5, 1830	....
Cracking and grinding mill	W. Beal, jr., and B. S. Hale	Norway, Me., and Lowell, Mass.	Dec. 17, 1846	4, 895
Cracklings cutting machine	A. Smith	Cincinnati, Ohio	Feb. 5, 1867	61, 884
Cracklings, &c., Cutting-machine for reducing	A. Smith	Cincinnati, Ohio	Nov. 26, 1867	71, 545
Cracklings from roasted pork, Cutting-tools for the manufacture of.	L. F. Lannay	Baltimore County, Md	Apr. 2, 1872	125, 137

Index of patents issued from the United States Patent Office from 1790 *to* 1873, *inclusive*—Continued.

Invention.	Inventor.	Residence.	Date.	No.
Cradle	W. Bedle	Keyport, N. J	June 5, 1866	55, 227
Cradle	J. B. Charlton	Kalamazoo, Mich	Apr. 4, 1871	113, 497
Cradle	F. Chichester	Milwaukee, Wis	July 22, 1873	141, 033
Cradle	P. Cooper	Hempstead, N. Y	Mar. 27, 1815	....
Cradle	D. Cox	Cincinnati, Ohio	Feb. 5, 1867	61, 720
Cradle	W. T. Doremus	New York, N. Y	Apr. 29, 1873	138, 320
Cradle	A. Dick	Buffalo, N. Y	Jan. 23, 1866	52, 146
Cradle	D. A. Dunham	Pilatka, Fla	Oct. 29, 1867	70, 179
Cradle	W. H. Earnest	Clarksburgh, Va	May 20, 1862	35, 307
Cradle	W. H. Earnest	Parkersburgh, W. Va	June 25, 1872	128, 375
Cradle	C. A. Fenner	Mystic River, Conn	Nov. 11, 1873	144, 391
Cradle	M. Griffin	Brooklyn, N. Y	Jan. 7, 1873	134, 661
Cradle	L. Heywood	Gardner, Mass	Jan. 21, 1873	135, 117
Cradle	L. and A. R. Hill	Alexandria, Va	Jan. 28, 1868	73, 892
Cradle	S. W. Knowles	New Haven, Conn	July 2, 1867	66, 361
Cradle	R. W. Myers	Clarksville Post-Office, N. J.	Feb. 28, 1871	112, 271
Cradle	A. H. Ordway	Haverhill, Mass	Jan. 10, 1871	110, 931
Cradle	D. O. Parker	Liverpool, Nova Scotia	Aug. 8, 1871	117, 809
Cradle	S. Pope	Windsor, Conn	June 15, 1813	....
Cradle	D. Sonder	Houston, Ohio	Apr. 15, 1873	137, 868
Cradle	L. Sperry and L. Robinson	East Windsor Hill and New Haven, Conn.	July 20, 1869	92, 896
Cradle	A. Spiegel	Indianapolis, Ind	Oct. 5, 1869	95, 530
Cradle	H. H. Wiggers	Cincinnati, Ohio	Aug. 13, 1872	130, 554
Cradle	F. R. Wolfinger	Vermont, Ill	July 5, 1864	43, 448
Cradle and baby-walker, Circular swinging	W. M. Messick	Louisville, Ky	July 30, 1867	67, 331
Cradle and chair	A. Berny	Williamsburgh, N. Y	July 3, 1866	55, 990
Cradle and chair, Combination of	A. Hicks	Flushing, N. Y	May 10, 1864	42, 730
Cradle and chair, Combined	F. E. Coomes	Berlin, Wis	July 31, 1866	56, 718
Cradle and chair rocker	S. Simmons	Baltimore, Md	Dec. 21, 1819	....
Cradle and chair, Propelling	E. Whitman, jr	Winthrop, Me	Mar. 27, 1835	....
Cradle and rocking-chair combined	E. Hambujer	Detroit, Mich	Feb. 4, 1873	135, 425
Cradle and tête-à-tête	G. H. Hazlewood	Boston, Mass	July 5, 1853	9, 829
Cradle, Automatic	D. Alger	Bryon, Mich	Sept. 6, 1870	107, 148
Cradle, Automatic	S. G. Delano	Grand Blanc, Mich	Sept. 1, 1868	81, 757
Cradle, Automatic	S. G. Delano	Argentine, Mich	Mar. 15, 1870	100, 735
Cradle, Automatic	I. S. Goodman	Winterset, Iowa	Apr. 22, 1873	138, 144
Cradle, Automatic	W. V. Van Dervoort and R. B. Walker.	New Antioch, Ohio	June 10, 1873	139, 838
Cradle-chair	J. H. Havens	Lewiston, N. Y	Aug. 5, 1862	36, 091
Cradle-chair	M. Studley	South Yarmouth, Mass	Mar. 2, 1869	87, 378
Cradle, Child's	J. L. Riter	Brownsville, Ind	Jan. 16, 1872	122, 737
Cradle, Child's	L. K. Selden	Haddam, Conn	Apr. 10, 1860	27, 835
Cradle, Child's	W. J. Stowell	Baltimore, Md	Feb. 21, 1871	111, 989
Cradle, crib, and standing stool combined	C. E. Nurse	Chesterfield Factory, N. H	Nov. 19, 1872	133, 169
Cradle, Fleecing	J. K. Alwood	Delta, Ohio	Nov. 3, 1868	83, 754
Cradle, Folding	C. Klein	Albany, N. Y	Feb. 25, 1868	74, 917
Cradle, Folding	J. A. Latham and G. W. Tileston.	New Haven, Conn	Aug. 23, 1864	43, 947
Cradle, Folding	T. W. Moore	New York, N. Y	July 11, 1871	116, 856
Cradle, Folding	L. K. Selden	Haddam, Conn	May 24, 1859	24, 142
Cradle, Hydrostatic steam	C. Miner	Lyme, Conn	Nov. 16, 1827	....
Cradle, Infant's	T. C. Ball	Keene, N. H	Nov. 16, 1858	22, 056
Cradle, Infant's	S. F. Brooks	Weston, Mass	Apr. 24, 1860	27, 964
Cradle or crib	E. N. Cutter	Chicago, Ill	Apr. 6, 1869	88, 553
Cradle or crib	J. M. Read	New York, N. Y	Feb. 27, 1830	....
Cradle or crib, Folding	M. McNamara	Philadelphia, Pa	Jan. 21, 1873	135, 138
Cradle or crib, Portable	D. M. Reynolds	Chicago, Ill	Nov. 8, 1870	109, 030
Cradle, Portable	W. R. Evans	Philadelphia, Pa	Sept. 12, 1871	118, 918
Cradle, Portable	W. S. Harris	Trenton, N. J	Dec. 30, 1873	146, 069
Cradle, &c., rocker	R. A. Jackson	Alliance, Ohio	June 20, 1871	116, 061
Cradle-rocker	P. Power	Chicago, Ill	Oct. 8, 1867	69, 698
Cradle-rocker	H. R. Taylor	Roxbury, Mass	Jan. 16, 1843	2, 915
Cradle, Rocking	W. A. N. Long	Fisherville, N. H	Aug. 13, 1861	33, 045
Cradle, Rocking	W. D. Tewksbury	Cuylersville, N. Y	June 7, 1859	24, 340
Cradle, Self-moving	A. Buchenberger	New York, N. Y	Nov. 3, 1829	....
Cradle, Self-rocking	C. H. Helmkamp	Reading, Ohio	Feb. 9, 1864	41, 507
Cradle, Self-rocking	C. Holtz	Saint Louis, Mo	May 27, 1873	139, 247
Cradle, Self-rocking	B. Brazelle	Nashville, Ill	May 15, 1866	54, 815
Cradle, Self-rocking	D. Walker	Newark, N. J	Feb. 25, 1862	34, 535
Cradle, Self-rocking	H. G. Williams	Hamilton, Iowa	Mar. 7, 1865	46, 744
Cradle, Sofa	H. A. Axtell	Westfield, Mass	Feb. 25, 1868	74, 876
Cradle, Spring	F. Chichester	Milwaukee, Wis	July 22, 1873	141, 032
Cradle, Spring-rocking	J. B. Malbert and A. Chevirou.	Saint Louis, Mo	May 18, 1858	20, 284
Cradle, stool, and chair	J. B. Warren	Davenport, Mass	June 5, 1866	55, 401
Cradle, Swing	P. P. Carroll	Washington, D. C	Apr. 14, 1868	76, 601
Cradle, Swing	Z. Mills	Hartford, Conn	July 17, 1806	....
Cradle, Swinging	S. W. Knowles	Middletown, Conn	Oct. 28, 1851	8, 468
Cradle, Swinging	J. McKinney	West Chester, Ohio	June 13, 1831	....
Cradle, Swinging	L. F. Whitaker	Raleigh, N. C	Oct. 21, 1851	8, 461
Cradle, Wire	L. Chevallier and R. Brass	Williamsburgh, N. Y., and Waterbury, Conn.	Jan. 11, 1870	98, 742
Cradles to rocking-chairs, Coupling for connecting.	J. Reeves	Cincinnati, Ohio	Sept. 9, 1873	142, 583
Cranberry-gatherer	W. Hall	Dennis, Mass	Sept. 8, 1868	81, 897
Cranberry-gatherer	E. D. Miller	Dorchester, Mass	Nov. 20, 1866	59, 857
Cranberry-gatherer	G. Shove	Yarmouth, Mass	Mar. 7, 1865	46, 760
Cranberry-gatherer	G. Shove	Yarmouthport, Mass	Jan. 22, 1867	61, 476
Cranberry-gatherer	C. Thacher	Yarmouth, Mass	June 6, 1865	48, 136
Cranberry-picker	J. P. Prickett	Medford, N. J	Mar. 22, 1870	101, 040
Cranberry-picker	J. Weston	Duxbury, Mass	Dec. 30, 1873	145, 979
Cranberry-separator	D. Perham	Tyngsborough, Mass	Jan. 19, 1858	19, 151
Cranberry-winnower	P. Flanders	Lowell, Mass	Apr. 4, 1854	10, 736
Cranberries for preservation, Putting up	A. Sampson	Providence, R. I	Dec. 2, 1862	37, 058
Cranberries, Machine for cleaning and assorting	G. L. Merrill	Chicago, Ill	July 23, 1867	67, 130
Crane	A. S. Batten	Topsham, Vt	Dec. 3, 1867	71, 682
Crane	H. Bradford	New York, N. Y	July 8, 1834	....
Crane	R. Briggs	Philadelphia, Pa	July 15, 1873	140, 882

Index of patents issued from the United States Patent Office from 1790 *to* 1873, *inclusive*—Continued.

Invention.	Inventor.	Residence.	Date.	No.
Crane	B. J. Burnett	New York, N. Y	Dec. 25, 1855	13, 976
Crane	B. J. Burnett	Mount Vernon, N. Y	Feb. 7, 1865	46, 213
Crane	F. Farrel	Ansonia, Conn	May 13, 1873	138, 876
Crane	G. Hunziker	Summit, Miss	July 16, 1872	129, 282
Crane	E. Marsh	Oswego, N. Y	Feb. 12, 1836	....
Crane	J. W. Middleton	Philadelphia, Pa	Mar. 21, 1871	112, 829
Crane	J. L. Pennock	Coatesville, Pa	Dec. 2, 1873	145, 234
Crane	F. Rumpf	Cold Spring, N. Y	Mar. 6, 1866	53, 044
Crane	G. Sherwood	Erie, Pa	June 30, 1836	....
Crane	J. F. Smith	Portsmouth, Va	July 10, 1860	29, 109
Crane	C. Williams	New York, N. Y	Aug. 18, 1868	81, 317
Crane, Balance	L. Henry	Paris, France	Nov. 9, 1844	3, 813
Crane, Blacksmith's	W. Maher	Slack, Ky	Dec. 23, 1856	16, 283
Crane, Compensating forge	T. Morris	Clarbeston, England	Nov. 5, 1867	70, 455
Crane, Dredging	G. Wood and J. King	Philadelphia, Pa	Nov. 9, 1858	22, 052
Crane, Elevating	J. T. Wright	Nashua, N. H	Aug. 22, 1865	49, 579
Crane for loading or discharging goods on board of vessels, Labor-saving	T. Godwin	New York, N. Y	Oct. 2, 1838	953
Crane for raising brick, Portable	E. Mann and G. Hill	Rochester, N. Y	July 21, 1827	....
Crane, Hoisting	J. Y. Parce	Fairport, N. Y	July 26, 1859	24, 912
Crane, Hydraulic	D. S. Hines	Brooklyn, N. Y	July 23, 1867	67, 113
Crane, Hydraulic	S. K. Wellman	Nashua, N. H	July 7, 1868	79, 710
Crane, Portable	L. A. Beardsley	South Edmeston, N. Y	June 25, 1861	32, 608
Crane, Portable	S. R. Marshall	Wilkesbarre, Pa	Jan. 5, 1864	41, 161
Crane, Portable	C. Snyder and S. M. Smith	Hawley, Pa	Oct. 9, 1860	30, 358
Crane, Power	W. F. Durfee	New Bedford, Mass	Aug. 11, 1868	80, 930
Crane, Rotary	J. S. Coffinan	Greenville, Ind	Dec. 31, 1867	72, 801
Crane, Yard and tank	L. Y. Ketcham and J. Taynton	Port Jervis, N. Y	Feb. 15, 1870	99, 912
Crank	C. T. Moore	Gilmanton, N. H	Apr. 27, 1869	89, 423
Crank	A. Shedlock	New York, N. Y	July 16, 1872	128, 981
Crank, Anti-friction	B. S. Oliver	Salem, Mass	Mar. 9, 1821	....
Crank-box	G. Westinghouse	Schenectady, N. Y	Mar. 20, 1860	27, 588
Crank-brace for augers, Adjustable	J. Gourlay	Ogdensburgh, N. Y	Dec. 18, 1855	13, 943
Crank-connection	E. R. Cole	Pawtucket, R. I	Aug. 20, 1867	67, 957
Crank-engine for raising and throwing water	J. Clap	Montague, Mass	Nov. 21, 1810	....
Crank-expander	L. Swenson	North Cape, Wis	July 30, 1872	129, 996
Crank, friction-wheel, and brake, Combined	R. M. Van Sickler	New York, N. Y	Oct. 8, 1867	69, 727
Crank-gearing	T. J. McGowan	Cincinnati, Ohio	July 25, 1871	117, 312
Crank-heating apparatus	J. Miller	New York, N. Y	Apr. 15, 1873	137, 944
Crank-indicators, Arrangement of machinery for actuating the.	S. B. Hutchins	Oswegatchie, N. Y	June 3, 1851	8, 131
Crank-motion	W. Bricknell	Hartford, Me	Sept. 3, 1867	68, 482
Crank-motion	E. Quinn	Brooklyn, N. Y	June 27, 1871	116, 487
Crank-motion	T. Taylor	New Orleans, La	July 23, 1867	67, 001
Crank-movement	H. C. Bradford	Providence, R. I	Jan. 21, 1873	135, 073
Crank-pin box	T. Welch	Churchville, N. Y	Aug. 1, 1865	49, 185
Crank pins, Apparatus for turning locomotive	W. Blythe and N. Hayes	Alexandria, Va	Apr. 14, 1868	76, 702
Crank-pins, Machine for turning	H. S. Smith and W. D. Whitmore.	Bloomington, Ill	July 5, 1870	105, 007
Crank-pins, Machine for turning	M. G. Wood	Boston, Mass	Apr. 18, 1871	113, 959
Crank-pins of locomotives, Machine for returning	N. Wright	Cleveland, Ohio	Feb. 15, 1870	99, 993
Crank, ratchet, and brake, Combined	R. B. McElrath	Newburgh, N. Y	June 13, 1871	115, 881
Crank, Serial	C. F. Ritchel	Chicago, Ill	Aug. 4, 1868	80, 769
Crank-shaft eccentric	J. F. Haskins	Fitchburgh, Mass	Apr. 1, 1873	137, 441
Crank, Substitute	A. Brooks	Crawford County, Ind	Aug. 3, 1858	21, 061
Crank-wheel motion	J. Wallace	Columbia, S. C	Sept. 25, 1824	....
Crank-wrist	C. B. Garlinghouse	Allensville, Ind	June 30, 1863	39, 034
Crank-wrist	J. M. Long	Hamilton, Ohio	Apr. 21, 1863	38, 233
Crank-wrist connection	J. Clayton	Brooklyn, N. Y	May 2, 1865	47, 522
Cranks by crank-pins, Mode of connecting	F. E. Sickels	New York, N. Y	Sept. 19, 1845	4, 199
Cranks on rods, Machine for bending	E. Lord	Todmorden, Great Britain	Mar. 13, 1866	53, 242
Cranks over dead-points, Carrying	F. Glass	Knightstown, Ind	Jan. 26, 1864	41, 373
Cranks to machinery, Attaching	A. Westcott	Syracuse, N. Y	May 23, 1865	47, 885
Cranks, Wheel used in machinery instead of	J. Steadwell, 3d	Carmel, N. Y	Nov. 25, 1823	....
Crate: *See* Folding-crate. Fruit-crate. Fruit-box crate. Peach-crate. Sewing-machine crate.				
Crate, Folding	L. A. Lindsey	Jackson, Miss	Mar. 1, 1870	100, 299
Crate, Folding	F. R. Van Dake	Jackson, Miss	Feb. 15, 1870	99, 977
Cravat	O. Ernst	New York, N. Y	Mar. 27, 1866	53, 428
Cravat-holder	J. N. Thomson	North Attleborough, Mass	June 27, 1871	116, 510
Cravat, Vulcanized rubber	W. W. Beach	New York, N. Y	July 19, 1864	43, 620
Crayon, Composition	W. Compton	New York, N. Y	June 8, 1869	91, 090
Crayon composition	I. N. Peirce	Boston, Mass	Dec. 20, 1864	45, 518
Crayon-holder	A. F. Howard	Waltham, Mass	Apr. 15, 1873	137, 844
Crayon-holder	R. Wright	New York, N. Y	July 28, 1868	80, 378
Crayon-holder, Tailors'	J. A. Gooch	Biddeford, Me	Aug. 20, 1872	130, 634
Crayon, Rubber	D. F. Pond	New Haven, Conn	Sept. 21, 1852	9, 277
Crayon-sharpener, Tailors'	R. R. Miles	Wabash, Ind	Dec. 21, 1869	98, 085
Crayons, Manufacture of nitrate of silver	S. P. Wheeler	Bridgeport, Conn	Nov. 22, 1859	26, 223
Cream-freezer	E. S. Farson	Philadelphia, Pa	Mar. 23, 1858	19, 733
Cream-freezer	E. C Seaman	Philadelphia, Pa	Oct. 3, 1848	5, 821
Cream-freezer	S. W. Smith	Brooklyn, N. Y	Mar. 15, 1859	23, 271
Cream-freezer	E. S. Torrey	New York, N. Y	Feb. 5, 1867	61, 895
Cream from milk, Extracting	S. Davis	New York, N. Y	Oct. 1, 1830	....
Cream from whey, Method of extracting	K. Egger	South Cortland, N. Y	Sept. 25, 1866	58, 232
Cream-beater	J. C. Beddol and J. S. Coon	Branchport, N. Y	Mar. 22, 1870	101, 086
Cream-paste press and strainer	L. Bishop	Cortlandville, N. Y	Feb. 20, 1866	52, 661
Cream, Process of preparing	C. D. Birdseye	New York, N. Y	Sept. 17, 1850	7, 644
Cream-saver	O. Abell	Witoka, Minn	June 18, 1872	128, 000
Cream saver	S. E. Mallett	Corry, Pa	Aug. 25, 1868	81, 519
Creeper	L. Witting	Philadelphia, Pa	Jan. 12, 1858	19, 109
Cresset or barrel-heater	W. B. Geddis	Rochester, N. Y	Mar. 5, 1867	62, 540
Crevasses, Method of stopping	L. A. Gossin	La Fourche Parish, La	Jan. 14, 1868	73, 318
Crib	W. B. Carpenter	West Topsham, Vt	Aug. 19, 1873	141, 918

Index of patents issued from the United States Patent Office from 1790 *to* 1873, *inclusive*—Continued.

Invention.	Inventor.	Residence.	Date.	No.
Crib and bedstead	G. T. Palmer	Brooklyn, N. Y	May 19, 1868	78, 123
Crib and bedstead, Extension	C. H. Hudson	New York, N. Y	Nov. 30, 1869	97, 403
Crib and chair	J. E. Small	Berlin, Wis	Oct. 23, 1866	59, 687
Crib and cradle	W. H. Earnest	Parkersburgh, W. Va	June 14, 1870	104, 288
Crib and cradle	H. W. Eastman	Baltimore, Md	Jan. 31, 1865	46, 091
Crib and cradle combined, Folding	J. B. Brolaski	Saint Louis, Mo	Sept. 3, 1872	131, 049
Crib and cradle, Folding	D. M. Reynolds	Chicago, Ill	Mar. 15, 1870	100, 925
Crib and walking-stool	S. S. Burr	Dedham, Mass	Jan. 1, 1867	60, 684
Crib, Child's	J. Batley	Orange, N. J	Nov. 5, 1872	132, 745
Crib, Child's	D. Cox	Cincinnati, Ohio	Mar. 26, 1872	124, 884
Crib, Child's	G. W. Ennis	Orange, N. J	Mar. 14, 1871	112, 570
Crib, Child's	W. L. Gerard	Fort Wayne, Ind	Dec. 11, 1866	60, 357
Crib, Child's	J. D. Lewis	Toronto, Canada	Dec. 2, 1873	145, 218
Crib, Child's	A. R. Swartz	Carlisle, Pa	May 11, 1869	89, 953
Crib, Extension	S. S. Burr	Dedham, Mass	Sept. 28, 1869	95, 318
Crib, Folding	A. J. Bettridge	North Bridgewater, Mass	Mar. 26, 1872	124, 877
Crib, Folding	C. Kilburn	Philadelphia, Pa	Jan. 14, 1873	134, 895
Crib or cradle	L. A. Chichester	Poughkeepsie, N. Y	Oct. 12, 1869	95, 768
Crib or cradle	W. T. Hazard	Randolph, Mass	May 2, 1871	144, 292
Crib or hammock, Swinging	D. O'Grady	Charleston, Ill	Mar. 25, 1873	137, 235
Crib, Reversible	A. E. Eaton	Portland, Me	May 23, 1871	115, 042
Crib, Traveling	S. L. Mercer	Washington, D. C	Sept. 24, 1872	131, 698
Cribs or cradles, Means of rocking	J. S. Ryan	Berlin, Wis	Jan. 1, 1867	60, 793
Cribbage-board, &c	J. Gill	New York, N. Y	Dec. 22, 1863	40, 999
Cribbing-preventer	B. J. Davis and I. S. Cramer	Sergeantsville, N. J	Mar. 10, 1868	75, 382
Cribbing-preventer	M. H. Sullivan	Providence, R. I	May 19, 1868	78, 155
Cricket and commode	J. C. Knowles	New Bedford, Mass	May 31, 1870	103, 754
Cricket-bat	M. Doherty	Boston, Mass	Feb. 22, 1859	23, 017
Cricket-wicket	W. Hanlon	Philadelphia, Pa	July 23, 1861	32, 869
Crimping and fluting machine	R. Werner	Hoboken, N. J	Jan. 7, 1873	134, 621
Crimping and fluting machine	R. Werner	Hoboken, N. J	June 24, 1873	140, 326
Crimping-brake	J. Howe	Milford, Mass	Aug. 31, 1869	94, 213
Crimping clamp	L. Hill	North Brookfield, Mass	Aug. 25, 1868	81, 503
Crimping-clamp	J. Kunstler	Collinsville, Conn	July 25, 1871	117, 304
Crimping-clamp	P. A. Schoellhorn	Buffalo, N. Y	Aug 19, 1873	141, 956
Crimping-forms, Machine for shaping	J. H. Jellison	Milford, Mass	Sept. 19, 1865	50, 074
Crimping-machine	D. Bissell	Detroit, Mich	Aug. 28, 1860	29, 757
Crimping-machine	W. Butterfield	Boston, Mass	Mar. 8, 1870	100, 498
Crimping-machine	S. G. Cabell	Quincy, Ill	July 17, 1866	56, 365
Crimping-machine	L. Crevissier and L. Lecamp	Reims, France	Oct. 29, 1872	132, 637
Crimping-machine	J. P. Jamison	New York, N. Y	May 15, 1866	54, 735
Crimping-machine	S. W. Jamison	New York, N. Y	Feb. 15, 1870	99, 906
Crimping-machine	J. Joslyn	Canton, N. Y	Feb. 19, 1867	62, 208
Crimping-machine	M. R. Lemman and W. A. L. Kirk.	Hamilton, Ohio	Sept. 26, 1871	119, 234
Crimping-machine	L. P. Lum	Newburgh, N. Y	Dec. 9, 1873	145, 303
Crimping-machine	R. A. York	Reading, Mich	Apr. 7, 1868	76, 576
Crimping-pin	C. N. and A. C. Tyler	Buffalo, N. Y	Nov. 10, 1868	83, 892
Crinoline-clip	H. Fletcher	London, England	Apr. 29, 1862	35, 091
Crocheting and knitting needles, Machine for forming barbs of.	J. P. Tirrell	North Bridgewater, Mass	Apr. 2, 1867	63, 442
Crockery stilts	P. Pointon	Trenton, N. J	Oct. 13, 1863	40, 310
Crockery-ware, Heated metallic mold for forming.	E. Leak, H. Moore, and J. Taylor.	Trenton, N. J	May 21, 1872	127, 074
Cromamometro	P. Pettinos	Philadelphia, Pa	Mar. 3, 1829	....
Croquet, Apparatus for parlor	A. P. Eastman	Washington, D. C	Nov. 8, 1870	109, 120
Croquet, Apparatus for parlor	W. S. Messinger	Roxbury, Mass	May 29, 1866	55, 139
Croquet-arch	F. M. Clarke	Washington, D. C	Aug. 8, 1871	117, 865
Croquet-ball, Rubber	J. H. Tuttle	East Hampton, Mass	Jan. 23, 1872	122, 926
Croquet-board	J. Federhen	Boston, Mass	Nov. 6, 1866	59, 376
Croquet-boards, Method of mounting	H. R. Heyl	Philadelphia, Pa	June 14, 1870	104, 151
Croquet-mallet	S. Byrnes	Boston, Mass	Nov. 21, 1865	51, 016
Croquet-mallet	E. A. Ross	Albany, N. Y	Mar. 4, 1873	136, 388
Croquet-wicket	F. W. Smith, jr	Bridgeport, Conn	Mar. 30, 1869	88, 335
Croquet-wicket driver	E. A. Barker	Providence, R. I	Aug. 26, 1873	142, 072
Croqueterie	L. and M. Bradley	Springfield, Mass	May 22, 1866	54, 848
Croqueterie	G. L. Morse	Harrison, N. J	Feb. 26, 1867	62, 495
Cross-bar lock for doors, &c	J. E. Hanger	Staunton, Va	June 16, 1868	78, 960
Cross-bow	E. C. H. Nye	Acushnet, Mass	Mar. 26, 1867	63, 172
Cross-head	J. West	Bethlehem, Pa	May 1, 1866	54, 457
Cross-head shifter	C. R. Joyce	Alexandria, Va	Feb. 8, 1870	99, 686
Cross, Memorial	E. W. Hall	New York, N. Y	Feb. 13, 1872	123, 694
Crosses, Mode of mounting ornamental	W. B. Bennett	Providence, R. I	Aug. 17, 1869	93, 664
Croup and other diseases, Apparatus for treating	G. Déclat	Paris, France	Dec. 7, 1869	97, 613
Crout-cutter	J. G. Schwarz	Indianapolis, Ind	Aug. 31, 1869	94, 244
Crow and tamping bar	A. Wright and A. F. Tew	Westfield, N. Y	May 6, 1873	138, 599
Crow-bar, Compound	I. J. Cole	Piermont, N. Y	Jan. 23, 1855	12, 288
Crow-killer	N. J. Tilghman	Salisbury, Md	July 5, 1853	9, 835
Croze and howel, Cooper's	A. Busenger	Mount Solon, Va	Oct. 3, 1871	119, 570
Croze, Cooper's	J. F. Applegate and C. Feiock	New Albany, Ind	Apr. 25, 1871	114, 089
Croze, Cooper's	V. Applegate, M. P. Jacobs, and S. F. Roby.	Harrison County, Ind	Feb. 28, 1871	112, 205
Croze, Cooper's	J. Bailey	Springport, Ind	June 17, 1873	139, 852
Croze, Cooper's	C. O. Cook	Rockford, Ill	Aug. 11, 1868	80, 9[illegible]7
Croze, Cooper's	J. C. Hofer	Bellaire, Ohio	June 9, 1868	78, 740
Crozing-knives, Method of operating	G. Finn	Oswego, N. Y	Sept. 20, 1859	25, 498
Crozing-machine	V. W. Houck	Buffalo, N. Y	June 10, 1862	38, 519
Crozing-machine	W. R. Middleton	Cleveland, Ohio	June 13, 1871	115, 974
Crozing-machine	A. Wilbur	Lancaster, Pa	Mar. 21, 1854	10, 684
Crucible and metal-heating furnace	B. A. M[illegible]son	New York, N. Y	Dec. 3, 1872	133, 538
Crucible, Black-lead	G. Nimmo	Jersey City, N. J	May 31, 1864	42, 959
Crucible for melting iron and steel	J. E. Atwood	Pittsburgh, Pa	Oct. 8, 1870	108, 084
Crucible for melting iron, steel, &c	W. F. Dunbarr	Pittsburgh, Pa	Jan. 9, 1872	122, 585
Crucible for melting metals, &c	J. L. North	Ansonia, Conn	Feb. 27, 1872	124, 076
Crucible for melting metals	E. R. Payle	Great Bend, Pa	Mar. 23, 1869	88, 072
Crucible for melting metals, &c	R. Yeilding	Detroit, Mich	Nov. 7, 1871	120, 807
Crucible for metallic baths	B. S. Stokes	Manchester, N. H	July 25, 1865	49, 009

50 P

Index of patents issued from the United States Patent Office from 1790 *to* 1873, *inclusive*—Continued.

Invention.	Inventor.	Residence.	Date.	No.
Crucible-making machine	S. R. Thompson	Portsmouth, N. H	Nov. 27, 1866	60, 090
Crucible-mold	T. G. French	Jersey City, N. J	Nov. 7, 1865	50, 812
Crucible-repairing process	W. F. Sherman	Bucksport, Me	Feb. 16, 1869	87, 075
Crucible-stand for fusing metals	J. C. McManus	Providence, R. I	June 14, 1870	104, 179
Crucibles and in melting steel, Mode of repairing plumbago	N. Washburn	Worcester, Mass	July 13, 1869	92, 676
Crucibles and other articles of earthenware, Mode of forming.	J. Akrill	Williamsburgh, N. Y	Oct. 26, 1852	9, 351
Crucibles and potter's ware, Molding	A. Newkumet	Philadelphia, Pa	Jan. 26, 1869	86, 243
Crucibles, Apparatus for making plumbago	W. Smith	Pittsburgh, Pa	Nov. 3, 1863	40, 506
Crucibles, Apparatus for molding	J. L. Presby	Taunton, Mass	Apr. 24, 1866	54, 204
Crucibles, Drying and preparing	G. Nimmo	Jersey City, N. J	July 11, 1865	48, 713
Crucibles, glass-melting pots, &c., Composition for making.	W. A. Fischer	Allegheny City, Pa	Nov. 7, 1871	120, 579
Crucibles, Machine for making	J. Winkle	Pittsburgh, Pa	Jan. 12, 1869	85, 775
Crucibles, Making	J. Dalliba	Watervliet, N. Y	Sept. 26, 1823	....
Crucibles, Manufacture of	A. K. Eaton	Piermont, N. Y	Sept. 14, 1869	94, 726
Crucibles, Manufacture of	G. Nimmo	Jersey City, N. J	Aug. 1, 1865	49, 141
Crucibles, Molding	G. Nimmo	Jersey City, N. J	Aug. 1, 1865	49, 140
Cruet	T. H. Mead	Boston, Mass	Jan. 4, 1870	98, 511
Cruet or bottle for caster	J. O. Mead	Philadelphia, Pa	Feb. 15, 1859	22, 970
Cruet or bottle, Vinegar	G. W. and G. H. Simmons	Bennington, Vt	May 17, 1859	24, 083
Cruet or decanter	A. H. Newton	Worcester, Mass	Apr. 8, 1862	34, 899
Cruet-stand	J. W. Ells	Pittsburgh, Pa	Feb. 21, 1871	111, 920
Crumb-remover	A. B. Hoffman	Roxbury, Mass	Nov. 27, 1866	60, 009
Crupper	F. Howes	Boston, Mass	May 30, 1865	47, 953
Crupper, Horse	P. A. La France	Elmira, N. Y	Feb. 23, 1869	87, 269
Crupper, Spring	E. Powell	Conneautville, Pa	Jan. 1, 1867	60, 784
Crusher: *See* Bark-crusher. Beef-steak crusher. Cane-crusher. Clod-crusher. Corn and cob crusher. Culinary crusher. Drug-crusher. Fruit and vegetable crusher. Grape-crusher. Ice-crusher. Meat-crusher. Ore-crusher. Quartz-crusher. Rock and ore crusher. Stalk-crusher. Stone-crusher. Vegetable-crusher.				
Crusher and press for culinary purposes	G. B. Fowler	Brooklyn, N. Y	Mar. 4, 1873	136, 498
Crusher, cultivator, and harrow, Combined	J. B. McClean and C. A. Mayes	Franklin, Ky	Dec. 31, 1872	1[illegible], 388
Crusher, harrow, and roller combined	J. Simpson	Charleston, Ill	Nov. 24, 1868	84, 386
Crushing and baling machine	J. Price, jr	Petaluma, Cal	Nov. 28, 1865	51, 212
Crushing and grinding machine	J. W. Rutter	Saint Louis, Mo	Mar. 23, 1869	88, 216
Crushing and grinding mill	J. Weigle	Swan Station, Pa	Feb. 6, 1855	12, 356
Crushing and grinding mill	A. P. Norton	Pittsburgh, Pa	Apr. 25, 1848	5, 533
Crushing and grinding rock, phosphates, &c., Machine for.	F. J. Kimball	Philadelphia, Pa	May 2, 1871	114, 303
Crushing and pressing machine	C. and O. Waste	Cameron, Ill	June 7, 1864	43, 054
Crushing-machine	J. Rowe	Athens, Ala	Apr. 24, 1840	1, 560
Crushing machine, Rock, ore, &c	W. F. Goodwin and C. R. Squire	East New York and New York, N. Y.	Oct. 8, 1867	69, 656
Crushing-mill	J. W. Smith	Columbus, Ga	Mar. 18, 1873	137, 035
Crushing mill, Apple, sugar cane, &c	J. H. Ellis	Brooklyn, Pa	Feb. 4, 1862	34, 296
Crushing-mill, Pendulum	J. Hart	Sweden Centre, N. Y	Nov. 8, 1870	109, 006
Crush-mills, Flask for casting stamp-shoes for	H. Bolthoff	Central City, Colo	Oct. 25, 1870	108, 556
Crushing-press	E. Chipman	New York, N. Y	Oct. 20, 1863	40, 325
Crushing, rolling, and kneading machine	C. Bates	Kingston, Mass	Aug. 7, 1866	56, 877
Crutch	G. T. Allamby and J. G. Bugbee	Bangor, Me	Apr. 18, 1865	47, 265
Crutch	G. T. Allamby and J. G. Bugbee	Bangor, Me	Dec. 26, 1865	51, 677
Crutch	A. Bickel	Philadelphia, Pa	Jan. 17, 1860	26, 829
Crutch	A. Bickel	Philadelphia, Pa	May 16, 1865	47, 695
Crutch	S. A. Bracket	Boston, Mass	Dec. 31, 1872	134, 351
Crutch	A. E. Brown	Baltimore, Md	June 30, 1868	79, 305
Crutch	L. Crandall	Plainfield, N. J	Oct. 27, 1863	40, 443
Crutch	L. Crandall	New York, N. Y	May 21, 1872	127, 028
Crutch	H. G. Davis	New York, N. Y	Jan. 13, 1863	37, 387
Crutch	J. S. Gallagher, jr	Washington, D. C	Jan. 4, 1853	9, 518
Crutch	T. E. Gordon	Cleveland, Ohio	Nov. 29, 1864	45, 242
Crutch	T. E. Gordon	Brooklyn, Ohio	Jan. 3, 1865	45, 709
Crutch	J. A. Lobb	Independence, Mo	May 12, 1868	77, 824
Crutch	E. T. Pearl	Milwaukee, Wis	Nov. 28, 1871	121, 254
Crutch	J. C. Rhodes	Stillwater, Minn	Jan. 14, 1868	73, 386
Crutch	D. Ring	Damariscotta, Me	Sept. 1, 1863	39, 751
Crutch	R. W. Ware	Chicago, Ill	Aug. 21, 1866	57, 416
Crutch	J. D. W. Wemple	Albany, N. Y	Sept. 8, 1863	39, 854
Crutch	J. Whittemore	South Reading, Mass	Oct. 21, 1862	36, 743
Crutch	P. R. Wimer	Trenton, N. J	May 10, 1870	102, 901
Crutch-foot, Revolving	J. G. Bugbee	Bangor, Me	Aug. 15, 1865	49, 371
Crutch-handle	S. Kreger	Philadelphia, Pa	July 4, 1871	116, 603
Crutch or perambulator, Wheel	S. A. Darrack	Orange, N. J	Aug. 6, 1872	130, 283
Cryptographic alphabet	E. H. Hawley	Signal Corps, Army of Potomac.	July 11, 1865	48, 681
Crystal-cutting machine	P. Pryibil	New York, N. Y	Sept. 23, 1862	36, 548
Crystal fountain	J. C. Johnson	Louisville, Ky	Apr. 28, 1868	77, 290
Crystallized metallic surfaces, Protecting and beautifying.	H. M. Johnston	New York, N. Y	July 19, 1870	105, 576
Crystallized salts upon glass, mica, &c., Preserving and beautifying.	O. S. Follet	New York, N. Y	July 19, 1870	105, 560
Cue-cutter	J. Huber	Saint Louis, Mo	May 10, 1870	102, 821
Cue-trimmer	D. Aldrich	New York, N. Y	May 5, 1868	77, 436

Index of patents issued from the United States Patent Office from 1790 *to* 1873, *inclusive*—Continued.

Invention.	Inventor.	Residence.	Date.	No.
Cuff	L. H. Foy	New Haven, Conn	Aug. 27, 1872	130, 801
Cuff	I. Levine	New York, N. Y	Mar. 5, 1867	62, 648
Cuff	F. E. Mack	Albany, N. Y	Dec. 30, 1873	145, 957
Cuff	I. M. Post	Philadelphia, Pa	Mar. 11, 1873	136, 760
Cuff-fastener	A. Douglas	English Neighborhood, N.J	Apr. 19, 1864	42, 434
Cuff-holder	G. W. James	Jersey City, N. J	Oct. 28, 1873	144, 101
Cuff, Reversible	L. H. Foy	New Haven, Conn	Apr. 15, 1873	137, 907
Cuff-supporter	T. Cogswell	Boston, Mass	Mar. 22, 1870	100, 985
Cuffs, Fabric for	H. H. Thayer and W. H. Hart, jr	Philadelphia, Pa	May 2, 1871	114, 490
Culinary apparatus	R. H. Cazier	Philadelphia, Pa	July 22, 1873	141, 114
Culinary apparatus	J. S. Field	Brooklyn, N. Y	Sept. 8, 1868	81, 887
Culinary apparatus	I. Former	Grafton, Va	Oct. 2, 1860	30, 214
Culinary apparatus	G. B. Isham	Burlington, Vt	May 12, 1868	77, 884
Culinary apparatus	T. W. Moore	New York, N. Y	Jan. 21, 1868	73, 630
Culinary apparatus	F. Morandi	Malden, Mass	Mar. 31, 1868	76, 231
Culinary apparatus	W. W. S. Orbeton	Bradford, Mass	July 28, 1868	80, 303
Culinary apparatus	V. M. Thomas	Brandon, Vt	July 28, 1868	80, 315
Culinary apparatus	J. Van	Cincinnati, Ohio	Aug. 23, 1870	106, 745
Culinary apparatus	B. Wardwell	Providence, R. I	May 4, 1869	89, 613
Culinary apparatus	H. A. Zopff	Milwaukee, Wis	May 5, 1868	77, 702
Culinary apparatus, Steam	C. I. Paine	Young America, Ill	Jan. 18, 1870	98, 881
Culinary baking apparatus	P. Wilcox	Springfield, Mass	Feb. 18, 1829	....
Culinary boiler	E. K. Ames	Chicago, Ill	Feb. 2, 1869	86, 488
Culinary boiler	A. Anderson	London, Canada	Feb. 13, 1872	123, 662
Culinary boiler	G. W. Bliss	Brooklyn, N. Y	Mar. 1, 1870	100, 361
Culinary boiler	P. Boesn and M. Bedessem	Kenosha, Wis	Mar. 28, 1871	113, 011
Culinary boiler	J. Bowlin	Charlestown, Mass	Dec. 17, 1872	133, 918
Culinary boiler	I. S. Bunnell	Carbondale, Pa	May 10, 1870	102, 765
Culinary boiler	F. M. Carnes	Rochester, N. Y	Mar. 15, 1870	100, 853
Culinary boiler	J. H. Corey	New York, N. Y	Oct. 14, 1873	143, 673
Culinary boiler	W. H. Crosby	Washington, D. C	Sept. 30, 1862	36, 558
Culinary boiler	T. Daro	Osceola, Iowa	July 30, 1861	32, 964
Culinary boiler	F. W. Dembois	East Saginaw, Mich	Mar. 27, 1866	53, 421
Culinary boiler	J. D. Durham	Dalston, England	Feb. 20, 1872	123, 876
Culinary boiler	S. S. Fitch	New York, N. Y	Apr. 8, 1873	137, 604
Culinary boiler	B. French	Rochester, N. Y	Dec. 12, 1871	121, 770
Culinary boiler	J. Gibbs	Opelousas, La	Feb. 20, 1872	123, 820
Culinary boiler	W. H. Henderson	Franklin, Ind	Sept. 3, 1867	68, 564
Culinary boiler	T. D. Ingersoll	Monroe, Mich	Mar. 26, 1861	31, 807
Culinary boiler	I. Kinney	London, Canada	Aug. 27, 1872	130, 921
Culinary boiler	R. B. Lewis	Quincy, Ill	Mar. 25, 1873	137, 140
Culinary boiler	S. P. Loomis	Philadelphia, Pa	Feb. 2, 1869	86, 428
Culinary boiler	L. McLellan	Gorham, Me	Apr. 27, 1869	89, 419
Culinary boiler	F. Meyer	New York, N. Y	May 30, 1871	115, 338
Culinary boiler	O. Poole	Detroit, Mich	Feb. 11, 1868	74, 419
Culinary boiler	T. T. Prosser	Chicago, Ill	July 24, 1866	56, 609
Culinary boiler	R. Russell	New Bedford, Mass	Jan. 2, 1872	122, 407
Culinary boiler	S. E. Saul	New York, N. Y	May 22, 1866	54, 964
Culinary boiler	J. R. Stafford	Cleveland, Ohio	June 12, 1847	5, 153
Culinary boiler	P. L. Suine	Shirleysburgh, Pa	June 30, 1863	39, 077
Culinary boiler	J. S. Totten	Lebanon, Ohio	Nov. 2, 1869	96, 509
Culinary boiler	I. H. West and T. L. Camp	Evans, N. Y	Feb. 18, 1868	74, 647
Culinary boiler	R. C. Whitehouse	Hogdon's Mills, Me	July 25, 1871	117, 356
Culinary boiler	F. Wilcox	Newark, N. J	Apr. 20, 1869	89, 189
Culinary boiler	J. Zimmerman	Royalton Centre, N. Y	Dec. 17, 1867	72, 354
Culinary-boiler cover	P. J. and J. Abbott	Dexter, Me	Oct. 11, 1870	108, 082
Culinary boiler, Portable	A. W. Spencer	Cazenovia, N. Y	June 19, 1835	....
Culinary cabinet	J. Billings	Brighton, Mass	Mar. 20, 1866	53, 260
Culinary fixtures for anthracite coal, Construction of	J. F. Walters	Philadelphia, Pa	June 8, 1827	....
Culinary fork and spoon	A. Hills	Naugatuck, Conn	Apr. 10, 1860	27, 802
Culinary furnace	J. Reed	Marshfield, Mass	Jan. 5, 1831	....
Culinary pot	J. D. Flansburgh	Philadelphia, Pa	Jan. 21, 1862	34, 202
Culinary pot	J. S. Kidd and M. Melville	Brooklyn, N. Y	July 16, 1872	129, 034
Culinary sink	Z. Hunt	Hudson, N. Y	July 10, 1866	56, 225
Culinary uses, Compound for	H. W. Bradley	Binghamton, N. Y	Jan. 3, 1871	110, 626
Culinary uses, Shortening for	H. W. Bradley	Plainfield, N. J	Oct. 17, 1871	120, 026
Culinary utensil	H. G. Dunkelberger	Shamokin, Pa	Nov. 11, 1873	144, 518
Culinary utensils for broiling and frying	S. Lee	Taunton, Mass	June 11, 1872	127, 900
Culinary vessel	J. C. Nobles	Ilion, N. Y	Nov. 7, 1871	120, 769
Culinary vessel	W. A. Barlow	Chicago, Ill	Dec. 16, 1873	145, 550
Culinary vessel	W. H. Bennett	New York, N. Y	Jan. 21, 1868	73, 568
Culinary vessel	W. H. Bloom	Tiffin, Ohio	Apr. 25, 1871	113, 971
Culinary vessel	W. J. Burnett	Cairo, Ill	Apr. 9, 1872	125, 538
Culinary vessel	J. H. Chappell	New York, N. Y	Jan. 31, 1871	111, 317
Culinary vessel	S. W. M. Chattaway	Middletown, Conn	June 6, 1871	115, 703
Culinary vessel	E. Clark	Buffalo, N. Y	July 26, 1870	105, 779
Culinary vessel	C. E. Corbett	Binghamton, N. Y	Mar. 15, 1870	100, 863
Culinary vessel	H. L. Dunckloe	Boston, Mass	Apr. 7, 1868	76, 310
Culinary vessel	C. Estabrooks	Calais, Me	Mar. 29, 1870	101, 244
Culinary vessel	C. W. Fuller	Earlville, Ill	June 2, 1868	78, 587
Culinary vessel	C. W. Hermance	Schuylerville, N. Y	May 17, 1870	103, 180
Culinary vessel	L. Hermance	Lansingburgh, N. Y	Mar. 21, 1871	112, 916
Culinary vessel	B. M. Hermance	Troy, N. Y	Dec. 13, 1870	110, 039
Culinary vessel	C. Jessup	New Haven, Conn	Mar. 7, 1871	112, 352
Culinary vessel	C. A. Johnson	Des Moines, Iowa	July 7, 1868	79, 574
Culinary vessel	A. C. Kasson	Milwaukee, Wis	Nov. 17, 1868	84, 194
Culinary vessel	G. Landrine	Jersey City, N. J	Feb. 22, 1870	100, 045
Culinary vessel	S. Lee	Taunton, Mass	Aug. 29, 1871	118, 402
Culinary vessel	A. F. Marston	Clinton, La	Sept. 1, 1868	81, 658
Culinary vessel	O. M. Mitchell	Marathon, N. Y	July 20, 1869	92, 867
Culinary vessel	F. Morandi	Malden, Mass	Jan. 31, 1871	111, 369
Culinary vessel	W. H. Murch	Portland, Me	Apr. 4, 1871	113, 442
Culinary vessel	G. L. Page	Wallingford, Conn	July 16, 1872	129, 293
Culinary vessel	J. W. Patterson	Cincinnati, Ohio	Feb. 4, 1868	74, 123
Culinary vessel	H. Poole	Richmond, Ind	Aug. 25, 1868	81, 534
Culinary vessel	E. Ripley	Troy, N. Y	Jan. 5, 1864	41, 095
Culinary vessel	J. C. Smith	Rochester, N. Y	May 3, 1870	102, 608
Culinary vessel	H. Zachgo	South Brooklyn, N. Y	June 22, 1869	91, 697

Index of patents issued from the United States Patent Office from 1790 *to* 1873, *inclusive*—Continued.

Invention.	Inventor.	Residence.	Date.	No.
Culinary vessel, Nickel-lined	S. C. Moore	Boston, Mass	July 6, 1869	92, 337
Culinary vessel, Steam	C. Waterman	Providence, R. I	Nov. 2, 1869	96, 518
Culinary vessels, Pivoted lid for	J. H. McConnell	Beaver Falls, Pa	Nov. 26, 1872	133, 326
Culinary vessels, Sheet-copper plate for	A. O'Neil	Portsmouth, Ohio	Aug. 27, 1867	68, 331
Cultivating and improving earth	J. Hall	....	Nov. 19, 1814	....
Cultivating and tilling the ground	J. D. Prescott	Chesterville, Me	May 15, 1834	....
Cultivating corn and beans, Machine for	E. Spooner	....	Jan. 25, 1799	....
Cultivating-hook	J. F. Leitch	Oxford, N. Y	June 7, 1870	104, 042
Cultivating implement, Garden	D. Mack	Barnesville, Kans	Nov. 25, 1873	144, 912
Cultivating land by steam	J. Fowler, jr	Cornhill, England	Jan. 10, 1865	45, 892
Cultivating-machine	C. G. Grabo	Greenfield, Mich	May 26, 1863	38, 676
Cultivating-machine	W. F. Quimby and G. G. Lobdell.	Stanton and Wilmington, Del.	Apr. 7, 1863	38, 124
Cultivating machine, Cotton	W. Altick	Dayton, Ohio	Apr. 23, 1867	64, 057
Cultivating machine, Cotton	W. P. Sample	Bedford County, Tenn	Sept. 3, 1831	....
Cultivator	H. A. Adams	Sandwich, Ill	May 31, 1870	103, 537
Cultivator	J. Adams	Manteno, Ill	June 21, 1870	104, 399
Cultivator	W. Adams	Detroit, Mich	Aug. 3, 1858	21, 055
Cultivator	A. Agnew and W. Morrison	Chester County and Chadd's Ford, Pa.	July 10, 1860	29, 043
Cultivator	M. Alden	Auburn, N. Y	May 10, 1859	2[illegible], 886
Cultivator	J. T. D. Alexander	Maryenna, Tex	Jan. 15, 1861	31, 101
Cultivator	D. R. Allen	Cumberland, Me	Feb. 26, 1867	62, 385
Cultivator	A. H. Allison	Charlottesville, Ind	Jan. 29, 1867	61, 649
Cultivator	A. H. Allison	Charlottesville, Ind	Oct. 15, 1867	69, 743
Cultivator	A. H. Allison	Charlottesville, Ind	Sept. 15, 1868	82, 060
Cultivator	J. H. Allison	Eureka, Ill	May 7, 1867	64, 469
Cultivator	P. H. Allstott	Jeffersonville, Ind	July 18, 1865	48, 783
Cultivator	C. Alvord	Westford, Wis	Dec. 15, 1868	84, 931
Cultivator	C. Alvord	Courtland, Wis	Apr. 26, 1870	102, 201
Cultivator	W. D. Ament	Muscatine, Iowa	Jan. 10, 1865	45, 807
Cultivator	W. D. Ament	Muscatine, Iowa	July 25, 1865	48, 884
Cultivator	A. Anderson	London, Canada	Sept. 18, 1866	58, 188
Cultivator	J. H. and E. H. Anderson	Easton, Md	Nov. 27, 1860	30, 709
Cultivator	A. P. Anderson and B. Edwards	Princeton, Ill	July 10, 1866	56, 157
Cultivator	W. W. Andrew	La Porte, Ind	Mar. 5, 1872	124, 241
Cultivator	W. J. Andrews	Columbia, Tenn	Sept. 11, 1866	57, 841
Cultivator	W. J. Andrews	Columbia, Tenn	Feb. 26, 1867	62, 386
Cultivator	J. and G. W. Ansley	Marengo, Mich	Nov. 28, 1871	121, 267
Cultivator	B. Anyan	Fitchville, Ohio	Mar. 24, 1868	75, 826
Cultivator	J. Armstrong	Elmira, Ill	Dec. 26, 1865	51, 680
Cultivator	J. Armstrong, jr	Elmira, Ill	Feb. 19, 1867	62, 109
Cultivator	T. Arndt	Mount Joy, Pa	Nov. 24, 1868	84, 338
Cultivator	O. J. Arnold	Mount Ida, Wis	Feb. 26, 1867	62, 387
Cultivator	H. B. Arnoldt and J. Grimm	Saint Louis, Mo	Feb. 4, 1868	74, 031
Cultivator	W. J. Arrington	Louisville, Ga	Aug. 15, 1871	117, 961
Cultivator	J. N. Arvin	Valparaiso, Ind	July 24, 1866	56, 511
Cultivator	J. Austin	Rockford, Ill	Mar. 15, 1864	41, 899
Cultivator	I. Avery	Ottawa, Ill	July 17, 1866	56, 344
Cultivator	R. H. Avery	Galesburgh, Ill	Dec. 27, 1870	110, 419
Cultivator	R. H. Avery	Galesburgh, Ill	May 28, 1872	127, 293
Cultivator	J. Ayres and M. F. Hunt	Bushnell, Ill	July 23, 1872	129, 642
Cultivator	D. C. Baker	Fulton, N. Y	May 13, 1873	138, 838
Cultivator	J. M Baker	Fayetteville, Tex	Sept. 7, 1869	94, 542
Cultivator	N. Baker	Flowerfield, Mich	Aug. 15, 1848	5, 715
Cultivator	W. T. Baker	Lancaster, Tex	Nov. 2, 1869	96, 379
Cultivator	L. Baldwin	Stone Mills, N. Y	Apr. 8, 1873	137, 649
Cultivator	P. O. Baldwin	Spring Lake, Mich	July 18, 1871	117, 034
Cultivator	W. M. Ball	Morristown, Ind	Apr. 16, 1867	63, 830
Cultivator	W. M. Ball	Morristown, Ind	July 23, 1867	66, 934
Cultivator	T. J. Ball and J. Post	Pittsfield, Mich	Apr. 6, 1852	8, 850
Cultivator	J. T. Baltimore	Marble Rock, Iowa	Dec. 31, 1867	72, 780
Cultivator	W. Bancroft	Whiteford, Ohio	Nov. 14, 1854	11, 924
Cultivator	J. Banks	Dadeville, Ala	Mar. 30, 1858	19, 742
Cultivator	W. Bankson	Mount Pleasant, Iowa	Feb. 28, 1865	46, 537
Cultivator	I. Barber, jr	La Porte, Ind	Jan. 3, 1865	45, 687
Cultivator	I. Barber	La Porte, Ind	Dec. 3, 1867	71, 834
Cultivator	J. A. Bardel	Freeport, Ill	Sept. 12, 1865	49, 845
Cultivator	J. H. Barley	Longwood, Mo	Sept. 4, 1866	57, 660
Cultivator	J. H. Barley	Sedalia, Mo	Sept. 24, 1867	69, 162
Cultivator	H. Barnes	Burlington, Wis	May 1, 1866	54, 280
Cultivator	N. Barnes	East Hampton, N. Y	Sept. 10, 1840	1, 779
Cultivator	M. Barnett and E. Wood	Hardinsburgh, Ind	Nov. 12, 1867	70, 779
Cultivator	F. Barney	Bloomington, Ill	July 12, 1854	43, 470
Cultivator	A. S. Barnwell	Savannah, Ga	Mar. 12, 1867	62, 808
Cultivator	M. J. Barr	Centreville, Ind	Mar. 5, 1872	124, 316
Cultivator	O. Barr and F. F. Cox	Beloit, Wis	May 15, 1866	54, 669
Cultivator	F. M. Barrier	Stevenson, Ala	Feb. 4, 1868	73, 945
Cultivator	H. Barsalow	Saint Anne, Ill	Jan. 8, 1867	61, 040
Cultivator	L. B Barton	Metamora, Ill	Apr. 25, 1865	47, 380
Cultivator	L. B. Barton	Metamora, Ill	Oct. 17, 1865	50, 439
Cultivator	W. E. Bates	Elmore, Ill	May 16, 1865	47, 693
Cultivator	I. Bates, A. Wood, and D. Wells	Adams, N. Y	May 28, 1842	2, 647
Cultivator	J. W. and L. Batson	Clarksville, Md	May 24, 1859	24, 089
Cultivator	J. N. Baumann	Mascatine, Iowa	July 29, 1862	35, 985
Cultivator	W. T. Bazemore	Bibb County, Ga	Aug. 29, 1854	11, 593
Cultivator	C. Beach and T. Brown	Jacksontown, Ohio	Feb. 12, 1861	31, 367
Cultivator	T. Beale	New Milford, Ill	Oct. 9, 1866	58, 578
Cultivator	H. Bean and J. D. Tyson	Schuylkill and Lower Providence, Pa.	Oct. 15, 1867	69, 7[illegible]0
Cultivator	E. C. Bean and F. N. Welden	Rockford, Ill	Nov. 2, 1869	96, [illegible]82
Cultivator	G. Beeching	Augusta, N. Y	Oct. 17, 1848	5, 859
Cultivator	J. Behel	Rockford, Ill	Feb. 18, 1873	135, 964
Cultivator	C. Belden	Middlebury, Ohio	Feb. 13, 1866	52, 515
Cultivator	H. M. Belden	Farmington, Ohio	Dec. 4, 1860	30, 796
Cultivator	A. C. Belt	Goresville, Va	Nov. 12, 1867	70, 785
Cultivator	I. A. Benedict	West Springfield, Pa	June 15, 1869	91, 303
Cultivator	D. G. Benner	Holmesville, Ohio	Feb. 8, 1870	99, 625

Index of patents issued from the United States Patent Office from 1790 *to* 1873, *inclusive*—Continued.

Invention.	Inventor.	Residence.	Date.	No.
Cultivator	A. Bennett	Rockford, Ill	Jan. 14, 1868	73, 224
Cultivator	J. S. and W. Benson	Lebanon, Pa	Sept. 3, 1867	68, 549
Cultivator	L. B. Benton	Penn Yan, N. Y	Nov. 27, 1860	30, 711
Cultivator	J. Bergen	Plain Township, Ohio	Aug. 28, 1866	57, 619
Cultivator	J. Bergen	Canton, Ohio	Apr. 23, 1867	64, 061
Cultivator	T. F. Bertrand and P. Sames	Rockford, Ill	Apr. 24, 1866	54, 099
Cultivator	T. F. Bertrand and P. Sames	Rockford, Ill	Jan. 1, 1867	60, 916
Cultivator	J. T. Bever	Bethel, Ill	June 27, 1865	48, 358
Cultivator	J. T. Bever	Bethel, Ill	Dec. 5, 1865	51, 286
Cultivator	C. Billups	Norfolk, Va	May 7, 1872	126, 513
Cultivator	C. Billups	Norfolk, Va	Jan. 21, 1873	135, 070
Cultivator	C. Bird	Ackley, Iowa	Mar. 29, 1870	101, 216
Cultivator	J. C. Bird	Rising Sun, Md	June 11, 1867	65, 719
Cultivator	A. M. Black	Auburn, Ill	Nov. 11, 1862	36, 889
Cultivator	A. M. Black	Auburn, Ill	July 3, 1866	55, 993
Cultivator	T. Black	Princeville, Ill	Aug. 28, 1860	29, 758
Cultivator	W. R. Blanchard	Hertford, N. C	Jan. 26, 1869	86, 205
Cultivator	B. C. Blomsten	Waupaca, Wis	Aug. 22, 1871	118, 186
Cultivator	A. R. Blood, A. Hathaway, and V. R. Beach.	Independence, Iowa	June 2, 1868	78, 417
Cultivator	A. R. Blood, A. Hathaway, and V. R. Beach.	Independence, Iowa	June 30, 1868	79, 304
Cultivator	D. G. Blue	Winfield, Iowa	Jan. 6, 1863	37, 271
Cultivator	J. Bohan	New Hartford, Iowa	Oct. 12, 1869	95, 762
Cultivator	J. W. Booker	Fairmount, Ill	May 26, 1863	38, 651
Cultivator	J. W. Boosinger	Marino, Ill	Sept. 4, 1866	57, 668
Cultivator	E. Boughton	East Bloomfield, N. Y	Jan. 31, 1854	10, 467
Cultivator	A. Bouton	Napa, Cal	Oct. 3, 1865	50, 217
Cultivator	H. W. Bowen	Providence, R. I	June 4, 1872	127, 453
Cultivator	J. Bower	Dayton, Ohio	Apr. 19, 1870	101, 976
Cultivator	H. Bowers	New Hudson, Mich	Aug. 27, 1861	33, 129
Cultivator	D. W. Bowman	Tippecanoe City, Ohio	Dec. 5, 1871	121, 484
Cultivator	J. C. Boyd	Milroy, Ind	Jan. 14, 1868	73, 291
Cultivator	H. Boys	Rushville, Ind	May 28, 1867	65, 158
Cultivator	B. C. Bradley	Chicago, Ill	Feb. 4, 1873	135, 401
Cultivator	G. Bradley	Rockford, Ill	June 11, 1872	127, 674
Cultivator	S. Brady	Salona, Pa	Apr. 6, 1842	2, 540
Cultivator	B. F. Brato	New Scotland, N. Y	Mar. 4, 1873	136, 409
Cultivator	M. Breneman	East Donegal Township, Pa.	Jan. 29, 1867	61, 512
Cultivator	J. Brewer	Albany, Ill	May 16, 1865	47, 699
Cultivator	J. Brewer	Albany, Ill	Aug. 1, 1865	49, 075
Cultivator	E. Briggs	Medina, Ohio	July 17, 1860	29, 136
Cultivator	E. Briggs	Cleveland, Ohio	July 29, 1873	141, 199
Cultivator	T. E. C. Brinly	Louisville, Ky	Sept. 25, 1860	30, 119
Cultivator	T. E. C. Brinly	Louisville, Ky	June 20, 1871	116, 147
Cultivator	A. C. Brinser	Middletown, Pa	Aug. 24, 1869	94, 067
Cultivator	J. H. Brinton	Thornbury Township, Pa.	Dec. 15, 1868	84, 935
Cultivator	H. C. Bristol	Ravenna, Ohio	Apr. 9, 1867	63, 698
Cultivator	J. T. Brittain	Springfield, Ohio	Oct. 17, 1871	120, 028
Cultivator	S. W. Brock	Niantic, Ill	Nov. 23, 1869	97, 032
Cultivator	G. W. Bronson	Ottawa, Ill	Jan. 17, 1871	111, 037
Cultivator	J. E. Brooks	Gooding's Grove, Ill	Dec. 24, 1867	72, 598
Cultivator	R. M. Brooks	Greenville, Ga	June 26, 1860	28, 829
Cultivator	W. Brooks	Lexington, Ga	Nov. 5, 1872	132, 796
Cultivator	R. Brotten	Oskaloosa, Iowa	Sept. 10, 1861	33, 235
Cultivator	F. E. Brown	Hightstown, N. J	Mar. 25, 1862	34, 732
Cultivator	G. W. Brown	Tylersville, Ill	June 5, 1849	6, 511
Cultivator	G. W. Brown	Galesburgh, Ill	Aug. 28, 1860	29, 762
Cultivator	J. Brown	Lawn Ridge, Ill	Nov. 14, 1854	11, 929
Cultivator	W. P. Brown	Malta, Ohio	July 9, 1872	128, 701
Cultivator	M. Bruner, jr	Fremont, Ohio	Mar. 15, 1870	100, 720
Cultivator	R. C. Buckley	Peoria, Ill	Dec. 24, 1872	134, 248
Cultivator	M. H. Bucknall	Darien, Wis	Sept. 11, 1866	57, 856
Cultivator	C. J. Buckner	Paxton, Ill	Feb. 23, 1864	41, 677
Cultivator	R. Bulleck	South Mills, N. C	July 10, 1866	56, 173
Cultivator	R. I. Burbank	Boston, Mass	Feb. 2, 1869	86, 502
Cultivator	J. M. Burke	Dansville, N. Y	Nov. 15, 1864	45, 019
Cultivator	J. Burnham	La Salle, Ill	Feb. 4, 1868	74, 044
Cultivator	J. Burnham and W. C. Lathrop	La Salle, Ill	Sept. 11, 1866	57, 858
Cultivator	J. Burns	Franklin, Ohio	July 28, 1863	39, 337
Cultivator	W. J. Burton	Turtle, Wis	Sept. 26, 1865	50, 093
Cultivator	N. Buttler	Otterville, Mo	Aug. 10, 1869	93, 412
Cultivator	S. S. Bushnel	Horicon, Wis	Jan. 14, 1873	134, 728
Cultivator	W. Bushnell	Easton, Pa	Mar. 27, 1860	27, 614
Cultivator	E. T. Bussell	Indianapolis, Ind	July 23, 1872	129, 712
Cultivator	H. F. Byerly	Clinton, Ill	May 22, 1866	54, 854
Cultivator	J. E. Byers	Butler, Pa	Mar. 5, 1872	124, 320
Cultivator	S. M. Cain and W. Stelfox	Austin, Tex	June 4, 1861	32, 468
Cultivator	G. Calkins	El Paso, Ill	Sept. 5, 1865	49, 715
Cultivator	J. F. Cameron	Livingston County, Mo	June 26, 1860	28, 841
Cultivator	J. Canfield	Sabula, Iowa	July 26, 1864	43, 635
Cultivator	J. Canfield and C. Hess	Washington and Lyons, Iowa.	Mar. 27, 1866	53, 408
Cultivator	T. F. Capp	Bloomington, Ill	May 23, 1871	115, 159
Cultivator	A. Carey	Rome, Ga	Feb. 14, 1860	27, 106
Cultivator	P. S. Carhart	Collamer, N. Y	June 10, 1862	35, 505
Cultivator	P. S. Carhart	Collamer, N. Y	May 9, 1865	47, 618
Cultivator	J. H. Carlow	Kidder, Mo	Dec. 27, 1870	110, 548
Cultivator	A. F. Carlson	Attica, Ind	Jan. 30, 1872	123, 235
Cultivator	D. F. Carr	East Union Township, Ohio.	June 8, 1869	91, 084
Cultivator	H. Carr	Wooster, Ohio	Mar. 8, 1870	100, 499
Cultivator	H. Carr	Wooster, Ohio	Mar. 8, 1870	100, 500
Cultivator	H. Carr	Wooster, Ohio	Mar. 8, 1870	100, 501
Cultivator	N., jr., and J. Carr	Monmouth, Ill	July 23, 1861	32, 858
Cultivator	N., jr., and J. Carr	Monmouth, Ill	Jan. 5, 1869	85, 509
Cultivator	C. H. and S. E. Carrington	Weymouth, Ohio	Oct. 12, 1858	21, 739

Index of patents issued from the United States Patent Office from 1790 *to* 1873, *inclusive*—Continued.

Invention.	Inventor.	Residence.	Date.	No.
Cultivator	N. C. Carter	Union City, Ind	Oct. 9, 1860	30, 295
Cultivator	J. Case	La Fayette, Ind	Feb. 2, 1864	41, 423
Cultivator	J. Case	Springfield, Ohio	Apr. 17, 1866	53, 947
Cultivator	J. Case	La Fayette, Ind	Jan. 31, 1871	111, 432
Cultivator	A. B. Cass	Muscatine, Iowa	June 24, 1862	35, 668
Cultivator	A. B. Cass	Chicago, Ill	Jan. 3, 1865	45, 700
Cultivator	L. J. Caswell	Scott Township, Ind	Nov. 6, 1866	59, 358
Cultivator	N. A. Cates	Thorndike, Me	Oct. 1, 1867	69, 314
Cultivator	W. W. Cato	Hicksford, Va	June 25, 1872	128, 369
Cultivator	I. N. Cauthorn	Carthage, Ill	Jan. 14, 1873	134, 732
Cultivator	R. S. Cavett	Bedias, Tex	Nov. 18, 1873	144, 740
Cultivator	J. Caylor	Fairview, Ind	July 15, 1873	140, 885
Cultivator	M. and J. Caywood	Peoria County, Ill	Feb. 16, 1869	86, 905
Cultivator	I. H. Chappell	Lawrence, Kans	Apr. 2, 1872	125, 271
Cultivator	I. H. Chappell and J. Montgomery.	Decatur, Ill	Dec. 1, 1868	84, 611
Cultivator	J. Charlton	Allegheny, Pa	June 26, 1860	28, 833
Cultivator	E. Children	Liberty, Wis	Oct. 2, 1866	58, 380
Cultivator	E. Children	Lancaster, Wis	Feb. 12, 1867	62, 004
Cultivator	J. G. Christopher	Byron, Ill	Apr. 10, 1860	27, 776
Cultivator	A. L. Chubb	Grand Rapids, Mich	Jan. 4, 1870	98, 560
Cultivator	D. Churchill	Ionia, Ill	Jan. 7, 1868	72, 975
Cultivator	D. Churchill and S. C. Brewer	Ionia, Ill	Oct. 17, 1865	50, 453
Cultivator	C. Clark	Andersonville, Ga	July 3, 1860	28, 968
Cultivator	C. A. Clark	Bloomfield, Iowa	Nov. 27, 1860	30, 720
Cultivator	C. M. Clark	Seward, Nebr	Apr. 23, 1872	125, 936
Cultivator	M. M. Clark	Industry, Ill	Dec. 15, 1863	40, 909
Cultivator	W. F. Clark	Hagaman's Mills, N. Y	Feb. 5, 1867	61, 805
Cultivator	G. D. Cleaveland	Flint, Ind	Sept. 10, 1872	131, 150
Cultivator	G. M. Clements	Kenduskeag, Me	Nov. 11, 1862	36, 894
Cultivator	A. P. Clements and J. C. Nealey	Monroe, Me	Apr. 26, 1870	102, 223
Cultivator	J. H. Clifton	Newcastle, Pa	Sept. 15, 1868	82, 089
Cultivator	L. Clifton	Barry, Ill	Nov. 10, 1868	83, 931
Cultivator	B. M. Close	West Camden, N. Y	June 15, 1869	91, 212
Cultivator	I. Cobb	Westminster, Vt	Dec. 7, 1829	....
Cultivator	B. C., T. W., and J. M. Cochran	Pana, Ill	June 18, 1867	65, 875
Cultivator	C. A. Cogswell	Maquoketa, Iowa	May 26, 1868	78, 186
Cultivator	D. C. Colby	Claremont, N. H	Nov. 11, 1862	36, 895
Cultivator	J. H. Coleman	Columbia, Mo	Jan. 19, 1869	86, 003
Cultivator	J. Collins	Farmington, Ill	Feb. 18, 1862	34, 406
Cultivator	A. B. Colver and J. Priest	Albany, Oreg	Jan. 28, 1873	135, 264
Cultivator	T. S. Cone and H. S. Potter	Oneida, Ill	May 28, 1861	32, 413
Cultivator	J. H. Conley	Moingona, Iowa	May 16, 1871	114, 767
Cultivator	A. Connelley	Milan, Ind	Mar. 23, 1869	88, 136
Cultivator	J. W. Connely	Charleston, Ill	Feb. 19, 1867	62, 185
Cultivator	J. W. Connely	Charleston, Ill	Sept. 24, 1867	69, 186
Cultivator	L. W. and R. G. Conner	Troy, Iowa	Mar. 28, 1871	113, 019
Cultivator	G. W. Conolly	Rochester, N. Y	Aug. 2, 1864	43, 671
Cultivator	I. Constant	Buffalo Heart Grove, Ill	Nov. 4, 1851	8, 483
Cultivator	A. M. Cook	Chicago, Ill	Feb. 9, 1864	41, 569
Cultivator	G. W. Cook	Macon, Ill	July 14, 1868	79, 956
Cultivator	J. Cook	Collinsville, Ohio	Oct. 2, 1866	58, 383
Cultivator	P. Conrod	Keithsburgh, Ill	June 16, 1863	38, 884
Cultivator	A. Cooper	Macomb, Ill	Dec. 23, 1873	145, 848
Cultivator	I. Cooper	Saybrook, Ohio	May 14, 1861	32, 270
Cultivator	N. B. Cooper	Gratis, Ohio	Aug. 12, 1862	36, 139
Cultivator	J. Copeland	Quasqueton, Iowa	Dec. 12, 1865	51, 428
Cultivator	T. R. Cormick	Cap Au Gris, Mo	July 21, 1863	39, 270
Cultivator	W. T. Coulter, G. F. Trabue, and W. A. Lowery.	Hardinsburgh, Ind	Nov. 24, 1868	84, 413
Cultivator	S. Cowan	Bloomfield, Iowa	Aug. 18, 1863	39, 553
Cultivator	B. S. Cox	Paulsborough, N. J	Jan. 4, 1870	98, 471
Cultivator	B. S. Cox	Paulsborough, N. J	Oct. 15, 1872	132, 201
Cultivator	J. Cox and J. A. Throp	Three Rivers, Mich	Mar. 19, 1861	31, 702
Cultivator	J. Cox and J. A. Throp	Three Rivers, Mich	Aug. 16, 1864	43, 836
Cultivator	R. D. Craft	La Porte, Ind	June 22, 1869	91, 718
Cultivator	A. Crafts and E. Weeks	Auburn, Ohio	Jan. 8, 1850	6, 997
Cultivator	R. Craig	State Line City, Ind	Mar. 6, 1860	27, 406
Cultivator	C. C. Creek	Liberty, Ind	Aug. 27, 1867	68, 290
Cultivator	S. Crossley	Rock Island, Ill	Mar. 19, 1872	124, 724
Cultivator	J. Crowther	Oxford, Mich	Mar. 3, 1868	75, 127
Cultivator	S. Crutcher	Little Mount, Ky	Nov. 4, 1873	144, 321
Cultivator	D. Culver	Kingston, Pa	July 9, 1872	128, 860
Cultivator	W. H. Cummings	Boonesborough, Iowa	Aug. 20, 1872	130, 700
Cultivator	J. Cunningham	Marshall, Mo	Jan. 18, 1859	22, 630
Cultivator	H. W. Curtis	Worcester, Mass	Apr. 24, 1866	54, 122
Cultivator	J. Custer	Sandusky, Ohio	June 26, 1866	55, 826
Cultivator	W. Custer	Shannondale, Ind	Oct. 20, 1868	83, 259
Cultivator	D. P. Daggett	Palmyra, N. Y	Dec. 15, 1857	18, 840
Cultivator	W. P. Dale	Agricultural College, Pa	Mar. 11, 1873	136, 708
Cultivator	C. H. Dana	West Lebanon, N. H	July 25, 1854	11, 361
Cultivator	C. Daniel	Lamonte, Mo	Aug. 28, 1866	57, 484
Cultivator	J. Danner	Milton, Ill	Dec. 23, 1862	37, 219
Cultivator	J. H. Davey	Rockford, Ill	June 30, 1868	79, 450
Cultivator	E. Davies, jr	Carthage, Ill	Sept. 17, 1867	68, 848
Cultivator	D. Davis	Fredericksburgh, Va	July 17, 1835	....
Cultivator	D. M. Davis	Ashbury, Ill	Aug. 23, 1864	43, 901
Cultivator	F. Davis	Lima, Ohio	Jan. 3, 1860	26, 656
Cultivator	J. Davis	Allegheny, Pa	July 5, 1864	43, 395
Cultivator	J. R. Davis	Bloomfield, Iowa	Dec. 15, 1863	40, 915
Cultivator	C. H. Dawson	Jacksonville, Ill	Mar. 8, 1859	23, 159
Cultivator	S. Day	Delavan, Ill	Nov. 10, 1868	83, 838
Cultivator	W. Day	Morristown, N. J	Feb. 23, 1869	87, 151
Cultivator	C. Debolt	Ottawa, Ill	Oct. 9, 1860	30, 302
Cultivator	I. Denham	Lanesfield, Kans	Oct. 3, 1865	50, 229
Cultivator	D. Dennett	Buxton, Me	Dec. 19, 1865	51, 567
Cultivator	E. W. Dennis	Peoria, Ill	Apr. 7, 1868	76, 411
Cultivator	O. H. Dennis	Altona, Ill	May 17, 1859	24, 013

Index of patents issued from the United States Patent Office from 1790 to 1873, inclusive, &c.—Continued.

Invention.	Inventor.	Residence.	Date.	No.
Cultivator	E. M. Dever and I. C. Pratt	Peoria, Ill	May 10, 1864	42, 646
Cultivator	G. W. Deweese	Lima, Ohio	Apr. 7, 1868	76, 412
Cultivator	C. B. Deyo	Marengo, Ill	Feb. 13, 1866	52, 542
Cultivator	E. F. Dhart	Swan Creek, Ill	Sept. 24, 1867	69, 081
Cultivator	R. D. Dodge	Adel, Iowa	June 24, 1862	35, 673
Cultivator	E. Doolittle	Pawnee, Ill	Jan. 7, 1868	73, 172
Cultivator	G. W. Doolittle	Lincoln, Ill	Oct. 2, 1866	58, 389
Cultivator	W. C. Doss	Lavaca, Tex	May 10, 1859	23, 906
Cultivator	W. D. Dorsey	Decatur, Ill	Apr. 3, 1860	27, 703
Cultivator	W. D. Dorsey	Decatur, Ill	Apr. 28, 1863	38, 295
Cultivator	J. W. Doud	Forestville, Iowa	Jan. 7, 1868	73, 173
Cultivator	J. W. Doud	Ward's Corner, Iowa	July 1, 1873	140, 484
Cultivator	L. H. Doyle	Waterloo, Iowa	July 9, 1861	32, 760
Cultivator	L. H. Doyle	Waterloo, Iowa	Dec. 9, 1862	37, 089
Cultivator	W. A. Dryden	Monmouth, Ill	Jan. 15, 1861	31, 112
Cultivator	W. A. Dryden	Monmouth, Ill	Dec. 29, 1868	85, 292
Cultivator	W. A. Dryden	Monmouth, Ill	Jan. 10, 1871	110, 836
Cultivator	W. A. and C. E. Dryden	Monmouth, Ill	July 30, 1867	67, 173
Cultivator	W. A. Dryden and J. M. Turnbull.	Monmouth, Ill	Sept. 14, 1869	94, 725
Cultivator	J. B. Duane	Schenectady, N. Y	Jan. 4, 1859	22, 494
Cultivator	W. Duffner	Petersburgh, Ind	Dec. 10, 1867	72, 004
Cultivator	J. K. Dugdale	Richmond, Ind	May 13, 1862	35, 223
Cultivator	J. Dundas	Little Rock, Ill	Feb. 8, 1859	22, 859
Cultivator	A. P. Durant	Atlanta, Ill	May 31, 1864	42, 932
Cultivator	G. M. Dwight	Oregon, Ill	Dec. 15, 1868	85, 001
Cultivator	S. Dwight	Byron, Ill	Feb. 5, 1861	31, 305
Cultivator	S. Dwight	Rockford, Ill	Apr. 3, 1866	53, 592
Cultivator	W. Dysert	Gettysburgh, Pa	Aug. 28, 1846	4, 725
Cultivator	W. Dyzert	Gettysburgh, Pa	Aug. 16, 1844	3, 709
Cultivator	D. S. Early	Hummelstown, Pa	Oct. 6, 1868	82, 814
Cultivator	D. S. Early	Hummelstown, Pa	Mar. 2, 1869	87, 400
Cultivator	N. Earlywine	Centreville, Iowa	June 4, 1872	127, 469
Cultivator	C. Eastburn	Spencer County, Ky	May 31, 1859	24, 203
Cultivator	J. S. Eastman	Baltimore, Md	June 30, 1836	....
Cultivator	D. B. Eberly	Pine Village, Ind	Oct. 10, 1871	119, 750
Cultivator	D. B. Eberly	Pine Village, Ind	Dec. 16, 1873	145, 636
Cultivator	R. N. Eby	Upper Leacock Township, Pa.	Aug. 27, 1867	68, 056
Cultivator	D. Edelman	Madison, Ind	Aug. 1, 1871	117, 524
Cultivator	D. Edwards	Marong, Australia	Mar. 28, 1870	113, 148
Cultivator	D. Edwards	Melbourne, Australia	Feb. 18, 1873	136, 047
Cultivator	I. Edwards	Paoli, Ind	Sept. 19, 1846	4, 762
Cultivator	G. Ekstrand and A. P. Cassel	Wataga, Ill	Aug. 23, 1865	49, 512
Cultivator	A. Eldred	Oppenheim, N. Y	Dec. 20, 1845	4, 320
Cultivator	T. E. Ellett	Monmouth, Ill	July 3, 1866	56, 022
Cultivator	J. L. Ellis	Concord, Ill	Nov. 18, 1862	36, 945
Cultivator	T. J. Ellis	Decatur, Ill	Aug. 15, 1871	118, 000
Cultivator	R. Ellwood and R. L. Pitcher	Sycamore, Ill	Oct. 29, 1872	132, 527
Cultivator	R. Ellwood and R. L. Pitcher	Sycamore, Ill	July 1, 1873	140, 353
Cultivator	B. M. Ely	Perry, Mo	Mar. 2, 1869	87, 401
Cultivator	C. W. Emerson	Albany, N. Y	Apr. 23, 1861	32, 128
Cultivator	E. Emmert	Franklin Grove, Ill	July 31, 1860	29, 368
Cultivator	J. Endsley and E. Fletcher	Abington, Ind	May 18, 1858	20, 260
Cultivator	G. A. Erickson	Swede Bend, Iowa	Sept. 1, 1863	39, 724
Cultivator	J. W. Ernst	Heidelburgh, Pa	Nov. 19, 1867	71, 152
Cultivator	C. Escudier	Iberia Parish, La	Oct. 3, 1871	119, 588
Cultivator	A. Eshleman	Martinsville, Pa	Dec. 6, 1870	109, 812
Cultivator	G. Essington	Plainfield, Ill	Feb. 8, 1859	22, 860
Cultivator	G. Esterly	Heart Prairie, Wis	Apr. 22, 1856	14, 715
Cultivator	G. W. Esterly and J. Van De Water.	Whitewater, Wis	Oct. 1, 1872	131, 861
Cultivator	O. Etnier	Mount Union, Pa	Apr. 23, 1867	64, 086
Cultivator	S. P. Etter	Scotland, Pa	Sept. 18, 1866	58, 182
Cultivator	D. Z. Evans	Town Point, Md	Dec. 26, 1871	122, 240
Cultivator	C. A. Ewick	Rushville, Ind	Oct. 29, 1867	70, 328
Cultivator	J. F. Eylar	Scott, Ohio	Apr. 24, 1860	27, 975
Cultivator	J. Faning and F. Legler	Burlington, Iowa	Nov. 7, 1871	120, 732
Cultivator	J. P. Farnutzer	Fond du Lac, Wis	Apr. 30, 1867	64, 262
Cultivator	C. K. Farr	Hinds County, Miss	May 9, 1854	10, 886
Cultivator	C. K. Farr	Auburn, Miss	Aug. 1, 1854	11, 454
Cultivator	G. Fawcett	Farmington, Ill	Apr. 30, 1872	126, 276
Cultivator	J. W. Fawkes	Decatur, Ill	Jan. 24, 1865	45, 987
Cultivator	J. Ferguson	Huntley Grove, Ill	Nov. 30, 1869	97, 377
Cultivator	J. Fernald	Frankfort, Ind	Nov. 21, 1865	51, 031
Cultivator	B. F. Field	Sheboygan Falls, Wis	Sept. 29, 1863	40, 095
Cultivator	B. F. Field	Sheboygan Falls, Wis	Sept. 29, 1863	40, 096
Cultivator	J. Fink	Baldwinsville, N. Y	Dec. 24, 1861	33, 985
Cultivator	R. A. Fish	Worcester, Mass	Aug. 12, 1873	141, 707
Cultivator	W. D. Fisher	Freeport, Ill	May 1, 1866	54, 317
Cultivator	O. F. Fitch	Morristown, Ind	June 26, 1860	38, 843
Cultivator	J. S. Fleming	Island Creek, Ohio	Aug. 29, 1871	118, 522
Cultivator	G. A. Forsgard	Houston, Tex	Sept. 10, 1872	131, 160
Cultivator	W. J. Forshee	Indianapolis, Ind	Oct. 6, 1857	18, 330
Cultivator	J. P. Fostevin	Racine, Wis	Sept. 19, 1865	50, 052
Cultivator	J. H. Frampton	Hopewell, Ohio	Sept. 13, 1859	25, 403
Cultivator	J. Frank	Webster City, Iowa	Aug. 6, 1867	67, 522
Cultivator	J. Frank	Webster City, Iowa	Feb. 18, 1868	74, 678
Cultivator	J. H. Frank	Millheim, Pa	Sept. 30, 1873	143, 338
Cultivator	J. T. Frankeberger	Hensly, Ill	Dec. 24, 1867	72, 622
Cultivator	D. D. Franklin	Flora, Ill	Aug. 10, 1869	93, 611
Cultivator	W. Frantz	Piqua, Ohio	Jan. 7, 1868	73, 087
Cultivator	N. W. Fraser and A. J. McLellan.	La Porte, Ind	Aug. 10, 1858	21, 128
Cultivator	P. F. Freeland	Newark, Ill	Aug. 9, 1859	25, 006
Cultivator	J. C. French	Monmouth, Ill	Nov. 6, 1866	59, 381
Cultivator	J. C. French	Monmouth, Ill	Mar. 16, 1869	87, 923
Cultivator	A. Friberg	Moline, Ill	May 14, 1867	64, 657

Index of patents issued from the United States Patent Office from 1790 *to* 1873, *inclusive*—Continued.

Invention.	Inventor.	Residence.	Date.	No.
Cultivator	A. Friberg	Moline, Ill	June 11, 1872	127, 757
Cultivator	J. Fridy	West Donegal Township, Pa.	Oct. 16, 1866	58, 805
Cultivator	E. W. Fuller	Martinsville, La	Jan. 22, 1861	31, 163
Cultivator	B. and C. Furnas	Ononwa, Iowa	Nov. 18, 1862	36, 948
Cultivator	W. Furnas	Ononwa, Iowa	Feb. 16, 1864	41, 614
Cultivator	C. Furst	Chicago, Ill	May 30, 1871	115, 459
Cultivator	L. M. Ganong	Friar's Point, Miss	Mar. 4, 1873	136, 500
Cultivator	H. D. Ganse	Freehold, N. J	Mar. 27, 1855	12, 589
Cultivator	H. D. Ganse	Freehold, N. J	Aug. 26, 1856	15, 606
Cultivator	C. Gardner	Hoosick, N. Y	Mar. 19, 1861	31, 710
Cultivator	J. M. Garnett	Loretto, Va	Feb. 3, 1836	....
Cultivator	G. Garrett	Elkhart City, Ill	June 9, 1868	78, 799
Cultivator	W. K. Garrison	Abingdon, Ill	Jan. 29, 1867	61, 661
Cultivator	R. Garter	Grand Rapids, Mich	Dec. 31, 1867	72, 835
Cultivator	R. R. Gaskill	Wyanet, Ill	Oct. 7, 1862	36, 609
Cultivator	H. A. Gaston	Stockton, Cal	May 19, 1868	78, 080
Cultivator	I. N. Gates	Burnside, Ill	Nov. 23, 1869	97, 073
Cultivator	W. Geahr	New Holland, Pa	Sept. 4, 1866	57, 699
Cultivator	J. B. Geisinger and D. H. S. Williams.	Montville, Ohio	Dec. 18, 1860	30, 963
Cultivator	J. Gerber	Rockford, Ill	Aug. 16, 1870	106, 478
Cultivator	J. Gerber	Rockford, Ill	Oct. 18, 1870	108, 471
Cultivator	J. Gerber and H. Brown	Rockford, Ill	Apr. 4, 1871	113, 511
Cultivator	J. Gibbs	Newark, Ohio	Dec. 1, 1857	18, 739
Cultivator	H. H. Gibson	Quincy, Ill	Oct. 15, 1872	132, 277
Cultivator	G. T. Gifford	Monmouth, Ill	Sept. 4, 1866	57, 700
Cultivator	I. B. Gilbert	Lewisville, Ind	Jan. 12, 1869	85, 736
Cultivator	J. R. Gilbert and S. R. Weston	Starkville and Dawson, Ga	Sept. 4, 1860	29, 876
Cultivator	J. G. B. Gill	Chester Court-House, S. C	Jan. 12, 1869	85, 812
Cultivator	H. Gilliard	Mount Hope, Wis	Dec. 27, 1859	26, 581
Cultivator	E. S. Gillies	Albany, Wis	June 20, 1865	48, 271
Cultivator	D. C. Gilliland	Brownsville, Ohio	Dec. 24, 1861	33, 988
Cultivator	J. Gilpatric	Biddeford, Me	Feb. 26, 1867	62, 405
Cultivator	J. H. Given, H. Hutsonpiller, and C. Gilbert.	Des Moines, Iowa	Mar. 7, 1865	46, 657
Cultivator	S. M. Goff	East Addison, Vt	Feb. 12, 1861	31, 382
Cultivator	S. Goldsmith	Wataga, Ill	Aug. 14, 1860	29, 583
Cultivator	A. Gordon	Rochester, N. Y	Apr. 9, 1867	63, 717
Cultivator	M. L. Gorham	Rockford, Ill	Dec. 5, 1871	121, 613
Cultivator	M. L. Gorham	Rockford, Ill	Oct. 1, 1872	131, 818
Cultivator	O. P. Goslee	Glastenbury, Conn	Apr. 2, 1861	31, 884
Cultivator	E. M. Graham	Vernon, La	May 20, 1873	139, 001
Cultivator	H. J. Graham	Monmouth, Ill	Nov. 5, 1867	70, 430
Cultivator	J. L. Graham	Bentley Station, Ill	Aug. 16, 1870	106, 354
Cultivator	B. A. Grant	Mount Pleasant, Iowa	Dec. 5, 1865	51, 306
Cultivator	I. A. Green	Henry, Ill	Mar. 11, 1862	34, 630
Cultivator	W. W. Green	Chelsea, Ill	Mar. 6, 1860	27, 363
Cultivator	T. Green and J. Sommer	Metamora, Ill	Feb. 11, 1868	74, 344
Cultivator	E. S. Gregory	Lockport, N. Y	Aug. 10, 1869	93, 530
Cultivator	W. H. Griffith	Lockhart, Tex	July 23, 1872	129, 730
Cultivator	A. M. Griswold	Momence, Ill	July 30, 1867	67, 295
Cultivator	A. M. Griswold	Momence, Ill	Oct. 27, 1868	83, 487
Cultivator	A. Grohmann	South Saginaw, Mich	Mar. 23, 1869	88, 034
Cultivator	G. Gross, jr	Germantown, Ohio	Sept. 26, 1848	5, 800
Cultivator	J. Gross	Manilla, Iowa	Apr. 1, 1862	34, 828
Cultivator	J. Gross and J. C. Tunison	Decatur, Ill	Dec. 10, 1867	72, 027
Cultivator	A. F. Grove	James Creek, Pa	Nov. 13, 1866	59, 592
Cultivator	S. Gulick	Kline's Grove, Pa	Feb. 14, 1865	46, 349
Cultivator	J. and S. Gum	Marseilles, Ill	Dec. 18, 1860	30, 966
Cultivator	J. and S. Gum	Marseilles, Ill	June 18, 1861	32, 560
Cultivator	D. Guptail	Elgin, Ill	Oct. 15, 1867	69, 801
Cultivator	J. M. Gustin	Wilmington, Ohio	Aug. 12, 1873	141, 786
Cultivator	J. Guyer	Westport, Conn	Mar. 13, 1860	27, 445
Cultivator	C. S. Gwinnup	Milroy, Ind	Feb. 26, 1867	62, 326
Cultivator	W. G. Halburt	Columbus, Miss	Jan. 7, 1873	134, 662
Cultivator	C. M. and D. E. Hall	Uniontown, Ill	Mar. 13, 1860	27, 627
Cultivator	D. E. Hall	Abingdon, Ill	Nov. 10, 1857	18, 587
Cultivator	S. Hall	Russellville, Ky	Nov. 14, 1865	50, 930
Cultivator	T. J. Hall	Bryan, Tex	Sept. 28, 1869	95, 338
Cultivator	J. H. Hamilton	Stevenson, Ala	Sept. 20, 1870	107, 484
Cultivator	A. P. Hammon, J. H. and S. Lincoln, and T. W. Hammon.	Montfort, Wis	Jan. 1, 1867	60, 722
Cultivator	J. R. Hand	College Corner, Ohio	Feb. 4, 1868	74, 082
Cultivator	J. R. Hand	Billingsville, Ind	Apr. 13, 1869	88, 868
Cultivator	R. Haney and J. S. Estes	Peoria, Ill	Aug. 24, 1869	94, 106
Cultivator	M. E. Hanover and D. D. Bailey.	Lamoille, Ill	June 30, 1868	79, 344
Cultivator	J. Harge	Shiloh, Ill	Mar. 1, 1864	41, 769
Cultivator	W. O. Hargrave	Ripon, Wis	Jan. 7, 1868	73, 094
Cultivator	A. A. Harmon	Olney, Ill	Nov. 17, 1868	84, 184
Cultivator	J. Harris	Janesville, Wis	Feb. 23, 1869	87, 101
Cultivator	N. J. Harris	Meredosia, Ill	July 25, 1871	117, 279
Cultivator	V. P. Harris	Greensburgh, Ind	Oct. 11, 1870	108, 260
Cultivator	J. O. Harris and W. F. Slewder	Ottawa, Ill	Feb. 14, 1860	27, 125
Cultivator	A. Harrison	Blissfield, Mich	Sept. 2, 1845	4, 170
Cultivator	A. T. Harrison	Clinton, Ill	May 8, 1866	54, 534
Cultivator	N. S. Harryman	Frankfort, Ind	Feb. 11, 1862	34, 362
Cultivator	C. A. Harper	Wheeling, Ind	Jan. 7, 1868	73, 181
Cultivator	C. A. Harper	Wheeling, Ind	Dec. 8, 1868	84, 823
Cultivator	J. Harper	Hillsborough, Iowa	Mar. 28, 1865	47, 017
Cultivator	G. D. Hart	Lycoming County, Pa	Apr. 2, 1867	63, 384
Cultivator	G. D. Hart	Muncy, Pa	May 26, 1868	78, 203
Cultivator	V. Harwell	Walker County, Ga	June 5, 1860	28, 576
Cultivator	J. Haskell	Lisbon, Me	Feb. 26, 1867	62, 329
Cultivator	M. Haskins and D. B. Hart	Mentor, Ohio	July 9, 1867	66, 491
Cultivator	G. F. Hassenpflug and G. Barnhart.	Green Township, Ohio	Apr. 4, 1865	47, 105

Index of patents issued from the United States Patent Office from 1790 *to* 1873, *inclusive*—Continued.

Invention.	Inventor.	Residence.	Date.	No.
Cultivator	J. W. Hatcher	Bethesda, Tenn	Oct. 24, 1871	120, 274
Cultivator	L. D. Haughey	Atlanta, Ill	Mar. 7, 1865	46, 666
Cultivator	L. Haverstick	Manor, Pa	Nov. 25, 1873	144, 846
Cultivator	L. E. Hawkins	Sangamon, Ill	Aug. 14, 1860	29, 592
Cultivator	A. W. Hawley	Milan, Ohio	Dec. 22, 1857	18, 900
Cultivator	W. H. Haworth	Towanda, Ill	Aug. 27, 1861	33, 176
Cultivator	G. J. Hayes	Ionia, Mich	Mar. 2, 1869	87, 492
Cultivator	C. W. S. Heaton	Salem, Ill	Mar. 12, 1861	31, 665
Cultivator	C. W. S. Heaton	Belleville, Ill	Jan. 20, 1863	37, 474
Cultivator	C. W. S. Heaton	Belleville, Ill	Apr. 21, 1863	38, 261
Cultivator	C. W. S. Heaton	Salem, Ill	Aug. 11, 1863	39, 528
Cultivator	H. I. Heaton	Peoria, Ill	Dec. 16, 1862	37, 166
Cultivator	T. Heermans	Sumner, Tenn	Mar. 8, 1859	23, 170
Cultivator	C. Hefft	Tazewell County, Ill	Jan. 28, 1868	73, 891
Cultivator	A. T. Heflin	Monmouth, Ill	May 14, 1867	64, 668
Cultivator	A. T. Heflin	Monmouth, Ill	Sept. 22, 1868	82, 406
Cultivator	J. M. Heiges	York, Pa	Jan. 7, 1873	134, 665
Cultivator	S. L. Heisey	West Donegal, Pa	Aug. 6, 1867	67, 430
Cultivator	J. Helm	Hockheim, Tex	Apr. 22, 1873	138, 085
Cultivator	R. H. Henry	Monmouth, Ill	Jan. 5, 1869	85, 662
Cultivator	S. Henry	Chenoa, Ill	Feb. 14, 1865	46, 355
Cultivator	I. Henton	Shelbyville, Ill	Mar. 6, 1866	52, 998
Cultivator	I. Henton	Shelbyville, Ill	July 13, 1869	92, 529
Cultivator	J. B. Herman	Mount Vernon, Iowa	Oct. 23, 1866	59, 012
Cultivator	J. T. Herndon	Bancroft, Mo	Jan. 28, 1868	73, 805
Cultivator	J. B. Herr	West Tampeter Township, Pa.	Oct. 23, 1866	59, 013
Cultivator	S. H. Herrick	Grinnell, Iowa	July 2, 1867	66, 340
Cultivator	T. Hicks	Pecatonica, Ill	Feb. 9, 1869	86, 750
Cultivator	G. W. Hildreth	Lockport, N. Y	May 21, 1861	32, 366
Cultivator	P. Hildreth	Beloit, Wis	Mar. 27, 1866	53, 445
Cultivator	J. H. Hill	Clinton, Ill	June 23, 1868	79, 119
Cultivator	J. B. Hinckley	Nacogdoches County, Tex.	Feb. 18, 1873	135, 912
Cultivator	J. Hinds and J. Gee	Conologue, Ill	Dec. 22, 1868	85, 095
Cultivator	C. Hoagland	Delavan, Ill	Mar. 24, 1868	75, 911
Cultivator	S. Hoake	Frederick, Md	Mar. 27, 1860	27, 632
Cultivator	J. C. Hoffeditz	Mercersburgh, Pa	Jan. 1, 1867	60, 892
Cultivator	S. Hoffheins	Hamilton Township, Pa	Apr. 24, 1866	54, 160
Cultivator	A. Hoffman and H. W. Limebeck.	Half Day, Ill	Nov. 19, 1861	33, 740
Cultivator	S. B. Hoisington	Galesburgh, Ill	Aug. 9, 1870	106, 161
Cultivator	L. M. Holland	Galesburgh, Ill	Apr. 14, 1868	76, 634
Cultivator	J. Hollinger	Millersburgh, Ohio	Sept. 4, 1866	57, 719
Cultivator	J. Hollinger	Millersburgh, Ohio	May 21, 1867	64, 808
Cultivator	J. Hollingsworth	Chicago, Ill	May 9, 1865	47, 641
Cultivator	C. Holman	Cameron, Ill	Mar. 27, 1866	53, 446
Cultivator	B. Holtz and W. Enoch	Springfield, Ohio	June 20, 1865	48, 281
Cultivator	L. Homrighouse	Baltimore, Ohio	Sept. 27, 1870	107, 777
Cultivator	H. T. Hooker	Skaneatoles, N. Y	Dec. 15, 1863	40, 935
Cultivator	H. Hoover	Hemlo, Ill	Sept. 11, 1866	57, 906
Cultivator	W. A. Hopkins	Vicksburgh, Miss	June 29, 1858	20, 712
Cultivator	S. G. Horming	Mount Carroll, Ill	June 6, 1865	48, 066
Cultivator	J. Houck	Clinton, Ind	Feb. 2, 1858	19, 248
Cultivator	H. Howe	Darlington, Wis	June 6, 1865	48, 068
Cultivator	H. Howe	Oneonta, N. Y	Mar. 19, 1867	63, 050
Cultivator	H. Howe	Oneonta, N. Y	Dec. 17, 1867	72, 297
Cultivator	H. Howe	Oneonta, N. Y	Nov. 8, 1870	109, 129
Cultivator	W. H. Howell	Ewingsville, N. J	Dec. 26, 1865	51, 721
Cultivator	D. C. Hubbard	Okolona, Miss	July 6, 1858	20, 798
Cultivator	S. Hubbard and J. Graves	Wilmington, Vt	June 21, 1823	....
Cultivator	E. S. Huff	Zanesville, Ohio	Aug. 28, 1860	29, 789
Cultivator	J. Huff	Young America, Ill	Jan. 26, 1869	86, 160
Cultivator	M. H. Hullinger	Granville, Ill	Feb. 2, 1864	41, 435
Cultivator	M. H. Hullinger	Granville, Ill	Mar. 20, 1866	53, 303
Cultivator	J. M. Hume	Colchester, Ill	May 21, 1867	64, 878
Cultivator	A. Hunt	Macomb, Ill	Sept. 28, 1869	95, 352
Cultivator	A. Hunt	Macomb, Ill	Apr. 4, 1871	113, 520
Cultivator	H. C. Hunt	Amboy, Ill	Nov. 13, 1866	59, 720
Cultivator	G. E. Hutchinson	Cleveland, Ohio	Apr. 16, 1872	125, 681
Cultivator	G. L. Hutchinson	White Rock, Ill	Jan. 16, 1866	52, 049
Cultivator	B. S. Hyers	Pekin, Ill	Apr. 27, 1869	89, 409
Cultivator	B. S. Hyers	Pekin, Ill	Jan. 18, 1870	98, 970
Cultivator	N. Ide	Shelby, N. Y	Apr. 18, 1846	4, 459
Cultivator	J. Imel	Liberty, Ind	Jan. 2, 1855	12, 163
Cultivator	C. B. Ingersoll	Morris, Ill	Nov. 25, 1862	36, 998
Cultivator	J. W. Ingle and R. H. Wright	Livingston, Ill	Mar. 7, 1865	46, 675
Cultivator	H. Ingraham	Naples, N. Y	Dec. 27, 1864	45, 612
Cultivator	H. Ingraham	Naples, N. Y	Aug. 1, 1865	49, 111
Cultivator	H. Ingraham	Naples, N. Y	Nov. 21, 1865	51, 055
Cultivator	H. Ingraham	Naples, N. Y	July 9, 1867	66, 495
Cultivator	N. L. Isgrigg	Moore's Hill, Ind	Feb. 22, 1870	100, 040
Cultivator	J. B. Jay	Arlington, Ill	Apr. 6, 1869	88, 638
Cultivator	P. R. Jenkins	Cottonville, Iowa	Oct. 17, 1871	120, 073
Cultivator	C. M. Jenne	Young America, Ill	Oct. 18, 1864	44, 729
Cultivator	C. M. Jenne	Young America, Ill	July 18, 1865	48, 817
Cultivator	C. M. Jenne	Young America, Ill	Oct. 1, 1867	69, 442
Cultivator	J. W. Jessop	Harveysburgh, Ohio	Dec. 29, 1868	85, 387
Cultivator	G. Jessup	Shortsville, N. Y	Nov. 5, 1872	132, 764
Cultivator	F. C. Jewell	Rahway, N. J	Dec. 13, 1870	110, 046
Cultivator	T. Jobe	Clarksville, Ohio	Feb. 5, 1867	61, 836
Cultivator	C. H. Johnson	Morristown, N. J	July 20, 1869	92, 835
Cultivator	J. P. Johnson	Macon, Ill	Dec. 3, 1867	71, 623
Cultivator	M. Johnson	Three Rivers, Mich	July 19, 1870	105, 460
Cultivator	W. D. Johnson	Raleigh, N. C	Sept. 13, 1859	25, 416
Cultivator	I. B. Jones	Xenia, Ohio	Aug. 12, 1862	36, 158
Cultivator	E. P. Jones and J. L. Harrell	Hertford, N. C	Sept. 12, 1871	118, 946
Cultivator	H. P. Jordan	Victoria, Tex	Apr. 23, 1872	125, 961
Cultivator	W. H. Jordan	Roseville, Ind	Oct. 28, 1862	36, 785

Index of patents issued from the United States Patent Office from 1790 to 1873, inclusive—Continued.

Invention.	Inventor.	Residence.	Date.	No.
Cultivator	W. T. Jordan	Newnan, Ga	Nov. 28, 1871	121, 381
Cultivator	R. F. Joynes	Bristol, R. I	June 4, 1861	32, 479
Cultivator	E. Julier	Beverly, Ohio	Mar. 13, 1860	27, 450
Cultivator	A. Keck	Montgomery, Ill	Jan. 10, 1865	45, 833
Cultivator	P. H. Keeks	Morgantown, Va	May 31, 1853	9, 754
Cultivator	J. Keezer	Chillicothe, Ohio	June 18, 1861	32, 567
Cultivator	A. M. Keith	Kosciusko, Miss	Sept. 13, 1859	25, 419
Cultivator	J. H. B. Keller	Chambersburgh, Pa	Oct. 27, 1868	83, 509
Cultivator	L. W. Kelley	Brunswick, Ohio	May 11, 1858	20, 207
Cultivator	W. H. Kelly	Onondaga County, N. Y	Mar. 4, 1862	34, 578
Cultivator	A. H. Kennedy	Oberlin, Ohio	Apr. 4, 1871	113, 306
Cvltivator	B. F. Kessler	Wilmington, Ill	Jan. 16, 1866	52, 053
Cultivator	J. Kessler	York County, Pa	Jan. 29, 1867	61, 622
Cultivator	W. Kiddoo	Keithsburgh, Ill	Oct. 30, 1866	59, 231
Cultivator	A. B. King	Camden, Ohio	May 7, 1867	64, 429
Cultivator	A. B. King	Camden, Ohio	Nov. 23, 1869	97, 201
Cultivator	J. R. King	Raleigh, Tenn	Dec. 27, 1859	26, 597
Cultivator	M. D. King	King's Ferry, N. Y	July 9, 1872	128, 734
Cultivator	W. H. L. King	Princeton, Iowa	Sept. 26, 1865	50, 141
Cultivator	T. and R. Kinghorn	Morgan, Ohio	June 26, 1860	28, 870
Cultivator	H. R. Kinney	Portsmouth, Ohio	Jan. 3, 1860	26, 682
Cultivator	J. Kirkman	Peoria, Ill	Dec. 27, 1864	45, 615
Cultivator	W. Kleffel	Maple Creek, Neb	May 14, 1872	126, 815
Cultivator	J. G. Knapp and S. D. Libby	Madison and Blooming Grove, Wis.	Jan. 25, 1870	99, 208
Cultivator	E. H. Knight	Unadilla, Mich	May 7, 1867	64, 542
Cultivator	J. M. Knox	Rensselaer, Ind	Apr. 15, 1873	137, 933
Cultivator	S. A. Knox	Worcester, Mass	Mar. 13, 1855	12, 536
Cultivator	J. Koehn	Canton, Ohio	June 18, 1867	65, 918
Cultivator	P. Kribs	Jefferson Furnace, Pa	July 5, 1859	24, 644
Cultivator	H. K. Krieble	Lansdale, Pa	Feb. 25, 1873	136, 249
Cultivator	G. W. Kring	Fairbury, Ill	Jan. 5, 1869	85, 675
Cultivator	C. and P. G. Krogh	Krohville, Wis	Dec. 10, 1872	133, 865
Cultivator	S. A. Kroner	New Britain, Pa	Nov. 5, 1867	70, 578
Cultivator	O. Kugler	Raritan, N. J	July 22, 1873	141, 145
Cultivator	O. Kugler	Three Bridges, N. J	July 22, 1873	141, 146
Cultivator	H. P. Kynett	Lisbon, Iowa	Aug. 1, 1871	117, 547
Cultivator	J. Lacey	Chicago, Ill	Feb. 23, 1864	41, 709
Cultivator	J. Lacey	Chicago, Ill	Feb. 23, 1864	41, 743
Cultivator	J. Lacey	Chicago, Ill	July 4, 1865	48, 627
Cultivator	J. Lacey	Chicago, Ill	Apr. 10, 1866	53, 837
Cultivator	H. Laird	Mechanicsburgh, Pa	May 24, 1870	103, 476
Cultivator	H. J. Lake	Conquest, N. Y	Nov. 27, 1860	30, 737
Cultivator	A. Lamb	Skaneateles, N. Y	Feb. 6, 1866	52, 421
Cultivator	H. Landes	Bath, Pa	Mar. 23, 1869	88, 045
Cultivator	W. B. Lane and W. Coultor	Organ Spring, Ind	Feb. 26, 1867	62, 344
Cultivator	J. B. Lang	Ithaca, N. Y	July 30, 1872	129, 894
Cul'ivator	G. Large	Rosemond, Ill	Jan. 5, 1864	41, 159
Cultivator	J. T. W. Larrabee	Newton, Ind	Mar. 19, 1872	124, 831
Cultivator	G. W. Lawbaugh and J. Williams.	Shanesville, Ohio	Aug. 13, 1861	33, 044
Cultivator	L. Leber	Springfield, Ill	Aug. 21, 1860	29, 704
Cultivator	G. Lechtenthaler	Limestoneville, Pa	July 25, 1854	11, 379
Cultivator	T. M. Lee	Broad Ford, Va	Oct. 12, 1858	21, 763
Cultivator	Z. W. and E. D. Lee	Blakeley, Ga	July 31, 1860	29, 380
Cultivator	R. A. Leeper and Z. B. Kidder.	San José, Ill	Feb. 12, 1861	31, 393
Cultivator	A. B. Lefler	Canton, Ind	Jan. 22, 1861	31, 178
Cultivator	F. C. Leffler	Highland Township, Iowa	July 25, 1865	48, 959
Cultivator	A. Leigh	Clinton Station, N. J	Apr. 14, 1863	38, 171
Cultivator	A. Leonard	Newell's Run, Ohio	Apr. 15, 1873	137, 782
Cultivator	M. Lewellin	Bergen, N. Y	Mar. 25, 1873	137, 221
Cultivator	J. Lewis	Washington, D. C	July 12, 1870	105, 225
Cultivator	W. Lewis	Oxford, N. C	Sept. 23, 1873	143, 019
Cultivator	C. Lidren	Aurora, Ill	Jan. 31, 1865	46, 116
Cultivator	J. R. Little	Galesburgh, Ill	Mar. 30, 1869	88, 311
Cultivator	J. R. Little	Galesburgh, Ill	Sept. 6, 1870	107, 069
Cultivator	J. R. Little	Galesburgh, Ill	Oct. 4, 1870	108, 037
Cultivator	J. B. Livezey	Clarksborough, N. J	July 10, 1860	29, 087
Cultivator	J. H. Lockie	Humphrey, N. Y	Oct. 26, 1869	96, 126
Cultivator	I. Long	Terre Haute, Ind	Sept. 7, 1858	21, 428
Cultivator	P. Long	Penn Township, Pa	May 27, 1873	139, 320
Cultivator	I. Lord and S. Woodman	Saco, Me	Feb. 12, 1867	61, 943
Cultivator	W. C. Lostutter and S. Wolcott.	Rising Sun, Ind	July 31, 1860	29, 391
Cultivator	J. P. Lotz	Lacon, Ill	Jan. 4, 1870	98, 604
Cultivator	I. Low	East Fairfield, Ohio	Nov. 15, 1870	109, 229
Cultivator	M. F. Lowth and T. J. Howe	Owatonna, Minn	Apr. 23, 1867	64, 119
Cultivator	M. F. Lowth and T. J. Howe	Owatonna, Minn	Sept. 22, 1868	82, 423
Cultivator	J. Lueth	Kankakee, Ill	Sept. 7, 1869	94, 497
Cultivator	G. H. Lund	Mackford, Wis	Sept. 17, 1872	131, 404
Cultivator	W. Lyman, jr	Malone, N. Y	May 27, 1862	35, 422
Cultivator	E. P. Lynch	Davenport, Iowa	Sept. 14, 1869	94, 903
Cultivator	E. P. Lynch	Davenport, Iowa	Sept. 23, 1873	143, 172
Cultivator	T. Mabbett, sr	Vineland, N. J	May 10, 1870	102, 841
Cultivator	I. B. Mahon	Marion, Ohio	May 19, 1863	38, 593
Cultivator	I. B. Mahon	Dunkirk, Ohio	Jan. 29, 1867	61, 674
Cultivator	I. B. Mahon	Dunkirk, Ohio	Sept. 17, 1867	69, 003
Cultivator	I. B. Mahon	Dunkirk, Ohio	Dec. 20, 1870	110, 256
Cultivator	I. B. Mahon	Dunkirk, Ohio	Dec. 20, 1870	110, 257
Cultivator	P. Maier	Mapleton, Wis	June 13, 1871	115, 875
Cultivator	J. Mallon	Lockport, Ill	Oct. 27, 1868	83, 519
Cultivator	J. Mallon and H. Von Phul, jr.	Holly Wood, La	Dec. 12, 1871	121, 794
Cultivator	H. Mann	San Francisco, Cal	July 14, 1857	17, 797
Cultivator	H. Mann	East Attleborough, Mass	Dec. 28, 1858	22, 437
Cultivator	A. J. Manny	Freeport, Ill	Sept. 19, 1865	50, 018
Cultivator	A. M. Manny	Lena, Ill	Nov. 21, 1871	121, 114
Cultivator	A. M. Manny	Lena, Ill	Nov. 21, 1871	121, 115
Cultivator	J. P. Manny	Rockford, Ill	June 3, 1873	139, 471

Index of patents issued from the United States Patent Office from 1790 *to* 1873, *inclusive*—Continued.

Invention.	Inventor.	Residence.	Date.	No.
Cultivator	T. J. Marinus	Independence, Iowa	Mar. 16, 1869	87,951
Cultivator	J. Markel	Monticello, Ill	Mar. 19, 1861	31,725
Cultivator	A. S. Markham	Monmouth, Ill	Aug. 4, 1863	39,412
Cultivator	A. S. Markham	Bushnell, Ill	Feb. 6, 1866	52,429
Cultivator	D. and A. S. Markham and D. Eldred.	Monmouth, Ill	Mar. 8, 1859	23,182
Cultivator	C. Marsh, 2d	Natchez, Miss	Aug. 13, 1872	130,384
Cultivator	C. Marsh, 2d	Natchez, Miss	Nov. 26, 1872	133,467
Cultivator	R. Marsh	Steubenville, Ohio	Apr. 25, 1865	47,439
Cultivator	W. W. Marsh and H. McIntyre.	Sycamore, Ill	July 16, 1872	128,969
Cultivator	T. J. Martin	Willow Hill, Ill	Jan. 26, 1869	86,170
Cultivator	R. E. Mason	Norway, Ill	July 2, 1872	128,497
Cultivator	W. May	Winchester, Ohio	Oct. 16, 1860	30,447
Cultivator	L. D. McClintick	Glenwood, Iowa	Dec. 22, 1868	85,233
Cultivator	R. McCorkell	Philadelphia, Pa	Oct. 3, 1865	50,257
Cultivator	R. McCorkell	Philadelphia, Pa	Aug. 4, 1868	80,556
Cultivator	W. McCormick	Muscatine, Iowa	May 15, 1866	54,751
Cultivator	W. J. McCoy	Cartersville, Ga	Nov. 27, 1860	30,744
Cultivator	A. S. McDermott	Ogden, Iowa	Feb. 13, 1872	123,715
Cultivator	T. W. McDill	Oquawka, Ill	Aug. 21, 1860	29,707
Cultivator	J. C. McDonald	Nevada, Iowa	Apr. 8, 1873	137,703
Cultivator	T. E. McDonald	New Brunswick, N. J	Nov. 24, 1868	84,430
Cultivator	A. S. McDonell	Osgood Township, Canada	Nov. 4, 1873	144,346
Cultivator	E. McEwen	Lisbon, Ill	Aug. 22, 1865	49,540
Cultivator	P. McGlew	Des Moines, Iowa	Feb. 9, 1864	41,523
Cultivator	J. McIlvain	Tennessee, Ill	May 18, 1869	90,112
Cultivator	K. McKinnon	Pleasant Hill, Ala	Feb. 25, 1873	136,254
Cultivator	D. McNabb	Moscow, Mich	Jan. 3, 1865	45,730
Cultivator	D. McNeely and C. J. Cady	Spurgeon, Ind	Sept. 1, 1868	81,807
Cultivator	T. McQuiston	Morning Sun, Ohio	Oct. 18, 1859	25,843
Cultivator	H. S. Mead	Gloversville, N. Y	July 4, 1865	48,575
Cultivator	C. E. Mead and G. E. Stevenson	Denmark, Iowa	Aug. 4, 1863	39,450
Cultivator	C. F. Megquier	Eureka, Ill	Mar. 12, 1867	62,868
Cultivator	R. M. Melton	Criglersville, Va	May 31, 1859	24,227
Cultivator	A. Merrill	Ingersoll, Canada	June 11, 1872	127,785
Cultivator	N. Messenger	Newark, Ill	Nov. 27, 1869	30,745
Cultivator	W. Mettler	Frankfort, Ill	June 14, 1864	43,123
Cultivator	I. Miers	Clay Lick, Ohio	Dec. 11, 1860	30,926
Cultivator	J. Millard	Winslow, Ind	Dec. 29, 1868	85,467
Cultivator	E. and B. Miller	Rising Sun, Ind	Sept. 13, 1859	25,432
Cultivator	G. D. Miller	Lovington, Ill	Nov. 15, 1864	45,066
Cultivator	I. Miller	Worth, Mich	July 26, 1870	105,828
Cultivator	W. Millerton	Jacksonville, Ill	Mar. 4, 1873	136,477
Cultivator	J. Mills	Reading, Ill	May 9, 1865	47,655
Cultivator	J. Mills	Johnstown, Wis	Feb. 18, 1873	135,997
Cultivator	J. R. Mills	Bloomfield, Iowa	Jan. 5, 1864	41,086
Cultivator	S. G. Mills	Des Moines, Iowa	Jan. 23, 1866	52,184
Cultivator	E. Minnich	McKee's Half Falls, Pa	Feb. 14, 1865	46,376
Cultivator	J. R. Minter	Unionville, S. C	Feb. 6, 1872	123,410
Cultivator	F. and P. A. Misner	Fox, Ill	Jan. 3, 1860	26,695
Cultivator	S. H. Mitchell	El Paso, Ill	Dec. 1, 1863	40,766
Cultivator	S. H. Mitchell	El Paso, Ill	June 14, 1870	104,334
Cultivator	P. Monaghan	Camac, Ga	Dec. 27, 1859	26,606
Cultivator	J. B. Moody	Pembroke, Ky	Apr. 27, 1869	89,422
Cultivator	J. B. Moody	Louisville, Ky	July 12, 1870	105,358
Cultivator	W. A. Moody	Montezuma, Iowa	Sept. 3, 1867	68,525
Cultivator	G. Moore	Moline, Ill	Sept. 10, 1867	68,643
Cultivator	G. Moore	Moline, Ill	July 2, 1872	128,499
Cultivator	M. H. Moore and A. Satterwhite.	Rome, Ga	Nov. 27, 1860	30,748
Cultivator	J. B. Moorhead and T. A. and G. G. Pool.	Bellefontaine, Ohio	Sept. 3, 1861	33,208
Cultivator	B. S. Morgan	Delhi, Iowa	Oct. 5, 1858	21,690
Cultivator	B. S. Morgan	Delhi, Iowa	Oct. 11, 1859	25,754
Cultivator	A. H. Morrel	Marlin, Tex	Apr. 10, 1855	12,690
Cultivator	J. E. Morrison	Washington, D. C	Apr. 24, 1866	54,191
Cultivator	I. J. Morrow	Everton, Ind	Sept. 21, 1869	95,035
Cultivator	J. M. Morse	Sandwich, Ill	Oct. 1, 1867	69,468
Cultivator	S. Mowry	Womelsdorf, Pa	Aug. 9, 1859	25,031
Cultivator	J. Mumford and J. W. Wilson	Clarksburgh, Ohio	May 28, 1861	32,431
Cultivator	T. Murphey	Cincinnati, Ohio	Feb. 14, 1860	27,144
Cultivator	J. Murphy	Albany, Ga	July 16, 1867	66,871
Cultivator	W. H. Murrey	Brodhead, Wis	May 14, 1872	126,828
Cultivator	B. F. Muschert	Morrisville, Pa	July 8, 1873	147,724
Cultivator	A. H. Myers	Hermon, Ill	Aug. 8, 1871	117,803
Cultivator	J. Neff, jr	Pultney, N. Y	May 8, 1860	28,191
Cultivator	J. Neff, jr	Pultney, N. Y	Mar. 3, 1868	75,185
Cultivator	J. Neff, jr	Pultney, N. Y	Sept. 20, 1870	107,526
Cultivator	J. Neidich and E. R. Girvin	Lancaster County, Pa	Nov. 27, 1860	30,751
Cultivator	O. S. Neisler	Indianola, Iowa	Jan. 2, 1872	122,400
Cultivator	R. Neison	West Point, Ind	Jan. 15, 1844	3,406
Cultivator	J. B. Netherland	Near Louisville, Ga	Mar. 6, 1860	27,376
Cultivator	W. Nevins	Irving, N. Y	Nov. 25, 1862	37,005
Cultivator	E. Newlon	Monmouth, Ill	Aug. 27, 1867	68,104
Cultivator	D. J. Noble	New Boston, Ill	Mar. 20, 1866	53,326
Cultivator	J. S. Nolen	Paulsborough, N. J	Oct. 3, 1871	119,639
Cultivator	D. Norman	Crawfordsville, Ind	July 16, 1872	129,420
Cultivator	C. P. Norton	Roseville, Ill	Jan. 22, 1867	61,450
Cultivator	C. P. Norton	Prairie City, Iowa	Oct. 18, 1870	108,384
Cultivator	W. Notman	Deerfield, Ohio	Mar. 8, 1870	100,655
Cultivator	A. B. C. Nusbaum	Sacramento, Cal	Feb. 22, 1870	100,183
Cultivator	A. T. Odell	Royalton, N. Y	July 17, 1847	5,195
Cultivator	W. H. Older	Packwaukee, Wis	Jan. 26, 1864	41,389
Cultivator	A. W. Olds	Green Oak, Mich	Oct. 21, 1862	36,724
Cultivator	H. Ogborn	Green's Fork, Ind	July 10, 1860	29,094
Cultivator	H. Ogborn and G. Taylor	Green's Fork and Richmond, Ind.	July 28, 1857	17,909

Index of patents issued from the United States Patent Office from 1790 *to* 1873, *inclusive*—Continued.

Invention.	Inventor.	Residence.	Date.	No.
Cultivator	B. F. Osborn	Nashville, Tenn	Aug. 30, 1870	106, 864
Cultivator	J. D. Osborn	Goshen, Ind	Nov. 29, 1864	45, 264
Cultivator	H. W. Ostrom	Grand Rapids, Mich	June 7, 1870	103, 918
Cultivator	G. W. Owens	Fairfield, Iowa	Aug. 29, 1871	118, 549
Cultivator	W. J. Oxer	Williamsport, Ind	Feb. 12, 1867	62, 060
Cultivator	L. Packard	Galesburgh, Ill	Aug. 9, 1859	25, 037
Cultivator	J. S. Pardon	Summerfield, Ill	July 29, 1862	36, 019
Cultivator	J. G. Page	Rockford, Ill	Aug. 22, 1865	49, 547
Cultivator	I. B. Palamountain	Tarborough, N. C	May 10, 1859	23, 942
Cultivator	I. A. Palmer	Monmouth, Ill	Feb. 14, 1865	46, 383
Cultivator	I. A. Palmer	Monmouth, Ill	Sept. 10, 1867	68, 784
Cultivator	I. A. Palmer	Monmouth, Ill	Dec. 29, 1868	85, 471
Cultivator	C. S. Pangborn and G. W. Beers.	Onarga, Ill	Apr. 3, 1866	53, 663
Cultivator	W. Y. Parker	Verona, Miss	Feb. 11, 1873	135, 726
Cultivator	R. B. and J. R. Parks	Neponset, Ill	Jan. 8, 1867	61, 091
Cultivator	R. B. and J. R. Parks	Neponset, Ill	June 22, 1869	91, 661
Cultivator	E. Parmele and G. Curkendall	Davenport, Iowa, and Moline, Ill.	July 23, 1872	129, 859
Cultivator	E. Parmele and R. N. Patterson.	Davenport, Iowa	May 15, 1866	54, 763
Cultivator	J. Paterson	Medina, N. Y	Apr. 17, 1847	5, 075
Cultivator	D. Pattee	Ypsilanti, Mich	June 20, 1848	5, 639
Cultivator	J. H. Pattee	Monmouth, Ill	Mar. 5, 1872	124, 218
Cultivator	J. H. Pattee	Monmouth, Ill	Jan. 21, 1873	135, 148
Cultivator	E. C. Patterson	Chicago, Ill	Jan. 17, 1865	45, 934
Cultivator	D. H. Paul	De Witt, Iowa	July 6, 1869	92, 350
Cultivator	J. J. Paxson	Middletown, Ind	Mar. 6, 1860	27, 378
Cultivator	R. L. Payne	Riceville, Va	Aug. 30, 1870	106, 956
Cultivator	S. G. Peabody	Champaign, Ill	Dec. 31, 1867	72, 889
Cultivator	S. G. Peabody	Champaign, Ill	Dec. 1, 1868	84, 575
Cultivator	J. C. Pearl	Mendota, Ill	Oct. 12, 1869	95, 831
Cultivator	H. N. Pease	Toledo, Ohio	Oct. 4, 1870	107, 954
Cultivator	E. Peck	Chicago, Ill	Oct. 22, 1867	70, 111
Cultivator	J. Peeler	Tallahassee, Fla	June 21, 1859	24, 486
Cultivator	L. D. Pelton and J. Barrow	Harrison, Ohio	June 18, 1867	65, 938
Cultivator	W. C. Percy	Bayou Sara, La	June 4, 1872	127, 508
Cultivator	F. Perez	Havana, Cuba	Sept. 30, 1873	143, 380
Cultivator	C. D. Perkins	Princeville, Ill	Sept. 3, 1872	131, 066
Cultivator	H. H. Perkins	Osceola, Ill	Apr. 1, 1873	137, 478
Cultivator	A. S. Perrigo	Sandwich, Ill	Oct. 5, 1869	95, 505
Cultivator	F. L. Perry	Canandaigua, N. Y	June 29, 1869	91, 963
Cultivator	F. L. Perry	Canandaigua, N. Y	Nov. 2, 1869	96, 344
Cultivator	F. L. Perry	Canandaigua, N. Y	Oct. 10, 1871	119, 786
Cultivator	G. Perry	Muscatine, Iowa	Apr. 10, 1866	53, 867
Cultivator	C. B. Pettengill	Hebron, Me	Dec. 17, 1867	72, 227
Cultivator	E. Phifer	Trenton, N. J	May 23, 1865	47, 904
Cultivator	E. Phifer	Trenton, N. J	May 7, 1867	64, 563
Cultivator	E. Phifer	Trenton, N. J	June 30, 1868	79, 387
Cultivator	W. W. Philler	Port Byron, Ill	Nov. 13, 1866	59, 643
Cultivator	J. W. Philp	Humboldt, Tenn	June 28, 1870	104, 763
Cultivator	H. L. Pigg	Knobnoster, Mo	July 2, 1872	128, 653
Cultivator	E. W. Pike	Galesburgh, Ill	Oct. 29, 1867	70, 258
Cultivator	W. H. Platt	Dayton, Ohio	Mar. 18, 1873	137, 024
Cultivator	T. Poling	Guthrie, Iowa	Aug. 13, 1872	130, 440
Cultivator	O. M. Pond	Independence, Iowa	Mar. 25, 1873	137, 094
Cultivator	T. W. Poole	Brunswick, Ohio	Sept. 28, 1858	21, 625
Cultivator	M. Porter and C. E. and G. F. Jenkins.	Terre Haute, Ill	Aug. 28, 1866	57, 562
Cultivator	J. Potts	Bridgeport, W. Va	Feb. 19, 1867	62, 223
Cultivator	T. J. Potts and P. C. Yost	Hamilton, Ill	Apr. 18, 1865	47, 332
Cultivator	J. Powell	Sullivan, Ill	Mar. 30, 1869	88, 409
Cultivator	E. Pratt	Grand Detour, Ill	Oct. 18, 1864	44, 747
Cultivator	A. Preston	Unionville, Ohio	May 17, 1859	24, 053
Cultivator	H. Preston	Oxfordville, Wis	July 28, 1868	80, 502
Cultivator	W. Rice	Goldsborough, N. C	June 6, 1854	11, 008
Cultivator	W. Rice	Mount Olive, N. C	Feb. 12, 1861	31, 400
Cultivator	G. W. Prugh and W. H. Beard	Armington, Ill	Feb. 20, 1866	52, 743
Cultivator	I. N. Pyle	Decatur, Ind	Nov. 15, 1859	26, 121
Cultivator	I. N. Pyle	Pleasant Mills, Ind	Apr. 25, 1871	114, 040
Cultivator	J. A. Quick	South Danville, N. Y	May 4, 1869	89, 791
Cultivator	W. F. Quinby	Stanton, Del	Mar. 19, 1861	31, 738
Cultivator	A. Ralston	West Middletown, Pa	Sept. 2, 1845	4, 171
Cultivator	N. A. Rand	Winslow, Ill	July 7, 1868	79, 598
Cultivator	H. C. Ravenscraft	Kingwood, Va	Nov. 27, 1860	30, 758
Cultivator	W. B. Read	Gallatin, Tenn	Jan. 24, 1871	111, 250
Cultivator	J. Rebman	Binkley's Bridge, Pa	Nov. 15, 1870	109, 247
Cultivator	J. Rebman	Manheim Township, Pa	May 7, 1872	126, 412
Cultivator	J. E. Reed	Mineville, N. Y	June 6, 1871	115, 771
Cultivator	S. Reed	Rising Sun, Md	June 16, 1868	79, 001
Cultivator	T. M. Reed	Germantown, Ohio	Oct. 18, 1870	108, 392
Cultivator	E. Reese	Eutaw, Ala	Aug. 15, 1871	118, 053
Cultivator	F. Reese	Wilsonville, Ala	Dec. 17, 1872	134, 099
Cultivator	J. Reichard	Fayetteville, Pa	Aug. 18, 1868	81, 108
Cultivator	J. K. Reiner	Line Lexington, Pa	Oct. 2, 1866	58, 476
Cultivator	L. Repp	Tiffin, Ohio	Mar. 19, 1867	62, 971
Cultivator	J. H. Reynerson	Pleasant Plain, Iowa	Apr. 2, 1867	63, 426
Cultivator	J. H. Reynerson	Pleasant Plain, Iowa	Mar. 17, 1868	75, 647
Cultivator	E. D. and O. B. Reynolds	North Bridgewater, Mass	Dec. 24, 1872	134, 166
Cultivator	P. B. and L. C. Reynolds	Prophetstown, Ill	Feb. 24, 1863	37, 789
Cultivator	W. Rhodes and M. Porter	Lovington, Ill	May 2, 1865	47, 568
Cultivator	H. Rice	Springfield, Ohio	Feb. 13, 1866	52, 606
Cultivator	R. Rice	Georgetown, Ill	Apr. 28, 1863	38, 337
Cultivator	J. C. Rich	Penfield, N. Y	Dec. 11, 1866	60, 422
Cultivator	G. R. Richardson and J. Bebel	Earlville and Rockford, Ill	June 3, 1873	139, 478
Cultivator	J. C. Rickerd	Lewisville, Ind	Feb. 4, 1868	74, 138
Cultivator	J. J. Rider	Wilton Junction, Iowa	Nov. 22, 1864	45, 177
Cultivator	M. Rigell	Dawson, Ga	Aug. 14, 1860	29, 618

Index of patents issued from the United States Patent Office from 1790 *to* 1873, *inclusive*—Continued.

Invention.	Inventor.	Residence.	Date.	No.
Cultivator	W. S. Riggs	Hightstown, N. J	Mar. 19, 1861	31,742
Cultivator	J. Righter	Clarksburgh, Va	Dec. 22, 1857	18,928
Cultivator	R. B. Robbins	Adrian, Mich	Aug. 5, 1873	141,462
Cultivator	C. Roberts	Three Rivers, Mich	Oct. 28, 1862	36,859
Cultivator	C. Roberts	Three Rivers, Mich	Nov. 25, 1862	37,009
Cultivator	C. Roberts	Three Rivers, Mich	Nov. 25, 1862	37,010
Cultivator	C. Roberts	Three Rivers, Mich	Jan. 10, 1865	45,860
Cultivator	C. Roberts	Three Rivers, Mich	Jan. 10, 1865	45,861
Cultivator	C. Roberts	Three Rivers, Mich	June 27, 1865	48,445
Cultivator	C. S. Roberts	Lyons, Iowa	Nov. 6, 1866	59,454
Cultivator	E. B. Roberts	Rochester, N. Y	Mar. 17, 1868	75,578
Cultivator	T. B. Roberts	Franklin, Ill	June 20, 1871	116,100
Cultivator	T. A. Robertson	Friendship, Md	Oct. 27, 1857	18,520
Cultivator	T. A. Robertson	Washington, D. C	Mar. 29, 1859	23,395
Cultivator	H. H. Robertson and C. G. Carr	Kingston, Mo	Nov. 6, 1860	30,589
Cultivator	L. Robinson	West Cambridge, Mass	Sept. 30, 1856	15,819
Cultivator	W. R. Robinson	Mattoon, Ill	Aug. 27, 1872	130,869
Cultivator	S. Rockafellow	Muscatine, Iowa	Aug. 25, 1863	39,703
Cultivator	A. Roden	Mumford, Ala	Dec. 23, 1873	145,901
Cultivator	W. Rodgers	Lynnville, Ind	Oct. 6, 1868	82,753
Cultivator	D. B. Rogers	Seneca Falls, N. Y	Jan. 16, 1849	6,037
Cultivator	D. B., S., and L. Rogers	Pittsburgh, Pa	Mar. 9, 1858	19,584
Cultivator	M. L. Rogers	Spring, Pa	Dec. 27, 1859	26,618
Cultivator	T. B. Rogers	Weathersfield, Conn	Apr. 2, 1867	63,430
Cultivator	J. Root	Hartland, N. Y	Aug. 23, 1870	106,728
Cultivator	H. M. Rose	Clinton, Ill	Jan. 24, 1871	111,256
Cultivator	J. J. Rose	Elmwood, Ill	Aug. 17, 1869	93,749
Cultivator	A. W. Ross	Northfield, Mass	Oct. 30, 1866	59,269
Cultivator	H. S. Ross	Millville, Ohio	Apr. 19, 1870	102,045
Cultivator	A. P. Routt	Liberty Mills, Va	Apr. 30, 1867	64,370
Cultivator	A. P. Routt	Liberty Mills, Va	July 14, 1868	80,015
Cultivator	J. S. and I. Rowell	Beaver Dam, Wis	July 3, 1866	56,102
Cultivator	J. E. Rowland	Hagerstown, Md	May 7, 1867	64,576
Cultivator	J. Rue	Englishtown, N. J	Aug. 9, 1859	25,048
Cultivator	J. Rue	Englishtown, N. J	Apr. 30, 1872	126,156
Cultivator	R. Rust	Odessa, Del	May 20, 1873	139,193
Cultivator	S. A. Sabin	Pecatonica, Ill	Oct. 5, 1869	95,520
Cultivator	N. F. Sandelin	New York, N. Y	Feb. 27, 1872	124,014
Cultivator	J. R. Sanders	Davenport, Iowa	Oct. 1, 1872	131,908
Cultivator	R. Sandiford	Joliet, Ill	Dec. 1, 1868	84,649
Cultivator	J. W. Sanford	Byron, Ill	Dec. 3, 1867	71,794
Cultivator	J. Sattison	Ripley Township, Ohio	Jan. 3, 1871	110,682
Cultivator	M. Sattley	Taylorville, Ill	Feb. 14, 1871	111,781
Cultivator	W. G. Savage	Clinton, Ill	June 6, 1865	48,102
Cultivator	J. Savill	Monmouth, Ill	Feb. 20, 1866	52,754
Cultivator	R. Sawyer	Wales, Me	Aug. 10, 1858	21,170
Cultivator	A. Sawyer and H. Barnes	Burlington, Wis	Feb. 25, 1862	34,528
Cultivator	E. H. Sawyers	Orleans, Iowa	Jan. 10, 1865	45,866
Cultivator	E. H. Sawyers	West Grove, Iowa	Feb. 24, 1863	37,775
Cultivator	C. H. Sayre	Utica, N. Y	Aug. 25, 1857	18,073
Cultivator	G. H. Schanck	Libertyville, Ill	Sept. 8, 1863	39,837
Cultivator	J. D. Scheetz and R. Adams	Robesonia, Pa	May 7, 1867	64,580
Cultivator	H. Schreiner, jr	Berrysburgh, Pa	July 14, 1857	17,821
Cultivator	J. Schröder	Kickapoo, Ill	Sept. 24, 1867	69,225
Cultivator	C. Schwanger	Mount Joy Township, Pa	Jan. 12, 1869	85,862
Cultivator	M. Schwartz	Canterbury, N. H	Jan. 30, 1872	123,128
Cultivator	T. S. Scoville	New York, N. Y	Mar. 6, 1860	27,388
Cultivator	W. Seely	Chillicothe, Ill	Oct. 11, 1859	25,764
Cultivator	E. S. Seger and J. C. Ormiston	Erie, Ill	Oct. 30, 1866	59,279
Cultivator	G. and J. Seibert	Ashley, Ill	Sept. 29, 1868	82,646
Cultivator	J. B. Sexton	Pella, Iowa	Jan. 14, 1868	73,392
Cultivator	J. B. Sexton	Pella, Iowa	Apr. 13, 1869	88,915
Cultivator	J. B. Sexton	Pella, Iowa	Nov. 22, 1870	109,554
Cultivator	W. H. and L. Seymour	Weymouth, Ohio	Sept. 11, 1860	30,000
Cultivator	S. B. Shank	Millersville, Pa	Aug. 15, 1871	118,159
Cultivator	J. Shannon	Dakota, Wis	Aug. 14, 1860	29,626
Cultivator	D. W. Shares	Hamden, Conn	Aug. 1, 1854	11,460
Cultivator	A. Shaw	Monmouth, Ill	June 29, 1869	91,876
Cultivator	A. Shaw	Monmouth, Ill	Nov. 30, 1869	97,319
Cultivator	S. C. Sheller	Lewisburgh, Pa	Feb. 13, 1872	123,583
Cultivator	J. Shepard	Newport, Me	June 29, 1869	91,973
Cultivator	J. Sherrill	Harrisburgh, Oreg	Jan. 7, 1873	134,615
Cultivator	A. T. Sherwood	Amador, Cal	Oct. 1, 1872	131,909
Cultivator	L. Sherwood	Marine, Ill	Jan. 3, 1865	45,758
Cultivator	T. N. Sherwood	Dunlapsville, Ind	Jan. 23, 1866	52,213
Cultivator	N. S. Shields	Rockford, Ill	Aug. 23, 1870	106,733
Cultivator	J. Simpson	Cordova, Ill	Nov. 16, 1869	96,979
Cultivator	M. P. Simpson	Rosemond, Ill	May 2, 1871	114,483
Cultivator	M. P. Simpson and J. P. Ellacott	Pana and Shelbyville, Ill	July 1, 1873	140,437
Cultivator	Z. B. Sims	Bonham, Tex	Jan. 21, 1873	135,165
Cultivator	J. E. Sisson	Bastrop, La	Dec. 16, 1873	145,535
Cultivator	J. H. Skelly	Aroma, Ill	July 21, 1868	80,094
Cultivator	M. H. Skiff	Cornwall Bridge, Conn	Dec. 8, 1863	40,859
Cultivator	H. M. Skinner	Rockford, Ill	Oct. 18, 1870	108,398
Cultivator	J. B. Skinner	Rockford, Ill	Jan. 23, 1866	52,217
Cultivator	J. B. Skinner	Rockford, Ill	Dec. 21, 1869	98,112
Cultivator	J. B. Skinner	Rockford, Ill	Mar. 15, 1870	100,812
Cultivator	J. B. Skinner	Rockford, Ill	July 23, 1872	129,759
Cultivator	D. S. Slater	Poynett, Wis	Mar. 3, 1868	75,211
Cultivator	D. Slaughter	West Hempfield Township, Pa.	Mar. 2, 1869	87,373
Cultivator	S. Sloan	Kewanee, Ill	Apr. 5, 1864	42,232
Cultivator	S. W. Slocum and E. Phillips	Fulton City, Ill	Apr. 26, 1864	42,513
Cultivator	G. Slusser	Hillsborough, Ohio	Dec. 16, 1873	145,690
Cultivator	J. Smalley	Bound Brook, N. J	Mar. 29, 1859	23,402
Cultivator	A. Smith	Westfield, Ohio	June 14, 1859	24,411
Cultivator	A. C. Smith	Fayetteville, N. C	Oct. 17, 1871	120,113
Cultivator	A. C. Smith	Fayetteville, N. C	Dec. 16, 1873	145,691

Index of patents issued from the United States Patent Office from 1790 *to* 1873, *inclusive*—Continued.

Invention.	Inventor.	Residence.	Date.	No.
Cultivator	G. Smith	Baltimore, Md	Mar. 27, 1860	27,654
Cultivator	G. H. Smith	Des Moines, Iowa	Sept. 13, 1870	107,416
Cultivator	H. B. Smith	Eureka, Ill	Sept. 1, 1863	39,760
Cultivator	H. B. Smith	Eureka, Ill	June 5, 1866	55,381
Cultivator	I. R. Smith	Elgin, Ill	Apr. 24, 1860	28,016
Cultivator	J. A. Smith	Lacon, Ill	Oct. 26, 1869	96,279
Cultivator	J. D. Smith	Peoria, Ill	Apr. 26, 1864	42,514
Cultivator	N. E. Smith	Springdale, Iowa	Aug. 25, 1863	39,686
Cultivator	N. S. Smith	Buffalo, N. Y	Aug. 31, 1858	21,377
Cultivator	P. E. Smith	Scotland Neck, N. C	Dec. 20, 1870	110,302
Cultivator	P. W. Smith	Abingdon, Ill	Sept. 10, 1867	68,662
Cultivator	W. Smith	Boonville, Ind	July 27, 1869	93,017
Cultivator	W. D. Smith	Homerville, Ga	Nov. 26, 1872	133,387
Cultivator	W. E. Smith	Oquawka, Ill	July 23, 1867	67,078
Cultivator	W. H. Smith	Wyanet, Ill	Jan. 15, 1861	31,132
Cultivator	F. L. Smithson	Mecklenburgh County, Va	Apr. 3, 1855	12,653
Cultivator	W. Smook	Nine Eagles, Iowa	June 29, 1869	91,981
Cultivator	S. Snider	Taylorsville, Ky	Nov. 7, 1871	120,789
Cultivator	J. Snyder	Rock Lick, W. Va	Feb. 11, 1868	74,441
Cultivator	E. M. Sorley	Neenah, Wis	July 10, 1866	56,286
Cultivator	J. W. Spangler	Jackson Township, Pa	July 18, 1871	117,215
Cultivator	J. W. Spangler	York, Pa	Mar. 26, 1872	125,093
Cultivator	A. J. Sparks	Wyanet, Ill	Dec. 15, 1863	40,959
Cultivator	S. T. Spaulding	North Cohocton, N. Y	Dec. 21, 1869	98,202
Cultivator	J. A. Spear, jr	Manchester, Pa	Apr. 9, 1861	32,010
Cultivator	A. B. Spies	Sterling, Ill	Dec. 1, 1868	84,588
Cultivator	P. Sprague	Pecatonica, Ill	May 4, 1869	89,801
Cultivator	R. H. Springstead	Constantine, Mich	Oct. 20, 1863	40,367
Cultivator	A. B. Springsteen	Schodack Landing, N. Y	May 21, 1872	126,991
Cultivator	D. S. Stafford	Decatur, Ill	Jan. 15, 1861	31,133
Cultivator	D. S. Stafford	Decatur, Ill	Jan. 6, 1863	37,309
Cultivator	D. S. Stafford	Decatur, Ill	Sept. 17, 1867	68,910
Cultivator	F. Stamm	Lancaster, Pa	Mar. 19, 1861	31,753
Cultivator	J. K. Staman	Mifflin, Ohio	Jan. 10, 1860	26,796
Cultivator	A. F. and T. M. Stansbury	Lewiston, Ill	Mar. 12, 1867	62,898
Cultivator	A. Stark	Topeka, Kans	Sept. 18, 1866	58,147
Cultivator	E. Starr	Royal Oak, Mich	July 10, 1866	56,288
Cultivator	W. H. Startzman	Big Lick, Va	Oct. 27, 1868	83,564
Cultivator	C. C. Stearns	Homer, Ill	Aug. 4, 1863	39,428
Cultivator	C. E. Steller	Chicago, Ill	Dec. 10, 1867	72,107
Cultivator	L. Stevens	Dover, Ky	Nov. 27, 1860	30,771
Cultivator	T. S. Stevens	Pepperell, Mass	Oct. 19, 1858	21,857
Cultivator	U. T. Stewart	Fayette County, Tenn	June 18, 1867	65,961
Cultivator	W. L. Stewart	Rushville, Ind	Dec. 29, 1868	85,488
Cultivator	G. Stiber	Cogan Station, Pa	June 4, 1872	127,658
Cultivator	A. F. Stillwell	Fayette, Iowa	Sept. 4, 1866	57,792
Cultivator	G. B. St. John	Kalamazoo, Mich	July 25, 1865	49,008
Cultivator	G. B. St. John	Brooklyn, Mich	Dec. 8, 1868	84,776
Cultivator	G. B. St. John	Kalamazoo, Mich	Apr. 5, 1870	101,536
Cultivator	W. W. St. John	Saint Louis, Mo	Nov. 21, 1865	51,096
Cultivator	A. D. Stocking	Dowagiac, Mich	May 29, 1866	55,175
Cultivator	G. W. Stockton	Oquawka, Ill	May 14, 1867	64,721
Cultivator	J. C. Stoddard	Worcester, Mass	Mar. 29, 1859	23,407
Cultivator	J. C. Stoddard	Worcester, Mass	June 21, 1859	24,500
Cultivator	M. Stoll	Conestoga Township, Pa	Mar. 28, 1871	113,109
Cultivator	M. Stoll	Conestoga Township, Pa	Aug. 13, 1872	130,393
Cultivator	O. Stone	Ionia, Mich	May 26, 1868	78,243
Cultivator	A. F. Stoner	West Unity, Ohio	Nov. 10, 1868	84,016
Cultivator	C. E. Storrs, W. E. Keyes, and D. W. Jones.	Grandville, Mich	Dec. 24, 1867	72,560
Cultivator	I. Stout	Tremont, Ill	Apr. 16, 1861	32,092
Cultivator	I. and S. Stout	Tremont, Ill	Dec. 1, 1863	40,776
Cultivator	A. J. Stover	Sandyville, Iowa	Feb. 27, 1866	52,905
Cultivator	D. C. Stover	Lanark, Ill	July 10, 1866	56,289
Cultivator	D. C. Stover	Lanark, Ill	Mar. 9, 1869	87,724
Cultivator	D. C. Stover	Lanark, Ill	Nov. 1, 1870	108,945
Cultivator	J. G. Stowe	Bloomington, Ill	June 11, 1872	127,935
Cultivator	J. G. Stowe	Bloomington, Ill	Nov. 12, 1872	133,067
Cultivator	W. Strieby	Wagontown, Pa	Mar. 12, 1861	31,683
Cultivator	J. C. Stroud	Lockhart, Tex	Sept. 29, 1868	82,562
Cultivator	W. D. Stroud	Oshkosh, Wis	Mar. 21, 1871	112,862
Cultivator	J. Stryker	Six-Mile Run, N. J	Apr. 17, 1855	12,744
Cultivator	E. E. Stubbs	West Elkton, Ohio	Aug. 13, 1867	67,817
Cultivator	J. Summers	Raleigh, Va	Nov. 24, 1857	18,714
Cultivator	B. J. Svenson	Manor Station, Tex	Aug. 20, 1872	130,765
Cultivator	J. Swart	Hoffman's Ferry, N. Y	Feb. 23, 1864	41,722
Cultivator	M. Sweet	Richland, Ind	Sept. 10, 1867	68,803
Cultivator	J. W. Swickard	Galva, Ill	Feb. 18, 1873	136,108
Cultivator	C. W. Taliaferro	Keithsburgh, Ill	Nov. 11, 1862	36,922
Cultivator	J. E. Tate	Columbia, Tenn	Apr. 23, 1867	64,165
Cultivator	A. C. Taylor	North Fairfield, Ohio	Nov. 7, 1871	120,794
Cultivator	C. F. Taylor	Vassalborough, Me	Feb. 25, 1868	74,775
Cultivator	J. W. Taylor	Ashland, Va	Feb. 12, 1861	31,416
Cultivator	W. Taylor	Mansfield, Mass	Feb. 11, 1873	135,736
Cultivator	W. A. Taylor and W. W. Graves.	Fort Adams, Miss	Aug. 14, 1860	29,637
Cultivator	H. M. Teasdale	Dansville, N. Y	June 20, 1865	48,324
Cultivator	D. C. Teller	Terre Haute, Ind	Feb. 20, 1866	52,770
Cultivator	E. Terrill	Cold Water, Mich	June 23, 1868	79,161
Cultivator	R. Thayer and J. McClelland	Pittsburgh, Pa	Oct. 10, 1865	50,403
Cultivator	C. Thede	Aledo, Ill	Apr. 29, 1873	138,451
Cultivator	J. Thirlwell	Galesburgh, Ill	Jan. 14, 1859	24,418
Cultivator	J. S. Thomas	Mifflintown, Pa	Mar. 28, 1871	113,223
Cultivator	J. H. Thomas and P. P. Mast	Springfield, Ohio	Mar. 28, 1865	47,055
Cultivator	J. H. Thomas and P. P. Mast	Springfield, Ohio	Jan. 16, 1866	52,093
Cultivator	J. H. Thomas, P. P. Mast, and T. Harding.	Springfield, Ohio	Dec. 12, 1865	51,494
Cultivator	A. Thompson	Ottawa, Ill	July 23, 1872	129,693

Index of patents issued from the United States Patent Office from 1790 *to* 1873, *inclusive*—Continued.

Invention.	Inventor.	Residence.	Date.	No.
Cultivator	J. J. Thompson	Columbus, Ohio	July 4, 1871	116, 776
Cultivator	W. L. Thompson	Rockville, Ind	Sept. 24, 1872	131, 720
Cultivator	J. J. Thompson and V. F. Collier.	Richwood, Ohio	Oct. 13, 1868	83, 111
Cultivator	P. W. Thomson	Truro, Ill	Feb. 9, 1864	41, 550
Cultivator	T. Thorley	Southfield, Mich	Sept. 15, 1868	82, 180
Cultivator	J. A. Throop and J. Cox	Three Rivers, Mich	Jan. 27, 1863	37, 532
Cultivator	J. B. Tibbets	Portland, Mich	Aug. 9, 1870	106, 235
Cultivator	E. S. Tichenor	Jacksonville, N. Y	Aug. 12, 1862	36, 180
Cultivator	H. H. Tietjens	Lyons, Iowa	Sept. 3, 1867	68, 469
Cultivator	H. Tilden	Davenport, Iowa	Aug. 6, 1872	130, 337
Cultivator	B. Tinkham	Cameron, Ill	Dec. 11, 1860	30, 897
Cultivator	J. B. Tipton	Peoria, Ill	Feb. 16, 1869	87, 080
Cultivator	L. K. Tipton	Easton, Mo	Aug. 13, 1872	130, 454
Cultivator	J. C. Tobias and W. N. Bates	El Paso, Ill	Jan. 26, 1869	86, 329
Cultivator	G. W. Tolhurst	Liverpool, Ohio	Jan. 4, 1859	22, 520
Cultivator	F. W. Tolley	Coxsackie, N. Y	July 9, 1872	128, 827
Cultivator	F. W. Tolley	Coxsackie, N. Y	Dec. 31, 1872	134, 446
Cultivator	S. A. Tombs	Ashley, Mo	May 10, 1864	42, 737
Cultivator	J. H. Tomlinson	Mount Carroll, Ill	Nov. 7, 1871	120, 684
Cultivator	A. Tompkins	Paris, Ill	Aug. 29, 1871	118, 562
Cultivator	Z. Toms and L. W. McMullan	Hertford, N. C	Apr. 30, 1872	126, 165
Cultivator	J. P. Testevin	Racine, Wis	Aug. 18, 1863	39, 597
Cultivator	P. R. Totten	Adams, Ill	Oct. 27, 1868	83, 569
Cultivator	A. C. Tower	Mendota, Ill	Jan. 14, 1873	134, 824
Cultivator	J. Townsend	Head of Sassafras, Md	Dec. 5, 1865	51, 365
Cultivator	F. Trigalet	Astoria, N. Y	Oct. 22, 1872	132, 504
Cultivator	A. G. Tucker	Richview, Ill	July 5, 1864	43, 441
Cultivator	W. Tucker	Blackstone, Mass	Oct. 12, 1858	21, 787
Cultivator	J. B. Turner	Jacksonville, Ill	Mar. 12, 1861	31, 682
Cultivator	J. B. Turner	Jacksonville, Ill	Dec. 3, 1861	33, 860
Cultivator	T. Turner	Marysville, Ohio	Dec. 14, 1858	22, 316
Cultivator	L. G. Tuttle	North Haven, Conn	Feb. 19, 1867	62, 302
Cultivator	S. D. Tuttle and J. H. Gans	Eaton, Ohio	Oct. 8, 1867	69, 725
Cultivator	J. W. Tyson	Lower Providence, Pa	Aug. 14, 1866	57, 222
Cultivator	J. W. Tyson	Lower Providence, Pa	Feb. 26, 1867	62, 511
Cultivator	C. A. Uhl	Millersburgh, Ohio	June 24, 1862	35, 718
Cultivator	F. J. Underwood	Rock Island, Ill	Dec. 29, 1868	85, 412
Cultivator	P. C. Van Brocklin	Buffalo, N. Y	Mar. 24, 1863	37, 988
Cultivator	G. W. Van Brunt	Horicon, Wis	Jan. 26, 1869	86, 261
Cultivator	E. W. Vangundy	Galesburgh, Ill	Feb. 2, 1864	41, 454
Cultivator	J. Van Horn	Plainfield, Ill	July 22, 1862	35, 961
Cultivator	R. P. Van Horn	Jacksontown, Ohio	Mar. 27, 1855	12, 609
Cultivator	R. P. Van Horne	Gratiot, Ohio	May 29, 1860	28, 523
Cultivator	H Van Meter	Macomb, Ill	May 18, 1869	90, 208
Cultivator	F. Veal	Hallettsville, Tex	June 21, 1859	24, 597
Cultivator	W. F. Veber	Bowling Green, Ohio	Apr. 2, 1861	31, 917
Cultivator	W. H. Vick	Holly Springs, Miss	May 14, 1872	126, 658
Cultivator	J. Vowles	New Hudson, Mich	Feb. 14, 1860	27, 174
Cultivator	J. Vowles	New Hudson, Mich	May 21, 1861	32, 391
Cultivator	J. Vowles	Milford, Mich	Nov. 10, 1868	84, 029
Cultivator	J. Waddell	Liberty, Ind	Sept. 19, 1871	119, 206
Cultivator	H. Wadsworth	Duxbury, Mass	Aug. 3, 1869	93, 374
Cultivator	C. L. Waffle	Sharon Centre, Ohio	July 26, 1870	105, 745
Cultivator	G. Waggoner	New Kingston, Pa	Jan. 14, 1873	134, 949
Cultivator	T. Waite	Plymouth, Ohio	Nov. 17, 1868	84, 238
Cultivator	L. Walker	Victoria, Tex	May 23, 1871	115, 138
Cultivator	L. B. Walker	Chicago, Ill	Sept. 12, 1865	49, 938
Cultivator	W. T. Walker	Fontenoy Mills, Ga	May 13, 1873	138, 964
Cultivator	E. Walker and J. J. Piatt	La Porte, Ind	Aug. 31, 1869	94, 456
Cultivator	E. Walker and J. J. Piatt	La Porte, Ind	Oct. 26, 1869	96, 290
Cultivator	E. Walker and A. M. Weed	La Porte, Ind	Oct. 29, 1867	70, 381
Cultivator	W. Walton	East Palestine, Ohio	June 2, 1868	78, 626
Cultivator	B. F. Ward	Indian Springs, Ga	Jan. 4, 1870	98, 650
Cultivator	C. Warner	Monroe, Ohio	Mar. 26, 1872	124, 922
Cultivator	J. Warner	Reading, Pa	Mar. 13, 1849	6, 167
Cultivator	A. Warren	Westport, Conn	Aug. 9, 1859	25, 066
Cultivator	G. W. Warren	Macomb, Ill	July 10, 1866	56, 295
Cultivator	L. B. Waterman	Chicago, Ill	May 13, 1862	35, 282
Cultivator	L. B. Waterman	Chicago, Ill	Nov. 25, 1862	37, 019
Cultivator	L. B. Waterman	Chicago, Ill	June 21, 1864	43, 268
Cultivator	W. M. Watkins	Talcott, Va	Nov. 28, 1871	121, 439
Cultivator	C. H. Watson	Washington, D. C	July 2, 1872	128, 685
Cultivator	C. H. Watson	Washington, D. C	July 2, 1872	128, 686
Cultivator	W. T. Watson	Nottingham, Md	Dec. 11, 1866	60, 449
Cultivator	H. J. Wattles	Rockford, Ill	Apr. 6, 1869	88, 758
Cultivator	H. J. Wattles	Rockford, Ill	Aug. 10, 1869	93, 651
Cultivator	H. J. Wattles	Rockford, Ill	Dec. 7, 1869	97, 573
Cultivator	S. Way	La Porte, Ind	Nov. 24, 1868	84, 449
Cultivator	T. U. Webb	Springfield, Ill	May 29, 1866	55, 185
Cultivator	N. G. Webber	East Springfield, Pa	May 10, 1870	102, 983
Cultivator	H. H. Webster	Claremont, N. H	Aug. 29, 1865	49, 667
Cultivator	W. S. Weir, jr	Monmouth, Ill	May 28, 1861	32, 442
Cultivator	W. S. Weir, jr	Monmouth, Ill	Dec. 23, 1862	37, 251
Cultivator	W. S. Weir, jr	Monmouth, Ill	Mar. 13, 1866	53, 205
Cultivator	S. G. Welch	Athens, Ill	Feb. 9, 1864	4[illegible]
Cultivator	H. Weld	Black Walnut, Ill	Oct. 10, 1871	119, 904
Cultivator	F. N. Welden	Rockford, Ill	Mar. 21, 1871	112, 994
Cultivator	C. Wells	Sandwich, Ill	Jan. 26, 1869	86, 262
Cultivator	C. C. Wells	Lyons, Iowa	Jan. 30, 1866	52, 349
Cultivator	E. Wells	Auburn, Miss	Aug. 28, 1860	29, 836
Cultivator	H. Wells	Walnut Grove, Ill	June 21, 1859	24, 514
Cultivator	P. F. Wells	Milford, Mich	June 17, 1873	139, 985
Cultivator	W. J. Wells	Sidney, Ohio	June 22, 1869	91, 802
Cultivator	N. Werts	Magnolia, Ill	May 3 1870	102, 631
Cultivator	P. L. West	Bath, Ill	Apr. 2, 1867	63, 447
Cultivator	L. Wetherell	Worcester, Mass	Dec. 22, 1857	18, 939
Cultivator	C. L. Whaite	Waverly, Pa	Sept. 6, 1870	107, 142

Index of patents issued from the United States Patent Office from 1790 *to* 1873, *inclusive*—Continued.

Invention.	Inventor.	Residence.	Date.	No.
Cultivator	E. P. Wheeler	Nebraska City, Nebr	Apr. 10, 1866	53, 911
Cultivator	N. Whitehall	Rob Roy, Ind	Oct. 27, 1857	18, 530
Cultivator	J. Whiteside and H. F. Crabill	Fuller's Corners, Ind	Nov. 22, 1859	26, 216
Cultivator	S. M. Whiting	Galesburgh, Ill	Jan. 15, 1867	61, 294
Cultivator	J. M. Whiting	Bolton, Mass	Mar. 1, 1859	23, 135
Cultivator	E. Wiard	Louisville, Ky	Mar. 4, 1873	136, 574
Cultivator	J. Widman	Panola, Ill	Jan. 7, 1868	73, 217
Cultivator	T. Wiles and J. M. Ginnis	Muscatine, Iowa	Jan. 3, 1865	45, 782
Cultivator	J. Wilhelm	Muscatine, Iowa	Feb. 9, 1864	41, 562
Cultivator	L. H. Wilkinson	Michigan City, Ind	Jan. 1, 1869	90, 905
Cultivator	E. Wilcox	Delhi, Iowa	Dec. 15, 1863	40, 973
Cultivator	C. Willard	Newtown, Pa	Feb. 5, 1867	61, 906
Cultivator	A. Williams	Berea, Ohio	June 21, 1864	43, 249
Cultivator	J. M. Williams	Greenville, Ga	June 26, 1860	28, 929
Cultivator	W. Willmot	Wilmington, Del	Nov. 30, 1858	22, 215
Cultivator	F. O. Wilson	Mount Olive, N. C	Mar. 6, 1860	27, 402
Cultivator	J. Wilson	Somerford, Ohio	July 23, 1867	67, 093
Cultivator	J. A. Wilson	Hamburgh, Iowa	Dec. 28, 1869	98, 326
Cultivator	W. C. Wilson	Brunswick, Ill	Nov. 7, 1871	120, 692
Cultivator	W. I. Wilson	Franklin, Ind	May 24, 1859	24, 171
Cultivator	B. W. Wingo	Chillicothe, Mo	Nov. 25, 1873	145, 038
Cultivator	A. Q. Withers	Red Banks, Miss	Dec. 1, 1857	18 785
Cultivator	B. Witter	Sherrill's Mount, Iowa	Feb. 11, 1873	135, 872
Cultivator	F. Wolf	Brooklyn, N. Y	Aug. 14, 1860	29, 644
Cultivator	J. Wood	Wedowee, Ala	Apr. 16, 1872	125, 872
Cultivator	J. F. Wood	Houma, La	Sept. 25, 1860	30, 173
Cultivator	J. A. and S. S. Woodward and T. Mason.	Sandwich, Ill	Sept. 15, 1868	82, 191
Cultivator	J. A. and S. S. Woodward and T. Mason.	Sandwich, Ill	June 29, 1869	91, 894
Cultivator	R. Wottring	Prospect, Ohio	Apr. 5, 1870	101, 695
Cultivator	G. W. N. Yost	Port Gibson, Miss	Mar. 20, 1855	12, 571
Cultivator	G. W. N. Yost	Yellow Springs, Ohio	Aug. 28, 1860	29, 849
Cultivator	G. W. N. Yost	Yellow Springs, Ohio	Sept. 4, 1860	29, 934
Cultivator	A. Young	Millstadt, Ill	Nov. 6, 1866	59, 499
Cultivator	B. F. Young	Toulon, Ill	May 8, 1866	54, 637
Cultivator	B. F. Young	Toulon, Ill	Feb. 16, 1869	87, 019
Cultivator	B. F. Young	Toulon, Ill	Nov. 15, 1870	109, 363
Cultivator	J. Young	Joliet, Ill	June 7, 1859	24, 348
Cultivator	S. L. Young	Scottville, Ill	Feb. 25, 1873	136, 297
Cultivator	W. B. Young	Chicago, Ill	Sept. 10, 1867	68, 679
Cultivator	L. G. Youngs	Wilmington, Ill	July 11, 1865	48, 758
Cultivator	W. P. Zane	Woolwich, N. J	Mar. 27, 1855	12, 611
Cultivator	G. W. Zeigler	Tiffin, Ohio	Mar. 13, 1866	53, 212
Cultivator	G. W. Zeigler	Maumee City, Ohio	Feb. 9, 1869	86, 794
Cultivator	J. P. Zeller	South Bend, Ind	July 13, 1869	92, 686
Cultivator	J. Zimmerman	Oswego, Ill	July 29, 1856	15, 453
Cultivator and chopper	Z. Doolittle and A. M. Crowder.	Houston Factory, Ga	Feb. 18, 1868	74, 519
Cultivator and corn-mill, Combined	C. L. Wilcox	Wayne Township, Ohio	July 12, 1870	105, 285
Cultivator and corn-stalk cutter, Combined	S. T. Miller	Empire Prairie, Mo	Jan. 2, 1872	122, 479
Cultivator and ditcher, Combined	N. Hawkes	Appleton, Me	Oct. 16, 1866	58, 819
Cultivator and grain-drill, Combined	J. Gire	Tipton, Ill	Sept. 13, 1870	107, 359
Cultivator and grain-drill, Combined adjustable	T. Lumsdon	Waterford, Ohio	Sept. 6, 1870	107, 186
Cultivator and gang-plow	I. B. Mahon	Dunkirk, Ohio	Mar. 24, 1868	75, 941
Cultivator and gang-plow, Wheel	W. Hammond	Marshall, Mich	May 29, 1866	55, 093
Cultivator and harrow	S. Conrad	Petaluma, Cal	Apr. 7, 1868	76, 578
Cultivator and harrow	E. T. Russel	Indianapolis, Ind	Aug. 9, 1870	106, 118
Cultivator and harrow	T. Short	Fairmount, Ill	Feb. 7, 1865	46, 274
Cultivator and harrow, Combined	H. Benedict	Detroit, Mich	July 27, 1869	93, 042
Cultivator and harrow, Combined	E. Emmert	Franklin Grove, Ill	Aug. 17, 1869	93, 692
Cultivator and harrow, Combined	J. Maxton	Saybrook, Ill	Feb. 14, 1871	111, 857
Cultivator and harrow, Combined	E. D. and O. B. Reynolds	North Bridgewater, Mass	Jan. 24, 1865	46, 025
Cultivator and harrow, Combined	C. Rich and O. L. Neisler	Poughkeepsie, N. Y	Jan. 21, 1868	73, 547
Cultivator and harrow, Combined rotary	H. T. Taplin	South New Market, N. H	Sept. 28, 1869	95, 394
Cultivator and harrow teeth	R. West and H. F. Paul	Concord, N. H	Oct. 8, 1867	69, 731
Cultivator and hoe, Combined	H. P. Eckler	Catskill, N. Y	June 2, 1868	78, 442
Cultivator and horseshoe	J. W. Blake	Jefferson, Wis	Nov. 28, 1871	121, 228
Cultivator and manure-drag, Combined	P. H. Stauffer	Lehighton, Pa	Jan. 19, 1869	86, 110
Cultivator and other teeth, Friction-block for attaching.	W. Workman and J. Hitchcock	Ripon, Wis	Dec. 13, 1870	110, 103
Cultivator and planter	E. M. Wright	Wilmington, Ohio	Aug. 1, 1865	49, 204
Cultivator and planter, Combined	B. Anyan	Fitchville, Ohio	Apr. 20, 1869	89, 113
Cultivator and planter combined	P. Burress	Braidwood, Ill	Jan. 3, 1871	110, 736
Cultivator and planter, Combined	S. B. Conover	New York, N. Y	Apr. 2, 1867	63, 476
Cultivator and planter combined	C. L. Lee	Fitchville, Ohio	June 23, 1868	79, 236
Cultivator and planter combined	E. Spangler	York, Pa	Jan. 16, 1872	122, 861
Cultivator and plow	W. H. Damron, R. H. Massey, and L. F. Whitman.	Macomb, Ill	Jan. 7, 1868	73, 081
Cultivator and plow	S. F. Seely	Sylvania, Ohio	Aug. 6, 1867	67, 595
Cultivator and plow	S. F. Seely	Whiteford, Mich	Dec. 15, 1868	84, 911
Cultivator and plow	L. R. Wright	Troy, N. Y	Dec. 3, 1872	133, 614
Cultivator and plow combined	L. R. Wright	Troy, N. Y	Aug. 11, 1868	81, 054
Cultivator and plow, Combined	I. Young	Byhalia, Miss	Feb. 12, 1867	61, 980
Cultivator and plow, Cotton	J. R. Thomas	Mifflin, Pa	Nov. 22, 1870	109, 558
Cultivator and plow shovel fastener	J. Pierpont and S. S. Tuttle	La Harpe, Ill	Oct. 18, 1870	108, 512
Cultivator and plow, Wheeled	S. Fisher	Hightstown, N. J	Oct. 5, 1869	95, 453
Cultivator and potato-digger	C. P. Goss	Saint Johnsbury, Vt	May 27, 1862	35, 371
Cultivator and potato-digger	J. G. Lacy	Eureka, Wis	Mar. 26, 1872	125, 057
Cultivator and potato digger, Combined	M. and J. W. Chandler	East Corinth, Me	July 4, 1865	48, 616
Cultivator and potato-digger, Combined	M. Darling and H. Gray	Marathon, N. Y	Apr. 28, 1868	77, 176
Cultivator and potato-digger, Combined	J. D C. Outwater	Newark, N. J	Nov. 26, 1867	71, 525
Cultivator and potato-plow, Corn	J. Kurtz	Clinton Township, Pa	July 16, 1867	66, 717
Cultivator and roller, Combined	L. G. and E. E. Reed	Stark County, Ill	June 21, 1870	104, 498
Cultivator and seed-planter	D. B. Morgan	Washington, Ohio	Feb. 9, 1869	86, 776
Cultivator and seed-planter	R. H. Springsteed	Wooster, Ohio	Feb. 12, 1845	3, 901
Cultivator and seed-planter, Combined	D. E. Holt	Wilkinson County, Miss	Nov. 2, 1869	96, 322
Cultivator and seeder	L. Bishop	Talladega, Ala	Mar. 24, 1868	75, 845
Cultivator and seeder	C. Lobdell	Fort Hill, Ill	Dec. 1, 1868	84, 499

Index of patents issued from the United States Patent Office from 1790 *to* 1873, *inclusive*—Continued.

Invention.	Inventor.	Residence.	Date.	No.
Cultivator and seeder	C. E. Miller	Amelia, Ohio	Jan. 19, 1864	41, 314
Cultivator and seeder	T. L. Ray	Flora, Ill	Oct. 11, 1864	44, 658
Cultivator and seeder, Combined	M. Baer	Logansport, Ind	July 25, 1871	117, 361
Cultivator and seeder, Combined	A. Dodge	Georgetown, D. C	Apr. 17, 1866	53, 960
Cultivator and seeder, Combined	J. Lewis	Washington, D. C	Nov. 22, 1870	109, 432
Cultivator and seeder, Combined	A. S. Markham	Bushnell, Ill	Oct. 29, 1867	70, 345
Cultivator and seeder, Combined	C. Norwood	Bloomington, Ill	May 30, 1865	47, 975
Cultivator and seeder, Combined	R. J. Robeson and W. Nash	Oskaloosa, Iowa	Nov. 1, 1870	108, 823
Cultivator and seeder, Combined	S. C. Schofield	Chicago, Ill	Oct. 26, 1869	96, 271
Cultivator and seeding-machine	C. Denton	Pekin, Ill	Mar. 27, 1866	53, 525
Cultivator and seeding-machine, Combined	C. Churchill	New Hartford, Iowa	Dec. 31, 1867	72, 799
Cultivator and seeding-machine, Combined	A. P. Durant	Atlanta, Ill	May 20, 1862	35, 306
Cultivator and shovel-plow	T. F. Hamilton	Geneseo, Ill	Aug. 22, 1871	118, 362
Cultivator and shovel-plow	G. W. Parsons and W. S. Finney.	Harrisburgh, Pa	May 16, 1871	114, 964
Cultivator and stalk-cutter	J. G. Johnson	Carthage, Ill	July 20, 1869	92, 834
Cultivator and stalk-cutter, Combined	E. F. Dehart	Swan Creek, Ill	Jan. 5, 1869	85, 570
Cultivator and sulky-plow	J. H. Barringer	Hillsborough, Ill	Jan. 8, 1867	61, 039
Cultivator and weeder	S. M. Marshall and J. W. Coburn.	Dracut, Mass	Oct. 3, 1838	955
Cultivator and weeder, Hand	W. G. Comstock	East Hartford, Conn	June 1, 1869	90, 639
Cultivator and weeder, Root	C. Jarvis	Ellsworth, Me	Jan. 10, 1865	45, 831
Cultivator and weeding-machine	M. Johnson	Three Rivers, Mich	May 23, 1871	115, 213
Cultivator-bar elevator	J. S. and I. Rowell	Beaver Dam, Wis	June 2, 1868	78, 484
Cultivator-blades, Mode of attaching	J. L. Fountain	New Milford, Ill	May 8, 1866	54, 522
Cultivator, Bog-cutting	E. L. Freeman	Ann Arbor, Mich	June 21, 1853	9, 796
Cultivator, Combined corn and cotton	W. C. Gaines	Salem, Va	June 27, 1871	116, 425
Cultivator, Combined double-shovel and two-horse	S. G. Rayl	Agency City, Iowa	Nov. 16, 1869	96, 938
Cultivator, Combined harrow and shovel	A. B. Baum	Grantville, Pa	July 26, 1870	105, 770
Cultivator, Corn	W. R. Adams	Independence, Mo	Mar. 24, 1868	75, 718
Cultivator, Corn	J. B. Baker	Onondaga, N. Y	Mar. 31, 1857	16, 906
Cultivator, Corn	S. Bell and G. W. Bronson	La Salle County, Ill	May 4, 1869	89, 729
Cultivator, Corn	N. G. Blauser	Etna, Ohio	Aug. 19, 1873	141, 988
Cultivator, Corn	P. F. Brittain	Geneseo, Ill	Aug. 20, 1867	67, 949
Cultivator, Corn	G. D. Brown	Lebanon, Ill	May 30, 1871	115, 427
Cultivator, Corn	A. Campbell	Oxford, Ind	June 2, 1868	78, 424
Cultivator, Corn	A. Canfield	Lyons City, Iowa	Aug. 27, 1867	68, 165
Cultivator, Corn	J. Chapman	Linn County, Iowa	Sept. 12, 1865	49, 856
Cultivator, Corn	J. Clements	Blooming Grove, Ind	Sept. 27, 1870	107, 760
Cultivator, Corn	W. Emmons and D. A. Wells	Sandwich, Ill	Aug. 10, 1869	93, 605
Cultivator, Corn	I. Emrick	Vernon, Mich	Feb. 4, 1873	135, 414
Cultivator, Corn	J. C. Erwood	Vernon, Ind	Mar. 1, 1870	100, 277
Cultivator, Corn	C. Flory	East Donegal, Pa	Oct. 22, 1867	69, 981
Cultivator, Corn	W. Gilman	Ottawa, Ill	Sept. 13, 1870	107, 357
Cultivator, Corn	A. J. Grush	Springfield, Ill	Nov. 16, 1869	96, 801
Cultivator, Corn	J. Harper	Salem, Iowa	Mar. 28, 1865	47, 016
Cultivator, Corn	J. C. Holmes	Wyoming, Pa	Dec. 14, 1869	97, 921
Cultivator, Corn	N. S. Johnson	Maquoketa, Iowa	Feb. 4, 1868	73, 979
Cultivator, Corn	A. Kinyon	Amboy, Ill	Dec. 20, 1864	45, 503
Cultivator, Corn	A. Martin	Oquawka, Ill	Aug. 6, 1867	67, 441
Cultivator, Corn	L. B. Moore	Janesville, Wis	Sept. 4, 1866	57, 752
Cultivator, Corn	D. J. Noble	New Boston, Ill	Sept. 18, 1866	58, 125
Cultivator, Corn	W. H. Parlin	Canton, Ill	Sept. 10, 1867	68, 648
Cultivator, Corn	H. S. Potter	Fairfield, Iowa	Aug. 28, 1866	57, 563
Cultivator, Corn	E. F. Rate	Cedar County, Iowa	Oct. 13, 1868	83, 093
Cultivator, Corn	W. N. Rhinehart and H. Felker	Miami City, Ohio	Feb. 5, 1867	61, 760
Cultivator, Corn	R. B. Robbins	Adrian, Mich	Feb. 23, 1869	87, 296
Cultivator, Corn	S. B. Shank	Manor Township, Pa	Jan. 19, 1869	85, 968
Cultivator, Corn	J. B. Smith	Norfolk, Va	Apr. 15, 1839	1, 121
Cultivator, Corn	G. Sprague	Spring Hill, Kans	Apr. 30, 1867	64, 376
Cultivator, Corn	L. O. Stevens	Pekin, Ill	Oct. 9, 1866	58, 693
Cultivator, Corn	J. S. Stukey	Sugar Grove, Ohio	Feb. 6, 1866	52, 462
Cultivator, Corn	C. W. Taliaferro	Keithsburgh, Ill	July 3, 1866	56, 122
Cultivator, Corn	D. W. Travis	Enfield, N. Y	Dec. 22, 1868	85, 189
Cultivator, Corn	D. W. Travis	Enfield, N. Y	Oct. 26, 1869	96, 167
Cultivator, Corn	D. Wilde	Washington, Iowa	Dec. 20, 1864	45, 549
Cultivator, Corn	M. Wilson	Marquette, Wis	Sept. 10, 1867	68, 678
Cultivator, Corn and cotton	G. T. Bennett	Mount Olive, N. C	Apr. 24, 1860	27, 962
Cultivator, Corn and cotton	J. W. Milroy	Galveston, Ind	Feb. 4, 1868	73, 988
Cultivator, Corn and cotton	R. F. Patton	Quincy, Ohio	July 13, 1869	92, 641
Cultivator, Corn and cotton	J. H. Robinson	Selma, Ala	Sept. 21, 1869	95, 142
Cultivator, Cotton	J. Adams	Clarksville, Tex	Aug. 13, 1867	67, 700
Cultivator, Cotton	R. N. Adams	Greenfield, Ohio	Apr. 2, 1867	63, 451
Cultivator, Cotton	S. W. Akin	Maury County, Tenn	Mar. 20, 1849	6, 204
Cultivator, Cotton	W. J. Andrews	Columbia, Tenn	Mar. 22, 1870	101, 077
Cultivator, Cotton	W. Baker	Memphis, Tenn	July 16, 1872	129, 081
Cultivator, Cotton	F. L. Bates	Bremond, Tex	May 6, 1873	138, 555
Cultivator, Cotton	G. W. Beard	Canton, Miss	Aug. 9, 1859	24, 983
Cultivator, Cotton	N. Bell and H. Winfield	Pantego Township, N. C	Jan. 7, 1873	134, 632
Cultivator, Cotton	J. C. Bethea	Blakely, Ga	Feb. 5, 1867	61, 705
Cultivator, Cotton	W. W. Blair	Lebanon, Tenn	June 19, 1866	55, 607
Cultivator, Cotton	I. W. Burch	Fayette, Miss	Dec. 14, 1869	97, 870
Cultivator, Cotton	M. B. Camp	Riley Centre, Kans	Jan. 9, 1872	122, 515
Cultivator, Cotton	C. Cannaday	Indianapolis, Ind	Jan. 4, 1859	22, 487
Cultivator, Cotton	C. Casey	Goldsborough, N. C	Mar. 27, 1860	27, 616
Cultivator, Cotton	C. W. Chambers and I. Washam	Talladega, Ala	June 25, 1867	66, 128
Cultivator, Cotton	T. Dale	Russellville, Ky	Sept. 19, 1871	119, 015
Cultivator, Cotton	S. C. Darden	Connersville, Miss	June 1, 1869	90, 734
Cultivator, Cotton	T. H. Dodge	Washington, D. C	July 17, 1860	29, 147
Cultivator, Cotton	R. I. Draughon	Claiborne, Ala	Nov. 9, 1869	96, 562
Cultivator, Cotton	E. Eneto	Catahoula Parish, La	Sept. 7, 1869	94, 481
Cultivator, Cotton	D. P. Forney	Jacksonville, Ala	Oct. 20, 1857	18, 442
Cultivator, Cotton	A. M. and B. H. Foster	Hallettsville, Tex	Dec. 18, 1866	60, 625
Cultivator, Cotton	L. M. Ganong	Friar's Point, Miss	July 12, 1870	105, 326
Cultivator, Cotton	R. J. Gatling	Indianapolis, Ind	July 3, 1860	28, 978
Cultivator, Cotton	C. Gibbon	Hicksford, Va	July 30, 1867	67, 289
Cultivator, Cotton	N. A. H. Goddin	Wilson, N. C	Dec. 4, 1860	30, 810
Cultivator, Cotton	E. H. and E. B. Goelet	Goldsborough, N. C	Dec. 24, 1867	72, 479

Index of patents issued from the United States Patent Office from 1790 *to* 1873, *inclusive*—Continued.

Invention.	Inventor.	Residence.	Date.	No.
Cultivator, Cotton	A. J. Going	Clinton, La	Apr. 6, 1869	88, 627
Cultivator, Cotton	W. W. Golsan	Autaugaville, Ala	Sept. 4, 1860	29, 877
Cultivator, Cotton	N. Gotten	Union Depot, Tenn	Jan. 1, 1867	60, 879
Cultivator, Cotton	J. A. Hall	Columbus, Ohio	Oct. 30, 1866	59, 215
Cultivator, Cotton	J. M. Hall	Warrenton, Ga	Apr. 21, 1857	17, 091
Cultivator, Cotton	J. M. Hall	Warrenton, Ga	Jan. 18, 1859	22, 647
Cultivator, Cotton	J. A. Hartsfield	Kinston, N. C	July 17, 1860	29, 166
Cultivator, Cotton	F. E. Heiway and J. J. Walls	Hazlehurst, Miss	June 25, 1872	128, 393
Cultivator, Cotton	L. Henderson	Manson, N. C	May 19, 1868	78, 088
Cultivator, Cotton	R. B. Henderson	Warren County, N. C	Mar. 26, 1867	63, 246
Cultivator, Cotton	J. Hinman and D. S. French	Watertown, Mass., and Marietta, Ga.	July 10, 1860	29, 127
Cultivator, Cotton	W. F. Johnson	Wetumpka, Ala	June 5, 1860	28, 583
Cultivator, Cotton	M. B. Lamar	Atlanta, Ga	Aug. 22, 1871	118, 371
Cultivator, Cotton	P. M. Leatherman	Woodville, Miss	Oct. 11, 1870	108, 159
Cultivator, Cotton	W. McCracken	Bainbridge, Ind	Mar. 5, 1867	62, 660
Cultivator, Cotton	J. L. Middlebrooks	Salem, Ga	Aug. 7, 1860	29, 507
Cultivator, Cotton	E. H. Nelson	Gainesville, Ala	Sept. 2, 1873	142, 501
Cultivator, Cotton	T. Newcomb and G. W. Byrd	Smith's Fork, Tenn	Jan. 3, 1860	26, 699
Cultivator, Cotton	R. H. Purnelle	Beulah, Miss	Oct. 3, 1871	119, 644
Cultivator, Cotton	G. W. Rice	Demopolis, Ala	Apr. 16, 1861	32, 082
Cultivator, Cotton	M. Rigell and W. D. Ivey	Dawson and Milford, Ga	July 17, 1860	29, 196
Cultivator, Cotton	W. J. Rivers	Sumter District, S. C	June 28, 1859	24, 580
Cultivator, Cotton	A. A. Roberts and B. Davis	La Grange, Ga	May 26, 1857	17, 391
Cultivator, Cotton	N. Rogers	Thomas County, Ga	Nov. 27, 1860	30, 763
Cultivator, Cotton	W. A. Rogers	Sommerville, Ala	Apr. 1, 1842	2, 526
Cultivator, Cotton	J. C. Sellers	Woodville, Miss	Sept. 25, 1860	30, 163
Cultivator, Cotton	N. F. Sandelin	Mott Haven, N. Y	Mar. 26, 1872	125, 087
Cultivator, Cotton	J. Shaw	Richland, Ga	Jan. 13, 1857	16, 401
Cultivator, Cotton	A. Smith	Ashville, Ala	July 6, 1858	20, 823
Cultivator, Cotton	M. Snow	Auburn, Miss	Mar. 27, 1860	27, 659
Cultivator, Cotton	J. Speer	Hazlehurst, Miss	July 31, 1860	29, 413
Cultivator, Cotton	H. G. Street	Liberty, Miss	Nov. 27, 1860	30, 773
Cultivator, Cotton	R. A. Vick	Byhalia, Miss	Oct. 20, 1857	18, 478
Cultivator, Cotton	J. R. Wallace and B. A. McClain	Murfreesborough, Tenn	Apr. 9, 1867	63, 767
Cultivator, Cotton	G. W. N. Yost	Yellow Springs, Ohio	July 17, 1860	29, 211
Cultivator, Cotton	C. Zocher	Augusta, Ga	June 10, 1873	139, 750
Cultivator, Cotton and cane	T. E. Shannon	Woodville, Miss	July 21, 1857	17, 849
Cultivator, Cotton and corn	M. Reed	Little Rock, Ark	Oct. 18, 1870	108, 518
Cultivator-coupling	J. Pierpont	La Harpe, Ill	Oct 8, 1867	69, 697
Cultivator-coupling	S. M. Whitney	Galesburgh, Ill	Nov. 13, 1866	59, 698
Cultivator, Device for steering	S. Lapham	Salem, Ohio	Nov. 1, 1853	10, 197
Cultivator, Double-shovel	S. B. Forbes	New Cumberland, W. Va	May 5, 1868	77, 474
Cultivator draft-hook	A. Adams	Sandwich, Ill	June 10, 1873	139, 752
Cultivator drag-bar	C. Alvord	Courtland, Wis	Oct. 20, 1868	83, 235
Cultivator, Equalizing	M. Eichholtz	Troy, Ohio	Apr. 6, 1869	88, 557
Cultivator, Field and garden	E. L. Dorsey	Union, Ind	June 5, 1866	55, 256
Cultivator, Finishing	B. Johnston	New Iberia, La	Apr. 5, 1870	101, 468
Cultivator for dirting cotton	J. S. Smith	Helena, Ark	Jan. 26, 1869	86, 185
Cultivator-frames, Attaching teeth to	G. W. Zeigler	Tiffin, Ohio	Oct. 2, 1866	58, 533
Cultivator-frames to wagon axle-trees, Attachment of.	D. Fuller	Fullersburgh, Ill	Nov. 8, 1870	108, 996
Cultivator, Gang	C. Belden	Middlebury, Ohio	Jan. 2, 1866	51, 790
Cultivator, Garden	J. H. Chapman	Newton, Iowa	Mar. 30, 1869	88, 275
Cultivator, Garden	J. M. Culver	Gilbertsville, Iowa	May 4, 1869	89, 634
Cultivator, Garden	J. A. Hall	Columbus, Ohio	Oct. 16, 1866	58, 814
Cultivator, Garden	C. F. Ruggles	Henderson, Ky	May 30, 1871	115, 526
Cultivator, Garden	G. W. Smith	Mount Olivet, Ky	May 21, 1867	64, 917
Cultivator, Garden	I. B. Smith	Norfolk, Va	Apr. 10, 1839	1, 117
Cultivator, Garden	W. S. Spratt	Allegheny City, Pa	Feb. 9, 1869	86, 879
Cultivator, Garden or hand	M. D. Cone and A. N. Douglass	Port Gibson, N. Y	Feb. 26, 1867	62, 317
Cultivator, Garden plow	C. A. Harris	Austin, Ark	Oct. 15, 1867	69, 803
Cultivator guard-attachment	J. Armstrong, jr	Elmira, Ill	Apr. 13, 1869	88, 940
Cultivator guard-attachment	T. B. McConaughey	Newark, Del	Sept. 4, 1866	57, 747
Cultivator, Hand	L. L. Beach	Mount Upton, N. Y	Dec. 28, 1869	98, 337
Cultivator, Hand	R. Blum	Champaign, Ill	Apr. 16, 1867	63, 840
Cultivator, Hand	D. Boggs and H. Rohs	Cynthiana, Ky	Sept. 26, 1871	119, 261
Cultivator, Hand	N. B. Chase and C. W. Saunders.	Wilkinsonville, Mass	Mar. 6, 1855	12, 478
Cultivator, Hand	E. Clark	Rushville, Ind	Oct. 19, 1869	95, 986
Cultivator, Hand	P. S. Clinger	Conestoga Centre, Pa	Apr. 3, 1860	27, 694
Cultivator, Hand	S. A. Conant	Centralia, Ill	Dec. 2, 1873	145, 153
Cultivator, Hand	L. J. Dawdy	Hamburgh, Iowa	Feb. 25, 1873	136, 220
Cultivator, Hand	L. Duval	Big Spring, Ky	Feb. 8, 1870	99, 543
Cultivator, Hand	R. B. Fitts and W. Thackara	Philadelphia, Pa	Aug. 18, 1863	39, 560
Cultivator, Hand	J. H. Gill	Mount Pleasant, Ohio	July 27, 1869	93, 080
Cultivator, Hand	W. C. Goodwin	Hamden, Conn	Dec. 10, 1867	72, 018
Cultivator, Hand	J. D. and A. M. Halsted	Rye, N. Y	May 20, 1862	35, 313
Cultivator, Hand	E. E. Hawley	Middletown, Conn	Dec. 5, 1848	5, 956
Cultivator, Hand	W. G. Jones	Marshall, Tex	Feb. 27, 1872	124, 140
Cultivator, Hand	D. C. Jordon	Centre Port, N. Y	May 22, 1860	28, 376
Cultivator, Hand	E. G. Mathews	Newton, Mass	June 8, 1869	91, 144
Cultivator, Hand	J. Naugle	Mooresville, Ind	Mar. 21, 1865	46, 926
Cultivator, Hand	J. A. Robinson	Poplin, N. H	Feb. 20, 1855	12, 428
Cultivator, Hand	A. W. Ross	Northfield, Mass	Nov. 25, 1873	144, 927
Cultivator, Hand	G. W. Rue	Hamilton, Ohio	Mar. 25, 1873	137, 098
Cultivator, Hand	J. Scheiblein and J. Heitzman	Philadelphia, Pa	Dec. 15, 1868	84, 910
Cultivator, Hand	G. Smith	Omaha City, Nebr	Jan. 16, 1866	52, 083
Cultivator, Hand	B. Taylor	Forestville, Minn	Aug. 11, 1868	81, 034
Cultivator, Hand garden	P. Byrns	Mindoro, Wis	July 13, 1869	92, 581
Cultivator, Hand-hoe	W. Goodwin	Marblehead, Mass	Mar. 19, 1872	124, 810
Cultivator, Harrow	F. Mishwitz	Brooklyn, N. Y	Dec. 7, 1869	97, 680
Cultivator, Harrow	H. W. Ostrom	Grand Rapids, Mich	Sept. 24, 1867	69, 239
Cultivator-hoe	J. H. Foster	Charlottesville, Va	Aug. 17, 1869	93, 869
Cultivator, Horse-hoe	A. Webb	Bangor, Me	Aug. 8, 1865	49, 354
Cultivator-joint	W. A. Dryden	Monmouth, Ill	June 22, 1869	91, 727
Cultivator-joint and coupling	W. H. Edwards	Moline, Ill	Nov. 10, 1868	83, 944

Index of patents issued from the United States Patent Office from 1790 *to* 1873, *inclusive*—Continued.

Invention.	Inventor.	Residence.	Date.	No.
Cultivator, marker, and cover, Combined	H. J. Coyle	Buffalo, N. Y	Aug. 15, 1871	117, 989
Cultivator, Meadow	F. P. Devenport	Carthage, Ill	Feb. 28, 1871	112, 130
Cultivator, Two-winged shifting-tooth	W. Beach	Philadelphia, Pa	Oct. 25, 1832	....
Cultivator or hoe-harrow	N. J. Shull	Bensalem, Pa	Nov. 26, 1836	....
Cultivator or hoe-harrow	N. J. Shull	Bensalem Township, Bucks County, Pa.	Nov. 26, 1836	88
Cultivator or hoe-harrow, &c., Teeth for	W. Beach	Philadelphia, Pa	Nov. 8, 1825	....
Cultivator-plow	C. C. Baum	Oxford, Iowa	Dec. 26, 1865	51, 682
Cultivator-plow	G. G. Black	Crossinville, Ohio	July 14, 1857	17, 777
Cultivator-plow	V. Bolis	Saint Mary's Parish, La	Sept. 27, 1870	107, 754
Cultivator-plow	M. Crenshaw	Springfield, Tex	Mar. 25, 1856	14, 533
Cultivator-plow	D. Culver	Kingston, Pa	May 23, 1871	115, 033
Cultivator-plow	J. Doak	Keithsburgh, Ill	Nov. 29, 1864	45, 231
Cultivator-plow	J. R. Finley	Delphi, Ind	May 2, 1865	47, 534
Cultivator-plow	W. O. Gibson	Charleston, S. C	Oct. 23, 1866	59, 003
Cultivator-plow	J. S. Gilmore	Millersburgh, Ill	Jan. 23, 1866	52, 159
Cultivator-plow	W. Gowen	Bartlett, Tenn	Feb. 21, 1871	111, 925
Cultivator-plow	G. W. Hatfield	Holton, Ind	Feb. 5, 1867	61, 828
Cultivator, Plow	L. Homrighouse	Baltimore, Md	May 3, 1870	102, 543
Cultivator, Plow	E. S. Huff	Zanesville, Ohio	June 29, 1869	91, 847
Cultivator-plow	M. J. Hunt	Cincinnati, Ohio	Sept. 30, 1842	2, 792
Cultivator-plow	W. S. Hyde	Townsend, Ohio	June 21, 1853	9, 798
Cultivator-plow	A. J. Lewis	Pittsburgh, Pa	June 8, 1869	91, 031
Cultivator-plow	W. Looker	Graham, Mo	Mar. 9, 1869	87, 690
Cultivator-plow	N. McKay	Columbia, Mo	Aug. 17, 1869	93, 730
Cultivator-plow	K. McKinnon	Pleasant Hill, Ala	Dec. 2, 1873	145, 222
Cultivator-plow	J. Meyer	Linden Hall, Pa	Nov. 11, 1862	36, 909
Cultivator-plow	J. G. Miner	Nashville, Tenn	June 28, 1870	104, 754
Cultivator-plow	T. H. Miner and S. Heavenridge.	Greenfield, Ind	Mar. 20, 1866	53, 322
Cultivator-plow	W. D. Nichols	Chicago, Ill	Sept. 11, 1866	57, 952
Cultivator-plow	J. Singer	Mendota, Ill	Jan. 31, 1871	111, 391
Cultivator-plow	W. H. Startzman	Big Lick, Va	Sept. 3, 1867	68, 393
Cultivator-plow	W. W. Stillman	Mount Hawley, Ill	Aug. 7, 1866	57, 007
Cultivator-plow	L. Strickland	Talleyrand, Iowa	Jan. 23, 1866	52, 222
Cultivator-plow	L. S. Tewell	Elbinsville, Pa	May 9, 1871	114, 726
Cultivator-plow	M. Tolle	Newport, Ky	June 16, 1857	17, 594
Cultivator-plow	L. M. Whitman	Weedsport, N. Y	Oct. 11, 1853	10, 123
Cultivator-plow	S. A. Wray	Greenfield, Ind	Jan. 1, 1867	60, 982
Cultivator-plow	W. E. Wycho	Brookville, N. C	Jan. 8, 1856	14, 075
Cultivator-plow	W. E. Wycho	Brookville, N. C	Feb. 26, 1856	14, 333
Cultivator-plow axle, Wheeled	G. W. C. Gillespie	Burlington, Iowa	Sept. 9, 1851	8, 348
Cultivator-plow, Double	P. Coonrod	Keithsburgh, Ill	Dec. 24, 1867	72, 456
Cultivator-plow fender	W. E. Moore	Crawfordsville, Ind	May 25, 1869	90, 376
Cultivator-plow, harrow, and roller, Combined	S. C. Thornton	Macomb, Tex	Nov. 3, 1868	83, 675
Cultivator-point	R. Creswell, jr	Chambersburgh, Pa.	Sept. 5, 1848	5, 755
Cultivator, Potato and corn	J. M. Davidson	Pulaski, Pa	Mar. 16, 1869	87, 914
Cultivator-rake	J. T. Van Wyck	Poughkeepsie, N. Y	Nov. 8, 1870	109, 082
Cultivator, Reversible	S. G. Tufts	Mainville, Ohio	June 15, 1869	91, 497
Cultivator, Revolving	W. A Estes	South China, Me	Sept. 7, 1869	94, 482
Cultivator, Revolving	A. J. Stephens	El Dorado, Wis	Mar. 9, 1869	87, 721
Cultivator, Revolving	G. Whitlock	Crown Point, N. Y	July 10, 1841	2, 163
Cultivator, Rice	G. W. Cooper	Ogeechee, Ga	June 18, 1867	65, 877
Cultivator, Rice	G. W. Cooper	Ogeechee, Ga	Aug. 4, 1868	80, 604
Cultivator, Rotary	E. T. Bussell	Shelbyville, Ind	June 15, 1858	20, 605
Cultivator, Rotary	G. Collins	Fremont, Nebr	Mar. 5, 1872	124, 332
Cultivator, Rotary	C. Comstock	Milwaukee, Wis	Feb. 26, 1861	31, 531
Cultivator, Rotary	M. Decelle	Newburgh, Ohio	June 11, 1872	127, 746
Cultivator, Rotary	B. F. Field	Sheboygan Falls, Wis	July 19, 1859	24, 799
Cultivator, Rotary	G. B. Field	Saint Louis, Mo	Mar. 14, 1854	10, 624
Cultivator Rotary	J. C. Fitzgerald	Willet, N. Y	Dec. 4, 1866	60, 164
Cultivator, Rotary	H. M. Johnson	Carlisle, Pa	June 27, 1854	11, 162
Cultivator, Rotary	G. F. Lynch	Milwaukee, Wis	Aug. 4, 1868	80, 643
Cultivator, Rotary	S. Mahurin	Clayton, Ill	Oct. 20, 1868	83, 187
Cultivator, Rotary	R. McKinley	Hyde Park, N. Y	May 20, 1873	139, 013
Cultivator, Rotary	J. W. Milroy	Haywood, Cal	Jan. 21, 1873	135, 002
Cultivator, Rotary	C. N. Poundstone	Livonia, Ill	Feb. 11, 1873	135, 664
Cultivator, Rotary	P. E. Royse	New Albany, Ind	Feb. 17, 1852	8, 747
Cultivator, Rotary	P. Shaw	Abington, Mass	Mar. 14, 1854	10, 646
Cultivator, Rotary	J. D. Starritt	Chicago, Ill	Nov. 11, 1873	144, 419
Cultivator, Rotary	A. Thompson	Ottumwa, Iowa	Sept. 25, 1866	58, 319
Cultivator, Rotary	J. Young	Joliet, Ill	June 28, 1859	24, 597
Cultivator, Rotary root-digging	S. Snow and A. Hine	Fayetteville and La Fayette, N. Y.	Oct. 11, 1853	10, 113
Cultivator, Rotating	T. Uehling	Logan, Neb	Oct. 19, 1869	95, 956
Cultivator, Rotating-tooth	J. Densmore	Holley, N. J	Dec. 3, 1867	71, 589
Cultivator, scraper, and chopper, Cotton	J. H. W. Young	Henderson, Tex	Dec. 27, 1870	110, 531
Cultivator, Seed-planting	G. Phillips	Philadelphia, Pa	Nov. 15, 1853	10, 236
Cultivator, seeder, and stalk-cutter, Combined	J. and W. Whait	Independence, Iowa	Feb. 20, 1872	123, 959
Cultivator, Seeding	A. P. Durant	Atlanta, Ill	July 16, 1861	32, 825
Cultivator, Seeding	J. B. Ewell	Baltimore, Md	Aug. 20, 1867	67, 860
Cultivator, Seeding	T. A. Galt	Sterling, Ill	Dec. 11, 1860	30, 876
Cultivator, Seeding	J. Goodman and S. Rote	Lancaster, Pa	Jan. 15, 1861	31, 118
Cultivator, Seeding	H. Hutchinson	Three Rivers, Mich	May 21, 1867	64, 981
Cultivator, Seeding	J. Reichard	Guilford Township, Pa	Dec. 16, 1833	....
Cultivator, Seeding	C. T. Settle	San José, Cal	Feb. 26, 1861	31, 564
Cultivator, Seeding	N. S. Thompson	Richmond, Ind	May 16, 1871	114, 881
Cultivator, Seeding	S. D. Tracy	Vernon, N. Y	Dec. 27, 1859	26, 630
Cultivator, Seeding	N. Whitchall	Newtown, Ind	May 17, 1859	24, 071
Cultivator-shovels, Attachment for	D. C. Stover	Dayton, Ohio	Apr. 14, 1868	76, 647
Cultivator, Steam	A. J. Stevens	San Francisco, Cal	Aug. 10, 1869	93, 494
Cultivator, Sugar-cane	A. Trouard	New Orleans, La	Jan. 21, 1873	135, 174
Cultivator, Sulky	F. G. Blauser	Etna, Ohio	July 26, 1870	105, 630
Cultivator, Sulky	E. S. Easterday	Nokomis, Ill	Feb. 25, 1868	74, 754
Cultivator, Sulky	F. Farnsworth	Frankfort, Ill	Apr. 12, 1870	101, 720
Cultivator, Sulky	O. L. Gaylord	Plainfield, Ill	Oct. 12, 1869	95, 790
Cultivator, Sulky	W. Harvey	Volga City, Iowa	July 7, 1868	79, 570
Cultivator, Sulky	P. Hewitt	Farmland, Ind	Oct. 31, 1871	120, 435

Index of patents issued from the United States Patent Office from 1790 *to* 1873, *inclusive*—Continued.

Invention.	Inventor.	Residence.	Date.	No.
Cultivator, Sulky	H. P. Jordan	Victoria, Tex	Jan. 10, 1871	110,853
Cultivator, Sulky	R. B. Robbins	Adrian, Mich	Mar. 8, 1871	112,496
Cultivator, Sulky	R. B. Robbins	Adrian, Mich	Nov. 9, 1869	96,733
Cultivator, Sulky	J. Robinson	Plainfield, Ill	June 22, 1869	91,566
Cultivator, Sulky	I. Welty	Olney, Ill	July 21, 1868	80,102
Cultivator, Sulky	N. Whitehall	Newtown, Ind	Aug. 29, 1871	118,567
Cultivator, Sulky	N. Wilson	Saint Louis, Mich	June 29, 1869	92,135
Cultivator-teeth	G. C. Aiken	Nashua, N. H	Feb. 14, 1860	27,092
Cultivator-teeth	G. C. Aiken	Nashua, N. H	Apr. 24, 1860	27,956
Cultivator-teeth	W. Beach	Philadelphia, Pa	Apr. 13, 1826	....
Cultivator-teeth	S. Beckwith	Oshkosh, Wis	Mar. 15, 1870	100,713
Cultivator-teeth	J. Birdsell	Hamorton, Pa	Nov. 9, 1844	3,819
Cultivator-teeth	M. Bucklin	Grafton, N. H	Feb. 2, 1858	19,234
Cultivator-teeth	N. Chappell	Lima, N. Y	Dec. 3, 1867	71,581
Cultivator-teeth	J. P. Cramer	Schuylerville, N. Y	Jan. 6, 1857	16,364
Cultivator-teeth	G. Custer	Monroe, Mich	Dec. 2, 1862	37,071
Cultivator-teeth	L. Dayley	Minaville, N. C	Aug. 22, 1871	118,208
Cultivator-teeth	D. Dean	Brighton, Mich	June 30, 1868	79,451
Cultivator-teeth	J. D. De Turk	Exeter, Pa	Mar. 17, 1868	75,669
Cultivator-teeth	H. Francisco	Lake Mills, Wis	Mar. 7, 1865	46,654
Cultivator-teeth	E. L. Freeman	Brownville, N. Y	Sept. 8, 1857	18,174
Cultivator-teeth	E. L. Freeman	Williamstown, N. Y	Apr. 20, 1869	89,137
Cultivator-teeth	H. F. French	Boston, Mass	Aug. 17, 1869	93,695
Cultivator-teeth	W. P. and T. H. Ford	Concord, N. H	Feb. 15, 1859	22,946
Cultivator-teeth	F. R. Forsythe	Cape Vincent, N. Y	Aug. 4, 1857	17,925
Cultivator-teeth	H. B. Hammon	Bristolville, Ohio	Apr. 10, 1860	27,797
Cultivator-teeth	B. F. Hisert	Norton Hill, N. Y	Sept. 3, 1867	68,440
Cultivator-teeth	J. S. Honey	Hartford, Ohio	Apr. 17, 1849	6,336
Cultivator-teeth	W. H. Kelly	Lysander, N. Y	Oct. 27, 1863	40,414
Cultivator-teeth	L. Lamborn	Kennett's Square, Pa	Mar. 26, 1850	7,220
Cultivator-teeth	M. F. Lowth and T. J. Howe	Owatonna, Minn	Mar. 10, 1868	75,436
Cultivator-teeth	D. C. Matteson and T. P. Williamson	Stockton, Cal	Apr. 9, 1867	63,647
Cultivator-teeth	G. Maynard	Ilion, N. Y	June 28, 1859	24,568
Cultivator-teeth	W. Morrison	Chadd's Ford, Pa	Apr. 16, 1861	32,077
Cultivator-teeth	E. B. Pratt	Monroe, Wis	July 20, 1869	92,880
Cultivator-teeth	W. B. Ready	Sacramento, Cal	July 28, 1868	80,503
Cultivator-teeth	D. B. Rogers	Pittsburgh, Pa	May 8, 1860	28,198
Cultivator-teeth	D. B. Rogers	Stafford, N. Y	Nov. 1, 1845	4,245
Cultivator-teeth	L. Rogers	Pittsburgh, Pa	Feb. 4, 1868	74,004
Cultivator-teeth	H. Sanders	Utica, N. Y	Nov. 29, 1859	26,297
Cultivator-teeth	C. H. Sayre	Utica, N. Y	Oct. 20, 1857	18,471
Cultivator-teeth	C. H. Sayre	Utica, N. Y	June 19, 1860	28,780
Cultivator-teeth	C. H. Sayre and G. Klinck	Utica, N. Y	Feb. 12, 1856	14,254
Cultivator-teeth	J. Stockdale	Ypsilanti, Mich	Jan. 30, 1855	12,332
Cultivator-teeth	G. F. Stroud	Oshkosh, Wis	July 29, 1873	141,400
Cultivator-teeth	J. Turner and T. P. Smith	Sunapee, N. H	June 26, 1860	28,945
Cultivator-teeth	B. Van Bracklin	Le Roy, N. Y	July 20, 1869	92,910
Cultivator-teeth, Adjustable	W. M. Hurlburt	Winona, Minn	Jan. 26, 1869	86,306
Cultivator-teeth, Die for cutting and forming	D. B. Rogers	Stafford, N. Y	Nov. 8, 1845	4,265
Cultivator-teeth, Hanging	J. Fowler and F. M. Bacon	Watertown, Wis	Mar. 28, 1865	47,008
Cultivator-teeth, Machine for forming	D. B. Rogers	Pittsburgh, Pa	Mar. 28, 1854	10,706
Cultivator-teeth, Machine for pointing blanks for	J. Pedder and G. Abel	West Pittsburgh, Pa	Mar. 7, 1871	112,374
Cultivator-teeth, Manufacture of	J. Behel	Rockford, Ill	June 3, 1873	139,535
Cultivator-teeth, Mode of attaching	J. C. Hoffeditz	Mercersburgh, Pa	Jan. 1, 1867	60,893
Cultivator-teeth, Operating	T. W. Hammon	Montfort, Wis	Dec. 27, 1864	45,671
Cultivator-teeth, Plate for blanks of	W. H. Singer	Pittsburgh, Pa	Nov. 30, 1869	97,451
Cultivator-teeth, Rolled steel plates for making	W. W. and D. D. Skinner	Des Moines, Iowa	Sept. 26, 1871	119,419
Cultivator-teeth, Spring	H. Francisco	White Water, Wis	Nov. 5, 1861	33,641
Cultivator-teeth to beams, Attaching	M. F. Lowth and O. H. Porter	Wabasha, Minn	July 18, 1871	117,692
Cultivator, Vine, &c	J. Mason	Union, N. J	May 28, 1842	2,650
Cultivator, Walking	A. Friberg	Moline, Ill	Feb. 7, 1871	111,627
Cultivator, Walking	E. P. Lynch and H. R. Raff	Davenport, Iowa	Sept. 7, 1869	94,623
Cultivator, Walking	J. Vanluvanee and H. Smith	Moline, Ill	Mar. 21, 1871	112,990
Cultivator weed-cutter	C. Rodger	Montpelier, Vt	June 25, 1850	7,463
Cultivator, Wheel	D. S. Billings	Conneaut, Pa	Feb. 1, 1848	5,429
Cultivator, Wheel	G. Bradley	Rockford, Ill	Dec. 9, 1873	145,331
Cultivator, Wheel	W. F. and G. Coulter and J. A. Lanery	Hardinsburgh, Ind	Mar. 16, 1869	87,824
Cultivator, Wheel	A. P. Durant and D. M. Buckley	Atlanta, Ill	Feb. 28, 1865	46,550
Cultivator, Wheel	N. Earlywine	Centreville, Iowa	Jan. 2, 1872	122,373
Cultivator, Wheel	J. Eshleman	Canaan Centre, Ohio	Aug. 2, 1870	106,039
Cultivator, Wheel	E. D. Hatch	Oconomowoc, Wis	Aug. 23, 1870	106,579
Cultivator, Wheel	J. F. Matchet and P. W. Smith	Paris, Mo	Oct. 14, 1873	143,631
Cultivator, Wheel	W. M. Pitts	Holden, Mo	Sept. 26, 1871	119,404
Cultivator, Wheel	J. H. Randolph, jr	Bayou Goula, La	May 13, 1873	138,931
Cultivator, Wheel	S. Rockafellow	Moline, Ill	Feb. 23, 1872	126,092
Cultivator, Wheel	F. P. Root	Sweden, N. Y	June 8, 1852	9,003
Cultivator, Wheel	T. C. Sebring	Milford, Mich	Dec. 5, 1871	121,670
Cultivator, Wheel	W. A. Sisson	Sheffield, Ill	Aug. 27, 1867	68,124
Cultivator, Wheel	W. H. Strong	Seneca County, Ohio	Dec. 30, 1873	146,030
Cultivator, Wheel	J. A. Viars	Sherman, Tex	Sept. 19, 1871	119,205
Cultivator, Wheeled	S. H. Dwight and W. B. Chambers	Decatur, Ill	Mar. 29, 1870	101,240
Cultivators, Insect-destroying attachment for	C. T. Hurd	Victoria, Tex	Dec. 30, 1873	145,949
Cultivators, Shovel-teeth for	T. Harding	La Fayette, Ind	July 19, 1870	105,570
Culvert	C. McIntire	Easton, Pa	Sept. 16, 1862	36,472
Culvert, Iron	M. G. Freeman	Wenona, Ill	Dec. 6, 1870	109,886
Culvert, Iron	M. G. Freeman	Bloomington, Ill	May 9, 1871	114,662
Cup: *See* Breast-cup. Dentists' impression-cup. Drinking-cup. Egg-cup. Ejecting-cup. Elevator-cup. Eye-cup.				

Index of patents issued from the United States Patent Office from 1790 *to* 1873, *inclusive*—Continued.

Invention.	Inventor.	Residence.	Date.	No.
Cup—Continued.				
See Grease-cup.				
Ink-cup.				
Lubricating-cup.				
Molasses-cup.				
Mucilage-cup.				
Nursery-cup.				
Oil-cup.				
Soap-cup.				
Sponge-cup.				
Surgical cup.				
Teat-cup.				
Tin cup.				
Cup and bell	T. Leach	Taunton, Mass	Aug. 2, 1870	106, 066
Cup and saucer, Metallic Columbian	J. Love	Baltimore, Md	June 14, 1814	....
Cup for effervescing drinks	A. Rottanzi	San Francisco, Cal	July 7, 1868	79, 689
Cups, Device for holding lids to	P. I. Schopp	Louisville, Ky	Aug. 10, 1869	93, 562
Cupboard and extension-table combined	B. F. Partridge	Syracuse, N. Y	Feb. 4, 1873	135, 440
Cupboard and sink	A. Iske	Lancaster, Pa	Aug. 7, 1860	29, 493
Cupboard and table	J. C. Mack	Bristol, Conn	Sept. 22, 1868	82, 426
Cupboard-catch	P. D. F. Goeney	Albany, N. Y	Sept. 15, 1868	82, 108
Cupboard-catch	I. Ottner	New Britain, Conn	Nov. 5, 1872	132, 771
Cupboard, Portable	J. L. Prescott	North Berwick, Me	Nov. 6, 1866	59, 516
Cupboard, Revolving	W. Wright	Bloomfield, N. J	Dec. 14, 1869	97, 980
Cupola and blast furnace	J. R. Grout	Detroit, Mich	July 31, 1866	56, 746
Cupola and blast furnace	D. W. Hendrickson	Red Bank, N. J	Aug. 13, 1872	130, 370
Cupola and blast furnace	C. Truesdale	Cincinnati, Ohio	Aug. 25, 1868	81, 561
Cupola and other furnace	A. Cowan and R. H. Starr	New Haven, Conn	July 9, 1867	66, 465
Cupola and other furnace	P. W. McKenzie and C. W. Isbell.	Jersey City, N. J., and New York, N. Y.	May 29, 1866	55, 204
Cupola and other furnace	L. Quincke	Joliet, Ill	Oct. 7, 1873	143, 463
Cupola and other melting and smelting furnace	J. Absterdam	New York, N. Y	Feb. 9, 1869	86, 795
Cupola and other metallurgic furnaces	O. Bolton, jr	Pittsburgh, Pa	Mar. 25, 1873	137, 125
Cupola, blast, and smelting furnace	H. Fayette	Portchester, N. Y	Oct. 29, 1867	70, 329
Cupola-furnace	F. C. Adams	Cincinnati, Ohio	May 12, 1868	77, 795
Cupola-furnace	R. Barckley	Philadelphia, Pa	Aug. 4, 1863	39, 372
Cupola-furnace	N. Burdick	Albany, N. Y	June 16, 1868	78, 924
Cupola-furnace	A. G. Cook	Burlington, Vt	June 13, 1871	115, 823
Cupola-furnace	J. Dougherty	Philadelphia, Pa	May 14, 1867	64, 645
Cupola-furnace	J. Dougherty	Philadelphia, Pa	May 2, 1871	114, 422
Cupola-furnace	J. H. Eddy	Taunton, Mass	Aug. 4, 1868	80, 537
Cupola-furnace	J. Howarth	Salem, Mass	Jan. 14, 1868	73, 333
Cupola-furnace	J. and T. Insull	New Haven, Conn	May 8, 1866	54, 552
Cupola-furnace	A. A. Lincoln	Norton, Mass	Oct. 31, 1865	50, 769
Cupola-furnace	P. W. Mackenzie	Jersey City, N. J	Aug. 25, 1857	18, 051
Cupola-furnace	P. W. Mackenzie	Blauveltville, N. Y	May 6, 1873	138, 510
Cupola-furnace	J. B. Pearse	Swatara Township, Pa	Apr. 22, 1873	138, 184
Cupola-furnace	A. Pevy	Lowell, Mass	Oct. 24, 1865	50, 623
Cupola-furnace	C. Truesdale	Cincinnati, Ohio	May 1, 1866	54, 470
Cupola-furnace	C. Truesdale	Cincinnati, Ohio	Dec. 11, 1866	60, 440
Cupola-furnace	H. Warral	New York	Dec. 31, 1821	....
Cupola-furnace for melting iron	I. D. Marshbank	Harrisburgh, Pa	July 16, 1872	129, 151
Cupola or blast furnace	A. G. Cook	Burlington, Vt	Feb. 20, 1866	52, 684
Cupping	L. Tillotson	Thompson, Ohio	Aug. 26, 1856	15, 626
Cupping and breast glass	W. S. Thomas	Norwich, N. Y	Mar. 16, 1852	8, 809
Cupping-apparatus	W. D. Hooper	Liberty, Va	Sept. 17, 1867	68, 985
Cupping-apparatus	M. Mattson	New York, N. Y	Aug. 13, 1867	67, 663
Cupping-instrument	R. J. Dodd	Philadelphia, Pa	Apr. 13, 1844	3, 537
Cupping-instrument	E. J. Leyburn	Lexington, Va	Sept. 10, 1867	68, 630
Cupping-instrument	S. McLean	Reynale's Basin, N. Y	Aug. 19, 1856	15, 568
Curb and gutter, Combined metallic street	W. E. Worthen	New York, N. Y	May 10, 1859	23, 973
Curb-bit	W. C. Baker	New York, N. Y	Jan. 23, 1866	52, 125
Curb-bit	T. S. Smith	Lowell, Mass	Oct. 13, 1863	40, 312
Curb, Excavating and well-boring	J. Cowperthwaite, sr	....	Apr. 13, 1809	....
Curb for street, road, &c	O. Faurot and W. P. Harris	Brooklyn, N. Y	Apr. 14, 1868	76, 614
Curbing	J. Miller	Pittsburgh, Pa	Sept. 3, 1867	68, 379
Curbing, Street	D. Herr	Lockhaven, Pa	Apr. 16, 1872	125, 814
Curculio-catcher	F. J. Claxton and C. D. Stevens	Saint Louis, Mo	Apr. 18, 1871	113, 855
Curculio-catcher	M. M. Hooton	Clinton County, Ill	July 12, 1870	105, 333
Curculio-trap	J. Smith	New Market, Ohio	Jan. 1, 1867	60, 951
Curd-agitator	D. C. Hall	Barnes' Corners, N. Y	June 22, 1869	91, 622
Curd-agitator	J. H. Maydole	Eaton, N. Y	Dec. 1, 1863	40, 764
Curd-agitator	B. G. Swain	Colden, N. Y	Sept. 13, 1870	107, 423
Curd-breaker	P. Crary	Lowville, N. Y	Jan. 21, 1868	73, 508
Curd-cutter	F. G. Abbey	Sandisfield, Mass	Sept. 6, 1864	44, 058
Curd-cutter	J. Crosby	Rome, N. Y	Mar. 8, 1864	41, 833
Curd-cutter	J. B. Lyons	Milton, Conn	Apr. 5, 1864	42, 209
Curd-cutter	J. H. Maydole	Eaton, N. Y	Oct. 18, 1864	44, 733
Curd-cutter	C. Wadsworth	East Livermore, Me	Oct. 3, 1865	50, 290
Curd-grinder	C. W. Terpening	Geneseo, Ill	Aug. 17, 1869	93, 768
Curd-mill	J. Macadam	Little Falls, N. Y	June 30, 1868	79, 365
Curd-mill	W. Ralph	Utica, N. Y	July 21, 1868	80, 089
Curing provisions	D. E. Somes	Biddeford, Me	Nov. 13, 1868	30, 658
Curl, Artificial	J. Graham	New York, N. Y	Mar. 11, 1873	136, 720
Curling-iron	J. O. Bentley and J. Jackson	Philadelphia, Pa	Oct. 11, 1870	108, 234
Curling-iron	H. Christian	New York, N. Y	Sept. 26, 1865	50, 095
Curling-iron	S. E. Condon	Williamsburgh, N. Y	Feb. 25, 1868	74, 800
Curling-iron	H. D. Jennings	Ilion, N. Y	July 4, 1865	48, 626
Curling-iron	J. S. Morgan	Brooklyn, N. Y	Nov. 11, 1873	144, 471
Curling-iron	L. Rosenstein and S. Feder	Memphis, Tenn	July 22, 1873	141, 079
Curling-iron	J. H. Williams	Middletown, Conn	July 16, 1872	129, 445
Curling-pin, Hair	J. Hall	Watertown, Mass	Feb. 20, 1872	123, 778
Curling-rod for paper cigar-lighters	W. D. Young	South Pittsburgh, Pa	Apr. 5, 1870	101, 561
Currency and stamp box	L. L. Tower	Cambridgeport, Mass	July 7, 1863	39, 184
Currency note, Diagram for testing the value of mutilated.	L. Fox	New York, N. Y	Aug. 1, 1865	49, 099
Current and paddle wheel	J. H. Hanchett	Beloit, Wis	Apr. 7, 1857	16, 975
Current and tide mill	H. Allen	Fayette County, Tenn	Dec. 30, 1820	....

Index of patents issued from the United States Patent Office from 1790 *to* 1873, *inclusive*—Continued.

Invention.	Inventor.	Residence.	Date.	No.
Current and tide wheel	A. Madison	Detroit, Mich	July 10, 1829	....
Current-changing apparatus	C. C. Hare	Kansas City, Mo	June 8, 1869	91, 126
Current-mill	G. H. D. Gray	Southampton, Va	Sept. 25, 1822	....
Current-mill	J. Wallace	Hartford, Ky	Sept. 11, 1829	....
Current-reversers and circuit-breakers	J. E. Smith	New York, N. Y	July 16, 1872	129, 607
Current-wheel	P. Chesley	Candia, N. H	Oct. 28, 1856	15, 970
Current-wheel	J. Clarke	....	Dec. 31, 1793	....
Current-wheel	J. Dennison	Hillsborough, N. H	July 20, 1869	92, 809
Current-wheel	C. Morehouse	Wayland, N. Y	May 16, 1871	114, 959
Current-wheel	W. S. Smith	Cedar Rapids, Iowa	Mar. 27, 1855	12, 606
Current-wheel	W. Tuder	Moffettown, Tex	June 6, 1871	115, 660
Current-wheel	C. Weeke	Saint Charles, Mo	July 29, 1873	141, 301
Current-wheel	E. A. White	Boston, Mass	Feb. 8, 1870	99, 614
Current-wheel and condensing-engine, Combined	A. Spear	Cape Elizabeth, Me	Mar. 15, 1870	100, 946
Current-wheel, Apparatus for	J. Secor	Saint Louis, Mo	Feb. 20, 1849	6, 132
Current-wheel, Hydraulic	W. P. Wing	Greenwich, Mass	Sept. 22, 1837	403
Currents, Means for creating artificial	E. Bantz	Baltimore, Md	June 17, 1873	139, 854
Currier's arm or grain-board	A. Chase	Weare, N. H	Apr. 5, 1864	42, 165
Currier's beam and knife	J. D. Willoughby	Carlisle, Pa	Aug. 17, 1852	9, 207
Currier's beam, Constructing the face of	I. Lindsey	Charlestown, Mass	Jan. 27, 1841	1, 955
Currier's bench, Clamp for holding leather to the	J. Shimer	Bronson, Mich	May 26, 1868	78, 334
Currier's knife	T. C. Barr	Clark County, Ky	Jan. 28, 1833	....
Currier's knife	G. Featherston	Au Sable Forks, N. Y	Jan. 6, 1863	37, 285
Currier's knife	L. A. Gignac	Troy, N. Y	Aug. 31, 1869	94, 197
Currier's knife	J. Glenn and J. Herd	Urbana, Ohio	Dec. 16, 1833	....
Currier's knife	I. H. Harrington	Albany, Y. Y	June 26, 1828	....
Currier's knife	J. P. Hawks	Troy, N. Y	Jan. 9, 1866	51, 942
Currier's knife	W. P. Moses	Exeter, N. H	June 5, 1860	28, 594
Currier's knife	F. Palmer	Littleton, N. H	Feb. 17, 1826	....
Currier's knife	S. Parsons	Parsonsfield, Mass	Oct. 25, 1810	....
Currier's knife	D. Tomlinson	Brookfield, Conn	July 6, 1820	....
Currier's knife and double trimmer	L. Townsend	Farmington, Me	Jan. 16, 1835	....
Currier's knife for shaving leather	J. Batchelder	Lancaster, N. H	Nov. 3, 1825	....
Curriers' knives, Constructing and grinding	S. Brooks	New York	Nov. 13, 1826	....
Curriers' knives, Grinding	H. Cunningham	Albany, N. Y	Oct. 12, 1869	95, 778
Curriers' knives, Machine for sharpening	J. Bachelder	Lancaster, N. H	Nov. 9, 1824	....
Curriers' scourer	J. Hankey	North Cambridge, Mass	Feb. 6, 1866	52, 491
Curriers' slicker	G. T. Collins	North Eastham, Mass	June 6, 1871	115, 709
Curriers' slicker	D. Peters and J. W. Pauly	Keokuk, Iowa	Feb. 12, 1867	62, 064
Curriers' slicker, Whitening	D. Peters and W. D. Wilson	Keokuk, Iowa	Apr. 19, 1864	42, 397
Curriers' tools	J. T. Barnstead	Peabody, Mass	Feb. 21, 1871	111, 901
Curriers' tools	C. A. Gardner and J. A. Enos	Peabody, Mass	Apr. 8, 1873	137, 671
Curry-comb	W. F. Arnold	Winthrop, Conn	Oct. 23, 1866	59, 118
Curry-comb	J. M. Baker	Marshfield, Ohio	Sept. 21, 1869	94, 991
Curry-comb	H. L. Baldwin	Branford, Conn	June 11, 1861	32, 505
Curry-comb	J. H. Baringer, jr	Hillsborough, Ill	Mar. 3, 1868	74, 974
Curry-comb	W. Beach	Philadelphia, Pa	Mar. 13, 1849	6, 181
Curry-comb	C. B. Bristol	New Haven, Conn	Mar. 1, 1864	41, 755
Curry-comb	C. B. Bristol	New Haven, Conn	Nov. 3, 1868	83, 757
Curry-comb	J. Chaumont	Woodhaven, N. Y	June 27, 1571	116, 268
Curry-comb	E. L. Evans	Providence, R. I	Nov. 25, 1856	16, 115
Curry-comb	E. L. Evans	Providence, R. I	Jan. 26, 1858	19, 188
Curry-comb	J. Filson, jr	Racine, Ohio	Feb. 6, 1872	123, 469
Curry-comb	F. N. Frost	New Britain, Conn	Nov. 27, 1866	59, 992
Curry-comb	N. C. Harris	Poultney, Vt	July 5, 1864	43, 405
Curry-comb	N. C. Harris and A. Butler	Poultney, Vt	Oct. 6, 1857	18, 337
Curry-comb	D. E. Hayward	Malden, Mass	July 16, 1872	129, 224
Curry-comb	A. Hotchkiss	Sharon, Conn	Mar. 13, 1849	6, 178
Curry-comb	A. A. and A. Hotchkiss	Sharon, Conn	July 8, 1856	15, 294
Curry-comb	J. E. Insley	Philadelphia, Pa	June 22, 1869	91, 637
Curry-comb	L. P. Jenks	Boston, Mass	July 13, 1869	92, 454
Curry-comb	J. Jones	Bristol, Conn	Aug. 28, 1847	5, 263
Curry-comb	W. P. Kellogg	Troy, N. Y	July 2, 1872	128, 632
Curry-comb	W. P. Kellogg and M. Sweet	Lansingburgh and Troy, N. Y.	Sept. 24, 1867	69, 100
Curry-comb	L. Knapp	Woodhaven, N. Y	Mar. 1, 1870	100, 417
Curry-comb	J. W. Latcher	Albany, N. Y	July 21, 1868	80, 190
Curry-comb	W. E. Lawrence	New York, N. Y	Dec. 27, 1870	110, 576
Curry-comb	W. E. Lawrence	New York, N. Y	June 6, 1871	115, 733
Curry-comb	H. Mithoff	Columbus, Ohio	Aug. 17, 1869	93, 782
Curry-comb	S. A. Morton	Wadesborough, N. C	Dec. 23, 1873	145, 891
Curry-comb	B. F. Neal	Poultney, Vt	Oct. 6, 1863	40, 179
Curry-comb	E. M. Noyes	Binghamton, N. Y	Sept. 17, 1867	69, 016
Curry-comb	R. D. Porter	Zanesville, Ohio	Dec. 10, 1861	33, 904
Curry-comb	A. H. Reid	Brandywine Manor, Pa	Dec. 2, 1873	145, 242
Curry-comb	B. W. Remington	Providence, R. I	Feb. 11, 1868	74, 423
Curry-comb	J. W. Rockwell	Ridgefield, Conn	May 26, 1863	38, 696
Curry-comb	J. W. Rockwell	Richfield, Conn	Dec. 15, 1863	40, 946
Curry-comb	C. W. Saladee	Putnam, Ohio	Dec. 27, 1864	45, 640
Curry-comb	C. W. Saladee	Putnam, Ohio	Mar. 7, 1865	46, 710
Curry-comb	R. C. Shippey	Union, N. Y	Aug. 20, 1872	130, 755
Curry-comb	M. Sweet	Troy, N. Y	Oct. 21, 1862	36, 736
Curry-comb	M. Sweet	Troy, N. Y	June 12, 1866	55, 553
Curry-comb	M. Sweet	Troy, N. Y	Apr. 20, 1869	89, 182
Curry-comb	J. W. Trussell	Troy, N. Y	Nov. 25, 1873	145, 033
Curry-comb	J. E. Yager	Barboursville, Va	Nov. 23, 1869	97, 258
Curry-comb	S. J. Wheeler	New Britain, Conn	Jan. 22, 1861	31, 199
Curry-comb	W. Wheeler	West Poultney, Vt	Apr. 25, 1846	4, 470
Curry-comb	N. Whipple	Ledyard, Conn	Oct. 29, 1872	132, 551
Curry-comb	T. Wilkinson	Cambridge, N. Y	Aug. 16, 1844	3, 706
Curry-comb and brush	H. C. Smith	Coxsackie, N. Y	Oct. 3, 1871	119, 659
Curry-combs, Construction of	W. Wheeler	Troy, N. Y	Mar. 1, 1853	9, 605
Curry-combs, Cutting the bars and teeth of	W. Wheeler	West Poultney, Vt	Oct. 25, 1853	10, 166
Curry-combs, Method of casting the backs upon the teeth of	J. M. Gardner	Troy, N. Y	Mar. 18, 1851	7, 986
Curry-combs, Mode of making	N. C. Sandford	Meriden, Conn	Nov. 3, 1838	997
Curry-combs, Riveting	B. B. Hotchkiss	Sharon, Conn	Jan. 1, 1861	31, 064
Currying and leather-dressing machine	R. P. Boyce	Erata, Miss	Apr. 17, 1860	27, 885

Index of patents issued from the United States Patent Office from 1790 *to* 1873, *inclusive*—Continued.

Invention.	Inventor.	Residence.	Date.	No.
Currying and tempering knife	D. S. Delano	Cornwall, Conn	Apr. 6, 1833	....
Currying cattle, Cards for	C. S. Dickerman	Lansingburgh, N. Y	Feb. 9, 1858	19, 288
Currying, Process for preparing stuffing for	C. L. Morehouse	Cleveland, Ohio	June 5, 1866	55, 426
Curtain-cord fastener	J. P. Arnold	Philadelphia, Pa	May 27, 1873	139, 228
Curtain-cord fastener	C. Gammel	Utica, N. Y	May 13, 1873	138, 878
Curtain	R. Neuninger and F. Brauer	Newark, N. J	Feb. 21, 1871	112, 067
Curtain and carpet fastener	P. Miles	New York, N. Y	Mar. 30, 1869	88, 501
Curtain and map fixture	J. W. Burns	Medway, Ohio	Jan. 25, 1870	99, 151
Curtain and shawl stretcher	J. Nicklin	Cleveland, Ohio	Dec. 21, 1869	98, 094
Curtain-brake	T. S. Baylie and G. H. Maurer	Washington, D. C	Jan. 3, 1871	110, 726
Curtain-clasp	B. F. Watson and A. Shepard	Bridgeport, Ill	Nov. 24, 1868	84, 448
Curtain-clasp	J. G. Whittier and T. M. Powell	Attica, Ind	Sept. 26, 1865	50, 193
Curtain-cord bracket	T. L. Pye	New York, N. Y	Dec. 18, 1860	30, 985
Curtain-cord clamp	G. W. Bishop	Saratoga, N. Y	May 21, 1872	127, 016
Curtain-cord fastener	H. Lull	Hoboken, N. J	May 27, 1873	139, 404
Curtain-cord rack	W. D. Ludlow	New York, N. Y	Jan. 14, 1873	134, 812
Curtain-cord retainer	H. Holcroft	Media, Pa	May 9, 1871	114, 560
Curtain-cord tightener	J. E. Baum	Philadelphia, Pa	Aug. 30, 1870	106, 770
Curtain-cord tightener	W. H. Betts	Brooklyn, N. Y	Feb. 9, 1869	86, 634
Curtain-cord tightener	T. C. Lippincott	Philadelphia, Pa	Aug. 27, 1867	68, 092
Curtain-cord tightener	J. O. Montignani	Albany, N. Y	Jan. 12, 1864	41, 231
Curtain, Electro-magnetic burglar-proof	E. Holmes and H. C. Roome	Brooklyn, N. Y., and Jersey City, N. J.	Nov. 14, 1871	120, 875
Curtain-eyelet	J. Starkey	Portland, Me	Oct. 30, 1866	59, 320
Curtain-fastener	J. F. A. Blätterlein	West Meriden, Conn	July 29, 1873	141, 313
Curtain-fastener, Reversible	H. Binder	Saint Louis, Mo	Sept. 12, 1871	118, 781
Curtain-fastening	J. R. Cook	Winsted, Conn	Aug. 15, 1865	49, 381
Curtain fastening, Window	H. Guyer	Albany, N. Y	Mar. 11, 1851	7, 971
Curtain-fixture	J. D. Ayers	East Greensborough, Vt	June 22, 1869	91, 591
Curtain-fixture	A. C. Babcock	New Haven, Conn	Jan. 11, 1860	26, 824
Curtain-fixture	J. B. Bailey	New York, N. Y	May 23, 1865	47, 891
Curtain-fixture	J. B. Bailey	New York, N. Y	June 12, 1866	55, 454
Curtain-fixture	J. B. Bailey	New York, N. Y	Feb. 23, 1869	87, 234
Curtain-fixture	H. O. Baker	New York, N. Y	July 3, 1866	55, 978
Curtain-fixture	T. C. Baldwin	Newton, Mass	Nov. 30, 1858	22, 153
Curtain-fixture	A. P. Barlow	Claremont, N. H	Dec. 3, 1867	71, 679
Curtain-fixture	J. H. Barnes and T. W. Brown	Brooklyn, N. Y	Apr. 3, 1866	53, 724
Curtain-fixture	J. E. Baum	Philadelphia, Pa	July 18, 1871	117, 037
Curtain-fixture	J. E. Baum	Philadelphia, Pa	July 18, 1871	117, 038
Curtain-fixture	J. E. Baum	Philadelphia, Pa	Sept. 26, 1871	119, 299
Curtain-fixture	R. Beal	Commerce, Mich	Nov. 1, 1870	108, 752
Curtain-fixture	G. T. Beardsley	Ithaca, N. Y	June 30, 1868	79, 435
Curtain-fixture	G. W. Beers	Bridgeport, Conn	Apr. 1, 1873	137, 405
Curtain-fixture	H. Binder	Saint Louis, Mo	Sept. 17, 1872	131, 328
Curtain-fixture	E. T. Briggs	Boston, Mass	Sept. 3, 1867	68, 552
Curtain-fixture	E. T. Briggs	Boston, Mass	Feb. 20, 1872	123, 861
Curtain-fixture	J. G. Brothwell	Wolcottville, Conn	Dec. 6, 1870	109, 800
Curtain-fixture	E. Brown	Waterbury, Conn	Apr. 3, 1860	27, 686
Curtain-fixture	S. S. Brown	Woonsocket, R. I	Oct. 6, 1868	82, 796
Curtain-fixture	W. Brown	West Cambridge, Mass	Feb. 18, 1868	74, 661
Curtain-fixture	C. M. Brown and C. L. Gates	Hartford, Conn	Feb. 14, 1871	111, 723
Curtain-fixture	C. Buckley	Meriden, Conn	July 11, 1871	116, 929
Curtain-fixture	C. Buckley	Meriden, Conn	Jan. 2, 1872	122, 356
Curtain-fixture	C. Buckley	West Meriden, Conn	Feb. 18, 1873	136, 030
Curtain-fixture	W. N. Bulkley	Brooklyn, N. Y	Oct. 3, 1871	119, 568
Curtain-fixture	T. Burgen	Rutland, Vt	Feb. 15, 1870	99, 837
Curtain-fixture	H. H. Burritt	Newark, N. J	Sept. 24, 1872	131, 496
Curtain-fixture	H. H. Burritt	Newark, N. J	Oct. 7, 1873	143, 494
Curtain-fixture	H. H. Burritt	Belleville, N. J	Dec. 23, 1873	145, 785
Curtain-fixture	N. Campbell	Rochester, N. Y	May 16, 1871	114, 917
Curtain-fixture	N. Campbell	Rochester, N. Y	May 16, 1871	114, 918
Curtain-fixture	N. Campbell	Rochester, N. Y	Oct. 10, 1871	119, 740
Curtain-fixture	N. Campbell	Rochester, N. Y	Sept. 3, 1872	130, 977
Curtain-fixture	W. Campbell	New York, N. Y	Apr. 18, 1871	113, 852
Curtain-fixture	R. Cassady	Newport, N. J	Feb. 9, 1869	86, 810
Curtain-fixture	H. W. Chace	Fall River, Mass	Oct. 8, 1861	33, 461
Curtain-fixture	J. Chace	Rochester, N. Y	Mar. 24, 1868	75, 860
Curtain-fixture	H. N. Chapman	Washington, D. C	Mar. 16, 1869	87, 757
Curtain-fixture	D. G. Chase	Boston, Mass	June 4, 1872	127, 565
Curtain-fixture	J. Chase and W. S. Loughborough.	Rochester, N. Y	Apr. 25, 1865	47, 392
Curtain-fixture	A. M. Cheney	Charlotte, Mich	Apr. 20, 1869	89, 126
Curtain-fixture	D. Clagett	Hagerstown, Md	Mar. 5, 1872	124, 330
Curtain-fixture	H. Clayton	Lexington, Ky	Sept. 26, 1871	119, 321
Curtain-fixture	W. Cleveland	New York, N. Y	July 24, 1860	29, 242
Curtain-fixture	B. F. Cloud	Philadelphia, Pa	May 11, 1869	89, 917
Curtain-fixture	W. C. Clover	Brooklyn, N. Y	Nov. 1, 1870	108, 761
Curtain-fixture	W. R. Cole	Baltimore, Md	Dec. 17, 1872	133, 921
Curtain-fixture	M. Converse	Jordan, N. Y	May 28, 1867	65, 058
Curtain-fixture	H. T. Cooper	New York, N. Y	June 15, 1869	91, 422
Curtain-fixture	J. M. Corns	Black Rock, N. Y	Feb. 18, 1868	74, 508
Curtain-fixture	G. B. Cowles	Bridgeport, Conn	Jan. 21, 1873	134, 980
Curtain-fixture	J. Crandell and P. W. Smith	Chicopee, Mass	July 13, 1869	92, 428
Curtain-fixture	J. P. Crawford	Carmichael's, Pa	Dec. 21, 1869	98, 039
Curtain-fixture	W. R. P. Cross	Portland, Me	Aug. 14, 1866	57, 096
Curtain-fixture	J. Cunningham	Philadelphia, Pa	Mar. 12, 1867	62, 824
Curtain-fixture	T. Curley	Troy, N. Y	Mar. 24, 1868	75, 869
Curtain-fixture	J. W. Currier and J. M. Thompson.	Holyoke, Mass	Nov. 3, 1857	18, 536
Curtain-fixture	J. David	New York, N. Y	Sept. 24, 1867	69, 189
Curtain-fixture	J. David	New York, N. Y	Aug. 18, 1868	81, 258
Curtain-fixture	A. S. Dickinson	Washington, D. C	Dec. 29, 1868	85, 433
Curtain-fixture	A. S. Dickinson	New York, N. Y	Oct. 19, 1869	95, 993
Curtain-fixture	L. Dodge	Syracuse, N. Y	June 29, 1869	91, 923
Curtain-fixture	E. Doen	New Britain, Conn	Apr. 9, 1867	63, 621
Curtain-fixture	J. Doyle	Hoboken, N. J	July 20, 1869	92, 710
Curtain-fixture	J. Doyle	Hoboken, N. J	Sept. 27, 1870	107, 764
Curtain-fixture	L. J. Earll	Union City, Pa	July 15, 1873	140, 901

Index of patents issued from the United States Patent Office from 1790 *to* 1873, *inclusive*—Continued.

Invention.	Inventor.	Residence.	Date.	No.
Curtain-fixture	C. Eaton	New York, N. Y	Nov. 28, 1871	121, 342
Curtain-fixture	C. Eaton	New York, N. Y	Oct. 22, 1872	132, 453
Curtain-fixture	M. R. Fenton	Washington, D. C	June 25, 1867	66, 010
Curtain-fixture	H. Fininley	New York, N. Y	Dec. 29, 1868	85, 295
Curtain-fixture	C. Fisher	Milton, Mass	Jan. 31, 1860	26, 980
Curtain-fixture	A. C. Flint	Boston, Mass	Nov. 3, 1863	40, 466
Curtain-fixture	J. W. Foard	San Francisco, Cal	July 20, 1869	92, 812
Curtain-fixture	C. H. Fowler	West Roxbury, Mass	May 28, 1867	65, 067
Curtain-fixture	C. E. Fritts	Oneonta, N. Y	May 11, 1869	89, 926
Curtain-fixture	C. E. Fritts	Oneonta, N. Y	May 6, 1873	138, 493
Curtain-fixture	G. P. Fuller	Philadelphia, Pa	Sept. 28, 1869	95, 218
Curtain-fixture	G. P. Fuller	Humphrey, N. Y	May 17, 1870	103, 167
Curtain-fixture	G. Gatty	New York, N. Y	Apr. 16, 1861	32, 062
Curtain-fixture	A. F. Gerald	Kendall's Mills, Me	Oct. 6, 1868	82, 824
Curtain-fixture	A. F. Gerald	Fairfield, Me	Sept. 17, 1872	131, 346
Curtain-fixture	H. B. Gingrich	Bradford, Ohio	Dec. 3, 1872	133, 641
Curtain-fixture	A. J. Goodrich	Wolcottville, Conn	Jan. 16, 1872	122, 826
Curtain-fixture	N. S. Graves	Boston, Mass	Aug. 11, 1857	17, 967
Curtain-fixture	J. Gray	Medford, Mass	Nov. 28, 1871	121, 242
Curtain-fixture	W. D. Gridley	New Britain, Conn	Mar. 24, 1868	75, 750
Curtain-fixture	L. B. Gusman	Philadelphia, Pa	Feb. 17, 1857	16, 673
Curtain-fixture	T. Hagerty	Richmond, Va	Feb. 27, 1872	124, 131
Curtain-fixture	J. F. Hall	Bangor, Me	Mar. 9, 1858	19, 560
Curtain-fixture	J. F. Hall	Bangor, Me	May 22, 1860	28, 363
Curtain-fixture	J. F. Hall	Bangor, Me	Sept. 4, 1860	29, 935
Curtain-fixture	A. N. Hallowell and H. S. Rue	Philadelphia, Pa	Oct. 1, 1872	131, 753
Curtain-fixture	B. Handforth	Chicago, Ill	Oct. 23, 1866	59, 009
Curtain-fixture	B. Handforth	Chicago, Ill	Nov. 10, 1868	83, 957
Curtain-fixture	O. Hanks	Cincinnati, Ohio	Aug. 27, 1867	68, 189
Curtain-fixture	T. G. Harold	Brooklyn, N. Y	Mar. 5, 1861	31, 643
Curtain-fixture	T. G. Harold and G. L. Kelty	Brooklyn and New York, N. Y.	Dec. 11, 1860	30, 878
Curtain-fixture	S. Hartshorn	New York, N. Y	Oct. 11, 1864	44, 624
Curtain-fixture	S. Hartshorn	New York, N. Y	July 9, 1872	128, 798
Curtain-fixture	S. F. Hay	New York, N. Y	July 30, 1872	129, 889
Curtain-fixture	W. B. Hazzard	Philadelphia, Pa	June 18, 1872	127, 975
Curtain-fixture	S. and M. Henry	Chenoa, Ill	Dec. 23, 1873	145, 868
Curtain-fixture	C. F. Herrick	Independence, Iowa	Aug. 20, 1867	67, 876
Curtain-fixture	J. J. Hessler	Reading, Pa	June 25, 1867	66, 084
Curtain-fixture	A. Hicks	Factoryville, N. Y	Dec. 6, 1864	45, 374
Curtain-fixture	W. C. Hicks	Summit, N. J	July 2, 1872	128, 489
Curtain-fixture	R. E. Hitchcock	Waterbury, Conn	Dec. 28, 1869	98, 261
Curtain-fixture	F. Hobart	Mount Pleasant, Iowa	Oct. 17, 1871	119, 983
Curtain-fixture	J. B. Holmes, jr	New York, N. Y	Oct. 4, 1859	25, 644
Curtain-fixture	M. G. Imbach	Bethlehem, Pa	Dec. 28, 1869	98, 384
Curtain-fixture	C. R. Jenkins	Philadelphia, Pa	Jan. 28, 1868	73, 811
Curtain-fixture	A. D. and E. M. Judd	New Haven, Conn	Apr. 1, 1873	137, 450
Curtain-fixture	E. M. Judd	New Britain, Conn	Jan. 29, 1861	31, 246
Curtain-fixture	E. M. Judd	New Britain, Conn	Oct. 20, 1863	40, 381
Curtain-fixture	E. M. Judd	New Haven, Conn	Dec. 19, 1865	51, 594
Curtain-fixture	E. M. Judd	Wolcottville, Conn	Mar. 5, 1867	62, 635
Curtain-fixture	H. L. Judd	New Britain, Conn	Dec. 13, 1864	45, 413
Curtain-fixture	J. W. King	New York, N. Y	Aug. 24, 1869	94, 006
Curtain-fixture	I. Kinman	Freeport, Ill	May 12, 1868	77, 890
Curtain-fixture	G. R. Kelsey	West Haven, Conn	Nov. 12, 1861	33, 708
Curtain-fixture	G. L. Kelty and T. G. Harold	New York and Brooklyn, N. Y.	Mar. 6, 1860	27, 410
Curtain-fixture	W. C. Kennedy	Commerce, Mich	Mar. 21, 1871	112, 814
Curtain-fixture	S. Ker	Washington, D. C	Feb. 4, 1873	135, 562
Curtain-fixture	A. H. Knapp	Newton Centre, Mass	Jan. 1, 1867	60, 908
Curtain-fixture	A. H. Knapp	Newton Centre, Mass	May 25, 1869	90, 366
Curtain-fixture	A. H. Knapp	Newton Centre, Mass	Sept. 5, 1871	118, 725
Curtain-fixture	A. H. Knapp	Newton Centre, Mass	July 30, 1872	129, 893
Curtain-fixture	A. A. Knapp and G. W. Bailey	Newton Centre and Boston, Mass.	Apr. 26, 1870	102, 409
Curtain-fixture	C. F. Knauer	Pittsburgh, Pa	Jan. 15, 1867	61, 212
Curtain-fixture	C. F. Knauer	Pittsburgh, Pa	Jan. 21, 1868	73, 612
Curtain-fixture	E. B. Lake	Bridgeport, N. J	July 23, 1867	66, 970
Curtain-fixture	W. A. Lamberson and T. O. Morton.	New York, N. Y	Jan. 30, 1866	52, 296
Curtain-fixture	B. Landon	Canton, Pa	Nov. 5, 1872	132, 726
Curtain-fixture	A. E. Lazell	West Meriden, Conn	June 10, 1873	139, 719
Curtain-fixture	C. Leo and J. Pandler	Washington, D. C	June 25, 1867	66, 094
Curtain-fixture	J. D. Legg	Long Eddy, N. Y	Aug. 18, 1868	81, 280
Curtain-fixture	J. D. Legg	Long Eddy, N. Y	Sept. 19, 1871	119, 158
Curtain-fixture	J. D. and I. W. Legg	Long Eddy, N. Y	May 5, 1868	77, 499
Curtain-fixture	M. Loeb	Chicago, Ill	Nov. 30, 1869	97, 304
Curtain-fixture	D. E. Long	Pawtucket, R. I	Aug. 4, 1868	80, 750
Curtain-fixture	J. S. Lovejoy	Washington, D. C	Jan. 4, 1870	98, 508
Curtain-fixture	T. Lovell	Cincinnati, Ohio	Apr. 23, 1872	125, 966
Curtain-fixture	A. Lovie	Philadelphia, Pa	Dec. 15, 1868	85, 016
Curtain fixture	H. and A. Lovie	Philadelphia, Pa	Feb. 5, 1867	61, 745
Curtain-fixture	H. and A. Lovie	Philadelphia, Pa., and Prussia.	Oct. 15, 1867	69, 823
Curtain-fixture	T. Lyons	Brooklyn, N. Y	Oct. 22, 1867	70, 099
Curtain-fixture	H. E. Marchand	Pittsburgh, Pa	Nov. 4, 1873	144, 342
Curtain-fixture	T. J. Marinus	Independence, Iowa	Jan. 7, 1868	73, 108
Curtain-fixture	J. Y. Marsh	New York, N. Y	Feb. 26, 1861	31, 550
Curtain-fixture	M. S. Marshall	Somerville, Mass	Feb. 16, 1869	86, 933
Curtain-fixture	W. W. Massey	Baltimore, Md	Dec. 16, 1873	145, 669
Curtain-fixture	E. Mentz	Philadelphia, Pa	May 1, 1866	54, 384
Curtain-fixture	W. T. Mersereau	Newark, N. J	Oct. 8, 1867	69, 572
Curtain-fixture	L. E. Michell	Cincinnati, Ohio	Aug. 4, 1868	80, 650
Curtain-fixture	P. Miles	Hartford, Conn	May 15, 1855	12, 866
Curtain-fixture	P. Miles	Hartford, Conn	Aug. 26, 1856	15, 615
Curtain-fixture	P. Miles	New York, N. Y	Sept. 26, 1865	50, 149
Curtain-fixture	P. Miles	New York, N. Y	Mar. 26, 1867	63, 169
Curtain-fixture	J. P. Miller	Somerset, Pa	May 26, 1868	78, 311
Curtain-fixture	J. Montgomery	Marseilles, Ill	May 24, 1870	103, 353

Index of patents issued from the United States Patent Office from 1790 *to* 1873, *inclusive*—Continued.

Invention.	Inventor.	Residence.	Date.	No.
Curtain-fixture	J. A. Morrison	Pittsburgh, Pa	Jan. 12, 1869	85, 751
Curtain-fixture	C. C. Moore	New York, N. Y	Dec. 9, 1873	145, 359
Curtain-fixture	B. Moser	Brooklyn, N. Y	Jan. 12, 1869	85, 842
Curtain-fixture	B. Moser	Philadelphia, Pa	May 25, 1869	90, 571
Curtain-fixture	B. Moser	Waltham, Mass	May 16, 1871	114, 843
Curtain-fixture	B. Moser	Waltham, Mass	June 27, 1871	116, 343
Curtain-fixture	M. H. Mosman	Waterbury, Conn	Nov. 22, 1870	109, 539
Curtain-fixture	G. W. Nell	Philadelphia, Pa	June 5, 1866	55, 344
Curtain-fixture	G. W. Nell	Philadelphia, Pa	May 11, 1869	89, 883
Curtain-fixture	P. H. Niles	Boston, Mass	Jan. 2, 1855	12, 150
Curtain-fixture	P. H. Niles	Boston, Mass	Sept. 18, 1855	13, 588
Curtain-fixture	J. Norman	Brooklyn, N. Y	July 4, 1871	116, 624
Curtain-fixture	J. L. Oliver	Boston, Mass	Nov. 15, 1870	109, 241
Curtain-fixture	P. O'Thayne	New York, N. Y	Jan. 12, 1869	85, 845
Curtain-fixture	P. O'Thayne and D.W. Canfield	New York, N. Y	Jan. 12, 1869	85, 846
Curtain-fixture	C. C. Parker	Brooklyn, N. H	Apr. 16, 1867	63, 934
Curtain-fixture	F. G. Peoble	New York, N. Y	Oct. 4, 1870	107, 956
Curtain-fixture	H. H. Phillips	Buffalo, N. Y	Feb. 27, 1872	124, 153
Curtain-fixture	H. H. Phillips	Buffalo, N. Y	Feb. 27, 1872	124, 154
Curtain-fixture	P. W. Phillips	Salem, Mass	Feb. 21, 1871	111, 967
Curtain-fixture	P. W. Phillips	Salem, Mass	Apr. 25, 1871	114, 036
Curtain-fixture	P. W. Phillips	Salem, Mass	Nov. 14, 1871	120, 997
Curtain-fixture	P. W. Phillips	Salem, Mass	Apr. 1, 1873	137, 480
Curtain-fixture	H. Polley	San Francisco, Cal	Sept. 10, 1872	131, 299
Curtain-fixture	L. C. Prindle	Chicago, Ill	May 16, 1871	114, 852
Curtain-fixture	R. B. Prindle	Norwich, N. Y	June 29, 1869	92, 094
Curtain-fixture	S. S. Putnam	Boston, Mass	Oct. 3, 1854	11, 757
Curtain-fixture	S. S. Putnam	Dorchester, Mass	Mar. 5, 1861	31, 623
Curtain-fixture	S. S. Putnam	Dorchester, Mass	July 1, 1862	35, 779
Curtain-fixture	S. S. Putnam	Dorchester, Mass	Sept. 2, 1862	36, 366
Curtain-fixture	S. S. Putnam	Dorchester, Mass	Feb. 4, 1868	74, 135
Curtain-fixture	S. S. Putnam	Dorchester, Mass	Jan. 19, 1869	86, 100
Curtain-fixture	W. Rice	Philadelphia, Pa	Jan. 24, 1860	26, 925
Curtain-fixture	T. C. Richards	Milwaukee, Wis	Mar. 4, 1862	34, 593
Curtain-fixture	C. J. Roberts	Chicago, Ill	Jan. 5, 1869	85, 695
Curtain-fixture	C. Robin	Chester, Conn	Mar. 7, 1871	112, 383
Curtain-fixture	A. Roelofs	Philadelphia, Pa	Oct. 24, 1871	120, 168
Curtain-fixture	A. Roelofs	Philadelphia, Pa	Oct. 31, 1871	120, 538
Curtain-fixture	A. Roelofs	Philadelphia, Pa	May 14, 1872	126, 835
Curtain-fixture	A. Roelofs	Philadelphia, Pa	July 16, 1872	129, 172
Curtain-fixture	F. Root	Chelsea, Mass	May 17, 1870	103, 084
Curtain-fixture	F. Root	Hartford, Conn	Aug. 9, 1870	106, 211
Curtain-fixture	F. Root	Hartford, Conn	Oct. 11, 1870	108, 190
Curtain-fixture	C. Rose	Allentown, Pa	Jan. 8, 1867	61, 106
Curtain-fixture	L. Ross	Springfield, Mass	Dec. 11, 1866	60, 426
Curtain-fixture	L. L. Sawyer	San Francisco, Cal	July 11, 1871	116, 906
Curtain-fixture	L. J. Schaefer	Philadelphia, Pa	Mar. 31, 1868	76, 252
Curtain-fixture	F. B. Scott	Lancaster, N. Y	Feb. 27, 1872	124, 088
Curtain-fixture	F. B. Scott	Lancaster, N. Y	May 28, 1872	127, 274
Curtain-fixture	W. E. Scranton	New Haven, Conn	Oct. 25, 1870	108, 734
Curtain-fixture	J. Shorey	Lowell, Mass	Aug. 11, 1868	81, 019
Curtain-fixture	J. Shorey	Lowell, Mass	Oct. 22, 1872	132, 376
Curtain-fixture	J. Shorey and F. H. Butler	Lowell, Mass	Dec. 28, 1869	98, 307
Curtain-fixture	D. C. Smart	Cambridgeport, Mass	Sept. 12, 1854	11, 683
Curtain-fixture	J. Smith	New York, N. Y	Apr. 3, 1860	27, 747
Curtain-fixture	R. L. Smith	Wolcottville, Conn	Aug. 16, 1870	106, 416
Curtain-fixture	W. R. Smith	Seaforth, Canada	Nov. 7, 1871	120, 787
Curtain-fixture	L. Smith and S. Foster, jr	Des Moines, Iowa	Nov. 24, 1868	84, 443
Curtain-fixture	H. C. Spalding	Brooklyn, N. Y	Feb. 22, 1859	23, 047
Curtain-fixture	J. Stephens	New York, N. Y	July 1, 1856	15, 258
Curtain-fixture	J. Stephens	Fairview, Ohio	Nov. 15, 1870	109, 266
Curtain-fixture	J. Stevens and W. B. Fay	Chicopee Falls, Mass	May 1, 1866	54, 434
Curtain-fixture	T. Stewart	Philadelphia, Pa	Nov. 29, 1870	109, 683
Curtain-fixture	J. S. Stewart and S. B. Pierce	Homer, N. Y	July 24, 1866	56, 630
Curtain-fixture	C. F. Stock	Peoria, Ill	Feb. 13, 1872	123, 591
Curtain-fixture	A. Studley	Natick, Mass	Mar. 3, 1868	75, 072
Curtain-fixture	T. Symonds	Portland, Me	Apr. 22, 1873	138, 054
Curtain-fixture	W. H. Tambling	Eleroy, Ill	Jan. 10, 1871	110, 939
Curtain-fixture	J. B. Tarr	Chicago, Ill	Apr. 3, 1866	53, 703
Curtain-fixture	J. W. Taylor, jr	Dubuque, Iowa	Nov. 27, 1866	60, 087
Curtain-fixture	C. M. Thielcke	Chicago, Ill	Aug. 30, 1870	106, 890
Curtain-fixture	L. H. Thomas	Waterbury, Vt	Apr. 2, 1867	63, 440
Curtain-fixture	H. L. Traphagen	New York, N. Y	Feb. 18, 1873	135, 950
Curtain-fixture	H. H. Trenor	New York, N. Y	Aug. 22, 1865	49, 571
Curtain-fixture	A. E. Tripp	Springfield, Ohio	Aug. 23, 1870	106, 637
Curtain-fixture	L. A. Tripp	Middletown, N. Y	Feb. 19, 1867	62, 235
Curtain-fixture	L. A. Tripp and S. M. Boyd	New York, N. Y	Jan. 19, 1869	86, 044
Curtain-fixture	J. and W. Turnbull	Vancouver, Wash	Mar. 1, 1870	100, 341
Curtain-fixture	E. Turner	Wolcottsville, N. Y	May 2, 1871	114, 494
Curtain-fixture	H. Voigt	Buffalo, N. Y	July 23, 1867	67, 086
Curtain-fixture	R. Vose	New York, N. Y	Jan. 31, 1871	111, 405
Curtain-fixture	F. Walker	New Orleans, La	July 15, 1873	140, 976
Curtain-fixture	H. K. Warner and C. E. Smith	Rochester, Minn	Dec. 23, 1873	145, 821
Curtain-fixture	T. N. Webb	Baltimore, Md	Aug. 15, 1871	118, 080
Curtain-fixture	T. N. Webb	Baltimore, Md	Aug. 15, 1871	118, 081
Curtain-fixture	T. N. Webb	Baltimore, Md	Dec. 26, 1871	122, 294
Curtain-fixture	W. J. Wells	Pittsburgh, Pa	Sept. 10, 1872	131, 318
Curtain-fixture	I. B. Werner	Rossville, Ill	Sept. 24, 1872	131, 643
Curtain-fixture	W. A. Wheeldon	Chicago, Ill	Feb. 25, 1873	136, 195
Curtain-fixture	C. H. Wheeler	Boston, Mass	Apr. 14, 1857	17, 059
Curtain-fixture	G. M. White	New Haven, Conn	Aug. 7, 1866	57, 053
Curtain-fixture	G. M. White and C. S. Meeker	New Haven, Conn	June 2, 1868	78, 628
Curtain-fixture	L. White	Hartford, Conn	Jan. 15, 1856	14, 123
Curtain-fixture	L. White	Hartford, Conn	Nov. 15, 1859	26, 146
Curtain-fixture	L. Whitehead	Buffalo, N. Y	Dec. 15, 1857	18, 878
Curtain-fixture	J. S. Whitney	Lowell, Mass	Apr. 26, 1870	102, 344
Curtain-fixture	J. G. Whitwell	New York, N. Y	Sept. 25, 1860	30, 172
Curtain-fixture	F. Wieterich and K. Hagen	New York, N. Y	Sept. 2, 1856	15, 676

Index of patents issued from the United States Patent Office from 1790 *to* 1873, *inclusive*—Continued.

Invention.	Inventor.	Residence.	Date.	No.
Curtain-fixture	W. C. Wilcox	Waltham, Mass	May 30, 1871	115, 402
Curtain-fixture	J. H. Wilhelm	Chicago, Ill	July 26, 1870	105, 871
Curtain-fixture	J. H. Wilhelm	Chicago, Ill	Nov. 8, 1870	109, 087
Curtain-fixture	H. Wocher and B. Geiger	Philadelphia, Pa	Dec. 31, 1867	72, 767
Curtain-fixture	H. Wocher and B. Geiger	Philadelphia, Pa	Dec. 31, 1867	72, 768
Curtain-fixture	J. F. Wollensak	Chicago, Ill	Apr. 16, 1872	125, 712
Curtain-fixture	J. F. Wollensak	Chicago, Ill	Apr. 16, 1872	125, 870
Curtain-fixture	J. F. Wollensak	Chicago, Ill	Nov. 25, 1873	145, 040
Curtain-fixture	W. H. Woods	Philadelphia, Pa	Dec. 10, 1867	72, 150
Curtain-fixture	W. H. Woods	Philadelphia, Pa	Aug. 4, 1868	80, 793
Curtain-fixture	T. K. Work	Hartford, Conn	Apr. 20, 1858	20, 013
Curtain-fixture	J. Wyatt	Philadelphia, Pa	Jan. 4, 1870	98, 654
Curtain-fixture	W. P. Yates	Elmira, N. Y	Sept. 27, 1870	107, 747
Curtain-fixture	A. Young	Philadelphia, Pa	Mar. 24, 1868	75, 821
Curtain-fixture	J. L. Young	New York, N. Y	May 14, 1872	126, 666
Curtain-fixture	W. H. and L. Young	Boston, Mass	Nov. 3, 1868	83, 680
Curtain-fixture rack	J. Pusey	Philadelphia, Pa	Apr. 1, 1873	137, 320
Curtain-fixture, Self winding and balancing	F. C. D. McKay	Elmira, N. Y	Apr. 19, 1870	102, 142
Curtain fixture, Spring	J. Shorey	Lowell, Mass	July 26, 1870	105, 854
Curtain fixture, Window	R. Ballou, jr., and B. F. Hooper	Albany, N. Y	Apr. 7, 1857	16, 900
Curtain fixture, Window	J. Gibbs	Brooklyn, N. Y	May 19, 1863	38, 579
Curtain fixture, Window	N. H. McLean	United States Army	Oct. 2, 1860	30, 236
Curtain fixture, Window	P. Miles	Hartford, Conn	Apr. 7, 1857	16, 989
Curtain fixture, Window	P. Miles	New Britain, Conn	June 21, 1859	24, 479
Curtain fixture, Window	G. L. Miller	De Witt, N. Y	May 5, 1868	77, 638
Curtain fixture, Window	S. S. Putnam	Boston, Mass	Apr. 15, 1851	8, 041
Curtain fixture, Window	A. W. Tanner and O. P. Gorton	Paw Paw, Mich	Apr. 3, 1860	27, 749
Curtain fixture, Window	T. C. Williams	Randolph, Wis	Mar. 21, 1871	112, 876
Curtain-fixtures, Cord-tightener for	A. Carter	New York, N. Y	June 8, 1869	90, 922
Curtain-fixtures, Cord-tightener for	A. S. Dickinson	New York, N. Y	Oct. 19, 1869	95, 994
Curtain-fixtures, Cord-tightener for	E. M. Judd	New Britain, Conn	Aug. 5, 1862	36, 094
Curtain-fixtures, Cord-tightener for	H. L. Judd	Brooklyn, N. Y	Mar. 23, 1869	88, 179
Curtain-fixtures, Cord-tightener for	H. L. Judd	Brooklyn, N. Y	Feb. 4, 1873	135, 561
Curtain-fixtures, Cord-tightener for	E. Turner	Wolcottville, Conn	Dec. 21, 1869	98, 209
Curtain-fixtures, Self-holding clamp for	F. C. Payne	New York, N. Y	Sept. 15, 1863	39, 949
Curtain-holder	G. W. Gount, P. P. Reister, A. L. Keeports, and W. Yount.	Littlestown, Pa	Jan. 25, 1870	99, 271
Curtain holder, Window	J. S. and J. O. Burch	Buffalo, N. Y	Aug. 31, 1869	94, 393
Curtain-hook	H. L. Judd	Brooklyn, N. Y	June 10, 1873	139, 676
Curtain or shade fixture	W. Campbell	New York, N. Y	Oct. 11, 1864	44, 602
Curtain-rack	J. F. Calhoun	Wolcottville, Conn	May 24, 1859	24, 097
Curtain-rack	F. and W. Schmidt	Cincinnati, Ohio	Oct. 3, 1871	119, 536
Curtain-roller	C. M. Fairman and J. A. Henderson.	Pittsburgh, Pa	Oct. 1, 1872	131, 864
Curtain-roller	C. Fisher	Milton, Mass	May 26, 1857	17, 368
Curtain-roller	P. Miles	Hartford, Conn	Mar. 3, 1857	16, 741
Curtain-roller	D. H. Chamberlain	West Roxbury, Mass	Aug. 21, 1855	13, 481
Curtain-roller	D. H. Chamberlain and J. Hartshorn.	Boston, Mass	Jan. 23, 1855	12, 271
Curtain-roller	D. N. B. Coffin, jr	Newton, Mass	Oct. 6, 1857	18, 323
Curtain-roller	F. W. Urann	Saxonville, Mass	Mar. 13, 1855	12, 524
Curtain-roller, Extension	T. Van Wagoner	Newark, N. J	Jan. 4, 1870	98, 649
Curtain-roller for windows, Adjustable	E. S. Clark	Suffolk County, Mass	Feb. 19, 1850	7, 098
Curtain-roller holder	B. G. Fitzhugh	Frederick, Md	Apr. 22, 1873	138, 014
Curtain-roller, Spring	E. M. Judd	Wolcottville, Conn	Sept. 28, 1869	95, 232
Curtain-roller, Spring	B. B. Webster	Boston, Mass	May 15, 1855	12, 881
Curtain-roller stop	R. Wangeman	Chicago, Ill	Jan. 4, 1870	98, 532
Curtain roller, Window	W. Gorton	New York, N. Y	July 18, 1871	117, 068
Curtain roller, Window	W. W. Grier	Hulton, Pa	May 13, 1873	138, 749
Curtain-rollers, Fixture for	J. Hartshorn and D. H. Chamberlain.	Boston, Mass	Apr. 3, 1855	12, 661
Curtain-rollers, Fixture for	C. H. Wheeler	Boston, Mass	Apr. 7, 1857	17, 006
Curtain-rollers, Fixture for	L. White	Hartford, Conn	July 28, 1857	17, 911
Curtain-rollers, Hub or spool for	F. Pilling	Washington, D. C	Mar. 27, 1866	53, 480
Curtain screw and key, Window	H. Andrew	New York, N. Y	Mar. 6, 1822	
Curtain slide, Window	G. Trinks	Jersey City, N. J	June 26, 1860	28, 922
Curtain-support	C. F. Herrick	Independence, Iowa	Apr. 2, 1867	63, 386
Curtain suspension, Window	G. H. Marden	Charlestown, Mass	Oct. 17, 1848	5, 868
Curtain-weight, Adjustable	W. F. Shaw	Boston, Mass	Feb. 23, 1869	87, 209
Curtain, Window	G. Butterfield and D. Bowker	Boston, Mass	Oct. 16, 1860	30, 385
Curtain, Window	H. Foster	Port Jervis, N. Y	Feb. 13, 1866	52, 555
Curtain, Window	D. G. Morgan	Jordan, N. Y	July 30, 1867	67, 337
Curtain, Window	W. H. Morrison	Indianapolis, Ind	Oct. 9, 1866	58, 668
Curtain, Window and bed	W. F. Phyfe	New York, N. Y	Feb. 19, 1830	
Curtains, Apparatus for operating window	J. Stephens and J. Collins	Fairview, Ohio	July 19, 1870	105, 508
Curtains, blinds, and maps, Mode of hanging	J. F. Landis	Harrisburgh, Pa	Feb. 13, 1866	52, 577
Curtains, Cord-tightener for window	M. Hey	Philadelphia, Pa	Nov. 21, 1865	51, 045
Curtains, Manufacture of window and bed	S. Abbot and J. Prentis	Chester, Mass	Aug. 23, 1825	
Curtains, Mode of hanging window	H. Aiken	Philadelphia, Pa	Oct. 19, 1869	95, 965
Curtains, Spring-roller for	J. and J. Hartshorn	Boston, Mass	May 1, 1855	12, 792
Curtains, Spring-roller for window	B. Bray	Salem, Mass	Sept. 5, 1854	11, 638
Curved pipes, Mold for casting	N. Thompson	Brooklyn, N. Y	June 25, 1872	128, 204
Curved pipes, Mold for casting	S. Williams	Foxborough, Mass	May 15, 1866	54, 826
Cushion:				
See Air-cushion.				
Billiard-cushion.				
Billiard-table cushion.				
Car-seat cushion.				
Elastic cushion.				
Elliptic cushion.				
Hydraulic cushion.				
Lubricating-cushion.				
Mop-cushion.				
Needle-cushion.				
Pin-cushion.				
Rubber cushion.				
Seat-cushion.				
Sleeping-cushion.				

Index of patents issued from the United States Patent Office from 1790 to 1873, inclusive—Continued.

Invention.	Inventor.	Residence.	Date.	No.
Cushion—Continued: *see* Sofa-cushion. Spring-cushion. Spring carriage-cushion.				
Cushion, mattress, &c	T. H. O'Brien	Providence, R. I	Oct. 4, 1870	108, 043
Cushion or mattress	L. Bannoefer	Philadelphia, Pa	Nov. 27, 1866	59, 945
Cushion-spring	J. W. Evans	New York, N. Y	Mar. 26, 1861	31, 793
Cushions, mattresses, &c., Apparatus for diffusing vapor through.	W. Welch	Montreal, Canada	Feb. 15, 1870	99, 986
Cuspadore	E. A. Heath	New York, N. Y	Oct. 10, 1871	119, 705
Cuspadore	E. A. Heath	New York, N. Y	Oct. 10, 1871	119, 706
Cutlery	J. Baldwin	Northampton, Mass	Sept. 24, 1867	69, 157
Cutlery	C. L. Butler	Greenfield, Mass	Dec. 19, 1865	51, 648
Cutlery	W. T. Clement	Northampton, Mass	Nov. 10, 1868	83, 831
Cutlery	R. E. Curtis	Great Bend, Pa	Apr. 28, 1868	77, 175
Cutlery	E. Day	Chicago, Ill	July 21, 1868	80, 062
Cutlery	R. H. Fisher	West Meriden, Conn	June 23, 1868	79, 061
Cutlery	D. Fitzpatrick	West Winsted, Conn	Feb. 13, 1866	52, 552
Cutlery	M. W. Lyman	Chicago, Ill	Jan. 17, 1871	110, 986
Cutlery	S. Mason	Beaver Falls, Pa	June 30, 1868	79, 370
Cutlery	W. C. Mason	Beaver Falls, Pa	June 30, 1868	79, 371
Cutlery	T. McGrah	Sheffield, England	Mar. 5, 1867	62, 661
Cutlery	J. H. Nichols and W. Bower	Beaver Falls, Pa	Apr. 26, 1870	102, 306
Cutlery	H. T. Reeves	Beaver Falls, Pa	Nov. 7, 1871	120, 774
Cutlery	W. W. Robinson	Ripon, Wis	July 3, 1866	56, 099
Cutlery	M. Rubel	Chicago, Ill	May 26, 1868	78, 328
Cutlery	M. Rubel	Chicago, Ill	Jan. 26, 1869	89, 252
Cutlery	H. Sanderson	Sheffield, England	May 28, 1867	65, 123
Cutlery	W. Sanderson	New York, N. Y	June 18, 1867	65, 952
Cutlery	W. Sanderson	New York, N. Y	Aug. 10, 1869	93, 560
Cutlery	A. L. Taylor	Springfield, Vt	July 21, 1868	80, 238
Cutlery	W. D. Woods	Bennington, N. H	Oct. 6, 1868	82, 779
Cutlery and tool handle	J. T. Haviland	San Francisco, Cal	Dec. 20, 1870	110, 358
Cutlery, Attaching handles to	M. Chapman	Greenfield, Mass	Jan. 4, 1859	22, 527
Cutlery, Attaching handles to	M. Chapman	Greenfield, Mass	Dec. 20, 1859	26, 478
Cutlery, Attaching handles to	J. Flood	New Haven, Conn	June 9, 1868	78, 796
Cutlery, Attaching handles to	J. W. Gardner	Shelburne Falls, Mass	Dec. 23, 1862	37, 225
Cutlery, Attaching handles to	J. W. Gardner	Shelburne Falls, Mass	Oct. 5, 1869	95, 457
Cutlery, Attaching handles to	J. W. Gardner	Shelburne Falls, Mass	June 7, 1870	103, 867
Cutlery, Attaching handles to	S. Mason and E. Binns	Beaver Falls, Pa	Apr. 20, 1869	89, 059
Cutlery, Casting handles of table	N. S. Clement	New Britain, Conn	Apr. 6, 1869	88, 544
Cutlery cleaning and polishing machine	M. N. Armstrong	Williamsburgh, N. Y	Jan. 24, 1842	2, 435
Cutlery, Construction of table	A. E. Elmer	Windsor, Vt	Feb. 16, 1869	87, 032
Cutlery, Device for grinding	J. P. Curtiss	New Britain, Conn	Dec. 3, 1867	71, 586
Cutlery, edge-tools, &c., Substance for making	T. H. Jenkins	New York, N. Y	Dec. 26, 1865	51, 724
Cutlery, Fastening handles to	E. G. Ost	Shelburne Falls, Mass	Feb. 15, 1870	99, 785
Cutlery, Forging	H. B. Harvey	West Meriden, Conn	Nov. 26, 1867	71, 482
Cutlery-grinding apparatus	W. Fosket	Meriden, Conn	Feb. 11, 1868	74, 214
Cutlery grinding and polishing machine	J. Dodge	Waterford, N. Y	July 21, 1863	39, 317
Cutlery-grinding machine	R. S. Gladwin	Meriden, Conn	July 17, 1866	56, 403
Cutlery-handle	J. D. Frary	New Britain, Conn	Dec. 28, 1869	98, 369
Cutlery-handle	M. Chapman	Greenfield, Mass	Aug. 7, 1860	29, 465
Cutlery-handle	J. W. Gardner	Shelburne Falls, Mass	May 3, 1859	23, 837
Cutlery-handle	T. D. Lakin	Hancock, N. H	Aug. 28, 1866	57, 521
Cutlery-handle blank	I. G. Hotchkiss	Naugatuck, Conn	Feb. 16, 1869	86, 983
Cutlery, Handle for table and other	M. Chapman	Greenfield, Mass	Sept. 13, 1870	107, 223
Cutlery-handle, Metallic	L. S. White	Waterbury, Conn	Mar. 27, 1866	53, 546
Cutlery handle, Pocket	S. Barnes	New Haven, Conn	Feb. 11, 1868	74, 279
Cutlery-handle, Securing	R. H. Fisher	Beverly, N. J	Apr. 10, 1860	27, 790
Cutlery handle, Table	R. H. Fisher	Beaver Falls, Pa	Mar. 16, 1869	87, 767
Cutlery handle, Table	J. W. Gardner	Shelburne Falls, Mass	Feb. 1, 1859	22, 795
Cutlery handles, Construction of table	W. Sanderson	New York, N. Y	June 9, 1868	78, 834
Cutlery, Manufacture of	G. Parr	Buffalo, N. Y	Nov. 27, 1866	60, 048
Cutlery, Manufacture of blades for pocket	W. H. and G. W. Miller	Meriden, Conn	Aug. 2, 1870	106, 073
Cutlery, Manufacture of bolster for	J. D. Frary	New Britain, Conn	Apr. 4, 1871	113, 648
Cutlery, Manufacture of table	J. W. Gardner	Shelburne Falls, Mass	Mar. 27, 1866	53, 529
Cutlery, Manufacture of table	A. McGuire	Winsted, Conn	Aug. 9, 1864	43, 785
Cutlery, Manufacture of table	F. W. Presber and P. Shiober	Winchester, Conn	May 21, 1864	42, 872
Cutlery, Manufacture of table	L. Rice	West Winsted, Conn	Aug. 30, 1864	44, 056
Cutlery, &c., Metallic compound for coating	J. Zimmer	Cleveland, Ohio	Jan. 21, 1873	135, 028
Cutlery, Method of attaching the tangs to handles of table.	D. N. Ropes	Meriden, Conn	May 29, 1849	6, 482
Cutlery, Method of cleaning and polishing	W. Vine	New York, N. Y	Feb. 28, 1844	3, 458
Cutlery, Mode of attaching handles to table	J. W. Gardner	Shelburne Falls, Mass	Mar. 5, 1867	62, 626
Cutlery, &c., Plating scales with hard rubber for the manufacture of.	F. Beals	New Haven, Conn	Dec. 15, 1868	84, 932
Cutlery, Pocket	J. Carreer	Southington, Conn	Dec. 22, 1868	85, 211
Cutlery, Pocket	P. S. Hoe	New York, N. Y	Nov. 12, 1867	70, 718
Cutlery, Pocket	D. R. Hundley	Mountain Home, Ala	Oct. 25, 1870	108, 596
Cutlery, Pocket	W. H. and G. W. Miller	Meriden, Conn	May 24, 1870	103, 352
Cutlery, Pocket	F. B. Perry	Northampton, Mass	Nov. 19, 1867	71, 211
Cutlery, Pocket	D. E. Smith	Bronxville, N. Y	July 6, 1869	92, 217
Cutlery-sharpening implement	A. Thayer	Albany, N. Y	June 9, 1868	78, 771
Cutlery, spoons, &c., Machine for producing uniform twist in table.	E. W. Sperry	Wolcottville, Conn	Jan. 5, 1869	85, 542
Cutlery, Table	M. Chapman	Greenfield, Mass	Nov. 5, 1867	70, 525
Cutlery, Table	W. Clayton	Bristol, Conn	July 28, 1868	80, 334
Cutlery, Table	E. G. Durant	Northampton, Mass	Oct. 18, 1870	108, 463
Cutlery, Table	J. W. Gardner	Shelburne Falls, Mass	Mar. 6, 1860	27, 357
Cutlery, Table	J. W. Gardner	Shelburne Falls, Mass	Sept. 22, 1863	40, 031
Cutlery, Table	W. Hubbard	Meriden, Conn	Apr. 16, 1867	63, 795
Cutlery, Table	E. G. Lamson	Windsor, Vt	Mar. 22, 1870	101, 139
Cutlery, Table	S. Mason	Beaver Falls, Pa	Mar. 16, 1869	87, 786
Cutlery, Table	S. Mason and E. Binns	Beaver Falls, Pa	Mar. 16, 1869	87, 787
Cutlery, Table	C. McDonald	Ottawa, Ill	Jan. 21, 1873	135, 136
Cutlery, Table	N. Miles	Buckland, Mass	Feb. 7, 1865	46, 304
Cutlery, Table	J. H. Nichols and W. Bower	Beaver Falls, Pa	Jan. 25, 1870	99, 104
Cutlery, Table	C. L. Robertson	Providence, R. I	Apr. 13, 1869	88, 810

Index of patents issued from the United States Patent Office from 1790 to 1873, inclusive—Continued.

Invention.	Inventor.	Residence.	Date.	No.
Cutlery, Table	M. Smith	Meriden, Conn	Oct. 3, 1848	5, 827
Cutlery, Table	J. Stott	Philadelphia, Pa	Apr. 2, 1867	63, 439
Cutlery, Table	W. D. Woods	Bennington, N. H	Apr. 2, 1867	63, 598
Cut-nail machine	W. Haddock	Pittsburgh, Pa	Nov. 25, 1873	144, 845
Cut-nail machine	E. A. Kimball	Abington, Mass	Dec. 16, 1873	145, 504
Cut-nail machine	J. Russell	Providence, R. I	Nov. 4, 1873	144, 229
Cut-nail machine	J. P. Sherwood	Fort Edward, N. Y	Aug. 26, 1851	8, 326
Cut nails and brads from rolled iron, Making cold	J. Elgar		Dec. 16, 1803	
Cut nails, cut points, and cut brads, Manufacturing	J. Perkins	Boston, Mass	July 17, 1810	
Cut nails from iron-hoops, &c., rendered tough	N. Kent		May 1, 1801	
Cut nails from Muntz's metal	S. L. Crocker	Taunton, Mass	Apr. 17, 1849	6, 354
Cut nails, Heading	J. Davey	Fairhaven, Vt	Apr. 7, 1814	
Cut nails, Machine for heading	S. Wilmot, jr	New Haven, Conn	Apr. 21, 1809	
Cut nails, Machine for making	D. J. Farmer	Wheeling, W. Va	Aug. 31, 1869	94, 194
Cut nails, Manufacturing	P. Cliff		Nov. 16, 1796	
Cut nails, Manufacturing	D. French		Dec. 23, 1796	
Cut nails while being headed, Device for holding	D. Savery	Wheeling, W. Va	Sept. 22, 1868	82, 354
Cut-off	H. Allen	New York, N. Y	Aug. 29, 1848	5, 745
Cut-off	F. E. Sickels	New York, N. Y	Feb. 24, 1852	8, 760
Cut-off	F. B. Stevens	Weehawken, N. J	Dec. 3, 1861	33, 858
Cut-off, Adjustable	S. H. Gilman	Cincinnati, Ohio	Mar. 18, 1851	7, 987
Cut-off, Adjustable	J. King	Bordentown, N. J	Mar. 20, 1849	6, 209
Cut-off and horse-power indicator, Adjustable	A. Stuckenrath	New York, N. Y	May 1, 1866	54, 439
Cut-off and regulating cock, Gas	C. E. Seal	Winchester, Va	July 1, 1873	140, 549
Cut-off and regulator valve	R. Stewart	Elmira, N. Y	May 19, 1863	38, 610
Cut-off and reversing valve-gear for engines	R. M. Fryer	Nashville, Tenn	Feb. 11, 1873	135, 794
Cut-off and steam-stop of rotary engines	J. W. Webb	Ledyard, N. Y	May 15, 1849	6, 448
Cut-off and steam valve	A. Kendall	Cleveland, Ohio	Apr. 12, 1870	101, 886
Cut-off and steam valves, Method of connecting the action of	B. H. Bartol	Cold Spring, N. Y	Sept. 20, 1844	3, 755
Cut-off and working the valves of steam-engines	G. H. Corliss	Providence, R. I	Mar. 10, 1849	6, 162
Cut-off apparatus, Steam-engine	R. Miller	Pittsburgh, Pa	Nov. 29, 1859	26, 281
Cut-off apparatus, Steam-engine	A. S. Walbridge	Malone, N. Y	Sept. 10, 1861	33, 274
Cut-off apparatus, Steam-engine	D. A. Woodbury	Rochester, N. Y	May 31, 1870	103, 698
Cut-off apparatus, Variable	T. May	Brooklyn, N. Y	Nov. 8, 1870	109, 137
Cut-off arrangement for steam-valves	J. Hornig	Newark, N. J	Nov. 22, 1859	26, 186
Cut-off attachment to slide-valves	T. Sault	New Haven, Conn	Mar. 28, 1871	113, 101
Cut-off, Automatic water	D. F. Sweet	Otsego, Mich	Feb. 8, 1870	99, 727
Cut-off, Automatic water-spout	E. Stewart	Fort Madison, Iowa	Mar. 28, 1871	113, 108
Cut-off, Blast-furnace	H. Davis	Newport, Ky	Apr. 18, 1871	113, 745
Cut-off, Cistern	F. Fischer	Quincy, Ill	Dec. 13, 1870	110, 128
Cut-off, Cistern	G. W. Howell	Covington, Ky	Sept. 9, 1873	142, 569
Cut-off, Cistern	J. P. Watson	Rochester, Minn	Mar. 1, 1870	100, 474
Cut-off, Cistern	C. Wuerz	Kimmswick, Mo	Sept. 16, 1873	142, 832
Cut-off, Electro-magnetic-engine	L. H. McCullough	Richmond, Ind	Feb. 26, 1867	62, 352
Cut-off for cistern-leaders	W. N. Hicks and F. Welker	Saint Louis, Mo	Nov. 27, 1866	60, 005
Cut-off for cisterns, Rain-water	X. Amoun	Sidney, Ohio	Sept. 14, 1869	94, 694
Cut-off for cisterns, Water	J. R. Manny	Chicago, Ill	Oct. 4, 1870	107, 936
Cut-off for fire-plug systems	F. W. Eames	Grand Rapids, Mich	Feb. 18, 1873	135, 976
Cut-off for oscillating-engines	W. Craig	Binghamton, N. Y	Oct. 15, 1861	33, 477
Cut-off for pipes	J. H. Perkins	Omaha, Nebr	Nov. 2, 1869	96, 478
Cut-off for rain-water pipes	C. Avery and J. W. Wetmore	Erie, Pa	July 25, 1871	117, 493
Cut-off for relays and other electro-magnetic instruments.	F. M. Perry	Barton, Vt	Aug. 2, 1870	105, 975
Cut-off for water-conductors	E. B. Armstrong	Columbus, Ohio	Sept. 10, 1867	68, 682
Cut-off for water-conductors	J. Ash	Sterling, Ill	Sept. 19, 1865	49, 960
Cut-off for water-conductors	H. Myers, jr	McLean, Ill	June 13, 1871	115, 977
Cut-off for water-spouts	H. W. Mosher	Aurora, Ill	Oct. 1, 1867	69, 359
Cut-off for engines of water-works, Variable	B. Holly	Lockport, N. Y	Apr. 25, 1871	114, 010
Cut-off gear	G. H. Corliss	Providence, R. I	July 29, 1851	8, 253
Cut-off gear for puppet-valve engines, Adjustable	H. Allen and D. G. Wells	New York, N. Y	Feb. 15, 1853	9, 582
Cut-off gear, Steam-engine	E. R. Arnold	Providence, R. I	May 17, 1859	23, 998
Cut-off gear, Steam-engine	J. Broughton	New York, N. Y	Dec. 21, 1858	22, 344
Cut-off gear, Steam-engine	C. P. Buckingham	Mount Vernon, Ohio	Aug. 23, 1859	25, 174
Cut-off gear, Steam-engine	P. W. Gates, D. R. Fraser, and T. Chalmers.	Chicago, Ill	Dec. 21, 1858	22, 361
Cut-off gear, Steam-engine	P. W. Gates, D. R. Fraser, and T. Chalmers.	Chicago, Ill	July 5, 1859	24, 624
Cut-off gear, Steam-engine	O. Leonard	Somerville, Mass	Mar. 18, 1856	14, 486
Cut-off gear, Steam-engine	A. K. Rider	Hydeville, Vt	Dec. 24, 1861	34, 013
Cut-off gear, Steam-engine	J. B. Root	New York, N. Y	Oct. 12, 1869	95, 838
Cut-off gear, Steam-engine	H. Withington	Philadelphia, Pa	Sept. 20, 1859	25, 541
Cut-off gear, Steam engine variable	A. Foster and N. Sutton	New York, N. Y	July 19, 1859	24, 801
Cut-off gear, Steam-engine variable	A. L. Holley	New York, N. Y	Apr. 19, 1859	23, 684
Cut-off gear, Steam-engine variable	B. Hotchkiss	New Haven, Conn	Apr. 19, 1859	23, 685
Cut-off gear, Steam-engine variable	J. Tremper	Buffalo, N. Y	Dec. 2, 1862	37, 063
Cut-off gear, Steam-engine variable	W. W. Wade	Springfield, Mass	Dec. 11, 1855	13, 934
Cut-off gear, Steam-engine variable	D. A. Woodbury	Rochester, N. Y	Apr. 19, 1859	23, 737
Cut-off gear, Variable	J. E. McKay	New York, N. Y	Sept. 12, 1871	118, 958
Cut-off, Governor	W. McCammon	Albany, N. Y	May 22, 1849	6, 462
Cut-off, Governor variable	H. Waterman	New York, N. Y	Mar. 4, 1851	7, 964
Cut-off, Hydrant	E. Bailey	Baltimore, Md	Aug. 26, 1862	36, 319
Cut-off motion for puppet-valves	S. H. Gilman	Cincinnati, Ohio	Dec. 10, 1850	7, 830
Cut-off, Piston-valve	G. McKay	Pittsfield, Mass	Apr. 17, 1849	6, 324
Cut-off, Rain-water	J. Abercrombie and E. D. Miner.	Morrisania, N. Y	Aug. 13, 1872	130, 400
Cut-off, Rain-water	L. Baltz	Saint Louis, Mo	Aug. 13, 1872	130, 352
Cut-off, Rain-water	D. W. Doty	Aurora, Ill	May 29, 1866	55, 072
Cut-off, Rain-water	E. Fleming	Ann Arbor, Mich	Aug. 17, 1869	93, 694
Cut-off, Rain-water	R. S. Laird and W. F. Stone	Sandwich, Ill	Oct. 20, 1868	83, 176
Cut-off, Rain-water	T. Leo	Cincinnati, Ohio	Apr. 16, 1872	125, 742
Cut-off, Rain-water	B. Rein	Marietta, Ohio	Aug. 15, 1871	118, 054
Cut-off, Rain water	C. and W. Scales	New Albany, Ind	Sept. 3, 1872	131, 121
Cut-off, Rain-water	J. Spear	Carbondale, Ill	Sept. 29, 1868	82, 653
Cut-off, Rain-water	J. Van Norman and W. Young	Easton, Pa	Nov. 3, 1868	83, 808
Cut-off, Rain-water	G. W. Wetmore	Erie, Pa	Mar. 25, 1873	137, 268
Cut-off regulator, Steam-engine	H. A. Luttgens	Paterson, N. J	Dec. 12, 1854	12, 064
Cut-off, Steam-engine	J. F. Allen	New York, N. Y	Mar. 10, 1857	16, 781

Index of patents issued from the United States Patent Office from 1790 *to* 1873, *inclusive*—Continued.

Invention.	Inventor.	Residence.	Date.	No.
Cut-off, Steam-engine	H. Allen and D. G. Wells	New York, N. Y	June 21, 1853	9,792
Cut-off, Steam-engine	C. Carr	Boston, Mass	Apr. 27, 1869	89,289
Cut-off, Steam-engine	S. Dunbar	New York, N. Y	June 1, 1869	90,643
Cut-off, Steam-engine	T. Hansbrow	Sacramento, Cal	Jan. 12, 1869	85,817
Cut-off, Steam-engine	H. O. Lothrop	Milford, Mass	Mar. 3, 1868	75,834
Cut-off, Steam-engine	J. McPherson	Brooklyn, N. Y	June 30, 1868	79,375
Cut-off, Steam-engine	J. H. Paine	Hartford, Conn	Jan. 24, 1865	46,020
Cut-off, Steam-engine	G. W. Rawson	Cambridgeport, Mass	Nov. 12, 1867	70,743
Cut-off, Steam-engine	G. W. Rawson	Cambridgeport, Mass	Oct. 6, 1868	82,751
Cut-off, Steam-engine	G. J. Roberts	Dayton, Ohio	Sept. 29, 1868	82,556
Cut-off, Steam-engine	A. P. Samuel	New York, N. Y	Jan. 19, 1858	19,154
Cut-off, Steam-engine	J. S. Shapter	New York, N. Y	Apr. 15, 1856	14,699
Cut-off, Steam-engine	A. Stuckenrath	New York, N. Y	Jan. 1, 1867	60,804
Cut-off, Steam-engine	W. Watts and F. A. Phelps	Newark, N. J	Jan. 10, 1871	110,943
Cut-off, Steam-engine	J. Widmer	New Haven, Conn	Aug. 31, 1858	21,399
Cut-off, Steam-engine	D. A. Woodbury	Rochester, N. Y	Apr. 5, 1859	23,521
Cut-off, Steam-engine	W. Wright	New York, N. Y	Oct. 10, 1871	119,908
Cut-off, Steam-engine adjustable	A. Hartupee and J. Morrow	Pittsburgh, Pa	Sept. 2, 1856	15,630
Cut-off, Steam-engine adjustable	H. J. and T. Hawkins	Mobile, Ala	June 24, 1856	15,181
Cut-off, Steam-engine adjustable	J. Rees	Pittsburgh, Pa	May 9, 1871	114,601
Cut-off, Steam-engine adjustable	W. Wright	Hartford, Conn	Nov. 25, 1856	16,132
Cut-off, Steam-engine automatic	D. A. Woodbury	Rochester, N. Y	Sept. 27, 1870	107,746
Cut-off, Steam-engine-governor	J. Felber	Saint Louis, Mo	Jan. 29, 1867	61,528
Cut-off, Steam-engine-governor	G. Milbank	Chillicothe, Mo	Jan. 25, 1870	99,220
Cut-off, Steam-engine variable	A. Crosby	Fredonia, N. Y	Jan. 19, 1858	19,134
Cut-off, Steam-engine variable	W. B. Cross	Sacramento, Cal	Jan. 24, 1871	111,180
Cut-off, Steam-engine variable	W. B. Cross	Sacramento, Cal	Aug. 8, 1871	117,747
Cut-off, Steam-engine variable	A. Crumbie and R. D. Briggs	Brooklyn, N. Y	May 3, 1859	23,830
Cut-off, Steam-engine variable	D. Fellenbaum	Lancaster, Pa	June 5, 1860	28,632
Cut-off, Steam-engine variable	C. H. Reynolds	Lewiston, Me	Sept. 16, 1856	15,745
Cut-off, Steam-engine variable	M. C. Taylor	Grass Valley, Cal	Dec. 21, 1869	98,122
Cut-off, Steam-engine variable	W. Wright	New York, N. Y	May 20, 1873	139,224
Cut-off valve	J. M. Albertson	New London, Conn	Oct. 10, 1865	50,320
Cut-off valve	H. Allen	New York, N. Y	Mar. 20, 1847	5,025
Cut-off valve	G. H. Babcock and S. Wilcox, jr	Providence, R. I	Apr. 24, 1866	54,090
Cut-off valve	H. H. Grame	New York, N. Y	Mar. 20, 1847	5,026
Cut-off valve	L. Griswold and G. Caul	Portland and York, Wis	July 23, 1867	67,043
Cut-off valve	J. L. Howes	Newark, N. J	Apr. 24, 1866	54,153
Cut-off valve	C. H. Parshall	Detroit, Mich	June 28, 1864	43,334
Cut-off valve	A. K. Rider	Lydeville, Vt	May 6, 1862	35,176
Cut-off valve	I. M. Scott and W. R. Eckart	San Francisco, Cal	June 25, 1867	66,046
Cut-off valve	R. Stewart	Elmira, N. Y	Jan. 23, 1866	52,221
Cut-off valve	D. Stoddart	Cincinnati, Ohio	May 29, 1855	12,966
Cut-off valve, Adjustable	G. W. Smith	New Haven, Conn	Dec. 26, 1871	122,198
Cut-off valve, Balance	B. F. McKinley	Falmouth, Ky	June 12, 1866	55,518
Cut-off-valve check for steam-engines	W. Wright	Hartford, Conn	June 21, 1856	15,208
Cut-off-valve gear	A. W. Almqvist and F. W. Ofeldt	New York, N. Y	Feb. 8, 1870	99,318
Cut-off-valve gear	W. Dawes	Leeds, England	Nov. 2, 1869	96,400
Cut-off-valve gear	G. W. Fisher and H Reid	Saint Louis, Mo	Dec. 20, 1870	110,223
Cut-off-valve gear	A. W. Foster, jr	Pittsburgh, Pa	Jan. 2, 1866	51,821
Cut-off-valve gear	A. Kendall	Buffalo, N. Y	May 19, 1868	77,986
Cut-off-valve gear	K. H. Loomis	Baltimore, Md	Aug. 8, 1865	49,284
Cut-off-valve gear	W. McClintock	Wilmington, Del	Oct. 3, 1865	50,304
Cut-off-valve gear	W. G. Pike	Philadelphia, Pa	Nov. 20, 1866	59,777
Cut-off-valve gear	J. T. Rich	Philadelphia, Pa	Apr. 3, 1866	53,680
Cut-off-valve gear	J. B. Schenck	Ansonia, Conn	Apr. 17, 1855	12,729
Cut-off-valve gear	S. Stanton	Newburgh, N. Y	July 14, 1868	80,025
Cut-off-valve gear	R. Stewart	Elmira, N. Y	May 19, 1863	38,611
Cut-off-valve gear	R. Stewart	Elmira, N. Y	June 30, 1863	39,075
Cut-off-valve gear	C. W. Wailey	New Orleans, La	Jan. 11, 1870	98,724
Cut-off-valve gear	S. H. Whitmore	Decatur, Ill	Mar. 28, 1871	113,232
Cut-off-valve gear	W. Wright	New York, N. Y	Mar. 24, 1868	76,027
Cut-off-valve gear	J. N. Wrigley and G. Smith	Newark, N. J	Oct. 1, 1867	69,526
Cut-off valve, Governor	K. H. Loomis	Baltimore, Md	Aug. 23, 1864	43,920
Cut-off-valve motion	S. W. Rogers	Baltimore, Md	Dec. 21, 1852	9,488
Cut-off-valve motion	F. B. Stevens	Weehawken, N. J	Dec. 3, 1861	33,855
Cut-off valve, Oscillating engine	H. E. Canfield	New York, N. Y	Oct. 9, 1855	13,637
Cut-off valve, Rotary balanced	P. Shellenback and F. Brilmayer	Hamilton, Ohio	Mar. 11, 1873	136,622
Cut-off valve, Sliding	S. P. Winne	Albany, N. Y	Apr. 10, 1849	6,306
Cut-off valve, Steam	R. Sanderson	Cleveland, Ohio	July 28, 1868	80,509
Cut-off valve, Steam	W. M. Stevenson	Sharon, Pa	Nov. 26, 1867	71,547
Cut-off-valve gear and valve	G. E. Noyes	Washington, D. C	July 5, 1870	105,119
Cut-off-valve gear and valve, Variable	W. Brown	Hoboken, N. J	Apr. 26, 1870	102,367
Cut off-valve gear, Regulating	S. W. Robinson	Champaign, Ill	May 16, 1871	114,861
Cut-off-valve gear, Steam-engine	H. Allen	New York, N. Y	Dec. 15, 1857	18,837
Cut-off-valve gear, Steam-engine	W. L. Colborne	Elmira, N. Y	Mar. 1, 1864	41,810
Cut-off-valve gear, Steam-engine	P. W. Gates, D. R. Fraser, and T. Chalmers	Chicago, Ill	Oct. 5, 1858	21,668
Cut-off-valve gear, Steam-engine	J. F. Hamilton	Pittsburgh, Pa	July 14, 1863	39,228
Cut-off-valve gear, Steam-engine	J. Montfort	Newburgh, N. Y	Sept. 12, 1871	118,873
Cut-off-valve gear, Steam-engine	C. W. Wailey	New Orleans, La	Sept. 15, 1868	82,184
Cut-off-valve gear, Steam-engine	W. Wright	New York, N. Y	Nov. 20, 1866	59,886
Cut-off-valve gear, Steam-engine	W. Wright	Danvers Centre, Mass	Mar. 12, 1867	62,797
Cut-off-valve gear, Steam-engine variable	M. W. Baldwin	Philadelphia, Pa	Sept. 13, 1853	10,007
Cut off-valve gear, Steam-engine variable	J. F. Hamilton	Pittsburgh, Pa	July 14, 1863	39,229
Cut-off-valve gear, Steam-engine variable	H. O. Perry	Buffalo, N. Y	Mar. 21, 1865	46,932
Cut-off-valve gear, Steam-engine variable	W. Wright	New York, N. Y	Nov. 20, 1866	59,887
Cut-off-valve gear, Variable	J. L. Dickinson	Dubuque, Iowa	Sept. 3, 1867	68,492
Cut-off-valve gear, Variable	G. E. Long	Harrisburgh, Pa	June 7, 1870	103,804
Cut-off-valve gear, Variable	N. K. Lynch	New York, N. Y	Apr. 5, 1870	101,634
Cut-off valve, Steam-engine	H. Allen	New York	Aug. 21, 1841	2,227
Cut-off valve, Steam-engine	H. Allen	New York	Apr. 30, 1842	2,597
Cut-off valve, Steam-engine	E R. Arnold	Providence, R. I	Nov. 1, 1859	25,936
Cut-off valve, Steam-engine	J. Broughton	New York, N. Y	Dec. 3, 1861	33,821
Cut-off valve, Steam-engine	B. Bunce	New York, N. Y	Oct. 19, 1858	21,813
Cut-off valve, Steam-engine	A. S. Cameron	New York, N. Y	Feb. 15, 1859	22,935

Index of patents issued from the United States Patent Office from 1790 *to* 1873, *inclusive*—Continued.

Invention.	Inventor.	Residence.	Date.	No.
Cut-off valve, Steam-engine	I. M. Colman	Milwaukee, Wis	Nov. 30, 1858	22, 164
Cut-off valve, Steam-engine	G. Frost	Brooklyn, N. Y	Sept. 25, 1860	30, 138
Cut-off valve, Steam-engine	N. T. Greene	Bridgeport, Conn	Mar. 13, 1855	12, 507
Cut-off valve, Steam-engine	J. Jackman, jr	Newburyport, Mass	Aug. 24, 1858	21, 300
Cut-off valve, Steam-engine	W. A. Lighthall	Albany, N. Y	Nov. 26, 1840	1, 870
Cut-off valve, Steam-engine	S. McCarter	Norristown, Pa	Aug. 22, 1871	118, 340
Cut-off valve, Steam-engine	S. Parks, jr	Brooklyn, N. Y	June 11, 1842	2, 662
Cut-off valve, Steam-engine	F. Perry	Newark, N. J	July 31, 1855	13, 359
Cut-off valve, Steam-engine	G. H. Reynolds	New York, N. Y	Dec. 6, 1859	26, 400
Cut-off valve, Steam-engine	T. Rodgers	Paterson, N. J	May 1, 1845	4, 028
Cut-off valve, Steam-engine	C. B. Sheller	Bellefontaine, Ohio	Aug. 13, 1872	130, 541
Cut-off valve, Steam-engine	R. L. and F. B. Stevens	New York, N. Y	Jan. 25, 1841	1, 950
Cut-off valve, Steam-engine	J. D. Whelpley	Boston, Mass	Mar. 1, 1864	41, 800
Cut-off valve, Steam-engine	G. S. Young	Clearfield, Pa	Jan. 3, 1871	110, 813
Cut-off valve, Steam-engine variable	I. M. Colman	Milwaukee, Wis	Apr. 12, 1859	23, 553
Cut-off valve, Variable	L. Eikenberry	Philadelphia, Pa	Apr. 1, 1862	34, 821
Cut-off, Variable	W. G. Pike	Philadelphia, Pa	Nov. 21, 1865	51, 081
Cut-off, Variable	J. Randles	Jersey City, N. J	Mar. 22, 1870	101, 162
Cut-off valves, Arrangement of means for operating steam-engine.	H. E. Canfield	New York, N. Y	Apr. 15, 1856	14, 649
Cut-off valves, Device for operating	K. H. Loomis	New York, N. Y	May 9, 1871	114, 574
Cut-off valves, Device for operating steam-engine	W. W. W. Wood and H. Howson.	Philadelphia, Pa	July 5, 1859	24, 707
Cut-off valves, Operating	S. Barber	New York, N. Y	May 22, 1847	5, 129
Cut-off valves, Operating	H. T. Peak	Charleston, S. C	Sept. 25, 1847	5, 310
Cut-off valves, Means of operating	W. A. Foster	Fitchburgh, Mass	Mar. 18, 1862	34, 679
Cut-off valves, Method of operating	G. B. McDonald	Louisville, Ky	Jan. 5, 1864	41, 083
Cut-off valves, Method of operating steam-engine	J. Cochrane	Baltimore, Md	Apr. 16, 1845	4, 002
Cut-off valves, Method of operating steam-engine	W. Wright	Hartford, Conn	June 30, 1863	39, 089
Cut-off valves, Mode of tripping	F. E. Sickels	New York, N. Y	Sept. 19, 1845	4, 201
Cut-off valves, Operating steam-engine	T. Ashcroft	Dorchester, Mass	June 13, 1854	11, 055
Cut-off valves, Operating steam-engine	W. Lowe	Hartford, Conn	July 11, 1854	11, 294
Cut-off valves, Operating steam-engine	G. H. Reynolds	Medford, Mass	Feb. 3, 1857	16, 570
Cut-off valves, Operating steam-engine	W. Wright	Hartford, Conn	Jan. 3, 1854	10, 398
Cut-off valves, Operating steam-engine	W. Wright	Hartford, Conn	June 24, 1856	15, 207
Cut-off, Water	R. M. Bixby	Iowa City, Iowa	Feb. 14, 1871	111, 720
Cut-off, Water	J. W. Burkholder	Rushford, Minn	Feb. 27, 1872	124, 033
Cut-off, Water	W. H. Lilley	Hannibal, Mo	Apr. 9, 1872	125, 581
Cut-off, Water	P. B. Peters	Marietta, Ohio	Dec. 19, 1871	121, 960
Cut-off, Water	W. Phipps	Milwaukee, Wis	Aug. 29, 1871	118, 639
Cut-off, Water-pipe	F. H. Goddard	Omaha, Nebr	Feb. 27, 1872	124, 053
Cut-off with secondary toe No. 1, Adjustable lever	H. Allen	New York, N. Y	Feb. 6, 1849	6, 093
Cut-off with secondary toe No. 2, Adjustable lever	H. Allen	New York, N. Y	Feb. 6, 1849	6, 092
Cut-offs, Means of regulating and working steam-valves as.	C. H. Brown and C. Burleigh	Fitchburgh, Mass	Jan. 15, 1856	14, 125
Cut-offs, Means of regulating steam-engine variable	H. S. Hopkins	Providence, R. I	Mar. 25, 1856	14, 545
Cutter:				
See Angle-iron cutter.				
Apple cutter.				
Bait and vegetable cutter.				
Bait or meat cutter.				
Band-cutter.				
Barrel-head cutter.				
Beef and vegetable cutter.				
Belt-cutter.				
Bias-cutter.				
Billiard-cue cutter.				
Biscuit-cutter.				
Blacking-cutter.				
Blind-slat cutter.				
Bog-cutter.				
Bolt-cutter.				
Bolt and rivet cutter.				
Bolt and rod cutter.				
Boot-pack cutter.				
Bread-cutter.				
Broom-corn cutter.				
Bung-cutter.				
Butter-cutter.				
Button-hole cutter.				
Cabbage-cutter.				
Cake-cutter.				
Candy-cutter.				
Carpet-rag cutter.				
Cheese-cutter.				
Cigar-cutter.				
Cigar-tip cutter.				
Cigar-tuck cutter.				
Circular cutter.				
Circular and elliptical cutter.				
Corn and cob cutter.				
Corn-cake cutter.				
Corn-cob cutter.				
Corn-stalk cutter.				
Crout-cutter.				
Cue-cutter.				
Curd-cutter.				
Cylindrical cutter.				
Die-cutter.				
Doughnut-cutter.				
Dovetail-cutter.				
Dried-beef cutter.				
Feed-cutter.				
File-cutter.				
Fish-bait cutter.				
Fodder-cutter.				
Gear-cutter.				

Index of patents issued from the United States Patent Office from 1790 *to* 1873, *inclusive*—Continued.

Invention.	Inventor.	Residence.	Date.	No.
Cutter—Continued.				
See Glass-cutter.				
Grain-cutter.				
Hand-sole cutter.				
Harvester-cutter.				
Heel-cutter.				
Hemp-cutter.				
Hoop-lock cutter.				
Ice-cutter.				
Key-cutter.				
Key-hole cutter.				
Key-seat cutter.				
Lath-cutter.				
Leather-cutter.				
Lumber-cutter.				
Lumber tonguing and grooving cutter.				
Meat-cutter.				
Meat and vegetable cutter.				
Metal-cutter.				
Metallic-bar cutter.				
Molding-cutter.				
Molding-machine cutter.				
Nail-cutter.				
Operating cutter.				
Paper-cutter.				
Paper-box cutter.				
Pasteboard cutter.				
Pastry-cutter.				
Peach-cutter.				
Peg-cutter.				
Photographic-print cutter.				
Picket-cutter.				
Pipe-cutter.				
Pipe and rod cutter.				
Planing-cutter.				
Plug-cutter.				
Potato-cutter.				
Rag-cutter.				
Rattan-cutter.				
Relisher and wedge cutter.				
Revolving cutter.				
Ring-twine cutter.				
Rivet-cutter.				
Rock-channeling-machine cutter.				
Root-cutter.				
Rotary cutter.				
Sausage-cutter.				
Screw-cutter.				
Screw-thread cutter.				
Segment-cutter.				
Sewing-machine cutter.				
Sewing-machine-thread cutter.				
Shaft and pipe cutter.				
Sheet-iron cutter.				
Shingle-cutter.				
Shingle-band cutter.				
Shoe-lacing cutter.				
Slaw-cutter.				
Snuff-cutter.				
Soap-cutter.				
Sod-cutter.				
Sole-cutter.				
Stalk-cutter.				
Stave-cutter.				
Stencil-plate cutter.				
Stone-cutter.				
Stone-molding cutter.				
Straw-cutter.				
Stubble-cutter.				
Sugar-cutter.				
Thread-cutter.				
Tin-bottom cutter.				
Tobacco-cutter.				
Tobacco-plant cutter.				
Tonguing and grooving cutter.				
Tube-cutter.				
Tube-hole cutter.				
Twine-cutter.				
Twine or thread cutter.				
Vegetable-cutter.				
Veneer-cutter.				
Vine-cutter.				
Washer-cutter.				
Weed-cutter.				
Well-casing cutter.				
Welt and strap cutter.				
Wire cutter.				
Wrapper-cutter.				
Wrench and bolt cutter.				
Cutter-bars in grinding, Device for holding	W. H. Daniels	Bryan, Ohio	Apr. 22, 1873	138,136
Cutter-bench and knee, Bent	E. Milner	Strathroy, Canada	Nov. 21, 1871	121,058
Cutter-bits for rifling-machines, Apparatus for grinding.	D. Slate	Hartford, Conn	Feb. 16, 1864	41,646
Cutter, grater, and sharpener	E. Culver	Shelburne Falls, Mass	May 28, 1867	65,177
Cutter-head	D. C. Allen	Concord, N. H.	Aug. 12, 1873	141,744
Cutter-head	E. Benjamin	Chicago, Ill	Sept. 9, 1873	142,669
Cutter-head	M. W. Clark	Worcester, Mass	July 27, 1869	93,056
Cutter-head	M. W. Clark	Worcester, Mass	Apr. 26, 1870	102,222

Index of patents issued from the United States Patent Office from 1790 *to* 1873, *inclusive*—Continued.

Invention.	Inventor.	Residence.	Date.	No.
Cutter-head	J. F. W. Erdmann	Philadelphia, Pa	July 15, 1873	140, 905
Cutter-head	W. G. Farmer	Burlington, Vt	Oct. 6, 1868	82, 699
Cutter-head	S. Fawcett	Rochester, N. Y	Sept. 15, 1868	82, 211
Cutter-head	H. Fletcher	Louisville, Ky	Oct. 14, 1873	143, 565
Cutter-head	J. Gage	Henniker, N. H	Sept. 7, 1869	94, 580
Cutter-head	E. B. Hayes	Vergennes, Vt	Aug. 22, 1871	118, 365
Cutter-head	J. Kindleberger and W. A. Arnold.	San Francisco, Cal	Oct. 12, 1869	95, 809
Cutter-head	M. Lehman	Cincinnati, Ohio	Aug. 10, 1869	93, 628
Cutter-head	T. Long	Cerro Gordo, Ill	Nov. 26, 1872	133, 463
Cutter-head	C. E. McBeth	Hamilton, Ohio	Oct. 3, 1871	119, 632
Cutter-head	R. N. Meriam	Worcester, Mass	Dec. 28, 1869	98, 396
Cutter-head	D. W. Perry	Wilkesbarre, Pa	Nov. 15 1870	109, 244
Cutter-head	C. Richards and W. Curtiss	Cleveland, Ohio	June 15, 1869	91, 269
Cutter-head	G. Rowe and S. W. Nelson	Worcester, Mass	July 7, 1868	79, 690
Cutter-head	E. A. Rowley	Williamsport, Pa	Apr. 9, 1872	125, 618
Cutter-head	A. D. Sherar	Baltimore, Md	Apr. 2, 1872	125, 340
Cutter-head	A. H. Shipman	Arcadia, N. Y	Aug. 19, 1873	142, 048
Cutter-head	G. E. Somers	Waterbury, Conn	Aug. 9, 1870	106, 291
Cutter-head	A. L. Sweet	Norwich, Conn	Apr. 4, 1871	113, 464
Cutter-head	H. Thompson	Worcester, Mass	Dec. 21, 1869	98, 124
Cutter-head	A. Van Vleck	Jordan, N. Y	Feb. 20, 1872	123, 800
Cutter-head	J. V. Woolsey	Sandusky, Ohio	Aug. 8, 1871	117, 850
Cutter-head	E. S. Wright	New York, N. Y	Sept. 1, 1868	81, 859
Cutter-head and table-rest for cutting irregular forms.	J. P. Grosvenor	Lowell, Mass	May 25, 1858	20, 345
Cutter-head for dressing moldings	J. Temple	Terre Haute, Ind	Dec. 3, 1867	71, 817
Cutter-head for irregular form	D. Dunlap	Concord, N. H	Aug. 7, 1855	13, 386
Cutter-head for matching boards, Rotary	G. Greenwood	Lawrence, Mass	Feb. 18, 1873	135, 907
Cutter-head or moldings	J. Whitworth	Cleveland, Ohio	Dec. 3, 1867	71, 670
Cutter-head, Rotary	I. P. Tice	Baltimore, Md	Dec. 6, 1859	26, 383
Cutter-heads, Method of securing knife to	W. D. Hooker	Dedham, Mass	May 13, 1856	14, 871
Cutter-heads, pulleys, &c., Fastening	J. Du Bois and E. F. Bengler	Williamsport, Pa	Mar. 29, 1870	101, 238
Cutter-stock	J. Peace	Camden, N. J	Jan. 3, 1865	45, 742
Cutters for turning, Arrangement of	M. Roberts	South Levant, Me	Aug. 23, 1853	9, 957
Cutters in their heads for irregular forms, Method of operating.	J. Fear	Chicago, Ill	June 17, 1856	15, 153
Cutting and bending sheet-metal, Machine for	J. R. Maitland	Little Rock, Ark	May 2, 1871	114, 311
Cutting and coring knife, Apple	C. D. House	Lake Village, N. H	Feb. 2, 1869	86, 401
Cutting and grasping shears	S. W. Valentine	Boston, Mass	Aug. 1, 1865	49, 178
Cutting and grinding apparatus	P. Miles	New Haven, Conn	Jan. 8, 1861	31, 098
Cutting and polishing compound	J. P. Hall	New York, N. Y	July 27, 1869	92, 962
Cutting-blocks, Machine for leveling	A. Davis	Oxford, Mass	Sept. 12, 1871	118, 912
Cutting-board	R. C. Hussey	Milford, Mass	Aug. 28, 1866	57, 513
Cutting-box	W. Green	Kinzua, Pa	Mar. 6, 1866	52, 992
Cutting-box	C. Sewerkrop	Louisville, Ky	Aug. 7, 1860	29, 524
Cutting-box	W. Willis	South Carolina	Aug. 24, 1822	....
Cutting cavities, spherical, ellipsoidal, &c., Machine for.	I. B. Hartwell	Woodstock, Vt	July 3, 1855	13, 169
Cutting, grinding, and polishing tools, Manufacture of.	A. K. Eaton	Piermont, N. Y	July 12, 1870	105, 320
Cutting irregular forms, Feeding-apparatus for machines for.	C. P. Bailey	Zanesville, Ohio	Dec. 19, 1854	12, 088
Cutting irregular forms in wood	D. George and H. Robertson	Granville, Ohio	Oct. 24, 1848	5, 873
Cutting irregular forms, Machine for	A. Aldrich	Princeton, Mass	Sept. 26, 1854	11, 738
Cutting irregular forms, Machine for	A. Babbett	Auburn, N. Y	June 19, 1855	13, 076
Cutting irregular forms, Machine for	I. S. Barber	Boston, Mass	May 15, 1855	12, 884
Cutting irregular forms, Machine for	J. W. Campbell	New York, N. Y	June 13, 1871	115, 820
Cutting irregular forms, Machine for	W. N. Oakes	Dana, Mass	June 8, 1858	20, 505
Cutting irregular forms, Machine for	O. L. Reynolds	Dover, N. H	Aug. 15, 1854	11, 533
Cutting irregular forms, Machine for	J. Russell	Philadelphia, Pa	Jan. 3, 1854	10, 369
Cutting irregular forms, Machine for	C. Spofford	Amesbury, Mass	Oct. 7, 1856	15, 859
Cutting irregular forms, Machine for	H. D. Stover	Boston, Mass	Aug. 31, 1858	21, 379
Cutting irregular forms, Machine for	H. D. Stover and J. W. Ricknell	Boston, Mass	Mar. 11, 1856	14, 421
Cutting irregular forms, Machine for	I. P. Tice	Baltimore, Md	May 24, 1859	24, 163
Cutting irregular forms, Machine for	W. Wadleigh	Hill, N. H	Jan. 2, 1855	12, 174
Cutting irregular forms, Machine for	P. H. Wait	Barkersville, N. Y	Aug. 28, 1855	13, 511
Cutting-machine	W. H. Johnson	Springfield, Mass	May 19, 1868	77, 985
Cutting-machine	M. H. Merriam and E. L. Norton	Charlestown, Mass	June 5, 1866	55, 336
Cutting-machine, Reversing	S. D. Tripp	Lynn, Mass	Sept. 1, 1868	81, 707
Cutting-machine, Rotary	J. J. Butler	Cincinnati, Ohio	Dec. 11, 1866	60, 341
Cutting objects with straight sides and semicircular ends, Machine for.	C. W. Packer	Philadelphia, Pa	Dec. 20, 1864	45, 565
Cutting or lap board	N. O'Donnell	Cincinnati, Ohio	Sept. 13, 1870	107, 285
Cutting polygonal surfaces in timber, Machine for	E. Unger	Dayton, Ohio	Dec. 20, 1853	10, 346
Cutting-press	N. J. Simonds	Woburn, Mass	May 23, 1871	115, 118
Cutting, punching, and bending machine	C. Wright	Newark, N. J	Apr. 12, 1864	42, 325
Cutting, punching, and upsetting, Compound tool for.	A. A. Kent	Lyons, Iowa	Nov. 19, 1867	71, 181
Cutting-shears	R. O. Wood	Niagara Falls, N. Y	Aug. 22, 1871	118, 419
Cutting thin material, Method of	A. Delkescamp	Brooklyn, N. Y	Mar. 19, 1872	124, 669
Cutting-tool	B. F. Allen	Boston, Mass	Feb. 13, 1872	123, 604
Cutting-tool	G. L. Jaeger	New York, N. Y	Dec. 17, 1867	72, 400
Cutting-tool	M. J. McIlyn	Roxbury, Mass	Oct. 8, 1867	69, 689
Cyanogen and iron, Compound of	H. Halvorson	Cambridge, Mass	June 7, 1864	43, 022
Cylinder and cone, Casting chilled	J. Harley	Pittsburgh, Pa	Mar. 3, 1835	....
Cylinder, Apparatus for straightening	T. F. Hammer	Branford, Conn	Apr. 23, 1872	125, 892
Cylinder boat	A. Kendall	Washington, D. C	Sept. 2, 1834	....
Cylinder-boring apparatus	L. B. Flanders	Philadelphia, Pa	June 25, 1867	66, 011
Cylinder, Co-operating frictionless	J. P. Sawin	Roxbury, Mass	Jan. 24, 1811	....
Cylinder engine, Revolving	J. Allonas and W. Bauman	Mansfield, Ohio	Aug. 29, 1871	118, 503
Cylinder engine, Revolving	J. S. Foster	Virginia, Nev	Nov. 28, 1865	51, 166
Cylinder engine, Revolving	C. F. Ruset	Communipaw, N. J	Oct. 16, 1866	58, 891
Cylinder engine, Revolving	C. Scott and W. H. Morton	Hamilton, Ohio	Aug. 20, 1867	68, 008
Cylinder engine, Rotating	R. L. Cohen	Philadelphia, Pa	Mar. 14, 1871	112, 688
Cylinder engine, Triple	P. Brotherhood	Notting Hill, England	Dec. 23, 1873	145, 719
Cylinder, Expanding	P. Maltby	Kent, Ohio	Dec. 4, 1866	60, 214
Cylinder for drying paper, warp, thread, &c., Drying	M. A. Furbush	Philadelphia, Pa	Oct. 4, 1864	44, 524

Index of patents issued from the United States Patent Office from 1790 *to* 1873, *inclusive*—Continued.

Invention.	Inventor.	Residence.	Date.	No.
Cylinder for machine-cards	C. E. Brownell	East Haddam, Conn	Mar. 25, 1862	24, 734
Cylinder for smoothing walks, &c	J. Giles and C. B. Tompkins	Dryden and Ulysses, N. Y.	Nov. 15, 1859	26, 100
Cylinder for spreaders, cotton-gins, &c., Brush	A. M. Laupher	Gloucester, N. J	Sept. 31, 1858	21, 568
Cylinder-heads, Machine for grinding	J. Shirrell	Paterson, N. J	Sept. 16, 1873	142, 874
Cylinder, Hydraulic	D. Fitzgerald	New York, N. Y	Dec. 16, 1862	37, 195
Cylinder, Magnetic	S. Browning	Franconia, N. H	Nov. 25, 1814	......
Cylinder mill for grinding corn and other grain	H. W. Pitts	Wilsonville, Ala	July 1, 1840	1, 670
Cylinder mill for granulating corn, powder, bark, &c.	J. Wilson	New London, Conn	July 23, 1841	2, 192
Cylinder, Mixing and drying	L. B. Pitcher	Salina, N. Y	Nov. 12, 1867	70, 742
Cylinder, Multiplying reacting hollow	T. Powell	New York, N. Y	Dec. 3, 1813	....
Cylinder-press fan-fly attachment	P. A. Cotter	Boston, Mass	Apr. 8, 1873	137, 597
Cylinder, Pulverizing and mixing	W. Coggeshall and J. W. Stanley.	Springfield, Ohio., and Chicago, Ill.	July 13, 1869	92, 585
Cylinder, Steam	W. Corliss	Providence, R. I	Dec. 31, 1872	134, 362
Cylinder, Steam-drying	J. Booth	Pawtucket, R. I	Mar. 31, 1857	16, 905
Cylinder, Steam-drying	H. W. Butterworth	Philadelphia, Pa	June 25, 1867	66, 075
Cylinders, Apparatus for boring	S. R. Wilmot	Bridgeport, Conn	Sept. 20, 1864	44, 296
Cylinders, Apparatus for sizing glass	L. B. Flanders	Philadelphia, Pa	Nov. 10, 1868	84, 040
Cylinders, Arrangement for ports in steam	B. Eaton	Roanoke, Ind	Apr. 28, 1857	17, 142
Cylinders, Boring and squaring off	J. C. Chapman	Charlestown, Mass	Jan. 13, 1863	37, 384
Cylinders, Boring-bar for facing the ends of	J. Flower	Detroit, Mich	Dec. 26, 1871	122, 243
Cylinders, Casting copper	F. Adams	Somerville, Mass	Aug. 2, 1859	24, 915
Cylinders, Casting hollow	J. W. Brittin	Black Rock, Conn	Jan. 25, 1870	99, 144
Cylinders, Casting toothed	H. W. Cornell	Owego, N. Y	Sept. 5, 1871	118, 693
Cylinders, Device for cutting section of annular	J. O. Joyce	Dayton, Ohio	Dec. 8, 1868	84, 697
Cylinders, Lubricator for steam-engine	J. Henwood	New York, N. Y	Mar. 10, 1857	16, 796
Cylinders, Machine for boring and facing	J. MacDonald	Boston, Mass	Oct. 21, 1873	143, 917
Cylinders, Machine for boring curved	W. Wright	New York, N. Y	May 3, 1864	42. 616
Cylinders, Machine for cutting teeth on	S. B. Dean, W. T. Nicholson, and G. Ames.	Boston, Mass., Providence, R. I, and Oswego, N. Y.	Aug. 13, 1872	130, 361
Cylinders, Machine for facing	T. M. Henderson and F. L. McDonald.	Omaha, Nebr	Dec. 2, 1873	145, 103
Cylincers, Machine for making wire	C. H. Latham	Lowell, Mass	Apr. 18, 1871	113, 779
Cylinders, Machine for polishing the inner surfaces of.	T. Goodrum	Providence, R. I	July 16, 1872	129, 402
Cylinders, Machine for turning	J. M. Poole	Wilmington, Del	July 7, 1868	79, 683
Cylinders, Machine for turning	G. Sibley	Troy, N. H	July 3, 1860	29, 014
Cylinders, Manner of mounting hollow revolving	L. B. Pitcher	Salina, N. Y	Sept. 20, 1870	107, 534
Cylinders, Method of forming	H. Willard	Grand Rapids, Mich	May 10, 1870	103, 001
Cylinders, Method of lowering	G. R. Bramhall	Chicago, Ill	June 16, 1868	78, 860
Cylinders, Mode of making toothed	J. L. Tuttle	Lawrence, Mass	Oct. 30, 1849	6, 840
Cylinders, pulleys, &c., Mode of balancing	W. Kitson	Lowell, Mass	Dec. 20, 1870	110, 247
Cylinders, Repairing cast-iron	S. Falkenbury	Susquehannah Depot, Pa	June 22, 1858	20, 635
Cylinders to be polished, Clamp for holding	G. Williamson	Newark, N. J	Nov. 13, 1860	30, 660
Cylindrical boiler	P. M. Hackley	Hudson, N. Y	Oct. 9, 1813	....
Cylindrical box	E. Waters	Troy, N. Y	Jan. 30, 1855	12, 335
Cylindrical boxes, Machine for manufacturing	H. S. Smith, E. Hanson, and M. S. Richardson.	Rutland, Vt	Apr. 7, 1857	17, 001
Cylindrical brake	S. Cram	New York, N. Y	June 2, 1836	....
Cylindrical cutter for leather, &c	J. H. Golding	Liverpool, England	Dec. 22, 1868	85, 085
Cylindrical cutting-knives, Method of sharpening	J. H. and A. T. Goodell	New York, N. Y	May 1, 1860	28, 074
Cylindrical mold for rubber-goods, Machine for filling.	J. W. Cobb	Melrose, Mass	June 18, 1867	65, 794
Cylindrical or tapering sticks, Tool for cutting	G. Davis	Duquesne, Pa	July 13, 1858	20, 866
Cylindrical structures, Construction of double	D. L. Bartlett and G. H. Johnson.	Baltimore, Md	Aug. 28, 1866	57, 462
Cyphering-machine	S. J. Kelso	Detroit, Mich	Sept. 25, 1866	58, 347
D.				
Daguerreotype-apparatus	J. Brown	New York, N. Y	Nov. 15, 1853	10, 225
Daguerreotype-apparatus	W., W. H. and H. J. Lewis	New York, N. Y	Nov. 11, 1851	8, 513
Daguerreotype-apparatus for gilding plates	W. and W. H. Lewis	New York, N. Y	May 8, 1849	6, 431
Daguerreotype-apparatus for panoramic views	I. Van Bunschoten, J. G. Woodbridge, and W. Mann.	New York, N. Y	Apr. 17, 1849	6, 357
Daguerreotype-case	R. Hill	New York, N. Y	June 18, 1861	32, 562
Daguerreotype-case	I. F. Mascher	Philadelphia, Pa	Mar. 8, 1853	9, 611
Daguerreotype-case hinges, Fastening for	S. Peck	New Haven, Conn	Feb. 5, 1856	14, 202
Daguerreotype-case, Monumental	J. Bergstresser	Berrysburgh, Pa	Feb. 8, 1859	22, 850
Daguerreotype-cases, &c., Apparatus for the manufacture of.	H. T. Anthony and F. Phoebus	New York, N. Y	Mar. 23, 1854	10, 953
Daguerreotype-cases, Manufacture of	H. Halvorson	Cambridge, Mass	Aug. 7, 1855	13, 410
Daguerreotype-cases, Manufacture of	S. Peck	New Haven, Conn	Oct. 3, 1854	11, 758
Daguerreotype-cases, Mold for making	J. L. Baldwin	Newark, N. J	Feb. 11, 1862	34, 344
Daguerreotype-cases, &c., Process for ornamenting	J. F. Mascher	Philadelphia, Pa	Feb. 10, 1857	16, 600
Daguerreotype face-plates or mats, Machine for beveling and polishing the inner edges of.	E. Brown	Waterbury, Conn	July 3, 1855	13, 196
Daguerreotype-mat	J. Dean	Worcester, Mass	Dec. 24, 1861	34, 035
Daguerreotype-picture	C. J. Anthony	Pittsburgh, Pa	Jan. 1, 1851	7, 865
Daguerreotype-picture	H. E. Insley	New York, N. Y	Jan. 6, 1852	8, 633
Daguerreotype-picture case	A. F. Stiles	Southbury, Conn	Jan. 22, 1850	7, 041
Daguerreotype-pictures, Coloring	D. Davis, jr	Boston, Mass	Oct. 22, 1842	2, 826
Daguerreotype-pictures, Coloring	W. Thompson	Philadelphia, Pa	May 12, 1843	3, 085
Daguerreotype-plate buffing apparatus	W. and W. H. Lewis	New York, N. Y	July 22, 1851	8, 235
Daguerreotype-plate holder	P. H. Benedict	Syracuse, N. Y	Jan. 31, 1854	10, 466
Daguerreotype-plate holder	D. N. B. Coffin, jr	Lynn, Mass	Feb. 6, 1855	12, 344
Daguerreotype-plate holder	M. Finley	Canandaigua, N. Y	Oct. 4, 1853	10, 093
Daguerreotype-plate holder	J. Hill	Skaneateles, N. Y	Aug. 22, 1854	11, 565
Daguerreotype-plate holder	R. Knecht	Easton, Pa	Feb. 7, 1854	10, 508
Daguerreotype-plate holder	G. Mallory	New York, N. Y	Sept. 17, 1850	7, 655
Daguerreotype-plate holder	S. Peck	New Haven, Conn	Apr. 30, 1850	7, 326
Daguerreotype-plate holder	D. Shive	Philadelphia, Pa	Oct. 9, 1855	13, 665
Daguerreotype-plate-polishing machine	D. Shive	Philadelphia, Pa	Mar. 20, 1855	12, 560
Daguerreotype-plate vise	S. S. Day	New York, N. Y	Oct. 23, 1855	13, 701
Daguerreotype-plates, Apparatus for cleaning and buffing.	T. Longking	Brooklyn, N. Y	Jan. 31, 1854	10, 475
Daguerreotype-plates, Apparatus for holding	W. and W. H. Lewis	New York, N. Y	Oct. 23, 1849	6, 819

Index of patents issued from the United States Patent Office from 1790 *to* 1873, *inclusive*—Continued.

Invention.	Inventor.	Residence.	Date.	No.
Daguerreotype-plates, Apparatus for polishing	B. F. Upton	Bath, Me	Sept. 19, 1854	11, 709
Daguerreotype-plates, Block for holding	A. Beckers	New York, N. Y	Oct. 23, 1849	6, 812
Daguerreotype-plates, Box for coating	W. and W. H. Lewis	New York, N. Y	Nov. 15, 1853	10, 233
Daguerreotype-plates, Box for coating	J. H. Tompkins	Buffalo, N. Y	Jan. 15, 1856	14, 122
Daguerreotype-plates, Coloring	J. B. Isenring	Canton of St. Gall, Switzerland.	Jan. 30, 1846	4, 369
Daguerreotype-plates, Coloring	F. Langenheim	Philadelphia, Pa	Jan. 30, 1846	4, 370
Daguerreotype-plates, Machine for cleaning	C. Ketcham	Penn Yan, N. Y	June 29, 1858	20, 718
Daguerreotype-plates, Machine for polishing	T. Duryea	Williamsburgh, N. Y	June 15, 1852	9, 018
Daguerreotypes, Camera for taking stereoscopic and other.	S. A. Holmes	Brooklyn, N. Y	May 30, 1854	10, 987
Daguerreotypes, Coloring	W. A. Pratt	Alexandria, D. C	Mar. 14, 1846	4, 423
Daguerreoptyes, Coloring	B. R. Stevens and L. Morse	Lowell, Mass	Mar. 28, 1842	2, 522
Daguerreotypes for stereoscopes, Taking	A. S. Southworth and J. J. Hawes.	Boston, Mass	July 11, 1854	11, 304
Daguerreotypes, Gilding	C. L'Homdieu	Charleston, S. C	Oct. 26, 1852	9, 354
Daguerreotypes in monumental stones, Securing	S. Jenkins	West Cambridge, Mass	Mar. 11, 1851	7, 974
Daguerreotypes, Taking	J. A. Whipple	Boston, Mass	Jan. 23, 1849	6, 056
Daguerreotyping	W. Yarnall	Newark, Ohio	Dec. 28, 1852	9, 511
Daguerreotyping, Mercury bath for	B. F. Upton	Bath, Me	Apr. 12, 1853	9, 666
Dairy-apparatus	J. A. Whitney	New York, N. Y	Aug. 17, 1869	93, 936
Dairy-can	L. A. Sunderland	Chagrin Falls, Ohio	Aug. 6, 1867	67, 607
Dairy-cooler	D. Whitmer	Paradise, Pa	Dec. 7, 1826	....
Dairy-heater for heating water	G. W. McCammon and D. H. Burrell.	Manheim and Little Falls, N. Y.	May 16, 1781	114, 836
Dairy-house	L. D. Yerks	Downington, Pa	Mar. 27, 1866	53, 516
Dam	J. Du Bois	Williamsport, Pa	Sept. 2, 1862	36, 342
Dam, Adjustable	J. A. Wood	Pittsburgh, Pa	July 11, 1871	117, 028
Dam and level	B. Britten	Galena, Ill	Sept. 11, 1866	57, 852
Dam or water-weir, Adjustable	M. S. Wheaton	Riga, N. Y	Apr. 3, 1849	6, 266
Dam, Portable and adjustable still-water	S. Lewis	Brooklyn, N. Y	July 28, 1868	80, 492
Dam, River	P. Magrath	Philadelphia, Pa	Oct. 10, 1829	....
Dam, Self-acting	H. Werner	Louisville, Ky	Jan. 21, 1873	135, 023
Dam, Still-water adjustable	S. Lewis	Brooklyn, E. D., N. Y	Jan. 5, 1869	85, 598
Dams, Building	S. J. Burr	Chambersburgh, Pa	Feb. 28, 1833	....
Dams, Mode of constructing	W. P. Craig	Newport, Ky	July 8, 1856	15, 317
Dams, Mode of constructing	J. M. Syme	Richmond, Va	Feb. 22, 1830	....
Damask hair-seating, Figured	S. Ross	Camden, N. J	Sept. 18, 1841	2, 262
Damper	F. Bleier	Pittsburgh, Pa	Jan. 15, 1860	7, 015
Damper	E. and J. Bourne	Pittsburgh, Pa	Mar. 24, 1863	37, 947
Damper	S. R. Brann	Hillsborough, Ill	June 10, 1862	35, 500
Damper	M. C. Burleigh	Somersworth, N. H	July 12, 1870	105, 167
Damper	G. Chilsom	Boston, Mass	Apr. 29, 1862	35, 080
Damper	D. B. Cox	Troy, N. Y	Aug. 11, 1868	80, 920
Damper	A. E. Elmer	Springfield, Mass	Oct. 24, 1865	50, 569
Damper	I. L. Frankem	Indianapolis, Ind	Oct. 15, 1867	69, 791
Damper	J. W. Freer	Pittston, Pa	Jan. 31, 1871	111, 336
Damper	W. Hailes	Albany, N. Y	July 28, 1868	80, 476
Damper	E. C. Harrison	New York, N. Y	May 26, 1863	38, 678
Damper	W. B. Hayden	Columbus, Ohio	Sept. 26, 1871	119, 270
Damper	F. M. Hubbard	Protection, N. Y	Mar. 31, 1863	38, 045
Damper	J. G. Jennings	Cleveland, Ohio	Nov. 15, 1864	45, 045
Damper	W. Johnson	Milwaukee, Wis	Sept. 26, 1865	50, 133
Damper	M. W. Kidder	Lowell, Mass	Feb. 26, 1867	62, 341
Damper	J. Kinckerbocker	Hartford, Conn	July 11, 1865	48, 695
Damper	J. W. Martin	Milton, Mass	Mar. 22, 1864	42, 049
Damper	S. Munson	Joliet, Ill	Feb. 16, 1864	41, 636
Damper	W. W. Paxson	Point Pleasant, Pa	Jan. 8, 1867	61, 093
Damper	N. R. Ramsey	Orange, Mass	June 27, 1865	48, 491
Damper	H. Raymond	Racine, Wis	Aug. 9, 1864	43, 794
Damper	J. C. Rhodes	Stillwater, Minn	July 21, 1868	80, 223
Damper	W. Sanford	Brooklyn, N. Y	May 6, 1862	35, 179
Damper	J. F. Stafford	North Granville, N. Y	Nov. 19, 1867	71, 077
Damper	C. C. F. Stender	Chicago, Ill	Mar. 8, 1864	41, 869
Damper	L. C. Taber	Eaton, N. Y	Feb. 23, 1869	87, 221
Damper	G. Tainter	Watertown, Mass	Oct. 14, 1862	36, 679
Damper	L. S. Taylor	Sigel, Mo	Mar. 21, 1871	112, 863
Damper	H. B. Thomas	Racine, Wis	Apr. 8, 1862	34, 925
Damper	A. Tracy	Paris Hill, Me	May 23, 1871	115, 135
Damper	J. P. Tuttle	Warren, Ohio	Mar. 8, 1870	100, 692
Damper	P. Verbeck and O. T. Walker	Neenah, Wis	June 2, 1863	38, 776
Damper	N. W. Wheeler	Ripon, Wis	Feb. 2, 1864	41, 457
Damper and handle for anthracite coal stove	E. Nott	Schenectady, N. Y	June 29, 1833	....
Damper and register, Ventilating	W. J. Towne	Newton, Mass	Aug. 30, 1864	44, 030
Damper and shelf, Stove-pipe	E. H. Clinton and W. H. Lavinia	Chicago, Ill	May 23, 1871	115, 025
Damper and stove-pipe collar combined	A. L. Shontz	Quincy, Ill	Jan. 30, 1872	123, 298
Damper and valve regulator, Electro-magnetic	G. M. Sternberg	Fort Riley, Kans	Mar. 1, 1870	100, 462
Damper and ventilator	J. H. Littlefield	Cambridge, Mass	Sept. 12, 1865	49, 899
Damper and ventilator	J. L. Skinner	Amboy, Ill	Aug. 5, 1873	141, 601
Damper and ventilator, Combined	A. Anderson	London, Canada	Dec. 17, 1867	72, 261
Damper and ventilator, Stove-pipe	A. R. Burdick	Racine, Wis	Mar. 1, 1870	100, 369
Damper and ventilator, Thermo regulator for	J. N. Adams	Olathe, Kan	July 30, 1872	130, 002
Damper, Automatic	G. A. Townsend	Hornellsville, N. Y	Aug. 13, 1867	67, 687
Damper, Chimney	P. Baker	Oakland, Md	Apr. 4, 1871	113, 245
Damper, Chimney	A. Campbell	Philadelphia, Pa	Apr. 21, 1857	17, 077
Damper, Chimney	T. F. Engelbrecht	New York, N. Y	July 29, 1856	15, 458
Damper, Cooking-stove	H. L. Sheperd	Dayton, Ohio	Aug. 27, 1850	7, 607
Damper, Cooking-stove	L. L. Thomas	Dighton, Mass	July 19, 1859	24, 849
Damper die, Stove-pipe	J. Van Hagan	Chicago, Ill	Oct. 6, 1868	82, 771
Damper, Fire-place	J. Bradford	Charlotte, N. C	Oct. 8, 1872	131, 994
Damper, Fire-place	J. Bridgham	New York, N. Y	May 21, 1872	126, 927
Damper for air-tight stoves, Self-acting	S. P. Lyon	Farmington, Mich	Nov. 15, 1853	10, 234
Damper for chimneys, cranks, and wheels	J. Reilly and J. Flanagan	Waynesburgh, Pa	Mar. 10, 1827	....
Damper for fire-places, Adjustable	S Albertson	New York, N. Y	Nov. 20, 1866	59, 789
Damper for flat-iron heater	G. R. Moore	Lyons, Iowa	Mar. 5, 1867	62, 557
Damper for flues	J. Liming	Philadelphia, Pa	Dec. 20, 1864	45, 508
Damper for heating-drums, Adjustable	A. J. Lovejoy	Augusta, Me	Nov. 12, 1872	132, 913
Damper for hot-air furnaces	A. H. Mershon	Philadelphia, Pa	May 5, 1868	77, 512

Index of patents issued from the United States Patent Office from 1790 *to* 1873, *inclusive*—Continued.

Invention.	Inventor.	Residence.	Date.	No.
Damper for hot-air furnaces	A. C. Warren	Concord, N. H	Feb. 25, 1873	136, 291
Damper for hot-air furnaces, Self-adjusting	E. Barrows, jr	Brooklyn, N. Y	Mar. 23, 1858	19, 678
Damper for multitubular steam-boilers	J. R. Robinson	Boston, Mass	Mar. 19, 1861	31, 744
Damper for steam-boilers	J. R. Robinson	Boston, Mass	June 11, 1861	32, 533
Damper for sugar-furnaces	J. Jordon	Boston, Mass	Dec. 27, 1833	....
Damper for windows, Fire	M. J. Barwick	New York, N. Y	June 17, 1873	139, 999
Damper, Grate	J. O'Brien	New York, N. Y	Dec. 15, 1857	18, 885
Damper guard, Stove	R. R. Howell	Fostoria, Ohio	July 9, 1872	128, 880
Damper, Illuminating	J. H. Keyser	New York, N. Y	Sept. 15, 1868	82, 228
Damper in steam-boiler	H. McDonough	New York, N. Y	June 25, 1867	66, 161
Damper, Operating stove	O. Paddock	Watertown, N. Y	Feb. 18, 1862	34, 446
Damper or draft-regulator for stove	S. Oppenheimer	Peru, Ind	Dec. 11, 1866	60, 412
Damper, Oven	J. P. Sherwood	Fort Edwards, N. Y	Oct. 10, 1854	11, 794
Damper-regulator	B. Fitts	Worcester, Mass	Jan. 21, 1873	135, 103
Damper-regulator	J. How and C. W. Copeland	Brooklyn, N. Y	Feb. 2, 1858	19, 249
Damper-regulator	J. H. Murrill	Baltimore, Md	Oct. 4, 1870	107, 948
Damper-regulator	J. F. Neall and W. Myers	Philadelphia, Pa	Nov. 6, 1866	59, 430
Damper-regulator	W. Noyes	New York, N. Y	Dec. 13, 1864	45, 429
Damper regulator and indicator, Steam	C. H. Ford	Baltimore, Md	Jan. 16, 1866	52, 114
Damper regulator, Fire	P. Lamb	San Francisco, Cal	June 21, 1864	41, 213
Damper regulator, Fire	W. Webster	Morrisania, N. Y	Aug. 19, 1862	36, 252
Damper regulator, Steam-boiler	W. Webster	Morrisania, N. Y	Feb. 17, 1857	16, 664
Damper regulator, Steam-boiler	P. White	Brooklyn, N. Y	June 9, 1857	17, 533
Damper regulator, Steam-pressure	E. B. Beach	West Meriden, Conn	Oct. 8, 1872	131, 992
Damper regularor, Stove	L. Boore	Buffalo, N. Y	Mar. 26, 1872	124, 931
Damper, Self-regulating	C. H. Lavis	Philadelphia, Pa	June 20, 1865	48, 291
Damper, Stove	G. Asmus	Portage, Mich	Oct. 3, 1865	50, 216
Damper, Stove	G. Cessford	Utica, N. Y	Mar. 11, 1862	34, 660
Damper, Stove	E. F. Cook	Omaha, Nebr	Dec. 30, 1873	145, 989
Damper, Stove	A. Cowan	Scranton, Pa	July 9, 1872	128, 859
Damper, Stove	E. T. Duke	Plattsmouth, Nebr	Nov. 26, 1867	71, 368
Damper, Stove	H. H. Huntley	Quincy, Ill	Nov. 18, 1873	144, 676
Damper, Stove	L. W. Langdon	Northampton, Mass	Nov. 30, 1869	97, 414
Damper, Stove	E. Lohsand	La Porte, Ind	May 2, 1871	114, 453
Damper, Stove	H. Mallory	Milwaukee, Wis	June 15, 1869	91, 245
Damper, Stove	J. Smith and S. C. Brown	Richmond, Ind	Mar. 12, 1867	62, 896
Damper, Stove	G. W. Walker	Boston, Mass	June 19, 1866	55, 451
Damper, Stove	J. D. Willoughby	Washington, D. C	Feb. 4, 1873	135, 611
Damper, Stove	R. Worster	Central Falls, R. I	Oct. 28, 1873	144, 043
Damper, Stove self-regulating	B. Owen	Seneca Falls, N. Y	June 19, 1849	6, 546
Damper, Stove-pipe	L. O. Allen	Gardiner, Me	Dec. 15, 1868	84, 930
Damper, Stove-pipe	I. C. and A. B. Allerton	Aztalan, Wis	Sept. 12, 1865	51, 409
Damper, Stove-pipe	T. K. Anderson	Hornellsville, N. Y	Mar. 26, 1867	63, 196
Damper, Stove-pipe	T. K. Anderson	Hornellsville, N. Y	June 8, 1869	90, 912
Damper, Stove-pipe	J. Ash	Sterling, Ill	Oct. 17, 1871	119, 911
Damper, Stove-pipe	H. Baker	Lancaster, Pa	Jan. 25, 1870	99, 048
Damper, Stove-pipe	J. M. Baker	Aurora, Ill	Oct. 19, 1869	95, 967
Damper, Stove-pipe	R. R. Ball	West Meriden, Conn	Sept. 24, 1872	131, 591
Damper, Stove-pipe	J. Barton	Battle Creek, Mich	Feb. 13, 1866	52, 514
Damper, Stove-pipe	N. A. Boynton	New York, N. Y	July 4, 1871	116, 675
Damper, Stove-pipe	J. Bradshaw and S. C. Wilson	Albion, N. Y	June 6, 1865	48, 046
Damper, Stove-pipe	R. M. Breckenridge	West Meriden, Conn	Aug. 7, 1866	56, 891
Damper, Stove pipe	H. C. Brown	Buffalo, N. Y	May 30, 1865	47, 923
Damper, Stove-pipe	E. C. Chapman	Lacon, Ill	Nov. 4, 1873	144, 192
Damper, Stove-pipe	D. A. Cleaveland	Providence, R. I	Sept. 3, 1872	130, 979
Damper, Stove-pipe	A. Colton	Sycamore, Ill	Mar. 24, 1868	75, 863
Damper, Stove-pipe	B. F. Cowan	New York, N. Y	July 17, 1866	56, 379
Damper, Stove-pipe	E. Cox and A. W. Potter	Monroe, Wis	Aug. 6, 1867	67, 415
Damper, Stove-pipe	E. K. Dean	Bangor, Me	Feb. 18, 1873	136, 042
Damper, Stove-pipe	D. De Garmo	Rochester, N. Y	Jan. 29, 1867	61, 613
Damper, Stove-pipe	W. H. Deily	Sycamore, Ill	Oct. 20, 1868	83, 139
Damper, Stove-pipe	N. J. Eldred	Chicago, Ill	Sept. 25, 1866	58, 233
Damper, Stove-pipe	J. Emmert	Chicago, Ill	May 20, 1873	138, 997
Damper, Stove-pipe	L. S. Enos	Almond, N. Y	July 14, 1868	79, 817
Damper, Stove-pipe	C. R. Everson	Palmyra, N. Y	Dec. 4, 1866	60, 160
Damper, Stove-pipe	A. V. and A. F. Fletcher	Athol, Mass	June 6, 1865	48, 058
Damper, Stove-pipe	J. Fowler	Watertown, Wis	Aug. 29, 1865	49, 619
Damper, Stove-pipe	J. Fraser and O. S. Garretson	Buffalo, N. Y	Dec. 18, 1866	60, 498
Damper, Stove-pipe	B. French	Rochester, N. Y	Aug. 8, 1871	117, 762
Damper, Stove-pipe	E. M. Gardner	Nantucket, Mass	Apr. 18, 1865	47, 293
Damper, Stove-pipe	W. T. Gray	Galesburgh, Ill	May 7, 1867	64, 415
Damper, Stove-pipe	D. L. Grover	Groton, N. Y	Apr. 3, 1866	53, 695
Damper, Stove-pipe	W. Hailes and P. Finkle	Albany, N. Y	Sept. 10, 1867	68, 738
Damper, Stove-pipe	E. R. Hall and D. A. Keyes	Norfolk, Conn	May 16, 1871	114, 806
Damper, Stove-pipe	G. B. Halsted	New York, N. Y	Nov. 12, 1867	70, 836
Damper, Stove-pipe	R. Ham	Troy, N. Y	Sept. 28, 1869	95, 340
Damper, Stove-pipe	B. I. Harris	Harrisburgh, Pa	Sept. 25, 1866	58, 251
Damper, Stove-pipe	J. Healey, jr	Detroit, Mich	July 7, 1868	79, 758
Damper, Stove-pipe	R. M. Hermance	Half Moon, N. Y	May 3, 1870	102, 539
Damper, Stove-pipe	T. Hessenbruch	Philadelphia, Pa	Jan. 19, 1869	85, 931
Damper, Stove-pipe	M. Hicks	Richmond, Ill	May 29, 1866	55, 101
Damper, Stove-pipe	R. Hillson	Albany, N. Y	Jan. 30, 1872	123, 171
Damper, Stove-pipe	G. Hollinger and S. H. Fry	Rothsville, Pa	Apr. 26, 1870	102, 266
Damper, Stove-pipe	J. L. Howard	Hartford, Conn	Mar. 7, 1865	46, 670
Damper, Stove-pipe	Z. Hunt	Hudson, N. Y	July 16, 1861	32, 834
Damper, Stove-pipe	J. A. Jacobs	Pittsfield, N. H	July 24, 1866	56, 566
Damper, Stove-pipe	J. Johnson	Atkinson, Ill	July 14, 1868	79, 836
Damper, Stove-pipe	E. Kabisius	Davenport, Iowa	Apr. 2, 1867	63, 395
Damper, Stove-pipe	C. Kathan	Hardin, Iowa	July 25, 1865	48, 952
Damper, Stove-pipe	W. J. Keep	Troy, N. Y	Mar. 8, 1870	100, 641
Damper, Stove-pipe	W. J. Keep	Troy, N. Y	Apr. 26, 1870	102, 407
Damper, Stove-pipe	W. J. Keep	Troy, N. Y	Dec. 12, 1871	121, 877
Damper, Stove-pipe	J. C. Kennedy	Chicago, Ill	Oct. 6, 1868	82, 848
Damper, Stove-pipe	H. Kipe	Thornbury, Pa	Apr. 4, 1865	47, 111
Damper, Stove-pipe	W. H. Lutz	Lancaster, Pa	Feb. 28, 1871	112, 260
Damper, Stove-pipe	E. Mackwitz and W. Frankfurth.	Milwaukee, Wis	Jan. 24, 1865	46, 007
Damper, Stove-pipe	D. Manuel	Boston, Mass	Dec. 17, 1867	72, 212

Index of patents issued from the United States Patent Office from 1790 *to* 1873, *inclusive*—Continued.

Invention.	Inventor.	Residence.	Date.	No.
Damper, Stove-pipe	M. S. Marshall	Melrose, Mass	Mar. 5, 1867	62,655
Damper, Stove-pipe	S. Marvin	South Royalston, Mass	Apr. 10, 1866	53,925
Damper, Stove-pipe	J. C. Merritt	Wyoming, N. Y	Mar. 6, 1866	53,024
Damper, Stove-pipe	B. F. Miller	New York, N. Y	Aug. 7, 1866	56,975
Damper, Stove-pipe	R. S. Miller	Battle Creek, Mich	Aug. 28, 1866	57,544
Damper, Stove-pipe	M. F. Moody	Andover, N. H	Oct. 8, 1872	131,963
Damper, Stove pipe	J. A. Noble	Florence, Mass	Sept. 6, 1864	44,109
Damper, Stove-pipe	W. H. Nutting	Orange, Mass	July 31, 1866	56,789
Damper, Stove-pipe	S. R. Nye	Barre, Mass	Apr. 24, 1866	54,197
Damper, Stove-pipe	H. Ogborn	Richmond, Ind	Nov. 26, 1867	71,524
Damper, Stove-pipe	H. Ogborn and A. T. Chapin	Richmond, Ind	Aug. 21, 1866	57,368
Damper, Stove-pipe	E. Parker	Marlow, N. H	May 22, 1866	55,017
Damper, Stove-pipe	E. Parker	Marlow, N. H	Apr. 23, 1867	64,136
Damper, Stove-pipe	F. D. Pastorious	Philadelphia, Pa	Aug. 11, 1868	80,832
Damper, Stove-pipe	W. V. Perry	Burnett, Wis	Mar. 5, 1867	62,559
Damper, Stove-pipe	J. M. Read	Boston, Mass	Nov. 18, 1873	144,634
Damper, Stove-pipe	C. Reed	Beaver Dam, Wis	June 4, 1872	127,516
Damper, Stove-pipe	W. F. Rossman	Hudson, N. Y	Aug. 16, 1870	106,410
Damper, Stove-pipe	R. S. Sanborn and W. Bennett	Ripon, Wis	Apr. 10, 1866	53,886
Damper, Stove-pipe	D. Sanders	Milwaukee, Wis	Feb. 16, 1869	86,943
Damper, Stove-pipe	D. Sanders	Milwaukee, Wis	June 28, 1870	104,889
Damper, Stove-pipe	H. J. Sayers	Salina, Pa	Apr. 6, 1864	88,744
Damper, Stove-pipe	G. E. Smith	Racine, Wis	Nov. 8, 1869	44,981
Damper, Stove-pipe	J. Spear	Philadelphia, Pa	Mar. 12, 1872	124,456
Damper, Stove-pipe	W. X. Stevens and W. E. Puffer	Worcester and Lexington, Mass.	Apr. 16, 1867	63,959
Damper, Stove-pipe	W. W. St. John	Saint Louis, Mo	Feb. 6, 1866	52,460
Damper, Stove-pipe	D. and S. Sweeney	Constableville, N. Y	May 22, 1866	54,976
Damper, Stove-pipe	G. Tamkin	Newburgh, N. Y	Sept. 29, 1868	82,565
Damper, Stove-pipe	W. Taylor	Lowell, Mass	May 31, 1870	103,686
Damper, Stove-pipe	I. Van Hagen	Chicago, Ill	Sept. 21, 1869	94,986
Damper, Stove-pipe	W. Wasson and G. W. Dungan	Genoa, Nev	Aug. 13, 1872	130,456
Damper, Stove-pipe	D. A. White	Chagrin Falls, Ohio	June 16, 1868	79,041
Damper. Stove-pipe	G. W. Wiseman	Sycamore, Ill	Dec. 17, 1867	72,437
Damper valve, Stove-pipe	G. B. Wiseman	Sycamore, Ill	May 21, 1867	65,033
Damper, Ventilating	N. A. Boynton	New York, N. Y	May 5, 1863	38,370
Damper, Ventilating	G. Tainter	Watertown, Mass	May 13, 1862	35,269
Damper, Ventilating and check-draft	J. A. Lawson	Troy, N. Y	Feb. 7, 1865	46,249
Dampers for cooking-stoves, Arrangement of	W. E. Hayes	Geneva, N. Y	Apr. 22, 1856	14,720
Dampers in rotary stoves, Arrangement of	W. W. Hill	Greenport, N. Y	June 6, 1854	11,010
Dampers in steam-heating apparatus, Method of operating.	J. J. Smith	Elizabeth, N. J	Aug. 20, 1861	33,107
Dampers of furnaces, Operating	D. Treadwell	Cambridge, Mass	Aug. 22, 1854	11,583
Dampers of steam-boilers by the pressure of the steam, Regulating the.	P. Clark	Rahway, N. J	Jan. 3, 1854	10,387
Damping-apparatus	P. Hill	Philadelphia, Pa	Feb. 5, 1867	61,833
Damping-trough	H. T. Davis	New Cross, Great Britain	Dec. 1, 1868	84,538
Dancer, Automatic	J. E. Atwood and C. P. Stimets	Trenton, N. J., and New York, N. Y.	Sept. 27, 1864	44,378
Dancer, Automatic	C. Chinnock	Brooklyn, N. Y	Oct. 17, 1865	50,452
Dancer, Automatic	T. N. and J. N. Crow	Mott Haven, N. Y	Dec. 1, 1863	40,740
Dancer, Automatic tight-rope	W. Humans	Boston, Mass	Nov. 12, 1867	70,850
Dancer, Automaton	I. S. Clough and V. Fountain, jr	Brooklyn and North Shore, N. Y.	Aug. 9, 1864	43,759
Dancer, Automaton	W. Nunns	New York, N. Y	May 31, 1864	42,962
Dash-board	J. S. Campbell	Bridgeport, Conn	Aug. 12, 1873	141,758
Dash-board and rein-holder	P. Verplanck, jr	Binghamton, N. Y	Mar. 24, 1868	76,007
Dash-board bag	S. Hipkiss	Charlestown, Mass	July 1, 1873	140,416
Dash-wheel for washing and bleaching, Use of the	J. Wallace, jr	Glasgow, North Britain	Sept 30, 1856	15,836
Dating-machine	G. J. Hill	Buffalo, N. Y	June 26, 1860	28,861
Davit and winch, Ship's	D. P. Nickerson	Cleveland, Ohio	Mar. 26, 1867	63,289
Davit-fall-block hook	W. R. Satterly	Port Jefferson, N. Y	Sept. 18, 1866	58,142
Davit-ring, Self-releasing	A. Guild and W. H. Pierce	Middletown, Conn	Oct. 18, 1870	108,353
Davit, Ship's	W. Crosthwait	Buffalo, N. Y	Oct. 8, 1872	131,941
Davit, Ship's	L. F. Frazee	South Amboy, N. J	July 30, 1867	67,282
Davit, Ship's	S. Gill and D. C. Woods	San Pablo and San Francisco, Cal.	Dec. 8, 1868	84,742
Davit, Ship's	C. G Meinhardt	Altoona, Pa	Aug. 11, 1868	80,869
Davit, Ship's	C. Perley	New York, N. Y	Jan 27, 1852	8,692
Davit, Ship's	J. A. Whiting	Baltimore, Md	Aug. 20, 1872	130,678
Davits, Device for detaching boats from	E. H. Sheffield and E. P. Palmer.	Stonington, Conn., and New York, N. Y.	Apr. 10, 1866	53,928
Davits, Tripping-block for boat's	C. Perley	New York, N. Y	Nov. 2, 1858	21,979
Dead center, Device for overcoming	J. Coy	Oswego, N. Y	May 7, 1872	126,526
Dead-center in cranks, Means for avoiding the	T. Williams	Providence, R. I	Apr. 2, 1861	31,926
Dead-center lift	J. J. Gorman	Cincinnati, Ohio	Jan. 31, 1865	46,102
Dead-eye blocks, Machine for making	T. Blanchard	United States	Aug. 10, 1836	7
Dead-point in cranks, Engine for overcoming	J. Griffin	Louisville, Ky	June 11, 1861	32,575
Dead-point in cranks, Machine for overcoming	J. P. Cooper	Finleyville, Pa	Apr. 3, 1860	27,698
Dead-point in cranks, Mode of arranging the cylinder in double-cylinder engines for overcoming.	C. S. Ferris	Courtland, N. Y	July 1, 1840	1,667
Dead-spindle	H. G. Davis	Northborough, Mass	Sept. 9, 1835	....
Decanter-stopper, Self-acting	L. Loeffler	East Cambridge, Mass	May 29, 1866	55,124
Decarbonizing furnace	S. H. Whitaker	Covington, Ky	Oct. 30, 1866	59,301
Deck and side light for ship	E. S. Hidden	New York, N. Y	Mar. 29, 1864	42,087
Deck and side light for vessel	C. Perley	New York, N. Y	July 18, 1865	48,836
Deck and side light of vessels, Fastening for	S. Winter	Boston, Mass	Mar. 22, 1864	42,058
Deck and side lights, Means of closing ship's	E. B. Vannevar	Boston, Mass	May 30, 1865	48,033
Deck-light	I. M. Bearse	Boston, Mass	Feb. 25, 1873	136,299
Deck-light	E. S. Hidden	New York, N. Y	Nov. 3, 1863	40,479
Deck-light	H Lanergan	East Cambridge, Mass	Jan. 29, 1861	31,247
Deck-light for vessels	J. Sutton and J. Gregory	New York, N. Y	Apr. 28, 1863	38,342
Deck light, Ship's	G. Gray	Lynn, Mass	Mar. 26, 1825	....
Decoctions, Apparatus for making	W. Adamson	Philadelphia, Pa	Sept. 6, 1859	25,311
Decoloring compound, Artificial	F. Gerau	New York, N. Y	May 20, 1856	14,911
Decolorizer, Compound used as	P. M. Belton	Brooklyn, N. Y	Aug. 14, 1860	29,560
Decorative slab from plastic materials	E. Robbins	Somers Town, England	Feb. 1, 1870	99,479
Decoy-duck	J. Foster	Philadelphia, Pa	Aug. 3, 1869	93,293

Index of patents issued from the United States Patent Office from 1790 to 1873, inclusive—Continued.

Invention.	Inventor.	Residence.	Date.	No.
Delaine, Process of manufacturing	J. Marland	West Bridgewater, Mass	Sept. 9, 1856	15, 703
Delineator for giving fac-simile	J. Wickes	New York, N. Y	Sept. 9, 1825	....
Demijohn	G. W. and S. W. Foster	Charlestown, Mass	Apr. 2, 1872	125, 187
Dental anæsthetic-instrument	E. Cutter	Woburn, Mass	Nov. 13, 1866	59, 562
Dental and surgical instruments, Handle for	H. T. Fogg	San Paulo, Brazil	Sept. 1, 1868	81, 616
Dental apparatus	W. H. Dibble	Bordentown, N. J	Oct. 17, 1865	50, 461
Dental apparatus	W. H. Dibble	Bordentown, N. J	Apr. 9, 1867	63, 709
Dental apparatus for casting plates for artificial teeth.	J. A. Loomis and C. F. Moll	Carthage, Ill., and San Francisco, Cal.	Apr. 19, 1870	102, 019
Dental apparatus for relief of pain while operating	N. Washburn	Bridgewater, Mass	Dec. 6, 1859	26, 388
Dental articulating-cup	C. Von Bonhorst	Lancaster, Ohio	June 1, 1869	90, 706
Dental articulator	L. Hoffstadt	Philadelphia, Pa	Aug. 22, 1871	118, 242
Dental articulator	G. F. Schaffer	New York, N. Y	Feb. 8, 1870	99, 598
Dental blow-pipe	J. Thompson	North Bridgewater, Mass	Sept. 7, 1852	5, 2[illegible]4
Dental crystalline-gold, Manufacture of	A. J. Watts	Utica, N. Y	Dec. 4, 1860	30, 847
Dental drill	J. W. Baxter	Vevay, Ind	May 20, 1873	139, 039
Dental drill	G. V. Black	Jacksonville, Ill	Aug. 8, 1871	117, 732
Dental drill	H. F. Bryant	Marathon, N. Y	Nov. 26, 1867	71, 361
Dental drill	W. S. Elliott	Goshen, N. Y	Feb. 13, 1872	123, 559
Dental drill	W. S. Elliott	Goshen, N. Y	Sept. 10, 1872	131, 156
Dental drill	W. H. Gates	Louisville, Ky	Oct. 9, 1866	58, 631
Dental drill	A. Hartman	Murfreesborough, Tenn	Aug. 22, 1871	118, 237
Dental drill	C. Poor	Dubuque, Iowa	Aug. 22, 1871	118, 268
Dental drill	W. M. Reynolds	New York, N. Y	May 28, 1872	127, 269
Dental drill	J. J. Ross	Memphis, Tenn	June 4, 1872	127, 518
Dental drill	P. Soper	London, Canada	Mar. 13 1866	53, 245
Dental drill	K. Spencer	Athens, Ga	Oct. 17, 1848	5, 866
Dental drill	L. D. Walter	Fort Plain, N. Y	May 15, 1847	5, 121
Dental drill, Automatic	M. I. Gallager	Savannah, Ga	Jan. 21, 1873	135, 109
Dental drilling-machine	C. E. Edwards	Philadelphia, Pa	Dec. 2, 1873	145, 098
Dental engine	C. M. Curtis	Philadelphia, Pa	Apr. 29, 1873	138, 318
Dental engine	J. B. Morrison	Saint Louis, Mo	Feb. 7, 1871	111, 667
Dental file holder and polisher	H. Lawrence	New Orleans, La	May 23, 1871	115, 070
Dental filling	C. E. Blake	San Francisco, Cal	Dec. 9, 1873	145, 275
Dental fillings, Porcelain blocks for	C. H. Mack	New York, N. Y	May 20, 1873	139, 012
Dental fillings, Securing	C. H. Mack	Portland, Oreg	May 2, 1871	114, 454
Dental forceps	H. J. Batchelder	West Fairlee, Vt	July 1, 1856	15, 215
Dental forceps	E. Bourne	New Bedford, Mass	Sept. 25, 1849	6, 741
Dental forceps	J. C. Burch	Evansville, Ind	Sept. 9, 1851	8, 351
Dental forceps	J. D. Chevalier	New York, N. Y	Oct. 22, 1872	132, 354
Dental forceps	J. G. Coates	Big Lick, Va	Sept. 16, 1856	15, 730
Dental forceps	N. A. Durham	Duquoin, Ill	Dec. 5, 1871	121, 599
Dental forceps	N. A. Durham	Duquoin, Ill	Dec. 12, 1871	121, 858
Dental forceps	C. G. French	Springfield, Ill	Dec. 2, 1873	145, 058
Dental forceps	L. G. Haskins	Newport, N. Y	Dec. 19, 1871	122, 012
Dental forceps	P. N. Jacobus	Montague, N. J	Dec. 26, 1871	122, 254
Dental forceps	J. A. McClelland	Louisville, Ky	Apr. 21, 1857	17, 107
Dental forceps	S. Woolverton	Trenton, N. J	Mar. 17, 1868	75, 716
Dental gold, Manufacture of	R. S. Williams	New York, N. Y	July 15, 1873	140, 984
Dental hammer. *See* Hammer.				
Dental hydraulic-cup	J. Harrison	Jamestown, N. Y	Aug. 26, 1851	8, 312
Dental impression-cup	O. B. Buttles	Milwaukee, Wis	June 12, 1866	55, 465
Dental impression cup	R. V. Jenks	Paterson, N. J	Dec. 21, 1869	98, 066
Dental impression-cup	G. McDonald	Athens, Ga	Sept. 21, 1869	95, 126
Dental impression-cup	G. T. Schaffer	New York, N. Y	Mar. 20, 1866	53, 347
Dental impression-cup	C. L. Wuestenberg	Pittsburgh, Pa	June 1, 18[illegible]9	90, 802
Dental impression-cup and suction-mold	G. H. Hurd	Memphis, Tenn	Apr. 27, 1869	89, 316
Dental impression-mold, Construction of	W. C. Smith	Warrensburgh, Mo	July 5, 1870	105, 008
Dental instrument	C. H. Dubs	Natchez, Miss	Oct. 17, 1848	5, 865
Dental instrument	C H Mack	Portland, Oreg	Aug. 8, 1871	117, 904
Dental instrument	W. R. Pomeroy	Millersburg, Ohio	May 25, 1869	90, 388
Dental instrument	I A. Salmon	Boston, Mass	Feb. 26, 1867	62, 504
Dental instrument	S C. Taylor	Toledo, Ohio	Feb. 18, 1868	74, 629
Dental jaw-brace	G. H. Hurd	Memphis, Tenn	Feb. 16, 1869	86, 922
Dental lathe	E. C. Risbel	White Haven, Pa	Jan. 10, 1871	110, 869
Dental mallet	J. A. Bidwell	Chicago, Ill	May 31, 1870	103, 706
Dental mallet	J. A. Harris	Pontiac, Mich	Oct. 17, 1865	50, 468
Dental mallet	C. Poor	Dubuque, Iowa	Sept. 18, 1866	58, 133
Dental mallet	J. N. Scranton and H. H. Parsons	Bennington, Vt., and Hoosick Falls, N. Y.	Oct. 24, 1865	50, 633
Dental mallet, Automatic	H. Hodge and J. P. Noyes	Binghamton, N. Y	July 23, 1867	67, 114
Dental models, Method of obtaining	L. Stuck	Bryan, Ohio	Sept. 29, 1868	82, 563
Dental mold	G. H. Hurd	Saint Louis, Mo	Sept. 4, 1866	57, 726
Dental mouth-meter	C. Von Bonhorst	Lancaster, Ohio	June 1, 1869	90, 705
Dental operations, Application of electricity in	W. G. A. Bomvill	Dover, Del	Feb. 8, 1859	22, 851
Dental operations, Applying electricity in	W. G. Oliver	Buffalo, N. Y	Apr. 19, 1859	23, 697
Dental pin	P. Crans, jr	Philadelphia, Pa	June 28, 1870	104, 835
Dental pins, Machine for heating	W. A. Duff and J. J. Griffith	Philadelphia, Pa	Mar. 14, 1865	46, 786
Dental pins, Manufacture of	F. W. Smith	Philadelphia, Pa	Mar. 4, 1862	34, 616
Dental plate	J. A. McClelland	Louisville, Ky	Aug. 11, 1863	39, 538
Dental plate	J. A. McClelland	Louisville, Ky	June 1, 1869	90, 765
Dental plate	E. J. Merick	Rochester, N. Y	July 23, 1867	67, 129
Dental plate	S. Purvine and H. Smith	Salem, Oreg	Aug. 29, 1871	118, 484
Dental plate	L. R. Streeter	Chelsea, Mass	Apr. 20, 1869	89, 253
Dental plate	G. W. Tripp	Auburn, N. Y	Aug. 4, 1862	39, 434
Dental plate	H. Twitchell	Pulaski, N. Y	Apr. 6, 1869	88, 682
Dental plate and teeth	R. E. Burlan	Lewisburgh, Pa	Feb. 6, 1872	123, 451
Dental plate, Atmospheric	N. T. Folsom	Laconia, N. H	Jan. 1, 1867	60, 871
Dental plate atmospheric attachment	J. P. Gillespie	San Francisco, Cal	June 13, 1871	115, 951
Dental plate, Atmospheric pressure	M. Levett	New York, N. Y	Apr. 6, 1858	19, 858
Dental plate atmospheric pressure attachment	J. B. Beers	San Francisco, Cal	Jan. 24, 1871	111, 168
Dental plate, Composition	A. Hill	Norwalk, Conn	July 27, 1869	93, 086
Dental plates and other articles, Composition for molds and models in casting.	S. Lawrence	Lowell, Mass	Aug. 31, 1869	94, 324
Dental plates and other purposes, Vulcanizing rubber for.	C. M. Kelsey	Mount Vernon, Ohio	Aug. 10, 1869	93, 623
Dental plates, Apparatur for molding	J. W., jr., and I. S. Hyatt	Albany, N. Y	Dec. 5, 1871	121, 522

Index of patents issued from the United States Patent Office from 1790 *to* 1873, *inclusive*—Continued.

Invention.	Inventor.	Residence.	Date.	No.
Dental plates, Casting	J. U. L. Fremster	Greencastle, Ind	Oct. 11, 1870	108. 245
Dental plates, Composition for	G. F. J. Colburn	Newark, N. J	July 23, 1867	67, 025
Dental plates, Composition for	L. R. Streeter	Chelsea, Mass	Mar. 23, 1869	88, 260
Dental plates, Flask for casting	S. Lawrence	Lowell, Mass	Aug. 31, 1869	94, 323
Dental plates from pyroxyline	I. S. J. W. Hyatt, jr., and J. A. Perkins.	Albany, N. Y	Mar. 28, 1871	113, 055
Dental plates from pyroxyline, Manufacture of	J. Brockway	Albany, N. Y	April 18, 1871	113, 736
Dental plates, Lathe-attachment for finishing	E. H. Danforth	Jamestown, N. Y	Jan. 11, 1859	22, 548
Dental plates, Machine for polishing	E. A. Mayor	Owego, N. Y	Aug. 6, 1872	130, 304
Dental plates, Manufacture of	F. M. Shields	Sacramento, Cal	Sept. 26, 1871	119, 245
Dental plates, &c., Material for	J. A. McClelland	Louisville, Ky	Apr. 28, 1868	77, 304
Dental plates, Mode of connecting artificial teeth with.	H. Crane	New York, N. Y	Feb. 16, 1869	86, 972
Dental plates, Mode of forming air-chamber in	M. A. Boughton	Norwalk, Conn	Jan. 31, 1871	111, 429
Dental plates, Preparing an application of pyroxyline for.	R. H. Winsborough	Saint Louis, Mo	April 25, 1871	114, 242
Dental plates, Vulcanized rubber for	C. M. Kelsey	Mount Vernon, Ohio	Nov. 21, 1871	121, 174
Dental plugger	J. T. Codman	Boston, Mass	Dec. 2, 1873	145, 051
Dental plugger	W. F. Griswold	Leavenworth, Kans	Apr. 9, 1872	125, 452
Dental plugger	C. M. Hooker	Hartford, Conn	Sept. 25, 1866	58, 257
Dental plugger	W. G. Redman	Louisville, Ky	Jan. 22, 1867	61, 460
Dental plugger	W. D. Stillman	West Winfield, N. Y	Aug. 27, 1872	130, 954
Dental plugger and burring-tool combined	I. M. Seaman	Buffalo, N. Y	Sept. 3, 1872	131, 123
Dental plugger, Pneumatic	E. A. Hyde	Ann Arbor, Mich	June 29, 1869	91, 849
Dental plugging-instrument	J. N. Scranton and H. A. Parsons	Bennington, Vt., and Hoosick Falls, N. Y.	June 1, 1869	90, 879
Dental plugging-instrument	G. B. Snow and T. G. Lewis	Buffalo, N. Y	Oct. 30, 1866	59, 284
Dental plugging-instrument	G. B. Snow and T. G. Lewis	Buffalo, N. Y	Nov. 20, 1866	59, 784
Dental plugging-instrument, Automatic	G. B. Snow and T. G. Lewis	Buffalo, N. Y	June 23, 1868	79, 270
Dental self-feeding plugging-tool	M. Burchardt	Berlin, Prussia	Oct. 10, 1865	50, 428
Dental substitute	G. W. Cool	Portland, Oreg	Dec. 3, 1867	71, 707
Dental swage, Adjustable	E. H. Danforth	Jamestown, N. Y	Mar. 22, 1859	23, 293
Dental tongue-holder	F. M. Osborn	Port Chester, N. Y	June 28, 1870	104, 874
Dental tongue-holder	F. M. Osborn	Port Chester, N. Y	Aug. 22, 1871	118, 386
Dental tool	C. P. Grout	New York, N. Y	Apr. 22, 1873	138, 150
Dental tools for separating teeth	R. Arthur	Baltimore, Md	Dec. 3, 1872	133, 617
Dental turnkey	H. Todd	Columbus, Ohio	May 9, 1846	4, 506
Dental use, Apparatus for packing rubber for	F. C. Brown	Palmyra, N. Y	Sept. 19, 1865	49, 969
Dental use, Compound for	F. Smith	Schenectady, N. Y	June 4, 1872	127, 656
Dental use, Diamond-pointed drill for	J. P. Gillespie	Louisville, Ky	Apr. 1, 1873	137, 434
Dental use, Gold for	R. S. Williams	New York, N. Y	Apr. 30, 1872	126, 242
Dental use, Making crystal shred gold for	E. Lamm	New Orleans, La	June 4, 1867	65, 398
Dental use, Manufacture of gold-foil for	U. K. Mayo	Boston, Mass	Nov. 1, 1870	108, 806
Dental use, Manufacture of rubber for	I. Woolworth	New Haven, Conn	Dec. 19, 1865	51, 642
Dental use, Metallic foil for	C. E. Blake	San Francisco, Cal	Dec. 9, 1873	145, 274
Dental use, Method of preparing gold for	E. G. Kearsing	New York, N. Y	Dec. 12, 1865	51, 459
Dental use, Method of preparing gold for	E. Lamm	New Orleans, La	July 31, 1866	56, 765
Dental use, Preparing gold for	G. J. Pack	New York, N. Y	May 17, 1870	103, 227
Dental use, Preparing gold for	G. J. Pack	New York, N. Y	May 14, 1872	126, 830
Dental use, Preparing gold for	R. S. Williams	New York, N. Y	June 21, 1870	104, 524
Dental use, Preparing gold for	R. S. Williams	New York, N. Y	Apr. 8, 1873	137, 747
Dental use, Process for preparing gold for	E. G. and L. Kearsing	Spring Valley, N. Y	Dec. 19, 1871	122, 029
Dental use, Rubber for	E. L. Simpson	Bridgeport, Conn	Oct. 16, 1866	58, 901
Dental vulcanizer, Safety-valve for	F. R. Moorhead	Chandlersville, Ohio	July 5, 1870	105, 115
Dental vulcanizing-heater	D. J. Peer	Rochester, N. Y	Apr. 3, 1866	53, 666
Dentifrice	J. G. Cook	Lewiston, Me	Jan. 22, 1867	61, 320
Dentifrice	O. Danforth	Bibb County, Ga	Feb. 14, 1871	111, 821
Dentifrice-paste	G. F. J. Colburn	Newark, N. J	Dec. 22, 1868	85, 166
Dentifrice, Vegetable	E. H. Reid	Clarkesville, Ga	Mar. 1, 1834	....
Dentist's and barber's chair	R. W. and G. W. Archer	Rochester, N. Y	July 9, 1872	128, 775
Dentist's and barber's chair	A. T. Boon and J. B. Finchure	Galesburgh, Ill	Aug. 4, 1868	80, 589
Dentist's and barber's chair	F. J. Coates	Cincinnati, Ohio	Oct. 15, 1872	132, 255
Dentist's and barber's chair	A. Gebhard and J. Blodan	Indianapolis, Ind	June 27, 1871	116, 427
Dentist's and barber's chair	O. C. White	Hopkinton, Mass	Nov. 14, 1871	120, 919
Dentist's and barber's chair, Head-rest for	R. W. Archer	Rochester, N. Y	Aug. 17, 1869	93, 662
Dentist's and surgeon's chair	F. Searle	Springfield, Mass	Mar. 26, 1850	7, 224
Dentist's chair	A. M. Asay	Philadelphia, Pa	Apr. 23, 1850	7, 299
Dentist's chair	A. M. Asay	Philadelphia, Pa	Feb. 7, 1854	10, 490
Dentist's chair	W. M. Butler	San Francisco, Cal	Dec. 19, 1865	51, 553
Dentist's chair	W. M. Butler	Louisville, Ky	Aug. 16, 1870	106, 463
Dentist's chair	A. M. Holmes	Morrisville, N. Y	Sept. 14, 1858	21, 562
Dentist's chair	A. W. Morrison	Saint Louis, Mo	Aug. 13, 1872	130, 525
Dentist's chair	D. W. Perkins	Rome, N. Y	Aug. 7, 1855	13, 396
Dentist's chair	I. A. Salmon	Boston, Mass	June 5, 1866	55, 368
Dentist's chair	R. A. Stratton	Philadelphia, Pa	May 29, 1855	12, 972
Dentist's chair	V. Van Vleck	New York, N. Y	Nov. 20, 1860	30, 706
Dentist's chair	J. O. Whitcomb	New York, N. Y	Oct. 3, 1865	50, 291
Dentist's chair	O. C. White	Hopkinton, Mass	Mar. 12, 1867	62, 794
Dentist's chair	O. C. White	Hopkinton, Mass	July 30, 1872	130, 093
Dentist's chair	O. C. White and A. T. Ashmead	Hopkinton, Mass., and Hartford, Conn.	Oct. 6, 1868	82, 776
Dentist's chair, Folding	C. M. Adams	Canton, Miss	June 21, 1870	104, 398
Dentist's chairs, Construction of	J. Ask	Lyons, N. Y	Sept. 4, 1860	29, 936
Dentist's chairs, Construction of	N. C. Lewis, jr	Boston, Mass	Oct. 4, 1859	25, 702
Dentist's chairs, Head-rest for	W. W. Evans	Washington, D. C	Dec. 31, 1872	134, 424
Dentist's chairs, Stool for	T. B. Downs and W. D. Morris	Jefferson City, Mo	May 13, 1873	138, 796
Dentist's clamp	C. E. Blake	San Francisco, Cal	Apr. 29, 1873	138, 370
Dentist's flask	C. Bailey	Kinston, N. C	Apr. 8, 1873	137, 589
Dentist's flask	C. P. Bellows	Gloversville, N. Y	Dec. 15, 1868	84, 988
Dentist's flask	G. E. Donham	East Abington, Mass	Mar. 3, 1868	75, 000
Dentist's flask	G. E. Hays	Buffalo, N. Y	Feb. 4, 1868	73, 974
Dentist's flask	L. R. Streeter	Chelsea, Mass	Mar. 23, 1869	88, 229
Dentist's furnace	E. A. L. Roberts	New York, N. Y	July 19, 1859	24, 823
Dentist's grinding and polishing wheel	J. K. Merrick	Odell, Ill	Oct. 12, 1869	95, 823
Dentist's instrument-stand	J. J. Rop	Hernando, Miss	Apr. 4, 1871	113, 571
Dentist's lamp for vulcanizing	G. E. Hayes	Buffalo, N. Y	Dec. 1, 1863	40, 750
Dentist's lamp-heater	J. C. House	Lowville, N. Y	Oct. 8, 1867	69, 670
Dentist's lamp-stove	S. P. Hildreth	Mount Vernon, Ohio	Oct. 16, 1866	58, 822

Index of patents issued from the United States Patent Office from 1790 *to* 1873, *inclusive*—Continued.

Invention.	Inventor.	Residence.	Date.	No.
Dentists, Mold for metal die used by	F. Y. Clark	Savannah, Ga	May 22, 1860	28, 348
Dentist's operating-chair	G. W. Tripp	Auburn, N. Y	Jan. 5, 1858	19, 052
Dentist's pattern-plate	W. M. Wright	Pittsburgh, Pa	June 29, 1858	20, 754
Dentist's rest	R. F. Hunt	Washington, D. C	Nov. 22, 1870	109, 411
Dentist's saliva-pump	C. Newton	New York, N. Y	Sept. 27, 1825	......
Dentist's tool-holder	G. F. Foote	New York, N. Y	May 22, 1866	54, 882
Dentist's tool-rack	G. E. Hayes	Buffalo, N. Y	Nov. 11, 1873	144, 539
Dentist's tool-rack	I. A. Salmon	Boston, Mass	Feb. 26, 1867	62, 368
Dentist's use, Lathe-bath and sponge-holder for	D. Murlless	Holyoke, Mass	Nov. 2, 1869	96, 467
Dentist's use, Vulcanizing-vessel for	G. E. Hayes	Buffalo, N. Y	Apr. 3, 1866	53, 612
Dentist's vulcanizer	C. H. James	Cincinnati, Ohio	Aug. 7, 1866	56, 945
Dentists, Vulcanizing-apparatus for	J. L. McDermut	New York, N. Y	Oct. 4, 1864	44, 541
Dentist's vulcanizing-flask	H. F. Clark	Poughkeepsie, N. Y	Apr. 2, 1867	63, 470
Dentist's vulcanizing-flask	L. W. Dowlin	Sherbrooke, Canada	Jan. 15, 1867	61, 174
Dentist's vulcanizing-flask	L. Hoffstadt	Philadelphia, Pa	Aug. 14, 1866	57, 135
Dentist's vulcanizing-flask	E. T. Starr	Philadelphia, Pa	Aug. 14, 1866	57, 210
Dentistry	W. Ballard	New York, N. Y	Jan. 16, 1866	52, 012
Dentistry	J. Johnson	Saco, Me	July 19, 1864	43, 588
Dentistry	E. C. Smith and D. F. Wilcox	Greenville, N. Y	May 12, 1868	77, 773
Denture, Artificial	F. C. Brown	Palmyra, N. Y	May 7, 1872	126, 517
Denture, Artificial	S. C. Taylor	Monroe, Mich	Sept. 26, 1865	50, 186
Deodorizer for privy-seats	N. Clifford and A. N. Bell	Brooklyn, N. Y	May 21, 1867	64, 841
Deodorizing air and gases in fat-rendering, bone-boiling, &c.	A. and E. Lister and C. J. Eames.	Newark, N. J	Nov. 29, 1870	109, 638
Deodorizing and fertilizing compound	J. M. Loewenstein	New Orleans, La	Mar. 26, 1872	124, 901
Deodorizing and fertilizing materials	J. E. Dotch	Washington, D. C	Feb. 27, 1872	124, 041
Deodorizing and improving alcoholic and vinous liquids.	L. Bradley	Jersey City, N. J	Oct. 25, 1870	108, 558
Deodorizing and purifying sewerage	C. Rawson, P. Ovenden, J. Wylde, W. McCree, and H. Hill.	London, Surrey County, Leamington, Leyton, and Hastings, England.	Aug. 29, 1871	118, 485
Deodorizing and treating offal, Apparatus and process for.	J. J. Storer	Boston, Mass	Sept. 3, 1872	131, 131
Deodorizing-apparatus for water-closets	A. Jordan	Washington, D. C	Nov. 14, 1871	120, 979
Deodorizing-apparatus for water-closets	P. S. Luther	Hartford, Conn	June 29, 1869	91, 855
Deodorizing-apparatus for water-closets	H. Moule and H. J. Girdlestone	Fordington and London, England.	June 15, 1869	91, 474
Deodorizing composition	A. Rankin	New York, N. Y	Nov. 28, 1865	51, 216
Deodorizing compound	R. Fish	Washington, D. C	Aug. 10, 1869	93, 607
Deodorizing, desiccating, and mixing manure, Apparatus for.	H. S. Firman	New York, N. Y	Dec. 8, 1868	84, 686
Deodorizing excrement	P. N. Goux	Paris, France	Oct. 10, 1871	119, 756
Deodorizing gases from lard-boiling, &c	W. H. McNeill	West Orange, N. J	Dec. 26, 1871	122, 273
Deodorizing hydrocarbon oils, Process for	R. Gaggin	Erie, Pa	Aug. 22, 1871	118, 359
Deodorizing India rubber, gutta-percha, &c	E. De la Granja	Boston, Mass	Dec. 17, 1867	72, 272
Deodorizing offal	A. and E. Lister	Newark, N. J	Feb. 27, 1866	52, 863
Deodorizing oil obtained from acid-tar of oil-refineries.	R. Gaggin	Erie, Pa	May 6, 1873	138, 629
Deodorizing oils and fats, Process for	O. Loew and J. E. Dotch	New York, N. Y	Nov. 26, 1872	133, 322
Deodorizing night-soil, &c	J. E. Dotch	Washington, D. C	Apr. 23, 1872	125, 886
Deodorizing water-closets	G. E. Waring, jr	Newport, R. I	June 1, 1869	90, 709
Deoxodizing-furnace for iron ore	A. W. Honsinger	Rome, N. Y	Jan. 4, 1870	98, 496
Depilating animal carcasses, Apparatus for	D. H. Sherman	Jersey City, N. J	Oct. 28, 1873	144, 150
Depressor and atomizer	O. A. Shultz	Chicago, Ill	June 16, 1868	79, 015
Depth-gage	I. A. Hurd	Boston, Mass	July 2, 1867	66, 239
Depth of water indicator for vessels	H. B. Sommers	Ithaca, N. Y	Dec. 10, 1850	7, 826
Depth of water register for vessel's hold	N. Edwards	Chittenden County, Vt	Mar. 5, 1850	7, 138
Depthing-tool	A. Rush	Fairfield, Iowa	Dec. 6, 1864	45, 348
Depurator	W. Curran	Saint Louis, Mo	Feb. 23, 1869	87, 247
Depurator	W. Curran	Saint Louis, Mo	Mar. 15, 1870	100, 867
Depurator	S. C. Frink	Indianapolis, Ind	July 26, 1870	105, 666
Depurator	S. C. Frink and L. D. Harlan	Indianapolis, Ind	Dec. 14, 1869	97, 768
Depurator	F. C. Leland and F. W. Poland	Lowell, Mass	Apr. 4, 1871	113, 536
Depurator	L. W. Werner	Saint Louis, Mo	Dec. 31, 1872	134, 406
Depurator for the teeth and gums	J. D. Wingate	Carbondale, Pa	Feb. 4, 1873	135, 612
Depurator, Liquid	W. Needham and J. Kite	Vauxhall, England	July 13, 1869	92, 465
Dermopathic-instrument	J. Firmenich	Buffalo, N. Y	Mar. 18, 1862	34, 677
Derrick	H. S. Blood	New Orleans, La	Mar. 26, 1872	124, 878
Derrick	A. Campbell	Downierville, Cal	Dec. 29, 1868	85, 279
Derrick	J. S. Clarke	New Orleans, La	Oct. 22, 1872	132, 442
Derrick	F. Donald and G. S. Newton	Waupum, Wis	Feb. 11, 1873	135, 785
Derrick	J. B. Drake and W. H. Hutson	Montoursville, Pa	Nov. 10, 1868	83, 938
Derrick	E. Duchamp	Saint Martinsville, La	Sept. 20, 1859	25, 494
Derrick	F. M. Everingham	Lafayette, N. Y	Oct. 8, 1867	69, 552
Derrick	S. S. Fertig	Titusville, Pa	Aug. 20, 1872	130, 706
Derrick	C. Fricke	Mobile, Ala	Apr. 28, 1868	77, 271
Derrick	S. Hill and C. M. Dupuy, jr	Jersey City, N. J., and Rondout, N. Y.	June 15, 1852	9, 025
Derrick	J. B. Holmes	Boston, Mass	Feb. 21, 1854	10, 544
Derrick	W. M. and G. L. Howland	Topsham, Me	Oct. 3, 1871	119, 612
Derrick	J. S. Lester and L. G. Jennings	La Fayette, Ind	Apr. 31, 1867	64, 336
Derrick	C. S. Lockwood	Newburgh, N. Y	Aug. 25, 1868	81, 385
Derrick	N. Matlick	Williamstown, Mo	Apr. 27, 1869	89, 416
Derrick	D. J. McDonald	Gold Hill, Nev	Dec. 10, 1867	72, 064
Derrick	E. Mingay	Boston, Mass	July 17, 1855	13, 269
Derrick	J. W. Piper and W. J. and J. S. Hanger.	Chicago and Taylor, Ill	Nov. 23, 1869	97, 114
Derrick	W. J. Perkins	Louisville, Ky	May 7, 1872	126, 484
Derrick	A. K. Richmond	Boston, Mass	Dec. 23, 1873	145, 899
Derrick	J. E. Serrell	New York, N. Y	Sept. 9, 1873	142, 740
Derrick	J. Sheldon	Chicago, Ill	May 5, 1868	77, 541
Derrick	A. B. Sprout	Picture Rocks, Pa	Sept. 17, 1867	68, 909
Derrick	S. Turner	Onarga, Ill	Dec. 13, 1864	45, 445
Derrick	J. E. Walsh	New York, N. Y	Apr. 22, 1873	138, 215
Derrick	D. D. Winant	Brooklyn, N. Y	Feb. 20, 1866	52, 777
Derrick and crane	O. C. Brown	Iberia, Ohio	Oct. 8, 1872	131, 934
Derrick and crane	J. W. Kennedy	Saint Louis, Mo	Jan. 7, 1873	134, 677
Derrick and horse-power	D. Woodbury	Rochester, N. Y	Jan. 10, 1865	45, 890

Index of patents issued from the United States Patent Office from 1790 *to* 1873, *inclusive*—Continued.

Index of patents issued from the United States Patent Office from 1790 *to* 1873, *inclusive*—Continued.

Invention.	Inventor.	Residence.	Date.	No.
Desk, Fire-proof	M. B. Bigelow and A. Hardy	Boston, Mass	June 28, 1859	24, 534
Desk, Folding	A. Chandler	Davenport, Iowa	Apr. 6, 1869	88, 609
Desk, Folding	E. W. Gilles and J. Wendell	Oswego, N. Y	Mar. 22, 1870	101, 118
Desk, Folding	H. E. Gillet	Oswego, N. Y	Apr. 26, 1870	102, 249
Desk, Folding	T. W. Heitz	Quincy, Ill	Oct. 29, 1867	70, 339
Desk, Folding	J. F. McNel	Philadelphia, Pa	Aug. 15, 1865	49, 428
Desk, Folding	J. Milwain	Nashville, Tenn	Jan. 24, 1871	111, 230
Desk, Folding school	E. Convers	Oswego, N. Y	June 14, 1870	104, 116
Desk, Folding school	S. F. Estell	Richmond, Ind	Oct. 26, 1869	96, 096
Desk for chair, &c., Adjustable	S. C. Ripley	Portland, Me	Oct. 22, 1872	132, 494
Desk for school-rooms, Arrangement of	H. G. Eastman	Poughkeepsie, N. Y	Sept. 6, 1864	44, 082
Desk for school-teacher, &c	W. C. Carter and J. P. Emery	Galva, Ill	Sept. 26, 1871	119, 316
Desk, Hand	M. C. Stebbins	Springfield, Mass	Oct. 8, 1872	132, 030
Desk joint, School	C. U. Crandall	Sterling, Ill	May 9, 1871	114, 649
Desk joint, School	T. A. Galt and G. S. Tracy	Sterling, Ill	Sept. 5, 1871	118, 773
Desk joint, School	T. Gregg	Danville, Pa	Oct. 3, 1871	119, 515
Desk-lid, Prop	H. R. Russell	Woodbury, N. J	June 4, 1872	127, 519
Desk, Night-reading	J. Rogowiski	New York, N. Y	Apr. 23, 1861	32, 148
Desk, Office	H. Mott	Troy, N. Y	Sept. 26, 1871	119, 390
Desk or seat joint	L. and W. F. Sylla	Elgin, Ill	May 30, 1871	115, 383
Desk or table, Recording	W. B. C. Stirling	Batavia, Ohio	July 13, 1869	92, 550
Desk, Pendent reading	G. F. Perkins	San Francisco, Cal	Dec. 12, 1871	121, 810
Desk, Portable writing	W. Bothe	Williamsburgh, N. Y	June 14, 1870	104, 255
Desk, Portable writing	W. H. Lochman	York, Pa	Mar. 29, 1859	23, 379
Desk, Reading	E. Kast	Waterbury, Conn	May 22, 1866	54, 919
Desk, Reading	J. Moessinger	New York, N. Y	Sept. 28, 1869	95, 369
Desk, Reading and writing	C. Pretsch	Trenton, N. J	Apr. 10, 1860	27, 831
Desk, Revolving	C. Hope	Springfield, Mass	June 12, 1866	55, 492
Desk, School	H. L. Andrews	Chicago, Ill	Sept. 15, 1868	82, 061
Desk, School	W. Blackburn	Manchester, Great Britain	June 11, 1872	127, 839
Desk, School	J. E. Blair	New Haven, Conn	Apr. 16, 1867	63, 839
Desk, School	W. M. Brooke	Eaton, Ohio	Dec. 26, 1871	122, 221
Desk, School	J. D. Brown	Madisonville, Ohio	Feb. 15, 1870	99, 832
Desk, School	A. Chase	North Weare, N. H	Sept. 11, 1860	30, 020
Desk, School	J. W. Childs	Kansas City, Mo	June 3, 1873	139, 543
Desk, School	S. Cox and W. W. Fanning	Richmond, Ind	Jan. 21, 1873	135, 089
Desk, School	W. E. Doyle	Eaton, Ohio	Nov. 15, 1870	109, 304
Desk, School	W. P. Erwin and T. A. Dugdale	Richmond, Ind	Mar. 1, 1870	100, 275
Desk, School	W. N. Foster	Indianapolis, Ind	July 9, 1872	128, 871
Desk, School	J. H. French	Burlington, Vt	June 13, 1871	115, 839
Desk, School	E. W. Gilles and J. Wendell	Oswego, N. Y	Jan. 19, 1869	85, 924
Desk, School	B. N. Hemenway	Rockland, Me	July 16, 1872	129, 559
Desk, School	C. J. Higgins	Indianapolis, Ind	Oct. 21, 1873	143, 760
Desk, School	G. W. Hildreth	Lockport, N. Y	Feb. 18, 1868	74, 688
Desk, School	A. O. Huffman	Springfield, Ohio	Aug. 1, 1871	117, 633
Desk, School	A. J. Hull	Sterling, Ill	Feb. 1, 1870	99, 440
Desk, School	A. Hutchinson	Philadelphia, Pa	Apr. 27, 1869	89, 484
Desk, School	W. Johnson	Topsham, Me	Dec. 26, 1865	51, 727
Desk, School	J. Long and E. Convers	Oswego, N. Y	July 18, 1871	117, 090
Desk, School	H. S. McRae	Muncie, Ind	Dec. 24, 1867	72, 662
Desk, School	J. Mealey	Fairville, New Brunswick	Oct. 27, 1868	83, 521
Desk, School	H. B. Osborne and N. W. Hammon.	Des Moines, Iowa	June 27, 1871	116, 477
Desk, School	J. Peard	New York, N. Y	Feb. 2, 1869	86, 440
Desk, School	J. Peard	New York, N. Y	May 23, 1871	115, 232
Desk, School	J. F. Piehl	Richmond, Ind	Aug. 16, 1870	106, 403
Desk, School	I. N. Peirce	Philadelphia, Pa	Dec. 5, 1871	121, 543
Desk, School	J. F. Prehl	Richmond, Ind	Apr. 26, 1870	102, 317
Desk, School	C. H. Bresbrey	Sterling, Ill	Jan. 21, 1873	135, 154
Desk, School	J. S. Rankin	Madison, Ind	Feb. 18, 1862	34, 448
Desk, School	A. E. Roberts	Des Moines, Iowa	Aug. 17, 1869	93, 907
Desk, School	A. E. Roberts	Des Moines, Iowa	Jan. 11, 1870	98, 801
Desk, School	C. H. Roberts	Geneva, Ohio	May 3, 1870	102, 713
Desk, School	J. Russel	Plymouth, Ind	July 25, 1871	117, 467
Desk, School	A. Schlag	Brooklyn, N. Y	Oct. 10, 1871	119, 794
Desk, School	C. W. Sherwood	Chicago, Ill	Apr. 5, 1870	101, 670
Desk, School	W. A. Slaymaker	Atlanta, Ga	Feb. 20, 1872	123, 796
Desk, School	W. A. Slaymaker	Atlanta, Ga	Feb. 20, 1872	123, 797
Desk, School	J. Smith	Richmond, Ind	Feb. 26, 1867	62, 375
Desk, School	J. Smith	Richmond, Ind	Mar. 1, 1870	100, 334
Desk, School	J. Smith	Richmond, Ind	Aug. 15, 1871	118, 161
Desk, School	W. H. Soper	Baltimore, Md	Mar. 31, 1863	38, 064
Desk, School	E. I. Stearns	Cambridge, Md	Apr. 14, 1868	76, 839
Desk, School	R. A. Thompson	Beaver Falls, Pa	Dec. 3, 1872	133, 551
Desk, School	D. G. Venable	Christiansburgh, Ky	Mar. 25, 1873	137, 263
Desk, School	A. S. Vorse	Des Moines, Iowa	Nov. 16, 1869	97, 005
Desk, School	F. A. Wilber	Wabash, Ind	July 15, 1873	140, 979
Desk, School	E. Wilson	New Brighton, Pa	Dec. 13, 1870	110, 101
Desk, School	W. S. Wooton	Richmond, Ind	Nov. 10, 1868	83, 896
Desk seat, School	C. Perley	New York, N. Y	Mar. 30, 1858	19, 791
Desk seat, School	A. S. Vorse	Des Moines, Iowa	June 28, 1870	104, 906
Desk, table, and shelf combined	L. H. Morrill and E. G. P. Smith	Falmouth and Portland, Me	Dec. 12, 1871	121, 886
Desk, Wall	T. Cogswell	Boston, Mass	Oct. 29, 1872	132, 632
Desk, Writing	C. H. Bergmann	New York, N. Y	Feb. 5, 1856	14, 217
Desk, Writing	J. W. Fiester	New Lexington, Ohio	Aug. 24, 1858	21, 249
Desk, Writing	J. H. Grimsley and P. I. Ankney.	New Lexington, Ohio	June 8, 1858	20, 487
Desk, Writing	W. Hoper	New Haven, Conn	Feb. 8, 1870	99, 672
Desk, Writing	E. Hughes	McCartysville, Cal	May 1, 1860	28, 086
Desk, Writing	S. Luther	Boston, Mass	June 19, 1838	786
Desk, Writing	C. Monson	New Haven, Conn	Feb. 4, 1862	34, 312
Desk, Writing	A. J. Ritter	Rahway, N. J	July 1, 1862	35, 781
Desk, Writing	F. Robbin	Hudson City, N. J	Nov. 16, 1869	96, 996
Desk, &c., Writing	D. Schafer	Parkersburgh, W. Va	Nov. 18, 1873	144, 636
Desk, Writing	E. Scheel	New York, N. Y	Oct. 25, 1870	108, 635
Desk, Writing	J. S. Watson	Newton, Mass	Aug. 16, 1864	43, 876
Desk, Writing	W. G. Wolf	Philadelphia, Pa	July 31, 1855	13, 371
Desk, Writing and drawing	W. W. Levering	New York, N. Y	Aug. 4, 1868	80, 749

Index of patents issued from the United States Patent Office from 1790 *to* 1873, *inclusive*—Continued.

Invention.	Inventor.	Residence.	Date.	No.
Desks, Attachment for school	D. I. Stagg	New York, N. Y	Oct. 1, 1867	69, 501
Desks, Device for supporting and connecting school	J. L. Rankin	Minneapolis, Minn	Dec. 5, 1871	121, 471
Desks in school-room, Arrangement of	V. Woodcock	Swanzey, N. H	Mar. 6, 1855	12, 497
Desks, seats, &c., to floors, Device for fastening	J. D. McAuliff	Saint Louis, Mo	Nov. 8, 1870	109, 031
Desks, System of school	S. L. Wilkinson	Cross Plains, Tenn	Sept. 18, 1860	30, 102
Desulphurizing and reducing furnace, Ore	J. Maunton	New York, N. Y	Nov. 12, 1867	70, 873
Desulphurizing furnace, Ore	W. Brückner	San Francisco, Cal	Dec. 4, 1866	60, 134
Desulphurizing furnace, Ore	W. Brückner	San Francisco, Cal	June 11, 1867	65, 538
Desulphurizing furnace, Ore	L. G. Marshall	Philadelphia, Pa	Sept. 1, 1863	39, 786
Desulphurizing furnace, Ore	C. A. Stelefeldt	New York, N. Y	June 14, 1864	43, 140
Desulphurizing furnace, Ore	T. D. Worrall	Central City, Colo	July 31, 1866	56, 842
Desulphurizing furnace, Steel and other wire	A. Cary	New York, N. Y	Dec. 1, 1868	84, 534
Desulphurizing metals and ores	L. G. Marshall	New York, N. Y	Apr. 19, 1864	42, 441
Detaching-block	T. J. Harte	New York, N. Y	May 24, 1870	103, 455
Detaching-hook	J. Bozorth	Camden, N. J	June 21, 1870	104, 547
Detaching-hook	J. O. Lord, jr	Middletown, Conn	Nov. 15, 1870	109, 328
Detaching-hook	J. W. Tuttle and J. Peterson	Rochester, N. Y	Apr. 19, 1870	102, 067
Detaching-hook for nautical use	J. M. Brooke	United States Navy	May 28, 1861	32, 408
Detective-register for watchman	P. H. Duffy	Somerset, Ohio	Nov. 29, 1859	26, 260
Detector:				
See Bank-note detector. Coin-detector. Egg-detector. Fire-detector. High and low water detector. Low-water detector. Pick-pocket detector. Steam-boiler detector.				
Detents, Tripping mechanical	S. Chester and C. T. Chester	New York, N. Y., and Englewood, N. J.	Mar. 23, 1869	88, 010
Detergent	S. Coburn	Stamford, Conn	July 5, 1864	43, 393
Detergent compound	W. Berrey	Boston, Mass	Mar. 15, 1870	100, 844
Detergent purposes, Composition for	A. Lovis	Boston, Mass	Nov. 8, 1859	26, 072
Detergent, Vegetable pulmonic	G. Rogers	Northampton, Mass	Dec. 31, 1808	....
Detergents, Manufacture of	S. Coburn	Stamford, Conn	Oct. 10, 1865	50, 336
Developing-stick	T. C. Roche	Williamsburgh, N. Y	Feb. 20, 1866	52, 748
Devulcanizing India rubber	S. Beer	New York, N. Y	May 29, 1855	12, 983
Dial, Sun	P. Fléchet	Paris, France	May 13, 1862	35, 225
Dial, Sun	J. P. Gardner	Columbia, Tenn	Dec. 5, 1843	3, 370
Dial, Sun	J. Scott	Portland, Me	June 5, 1849	6, 506
Dial, Steam-gage	E. H. Ashcroft	Lynn, Mass	July 23, 1867	67, 096
Dials to ascertain time, Combination of the needle and sun.	C. R. M. Pohlé	Richmond, Va	July 27, 1858	21, 020
Dials, Transmitting time-movement to distant	H. J. Wenzel	San Francisco, Cal	July 8, 1873	140, 661
Diamond-gage	W. Shumard	Richmond, Ind	Jan. 28, 1873	135, 249
Diamond-holder	G. D. Dunham	Chicago, Ill	Mar. 22, 1870	101, 111
Diamond-holder	J. E. Karelson	New York, N. Y	July 10, 1866	56, 231
Diamond-key	B. F. Southgate	Bridgewater, Vt	Sept. 3, 1867	68, 538
Diamond-setting	F. J. Herpers	Newark, N. J	Sept. 3, 1872	131, 058
Diamonds, Method of setting black	T. W. Baxter	Chicago, Ill	Jan. 21, 1873	134, 968
Diamonds, Setting	J. Dickinson	Phila[illegible]elphia, Pa	Nov. 30, 183[illegible]	....
Diamonds, &c., Setting	I. Lindsley	Providence, R. I	Sept. 29, 1857	18, 288
Diamonds, Setting and adjusting glaziers'	M. Kleeman	Columbus, Ohio	May 9, 1865	47, 645
Diaper	J. C. Hempel	Baltimore, Md	June 15, 1869	91, 334
Diaper	A. M. Hughes	Hudson City, N. J	Nov. 22, 1870	109, 410
Diaper, Child's	M. A. Moore	Lisbon, Ill	Dec. 8, 1868	84, 703
Diaper or shawl pin	J. G. Klinger	Jersey City, N. J	Feb. 2, 1858	19, 280
Diaper-pin	J. Heilmann	New York, N. Y	July 21, 1857	17, 857
Diaper-pin	W. H. Hockensmith	Bridgeport, Conn	Aug. 29, 1871	118, 533
Diaper-pin	H. S. Lesher	Brooklyn, N. Y	Oct. 2, 1860	30, 232
Diaper-pin	J. Rabbeth	Mansfield, Conn	Jan. 21, 1847	4, 938
Diaper-pin	J. E. Rabbeth	East Hartford, Conn	July 11, 1854	11, 272
Diaper-pin	I. W. Stewart	New York, N. Y	Aug. 16, 1870	106, 422
Diaper-pin	A. Wanner	Hoboken, N. J	Aug. 30, 1864	44, 031
Diapers, Substitute for infants'	J. H. Hall	Kittaning, Pa	Feb. 23, 1858	19, 418
Dice apparatus, Mechanical	A. Klingenberg	Baltimore, Md	Nov. 21, 1871	121, 110
Dice-box	E. W. Quincy	Lacon, Ill	Dec. 11, 1866	60, 421
Dice-box	J. Twamly	Troy, N. Y	Oct. 14, 1873	143, 599
Dice-box	J. E. Zender	New York, N. Y	Nov. 12, 1867	70, 732
Dice, Instrument for throwing	B. F. Bee	Harwick, Mass	Sept. 5 1865	49, 700
Dice, &c., Tool for marking	C. B. Rogers	Deep River, Conn	May 2, 1865	47, 571
Die:				
See Auger-die. Auger-bit die. Auger-blank die. Axle-clip trimming and straightening die. Axle-forming die. Axle-nut die. Bead-forming die. Bit and auger die. Blank-forming die. Blind-shaping die. Bolt-die. Bolt-heading die. Bolt-threading die. Box-stamping die. Buckle-closing die. Bullet-cutting die. Bullet-making die. Bunter-shape swaging and forming die. Button-molding die. Can-making die. Carriage-clip die. Carriage-clip-swaging die. Carriage-head block-plate die. Carriage-shackle die. Carriage-shackle-eye die. Carriage-shackle-eye-forging die. Carriage-shaft-shackle die. Carriage-spring-head-bar die. Cartridge-shell die. Chord-bar die. Chord-bar-head die. Clinch-ring die. Clinching-die. Clock-collet die. Collar-die. Cotton-tie-forming die. Damper die. Design-die. Draw-bar-follower die. Draw-head-face-plate die. Electrotype-die. Elliptic-spring die. Eye-bolt-forging die. Eyelet-forming die. Felly-plate die. Felly-plate-making die. Fifth-wheel die. Fifth-wheel-head-forging die.				

Index of patents issued from the United States Patent Office from 1790 to 1873, inclusive—Continued.

Invention.	Inventor.	Residence.	Date.	No.
Die—Continued. *See* Finishing-die. Flange-turning die. Furniture-nail die. Hammer-die. Hammer-claw die. Hammer-forging die. Hammer-swaging die. Harness-blind die. Harness-blind-shaping die. Harness-tooth die. Hat-box-cutting die. Hat-forming die. Hat-pressing die. Hatter-iron-making die. Heel-die. Hoe and pick die. Horseshoe-die. Horseshoe-calk die. Kettle-die. Key-blank die. Key-blank-making die. King-bolt die. King-bolt-forging die. King-bolt-formingdie. King-bolt-head die. King-bolt-trimming die. Knife-die. Knob-die. Lead-die. Lead-pipe die. Link-welding die. Locket-die. Mattock, hoe, &c., swaging die. Metal-die. Metal cupping and raising die. Metal-raising die. Mold-board-bending die. Nail-machine-grinding die. Nozzle-bending die. Nut-machine die. Ox-shoe die. Ox-shoe-forging die. Paper-collar-cutting die. Perch-iron die. Pistol-frame die. Plier-joint die. Plier-making die. Plow-brace die. Plow mold-board die. Punching-die. Roller-die. Screw-capping die. Screw-cutting die. Screw-threading die. Shackle-die. Shears-die. Shears-bolt die. Shears-bow die. Shears-bow-forming die. Sheet-metal-box-cover die. Sheet-metal-ware die. Shovel-die. Shovel-making die. Shuttle-tip die. Skelping-die. Sleeve-die. Soap-bar die. Sole-die. Spike-head die. Spike-machine die. Spoon-blank-cutting die. Spring-calipers die. Square-forging die. Stay-end die. Straw-goods die. Tea-kettle-bail die. Thill-iron die. Thrashing-machine-teeth die. Tin-ware-stamping die. Tinners' die. Tube-punching die. Tube skelp die. Tube-thread die. Type-wheel die. Upsetting-die. Vise-box die. Washer-die. Washer-making die. Watch-die. Watch-case die. Watch-case-swaging die. Watch-hand-swaging die. Whiffletree T-boltdie. Wire-die. Wire-drawing die. Wrench-bar die. Wrench-head die. Wrench-head-forging die. Wrench-swaging die.				
Die	R. Brayton	Buffalo, N. Y	Jan. 13, 1857	16,372
Die	L. Wetherell	Boston, Mass	Feb. 19, 1867	62,174
Die and plunger	J. H. Cole	Millbury, Mass	Feb. 15, 1870	99,848
Die and plunger	H. G. Williams	Providence, R. I	July 14, 1868	80,042
Die and punch	T. G. Arnold	New York, N. Y	Nov. 3, 1868	83,586
Die and punch, Method of holding and adjusting	P. E. Austin	New Haven, Conn	Dec. 1, 1868	84,468
Die and tap	A. Lemont	Pittsburgh, Pa	Jan. 29, 1830	....
Die cutter stock	H. C. Meyer	Flushing, N. Y	May 28, 1872	127,257
Die-cutting machine	W. Newsham	Philadelphia, Pa	July 5, 1870	104,985
Die for stamping polished blanks or shells for buttons, &c., Bright.	W. B. Dunbar	Waterbury, Conn	Oct. 31, 1839	1,392
Die-forming press	M. H. Stein	New York, N. Y	June 2, 1863	38,767
Die-holder for screen-press	J. McWilliams	Providence, R. I	Aug. 3, 1869	93,215
Die-mold for composition articles	I. Smith	New York, N. Y	Aug. 8, 1871	117,826
Die-operating mechanism	H. Waters	Northbridge, Mass	Jan. 1, 1857	60,973
Die-plate	F. D. Bliss	New Bedford, Mass	Jan. 28, 1873	135,314
Die-plate	J. D. Driggs	New Bedford, Mass	Oct. 8, 1867	69,644
Die-press	W. Burke	Brooklyn, N. Y	Jan. 25, 1870	99,149
Die-press	J. Mays and E. W. Bliss	Brooklyn, N. Y	Jan. 28, 1868	73,823
Die-rolling machine	H. Waters	Northbridge, Mass	Apr. 15, 1873	137,984
Die spike-machinery, Reciprocating	M. Belknap	Canton, Mass	Nov. 9, 1852	9,397
Die-stock	W. and J. Holroyd	Waterford, N. Y	Nov. 21, 1865	51,048
Die-stock	J. Koberle	Bavaria	Aug. 29, 1869	49,687
Die-stock	J. F. Sharer	New York, N. Y	June 2, 1857	17,453
Die-stock	S. P. M. Tasker	Philadelphia, Pa	July 26, 1870	105,861
Die-stock	J. Teachout	Waterford, N. Y	June 30, 1857	17,707
Die stock	J. Teachout	Waterford, N. Y	Mar. 27, 1860	27,657
Die-work as a substitute for etching, &c	A. Brewster	Frankfort, Pa	July 15, 1813	....
Die-work on steel, Mode of impressing	J. Perkins and G. Murray	Newburyport, Mass., and Philadelphia, Pa.	June 25, 1813	....
Dies, Construction of	H. W. Hayden	Waterbury, Conn	June 17, 1851	8,159
Dies, Formation of	T. Hollister	Cornwall, Conn	May 9, 1848	5,554
Dies, Hardening	E. W. Sperry	Wolcottville, Conn	Feb. 2, 1869	86,467
Dies, Manufacture of	F. W. Arvine	Fair Haven, Conn	Mar. 12, 1872	124,414
Dies, Press for operating, bending, and shaping	W. D. Mendenhall	Farmington, Ill	July 27, 1869	93,107
Diet, Compound to be used as an article of	C. G. Baylor	Quincy, Mass	Mar. 8, 1870	100,587
Diet, Compound to be used as an article of	W. D. St. Clair	Chicago, Ill	Feb. 22, 1870	100,081
Digester for treating bones, Steam	W. Perry	North Bridgewater, Mass	Feb. 26, 1867	62,459

Index of patents issued from the United States Patent Office from 1790 to 1873, inclusive—Continued.

Invention.	Inventor.	Residence.	Date.	No.
Digger: *See* Garden-digger. Peanut-digger. Peat-digger. Post-hole digger. Potato-digger. Rotary-digger. Stone and root digger. Tree-digger.				
Digging-machine	N. Badger	Shelbyville, Ky	Feb. 25, 1862	34, 473
Digging-machine	A. A. Garver	Mechanicsburgh, Pa	May 22, 1860	28, 359
Digging-machine	J. Mitchell	Oceola, Iowa	Oct. 13, 1857	18, 404
Digging-machine	C. H. Stratton	Munroetown, Pa	Jan. 10, 1865	45, 877
Digging-machine	I. P. Tice	New York, N. Y	Jan. 31, 1871	111, 404
Digitorium	M. Marks	London, England	Aug. 8, 1871	117, 791
Dike-core	J. P. Culver	Jersey City, N. J	Nov. 14, 1871	120, 943
Dikes and embankments against the ravages of animals, &c., Protecting.	S. Gardner	New York, N. Y	Sept. 20, 1870	107, 608
Dikes and levees, Construction of	L. S. Robbins	New York, N. Y	Mar. 12, 1867	62, 889
Dikes, levees, and embankments, Construction of	J. C. Schooley	New York, N. Y	Dec. 31, 1867	72, 913
Diking-sheet frame	J. S. Pierson	New York, N. Y	Nov. 14, 1841	120, 896
Dining and ironing table and quilting-frame	T. Elkins	Albany, N. Y	Feb. 22, 1870	100, 020
Dining and other tables	A. Kinkead	Washington County, Ohio	Oct. 26, 1858	21, 885
Dining-chair, Child's	A. Smith	Perrysburgh, Ohio	Oct. 18, 1870	108, 536
Dining-room fixed at the end of vessels	B. Maillefert and L. Hayden	New York, N. Y	Jan. 5, 1864	41, 078
Dining-table	E. H. Bleebaum and C. H. Nagel	Saint Charles, Mo	Sept. 22, 1868	82, 375
Dining-table	D. Boardman	Columbus, Ind	Nov. 8, 1870	109, 107
Dining-table	M. P. Boyd	Unionville, S C	Aug. 16, 1870	106, 460
Dining-table	R. C. Case	Guilderland, N. Y	Nov. 1, 1870	108, 878
Dining-table	J. H. and L. Drane	Eminence, Ky	June 27, 1871	116, 419
Dining-table	S. R. Garner	Independence, Iowa	Mar. 7, 1871	112, 441
Dining-table	J. L. Knight	Tracy Creek, N. Y	May 31, 1870	103, 625
Dining table	A. Land	Hillsdale, Mich	Apr. 15, 1873	137, 779
Dining-table	G. L. Motter	Bloomington, Ill	Mar. 4, 1873	136, 381
Dining-table	J. C. Nichols	Woburn, Mass	Aug. 21, 1849	6, 665
Dining-table	M. Pirz	East New York, N. Y	Dec. 31, 1867	72, 896
Dining-table	B. Welteck	New York, N. Y	June 11, 1872	127, 720
Dining-table, Caloric	H. L. B. Lewis	New York, N. Y	Sept. 27, 1845	4, 207
Dining-table, Extension	D. T. Robinson	Boston, Mass	Aug. 10, 1869	93, 557
Dining-table, Revolving	R. Wilson	Rees Corners, Md	July 6, 1869	92, 413
Dining-table, Self-waiting	L. Pusey	Patterson, Pa	June 14, 1853	9, 783
Dinner-can	A. A. Arnold	Clyde, Ohio	June 17, 1873	139, 851
Dinner-can	J. H. Murphy	Boston, Mass	May 24, 1864	42, 865
Dinner-pot	A. F. Wolf	Beaver Falls, Pa	Mar. 19, 1872	124, 775
Dipper-handles, Means of attaching	J. B. Wood	Cranston, R. I	Jan. 7, 1868	73, 066
Direct-acting compound engine	W. M. Henderson	Philadelphia, Pa	Aug. 2, 1870	105, 941
Direct-acting engine	G. F. Blake	Boston, Mass	Jan. 1, 1867	60, 852
Direct-acting engine	A. S. Cameron	New York, N. Y	May 3, 1870	102, 486
Direct-acting engine	A. Campbell and C. B. Hardick	Brooklyn, N. Y	Apr. 26, 1864	42, 527
Direct-acting engine	C. P. Deane	Springfield, Mass	Apr. 26, 1870	102, 234
Direct-acting engine	T. Hanson	New York, N. Y	Dec. 1, 1863	40, 749
Direct-acting engine	T. Hanson	New York, N. Y	June 20, 1871	116, 051
Direct-acting engine	W. D. Hooker	San Francisco, Cal	Aug. 18, 1868	81, 168
Direct-acting engine	B. M. Johnson	Brooklyn, N. Y	Sept. 19, 1871	119, 088
Direct-acting engine	S. F. Shelbourne and C. E. Emery	New York and Brooklyn, N. Y.	Dec. 6, 1870	109, 951
Direct-acting engine	W. J. Stevens	New York, N. Y	Dec. 6, 1870	109, 963
Direct-acting engine	J. Storer	New York, N. Y	Sept. 7, 1869	94, 665
Direct-acting engine	L. Winterbauer	New York, N. Y	Apr. 14, 1863	38, 193
Direct-acting steam-engine	J. Bailey	Quincy, Ill	Mar. 18, 1873	136, 806
Direct-acting steam-engine	H. A. Benson and W. Avery	Warren, Mass	June 4, 1872	127, 451
Direct-acting steam-engine	C. P. Deane	Springfield, Mass	Dec. 5, 1871	121, 451
Direct-acting steam-engine	G. H. and C. P. Deane and J. B. Gardiner.	Springfield, Mass	Mar. 9, 1869	87, 550
Direct-acting steam-engine	W. B. Hayden	Columbus, Ohio	Sept. 28, 1869	95, 225
Direct-acting steam-engine	W. D. Hooker	San Francisco, Cal	July 16, 1872	129, 345
Direct-acting steam-engine	J. B. Smith	Dunmore, Pa	Mar. 19, 1872	124, 862
Direct-acting steam-engine	T. Thatcher	Danville, Pa	Dec. 1, 1863	40, 778
Dirk-knife	A. Henninger	New Haven, Conn	July 11, 1865	48, 685
Dirk-knife, Spring	C. Hibbard	Chicago, Ill	Sept. 11, 1866	57, 902
Discharge pipe and nozzle	A. Lovie	Albany, N. Y	Aug. 27, 1872	130, 927
Disengaging-hook	A. W. Roberts	Hartford, Conn	Oct. 25, 1859	25, 915
Dish and clothes washer	G. Williamson	Goldsborough, Pa	Mar. 23, 1869	88, 251
Dish and vegetable washer	J. N. Paddack	Oswego, N. Y	Sept. 24, 1867	69, 240
Dish, Baking	B. Harrington	China, Me	July 9, 1872	128, 725
Dish, Baking	H. C. Wilcox	West Meriden, Conn	Feb. 9, 1869	86, 791
Dish, Butter	N. Lawrence	Taunton, Mass	Apr. 14, 1868	76, 639
Dish, Butter	D. T. Lyon	West Meriden, Conn	Oct. 15, 1867	69, 824
Dish, Butter	W. M. Whittaker	Wallingford, Conn	Dec. 4, 1866	60, 308
Dish, Carving	E. P. Bernard	New York, N. Y	Apr. 30, 1872	126, 253
Dish, Carving	C. W. Sykes	Suffield, Conn	Aug. 17, 1869	93, 844
Dish-cleaner	R. T. Osgood	Orland, Me	Sept. 24, 1872	131, 555
Dish-cloth holder	W. J. Johnson	Newton Corner, Mass	Feb. 21, 1860	27, 225
Dish-cloth holder	J. T. Walker	Albany, N. Y	July 21, 1868	80, 100
Dish-cover	H. S. and F. M. Goff	Middletown, Conn	July 14, 1868	79, 824
Dish-cover	A. J. Ohmer	Hamilton, Ohio	Mar. 18, 1873	136, 856
Dish-cover	W. H. White	Kent Island, Md	June 11, 1867	65, 626
Dish-cover, Refrigerating	O. Marland	Boston, Mass	Jan. 12, 1864	41, 228
Dish-covers, Forming wire-cloth	L. H. Allen	Amherst, Mass	June 4, 1861	32, 457
Dish-covers, Machine for making wire	W. Lincoln	Oakham, Mass	Oct. 9, 1855	13, 651
Dish, Covered	W. A. Fenn	West Meriden, Conn	May 26, 1868	78, 366
Dish-drainer	C. Britain	Saint Joseph, Mich	Jan. 14, 1864	43, 088
Dish-drainer	W. H. Gould	Manchester, N. H	Aug. 12, 1873	141, 643
Dish-drainer	H. F. Pond	Franklin, Mass	Nov. 9, 1869	96, 725
Dish-drainer	H. R. Richmond	New Plymouth, New Zealand.	Feb. 27, 1872	124, 085
Dish drainer and drier	R. W. Stone and H A. Kendrick	Rowe, Mass	Mar. 6, 1866	53, 055
Dish, Earthenware	A. and T. Vail	Berlin, Wis	July 13, 1858	20, 906
Dish-fastener	C. R. Freet	Upper Strasburgh, Pa	July 26, 1870	105, 794
Dish, Glass	J. S. and T. B. Atterbury	Pittsburgh, Pa	Oct. 29, 1872	132, 558
Dish-heater	W. Brand	Burlington, Iowa	Aug. 11, 1863	39, 459
Dish-heater	S. S. Fitch	New York, N. Y	July 15, 1873	140, 769

Index of patents issued from the United States Patent Office from 1790 *to* 1873, *inclusive*—Continued.

Invention.	Inventor.	Residence.	Date.	No.
Dish-holder	T. M. Hubbard	Ripon, Wis	July 16, 1867	66, 842
Dish-mop	A. S. Hadley	Boston, Mass	Dec. 11, 1866	60, 364
Dish-pan	S. Lafferty	Chicago, Ill	May 27, 1873	139, 252
Dish-pan	J. Vandercar	Brooklyn, N. Y	July 5, 1864	43, 442
Dish pan and drainer	F. Bucknam	Portland, Me	Apr. 2, 1867	63, 361
Dish-rack	W. H. Duffett	Rochester, N. Y	Apr. 18, 1871	113, 862
Dish-rack	J. M. Rudiger	Brooklyn, N. Y	Jan. 16, 1872	122, 855
Dish-rack	E. A. Sawyer	Portland, Me	Oct. 27, 1868	83, 413
Dish, Soap	J. Cundy	Philadelphia, Pa	Feb. 16, 1864	41, 606
Dish-stand	W. F. Collier	Worcester, Mass	Aug. 23, 1870	106, 552
Dish-stand	I. W. Lamb	Rochester, N. Y	Feb. 13, 1866	52, 576
Dish-stand	D. Sherwood	Lowell, Mass	Apr. 27, 1869	89, 440
Dish-stand	H. C. Wilcox	West Meriden, Conn	Apr. 12, 1870	101, 797
Dish-stand, Table	F. Gresjean	New York, N. Y	July 8, 1873	140, 623
Dish-stand, Wire	G. D. Dudley	Lowell, Mass	Mar. 19, 1872	124, 798
Dish-stand, Wire	E. P. Woods and D. Sherwood	Lowell, Mass	Dec. 31, 1867	72, 770
Dish-stands, &c., Machine for making wire	E. P. Woods and D. Sherwood	Lowell, Mass	Nov. 12, 1867	70, 770
Dish-washer	C. Bartlett	Providence, R. I	Dec. 2, 1873	145, 042
Dish-washer	F. E. Clarke	Flint, Mich	Dec. 7, 1869	97, 634
Dish-washer	W. H. Emerson	Dixon, Ill	June 22, 1869	91, 529
Dish-washer	W. H. Emory	Ashburnham, Mass	Sept. 19, 1871	119, 085
Dish-washer	R. and R. D. S. Filson and J. D. Cope.	Xenia, Ill	Dec. 27, 1870	110, 559
Dish-washer	M. Hobson	Williamsburgh, Mo	Mar. 22, 1870	101, 129
Dish-washer	J. A. Hotchkiss and R. Eaves	Derby, Conn	July 18, 1865	48, 814
Dish-washer	M. E. Lewis	Mansfield, Ohio	Nov. 14, 1871	120, 886
Dish-washer, &c	W. M. Long	Moline, Ill	Sept. 17, 1872	131, 451
Dish-washer	C. Messinger	Cleveland, Ohio	Nov. 24, 1868	84, 431
Dish-washer	M. K. Morris	Louisville, Ky	May 7, 1872	126, 566
Dish-washer	S. D. Moxley	Keeseville, N. Y	May 14, 1872	126, 735
Dish-washer	E. and J. S. B. Norton	Boston, Mass	Nov. 12, 1867	70, 883
Dish-washer	M. S. Orton and P. B. Stiles	Galesburgh, Ill	Mar. 8, 1870	100, 657
Dish-washer	G. Richards and L. Alexander	Cummington and Shelburne Falls, Mass.	Oct. 13, 1863	40, 280
Dish-washer	J. J. Sawyer	Woodstock, Conn	Oct. 16, 1866	58, 895
Dish-washer	C. H. Sterling	Gambier, Ohio	Aug. 20, 1872	130, 761
Dish-washer	J. A. Strong	North Wolcott, Vt	Oct. 5, 1869	95, 618
Dish-washer	W. L. Thompson	Stanstead, Canada	Oct. 17, 1871	119, 953
Dish-washer	A. W. Thornton	Mendocino, Cal	Dec. 10, 1872	133, 811
Dish-washer	H. B. Todd	Plymouth, Conn	May 2, 1871	114, 367
Dish-washer	W. and S. B. Way and S. C. Pomeroy.	South Butler, N. Y	Apr. 9, 1867	63, 677
Dish washer	G. A. Wells	Luzerne, N. Y	June 14, 1870	104, 235
Dish washing and drying machine	A. W. Ward	Fishkill, N. Y	July 23, 1867	67, 088
Dish-washing machine	L. A. Alexander	Colerain, Mass	Nov. 21, 1865	51, 000
Dish-washing machine	A. M. and J. I. D. Bristol	Detroit, Mich	Nov. 3, 1863	40, 457
Dish-washing machine	D. Guptail	Elgin, Ill	Apr. 20, 1869	89, 216
Dish-washing machine	G. Richards	Cummington, Mass	Jan. 15, 1867	61, 256
Dish-washing machine	H. C. Robertson	East Saginaw, Mich	Aug. 1, 1871	117, 568
Dish-washing machine	S. S. Tupper	Churchville, N. Y	July 26, 1870	105, 742
Dish-washing machine	J. Usher	West Albany, N. Y	Jan. 21, 1873	135, 176
Dish-washing machine	J. Wheeler	Athol, Mass	Mar. 27, 1866	53, 511
Dish-washing machine	C. H. Williams	Syracuse, N. Y	Oct. 7, 1873	143, 484
Dish-washing machine	L. R. Witherell	Galesburgh, Ill	Sept. 28, 1869	95, 400
Dish-washing machine	L. R. and E. A. Witherell	Galesburgh, Ill	Dec. 22, 1868	85, 155
Dish-washing machine	C. Woodruff	Antioch, Cal	Feb. 6, 1872	123, 434
Dishes, Apparatus for drying	C. W. Schroeder	New York, N. Y	Oct. 23, 1866	59, 083
Dishes, knives and forks, &c., Machine for washing	C. M. Leland	Central City, Colo	July 6, 1869	92, 323
Disinfectant	L. Broad	Saint Louis, Mo	Sept. 18, 1866	58, 163
Disinfectant-compound	J. Hilton	New York, N. Y	July 29, 1873	141, 274
Disinfectant-package	W. P. Tenny	Boston, Mass	Sept. 16, 1873	142, 963
Disinfectant or ozone generator	W. H. Ford and S. Logan	New Orleans, La	Dec. 29, 1868	85, 297
Disinfectants, Apparatus for vaporizing and atomizing.	E. S. De Luce and H. M. Wells	United States Navy	June 25, 1872	128, 368
Disinfecting and antiseptic compound	J. Strigel	Louisville, Ky	July 23, 1867	67, 082
Disinfecting and deodorizing compound	H. G. Dayton	Dayton, Ohio	Nov. 30, 1869	97, 469
Disinfecting and embalming fluid	H. C. Coffman	Washington Court-House, Ohio.	May 28, 1867	65, 174
Disinfecting and preserving, Composition for	J. Hickson and L. L. Wilkinson	Auburn, N. Y	May 1, 1866	54, 345
Disinfecting and purifying hospitals, camps, &c., Composition for.	J. L. Kidwell	Georgetown, D. C	June 2, 1863	38, 748
Disinfecting and ventilating burial-vault	B. F. Lyford	San Francisco, Cal	Jan. 31, 1871	111, 358
Disinfecting-apparatus	J. M. Scudder	Cincinnati, Ohio	Apr. 24, 1866	54, 221
Disinfecting bone-boiling establishments, Mode of	D. E. Contaret	New York, N. Y	Aug. 14, 1866	57, 093
Disinfecting buildings, ships, &c., Process of	H. M. Wells	New York, N. Y	Oct. 24, 1871	120, 355
Disinfecting-composition	F. Hoffman and R. Wendler	Brooklyn, N. Y	May 22, 1866	54, 907
Disinfecting-compound	J. Gamage	London, England	Nov. 26, 1872	133, 430
Disinfecting-compound	J. Le Doyen	Paris, France	Dec. 24, 1844	5, 403
Disinfecting-compound	J. W. Lee and J. W. Davis	Washington, D. C	Dec. 9, 1873	145, 433
Disinfecting-compound	H. Napier	Elizabeth, N. J	Aug. 14, 1866	57, 174
Disinfecting-compound	O. Oldberg	Washington, D. C	Aug. 1, 1871	117, 671
Disinfecting compound	L. S. Robbins	New York, N. Y	Mar. 1, 1870	100, 327
Disinfecting-compound	C. A. Seely and C. J. Eames	New York, N. Y	Feb. 18, 1868	74, 608
Disinfecting-compound	E. Süvern	Halle, Prussia	Sept. 17, 1867	69, 043
Disinfecting-compound	H. A. Tilden	New Lebanon, N. Y	Sept. 26, 1871	119, 250
Disinfecting-compound	H. A. Tilden	New Lebanon, N. Y	Dec. 12, 1871	121, 913
Disinfecting-compound	G. Vique, sr	Bordeaux, France	Apr. 18, 1871	113, 820
Disinfecting fecal matter	D. E. Contaret	Boston, Mass	Jan. 8, 1856	14, 053
Disinfecting foul air in vessels, Apparatus for	A. Peteler	New Brighton, N. Y	Apr. 9, 1861	31, 996
Disinfecting noxious vapors from rendering-houses, hospitals, &c., Mode of.	R. B. Lockwood	New York, N. Y	Dec. 11, 1866	60, 394
Disinfecting noxious vapors, Process for	W. Adamson	Philadelphia, Pa	Feb. 14, 1865	46, 317
Disinfecting-powder	H. G. Dayton	Maysville, Ky	Aug. 5, 1873	141, 540
Disinfecting rooms, ships, &c., Process of	E. Dumplemann	Washington, D. C	Nov. 26, 1867	71, 467
Disinfecting soap-boiling establishments	S. Strunz	Pittsburgh, Pa	May 3, 1873	138, 954
Disinfecting vessels, Apparatus for	E. H. Covel	New York, N. Y	Apr. 26, 1864	42, 464
Disinfecting water-closets, urinals, gutters, &c	A. G. Brown	Southwark, England	Sept. 17, 1872	131, 422
Disinfector	J. D. C. Outwater	New York, N. Y	Aug. 28, 1866	57, 559

Index of patents issued from the United States Patent Office from 1790 *to* 1873, *inclusive*—Continued.

Invention.	Inventor.	Residence.	Date.	No.
Disintegrating-mill	G. B. Davis	Baltimore, Md	Dec. 14, 1869	97, 890
Disintegrating substances, Apparatus for	C. G. C. Simpson	Montreal, Canada	Aug. 8, 1871	117, 824
Disintegrator, Rotary	H. Dusch	Baltimore, Md	Oct. 25, 1870	108, 692
Disk, bolt, and rivet machine, Rotating	J. G. Day	Brooklyn, N. Y	July 3, 1849	6, 578
Disks, Machine for cutting out and flanging metallic	G. W. Bentley	Brooklyn, N. Y	Feb. 13, 1872	123, 667
Disks, Machinery for cutting and bending metallic	E. Savage	Berlin, Conn	Aug. 30, 1853	9, 982
Disks, Mode of securing cutters to rotary	J. Newton	New York, N. Y	June 19, 1855	13, 096
Disks, rivets, &c., Machine for molding metal	P. L. Higley	Cincinnati, Ohio	May 11, 1869	89, 866
Dislocations, Apparatus for reducing	G. O. Jarvis	Portland, Conn	Sept. 14, 1843	3, 263
Distance between itself and the target without chaining, Instrument for ascertaining the.	B. De Villeroi	Philadelphia, Pa	Mar. 22, 1859	23, 294
Distance-indicator for railway	S. O. Schoonmaker	Wright, N. Y	Sept. 22, 1863	40, 066
Distillates, Apparatus for cooling	H. G. Dayton	Maysville, Ky	Oct. 18, 1864	44, 712
Distillation	J. W. Alder	Pennsborough, Pa	Apr. 19, 1814	....
Distillation	J. F. Collins	New York, N. Y	Oct. 30, 1866	59, 187
Distillation	J. Dimond	Philadelphia, Pa	Dec. 28, 1808	....
Distillation	W. Richardson	Kingston, N. Y	June 15, 1816	....
Distillation	H. B. Sinks	Cincinnati, Ohio	Mar. 29, 1870	101, 388
Distillation and other purposes, Mode of fermenting liquids for.	R. D'Heureuse	San Francisco, Cal	Aug. 6, 1867	67, 512
Distillation, Apparatus and process of	G. S. Williamson	Gallatin, Tenn	Sept. 6, 1870	107, 147
Distillation, Apparatus for continuous	C. H. Budd	Philadelphia, Pa	Mar. 9, 1869	87, 537
Distillation, Apparatus for continuous	W. G. W. Jaeger	Baltimore, Md	May 1, 1866	54, 358
Distillation, Apparatus for cooling mash for	T. Whitemell	Halifax County, N. C	Sept. 2, 1815	....
Distillation, Apparatus for destructive	L. Atwood	Brooklyn, N. Y	Dec. 28, 1858	22, 407
Distillation, Apparatus for destructive	L. Atwood	Brooklyn, N. Y	Feb. 22, 1859	23, 006
Distillation, Apparatus for destructive	L. Atwood	Brooklyn, N. Y	Mar. 29, 1859	23, 337
Distillation, Apparatus for treating grain for	A. Woolner	Louisville, Ky	June 10, 1873	139, 749
Distillation, &c., Application of steam in	H. Kelly	Brooklyn, N. Y	Feb. 16, 1816	....
Distillation by steam in wooden or other stills	S. Brown, and E. and T. West	....	July 8, 1803	....
Distillation, Condensation of vapors in	N. Blanche	New York, N. Y	Mar. 2, 1811	....
Distillation for hydrocarbon oils	J. J. Johnston	Allegheny, Pa	Apr. 9, 1861	31, 982
Distillation, Method of	V. B. Ryerson	New York, N. Y	May 7, 1861	32, 254
Distillation, &c., Mode of cooling the mash used in the process of.	A. D. Ward	Minerva, Ky	Nov. 7, 1840	1, 850
Distillation of bromine and iodine	D. Alter	Freeport, Pa	Mar. 19, 1867	62, 988
Distillation of coal, Apparatus for	H. P. Gengembre	Allegheny, Pa	Mar. 20, 1860	27, 542
Distillation of coal-oils	B. Garvey	New York, N. Y	July 17, 1860	29, 218
Distillation of coal-oils	D. S. Stombs and J. Brace	Newport, Ky., and Point Creek, Va.	Apr. 10, 1860	27, 842
Distillation of coal-oils, Apparatus for	L. Atwood	New York, N. Y	Apr. 10, 1860	27, 768
Distillation of fresh water from salt water	A. Normandy	France	Oct. 5, 1858	21, 693
Distillation of hydrocarbon oils	L. Atwood	New York, N. Y	Apr. 10, 1860	27, 767
Distillation of hydrocarbon oils	H. Grogan and G. T. Lape	New York, N. Y	May 11, 1869	89, 988
Distillation of hydrocarbon oils	F. McCarty	Smith's Ferry, Pa	June 29, 1869	91, 953
Distillation of hydrocarbon oils	J. Merrill	Boston, Mass	July 2, 1861	32, 704
Distillation of oils from resin	S. Frazer	Galena, Ill	June 12, 1860	28, 663
Distillation of petroleum	A. Millochau	New York, N. Y	Mar. 13, 1866	53, 167
Distillation of petroleum, &c., Apparatus for the continuous.	J. I. Vaughn	London, England	Aug. 29, 1869	49, 689
Distillation of salt water, Ship's galley for	E. Hutchinson	Baltimore, Md	May 20, 1839	1, 156
Distillation of spirits of turpentine, Apparatus for	J. Jennings	New York, N. Y	Aug. 27, 1835	....
Distillation of tar and other substances, Apparatus for.	L. S. Fales	Boston, Mass	Jan. 23, 1866	52, 151
Distillation of wood, &c., Apparatus for destructive	L. Atwood	Brooklyn, N. Y	Dec. 28, 1858	22, 408
Distillery	H. Becker	Warwick Township, Pa	June 29, 1833	....
Distillery	H. H. Kirk	Springfield, Tenn	Feb. 4, 1868	74, 098
Distillery and brewery boiler	B. Eggleston, jr	Princetown, N. Y	May 27, 1805	....
Distillery and kitchen range	W. Gamble	Washington, D. C	Apr. 18, 1811	....
Distillery-boiler	T. Pierce	Hartwick, N. Y	Feb. 27, 1819	....
Distillery-furnace, Fire-proof	J. Miller	Northampton, Pa	Mar. 13, 1823	....
Distilleries, Mashing-machinery for	W. Whitney	Rochester, N. Y	Jan. 19, 1826	....
Distilleries, Refrigerator for	L. C. and P. Rodman	Baltimore, Md	Jan. 6, 1826	....
Distilling	J. M. Aiken	Philadelphia, Pa	Aug. 30, 1827	....
Distilling	E. Barnum and B. Brooks	New Marlborough, Mass	July 13, 1808	....
Distilling	J. Bates	Hartford, Conn	Jan. 26, 1813	....
Distilling	W. H. Bayless	New York, N. Y	May 29, 1847	5, 136
Distilling	J. Cairon	New York, N. Y	Jan. 10, 1831	....
Distilling	J. Cairon	Boston, Mass	Aug. 22, 1831	....
Distilling	I. Carpenter and J. Roe	New York, N. Y	Jan. 29, 1824	....
Distilling	O. Carrier	Enfield, Conn	Jan. 18, 1813	....
Distilling	J. Carzo	New York, N. Y	Mar. 18, 1819	....
Distilling	W. J. Cocke	Surry County, Va	Oct. 30, 1827	....
Distilling	W. Cook	Southport, N. Y	Dec. 7, 1829	....
Distilling	F. S. Cozzens	New York, N. Y	July 27, 1822	....
Distilling	A. Dunlap	Boston, Mass	May 3, 1811	....
Distilling	C. F. Fisher	York, Pa	Apr. 24, 1830	....
Distilling	T. Gallaher	Liverpool, Pa	Dec. 14, 1830	....
Distilling	M. Garber, sr	Staunton, Va	July 13, 1810	....
Distilling	J. J. Giraud	Baltimore, Md	June 14, 1811	....
Distilling	P. Griener	Brandywine, Pa	Apr. 17, 1822	....
Distilling	N. Hart	Easton, Pa	Oct. 29, 1814	....
Distilling	S. Harwood, 3d	Braintree, N. Y	Apr. 15, 1826	....
Distilling	J. L. Jencks	Sackett's Harbor, N. Y	May 2, 1831	....
Distilling	L. Johnston	Easton, Pa	Nov. 9, 1832	....
Distilling	A. R. Kerr and H. Hoover	Waynesborough, Pa	July 1, 1836	....
Distilling	T. Lawes and P. Grosjean	Louisville, Ky	July 30, 1828	....
Distilling	J. Lusk	Butler County, Ohio	Dec. 22, 1827	....
Distilling	M. McDonald	Fayette County, Pa	Feb. 19, 1823	....
Distilling	J. Miller	Lancaster County, Pa	Mar. 2, 1811	....
Distilling	J. Miller	Lancaster, Pa	Feb. 16, 1832	....
Distilling	S. Oliver	Northampton, Pa	Aug. 4, 1841	2, 207
Distilling	A. Putnam	....	Jan. 29, 1791	....
Distilling	N. Read	....	Aug. 26, 1791	....
Distilling	G. Riley	New York, N. Y	May 29, 1847	5, 133
Distilling	P. Swartz, jr	Muncy, Pa	June 25, 1836	....
Distilling	E. Talmage	Lancaster, Ky	July 8, 1816	....

Index of patents issued from the United States Patent Office from 1790 *to* 1873, *inclusive*—Continued.

Invention.	Inventor.	Residence.	Date.	No.
Distilling	W. M. B. Wollias and H. P. Barlow.	Oneida County, N. Y	May 6, 1814	
Distilling	P. Woods	Frederick County, Md	Sept. 29, 1818	
Distilling	L. W. Wright	London, England	Sept. 28, 1831	
Distilling acid and naphtha from resin	L. S. Robbins	New York, N. Y	Nov. 4, 1851	8, 490
Distilling alcohol	J. T. Heard	Boston, Mass	Sept. 9, 1843	3, 256
Distilling alcohol, &c., Apparatus for	P. L. Howlett	Springfield, Ill	Dec. 16, 1862	37, 167
Distilling alcoholic liquors	S. F. Van Choat	Boston, Mass	Nov. 9, 1869	96, 640
Distilling alcoholic spirits	H. Fake	Chicago, Ill	Dec. 3, 1872	133, 523
Distilling alcoholic spirits and liquors	J. Dennis, jr	Washington, D. C	Aug. 10, 1869	93, 523
Distilling and bleaching oils	C. J. T. Burcey	Black Rock, Conn	Jan. 16, 1872	122, 810
Distilling and brewing, Treating grain for	A. Woolner	Louisville, Ky	Feb. 27, 1872	124, 188
Distilling and concentrating liquids, Apparatus for	C. C. Parsons	New York, N. Y	Jan. 17, 1871	110, 997
Distilling and condensing apparatus	J. K. Stafford	Brooklyn, N. Y	Apr. 25, 1854	10, 813
Distilling and employing the residuum advantageously.	I. Jennings	New York, N. Y	June 13, 1831	
Distilling and evaporating extracts, saline solutions, &c., Apparatus for.	T. Steers, jr	Richmond, Va	July 12, 1870	105, 381
Distilling and evaporating liquids	P. T. Badoux	New York, N. Y	Jan. 29, 1867	61, 651
Distilling and evaporation	A. Matthews	Island Creek Township, Ohio.	June 13, 1831	
Distilling and producing fresh potable water, Apparatus for.	W. A. Gray	New York, N. Y	May 25, 1869	90, 444
Distilling and purifying liquors, Apparatus for	F. M. Young	Nashville, Tenn	May 24, 1870	103, 535
Distilling and purifying spirits, Apparatus for	D. Woodard	Springfield, Tenn	May 11, 1869	89, 961
Distilling and purifying turpentine from wood	J. D. Stanley	Baltimore, Md	Aug. 20, 1872	130, 598
Distilling and rectifying apparatus	C. Gresinchna	New York, N. Y	Jan. 7, 1868	73, 092
Distilling and rectifying petroleum, Apparatus for.	C. Stott	San Francisco, Cal	Aug. 27, 1867	68, 257
Distilling and rectifying spirits	C. Falkman	Stockholm, Sweden	Nov. 20, 1849	6, 881
Distilling and rectifying spirits, Apparatus for	A. Foubert	New York, N. Y	Aug. 20, 1867	67, 863
Distilling and rectifying spirits, Apparatus for	G. Kaiser	New York, N. Y	Sept. 7, 1869	94, 611
Distilling and rectifying spirits, Apparatus for re	A. Noteman	Toledo, Ohio	Apr. 19, 1870	102, 033
Distilling and rectifying spirituous liquors, Apparatus for.	M. Newmann	New York, N. Y	Mar. 5, 1867	62, 670
Distilling and rectifying whisky and other spirits, Apparatus for.	E. F. Prentiss and R. A. Robertson.	Philadelphia, Pa., and Liverpool, England.	Mar. 1, 1864	41, 819
Distilling and rectifying whisky, Apparatus for	E. F. Prentiss and R. A. Robertson.	Philadelphia, Pa	June 27, 1865	48, 436
Distilling and refining apparatus	J. Sherer and A. Killian	Lancaster, Pa	June 17, 1811	
Distilling and refining oils, Apparatus for	A. Foubert	Buffalo, N. Y	Aug. 29, 1871	118, 602
Distilling and refining oils, wines, and other liquids	A. Foubert	New York, N. Y	Dec. 4, 1866	60, 166
Distilling and refining petroleum, &c., Apparatus for.	J. Ellis and E. C. Kattell	New York and Binghamton, N. Y.	Apr. 16, 1867	63, 789
Distilling and refining petroleum, Apparatus for	C. G. Howell	Corning, N. Y	July 16, 1867	66, 841
Distilling and separating oils, fats, and glue, Apparatus for.	C. A. Seely	New York, N. Y	Feb. 23, 1869	87, 207
Distilling and treating alcoholic spirits	G. Clark	Buffalo, N. Y	Oct. 26, 1869	96, 201
Distilling and wooden still	J. J. Giraud	Baltimore, Md	Aug. 3, 1813	
Distilling-apparatus	A. Blood	Boston, Mass	July 16, 1816	
Distilling apparatus	A. Boucherie	Philadelphia, Pa	Jan. 30, 1809	
Distilling-apparatus	W. Chamberlin	Vermont	Mar. 17, 1810	
Distilling-apparatus	J. A. Coffey	London, England	Dec. 18, 1866	60, 477
Distilling-apparatus	W. Corfield	Philadelphia, Pa	Dec. 29, 1868	85, 286
Distilling-apparatus	W. Corfield	Philadelphia, Pa	Dec. 29, 1868	85, 287
Distilling-apparatus	H. G. Dayton	Maysville, Ky	Aug. 25, 1863	39, 635
Distilling-apparatus	C. Delescluze	New York, N. Y	Oct. 12, 1852	9, 317
Distilling-apparatus	S. De Witt	Albany, N. Y	Jan. 30, 1833	
Distilling-apparatus	S. R. Divine and C. A. Seely	New York, N. Y	May 29, 1866	55, 071
Distilling-apparatus	J. C. Douglass	Troy, N. Y	Nov. 26, 1825	
Distilling-apparatus	H. Drüding	Brieg, Prussia	June 25, 1872	128, 291
Distilling-apparatus	J. T. Dwyer	Nashville, Tenn	Nov. 19, 1833	
Distilling-apparatus	J. T. Dwyer	Nashville, Tenn	Oct. 14, 1834	
Distilling-apparatus	H. F. Fisher	Philadelphia, Pa	Sept. 12, 1821	
Distilling-apparatus	C. L. Fleischmann	Washington, D. C	May 4, 1869	89, 749
Distilling-apparatus	A. Foubert	New York, N. Y	Nov. 19, 1867	71, 156
Distilling-apparatus	J. Frageser and I. Illofsky	New York, N. Y	Sept. 3, 1867	68, 470
Distilling apparatus	C. F. Frederici	New York, N. Y	July 11, 1865	48, 672
Distilling-apparatus	N. Goodsell	Paris, N. Y	June 13, 1816	
Distilling-apparatus	T. Grundmann	Cleveland, Ohio	Dec. 3, 1867	71, 744
Distilling-apparatus	C. H. Hall and J. Ellis	New York, N. Y	Oct. 16, 1866	58, 813
Distilling-apparatus	H. Halvorson	Boston, Mass	May 2, 1854	10, 850
Distilling-apparatus	A. Heistand	York Town, Pa	Nov. 27, 1805	
Distilling-apparatus	I. Hoffman	Shawangunk, N. Y	Dec. 31, 1813	
Distilling-apparatus	G. Hunziker	Summit, Miss	Mar. 18, 1873	136, 921
Distilling-apparatus	F. Kalisky	Philadelphia, Pa	Dec. 14, 1819	
Distilling-apparatus	P. Kessler	Belleville, Ill	Mar. 1, 1859	23, 089
Distilling-apparatus	J. Kunze	Chatsworth, Ill	Apr. 9, 1872	125, 463
Distilling-apparatus	L. Lecesne	Belleville, N. J	Dec. 4, 1811	
Distilling-apparatus	A. A. Meyendorff	New York, N. Y	June 9, 1868	78, 678
Distilling-apparatus	C. Otis	Tunkhannock, Pa	Feb. 16, 1831	
Distilling-apparatus	L. Pray	Charlestown, Mass	Jan. 8, 1867	61, 098
Distilling-apparatus	G. Riley	New York, N. Y	Apr. 17, 1849	6, 317
Distilling-apparatus	J. D. Riley	Cincinnati, Ohio	Apr. 28, 1868	77, 216
Distilling-apparatus	D. Savalle	Paris, France	June 23, 1868	79, 260
Distilling-apparatus	H. A. Schesch	Brooklyn, N. Y	Apr. 24, 1866	54, 218
Distilling-apparatus	J. Sloan	Pittsburgh, Pa	Jan. 17, 1860	26, 877
Distilling-apparatus	U. Swetland	Kingston, Pa	Nov. 18, 1822	
Distilling-apparatus	A. H. Tait and J. W. Avis	New York, N. Y	Mar. 20, 1866	53, 359
Distilling-apparatus	A. Tobey	Alford, Mass	June 21, 1810	
Distilling-apparatus	A. Webster	Seneca Falls, N. Y	June 2, 1868	78, 498
Distilling-apparatus	C. E. Werner	New Castle, Ill	Jan. 24, 1854	10, 463
Distilling-apparatus	E. Werner	Canton, Ill	Sept. 26, 1871	119, 436
Distilling-apparatus	J. M. Weyand	Saint Louis, Mo	May 3, 1870	102, 632
Distilling-apparatus	F. W. Willard	New York, N. Y	Mar. 13, 1860	27, 503
Distilling-apparatus and boiler	J. Lovatt	Philadelphia, Pa	Mar. 17, 1829	
Distilling-apparatus, Combination	L. Wolff	Chicago, Ill	Apr. 5, 1870	101, 555
Distilling-apparatus, Construction of	J. Sloan	Pittsburgh, Pa	Oct. 4, 1859	25, 705
Distilling, Apparatus for and mode of	A. Weaver	Adams County, Pa	Apr. 23, 1807	

Index of patents issued from the United States Patent Office from 1790 to 1873, inclusive—Continued.

Index of patents issued from the United States Patent Office from 1790 *to* 1873, *inclusive*—Continued.

Invention.	Inventor.	Residence.	Date.	No.
Distilling petroleum, Apparatus for	A. Krensler	New Lebanon, N. Y	Oct. 10, 1865	50, 368
Distilling petroleum, &c., Apparatus for	O. Lugo	New York, N. Y	Sept 18, 1866	58, 113
Distilling petroleum, Apparatus for	J. Miller	Allegheny City, Pa	Apr. 21, 1868	77, 070
Distilling petroleum, &c., Apparatus for	A. Millochan	New York, N. Y	Mar. 21, 1865	46, 923
Distilling petroleum, Apparatus for	E. F. Prentiss and R. A. Robertson.	Philadelphia, Pa	June 27, 1865	48, 435
Distilling petroleum, Apparatus for	W. B. Snow	Brooklyn, N. Y	Aug. 20, 1872	130, 668
Distilling petroleum, &c., Apparatus for	A. H. Tait and J. W. Avis	New York, N. Y	Mar. 19, 1867	63, 115
Distilling petroleum, &c., Apparatus for	C. M. Warren	Boston, Mass	Apr. 11, 1865	47, 235
Distilling petroleum, oils, and other substances, Process of.	O. Lugo and T. O. L. Shrader	New York, N. Y	Dec. 11, 1866	60, 396
Distilling petroleum, Process for	R. A. Chesebrough	New York, N. Y	June 27, 1865	48, 367
Distilling petroleum, Process for	A. Dubreuil	Baltimore, Md	Nov. 28, 1865	51, 156
Distilling petroleum, Process of	L. S. Fales	Boston, Mass	Sept. 5, 1865	49, 739
Distilling petroleum, Retort for	G. H. S. Duffus	New Orleans, La	Jan. 31, 1865	46, 088
Distilling petroleum, Retort for	G. H. S. Duffus	New Orleans, La	Jan. 31, 1865	46, 089
Distilling petroleum, Retort for	G. H. S. Duffus	New Orleans, La	Jan. 31, 1865	46, 090
Distilling pine wood	J. A. Matlocks	Swansborough, N. C	Apr. 3, 1866	53, 641
Distilling pine wood	T. W. Wheeler	New Berne, N. C	July 5, 1870	105, 019
Distilling pine wood, &c., Apparatus for	S. L. Cole	Burlington, Vt	May 19, 1863	38, 560
Distilling pine wood, Apparatus for	D. F. Mellen	Manchester, N. H	May 5, 1868	77, 636
Distilling pine wood, Apparatus for	W. Messau	Atlanta, Ga	July 23, 1872	129, 849
Distilling pure alcoholic spirits	C. Andersen	Brooklyn, N. Y	Oct. 14, 1873	143, 654
Distilling, rectifying, &c	J. Whips	Jefferson County, Ky	Apr. 22, 1816	....
Distilling resin-oils, Process for	H. Halvorson	Boston, Mass	May 2, 1854	10, 849
Distilling resin-oils, Process of	M. Page	Williamsburgh, N. Y	May 24, 1853	9, 752
Distilling resin-oils, Process for	J. Riley and W. Allen	Southfield, N. Y	Mar. 22, 1853	9, 627
Distilling rock-oils	A. Thirault	New York, N. Y	Mar. 8, 1864	41, 871
Distilling rock-oils and other hydrocarbons, Apparatus for.	E. F. Prentiss and R. A. Robertson.	Philadelphia, Pa., and Liverpool, England.	Mar. 8, 1864	41, 858
Distilling salt-water, Caboose adapted for	M. Rocher	Nantes, France	Aug. 28, 1841	2, 232
Distilling sea-water, Apparatus for	J. Ericsson and R. B. Forbes	New York, N. Y., and Boston, Mass.	Oct. 23, 1849	6, 815
Distilling sea-water, Apparatus for	G. S. G. Spencer	Boston, Mass	July 3, 1860	29, 015
Distilling spirits	R. Blaikie	New York, N. Y	Apr. 27, 1821	....
Distilling spirits	D. Ilsley	....	May 14, 1803	....
Distilling spirits and other liquids, Apparatus for	F. Haeck	Brussels, Belgium	Dec. 5, 1865	51, 403
Distilling spirits and other liquids, Apparatus for condensing in.	H. G. Dayton and J. Christie	Maysville, Ky., and Atlanta, Ill.	Dec. 1, 1868	84, 479
Distilling spirits, Apparatus for	E. D. Bannister	Saint Louis, Mo	Mar. 30, 1869	88, 434
Distilling spirits, Apparatus for	H. G. Dayton	Maysville, Ky	Apr. 3, 1866	53, 581
Distilling spirits, Apparatus for	A. Foubert	New York, N. Y	Aug. 20, 1867	67, 864
Distilling spirits, Apparatus for	F. Haeck	Brussels, Belgium	Sept. 29, 1868	82, 519
Distilling spirits, Apparatus for	C. S. Hutchinson	Burlington, N. J	Aug. 4, 1868	80, 740
Distilling spirits, Apparatus for	G. Kleiner	Georgetown, Mo	Dec. 19, 1871	122, 032
Distilling spirits, Apparatus for	A. Kreusler and W. T. Pelton	New Lebanon, N. Y	Nov. 7, 1865	50, 876
Distilling spirits, Apparatus for	F. M. Young	Nashville, Tenn	May 3, 1870	102, 745
Distilling spirits by steam	W. Avery	Pompey, N. Y	May 13, 1825	....
Distilling spirits from corn-stalks	B. Allison	Philadelphia, Pa	July 6, 1809	....
Distilling spirits from grain	W. H. Ford, J. D. Burns, and L. C. Clarke.	New Orleans, La	Aug. 11, 1868	8[illegible], 860
Distilling spirits from grain and fruit	J. Hugus	Westmoreland County, Pa.	May 17, 1828	....
Distilling spirits, Method of	A. Whiston	Staunton, Va	Sept. 28, 1825	....
Distilling spirits of turpentine	C. J. Meinicke	New York, N. Y	July 30, 1850	7, 528
Distilling spirits of turpentine, Apparatus for	D. Cashwell	Fayetteville, N. C	Nov. 19, 1867	70, 956
Distilling spirits of turpentine, Apparatus for	D. Reid	Washington, N. C	May 25, 1858	20, 371
Distilling spirits, Process of	J. Ellingwood	Owensborough, Ky	Oct. 5, 1869	95, 574
Distilling spirits, Process of	C. B. Jarvis	New York, N. Y	Apr. 27, 1869	89, 318
Distilling spirituous liquors	W. J. Cocke	Cabin Point, Va	Feb. 4, 1828	....
Distilling spirituous liquors	J. Simpson	....	Mar. 4, 1794	....
Distilling spirituous liquids, Apparatus for	O. Lugo	New York, N. Y	Jan. 21, 1868	73, 539
Distilling spirituous liquors, Apparatus for	W. Schilling	Baltimore, Md	Mar. 10, 1868	75, 470
Distilling, Steam	B. Barr	Strasburgh Township, Lancaster County, Pa.	Apr. 5, 1828	....
Distilling together spirits of turpentine and alcoholic liquids.	W. Corfield	Chicago, Ill	Feb. 25, 1873	136, 137
Distilling-tub for essential oils	B. P. Van Marter	Lyons, N. Y	Jan. 19, 1869	86, 115
Distilling turpentine	D. Cashwell	Wilmington, N. C	May 10, 1870	102, 774
Distilling turpentine	R. F. Smith	Charleston, S. C	Oct. 2, 1847	5, 320
Distilling turpentine, Apparatus for	L. Bellingrath, jr	Fayetteville, N. C	June 1, 1858	20, 465
Distilling turpentine, &c., Apparatus for	C. [illegible] T. Burcey	Black Rock, Conn	May 30, 1871	115, 429
Distilling turpentine, Apparatus for	A. K. Lee	Galveston, Tex	Aug. 1, 1871	117, 549
Distilling turpentine, Apparatus for	A. K. Lee	Galveston, Tex	Sept. 24, 1872	131, 550
Distilling turpentine, Apparatus for	A. H. Van Bokkelen	Wilmington, N. C	Aug. 22, 1871	118, 305
Distilling turpentine, Apparatus for	J. E. Winants and J. F. Griffen	New York, N. Y	May 28, 1867	65, 147
Distilling turpentine from wood	G. R. H. Leffler	Baltimore, Md	Sept. 27, 1864	44, 435
Distilling turpentine, tar, &c	W. A. Rapp	New York, N. Y	Dec. 4, 1815	....
Distilling volatile hydrocarbons and other substances, Apparatus for.	C. M. James	New York, N. Y	June 26, 1869	86, 232
Distilling whisky and other spirits	J. S. Oliver and E. Harris	New York, N. Y	Oct. 19, 1869	96, 029
Distilling whisky and other spirits, Apparatus for	H. C. Dayton	Maysville, Ky	Feb. 16, 1869	87, 029
Distilling whisky from corn	D. Samson	Perrysburgh, N. Y	Oct. 1, 1830	....
Distilling with cast-iron stills, Mode of	J. Coppinger	Beaufort, S. C	Nov. 21, 1809	....
Distilling wood, &c., Portable apparatus for	G. E. Mills	New York, N. Y	Mar. 29, 1864	42, 101
Distributing-pipe, Hot-air	H. C. Crehore	Boston, Mass	Jan. 31, 1871	111, 483
Distributing table	G. Whitaker	Lewistown, Ill	Nov. 20, 1866	59, 883
Ditches, Construction of	T. K. Grube	Napoleon, Ohio	Aug. 23, 1870	106, 690
Ditches, Covering for blind	T. M. C. Lutes	New Mount Pleasant, Ind	Mar. 9, 1869	87, 094
Ditches, Machine for cutting open	J. N. Smith and W. O. Buckley	Washington, Ill	Aug. 11, 1868	80, 880
Ditcher	W. Robbins	Hancock County, Ill	June 22, 1869	91, 771
Ditcher	C. F. Woodruff	Newbern, Tenn	Feb. 22, 1870	100, 231
Ditcher and grader	E. L. Foreman	Rantoul, Ill	Nov. 23, 1869	97, 183
Ditcher and grader	J. H. Martin and C. D. Bradshaw.	Danville, Ill	Sept. 13, 1870	107, 393
Ditcher and grader	J. G. Sisson and L. Delana	Arcola, Ill	Feb. 22, 1870	100, 199
Ditcher and pipe-layer combined	J. I. Mettler	Mendota, Ill	July 25, 1871	117, 441
Ditching and boring machine	I. B. Jones	Xenia, Ohio	Oct. 6, 1868	82, 846
Ditching and embanking earth, Machine for	H. Cleveland	Fort Wayne, Ind	Dec. 31, 1842	2, 897

Index of patents issued from the United States Patent Office from 1790 *to* 1873, *inclusive*—Continued.

Invention.	Inventor.	Residence.	Date.	No.
Ditching and embanking machine	W. C. Bussey	Rock Grove, Ill	Sept. 3, 1846	4, 740
Ditching and embanking machine	L. Thorn	Washington, D. C	Oct. 10, 1838	975
Ditching and grading machine	F. H. De Tray	Odin, Ill	Jan. 21, 1868	73, 441
Ditching and grading machine	I. and J. Hoskins	Wilmington, Ohio	Oct. 25, 1859	25, 899
Ditching and grading machine	F. M. Howard and D. W. Avery	Saint Paul, Ind	May 5, 1868	77, 487
Ditching and grading machine	L. D. Noble	Cerro Gordo, Ill	Apr. 1, 1873	137, 318
Ditching and grading machine	W. J. Wanchope	Brookfield, Ill	Feb. 19, 1867	62, 171
Ditching and grading machine	H. A. Winter	Windsor, Ill	Nov. 8, 1870	109, 091
Ditching and grading machine	W. S. Worley	Tuscola, Ill	Feb. 5, 1867	61, 908
Ditching and hedging machine	W. Stacy	Hardin County, Iowa	July 26, 1870	105, 858
Ditching and tile-laying machine	B. P. Foster and W. H. Chaffee	Flint, Mich	Oct. 15, 1861	33, 506
Ditching and tile-laying machine	M. M. Hooton	Centralia, Ill	Feb. 6, 1872	123, 479
Ditching and tile-laying machine, Combined	O. W. Voorhis, S. M. Mapes, and W. M. Voorhis.	Lawrence, Ill	May 31, 1870	103, 801
Ditching, grading, &c., Machine for	W. Provines	Columbus, Mo	Jan. 4, 1859	22, 512
Ditching-machine	I. V. Adair	Varick, N. Y	Nov. 12, 1867	70, 772
Ditching-machine	P. W. Adaire	Hays' Creek, Miss	June 5, 1860	28, 544
Ditching-machine	J. S. Anderson and J. B. Cooley	Clark's Hill, Ind	Sept. 7, 1869	94, 539
Ditching-machine	A. S. Ballard	Mount Pleasant, Iowa	Aug. 14, 1860	29, 647
Ditching-machine	J. Ballard and T. J. Magee	New Antioch and Cincinnati, Ohio.	Sept. 4, 1866	57, 814
Ditching-machine	J. W. Barcroft	Friendship, Va	Oct. 25, 1859	25, 875
Ditching-machine	J. W. Barcroft	Friendship, Va	Mar. 13, 1860	27, 419
Ditching-machine	E. Barnes	Chelsea, Mich	May 19, 1868	77, 949
Ditching-machine	C. Bartholomew	Ætna, N. Y	Sept. 14, 1869	94, 696
Ditching-machine	I. A. Benedict and G. W. Cummings.	West Springfield, Pa., and Conneaut, Ohio.	May 15, 1860	28, 247
Ditching-machine	I. A. Benedict and G. W. Cummings.	Conneaut, Ohio	Mar. 12, 1861	31, 653
Ditching-machine	H. Benett	Linden, Cal	Nov. 9, 1869	96, 540
Ditching-machine	S. Bentley	Green Oak, Mich	Aug. 10, 1869	93, 401
Ditching-machine	U. Blickensderfer	Springfield, Pa	Aug. 23, 1870	106, 653
Ditching-machine	I. Boas	New Orleans, La	May 2, 1871	114, 395
Ditching-machine	J. C. Boyd	Rushville, Ind	Mar. 20, 1866	53, 264
Ditching-machine	C. M. Brown	Baltimore, Md	June 10, 1873	139, 765
Ditching-machine	M. E. Burtless	Seneca Falls, N. Y	May 25, 1869	90, 495
Ditching-machine	E. T. Bussell	Indianapolis, Ind	Dec. 12, 1871	121, 846
Ditching-machine	C. Bymer and J. Imlay	Greensburgh, Ind	Nov. 26, 1867	71, 275
Ditching-machine	J. Calliham	Baton Rouge, La	Mar. 8, 1870	100, 597
Ditching-machine	H. Carter	Aylmer, Canada	Nov. 23, 1869	97, 164
Ditching-machine	H. Carter	Aylmer, Canada	Nov. 7, 1871	120, 711
Ditching-machine	H. Carter	Aylmer, Canada	Apr. 2, 1872	125, 167
Ditching-machine	W. Cline, jr	Clayton, Ind	Dec. 7, 1869	97, 606
Ditching-machine	R. Conarroe	Camden, Ohio	Nov. 19, 1867	70, 960
Ditching-machine	R. Conarroe	Camden, Ohio	July 20, 1869	92, 707
Ditching-machine	T. R. Cook	West Newton, Ind	Apr. 17, 1866	53, 950
Ditching-machine	A. W. Cox	Dublin, Ind	May 3, 1864	42, 563
Ditching-machine	A. W. Cox	Dublin, Ind	Aug. 8, 1865	49, 235
Ditching-machine	I. R. Crane	Warsaw, Mo	Dec. 27, 1859	26, 566
Ditching-machine	W. Crawford	Streator, Ill	Aug. 10, 1869	93, 419
Ditching-machine	R. Cummings	Lima, Ind	July 14, 1845	4, 113
Ditching-machine	W. H. Dalbey	Clarksburgh, Ind	Aug. 8, 1865	49, 239
Ditching-machine	A. C. Decker	Bushnell, Ill	Mar. 31, 1868	76, 172
Ditching-machine	O. Doolittle	Dansville, N. Y	Sept. 23, 1862	36, 511
Ditching-machine	O. Doolittle and H. Eldridge	Dansville, N. Y	Feb. 12, 1861	31, 376
Ditching-machine	T. B. Fagan	Mendon, Ohio	May 26, 1868	78, 198
Ditching-machine	J. W. Fauver	Augusta County, Va	Aug. 26, 1873	142, 222
Ditching-machine	H. Felthoff and L. D. Tingley	Prince William, Ind	May 25, 1869	90, 517
Ditching-machine	L. W. Fisher	Rockville, Ind	Dec. 17, 1872	133, 974
Ditching-machine	E. L. Foreman	Rantoul, Ill	Apr. 21, 1868	77, 024
Ditching-machine	R. G. Forsyth	Clayton, Ind	May 31, 1870	103, 595
Ditching-machine	O. and O. S. Foster	Durhamville, N. Y	Oct. 8, 1872	131, 947
Ditching-machine	C. Freese	Aurelius, N. Y	Apr. 3, 1866	53, 737
Ditching-machine	A. A. Fuselier	Algiers, La	Feb. 4, 1868	74, 074
Ditching-machine	S. F. Gard	New Orleans, La	Oct. 11, 1870	108, 248
Ditching-machine	W. Gause	Greensborough, Ind	Feb. 11, 1868	74, 338
Ditching-machine	A. Gifford and I. Seright	Milroy, Ind	Sept. 17, 1867	68, 975
Ditching-machine	H. Gonellaz	Vermillionville, La	July 15, 1873	140, 820
Ditching-machine	O. F. Hale	Irvington, Iowa	Oct. 10, 1871	119, 759
Ditching-machine	H. L. Hall	Buffalo, N. Y	Dec. 7, 1869	97, 504
Ditching-machine	E. Heath	Fowlerville, N. Y	Oct. 2, 1866	58, 413
Ditching-machine	M. C. and G. B. Higgins	Flemington, N. J	June 14, 1870	104, 153
Ditching-machine	E. and B. Holmes	Buffalo, N. Y	Oct. 13, 1857	18, 398
Ditching-machine	W. T. Hoskins	Livia, Ky	Feb. 11, 1873	135, 807
Ditching-machine	J. W. Humphreys	La Fayette, Ind	Jan. 21, 1873	134, 991
Ditching-machine	J. W. Humphreys	Oxford, Ind	Dec. 23, 1873	145, 736
Ditching-machine	H. C. Ingraham	Tecumseh, Mich	Oct. 23, 1866	59, 028
Ditching-machine	H. C. Ingraham	Tecumseh, Mich	Dec. 17, 1867	72, 399
Ditching-machine	G. E. Inman	Buffalo, N. Y	Nov. 22, 1859	26, 189
Ditching-machine	G. Ives	Detroit, Mich	July 9, 1861	32, 772
Ditching-machine	G. Jensen	Brooklyn, N. Y	Oct. 16, 1866	58, 834
Ditching-machine	S. F. Jones	Saint Paul, Ind	Aug. 8, 1865	49, 276
Ditching-machine	N. Kidder	Moscow, Iowa	June 24, 1862	35, 736
Ditching-machine	J. King	Indianapolis, Ind	Feb. 18, 1868	74, 540
Ditching-machine	A. La Tourrette	Waterloo, N. Y	Oct. 8, 1867	69, 682
Ditching-machine	N. B. Lewis	Hopewell, N. Y	Sept. 14, 1869	94, 901
Ditching-machine	P. Lugenbell	Greensburgh, Ind	Aug. 14, 1866	57, 160
Ditching-machine	P. Lugenbeil	Greensburgh, Ind	Apr. 20, 1869	89, 227
Ditching-machine	P. Lugenbell and J. S. Armstrong.	Greensburgh, Ind	Nov. 21, 1865	51, 067
Ditching-machine	J. Marsh	Seneca, Ill	Oct. 20, 1868	83, 296
Ditching-machine	J. H. Marshall and O. E. Mann	Lockport and Somerset, N. Y.	Nov. 27, 1866	60, 025
Ditching-machine	E. C. Martin	Muscatine, Iowa	Feb. 26, 1861	31, 551
Ditching-machine	J. Masters	Waukegan, Ill	May 22, 1860	28, 387
Ditching-machine	J. Masters	Waukegan, Ill	Apr. 14, 1868	76, 788
Ditching-machine	C. Metheny	Greensburgh, Ind	June 25, 1867	66, 139
Ditching-machine	R. C. Mauck	Harrisonburgh, Va	Mar. 13, 1855	12, 514

Index of patents issued from the United States Patent Office from 1790 *to* 1873, *inclusive*—Continued.

Invention.	Inventor.	Residence.	Date.	No.
Ditching-machine	J. W. McAlister and J. C. Roffenberger.	Jacksonville, Ill	Feb. 27, 1872	124, 074
Ditching-machine	J. W. McGehee	Fayetteville, Tex	Nov. 16, 1869	96, 824
Ditching-machine	S. P. McKelvy	Farmer City, Ill	Apr. 5, 1870	101, 640
Ditching-machine	W. D. McKinney	Marion, Ind	May 4, 1869	89, 676
Ditching-machine	J. W. Metz	Stouts, Ohio	Oct. 3, 1871	119, 633
Ditching-machine	H. E. Moon and J. Doan	Wilmington, Ohio	Oct. 16, 1866	58, 871
Ditching-machine	J. W. Morrill	Hampton Falls, N. H	May 10, 1853	9, 709
Ditching-machine	G. W. Nevill	Richmond, Va	Jan. 25, 1870	99, 102
Ditching-machine	G. W. Nevill	Richmond, Va	Jan. 30, 1872	123, 286
Ditching-machine	G. W. Nevill	Richmond, Va	Mar. 11, 1873	136, 752
Ditching-machine	W. A. Nichols	West Liberty, Iowa	Mar. 31, 1868	76, 237
Ditching-machine	L. D. Noble	Cerro Gordo, Ill	June 21, 1870	104, 631
Ditching-machine	P. O'Connor and M. Collins	Decatur, Ill	July 14, 1868	79, 851
Ditching-machine	J. C. Osgood	Troy, N. Y	Sept. 27, 1870	107, 710
Ditching-machine	R. R. Osgood	Troy, N. Y	Sept. 20, 1870	107, 529
Ditching-machine	A. B. Overbaugh	Newark, N. J	Mar. 2, 1869	87, 357
Ditching-machine	E. Owen	La Porte, Ind	Sept. 24, 1844	3, 757
Ditching-machine	J. A. Parsons	Cleveland, Ohio	July 12, 1870	105, 364
Ditching-machine	W. M. Perkins	La Fontaine, Ind	Jan. 2, 1866	51, 859
Ditching-machine	W. Pierce	Truxton, N. Y	Mar. 8, 1870	100, 664
Ditching-machine	R. C. Pratt	Canandaigua, N. Y	July 19, 1853	9, 860
Ditching-machine	J. P. Rees and R. A. Graham	Greensburgh, Ind	May 15, 1866	54, 823
Ditching-machine	J. R. Remington	Lowndes County, Ala	May 28, 1846	4, 539
Ditching-machine	B. Rhett	Abbeville, S. C	July 18, 1871	117, 235
Ditching-machine	L. Rickard	Danville, Ill	Nov. 17, 1868	84, 136
Ditching-machine	J. W. Roberts	Hartford City, Ind	Nov. 15, 1870	109, 251
Ditching-machine	D. Sawyer	Webster, Ohio	Oct. 23, 1866	59, 140
Ditching-machine	F. B. Scott	Buffalo, N. Y	Jan. 24, 1860	26, 934
Ditching-machine	W. R. Selfridge	Greensburgh, Ind	July 21, 1868	80, 092
Ditching-machine	W. Y. Singleton	Springfield, Ill	May 28, 1846	4, 535
Ditching-machine	J. H. Snyder	Killbuck, Ill	Apr. 11, 1865	47, 229
Ditching-machine	A. Spencer	Grampian Hills, Pa	Nov. 12, 1872	132, 929
Ditching-machine	R. Starbuck	Wilmington, Ohio	Feb. 4, 1873	135, 605
Ditching-machine	N. Starbuck	Wilmington, Ohio	Aug. 1, 1865	49, 166
Ditching-machine	N. Starbuck	Wilmington, Ohio	June 18, 1867	65, 841
Ditching-machine	A. J. Stephens	Milford, Ill	Aug. 2, 1870	105, 995
Ditching-machine	J. Stevens	Chicago, Ill	Aug. 7, 1866	57, 050
Ditching-machine	G. H. Stevenson	Washington, Ohio	May 12, 1868	77, 930
Ditching-machine	B. T. Stowell	Waddam's Grove, Ill	Aug. 22, 1848	5, 719
Ditching machine	T. J. Stratton	Waterloo, N. Y	Jan. 15, 1856	14, 117
Ditching-machine	G. Sullivan	West Liberty, Ohio	Jan. 8, 1867	61, 114
Ditching-machine	F. Taylor	Indianapolis, Ind	Nov. 14, 1871	120, 836
Ditching-machine	E. W. Thomas	Chicago, Ill	Mar. 27, 1847	5, 042
Ditching-machine	S. Thrailkill	La Fayette, Ind	Sept. 10, 1846	4, 751
Ditching-machine	B. Tobias	Washington, Ill	May 27, 1862	35, 403
Ditching-machine	S. E. Todd	Brooklyn, N. Y	Nov. 12, 1872	133, 069
Ditching-machine	J. Valentine	Buffalo, N. Y	Dec. 12, 1871	121, 737
Ditching-machine	H. Vannatta	Jefferson, Ill	Oct. 11, 1870	108, 217
Ditching-machine	J. Vaughn and E. Chamness	Miami County and Grant County, Ind.	Apr. 7, 1868	76, 359
Ditching-machine	I. S. Weaver	Dayton, Ohio	July 10, 1866	56, 299
Ditching-machine	C. O., D., and E. West, J. R. Smith, J. Carey, G. Janney, R. Hunt, A. Hackett, and J. Garner.	Martinsville, Ohio	May 15, 1860	28, 320
Ditching-machine	J. W. and M. H. Weston	Windsor, Ill	Nov. 30, 1869	97, 464
Ditching-machine	D. Whisler	Union Township, Ohio	Dec. 31, 1867	72, 953
Ditching-machine	A. H. and T. S. Whitacre	Morrow, Ohio	Dec. 10, 1867	72, 140
Ditching-machine	D. Whitesell	Mattoon, Ill	Sept. 19, 1871	119, 209
Ditching-machine	G. W. Wiggin	Exeter, N. H	June 7, 1864	43, 060
Ditching-machine	I. M. Williams	Blanchester, Ohio	Feb. 18, 1868	74, 653
Ditching-machine	S. S. Wood	Brooklyn, N. Y	Nov. 22, 1870	109, 480
Ditching-machine	S. S. Wood	Brooklyn, N. Y	Aug. 8, 1871	117, 848
Ditching-machine	A. Woolfolk	Iberville Parish, La	Mar. 6, 1860	27, 404
Ditching-machine	E. Worth and C. A. Davis	Oswego, N. Y	Jan. 21, 1868	73, 560
Ditching machine, Mole	I. Hodgson	New Michigan, Ill	July 24, 1860	29, 269
Ditching machine, Mole	A. Peterson	Stockwell, Ind	Aug. 23, 1870	106, 721
Ditching machine, Railway	W. Chadwick and S. I. B. Anderson.	Terre Haute, Ind	Nov. 2, 1858	21, 942
Ditching-machine, Steam	A. J. Dye	New Orleans, La	Mar. 22, 1870	101, 112
Divan and bed	H. Buckler	New York, N. Y	June 11, 1867	65, 640
Dividers	A. A. Cook	Milford, Mass	Dec. 12, 1871	121, 850
Dividers	E. S. Fisher	Boston, Mass	Nov. 26, 1867	71, 370
Dividers	H. Gerecke	Carlstadt, N. J	June 11, 1872	127, 686
Dividers	C. M. Nichols	West Greenwich, R. I	Oct. 10, 1871	119, 875
Dividers	S. A. Shurtleff	Taunton, Mass	Sept. 26, 1865	50, 173
Dividers	O. E. Weatherhead	Winchendon, Mass	Dec. 17, 1867	72, 433
Dividers	H. Whiting	New York, N. Y	Apr. 30, 1867	64, 391
Dividers and calipers	G. W. Lane	Plantsville, Conn	Nov. 1, 1870	108, 799
Dividers and calipers	G. L. McKnight	Worcester, Mass	Apr. 30, 1867	64, 240
Dividers and calipers	S. Sawyer	Fitchburgh, Mass	Apr. 9, 1867	63, 656
Dividers and calipers	E. S. Scripture	Brooklyn, N. Y	Jan. 7, 1868	73, 126
Dividers, Extension	G. C. Miller	Detroit, Mich	Nov. 11, 1873	144, 468
Dividers, Mathematical	J. E. Earle	Leicester, Mass	Jan. 5, 1858	19, 058
Dividers, Mathematical	A. Schaefer	New York, N. Y	Mar. 9, 1858	19, 589
Dividers or compasses	D. H. Chamberlain	Boston, Mass	Apr. 9, 1850	7, 257
Dividers or measuring-compasses	C. Reiffel and N. Thorn	New York, N. Y	Nov. 21, 1848	5, 929
Dividers, Pencil-attachment for	W. Schollhorn	New Haven, Conn	June 17, 1873	140, 081
Dividers, Proportional	H. M Parkhurst	Perth Amboy, N. J	Dec. 25, 1855	13, 993
Dividers, Spring	J. W. Strange	Bangor, Me	Sept. 11, 1860	30, 009
Dividing-engine, Circular and straight-lined	R. Tyler	Philadelphia, Pa	Sept. 10, 18[illegible]8	....
Dividing-engine, Variable dial for	W. H. Brown	Worcester, Mass	Jan. 15, 1856	14, 082
Diving-apparatus	T. C. McKeen	Dunkirk, N. Y	Sept. 29, 1863	40, 114
Diving-apparatus	T. C. McKeen	Irvington, N. J	June 11, 1867	65, 760
Diving-apparatus	W. H. Taylor	New York	Jan. 20, 1838	578
Diving-apparatus	G. Williamson	Brooklyn, N. Y	Sept. 22, 1857	18, 260
Diving-apparatus	C. Wilson	Bridgeport, Conn	Sept. 19, 1871	119, 210

Index of patents issued from the United States Patent Office from 1790 *to* 1873, *inclusive*—Continued.

Invention.	Inventor.	Residence.	Date.	No.
Diving-bell	H. C. Billings	Brooklyn, N. Y	Dec. 14, 1869	97, 862
Diving-bell	E. W. Foreman	New Rochelle, N. Y	Aug. 23, 1853	9, 965
Diving-bell	B. Maillefert	Astoria, N. Y	Mar. 30, 1858	19, 785
Diving-bell	J. R. Wooster	Baltimore, Md	Apr. 24, 1849	6, 397
Diving-bell, Deep-sea	J. A. Richards and I. W. Wolcott.	Boston, Mass	Apr. 3, 1849	6, 250
Diving-dress	C. Hall	Connecticut	Dec. 24, 1810	....
Diving-machine	R. Tripe	Dover, N. H	Apr. 1, 1806	....
Diving-suit	W. C. Davison and D. Clark	Pittsford, N. Y	July 26, 1824	....
Diving-suit	F. Smith and L. S. Steel	Norfolk, Va	Apr. 23, 1834	....
Diving suit	N. Wolcott	Sidney, N. Y	Apr. 17, 1834	....
Diving-suit, Elastic	L. Norcross	Dixfield, Me	June 14, 1834	....
Divitials and preventing forgery, Making	C. S. Rafinesque	Lexington, Ky	Aug. 23, 1825	....
Dock and wharf fender	J. Moomey	Clinton, Iowa	June 19, 1860	28, 765
Dock, Buoyant	M. Isnard	New York, N. Y	June 22, 1826	....
Dock, Dry	G. A. Albertson	New York, N. Y	Mar. 14, 1871	112, 525
Dock, Dry	D. Brown	New York, N. Y	Feb. 11, 1832	....
Dock, Dry	R. Bulkley	New York, N. Y	Aug. 28, 1821	....
Dock, Dry	G. H. Ferris	Brooklyn, N. Y	June 28, 1870	104, 843
Dock, Dry	J. L. Gilbert	New York, N. Y	May 12, 1840	1, 606
Dock, Dry	J. Houston, A. Hinman, and J. Ingraham.	Buffalo, N. Y	June 22, 1836	....
Dock, Dry	C. F. Johnson	Tioga, N. Y	Mar. 6, 1840	1, 506
Dock, Dry	W. Jones	New York, N. Y	May 3, 1870	102, 554
Dock, Dry	C. Krogh	Kroghsville, Wis	Sept. 8, 1863	39, 818
Dock, Dry	I. J. Merritt	New York, N. Y	Dec. 10, 1867	72, 066
Dock, Dry	J. W. Munger and W. O. Jones	Portland, Me	Aug. 28, 1866	57, 550
Dock, Dry	A. Place	New York, N. Y	Apr. 1, 1826	....
Dock, Dry	J. Richardson	Germantown, Va	Feb. 23, 1869	87, 291
Dock, Dry	J. Ryan	Saint Louis, Mo	Oct. 10, 1865	50, 390
Dock, Dry	E. Selden	Haddam, Conn	July 30, 1829	....
Dock, Dry	J. E. Simpson	East Boston, Mass	Dec. 5, 1854	12, 032
Dock, Dry	H. K. Wagner	Saint Louis, Mo	Nov. 10, 1846	4, 842
Dock, Floating	J. Campbell	London, England	Nov. 9, 1869	96, 672
Dock, Floating	S. Janicki	St. Petersburg, Russia	Feb. 6, 1872	123, 402
Dock, Floating	S. Janicki	St. Petersburg, Russia	Apr. 30, 1872	126, 146
Dock, Floating	A. R. McNair	Saint Louis, Mo	Sept. 17, 1872	131, 365
Dock, Floating	E. Turner	Baltimore, Md	Apr. 25, 1865	47, 501
Dock, Floating	H. Van Keuren	Jersey City, N. J	July 18, 1871	117, 223
Dock, Floating	O. T. Williams	Smithland, Ky	Feb. 24, 1852	8, 765
Dock, Floating dry	J. Adamson	Boston, Mass	Dec. 13, 1816	....
Dock, Floating dry	J. Barron	Philadelphia, Pa	July 17, 1837	272
Dock, Floating dry	A. Brux	Augusta, Ga	Nov. 6, 1818	....
Dock, Floating dry	J. R. Campbell and J. S. Withington.	Boston, Mass	Nov. 28, 1835	....
Dock, Floating dry	E. Covenhoven	Greenburgh, N. Y	Oct. 30, 1821	....
Dock, Floating dry	D. Dodge and P. Burgess	New York, N. Y	Oct. 9, 1841	2, 281
Dock, Floating dry	J. Floyd	Kittery, Me	Aug. 17, 1826	....
Dock, Floating dry	J. G. Gilbert	New York, N. Y	Mar. 25, 1840	1, 524
Dock, Floating dry	J. G. Gilbert	New York, N. Y	July 28, 1842	2, 742
Dock, Floating dry	J. Hawes	Cayuga County, N. Y	Apr. 22, 1835	....
Dock, Floating dry	S. Hill	Jersey City, N. J	Feb. 1, 1842	2, 442
Dock, Floating dry	S. Loveland	Oswego, N. Y	Feb. 5, 1847	4, 954
Dock, Floating dry	J. T. Martin	New York, N. Y	Mar. 19, 1840	1, 518
Dock, Floating dry	R. Moody and S. D. Dakin	New York, N. Y	Nov. 24, 1843	3, 351
Dock, Floating dry	R. Porter	Bellerica, Mass	Nov. 14, 1835	....
Dock, Floating dry	S. Rose	New York, N. Y	June 15, 1812	....
Dock, Floating dry	J. Thomas	Saint Louis, Mo	Mar. 26, 1834	....
Dock, Floating dry	J. Thomas	New York, N. Y	Dec. 20, 1837	522
Dock, Floating dry	J. Thomas	New York, N. Y	June 26, 1841	2, 149
Dock, Floating dry	W. Thomas	Saint Louis, Mo	May 19, 1840	1, 609
Dock, Floating graving	T. Cunningham	Pittsburgh, Pa	Oct. 1, 1830	....
Dock, Floating screw	S. F. Stinchfield	New Orleans, La	Apr. 27, 1832	....
Dock, Floating sectional dry	J. Seely	Buffalo, N. Y	Feb. 24, 1857	16, 696
Dock, Floating tide	W. Pickard	Jersey City, N. J	July 26, 1870	105, 725
Dock for cleansing the bottoms of vessels, Floating dry.	W. Rhodes	New York, N. Y	May 16, 1808	....
Dock for raising and removing vessels, Floating dry.	J. S. Gilbert	New York, N. Y	Sept. 19, 1840	1, 792
Dock for repairing vessels, Dry	C. Bergh	New York, N. Y	Apr. 29, 1825	....
Dock for repairing vessels, &c., Floating dry	W. R. Lowcree	New York, N. Y	June 23, 1825	....
Dock, Fresh-water dry	L. H. Clarke and L. M. Wiss	New York, N. Y	Dec. 22, 1825	....
Dock, Graving	W. A. Kenrick and G. H. Whitcher.	Boston, Mass	Dec. 20, 1859	26, 501
Dock, Hydraulic	Z. Ring	New York, N. Y	Feb. 13, 1836	....
Dock, Hydrostatic suspension	T. Evans and J. Parsons	New York, N. Y	May 13, 1831	....
Dock indicator, Dry	P. F. Campbell	Jersey City, N. J	July 31, 1866	56, 702
Dock, Lifting	Z. P. Leach	Danbury, Conn	Jan. 3, 1865	45, 724
Dock, Marine dry	H. I. Crandall	New Bedford, Mass	June 12, 1860	28, 658
Dock, Marine elevating	E. Buck, H. Crehore, R. Gerry, and A. Bayard.	Boston, Mass	July 11, 1825	....
Dock, Rotary dry	J. Webb	New York, N. Y	May 3, 1817	....
Dock, Screw	J. C. Ely	New York, N. Y	Jan. 28, 1829	....
Dock, Screw	E. Turner	Rochester, N. Y	Oct. 10, 1829	....
Dock, Sectional dry	S. Loveland	Astoria, N. Y	Mar. 7, 1854	10, 600
Dock, Ship-railway	J. Thomas	New York, N. Y	Feb. 24, 1826	....
Docks and harbors, Machine for clearing	S. Colver	....	Dec. 14, 1798	....
Docks and marine-railway, Adjustable cradle for dry	W. Van Deusen	Philadelphia, Pa	Dec. 14, 1858	22, 317
Docks, Basin to be used in connection with floating dry.	R. Moody and S. D. Dakin	New York, N. Y	Sep. 17, 1844	3, 745
Docks, Bilge-supporter for holding vessels in	H. I. Crandall	Boston, Mass	Dec. 19, 1854	12, 093
Docks, Building	A. W. Thompson and J. Pattison	New York, N. Y	Mar. 4, 1873	136, 560
Docks, Carrying and lifting trunk	J. Barron	Norfolk, Va	Aug. 2, 1826	....
Docks, &c., Construction of	S. J. Seely	New York, N. Y	Jan. 31, 1865	46, 146
Docks, Erecting dry	J. Gardiner	....	Dec. 3, 1802	....
Docks, Machine for cleaning out	J. Greenleaf	....	July 13, 1802	....
Docks, Method of holding vessel by the keel in dry and other	J. Smith	Neponset Village, Mass	Dec. 19, 1854	12, 104

Index of patents issued from the United States Patent Office from 1790 *to* 1873, *inclusive*—Continued.

Invention.	Inventor.	Residence.	Date.	No.
Docks, Mode of adjusting vessel upon the keel-block of dry sectional or railway.	H. I. Crandall	East Boston, Mass	Nov. 14, 1854	11, 932
Docks, Mode of constructing projecting	M. Rogers	New York	Jan. 7, 1817	....
Docks or harbors, Machine for cleaning	P. Zacharie	....	Nov. 24, 1791	....
Document case	C. S. Trevitt	Washington, N. C	May 30, 1871	115, 542
Document holder and filer	M. L. M. Hussey	New York, N. Y	Aug. 7, 1866	56, 941
Dog kennel or house	S. S. Bent	Port Chester, N. Y	Jan. 5, 1869	85, 557
Dog-power	F. Cole	Conesus, N. Y	July 14, 1863	39, 263
Dog-power	A. W. Hager and J. H. S. Grove	Waverly, Iowa	Nov. 24, 1868	84, 354
Dog-power	A. Tieman	New York	Apr. 27, 1818	....
Dog-power, Operating machinery by	D. C. Slater	Laurens, N. Y	June 7, 1859	24, 338
Doll	M. Kintzback	Philadelphia, Pa	Oct. 5, 1869	95, 489
Doll	J. Lacman	Philadelphia, Pa	Apr. 4, 1871	113, 532
Doll	H. C. Work	Brooklyn, N. Y	July 8, 1873	140, 605
Doll, Creeping	G. P. Clarke	New York, N. Y	Aug. 29, 1871	118, 435
Doll, Creeping	R. J. Clay	New York, N. Y	Mar. 14, 1871	112, 550
Doll, Fancy	D. Checkeni	Marion, Conn	Feb. 20, 1866	52, 782
Doll-head	G. Benda	Coburg, Germany	July 16, 1872	129, 086
Doll-heads and other toys, Mode of constructing	L. E. Sallee	Decatur, Ill	Feb. 7, 1865	46, 270
Doll-heads, Constructing	L. Greiner	Philadelphia, Pa	Mar. 30, 1858	19, 770
Doll-heads, Construction of	G. H. Hawkins	New York, N. Y	Sept. 8, 1868	81, 999
Doll-heads, Manufacture of	G. H. Hawkins	New York, N. Y	Jan. 5, 1869	85, 589
Doll-joint	J. A. H. Ellis	Springfield, Vt	May 20, 1873	139, 130
Doll, Walking	A. W. Nicholson	Brooklyn, N. Y	Mar. 23, 1869	88, 197
Dolls, Arms for	C. F. Blakeslee	New York, N. Y	Jan. 3, 1865	45, 691
Dolls, Manufacture of	F. E. Darrow	Bristol, Conn	May 1, 1866	54, 201
Dolls, Process for manufacturing	W. Rumbold	Saint Louis, Mo	June 17, 1862	35, 630
Dome	I. F. Walker	Central Falls, R. I	Nov. 4, 1873	144, 373
Dome, bridge, &c., Mode of uniting timber for	W. Armesley	Albany, N. Y	Nov. 6, 1830	....
Domestic boiler	F. Till	Reading, Pa	Dec. 19, 1871	121, 973
Domino	J. W. Hyatt, jr	Albany, N. Y	June 15, 1869	91, 234
Domino	B. Louinean	Sables d'Olonnes, France	Oct. 14, 1873	143, 703
Domino	W. X. Stevens	East Brookfield, Mass	June 17, 1873	139, 928
Dominos, Manufacture of	J. W. Hyatt, jr	Albany, N. Y	June 15, 1869	91, 235
Dominos, &c., Treatment of wood for the manufacture of.	G. H. Chinnock	Brooklyn, N. Y	Dec. 10, 1872	133, 697
Donkey, Mechanical	A. and W. Shedlock	New York, N. Y	Feb. 25, 1868	74, 772
Door	E. R. Ball	Oswego, N. Y	Apr. 5, 1832	....
Door	B. F. Barker	Belfast, Me	June 20, 1871	116, 010
Door	O. C. Hill	Malone, N.Y	June 19, 1855	13, 090
Door	G. M. McMahan	Mount Sterling, Ky	Apr. 14, 1868	76, 790
Door-alarm	H. Behn	New York, N. Y	Oct. 2, 1860	30, 193
Door-alarm	H. Curtis and A. Tufts	Charlestown, Mass	Apr. 9, 1861	31, 957
Door and blind fastening	D. Bull	Amboy, Ill	Sept. 17, 1867	68, 947
Door and chest lock, Construction of	R. Wilson	Burdett, N. Y	May 10, 1838	734
Door and gate bolt	J. Smith	Southold, N. Y	Dec. 2, 1873	145, 131
Door and gate closer	H. N. Conklin	Indianapolis, Ind	Oct. 6, 1868	82, 804
Door and gate fastening, Barn	L. B. Hayes and W. Norris	Greene, N. Y	Nov. 5, 1867	70, 562
Door and gate spring	S. L. Bean and L. Mills	Galesburgh, Ill	Mar. 4, 1873	136, 482
Door and gate spring	J. T. Foster	Jersey City, N. J	Apr. 15, 1873	137, 770
Door and gate spring	J. C. Gould	Boonton, N. J	Oct. 2, 1866	58, 405
Door and gate spring	P. Kern	Dayton, Ohio	June 20, 1871	116, 196
Door and gate spring	C. N. Owen	Salem, Ohio	Apr. 8, 1873	137, 619
Door and gate spring	C. W. Saladee	Saint Catharine's, Canada	Feb. 20, 1872	123, 843
Door and gate spring	J. Stephenson	Canandaigua, N. Y	Jan. 1, 1867	60, 954
Door and gate spring	E. Stinson	Montpelier, Vt	Nov. 19, 1867	71, 081
Door and gate spring	M. F. Taber	Salem, Ohio	July 4, 1871	116, 644
Door and gate spring	S. D. Tuttle	Eaton, Ohio	Oct. 1, 1872	131, 914
Door and other locks	A. Prutzmann	Philadelphia, Pa	Sept. 5, 1840	1, 773
Door and other locks	C. F. Voorkies	Newark, N. J	June 9, 1843	3, 125
Door and other locks	R. Wilcox	New York	Apr. 20, 1824	....
Door and other locks, Manner of closing and opening the key-hole of.	D. Evans	Philadelphia, Pa	July 10, 1841	2, 166
Door and package holder	J. K. McDonald	Newark, N. J	Mar. 31, 1868	76, 224
Door and safe lock	J. Gillingham	Turner, Me	Sept. 8, 1868	81, 988
Door and sash clamp	E. F. Dunaway	Cincinnati, Ohio	Mar. 24, 1868	75, 880
Door and sash guide, Sliding	G. L. Waitt	Philadelphia, Pa	May 9, 1871	114, 731
Door and shutter	S. G. Cabell	Quincy, Ill	Nov. 13, 1866	59, 553
Door and shutter bolt	J. Feldman	New York, N. Y	Mar. 21, 1865	46, 891
Door and shutter bolt	G. B. Green	Philadelphia, Pa	June 21, 1870	104, 449
Door and shutter fastener	J. Anser	Mount Vernon, N. Y	Dec. 15, 1868	84, 984
Door and shutter fastening and buffer, Combined	W. C. Wendell	Philadelphia, Pa	June 27, 1871	116, 379
Door and shutter, Metallic	C. K. Marshall	New Orleans, La	May 26, 1868	78, 218
Door and shutter spring	L. Bommer	New York, N. Y	Mar. 31, 1863	38, 023
Door and trunk lock	A. Beals	Exeter, N. H	Jan. 26, 1830	....
Door and window bolt	G. Smith	Philadelphia, Pa	Dec. 18, 1839	1, 435
Door and window fastener	W. I. Corthell and P. Richards	Boston, Mass	Nov. 12, 1867	70, 699
Door and window fastener	J. Z. Davis	San Francisco, Cal	May 23, 1871	115, 176
Door and window fastener	H. Wilkinson	Newburgh, N. Y	Sept. 13, 1864	44, 245
Door and window frames, Machine for making	W. W. Maughlin	Baltimore, Md	May 14, 1867	64, 779
Door and window guard	J. W. White	Weymouth, Mass	Dec. 23, 1873	145, 772
Door and window locking device	A. H. Boyd	Rockville, Mass	Oct. 15, 1867	69, 753
Door and window tightener and fastener	D. Conlon	Portland, Me	Jan. 12, 1869	85, 729
Door apparatus, Sliding	J. Capron	New York, N. Y	May 17, 1870	103, 139
Door-bell	J. Harrison	East Hampton, Conn	Apr. 22, 1873	138, 151
Door-bell	W. M. Preston	Roxbury, N. Y	Sept. 2, 1873	142, 412
Door-bolt	G. T. Allamby	Bangor, Me	Aug. 28, 1866	57, 616
Door-bolt	S. D. Arnold	New Britain, Conn	Apr. 29, 1873	138, 360
Door, &c., bolt	W. F. Arnold and O. L. Steele	New Britain, Conn	Apr. 20, 1869	89, 191
Door-bolt	N. W. Bonney	Victoria, Tex	June 26, 1860	28, 827
Door-bolt	C. Chevallier	New York, N. Y	Aug. 1, 1865	49, 085
Door-bolt	J. H. Cohen, W. A. Pennoyer, and W. H. Crosby.	Catskill, N. Y	Aug. 13, 1872	130, 483
Door-bolt	J. M. Crosby	Norwalk, Ohio	May 5, 1857	17, 204
Door-bolt	F. Engelbrecht	Memphis, Tenn	May 16, 1871	114, 782
Door-bolt	L. J. Evans	Binghamton, N. Y	Nov. 7, 1871	120, 729
Door-bolt	A. P. Floyd	Niagara Falls, N. Y	Nov. 21, 1865	51, 034
Door-bolt	B. E. Fowler	Hartford, Conn	Jan. 15, 1867	61, 185

Index of patents issued from the United States Patent Office from 1790 *to* 1873, *inclusive*—Continued.

Invention.	Inventor.	Residence.	Date.	No.
Door-bolt	W. H. Hart	New Britain, Conn	July 4, 1865	48, 555
Door-bolt	W. H. Hart	New Britain, Conn	Sept. 26, 1865	50, 120
Door-bolt	W. H. Hart	New Britain, Conn	May 31, 1870	103, 606
Door-bolt	L. G. Hoffman	Waterford, N. Y	Sept. 6, 1859	25, 335
Door-bolt	A. G. Hofstatter	New York, N. Y	Apr. 15, 1873	137, 841
Door-bolt	C. C. Jones	Portland, Me	Dec. 17, 1867	72, 302
Door-bolt	J. Jones	New York, N. Y	Mar. 25, 1873	137, 211
Door-bolt	J. Levy	New York, N. Y	Feb. 1, 1870	99, 330
Door-bolt	D. McArthur	New Haven, Conn	Nov. 1, 1870	108, 920
Door-bolt	M. McGonnigle	Allegheny City, Pa	June 20, 1865	48, 297
Door-bolt	C. G. Page	Washington, D. C	Dec. 20, 1859	26, 518
Door-bolt	J. E. Parker	West Meriden, Conn	Aug. 8, 1865	49, 296
Door-bolt	A. Pelham	Plymouth, Mich	Mar. 18, 1873	136, 861
Door-bolt	G. A. Pridham	Newark, N. J	Nov. 12, 1867	70, 895
Door-bolt	R. B. Prindle	Norwich, N. Y	July 19, 1870	105, 489
Door-bolt	B. Russell	Brooklyn, N. Y	Apr. 9, 1861	32, 002
Door-bolt	J. B. Sargent	New Haven, Conn	June 6, 1871	115, 645
Door-bolt	J. B. Sargent	New Haven, Conn	June 18, 1872	128, 074
Door-bolt	A. H. Sherwood	Southport, Conn	Sept. 17, 1867	69, 033
Door-bolt	H. S. Smith	Brooklyn, N. Y	Feb. 10, 1863	37, 646
Door-bolt	S. B. Swartz and J. M. Opdycke	Lumberville, Pa	June 8, 1869	91, 180
Door-bolt	A. F. Warren	Brooklyn, N. Y	June 29, 1869	92, 130
Door-bolt	A. Westcott	Syracuse, N. Y	June 2, 1857	17, 464
Door-bolt	A. Westcott	Syracuse, N. Y	Mar. 7, 1865	46, 740
Door-bolt	W. Wheeler	Troy, N. Y	Oct. 23, 1847	5, 338
Door-bolt	S. R. Wilmot	Wartertown, Conn	June 2, 1857	17, 474
Door-bolt	G. M. Wood	Decatur, Ill	Aug. 14, 1866	57, 241
Door-bolt	J. Woolman	Philadelphia, Pa	Apr. 6, 1858	19, 891
Door-bolt	J. S. R. Wright	Nichols, N. Y	Apr. 15, 1873	137, 994
Door-bolt and lock	C. Sulzman	Waterford, N. Y	Apr. 14, 1868	76, 671
Door-bolt and weather-strip	A. Newcomb	Shipman, Ill	Jan. 26, 1869	86, 242
Door-bolt, Automatic	A. McKay	Montreal, Canada	Dec. 27, 1870	110, 486
Door bolt, Barn	W. Campbell	Belleville, Mich	May 21, 1872	127, 024
Door bolt, Barn	M. R. Green	Warwick, N. Y	Oct. 4, 1870	108, 017
Door-bolt, Cylindrical	C. G. Page	Washington, D. C	July 21, 1857	17, 843
Door-bolt for safes, &c	O. Gallagher	Boston, Mass	Sept. 14, 1869	94, 735
Door-bolt, Signal	C. Page	West Meriden, Conn	May 17, 1859	24, 051
Door-bolt, Spring	G. F. Atkinson	Seymour, Conn	Oct. 29, 1867	70, 149
Door-bolts, Adjustible keeper for	G. W. Davis	Brooklyn, N. Y	Jan. 26, 1869	86, 217
Door-bolts, Locking cylindrical	C. G. Page	Washington, D. C	July 14, 1857	17, 808
Door buffer and catch	A. A. Veer	Delaware, Ohio	Nov. 29, 1870	109, 692
Door-button	G. F. Beardsley	Binghamton, N. Y	Nov. 28, 1871	121, 271
Door-button	O. F. Fogelstrand	Kensington, Conn	Jan. 28, 1873	135, 215
Door-button	T. Lincoln and G. Hubbard	New Haven, Conn	Mar. 23, 1869	88, 166
Door-button	W. E. Sparks	New Haven, Conn	Mar. 24, 1868	75, 996
Door-button	H. Underwood	Tolland, Conn	Sept. 27, 1864	44, 474
Door-call	W. E. Sparks	New Haven, Conn	July 2, 1872	128, 565
Door-catch	A. Blood, jr	Independence, Iowa	Nov. 19, 1867	70, 945
Door-catch	J. M. Crosby	Norwalk, Ohio	June 9, 1857	17, 490
Door-catch	W. H. Fowler	Newburgh, N. Y	Nov. 6, 1866	59, 380
Door-catch	R. V. Phillips	Council Bluffs, Iowa	Nov. 15, 1870	109, 342
Door-catch and cushion	S. Wagner	Galion, Ohio	May 4, 1869	89, 819
Door-check	C. R. Anderson	Saint Louis, Mo	Mar. 14, 1871	112, 673
Door-check	J. Bader	Olathe, Kans	Nov. 4, 1873	144, 246
Door-check	C. Bird	Lower Merion Township, Pa	Feb. 28, 1871	112, 210
Door-check	W. O. Clough	Lexington, Ky	May 7, 1872	126, 445
Door-check	L. Goodyear	Trumansburgh, N. Y	Aug. 5, 1873	141, 435
Door-check	A. Hanna	Dover, Ky	Jan. 21, 1873	135, 115
Door-check	L. S. Hicks	Peoria, Ill	Mar. 7, 1871	112, 455
Door-check	G. C. Idly	Burlingame, Kans	Mar. 11, 1873	136, 731
Door-check	J. P. Israel and D. W. McLane	Oil City, Pa	June 24, 1873	140, 139
Door-check	W. H. Johnson, sr	Clayton, Ind	Nov. 16, 1869	96, 924
Door-check	J. and A. Kolb	Oxford, Ind	Jan. 28, 1873	135, 346
Door-check	H. N. H. Lugrin	Chelsea, Mass	Jan. 17, 1871	110, 985
Door-check	J. A. McNabb	Olathe, Kans	Aug. 5, 1873	141, 577
Door-check	G. W. Pagett	Oxford, Ind	June 6, 1871	115, 768
Door-check	M. R. Perkins	Portsmouth, N. H	Nov. 4, 1873	144, 222
Door-check	S. Peters and C. D. Eisaman	Penn Station, Pa	Apr. 30, 1872	126, 328
Door-check	J. Pool	Elizabeth City, N. C	Oct. 31, 1871	120, 533
Door-check	B. Poulson	Forte Wayne, Ind	Mar. 25, 1873	137, 237
Door-check	G. Ramsay	Clyde, Ohio	Oct. 8, 1872	131, 970
Door-check	G. E. Rittenhouse	Akron, Ohio	May 20, 1873	139, 082
Door-check	G. Rohrbaker	Penn Station, Pa	Jan. 7, 1873	134, 612
Door-check	D. C. Smart	Cambridgeport, Mass	Aug. 15, 1871	118, 063
Door-check	H. D. Weever	Mount Vernon, Ind	July 23, 1872	129, 875
Door-check	C. P. Young	Attleborough, Miss	Nov. 8, 1870	109, 096
Door check and holder	S. L. Hart	Menasha, Wis	May 17, 1870	103, 044
Door check and retainer	G. H. Worster	Athol, Mass	May 6, 1873	138, 551
Door-clamp	H. O. Hooper	Diamond Springs, Cal	July 13, 1869	92, 531
Door-clamp	H. O. Hooper	Diamond Springs, Cal	Mar. 7, 1871	112, 342
Door-closing apparatus	M. T. Cooper	Ballston Spa, N. Y	Apr. 6, 1852	8, 855
Door-closing apparatus	H. F. Shaw	West Roxbury, Mass	Aug. 19, 1873	141, 896
Door-closing device	D. I. Stagg	New York, N. Y	Jan. 7, 1862	34, 075
Door-closing fixture	W. Wilson	Northampton, Mass	May 16, 1848	5, 579
Door-closing mechanism	H. Smith	Boston, Mass	Nov. 13, 1866	59, 667
Door-directory	L. Burger	Springfield, Ill	May 5, 1868	77, 450
Door, Double-acting	W. Rippon	Providence, R. I	July 6, 1852	9, 102
Door-fastener	L. C. Bignall	Lockport, N. Y	May 31, 1864	42, 924
Door-fastener	H. Burt	Newark, N. J	Aug. 16, 1859	25, 090
Door-fastener	J. M. Clark	Lancaster, Pa	Dec. 22, 1868	85, 165
Door-fastener	E. H. Crane	Jonesville, Mich	Feb. 21, 1865	46, 451
Door-fastener	L. Crofoot	Syracuse, N. Y	Nov. 11, 1856	16, 048
Door-fastener	W. F. Davis and C. E. Broad	Boston and Milton, Mass	Apr. 27, 1869	89, 295
Door-fastener	G. V. Hazard	Torrey, N. Y	Dec. 20, 1859	26, 494
Door-fastener	W. A. Howard	Dugway, N. Y	Sept. 12, 1871	118, 942
Door-fastener	H. M. Jones	West Meriden, Conn	Sept. 28, 1869	95, 231
Door-fastener	S. P. Kittle	Buffalo, N. Y	June 7, 1853	9, 765
Door fastener	J. Letort	Wytheville, Va	Dec. 23, 1856	16, 282

Index of patents issued from the United States Patent Office from 1790 *to* 1873, *inclusive*—Continued.

Invention.	Inventor.	Residence.	Date.	No.
Door-fastener	F. C. Levalley	Warnerville, N. Y	Dec. 10, 1867	72, 053
Door-fastener	J. Lightfoot	Cold Spring, Ky	May 8, 1860	28, 186
Door-fastener	G. H. Lindner	Hoboken, N. J	Apr. 8, 1856	14, 594
Door-fastener	F. McDonough	Chicago, Ill	Nov. 6, 1866	59, 431
Door-fastener	D. E. McDougall	Troy, N. Y	May 31, 1853	9, 753
Door-fastener	J. H. McElroy and J. H. Holly	Warwick, N. Y	Dec. 29, 1868	85, 321
Door-fastener	G. W. McGill	Buffalo, N. Y	Apr. 13, 1858	19, 937
Door-fastener	J. A. Morris	Greenbush, N. Y	July 4, 1871	116, 621
Door-fastener	E. P. Moulton	Baltimore, Md	Apr. 29, 1856	14, 773
Door-fastener	H. Orcutt	Amherst, Wis	Aug. 12, 1873	141, 724
Door-fastener	G. F. Perkins and S. F. Gibbs	Holyoke, Mass	May 5, 1868	77, 651
Door-fastener	W. Quayle	Warsaw, Ill	May 11, 1869	89, 942
Door-fastener	J. O. Reilley	Baltimore, Md	Dec. 22, 1868	85, 243
Door-fastener	W. J. Ross	Worcester, Mass	Dec. 8, 1868	84, 767
Door-fastener	G. W. Sayre	Pisgah, Ohio	Aug. 29, 1865	49, 656
Door-fastener	W. H. Smith	New York, N. Y	May 6, 1856	14, 834
Door-fastener	H. N. Taft	Sag Harbor, N. Y	May 14, 1867	64, 808
Door-fastener	G. E. Thompson	New Haven, Conn	Feb. 6, 1866	52, 469
Door-fastener	G. Yates	West Dresden, N. Y	Dec. 28, 1858	22, 469
Door-fastener, Adjustable	L. P. Barnes	Fitchburgh, Mass	Jan. 10, 1871	110, 821
Door-fastener and key-ring combined	B. H. Melendy	Manchester, N. H	May 17, 1870	103, 068
Door fastener and pocket-knife combined	B. F. Porter	Manchester, N. H	Nov. 5, 1867	70, 609
Door-fastener, Mortise-latch	L. Foster	Boston, Mass	Aug. 28, 1841	2, 231
Door-fastener, Portable	B. R. Eames	South Newry, Me	Apr. 10, 1855	12, 675
Door-fastener, Portable	G. W. Griswold	Carbondale, Pa	Sept. 5, 1854	11, 646
Door-fastener, Portable	E. H. Janney and E. J. Hamilton.	Fairfax, Va	June 5, 1866	55, 305
Door-fastener, Portable	L. C. Johnson	Buffalo, N. Y	June 28, 1859	24, 603
Door-fastener, Portable	J. Pepper	Lake Village, N. H	Aug. 6, 1867	67, 578
Door-fastening	M. Bennett	Kilbourne City, Wis	Jan. 1, 1867	60, 673
Door-fastening	A. Call	Springfield, Mass	Mar. 7, 1846	4, 407
Door-fastening	J. Decker	Sparta, N. J	Mar. 5, 1867	62, 532
Door-fastening	C. Frost	Waterbury, Conn	July 26, 1859	24, 859
Door-fastening	W. Hartsfield	Thomaston, Ga	July 5, 1859	24, 632
Door-fastening	L. G. Hoffman	Waterford, N. Y	Nov. 22, 1859	26, 185
Door-fastening	N. Hornady	West Elkton, Ohio	Nov. 12, 1867	70, 846
Door-fastening	F. H. and A. J. Illingworth	Weston, Mass	Jan. 16, 1866	52, 050
Door-fastening	J. C. Palmer	East Haddam, Conn	Oct. 11, 1845	4, 229
Door-fastening	R. Peck	Cortlandville, N. Y	Jan. 15, 1856	14, 112
Door-fastening	S. M. Pye	Acquackanocnk, N. J	Mar. 28, 1848	5, 492
Door-fastening	F. Reed	Brattleborough, Vt	Nov. 13, 1866	59, 653
Door-fastening	C. Washburn	Bridgewater, Mass	Apr. 18, 1832	....
Door-fastening and alarm	A. F. Kitchen	Shelton Depot, S. C	Nov. 24, 1868	84, 362
Door-fastening and alarm, Combined	O. Fisher	Smyrna, Del	June 6, 1871	115, 724
Door-fastening and knife	A. W. Hall	New York, N. Y	July 23, 1867	67, 044
Door fastening, Barn	A. D. Wright and A. Roys	Belleville, Mich	Jan. 21, 1873	135, 027
Door fastening, Chamber	J. P. Frazer	New York, N. Y	Sept. 30, 1862	36, 563
Door fastening, Double	G. H. Lindner	Hoboken, N. J	June 15, 1858	20, 570
Door, Fastening for folding	E. L. Roberts	Brooklyn, N. Y	Mar. 15, 1859	23, 264
Door fastening, Gate and barn	W. W. Peck	Cassopolis, Mich	Dec. 24, 1867	72, 536
Door-fastening, Mortise	L. Foster	Boston, Mass	Feb. 25, 1831	....
Door-fastening, Portable	D. Conlon	Portland, Me	June 19, 1866	55, 624
Door-fastening, Portable	L. S. Enos	Almond, N. Y	June 12, 1866	55, 477
Door-fastening, Spring-catch	J. Buck	Bucksport, Me	Sept. 28, 1831	....
Door-fastenings, Mode of operating the bolt of	A. Bingham	Boston, Mass	June 5, 1844	3, 611
Door-fender	W. Cole and I. Johnson	Randolph, Mass	Mar. 27, 1829	....
Door-fender	S. Durfee	Providence, R. I	Oct. 1, 1830	....
Door for buildings, Safety	C. Hesse	Champaign, Ill	Aug. 24, 1869	94, 109
Door for churches, Safety	A. H. Wagner	Pimlico, England	May 10, 1864	42, 719
Door for guarding against cold	D. Williams, jr	Colchester, Conn	Sept. 11, 1828	....
Door for steam-boilers, Water	I. W. Ayres	New York, N. Y	Oct. 31, 1848	5, 888
Door flush-bolt	S. D. Arnold	New Britain, Conn	June 10, 1873	139, 647
Door gong	C. W. Penfield	New Britain, Conn	Oct. 28, 1873	143, 996
Door guard	C. W. Gochwind	Port Republic, N. J	May 17, 1870	103, 042
Door guard	N. C. Perry and G. S. Gladding	Chester, Conn	Feb. 6, 1866	52, 497
Door guard	J. Tinkey	New Haven, Conn	Oct. 16, 1866	58, 916
Door guard, Elastic	W. N. Clark	Chester, Conn	Nov. 17, 1857	18, 627
Door guard, Elastic	D. E. Peck	Burlington, Conn	Apr. 26, 1870	102, 427
Door hanger	A. C. Arnold	Norwalk, Conn	July 23, 1872	129, 777
Door hanger	S. L. Bignall	Chicago, Ill	Oct. 14, 1873	143, 557
Door hanger	T. Kent and J. S. Barker	Waukegan, Ill	Aug. 8, 1871	117, 894
Door hanger	A. K. Rider	Walden, N. Y	July 29, 1873	141, 382
Door hanger	S. P. Robinson	Canterbury, Conn	June 7, 1870	104, 064
Door hanger and rail	T. F. Hamilton	Geneseo, Ill	Jan. 31, 1871	111, 342
Door hanger, Barn	W. R. Axe	Rockton, Ill	Mar. 1, 1870	100, 351
Door hanger, Barn	J. A. Cauldwell	Watkins, N. Y	July 2, 1872	128, 590
Door hanger, Barn	W. W. Soden	Unadilla, N. Y	July 16, 1872	129, 065
Door hanger, Sliding	C. B. Clark	Buffalo, N. Y	June 11, 1872	127, 846
Door hanger, Sliding	G. Rumsey	Watkins, N. Y	Apr. 4, 1871	113, 697
Door, Hatchway	M. S. Driggs	Brooklyn, N. Y	May 22, 1866	54, 874
Door-holder	G. C. Bunsen	Belleville, Ill	Sept. 1, 1868	81, 746
Door-holder	J. K. Clark	Mount Pleasant, Iowa	July 28, 1868	80, 390
Door-holder	C. J. Fisher	Waukon, Iowa	Nov. 12, 1867	70, 823
Door-holder	J. Hale	Scranton, Pa	Oct. 29, 1867	70, 333
Door-holder	J. J. Harris and I. H. Mosher	Greene, N. Y	June 11, 1867	65, 566
Door-holder	E. Huddart	Prairie du Lac, Wis	July 9, 1867	66, 591
Door-holder	E. Manley	Marion, N. Y	Mar. 16, 1869	87, 785
Door-holder	W. A. Messler	Eureka, Ill	Sept. 24, 1867	69, 235
Door-holder	E. Morris	Burlington, N. J	June 19, 1849	6, 549
Door-holder	W. Quayle	Warsaw, Ill	May 14, 1867	64, 704
Door-holder	O. Sliker	Lincoln, Ill	June 29, 1869	91, 978
Door-holder	G. Wells	Bethel, Conn	Dec. 3, 1867	71, 828
Door-holder	J. S. White	Prescott, Wis	Apr. 20, 1869	89, 101
Door holder or check	O. Sliker	Lincoln, Ill	Nov. 29, 1870	109, 771
Door-holder, Spring	J. B. Okey	Indianapolis, Ind	Jan. 28, 1868	73, 829
Door, Illuminating	T. Hyatt	New York, N. Y	Dec. 2, 1873	145, 183
Door indicator	A. Hadley	Washington, D. C	May 26, 1868	78, 278
Door indicator	F. E. Mills	San Francisco, Cal	May 21, 1867	64, 894

Index of patents issued from the United States Patent Office from 1790 *to* 1873, *inclusive*—Continued.

Invention.	Inventor.	Residence.	Date.	No.
Door, Iron	L. Hover	Chicago, Ill	Oct. 13, 1868	83, 062
Door-key	W. H. Andrews	New Haven, Conn	Mar. 23, 1869	88, 113
Door-key	J. Brady	Branford, Conn	June 7, 1870	103, 837
Door-key	J. Brady	Branford, Conn	June 28, 1870	104, 823
Door-key	C. C. Carpenter	Huntsville, Ala	Feb. 28, 1871	112, 123
Door-key	J. Collins	Hohokus Township, N. J	Dec. 9, 1873	145, 401
Door-key	H. H. Elwell	South Norwalk, Conn	Oct. 18, 1870	108, 466
Door-key	F. Greene	Troy, Pa	June 30, 1868	79, 466
Door-key	E. Parker	New Britain, Conn	May 4, 1869	89, 596
Door-key attachment	D. E. Campbell	Boston, Mass	Apr. 30, 1867	64, 281
Door-key fastener	S. Macferran	Philadelphia, Pa	July 3, 1866	56, 071
Door-key, Folding	J. Seibert	Pittsburgh, Pa	Feb. 4, 1873	135, 609
Door-key guard	H. A. Adams	New York, N. Y	Feb. 9, 1869	86, 797
Door-key guard, Safety	W. K. Marvin	New York, N. Y	May 5, 1868	77, 633
Door-keys from being turned, Device for preventing	A. Westcott	Syracuse, N. Y	Feb. 10, 1863	37, 665
Door-knob fastening	W. H. Mackrell	New York, N. Y	Oct. 30, 1847	5, 345
Door-knobs, Manufacture of	J. Ottner	Bridgeport, Conn	May 13, 1873	138, 758
Door-knobs, Shank for mineral	J. Laird	Cincinnati, Ohio	May 22, 1849	6, 473
Door-knocker with brass plate, Cast-iron	I. Wilson	New London, Conn	Mar. 11, 1831	....
Door-latch	W. T. Munger	New Britain, Conn	Dec. 6, 1870	109, 834
Door-latch	J. H. Vickers	Norwich, Conn	May 31, 1870	103, 819
Door-lock	C. Adams	Pittsburgh, Pa	July 3, 1860	28, 949
Door-lock	H. Ahrend	New York, N. Y	Jan. 12, 1869	85, 776
Door-lock	E. Allen and J. Brady	Norwich, Conn	Sept. 3, 1867	68, 334
Door-lock	W. H. Andrews	New Haven, Conn	Apr. 5, 1870	101, 564
Door-lock	S. Andrews	Perth Amboy, N. J	Jan. 11, 1836	....
Door-lock	T. B. Atterbury	Pittsburgh, Pa	June 2, 1857	17, 412
Door-lock	J. Atwater	New Haven, Conn	July 24, 1846	4, 659
Door-lock	J. R. Baker	Jersey City, N. J	Apr. 30, 1872	126, 248
Door-lock	D. Ball	Kingsbury, N. Y	July 12, 1838	833
Door-lock	F. H. Bartholomew	New York, N. Y	Mar. 24, 1867	75, 838
Door-lock	T. Bartholomew	New York, N. Y	Apr. 3, 1829	....
Door-lock	C. H. Beatty	Wheeling, Va	Oct. 14, 1851	8, 426
Door-lock	J. Behel	Rockford, Ill	Feb. 11, 1868	74, 283
Door-lock	J. Brady	Branford, Conn	Nov. 7, 1871	120, 704
Door-lock	J. Brady	Brooklyn, N. Y	Sept. 24, 1872	131, 654
Door-lock	E. W. Brettell	Newark, N. J	Mar. 26, 1867	63, 204
Door-lock	J. Brown and G. W. Robinson	Providence, R. I	Feb. 20, 1827	....
Door-lock	J. H. Butterworth	Dover, N. J	Apr. 11, 1846	4, 452
Door-lock	W. Cayce	Franklin, Tenn	Aug. 1, 1854	11, 412
Door-lock	S. L. Chase	New York, N. Y	Mar. 26, 1867	63, 214
Door-lock	H. Clarke	Baltimore, Md	July 20, 1869	92, 796
Door-lock	A. Conant	Lowell, Mass	Mar. 12, 1836	....
Door-lock	J. H. Davis	Lumberville, Pa	Mar. 7, 1846	4, 403
Door-lock	W. P. Dodson	Philadelphia, Pa	Mar. 12, 1872	124, 424
Door-lock	H. H. Elwell	South Norwalk, Conn	Feb. 18, 1873	136, 049
Door-lock	J. B. Erb	Strasburgh, Pa	Apr. 22, 1856	14, 714
Door-lock	P. S. Felter	Cincinnatus, N. Y	Mar. 31, 1868	76, 066
Door-lock	W. D. Field	Providence, R. I	Apr. 28, 1868	77, 267
Door-lock	E. Finney	Cleveland, Ohio	June 18, 1839	1, 173
Door-lock	C. Fleischel and W. C. Bussey	San Francisco, Cal	Dec. 8, 1868	84, 737
Door-lock	M. B. Foote	Northampton, Mass	Dec. 1, 1868	84, 484
Door-lock	M. B. Foote	Northampton, Mass	May 4, 1869	89, 753
Door-lock	E. P. Fowler and C. J. Clements	Brooklyn and Mott Haven, N. Y.	June 22, 1869	91, 733
Door-lock	V. Frazee	San Francisco, Cal	Sept. 3, 1872	131, 093
Door-lock	S. Frye	Monongahela City, Pa	Apr. 30, 1861	32, 218
Door-lock	J. E. A. Gibbs	Steele's Tavern, Va	June 2, 1868	78, 449
Door-lock	H. R. Gillingham	Baltimore, Md	Sept. 10, 1867	67, 622
Door-lock	C. G. Gumpel	Leicester Square, England	Nov. 16, 1869	96, 802
Door-lock	F. Gyss	New York, N. Y	Oct. 10, 1871	119, 758
Door-lock	J. J. Hamilton	Newcastle, Ind	Apr. 27, 1858	20, 063
Door-lock	R. C. Harrington	Newark, N. J	June 16, 1868	78, 962
Door-lock	W. I. and J. W. Harris	Newport, N. Y	May 21, 1867	64, 975
Door-lock	J. S. Hoard and V. O. Spencer	Mansfield, Pa	Feb. 8, 1859	22, 872
Door-lock	E. B. Horn	Boston, Mass	Sept. 25, 1849	6, 733
Door-lock	H. Jackson	New York, N. Y	Dec. 24, 1867	72, 499
Door-lock	J. W. Jones	Paducah, Ky	May 11, 1869	89, 931
Door-lock	D. C. Jordon, sr	Brooklyn, N. Y	Mar. 12, 1867	62, 753
Door-lock	F. Just	Buffalo, N. Y	Feb. 12, 1867	61, 036
Door-lock	J. Kinger	Pittsburgh, Pa	Nov. 13, 1860	30, 654
Door-lock	J. H. Kinsman	Salem, Mass	June 27, 1871	116, 452
Door-lock	J. Kinzer	Pittsburgh, Pa	Sept. 14, 1858	21, 504
Door-lock	J. C. Kline	Pittsburgh, Pa	June 12, 1855	13, 037
Door-lock	M. and J. Knapp	Hudson City, N. J	Nov. 5, 1867	70, 576
Door-lock	C. Knauer	Birmingham, Pa	June 17, 1856	15, 136
Door-lock	T. Kromer	Freiburg, Baden	July 1, 1873	140, 377
Door-lock	J. Kyle	New York, N. Y	May 18, 1832	....
Door-lock	J. Kyle	Ramapo, N. Y	Sept. 16, 1833	....
Door-lock	J. Kyle	Ramapo, N. Y	Sept. 16, 1833	....
Door-lock	F. F. Landis	Lancaster, Pa	Mar. 5, 1867	62, 545
Door-lock	A. Leich	Brooklyn, N. Y	Mar. 5, 1867	62, 645
Door-lock	J. Linder	Seneca Falls, N. Y	June 28, 1870	104, 749
Door-lock	H. Lockwood	New York, N. Y	May 1, 1860	28, 092
Door-lock	W. Maguire	Cincinnati, Ohio	Jan. 15, 1850	7, 026
Door-lock	J. R. Marston	New York, N. Y	June 15, 1858	20, 571
Door-lock	W. Maurer	New York, N. Y	May 29, 1855	12, 957
Door-lock	J. McClory	New York, N. Y	Mar. 18, 1836	....
Door-lock	J. McClory	New York, N. Y	July 2, 1836	....
Door-lock	R. McDowell	Lambertville, N. J	Apr. 6, 1869	88, 577
Door-lock	A. McKinnon	New York, N. Y	Aug. 16, 1845	4, 151
Door-lock	D. V. Miller	Weedsport, N. Y	Apr. 20, 1869	89, 161
Door-lock	J. F. Milligan	Saint Louis, Mo	June 1, 1869	90, 864
Door-lock	W. Moore	Williamsburgh, N. Y	Sept. 14, 1852	9, 265
Door-lock	W. T. Munger	New Britain, Conn	Apr. 18, 1871	113, 910
Door-lock	H. Norton	Delton, Wis	Mar. 17, 1868	75, 569
Door-lock	G. Oates	Charleston, S. C	Sept. 2, 1845	4, 175
Door-lock	T. A. Olson	Beloit, Wis	June 20, 1871	116, 214

Index of patents issued from the United States Patent Office from 1790 *to* 1873, *inclusive*—Continued.

Invention.	Inventor.	Residence.	Date.	No.
Door-lock	E. Parker	New Britain, Conn	July 16, 1872	129, 587
Door-lock	J. E. Parker	West Meriden, Conn	Nov. 6, 1860	30, 586
Door-lock	W. Parr and J. F. Fowler	New York, N. Y	Nov. 19, 1833	....
Door-lock	A. Patterson	Pittsburgh, Pa	Apr. 8, 1856	14, 618
Door-lock	N. Petré	New York, N. Y	Sept. 7, 1869	94, 639
Door-lock	E. P. Porter and G. W. Hallett	Waterford, N. Y	Mar. 26, 1867	63, 295
Door-lock	E. P. Porter and G. W. Hallett	Waterford, N. Y	Nov. 26, 1867	71, 411
Door-lock	S. M. Pye	Acquackanonck, N. J	Mar. 13, 1849	6, 184
Door-lock	W. Pye	New York, N. Y	Apr. 28, 1818	....
Door-lock	J. M. Quimby and A. S. Dyer	Westbrook and Cape Elizabeth, Me.	Feb. 21, 1871	112, 076
Door-lock	W. Reynolds	Greenbriar County, Va	May 9, 1848	5, 557
Door-lock	B. F. Roberts	Lacona, Iowa	Jan. 17, 1871	111, 005
Door-lock	P. Rodgers	Philadelphia, Pa	Sept. 25, 1840	1, 796
Door-lock	A. Roff	New York, N. Y	July 1, 1836	....
Door-lock	R. Schade	New York, N. Y	Nov. 26, 1867	71, 534
Door-lock	I. P. Sherwood	Sandy Hill, N. Y	Dec. 17, 1842	2, 886
Door-lock	J. C. Silvy	New Orleans, La	June 12, 1855	13, 050
Door-lock	B. Smith	Canton, Conn	Apr. 13, 1836	....
Door-lock	D. M. Smith	Springfield, Vt	July 14, 1846	4, 635
Door-lock	J. G. Spathelf	Sandusky, Ohio	July 28, 1868	80, 369
Door-lock	M. R. Stephenson	Boston, Mass	July 13, 1852	9, 126
Door-lock	W. Stephenson	Cincinnati, Ohio	Sept. 12, 1848	5, 758
Door-lock	W. Stephenson	Cincinnati, Ohio	Sept. 12, 1848	5, 766
Door-lock	C. I. Stewart	Baltimore, Md	Sept. 12, 1871	118, 828
Door-lock	B. Van Dyke	Chicago, Ill	Aug. 20, 1872	130, 609
Door-lock	R. Vollschwitz	New York, N. Y	Jan. 1, 1867	60, 970
Door-lock	N. Warren	Wilmington, Del	Nov. 21, 1871	121, 142
Door-lock	W. Warwick	Birmingham, Pa	Mar. 13, 1855	12, 526
Door-lock	J. Weimar	New York, N. Y	Dec. 12, 1854	12, 081
Door-lock	J. Welsh	Canton, Ohio	Jan. 31, 1871	111, 499
Door-lock	W. P. Wentworth	Detroit, Mich	June 25, 1867	66, 059
Door-lock	J. L. Whetstone	Cincinnati, Ohio	July 20, 1846	4, 640
Door-lock	T. Whitehouse	Boston, Mass	Sept. 8, 1837	377
Door-lock	T. Whitehouse	Boston, Mass	June 14, 1838	783
Door-lock	A. F. Whiting	Bath, Me	Feb. 6, 1872	123, 531
Door-lock	L. Whitney	Toledo, Ohio	June 8, 1858	20, 524
Door-lock	J. T. Williams	Chicago, Ill	July 11, 1871	116, 907
Door-lock	A. Wolfe	Pittsburgh, Pa	Apr. 18, 1831	....
Door-lock	W. E. Woodbridge	New York, N. Y	July 14, 1846	4, 630
Door-lock	L. L. Woolley	Medford, Mass	May 19, 1868	78, 038
Door-lock	T. B. Worrell	Frankford, Pa	July 13, 1869	92, 502
Door-lock	L. Yale	Springfield, Mass	June 13, 1844	3, 630
Door-lock	L. Yale	Newport, N. Y	Oct. 18, 1853	10, 144
Door-lock-alarm attachment	J. Schneider	Rochester, N. Y	May 1, 1855	12, 784
Door lock and bolt, Sliding	T. Whaley	New York, N. Y	Nov. 2, 1821	....
Door lock and key	G. M. Zahm	Lancaster, Pa	May 26, 1842	2, 638
Door lock and latch	E. Halley	Branford, Conn	Sept. 1, 1863	39, 770
Door lock and latch	N. and C. Hunt	Cleveland, Ohio	July 29, 1839	1, 268
Door lock and latch	W. T. Mungeo	Branford, Conn	July 7, 1863	39, 203
Door lock and latch	G. W. Wilson	Nashua, N. H	June 11, 1841	2, 123
Door lock and latch, Sliding	E. J. Kehoe	New York, N. Y	Nov. 15, 1870	109, 220
Door-lock and other fastening	J. R. and H. C. Cambell	Charlestown, Mass	Dec. 28, 1835	....
Door-lock bolt	E. Parker	West Meriden, Conn	Feb. 7, 1860	27, 064
Door-lock, Burglar-alarm	E. Tracy	Kansas City, Mo	Dec. 3, 1867	71, 822
Door-lock by a combined key and gage, also a thief detector.	F. C. Goffin	Philadelphia, Pa	Mar. 10, 1849	6, 165
Door-lock by which one key-hole serves for two distinct keys.	A. Call	Springfield, Mass	Feb. 13, 1849	6, 109
Door-lock, Combination	M. R. Stephenson and O. Edwards.	Boston, Mass	Apr. 17, 1844	3, 543
Door-lock, Combination safety	S. Yale and C. Wilson	Springfield, Mass	Oct. 20, 1843	3, 312
Door-lock, Combination tumbler	R. M. Tuttle	Newark, N. J	Dec. 5, 1842	2, 869
Door-lock, Compound	G. Hubert	Lancaster, Pa	July 23, 1867	67, 116
Door-lock, Divided-bolt	J. Kyle	New York, N. Y	Aug. 15, 1848	5, 708
Door-lock, Escutcheon latch and bolt	P. E. W. and J. A. Blake	New Haven, Conn	Dec. 31, 1833	....
Door-lock, Extension-bit guard-key for	W. Damerel	Brooklyn, N. Y	May 9, 1854	10, 883
Door-lock guard	W. Ballauff and F. Wurth	Cincinnati, Ohio	Mar. 6, 1855	12, 476
Door lock, Jail	E. Jacobs	Cincinnati, Ohio	Aug. 23, 1864	43, 915
Door-lock keeper	G. W. DaCunha	New York, N. Y	May 21, 1867	64, 8?7
Door-lock key	T. K. Webster	Lawrence, Mass	Nov. 17, 1857	18, 654
Door-lock key, Swivel-nibbed	A. C. Harig	Louisville, Ky	Mar. 1, 1853	9, 599
Door-lock, night-latch, &c	J. McClory	New York, N. Y	June 14, 1837	215
Door lock or latch	W. Hall	Chelsea, Mass	Oct. 18, 1843	3, 308
Door lock or latch	T. L. Littlefield	Philadelphia, Pa	Nov. 21, 1843	3, 343
Door lock or latch, Compound lever graduating	S. Noyes	Beverly, Mass	Feb. 20, 1843	2, 963
Door-lock or spring-catch	R. J. Byram	Boston, Mass	May 31, 1832	....
Door-lock, Portable	E. G. F. Arndt	Rondout, N. Y	Sept. 18, 1860	30, 035
Door-lock, Portable	J. W. Webb	Washington, D. C	Feb. 7, 1854	10, 511
Door lock, Prison	L. M. Ham	Boston, Mass	May 4, 1869	89, 830
Door-lock, Protector-slide for	G. F. I. Colburn	Newark, N. J	Feb. 27, 1849	6, 142
Door-lock, Safety	W. Stillman	Westerly, R. I	Sept. 14, 1839	1, 323
Door-lock, Sliding	A. W. Cram	Saint Louis, Mo	May 20, 1873	139, 118
Door-lock, Sliding	J. Davidson	Albany, N. Y	Nov. 1, 1870	108, 767
Door-lock strike or keeper	J. Scott	Philadelphia, Pa	Apr. 22, 1873	138, 048
Door-locks, Bolt-attachment to	W. H. Andrews	New Haven, Conn	Dec. 10, 1867	71, 944
Door-locks for banks, vaults, &c., Mode of constructing.	J. McClory	New York, N. Y	June 19, 1838	787
Door-locks, Keeper for	S. B. Williams	Leavenworth City, Kans	Dec. 19, 1865	51, 639
Door-locks, Keeper for right and left hand	C. Adams	Oak Hill, N. Y	Feb. 24, 1857	16, 676
Door locks or latches, Check-bolt of	A. Bingham	Boston, Mass	Oct. 17, 1842	2, 719
Door-locks, Safety key-holder for	F. J. May	Morrisania, N. Y	Mar. 12, 1867	62, 865
Door-mat	N. Berkeley	Aldie, Va	Apr. 4, 1871	113, 389
Door-mat	J. J. Diehl	Idaville, Pa	Feb. 2, 1869	86, 512
Door-mat	P. W. Neefus	New York, N. Y	May 30, 1871	115, 345
Door-mat	A. P. Noyes	Middleton, Mass	June 7, 1870	103, 916
Door-mat	F. V. Noyes	Mattoon, Ill	Sept. 5, 1865	49, 780
Door-mat	J. V. Oldaker	Atlanta, Ill	July 9, 1872	128, 897

Index of patents issued from the United States Patent Office from 1790 *to* 1873, *inclusive*—Continued.

Invention.	Inventor.	Residence.	Date.	No.
Door-mat	W. Young, jr	Franklin, Mass	July 28, 1868	80, 379
Door-mat, India-rubber	E. M. Chaffee	Providence, R. I	Feb. 16, 1858	19, 347
Door-mat, Metallic and elastic	P. W. Neefus	New York, N. Y	Nov. 29, 1870	109, 650
Door-numbers, Casting	J. T. Fuller	Louisville, Ky	Apr. 10, 1860	27, 861
Door or partition for separating rooms, &c., Drop	G. Kilburn	Walpole, N. H	Dec. 31, 1838	1, 052
Door or shutter fastener	W. Fields	Wilmington, Del	Feb. 20, 1872	123, 816
Door or shutter, Metallic	A. B. Mullett and B. Oertly	Washington, D. C	July 6, 1869	92, 205
Door-panel	L. W. Kimball	Pittsford, Vt	Aug. 11, 1868	80, 972
Door-panels, Composition for	R. B. Andrews	Poland, Me	Nov. 9, 1869	96, 655
Door-plate	J. W. Bliss	Hartford, Conn	July 13, 1858	20, 859
Door-plate	W. A. Caron	Springfield, Mass	Dec. 12, 1871	121, 703
Door-plate	J. H. Grout and F. M. Ray	New York, N. Y	Mar. 20, 1844	3, 496
Door-plate	J. S. Richardson	Boston, Mass	Oct. 15, 1836	56
Door-plate	J. S. Richardson	Boston, Mass	Oct. 15, 1836	....
Door-plate	E. I. Sause	New York	Aug. 11, 1843	3, 216
Door-plate and alarm	C. H. Miller	Buffalo, N. Y	Mar. 16, 1869	87, 958
Door-plate and bell-alarm	W. G. Brady	Lowell, Mass	June 29, 1869	91, 820
Door-plate and card-receiver	S. A. Baldwin	Waterbury, Conn	Sept. 9, 1862	36, 388
Door-plate and indicator	T. M. and W. F. Tobin	Middlebury, Vt	Apr. 1, 1873	137, 508
Door-plate and letter-box	E. A. Hopkins	Minneapolis, Minn	Dec. 24, 1867	72, 493
Door-plate and letter-box, Combined	J. T. Green	Marquette, Wis	Oct. 15, 1867	69, 800
Door-plate and letter-chute, Combined	B. Morningstar	Pittsburgh, Pa	Apr. 15, 1873	137, 946
Door-plate, Glass	D. Montague and J. Townsend	New Bedford, Mass., and Gardiner, Me.	May 22, 1860	28, 396
Door-plate, Index	N. Ames	Saugus Centre, Mass	July 31, 1860	29, 430
Door-plate, letter-box, and bell-pull combined	T. Thompson	Cleveland, Ohio	Oct. 22, 1872	132, 378
Door-plates and signs of separate types or cutters, Method of making.	E. Morris	Philadelphia, Pa	Apr. 25, 1844	3, 565
Door-plates, Casting	J. A. Pease	Philadelphia, Pa	Aug. 14, 1847	5, 243
Door-plates, Making and preparing	W. C. Austin	Greensville, Va	Jan. 31, 1837	113
Door-plates, &c., Number for	J. T. Smith	Washington, D. C	Jan. 18, 1870	99, 019
Door-retainer	C. T. Gravatt	Philadelphia, Pa	Mar. 8, 1870	100, 616
Door-retainer	G. W. Perry and J. D. Billins	Wilmington, Del	Dec. 8, 1868	84, 756
Door-register	J. G. Miller	Swanton, Md	Mar. 16, 1858	19, 646
Door, safe, &c., Burglar-proof	G. Little	Rutherford Park, N. J	Apr. 1, 1873	137, 456
Door-securer	D. Arndt	Cleveland, Ohio	Dec. 19, 1871	121, 980
Door-securer	B. F. Baer	Lancaster, Pa	May 23, 1871	115, 012
Door-securer	W. H. Caldwell	Wheeling, W. Va	Mar. 7, 1871	112, 320
Door-securer	B. H. Melendy	Amherst, N. H	Mar. 12, 1872	124, 503
Door-securer	G. B. Pharo	Philadelphia, Pa	Nov. 12, 1872	132, 922
Door-securer	W. H. Phipps	Poquonock, Conn	Nov. 4, 1873	144, 223
Door-securer	S. A. Pool	Memphis, Tenn	May 21, 1872	126, 903
Door-securer and key-ring, Combined	J. P. Tuck	Houlton, Me	Nov. 18, 1873	144, 642
Door, Self-closing	J. C. Harkness	Washington, D. C	Oct. 12, 1858	21, 754
Door-sheave	R. G. Hatfield	New York, N. Y	June 21, 1864	43, 205
Door sheave, Sliding	M. L. Deering	New York, N. Y	Mar. 2, 1869	87, 329
Door sheave, Sliding	M. L. Deering	New York, N. Y	May 25, 1869	90, 345
Door sheave, Sliding	R. G. Hatfield	New York, N. Y	May 5, 1863	38, 387
Door-sill	D. Hitchcock and D. S. Trout	Arcola, Ill	Oct. 12, 1869	95, 799
Door-sill	J. Johnston and E. O. Marlow	Brodhead, Wis	June 14, 1870	104, 321
Door-sill, Adjustable	M. Armstrong	Girard, Ill	July 26, 1870	105, 623
Door-sill, Adjustable	J. H. Morris	Philadelphia, Pa	Mar. 30, 1869	88, 502
Door-sill gutter	J. A. Hemberger	Reading, Ohio	Oct. 26, 1869	96, 233
Door-sill, Self-adjusting	G. C. Bigelow	Worcester, Mass	Mar. 23, 1858	19, 673
Door-sills and door-strips, Arrangement of	H. Tryon	Steuben, Pa	May 5, 1857	17, 242
Door, Sliding	J. Capron	New York, N. Y	Mar. 1, 1870	100, 373
Door, Sliding	L. A. Cook	Concord, Mich	Nov. 1, 1870	108, 763
Door, Sliding	W. T. Forsyth	Philadelphia, Pa	Feb. 12, 1844	3, 428
Door, Sliding	J. More	New York, N. Y	Jan. 31, 1871	111, 468
Door, Sliding	E. Prudhomme and P. M. Leprohon.	New York, N. Y	May 18, 1869	90, 193
Door, Sliding	W. A. Waterhouse	Liverpool, N. Y	Mar. 22, 1870	101, 194
Door-spring	W. Allen	Oswego, N. Y	July 5, 1870	105, 025
Door-spring	W. Badger, jr	North Chelsea, Mass	Mar. 22, 1864	41, 971
Door-spring	G. L. Bailey	Portland, Me	Apr. 15, 1856	14, 686
Door-spring	G. L. Bailey	Portland, Me	Apr. 21, 1857	17, 070
Door-spring	A. T. Ballantine	Titusville, Pa	Apr. 19, 1870	102, 197
Door-spring	B. F. Barker	San Francisco, Cal	Mar. 27, 1866	53, 391
Door-spring	J. Barkley	Weston, Mo	Jan. 11, 1859	22, 540
Door-spring	W. S. Barlow	Paterson, N. J	Nov. 17, 1868	84, 119
Door-spring	O. D. Barrett	Cleveland, Ohio	Sept. 27, 1859	25, 602
Door-spring	A. Barton	Syracuse, N. Y	Apr. 1, 1856	14, 583
Door-spring	A. S. Blake	Waterbury, Conn	May 3, 1859	23, 819
Door-spring	J. O. Blythe	Germantown, Pa	Apr. 2, 1861	31, 862
Door-spring	J. Boyd and J. Belford	Philadelphia, Pa	Oct. 16, 1860	30, 383
Door-spring	J. Broughton	Chicago, Ill	Aug. 19, 1856	15, 555
Door-spring	J. Broughton	Chicago, Ill	Jan. 6, 1857	16, 324
Door-spring	I. Buckman, jr	Williamsburgh, N. Y	Nov. 5, 1872	132, 710
Door-spring	C. Burnham	Philadelphia, Pa	Dec. 24, 1867	72, 449
Door-spring	L. Burwell	Berlin, Conn	Nov. 25, 1829	....
Door-spring	A. F. Chatman	New York, N. Y	Jan. 27, 1857	16, 512
Door-spring	H. Cody	New York, N. Y	Nov. 4, 1873	144, 256
Door-spring	J. M. Connel	Newark, Ohio	Dec. 18, 1866	60, 481
Door-spring	J. M. Connel	Newark, Ohio	Feb. 9, 1869	86, 815
Door-spring	J. J. Corvell	Newark, N. J	May 28, 1872	127, 311
Door-spring	S. Cutler	Cincinnati, Ohio	Mar. 18, 1873	136, 974
Door-spring	D. Dick	New York, N. Y	June 3, 1873	139, 453
Door-spring	F. Dodge	Syracuse, N. Y	Sept. 21, 1869	94, 949
Door-spring	R. B. Donaldson	Washington, D. C	Oct. 30, 1860	30, 531
Door-spring	W. Duncan	Lebanon, N. H	Feb. 23, 1869	87, 095
Door-spring	W. Duryea	Glen Cove, N. Y	Aug. 11, 1868	80, 931
Door-spring	I. Eaton	Boston, Mass	Feb. 24, 1830	....
Door-spring	S. Elliott	Richmond, Ind	June 22, 1869	91, 528
Door-spring	C. Ellis	Boston, Mass	Dec. 15, 1843	3, 376
Door-spring	B. G. Fitzhugh	Frederick, Md	Mar. 1, 1870	100, 388
Door-spring	O. V. Flora	Madison, Ind	June 15, 1869	91, 222
Door-spring	J. T. Folwell	Camden, N. J	June 7, 1870	103, 859
Door-spring	H. S. Frost	Watertown, Conn	Aug. 6, 1867	67, 525

Index of patents issued from the United States Patent Office from 1790 *to* 1873, *inclusive*—Continued.

Invention.	Inventor.	Residence.	Date.	No.
Door-spring	F. Gardner	Boston, Mass	Jan. 2, 1872	122, 316
Door-spring	G. Geer	Plainville, Conn	Mar. 4, 1873	136, 371
Door-spring	W. Gilfillan	Syracuse, N. Y	July 30, 1867	67, 290
Door-spring	W. Gilfillan	Syracuse, N. Y	Apr. 6, 1869	88, 625
Door-spring	J. S. Gray	New York, N. Y	Jan. 11, 1859	22, 554
Door-spring	W. M. Gray	Brooklyn, N. Y	Dec. 5, 1871	121, 507
Door-spring	W. M. Gray	Brooklyn, N. Y	Dec. 5, 1871	121, 508
Door-spring	G. W. Griswold	Carbondale, Pa	Apr. 15, 1856	14, 691
Door-spring	L. J. Higgins	Mount Desert, Me	Apr. 1, 1873	137, 367
Door-spring	L. Hillebrand	Philadelphia, Pa	Dec. 3, 1867	71, 616
Door-spring	L. Hillebrand	Philadelphia, Pa	Jan. 26, 1869	86, 228
Door-spring	H. Hochstrasser and A. Masson	Philadelphia, Pa	Feb. 3, 1852	8, 704
Door-spring	A. D. Hoffman	Chicago, Ill	Feb. 18, 1873	135, 914
Door-spring	G. L. Hudson	Connecaut, Ill	Feb. 8, 1859	22, 874
Door-spring	H. Hughes	Utica, N. Y	July 16, 1867	66, 843
Door-spring	S. W. Huntington	Augusta, Me	June 23, 1868	79, 125
Door-spring	M. Jincks	Wallace, N. Y	Sept. 20, 1870	107, 616
Door-spring	W. M. Kellie	Chicago, Ill	Mar. 18, 1873	136, 923
Door-spring	W. F. Kells	San Francisco, Cal	Oct. 11, 1870	108, 268
Door spring	F. Kellsey	Middletown, Conn	June 27, 1848	5, 654
Door-spring	D. C. King	Boston, Mass	July 9, 1872	128, 891
Door-spring	J. Losee	Peekskill, N. Y	July 16, 1872	129, 574
Door-spring	J. J. Mackey	South Brooklyn, N. Y	Dec. 3, 1867	71, 772
Door-spring	J. F. Mason and J. Johnson	Newark, N. J., and Brooklyn, N. Y.	Apr. 16, 1867	63, 914
Door-spring	J. Maxon	De Ruyter, N. Y	Sept. 19, 1848	5, 784
Door-spring	T. J. Mayall	Roxbury, Mass	Dec. 28, 1858	22, 441
Door-spring	A. Mishler	New York, N. Y	Apr. 19, 1870	102, 029
Door-spring	E. L. Morse	Saint Louis, Mo	Mar. 16, 1869	87, 867
Door-spring	E. D. Morton	Cuba, N. Y	Nov. 2, 1869	96, 470
Door spring	J. M. Newton	Norwich, Conn	July 16, 1867	66, 873
Door-spring	C. W. Oldham	Leipsic, Ind	July 8, 1873	140, 638
Door-spring	C. A. Peck	New York, N. Y	Dec. 29, 1857	18, 987
Door-spring	T. Peck	Syracuse, N. Y	May 22, 1847	5, 124
Door-spring	T. Peck	Syracuse, N. Y	Oct. 17, 1848	5, 864
Door-spring	J. Post	Newark, N. J	June 12, 1860	28, 689
Door-spring	I. Powars	Waukegan, Ill	Jan. 26, 1869	86, 318
Door-spring	L. C. Prindle	Chicago, Ill	Feb. 4, 1868	73, 999
Door-spring	F. H. Richards	New Britain, Conn	Nov. 25, 1875	144, 926
Door-spring	W. T. Root	Geneva, N. Y	July 21, 1863	39, 308
Door-spring	W. Ross	Baltimore, Md	Apr. 13, 1869	88, 985
Door-spring	W. T. Rossiter	Lincoln, Nebr	Dec. 2, 1873	145, 244
Door-spring	C. W. Saladee	Newark, Ohio	Apr. 30, 1867	64, 372
Door-spring	C. W. Saladee	Newark, Ohio	Nov. 12, 1867	70, 903
Door-spring	S. Sawyer	Boston, Mass	Jan. 21, 1841	1, 938
Door-spring	R. Scheidler	Newark, Ohio	Oct. 23, 1866	59, 082
Door spring	R. Schrader	Indianapolis, Ind	Dec. 10, 1867	72, 089
Door-spring	J. Shaw, jr	Hinckley, Ohio	July 20, 1846	4, 641
Door-spring	J. Simpson	Newark, Ohio	Nov. 2, 1869	96, 493
Door-spring	D. G. Smith	Carbondale, Pa	Feb. 26, 1856	14, 326
Door-spring	P. Smith	Newport, Ky	Aug. 3, 1869	93, 359
Door-spring	W. W. Smith and B. Mulliken, jr.	New York, N. Y	Nov. 13, 1840	1, 854
Door-spring	W. H. Stafford	New York, N. Y	Dec. 6, 1870	109, 962
Door-spring	F. Stemmler	East New York, N. Y	Apr. 23, 1872	125, 995
Door-spring	E. Stimson	Montpelier, Vt	July 13, 1869	92, 486
Door-spring	L. Thomas	Allegheny City, Pa	Mar. 3, 1857	16, 759
Door-spring	T. Thorpe	West Cambridge, Mass	Dec. 7, 1837	506
Door-spring	A. Tittman	Evansville, Ind	July 1, 1873	140, 446
Door-spring	E. P. Torrey and W. B. Tilton	New York, N. Y	Sept. 8, 1857	18, 164
Door-spring	J. L. Tucker	Laconia, N. H	June 8, 1869	91, 184
Door-spring	T. Van Kannel	Cincinnati, Ohio	July 9, 1867	66, 538
Door-spring	M. L. Webster	Albany, N. Y	May 20, 1873	139, 037
Door-spring	A. Westcott	Syracuse, N. Y	Oct. 1, 1850	7, 692
Door-spring	A. Westcott	Spracuse, N. Y	Nov. 6, 1855	13, 770
Door-spring	F. S. Willcox	Bridgeport, Conn	Feb. 2, 1869	86, 482
Door-spring	W. Wilson	Greenfield, Mass	July 17, 1838	845
Door-spring	A. Wiswall	New York, N. Y	Aug. 14, 1866	57, 240
Door-spring	L. R. Witherell	Galesburgh, Ill	May 2, 1871	114, 379
Door-spring	W. H. Worcester and E. F. Jones	Farmington, N. H	Aug. 30, 1864	44, 034
Door spring and hinge	A. Wiswall	New York, N. Y	July 16, 1867	66, 927
Door spring and retainer combined	C. Bird	Lower Merion Tp., Pa	Oct. 8, 1872	132, 046
Door-spring bracket	A. J. Walker	New York, N. Y	Oct. 7, 1856	15, 864
Door-spring for closing doors, gates, &c	G. Barton, jr	Shaftsbury, Vt	July 1, 1840	1, 668
Door-spring, India-rubber	B. G. Fitzhugh	Sykesville, Md	Jan. 7, 1868	72, 992
Door-spring, Rubber	J. B. Hayden	Schaghticoke, N. Y	June 7, 1870	104, 027
Door, Spring wire	J. Codman	Boston, Mass	Aug. 17, 1835	......
Door springs and levers, Arrangement of	W. B. Barnard	Bristol, Conn	Apr. 9, 1850	7, 255
Door-springs, Vertical wire for	J. Codman	Boston. Mass	Dec. 28, 1832	......
Door-stay	A. H. Platt	Yellow Springs, Ohio	Aug. 5, 1856	15, 493
Door-stop	M. V. Doyle and J. Behel	Rockford, Ill	May 23, 1871	115, 038
Door-stop	W. H. Fahrney	Rockford, Ill	May 31, 1870	103, 729
Door-stop	W. H. Fahrney	Rockford, Ill	Dec. 13, 1870	110, 036
Door-stop	T. Hazard and J. M. Richardson	Wilmington, Ohio	Feb. 5, 1867	61, 830
Door-stop	G. W. Hunt	Winchendon, Mass	May 28, 1867	65, 083
Door-stop	W. May	Binghamton, N. Y	Nov. 3, 1868	83, 650
Door-stop	A. G. Stevens	Manchester, N. H	Apr. 21, 1868	77, 122
Door-stop	P. L. Weimer	Lebanon, Pa	Oct. 29, 1867	70, 302
Door-stop	I. J. Wells	Willmar, Minn	July 4, 1871	116, 654
Door-stop	L. C. Wemple	Rockford, Ill	Nov. 15, 1870	109, 281
Door stop and latch	C. L. Willis	Washington, D. C	June 25, 1867	66, 198
Door-straightener	O. C. Ross	Penfield, N. Y	July 14, 1868	79, 862
Door-strip	G. W. Carpender	Jarvis, Ind	May 7, 1867	64, 486
Door-strip	J. W. Kramer	Bloomsburgh, Pa	Aug. 30, 1870	106, 875
Door-strip, Metallic	A. D. Smith	Grafton, Ohio	May 25, 1869	90, 400
Door, Temporary folding	W. M. O'Brien	San Francisco, Cal	Sept. 3, 1872	131, 114
Door-threshold	C. Loring	South Braintree, Mass	Nov. 21, 1865	51, 066
Door-threshold	O. G. Thomas	Taunton, Mass	Apr. 29, 1873	138, 300

Index of patents issued from the United States Patent Office from 1790 *to* 1873, *inclusive*—Continued.

Invention.	Inventor.	Residence.	Date.	No.
Door, Trap	G. Runge	Philadelphia, Pa	July 11, 1854	11,254
Door, Ventilating	T. R. Timby	Saratoga Springs, N. Y	June 4, 1867	65,451
Doors, Adjustable hasp and hook for	W. Bisbee and F. G. Hearn	Yreka, Cal	Dec. 31, 1867	72,784
Doors and gates, Closing	S. Stewart	Philadelphia, Pa	Sept. 11, 1860	30,005
Doors and gates, Device for closing	S. P. Griffin and B. M. Harrod	New Orleans, La	Nov. 19, 1872	133,221
Doors and gates, Spring for shutting	I. S. Richardson	Boston, Mass	Oct. 20, 1837	433
Doors and gates, Weight and lever attachment for	A. S. Blake	Waterbury, Conn	July 29, 1862	35,988
Doors and sashes, Machine for laying out	S. C. Ellis	Jersey City, N. J	Feb. 15, 1870	99,866
Doors and windows, Mode of hanging	A. B. Carpenter	New York, N. Y	Sept. 19, 1845	4,200
Doors and windows, Tightening	S. Hayward	Plainfield, Mass	Oct. 17, 1829	....
Doors and windows water-tight, Method of rendering.	W. C. Fuller	London, Great Britain	Apr. 18, 1865	47,368
Doors, Apparatus for closing	D. Ball	Albany, N. Y	Feb. 1, 1847	4,947
Doors, Arrangement of spring and spring-catch for closing.	J. Clark	North Hadley, Mass	July 25, 1854	11,358
Doors, &c., Attachment for opening and closing	A. W. Webster	Waterbury, Conn	May 25, 1858	20,381
Doors, Automatic catch for sliding	A. W. Gibbs	Norwich, Conn	Dec. 16, 1873	145,644
Doors, &c., being too tight, Preventing	D. Fraser	New York, N. Y	Dec. 12, 1825	....
Doors, Bolt for double	D. B. Conklin	Hardwick, N. J	Mar. 12, 1872	124,422
Doors, Bolt-mechanism for prison	T. R. and J. Pullis	Saint Louis, Mo	Apr. 22, 1873	138,099
Doors, Bolt-work for	J. Sargent	Rochester, N. Y	July 9, 1872	128,816
Doors, Closing	C. Perley	New York, N. Y	Feb. 24, 1863	37,770
Doors, Combined latch and lock for sliding	J. Capron	New York, N. Y	Nov. 15, 1870	109,298
Doors, Construction of	W. C. James	Fishersville, N. H	July 18, 1871	117,080
Doors, Construction of	W. W. J. Toussaint	Boston, Mass	July 15, 1873	140,799
Doors, Device for closing	T. Peck	Syracuse, N. Y	Apr. 10, 1847	5,058
Doors, Device for closing	R. F. Stevens	Syracuse, N. Y	Apr. 10, 1847	5,061
Doors, Device for holding open	J. B. Sweetland	Pontiac, Mich	Oct. 18, 1870	108,534
Doors, Device for opening and closing double	G. C. Gooch and T. B. Jeffery	Chicago, Ill	Feb. 16, 1869	86,981
Doors, Elastic stud for	A. Eliaers	Boston, Mass	Jan. 24, 1865	45,984
Doors, Fastening for jail	E. Jacobs	Cincinnati, Ohio	Nov. 15, 1859	26,108
Doors, Fastening for sliding	E. W. Staples, jr	Norwich, Conn	July 22, 1873	141,019
Doors, gates, &c., Apparatus for closing	G. Barton	Waterford, N. Y	Sept. 23, 1843	3,280
Doors, gates, &c., Closing	O. Davidson	Ballston Spa, N. Y	Mar. 30, 1835	....
Doors, gates, &c., Device for closing	L. S. Deming	Newington, Conn	Jan. 1, 1867	60,703
Doors, gates, &c., Spring for	R. Espey	Saint Louis, Mo	Jan. 21, 1873	135,192
Doors, Guard-fastener for	E. C. Cochrane	Buffalo, N. Y	July 7, 1868	79,550
Doors, Guide for fitting locks to	F. P. Pfleghar	New Haven, Conn	May 18, 1869	90,299
Doors Hanging	G. Heegler	San Francisco, Cal	Jan. 7, 1873	134,542
Doors, Hanging	A. Hitchcock	New York, N. Y	Dec. 22, 1863	41,006
Doors, Hanging	G. W. Holly	Low Moor, Iowa	Oct. 16, 1866	58,827
Doors, Hanging	A. W. Morse	Eaton, N. Y	June 9, 1857	17,513
Doors, Hanging	G. W. Wilson	Nashua, N. H	July 10, 1840	1,678
Doors, Hanging and fastening	C. W. Earl	Elk River, Minn	Apr. 13, 1869	88,857
Doors, Hanging double	C. E. Brown	New York, N. Y	Jan. 8, 1856	14,047
Doors, Hanging sliding	A. J. Culver	White Hall, Ill	June 29, 1869	91,916
Doors, Hanging sliding	G. M. Darley	Nebraska City, Nebr	Nov. 26, 1872	133,359
Doors, Hanging sliding	G. F. Prindle	Stockbridge, Mass	July 9, 1872	128,903
Doors, Hook-catch for	C. B. Richards	Brooklyn, N. Y	May 8, 1860	28,241
Doors, &c., Machine for relishing	F. D. Green	Williamsport, Pa	Mar. 4, 1873	136,505
Doors, &c., Machinery and art of locking	J. Dillingham	Turner, Me	June 2, 1825	....
Doors, Method of mounting porcelain roses for	J. Bell	New York, N. Y	Apr. 3, 1849	6,280
Doors on the inside, Fastening	B. H. Green	Princeton, N. J	June 11, 1841	2,121
Doors open, Device for holding	W. W. Green, jr	Janesville, Wis	Nov. 24, 1868	84,352
Doors open, Holding	A. D. Witzleben	Washington, D. C	Aug. 28, 1860	29,770
Doors, Operating bolt and lock for controlling series of.	D. I. Stagg	Hoboken, N. J	June 13, 1854	11,093
Doors or shutters, Attachment for opening and closing.	W. Post	Flushing, N. Y	Feb. 18, 1851	7,940
Doors or windows, Guard for nursery	A. Howard	Milford, Mass	May 28, 1872	127,166
Doors, Rail for sliding	J. Collins	Bergen County, N. J	Dec. 16, 1873	145,630
Doors, &c., Retaining-device for	L. F. Howell	Camden, N. J	Nov. 10, 1868	83,967
Doors, safe-walls, vaults, &c., Burglar-proof plates for.	L. Yale, jr	Newport, N. Y	Oct. 19, 1852	9,350
Doors, Sheave and rail for sliding	T. M. Lyons	New York, N. Y	May 30, 1871	115,333
Doors, Spring catch and stop for	C. W. Barnes	Janesville, Wis	May 26, 1868	78,355
Doors, Spring-catch for	W. Glue	Muskegon, Mich	Jan. 24, 1871	111,196
Doors, Spring-catch for	J. C. Plumer	Boston, Mass	Mar. 7, 1865	46,697
Doors, Spring for closing	L. Evans	Fayetteville, N. Y	Apr. 18, 1848	5,515
Doors, Spring for closing	R. T. Knight	Philadelphia, Pa	Nov. 6, 1866	59,414
Doors, stair-rails, lasts, &c., Fastening for	W. Sellers	New York, N. Y	May 31, 1864	42,994
Doors, stiles, &c., Mortising	A. Whitmarsh	East Bridgewater, Mass	July 30, 1833	....
Doors to prevent rain from being forced under them by wind, &c., Method of hanging.	E. C. Tilson	Thomaston, Me	Jan. 9, 1838	571
Doors, &c., Turn-button for	P. Bradford	New Haven, Conn	Oct. 3, 1871	119,499
Doors, Water-excluding attachment for	A. Kirkpatrick	Newark, N. J	Dec. 14, 1840	1,901
Doors, Water-table for	N. Briggs	Windham, Vt	June 17, 1809	....
Doors, Water-table for	D. Dulkely	Hampton, Conn	June 14, 1834	....
Doors, Water-table for	J. Burt, jr	Tiverton, R. I	Jan. 24, 1834	....
Doors, windows, &c., Rolling screen for	W. G. Perkins	Walden, Vt	June 11, 1867	65,692
Double and single tree fastening for carriages	J. Ingels	Milton, Ind	May 10, 1870	102,940
Double and whiffle tree coupling. Open link for	N. C. Sample	Penningtonville, Pa	Jan. 17, 1871	111,007
Double-centered joint, butt, or hinge	E. Hedge	Hartford, Conn	Nov. 23, 1837	473
Double-cooler	J. Van Duzer	Otisville, N. Y	Mar. 23, 1869	88,098
Double-cylinder boiler for hot-water apparatus	W. Beebe	New York, N. Y	Nov. 14, 1854	11,926
Double gate	J. S. Brown	Washington, D. C	Aug. 10, 1852	9,176
Double-headed wrench	J. J. Love	New York, N. Y	Oct. 30, 1866	59,242
Double sliding or turning gate	R. Fleming	Victory, N. Y	Apr. 28, 1868	77,367
Double-tree	H. L. Bowen	Belvidere, Ill	Oct. 8, 1872	132,048
Double-tree	C. C. Bradley	Brodhead, Wis	Dec. 3, 1861	33,820
Double-tree	W. Dowell	Hicksville, Ohio	June 23, 1863	38,952
Double-tree	M. Durnell and W. Milner	Leesburgh, Ohio	Apr. 25, 1871	114,116
Double-tree	A. W. Green	South Dansville, N. Y	Oct. 15, 1872	132,281
Double-tree	J. B. Hough	Lebanon, Ohio	Mar. 19, 1867	62,957
Double-tree	D. W. Kauffman	Sterling, Ill	Apr. 18, 1871	113,895
Double-tree	A. Lomax	La Porte, Ind	Oct. 10, 1871	119,777
Double-tree	W. Martin	Clarence, Iowa	Sept. 25, 1873	143,173
Double-tree	H. Palmer and A. N. Case	Kingsville, Ohio	Aug. 11, 1868	80,872

Index of patents issued from the United States Patent Office from 1790 *to* 1873, *inclusive*—Continued.

Invention.	Inventor.	Residence.	Date.	No.
Double-tree	H. W. Palmer	Kingsville, Ohio	Apr. 13, 1869	88, 896
Double-tree	M. V. B. Williamson	Jamesport, N. Y	Feb. 11, 1868	74, 471
Double-tree, Carriage	J. Hoover	Manchester, Md	Mar. 21, 1865	46, 904
Double-tree-clevis hook	W. W. Bently	Lee Township, Mich	Mar. 21, 1871	112, 888
Double-tree, Compound	J. Wykoff	Grant City, Mo	Oct. 6, 1868	82, 781
Double-tree draft-equalizer	M. V. B. Williamson	Jamesport, N. Y	Feb. 11, 1868	74, 470
Double-tree, Equalizing	E. Griswold, J. B. Cramer, and W. Blay.	Helena, Mont	Feb. 11, 1868	74, 347
Double-tree fastener	D. Werst	South Bend, Ind	Dec. 13, 1870	110, 095
Double-walled coolers, Construction of	J. O dfield	Thompsonville, Conn	Feb. 23, 1869	87, 283
Doubling and spooling machine, Stopping-mechanism for.	J. Arnold	Pawtucket, R. I	May 24, 1870	103, 277
Doubling and twisting machine, Stopping-mechanism for.	W. Cockcroft and R. Ackroyd	Chester, Pa	Sept. 2, 1873	142, 374
Doubling, twisting, and reeling	G. Levan	Gap, Pa	July 20, 1846	4, 649
Doubling, twisting, and reeling machine	H. E. and J. Haight	New York, N. Y	Aug. 30, 1813	....
Douche-bath	M. Mattson	Boston, Mass	June 3, 1862	35, 458
Douche, Electro-nasal	S. E. Adams	Springfield, Ohio	Nov. 22, 1870	109, 367
Douche, Nasal	W. B. Snyder	Bridgeport, Conn	June 25, 1872	128, 257
Dough and cake mixer	T. Holmes	Williamsburgh, N. Y	Sept. 6, 1870	107, 050
Dough and cutting crackers, &c., Machine for plaiting.	I. M. Heagle	New Haven, Conn	Apr. 13, 1838	689
Dough and paste, Breaking	D. Pettibone	....	Nov. 16, 1797	....
Dough and paste, Liquid for raising	A. and G. Sauer and L. Cachal	Paris, France	Aug. 9, 1870	106, 213
Dough and sponge raiser	W. Pearce	McLean County, Ill	July 7, 1868	79, 680
Dough, Apparatus for aërating	E. Fitzgerald	New York, N. Y	Jan. 3, 1865	45, 706
Dough, Apparatus for raising	T. Stockton	North Chenango, Pa	Mar. 28, 1865	47, 050
Dough, Apparatus for rolling and spreading	G. F. Fessenden	West Cambridge, Mass	Feb. 26, 1867	62, 323
Dough apportioning, expanding, and shaping apparatus for manufacture of bread.	J. Perry	Brooklyn, N. Y	May 26, 1868	78, 232
Dough-board	H. F. Morse	Manchester, N. H	Apr. 2, 1872	125, 208
Dough-board	N. B. Petterson	McGregor, Iowa	Oct. 31, 1871	120, 394
Dough-box for cake-machine	D. M. Holmes	Williamsburgh, N. Y	Feb. 9, 1869	86, 752
Dough, Breaking and kneading	I. Cole	Cincinnati, Ohio	Dec. 12, 1848	5, 959
Dough-breaking machine	C. Barnard	Nantucket County, Mass	Apr. 17, 1810	....
Dough-breaking machine	L. Folger	....	Nov. 1, 1804	....
Dough-breaking machine	L. Shaw	Bath, Me	May 26, 1843	3, 102
Dough, crushing sugar, &c., Machine for rolling	G. Perkins	Burlington, Vt	Apr. 23, 1867	64, 029
Dough-cutter and rolling-pin, Combined	F. E. Chadwick	Gardiner, Me	July 2, 1872	128, 462
Dough-dresser, Rotary	G. H. Cross	Montpelier, Vt	June 11, 1867	65, 649
Dough for biscuit, &c., Preparing	J. R. Treadwell	Brooklyn, N. Y	Sept. 15, 1863	39, 972
Dough for bread, Apparatus for raising	J. Johnson	New York, N. Y	Oct. 5, 1858	21, 683
Dough for molding crackers, Machine for preparing	F. C. Treadwell, jr	New York, N. Y	May 13, 1856	14, 889
Dough into loaves or crackers, Machine for molding and shaping.	W. Hotine	Brooklyn, N. Y	Sept. 11, 1866	57, 908
Dough-kneader	J. H. Barr and J. H. Smith	Roanoke, Ind	July 12, 1870	105, 293
Dough-kneader	L. Bell	Washington, D. C	Dec. 10, 1872	133, 823
Dough-kneader	H. H. Hawes	Mount Meridian, Va	Mar. 14, 1871	112, 707
Dough-kneader	C. C. Johnson	Springfield, Vt	July 2, 1867	66, 351
Dough-kneader	H. P. Jones	Davenport, Iowa	Jan. 15, 1867	61, 206
Dough-kneader	F. C. King	Portland, Me	July 25, 1865	48, 979
Dough-kneader	S. H. Lombard	Winona, Minn	May 19, 1868	78, 106
Dough-kneader	J. C. Loveland	Springfield, Vt	Jan. 16, 1866	52, 062
Dough-kneader	E. Mathers	Harrisville, W. Va	Jan. 23, 1872	122, 902
Dough-kneader	W. B. Morrison	Muskegon, Mich	Oct. 1, 1867	69, 467
Dough-kneader	A. J. Palmer	Brooklyn, N. Y	Aug. 9, 1864	43, 791
Dough-kneader	P. W. Robinson	New Bedford, Mass	July 30, 1867	67, 353
Dough-kneader	A. P. Routt	Orange Court-House, Va	Aug. 7, 1866	56, 995
Dough-kneader	G. W. Sanders	Springfield, Mass	June 19, 1866	55, 718
Dough-kneader	C. B. Sawyer	Fitchburgh, Mass	July 13, 1869	92, 479
Dough-kneader	F. Thrall	Oshkosh, Wis	June 8, 1869	91, 054
Dough-kneader	W. Tyler	Georgetown, D. C	May 16, 1871	114, 993
Dough-kneader	C. I. Wilmans and W. J. Wolfe	Olney, Ill	June 9, 1868	78, 778
Dough-kneader and meat-pounder, &c	P. Perry	Charlestown, Mass	July 3, 1866	56, 091
Dough kneader and roller	W. A. Snow	Killingworth, Conn	June 25, 1872	128, 333
Dough-kneading machine	G. R. Baker	Brooklyn, N. Y	Oct. 10, 1865	50, 322
Dough-kneading machine	H. Berdan	New York, N. Y	Sept. 15, 1857	18, 180
Dough-kneading machine	S. Emmore	Stouchsburgh, Pa	Dec. 3, 1867	71, 723
Dough-kneading machine	J. S. Fisher and S. W. Talbot	Dedham, Mass	Apr. 23, 1822	....
Dough-kneading machine	S. Nixon	Prince George's County, Va	Feb. 28, 1818	....
Dough-kneading machine	J. L. Rolland	Paris, France	Jan. 9, 1855	12, 217
Dough-kneading machine	N. C. Willett	Jonesborough, Tenn	Dec. 28, 1832	....
Dough-machine	O. B. Fuller	Newark, N. J	July 8, 1873	140, 695
Dough-machine	D. and T. Shackford	West Brook, N. Y	Mar. 2, 1836	....
Dough, Machine for breaking or working	J. W. Post	Baltimore, Md	Mar. 14, 1840	1, 516
Dough, Machine for feeding the flour, mixing the materials, and kneading.	J. Hecker and W. Hotine	New York, N. Y	Nov. 24, 1857	18, 723
Dough, Machine for making	G. Richards	Stonington, Conn	Feb. 14, 1806	....
Dough, Machine for sheeting	D. B. Fuller	Philadelphia, Pa	Mar. 12, 1872	124, 431
Dough, Machine for sheeting	O. B. Fuller	Newark, N. J	Nov. 18, 1873	144, 666
Dough, Machine for sheeting	J. H. Shrote	Baltimore, Md	July 25, 1871	117, 474
Dough making and kneading machine	S. M. Ridgaway	Saint Michael's, Md	July 1, 1856	15, 254
Dough, Method of kneading	H. N. Rider	Adams, Mass	Feb. 19, 1850	7, 105
Dough-mixer	C. Chavanne	New Orleans, La	Oct. 9, 1866	58, 596
Dough-mixer	W. E. Damant	West Hoboken, N. J	June 25, 1872	128, 288
Dough-mixer	F. Grenier	Beroserac, France	Oct. 6, 1868	82, 710
Dough-mixer	R. Kent	Portland, Me	Feb. 6, 1872	123, 403
Dough-mixer	A. E. Muth	Cincinnati, Ohio	Mar. 26, 1872	125, 072
Dough-mixer	J. M. Stanyan	Milford, N. H	Oct. 9, 1866	58, 691
Dough-mixer	S. J. Talbott	Milford, N. H	Dec. 18, 1866	60, 672
Dough mixer and roller	J. Bailie and J. Gervers	Cincinnati, Ohio	Jan. 22, 1867	61, 307
Dough-mixer, Revolving	T. Holmes	Williamsburgh, N. Y	June 15, 1869	91, 335
Dough-mixer, Revolving	T. Holmes	Williamsburgh, N. Y	Sept. 21, 1869	95, 021
Dough-mixing	E. Fitzgerald	New York, N. Y	Oct. 8, 1861	32, 432
Dough mixing and kneading machine	E. Edwards	London, England	Feb. 25, 1873	136, 144
Dough mixing and kneading machine	W. Wells	Middleton, Mass	July 5, 1864	43, 415
Dough-mixing machine	G. Clark, jr., and L. P. Jenks	Dorchester and Boston, Mass.	Feb. 20, 1866	52, 078

Index of patents issued from the United States Patent Office from 1790 *to* 1873, *inclusive*—Continued.

Invention.	Inventor.	Residence.	Date.	No.
Dough-mixing machine	J. Davidson	Xenia, Ohio	May 25, 1869	90, 509
Dough-mixing machine	W. Hotine	Brooklyn, N. Y	Jan. 8, 1861	31, 082
Dough, &c., Mixing or breaking	H. Ball	Cincinnati, Ohio	Feb. 27, 1847	4, 981
Dough, paste, &c., Machine for making	E. Stevens	London, England	Oct. 20, 1863	40, 370
Dough-raiser, Automatic	J. Stark	Thomasville, Ga	May 25, 1869	90, 471
Dough, Raising	J. Perry and E. Fitzgerald	New York, N. Y	Mar. 9, 1858	19, 610
Dough raising and kneading machine	G. Scott	Steubenville, Ohio	Nov. 27, 1860	30, 764
Dough-raising apparatus	S. V. Dodge	De Soto, Iowa	Apr. 9, 1872	125, 445
Dough-raising apparatus	W. Leas	Kokomo, Ind	Jan. 9, 1866	51, 949
Dough-raising trough	H. L. McKean	Allegheny, Pa	Mar. 7, 1865	46, 688
Dough-roller	D. B. Baker	Rollersville, Ohio	Dec. 19, 1865	51, 539
Dough-roller	W. Long	Watertown, N. Y	May 26, 1868	78, 300
Dough roller and cutter	W. F. Rippon	Providence, R. I	May 14, 1872	126, 833
Dough, Roller for pressing	F. J. Rice and G. W. Hayward	Providence, R. I	July 3, 1860	29, 606
Dough rolling and cutting machine	I. S. Schuyler	New York, N. Y	Apr. 13, 1858	19, 968
Dough-rolling machine	H. Goodwin and C. H. Bennett, 2d.	South Berwick Junction, Me.	May 4, 1869	89, 653
Dough-rolling machine	J. Hecker and W. Hotine	New York, N. Y	Mar. 22, 1859	23, 301
Dough-rolling machine	J. McCollum	New York, N. Y	Dec. 1, 1857	18, 758
Dough under pressure, Apparatus for measuring out and discharging.	J. Perry	Brooklyn, N. Y	July 8, 1862	35, 837
Dough-worker	W. R. Pool	Havana, Ala	May 24, 1870	103, 366
Doughnut-cutter	J. F. Blondel	Thomaston, Me	July 9, 1872	128, 783
Doughnut-mold	G. Machlet	Newark, N. J	Mar. 25, 1873	137, 142
Dovetail and tenon cutting machine	T. J. Wells	New York, N. Y	July 8, 1841	2, 158
Dovetail-cutter	J. C. Hursell	Boston, Mass	Aug. 13, 1867	67, 654
Dovetail-joint for wood, &c	F. S. Barnard	New York, N. Y	Apr. 12, 1859	23, 542
Dovetail-joint, Sliding	G. B. Raymond		Mar. 26, 1816	
Dovetail key-cutter	A. P. Hughes	Philadelphia, Pa	Sept. 18, 1855	13, 574
Dovetail-marker	J. Evans	Philadelphia, Pa	Apr. 21, 1868	77, 018
Dovetail-marking device	G. Ashby	Decatur, Ill	Dec. 16, 1873	145, 477
Dovetail-molding device	A. L. Finch	Sing Sing, N. Y	Apr. 2, 1872	125, 186
Dovetail-molding tool	B. McEnally and E. Farrell	Detroit, Mich	Nov. 30, 1869	97, 368
Dovetail-moldings, Machine for cutting	S. Withington	Saint Louis, Mo	Nov. 30, 1858	22, 222
Dovetail-mortises, Machine for making	T. D. White	Cincinnati, Ohio	Apr. 21, 1868	77, 149
Dovetails, Adjustable gage for	J. S. L. Babbs and A. H. Ray	Boston, Mass., and Providence, R. I.	Dec. 15, 1857	18, 838
Dovetails and their grooves, Machine for cutting	E. G. Matthews	Clear Water, Minn	Feb. 10, 1857	16, 627
Dovetailing-board	A. Davis	Lancaster, Mass	Sept. 6, 1833	
Dovetailing-machine	J. S. L. Babbs	New Albany, Ind	June 5, 1866	55, 223
Dovetailing-machine	J. S. L. Babbs	New Albany, Ind	Jan. 1, 1867	60, 843
Dovetailing-machine	J. Bain and S. C. Brown	Richmond, Ind	Oct. 16, 1860	30, 382
Dovetailing-machine	H. H. Bashore	Philadelphia, Pa	Mar. 8, 1870	100, 704
Dovetailing-machine	J. Bell	Harlem, N. Y	Oct. 23, 1855	13, 696
Dovetailing-machine	M. T. Boult	Battle Creek, Mich	Oct. 8, 1872	131, 932
Dovetailing-machine	W. G. Branch, J. A. Haseltine, and W. and C. F. Branch.	Pomeroy, Ohio	Sept. 19, 1871	119, 113
Dovetailing-machine	T. H. Burley	Cincinnati, Ohio	Jan. 2, 1855	12, 122
Dovetailing-machine	T. H. Burley	New York, N. Y	Jan. 3, 1860	26, 647
Dovetailing-machine	E. Coffin	Indianapolis, Ind	Feb. 5, 1861	31, 301
Dovetailing-machine	T. Cullen	Blackstone, Mass	Apr. 15, 1873	137, 830
Dovetailing-machine	A. Davis	Lowell, Mass	Nov. 28, 1871	121, 278
Dovetailing-machine	A. Davis	Lowell, Mass	May 27, 1873	139, 299
Dovetailing-machine	A. and A. Davis	Lowell, Mass	Feb. 26, 1856	14, 307
Dovetailing-machine	J. Dill	Grand Rapids, Mich	Aug. 30, 1870	106, 922
Dovetailing-machine	J. Dill	Boston, Mass	Nov. 19, 1872	133, 143
Dovetailing-machine	H. H. Evarts	Chicago, Ill	Jan. 3, 1871	110, 642
Dovetailing-machine	H. H. Evarts	Chicago, Ill	June 7, 1870	104, 001
Dovetailing machine	J. P. Flanders	Vergennes, Vt	Nov. 15, 1870	109, 194
Dovetailing-machine	A. S. Gear and B. F. Dunklee	Boston, Mass., and Concord, N. H.	Apr. 2, 1872	125, 282
Dovetailing-machine	R. J. Gould	Newark, N. J	Aug. 11, 1868	80, 942
Dovetailing-machine	F. D. Green	Williamsport, Pa	Feb. 25, 1873	136, 236
Dovetailing-machine	C. S. Griffin and J. W. Wilkins	Stockton, Me	Nov. 8, 1870	109, 123
Dovetailing-machine	C. S. Griffin and J. W. Wilkins	Chelsea, Me	June 20, 1871	116, 178
Dovetailing-machine	H. J. and H. J. Hale, jr	Indianapolis, Ind	Mar. 3, 1863	37, 812
Dovetailing-machine	J. J. Haley	Philadelphia, Pa	Sept. 4, 1855	13, 522
Dovetailing-machine	W. T. Hamilton	Dublin, Ireland	Nov. 11, 1873	144, 536
Dovetailing-machine	S. E. Hartwell	New Albany, Ind	Mar. 22, 1864	41, 982
Dovetailing machine	J. E. Haskell	Baltimore, Md	Mar. 4, 1873	136, 374
Dovetailing-machine	E. Heath	San Francisco, Cal	July 21, 1863	39, 230
Dovetailing-machine	E. Heath	San Francisco, Cal	May 16, 1871	114, 814
Dovetailing-machine	E. Heath	San Francisco, Cal	June 14, 1870	104, 147
Dovetailing-machine	H. W. Jelliff	Appleton, Ohio	June 12, 1860	28, 672
Dovetailing-machine	E. L. Jones and M. E. Carter	Saint Louis, Mo	Aug. 20, 1861	33, 087
Dovetailing-machine	D. Jordan	Charlestown, Mass	Feb. 1, 1870	99, 446
Dovetailing-machine	D. Jordan and J. Dill	Charlestown, Mass., and Grand Rapids, Mich.	Apr. 19, 1870	102, 011
Dovetailing-machine	D. A. King and T. Norris	Lexington, Ky	Jan. 22, 1861	31, 173
Dovetailing-machine	T. E., A., and E. King	Cherry Valley, Ohio	Sept. 14, 1858	21, 503
Dovetailing-machine	C. B. Knapp and N. S. Clement	Waterloo, Wis., and Northampton, Mass.	Jan. 2, 1872	122, 390
Dovetailing-machine	C. F. Kuhnle	Washington, D. C	Dec. 15, 1868	84, 884
Dovetailing-machine	W. A. McDonald	Mott Haven, N. Y	Feb. 15, 1859	22, 967
Dovetailing-machine	W. A. McDonald	Mott Haven, N. Y	Sept. 13, 1859	25, 431
Dovetailing-machine	W. F. Moody	Chicago, Ill	Apr. 1, 1873	137, 515
Dovetailing-machine	C. Oblemacher and O. Kromer	Sandusky, Ohio	Mar. 9, 1869	87, 586
Dovetailing-machine	L. A. Orcutt	Albany, N. Y	July 8, 1856	15, 301
Dovetailing-machine	O. J. Pennell and G. Zimmer	Williamsport, Pa	Nov. 7, 1871	120, 594
Dovetailing-machine	J. Phillips, jr	Chicago, Ill	Aug. 3, 1869	93, 225
Dovetailing-machine	D. Pomroy	San Francisco, Cal	Apr. 4, 1871	113, 560
Dovetailing-machine	J. B. Ritchey	Pomeroy, Ohio	May 16, 1871	114, 859
Dovetailing-machine	J. B. Ritchey	Pomeroy, Ohio	July 25, 1871	117, 332
Dovetailing-machine	J. B. Schmidt	Salem, Va	Nov. 29, 1870	109, 674
Dovetailing-machine	J. B. Schmidt	Salem, Va	Nov. 29, 1870	109, 675
Dovetailing-machine	J. M. Seymour	Newark, N. J	Mar. 7, 1871	112, 502
Dovetailing-machine	W. E. Sibley	Weston, Mass	Dec. 6, 1864	45, 351
Dovetailing-machine	W. E. Sibley	Weston, Mass	May 31, 1870	103, 670

Index of patents issued from the United States Patent Office from 1790 *to* 1873, *inclusive*—Continued.

Invention.	Inventor.	Residence.	Date.	No.
Dovetailing-machine	P. A. B. Triacca	Stamford, Conn	Aug. 13, 1872	130, 548
Dovetailing-machine	A. C. Van Alstine	New York, N. Y	July 22, 1873	141, 096
Dovetailing-machine	J. R. Van Epps	Albany, N. Y	Apr. 19, 1870	102, 069
Dovetailing-machine	T. D. White	Cincinnati, Ohio	Apr. 21, 1868	77, 148
Dovetailing-machine	D. Whitlock	Newark, N. J	Jan. 30, 1872	123, 137
Dovetailing-machine	E. Wight	Philadelphia, Pa	Mar. 11, 1856	14, 427
Dovetailing-machine	R. Wolf	Burlington, Iowa	Mar. 10, 1868	75, 506
Dovetailing-machine	C. Young	Auburn, N. Y	July 16, 1867	66, 763
Dovetailing-machine, Cutter for	J. C. Hursell	Boston, Mass	June 19, 1866	55, 661
Dovetailing-machine, Cutter for	D. Jordan	Charlestown, Mass	May 31, 1870	103, 750
Dovetailing-machine cutters, Method of operating	J. Bell	Harlem, N. Y	July 10, 1860	29, 051
Dovetailing machine, Miter	F. A. Gleason	Rome, N. Y	Mar. 17, 1863	37, 910
Dovetailing machine, Miter	F. A. Gleason	New York, N. Y	Aug. 9, 1864	43, 767
Dovetailing machine, Square-joint	W. Perrin	Lowell, Mass	Mar. 24, 1841	2, 014
Dovetailing-machine table	J. Dill	Grand Rapids, Mich	July 5, 1870	104, 943
Dovetailing rotary cutters in their heads, Method of	G. H. Mallory	New York, N. Y	Jan. 5, 1858	19, 035
Dovetailing-tool	G. W. Billings	Cleveland, Ohio	Feb. 23, 1858	19, 406
Dovetailing-tool	A. P. Hughes	Philadelphia, Pa	Feb. 21, 1854	10, 548
Dowel-brad, Double headed and pointed	J. Sowle	Boston, Mass	June 27, 1871	116, 367
Dowel-gage	J. Er	Cleveland, Ohio	Feb. 6, 1872	123, 337
Dowel-hoop for cooperage	A. W. Ballow	Saint Charles, Mich	Mar. 19, 1872	124, 656
Dowel-pins, Machine for making	M. Everts	Girard Township, Pa	Feb. 4, 1873	135, 416
Dowel-pins, Machine for making wooden	A. H. Boyd	Saco, Me	Apr. 20, 1858	20, 016
Doweling	P. Jones	Newark, N. J	Apr. 1, 1862	34, 835
Doweling-bit used in ship-building	J. Thomas	Washington, D. C	Apr. 2, 1825	....
Doweling heading for cooperage, Machine for	R. Hunt	Ontario County, N. Y	Dec. 11, 1820	....
Doweling-instrument	W. Bowhay	Philadelphia, Pa	Oct. 14, 1816	....
Doweling-machine, Cooper's	J. German	Oriskany Falls, N. Y	Feb. 10, 1863	37, 619
Draft and hold-back attachment	W. H. Chamberlin	Medina, N. Y	Jan. 21, 1870	104, 557
Draft and shaft tug	H. Bowers	Albany, N. Y	May 5, 1868	77, 575
Draft-attachment	M. Adsit	Forest, N. Y	May 5, 1868	77, 433
Draft-attachment	C. W. Conolly	Rochester, N. Y	July 3, 1866	56, 012
Draft-attachment for horse	C. C. Cole	Phelps, N. Y	Jan. 4, 1870	98, 563
Draft-attachment for horse	E. Sanford	Meriden, Conn	Nov. 26, 1867	71, 415
Draft-bar	D. and M. Foreman	Dalton, Ohio	Apr. 14, 1868	76, 737
Draft-bar, Railway	R. Fiegel	Montgomery County, Pa	Apr. 4, 1865	47, 098
Draft-chain, whiffletree, &c., Hook for	V. B. Paul	Morrill, Me	Sept. 10, 1872	131, 224
Draft-device for three horses	O. W. Jones	Columbus, Wis	Feb. 21, 1871	111, 944
Draft-equalizer	J. Averill and E. S. Fitch	Champlain and Movers, N. Y.	Jan. 28, 1868	73, 864
Draft-equalizer	J. P. Beckenbaugh	Springfield, Ill	Oct. 28, 1873	144, 052
Draft-equalizer	E. H. Blake	Coatsburgh, Ill	Dec. 30, 1873	145, 983
Draft-equalizer	O. N. Collins and P. B. Stiles	Cedar Rapids, Iowa	Dec. 9, 1873	145, 474
Draft-equalizer	W. W. Hinman	Elkhart, Ill	Oct. 14, 1873	143, 696
Draft-equalizer	W. McClelland, sr	Fowler, Ill	Dec. 30, 1873	146, 011
Draft-equalizer	G. A. Mosher	Champlain, N. Y	Sept. 1, 1868	81, 669
Draft-equalizer	J. Parker	Pontiac, Mich	Aug. 12, 1873	141, 813
Draft-equalizer	W. M. Perkins and T. F. Vandergift.	La Fontaine, Ind	Oct. 25, 1870	108, 727
Draft-equalizer	S. Shadduck	Elk River Township, Iowa.	Sept. 22, 1868	82, 443
Draft-equalizer	I. Starr	Prairieville, Mich	Feb. 9, 1869	86, 708
Draft-equalizer	W. Stevenson	Neponset, Ill	May 16, 1871	114, 988
Draft-equalizer	S. H. Smith	North Adams, Mich	Feb. 23, 1869	87, 305
Draft-equalizer	R. Walker and G. Trumbull	Batavia, N. Y	Dec. 15, 1868	85, 639
Draft-equalizer	S. H. Wheeler	Dowagiac, Mich	May 4, 1869	89, 614
Draft-equalizer for horse-power	A. Stewart	Troy, Wis	May 28, 1867	65, 297
Draft-equalizer for wagons	L. Kendle, G. Gates, and J. M. Orput.	Rochelle, Ill	Nov. 5, 1872	132, 725
Draft equalizer, Three-horse	H. F. Jerauld	Vandalia, Ill	Mar. 14, 1871	112, 715
Draft-equalizing attachment	J. Wilkinson	Prophetstown, Ill	Aug. 11, 1863	39, 517
Draft-evener	R. Bunker	Hudson, Wis	Apr. 1, 1873	137, 286
Draft for furnaces, Hot-air	E. Boughton	South Norwalk, Conn	Nov. 4, 1873	144, 249
Draft-hook, Detachable	J. Nicholson	Monticello, Ind	Dec. 5, 1871	121, 464
Draft in flues, furnaces, &c., Machine for creating	T. Fairbanks	Saint Johnsbury, Vt	May 26, 1843	3, 100
Draft in smoke-pipes, Using exhaust steam for increasing.	R. Winans	Baltimore, Md	Apr. 10, 1847	5, 056
Draft-link, Spring	B. Richards	North Industry, Ohio	Feb. 9, 1869	86, 863
Draft-plate	G. Smith	Providence, R. I	Apr. 16, 1867	63, 954
Draft-promoter	B. A. Haycock	Richland, Iowa	May 2, 1871	114, 291
Draft-regulator	J. W. Branham	Franklin, Ind	Mar. 31, 1868	76, 045
Draft regulator	C. A. Harper	Burlington, N. J	July 16, 1872	129, 551
Draft-regulator	E. Harrington	Boston, Mass	Sept. 6, 1864	44, 091
Draft-regulator	A. L. Ide	Springfield, Mass	July 11, 1871	116, 962
Draft-regulator	J. J. Smith and S. Wood	Cleveland, Ohio	Nov. 2, 1869	96, 494
Draft-regulator	H. E. Turner	Boston, Mass	Feb. 24, 1863	37, 781
Draft-regulator	J. Woodruff	Rahway, N. J	July 9, 1872	128, 836
Draft regulator and ventilator	G. Chilson	Boston, Mass	Aug. 23, 1864	43, 897
Draft-regulator for heating-apparatus	R. E. Deane	Brooklyn, N. Y	June 8, 1869	90, 934
Draft-regulator for warming-apparatus	J. Brown and C. R. Ellis	New York and Brooklyn, N. Y.	Apr. 3, 1860	27, 687
Draft-regulator, Hot-air-furnace	F. E. Chatard, jr	Baltimore, Md	May 7, 1872	126, 377
Draft-regulator, Hot-air-furnace	S. J. Gold	Cornwall, Conn	June 18, 1872	128, 035
Draft-regulator, Locomotive	P. H. Corlett	West Manchester, Pa	Nov. 10, 1863	40, 555
Draft-regulator, Steam-boiler	P. E. Chase	Philadelphia, Pa	Oct. 14, 1856	15, 870
Draft-regulator, Steam-boiler	H. N. Winans	New York, N. Y	Nov. 8, 1864	44, 992
Draft-regulator, Steam-boiler-furnace	E. B. Beach	West Meriden, Conn	Feb. 13, 1872	123, 608
Draft-regulator, Stove	E. Foote, jr	Seneca Falls, N. Y	May 26, 1842	2, 636
Draft-regulator, Stove and furnace	J. Briggs	Roxbury, Mass	Feb. 16, 1864	41, 598
Drafting-attachment	T. Evans	Newark, N. J	Dec. 3, 1867	71, 595
Drafting-instrument	J. C. Moore	Belmont County, Ohio	Dec. 30, 1833	....
Draftsman, Adjustable curve for use of	S. K. Kirby	East Saginaw, Mich	June 7, 1870	103, 896
Drag	J. W. Newton	Geneva, Wis	Nov. 16, 1869	96, 929
Drag and cultivator combined	H. H. Christie	Perch River, N. Y	Nov. 11, 1862	36, 892
Drag and hook, Dung	H. W. Weiss	Quakertown, Pa	Nov. 24, 1868	84, 452
Drag for removing stones, &c., from the bottoms of rivers, lakes, &c.	P. L. Lyme	New York, N. Y	Oct. 31, 1839	1, 386
Drag, Ground	B. J. McAfee and J. H. Wirt	Delphia, Ind	Sept. 11, 1866	57, 939
Drag-hook	J. Parish	Chicago, Ill	Dec. 24, 1867	72, 671

Index of patents issued from the United States Patent Office from 1790 *to* 1873, *inclusive*—Continued.

Invention.	Inventor.	Residence.	Date.	No.
Drag, Marine	J. Faunce	Washington, D. C	Feb. 22, 1870	100, 021
Drag-rake	G. H. Hackett	North Tunbridge, Vt	Jan. 18, 1870	98, 954
Drag-rake	H. F. Morton	West Sumner, Me	Mar. 30, 1869	88, 325
Drag-rake, Hand	E. Brown	Kennebunk, Me	Nov. 15, 1870	109, 294
Drag, Sea	S. Curtis	Lynn, Mass	Aug. 31, 1869	94, 402
Drag, Sea	J. Edson	Boston, Mass	Aug. 31, 1869	94, 191
Drag, Steam	G. Bradley	Paterson, N. J	Nov. 11, 1856	16, 044
Drain	G. R. Moore	Lyons, Iowa	Feb. 11, 1873	135, 723
Drain	G. W. Smith	Springfield, N. J	Feb. 9, 1864	41, 542
Drain	G. W. Smith	Springfield Township, N. J.	Nov. 15, 1864	45, 089
Drain and sewer pipe molding machine	D. Copeland, jr	Rochester, N. Y	May 23, 1871	115, 030
Drain and water pipe	W. P. Kirkland	San Francisco, Cal	Apr. 14, 1868	76, 778
Drain and water pipe	G. H. Titcomb and J. P. Culver	Jersey City, N. J	May 3, 1870	102, 623
Drain, Arched	G. R. Moore	Lyons, Iowa	July 16, 1872	129, 578
Drain-pipe	S. Carlton	Lynn, Mass	May 4, 1869	89, 630
Drain-pipe	T. J. Mayall	Roxbury, Mass	June 21, 1859	24, 476
Drain-pipe	W. G. Monk	Brooklyn, E. D., N. Y	Feb. 11, 1873	135, 721
Drain-pipe	G. Richardson	Milwaukee, Wis	Sept. 6, 1870	107, 103
Drain-pipe machine	H. Bissell	Hartford, Conn	July 11, 1871	116, 920
Drain-pipe machine	I. C. Bryant	Washington, D. C	Nov. 23, 1869	97, 035
Drain-pipe machine	A. J. Davis	Newark, N. J	Nov. 21, 1871	121, 160
Drain-pipe machine	C. W. Kennedy	Brooklyn, E. D., N. Y	July 11, 1871	116, 839
Drain-pipe machine	P. McIntyre	Norwick, Conn	Dec. 7, 1869	97, 668
Drain-pipe machine	B. S. Pierce and M. R. Pierce	New Bedford and Mansfield, Mass.	Apr. 19, 1859	23, 703
Drain-pipe machine	M. R. Pierce	New York, N. Y	Nov. 14, 1871	120, 999
Drain-pipe machine	G. Richardson	Milwaukee, Wis	Sept. 12, 1871	118, 880
Drain-pipe machine	J. W. Stockwell	Portland, Me	June 27, 1871	116, 371
Drain-pipe machine	J. W. Stockwell	Portland, Me	July 4, 1871	116, 643
Drain-pipe mold	J. S. Roake	Williamsburgh, N. Y	Sept. 17, 1872	131, 375
Drain-pipes, Apparatus for carrying	D. W. Brown	Woodbridge, N. J	Mar. 14, 1871	112, 538
Drain-pipes, &c., Apparatus for mixing and preparing material for manufacture of.	J. A. Middleton	Williamsburgh, N. Y	Sept. 17, 1872	131, 366
Drain-pipes, Device for the manufacture of	J. W. Stockwell	Portland, Me	Mar. 19, 1872	124, 702
Drain-pipes, Flask for	E. Dayton	Meriden, Conn	Nov. 29, 1864	45, 229
Drain-pipes, Machine and mold for	P. McIntyre	Hartford, Conn	Oct. 15, 1872	132, 169
Drain-pipes, Machine for making	A. Müller	Jersey City, N. J	Sept. 16, 1873	142, 930
Drain-pipes, Machine for making	A. Skinner	San Francisco, Cal	May 12, 1868	77, 925
Drain-pipes, Machine for making composition	R. Skinner and R. Gaines	San Francisco, Cal	Aug. 9, 1870	106, 290
Drain-pipes, Manufacture of	F. Dickerson, jr	Hartford, Conn	June 25, 1872	128, 369
Drain pipes, tiles, &c., Composition for the manufacture of.	E. J. Eames	New York, N. Y	Apr. 2, 1872	125, 125
Drain roller and molder combined	F. B. Fournier	Berea, Ohio	Feb. 4, 1862	34, 327
Drain, Sediment	G. R. Moore	Lyons, Iowa	Mar. 11, 1873	136, 608
Drain-tile	A. Newkumet	Philadelphia, Pa	Apr. 16, 1861	32, 079
Drain-tile	E. W. Rowe	Brewer, Me	July 3, 1860	29, 040
Drain-tile-laying apparatus	G. W. Nevill	Richmond, Va	Mar. 11, 1873	136, 751
Drain-tile machine	J. Daines	Birmingham, Mich	June 14, 1859	24, 379
Drain-tile machine	G. Graessle	Hamilton, Ohio	Aug. 14, 1860	29, 586
Drain-tile machine	J. Hotchkiss	Yellow Springs, Ohio	Mar. 27, 1860	27, 669
Drain-tile machine	H. Knight	Brooklyn, N. Y	Aug. 18, 1863	39, 579
Drain-tile machine	T. Maycock	Buffalo, N. Y	Nov. 4, 1856	16, 0[illegible]5
Drain-tile machine	S. M. Smith and C. Winegar	Union Springs, N. Y	Jan. 10, 1860	26, 793
Drain-tile mold	J. J. Alvord	Tecumseh, Mich	Aug. 25, 1863	39, 621
Drain-tiles, Apparatus for laying	B. B. Briggs	Sharon, Ohio	Oct. 4, 1859	25, 624
Drain-tiles, Bottom-plate for	J. Parsons	Cleveland, Ohio	Aug. 7, 1860	29, 516
Drain-tiles, Casting	J. Coy	Oswego, N. Y	May 10, 1864	42, 643
Drain-tiles, Mode of laying	H. F. Baker	Centreville, Ind	May 1, 1860	28, 050
Drain-trap	J. C. I. Sturm	Buffalo, N. Y	Jan. 16, 1872	122, 866
Drain-tube	J. McMillan	Perinton, N. Y	Aug. 23, 1870	106, 709
Drain, Underground	S. H. Warner	Darbyville, Ohio	Nov. 22, 1870	109, 474
Drain, Waste-water	C. H. Parker and G. N. Copeland.	Cortland, N. Y	July 2, 1867	66, 380
Drain-water pipes, Machine for making	C. Collier	Charlestown, Mass	Apr. 16, 1867	63, 784
Drains, Apparatus for suppressing effluvia from	W. Bryent	Boston, Mass	Aug. 21, 1866	57, 284
Drains, Construction of cement	B. Livermore	Hartland, Vt	May 1, 1860	28, 091
Drains, Lining underground	J. C. Miller, S. A. Clemens, and G. H. Clemens.	Irwin, Ohio, Rockford, Ill., and Urbana, Ohio.	Oct. 4, 1859	25, 7[illegible]3
Drains, Pen-stock for underground	D. A. Parks	Fairview, Ill	Mar. 10, 1868	75, 295
Drains with cement, Lining underground	A. Watson	London, Ohio	Feb. 28, 1860	27, 324
Drainer, Pipe	A. Brigham	Lawrence, Mass	May 5, 1863	38, 371
Draining and pipe-laying machine	I. C. Pratt	Morton, Ill	Jan. 3, 1860	26, 708
Draining-apparatus	J. Roy	New Orleans, La	May 11, 1869	89, 946
Draining cellars	E. S. Dickinson and J. L. Peake	New York, N. Y	July 18, 1871	117, 156
Draining cellars, Sink-apparatus for	A. Knacker	Meadville, Pa	Apr. 12, 1870	101, 744
Draining-machine	M. Bucklin	Grafton, N. H	Aug. 2, 1859	24, 928
Draining-machine	J. Cole and A. L. O. Wall	De Witt, Ill	Nov. 11, 1856	16, 046
Draining-machine	A. P. Routt	Somerset, Va	July 14, 1857	17, 809
Draining-machine	A. P. Routt	Liberty Mills, Va	Jan. 15, 1867	61, 263
Draining-machine, Centrifugal	W. Richardson	New Orleans, La	Sept. 27, 1853	10, 000
Draining machine, Underground	A. Miller	Mount Pleasant, Iowa	Aug. 9, 1859	25, 027
Drapery-hook	E. Carrington	West Meriden, Conn	Oct. 15, 1867	69, 766
Draw-bar	W. Kotzum	Aurora, Ind	June 29, 1869	92, 062
Draw-bar and bumper, Elastic	T. J. Mayall	Roxbury, Mass	Jan. 11, 1859	22, 6[illegible]7
Draw-bar, Railway	D. S. Beals	Adrian, Mich	Aug. 10, 1869	93, 584
Draw-bars of railway-couplings, Die for making followers for.	J. T. Wilson	Pittsburgh, Pa	Aug. 8, 1871	117, 953
Draw-bars or buffers, Method of making	J. T. Wilson	Pittsburgh, Pa	Aug. 22, 1871	118, 322
Draw-bolts, Blank for	D. B. Oliver	McClure Township, Pa	Mar. 11, 1873	136, 757
Draw-bridge	N. Macneale	Cincinnati, Ohio	Mar. 15, 1870	100, 910
Draw-bridge signal, Railway	S. L. Spofford	Philadelphia, Pa	July 10, 1855	13, 235
Draw-bridge signals, Connection for	T. S. Hall	Stamford, Conn	June 1, 1869	90, 743
Draw-head face-plates for railway-couplings, Die for making.	J. T. Wilson	Pittsburgh, Pa	Aug. 8, 1871	117, 954
Draw-head plates, Bending and punching	P. L. Weimer	Lebanon, Pa	Oct. 31, 1865	50, 756
Draw-heads, Regulating the speed of	H. MacLean	Paterson, N. J	Oct. 23, 1847	5, 341
Draw-heads, Stop-motion for	B. O. Paige	Lowell, Mass	Mar. 3, 1863	37, 823
Draw-heads, Stop-motion for railway	B. O. Paige	Lowell, Mass	Feb. 12, 1861	31, 398

Index of patents issued from the United States Patent Office from 1790 *to* 1873, *inclusive*—Continued.

Invention.	Inventor.	Residence.	Date.	No.
Draw-heads while in motion, Mode of changing the gearing of.	A. Jenks	Bridesburgh, Pa	Dec. 11, 1849	6, 938
Draw-hook and buffer, Self-coupling	P. G. Gardiner	New York, N. Y	May 23, 1871	115, 050
Draw-plate	J. O. Kane	New York, N. Y	July 2, 1867	66, 248
Drawer	B. J. Greely	Boston, Mass	Apr. 22, 1873	138, 017
Drawer	I. A. Howe	Boston, Mass	Aug. 8, 1871	117, 885
Drawer-alarm	W. B. Card	Sag Harbor, N. Y	Jan. 10, 1860	26, 813
Drawer-alarm	F. H. Purington	Willimantic, Conn	Jan. 22, 1861	31, 188
Drawer, Bureau	M. Fitzgibbons	New York, N. Y	Aug. 24, 1869	94, 096
Drawer catch, Money	S. Hubbell, jr	West Salem, Ohio	July 14, 1868	79, 981
Drawer, Closet, bureau, &c	H. R. Taylor	Roxbury, Mass	Apr. 27, 1858	20, 100
Drawer-fastening	J. Schweinfurt	Philadelphia, Pa	Oct. 8, 1872	132, 028
Drawer-fastening	J. Serrill	Philadelphia, Pa	Dec. 19, 1865	51, 625
Drawer-guide	G. S. and H. Curtis	Chicago, Ill	July 20, 1869	92, 798
Drawer-handle	J. Smith	Brockport, N. Y	Apr. 13, 1869	88, 817
Drawer-handle	C. A. Stock	New York, N. Y	Dec. 6, 1870	109, 964
Drawer-lock	A. G. Burton	Rochester, N. Y	Mar. 24, 1868	75, 854
Drawer-lock	E. L. Gaylord	Terryville, Conn	Jan. 1, 1867	60, 874
Drawer-lock	E. G. Gory	Cincinnati, Ohio	Apr. 22, 1873	138, 148
Drawer-lock	I. Robbins	Hughesville, Pa	Mar. 2, 1869	87, 514
Drawer-lock	E. Skinner	Sandwich, N. H	Apr. 13, 1830	
Drawer-locking device	L. Renker	Hoboken, N. J	Aug. 5, 1873	141, 461
Drawer or till alarm	F. H. Purington	Willimantic, Conn	Dec. 13, 1864	45, 435
Drawer-pull	C. S. and E. A. Barnard	West Meriden, Conn	Feb. 11, 1873	135, 754
Drawer-pull	H. Herlt	New York, N. Y	Feb. 6, 1872	123, 398
Drawer-pull	J. Kintz	West Meriden, Conn	Mar. 21, 1871	112, 816
Drawer-pull	C. H. Pierpent	West Meriden, Conn	Jan. 24, 1871	111, 243
Drawer-pull	W. E. Sparks	New Haven, Conn	Jan. 30, 1872	123, 301
Drawer pull and label, Combined	J. Quinlan	New York, N. Y	June 22, 1869	91, 810
Drawer pull and label, Combined	C. H. Robinson	Greenwich, N. Y	June 29, 1869	92, 102
Drawer, Slide	J. L. Chapman	West Roxbury, Mass	May 3, 1870	102, 489
Drawer, Slide	J. S. Gibbons	Philadelphia, Pa	Apr. 18, 1871	113, 871
Drawer-support	J. Baggs	Easton, Md	Nov. 12, 1872	133, 005
Drawers	J. Bellamy	New York, N. Y	Nov. 19, 1872	133, 138
Drawers	H. Heath	New York, N. Y	Feb. 4, 1868	73, 975
Drawers	O. Jenkins	Boston, Mass	June 22, 1842	2, 690
Drawers	F. Rose	Boston, Mass	Mar. 18, 1873	136, 869
Drawers	J. Ware	North Hoboken, N. J	Oct. 3, 1865	50, 308
Drawers, Cloth	J. Dyson	New Britain, Conn	Oct. 20, 1868	83, 141
Drawers, Cloth	H. Heath	New York, N. Y	Apr. 28, 1868	77, 189
Drawers, Cloth	H. P. Wetmore and J. G. Hitchcock.	Elizabeth, N. J., and New York, N. Y.	Nov. 17, 1868	84, 073
Drawers, Device for cutting out bands and fronts of.	L. Bennet	Amsterdam, N. Y	Mar. 3, 1868	74, 977
Drawers, Device for locking	C. E. Gould	Northampton, Mass	July 16, 1872	129, 404
Drawers, Device for locking a series of	W. F. Daly	Peru, Ind	July 1, 1873	140, 481
Drawers, Device for locking a series of	C. A. Stock	New York, N. Y	Apr. 1, 1873	137, 391
Drawers, Device for supporting	C. F. Langford	Brooklyn, N. Y	Dec. 26, 1871	122, 178
Drawers for wearing-apparel	H. Brewer	New York, N. Y	Feb. 28, 1822	
Drawers, Locking	E. Brown	Lynchburgh, Va	Oct. 28, 1835	
Drawers, Men's	E. L. Closse	Cleveland, Ohio	Aug. 19, 1873	142, 000
Drawers, Men's	K. V. R. Lansingh, jr	Albany, N. Y	Nov. 28, 1871	121, 250
Drawers-stretching frame	J. Dyson	New Britain, Conn	Aug. 18, 1868	81, 263
Drawers-supporter	C. F. Langford	Brooklyn, N. Y	Jan. 23, 1872	123, 027
Drawers, Supporter for men's	E. K. Cleaveland	Boston, Mass	Apr. 15, 1873	137, 761
Drawers, Supporting furniture	H. R. Taylor	Roxbury, Mass	Feb. 21, 1860	27, 247
Drawing and camera table	J. B. Stackpole	Boston, Mass	Nov. 17, 1863	40, 647
Drawing apparatus, Perspective	A. Richter	New York, N. Y	Nov. 16, 1852	9, 409
Drawing-board	H. W. Chamberlin	Pittsfield, Mass	Dec. 25, 1849	6, 967
Drawing-board	C. G. Collins	New York, N. Y	June 4, 1872	127, 573
Drawing-board	J. B. Franklin	New York, N. Y	Aug. 8, 1871	117, 761
Drawing-board	I. P. Hansell	Springfield, Ill	Aug. 31, 1858	21, 336
Drawing-board	A. Hitchcock	New York, N. Y	June 3, 1873	139, 507
Drawing-board	T. H. Kane	New York, N. Y	Jan. 7, 1873	134, 550
Drawing-board	W. Keuffel and H. Esser	Hoboken, N. J	May 13, 1873	138, 896
Drawing-board	H. H. Meyer	Denver, Colo	May 27, 1873	139, 411
Drawing-board	L. F. Schwenkel	New York, N. Y	Mar. 26, 1872	125, 089
Drawing-board, Symmetrical	C. D. Billman	Louisville, Ky	Oct. 24, 1865	50, 583
Drawing-board trestle	J. H. Harden	Philadelphia, Pa	Dec. 2, 1873	145, 174
Drawing-boards, Ruler-attachment for	T. Bergner	Philadelphia, Pa	Apr. 18, 1871	113, 726
Drawing-clamp	J. Bouniol	Philadelphia, Pa	Feb. 4, 1868	73, 947
Drawing, Device for teaching	A. C. Covell	New York, N. Y	May 27, 1873	139, 237
Drawing-frame	S. Brooks and J. Standish	West Gorton, England	July 16, 1872	128, 999
Drawing-frame	G. Draper	Hopedale, Mass	Apr. 18, 1871	113, 752
Drawing-frame	G. Draper	Hopedale, Mass	Dec. 27, 1870	110, 556
Drawing-frame	J. T. Harris	Richmond, R. I	July 2, 1872	128, 618
Drawing-frame	O. P. Hussey	Nashna, N. H	Sept. 14, 1869	94, 752
Drawing-frame	C. P. Leavitt	New York, N. Y	Nov. 22, 1870	109, 430
Drawing-framo	J. McDonald	Concord, N. C	Oct. 1, 1872	131, 766
Drawing-frame	B. Moon	Coventry, R. I	July 18, 1871	117, 098
Drawing-framo	J. Pray and C. Stafford	East Killingly, Conn	Nov. 12, 1846	4, 847
Drawing-frame	G. E. Taft	Northbridge, Mass	Apr. 25, 1871	114, 064
Drawing-framo	T. S. Winn	Lawrence, Mass	Sept. 6, 1870	107, 146
Drawing-frame for drawing fibrous material	S. C. Durgin	Holyoke, Mass	Jan. 25, 1859	22, 768
Drawing-frame for hemp, &c	G. Davis and J. R. Hoover	Elizabethport, N. J	Aug. 9, 1870	106, 130
Drawing-frame for flax, hemp, &c	C. Wall and J. Stewart	New York and Brooklyn, N. Y.	Feb. 1, 1870	99, 503
Drawing-frame regulator	S. J. Whitton	Coleraine, Mass	Feb. 9, 1869	86, 719
Drawing-frame roll	J. M. Stone	North Andover, Mass	May 9, 1865	47, 667
Drawing-frames, Mode of operating rolls in	J. Chase and J. M. Stone	Worcester and North Andover, Mass.	Mar. 29, 1864	42, 076
Drawing-frames, Stop-motion for	J. S. Casey	Voluntown, Conn	Oct. 12, 1869	95, 767
Drawing-frames, Stop-motion for	L. Cutting	Lowell, Mass	May 15, 1834	
Drawing-frames, Stop-motion for	C. Danforth	Paterson, N. J	Jan. 9, 1849	6, 014
Drawing-frames, &c., Stop-motion for	A. I. Earle	Valley Falls, R. I	May 13, 1873	138, 868
Drawing-frames, Stop-motion for	D. W. Hayden	Wauregan, Conn	Feb. 20, 1872	123, 826
Drawing-frames, Stop-motion for	H. G. Williams	Warren, R. I	May 21, 1861	32, 393
Drawing-frames, Stop-motion for	P. J. Wright and J. Thompson	Holyoke, Mass	May 27, 1873	139, 447
Drawing-frames, Stopping-mechanism for	J. C. Taft	Pawtucket, R. I	Oct. 28, 1873	144, 162

Index of patents issued from the United States Patent Office from 1790 *to* 1873, *inclusive*—Continued.

Invention.	Inventor.	Residence.	Date.	No.
Drawing-frames, &c., Top-roll for	H. T. Potter	Norwich, Conn	Sept. 2, 1873	142, 509
Drawing-instrument	E. W. Ellsworth	East Windsor, Conn	June 7, 1845	4, 070
Drawing-instrument	J. P. Jamison	New York, N. Y	June 18, 1861	32, 566
Drawing-instrument	W. W. Wythes	Philadelphia, Pa	July 27, 1858	21, 041
Drawing-knife	J. H. Atwater	Oshtemo, Mich	June 18, 1870	98, 003
Drawing-knife	C. C. Barton	Rochester, N. Y	June 21, 1870	104, 539
Drawing-knife	W. Brady	Mount Joy, Pa	Mar. 5, 1872	124, 246
Drawing-knife	M. Brooks	Chicago, Ill	Dec. 16, 1873	145, 485
Drawing-knife	T. M. Clarke	Winsted, Conn	Nov. 21, 1871	121, 084
Drawing-knife	E. Parker	Chambersburgh, Pa	Sept. 9, 1873	142, 720
Drawing-knife	E. Richards	Hingham, Mass	June 28, 1836	....
Drawing-knife	J. C. Smead	Huntington, Ohio	Nov. 19, 1872	133, 126
Drawing-knife	H. C. Smith	Westville, Conn	July 9, 1872	128, 821
Drawing-knife	A. M. Steele	Danbury, Conn	Jan. 30, 1872	123, 206
Drawing-knife	R. N. Watrous	Charlestown, Ohio	Dec. 15, 1857	18, 877
Drawing-machine roller	F. and G. G. Crague	Lewiston, Me	Apr. 28, 1868	77, 173
Drawing-machinery, Applying pressure to top-rolls of.	N. E. Hale	Nashua, N. H	Nov. 8, 1859	26, 031
Drawing metals, Apparatus for	L. Christoph, W. Hanksworth, and G. P. Harding.	Paris, France, Gartness, North Britain, and Chiswick, England.	July 21, 1868	80, 057
Drawing perspective mechanically	S. De Witt	Albany, N. Y	Apr. 30, 1813	....
Drawing rods and shafting, Machine for cold	G. H. Billings	Cincinnati, Ohio	Aug. 13, 1872	130, 465
Drawing-roller	D. Hussey	Nashua, N. H	May 15, 1866	54, 732
Drawing-roller	S. P. Spencer	Lancaster, Pa	June 29, 1858	20, 766
Drawing-roller cleaner	D. Crowley	Philadelphia, Pa	Feb. 11, 1868	74, 202
Drawing-roller regulator	W. Hayden	Windham, Conn	Mar. 12, 1850	7, 165
Drawing-rollers, Machine for rolling cots on	W. C. Joslin	Putnam, Conn	Mar. 31, 1868	76, 199
Drawing-rollers, Mode of lubricating	F. Hardenburg	Providence, R. I	June 25, 1872	128, 224
Drawing-rollers, Wiper for	J. M. Dunham	Holyoke, Mass	Nov. 5, 1872	132, 714
Drawing scrolls, Instrument for	E. E. Stebbins	Meadville, Pa	Apr. 22, 1873	138, 053
Drawing-stand	W. Bell	Buffalo, N. Y	Oct. 31, 1871	120, 364
Drawing-table	J. L. Ross and F. C. Hanson	Boston and Charlestown, Mass.	Dec. 26, 1871	122, 134
Drawing-table and desk, Combined	J. A. Wilkens	Indianapolis, Ind	Dec. 9, 1873	145, 378
Drawings, Instrument for hatch-lining	E. K. Haynes	Hanover, N. H	Dec. 10, 1867	72, 036
Drawings, Machine for making perspective	R. Lyons	New Rumley, Ohio	June 14, 1834	....
Dray	C. S. Martin	Milwaukee, Wis	Apr. 30, 1867	64, 346
Dray	E. Warren and T. Brangwin	Ceresco, Mich	Apr. 14, 1868	76, 856
Dray	F. Van Doren	Adrian, Mich	July 2, 1867	66, 426
Dray-skid	E. H. Boswell	Philadelphia, Pa	Jan. 5, 1864	41, 054
Dredge	E. B. Bishop	San Francisco, Cal	Apr. 22, 1873	137, 998
Dredge, Bail	N. A. Williams	Warwick, R. I	Jan. 2, 1872	122, 423
Dredge-box	H. M. Clark	Toledo, Ohio	Oct. 1, 1872	131, 810
Dredge box	P. F. Cooley	Pittsfield, Mass	Oct. 1, 1872	131, 744
Dredge-box	J. Dalzell	Birmingham, Pa	Nov. 26, 1872	133, 307
Dredge-box	W. S. Potwin	Chicago, Ill	Feb. 20, 1872	123, 792
Dredge-box	G. W. Putnam	Peterborough, N. Y	June 4, 1867	65, 430
Dredge-box	T. Smith	Cleveland, Ohio	Jan. 21, 1873	135, 048
Dredge-box	C. F. Spencer	Cleveland, Ohio	Oct. 24, 1871	120, 339
Dredge-box	A. F. Tripp	Buffalo, N. Y	Aug. 16, 1870	106, 430
Dredge-box	T. Williams	Boston, Mass	July 9, 1867	66, 661
Dredge-box, cake-cutter, and grater	S. Cooke	Bayonne City, N. J	Apr. 26, 1870	102, 225
Dredge-box with grater and cake-cutter attached	G. D. Bayley	Lebanon, N. H	Feb. 17, 1863	37, 716
Dredge, Salt and pepper	D. C. Ripley	Pittsburgh, Pa	Sept. 2, 1873	142, 351
Dredger	A. C. Booth	Portland, Me	Apr. 29, 1873	138, 227
Dredger	T. J. Clepper	Columbia, Pa	Nov. 26, 1872	133, 303
Dredger	J. F. Morse	Oshkosh, Wis	Sept. 9, 1873	142, 577
Dredger	R. G. Packard	Brooklyn, N. Y	Jan. 14, 1873	134, 817
Dredger	T. Symonds	Portland, Me	Feb. 25, 1873	136, 187
Dredger	T. Symonds	Portland, Me	Apr. 29, 1873	138, 295
Dredging and excavating machine	W. Atkinson	Brooklyn, N. Y	July 7, 1863	39, 194
Dredging and excavating machine	W. H. Pearson	Philadelphia, Pa	Mar. 22, 1870	101, 157
Dredging-apparatus	E. Bazin	Paris, France	Sept. 30, 1873	143, 269
Dredging-apparatus	B. and D. Hughes	Rochester, N. Y	Sept. 21, 1869	95, 114
Dredging-apparatus	C. A. Scanlan	Charleston, S. C	Apr. 19, 1870	102, 049
Dredging-boat for excavating rivers	E. L. Brady	New Orleans, La	Dec. 17, 1867	72, 360
Dredging boat, Harbor	W. H. Nobles	Saint Paul, Minn	June 5, 1866	55, 346
Dredging-boat, Steam	W. H. Nobles	Saint Paul, Minn	June 5, 1866	55, 347
Dredging-can	D. W. Pepper	Philadelphia, Pa	Apr. 26, 1870	102, 428
Dredging-machine	E. B. Bishop	Shreveport, La	Apr. 13, 1858	19, 908
Dredging-machine	A. Blood, sr	Norfolk, Va	Aug. 11, 1857	17, 959
Dredging-machine	A. Boschke	Boston, Mass	Sept. 22, 1868	82, 376
Dredging-machine	A. Boschke	San Francisco, Cal	Aug. 12, 1873	141, 752
Dredging-machine	T. Byrne	New York, N. Y	Sept. 11, 1866	57, 859
Dredging-machine	D. Carmichael and J. C. Osgood	Brooklyn and Chittenango, N. Y.	May 30, 1846	4, 547
Dredging-machine	O. Chanute and G. L. Morison	Kansas City, Mo	Jan. 18, 1870	98, 848
Dredging-machine	W. A. Collins	Bloomfield, N. J	Dec. 23, 1873	145, 723
Dredging-machine	D. C. Cregier	Chicago, Ill	June 30, 1868	79, 448
Dredging-machine	J. Du Bois	Williamsport, Pa	Aug. 18, 1868	81, 076
Dredging-machine	W. Easby	Washington, D. C	Aug. 25, 1840	1, 727
Dredging-machine	J. Ebbert	Chicago, Ill	June 27, 1871	116, 282
Dredging-machine	C. H. Fondé	Mobile, Ala	Apr. 17, 1855	12, 720
Dredging-machine	C. H. Fondé and T. B. Lyons	Mobile, Ala	Mar. 21, 1854	10, 668
Dredging-machine	H. Gonellaz	Houma, La	Aug. 6, 1872	130, 213
Dredging-machine	H. Gonellaz	Vermillionville, La	July 15, 1873	140, 821
Dredging-machine	L. J. Gonyo	North Buffalo, N. Y	June 4, 1872	127, 595
Dredging-machine	A. J. Gove	San Francisco, Cal	Nov. 10, 1868	83, 845
Dredging-machine	A. J. Gove	San Francisco, Cal	Sept. 24, 1872	131, 608
Dredging-machine	J. Hamilton	New York, N. Y	Mar. 30, 1852	8, 840
Dredging-machine	D. S. Howard	Lyonsdale, N. Y	Jan. 9, 1855	12, 201
Dredging-machine	D. S. Howard	Lyons Falls, N. Y	Jan. 21, 1870	104, 594
Dredging-machine	J. Johnson	Saco, Me	Aug. 7, 1866	56, 948
Dredging-machine	S. H. Long	Alton, Ill	Mar. 26, 1861	31, 811
Dredging-machine	W. H. Lotz	Chicago, Ill	Jan. 9, 1872	122, 529
Dredging-machine	J. McClean	New Orleans, La	Apr. 12, 1870	101, 898
Dredging-machine	J. R. McClintock and J. K. Scott	New Orleans, La	Jan. 15, 1867	61, 227

Index of patents issued from the United States Patent Office from 1790 *to* 1873, *inclusive*—Continued.

Invention.	Inventor.	Residence.	Date.	No.
Dredging-machine	J. H. McLean	Saint Louis, Mo	July 9, 1867	66, 608
Dredging-machine	A. Menge	Point à la Hache, La	July 12, 1859	24, 750
Dredging-machine	A. Minard	New York, N. Y	Sept. 28, 1858	21, 613
Dredging-machine	G. Mitchell	Philadelphia, Pa	July 5, 1870	104, 980
Dredging-machine	J. H. Newcomb	Port Norris, N. J	May 20, 1862	35, 324
Dredging-machine	W. H. Nobles	Saint Paul, Minn	Aug. 7, 1866	56, 984
Dredging-machine	R. R. Osgood	Troy, N. Y	June 28, 1870	104, 757
Dredging-machine	R. G. Packard	Brooklyn, N. Y	Oct. 1, 1872	131, 825
Dredging-machine	E. Platt	Charleston, S. C	July 18, 1871	117, 109
Dredging-machine	W. D. Robertson	San Francisco, Cal	May 24, 1870	103, 373
Dredging-machine	J. Stewart	New London, Conn	Dec. 28, 1858	22, 458
Dredging-machine	W. T. Thelin	Baltimore, Md	Apr. 2, 1872	125, 351
Dredging-machine	I. D. Vandecar	Chicago, Ill	Apr. 23, 1867	64, 169
Dredging-machine	I. D. Vandecar	Chicago, Ill	Oct. 10, 1871	119, 901
Dredging-machine	J. L. Vergniais	Paris, France	July 30, 1867	67, 384
Dredging-machine	N. A. Williams	Warwick, R. I	May 28, 1872	127, 397
Dredging machine bucket	T. and A. Walsh	New York, N. Y	Jan. 21, 1868	73, 678
Dredging-machine-dipper handles, Mode of fastening racks of.	R. R. Osgood	Troy, N. Y	Sept. 30, 1873	143, 247
Dredging machine, Harbor and river	A. J. Gove	San Francisco, Cal	Feb. 21, 1865	46, 463
Dredging-machine, Hydraulic	R. S. Elliott	Saint Louis, Mo	Sept. 28, 1869	95, 213
Dredging-machine, Pneumatic	A. F. Du Faur and C. H. Campbell.	Newark, N. J., and New York, N. Y.	Nov. 12, 1872	133, 022
Dredging-machine, Rotary	J. Molyneux	Bordentown, N. J	Oct. 4, 1859	25, 704
Dredging machine, Sand	J. T. Clarkson	Chicago, Ill	Mar. 26, 1872	125, 023
Dredging-machines, Method of directing the scoops in.	J. Callaghan	New Bedford, Mass	Jan. 16, 1849	6, 029
Dredging or excavating machine	O. Allen	Norwich, Conn	May 1, 1845	4, 020
Dredging-scoop	A. C. Ellithorpe	Chicago, Ill	June 20, 1871	116, 171
Dredging, Spice and pepper box	G. W. Putnam	Peterborough, N. Y	Nov. 5, 1867	70, 618
Dress and satchel holder combined	G. McFadden	Thomaston, Conn	July 21, 1868	80, 196
Dress and skirt protector	A. H. Graton	Lawrence, Kans	Nov. 16, 1869	96, 797
Dress-body lining, Lady's	S. Moschcowitz	New York, N. Y	Jan. 24, 1871	111, 236
Dress, Boy's	C. Herwick	New York, N. Y	May 16, 1826	....
Dress-cutting, System of	H. M. Carpenter	Grand Rapids, Mich	Sept. 4, 1866	57, 837
Dress-cutting, System of	C. Dittenhafer	Canton, Ohio	July 17, 1866	56, 383
Dress, Diving	J. R. Campbell	Boston, Mass	Nov. 30, 1835	....
Dress-elevator	M. Dewey	New Albany, Ind	July 16, 1872	129, 399
Dress-elevator	H. Essex and J. Johnson	West Haverstraw and Brooklyn, N. Y.	June 26, 1866	55, 842
Dress-elevator	M. Fox	New York, N. Y	Feb. 11, 1873	135, 703
Dress-elevator	G. Kammerl and D. L. Bollermann.	New York, N. Y	Aug. 28, 1866	57, 519
Dress-elevator	G. W. Keller	Philadelphia, Pa	Nov. 5, 1867	70, 575
Dress-elevator	S. A. Moody	New York, N. Y	Sept. 11, 1866	57, 950
Dress-elevator	I. Nathan	New Haven, Conn	Mar. 20, 1866	53, 324
Dress-elevator	T. V. Phelps	Worcester, Mass	July 10, 1866	56, 341
Dress-elevator	W. E. Stein	New York, N. Y	Mar. 20, 1860	27, 578
Dress-elevator	C. Tage	Philadelphia, Pa	Nov. 11, 1873	144, 576
Dress-facing	W. H. Gallup	Troy, N. Y	Apr. 29, 1873	138, 326
Dress-facing	J. A. Mackee	Boston, Mass	Jan. 10, 1865	45, 849
Dress-frame, Lady's	J. R. Palmenberg	New York, N. Y	Jan. 10, 1860	26, 781
Dress-goods holder	A. S. Grant	Rochester, N. Y	Mar. 26, 1872	124, 948
Dress-hook	M. A. Keilig	Boston, Mass	Dec. 31, 1867	72, 862
Dress-hook, Self-fastening	J. W. Strange	Bangor, Me	May 8, 1860	28, 213
Dress, Jubilee stock	W. J. Cantolo and R. M. Kerrison.	New York, N. Y	Aug. 30, 1826	....
Dress, Lady's	H. and E. S. Judson	Brooklyn, N. Y	June 10, 1873	139, 677
Dress, Lady's	A. Kelley	New York, N. Y	Nov. 14, 1871	120, 981
Dress-looping clasp, Lady's	H. H. Cole	New York, N. Y	Feb. 27, 1866	52, 822
Dress measuring and fitting apparatus	P. A. La Ment	New York, N. Y	Aug. 14, 1866	57, 254
Dress, Mode of attaching trimming to articles of	J. Sims	Liverpool Road, England	Oct. 5, 1869	95, 525
Dress-pattern	E. P. Smith	Chicago, Ill	Apr. 19, 1873	137, 967
Dress-protector	A. Herrmann	New York, N. Y	July 1, 1873	140, 415
Dress protector	E. Higgins	Boston, Mass	Aug. 5, 1862	36, 125
Dress-protector	T. Himes	New Albany, Ind	June 30, 1868	79, 350
Dress-protector	F. Wittram	San Francisco, Cal	Mar. 22, 1870	101, 203
Dress-protector, Lady's	T. D. Day	New York, N. Y	Feb. 7, 1865	46, 218
Dress-protector, &c., Fabric for	J. McMullen	Brooklyn, N. Y	Apr. 1, 1873	137, 311
Dress-shield	B. M. Hotchkiss	Naugatuck, Conn	Nov. 1, 1870	108, 908
Dress-shield	I. M. Post	Philadelphia, Pa	July 1, 1873	140, 538
Dresses, Apparatus for obtaining the measure for ladies'.	C. E. McDonald	Indianapolis, Ind	Nov. 27, 1866	60, 028
Dresses, Cutting ladies'	H. Segar	Macon, Ga	Jan. 28, 1846	4, 367
Dresses, Fastening for ornaments on	D. B. Howell	New York, N. Y	May 5, 1863	38, 390
Dresses, Fitting ladies'	S. S. Richardson	Baldwin, Me	Apr. 4, 1844	3, 522
Dresses, Frame for finishing ladies'	J. R. Williams	Baltimore, Md	Mar. 3, 1824	....
Dresses, Instrument for drafting ladies'	H. A. Fowler	Afton, N. Y	May 13, 1862	35, 226
Dresses, Method of finding waist and chest measurement of ladies'.	M. M. Turner	North Fairfield, Ohio	Feb. 14, 1865	46, 409
Dresses, &c., Taking measure and drafting for the cutting out of ladies'.	A. A. Tenther	Philadelphia, Pa	Jan. 23, 1841	1, 944
Dressing-case	H. W. Eastman	Baltimore, Md	June 29, 1869	91, 830
Dressing-case and bath-tub	C. A. Staples	Boston, Mass	Sept. 10, 1867	68, 8[illegible]2
Dressing-case. Portable	J. Russell	Boston, Mass	Apr. 7, 1863	38, 130
Dressing-combs of wood, Manufacturing	N. Bushnell	Middletown, Conn	Apr. 14, 1829	....
Dressing conical tapering surfaces, Machine for	P. Peckham	Petersham, Mass	July 3, 1855	13, 180
Dressing-frames, Composition roll for	R. Collier	Laurel, Md	Aug. 15, 1871	117, 985
Dressing irregular forms, Machine for	A. Cary	Worcester, Mass	Nov. 5, 1850	7, 750
Dressing-roller	B. R. Cotton	Lewiston, Me	Dec. 10, 1867	71, 994
Dressing sticks to polygonal forms, Machine for	J. W. Killam	East Wilton, N. H	Jan. 22, 1856	14, 136
Drier: *See* Dryer.				
Drift	J. Eglin	Manchester, England	Feb. 19, 1867	62, 123
Drill: *See* Boring-drill. Bow-drill. Brace-drill. Chuck-drill. Dental drill. Dentist's drill.				

Index of patents issued from the United States Patent Office from 1790 *to* 1873, *inclusive*—Continued.

Invention.	Inventor.	Residence.	Date.	No.
Drill—Continued. *See* Expanding drill. Grain-drill. Guano and seed drill. Hand-drill. Jeweler's drill. Machine-drill. Metal-drill. Mining-drill. Oil-well drill. Planter-drill. Pneumatic drill. Power and hand drill. Ratchet-drill. Reservoir-drill. Rock-drill. Seed-drill. Self-feeding drill. Steam-drill. Stone-drill. Stone-channeling drill. Suction-drill. Tapering drill. Twist-drill. Upright drill. Well-drill. Well-boring drill. Wheat-drill.				
Drill	A. E. Allen	Perch River, N. Y	Sept. 3, 1872	131, 074
Drill	C. H. Amidon	Miller's Falls, Mass	Dec. 24, 1872	134, 237
Drill	L. Andrews	Biddeford, Me	Jan. 15, 1867	61, 134
Drill	H. and D. L. Bates	Dayton, Ohio	July 13, 1869	92, 419
Drill	T. V. Boyden	Bridgeport, Conn	Feb. 28, 1871	112, 115
Drill	G. F. Case	New York, N. Y	Feb. 12, 1867	62, 003
Drill	R. Dudgeon	New York, N. Y	Aug. 2, 1864	43, 673
Drill	F. Glasser	Mystic Bridge, Conn	Sept. 1, 1868	81, 769
Drill	H. Hufendeck	Saint Louis, Mo	Jan. 1, 1867	60, 895
Drill	C. W. Le Count	Norwalk, Conn	Dec. 22, 1868	85, 107
Drill	H. Loftie and E. Hinman	Syracuse, N. Y	Nov. 21, 1865	51, 065
Drill	L. G. Marshall	Mokena, Ill	July 18, 1865	48, 819
Drill	L. G. Marshall	Mokena, Ill	July 18, 1865	48, 872
Drill	J. M. May	Janesville, Wis	Aug. 1, 1865	49, 129
Drill	C. L. Noé	Bergen Point, N. J	Mar. 14, 1865	46, 815
Drill	M. Nottingham and W. Duncan.	Vinton, Iowa	Nov. 13, 1866	59, 631
Drill	A. Shiland	West Troy, N. Y	Mar. 21, 1865	46, 949
Drill	W. Stivers	New York, N. Y	Feb. 9, 1864	41, 546
Drill	G. C. Taft	Worcester, Mass	Feb. 28, 1860	27, 320
Drill	G. C. Taft	Worcester, Mass	June 28, 1864	43, 372
Drill	A. Thompson	Burlington, Vt	Apr. 19, 1870	102, 066
Drill	F. Vestor	Newark, N. J	Mar. 24, 1868	75, 816
Drill	D. Warner	Port Clinton, Ohio	Aug. 13, 1867	67, 825
Drill	R. G. Wells	Plumer, Pa	July 4, 1865	48, 609
Drill	E. S. Young and A. Whipple	Whitingsville, Mass	Sept. 10, 1867	68, 827
Drill and bit stock	C. H. Amidon	Miller's Falls, Mass	July 1, 1873	140, 451
Drill and blacksmith's tongs, Combined	F. Nevergold and G. Stackhouse.	Pittsburgh, Pa	June 19, 1866	55, 696
Drill and counter sink	P. A. Whitney	Woodstock, Vt	Feb. 25, 1868	74, 870
Drill and crane attachment	I. S. Lauback	New York, N. Y	Apr. 17, 1866	53, 992
Drill and cultivator teeth, Securing	J. H. Thomas and P. P. Mast	Springfield, Ohio	July 12, 1870	105, 387
Drill and fertilizer, Combined	G. E. Cooper	Baltimore, Md	June 5, 1866	55, 243
Drill and holder	I. McLaughlin	East Arlington, Vt	Oct. 18, 1870	108, 374
Drill and sand-pump	E. R. Morrison	New York, N. Y	Nov. 15, 1864	45, 068
Drill and saw-gummer, Combined	W. C. Marr	Peru, Wis	July 27, 1869	92, 983
Drill and seeder, Combined	J. E. Buxton	Owatonna, Minn	July 6, 1869	92, 262
Drill and seeder, Combined	J. E. Buxton	Owatonna, Minn	Mar. 14, 1871	112, 540
Drill and seeding-machine, Combined	J. E. Buxton	Owatonna, Minn	Aug. 16, 1870	106, 320
Drill-bit	W. W. Grier and R. H. Boyd	Hulton, Pa	May 23, 1865	47, 812
Drill-bit	S. A. Morse	East Bridgewater, Mass	Apr. 7, 1863	38, 119
Drill-bit and reamer	P. M. Ward	Cow Run, Ohio	Nov. 21, 1871	121, 223
Drill-coupling	E. E. and C. T. Packer	Philadelphia, Pa	June 26, 1866	55, 895
Drill, Cylinder	C. S. Pattison	North Adams, Mass	Apr. 25, 1871	114, 193
Drill-extractor	D. Kunkel	Oregon, Mo	Aug. 26, 1873	142, 244
Drill-frame	G. C. Taft	Worcester, Mass	Nov. 27, 1860	30, 774
Drill-gage	A. C. Trafton	Worcester, Mass	June 3, 1873	139, 487
Drill-gage	W. C. Wells	Newark, N. J	Nov. 28, 1865	51, 248
Drill-gage	W. C. Wells	Newark, N. J	Mar. 31, 1868	76, 123
Drill gage, Machine	E. G. Parkhurst	Hartford, Conn	Oct. 1, 1872	131, 775
Drill-guide	J. F. Case	Windsor, Vt	Mar. 22, 1870	101, 095
Drill-head	W. W. St. John	Syracuse, N. Y	Jan. 9, 1866	51, 980
Drill-holder	T. K. Bacon	Norwich, Conn	May 26, 1868	78, 251
Drill-holder	C. Burleigh	Fitchburgh, Mass	July 28, 1868	80, 386
Drill-holder	W. Hall, jr	North Adams, Mass	July 28, 1868	80, 406
Drill holes, Device for charging	F. X. Lavalle	Auburn, Cal	Nov. 12, 1872	133, 040
Drill-jar	J. C. Eastman	Titusville, Pa	July 16, 1867	66, 816
Drill-jar	E. Guillod	Titusville, Pa	Nov. 24, 1868	84, 353
Drill-jar	R. McMullen	Titusville, Pa	Apr. 1, 1873	137, 378
Drill-jar	C. A. Read	Lockport, N. Y	Nov. 28, 1865	51, 217
Drill-jars, Construction of	E. Guillod	Titusville, Pa	June 16, 1868	78, 958
Drill, Machine	J. Conner and T. Newby	Richmond, Ind	Aug. 7, 1855	13, 383
Drill or pump-rod coupling	J. R. Cross	Chicago, Ill	Aug. 15, 1865	49, 386
Drill or well tube	J. Hutchins	Elmira, N. Y	Nov. 13, 1866	59, 608
Drill-press	J. M. Cullen and A. J. Baird	Pittsburgh, Pa	Oct. 27, 1868	83, 366
Drill-rest	C. Teachout	Waterford, N. Y	June 19, 1860	28, 791
Drill-rod attachment	R. S. Torrey	Bangor, Me	Nov. 7, 1865	50, 857
Drill-rod coupling	R. A. Clark	Petrolia City, Pa	Aug. 12, 1873	141, 694
Drill-rod coupling	W. H. Downing	Shamburgh, Pa	Nov. 5, 1872	132, 755
Drill, roller, and cultivator, Combined	T. S. Mills	Kendallsville, Ind	Jan. 14, 1868	73, 365
Drill-shaft, Feeding	G. C. Taft	Worcester, Mass	Mar. 24, 1857	16, 900
Drill-sharpener	E. W. Walton	Drytown, Cal	Mar. 3, 1868	75, 084
Drill-spring for quarrying stone, &c	E. G. Lamson	Shelburne Falls, Mass	Mar. 26, 1867	63, 262
Drill-stock	M. S. Brooks	Chester, Conn	May 17, 1859	24, 005
Drill-stock	C. M. Daboll	New London, Conn	Aug. 11, 1868	80, 812
Drill-stock	M. Hainque	San Francisco, Cal	June 23, 1868	79, 115
Drill-stock	D. F. Hartford	Boston, Mass	Apr. 17, 1866	54, 069
Drill-stock	W. H. Rand	Brooklyn, N. Y	Apr. 4, 1871	113, 344
Drill-stock, Geared	G. Page	Keene, N. H	May 8, 1838	730
Drill-teeth	S. Black	West Alexandria, Ohio	Mar. 4, 1873	136, 408
Drill-teeth setting	P. I. and P. Schmitt	Waterloo, Ill	Feb. 16, 1869	87, 074
Drill, Well	W. Tingley	New York, N. Y	Mar. 26, 1867	63, 338
Drills, Feed-motion for	G. F. Case	New York, N. Y	Nov. 27, 1866	59, 963

Index of patents issued from the United States Patent Office from 1790 *to* 1873, *inclusive*—Continued.

Invention.	Inventor.	Residence.	Date.	No.
Drills, Gearing for operating	A. Blatchly	San Francisco, Cal	May 16, 1871	114, 754
Drills, Machine for operating	J. W. Stockwell	Portland, Me	Apr. 1, 1873	137, 504
Drills, Mode of mounting	H. Haupt	Cambridge, Mass	May 2, 1865	47, 541
Drilling and babbiting jig	J. Underwood	Muscatine, Iowa	Oct. 29, 1867	70, 294
Drilling and bolt-tapping machine	C. W. Coe	Fentonville, Mich	Jan. 19, 1869	86, 001
Drilling and boring machine	H. Haupt	Cambridge, Mass	May 23, 1865	47, 819
Drilling and boring machine	S. W. Shryock	Hopkinsville, Ky	Nov. 6, 1855	13, 766
Drilling and driving machine	I. M. Rose	New York, N. Y	Mar. 13, 1866	53, 189
Drilling and hoisting machine	W. C. McGill and A. J. Gibson	Cincinnati, Ohio	Mar. 6, 1866	53, 022
Drilling and milling machine	W. D. Sloan	New York, N. Y	Sept. 29, 1857	18, 305
Drilling and pumping apparatus	M. T. McCormick	Meadville, Pa	July 2, 1867	66, 372
Drilling and pumping machinery, Standard jack-post for.	W. W. Eastman and W. H. H. Morris.	Meadville, Pa	Sept. 9, 1873	142, 619
Drilling-and screw-cutting machine	J. P. Heacock	Marlborough, Ohio	Nov. 27, 1855	13, 845
Drilling-and screw-cutting machinery	C. W. Coe	Corunna, Mich	Jan. 20, 1863	37, 433
Drilling-apparatus	J. Fanning	New York, N. Y	July 2, 1867	66, 229
Drilling-apparatus	A. J. Fullam	Springfield, Vt	July 30, 1867	67, 284
Drilling-apparatus	S. Lauchli	Saint Louis, Mo	June 1, 1869	90, 670
Drilling-apparatus	J. Y. Smith	Pittsburgh, Pa	Mar. 26, 1867	63, 319
Drilling-apparatus, Submarine	S. Lewis	Williamsburgh, N. Y	June 7, 1870	103, 899
Drilling, Coupling-tool for	J. R. Moore	Brooklyn, N. Y	Mar. 28, 1865	47, 031
Drilling-instrument	N. Barnum and G. C. Schreiber	Saint Louis, Mo	June 25, 1867	65, 991
Drilling-machine	M. M. Ammidown	Boston, Mass	Dec. 4, 1866	60, 114
Drilling-machine	T. P. Bashford	Decatur, Mich	Feb. 27, 1866	52, 815
Drilling-machine	G. W. Bishop	Stamford, Conn	Oct. 8, 1867	69, 533
Drilling-machine	P. Blaisdell	Worcester, Mass	Jan. 28, 1873	135, 313
Drilling-machine	J. Button	Springfield, Mass	Nov. 14, 1865	50, 985
Drilling-machine	C. W. Coe	Ashtabula, Ohio	Dec. 7, 1852	9, 441
Drilling-machine	J. Cumming	Boston, Mass	Oct. 25, 1859	25, 886
Drilling-machine	W. H. Elliot	New York, N. Y	June 18, 1867	65, 802
Drilling-machine	W. and J. Gardam	Williamsburgh, N. Y	Febr 20, 1872	123, 886
Drilling-machine	A. Gordon	New York, N. Y	Apr. 19, 1864	42, 365
Drilling-machine	W. D. Grimshaw	Newark, N. J	Sept. 3, 1867	68, 362
Drilling-machine	J. Hale	Scranton, Pa	Oct. 26, 1869	96, 227
Drilling-machine	E. Hall	Byron, N. Y	Aug. 29, 1839	1, 305
Drilling-machine	A. Hatch	New Haven, Conn	Nov. 21, 1865	51, 113
Drilling-machine	J. G. Hirzel	Wilmington, Del	Mar. 13, 1866	53, 145
Drilling-machine	T. M. Howard	Charlestown, Pa	Apr. 17, 1866	53, 981
Drilling-machine	A. P. Jackson and L. Thompson.	Memphis, Ind	Nov. 28, 1865	51, 189
Drilling-machine	G. Koch	Cass, Pa	Sept. 12, 1871	118, 950
Drilling-machine	I. S. Lauback	New York, N. Y	Feb. 21, 1865	46, 478
Drilling-machine	J. Lemman	Cincinnati, Ohio	Aug. 8, 1871	117, 896
Drilling-machine	W. Lyon	New York, N. Y	Jan. 31, 1865	46, 123
Drilling-machine	H. Martin	Duncan, Pa	May 6, 1873	138, 570
Drilling-machine	A. Morgan	Wooster, Ohio	May 30, 1844	3, 609
Drilling-machine	A. Morgan	Massillon, Ohio	May 15, 1847	5, 116
Drilling-machine	N. A. Morlan	Salem, Ohio	Dec. 31, 1872	134, 392
Drilling-machine	W. Morton	Woodhull, N. Y	Mar. 22, 1864	42, 011
Drilling-machine	J. Moulton	Boston, Mass	Mar. 14, 1865	46, 813
Drilling-machine	R. Nutty	New York, N. Y	Sept. 18, 1866	58, 175
Drilling-machine	W. F. Parker	Andover, Mass	Apr. 30, 1867	64, 357
Drilling-machine	C. P. Philippi	Crown Point, Ind	June 23, 1863	38, 981
Drilling-machine	W. Sellers	Philadelphia, Pa	July 2, 1872	128, 665
Drilling-machine	F. Shaller	Hudson, N. Y	June 26, 1866	55, 918
Drilling-machine	J. Smith	New Haven, Conn	May 24, 1870	103, 515
Drilling-machine	R. H. Springsteed	Wooster, Ohio	Feb. 20, 1843	2, 961
Drilling-machine	G. C. Taft	Worcester, Mass	Apr. 18, 1871	113, 815
Drilling-machine	R. A. Thomas	Damascus, Cal	Aug. 7, 1866	57, 011
Drilling-machine	W. H. Thorne	Philadelphia, Pa	June 3, 1873	139, 629
Drilling-machine	W. H. Thorne and I. M. De Haven.	Philadelphia, Pa	Sept. 16, 1873	142, 966
Drilling-machine	A. and C. Van Haagen	Philadelphia, Pa	Apr. 23, 1872	126, 111
Drilling-machine	D. Warner, W. F. Peiffer, and A. F. Lepper.	Port Clinton, Ohio	Aug. 13, 1867	67, 826
Drilling-machine	W. C. Whipple	New Haven, Conn	July 13, 1869	92, 682
Drilling-machine	E. J. Worcester	Worcester, Mass	Feb. 15, 1870	99, 803
Drilling-machine	E. J. Worcester	Worcester, Mass	Feb. 4, 1873	135, 613
Drilling-machine	E. J. Worcester and A. F. Prentice.	Worcester, Mass	May 21, 1872	127, 132
Drilling-machine carriage	C. Burleigh	Fitchburgh, Mass	July 28, 1868	80, [illegible]87
Drilling-machine-cutter head	E. Weicke	Philadelphia, Pa	Aug. 26, 1873	142, 133
Drilling machine, Hand	R. Daniels	Woodstock, Vt	Sept. 21, 1852	9, 271
Drilling machine, Hand	T. J. Sloan	New York, N. Y	June 25, 1872	128, 430
Drilling machine, Metal	W. H. Judson	Titusville, Pa	July 23, 1872	129, 831
Drilling machine, Metal	J. C. Keller	Philadelphia, Pa	July 15, 1873	140, 9[illegible]5
Drilling-machine, Portable	W. H. Thorne	Philadelphia, Pa	Apr. 25, 1871	114, 229
Drilling machine, Radial	G. A. Gray, jr	Cincinnati, Ohio	Dec. 14, 1869	97, 908
Drilling-machine, Steam	J. W. Fowle	Boston, Mass	Mar. 11, 1851	7, 972
Drilling-machine, Subaqueous	S. Lewis	Brooklyn, N. Y	Jan. 5, 1869	85, 597
Drilling-machine table	T. Reaney	Chester, Pa	Jan. 17, 1871	111, 084
Drilling-machine, Adjustable feed-gear for	A. R. Morrill and H. Baldwin	Nashville, N. H	Aug. 27, 1850	7, 604
Drilling metal, Machine for	G. C. Taft	Worcester, Mass	Feb. 1, 1870	99, 495
Drilling or tapping instruments, Stock for	G. Bunch	Bonnot's Mill, Mo	May 20, 1873	139, 042
Drilling, riveting, and watch-jeweling apparatus	C. Hopkins	Philadelphia, Pa	Jan. 4, 1870	98, 497
Drilling-tool, Portable	C. Van Haagen	Philadelphia, Pa	Dec. 20, 1870	110, 405
Drinking-cup	B. Adler	New York, N. Y	Dec. 7, 1869	97, 583
Drinking-cup	L. Grosholz	Philadelphia, Pa	Nov. 2, 1858	21, 955
Drinking-cup	A. Millar	Roxbury, Mass	Jan. 8, 1867	61, 084
Drinking-cup	J. S. Ostrander	Albany, N. Y	July 1, 1862	35, 777
Drinking-cup, Invalid	M. P. Codman	Boston, Mass	Nov. 14, 1865	50, 906
Drinking-cup, Pocket	J. S. Towndrow	Moline, Ill	Oct. 20, 1868	83, 341
Drinking-cup, Telescopic	P. H. Niles	Boston, Mass	June 5, 1860	28, 597
Drinking-cups, Mustache-shield for	J. J. Greenough	Syracuse, N. Y	Nov. 18, 1873	144, 614
Drinking-fountain, Poultry	G. H. Lomax	Somerville, Mass	Oct. 1, 1867	69, 351
Drinking-glass holder	J. V. Snider	Philadelphia, Pa	Mar. 21, 1871	112, 974
Drinking-glasses, Manufacture of	J. L. and T. B. Atterbury	Pittsburgh, Pa	Oct. 17, 1865	50, 437
Drinking-tube, Invalid	E. Chapin	Saint Louis, Mo	May 24, 1870	103, 299

Index of patents issued from the United States Patent Office from 1790 *to* 1873, *inclusive*—Continued.

Invention.	Inventor.	Residence.	Date.	No.
Drinking-tube, Invalid	E. Chapin	Saint Louis, Mo	May 24, 1870	103, 300
Drinking-vessel cover	J. Henermann	Davenport, Iowa	May 25, 1869	90, 539
Drinks, Apparatus for mixing	W. Harnett	Brooklyn, N. Y	Dec. 24, 1872	134, 274
Drinks from fruit, Manufacture of effervescent	A. Meucci	Clifton, N. Y	Jan. 3, 1872	122, 478
Drip-collecting device	W. A. Harris	Providence, R. I	Mar. 11, 1873	136, 597
Drip-conductor	J. G. Widmann	Yonkers, N. Y	June 3, 1873	139, 641
Dripping-pan	A. Reid	Buffalo, N. Y	Aug. 16, 1870	106, 506
Drive-well tube	J. M. Mott	Chicago, Ill	Feb. 22, 1870	100, 179
Driver, Friction	J. T. Jones	New York, N. Y	Mar. 3, 1868	75, 023
Driver, Friction	J. T. Jones	New York, N. Y	Mar. 3, 1868	75, 024
Driving-bit	E. S. Dawson	Syracuse, N. Y	Sept. 24, 1867	69, 079
Driving-bit	D. Hale	Roston, Mass	Sept. 10, 1867	67, 623
Driving-bit	C. Huie	New York, N. Y	May 14, 1872	126, 704
Driving-hoop	T. Lucey	Salem, Mass	Sept. 22, 1868	82, 425
Driving-lines	L. D. Woodmansee	Dayton, Ohio	Mar. 17, 1868	75, 614
Driving-power, Machinery	S. P. W. Douglass	Williamson, N. Y	May 22, 1841	2, 104
Driving-wheel of locomotive-engines	J. F. Elliott	New Haven, Conn	Apr. 20, 1858	19, 986
Driving-wheel of locomotives for ascending inclined planes.	J. Morss	Washington, D. C	Sept. 5, 1854	11, 650
Driving-wheel of portable steam-engines and agricultural implements, &c.	G. W. Barnett	Springfield, Ohio	May 25, 1858	28, 318
Driving-wheel of steam drags or propellers	G. W. N. Yost	Pittsburgh, Pa	June 3, 1856	15, 049
Driving-wheels, Method of connecting the wheels of locomotive steam-engines to render them.	H. Hinckley	Boston, Mass	Apr. 1, 1845	3, 981
Driving-wheels of locomotive-engines, Applying	A. M. Eastwich	Philadelphia, Pa	Nov. 20, 1837	471
Driving-wheels of locomotives, Method of arranging galvano-electro helices for magnetizing.	O. D. Vosmus	Boston, Mass	Apr. 12, 1859	23, 648
Driving-wheels of steam vehicles, plows, &c., Giving adhesion to.	J. T. Price	Rockville, Ind	Apr. 13, 1858	19, 947
Drop-light and hanger	G. F. Blaisse and W. F. Crites	Philadelphia, Pa	Nov. 4, 1873	144, 309
Drop-light and hanger	W. Stachlen	Brooklyn, N. Y	Dec. 30, 1873	146, 104
Drop-light, Center	C. Deavs	New York, N. Y	Dec. 16, 1873	145, 632
Drop-light, Center-slide	C. Deavs	New York, N. Y	May 20, 1873	139, 123
Drop-light, Chandelier	R. Cornelius	Philadelphia, Pa	July 1, 1873	140, 347
Drop-light, Chandelier	R. Gornelius	Philadelphia, Pa	July 1, 1873	140, 348
Drop light, Chandelier	N. W. Williames	Philadelphia, Pa	July 1, 1873	140, 565
Drop-light coupling	R. S. Roeschlaub	Quincy, Ill	May 21, 1872	127, 105
Drop-light fixture	S. B. H. Vance and E. M. Smith.	New York, N. Y	May 29, 1866	55, 212
Drop-light, Gasolier	C. Deavs	New York, N. Y	July 19, 1870	105, 435
Drop-light joint	T. G. Arnold	New York, N. Y	June 5, 1860	28, 548
Drop-light of gasaliers, Sustaining-device for center	C. Deaves	New York, N. Y	Aug. 22, 1871	118, 349
Drop-light standard	J. Cunningham	West Meriden, Conn	May 30, 1871	115, 442
Drop-light standard	J. Horton	New York, N. Y	June 14, 1870	104, 155
Drop-lights, Sliding gas-joints for extension	C. Deavs	New York, N. Y	May 30, 1871	115, 447
Drop-pipe, Rotating	G. C. Morgan	Chicago, Ill	Sept. 26, 1871	119, 388
Drop-press	J. Duff	Peoria, Ill	June 16, 1868	78, 867
Drop-press	T. Gaillard	Brooklyn, N. Y	Apr. 9, 1872	125, 386
Drop-press	H. C. Gladding	Providence, R. I	Jan. 3, 1865	45, 792
Drop-press	W. F. Goulding and F. Cheney	Providence, R. I., and Hartford, Conn.	Sept. 16, 1862	36, 459
Drop-press	W. C. Hicks	New York, N. Y	Jan. 20, 1863	37, 445
Drop-press	B. Hotchkiss	New Haven, Conn	Feb. 17, 1863	37, 692
Drop-press	N. P. Maker	Providence, R. I	May 25, 1869	90, 456
Drop-press	J. P. Noyes	Binghamton, N. Y	Oct. 16, 1866	58, 880
Drop-press	M. Peck	New Haven, Conn	Nov. 25, 1851	8, 548
Drop-press	M. Peck	New Haven, Conn	May 26, 1857	17, 411
Drop-press	M. and C. Peck	New Haven, Conn	Sept. 4, 1860	29, 910
Drop-press	S. Remington	Ilion, N. Y	Dec. 1, 1863	40, 709
Drop-press	J. C. Rhodes	South Abington, Mass	July 16, 1867	66, 884
Drop-press	N. C. Stiles and J. S. Miller	Meriden, Conn., and Springfield, Mass.	Nov. 19, 1867	71, 080
Drop press	W. Wilson, jr	Brandywine, Del	Aug. 11, 1857	18, 004
Drop press and hammer lifting device	C. Peck	New Haven, Conn	June 8, 1869	91, 159
Drop press and trip-hammer	L. L. Whitlock	New York, N. Y	Aug. 22, 1871	118, 317
Drop-press strap	C. McBurney	Roxbury, Mass	Oct. 20, 1863	40, 349
Drop-weight-lifting machine	L. L. Whitlock	New York, N. Y	Aug. 22, 1871	118, 316
Dropper: *See* Corn-dropper. Corn and fertilizer dropper. Harvester-dropper. Hoe seed-dropper. Medicine-dropper. Seed-dropper. Seed and manure dropper.				
Drub, Universal	S. Felton	Holmes County, Ohio	July 22, 1828	....
Drug-crusher, Portable	H. C. Becker	New York, N. Y	Aug. 14, 1866	57, 071
Drugs, &c., Machine for pulverizing	I. Eddy	Boston, Mass	Dec. 31, 1823	....
Drum	J. Mason	Louisville, Ky	June 30, 1863	39, 058
Drum and grate for stoves and furnaces, Hot-air	B. F. Campbell	Boston, Mass	July 9, 1872	128, 709
Drum and oven, Combined	G. F. Reinhardt	Lincoln, Ill	July 13, 1869	92, 543
Drum and oven, Stove-pipe	J. Beebe	Chicago, Ill	Mar. 6, 1866	53, 077
Drum attachment for furnace, Heating	W. Duryea and W. Ennis	Glen Cove and Hudson, N. Y.	Apr. 30, 1867	64, 293
Drum, Clip	F. Pelzer	Kohlscheid, Prussia	Oct. 8, 1872	132, 099
Drum evaporator	D. Wolf	Easton, Kans	Aug. 18, 1868	81, 236
Drum for coal-stoves, Hot-air	G. J. Bentley	Michigan City, Mich	Apr. 26, 1870	102, 210
Drum for heating apartments	W. Frazier	Brooklyn, N. Y	Apr. 30, 1840	1, 571
Drum for hot-air furnace	J. H. Keyser	New York, N. Y	Oct. 6, 1868	82, 723
Drum, Heating	J. E. Bartlett	Boston, Mass	Aug. 12, 1873	141, 621
Drum, Heating	S. M. Bayard	Ionia, Mich	June 15, 1869	91, 301
Drum, Heating	J. Hall	Pleasant Hill, Ill	Oct. 1, 1872	131, 875
Drum, Heating	T. Jefferis	Council Bluffs, Iowa	June 29, 1869	91, 940
Drum, Heating	M. W. Lester	Chicago, Ill	July 16, 1872	129, 147
Drum, Heating	F. Proudfoot	Toronto, Canada	Dec. 2, 1873	145, 237
Drum, Heating	J. Reynolds	Philadelphia, Pa	May 10, 1870	102, 866
Drum, Heating	C. W. Servoss	Chicago, Ill	Apr. 19, 1870	102, 053
Drum, Heating	C. W. Servoss	Chicago, Ill	Aug. 8, 1871	117, 820
Drum, Heating	O. D. Spalding	Mankato, Minn	Nov. 11, 1873	144, 573
Drum, Heating	I. P. Tice	New York, N. Y	Oct. 21, 1873	143, 795

Index of patents issued from the United States Patent Office from 1790 *to* 1873, *inclusive*—Continued.

Index of patents issued from the United States Patent Office from 1790 *to* 1873, *inclusive*—Continued.

Invention.	Inventor.	Residence.	Date.	No.
Dryer—Continued.				
See. Fruit-dryer. Glue-dryer. Grain-dryer. Hop-dryer. Lead-dryer. Lumber-dryer. Malt-dryer. Offal-dryer. Paper-dryer. Photograph-dryer. Poudrette-dryer. Salt-dryer. Sand and gravel dryer. Steam dryer. Sugar-dryer. Sugar and salt dryer. Tan-dryer. Tobacco-dryer. Towel dryer. Wool-Dryer. Yeast-cake dryer.				
Dryer	H. W. Adams and S. S. Bacon	Boston, Mass	July 4, 1871	116, 531
Dryer	H. W. Adams and S. S. Bacon	Boston, Mass	July 4, 1871	116, 532
Dryer	R. N. Allen	Pittsford, Vt	Dec. 24, 1867	72, 583
Dryer	C. E. Ashcroft	Boston, Mass	Feb. 9, 1869	86, 625
Dryer	E. H. Ashcroft	Boston, Mass	July 7, 1868	79, 623
Dryer	D. Barker	Northfleet, England	Mar. 3, 1868	75, 113
Dryer	J. Brakeley	Bordentown, N. J	May 12, 1868	77, 712
Dryer	J. Butterworth	Philadelphia, Pa	May 6, 1873	138, 475
Dryer	S. L. Cheyney	Wooster, Ohio	Apr. 28, 1868	77, 253
Dryer	S. L. Cheyney	Springfield, Ohio	Oct. 24, 1871	120, 242
Dryer	A. W. Cox	Indianapolis, Ind	Apr. 26, 1870	102, 230
Dryer	A. W. Cox and W. Gause	Indianapolis, Ind	Jan. 4, 1870	98, 470
Dryer	C. Crane	Boston, Mass	Sept. 1, 1868	81, 606
Dryer	L. J. Crow and G. Sanderson	Fredericksburgh, Ohio	Apr. 28, 1868	77, 362
Dryer	E. Drevet	New York, N. Y	June 27, 1871	116, 279
Dryer	E. Foote and M. P. Smith	East Bloomfield, N. Y., and Baltimore, Md.	Mar. 26, 1872	124, 944
Dryer	H. Garrett	Linneus, Mo	Jan. 25, 1870	99, 182
Dryer	W. A. Gibbs and A. Borwick	Sewardstone and London, England.	Jan. 7, 1873	134, 659
Dryer	T. S. Harrison	Philadelphia, Pa	Apr. 5, 1870	101, 458
Dryer	H. Henry	Halbert's Bluff, Ind	May 26, 1868	78, 285
Dryer	C. H. Hersey	Boston, Mass	Apr. 25, 1871	114, 137
Dryer	J. B. Johnson	Indianapolis, Ind	Mar. 10, 1868	75, 277
Dryer	C. Kaibel	Sacramento City, Cal	Feb. 9, 1869	86, 840
Dryer	R. Kidd	Montezuma, Ind	July 23, 1872	129, 736
Dryer	I. B. Kinkead	Watertown, Ohio	May 31, 1870	103, 622
Dryer	A. W. J. Mason	New Orleans, La	Oct. 31, 1871	120, 447
Dryer	O. F. Mayhew	Indianapolis, Ind	Sept. 21, 1869	94, 967
Dryer	P. Mickel	Milford, N. Y	June 14, 1870	104, 333
Dryer	J. P. Miller	Somerville, N. J	Nov. 15, 1870	109, 234
Dryer	C. A. Moffat	Indianapolis, Ind	Oct. 25, 1870	108, 616
Dryer	J. E. Rice	Moline, Ill	Aug. 9, 1870	106, 205
Dryer	E. Y. Robbins	Cincinnati, Ohio	July 19, 1864	43, 603
Dryer	M. P. Smith	Baltimore, Md	Feb. 1, 1870	99, 488
Dryer	M. P. Smith	Baltimore, Md	Sept. 13, 1870	107, 417
Dryer	M. P. Smith	Baltimore, Md	Apr. 2, 1872	125, 344
Dryer	E. Trowbridge and J. M. Jones	Detroit, Mich	Oct. 4, 1870	107, 982
Dryer	J. Turner	Chicago, Ill	Dec. 12, 1871	121, 915
Dryer	C. H. Wakelee	San Francisco, Cal	Oct. 10, 1871	119, 903
Dryer	J. M. Ward	Oxford, Ohio	Nov. 16, 1869	97, 006
Dryer	G. W. White and L. E. Wentworth.	Malden and Melrose, Mass	May 3, 1870	102, 742
Dryer	W. E. Wright	Rome, N. Y	July 23, 1872	129, 775
Dryer and evaporator	C. Alden	Newburgh, N. Y	Mar. 15, 1870	100, 835
Drying and burning kiln	J. Buhrer	Munich, Bavaria	Sept. 29, 1868	82, 488
Drying and desiccating apparatus	H. G. Bulkley	New York, N. Y	Oct. 22, 1867	69, 964
Drying and oxidizing colored goods	J. C. Kempton	Manayunk, Pa	Sept. 2, 1851	8, 334
Drying and preserving animal and vegetable substances, Process and apparatus for.	C. Alden	Newburgh, N. Y	Dec. 5, 1871	121, 569
Drying and ventilating apparatus	J. Royal	Rochelle, Ill	Feb. 4, 1868	74, 149
Drying-apparatus	D. K. Boswell	Corinth, Miss	Nov. 14, 1865	59, 895
Drying-apparatus	J. O. Mellen	Saint Louis, Mo	Apr. 2, 1867	63, 412
Drying-apparatus	F. I. Norton	Tremont, Ohio	Apr. 28, 1868	77, 205
Drying-apparatus	A. Stevens	West Milton, Ohio	July 31, 1866	56, 823
Drying-chamber	J. E. Tourné	New Orleans, La	Oct. 16, 1860	30, 436
Drying cloth	R. L. Hawes	Worcester, Mass	Oct. 3, 1854	11, 748
Drying-cylinder for fibrous manufactures	H. W. Peaslee	Malden Bridge, N. Y	Dec. 2, 1856	16, 149
Drying-cylinder, Steam	W. C. Collier	Salford, England	Jan. 14, 1873	134, 786
Drying-cylinders by steam, Mode of heating	A. P. Pitkin	Hartford, Conn	July 19, 1859	24, 819
Drying fibrous substances, Machine for	J. Essex	North Bennington, Vt	May 31, 1859	24, 205
Drying-frame, Lace-curtain, &c	S. Short	Cincinnati, Ohio	Dec. 23, 1873	145, 912
Drying furnace and oven	J. K. Caldwell	Allegheny City, Pa	Mar. 30, 1869	88, 444
Drying-house	J. J. Allen	Philadelphia, Pa	Mar. 26, 1872	124, 998
Drying-house	H. B. Gallup and C. Wood	Watertown, Wis	Aug. 14, 1866	57, 117
Drying house and oven	D. Stouder	Dayton, Ohio	Mar. 26, 1867	63, 327
Drying-house for drying fruit	S. Strong	Wilks Township, Ohio	Sept. 2, 1811	....
Drying-house for fruit, &c	L. A. Oellig	Martinsburgh, Pa	Jan. 21, 1868	73, 637
Drying-kiln	H. G. Bulkley	Kalamazoo, Mich	Feb. 13, 1866	52, 524
Drying-kiln	B. R. Hawley	Normal, Ill	Nov. 17, 1868	84, 117
Drying-machine	N. E. Chaffee	Ellington, Conn	Feb. 20, 1849	6, 119
Drying-room	R. Dalrymple	Galt, Canada	Oct. 10, 1871	119, 747
Duck-call	E. Fisher	Detroit, Mich	May 10, 1870	102, 799
Duck-shooting boat	R. Bogle	Rock Hall, Md	May 5, 1857	17, 192
Ducks, Mode of catching	W. Coffield	Norfolk, Va	Jan. 18, 1830	....
Ducts or natural passages for animal fluid, Instrument for obliterating strictures in.	G. N. Palmer	Greene, N. Y	Sept. 10, 1867	68, 647
Dulcimer	E. Durand	Norwich, Conn	Dec. 31, 1867	72, 824
Dulcimer	J. Low	Clinton, Mass	June 19, 1860	28, 811
Dumb-bell	E. Ballou	Zanesville, Ohio	Apr. 25, 1871	113, 966
Dumb-bell	D. P. Butler	Boston, Mass	July 4, 1865	48, 514
Dumb-bell	D. F. Savage	Boston, Mass	May 29, 1860	28, 505
Dumb-bell, Graduated	G. B. Windship	Boston, Mass	Feb. 14, 1865	46, 413
Dumb-jockey, the cross and saddle-tree being made of gutta-percha.	S. Blackwell	Middlesex County, England.	Mar. 18, 1856	14, 438
Dumb-waiter	T. B. Bryson	Newcastle, Pa	Oct. 15, 1867	69, 759

Index of patents issued from the United States Patent Office from 1790 *to* 1873, *inclusive*—Continued.

Invention.	Inventor.	Residence.	Date.	No.
Dumb-waiter	A. Cannon, jr	Poughkeepsie, N. Y	May 25, 1869	90, 422
Dumb-waiter	L. Carrier	New York, N. Y	Dec. 3, 1872	133, 561
Dumb-waiter	W. H. Elliott	Boston, Mass	May 24, 1870	103, 313
Dumb-waiter	R. W. Lawrence	New York, N. Y	Sept. 11, 1866	57, 928
Dumb-waiter	A. Murtaugh	New York, N. Y	Dec. 4, 1860	30, 831
Dumb-waiters, Pulley arrangement for	A. Murtaugh	New York, N. Y	Apr. 3, 1855	12, 640
Dummy-engine	J. Comly	Philadelphia, Pa	Apr. 1, 1873	137, 421
Dummy-engine	M. H. Kollock	Philadelphia, Pa	Mar. 25, 1873	137, 216
Dummy-engine	T. C Robinson	Mystic River, Conn	Jan. 9, 1872	122, 534
Dummy-engine	C. G. Spengler	Hoboken, Ga	Aug. 22, 1871	118, 291
Dummy or traction engine	A. A. Wilder	Detroit, Mich	Mar. 18, 1873	136, 886
Dumping and loading machine, Portable	W. Goff	Big Flats, N. Y	Oct. 29, 1867	70, 196
Dumping-apparatus	F. Ficht	Isle Royal Mine, Mich	Sept. 27, 1864	44, 412
Dumping-apparatus	R. M. McGrath	La Fayette, Ind	June 6, 1871	115, 759
Dumping-apparatus	G. W. Reed	Middlesex, Pa	June 3, 1873	139, 613
Dumping-apparatus	L. B. Stilson and J. G. Payson	Minneapolis, Minn	Nov. 29, 1870	109, 776
Dumping-box for agricultural purposes	J. Van Doren	Farm Ridge, Ill	Mar. 16, 1858	19, 663
Dumping-machine	G. W. and W. S. Hough	Galva, Ill	June 28, 1870	104, 736
Dumping-machine	B. Walton	Farisburgh, Ill	Nov. 23, 1869	97, 252
Dumping-platform	J. Atkinson	Cameron, Tex	Feb. 11, 1873	135, 683
Dumping platform	R. M. Fish	Glenwood, Iowa	Apr. 5, 1870	101, 451
Dumping-platform	W. W. Hinman	Elkhart, Ill	Apr. 29, 1873	138, 400
Dumping-platform	S. C. Kenago	Kankakee, Ill	Oct. 20, 1868	83, 288
Dumping-platform	F. Peteler	Bloomington, Minn	Sept. 9, 1873	142, 724
Dumping-platform	N. Swickard	Galva, Ill	July 16, 1872	129, 618
Dumping-platform	D. A. Wells	Sandwich, Ill	Aug. 13, 1872	130, 551
Dumping-tub	W. H. Brown	Erie, Pa	Mar. 3, 1863	37, 808
Dumping-tub	J. S. Evans	Berkley, Mass	Sept. 7, 1869	94, 483
Dumping-tub hook	J. R. Thorne	Waldoborough, Me	Nov. 15, 1870	109, 274
Dumping-wagon	R. W. Green	Bradford, Pa	Aug. 11, 1863	39, 478
Dung-forks, Device for convertible	E. H. Dawes	Litchfield, Me	Oct. 25, 1853	10, 148
Dung-forks, Making four-tined	M. Stevens	New Haven, Conn	Apr. 16, 1824	....
Dung-hook	J. G. Good	Raps, Pa	Apr. 16, 1867	63, 878
Duplex wrench	A. B. Davis	Philadelphia, Pa	Aug. 24, 1869	94, 085
Duplex wrench	A. B. Davis	Philadelphia, Pa	Aug. 9, 1870	106, 129
Durogel, Manufacture of	C. C. Peck and F. E. Engelhardt	New York, N. Y	June 4, 1867	65, 425
Dust-pan	A. Brigham	Cold Brook, Mass	July 23, 1867	67, 019
Dust-pan	D. C. Colby	Washington, D. C	Apr. 28, 1868	77, 258
Dust-pan	S. E. Condon	Brooklyn, N. Y	Feb. 25, 1868	74, 801
Dust-pan	W. M. Conger	Newark, N. J	Aug. 22, 1871	118, 343
Dust-pan	W. M. Conger	Newark, N. J	Feb. 6, 1872	123, 331
Dust-pan	W. M. Conger	Newark, N. J	July 30, 1872	129, 935
Dust-pan	F. L. Daniels	Boston, Mass	Nov. 30, 1869	97, 276
Dust-pan	F. L. Daniels	Boston, Mass	July 12, 1870	105, 315
Dust-pan	F. L. Daniels and J. Russell	Boston, Mass	Apr. 25, 1871	113, 985
Dust-pan	O. C. Forsyth, jr	Newburgh, N. Y	Dec. 23, 1873	145, 792
Dust-pan	T. G. Harold	Brooklyn, N. Y	Mar. 1, 1864	41, 771
Dust-pan	A. B. Hoffman	Roxbury, Mass	Oct. 16, 1866	58, 825
Dust-pan	G. H. Horstman	Philadelphia, Pa	May 21, 1861	32, 368
Dust-pan	R. S. Jennings	Philadelphia, Pa	Mar. 12, 1872	124, 584
Dust-pan	T. E. McNeil	Philadelphia, Pa	July 6, 1858	20, 811
Dust-pan	J. B. Morgan	Davenport, Iowa	Sept. 19, 1871	119, 042
Dust-pan	W. Musgrove	New York, N. Y	Oct. 22, 1872	132, 367
Dust-pan	W. S. Potwin	Chicago, Ill	Oct. 15, 1872	132, 176
Dust-pan	J. H. Rohrman	Philadelphia, Pa	June 7, 1859	24, 331
Dust-pan	T. F. Rooney	Chicago, Ill	May 2, 1871	114, 341
Dust-pan	P. A. Schanck	Matawan, N. J	July 20, 1869	92, 754
Dust-pan	M. Vanderhoven	Utica, N. Y	July 30, 1867	67, 232
Dust-pan	W. Westlake	Chicago, Ill	Aug. 15, 1871	118, 084
Dust-pan	L. F. Wheaton	Madison, Conn	May 26, 1868	78, 406
Dust-pan	H. Whittemore	Orangetown, N. Y	Feb. 21, 1871	112, 102
Dust pan and brush	C. H. Parker and G. Burnham	Waltham, Mass	July 4, 1865	48, 582
Dust pan and brush	C. H. Parker and G. Burnham	Waltham, Mass	Oct. 3, 1865	50, 270
Dust-receptacle	C. Butterfield	West Waterville, Me	Feb. 12, 1867	61, 999
Duster	G. M. Smith	Louisville, Ky	Jan. 28, 1873	135, 376
Duster, Feather	C. L. W. Baker	Camden, N. J	Nov. 18, 1873	144, 728
Duster, Feather	M. A. Goodenough	New York, N. Y	Apr. 28, 1868	77, 278
Duster, Feather	M. A. Goodenough	New York, N. Y	Jan. 11, 1870	98, 759
Dye, Aniline	B. Block	Soultz, France	July 14, 1868	79, 942
Dye, Aniline	J. Lambert, jr	New York, N. Y	Sept. 15, 1868	82, 129
Dye for coloring wool	G. W. Talbot	Providence, R. I	Feb. 1, 1870	99, 496
Dye-stuff	C. E. and M. E. Fox	Gilroy, Cal	Sept. 8, 1868	81, 992
Dye-stuffs, bark, &c., Cutting	A. Broad	Litchfield, Conn	June 9, 1814	....
Dye-stuffs from spent matter, Preparation of	F. Pfanner	Providence, R. I	Sept. 13, 1845	4, 192
Dye-stuffs, Machine for cutting and shaving	B. Swift	Washington, N. Y	Aug. 10, 1836	....
Dye-stuffs, Preparing vegetable	F. E. Schmidt	New York, N. Y	July 15, 1856	15, 361
Dye-tub	T. Sampson	Providence, R. I	Nov. 8, 1870	109, 059
Dye-vat	T. E. Rogers	Dexter, Me	Mar. 8, 1870	100, 670
Dye-wood and dye-stuff cutting and shaving machine.	B. Swift	United States	Aug. 10, 1836	10
Dye-wood cutter, Self-feeding	A. Foster	Rochester, N. Y	Dec. 9, 1828	....
Dye-wood, Cutting and separating	G. W. Pearson and D. Coburn	Lowell, Mass	Feb. 18, 1868	74, 586
Dye-wood-cutting machine	M. Hurd	Augusta, N. Y	July 22, 1831	....
Dye-wood-cutting machine	L. H. Moseley	Poughkeepsie, N. Y	June 22, 1837	242
Dye-woods and bark, Machine for reducing and cutting.	A. McMillen	Bedford, N. H	Dec. 26, 1837	532
Dye woods, Machine for cutting	E. Converse	Dayton, Ohio	Jan. 10, 1821	....
Dye woods, Machine for cutting	O. E. Pray	Portsmouth, N. H	Jan. 21, 1868	73, 647
Dye-woods, Machine for cutting	J. Richards, 3d	Norfolk, Conn	Aug. 13, 1810	....
Dye-woods, Machine for cutting and chipping	E. Morris	Bloomfield, N. J	Sept. 27, 1825	....
Dye-woods, Machine for grinding, sawing, or rasping.	J. Mathews	Philadelphia, Pa	Aug. 13, 1805	....
Dye-woods, Machine for grinding, sawing, and rasping.	J. Mathews	Philadelphia, Pa	Feb. 6, 1807	....
Dye-woods, Machine for rasping	J. Reed	Boston, Mass	June 3, 1808	....
Dye-woods, Machine for rasping and cutting	B. Swift	Washington, N. Y	Feb. 1, 1817	....
Dye-woods, Machinery for rasping	C. W. Roberts and J. Hambley	Philadelphia, Pa	Aug. 21, 1847	5, 251
Dye-woods, Mode of extracting color from	L. Kent	Dorset, Vt	Sept. 27, 1838	951

Index of patents issued from the United States Patent Office from 1790 to 1873, inclusive—Continued.

Invention.	Inventor.	Residence.	Date.	No.
Dye-woods, &c., Rasping and grinding	J. Broad	Springfield, Mass	Mar. 1, 1814	....
Dye-woods, Rasping or sawing	S. Stone	Enosburgh, Vt	May 3, 1811	....
Dyes and colors, Manufacture of	G. H. Reed	Boston, Mass	May 22, 1866	54, 957
Dyes and colors, Preparation of	M. Howe and H. R. Stevens	Boston, Mass	Oct. 13, 1863	40, 263
Dyes and colors, Preparation and manufacture of	G. H. Reed	Boston, Mass	Oct. 17, 1865	50, 495
Dyes by steam, Mode of manufacturing	R. Wood	Erin, N. Y	Aug. 25, 1829	....
Dyes from aniline, Manufacture of	R. Pinkney	London, England	May 21, 1872	127, 102
Dyes, ink, &c., from aniline, Production of colors for.	R. Pinkney	London, England	Aug. 23, 1870	106, 616
Dyes made from aniline, &c., from portions of fabric, Removing.	J. Lambert, jr	New York, N. Y	Nov. 8, 1870	109, 025
Dyes, Manufacture of madder	T. Bristow	Cranston, R. I	Mar. 1, 1870	100, 365
Dyes, Preparation of	J. Reynolds	San Francisco, Cal	Jan. 28, 1868	73, 756
Dyes, Putting up bluing and other	E. L. Molineaux	New York, N. Y	Dec. 24, 1867	72, 524
Dyer's and bleacher's implement	H. W. Holly	Norwich, Conn	Jan. 14, 1868	73, 331
Dyer's vat	H. Champenois	New York, N. Y	Oct. 5, 1869	95, 425
Dyer's vat	W. Vine and W. H. Jubb	Norwalk, Conn	Mar. 3, 1868	75, 081
Dyers' wood, Machine for cutting	E. Hubbel	Middlebury, Vt	June 27, 1809	....
Dyeing	J. P. Derby	Amesbury, Mass	Oct. 21, 1856	15, 959
Dyeing	H. Hibbard	Attica, N. Y	May 2, 1843	3, 068
Dyeing	P. Magennis	Paterson, N. J	Apr. 21, 1838	703
Dyeing	S. Mallard	Staten Island, N. Y	Mar. 27, 1849	6, 242
Dyeing and bleaching machine	J. Young	New York, N. Y	Aug. 18, 1863	39, 609
Dyeing and bleaching yarn and thread, Apparatus for.	W. H. Elliot and I. Osgood	New York and Utica, N. Y	Mar. 31, 1868	76, 178
Dyeing and embossing table and piano covers, Mode of.	A. Jack	Milton, N. H	Sept. 24, 1867	69, 098
Dyeing and finishing reel for silk and velvet woven fabrics.	E. Mafat	New York, N. Y	Aug. 30, 1870	106, 844
Dyeing and finishing, Silk	A. Stearns and W. Barrett	Boston, Mass	Sept. 2, 1818	....
Dyeing and finishing silk goods, Machine for	W. Barrett	....	June 27, 1809	....
Dyeing and printing a black color on fabrics with aniline compounds.	J. Lightfoot	Accrington, England	May 19, 1863	38, 589
Dyeing and printing, Compound to be used as a mordant in.	F. S. Dumont	New York, N. Y	Sept. 7, 1869	94, 581
Dyeing and printing, Material called ole-izerine for.	A. Paraf	New York, N. Y	Jan. 17, 1871	110, 994
Dyeing and printing, Mode of producing black in	A. Paraf	New York, N. Y	Sept. 24, 1867	69, 121
Dyeing and printing, Preparing coloring-matters for.	A. W. Hoffmann	Middlesex, England	June 7, 1864	43, 066
Dyeing and printing textile fabrics	J. Lightfoot	Burnley, England	Feb. 7, 1871	111, 654
Dyeing and printing textile fabrics and in compounds therefor.	A. Paraf	Mulhouse, France	Mar. 19, 1867	63, 084
Dyeing and printing with aniline colors	R. H. Gratrix	Salford, England	Jan. 5, 1864	41, 066
Dyeing and printing with aniline colors	N. Loyd and J. G. Dale	Accrington, England	Apr. 1, 1862	34, 840
Dyeing and tanning, Preparing quercitron or black-oak bark for.	N. Harper	Frankfort, Pa	Oct. 30, 1810	....
Dyeing and washing fibrous materials, Apparatus for.	C. G. Sargent	Graniteville, Mass	Jan. 14, 1873	134, 935
Dyeing-apparatus	C. T. Appleton	Roxbury, Mass	Mar. 21, 1854	10, 677
Dyeing-apparatus	E. Brierley	Lowell, Mass	Dec. 11, 1849	6, 932
Dyeing-apparatus	G. M. Rohrbacher	Philadelphia, Pa	May 7, 1872	126, 578
Dyeing-apparatus	M. Waterhouse	Passaic, N. J	June 2, 1868	78, 559
Dyeing black, Process of	J. Gee	West New Brighton, N. Y	Dec. 7, 1869	97, 497
Dyeing black with aniline colors	L. Jarossen and J. J. Muller-Pack.	Lille, France, and Basel, Switzerland.	Dec. 17, 1872	134, 066
Dyeing blue	J. Percy	....	Mar. 3, 1800	....
Dyeing blue, Process for	E. Swiney	Andover, Mass	Nov. 4, 1851	8, 494
Dyeing-composition	F. Graupner	Evansville, Ind	Aug. 16, 1870	106, 479
Dyeing, Composition of the pastel-vat to be used in	H. N. Barrow	East Windsor, Conn	Dec. 5, 1848	5, 947
Dyeing-compound	F. Graupner	Evansville, Ind	Aug. 1, 1871	117, 620
Dyeing-compound	F. G. Vetteroke	New York, N. Y	July 26, 1853	9, 890
Dyeing cotton, &c	H. Haigh and R. Heaton	Huddersfield, England	Jan. 5, 1864	41, 153
Dyeing cotton in the staple	J. R. Stewart	New York, N. Y	Nov. 11, 1831	....
Dyeing cotton, &c., Mode of	A. J. J. d'Andiran	Mulhouse, France	Jan. 19, 1869	85, 912
Dyeing door-mats	R. Shaler	Madison, Conn	July 22, 1851	8, 249
Dyeing, &c., Extract of bark for	S. Downing	....	June 12, 1801	....
Dyeing, Extracting the effective matter in bark, &c., for.	T. Bedwell and W. Mitchell	....	June 7, 1803	....
Dyeing, Extracting the essence of bark for	S. Downing	....	Apr. 19, 1802	....
Dyeing fabric	F. G. Graupner	Evansville, Ind	June 3, 1873	139, 573
Dyeing fabrics, Apparatus for	T. M. Drown	Philadelphia, Pa	Jan. 10, 1871	110, 907
Dyeing fabrics with naphtylamine colors	F. Lamy, jr	Deville-les-Rouen, France	Dec. 17, 1872	134, 076
Dyeing felt caps, &c., Device for	J. McFarlane	Matteawan, N. Y	May 24, 1864	42, 915
Dyeing felt hats and caps	J. T. Waring	Yonkers, N. Y	Aug. 19, 1873	142, 064
Dyeing fibrous and textile materials, Apparatus for.	C. Corron	St. Etienne, France	Aug. 6, 1872	130, 280
Dyeing hair on seal-skins, &c	J. Herring	New York, N. Y	Nov. 16, 1826	....
Dyeing hair, wool, &c	D. Williams	Albany, N. Y	Mar. 14, 1846	4, 416
Dyeing hats	I. Taylor	Trenton, N. J	Aug. 27, 1824	....
Dyeing hats, Apparatus used in	M. Burt	Warwick, N. Y	Nov. 8, 1825	....
Dyeing in various colors for manufacture of Scotch plaids, &c., Frame for.	C. Barton	Paterson, N. J	Feb. 15, 1870	99, 750
Dyeing, Iron liquor as a mordant for	J. D. Prince	Lowell, Mass	Apr. 24, 1841	2, 060
Dyeing machine, Silk	N. Mary, sr	Philadelphia, Pa	Aug. 11, 1857	17, 974
Dyeing madder-colors	F. A. Gatty	Accrington, England	May 20, 1873	139, 056
Dyeing, Manufacturing of prussiate of potash and soda for.	F. Fossard	Philadelphia, Pa	Nov. 7, 1835	....
Dyeing &c., Mode of treating fish-water for use in	J. B. Herreshoff	Bristol, R. I	Dec. 15, 1863	40, 933
Dyeing, Mordant for	R. O. Burgess and S. LaRhett	Providence, R. I	Nov. 25, 1873	144, 952
Dyeing, Mordant for	G. A. Hagemann	Copenhagen, Denmark	Oct. 7, 1873	143, 449
Dyeing nankeen, Mode of	A. G. Trott	New York, N. Y	Feb. 11, 1825	....
Dyeing piece-goods, Apparatus for	H. Burrows	Lowell, Mass	Mar. 3, 1868	74, 985
Dyeing, &c., Preparing quercitron or black-oak bark for.	T. Benger	....	Jan. 25, 1804	....
Dyeing-press	J. Holt	Lowell, Mass	July 19, 1870	105, 455
Dyeing-process	C. T. Appleton	Roxbury, Mass	May 30, 1854	10, 978
Dyeing-process	C. T. Appleton	Roxbury, Mass	Mar. 21, 1854	10, 664

Index of patents issued from the United States Patent Office from 1790 *to* 1873, *inclusive*—Continued.

Invention.	Inventor.	Residence.	Date.	No.
Dyeing silk	T. Harrison and R. Pierpont	New York, N. Y	Oct. 18, 1814	....
Dyeing textile fabrics with aniline colors	I. O. Iverson	Madison, Wis	Oct. 27, 1868	83, 502
Dyeing with alkaline prussiate	F. Fossard	Pittsburgh, Pa	Dec. 14 1832	....
Dyeing with alkaline prussiates and manufacturing potash.	F. Fossard	Philadelphia, Pa	Apr. 23 1834	....
Dyeing with aniline black	J. Higgen	Manchester, England	Apr. 22, 1873	138, 155
Dyeing with indigo	L. Scala	Genoa, Italy	July 23, 1872	129, 753
Dyeing with madder-colors	A. C. and A. Duncan	Manchester, England	June 18, 1872	128, 027
Dyeing wool, Process of	F. Fossard	Philadelphia, Pa	Apr. 21, 1838	702
Dyeing wool, silk, &c., with aniline colors	R. H. Gratix	New York, N. Y	Apr. 28, 1863	38, 306
Dyeing woolen goods	W. W. Sanborn	Lewiston, Me	Oct. 18, 1870	108, 523
Dyeing yarn, &c	A. Paraf	Mulhouse, France	Feb. 27, 1866	52, 942
Dyeing yarn from the beam, Machine for	W. Spencer	Lowell, Mass	Sept. 25, 1838	947
Dyeing yarn, Machinery for	W. A. Burke	Manchester, N. H	May 30, 1844	3, 608
Dyeing yarn parti-colored	D. B. Hinman	Philadelphia, Pa	July 26, 1853	9, 887
Dyeing yarn parti-colored	D. B. Kerr	New York, N. Y	Mar. 23, 1858	19, 701
Dynamic machine	L. C. Errani and R. Anders	Liege, Belgium	June 17, 1873	140, 021
Dynamometer	G. W. Bigelow	New Haven, Conn	Nov. 25, 1873	144, 945
Dynamometer	J. Emerson	Lowell, Mass	July 7, 1868	79, 561
Dynamometer	J. Emerson	Lowell, Mass	July 7, 1868	79, 562
Dynamometer	J. Emerson	Lowell, Mass	Dec. 21, 1869	98, 043
Dynamometer	J. Emerson	Lowell, Mass	June 27, 1871	116, 285
Dynamometer	G. and J. W. Gibbs	Canton, Ohio	Aug. 26, 1856	15, 608
Dynamometer	G. Juengst	New York, N. Y	Dec. 22, 1857	18, 908
Dynamometer	C. Neer	Albany, N. Y	July 12, 1859	24, 753
Dynamometer	C. Neer	Brooklyn, N. Y	Jan. 15, 1867	61, 237
Dynamometer	J. W. Sutton	Portland, Oreg	Dec. 21, 1869	98, 205
Dynamometer	W. Tucker	Blackstone, Mass	Dec. 21, 1858	22, 388
Dynamometer	A. Warren and E. Damon, jr	Boston, Mass	June 26, 1860	28, 925
Dynamometer, Recording	L. Miller	Akron, Ohio	May 21, 1872	127, 088
Dynamometer, Registering	W. B. Leonard	New York, N. Y	Dec. 19, 1854	12, 099
Dynamometer-wrench	H. R. Leonard	Portland, Oreg	June 11, 1872	127, 902
E.				
Eagle-chair	W. I. Weaver	New York, N. Y	June 14, 1816	....
Ear-cover	M. Stone	Vermillion, Ohio	June 10, 1873	139, 831
Ear-drop lobe-attachment	L. L. Northrup	Johnston, R. I	Oct. 3, 1871	119, 536
Ear-drop suspender	L. Weed	Norwalk, Conn	Apr. 27, 1869	89, 452
Ear-muff	S. Goge	New York, N. Y	Dec. 2, 1873	145, 168
Ear-muff	C. Sedgwick	New York, N. Y	Apr. 2, 1872	125, 339
Ear-protector	M. Isidor	New York, N. Y	May 13, 1873	138, 894
Ear-ring	G. Haberland	Bloomington, Ill	Sept. 27, 1870	107, 679
Ear-ring	L. L. Northrup	Olneyville, R. I	Jan. 2, 1872	122, 328
Ear-ring supporter	J. P. Tryner	Bloomington, Ill	Aug. 20, 1872	130, 771
Ear-rings, Device for piercing and lining ears for the reception of.	W. C. Edge	Newark, N. J	Mar. 28, 1871	113, 041
Ear-rings, Fastening for	G. E. Higgins	Syracuse, N. Y	May 16, 1854	10, 921
Ear-trumpet	T. H. Stilwell	New York, N. Y	June 2, 1868	78, 493
Ear-trumpets, Construction of	E. G. Hyde	Camptown, N. J	May 29, 1855	12, 951
Ears, Device for applying remedies to the	J. Fanyon	Bridgeport, Conn	June 13, 1871	115, 944
Ears, Method of attaching ornaments to the	W. B. Carpenter	Brooklyn, N. Y	June 8, 1858	20, 480
Ears, &c., Surgical instrument for examining the	H. Le Riemondie	New Orleans, La	Feb. 8, 1853	9, 581
Earth and sand, Raising and removing	C. Barnard	Newlin, Pa	July 14, 1826	....
Earth and stone, Machine for removing	S. Davis, jr	North Dartmouth, Mass	Feb. 22, 1831	....
Earth-borer	M. C. Chamberlin	Warsaw, N. Y	Jan. 30, 1866	52, 267
Earth borer and elevator	P. Dow	Philadelphia, Pa	Dec. 25, 1849	6, 970
Earth-borer for post-holes, &c	A. S. Ballard	Mount Pleasant, Iowa	Sept. 25, 1860	30, 175
Earth-boring implement	D. Gordon	Evansville, Ind	Oct. 25, 1859	25, 896
Earth-boring implement	C. N. White	Concord, N. Y	Apr. 10, 1855	12, 706
Earth-boring instrument	W. T. Huntington	Washington, D. C	Jan. 12, 1869	85, 741
Earth-boring machine	W. H. Bouser	Paris, Ill	June 10, 1873	139, 761
Earth-boring machine	J. Burns	Anamosa, Iowa	Aug. 19, 1873	141, 916
Earth-boring machine	J. R. Failing	Canajoharie, N. Y	June 13, 1827	....
Earth-boring machine	J. R. Failing	Canajoharie, N. Y	Aug. 25, 1828	....
Earth-boring machine	I. G. Manley and F. Wedge	Zanesville, Ohio	Feb. 19, 1861	31, 469
Earth-boring machine	S. R. Owen	Stewartville, Mo	Nov. 25, 1873	145, 007
Earth-boring machine	J. E. Race	Chicago, Ill	July 21, 1868	80, 217
Earth-boring machine	W. H. Salyer	Hamburgh, Iowa	July 8, 1873	140, 595
Earth-boring machine	C. Vernier	Stryker, Ohio	May 21, 1872	127, 124
Earth-boring machine	G. Wilson and G. H. Baisley	Hamilton, Mo	July 22, 1873	141, 097
Earth-cabinet	W. H. Bliss	Newport, R. I	Sept. 5, 1871	118, 681
Earth chamber-vessel	G. G. Baldwin	Milford, Conn	May 10, 1870	102, 750
Earth chamber-vessel	W. H. Bliss	Newport, R. I	May 3, 1870	102, 480
Earth-closet	J. A. August	Hot Springs, Va	Apr. 16, 1872	125, 781
Earth-closet	A. F. Baird	Pimlico, England	Nov. 16, 1869	96, 767
Earth-closet	W. J. Bradshaw	Cleveland, Ohio	June 20, 1871	116, 015
Earth-closet	W. J. Bradshaw	Cleveland, Ohio	Oct. 31, 1871	120, 367
Earth-closet	H. C. Bull	New Orleans, La	Dec. 26, 1871	122, 103
Earth-closet	R. A. Cannell	New Orleans, La	July 5, 1870	105, 139
Earth-closet	R. A. Cannell	New Orleans, La	May 23, 1871	115, 024
Earth-closet	H. Clark	Baltimore, Md	Nov. 5, 1872	132, 802
Earth-closet	W. R. C. Clark	New Orleans, La	Mar. 22, 1870	101, 098
Earth-closet	W. R. C. Clark	New Orleans, La	May 3, 1870	102, 494
Earth-closet	W. R. C. Clark	New Orleans, La	May 3, 1870	102, 495
Earth closet	W. R. C. Clark	New Orleans, La	July 5, 1870	105, 045
Earth-closet	L. G. Clock	Manchester, N. H	June 14, 1870	104, 270
Earth-closet	L. G. Clock	Manchester, N. H	Sept. 20, 1870	107, 451
Earth-closet	D. B. Collins	Richmond, Va	Dec. 5, 1871	121, 489
Earth-closet	R. A. Cowell	Cleveland, Ohio	Nov. 1, 1870	108, 885
Earth-closet	R. A. Cowell	Cleveland, Ohio	June 6, 1871	115, 580
Earth-closet	A. W. Davis	Wilmington, Del	Mar. 19, 1872	124, 725
Earth-closet	M. E. Doolittle	Hartford, Conn	Sept. 12, 1871	118, 795
Earth-closet	J. A. Drake	New Orleans, La	May 17, 1870	103, 029
Earth-closet	J. A. Drake	New Orleans, La	July 5, 1870	105, 053
Earth-closet	J. A. Drake	New Orleans, La	Aug. 23, 1870	106, 564
Earth-closet	J. A. Drake	New Orleans, La	Aug. 23, 1870	106, 565
Earth-closet	J. A. Drake	New Orleans, La	Aug. 23, 1870	106, 566

Index of patents issued from the United States Patent Office from 1790 *to* 1873, *inclusive*—Continued.

Invention.	Inventor.	Residence.	Date.	No.
Earth-closet	J. A. Drake and W. R. C. Clark	New Orleans, La	Apr. 12, 1870	101, 717
Earth-closet	B. Ferris	Wilmington, Del	Apr. 4, 1871	113, 411
Earth-closet	J. A. French	Milwaukee, Wis	June 14, 1870	104, 296
Earth-closet	B. A. G. Fuller	West Roxbury, Mass	Dec. 7, 1869	97, 495
Earth-closet	H. J. and J. W. Girdlestone	London, England	Sept. 13, 1870	107, 358
Earth-closet	E. Griffith	Wilmington, Del	Feb. 21, 1871	111, 926
Earth-closet	D. C. Hartman	Baltimore, Md	Feb. 14, 1871	111, 842
Earth-closet	C. C. Haskins	New Albany, Ind	Sept. 30, 1873	143, 239
Earth-closet	C. D. Holmes	Boston, Mass	Oct. 3, 1871	119, 610
Earth-closet	A. A. Jaqua	New York, N. Y	Feb. 20, 1872	123, 780
Earth-closet	A. A. Jaqua	New York, N. Y	June 4, 1872	127, 606
Earth-closet	G. B. Jewett	Salem, Mass	Apr. 19, 1870	102, 128
Earth-closet	G. B. Jewett	Salem, Mass	June 14, 1870	104, 319
Earth-closet	G. B. Jewett	Salem, Mass	July 26, 1870	105, 803
Earth-closet	W. A. Jordan	New Orleans, La	June 27, 1871	116, 320
Earth-closet	W. A. Jordan	New Orleans, La	July 16, 1872	129, 480
Earth-closet	B. L. Kent	West Chester, Pa	Jan. 16, 1872	122, 727
Earth-closet	B. L. Kent	Coatesville, Pa	Apr. 9, 1872	125, 575
Earth-closet	B. L. Kent	Coatesville, Pa	Feb. 11, 1873	135, 817
Earth-closet	C. Kieffer and J. R. D. Seeds	Wilmington, Del	Aug. 23, 1870	106, 593
Earth-closet	J. M. Loewenstein	New Orleans, La	Sept. 26, 1871	119, 376
Earth-closet	J. M. Loewenstein	New Orleans, La	Dec. 26, 1871	122, 123
Earth-closet	B. L. Mack	Essex, Conn	Mar. 18, 1873	137, 013
Earth-closet	A. Mallory	Mystic Bridge, Conn	Sept. 24, 1872	131, 694
Earth-closet	P. Malone	New Orleans, La	Jan. 17, 1871	110, 989
Earth-closet	J. Megratten	Wilmington, Del	Mar. 28, 1871	113, 186
Earth-closet	H. Moule and J. Brannehr	Fordington and Exeter, England.	May 16, 1871	114, 960
Earth-closet	S. D. Newbro	Lansing, Mich	Mar. 14, 1871	112, 620
Earth-closet	W. H. Newton	Newport, R. I	Sept. 27, 1870	107, 799
Earth-closet	N. P. Rider	Mandeville, La	May 14, 1872	126, 745
Earth-closet	G. W. Roberts	Wilmington, Del	Nov. 29, 1870	109, 667
Earth-closet	G. W. Roberts and J. H. Graham	Wilmington, Del	Apr. 30, 1872	126, 155
Earth-closet	I. S. and H. R. Russell	New Market, Md., and Woodbury, N. J.	Mar. 25, 1873	137, 099
Earth-closet	I. S. and H. R. Russell	New Market, Md., and Woodbury, N. J.	Dec. 23, 1873	145, 756
Earth-closet	H. Sherman	Waverly, Pa	Oct. 18, 1870	108, 396
Earth-closet	H. Sherman	Waverly, Pa	Jan. 16, 1872	122, 784
Earth-closet	J. G. Smith	Saint Louis, Mo	Dec. 10, 1872	133, 899
Earth-closet	R. R. Strain	San Francisco, Cal	Nov. 21, 1871	121, 068
Earth-closet	E. W. C. Vanderveer	Linden, N. J	Nov. 15, 1870	109, 276
Earth-closet	G. H. Vroom	Zanesville, Ohio	Nov. 12, 1872	133, 071
Earth closet	C. A. Wakefield	Pittsfield, Mass	May 17, 1870	103, 260
Earth-closet	C. A. Wakefield	Pittsfield, Mass	May 23, 1871	115, 256
Earth-closet	C. A. Wakefield	Pittsfield, Mass	Dec. 3, 1872	133, 685
Earth-closet	C. A. Wakefield	Pittsfield, Mass	June 17, 1873	140, 099
Earth-closet	R. S. Williams	Norristown, Pa	Apr. 2, 1872	125, 156
Earth closet	R. S. Williams	Norristown, Pa	Apr. 2, 1872	125, 370
Earth-closet	R. S. Williams	Norristown, Pa	Jan. 21, 1873	135, 026
Earth-closet	J. Wood	Martinsville, Ohio	Aug. 9, 1870	106, 244
Earth-closet	J. L. Young	New York, N. Y	June 4, 1872	127, 540
Earth-closet	J. L. Young	New York, N. Y	Feb. 4, 1873	135, 504
Earth-closet	J L. Young	New York, N. Y	Dec. 30, 1873	146, 119
Earth closet, Dry	W. H. Grove	Philadelphia, Pa	May 2, 1871	114, 434
Earth-closet, Portable	A. Panyard	Massillon, Ohio	Apr. 1, 1873	137, 319
Earth-closets, Portable dumping-hod for	E. W. C. Vanderveer	Elizabeth, N. J	Apr. 4, 1871	113, 364
Earth-conveyor	N. Russell	Harrison, Ohio	Dec. 24, 1867	72, 542
Earth, Endless-conveyor for removing	S. Falwell	Memphis, Tenn	Jan. 11, 1859	22, 559
Earth, Excavating and removing	N. Currier	Methuen, Mass	May 29, 1835	....
Earth, Machine for pulverizing	W. M. Bush	Greensburgh, Ind	Jan. 5, 1869	85, 639
Earth, Machine for raising and removing	J. Platt	Albany, N. Y	May 4, 1805	....
Earth, Machine for raising and removing	J. Platt	Albany, N. Y	May 4, 1805	....
Earth, &c., Machine for removing	W. H. Doll	Harrisburgh, Pa	May 29, 1826	....
Earth, Machine for removing	P. Reading	Trenton, N. J	June 1, 1826	....
Earth, &c., Machine for removing	J. Ring	Ogden, N. Y	July 1, 1840	1, 669
Earth, Machine for removing	J. Welsh	Boston, Mass	May 6, 1805	....
Earth-moving machine	J. Cowdon	New Orleans, La	Nov. 10, 1857	18, 573
Earth, mud, &c., Machine for raising	S. Collins	New York, N. Y	Sept. 26, 1826	....
Earth-pulverizer	J. W. Pence	Clayton, Ohio	Sept. 13, 1870	107, 287
Earth-removing apparatus	I. L. Skinner and S. F. Tooker	Hartford, Conn	Mar. 23, 1820	....
Earth scraping and loading machine	A. Ward	New Michigan, Ill	Mar. 9, 1869	87, 736
Earth, stones, &c., Concentrating the volatile parts of calcareous.	J. Fowler	....	Nov. 16, 1796	....
Earth to be excavated or removed, Machine for loosening.	W. H. Butler	Chicago, Ill	Sept. 3, 1867	68, 411
Earth-works, Machine for building	H. Morey	Cameron, Tex	Dec. 2, 1873	145, 119
Earthen covers, Molding	W. S. Thompson	Rochester, N. Y	June 25, 1872	128, 437
Earthen or cement pipe mold	C. M. Peirce, jr	New Bedford, Mass	Aug. 27, 1861	33, 161
Earthen or cement pipes for conveying water, Construction of.	C. Stearns	Springfield, Mass	May 8, 1839	1, 147
Earthen-pipe mold	P. McIntyre	Hartford, Conn	Apr. 22, 1873	138, 035
Earthen-pipe mold	P. McIntyre	Hartford, Conn	Aug. 26, 1873	142, 168
Earthen pipes, Machine for making curved	R. Connable	Jackson, Mich	Oct. 14, 1873	143, 670
Earthenware kiln	J. Hassell	Elizabethtown, N. J	Oct. 21, 1815	....
Earthenware, Machine for making	C. W. Saladee	Putnam, Ohio	Mar. 28, 1865	47, 043
Earthenware, Manufacture of ornamental	C. L. Fleishmann	Washington, D. C	July 2, 1872	128, 479
Earthenware, Ornamenting baked	R. B. Beech	Kensington, Pa	June 3, 1851	8, 140
Earthenware pipes, Machine for making	J. Bingham	Philadelphia, Pa	Oct. 21, 1873	143, 870
Earthenware pipes, Process of making curved	R. Connable	Jackson, Mich	Oct. 14, 1873	143, 671
Earthenware-shaping apparatus	J. H. Baddeley	Greensborough, Pa	Nov. 9, 1869	96, 537
Earthenware, Stilts for burning	P. Painton	Trenton, N. J	July 28, 1863	39, 356
Easel	E. G. Chormann	Philadelphia, Pa	Dec. 10, 1872	133, 759
Easel	N. Johnson	New York, N. Y	Jan. 16, 1872	122, 725
Easel	G. Munger and J. W. Schermerhorn.	New York, N. Y	Mar. 29, 1870	101, 377
Easel, Artist's	F. W. Bacon	New York, N. Y	Mar. 23, 1869	88, 256
Easel, Artist's	G. W. King	Perth Amboy, N. J	Oct. 6, 1863	40, 171

Index of patents issued from the United States Patent Office from 1790 to 1873, inclusive—Continued.

Invention.	Inventor.	Residence.	Date.	No.
Easel, Carriage-painter's	B. Irons	Columbus, Wis	May 18, 1869	90, 105
Easel, Coach-painter's	D. R. Harris	South New Berlin, N. Y	Mar. 28, 1871	113, 049
Easel, Folding	R. Wright	Brooklyn, N. Y	June 20, 1871	116, 133
Easel, Painter's	P. Dechause	New York, N. Y	Dec. 10, 1867	71, 858
Easel, Painter's	G. Gillett	Little York, N. Y	Sept. 15, 1857	18, 198
Easel, Studio	J. C. Forbes	Toronto, Canada	Nov. 28, 1871	121, 240
Easy-chair	A. Clarke	New York, N. Y	May 1, 1849	6, 416
Easy-chair	J. H. Devereux	Alexandria, Va	May 17, 1864	42, 753
Easy-chair	J. D. Finney	Keene, N. H	May 8, 1823	....
Easy-chair	E. Foster	Hartford, Conn	Aug. 23, 1859	25, 188
Easy-chair	B. F. Hays	Pittsfield, Mass	Dec. 17, 1834	....
Easy-chair	D. Mareau	Hubbardstown, Mass	Aug. 8, 1868	81, 282
Easy-chair	W. C. Poppendieche	New York, N. Y	Apr. 12, 1870	101, 764
Easy-chair	D. S. Rice	Portland, Me	May 21, 1872	126, 984
Easy-chair	A. Wood	Charlestown, Va	June 28, 1836	....
Easy-chair, Folding	C. C. Schmitt and R. Wodrich	New York, N. Y	Oct. 6, 1868	82, 754
Easy-chair for invalids, &c	P. O'Neil	Brooklyn, N. Y	Sept. 23, 1851	8, 377
Easy-motion and pavement-saving wheel	F. Varela	New York, N. Y	July 20, 1831	....
Eave-gutter for houses	G. W. Wheatly	Harrodsburgh, Ky	Mar. 13, 1855	12, 527
Eave-protector	J. J. Lovell	New York, N. Y	May 25, 1869	90, 454
Eave-trough	J. P. Abbott	Cleveland, Ohio	June 19, 1866	55, 595
Eave-trough	W. Adel	Rockton, Ill	Dec. 28, 1869	98, 328
Eave-trough	J. R. Baker	Kendallville, Ind	Nov. 19, 1872	133, 186
Eave-trough	J. P. Dauth	Reading, Pa	Dec. 31, 1867	72, 813
Eave-trough	N. J. Eldred	Elk Horn, Wis	Aug. 20, 1861	33, 076
Eave-trough	F. J. Emery	Springfield, Ill	Jan. 31, 1865	46, 093
Eave-trough	J. Jacoby	Doylestown, Ohio	Apr. 17, 1866	53, 984
Eave-trough	P. F. Kiblinger	Millersburgh, Ind	Nov. 18, 1873	144, 770
Eave-trough	T. C. Moore	Marion, Ind	Feb. 6, 1866	52, 438
Eave-trough	J. Reinig	Fond du Lac, Wis	Sept. 1, 1868	81, 818
Eave-trough	G. M. Selden	Troy, N. Y	Dec. 18, 1860	30, 934
Eave-trough	W. Stine	Elmore, Ohio	June 2, 1868	78, 617
Eave-trough	W. Yapp	Cleveland, Ohio	Sept. 4, 1866	57, 813
Eave-trough and conductor	K. B. Miller	Utica, N. Y	May 30, 1871	115, 340
Eave trough and gutter machine	J. Lee	Wellsville, Ohio	Oct. 8, 1850	7, 704
Eave-trough and lightning-rod, Combined	J. W. Hankenson and W. Baker	Minneapolis, Minn	Oct. 18, 1870	108, 354
Eave-trough attachment	F. M. Buckles	Altona, Ill	June 29, 1869	91, 823
Eave-trough brace	W. H. Henderson	Franklin, Ind	May 4, 1858	20, 155
Eave-trough bracket	J. W. Gillespie	Alliance, Ohio	Apr. 6, 1869	88, 626
Eave-trough bracket	J. Marshall	Hartland, Mich	Sept. 3, 1867	68, 765
Eave-trough bracket	W. Yapp	Cleveland, Ohio	Aug. 15, 1865	49, 466
Eave-trough bracket and cornice	J. N. Ball	Buffalo, N. Y	July 30, 1867	67, 155
Eave-trough fastener	L. Cook	Shreveport, La	Jan. 3, 1871	110, 633
Eave-trough fastener	M. Henney and W. B. Rager	North Manchester, Ind	Nov. 1, 1870	108, 906
Eave-trough fastening	J. P. Abbott	Cleveland, Ohio	June 18, 1872	128, 089
Eave-trough fastening	P. Ahn	Brandon, Vt	Dec. 10, 1867	71, 941
Eave-trough fastening	W. H. Hammond	Syracuse, Mo	Aug. 19, 1873	142, 016
Eave-trough former	L. Granger and L. Phillips	Memphis, Mich	July 20, 1869	92, 720
Eave-trough hanger	J. P. Abbott	Cleveland, Ohio	July 19, 1870	105, 404
Eave-trough hanger	J. P. Abbott	Cleveland, Ohio	Jan. 21, 1873	135, 056
Eave-trough hanger	D. Aiter	Ashland, Ohio	Dec. 1, 1868	84, 467
Eave-trough hanger	T. W. Bailey	Savannah, Ohio	Sept. 16, 1873	142, 758
Eave-trough hanger	H. S. Bishop	Cleveland, Ohio	July 2, 1872	128, 457
Eave-trough hanger	D. Dimmick	Orwell, Pa	June 18, 1872	128, 128
Eave-trough hanger	J. J. Kaufman	Ashland, Ohio	Aug. 2, 1870	105, 947
Eave-trough hanger	R. A. Lucas	Wooster, Ohio	Apr. 26, 1870	102, 412
Eave-trough hanger	T. F. Palm	Toledo, Ohio	Sept. 30, 1873	143, 375
Eave-trough hanger	H. B. Todd	Plymouth, Conn	Feb. 18, 1873	136, 109
Eave-trough hanger	T. G. Williams	Akron, Ohio	Nov. 4, 1873	144, 299
Eave-trough hanging	H. M. Gilbert and F. Elberson	Ada, Ohio	July 28, 1868	80, 473
Eave-trough-making machine	L. Mann	Ionia, Mich	Apr. 17, 1860	27, 916
Eave-trough-sawing machine	J. Wing	Hancock, Vt	Mar. 17, 1838	635
Eave-trough support	T. F. Morrison	Findley, Ohio	Dec. 30, 1873	146, 014
Eave-trough support	J. D. Pierce	Milwaukee, Wis	Dec. 24, 1872	134, 163
Eave-trough supporter	A. G. Perry	Clyde, Ohio	May 18, 1869	90, 122
Eave-trough supporter	B. Prugh and H. Austry	Grant City, Mo	Apr. 9, 1872	125, 483
Eave-trough suspender	T. F. Palm	Toledo, Ohio	Apr. 20, 1869	89, 068.
Eave troughs and pipings, Process for manufacturing wooden.	S. T. Field	Worcester, Mass	Feb. 19, 1861	31, 449
Eave-troughs, Apparatus for suspending	J. A. Watrous	Green Spring, Ohio	Sept. 1, 1857	18, 113
Eave-troughs, Connecting sheet-metal for	W. M. Phelps	Marshall, Mich	Oct. 28, 1862	36, 855
Eave-troughs, Finishing	C. A. Codding	Battle Creek, Mich	Oct. 11, 1864	44, 605
Eave-troughs, Machine for forming	J. Brett	Memphis, Mich	Sept. 15, 1868	82, 077
Eave-troughs, Machine for forming	A. Calkins and W. Tower	Almont, Mich	Mar. 19, 1867	63, 012
Eave-troughs, Machine for making	O. E. Mallory	Castile, N. Y	Jan. 1, 1856	14, 025
Eave-troughs, Machine for making	O. W. Noble	Darlington, Wis	May 15, 1866	54, 758
Eave-troughs, Machine for making sheet-metal	S. A. Scofield and E. Churchill	Morenci, Mich	Dec. 15, 1863	40, 951
Eave-troughs, Machine for making wooden	A. T. Stearns	Dorchester, Mass	Apr. 2, 1867	63, 572
Eave-troughs, Machine for manufacturing	S. Yates	Clarence, Iowa	Aug. 28, 1866	57, 615
Eave-troughs, Making	L. Pierson	Jeffersonville, Ind	June 26, 1868	28, 901
Eave-troughs, Suspending	C. D. Woodruff	Toledo, Ohio	Mar. 7, 1854	10, 606
Eave-troughs to houses, Method of attaching	W. R. Wallis	Alliance, Ohio	June 11, 1867	65, 779
Eave-troughs, while soldering them, Device for holding.	E. Wilkinson, jr	Mansfield, Ohio	Aug. 14, 1866	57, 237
Eccentric	J. C. Butterfield	Chicago, Ill	Sept. 16, 1873	142, 898
Eccentric	J. C. Wells	Warren, Pa	Sept. 21, 1869	95, 174
Eccentric, Adjustable	J. B. Strickland	Scranton, Pa	May 21, 1867	64, 922
Eccentric, Adjustable	D. F. Walker	Bowling Green, Ky	Mar. 7, 1865	46, 737
Eccentric adjustment	J. M. Stone	North Andover, Mass	Feb. 7, 1865	46, 278
Eccentric, Variable	T. Keeler and G. S. Avery	Danbury, Conn	Apr. 28, 1868	77, 197
Eccentrics, Mechanism for actuating adjustable	M. Stubbs	Cincinnati, Ohio	Apr. 6, 1852	8, 863
Edge-burnishing machine for boot and shoe soles	A. C. Carey	Malden, Mass	July 16, 1872	129, 457
Edge-burnishing machine for boot and shoe soles	F. Curtis	Boston, Mass	Aug. 6, 1872	130, 109
Edge-burnishing machine for boot and shoe soles	S. H. Hodges	Lynn, Mass	July 23, 1872	129, 825
Edge-burnishing machine, Sole	A. C. Carey	Malden, Mass	Sept. 17, 1872	131, 425
Edge-burnishing tool, Welt	M. J. Ferren	Stoneham, Mass	Apr. 15, 1873	137, 903
Edge-finishing machine for boot and shoe soles	L. Cote	Saint Hyacinth, Quebec, Canada.	June 21, 1870	104, 560

Index of patents issued from the United States Patent Office from 1790 *to* 1873, *inclusive*—Continued.

Invention.	Inventor.	Residence.	Date.	No.
Edge-finishing tool	J. B. Blanchard	Marlborough, Mass	Apr. 7, 1868	76, 391
Edge-finishing tool, Sole	F. M. Schmitt	Jamaica Plains, Mass	Dec. 18, 1866	60, 563
Edge-gage, Feather	G. G. Townsend	Rochester, N. Y	Sept. 23, 1856	15, 789
Edge-iron for shoemakers	E. D. Beales	Gallipolis, Ohio	June 21, 1870	104, 540
Edge-key	E. Campbell	Bath, Me	Apr. 30, 1861	30, 230
Edge-key for boots	G. C. Todd	Lynn, Mass	Dec. 7, 1858	22, 248
Edge-key for making and polishing the edge of boot and shoe soles.	G. C. Todd	Lynn, Mass	Nov. 25, 1856	16, 128
Edge-key handle	R. A. Woodberry	Beverly, Mass	May 31, 1870	103, 812
Edge-parer, Boot and shoe	W. Frederick	Ashland, Pa	Aug. 28, 1866	57, 493
Edge-plane	C. P. Bigelow	Clinton, Mass	Mar. 30, 1869	88, 264
Edge-plane	J. H. Conklin	Yorktown, N. Y	Dec. 27, 1864	45, 669
Edge-plane	C. D. McAuley	Carthage, Ohio	Feb. 18, 1868	74, 561
Edge-plane	S. Miller	Urbana, Ohio	Sept. 18, 1866	58, 123
Edge-plane	M. Newman	Unadilla, N. Y	May 30, 1865	47, 973
Edge-plane	J. E. Plummer	Binghamton, N. Y	Nov. 12, 1867	70, 894
Edge-plane	H. Sauerbier	Newark, N. J	July 19, 1859	24, 825
Edge-plane for boot-soles	C. Coti	Marlborough, Mass	Apr. 6, 1869	88, 551
Edge-plane for boots, &c	F. Buxton and G. Crosby	Lake Village, N. H	June 23, 1868	79, 203
Edge-plane for boots and shoes	W. Bayhouse	Portland, Oreg	Jan. 22, 1867	61, 384
Edge-plane for boots and shoes	A. B. Clark	Auburn, Mass	Feb. 5, 1867	61, 804
Edge-plane for boots and shoes	P. S. Foster	Richmond, Me	May 4, 1869	89, 754
Edge-plane for boots and shoes	J. C. Grün	Peoria, Ill	Feb. 27, 1866	52, 845
Edge-plane for boots and shoes	E. S. Snell	North Bridgewater, Mass	Apr. 10, 1860	27, 840
Edge-plane for boots and shoes	B. Tolman	Pembroke, Mass	June 21, 1859	24, 526
Edge-plane for trimming boot and shoe soles	I. A. Dunham	North Bridgewater, Mass	Sept. 22, 1857	18, 237
Edge-plane for trimming boot and shoe soles	C. Warren	Putnam, Conn	July 28, 1857	17, 905
Edge-plane for trimming soles and welts of boots and shoes.	B. J. Tayman	Philadelphia, Pa	May 20, 1873	139, 034
Edge-plane for trimming soles of boots, &c	J. Brooks and J. H. Sanford	North Bridgewater, Mass	Mar. 31, 1863	38, 026
Edge-plane, Shoemaker's	F. F. Baumann	Cambridge, Mass	Jan. 28, 1873	135, 308
Edge-plane, Shoemaker's	N. Bucher	Weedsport, N. Y	Nov. 2, 1852	9, 364
Edge-plane, Shoemaker's	I. A. Dunham	North Bridgewater, Mass	June 24, 1856	15, 176
Edge-plane, Shoemaker's	A. P. Hazard	North Bridgewater, Mass	July 19, 1870	105, 452
Edge-plane, Shoemaker's	A. P. Hazard	North Bridgewater, Mass	Sept. 20, 1870	107, 491
Edge-plane, Shoemaker's	C. E. Hersey	East Stoughton, Mass	Sept. 6, 1864	44, 093
Edge-plane, Shoemaker's	D. W. Horton	Petersburgh, Ind	Oct. 17, 1854	11, 808
Edge-plane, Shoemaker's	A. J. Parker	Lynn, Mass	Dec. 5, 1871	121, 465
Edge-plane, Shoemaker's	J. H. Sandford	North Bridgewater, Mass	Apr. 19, 1870	102, 048
Edge plane, Sole, (*See also* Sole)	M. Packard	North Easton, Mass	June 9, 1868	78, 758
Edge-setting tool, Sole	J. H. Morrison	Marlborough, Mass	Feb. 18, 1873	136, 087
Edge, Straight	S. Darling	Bangor, Me	Jan. 7, 1868	73, 082
Edge-tool sharpener	J. W. Wood	Watertown, N. Y	July 24, 1860	29, 336
Edge-tools, Composition for sharpening	G. L. Witsil	Philadelphia, Pa	Mar. 24, 1868	76, 025
Edge-tools, Grinding	G. C. Eaton	Lockport, N. Y	Feb. 10, 1863	37, 616
Edge-tools, Grinding	S. D. McLelland	McGregor, Iowa	July 12, 1864	43, 518
Edge-tools, Machine for holding and grinding	J. Richardson	Turner, Me	Apr. 3, 1866	53, 747
Edge-tools, Making	W. White	Newark, N. J	Dec. 28, 1858	22, 466
Edge-tools, Manufacture of	S. W. Collins	Canton, Conn	Nov. 20, 1860	30, 668
Edge-tools, Manufacture of	R. C. Grover	Newton, Mass	Oct. 6, 1868	82, 711
Edge-tools, Process of hardening	L. W. Stuart	Hawley, Pa	July 1, 1873	140, 390
Edge trimming and burnishing machine, Jack-center for.	T. M. Orr and A. R. Sears	North Bridgewater, Mass	Nov. 11, 1873	144, 560
Edge trimming and setting machine, Boot and shoe.	S. H. Hodges	Lynn, Mass	Mar. 19, 1872	124, 744
Edge-trimming machine for boots and shoes	R. C. Lambert	Raynham, Mass	Aug. 11, 1868	80, 828
Edge-trimming tool, Sole	I. R. Rogers	Lynn, Mass	Feb. 18, 1873	136, 096
Edges of boot and shoe soles, Burnishing-machine for setting the.	S. H. Hodges	Lynn, Mass	July 23, 1872	129, 663
Edging and ripping machine	E. C. Dicey	Whitehall, Mich	July 16, 1872	129, 400
Edging boards, Machine for	S. H. Richardson	Bangor, Me	Jan. 16, 1872	122, 780
Edging-gage for shoemakers, Feather	J. Jenkins	Andover, Mass	July 22, 1851	8, 247
Edging leather straps, Machine for	J. Barnes	Franklin, N. Y	Sept. 6, 1853	9, 986
Edging-machine	H. E. Bradt	Manistee, Mich	Apr. 4, 1871	113, 487
Edging-machine	L. Fay	Cincinnati, Ohio	Sept. 3, 1861	33, 190
Edging-machine	O. H. Gromberg and W. M. Ferry.	Ferrysburgh and Grand Haven, Mich.	May 20, 1873	139, 142
Edging-machine	E. H. Stearns	Erie, Pa	Jan. 17, 1871	111, 093
Edging-machine	E. H. Stearns	Erie, Pa	Sept. 30, 1873	143, 264
Edging machine, Feather	L. Goddu	Braintree, Mass	Sept. 20, 1864	44, 300
Edging-machine for turning the edges of tin, copper, or sheet-iron.	J. Woolley	New York, N. Y	Mar. 16, 1831	......
Edging metals, Machine for	W. Crossley	Chicago, Ill	Oct. 27, 1868	83, 365
Edging soles, Machine for feather	A. S. Libby	Lawrence, Mass	June 4, 1872	127, 618
Edging tin plates, sheet-iron, sheathing-copper, &c	C. F. Fisher	York, Pa	Feb. 28, 1833	......
Edging-tool for boot and shoe soles	T. Smiley	Albia, Iowa	Apr. 13, 1869	88, 920
Edging-tool, Harness-maker's	O. W. Morley	Tarrytown, N. Y	Sept. 7, 1869	94, 629
Edging-tool, Harness-maker's	F. M. Patterson and H. P. Miller.	Seymour, Ind	July 12, 1870	105, 242
Edging-tool, Tinman's	W. H. Henderson	Franklin, Ind	May 1, 1866	54, 342
Edible composition	D. Fobes	Boston, Mass	May 21, 1867	64, 856
Education-table	E. Allen	Windham, Conn	May 1, 1849	6, 407
Eel-pot	G. D. Allen	New York, N. Y	Oct. 13, 1868	82, 913
Egg and cake beater	J. W. Condon	Logansport, Ind	July 15, 1873	140, 891
Egg and cake beater	H. S. Maltby	Cincinnati, Ohio	Oct. 18, 1870	108, 498
Egg and cream beater	F. Oakley	London, England	Jan. 29, 1867	61, 679
Egg and fruit carrier	I. R. Amsden	Buffalo, N. Y	Jan. 26, 1869	86, 267
Egg and fruit carrier	W. J. Clark	Lena, Ill	Mar. 21, 1871	112, 784
Egg and fruit carrier	J. T. Cornforth	Kansas City, Mo	Aug. 15, 1871	117, 988
Egg-beater	L. B. Alden	Cincinnati, Ohio	July 31, 1866	56, 845
Egg-beater	W. N. Angus	Morristown, N. J	Apr. 21, 1868	76, 970
Egg-beater	V. G. Arnold	Providence, R. I	Oct 16, 1866	58, 750
Egg-beater	F. Ashley	New York, N. Y	May 1, 1860	28, 047
Egg-beater	F. Ashley	New York, N. Y	June 26, 1866	55, 802
Egg-beater	U. Baker	Brooklyn, N. Y	Oct. 23, 1860	30, 453
Egg-beater	L. T. Blake	New Haven, Conn	July 28, 1868	80, 440
Egg-beater	A. R. Blasse	Westminster, Md	Feb. 13, 1866	52, 518
Egg-beater	G. E. Bridger	Milwaukee, Wis	Aug. 27, 1867	68, 037

Index of patents issued from the United States Patent Office from 1790 *to* 1873, *inclusive*—Continued.

Invention.	Inventor.	Residence.	Date.	No.
Egg-beater	C. H. Butterfield	Sturbridge, Mass	Oct. 16, 1866	58, 770
Egg-beater	G. G. Carver	Roxbury, Mass	Dec. 3, 1867	71, 696
Egg-beater	D. B. Clayton	Columbia, S. C	Aug. 15, 1871	117, 982
Egg-beater	M. G. Crane	Boston, Mass	July 4, 1865	48, 525
Egg-beater	M. G. Crane	Boston, Mass	June 19, 1866	55, 625
Egg-beater	W. O. Crocker	Laconia, N. H	Sept. 24, 1872	131, 600
Egg-beater	J. Dane, jr	Newark, N. J	Jan. 23, 1872	122, 997
Egg-beater	J. Davis	Schenectady, N. Y	July 17, 1866	56, 382
Egg-beater	G. K. Dearborn	Pawtucket, R. I	July 26, 1870	105, 655
Egg-beater	C. M. Drennan	Boston, Mass	Sept. 18, 1866	58, 165
Egg-beater	H. F. Drott	Cumberland, Md	Sept. 18, 1860	30, 053
Egg-beater	T. Earle	Smithfield, R. I	July 7, 1863	39, 134
Egg-beater	T. Earle	Valley Falls and Smithfield, R. I.	Apr. 24, 1866	54, [illegible]34
Egg-beater	T. Earle	Valley Falls, R. I	Jan. 25, 1870	99, 173
Egg-beater	T. Earle	Smithfield, R. I	July 5, 1870	105, 057
Egg-beater	T. Earle and G. K. Dearborn	Valley Falls, Smithfield, and Pawtucket, R. I.	Sept. 27, 1870	107, 673
Egg-beater	H. D. and J. T. Felthouse	Philadelphia, Pa	Mar. 27, 1866	53, 429
Egg-beater	H. G. and A. C. Fougen	Cape Girardeau, Mo	Nov. 30, 1869	97, 379
Egg-beater	E. Hadley	Chicopee Falls, Mass	May 6, 1873	138, 647
Egg-beater, &c	W. H. Haines	Newark, N. J	Feb. 15, 1870	99, 883
Egg-beater	W. Hart	Philadelphia, Pa	Mar. 12, 1861	31, 663
Egg-beater	J. B. Heich	Cincinnati, Ohio	Dec. 15, 1857	18, 849
Egg-beater	H. P. Hood	Indianapolis, Ind	Aug. 6, 1872	130, 297
Egg-beater	J. M. Jay	Canton, Ohio	Feb. 7, 1860	27, 054
Egg-beater	J. M. Jay and J. Danner	Canton, Ohio	Apr. 17 1860	27, 908
Egg-beater	H. F. Jenks and T. Marsh	Pawtucket, R. I	June 13, 1871	115, 862
Egg-beater	S. F. Jones	Saint Paul, Ind	May 3, 1859	23, 843
Egg-beater	F. L. King	Worcester, Mass	Jan. 2, 1866	51, 839
Egg-beater	P. Klepper	Centralia, Ill	July 16, 1867	66, 855
Egg-beater	F. Krandelt	San Francisco, Cal	Feb. 22, 1870	100, 155
Egg-beater	E. B. Kunkle	Fort Wayne, Ind	Sept. 5, 1871	118, 727
Egg-beater	L. Laurie	Washington, D. C	Dec. 21, 1869	98, 168
Egg-beater	H. W. Louden	Ephratah, Pa	Feb. 25 1866	74, 837
Egg-beater	D. D. Mackay	Whitestone, N. Y	Dec. 29, 1868	85, 460
Egg-beater	T. Marsh	Pawtucket, R. I	Sept. 20, 1870	107, 515
Egg-beater	T. Marsh and J. Berney	Pawtucket, R. I	June 14, 1870	104, 174
Egg-beater	T. Marsh and J. Berney	Pawtucket, R. I	Aug. 9, 1870	106, 182
Egg-beater	T. McBean	Fowlerville, N. Y	May 24, 1859	24, 134
Egg-beater	J. P. McLean and P. A. Morley	Brooklyn, N. Y	June 19, 1860	28, 760
Egg-beater	P. Mihan	Boston, Mass	Mar. 23, 1858	19, 738
Egg-beater	H. Miller	Cincinnati, Ohio	Dec. 1, 1857	18, 759
Egg-beater	H. Miller	Cincinnati, Ohio	Feb. 6, 1872	123, 353
Egg-beater	N. C. Miller	Stroudsburgh, Pa	Feb. 1, 1870	99, 337
Egg-beater	N. C. Miller	Stroudsburgh, Pa	Apr. 22, 1873	138, 094
Egg-beater	J. F. Monroe and E. P. Monroe	Fitchburgh, Mass., and New York, N. Y.	Apr. 19, 1859	23, 694
Egg-beater	D. Munson	Indianapolis, Ind	Mar. 5, 1872	124, 375
Egg-beater	D. Munson	Indianapolis, Ind	June 17, 1873	140, 067
Egg-beater	W. T. Nicholson	Providence, R. I	July 23, 1861	32, 886
Egg-beater	W. T. Nicholson and T. Earle	Providence and Smithfield, R. I.	Sept. 25, 1860	30, 152
Egg-beater	J. L. Nicolai	Chicago, Ill	Apr. 26, 1859	23, 814
Egg-beater	S. B. Pangborn and G. H. Griffin.	Boston, Mass	May 15, 1866	54, 761
Egg-beater	C. R. Peirce	Philadelphia, Pa	Aug. 20, 1872	130, 591
Egg-beater	W. H. Peirce	Bangor, Me	Mar. 24, 1868	75, 787
Egg-beater	C. Pinder	Lowell, Mass	Oct. 16, 1866	58, 882
Egg-beater	A. M. Robinson	Boston, Mass	May 15, 1866	54, 776
Egg-beater	J. F. Rote	Reading, Pa	Nov. 11, 1873	144, 567
Egg-beater	W. Saladee and E. M. Luckett	Philadelphia, Pa	May 3, 1864	42, 603
Egg-beater	P. Schildecker	Pittsburgh, Pa	Oct. 6, 1863	40, 188
Egg-beater	C. F. A. Seitz	Philadelphia, Pa	Apr. 6, 1869	88, 672
Egg-beater	D. Shive	Philadelphia, Pa	July 29, 1862	36, 030
Egg-beater	W. B. Smith	New York, N. Y	Dec. 26, 1865	51, 758
Egg-beater	D. M. Swartz	Lewisburgh, Pa	Oct. 11, 1870	108, 203
Egg-beater	H. Tilden	Boston, Mass	Aug. 1, 1865	49, 176
Egg-beater	S. Walker	Boston, Mass	Jan. 24, 1860	26, 958
Egg-beater	D. Webster	Washington, D. C	Dec. 10, 1867	72, 136
Egg-beater	W. Weckersham	Boston, Mass	Apr. 9, 1867	63, 774
Egg-beater	L. Williams	Terrysville, Conn	Jan. 4, 1870	98, 533
Egg-beater	M. T. Williams	Milwaukee, Wis	May 21, 1867	64, 928
Egg-beater	T. Williams	Providence, R. I	May 31, 1870	103, 811
Egg-beater	S. C. Wilson	Central Falls, R. I	Mar. 10, 1868	75, 340
Egg-beater and liquor-mixer	E. C. Strange	Taunton, Mass	Aug. 28, 1866	57, 596
Egg beater and stirrer	C. Lehman	Hartford, Conn	Mar. 29, 1870	101, 281
Egg-beater, cake-cutter, and nutmeg-grater	S. C. Moore	Boston, Mass	May 1, 1866	54, 388
Egg beater or agitator	J. W. Bliss	Hartford, Conn	Dec. 6, 1864	45, 309
Egg beater or churn	J. J. Parker	Marietta, Ohio	Aug. 9, 1859	25, 038
Egg-beater or ice cream freezer	J. Pyne and W. Burr	Harrisburgh, Pa	Nov. 15, 1859	26, 123
Egg-beater, Rotary	R. Collier	Baltimore, Md	Dec. 23, 1856	16, 267
Egg-boiler	F. Ashley	New York, N. Y	Aug. 1, 1865	49, 062
Egg-boiler	P. Malapert and E. A. Des Courtis.	Poitiers, France, and New York, N. Y.	Oct. 24, 1865	50, 669
Egg-boiler	A. Sharlow	Fort Lee, N. J	Apr. 11, 1865	47, 228
Egg-boiling apparatus	I. Dimock	Florence, Mass	Oct. 20, 1868	83, 264
Egg-box	J. D. Michael	Baltimore, Md	Jan. 4, 1870	98, 609
Egg-carrier	J. R. Asher	Oskaloosa, Iowa	Sept. 6, 1870	106, 983
Egg-carrier	J. A. Beam	California, Mo	July 15, 1873	140, 807
Egg-carrier	W. Bramwell	Toledo, Ohio	Aug. 13, 1872	130, 469
Egg-carrier	A. H. Bryant	Chicago, Ill	Mar. 22, 1870	101, 092
Egg-carrier	A. H. Bryant	Chicago, Ill	Mar. 22, 1870	101, 093
Egg-carrier	A. H. Bryant	Chicago, Ill	June 14, 1870	104, 261
Egg-carrier	A. H. Bryant	New York, N. Y	July 16, 1872	129, 313
Egg-carrier	A. H. Bryant	New York, N. Y	Dec. 17, 1872	134, 031
Egg-carrier	A. H. Bryant	Chicago, Ill	June 3, 1873	139, 540
Egg-carrier	W. J. Clark	Lena, Ill	Mar. 15, 1870	100, 857

Index of patents issued from the United States Patent Office from 1790 to 1873, inclusive—Continued.

Invention.	Inventor.	Residence.	Date.	No.
Egg-carrier	G. Dorn	Albany, N. Y	Aug. 18, 1868	81, 151
Egg-carrier	G. Dorn and J. Shibley	Albany, N. Y	Apr. 20, 1869	89, 133
Egg-carrier	W. Duchemin	Charlottetown, Prince Edward Island.	June 27, 1871	116, 280
Egg-carrier	D. A. Fanghaenel	Kansas City, Mo	July 9, 1872	128, 793
Egg-carrier	E. P. Herrick	Chicago, Ill	Jan. 33, 1872	122, 889
Egg-carrier	G. M. Huston	San Francisco, Cal	Nov. 26, 1872	133, 315
Egg-carrier	G. M. Huston	Zanesville, Ohio	July 8, 1873	140, 579
Egg-carrier	G. M. Huston	Zanesville, Ohio	July 8, 1873	140, 580
Egg-carrier	P. P. Josef	Buffalo, N. Y	Apr. 6, 1869	88, 641
Egg-carrier	P. P. Josef	Buffalo, N. Y	Oct. 26, 1869	96, 119
Egg-carrier	E. E. Joseff	Saint Louis, Mo	Aug. 16, 1870	106, 369
Egg-carrier	W. A. Laverty	Philadelphia, Pa	Dec. 9, 1873	145, 431
Egg-carrier	E. L. Mueller	Saint Louis, Mo	Apr. 23, 1872	125, 977
Egg-carrier	E. L. Mueller	Saint Louis, Mo	Apr. 15, 1873	137, 791
Egg-carrier	A. Selkirk	Albany, N. Y	Apr. 20, 1869	89, 174
Egg-carrier	C. J. Simmons	Kansas City, Mo	Sept. 16, 1873	142, 952
Egg-carrier	S. H. Smith	North Adams, Mich	May 28, 1872	127, 379
Egg-carrier	S. H. Smith	North Adams, Mich	May 27, 1873	139, 431
Egg-carrier	J. L. Stevens	Chicago, Ill	Oct. 1, 1872	131, 911
Egg-carrier	J. L. Stevens	New York, N. Y	Dec. 31, 1872	134, 495
Egg-carrier	W. O. Strong	Ypsilanti, Mich	July 9, 1872	128, 920
Egg-carrier	W. D. Taber	Buffalo, N. Y	Nov. 12, 1872	132, 937
Egg-carrier	C. Tennant	Dublin, Md	Nov. 7, 1871	120, 795
Egg-carrier	F. M. Wade	San Francisco, Cal	Dec. 2, 1873	145, 137
Egg-carrier	W. Weis	Saint Paul, Minn	Dec. 30, 1873	145, 038
Egg-carrier, Suspension	A. H. Bryant	Wilmington, Del	Mar. 17, 1868	75, 623
Egg-carriers, Pocket for	A. H. Bryant	Philadelphia, Pa	June 22, 1869	91, 516
Egg-carriers, Safety-attachment for	A. H. Bryant	Wilmington, Del	Sept. 1, 1868	81, 593
Egg-cooker	W. Loucks	Schoharie, N. Y	June 13 1865	48, 190
Egg-cup	C. Hellen	Washington, D. C	Oct. 8, 1867	6[illegible], 665
Egg-cup	C. D. P. Watters	New York, N. Y	Apr. 21, 1868	77, 140
Egg-cup and tongs	C. Hellen	Washington, D. C	Sept. 17, 1867	68, 984
Egg-cup, Spring	H. G. Batty	Springfield, Mass	Feb. 14, 1860	27, 095
Egg-cutter	F. L. King	Worcester, Mass	June 18, 1867	65, 916
Egg-detector	F. J. Eisenman	Chicago, Ill	Oct. 26, 1869	96, 693
Egg-detector	A. Sahlstrom and P. Rohdin	Chicago, Ill	June 27, 1871	116, 501
Egg-detector	A. F. Summers and C. Nye	Peoria, Ill	Mar. 19, 1867	62, 979
Egg-frier	A. Overbagh	Hudson, N. Y	Nov. 1, 1864	44, 886
Egg-hatching apparatus	T. Carter	Covington, Ky	Mar. 8, 1864	41, 830
Egg-hatching apparatus	P. Degive	New York, N. Y	Mar. 26, 1867	63, 146
Egg-holder	F. Arnold	Haddam, Conn	Aug. 14, 1855	13, 414
Egg-holder	A. Brown	Springfield, Vt	Aug. 2, 1870	105, 901
Egg-holder	F. R. Harbaugh	Philadelphia, Pa	Oct. 20, 1868	83, 281
Egg-holder	J. Nathan	Washington, D. C	Oct. 29, 1867	70, 350
Egg-holder	R. M. Washburn	Burlington, Iowa	July 16, 1872	129, 632
Egg-holder	F. Wegrather	Chicago, Ill	Apr. 3, 1866	53, 712
Egg holder and packer	O. T. Bedell	New York, N. Y	July 4, 1865	48, 507
Egg-inspector	A. Jewett	Sanford's Corners, N. Y	July 30, 1872	130, 054
Egg-packing	G. Ruston	Freeport, Ill	Apr. 19, 1870	102, 047
Egg-packing box	N. L. Janney	Wilmington, Del	Oct. 3, 1871	119, 613
Egg-pan	N. Waterman	Boston, Mass	Apr. 5, 1859	23, 517
Egg-poaching pan	M. M. Crutchfield	Fayette Corner, Tenn	Nov. 19, 1872	133, 205
Egg-preserving frame	C. A. Erskine	Palermo Centre, Me	Feb. 4, 1868	73, 960
Egg-preserving process	A. Wadgymar	Saint Louis, Mo	Nov. 5, 1867	70, 655
Egg stand and boiler	E. P. Woods and D. Sherwood	Lowell, Mass	Nov. 12, 1867	70, 769
Egg-tester	F. B. Seeley	Johnson's Creek, N. Y	Aug. 21, 1866	57, 389
Eggs, Apparatus for assorting	H. Burt	Newark, N. J	Nov. 30, 1858	22, 161
Eggs, Apparatus for desiccating	C. A. Lamont	New York, N. Y	Oct. 10, 1865	50, 421
Eggs, &c., Apparatus for desiccating	J. B. Thompson	New York, N. Y	Mar. 20, 1866	53, 361
Eggs, Box for packing	E. M. Coombs	Memphis, Ind	Oct. 10, 1865	50, 341
Eggs, Box for transporting	G. A. Wells	Oskaloosa, Iowa	May 17, 1870	103, 111
Eggs, Case for transporting	J. L. and G. W. Stevens	San Francisco, Cal	Feb. 26, 1867	62. 378
Eggs, churning, &c., Apparatus for beating	W. Borrman	Cincinnati, Ohio	Apr. 27, 1858	20, 032
Eggs, &c., Desiccating	T. H. Quick	New York, N. Y	Nov. 21, 1865	51, 084
Eggs, Device for packing and transporting	B. Illingworth	Freeport, Ill	Mar. 8, 1870	100, 633
Eggs, Device for transporting	A. H. Bryant	Chicago, Ill	Mar. 21, 1871	112, 778
Eggs for transportation, Device for packing	A. S. Smith	Lawrence, Mass	Nov. 23, 1869	97, 129
Eggs, Mode of keeping	B. D. Atwell and G. H. Crawford.	Portage City, Wis	June 25, 1867	65, 988
Eggs, Mode of transporting	H. Williard	Grand Rapids, Mich	July 25, 1871	117, 496
Eggs, &c., Packing	A. Thomas	Ulysses, N. Y	Feb. 11, 1868	74, 257
Eggs, Process of preserving	H. Scheffer	Saint Louis, Mo	Apr. 30, 1867	64, 256
Egyptian lock	A. O. Stansbury	New York, N. Y	Feb. 11, 1807	....
Ejecting cup, Oil	H. E. Stager	Milwaukee, Wis	Sept. 26, 1865	50, 183
Ejector	H. Coll	Millvale Borough, Pa	Dec. 20, 1870	110, 205
Ejector	G. W. Glass	New Brighton, Pa	July 20, 1869	92, 718
Ejector	G. Hibberd	Wheeling, W. Va	July 29, 1873	141, 349
Ejector	W. B. Mack	Boston, Mass	June 10, 1873	139, 799
Ejector	J. Nixon	Pittsburgh, Pa	July 5, 1870	104, 986
Ejector	T. H. Schriber	Evansville, Ind	Nov. 22, 1870	109, 553
Ejector, Air	J. Y. Smith	Pittsburgh, Pa	Mar. 11, 1873	136, 779
Ejector and steam condenser	A. Barclay	Kilmarnock, North Britain	Aug. 16, 1870	106, 452
Ejector, Artesian well	M. Lytle	Oil City, Pa	Jan. 23, 1872	122, 970
Ejector, Centrifugal hydro	H. W. and R. Lafferty	Gloucester, N. J	Apr. 21, 1868	77, 054
Ejector, Fluid	R. McGrath	Philadelphia, Pa	May 9, 1865	47, 654
Ejector, Fluid	J. Ryan	Saint Louis, Mo	Mar. 12, 1867	62, 893
Ejector, Fluid	J. Wood	Red Bank, N. J	July 18, 1865	48, 861
Ejector for deep wells	J. Blackie	Washington, D. C	Nov. 14, 1865	50, 893
Ejector for forcing liquids	J. T. Hancock	West Roxbury, Mass	Dec. 5, 1871	121, 515
Ejector for oil-wells	J. D. Angier and F. Crocker	Titusville, Pa	Oct. 11, 1864	44, 587
Ejector for oil-wells	J. D. Angier and F. Crocker	Titusville, Pa	Dec. 13, 1864	45, 463
Ejector for oil-wells	G. M. Mowbray	Titusville, Pa	Oct. 11, 1864	44, 646
Ejector for oil-wells	G. M. Mombray	Titusville, Pa	Nov. 1, 1864	44, 878
Ejector for oil-wells	G. M. Mowbray	Titusville, Pa	Dec. 13, 1864	45, 464
Ejector for oil-wells	G. M. Mowbray	Titusville, Pa	Jan. 10, 1865	45, 849
Ejector for oil-wells	G. M. Mowbray	Titusville, Pa	Feb. 21, 1865	46, 485
Ejector for oil-wells, Oil	T. B. Gunning	New York, N. Y	Nov. 22, 1864	45, 153

Index of patents issued from the United States Patent Office from 1790 *to* 1873, *inclusive*—Continued.

Invention.	Inventor.	Residence.	Date.	No.
Ejector for oil-wells, Oil	W. Reed	Pittsburgh, Pa	Dec. 31, 1872	134, 397
Ejector for refuse matter from steam-vessels	J. Palmer	Sandisfield, Mass	Sept. 26, 1865	50, 153
Ejector for steam-boiler furnaces	J. N. Snowdon and H. Wilkins	Brownsville, Pa	June 13, 1865	48, 218
Ejector for steam-vessels, Ash	G. P. Hunt	United States Navy	Dec. 3, 1872	133, 535
Ejector for steam-vessels, Refuse	J. Brown, jr., and S. R. Brooks	New York, N. Y., and Saint Louis, Mo.	Jan. 12, 1864	41, 192
Ejector, Insect-powder	S. Rose and N. Goldsmith	Cincinnati, Ohio	Nov. 29, 1870	109, 762
Ejector, Liquid	A. Brear	Saugatuck, Conn	Aug. 20, 1865	49, 602
Ejector, Oil	R. Boeklen	Brooklyn, N. Y	Nov. 21, 1865	51, 068
Ejector, Oil	A. Brear	Saugatuck, Conn	May 23, 1865	47, 793
Ejector, Oil	E. Crooker	Buffalo, N. Y	Apr. 25, 1865	47, 399
Ejector, Oil	W. R. Greenleaf	Buffalo, N. Y	Mar. 28, 1865	47, 011
Ejector, Oil	W. R. Greenleaf	Buffalo, N. Y	June 13, 1865	48, 170
Ejector, Oil	W. W. Hubbell	Philadelphia, Pa	Oct. 31, 1865	50, 710
Ejector, Oil	G. E. Mills	New York, N. Y	Apr. 25, 1865	47, 444
Ejector, Oil	G. M. Mowbray	Titusville, Pa	Mar. 21, 1865	46, 925
Ejector, Oil	F. S. Pease	Buffalo, N. Y	Mar. 21, 1865	46, 931
Ejector, Oil	F. S. Pease	Buffalo, N. Y	Mar. 28, 1865	47, 034
Ejector, Oil	S. F. Schoonmaker	New York, N. Y	Apr. 11, 1865	47, 226
Ejector, Oil	S. F. Schoonmaker	New York, N. Y	Apr. 11, 1865	47, 227
Ejector, Oil	H. Searl	Rochester, N. Y	Mar. 14, 1865	46, 824
Ejector, Oil	H. Searle	Rochester, N. Y	Jan. 29, 1867	61, 571
Ejector, Oil	J. Y. Smith	Alexandria, Va	May 23, 1865	47, 871
Ejector, Oil	J. Y. Smith	Alexandria, Va	June 6, 1865	48, 106
Ejector, Oil	L. W. Turrell, S. Stanton, and L. C. Ward.	Newburgh, N. Y	Apr. 4, 1865	47, 174
Ejector, Oil	G. L. Witsil and E. Burke	Philadelphia, Pa	Apr. 4, 1865	47, 148
Ejector, Perfume	C. L. Fehrenson	New York, N. Y	Apr. 12, 1870	101, 848
Ejector, Sand	E. W. Poston	Fort Wayne, Ind	Aug. 6, 1867	67, 580
Ejector, Sand	J. Thayer	Topeka, Kans	Apr. 1, 1873	137, 507
Ejector, Sand and seed	M. Christiansen	Winneconne, Wis	May 23, 1871	115, 164
Ejector, Steam	N. L. Chappell	New York, N. Y	Aug. 6, 1867	67, 413
Ejector, Steam air	J. Y. Smith	Pittsburgh, Pa	Mar. 11, 1873	136, 780
Ejector, Steam and air	S. E. Hewes	Albany, N. Y	Oct. 30, 1866	59, 221
Ejector, Steam-operated water	H. Coll	Millville Borough, Pa	June 8, 1869	90, 930
Ejector, Steam water	R. D. and W. F. Cox	Philadelphia, Pa	May 7, 1872	126, 525
Ejector, Steam water	J. Habermehl and H. Kleiman	Allegheny, Pa	Mar. 26, 1872	124, 895
Ejector, Steam water	H. S. Ross	New York, N. Y	May 26, 1868	78, 395
Ejector, Water	N. L. Chappell	New York, N. Y	Aug. 29, 1865	49, 603
Ejector, Water	H. Coll	Millvale, Pa	Oct. 21, 1873	143, 884
Ejector, Water	T. J. Jones	Madison, N. J	May 7, 1867	64, 539
Ejector, Water	H. S. Lansdell	New York, N. Y	Mar. 26, 1867	63, 264
Elastic bands, Clasp for	R. P. Staats	New York, N. Y	Dec. 2, 1873	145, 073
Elastic chair	S. Gragg	Boston, Mass	Aug. 31, 1808	....
Elastic clamp for shoemakers, &c	T. R. Hoyt	Goffstown, N. H	Dec. 6, 1817	....
Elastic coupling for mill-shafting, &c	W. S. Reeder	Saint Louis, Mo	Oct. 13, 1857	18, 412
Elastic cups, dippers, &c., Manufacture of	T. Smith, jr	Boston, Mass	Dec. 16, 1862	37, 181
Elastic cushion for horses' feet	J. Haseltine and C. L. Wheeler	Melrose and Cambridge, Mass.	Sept. 21, 1869	95, 107
Elastic cushion for piercing implements	B. D. Sanders	Wellsburgh, W. Va	Apr. 5, 1864	42, 228
Elastic fabric	H. Hynes	New York, N. Y	Mar. 7, 1865	46, 674
Elastic fabric	J. W. Newell	New Brunswick, N. J	Aug. 24, 1858	21, 270
Elastic fabrics, Apparatus for the manufacture of	C. A. Ensign	Naugatuck, Conn	Aug. 30, 1870	106, 924
Elastic gate, Self-adjusting	P. S. Reist	Oregon, Pa	Oct. 8, 1867	69, 704
Elastic goods	E. Brown	Rindge, N. H	Sept. 26, 1854	11, 716
Elastic hollow molded articles, Manufacture of	D. D. Parmelee	Salem, Mass	Jan. 17, 1860	26, 864
Elastic mold	T. Taylor	Washington, D. C	Jan. 29, 1867	61, 641
Elastic or yielding roller, Driving gear of	L. M. Woodcock	Auburn, N. Y	Aug. 6, 1872	130, 349
Elastic roller	L. R. Streeter	Chelsea, Mass	Apr. 19, 1864	42, 415
Elastic-rubber straps, Manufacture of	C. Goodyear, jr	New York, N. Y	May 26, 1863	38, 674
Elastic seat, Portable adjustable	H. Perkins	Mansfield, Mass	Sept. 29, 1868	82, 636
Elastic shirred goods, Machinery for making	R. Solis	New Brunswick, N. J	Mar. 26, 1861	31, 832
Elastic-spring cushion, &c	S. Blair	New Haven, Conn	Aug. 1, 1823	....
Elastic springs, Manufacture of	S. G. Randall	Providence, R. I	Aug. 21, 1866	57, 377
Elastic strap for garments	J. W. Boughton	Chicago, Ill	Dec. 4, 1866	60, 131
Elastic supporter, Ladies'	G. C. Stillson	Derby, Conn	July 11, 1871	116, 882
Elastic-tube clasp	E. A. Day	Oberlin, Ohio	Dec. 17, 1872	134, 038
Elastic tubes, Regulating-clasp for	W. Bunce	Oberlin, Ohio	Mar. 28, 1871	113, 016
Elastic washer	C. Dittman	Leacock, Pa	July 2, 1872	128, 602
Elastic washer	J. P. Verre	Philadelphia, Pa	Dec. 26, 1871	122, 141
Elbow-joint band	S. M. Parse	Newark, N. J	Nov. 11, 1862	36, 911
Elbows, Manufacture of curved	F. G. and W. F. Niedringhaus	Saint Louis, Mo	Jan. 12, 1869	85, 843
Electric alarm	C. T. Mason	Sumter, S. C	May 11, 1869	89, 936
Electric and vapor chair	M. A. Hayward	Brooklyn, N. Y	Sept. 26, 1871	119, 230
Electric bath	M. W. House	Cleveland, Ohio	Feb. 18, 1862	34, 425
Electric bath	M. W. House	Cleveland, Ohio	May 5, 1863	38, 389
Electric battery	L. Bastet	Tarrytown, N. Y	Sept. 26, 1871	119, 298
Electric battery	T. Chutaux	Paris, France	July 5, 1870	105, 042
Electric battery	T. Chutaux	Paris, France	July 5, 1870	105, 043
Electric battery	V. Himmer	New York, N. Y	Oct. 10, 1871	119, 763
Electric battery for telegraphing and other purposes.	D. M. Cook	Mansfield, Ohio	Apr. 4, 1871	113, 399
Electric battery, Compound switch for	J. Kidder	New York, N. Y	July 26, 1870	105, 697
Electric currents, Apparatus for regulating and measuring the intensity of.	J. Lacassagne and R. Thiers	Lyons, France	Mar. 16, 1858	19, 642
Electric currents, Method of integrating inconstant.	C. Kirchhof	New York, N. Y	Feb. 26, 1861	31, 545
Electric fire and burglar alarm	E. Fontaine	Fort Wayne, Ind	Aug. 17, 1869	93, 816
Electric light	A. A. Meynial	New York, N. Y	Feb. 20, 1872	123, 923
Electric light	J. F. May	London, England	Oct. 8, 1861	33, 457
Electric light	J. F. May	London, England	Oct. 8, 1861	33, 458
Electric light, Producing the	E. L. C. d'Ivernois	Paris, France	May 9, 1871	114, 652
Electric machine	A. L. Fleury	New York, N. Y	July 14, 1868	79, 819
Electric machine, Frictional	R. Cornelius	Philadelphia, Pa	May 21, 1861	32, 354
Electric switch	S. Gardiner, jr	New York, N. Y	Nov. 19, 1867	71, 158
Electrical apparatus, Connecting-post for	T. Wishart	Clayton, Del	Apr. 15, 1873	137, 810
Electrical apparatus, Construction of	T. Brown	Albany, N. Y	Dec. 20, 1816	....

Index of patents issued from the United States Patent Office from 1790 *to* 1873, *inclusive*—Continued.

Invention.	Inventor.	Residence.	Date.	No.
Electrical apparatus, Keys for use with	J. Olmsted	Providence, R. I	Dec. 10, 1872	133, 797
Electrical apparatus, Pole-changer for	J. E. Smith	New York, N. Y	June 11, 1872	127, 809
Electrical apparatus, Portable	F. H. Varley	London, England	Apr. 29, 1873	138, 455
Electrical apparatus, Screw-post for	S. E. Field	San Francisco, Cal	July 8, 1873	140, 618
Electrical bath	C. Winterburn and W. Kent	Cincinnati, Ohio	July 14, 1868	79, 929
Electrical-current breaker, Automatic	C. Robinson and C. T. Chester.	New York, N. Y	Jan. 1, 1856	14, 032
Electrical heating apparatus	G. B. Simpson	Washington, D. C	Sept. 20, 1859	25, 532
Electrical indicator	S. S. Laws	New York, N. Y	Dec. 31, 1867	72, 742
Electrical indicator	G. Little	Rutherford Park, N. J	Apr. 9, 1872	125, 586
Electrical indicator for elevators	J. H. Corey	New York, N. Y	Apr. 1, 1872	137, 422
Electrical machine	E. S. Blake	Allegheny County, Pa	Mar. 28, 1848	5, 485
Electrical machine	H. J. Smith	Boston, Mass	Aug. 10, 1869	93, 563
Electrical machine, Holtz	E. S. Ritchie	Brookline, Mass	Feb. 4, 1868	74, 139
Electrical machines from moisture, Protecting frictional.	C. A. Seely	New York, N. Y	Dec. 13, 1859	26, 445
Electrical-pole changer	J. E. Smith	New York, N. Y	July 23, 1872	129, 867
Electrical regulator for transmitting-instruments	T. A. Edison	Newark, N. J	Sept. 9, 1873	142, 688
Electrical vacuum and vapor treatment, Apparatus for.	M. H. Utley	Montreal, Canada	May 23, 1871	115, 137
Electricity, Apparatus for obtaining light by frictional.	M. Wesolowski	New York, N. Y	Jan. 29, 1861	31, 273
Electricity as a remedial agent, Apparatus for using.	G. Munroe	Philadelphia, Pa	Feb. 28, 1871	112, 270
Electricity, Method of utilizing atmospheric	H. C. Vion	Paris, France	June 19, 1860	28, 793
Electricity, Remedial application of	M. W. House	Cleveland, Ohio	Sept. 1, 1863	39, 733
Electrifying-machine	E. Cole	Richmond, Ohio	July 22, 1843	3, 191
Electro and permanent magnets to render telegraphing-magnets easy of adjustment, Combination of.	E. F. Barnes	Brooklyn, N. Y	July 20, 1858	20, 930
Electro-bathing apparatus	W. W. Karshner	Cincinnati, Ohio	Jan. 25, 1859	22, 733
Electro-deposition of metals	I. Adams, jr	Boston, Mass	Mar. 22, 1870	100, 961
Electro-gilding iron	H. Tucker	Newton, Mass	June 1, 1869	90, 893
Electro-heating apparatus	W. L. Burton	Richmond, Va	Mar. 23, 1869	88, 006
Electro-magnet	S. G. Cabell	Quincy, Ill	June 25, 1867	66, 001
Electro-magnet	C. T. Chester	New York, N. Y	Sept. 4, 1860	29, 862
Electro-magnet	W. E. Davis	Jersey City, N. J	Nov. 9, 1869	96, 554
Electro-magnet	M. S. Frost	New York, N. Y	May 24, 1870	103, 440
Electro-magnet	A. G. Holcomb	New York, N. Y	June 4, 1861	32, 478
Electro-magnet	J. S. Jenness	Bangor, Me	July 23, 1861	32, 874
Electro-magnet	H. M. Paine	Newark, N. J	May 10, 1870	102, 856
Electro-magnet	H. M. Paine	Newark, N. J	May 17, 1870	103, 230
Electro-magnet	E. Provost	New York, N. Y	Sept. 19, 1871	119, 176
Electro-magnet	W. W. Smith	Cincinnati, Ohio	Aug. 16, 1870	106, 418
Electro-magnet	I. P. Tice	New York, N. Y	Apr. 2, 1872	125, 151
Electro-magnet circuit	J. E. Smith	New York, N. Y	Apr. 8, 1873	137, 730
Electro-magnet sector	H. M. Paine	Newark, N. J	May 31, 1870	103, 768
Electro-magnets, Construction of	H. M. Paine	Newark, N. J	May 17, 1870	103, 231
Electro-magnets, Induction-coil for	J. B. Lyon and A. Doll	Cleveland, Ohio	Oct. 2, 1866	58, 439
Electro-magnets, Mode of changing the poles of	N. Walkly	Tuscaloosa, Ala	June 27, 1838	809
Electro magnetic adjuster	T. A. Edison	Newark, N. J	Jan. 14, 1873	134, 868
Electro-magnetic alarm	J. G. Butler	New York, N. Y	July 6, 1869	92, 260
Electro-magnetic alarm	M. G. Crane	Newton, Mass	Aug. 11, 1868	80, 922
Electro-magnetic alarm	W. B. Guernsey	Jersey City, N. J	Apr. 30, 1872	126, 287
Electro-magnetic alarm	T. S. Hall	Stamford, Conn	July 19, 1870	105, 447
Electro magnetic alarm	A. R. Pope	Somerville, Mass	June 21, 1853	9, 802
Electro-magnetic alarm for railway-car	W. Gillett	Ypsilanti, Mich	Aug. 31, 1869	94, 198
Electro-magnetic apparatus	H. N. Baker	Binghamton, N. Y	Sept. 4, 1860	29, 850
Electro-magnetic apparatus	S. Gardiner, jr	New York, N. Y	July 11, 1871	116, 944
Electro-magnetic apparatus	J. Kidder	New York, N. Y	Sept. 18, 1860	30, 068
Electro-magnetic apparatus	G. Little	Rutherford Park, N. J	Dec. 26, 1871	122, 266
Electro-magnetic apparatus	J. W. Powell	New York, N. Y	Mar. 26, 1872	125, 0.8
Electro-magnetic apparatus	R. Sayer	New York, N. Y	July 23, 1872	129, 752
Electro-magnetic apparatus, Circuit-closer for	M. G. Farmer	Salem, Mass	May 14, 1872	126, 627
Electro-magnetic apparatus with tooth-forceps, Mode of connecting.	J. J. Clark	Philadelphia, Pa	Nov. 16, 1858	22, 063
Electro-magnetic-bathing apparatus	J. Young	New York, N. Y	May 14, 1861	32, 332
Electro-magnetic battery	P. Bruso	Erie, Pa	Apr. 16, 1867	63, 848
Electro-magnetic batteries to car-brakes, Application of.	S. D. Carpenter	Madison, Wis	Jan. 19, 1858	19, 132
Electro-magnetic burglar-alarms, Automatic circuit-closer for.	J. P. Snyder	Brooklyn, N. Y	Sept. 13, 1870	107, 301
Electro-magnetic currents constant or intermittent, Device for making.	M. Marshall	Lowell, Mass	Aug. 9, 1859	25, 023
Electro-magnetic engine	T. C. Avery	New York, N. Y	Feb. 25, 1851	7, 950
Electro-magnetic engine	A. P. Berlioz	Paris, France	Oct. 16, 1866	58, 960
Electro magnetic engine	H. S. Daggett	La Fayette, Ind	Jan. 9, 1872	122, 572
Electro-magnetic engine	A. J. B. De Morat	Philadelphia, Pa	July 28, 1868	80, 463
Electro magnetic engine	A. E. Dupas	New Orleans, La	Aug. 17, 1869	93, 689
Electro-magnetic engine	M. G. Farmer	Salem, Mass	May 14, 1872	126, 628
Electro-magnetic engine	C. J. B. Gaume	Davenport, Iowa	Apr. 2, 1867	63, 380
Electro-magnetic engine	C. J. B. Gaume	New York, N. Y	Mar. 16, 1869	87, 835
Electro-magnetic engine	C. V. Gaume	Williamsburgh, N. Y	Jan. 23, 1872	122, 944
Electro-magnetic engine	J. S. Gustin	Trenton, N. J	Sept. 28, 1852	9, 291
Electro-magnetic engine	J. S. Gustin	Trenton, N. J	Oct. 12, 1852	9, 320
Electro-magnetic engine	S. Jones	New Orleans, La	Nov. 21, 1871	121, 173
Electro-magnetic engine	J. H. Lillie	Joliet, Ill	Apr. 16, 1850	7, 287
Electro-magnetic engine	J. Neff	Philadelphia, Pa	Jan. 7, 1851	7, 889
Electro-magnetic engine	W. H. Odell	Yonkers, N. Y	July 23, 1872	129, 857
Electro-magnetic engine	C. G. Page	Washington, D. C	Jan. 31, 1854	10, 480
Electro-magnetic engine	H. M. Paine	Newark, N. J	May 17, 1870	103, 228
Electro-magnetic engine	L. C. Stuart	New York, N. Y	June 2, 1868	78, 619
Electro-magnetic engine	W. G. Thornton	Victoria, Tex	Apr. 9, 1872	125, 504
Electro-magnetic engine	J. P. Tirrel	Charlestown, Mass	Mar. 31, 1870	103, 798
Electro-magnetic engine	J. P. Tirrel	Charlestown, Mass	Aug. 29, 1871	118, 561
Electro-magnetic engine	M. Vergnes	New York, N. Y	Apr. 15, 1856	14, 682
Electro-magnetic engine	M. Vergnes	New York, N. Y	Oct. 2, 1860	30, 272
Electro-magnetic engine	W. Wickersham	Boston, Mass	Oct. 15, 1867	69, 880

Index of patents issued from the United States Patent Office from 1790 *to* 1873, *inclusive*—Continued.

Invention.	Inventor.	Residence.	Date.	No.
Electro-magnetic engine	W. Wickersham	Boston, Mass	June 2, 1868	78, 629
Electro-magnetic engine	W. Wickersham	Boston, Mass	Mar. 19, 1872	124, 868
Electro-magnetic engine	F. Yeiser	Lexington, Ky	Aug. 3, 1858	21, 105
Electro-magnetic gate and signal-apparatus for railways.	W. Robinson	Brooklyn, N. Y	July 19, 1870	105, 493
Electro-magnetic gate-operating apparatus	W. Robinson	Brooklyn, N. Y	July 19, 1870	105, 494
Electro-magnetic helix	M. Vergnes	New York, N. Y	Oct. 2, 1860	30, 271
Electro-magnetic indicator	W. D. Smith	Washington, D. C	Jan. 31, 1871	111, 394
Electro-magnetic indicator for burglar-alarms, &c	J. P. Snyder	Brooklyn, N. Y	May 24, 1870	103, 383
Electro-magnetic instrument	L. L. Duerden	Brooklyn, N. Y	July 25, 1871	117, 268
Electro-magnetic lock	H. Arden	Saint Louis, Mo	Nov. 8, 1870	108, 952
Electro-magnetic lock	J. C. Smith	Brooklyn, N. Y	Dec. 21, 1869	98, 114
Electro-magnetic machine	W. H. Burnap and J. A. Bradshaw.	Lowell, Mass	Mar. 8, 1859	23, 214
Electro-magnetic machine, &c	T. Cook	New York, N. Y	Aug. 25, 1840	1, 735
Electro-magnetic machine	A. E. Dupas	New Orleans, La	Feb. 1, 1870	99, 300
Electro-magnetic machine	T. Hall	Boston, Mass	June 21 1859	24, 459
Electro-magnetic machine	J. Kidder	New York, N. Y	Aug. 10 1869	93, 625
Electro-magnetic machine	J. W. Powell	New York, N. Y	May 30, 1871	115, 518
Electro-magnetic machine for shocks	S. B. Smith	New York, N. Y	June 4, 1850	7, 420
Electro-magnetic machines, Commutator for	V. Barjon	New York, N. Y	July 16, 1872	129, 085
Electro-magnetic meter	S. Gardiner, jr	New York, N. Y	Oct. 29, 1872	132, 569
Electro-magnetic motor	J. S. Camacho	Havana, Cuba	July 16, 1872	129, 000
Electro-magnetic motor	S. C. Carter	Richmond, Ind	May 13, 1873	138, 855
Electro-magnetic motor	L. Finger	Cambridge, Mass	July 26, 1870	105, 663
Electro-magnetic motor	L. T. Lindsey	Jackson, Tenn	June 29, 1869	92, 066
Electro-magnetic motor	L. T. Lindsey	Jackson, Tenn	May 3, 1870	102, 562
Electro-magnetic motor	L. T. Lindsey	Jackson, Tenn	Aug. 16, 1870	106, 493
Electro-magnetic motor	G. Little	Rutherford Park, N. J	Nov. 2, 1869	96, 332
Electro-magnetic motor	H. M. Paine	Newark, N. J	Mar. 21, 1871	112, 841
Electro-magnetic motor	W. H. Richardson	Albany, N. Y	May 28, 1872	127, 369
Electro-magnetic motor	A. Schreiber	Brooklyn, N. Y	Sept. 17, 1872	131, 377
Electro-magnetic motor	J. Taggart	Boston, Mass	June 11, 1872	127, 810
Electro-magnetic motor	M. H. Utley and A. Ross	Montreal, Canada	Oct. 10, 1871	119, 899
Electro-magnetic regulator	F. F. A. Achard	Paris, France	Sept. 5, 1865	49, 842
Electro-magnetic separator	A. H. Balch and W. D. E. Nelson.	Montreal, Canada	June 6, 1871	115, 561
Electro-magnetic separator	A. Ross	Montreal, Canada	Jan. 2, 1872	122, 493
Electro-magnetic signal	S. F. B. Morse	New York, N. Y	June 20, 1840	1, 647
Electro-magnetic-signal apparatus	A. Hahl	Washington, D. C	Feb. 28, 1871	112, 242
Electro-magnetic-signal apparatus	G. B. Hicks	Cleveland, Ohio	Aug. 24, 1869	93, 993
Electro-magnetic-signal apparatus for railway-crossings, &c.	W. Robinson	Brooklyn, N. Y	Nov. 22, 1870	109, 549
Electro-magnetic watchman's register	H. D. Sheppard	New York, N. Y	Apr. 9, 1872	125, 624
Electro-medical battery	H. Fritz	Cleveland, Ohio	Feb. 25, 1868	74, 905
Electromotor escapement	T. A. Edison	New York, N. Y	May 17, 1870	103, 035
Electromotors, Armature for	S. Jones	New Orleans, La	Aug. 29, 1871	118, 538
Electrodes, Fibrous covering for spiral	E. Maynard	Brooklyn, N. Y	Feb. 8, 1859	22, 922
Electrophorus	R. Cornelius	Philadelphia, Pa	May 21, 1861	32, 353
Electrophorus	D. F. Launy	Philadelphia, Pa	Aug. 23, 1811	....
Electro-photo damaskening and enameling	A. G. Morvan	New York, N. Y	Oct. 4, 1870	108, 041
Electroplated rollers, Constructing	J. W. Wilcox	West Roxbury, Mass	Apr. 12, 1859	23, 633
Electroplating	J. P. Woodworth	Brooklyn, N. Y	Nov. 17, 1868	84, 243
Electroplating and gilding cast iron	H. Tucker	Newton, Mass	June 1, 1869	90, 894
Electroplating and platedware	H. W. Wright	Taunton, Mass	June 30, 1868	79, 427
Electroplating-apparatus	W. Gates	New Haven, Conn	July 28, 1868	80, 402
Electroplating-apparatus	H. W. Wright	Taunton, Mass	Mar. 22, 1870	101, 075
Electroplating-frame	W. H. Watrous	Hartford, Conn	June 2, 1868	78, 497
Electroplating iron and other metals with copper, Process of.	J. E. Walcott	Boston, Mass	Feb. 18, 1862	34, 470
Electroplating iron, steel, &c., Process of	C. Beslay	Paris, France	Oct. 21, 1862	36, 750
Electroplating iron with copper, &c., Apparatus for.	A. L. Freeman	South Boston, Mass	July 16, 1872	129, 124
Electroplating letters and numbers on metallic plates for signs, &c.	J. J. Pratt	New York, N. Y	Mar. 28, 1871	113, 090
Electroplating steel wires for piano-strings, &c., Mode of.	M. Miller, jr	Vienna, Austria	Mar. 11, 1862	34, 640
Electroplating the interior of pipes and tubes with silver, nickel, &c.	D. D. Parmelee	New York, N. Y	Apr. 25, 1871	114, 191
Electroplating with alloys of gold	A. Berthoud	New York, N. Y	Nov. 20, 1860	30, 663
Electroplating with antimony	J. S. Howard	Mansfield, Mass	Feb. 22, 1870	100, 038
Electroplating with brass and other alloys	S. Rust, jr	Cincinnati, Ohio	Dec. 21, 1869	98, 110
Electroplating with copper, &c, the surfaces of mirrors, &c.	J. Von Liebig	Munich, Bavaria	Nov. 12, 1861	33, 721
Electroplating with nickel	I. Adams, jr	Boston, Mass	Apr. 4, 1871	113, 612
Electroplating with nickel and other metals	G. W. Beardslee	Brooklyn, N. Y	July 30, 1872	129, 881
Electroplating with nickel, Mode of	I. Adams, jr	Boston, Mass	May 25, 1869	90, 332
Electroplating with nickel, Process of	W. H. Remington	Boston, Mass	Oct. 6, 1868	82, 877
Electroplating with tin	J. E. Bingham	Sheffield, Great Britain	June 13, 1871	115, 926
Electro-pneumatic dispatch-transmitter	C. F. Varley	London, England	June 9, 1868	78, 845
Electrotype and stereotype plates, Manufacture of curved.	H. and H. W. Lovejoy and J. H. Ferguson.	New York, N. Y	Jan. 19, 1869	86, 021
Electrotype-backing pan	W. A. Leggo	Quebec, Canada	Aug. 4, 1863	39, 410
Electrotype die or mold for molding plastic material.	D. Scrymgeour	Foxborough, Mass	Feb. 7, 1871	111, 688
Electrotype-mold	S. P. Knight	Brooklyn, N. Y	May 2, 1871	114, 447
Electrotype-molds, Coating	S. P. Knight	Brooklyn, N. Y	Sept. 10, 1872	131, 169
Electrotype-molds, Machine for coating	H. Lovejoy and R. Wheeler	Brooklyn, N. Y	Sept. 14, 1858	21, 509
Electrotype-molds with plumbago, Machine for coating surface of.	S. D. Tucker	New York, N. Y	Dec. 29, 1868	85, 411
Electrotype-plates, Method of backing	A. H. Jocelyn	New York, N. Y	July 7, 1857	17, 741
Electrotype-plates, Mode of backing	W. Filmer and E. Bookhout	New York, N. Y	Dec. 2, 1856	16, 141
Electrotype-plates, Mode of forming curved	W. H. Elliot	Plattsburgh, N. Y	May 3, 1859	23, 836
Electrotype-plates, Production of	S. P. Knight	New York, N. Y	May 25, 1858	20, 353
Electrotype-printing block	T. Crossley	Rockville, Conn	Nov. 1, 1859	25, 953
Electrotypes, Forming curved	A. Judson	Brooklyn, N. Y	Aug. 6, 1872	130, 140
Electrotyping	J. A. Adams	Brooklyn, N. Y	Apr. 19, 1870	102, 077
Electrotyping	W. A. Leggo	Montreal, Canada	Oct. 3, 1871	119, 622

Index of patents issued from the United States Patent Office from 1790 *to* 1873, *inclusive*—Continued.

Invention.	Inventor.	Residence.	Date.	No.
Electrotyping	G. Mathiot	Washington, D. C	Dec. 10, 1850	7, 821
Electrotyping-battery	P. S. Hoe	New York, N. Y	Jan. 25, 1870	99, 192
Electrotyping iron and steel with silver	A. Law	Kingston, Canada	Nov. 29, 1870	109, 633
Electrotyping-machine	J. A. Adams	Brooklyn, N. Y	Sept. 4, 1855	13, 516
Electrotyping, Method of etching plates for	A. and H. T. Dawson	London, England	July 22, 1873	140, 995
Electrotyping purposes, Process of obtaining mold for.	W. A. Leggo	Montreal, Canada	May 30, 1871	115, 490
Electrotyping, Surface conductor for	S. Hallock	New York, N. Y	Apr. 2, 1867	63, 512
Elevated way	H. W. Farley	Oswego, Ill	Apr. 8, 1873	137, 667
Elevated way	H. W. Farley	Oswego, Ill	Dec. 16, 1873	145, 638
Elevating and conveying device	W. Louden	Fairfield, Iowa	Sept. 24, 1867	69, 107
Elevating and transporting device	E. B. Coffin	Olneyville, R. I	June 28, 1864	43, 291
Elevating and weighing apparatus	J. H. Brookmire	Saint Louis, Mo	Mar. 23, 1869	88, 124
Elevating-apparatus	P. R. Berry	Youngstown, Ohio	June 14, 1870	104, 102
Elevating-apparatus	M. A. Blakley and J. Cahill	Chattanooga, Tenn	Feb. 4, 1873	135, 511
Elevating-block	W. H. Hawley	Utica, N. Y	Sept. 17, 1867	68, 874
Elevating-jack	S. Lauchli	Saint Louis, Mo	June 28, 1864	43, 369
Elevating-machine	G. A. Dupuis	Detroit, Mich	July 1, 1873	140, 485
Elevating-machine	D. L. Miller	Madison, N. J	Feb. 18, 1862	34, 440
Elevating power-engine and compressing-machine for raising vessels, &c.	B. Bruff	Rochester, N. Y	Sept. 13, 1831	....
Elevator: *See* Balance-elevator. Barrel and box elevator. Beer-elevator. Bucket-elevator. Building-elevator. Car-elevator. Car-body elevator. Chain-elevator. Coal-elevator. Corn-elevator. Cultivator-bar elevator. Dress-elevator. Fireman's elevator. Fluid-elevator. Fluid or grain elevator. Freight-elevator. Gear-elevator. Grain-elevator. Hay-elevator. Hod-elevator. Hog-elevator. Hose-elevator. Hydraulic elevator. Hydraulic-power elevator. Ice-elevator. Inclined-plane elevator. Last-block elevator. Liquid-elevator. Merchandise-elevator. Millstone-elevator. Mortar and brick elevator. Passenger and freight elevator. Patient-elevator. Peat-elevator. Platform-elevator. Pneumatic elevator. Portable elevator. Rotary fluid-elevator. Sash-elevator. Scaffold-elevator. Self-elevator. Sirup-pan elevator. Skirt-elevator. Sorghum-elevator. Steam-elevator. Store-house elevator. Straw-elevator. Sucker-rod elevator. Tailing-elevator. Telescopic-platform elevator. Tobacco-elevator. Wall-elevator. Warehouse-elevator. Water-elevator. Wind-elevator. Wool-elevator.				
Elevator	E. H. Ashcroft	Lynn, Mass	Nov. 5, 1867	70, 387
Elevator	E. H. Ashcroft and J. R. Brown	Boston, Mass	Aug. 25, 1868	81, 325
Elevator	L. Atwood	New York, N. Y	May 28, 1872	127, 138
Elevator	C. W. Baldwin	Boston, Mass	Nov. 19, 1867	70, 941
Elevator	C. W. Baldwin	Boston, Mass	Nov. 15, 1870	109, 169
Elevator	C. W. Baldwin	Boston, Mass	Feb. 20, 1872	123, 761
Elevator	J. S. Baldwin	Newark, N. J	Nov. 12, 1867	70, 777
Elevator	J. S. Baldwin	Newark, N. J	Apr. 14, 1868	76, 692
Elevator	J. S. Baldwin	Newark, N. J	Apr. 14, 1868	76, 693
Elevator	J. S. Baldwin	Newark, N. J	May 20, 1873	138, 985
Elevator	J. M. Bean	Watertown, Mass	Mar. 11, 1873	136, 580
Elevator	A. Betteley	Boston, Mass	May 3, 1859	23, 818
Elevator	J. Bishop	Austin, Tex	June 13, 1871	115, 813
Elevator	V. C. Blair	Wheatland, Pa	June 6, 1871	115, 683
Elevator	A. Blass and D. Brown	Brooklyn, N. Y	Dec. 31, 1872	134, 416
Elevator	J. H. Blohm	New York, N. Y	Feb. 4, 1873	135, 398
Elevator	C. D. Bois	Fishkill Landing, N. Y	Mar. 18, 1873	136, 978
Elevator	E. Boyden	Lowell, Mass	Sept. 9, 1873	142, 555
Elevator	P. Brand	Springfield, Ill	July 28, 1868	80, 445
Elevator	W. D. Brooks	Bethany, Pa	Dec. 8, 1868	84, 794
Elevator	P. Byrne	Nashville, Tenn	Oct. 3, 1871	119, 572
Elevator	P. Byrne	Nashville, Tenn	Oct. 1, 1872	131, 809
Elevator	S. B. Castle	Cortland, N. Y	Mar. 10, 1868	75, 366
Elevator	D. H. Chamberlain	West Roxbury, Mass	June 20, 1871	116, 156
Elevator	T. F. Christman	Wilson, N. C	Oct. 9, 1866	58, 715
Elevator	G. R. Clarke	New York, N. Y	June 9, 1868	78, 646
Elevator	C. W. Collyer	Marblehead, Mass	July 1, 1873	140, 473
Elevator	A. W. Cram	Litchfield, Ill	June 17, 1873	140, 017
Elevator	A. B. Darling and J. Bones	New York, N. Y	May 21, 1872	126, 935
Elevator	J. G. Drew	Boston, Mass	Aug. 6, 1872	130, 112
Elevator	W. Edson	Boston, Mass	Dec. 7, 1869	97, 489
Elevator	W. Elmes	Georgetown, D. C	Oct. 22, 1872	132, 459
Elevator	Z. C. Favor	Chicago, Ill	Mar. 14, 1871	112, 573
Elevator	C. R. Foreman	West Branch, N. Y	Sept. 6, 1870	107, 028
Elevator	P. Griffhorn	Akron, Ohio	Feb. 6, 1872	123, 391
Elevator	W. Hamilton	Allegheny City, Pa	June 28, 1870	104, 731
Elevator	M. Hanford	Boston, Mass	Feb. 1, 1870	99, 433
Elevator	M. Hanford	Boston, Mass	Mar. 26, 1872	124, 952
Elevator	M. Hanford	Boston, Mass	Dec. 24, 1872	134, 273
Elevator	D. D. Hanson	Weare, N. H	July 19, 1870	105, 449
Elevator	O. P. Hatfield	New York, N. Y	Mar. 4, 1862	34, 572
Elevator	A. G. Hawkes	Baltimore, Md	July 16, 1872	129, 339
Elevator	A. C. Herron	Boston, Mass	Apr. 22, 1873	138, 154
Elevator	E. Hicks	North Hempstead, N. Y	Mar. 26, 1867	63, 248

Index of patents issued from the United States Patent Office from 1790 *to* 1873, *inclusive*—Continued.

Invention.	Inventor.	Residence.	Date.	No.
Elevator	N. D. Hinman	Pleasant Vale, Conn	Nov. 29, 1864	45, 245
Elevator	J. E. Hollister	Calais, Vt	Dec. 8, 1868	84, 744
Elevator	E. T. Hope	Philadelphia, Pa	Aug. 18, 1868	81, 276
Elevator	G. W. Hubbard	Philadelphia, Pa	Sept. 23, 1873	143, 013
Elevator	A. B. Hunt	Matteson, Mich	Oct. 27, 1868	83, 385
Elevator	G. Joslin	Boston, Mass	June 23, 1868	79, 129
Elevator	J. T. Ketchledge	Burns, Mich	Sept. 14, 1869	94, 896
Elevator	D. Knowles	Philadelphia, Pa	Sept. 10, 1872	131, 170
Elevator	A. Lawton	Philadelphia, Pa	Aug. 30, 1870	106, 841
Elevator	J. S. Lester	Knoxville, Tenn	July 20, 1869	92, 847
Elevator	W. Livingstone	Brooklyn, N. Y	Aug. 13, 1872	130, 509
Elevator	W. Livingstone and W. F. Holske.	Brooklyn, N. Y	Jan. 16, 1872	122, 839
Elevator	W. Lowden	Cedar Township, Iowa	Nov. 17, 1868	84, 127
Elevator	G. B. Lowe	Jamesville, N. Y	Aug. 8, 1871	117, 789
Elevator	J. Macomb	Chicago, Ill	May 30, 1871	115, 335
Elevator	J. Macomb	Chicago, Ill	Aug 29, 1871	118, 468
Elevator	M. Mageean and G. W. Marks.	Chicago, Ill	Apr. 29, 1873	138, 337
Elevator	J. F. Marsh	Littleton, N. H	Apr. 15, 1873	137, 940
Elevator	W. K. Marvin	New York, N. Y	Nov. 15, 1870	109, 331
Elevator	G. McKinzie	Zanesville, Ohio	Nov. 15, 1870	109, 232
Elevator	P. W. Mellen	Saint Louis, Mo	Apr. 1, 1873	137, 464
Elevator	N. L. Milburn	Saint Louis, Mo	Sept. 29, 1868	82, 540
Elevator	C. E. Moore	Boston, Mass	May 2, 1871	114, 460
Elevator	C. E. Moore	Boston, Mass	Oct. 3, 1871	119, 635
Elevator	W. A. Morrison	Cambridge, Mass	Apr. 15, 1873	137, 789
Elevator	A. B. Nimbs	Buffalo, N. Y	Jan. 10, 1865	45, 851
Elevator	C. R. Otis	Yonkers, N. Y	Oct. 1, 1872	131, 896
Elevator	C. R. Otis	Yonkers, N. Y	Oct. 1, 1872	131, 897
Elevator	F. B. Perkins	Boston, Mass	Sept. 26, 1871	119, 401
Elevator	H. G. Porter	Grand Rapids, Mich	June 29, 1869	92, 092
Elevator	J. J. Rea	Cadiz, Ohio	Oct. 20, 1868	83, 319
Elevator	J. Reedy	Chicago, Ill	July 30, 1872	130, 073
Elevator	W. R. Rightor	Helena, Ark	June 17, 1873	140, 076
Elevator	T. H. Rudiger	Lawrence, Kans	Sept. 27, 1870	107, 726
Elevator	W. Sawyer	Lowell, Mass	Oct. 31, 1865	50, 778
Elevator	G. Scott	Louisville, Ky	Aug. 18, 1868	81, 299
Elevator	G. Scott	Louisville, Ky	June 22, 1869	91, 775
Elevator	G. Scott	New Orleans, La	Nov. 29, 1870	109, 676
Elevator	G. Scott	New Orleans, La	Aug. 27, 1872	130, 824
Elevator	A. Shoemaker and J. R. Gearhart.	Marion, Pa	Feb. 9, 1869	86, 703
Elevator	T. B. Simonton	New York, N. Y	Nov. 24, 1868	84, 385
Elevator	D. F. Skinner and J. Arnold	Albany, N. Y	Nov. 7, 1871	120, 676
Elevator	H. Spiro	Knoxville, Tenn	July 7, 1868	79, 697
Elevator	F. Stein and H. Haering	New York, N. Y	Dec. 21, 1869	98, 203
Elevator	H. S. Stewart	Yreka, Cal	Dec. 12, 1871	121, 822
Elevator	H. C. Stouffer	Salem, Ohio	Mar. 29, 1870	101, 457
Elevator	J. B. Sweetland	Pontiac, Mich	Oct. 28, 1873	144, 161
Elevator	G. C. Timpe	New Orleans, La	Nov. 15, 1870	109, 275
Elevator	G. C. Timpe	New Orleans, La	Aug. 22, 1871	118, 300
Elevator	G. C. Timpe	New Orleans, La	Aug. 22, 1871	118, 301
Elevator	G. C. Timpe	New Orleans, La	Feb. 4, 1873	135, 454
Elevator	O. Tufts	Boston, Mass	May 28, 1861	32, 441
Elevator	O. Tufts	Boston, Mass	Dec. 11, 1866	60, 441
Elevator	O. Tufts	Boston, Mass	Dec. 11, 1866	60, 442
Elevator	O. Tufts	Boston, Mass	Oct. 21, 1873	143, 944
Elevator	O. Tufts, jr	Boston, Mass	Feb. 16, 1869	87, 083
Elevator	R. M. Van Sickler	New York, N. Y	Feb. 12, 1867	62, 098
Elevator	J. Walker	Kansas City, Mo	Oct. 15, 1867	69, 871
Elevator	J. C. and J. W. Wandell	New York, N. Y	Mar. 6, 1866	53, 064
Elevator	J. D. Warner	Brooklyn, N. Y	Jan. 16, 1872	122, 791
Elevator	J. J. Weber	Saint Clair, Pa	Jan. 24, 1871	111, 285
Elevator	J. Westover	Taylor, Ill	July 21, 1868	80, 103
Elevator	C. Whittier	Boston, Mass	Dec. 24, 1872	134, 179
Elevator	F. Wicks	Decatur, Ill	Nov. 29, 1870	109, 787
Elevator	G. Williams	Sterling, Cal	July 17, 1866	56, 481
Elevator	G. G. Winans	Scranton, Pa	Feb. 15, 1870	99, 802
Elevator	M. L. Wyman	Melrose, Mass	Mar. 15, 1870	100, 832
Elevator	J. Yost	White Deer Township, Pa.	June 8, 1869	91, 193
Elevator and carrier	S. W. Lackore	Worth, Ill	Mar. 7, 1871	112, 357
Elevator and carrier	H. E. Plumb	Monroe, Conn	Feb. 17, 1863	37, 704
Elevator and conveyer	L. Y. Myers	Roanoke, Ind	Nov. 24, 1868	84, 436
Elevator and conveyer	T. J. Powell	Naples, N. Y	May 24, 1870	103, 367
Elevator and conveyer	T. J. Powell	Naples, N. Y	Feb. 14, 1871	111, 869
Elevator and conveyer	W. F. Shanks	Louisville, Ky	July 16, 1872	129, 298
Elevator and conveyer, Combined	T. J. Powell	Naples, N. Y	Oct. 11, 1870	108, 183
Elevator and distributer	T. Shanks	Baltimore, Md	Dec. 6, 1870	109, 950
Elevator and dumper, Portable	W. H. Herriott	Brimfield, Ill	Dec. 30, 1873	146, 002
Elevator-belt tightener	W. Merson	Danbury, Conn	July 23, 1872	129, 745
Elevating-block	W. H. Hawley	Utica, N. Y	Aug. 27, 1867	68, 193
Elevator-boxes, Machine for making	W. L. Young	Marthasville, Mo	Sept. 24, 1872	131, 648
Elevator-brake	F. P. Canfield	Boston, Mass	Jan. 7, 1873	134, 640
Elevator-brake	M. G. and C. L. Gill	Baltimore, Md	July 16, 1872	129, 546
Elevator-brake	T. Thorn	Saint Clair, Pa	Oct. 10, 1871	119, 800
Elevator-brake	T. Thorn	Saint Clair, Pa	July 16, 1872	129, 625
Elevator-bucket	J. S. Brooks	Rochester, N. Y	Dec. 23, 1862	37, 215
Elevator-bucket	J. S. Brooks	Rochester, N. Y	Nov. 24, 1863	40, 671
Elevator-bucket	C. Camp	Buffalo, N. Y	Oct. 9, 1866	58, 595
Elevator-bucket	H. Dorer and J. Storms	Buffalo, N. Y	July 17, 1866	56, 386
Elevator-bucket	J. Magee	Chicago, Ill	Dec. 19, 1865	51, 603
Elevator-bucket	J. Pfitzinger	Buffalo, N. Y	May 18, 1869	90, 189
Elevator-bucket	N. C. Staples	Lynchburgh, Va	June 29, 1833	....
Elevator-buckets, Construction of	N. Hawkins	Chicago, Ill	Jan. 19, 1869	85, 930
Elevator-buckets, Manufacture of	A. B. Nimbs	Buffalo, N. Y	May 10, 1864	42, 734
Elevator-cup	J. H. Gibbens	Saint Paul, Minn	Oct. 15, 1872	132, 276
Elevator-cup	A. A. Vitt	Union, Mo	Aug. 15, 1871	118, 076
Elevator-cup for flouring mills	L. B. Prindle	Litchfield, Conn	Apr. 29, 1862	35, 111

Index of patents issued from the United States Patent Office from 1790 *to* 1873, *inclusive*—Continued.

Invention.	Inventor.	Residence.	Date.	No.
Elevator for the sick	J. Elliot	Newbury, Mass	Feb. 15, 1811	....
Elevator-guide	C. R. Otis	Yonkers, N. Y	Jan. 7, 1873	134, 698
Elevator-guide	O. Tufts	Boston, Mass	Dec. 11, 1866	60, 443
Elevator-indicator, Electric	E. Holmes	Brooklyn, N. Y	Dec. 5, 1871	121, 620
Elevator-leg	G. H. Johnson	Buffalo, N. Y	Feb. 16, 1869	86, 926
Elevator-leg	G. H. Johnson	Buffalo, N. Y	Feb. 16, 1869	86, 927
Elevator stop-motion	H. E. Bathrick	Boston, Mass	Apr. 2, 1872	125, 256
Elevators, Apparatus for indicating the position of	W. S. Auchincloss	New York, N. Y	June 21, 1870	104, 535
Elevators, Automatic safety-lock for	G. C. Timpe	New Orleans, La	Feb. 4, 1873	135, 453
Elevators, Safety-device for	P. P. Lane	Cincinnati, Ohio	June 18, 1872	128, 152
Elevators, Safety-device for	T. Stebins	San Francisco, Cal	Oct. 8, 1872	132, 112
Elevators, Safety-platform for	R. Dunbar	Buffalo, N. Y	June 24, 1873	140, 190
Elixir of life	J. Bucco	Baltimore, Md	Mar. 29, 1817	....
Elixir or cough-drop, Vegetable	S. Cooley	....	Nov. 12, 1803	....
Elixir, Restorative	H. Frink	Northampton, Mass	Jan. 6, 1812	....
Ellipses, Instrument for describing	J. B. Atwater	Chicago, Ill	June 2, 1863	38, 720
Ellipses, Instrument for drawing	F. Bowly	Winchester, Va	Jan. 14, 1868	73, 290
Ellipses, Instrument for drawing	A. Warr	Lockport, N. Y	Mar. 19, 1867	63, 123
Ellipses, Machine for cutting	W. G. Merrell	Auburn, N. Y	Jan. 10, 1854	10, 412
Ellipses, Trammel for	C. Crow	Onargo, Ill	Mar. 27, 1866	53, 524
Ellipsograph	H. M. Albee	Webster, Mass	Dec. 18, 1866	60, 609
Ellipsograph	A. W. Browne	Bloomfield, N. J	May 14, 1872	126, 782
Ellipsograph	J. W. Campbell	Brooklyn, N. Y	Dec. 9, 1856	16, 175
Ellipsograph	E. G. Chormann	Philadelphia, Pa	Dec. 21, 1858	22, 347
Ellipsograph	R. E. Harte	Marietta, Ohio	Dec. 4, 1860	30, 816
Ellipsograph	H. Smith	Dayton, Oreg	June 22, 1869	91, 681
Ellipsograph	T. Williams and W. C. Joslyn	Fisherville, Conn	Feb. 8, 1859	22, 910
Elliptic spring	R. Gray	Litchfield, Ill	July 16, 1867	66, 702
Elliptic spring	F. Keeler	Bridgeport, Conn	Feb. 15, 1870	99, 776
Elliptic spring	E. C. Lewis	Auburn, N. Y	Aug. 27, 1867	68, 217
Elliptic spring	W. A. Sweet	Syracuse, N. Y	Nov. 30, 1869	97, 458
Elliptic spring	R. Vose	New York, N. Y	May 5, 1863	38, 432
Elliptic-spring clip	W. Evans	Pittsburgh, Pa	Jan. 25, 1870	99, 074
Elliptic spring for carriages	E. M. Chaffee	Providence, R. I	Feb. 5, 1867	61, 712
Elliptic spring for vehicles	R. Halloran	New York, N. Y	Feb. 6, 1872	123, 396
Elliptic-spring support	E. Eves	Millville, Pa	Nov. 30, 1869	97, 370
Elliptic-spring support	J. J. Unsworth	Washington, D. C	Aug. 24, 1869	94, 150
Elliptic springs, Confining the ends of	R. Vose	New York, N. Y	Dec. 15, 1863	40, 968
Elliptic springs, Die for making heads for	J. Palmer	Concord, N. H	Sept. 3, 1867	68, 454
Elliptic springs, Ear-blank for	W. Evans	Pittsburgh, Pa	Apr. 13, 1869	88, 861
Elliptic springs for carriages, &c., Construction of	M. Tuells	Penn Yan, N. Y	July 9, 1838	828
Elliptic springs, Machine for bending	J. Gatchell	Rahway, N. J	Nov. 3, 1868	83, 625
Elliptic springs, Machine for forming	J. B. Cleveland and H. C. Guildersleive.	Newark, N. J	June 14, 1870	104, 114
Elliptic springs, Machine for forming and tempering.	G. S. Long	Bridgeport, Conn	Dec. 10, 1867	72, 055
Elliptic springs, Machine for punching the leaves of	G. Hopson	Bridgeport, Conn	Mar. 8, 1870	100, 630
Elliptic springs, Machine for setting and fitting	G. I. Neviel	Philadelphia, Pa	Sept. 20, 1839	1, 333
Elliptic springs, Machine for straightening	J. W. Gray and C. H. Curtis	Bridgeport, Conn	Feb. 14, 1865	46, 421
Elliptic springs, Machine for welding ears on carriage.	A. Richards and J. Jones	Concord, N. H	Apr. 9, 1872	125, 485
Elliptic springs, Making the eyes of	W. T. Richards	Bridgeport, Conn	Aug. 27, 1867	68, 113
Elliptic springs to vehicles, Connecting	J. W. Lawrence	New York, N. Y	Dec. 13, 1859	26, 461
Elliptic springs, Welding the ears of	J. Palmer	Concord, N. H	May 26, 1868	78, 230
Elliptical spindles, Grinder for	J. Wheaton	Providence, R. I	May 28, 1834	....
Elliptical spring	D. A. Edwards	Boston, Mass	Nov. 16, 1841	2, 360
Elliptical-spring joints, Machinery for forming	W. T. Richards	New Haven, Conn	Aug. 26, 1851	8, 325
Elliptical-spring sockets, Machine for forming	W. T. Richards	Poultney, Vt	Nov. 16, 1841	2, 367
Elliptical springs for carriages, &c., Mode of constructing.	G. B. Robinson	Pawlet, Vt	Oct. 3, 1838	961
Elliptical steel-spring	C. Hinkle	Lehigh County, Pa	Nov. 12, 1831	....
Embalming	T. Holmes	Williamsburgh, N. Y	Dec. 10, 1861	33, 885
Embalming	B. F. Lyford	San Francisco, Cal	Jan. 24, 1871	111, 222
Embalming and preserving animal substances, Mode of.	L. Brunetti	Rovigne, Italy	Oct. 1, 1867	69, 312
Embalming and preserving dead bodies	E. De la Granja	Boston, Mass	July 30, 1867	67, 170
Embalming birds	S. A. Morey	Grand Rapids, Mich	Apr. 16, 1872	125, 685
Embalming bodies	G. W. Scollay	Saint Louis, Mo	Jan. 22, 1867	61, 472
Embalming composition	J. C. Sickle	Philadelphia, Pa	Mar. 24, 1868	75, 992
Embalming dead bodies	W. Iddings	Warren, Ohio	Nov. 6, 1860	30, 576
Embalming dead bodies, Compound for	E. H. Crane	Burr Oak, Mich	Sept. 1, 1868	81, 755
Embalming-fluid	F. A. Hutton	Washington, D. C	June 2, 1863	38, 747
Embalming human bodies, Fluid compound for	W. E. Chenoweth	Baltimore County, Md	Nov. 18, 1873	144, 602
Embankment, levee, &c., Method of forming	D. Green	Dalton, Ga	June 11, 1850	7, 425
Embossing	R. J. Chute	Philadelphia, Pa	Jan. 9, 1872	122, 569
Embossing and compressing machine, Hydraulic	J. Robertson	Brooklyn, N. Y	Dec. 3, 1872	133, 543
Embossing and finishing woven fabrics	W. Ralston	Manchester, England	Nov. 1, 1859	25, 980
Embossing and perforating paper, &c., Machine for.	C. Lang	New York, N. Y	Mar. 26, 1867	63, 263
Embossing and printing machine	S. W. Lowe	Philadelphia, Pa	Apr. 29, 1856	14, 789
Embossing and printing press	S. J. Smith and C. Loekle	New York, N. Y	July 7, 1857	17, 703
Embossing and seal press	B. B. Hill	Chicopee, Mass	May 23, 1865	47, 821
Embossing and seal press	G. B. Sargent	Boston, Mass	Sept. 27, 1864	44, 459
Embossing articles of wearing-apparel, Machine for	G. W. Ray	Springfield, Mass	Mar. 26, 1867	63, 177
Embossing bonnets and hats, Apparatus for	H. E. West	Attleborough, Mass	July 25, 1865	49, 049
Embossing brass tubes, Machinery for	D. F. Sanford	New York, N. Y	Nov. 27, 1866	60, 067
Embossing capsules, Machine for	W. Betts	No. 1 Wharf Road, City Road, England.	Sept. 13, 1870	107, 329
Embossing cloth	J. E. Pollard	Franklin, Mass	Nov. 19, 1867	71, 213
Embossing consecutive numbers, Machine for	L. Henser	Boston, Mass	Jan. 1, 1867	60, 726
Embossing designs on metal for jewelry, Process of	W. Riker	Newark, N. J	Mar. 13, 1860	27, 474
Embossing fabrics, Implement for	J. W. McKee	Brooklyn, E. D., N. Y	Dec. 19, 1871	122, 044
Embossing-machine	J. C. Arms	Northampton, Mass	Dec. 4, 1866	60, 115
Embossing napkin-rings, Machine for	E. H. Eldridge and T. Leach	Taunton, Mass	May 8, 1866	54, 515
Embossing-press	G. Clisbee	Marlborough, Mass	Apr. 22, 1873	138, 130
Embossing-press	A. Komp	New York, N. Y	Jan. 23, 1872	123, 026
Embossing-press	J. C. Merriam and W. N. Weeden.	Boston, Mass	July 10, 1866	56, 244
Embossing-press	J. M. Willbur	Cleveland, Ohio	Aug. 31, 1869	94, 368

Index of patents issued from the United States Patent Office from 1790 *to* 1873, *inclusive*—Continued.

Invention.	Inventor.	Residence.	Date.	No.
Embossing-press for linen and other fabrics	L. H. Olmsted	New York, N. Y	Apr. 9, 1872	125, 610
Embossing-press gage	W. Richards, jr	Cincinnati, Ohio	May 19, 1868	78, 130
Embossing-press, Rotary	J. M. Willbur	Cleveland, Ohio	Sept. 22, 1868	82, 461
Embossing wood, Mode of	H. May	Bridgeport, Conn	Oct. 24, 1865	50, 608
Embroidering-machine	H. Berger	Marthalen, Switzerland	Sept. 28, 1869	95, 186
Embroidering machine	J. Einhorn	New York, N. Y	July 14, 1868	79, 901
Embroidering-machine	A. Heaven and R. Smith	Manchester, England	Apr. 28, 1863	38, 358
Embroidery and sewing stand	W. H. Trowbridge	Saginaw, Mich	Sept. 28, 1858	21, 633
Embroidery-holder	H. Gundaker	Lancaster, Pa	May 3, 1870	102, 537
Embroidery, Imitation metal	J. S. Smith, jr	New York, N. Y	Apr. 8, 1862	34, 907
Embroidery, Imitation of	B. Müller	Fulda, Germany	Dec. 19, 1865	51, 668
Embroidery-patterns, Apparatus for transferring	C. Bordas	New York, N. Y	Oct. 21, 1873	143, 872
Emery-cleaning machine	J. H. Hawes and G. H. Bliss	Boston and West Stockbridge, Mass.	Apr. 28, 1868	77, 281
Emery-cloth, polishing-wheels, &c., Composition for the manufacture of.	L. Francis	New York, N. Y	Jan. 7, 1868	72, 994
Emery-cloth, Substitute for	T. J. Mayall	Roxbury, Mass	Apr. 10, 1860	27, 817
Emery for grinding and polishing tools, Composition of.	T. J. Mayall	Roxbury, Mass	Oct. 18, 1859	25, 841
Emery from foreign substances, Process of separating crude.	N. C. Sawyer	Boston, Mass	Oct. 2, 1866	58, 487
Emery-grinder, Table for	J. L. Jackson	New York, N. Y	Aug. 15, 1871	118, 017
Emery-grinder, Table for	J. L. Jackson	New York, N. Y	Dec. 26, 1871	122, 253
Emery-grinding machine	H. S. Lucas	Chester, Mass	Feb. 4, 1873	135, 482
Emery or sand-paper holder	E. R. Barnes	Brookfield, Conn	Oct. 13, 1863	40, 231
Emery polishing-stick	G. C. Taft	Worcester, Mass	May 30, 1871	115, 384
Emery polishing-wheel, &c	W. P. Van Kleeck	Charlestown, Mass	June 14, 1870	104, 231
Emery sticks and wheels, Composition for	T. J. Mayall	Roxbury, Mass	May 17, 1859	24, 039
Emery-vulcanite or hard-rubber compounds, Preparing.	T. J. Mayall	Boston, Mass	Apr. 9, 1872	125, 600
Emery-wheel	T. Harding	La Fayette, Ind	Jan. 17, 1871	111, 057
Emery-wheel	W. S. Jarboe	New York, N. Y	May 14, 1872	126, 706
Emery-wheel	W. A. Johnston	New York, N. Y	July 8, 1873	140, 630
Emery-wheel	T. Nelson	West Troy, N. Y	Nov. 1, 1864	44, 918
Emery-wheel	J. L. Otis	Leeds, Mass	Mar. 8, 1870	100, 659
Emery-wheel	A. M. Sawyer	Athol, Mass	Jan. 5, 1869	85, 537
Emery-wheel	J. Tyzick	Saint John's, Canada	Sept. 17, 1872	131, 481
Emery-wheel	W. T. Vose	Newtonville, Mass	May 7, 1872	126, 597
Emery-wheel clamp	E. A. Süwerkrop	Washington, D. C	Mar. 22, 1870	101, 158
Emery-wheel-cleaning machine	S. A. and H. Whipple	Shaftsbury, Vt., and Port Richmond, N. Y.	Oct. 14, 1856	15, 912
Emery-wheel cowl	C. Heaton	New York, N. Y	Feb. 27, 1872	124, 134
Emery-wheel for grinding and polishing saws, &c	G. L. Benton	Rochester, N. Y	Nov. 5, 1867	70, 393
Emery-wheels and artificial stone, Manufacture of.	E. C. Merrill	Charleston, Vt	Apr. 4, 1871	113, 439
Emery-wheels and grinding-surfaces, Forming	G. E. Vanderburgh	Mamaroneck, N. Y	Jan. 7, 1862	34, 123
Emery-wheels and oil-stones, Compound for	N. B. Hadley and R. J. Costain	Northampton, Mass	Sept. 21, 1869	94, 955
Emery-wheels and other abrading implements, Composition for.	E. C. Merrill and A. W. Willard.	Charleston, Vt	Oct. 12, 1869	95, 824
Emery wheels and sticks, Manufacture of	T. J. Mayall	Roxbury, Mass	Jan. 11, 1859	22, 606
Emery-wheels, Clamp for girding	H. S. Vrooman	Springfield, Mass	Nov. 5, 1850	7, 761
Emery-wheels, Machine for cleaning	J. Chandler	Collinsville, Conn	Jan. 7, 1862	34, 104
Emery-wheels, &c., Machine for molding	J. S. Elliott	Chelsea, Mass	July 23, 1872	129, 801
Emery-wheels, Making	J. D. Alvord	Bridgeport, Conn	Oct. 2, 1860	30, 189
Emery-wheels, Manufacture of	J. F. Wood	Boston, Mass	Dec. 13, 1870	110, 102
Emery-wheels, &c., Mode of finishing and turning	C. Marsh	Bridgeport, Conn	Apr. 9, 1869	88, 725
Emery-wheels, Mode of forming	C. G. Marshall	Florence, Mass	June 18, 1867	65, 924
Emery-wheels, Process of making	T. Nelson	West Troy, N. Y	Mar. 6, 1866	53, 032
Emery with caoutchouc, Method of combining	T. J. Mayall	Roxbury, Mass	Oct. 11, 1859	25, 747
Enamel	T. L. Oest	Berlin, Prussia	June 27, 1865	48, 500
Enamel, Composition of	J. G. Dunn and A. F. Howes	Lawrenceburgh, Ind	Sept. 7, 1852	9, 250
Enamel for clay gas-retorts, burners, tiles, &c	D. W. Clark	Chicago, Ill	Mar. 15, 1870	100, 725
Enamel for covering hoop-skirt springs	W. S. Ryerson	Philadelphia, Pa	Feb. 12, 1867	62, 074
Enamel for iron	C. Stumer	New York, N. Y	July 25, 1848	5, 681
Enamel for leather	C. W. Held	Brooklyn, N. Y	Feb. 11, 1862	34, 366
Enamel for leather	S. A. Hickel	Spencer, Pa	Nov. 26, 1867	71, 485
Enamel or glaze for pottery, bricks, tiles, &c	W. S. Thomas	Carbon Cliff, Ill	Nov. 9, 1869	96, 634
Enamel, paint, &c., Composition for	M. W. Brown	Morrisania, N. Y	Sept. 5, 1865	49, 708
Enamel to be applied to metals, &c	W. J. Cheyney and E. F. Dieterichs.	Wallingford and Philadelphia, Pa.	Oct. 1, 1867	69, 318
Enameled-metal comb	C. Foster	Wappinger's Falls, N. Y	July 7, 1868	79, 747
Enameled metal, Manufacture of articles of	G. A. Burrough	Providence, R. I	May 30, 1871	115, 278
Enameling and coating articles with rubber, gutta-percha, &c.	P. Finley	New York, N. Y	Apr. 30, 1872	126, 195
Enameling bricks, Compound for	D. W. Clark	Chicago, Ill	Jan. 31, 1871	111, 318
Enameling cast-iron	G. W. Holley	Niagara, N. Y	Mar. 10, 1857	16, 798
Enameling checkers, Apparatus for	I. S., J. W., and C. M. Hyatt	Albany, N. Y	July 9, 1872	128, 729
Enameling cloth, leather, &c., Machine for	L. L. Allen	Hallowell, Me	Sept. 3, 1872	130, 968
Enameling elliptical frames, Machine for	G. W. and H. H. Ferguson	New York, N. Y	June 21, 1864	43, 189
Enameling hard rubber, gutta-percha, &c., Process of.	A. W. and I. C. Monroe	Rahway, N. J., and Brooklyn, N. Y.	Apr. 2, 1867	63, 553
Enameling hollow ware, Composition for	C. E. and C. H. Paris	Paris, France	Mar. 5, 1850	7, 145
Enameling iron and steel	B. Baugh	Chadwick, England	Dec. 28, 1869	98, 336
Enameling iron and steel	J. G. Dreyfus	New York, N. Y	Mar. 2, 1869	87, 475
Enameling iron pipes and hollow ware	E. Pierce	Philadelphia, Pa	June 23, 1857	17, 635
Enameling iron, Process for	C. F. Thomin and C. Stumer	Cincinnati, Ohio	Oct. 17, 1854	11, 815
Enameling, japanning, and inlaying, Preparing metallic substances for.	D. Rait	New York, N. Y	Aug. 30, 1864	44, 046
Enameling jewelry and other articles	G. Krebs	New York, N. Y	Apr. 30, 1872	126, 308
Enameling-machine	H. R. Hall	Philadelphia, Pa	Apr. 28, 1868	77, 187
Enameling moldings, Apparatus for	B. McEachren	San Francisco, Cal	Sept. 26, 1865	58, 146
Enameling moldings, Machine for	G. Boos	New York, N. Y	Dec. 18, 1860	30, 954
Enameling moldings, Machine for	J. Johnson	Boston, Mass	June 9, 1868	78, 747
Enameling moldings, Machine for	J. Johnson	Boston, Mass	Dec. 5, 1871	121, 628
Enameling moldings, Machine for	R. Marcher	New York, N. Y	July 26, 1859	24, 879
Enameling moldings, Machine for	T. Moore	Boston, Mass	Nov. 7, 1871	120, 659
Enameling moldings, Machine for	R. Ten Eyck, jr	Brooklyn, N. Y	Apr. 24, 1860	28, 022
Enameling moldings, &c., Machinery for	R. Marcher	Cornwall, N. Y	Oct. 21, 1851	8, 448

Index of patents issued from the United States Patent Office from 1790 *to* 1873, *inclusive*—Continued.

Invention.	Inventor.	Residence.	Date.	No.
Enameling paper, cloth, card-board, &c., Composisition for.	M. W. Brown	New York, N. Y	Feb. 9, 1869	86, 639
Enameling paper, Machine for	M. H. Gardner	New York, N. Y	May 19, 1868	78, 079
Enameling photographic pictures, Apparatus for	N. Weston	San Francisco, Cal	Dec. 10, 1867	72, 133
Enameling picture-frames, &c	R. Marcher	New York, N. Y	Aug. 14, 1860	29, 609
Enameling picture-frames, &c., Tool for	J. Sperry	New York, N. Y	July 10, 1860	29, 122
Enameling sheet-iron, Apparatus for	W. Harris and D. Hall	Chicago, Ill	May 31, 1870	103, 741
Enameling stone and earthen ware	J. H. Giles	New York, N. Y	May 4, 1869	89, 574
Enameling wood and other solid materials with hard rubber.	P. Finley	Memphis, Tenn	Aug. 10, 1869	93, 606
Enema-chair	W. Laighton	Portsmouth, N. H	Aug. 8, 1846	4, 684
Enema-giving apparatus	B. T. Babbitt	New York, N. Y	Mar. 17, 1857	16, 822
Engine: *See* Air-engine. Air and gas engine. Air-compressing engine. Ammonia-engine. Ammonia-gas engine. Ammoniacal engine. Atmospheric engine. Atmospheric steam-engine. Beam-engine. Beating-engine. Blowing-engine. Boring-engine. Caloric engine. Carbonic-acid engine. Carding-engine. Chloride of calcium engine. Compound-engine. Compound steam-engine. Compressed air engine. Condensing-engine. Crank-engine. Cylinder-engine. Dental engine. Direct-acting engine. Direct-acting compound steam-engine. Direct-acting steam-engine. Drum-engine. Dummy-engine. Electro-magnetic engine. Exhaust-steam engine. Expansion engine. Explosive engine. Fire-engine. Fire-extinguishing engine. Garden-engine. Gas-engine. Gas-explosive engine. Gear-cutting engine. Gunpowder-engine. Hand-engine. Heated-liquid engine. High and low pressure engine. Hoisting-engine. Horizontal engine. Horse-power engine. Hot-water engine. Hydraulic engine. Hydrostatic engine. Knapsack-engine. Link-motion engine. Locomotive-engine. Marine-engine. Motive-power engine. Motor-engine. Non-condensing engine. Oscillating engine. Oscillating steam-engine. Paper-pulp engine. Paper-rag engine. Piston-engine. Pneumatic engine. Pneumo-hydraulic engine. Propeller-engine. Propulsion-engine. Pumping-engine. Rag or paper engine. Reacting engine. Reacting steam-engine. Reciprocating-engine. Reciprocating steam-engine. Rose-engine. Rosette-engine. Rotary engine. Rotary-cylinder engine. Rotary steam-engine. Rotating cylinder-engine. Stationary engine. Steam-engine. Steam and air engine. Steam and caloric engine. Steam-hammer engine. Traction-engine. Traveling engine. Triple-cylinder engine. Trunk-engine. Turning-engine. Two-beam engine. Vacuum-engine. Vapor-engine. Vertical engine. Water-engine.				
Engine	J. Idler	Philadelphia, Pa	July 31, 1819	....
Engine	T. C. Robinson and C. W. Clift	Mystic Bridge, Conn	Mar. 11, 1873	136, 764
Engine and pump	O. P. Lewis	Cincinnati, Ohio	Nov. 28, 1871	121, 388
Engine-boiler and superheater, Combined	F. B. Blanchard	Spuyten Duyvil, N. Y	Mar. 1, 1870	100, 359
Engine by bi-sulphuret of carbon, Actuating	B. Hughes	Rochester, N. Y	Aug. 22, 1854	11, 553
Engine for raising weights	A. Holmes	Boston, Mass	Oct. 21, 1824	....
Engine-furnace Air-heating apparatus for	J. H. Shotwell	Rahway, N. J	Nov. 26, 1861	33, 801
Engine indicator	C. W. F. Krausch	Chicago, Ill	Sept. 9, 1862	36, 411
Engine operated by heated liquid	J. S. Baldwin	Newark, N. J	Dec. 5, 1871	121, 479
Engine operated by heated liquid	J. S. Baldwin	Newark, N. J	Dec. 5, 1871	121, 480
Engine operated by heated liquid	J. S. Baldwin	Newark, N. J	Dec. 5, 1871	121, 481
Engine-power, Augmenting	A. Ochler	Eastville, Va	Mar. 30, 1835	....
Engine smoke-stack	T. B. Phoebus	Memphis, Tenn	Nov. 21, 1871	121, 062
Engine-turning machine	A. Schwitler	New York, N. Y	Sept. 1, 1863	39, 755
Engines, Applying power to the cranks of	T. Stewart	Philadelphia, Pa	Oct. 26, 1858	21, 911
Engines, Combined quarter-connection and parallel motion for.	A. J. L. Loretz	Brooklyn, N. Y	Nov. 25, 1873	144, 852
Engines, Crank-motion for	J. Smith and G. Joithe	Newark, N. J	June 14, 1870	104, 367
Engines, Device for controlling	J. J. L. Farcot	Saint Ouen, (Seine,) France	Dec. 29, 1868	85, 439
Engines for using steam expansively, Arrangement of.	J. Ericsson	New York, N. Y	Nov. 6, 1849	6, 844
Engines, Holding-keys for strap-connections for	T. Cook	Washington, D. C	Apr. 19, 1859	23, 743
Engines, Mechanism for reversing	G. W. Bishop	Brooklyn, N. Y	Nov. 18, 1873	144, 731
Engines, Method of lubricating	J. Marks	Boston, Mass	Oct. 16, 1860	30, 416
Engines off their centers, Starting	A. Sims	New York, N. Y	July 9, 1867	66, 527
Engines, Utilizing the exhaust steam of	E. Körting	Berlin, Prussia	Mar. 26, 1872	125, 056
Engraver, Pantographic	J. Hope	Providence, R. I	Nov. 19, 1867	71, 010
Engraver's plate	T. Bardon	Brooklyn, N. Y	Aug. 25, 1868	81, 461
Engraver's ring-clamp	T. R. Hopkins	Petersburgh, Va	June 29, 1858	20, 711
Engraving	J. Hutton and G. Fairman		Jan. 8, 1802	....
Engraving	H. S. Ingersoll	Lansing, Mich	Dec. 10, 1872	133, 860

Index of patents issued from the United States Patent Office from 1790 *to* 1873, *inclusive*—Continued.

Invention.	Inventor.	Residence.	Date.	No.
Engraving and carving machine	T. W. Minter	New York, N. Y	Oct. 29, 1872	132, 594
Engraving and carving machine	T. W. Minter	New York, N. Y	Feb. 18, 1873	135, 998
Engraving and chasing articles of metal	T. Lippiatt	Orange, N. J	May 10, 1870	102, 950
Engraving and printing, Making and preparing metallic plates for.	D. H. Mason	Philadelphia, Pa	May 17, 1822	....
Engraving and printing to prevent counterfeits	G. Murray	Philadelphia, Pa	Feb. 13, 1810	....
Engraving bank-notes	B. Chambers	Washington, D. C	June 12, 1847	5, 155
Engraving bank-notes	W. L. Ormsby	Jersey City, N. J	May 16, 1865	47, 744
Engraving bank-notes, &c., Style of	J. Macdonough	New York, N. Y	Oct. 23, 1860	30, 488
Engraving calico-printers' rollers, Machine for	J. and T. Hope	Providence. R. I	Aug. 21, 1855	13, 462
Engraving copper, &c	V. Q. Wedikind	Philadelphia, Pa	Oct. 2, 1866	58, 516
Engraving copper cylinders, Machine for	B. L. Phillips	Providence, R. I	July 3, 1860	29, 002
Engraving copper, &c., Process for	A. F. Burson	Mount Blanchard, Ohio	Nov. 29, 1864	45, 224
Engraving cylinders, Machine for	R. Muckett and W. Rigby	Salford, Great Britain	May 12, 1857	17, 290
Engraving-machine	E. Allen	Grafton, Mass	Jan. 16, 1843	2, 912
Engraving-machine	J. B. Blair	Alton, Ill	May 24, 1853	9, 743
Engraving-machine	C. J. Coulter	Seville, Ohio	May 31, 1870	103, 576
Engraving-machine	J. C. Guerrant and B. J. Field	Leaksville, N. C	Nov. 5, 1867	70, 553
Engraving-machine	J. C. Guerrant and B. J. Field.	Leaksville, N. C	Nov. 3, 1868	83, 708
Engraving-machine	J. S. Ives	Morrisania, N. Y	Dec. 23, 1862	37, 235
Engraving-machine	J. D. Lathrop	New York, N. Y	June 28, 1870	104, 744
Engraving-machine	J. C. Spencer	Phelps, N. Y	Feb. 15, 1870	99, 794
Engraving-machine, Apparatus for supporting and adjusting graver.	J. Hope	Providence, R. I	June 8, 1858	20, 528
Engraving-machine, Device for pentagraphic	J. Hope	Providence, R. I	Mar. 9, 1858	19, 607
Engraving-machinery	J. C. Guerrant and B. J. Field.	Leaksville, N. C	Dec. 18, 1866	60, 506
Engraving metallic plates, Apparatus for	W. L. Ormsby	Jersey City, N. J	May 16, 1865	47, 745
Engraving or printing upon glass, Process of	M. D. and L. W. Whipple	Somerville, Mass	June 27, 1854	11, 189
Engraving rollers, &c., Machine for	W. Shields	Manchester, England	May 15, 1860	28, 332
Engraving-surface	I. Taylor	Stanford Rivers, England	June 1, 1852	8, 991
Engraving, Transfer	R. Meale	Brooklyn, N. Y	Aug. 31, 1869	94, 432
Engravings, &c., Binding	W. T. Anderson	Brooklyn, N. Y	Oct. 2, 1860	30, 277
Engravings, &c., Process for reducing copies of	J. A. F. Lair	Paris, France	Oct. 15, 1861	33, 485
Entrail-cleaning machine	J. A. Huss	Louisville, Ky	Nov. 24, 1868	84, 358
Entry-light	C. W. Felt	Salem, Mass	Jan. 9, 1855	12, 200
Envelope	E. L. Barrett	Springfield, Ohio	Oct. 24, 1865	50, 549
Envelope	S. D. Bates	Boston, Mass	Dec. 26, 1871	122, 212
Envelope	H. C. Bristol	Saint Clair, Mich	Mar. 8, 1864	41, 828
Envelope	R. S. Clark	Great Bend, Pa	Apr. 7, 1868	76, 303
Envelope	W. B. Coates	Philadelphia, Pa	Aug. 5, 1856	15, 475
Envelope	C. Crowell	Syracuse, N. Y	Apr. 16, 1872	125, 664
Envelope	B. C. Davis	Binghamton, N. Y	Sept. 6, 1870	107, 106
Envelope	F. W. Eberman	West Salem, Ill	Nov. 9, 1869	96, 566
Envelope	E. S. Ellis	Trenton, N. J	Mar. 14, 1871	112, 568
Envelope	H. Everdell	New York, N. Y	May 14, 1867	64, 753
Envelope	E. Fitzki	Washington, D. C	May 14, 1867	64, 653
Envelope	J. C. Gaston	Cincinnati, Ohio	Dec. 31, 1867	72, 836
Envelope	J. C. Gaston	Cincinnati, Ohio	Feb. 23, 1869	87, 253
Envelope	L. Giebrich	Ottumwa, Iowa	July 1, 1873	140, 496
Envelope	L. Giebrich	Ottumwa, Iowa	Sept. 23, 1873	143, 136
Envelope	J. Gray	Raymond, Miss	Mar. 26, 1861	31, 801
Envelope	H. K. Gregg	Baltimore, Md	May 9, 1871	114, 672
Envelope	J. W. Groomes	Portsmouth, Ohio	June 20, 1871	116, 180
Envelope	G. P. Hachenberg	Hudson, N. Y	June 15, 1869	91, 331
Envelope	E. Harmon	Washington, D. C	Nov. 20, 1855	13, 838
Envelope	W. E. Haskins	New York, N. Y	July 23, 1867	67, 111
Envelope	B. J. Hoffacker	Melrose, N. Y	June 1, 1869	90, 663
Envelope	J. W. Huffington and A. Buckman.	Brooklyn, N. Y	Dec. 24, 1872	134, 142
Envelope	R. S. Jennings	New York, N. Y	May 21, 1867	64, 879
Envelope	A. A. C. Klaucke and J. Fraser.	Washington, D. C., and New York, N. Y.	Apr. 6, 1869	88, 722
Envelope	R. T. Knight	Philadelphia, Pa	June 24, 1856	15, 185
Envelope	S. Kuh	Jefferson, Iowa	June 24, 1873	140, 204
Envelope	R. K. Kuhn and T. O. Atkinson	Doylestown, Pa	Feb. 11, 1873	135, 819
Envelope	P. Lockwood	Auburn, Ind	Apr. 25, 1871	114, 161
Envelope	R. Magee	Philadelphia, Pa	Nov. 20, 1866	59, 849
Envelope	G. H. Mathews	New York, N. Y	Dec. 1, 1868	84, 501
Envelope	W. F. McCrary	Baker City, Oreg	Apr. 30, 1872	126, 316
Envelope	C. E. McMahan	Elizabeth, N. J	Aug. 8, 1871	117, 795
Envelope	B. Morison	Philadelphia, Pa	June 19, 1860	28, 767
Envelope	J. B. Murray	New York, N. Y	Dec. 18, 1860	30, 980
Envelope	S. E. Pettee	Philadelphia, Pa	Mar. 22, 1859	23, 309
Envelope	C. Pink and M. Silverberg	Cairo, Ill	June 3, 1873	139, 475
Envelope	C. R. M. Pohlé	Richmond, Va	Apr. 28, 1868	77, 316
Envelope	C. R. M. Pohlé	Richmond, Va	Dec. 8, 1868	84, 840
Envelope	J. Reckendorfer and J. C. Richard.	New York and Brooklyn, N. Y.	July 9, 1861	32, 813
Envelope	C. W. Saladee	Circleville, Ohio	Apr. 27, 1869	89, 507
Envelope	F. M. Shields	Macon, Miss	Jan. 7, 1868	73, 203
Envelope	E. J. Smith	Washington, D. C	May 16, 1871	114, 871
Envelope	G. W. Starr	Washington, D. C	Dec. 22, 1868	85, 253
Envelope	R. S. Stubbs	Lisbon, N. H	Jan. 3, 1871	110, 798
Envelope	M. Saylor	Buffalo, N. Y	July 11, 1871	117, 015
Envelope	J. P. Thompson	Philadelphia, Pa	Apr. 25, 1871	114, 228
Envelope	S. Ullman	New York, N. Y	Feb. 25, 1868	74, 867
Envelope	S. Ullman	New York, N. Y	Sept. 8, 1868	81, 962
Envelope	S. Ullman	New York, N. Y	Sept. 8, 1868	81, 963
Envelope	J. B. Wheeler	Neville, Ohio	July 21, 1868	80, 257
Envelope	S. L. Wiegand	Philadelphia, Pa	Mar. 22, 1864	42, 035
Envelope	J. W. Wilcox	New York, N. Y	Apr. 8, 1862	34, 927
Envelope	C. C. Woolworth	New York, N. Y	Mar. 1, 1864	41, 804
Envelope and letter-sheet combined	J. B. Anderson	Wakefield, Mass	Jan. 16, 1872	122, 694
Envelope and letter sheet combined	C. Schweizer	Boston, Mass	Sept. 10, 1872	131, 184
Envelope and letter-sheet combined	C. Rowland	Clinton, Ill	Dec. 19, 1865	51, 623
Envelope-blanks, Gumming and feeding	J. B. Duff	Patchogue, N. Y	Dec. 13, 1864	45, 397
Envelope, Card	C. Rowland	Washington, D. C	Aug. 8, 1871	117, 818

Index of patents issued from the United States Patent Office from 1790 *to* 1873, *inclusive*—Continued.

Index of patents issued from the United States Patent Office from 1790 *to* 1873, *inclusive*—Continued.

Invention.	Inventor.	Residence.	Date.	No.
Equalizer	G. W. N. Yost	Corry, Pa	Mar. 9, 1869	87, 612
Equalizer for double-trees, Draft	R. F. Judson	Kalamazoo, Mich	Apr. 7, 1868	76, 466
Equalizer or power-regulator	A. Gregory	Brooklyn, N. Y	Sept. 9, 1851	8, 345
Equalizer, Spring	H. Davis	Berlin, Wis	Oct. 28, 1873	143, 966
Equalizer, Three-horse	E. F. Avery and H. B. Leckenby	Dowagiac, Mich	Feb. 2, 1869	86, 491
Equalizer, Three-horse	F. E. Barr	Albion, N. Y	June 8, 1869	90, 915
Equalizer, Three-horse	J. Blackwood	Lithopolis, Ohio	Mar. 12, 1872	124, 537
Equalizer, Three-horse	W. P. Brooks	Bloomington, Ill	Aug. 10, 1869	93, 593
Equalizer, Three-horse	J. E. Coveney	Buchanan, Mich	Mar. 2, 1869	87, 471
Equalizer, Three-horse	G. Cramton	Marshall, Mich	Feb. 4, 1868	74, 053
Equalizer, Three-horse	G. Cramton	Marshall, Mich	Sept. 14, 1869	94, 718
Equalizer, Three-horse	G. Cramton and P. A. Spicer	Marshall, Mich	July 21, 1868	80, 060
Equalizer, Three-horse	W. Haistings, sr	Fowler, Ill	June 24, 1873	140, 268
Equalizer, Three-horse	T. Hoadley	Toulon, Ill	Aug. 19, 1873	141, 875
Equalizer, Three-horse	A. March	Taylor, Ill	Mar. 19, 1872	124, 692
Equalizer, Three-horse	E. K. Parish	Shelbyville, Ind	July 16, 1872	129, 050
Equalizer, Three-horse	J. C. Pfeil	Arenzville, Ill	Oct. 11, 1870	108, 179
Equalizer, Three-horse	Z. B. Sims	Bonham, Tex	Aug. 31, 1869	94, 355
Equalizer, Three-horse	A. L., G. J., and T. N. Thomas	Lee's Summit, Mo	May 21, 1872	126, 998
Equalizer, Three-horse	J. T. Thornton	Kewanee, Ill	Mar. 1, 1870	100, 469
Equalizer, Three-horse	L. Warren	Dwight, Ill	July 11, 1871	117, 021
Equalizer, Three-horse	E. M. Wright	Castile, N. Y	July 13, 1869	92, 503
Equalizer, Three-horse-draft	E. J. Toof	Fort Madison, Iowa	Dec. 19, 1865	51, 632
Equalizer, Two-horse	Z. B. Sims	Bonham, Tex	Aug. 2, 1870	106, 084
Equalizing-bars, Die for bending	A. E. Barnard	Akron, Ohio	Feb. 9, 1869	86, 629
Eraser	H. T. Cushmann	North Bennington, Vt	May 17, 1870	103, 149
Eraser	J. M. Hicks	Boston, Mass	May 14, 1861	32, 288
Eraser	A. H. Hook and H. B. Adams	New York, N. Y	July 17, 1866	56, 415
Eraser	W. A. Morse and J. G. Powell	Philadelphia, Pa	June 16, 1868	78, 887
Eraser	A. G. Shaver	New Haven, Conn	Jan. 24, 1865	46, 032
Eraser	R. Smith	Bangor, Me	Aug. 7, 1866	57, 004
Eraser and burnisher	S. R. Andres	Troy, N. Y	Aug. 21, 1866	57, 273
Eraser and burnisher	A. G. Shaver	New Haven, Conn	Aug. 22, 1865	49, 558
Eraser and burnisher	A. G. Shaver	New Haven, Conn	Oct. 9, 1866	58, 684
Eraser and burnisher, Combined	A. G. Shaver	New Haven, Conn	Aug. 22, 1865	49, 559
Eraser and eraser-sharpener, Combination of	J. Gault	Boston, Mass	Sept. 17, 1861	33, 304
Eraser and letter-opener	G. C. Barney	Philadelphia, Pa	Oct. 1, 1867	69, 388
Eraser and pen-handle combined	W. A. Morse and J. G. Powell	Philadelphia, Pa	Feb. 26, 1867	62, 496
Eraser and pencil-sharpener	A. G. Shaver	Hartford, Conn	Mar. 8, 1859	23, 196
Eraser and pencil-sharpener combined	C. D. Smith	Washington, D. C	Oct. 2, 1866	58, 558
Eraser-attachment for pencil, &c	G. H. Richards	New York, N. Y	Feb. 22, 1870	100, 189
Eraser, Blackboard	F. G. Johnson	Brooklyn, N. Y	June 18, 1872	128, 149
Eraser, Blackboard	W. S. Read	Oakland, Cal	Feb. 4, 1873	135, 487
Eraser, Chalk	G. Munger	New Haven, Conn	Nov. 5, 1861	33, 684
Eraser for pencils, Detachable	W. K. Evans	New York, N. Y	May 14, 1872	126, 792
Eraser-holder	W. P. Patton	Harrisburgh, Pa	Aug. 21, 1866	57, 370
Eraser, Ink	J. W. Tallmage	New York, N. Y	Jan. 16, 1872	122, 867
Eraser, Rubber	W. N. Bartholomew	Newton Centre, Mass	Dec. 15, 1868	84, 985
Eraser, Rubber	W. N. Bartholomew	Newton Centre, Mass	Dec. 19, 1871	121, 982
Eraser, Rubber	M. D. Converse and F. A. Bates	London, Ohio, and Boston, Mass.	June 28, 1870	104, 831
Eraser, Rubber	E. W. Frost	Brooklyn, N. Y	Apr. 1, 1873	137, 299
Eraser, Rubber	S. D. Hovey	Brooklyn, N. Y	Aug. 17, 1869	93, 823
Eraser, Rubber	T. H. Müller	Yonkers, N. Y	Mar. 5, 1872	124, 374
Eraser, Rubber	G. Stackpole	Elizabeth, N. J	Nov. 4, 1873	144, 364
Eraser, Vulcanized rubber pencil-mark	T. H. Müller	Yonkers, N. Y	Jan. 23, 1872	122, 904
Escape-pipe, Condensing	B. F. Smith	New Orleans, La	Sept. 12, 1871	118, 885
Escapement	W. C. Kellum	San Francisco, Cal	Sept. 1, 1868	81, 789
Escapement	W. C. Kellum	San Francisco, Cal	Sept. 8, 1868	81, 910
Escapement	W. N. Manning	Rockport, Mass	May 19, 1863	38, 594
Escapement	J. V. D. Patch	Brownville, Nebr	July 21, 1868	80, 209
Escapement, Duplex	C. E. Jacot	New York, N. Y	July 27, 1852	9, 150
Escapements, Arrangement of dead-beat	D. J. Mozart	Yellow Springs, Ohio	Aug. 9, 1859	25, 034
Escritoir, Portable	W. G. Mitchell	Holliston, Mass	Jan. 24, 1871	111, 231
Esophagus-tube	N. Q. Munger	Brookfield Centre, Wis	July 10, 1860	29, 092
Essence-extracting apparatus	G. Bantz	Frederick, Md	Feb. 9, 1869	86, 803
Essences, Mode of extracting	J. C. Walker	Waco Village, Tex	Aug. 13, 1867	67, 824
Essences, Vessel for extracting	O. Ernst	New York, N. Y	July 1, 1862	35, 747
Etching-grounds, Mode of producing	R. Gottgetreu	Munich, Bavaria	Aug. 28, 1866	57, 651
Etching stones, Composition for	A. Hoen	Baltimore, Md	Apr. 24, 1860	27, 981
Ether, Apparatus for administering	L. Roper	Philadelphia, Pa	Oct. 10, 1848	5, 850
Ether, Process of manufacturing sulphuric	F. Renz	Poughkeepsie, N. Y	Aug. 11, 1868	80, 835
Evaporating alkaline solutions, &c., Furnace for	M. L. Keen	Jersey City, N. J	Nov. 18, 1873	144, 682
Evaporating and clarifying pan	C. Jacobs	Columbus, Ohio	Aug. 6, 1861	32, 998
Evaporating and distilling apparatus	W. R. King	Yellow Springs, Ohio	Jan. 7, 1862	34, 062
Evaporating and distilling apparatus	W. P. Wheeler	Louisville, Ky	Aug. 8, 1865	49, 328
Evaporating and distilling by solar heat	N. W. Wheeler and W. W. Evans.	Brooklyn and New Rochelle, N. Y.	May 3, 1870	102, 633
Evaporating and distilling liquids	J. Adair and H. W. C. Tweddle.	Pittsburgh, Pa	July 17, 1866	56, 343
Evaporating-furnace	J. Richardson		Sept. 13, 1802	....
Evaporating-furnace	J. Richardson		Apr. 4, 1803	....
Evaporating furnace, Salt	J. Colquhoun	Charleston, Va	Feb. 6, 1834	....
Evaporating furnace, Sugar-juice	L. Lefebvre	New Orleans, La	Nov. 23, 1858	22, 126
Evaporating furnace, Sugar-juice	F. Roy	Saint Bernard Parish, La	Dec. 14, 1858	22, 307
Evaporating-kettle furnaces, Arch for	E. Laass	Syracuse, N. Y	June 2, 1868	78, 527
Evaporating-pan	H. O. Ames	New Orleans, La	Oct. 16, 1860	30, 413
Evaporating-pan	H. F. Bartlett	La Grange, Mo	Sept. 5, 1865	49, 694
Evaporating-pan	G. Bez	Mokena, Ill	May 2, 1865	47, 511
Evaporating-pan	S. P. Dyer	Prairie Depot, Ohio	June 11, 1867	65, 656
Evaporating-pan	J. J. Mapes and W. A. Cox	New York, N. Y	Jan. 7, 1846	4, 352
Evaporating-pan	S. Page	McAllisterville, Pa	June 25, 1867	66, 037
Evaporating-pan	G. W. Storer	Philadelphia, Pa	June 3, 1873	139, 625
Evaporating-pan	G. W. Storer	Philadelphia, Pa	Oct. 21, 1873	143, 939
Evaporating-pan	G. W. Storer	Philadelphia, Pa	Oct. 28, 1873	144, 158
Evaporating-pan	E. E. Stubbs and T. C. Davis	West Elkton, Ohio	July 16, 1867	66, 750
Evaporating-pan	D. Watson	Mexico, Mexico	Oct. 14, 1873	143, 649

Index of patents issued from the United States Patent Office from 1790 *to* 1873, *inclusive*—Continued.

Invention.	Inventor.	Residence.	Date.	No.
Evaporating-pan	J. A. Webb and C. Cory	Madison, N. J., and Lima, Ind.	Apr. 9, 1867	63, 678
Evaporating-pan	N. Willey	South Windsor, Conn	Sept. 10, 1867	68, 821
Evaporating-pan	J. B. Williams	Glastenbury, Conn	June 29, 1869	91, 890
Evaporating-pan	J. B. Williams	Glastenbury, Conn	June 27, 1871	116, 524
Evaporating pan and furnace	A. Kolb	Steubenville, Ohio	Jan. 14, 1825	....
Evaporating pan and furnace	L. Scott	Sinking Spring, Ohio	Sept. 21, 1869	95, 049
Evaporating pan and plant for salt-manufacture	G. W. Storer	Philadelphia, Pa	Oct. 28, 1873	144, 159
Evaporating pan, Cane-juice	D. M. Cook	Mansfield, Ohio	June 22, 1858	20, 631
Evaporating pan, Cane-juice	C. A. Desobry	Plaquemine, La	Nov. 8, 1859	26, 024
Evaporating-pan for saccharine juices	E. D. Foss	Maineville, Ohio	Feb. 25, 1862	34, 484
Evaporating-pan for saccharine juices	J. V. Harter	Plymouth, Ill	Dec. 17, 1861	33, 942
Evaporating-pan for saccharine juices	J. M. Moss	Waverly, Iowa	May 20, 1862	35, 350
Evaporating-pan for saccharine juices	D. B. Neal	Mount Gilead, Ohio	Mar. 11, 1862	34, 644
Evaporating-pan for saccharine juices	W. E. Prall	Maineville, Ohio	Feb. 18, 1862	34, 469
Evaporating-pan for saccharine liquids	O. N. Brainerd	Marion, Iowa	Jan. 28, 1862	34, 236
Evaporating-pan for saccharine liquids	F. G. Butler	Bellows Falls, Vt	Mar. 7, 1871	112, 319
Evaporating-pan for saccharine liquids	P. W. Gates	Chicago, Ill	Oct. 28, 1862	36, 881
Evaporating-pan for saccharine liquids	G. Stump	New York, N. Y	July 8, 1862	35, 844
Evaporating-pan for sorghum-juice	N. Z. Potter	Uniontown, Ill	June 9, 1863	38, 839
Evaporating-pan for sugar	H. F. Bartlett	La Grange, Mo	Oct. 18, 1864	44, 698
Evaporating-pan for sugar and sirup	L. Megowan	Upper Alton, Ill	June 21, 1864	43, 220
Evaporating-pan for sugar-juices	D. M. Cook	Mansfield, Ohio	Apr. 14, 1863	38, 152
Evaporating-pan for sugar, salt, &c	L. R. Cornell	Brooklyn, N. Y	Feb. 11, 1873	135, 630
Evaporating pan, Steam	T. C. Bartle and C. F. Putney	Independence, Iowa	Dec. 27, 1864	45, 667
Evaporating pan, Sugar	C. B. Darrow	Orland, Ind	Nov. 3, 1863	40, 460
Evaporating pan, Sugar	S. H. Gilman	New Orleans, La	Sept. 9, 1856	15, 694
Evaporating pan, Sugar	H. F. Schroder	Cincinnati, Ohio	Dec. 18, 1866	60, 564
Evaporating pan, Sugar-juice	W. Hedges	Chicago, Ill	Nov. 29, 1859	26, 325
Evaporating-pan with cellular boiler	D. M. Cook	Mansfield, Ohio	Feb. 24, 1863	37, 736
Evaporating-pan with tubular boiler	D. M. Cook	Mansfield, Ohio	Feb. 24, 1863	37, 737
Evaporating-pans, Apparatus for heating	H. O. Ames	New Orleans, La	Aug. 9, 1859	24, 978
Evaporating-pans, Apparatus for heating	E. Skelly	Plaquemine, La	Aug. 9, 1859	25, 052
Evaporating-pans, Cellular or tubular boiler for	D. M. Cook	Mansfield, Ohio	Feb. 24, 1863	37, 735
Evaporating-pans, Device to regulate the flow of sap to.	J. Thomas	Hardwick, Vt	Sept. 6, 1870	107, 124
Evaporating-pans for saccharine juices, &c., Construction of.	T. J. Price	Industry, Ill	Jan. 28, 1862	34, 264
Evaporating-pans furnaces, Arch bar and support for constructing.	G. S. Deane	Grand Rapids, Mich	Oct. 15, 1867	69, 781
Evaporating-pans, &c., Method of inserting tubes in.	G. H. Thomas	Kingston, Mass	Nov. 20, 1855	13, 832
Evaporating pans or boilers, Feeder for	S. A. Mitchell	Alstead Centre, N. H	Apr. 16, 1867	63, 925
Evaporating-vessel	J. P. Hale	Kanawha Court-House, Va	Nov. 22, 1859	26, 182
Evaporating-vessels, Arrangement of steam-coils in.	H. O. Ames	New Orleans, La	June 29, 1858	20, 687
Evaporation	T. Arnold	....	Mar. 5, 1806	....
Evaporation	T. Bedwell and B. Henfrey	....	Feb. 12, 1801	....
Evaporation and vaporization	M. S. Bringier	Ascension Parish, La	Nov. 12, 1867	70, 690
Evaporator: *See* Brine-evaporator. Cane-juice evaporator. Compound evaporator. Fluid-evaporator. Hot-air-pipe evaporator. Liquid-evaporator. Medicine-evaporator. Portable evaporator. Rotary evaporator. Saccharine-juice evaporator. Saccharine-liquid evaporator. Salt-evaporator. Salt-water evaporator. Sap-evaporator. Sorghum-evaporator. Steam-heated evaporator. Sugar-evaporator. Sugar-juice evaporator. Sugar-pan evaporator. Vacuum-evaporator.				
Evaporator	C. Alden	New York, N. Y	Oct. 4, 1859	25, 614
Evaporator	P. J. Badoux	New York, N. Y	June 9, 1868	78, 639
Evaporator	A. Balding	Madison, Ind	Aug. 28, 1866	57, 459
Evaporator	J. Beechley	Dayton, Ohio	Mar. 6, 1866	52, 952
Evaporator	J. C. Bell	Pawnee City, Nebr	Dec. 26, 1865	51, 683
Evaporator	J. Bogue	Auburn, Wis	Sept. 12, 1865	49, 851
Evaporator	S. Bowerman	Battle Creek, Mich	Dec. 20, 1864	45, 470
Evaporator	W. Canning	New York, N. Y	May 23, 1865	47, 795
Evaporator	B. F. Cauffman	Millerstown, Pa	Sept. 1, 1868	81, 752
Evaporator	E. Chitister	Chatham, Iowa	Jan. 12, 1869	85, 791
Evaporator	J. Cook	Wellsville, N. Y	Nov. 14, 1871	120, 859
Evaporator	J. Cooper	Mount Vernon, Ohio	Oct. 9, 1866	58, 607
Evaporator	S. P. Dyer	Ankney Town, Ohio	May 2, 1871	114, 278
Evaporator	A. S. Eddy	Smithville, N. Y	Aug. 21, 1866	57, 301
Evaporator	J. H. Elward	Polo, Ill	Feb. 6, 1866	52, 402
Evaporator	N. Evinger	Terre Haute, Ind	July 28, 1868	810, 342
Evaporator	F. Farquahar and R. E. Doan	Wilmington, Ohio	Sept. 25, 1866	58, 236
Evaporator	H. C. Gilbert	Cambridge, Vt	Feb. 12, 1867	61, 025
Evaporator	S. D. Gilson	Syracuse, N. Y	Oct. 25, 1870	108, 701
Evaporator	L. R. Gleason	Dundee, N. Y	Mar. 27, 1866	53, 438
Evaporator	F. M. Harris	Winnamac, Ind	Jan. 2, 1866	51, 828
Evaporator	J. Harris	Janesville, Wis	Nov. 24, 1868	84, 277
Evaporator	S. T. Harrison	Baltimore, Md	Dec. 31, 1838	1, 056
Evaporator	B. R. Hawley	Normal, Ill	May 1, 1866	54, 340
Evaporator	R. Hawley, jr	Detroit, Mich	Jan. 24, 1871	111, 121
Evaporator	G. W. L. Hazen	Franklin, Ind	Apr. 17, 1866	53, 975
Evaporator	W. H. Isaacs	Terre Haute, Ind	Aug. 21, 1866	57, 327
Evaporator	D. Kinzer	Sardinia, Ohio	Sept. 11, 1866	57, 923
Evaporator	H. Lighty	Attica, Ind	June 4, 1867	65, 404
Evaporator	J. and S. W. Little	Patoka, Ind	Aug. 28, 1866	57, 523
Evaporator	F. A. Lord	Aurora, N. Y	May 30, 1865	47, 966
Evaporator	F. M. Love	Waldron, Ind	July 4, 1865	48, 628
Evaporator	N. R. Martin	Canandaigua, N. Y	Aug. 9, 1870	106, 270
Evaporator	S. B. Maulsby	Muncie, Ind	Mar. 20, 1866	53, 318

Index of patents issued from the United States Patent Office from 1790 *to* 1873, *inclusive*—Continued.

Invention.	Inventor.	Residence.	Date.	No.
Evaporator	S. B. Maulsby	Muncie, Ind	July 24, 1866	56, 585
Evaporator	J. McCracken	Bloomfield, N. J	Mar. 13, 1855	12, 516
Evaporator	J. A. McKinney	Griggsville, Ill	Jan. 8, 1867	61, 061
Evaporator	C. and D. Mercer	Strickersville, Pa	Mar. 13, 1866	53, 229
Evaporator	F. Michael	Gratis, Ohio	Feb. 19, 1867	62, 147
Evaporator	J. E. Moeller	Terre Haute, Ind	Nov. 28, 1865	51, 206
Evaporator	R. C. Nourse	Corydon, Ind	Sept. 11, 1866	57, 954
Evaporator	S. Page	McAllisterville, Pa	Oct. 9, 1866	58, 671
Evaporator	M. Pake	Dorchester, Ill	Sept. 15, 1863	39, 948
Evaporator	I. H. Palmer	Lodi, Wis	July 25, 1865	48, 990
Evaporator	W. H. Parmelee	Hopkins, Mich	Nov. 15, 1864	45, 072
Evaporator	D. Reeves	South Pass, Ill	Apr. 10, 1866	53, 873
Evaporator	D. Reynolds	Albany, N. Y	June 15, 1869	91, 485
Evaporator	J. F. Riggs	Saint Joseph, Mo	July 3, 1866	56, 097
Evaporator	T. and J. M. Scantlin	Evansville, Ind	July 25, 1865	48, 982
Evaporator	I. Sherman	Cleveland, Ohio	May 22, 1860	28, 415
Evaporator	A. W. Shidler	South Bend, Ind	Aug. 31, 1869	94, 249
Evaporator	H. Staude and A. Traver	Troy, N. Y	Oct. 8, 1872	131, 979
Evaporator	H. Stoller	Watertown, Ohio	May 11, 1869	89, 951
Evaporator	J. J. Stout	Greensburgh, Ind	Jan. 8, 1867	61, 112
Evaporator	J. Sutton	New York, N. Y	Jan. 3, 1860	26, 717
Evaporator	E. W. Taylor	Franklin, Ind	July 17, 1866	56, 464
Evaporator	T. Thomasson	Keoga, Ill	Apr. 24, 1866	54, 231
Evaporator	S. M. Williams	Pine Village, Ind	June 11, 1867	65, 714
Evaporator	W. S. Worthington	Newtown, N. Y	Jan. 11, 1859	22, 601
Evaporator	J. E. Youngman	Rockford, Ill	Sept. 25, 1866	58, 331
Evaporator	A. Youngs	Berlin, Mich	May 3, 1870	102, 643
Evaporator and condenser	E. Lynch	Brooklyn, N. Y	July 18, 1848	5, 668
Evaporator and cooler	H. Koehly, jr	Potosi, Mo	Mar. 13, 1866	53, 226
Evaporator and drier	W. Kendrick	New York, N. Y	Apr. 24, 1866	54, 173
Evaporator and steam-engine	D. Heath	Philadelphia, Pa	July 26, 1816	....
Evaporator and still	M. H. Powers	Pike County, Ind	June 14, 1870	104, 351
Evaporator, Compound	J. A. Wadsworth	Portsmouth, R. I	Nov. 23, 1825	....
Evaporator-furnace	W. Barrett	Malden, Mass	Nov. 19, 1833	....
Evaporator-furnace	M. P. Hays	Seaforth, Canada	Dec. 24, 1872	134, 277
Evaporator-furnace	T. Spencer	Syracuse, N. Y	July 25, 1848	5, 676
Evaporator furnace and fire-place	P. Tomlinson	Derby, Conn	Mar. 7, 1815	....
Evaporator furnace or fire-arch	S. Berry	Grand Rapids, Mich	Nov. 17, 1863	40, 599
Evaporators, Adjuster for	J. A. De Tar	Lanesfield, Kans	Mar. 27, 1866	53, 422
Evaporators, Automatic feeder for	J. Smead	East Wallingford, Vt	May 5, 1868	77, 666
Evaporators, Construction of	N. Bourne	Peosto, Iowa	Oct. 4, 1859	25, 623
Evaporators, Construction of	J. B. Dagne	Ashley, Ohio	Oct. 18, 1859	25, 813
Evaporators, Construction of	T. J. Price	Industry, Ill	May 15, 1860	28, 304
Evener	M. Terrill	Star Prairie, Wis	July 18, 1871	117, 123
Evener, Three-horse	B. W. Sutherlen	Fillmore, Minn	Feb. 11, 1873	135, 861
Evener, Two-horse	J. Sturgis	Minneapolis, Minn	Jan. 14, 1873	134, 946
Earth, Machine for excavating and conveying	J. A. Sprague	Dayton, Ohio	Oct. 15, 1850	7, 723
Excavating and ditching machine	M. M. Stewart and J. D. M. Russell	Wayfield, Ky	Jan. 30, 1872	123, 303
Excavating and ditching machine	B. F. Stowell	Quincy, Ill	Mar. 10, 1863	37, 878
Excavating and dredging	W. S. Smith	Oak Park, Ill	Apr. 9, 1867	63, 661
Excavating and dredging machine	O. Allen	Norwich, Conn	May 8, 1849	1, 591
Excavating and dredging machine	J. R. Anderson	Chicago, Ill	Feb. 3, 1857	16, 519
Excavating and dredging machine	C. Willey, jr	Chicago, Ill	Feb. 10, 1852	8, 731
Excavating and embanking ditches, Machine for	G. Page	Keene, N. H	Oct. 26, 1838	993
Excavating and grading machine	P. T. Mayne	Keosaugua, Iowa	July 17, 1860	29, 183
Excavating and grading machine	W. P. Miller	Marysville, Cal	Aug. 2, 1859	24, 946
Excavating and grading machine	Z. N. Morrel	Cameron, Tex	July 19, 1859	24, 816
Excavating and moving earth, Machine for	A. W. Cady	Sullivan, N. Y	Apr. 29, 1856	14, 762
Excavating-apparatus	P. W. Clark	Oblong, N. Y	May 3, 1870	102, 492
Excavating canals, ditches, &c	W. Graham	New Orleans, La	Sept. 5, 1831	....
Excavating canals, Machine for	L. Forrester	Bridgefield, Conn	May 10, 1826	....
Excavating-cart	J. King	Oswego, N. Y	Nov. 21, 1871	121, 108
Excavating earth, Inclined elevating-box wheel for	J. Rowe	Triana, Ala	Feb. 15, 1838	602
Excavating from rivers	S. Russell	Buffalo, N. Y	Apr. 28, 1836	....
Excavating-machine	S. Achenbach	Orangeville, Pa	June 11, 1872	127, 671
Excavating-machine	J. A. Bailey	Detroit, Mich	July 13, 1869	92, 508
Excavating-machine	J. A. Bailey	Detroit, Mich	Aug. 2, 1870	105, 883
Excavating-machine	C. Bishop	Norwalk, Ohio	Mar. 30, 1852	8, 836
Excavating-machine	D. Brown	Southampton, Ill	Apr. 30, 1872	126, 178
Excavating-machine	T. Claton	Shelbyville, Ind	Dec. 1, 1837	500
Excavating-machine	R. W. Davis	Sonora, N. Y	Aug. 15, 1871	117, 993
Excavating-machine	W. H. Elliot	New York, N. Y	Nov. 23, 1869	97, 068
Excavating-machine	P. W. Hamel	San Francisco, Cal	Feb. 23, 1869	87, 168
Excavating-machine	W. Hamilton	South Paris, Me	May 12, 1863	38, 497
Excavating-machine	W. M. Hansen	Stockton, Cal	May 31, 1870	103, 740
Excavating-machine	J. M. Hughes and A. J. Mapes	Independence, Mo	Feb. 21, 1871	111, 940
Excavating-machine	W. S. Lane	Cairo, Ill	July 30, 1872	130, 059
Excavating-machine	W. R. Maffet	Wilkesbarre, Pa	Aug. 17, 1858	21, 206
Excavating-machine	G. S. Manning	Springfield, Ill	July 17, 1860	29, 182
Excavating-machine	T. R. Markillie	Winchester, Ill	Dec. 27, 1859	26, 601
Excavating-machine	M. Newman, 2d	Lanesborough, Pa	Nov. 19, 1850	7, 787
Excavating-machine	B. W. Remy	Brookville, Ind	Oct. 21, 1851	8, 453
Excavating-machine	J. Robertson	Glasgow, Scotland	July 21, 1868	80, 225
Excavating-machine	N. Saunders and F. T. Sherman	Chicago, Ill	June 8, 1858	20, 511
Excavating-machine	J. J. Savage	New York, N. Y	Jan. 8, 1856	14, 068
Excavating-machine	C. Schott and J. C. Baldwin	Nashville, Tenn	Apr. 19, 1859	23, 713
Excavating-machine	G. D. Stillson	Rochester, N. Y	Nov. 14, 1854	11, 949
Excavating-machine	G. D. Stillson	Rochester, N. Y	Apr. 19, 1859	23, 723
Excavating-machine	A. Taggart	Warrenton, Mo	June 16, 1857	17, 595
Excavating-machine	M. B. True	Newburyport, Mass	Sept. 18, 1860	30, 098
Excavating-machine	W. F. Wickersham	Springfield, Ill	June 25, 1861	32, 660
Excavating-machine	C. Williams	Jackson, Tenn	Apr. 3, 1855	12, 651
Excavating-machine	E. Williams	Covington, Ky	July 17, 1855	13, 282
Excavating-machine	E. H. Williams	Clermont, Iowa	June 13, 1871	115, 998
Excavating-machine	E. H. and D. R. W. Williams	Grand Meadow, Iowa., and Werner, Wis.	Oct. 1, 1867	69, 378

Index of patents issued from the United States Patent Office from 1790 *to* 1873, *inclusive*—Continued.

Invention.	Inventor.	Residence.	Date.	No.
Excavating-machine	C. Winegar	Union Springs, N. Y	Aug. 28, 1866	57, 611
Excavating machine, Coal	J. Borton	Antrim, Ohio	Aug. 14, 1868	76, 704
Excavating machine, Coal	H. Wilverth	Caseyville, Ky	Jan. 3, 1860	26, 726
Excavating machine, Ditch	H. Aiken	Franklin, N. H	Feb. 1, 1842	2, 440
Excavating-machine for ditches, canals, &c	J. Hanchett	Coldwater, Mich	Feb. 28, 1840	1, 502
Excavating-machine for ditching, &c	G. W. Cherry	Washington, D. C	Jan. 16, 1839	1, 069
Excavating-machine, Mode of operating	J. A. H. Ellis and A. Gordon	Rochester, N. Y	July 18, 1854	11, 323
Excavating-machine, Submarine	J. C. Osgood	Troy, N. Y	May 22, 1855	12, 919
Excavating mud, Borer for	M. H. Ford	New York, N. Y	Oct. 4, 1859	25, 636
Excavating, plowing, and grading machines	E. H. Williams and D. R. W. Williams.	Clermont, Iowa, and Werner, Wis.	Apr. 15, 1862	35, 005
Excavating rock, Machinery for	J. C. Osgood	Troy, N. Y	Feb. 17, 1857	16, 652
Excavating-scoop	O. P. Kniffin	Clinton, Conn	Nov. 8, 1870	109, 132
Excavating-shovel	T. Pierce	Hartwick, N. Y	Mar. 3, 1825	....
Excavating, Softening frozen ground for	A. Derrom	Paterson, N. J	Feb. 6, 1872	123, 384
Excavating tunnels and cuttings, Sinking shafts and.	J. Shelley and M. C. Bullock	Mahanoy and Pottsville, Pa.	May 23, 1871	115, 115
Excavating under water, Method of	A. Duvall	Baltimore, Md	Mar. 3, 1868	75, 003
Excavating under water, Method of	A. Duvall	Baltimore, Md	Mar. 3, 1868	75, 004
Excavating-vehicle	J. P. Smith	Cherry Hill, Pa	Apr. 28, 1868	77, 329
Excavation, Curbing for	H. Whitestone	Louisville, Ky	Jan. 10, 1871	110, 882
Excavator	S. B. Alger	Oswego, N. Y	Dec. 24, 1872	134, 187
Excavator	A. J. Bartlett	Romulus, N. Y	Nov. 13, 1860	30, 610
Excavator	J. Bartoo	East Aurora, N. Y	June 4, 1861	42, 494
Excavator	H. H. Beard	Friar's Point, Miss	Aug. 17, 1869	93, 796
Excavator	J. Bourbin	San Francisco, Cal	Oct. 14, 1856	15, 875
Excavator	J. Bradley	Cedar Falls, Iowa	Aug. 7, 1866	57, 038
Excavator	H. Brown	Lowell, Mass	Aug. 25, 1868	81, 334
Excavator	Z. Butt	Lincolnton, N. C	Sept. 15, 1857	18, 185
Excavator	W. J. Carroll	Natchez, Miss	June 6, 1871	115, 700
Excavator	O. S. Chapman	Canton, Mass	Apr. 16, 1867	63, 857
Excavator	D. Close	Harmonsburgh, Pa	July 5, 1864	43, 392
Excavator	D. Comstock	Lockport, N. Y	Mar. 15, 1825	....
Excavator	J. Cowden and D. Brown	La Prairie Centre and Akron, Ill.	Oct. 12, 1869	95, 658
Excavator	J. M. Curless	Cedar Rapids, Iowa	May 6, 1873	138, 485
Excavator	S. S. Curtis	Croton Corners, N. Y	Dec. 14, 1858	22, 279
Excavator	J. P. T. Davis	New Trenton, Ind	Sept. 12, 1871	118, 793
Excavator	J. M. Dunn	Erin, Miss	Sept. 26, 1871	119, 334
Excavator	H. W. Farley	Hannibal, Mo	July 11, 1865	48, 669
Excavator	D. Gilmore and W. W. Forrest	Peotone, Ill	Jan. 3, 1871	110, 759
Excavator	J. T. Ham	Liberty, Ind	Feb. 4, 1873	135, 475
Excavator	W. Hamilton	Saint Catherine, Mo	Sept. 13, 1859	25, 408
Excavator	B. Hancock	Troy, N. Y	Oct. 16, 1855	13, 680
Excavator	J. P. Hayes	Hennepin, Ill	Dec. 4, 1860	30, 819
Excavator	J. Hodges	Bagshot, England	May 23, 1865	47, 908
Excavator	M. M. Hodgman	Weymouth, Mass	Apr. 18, 1871	113, 883
Excavator	M. M. Hodgman	Weymouth, Mass	Oct. 8, 1872	131, 954
Excavator	T. Hutchinson	Green Point, N. Y	Aug. 6, 1861	32, 997
Excavator	D. Judd	Hinsdale, N. Y	July 10, 1866	56, 229
Excavator	D. Judd	Hinsdale, N. Y	Nov. 18, 1873	144, 679
Excavator	A. Kirby	Paris, Ill	Apr. 30, 1861	32, 194
Excavator	J. Lee	Galesburgh, Ill	Feb. 9, 1869	86, 678
Excavator	J. R. Lewis	Piper City, Ill	Dec. 14, 1869	97, 783
Excavator	A. P. Lomax	Warsaw, Ill	Mar. 18, 1873	137, 011
Excavator	C. A. Mann, jr	Pike, N. Y	May 27, 1856	14, 966
Excavator	D. McNabb	Moscow, Mich	Dec. 8, 1863	40, 850
Excavator	E. B. Meatyard	Chicago, Ill	May 14, 1872	126, 729
Excavator	S. Miller and E. Claringdon	Waterloo, N. Y	May 23, 1871	115, 084
Excavator	J. Milroy	Edinburgh, Great Britain	Apr. 23, 1867	64, 023
Excavator	J. Molyneux	Bordentown, N. J	Jan. 1, 1867	60, 774
Excavator	S. G. L. Morron	Linn, Mo	Sept. 30, 1856	15, 813
Excavator	B. A. Oliver	Bunker Hill, Ill	Mar. 18, 1873	136, 936
Excavator	J. C. Osgood	Troy, N. Y	July 4, 1865	48, 581
Excavator	J. C. Osgood	Troy, N. Y	Apr. 4, 1871	113, 691
Excavator	E. Phelps	Hendersonville, Ill	June 6, 1854	11, 028
Excavator	A. E. Pierce	Gilroy, Cal	Nov. 9, 1869	96, 724
Excavator	W. Provines	Columbia, Mo	Jan. 13, 1857	16, 397
Excavator	W. Randall	Uxbridge, Canada	Apr. 2, 1861	31, 905
Excavator	C. H. Sage and S. B. Alger	Norwich, N. Y	Nov. 29, 1870	109, 764
Excavator	F. W. Schultz	Mount Pleasant, Iowa	Jan. 21, 1873	135, 162
Excavator	B. Slusser	Sidney, Ohio	Dec. 4, 1866	60, 268
Excavator	B. Slusser	Sidney, Ohio	Dec. 10, 1867	72, 098
Excavator	B. Slusser	Sidney, Ohio	June 28, 1870	104, 782
Excavator	A. B. Smith	Denison, Tex	May 6, 1873	138, 539
Excavator	J. D. Smith	Panton, Vt	Jan. 12, 1858	19, 104
Excavator	S. W. Soule	Oswego, N. Y	July 10, 1855	13, 234
Excavator	S. W. Soule	Saint Louis, Mo	Apr. 28, 1857	17, 174
Excavator	B. T. Stowell	Quincy, Ill	Dec. 17, 1867	72, 336
Excavator	B. T. Stowell	Quincy, Ill	Nov. 17, 1868	84, 250
Excavator	B. T. Stowell	Quincy, Ill	Mar. 28, 1871	113, 221
Excavator	J. W. Swickard	Galva, Ill	July 6, 1869	92, 224
Excavator	T. Symonds	Portland, Mo	Feb. 14, 1871	111, 787
Excavator	T. Symonds	Portland, Me	May 16, 1871	114, 878
Excavator	I. D. Vandecar	Chicago, Ill	Apr. 23, 1867	64, 168
Excavator	B. R. Wehner	Mankato, Minn	Oct. 19, 1869	95, 961
Excavator	J. F. Willey	Fredonia, N. Y	Nov. 11, 1856	16, 031
Excavator	G. W. Williams	Corning, N. Y	Jan. 2, 1872	122, 344
Excavator	C. F. Woodruff	Newbern, Tenn	Aug. 4, 1868	80, 696
Excavator and ditching-plow	C. A. Robbins	Iowa City, Iowa	Nov. 14, 1854	11, 948
Excavator and potato-digger	B. O. Warren	Elkhart, Ind	Feb. 12, 1867	61, 963
Excavator and self-loading cart	M. Alden and W. T. Boyd	Northumberland, Pa	July 20, 1831	....
Excavator, Canal	I. L. Skinner	Hartford, Conn	May 3, 1820	....
Excavator-carrier	J. Williams	Hemmingford, Canada	May 27, 1873	139, 446
Excavator, Channel	R. Gamble, jr	Tallahassee, Fla	Nov. 13, 1860	30, 626
Excavator, Ditch	G. W. Cherry	Washington, D. C	Mar. 26, 1841	2, 017
Excavator, Earth	J. P. Barker	Wayne, Ohio	Feb. 8, 1859	22, 847
Excavator, Earth	C. Colby	Wilson, N. Y	June 30, 1857	17, 669

Index of patents issued from the United States Patent Office from 1790 to 1873, inclusive—Continued.

Invention.	Inventor.	Residence.	Date.	No.
Excavator, Earth	D. C. Lockwood	New Windsor, N. Y	Mar. 31, 1841	2, 025
Excavator, Earth	J. W. Myers	Lyons, Iowa	Oct. 25, 1870	108, 723
Excavator, Earth	J. Taggart	Roxbury, Mass	July 4, 1854	11, 242
Excavator, Floating	H. W. Campbell	Lockport, N. Y	Jan. 22, 1828	....
Excavator, Floating	A. Hawley	Milwaukee, Wis	Aug. 29, 1848	5, 743
Excavator, Floating	W. Morrison and G. Tomb	Jersey Shore, Pa	Aug. 25, 1830	....
Excavator, Floating	A. Watson	Pendleton, N. Y	Jan. 18, 1830	....
Excavator for ditching, embanking, and draining prairie-land.	C. K. Bartlett	Geneseo, Ill	Mar. 23, 1842	2, 512
Excavator for excavating and removing earth, Crane.	W. S. Otis	Philadelphia, Pa	Feb. 24, 1839	1, 089
Excavator for railways, Revolving snow	J. Urmy	Wilmington, Del	Nov. 10, 1857	18, 615
Excavator for water-courses having currents	N. Van Deventer	New Albany, Ind	Oct. 8, 1861	33, 460
Excavator, Inclined-plane	D. Marvin	Canandaigua, N. Y	Sept. 2, 1831	....
Excavator or digging-machine	F. J. Vandervinne	Brussels, Belgium	July 2, 1867	66, 425
Excavator or drag for removing mud, &c., in the beds of rivers.	D. Vermillion	Washington, D. C	Nov. 9, 1844	3, 818
Excavator or dredging-machine for rivers, canals, &c., Scoop.	J. Smith	Mansfield, Ohio	Aug. 24, 1844	3, 718
Excavator or self-loading cart	W. Beach	Philadelphia, Pa	Feb. 5, 1828	....
Excavator or shovel	W. T. Nichols	Rutland, Vt	Mar. 24, 1868	75, 783
Excavator, Post-hole	J. D. Owen	Carlinville, Ill	Nov. 26, 1861	33, 814
Excavator, Railway	E. O. Baxter	Foreston, Ill	Sept. 6, 1859	25, 314
Excavator, Railway snow	F. G. Johnson	Brooklyn, N. Y	Aug. 27, 1872	130, 807
Excavator, Railway snow	S. Y. Ludlum	Oyster Bay, N. Y	June 16, 1857	17, 580
Excavator, Roads, &c	N. Parkins	Frederick County, Va	Jan. 1, 1847	4, 917
Excavator, Rotary	J. Deveraux	Marshall, Mich	Aug. 11, 1868	80, 813
Excavator, Rotary	D. Judd	Hinsdale, N. Y	June 10, 1856	15, 102
Excavator, Rotary	G. H. Moore	Rochester, N. Y	Oct. 3, 1857	18, 551
Excavator, Screw	R. Montgomery	New York, N. Y	May 7, 1850	7, 346
Excavator, Screw	R. Montgomery	New York, N. Y	May 17, 1859	24, 043
Excavator, Self-acting bar	G. T. Beauregard	New Orleans, La	Oct. 25, 1853	10, 147
Excavator, Sewer	F. W. Slater	Bay City, Mich	Jan. 18, 1870	99, 016
Excavator, Snow	M. V. Nobles	Elmira, N. Y	Oct. 29, 1872	132, 684
Excavator, Steam	W. G. Goodale and R. L. T. Marsh	Centralia, Ill	Dec. 20, 1859	26, 490
Excavator, Submarine	I. R. Benjamin	New York, N. Y	Aug. 2, 1864	43, 664
Excavator, Submarine	W. P. Brayton and J. Hamilton	New York, N. Y	Jan. 8, 1839	1, 063
Excavator, Submarine	A. Duvall	Baltimore, Md	Jan. 26, 1869	86, 290
Excavator, Submarine	T. Jones	Washington, D. C	July 25, 1871	117, 298
Excavator, Submarine	W. Kennish	Brooklyn, N. Y	May 12, 1857	17, 306
Excavator, Submarine	R. R. and R. R. Osgood	Troy, N. Y	Oct. 17, 1871	119, 992
Excavator, Submarine	G. V. Sheffield	Boston, Mass	July 11, 1871	116, 876
Excavator, Tunnel	T. A. and A. F. Fisher	Beardstown, Ill	Feb. 4, 1868	74, 069
Excavators and dredgers, Mode of operating	H. McCarty	Pittsburgh, Pa	Apr. 1, 1845	3, 978
Excavators, Dirt-loading apparatus for	W. Cooper	Mount Gilead, Ohio	Apr. 3, 1860	27, 699
Excelsior-machine	D. F. Brackett	Bangor, Me	Sept. 10, 1872	131, 147
Excelsior-machine	G. Brooks and S. Clements	Detroit, Mich	Mar. 24, 1868	75, 728
Excelsior-machine	J. Felber	Saint Louis, Mo	Nov. 14, 1871	120, 866
Excelsior-machine	W. H. Mayo	Orono, Me	July 16, 1872	128, 970
Excelsior-machine	W. H. Mayo	Orono, Me	Mar. 4, 1873	136, 529
Excelsior-machine	G. H. Smith	Guilford, Me	Aug. 22, 1871	118, 289
Excursion-chair	D. O. Parker	Liverpool, Canada	Aug. 29, 1871	118, 480
Exercising-apparatus	B. F. Brady	New York, N. Y	Apr. 16, 1867	63, 846
Exercising-apparatus	H. E. Eastman	Green Bay, Wis	Jan. 7, 1873	134, 527
Exercising-apparatus	G. W. S. Hall	Baltimore, Md	Feb. 18, 1868	74, 683
Exercising-apparatus	G. H. Taylor	New York, N. Y	Mar. 3, 1868	75, 217
Exercising-apparatus	G. H. Taylor	New York, N. Y	Mar. 3, 1868	75, 218
Exercising-chair	S. Chapin	Ashland, Ohio	Mar. 26, 1850	7, 210
Exercising-chair	J. Stevens	Chicopee Falls, Mass	Aug. 29, 1854	11, 622
Exercising-chair	J. A. Wroe	Hagerstown, Md	Aug. 8, 1868	82, 056
Exercising chair and scale, Child's	T. Shedd and F. Glockner	Williamsburgh, N. Y	Nov. 21, 1865	51, 091
Exercising-chair, Infantine	J. Sawin, D. J. Goodspeed, and J. H. Minott.	Gardner, Mass	Dec. 15, 1857	18, 873
Exercising-club	J. L. Dibble	New York, N. Y	Apr. 23, 1867	64, 081
Exercising-club	C. E. Biester	New York, N. Y	June 13, 1871	115, 856
Exercising-device	J. E. Austin	Philadelphia, Pa	June 24, 1873	140, 237
Exercising-lift	R. Forward	Cincinnati, Ohio	May 14, 1872	126, 796
Exercising-machine	S. M. Barnett	New York, N. Y	Apr. 15, 1873	137, 876
Exercising-machine	J. Elliott	Newark, N. J	Sept. 2, 1845	4, 173
Exercising-machine	O. Halstead	New York, N. Y	Mar. 13, 1844	3, 480
Exercising-machine	D. Harrington	Philadelphia, Pa	Apr. 23, 1831	....
Exercising-machine	C. Kolle	New York, N. Y	Jan. 28, 1873	135, 347
Exercising-machine	R. Shaler	Madison, Conn	June 17, 1873	139, 924
Exercising-machine	C. F. Taylor	New York, N. Y	Dec. 8, 1863	40, 865
Exercising-machine	C. F. Taylor	New York, N. Y	Apr. 26, 1864	42, 516
Exercising-machine	C. F. Taylor	New York, N. Y	Dec. 27, 1864	45, 652
Exercising-machine	T. P. Thorpe	New York, N. Y	May 30, 1865	47, 999
Exercising-machine	T. P. Thorpe	New York, N. Y	Apr. 10, 1866	53, 900
Exercising-machine	L. D. Tice	New York, N. Y	Apr. 1, 1873	137, 394
Exercising-machine, Child's	G. W. Tuttle	New York, N. Y	Sept. 4, 1847	5, 273
Exercising-machine, Elastic	R. L. Hinsdale	New York, N. Y	May 3, 1853	9, 695
Exercising-machine, Infant's	J. S. Brown	New York, N. Y	Mar. 31, 1863	38, 028
Exhaust, Atmospheric air or gas	R. W. Sievier	Upper Halloway, England	July 17, 1860	29, 226
Exhaust device for steam-engines, Variable	J. Barney	Chicago, Ill	July 19, 1859	24, 785
Exhaust for locomotive-engines, Variable	J. Dykeman	Greenbush, N. Y	July 3, 1860	28, 976
Exhaust for locomotive-engines, Variable	O. Stewart	East Cambridge, Mass	Oct. 17, 1871	120, 120
Exhaust for locomotive steam-engines, Variable	C. B. Knowles	Nashville, Tenn	July 30, 1872	130, 057
Exhaust for locomotives, Variable	J. Dykeman and J. Bolton	Greenbush, N. Y	July 12, 1864	43, 484
Exhaust for locomotives, Variable	R. McDowell	Lambertsville, N. J	Aug. 18, 1863	39, 583
Exhaust for non-condensing engines, Variable	J. H. Baker	Saratoga Springs, N. Y	Mar. 24, 1868	75, 723
Exhaust for steam-engines, Condensed-steam	W. H. Wheatland	Newark, N. J	Dec. 5, 1871	121, 697
Exhaust for steam-engines, Variable	W. M. Hurlbert	Northfield, Vt	Sept. 20, 1859	25, 509
Exhaust in locomotive-engines, Mode of regulating the.	T. B. Quigley	Galion, Ohio	July 5, 1859	24, 661
Exhaust, Locomotive steam	T. Davies	Cleveland, Ohio	Oct. 29, 1872	132, 565
Exhaust-mechanism for locomotive-engines	W. A. Carns	Malden, Mass	Sept. 26, 1871	119, 219
Exhaust-nozzle for steam-engines	Richard Norris	Harrisburgh, Pa	Nov. 24, 1868	84, 370
Exhaust-nozzle-valve device	A. Onslow	Jersey City, N. J	Aug. 10, 1869	93, 470

Index of patents issued from the United States Patent Office from 1790 *to* 1873, *inclusive*—Continued.

Invention.	Inventor.	Residence.	Date.	No.
Exhaust of caloric engines, Utilizing the	P. Shaw	Boston, Mass	Oct. 15, 1861	33, 497
Exhaust of locomotive-engines, Variable	W. S. G. Baker	Chicago, Ill	May 17, 1859	23, 999
Exhaust of locomotive-engines, Variable	S. L. Hay	Reading, Mass	Oct. 9, 1855	13, 648
Exhaust of locomotives, Means for directing the	R. Hale	Roxbury, Mass	May 5, 1857	17, 215
Exhaust of steam-engines, Regulating	J. Thierry	Detroit, Mich	June 26, 1860	28, 918
Exhaust-pipe for steam-engines	R. Hale	Roxbury, Mass	Sept. 13, 1859	25, 407
Exhaust-pipe, Variable	W. P. Parrott and S. H. Head	Boston, Mass	Feb. 1, 1859	22, 819
Exhaust-pipe, Variable	J. Patrick	Chicago, Ill	Feb. 1, 1859	22, 820
Exhaust-regulator for locomotives, Rotary	E. R. Addison	Baltimore, Md	Oct. 13, 1857	18, 373
Exhaust-regulator, Steam	J. Shackleton	Rahway, N. J	Dec. 1, 1868	84, 586
Exhaust-valve for steam and air cylinders	G. Westinghouse, jr	Pittsburgh, Pa	Jan. 9, 1872	122, 544
Exhauster, Barometric vacuum	J. Gordon and J. Archbald	San Francisco, Cal	Sept. 17, 1867	68, 979
Exhausting ventilator and chimney-cowl	J. W. C. Anderson	New York, N. Y	Jan. 14, 1868	73, 280
Exhibiting case, Spool	J. D. Cutter	Brooklyn, N. Y	Feb. 11, 1873	135, 782
Exhibiting dry goods, Device for	J. J. Bisel	Williamsport, Pa	July 16, 1872	128, 943
Exhibiting hymns, &c., Apparatus for	H. V. Edmond	Norwich, Conn	July 30, 1867	67, 177
Exhibiting hymns, Apparatus for	H. V. Edmond	Norwich, Conn	Apr. 13, 1869	88, 947
Expanding and folding wheel	H. Steward	Clark County, Ind	Jan. 24, 1811	....
Expanding bit	C. L. Barnes	New York, N. Y	Nov. 16, 1852	9, 398
Expanding bit	H. Stone	Blackstone, Mass	Dec. 28, 1858	22, 474
Expanding die	B. T. Loomis	New York, N. Y	Aug. 20, 1867	67, 993
Expanding drill	F. Gleason	Philadelphia, Pa	July 4, 1865	48, 548
Expanding drill	T. Prosser	New York, N. Y	Jan. 25, 1853	9, 562
Expanding drill	J. L. Sayles	Gloucester, R. I	Dec. 29, 1868	85, 334
Expanding tool	J. Greenhalgh, jr	Burville, R. I	Feb. 23, 1858	19, 416
Expansible bit	C. L. Adancourt	Troy, N. Y	Aug. 27, 1850	7, 589
Expansion-bolt	D. L. Bartlett	Baltimore, Md	Apr. 1, 1873	137, 338
Expansion-drill	G. Mackinnon	Millbury, Mass	Oct. 15, 1867	69, 825
Expansion-engine	C. G. Wilson	Brooklyn, N. Y	June 21, 1870	104, 526
Expansive bit	W. A. Clark	Bethany, Conn	Sept. 28, 1858	21, 597
Expansive bit	W. A. Clark	New Haven, Conn	July 29, 1873	141, 324
Expansive bit	E. Ford	Westville, Conn	Oct. 8, 1872	131, 946
Expansive bit	A. Hall	New York, N. Y	Apr. 14, 1857	17, 038
Expansive bit	A. Weeks	South Boston, Mass	May 2, 1854	10, 872
Expansive bit for wood-boring	W. A. Ives	New Haven, Conn	Oct. 13, 1868	82, 956
Expansive bits, Method of seating the movable cutter in.	W. A. Clark	Bethany, Conn	May 11, 1858	20, 192
Exploding by electricity, Apparatus for	J. B. Dowse	Lockport, Ill	Aug. 27, 1867	68, 055
Explosive agent, xyloglodine	C. Dittmar	Charlottenburg, Prussia	Jan. 25, 1870	99, 069
Explosive agents, Manufacture of xyloglodine and other.	C. Dittmar	Charlottenburg, Prussia	Jan. 25, 1870	99, 070
Explosive composition	E. Harrison	New York, N. Y	Feb. 9, 1864	41, 578
Explosive compound	O. H. Bandisch	Berlin, Prussia	May 11, 1869	89, 910
Explosive compound	T. S. Beach	New York, N. Y	May 13, 1873	138, 841
Explosive compound	C. Dittmar	Charlottenburg, Prussia	Jan. 18, 1870	98, 854
Explosive compound	C. Dittmar	Boston, Mass	Dec. 9, 1873	145, 403
Explosive compound	E. Gomez	New York, N. Y	Feb. 16, 1869	86, 980
Explosive compound	E. Gomez	New York, N. Y	Dec. 26, 1871	122, 245
Explosive compound	J. Hafenegger	San Francisco, Cal	Sept. 8, 1868	81, 894
Explosive compound	J. Hafenegger	San Francisco, Cal	Dec. 20, 1870	110, 355
Explosive compound	J. Hafenegger	San Francisco, Cal	Feb. 7, 1871	111, 642
Explosive compound	H. Halvorson	Cambridge, Mass	Jan. 7, 1864	43, 621
Explosive compound	W. Mills	New York, N. Y	Oct. 26, 1869	96, 248
Explosive compound	W. Mills	New York, N. Y	Feb. 28, 1871	112, 163
Explosive compound	A. Nobel	New York, N. Y	Aug. 14, 1866	57, 175
Explosive compound	A. Nobel	Hamburg, Germany	May 26, 1868	78, 317
Explosive compound	A. Nobel	Hamburg, Germany	Aug. 5, 1873	141, 455
Explosive compound	J. H. Norrbin and J. Ohlsson	Stockholm, Sweden	Aug. 5, 1873	141, 585
Explosive compound	E. A. L. Roberts	Titusville, Pa	Nov. 7, 1871	120, 776
Explosive compound	T. P. Shaffner	Louisville, Ky	Aug. 17, 1869	93, 753
Explosive compound	T. P. Shaffner	Louisville, Ky	Aug. 17, 1869	93, 754
Explosive compound	T. P. Shaffner	Louisville, Ky	Dec. 28, 1869	98, 427
Explosive compound	T. P. Shaffner	Louisville, Ky	June 10, 1873	139, 738
Explosive compound	T. Varney	San Francisco, Cal	June 10, 1873	139, 746
Explosive compound	C. W. Volney	Boston, Mass	Mar. 5, 1872	124, 397
Explosive compound for use in fire-arm, blasting, &c.	T. P. Shaffner	Louisville, Ky	Aug. 17, 1869	93, 752
Explosive compound from gun-cotton	R. Punshon	Newcastle-upon Tyne, England.	Mar. 12, 1872	124, 510
Explosive compound or giant-powder	E. Judson	San Francisco, Cal	June 3, 1873	139, 468
Explosive engine	J. M. Welbourn	Caledonia, Ohio	Sept. 16, 1873	142, 880
Explosive powder	G. Designoble and J. Casthelaz	France	Mar. 31, 1868	76, 173
Explosive powder	F. M. Ruschhaupt	New York, N. Y	June 16, 1868	79, 010
Explosive substances and process of manufacturing.	J. B. Muschamp	Kensington, Great Britain.	June 25, 1872	128, 450
Express-bag, &c., Lock for	E. A. Locke and W. B. Mason	Boston, Mass	Feb. 2, 1869	86, 560
Express-signal	C. H. Seawell	Saint Louis, Mo	Oct. 6, 1868	82, 756
Extender	A. Bisbee	North Yarmouth, Me	Jan. 27, 1824	....
Extension-bit	H. P. Chapman	Essex, Conn	Nov. 23, 1869	97, 166
Extension-bit	J. P. Rollins	Boston, Mass	Dec. 25, 1855	13, 938
Extension-bracket	W. S. Elliott	Goshen, N. Y	June 18, 1872	127, 967
Extension-chair	S. J. Anderson and N. Richardson.	Erieville, N. Y	Feb 17, 1857	16, 635
Extension-chair	N. C. O. and A. Collignon	Closter, N. J	June 27, 1871	116, 271
Extension-chair	F. W. Lange	Chicago, Ill	Sept. 7, 1869	94, 615
Extension-chair	L. F. Schwenkel	New York, N. Y	Nov. 7, 1871	120, 780
Extension-chair	J. H. Travis	Charlestown, Mass	July 23, 1872	129, 873
Extension-chair	B. H. Zinn	New York, N. Y	Apr. 7, 1868	76, 577
Extension-elevator	P. Porter	Hooksett, N. H	Oct. 6, 1857	18, 353
Extension-gate	C. S. Snead	Louisville, Ky	July 23, 1867	67, 143
Extension-platform	A. Morse	Portland, Me	May 7, 1861	32, 265
Extension-slide	J. Dourson	Columbus, Ohio	Mar. 26, 1872	125, 034
Extension-table	J. J. Arnaud	Boston, Mass	May 28, 1872	127, 291
Extension-table	H. Bachman	Philadelphia, Pa	Mar. 30, 1869	88, 433
Extension-table	A. Bader	New York, N. Y	Dec. 7, 1858	22, 224
Extension-table	M. Bancroft	Montague, Mass	Sept. 13, 1870	107, 215
Extension-table	W. Beale	Keyport, N. J	Apr. 10, 1866	53, 774
Extension-table	J. M. Blaisdell	Sanbornton, N. H	Apr. 20, 1869	89, 266
Extension-table	J. M. Blaisdell	Sanbornton, N. H	Jan. 16, 1872	122, 800

Index of patents issued from the United States Patent Office from 1790 *to* 1873, *inclusive*—Continued

Invention.	Inventor.	Residence.	Date.	No.
Extension-table	W. J. Boda	Dayton, Ohio	Jan. 4, 1870	98, 465
Extension-table	C. Briggs	Roxbury, Mass	Sept. 9, 1845	4, 185
Extension-table	C. Briggs	Roxbury, Mass	Sept. 1, 1843	3, 249
Extension-table	N. Carl	Cincinnati, Ohio	Jan. 8, 1867	60, 996
Extension-table	G. Chelini	Washington, D. C	Mar. 23, 1869	88, 132
Extension-table	A. F. Chubbuck	Casnovia, Mich	Dec. 2, 1873	145, 049
Extension-table	B. Clark	Oriskany Falls, N. Y	Jan. 6, 1857	16, 350
Extension-table	C. B. Clark	Mount Pleasant, Iowa	Dec. 1, 1857	18, 733
Extension-table	M. Coleman	Ionia, Mich	Mar. 11, 1873	136, 705
Extension-table	E. A. Curley	Westport, Conn	Jan. 15, 1856	14, 093
Extension-table	E. A. Curley	Westport, Conn	Dec. 22, 1857	18, 891
Extension-table	J. P. Curry	Vincennes, Ind	Sept. 21, 1869	95, 003
Extension-table	J. B. Curtis	Port Henry, N. Y	Nov. 6, 1866	59, 367
Extension-table	A. Dietsch	Frankfort Station, Ill	Apr. 26, 1870	102, 235
Extension-table	J. Dourson	Columbus, Ohio	June 8, 1869	91, 099
Extension-table	J. Dourson	Columbus, Ohio	Oct. 26, 1869	96, 209
Extension-table	T. E. Ellison	Albany, N. Y	Dec. 20, 1870	110, 220
Extension-table	W. Farson	Philadelphia, Pa	Jan. 18, 1870	98, 942
Extension-table	G. F. Folsom	Roxbury, Mass	May 21, 1867	64, 857
Extension-table	T. Franck	New York, N. Y	Apr. 10, 1849	6, 362
Extension-table	L. Freeman	New York, N. Y	Mar. 23, 1869	88, 028
Extension-table	T. Gray	Philadelphia, Pa	Mar. 8, 1859	23, 219
Extension-table	H. Gross	Tiffin, Ohio	Nov. 17, 1857	18, 636
Extension-table	J. Haines	West Middlebury, Ohio	Mar. 20, 1855	12, 5 8
Extension-table	T. Q. Hall	Fairfield, Iowa	Feb. 5, 1861	31, 312
Extension-table	F. Hamblin	Madrid Springs, N. Y	June 15, 1869	91, 332
Extension-table	E. Hambujer	Detroit, Mich	Apr. 15, 1873	137, 917
Extension-table	A. Hanson	San Francisco, Cal	Feb. 6, 1872	123, 397
Extension-table	W. Heerdt	New York, N. Y	June 8, 1858	20, 489
Extension-table	G. H. Henkel	Germantown, Ohio	Jan. 23, 1872	122, 946
Extension-table	A. Herzog	New York, N. Y	Feb. 25, 1873	136, 243
Extension-table	M. Hofmann	Darlington, Wis	Jan. 28, 1873	135, 274
Extension-table	F. Hoguet	Philadelphia, Pa	Feb. 25, 1851	7, 954
Extension-table	F. Huber	Franklin, Ind	May 28, 1872	127, 168
Extension-table	A. Iske	Lancaster, Pa	Feb. 7, 1865	46, 240
Extension-table	A. Iske	Lancaster, Pa	Apr. 5, 1859	23, 469
Extension-table	G. Lauter and J. Kautz	Vincennes, Ind	Sept. 11, 1866	57, 927
Extension-table	C. P. Lenz	Poughkeepsie, N. Y	Sept. 7, 1869	94, 617
Extension-table	C. P. Lenz	Poughkeepsie, N. Y	Mar. 15, 1870	100, 776
Extension-table	G. S. Manning	Danville, Ill	Jan. 12, 1869	85, 836
Extension-table	S. H. Martin	Mount Vernon, N. Y	May 6, 1873	138, 571
Extension-table	J. J. McKnight	Tarrytown, N. Y	Aug. 1, 1871	117, 659
Extension-table	F. Menzer	Flint, Mich	May 2, 1871	114, 319
Extension-table	E. Metz	Rochester, N. Y	Sept. 16, 1862	36, 496
Extension-table	L. Meyer	Columbus, Ga	Nov. 15, 1859	26, 116
Extension-table	C. Monson	New Haven, Conn	Jan. 14, 1862	34, 160
Extension-table	L. Munzer	Goodrich, Mich	Nov. 7, 1871	120, 700
Extension-table	G. Munzinger	Brooklyn, N. Y	Dec. 4, 1860	30, 823
Extension-table	F. R. Osgood	Roxbury, Mass	Jan. 2, 1866	51, 855
Extension-table	J. Pleukharp	Columbus, Ohio	May 14, 1872	126, 831
Extension-table	E. Pond, jr	Woonsocket, R. I	Mar. 12, 1872	124, 447
Extension-table	G. Pratt	Boston, Mass	Nov. 7, 1848	5, 905
Extension-table	G. Pratt	Boston, Mass	June 8, 1858	20, 530
Extension-table	A. E. Preston	Battle Creek, Mich	Oct. 15, 1867	69, 937
Extension-table	A. Reed	Chicago, Ill	Mar. 25, 1873	137, 148
Extension-table	W. Reichenbach and F. Roschdiantzky.	Chicago, Ill	Mar. 1, 1870	100, 446
Extension-table	E. Richards	New York, N. Y	Apr. 15, 1843	3, 050
Extension-table	C. Rieger	Morrisania, N. Y	Aug. 19, 1873	141, 954
Extension-table	S. M. Rounds	Somerset, Mass	July 23, 1861	32, 894
Extension-table	J. M. Sackman	Ridgeville, Ind	Sept. 9, 1873	142, 586
Extension-table	T. P. Sherborne	Philadelphia, Pa	June 26, 1849	6, 557
Extension-table	J. Sherman	Burlington, N. J	Aug. 31, 1869	94, 447
Extension-table	E. F. Shoenberger	Pittsburgh, Pa	Nov. 19, 1850	7, 789
Extension-table	L. Showalter	Beetown, Wis	June 25, 1872	128, 330
Extension-table	J. Simensen	Hermon, N. Y	June 29, 1869	91, 974
Extension-table	F. Souweine	New York, N. Y	May 9, 1871	114, 722
Extension-table	B. D. Sutlief	Wallingford, Conn	Jan. 19, 1869	86, 113
Extension-table	L. Thorn	Philadelphia, Pa	Mar. 25, 1851	7, 997
Extension-table	S. Tilton	Alton, N. H	Apr. 5, 1870	101, 545
Extension-table	W. Valentin	New York, N. Y	July 1, 1873	140, 392
Extension-table	S. E. Wales	Lebanon, N. H	Feb. 6, 1872	123, 372
Extension-table	S. E. Wales	Oxford, N. H	Apr. 1, 1873	137, 516
Extension-table	F. R. Wolfinger	Chicago, Ill	Nov. 5, 1867	70, 668
Extension-table	F. R. Wolfinger and J. Barrett	Chicago, Ill	Oct. 20, 1868	83, 350
Extension-table and settee	M. Debzell	Wabash, Ind	Sept. 20, 1870	107, 463
Extension-table, Convertible	M. Quigley	Watertown, Wis	Apr. 27, 1858	20, 088
Extension-table, Fall-leaf	J. Dourson	Columbus, Ohio	Mar. 16, 1869	87, 829
Extension-table rail	J. Letz	Brooklyn, N. Y	May 21, 1872	126, 972
Extension-table, Revolving	F. Menzer	Flint, Mich	Apr. 16, 1872	125, 827
Extension-table roller slide	J. Dourson	Columbus, Ohio	Dec. 28, 1869	98, 369
Extension-table slide	E. P. Allyn	North Canaan, Conn	Apr. 25, 1865	47, 374
Extension-table slide	J. F. Birchard	Milwaukee, Wis	June 19, 1866	55, 606
Extension-table slide	M. E. Carter and E. Mets	Rochester, N. Y	Sept. 6, 1864	44, 073
Extension-table slide	W. Denoghue	Philadelphia, Pa	Aug. 16, 1870	106, 340
Extension-table slide	G. Finkbeiner	Syracuse, N. Y	Feb. 4, 1873	135, 418
Extension-table slide	M. Fleck	Milwaukee, Wis	Jan. 25, 1870	99, 075
Extension-table slide	S. R. Garner	Independence, Iowa	Mar. 26, 1872	124, 947
Extension-table slide	S. J. Genung	Waterloo, N. Y	Sept. 7, 1869	94, 486
Extension-table slide	N. Jenkins	New York, N. Y	Mar. 3, 1868	75, 022
Extension-table slide	J. King	Oswego, N. Y	Nov. 4, 1873	144, 276
Extension-table slide	P. Marx	Buffalo, N. Y	Aug. 20, 1872	130, 731
Extension-table slide	E. Metz	Rochester, N. Y	Nov. 12, 1867	70, 879
Extension-table slide	S. B. Nash	Buffalo, N. Y	May 23, 1871	115, 087
Extension-table slide	H. Olds	Syracuse, N. Y	Sept. 10, 1867	68, 782
Extension-table slide	H. Olds	Syracuse, N. Y	June 14, 1870	104, 340
Extension-table slide	J. Pleukharp	Columbus, Ohio	Dec. 26, 1871	122, 278
Extension-table slide	O. E. Sanford	La Porte, Ind	Aug. 31, 1869	94, 243

Index of patents issued from the United States Patent Office from 1790 *to* 1873, *inclusive*—Continued.

Invention.	Inventor.	Residence.	Date.	No.
Extension-table slide	A. H. Shipman	Arcadia, N. Y	Nov. 2, 1869	96, 533
Extension-table slide	A. P. Shute and J. F. Jackson	Charlestown, Mass	Oct. 22, 1867	70, 127
Extension-table slide	S. Stilwell	Waterloo, N. Y	Sept. 20, 1870	107, 636
Extension-table slide	J. W. Teift	Buffalo, N. Y	June 22, 1869	91, 579
Extension-table slide	G. W. Townsend	Hubbardston, Mich	Jan. 7, 1873	134, 711
Extension-table slide	A. Zeh, G. P. Livingston, and P. V. W. Cullings.	Gallupsville, N. Y	Oct. 7 1873	143, 554
Extension-table slides, Tool for making	S. J. Moore and G. A. Buckman.	Ogdensburgh, N. Y	May 10, 1870	102, 850
Extension-table tops, Machine for making	R. G. Utley	Boston, Mass	Feb. 25, 1873	136, 193
Extension-tables, Making slides of	C. F. Hobe	New York, N. Y	June 22, 1841	2, 135
Extract of barley-malt	M. Wesselhoeft	Baltimore, Md	Oct. 6, 1868	82, 909
Extract of fruit	R. Carpenter	Medford, Mass	Sept. 13, 1859	25, 384
Extract of sea-clams	B. G. Noble	New York, N. Y	July 9, 1867	66, 616
Extracts and decoctions from coffee, tea, &c., Apparatus for making.	L. Brauer	Washington, D. C	Mar. 15, 1870	100, 849
Extracts and essences, Apparatus for making	E. E. Burrough	Baltimore, Md	Nov. 10, 1868	83, 922
Extracts, Apparatus for concentrating	T. W. Johnson	New York, N. Y	Sept. 1, 1868	81, 643
Extracts, &c., Apparatus for evaporating and concentrating bark.	T. W. Johnson and A. W. Goodell.	New York, N. Y	Nov. 1, 1870	108, 793
Extracts, Apparatus for leaching and concentrating bark.	P. M. Church	Sault de Ste. Marie, Mich	July 1, 1873	140, 469
Extracts, Apparatus for making	W. Class and E. Reubenow	Cincinnati, Ohio	Mar 22, 1864	41, 974
Extracts, Apparatus for making	J. Miller	Upton, Canada East	Jan. 23, 1866	52, 253
Extracts, Apparatus for making	L. Smith	Erie, Pa	June 6, 1865	48, 107
Extracts, Apparatus for making	A. Steers	Medina, N. Y	Mar. 11, 1856	14, 418
Extracts, Apparatus for making	A. Steers	New York, N. Y	Mar. 12, 1867	62, 901
Extracts from animal and vegetable substances, Apparatus for making.	J. Chilcott	Brooklyn, N. Y	Dec. 27, 1864	45, 584
Extracts from bark and other materials, Apparatus for making.	J. W. Jones	Cumberland, Md	Nov. 5, 1867	70, 439
Extracts from bark, &c., Apparatus for making	F. W. Perry and J. H. Pierce	Woburn, Mass	May 22, 1866	54, 945
Extracts from bark, Obtaining	W. G. Fessenden	Walpole, N. H	Oct. 20, 1812	....
Extracts from dye-woods, Apparatus for obtaining	I. B. Kirby	Providence, R. I	Jan. 2, 1872	122, 467
Extracts from sumac, Manufacture of	T. Steers, jr., and J. R. Sedgwick.	Richmond, Va	Feb. 13, 1872	123, 590
Extracts from tan-bark, Apparatus for making	S. W. Pingree	Lawrence, Mass	Oct. 24, 1865	50, 626
Extracts from vegetable and animal substances, Apparatus for making.	L. Brauer	Philadelphia, Pa	Apr. 18, 1871	113, 844
Extracts from vegetables, &c., Apparatus for obtaining.	J. Chilcott	Brooklyn, N. Y	Apr. 25, 1865	47, 393
Extracts from vegetables, Liquid	G. De Villepoix and J. F. Bonneterre.	Abbeville, Somme, and Paris, France.	May 12, 1868	77, 805
Extracts, Making	T. Close and J. C. Sandford	Rye, N. Y	Mar. 18, 1836	....
Extracts, Making vegetable	B. Brandeth	New York, N. Y	Jan. 20, 1843	2, 920
Extracts, Making vegetable	T. J. Covell	Bergen, N. J	Feb. 13, 1872	123, 679
Extracts, Manufacture of fluid	L. D. Puy	Grand Rapids, Mich	Feb. 6, 1872	123, 336
Extracts, Mode of obtaining	B. G. Martin	Philadelphia, Pa	Mar. 14, 1865	46, 809
Extracts of bark, &c., Apparatus for concentrating	T. W. Johnson	New York, N. Y	July 13, 1869	92, 455
Extracts of bark, &c., Apparatus for evaporating	G. W. Klein	Boston, Mass	Dec. 15, 1838	1, 035
Extracts of bark, Making	J. Biddis and T. Bedwell	....	Aug. 10, 1791	....
Extracts of bark, &c., Process and apparatus for manufacture of.	J. Pickles	Wigan, England	Apr. 13, 1869	88, 807
Extracts, Preparation of desiccated vegetable	W. J. Rand	Brooklyn, N. Y	July 11, 1865	48, 719
Extracts, Process of making	J. Robert	Seelowitz, Austria	Oct. 30, 1866	59, 330
Extracts, Process of making	N. S. Thomas	Painted Post, N. Y	Aug. 14, 1866	57, 217
Extracts, Process of making concentrated fluid	N. S. Thomas	Painted Post, N. Y	Jan. 31, 1865	46, 156
Extracts under pressure, Apparatus for making	A. A. Burlingame	New York, N. Y	Apr. 9, 1861	31, 951
Extracting process and apparatus	G. W. Sylvester	Belleville, N. J	Apr. 16, 1872	125, 856
Extracting tanning matter from bark, Apparatus for.	N. S. Thomas	Painted Post, N. Y	Aug. 14, 1866	57, 218
Extractor: *See* Bolt-extractor. Bung-extractor. Cartridge-extractor. Cartridge-shell extractor. Cheese-skipper extractor. Cork-extractor. Drill-extractor. Hop-extractor. Kettle-molding extractor. Madder-extractor. Nail-extractor. Obstetrical extractor. Oil-tool extractor. Peach-stone extractor. Root-extractor. Spike-extractor. Stone extractor. Stump-extractor. Tack-extractor. Tooth-extractor.				
Eye and lung protector	G. A. Crofutt	New York, N. Y	Dec. 9, 1873	145, 337
Eye, Artificial	A. Boissonneau	Paris, France	June 19, 1866	55, 793
Eye-bolt die	C. Norton	New Haven, Conn	July 24, 1866	56, 599
Eye-bolt-forging die	F. Leonard	Cleveland, Ohio	June 16, 1868	78, 977
Eye-bolts or links without welding, Method of making.	G. H. Sellers	Phœnixville, Pa	Sept. 29, 1868	82, 559
Eye-cup	B. K. Maltby	Cincinnati, Ohio	July 14, 1868	79, 847
Eye-cup	B. F. Stephens	Brooklyn, N. Y	Dec. 10, 1867	72, [illegible]
Eye-cup	J. M. Winslow	Rochester, N. Y	Aug. 13, 1867	67, 832
Eye-glass	A. D. Ansell	Hartford, Conn	May 27, 1873	139, 353
Eye-glass	J. Cadman	Chatham Village, N. Y	June 14, 1872	127, 459
Eye-glass	I. Clements	Fort Ann, N. Y	June 6, 1871	115, 574
Eye-glass	E. M. Cole	Southbridge, Mass	Jan. 7, 1868	72, 978
Eye-glass	J. J. Crispin	Providence, R. I	Dec. 3, 1867	71, 584
Eye-glass	G. M. Cummings	Providence, R. I	July 30, 1867	67, 167
Eye-glass	A. H. Daniels	Hartford Conn	May 26, 1868	78, 190
Eye-glass	S. Greacen	Rye, N. Y	July 15, 1873	140, 912
Eye-glass	E. K. Josselyn	Cambridge, Mass	Jan. 8, 1867	61, 073
Eye-glass	E. Maynard	Tarrytown, N. Y	Aug. 7, 1866	56, 967
Eye-glass	J. K. McDonald	Newark, N. J	Feb. 4, 1868	74, 109
Eye-glass	J. Prentice	New York, N. Y	Jan. 8, 1867	61, 099
Eye-glass	M. Risley	Springfield, Mass	Aug. 26, 1873	142, 277
Eye-glass	R. Straubel	Williamsburgh, N. Y	July 27, 1869	93, 020

Index of patents issued from the United States Patent Office from 1790 *to* 1873, *inclusive*—Continued.

Invention.	Inventor.	Residence.	Date.	No.
Eye-glass	A. Süs	Edgewater, N. Y	July 23, 1872	129, 765
Eye-glass	E. Want	New Haven, Conn	Jan. 15, 1867	61, 289
Eye-glass	E. Want	New Haven, Conn	Sept. 1, 1868	81, 849
Eye-glass	L. B. Winslow	New York, N. Y	Oct. 29, 1872	132, 612
Eye-glass and spectacles	J. J. Bausch	Rochester, N. Y	Jan. 14, 1868	73, 285
Eye-glass and spectacles	H. Lomb	New York, N. Y	Dec. 3, 1867	71, 770
Eye-glass attachment	J. Dorn	New York, N. Y	Apr. 7, 1868	76, 420
Eye-glass, Double	J. Federhen and W. C. Sherman	Boston, Mass	Oct. 8, 1867	69, 554
Eye glass holder	G. Sickels	Boston, Mass	June 14, 1870	104, 216
Eye-glass, Spring	L. Black	Detroit, Mich	Oct. 19, 1869	95, 872
Eye-glass supporter	T. C. Rice	Worcester, Mass	July 16, 1872	129, 170
Eye glass suspender	S. F. Merritt	New York, N. Y	Oct. 16, 1866	58, 867
Eye-glass suspender	S. F. Merritt	Springfield, Mass	Jan. 9, 1872	122, 629
Eye-glass, Device for securing	A. W. Roberts	Hartford, Conn	June 30, 1868	79, 394
Eye-protector	D. Everett	Attleborough, Mass	Jan. 12, 1864	41, 209
Eye-protector	L. Morse	North Attleborough, Mass	Nov. 29, 1864	45, 263
Eye-shading apparatus	F. H. Jones	Federalsburgh, Md	Aug. 18, 1857	18, 015
Eye-sirup	W. C. Hall and C. Moore	California, Mo	Aug. 3, 1869	93, 300
Eye-wash	R. C. Fisher	Belleville, N. Y	July 15, 1873	140, 768
Eye-wash	H. Whiteley	Pittsburgh, Pa	Apr. 30, 1872	126, 363
Eye-water	M. Noll	New York, N. Y	June 26, 1866	55, 889
Eye-water	M. Pike	Cornish, N. H	Feb. 21, 1865	46, 494
Eye-water	J. Roemheld	Chicago, Ill	Aug. 11, 1868	81, 008
Eyes, Apparatus for treating the	M. F. Potter	Kanesville, Ill	Oct. 21, 1873	143, 928
Eyes, Instrument for modifying focal length of the	D. Parish	New York, N. Y	Dec. 18, 1855	13, 953
Eyes, Shade for protecting the	J. F. Spence	Brooklyn, N. Y	Oct. 16, 1866	58, 907
Eyelet	G. B. Brayton	Providence, R. I	Aug. 6, 1867	67, 491
Eyelet	T. Garrick	Providence, R. I	June 7, 1870	104, 113
Eyelet	R. Leavitt	Melrose, Mass	Jan. 23, 1866	52, 179
Eyelet	E. Parker	Middletown, Conn	Aug. 23, 1864	43, 954
Eyelet	G. W. Printice	Providence, R. I	Sept. 1, 1868	81, 684
Eyelet	J. F. Richards	Attleborough, Mass	Mar. 13, 1866	53, 234
Eyelet	C. D. Smith	Washington, D. C	Feb. 13, 1866	52, 614
Eyelet	S. W. Young	Providence, R. I	Apr. 22, 1873	138, 221
Eyelet-batten, Self-acting	S. Land	Philadelphia, Pa	Apr. 23, 1867	64, 016
Eyelet-blanks, Machine for making	S. W. Young	Providence, R. I	Jan. 23, 1866	52, 240
Eyelet-blanks, Manufacture of	W. R. Landfear	Hartford, Conn	Jan. 17, 1871	110, 979
Eyelet-casting machine	J. M. Osgood	Somerville, Mass	May 5, 1868	77, 647
Eyelet-cutting machine	G. B. Brayton	Providence, R. I	Dec. 8, 1868	84, 673
Eyelet-fastening	W. W. Wilcox	Middletown, Conn	Nov. 5, 1867	70, 488
Eyelet-fastening for ladies' skirts	W. S. Thomson	New York, N. Y	Sept. 21, 1858	21, 581
Eyelet for attaching buttons to textile fabrics	C. M. Platt	Waterbury, Conn	Aug. 29, 1871	118, 640
Eyelet for fastening buttons	S. M. Porter	New York, N. Y	Aug. 2, 1870	105, 978
Eyelet-forming die	D. K. Hoxsie	Providence, R. I	Aug. 30, 1870	106, 938
Eyelet-machine	C. W. Clewley	Cranston, R. I	June 23, 1868	79, 105
Eyelet-machine	O. D. Critchett	Stoneham, Mass	Aug. 12, 1862	36, 191
Eyelet-machine	W. R. Landfear	Hartford, Conn	Mar. 6, 1866	53, 080
Eyelet-machine	H. L. Lipman	Philadelphia, Pa	June 6, 1854	11, 027
Eyelet-machine	H. L. Lipman	Philadelphia, Pa	July 11, 1854	11, 260
Eyelet-machine	H. L. Lipman	Philadelphia, Pa	July 25, 1854	11, 380
Eyelet-machine	T. K. Reed and H. F. Packard	East and North Bridgewater, Mass	July 22, 1862	35, 952
Eyelet-machine	S. J. Smith	New York, N. Y	Apr. 16, 1861	32, 088
Eyelet-machine	S. N. Smith	Providence, R. I	Dec. 27, 1870	110, 506
Eyelet-machine	W. Steinmetz	Philadelphia, Pa	Apr. 17, 1860	27, 934
Eyelet-machine	H. D. Walcott	Boston, Mass	Mar. 27, 1860	27, 674
Eyelet-machine	H. D. Walcott	Boston, Mass	Apr. 15, 1862	35, 008
Eyelet-machine	I. E. Wilson and J. Lowe	Providence, R. I	Apr. 24, 1866	54, 249
Eyelet-machines, Machine for feeding stock to	T. Garrick	Providence, R. I	Jan. 21, 1870	104, 443
Eyelet-making	W. R. Landfear	Hartford, Conn	June 5, 1866	55, 421
Eyelet-making implement	D. K. Hoxsie	Providence, R. I	Feb. 25, 1868	74, 758
Eyelet-making machine	S. W. Adams	Providence, R. I	Mar. 26, 1867	63, 1[illegible]
Eyelet-making machine	H. C. Bradford	Providence, R. I	July 6, 1869	92, 254
Eyelet-making machine	E. B. Butler	New Britain, Conn	Aug. 7, 1866	56, 807
Eyelet-making machine	H. L. Churchill and J. D. Robinson	Taunton, Mass	Sept. 30, 1873	143, 274
Eyelet-making machine	A. Delkescamp	Brooklyn, N. Y	Nov. 2, 1869	96, 401
Eyelet-making machine	T. Garrick	Providence, R. I	Apr. 10, 1866	53, 807
Eyelet-making machine	T. Garrick	Providence, R. I	July 6, 1869	92, 185
Eyelet-making machine	T. Garrick	Providence, R. I	Oct. 17, 1871	119, 979
Eyelet-making machine	L. E. Hicks	Berlin, Conn	Dec. 17, 1850	7, 839
Eyelet-making machine	D. K. Hoxsie	Providence, R. I	Dec. 10, 1867	72, 044
Eyelet-making machine	E. E. Marsh	Providence, R. I	May 1, 1866	54, 468
Eyelet-making machine	J. C. Rhodes	South Abington, Mass	Oct. 3, 1871	119, 647
Eyelet-making machine	J. F. Richards	Providence, R. I	Oct. 4, 1864	44, 555
Eyelet-making machine	L. Richards	Providence, R. I	Jan. 1, 1867	60, 939
Eyelet-making machine	S. W. Young	Providence, R. I	May 21, 1867	65, 035
Eyelet-making machine	S. W. Young	Providence, R. I	May 21, 1867	65, 036
Eyelet-setting machinery	A. B. Edmands	Saugus, Mass	July 29, 1873	141, 211
Eyelet-stock	J. W. Hoard	Bristol R. I	May 8, 1866	54, 646
Eyelet-stocks, Machine for forming	F. Garrick	Providence, R. I	June 21, 1870	104, 442
Eyelet-stocks, Manufacture of	S. N. Smith	Providence, R. I	Mar. 21, 1871	112, 973
Eyelet, Tin-coated	A. I. Upson	New York, N. Y	Aug. 31, 1869	94, 455
Eyelets and apparatus for setting, Manufacture of	A. B. Edmands	Saugus, Mass	Mar. 5, 1872	124, 346
Eyelets and the preparation of stock for the same, Machine for forming and cutting	S. W. Young	Providence, R. I	Apr. 19, 1870	102, 195
Eyelets, Composition-metal for	G. B. Brayton	Boston, Mass	May 11, 1869	89, 847
Eyelets, Device for separating	S. N. Smith and S. W. Young	Providence, R. I	Feb. 21, 1871	112, 086
Eyelets, Machine for cutting out the end of	D. K. Hoxsie	Providence, R. I	Aug. 30, 1870	106, 939
Eyelets, Machine for inserting	W. H. Rodgers	New York, N. Y	Nov. 15, 1859	26, 134
Eyelets, Method of Making	G. B. Brayton	Boston, Mass	Dec. 31, 1867	72, 790
Eyeleted brace	S. J. Shaw	Marlborough, Mass	Oct. 16, 1866	58, 954
Eyeleting-machine	N. Ames and J. E. Gowen	Saugus Centre and Stoneham, Mass.	May 14, 1867	64, 734
Eyeleting-machine	O. G. Critchett	Stoneham, Mass	Jan. 2, 1872	122, 366
Eyeleting-machine	A. Dawes	Hudson, Mass	May 20, 1873	139, 048
Eyeleting-machine	L. De Forest	Birmingham, Conn	Jan. 13, 1863	37, 417
Eyeleting machine	T. B. De Forest	Birmingham, Conn	Jan. 13, 1863	37, 418

Index of patents issued from the United States Patent Office from 1790 *to* 1873, *inclusive*—Continued.

Invention.	Inventor.	Residence.	Date.	No.
Eyeleting-machine	A. Delkescamp	New York, N. Y	Dec. 5, 1871	121, 495
Eyeleting-machine	L. Goddu	Boston, Mass	July 23, 1872	129, 812
Eyeleting-machine	L. Hall	Boston, Mass	May 14, 1867	64, 761
Eyeleting-machine	P. Harlow	Hudson, Mass	Nov. 27, 1866	60, 0[illegible]0
Eyeleting-machine	H. Juge	New York, N. Y	Apr. 16, 1867	63, 904
Eyeleting-machine	J. Keith	New Bedford Mass	Jan. 19, 1864	41, 303
Eyeleting machine	A. Komp	New York, N. Y	June 30, 1868	79, 482
Eyeleting-machine	A. Komp	New York, N. Y	Jan. 3, 1871	110, 767
Eyeleting-machine	H. L. Lipman	Philadelphia, Pa	Jan. 3, 1865	45, 727
Eyeleting machine	A. A. Reed	North Bridgewater, Mass	Apr. 10, 1866	53, 926
Eyeleting-machine	T. K. Reed	North Bridgewater, Mass	Aug. 9, 1864	43, 816
Eyeleting machine	J. F. Sargent	Boston, Mass	Jan. 6, 1863	37, 306
Eyeleting-machine	J. F. Sargent	Boston, Mass	Aug. 27, 1863	39, 705
Eyeleting-machine	J. F. Sargent	Boston, Mass	Jan. 5, 1864	41, 125
Eyeleting-machine	J. F. Sargent	Melrose, Mass	Aug. 3, 1869	93, 353
Eyeleting-machine	E. Shaw	Milwaukee, Wis	Apr. 19, 1870	102, 054
Eyeleting-machine	G. Shipman	West Bridgewater, Mass	Aug. 21, 1866	57, 446
Eyeleting-machine	J. E. Wiggin	Stoneham, Mass	May 21, 1872	126, 916
Eyeleting-machine	G. Wunderlick	Philadelphia, Pa	Nov. 21, 1871	121, 224
Eyeleting-machine for attaching buttons to garments.	E. J. Warner	Newark, N. J	Sept. 24, 1867	69, 284

F.

Fabric:

See Bleached fabric.
Carpet-fabric.
Cellular fabric.
Corrugated fabric.
Elastic fabric.
Felted fabric.
Felted tufted fabric.
Fiber and gum fabric.
Figured fabric.
Fire proof fabric.
Flocked fabric.
Fringed fabric.
Fur-coated fabric.
Gathered fabric.
Hat and bonnet fabric.
Hydrofuze fabric.
India-rubber fabric.
Knit fabric.
Knitted medicated fabric.
Metallic fabric.
Netted or laced fabric.
Palm-leaf fabric.
Pile-fabric.
Plain and figured fabric.
Rubber fabric.
Spring-fabric.
Terry fabric.
Textile fabric.
Tubing-fabric.
Tubular fabric.
Tufted fabric.
Warp-net fabric.
Water-proof fabric.
Water-proof furze fabric
Water-proofing fabric.
Wire fabric
Woolen fabric.
Woven fabric.
Woven tuck fabric.

Invention.	Inventor.	Residence.	Date.	No.
Fabric	A. Forot	Paris, France	Aug. 16, 1859	25, 107
Fabric	C. Roder	Philadelphia, Pa	Oct. 1, 1872	131, 906
Fabric for bags, roofs, &c	H. W. Johns	New York, N. Y	Apr. 9, 1872	125, 573
Fabric for head-covering	E. Arnheim	New York, N. Y	Aug. 2, 1870	106, 024
Fabric for head-covering	H. Loewenberg	New York, N. Y	Mar. 12, 1872	124, 599
Fabric for wrapping and packing	J. A. Turner	Manchester, Great Britain	Aug. 6, 1872	130, 340
Fabric from fibrous sheets and hard rubber	R. O. Lowrey	Salem, N. Y	June 15, 1869	91, 458
Fabric opening, smoothing, and guiding machine	W. Birch	Manchester, England	Mar. 25, 1873	137, 169
Fabric or paper cloth, Imitation	J. H. Newton	Holyoke, Mass	July 20, 1869	92, 743
Fabric, Plaiting	W. Fuzzard	Chelsea, Mass	Jan. 19, 1869	85, 922
Fabric-pressing machine	G. H. Mussey and W. B. Leachman.	Leeds, England	Jan. 24, 1871	111, 141
Fabric-shirring machine	A. Hecht	New York, N. Y	June 7, 1870	104, 029
Fabric-stretching machine	I. E. Palmer	Hackensack, N. J	Mar. 30, 1869	88, 505
Fabric to be used as a substitute for japanned leather.	J. Fletcher	Newark, N. J	Aug. 21, 1866	57, 307
Fabrics and introducing flat skirt-wires therein, Instrument for puncturing.	M. Fishel	New York, N. Y	June 5, 1866	55, 267
Fabrics, &c., Apparatus for discharging extraneous coloring-matter from.	B. G. Brooks	Manchester, N. H	Oct. 3, 1871	119, 503
Fabrics, Coating and metallizing	R. Nöggerath	Paris, France	Dec. 24, 1867	72, 601
Fabrics, Composition for making designs upon	R. L. Jones	Sacramento, Cal	Sept. 15, 1868	82, 122
Fabrics, Fluid for extracting grease from	J. B. Wilson	Philadelphia, Pa	Dec. 19, 1871	122, 094
Fabrics from vegetable and animal fibers, Manufacture of useful and ornamental.	E. Pavy	Paris, France	June 21, 1870	104, 638
Fabrics impervious to gas, Composition to render	G. L. Burnham	Providence, R. I	Oct. 31, 1871	120, 368
Fabrics, Machine for cutting	W. J. Cussen	Richmond, Va	Dec. 10, 1872	133, 700
Fabrics, Machine for disintegrating	M. Marshall	Lowell, Mass	Sept. 30, 1873	143, 290
Fabrics, Machine for disintegrating	M. Marshall	Lowell, Mass	Nov. 18, 1873	144, 685
Fabrics, Machine for drying and stretching	O. C. Sweet	Albany, N. Y	Sept. 29, 1868	82, 564
Fabrics, Machine for scouring and washing	B. and F. Bates	Sowerby Bridge, Halifax, England.	Jan. 28, 1870	104, 818
Fabrics, Method of making dies for figures in press-dyed.	J. Holt	Lowell, Mass	Mar. 26, 1867	63, 159
Fabrics, Mode of ornamenting	W. Swan	New York, N. Y	May 19, 1868	78, 156
Fabrics, &c., Preventing mildew and decay in	W. A. Torrey	Mount Clair, N. J	Apr. 26, 1870	102, 450
Fabrics, Renovating faded	R. H. Klander	Philadelphia, Pa	July 24, 1866	56, 574
Fabrics, Singeing-machine for	P. McEwen and W. McKenzie	Jersey City and Hudson City, N. J.	Oct. 27, 1868	83, 395
Fabrics to render them water-proof, Treating	C. Tappan	Wakefield, Mass	May 31, 1870	103, 799
Fabrics uninflammable, Rendering	D. Nicoll	London, England	Aug. 26, 1873	142, 267
Fabrics with button-hole therein, Mode of weaving	J. Connor	Boston, Mass	Apr. 4, 1865	47, 151
Fabrics with fluid or semi-fluid substances, Apparatus for coating.	G. Adamson	Philadelphia, Pa	Jan. 1, 1867	60, 600
Fabrics with parkesine, Coating	J. Lewthwaite	London, England	May 17, 1870	103, 209
Fagot for beams	W. W. Miller	Safe Harbor, Pa	Sept 24, 1867	69, 237
Fagot for beams	G. Walters and T. Shaffer	Phœnixville, Pa	Mar. 17, 1868	75, 712
Fagot for wrought-metal cannon, hydraulic pumps, &c.	S. J. Reeves	Philadelphia, Pa	Dec. 9, 1862	37, 168
Fagot, Kindling	C. R. Jacobi	Green Point, N. Y	July 12, 1870	105, 213
Fagots, Construction of	F. W. Webb	Crewe, England	Mar. 28, 1865	47, 077

Index of patents issued from the United States Patent Office from 1790 *to* 1873, *inclusive*—Continued.

Invention.	Inventor.	Residence.	Date.	No.
Fall-leaf table	W. Caldwell	Bryan, Ohio	May 10, 1870	102, 771
Fall-leaf table	J. S. Rankin	Detroit, Mich	May 5, 1868	77, 655
Family-mill	D. Flagg, jr	Gardiner, Me	Feb. 23, 1826	....
Fan	S. Ainsworth	Saratoga Springs, N. Y	Apr. 21, 1868	76, 875
Fan	G. Anton	Philadelphia, Pa	Jan. 16, 1866	52, 109
Fan	O. Brück	New York, N. Y	Nov. 19, 1867	70, 952
Fan	O. Brück	New York, N. Y	Aug. 31, 1869	94, 390
Fan	O. Brück	New York, N. Y	Oct. 12, 1869	95, 764
Fan	O. Brueck	New York, N. Y	Oct. 25, 1870	108, 681
Fan	G. Brueck	New York, N. Y	Apr. 1, 1873	137, 413
Fan	A. B. Hancock	Suspension Bridge, N. Y	Nov. 24, 1868	84, 276
Fan	N. Harper	Newark, N. J	Sept. 25, 1866	58, 250
Fan	T. W. Hawkins	New Haven, Conn	Dec. 31, 1867	72, 372
Fan	T. W. Hawkins	New Haven, Conn	June 1, 1869	90, 748
Fan	L. Hill	North Brookfield, Mass	Apr. 23, 1867	64, 013
Fan	J. L. Jackson	New York, N. Y	Apr. 2, 1867	63, 389
Fan	F. Koppenfels and G. Brueck	New York, N. Y	Apr. 2, 1867	63, 396
Fan	W. Lucas	New Haven, Conn	Sept. 17, 1867	68, 890
Fan	C. C. Lusby	Philadelphia, Pa	Dec. 16, 1873	145, 666
Fan	G. Mallory	Watertown, Conn	Apr. 24, 1866	54, 184
Fan	J. McLoughlin	Morrisania, N. Y	July 23, 1872	129, 848
Fan	O. R. Nitsch	New York, N. Y	June 8, 1869	91, 156
Fan	O. R. Nitsch	New York, N. Y	Sept. 7, 1869	94, 633
Fan	A. K. Rich and J. B. Thurston	New York, N. Y	Sept. 3, 1872	131, 026
Fan	B. M. Smith	New York, N. Y	Nov. 28, 1865	51, 228
Fan	H. B. Smith	Essex, Conn	May 19, 1868	78, 145
Fan and air-circulator	J. D. Wright	Bergen, N. J	Jan. 26, 1869	86, 336
Fan and caster-stand, Table	N. H. Tilman and D. G. Good	Arcanum, Ohio	Apr. 28, 1868	77, 415
Fan and fly-brush combined	H. Mee	Crown Point, Ind	Sept. 12, 1871	118, 870
Fan and fly-brush, Rotating	O. Matcalf	Orleans, Ind	Sept. 13, 1870	107, 396
Fan and fly-driver	F. M. Hunt	Clinton, Ga	Mar. 21, 1871	112, 921
Fan and parasol	H. H. White	West River, Md	May 15, 1866	54, 799
Fan and parasol combined	J. Brooks	Boston, Mass	Mar. 15, 1870	100, 719
Fan and parasol combined	G. Mallory	Bridgeport, Conn	Oct. 29, 1867	70, 344
Fan and parasol, Combined	C. St. John	New York, N. Y	Nov. 11, 1873	144, 575
Fan and screen in cleaning grain for grinding	J. Peyton	Orange City, Va	Nov. 7, 1825	....
Fan attachment, Spring	J. Carey	Victoria, Mo	July 13, 1869	92, 513
Fan attachment, Table	S. S. Binkard and R. H. Boal	Urbana, Ohio	July 11, 1871	116, 919
Fan attachment, Table	J. E. Mansker	Clinton, La	Mar. 2, 1869	87, 417
Fan, Automatic	D. Aaron	San Francisco, Cal	June 15, 1869	91, 297
Fan, Automatic	J. Beck	New York, N. Y	May 12, 1868	77, 709
Fan, Automatic	J. M. Belcour	Paris, France	June 25, 1872	128, 279
Fan, Automatic	G. C. Bovey	Cincinnati, Ohio	Apr. 4, 1871	113, 620
Fan, Automatic	G. H. Briggs	Montgomery, Ala	July 26, 1870	105, 772
Fan, Automatic	C. F. Burleigh	Tuftonborough, N. H	Dec. 28, 1869	98, 347
Fan, Automatic	J. D. Bush	Elyton, Ala	Aug. 26, 1873	142, 081
Fan, Automatic	W. B. Campbell	Selma, Ala	Nov. 11, 1873	144, 505
Fan, Automatic	G. F. Case	Claremont, N. H	July 2, 1872	128, 589
Fan, Automatic	C. H. Clark	Hartford, Conn	Feb. 4, 1873	135, 524
Fan, Automatic	F. O. Degener	New York, N. Y	Oct. 25, 1859	25, 892
Fan, Automatic	C. Dieringer and M. Lindamann.	Cincinnati, Ohio	July 13, 1869	92, 589
Fan, Automatic	E. Duffner	Vicksburgh, Miss	May 13, 1873	138, 741
Fan, Automatic	J. R. Dunn and G. B. Burroughs.	Queens County and Brooklyn, N. Y.	May 4, 1869	89, 566
Fan, Automatic	W. Fay	New Orleans, La	Mar. 25, 1873	137, 189
Fan, Automatic	W. D. Hall	Memphis, Tenn	Sept. 26, 1871	119, 351
Fan, Automatic	W. D. Hall	Memphis, Tenn	Feb. 6, 1872	123, 476
Fan, Automatic	W. D. Hall	Memphis, Tenn	Apr. 30, 1872	126, 292
Fan, Automatic	W. D. Hall	Memphis, Tenn	Feb. 18, 1873	136, 044
Fan, Automatic	A. P. Heidt	New York, N. Y	Jan. 7, 1873	134, 543
Fan, Automatic	H. Hoffman	New York, N. Y	July 5, 1859	24, 638
Fan, Automatic	F. W. Jones	Orangeburgh, S. C	Apr. 8, 1873	137, 687
Fan, Automatic	W. Lawrence and J. Sanders	New Albany, Ind	Jan. 7, 1873	134, 605
Fan, Automatic	J. Lehner	Galena, Ill	May 6, 1873	138, 567
Fan, Automatic	M. Lochner	Newark, N. J	Oct. 24, 1871	120, 293
Fan, Automatic	W. O. Loeffler	New York, N. Y	July 9, 1867	66, 507
Fan, Automatic	J. A. W. Lundborg	San Francisco, Cal	Feb. 26, 1867	62, 431
Fan, Automatic	J. Maltry	Morrisania, N. Y	May 11, 1869	90, 009
Fan, Automatic	H. T. McCormick	Selma, Ala	Apr. 15, 1873	137, 785
Fan, Automatic	J. McLain	Saint Mary's, Ohio	Jan. 7, 1862	34, 066
Fan, Automatic	J. Naugle	Mooresville, Ind	Mar. 23, 1869	88, 062
Fan, Automatic	J. B. Powell	Philadelphia, Pa	Sept. 6, 1859	25, 368
Fan, Automatic	J. B. Powell	Philadelphia, Pa	Oct. 4, 1864	44, 553
Fan, Automatic	D. Ramler	Union Deposit, Pa	June 28, 1870	104, 768
Fan, Automatic	L. Rebstock and N. Reimel	Philadelphia, Pa	June 9, 1857	17, 517
Fan, Automatic	P. H. Reichhardt and M. Schnapp.	Brunswick, Mo	Apr. 29, 1873	138, 345
Fan, Automatic	J. Schnell and P. Schmidt	Waterloo, Ill	Oct. 25, 1870	108, 637
Fan, Automatic	C. B. Smith	Griffin, Ga	Feb. 28, 1871	112, 293
Fan, Automatic	G. C. Steinhauer	Indianapolis, Ind	Mar. 30, 1869	88, 343
Fan, Automatic	E. D. Swartwout	Chicago, Ill	July 25, 1871	117, 346
Fan, Automatic	B. D. Thompson	New York, N. Y	May 2, 1871	114, 491
Fan, Automatic	S. J. Tucker and J. H. Rose	Richmond, Va	Mar. 22, 1870	101, 188
Fan, Automatic	O. Vanorman	Fond du Lac, Wis	Sept. 23, 1873	143, 206
Fan, Automatic	L. A. Walton	Byhalia, Miss	Sept. 12, 1871	118, 832
Fan, Automatic	T. Welch	Philadelphia, Pa	May 6, 1873	138, 720
Fan, Automatic	J. B. Williamson	Louisville, Ky	Feb. 27, 1872	124, 103
Fan, Automatic	S. E. Winslow	Kensington, Pa	Nov. 9, 1852	9, 395
Fan, Automatic	G. W. Zeigler	Tiffin, Ohio	Apr. 19, 1859	23, 739
Fan, Automatic or musquito	C. A. Gale	Boston, Mass	Apr. 10, 1860	27, 862
Fan, Bed and table	W. H. Downs	Jeffersonville, Ind	Sept. 19, 1871	119, 128
Fan blast-regulator	D. Garver	Ringgold, Md	May 9, 1871	114, 547
Fan, Blowing	T. Wallace and H. Backmaster	Philadelphia, Pa	June 6, 1854	11, 047
Fan, brush, and rack	B. Poulson	Fort Wayne, Ind	Dec. 18, 1866	60, 554
Fan, Buckwheat	A. Platt	Waterbury, Conn	Jan. 13, 1852	8, 659
Fan-chair	D. Linzio	Petersham, Mass	Apr. 10, 1849	6, 307
Fan, Electro-magnetic	G. Stevens and J. W. Moyle	Cincinnati, Ohio	July 4, 1871	116, 770

Index of patents issued from the United States Patent Office from 1790 *to* 1873, *inclusive*—Continued.

Invention.	Inventor.	Residence.	Date.	No.
Fan, Exhaust	R. Cook	Saratoga Springs, N. Y	Nov. 12, 1861	33, 693
Fan, Exhaust	J. V. Merrick	Philadelphia, Pa	June 13, 1854	11, 071
Fan, Fly	G. A. Goodrich and P. Miller.	Hope, Ohio	Feb. 27, 1872	124, 054
Fan, Fly	J. G. Schwemmer and T. Mueller.	Philadelphia, Pa	Oct. 9, 1866	58, 683
Fan, Fly-expelling	W. R. Fowler	Anne Arundel County, Md	Dec. 1, 1863	40, 746
Fan, Folding	T. S. Thorn	South Amboy, N. J	Mar. 10, 1868	75, 316
Fan for apartments, Revolving	L. Stein	New York, N. Y	Dec. 19, 1854	12, 106
Fan for bed-chambers, dining-rooms, &c., moved by mechanism.	J. Barron	Norfolk, Va	Nov. 27, 1830	....
Fan for furnaces, gas-works, &c , Rotary blowing	H. Aland	London, England	Mar. 2, 1869	87, 456
Fan for ventilating mines, Cross-paddle propeller	D. Rissinger	Mahanoy City, Pa	May 27, 1873	139, 330
Fan, Grain	P. Bailey	Falls Township, Pa	Mar. 13, 1860	27, 417
Fan, Grain	G. Gocwey	Philadelphia, Pa	Jan. 10, 1860	26, 760
Fan, Grain	O. Lindsay and R. F. Strean	Washington, Pa	Nov. 29, 1859	26, 273
Fan, Grain	J. McPhail	Charles City, Iowa	Mar. 1, 1870	100, 454
Fan, Grain	I. Pennington	Tiffin, Ohio	Feb. 1, 1870	99, 469
Fan, House	J. and A. Bloom	New Brunswick, N. J., and New York, N. Y.	Sept. 3, 1867	68, 483
Fan, House	E. Marquam		Mar. 28, 1803	....
Fan, Lady's	S. A. Grant	Burlington, N. J	Aug. 14, 1866	57, 253
Fan, Lady's	F. B. Scott	Lancaster, N. Y	Apr 16, 1867	63, 817
Fan, Lady's	B. Todd	Reading, Pa	Aug. 28, 1866	57, 598
Fan, Lady's	J. and I. N. Todd	Madison, Ind	Sept. 13, 1864	44, 237
Fan, Lady's	T. Welham	Washington, D. C	Apr. 3, 1866	53, 714
Fan, Mechanical	J. Barron	Norfolk, Va	June 13, 1831	....
Fan-mill	I. T. Grant	Schaghticoke, N. Y	July 10, 1845	4, 105
Fan-mill	W. C. Hawley	Brookfield, Conn	Oct. 1, 1830	....
Fan-mill	F. H. Plymate	Blue Earth County, Minn	Sept. 19, 1871	119, 174
Fan, Musquito	J. M. Beverly	Chicago, Ill	Aug. 15, 1871	117, 969
Fan or brush, Automatic table	R. E. Tclar and W. D. Orr	Newnan, Ga	Aug. 9, 1870	106, 236
Fan-power	W. E. Wilcox	Saint Louis, Mo	Dec. 13, 1864	45, 447
Fan, Reversible screw	W. H. Goyne	Shamokin, Pa	Dec. 10, 1872	133, 772
Fan, Rocking-chair	O. Brueck	Union Hill, N. J	May 20, 1873	139, 112
Fan, Rocking-chair	O. Matzke	Durant, Miss	Nov. 19, 1872	133, 164
Fan, Rocking-chair	L. T. Simon	New York, N. Y	Aug. 17, 1869	93, 916
Fan, Rotary	I. S. Eastman	Madison, Wis	Jan. 14, 1873	134, 740
Fan, Rotary	G. Leach	Elmira, N. Y	May 23, 1865	47, 838
Fan, Rotating	I. S. Eastman	Madison, Wis	Mar. 31, 1868	76, 174
Fan, Rotating	J. H. Reynerson	Pleasant Plain, Iowa	Aug. 25, 1868	81, 539
Fan, Self-acting fly	W. D. Harrell and H. M. Hall	Osgood, Ind	Oct. 15, 1867	69, 802
Fan, Spring	O. Brueck	New York, N. Y	Oct. 11, 1870	108, 236
Fan-sticks, Machine for making	E. S. Hunt	Weymouth, Mass	Oct. 4, 1870	107, 913
Fan, Suction	C. R. Patterson	Pittston, Pa	Aug. 6, 1872	130, 310
Fan, Suction and blast	C. R. Patterson	Pittston, Pa	Oct. 24, 1871	120, 317
Fan, Table	J. C. McEwen	Micanopy, Fla	Dec. 20, 1870	110, 381
Fan, Table	W. A. McReynolds	Elkton, Ky	Aug. 6, 1867	67, 562
Fan, Table	A. R. Traber	Saint Martinsville, La	Jan. 29, 1861	31, 269
Fan, table-caster, and lamp-stand, Automatic	T. W. Carmichael	Indianapolis, Ind	Feb 11, 1868	74, 303
Fan, Wheat	W. Adams	Virginia	Mar. 1, 1816	....
Fan, Wheat	J. Bamborough	Lancaster, Pa	Mar. 20, 1847	5, 031
Fan, Wheat	J. Deakyne	Petersburgh, Va	Sept. 13, 1833	....
Fan, Wheat	G. Hoffman	Fredericktown, Md	Aug. 21, 1829	....
Fan, Wheat	J. Hollingsworth	Zanesville, Ohio	Apr. 1, 1851	8, 008
Fan, Wheat	J. Montgomery and J. Montgomery.	Lancaster, Pa., and Baltimore, Md.	June 12, 1855	13, 062
Fan, Wheat	W. Stanley	Jamestown, N. C	Nov. 18, 1844	3, 829
Fan, Wheat	D. Watkins	Port Republic, Va	Feb. 2, 1844	3, 423
Fan, Wheat	P. H. Watson	Rockford, Ill	June 6, 1848	5, 616
Fan, Wheat	S. Weaver	Frederick County, Md	Mar. 11, 1816	....
Fan, Wheat	J. White	Barnesville, Ohio	Apr. 1, 1851	8, 013
Fan-wheel, Rotary	T. H. Walton	Ashland, Pa	Sept. 10, 1872	131, 238
Fans, Apparatus for binding circular paper or other	R. T. Smith	Nashua, N. H	Nov. 20, 1866	59, 783
Fans, Apparatus for operating	W. M. Bruton	Baltimore, Md	July 4, 1871	116, 788
Fans, Device for opening and closing	G. Bordes	New York, N. Y	Oct. 11, 1870	108, 096
Fans, Device for operating hand	W. A. Ireland	New York, N. Y	Sept. 20, 1870	104, 501
Fans, Escapement movement for automatic	D. J. Mozart	Xenia, Ohio	Oct. 14, 1856	15, 889
Fans, Machine for folding paper	R. T. Smith	Nashua, N. H	Nov. 20, 1866	59, 867
Fans, Machine for manufacturing webbing for ladies'.	J. W. White	Weymouth, Mass	June 1, 1869	90, 711
Fans, Manufacture of	E. S. Hunt	Weymouth, Mass	Dec. 15, 1868	84, 882
Fans, Manufacture of portable	J. C. Hall	Fayette, Miss	Dec. 21, 1858	22, 366
Fanning and rocking chair	T. Kerr	York, Pa	Aug. 11, 1868	80, 970
Fanning and smut mill	H. Littlefield	Lewis, Iowa	Mar. 15, 1870	100, 908
Fanning and winnowing mill	B. Atwell	Burlington, N. Y	Sept. 19, 1808	....
Fanning-apparatus	L. C. England	Philadelphia, Pa	Feb. 28, 1871	112, 232
Fanning-chair	A. R. Hobbs and N. F. Wright	Elizabethport, N. J	Apr. 7, 1868	76, 452
Fanning machine	E. P. Doremus	Washington, La	Feb. 21, 1871	111, 917
Fanning-machine	G. F. Evans	Chelsea, Mass	Aug. 25, 1868	81, 353
Fanning-machine	D. Flanders and C. Rathburn	Fort Covington, N. Y	Feb. 13, 1836	....
Fanning-mill	C. Altringer	Racine, Wis	May 7, 1872	126, 371
Fanning-mill	J. Ashton	Red Wing, Minn	July 20, 1869	92, 774
Fanning-mill	H. R. Averill	New Oregon, Iowa	Nov. 8, 1870	108, 953
Fanning-mill	B. Barney	Time, Ill	Mar. 7, 1871	112, 407
Fanning-mill	T. S. Barnum	Sharon, Conn	Jan. 15, 1812	....
Fanning-mill	E. Bless	Minerva, Ky	Dec. 17, 1850	7, 849
Fanning-mill	L. M. Boardman	Ottawa, Minn	Aug. 26, 1873	142, 197
Fanning-mill	F. E. Bowen	Knightstown, Ind	July 25, 1871	117, 374
Fanning-mill	J. J. Bradner	Pine Creek, N. Y	July 30, 1867	67, 260
Fanning-mill	L. Bronson	Buffalo, N. Y	Dec. 20, 1870	110, 196
Fanning-mill	H. Bruggeman	Petersburgh, Ind	June 22, 1869	91, 600
Fanning-mill	J. K. Buck	Winona, Minn	Apr. 11, 1865	47, 186
Fanning-mill	G. E. Clarke	Racine, Wis	Sept. 27, 1870	107, 759
Fanning-mill	G. E. Clarke	Racine, Wis	Mar. 14, 1871	112, 637
Fanning-mill	G. E. Clarke	Kenosha, Wis	Jan. 7, 1873	134, 643
Fanning-mill	D. Clinton	New Haven, Conn	Nov. 29, 1832	....
Fanning-mill	D. Clow	Port Byron, N. Y	June 16, 1846	4, 582
Fanning-mill	D. Collins	Zanesfield, Ohio	Nov. 21, 1871	121, 085

Index of patents issued from the United States Patent Office from 1790 *to* 1873, *inclusive*—Continued.

Invention.	Inventor.	Residence.	Date.	No.
Fanning-mill	B. Cortrite	Norwalk, Ohio	Apr. 12, 1870	101, 713
Fanning-mill	L. M. Crosby	Ashtabula, Ohio	May 2, 1871	114, 416
Fanning-mill	A. B. Culver	Westfield, N. Y	July 16, 1867	66, 803
Fanning-mill	H. W. Curtis	Lockport, Ill	Aug. 28, 1866	57, 483
Fanning-mill	L. H. Decker	Sauk Centre, Minn	Mar. 25, 1873	137, 185
Fanning-mill	L. H. Decker	Grove Lake, Minn	Sept. 23, 1873	143, 127
Fanning-mill	E. P. Dickey	Racine, Wis	June 8, 1869	90, 936
Fanning-mill	J. Drummond	Trenton, Mo	Feb. 20, 1872	123, 814
Fanning-mill	C. K. Ehle	Greenbush, Wis	Aug. 7, 1866	56, 912
Fanning-mill	L. Ensign	Millburn, N. Y	June 17, 1862	35, 594
Fanning-mill	A. Erwin	Jefferson, Md	Sept. 30, 1839	1, 354
Fanning-mill	F. Eves	Fountain City, Wis	Sept. 26, 1871	119, 340
Fanning-mill	A. Fanckboner	Schoolcraft, Mich	May 2, 1865	47, 533
Fanning-mill	L. Farnham and J. Mosher	Delta, Mich	May 4, 1869	89, 643
Fanning-mill	S. Fitch	Homer, N. Y	Oct. 29, 1814	....
Fanning-mill	S. Fitch	Edmeston, N. Y	Jan. 6, 1832	....
Fanning-mill	S. Foster, jr	Des Moines, Iowa	July 20, 1869	92, 814
Fanning-mill	J. Frary	Southampton, Mass	Feb. 17, 1829	....
Fanning-mill	J. W. Free	Richmond, Ind	Feb. 27, 1866	52, 840
Fanning-mill	D. A. Fulk and L. B. McLain	Hookstown and Lisbon, Ohio.	Oct. 6, 1843	3, 294
Fanning-mill	E. M. Gilbert	Kasson, Minn	Oct. 7, 1873	143, 506
Fanning-mill	R. Gipson	Shelby, Ohio	Mar. 14, 1871	112, 584
Fanning-mill	J. Goetz	West Bend, Wis	Aug. 1, 1871	117, 735
Fanning-mill	A. Hall and J. Faulkner	Dansville, N. Y	Feb. 25, 1862	34, 488
Fanning-mill	J. W. Hunter, M. L. Hunt, and S. Holman.	Oakland County, Mich	Dec. 18, 1832	....
Fanning-mill	J. Hutchins	Syracuse, Iowa	Nov. 7, 1871	120, 745
Fanning-mill	J. W. Johnson	Port Treverton, Pa	Apr. 29, 1873	138, 407
Fanning-mill	D. Kane	Tivoli, Iowa	Aug. 30, 1870	106, 83[illegible]
Fanning-mill	H. Kelly and W. Franklin	Decorah, Iowa	Dec. 15, 1863	40, 937
Fanning-mill	J. M. Kendall and J. Peel	Madelia, Minn	July 30, 1872	129, 965
Fanning-mill	T. B. Kirkwood	Dublin, Ind	Aug. 17, 1869	93, 721
Fanning-mill	G. Leach	Elmira, N. Y	May 23, 1865	47, 839
Fanning-mill	E. Lindsley	Neenah, Wis	Sept. 8, 1868	82, 011
Fanning-mill	S. McMillan	Fletcher, Ohio	Feb. 18, 1868	74, 567
Fanning-mill	E. Michael	La Porte, Ind	May 25, 1869	90, 570
Fanning-mill	F. Miles	Rochester, N. Y	June 10, 1862	35, 536
Fanning-mill	J. Miller	Canton, Ohio	June 3, 1862	35, 461
Fanning-mill	J. Miller	Canton, Ohio	June 3, 1862	35, 462
Fanning-mill	J. Miller	Canton, Ohio	June 3, 1862	35, 463
Fanning-mill	S. Miller and I. J. Chase	Barrington, Ill	July 30, 1867	67, 206
Fanning-mill	J. Mumma	Middletown, Ohio	June 12, 1866	55, 526
Fanning-mill	D. Neefus	Flatlands, N. Y	Sept. 22, 1823	....
Fanning-mill	A. Niebel	Tiffin, Ohio	June 11, 1872	127, 912
Fanning-mill	H. Ogborn	Richmond, Ind	Aug. 16, 1870	106, 395
Fanning-mill	H. Ogborn	Richmond, Ind	Jan. 31, 1871	111, 375
Fanning-mill	L. Peck	Brookfield, Conn	Aug. 13, 1824	....
Fanning-mill	C. Peterson	Red Wing, Minn	Oct. 4, 1870	108, 049
Fanning-mill	O. Pinney and J. Olmested	Caledonia, N. Y	Nov. 7, 1826	....
Fanning-mill	J. F. Pool	Monroe, Wis	Jan. 19, 1869	86, 099
Fanning-mill	J. P. Preston	Monroe, Wis	Oct. 20, 1868	83, 312
Fanning-mill	P. Prine and L. Huestis	Auburn, N. Y	Feb. 23, 1832	....
Fanning-mill	B. F. Randell	Des Moines, Iowa	Mar. 9, 1869	87, 706
Fanning-mill	W. C. Ray and G. Leigh	Pleasant Run and Clinton Station, N. J.	May 19, 1868	78, 008
Fanning-mill	J. E. Rice	Oneida, Ill	Feb. 1, 1859	22, 825
Fanning-mill	G. Richards and D. Stickland	Richland Centre, Wis	Oct. 13, 1868	83, 096
Fanning-mill	J. Roberts	Penn's Square Post-Office, Pa.	May 28, 1850	7, 400
Fanning-mill	B. F. Roe	Nebraska City, Nebr	Sept. 11, 1860	29, 998
Fanning-mill	J. L. Runk and B. H. Sharp	Nashville, Ill	Apr. 5, 1870	101, 514
Fanning-mill	F. Sauer and J. Coerver	Waterloo, Ill	Dec. 20, 1870	110, 291
Fanning-mill	D. Sears	Franklin, N. Y	Mar. 24, 1830	....
Fanning-mill	H. H. Seeley	Hudson, Mich	Sept. 29, 1868	82, 558
Fanning-mill	H. H. Seeley	Hudson, Mich	May 16, 1871	114, 977
Fanning-mill	H. F. Seibert	Brady's Bend, Pa	Apr. 13, 1869	88, 913
Fanning-mill	L. Shultz	Upper Sandusky, Ohio	June 19, 1866	55, 725
Fanning-mill	A. W. Smith	Dudleyville, Ala	Jan. 21, 1868	73, 469
Fanning-mill	S. Snedeker	Johnstown, N. Y	Apr. 27, 1810	....
Fanning-mill	H. A. Snyder	Shullsburgh, Wis	Sept. 8, 1868	81, 955
Fanning-mill	J. Soper	Windsor, Conn	Dec. 3, 1814	....
Fanning-mill	W. Stoddard	Winona, Minn	Sept. 8, 1868	81, 957
Fanning-mill	H. K. Stoner	West Lampeter, Pa	Mar. 26, 1872	124, 918
Fanning-mill	E. Tush	Manchester, Iowa	May 17, 1864	42, 808
Fanning-mill	H. W. Veregge	Richmond, Ind	Feb. 7, 1865	46, 312
Fanning-mill	W. W. Wait	Richmond, Ind	Mar. 23, 1869	88, 241
Fanning-mill	E. Walker	Springfield Four-Corners, Pa.	Sept. 20, 1827	....
Fanning-mill	J. Weidman	Littlestown, Pa	May 28, 1850	7, 405
Fanning-mill	N. Wells	Milford, Pa	Sept. 11, 1833	....
Fanning-mill	B. C. White	Richmond, Ind	Jan. 24, 1865	46, 039
Fanning-mill	L. L. Willson	Denmark, Mich	Nov. 5, 1872	132, 784
Fanning-mill	B. Wright and J. C. Hogaboam	Hudson, Mich	May 7, 1872	126, 616
Fanning-mill	P. Young	Austin, Minn	May 16, 1871	114, 898
Fanning-mill and grain-separator	H. Ogborn	Richmond, Ind	Jan. 3, 1865	45, 796
Fanning-mill and grain-separator	H. Ogborn	Richmond, Ind	Mar. 8, 1870	100, 552
Fanning-mill and grain-separator	D. Wilcox	Chariton, Iowa	Aug. 24, 1869	94, 052
Fanning-mill and grain-separator	D. C. Hill	Red Wing, Minn	Oct. 8, 1872	131, 953
Fanning-mill and wheelbarrow combined	J. Wormeldorff	Warsaw, Ind	Feb. 2, 1869	86, 618
Fanning-mill attachment	P. Austin	Medina, Wis	Aug. 3, 1869	93, 166
Fanning mill-elevator attachment	N. Hinman	Sparta Centre, Mich	Apr. 27, 1869	89, 406
Fanning-mill feeding-device	N. Kibler	Milton, Ill	Oct. 11, 1870	108, 154
Fanning-mill for cleaning grain	C. O. Guernsey	Russia, N. Y	Oct. 12, 1844	3, 794
Fanning-mill for cleaning grain	T. W. Jessup	Fredericktown, Md	June 18, 1811	....
Fanning-mill for cleaning grain	E. Walker	Springville, Pa	Mar. 26, 1825	....
Fanning-mill for cleaning wheat, &c	B. D. Beecher	New Haven, Conn	May 30, 1816	....
Fanning-mill for grain, &c	S. Dodge	Cleveland, Ohio	Feb. 9, 1808	....

Index of patents issued from the United States Patent Office from 1790 *to* 1873, *inclusive*—Continued.

Invention.	Inventor.	Residence.	Date.	No.
Fanning-mill for grain, &c	D. Donoghoe	New York	Apr. 16, 1821	....
Fanning-mill for grain or clover-seed, &c	O. Barrett, jr	Sandy Hill, N. Y	Mar. 23, 1808	....
Fanning-mill, grain and seed separator	H. Ogborn	Richmond, Ind	Nov. 12, 1867	70, 885
Fanning-mill or machine for winnowing grain	D. Philips and A. Jackson	Georgetown, Pa., and Franklin Mills, Va.	May 4, 1841	2, 080
Fanning-mill shakers, Attachment to	J. Van Houten	Mount Morris, N. Y	Mar. 29, 1864	42, 132
Fanning-mill shoes, Device for balancing	W. Crain	Millgrove, Ind	Sept. 20, 1870	107, 459
Fanning-mill, Adjusting-screw for the legs of	H. Wolf	Avon, Pa	May 14, 1867	64, 728
Fanning-mills, Bag-filler for	J. C. Gephart	Dowagiac, Mich	June 14, 1870	104, 297
Fare-box	H. Baranger	Saint Louis, Mo	Jan. 9, 1872	122, 549
Fare-box	H. Baranger	Saint Louis, Mo	May 13, 1873	138, 839
Fare-box	H. Baranger	Saint Louis, Mo	July 8, 1873	140, 669
Fare-box	W. B. Bartram	Norwalk, Conn	Jan. 22, 1861	31, 204
Fare-box	A. H. Bugher	Cincinnati, Ohio	Aug. 1, 1865	49, 078
Fare-box	A. H. Bugher	Cincinnati, Ohio	Aug. 1, 1865	49, 079
Fare-box	A. H. Bugher	Cincinnati, Ohio	Aug. 1, 1865	49, 080
Fare-box	T. L. Johnson	Louisville, Ky	Oct. 14, 1873	143, 698
Fare-box	S. H. Little	Rosemond, Ill	Sept. 30, 1873	143, 360
Fare-box	W. H. McLellan	New Orleans, La	Apr. 16, 1867	63, 864
Fare-box	C. Newman	San Francisco, Cal	Apr. 16, 1872	125, 836
Fare-box	Z. I. Pratt	Chicago, Ill	Mar. 18, 1873	136, 865
Fare-box	J. B. Slawson	New Orleans, La	July 28, 1857	17, 899
Fare-box	J. B. Slawson	New Orleans, La	Jan. 29, 1861	31, 262
Fare-box	J. B. Slawson	New Orleans, La	Aug. 7, 1866	57, 000
Fare-box	J. B. Slawson	New York, N. Y	June 11, 1872	127, 808
Fare-box	J. B. Slawson	New York, N. Y	Oct. 29, 1872	132, 698
Fare-box	J. B. Slawson	New York, N. Y	Dec. 24, 1872	134, 321
Fare-box	R. D. O. Smith	Washington, D. C	July 15, 1873	140, 959
Fare-box	J. F. Winchell	Springfield, Ohio	June 13, 1871	115, 999
Fare-box	J. F. Winchell	Springfield, Ohio	Dec. 12, 1871	121, 920
Fare-box	J. F. Winchell	Springfield, Ohio	Feb. 18, 1873	136, 118
Fare-box	J. F. Winchell	Springfield, Ohio	July 15, 1873	140, 985
Fare-box, Car	B. F. Grimes	Memphis, Tenn	Sept. 12, 1871	118, 927
Fare-box, Car and omnibus	J. B. Slawson	New Orleans, La	Sept. 24, 1867	69, 263
Fare-box, City-car and omnibus	J. Blackadder	New Orleans, La	Sept. 24, 1867	69, 166
Fare-box, Omnibus	I. S. Reeves	New Orleans, La	Feb. 23, 1858	19, 471
Fare-box, Omnibus, &c	J. B. Slawson	New Orleans, La	Aug. 31, 1858	21, 372
Fare-box, Omnibus, &c	W. H. Young	Chicago, Ill	June 21, 1870	104, 530
Fare-box, Passenger-car	H. Baranger	Saint Louis, Mo	June 28, 1870	104, 816
Fare-box, Passenger-car	J. E. Woodruff	Buffalo, N. Y	Mar. 31, 1868	76, 290
Fare-box, Portable	A. Bradley	New Orleans, La	Dec. 27, 1870	110, 428
Fare-box, Portable	J. S. Hagerty	Baltimore, Md	June 11, 1872	127, 869
Fare-box, Portable	W. J. Hooper	Baltimore, Md	Aug. 13, 1872	130, 499
Fare-box, Portable	W. L. May	Philadelphia, Pa	June 27, 1871	116, 466
Fare-box, Portable	J. W. Prendergast	New York, N. Y	Mar. 5, 1872	124, 287
Fare-box, Portable	J. C. Schooley	New York, N. Y	Mar. 26, 1872	125, 088
Fare-box, Portable	J. C. Schooley	New York, N. Y	Sept. 24, 1872	131, 710
Fare-box, Railway	J. H. Phares	Zionsville, Ind	Apr. 27, 1869	89, 337
Fare-box, Railway-car	G. C. Hathorn	New York, N. Y	Mar. 15, 1870	100, 758
Fare-box, Railway-car	R. H. Long	Philadelphia, Pa	Apr. 6, 1869	88, 648
Fare-box, Railway-car	W. G. Raoul	Independence, La	Feb. 1, 1870	99, 351
Fare-box, Railway-car, &c	H. Tupper	Buffalo, N. Y	Mar. 19, 1861	31, 755
Fare-box, Registering	T. L. Johnson	Louisville, Ky	Oct. 29, 1872	132, 535
Fare-box, Street-car	W. W. Wormood	Dubuque, Iowa	Feb. 8, 1870	99, 616
Fare-box, Street-car	W. H. Young	Chicago, Ill	Feb. 15, 1870	99, 804
Fare-box, Vehicle	J. B. Slawson	New York, N. Y	July 5, 1870	105, 005
Fare on street-railway cars, Mode of collecting	J. H. Dennis	Louisville, Ky	Dec. 17, 1861	33, 928
Fare-receiver, Registering	W. G. Smoot	Washington, D. C	Aug. 18, 1868	81, 223
Fare-recorder for cars, &c	G. R. Metten and O. S. Pease	Cleveland and Xenia, Ohio.	Jan. 3, 1871	110, 770
Fare-recorder for cars	O. S. Pease	Xenia, Ohio	June 7, 1870	104, 059
Fare-register	F. Blackburn and G. W. Woodside.	Philadelphia, Pa	Mar. 15, 1870	100, 715
Fare-register	C. A. Calvert	Manchester, Great Britain.	Dec. 20, 1870	110, 339
Fare-register, Railway	S. F. Covington	Cincinnati, Ohio	May 5, 1868	77, 593
Fare-registering machine	M. W. Helton	Bloomington, Ind	July 24, 1860	29, 274
Fare taken on public conveyances, Apparatus for ascertaining the.	D. F. Haasz	Philadelphia, Pa	Feb. 19, 1861	31, 513
Fare-ticket	T. A. Jebb	Buffalo, N. Y	July 2, 1872	128, 629
Farinaceous substances, Apparatus for desiccating and torrefying.	F. Huckins and E. C. R. Walker	Roxbury, Mass	Mar. 19, 1861	31, 763
Farm-gate	G. W. Baker	Neponset, Ill	Mar. 29, 1859	23, 339
Farm-gate	M. Barthel	San Francisco, Cal	July 18, 1871	117, 143
Farm-gate	J. Baughman	Suffield Township, Ohio	June 29, 1869	91, 816
Farm-gate	G. F. Bissell	Oneonta, N. Y	Nov. 16, 1869	96, 771
Farm-gate	G. W. Blackwell	Lebanon, Ind	July 28, 1868	80, 439
Farm-gate	C. S. Bonney	Penn Yan, N. Y	Sept. 15, 1868	82, 075
Farm-gate	G. C. Bovey	Chillicothe, Ohio	Nov. 27, 1860	30, 784
Farm-gate	J. W. Brewster	West Laurens, N. Y	July 9, 1867	66, 454
Farm-gate	W. Brown	Addison, Mich	Mar. 17, 1868	75, 517
Farm-gate	W. S. Brown	Norwood, Ill	Oct. 7, 1873	143, 493
Farm-gate	E. and A. Buckman	East Greenbush, N. Y	Jan. 29, 1867	61, 605
Farm-gate	M. Burtless	Seneca Falls, N. Y	July 8, 1873	140, 612
Farm-gate	A. L. Butler	Ripon, Wis	Aug. 25, 1868	81, 337
Farm-gate	H. F. Butler	Troy, Mich	Feb. 25, 1868	74, 748
Farm-gate	J. W. Byers	Mechanicsburgh, Pa	May 25, 1869	90, 496
Farm-gate	J. Campbell and A. D. Krewson	Harrison, Ohio	Apr. 2, 1867	63, 363
Farm-gate	E. P. H. Capron	Springfield, Ohio	Apr. 28, 1868	77, 251
Farm-gate	W. D. Carlton	Morrisville, N. C	July 25, 1871	117, 381
Farm-gate	J. Case	Springfield, Ohio	May 29, 1866	55, 058
Farm-gate	L. Charles	Clear Spring, Md	Sept. 8, 1868	81, 982
Farm-gate	J. A. Cheatham	Nashville, Tenn	Oct. 23, 1866	58, 983
Farm-gate	W. D. Clark	Ottawa, Ill	Jan. 7, 1868	72, 976
Farm-gate	C. N. Cole	Pleasant Valley, N. Y	May 13, 1856	14, 851
Farm-gate	T. Collier	Springfield, Ohio	Aug. 13, 1867	67, 723
Farm-gate	S. B. Cooper	Beloit, Wis	Apr. 16, 1867	63, 861
Farm-gate	A. W. Cox	Indianapolis Ind	July 2, 1867	66, 300
Farm-gate	W M. Crawford	Ashland, Ohio	Apr. 16, 1867	63, 862
Farm-gate	J. Curtis	Truro, Ill	Apr. 28, 1868	77, 174

Index of patents issued from the United States Patent Office from 1790 *to* 1873, *inclusive*—Continued.

Invention.	Inventor.	Residence.	Date.	No.
Farm-gate	J. David	East Enterprise, Ind	June 23, 1868	79, 109
Farm-gate	E. B. Decker	Carrollton, Ill	Aug. 5, 1873	141, 497
Farm-gate	L. S Deming	Newington, Conn	Jan. 2, 1866	51, 811
Farm-gate	J. Dickason	Vevay, Ind	Feb. 5, 1867	61, 725
Farm-gate	J. Dickason	Vevay, Ind	June 21, 1870	104, 435
Farm-gate	J. Dickason and G. W. D. Culp	Vevay and Moore's Hill, Ind.	Jan. 4, 1870	98, 573
Farm-gate	A. Dietz	Raritan, N. J	Mar. 2, 1858	19, 499
Farm-gate	E. Easton	Prairieville, Mich	Aug. 18, 1868	81, 0[illegible]7
Farm-gate	W. Elliott	Stockport, N. Y	June 12, 1866	55, 4[illegible]6
Farm-gate	J. W. Epperson	Woodhull, Ill	June 25, 1867	66, 008
Farm-gate	G. J. Fiedler	Danby, Ill	July 26, 1870	105, 662
Farm-gate	G. W. Fox	Saint Joseph County, Mich	July 16, 1867	66, 823
Farm-gate	D. C. Frazeur and W. D. Cocklin.	Sidonsburgh, Pa	June 22, 1869	91, 735
Farm-gate	F. Gay	Bedford, Ohio	July 24, 1866	56, 550
Farm-gate	F. Gay	Bedford, Ohio	Sept. 4, 1866	57, 6[illegible]8
Farm-gate	G. Gibbs	Fairview, Ind	Sept. 22, 1868	82, 3[illegible]8
Farm-gate	L. Gibbs and H. M. Shaw	Fremont, Ohio	Jan. 2, 1866	51, 824
Farm-gate	C. E. Gillespie	Edwardsville, Ill	Dec. 17, 1872	133, 980
Farm-gate	N. J. Glover	Waveland, Ind	Oct. 1, 1867	6[illegible], 337
Farm-gate	S. Goewey	Dormansville, N. Y	July 16, 1867	6[illegible], 8[illegible]9
Farm-gate	C. E. Goodwin	Portland, Mich	Feb. 18, 1868	74, 5[illegible]9
Farm-gate	O. Graham	Lima, N. Y	Nov. 5, 1867	70, 548
Farm-gate	H. Gray and W. A. Bury	Goose Isle, Mich	Mar. 26, 1861	31, 800
Farm-gate	M. Gunshenan	New York, N. Y	Apr. 19, 1870	101, 998
Farm-gate	T. F. Hall	Circleville, Ohio	June 1, 1869	90, 839
Farm-gate	W. D. Harrah	Davenport, Iowa	Sept. 20, 1864	44, 3[illegible]6
Farm-gate	C. L. Harsen and M. R. Brailey	Norwalk, Ohio	May 1, 1855	12, 790
Farm-gate	C. Hart	Farmington, Ill	June 29, 1869	92, 046
Farm-gate	C. Hart	Farmington, Ill	Mar. 8, 1870	100, 620
Farm-gate	H. P. Haskins	Roscoe, Ill	Apr. 4, 1871	113, 657
Farm-gate	A. Hathaway	Prairie du Sac, Wis	Aug. 9, 1870	106, 156
Farm-gate	W. C. Hender	Miami, Ohio	June 30, 1863	39, 044
Farm-gate	H. A. Henderson	Avoca, N. Y	Mar. 24, 1868	75, 756
Farm-gate	W. G. Hermance	Albany, N. Y	Feb. 20, 1866	52, 713
Farm-gate	E. Hill, C. Ostrander, and H. A. Spink.	Bainbridge, Mich	Apr. 6, 1869	88, 569
Farm-gate	V. W. Horton	Palmyra, N. Y	May 19, 1868	78, 095
Farm-gate	J. G. Hunt	Cincinnati, Ohio	Apr. 18, 1865	47, 307
Farm-gate	T. W. Johnson	Granger, Ohio	June 9, 1868	78, 670
Farm-gate	J. Kelsey and J. McLain	Saint Mary's, Ohio	Feb. 26, 1867	62, 426
Farm-gate	H. H. Kelty	Northfield, Ohio	July 9, 1867	66, 501
Farm-gate	D. L. Koons	Trimble, Ohio	Jan. 5, 1869	85, 674
Farm-gate	I. L. Landis	Lancaster, Pa	Jan. 7, 1868	73, 016
Farm-gate	A. Larowe	Cohocton, N. Y	Dec. 18, 1866	60, 547
Farm-gate	J. Lee	Galesburgh, Ill	May 23, 1865	47, 840
Farm-gate	J. Lee	Galesburgh, Ill	June 26, 1866	55, 876
Farm-gate	W. Lucus	Olive Green, Ohio	Nov. 25, 1873	144, 994
Farm-gate	H. B. Lum	Sandusky, Ohio	May 22, 1855	12, 914
Farm-gate	D. F. Luse	Spring Mills, Pa	May 29, 1866	55, 129
Farm-gate	J. Martin	New Oxford, Pa	Mar. 21, 1865	46, 920
Farm-gate	J. Mayben	Milroy, Pa	May 3, 1870	102, 569
Farm-gate	D. McCurdy	Ottawa, Ohio	Aug. 28, 1866	57, 537
Farm-gate	R. W. McFarland	Monticello, Wis	Nov. 13, 1866	59, 621
Farm-gate	W. McGuire	Chess Springs, Pa	Aug. 25, 1868	81, 521
Farm-gate	H. D. Mead	Wayne, N. Y	Sept. 11, 1866	57, 946
Farm-gate	A. T. Morris	Seal, Ohio	Mar. 30, 1869	88, 323
Farm-gate	D. Mougey	Marshallsville, Ohio	Oct. 20, 1868	83, 197
Farm-gate	J. T. Maxley	Owasso, Mich	Apr. 27, 1869	89, 424
Farm-gate	H. W. Mullennex	Alpine, N. Y	May 13, 1873	138, 918
Farm-gate	F. Müller	Mokena, Ill	Mar. 6, 1866	53, 084
Farm-gate	J. C. Murphy	Mendota, Ill	Apr. 10, 1866	53, 856
Farm-gate	J. H. and P. J. Murphy	Abingdon, Ill	Mar. 15, 1870	100, 787
Farm-gate	D. S. Neal	Lynn, Mass	Mar. 26, 1867	63, 288
Farm-gate	D. A. Neidig	Paris, Ohio	Dec. 30, 1873	146, 015
Farm-gate	W. Newlove	Penn Yan, N. Y	Nov. 23, 1858	22, 131
Farm-gate	E. Nicholson	East Rockport, Ohio	Aug. 11, 1863	39, 491
Farm-gate	J. H. Nonamaker	Middletown, Pa	Apr. 23, 1867	64, 133
Farm-gate	C. Ostrander	Lodi, Wis	Dec. 21, 1869	98, 185
Farm-gate	H. Palmerlee	Grand Rapids, Mich	Jan. 26, 1869	86, 315
Farm-gate	E. H. Peck	Brownhelm, Ohio	Dec. 11, 1866	60, 415
Farm-gate	D. Phillips	Shaftsbury, Vt	Nov. 7, 1854	11, 905
Farm-gate	H. Piper	Haskins, Ohio	May 10, 1870	102, 859
Farm-gate	J. Pool	Elizabeth City, N. C	July 12, 1870	105, 366
Farm-gate	A. J. Potter	Omaha, Nebr	Dec. 29, 1868	85, 474
Farm-gate	J. H. Reinhart	McKay, Ohio	Apr. 23, 1867	64, 034
Farm-gate	C. Rich	Marshallsville, Ohio	May 5, 1868	77, 658
Farm-gate	J. C. Rohrer	Gomer, Ohio	Nov. 4, 1873	144, 291
Farm-gate	J. Root	Cass County, Mich	Sept. 1, 1868	81, 820
Farm-gate	C. W. Saladee	Saint Catharine's, Canada	Aug. 16, 1870	106, 411
Farm-gate	S. Scott	Yano, Ohio	Dec. 21, 1869	98, 195
Farm-gate	E. C. Sears	Crystal Lake, Ill	Apr. 9, 1867	63, 757
Farm-gate	O. E. Seymour	Madison, Ind	Dec. 1, 1868	84, 512
Farm-gate	H. S. Shisler	Manheim Township, Pa	Aug. 11, 1868	81, 017
Farm-gate	D. Shockey	Waynesborough, Pa	Dec. 15, 1868	85, 033
Farm-gate	D. Shockey	Waynesborough, Pa	Oct. 5, 1869	95, 524
Farm-gate	S. A. Skinner	Derby, Vt	Oct. 9, 1855	13, 658
Farm-gate	H. R. Sloat	Sloatsburgh, N. Y	July 9, 1861	32, 793
Farm-gate	W. F. Smelley	Vevay, Ind	May 30, 1865	47, 994
Farm-gate	A. D. Smith	Grafton, Ohio	Mar. 19, 1867	62, 975
Farm-gate	A. J. Smith and G. S. Hudson	Ellisburgh, N. Y	Feb. 20, 1866	52, 759
Farm-gate	G. Smith	Providence, R. I	Jan. 26, 1869	86, 184
Farm-gate	R. M. Smith	La Fargeville, N. Y	Mar. 30, 1869	88, 339
Farm-gate	B. Snyder	Clinton, Wis	Dec. 1, 1868	84, 653
Farm-gate	H. Snyder	Wooster, Ohio	Mar. 6, 1866	53, 053
Farm-gate	G. W. States and A. W. Lutts	Norwalk, Ohio	Sept. 24, 1867	69, 138
Farm-gate	T. Steers	Milton, Wis	July 15, 1873	140, 960

Index of patents issued from the United States Patent Office from 1790 *to* 1873, *inclusive*—Continued.

Invention.	Inventor.	Residence.	Date.	No.
Farm-gate	J. G. Talbot	Sloansville, N. Y	June 11, 1867	65, 707
Farm-gate	J. G. Talbot	Sloansville, N. Y	Mar. 9, 1869	87, 600
Farm-gate	J. Tanner	Hebron, Ky	Feb. 2, 1869	86, 603
Farm-gate	L F. Tanner	Milan, Ind	Aug. 25, 1868	81, 558
Farm-gate	A. Taylor	New Hartford, Conn	June 16, 1868	79, 025
Farm-gate	G. Taylor	Richmond, Ind	June 24, 1856	15, 213
Farm-gate	A. C. Teel	Girard, Ill	Dec. 1, 1863	40, 777
Farm-gate	F. F. Terry	Port Gibson, N. Y	Nov. 20, 1866	59, 873
Farm-gate	C. W. Todd	Spring Arbor, Mich	June 8, 1869	90, 971
Farm-gate	J. A. Treat	Tallmadge. Ohio	Oct. 12, 1858	21, 785
Farm-gate	S. Vreeland	Cuba, N. Y	July 20, 1869	92, 914
Farm-gate	J. B. Webb	Muscatine, Iowa	June 4, 1867	65, 519
Farm-gate	B. Werrich and J. Smith	Middleburgh, Ind	Apr. 21, 1868	77, 142
Farm-gate	J. W. Westbrooks and A. J. Clemmons.	Aberdeen, Miss	May 20, 1873	139, 219
Farm-gate	T. B. Wickham	Granville, Ohio	Feb. 5, 1867	61, 785
Farm-gate	T. B. Wickham	Granville, Ohio	Sept. 29, 1868	82, 668
Farm-gate	W. H. Wright	Rochester, N. Y	Mar. 1, 1870	100, 484
Farm-gate	G. Yeomans	Romulus, Mich	Jan. 12, 1869	85, 886
Farm-gate	I. N. Young	Swann, Ind	July 16, 1867	66, 764
Farm-gate, Approach-opening	C. W. Smart	Watertown, N. Y	Dec. 22, 1857	18, 932
Farm-gate, Iron	W. F. Whitney	Milwaukee, Wis	Jan. 12, 1869	85, 882
Farm-gate, Self-acting	E. Dunbar	Philadelphia, Pa	Mar. 4, 1856	14, 351
Farm-gate, Sliding	T. Ellison	Abingdon, Ill	July 20, 1869	92, 805
Farm-gates by approaching vehicles, Method of operating.	A. J. Hamilton	Kewanee, Ill	Mar. 8, 1859	23, 169
Farm-gates by hand, Mode of opening and closing.	G. Yates	West Dresden, N. Y	Apr. 19, 1859	23, 738
Farm-gates, Closing	T. B. Hand	Madison, Ind	Oct. 20, 1857	18, 449
Farm-gates, Device for raising or lowering	D. E. Fenn	Tallmadge, Ohio	Mar. 10, 1857	16, 791
Farm-gates, Hanging	J. Filson	Milroy, Pa	Feb. 8, 1853	9, 576
Farm-gates, Hinging	I. S. Rowland	West Earl, Pa	Jan. 13, 1857	16, 400
Farm-gates, Hanging and elevating	J. F. Downing	Erie, Pa	Apr. 15, 1856	14, 689
Farm-gates, Hanging and latching	J. Kinman	Freeport, Ill	Apr. 25, 1865	47, 429
Farm-gates, Opening and closing	J. A. Ayres	Hartford, Conn	Jan. 22, 1856	14, 131
Farm-gates, Opening and closing	W. F. C. Beattie	Cornwall, N. Y	May 18, 1858	20, 247
Farm-gates, Opening and closing	W. T. Boggs	Cincinnati, Ohio	Oct. 19, 1858	21, 811
Farm-gates, Opening and closing	B. M. Dorr	Kewanee, Ill	July 5, 1859	24, 619
Farm-gates, Opening and closing	D. E. Fenn	Tallmadge, Ohio	Oct. 14, 1856	15, 881
Farm-gates, Opening and closing	W. G. Hermance	Geneva, N. Y	Nov. 9, 1858	22, 023
Farm-gates, Opening and closing	W. Sherwood	Beloit, Wis	June 30, 1857	17, 699
Farm-gates, Opening and closing	D. Warren	Gettysburgh, Pa	June 21, 1859	24, 513
Farm-gates, Operating	J. H. Butler and P. G. Van Houten.	Cohocton, N. Y	July 12, 1859	24, 717
Farm-gates, Operating	J. K. Weber	Seneca Falls, N. Y	Oct. 9, 1855	13, 673
Farm-gates, Operating	C. Winegar	Union Springs, N. Y	Aug. 26, 1856	15, 631
Farm-gates, Raising, lowering, and operating	C. Hunter and N. Isham	Norwalk. Ohio	Aug. 12, 1856	15, 518
Farmer's boiler	G. H. Buckley	Quincy, Ill	July 25, 1871	117, 254
Farmer's boiler	P. Colvin	Pecatonica, Ill	Nov. 25, 1873	144, 890
Farmer's boiler	M. Ellis	South Carver, Mass	Apr. 28, 1863	38, 299
Farmer's boiler	J. H. Hunter	Pennington Point, Ill	Dec. 13, 1870	110, 139
Farmer's boiler	A. N. Merrill	Batavia, Ill	Jan. 18, 1870	98, 988
Farmer's boiler	A. N. Merrill	Batavia, Ill	May 31, 1870	103, 639
Farmer's boiler	A. B. Nott	Fairhaven, Mass	Jan. 21, 1873	135, 005
Farmer's boiler	W. M. Pryor and R. Ludwick	Kellogg Iowa	July 4, 1871	116, 753
Farmer's boiler	G. Stevenson	Zionsville, Ind	Aug. 15, 1871	118, 068
Farmer's boiler	R. W. Thickens	Batavia, Ill	July 26, 1870	105, 740
Farmer's boiler	R. W. Thickens and D. R. Sperry.	Batavia, Ill	Mar. 28, 1871	113, 222
Farrier's clinching-tool	S. Ogden	Sicily, Ohio	Apr. 23, 1872	126, 078
Farrier's tool	E. Warren and W. Johnston	Marshall, Mich	May 24, 1864	42, 918
Fat, lard, &c., Machine for cutting	C. Forschner	New York, N. Y	Aug. 14, 1866	57, 111
Fat, Machine for cutting	W. E. Boulger	Janesville, Wis	July 3, 1860	28, 960
Fat, Machine for cutting	J. M. Hunter	New York, N. Y	May 8, 1860	28, 179
Fat, Machine for cutting	A. Pfaff	Baltimore, Md	June 28, 1870	104, 878
Fat, Machine for cutting up	F. Miller and J. N. McIntire	New York, N. Y	Mar. 15, 1864	41, 963
Fats and oils from grains, &c., Process and apparatus for separating.	E. S. Hutchinson	Baltimore, Md	Apr. 2, 1872	125, 300
Fats and oils, Hardening	C. W. Schindler	New York, N. Y	Nov. 5, 1850	7, 760
Fats into fatty acids and glycerine, Method of decomposing.	R. A. Tilghman	Philadelphia, Pa	May 15, 1860	28, 315
Fats, Process for decomposing	R. A. Wright and L. J. Fouché.	Paris, France	Jan. 25, 1859	22, 765
Fats, Purifying and separating	A. Paraf	New York, N. Y	Apr. 8, 1873	137, 564
Fats, Saponifying	G. F. Wilson and G. Payne	Belmont, Vauxhall, England.	June 17, 1856	15, 158
Fatty matter from residuum, Obtaining	D. Thain and W. Jackson	Philadelphia, Pa	Jan. 10, 1860	26, 799
Fatty matter from vegetable substances, Apparatus for separating.	T. Sim	Baltimore, Md	Dec. 12, 1871	121, 903
Fatty matter, Process for extracting	E. Deiss	Paris, France	Apr. 27, 1858	20, 048
Fatty matter, Treating	L. L. A. E. P. De la Peyrouse	Paris, France	Nov. 21, 1871	121, 162
Fatty material, Purifying	J. B. Moinier and P. H. Bontigny.	Paris, France	Feb. 8, 1853	9, 572
Fatty substances, Hardening	B. C. Tilghman	Philadelphia, Pa	Jan. 11, 1859	22, 593
Fatty substances, Process and apparatus for extracting.	C. F. A. Simonin	Philadelphia, Pa	Sept. 19, 1871	119, 188
Faucet	J. H. Alexander	Geneva, N. Y	Dec. 19, 1871	121, 978
Faucet	C. E. Allan	Boston, Mass	Nov. 27, 1866	59, 939
Faucet	L. L. Alrich	Carthage, Miss	Sept. 25, 1860	30, 110
Faucet	J. Ashcroft	New York, N. Y	Apr. 5, 1870	101, 410
Faucet	F. M. Bachman and S. Ricker	Fredericksburgh, Pa	Mar. 8, 1870	100, 489
Faucet	A. Bain	New York, N. Y	Nov. 15, 1864	45, 012
Faucet	W. Ball	Cabotville, Mass	Feb. 1, 1848	5, 431
Faucet	S. Barker	Hartford, Conn	May 3, 1859	23, 817
Faucet	T. W. Bartholomew	New York, N. Y	Feb. 7, 1871	111, 569
Faucet	D. L. and R. Bollerman	New York, N. Y	Feb. 2, 1869	86, 498
Faucet	R. M. Bouton	West Troy, N. Y	Apr. 18, 1854	10, 800
Faucet	C. K. Bradford	Linn, Mass	Apr. 19, 1859	23, 658
Faucet	A. Brinckmann	New York, N. Y	May 28, 1867	65, 160
Faucet	J. Broughton	Chicago, Ill	Sept. 8, 1863	39, 795

Index of patents issued from the United States Patent Office from 1790 to 1873, inclusive—Continued.

Invention.	Inventor.	Residence.	Date.	No.
Faucet	J. Broughton	New York, N. Y	Nov. 8, 1864	44, 933
Faucet	J. Broughton	New York, N. Y	Sept. 21, 1869	95, 077
Faucet	H. L. and J. A. Buckwalter	Kimberton, Pa	Oct. 9, 1866	58, 592
Faucet	J. Bulger	Port Sherman, Mich	Mar. 15, 1870	100, 721
Faucet	G. F. Burkhardt	Roxbury, Mass	Oct. 11, 1864	44, 596
Faucet	M. Burnett	Boston, Mass	June 18, 1867	65, 791
Faucet	M. Burnett	Boston, Mass	Dec. 5, 1871	121, 487
Faucet	E. Candler	London, England	Sept. 25, 1866	58, 356
Faucet	I. Carey	Morristown, N. J	May 10, 1870	102, 773
Faucet	W. P. Clark	Medford, Mass	Nov. 2, 1869	96, 394
Faucet	W. F. Class and L. W. Sapp	Cleveland, Ohio	Oct. 25, 1870	108, 568
Faucet	W. Cleveland	Orange, N. J	Sept. 25, 1860	30, 122
Faucet	W. Cleveland	Orange, N. J	Aug. 8, 1871	117, 866
Faucet	W. Cleveland	Orange, N. J	Mar. 12, 1872	124, 546
Faucet	J. S. Clute and H. W. and W. Frissler.	Cleveland, Ohio	Apr. 4, 1871	113, 630
Faucet	D. N. B. Coffin, jr	Newton, Centre, Mass	June 16, 1857	17, 604
Faucet	T. M. Coffin	Plymouth, Mass	Oct. 9, 1866	58, 600
Faucet	W. S. Cooper	Philadelphia, Pa	Oct. 23, 1866	59, 122
Faucet	W. S. Cooper	Philadelphia, Pa	May 17, 1870	103, 145
Faucet	G. T. Dalton	New York, N. Y	May 25, 1869	90, 343
Faucet	J. S. Davison	Cranberry, N. J	Apr. 16, 1861	32, 053
Faucet	J. M. A. Dow	Chicago, Ill	Feb. 22, 1870	100, 126
Faucet	A. Doll and C. Elling	Cleveland, Ohio	Nov. 11, 1873	144, 516
Faucet	J. H. Dorst	New Albany, Ind	Jan. 11, 1870	98, 749
Faucet	C. A. Douglas	Franklin, N. Y	Nov. 15, 1870	109, 191
Faucet	D. Drawbaugh	Eberly's Mill, Pa	Nov. 20, 1866	59, 792
Faucet	D. Drawbaugh	Eberly's Mill, Pa	Nov. 20, 1866	59, 793
Faucet	E. Duchamp	Saint Martinsville, La	Sept. 13, 1859	25, 397
Faucet	A. Eggleston	Fall River, Mass	June 14, 1870	104, 128
Faucet	J. Fahrney	Boonsborough, Md	Sept. 4, 1866	57, 818
Faucet	J. Farnan	Cleveland, Ohio	Sept. 18, 1860	30, 055
Faucet	J. Flattery	Brooklyn, N. Y	July 24, 1860	29, 263
Faucet	W. Fowler	New York, N. Y	May 8, 1855	12, 817
Faucet	A. Fuller	Boston, Mass	Oct. 16, 1855	13, 677
Faucet	A. Fuller	Cincinnati, Ohio	Aug. 30, 1859	25, 253
Faucet	A. Fuller	Cincinnati, Ohio	Feb. 18, 1862	34, 419
Faucet	H. Getty	Brooklyn, N. Y	July 6, 1858	20, 788
Faucet	J. Goodridge	Boston, Mass	July 29, 1856	15, 459
Faucet	J. Goodridge	Boston, Mass	Sept. 9, 1856	15, 719
Faucet	A. J. Gove	San Francisco, Cal	Apr. 29, 1862	35, 094
Faucet	R. Graham	Brooklyn, N. Y	Mar. 26, 1861	31, 799
Faucet	D. W. Green	Port Chester, N. Y	Mar. 23, 1869	88, 032
Faucet	J. Grundy	Stoneham, Mass	Apr. 12, 1864	42, 286
Faucet	O. Hanks	Cincinnati, Ohio	Nov. 29, 1870	109, 730
Faucet	A. S. Hart	Buffalo, N. Y	Jan. 17, 1860	26, 844
Faucet	I. W. Harvey	Norwich, Conn	June 7, 1870	104, 025
Faucet	J. Hayden, jr	Haydenville, Mass	Jan. 26, 1869	86, 225
Faucet	W. H. Hedges	Newark, N. J	Feb. 21, 1871	112, 8[illegible]5
Faucet	J. Heine and J. Vonficht	Toledo, Ohio	Apr. 19, 1870	102, 120
Faucet	T. Hersee and P. J. Bourgnon	Buffalo, N. Y	Oct. 4, 1859	25, 643
Faucet	W. B. Hersman	Richmond, Va	July 23, 1872	129, 823
Faucet	P. Hille	Union, N. J	Oct. 28, 1873	144, 097
Faucet	J. Hills	Haydensville, Mass	Dec. 6, 1870	109, 902
Faucet	N. Hotz	Green Point, Brooklyn, N. Y	June 11, 1872	127, 883
Faucet	W. H. Humphrey	Lansingburgh, N. Y	July 23, 1867	67, 056
Faucet	G. R. Huntley	Taunton, Mass	Sept. 11, 1866	57, 910
Faucet	G. R. Huntley	Taunton, Mass	Mar. 24, 1868	75, 918
Faucet	J. Jahrans and J. G. Bickel	Buffalo, N. Y	June 3, 1862	35, 450
Faucet	N. Jenkins	Boston, Mass	Aug. 22, 1865	49, 527
Faucet	T. J. Jones and T. L. Webster.	Summit, N. J., and Brooklyn, N. Y.	May 7, 1867	64, 427
Faucet	A. D. King and J. W. King	Granville Corners, Mass., and Bridgeport, Conn.	Nov. 4, 1873	144, 208
Faucet	J. Knoche	Cincinnati, Ohio	June 21, 1870	104, 602
Faucet	J. Knoche	Cincinnati, Ohio	June 27, 1871	116, 326
Faucet	L. J. Knowles	Warren, Mass	June 2, 1857	17, 433
Faucet	B. F. Kraft	Reading, Pa	Sept. 15, 1868	82, 232
Faucet	A. W. P. Ladd	San Francisco, Cal	July 2, 1861	32, 699
Faucet	J. Laing	Hoboken, N. J	May 28, 1867	65, 238
Faucet	J. Leitch	Buffalo, N. Y	Dec. 15, 1863	40, 939
Faucet	J. H. Lord	San Francisco, Cal	July 26, 1870	105, 818
Faucet	J. R. Mackay	Meriden, Conn	Feb. 7, 1871	111, 659
Faucet	J. Marchbank	Lansingburgh, N. Y	Jan. 28, 1868	73, 822
Faucet	J. Marchbank and W. H. Humphrey.	Lansingburgh, N. Y	Nov. 6, 1866	59, 426
Faucet	J. Matthews, jr	New York, N. Y	June 27, 1865	48, 421
Faucet	W. McKay	Newburyport, Mass	June 7, 1870	104, 050
Faucet	J. McKenna	Pittsburgh, Pa	Sept. 16, 1862	36, 473
Faucet	J., A., and T. McKenna	Pittsburgh, Pa	Nov. 4, 1873	144, 213
Faucet	F. Meyrose	Saint Louis, Mo	June 14, 1864	43, 125
Faucet	W. Morgenstern	New York, N. Y	July 12, 1870	105, 360
Faucet	O. F. Morrill	Chelsea, Mass	Dec. 4, 1866	60, 223
Faucet	A. J. Morse	Melrose, Mass	Oct. 25, 1864	44, 813
Faucet	R. Murray	Boston, Mass	Jan. 17, 1865	45, 949
Faucet	J. Neumann	New York, N. Y	Apr. 30, 1861	32, 201
Faucet	C. B. O'Sullivan	New Orleans, La	Feb. 28, 1871	112, 173
Faucet	S. W. and J. F. Palmer	Auburn, N. Y	Aug. 3, 1869	93, 2[illegible]2
Faucet	E. Parks	Winchendon, Mass	July 23, 1861	32, 888
Faucet	G. G. Percival	Brooklyn, N. Y	July 25, 1865	48, 995
Faucet	S. Pfleger	Reading, Pa	Mar. 7, 1871	112, 487
Faucet	J. Phelps	Owego, N. Y	Sept. 24, 1867	69, 124
Faucet	W. Pinkerman	Bridgeport, N. Y	Aug. 18, 1863	39, 585
Faucet	J. Powell	Cincinnati, Ohio	Mar. 22, 1859	23, 310
Faucet	J. Powell	Cincinnati, Ohio	Sept. 6, 1859	25, 349
Faucet	A. D. Puffer	Boston, Mass	June 28, 1870	104, 880
Faucet	A. Putnam, jr	Saratoga Springs, N. Y	Nov. 1, 1870	108, 824
Faucet	G. W. Randall	Boston, Mass	Apr. 5, 1859	23, 533

Index of patents issued from the United States Patent Office from 1790 to 1873, inclusive—Continued.

Invention.	Inventor.	Residence.	Date.	No.
Faucet	J. Regester	Baltimore, Md	Apr. 9, 1867	63, 748
Faucet	E. Ripley	Troy, N. Y	Mar. 14, 1854	10, 641
Faucet	F. Roach	Boston, Mass	Sept. 8, 1868	81, 948
Faucet	M. Robbins and J. Powell	Cincinnati, Ohio	Dec. 21, 1858	22, 402
Faucet	A. Rooker	London, England	June 16, 1868	78, 897
Faucet	J. Schaefer and G. Schock	New York, N. Y	July 12, 1870	105, 258
Faucet	H. Schnantz and H. Bremenkamp.	Cincinnati, Ohio	Nov. 15, 1864	45, 085
Faucet	C. Schullian	New York, N. Y	July 3, 1866	56, 105
Faucet	E. Scrannage, jr	Melrose, Mass	May 6, 1873	138, 700
Faucet	M. Scrannage and W. H. Bate	Medford and East Somerville, Mass.	Dec. 20, 1870	110, 292
Faucet	A. D. Smith	Grafton, Ohio	Oct. 26, 1869	96, 158
Faucet	A. D. Smith	Grafton, Ohio	Nov. 28, 1871	121, 430
Faucet	D. P. Smith	Salem, N. J	Aug. 18, 1868	81, 305
Faucet	J. N. Smith	Jersey City, N. J	Mar. 14, 1865	46, 862
Faucet	J. N. Smith	Jersey City, N. J	Nov. 13, 1866	59, 672
Faucet	J. N. Smith	Jersey City, N. J	July 9, 1872	128, 762
Faucet	T. Somerville	Washington, D. C	Apr. 5, 1870	101, 533
Faucet	C. W. Stearns	Springfield, Mass	July 22, 1851	8, 237
Faucet	E. Stebbins	Chicopee, Mass	July 9, 1861	32, 797
Faucet	E. A. Sterry	Norwich Town, Conn	June 12, 1855	13, 047
Faucet	F. P. Stiker	Buffalo, N. Y	Aug. 20, 1867	67, 925
Faucet	J. T. Stilwell	Dowagiac, Mich	Aug. 6, 1867	67, 605
Faucet	S. C. Stokes	Manchester, N. H	Oct. 15, 1867	69, 859
Faucet	H. Strater, jr	Boston, Mass	Mar. 7, 1865	46, 726
Faucet	H. Strater, jr	Boston, Mass	Mar. 7, 1865	46, 727
Faucet	H. Strater, jr	Boston, Mass	Mar. 7, 1865	46, 728
Faucet	J. R. Street and S. M. Davis	Washington, D. C	Nov. 27, 1866	60, 082
Faucet	I. C. Tate	New London, Conn	June 12, 1860	28, 699
Faucet	G. Taylor	New York, N. Y	May 24, 1870	103, 523
Faucet	S. R. Thompson	Portsmouth, N. H	Nov. 11, 1873	144, 422
Faucet	T. J. Thorn and J. Dennis, jr	Skaneateles, N. Y., and Washington, D. C.	Aug. 14, 1866	57, 220
Faucet	D. H. Thorp	Chelsea, Mass	June 19, 1860	28, 819
Faucet	H. B. Tiffany	Medina, Ohio	Aug. 2, 1870	106, 000
Faucet	R. Tilly	Brooklyn, N. Y	June 21, 1870	104, 663
Faucet	J. W. Trafton	Springfield, Mass	July 23, 1872	129, 872
Faucet	W. A. Traver	Rhinebeck, N. Y	Oct. 8, 1872	132, 036
Faucet	W. H. Trissler	Cleveland, Ohio	May 3, 1870	102, 624
Faucet	J. E. Tucker	Boston, Mass	Nov. 12, 1867	70, 919
Faucet	J. E. Tucker	Boston, Mass	Dec. 22, 1868	85, 257
Faucet	C. Utter and G. E. Bruster	Newark, N. J	Aug. 1, 1871	117, 699
Faucet	H. Varwig	Cincinnati, Ohio	Apr. 15, 1873	137, 981
Faucet	C. T. Vose	Stapleton, N. Y	Aug. 6, 1872	130, 341
Faucet	C. Weaver	Easton, Pa	Oct. 8, 1867	69, 730
Faucet	W. Weaver	Nashua, N. H	Nov. 2, 1869	96, 519
Faucet	D. Wellington	Boston, Mass	Apr. 26, 1870	102, 341
Faucet	H. G. Whitaker	West Brattleborough, Vt	May 21, 1872	127, 128
Faucet	J. White	Philadelphia, Pa	Oct. 28, 1873	144, 175
Faucet	N. P. Whittelsey	Meriden, Conn	July 6, 1858	20, 853
Faucet	F. Wieshofer	Fremont, Ohio	Dec. 13, 1870	110, 099
Faucet	J. Wilcox	Thompsonville, Conn	Mar. 19, 1867	63, 127
Faucet	W. C. Wise and J. Ashman	Chelsea, Mass	Feb. 21, 1871	112, 000
Faucet	M. Woodbury	Boston, Mass	Mar. 11, 1856	14, 429
Faucet	C. T. Woodman	Boston, Mass	Feb. 16, 1864	41, 659
Faucet	W. E. Worthen	New York, N. Y	Apr. 22, 1862	35, 054
Faucet	E. Young	Cleveland, Ohio	June 28, 1870	104, 811
Faucet	M. Zimmerman	Earl Township, Pa	Jan. 5, 1869	85, 717
Faucet	O. Zwietusch	Milwaukee, Wis	July 16, 1872	129, 263
Faucet, Alarm	T. M. Biddle	Fort Wayne, Ind	Dec. 7, 1869	97, 594
Faucet and valve, Grinding	F. Shaw	Philadelphia, Pa	June 13, 1865	48, 216
Faucet and vent	J. Jahraus	Buffalo, N. Y	Sept. 22, 1863	40, 044
Faucet and vent, Combined beer	J. G. Bickel	Buffalo, N. Y	May 24, 1864	42, 828
Faucet and vent, Combined beer	J. Miller	Buffalo, N. Y	May 10, 1864	42, 676
Faucet, Anti-frost	F. H. Bartholomew	New York, N. Y	Nov. 11, 1856	16, 043
Faucet-attachment	J. Church	Saint Louis, Mo	Sept. 23, 1873	143, 062
Faucet-attachment	E. L. Dunbar	Bay City, Mich	July 22, 1873	141, 040
Faucet-attachment	G. Johnson and W. H. Milliken	San Francisco, Cal	Dec. 3, 1867	71, 622
Faucet-attachment, Self-closing	R. McConnell, W. Truesdell, and F. Mertsheimer.	Omaha, Nebr	Sept. 30, 1873	143, 291
Faucet-attachment to cans	J. H. Garrigan and F. L. Hall	Sacramento, Cal., and Reno, Nev.	Nov. 30, 1869	97, 290
Faucet, Balance-gate	E. Ripley	Troy, N. Y	May 8, 1855	12, 830
Faucet, Basin	J. Benson	Yonkers, N. Y	June 23, 1868	79, 190
Faucet, Basin	J. Chambers	Boston, Mass	Dec. 24, 1867	72, 453
Faucet, Basin	W. P. Clark	Charlestown, Mass	Aug. 2, 1864	43, 736
Faucet, Basin	W. Gordon	Philadelphia, Pa	May 28, 1872	127, 341
Faucet, Basin	J. Hills	Haydenville, Mass	Aug. 14, 1866	57, 134
Faucet, Basin	W. C. Marshall and H. W. Smith	Hartford, Conn	June 9, 1857	17, 511
Faucet, Basin	F. Roach	Boston, Mass	Dec. 3, 1867	71, 790
Faucet, Basin	R. P. Ross	Bethlehem, Pa	Mar. 10, 1868	75, 464
Faucet, Basin	E. Stebbins	Chicopee, Mass	May 19, 1857	17, 342
Faucet, Beer	T. Ahrens	Louisville, Ky	Aug. 2, 1870	106, 020
Faucet, Beer	J. C. Baer	Cincinnati, Ohio	Apr. 24, 1866	54, 091
Faucet, Beer	C. Bourgeois	Buffalo, N. Y	July 16, 1872	129, 090
Faucet, Beer	C. Brown and C. McGhie	Chicago, Ill	July 17, 1866	56, 357
Faucet, Beer	P. F. Donnelly	San Francisco, Cal	July 30, 1872	129, 938
Faucet, Beer	O. T. Earle	Norwalk, Conn	Aug. 26, 1873	142, 090
Faucet, Beer	J. Firmenich	Buffalo, N. Y	Jan. 2, 1866	51, 820
Faucet, Beer	J. Firmenich	Buffalo, N. Y	Mar. 20, 1866	53, 283
Faucet, Beer	J. Firmenich	Buffalo, N. Y	May 15, 1866	54, 707
Faucet, Beer	A. Hallowell	Lowell, Mass	June 20, 1865	48, 273
Faucet, Beer	J. Jahraus	Buffalo, N. Y	May 1, 1866	54, 359
Faucet, Beer	C. Jakob	New Orleans, La	Oct. 4, 1870	108, 025
Faucet, Beer	F. Manz	Allegheny City, Pa	Apr. 12, 1870	101, 966
Faucet, Beer	T. Marsh	Smithfield, R. I	Mar. 12, 1867	62, 864
Faucet, Beer	J. Miller	Buffalo, N. Y	Apr. 25, 1865	47, 442

Index of patents issued from the United States Patent Office from 1790 *to* 1873, *inclusive*—Continued.

Invention.	Inventor.	Residence.	Date.	No.
Faucet, Beer	L. Mullenhoff	Buffalo, N. Y	May 14, 1872	126, 736
Faucet, Beer	L. Poh	Buffalo, N. Y	July 4, 1865	48, 588
Faucet, Beer	A. D. Puffer	Somerville, Mass	Feb. 9, 1869	86, 861
Faucet, Beer	J. M. Stark	Buffalo, N. Y	Feb. 18, 1868	74, 625
Faucet, Beer	E. Stirrot	Buffalo, N. Y	Apr. 3, 1866	53, 092
Faucet, Beer	F. J. Walz and C. Steck	Hudson, N. J	Mar. 3, 1868	75, 085
Faucet, Beer and ale	J. Deasey	Fall River, Mass	Nov. 11, 1873	144, 447
Faucet, Boring	J. R. Lawrence and J. G. Johnson.	Cutler, Me	Oct. 6, 1868	82, 851
Faucet, Boring	S. McGee	Madison, N. J	Mar. 3, 1868	75, 177
Faucet, Boring	A. Weed	Boston, Mass	Feb. 25, 1868	74, 961
Faucet, Boring	A. Weed	Boston, Mass	Feb. 16, 1869	86, 956
Faucet, Bottle	H. Fischer	Lanesville, Ind	Nov. 1, 1870	108, 898
Faucet, Bottle	W. I. Luther	Rochester, N. Y	Mar. 17, 1868	75, 557
Faucet, Bottle	J. Sargent and L. F. Munger	Rochester, N. Y	Nov. 21, 1871	121, 201
Faucet, Bung	G. D. Lee	Brookhaven, N. Y	Dec. 9, 1873	145, 432
Faucet, Casting	O. T. Wood	Pittsburgh, Pa	May 25, 1858	20, 395
Faucet, Compound	W. S. Bate	Philadelphia, Pa	July 22, 1873	141, 102
Faucet, Compression basin	W. Gordon	Philadelphia, Pa	Feb. 4, 1873	135, 541
Faucet-connection	T. H. Brady	New Britain, Conn	Nov. 9, 1869	96, 545
Faucet-coupling	O. Salgee	Brooklyn, N. Y	Sept. 26, 1871	119, 243
Faucet, Diaphragm	W. Blake	Boston, Mass	Nov. 6, 1866	59, 346
Faucet, Double	E. Sauter	Hartford, Conn	Aug. 10, 1869	93, 561
Faucet, Filter	R. B. Coar	Jersey City, N. J	Aug. 27, 1867	68, 170
Faucet, Filtering	L. Finger	Boston, Mass	Nov. 20, 1855	13, 836
Faucet, Filtering	G. H. Fox and H. J. Siller	Boston and East Cambridge, Mass.	Dec. 16, 1856	16, 232
Faucet, Filtering	G. Hillegass	Philadelphia, Pa	May 1, 1866	54, 347
Faucet, Flexible-lined	J. Broughton	New York, N. Y	Oct. 4, 1864	44, 510
Faucet, Fluid	J. Hollely	Brooklyn, N. Y	May 29, 1855	12, 950
Faucet for beer and other barrels	S. Thompson	Schaghticoke, N. Y	Jan. 17, 1871	111, 018
Faucet for bottles	J. Hiney	Hartford, Conn	Dec. 11, 1860	30, 920
Faucet for discharging liquids, Ventilating	J. W. McKee	Brooklyn, N. Y	Mar. 30, 1869	88, 402
Faucet for drawing liquor from casks	I. Ives	Bristol, Conn	Apr. 14, 1808	....
Faucet for filling barrels, Self-closing	S. C. Catlin	Cleveland, Ohio	Feb. 16, 1869	86, 970
Faucet for measuring liquids	J. Cross	New London, Ohio	Mar. 14, 1854	10, 633
Faucet for measuring liquids	J. B. Larwill and J. Cross	Bucyrus, Ohio	Mar. 14, 1854	10, 638
Faucet for oil, &c	J. D. Frary	New Britain, Conn	Feb. 28, 1865	46, 555
Faucet for stove-reservoirs	J. B. Crowley	Cincinnati, Ohio	Nov. 12, 1867	70, 815
Faucet-holes, Bushing for	S. R. Thompson	Portsmouth, N. H	Aug. 5, 1873	141, 473
Faucet, Liquid measuring and registering	E. W. Scott	Wauregan, Conn	Feb. 9, 1869	86, 700
Faucet-lock	V. L. Maxwell	Wilkesbarre, Pa	Apr. 26, 1870	102, 290
Faucet, Measure	G. Hubbard	Sandisfield, Mass	Aug. 25, 1863	39, 654
Faucet, Measure	M. W. Nalton	Utica, N. Y	Mar. 13, 1860	27, 465
Faucet Measure	A. Vrooman	Kokomo, Ind	Feb. 13, 1866	52, 628
Faucet measure and funnel combined	T. McMahon	Williamsburgh, N. Y	Feb. 1, 1870	99, 454
Faucet measure and indicator	V. Squarza	San Francisco, Cal	Jan. 19, 1864	41, 390
Faucet measure, Graduated	G. H. Henkel	Middletown, Ohio	July 4, 1865	48, 556
Faucet, Measuring	G. K. Babcock	Utica, N. Y	Apr. 3, 1860	27, 679
Faucet, Measuring	J. G. Baker	Philadelphia, Pa	July 10, 1866	56, 342
Faucet, Measuring	E. Bigelow	Springfield, Mass	Feb. 22, 1859	23, 008
Faucet, Measuring	E. Bigelow	Springfield, Mass	May 1, 1866	54, 282
Faucet, Measuring	T. B. Bishop	New York, N. Y	Sept. 28, 1869	95, 308
Faucet, Measuring	O. B. Blake and O. E. Colony	Keene, N. H	Aug. 11, 1868	80, 852
Faucet, Measuring	E. T. Bussell	Covington, Ky	Oct. 4, 1859	25, 627
Faucet, Measuring	J. R. Byler and G. W. Seusenich	Beartown, Pa	May 11, 1852	8, 937
Faucet, Measuring	J. F. De Navarro	New York, N. Y	July 6, 1869	92, 287
Faucet, Measuring	E. Fitzgerald	New York, N. Y	Dec. 10, 1867	71, 865
Faucet, Measuring	F. C. Heiser	Brooklyn, N. Y	Aug. 30, 1870	106, 816
Faucet, Measuring	W. W. Hollman	Eddyville, Ky	Mar. 1, 1859	23, 143
Faucet, Measuring	A. Houpt and J. K. Griffith	Reading, Pa	Aug. 6, 1861	32, 996
Faucet, Measuring	G. Hubbard	Montville, Mass	July 6, 1858	20, 799
Faucet, Measuring	G. Hubbard	Montville, Mass	Oct. 9, 1860	30, 321
Faucet, Measuring	I. Kinman	Freeport, Ill	May 3, 1859	23, 845
Faucet, Measuring	T. McGirr	Richmond, Ind	June 20, 1865	48, 296
Faucet, Measuring	E. A. Palmer	Clayville, N. Y	Apr. 22, 1856	14, 734
Faucet, Measuring	T. S. Reeve	Chicago, Ill	July 28, 1868	80, 307
Faucet, Measuring	F. Saunders	Aberdeen, Miss	Feb. 18, 1868	74, 605
Faucet Measuring	J. Schalk, jr	Guttenberg, N. J	Oct. 21, 1873	143, 850
Faucet Measuring	J. Smith and G. B. Griffin	Cincinnati, Ohio, and Madison, Wis.	June 21, 1859	24, 498
Faucet, Measuring	J. D. Smith	New York, N. Y	May 12, 1868	77, 928
Faucet, Measuring	J. N. Smith	Jersey City, N. J	June 20, 1865	48, 318
Faucet, Measuring	D. S. Spafford and G. Elsey	Morrison, Ill	July 2, 1867	66, 406
Faucet, Measuring	O. L. Wheeler	Lewiston, Me	Aug. 11, 1868	80, 847
Faucet, Measuring	S. H. Wheeler	Dowagiac, Mich	July 11, 1865	48, 778
Faucet, Measuring	S. S. Wiles	Santa Clara, Cal	Nov. 27, 1866	60, 104
Faucet, Molasses	H. D. Blake	New Britain, Conn	Jan. 23, 1866	52, 241
Faucet, Molasses	J. Dudley	Fall River, Mass	Feb. 1, 1848	5, 430
Faucet, Molasses	J. and S. Fahrney	Boonsborough, Md	Sept. 22, 1863	40, 029
Faucet, Molasses	D. D. Hanson	Weare, N. H	Feb. 1, 1848	5, 427
Faucet, Molasses	W. H. Hartman	Fostoria, Ohio	Feb. 20, 1866	52, 712
Faucet, Molasses	C. W. Peckham	New Haven, Conn	Feb. 10, 1836	....
Faucet, Molasses	E. Stebbins	Cabotville, Mass	Feb. 1, 1848	5, 428
Faucet or gate, Molasses	C. Woodyear	Philadelphia, Pa	Feb. 5, 1834	....
Faucet or supply-cock	E. F. Shoenberger	Philadelphia, Pa	May 16, 1871	114, 981
Faucet or trap	A. L. Webster	New York, N. Y	Aug. 2, 1870	106, 007
Faucet, Permutation-lock	W. F. Jones	Baltimore, Md	Oct. 11, 1870	108, 153
Faucet-plug	G. Howland and E. T. Ford	Brunswick and Stillwater, N. Y.	July 20, 1869	92, 725
Faucet, Plugged	W. Jones	New York, N. Y	May 13, 1812	....
Faucet, Protected	P. A. Schwarz	Boston, Mass	Dec. 17, 1872	134, 102
Faucet, Rotary measuring	J. G. Baker and W. Harbster	Philadelphia and Reading, Pa.	Sept. 3, 1867	68, 546
Faucet, Rotary measuring	W. H. Laubach	Philadelphia, Pa	Aug. 8, 1871	117, 895
Faucet, Self-balancing and self-closing	E. Osgood	Boston, Mass	Apr. 21, 1863	38, 269
Faucet, Self-closing	W. H. Bate	Charlestown, Mass	Aug. 26, 1873	142, 192
Faucet, Self-closing	A. Brinckmann	New York, N. Y	Sept. 21, 1869	94, 998

Index of patents issued from the United States Patent Office from 1790 to 1873, inclusive—Continued.

Invention.	Inventor.	Residence.	Date.	No.
Faucet, Self-closing	A. Brinckmann	New York, N. Y	June 24, 1873	140, 183
Faucet, Self-closing	A. and E. Buckman	Brooklyn, N. Y	Apr. 22, 1873	138, 127
Faucet, Self-closing	M. S. Clark	New York, N. Y	Feb. 4, 1873	135, 407
Faucet, Self closing	J. Hayden, jr	Haydensville, Mass	Aug. 15, 1871	118, 012
Faucet, Self-closing	H. F. King	New York, N. Y	Aug. 31, 1869	94, 419
Faucet, Self-closing	C. Schultz and T. Warker	New York, N. Y	Mar. 8, 1870	100, 561
Faucet, Self-closing	J. W. Trafton	Chicopee Falls, Mass	Sept. 23, 1873	143, 042
Faucet, Self-closing compression	E. Noble	North Haven, Conn	Aug. 16, 1870	106, 394
Faucet, Self-inserting	S. N. Haight	Bedford Station, N. Y	June 5, 1866	55, 286
Faucet, Siphon	T. W. Plum	London, England	Mar. 3, 1868	75, 191
Faucet, Spring-lever	C. Goodyear	Philadelphia, Pa	Mar. 16, 1832	....
Faucet, Stop	W. Cleveland	Orange, N. J	Mar. 20, 1866	53, 271
Faucet, Swing-nose basin	M. and W. Scrannage and W. H. Bate.	Boston, Mass	Aug. 27, 1867	68, 123
Faucet, Vented	H. and J. Schild	New York, N. Y	May 21, 1867	65, 016
Faucet, Ventilating	C. Cleveland	Ashfield, Mass	Aug. 14, 1855	13, 424
Faucet, Wash-basin	D. Wellington	Boston, Mass	Jan. 20, 1863	37, 478
Faucet, Wash-stand	W. S. Bate	Philadelphia, Pa	Dec. 16, 1873	145, 609
Faucet, Water	P. A. Mayor	New York, N. Y	Dec. 27, 1870	110, 484
Faucet, Weighing	D. Lesh, jr	Liverpool, Pa	Apr. 5, 1870	101, 633
Faucet, Weighing	C. H. McAleer and J. Shively	Canton, Ohio	June 10, 1862	35, 530
Faucet-weighing attachment	J. Brown	Lawn Ridge, Ill	Nov. 13, 1855	13, 776
Faucet-weighing attachment	L. C. Fisher and A. D. Holliday.	El Paso, Ill	Oct. 1, 1867	69, 425
Faucets, Bush for	O. Netzow and J. F. Heck	Baltimore, Md	Feb. 20, 1872	123, 789
Faucets, Device for locking	H. Getty	Brooklyn, N. Y	Sept. 1, 1857	18, 091
Faucets into fluids under pressure, Method of inserting.	P. Mihan	Boston, Mass	July 29, 1856	15, 430
Faucets, Machine for reaming	W. Read	New York, N. Y	May 23, 1846	4, 534
Faucets, Method of manufacturing	W. Westlake	Brooklyn, N. Y	July 9, 1867	66, 656
Faucets, Method of manufacturing	W. Westlake	Brooklyn, N. Y	July 9, 1867	66, 657
Faucets of water-coolers, Arrangement of means for making tight joints around.	J. S. Clark	Philadelphia, Pa	Oct. 19, 1858	21, 819
Faucets to pipes, Coupling	N. F. Weston	Boston, Mass	July 9, 1867	66, 659
Faucets, Tool for inserting and withdrawing	K. A. Wattendorf	New York, N. Y	May 27, 1873	139, 443
Faucets, Valvular arrangement for	E. Hamilton	Chicago, Ill	June 23, 1857	17, 624
Faucets, &c., Valvular arrangement in	J. C. Macdonald	Cincinnati, Ohio	Aug. 11, 1857	17, 973
Faucets, Waste-way in	J. E. Boyle	Richmond, Va	Apr. 21, 1857	17, 074
Feather-cleaner	W. Mills	New Athens, Ohio	Oct. 29, 1861	33, 594
Feather cleaning and dressing machine	S. Swett, jr	Readfield, Me	July 31, 1837	330
Feather cleaning and drying machine	R. B. Lewis	Hallowell, Me	June 27, 1840	1, 655
Feather cleaning and purifying machine	S. G. Ladd	Hallowell, Me	Sept. 22, 1838	939
Feather-cleaning machine	H. J. Beckwith	Chicopee, Mass	May 5, 1868	77, 571
Feather-cleaning machine	J. H. Sardam	Wellington, Ohio	June 4, 1867	65, 438
Feather-cleaning machine	T. Taylor	Washington, D. C	Sept. 1, 1868	81, 841
Feather-cleaning machine	C. Toupet	New York, N. Y	Oct. 15, 1829	....
Feather cleansing and renovating machine	H. B. Steele	West Winstead, Conn	Apr. 14, 1868	76, 840
Feather-dresser	S. Keplinger	Baltimore, Md	Feb. 12, 1836	....
Feather-dresser	F. P. Knowlton	Clermont, N. H	July 2, 1836	....
Feather-dresser	S. Orr	Springfield, Ohio	Apr. 9, 1861	31, 993
Feather-dressing	B. P. Coston	Philadelphia, Pa	June 28, 1836	....
Feather-dressing	G. Reynolds	East Hartford, Conn	May 23, 1836	....
Feather-dressing	B. and A. Todd	Marietta, Ohio	May 6, 1836	....
Feather-dressing	E. Wilbur	Geneva, N. Y	Mar. 18, 1836	....
Feather dressing and cleaning machine	O. Badger	Otsego, N. Y	Apr. 22, 1835	....
Feather dressing and purifying machine	B. Smith	Shodiack, N. Y	Nov. 23, 1835	....
Feather dressing and renovating machine	G. W. Peabody and O. L. Cowles.	East Hampton and Westfield, Mass.	Aug. 6, 1867	67, 449
Feather-dressing machine	A. Bailey	East Poultney, Vt	Oct. 27, 1857	18, 493
Feather-dressing machine	S. W. Bevans	Plymouth, Conn	Apr. 21, 1868	76, 982
Feather-dressing machine	A. B. Morey and W. Scarlett	Aurora, Ill	July 1, 1862	35, 773
Feather-dressing machine	G. Reynolds	East Hartford, Conn	Oct. 17, 1835	....
Feather-dressing machine	A. Washburn and J. N. Van Sickle.	Medina, Ohio	June 11, 1867	65, 782
Feather drying, whipping, and cleansing machinery	N. L. Manning	Boston, Mass	Apr. 16, 1841	2, 053
Feather dusters, Manufacture of	C. F. Shourds	New York, N. Y	Apr. 20, 1869	89, 176
Feather purifying and renovating machine	C. Turner and J. A. Jackson	Triangle, N. Y	Dec. 8, 1863	40, 871
Feather renovating and dressing	A. C. Sanford	Plymouth, Conn	July 14, 1868	80, 017
Feather-renovating machine	J. S. Peasley	Providence, R. I	Oct. 22, 1867	70, 110
Feather-renovator	T. J. Adams	Ansonia, Conn	Nov. 26, 1872	133, 348
Feather-renovator	C. E. Barber and W. Dean	Central Village, Conn	July 4, 1871	116, 535
Feather-renovator	W. T. Beauchamp	Grenada, Miss	Oct. 15, 1872	132, 236
Feather-renovator	J. A. Bell	Tyrone, Pa	Feb. 7, 1871	111, 606
Feather-renovator	E. Bickell and M. F. Noracouk	Milton, Pa	Oct. 4, 1870	107, 999
Feather-renovator	L. Blair	Painesville, Ohio	Mar. 9, 1869	87, 534
Feather-renovator	A. Bond	Chicopee, Mass	Sept. 15, 1868	82, 200
Feather-renovator	J. B. Booker and M. C. Green	Chicago and Paris, Ill	July 16, 1872	129, 390
Feather-renovator	S. A. Boyett	Grenada, Miss	Feb. 4, 1873	135, 516
Feather-renovator	E. Colvin	Paulet, Vt	Feb. 23, 1869	87, 145
Feather-renovator	A. D. Cook and J. Graves	New Madrid, Mo	Feb. 22, 1870	100, 120
Feather-renovator	R. B. Cooper	Monticello, N. Y	Oct. 7, 1873	143, 4[illegible]7
Feather-renovator	B. F. Cramer	Tyrone, Pa	May 30, 1871	115, 440
Feather-renovator	J. Cyester	Osborn, Ohio	May 4, 1869	89, 740
Feather-renovator	W. F. Daugherty	Wellington, Ohio	Aug. 4, 1868	80, 610
Feather-renovator	L. Dimick	Ellsworth, N. Y	July 16, 1872	129, 325
Feather-renovator	W. H. Elliot	New York, N. Y	Dec. 8, 1868	84, 809
Feather-renovator	L. S. Enos	Almond, N. Y	Sept. 23, 1873	143, 130
Feather-renovator	C. H. Farnham	Canterbury, Conn	June 22, 1869	91, 731
Feather-renovator	J. Garrett and J. E. Rauch	Selin's Grove, Pa	Mar. 28, 1871	113, 157
Feather-renovator	R. H. Graves and H. L. Crandell.	McGranville, N. Y	Jan. 5, 1869	85, 654
Feather-renovator	W. H. Groff	Mahanoy City, Pa	Apr. 29, 1873	138, 327
Feather-renovator	C. E. Hendrick	Chicopee, Mass	July 14, 1868	79, 975
Feather-renovator	C. E. Hendrick	Chicopee, Mass	Aug 25, 1868	81, 369
Feather-renovator	C. Kendall	Beloit, Wis	Nov. 5, 1872	132, 838
Feather-renovator	W. G. Lumbard	Georgetown, Ill	Oct. 11, 1870	108, 161
Feather-renovator	C. E. Macon and G. F. Bell	Wellington, Ohio	July 7, 1868	79, 668
Feather-renovator	W. McArthur	Philadelphia, Pa	July 11, 1865	48, 702

Index of patents issued from the United States Patent Office from 1790 *to* 1873, *inclusive*—Continued.

Invention.	Inventor.	Residence.	Date.	No.
Feather-renovator	E. N. McKimm and J. R. Gearhart.	Lathrop, Mo	Jan. 14, 1873	134, 914
Feather-renovator	A. McKissick and C. M. French	Jordan and Weedsport, N. Y.	Apr. 15, 1862	34, 975
Feather-renovator	J. C. Moorehead and W. W. Elliott.	New Madrid, Mo	Apr. 21, 1868	77, 075
Feather-renovator	M. K. Morris	Council Bluffs, Iowa	Oct. 4, 1870	107, 944
Feather-renovator	O. J. Pennell	Williamsport, Pa	May 29, 1860	28, 500
Feather-renovator	J. W. Perry	Perrysburgh, N. Y	Aug. 17, 1869	93, 901
Feather-renovator	J. W. Post and R. Collier	Baltimore, Md	Mar. 2, 1836	......
Feather-renovator	J. B. Riley	Muncy, Pa	Mar. 25, 1873	137, 240
Feather-renovator	H. H. Robbins	Lynn, Mass	Aug. 18, 1868	81, 204
Feather-renovator	J. C. Rose and J. F. Silversmith.	Albany, N. Y	June 20, 1871	116, 101
Feather-renovator	J. E. Schooler	Chillicothe, Mo	Dec. 23, 1873	145, 759
Feather-renovator	J. T. Sheldon	Chicopee, Mass	Feb. 7, 1871	111, 576
Feather-renovator	S. B. Shoemaker	Willoughby, Ohio	Nov. 28, 1871	121, [illegible]57
Feather-renovator	S. G. Thanhauser	Baltimore, Md	May 20, 1873	139, 211
Feather-renovator	U. B. Waddle	Cleveland, Ohio	Nov. 26, 1867	71, 555
Feather-renovator	J. Wellfare and F. Champagne	Aurora, Ill	Oct. 24, 1871	120, 174
Feather-renovator and cleaner	O. C. Monroe	Poultney, Vt	Sept. 24, 1867	69, 114
Feather washer and drier	J. Mallory	Penn Yan, N. Y	Mar. 15, 1870	100, 911
Feathers, Apparatus for cleaning and renovating	J. R. Morrison	East Springfield, Ohio	Oct. 15, 1861	33, 489
Feathers, Cleaning	D. K. Hall	New York, N. Y	Feb. 12, 1836	....
Feathers, Machine for dressing	R. Glore	Nashville, Tenn	July 20, 1869	92, 818
Feathers, Machine for dressing	G. Reynolds	East Hartford, Conn	Feb. 7, 1834	....
Feathers, Machine for washing and dressing	J. W. Howlet	Greensborough, N. C	Oct. 5, 1838	965
Feathers, Made	A. E. Woolf	New York, N. Y	Mar. 18, 1873	136, 891
Feathers, Manufacture of ornamental	T. E. Schmidt	Hoboken, N. J	June 18, 1867	65, 955
Feathers, Mode of disinfecting	J. W. Howlett	Greensborough, N. C	Oct. 4, 1859	25, 647
Feed and delivery apron	P. R. Mansfield	Lancaster, Mass	Mar. 25, 1873	137, 224
Feed and other rollers, Wiping-apparatus for	L. Crawford	Holyoke, Mass	Sept. 27, 1870	107, 667
Feed and straw cutter	A. P. Chapin	Chicopee Falls, Mass	Sept. 3, 1867	68, 412
Feed and water trough, Combined	J. Sherman	Coopersville, Mich	June 7, 1870	103, 935
Feed-attachment for machinery	S. Brown	Philadelphia, Pa	Dec. 22, 1868	85, 064
Feed-bag	J. Becher and W. Tustin	Philadelphia, Pa	Feb. 23, 1864	41, 670
Feed-bag	C. Chinnock	Brooklyn, N. Y	Sept. 15, 1868	82, 088
Feed-bag	T. Fisler	Camden, N. J	Mar. 18, 1862	34, 715
Feed-bag	H. Pennie and C. Chinnock	New York, N. Y	Apr. 25, 1865	47, 498
Feed-bag	F. J. Simeon	Brooklyn, N. Y	June 19, 1866	55, 726
Feed-bag	J. Vandercar	Brooklyn, N. Y	June 25, 1867	66, 190
Feed-bag	W. B. Wait	Greenwood, Mass	Jan. 19, 1864	41, 346
Feed-bag for horses	T. Adams	Jersey City, N. J	Aug. 12, 1873	141, 686
Feed-bag for horses	A. T. Ballentine	New York, N. Y	Apr. 18, 1865	47, 270
Feed-bag for horses	W. A. Hough	South Butler, N. Y	Mar. 7, 1871	112, 458
Feed-bag for horses and other animals	R. B. Fitts	Philadelphia, Pa	Sept. 17, 1861	33, 318
Feed-bag for horses or other animals	W. B. Wait	Greenwood, Mass	Dec. 23, 1862	37, 262
Feed-box	J. Hawse	Wolcott, Vt	June 8, 1869	91, 013
Feed-box	W. S. Shaw and M. B. Gould	Buffalo, N. Y	Nov. 14, 1871	120, 906
Feed-box and stanchion, Combined	W. I. and J. W. Harris	Newport, N. Y	May 21, 1872	126, 886
Feed-box, Folding	J. L. Edwards	Cochranville, Pa	Jan. 14, 1873	134, 869
Feed-box for animals, Automatic	A. Goodyear, 2d	Hamden, Conn	Nov. 16, 1858	22, 076
Feed-box, Ration	J. Hayden	Exeter, Wis	July 24, 1866	56, 557
Feed-changing device	R. L. Nelson	Mexico, N. Y	Feb. 18, 1868	74, 578
Feed-cutter	T. P. Allen	Gowanda, N. Y	Mar. 17, 1868	75, 558
Feed-cutter	W. F. Altfather	Johnstown, Pa	Oct. 23, 1866	58, 967
Feed-cutter	W. S. Bartle and J. Garlock	Newark, N. Y	Mar. 25, 1873	137, 108
Feed-cutter	J. H. Bradley	Hillsborough, Ohio	Jan. 17, 1871	111, 035
Feed-cutter	H. A. Buck	Fredonia, N. Y	Feb. 28, 1871	112, 117
Feed cutter	C. H. Cain	Dayton, Ohio	May 3, 1870	102, 485
Feed-cutter	J. Criley and W. Gilbreath	Shiloh Hill and Rockwood, Ill.	Feb. 14, 1871	111, 819
Feed-cutter	W. Dahlem	Madison, Ind	Jan. 10, 1871	110, 834
Feed-cutter	C. R. Donner	Sonora, Cal	Oct. 11, 1870	108, 118
Feed-cutter	C. R. Donner	Sonora, Cal	Aug. 1, 1871	117, 521
Feed-cutter	M. Fletcher	Louisville, Ky	Aug. 27, 1861	33, 137
Feed-cutter	W. Gale	Peekskill, N. Y	Nov. 30, 1869	97, 384
Feed-cutter	F. E. Garner	Cornwall, Conn	Oct. 11, 1870	108, 249
Feed-cutter	G. W. Hathaway	Tioga, Pa	Dec. 4, 1860	30, 817
Feed-cutter	H. Helm	Pittsburgh, Pa	June 11, 1867	65, 571
Feed-cutter	S. Holl	Reading, Pa	July 16, 1872	129, 562
Feed-cutter	W. Hutchins	Paw Paw, Mich	Dec. 6, 1870	109, 822
Feed-cutter	C. Kemper	Hermann, Mo	Jan. 17, 1871	111, 065
Feed-cutter	J. Massey	New York, N. Y	Oct. 23, 1866	59, 043
Feed-cutter	R. McCain	Rootstown, Ohio	Jan. 14, 1862	34, 154
Feed-cutter	J. B. and W. McClinton	Galion, Ohio	Feb. 28, 1871	112, 265
Feed-cutter	N. McLeod	Clio, S. C	Nov. 10, 1868	83, 984
Feed-cutter	J. J. Parker	Marietta, Ohio	Oct. 11, 1864	44, 650
Feed-cutter	G. Parnell	Ontario, N. Y	Jan. 18, 1870	98, 997
Feed-cutter	H. Peterson	Red Wing, Minn	Dec. 7, 1869	97, 687
Feed-cutter	S. Pettibone	Corunna, Mich	Mar. 13, 1866	53, 179
Feed-cutter	J. P. Randolph	Marietta, Ohio	Dec. 28, 1869	98, 414
Feed-cutter	W. H. Rosser and J. Stiver	Mill Hall, Pa	Feb. 1, 1870	99, 352
Feed-cutter	J. Seaman	Chicago, Ill	Apr. 4, 1871	113, 579
Feed-cutter	F. Sims	Ridgeville, Ind	July 13, 1869	92, 548
Feed-cutter	G. Small	Clayton, Mich	Sept. 24, 1867	69, 133
Feed-cutter	J. R. Whittemore	Chicopee Falls, Mass	Feb. 7, 1871	111, 594
Feed-cutter and box	A. B. King	Camden, Ohio	Oct. 9, 1866	58, 649
Feed-cutter and thrasher	N. McLeod	Clio, S. C	Feb. 15, 1870	99, 931
Feed-cutters, Adjusting knife of	J. R. Whittemore	Chicopee Falls, Mass	July 30, 1861	32, 936
Feed for horses and cattle, Cutting	E. H. Porter	Lincolnton, N. C	Mar. 14, 18[illegible]4	....
Feed for horses, &c., Concentrated	G. Jaques, D. F. White, and J. Stowell.	Somerville and Charlestown, Mass.	Jan. 19, 1864	41, 301
Feed-gates for mills, Method of regulating	C. Dare	Cincinnati, Ohio	Feb. 12, 1856	14, 227
Feed-grinder	M. Gore	Ottawa, Ill	Feb. 7, 1871	111, 530
Feed-guide, Platen	E. L. Megill	Brooklyn, N. Y	Mar. 21, 1871	112, 827
Feed-hopper	J. Mattison	Oswego, N. Y	Feb. 15, 1870	99, 926
Feed-manger	C. E. Steller	McGregor, Iowa	Nov. 22, 1864	45, 190

Index of patents issued from the United States Patent Office from 1790 to 1873, inclusive—Continued.

Invention.	Inventor.	Residence.	Date.	No.
Feed-mill	Z. S. Cracraft	Ottawa, Ill	Oct. 31, 1871	120, 562
Feed-mill	G. W. Gibson	Dryden, N. Y	May 21, 1872	126, 883
Feed-mill	J. W. Myers	Lyons City, Iowa	Dec. 26, 1871	122, 129
Feed-rack	J. W. Blanchard	Rutland, Wis	Mar. 5, 1867	62, 522
Feed-rack	E. Gratten	Williamstown, Mich	May 14, 1867	64, 759
Feed-rack	J. L. Rhodeback	Newway, Ohio	Aug. 27, 1872	130, 867
Feed-rack	J. Robinson	Carmel, Me	Jan. 23, 1872	122, 967
Feed-rack	W. and H. Sias	Henderson, N. Y	July 19, 1864	43, 609
Feed-rack	F. G. L. Struve	Jefferson, Wis	Mar. 25, 1862	34, 793
Feed-rack	J. M. Van Nest	Clayton, Iowa	Apr. 25, 1865	47, 472
Feed-rack	M. Workman	Washington Township, Ohio.	July 14, 1868	79, 886
Feed rack and trough combined	D. Close	Harmonsburgh, Pa	May 31, 1864	42, 927
Feed-rack for stock	J. C. Ramsey	Le Roy, Ohio	Aug. 27, 1867	68, 111
Feed-rack, Portable	E. Farquhar	Ankenytown, Ohio	Feb. 28, 1871	112, 133
Feed-rack, Portable	C. W. Lamb	Columbia City, Ind	Apr. 3, 1866	53, 634
Feed-regulator	W. F. H. Daniels	Belleville, Ohio	Dec. 13, 1870	110, 015
Feed-regulator for liquids	H. Seyter	Vaihingen, Würtemberg	Nov. 14, 1871	121, 010
Feed-regulator, Steam-boiler	R. Berryman	Hartford, Conn	Nov. 19, 1872	133, 189
Feed-regulator, Steam-boiler	L. Thorn	New York, N. Y	May 25, 1858	20, 380
Feed-roller	H. R. Crowe	Carondelet, Mo	Mar. 12, 1867	62, 822
Feed-rollers, Method of operating yielding	J. H. Brinton	West Chester, Pa	Feb. 15, 1859	22, 931
Feed-trough	G. M. Goss	Bloomfield, Iowa	Jan. 23, 1872	123, 012
Feed-trough	A. Simkins	Algansee, Mich	July 23, 1872	129, 687
Feed trough and rack, Combined	J. Depne	California, Mich	Mar. 31, 1868	76, 061
Feed trough and rack for sheep, cattle, and horses	J. D. McBride	Mansfield, Ohio	Jan. 14, 1868	73, 426
Feed-trough, Folding	W. N. Shellabarger	Union, Ohio	May 18, 1869	90, 129
Feed-trough guard	E. Hovenden	Bushnell, Ill	Jan. 24, 1871	111, 122
Feed-water and blow-off apparatus for steam-boilers	J. Frick	Philadelphia, Pa	Dec. 14, 1858	22, 284
Feed-water apparatus	J. Kindel	Wilmington, Ohio	Feb. 7, 1871	111, 650
Feed-water apparatus	J. H. Pease	Reading, Pa	Apr. 10, 1866	53, 864
Feed-water apparatus	G. A. Reidel	Philadelphia, Pa	Sept. 19, 1865	50, 033
Feed-water apparatus	G. I. Washburn	Worcester, Mass	Sept. 12, 1865	49, 941
Feed-water apparatus	J. Wozniakowski	St. Petersburg, Russia	Sept. 17, 1872	131, 490
Feed-water apparatus for locomotive-engines	R. A. Wilder	Schuylkill Haven, Pa	Mar. 27, 1860	27, 662
Feed-water apparatus for steam-boilers, Heating	T. Sloan	Saint Louis, Mo	May 6, 1856	14, 835
Feed-water apparatus of steam-boilers, Means for controlling.	B. F. Bee	Wareham, Mass	July 15, 1856	15, 324
Feed-water apparatus, Steam-boiler	T. Armitage	Philadelphia, Pa	Oct. 4, 1859	25, 617
Feed-water apparatus, Steam-boiler	W. Barnes	Troy, N. Y	Sept. 6, 1859	25, 360
Feed-water apparatus, Steam-boiler	B. F. Bee	Harwich, Mass	Aug. 1, 1854	11, 433
Feed-water apparatus, Steam-boiler	R. Berryman	Hartford, Conn	Feb. 11, 1873	135, 757
Feed-water apparatus, Steam-boiler	W. P. Curry	Vincennes, Ind	Oct. 18, 1859	25, 811
Feed-water apparatus, Steam-boiler	J. Densmore	Blooming Valley, Pa	Sept. 18, 1855	13, 567
Feed-water apparatus, Steam-boiler	J. W. Doughty	New York, N. Y	July 16, 1861	32, 824
Feed-water apparatus, Steam-boiler	T. Firth	Cincinnati, Ohio	Feb. 5, 1856	14, 191
Feed-water apparatus, Steam-boiler	C. G. Fisher	Washington, D. C	Oct. 10, 1871	119, 835
Feed-water apparatus, Steam-boiler	B. Fitts	Worcester, Mass	Mar. 28, 1854	10, 695
Feed-water apparatus, Steam-boiler	L. X. Gargan	Paris, France	Apr. 16, 1861	32, 061
Feed-water apparatus, Steam-boiler	H. Giffard	Paris, France	Apr. 24, 1860	27, 979
Feed-water apparatus, Steam-boiler	J. Hibbard	Hermitage, N. Y	Jan. 17, 1860	26, 847
Feed-water apparatus, Steam-boiler	W. A. Lighthall	New York, N. Y	Apr. 9, 1861	31, 988
Feed-water apparatus, Steam-boiler	E. Pierce	Cincinnati, Ohio	June 12, 1860	28, 685
Feed-water apparatus, Steam-boiler	G. W. Rains	Newburgh, N. Y	Apr. 24, 1860	28, 011
Feed-water apparatus, Steam-boiler	H. C. Sargeant	Cincinnati, Ohio	June 13, 1854	11, 095
Feed-water apparatus, Steam-boiler	W. C. Selden	Brooklyn, N. Y	Sept. 19, 1871	119, 185
Feed-water apparatus, Steam-boiler	J. B. Thompson	Warrenton, Ga	Aug. 30, 1859	25, 290
Feed-water apparatus, Steam-boiler	A. J. Vandegrift	Delaware, Ohio	Feb. 17, 1857	16, 662
Feed-water apparatus, Steam-boiler	A. Winkler	St. Petersburgh, Russia	Sept. 17, 1872	131, 489
Feed-water apparatus, Steam-boiler	C. and G. M. Woodward	New York, N. Y	Apr. 10, 1860	27, 853
Feed-water apparatus, Steam-boiler	J. W. Youman	Mobile, Ala	Nov. 5, 1872	132, 888
Feed-water arrangement for steam-boilers	T. Snowdon	Pittsburgh, Pa	Apr. 3, 1860	27, 743
Feed-water attachment to steam-engines	L. Martin	New York, N. Y	Dec. 22, 1857	18, 919
Feed-water connecting-pipe, Locomotive	C. A. Peavey	Joliet, Ill	May 24, 1870	103, 494
Feed-water device for boilers	W. F. Duerr	Newark, N. J	Apr. 20, 1869	89, 208
Feed-water device for boilers	J. D. Otis	Peoria, Ill	Feb. 2, 1869	86, 580
Feed-water device for boilers, Automatic	J. A. Davis	Watertown, N. Y	Feb. 2, 1869	86, 372
Feed-water filtering-heater for boilers	D. Wineland	McComb, Ohio	Apr. 27, 1869	89, 366
Feed-water for steam-boilers, Heating	W. A. Lighthall	New York, N. Y	July 4, 1871	116, 727
Feed-water for steam-engines, Heating	F. B. Stevens	New York, N. Y	July 1, 1862	35, 789
Feed-water for steam-engines, Method of heating	F. B. Stevens	New York, N. Y	June 24, 1862	35, 714
Feed-water for steam-engines, Valve for heating	F. B. Stevens	New York, N. Y	July 1, 1862	35, 788
Feed-water for steam-generators, Apparatus for heating and purifying.	J. S. Hooton	New Carlisle, Ind	Mar. 3, 1868	75, 163
Feed-water heater	H. Anderson	Peoria, Ill	Oct. 4, 1870	107, 850
Feed-water heater	J. V. Beekman	Brooklyn, N. Y	Sept. 23, 1873	142, 983
Feed-water heater	R. Berryman	Hartford, Conn	Oct. 29, 1872	132, 518
Feed-water heater	H. F. Boody and E. P. Merrill	Portland, Me	Jan. 7, 1873	134, 634
Feed-water heater	W. Crighton, W. Wills, and L. Bustetter.	Fort Wayne, Ind	June 11, 1867	65, 547
Feed-water heater	W. B. Cross	Sacramento City, Cal	Oct. 17, 1865	50, 459
Feed-water heater	J. Fairclough	Saint Joseph, Mo	Nov. 30, 1869	97, 371
Feed-water heater	C. E. Frazier	Baltimore, Md	June 10, 1873	139, 665
Feed-water heater	J. Gates	Portland, Oreg	June 18, 1872	128, 033
Feed-water heater	J. G. Goesel	Saint Louis, Mo	Sept. 3, 1867	68, 433
Feed-water heater	C. S. S. Griffing	Salem, Ohio	Apr. 25, 1871	114, 132
Feed-water heater	J. H. Hale and A. C. Whitney	Boston, Mass	Dec. 2, 1873	145, 059
Feed-water heater	R. W. Hale	Boston, Mass	Oct. 7, 1862	36, 614
Feed-water heater	G. Hasecoster and I. Stephens	Richmond, Ind	Sept. 18, 1866	58, 099
Feed-water heater	N. Jones	Buffalo, N. Y	Oct. 29, 1872	132, 585
Feed-water heater	P. M. Kafer and J. M. De Lacy	Trenton, N. J	May 7, 1867	64, 540
Feed-water heater	J. F. Morse	Oshkosh, Wis	June 14, 1870	104, 187
Feed-water heater	G. M. Mullen	Baltimore, Md	Mar. 5, 1872	124, 373
Feed-water heater	J. Nicholson	Allegheny City, Pa	May 22, 1866	54, 940
Feed-water heater	J. Nicholson	Allegheny City, Pa	Oct. 8, 1867	69, 576
Feed-water heater	R. Poole	Baltimore, Md	Apr. 25, 1865	47, 599
Feed-water heater	L. B. Powelson	Pittsburgh, Pa	Oct. 27, 1868	83, 543
Feed-water heater	G. W. Richardson	Troy, N. Y	Dec. 16, 1873	145, 591

Index of patents issued from the United States Patent Office from 1790 *to* 1873, *inclusive*—Continued.

Invention.	Inventor.	Residence.	Date.	No.
Feed-water heater	W. Sambrook	Liverpool, England	Dec. 30, 1873	146, 024
Feed-water heater	J. R. Sees	New York, N. Y	Apr. 26, 1864	42, 538
Feed-water heater	T. Shipton	Newark, N. J	May 19, 1868	78, 140
Feed-water heater	T. D. Simpson	Mount Vernon, Ohio	Apr. 4, 1871	113, 355
Feed-water heater	E. R. Stilwell	Dayton, Ohio	July 23, 1867	66, 998
Feed-water heater	S. Stucky	New Albany, Ind	July 28, 1868	80, 516
Feed-water heater	G. Wales	Brooklyn, N. Y	Jan. 21, 1873	135, 181
Feed-water heater	W. E. Walsh	Jersey City, N. J	Dec. 26, 1871	122, 204
Feed-water heater	G. I. Washburn	Worcester, Mass	Feb. 25, 1868	74, 959
Feed-water heater	G. Waters	Cincinnati, Ohio	Aug. 30, 1870	106, 972
Feed-water heater	P. C. Wortman	Meadville, Pa	Aug. 17, 1869	93, 790
Feed-water heater and circulator combined	E. L. Jones	Memphis, Tenn	Jan. 24, 1871	111, 215
Feed-water heater and condenser	R. Berryman	Hartford, Conn	Feb. 11, 1873	135, 756
Feed-water heater and condenser	T. E. McNeill and R. N. Pratt	New York, N. Y	June 17, 1873	139, 908
Feed-water heater and condenser	L. C. Wyatt	Baltimore, Md	Aug. 6, 1872	130, 351
Feed-water heater and filter	J. Armstrong	Bucyrus, Ohio	Sept. 8, 1868	81, 971
Feed-water heater and filter	J. Armstrong	Toledo, Ohio	Dec. 31, 1872	134, 450
Feed-water heater and filter	D. E. Shaw	Chatsworth, Ill	May 17, 1870	103, 243
Feed-water heater and filter	E. R. Stilwell	Dayton, Ohio	Oct. 4, 1864	44, 561
Feed-water heater and filter	E. R. Stilwell	Dayton, Ohio	June 28, 1870	104, 789
Feed-water heater and purifier	R. K. McMurry	West New Brighton, N. Y	Oct. 15, 1872	132, 170
Feed-water heater and purifier	S. J. Sadler and H. Volmar	Cleveland, Ohio	Aug 5, 1873	141, 517
Feed-water heater and regulator	R. Berryman	Hartford, Conn	July 30, 1872	130, 109
Feed-water heater and steam-condenser	B. N. and D. W. Payne	Corning, N. Y	Aug. 20, 1872	130, 656
Feed-water heater for boilers	H. O. Perry	Buffalo, N. Y	June 30, 1868	79, 385
Feed-water heater for boilers	E. R. Stilwell	Dayton, Ohio	Aug. 18, 1868	81, 117
Feed-water heater for boilers	C. Webster	New Haven, Conn	Apr. 21, 1868	76, 961
Feed-water heater for boilers	H. Wigley	New Albany, Ind	Dec. 7, 1869	97, 737
Feed-water heater for locomotives	S. F. Allen	Chicago, Ill	Feb. 16, 1864	41, 591
Feed-water heater for locomotives	B. Crawford	Pittsburgh, Pa	June 2, 1863	38, 730
Feed-water heater for locomotives	P. S. Ebbert	Chicago, Ill	Feb. 5, 1856	14, 187
Feed-water heater for locomotives	B. Garvin and R. J. Pettibone	Oshkosh, Wis	Dec. 3, 1867	71, 604
Feed-water heater for locomotives	J. S. Hooton	New Carlisle, Ind	July 12, 1870	105, 207
Feed-water heater for locomotives	I. P. Magoon	Saint Johnsbury, Vt	Mar. 29, 1870	101, 287
Feed-water heater for locomotives	E. Moyel	Wyandotte, Kans	Feb. 4, 1873	135, 438
Feed-water heater for locomotives	D. Pollock	Lancaster, Pa	Jan. 19, 1864	41, 319
Feed water heater for locomotives	J. R. Sees	New York, N. Y	Apr. 26, 1864	42, 539
Feed-water heater for locomotives	W. H. Standeford	Stewartsville, Mo	Aug. 20, 1872	130, 759
Feed-water heater for locomotive-engines	D. Matthew	Philadelphia, Pa	July 17, 1855	13, 270
Feed-water heater for locomotive-engines	J. R. Sees	New York, N. Y	Nov. 11, 1856	16, 071
Feed-water heater for steam-boilers	M. W. Baldwin and D. Clark	Philadelphia and Schuylkill Haven, Pa.	Oct. 12, 1852	9, 312
Feed-water heater for steam-boilers	R. Berryman	Hartford, Conn	June 6, 1871	115, 682
Feed-water heater for steam-boilers	R. Berryman	Hartford, Conn	Apr. 9, 1872	125, 526
Feed-water heater for steam-boilers	R. C. Bristol	Chicago, Ill	Feb. 24, 1863	37, 731
Feed-water heater for steam-boilers	J. T. Brooks	New Albany, Ind	May 24, 1859	24, 094
Feed-water heater for steam-boilers	J. Codling, jr., and J. McCunniff	Fairbanks, Iowa	Feb. 28, 1860	27, 271
Feed-water heater for steam-boilers	W. C. Drum	Belle Vernon, Pa	June 26, 1860	28, 840
Feed-water heater for steam-boilers	S. W. Franco	Brooklyn, N. Y	Aug. 6, 1872	130, 122
Feed-water heater for steam-boilers	B. Garvin	Oshkosh, Wis	Nov. 14, 1871	120, 959
Feed-water heater for steam-boilers	A. M. Granger	Saint Louis, Mo	Jan. 26, 1864	41, 374
Feed-water heater for steam-boilers	B. A. Hopkins	Sodus, N. Y	Oct. 20, 1868	83, 161
Feed-water heater for steam-boilers	W. A. Lighthall	New York, N. Y	Feb. 7, 1865	46, 252
Feed-water heater for steam-boilers	D. Lordon	Memphis, Tenn	Sept. 6, 1870	107, 185
Feed-water heater for steam-boilers	L. E. C. Martin	London, England	Aug. 2, 1864	43, 750
Feed-water heater for steam-boilers	W. W. Martin	Allegheny, Pa	June 9, 1863	38, 870
Feed-water heater for steam-boilers	J. Rodgers	Clarington, Ohio	May 21, 1872	126, 988
Feed-water heater for steam-boilers	J. R. Sees	New York, N. Y	Aug. 5, 1856	15, 494
Feed-water heater for steam-boilers	S. T. Taylor	Charleston, S. C	Sept. 26, 1871	119, 428
Feed-water heater for steam-boilers	J. F. Taylor	Baltimore, Md	May 13, 1873	138, 957
Feed-water heater for steam-boilers	J. M. White	New York, N. Y	Aug. 30, 1859	25, 296
Feed-water heater for steam-boilers	D. Whitlock	Newark, N. J	July 12, 1870	105, 397
Feed-water heater for steam-boilers	R. Wilson	Columbus City, Iowa	July 3, 1855	13, 193
Feed-water heater for steam-engines	J. Armstrong	Bucyrus, Ohio	June 22, 1869	91, 700
Feed-water heater for steam fire-engines	W. A. Brickill	New York, N. Y	Aug. 18, 1868	81, 132
Feed-water heater for steam-generators	G. Candee	Berlin Heights, Ohio	May 5, 1868	77, 454
Feed-water heater for steam-generators	R. Eaton	Kentish Town, England	Feb. 2, 1869	86, 515
Feed-water heater for steam-generators	R. R. Fenner	Urbana, Ill	Oct. 27, 1868	83 370
Feed-water heater for steam-generators	E. B. Johnson	Chicago, Ill	Feb. 8, 1870	99, 573
Feed-water heater for steam-generators	G. W. Mack	Hamtramck, Mich	Mar. 31, 1868	76, 217
Feed-water heater for steam-generators	D. F. McKim	Austin, Nev	Dec. 22, 1868	85, 116
Feed-water heater for steam-generators	H. S. Saroni	Marietta, Ohio	Aug. 28, 1866	57, 576
Feed-water heater for steam-generators	H. N. Waters	Hartford, Conn	Feb. 18, 1868	74, 735
Feed-water heater for steam-generators	H. N. Waters	Meriden, Conn	Apr. 23, 1872	125, 918
Feed-water heater, Hollow grate	G. W. Jones	Nashville, Tenn	July 18, 1871	117, 176
Feed-water heaters and generators, Series of	J. Goulding	Worcester, Mass	June 25, 1872	128, 300
Feed-water heaters for steam generators, Filtering	B. F. Wilson	Geddes, N. Y	Apr. 20, 1869	89, 106
Feed-water of locomotives, &c., Apparatus for heating.	I. P. Magoon	Saint Johnsbury, Vt	Sept. 7, 1852	9, 251
Feed-water of steam-boilers, Apparatus for heating and purifying.	J. Guhmann	Rochester, N. Y	Mar. 15, 1859	23, 244
Feed-water of steam-boilers, Device for heating	S. Lamon and W. S. Gaskill	Van Wert, Ohio	Apr. 12, 1859	23, 588
Feed-water pipe	J. Doyle	Baltimore, Md	Jan. 3, 1871	110, 753
Feed-water pipes in the beds of steam-engines, Arrangement of.	H. W. Bill	Cuyahoga Falls, Ohio	Nov. 3, 1857	18, 532
Feed-water purifier for steam-generators	H. K. Hazlett	Saint Louis, Mo	Feb. 22, 1870	100, 144
Feed-water regulator	R. Berryman	Hartford, Conn	Apr. 9, 1872	125, 527
Feed-water regulator	G. E. Chenoweth	Baltimore, Md	Feb. 26, 1867	62, 474
Feed-water regulator	E. C. Fernald	Flatbush, N. Y	Apr. 8, 1873	137, 541
Feed-water regulator	N. Nolan	New York, N. Y	Nov. 21, 1871	121, 122
Feed-water regulator	J. B. Root	New York, N. Y	Aug. 5, 1873	141, 592
Feed-water regulator and low-water alarm	A. W. Morrell	Niles, Mich	Apr. 12, 1870	101, 756
Feed-water regulator and low-water alarm for steam-boilers.	W. Painter	Baltimore, Md	June 11, 1872	127, 917
Feed-water regulator and low-water alarm for steam-boilers.	J. B. Smith	Milwaukee, Wis	Apr. 23, 1872	125, 993
Feed-water regulator, Boiler	C. H. Gould	Cincinnati, Ohio	June 25, 1867	66, 018
Feed-water regulator, Boiler	J. K. P. Nourse	West Medway, Mass	Nov. 10, 1868	83, 993

Index of patents issued from the United States Patent Office from 1790 *to* 1873, *inclusive*—Continued.

Invention.	Inventor.	Residence.	Date.	No.
Feed-water regulator for boilers, Alarm	N. L. Smith	Derby, Conn	May 11, 1869	89, 949
Feed-water regulator for steam-boilers	R. Berryman	Hartford, Conn	Sept. 5, 1871	118, 679
Feed-water regulator for steam-boilers	R. E. Bond	Detroit, Mich	Oct. 18, 1864	44, 702
Feed-water regulator for steam-boilers	J. Stowell	Charlestown, Mass	Mar. 20, 1860	27, 601
Feed-water to steam-boilers, Admission of	T. Roberts	Baltimore, Md	Apr. 25, 1871	114, 202
Feed-water to steam-boilers, Apparatus for regulating the supply of.	A. Jacobs	Ithaca, N. Y	May 23, 1854	10, 963
Feed-wheel as substitute for ratchets and pawls	O. C. Phelps	New York, N. Y	Apr. 4, 1865	47, 126
Feed wheel-operating mechanism	H. A. M. Harris	Philadelphia, Pa	July 16, 1872	129, 131
Feeder, Calf	W. C. Dodge	Washington, D. C	Aug. 23, 1864	43, 902
Feeder, Fowl	J. Richardson	Ballston Spa, N. Y	Apr. 12, 1870	101, 766
Feeder, Portable stock	J. M. Spencer	La Plata, Mo	Apr. 29, 1873	138, 351
Feeder, Stock	C. M. Hall	Yates City, Ill	May 13, 1873	138, 801
Feeder, Stock	T. W. Peirce	Richfield, Minn	Feb. 21, 1865	46, 493
Feeder, Stock and poultry	G. Bowerman	Napoleon, Ohio	Nov. 5, 1867	70, 401
Feeder, Swine	N. Stockwell	Windsor, N. Y	June 29, 1869	91, 881
Feeder, Swing sheep	A. Putnam	Vernon, Big Bend Post-Office, Wis.	Apr. 14, 1868	76, 810
Feeding-apparatus, Automatic	R. B. Ruggles	Hartford, Conn	Jan. 23, 1872	122, 914
Feeding chickens, Apparatus for	S. W. Abbee	Walpole, N. H	Sept. 7, 1852	9, 244
Feeding-door for animal-pens	B. C. Scott	Paxton, Ill	Aug. 3, 1869	93, 234
Feeding rack and trough combined, Stock	A. Ralston	West Middletown, Pa	May 13, 1862	35, 259
Feeding rack, Cattle	G. W. Balding	Angola, Ind	Oct. 8, 1867	69, 608
Feeding rack, Sheep	J. C. Colflesh	Delaware, Ohio	Aug. 4, 1868	80, 603
Feeding rack, Sheep	M. S. Every	Bridgewater, Mich	July 3, 1866	56, 024
Feeding stock, Compound for	C. G. Otis	Troy, N. Y	Oct. 30, 1866	59, 255
Feeding swine, Apparatus for	N. Stockwell	Onaquaga, N. Y	Jan. 11, 1870	98, 718
Feeding-trough	R. Chesnut	Richmond, Ind	Aug. 28, 1866	57, 477
Feeding trough, Animal	J. N. Gray	Lynn, Mass	May 24, 1864	42, 909
Feeding-trough for stock	B. Arnold	Arba, Ind	July 10, 1866	56, 158
Feeding trough, Hog	J. H. McElrath and L. M. Houghton.	Princeton, Ill	Aug. 20, 1872	130, 735
Feeding trough, Horse	A. D. Barrett	Cambridgeport, Mass	Apr. 13, 1869	88, 768
Feeding trough, Sheep	C. Aulls	Bridgewater, Mich	Apr. 9, 1867	63, 688
Feet, Taking impressions of	J. E. A. Rillot	San José, Cal	Nov. 22, 1864	45, 178
Feldspar to obtain useful products, Treating	G. E. Vanderburgh	Mamaroneck, N. Y	July 12, 1864	43, 534
Fellies and spokes in carriage-wheels, Mode of securing ends of.	J. Switzer	Lynn, Mass	Mar. 10, 1868	75, 314
Fellies and tightening spokes, Expanding	A. N. Towne	Chicago, Ill	Jan. 21, 1868	73, 476
Fellies, Bending	A. W. Johnson	Saint George's, Del	Nov. 11, 1851	8, 511
Fellies, Bending	T. Kimball	Salem, N. H	Jan. 16, 1832	....
Fellies, Bending	E. Reynolds	Haddonfield, N. J	July 17, 1835	....
Fellies by steaming and bending, Method of making.	M. Blakeslee	Canaan, Conn	July 29, 1829	....
Fellies for wheels, Machine for rounding	H. A. Gore	Goshen, Ind	Aug. 30, 1870	106, 931
Fellies, Guide for doweling wheel	W. C. Dean	Jacksonville, N. Y	Oct. 4, 1853	10, 092
Fellies in wheels, Mode of tightening	A. Stoner	Mount Joy, Pa	Jan. 13, 1857	16, 408
Fellies, Mode of securing	M. J. Mellyn	Roxbury, Mass	Dec. 24, 1867	72, 663
Fellies of carriage-wheels, Machinery for shaping the inner sides of.	R. A. Henry	Barre, Mass	Nov. 21, 1842	2, 860
Fellies of wagon-wheels, Machine for dressing the.	A. P. Odholm	Bridgeport, Conn	Nov. 27, 1866	60, 040
Fellies of wheels, Mode of connecting	J. Eveland	Elizabeth City, N. J	Oct. 28, 1862	36, 774
Fellies, Sawing and boring	W. W. Forwood	Abingdon, Md	Nov. 19, 1833	....
Fellies, Sawing and boring	J. Hamilton	New York, N. Y	Apr. 29, 1833	....
Fellies, &c., Sawing wood for	B. Ruggles	Poultney, Vt	June 29, 1826	....
Fellies, Securing the ends of	H. and H. Inman	Amsterdam, N. Y	Nov. 5, 1867	70, 438
Fellies, Tightening	H. Thompson	Palmyra, Wis	Aug. 2, 1864	43, 722
Fellies to wheels, Machine for fitting	F. H. Brinkkotter	Callahan's Ranch, Cal	Mar. 30, 1869	88, 267
Fellies with oil, Apparatus for saturating	J. R. Fans	Espy, Pa	Aug. 30, 1870	106, 927
Fellies, spokes, &c., Apparatus for oiling	P. E. Bromby	Espy, Pa	Feb. 7, 1871	111, 511
Felling apparatus, Tree	M. R. Fory	New York, N. Y	June 1, 1869	90, 834
Felling trees, &c	J. Hamilton	New York, N. Y	June 26, 1835	....
Felling trees	P. Johnson	Whitney's Point, N. Y	May 15, 1870	28, 280
Felling trees by hand, Machine for	E. T. Miller	Chelsea, Mass	June 9, 1857	17, 512
Felling trees by saws, Method of	G. C. Ehrsam	New York, N. Y	June 24, 1856	15, 178
Felling trees, Machine for	H. J. Beard	New Sharon, Me	Oct. 25, 1870	108, 675
Felling trees, Machine for	T. Durden	Montgomery, Ala	Sept. 18, 1855	13, 568
Felling trees, Machine for	A. Edwards	New Haven, Conn	Mar. 24, 1868	75, 882
Felling trees, Machine for	M. R. Fory	New York, N. Y	Sept. 22, 1868	82, 303
Felling trees, Machine for	J. S. Foster	Vallicita, Cal	July 2, 1861	32, 688
Felling trees, Machine for	E. Mathers	Morgantown, Va	Mar. 18, 1856	14, 462
Felling trees, Machine for	E. R. Morrison	New York, N. Y	June 13, 1871	115, 975
Felling trees, Method of	S. Ingersoll	Green Point, N. Y	Oct. 14, 1856	15, 913
Felling trees, Saw for	F. Bauschtliker	Washington, D. C	Oct. 6, 1868	82, 789
Felly	W. L. Perry and A. J. Mathews	Hartwell, Ga	Apr. 15, 1873	137, 955
Felly-bending machine	J. Compton	Elmira, N. Y	Sept. 15, 1863	39, 887
Felly-bending machine	T. Cox	Lancaster, Pa	July 4, 1854	11, 209
Felly-bending machine	A. Hemenway	Cleveland, Ohio	May 1, 1860	28, 080
Felly-bending machine	J. L. Mann	Ravenna, Ohio	Aug. 31, 1858	21, 351
Felly bending machine	S. Moyer	Shinersville, Pa	Mar. 20, 1860	27, 560
Felly-bending machine	D. A. Sprinkle	Leoti, Ind	Mar. 8, 1870	100, 685
Felly-bending machine, Wood	G. A. Brown	Newfane, N. Y	Mar. 15, 1859	23, 227
Felly-boring and spoke-tenoning bit	H. McGrath	Meig's Creek, Ohio	Jan. 15, 1856	14, 105
Felly, Carriage-wheel	M. Turley	Council Bluffs, Iowa	Feb. 13, 1872	123, 750
Felly-clamp and spoke-support for carriage-wheels	J. C. Plumer	Boston, Mass	Dec. 19, 1865	51, 620
Felly-clip for vehicle-wheels	D. Grim	Pittsburgh, Pa.	June 20, 1871	116, 050
Felly coupling, Carriage	H. Austin	East Liberty, Ohio	May 8, 1866	54, 485
Felly coupling, Wheel	C. Cheney	Milford, Mass	Aug. 2, 1870	105, 904
Felly cutting and dressing machine	S. Church	Amherst, Mass	Apr. 25, 1810	....
Felly-cutting machine	J. and L. Adams	Hadley, Mass	July 9, 1850	7, 485
Felly-cutting machine	J. and L. Adams and L. H. Moore.	Hadley and Leverett, Mass	June 12, 1849	6, 521
Felly-cutting machine	Bradley and Worthley	Phillips, Me	Oct. 14, 1835	....
Felly-cutting machine	Brown and Barker	Phillips, Me	Oct. 14, 1835	....
Felly-cutting machine	J. Goulding	Leicester, Mass	Feb. 28, 1811	....
Felly-cutting machine	B. L. Greenough	Lebanon, N. H	Dec. 22, 1824	....
Felly-cutting machine	W. A. Lewis and G. W. Butler	Joliet, Ill	Nov. 16, 1869	96, 818
Felly-cutting machine	I. S. Moon	Bennington, Vt	Sept. 10, 1872	131, 292
Felly dowel-pin	E. D. Tyler	Gibson, Pa	Apr. 28, 1868	77, 337

Index of patents issued from the United States Patent Office from 1790 to 1873, inclusive—Continued.

Invention.	Inventor.	Residence.	Date.	No.
Felly-doweling machine	J. P. O'Brien	Kewanee, Ill	July 30, 1872	129, 979
Felly-dressing machine	W. M. Bullock	Marcy, Ind	Sept. 16, 1856	15, 727
Felly-dressing machine	H. Kurtz	Washington, D. C	Jan. 11, 1870	98, 696
Felly-dressing machine	D. J. Marston	Amesbury, Mass	Apr. 25, 1871	114, 169
Felly-dressing machine	W. H. Rodeheaver	Miamisburgh, Ohio	Oct. 11, 1870	108, 1[illegible]9
Felly-dressing machine	W. H. Rodeheaver	Miamisburgh, Ohio	July 14, 1868	80, 013
Felly-dressing machine	C. W. Wyatt	New York, N. Y	Dec. 12, 1854	12, 082
Felly-finishing tool	C. H. Denison	Guilford, Vt	Dec. 6, 1859	26, 392
Felly fitting and boring machine	W. L. Perry	Jonesville, S. C	Oct. 10, 1871	119, 880
Felly, Hollow metallic rim or	S. R. Bryant	Waterford, Pa	June 28, 1870	104, 824
Felly joint, Carriage-wheel	F. M. Gibson	Chelsea, Mass	Feb. 5, 1861	31, 309
Felly joint, clip, and ferrule	P. Jones	Newark, N. J	Jan. 28, 1868	73, 903
Felly-joint coupling	S. A. Garrison and D. C. Morey	Chelsea, Mass	Feb. 26, 1856	14, 311
Felly-joints, Mode of securing	J. W. Lawrence	New York, N. Y	Sept. 17, 1867	68, 999
Felly-machine	H. H. Dean	Adrian, Mich	May 9, 1854	10, 884
Felly-machine	C. H. Denison	Brattleborough, Vt	Feb. 19, 1861	31, 443
Felly-machine	F. H. Mallett	New Haven, Conn	July 17, 1860	29, 2[illegible]3
Felly-machine	R. Massey	Philadelphia, Pa	Oct. 6, 1863	40, 177
Felly-manufacturing machine	A. B. Richmond	Meadville, Pa	May 27, 1856	14, 987
Felly-mill	S. Church	Amherst, Mass	May 4, 1805	....
Felly of wheel for trucks, &c	G. Andrews	Tolland, Conn	Oct. 24, 1828	....
Felly-planing machine	A. W. Fox	Athens, Pa	Apr. 8, 1856	14, 604
Felly-planing machine	W. W. Johnson	Clifford, Pa	Dec. 18, 1855	13, 947
Felly-plate	C. D. Everett	Cleveland, Ohio	May 6, 1873	138, 624
Felly-plate	C. D. Everett and A. Baldwin	Cleveland, Ohio	Oct. 8, 1872	132, 065
Felly-plate	F. B. Morse	Plantsville, Conn	May 30, 1871	115, 504
Felly-plate	F. B. Morse	Plantsville, Conn	July 2, 1872	128, 558
Felly-plate	H. Sylvester	Saint Louis, Mo	Apr. 8, 1873	137, 571
Felly-plate for carriage-wheels	F. B. Morse	Plantsville, Conn	May 17, 1870	103, 273
Felly-plate-making die	A. N. Clark	Plainville, Conn	Jan. 24, 1871	111, 177
Felly-plates, Die for forming	F. B. Morse	Plantsville, Conn	Apr. 16, 1872	125, 751
Felly-plates, Die for the manufacture of	L. C. Clark	Plantsville, Conn	July 9, 1872	128, 790
Felly-sawing machine	D. Bowen	Wadesville, Va	July 1, 1856	15, 216
Felly-sawing machine	S. and W. H. Brook	Rushville, Ohio	May 6, 1856	14, 802
Felly-sawing machine	W. Carr	Logansport, Ind	Jan. 26, 1869	86, 279
Felly-sawing machine	A. Colby	Sharon, Vt	Oct. 15, 1830	....
Felly-sawing machine	P. Collier	Catskill, N. Y	May 20, 1826	....
Felly-sawing machine	D. D. Hansom	Weare, N. H	Oct. 20, 1830	....
Felly-sawing machine	E. Rhodes	Erie, Pa	Sept. 21, 1869	95, 140
Felly-sawing machine	W. E. Sheffield	New York, N. Y	Dec. 20, 1809	....
Felly-sawing machine	J. B. Zimmerman	Fort Seneca, Ohio	May 14, 1872	126, 768
Felly-sawing machine, Wagon	N. W. Graves	Winnebago, Ill	Feb 26, 1867	62, 408
Felly-sawing machine, Wheel	S. Fahrney	Washington County, Md	Dec. 9, 1828	....
Felly-sawing mill	I. Sheetz	Taneytown, Md	May 20, 1842	2, 632
Felt fabrics, Machine for disintegrating waste	J. T. Greene	Brooklyn, N. Y	Apr. 12, 1859	23, 643
Felt for bottoms of vessels, &c	T. R. Williams	Newport, R. I	May 22, 1830	....
Felt for cloth, padding, carpets, &c., Manufacturing	J. Barker and L. Kinsley	Greene County, N. Y	Aug. 29, 1829	....
Felt for weather-strips, packings, &c., Process of preparing.	F. Siering	New York, N. Y	Dec. 23, 1873	145, 913
Felt goods, Manufacturing seamless	J. H. Bloodgood	New York, N. Y	Feb. 6, 1855	12, 343
Felt, Machinery for manufacturing sheathing	J. B. Hyde	Newark, N. J	May 29, 1860	28, 489
Felt, Machinery for the manufacture of	M. D. Whipple	Cambridge, Mass	Oct. 12, 1869	95, 862
Felt, Machinery for the manufacture of	M. D. Whipple	Cambridge, Mass	Oct. 12, 1869	95, 863
Felt, Manufacture of	S. M. Allen	Boston, Mass	Feb. 3, 1863	37, 559
Felt, Manufacture of roofing and sheathing	W. P. Arnold	New York, N. Y	Aug. 20, 1872	130, 615
Felt of wool without spinning or weaving, Making	L. Van Hoesen	Norwalk, Conn	June 27, 1829	....
Felt skirts, &c., Ornamenting	J. W. Blackham	Brooklyn, N. Y	Sept. 9, 1873	142, 554
Felt washer	W. Cole	Lee, Mass	Jan. 23, 1833	....
Felted and other goods and fabrics, Process of finishing	T. Crossley	Bridgeport, Conn	Jan. 29, 1867	61, 520
Felted articles, Manufacture of hollow	C. W. and H. E. Palmer and C. Houghton.	Lynn and Boston, Mass	July 26, 1870	105, 836
Felted fabric	W. E. Bloodgood	Rahway, N. J	July 9, 1872	128, 844
Felted fabric	T. Crossley	Bridgeport, Conn	Feb. 2, 1869	86, 510
Felted fabric	T. Demuth	Danbury, Conn	Apr. 4, 1871	113, 274
Felted fabric	H. Hayward	New York, N. Y	July 21, 1868	80, 263
Felted fabric	M. A. Johnson	Lowell, Mass	Jan. 5, 1864	41, 073
Felted fabric	M. A. Johnson	Lowell, Mass	Jan. 28, 1868	73, 727
Felted fabric	J. E. Pollard	Franklin City, Mass	Feb. 21, 1871	111, 968
Felted fabric	S. P. Siver	Danbury, Conn	Mar. 8, 1870	100, 563
Felted fabric	E. Waite	Franklin City, Mass	Aug. 8, 1865	49, 353
Felted fabric	E. Waite	Franklin, Mass	June 11, 1872	127, 813
Felted fabric	J. T. Waring	Yonkers, N. Y	Oct. 6, 1868	82, 904
Felted fabric for bonnets, Woven	R. S. Gillespie and F. Ziesing	New York, N. Y	Feb. 27, 1872	124, 191
Felted fabrics, Manufacture of	E. D. McCracken	New York, N. Y	Aug. 1, 1865	49, 131
Felted fabrics, Manufacture of	E. Waite	South Natick, Mass	Mar. 14, 1865	46, 837
Felted fabrics, Removing vegetable fiber from	J. T. Waring	Yonkers, N. Y	Aug. 19, 1873	142, 063
Felted tufted fabric	J. T. Waring	Yonkers, N. Y	Nov. 24, 1868	84, 325
Felting, Bat for	L. W. Boynton	South Coventry, Conn	Apr. 29, 1851	8, 068
Felting bats, Machine for forming	J. H. Bloodgood	New York, N. Y	Jan. 20, 1857	16, 431
Felting, Composition	L. S. Stimson	Lowell, Mass	Sept. 19, 1871	119, 059
Felting-compound	L. E. Hopkins	Brooklyn, N. Y	Aug. 19, 1856	15, 563
Felting for coats, hats, &c	M. Osborne	New York, N. Y	May 28, 1842	2, 646
Felting-machine	W. J. Benedict and J. Wylie	South Norwalk, Conn	Aug. 18, 1868	81, 244
Felting-machine	J. W. Blackham	Brooklyn, N. Y	Sept. 21, 1869	94, 939
Felting-machine	J. H. Bloodgood and M. A. Johnson.	New York, N. Y., and Lowell, Mass.	Nov. 15, 1864	45, 017
Felting-machine	H. Brisco and J. W. Blackham	Brooklyn, N. Y	June 1, 1869	90, 633
Felting-machine	G. N. Bronson	New Milford, Conn	Apr. 16, 1861	32, 042
Felting-machine	A. Cattaneo	Newark, N. J	Aug. 18, 1868	81, 252
Felting-machine	R. Eickemeyer	Yonkers, N. Y	Mar. 16, 1869	87, 763
Felting-machine	R. Eickemeyer	Yonkers, N. Y	June 22, 1869	91, 729
Felting-machine	R. Eickemeyer	Yonkers, N. Y	Oct. 11, 1870	108, 121
Felting-machine	R. Eickemeyer	New York, N. Y	Nov. 21, 1871	121, 045
Felting-machine	F. S. Jennings	Danbury, Conn	Jan. 18, 1870	98, 871
Felting-machine	C. P. Ladd	New York, N. Y	Dec. 27, 1870	110, 574
Felting-machine	C. P. Ladd	Bloomfield, N. J	Mar. 19, 1872	124, 828
Felting-machine	W. B. Lodge and H. Platner	Danbury, Conn	Nov. 26, 1867	71, 516

Index of patents issued from the United States Patent Office from 1790 *to* 1873, *inclusive*—Continued.

Invention.	Inventor.	Residence.	Date.	No.
Felting-machine	W. A. Lyon	Danbury, Conn	July 9, 1867	66, 603
Felting-machine	S. S. Middlebrook	Sandy Hook, Conn	June 4, 1867	65, 413
Felting-machine	C. Mossant	Bourg du Péage, France	June 16, 1868	78, 991
Felting-machine	L. Robinson, L. Conine, and N. F. and D. W. Hyatt.	Matteawan, N. Y	June 22, 1869	91, 670
Felting-machine	E. Waite	Lawrence, N. Y	Sept. 22, 1863	40, 087
Felting-machine	E. Waite	South Natick, Mass	May 3, 1864	42, 611
Felting-machine	E. Waite	South Natick, Mass	June 14, 1864	43, 164
Felting-machine	E. Waite	South Natick, Mass	June 4, 1867	65, 455
Felting, Machine for crossing bats for	A. C. Arnold	Norwalk, Conn	Oct. 22, 1867	70, 065
Felting, Machine for crossing fibers in forming bats for.	L. Robinson	Matteawan, N. Y	July 20, 1869	92, 750
Felting-machinery	J. H. Bloodgood and M. A. Johnson.	New York, N. Y., and Lowell, Mass.	Mar. 6, 1860	27, 345
Felting, Machinery for forming bats for	T. B. Butler	Norwalk, Conn	Aug. 10, 1858	21, 164
Felting, wadding, &c., Machine for forming bats for	E. Waite	Franklin, Mass	June 4, 1867	65, 456
Female-supporter	A. D. Reeves	Portland, Me	Apr. 1, 1862	34, 845
Fence	G. W. Adams	Rochester, N. Y	Oct. 1, 1867	69, 299
Fence	G. Albro	Columbus, Pa	Aug. 5, 1873	141, 532
Fence	E. Allen	Honeoye, N. Y	July 16, 1872	129, 305
Fence	B. F. Allison	West Dayton, Iowa	Feb. 24, 1863	37, 729
Fence	A. M. Alpin	Chetopah, Kans	Feb. 20, 1872	123 854
Fence	W. Altick and F. P. Grimes	Dayton, Ohio	Mar. 14, 1871	112, 6[illegible]2
Fence	D. B. Ayres	Brooklyn, Mich	Aug. 10, 1869	93, 397
Fence	C. M. Ballard and M. Morehouse.	Johnsbury, N. Y	Jan. 10, 1871	110, 888
Fence	H. M. Barber	Franklin Station, Ohio	Feb. 7, 1871	111, 508
Fence	A. T. Barnes	Seneca, N. Y	Jan. 5, 1869	85, 506
Fence	T. Barnes	Wayne, Mich	July 13, 1869	92, 509
Fence	H. Bartholomew	Dover Centre, Ohio	Oct. 22, 1867	69, 961
Fence	W. Bartlett	Little Hocking, Ohio	Aug. 16, 1871	106, 455
Fence	A. C. Betts	Troy, N. Y	Mar. 12, 1872	124, 477
Fence	B. Billings	Lyons, Iowa	Dec. 4, 1863	60, 127
Fence	I. Blackaby	Civer, Ill	Dec. 21, 1869	98, 016
Fence	I. Boone	Troy, Ohio	July 23, 1867	67, 017
Fence	L. H. Bowlus	Knoxville, Tenn	Aug. 20, 1867	67, 944
Fence	W. J. Brainard	Hamilton, N. Y	Dec. 28, 1847	5, 406
Fence	R. W. Brockway and H. Frederick.	Akron, Ohio	July 21, 1868	80, 054
Fence	C. E. Brown	Pamelia, N. Y	Dec. 5, 1871	121, 448
Fence	F. G. Brown	Chapel Hill, Tex	June 4, 1872	127, 558
Fence	M. Brown and O. J. Shannon	Fond du Lac and Fairwater, Wis.	Feb. 28, 1865	46, 541
Fence	W. H. Brown	Stockwell, Ind	Aug. 7, 1866	56, 895
Fence	J. H. Buckman	Cartersville, Ga	Apr. 16, 1872	125, 845
Fence	J. Bundy	West Liberty, Iowa	Oct. 30, 1866	59, 176
Fence	J. S. Burch	Buffalo, N. Y	Oct 19, 1869	95, 982
Fence	T. L. Burk	Greensburgh, Ind	July 21, 1868	80, 131
Fence	H. Burrows	Georgetown, D. C	Sept. 11, 1860	30, 021
Fence	T. R. Byrnes	Washington, D. C	Dec. 26, 1865	51 691
Fence	J. Card	Gainesville, N. Y	Feb. 17, 1852	8, 735
Fence	J. Carr	Emerald Post-Office, Ohio	July 13, 1869	92, 582
Fence	I. D. Carter	Wilson, N. Y	Jan. 26, 1869	86, 280
Fence	J. M. Chaplin	Middleport, Conn	Oct. 13, 1868	83, 038
Fence	J. W. Cherry	Carthage, Ill	July 11, 1870	105, 303
Fence	J. W. Cherry	Carthage, Ill	Dec. 12, 1871	121, 752
Fence	E. S. Clapp and E. Blanchard	Montague and Amherst, Mass.	Apr. 5, 1864	42, 166
Fence	G. R. Clark	Livonia, N. Y	Mar. 12, 1867	62, 732
Fence	J. K. and C. B. Clark	Mount Pleasant, Ohio	Mar. 21, 1865	46, 881
Fence	L. N. Clark	Brighton, Mich	May 23, 1871	115, 165
Fence	A. J. Clemmons and J. W. Westbrooks.	Aberdeen, Miss	Dec. 10, 1872	133, 831
Fence	T. Coffield	Natrona, Pa	Mar. 29, 1870	101, 351
Fence	T. C. Collins	Little Hockhocking, Ohio	Jan. 10, 1871	110, 899
Fence	J. Comstock	Greenfield, Ind	Oct. 4, 1870	107, 879
Fence	S. P. Coon	Milwaukee, Wis	July 11, 1870	105, 307
Fence	F. K. Cosgrove and R. Westerman.	Fort Wayne, Ind	Jan. 20, 1863	37, 434
Fence	E. Cozad	East Cleveland, Ohio	Mar. 27, 1866	53, 418
Fence	E. Crandal	Marshalltown, Iowa	Nov. 26, 1872	133, 358
Fence	S. Crocker	Fredonia Post-Office, Iowa	Sept. 11, 1866	57, 872
Fence	J. M. Crull	Noblesville, Ind	Aug. 17, 1869	93, 860
Fence	H. J. Culp	Goshen, Ind	Aug 4, 1868	80, 609
Fence	P. Davis	Newport News, Va	June 29, 1869	91, 918
Fence	H. H. Dennis	Steam Mill, Pa	Nov. 27, 1855	13, 844
Fence	S. Denton	Penn Yan, N. Y	Feb. 21, 1860	27, 209
Fence	B. G. Devoe	Fredericktown, Ohio	Dec. 12, 1871	121, 8[illegible]5
Fence	B. G. Devoe, T. Rogers, and J. C. Beals.	Fredericktown, Ohio, and Searsport, Me.	Mar. 5, 1872	124, 342
Fence	H. Deyoe	Machias, N. Y	June 13, 1871	115, 8[illegible]0
Fence	M. Dickle	Wellersburgh, Pa	Feb. 27, 1866	52, 828
Fence	B. K. Dorwart and W. J. Hines.	Lancaster, Pa., and Frederick, Md.	Sept. 24, 1867	69, 191
Fence	B. K. Dorwart and G. F. Rote, jr	Lancaster, Pa	Nov. 19, 1867	71, 146
Fence	B. K. Dorwart and G. F. Rote, jr	Lancaster, Pa	Nov. 19, 1867	71, 147
Fence	J. G. Downer	Auburn, N. Y	Nov. 9, 1869	96, 561
Fence	J. T. Drummond	Mount Pleasant, Iowa	Apr. 18, 1871	113, 753
Fence	C. E. Easton	Cedarville, N. Y	Oct. 7, 1862	36, 605
Fence	J. Edmunds	South Adams, Mass	Mar. 6, 1866	52, 981
Fence	O. L. Edwards and N. Gabel	Gratis, Preble County, Ohio	Jan. 28, 1862	34, 246
Fence	A. Ellis and O. Albertson	Salem, Ohio	Dec. 24, 1867	72, 469
Fence	F. Ellis	La Fayette, Ohio	May 7, 1867	64, 509
Fence	E. Ely	Lockport, N. Y	May 9, 1871	114, 543
Fence	D. S. Evans	Richmond, Ind	Oct. 30, 1866	59, 199
Fence	O. J. Everson	Lake City, Minn	May 19, 1868	77, 967
Fence	E. Fales	Glenwood, Mo	Sept 6, 1870	107, 020
Fence	E. Fales	Glenwood, Mo	Apr. 16, 1872	1[illegible]5, 880

Index of patents issued from the United States Patent Office from 1790 *to* 1873, *inclusive*—Continued.

Invention.	Inventor.	Residence.	Date.	No.
Fence	A. Fanckboner	Schoolcraft, Mich	Oct. 13, 1863	40, 253
Fence	A. Faulkner	Mount Pleasant, Iowa	Jan. 10, 1871	110, 910
Fence	O. F. A. Faulkner	Mount Pleasant, Iowa	Feb. 14, 1871	111, 831
Fence	R. J. Flanner	Plainfield Township, Mich	Nov. 29, 1870	109, 606
Fence	B. Force	Mount Pleasant, Iowa	Aug. 27, 1867	68, 177
Fence	J. Fox	Bucyrus, Ohio	Jan. 11, 1870	98, 682
Fence	E. L. Fraker	Oshkosh, Wis	Mar. 2, 1869	87, 336
Fence	A. A. Garver	Albion, Iowa	May 21, 1872	126, 950
Fence	M. J. Gaskill	Pleasant Plain, Ohio	Feb. 25, 1868	74, 908
Fence	M. J. Gaskill	Pleasant Plain, Ohio	Mar. 9, 1869	87, 558
Fence	G. L. Gavett	Sandstone, Mich	July 16, 1867	66, 826
Fence	W. Gibson	Fort Wayne, Ind	May 13, 1862	35, 238
Fence	T. Glover	Woodbury, N. J	Dec. 11, 1866	60, 350
Fence	J. Godfrey	Allegheny City, Pa	Aug. 31, 1869	94, 199
Fence	S. Good	Greenville, Ohio	Dec. 3, 1867	71, 736
Fence	E. C. Gordon	Sevastopol, Ind	Dec. 4, 1866	60, 174
Fence	E. C. Gordon	Sevastopol, Ind	May 28, 1867	65, 209
Fence	J. Gray	Raymond, Miss	Nov. 11, 1873	144, 534
Fence	I. M. Greene, sr	Clinton, Ill	Nov. 5, 1867	70, 549
Fence	C. S. S. Griffing	Ashtabula, Ohio	May 24, 1864	42, 848
Fence	C. S. S. Griffing	Geneva, Ohio	Mar. 12, 1867	62, 840
Fence	H. A. Grover	North Cohocton, N. Y	July 13, 1869	92, 442
Fence	C. Guthrie	Peoria, N. Y	Sept. 3, 1872	130, 991
Fence	S. W. Hall	Elmira, N. Y	Dec. 10, 1872	133, 853
Fence	T. Harrison	La Fayette, Wis	Aug. 3, 1869	93, 198
Fence	D. Harvey	Jackson Township, Iowa	Apr. 11, 1865	47, 203
Fence	J. Hatfield	Ogden, Ind	Jan. 6, 1863	37, 372
Fence	C. A. Haviland	Davenport, Iowa	Dec. 3, 1867	71, 750
Fence	W. D. Hillis	Elgin, Ill	Apr. 3, 1866	53, 616
Fence	W. D. Hillis	Elgin, Ill	June 23, 1868	79, 121
Fence	W. D. Hillis	Elgin, Ill	Dec. 20, 1870	110, 234
Fence	C. N. Hitchcock, and H. P. T. Wilson.	Canton, Miss	Nov. 8, 1870	109, 127
Fence	E. Hollinger	New Haven, Conn	Mar. 14, 1865	46, 799
Fence	H. G. Hood	Harlan, Ind	July 14, 1863	39, 231
Fence	T. J. Hubbard	Hamilton, N. Y	Dec. 28, 1847	5, 407
Fence	W. D. Hunt	Scott, N. Y	July 23, 1867	67, 117
Fence	G. W. Hunter	Versailles, Ind	Nov. 2, 1869	96, 435
Fence	C. B. Hunting	Clinton, Ill	Feb. 20, 1866	52, 717
Fence	F. W. Huxford	Boonesborough, Iowa	July 30, 1867	67, 308
Fence	P. J. Hynes	Stoughton, Wis	Aug. 29, 1871	118, 535
Fence	A. Jackson	Clifton Springs, N. Y	Jan. 16, 1866	52, 051
Fence	J. B. Johnson	Laurel, Ind	Dec. 17, 1867	72, 402
Fence	N. Johnson	Jasper, N. Y	Oct. 1, 1867	69, 444
Fence	N. Johnson	Jasper, N. Y	Oct. 1, 1867	69, 445
Fence	D. Johnston	Cranberry, Ohio	Dec. 14, 1869	97, 926
Fence	L. P. Judson	Rose, N. Y	Aug. 15, 1871	118, 135
Fence	D. Kaufman	Boiling Springs, Pa	Sept. 17, 1867	68, 991
Fence	D. Kaufman	Boiling Springs, Pa	Jan. 21, 1868	73, 611
Fence	M. Kelly	New York, N. Y	Feb. 11, 1868	74, 379
Fence	J. E. Kendeigh	Amherst, Ohio	Mar. 13, 1866	53, 153
Fence	J. Kerr	Corsicana, Tex	Feb. 15, 1870	99, 911
Fence	G. Kicherer	Brooklyn, N. Y	Oct. 2, 1866	58, 432
Fence	T. E. King	Ashtabula, Ohio	May 5, 1863	38, 396
Fence	T. E. King	Painesville, Ohio	June 26, 1866	55, 874
Fence	T. E. King	Painesville, Ohio	Feb. 19, 1867	62, 209
Fence	W. F. King	Gonzales County, Tex	Sept. 23, 1873	143, 161
Fence	E. Kirk	Sharon, Pa	May 10, 1870	102, 834
Fence	J. J. Knight	Long Point, Ill	June 6, 1871	115, 742
Fence	A. Kull, jr	Bloomfield, Wis	Nov. 16, 1869	96, 814
Fence	E. Kyes	Nunda, N. Y	May 21, 1872	127, 071
Fence	J. A. Kysor	Leon, N. Y	June 27, 1871	116, 329
Fence	I. Lackey	Lebanon, Ohio	Dec. 10, 1867	71, 888
Fence	H. H. Landis	Lancaster, Pa	Aug. 29, 1871	118, 461
Fence	I. L. Landis	Lancaster, Pa	June 18, 1867	65, 819
Fence	I. L. Landis	Lancaster, Pa	Feb. 6, 1872	123, 487
Fence	I. L. Landis	Lancaster, Pa	Feb. 6, 1872	123, 488
Fence	I. L. Landis	Lancaster, Pa	July 23, 1872	129, 837
Fence	A. Lapham	Farmington, Mich	Aug. 25, 1868	81, 513
Fence	H. Latshaw	McKnightstown, Pa	Sept. 26, 1871	119, 372
Fence	J. E. Layton	New Wilmington, Pa	Oct. 22, 1867	70, 097
Fence	C. G. Lazear	Norwalk, Ohio	Nov. 27, 1866	60, 020
Fence	L. Leavenworth	Trumansburgh, N. Y	Oct. 30, 1849	6, 831
Fence	C. Lee	Winchester, Ohio	Sept. 4, 1866	57, 735
Fence	C. Lee	Sandy Post-Office, Ohio	Apr. 7, 1868	76, 475
Fence	J. C. Leonard	Union City, Mich	Feb. 12, 1867	61, 942
Fence	I. N. Lerick	San Antonio, Tex	July 23, 1872	129, 738
Fence	L. E. Lockling	Perrysburgh, N. Y	Oct. 16, 1866	58, 848
Fence	L. E. Lockling and N. N. Whitaker.	Perrysburgh and Sheridan, N. Y.	June 7, 1870	103, 903
Fence	O. Love	Saxenburgh, Pa	Oct. 20, 1868	83, 184
Fence	C. Lowe	Randolph, N. H	Nov. 16, 1869	96, 934
Fence	W. Mallary	Bucyrus, Ohio	Oct. 5, 1869	95, 596
Fence	C. Maltby	Glenwood, N. Y	June 18, 1872	128, 157
Fence	H. H. Margeson	San Francisco, Cal	Feb. 22, 1870	100, 169
Fence	J. Markley	Bucyrus, Ohio	Oct. 12, 1869	95, 820
Fence	C. C. Mather	Burlington, N. Y	Nov. 6, 1866	59, 427
Fence	J. B. Mattern	Matternsville, Pa	June 25, 1872	128, 409
Fence	N. Maxson	Wilmington, Ohio	Oct. 6, 1868	82, 733
Fence	J. McConnell	Tyro, Ohio	Mar. 1, 1870	100, 431
Fence	J. W. McCormick	Youngstown, N. Y	Mar. 30, 1869	88, 401
Fence	D. McCurdy	Ottawa, Ohio	Aug. 9, 1870	106, 183
Fence	R. McFarlane	Dane, Wis	May 18, 1869	90, 280
Fence	J. M. McKee	Mount Vernon, Ohio	July 6, 1869	92, 334
Fence	J. M. McKee	Hunt's Station, Ohio	May 24, 1870	103, 483
Fence	J. McKnight	Romulus, N. Y	Mar. 12, 1872	124, 502
Fence	H. McMullin	Batesville, Ark	Nov. 19, 1872	133, 165
Fence	B. F. Mears	Washington, Ind	Nov. 14, 1871	120, 989

Index of patents issued from the United States Patent Office from 1790 to 1873, inclusive—Continued.

Invention.	Inventor.	Residence.	Date.	No.
Fence	R. B. Meeker	Sanford's Corners, N. Y	Dec. 12, 1871	121, 797
Fence	M. D. Messler	New Lebanon, Ohio	Oct. 1, 1867	69, 462
Fence	W. A. Middleton	Harrisburgh, Pa	July 30, 1867	67, 332
Fence	W. A. Middleton	Harrisburgh, Pa	Nov. 1, 1870	108, 925
Fence	U. D Mibills	Fond du Lac, Wis	Nov. 8, 1870	109, 056
Fence	G. S. Mills	Johnson, Vt	Mar. 1, 1870	100, 310
Fence	C. Milner	Des Moines, Iowa	Nov. 9, 1869	96, 719
Fence	D. Mitchel	New Berlin, Pa	Mar. 15, 1870	100, 919
Fence	S. H Mitchell	El Paso, Ill	June 26, 1866	55, 883
Fence	J. Moore	Pittsburgh, Pa	June 30, 1857	17, 692
Fence	L. Moore	Baraboo, Wis	Apr. 25, 1871	114, 178
Fence	L. Moore	Baraboo, Wis	Mar. 26, 1872	125, 071
Fence	T. Morris	McGregor, Iowa	June 4, 1867	65, 415
Fence	I. J. Morrow	Everton, Ind	Aug. 3, 1869	93, 332
Fence	J. Morton	Thornville Mills, Mich	Feb. 21, 1871	112, 064
Fence	H. B. Myers	Schoolcraft, Mich	Nov. 29, 1894	45, 298
Fence	W. Neely	Sandy, Ohio	Aug. 21, 1866	57, 366
Fence	W. Nevins	Lyons, N. Y	June 6, 1865	48, 086
Fence	A. M. Nichol	Granville, Ohio	Sept. 24, 1867	69, 116
Fence	E Odell	Winterset, Iowa	Aug. 7, 1866	56, 985
Fence	A. W. Olds	Green Oak, Mich	June 5, 1866	55, 352
Fence	A. W. Olds	Green Oak, Mich	July 17, 1866	56, 441
Fence	E. F. Olds and W. Clark	Brighton and Green Oak, Mich.	Jan. 14, 1868	73, 257
Fence	F. W. Owens	Granville, Ohio	Sept. 6, 1870	107, 095
Fence	C. H. Paine	Providence, R. I	June 11, 1867	65, 592
Fence	P. C. Pearson	Louisville, Ky	July 11, 1871	116, 989
Fence	D. L. Pettegrew	Claremont, N. H	July 11, 1865	48, 774
Fence	W. Pettengell	Painesville, Ohio	Aug. 20, 1867	67, 902
Fence	L. Philips	Eau Claire, Wis	Sept. 20, 1870	107, 533
Fence	T. E. Phillips	Coatesville, Ind	Mar. 2, 1869	87, 364
Fence	S. B. Pierce	Homer, N. Y	Aug. 4, 1868	80, 661
Fence	J. M. Pitts	Sumter, S. C	Oct. 30, 1860	30, 544
Fence	S. S. Porter	Broad Ford, Pa	July 25, 1871	117, 325
Fence	A. W. Pratt	Pultneyville, N. Y	Mar. 26, 1867	63, 296
Fence	M. D. Pratt	Copley, Ohio	Jan. 14, 1868	73, 260
Fence	S. M. Prentice	Aurora, Ill	Aug. 31, 1869	94, 258
Fence	R. Prouty	Springfield, Iowa	Feb. 20, 1866	52, 795
Fence	H. B. Ramsey	Rockville, Ind	Aug. 13, 1872	130, 441
Fence	T. D. Read	Aberdeen, Ind	Sept. 10, 1867	68, 790
Fence	W. Reed	Wayne, N. Y	Apr. 30, 1867	64, 363
Fence	J. J. Reicherts	Delaware, Ohio	Jan. 12, 1869	85, 852
Fence	J. B. Reyman	Dubuque, Iowa	May 22, 1855	12, 921
Fence	D. Rhodes	Fredericktown, Mo	Sept. 19, 1871	119, 047
Fence	J. Richard	Columbiaville, Mich	Mar. 30, 1869	88, 412
Fence	R. A. Riggs	Salem, Oreg	May 7, 1872	126, 413
Fence	S. Riley	Kenton, Ohio	Oct. 5, 1869	95, 518
Fence	J. Riordan	Six Mile, Ind	July 20, 1869	92, 886
Fence	E. C. Roberts	Salem, Mich	June 11, 1867	65, 694
Fence	T. D. Roberts	Nekimi, Wis	Aug. 27, 1872	130, 823
Fence	J. Rohrer	Springfield, Ohio	Aug. 15, 1871	118, 156
Fence	W. P. Rollo	Holland Patent, N. Y	Apr. 16, 1872	125, 761
Fence	S. H. Rose	Wheeler, N. Y	Sept. 25, 1866	58, 300
Fence	H. S. Ross	Cincinnati, Ohio	Sept. 13, 1853	10, 015
Fence	B. Rowell	Elmira, N. Y	Sept. 18, 1866	58, 193
Fence	B. Rowell	Byersville, N. Y	June 7, 1870	104, 065
Fence	J. R. Rowley	Fabius, N. Y	Mar. 19, 1867	63, 100
Fence	J. W. Sanders	Ripon, Wis	May 28, 1867	65, 284
Fence	S. Saunders	Fort Plain, N. Y	Feb. 13, 1866	52, 611
Fence	C Seabaugh	San Antonio, Tex	Aug. 28, 1866	57, 581
Fence	I. R. Shank	Buffalo, Va	Mar. 31, 1863	38, 063
Fence	J. W. Shankland	Summerfield, Ohio	Sept. 25, 1866	58, 308
Fence	N. L. Shaw	Wilson, N. Y	Apr. 21, 1868	77, 109
Fence	A. Sheldon	Greenwich Station, Ohio	Jan. 28, 1868	73, 761
Fence	W. B. Shelton	Congruity, Pa	Dec. 18, 1866	60, 576
Fence	P. L. Sherman	Geneseo Township, Iowa	Sept. 13, 1870	107, 297
Fence	W. W. Sherman	Saint Charles County, Mo	Jan. 17, 1871	111, 090
Fence	A. D. Smith and E. Stow	Townsend Station, Ohio	Mar. 24, 1868	75, 994
Fence	A. H. Smith	Elkhorn, Wis	Aug. 22, 1871	118, 398
Fence	D. N. Smith and E. F. Olds	Salem and Lyon, Mich	Dec. 24, 1867	72, 693
Fence	R A. Smith	Newburyport, Mass	Mar. 11, 1862	34, 650
Fence	F. F. Sommer	Detroit, Mich	June 29, 1869	92, 118
Fence	J. Southwick	Brant, N. Y	Sept. 1, 1868	81, 836
Fence	A. B Sprout	Picture Rocks, Pa	Sept. 3, 1872	131, 038
Fence	S. Stanbro	Northville, Mich	Aug. 8, 1865	49, 313
Fence	T. Stanford	Noblesville, Ind	Apr. 13, 1869	88, 819
Fence	J. Stevens	Northumberland, N. Y	July 20, 1846	4, 650
Fence	H. M. Stoker	Watson, Ill	Apr. 30, 1867	64, 379
Fence	J. Stone and S. Blocker, sr	Plattsburgh, Mo	July 31, 1866	56, 826
Fence	J. H. Stone	Chapel Hill, Tex	Mar. 12, 1872	124, 516
Fence	N. M. Stratton	New York, N. Y	Oct. 23, 1860	30, 507
Fence	C. H. Strowger	Webster, N. Y	Oct. 31, 1871	120, 546
Fence	C. H Strowger	Webster, N. Y	May 28, 1872	127, 282
Fence	I. Subers	Philadelphia County, Pa	Feb. 19, 1850	7, 108
Fence	W. W. Sullivan	Liberty, Ind	Dec. 13, 1870	110, 170
Fence	J. B. Tedrow	Chillicothe, Ohio	Mar. 9, 1869	87, 729
Fence	J. W. Teller and W. Townsend.	Lapeer, Mich	Feb. 28, 1871	112, 194
Fence	D. Terry	Wakeman, Ohio	Aug. 21, 1866	57, 408
Fence	J. Thomas	Mount Union, Ohio	May 21, 1867	65, 025
Fence	J. D. Tifft	Cuyahoga Falls, Ohio	Oct. 3, 1871	119, 670
Fence	A. Todd, jr	Pultneyville, N. Y	Nov. 26, 1867	71, 340
Fence	A. Todd, jr	Pultneyville, N. Y	Feb. 4, 1868	74, 017
Fence	A. Todd, jr	Pultneyville, N. Y	Feb. 4, 1868	74, 018
Fence	W. H Trimble	Hillsborough, Ohio	Apr. 27, 1869	89, 521
Fence	M. I. Turck	Schodack, N. Y	Jan. 5, 1869	85, 710
Fence	S. P Tuttle	Decatur, Mich	Dec. 4, 1866	60, 286
Fence	W. Tuttle, jr	Dowagiac, Mich	Sept. 11, 1866	58, 003

Index of patents issued from the United States Patent Office from 1790 *to* 1873, *inclusive*—Continued.

Invention.	Inventor.	Residence.	Date.	No.
Fence	D. M. Tyler	Union Township, Ind	July 5, 1870	105,143
Fence	I. Vanamberg	Watertown, N. Y	Dec. 20, 1843	3,388
Fence	J. H. Van Dorn	Akron, Ohio	Apr. 30, 1872	126,167
Fence	M. Van Wormer	Troy, Ohio	Feb. 15, 1870	99,796
Fence	M. Van Wormer	Troy, Ohio	June 6, 1871	115,663
Fence	J. Waddle	Bakerstown, Pa	Feb. 28, 1871	112,198
Fence	J. F. Warner	Oskaloosa, Iowa	Feb. 13, 1866	52,629
Fence	D. H. Weaver	North Liberty, Ind	June 25, 1872	128,343
Fence	R. M. Weider and J. Meals	Carthage, Ill	Sept. 12, 1871	118,888
Fence	J. L. Wellington	Dansville, N. Y	July 20, 1869	92,917
Fence	I. M. West	Wilmington, Ohio	Aug. 23, 1870	106,640
Fence	T. Westerman	Clinton Township, Pa	Aug. 31, 1869	94,262
Fence	R. H. White	Billingsville, Ind	Apr. 30, 1872	126,362
Fence	J. Whiteside	Coesse, Ind	Sept. 11, 1866	58,013
Fence	H. Wicker	Olean, N. Y	Oct. 19, 1869	95,963
Fence	B. Williams	Williamsburgh, Ohio	June 4, 1872	127,536
Fence	S. P. Williams	Sheridan, N. Y	May 22, 1866	54,989
Fence	S. P. Williams	Sheridan, N. Y	Apr. 2, 1867	63,594
Fence	W. T. Willie	Independence, Tex	Aug. 20, 1872	130,682
Fence	S. A. Wood	Cardington, Ohio	Nov. 16, 1869	96,859
Fence	T. C. Wood	Augusta, Mich	July 4, 1871	116,657
Fence	W. D. Woodruff	Phelps, N. Y	Sept. 5, 1865	49,820
Fence	O. H. Woodworth	Upper Marlborough, Md	Nov. 27, 1860	30,780
Fence	O. H. Woodworth	Columbia City, Ind	Mar. 21, 1865	46,964
Fence	N. Woolsey	Ottawa, Ill	Oct. 11, 1870	108,226
Fence	W. P. Wright	Winamac, Ind	May 17, 1870	103,270
Fence	E. York	Windsor, Ill	May 1, 1866	54,459
Fence	P. C. Yost	Carthage, Ill	Oct. 24, 1871	120,178
Fence	J. Q. A. Youkey and F. M. Rawson.	Frankfort, Ind	Mar. 23, 1869	88,252
Fence adaptable to uneven ground	G. R. McIlroy	Covington, Ky	Feb. 10, 1857	16,598
Fence, Adjustable picket	J. S. Anderson	Flintville, Wis	Jan. 7, 1873	134,624
Fence and gate	E. Muirheid	Greenfield, Ohio	May 3, 1870	102,576
Fence and gate, Combined	C. S. S. Griffing	Geneva, Ohio	Apr. 23, 1867	64,095
Fence and gate combined, Field	J. C. Lee	Seville, Ohio	Oct. 24, 1865	50,605
Fence and pen, Worm	J. Will	Bryan, Ohio	Jan. 14, 1868	73,420
Fence and trellis hook	D. S. Humphrey	East Townsend, Ohio	Dec. 31, 1867	72,856
Fence and trellis post	S. Lamont	Pittsburgh, Pa	Mar. 17, 1868	75,636
Fence-bars, Bracket for	P. Cope	Perryopolis, Pa	Dec. 24, 1872	134,256
Fence-board-gage holder	D. Bordner	Canton, Ohio	Apr. 27, 1869	89,281
Fence-builder	J. M. Kirkpatrick	Utica, Ohio	Jan. 19, 1869	86,081
Fence, Combined wire and stone	H. C. Wire	Wilmington, Ohio	May 10, 1870	102,902
Fence, Farm	C. Abbott	Iowa City, Iowa	June 22, 1869	91,585
Fence, Farm	T. G. Beecher	Beaver Dam, N. Y	Nov. 1, 1859	25,944
Fence, Farm	J. S. Bettis	Hanover, N. Y	Aug. 14, 1866	57,073
Fence, Farm	V. Calkins	Varysburgh, N. Y	Jan. 26, 1869	86,133
Fence, Farm	D. S. Humphrey	East Townsend, Ohio	Oct. 15, 1867	69,809
Fence, Farm	W. Jasper	Columbia, Ohio	Feb. 16, 1869	86,924
Fence, Farm	H. A. Kephart	Fletcher, Ohio	Dec. 24, 1867	72,504
Fence, Farm	P. Kidney	Olmstead Falls, Ohio	July 12, 1870	105,221
Fence, Farm	W. S. McKenzie	Rockwell, Tex	July 29, 1873	141,284
Fence, Farm	E. G. McMillan	Norwalk, Ohio	Nov. 10, 1868	83,871
Fence, Farm	T. W. Owens	Granville, Ohio	July 12, 1870	105,249
Fence, Farm	C. W. Reeder	Trenton, Mo	July 6, 1869	92,359
Fence, Farm	J. K. Staman	Mansfield, Ohio	Mar. 9, 1869	87,597
Fence, Farm	E. Stiles	Cleveland, Ohio	Oct. 15, 1867	69,858
Fence, Farm	S. P. Williams	Sheridan, N. Y	Dec. 10, 1867	72,141
Fence, Farm	E. M. Woodruff	Washington, D. C	July 12, 1864	43,542
Fence, Field	T. H. Bellard	Colbrook, Ohio	Oct. 29, 1867	70,153
Fence, Field	S. H. Bennett	Belleville, Pa	Jan. 13, 1857	16,369
Fence, Field	P. S. Carhartt	Collomer, N. Y	Mar. 2, 1858	19,491
Fence, Field	T. J. Carleton and S. Post	York, Ohio	Jan. 29, 1856	14,152
Fence, Field	S. Cheney	Kiantone, N. Y	Jan. 25, 1859	22,702
Fence, Field	D. S. Curtiss	Madison, Wis	Jan. 25, 1859	22,709
Fence, Field	F. Dickinson	Geneva, Ohio	May 14, 1867	65,641
Fence, Field	J. Drown	Huron, N. Y	Feb. 16, 1858	19,353
Fence, Field	A. Frankboner	Schoolcraft, Mich	Nov. 20, 1866	59,900
Fence, Field	B. Gabriel	Elmira, N. Y	Apr. 20, 1858	19,990
Fence, Field	I. A. Gormly	Bucyrus, Ohio	Jan. 7, 1868	73,090
Fence, Field	I. A. Gormly	Bucyrus, Ohio	Apr. 14, 1868	76,745
Fence, Field	J. Haines	West Middleburgh, Ohio	Oct. 18, 1859	25,821
Fence, Field	J. Heacock	Marlborough, Ohio	June 11, 1867	65,670
Fence, Field	D. M. Heikes	York County, Pa	Aug. 3, 1858	21,073
Fence, Field	T. Hoge	Waynesburgh, Pa	June 15, 1858	20,560
Fence, Field	C. Horton	Phelps, N. Y	Aug. 3, 1858	21,074
Fence, Field	D. S. Humphrey	East Townsend, Ohio	Jan. 7, 1868	73,011
Fence, Field	M. Ingersoll	Elyria, Ohio	June 25, 1867	66,027
Fence, Field	I. G. Inskoop	West Middleburgh, Ohio	Mar. 12, 1861	31,667
Fence, Field	J. H. Jones and N. W. Smith	Lebanon, Ohio	Mar. 9, 1858	19,566
Fence, Field	D. W. Keefer	Leechburgh, Pa	June 15, 1869	91,344
Fence, Field	E. King	Dunkirk, N. Y	Sept. 21, 1869	94,963
Fence, Field	P. W. Kniskern	Monee, Ill	Jan. 24, 1865	46,052
Fence, Field	J. W. Larmore	Harrison, Ohio	July 31, 1866	56,766
Fence, Field	W. H. Leech	Dunlapville, Ind	Oct. 21, 1862	36,719
Fence, Field	E. E. Lewis	Geneva, N. Y	Apr. 27, 1858	20,071
Fence, Field	J. B. Mitchell	Wayne, N. Y	Oct. 19, 1858	21,843
Fence, Field	A. W. Olds	Green Oak, Mich	Mar. 26, 1867	63,290
Fence, Field	D. R. Prindle	East Bethany, N. Y	Apr. 25, 1854	10,829
Fence, Field	S. Rains	Lancaster County, Va	Apr. 7, 1857	16,996
Fence, Field	J. B. Reyman	Salem, Ind	Mar. 25, 1856	14,518
Fence, Field	B. Rowells	Ossian, Ohio	Apr. 6, 1858	19,873
Fence, Field	D. Sattler	Mifflin, Ohio	Jan. 25, 1870	99,112
Fence, Field	F. L. Sexton	Wellington, Ohio	Nov. 22, 1864	45,184
Fence, Field	S. G. Tufts	Maineville, Ohio	Apr. 1, 1856	14,581
Fence, Field	J. L. Wentworth	Spread Eagle, Pa	Oct. 25, 1859	25,925
Fence, Field	W. I. Young	Le Roy, N. Y	July 12, 1864	43,544
Fence, Flexible	M. P. Coons	Lansingburgh, N. Y	July 29, 1851	8,253

Index of patents issued from the United States Patent Office from 1790 *to* 1873, *inclusive*—Continued.

Invention.	Inventor.	Residence.	Date.	No.
Fence, Floating	J. Pitcher	Mount Vernon, Ind	Aug. 27, 1867	68, 232
Fence, Flood	W. F. Auxier	Mason City, Ill	Aug. 3, 1869	93, 161
Fence, Flood	W. C. Barber	Van Wert, Ga	Aug. 10, 1869	93, 398
Fence, Flood	D. P. Bird	Richwood, Ohio	Dec. 29, 1868	85, 271
Fence, Flood	Z. Dowden and C. T. Anderson	Clarksburgh, Md	Mar. 23, 1869	88, 147
Fence, Flood	G. W. Duncan	Columbia, Mo	Dec. 16, 1873	145, 493
Fence, Flood	R. S. Gilcrest	De Graff, Ohio	Feb. 20, 1872	123, 889
Fence, Flood	C. R. Hunter	Douglas, Ill	Feb. 28, 1871	112, 250
Fence, Flood	W. R. McFarland	Paris, Tenn	May 21, 1872	127, 083
Fence, Flood	D. J. Miller	Indianapolis, Ind	July 12, 1870	105, 230
Fence, Flood	H. W. Nichols	Worthfield, Ind	Dec. 10, 1872	133, 795
Fence, Flood	A. Orvis	Ellington, Iowa	May 27, 1873	139, 418
Fence, Flood	H. Reichert	Shippensburgh, Pa	Feb. 27, 1849	6, 138
Fence, Flood	J. L. Seat	Nashville, Tenn	Dec. 19, 1871	122, 067
Fence, Flood	J. Sourbeer	Mount Joy Township, Pa	Jan. 30, 1849	6, 075
Fence, Flood	J. A. Swope	Germany, Pa	Oct. 17, 1848	5, 857
Fence, Flood	D. C. Wilkinson	Sidney, Ohio	Nov. 6, 1860	30, 599
Fence, Flood	J. L. Wines	Hebardsville, Ohio	Sept. 19, 1871	119, 211
Fence, Flood	J. B. Wolfe	Marion, Ohio	Jan. 23, 1872	123, 068
Fence, Flood	V. Wood	Richmond, Ind	June 2, 1868	78, 633
Fence for collecting rain-water for stock	L. Howe	Alamo, Mich	Feb. 18, 1868	74, 690
Fence for crossing streams	W. McFarlin	Jackson, Ill	June 23, 1868	79, 141
Fence for poultry-yard	H. W. Rutt	Reedsburgh, Ohio	Apr. 21, 1868	77, 101
Fence for poultry-yard	W. P. Thomas	Whitewater, Ind	Aug. 25, 1857	18, 064
Fence for preventing injury by floods	W. Miller	Orrstown, Pa	Oct. 2, 1847	5, 313
Fence for rolling ground, Farm	E. D. Foss	Mainville, Ohio	Aug. 19, 1856	15, 561
Fence for sheep-fold	A. P. Hopkins	Bentleysville, Pa	Oct. 14, 1862	36, 651
Fence for stock-pens, Portable prairie	T. Hoge	Waynesburgh, Pa	Dec. 9, 1856	16, 181
Fence foundation	T. W. Welch and G. B. Starbird	Mechanicsburgh, Pa	July 28, 1868	80, 318
Fence-gage	W. V. Van Syckel	Joshua, Ill	May 18, 1869	90, 138
Fence-gate	J. Bailey	Leatherwood, Ohio	Jan. 15, 1850	7, 013
Fence-gate	A. G. Barnard	Seville, Ohio	May 8, 1866	54, 487
Fence-gate	J. S. Benedict	Bedford, Ohio	Mar. 27, 1866	53, 394
Fence-gate	J. S. Benedict	Bedford, Ohio	Oct. 2, 1866	58, 369
Fence-gate	W. W. Bratt	Ottawa, Ill	Dec. 11, 1866	60, 331
Fence-gate	N. Burch	North Fairfield, Ohio	Sept. 3, 1867	68, 553
Fence-gate	J. S. Jewett	Ottawa, Ill	May 5, 1868	77, 492
Fence-gate	J. S. Jewett	Ottawa, Ill	Sept. 1, 1868	81, 640
Fence-gate	F. Raymond and A. Miller	Cleveland, Ohio	Jan. 10, 1865	45, 858
Fence-gate	F. Raymond and A. Miller	Cleveland, Ohio	June 20, 1865	48, 309
Fence-gate	F. Raymond and A. Miller	Cleveland, Ohio	June 26, 1866	55, 906
Fence-gate	M. L. Salyards	Troy Grove, Ill	Mar. 19, 1867	63, 103
Fence-gate	W. F. Veber	Perrysburgh, Ohio	Apr. 23, 1867	64, 171
Fence-gate	B. J. Wheelock	Bedford, Ohio	Nov. 6, 1866	59, 492
Fence gate and gateway	A. Hood	New York, N. Y	Dec. 16, 1845	4, 307
Fence gate, Iron	C. T. Bush	Oneonta, N. Y	Apr. 22, 1873	138, 071
Fence gate post	E. Humphreys	Samsville, Ill	July 13, 1869	92, 451
Fence, Hedge	A. Belt	Newton, Iowa	Mar. 15, 1870	100, 843
Fence, Hedge	S. N. Caldwell	Pilot Grove, Ind	Mar. 30, 1869	88, 445
Fence hook, Wire	A. J. Gill	Denver, Colo	Mar. 5, 1872	124, 349
Fence, Hurdle	C. C. Cole	Rushville, N. Y	Dec. 2, 1851	8, 555
Fence, Iron	C. T. Bush	Middleburgh, N. Y	July 13, 1869	92, 579
Fence, Iron	C. T. Bush	Oneonta, N. Y	Mar. 18, 1873	136, 966
Fence, Iron	M. P. Coons	Brooklyn, N. Y	Apr. 18, 1854	10, 781
Fence, Iron	S. Crowell	Philadelphia, Pa	Oct. 11, 1870	108, 112
Fence, Iron	D. I. De Groat	Newburgh, N. Y	June 15, 1869	91, 310
Fence, Iron	B. G. Devoe	Fredericktown, Ohio	July 15, 1873	140, 897
Fence, Iron	A. Ferry	Waterbury, Conn	Nov. 24, 1868	84, 318
Fence, Iron	W. S. Fuller	Millbury, Mass	Apr. 7, 1857	17, 010
Fence, Iron	J. Gorr	Erie, Pa	Dec. 3, 1872	133, 528
Fence, Iron	P. Hedl	New York	Dec. 18, 1828	....
Fence, Iron	B. F. Miller	New York, N. Y	Nov. 29, 1853	10, 273
Fence, Iron	T. Rogers	Fredericktown, Ohio	Nov. 26, 1872	133, 489
Fence, Iron	T. Rogers	Kenton, Ohio	Dec. 23, 1873	145, 902
Fence, Iron	T. Rogers and B G. Devoe	Kenton, Ohio	Dec. 23, 1873	145, 903
Fence, Iron	S. Sellers and W. Beschke	Philadelphia, Pa	May 7, 1872	126, 417
Fence, Iron	J. B. Wickersham	New York, N. Y	July 1, 1851	8, 189
Fence, Iron	J. B. Wickersham	New York, N. Y	Mar. 9, 1852	8, 793
Fence, Iron	J. B. Wickersham	Philadelphia, Pa	Jan. 21, 1873	135, 188
Fence, Iron	J. B. Wickersham and H. Jenkins.	Brooklyn, N. Y	Aug. 16, 1859	25, 166
Fence, Iron	O. Wilson	Middleburgh, N. Y	Feb. 27, 1872	124, 105
Fence, Iron hurdle	M. P. Coons	Lansingburgh, N. Y	Oct. 17, 1848	5, 863
Fence, Iron picket	M. Walker, sr	Philadelphia, Pa	July 11, 1854	11, 315
Fence-jack	C. Lewis	Nelson, Ohio	Nov. 6, 1866	59, 421
Fence key, Wire	S. B. Hewett, jr	Eagle Grove, Iowa	Mar. 24, 1868	75, 759
Fence, Lattice iron	A. Betteley	Boston, Mass	June 1, 1858	20, 400
Fence-machine	J. H. Evans	Dallas, Ky	Dec. 30, 1873	145, 996
Fence, Metal	H. Noblit	Philadelphia, Pa	Sept. 3, 1861	33, 211
Fence, Metallic	W. Bush	Harrisburgh, Pa	Aug. 3, 1858	21, 064
Fence, Metallic	M. Kelly	New York, N. Y	Nov. 17, 1868	84, 062
Fence, Multigrade iron	M. P. Coons	Brooklyn, N. Y	Nov. 14, 1854	11, 931
Fence of wire, cords, or twine, and seines or nets of wire.	C. Hall	Meriden, Conn	Nov. 27, 1829	....
Fence, Panel	C. W. Sproull	Rome, Ga	July 7, 1868	79, 698
Fence-panel adjuster	F. M. Ranous	Yreka, Cal	July 2, 1872	128, 563
Fence, Picket	G. W. T. Grant	Winona County, Minn	Mar. 5, 1861	31, 594
Fence, Picket	H. N. Hill	Pontiac, Mich	Sept. 14, 1869	94, 824
Fence, Picket	R. H. McGinty	Moulton, Tex	Oct. 14, 1873	143, 632
Fence, Picket	W. Most	Greenville, N. J	May 6, 1873	138, 573
Fence, Picket	J. Willhite	Pilot Point, Tex	Dec. 24, 1872	134, 235
Fence-picket, Corrugated	B. F. Miller	New York, N. Y	July 26, 1864	43, 644
Fence-pickets, Cutting	J. Tichenor, S. Goodrich, and G. A. Hart.	Ithaca, N. Y	June 22, 1836	....
Fence-pickets, Machine for cutting the heads of	A. Burnham	Revere, Mass	Nov. 4, 1873	144, 187
Fence-pickets, Machine for dressing	W. and J. F. Nuelle	Saint Louis, Mo	Dec. 27, 1870	110, 586
Fence-pickets, Machine for sharpening	H. F. Bond	Waltham, Mass	July 30, 1861	32, 960
Fence-pickets, Machine for sharpening	J. A. Montgomery	Columbus, Ohio	Feb. 26, 1867	62, 355

Index of patents issued from the United States Patent Office from 1790 *to* 1873, *inclusive*—Continued.

Invention.	Inventor.	Residence.	Date.	No.
Fence-pickets, &c., Machine for turning	E. Briggs	Perry, N. Y	July 20, 1842	2, 734
Fence, Portable	A. Armitage and J. H. Olmsted	Phelps Township and Arcadia, N. Y.	Nov. 9, 1869	96, 536
Fence, Portable	J. Augspurger	Trenton, Ohio	Apr. 16, 1867	63, 825
Fence, Portable	J. Augspurger	Trenton, Ohio	Apr. 16, 1867	63, 826
Fence, Portable	J. Augspurger	Trenton, Ohio	Apr. 16, 1867	63, 827
Fence, Portable	J. Augspurger	Trenton, Ohio	Apr. 16, 1867	63, 828
Fence, Portable	J. Augspurger	Trenton, Ohio	Apr. 16, 1867	63, 829
Fence, Portable	J. Augspurger	Trenton, Ohio	July 7, 1868	79, 624
Fence, Portable	G. F. Becher	Brooklyn, N. Y	Aug. 12, 1873	141, 750
Fence, Portable	J. Bickhart	Harlan, Ind	June 17, 1862	35, 581
Fence, Portable	J. W. Blodgett	Three Rivers, Mich	Apr. 21, 1863	28, 214
Fence, Portable	L. W. Bosart	Saint Marie, Ill	June 9, 1868	78, 783
Fence, Portable	L. W. Bosart	Saint Marie, Ill	Nov. 10, 1868	83, 911
Fence, Portable	B. F. Brattain	Noblesville, Ind	July 21, 1868	80, 052
Fence, Portable	J. Breneman	Mount Joy, Pa	July 31, 1866	56, 695
Fence, Portable	A. Brooker	Atalissa, Iowa	May 29, 1866	55, 051
Fence, Portable	P. M. Brown	Carrollton, Ill	Dec. 13, 1859	26, 413
Fence, Portable	R. J. Brown	Perry, Pa	Aug. 31, 1858	21, 315
Fence, Portable	S. Bryan	Jefferson, Wis	Oct. 17, 1865	50, 446
Fence, Portable	S. G. Burke	Chambers Court-House, Ala	July 29, 1873	141, 202
Fence, Portable	B. and V. Calkins	Varysburgh, N. Y	Apr. 2, 1867	63, 362
Fence, Portable	G. W. Campbell	Pendleton, Ind	Oct. 29, 1867	70, 162
Fence, Portable	J. T. Campbell	Rockville, Ind	Apr. 16, 1867	63, 853
Fence, Portable	G. S. Carlisle	Columbus City, Iowa	Sept. 4 1866	57, 672
Fence, Portable	Z. Castaline	Baconsburgh, Ohio	Dec. 3, 1867	71, 697
Fence, Portable	P. Chandler	Olney, Ill	June 25, 1867	66, 129
Fence, Portable	P. Chandler	Olney, Ill	Aug. 27, 1867	68, 166
Fence, Portable	J. M. Clark	Lancaster, Pa	Nov. 26, 1867	71, 278
Fence, Portable	F. C. Class	Roanoke, Ind	Oct. 30, 1866	59, 185
Fence, Portable	J. Closs	Decatur, Ind	Oct. 26, 1869	96, 084
Fence, Portable	W. F. Converse	Harrison, Ohio	May 5, 1868	77, 589
Fence, Portable	C. S. Coolidge and J. A. Rollins	Jersey Mills, Pa	Dec. 29, 1868	85. 285
Fence, Portable	W. Corson	Camden, Ohio	June 9, 1868	78, 789
Fence, Portable	W. Crumb	Coloma, Mich	Oct. 4, 1870	107, 883
Fence, Portable	H. M. Dake	Nunda, N. Y	Feb. 25, 1873	136, 217
Fence, Portable	T. Donohoo	Richmond, Mo	Oct. 31, 1871	120, 506
Fence, Portable	J. C. Duncan	Olney, Ill	May 14, 1867	64, 648
Fence, Portable	P. S. Dusenbury	Boscobel, Wis	Jan. 8, 1867	61, 057
Fence, Portable	J. S. Edgar	Janesville, Wis	Jan. 22, 1867	61, 524
Fence, Portable	E. Gale	Kendall, Ill	Nov. 25, 1862	36, 996
Fence, Portable	J. E. Garlington	Chambers Court-House, Ala.	Mar. 18, 1873	136, 989
Fence, Portable	L. Gates	Mount Vernon, Ohio	May 13, 1873	138, 747
Fence, Portable	M. F. Gibbs	Livonia, N. Y	June 4, 1867	65, 372
Fence, Portable	A. C. Gilmore	Centralia, Ill	Oct. 22, 1872	132, 461
Fence, Portable	N. J. Glover	Waveland, Ind	Oct. 8, 1867	69, 654
Fence, Portable	N. J. Glover	Waveland, Ind	Sept. 21, 1869	94, 953
Fence, Portable	W. P. Goff	Yorkville, Wis	Mar. 30, 1869	88, 469
Fence, Portable	C. S. S. Griffing	Unionville, Ohio	Apr. 28, 1868	77, 371
Fence, Portable	F. W. Groff	Indianapolis, Ind	Apr. 13, 1869	88, 782
Fence, Portable	R. Haynes	Oberlin, Ohio	Apr. 7, 1863	38, 108
Fence, Portable	L. and S. D. Hazlett	Winfield Township, Pa	Nov. 16, 1869	96, 805
Fence, Portable	L. F. Henderson	Freeport, Ill	Jan. 7, 1868	73, 098
Fence, Portable	C. R. Hight	Geneva, Ill	June 1, 1869	90, 751
Fence, Portable	J. Hoffman	Hixton, Wis	Sept. 3, 1872	131, 000
Fence, Portable	N. Hornaday	West Elkton, Ohio	Aug. 19, 1862	36, 215
Fence, Portable	O. Huffman	Lucieville, Nebr	June 24, 1873	140, 273
Fence, Portable	J. C. Hughes	Robinson, Ill	Sept. 24, 1867	69, 214
Fence, Portable	G. H. Hume	Paola, Kans	Oct. 29, 1872	132, 534
Fence, Portable	E. Hunt	Hartford, Ind	Aug. 30, 1870	106, 826
Fence, Portable	A. Jewett	Sanford's Corners, N. Y	Oct. 3, 1871	119, 614
Fence, Portable	C. E. Johnson	San Francisco, Cal	Sept. 14, 1869	94, 828
Fence, Portable	R. Johnson	Griffin, Ga	Dec. 23, 1873	145, 875
Fence, Portable	S. Keller	Elizabethtown, Pa	Mar. 17, 1868	75, 551
Fence, Portable	J. Kennel	Morton, Ill	July 5, 1864	43. 415
Fence, Portable	J. Killian	Marshall, Iowa	Oct. 20, 1863	40, 342
Fence, Portable	A. Labair	Pewaukee, Wis	Dec. 31, 1867	72, 863
Fence, Portable	P. Lambkin	Saint Albans, Vt	Jan. 5, 1869	85, 595
Fence, Portable	I. L. Landis	Lancaster, Pa	Apr. 30, 1867	64, 335
Fence, Portable	J. Lefeber	Wayne County, Ind	Apr. 16, 1867	63, 801
Fence, Portable	J. Leonard	Basil, Ohio	June 16, 1868	78, 979
Fence, Portable	S. Leonard, jr	Fairfield County, Conn	Dec. 3, 1867	71, 767
Fence, Portable	A. Love	Saxonburgh, Pa	Dec. 7, 1869	97, 538
Fence, Portable	J. M. May and E. B. Godfrey	Janesville and Oshkosh, Wis.	July 11, 1865	48, 701
Fence, Portable	P. McCollum	Fayette, Mo	June 22, 1869	91, 651
Fence, Portable	G. R. McIlroy	Oakdale, Ind	Sept. 30, 1856	15, 812
Fence, Portable	J. J. McMaken	Middletown, Iowa	Nov. 12, 1872	132, 916
Fence, Portable	G. McQuisten	Cardington, Ohio	Dec. 3, 1872	133, 658
Fence, Portable	S. Miles	Fabius, N. Y	Aug. 6, 1867	67, 564
Fence, Portable	E. D. Montrose	Nashua, Iowa	May 15, 1866	54, 754
Fence, Portable	W. Morrison	Carlisle, Pa	June 9, 1857	17, 514
Fence, Portable	A. Mosher	Canton, Mo	Aug. 5, 1873	141, 584
Fence, Portable	T. Nevison	Morgan, Ohio	May 18, 1869	90, 117
Fence, Portable	H. W. and R. P. Nichols	Northfield, Ind	Sept. 30, 1873	143, 372
Fence, Portable	J. W. Norman	Eugene, Ind	Aug. 4, 1868	80, 657
Fence, Portable	A. W. Olds	Green Oak Station, Mich	Apr. 15, 1878	137, 949
Fence, Portable	A. H. Palmer	Skaneateles, N. Y	Nov. 8, 1864	44, 967
Fence, Portable	L. P. Pease	McCordsville, Ind	Apr. 21, 1868	77, 087
Fence, Portable	D. K. Peterson	Williamsburgh, Ohio	Nov. 19, 1872	133, 116
Fence, Portable	D. Philips	Cordova, Ill	May 18, 1869	90, 300
Fence, Portable	W. W. Potts	Swedeland, Pa	Sept. 16, 1873	142, 865
Fence, Portable	P. M. Purdy	Haysville, Ohio	Feb. 19, 1850	7, 103
Fence, Portable	J. Reber	Shoemakerville, Pa	Apr. 21, 1863	38, 241
Fence, Portable	J. Reedy	Toledo, Iowa	May 15, 1866	54, 772
Fence, Portable	F. Richter	Orange, Ohio	Aug. 27, 1861	33, 163
Fence, Portable	J. R. Robbins	Buttsville, Mo	Dec. 3, 1872	133, 542

Index of patents issued from the United States Patent Office from 1790 *to* 1873, *inclusive*—Continued.

Invention.	Inventor.	Residence.	Date.	No.
Fence, Portable	W. E. Roberts	North Coventry, Pa	Mar. 31, 1868	76, 102
Fence, Portable	G. Robinson	Chillicothe, Mo	Nov. 4, 1873	144, 228
Fence, Portable	H. P. Ross	Hastings, N. Y	Nov. 10, 1863	40, 574
Fence, Portable	C. Rowland	Clinton, Ill	Jan. 16, 1866	52, 080
Fence, Portable	R. Samuel	Walden, N. Y	May 26, 1868	78, 329
Fence, Portable	A. H. Scott	Concord, N. C	Mar. 16, 1869	87, 976
Fence, Portable	H. Sinclair	New York, N. Y	Feb. 7, 1871	111, 578
Fence, Portable	H. D. Smalley	New Baltimore, Ohio	May 5, 1868	77, 544
Fence, Portable	J. O. Smith	Reiley, Ohio	Aug. 2, 1870	106, 088
Fence, Portable	S. C. H. Smith	Belpre, Ohio	Mar. 30, 1869	88, 523
Fence, Portable	F. Sproul	Doniphan, Kans	Mar. 28, 1871	113, 105
Fence, Portable	J. K. Staman	Mifflin, Ohio	June 26, 1866	55, 926
Fence, Portable	H. A. Stewart	Minneapolis, Minn	Feb. 4, 1868	74, 166
Fence, Portable	J. W. Suidter	Sharon, Wis	Apr. 9, 1867	63, 764
Fence, Portable	G. D. Sweigert	Martic Township, Pa	Dec. 10, 1867	72, 113
Fence, Portable	B. L Taylor	Marlin, Tex	Nov. 18, 1873	144, 641
Fence, Portable	C. A. Thomas	Bellbuckle, Tenn	Oct. 28, 1873	144, 165
Fence, Portable	J. Thompson	Williamsburgh, N. Y	May 15, 1866	54, 794
Fence, Portable	J. B. Tillinghast	Racine, Ohio	Apr. 7, 1863	38, 131
Fence, Portable	D. Unthank	Spiceland, Ind	Jan. 8, 1867	61, 123
Fence, Portable	C. Van De Mark	Oak's Corners, N. Y	Mar. 24, 1863	37, 989
Fence, Portable	W. M. Wallace	Cameron, Ill	July 3, 1860	29, 024
Fence, Portable	J. M. Wallis	Milton, Iowa	July 1, 1862	35, 793
Fence, Portable	D. S. Watts	Canton, Miss	Mar. 11, 1873	136, 630
Fence, Portable	J. W. Westbrooks and A. J. Clemmons.	Aberdeen, Miss	Nov. 26, 1872	133, 510
Fence, Portable	T. B. Wickham	Granville, Ohio	May 12, 1868	77, 942
Fence, Portable	H. Willard	Ripon, Wis	July 14, 1868	79, 884
Fence, Portable	H. C. Wilson	West Elkton, Ohio	Mar. 30, 1869	88, 427
Fence, Portable	T. L. Wiswell	Olathe, Kans	July 8, 1873	140, 752
Fence, Portable	G. C. Wright	Westfield, Ohio	Oct. 23, 1866	59, 114
Fence, Portable	E. York	Windsor, Ill	Mar. 5, 1867	62, 718
Fence, Portable extension	A. W. Overholser	Duchoyquet Township, Ohio.	Feb. 11, 1873	135, 837
Fence, Portable farm	H. C. Foote	Jersey City, N. J	Dec. 17, 1861	33, 937
Fence, Portable field	W. B. Burnett	Lyons, N. Y	Dec. 23, 1856	16, 265
Fence, Portable field	P. S. Carhart	Collamer, N. Y	Sept. 21, 1858	21, 549
Fence, Portable field	E. Cole	Fairfield, Mich	May 5, 1857	17, 201
Fence, Portable field	D. Denham	Virden, Ill	Dec. 17, 1861	33, 927
Fence, Portable field	J. J. Friend	Altona, Ill	Jan. 1, 1867	60, 873
Fence, Portable field	T. B. Garside	Danville, Iowa	Aug. 2, 1859	24, 930
Fence, Portable field	E. C. Goddard	Unionville, Ohio	Sept. 17, 1867	68, 976
Fence, Portable field	C. S. S. Griffing	Ashtabula, Ohio	May 24, 1864	42, 849
Fence, Portable field	C. S. S. Griffing	Ashtabula County, Ohio	July 16, 1867	66, 705
Fence, Portable field	M. Hall	Richfield, Ohio	May 29, 1866	55, 091
Fence, Portable field	J. G. Hunt	Reading, Ohio	Dec. 16, 1856	16, 236
Fence, Portable field	J. B. Johnson	Linden, Ind	Aug. 24, 1858	21, 260
Fence, Portable field	B. F. Lyon	Pleasantville, Pa	June 24, 1856	15, 188
Fence, Portable field	G. B. Mallette	Millport, N. Y	Mar. 5, 1861	31, 611
Fence, Portable field	O. H. P. Orendorff	Bloomington, Ill	Nov. 26, 1861	33, 792
Fence, Portable field	T. B. Page	Laurel, Ohio	Dec. 15, 1857	18, 858
Fence, Portable field	L. S. Robison	Gypsum, N. Y	Apr. 20, 1858	20, 005
Fence, Portable field	J. Rowe	Tampa Bay, Fla	Mar. 25, 1856	14, 519
Fence, Portable field	H. F. Stanard	Wayne, Mich	Dec. 22, 1857	18, 934
Fence, Portable field	S. G. Tufts	Mainville, Ohio	May 12, 1857	17, 302
Fence, Portable field	A. B. and M. Vandemark	Phelps, N. Y	Sept. 14, 1858	21, 529
Fence, Portable field	W. Wilson, jr	Raymond, Ill	July 13, 1869	92, 553
Fence, Portable flood	J. B. Stoner	Lacon, Ill	Oct. 15, 1867	69, 861
Fence, Portable folding	A. M. Olds	New York, N. Y	Oct. 6, 1868	82, 865
Fence, Portable gate	J. W. Curtis	Bath, N. Y	Aug. 23, 1870	106, 670
Fence, Portable picket	G. Gross	Buffalo, N. Y	Dec. 20, 1864	45, 490
Fence, Portable picket	G. W. C. Jarvis and C. Graves	Lapeer, Mich	July 20, 1869	92, 727
Fence, Portable picket	A. L. Thorp	Vandalia, Mich	July 17, 1866	56, 465
Fence, Portable wire	L. W. Bosart	Saint Marie, Ill	Mar. 31, 1868	76, 151
Fence-post	C. Ayres	Farmington Centre, Wis	Aug. 15, 1871	117, 963
Fence-post	J. M. Beebe	Cassadaga, N. Y	Mar. 4, 1873	136, 406
Fence-post	R. E. Bowen	Colden, N. Y	Dec. 29, 1868	85, 360
Fence-post	M. K. Butterfield	Eddyville, N. Y	Sept. 21, 1869	95, 178
Fence-post	M. K. Butterfield	Eddyville, N. Y	Feb. 1, 1870	99, 288
Fence-post	S. A. Darrach	Newburgh, N. Y	Aug. 2, 1870	106, 035
Fence-post	H. T. Dewey	Sandusky, Ohio	May 10, 1859	23, 905
Fence-post	H. N. Dunbar	Mentor, Ohio	June 11, 1872	127, 749
Fence-post	H. O. Elmer	Sand Bank, N. Y	Aug. 5, 1873	141, 499
Fence-post	R. M Filson	Willsborough, N. Y	Dec. 20, 1870	110, 221
Fence-post	D. Fisher	Fair Haven, Ohio	Aug. 31, 1869	94, 195
Fence-post	H. K. Flinchbaugh	Conestoga Centre, Pa	Mar. 3, 1868	75, 144
Fence-post	A. M. Freeman, C. P. Idell, and B. Vanderhoven.	Metuchen, N. J	Apr. 2, 1872	125, 189
Fence-post	J. Gibbs	Fremont, Ohio	Sept. 16, 1873	142, 910
Fence-post	A. J. Gill	Denver, Colo	Apr. 18, 1871	113, 872
Fence-post	E. S. Goodrich	Oakland, Wis	Apr. 13, 1869	88, 866
Fence-post	A. W. Gore	Manhattan, Kans	July 2, 1867	66, 321
Fence-post	B. S. Haviland	Fort Dodge, Iowa	Jan. 1, 1867	60, 889
Fence-post	W. D. Hopgood	Henderson, Ky	Jan. 23, 1872	122, 947
Fence-post	W. Hunter	Detroit, Mich	Oct. 23, 1866	59, 023
Fence-post	G. Ipe	Kent, Ohio	Apr. 9, 1867	63, 725
Fence-post	J. F. Keeler	Pittsburgh, Pa	Mar. 19, 1872	124, 686
Fence-post	J. E. and A. H. Kendeigh	Amherst, Ohio	Oct. 8, 1867	69, 680
Fence-post	R. Ketcham	South Dansville, N. Y	Feb. 5, 1867	61, 838
Fence-post	E. King	Dunkirk, N. Y	Sept. 16, 1873	142, 795
Fence-post	O. L. Larkin	Otto, N. Y	Aug. 16, 1870	106, 375
Fence-post	C. Losee	Perrysburgh, N. Y	Sept. 21, 1869	95, 123
Fence-post	W. S. Mayo	New York, N. Y	Sept. 17, 1861	33, 310
Fence-post	P. McDuff	Atchison, Kans	Apr. 21, 1868	77, 066
Fence-post	R. Merrill	Elmira, N. Y	Apr. 6, 1858	19, 863
Fence-post	W. A. Middleton	Harrisburgh, Pa	Aug. 24, 1869	94, 124
Fence-post	W. A. Middleton	Harrisburgh, Pa	Oct. 24, 1871	120, 308
Fence-post	F. Miller	Warsaw, N. Y	Sept. 24, 1872	131, 624

Index of patents issued from the United States Patent Office from 1790 *to* 1873, *inclusive*—Continued.

Invention.	Inventor.	Residence.	Date.	No.
Fence-post	E. G. Nichols	Beaufort, S. C	June 1, 1869	90, 773
Fence-post	D. Oliver	Oxford, Ohio	Aug. 6, 1867	67, 446
Fence-post	J. A. Otis	Watertown, N. Y	Apr. 25, 1871	114, 189
Fence-post	H. S. Palmer	Norvell, Mich	May 21, 1872	127, 099
Fence-post	J. Palmer	Painesville, Ohio	Aug. 9, 1864	43, 790
Fence-post	G. R. Patton	Juda, Wis	Apr. 7, 1868	76, 515
Fence-post	C. Putman and L. S. Totman	Cassadaga, N. Y	June 18, 1872	127, 987
Fence-post	R. Ramsey	New Wilmington, Pa	Dec. 10, 1867	72, 086
Fence-post	I. D. Richards and H. D. Snyder	Carbondale, Pa	May 12, 1868	77, 842
Fence-post	H. S. Ross	Millville, Ohio	Dec. 16, 1873	145, 528
Fence-post	J. Scott	Antwerp, N. Y	Oct. 28, 1873	144, 035
Fence-post	W. H. Shay	Sylvania, Ohio	Dec. 10, 1867	72, 094
Fence-post	C. J. Shuttleworth	Springfield, N. Y	Aug. 2, 1870	105, 988
Fence-post	C. R. Smith	Haverhill, N. H	Feb. 9, 1864	41, 541
Fence-post	H. Vail	Cortland, N. Y	Feb. 1, 1833	......
Fence-post	G. Vanauken	Phelps, N. Y	Sept. 15, 1863	39, 973
Fence-post	G. Webb	Lewiston, Me	Feb. 2, 1869	86, 476
Fence-post base	A. B. Drake	Painesville, Ohio	Oct. 15, 1872	132, 259
Fence-post, Cast-iron	P. Stewart	New Lebanon, N. Y	Mar. 1, 1859	23, 140
Fence-post driver	W. S. Graves	Oberlin, Ohio	Sept. 1, 1868	81, 771
Fence-post driver	J. D. Israel	Utica, Iowa	Aug. 11, 1868	80, 962
Fence-post driver	I. J. Parker	Buffalo Grove, Iowa	July 28, 1868	80, 364
Fence-post driver, Portable	W. Carns	New Cumberland, Ohio	May 31, 1870	103, 716
Fence-post excavator	R. P. Adams	Clinton, Ill	May 23, 1854	10, 952
Fence-post, Iron	J. W. Jenkins	Greenport, N. Y	Aug. 9, 1853	9, 921
Fence post, Iron	M. M. Manly	Philadelphia, Pa	May 7, 1872	126, 406
Fence-post, Iron	W. Merrell	Kent, Ohio	Nov. 10, 1868	84, 985
Fence-post, Metallic	W. A. Middleton	Harrisburgh, Pa	Feb. 16, 1869	86, 935
Fence-post pedestal	G. W. Hatch	Garrettsville, Ohio	May 7, 1867	64, 417
Fence-post pedestal	J. Robbins	Amherst, Ohio	Sept. 17, 1867	68, 902
Fence post, Picket	A. M. Freeman, C. P. Idell, and B. Vanderhoven.	Metuchen, N. J	Nov. 22, 1870	109, 402
Fence-post, Portable	D. M. Graham	Evansville, Ind	Dec. 10, 1867	72, 022
Fence-post socket	J. S. Blood and J. W. Miller	Newport, N. H	July 3, 1860	28, 958
Fence-post socket	G. W. and J. B. Durant	Bryan, Tex	Sept. 9, 1873	142, 687
Fence-post socket	G. Unger	Danville, Pa	May 25, 1869	90, 611
Fence-post stub	G. Lakins	East Norwalk, Ohio	July 29, 1873	141, 362
Fence posts and rails, Machine for mortising and sharpening.	J. A. Snyder	Georgetown, Pa	Jan. 28, 1868	73, 844
Fence posts and ties, Construction of iron	J. B. Wickersham	New York, N. Y	Sept. 16, 1856	15, 750
Fence-posts, Boring-machine for	R. Weems	......	Mar. 16, 1801	......
Fence-posts, Construction of	M. Krumm, jr	Columbus, Ohio	Apr. 14, 1868	76, 637
Fence-posts, Device for bracing and ventilating	C. R. Smith	Haverhill, N. H	Oct. 11, 1859	25, 768
Fence-posts, Device for driving	J. Anderson	Waukesha, Wis	Feb. 27, 1866	52, 811
Fence-posts, Device for securing ends of wire in	W. G. Lavers	New York, N. Y	July 25, 1854	11, 378
Fence-posts, Driving-machine for	D. M. Wotson	Albia, Iowa	July 16, 1872	129, 442
Fence-posts, Machine for boring	J. Agnew	Bath, Pa	Dec. 26, 1865	51, 676
Fence-posts, Machine for boring	J. Temple	Birmingham, Pa	May 1, 1855	12, 808
Fence-posts, Method of attaching the cappings to	R. S. Cadwell	Andover, Ohio	June 14, 1859	24, 373
Fence-posts, Method of constructing	F. G. Johnson	Brooklyn, N. Y	Jan. 27, 1857	16, 486
Fence-posts, Method of driving	G. E. West	Indianapolis, Ind	Aug. 14, 1866	57, 231
Fence-posts, Method of fastening wires to	Z. Knapp	Pittston, Pa	Oct. 24, 1848	5, 864
Fence-posts, Mode of constructing iron	H. S. Brooks and J. S. Lehman	Martickville, Pa	June 2, 1868	78, 572
Fence-posts, Setting	H. W. Clarke	Newport, R. I	Oct. 16, 1866	58, 776
Fence-posts, Setting	W. Fulkerson	Three Rivers, Mich	Sept. 27, 1870	107, 770
Fence, Rail	A. Frayer	Ripley, Ohio	Dec. 24, 1867	72, 473
Fence, Rail	J. W. Mathews	Killbourne, Ohio	Apr. 8, 1873	137, 701
Fence, Rail	E. G. Warner	Union Township, Ohio	Sept. 15, 1868	82, 186
Fence-rails, Machine for pointing	C. Yost	Intercourse, Pa	July 3, 1860	29, 030
Fence-rails, Splicing	D. W. Knowles	Hotchkissville, Conn	Oct. 28, 1873	144, 113
Fence, Self-locking rail	A. Bagley	Ypsilanti, Mich	Jan. 21, 1873	134, 967
Fence, Self-supporting	T. Flinn	Birmingham, Mich	Nov. 2, 1869	96, 411
Fence-stake	J. N. Pease	Panama, N. Y	Oct. 19, 1869	95, 932
Fence, Stream	J. Fryling	Fletcher, Ohio	Aug. 6, 1867	67, 526
Fence, Stream or river	H. A. Kephart	Fletcher, Ohio	Jan. 14, 1868	73, 345
Fence, Suspended portable	A. Skinner	Warren, Mich	Mar. 23, 1869	88, 090
Fence, Wire	P. S. Clinger	Conestoga Centre, Pa	Sept. 13, 1859	25, 387
Fence, Wire	S. F. Dexter	Auburn, N. Y	Aug. 19, 1833	......
Fence, Wire	G. W. Ensminger	Richland, Iowa	Dec. 8, 1868	84, 810
Fence, Wire	E. Gale	Pavilion, Ill	Aug. 18, 1863	39, 563
Fence, Wire	T. Hill, jr	Sturgis, Mich	June 18, 1872	128, 145
Fence, Wire	H. Jenkins	Pottsville, Pa	Feb. 13, 1849	6, 106
Fence, Wire	I. Knapp	Medina, N. Y	June 7, 1864	43, 032
Fence, Wire	G. and L. N. Lakins	East Norwalk and Toledo, Ohio.	Aug. 26, 1873	142, 246
Fence, Wire	J. A. Little	Cartersburgh, Ind	June 24, 1873	140, 147
Fence, Wire	A. H. Mendell	Adams, N. Y	Aug. 3, 1869	93, 326
Fence, Wire	W. H. Meriwether	Comal County, Tex	Nov. 8, 1853	10, 211
Fence, Wire	Z. Nicholson	Haddonfield, N. J	Apr. 25, 1871	114, 029
Fence, Wire	J. W. Norcross	Middletown, Conn	Jan. 10, 1865	45, 872
Fence, Wire	J. W. Rappleye	Farmer Village, N. Y	July 4, 1871	116, 755
Fence, Wire	J. W. Rappleye	Farmer Village, N. Y	Feb. 18, 1873	136, 094
Fence, Wire	J. B. Reyman	Bloomington, Ill	Sept. 29, 1857	18, 301
Fence, Wire	H. M. Rose	Waterman Station, Ill	May 13, 1873	138, 763
Fence, Wire	A. C. Sisson	Factoryville, Pa	Apr. 25, 1871	114, 057
Fence, Wire	L. B. Smith	Kent, Ohio	June 25, 1867	66, 182
Fence, Wire	T. H. Speakman	Philadelphia, Pa	Jan. 16, 1872	122, 862
Fence, Wire	C. A. Wakefield	Pittsfield, Mass	Mar. 14, 1871	112, 658
Fence, Wire	M., sr., M., jr., and D. S. Walker.	Philadelphia, Pa	Mar. 29, 1853	9, 642
Fence, Wire	B. Wilson and F. P. Grimes	Dayton, Ohio	Dec. 6, 1870	109, 858
Fence, Wire and picket	E. C. Patterson	Rochester, N. Y	July 14, 1868	79, 854
Fence, Wood	W. Riley	Madison County, Miss	Apr. 8, 1873	137, 723
Fence, Wood	D. G. Temple	Farmersville, La	Mar. 11, 1873	136, 679
Fence, Wood	R. F. Ward	Senatobia, Miss	Oct. 7, 1873	143, 478
Fences, Apparatus for building sod	C. W. Smith	Morrisville, N. Y	Nov. 23, 1869	97, 130
Fences, Apparatus for stretching wire	J. T. Maugham	Gatesville, Tex	Mar. 4, 1873	136, 528
Fences, Board-holder in making board	J. Wallmer	Goshen, Ind	Nov. 15, 1864	45, 098

Index of patents issued from the United States Patent Office from 1790 *to* 1873, *inclusive*—Continued.

Invention.	Inventor.	Residence.	Date.	No.
Fences, Bore or support for posts of field	O. Spencer	Jacksonburgh, Ohio	Jan. 13, 1857	16, 406
Fences, Brace-post for field	C. Quackenbush	Huron, N. Y	Nov. 30, 1858	22, 202
Fences, Device for connecting panels of field	R. Merrill	Elmira, N. Y	Feb. 23, 1858	19, 434
Fences, Device for connecting panels of portable field.	J. Haines	West Middleburgh, Ohio	Oct. 4, 1859	25, 641
Fences, Device for holding together panels of portable.	O. P. Moran	Haynesville, Mo	Aug. 9, 1859	25, 030
Fences, Device for straining wire	F. H. Crandall	Ontario, N. Y	Jan. 14, 1868	73, 302
Fences, Device for stretching wires of	W. H. Robinson and J. Bebel	Earlville, Ill	Sept. 13, 1864	44, 221
Fences, Device for tightening wire	P. S. Crawford	Union, Ill	Apr. 24, 1866	54, 119
Fences, Device for tightening wire	D. W. Eaton	North Ridge, N. Y	Aug. 24, 1869	93, 976
Fences, Device to allow for contraction and expansion in wire.	T. D. Burk	Chicago, Ill	Apr. 22, 1856	14, 751
Fences, Fastening for wire	W. E. Lockwood	Philadelphia, Pa	Jan. 14, 1868	73, 349
Fences, Flood-gate for	S. D. Hopkins	Brookville, Va	Nov. 20, 1849	6, 892
Fences in the posts, Method of fastening the rails of iron.	J. B. Wickersham	New York, N. Y	Jan. 13, 1857	16, 419
Fences, Iron post for wire	H. K. Flinchbaugh	Conestoga Centre, Pa	Mar. 3, 1868	75, 145
Fences, Iron railing for	S. Crowell	Philadelphia, Pa	May 23, 1865	47, 801
Fences, Machine for boring the posts for post-and-rail.	W. H. Shay	New York, N. Y	Nov. 25, 1839	1, 420
Fences, Machine for excavating and removing earth in making prairie.	J. Sawyer	New York, N. Y	Mar. 23, 1838	652
Fences, Machine for making picket	J. Moore and A. Kelly	Pittsburgh, Pa	Apr. 17, 1860	27, 923
Fences, Machine for making sod	H. L. F. Gavett	Jackson, Mich	Sept. 9, 1851	8, 341
Fences, Machine for making sod	J. Osgood	Blue Hill, Me	Aug. 24, 1869	94, 128
Fences, Machine for mortising posts and sharpening rails for.	W. Mace	New York, N. Y	Mar. 11, 1837	140
Fences, Method of allowing for expansion and contraction of wire.	O. Williams	Saint Louis, Mo	Sept. 7, 1858	21, 459
Fences, Method of clamping and unclamping panels of portable field.	W. B. Burnett	Lyons, N. Y	Apr. 21, 1857	17, 075
Fences, Method of compensating for expansion and contraction of metallic.	L. Eikenberry	Easton, Pa	May 10, 1859	23, 908
Fences, Method of connecting panels of field	S. F. Jones	Milford, Ind	July 7, 1857	17, 742
Fences, Method of connecting panels of field	W. D. Sheldon	Huron, N. Y	Jan. 19, 1858	19, 159
Fences, Method of connecting panels of portable field.	J. H. Bruen	Elmira, N. Y	Dec. 29, 1857	18, 952
Fences, Method of locking and supporting the panels of field.	E. West	Ogden, N. Y	Feb. 15, 1859	22, 994
Fences, Method of uniting and sustaining the panels of portable field.	I. D. Garlick	Lyons, N. Y	May 5, 1857	17, 210
Fences, Method of uniting panels of portable	C. Van De Mark	Oak's Corners, N. Y	June 2, 1857	17, 459
Fences, Mode of building and coating earth	C. A. Strong	Brooklyn, N. Y	May 13, 1862	35, 268
Fences, Mode of constructing prairie	I. Van Kersen	Kalamazoo, Mich	June 2, 1868	78, 622
Fences, Mode of fastening the paling to the rail in iron.	G. Hess	Easton, Pa	Nov. 23, 1852	9, 420
Fences, Mode of making combined wood and wire	G. Fletcher, sr	Greensburgh, Ind	Nov. 17, 1868	84, 180
Fences. Mode of securing to each other the panels of field.	C. P. Garlick and M. G. Blackstone.	Amador, Minn., and Mainville, Ohio.	Feb. 17, 1857	16, 675
Fences, &c., Molding and pressing clay for the construction of.	M. Wright	Tallytown, Pa	May 15, 1841	2, 093
Fences, Ornamental connection of the parts of iron	H. Jenkins	Cincinnati, Ohio	Jan. 13, 1852	8, 654
Fences, Post for field	J. Drown	Huron, N. Y	Jan. 25, 1859	22, 712
Fences, Post for field	H. G. Seekins	Elyria, Ohio	Mar. 23, 1858	19, 724
Fences, Rail for ornamental	E. M. Stigale	Philadelphia, Pa	Dec. 14, 1869	97, 984
Fences, Raising	T. J. Smith	Jackson, Mich	Nov. 17, 1868	84, 141
Fences, Repairing	E. Pitkin	East Hartford, Conn	Dec. 13, 1828	....
Fences, Rivet-clamp for wire	M. P. Coons	Brooklyn, N. Y	June 6, 1854	11, 012
Fences, telegraph-poles, &c., Composition post for	J. L. Boone	San Francisco, Cal	June 4, 1872	127, 552
Fences, Tool for holding and driving staples for wire.	A. C. Betts	Troy, N. Y	Aug. 7, 1866	56, 884
Fences, Triangular brace for locking the panels of field.	C. Van De Mark	Oak's Corners, N. Y	July 27, 1858	21, 037
Fences, Wire-stretcher for	D. J. Denmark and P. P. Hill	Vergil and Alto, Ill	May 21, 1872	126, 939
Fences, Wire-stretcher for	W. B. Hayden	Columbus, Ohio	Aug. 25, 1868	81, 367
Fences, Wire-stretcher for picket	B. F. Alkire	Williamsport, Ohio	Oct. 8, 1872	132, 040
Fences, Wire-tightener for wire	F. Fanning	Atchison, Kans	Apr. 5, 1870	101, 601
Fences, Wire-work for	A. Algoever	New York, N. Y	Jan. 6, 1863	37, 266
Fences, Yielding joint for portable	R. J. Brown	Perry, Pa	Dec. 9, 1856	16, 172
Fencing grounds, Mode of	O. Church	Friendship, N. Y	July 3, 1823	....
Fencing, Machine for making wire	B. Greening	Hamilton, Canada	July 25, 1871	117, 275
Fencing, Machine for manufacturing picket	W. W. Johnson	Clarksburgh, Va	May 17, 1859	24, 029
Fencing, Mode of making clay posts for	W. Cooley	Bolton, Conn	May 27, 1805	....
Fender: *See* Boot and shoe fender. Clod-fender. Cultivator-plow fender. Fire-fender. Gas-bracket fender. Grate-fender. Ice and snow fender. Iron fender. Locomotive-fender. Plow-fender. Ship-fender.				
Fender	G. F. Filley	Saint Louis, Mo	Nov. 4, 1873	144, 269
Fender and ash-sifter combined	W. C. Dobbins	Zanesville, Ohio	Aug. 26, 1873	142, 214
Fender and fire-screen, Combined	J. Miller and W. H. B. Flender	Washington, Pa	July 12, 1870	105, 231
Fender and gage-wheel, Combined	A. B. Thornton	New Berlin, Ill	Feb. 14, 1871	111, 790
Fermentation and distillation	J. E. Siebel	Chicago, Ill	Dec. 3, 1872	133, 677
Fermentation and purification of organic substances.	R. D'Heureuse	New York, N. Y	Feb. 28, 1871	112, 226
Fermentation, Vinous	C. C. Edday	Benton, Miss	Apr. 1, 1842	2, 535
Fermentation, Vinous	C. O. Wolpers	Cincinnati, Ohio	July 16, 1841	2, 169
Fermenting and distilling	J. Stowell	Manchester, N. H	Feb. 5, 1836	....
Fermenting and distilling spirits	I. Belnap	Millersburgh, Pa	July 20, 1827	....
Fermenting apple cider	W. Elder	New Brunswick, N. J	Aug. 21, 1822	....
Fermenting in close vessels, Vinous	A. Harvie and C. Guild	Cincinnati, Ohio	Apr. 25, 1854	10, 814
Fermenting mash	C. H. Frings	Centreton, Mo	June 20, 1871	116, 043
Fermenting-tanks, Preventing waste of alcohol in	C. H. Frings	Centreton, Mo	June 20, 1871	116, 044
Fernery	C. L. Osborn	New York, N. Y	Sept. 28, 1869	95, 255
Ferrotype card-mount	J. H. Daniels	Boston, Mass	Aug. 9, 1864	43, 761

Index of patents issued from the United States Patent Office from 1790 *to* 1873, *inclusive*—Continued.

Invention.	Inventor.	Residence.	Date.	No.
Ferrotype-plate	H. M. Hedden	Worcester, Mass	Mar. 1, 1870	100, 291
Ferrule	S. N. Chapin	New Britain, Conn	Aug. 31, 1869	94, 280
Ferrule	T. W. Detray	Montpelier, Vt	May 29, 1860	28, 458
Ferrule	C. E. Green and J. H. Bodwell	Newark, N. J	Sept. 2, 1873	142, 461
Ferrule	S. E Jeralds	Cheshire, Conn	Dec. 30, 1873	145, 950
Ferrule	D. Moore	Brooklyn, N. Y	Nov. 7, 1871	120, 763
Ferrule	W. H. Rodden	Toronto, Canada	Feb. 7, 1871	111, 573
Ferrule	D. G. Smith	Columbus, Ohio	Apr. 18, 1871	113, 805
Ferrule, Brush	W. F. Lorey	Mendon, N. Y	Mar. 11, 1873	136, 605
Ferrule for boiler-tubes	E. Lawton and T. J. Jones	New York, N. Y., and Summit, N. J.	Apr. 2, 1867	63, 399
Ferrule-making machine, Wire	H. O. Lothrop	Milford, Mass	Oct. 19, 1869	95, 918
Ferrule, Metal socket	T. H. Windle	Westchester, Pa	May 7, 1867	64, 613
Ferrule-tapering apparatus	J. L. Parker	Worcester, Mass	June 27, 1871	116, 479
Ferrules, Machine for forming	W. L. Newsham	Philadelphia, Pa	Dec. 17, 1872	134, 092
Ferrules, Machine for making	R. Briggs	Philadelphia, Pa	Dec. 21, 1869	98, 020
Ferrules, Machine for making	J. Stever and J. A. Way	Bristol, Conn	May 28, 1867	65, 132
Ferrules, Machinery employed in the manufacture of coiled wire.	W. T. Richards	New Haven, Conn	Sept. 14, 1852	9, 262
Ferrules, Manufacture of	A. Shaw	Philadelphia, Pa	Dec. 10, 1867	72, 093
Ferrules, Manufacture of wire	W. T. Richards	New Haven, Conn	Nov. 2, 1852	9, 369
Ferrules, Manufacturing	S. E. Jeralds, H. A. Nettleton, and E. R. Lawton.	West Cheshire, Conn	Sept. 12, 1871	118, 858
Ferrules to handles, Mode of attaching	A. L. Carrier	Washington, D. C	Nov. 12, 1867	70, 694
Ferruling machine, Ring	J. Siddons	Rochester, N. Y	Nov. 24, 1868	84, 311
Ferry-boat	M. D. Brown	Buffalo, Va	Oct. 1, 1830	....
Ferry-boat	H. Clenny	Gallatin, Tenn	June 20, 1871	116, 024
Ferry-boat	T. Cohoon	Pittsfield, Mass	June 25, 1813	....
Ferry-boat for trains of cars	F. Cass	New Orleans, La	Oct. 21, 1873	143, 808
Ferry-boat guard	D. Fitzgerald, T. Rogers, and W. C. Walker.	New York, N. Y	Dec. 19, 1854	12, 094
Ferry-boat locking-apparatus	J. L. Canham	Newark, N. J	Apr. 16, 1867	63, 855
Ferry-boats, Means of stopping and starting	J. Rowland	Brooklyn, N. Y	May 14, 1867	64, 710
Ferry-boats, Operating	J. C. Day	Jersey City, N. J	Nov. 24, 1857	18, 683
Ferry-boats or flying bridges, Means of guiding line.	E. W. Quincy and W. Fisher	Lacon, Ill	Apr. 21, 1868	76, 943
Ferry-boats, Tram-way for	W. A. Jordan	Thibodeaux, La	Aug. 5, 1856	15, 487
Ferrying and draying	N. W. Wheeler	Brooklyn, N. Y	Apr. 25, 1865	47, 479
Fertilizer	L. C. Abernathy	Burlington, Ky	Aug. 18, 1829	....
Fertilizer	J. Althouse	Cross Roads, Pa	May 12, 1868	77, 860
Fertilizer	A. F. Andrews	New Haven, Conn	Aug. 19, 1873	141, 848
Fertilizer	J. W. Bitner	Downsville, Md	Dec. 3, 1867	71, 689
Fertilizer	J. R. Black	Ninety Six, S. C	Apr. 23, 1872	125, 927
Fertilizer	S. A. Burkholder and G. W. Wilson.	Bendersville, Pa	Mar. 30, 1869	88, 443
Fertilizer	W. G. Busey	Georgetown, D. C	Apr. 21, 1868	76, 991
Fertilizer	J. Commins	Charleston, S. C	Feb. 1, 1870	99, 294
Fertilizer	J. Commins	Charleston, S. C	Mar. 15, 1870	100, 729
Fertilizer	B. R. Croasdale	Philadelphia, Pa	Aug. 30, 1870	109, 918
Fertilizer	J. P. Crutchfield	Fayette Corner, Tenn	May 21, 1872	126, 933
Fertilizer	S. O. Doris	Philadelphia, Pa	Dec. 24, 1861	34, 039
Fertilizer	L. S. Fales	Tarrytown, N. Y	Dec. 3, 1867	71, 725
Fertilizer	L. S. Fales	New York, N. Y	Mar. 30, 1869	88, 466
Fertilizer	R. Fish	Washington, D. C	July 20, 1869	92, 810
Fertilizer	J. and A. Fox	Avoca, N. Y	Mar. 12, 1872	124, 487
Fertilizer	W. H. H. Glover	New York, N. Y	July 26, 1864	43, 639
Fertilizer	J. Gould	Lexington, Mass	Feb. 27, 1866	52, 844
Fertilizer	W. C. Grimes	Ladiesburgh, Md	Dec. 10, 1867	72, 026
Fertilizer	W. D. Hall	Hamden, Conn	Dec. 20, 1859	26, 548
Fertilizer	L. Harper	Riceville, N. J	Nov. 22, 1859	26, 184
Fertilizer	L. Harper	Riceville, N. J	Jan. 31, 1860	26, 985
Fertilizer	L. Harper	Brooklyn, N. Y	May 27, 1862	35, 417
Fertilizer	H. A. Hogel	Brooklyn, N. Y	Mar. 22, 1870	101, 131
Fertilizer	J. and A. Hursh	Philadelphia, Pa	June 26, 1866	55, 871
Fertilizer	W. Lalor	Utica, N. Y	May 25, 1869	90, 367
Fertilizer	O. Lugo	New York, N. Y	Nov. 14, 1865	50, 940
Fertilizer	J. J. Mapes	Newark, N. J	Nov. 22, 1859	26, 196
Fertilizer	J. J. Mapes	Newark, N. J	Dec. 20, 1859	26, 507
Fertilizer	J. McDougall	London, England	Feb. 18, 1873	135, 995
Fertilizer	J. K. Moore	Millville, N. J	July 30, 1867	67, 335
Fertilizer	H. E. Pond	Franklin, Mass	Nov. 5, 1867	70, 608
Fertilizer	J. S. Ramsburgh	New Market, Md	May 12, 1868	77, 840
Fertilizer	F. C. Renner	Ladiesburgh, Md	Feb. 5, 1867	61, 870
Fertilizer	F. C. Renner	Ladiesburgh, Md	June 22, 1869	91, 667
Fertilizer	A. Rolland	Toulouse, France	Feb. 7, 1860	27, 072
Fertilizer	A. Smith	Cincinnati, Ohio	Jan. 1, 1867	60, 948
Fertilizer	A. Smith	Cincinnati, Ohio	May 5, 1868	77, 667
Fertilizer	A. Smith	Baltimore, Md	Mar. 23, 1869	88, 223
Fertilizer	F. W. Speyer	Hamburg, Germany	Jan. 25, 1870	99, 255
Fertilizer	L. Stephens	Philadelphia, Pa	May 29, 1860	28, 516
Fertilizer	J. W. Stubbs	Cheraw, S. C	Feb. 25, 1873	136, 277
Fertilizer	T. Taylor	Washington, D. C	Mar. 14, 1871	112, 653
Fertilizer	J. D. Whelpley	Boston, Mass	Sept. 12, 1865	49, 943
Fertilizer	J. Whitehill	Frederick, Md	Apr. 29, 1873	138, 458
Fertilizer	J. W. York	Nolensville, Tenn	Apr. 8, 1873	137, 586
Fertilizer and corn-planter combined	S. H. Wallize	Washingtonville, Pa	Dec. 10, 1867	71, 930
Fertilizer and distributer	C. Salvo	Columbus, Ga	Feb. 7, 1871	111, 685
Fertilizer and planter, Corn	J. M. Stoner	Greenville Lodge, Pa	June 22, 1869	91, 786
Fertilizer and seed-drill	T. B. McConaughey	Newark, Del	Jan. 26, 1869	86, 313
Fertilizer and seeding-machine	A. Putnam	Owego, N. Y	Mar. 7, 1871	112, 49[illegible]
Fertilizer, Artificial	H. E. Pond	Franklin, Mass	Aug. 6, 1867	67, 450
Fertilizer-attachment	C. C. Foster	Odessa, Del	Apr. 28, 1868	77, 269
Fertilizer-attachment	C. C. Foster	Odessa, Del	Sept. 28, 1869	95, 336
Fertilizer-desiccating machine	A. Smith	Baltimore, Md	May 4, 1869	89, 800
Fertilizer-distributer	M. W. Faubion	Parrottsville, Tenn	Sept. 2, 1873	142, 454
Fertilizer-distributer	B. Fickes	North Codorus Township, Pa.	Aug. 20, 1872	130, 707
Fertilizer-distributer	D. F. Halliburton	Rutherford Station, Tenn	Apr. 29, 1873	138, 398

Index of patents issued from the United States Patent Office from 1790 *to* 1873, *inclusive*—Continued.

Invention.	Inventor.	Residence.	Date.	No.
Fertilizer-distributer	J. Lytch	Laurinburgh, N. C	Nov. 11, 1873	144, 465
Fertilizer-distributer	J. A. Morton	New Orleans, La	May 30, 1871	115, 505
Fertilizer-distributer	J. J. Singleton	Forsyth, Ga	Oct. 11, 1870	108, 196
Fertilizer-distributer	W. F. White	Belchertown, Mass	Apr. 23, 1872	126, 118
Fertilizer-distributer	J. M. Wiltsie	Pittsford, N. Y	Feb. 21, 1865	46, 515
Fertilizer-distributer, Broadcast	J. P. Machen	Centreville, Va	June 6, 1871	115, 749
Fertilizer-distributer, corn and cotton-seed planter	R. M. Brooks	Woodbury, Ga	May 10, 1870	102, 910
Fertilizer, Distributing	H. M. Keith	Pontiac, Mich	Oct. 11, 1864	44, 635
Fertilizer distributing machine	J. F. Fisher	Greencastle, Pa	Dec. 15, 1868	84, 870
Fertilizer-distributing machine	S. Hoke	Mount Pleasant Township, Md.	Aug. 27, 1867	68, 077
Fertilizer-distributing machine	J. F. Keller	Hagerstown, Md	June 28, 1870	104, 854
Fertilizer-distributing machine	I. M. Reames	Oxford, N. C	Feb. 11, 1873	135, 846
Fertilizer-distributing machine	W. F. Weirick, J. C. Weller, and D. E. Rohr.	Charlestown, W. Va	Feb. 2, 1869	86, 477
Fertilizer from excrements	F. Wicke, J. Brönner, T. Petersen, and J. G. Zehfuss.	Frankfort, Prussia	Mar. 1, 1870	100, 347
Fertilizer from glue residuum	A. Van Haagen and W. Adamson.	Philadelphia, Pa	Feb. 15, 1870	99, 978
Fertilizer from offal	J. J. Storer	Boston, Mass	Sept. 30, 1873	143, 310
Fertilizer from sea-weed	J. G. Nickerson	Boston, Mass	July 20, 1869	92, 744
Fertilizer from sea-weed	U. S. Treat	Eastport, Me	Sept. 12, 1871	118, 987
Fertilizer of land, Process of preparing greens and marl as a.	C. Stearns	New York, N. Y	May 5, 1857	17, 237
Fertilizer or fish guano	O. Lugo	Baltimore, Md	Feb. 1, 1870	99, 452
Fertilizer or guano	O. Lugo	Baltimore, Md	Dec. 14, 1869	97, 939
Fertilizer or manure	G. F. Wilson	East Providence, R. I	Aug. 11, 1863	39, 519
Fertilizer-spreader	J. W. Thornburg	Woodstock, Va	Apr. 8, 1873	137, 736
Fertilizers and ammoniacal salts, Treating blood for the manufacture of.	J. J. Craven	Jersey City, N. J	Feb. 21, 1871	111, 910
Fertilizers and extracting oils and fats, Manufacture of.	O. Lugo	Baltimore, Md	Feb. 15, 1870	99, 924
Fertilizers and oil from fish, Manufacture of	O. Lugo	Baltimore, Md	May 3, 1870	102, 689
Fertilizers and other articles of manufacture, Machine for disintegrating.	T. Carr	Bristol, Great Britain	June 8, 1869	91, 085
Fertilizers and other materials, Machine for disintegrating, dispersing, and mixing.	T. Carr	Bristol, Great Britain	Aug. 10, 1869	93, 595
Fertilizers and other purposes, Treating blood for the preparation of.	H. A. Hogel	New York, N. Y	Mar. 8, 1870	100, 629
Fertilizers and to destroy offensive gases and vapors, Treating offal to produce.	J. J. Storer	Boston, Mass	Oct. 22, 1872	132, 498
Fertilizers, Apparatus for pulverizing animal matter for.	A. Smith	Cincinnati, Ohio	Apr. 2, 1872	125, 343
Fertilizers, Apparatus for treating animal matter for.	W. L. Bradley	Boston, Mass	Apr. 2, 1872	125, 260
Fertilizers, Apparatus for treating animal matter for.	H. A. Hogel	New York, N. Y	May 2, 1871	114, 508
Fertilizers, Composition for deodorizing and preparing.	T. Sewell	Washington, D. C	May 7, 1872	126, 418
Fertilizers, Composition of matter for disinfecting and preparing.	J. A. Thompson	Auburn, N. Y	July 9, 1867	66, 650
Fertilizers, Compound for	G. Bourgrade	New York, N. Y	Aug. 16, 1870	106, 313
Fertilizers, Cylinder for mixing	L. B. Pitcher	Salina, N. Y	July 26, 1870	105, 839
Fertilizers, &c., Deodorizing animal matter for	E. C. C. Stanford	Glasgow, Scotland	Apr. 15, 1873	137, 969
Fertilizers from animal matter, Process and apparatus for the manufacture of.	C. G. Bruce and M. J. Stein	New York, N. Y	Oct. 15, 1872	132, 244
Fertilizers from animal substances, Manufacture of.	O. Lugo	Baltimore, Md	Feb. 22, 1870	100, 163
Fertilizers from earth, &c., Preparing	S. Brown	New Oxford, Pa	Mar. 26, 1872	125, 017
Fertilizers from fish, &c., Manufacture of	O. Lugo	Baltimore, Md	June 14, 1870	104, 327
Fertilizers from night-soil, Manufacture of	D. J. Loewenstein	New Orleans, La	July 23, 1872	129, 739
Fertilizers, Machine for distributing	J. S. Edwards	Medford, N. J	Mar. 10, 1868	75, 252
Fertilizers, Machine for distributing	Z. N. Morrell	Cameron, Tex	Sept. 27, 1859	25, 574
Fertilizers, Machine for distributing	J. H. Thomas and P. P. Mast	Springfield, Ohio	Apr. 4, 1865	47, 138
Fertilizers, Machine for distributing	J. H. Thomas and P. P. Mast	Springfield, Ohio	Aug. 3, 1869	93, 368
Fertilizers, Machine for sowing	J. F. Keller	Greencastle, Pa	Jan. 8, 1861	31, 084
Fertilizers, Manufacture of	J. Commins	Charleston, S. C	Oct. 4, 1870	107, 878
Fertilizers, Manufacture of	J. Y. Diaz	Havana, Cuba	Mar. 15, 1870	100, 871
Fertilizers, Manufacture of	L. S. Fales	New York, N. Y	June 9, 1868	78, 730
Fertilizers, Manufacture of	D. A. T. Hoeven	Philadelphia, Pa	June 23, 1868	79, 160
Fertilizers, Manufacture of	C. P. Houghton	Georgetown, D. C	Nov. 1, 1870	108, 969
Fertilizers, Manufacture of	F. Klett	Philadelphia, Pa	Sept. 12, 1865	49, 891
Fertilizers, Manufacture of	W. I. Sapp	Baltimore, Md	Apr. 26, 1870	102, 438
Fertilizers, Manufacture of	T. Sim	Baltimore, Md	Aug. 23, 1870	106, 626
Fertilizers, Manufacture of	H. Stevens	Brazoria, Tex	Nov. 25, 1873	144, 877
Fertilizers, Manufacture of	E. Whitley	Murfreesborough, N. C	July 12, 1870	105, 283
Fertilizers, Manufacture of phosphatic	G. F. Wilson	East Providence, R. I	Mar. 10, 1868	75, 325
Fertilizers, Mode of treating mineral phosphates for the manufacture of.	J. Commins	Charleston, S. C	Feb. 25, 1868	74, 799
Fertilizers, Mode of treating mineral phosphates for the manufacture of.	J. Commins	Charleston, S. C	May 19, 1868	78, 061
Fertilizers, Preparation of	W. S. De Zeng	Geneva, N. Y	Nov. 5, 1867	70, 671
Fertilizers, Preparing	G. A. Leinau	Philadelphia, Pa	Mar. 12, 1867	62, 760
Fertilizers, Preparing ammoniated sulphuric acid for the manufacture of.	C. U. Shepard, jr	Charleston, S. C	Mar. 1, 1870	100, 457
Fertilizers, Preparing blood for	W. D. Craven	Jersey City, N. J	Feb. 18, 1873	136, 036
Fertilizers, Process for manufacturing	J. A. Manning	London, England	Jan. 16, 1872	122, 773
Fertilizers, Process for preparing	L. Reid	Barren Island, N. Y	Mar. 24, 1857	16, 882
Fertilizers, &c., Process for treating sewage and ammoniacal water for the production of.	T. Christy, jr., and A. Bobrownicki.	London, England	Mar. 25, 1873	137, 059
Fertilizers, Process of treating offal-gelatine, &c., for the manufacture of.	G. F. Wilson	East Providence, R. I	May 18, 1869	90, 328
Fertilizers to growing plants, Implement for distributing.	D. C. Colby	Claremont, N. H	June 13, 1865	48, 155
Fertilizers, Treating animal matter and manufacturing.	W. C. and R. G. Sillar and C. Rawson.	Blackheath, Bolton, and London, England.	Nov. 19, 1872	133, 125
Fertilizers, Treating animal matter for	H. A. Hogel and A. Edwards	New York, N.Y., and New Haven, Conn.	Nov. 5, 1872	132, 723
Fertilizers, Treating blood for manufacture of	L. S. Fales	New York, N. Y	Feb. 14, 1871	111, 734

Index of patents issued from the United States Patent Office from 1790 to 1873, inclusive—Continued.

Invention.	Inventor.	Residence.	Date.	No.
Fertilizers, Treating bones, horns, hoofs, &c., for manufacture of.	W. B. Johns	Philadelphia, Pa	Feb. 14, 1871	111, 851
Fertilizers, Treating offal and manufacturing	J. J. Storer	Boston, Mass	Jan. 28, 1873	135, 383
Fertilizers, Treating phosphate of lime for manufacture of.	N. A. Pratt	Charleston, S. C	Apr. 9, 1872	125, 613
Fertilizers, Treating refuse animal matter for manufacture of.	W. L. Bradley	Boston, Mass	Feb. 27, 1872	124, 112
Fertilizers, &c., Treating sewage for	H. H. Parish	Rome, Italy	Mar. 26, 1872	126, 074
Fertilizers, &c., Treatment of phosphates for the manufacture of.	N. A. Pratt and G. F. Lewis	Charleston, S. C., and Philadelphia, Pa.	May 21, 1872	126, 904
Fertilizing-composition	J. M. Gallacher	Roxbury, Mass	Apr. 1, 1862	34, 825
Fertilizing-compound	J. M. Deering	Boston, Mass	Apr. 23, 1872	125, 939
Fertilizing-compound	L. S. Fales	Tarrytown, N. Y	Dec 3, 1867	71, 724
Fertilizing-compound	W. B. Hamilton	New Orleans, La	Apr. 25, 1871	114, 133
Fertilizing-compound	J. M. Loewenstein	New Orleans, La	Oct. 18, 1870	108, 369
Fertilizing-compound	J. M. Loewenstein	New Orleans, La	Jan. 31, 1871	111, 357
Fertilizing-compound	E. N. McKimm and H. W. Bender.	Benderville, Pa	June 29, 1869	92, 077
Fertilizing-compound	L. S. Robbins	Brooklyn, N. Y	May 26, 1857	17, 392
Fertilizing-compound, Phosphate	D. Stewart	Port Penn, Del	May 11, 1869	90, 057
Fertilizing distributer	H. N. Sweeney	Worcester, Mass	Apr. 8, 1873	137, 734
Fertilizing purposes, Method of preparing bones for.	D. Stewart	Annapolis, Md	Oct. 11, 1859	25, 772
Fertilizing soil	J. B. Wilson	Townsend's Inlet, N. J	Sept. 23, 1873	143, 213
Fetter for cow's tail	C. F. Tolles	Nashua, N. H	Oct. 21, 1873	143, 943
Fiber and gum fabric	A. F. Bishop, J. M. Pendleton, and J. H. Aiken.	Norwalk, Conn., New York, N. Y., and Norwalk, Conn.	Sept. 1, 1868	81, 740
Fiber and other products from the maize plant, Mode of obtaining.	J. T. Harris	Tyngsborough, Mass	Aug. 31, 1869	94, 411
Fiber, Apparatus and process for treating animal and vegetable.	W. Adamson	Philadelphia, Pa	Sept. 5, 1871	118, 668
Fiber-cleaning machine	J. Brown	Bay Ridge, N. Y	July 4, 1871	116, 546
Fiber-cleaning machine	C. A. Dean	Boston, Mass	Aug. 29, 1871	118, 591
Fiber-cleaning machine	S. T. Lamb	Boston, Mass	June 17, 1873	140, 050
Fiber, Composition for preserving and water-proofing vegetable.	G. A. Cowles, J. P. Case, and V. Vieuow.	New York, N. Y	Sept. 20, 1864	44, 285
Fiber, Disintegrating	C. Heaton	New York, N. Y	Mar. 13, 1866	53, 247
Fiber, Disintegrating	C. Heaton	New York, N. Y	Mar. 13, 1866	53, 248
Fiber, Disintegrating and separating vegetable	G. E. Sellers	Seller's Landing, Ill	Feb. 9, 1864	41, 538
Fiber, Disintegrating vegetable	C. Heaton	New York, N. Y	Aug. 1, 1865	49, 106
Fiber, Disintegrating vegetable	R. W. Russell	New York, N. Y	Sept. 17, 1872	131, 465
Fiber, &c., Disintegration of vegetable substances for the separation of.	G. E. Sellers	Hardin County, Ill	Nov. 10, 1863	40, 576
Fiber-disintegrator	A. Berthet and P. Laberie	New Orleans, La	Dec. 16, 1873	145, 613
Fiber drier, Disintegrated	W. Adamson	Philadelphia, Pa	Nov. 29, 1870	109, 706
Fiber during manufacture, Mode of preventing mildew or injury to.	E. T. Rice	New York, N. Y	Oct. 27, 1868	83, 409
Fiber, Engine for reducing rags, &c., to	J. McCracken	Bloomfield, N. J	Aug. 21, 1866	57, 355
Fiber for stuffing mattress and cushion, Preparing vegetable.	W. Staufen	Prussia	Dec. 23, 1856	16, 293
Fiber for textile and other fabrics, Preparing vegetable.	H. Messmer	Newark, N. J	Aug. 20, 1867	67, 997
Fiber from bamboo, Preparing	P. Lichtenstadt	New York, N. Y	Feb. 16, 1864	41, 627
Fiber from bamboo, &c., Preparing	L. S. Robbins and J. A. Southmayd.	New York, N. Y., and Elizabeth, N. J.	Feb. 23, 1869	87, 295
Fiber from mulberry-tree, Method of separating	W. Holdmann	New York, N. Y	Aug. 4, 1868	80, 737
Fiber from pine-leaves for hygienic and other purposes.	A. Roque	Brire, France	Jan. 1, 1867	60, 940
Fiber from plants, Machinery for separating	J. A. De Brame	New York, N. Y	Dec. 2, 1862	37, 081
Fiber from plants, Machinery for separating	G. Sanford	New York, N. Y	June 24, 1862	35, 708
Fiber from seed, Machine for separating	A. B. Ely	Newton, Mass	Apr. 2, 1867	63, 373
Fiber from sisal grass and like substances, Machine for preparing.	G. E. Hopkins and W. B. Shedd	Boston, Mass	Dec. 20, 1870	110, 237
Fiber from waste felted fabrics, Obtaining	J. F. Greene	Brooklyn, N. Y	Apr. 12, 1859	23, 642
Fiber from wood and other substances, Separating	M. R. Fletcher	Cambridgeport, Mass	Feb. 11, 1868	74, 332
Fiber from woody portion of tropical plants, Machinery for separating.	J. Lilley	Birkenhead, England	Dec. 5, 1854	12, 025
Fiber, Machine for separating from the stalk and twisting woody.	H. W. Bowen	Providence, R. I	Oct. 20, 1863	40, 322
Fiber, Machine for treating vegetable	G. Sanford	New York, N. Y	Feb. 19, 1861	31, 479
Fiber, Machinery for cleaning vegetable	C. Brody	New York, N. Y	Sept. 24, 1861	33, 333
Fiber, Manufacturing Asclepias syriaca	M. Gerrish	Salem, Mass	Mar. 27, 1834	....
Fiber, Method of preserving vegetable	T. P. Shaffner	Louisville, Ky	June 5, 1866	55, 371
Fiber, Mode of treating and separating vegetable	J. R. Haskell	New York, N. Y	Mar. 19, 1867	63, 044
Fiber of banana, plantain, aloe, &c., Machine for preparing the.	F. Burke	Montserrat, West Indies	June 2, 1857	17, 420
Fiber of plants, Machine for preparing	E. J. y Patrullo	New York, N. Y	Jan. 15, 1867	61, 244
Fiber of straw, &c., Separating	A. S. Lyman	New York, N. Y	Nov. 24, 1863	40, 696
Fiber of tropical plants, Machinery for separating the.	E. J. y Patrullo	New York, N. Y	Apr. 28, 1863	38, 330
Fiber of various materials are united with adhesive mixtures, Machinery for the manufacture of stuffs in which.	T. R. Williams	Newport, R. I	Apr. 24, 1840	1, 559
Fiber, Plastic compound made from vegetable	W. H. Pierson	New Orleans, La	May 28, 1867	65, 267
Fiber, Preparation of vegetable	J. J. Stover	Portsmouth, N. H	Apr. 12, 1864	42, 319
Fiber, Preparation of vegetable	D. A. Wells	Cambridge, Mass	Apr. 4, 1854	10, 727
Fiber, Preparing and treating vegetable	C. Heaton	New York, N. Y	Sept. 3, 1867	68, 363
Fiber, Preparing vegetable	J. Blanc	New Orleans, La	Oct. 9, 1855	13, 636
Fiber, Process for preparing vegetable	C. J. Pownall	Addison Road, England	Apr. 5, 1853	9, 650
Fiber, Process for removing mineral, gummy, and resinous substances from vegetable.	A. Meucci	Clifton, N. Y	Mar. 28, 1865	47, 068
Fiber, Process of obtaining useful	D. Bickford	Boston, Mass	Oct. 15, 1867	69, 752
Fiber, Process of obtaining vegetable	W. Adamson	Philadelphia, Pa	Apr. 23, 1872	126, 006
Fiber, Process of obtaining vegetable	W. Adamson and C. F. A. Simonin.	Philadelphia, Pa	Aug. 8, 1871	117, 852
Fiber, Process of treating vegetable	P. Claussen	London, England	June 3, 1851	8, 134
Fiber, Process of treating vegetable	S. Knowles	Trenton, N. J	Feb. 14, 1854	10, 518
Fiber, Process of treating vegetable	E. T. Rice	New York, N. Y	June 29, 1869	92, 098

Index of patents issued from the United States Patent Office from 1790 *to* 1873, *inclusive*—Continued.

Invention.	Inventor.	Residence.	Date.	No.
Fiber, Process of treating vegetable substances to obtain.	B. C. Tilghman	Philadelphia, Pa	July 6, 1869	92, 229
Fiber, Reducing long staple	S. M. Allen	Woburn, Mass	Mar. 10, 1863	37, 846
Fiber, Separating animal from vegetable	J. Stuart	London, England	Sept. 27, 1870	107, 833
Fiber, Separating gummy and silicious matter from vegetable.	C. Heaton	New York, N. Y	Apr. 18, 1865	47, 301
Fiber, Separating vegetable	W. E. Woodbridge	Little Falls, N. Y	Sept. 15, 1863	39, 981
Fiber, Separating vegetable	W. E. Woodbridge	Little Falls, N. Y	June 24, 1873	140, 333
Fiber to pulp, Process of reducing wood	T. B. Armitage	New York, N. Y	June 10, 1873	139, 646
Fiber winding and twisting machine	H. Parmelee	Philadelphia, Pa	July 10, 1866	56, 258
Fibrous and porous materials, Impregnating	S. Gwynn	New York, N. Y	Feb. 21, 1865	46, 466
Fibrous and textile substances, Apparatus for washing and bleaching.	J. A. Jillson and H. Whinfield	Poughkeepsie and New York, N. Y.	Oct. 9, 1855	13, 650
Fibrous and textile substances in a vacuum for cleansing purposes, Method of treating.	J. A. Jillson and H. Whinfield	Poughkeepsie and New York, N. Y.	Sept. 15, 1857	18, 204
Fibrous-composition tube	R. W. Russell	New York, N. Y	Mar. 30, 1869	88, 518
Fibrous material	P. Higginbotham	Hernando, Fla	Nov. 19, 1867	71, 066
Fibrous materials, Combing	J. Heilmann	France	Nov. 29, 1853	10, 289
Fibrous materials from corn-stalks	J. A. Roth	Philadelphia, Pa	Feb. 16, 1864	41, 642
Fibrous materials, Lubricating-compound for use in the manufacture of.	C. Clark	Dayton, Ky	Jan. 5, 1869	85, 642
Fibrous materials, Machine for breaking, scutching, and separating.	E. Brasier	New Cross, England	May 17, 1870	103, 135
Fibrous materials, Machine for cleaning	C. G. Sargent	Graniteville, Mass	Dec. 3, 1861	33, 852
Fibrous materials, Machine for cleaning and blending.	A. J. Loiseau	Philadelphia, Pa	Aug. 6, 1867	67, 559
Fibrous materials, Machine for combing	C. Whipple	Providence, R. I	Apr. 19, 1859	23, 732
Fibrous materials, Machine for combing	M. D. Whipple	Charlestown, Mass	Mar. 17, 1857	16, 865
Fibrous materials, Machine for disintegrating and pulping.	J. C. Beach and J. Abbey	Bloomfield and Orange, N. J.	Apr. 16, 1867	63, 832
Fibrous materials, Machine for picking	O. Woodsworth, jr., and J. D. Page.	East Hartford, Conn	Mar. 9, 1858	19, 600
Fibrous materials, Machine for picking and opening.	S. Baxendale	Boston, Mass	Oct. 9, 1866	58, 711
Fibrous materials, Machine for reducing	R. Daniels	Woodstock, Vt	Jan. 22, 1861	31, 154
Fibrous materials, Machine for sizing	W. Fuzzard	Chelsea, Mass	Dec. 4, 1866	60, 167
Fibrous materials, Machine for surface-sizing	W. Fuzzard	Chelsea, Mass	Jan. 12, 1864	41, 214
Fibrous materials, Machine for surface-sizing	W. Fuzzard	Malden, Mass	Aug. 9, 1864	43, 765
Fibrous materials, Machinery for picking	R. Kitson	Lowell, Mass	Sept. 18, 1855	13, 578
Fibrous materials, Machinery for washing and drying.	C. G. Sargent	Graniteville, Mass	May 24, 1870	103, 506
Fibrous materials, Manufacturing sheets of	W. Fuzzard	Charlestown, Mass	Sept. 18, 1860	30, 058
Fibrous materials, Method of cleansing	J. Howarth	Salem, Mass	Mar. 17, 1857	16, 838
Fibrous materials, Method of reducing long staple	S. M. Allen	Niagara Falls, N. Y	Apr. 17, 1860	27, 878
Fibrous materials, Picker for	L. Ferguson	Lowell, Mass	Aug. 14, 1866	57, 109
Fibrous materials, Picking-cylinder of machine for disintegrating.	S. Boydon	Newark, N. J	Feb. 7, 1865	46, 294
Fibrous materials, Preparation of	J. Woodruff and F. Boyd	Quincy, Ill	May 17, 1870	103, 115
Fibrous materials, Surfacing	W. Fuzzard	Charlestown, Mass	June 19, 1860	28, 745
Fibrous materials to textile stock, Apparatus for reducing.	L. Dean	Fort Edward, N. Y	Aug. 9, 1870	106, 133
Fibrous materials to textile stock, Boiler for reducing.	L. Dean	Fort Edward, N. Y	Aug. 9, 1870	106, 135
Fibrous plants from pulpy matter, Machine for separating.	J. R. Beckwith	New Orleans, La	Sept. 12, 1865	51, 413
Fibrous plants, Machine for disintegrating	J. Evans	Newark, N. J	Sept. 26, 1865	50, 108
Fibrous plants, Method of utilizing waste extracts of.	G. E. Sellers	Seller's Landing, Ill	Jan. 22, 1867	61, 364
Fibrous plants, Treatment of	S. M. Allen	Niagara Falls, N. Y	Mar. 20, 1860	27, 507
Fibrous stock, Machine for working waste	A. W. Johnson	Worcester, Mass	Feb. 2, 1869	86, 409
Fibrous substances, Apparatus for washing	W. Adamson	Philadelphia, Pa	Mar. 5, 1867	62, 517
Fibrous substances, Drawing	J. B. Fuller	Norwich, Conn	Aug. 25, 1868	81, 489
Fibrous substances, Machine for cutting and working.	A. W. Hale	New York, N. Y	Dec. 17, 1867	72, 393
Fibrous substances, Machine for separating the pulp from.	G. Sanford	Bergen Point, N. J	Nov. 17, 1868	84, 070
Fibrous substances, Machinery for twisting	G. W. Pittman	Bushwick, N. Y	Jan. 25, 1859	22, 745
Fibrous substances, Mode of reducing vegetable	J. R. Haskell	New York, N. Y	Mar. 19, 1867	63, 043
Fid	H. H. Pember	New York, N. Y	Mar. 12, 1867	62, 880
Fid	S. H. Sugett	Eden, Me	Mar. 10, 1863	37, 879
Field-battery, Magazine	J. O. Whitcomb	New York, N. Y	Apr. 28, 1863	38, 350
Field-gates, Operating	A. J. Curtis	Frankfort, Mo	Oct. 18, 1859	25, 812
Field-press	E. J. Marsters	Shaw's Flat, Cal	Nov. 16, 1869	96, 822
Field-roller	W. W. Andrew	Grand Rapids, Mich	Nov. 10, 1868	83, 818
Field-roller	A. W. Brinkerhoff and A. J. Failor.	Upper Sandusky, Ohio	Sept. 2, 1862	36, 336
Field-roller	A. L. Chubb	Grand Rapids, Mich	June 30, 1868	79, 456
Field-roller	O. B. Colcord	Greenville, Ill	May 14, 1867	64, 748
Field-roller	G. H. Dow	Freeport, Ill	Nov. 14, 1871	120, 950
Field-roller	C. Dunham	Bedford, Ohio	Oct. 20, 1863	40, 380
Field-roller	R. Glover	Tonawanda, N. Y	Dec. 14, 1869	97, 905
Field-roller	A. S. Keagy	Harristown, Ill	Apr. 5, 1870	101, 626
Field-roller	J. M. Kelly	Ellison, Ill	Aug. 29, 1871	118, 616
Field-roller	G. Lindley	Chicago, Ill	May 31, 1859	24, 219
Field-roller	R. A. McConaughy	Ripley, Ohio	Sept. 6, 1870	107, 074
Field-roller	E. F. Olds	South Lyon, Mich	May 7, 1867	64, 559
Field-roller	J. C. Pease	Sycamore, Ohio	Jan. 8, 1861	31, 087
Field-roller	D. R. Prindle	East Bethany, N. Y	May 5, 1868	77, 523
Field-roller	A. Rogers	Freeport, Ill	Nov. 28, 1871	121, 424
Field-roller	W. M. Sunderland	Highgate, Vt	Dec. 15, 1863	40, 961
Field-roller	W. Westfall	Chelsea, Mich	Nov. 17, 1868	84, 150
Field-roller and furrowing-machine	M. M. Robbins	Centreville, Ind	Oct. 4, 1870	107, 056
Field-roller for cutting stalks and weeds	J. H. Gest	Batavia, Ohio	Dec. 14, 1852	9, 463
Fife	J. Pfaff	Philadelphia, Pa	Nov. 29, 1864	45, 270
Fife	J. W. Tanner	New York, N. Y	July 5, 1864	43, 458
Fife and flute	A. H. Stratton	New York, N. Y	May 2, 1865	47, 582
Fifth-wheel	A. Finley	Bainbridge, Ind	Dec. 5, 1871	121, 603
Fifth-wheel	J. Irving	New York, N. Y	Dec. 18, 1866	60, 634

Index of patents issued from the United States Patent Office from 1790 *to* 1873, *inclusive*—Continued.

Invention.	Inventor.	Residence.	Date.	No.
Fifth-wheel	J. Le Roy	Marathon, N. Y	Nov. 29, 1870	109, 636
Fifth-wheel	W. Munson	Abington, Pa	Mar. 23, 1869	88, 196
Fifth-wheel	J. Skeen	Mound City, Ill	May 23, 1871	115, 245
Fifth-wheel	R. D. Wilson	Pittston, Pa	Jan. 2, 1872	122, 425
Fifth-wheel and attachment	J. Skeen	Mound City, Ill	May 23, 1871	115, 246
Fifth-wheel and coupling for vehicles	E. W. Silsby	Ottumwa, Iowa	Sept. 26, 1871	119, 417
Fifth-wheel bender	G. W. Heckart	Columbiana, Ohio	Sept. 8, 1868	81, 902
Fifth-wheel-bending machine	G. W. Heckart	New Lisbon, Ohio	Oct. 5, 1869	95, 585
Fifth-wheel-bending machine	W. J. Jordan	New Lisbon, Ohio	Mar. 15, 1870	100, 903
Fifth-wheel die, Carriage	D. Wilcox	Birmingham, Conn	Oct. 29, 1872	132, 705
Fifth-wheel for carriages	E. H. Adams	Detroit, Mich	June 30, 1868	79, 429
Fifth-wheel for carriages	W. A. Collins	Bloomfield, N. J	July 5, 1870	104, 932
Fifth-wheel for carriages	D. D. Decker	Saugerties, N. Y	Nov. 16, 1869	96, 898
Fifth-wheel for carriages	J. Deeble	Plantsville, Conn	July 23, 1867	66, 956
Fifth-wheel for carriages	P. S. Eastman	Washington Mills, N. Y	May 9, 1871	114, 539
Fifth-wheel for carriages	R. Hoadly	Toulon, Ill	Dec. 14, 1869	97, 919
Fifth-wheel for carriages	D. A. Johnson	Boston, Mass	Apr. 9, 1872	125, 397
Fifth-wheel for carriages	J. Lawrence	Palmyra, N. Y	Dec. 10, 1867	72, 051
Fifth-wheel for carriages	H. A. Luttgens	Paterson, N. J	Jan. 14, 1873	134, 907
Fifth-wheel for carriages	J. A. Peck	Taunton, Mass	Nov. 23, 1869	97, 111
Fifth-wheel for carriages	H. Poth	Pittsburgh, Pa	Mar. 2, 1869	87, 429
Fifth-wheel for carriages	H. W. Ransom	Lawrenceburgh, Ind	Feb. 11, 1868	74, 422
Fifth-wheel for carriages	H. Sayler	Saint Paris, Ohio	Aug. 23, 1870	106, 731
Fifth-wheel for carriages	R. M. Stivers and G. W. V. Smith	New York, N. Y	Aug. 26, 1862	36, 310
Fifth-wheel for carriages	C. St. James	Pittsfield, Mass	Nov. 16, 1869	96, 846
Fifth-wheel for carriages	D. Weaver	Dayton, Ohio	Aug. 3, 1869	93, 376
Fifth-wheel for carriages	D. Wilcox	Birmingham, Conn	Aug. 3, 1869	93, 261
Fifth-wheel for carriages	E. Yeiser	Sheridan, Pa	Aug. 25, 1868	81, 452
Fifth-wheel for vehicles	G. A. Brice	Townville, Pa	July 8, 1873	140, 676
Fifth-wheel for vehicles	E. G. Cameron	Tiffin, Ohio	Mar. 23, 1869	88, 007
Fifth-wheel for vehicles	P. H. Cummins	Adams, N. Y	Aug. 22, 1871	118, 347
Fifth-wheel for vehicles	J. Du Bois	Kingston, N. Y	May 14, 1872	126, 790
Fifth-wheel for vehicles	H. T. Goodale	Clinton, Mass	Mar. 9, 1858	19, 558
Fifth-wheel for vehicles	J. R. McGuire	Ansonia, Conn	Dec. 30, 1873	145, 959
Fifth-wheel for vehicles	S. Moreland	Covington, Ky	May 21, 1872	127, 093
Fifth-wheel for vehicles	U. Reynolds	New York, N. Y	May 22, 1866	54, 958
Fifth-wheel for vehicles	J. P. Smith	Hillsborough, Ohio	May 23, 1871	115, 122
Fifth-wheel for wagons	J. B. Stuart	Bunker Hill, Ill	Apr. 30, 1867	64, 380
Fifth-wheel for wagons, Machine for bending	C. Kieser	Baltimore, Md	July 30, 1861	32, 947
Fifth-wheel head for carriages	R. R. Miller	Plantsville, Conn	Feb. 22, 1870	100, 177
Fifth-wheel-head-forging die	F. Van Patten	Auburn, N. Y	Nov. 29 1870	109, 781
Fifth-wheel heads, Die for manufacture of	F. Van Patten	Auburn, N. Y	Aug. 12, 1873	141, 682
Fifth-wheel-milling machine, Vehicle	F. Van Patten	Auburn, N. Y	Aug. 12, 1873	141, 683
Fifth-wheel of fire-engines and other vehicles	R. Poole	Baltimore, Md	Aug. 16, 1859	25, 164
Fifth-wheel of whiffletree attachment for carriages	F. Van Patten	Auburn, N. Y	Feb. 5, 1867	61, 776
Fifth-wheels, Bending	W. Morgey	Wilmington, Del	July 7, 1868	79, 677
Fifth-wheels for carriages, Bearing for	S. B. Smith	Salem, N. J	Apr. 14, 1868	76, 667
Fifth-wheels for carriages, &c., Manufacture of	D. Wilcox	Derby, Conn	Mar. 25, 1873	137, 274
Fifth-wheels, Keep and brace for	F. B. Morse	Plantsville, Conn	Mar. 21, 1871	112, 950
Fifth-wheels, Machine for forming	G. Feightner	Wooster, Ohio	Apr. 21, 1868	76, 899
Figured fabrics, Manufacturing	J. Smith	Shaefferstown, Pa	Aug. 4, 1834	....
File	P. Cinquini	West Meriden, Conn	Apr. 3, 1860	27, 691
File	J. H. Clark	Washington, D. C	July 5, 1870	105, 044
File	G. B. Cubberley	Milwaukee, Wis	June 2, 1868	78, 435
File	H. Disston	Philadelphia, Pa	Sept. 2, 1873	142, 445
File	H. A. Harvey	New York, N. Y	Oct. 18, 1864	44, 724
File	J. U. Houston	West Meriden, Conn	Jan. 19, 1858	19, 143
File	A. Hyland	Hingham, Mass	May 16, 1871	114, 824
File	J. B. Johnson	San Francisco, Cal	Apr. 29, 1873	138, 256
File	C. M. Nes	York, Pa	Dec. 10, 1872	133, 793
File	W. T. Nicholson	Providence, R. I	Sept. 11, 1866	58, 025
File	H. B. Nickerson	Boston, Mass	Mar. 17, 1868	75, 568
File	H. B. Nickerson	Boston, Mass	May 16, 1871	114, 962
File	I. N. Patten	Memphis, Tenn	Oct. 17, 1871	119, 947
File	G. M. Ramsay	New York, N. Y	Aug. 12, 1856	15, 525
File	A. Thompson	Norway, Me	Nov. 16, 1869	97, 002
File	A. Weed	Boston, Mass	Sept. 3, 1867	68, 584
File	M. D. Whipple	Cambridge, Mass	Apr. 1, 1862	34, 866
File	H. Young	Carey, Ohio	Sept. 17, 1867	68, 929
File and binder, Letter	E. Buell and J. W. Lilley	Columbus, Ohio	July 8, 1873	140, 610
File and binder, Paper	L. P. Keech	Brooklyn, N. Y	Sept. 2, 1873	142, 541
File and rasp	F. C. Curio	Lancaster, Pa	July 28, 1868	80, 460
File and rasp	H. Powers	Florence, Italy	Oct. 4, 1853	10, 088
File, Bill	C. W. Bond	Biddeford, Me	Nov. 10, 1868	83, 908
File, Bill and letter	A. J. Marshall	North Buffalo, N. Y	Jan. 7, 1873	134, 554
File, Bill and paper	W. H. Foye	Portland, Me	Dec. 16, 1873	145, 497
File, Bill and paper	T. Orton	Chicago, Ill	Dec. 2, 1873	145, 230
File, Bill and paper	G. T. Wolcott	Detroit, Mich	June 24, 1873	140, 177
File-blanks, Apparatus for grinding	S. O. Morse	Medford, Mass	May 5, 1863	38, 403
File-blanks, flyers, &c., Machine for rolling, shaping, and forging.	J. Dodge	Waterford, N. Y	May 1, 1866	54, 310
File-blanks, Grinding	A. B. Southwick	Ballard Vale, Mass	Feb. 3, 1863	37, 603
File-blanks, Machine for cutting teeth of	H. B. Nickerson	Boston, Mass	Nov. 5, 1867	70, 458
File-blanks, Machine for forging	W. T. Nicholson	Providence, R. I	Jan. 10, 1865	45, 850
File-blanks, Machine for grinding	J. S. Brown	Pawtucket, R. I.	June 7, 1864	43, 005
File-blanks, Machine for grinding	E. Norton	Boston, Mass	May 5, 1868	77, 646
File-blanks, Machine for grinding	R. G. Pine	Newark, N. J	Feb. 3, 1857	16, 552
File-blanks, Machine for rolling	P. D. Cummings	Portland, Me	Nov. 13, 1866	59, 561
File-blanks, Machine for rolling	J. B. Mignault	Chelsea, Mass	Mar. 6, 1866	53, 025
File-blanks, Machine for rolling	C. Spofford and A. B. Southwick.	Ballard Vale, Mass	May 5, 1863	38, 454
File-blanks, Machine for rolling	M. D. Whipple	Cambridge, Mass	May 31, 1864	42, 981
File-blanks, Machine for stripping	A. Marshall and A. B. Southwick.	Lawrence and Ballard Vale, Mass.	Sept. 1, 1863	39, 775
File-blanks, Machinery for grinding the edge of	H. E. Grandy and S. O. Morse	Ballard Vale and Medford, Mass.	Sept. 15, 1863	39, 992
File-blanks, Rolling	J. N. Aspinwall	Newark, N. J	May 13, 1856	14, 897
File-box, Paper	J. H. Bentley	Cambridge, Mass	June 10, 1873	139, 653

Index of patents issued from the United States Patent Office from 1790 *to* 1873, *inclusive*—Continued.

Invention.	Inventor.	Residence.	Date.	No.
File-clasp for document, &c	I. S. Richardson	Boston, Mass	Jan. 30, 1866	52, 323
File-cutter	G. F. Card and C. A. Studley	Bridgeport, Conn	Nov. 26, 1867	71, 362
File-cutter	P. J. Carlsson	Andovor, Mass	Jan. 17, 1871	110, 956
File cutting and making machine	C. Jackson	Butternuts, N. Y	May 28, 1813	....
File-cutting apparatus	S. A. Sutton	Pawtucket, R. I	July 30, 1867	67, 374
File-cutting engine	N. Starr	Middletown, Conn	Oct. 17, 1848	5, 869
File-cutting machine	L. Anderson	Kensington, Pa	Nov. 16, 1841	2, 365
File-cutting machine	J. K. Barker	Lawrence, Mass	Aug. 8, 1865	49, 214
File-cutting machine	M. B. Belknap	Brimfield, Mass	Jan. 16, 1812	....
File-cutting machine	M. B. Belknap	Worcester, Mass	June 13, 1812	....
File-cutting machine	E. Bernot	Paris, France	July 24, 1860	29, 236
File-cutting machine	E. Bucklin, jr	Pawtucket, R. I	Feb. 27, 1866	52, 926
File-cutting machine	E. Bucklin, jr	North Providence, R. I	Sept. 17, 1867	68, 946
File-cutting machine	T. Burr	Hastings, Mich	Mar. 20, 1860	27, 591
File-cutting machine	T. Burr	Battle Creek, Mich	Nov. 3, 1863	40, 534
File-cutting machine	A. Chambers	North Providence, R. I	Mar 13, 1866	53, 113
File-cutting machine	I. H. Coller	Poughkeepsie, N. Y	Feb. 24, 1857	16, 681
File-cutting machine	H. B. Corner	Pittsburgh, Pa	Sept. 4, 1866	57, 680
File-cutting machine	J. C. Cooke	Middletown, Conn	July 10, 1860	29, 130
File-cutting machine	J. C. Cooke	Middletown, Conn	Feb. 20, 1866	52, 804
File-cutting machine	M. G. Crane	Boston, Mass	Mar. 14, 1865	46, 780
File-cutting machine	J. E. Crisp	Charlestown, Mass	June 11, 1872	127, 854
File-cutting machine	J. D. Crocker	Norwich, Conn	Feb. 28, 1865	46, 545
File-cutting machine	G. Crosby	Baltimore, Md	Dec. 4, 1849	6, 922
File-cutting machine	J. Dodge	Manchester, England	Mar. 7, 1871	112, 430
File-cutting machine	A. B. Ely	Newton, Mass	Jan. 22, 1867	61, 410
File cutting machine	M. H. Fisher	Bridgeport, Conn	Jan. 13, 1863	37, 419
File-cutting machine	G. W. Fogg	South Dedham, Mass	Dec. 14, 1858	22, 329
File-cutting machine	I. Goodspeed	Norwich, Conn	Jan. 1, 1867	60, 878
File-cutting machine	W. Halliwell and L. Osborn	Poughkeepsie, N. Y	Aug. 4, 1857	17, 928
File-cutting machine	C. Hesser and A. Paxson	Philadelphia, Pa	Apr. 11, 1812	....
File-cutting machine	S. Hoke	Union City, Ind	Jan. 13, 1863	37, 398
File-cutting machine	H. Hotchkiss	Waterbury, Conn	July 24, 1855	13, 310
File-cutting machine	J. N. Jacobs	Worcester, Mass	Apr. 6, 1858	19, 854
File-cutting machine	W. F. James	Greenwich, N. Y	Nov. 19, 1812	....
File-cutting machine	J. Jervis	Baltimore, Md	Oct. 11, 1864	44, 633
File-cutting machine	J. Jervis	Baltimore, Md	Oct. 24, 1865	50, 595
File-cutting machine	J. Jervis	Baltimore, Md	Oct. 12, 1869	95, 804
File-cutting machine	A. F. Johnson and M. P. Griffin	Medford, Mass	Jan. 22, 1867	61, 341
File-cutting machine	W. McGregor	Manchester, England	Oct. 1, 1872	131, 767
File-cutting machine	J. B. Mignault	Boston, Mass	Jan. 28, 1868	73, 824
File-cutting machine	C. Miller and T. W. Decker	New York, N. Y	Apr. 12, 1859	23, 645
File-cutting machine	G. Miller	New York, N. Y	Apr. 3, 1866	53, 650
File-cutting machine	W. T. Nicholson	Providence, R. I	Apr. 5, 1864	42, 216
File-cutting machine	W. T. Nicholson	Providence, R. I	Apr. 5, 1864	42, 217
File-cutting machine	W. T. Nicholson	Providence, R. I	June 9, 1868	78, 681
File-cutting machine	J. L. Norton	Alum Bank, Pa	May 13, 1856	14, 881
File-cutting machine	E. O. Potter	Pawtucket, R. I	Nov. 8, 1864	44, 998
File-cutting machine	E. O. Potter	Pawtucket, R. I	Apr. 30, 1867	64, 396
File-cutting machine	A. N. Redman	Charlestown, Mass	Apr. 23, 1867	64, 033
File-cutting machine	J. Rieppel	Renovo, Pa	July 30, 1872	130, 076
File-cutting machine	J. Rotherham and J. Holden	Middletown, N. Y	May 8, 1866	54, 606
File-cutting machine	T. Schultz and C. Renne	Hoboken, N. J., and New York, N. Y.	June 1, 1869	90, 788
File-cutting machine	A. B. Southwick	Ballard Vale, Mass	Jan. 27, 1863	37, 552
File-cutting machine	S. A. Sutton	Dixon, Ill	Aug. 4, 1868	80, 679
File-cutting machine	J. H. Thompson	Paterson, N. J	Jan. 27, 1852	8, 697
File-cutting machine	T. E. Thurston	Newark, N. J	July 14, 1868	79, 878
File-cutting machine	W. Van Anden	Poughkeepsie, N. Y	July 7, 1857	17, 760
File-cutting machine	W. Van Anden	Poughkeepsie, N. Y	Aug. 14, 1860	29, 641
File-cutting machine	S. Vanstone	Providence, R. I	Apr. 29, 1862	35, 130
File-cutting machine	C. Vogel	New York, N. Y	Jan. 22, 1867	61, 486
File-cutting machine	C. Vogel	New York, N. Y	Jan. 21, 1873	135, 179
File-cutting machine	S. Walton	Ballard Vale, Mass	Sept. 10, 1867	68, 815
File-cutting machine	A. Weed	Boston, Mass	Mar. 14, 1865	46, 865
File-cutting machine	A. Weed	Boston, Mass	Mar. 13, 1866	53, 204
File-cutting machine	A. Weed	Boston, Mass	Feb. 20, 1872	123, 849
File-cutting machine	A. Weed	Boston, Mass	July 29, 1873	141, 500
File-cutting machine	M. D. Whipple	Charlestown, Mass	Feb. 1, 1859	22, 842
File-cutting machine	M. D. Whipple	Cambridge, Mass	Apr. 1, 1862	34, 865
File-cutting machine	M. D. Whipple	Cambridgeport, Mass	Jan. 27, 1863	37, 554
File-cutting machine	M. D. Whipple	Boston, Mass	Oct. 24, 1865	50, 647
File-cutting machine	S. Whipple	Albany, N. Y	Feb. 12, 1845	3, 914
File-cutting machines, Feeding-mechanism for	C. E. Moore	Boston, Mass	May 16, 1871	114, 957
File-cutting machinery	J. C. Blair	Pittsburgh, Pa	Apr. 27, 1852	8, 901
File-cutting machinery	J. W. Conklin, H. L. Sidman, and E. Whritner.	Ramapo, N. Y	Aug. 17, 1852	9, 194
File-cutting machinery	J. Crum	Ramapo, N. Y	July 1, 1851	8, 199
File-cutting machinery	M. H. Fisher	Bridgewater, Mass	Aug. 28, 1846	4, 728
File-cutting machinery	J. Hatch	Dedham, Mass	May 1, 1815	....
File cutting machinery	J. Hatch	Roxbury, Mass	Oct. 11, 1828	....
File-cutting machinery	R. Walker	Portsmouth, N. H	June 12, 1847	5, 149
File-fastener	E. P. McCeney	Washington, D. C	Aug. 11, 1868	80, 986
File for dressing metal	W. T. Nicholson	Providence, R. I	Sept. 27, 1864	44, 443
File for grooving rolls	H. L. Butts	Norwich, Conn	Apr. 14, 1868	76, 599
File-guiding machine	I. H. Spencer	Pawtucket, R. I	July 25, 1865	49, 042
File-griping handle	A. Weed	Boston, Mass	Feb. 6, 1872	123, 433
File-handle	H. K. Austin	Charlestown, Mass	Feb. 11, 1873	135, 684
File-handle	B. Boardman	Norwich, Conn	Dec. 1, 1868	84, 529
File-handle	W. W. Draper	Greenfield, Mass	Jan. 18, 1859	22, 635
File-handle	C. F. Hunter	Adrian, Mich	Aug. 30, 1864	43, 994
File-handle	D. Pfouts	Empire Mills, near Wincsburgh, Ohio.	Aug. 1, 1871	117, 677
File-handle	H. C. Storrs	New York, N. Y	Apr. 28, 1868	77, 332
File-handle	A. Weed	Boston, Mass	Sept. 3, 1867	68, 585
File handle, Surface	J. Weare	Fitchburgh, Mass	July 7, 1868	79, 709
File-holder	A. P. Brown	Worcester, Mass	Apr. 20, 1869	89, 019
File-holder	W. C. McGill	Cincinnati, Ohio	Dec. 12, 1865	51, 470

Index of patents issued from the United States Patent Office from 1790 *to* 1873, *inclusive*—Continued.

Invention.	Inventor.	Residence.	Date.	No.
File holder, Newspaper	W. Bright	Saint Louis, Mo	Jan. 21, 1873	134, 974
File-hook	G. W. Schramm	Brooklyn, N. Y	July 5, 1864	43, 432
File, Horse-tooth	J. P. Howell	Washingtonville, N. Y	May 5, 1863	38, 391
File, Letter	F. Ashley	New York, N. Y	Aug. 21, 1866	57, 274
File, Letter	F. Ashley	New York, N. Y	Oct. 1, 1867	69, 385
File, Letter	J. C. Hadden	New York, N. Y	Apr. 10, 1866	53, 817
File, Letter	J. W. Hauxhurst	New York, N. Y	Oct. 24, 1865	50, 580
File, Letter	J. H. Shipman	Yorkville, N. Y	Aug. 30, 1859	25, 282
File, Letter	A. E. Taylor	New Britain, Conn	Aug. 25, 1868	81, 559
File, Letter and music	R. B. Irwin	New York, N. Y	Dec. 6, 1864	45, 327
File, Letter and paper	W. C. Choate	Washington, D C	Mar. 13, 1866	53, 114
File, Letter-box	T. K. Sterrett and W. R. Farrell	Philadelphia, Pa	Oct. 30, 1866	59, 287
File, Letter or invoice	R. Boeklen	Brooklyn, N. Y	Oct. 24, 1865	50, 652
File-machine	E. B. Rollins	Poland, N. Y	May 17, 1870	103, 240
File-machine	G. S. Tiffany and H. Ingraham	Palmyra and Tecumseh, Mich.	Feb. 26, 1861	31, 581
File, Newspaper	J. H. Atwater	Providence, R. I	Nov. 10, 1863	40, 545
File, Newspaper	W. Burnet	Providence, R. I	Jan. 31, 1865	46, 072
File, Newspaper	G. Coope	New York, N. Y	Aug. 6, 1872	130, 197
File, Newspaper	J. W. Foard	San Francisco, Cal	May 1, 1866	54, 320
File, Newspaper	J. Frick	Philadelphia, Pa	Aug. 29, 1865	49, 620
File, Newspaper	L. P. McCarty	San Francisco, Cal	Feb. 18, 1868	74, 562
File, Newspaper	W. R. McNorton	Livingston, Ala	Aug. 20, 1872	130, 649
File, Newspaper	L. C. Prindle	Chicago, Ill	Aug. 10, 1869	93, 475
File, Newspaper	J. Robson	Chicago, Ill	Sept. 28, 1869	95, 380
File, Newspaper	R. K. Ville	New York, N. Y	July 2, 1872	128, 681
File, Newspaper	H. S. White	Newport, R. I	Jan. 22, 1861	31, 200
File, Newspaper	H. S. White	Newport, R. I	Apr. 2, 1861	31, 919
File or bill-holder	T. W. Brown	Boston, Mass	Apr. 25, 1854	10, 820
File or binder, Paper	B. J. Beck	Brooklyn, N. Y	July 6, 1869	92, 251
File or holder, Document	H. E. Woodbury	Washington, D. C	Aug. 8, 1854	11, 504
File or ready binder for filing pamphlets, letters, papers, &c.	I. Detterer	Philadelphia, Pa	May 22, 1841	2, 105
File, Pamphlet	R. M. Abercrombie	Rahway, N. J	Dec. 27, 1864	45, 570
File, Paper	J. Adair	Pittsburgh, Pa	Dec. 31, 1867	72, 711
File, Paper	S. Angell	Providence, R. I	Apr. 22, 1834	....
File, Paper	H. J. Asthalter	Pittsburgh, Pa	Oct. 24, 1871	120, 227
File, &c., Paper	A. Baker	Appleton, Wis	Apr. 18, 1871	113, 721
File, Paper	G. W. Billow	Shelby, Ohio	Jan. 14, 1873	134, 724
File, Paper	R. Boeklen	Brooklyn, N. Y	May 14, 1867	64, 624
File, Paper	J. W. Boughton	New York, N. Y	June 30, 1868	79, 441
File, Paper	W. Boyrer	New York, N. Y	June 21, 1870	104, 415
File, Paper	S. Brock	Brooklyn, N. Y	Jan. 21, 1868	73, 572
File, Paper	F. Bühle	Newark, N. J	Oct. 8, 1867	69, 539
File, Paper	H. Burgess	San Francisco, Cal	Oct. 12, 1869	95, 766
File, Paper	W. Burnet	New York, N. Y	Jan. 10, 1865	45, 813
File, Paper	J. and J. Cash, jr	Coventry, England	Aug. 30, 1870	102, 778
File, Paper	C. Chapman	Chicago, Ill	Oct. 17, 1871	119, 917
File, Paper	W. Z. W. Chapman	New York, N. Y	Mar. 30, 1858	19, 748
File, Paper	E. Clark	New York, N. Y	May 8, 1860	28, 234
File, Paper	W. R. Clough	Cambridge, Mass	Aug. 18, 1868	81, 253
File, Paper	L. Cohn	Montreal, Canada	Dec. 19, 1871	121, 993
File, Paper	W. A. Collord	Cincinnati, Ohio	Sept. 17, 1850	7, 648
File, Paper	L. B. Covert	Chicago, Ill	Apr. 23, 1867	64, 679
File, Paper	M. Craft	Bellaire, Ohio	Nov. 11, 1873	144, 512
File, Paper	E. H. Craige	Brooklyn, N. Y	Nov. 17, 1868	84, 172
File, Paper	G. Crandell	Washington, D. C	Apr. 16, 1867	63, 785
File, Paper	E. J. Crane	La Porte, Ind	May 10, 1870	102, 918
File, Paper	A. Day	Detroit, Mich	June 14, 1870	104, 122
File, Paper	P. W. Derham	Brooklyn, N. Y	July 20, 1869	92, 925
File, Paper	P. W. Derham	New York, N. Y	Aug. 26, 1873	142, 213
File, Paper	E. D. Dodd	Cincinnati, Ohio	Jan. 15, 1850	7, 018
File, Paper	G. W. Emerson	Chicago, Ill	Apr. 26, 1870	102, 237
File, Paper	G. W. Emerson	Chicago, Ill	Apr. 25, 1871	113, 991
File, Paper	T. C. Fahnestock	Cincinnati, Ohio	June 7, 1870	104, 002
File, Paper	W. Fallon	Washington, D. C	Nov. 12, 1867	70, 708
File, Paper	J. D. Field	Wataga, Ill	Dec. 22, 1868	85, 078
File, Paper	J. Fleischl	New York, N. Y	Jan. 1, 1867	60, 710
File, Paper	J. G. Floyd, jr	New York, N. Y	Jan. 31, 1871	111, 335
File, Paper	J. W. Foard	San Francisco, Cal	Jan. 2, 1872	122, 314
File, Paper	J. O. Foster	Pecatonica, Ill	Feb. 23, 1869	87, 161
File, Paper	J. M. D. France	Washington, D. C	Dec. 8, 1868	84, 738
File, Paper	E. K. Godfrey	New York, N. Y	Dec. 21, 1858	22, 363
File, Paper	S. E. Harrison	Jersey City, N. J	Apr. 23, 1872	126, 053
File, Paper	R. Henning	Ottawa, Ill	Apr. 22, 1873	138, 086
File, Paper	B. F. Herr	Livingston, Ala	Nov. 30, 1869	97, 397
File, Paper	A. Hockett	Wilmington, Ohio	Mar. 22, 1870	101, 130
File, Paper	L. P. Keech	Washington, D. C	Mar. 26, 1872	124, 961
File, Paper	L. P. Keech	New York, N. Y	Nov. 5, 1872	132, 836
File, Paper	J. W. Kinsley	Boston, Mass	Oct. 8, 1872	132, 085
File, Paper	G. Lautenschlager	New York, N. Y	July 4, 1865	48, 568
File, Paper	A. Liebenroth	New York, N. Y	May 22, 1860	28, 438
File, Paper	C. D. Lindsey	Cincinnati, Ohio	Apr. 15, 1873	137, 851
File, Paper	C. Mason	New York, N. Y	June 3, 1873	139, [illegible]92
File, Paper	J. Matthias	New York, N. Y	Oct. 22, 1872	132, 478
File, Paper	T. E. Moore	Columbus, Ohio	July 5, 1870	105, 114
File, Paper	E. Motz	Woodward, Pa	Jan. 21, 1873	135, 144
File, Paper	B. Ney and H. Hofheimer	Alexandria, Va	Oct. 27, 1868	83, 5[illegible]1
File, Paper	C. M. O'Hara	New York, N. Y	Jan. 30, 1872	123, 2[illegible]8
File, Paper	L. H. Olmsted	Brooklyn, N. Y	Dec. 1, 1868	84, 505
File, Paper	J. J. Parker	Marietta, Ohio	Nov. 29, 1859	26, 285
File, Paper	S. E. Pettee and C. A. Wolle	Bethlehem, Pa	Oct. 25, 1870	108, 623
File-Paper	J. P. Quarles	Richmond, Va	Apr. 19, 1870	102, 153
File, Baper	R. Rathbone	New York, N. Y	July 22, 1873	141, 170
File, Paper	A. S. Richards	Montgomery County, Md	June 15, 1869	91, 268
File, Paper	G. Rowe	London, England	Aug. 1, 1871	117, 688
File, Paper	W. W. Russell	Malden, Mass	Nov. 15, 1870	109, 253
File, Paper	F. C. Senseman	Philadelphia, Pa	Aug. 2, 1870	10[illegible], 987

Index of patents issued from the United States Patent Office from 1790 *to* 1873, *inclusive*—Continued.

Invention.	Inventor.	Residence.	Date.	No.
File, Paper	J. A. Shannon	Perrysburgh, Ohio	Dec. 5, 1871	121, 671
File, Paper	E. J. Smith and P. H. Cheever	Washington, D. C.	Apr. 14, 1868	76, 834
File, Paper	H. L. Smith	Cleveland, Ohio	June 7, 1853	9, 776
File, Paper	A. P. Stephens	Brooklyn, N. Y	Mar. 9, 1869	87, 598
File, Paper	D. A. Stiles	West Meriden, Conn	June 9, 1857	17, 526
File, Paper	M. Sullivan and J. Reedy	New York, N. Y	Mar. 2, 1869	87, 443
File, Paper	C. Tabor	Craftsbury, Vt	Sept. 27, 1870	107, 836
File, Paper	J. F. Tapley	Springfield, Mass	Feb. 14, 1871	111, 886
File, Paper	J. P. Terrell and S. G. Brett	Somerville, Mass	Feb. 9, 1869	86, 712
File, Paper	E. H. Thompson	Washington, D. C	Sept. 5, 1871	118, 757
File, Paper	S. Thompson	San Pedro, Cal	Nov. 3, 1863	40, 518
File, Paper	J. P. Tirrell and H. Whitney	Charlestown and Watertown, Mass.	Apr. 27, 1869	89, 358
File, Paper	C. W. West	Shiloh, N. J	Dec. 14, 1869	97, 999
File, Paper	F. W. Whitney	Brooklyn, N. Y	Nov. 8, 1870	109, 085
File, Paper	D. Winslow and P. D. Cummings.	Westbrook and Portland, Me.	Aug. 30, 1853	9, 979
File, Paper	J. F. Winter	Brooklyn, N. Y	July 15, 1873	140, 863
File, Paper	J. Wolfe	Washington, D. C	Dec. 10, 1867	72, 146
File, Paper	E. W. Woodruff and G. C. Green	Washington, D. C	Mar. 31, 1868	76, 287
File, Paper	E. W. Woodruff and G. C. Green	Washington, D. C	Apr. 14, 1868	76, 872
File, Paper	W. L. Woods	Washington, D. C	Aug. 12, 1862	36, 200
File, Paper	W. L. Woods	Washington, D. C	June 9, 1863	38, 868
File, Paper	W. L. Woods	Washington, D. C	Feb. 14, 1865	46, 415
File, Paper	W. L. Woods	Washington, D. C	Oct. 25, 1870	108, 746
File, Paper	T. P. Yates	Concord, N. H	Oct. 22, 1861	33, 554
File, Paper	S. W. Young	Providence, R. I	May 2, 1871	114, 504
File, Paper and letter	J. B. McEnally	Clearfield, Pa	Feb. 28, 1860	27, 302
File, Paper and letter	H. Riggs	Oxford, Conn	Dec. 12, 1865	51, 520
File, Portable	C. A. Cook	Chicago, Ill	Dec. 17, 1872	133, 923
File, Portfolio	P. W. Toy	New York, N. Y	June 22, 1858	20, 670
File, Portfolio paper	J. N. Jacobs	Worcester, Mass	June 19, 1860	28, 755
File, Prescription	A. D. Foster	Council Bluffs, Iowa	Apr. 29, 1873	138, 390
File, Rat-tail	R. Flint	Meriden, Conn	July 24, 1846	4, 660
File, Saw	W. Roberts	Blue Hill, Me	June 1, 1869	90, 784
File-stripping apparatus	T. Coldwell	Matteawan, N. Y	Sept. 11, 1866	57, 869
File-supporter	J. B. Woodruff and B. M. Townsend.	Washington, D. C., and Quincy, Ill.	Nov. 6, 1849	6, 858
Files and rasps, Composition for recutting	A. Van Camp	Washington, D. C	Mar. 9, 1869	87, 733
Files and rasps, Manufacture of	T. Sheehan	Dunkirk, N. Y	Feb. 5, 1861	31, 331
Files and rasps, Mode of hardening and repairing	C. A. Clavel	Paris, France	July 26, 1864	43, 658
Files, Compound for cleaning, biting, or sharpening damaged.	A. P. and E. Brittingham	New York, N. Y	July 27, 1829	....
Files, Construction of round and half-round	J. N. Jacobs	Worcester, Mass	Aug. 9, 1864	43, 775
Files, Cutting	M. H. Fisher	Sing Sing, N. Y	Feb. 5, 1856	14, 189
Files, Cutting	E. Gebbe	Northampton County, Pa	Oct. 10, 1811	....
Files, Cutting	S. Hawes	Bennington, Vt	May 11, 1814	....
Files, Cutting	C. Miller	New York, N. Y	Nov. 11, 1856	16, 064
Files, Cutting	C. and D. Platt	Sharon, Conn	Mar. 7, 1814	....
Files, Cutting round	M. D. Whipple	Charlestown, Mass	Oct. 7, 1856	15, 867
Files for papers, accounts, &c., Construction of screw-nuts for.	W. Mann	Philadelphia, Pa	July 3, 1840	1, 673
Files, Machine for grinding half-round	T. Smith and J. A. Stafford	Charlestown and Boston, Mass.	Sept. 1, 1863	39, 782
Files, Machine for manufacturing	L. and D. Anderson	Philadelphia, Pa	Apr. 20, 1812	....
Files, Manufacture of	M. D. Whipple	Charlestown, Mass	June 26, 1860	28, 947
Files, Method of making	T. S. Smith	Cincinnati, Ohio	June 21, 1870	104, 507
Files, Method of restoring	T. James	Newport, England	Feb. 13, 1872	123, 705
Files, &c., Method of sharpening	W. B. Gillett	Auburn, N. Y	Feb. 7, 1860	27, 046
Files, Mode of repairing	A. A. Dunk	Manchester, N. H	July 31, 1866	56, 734
Files, &c., Process and apparatus for hardening	S. Darling	Providence, R. I	July 12, 1870	105, 180
Files, Process of hardening	J. Russell	Sing Sing, N. Y	Feb. 6, 1866	52, 450
Files, Process of recutting	A. I. Ferguson	Sharon, Pa	Jan. 21, 1868	73, 590
Files, Process of recutting	X. Robert	Worcester, Mass	June 15, 1869	91, 271
Files, rasps, and sickles, Machine for cutting	S. G. White	Haverhill, Mass	July 11, 1812	....
Files, saw-blades, &c., Machine for tempering	J. Small	Saint Louis, Mo	Nov. 12, 1867	70, 755
Files, saws, &c., Machine for tempering	J. Small	Saint Louis, Mo	Aug. 15, 1865	49, 451
Files, Tip for saw	H. Disston	Philadelphia, Pa	Sept. 16, 1873	142, 900
Filing-case, Numerical	G. W. Bettesworth	Cedar Rapids, Iowa	Nov. 18, 1873	144, 593
Filing-machine	A. G. Burton and H. W. Covert	Rochester, N. Y	Nov 20, 1866	59, 741
Filing-machine	M. Fiedler	Rochester, N. Y	Mar. 10, 1868	75, 402
Filing-machine	T. H. Lindley	Taunton, Mass	June 18, 1867	65, 920
Filing papers, Safety-hook for	L. H. Beckwith	Port Jervis, N. Y	May 13, 1873	138, 782
Filings, Apparatus for separating metallic	J. Jonson	Baltimore, Md	Jan. 24, 1865	46, 005
Filling-frame, Cap for	J. Ripka	Manayunk, Pa	July 13, 1833	....
Filter	C. Andersen	Brooklyn, N. Y	Sept. 23, 1873	143, 113
Filter	E. Andries	Schaerbeek, Belgium	Mar. 28, 1865	47, 074
Filter	B. Arnold	East Greenwich, R. I	July 16, 1861	32, 815
Filter	W. W. Ayres	Worcester, Mass	Aug. 25, 1857	18, 031
Filter	T. Barrows	Brooklyn, N. Y	May 24, 1870	103, 280
Filter	C. F. Baxter	Boston, Mass	Jan. 31, 1860	26, 965
Filter	C. F. Baxter	Boston, Mass	Mar. 11, 1862	34, 620
Filter	J. Bean	Hudson, Mich	Nov. 15, 1870	109, 288
Filter	B. Best	Dayton, Ohio	Jan. 26, 1864	41, 357
Filter	B. Best	Dayton, Ohio	Mar. 27, 1866	53, 3[illegible]5
Filter	C. D. Birdseye	New York, N. Y	Mar. 26, 1850	7, 208
Filter	T. Bishop	Dobb's Ferry, N. Y	Dec. 31, 1842	2, 892
Filter	J. Brady	New York, N. Y	May 21, 1872	126, 926
Filter	J. Brown	San Francisco, Cal	Apr. 4, 1871	113, 491
Filter	J. R. Brown and W. A. Foskett	New Haven, Conn	Apr. 8, 1873	137, 653
Filter	A. Chabot	San Francisco, Cal	Dec. 8, 1863	40, 818
Filter	L. S. Chichester	New York, N. Y	May 29, 1860	28, 533
Filter	T. C. Clarke	Camden, N. J	June 12, 1855	13, 026
Filter	T. C. Clarke	Camden, N. J	Oct. 9, 1860	30, 300
Filter	W. T. Class	Cincinnati, Ohio	Sept. 13, 1864	44, 253
Filter	C. Cleminshaw	Troy, N. Y	Jan. 31, 1865	46, 079
Filter	D. N. B. Coffin, jr	Newton, Mass	Sept. 2, 1856	15, 646
Filter	M. Cooke and J. W. Watt	Sacramento, Cal	Oct. 22, 1872	132, 385

Index of patents issued from the United States Patent Office from 1790 *to* 1873, *inclusive*—Continued.

Invention.	Inventor.	Residence.	Date.	No.
Filter	G. Curtis	Springfield, Mass	Nov. 29, 1870	109, 592
Filter	G. Curtis	Springfield, Mass	Nov. 29, 1870	109, 593
Filter	F. J. Delker	Philadelphia, Pa	June 11, 1872	127, 681
Filter	J. Doering	Philadelphia, Pa	Jan. 22, 1867	61, 407
Filter	N. Downes	Syracuse, N. Y	July 10, 1866	56, 193
Filter	E. Duchamp	Saint Martinsville, La	Sept. 13, 1859	25, 398
Filter	J. B. Ellis	Washington, D. C	Aug. 26, 1873	142, 217
Filter	M. A. Espirat and E. Sause	Marseilles, France	Apr. 11, 1865	47, 251
Filter	J. M. Evarts	New Haven, Conn	July 15, 1873	140, 907
Filter	E. S. Farson	Philadelphia, Pa	May 31, 1870	103, 592
Filter	J. Fitch	Seneca Falls, N. Y	Mar. 22, 1859	23, 297
Filter	J. Fitch	Seneca Falls, N. Y	July 10, 1860	29, 069
Filter	H. Flad	Saint Louis, Mo	Mar. 20, 1866	53, 287
Filter	H. Flad	Saint Louis, Mo	Mar. 5, 1867	62, 538
Filter	J. Ford	Newburgh, N. Y	Feb. 23, 1869	87, 250
Filter	A. Fox	Poughkeepsie, N. Y	July 30, 1867	67, 281
Filter	L. W. W. Goodwyn	New Orleans, La	Dec. 24, 1867	72, 481
Filter	L. A. Gouch	Yonkers, N. Y	Oct. 25, 1864	44, 797
Filter	F. P. Griffiths	Philadelphia, Pa	May 22, 1866	54, 894
Filter	J. M. Hackney	Danville, Ky	May 17, 1870	103, 173
Filter	C. M. Halsted	Troy, N. Y	Nov. 17, 1863	40, 620
Filter	T. Hayes	Cambridge, Mass	Dec. 18, 1866	60, 512
Filter	F. Henshaw	Washington, D. C	Oct. 1, 1867	69, 433
Filter	B. Holly	Lockport, N. Y	Apr. 4, 1871	113, 516
Filter	L. Holms	Paterson, N. J	June 2, 1868	78, 524
Filter	P. Huerne	San Francisco, Cal	July 16, 1872	129, 136
Filter	P. Huerne	San Francisco, Cal	Jan. 28, 1873	135, 222
Filter	C. H. Jackson	Saint Louis, Mo	Dec. 29, 1868	85, 449
Filter	A. Jaminet	Saint Louis, Mo	Mar. 22, 1859	23, 302
Filter	L. P. Jenks	Boston, Mass	Feb. 5, 1861	31, 352
Filter	W. H. Jennison	New York, N. Y	Feb. 20, 1846	4, 386
Filter	W. H. Jennison	New York, N. Y	Mar. 7, 1846	4, 399
Filter	J. Kedzie	Rochester, N. Y	Jan. 10, 1854	10, 420
Filter	J. G. Lefler	Philadelphia, Pa	Jan. 5, 1864	41, 075
Filter	J. N. Lighthall	Joliet, Ill	Jan. 7, 1868	73, 105
Filter	W. Linton	Baltimore, Md	Nov. 29, 1859	26, 274
Filter	W. Linton	Baltimore, Md	June 27, 1871	116, 463
Filter	W. C. Long and H. A. Lowsbery	Lockport, N. Y	Aug. 25, 1868	81, 386
Filter	C. F. Mietzsch	Philadelphia, Pa	Oct. 16, 1866	58, 868
Filter	G. S. Neff	Rochester, N. Y	Oct. 21, 1873	143, 924
Filter	J. Nixon	Pittsburgh, Pa	July 5, 1870	104, 987
Filter	G. Norris	New York, N. Y	Apr. 30, 1861	32, 202
Filter	G. T. Palmer	Brooklyn, N. Y	Jan. 28, 1868	73, 751
Filter	G. O. Parkman and J. M. Trussell.	Lincolnville and Belfast, Me.	May 25, 1869	90, 383
Filter	J. D. Parrot	Morristown, N. J	Aug. 3, 1869	93, 339
Filter	W. C. Pettijohn	Ozark, Mo	Dec. 10, 1872	133, 720
Filter	J. S. Phillips	Philadelphia, Pa	Aug. 27, 1828	....
Filter	J. Porée	New Orleans, La	Apr. 18, 1848	5, 512
Filter	L. Raecke	New York, N. Y	Jan. 17, 1871	111, 001
Filter	W. Rice	Philadelphia, Pa	June 21, 1859	24, 489
Filter	A. J. Robinson	Troy, N. Y	Aug. 6, 1872	130, 316
Filter	C. C. Savery	Philadelphia, Pa	Dec. 17, 1872	133, 953
Filter	C. C. Savery	Philadelphia, Pa	June 17, 1873	139, 922
Filter	F. Shickle and E. Randols	Saint Louis, Mo	Mar. 5, 1867	62, 696
Filter	T. Simmons	Chicago, Ill	Apr. 11, 1865	47, 261
Filter	T. Simmons	Chicago, Ill	Nov. 6, 1866	59, 467
Filter	T. Simmons	Brooklyn, N. Y	Sept. 15, 1868	82, 255
Filter	T. C. Simonton	Paterson, N. J	June 26, 1860	28, 942
Filter	T. Stewart	Philadelphia, Pa	May 25, 1869	90, 405
Filter	C. Süssner	United States	Oct. 20, 1863	40, 369
Filter	H. N. Taft	Sag Harbor, N. Y	Dec. 26, 1871	122, 291
Filter	J. A. Thompson	Cayuga, N. Y	Aug. 11, 1857	17, 987
Filter	J. A. Thompson	Geneva, N. Y	Apr. 21, 1863	38, 270
Filter	T. P. Thompson	Charlestown, Mass	May 10, 1870	102, 881
Filter	L. Tilliers	West Morrisania, N. Y	Mar. 22, 1859	23, 325
Filter	J. P. A. Vollman	Bingen, Germany	Aug. 22, 1871	118, 306
Filter	M. W. Warne	Saint Louis, Mo	Oct. 9, 1860	30, 366
Filter	C. Warner	Green Point, N. Y	June 3, 1856	15, 027
Filter	J. Watts	New Orleans, La	Mar. 5, 1867	62, 714
Filter	W. H. Wiley	Fredonia, N. Y	Sept. 10, 1867	68, 675
Filter and cooler	J. S. Brooks	Rochester, N. Y	July 21, 1863	39, 271
Filter and cooler	G. B. Davis	Chicago, Ill	Oct. 20, 1863	40, 329
Filter and cooler	W. P. Dickinson	Reading, Pa	Dec. 26, 1865	51, 703
Filter and cooler	N. Downes	Syracuse, N. Y	Dec. 1, 1868	84, 482
Filter and cooler	H. M. Seavey	Chicago, Ill	Oct. 4, 1864	44, 558
Filter and cooler	J. C. Whitehill	Saint Louis, Mo	Mar. 5, 1867	62, 582
Filter and cooler, Combined	J. E. Cheney	Rochester, N. Y	May 19, 1863	38, 559
Filter and cooler, Combined	L. Scharff	Spring Mill, Pa	Dec. 12, 1865	51, 485
Filter and cooler combined	J. E. White	New York, N. Y	Apr. 26, 1870	102, 455
Filter and cooler combined	H. T. Woodman	Dubuque, Iowa	Oct. 2, 1866	58, 530
Filter and cooler, Water	L. Scharff	Spring Mill, Pa	June 11, 1872	127, 926
Filter and refrigerator	J. T. Craddock	Baltimore, Md	Dec. 31, 1845	4, 344
Filter-attachment for faucet	J. H. Wright	New York, N. Y	July 1, 1856	15, 263
Filter, Barrel	G. Armstrong	Liverpool, England	May 31, 1870	103, 540
Filter, Bone, coal, and other	H. Forstrick	New York, N. Y	Dec. 22, 1868	85, 256
Filter, Cistern	N. Gonner and H. Bader	Cape Girardeau, Mo	Feb. 11, 1868	74, 215
Filter, Cistern	G. W. Lampson	Waterloo, N. Y	Mar. 12, 1867	62, 757
Filter, Cistern	P. Laughlin	Danville, Ky	Mar. 1, 1870	100, 418
Filter, Cistern	P. Laughlin	Danville, Ky	May 17, 1870	103, 206
Filter, Cistern	B. B. Redfield	Lapeer, Mich	Mar. 1, 1870	100, 323
Filter, Cistern	R. W. Thompson	Mansfield, Ohio	Feb. 7, 1871	111, 701
Filter-cooler	S. M. Pike	Cincinnati, Ohio	Dec. 18, 1866	60, 553
Filter, Driving-pump	A. J. Sternberg	Butler, Ind	Aug. 13, 1872	130, 447
Filter, Faucet	H. G. Fuhrmann	Brooklyn, N. Y	July 28, 1868	80, 469
Filter, Faucet	M. P. Simons	Philadelphia, Pa	Feb. 22, 1870	100, 079
Filter, Feed-water	J. S. Hooton	New Carlisle, Ind	July 12, 1870	105, 209
Filter, Feed-water	G. Waters	Cincinnati, Ohio	Mar. 1, 1870	100, 344

Index of patents issued from the United States Patent Office from 1790 *to* 1873, *inclusive*—Continued.

Invention.	Inventor.	Residence.	Date.	No.
Filter for artesian wells	J. Clay and E. B. Torrey	Ithaca, N. Y	Oct. 31, 1865	50, 686
Filter for cane-juice	H. Bessemer	Baxter House, England	Mar. 8, 1853	9, 608
Filter for cane-juice, &c	E. Tuttle	Jeanerett, La	Aug. 6, 1872	130, 255
Filter for cane juice, oil, and other dense liquids	A. K. Lee	Galveston, Tex	Apr. 15, 1873	137, 849
Filter for drawing sirups. Siphon	C. N. Brock	Philadelphia, Pa	June 30, 1863	39, 031
Filter for hydrants, Self-cleaning	J. Raible, M. Reis, and J. Ritter	Chicago, Ill	Jan. 18, 1870	99, 002
Filter for oils	W. Cady	Marietta, Ohio	Jan. 1, 1867	60, 685
Filter for oils, &c	P. Halle	Philadelphia, Pa	June 13, 1865	48, 172
Filter for oils, acids, &c	J. Jowett	Brooklyn, N. Y	Oct. 21, 1873	143, 768
Filter for petroleum	G. W. Sylvester	Newark, N. J	Dec. 18, 1866	60. 593
Filter for pharmaceutists and others	A. B. Spencer	Rochester, N. Y	June 4, 1867	65, 515
Filter for refining sugar	R. W. Bender	New York, N. Y	Aug. 27, 1867	68, 157
Filter for saccharine and other liquids	H. Merrill	New York, N. Y	Oct. 6, 1868	82, 735
Filter for sirup	P. and H. A. Perdew	Seal, Ohio	Oct. 2, 1866	58, 472
Filter for sirup, &c., Bag	G. A. Gasper	Charlestown, Mass	Apr. 12, 1864	42, 291
Filter for steam-boilers, Arrangement of	E. Blunt	Brooklyn, N. Y	Aug. 14, 1849	6, 650
Filter for sugar, &c	J. Watson	Elizabethtown, N. J	Jan. 31, 1844	3, 419
Filter for wine, sirup, &c	J. Strauss	New York, N. Y	Nov. 22, 1870	109, 467
Filter, Hydrant	T. C Clarke	Camden, N. J	June 12, 1855	13, 027
Filter, Liquid	D. N. Denman	Millburn, N. J	May 5, 1863	38, 378
Filter, liquor-cooler, and refrigerator, Water	W. F. Nickels	Philadelphia, Pa	Feb. 22, 1870	100, 182
Filter, Nozzle	H. Houston	Pittsburgh, Pa	Jan. 26, 1869	86, 158
Filter, Petroleum	J. H. Smith	Pittsburgh, Pa	July 9, 1867	66, 645
Filter, Portable	H. A. Hall	Boston, Mass	May 21, 1861	32, 361
Filter, Portable	J. P. A. Havard and J. B. Bourgoise.	Paris, France	Feb. 25, 1862	34, 492
Filter, Portable floating	N. Waterman	Boston, Mass	June 12, 1855	13, 054
Filter-press	L. P. R. De Massy	Paris, France	Aug. 14, 1866	57, 265
Filter, Pressure	C. N. Brock	Philadelphia, Pa	July 2, 1867	66, 293
Filter, Pump	J. Christman	Syracuse, N. Y	Nov. 28, 1865	51, 145
Filter-pump	S. D. Richardson and T. S. Hughes.	Syracuse, N. Y	Jan. 23, 1866	52, 204
Filter-rack	E. C. Andrews	Seneca Falls, N. Y	Nov. 16, 1869	96, 765
Filter-regulator	R. Berryman	Hartford, Conn	July 30, 1872	130, 008
Filter, Reversible	J. D. Parrot	Morristown, N. J	Apr. 30, 1872	126, 325
Filter, Sirup	J. L. Smith	Tuscola, Ill	Apr. 3, 1866	53, 693
Filter, Sugar	C. E. Bertrand	New York, N. Y	Oct. 30, 1855	13, 740
Filter, Sugar	W. H. Merrick	Philadelphia, Pa	Apr. 7, 1868	76, 495
Filter-supporter	F. C. Hughes	Frankfort, Ky	July 5, 1870	104, 959
Filter, Thermo-udoric	G. Weissenborn	New York, N. Y	Oct. 2, 1855	13, 628
Filter, Turpentine	F. G. Richardson	Brooklyn, N. Y	Aug. 26, 1873	142, 276
Filter, Vacuum	T. Simmons	Chicago, Ill	Feb. 26, 1867	62, 505
Filter, Water	W. M. Conger	Newark, N. J	Mar. 4, 1873	136, 36[illegible]
Filter, Water	G. B. Davis	Chicago, Ill	Feb. 18, 1862	34, 411
Filter, Water	N. Downes	Syracuse, N. Y	Mar. 7, 1865	46, 646
Filter, Water	A. T. Dunshee	McKeesport, Pa	Sept. 24, 1861	33, 340
Filter, Water	A. T. Dunshee	Pittsburgh, Pa	June 29, 1869	91, 924
Filter, Water	F. Henshaw	Washington, D. C	Mar. 19, 1872	124, 741
Filter, Water	A. Jaminet	Florisant, Mo	Apr. 13, 1858	19, 929
Filter, Water	J. C. Jewett	Buffalo, N. Y	Nov. 16, 1869	96, 923
Filter, Water	J. Pearson	Sacramento, Cal	Sept. 9, 1873	142, 722
Filter, Water	A. J. Robinson	Troy, N. Y	Nov. 26, 1872	133, 488
Filter, Water	G. B. White	New York, N.Y	July 7, 1829	....
Filter, Water-cock	N. C. Wilder	Hartford Conn	May 3, 1870	102, 636
Filter, Water-cooler	C. Schneider	Newark, N. J	May 20, 1873	139, 085
Filter, Well	J. P. Spaulding	Williamsport, Pa	July 5, 1870	105, 009
Filter, Well and cistern	W. H. Wiley	Fredonia, N. Y	Dec. 4, 1866	60, 311
Filter, Well-point	D. A. Danforth and A. N. Chamberlain.	Elkhart, Ind	June 18, 1872	128, 126
Filter, Well-tube	W. A. Sharpe	Syracuse, N. Y	May 1, 1866	54, 417
Filter, Wine	C. W. Farciot	Kelley's Island, Ohio	Dec. 9, 1873	145, 288
Filter, Wine	A. F. Schmidt	Davenport, Iowa	Nov. 21, 1871	121, 065
Filters, Cleaning	J. Watson	Kingston, Jamaica	Dec. 28, 1847	5, 404
Filters, Composition for	W. H. Jennison	New York, N. Y	May 31, 1853	9, 760
Filters to supply-pipes, Method of attaching	J. Fernald	Boston, Mass	Jan. 6, 1857	16, 330
Filterer and purifier	R. A. Maingay	Pottsville, Pa	May 17, 1859	24, 036
Filtering and drinking tube, Pocket	A. Fessenden	Boston, Mass	Apr. 2, 1850	7, 238
Filtering and purifying spirits, Apparatus for	W. F. Bearns	Mount Pleasant, N. Y	Oct. 1, 1867	69, 390
Filtering and rectifying spirits, Apparatus for	C. W. Ackermann	Pekin, Ill	Jan. 21, 1873	135, 057
Filtering and ventilating apparatus for wells and cisterns.	B. B. Redfield	Pontiac, Mich	July 27, 1869	93, 121
Filtering-apparatus	L. Ayres	Baltimore, Md	July 8, 1834	....
Filtering-apparatus	C. Ballard	Worcester, Mass	Feb. 16, 1858	19, 335
Filtering-apparatus	J. P. Gruber	New York, N. Y	Apr. 3, 1866	53, 606
Filtering-apparatus	N. F. Rice	New Orleans, La	Feb. 1, 1859	22, 826
Filtering-apparatus	J. H. G. D. Wagner	Paris, France	May 29, 1860	28, 524
Filtering-apparatus, Pipe	T. S. Hudson	East Cambridge, Mass	Jan. 4, 1870	98, 596
Filtering burning-fluid	J. D. Kirkpatrick	Urbana, Ohio	Feb. 18, 1868	74, 698
Filtering collodion, Vial for	D. H. Cross	Bennington, Vt	June 21, 1870	104, 432
Filtering-cup	L. Jennings	Brooklyn, N. Y	Sept. 10, 1861	33, 281
Filtering-diaphragm, Self-regulating	W. H. Jennison	New York, N. Y	May 1, 1849	6, 408
Filtering liquids, Apparatus for	B. N. De Buffon	Paris, France	Apr. 14, 1857	17, 028
Filtering liquids, Apparatus for	T. R. Sinclaire	New York, N. Y	Nov. 14, 1871	120, 908
Filtering liquids, &c., Apparatus for	R. Stewart	Brooklyn, N. Y	Mar. 7, 1865	46, 724
Filtering liquids under pressure, Apparatus for	T. R. Sinclaire	New York, N. Y	July 6, 1869	92, 215
Filtering machine, Water	J. Wiseman	New York, N. Y	Aug. 20, 1834	....
Filtering-materials	L. Brandeis	Brooklyn, N. Y	Apr. 25, 1871	113, 973
Filtering-medium	W. Wickersham	Boston, Mass	July 15, 1856	15, 363
Filtering, Metallic medium for	O. C. Phelps	Boston, Mass	June 12, 1855	13, 070
Filtering petroleum, Apparatus for	R. A. Chesebrough	New York, N. Y	Aug. 8, 1865	49, 230
Filtering petroleum, Apparatus for	R. B. Douglass	Cleveland, Ohio	Sept. 24, 1867	69, 192
Filtering petroleum, sirup, and other liquids, Composition for.	W. Van Wyck	Belleville, N. J	May 28, 1867	65, 313
Filtering-pot	M. Freytag	Philadelphia, Pa	July 1, 1807	....
Filtering, Preparing charcoal for	G. W. Ferris	Quincy, Ill	July 10, 1866	56, 198
Filtering-press	L. P. R. De Massy	Paris, France	Nov. 21, 1865	51, 124
Filtering-press	L. P. R. De Massy	Paris, France	Nov. 28, 1865	51, 277
Filtering-press, Cylindrical	P. Du Rieux and E. Roettger	Lille, France	July 21, 1868	80, 157

Index of patents issued from the United States Patent Office from 1790 *to* 1873, *inclusive*—Continued.

Invention.	Inventor.	Residence.	Date.	No.
Filtering-sand for cider	I. Holmes	Leicester, N. Y	Aug. 12, 1856	15, 517
Filtering sirup and other liquid, Apparatus for	H. A. Tilden	New Lebanon, N. Y	July 25, 1865	49, 013
Filtering sirup, &c., Mode of treating bone-black for	J. O. Donner	Jersey City, N. J	Aug. 17, 1869	93, 865
Filtering-stopper	G. H. Mellen	Hartford, Conn	Oct. 8, 1861	33, 443
Filtering sugar, Treating bone-black for	C. B. Orvis	Saint Louis, Mo	Sept. 24, 1867	69, 118
Filtering-tube	D. and E. Moore	Brooklyn, N. Y	July 27, 1869	92, 988
Filtering volatile liquids, Apparatus for	W. Boyce	Tuscola, Ill	Dec. 28, 1869	98, 343
Filtering water, &c	J. Barron	United States Navy	Aug. 30, 1831	....
Filtering water	C. Hall	Norfolk, Va	Feb. 22, 1828	....
Filtering water, Apparatus and process for	J. Du Commun	New York, N. Y	Feb. 10, 1816	....
Filtering water, &c., Apparatus for	J. Mulhern	Saint Louis, Mo	July 31, 1849	6, 621
Filtering water, wine, &c	S. McCombs, J. Smith, and B. D. Galpin.	Baltimore, Md	June 24, 1806	....
Filtration-press for expressing liquids from substances.	W. Needham and J. Kite	Vauxhall, England	Aug. 11, 1857	17, 978
Fine-tooth comb, Making ivory	F. Bush and J. H. Pratt	Meriden, Conn	June 5, 1849	6, 492
Finger-bars, Machine for straightening	J. Corns	Akron, Ohio	Jan. 16, 1872	122, 815
Finger-exerciser	F. Wenzel	Saint Louis, Mo	Aug. 13, 1872	130, 457
Finger-exercising apparatus	A. C. Armengol	New York, N. Y	Feb. 9, 1869	86, 722
Finger-guard	W. J. Budington	Lancaster, Pa	July 16, 1872	129, 392
Finger-guard	L. Holmes	Green Point, N. Y	Apr. 4, 1871	113, 519
Finger-guard	G. H. Spencer	Cleveland, Ohio	Sept. 13, 1870	107, 420
Finger-guard for holding hot corn	H. Hebbard	New York, N. Y	Aug. 10, 1869	93, 436
Finger-nails, Instrument for cutting	C. C. E. Schuartz	Philadelphia, Pa	May 22, 1866	54, 966
Finger-ring	S. Bogert	New York, N. Y	Aug. 23, 1859	25, 172
Finger-ring	C. S. Ford	New York, N. Y	Apr. 27, 1869	89, 475
Finger-ring	J. S. Palmer	Providence, R. I	Dec. 27, 1870	110, 587
Finger-ring	W. H. Peckham	New York, N. Y	Sept. 29, 1868	82, 546
Finger-ring	G. W. Tinsley and E. W. Storer	Minneapolis, Minn	Aug. 15, 1871	118, 169
Finger-ring, Extension	S. Friend and G. Seiler	New York, N. Y	Dec. 21, 1858	22, 358
Finger-rings, Die for enlarging and sizing plain	G. Krementz	Newark, N. J	July 1, 1873	140, 422
Finger-rings, Die for manufacturing plain	G. Krementz	Newark, N. J	July 1, 1873	140, 423
Finger-rings, Instrument for expanding	L. Mason	Rochester, N. Y	Dec. 17, 1867	72, 410
Finger-rings, Machine for rolling stock for	J. S. Palmer	Providence, R. I	Mar. 26, 1872	124, 971
Finger-rings, Manufacture of sheet-metal	I. M. Porter	Providence, R. I	Oct. 2, 1860	30, 246
Finger, scarf, and napkin rings	L. Sauter	Jersey City, N. J	July 24, 1866	56, 618
Finishing-die in machine for making rings from sheet-metal.	C. W. Dickinson	Newark, N. J	July 25, 1854	11, 363
Fire-alarm	W. W. Andrews, J. Cummer, J. F. Gauweiler, and J. Stengel.	Croton, Mich	June 11, 1867	65, 526
Fire-alarm	W. A. Barnes	Bridgeport, Conn	May 6, 1873	138, 467
Fire-alarm	H. L. Brower	New York, N. Y	Oct. 17, 1871	120, 029
Fire-alarm	A. F. Cobb	Chapel Hill, Mo	Nov. 13, 1860	30, 613
Fire-alarm	J. Coulson	Oskaloosa, Iowa	Dec. 15, 1868	84, 997
Fire-alarm	J. Dinsmore	Millburn, Me	May 14, 1833	....
Fire-alarm	C. Dion	Montreal, Canada	Aug. 29, 1869	49, 686
Fire-alarm	C. Dion	Montreal, Canada	Apr. 3, 1866	53, 757
Fire-alarm	C. Dion	New York, N. Y	Apr. 6, 1869	88, 698
Fire-alarm	E. Eblin	Boston, Mass	Nov. 13, 1860	30, 624
Fire-alarm	A. Fontaine	Milwaukee, Wis	Nov. 6, 1866	59, 379
Fire-alarm	E. Fontaine and O. A. Simons	Fort Wayne, Ind	Nov. 13, 1866	59, 579
Fire-alarm	J. F. Gauweiler and J. Stengel	Croton, Mich	Feb. 11, 1868	74, 339
Fire-alarm	T. Goodwin	Exeter, N. H	Jan. 30, 1841	1, 956
Fire-alarm	W. D. Grimshaw	Newark, N. J	Feb. 28, 1860	27, 282
Fire-alarm	F. F. Herman	Grafton, Mich	Mar. 19, 1872	124, 680
Fire-alarm	C. D. Kubach	Philadelphia, Pa	June 26, 1866	55, 957
Fire-alarm	I. T. Pease	Thompsonville, Conn	Dec. 24, 1867	72, 672
Fire-alarm	I. T. Pease	Thompsonville, Conn	Feb. 23, 1869	87, 194
Fire-alarm	J. N. Pitts and J. E. Russell	Niagara Falls, N. Y	Oct. 10, 1871	119, 713
Fire-alarm	R. Porter	Billerica, Mass	Dec. 26, 1840	1, 915
Fire-alarm	R. Powers	Prescott, Mass	Apr. 24, 1866	54, 202
Fire-alarm	H. N. Shultz	Mechanicstown, Md	Apr. 4, 1871	113, 460
Fire-alarm	D. Tomlinson and H. S. Hopkins	Brookfield, Conn	June 12, 1847	5, 152
Fire-alarm	J. R. Tunnicliff	Van Hornesville, N. Y	Apr. 22, 1862	35, 050
Fire-alarm and circuit therefor, Electrical and thermostatic.	J. H. Guest	Brooklyn, N. Y	Oct. 14, 1873	143, 691
Fire-alarm and heat-detector	A. Ross	Brooklyn, N. Y	Mar. 10, 1863	37, 875
Fire-alarm and police-signal box	W. J. Philips	Philadelphia, Pa	Oct. 31, 1871	120, 395
Fire-alarm, Annunciating	A. and E. Fontaine	Fort Wayne, Ind	Oct. 8, 1867	69, 648
Fire-alarm apparatus	A. Allen	Rochester, N. Y	June 1, 1869	90, 806
Fire-alarm apparatus	S. D. Cooper	Hartford, Conn	Aug. 6, 1861	32, 980
Fire-alarm apparatus	B. Seymour and J. Whipple	Utica, N. Y	Apr. 2, 1835	....
Fire-alarm apparatus, Electro-magnetic	M. G. Farmer	Salem, Mass	Nov. 16, 1858	22, 071
Fire-alarm apparatus, Electro-magnetic	M. G. Farmer	Salem, Mass	Jan. 11, 1859	22, 553
Fire-alarm apparatus, Electro-magnetic	M. G. Farmer	Salem, Mass	Feb. 22, 1859	23, 060
Fire-alarm apparatus, Electro-magnetic	M. G. Farmer and W. F. Channing.	Salem and Boston, Mass	Mar. 8, 1859	23, 217
Fire-alarm, Automatic	H. L. Brown	Middletown, Conn	May 27, 1873	139, 292
Fire-alarm, Automatic	C. H. Lehnis	Philadelphia, Pa	Nov. 25, 1873	144, 991
Fire-alarm box, &c., Lock for	J. M. Fairchild	New Haven, Conn	Oct. 28, 1873	144, 079
Fire-alarm, Electric	E. A. Hill	Chicago, Ill	Dec. 12, 1871	121, 717
Fire-alarm, Electro-magnetic	H. Van Ausdall	Preble County, Ohio	Aug. 31, 1852	9, 240
Fire-alarm, Electro-magnetic	W. Whiting	Roxbury, Mass	Mar. 31, 1863	38, 074
Fire-alarm, Magnetic	A. Smith	Perrysburgh, Ohio	July 24, 1846	4, 661
Fire-alarm, Self-acting	I. S. Richardson	New Market, N. H	Aug. 15, 1831	....
Fire-alarm-signal box	C. E. Carpenter	Providence, R. I	Feb. 28, 1865	46, 542
Fire-alarm-signal box	G. Floyd	Cincinnati, Ohio	May 21, 1872	127, 041
Fire-alarm-signal box	F. Latta	Cincinnati, Ohio	Jan. 7, 1873	134, 552
Fire-alarm-signal box	G. W. Shawk	Cleveland, Ohio	Feb. 1, 1870	99, 358
Fire-alarm-signal box	G. Wright, M. Y. Holley, and H. R. Miles.	Washington, D. C	June 17, 1873	140, 106
Fire-alarm, Telegraph	J. B. Franz	Cleveland, Ohio	July 13, 1869	92, 598
Fire-alarm, Telegraphic	G. W. Shaw, S. C. Morley, and S. D. Cushman.	Cleveland and New Lisbon, Ohio.	Sept. 11, 1866	57, 981
Fire-alarm, Thermostat	W. B. Watkins	Jersey City, N. J	May 10, 1870	102, 982
Fire and burglar alarm	H. L. Bower	New York, N. Y	Aug. 22, 1871	118, 191
Fire and burglar alarm	J. L. Cheston	South Easton, Pa	Aug. 31, 1869	94, 282
Fire and burglar alarm	W. Henckler	Kirkwood, Mo	Apr. 30, 1872	126, 294

Index of patents issued from the United States Patent Office from 1790 *to* 1873, *inclusive*—Continued.

Invention.	Inventor.	Residence.	Date.	No.
Fire and burglar alarm	E. Middleton	Cleveland, Ohio	Oct. 9, 1866	58,662
Fire and burglar alarm	O. E. Pickett and R. S. Luce	North Auburn and Lawsville Centre, Pa.	Feb. 11, 1868	74,418
Fire and burglar alarm	D. Ward and R. S. Luce	Lawsville Centre, Pa	Nov. 7, 1865	50,863
Fire and light, Producing	I. Jennings	New York, N. Y	June 11, 1829	....
Fire and ventilating apparatus for ships	J. W. Richards	New York, N. Y	Feb. 1, 1859	22,897
Fire and water proof compositions for ceilings, walls, and floors.	L. A. Tartieré	New York, N. Y	May 13, 1873	138,956
Fire and water proofing paper, cloth, &c., Process for.	R. O. Lowrey	Salem, N. Y	Dec. 10, 1867	71,892
Fire and weather proof composition or artificial slate.	W. Blake	Sharon, Ohio	Mar. 28, 1848	5,490
Fire-annihilator	H. Baragwanath and M. Van Wisker.	New York, N. Y	Dec. 5, 1865	51,248
Fire-annihilator	C. T. Jerome	Minneapolis, Minn	July 9, 1867	66,498
Fire, Apparatus for barns, stables, &c., for rescuing horses and other stock from.	J. E. Hall	Cleveland, Ohio	Oct. 13, 1857	18,395
Fire, Apparatus to protect buildings from	S. M. Andrus	Bellevue, Mich	July 10, 1860	29,044
Fire, Apparatus to protect buildings from	T. Odion	Portsmouth, N. H	Sept. 29, 1857	18,295
Fire-arm	J. Adams	Cleveland, Ohio	Sept. 30, 1856	15,797
Fire-arm	S. Adams	Springfield, Mass	Oct. 3, 1838	960
Fire-arm	E. Allen	Worcester, Mass	July 3, 1855	13,154
Fire-arm	E. Allen	Worcester, Mass	Jan. 13, 1857	16,367
Fire-arm	E. Allen	Worcester, Mass	Mar. 13, 1860	27,415
Fire-arm	L. Bailey, J. B. Ripley, and W. B. Smith.	Portland, Me	Feb. 20, 1839	1,084
Fire-arm	E. Baldwinn	Templeton, Mass	July 11, 1854	11,283
Fire-arm	T. H. Barlow	Lexington, Ky	Jan. 16, 1855	12,230
Fire-arm	F. Beals	New Haven, Conn	Sept. 26, 1854	11,715
Fire-arm	F. Beals	New Haven, Conn	June 24, 1856	15,167
Fire-arm	F. B. E. Beaumont	Barnsley, England	June 3, 1856	15,032
Fire-arm	F. Beerstecher	Philadelphia, Pa	Sept. 25, 1855	13,592
Fire-arm	J. E. Blake	Norwich, Conn	June 25, 1867	66,072
Fire-arm	G. A. Blittkowskie	New York, N. Y	Apr. 28, 1857	17,136
Fire-arm	C. C. Brand	Norwich, Conn	July 29, 1862	35,989
Fire-arm	F. S. Brettell and J. B. Frisbie	Allegheny City, Pa	Feb. 10, 1857	16,575
Fire-arm	C. F. Brown	Warren, R. I	Sept. 18, 1860	30,045
Fire-arm	I. W. Brown	West Springfield, Mass	Aug. 8, 1854	11,470
Fire-arm	C. Buss	Marlborough, N. H	Apr. 25, 1854	10,821
Fire-arm	E. B. Butterfield	Brattleborough, Vt	Mar. 16, 1839	1,106
Fire-arm	S. Colt	Hartford, Conn	Feb. 25, 1836	....
Fire-arm	S. Colt	Paterson, N. J	Aug. 29, 1839	1,304
Fire-arm	S. Colt	Hartford, Conn	May 20, 1856	14,905
Fire-arm	T. Cook	New York, N. Y	Feb. 14, 1854	10,520
Fire-arm	A. and C. Daniels	Chester, Conn	Feb. 15, 1838	610
Fire-arm	J. C. Day	Hackettstown, N. J	Aug. 8, 1854	11,477
Fire-arm	J. C. Day	Hackettstown, N. J	Dec. 18, 1855	13,941
Fire-arm	J. C. Day	Hackettstown, N. J	Jan. 15, 1856	14,095
Fire-arm	S. Day	New York, N. Y	Oct. 8, 1840	1,810
Fire-arm	S. Day and S. Hall	New York, N. Y	Dec. 31, 1839	1,461
Fire-arm	J. A. De Brame	New York, N. Y	July 2, 1861	32,685
Fire-arm	R. Eastman	Brunswick, Me	Dec. 7, 1829	....
Fire-arm	D. Edwards	Zanesville, Ohio	Apr. 25, 1839	1,134
Fire-arm	J. Ells	Pittsburgh, Pa	Apr. 28, 1857	17,143
Fire-arm	E. Fisher and D. H. Chamberlain.	Springfield and Boston, Mass.	Apr. 17, 1837	168
Fire-arm	L. H. Gibbs	Oberlin, Ohio	Oct. 2, 1847	5,316
Fire-arm	J. W. Goodale	Amherst, Mass	June 1, 1869	90,741
Fire-arm	E. H. Graham	Biddeford, Me	Jan. 16, 1855	12,235
Fire-arm	E. H. Graham	Manchester, N. H	Sept. 16, 1856	15,734
Fire-arm	R. Graham	Brooklyn, N. Y	Aug. 16, 1864	43,881
Fire-arm	H. Gross	Tiffin, Ohio	May 22, 1855	12,906
Fire-arm	J. E. Halsey	New York, N. Y	July 8, 1856	15,292
Fire-arm	H. Harrington	Southbridge, Mass	July 29, 1837	297
Fire-arm	A. V. Hill	Carrollton, N. Y	May 28, 1861	32,421
Fire-arm	F. W. Hoffman	New York, N. Y	Aug. 12, 1856	15,516
Fire-arm	A. Holcomb	Litchfield, N. Y	Oct. 31, 1822	....
Fire-arm	J. Hollingsworth and R. S. Mershon.	Zanesville, Ohio	Feb. 27, 1855	12,470
Fire-arm	J. C. Howe	Milwaukee, Wis	Oct. 31, 1854	11,862
Fire-arm	W. W. Hubbell	Philadelphia, Pa	July 1, 1844	3,649
Fire-arm	W. Jenks	Columbia, S. C	May 25, 1838	747
Fire-arm	B. F. Joslyn	Worcester, Mass	Oct. 8, 1861	33,435
Fire-arm	G. Kesling	Lebanon, Ohio	June 3, 1856	15,041
Fire-arm	F. Klein	Newark, N. J	Apr. 10, 1855	12,681
Fire-arm	D. Knight	Salem, Ind	Aug. 8, 1854	11,483
Fire-arm	P. Lancaster	Burr Oak, Mich	Apr. 15, 1856	14,667
Fire-arm	E. Lefauchaux	Paris, France	Mar. 26, 1861	31,809
Fire-arm	A. Le Mat	New Orleans, La	Oct. 21, 1856	15,925
Fire-arm	A. Le Mat	New Orleans, La	Nov. 25, 1856	16,124
Fire-arm	G. Leonard	Shrewsbury, Mass	Aug. 9, 1853	9,922
Fire-arm	E. Lindner	New York, N. Y	May 26, 1857	17,382
Fire-arm	J. Lord	Minersville, Pa	June 12, 1860	28,677
Fire-arm	S. K. Lovewell	Gardner, Mass	Mar. 17, 1857	16,846
Fire-arm	W. W. Marston	New York, N. Y	Sept. 18, 1855	13,581
Fire-arm	W. McCord	Sing Sing, N. Y	Apr. 2, 1861	31,933
Fire-arm	L. A. Merriam	New York, N. Y	Jan. 19, 1869	86,091
Fire-arm	J. H. Merrill	Baltimore, Md	Jan. 8, 1856	14,077
Fire-arm	J. H. Merrill	Baltimore, Md	May 28, 1861	32,450
Fire-arm	J. H. Merrill	Baltimore, Md	May 28, 1861	32,451
Fire-arm	J. Merwin and E. P. Bray	New York, N. Y	Jan. 5, 1864	41,166
Fire-arm	D. Moore	Brooklyn, N. Y	Feb. 19, 1861	31,473
Fire-arm	W. H. Morrison	Marion County, Ind	Sept. 19, 1854	11,698
Fire-arm	F. Newbury	Albany, N. Y	Mar. 20, 1855	12,555
Fire-arm	F. Newbury	Albany, N. Y	Apr. 29, 1856	14,774
Fire-arm	F. D. Newbury	Albany, N. Y	Aug. 12, 1856	15,521
Fire-arm	F. D. Newbury	Albany, N. Y	Feb. 9, 1858	19,327
Fire-arm	A. N. Newton	Richmond, Ind	Aug. 12, 1856	15,522

Index of patents issued from the United States Patent Office from 1790 *to* 1873, *inclusive*—Continued.

Invention.	Inventor.	Residence.	Date.	No.
Fire-arm	C. V. Nickerson	Baltimore, Md	Jan. 27, 1852	8, 690
Fire-arm	H. S. North	Middletown, Conn	June 5, 1847	5, 141
Fire-arm	H. S. North	Middletown, Conn	June 17, 1856	15, 144
Fire-arm	G. F. and A. H. Palmié	Berlin, Prussia	Oct. 24, 1854	11, 835
Fire-arm	J. Peck	New Haven, Conn	May 16, 1854	10, 930
Fire-arm	A. D. Perry	Newark, N. J	Jan. 16, 1855	12, 244
Fire-arm	J. W. Plummer and J. Clark	Wayne Township, Ohio	May 17, 1832	....
Fire-arm	J. B. Porter	Girard, Pa	Aug. 4, 1832	....
Fire-arm	J. B. Read	Tuscaloosa, Ala	May 5, 1857	17, 233
Fire-arm	J. A. Reynolds	Elmira, N. Y	July 17, 1855	13, 292
Fire-arm	J. A. Reynolds	Elmira, N. Y	July 17, 1855	13, 293
Fire-arm	F. Ruggles	Hardwick, Mass	Nov. 24, 1826	....
Fire-arm	E. Savage and S. North	Middletown, Conn	July 30, 1844	3, 686
Fire-arm	J. Shaw, jr	Hinckley Township, Ohio	June 30, 1857	17, 698
Fire-arm	C. Slotterbek	San Francisco, Cal	Nov. 17, 1868	84, 224
Fire-arm	B. F. Smith	South Hadley, Mass	Dec. 5, 1839	1, 422
Fire-arm	H. Smith and D. B. Wesson	Norwich, Conn	Feb. 14, 1854	10, 535
Fire-arm	D. E. Somes	Washington, D. C	Aug. 18, 1863	39, 592
Fire-arm	G. H. Soule	Jersey City, N. J	July 15, 1856	15, 347
Fire-arm	N. Starr	Middletown, Conn	May 3, 1839	1, 141
Fire-arm	J. Stowell	Charlestown, Mass	May 8, 1855	12, 836
Fire-arm	J. L. Swan	Lowville, N. Y	Apr. 8, 1862	34, 911
Fire-arm	W. A. Sweet	Pompey, N. Y	Aug. 15, 1854	11, 536
Fire-arm	W. Thornton and J. Hatkill	Washington, D. C	May 21, 1811	....
Fire-arm	J. Warner	Springfield, Mass	June 24, 1856	15, 202
Fire-arm	E. Whitney	Whitneyville, Conn	Aug. 1, 1854	11, 447
Fire-arm	J. Widmer	Newark, N. J	Nov. 9, 1869	96, 751
Fire-arm	S. W. Wood	Cornwall, N. Y	Aug. 18, 1863	39, 619
Fire-arm	W. Wright	New York, N. Y	Nov. 7, 1854	11, 917
Fire-arm, Accelerating	A. S. Lyman	New York, N. Y	Feb. 3, 1857	16, 568
Fire-arm and ordnance	H. C. Fay	Lancaster, Mass	May 22, 1837	203
Fire arm applicable alike to small-arms and cannon.	A. S. Thistle	New Orleans, La	Aug. 1, 1838	865
Fire-arm barrels, Method of making	J. Pannabecker	Elizabeth Township, Pa	Aug. 6, 1850	7, 547
Fire-arm, Breech-loading	F. J. Abbey and J. H. Foster	Chicago, Ill	Apr. 25, 1871	114, 081
Fire-arm, Breech-loading	G. T. Abbey	Chicago, Ill	Mar. 16, 1869	87, 814
Fire-arm, Breech-loading	H. W. Adams	New York, N. Y	Sept. 19, 1854	11, 685
Fire-arm, Breech-loading	J. S. Adams	Taunton, Mass	Aug. 11, 1863	39, 455
Fire-arm, Breech-loading	J. S. Adams	Taunton, Mass	Sept. 27, 1864	44, 377
Fire-arm, Breech-loading	S. Albright	Ottawa, Ohio	May 5, 1863	38, 366
Fire-arm, Breech-loading	W. Aldrich	Cleveland, Ohio	May 12, 1863	38, 455
Fire-arm, Breech-loading	E. Allen	Worcester, Mass	Sept. 18, 1860	30, 033
Fire-arm, Breech-loading	E. Allen	Worcester, Mass	Aug. 22, 1865	49, 491
Fire-arm, Breech-loading	E. Allen	Worcester, Mass	Dec. 15, 1868	84, 929
Fire-arm, Breech-loading	E. S. Allin	Springfield, Mass	Sept. 19, 1865	49, 959
Fire-arm, Breech-loading	C. H. Alsop	Middletown, Conn	Apr. 7, 1868	76, 374
Fire-arm, Breech-loading	P. Altmair	Lewistown, Pa	July 12, 1859	24, 774
Fire-arm, Breech-loading	J. W. Armstrong and J. Taylor	Augusta, Ky	Nov. 25, 1862	37, 025
Fire-arm, Breech-loading	W. H. Arnold	Washington, D. C	Nov. 15, 1859	26, 076
Fire-arm, Breech-loading	J. N. Aronson	New York, N. Y	Nov. 13, 1866	59, 540
Fire-arm, Breech-loading	E. H. Ashcroft	Boston, Mass	May 26, 1863	38, 645
Fire-arm, Breech-loading	J. Aston	Hythe, England	May 13, 1873	138, 837
Fire-arm, Breech-loading	N. L. Babcock	New Haven, Conn	Mar. 20, 1860	27, 509
Fire-arm, Breech-loading	A. M. Bacon	Washington, D. C	July 31, 1866	56, 846
Fire-arm, Breech-loading	G. R. Bacon	Providence, R. I	July 21, 1863	39, 270
Fire-arm, Breech-loading	C. W. Baldwin	Boston, Mass	Jan. 19, 1869	85, 897
Fire-arm, Breech-loading	C. H. Ballard	Worcester, Mass	Nov. 5, 1861	33, 631
Fire-arm, Breech-loading	J. Barber and P. C. Reinfried	Bridesburgh, Pa	Mar. 15, 1859	23, 224
Fire-arm, Breech-loading	K. V. Barnekov	Cornwall, N. Y	June 14, 1870	104, 100
Fire-arm, Breech-loading	O. W. Bayley	Somerville, Mass	Apr. 22, 1862	35, 008
Fire-arm, Breech-loading	F. Beals	New Haven, Conn	June 28, 1864	43, 284
Fire-arm, Breech-loading	F. Beals	New Haven, Conn	Jan. 30, 1866	52, 258
Fire-arm, Breech-loading	S. Belden and J. F. Crabtree	Visalia, Cal	Dec. 29, 1868	85, 268
Fire-arm, Breech-loading	H. Berdan	New York, N. Y	Jan. 10, 1865	45, 899
Fire-arm, Breech-loading	H. Berdan	New York, N. Y	Jan. 9, 1866	51, 991
Fire-arm, Breech-loading	H. Berdan	New York, N. Y	Feb. 27, 1866	52, 925
Fire-arm, Breech-loading	H. Berdan	New York, N. Y	Dec. 22, 1868	85, 162
Fire-arm, Breech-loading	H. Berdan	New York, N. Y	Mar. 30, 1869	88, 436
Fire-arm, Breech-loading	H. Berdan	New York, N. Y	Apr. 5, 1870	101, 418
Fire-arm, Breech-loading	H. Berdan	New York, N. Y	Nov. 1, 1870	108, 869
Fire-arm, Breech-loading	H. Berg	Davenport, Iowa	Mar. 25, 1862	34, 729
Fire-arm, Breech-loading	A. J. Bergen	Brooklyn, N. Y	Feb. 26, 1867	62, 465
Fire-arm, Breech-loading	A. J. Bergen and D. Williamson	Brooklyn, N. Y	Nov. 22, 1864	45, 202
Fire arm, Breech-loading	C. E. Billings	Windsor, Vt	Apr. 24, 1866	54, 100
Fire-arm, Breech-loading	J. D. Blaker	Newtown, Pa	Aug. 10, 1869	93, 403
Fire-arm, Breech-loading	S. Bostwick and C. G. Sargent	Graniteville, Mass	Nov. 11, 1862	36, 891
Fire-arm, Breech-loading	P. Bourdereaux	New York, N. Y	Nov. 13, 1866	59, 706
Fire-arm, Breech-loading	P. Bourdereaux	New York, N. Y	July 29, 1873	141, 198
Fire-arm, Breech-loading	F. E. Boyd and P. S. Tyler	Boston, Mass	Jan. 21, 1868	73, 494
Fire-arm, Breech-loading	F. E. Boyd and P. S. Tyler	Boston, Mass	Apr. 6, 1869	88, 540
Fire-arm, Breech-loading	J. Boynton	East Hartford, Conn	Nov. 27, 1860	30, 714
Fire-arm, Breech-loading	I. Bradley	Hartford, Conn	Aug. 7, 1866	56, 899
Fire-arm, Breech-loading	C. C. Brand	Norwich, Conn	Apr. 28, 1863	38, 280
Fire-arm, Breech-loading	C. C. Brand	Norwich, Conn	June 23, 1863	38, 943
Fire-arm, Breech-loading	W. Briggs	Norristown, Pa	Apr. 6, 1869	88, 605
Fire-arm, Breech-loading	L. W. Broadwell	New Orleans, La	Aug. 22, 1865	49, 583
Fire-arm, Breech-loading	E. Brooks and G. Walker	Philadelphia, Pa	July 6, 1858	20, 776
Fire-arm, Breech-loading	J. Broughton	New York, N. Y	Apr. 14, 1868	76, 595
Fire-arm, Breech-loading	W. H. Brown	Worcester, Mass	Mar. 4, 1862	34, 561
Fire-arm, Breech-loading	J. Brownes	Prince Edward Island	Aug. 2, 1864	43, 733
Fire-arm, Breech-loading	H. Brügmann	Waterloo, Mich	July 16, 1872	129, 312
Fire-arm, Breech-loading	H. Büchner	New York, N. Y	May 2, 1871	114, 259
Fire-arm, Breech-loading	A. Burgess	New York, N. Y	Sept. 26, 1871	119, 218
Fire-arm, Breech-loading	A. Burgess	Owego, N. Y	June 11, 1872	127, 737
Fire-arm, Breech-loading	J. Burke	Courtland, Ill	May 15, 1866	54, 080
Fire-arm, Breech-loading	J. Burke	Syracuse, Ill	June 19, 1866	55, 613
Fire-arm, Breech-loading	A. E. Burnside	Bristol, R. I	Mar. 25, 1856	14, 491
Fire-arm, Breech-loading	B. Burton	Brooklyn, N. Y	Dec. 20, 1859	26, 475
Fire-arm, Breech-loading	B. Burton	Brooklyn, N. Y	Aug. 11, 1868	81, 059

Index of patents issued from the United States Patent Office from 1790 *to* 1873, *inclusive*—Continued.

Invention.	Inventor.	Residence.	Date.	No.
Fire-arm, Breech-loading	C. Callaghon	Great Britain	Feb. 25, 1868	74, 888
Fire-arm, Breech-loading	J. F. C. Carle	Hamburg, Germany	Feb. 27, 1866	52, 938
Fire-arm, Breech-loading	H. Carter and G. H. Edwards	Stepney, England	Jan. 19, 1869	85, 999
Fire-arm, Breech-loading	H. A. Castle	Ilion, N. Y	Nov. 4, 1873	144, 190
Fire-arm, Breech-loading	C. Chabot	Philadelphia, Pa	Apr. 4, 1865	47, 163
Fire-arm, Breech-loading	C. Chabot	Philadelphia, Pa	Sept. 5, 1865	49, 718
Fire-arm, Breech-loading	M. J. Chamberlin	Springfield, Mass	Feb. 14, 1871	111, 814
Fire-arm, Breech-loading	M. J. Chamberlin	Springfield, Mass	July 16, 1872	129, 393
Fire-arm, Breech-loading	M. J. Chamberlin	Springfield, Mass	Feb. 4, 1873	135, 405
Fire-arm, Breech-loading	M. J. and H. M. Chamberlin	Springfield, Mass	Jan. 8, 1867	60, 998
Fire-arm, Breech-loading	L. N. Chapin	New Lisbon, N. Y	May 17, 1864	42, 748
Fire-arm, Breech-loading	A. A. Chassepot	Paris, France	Nov. 23, 1869	97, 167
Fire-arm, Breech-loading	F. Clark	North Oxford, Mass	July 19, 1864	43, 571
Fire-arm, Breech-loading	F. Clark	Auburn, Mass	Jan. 3, 1865	45, 701
Fire-arm, Breech-loading	F. Clark	Auburn, Mass	Mar. 27, 1866	53, 522
Fire-arm, Breech-loading	N. S. Clement	Worcester, Mass	May 27, 1856	14, 949
Fire-arm, Breech-loading	N. S. Clement	New York, N. Y	Oct. 10, 1865	50, 334
Fire-arm, Breech-loading	J. J. Cloes	Liege, Belgium	Apr. 12, 1870	101, 826
Fire-arm, Breech-loading	J. W. Cochran	New York, N. Y	July 7, 1863	39, 120
Fire-arm, Breech-loading	J. W. Cochran	New York, N. Y	Dec. 22, 1863	40, 992
Fire-arm, Breech-loading	J. W. Cochran	New York, N. Y	Apr. 4, 1865	47, 088
Fire-arm, Breech-loading	J. W. Cochran	New York, N. Y	Apr. 25, 1865	47, 396
Fire-arm, Breech-loading	J. W. Cochran	New York, N. Y	Mar. 26, 1867	63, 217
Fire-arm, Breech-loading	J. W. Cochran	New York, N. Y	Mar. 17, 1868	75, 627
Fire-arm, Breech-loading	J. W. Cochran	New York, N. Y	Jan. 5, 1869	85, 645
Fire-arm, Breech-loading	J. W. Cochran	New York, N. Y	May 7, 1872	126, 446
Fire-arm, Breech-loading	C. C. Coleman	Worcester, Mass	May 13, 1862	35, 217
Fire-arm, Breech-loading	C. C. Coleman	Worcester, Mass	Nov. 6, 1866	59, 500
Fire-arm, Breech-loading	H. Conant	Hartford, Conn	Apr. 1, 1856	14, 554
Fire-arm, Breech-loading	I. B. Conklin	Baltimore, Md	Feb. 16, 1869	86, 971
Fire-arm, Breech-loading	J. A. Conover	New York, N. Y	July 24, 1869	56, 669
Fire-arm, Breech-loading	L. Conroy	New York, N. Y	Dec. 31, 1867	72, 803
Fire-arm, Breech-loading	L. Conroy	New York, N. Y	June 15, 1869	91, 421
Fire-arm, Breech-loading	L. Conroy	New York, N. Y	Dec. 2, 1873	145, 154
Fire-arm, Breech-loading	R. F. Cook	Potsdam, N. Y	July 24, 1860	29, 340
Fire-arm, Breech-loading	R. F. Cook	Watertown, N. Y	Mar. 10, 1863	37, 854
Fire-arm, Breech-loading	J. C. Cooke	Middletown, Conn	June 3, 1862	35, 488
Fire-arm, Breech-loading	J. R. Cooper	Birmingham, England	Dec. 15, 1868	84, 938
Fire-arm, Breech-loading	C. Cox	Coxville, N. C	Apr. 27, 1858	20, 041
Fire-arm, Breech-loading	C. Cox	Coxville, N. C	Apr. 10, 1860	27, 778
Fire-arm, Breech-loading	S. Crispin	New York, N. Y	Jan. 1, 1867	60, 698
Fire-arm, Breech-loading	S. Crispin	New York, N. Y	Feb. 5, 1867	61, 722
Fire-arm, Breech-loading	F. Curtis	Saugus Centre, Mass	Feb. 15, 1859	22, 940
Fire-arm, Breech-loading	F. Curtis	Newton, (Lower Falls,) Mass.	Sept. 17, 1861	33, 317
Fire-arm, Breech-loading	F. Curtis	Newton, (Lower Falls,) Mass.	Jan. 19, 1864	41, 281
Fire-arm, Breech-loading	F. S. Dangerfield	Auburn, N. Y	Sept. 3, 1872	130, 984
Fire-arm, Breech-loading	J. Davis	Buffalo, N. Y	Jan. 27, 1863	37, 544
Fire-arm, Breech-loading	J. Davis	Buffalo, N. Y	July 7, 1863	39, 198
Fire-arm, Breech-loading	J. Davis	Buffalo, N. Y	Apr. 26, 1864	42, 529
Fire-arm, Breech-loading	J. Davis	Buffalo, N. Y	Nov. 28, 1865	51, 258
Fire-arm, Breech-loading	J. Davis	Buffalo, N. Y	May 17, 1870	103, 154
Fire-arm, Breech-loading	J. M. Deprez	Liege, Belgium	Feb. 9, 1869	86, 739
Fire-arm, Breech-loading	M. L. M. Descontures	Paris, France	July 25, 1865	49, 057
Fire-arm, Breech-loading	F. V. Diaz	New York, N. Y	Sept. 7, 1869	94, 577
Fire-arm, Breech-loading	W. C. Dodge	Washington, D. C	Sept. 20, 1864	44, 290
Fire-arm, Breech-loading	W. C. Dodge	Washington, D. C	Feb. 13, 1866	52, 547
Fire-arm, Breech-loading	W. C. Dodge	Washington, D. C	Mar. 14, 1871	112, 763
Fire-arm, Breech-loading	W. C. Dodge	Washington, D. C	Apr. 4, 1871	113, 408
Fire-arm, Breech-loading	W. C. Dodge	Washington, D. C	May 9, 1871	114, 653
Fire-arm, Breech-loading	W. C. and P. T. Dodge	Washington, D. C	Mar. 14, 1871	112, 694
Fire-arm, Breech-loading	W. C. and P. T. Dodge	Washington, D. C	Aug. 22, 1871	118, 350
Fire-arm, Breech-loading	W. C. and P. T. Dodge	Washington, D. C	June 11, 1872	127, 683
Fire-arm, Breech-loading	J. D. Dougall	Westminster, Great Britain.	Sept. 5, 1865	49, 844
Fire-arm, Breech-loading	J. Duval	Laprairie, Canada	Mar. 14, 1871	112, 565
Fire-arm, Breech-loading	J. Duval	Laprairie, Canada	Jan. 30, 1872	123, 159
Fire-arm, Breech-loading	J. Duval	Montreal, Canada	Dec. 16, 1873	145, 494
Fire-arm, Breech-loading	G. H. Earnest	Springfield, Ohio	July 16, 1872	129, 115
Fire-arm, Breech-loading	W. H. Elliot	Plattsburgh, N. Y	May 13, 1862	35, 284
Fire-arm, Breech-loading	W. H. Elliot	Plattsburgh, N. Y	July 7, 1863	39, 136
Fire-arm, Breech-loading	W. H. Elliot	Plattsburgh, N. Y	Apr. 18, 1865	47, 372
Fire-arm, Breech-loading	W. H. Elliot	Plattsburgh, N. Y	May 23, 1865	47, 809
Fire-arm, Breech-loading	W. H. Elliot	New York, N. Y	Dec. 13, 1870	110, 024
Fire-arm, Breech-loading	W. H. Elliot	New York, N. Y	May 9, 1871	114, 540
Fire-arm, Breech-loading	W. H. Elliot	New York, N. Y	Dec. 5, 1871	121, 499
Fire-arm, Breech-loading	W. H. Elliot	New York, N. Y	Apr. 2, 1872	125, 127
Fire-arm, Breech-loading	W. C. Ellis	Springfield, Mass	Apr. 26, 1859	23, 762
Fire-arm, Breech-loading	J. Elson	Boston, Mass	May 14, 1867	64, 650
Fire-arm, Breech-loading	J. Elson	Boston, Mass	July 23, 1867	67, 033
Fire-arm, Breech-loading	J. Elson	Boston, Mass	Nov. 19, 1867	71, 149
Fire-arm, Breech-loading	J. Elson and W. R. Schaefer	Boston, Mass	Feb. 2, 1869	86, 378
Fire-arm, Breech-loading	A. B. Ely and E. C. Clay	Newton and Malden, Mass.	July 5, 1870	105, 058
Fire-arm, Breech-loading	F. H. Escherich	Baltimore, Md	June 2, 1868	78, 519
Fire-arm, Breech-loading	L. T. Fairbanks	Worcester, Mass	June 22, 1869	91, 616
Fire-arm, Breech-loading	G. H. Ferriss	Utica, N. Y	Oct. 10, 1871	119, 834
Fire-arm, Breech-loading	V. Fogerty	Boston, Mass	Feb. 2, 1869	86, 520
Fire-arm, Breech-loading	V. Fogerty	Boston, Mass	July 25, 1871	117, 398
Fire-arm, Breech-loading	G. P. Foster	Providence, R. I	Apr. 10, 1860	27, 874
Fire-arm, Breech-loading	G. P. and G. F. Foster	Mohawk, N. Y	July 17, 1866	56, 399
Fire-arm, Breech-loading	G. H. Fox	Boston, Mass	Jan. 4, 1870	98, 579
Fire-arm, Breech-loading	A. T. Freeman	Herkimer, N. Y	Jan. 16, 1872	122, 717
Fire-arm, Breech-loading	A. T. Freeman	Herkimer, N. Y	Dec 10, 1872	135, 770
Fire-arm, Breech-loading	M. J. Gallager	Savannah, Ga	July 17, 1860	29, 157
Fire-arm, Breech-loading	M. J. Gallager and W. H. Gladding.	Savannah, Ga	July 12, 1859	24, 730
Fire-arm, Breech-loading	L. Geiger	Hudson, N. Y	Jan. 27, 1863	37, 501

Index of patents issued from the United States Patent Office from 1790 to 1873, inclusive—Continued.

Invention.	Inventor.	Residence.	Date.	No.
Fire-arm, Breech-loading	S. Gerngross	Saint Louis, Mo	Dec. 20, 1870	110, 353
Fire-arm, Breech-loading	L. H. Gibbs	New York, N. Y	Jan. 8, 1856	14, 057
Fire-arm, Breech-loading	W. Golcher	Saint Paul, Minn	Mar. 30, 1869	88, 470
Fire-arm, Breech-loading	W. Golcher	Saint Paul, Minn	Oct. 19, 1869	95, 998
Fire-arm, Breech-loading	R. Gosham	New York, N. Y	Feb. 27, 1872	124, 056
Fire-arm, Breech-loading	T. P. Gould	Niagara Falls, N. Y	Jan. 3, 1860	26, 734
Fire-arm, Breech-loading	J. Goulding	Worcester, Mass	May 3, 1864	42, 573
Fire-arm, Breech-loading	G. B. Gray and J. H. Romans	Mount Vernon, Ohio	Mar. 21, 1871	112, 803
Fire-arm, Breech-loading	J. Gray	Medford, Mass	Nov. 8, 1864	44, 995
Fire-arm, Breech-loading	C. Green	Rochester, N. Y	Dec. 6, 1870	109, 890
Fire-arm, Breech-loading	J. D. Greene	Cambridge, Mass	Jan. 3, 1854	10, 391
Fire-arm, Breech-loading	J. D. Greene	Cambridge, Mass	June 27, 1854	11, 157
Fire-arm, Breech-loading	J. D. Greene	Cambridge, Mass	Nov. 17, 1857	18, 634
Fire-arm, Breech-loading	J. D. Greene	United States Army	Feb. 18, 1862	34, 422
Fire-arm, Breech-loading	J. D. Greene	Cambridge, Mass	Mar. 23, 1869	88, 161
Fire-arm, Breech-loading	A. Grillet	Philadelphia, Pa	Nov. 22, 1864	45, 152
Fire-arm, Breech-loading	H. Gross	Seneca County, Ohio	June 10, 1856	15, 072
Fire-arm, Breech-loading	H. Gross	Tiffin, Ohio	Aug. 30, 1859	25, 259
Fire-arm, Breech-loading	H. Gross	Tiffin, Ohio	Aug. 11, 1863	39, 479
Fire-arm, Breech-loading	H. Gross	Tiffin, Ohio	Aug. 25, 1863	39, 646
Fire-arm, Breech-loading	H. Gross	Tiffin, Ohio	May 31, 1864	42, 941
Fire-arm, Breech-loading	F. Gueury	Paris, France	Dec. 24, 1872	134, 200
Fire-arm, Breech-loading	G. Gundersen	Chicago, Ill	Dec. 30, 1873	145, 998
Fire-arm, Breech-loading	E. F. Gunn	Charleston, S. C	Sept. 10, 1867	68, 736
Fire-arm, Breech-loading	E. F. Gunn	Charleston, S. C	Dec. 29, 1868	85, 442
Fire-arm, Breech-loading	E. Gwyn and A. C. Campbell	Hamilton, Ohio	Oct. 21, 1862	36, 709
Fire-arm, Breech-loading	A. Hamilton	Broad Brook, Conn	Nov. 19, 1861	33, 769
Fire-arm, Breech-loading	H. Hammond	Providence, R. I	Oct. 25, 1864	44, 798
Fire-arm, Breech-loading	H. Hammond	Hartford, Conn	Mar. 14, 1871	112, 589
Fire-arm, Breech-loading	G. Hancock	Providence, R. I	Apr. 26, 1864	42, 471
Fire-arm, Breech-loading	J. Hanson	Raschliffe, near Huddersfield, England.	Nov. 29, 1870	109, 731
Fire-arm, Breech-loading	I. Hartshorn	Providence, R. I	Mar. 31, 1863	38, 042
Fire-arm, Breech-loading	H. W. Hayden	Waterbury, Conn	Dec. 20, 1864	45, 495
Fire-arm, Breech loading	J. S. Heath	London, England	May 13, 1873	138, 887
Fire-arm, Breech-loading	J. A. Heckenbach	Mayville, Wis	June 22, 1869	91, 624
Fire-arm, Breech-loading	A. Henry	Edinburgh, North Britain	Feb. 13, 1866	52, 654
Fire-arm, Breech-loading	A. Henry	Edinburgh, North Britain	Sept. 19, 1871	119, 145
Fire-arm, Breech-loading	A. Henry	Edinburgh, Scotland	Dec. 30, 1873	145, 944
Fire-arm, Breech-loading	W. C. Hicks	New York, N. Y	Mar. 1, 1864	41, 814
Fire-arm, Breech-loading	A. V. Hill	Hinsdale, N. Y	Aug. 2, 1859	24, 936
Fire-arm, Breech-loading	W. D. Hillis	Joliet, Ill	Sept. 20, 1864	44, 312
Fire-arm, Breech-loading	A. J. H. Hilton	Boston, Mass	July 16, 1867	66, 709
Fire-arm, Breech-loading	M. J. Hinden	Detroit, Mich	June 29, 1869	92, 048
Fire-arm, Breech-loading	C. B. Holden	Worcester, Mass	Apr. 1, 1862	34, 859
Fire-arm, Breech-loading	C. B. Holden	Worcester, Mass	Mar. 29, 1864	42, 139
Fire-arm, Breech-loading	G. L. Holt and J. C. Marshall	Springfield, Mass	Apr. 22, 1873	138, 157
Fire-arm, Breech-loading	H. H. Hopkins	Norwich, Conn	Sept. 23, 1873	143, 012
Fire-arm, Breech-loading	H. Hoppenau	Kansas City, Mo	Mar. 18, 1873	136, 998
Fire-arm, Breech-loading	B. B. Hotchkiss	New York, N. Y	Aug. 17, 1869	93, 822
Fire-arm, Breech-loading	B. B. Hotchkiss	New York, N. Y	Feb. 15, 1870	99, 898
Fire-arm, Breech-loading	B. B. Hotchkiss	New York, N. Y	Jan. 2, 1872	122, 465
Fire-arm, Breech-loading	C. Howard	New York, N. Y	Sept. 26, 1865	50, 125
Fire-arm, Breech loading	C. Howard	New York, N. Y	Oct. 10, 1865	50, 358
Fire-arm, Breech-loading	C. W. Howard	Hammonton, N. J	July 14, 1863	39, 232
Fire-arm, Breech-loading	S. Howard	Elyria, Ohio	Oct. 28, 1862	36, 779
Fire-arm, Breech-loading	F. W. Howe	Providence, R. I	Sept. 16, 1862	36, 466
Fire-arm, Breech-loading	F. W. Howe	Providence, R. I	Mar. 7, 1865	46, 671
Fire-arm, Breech-loading	W. W. Hubbell	Philadelphia, Pa	June 18, 1867	65, 812
Fire-arm, Breech-loading	D. Hug	New York, N. Y	Sept. 2, 1873	142, 396
Fire-arm, Breech-loading	C. Jackson and T. Goodrem	Providence, R. I	Mar. 7, 1863	37, 937
Fire arm, Breech loading	A. E. and P. J. Jarre	Paris, France	Apr. 15, 1873	137, 927
Fire-arm, Breech loading	B. H. Jenks	Bridesburgh, Pa	Feb. 25, 1868	74, 760
Fire-arm, Breech-loading	L. Jennings	New York, N. Y	Dec. 25, 1849	6, 973
Fire-arm, Breech-loading	W. Johnston	Cincinnati, Ohio	May 13, 1862	35, 241
Fire-arm, Breech-loading	W. Johnston	Cincinnati, Ohio	Nov. 1, 1864	44, 868
Fire-arm, Breech-loading	F. Jonas	McConnel's Grove, Ill	Oct. 2, 1860	30, 228
Fire-arm, Breech-loading	B. F. Joslyn	Worcester, Mass	Aug. 28, 1855	13, 507
Fire-arm, Breech-loading	B. F. Joslyn	Worcester, Mass	July 1, 1856	15, 240
Fire-arm, Breech-loading	B. F. Joslyn	Stonington, Conn	June 24, 1862	35, 688
Fire-arm, Breech-loading	B. F. Joslyn	Stonington, Conn	Aug. 4, 1863	39, 407
Fire-arm, Breech-loading	B. F. Joslyn	Stonington, Conn	Mar. 22, 1864	42, 000
Fire-arm, Breech-loading	B. F. Joslyn	Stonington, Conn	June 6, 1865	48, 073
Fire-arm, Breech-loading	B. F. Joslyn	Stonington, Conn	June 20, 1865	48, 288
Fire-arm, Breech-loading	B. F. Joslyn	Stonington, Conn	Jan. 2, 1866	51, 837
Fire-arm, Breech-loading	B. F. Joslyn	New York, N. Y	Nov. 15, 1870	109, 218
Fire-arm, Breech-loading	A. B. Kay	Newark, N. J	Nov. 22, 1870	109, 419
Fire-arm, Breech-loading	H. Kellogg	New Haven, Conn	May 20, 1862	35, 356
Fire-arm, Breech-loading	A. Krupp	Essen, Prussia	Aug. 9, 1864	43, 820
Fire-arm, Breech-loading	T. T. S. Laidley and C. A. Emery	United States Army and Springfield, Mass.	May 15, 1866	54, 743
Fire-arm, Breech-loading	W. R. Landfear	Hartford, Conn	Sept. 6, 1864	44, 099
Fire-arm, Breech-loading	R. S. Lawrence	Windsor, Vt	Jan. 6, 1852	8, 637
Fire-arm, Breech-loading	R. S. Lawrence	Hartford, Conn	Dec. 20, 1859	26, 504
Fire-arm, Breech-loading	R. S. Lawrence	Hartford, Conn	Apr. 6, 1869	88, 645
Fire-arm, Breech-loading	D. Leavitt	Chicopee, Mass	June 14, 1859	24, 394
Fire-arm, Breech-loading	J. Lee	Stevens Point, Wis	July 22, 1862	35, 941
Fire-arm, Breech-loading	J. Lee	Milwaukee, Wis	May 15, 1866	54, 744
Fire-arm, Breech-loading	J. Lee	Milwaukee, Wis	May 16, 1871	114, 951
Fire-arm, Breech-loading	J. Lee	Milwaukee, Wis	June 20, 1871	116, 068
Fire-arm, Breech-loading	J. Lee	Milwaukee, Wis	Jan. 2, 1872	122, 470
Fire-arm, Breech-loading	J. Lee	Milwaukee, Wis	Jan. 16, 1872	122, 772
Fire-arm, Breech-loading	T. Lee	New York, N. Y	Apr. 27, 1858	20, 073
Fire-arm, Breech-loading	T. Lee	Newark, N. J	Nov. 19, 1861	33, 745
Fire-arm, Breech-loading	J. Letort and H. S. Mathews	Wytheville, Va	Apr. 3, 1860	27, 723
Fire-arm, Breech-loading	E. Lindner	New York, N. Y	Mar. 29, 1859	23, 378
Fire-arm, Breech-loading	H. Lord	Hartford, Conn	Feb. 11, 1868	74, 387
Fire-arm, Breech-loading	O. D. Lull	Watkins, N. Y	June 16, 1863	38, 903

Index of patents issued from the United States Patent Office from 1790 to 1873, inclusive—Continued.

Invention.	Inventor.	Residence.	Date.	No.
Fire-arm, Breech-loading	J. Manton	Montreal, Canada	Aug. 1, 1871	117, 552
Fire-arm, Breech-loading	A. Marelli	Milan, Italy	May 27, 1873	139, 323
Fire-arm, Breech-loading	S. W. Marsh	Washington, D. C	Dec. 6, 1859	26, 362
Fire-arm, Breech-loading	S. W. Marsh	Washington, D. C	Nov. 5, 1861	33, 655
Fire-arm, Breech-loading	J. P. Marshall	Millbury, Mass	Oct. 4, 1859	25, 661
Fire-arm, Breech-loading	J. P. Marshall	Millbury, Mass	Apr. 29, 1862	35, 107
Fire-arm, Breech-loading	J. M. Mason	Washington, D. C	Mar. 7, 1871	112, 523
Fire-arm, Breech-loading	J. M. Mason	Washington, D. C	Aug. 8, 1871	117, 906
Fire-arm, Breech-loading	F. Maton	New York, N. Y	Nov. 14, 1854	11, 938
Fire-arm, Breech-loading	E. Maynard	Washington, D. C	May 27, 1851	8, 126
Fire-arm, Breech-loading	E. Maynard	Washington, D. C	Dec. 6, 1859	26, 364
Fire-arm, Breech-loading	E. Maynard	Washington, D. C	Oct. 30, 1860	30, 537
Fire-arm, Breech-loading	E. Maynard	Washington, D. C	June 27, 1865	48, 423
Fire-arm, Breech-loading	E. Maynard	Washington, D. C	Aug. 1, 1865	49, 130
Fire-arm, Breech-loading	E. Maynard	Washington, D. C	Feb. 2, 1869	86, 566
Fire-arm, Breech-loading	E. Maynard	New York, N. Y	Feb. 18, 1873	135, 928
Fire-arm, Breech-loading	J. E. McBeth	New Orleans, La	Jan. 14, 1868	73, 357
Fire-arm, Breech-loading	J. E. McBeth	New Orleans, La	Aug. 11, 1868	80, 985
Fire-arm, Breech-loading	R. McChesney	Ilion, N. Y	Oct. 2, 1866	58, 444
Fire-arm, Breech-loading	R. McChesney	Utica, N. Y	May 28, 1867	65, 103
Fire-arm, Breech-loading	J. McGoveren	New York, N. Y	Apr. 13, 1869	88, 890
Fire-arm, Breech-loading	J. V. Meigs	Washington, D. C	Oct. 21, 1862	36, 721
Fire-arm, Breech-loading	J. V. Meigs	Washington, D. C	May 22, 1866	54, 934
Fire-arm, Breech-loading	J. V. Meigs	Washington, D. C	Aug. 18, 1868	81, 100
Fire-arm, Breech-loading	D. F. Mellen	Manchester, N. H	Oct. 4, 1864	44, 545
Fire-arm, Breech-loading	J. Merlett	Boundbrook, N. J	Aug. 18, 1868	81, 283
Fire-arm, Breech-loading	L. A. Merriam	New York, N. Y	Feb. 16, 1869	87, 058
Fire-arm, Breech-loading	G. Merrill	East Orange, N. J	Oct. 17, 1871	119, 939
Fire-arm, Breech-loading	G. Merrill	East Orange, N. J	Oct. 17, 1871	119, 940
Fire-arm, Breech-loading	J. H. Merrill	Baltimore, Md	July 20, 1858	20, 954
Fire-arm, Breech-loading	J. H. Merrill	Baltimore, Md	Apr. 9, 1861	32, 032
Fire-arm, Breech-loading	J. H. Merrill	Baltimore, Md	Apr. 9, 1861	32, 033
Fire-arm, Breech-loading	J. H. Merrill	Baltimore, Md	Oct. 22, 1861	33, 536
Fire-arm, Breech-loading	J. H. Merrill	Baltimore, Md	Dec. 8, 1863	40, 884
Fire-arm, Breech-loading	I. M. Milbank	Greenfield Hill, Conn	Dec. 2, 1862	37, 048
Fire-arm, Breech-loading	I. M. Milbank	Greenfield Hill, Conn	Jan. 31, 1865	46, 125
Fire-arm, Breech-loading	I. M. Milbank	Greenfield Hill, Conn	Feb. 20, 1866	52, 734
Fire-arm, Breech-loading	I. M. Milbank	Greenfield Hill, Conn	June 12, 1866	55, 520
Fire-arm, Breech-loading	I. M. Milbank	Greenfield Hill, Conn	Jan. 8, 1867	61, 082
Fire-arm, Breech-loading	I. M. Milbank	Greenfield Hill, Conn	Feb. 5, 1867	61, 751
Fire-arm, Breech-loading	I. M. Milbank	Greenfield Hill, Conn	June 11, 1867	65, 585
Fire-arm, Breech-loading	I. M. Milbank	Greenfield Hill, Conn	Dec. 1, 1868	84, 566
Fire-arm, Breech-loading	I. M. Milbank	Greenfield Hill, Conn	Apr. 16, 1872	125, 829
Fire-arm, Breech-loading	I. M. Milbank	Greenfield Hill, Conn	Mar. 18, 1873	136, 850
Fire-arm, Breech-loading	W. H. Miller	West Meriden, Conn	Nov. 13, 1866	59, 723
Fire-arm, Breech-loading	W. H. and G. W. Miller	Meriden, Conn	May 23, 1865	47, 902
Fire-arm, Breech-loading	W. H. and G. W. Miller	West Meriden, Conn	Dec. 26, 1865	51, 739
Fire-arm, Breech-loading	W. H. and G. W. Miller	West Meriden, Conn	May 14, 1867	64, 786
Fire-arm, Breech-loading	J. K. Millner	New York, N. Y	Feb. 17, 1863	37, 723
Fire-arm, Breech-loading	E. M. Mix and H. B. Horton	Ithaca, N. Y	Jan. 19, 1864	41, 343
Fire-arm, Breech-loading	D. Moore	Brooklyn, N. Y	Dec. 3, 1861	33, 847
Fire-arm, Breech-loading	W. Morgenstern	Philadelphia, Pa	Nov. 29, 1864	45, 262
Fire-arm, Breech-loading	W. Morgenstern	Philadelphia, Pa	June 6, 1865	48, 133
Fire-arm, Breech-loading	W. Morgenstern	Hartford, Conn	Dec. 24, 1867	72, 526
Fire-arm, Breech-loading	W. Morgenstern	Philadelphia, Pa	Feb. 18, 1868	74, 712
Fire-arm, Breech-loading	W. Morgenstern	Hartford, Conn	June 23, 1868	79, 291
Fire-arm, Breech-loading	W. Morgenstern	New York, N. Y	Feb. 2, 1869	86, 434
Fire-arm, Breech-loading	W. Morgenstern	New York, N. Y	Feb. 23, 1869	87, 190
Fire-arm, Breech-loading	W. Morgenstern	New York, N. Y	Aug. 3, 1869	93, 320
Fire-arm, Breech-loading	W. Morgenstern and E. Morwitz.	Philadelphia, Pa	Nov. 10, 1863	40, 572
Fire-arm, Breech-loading	S. Morris and W. and P. Mauser.	Springfield, Mass., and Oberndorf, Würtemberg.	June 2, 1868	78, 603
Fire-arm, Breech-loading	G. W. Morse	Baton Rouge, La	Oct. 28, 1856	15, 995
Fire-arm, Breech-loading	G. W. Morse	Baton Rouge, La	June 8, 1858	20, 503
Fire-arm, Breech loading	M. Moses	Malone, N. Y	Sept. 30, 1862	36, 571
Fire-arm, Breech-loading	A. Muller	Paris, France	May 24, 1870	103, 488
Fire-arm, Breech-loading	F. Muller	Hartford, Conn	Feb. 4, 1868	74, 119
Fire-arm, Breech-loading	A. S. Munger	Chicopee Falls, Mass	Mar. 12, 1867	62, 873
Fire-arm, Breech-loading	S. and G. H. Needham	London, England	May 21, 1867	64, 999
Fire-arm, Breech-loading	R. Nenninger	Newark, N. Y	Mar. 28, 1871	113, 194
Fire-arm, Breech-loading	F. D. Newbury	New York, N. Y	Jan. 9, 1867	51, 959
Fire-arm, Breech-loading	J. D. S. Newell	Tensas Parish, La	Apr. 6, 1869	88, 730
Fire-arm, Breech-loading	J. D. S Newell	Tensas Parish, La	May 25, 1869	90, 381
Fire-arm, Breech-loading	A. N. Newton	Richmond, Ind	June 27, 1854	11, 198
Fire-arm, Breech-loading	A. N. Newton	Richmond, Ind	Sept. 19, 1854	11, 700
Fire-arm, Breech-loading	F. E. M. Nillus	Havre, France	May 7, 1872	126, 568
Fire-arm, Breech-loading	P. J. J. Noël	Paris, France	Dec. 22, 1868	85, 120
Fire-arm, Breech-loading	J. C. Nye	Cincinnati, Ohio	Oct. 28, 1862	36, 852
Fire-arm, Breech-loading	J. C. Nye	Cincinnati, Ohio	Jan. 6, 1863	37, 336
Fire-arm, Breech-loading	J. Oliphant	Uniontown, Pa	Jan. 13, 1863	37, 407
Fire-arm, Breech loading	W. Palmer	New York, N. Y	July 23, 1861	32, 887
Fire-arm, Breech-loading	W. Palmer	New York, N. Y	Dec. 22, 1863	41, 017
Fire-arm, Breech-loading	W. R. Pape	Newcastle-upon-Tyne, Great Britain.	Nov. 5, 1867	70, 463
Fire-arm, Breech-loading	W. R. Pape	Newcastle-upon-Tyne, England.	Nov. 24, 1868	84, 373
Fire-arm, Breech-loading	C. F. Payne	Gardner, Mass	May 10, 1864	42, 685
Fire-arm, Breech-loading	H. O. Peabody	Boston, Mass	July 22, 1862	35, 947
Fire-arm, Breech-loading	H. O. Peabody	Providence, R. I	Dec. 10, 1867	72, 076
Fire-arm, Breech-loading	H. O. Peabody	Providence, R. I	Apr. 14, 1868	76, 805
Fire-arm, Breech-loading	J. Percy	Albany, N. Y	Aug. 11, 1863	39, 494
Fire-arm, Breech-loading	C. Perley	New York, N. Y	Feb. 24, 1863	37, 764
Fire-arm, Breech-loading	A. D. Perry	Newark, N. J	Nov. 28, 1854	12, 001
Fire-arm, Breech-loading	M. Pidault and G. Elize dit Lagieze.	Paris, France	Sept. 10, 1867	68, 786
Fire-arm, Breech-loading	G. R. Pierce	Grand Rapids, Mich	Oct. 3, 1871	119, 474

Index of patents issued from the United States Patent Office from 1790 *to* 1873, *inclusive*—Continued.

Invention.	Inventor.	Residence.	Date.	No.
Fire-arm, Breech-loading	T. Poultney and S. Crispin	Baltimore, Md., and New York, N. Y.	May 14, 1867	64, 701
Fire-arm, Breech-loading	J. W. Preston	Newton, Mass	Feb. 5, 1867	61, 865
Fire-arm, Breech-loading	F. B. Prindle	New Haven, Conn	Nov. 28, 1865	51, 213
Fire-arm, Breech-loading	S. S. Rembert	Memphis, Tenn	Oct. 29, 1867	70, 264
Fire-arm, Breech-loading	S. S. Rembert	Memphis, Tenn	Feb. 18, 1868	74, 594
Fire-arm, Breech-loading	S. Remington	Ilion, N. Y	Feb. 9, 1869	86, 690
Fire-arm, Breech-loading	E. S. Renwick	New York, N. Y	Apr. 26, 1870	102, 434
Fire-arm, Breech-loading	T. Restell	London, England	Mar. 26, 1867	63, 303
Fire-arm, Breech-loading	T. Restell	Birmingham, England	May 20, 1873	139, 190
Fire-arm, Breech-loading	H. Reynolds	New Haven, Conn	May 8, 1866	54, 600
Fire-arm, Breech-loading	C. B. Richards	Hartford, Conn	Aug. 18, 1868	81, 290
Fire-arm, Breech-loading	W. Richards	Birmingham, England	July 14, 1863	39, 246
Fire-arm, Breech-loading	W. Richards	Birmingham, England	Oct. 10, 1865	50, 432
Fire-arm, Breech-loading	W. Richards	Birmingham, England	May 11, 1869	89, 889
Fire-arm, Breech-loading	W. Richards	Birmingham, England	June 22, 1869	91, 668
Fire-arm, Breech-loading	W. Richards	Birmingham, England	Dec. 3, 1872	133, 665
Fire-arm, Breech-loading	W. Richards	Birmingham, England	May 27, 1873	139, 422
Fire-arm, Breech-loading	G. J. Richardson	Philadelphia, Pa	Aug. 23, 1864	43, 929
Fire-arm, Breech-loading	J. Rider	Newark, Ohio	Sept. 13, 1859	25, 470
Fire-arm, Breech-loading	J. Rider	Newark, Ohio	Nov. 15, 1864	45, 123
Fire-arm, Breech-loading	J. Rider	Newark, Ohio	Jan. 3, 1865	45, 797
Fire-arm, Breech-loading	J. Rider	Newark, Ohio	Feb. 21, 1865	46, 532
Fire-arm, Breech-loading	J. Rider	Newark, Ohio	Mar. 27, 1866	53, 543
Fire-arm, Breech-loading	J. Rider	Newark, Ohio	Feb. 11, 1868	74, 428
Fire-arm, Breech-loading	J. Rider	Newark, Ohio	July 29, 1873	141, 383
Fire-arm, Breech-loading	J. Rider	Newark, Ohio	July 29, 1873	141, 384
Fire-arm, Breech-loading	B. S. Roberts	United States Army	Sept. 23, 1862	36, 531
Fire-arm, Breech-loading	B. S. Roberts	United States Army	Feb. 27, 1866	52, 867
Fire-arm, Breech-loading	B. S. Roberts	United States Army	June 11, 1867	65, 607
Fire-arm, Breech-loading	B. S. Roberts	United States Army	May 11, 1869	90, 024
Fire-arm, Breech-loading	W. H. Robertson and G. W. Simpson.	Hartford, Conn	Feb. 12, 1856	14, 253
Fire-arm, Breech-loading	W. H. Robertson and G. W. Simpson.	Hartford, Conn	Mar. 13, 1866	53, 187
Fire-arm, Breech-loading	O. M. Robinson	Upper Jay, N. Y	May 24, 1870	103, 504
Fire-arm, Breech-loading	O. M. Robinson	Plattsburgh, N. Y	Apr. 23, 1872	125, 988
Fire-arm, Breech-loading	E. K. Root	Hartford, Conn	June 4, 1867	65, 509
Fire-arm, Breech-loading	A. H. Rowe	Hartford, Conn	Apr. 5, 1864	42, 227
Fire-arm, Breech-loading	J. Ruler	Newark, Ohio	Dec. 8, 1863	40, 887
Fire-arm, Breech-loading	C. F. Russell	New Britain, Conn	May 14, 1872	126, 748
Fire-arm, Breech-loading	S. Rydbeck	Red Wing, Minn	June 28, 1870	104, 775
Fire-arm, Breech-loading	C. G. Saez	Madrid, Spain	Jan. 3, 1865	45, 801
Fire-arm, Breech-loading	E. L. Sargent	Watertown, N. Y	Mar. 1, 1870	100, 4[illegible]5
Fire-arm, Breech-loading	E. L. Sargent	Watertown, N. Y	June 21, 1870	104, 502
Fire-arm, Breech-loading	E. L. Sargent	Watertown, N. Y	Nov. 15, 1870	109, 255
Fire-arm, Breech-loading	A. Sayer	Naubuc, Conn	June 19, 1866	55, 719
Fire-arm, Breech-loading	J. Scharffe	New York, N. Y	Nov. 11, 1856	16, 070
Fire-arm, Breech-loading	J. P. Schenkl	Boston, Mass	Aug. 16, 1853	9, 943
Fire-arm, Breech-loading	J. P. Schenkl	Boston, Mass	June 23, 1857	17, 642
Fire-arm, Breech-loading	J. P. Schenkl	Worcester, Mass	Oct. 12, 1858	21, 802
Fire-arm, Breech-loading	H. A. Schesch	Ilion, N. Y	Apr. 9, 1872	125, 62[illegible]
Fire-arm, Breech-loading	G. W. Schofield	United States Army	June 14, 1870	104, 211
Fire-arm, Breech-loading	G. W. Schofield	United States Army	June 20, 1871	116, 225
Fire-arm, Breech-loading	F. Schopp	New York, N. Y	Nov. 28, 1865	51, 225
Fire-arm, Breech-loading	H. Schroder	New York, N. Y	June 25, 1861	32, 653
Fire-arm, Breech-loading	H. Schroeder, L. Salewski, and W. Schmidt.	Bloomington, Ill	Dec. 23, 1856	16, 288
Fire-arm, Breech-loading	C. D. Schubarth	Providence, R. I	July 23, 1861	32, 895
Fire-arm, Breech-loading	P. Schuler	Morris, Ind	Jan. 5, 1869	85, 616
Fire-arm, Breech-loading	P. Schuler	Morris, Ind	Nov. 1, 1870	108, 836
Fire-arm, Breech-loading	G. Schulz	Fort Madison, Iowa	May 11, 1869	89, 947
Fire-arm, Breech-loading	W. Scott and W. J. Matthews	Birmingham and Aston, England.	Nov. 25, 1873	144, 870
Fire-arm, Breech-loading	W. M. Scott	Birmingham, England	Nov. 1, 1870	108, 942
Fire-arm, Breech-loading	J. H. Sears	Brantford, Canada	Dec. 20, 1859	26, 526
Fire-arm, Breech-loading	J. H. Selwyn	Grasmere, England	Aug. 14, 1866	57, 269
Fire-arm, Breech-loading	C. Sharps	Philadelphia, Pa	Jan. 25, 1859	22, 752
Fire-arm, Breech-loading	C. Sharps	Philadelphia, Pa	July 9, 1861	32, 790
Fire-arm, Breech-loading	C. Sharps	Philadelphia, Pa	Oct. 29, 1861	33, 607
Fire-arm, Breech-loading	C. Sharps	Philadelphia, Pa	Feb. 12, 1867	62, 077
Fire-arm, Breech-loading	C. Sharps	Philadelphia, Pa	Apr. 8, 1873	137, 625
Fire-arm, Breech-loading	H. N. Sherman	Beloit, Wis	Nov. 25, 1873	144, 872
Fire-arm, Breech-loading	T. E. Shull	Millersburgh, Pa	Apr. 5, 1859	23, 505
Fire-arm, Breech-loading	B. F. Skinner and A. Plummer, jr.	Mystic Bridge, Conn	Feb. 18, 1862	34, 449
Fire-arm, Breech-loading	C. D. Skinner and D. Tryon	Haddam and Middletown, Conn.	Oct. 20, 1857	18, 472
Fire-arm, Breech loading	J. Smiles	Birmingham, England	Dec. 27, 1870	110, 505
Fire-arm, Breech-loading	D. Smith	Springfield, Mass	July 16, 1872	129, 433
Fire-arm, Breech-loading	D. Smith	Springfield, Mass	Apr. 22, 1873	138, 207
Fire-arm, Breech-loading	D. Smith and M. J. Chamberlin	Springfield, Mass	Mar. 7, 1871	112, 505
Fire-arm, Breech-loading	D. Smith and J. C. Marshall	Springfield, Mass	Aug. 5, 1873	141, 603
Fire-arm, Breech-loading	G. Smith	Buttermilk Falls, N. Y	Dec. 25, 1855	14, 001
Fire-arm, Breech-loading	G. Smith	Buttermilk Falls, N. Y	Aug. 5, 1856	15, 496
Fire-arm, Breech-loading	G. Smith	Buttermilk Falls, N. Y	June 23, 1857	17, 644
Fire-arm, Breech-loading	H. Smith	Norwich, Conn	Aug. 26, 1851	8, 317
Fire-arm, Breech-loading	I. Smith	New York, N. Y	Apr. 26, 1864	42, 542
Fire-arm, Breech-loading	W. H. Smith	Birmingham, Conn	Dec. 10, 1861	33, 907
Fire-arm, Breech-loading	W. H. Smith	Birmingham, Conn	Aug. 23, 1864	43, 957
Fire-arm, Breech-loading	W. S. Smoot	Washington, D. C	June 1, 1869	90, 792
Fire-arm, Breech loading	W. S. Smoot	Ilion, N. Y	June 20, 1871	116, 106
Fire-arm, Breech-loading	W. S. Smoot	Ilion, N. Y	Nov. 7, 1871	120, 788
Fire-arm, Breech-loading	W. S. Smoot	Ilion, N. Y	Nov. 12, 1872	133, 063
Fire-arm, Breech loading	W. T. Snedden	Johnstown, Pa	June 27, 1871	116, 363
Fire-arm, Breech-loading	W. T. Snedden	Johnstown, Pa	June 27, 1871	116, 364
Fire-arm, Breech-loading	C. E. Sneider	Baltimore, Md	Mar. 20, 1860	27, 600
Fire-arm, Breech-loading	C. E. Sneider	Baltimore, Md	Aug. 25, 1863	39, 707

Index of patents issued from the United States Patent Office from 1790 *to* 1873, *inclusive*—Continued.

Invention.	Inventor.	Residence.	Date.	No.
Fire-arm, Breech-loading	C. E. Sneider	Baltimore, Md	May 16, 1865	47, 755
Fire-arm, Breech-loading	C. E. Sneider	Baltimore, Md	Dec. 22, 1868	85, 252
Fire-arm, Breech-loading	J. Snider, jr	Philadelphia, Pa	Oct. 15, 1867	69, 941
Fire-arm, Breech-loading	W. Soper	Reading, England	June 14, 1870	104, 223
Fire-arm, Breech-loading	G. H. Soule	Jersey City, N. J	Apr. 3, 1855	12, 655
Fire-arm, Breech-loading	G. H. Soule	Jersey City, N. J	July 6, 1858	20, 825
Fire-arm, Breech-loading	A. Spellerberg	Philadelphia, Pa	July 30, 1861	32, 929
Fire-arm, Breech-loading	C. M. Spencer	South Manchester, Conn	Feb. 4, 1862	34, 319
Fire-arm, Breech-loading	C. M. Spencer	Hartford, Conn	Feb. 11, 1873	135, 671
Fire-arm, Breech-loading	S. F. Stanton	Manchester, N H	Apr. 29, 1856	14, 780
Fire-arm, Breech-loading	E. T. Starr	New York, N. Y	Sept. 14, 1858	21, 523
Fire-arm, Breech-loading	R. E. Stephens	Owen Sound, Canada	June 11, 1867	65, 704
Fire-arm, Breech-loading	G. R. Stetson	New Haven, Conn	July 4, 1871	116, 642
Fire-arm, Breech-loading	A. C. Stevens	Hudson, N. Y	May 4, 1869	89, 699
Fire-arm, Breech-loading	J. Stevens	Chicopee Falls, Mass	Sept. 6, 1864	44, 123
Fire-arm, Breech-loading	W. X. Stevens	Worcester, Mass	Jan. 12, 1864	41, 242
Fire-arm, Breech-loading	J. Stillman	Springfield, Mass	Oct. 17, 1865	50, 507
Fire-arm, Breech-loading	J. T. Stoakes	Champlain, N. Y	July 6, 1869	92, 393
Fire-arm, Breech-loading	W. M. Storm	New York, N. Y	July 8, 1856	15, 307
Fire-arm, Breech-loading	W. M. Storm	New York, N. Y	June 14, 1859	24, 414
Fire-arm, Breech-loading	W. M. Storm	New York, N. Y	Nov. 5, 1872	132, 740
Fire-arm, Breech-loading	S. Strong	Washington, D. C	Dec. 16, 1862	37, 208
Fire-arm, Breech-loading	S. Strong	Washington, D. C	May 19, 1863	38, 643
Fire-arm, Breech-loading	S. Strong	Washington, D. C	May 19, 1863	38, 644
Fire-arm, Breech-loading	T. L. Sturtevant	Boston, Mass	Sept. 19, 1865	50, 048
Fire-arm, Breech-loading	T. L. Sturtevant	Boston, Mass	Dec. 18, 1866	60, 592
Fire-arm, Breech-loading	I. Sutvan	Bridesburgh, Pa	Mar. 14, 1865	46, 866
Fire-arm, Breech-loading	J. F. Swinburn	Birmingham, England	Dec. 17, 1872	134, 014
Fire-arm, Breech-loading	J. C. Symmes	Watertown, Mass	Nov. 16, 1858	22, 094
Fire-arm, Breech-loading	T. D. Sympson, G. B. Gray, and J. H. Romans.	Mount Vernon, Ohio	Aug. 2, 1870	106, 083
Fire-arm, Breech-loading	J. P. Taylor	Elizabethton, Tenn	May 6, 1873	138, 711
Fire-arm, Breech loading	W. Terry	Birmingham, England	Oct. 14, 1862	36, 681
Fire-arm, Breech-loading	J. F. Thomas	Ilion, N. Y	Apr. 2, 1872	125, 229
Fire-arm, Breech-loading	J. F. Thomas	Ilion, N. Y	May 28, 1872	127, 386
Fire-arm, Breech-loading	D. C. Thrasher and B. F. Aiken	Freetown, Mass	July 16, 1867	66, 913
Fire-arm, Breech-loading	F. A. Thuer	East Hartford, Conn	July 12, 1870	105, 388
Fire-arm, Breech-loading	W. Tibbals	South Coventry, Conn	Nov. 28, 1865	51, 243
Fire-arm, Breech-loading	G. H. Tibbets	Augusta, Me	Feb. 13, 1872	123, 595
Fire-arm, Breech-loading	L. B. Tiebel	Hudson City, N. J	May 11, 1869	89, 955
Fire-arm, Breech-loading	F. Tiesing and C. Gerner	New Haven, Conn	Apr. 4, 1871	113, 470
Fire-arm, Breech-loading	F. Tiesing and C. Gerner	New Haven, Conn	Apr. 25, 1871	114, 230
Fire-arm, Breech-loading	G. H. Todd	Montgomery, Ala	July 27, 1869	93, 023
Fire-arm, Breech-loading	I. Townsend	Albany, N. Y	Jan. 29, 1861	31, 268
Fire-arm, Breech-loading	F. Townsend and N. S. Clement.	Albany, N. Y., and Worcester, Mass.	Sept. 6, 1864	44, 127
Fire-arm, Breech-loading	H. Underwood	Tolland, Conn	June 2, 1863	38, 772
Fire-arm, Breech-loading	H. Updegraff	Fort Laramie, Wyo	Sept. 19, 1871	119, 098
Fire-arm, Breech-loading	H. Updegraff	Smithfield, Ohio	Aug. 6, 1872	130, 165
Fire-arm, Breech-loading	S. F. Van Choate	Boston, Mass	May 11, 1869	89, 902
Fire-arm, Breech-loading	S. F. Van Choate	Boston, Mass	Aug. 24, 1869	94, 047
Fire-arm, Breech-loading	S. F. Van Choate	Boston, Mass	June 13, 1871	115, 911
Fire-arm, Breech-loading	S. F. Van Choate	Boston, Mass	Oct. 22, 1872	132, 505
Fire-arm, Breech-loading	A. L. Varney	Watertown, Mass	Mar. 30, 1869	88, 530
Fire-arm, Breech-loading	A. L. Varney	Watertown, Mass	Mar. 30, 1869	88, 531
Fire-arm, Breech-loading	A. L. Varney	Watertown, Mass	Sept. 28, 1869	95, 395
Fire-arm, Breech-loading	F. Vetterlin	Newhausen, Switzerland	Nov. 15, 1870	109, 277
Fire-arm, Breech-loading	F. J. Vittum and E. M. Stevens	Boston and Medford, Mass	Oct. 22, 1861	33, 569
Fire-arm, Breech-loading	J. Von der Poppenburg	Birmingham, England	Oct. 24, 1865	50, 670
Fire-arm, Breech loading	E. Von Jeinsen	New York, N. Y	Dec. 15, 1868	84, 922
Fire-arm, Breech-loading	E. Von Martini	Frauenfeld, Switzerland	May 25, 1869	90, 614
Fire-arm, Breech-loading	F. Von Martini	Frauenfeld, Switzerland	May 30, 1871	115, 546
Fire-arm, Breech-loading	F. Von Martini	Frauenfeld, Switzerland	Nov. 7, 1871	120, 800
Fire-arm, Breech-loading	F. Von Martini	Frauenfeld, Switzerland	Oct. 15, 1872	132, 222
Fire-arm, Breech-loading	H. Walker	Handsworth, England	Sept. 17, 1872	131, 484
Fire-arm, Breech-loading	J. M. Wampler	Loudoun County, Va	Mar. 6, 1860	27, 399
Fire-arm, Breech-loading	W. G. Ward	New York, N. Y	Aug. 31, 1869	94, 458
Fire-arm, Breech-loading	W. G. Ward	New York, N. Y	Dec. 7, 1869	97, 734
Fire-arm, Breech-loading	W. G. Ward	Edgewater, N. Y	Feb. 1, 1870	99, 504
Fire-arm, Breech-loading	W. G. Ward	Edgewater, N. Y	Feb. 21, 1871	111, 994
Fire-arm, Breech-loading	J. Warner	Springfield, Mass	Dec. 27, 1864	45, 660
Fire-arm, Breech-loading	J. Warner	Springfield, Mass	Feb. 23, 1864	47, 732
Fire-arm, Breech-loading	T. A. Washington	United States Army	Oct. 28, 1856	15, 990
Fire-arm, Breech-loading	A. T. Watson	Castleton, N. Y	Mar. 20, 1855	12, 567
Fire-arm, Breech-loading	J. B. Wayne	Birmingham, England	Aug. 15, 1871	118, 171
Fire-arm, Breech-loading	H. B. Weaver	South Windham, Conn	Oct. 16, 1855	13, 691
Fire-arm, Breech loading	T. W. Webley	Birmingham, England	June 11, 1867	65, 783
Fire-arm, Breech-loading	J. Wernal	Steyer, Austria	Feb. 18, 1868	74, 737
Fire-arm, Breech-loading	D. B. Wesson	Springfield, Mass	Dec. 17, 1867	72, 434
Fire-arm, Breech-loading	D. B. Wesson	Springfield, Mass	June 9, 1868	78, 847
Fire-arm, Breech-loading	F. Wesson	Worcester, Mass	Nov. 11, 1862	36, 925
Fire-arm, Breech-loading	F. Wesson	Worcester, Mass	May 31, 1870	103, 694
Fire-arm, Breech-loading	F. Wesson and N. S. Harrington	Worcester, Mass	Oct. 25, 1859	25, 926
Fire-arm, Breech-loading	H. F. Wheeler	Boston, Mass	Oct. 31, 1865	50, 760
Fire-arm, Breech-loading	H. F. Wheeler	Boston, Mass	June 19, 1866	55, 752
Fire-arm, Breech-loading	L. Wheelock	New Haven, Conn	Oct. 22, 1867	70, 141
Fire-arm, Breech-loading	A. M. White	Port Chester, N. Y	Apr. 18, 1865	47, 350
Fire-arm, Breech-loading	G. W. White	New York, N. Y	Feb. 4, 1862	34, 325
Fire-arm, Breech-loading	G. W. White	New York, N. Y	Jan. 6, 1863	37, 369
Fire-arm, Breech-loading	L. S. White	Waterbury, Conn	Jan. 6, 1863	37, 376
Fire-arm, Breech-loading	R. White	Hartford, Conn	Mar. 13, 1855	12, 528
Fire-arm, Breech-loading	R. White	Hartford, Conn	Mar. 13, 1855	12, 529
Fire-arm, Breech-loading	R. White	Hartford, Conn	Apr. 3, 1855	12, 638
Fire-arm, Breech-loading	A. E. Whitmore	Ilion, N. Y	Aug. 8, 1871	117, 843
Fire-arm, Breech-loading	A. E. Whitmore	Ilion, N. Y	Apr. 16, 1872	125, 775
Fire-arm, Breech-loading	E. Whitney	New Haven, Conn	Nov. 8, 1864	44, 991
Fire-arm, Breech-loading	E. Whitney	New Haven, Conn	Nov. 26, 1867	71, 349
Fire-arm, Breech loading	E. Whitney	New Haven, Conn	Mar. 21, 1871	112, 997

Index of patents issued from the United States Patent Office from 1790 *to* 1873, *inclusive*—Continued.

Invention.	Inventor.	Residence.	Date.	No.
Fire-arm Breech-loading	E. Whitney	New Haven, Conn	June 13, 1871	115, 997
Fire-arm, Breech-loading	E. Whitney	New Haven, Conn	Mar. 26, 1872	124, 994
Fire-arm, Breech-loading	E. Whitney, C. Gerner, and F. Tiesing.	New Haven, Conn	July 27, 1869	93, 149
Fire-arm, Breech-loading	E. Whitney and F. Tiesing	New Haven, Conn	July 16, 1872	129, 637
Fire-arm, Breech-loading	J. M. Whittemore	Augusta, Me	June 14, 1870	104, 387
Fire-arm, Breech-loading	J. M. Whittemore	Augusta, Me	Sept. 17, 1872	131, 487
Fire-arm, Breech-loading	J. M. Whittemore	Augusta, Me	Oct. 1, 1872	131, 921
Fire arm, Breech-loading	J. A. Wickmann	Oldenburg, Germany	Sept. 29, 1863	40, 151
Fire-arm, Breech-loading	J. D. Wilkinson	Plattsburgh, N. Y	Aug. 29, 1871	118, 5[illegible]9
Fire-arm, Breech-loading	D. Williamson	Brooklyn, N. Y	Mar. 21, 1865	46, 977
Fire-arm, Breech-loading	D. Williamson	New York, N. Y	Oct. 2, 1866	58, 525
Fire-arm, Breech-loading	D. Williamson	New York, N. Y	Mar. 16, 1869	87, 997
Fire-arm, Breech-loading	T. Wilson	Birmingham, England	July 14, 1868	80, 043
Fire-arm, Breech-loading	W. F. Wilson and H. Flather	Bridesburgh, Pa	Aug. 15, 1865	49, 463
Fire-arm, Breech-loading	F. Wohlgemuth	New York, N. Y	May 18, 1869	90, 214
Fire-arm, Breech-loading	H. H. Wolcott	Yonkers, N. Y	Nov. 27, 1866	60, 106
Fire-arm, Breech-loading	C. O. Wood	Worcester, Mass	Oct. 9, 1860	30, 372
Fire-arm, Breech-loading	C. O. Wood	Worcester, Mass	Jan. 1, 1861	31, 050
Fire-arm, Breech-loading	S. W. Wood	Cornwall, N. Y	Apr. 1, 1862	34, 854
Fire-arm, Breech-loading	F. G. Woodward	Worcester, Mass	Jan. 7, 1862	34, 084
Fire-arm, Breech-loading	E. S. Wright	New York, N. Y	Nov. 15, 1864	45, 126
Fire-arm, Breech-loading	A. Wyley	Birmingham, England	Nov. 24, 1868	84, 459
Fire-arm, Breech-loading	T. Yates	Milwaukee, Wis	Dec. 18, 1866	60, 607
Fire-arm, Breech-loading	J. Yglesias	New York, N. Y	May 9, 1871	114, 742
Fire-arm, Breech-loading	L. V. Young	Saint Louis, Mo	June 21, 1870	104, 682
Fire-arm, Breech-loading	G. Zeller	Brussels, Belgium	Mar. 18, 1873	136, 894
Fire-arm, Breech loading and magazine	J. S. Reeder	Canton, Ohio	Nov. 27, 1860	30, 760
Fire-arm, Breech-loading and other	J. W. Cochran	New York, N. Y	Nov. 29, 1859	26, 256
Fire-arm, Breech-loading magazine	J. Swyney	Charlestown, Mass	Aug. 21, 1855	13, 474
Fire-arm, Breech-loading repeating	C. Sharps	Philadelphia, Pa	Jan. 25, 1859	22, 753
Fire-arm, Breech-loading revolving	E. Claude	New York, N. Y	Dec. 21, 1858	22, 348
Fire-arm, Breech-loading revolving	F. A. Le Mat	New Orleans, La	Dec. 14, 1869	97, 780
Fire-arm, Double-barreled	E. Maynard	Tarrytown, N. Y	Oct. 20, 1868	83, 194
Fire-arm, Double-barreled	E. Whitney	New Haven, Conn	Oct. 23, 1866	59, 110
Fire-arm, Double-barreled breech-loading	W. H. Elliot	Plattsburgh, N. Y	Aug. 16, 1864	43, 840
Fire-arm, Double-barreled revolving	H. D. Ward	Pittsfield, Mass	Sept. 8, 1863	39, 850
Fire-arm lock	E. Allen	Grafton, Mass	Nov. 11, 1837	461
Fire-arm lock	W. H. Baker	Marathon, N. Y	Dec. 8, 1863	40, 809
Fire-arm lock	O. Blunt	New York, N. Y	Dec. 25, 1849	6, 966
Fire-arm lock	J. S. Butterfield	Philadelphia, Pa	Jan. 2, 1855	12, 124
Fire-arm lock	E. S. Chapin	Stafford Springs, Conn	July 17, 1837	274
Fire-arm lock	N. B. Cook	Chicago, Ill	Aug. 27, 1850	7, 596
Fire-arm lock	W. Frank	Mount Sterling, Ill	Sept. 10, 1861	33, 245
Fire-arm lock	P. Hiller	Mattapoisett, Mass	Apr. 30, 1861	32, 188
Fire-arm lock	J. P. Lindsay	New York, N. Y	Oct. 9, 1860	30, 332
Fire-arm lock	D. Moore	Brooklyn, N. Y	Dec. 2, 1873	145, 118
Fire-arm lock	J. Post	Newark, N. J	May 15, 1849	6, 453
Fire-arm lock	E. T. Starr	New York, N. Y	May 10, 1864	42, 697
Fire-arm lock	A. P. Stephens	Brooklyn, N. Y	Apr. 21, 1863	38, 249
Fire-arm lock	A. Tonks	Boston, Mass	Jan. 13, 1857	16, 411
Fire-arm lock	M. Tromly	Mount Vernon, Ill	Oct. 13, 1857	18, 418
Fire-arm lock	M. Tromly	Mount Vernon, Ill	July 12, 1859	24, 768
Fire-arm lock	A. Young	Philadelphia, Pa	June 14, 1870	104, 394
Fire-arm lock, Double-barreled	D. B. Wesson	Springfield, Mass	May 2, 1871	114, 374
Fire-arm lock, Repeating	J. R. Mock	Elizabethtown, Ky	May 31, 1859	24, 228
Fire-arm, Magazine	A. Assmus	Chicago, Ill	Dec. 16, 1873	145, 478
Fire-arm, Magazine	A. Ball	Worcester, Mass	Dec. 6, 1864	45, 307
Fire-arm, Magazine	S. G. Bayes	Wauseon, Ohio	Feb. 9, 1869	86, 723
Fire-arm, Magazine	J. H. Bean	Cincinnati, Ohio	Aug. 12, 1873	141, 624
Fire-arm, Magazine	P. Boynton	Canton, N. Y	Mar. 15, 1859	23, 226
Fire-arm, Magazine	P. Boynton	Canton, N. Y	Jan. 3, 1860	26, 646
Fire-arm, Magazine	G. W. Briggs	New Haven, Conn	Oct. 16, 1866	58, 937
Fire-arm, Magazine	A. Burgess	New York, N. Y	Sept. 19, 1871	119, 115
Fire-arm, Magazine	A. Burgess	Hartford, Conn	Jan. 7, 1873	134, 589
Fire-arm, Magazine	T. Cullen	San Francisco, Cal	Apr. 13, 1869	88, 853
Fire-arm, Magazine	J. Davis	Limestoneville, Pa	Feb. 28, 1871	112, 127
Fire-arm, Magazine	W. C. Dodge	Washington, D. C	Oct. 16, 1866	58, 790
Fire-arm, Magazine	J. B. Doolittle	Seymour, Conn	July 29, 1862	35, 996
Fire-arm, Magazine	W. H. Elliot	New York, N. Y	May 28, 1872	127, 323
Fire-arm, Magazine	D. Ellis	Whitestone, N. Y	Apr. 12, 1870	101, 845
Fire-arm, Magazine	V. Fogerty	Boston, Mass	Feb. 21, 1865	46, 459
Fire-arm, Magazine	V. Fogerty	Boston, Mass	Oct. 23, 1866	59, 126
Fire-arm, Magazine	V. Fogerty	Roxbury, Mass	Oct. 6, 1868	82, 819
Fire-arm, Magazine	H. K. Forbis	Danville, Ky	Mar. 21, 1871	112, 795
Fire-arm, Magazine	W. Gardner	Toledo, Ohio	Feb. 16, 1869	87, 038
Fire-arm, Magazine	J. Gray	Medford, Mass	July 4, 1865	48, 622
Fire-arm, Magazine	J. Gray	Medford, Mass	Apr. 17, 1866	54, 068
Fire-arm, Magazine	H. W. Hayden	Waterbury, Conn	Aug. 7, 1866	56, 939
Fire-arm, Magazine	B. T. Henry	New Haven, Conn	Oct. 16, 1860	30, 446
Fire-arm, Magazine	G. W. Hughes and J. G. Pusey	Providence, R. I	Aug. 15, 1865	49, 409
Fire-arm, Magazine	N. King	Bridgeport, Conn	May 22, 1866	55, 012
Fire-arm, Magazine	N. King	Bridgeport, Conn	Aug. 28, 1866	57, 636
Fire-arm, Magazine	E. C. Kirk and E. Sneider	Baltimore, Md	July 9, 1867	66, 526
Fire-arm, Magazine	J. L. Kirk	Mattoon, Ill	June 20, 1871	116, 066
Fire arm, Magazine	J. Kraffert	Berlin, Prussia	July 5, 1870	105, 093
Fire-arm, Magazine	T. W. Lane	Boston, Mass	Jan. 1, 1867	60, 910
Fire-arm, Magazine	G. D. Luce	New Orleans, La	Mar. 11, 1873	136, 660
Fire-arm, Magazine	J. Nichols	Limestone, N. Y	Sept. 2, 1862	36, 3[illegible]8
Fire-arm, Magazine	B. F. Parkinson	Washington, Pa	June 13, 1865	48, 201
Fire-arm, Magazine	J. Rider	Newark, Ohio	Aug. 15, 1871	118, 152
Fire-arm, Magazine	J. Rider	Newark Ohio	Aug. 15, 1873	141, 590
Fire-arm, Magazine	L. C. Rodier	Springfield, Mass	May 25, 1862	34, 776
Fire-arm, Magazine	L. C. Rodier and F. G. Bates	Springfield, Mass	Apr. 29, 1873	138, 439
Fire-arm, Magazine	J. Q. A. Scott	Pittsburgh, Pa	Aug. 12, 1862	36, [illegible]74
Fire-arm, Magazine	P. Sheckler	Orangeville, Ill	Apr. 2, 1867	63, 564
Fire-arm, Magazine	L. Sibert	Mount Solon, Va	May 14, 1861	32, 316
Fire-arm, Magazine	J. D. Smith	Bridgeport, Conn	Feb. 27, 1866	52, 933

Index of patents issued from the United States Patent Office from 1790 *to* 1873, *inclusive*—Continued.

Invention.	Inventor.	Residence.	Date.	No.
Fire-arm, Magazine	J. D. Smith	Bridgeport, Conn	Feb. 27, 1866	52, 934
Fire-arm, Magazine	J. N. Smith	Cincinaati, Ohio	Aug. 18, 1863	39, 591
Fire-arm, Magazine	C. M. Spencer	Boston, Mass	May 26, 1863	38, 702
Fire-arm, Magazine	C. M. Spencer	Boston, Mass	Oct. 9, 1866	58, 737
Fire-arm, Magazine	C. M. Spencer	Boston, Mass	Oct. 9, 1866	58, 738
Fire-arm, Magazine	E. Stabler	Sandy Springs, Md	Mar. 14, 1865	46, 828
Fire-arm, Magazine	E. L. Sturtevant	Boston, Mass	July 16, 1867	66, 751
Fire-arm, Magazine	A. Swingle and F. A. Huntington	San Francisco, Cal	Feb. 18, 1873	135, 947
Fire-arm, Magazine	L. Z. Terrill	Chicopee, Mass	May 4, 1869	89, 705
Fire-arm, Magazine	F. Vetterlin	Newhausen, Switzerland	Dec. 29, 1868	85, 494
Fire-arm, Magazine	H. F. Wheeler	Boston, Mass	June 25, 1867	66, 110
Fire-arm, Magazine	L. Wheelock	New Haven, Conn	Dec. 1, 1868	84, 598
Fire-arm, Magazine	J. A. Whitney	Maryland, N. Y	July 30, 1867	67, 242
Fire-arm, Magazine	O. F. Winchester	New Haven, Conn	Sept. 4, 1866	57, 808
Fire-arm, Magazine breech-loading	H. F. Wheeler	Boston, Mass	Feb. 7, 1865	46, 286
Fire-arm, Magazine for breech-loading	W. H. Elliot	New York, N. Y	Feb. 14, 1871	111, 827
Fire-arm, Magazine for self-loading	J. F. Appleby	Mazo Manie, Wis	Dec. 20, 1864	45, 466
Fire-arm, Magazine or self-loading	W. Fitzgerald	Boston, Mass	Jan. 17, 1865	45, 919
Fire-arm, Magazine or self-loading	J. Gray	Medford, Mass	Dec. 20, 1864	45, 560
Fire-arm, Magazine or self-loading	G. W. Hughes	Bloomington, Ill	Nov. 15, 1864	45, 043
Fire-arm, Magazine or self-loading	R. Roberts	Utica, N. Y	Dec. 27, 1864	45, 638
Fire-arm, Magazine or self-loading	L. Triplett	Columbia, Ky	Dec. 6, 1864	45, 361
Fire-arm, Magazine revolving	E. J. Frost	New York, N. Y	June 11, 1867	65, 742
Fire-arm, Many-barreled	W. J. Christy	Philadelphia, Pa	Sept. 18, 1866	58, 064
Fire-arm, Many-barreled	W. H. Elliot	Plattsburgh, N. Y	May 10, 1864	42, 648
Fire-arm, Many-barreled	W. H. Elliot	Plattsburgh, N. Y	May 10, 1864	42, 649
Fire-arm, Many-barreled	W. H. Elliot	Ilion, N. Y	Oct. 3, 1865	50, 232
Fire-arm, Many-barreled	W. H. Elliot	Ilion, N. Y	Dec. 12, 1865	51, 440
Fire-arm, Many-chambered	C. A. Bennett and P. F. Haviland	Waterville, Me	Feb. 15, 1838	603
Fire-arm, Many-chambered	C. Parkhurst	Lawrenceville, Pa	Sept. 25, 1837	409
Fire-arm, Many-chambered cylinder	J. W. Cochran	New York, N. Y	Apr. 29, 1837	183
Fire-arm, Many-chambered cylinder	J. W. Cochran	New York, N. Y	Mar. 8, 1837	188
Fire-arm, Many-chambered cylinder	E. Jaquith	Brattleborough, Vt	July 12, 1838	832
Fire-arm, Many-chambered cylinder	D. Leavitt	Cabotsville, Mass	Apr. 29, 1837	182
Fire-arm, Many-chambered cylinder	R. Nichols and E. Childs	Conway, Mass	Apr. 24, 1838	707
Fire-arm, Many-chambered cylinder	M. Nutting	Portland, Me	Apr. 25, 1838	713
Fire-arm, Many-chambered cylinder	T. F. Strong	Northampton, Mass	Apr. 21, 1838	698
Fire-arm, Many-chambered cylinder	O. W. Whittier	Enfield, N. H	May 30, 1837	216
Fire-arm, Many-chambered rotating-breech	S. Colt	Hartford, Conn	Feb. 24, 1857	16, 683
Fire-arm, Many-chambered rotating-breech	S. Colt	Hartford, Conn	Nov. 24, 1857	18, 678
Fire-arm percussion-lock	J. H. B. Latrobe	Howard County, Md	Feb. 26, 1856	14, 319
Fire-arm percussion-lock	O. Moses	Malone, N. Y	May 3, 1828	....
Fire-arm, Portable	A. O. H. P. Schorn	Murfreesborough, Tenn	Jan. 30, 1855	12, 328
Fire-arm, Portable	C. L. Stanislaus, Baron Heurteloup.	France	July 29, 1841	2, 203
Fire-arm, Portable	J. Tilton and W. Floyd	Rock House, Ohio	Mar. 3, 1857	16, 761
Fire-arm, Repeating	S. Colt	Hartford, Conn	Sept. 3, 1850	7, 613
Fire-arm, Repeating	C. Draeger	Indianapolis, Ind	Apr. 8, 1862	34, 922
Fire-arm, Repeating	H. J. Drew	Dixon, Ill	Mar. 14, 1871	112, 564
Fire-arm, Repeating	W. H. Elliot	Plattsburgh, N. Y	May 29, 1860	28, 460
Fire-arm, Repeating	A. C. Faivre	Meadville, Pa	Mar. 9, 1858	19, 553
Fire-arm, Repeating	H. Genhart	Liege, Belgium	Jan. 27, 1857	16, 477
Fire-arm, Repeating	J. Gray	Boston, Mass	Jan. 26, 1864	41, 375
Fire-arm, Repeating	B. Groomes	Cumberland Township, Pa.	Jan. 1, 1856	14, 017
Fire-arm, Repeating	A. Hall	New York, N. Y	June 10, 1856	15, 110
Fire-arm, Repeating	P. J. Jarre	Paris, France	June 24, 1862	35, 685
Fire-arm, Repeating	E. M. Judd	New Britain, Conn	Feb. 25, 1862	34, 504
Fire-arm, Repeating	G. Leonard	Shrewsbury, Mass	May 6, 1856	14, 820
Fire-arm, Repeating	E. Maher	New York, N. Y	May 6, 1862	35, 167
Fire-arm, Repeating	W. W. Marston	New York, N. Y	May 26, 1857	17, 386
Fire-arm, Repeating	H. H. McKenny and F. Goth.	Biddeford, Me	Feb. 15, 1859	22, 969
Fire-arm, Repeating	R. S. Mershon and J. Hollingsworth.	Zanesville, Ohio	Feb. 27, 1855	12, 471
Fire-arm, Repeating	W. H. Morris and C. L. Brown	New York, N. Y	Jan. 24, 1860	26, 919
Fire-arm, Repeating	C. S. Pettengill	New Haven, Conn	July 22, 1856	15, 388
Fire-arm, Repeating	F. B. Prindle	New Haven, Conn	Aug. 10, 1858	21, 149
Fire-arm, Repeating	J. N. Smith	Jersey City, N. J	June 10, 1862	35, 548
Fire-arm, Repeating	W. S. Smoot	Washington, D. C	Dec. 14, 1869	97, 821
Fire-arm, Repeating	E. T. Starr	New York, N. Y	May 10, 1864	42, 698
Fire-arm, Repeating	J. Stevens	Chicopee, Mass	Aug. 9, 1853	9, 929
Fire-arm, Repeating	J. Stevens	Chicopee Falls, Mass	Jan. 2, 1855	12, 189
Fire-arm, Repeating	C. C. Terrel	Shullsburgh, Wis	Feb. 16, 1858	19, 387
Fire-arm, Repeating	C. N. Tyler	Worcester, Mass	May 3, 1853	9, 701
Fire-arm, Repeating	L. Wheelock	New Haven, Conn	Jan. 31, 1871	111, 500
Fire-arm, Repeating	R. White	Hartford, Conn	Apr. 3, 1855	12, 648
Fire-arm, Repeating	R. White	Hartford, Conn	Apr. 3, 1855	12, 649
Fire-arm, Repeating magazine	J. C. Smith	Camden, N. J	Jan. 1, 1856	14, 034
Fire-arm, Repeating or many-chambered	H. and C. Daniels	Chester, Conn	Apr. 5, 1838	677
Fire-arm, Repeating single-barreled	D. B. Neal	Mount Gilead, Ohio	Feb. 27, 1855	12, 440
Fire-arm, Revolver	J Adams	Dalston, England	Nov. 6, 1860	30. 602
Fire-arm, Revolving	J. Adams	Strand, England	Dec. 29, 1868	85, 350
Fire-arm, Revolving	R. Adams	London, England	May 3, 1853	9, 694
Fire-arm, Revolving	E. Allen	Worcester, Mass	Dec. 15, 1857	18, 836
Fire-arm, Revolving	E. Allen	Worcester, Mass	Sept. 7, 1858	21, 400
Fire-arm, Revolving	E. Allen	Worcester, Mass	Nov. 9, 1858	22, 005
Fire-arm, Revolving	E. Allen	Worcester, Mass	July 3, 1860	28, 951
Fire-arm, Revolving	E. Allen	Worcester, Mass	Sept. 24, 1861	33, 328
Fire-arm, Revolving	E. Allen	Worcester, Mass	Oct. 22, 1861	33, 509
Fire-arm, Revolving	E. Allen	Worcester, Mass	Apr. 29, 1862	35, 067
Fire-arm, Revolving	C. H. Alsop	Middletown, Conn	Nov. 26, 1861	33, 770
Fire-arm, Revolving	C. R. Alsop	Middletown, Conn	July 17, 1860	29, 213
Fire-arm, Revolving	C. R. Alsop	Middletown, Conn	May 14, 1861	32, 333
Fire-arm, Revolving	C. R. Alsop	Middletown, Conn	Jan. 21, 1862	34, 226
Fire-arm, Revolving	C. R. Alsop	Middletown, Conn	Mar. 25, 1862	34. 803
Fire-arm, Revolving	T. K. Austin	New York, N, Y	Oct. 12, 1858	21, 730
Fire-arm, Revolving	T. Bailey	New Orleans, La	June 7, 1859	24, 274
Fire-arm, Revolving	F. Beals	New Haven, Conn	May 26, 1857	17, 359
Fire-arm, Revolving	F. Beals	New Haven, Conn	Sept. 14, 1858	21, 478

Index of patents issued from the United States Patent Office from 1790 *to* 1873, *inclusive*—Continued.

Invention.	Inventor.	Residence.	Date.	No.
Fire-arm, Revolving	W. H Bell	Washington, D. C	Mar. 20, 1860	27, 518
Fire-arm, Revolving	G. A. Blittkowski and F. W. Hoffman.	New York, N. Y	Apr. 22, 1856	14, 710
Fire-arm, Revolving	C. C. Brand	Norwich, Conn	Sept. 23, 1862	36, 505
Fire-arm, Revolving	C. C. Brand	Norwich, Conn	Apr. 28, 1863	38, 279
Fire-arm, Revolving	H. A. Briggs and S. S. Hopkins.	Norwich, Conn	Jan. 5, 1864	41, 117
Fire-arm, Revolving	G. C. Bunsen	Belleville, Ill	Dec. 26, 1865	51, 690
Fire-arm, Revolving	G. W. H. Calver	Burlington, N. J	May 17, 1870	103, 013
Fire-arm, Revolving	A. Christ	California, Ohio	Sept. 11, 1866	57, 865
Fire-arm, Revolving	F. G. Cochran	Saint Louis, Mo	July 4, 1871	116, 559
Fire-arm, Revolving	J. W. Cochran	New York, N. Y	Dec. 28, 1858	22, 412
Fire-arm, Revolving	J. W. Cochran	New York, N. Y	Nov. 10, 1863	40, 553
Fire-arm, Revolving	S. Colt	Hartford, Conn	May 4, 1858	20, 144
Fire-arm, Revolving	C. A. Converse and S. S. Hopkins.	Norwich, Conn	Aug. 28, 1866	57, 622
Fire-arm, Revolving	J. M. Cooper	Pittsburgh, Pa	Mar. 20, 1860	27, 526
Fire-arm, Revolving	J. M. Cooper	Pittsburgh, Pa	Sept. 4, 1860	29, 864
Fire-arm, Revolving	J. M. Cooper	Pittsburgh, Pa	Sept. 22, 1863	40, 021
Fire-arm, Revolving	S. Crispin	New York, N. Y	Oct. 3, 1865	50, 224
Fire-arm, Revolving	G. G. Crowell	Lime Rock, Conn	Apr. 17, 1866	53, 955
Fire-arm, Revolving	C. F. and J. E. De Dartein	Strasbourg, France	May 10, 1870	102, 782
Fire-arm, Revolving	W. C. Dodge	Washington, D. C	Jan. 24, 1865	45, 983
Fire-arm, Revolving	J. B. Doolittle	New Haven, Conn	Apr. 17, 1866	54, 065
Fire-arm, Revolving	B. K. Dorwart	Rockland, R. I	Sept. 2, 1873	142, 376
Fire-arm, Revolving	R. W. Drew	Lowell, Mass	Apr. 2, 1867	63, 450
Fire-arm, Revolving	W. H. Elliot	Plattsburgh, N. Y	Aug. 17, 1858	2[illegible], 188
Fire-arm, Revolving	W. H. Elliot	Plattsburgh, N. Y	May 29, 1860	28, 461
Fire-arm, Revolving	W. H. Elliot	Plattsburgh, N. Y	Oct. 1, 1861	33, 382
Fire-arm, Revolving	W. H. Elliot	Plattsburgh, N. Y	Feb. 7, 1865	46, 225
Fire-arm, Revolving	W. C. Ellis and J. N. White	Springfield, Mass	July 12, 1859	24, 726
Fire-arm, Revolving	W. C. Ellis and J. N. White	Springfield, Mass	July 21, 1863	39, 318
Fire-arm, Revolving	J. Ells	Pittsburgh, Pa	Apr. 25, 1854	10, 812
Fire-arm, Revolving	J. Ells	Pittsburgh, Pa	Apr. 14, 1857	17, 032
Fire-arm, Revolving	C. Foehl	Philadelphia, Pa	June 3, 1873	139, 461
Fire-arm, Revolving	S. Forehand and H. C. Wadsworth.	Worcester, Mass	June 27, 1871	116, 422
Fire-arm, Revolving	S. Forehand and H. C. Wadsworth.	Worcester, Mass	Oct. 14, 1873	143, 566
Fire-arm, Revolving	A. T. Freeman	Binghamton, N. Y	Dec. 9, 1862	37, 091
Fire-arm, Revolving	G. H. Gardner	New York, N. Y	May 16, 1865	47, 712
Fire-arm, Revolving	G. W. B. Gedney	New York, N. Y	July 29, 1862	35, 999
Fire-arm, Revolving	M. F. Geraghty	Jersey City, N. J	Aug. 25, 1863	39, 642
Fire-arm, Revolving	A. J. Gibson	Worcester, Mass	May 22, 1860	28, 437
Fire-arm, Revolving	A. J. Gibson	Worcester, Mass	July 10, 1860	29, 126
Fire-arm, Revolving	A. J. Gibson	Worcester, Mass	Oct. 9, 1860	30, 309
Fire-arm, Revolving	J. Gordon	San Francisco, Cal	July 16, 1872	129, 334
Fire-arm, Revolving	E. H. Graham	Yonkers, N. Y	Nov. 24, 1863	40, 687
Fire-arm, Revolving	H. Gross	Tiffin, Ohio	Dec. 3, 1861	33, 836
Fire-arm, Revolving	H. Gross	Tiffin, Ohio	Aug. 25, 1863	39, 645
Fire-arm, Revolving	J. Gruler and A. Rebetey	Norwich, Conn	Dec. 27, 1859	26, 641
Fire-arm, Revolving	A. Guerriero	Genoa, Italy	Apr. 11, 1865	47, 252
Fire-arm, Revolving	A. Hall	Danville, Iowa	Mar. 24, 1863	37, 961
Fire-arm, Revolving	F. H. Harrington	Springfield, Mass	June 15, 1858	20, 607
Fire-arm, Revolving	C. W. Harris	Pittsburgh, Pa	Sept. 1, 1863	39, 771
Fire-arm, Revolving	P. Haughian	New York, N. Y	Feb. 28, 1865	46, 562
Fire-arm, Revolving	W. C. Haynes	Melrose, Tex	Mar. 1, 1859	23, 087
Fire-arm, Revolving	B. R. Hill	Cranston, R. I	Feb. 15, 1870	99, 893
Fire-arm, Revolving	G. Holman	Waterville, N. Y	Mar. 3, 1868	75, 016
Fire-arm, Revolving	F. W. Hood	Worcester, Mass	Nov. 8, 1864	44, 953
Fire-arm, Revolving	F. W. Hood	Boston, Mass	July 4, 1871	116, 593
Fire-arm, Revolving	C. W. Hopkins	Norwich, Conn	May 27, 1862	35, 419
Fire-arm, Revolving	S. S. Hopkins	Norwich, Conn	Mar. 28, 1871	113, 053
Fire-arm, Revolving	J. C. Howe	Worcester, Mass	Feb. 17, 1863	37, 693
Fire-arm, Revolving	J. Jenkinson	Brooklyn, N. Y	Dec. 2, 1862	37, 075
Fire-arm, Revolving	B. F. Joslyn	Worcester, Mass	May 4, 1858	20, 160
Fire-arm, Revolving	B. F. Joslyn	Stonington, Conn	Aug. 4, 1863	39, 405
Fire-arm, Revolving	B. F Joslyn	Stonington, Conn	Aug. 4, 1863	39, 406
Fire-arm, Revolving	B. F. Joslyn	Stonington, Conn	Apr. 19, 1864	42, 379
Fire-arm, Revolving	B. F. Joslyn	Stonington, Conn	Feb. 7, 1865	46, 243
Fire-arm, Revolving	B. F. Joslyn	Stonington, Conn	June 20, 1865	48, 287
Fire-arm, Revolving	B. F. Joslyn	Stonington, Conn	Jan. 2, 1866	51, 836
Fire-arm, Revolving	B. F. Joslyn	New York, N. Y	Nov. 22, 187[illegible]	109, 417
Fire-arm, Revolving	B. F. Joslyn	New York, N. Y	May 30, 1871	115, 483
Fire-arm, Revolving	H. S. Josselyn	Roxbury, Mass	Jan. 23, 1866	52, 248
Fire-arm, Revolving	J. Kerr	Southwark, England	Aug. 4, 1863	39, 4[illegible]9
Fire-arm, Revolving	C. A. King	Springfield, Mass	Aug. 24, 1869	94, 003
Fire-arm, Revolving	M. Kinsey	Newark, N. J	June 8, 1858	20, 496
Fire-arm, Revolving	B. Kittridge	Cincinnati, Ohio	Mar. 8, 1864	41, 848
Fire-arm, Revolving	E. S. Leaycroft	Brooklyn, N. Y	Mar. 7, 1871	112, 471
Fire-arm, Revolving	E. S. Leaycroft	Brooklyn, N. Y	Mar. 7, 1871	112, 472
Fire-arm, Revolving	S. C. Lewis and F. P. Pfleghar	Whitneyville, Conn	Aug. 2, 1859	24, 942
Fire-arm, Revolving	B. T. Loomis	New York, N. Y	Feb. 13, 1866	52, 582
Fire-arm, Revolving	C. J. Lunberg and W. J. Phillips.	Saint Louis, Mo	Dec. 6, 1870	109, 914
Fire-arm, Revolving	J. M. Marlin	New Haven, Conn	July 1, 1873	140, 516
Fire-arm, Revolving	W. Mason	Ilion, N. Y	Nov. 21, 1865	51, 117
Fire-arm, Revolving	W. Mason	Ilion, N. Y	Mar. 27, 1866	53, 539
Fire-arm, Revolving	W. Mason	Hartford, Conn	July 2, 1872	128, 644
Fire-arm, Revolving	T. J. Mayall	Roxbury, Mass	Nov. 25, 1862	37, 004
Fire-arm, Revolving	J. C. Miller	Danville, Ky	Feb. 8, 1870	99, 693
Fire-arm, Revolving	D. Moore	Brooklyn, N. Y	Sept. 18, 1860	30, 079
Fire-arm, Revolving	D. Moore	Brooklyn, N. Y	Jan. 7, 1862	34, 067
Fire-arm, Revolving	D. Moore	Brooklyn, N. Y	Apr. 28, 1863	38, 321
Fire-arm, Revolving	J. L. Morse and E. W. Johnson	Columbus, Miss	June 20, 1871	116, 078
Fire-arm, Revolving	A. L. Munson	New Haven, Conn	Nov. 13, 1866	59, 629
Fire-arm, Revolving	F. Newbury	Albany, N. Y	June 12, 1855	13, 039
Fire-arm, Revolving	F. Newbury	Albany, N. Y	Sept. 18, 1855	13, 582

Index of patents issued from the United States Patent Office from 1790 to 1873, inclusive—Continued.

Invention.	Inventor.	Residence.	Date.	No.
Fire-arm, Revolving	F. Newbury	Albany, N. Y	Mar. 11, 1856	14,406
Fire-arm, Revolving	F. D. Newbury	Albany, N. Y	Mar. 23, 1858	19,739
Fire-arm, Revolving	F. D. Newbury	Albany, N. Y	June 29, 1858	20,765
Fire-arm, Revolving	F. D. Newbury	Albany, N. Y	Apr. 10, 1860	27,868
Fire-arm, Revolving	F. D. Newbury	Albany, N. Y	Oct. 23, 1860	30,494
Fire-arm, Revolving	H. S. North and E. Savage	Middletown and Cromwell, Conn.	Jan. 18, 1859	22,666
Fire-arm, Revolving	W. I. Page	Boston, Mass	June 21, 1870	104,636
Fire-arm, Revolving	W. Palmer	New York, N. Y	Sept. 28, 1858	21,623
Fire-arm, Revolving	W. Palmer	New York, N. Y	Mar. 8, 1864	41,857
Fire-arm, Revolving	C. S. Pettengill	New Haven, Conn	Jan. 4, 1859	22,511
Fire-arm, Revolving	W. H. Philip	Brooklyn, N. Y	Aug. 26, 1873	142,175
Fire-arm, Revolving	W. J. Pitt	Middletown, Conn	Jan. 7, 1862	34,093
Fire-arm, Revolving	K. H. Plass	New York, N. Y	Jan. 24, 1865	46,023
Fire-arm, Revolving	P. Polain	Brussels, Belgium	Mar. 27, 1866	53,548
Fire-arm, Revolving	L. W. Pond	Worcester, Mass	June 17, 1862	35,623
Fire-arm, Revolving	L. W Pond	Worcester, Mass	June 16, 1863	38,934
Fire-arm, Revolving	E A. Prescott	Worcester, Mass	Oct. 2, 1860	30,245
Fire-arm, Revolving	E. A. Raymond and C. Robitaille.	Brooklyn, N. Y	July 27, 1858	21,054
Fire-arm, Revolving	J. Reid	New York, N. Y	Apr. 28, 1863	38,336
Fire-arm, Revolving	J. Reid	Catskill, N. Y	Dec. 26, 1865	51,752
Fire-arm, Revolving	H. Reynolds	Springfield, Mass	May 10, 1864	42,688
Fire-arm, Revolving	C. B. Richards	Hartford, Conn	July 25, 1871	117,461
Fire-arm, Revolving	C. B. Richards	Hartford, Conn	Sept. 19, 1871	119,048
Fire-arm, Revolving	J. Rider	Newark, Ohio	Aug. 17, 1858	21,215
Fire-arm, Revolving	J. Rider	Newark, Ohio	May 3, 1859	23,861
Fire-arm, Revolving	J. Rider	Newark, Ohio	Nov. 28, 1865	51,269
Fire-arm, Revolving	C. Robitaille and F. Dahis	Brooklyn, N. Y	Aug. 2, 1864	43,709
Fire-arm, Revolving	L. C. Rodier	Springfield, Mass	July 11, 1865	48,775
Fire-arm, Revolving	H. S. Rogers	Willow Vale, N. Y	Oct. 28, 1862	36,861
Fire-arm, Revolving	M. L. Rood	Marshall, Mich	Nov. 22, 1853	10,259
Fire-arm, Revolving	E. K. Root	Hartford, Conn	Dec. 25, 1855	13,999
Fire-arm, Revolving	E. K. Root	Hartford, Conn	June 4, 1867	65,510
Fire-arm, Revolving	S. H. Roper	Roxbury, Mass	Apr. 10, 1866	53,881
Fire-arm, Revolving	J. Rupertus	Philadelphia, Pa	Apr. 19, 1859	23,711
Fire-arm, Revolving	J. Rupertus	Philadelphia, Pa	Dec. 2, 1862	37,059
Fire-arm, Revolving	J. Rupertus	Philadelphia, Pa	July 19, 1864	43,606
Fire-arm, Revolving	J. Rupertus	Philadelphia, Pa	Nov. 21, 1871	121,199
Fire-arm, Revolving	E. Savage and H. S. North	Cromwell and Middletown, Conn.	May 15, 1860	28,331
Fire-arm, Revolving	O. Schneeloch	Brooklyn, N. Y	Dec. 31, 1872	134,442
Fire-arm, Revolving	G. W. Schofield	United States Army	Apr. 22, 1873	138,047
Fire-arm, Revolving	C. Sharps	Philadelphia, Pa	Sept. 5, 1871	118,752
Fire-arm, Revolving	T. Shaw	Philadelphia, Pa	Dec. 24, 1861	34,032
Fire-arm, Revolving	F. P. Slocum	Brooklyn, N. Y	Jan. 27, 1863	37,551
Fire-arm, Revolving	F. P. Slocum	Brooklyn, N. Y	Apr. 14, 1863	38,204
Fire-arm, Revolving	A. Smith	Hartford, Conn	Dec. 24, 1861	34,016
Fire-arm, Revolving	H. Smith and D. B. Wesson	Springfield, Mass	July 5, 1859	24,666
Fire-arm, Revolving	H. Smith and D. B. Wesson	Springfield, Mass	June 16, 1863	38,921
Fire-arm, Revolving	H. Smith and D. B. Wesson	Springfield, Mass	Nov. 21, 1865	51,092
Fire-arm, Revolving	O. A. Smith	Middlefield, Conn	Jan. 28, 1873	135,377
Fire-arm, Revolving	O. A. Smith	Middlefield, Conn	Jan. 28, 1873	135,378
Fire-arm, Revolving	O. A. Smith	Middlefield, Conn	Apr. 15, 1873	137,968
Fire-arm, Revolving	W. S. Smoot	Ilion, N. Y	Oct. 21, 1873	143,855
Fire-arm, Revolving	C. E. Sneider	Baltimore, Md	Mar. 18, 1862	34,703
Fire-arm, Revolving	C. E. Sneider	Baltimore, Md	Feb. 28, 1865	46,612
Fire-arm, Revolving	A. Spelher	Philadelphia, Pa	Oct. 2, 1860	30,260
Fire-arm, Revolving	E. T. Starr	New York, N. Y	Jan. 15, 1856	14,118
Fire-arm, Revolving	E. T. Starr	New York, N. Y	Dec. 19, 1865	51,628
Fire-arm, Revolving	W. M. Storm	New York, N. Y	Mar. 11, 1856	14,420
Fire-arm, Revolving	F. A. Thuer	East Hartford, Conn	Sept. 15, 1868	82,258
Fire-arm, Revolving	W. Tibbals	South Coventry, Conn	June 19, 1866	55,743
Fire-arm, Revolving	W. Tibbals	South Coventry, Conn	July 17, 1866	56,466
Fire-arm, Revolving	A. C. Vaughan	Bedford, Pa	May 27, 1862	35,404
Fire-arm, Revolving	J. H. Vickers	Worcester, Mass	June 17, 1862	35,657
Fire-arm, Revolving	J. H. Vickers	Worcester, Mass	May 16, 1865	47,775
Fire-arm, Revolving	J. H. Vickers	Norwich, Conn	Aug. 21, 1866	57,448
Fire-arm, Revolving	J. Walch	New York, N. Y	Feb. 8, 1859	22,905
Fire-arm, Revolving	J. Warner	Springfield, Mass	July 28, 1857	17,904
Fire-arm, Revolving	D. B. Wesson	Springfield, Mass	Feb. 25, 1873	136,348
Fire-arm, Revolving	D. B. Wessen and C. A. King	Springfield, Mass	July 16, 1872	128,991
Fire-arm, Revolving	F. Wesson	Worcester, Mass	Dec. 15, 1868	84,976
Fire-arm, Revolving	F. Wesson	Worcester, Mass	June 13, 1871	115,916
Fire-arm, Revolving	J. A. Whalen	Brooklyn, N. Y	Apr. 22, 1862	35,052
Fire-arm, Revolving	R. White	Hartford, Conn	Apr. 13, 1858	19,961
Fire-arm, Revolving	R. White	Lowell, Mass	Nov. 29, 1864	45,290
Fire-arm, Revolving	R. White	Lowell, Mass	July 9, 1867	66,542
Fire-arm, Revolving	R. White	Lowell, Mass	Aug. 10, 1869	93,572
Fire-arm, Revolving	R. White	Lowell, Mass	Aug. 10, 1869	93,653
Fire-arm, Revolving	R. White	Lowell, Mass	Feb. 1, 1870	99,505
Fire-arm, Revolving	R. White	Lowell, Mass	Sept. 30, 1873	143,394
Fire-arm, Revolving	E. Whitney	New Haven, Conn	Jan. 9, 1866	51,985
Fire-arm, Revolving	E. Whitney	New Haven, Conn	May 23, 1871	115,258
Fire-arm, Revolving	D. Williamson	Brooklyn, N. Y	Jan. 5, 1864	41,184
Fire-arm, Revolving	D. Williamson	Brooklyn, N. Y	May 17, 1864	42,823
Fire-arm, Revolving	D. Williamson	Greenville, N. J	Mar. 18, 1873	137,043
Fire-arm, Revolving	D. Williamson	Greenville, N. J	Nov. 18, 1873	144,814
Fire-arm, Revolving	D. Williamson	Greenville, N. J	Nov. 18, 1873	144,815
Fire-arm, Revolving	S. W. Wood	Cornwall, N. Y	Nov. 18, 1862	36,984
Fire-arm, Revolving	S. W. Wood	Cornwall, N. Y	Mar. 1, 1864	41,803
Fire-arm, Revolving	S. W. Wood	Cornwall, N. Y	Sept. 20, 1864	44,363
Fire-arm, Revolving-breech	J. Ells	Pittsburgh, Pa	Aug. 1, 1854	11,419
Fire-arm, Revolving-breech	H. Iversen	New York, N. Y	Mar. 26, 1850	7,218
Fire-arm, Revolving-breech	H. S. North and C. D. Skinner	Middletown and Haddam, Conn.	June 1, 1852	8,982
Fire-arm, Revolving-breech	P. W. Porter	Memphis, Tenn	July 8, 1851	8,210
Fire-arm, Revolving-breech	J. Warner	Springfield, Mass	July 15, 1851	8,229

Index of patents issued from the United States Patent Office from 1790 *to* 1873, *inclusive*—Continued.

Invention.	Inventor.	Residence.	Date.	No.
Fire-arm, Revolving chambered	S. Colt	Hartford, Conn	Sept. 10, 1850	7, 629
Fire-arm, Revolving-hammer	G. Leonard, jr	Shrewsbury, Mass	July 9, 1850	7, 493
Fire-arm, Rifled	J. B. Atwater	Ripon, Wis	Mar. 6, 1860	27, 342
Fire-arm, Rifled	A. Henry	Edinburgh, North Britain	Oct. 10, 1871	119, 846
Fire-arm, Safety sliding-breech	C. Hartung	Beichlingen, Prussia	Nov. 13, 1849	6, 871
Fire-arm, Self-cocking	R. S. Mershon and J. Hollingsworth.	Philadelphia, Pa., and Zanesville, Ohio.	Sept. 8, 1863	39, 825
Fire-arm, Self-feeding breech-loading	A. Ball	Worcester, Mass	Aug. 16, 1864	43, 827
Fire-arm, Self loading	A. Ball	Worcester, Mass	June 23, 1863	38, 935
Fire-arm, Self-loading	N. W. Brewer	Williamsport, Pa	June 12, 1860	28, 646
Fire-arm, Self-loading	J. D. Moore	Zanesville, Ohio	Mar. 6, 1860	27, 374
Fire-arm, Self-loading	W. H. Rice	Windsor, Conn	May 19, 1863	38, 604
Fire-arm, Self-loading	C. M. Spencer	South Manchester, Conn	Mar. 6, 1860	27, 393
Fire-arm, Self-loading	C. M. Spencer	Boston, Mass	Jan. 17, 1865	45, 952
Fire-arm, Self-loading	R. Wilson	Macomb, Ill	Nov. 15, 1864	45, 105
Fire-arm, Self loading and priming	S. Day	New York, N. Y	Aug. 31, 1837	364
Fire-arm, Self-loading and self-capping repeating	M. M. Cass	Utica, N. Y	Sept. 26, 1848	5, 814
Fire-arm, Self priming	G. W. B. Gedney	New York, N. Y	Mar. 15, 1859	23, 241
Fire-arm with several stationary barrels and a revolving hammer.	G. Leonard, jr	Shrewsbury, Mass	Sept. 18, 1849	6, 723
Fire-arms, Adjustable back-sight for	C. Sharps	Philadelphia, Pa	July 23, 1861	32, 899
Fire-arms, Adjustable hammer for many-barreled	R. I. Howland and W. H. Elliot	Ilion, N. Y	Feb. 9, 1864	41, 510
Fire-arms, Adjustable hammer for revolving	A. Le Mat	New Orleans, La	June 7, 1859	24, 312
Fire-arms, Adjustable sight for	R. S. Lawrence	Hartford, Conn	Feb. 15, 1859	22, 958
Fire-arms, Adjustable stock of	C. W. Jones	Cheltenham, England	July 17, 1866	56, 506
Fire-arms and the lock and appurtenances of the same, Movable breech for.	B. Chambers	Washington, D. C	July 31, 1849	6, 612
Fire-arms, Apparatus for cooling repeating	J. A. Reynolds	Elmira, N. Y	July 17, 1855	13, 294
Fire-arms, Attached muzzle for	P. S. Newton	Hartford, Conn	June 1, 1843	3, 115
Fire-arms, Attaching bayonets to	H. Berdan	New York, N. Y	Jan. 10, 1865	45, 901
Fire-arms, Automatic primer for	J. Rupertus	Philadelphia, Pa	May 10, 1859	23, 952
Fire-arms, Automatic primer for	J. H. Wells	Brooklyn, N. Y	Dec. 24, 1861	34, 020
Fire-arms, Back-sight for	W. Conner	Rensselaerville, N. Y	Mar. 19, 1867	63, 022
Fire-arms, Back-sight for	H. Hammond	Hartford, Conn	Jan. 8, 1867	61, 007
Fire-arms, Back-sight for	J. B. Learock	Boston, Mass	Jan. 27, 1863	37, 512
Fire-arms, Back-sight for	E. Maynard	Washington, D. C	Oct. 4, 1859	25, 663
Fire-arms, Ball-screw for	J. J. Alises	Washington, D. C	Oct. 11, 1864	44, 586
Fire-arms, Ball-screw for	A. De Witzleben	Washington, D. C	Feb. 7, 1865	46, 220
Fire-arms, blasting, &c., Explosive compound for use in.	T. Taylor	Washington, D. C	Dec. 7, 1869	97, 566
Fire-arms, Cap-priming attachment to	E. D. Seely	Brookline, Mass	July 1, 1862	35, 783
Fire-arms, Capsule for preventing the soiling of	F. L. M. Dorvault	Paris, France	Apr. 25, 1865	47, 503
Fire-arms, Charger attached to	O. B. Percival and A. Smith	East Haddam, Conn, and New York, N. Y.	July 9, 1850	7, 496
Fire-arms, &c., Charger for	J. Johnson	Washington, D. C	Sept. 11, 1855	13, 547
Fire-arms, Charger for	T. H. Peavey	South Montaille, Me	June 27, 1854	11, 174
Fire-arms, Charger for	W. M. Storm	New York, N. Y	May 2, 1854	10, 846
Fire-arms, Combined back-sight and cartridge-retractor for.	G. W. Bowlby	Pontiac, Mich	May 21, 1867	64, 941
Fire-arms, Combined implement for detaching and replacing the parts of.	A. Grillet	Philadelphia, Pa	May 16, 1865	47, 715
Fire-arms, Concealed trigger for	J. Pecare and J. M. Smith	New York, N. Y	Dec. 4, 1849	6, 925
Fire-arms, Construction and mode of loading	T. McCarty	Elmira, N. Y	Mar. 11, 1837	147
Fire-arms, Continuous priming for	D. G. Rollin	New York, N. Y	Apr. 27, 1858	20, 129
Fire-arms, Cylinder-pin for revolving	W. H. Elliot	Plattsburgh, N. Y	May 16, 1865	47, 707
Fire-arms, Discharging breech-loading	H. Stanton	United States Army	Aug. 16, 1853	9, 950
Fire-arms, Expanding tampion for	T. K. Schermerhorn and J. Anderson.	Brooklyn, N. Y	Dec. 27, 1864	45, 641
Fire-arms, Expansible tampion for	G. R. Willmott	Meriden, Conn	Nov. 24, 1863	40, 720
Fire-arms, Feeder for repeating	L. W. Broadwell	Carlsruhe, Grand Duchy of Baden.	Dec. 20, 1870	110, 338
Fire-arms, Fitting lock-plate to stock of	G. Henry	Nazareth, Pa	Dec. 4, 1866	60, 188
Fire-arms, Fly tumbler-lock for	S. W. Marston	New York, N. Y	Jan. 7, 1851	7, 887
Fire-arms, Frame and stock for revolving	C. F. Galand	Paris, France	June 17, 1873	140, 028
Fire-arms, Gas-check for breech-loading	F. Curtis	Newton Lower Falls, Mass	Feb. 9, 1864	41, 489
Fire arms, Gas-check for breech-loading	J. M. Seymour	Boston, Mass	May 20, 1862	35, 354
Fire arms, Gas-check for breech-loading	J. C. Symmes	United States Ordnance Corps.	Sept. 8, 1863	39, 844
Fire-arms, Gas-check for revolving	J. Davis	Limestoneville, Pa	Oct. 22, 1872	132, 357
Fire-arms, Hammer for breech-loading	W. H. Elliot	New York, N. Y	Aug. 27, 1867	68, 292
Fire-arms, Hammer-guard to	C. Sharps	Philadelphia, Pa	Oct. 22, 1861	33, 546
Fire-arms, Hammer-guard for	B. Singleton	Portsmouth, Va	May 1, 1860	28, 109
Fire-arms, Handle-attachment to	E. Charlesworth	London, England	Oct. 3, 1865	50, 312
Fire-arms, Hook-attachment to bands of	I. Merrill	Springfield, Mass	Apr. 15, 1873	137, 786
Fire-arms, Loading and discharging	P. A. Morineau	Philadelphia, Pa	Oct. 10, 1832	
Fire-arms, Locking-apparatus of repeating	J. Stevens	Chicopee, Mass	Nov. 26, 1850	7, 802
Fire-arms, Locking-cylinder of revolving	T. Gibson	Yonkers, N. Y	Apr. 19, 1864	42, 435
Fire-arms, Lubricating	S. Colt	Hartford, Conn	Mar. 3, 1857	16, 716
Fire-arms, Lubricating-pellet for	S. W. Wood	Cornwall, N. Y	May 7, 1872	126, 614
Fire-arms, Lubricating-wad for	S. W. Wood	Cornwall, N. Y	May 7, 1872	126, 615
Fire-arms, Machine for boring chambers in the cylinders of.	E. K. Root	Hartford, Conn	Nov. 28, 1854	12, 002
Fire-arms, Magazine-hammer for	J. N. Ward	United States Army	July 1, 1856	15, 262
Fire-arms, Manner of discharging	J. Shaw	Philadelphia, Pa	Jan. 30, 1841	1, 958
Fire arms, Manufacture of the metallic parts of	I. Adams, jr	Boston, Mass	Dec. 21, 1869	98, 606
Fire-arms, Means for actuating movable parts of	T. Bailey	New Orleans, La.	June 14, 1859	24, 437
Fire-arms, Means for revolving the breeches of repeating.	J. Warner	Springfield, Mass	Jan. 7, 1851	7, 894
Fire-arms, Means of attaching cartridge magazine-blocks to.	H. Metcalfe	United States Army	Oct. 7, 1873	143, 415
Fire-arms, Method of attaching the cylinder in revolving.	D. H. Chamberlain	Boston, Mass	Apr. 23, 1850	7, 300
Fire-arms, Method of connecting the hammer with the cylinder of revolving.	E. Wesson	Hartford, Conn	Aug. 28, 1849	6, 669
Fire-arms, Method of converting muzzle into breech loading.	C. E. Sneider	Baltimore, Md	Jan. 24, 1865	46, 054
Fire-arms, Method of forming receiver for breech-block of.	E. G. W. Bartlett	Providence, R. I	Dec. 23, 1873	145, 717

Index of patents issued from the United States Patent Office from 1790 to 1873, inclusive—Continued.

Invention.	Inventor.	Residence.	Date.	No.
Fire-arms, Method of revolving the hammer of repeating.	C. Sharps	Washington, D. C	Dec. 18, 1849	6, 960
Fire-arms, Mode of altering flint-lock to percussion	J. N. Ward	United States Army	Jan. 27, 1857	16, 503
Fire-arms, Mode of loading	C. A. McEvoy	Richmond, Va	Mar. 26, 1861	31, 815
Fire-arms, Mode of overcoming the windage in	A. E. Burnside	Bristol, R. I	May 12, 1857	17, 261
Fire-arms, Nipple-guard of	J. M. Hill and R. D. Hay	Crooked Creek, N. C	Oct. 26, 1869	96, 112
Fire-arms, Nipple-guard of	B. Lilly	Birmingham, England	May 3, 1864	42, 621
Fire-arms, Nipple-guard of	D. W. Smith	Boston, Mass	Jan. 26, 1858	19, 213
Fire-arms, Nipple of	E. Maynard	Washington, D. C	Oct. 4, 1859	25, 654
Fire-arms, Nipple-primer for	L. H. Bradford	Boston, Mass	May 17, 1864	42, 741
Fire-arms, Patched ball for	M. Peck	New Haven, Conn	July 19, 1864	43, 601
Fire-arms, Percussion-cap holder for	R. S. Pickett	New Haven, Conn	Apr. 4, 1865	47, 127
Fire-arms, Percussion-cap holder for priming	L. R. Budd	Oskaloosa, Iowa	May 19, 1863	38, 557
Fire-arms, Percussion-pellet for	J. Rupertus	Philadelphia, Pa	Aug. 16, 1859	25, 142
Fire-arms, Powder and shot charger for	A. Hall	New York, N. Y	May 13, 1873	138, 751
Fire-arms, Primer for	A. N. Newton	Richmond, Ind	May 23, 1854	10, 950
Fire-arms, Priming	C. Sharps	Hartford, Conn	Oct. 5, 1852	9, 308
Fire-arms, Priming-repeating	G. R. Crooker	New York, N. Y	Oct. 20, 1857	18, 486
Fire-arms, Rammer connection for revolving	F. Beals	New Haven, Conn	Jan. 6, 1863	37, 329
Fire-arms, Rammer for many-chambered-breech	J. Kerr	London, England	Apr. 14, 1857	17, 044
Fire-arms, Rammer for revolving	C. R. Alsop	Middletown, Conn	Aug. 7, 1860	29, 538
Fire arms, Rammer for revolving	F. D. Newbury	Hudson City, N. J	Jan. 31, 1865	46, 131
Fire-arms, Rear-sight base for	F. W. Howe	Providence, R. I	Jan. 24, 1865	46, 000
Fire-arms, Removable rammer for revolving	H. S. North	Middletown, Conn	Apr. 6, 1858	19, 868
Fire-arms, Retractor for revolving	T. Lee	Westport, Conn	Dec. 26, 1871	122, 182
Fire-arms, Revolving block of revolving	C. Sharps	Philadelphia, Pa	Nov. 27, 1860	30, 765
Fire-arms, Rifling	E. G. Allen	Boston, Mass	June 30, 1863	39, 024
Fire-arms, Rifling	A. Frauth	Chemnitz, Saxony	Oct. 10, 1865	50, 433
Fire-arms, Rifling breech-loading	H. Berdan	New York, N. Y	Jan. 10, 1865	45, 898
Fire-arms, Safety-device for lock of	E. T. Starr	New York, N. Y	Dec. 20, 1864	45, 532
Fire-arms, Safety-guard for	B. P. Cutler	Boston, Mass	Mar. 31, 1868	76, 058
Fire-arms, Safety-guard for the hammers of	H. E. Gibbon	Brooklyn, N. Y	Jan. 31, 1865	46, 100
Fire-arms, Safety-nipple for	W. N. Rowe	Washington, D. C	Jan. 1, 1867	60, 791
Fire arms, Safety nipple-guard	J. Oliphant	Uniontown, Pa	Jan. 13, 1863	37, 406
Fire-arms, Safety-stop for revolving	W. Tileston	Georgetown, D. C	Sept. 6, 1864	44, 126
Fire-arms, Screw driver for	G. W. Schofield	United States Army	Oct. 3, 1871	119, 656
Fire-arms, Securing the base-pin of revolving	S. Remington	Ilion, N. Y	Mar. 17, 1863	37, 921
Fire-arms, Self-primer for	W. H. Bell	Washington, D. C	Jan. 18, 1859	22, 618
Fire-arms, Self-priming hammer for	A. F. Tait	Morrisania, N. Y	June 2, 1863	38, 770
Fire-arms, Sight for	H. W. Colvin	Pendleton County, Ky	Sept. 13, 1859	25, 389
Fire-arms, Sight for	W. McKibbin	Buck Valley, Pa	Sept. 15, 1863	39, 941
Fire-arms, Sight for	C. E. Sneider	Baltimore, Md	Dec. 7, 1869	97, 717
Fire-arms, Sight for	J. Warner	Springfield, Mass	Feb. 24, 1863	37, 782
Fire-arms, Sighting	A. F. Garretson	Mount Pleasant, Iowa	Oct. 13, 1863	40, 256
Fire-arms, Snap-ring for	J. Rider	Newark, Ohio	Feb. 11, 1868	74, 427
Fire-arms so as to prevent oxidation and corrosion, Mode of finishing.	J. Allen and S. P. Townsend	New York, N. Y., and New Providence, N. J.	Jan. 1, 1867	60, 915
Fire arms, Spring-power repeating	J. Gordon	New London, Conn	Dec. 31, 1867	72, 844
Fire-arms, Stand for testing	J. Lehnert	Louisville, Ky	Apr. 16, 1872	125, 743
Fire-arms, Swivel-loop for	E. Whitney, jr	New Haven, Conn	Apr. 15, 1873	137, 989
Fire arms, Swivel-loop for	O. F. Winchester	New Haven, Conn	Dec. 12, 1871	121, 835
Fire-arms, Tape primer for	T. T. S. Laidley	United States Army	Feb. 15, 1859	22, 957
Fire-arms, Telescopic sight for	J. M. Trowbridge	United States Army	Mar. 8, 1864	41, 874
Fire-arms, Tig for	D. A. Hopkins	Brooklyn, N. Y	Sept. 16, 1862	36, 464
Fire-arms, Tompion for	R. Kingsley	Springfield, Mass	Feb. 18, 1862	34, 430
Fire-arms, Tompion for	T. T. S. Laidley	United States Army	May 19, 1868	77, 988
Fire-arms, Tompion for	R. G. Shurtliff	Springfield, Mass	Feb. 10, 1863	37, 645
Fire-arms, Tompion for	A. Tracy	United States Army	Mar. 18, 1862	34, 705
Fire-arms, Tool for manufacture of	A. Rebetey	Norwich, Conn	May 10, 1859	23, 944
Fire-arms, Toothed segment-lock for	D. H. Chamberlain	Boston, Mass	May 14, 1850	7, 360
Fire-arms, Trigger-cover for	J. Birkenhead	Ilion, N. Y	Feb. 9, 1864	41, 472
Fire-arms, Trigger-protector for	B. H. Westerhood	Philadelphia, Pa	July 22, 1856	15, 397
Fire-arms with tin, Overlaying	S. Ladd	Waltham, Mass	Oct. 14, 1835	....
Fire-arrester	G. W. Cook	Geneseo, Ill	Apr. 16, 1872	125, 663
Fire-back and grate setting	R. T. Collis	Webster, Ohio	Aug. 6, 1872	130, 195
Fire-back for warming rooms, Iron	C. Harris	Boston, Mass	May 15, 1815	....
Fire-balk	H. H. Baker	New Market, N. J	Jan. 17, 1865	45, 956
Fire-bar	W. Batchelor	Winchester, England	Jan. 17, 1871	111, 031
Fire-bar and connecting-bearing, Tubular	R. J. Ellis	Liverpool, England	Dec. 30, 1873	145, 995
Fire beds and tuyeres, Construction jointly of	P. H and F. M. Roots	Connersville, Ind	Oct. 18, 1870	108, 519
Fire-board	G. W. and W. H. Metcalf	Baltimore, Md	Jan. 26, 1869	86, 240
Fire-box	R. Gay	Richmond, Va	Nov. 30, 1869	97, 387
Fire box and grate	J. J. Folts	Buffalo, N. Y	Feb. 16, 1858	19, 358
Fire-box, Smoke-consuming	G. H. Smith	Galesburgh, Ill	Dec. 14, 1869	97, 819
Fire-boxes, Smoke-consuming apparatus for	J. Durand	Columbus, Ohio	Oct. 10, 1871	119, 832
Fire, Canvas conductor to be used when houses are on.	S. Green	....	Mar. 28, 1792	....
Fire-cavern	A. Quincy	Boston, Mass	Mar. 20, 1811	....
Fire-chamber, Apparatus for clearing	G. R. Moore	Lyons, Iowa	Mar. 29, 1864	42, 102
Fire-chamber clearer	G. R. Moore	Lyons, Iowa	Jan. 17, 1865	45, 933
Fire, Closed blomary	J. Renton and J. H. Crane	Newark, N. J	Aug. 10, 1848	5, 702
Fire, Composition for coating wooden structures to protect them against.	A. Pirz	Long Island City, N. Y	Jan. 24, 1871	111, 148
Fire, Conveying warm air to	W. R. Miller	Hinsdale, N. Y	Dec. 31, 1833	....
Fire-cracker holder	C. Most	Bergen City, N. J	Aug. 23, 1870	106, 714
Fire-cracker holder	A. E. Peck	Brooklyn, N. Y	Oct. 26, 1869	96, 143
Fire-cracker pistol or holder	R. Hutcheson	Newark, N. J	Nov. 8, 1870	109, 014
Fire-cracker pistol, Revolving	J. H. Hawes and O. W. Brock	Monroeton, Pa	Oct. 4, 1870	108, 022
Fire-detector	W. C. Grimes	Philadelphia, Pa	Apr. 21, 1868	76, 911
Fire-detector with the alarm, Connecting	H. L. Brower	New York, N. Y	Nov. 15, 1870	109, 292
Fire, Device in the walls of buildings to prevent damage to goods by water in case of.	T. Estlack	Philadelphia, Pa	June 3, 1856	15, 002
Fire, Distributer for extinguishing	G. J. Orr	New York, N. Y	Nov. 18, 1873	144, 696
Fire-draft or regulator by atmospheric pressure	R. Mayo	Washington, D. C	Sept. 9, 1835	....
Fire-engine	J. Achman	Washington, D. C	Dec. 30, 1812	....
Fire engine	J. R. Adams	Port Jervis, N. Y	May 1, 1855	12, 773
Fire-engine	O. G. Adkins	Oswego, N. Y	July 20, 1852	9, 127
Fire-engine	A. F. Allen	Providence, R. I	Oct. 22, 1872	132, 426

Index of patents issued from the United States Patent Office from 1790 *to* 1873, *inclusive*—Continued.

Invention.	Inventor.	Residence.	Date.	No.
Fire-engine	J. B. Babcock	Marietta, Ohio	July 1, 1841	2, 150
Fire-engine	A. Barrett	Baltimore, Md	Feb. 18, 1841	1, 982
Fire-engine	G. Barton, jr	Waterford, N. Y	Aug. 16, 1844	3, 707
Fire-engine	G. Barton, jr., and L. Button	Waterford, N. Y	Sept. 19, 1846	4, 767
Fire-engine	J. Briggs, jr	St. Louis, Mo	Sept. 3, 1842	2, 770
Fire-engine	E. Bryant	New London, Conn	Mar. 28, 1820	....
Fire-engine	L. Button and R. Blake	Waterford, N. Y	Nov. 30, 1858	22, 162
Fire-engine	C. and W. C. Cleveland	New York and Ithaca, N. Y	Apr. 23, 1872	125, 883
Fire-engine	E. Daboll	Canaan, Conn	Apr. 12, 1828	....
Fire-engine	J. N. Dennisson	Newark, N. J	Feb. 7, 1765	46, 219
Fire-engine	J. J. Giraud	Baltimore, Md	Nov. 11, 1830	....
Fire-engine	C. W. Grannis	Collins, N. Y	Oct. 7, 1846	4, 796
Fire-engine	I. Hathaway	Walton, N. Y	Aug. 6, 1812	....
Fire-engine	E. Higgins	Saratoga, N. Y	Apr. 27, 1822	....
Fire-engine	J. Kersey	....	Apr. 13, 1797	....
Fire-engine	S. Lockwood and W. Loveland	Little Falls, N. Y	Apr. 16, 1822	....
Fire-engine	E. Marx	New York, N. Y	Dec. 20, 1845	4, 316
Fire-engine	A. Nudd	Exeter, N. H	Feb. 27, 1855	12, 441
Fire-engine	T. Odiorne	Portsmouth, N. H	Aug. 27, 1835	....
Fire-engine	J. Perkins	Newburyport, Mass	Mar. 23, 1813	....
Fire-engine	N. Pierce	Whitehall, N. Y	Feb. 23, 1831	....
Fire-engine	A. Pollock and J. Perkins	Boston, Mass	Aug. 6, 1812	....
Fire-engine	F. Ransom and D. L. Farnam	New York, N. Y	Apr. 17, 1847	5, 077
Fire-engine	J. Richardson, jr	Shrewsbury, Mass	July 24, 1818	....
Fire-engine	A. W. Roberts	Hartford, Conn	Jan. 23, 1855	12, 284
Fire-engine	G. Shalk and W. Tintoff	Lebanon, Pa	Sept. 23, 1826	....
Fire-engine	J. Smith, jr	New York, N. Y	May 20, 1807	....
Fire-engine	J. A. Sinclair	Bridgeport, Ohio	Oct. 28, 1873	144, 001
Fire-engine	S. Steward	....	Dec. 6, 1803	....
Fire-engine	J. B. Tarr	Albany, N. Y	Nov. 6, 1849	6, 859
Fire-engine	A. Warth	New York, N. Y	Aug. 1, 1854	11, 459
Fire-engine	J. Williams, jr	Salem, N. Y	May 11, 1839	1, 150
Fire-engine and lawn-sprinkler, Pneumatic	H. C. Neer	Park Ridge, N. J	Oct. 22, 1872	132, 407
Fire-engine and pump	J. N. Dennisson	Newark, N. J	Apr. 24, 1866	54, 247
Fire engine and water-pump	E. Williams and J. Collins	Falley Cross-Roads, Mass	June 20, 1823	....
Fire-engine and wrecking-pump, Floating	G. W. Talcott	Buffalo, N. Y	Oct. 6, 1868	82, 767
Fire-engine, Capstan	S. E. Hamlin	....	Aug. 30, 1799	....
Fire-engine, Chemical	I. H. Clark	Boston, Mass	June 1, 1869	90, 637
Fire-engine, Chemical	E. Gordon	Boston, Mass	Aug. 4, 1868	80, 542
Fire-engine, Chemical	R. Lapham and G. Clark, jr	Boston, Mass	May 28, 1867	65, 240
Fire-engine, Chemical	J. B. Stillson and J. A. Kley	Chicago, Ill	Sept. 17, 1872	131, 414
Fire-engine, Floating	J. C. Lang	Washington, D. C	Feb. 18, 1873	135, 922
Fire-engine heater, Steam	W. F. Shaw	Boston, Mass	Sept. 9, 1873	142, 589
Fire-engine, Horizontal	L. Holland	Belchertown, Mass	Mar. 11, 1824	....
Fire-engine, Horse-power	J. C. McCarthy	New York, N. Y	Nov. 2, 1869	96, 457
Fire-engine, Miniature steam	A. L. Dewey	Westfield, Mass	Aug. 22, 1871	118, 218
Fire-engine on locomotive	D. Williams	Syracuse, N. Y	Apr. 22, 1862	35, 053
Fire-engine pipe	J. Riley	Boston, Mass	Feb. 6, 1834	....
Fire-engine, Steam	N. S. Bean	Manchester, N. H	Jan. 15, 1861	31, 138
Fire-engine, Steam	L. Button and R. Blake	Waterford, N. Y	May 3, 1864	42, 557
Fire-engine, Steam	L. and T. E. Button	Waterford, N. Y	June 20, 1871	116, 151
Fire-engine, Steam	M. R. Clapp	Seneca Falls, N. Y	Jan. 7, 1862	34, 087
Fire-engine, Steam	E. R. and H. S. Cole	Pawtucket, R. I	July 7, 1868	79, 730
Fire-engine, Steam	E. R. and H. S. Cole	Pawtucket, R. I	Oct. 18, 1870	108, 452
Fire-engine, Steam	W. C. Davol, jr	Fall River, Mass	Oct. 21, 1873	143, 750
Fire-engine water-heater	P. M. Kafer and J. M. De Lacy	Trenton, N. J	Jan. 7, 1868	73, 015
Fire-engine water-heater	A. H. Perry	Boston, Mass	Oct. 22, 1872	132, 488
Fire-engines, Application of carbonic acid in	I. H. Clark	Boston, Mass	Dec. 1, 1868	84, 613
Fire-engines, Carriage for steam	A. B. Latta	Cincinnati, Ohio	May 22, 1855	12, 912
Fire-engines, Circulating water-heater for steam	H. V. Coleman	Chicago, Ill	Aug. 30, 1870	102, 782
Fire-engines, Coupling for uniting streams from	D. J. Tapley	Danvers, Mass	Dec. 17, 1872	134, 110
Fire-engines, Device for applying power to	G. Backstein	Philadelphia, Pa	Nov. 28, 1854	11, 987
Fire-engines, Electric signaling-apparatus for	W. H. Mumler	Boston, Mass	Feb. 6, 1872	123, 355
Fire-engines, Flue-blast for steam	J. Grabner	Warsaw, Ind	Jan. 14, 1873	134, 796
Fire-engines, Method of applying horse-power to	D. Russell	Lockport, N. Y	June 10, 1856	15, 089
Fire-engines, Method of working the lever of	S. Huse	Newburyport, Mass	Apr. 9, 1833	....
Fire-engines, Mode of applying water to	F. Ransom and U. Winman	New York, N. Y	Feb. 13, 1841	1, 980
Fire-engines, Operating	J. P., P., and G. Cowing	Seneca Falls, N. Y	Jan. 15, 1856	14, 089
Fire-engines, Operating	F. G. Smith	Columbia, Tenn	Sept. 12, 1854	11, 684
Fire-engines, Supplementary heater for steam	R. Gilbert and J. P. Topham	Rochester, N. Y	May 13, 1873	138, 880
Fire-engines, Supporting the carriage-bodies of	L. Button and R. Blake	Waterford, N. Y	Oct. 4, 1859	25, 628
Fire-escape	L. E. Ainsworth	Bolton, Canada	Sept. 23, 1873	143, 112
Fire-escape	E. Ale	Clearfield, Pa	July 4, 1871	116, 659
Fire-escape	W. B. Avery	Cambridge, Mass	June 5, 1860	28, 551
Fire-escape	H. O. Baker and J. McGill	New York, N. Y	May 22, 1860	28, 340
Fire-escape	A. T. Ballentine	New York, N. Y	June 28, 1864	43, 283
Fire-escape	P. W. Barnes	Albany, N. Y	Aug. 26, 1873	142, 141
Fire-escape	J. Bearns and A. Olsson	Brooklyn, N. Y	Mar. 19, 1872	124, 715
Fire-escape	G. W. Bishop and H. H. Smith	Baltimore, Md	Sept. 19, 1871	119, 008
Fire-escape	W. Breitenstein	New York, N. Y	Oct. 9, 1860	30, 291
Fire-escape	W. and G. H. Burditt	Boston, Mass	Feb. 1, 1870	99, 399
Fire-escape	O. F. Burton	New York, N. Y	Aug. 7, 1860	29, 542
Fire-escape	J. A. Chambers	Ogdensburgh, N. Y	July 3, 1866	56, 006
Fire-escape	R. Chandler	New York, N. Y	Nov. 8, 1864	44, 934
Fire-escape	L. M. Chipley	Saint Louis, Mo	Dec. 23, 1873	145, 844
Fire-escape	J. T. Commoss	New York, N. Y	Mar. 31, 1863	38, 078
Fire-escape	J. Cox	Brush Valley, Pa	June 27, 1846	4, 597
Fire-escape	C. W. Crosley	New York, N. Y	June 19, 1860	28, 740
Fire-escape	J. W. Davis and J. Vermillion	Washington, D. C	Oct. 31, 1871	120, 420
Fire-escape	J. Deckelmann and F. Spiess	New York, N. Y	Apr. 24, 1860	27, 972
Fire-escape	W. De Pew	Paris, Canada	May 2, 1871	114, 421
Fire-escape	T. S. Diblin	New York, N. Y	Sept. 3, 1867	68, 491
Fire-escape	C. Dieterich	Boston, Mass	Oct. 14, 1873	143, 677
Fire-escape	W. Gardner	Boston, Mass	Apr. 4, 1871	113, 509
Fire-escape	J. A. Griswold	Chicago, Ill	Aug. 30, 1870	106, 812
Fire-escape	J. C. Hancock and E. P. Richardson.	Charlestown and Somerville, Mass.	Aug. 8, 1871	117, 773
Fire-escape	J. M. Hancock	Lansing, Iowa	Apr. 5, 1859	23, 462

Index of patents issued from the United States Patent Office from 1790 *to* 1873, *inclusive*—Continued.

Invention.	Inventor.	Residence.	Date.	No.
Fire-escape	J. J. Hartmann	Saint Louis, Mo	July 16, 1872	129, 336
Fire-escape	E. Hawthorne	Mountain View, Cal	Jan. 7, 1868	73, 007
Fire-escape	W. Henley	Chicago, Ill	June 27, 1871	116, 441
Fire-escape	C. Herold	Pittsburgh, Pa	Oct. 8, 1872	132, 073
Fire-escape	J. Heuermann	Davenport, Iowa	July 23, 1867	66, 961
Fire-escape	J. Heuermann	Davenport, Iowa	Nov. 9, 1869	96, 698
Fire-escape	G. Heydrich	Philadelphia, Pa	Feb. 14, 1860	27, 127
Fire-escape	J. Hobbs	Columbus, Ind	Oct. 9, 1860	30, 318
Fire-escape	J. F. Hobson	Newburgh, Ohio	July 16, 1872	129, 410
Fire-escape	J. Hoeflinger	Carrollton, Mo	Apr. 4, 1871	113, 667
Fire-escape	J. J. Holwell	New York, N. Y	June 26, 1860	28, 862
Fire-escape	W. L. Horne	Batavia, Ill	July 17, 1866	56, 417
Fire-escape	E. J. Hudson	Golconda, Ill	Jan. 10, 1871	110, 851
Fire-escape	G. A. W. Hüttman and G. K. Kornelio.	Philadelphia, Pa	Mar. 10, 1849	6, 155
Fire-escape	J. Ivory	New York, N. Y	Mar. 14, 1871	112, 714
Fire-escape	L. Jewell	Stratham, N. Y	Jan. 22, 1861	31, 173
Fire-escape	C. J. and E. W. Jones	New Brighton, N. Y	Oct. 24, 1865	50, 596
Fire-escape	J. L. Jürgens	New Orleans, La	Sept. 22, 1868	82, 325
Fire-escape	C. P. Keenyon	Selma, N. C	Mar. 21, 1871	112, 928
Fire-escape	W. Kegg	Lasellsville, N. Y	Apr. 29, 1873	138, 410
Fire-escape	G. W. Keller	Philadelphia, Pa	Apr. 18, 1854	10, 807
Fire-escape	L. King	Bridgeport, Conn	May 22, 1860	28, 378
Fire-escape	L. Knocke	Davenport, Iowa	May 22, 1860	28, 380
Fire-escape	E. B. Larchar	New York, N. Y	Nov. 13, 1860	30, 633
Fire-escape	J. A. Law	Meredith, N. Y	Jan. 29, 1861	31, 248
Fire-escape	G. Laytor and H. Helmling	Baltimore, Md	Apr. 4, 1871	113, 311
Fire-escape	M. Lewis and J. C. Swenson	Williamsburgh, N. Y	Mar. 15, 1870	100, 777
Fire-escape	A. Lippmann	New York, N. Y	Apr. 24, 1860	27, 992
Fire-escape	I. Lohr	New York, N. Y	Feb. 16, 1864	41, 628
Fire-escape	R. Mackenzie and J. Cooper	New York, N. Y	June 4, 1867	65, 408
Fire-escape	H. Marshall	Atlanta, Ga	Dec. 10, 1872	133, 870
Fire-escape	J. Marx	Rochester, N. Y	Nov. 19, 1867	71, 030
Fire-escape	W. McCord	Sing Sing, N. Y	June 26, 1860	28, 880
Fire-escape	J. W. McKenzie	Brooklyn, N. Y	Nov. 12, 1861	33, 710
Fire-escape	I. Merritt	North Bridgewater, Mass	May 27, 1873	139, 410
Fire-escape	W. Miller	Boston, Mass	July 9, 1861	32, 778
Fire-escape	W. Miller	Boston, Mass	Sept. 6, 1870	107, 077
Fire-escape	C. C. Milton	San Francisco, Cal	May 6, 1873	138, 513
Fire-escape	H. Morohan	Brooklyn, N. Y	Nov. 13, 1860	30, 639
Fire-escape	E. R. Morrison	Washington, D. C	Jan. 28, 1873	135, 354
Fire-escape	S. Murset and E. Zuberbuhler	Philadelphia, Pa	Oct. 28, 1873	144, 122
Fire-escape	G. H. Nichols	Richmond, Va	Apr. 4, 1871	113, 329
Fire-escape	J. O'Brien	New York, N. Y	May 27, 1873	139, 416
Fire-escape	J. Paar	New York, N. Y	Mar. 31, 1868	76, 097
Fire-escape	J. W. Patten and G. P. Terry	Albany, N. Y	June 26, 1860	28, 898
Fire-escape	A. Pelham	Plymouth, Mich	July 29, 1873	141, 378
Fire-escape	S. Penfield	Hartford, Conn	Mar. 3, 1840	1, 505
Fire-escape	H. Poweison	New Brunswick, N. J	May 29, 1860	28, 501
Fire-escape	T. C. Rice	Worcester, Mass	Oct. 17, 1871	119, 997
Fire-escape	H. A. Richards	Chicago, Ill	Apr. 1, 1873	137, 483
Fire-escape	E. P. Richardson	Manchester, N. H	May 4, 1869	89, 686
Fire-escape	A. Rigny	New York, N. Y	May 7, 1867	64, 569
Fire-escape	A. Robinson	New York, N. Y	Apr. 7, 1868	76, 527
Fire-escape	W. Sawyer	Lowell, Mass	May 27, 1862	35, 413
Fire-escape	D. A. Scott and A. W. Hiltz	Calais, Me	Nov. 4, 1873	144, 361
Fire-escape	H. G. Sedgwick	Warsaw, Mo	May 7, 1872	126, 581
Fire-escape	H. T. Seely and W. M. Harrison.	Kenosha, Wis	July 16, 1872	129, 179
Fire-escape	F. Seymour	Cincinnati, Ohio	May 1, 1860	28, 095
Fire-escape	W. A. Sharp and G. Hollenbeck.	Tama City, Iowa	Nov. 14, 1871	121, 011
Fire-escape	G. H. Shaw	Phelps, N. Y	Apr. 22, 1873	138, 051
Fire-escape	A. Shute	Flushing, N. Y	Nov. 19, 1861	33, 757
Fire-escape	A. Shute	Flushing, N. Y	July 29, 1862	36, 032
Fire-escape	W. H. Simmons	Skaneateles, N. Y	May 18, 1869	90, 316
Fire-escape	G. C. Smith and F. M. Burrows	Baltimore, Md	Apr. 4, 1871	113, 357
Fire-escape	G. C. Smith and F. M. Burrows	Baltimore, Md	July 11, 1871	117, 007
Fire-escape	T. L. Sommeril	Juda, Wis	Mar. 21, 1871	112, 982
Fire-escape	O. Spear	Baltimore, Md	Feb. 2, 1869	86, 600
Fire-escape	J. W. Sprague	Rochester, N. Y	Jan. 22, 1861	31, 216
Fire-escape	J. Steger	New York, N. Y	Mar. 29, 1870	101, 393
Fire-escape	E. Sturel	New York, N. Y	Dec. 18, 1860	30, 939
Fire-escape	S. A. Swalm and C. C. Schmitt	New York, N. Y	Sept. 15, 1868	82, 176
Fire-escape	O. Sweeney	Brooklyn, N. Y	Aug. 24, 1858	21, 282
Fire-escape	J. A. Talpey	Somerville, Mass	June 3, 1873	139, 484
Fire-escape	J. A. Talpey	Somerville, Mass	July 22, 1873	141, 093
Fire-escape	T. Thompson	Baltimore, Md	Aug. 11, 1863	39, 505
Fire-escape	T. Thompson, jr	New York, N. Y	Aug. 25, 1868	81, 436
Fire-escape	J. J. Treanor	New York, N. Y	Dec. 12, 1871	121, 826
Fire-escape	W. W. Van Loan	Catskill, N. Y	Feb. 20, 1847	4, 971
Fire-escape	F. A. L. Von Ehren	New Orleans, La	Mar. 18, 1873	136, 883
Fire-escape	J. Wagner and J. Schmid	Philadelphia, Pa	June 25, 1867	66, 058
Fire-escape	L. Wahle	Davenport, Iowa	July 12, 1870	105, 280
Fire-escape	A. Warth	New York, N. Y	May 29, 1860	28, 525
Fire-escape	W. M. Watson	Tonica, Ill	Jan. 23, 1872	123, 066
Fire-escape	C. Wiedling	New York, N. Y	July 30, 1867	67, 239
Fire-escape	E. R. Wethered	London, England	Aug. 15, 1871	118, 172
Fire-escape	W. P. Withey	Hartford, Conn	May 12, 1840	1, 599
Fire-escape	R. Wyatt	Brooklyn, N. Y	June 20, 1865	48, 333
Fire escape and alarm	J. Fischer	New York, N. Y	May 28, 1867	65, 194
Fire escape and extinguisher	S. Welsh and T. Linacree	Albany, N. Y	Jan. 23, 1841	1, 943
Fire-escape and hose-elevator	W. H. Nobles	Saint Paul, Minn	Oct. 24, 1871	120, 211
Fire-escape attachment for horse-stalls	D. S. Neal	Lynn, Mass	July 24, 1860	29, 301
Fire-escape, Pocket	G. A. England	Ripon, Wis	Apr. 25, 1871	114, 119
Fire escape, Portable	H. C. Carrigan	New York, N. Y	Sept. 28, 1869	95, 321
Fire-escape, Portable	I. Gratius	Alexandria, Pa	Oct. 2, 1860	30, 219
Fire-escape, Portable	G. D. McCullen	New Orleans, La	Dec. 12, 1871	121, 796

Index of patents issued from the United States Patent Office from 1790 to 1873, inclusive—Continued.

Invention.	Inventor.	Residence.	Date.	No.
Fire-extinguisher	B. T. Babbitt	New York, N. Y	Dec. 17, 1872	134, 024
Fire-extinguisher	J. F. Babcock	Boston, Mass	Aug. 4, 1868	80, 701
Fire-extinguisher	E. Barrett	New York, N. Y	Mar. 12, 1872	124, 534
Fire-extinguisher	W. H. Bate and G. F. Pinkham	Medford and Cambridge, Mass.	Mar. 30, 1869	88, 359
Fire-extinguisher	W. F. Beasley	Louisville, Ky	July 16, 1872	129, 519
Fire-extinguisher	C. Blake	Boston, Mass	May 2, 1871	114, 256
Fire-extinguisher	G. Booth	Toronto, Canada	Nov. 18, 1873	144, 595
Fire-extinguisher	J. F. Boynton	Syracuse, N. Y	Sept. 17, 1867	68, 940
Fire-extinguisher	J. F. Boynton	Syracuse, N. Y	June 15, 1869	91, 304
Fire-extinguisher	J. F. Boynton	Syracuse, N. Y	June 15, 1869	91, 411
Fire-extinguisher	J. F. Boynton	Syracuse, N. Y	Nov. 16, 1869	96, 876
Fire-extinguisher	Z. Breed	Weare, N. H	June 22, 1869	91, 709
Fire-extinguisher	P. F. Carlier and A. A. C. Vignon.	Paris, France	Apr. 13, 1869	88, 844
Fire-extinguisher	G. Clark, jr	Boston, Mass	Sept. 22, 1868	82, 471
Fire-extinguisher	G. Clark, jr	Boston, Mass	Mar. 9, 1869	87, 544
Fire-extinguisher	G. Cowing	Seneca Falls, N. Y	Apr. 26, 1870	102, 229
Fire-extinguisher	C. A. Cox	Jeffersonville, Ind	Apr. 15, 1873	137, 895
Fire-extinguisher	A. Crane	Fortress Monroe, Va	Feb. 10, 1863	37, 610
Fire-extinguisher	R. O. Doremus	New York, N. Y	Feb. 19, 1867	62, 118
Fire-extinguisher	W. L. Drake	Evanston, Ill	Dec. 9, 1873	145, 405
Fire-extinguisher	W. L. Drake	Evanston, Ill	Dec. 9, 1873	145, 406
Fire-extinguisher	J. Duffy	Quincy, Ill	Apr. 2, 1872	125, 275
Fire-extinguisher	W. L. Ellsworth	Brooklyn, N. Y	Aug. 20, 1872	130, 626
Fire-extinguisher	D. M. Ford and J. A. Kley	Chicago, Ill	June 20, 1871	116, 041
Fire-extinguisher	J. Gardner	Bedford, Ind	Feb. 14, 1871	111, 836
Fire-extinguisher	J. Gardner	Louisville, Ky	Dec. 26, 1871	122, 244
Fire-extinguisher	J. Gardner	Louisville, Ky	Mar. 12, 1872	124, 565
Fire-extinguisher	H. Henly	Bloomington, Ind	July 16, 1872	129, 134
Fire-extinguisher	L. Herman	Detroit, Mich	July 12, 1870	105, 203
Fire-extinguisher	C. T. Holloway	Baltimore, Md	June 11, 1872	127, 770
Fire-extinguisher	S. B. Johnson	Philadelphia, Pa	Aug. 8, 1871	117, 891
Fire-extinguisher	E. Jones	Pierrepont, N. Y	Oct. 17, 1871	119, 931
Fire-extinguisher	E. Jones	Colton, N. Y	Jan. 30, 1872	123, 106
Fire extinguisher	W. Kitson	Lowell, Mass	Oct. 20, 1863	40, 343
Fire-extinguisher	F. Latta	Cincinnati, Ohio	Sept. 9, 1873	142, 637
Fire-extinguisher	W. H. Laubach	Philadelphia, Pa	Sept. 22, 1868	82, 421
Fire-extinguisher	C. L. Levey	New York, N. Y	Feb. 20, 1872	123, 783
Fire-extinguisher	S. M. Lillie	Elizabeth, N. J	Aug. 8, 1871	117, 900
Fire-extinguisher	C. Lippincott and J. Patterson.	Philadelphia, Pa	July 1, 1873	140, 512
Fire-extinguisher	S. C. Main	Boston, Mass	June 15, 1869	91, 459
Fire-extinguisher	J. H. Manning	Chicago, Ill	Oct. 17, 1871	119, 936
Fire-extinguisher	T. J. Martin	Dowagiac, Mich	Mar. 26, 1872	125, 063
Fire-extinguisher	H. S. Maxim	Brooklyn, N. Y	July 22, 1873	141, 062
Fire-extinguisher	H. L. McAvoy	Baltimore, Md	June 17, 1873	139, 906
Fire-extinguisher	J. C. Meehan	Springfield, Mass	Apr. 1, 1873	137, 379
Fire-extinguisher	W. Mullally	Boston, Mass	June 2, 1868	78, 636
Fire-extinguisher	G. W. Nichols	Chicago, Ill	Oct. 3, 1871	119, 638
Fire-extinguisher	W. M. Parker	Boston, Mass	Apr. 6, 1869	88, 583
Fire-extinguisher	W. M. Parker	Boston, Mass	May 3, 1870	102, 582
Fire-extinguisher	G. F. Pinkham	Cambridge, Mass	Apr. 26, 1870	102, 431
Fire-extinguisher	W. K. Platt	Camden, N. J	Apr. 1, 1873	137, 481
Fire-extinguisher	P. W. Pratt	Abington, Mass	Sept. 17, 1872	131, 370
Fire-extinguisher	E. Sander	Saint Louis, Mo	Oct. 12, 1869	95, 840
Fire-extinguisher	E. Sander	Saint Louis, Mo	Feb. 14, 1871	111, 877
Fire-extinguisher	A. J. Sparrow	Potsdam, N. Y	Dec. 17, 1872	134, 107
Fire-extinguisher	J. H. Steiner	Cincinnati, Ohio	Aug. 12, 1873	141, 825
Fire-extinguisher	J. B. Stillson	Chicago, Ill	May 27, 1873	139, 275
Fire-extinguisher	D. J. Tapley	Danvers, Mass	Aug. 5, 1873	141, 607
Fire-extinguisher	J. S. Tibbets	Jeffersonville, Ind	July 8, 1873	140, 744
Fire-extinguisher	J. S. Tibbets	Jeffersonville, Ind	Sept. 23, 1873	143, 203
Fire-extinguisher	T. Tripp	Chicago, Ill	Aug. 16, 1870	106, 517
Fire-extinguisher	W. P. Van Deursen	Cincinnati, Ohio	Dec. 6, 1870	109, 975
Fire-extinguisher	J. B. Van Dyne	Covington, Ky	July 12, 1870	105, 279
Fire-extinguisher	J. B. Van Dyne	Covington, Ky	Dec. 6, 1870	109, 976
Fire-extinguisher	J. B. Van Dyne	Covington, Ky	May 9, 1871	114, 627
Fire-extinguisher	J. B. Van Dyne	Louisville, Ky	Apr. 9, 1872	125, 634
Fire-extinguisher	C. G. Wheeler	Chicago, Ill	Jan. 25, 1870	99, 270
Fire-extinguisher and chimney-regulator	D. Shoemaker	Philadelphia, Pa	Mar. 27, 1812	....
Fire-extinguisher and chimney-sweeper	E. Paine	Philadelphia, Pa	Dec. 11, 1817	....
Fire-extinguisher and lightning-rod, Combined	N. Carl	Cincinnati, Ohio	July 2, 1872	128, 534
Fire-extinguisher, Anti-freezing	W. C. Bruson	Chicago, Ill	Oct. 21, 1873	143, 746
Fire-extinguisher, Automatic	E. H. Ashcroft	Boston, Mass	Nov. 11, 1873	144, 493
Fire-extinguisher, Automatic	R. Lapham	New York, N. Y	June 11, 1867	65, 682
Fire-extinguisher, Automatic	I. P. Tice	New York, N. Y	Oct. 21, 1873	143, 794
Fire-extinguisher, Boiler	J. D. Bresnihan	Montgomery, Ala	Apr. 22, 1873	138, 068
Fire-extinguisher, Boiler	T. R. Sinclaire	New York, N. Y	Sept. 19, 1871	119, 190
Fire-extinguisher, Chemical	E. Bigelow	Springfield, Mass	Nov. 29, 1870	109, 576
Fire-extinguisher, Chemical	J. W. Douglas	Middletown, Conn	Dec. 14, 1869	97, 894
Fire-extinguisher, Chemical	A. E. Hughes	Louisville, Ky	Sept. 2, 1873	142, 340
Fire-extinguisher, Chimney	D. Berrien	New York, N. Y	Aug. 21, 1823	....
Fire-extinguisher for buildings, Steam	J. A. Coleman	Providence, R. I	July 22, 1873	141, 034
Fire-extinguisher for houses	S. P. Lord, jr	....	Mar. 10, 1804	....
Fire-extinguisher for railway-cars, &c., Automatic	W. P. Van Deursen and W. C. Davis.	Cincinnati, Ohio	Aug. 2, 1870	106, 002
Fire-extinguisher for steam-boilers	A. G. Davids	Baltimore, Md	Feb. 20, 1872	123, 874
Fire-extinguisher for steam-boilers	W. E. Prall	Washington, D. C	Jan. 2, 1872	122, 489
Fire-extinguisher for use on railway-cars, Automatic.	H. C. Stewart and R. T. Bradley.	Cincinnati, Ohio	Mar. 29, 1870	101, 404
Fire-extinguisher, Portable	I. C. Andrews	New York, N. Y	Oct. 14, 1873	143, 605
Fire-extinguisher, Steam	J. Souther	Boston, Mass	June 16, 1868	79, 021
Fire-extinguisher, Steamship	D. Spooner	Lowell, Ohio	Sept. 24, 1867	69, 267
Fire-extinguishers, Acid-bottle for	J. C. Davison	Chicago, Ill	May 16, 1871	114, 775
Fire-extinguishers, Composition for use in	J. M. Muterse and H. G. De Valory.	Guérande, France	Sept. 21, 1869	95, 036
Fire, Extinguishing	C. Alden	Newburgh, N. Y	Oct. 30, 1866	59, 151
Fire, Extinguishing	R. B. Armitage	Philadelphia, Pa	July 8, 1856	15, 276

Index of patents issued from the United States Patent Office from 1790 to 1873, inclusive—Continued.

Invention.	Inventor.	Residence.	Date.	No.
Fire, Extinguishing	J. Autenrieth	Newark, N. J	Sept. 19, 1871	119, 104
Fire, Extinguishing	I. Clowes	Norfolk, Va	July 2, 1836	....
Fire, Extinguishing	J. R. Laurent	Milford, Pa	Nov. 20, 1866	59, 847
Fire, Extinguishing	W. C. Marshall	New York, N. Y	May 15, 1866	54, 748
Fire, Extinguishing	L. Pusey	Philadelphia, Pa	Feb. 12, 1856	14, 252
Fire-extinguishing apparatus	O. F. Burton	New York, N. Y	Feb. 11, 1873	135, 772
Fire-extinguishing apparatus	I. H. Clark	Boston, Mass	Feb. 1, 1870	99, 291
Fire-extinguishing apparatus	M. Dunn	Chelsea, Mass	Dec. 24, 1872	134, 132
Fire-extinguishing apparatus	C. T. Holloway	Baltimore, Md	Aug. 20, 1872	130, 716
Fire-extinguishing apparatus	R. Lapham	Boston, Mass	Sept. 1, 1868	81, 653
Fire-extinguishing apparatus	W. H. Phillips	North Brixton, Surrey, England.	Apr. 9, 1850	7, 269
Fire-extinguishing apparatus for vessels	V. E. Campbell	Sterling Centre, N. Y	Feb. 2, 1869	86, 360
Fire extinguishing apparatus for vessels	J. L. Stuart	New York, N. Y	May 21, 1861	32, 389
Fire-extinguishing composition	C. G. Mueller	New York, N. Y	Mar. 6, 1860	27, 375
Fire-extinguishing composition	E. F. Overdeer	Chattanooga, Tenn	Mar. 13, 1855	12, 519
Fire-extinguishing composition	W. P. Van Deursen	Cincinnati, Ohio	May 31, 1870	103, 800
Fire-extinguishing compound	R. Bulkley	New York, N. Y	Mar. 21, 1854	10, 658
Fire-extinguishing compound	T. Drew	Newton, Mass	Dec. 29, 1868	85, 434
Fire-extinguishing compound	E. A. Galbraith	Boston, Mass	Aug. 4, 1868	80, 720
Fire-extinguishing compound	E. Thayer	New York, N. Y	June 29, 1869	91, 882
Fire extinguishing compound	J. Upham	Salem, Mass	Nov. 4, 1851	8, 495
Fire-extinguishing compound	W. P. Van Duersen	Cincinnati, Ohio	Aug. 16, 1870	106, 518
Fire-extinguishing device	J. Lamm	Port Deposit, Md	Aug. 6, 1872	130, 226
Fire-extinguishing engine	J. B. Van Dyne	Louisville, Ky	May 28, 1872	127, 390
Fire-extinguishing water-pipe attachment for buildings.	T. Miller	New York, N. Y	Nov. 18, 1873	144, 690
Fire-fender	M. Benson	Cincinnati, Ohio	May 19, 1823	....
Fire-fender	M. Morgan, jr	New York, N. Y	July 22, 1844	3, 675
Fire-fender, grate, and andiron, Combined adjustable	W. N. Hall	Mexia, Tex	May 13, 1873	138, 885
Fire fender or guard	C. H. S. Schultz	Cincinnati, Ohio	Nov. 19, 1867	71, 224
Fire-fender to prevent spread of fire	E. Ruggles	Rochester, Mass	Feb. 27, 1821	....
Fire-fenders, Shaping	T. Thomas and R. Fuller	New York, N. Y	Nov. 19, 1832	....
Fire-hearth, &c., for vessels	J. Lamb	Amboy, N. J	Mar. 18, 1820	....
Fire-hearth range or galley	G. Youle	New York, N. Y	Mar. 19, 1819	....
Fire-heater	F. Strattner	Wilmington, Del	May 13, 1873	138, 952
Fire-hook	J. G. Ernst	Harrisburgh, Pa	Jan. 6, 1857	16, 329
Fire-hydrant, Extension	J. Fricker, jr	Cincinnati, Ohio	June 4, 1872	127, 473
Fire in buildings, Apparatus for extinguishing	J. D. Sutter	Chicago, Ill	Oct. 28, 1873	144, 039
Fire in buildings, Extinguishing	O. Lugo	Baltimore, Md	Dec. 21, 1869	98, 175
Fire in high buildings, Extinguishing	A. Watson	Washington, D. C	Dec. 23, 1873	145, 920
Fire in holds of ships, vessels, &c., Extinguishing	C. Godfrey	Brooklyn, N. Y	Sept. 23, 1862	36, 515
Fire in inaccessible places, Method of extinguishing	A. Stone	Philadelphia County, Pa	Dec. 5, 1854	12, 038
Fire in inflammable liquids, Apparatus for extinguishing.	H. Baker	Chicago, Ill	Mar. 26, 1872	124, 875
Fire in oil-tanks, &c., Method of extinguishing	J. W. Stanton	Brooklyn, N. Y	Dec. 2, 1873	145, 134
Fire in steam-vessels, Arrangement for extinguishing.	W. Arthur	Brooklyn, N. Y	Apr. 5, 1859	23, 435
Fire indicator and alarm	J. Fawcett	East Boston, Mass	Nov. 25, 1873	144, 895
Fire-iron	R. Willingham	New York, N. Y	June 8, 1821	....
Fire-kindler	R. Adams	East Enterprise, Ind	Feb. 4, 1863	135, 395
Fire-kindler	W. Altick	Dayton, Ohio	Apr. 30, 1872	126, 245
Fire-kindler	C. Batcheller	Des Moines, Iowa	Apr. 12, 1870	101, 704
Fire-kindler	A. Bushnell	Iona Island, N. Y	May 13, 1873	138, 852
Fire-kindler	G. S. Coleman	Alexandria, Va	Sept. 17, 1872	131, 428
Fire-kindler	J. C. Crumpton	Allegheny City, Pa	Sept. 23. 1873	143, 066
Fire-kindler	J. C. Crumpton	Allegheny City, Pa	Sept. 30, 1873	143, 277
Fire-kindler	E. Everett	Walpole, Mass	Dec. 17, 1872	133, 973
Fire-kindler	M. E. Ezell	Hatchechubbee, Ala	Mar. 9, 1869	87, 654
Fire-kindler	J. E. Finley, G. H. Hurd, and B. F. Tatem.	Memphis, Tenn	Aug. 8, 1871	117, 757
Fire-kindler	J. A. Fuller	Rockford, Ill	Nov. 2, 1869	96, 532
Fire-kindler	M. Gernsey	Middleburgh, N. Y	Feb. 11, 1873	135, 706
Fire-kindler	J. R. Hice	Salem, Ohio	May 23, 1871	115, 205
Fire-kindler	H. K. Horton	Winfield, Mich	Feb. 9, 1869	86, 838
Fire-kindler	C. E. Imlay	Brooklyn, N. Y	Oct. 1, 1872	131, 759
Fire-kindler	J. Kenney, sr	Baltimore, Md	Nov. 15, 1870	109, 324
Fire-kindler	A. B. King	Camden, Ohio	May 23, 1871	115, 216
Fire-kindler	A. Lodeman and M. Desenberg	Kalamazoo, Mich	Sept. 7, 1869	94, 621
Fire-kindler	J. W. Lowe	Ottumwa, Iowa	Feb. 9, 1869	86, 767
Fire-kindler	J. Y. Marks	Rochester, Pa	Jan. 28, 1873	135, 280
Fire-kindler	W. H. McCrary	Kingston, Ga	June 6, 1871	115, 757
Fire-kindler	J. McFarland	Clinton, Ill	June 23, 1868	79, 140
Fire-kindler	I. Morris	Clinton, Ill	Nov. 10, 1868	83, 988
Fire-kindler	A. S. Morse and E. A. Jefferies	Fort Wayne, Ind	June 14, 1870	104, 336
Fire-kindler	C. A. Nisbett	Pontiac, Mich	Mar. 4, 1873	136, 451
Fire-kindler	B. Pickering	Dayton, Ohio	May 28, 1872	127, 365
Fire-kindler	N. Rogers	Thomasville, Ga	Nov. 14, 1871	120, 898
Fire-kindler	R. P. Smith	Dubuque, Iowa	Oct. 10, 1871	119, 893
Fire-kindler	V. G. Tansey	Quincy, Ill	June 4, 1867	65, 448
Fire-kindler	V. G. Tansey	Indianapolis, Ind	July 28, 1868	80, 429
Fire-kindler	W. H. Thomas	Goshen, Ind	Nov. 5, 1872	132, 780
Fire-kindler	D. W. Thompson	Saint Joseph, Mo	Apr. 30, 1872	126, 347
Fire-kindler	H. Van Ausdall	Keokuk, Iowa	July 30, 1867	67, 382
Fire-kindler	S. F. Watson	Richmond, Ind	Mar. 19, 1872	124, 705
Fire-kindler	E. P. Wheeler	Corinth, Miss	Sept. 23, 1873	143, 048
Fire-kindler case	D. W. Thompson	Saint Joseph, Mo	July 2, 1872	128, 676
Fire-kindling	I. Bicknell	Cincinnati, Ohio	Feb. 9, 1869	86, 635
Fire-kindling	E. Buss	Springfield, Ohio	Sept. 3, 1872	130, 975
Fire-kindling	L. Dodge	Waterford, N. Y	Sept. 5, 1871	118, 700
Fire-kindling	G. W. Eldridge	South Chatham, Mass	Apr. 5, 1870	101, 597
Fire-kindling	G. W. Eldridge	South Chatham, Mass	May 17, 1870	103, 163
Fire-kindling	C. Gaudin, and Z. and J. Granier	San Francisco, Cal	July 14, 1868	79, 903
Fire-kindling	J. L. Hannum and S. H. Stebbins.	Berea, Ohio	June 14, 1870	104, 145
Fire-kindling	J. W. Kennedy	Plainfield, Conn	May 21, 1872	127, 068
Fire kindling	J. W. Still	San Francisco, Cal	Apr. 25, 1871	114, 219
Fire-kindling	W. B. Tucker	Baltimore, Md	Feb. 4, 1873	135, 607
Fire-kindling	W. F. Wenisch	New York, N. Y	July 31, 1866	56, 867

Index of patents issued from the Unit d States Patent Office from 1790 *to* 1873, *inclusive*—Continued.

Invention.	Inventor.	Residence.	Date.	No.
Fire-kindling and fuel	I. Bicknell	Cincinnati, Ohio	Jan. 7, 1868	72, 964
Fire-kindling composition	D. B. Andrews	Fort Wayne, Ind	Jan. 22, 1867	61, 378
Fire kindling composition	E. Bellinger	Mohawk, N. Y	Dec. 13, 1859	26, 408
Fire-kindling composition	M. Carstens	New York, N. Y	Mar. 20, 1866	53, 270
Fire-kindling composition	J. C. Crumpton	Allegheny City, Pa	Apr. 29, 1873	138, 382
Fire kindling composition	B. O'Reilly	New York, N. Y	Nov. 6, 1855	13, 758
Fire-kindling composition	W. C. Philbrick	Lynn, Mass	Jan. 28, 1868	73, 922
Fire-kindling composition	A. Reed	Louisville, Ky	Mar. 23, 1869	88, 075
Fire-kindling composition	J. Smith	Providence, R. I	Oct. 17, 1865	50, 503
Fire-kindling composition	A. Van Camp	Washington, D. C	Mar. 9, 1869	87, 734
Fire-kindling composition	W. P. Winkley	Des Moines, Iowa	Sept. 29, 1868	82, 506
Fire-kindling compound	J. S. Carroll	Covington, Ga	Oct. 8, 1872	131, 997
Fire-kindling compound	J. L. Hannum and S. H. Stebbins.	Berea, Ohio	Mar. 7, 1871	112, 337
Fire-kindling compound	S. L. Loomis and C. T. Shepherd.	Washington, D. C	Sept. 3, 1872	131, 011
Fire-kindling fagot	W. J. Wiggins and C. Stout	Saint Louis, Mo	June 7, 1870	103, 951
Fire-kindling material	L. T. Cheever	East Greenwich, R. I	Feb. 20, 1849	6, 125
Fire-kindling material	C. A. Rose	Columbus, Ga	Sept. 4, 1866	57, 774
Fire, Lehigh forge	J. Evans	New Haven, Conn	Jan. 5, 1864	41, 143
Fire-lighter	J. McCallum and J. Hartzell	Alliance, Ohio	Oct. 24, 1871	120, 206
Fire-lighter	J. R. Murphy	Chicago, Ill	Mar. 12, 1872	124, 505
Fire lighter	L. H. Whitney	Vallejo, Cal	Feb. 25, 1868	74, 782
Fire, Means of detecting and signaling	W. B. Watkins	Jersey City, N. J	Mar. 28, 1871	113, 120
Fire, Method of lighting, heating, and extinguishing.	J. Kidd	New York, N. Y	Jan. 23, 1872	122, 895
Fire, Method of removing and protecting stores in case of.	J. H. Page	Whitewater, Wis	Jan. 19, 1869	85, 954
Fire, Method of removing stores, &c., in case of	A. Blood, sr., and R. W. Brown	Norfolk, Va, and Washington, D. C.	Sept. 1, 1857	18, 118
Fire, Mode of kindling	W. H. Towers	Boston, Mass	Mar. 5, 1867	62, 704
Fire, Mode of preventing the progress of	B. Taylor		Mar. 23, 1794	......
Fire, Mode of protecting plastered walls and ceilings from.	P. Naylor	New York, N. Y	Feb. 22, 1839	1, 087
Fire, Mode of supplying water to buildings for the purpose of extinguishing.	I. Lowell	Pendleton, N. Y	Oct. 16, 1840	1, 489
Fire-place	T. C. Aldridge	Saint Louis, Mo	June 8, 1869	91, 059
Fire-place	A. C. Bacon and J. G. Jennings	Cleveland, Ohio	Dec. 22, 1863	40, 989
Fire-place	T. W. Baird	Bowling Green, Ky	Sept. 6, 1870	106, 985
Fire-place	T. F. Baker	Cincinnati, Ohio	June 15, 1869	91, 299
Fire-place	Bean and Skinner	Sandwich, N. H	June 12, 1835	......
Fire-place	J. S. Blair	Boston, Mass	May 17, 1864	42, 739
Fire-place	P. Brecher	Louisville, Ky	June 20, 1871	116, 146
Fire-place	W. Bryant	Boston, Mass	Apr. 19, 1864	42, 342
Fire-place	R. Buck	Acton, Me	July 1, 1836	......
Fire-place	W. Burgess	Middleborough, Mass	Mar. 12, 1836	......
Fire-place	T. F. Card	Cincinnati, Ohio	Apr. 17, 1860	27, 886
Fire-place	A. Carson	New York, N. Y	May 22, 1860	28, 347
Fire-place	A. E. Chamberlain and J. B. Crowley.	Cincinnati, Ohio	Dec. 3, 1867	71, 698
Fire-place	G. A. Clark	Farmington, Conn	Oct. 4, 1859	25, 629
Fire-place	W. B. Coates	Philadelphia, Pa	July 28, 1868	80, 455
Fire-place	B. F. Conley	Funnelton, W. Va	Nov. 23, 1869	97, 050
Fire-place	C. D. Cooper	Albany, N. Y	June 27, 1810	......
Fire-place	B. F. Cowan	Memphis, Tenn	Mar. 26, 1861	31, 785
Fire-place	J. M. Crockett	Newbern, Va	Oct. 12, 1869	95, 660
Fire-place	M. A. Cushing	Aurora, Ill	July 18, 1871	117, 053
Fire-place	A. D. Dailey	Terre Haute, Ind	Apr. 20, 1869	89, 2[illegible]3
Fire-place	T. C. Damborg	Philadelphia, Pa	July 16, 1872	128, 953
Fire-place	S. D. Dearman	Rock Hill, S. C	Apr. 23, 1872	125, 938
Fire-place	C. Dodge	Pittsburgh, Pa	Mar. 18, 1856	14, 447
Fire-place	J. Ervin, sr	Princeton, Ind	Nov. 3, 1868	93, 701
Fire-place	J. U. Fiester	Winchester, Ohio	June 4, 1867	65, 364
Fire-place	J. S. Ganson and C. T. Coit	Buffalo, N. Y	May 14, 1861	32, 283
Fire-place	J. L. Garlington	Snapping Shoals, Ga	July 8, 1873	140, 621
Fire-place	E. H. Gibbs	New York, N. Y	Dec. 14, 1869	97, 902
Fire-place	E. S. Greely	Dover, Me	Oct. 6, 1835	......
Fire place	C. B. Gregory	Beverly, N. J	Mar. 3, 1868	75, 155
Fire-place	C. B. Gregory	Beverly, N. J	Apr. 14, 1868	76, 750
Fire-place	G. Gridley	Newburyport, Mass	Mar. 14, 1808	......
Fire-place	E. Griffiths	Philadelphia, Pa	Mar. 6, 1820	......
Fire-place	W. D. Guseman	Morgantown, W. Va	Apr. 14, 1868	76, 751
Fire-place	J. Hackett	Louisville, Ky	Feb. 21, 1871	111, 929
Fire-place	J. Hackett	Louisville, Ky	July 25, 1871	117, 276
Fire-place	S. Hammond	Baltimore, Md	June 25, 1839	1, 197
Fire-place	E. Hampton	New York, N. Y	Feb. 23, 1869	87, 099
Fire-place	C. Harris and P. W. Zoiner	Cincinnati, Ohio	Apr. 16, 1867	63, 885
Fire-place	D. Hattan	Zanesville, Ohio	Aug. 4, 1868	80, 731
Fire-place	M. Haughey	Saint Louis, Mo	Aug. 13, 1872	130, 427
Fire-place	D. Hemingway	Leesburgh, Ky	Nov. 13, 1844	3, 821
Fire-place	J. R. Hendrickson	McKeesport, Pa	Sept. 24, 1861	33, 349
Fire-place	W. Hoyland	Newcastle, Pa	Nov. 18, 1873	144, 675
Fire-place	W. Hoyt	Brookville, Ind	June 3, 1825	......
Fire-place	J. M. Irwin	Pittsburgh, Pa	Sept. 16, 1873	142, 791
Fire-place	W. H. James	Cincinnati, Ohio	Apr. 25, 1865	47, 423
Fire-place	E. Jenks	Colebrook, Conn	Sept. 2, 1818	......
Fire-place	A. B. Johnson	Washington, Ind	July 26, 1870	105, 806
Fire-place	I. Kepler	Corry, Pa	Nov. 12, 1867	70, 858
Fire-place	W. M. Kepler	Cincinnati, Ohio	Aug. 26, 1873	142, 241
Fire-place	D. F. Launy	Philadelphia, Pa	Mar. 18, 1813	......
Fire-place	J. E. Layton	Pittsburgh, Pa	July 2, 1861	32, 700
Fire-place	E. Lester	Killingsworth, Conn	June 21, 1830	......
Fire-place	C. A. Littlefield	Covington, Ky	Sept. 11, 1860	29, 980
Fire-place	W. Lossie	Owensborough, Ky	Aug. 19, 1873	141, 937
Fire-place	J. Maggini	Baltimore, Md	Feb. 4, 1822	......
Fire-place	S. Martin	Detroit, Mich	Nov. 30, 1809	97, 307
Fire-place	T. McCleary	Blairsville, Pa	Nov. 13, 1866	59, 620
Fire-place	R. D. McDonald	Jersey City, N. J	Sept. 21, 1869	95, 030

Index of patents issued from the United States Patent Office from 1790 *to* 1873, *inclusive*—Continued.

Invention.	Inventor.	Residence.	Date.	No.
Fire-place	G. H. McElevey	Newcastle, Pa	Aug. 25, 1868	81, 389
Fire-place	W. T. McMillen	Cincinnati, Ohio	Dec. 4, 1866	60, 220
Fire-place	J. McMurtry	Fayette County, Ky	Jan. 22, 1861	31, 212
Fire-place	W. P. Miller	San Francisco, Cal	Feb. 12, 1867	62, 053
Fire-place	E. Mix	New Haven, Conn	Apr. 25, 1812	....
Fire-place	G. Moody	Piqua, Ohio	Jan. 30, 1866	52, 375
Fire-place	A. Moon	Bethlehem, Ind	Feb. 20, 1866	52, 735
Fire-place	J. Moore	Ergineth, Ireland	Apr. 5, 1870	101, 645
Fire-place	M. Moore	Bartlett, Tenn	Jan. 16, 1872	122, 775
Fire-place	E. Nott	Schenectady, N. Y	Feb. 3, 1819	....
Fire-place	C. W. Peale		Nov. 16, 1797	....
Fire-place	T. Phillips	Cadiz, Ohio	Oct. 11, 1870	108, 180
Fire-place	W. R. Prescott	Hallowell, Me	Mar. 19, 1836	....
Fire-place	F. Proudfoot	Toronto, Canada	June 10, 1873	139, 813
Fire-place	C. S. Rankin	Cincinnati, Ohio	Mar. 30, 1869	88, 509
Fire-place	A. G. Redway	Cincinnati, Ohio	May 7, 1867	64, 446
Fire-place	I. I. Richardson	Delaware, Ohio	Mar. 19, 1867	63, 098
Fire-place	W. D. Robb	New Philadelphia, Ohio	July 1, 1873	140, 543
Fire-place	E. Y. Robbins	Cincinnati, Ohio	July 19, 1864	43, 604
Fire-place	E. Y. Robbins	Cincinnati, Ohio	Sept. 10, 1867	68, 653
Fire-place	P. M. Roche	Cleveland, Ohio	Apr. 25, 1871	114, 045
Fire-place	F. M. Rogers	Cincinnati, Ohio	Apr. 10, 1866	53, 880
Fire-place	D. A. Ross	Cincinnati, Ohio	Sept. 8, 1863	39, 836
Fire-place	J. K. Ross	Lebanon, Ohio	Apr. 3, 1860	27, 741
Fire-place	W. Salisbury	Derby, Vt	Aug. 16, 1817	....
Fire-place	H. Saxton	Eden, N. Y	July 8, 1834	....
Fire-place	G. R. Scriven	Hanging Rock, Ohio	Feb. 6, 1872	123, 518
Fire-place	L. Shepherd	Northampton, Mass	Jan. 25, 1817	....
Fire-place	E. A. Skeele	Saint Louis, Mo	June 23, 1863	38, 991
Fire-place	E. Skinner	Sandwich, N. H	Mar. 12, 1836	....
Fire-place	H. E. Smith	Cincinnati, Ohio	Sept. 13, 1864	44, 228
Fire-place	J. Smith	Brantford, Canada	Feb. 28, 1871	112, 188
Fire-place	J. Smith	Pittsburgh, Pa	Jan. 2, 1872	122, 410
Fire-place	J. W. Smith and J. S. Gallaher, jr.	Washington, D. C	Mar. 6, 1855	12, 491
Fire-place	A. Snyder	Richmond, Va	Oct. 5, 1869	95, 529
Fire-place	S. Spalding	Colchester, Conn	Apr. 11, 1822	....
Fire-place	A. J. Sprague	Springfield, Mo	Mar. 16, 1869	87, 884
Fire-place	P. Sternberg	Montgomery County, N. Y	Mar. 20, 1811	....
Fire-place	P. Sternberg	Montgomery County, N. Y	Oct. 28, 1811	....
Fire-place	P. Sternberg	Montgomery County, N. Y	Nov. 19, 1811	....
Fire-place	D. and J. Stoner	West Overton, Pa	May 17, 1864	42, 804
Fire-place	J. C. Strong and L. C. McNeal	Buffalo, N. Y	Sept. 21, 1869	94, 984
Fire-place	R. P. Thomas	Sciotoville, Ohio	Dec. 12, 1871	121, 911
Fire-place	I. H. Upton	New York, N. Y	Nov. 6, 1866	59, 484
Fire-place	W. R. Warden	Boston, Mass	Aug. 3, 1858	21, 094
Fire-place	M. D. Wellman	Pittsburgh, Pa	May 7, 1867	64, 465
Fire-place	M. D. Wellman and J. Old	Pittsburgh, Pa	July 11, 1865	48, 752
Fire-place	J. W. Wetmore	Erie, Pa	Feb. 28, 1871	112, 199
Fire-place	E. Whiting	Great Barrington, Mass	June 18, 1810	....
Fire-place	A. Wilkin	Lucas County, Ohio	June 8, 1869	91, 190
Fire-place	J. E. Wood	Webster, Ohio	Apr. 25, 1871	114, 075
Fire-place and chimney	R. Bacon and E. Harris	Boston, Mass	Apr. 8, 1835	....
Fire-place and chimney	C. Blood	Washington County, Md	Apr. 7, 1825	....
Fire-place and chimney	D. Hemingway	Covington, Ky	July 17, 1860	29, 168
Fire-place and chimney for saving fuel	S. Morey	Philadelphia, Pa	Jan. 18, 1813	....
Fire-place and chimney-stack in buildings	H. R. Sawyer	New York, N. Y	Mar. 26, 1841	2, 016
Fire-place and furnace	E. B. Wilson	London, England	Nov. 15, 1864	45, 111
Fire-place and grate	C. Lane	Hingham, Mass	Dec. 15, 1835	....
Fire-place and grate, Open	R. M. Sherman	Fairfield, Conn	June 30, 1837	249
Fire-place and oven	J. Knight	Stoddard, N. H	Dec. 15, 1831	....
Fire-place and stove	C. Guernsey	Poultney, Vt	July 7, 1813	....
Fire-place and stove	E. Haskell	New London, Conn	June 25, 1813	....
Fire-place and stove	C. Neer	Troy, N. Y	May 31, 1853	9, 756
Fire-place and stove	E. W. Newton	Middletown, Conn	Dec. 3, 1834	....
Fire-place and stove	A. Pollock	Boston, Mass	Apr. 23, 1807	....
Fire-place and stove	F. Stevens	Springfield, Mass	Mar. 2, 1836	....
Fire-place and throat of chimney	C. W. Russell	Washington, D. C	Mar. 5, 1850	7, 149
Fire-place and warming buildings	J. Cox	Philadelphia, Pa	May 2, 1834	....
Fire-place back	J. C. Bard	New Orleans, La	Feb. 15, 1870	99, 748
Fire-place back	G. W. Cummings	Franklin, Pa	Apr. 22, 1873	138, 135
Fire-place called "The defiance," Construction of	E. Bartholomew and W. Church	Boston, Mass	Aug. 18, 1815	....
Fire-place, Cast-iron	A. Hayward	Easton, Mass	Sept. 25, 1834	....
Fire-place, Chimney funneled	A. Gerrish	Shopleigh, Me	Jan. 23, 1835	....
Fire-place, Close	H. G. Spafford	Hudson, N. Y	May 3, 1805	....
Fire-place, Close and open	J. C. Brush	Washington, D. C	Aug. 19, 1819	....
Fire-place, Columbia	R. Heterick		June 30, 1803	....
Fire-place, Cooking and baking	J. C. Howard	Howard's Valley, Conn	Oct. 27, 1835	....
Fire-place, Doric	J. Pierpont	Boston, Mass	Jan. 8, 1830	....
Fire-place, Double-draft	T. Rose		Jan. 23, 1804	....
Fire-place fender	C. C. Algeo	Pittsburgh, Pa	May 30, 1871	115, 265
Fire-place fender	C. C. Algeo	Pittsburgh, Pa	Nov. 21, 1871	121, 073
Fire-place fender	W. N. Hall	Springfield, Tex	Feb. 27, 1872	124, 132
Fire-place fender	E. Skinner	Sandwich, N. H	Apr. 19, 1822	....
Fire place fender	J. W. Truslow	Lewisburgh, Va	July 15, 1856	15, 362
Fire-place frame-work	J. L. Henderson	Covington, Ky	Oct. 22, 1867	70, 090
Fire-place front	E. A. Jackson	New York, N. Y	Nov. 11, 1873	144, 459
Fire-place, furnace, &c	J. W. Boot and W. Lyman	Boston, Mass	Dec. 29, 1826	....
Fire-place, Grate	J. Snyder	Philadelphia, Pa	June 12, 1835	....
Fire-place, Grated	A. Graham	Fredericktown, Md	Nov. 24, 1810	....
Fire-place heater	B. C. Bibb	Baltimore, Md	July 20, 1869	92, 781
Fire-place heater	S. S. Benk	New York, N. Y	Oct. 1, 1861	33, 412
Fire-place heater	F. L. Hedenberg	New York, N. Y	May 21, 1861	32, 364
Fire-place heater	W. C. Lesster	New York, N. Y	Jan. 29, 1867	61, 623
Fire-place heater	D. S. Quimby	Brooklyn, N. Y	Oct. 9, 1860	30, 349
Fire-place heater	D. S. Quimby, jr	Brooklyn, N. Y	June 8, 1869	90, 957
Fire-place heater	W. Sanford	Brooklyn, N. Y	Jan. 5, 1869	85, 614
Fire-place heater	W. Sanford	Brooklyn, N. Y	May 4, 1869	89, 693

Index of patents issued from the United States Patent Office from 1790 to 1873, inclusive—Continued.

Invention.	Inventor.	Residence.	Date.	No.
Fire-place heater	J. M. Thatcher	Bergen, N. J	Dec. 22, 1868	85, 255
Fire-place heater	J. M. Thatcher	Bergen, N. J	June 15, 1869	91, 287
Fire-place heater	J. M. Thatcher	Bergen, N. J	June 14, 1870	104, 376
Fire-place heater	H. H. Welch	Athens, Ohio	Aug. 8, 1865	49, 325
Fire-place heater, Base-burning	B. C. Bibb	Baltimore, Md	Sept. 14, 1869	94, 700
Fire-place heater, Base-burning	B. C. Bibb and P. Klotz	Baltimore, Md	Feb. 8, 1870	99, 525
Fire-place heater, Base-burning	J. H. Burtis	Brooklyn, N. Y	July 4, 1871	116, 680
Fire-place heater, Base-burning	E. S. Heath	Baltimore, Md	Jan. 3, 1871	110, 654
Fire-place heater, Base-burning	J. Jaeger	Tompkinsville, N. Y	Dec. 6, 1870	109, 909
Fire-place heater, Base-burning	P. Klotz	Baltimore, Md	Aug. 31, 1769	94, 320
Fire-place heater, Base-burning	P. Klotz	Baltimore, Md	Feb. 14, 1871	111, 753
Fire-place heater, Base-burning	W. Magill	Port Deposit, Md	Jan. 28, 1873	135, 278
Fire-place heater, Base-burning	J. Martino	Philadelphia, Pa	Mar. 8, 1870	100, 539
Fire-place heater, Base-burning	W. L. McDowell	Philadelphia, Pa	Nov. 21, 1871	121, 185
Fire-place heater, Base-burning	A. Murdock	Brooklyn, E. D., N. Y	Aug. 9, 1870	106, 191
Fire-place heater, Base-burning	J. S. Perry	Albany, N. Y	Jan. 14, 1873	134, 767
Fire-place heater, Base-burning	S. B. Sexton	Baltimore, Md	Dec. 14, 1869	97, 970
Fire-place heater, Base-burning	S. B. Sexton	Baltimore, Md	Mar. 19, 1872	124, 860
Fire-place heater, Base burning	G. B. Snider	New York, N. Y	June 27, 1871	116, 365
Fire-place heater, Base-burning	J. Spear	Philadelphia, Pa	Jan. 16, 1872	122, 863
Fire-place heater, Base-burning	W. E. Wood	Baltimore, Md	Aug. 1, 1871	117, 585
Fire-place-heater fender	D. Stuart and L. Bridge	Philadelphia, Pa	Feb. 8, 1870	99, 726
Fire-place heater or furnace	O. Collins	New York, N. Y	Apr. 30, 1867	64, 284
Fire-place lining	E. A. Jackson	New York, N. Y	Nov. 11, 1873	144, 460
Fire-place lining	A. J. Redwig	Cincinnati, Ohio	Feb. 4, 1873	135, 587
Fire-place lining	C. Truesdale	Cincinnati, Ohio	June 22, 1869	91, 689
Fire-place mantel and front	D. K. Innes and W. W. Magill	Cincinnati, Ohio	Oct. 31, 1871	4, 613
Fire-place mantel and front	D. K. Innes and W. W. Magill	Cincinnati, Ohio	July 25, 1871	117, 294
Fire-place, Metallic	J. F. Snider	Culpeper County, Va	July 18, 1854	11, 340
Fire-place, Open	M. D. Wellman	Pittsburgh, Pa	Dec. 18, 1866	60, 601
Fire-place or Franklin stove	J. Peckover	Cincinnati, Ohio	May 28, 1872	127, 265
Fire place or grate, Portable	J. Williamson	Washington, D. C	Nov. 8, 1836	74
Fire-place or open stove	J. F. Gould	Newburyport, Mass	Feb. 1, 1808	....
Fire-place or stove	J. E. Cayford	Milburn, Me	Dec. 31, 1833	....
Fire-place, Parlor	E. Backus	Brooklyn, N. Y	Sept. 25, 1847	5, 307
Fire-place, Parlor and kitchen	J. Hagerty	Monroe, Mich	Mar. 24, 1838	655
Fire-place, Portable	W. B. Johns	Georgetown, D. C	Dec. 24, 1861	33, 995
Fire-place, Reflecting	R. Jobson	Dudley, England	May 20, 1851	8, 101
Fire-place register	E. A. Tuttle	Brooklyn, N. Y	July 2, 1861	32, 728
Fire-place, Sheet-iron	J. Ingalls	Sanbornton, N. H	May 23, 1833	....
Fire-place, Sheet-iron	L. Mansfield	New Hartford, N. Y	May 29, 1833	....
Fire-place, Sheet-iron	G. Richards	Ashfield, Mass	Nov. 26, 1835	....
Fire-place, Steam	J. W. Cochran	Lowell, Mass	July 18, 1834	....
Fire-place to prevent smoking	H. Roberts	Delhi, N. Y	Apr. 30, 1840	1, 578
Fire-place warming-apparatus	C. Kalbfuss	New Richmond, Ohio	Aug. 13, 1867	67, 769
Fire-place with a flat funnel	A. Fisher		Feb. 19, 1807	....
Fire-place with gridiron attachment, Movable	J. W. Wetmore	Erie, Pa	Apr. 4, 1865	47, 176
Fire places and grates, Back-plate for	F. E. Pitts	Nashville, Tenn	Mar. 3, 1857	16, 768
Fire-places, Back-plate and chimney-throat for	J. E. Layton	Pittsburgh, Pa	Oct. 29, 1861	33, 591
Fire-places, Constructing flue of open	T. Whitson	New York, N. Y	June 14, 1838	784
Fire-places, Fire-back for	S. M. Echols	La Fayette, Ind	July 15, 1856	15, 331
Fire-places for burning coal, Building and altering	A. Terrell	Boston, Mass	Oct. 25, 1832	....
Fire-places, stoves, &c., Composition slab for lining.	J. Putnam	Salem, Mass	Aug. 20, 1835	....
Fire-places, Ornamental back for	W. H. Jackson	New York, N. Y	July 27, 1869	92, 974
Fire-plug	J. W. Baker	Parkersburgh, W. Va	Sept. 24, 1867	69, 156
Fire-plug	J. P. Cummings	Newport, Ky	July 14, 1868	79, 960
Fire-plug	J. Curran	Baltimore, Md	Feb. 8, 1870	99, 646
Fire-plug	J. Fricker	Cincinnati, Ohio	Oct. 3, 1865	50, 235
Fire-plug	J. P. Gallagher	Saint Louis, Mo	July 22, 1873	141, 131
Fire-plug	R. A. Hill	Washington, D. C	May 25, 1869	90, 540
Fire-plug	F. Latta	Cincinnati, Ohio	Aug. 20, 1872	130, 726
Fire-plug	J. L. Lowry	Pittsburgh, Pa	Feb. 22, 1859	23, 034
Fire-plug	J. McClelland	Washington, D. C	Sept. 27, 1864	44, 439
Fire-plug	J. McClelland	Washington, D. C	May 30, 1871	115, 495
Fire-plug	L. Moss	Philadelphia, Pa	Nov. 10, 1857	18, 595
Fire-plug	J. H. Rhodes	Brooklyn, N. Y	May 26, 1868	78, 393
Fire-plug and cistern combined	F. Latta and W. H. Hughes	Cincinnati, Ohio	Mar. 18, 1873	137, 006
Fire-plug and hydrant	A. F. Allen	Providence, R. I	Dec. 26, 1871	122, 097
Fire-plug and hydrant	J. M. Jorden	Baltimore, Md	Sept. 8, 1838	919
Fire-plug and lamp-post, Combined	D. Y. and J. H. Johns	Cincinnati, Ohio	Nov. 19, 1872	133, 230
Fire-plugs, Casting	W. M. and J. B. Ellis	Washington, D. C	Apr. 17, 1860	27, 896
Fire-poker	G. R. Moore	Pittsburgh, Pa	July 24, 1860	29, 298
Fire-pot for coal-stoves	D. G. Littlefield	Albany, N. Y	June 25, 1861	32, 635
Fire-pot for stoves	N. O. Bond	Needham, Mass	May 24, 1864	42, 831
Fire-pot for stoves, furnaces, &c	P. P. Stewart	Troy, N. Y	Mar. 28, 1865	47, 049
Fire-pot, Tinners'	F. M. Campbell and L. W. Brown.	Cleveland, Ohio	Nov. 22, 1870	109, 383
Fire-pot, Tinners'	C. W. Johnson	Neponset, Ill	Sept. 1, 1868	81, 644
Fire-pot, Tinsmiths'	W. Yapp	Cleveland, Ohio	Aug. 11, 1863	39, 521
Fire-pots, Iron lining for	E. A. Tuttle	Williamsburgh, N. Y	Nov. 8, 1870	109, 080
Fire-proof chest	J. Matthews	New York, N. Y	June 16, 1836	....
Fire-proof chest	J. Scott	Philadelphia, Pa	Nov. 12, 1830	....
Fire-proof chest or safe	D. Fitzgerald	New York, N. Y	June 1, 1843	3, 117
Fire-proof chests, Use of asbestos in manufacture of	J. Scott	Philadelphia, Pa	July 21, 1835	....
Fire-proof column, Double-cylinder	J. B. Cornell	New York, N. Y	Mar. 20, 1860	27, 528
Fire-proof composition	N. E. Blake	Almond, N. Y	Apr. 18, 1865	47, 275
Fire-proof composition for crucibles, &c	L. Held	New York, N. Y	July 12, 1864	43, 548
Fire-proof compound	R. Spencer	New York, N. Y	Nov. 17, 1868	84, 143
Fire proof compound for coating roofs, &c	R. W. Piper	Girard, Mich	Jan. 21, 1873	135, 152
Fire-proof, Compound for rendering substances	O. A. Tooker	Green Bay, Wis	July 2, 1872	128, 678
Fire-proof houses, Construction of	W. A. Berkey	Grand Rapids, Mich	Nov. 10, 1868	84, 044
Fire-proof iron chest	J. Delano	New York, N. Y	Aug. 13, 1834	....
Fire-proof iron chest	C. A. Gayler	New York, N. Y	Apr. 12, 1833	....
Fire-proof iron chest	C. A. Gayler	New York, N. Y	Apr. 3, 1835	....
Fire-proof packing for smoke and hot-air flues	J. B. Harris	Germantown, Ky	Nov. 26, 1867	71, 300
Fire-proof paper for roofs, &c	R. W. Piper	Girard, Mich	Jan. 21, 1873	135, 153
Fire-proof store, counting-room, &c	R. D. Curtis	Erie, Pa	Feb. 15, 1848	5, 445

Index of patents issued from the United States Patent Office from 1790 *to* 1873, *inclusive*—Continued.

Invention.	Inventor.	Residence.	Date.	No.
Fire-proof structure	H. H. Bryant	Boston, Mass	July 14, 1868	79,809
Fire-proof wrought-iron chest	J. Delano	New York, N. Y	Mar. 7, 1826	......
Fire, Protecting buildings against	W. McAllister	Lawrence, Mass	Nov. 18, 1873	144,625
Fire-regulator	J. Rozell	Brooklyn, N. Y	Sept. 29, 1863	40,147
Fire-regulator, Automatic	G. M. Eldridge	Philadelphia, Pa	Jan. 30, 1872	123,252
Fire-regulator for steam-boiler	J. M. Stiven	New York, N. Y	Aug. 5, 1862	36,128
Fire safety-line	C. A. Gregory	Montreal, Canada	July 29, 1873	141,269
Fire-screen	A. Chestnutwood	Davidsville, Pa	Aug. 8, 1871	117,863
Fire-screen	H. P. Gengembre	Pittsburgh, Pa	Aug. 29, 1865	49,622
Fire-screen	H. P. Gengembre	Pittsburgh, Pa	May 15, 1866	54,713
Fire-screen	C. Pierce	Salem, Mass	Apr. 29, 1829	......
Fire-screen and stand	H. O. Fritsch	New York, N. Y	Jan. 10, 1871	110,844
Fire shield	J. C. Clark	La Grange, Mich	Dec. 15, 1868	84,859
Fire-shield	J. Lee	Galesburgh, Ill	Dec. 11, 1866	60,390
Fire-shield	H. Rieger	Beaufort, N. C	Nov. 28, 1871	121,421
Fire shield, Camp	M. Saviers	Kansas City, Mo	May 24, 1864	42,879
Fire-shield, Portable	A. Dean	Ann Arbor, Mich	Aug. 8, 1871	117,749
Fire-shovel	I. W. Denning	Allegheny City, Pa	Mar. 21, 1871	112,789
Fire-shovel	F. M. Ketcham	Indianapolis, Ind	Sept. 23, 1873	143,018
Fire-shovel	S. Kyle	Hyde Park, Ill	Nov. 26, 1872	133,320
Fire-shovel	F. J. Niemöller	Rich Fountain, Mo	May 24, 1864	42,867
Fire-stop	E. Putnam		Aug. 24, 1802	......
Fire, Water-gun for extinguishing	H. Strait	Covington, Ky	Feb. 24, 1852	8,762
Fire-works, Machine for charging	T. Sharfenberg	Brooklyn, N. Y	Oct. 11, 1864	44,662
Fireman's and builder's elevator	A. M. Patrick	Long Lane, Mo	Feb. 13, 1872	123,642
Fireman's elevator	V. O'Bryan	Saint John's, Mich	May 19, 1868	78,122
Fireman's protector	C. D. Woodruff	Toledo, Ohio	Mar. 8, 1859	23,212
Fireman's signal	H. D. Treadwell	Elmira, N. Y	May 3, 1859	23,873
Fireman's trumpet	W. Staehlen	Williamsburgh, N. Y	July 20, 1858	20,961
Firemen, Machine for protecting	R. Bulkley	New York, N. Y	Mar. 29, 1821	......
Firing, Mechanical	S. Danks	Cincinnati, Ohio	June 27, 1871	116,275
Firkin	C. Alvord	Westford, Wis	Aug. 19, 1873	141,847
Firkins, barrels, &c., Device to attach to	A. T. Dunbar and A. McNaught	Alba, Pa	Aug. 13, 1867	67,737
Fish and animal matter to obtain oil, fats, &c., Treating	W. J. and T. Hooper	Baltimore, Md	Feb. 15, 1870	99,896
Fish and animal trap	J. T. Harcourt and G. W. Cottingham	Columbus, Tex	Sept. 17, 1872	131,439
Fish, Apparatus for curing and drying	B. Robinson	East Gloucester, Mass	July 11, 1865	48,723
Fish, Article of prepared cod	E. Crowell	New York, N. Y	Dec. 8, 1868	84,801
Fish-bait	G. T. Thorp	Philadelphia, Pa	Oct. 26, 1869	96,288
Fish-bait, Compound for	S. A. Goodman, jr	Jamestown, Tex	Jan. 21, 1873	135,113
Fish-bait cutter	V. Doane, jr	Harwich Port, Mass	Oct. 13, 1868	83,048
Fish-bait mill	W. McKay	Newburyport, Mass	July 16, 1872	129,576
Fish-bars, Machine for punching, shearing, and straightening	W. Morehouse	Buffalo, N. Y	Apr. 20, 1869	89,062
Fish, Catching	J. Ellicott		Mar. 25, 1795	......
Fish-catching apparatus	J. Garl	Suffield, Ohio	May 25, 1858	20,343
Fish-catching apparatus	A. Tiffany	Gibson, Pa	July 26, 1838	854
Fish, Conveying live	A. J. Smidth	Copenhagen, Denmark	Aug. 4, 1868	80,775
Fish, Curing and preserving	R. A. Adams	Cambridge, Mass	Nov. 23, 1869	97,145
Fish-cutter or bait-mill	N. Richardson	Gloucester, Mass	June 3, 1862	35,472
Fish-decoy	I. B. Quimby	East Boston, Mass	Nov. 21, 1865	51,120
Fish, Device for hatching the spawn of	S. Green	Rochester, N. Y	Sept. 17, 1867	68,871
Fish-dressing machine	F. Kelsey and F. H. Hosmer	Sandusky, Ohio	Sept. 16, 1873	142,918
Fish, &c., drier	W. J. and S. Hooper and O. Lugo	Baltimore, Md	Feb. 8, 1870	99,673
Fish-flake	J. Foster	Beverly, Mass	Aug. 20, 1867	67,970
Fish for food, Mode of preparing	G. H. Heron	Washington, D. C	Nov. 5, 1867	70,435
Fish for food, Process of preparing	J. Nickerson	Booth Bay, Me	Mar. 23, 1869	88,064
Fish for use, Putting up cod	B. F. Stephens	Brooklyn, N. Y	Mar. 16, 1869	87,986
Fish, Globe for	A. Ivers	New York, N. Y	Mar. 14, 1865	46,801
Fish-grappling spear	J. W. Knapp	Cross River, N. Y	Oct. 28, 1873	144,110
Fish-hatching apparatus	L. Stone	Charlestown, N. H	June 20, 1871	116,112
Fish-hook	B. F. Allen	Boston, Mass	Aug. 19, 1873	141,910
Fish-hook	F. T. Angers	Canastota, N. Y	Oct. 12, 1869	95,755
Fish-hook	F. Angilard	Royan, France	Aug. 27, 1867	68,027
Fish-hook	L. Arnold	Belchertown, Mass	Feb. 21, 1871	111,898
Fish-hook	J. B. Christian	Mount Carroll, Ill	June 30, 1868	79,446
Fish-hook	R. F. Cook	Troy, Ala	June 19, 1855	13,081
Fish-hook	C. O. Crosby	New Haven, Conn	Nov. 20, 1866	59,893
Fish-hook	W. Davis and J. Johnson	Brooklyn, N. Y	Dec. 19, 1865	51,651
Fish-hook	T. F. Engelbrecht and G. F. Skiff	Philadelphia, Pa	July 28, 1846	4,670
Fish-hook	R. A. Fish	Worcester, Mass	Apr. 28, 1868	77,365
Fish-hook	N. A. Gardiner, jr	Willett, N. Y	Sept. 20, 1864	44,368
Fish-hook	W. C. Goodwin	Hamden, Conn	Oct. 2, 1866	58,404
Fish-hook	M. Hiltz	Gloucester, Mass	Jan. 26, 1869	86,154
Fish-hook	J. Johnson	Brooklyn, N. Y	Aug. 21, 1847	5,256
Fish-hook	J. Johnson	Brooklyn, N. Y	Oct. 9, 1855	13,649
Fish-hook	J. Johnson and H. Howarth	Brooklyn, N. Y	Apr. 24, 1866	54,251
Fish-hook	F. Kemlo	Boston, Mass	Sept. 14, 1869	94,893
Fish-hook	F. Kemlo	Boston, Mass	Sept. 14, 1869	94,894
Fish-hook	F. Kemlo	Boston, Mass	Sept. 14, 1869	94,895
Fish-hook	B. Lee, jr	Williamsburgh, N. Y	Feb. 12, 1867	61,042
Fish-hook	A. I. Lenhart	New Brunswick, N. J	Nov. 12, 1867	70,868
Fish-hook	H. B. Livermore	Ashland, Pa	Jan. 9, 1866	51,951
Fish-hook	W. S. Morris	New York, N. Y	Feb. 12, 1861	31,396
Fish hook	S. Pendleton	New Haven, Conn	Aug. 21, 1847	5,255
Fish-hook	E. Pitcher	Brooklyn, N. Y	July 16, 1872	129,053
Fish-hook	H. Sigler	Houston, Tex	Apr. 11, 1854	10,761
Fish-hook	E. Sterling	Cleveland, Ohio	Nov. 12, 1867	70,913
Fish-hook, Double-lever	G. Crandell	Washington, D. C	Nov. 7, 1865	50,799
Fish-hook holder	L. Arnold	Belchertown, Mass	Aug. 8, 1871	117,719
Fish-hook, Spring	W. P. Blake	New York, N. Y	Aug. 15, 1848	5,710
Fish-hook, Spring	D. Ellis and C. T. Grilley	Naugatuck, Conn	Aug. 15, 1848	5,709
Fish-hook, Spring	D. Kidder	Franklin, N. H	Sept. 24, 1867	69,221
Fish-hook, Spring	J. King, jr	Fort Wayne, Ind	Nov. 20, 1866	59,844

Index of patents issued from the United States Patent Office from 1790 *to* 1873, *inclusive*—Continued.

Invention.	Inventor.	Residence.	Date.	No.
Fish-hook, Spring	E. Rhodes, jr., and J. W. Rhoades.	Clyde, Ohio	Jan. 1, 1867	60, 786
Fish-hooks and artificial bait, Attachment for	J. T. Buel	Whitehall, N. Y	Apr. 11, 1854	10, 771
Fish-hooks, Machine for making	C. O. Crosby	New Haven, Conn	Mar. 7, 1865	46, 644
Fish in warm weather, Mode of carrying	N. Robbins		Mar 11, 1802	....
Fish-nurseries	R. E Sabin	West Springfield, Mass	July 11, 1871	116, 995
Fish-plates, Fastening for	R. Anthony	Kingston, Pa	Jan. 9, 1872	122, 547
Fish, Preparing and preserving	W. Sharp	Portland, Me	Sept. 30, 1873	143, 386
Fish, Preparing, desiccating, and preserving	W. D. Cutler	PhiladelphiaPa.	Sept. 8, 1868	81, 987
Fish, Process of curing and putting up	J. Atwood, jr	Provincetown, Mass	May 25, 1869	90, [illegible]34
Fish, Process of extracting oil from	E. H. Woodward	New York, N. Y	Aug. 21, 1866	57, 427
Fish, Putting up salt mackerel and similar	E. A. Pharo	Philadelphia, Pa	Oct. 15, 1872	132, 316
Fish-scaling machine	N. B. White	Cecil County, Md	Nov. 26, 1867	71, 434
Fish, Serpentine spinner to catch	C. De Saxe	New York, N. Y	June 12, 1855	13, 068
Fish-spawn hatcher	M. G. Holton	Rochester, N. Y	Mar. 18, 1873	136, 834
Fish, Spinning bait for catching	J. T. Buel	Whitehall, N. Y	Apr. 6, 1852	8, 853
Fish to obtain oil and fertilizers, Process of treating.	A. Smith	Baltimore, Md	Jan. 25, 1870	99, 251
Fish to guano, &c., Apparatus for reducing	T. L. Robinson	Boston, Mass	Apr. 12, 1864	42, 310
Fish-trap	E. B. Beach	West Meriden, Conn	Dec. 22, 1868	85, 199
Fish-trap	D. Bowman	Tampico, Tenn	Mar. 8, 1859	23, 154
Fish-trap	R. Gray	Anson, Me	Jan. 18, 1859	22, 644
Fish-trap	F. Goodwin	Astoria, N. Y	Apr. 8, 1862	34, 887
Fish-trap	J. E Hammond	New Bedford, Mass	Apr. 4, 1871	113, 292
Fish-trap	C. E. Ketcham	Washington, D. C	Apr. 15, 1873	137, 930
Fish-trap	T. B McCaughan	Moscow, Tenn	Apr. 7, 1868	76, 489
Fish-trap	S. Pavonarius and C. C. Michtle	Philadelphia, Pa	Aug. 5, 1873	141, 588
Fish-trap	L. Van Hoesen	Westville, Conn	Dec. 9, 1856	16, 217
Fish, Trolling-bait for catching	R. Haskell	Painesville, Ohio	Sept. 20, 1859	25, 507
Fish-way	E A. Brackett	Winchester, Mass	Oct. 22, 1872	132, 349
Fish-way	A. Livermore	Ashland, Pa	Aug. 14, 1866	57, 159
Fish-way for dams	D. Steck	Hughesville, Pa	June 26, 1866	55, 929
Fish-weir	H. Emerson	Hancock	Aug. 14, 1811	....
Fishing-apparatus	P. H. Ferl and W. Larkins	Detroit, Mich	Aug. 7, 1866	56, 917
Fishing-apparatus	O. M. Fuller	Catasauqua, Pa	Jan. 30, 1872	123, 164
Fishing-apparatus	J. Koehler	New York, N. Y.	May 12, 1868	77, 893
Fishing-apparatus	J. Stetson	West Harwich, Mass	Nov. 3, 1868	83, 740
Fishing-bait, Mode of preserving	E E. Burnham	Gloucester, Mass	Dec. 15, 1868	84, 855
Fishing-bait, Preserving	T. D. Kellogg	New York, N. Y	Feb. 11, 1868	74, 3[illegible]8
Fishing-boat	J. Donn	Washington, D. C	Mar. 6, 1835	....
Fishing-implement	E. Horton	Bristol, Conn	Nov. 4, 1856	16, 014
Fishing-jack	M. D. Kirk and W. H. Belnap	Sturgis, Mich	July 20, 1869	92, 730
Fishing-jig	S. Albee	Wiscasset, Me	Nov. 3, 1868	83, 681
Fishing-lead	W. Smith	South Thomaston, Me	Apr. 1, 1856	14, 587
Fishing-line	F. E. Foster	New York, N. Y	Feb. 18, 1873	135, 900
Fishing-line float	E. Jewell	Louisville, Ky	July 9, 1872	128, 885
Fishing-line, Metallic	H. Camp	Covington, Ga	Sept. 5, 1871	118, 772
Fishing-line, Pivot	F. X. Monnier	Detroit, Mich	Feb. 23, 1869	87, 188
Fishing-line reel	A. Dougherty	Brooklyn, N. Y.	Feb. 9, 1864	41, 494
Fishing-line reel	D. Ellis	Waterbury, Conn	July 12, 1864	43, 485
Fishing-line reel	A. B. Hartill	New York, N. Y	Aug. 7, 1866	56, 937
Fishing-line reel	W. M. Stuart	Newark, N. J.	Aug. 29, 1865	49, 663
Fishing-line reel	W. H. Van Gieson	New York, N. Y	July 5, 1864	43, 400
Fishing-line sinker	L. A. Burnham	Gloucester, Mass	Sept. 25, 1866	58, 211
Fishing-line sinker	E. F. Decker	Southport, Me	Feb. 21, 1865	46, 453
Fishing-line sinker	J. R. Martin	Booth Bay, Me	July 31, 1866	56, 857
Fishing-line sinker	J. R. Martin	Booth Bay, Me	Jan. 29, 1867	61, 625
Fishing-line sinker	R T. Osgood	Orland, Me	Aug. 3, 1869	93, 220
Fishing-line sinker	W. H. Smith	New York, N. Y	May 12, 1868	77, 774
Fishing-line swivel	M. Hiltz	Gloucester, Mass	Dec. 10, 1867	71, 879
Fishing lines and other small cords, Machine for making.	P. Brooks	New Haven, Conn	Oct. 23, 1866	59, 120
Fishing-lines, Attaching float and sinker to	J. Ingrams	Troy, N. Y.	Feb. 8, 1870	99, 572
Fishing-reel	P. A. Altmaeir	Harrisburgh, Pa	Nov. 9, 1869	96, 652
Fishing-reel	W. Billinghurst	Rochester, N. Y	Aug. 9, 1859	24, 987
Fishing-reel	A. H. Fowler	Batavia, N. Y	June 18, 1872	128, 137
Fishing-reel	A. Hatch	New Haven, Conn	June 19, 1866	55, 653
Fishing-reel	G. Mooney	Providence, R. I	Jan. 14, 1873	134, 917
Fishing-reel	M. S. Palmer	New Bedford, Mass	Feb. 28, 1860	27, 205
Fishing-reel	J. J. Ross	Buffalo, N. Y	Oct. 12, 1869	95, 839
Fishing-reel	S. B. Terry	Waterbury, Conn	Nov. 14, 1871	121, 020
Fishing-reel	J. Von Hofe	Brooklyn, E. D., N. Y	Nov. 26, 1867	71, 344
Fishing-rod	R. N. Isaacs	New York, N. Y	Oct. 16, 1866	58, 833
Fishing-rod	J. B. McHarg	Rome, N. Y	Mar. 18, 1873	137, 015
Fishing-rod	W. N. Smith	Reading, Pa	July 8, 1873	140, 656
Fishing-rod	T. Tout	Cambridge, Mass	Sept. 26, 1871	119, 251
Fishing-rod and float	C. De Saxe	New York, N. Y	Apr. 18, 1854	10, 795
Fishing-rod, Hinged	J. H. Montrose	New York, N. Y	Dec. 24, 1867	72, 667
Fishing-rod holder	F. Senicur	Mount Sterling, Ky	Aug. 26, 1873	142, 126
Fishing-rod joint	W. J. Hubbard	Ansonia, Conn	Mar. 15, 1870	100, 895
Fishing-rod reel	J. A. Bailey	Jersey City, N. J	Aug. 5, 1856	15, 466
Fishing-rod reel	E. Deacon	Brooklyn, N. Y	Feb. 10, 1857	16, 626
Fishing-rod tip	J. V. Hofe	New York, N. Y	May 20, 1862	35, 339
Fishing-rod tip	J. C. Underwood and T. J. Bargis.	Richmond, Ind	May 18, 1858	20, 309
Fishing-rods, Attaching reels to	T. W. Cummings	New York, N. Y	July 12, 1864	43, 546
Fishing-rods, Guide-ring for	H. Pritchard	Brooklyn, N. Y	Oct. 4, 1859	25, 693
Fishing-stake	J. O. Campbell	Alpena, Mich	Nov. 25, 1873	144, 888
Fishing-tackle	J. T. Buel	Whitehall, N. Y	Apr. 22, 1856	14, 706
Fishing-tackle	W. D. Chapman	Theresa, N. Y	May 15, 1866	54, 684
Fishing-tackle	A. A. Dennett	New Brunswick, N. J	July 21, 1868	80, 151
Fishing-tackle	J. D. Leach and S. Hutchings	Penobscot, Me	Dec. 15, 1868	84, 885
Fishing-tackle	A. J. Lenhart	Trenton, N. J	Aug. 2, 1864	43, 694
Fishing-tackle	L. D. Lothrop	Dover, N. H	May 5, 1868	77, 628
Fishing-tackle	D. C Talbot	Holden, Mass	Mar. 3, 1868	75, 075
Fishing-tackle	F. Tellgmann	Stamford, Conn	Feb. 9, 1869	86, 786
Fishing-tackle for deep-sea fishing	W. Woodbury	Gloucester, Mass	July 7, 1863	39, 192
Fishing-torch	S. Bartholomew	Sturgis, Mich	Apr. 15, 1873	137, 877

Index of patents issued from the United States Patent Office from 1790 *to* 1873, *inclusive*—Continued.

Invention.	Inventor.	Residence.	Date.	No.
Fishing vessel and net	J. Wills, jr	Galloway, N. J	Dec. 17, 1814	....
Fistula, Instrument for treating	E. F. Garvin	New York, N. Y	Dec. 8, 1868	84, 815
Fixing, puddling, and boiler furnace	M. Z. Evans	Ormsby, Pa	Oct. 5, 1869	95, 450
Flag	A. Watson	Washington, D. C	Feb. 16, 1864	41, 656
Flag-halyard	W. Albert	Brooklyn, N. Y	Sept. 26, 1871	119, 292
Flag-hoisting apparatus	J. W. Mackenzie	San Francisco, Cal	May 7, 1872	126, 469
Flag, Signal, &c	J. Holt	Lowell, Mass	Apr. 26, 1870	102, 267
Flag, Signal	H. J. Rogers	Baltimore, Md	Jan. 2, 1855	12, 140
Flags, Apparatus for press-dyeing stars for	D. C. Farrington	Lowell, Mass	Mar. 12, 1872	124, 428
Flags, Apparatus for press-dyeing stripes for	D. C. Farrington	Lowell, Mass	Mar. 12, 1872	124, 427
Flail-cap	T. J. Hubbard	Hamilton, N. Y	Jan. 11, 1859	22, 557
Flange	D. Paterson	Jersey City, N. J	July 10, 1866	56, 326
Flange-turning die	A. W. Sangster	Buffalo, N. Y	Mar. 10, 1863	37, 876
Flange-union	A. A. Dame	Titusville, Pa	June 17, 1873	139, 877
Flanges, Tool for upsetting	J. Connolly	Newburgh, N. Y	Apr. 2, 1867	63, 474
Flanged and beaded hoops, Machine for making	J. Blood	Watertown, N. Y	Sept. 13, 1870	107, 216
Flanged pipes, Mold for casting	G. T. Sheldon	Chelmsford, Mass	Apr. 3, 1866	53, 690
Flanging-apparatus	E. Regan	Indianapolis, Ind	Feb. 8, 1870	99, 707
Flanging-machine	G. A. Bowers	Chicago, Ill	Mar. 26, 1872	124, 859
Flanging-machine	S. Lowen	Temperanceville, Pa	Aug. 3, 1869	93, 320
Flannel and other cloth, Machine for drying	D. M. Cummings and A. Hayes	Enfield, N. H	Sept. 27, 1864	44, 402
Flannel and other cloth, Wetting	J. W. Hale	Haverhill, Mass	Apr. 2, 1841	2, 028
Flannel, Process of finishing	S. Archer	Globe Village, Mass	Aug. 18, 1863	39, 539
Flash-light signal	W. Mitchell and J. J. Mayo	London and Sutton, England.	July 22, 1873	141, 010
Flash-light-signal recorder	M. Gustin	Troy, Pa	May 6, 1873	138, 498
Flask:				
See Car-wheel flash. Column-flask. Dentists' flask. Founders' flask. Kettle-molding flask. Liquor-flask. Molders' flask. Molding-flask. Pipe flask. Pocket-flask. Powder-flask. Vulcanizing-flask.				
Flask	W. T. Fry	Philadelphia, Pa	Dec. 5, 1865	51, 303
Flask and bottle	W. T. Fry	Philadelphia, Pa	Oct. 20, 1863	40, 338
Flask clamp, Foundery	C. C. Stewart	Oneonta, N. Y	May 10, 1870	102, 987
Flask, Guide	T. S. Brown	Poughkeepsie, N. Y	Apr. 5, 1870	101, 426
Flask or bottle	W. T. Fry	New York, N. Y	Aug. 11, 1868	80, 939
Flask or mold fastening	O. H. Burdick	Auburn, N. Y	Apr. 26, 1864	42, 543
Flask or retort	S. L. Geer	Norwich, Conn	June 21, 1864	43, 193
Flask-pin	B. B. Whaley	Brooklyn, N. Y	Mar. 28, 1865	47, 059
Flasks or molds, Slide and guide for	S. A. Traugh	Cincinnati, Ohio	Apr. 19, 1864	42, 419
Flat-boats, Launching	J. and E. Davis	Matildaville, Pa	Nov. 22, 1859	26, 168
Flat-bottom boat with movable keel	S. Buel	Burlington, Vt	July 7, 1810	....
Flat-bottom boats, Construction of	H. Haupt and J. Y. Smith	Cambridge, Mass., and Alexandria, Va.	July 25, 1865	48, 935
Flat-iron	J. Alexander	Brooklyn, N. Y	Feb. 13, 1866	52, 512
Flat-iron	A. Bachelder	Pelham, N. H	Aug. 1, 1871	117, 592
Flat-iron	T. Butlers	Concord, N. H	Feb. 13, 1866	52, 529
Flat-iron	J. Grüss	Cleveland, Ohio	Mar. 3, 1868	75, 156
Flat-iron	D. Lithgow	Philadelphia, Pa	Oct. 26, 1858	21, 891
Flat-iron	E. B. Robinson	Portland, Me	Sept. 18, 1866	58, 138
Flat-iron	P. T. Wilbur	Boston, Mass	July 9, 1872	128, 936
Flat-iron, Gas	A. Hallowell and A. T. Atherton.	Lowell, Mass	Oct. 26, 1869	96, 228
Flat-iron guard	J. C. Briggs	Concord, N. H	Feb. 5, 1861	31, 295
Flat-iron heater	M. D. Birge	Grand Rapids, Mich	July 16, 1872	129, 453
Flat-iron heater	J. F. Hall	Albia, Iowa	Nov. 4, 1873	144, 335
Flat-iron heater	A. Hallowell	Lowell, Mass	Mar. 17, 1868	75, 631
Flat-iron heater	G. R. Moore	Lyons, Iowa	Aug. 9, 1864	43, 786
Flat-iron heater	S. W. Smith	Addison, Vt	Mar. 24, 1868	75, 995
Flat-iron heater	W. C. Wren	Brooklyn, N. Y	Sept. 10, 1872	131, 202
Flat-iron heater	J. C. Wright and J. W. Sursa	Moline, Ill	July 15, 1873	140, 987
Flat-iron heater	J. H. Yates	Batavia, N. Y	Aug. 20, 1867	68, 024
Flat-iron holder	F. W. Brocksieper	New Britain, Conn	Dec. 27, 1864	45, 581
Flat-iron holder	F. Bruns	Cleveland, Ohio	Nov. 28, 1871	121, 273
Flat-iron holder and polisher	I. F. Brown	New London, Conn	Oct. 15, 1872	132, 137
Flat-iron polisher and holder	W. B. Mason	Boston, Mass	Mar. 8, 1870	100, 649
Flat-iron, Steam	C. C. Walworth	Boston, Mass	Dec. 21, 1852	9, 494
Flat or sad iron	L. Lincoln	Norton, Mass	June 28, 1870	104, 748
Flat or sad iron	W. Wilson	Greenfield, Mass	Mar. 27, 1835	....
Flavoring compound	W. Zeigler and J. H. Seal	New York, N. Y	Nov. 15, 1870	109, 364
Flax and cotton, Treating	C. W. and O. G. Newton	Edinburgh, Mo	Feb. 27, 1866	52, 877
Flax and hemp, Bleaching unrotted	W. Cumberland	New York, N. Y	Aug. 27, 1822	....
Flax and hemp brake	J. L. Boorum and C. D. Palmiter.	Homer, N. Y	July 5, 1864	43, 452
Flax and hemp brake	J. A. Dana	Cazenovia, N. Y	July 23, 1811	....
Flax and hemp brake	A. W. Hall	New York, N. Y	Nov. 22, 1864	45, 154
Flax and hemp brake	E. Rumsey	Christian County, Ky	Apr. 26, 1811	....
Flax and hemp, Breaking	T. Pullen	Lexington, Ky	June 20, 1816	....
Flax and hemp, Breaking and cleaning	A. Zellnor	Pulaski, Tenn	July 26, 1833	....
Flax and hemp breaking and cleaning machine	J. Godden	Pittsburgh, Iowa	Jan. 20, 1843	2, 922
Flax and hemp breaking and cleaning machine	W. McMillen	Ripley, Ohio	Sept 30, 1842	2, 796
Flax and hemp breaking and cleaning machine	O. Roberts		Apr. 12, 1804	....
Flax and hemp breaking and cleaning machinery	G. Sanford and J. E. Mallory	New York, N. Y	June 24, 1862	35, 710
Flax and hemp breaking and cleaning machinery	G. Sanford and J. E. Mallory	New York, N. Y	Sept. 16, 1862	36, 485
Flax and hemp breaking and cleaning machinery	G. Sanford and J. E. Mallory	New York, N. Y	Oct. 14, 1862	36, 674
Flax and hemp breaking and corn-shelling machine	R. Gillman	New York, N. Y	Nov. 5, 1824	....
Flax and hemp, Breaking and dressing	E. C. Chase	Jay, Me	Jan. 6, 1832	....
Flax and hemp, Breaking and dressing	F. Cox	Somerville, N. J	Dec. 4, 1823	....
Flax and hemp, Breaking and dressing	A. Zellnor	Giles County, Tenn	Oct. 25, 1832	....
Flax and hemp breaking and dressing machine	E. Christian	Philadelphia, N. Y	Feb. 8, 1828	....
Flax and hemp breaking and dressing machine	G. H. Rickets and J. Kinney, jr	Mount Pleasant, N. J	July 12, 1814	....
Flax and hemp breaking and dressing machine	L. Tibbitts	New Glasgow, Va	Oct. 22, 1831	....
Flax and hemp breaking and dressing machinery	B. M. Smith	Massillon, Ohio	Oct. 7, 1845	4, 219
Flax and hemp breaking and swingling	W. C. Davison	Pittsford, N. Y	June 22, 1824	....
Flax and hemp breaking and thrashing	N. G. Hayden	Harrodsburgh, Ky	Apr. 12, 1833	....
Flax and hemp breaking machine	F. M. Barnes	Lexington, Mo	Jan. 10, 1843	2, 905

Index of patents issued from the United States Patent Office from 1790 to 1873, inclusive—Continued.

Invention.	Inventor.	Residence.	Date.	No.
Flax and hemp breaking machine	G. W. Billings	New York, N. Y	Mar. 15, 1864	41, 903
Flax and hemp breaking machine	J. P. Fry	Pulaski, Tenn	Dec. 21, 1842	2, 889
Flax and hemp breaking machine	A. Forsyth	Columbia, Tenn	Jan. 9, 1838	550
Flax and hemp breaking machine	J. Hindo	Schenectady, N. Y	Sept. 5, 1854	11, 647
Flax and hemp breaking machine	D. Melville	Newport, R. I	Nov. 18, 1818	....
Flax and hemp breaking machine	N. P. Robinson	Fleming County, Ky	Aug. 31, 1810	....
Flax and hemp breaking machine	G. Sanford, J. E. Mallory, and C. P. Hayes.	New York, N. Y	Oct. 14, 1862	36, 675
Flax and hemp breaking machine	W. Van Luser	Warwick, N. Y	June 30, 1813	....
Flax and hemp breaking machinery	G. Sanford and J. E. Mallory	New York, N. Y	Mar. 25, 1862	34, 779
Flax and hemp breaking, scutching, or cleaning machine.	H. Johnson	Maysville, Ky	Mar. 4, 1843	2, 980
Flax and hemp by animal power, Machine for gathering or pulling.	W. Brittain and J. Silvers	New Hope, Pa	Nov. 25, 1838	1, 020
Flax and hemp by steam, Rotting	A. Chinn	Harrison County, Ky	Dec. 28, 1825	....
Flax and hemp, Cleaning and breaking	R. Miller	Glasgow, Ky	May 23, 1834	....
Flax and hemp cleaning and dressing machine	I. C., G. W., and C. E. Geisindorff.	Cincinnati, Ohio	Nov. 28, 1842	2, 864
Flax and hemp cleaning and hackling machine	C. Learned	Saint Louis, Mo	Oct. 22, 1842	2, 831
Flax and hemp, Cleaning and separating the fibers of.	G. W. Billings	New York, N. Y	Mar. 8, 1864	41, 826
Flax and hemp cleaning machine	A. Gärtner	New York, N. Y	Apr. 2, 1867	63, 499
Flax and hemp, Cleaning, softening, separating, and shortening the fibers of.	H. Hawley	Louisville, Ky	June 29, 1833	....
Flax and hemp dresser	E. H. Nichols and T. Fairbanks	Saint Johnsbury, Vt	Oct. 1, 1830	....
Flax and hemp, Dressing	L. S. Chichester	Brooklyn, N. Y	Apr. 11, 1854	10, 772
Flax and hemp dressing machine	T. S. and A. Barnum	New York, N. Y	Nov. 27, 1824	....
Flax and hemp dressing machine	R. S. Chappel	Pawlet, N. Y	Jan. 18, 1809	....
Flax and hemp dressing machine	W. Cumberland	New York, N. Y	July 9, 1822	....
Flax and hemp dressing machine	N. Goodsall	Paris, N. Y	Sept. 19, 1822	....
Flax and hemp dressing machine	H. Hawley	Louisville, Ky	June 4, 1833	....
Flax and hemp dressing machine	J Hines and W. Bain	Columbus, Ohio	Feb. 3, 1823	....
Flax and hemp dressing machine	C. G. Howard	Topeka, Kans	Sept. 6, 1864	44, 138
Flax and hemp dressing machine	E Kellogg	Palmyra, N. Y	May 11, 1824	....
Flax and hemp dressing machine	B. Lewis	Ligonia, Me	Jan. 28, 1824	....
Flax and hemp dressing machine	J. Macdonald	New York, N. Y	Aug. 31, 1822	....
Flax and hemp dressing machine	A. Smith and J. Olney	Westmoreland, N. Y	July 10, 1830	....
Flax and hemp dressing machine	J. C. Wenzle	Louisville, Ky	Jan. 17, 1828	....
Flax and hemp dressing machinery	F. Kellsey	Middletown, Conn	Nov. 26, 1824	....
Flax and hemp dressing machinery	G. Sanford	New York, N. Y	June 24, 1862	35, 709
Flax and hemp drying	G. W. Billings	New York, N. Y	Oct. 13, 1863	40, 236
Flax and hemp drying frame	G. W. Billings	New York, N. Y	Oct. 6, 1863	40, 155
Flax and hemp, Extracting vegetable matter from	S. Olcott	Harsimus, N. J	Dec. 3, 1828	....
Flax and hemp for spinning, Preparing	P. Antrim	Philadelphia, Pa	Nov. 25, 1814	....
Flax and hemp for spinning, Roving	G. Brown	Schatecoke, N. Y	June 16, 1809	....
Flax and hemp hackling machine	J. P. Arnold	Louisville, Ky	Jan. 4, 1853	9, 512
Flax and hemp hackling machine	F. Demasters	Shelbyville, Ky	Nov. 20, 1838	1, 012
Flax and hemp machine	D. Ball	Sandy Hill, N. Y	July 7, 1830	....
Flax and hemp machine	G. W. Billings	New York, N. Y	Mar. 15, 1864	41, 902
Flax and hemp machine	J. Dewey, jr	Troy, N. Y	Nov. 25, 1830	....
Flax and hemp machine	E. F. Hill	Fabias, N. Y	Feb. 11, 1809	....
Flax and hemp machine	R. McCormick	Rockbridge County, Va	Oct. 1, 1830	....
Flax and hemp machine	J. Rich, jr	Troy, N. Y	May 20, 1830	....
Flax and hemp machine	W. K. Scott	Sandy Hill, N. Y	Feb. 11, 1830	....
Flax and hemp, Machine for reducing the fibers of.	S. Olcott	Philadelphia, Pa	Apr. 11, 1840	1, 550
Flax and hemp, Manufacture of	R. Patterson	New Hartford, N. Y	Dec. 18, 1849	6, 958
Flax and hemp mill	B. Tyler	....	Feb. 26, 1799	....
Flax and hemp preparatory to the various processes of cleaning and separating the fibers, &c., Mode of preparing.	S. Olcott	New Hope, Pa	Mar. 31, 1840	1, 532
Flax and hemp, Retting	G. W. Billings	New York, N. Y	Mar. 8, 1864	41, 825
Flax and hemp scutching machine	G. Sanford and J. E. Mallory	New York, N. Y	Mar. 25, 1862	34, 781
Flax and hemp to make them resemble cotton, Treating.	J. P. Comly	Dayton, Ohio	Mar. 4, 1862	34, 619
Flax and hemp without rotting by water, Preparing.	W. Hickingbottom	New York, N. Y	July 12, 1816	....
Flax-bleaching machine	I. A. Roth and J. Lea	Philadelphia County, Pa	Apr. 18, 1854	10, 780
Flax-boll brake	B. S. Burgan	Congress, Ohio	Jan. 12, 1869	85, 725
Flax-brake	A. G. Bill	Cuyahoga Falls, Ohio	Aug. 31, 1869	94, 177
Flax-brake	J. Boyce	Wooster, Ohio	Sept. 14, 1869	94, 706
Flax-brake	J. C. Kurtz	Wooster, Ohio	June 27, 1871	116, 328
Flax-brake	M. B. Southwick	Mont Saint Hillaire, Canada.	July 25, 1871	117, 342
Flax-brake and swingler	S. Cowan	Bloomfield, Iowa	Sept. 29, 1863	40, 091
Flax breaking and cleaning machine	S. A. Clemens	Chicago, Ill	Nov. 6, 1866	59, 503
Flax breaking and cleaning machine	G. Sanford and J. E. Mallory	England and New York, N. Y.	Aug. 25, 1863	39, 680
Flax breaking and cleaning machine	G. B. Turner	Cuyahoga Falls, Ohio	Sept. 6, 1864	44, 128
Flax breaking and dressing machine	S. M. Allen	Woburn, Mass	June 30, 1863	39, 025
Flax breaking and dressing machine	J. Briggs	Schoharie, N. Y	Oct. 1, 1825	....
Flax breaking and dressing machine	S. A. Clemens	Springfield, Mass	Mar. 8, 1853	9, 609
Flax breaking and dressing machine	L. Rundell	Pike, N. Y	Sept. 27, 1864	44, 458
Flax-breaking machine	J. Cannon	....	Jan. 17, 1801	....
Flax-breaking machine	S. Davison	Romulus Township, N. Y.	May 17, 1822	....
Flax-breaking machine	J. Haues and L. Kohler	Millersburgh, Ind	Nov. 17, 1863	40, 621
Flax-breaking machine	A. S. Miller	Bluffton, Ind	June 9, 1868	78, 811
Flax-breaking machine	P. Reading	Trenton, N. J	Jan. 3, 1825	....
Flax-breaking machine	H. Schoonhoven	Pultney, N. Y	Dec. 11, 1827	....
Flax cleaning and dressing machine	J. E. Crowell	Chelsea, Mass	Aug. 5, 1862	36, 075
Flax-cleaning machine	C. Beach	Penn Yan, N. Y	Sept. 27, 1864	44, 387
Flax-cleaning machine	W. W. Whiddit	Richmond, Ind	May 28, 1867	65, 319
Flax &c., cleansing, dressing, and cutting machine	E Phillips	Blackstone, Mass	May 2, 1865	47, 604
Flax, Dressing	E. Mack	....	Mar. 21, 1806	....
Flax-dressing machine	D. S. Abbott	Ischua, N. Y	June 12, 1866	55, 446
Flax-dressing machine	J. Barlow	Granville, Mass	Aug. 23, 1809	....
Flax-dressing machine	F. Burd ck	Kortright, N. Y	Feb. 28, 1825	....
Flax-dressing machine	J. Haws	Hudson, N. Y	June 19, 1812	....
Flax-dressing machine	J. Hines and W. Bain	New York, N. Y	Aug. 12, 1826	....

Index of patents issued from the United States Patent Office from 1790 to 1873, inclusive—Continued.

Invention.	Inventor.	Residence.	Date.	No.
Flax-dressing machine	W. C. McBride	Somerville, N. J	Mar. 17, 1868	75, 559
Flax-dressing machine	W. Wheeler	Warren, N. Y	Mar. 26, 1825	....
Flax-dressing machinery	E. L. Norfolk	Salem, Mass	May 9, 1854	10, 876
Flax-dressing machinery	D. Warner, jr	South Hadley, Mass	Sept. 5, 1854	11, 654
Flax, &c., gathering and loading machine	G. W. Hatch	Parkman, Ohio	June 6, 1865	48, 064
Flax, &c., gathering and loading machine	G. W. Hatch	Parkman, Ohio	Dec. 4, 1866	60, 185
Flax, hemp, and Manila grass, Combing and separating fibers of	S. Couillard, jr	Boston, Mass	Oct. 19, 1836	....
Flax, hemp, and other fibrous materials, Mode of treating.	J. W. Burton and G. Pye	Eye and Ipswich, England	Dec. 8, 1857	18, 801
Flax, hemp, and other fibrous plants, Disintegrating	R. M. Russell	New York, N. Y	Aug. 6, 1867	67, 455
Flax, hemp, &c., Apparatus for separating fibers of	J. B. Fuller	Claremont, N. H	Mar. 1, 1864	41, 812
Flax, hemp, &c., breaking and cleaning machine	G. Sanford and J. E. Mallory	New York, N. Y	June 16, 1863	38, 916
Flax, hemp, &c., breaking and cleaning machine	G. Sanford and J. E. Mallory	New York, N. Y	Sept. 15, 1863	39, 962
Flax, hemp, &c., breaking machine	J. Millard	Kent, Conn	May 6, 1813	....
Flax, hemp, &c., breaking machine	J. L. F. Roumage	New York, N. Y	Aug. 6, 1829	....
Flax, hemp, &c., cutting and gathering machine	R. M. Couch	Lambertsville, N. J	July 16, 1841	2, 179
Flax, hemp, &c., Disintegrating and separating fibers of.	J. B. Fuller	Claremont, N. H	Mar. 1, 1864	41, 813
Flax, hemp, &c., Disintegrating or cottonizing	H. Burgess	Royer's Ford, Pa	Jan. 19, 1864	41, 276
Flax, hemp, &c., Fiber from	H. Burgess	Royer's Ford, Pa	Jan. 19, 1864	41, 275
Flax, hemp, &c., for spinning, Mode of preparing	J. Owings	Baltimore, Md	Mar. 5, 1812	....
Flax, hemp, &c., Mode of separating the fibers of	R. T. Shaw	New York, N. Y	Jan. 19, 1864	41, 352
Flax, hemp, &c., Plant used as a substitute for	C. Whitlow	New York, N. Y	Jan. 11, 1812	....
Flax, hemp, &c., Retting and disintegrating	R. T. Shaw	New York, N. Y	Jan. 19, 1864	41, 350
Flax, hemp, silk, tow, and wool, Combing and hackling.	J. and J. Westerman	New York, N. Y	Aug. 14, 1833	....
Flax-machine	J. Halladay, T. Eldridge, C. Gibbs, and J. D. Smith.	Hartford, N. Y	Mar. 4, 1830	....
Flax-machine	O. Wilde	Canaan, N. Y	Apr. 16, 1810	....
Flax, &c., Machine for drawing	J. Good	Brooklyn, E. D., N. Y	Oct. 5, 1869	95, 462
Flax, Machine for scutching and thrashing	M. Jerome	Dixon, Ill	June 8, 1869	90, 946
Flax, Machine for scutching tangled	W. C. McBride	Raritan, N. J	Nov. 29, 1864	45, 259
Flax, Machine for straightening and thrashing tangled.	S. A. Clemens	Chicago, Ill	Nov. 6, 1866	59, 502
Flax, Machine for thrashing	S. A. Clemens	Chicago, Ill	Nov. 6, 1866	59, 360
Flax, Machinery for preparing	J. B. Fuller	Claremont, N. H	Dec. 19, 1865	51, 652
Flax, Mode of treating	A. F. and J. H. Andrews	Avon, Conn	Apr. 23, 1867	64, 058
Flax or hemp breaking and dressing machinery	G. Sanford	New York, N. Y	Mar. 18, 1862	34, 697
Flax or hemp, Cylindrical frame for roving or spinning.	W. Gitton	New York, N. Y	Jan. 11, 1812	....
Flax or hemp dressing wheel	C. and W. A. Benton	Amenia, N. Y	May 22, 1816	....
Flax or hemp, Machine for cleaning unrotted or rotted.	W. Cumberland	New York, N. Y	Nov. 29, 1822	....
Flax, Picking and cleaning	A. H. Caryl	Sandusky, Ohio	Feb. 14, 1854	10, 513
Flax, Process for bleaching	I. A. Roth and J. Lea	Philadelphia County, Pa	Apr. 18, 1854	10, 808
Flax-puller	J. H. Bennett	East Bennington, Vt	Jan. 23, 1845	3 890
Flax-puller	L. S. Chichester	Brooklyn, N. Y	Nov. 16, 1852	9, 400
Flax-puller	B. M. Reeves	Franklin, Pa	Aug. 8, 1871	117, 926
Flax-puller	J. Smith	Troy, N. Y	May 10, 1870	102, 875
Flax-puller	S. W. Tyler	Troy, N. Y	July 18, 1871	117, 125
Flax-pulling machine	A. Burchard	Livingstonville, N. Y	Mar. 14, 1865	46, 857
Flax-pulling machine	J. Harrington	Menomonee, Wis	Jan. 22, 1867	61, 422
Flax-pulling machine	B. M. Reeves	Franklin, Pa	Mar. 28, 1871	113, 094
Flax-pulling machine	J. Sivers	Lambertsville, N. J	July 11, 1865	48, 731
Flax-pulling machine	S. W. Tyler	Troy, N. Y	Feb. 12, 1867	62, 090
Flax-pulling machine	S. W. Tyler	Troy, N. Y	Aug. 27, 1867	68, 132
Flax-scutching machine	H. Black	Lewisburgh, Ohio	June 5, 1866	55, 232
Flax-scutching machine	A. S. Miller	Bluffton, Ind	June 9, 1868	78, 810
Flax-scutching machinery	W. C. McBride	Raritan, N. J	Jan. 25, 1859	22, 738
Flax-seed-cleaning machine	P. Goltry	....	Apr. 24, 1804	....
Flax-seed, paint, &c., Grinding	A. Cross and E. Brown	Cazenovia, N. Y	Feb. 4, 1830	....
Flax-seeds, Machine for extracting	A. Hook	Searsmont, Me	Sept. 9, 1823	....
Flax-seeds, &c., Mill for grinding	G. L. Stearns	Boston, Mass	Aug. 17, 1838	886
Flax-spinning machine	L. Skeels	Worthington, Ohio	Feb. 6, 1866	52, 506
Flax-straw, Machine for preparing tow from tangled	G. F. Clemons	Springfield, Mass	July 7, 1863	39, 119
Flax-straw, Machine for straightening, breaking, and cleaning.	S. A. Clemens	Chicago, Ill	Nov. 6, 1866	59, 501
Flax-swingling machine	S. Achey	Heidelberg Township, Lebanon County, Pa.	Feb. 18, 1828	....
Flax, &c., to produce short fibers for spinning, Treating.	S. M. Allen	Woburn, Mass	Jan. 12, 1864	41, 185
Flea-powder	C. E. Jaycox	San Francisco, Cal	Mar. 30, 1869	88, 300
Fleece-bundling apparatus	J. Walton	Roseburgh, Oreg	July 20, 1869	92, 916
Fleece-folder	C. W. Rudgers	Brecksville, Ohio	Sept. 19, 1865	50, 040
Fleece-tying apparatus	S. Cooley	Caro, Mich	Nov. 16, 1869	96, 779
Flesh-fork	P. Fisher	Brooklyn, N. Y	June 27, 1871	116, 291
Flesh-fork	J. C. Klein	Birmingham, Pa	Feb. 19, 1867	62, 276
Flesh-fork and skimmer, Combination of	C. B. Bristol	Naugatuck, Conn	July 12, 1859	24, 716
Flesh, fruit, &c., Machinery for cutting	J. Buffington	Chester, Pa	July 5, 1833	....
Flesh hooks and forks, Manufacturing	M. V. Trask	Meriden, Conn	Aug. 11, 1863	39, 534
Flesh-offal, &c., Treating	W. Adamson and C. F. A. Simonin.	Philadelphia, Pa	Sept. 19, 1871	119, 000
Flexible boat, Division between the tubes of	E. T. Harr	New York, N. Y	Apr. 17, 1849	6, 363
Flexible coupling	N. W. Wheeler	Brooklyn, N. Y	June 25, 1867	66, 193
Flexible gate	J. M. Richardson	Elmira, N. Y	Nov. 12, 1872	133, 057
Flexible pipe for mining	A. Clark	Todd's Valley, Cal	Feb 7, 1865	46, 295
Flexible platform for giving motion to wheels and machinery.	J. Johnson, jr	Charleston, S. C	Nov. 22, 1809	....
Flexible tube, hose, &c., Manufacture of	I. B. Harris	Edinburgh, Scotland	May 24, 1864	42, 900
Flexible tube or hose	D. K. Hoxsie and T. L. Reed	Providence, R. I	Sept. 27, 1864	44, 425
Flexible tubes, Device for making curvatures in	A. Beckers	New York, N. Y	Nov. 29, 1864	45, 218
Flexible tubing	E. P. Gleason	New York, N. Y	Feb. 28, 1865	46, 558
Flexible tubing for illuminating-gas	W. B. S. Taylor	New York, N. Y	Feb. 21, 1865	46, 507
Flexible tubing or hose	T. L. Reed	Providence, R. I	Apr. 30, 1867	64, 362
Flexible tubings, Elastic connection for	W. B. S. Taylor	New York, N. Y	Oct. 28, 1873	144, 163
Flexible tubings, Manufacture of	D. K. Hoxsie and T. L. Reed	Providence, R. I	Nov. 21, 1865	51, 052
Flexible tubings, Manufacture of	D. K. Hoxsie and T. L. Reed	Providence, R. I	May 22, 1866	54, 909

Index of patents issued from the United States Patent Office from 1790 *to* 1873, *inclusive*—Continued.

Invention.	Inventor.	Residence.	Date.	No.
Flexible tubings, Manufacture of	W. B. S. Taylor	New York, N. Y	June 19, 1866	55, 740
Flexomanus	H. A. Nathans	Philadelphia, Pa	Dec. 15, 1857	18, 857
Float-gage, feed-regulator, &c., for steam-boilers, &c.	T. J. Sloan	New York, N. Y	Apr. 27, 1852	8, 912
Float or raft	A. Carson	Memphis, Tenn	June 18, 1867	65, 792
Floating-bag	G. Mitchell	London, England	Feb. 16, 1864	41, 632
Floating battery	A. B. Cooley	Philadelphia, Pa	Apr. 1, 1862	34, 867
Floating battery	P. Martin	Philadelphia, Pa	Aug. 11, 1841	2, 217
Floating battery	J. P. Taylor	Little Compton, R. I	Oct. 17, 1848	5, 854
Floating battery	E. A. Willis	Cold Spring, N. Y	Nov. 22, 1859	26, 219
Floating battery and light-house	J. Moody	York, England	Mar. 12, 1867	62, 870
Floating battery for ships, &c	J. Hyde	New York, N. Y	Dec. 23, 1862	37, 232
Floating battery or steamship	G. Stiles	Baltimore, Md	Apr. 4, 1815	....
Floating house or bathing-machine	H. Chevens	New York, N. Y	July 13, 1813	....
Floating-mill	J. A. Dorman	New York, N. Y	May 17, 1864	42, 756
Floating-mill and silent fisher	E. Ford	Charleston, S. C	Dec. 21, 1809	....
Floating-wheel	J. Owings	Baltimore, Md	Sept. 9, 1816	....
Floating-wheel for vessels	J. Spilman	Tonawanda, N. Y	July 9, 1867	66, 532
Flock and paper-stock cutting machine	J. N. Pitts	Blackstone, Mass	Jan. 29, 1856	14, 165
Flock-cleaning machine	R. H. Dawson	Rockville, Conn	July 8, 1873	140, 684
Flock-cloth dyed or printed	T. Crossly	Bridgeport, Conn	Jan. 31, 1865	46, 199
Flock-cutter	M. and C. H. Morse	Franklin, Mass	May 9, 1871	114, 588
Flock-cutting machine	J. Chase	Lowell, Mass	Oct. 14, 1862	36, 642
Flock-cutting machine, Reversible	J. Pitts	Millerville, Mass	Nov. 28, 1871	121, 415
Flock-duster	M. Waterhouse	Passaic, N. J	Jan. 7, 1868	73, 144
Flock for felting, Machine for preparing	L. W. Boynton	South Coventry, Conn	July 18, 1854	11, 318
Flock-grinder	E. T. Marble	Worcester, Mass	Mar. 26, 1872	124, 903
Flock-grinder	J. Waterhouse	Passaic, N. J	Mar. 12, 1872	124, 463
Flock-grinding machine	J. C. Fonda	Albany, N. Y	July 29, 1851	8, 261
Flock-machine	W. McAllister	Lawrence, Mass	Dec. 6, 1870	109, 920
Flock, Machine for cleaning and opening	W. C. Geer	Rockville, Conn	Oct. 25, 1859	25, 895
Flock, Machine for opening and cleaning	E. C. Brett	Great Barrington, Mass	Oct. 7, 1851	8, 404
Flock, Machine for preparing	L. W. Boynton	Worcester, Mass	Aug. 7, 1855	13, 380
Flock, Machine for preparing	J. R. Peters, jr	New York, N. Y	June 22, 1852	9, 059
Flock, Machine for sifting	J. F. Greene	Brooklyn, N. Y	Feb. 26, 1861	31, 574
Flock, Machinery for cutting	A. Parber	Stephentown, N. Y	Nov. 18, 1846	4, 857
Flock, Machinery for cutting	J. Tilton and E. Ritson	Northfield and Sanbornton, N. H.	May 15, 1860	28, 316
Flock to cloth, Apparatus for applying	D. and R. Pratt	Elmira, N. Y	Oct. 7, 1851	8, 405
Flock with flannel, Mode of incorporating	J. M. Pratt	Dudley, Mass	Sept. 5, 1848	5, 757
Flocked cloth, Dyeing, printing, and manufacture of water-proof.	T. Crossly	Bridgeport, Conn	Jan. 31, 1865	46, 200
Flocked fabric for hats, bonnets, &c	C. L. Mitchell	Westborough, Mass	Oct. 17, 1871	120, 084
Flocking-machines, Feeding-apparatus for	H. Turner	New York, N. Y	Jan. 21, 1868	73, 676
Flocculent substances, Press for bundling	D. Kellogg	Pittsfield, Mich	Oct. 12, 1852	9, 324
Flood-gate	A. H. Adams	Piqua, Ohio	Mar. 28, 1871	113, 001
Flood-gate	T. H. Breed	Dundee, Mich	Sept. 6, 1870	107, 159
Flood-gate	J. Campbell and A. Watson	London, Ohio	Sept. 27, 1870	107, 659
Flood-gate	J. W. Edgarton	Thornton, Ind	June 20, 1871	116, 170
Flood-gate	G. W. Flanders	Lynn, Mass	Apr. 8, 1856	14, 602
Flood-gate	E. H. Hancock	Augusta, Ga	Sept. 6, 1859	25, 330
Flood-gate	N. Hinckley	Marston's Mills, Mass	Nov. 29, 1870	109, 734
Flood-gate	B. S. Hort	Georgetown, S. C	Oct. 9, 1813	....
Flood-gate	R. Keese, D. T. Ward, and J. G. Wilkinson.	Cardington, Ohio	Sept. 3, 1861	33, 201
Flood-gate	H. A. Kephart	Fletcher, Ohio	Apr. 28, 1868	77, 384
Flood-gate	J. J. Kimball	Napierville, Ill	Feb. 16, 1869	86, 985
Flood-gate	J. J. Kimball	Napierville, Ill	Jan. 18, 1870	98, 979
Flood-gate	A. L. King	Farmersville, Ohio	Mar. 16, 1869	87, 944
Flood-gate	A. L. King	Farmersville, Ohio	Dec. 21, 1869	98, 071
Flood-gate	J. Leatherman	Napoleon, Ohio	Aug. 18, 1868	81, 180
Flood-gate	J. Macby	Portage, Wis	Aug. 7, 1866	56, 962
Flood-gate	A. Main	Delaware, Ohio	Mar. 30, 1869	88, 598
Flood-gate	C. B. McKinney	Houston, Ohio	Sept. 3, 1867	68, 767
Flood-gate	A. E. Noble	La Motte, Iowa	Apr. 5, 1870	101, 651
Flood-gate	A. Ralston	Carlisle, Pa	July 25, 1865	48, 977
Flood-gate	S. Rowland and T. C. Tipton	Williamsport, Ohio	Nov. 15, 1870	109, 252
Flood-gate	S. B. Shoup	Dayton, Ohio	Apr. 6, 1869	88, 673
Flood-gate	J. B. Stoner	Lacon, Ill	Oct. 15, 1867	69, 860
Flood-gate	H. O. Way	Thorntown, Ind	June 20, 1871	116, 247
Flood-gate, Adjustable	N. Tupper	Grand Blanc, Mich	Nov. 24, 1868	84, 321
Flood-gate for mill-dams	M. Cotton	Sardinia, N. Y	Mar. 21, 1865	46, 883
Flood-gate, Revolving	J. Du Bois	Williamsport, Pa	Jan. 17, 1865	45, 913
Flood-gate, Self-acting	G. B. Markham	Mead's Mills, Mich	Sept. 4, 1860	29, 896
Flood-gate, Self-operating	W. H. Allard and R. W. Thomas	Portage, Wis	Sept. 11, 1866	57, 839
Flood or waste gate	W. L. Clark	Cambria, Wis	July 16, 1867	66, 795
Flood-roller	W. J. Connell	West Unity, Ohio	June 22, 1869	91, 607
Floor	L. S. Wood	Marion, Iowa	July 15, 1873	140, 864
Floor and ceiling, Fire-proof	W. T. Butler	Chicago, Ill	July 29, 1873	141, 260
Floor and ceiling, Fire-proof	I. Hodgson and W. H. Brown	Indianapolis, Ind	July 30, 1872	129, 955
Floor and ceiling, Fire-proof	F. A. Petersen	New York, N. Y	Apr. 3, 1855	12, 642
Floor and chimney connection, Fire-proof	W. Neracher	Cleveland, Ohio	Apr. 22, 1873	138, 096
Floor and roof, Fire-proof	T. Hyatt	New York, N. Y	Dec. 2, 1873	145, 181
Floor and wall, Fire-proof	J. John	Chicago, Ill	Dec. 2, 1873	145, 211
Floor, Basement	E. S. Vaughan	Flatbush, N. Y	Apr. 8, 1873	137, 740
Floor-clamp	J. H. Baker	Saratoga Springs, N. Y	Apr. 28, 1868	77, 243
Floor-clamp	G. E. Banner	Newark, N. J	Apr. 14, 1868	76, 583
Floor-clamp	H. D. Barnes	Fair Haven, Conn	Nov. 26, 1867	71, 440
Floor-clamp	J. L. Bryant	Logansport, Ind	Sept. 12, 1865	49, 852
Floor-clamp	J. L. Clough	Suffield, Conn	Apr. 23, 1861	32, 120
Floor-clamp	W. Conner and C. W. Mitchell	Wilmington, Del	Dec. 10, 1867	71, 987
Floor-clamp	J. H. Ferriera	Newark, N. J	Oct. 6, 186-	82, 700
Floor-clamp	J. J. Foster	Belmont, Tex	Mar. 4, 1873	136, 428
Floor-clamp	J. A. Haase	Philadelphia, Pa	May 4, 1869	89, 577
Floor-clamp	E. A. Hall	Sugar Branch, Ind	May 5, 1868	77, 610
Floor-clamp	J. F. Hammond	Providence, R. I	July 30, 1867	67, 297
Floor-clamp	A. Lloyd	Mattoon, Ill	June 5, 1866	55, 424
Floor-clamp	F. S. Mack	Galesburgh, Ill	July 21, 1868	80, 079
Floor-clamp	D. Nettleton	Humbird, Wis	Sept. 20, 1870	107, 527

Index of patents issued from the United States Patent Office from 1790 *to* 1873, *inclusive*—Continued.

Invention.	Inventor.	Residence.	Date.	No.
Floor-clamp	D. Nevin	Georgetown, Colo	Feb. 7, 1871	111,560
Floor-clamp	H. W. Oliver	Whitneysville, Conn	Apr. 15, 1856	14,676
Floor-clamp	D. K. Peoples	Philadelphia, Pa	Nov. 24, 1863	40,727
Floor-clamp	G. B. Perkins	Utica, N. Y	Aug. 25, 1868	81,531
Floor-clamp	W. Partlock and J. H. Smith	Pleasant Grove and Toolesborough, Iowa.	Feb. 4, 1868	74,128
Floor-clamp	H. J. O. Reed	Salem, Mass	Oct. 28, 1873	144,140
Floor-clamp	J. G. Rogers	Miles, Mich	May 27, 1873	139,265
Floor-clamp	J. B. Spencer	Norwich, Conn	Dec. 21, 1869	98,116
Floor-clamp	O. Taff	Whitestone, N. Y	June 28, 1870	104,790
Floor-clamp	T. S. Urie	Hubbardston, Mich	Sept. 19, 1871	119,203
Floor-clamp	H. C. Wight	Worcester, Mass	July 13, 1858	20,913
Floor-clamp	J. D. Winslow	Wilmington, Del	Oct. 30, 1866	59,305
Floor-clamp	S. C. and S. Winslow	Worcester, Mass	May 15, 1866	54,805
Floor-clamp	G. Wood	Philadelphia, Pa	Mar. 8, 1870	100,700
Floor-cleaner	A. Armstrong	Newburgh, Ohio	Mar. 10, 1868	75,236
Floor-cloth: *See* oil-cloth.				
Floor-cloth	S. M. Allen	Woburn, Mass	Nov. 17, 1863	40,592
Floor-cloth	T. Griffin	Roxbury, Mass	June 18, 1867	65,904
Floor-cloth	S. Hawksworth	Doncaster, England	Apr. 26, 1864	42,479
Floor-cloth and carpeting	J. B. Meldrum	Paterson, N. J	July 30, 1867	67,330
Floor cloth and carpeting	J. B. Meldrum	Paterson, N. J	Nov. 19, 1867	71,034
Floor-cloth, Composition for	J. W. Harmon	Brooklyn, N. Y	Mar. 31, 1857	16,918
Floor-cloth, &c., Composition for sizing and stiffening.	N. B. Powers	Lansingburgh, N. Y	Oct. 28, 1862	36,794
Floor-cloth, &c., Composition for sizing for use in the manufacture of.	N. B. Powers	Lansingburgh, N. Y	Oct. 28, 1862	36,793
Floor-cloth from straw-board, Manufacture of	F. N. Davis	Beloit, Wis	Nov. 19, 1872	133,210
Floor-cloth, leather-cloth, &c., Mode of producing	R. O. Lowrey	Salem, N. Y	May 19, 1868	77,993
Floor-cloth, &c., Leather-paper for	E. Richmond	Brookline, Mass	June 28, 1864	43,340
Floor-cloth, Machine for printing	S. Savage	Lowell Mass	Mar. 2, 1852	8,778
Floor-cloth, Manufacture of	J. B. Hodgskin	New York, N. Y	Jan. 2, 1866	51,830
Floor-cloth, Manufacture of	G. F. Hopper	New York, N. Y	Jan. 2, 1866	51,832
Floor-cloth, Manufacture of	C. L. Laurence	New York, N. Y	Aug. 22, 1865	49,537
Floor-cloth, Manufacture of	J. H. Williams	Essex, Conn	July 7, 1868	79,712
Floor-cloth, Manufacture of rubber	H. W. Joslin	Jersey City, N. J	Feb. 7, 1871	111,549
Floor-cloth, Method of printing	J. Albro	Elizabeth, N. J	Nov. 15, 1859	26,075
Floor-cloth, &c., Printing	J. Marchbank	Lansingburgh, N. Y	Jan. 6, 1863	37,298
Floor-cloth, Roller for	R. Hoskin	Brooklyn, N. Y	May 28, 1867	65,223
Floor-covering	W. Howell, J. C. Finn, and C. A. Duy.	Philadelphia, Pa	Sept. 15, 1868	82,119
Floor-covering	C. Keen	Philadelphia, Pa	Sept. 18, 1866	58,171
Floor-covering	A. H. Platt	Yellow Springs, Ohio	Jan. 17, 1865	45,937
Floor-covering	A. H. Platt	Ann Arbor, Mich	Sept. 4, 1866	57,763
Floor-covering, roof, &c	D. L. Wolff	Chicago, Ill	June 20, 1871	116,128
Floor-covering, wainscoting, &c., Fabric for	M. Flurscheim	New York, N. Y	Nov. 10, 1868	83,948
Floor-coverings, Manufacture of	J. H. Spencer	Philadelphia, Pa	Oct. 2, 1866	58,497
Floor, Fire-proof	N. Cheney	New York, N. Y	Apr. 1, 1873	137,345
Floor, Fire-proof	J. B. Cornell	New York, N. Y	Feb. 15, 1859	22,939
Floor, Fire-proof	J. Dunseith	New York, N. Y	Aug. 22, 1871	118,220
Floor, Fire-proof	I. Hodgson and W. H. Brown	Indianapolis, Ind	July 23, 1872	129,827
Floor, Fire-proof	G. H. Johnson and W. Freeborn	Chicago, Ill	Oct. 15, 1872	132,292
Floor, Fire-proof tile	W. L. Drake	Evanston, Ill	July 1, 1873	140,352
Floor for buildings	H. M. and W. C. Smith	New York, N. Y	Aug. 10, 1869	93,646
Floor-gage	J. Fales	Cambridge, Mass	Sept. 14, 1869	94,814
Floor, Hollow tile	G. H. Johnson and B. Kreischer	New York, N. Y	Mar. 21, 1871	112,926
Floor-mat, India-rubber	T. J. Mayall	Roxbury, Mass	Dec. 24, 1861	34,001
Floor, Mosaic	G. G. Garibaldi	Buffalo, N. Y	Apr. 14, 1868	76,742
Floor, Mosaic	J. G. Kappes	New York, N. Y	Mar. 16, 1869	87,853
Floor, Mosaic	J. Stegmiller	New York, N. Y	Nov. 15, 1870	109,265
Floor-set	C. M. Shaw	Portland, Me	Nov. 2, 1869	96,355
Floor, Skating	W. L. Nelson	Saint Louis, Mo	Jan. 19, 1869	86,031
Floor, Tessellated	L. B. Hamilton	Boston, Mass	Nov. 1, 1870	108,781
Floor, Tessellated	J. F. Worth	Brooklyn, N. Y	Oct. 19, 1869	96,069
Floor-timber support	T. Voelckers	Boston, Mass	Mar. 18, 1873	136,947
Floor-warmer	C. Britain	Saint Joseph, Mich	Mar. 10, 1863	37,851
Floor, Water-proof	T. New	New York, N. Y	Apr. 18, 1871	113,787
Floors, ceilings, roofs, &c., Mode and material for constructing.	G. C. Bouziat	Vincennes, France	May 31, 1870	103,553
Floors, Clamp for laying	S. E. Parrish	New York, N. Y	Sept. 27, 1853	10,061
Floors, Construction of marquetry	B. H. Shedaker	Philadelphia, Pa	Jan. 19, 1858	19,174
Floors, Laying malting	C. Hollmann	Union Hill, N. J	May 24, 1870	103,333
Floors, Mosaic covering for	S. H. Pearce	Boston, Mass	June 15, 1869	91,364
Floors of houses, Machine for scrubbing or scouring.	S. B. Willard	Bloomfield, N. Y	Nov. 17, 1808	....
Floors, pavements, &c., Coating concrete and cement.	C. C. Hallock	Brooklyn, N. Y	Nov. 28, 1871	121,284
Floors, pavements, &c., Composition for	A. Solari	Louisville, Ky	Jan. 31, 1871	111,395
Floors, sidewalks, &c., Composition for	T. Landmann	Cincinnati, Ohio	May 11, 1869	89,933
Floors, walls, &c., Ornamental covering for	H. Whittemore	New York, N. Y	Nov. 2, 1869	96,523
Floors, Waxing	R. B. Walker	Claremont, N. H	May 12, 1868	77,784
Flooring	W. Baum	Hoboken, N. J	Feb. 8, 1870	99,522
Flooring	C. J. McAlister	Chicago, Ill	Apr. 5, 1870	101,638
Flooring-clamp	A. S. Blinn and D. W. Hewitt	Dubuque, Iowa	Aug. 14, 1866	57,078
Flooring-clamp	F. G. Lafayette	Middletown, Ohio	Jan. 19, 1869	85,939
Flooring-clamp	D. D. Mackay	Whitestone, N. Y	Sept. 1, 1868	81,803
Flooring-clamp	D. Nevin	Boulder City, Colo	Aug. 3, 1869	93,217
Flooring-clamp	S. B. Wood and W. S., R. Y. H., and A. W. Terry.	Hamburgh, Ark	Aug. 5, 1873	141,528
Flooring houses, Composition for	R. Robotham		Apr. 12, 1794	....
Flooring-sett	T. M. Richardson	Stockton, Me	Feb. 1, 1870	99,477
Flooring, wainscoting, and other purposes, Composition for.	S. Whitmarsh	Northampton, Mass	Jan. 4, 1870	98,652
Flooring, Wood-block for	F. Donbrava and J. Staib	Hartford, Conn	June 10, 1873	139,662
Floral bracket	E. M. Stigale	Philadelphia, Pa	Mar. 14, 1871	112,748
Floral ornament	H. J. Rogers	Saint Denis, Md	July 16, 1872	129,173
Flour	T. Carr	Bristol, Great Britain	Aug. 15, 1871	118,105

Index of patents issued from the United States Patent Office from 1790 *to* 1873, *inclusive*—Continued.

Invention.	Inventor.	Residence.	Date.	No.
Flour and grain elevator	H. Stanley	Saint Johnsbury, Vt	Oct. 13, 1863	40, 313
Flour and grist mill	A. J. Vandegrift	Covington, Ky	Sept. 13, 1870	107, 311
Flour and meal, Bolting	W. H. Akins	Berkshire, N. Y	Dec. 3, 1829	....
Flour and meal chest	E. M. Collis	Princeton, Ind	Aug. 27, 1872	130, 898
Flour and meal chest	T. J. Corr	Carlinville, Ill	Feb. 11, 1868	74, 200
Flour and meal chest	J. M. Dashiell	Decatur, Ill	Apr. 15, 1870	101, 438
Flour and meal for transportation, Method of preparing.	E. B. Larcher	New York, N. Y	July 11, 1865	48, 697
Flour and meal, Machine for manufacturing	O. Evans	Philadelphia, Pa	Jan. 22, 1808	....
Flour and meal, Manufacturing	O. Evans	....	Dec. 18, 1790	....
Flour and meal, Process for treating corn, &c., in the manufacture of.	W. Freudenau	Saint Louis, Mo	May 18, 1869	90, 253
Flour and middlings, Bolt for	B. F. Foreman and J. B. Speck	Upton, Pa	Apr. 1, 1873	137, 430
Flour and middlings purifier	E. N. Lacroix	Minneapolis, Minn	Sept. 9, 1873	142, 705
Flour and semolina, Manufacture of	G. A. Buchholz	London, England	Oct. 11, 1870	108, 102
Flour and semolina, Manufacture of	G. A. Buchholz	London, England	Oct. 11, 1870	108, 103
Flour, Apparatus for bolting	J. E. Madigan	Beloit, Wis	Mar. 21, 1865	46, 919
Flour, Apparatus for dressing	H. Cabanes	Bordeaux, France	Dec. 7, 1869	97, 600
Flour, &c., Apparatus for drying	J. Ballantine and A. Clark	Zanesville, Ohio	Mar. 4, 1839	1, 093
Flour-bolt	W. H. Akins	Ithaca, N. Y	Sept. 5, 1854	11, 637
Flour-bolt	R. H. Alexander	Plato, Ohio	Aug. 20, 1867	67, 836
Flour-bolt	W. H. Allen and W. Stoddard	Winona, Minn	May 11, 1869	89, 907
Flour-bolt	E. D. Auchey	Manheim, Pa	May 30, 1871	115, 412
Flour-bolt	W. Bashor	Johnson City, Tenn	Aug. 29, 1871	118, 508
Flour-bolt	E. Bateman	Frederick City, Md	June 18, 1867	65, 789
Flour-bolt	N. Baumann	Elmore, Ill	Sept. 15, 1857	18, 179
Flour-bolt	J. Beall and S. K. Shaffer	Decatur, Ill	Aug. 15, 1865	49, 365
Flour-bolt	S. H. Blossom and J. E. Huston	Buffalo, N. Y., and Hillsdale, Mich.	July 16, 1867	66, 783
Flour-bolt	J. C. Blythe	Perry, N. Y	Aug. 7, 1866	56, 887
Flour-bolt	A. T. Boon	Galesburgh, Ill	Dec. 6, 1864	45, 311
Flour-bolt	B. Boorman	Waukesha, Wis	May 14, 1867	64, 625
Flour-bolt	G. W. Brown	Jackson, Mich	Nov. 27, 1849	6, 897
Flour-bolt	J. Brown	Utica, N. Y	Dec. 19, 1865	51, 548
Flour-bolt	J. Brown	North Buffalo, N. Y	Dec. 31, 1872	134, 354
Flour-bolt	R. Buchanan	Sullivan County, Tenn	July 24, 1844	3, 680
Flour-bolt	D. T. Choat and H. Rich	Cedar Falls, Iowa	Aug. 26, 1873	142, 083
Flour-bolt	J. M. Clark	Philadelphia, Pa	July 26, 1859	24, 857
Flour-bolt	W. F. Cochrane	Springfield, Ohio	Jan. 1, 1867	60, 860
Flour-bolt	S. Cook	Adam's Basin, N. Y	July 22, 1851	8, 241
Flour-bolt	S. Cook	Adam's Basin, N. Y	Mar. 9, 1852	8, 786
Flour-bolt	J. C. Cookson	Lancaster, Pa	June 2, 1863	38, 783
Flour-bolt	M. Cosgro	Peoria, Ill	Dec. 3, 1867	71, 709
Flour-bolt	W. Craig	Uniontown, Pa	Jan. 7, 1868	73, 167
Flour-bolt	R. W. Cunningham	Chesterville, Ohio	Jan. 3, 1871	110, 6[illegible]5
Flour-bolt	E. Davies and J. Gerrard	Liverpool, Great Britain	May 21, 1872	126, 936
Flour bolt	W. Derwent, jr	Rockford, Ill	Mar. 19, 1867	62, 943
Flour-bolt	A. J. Dibble	Franklin, N. Y	Feb. 15, 1870	99, 861
Flour-bolt	E. V. Easley	Johnson City, Tenn	July 25, 1871	117, 395
Flour-bolt	J. Frickinger	Kingsville, Ohio	Oct. 11, 1870	108, 246
Flour-bolt	W. Gosshorn	Waterloo, Pa	Oct. 21, 1873	143, 821
Flour-bolt	E. Graham and I. N. Patten	Elizabethtown, Ky	Aug. 30, 1859	25, 256
Flour-bolt	H. Gross and J. B. Rumsey	Tiffin, Ohio	Apr. 2, 1867	63, 506
Flour-bolt	C. T. Hanna	Keokuk, Iowa	Dec. 27, 1870	110, 456
Flour-bolt	S. Hellebower	Alexandria, Va	July 11, 1865	48, 684
Flour-bolt	C. B. Horton	Sand Bank, N. Y	Aug. 18, 1868	81, 086
Flour-bolt	J. G. Humes	Gravios Mills, Mo	June 30, 1868	79, 354
Flour-bolt	J. E. Huston	Hillsdale, Mich	Aug. 29, 1865	49, 629
Flour-bolt	J. W. Johnson	Evansport, Ohio	Nov. 12, 1872	132, 965
Flour-bolt	J. H. Jones	Yellow Springs, Ohio	Aug. 23, 1870	106, 697
Flour-bolt	J. G. Kaufman	Nevada, Mo	Oct. 21, 1873	143, 910
Flour-bolt	E. H. Kellogg	Mukwonago, Wis	Feb. 4, 1868	73, 981
Flour-bolt	I. B. Ketchum	Rochester, Minn	Mar. 16, 1869	88, 792
Flour-bolt	I. B. Lewis	Belvidere, Ill	Apr. 16, 1872	125, 819
Flour-bolt	S. Lewis	Tiffin, Ohio	Oct. 10, 1865	50, 371
Flour-bolt	S. Lewis	Tiffin, Ohio	Nov. 26, 1867	71, 395
Flour-bolt	S. Lewis	Tiffin, Ohio	June 4, 1872	127, 617
Flour-bolt	J. Mallin	Chicago, Ill	Oct. 4, 1870	107, 935
Flour-bolt	D. Marsh	Fairfield, Conn	May 25, 1852	8, 970
Flour-bolt	S. G. McMurtry	West Urbana, Ill	Feb. 9, 1858	19, 303
Flour-bolt	S. C. Mendenhall	Richmond, Ind	Feb. 5, 1856	14, 199
Flour-bolt	S. C. Mendenhall and I. Conner	Richmond, Ind	July 29, 1856	15, 455
Flour-bolt	R. S. Mitchell and G. Z. Kessinger.	Elizabeth, Ind	May 11, 1869	90, 011
Flour-bolt	R. Mohler and J. Becker	Lancaster County, Pa	Sept. 8, 1863	39, 826
Flour-bolt	T. G. Morgan	Murfreesborough, Tenn	Oct. 10, 1871	119, 783
Flour-bolt	E. and A. H. Nordyke	Richmond, Ind	July 5, 1859	24, 656
Flour-bolt	D. N. M. Peregoy	Elizabethtown, Tenn	May 16, 1871	114, 966
Flour-bolt	H. N. Peterson	Peoria, Ill	Dec. 19, 1871	122, 054
Flour-bolt	J. M. Reed and W. B. Willis	Charlestown, Va	Jan. 29, 1850	7, 063
Flour-bolt	H. Reichert	Shippensburgh, Pa	July 22, 1862	35, 953
Flour-bolt	F. Bender	Etchells, England	Feb. 4, 1873	135, 588
Flour-bolt	A. N. Shultz	Sabillasville, Md	Sept. 1, 1868	81, 831
Flour-bolt	J. Skinner	Hadley, Mich	Aug. 9, 1870	106, 223
Flour-bolt	C. B. Slater	Blanchester, Ohio	Dec. 10, 1872	133, 805
Flour-bolt	A. R. Smith	Delaware, Ohio	Nov. 27, 1866	60, 073
Flour-bolt	G. T. and A. Smith	Minneapolis, Minn	Feb. 4, 1873	135, 496
Flour-bolt	J. C. Smith	Zanesfield, Ohio	Aug. 8, 1871	117, 938
Flour-bolt	S. A. Smith	Philadelphia, Pa	Mar. 10, 1868	75, 307
Flour-bolt	R. H. St. John	Bellefontaine, Ohio	Dec. 5, 1871	121, 681
Flour-bolt	F. S. Thayer	Troy, N. Y	Apr. 11, 1865	47, 233
Flour-bolt	T. M. Walker	Bellefontaine, Ohio	Mar. 28, 1871	113, 226
Flour-bolt	J. W. Walters	Tiffin, Ohio	May 7, 1867	64, 603
Flour-bolt	J. Wernz	Epolzheim, Bavaria	Oct. 1, 1872	131, 919
Flour-bolt	J. Wister	Greencastle, Pa	Aug. 26, 1862	36, 317
Flour-bolt and bran-duster	A. Burbank	Rochester, N. Y	Mar. 20, 1866	53, 268
Flour bolt and reel	J. R. Bradfield	Ada, Mich	Apr. 25, 1871	113, 972
Flour-bolt as applied to grinding-mills	S. E. Fitch and T. Sharp	Greenbush, N. Y	Jan. 13, 1857	16, 383

Index of patents issued from the United States Patent Office from 1790 *to* 1873, *inclusive*—Continued.

Invention.	Inventor.	Residence.	Date.	No.
Flour-bolt attachment	R. Turner	Rochester, N. Y	July 19, 1870	105, 618
Flour-bolt feeder	J. Boehm	Peru, Ohio	June 11, 1872	127, 673
Flour-bolt feeder	J. Cornwell	Kalamazoo, Mich	Nov. 12, 1867	70, 806
Flour-bolt feeder	J. Mallin	Chicago, Ill	June 29, 1869	92, 070
Flour-bolt feeder	E. J. Weaver	Sterling, Ill	Oct. 18, 1870	108, 417
Flour-bolt knocker	J. W. Bradley	Rocheport, Mo	July 5, 1870	105, 034
Flour-bolt knocker	E. B. Lowe	Bellefontaine, Ohio	Apr. 30, 1872	126, 312
Flour-bolt screen	D. Landis	Lancaster, Pa	Oct. 23, 1860	30, 483
Flour-bolt vibrator	C. E. Canan	Coldwater, Mich	Dec. 5, 1871	121, 585
Flour-bolt, Wire-cloth	F. B. Hunt and E. Nordyke	Richmond, Ind	Feb 6, 1855	12, 349
Flour-bolt, Feeding	S. Taggart	Indianapolis, Ind	Feb. 20, 1855	12, 422
Flour, Bolting	E. Bradfield	Rochester, N. Y	Sept. 15, 1846	4, 758
Flour, Bolting	J. H. Burk and T. W. Trussell.	New Market, Va	Jan. 30, 1872	123, 082
Flour-bolting	W. F. Cochrane	Springfield, Ohio	Jan. 6, 1863	37, 317
Flour-bolting	W. F. Cochrane	Springfield, Ohio	Jan. 6, 1863	37, 318
Flour-bolting	W. F. Cochrane	Springfield, Ohio	Jan. 6, 1863	37, 319
Flour-bolting	W. F. Cochrane	Springfield, Ohio	Jan. 6, 1863	37, 320
Flour-bolting	W. F. Cochrane	Springfield, Ohio	Jan. 6, 1863	37, 321
Flour-bolting	D. Geib	Mifflintown, Pa	Jan. 5, 1858	19, 024
Flour, Bolting	E. S. Snyder	Charlestown, Va	May 2, 1846	4, 490
Flour, &c., Bolting	J. Wright	Saint Louis, Mo	Feb. 23, 1864	47, 737
Flour bolting and dressing machine	J. Hean	Annville, Pa	Feb. 28, 1842	2, 471
Flour-bolting apparatus	L. Fagin and H. C. Hayman	Cincinnati, Ohio	Apr. 8, 1851	8, 025
Flour-bolting apparatus	L. C. A. Schmidt	Tiffin, Ohio	May 31, 1870	103, 784
Flour-bolting apparatus	D. Speck	Weaverton, Md	July 16, 1872	129, 611
Flour-bolting device	W. Halderman	Freeport, Ill	Aug. 7, 1860	29, 483
Flour-bolting machine	M. H. Collins	Chelsea, Mass	Oct. 25, 1859	25, 884
Flour-bolting machine	J. C. Cookson	Lancaster, Pa	Dec. 12, 1871	121, 708
Flour-bolting machinery	R. Mauck	Honeyville, Va	Dec. 26, 1845	4, 329
Flour-bolting machinery	B. D. Sanders	Halliday's Cove, Va	Aug. 24, 1858	21, 277
Flour-bolting process	L. G. Binkley	Baughman, Ohio	June 27, 1871	116, 260
Flour-bolting reel	F. B. Lewis	Tiffin, Ohio	May 30, 1871	115, 331
Flour-bolting reel	D. Shamp	Perry, N. Y	May 16, 1871	114, 980
Flour-bolting reel	A. L. Williams	Orth, Ind	May 10, 1870	103, 000
Flour-bolting reel	A. L. Williams	Orth, Ind	Jan. 24, 1871	111, 292
Flour-box	F. Monroe	Charlestown, Mass	July 16, 1867	66, 867
Flour by means of heated air, Kiln-drying	N. Tyson	Baltimore, Md	Aug. 3, 1831	....
Flour-chest	M. W. Hill	New York, N. Y	Aug. 15, 1865	49, 404
Flour-chest	I. R. Shank	Buffalo, Va	July 24, 1860	29, 319
Flour-chest and cupboard combined	T. J. Corr	Bloomington, Ill	Oct. 31, 1871	120, 496
Flour-cooler	H. B. Allis	Little Rock, Ark	Nov. 9, 1858	22, 006
Flour-cooler	W. W. Goff	Avoca, N. Y	Aug. 3, 1869	93, 297
Flour-cooler	Hebard, Catlin & Abell	Pomfret, N. Y	May 22, 1835	....
Flour-cooler	P. Johnson	Wauconda, Ill	Apr. 27, 1869	89, 485
Flour-cooler	J. Pope	Windham, Me	Feb. 5, 1836	....
Flour-cooler	J. S. Reynolds	Wauconda, Ill	Dec. 8, 1868	84, 842
Flour-cooler	A. and P. Staffer	Salt Creek, Ind	June 15, 1869	91, 381
Flour, Cooling and drying	G. B. Willison	Elizabeth, Pa	July 3, 1855	13, 192
Flour cooling and drying machine	S. N. Park and J. A. Staats	Somerville, N. J	May 28, 1861	32, 433
Flour dipper, measurer, and sifter	G. C. Carver	Roxbury, Mass	May 22, 1866	54, 857
Flour-dispenser	D. L. Johnson	Yorkville, Mich	Oct. 13, 1868	82, 958
Flour-dredge	E. A. Goodes	Philadelphia, Pa	Sept. 1, 1868	81, 770
Flour, Drying	H. Ely	Rochester, N. Y	June 6, 1854	11, 046
Flour-drying reel	W. H. Dole and D. R. Frazer	Chicago, Ill	June 9, 1863	38, 816
Flour, Elevating, cooling, and conveying	J. White and J. Bundy	Barnesville, Ohio	Dec. 10, 1850	7, 828
Flour, feed, and grain elevator	J. Rancy	Newcastle, Pa	May 5, 1868	77, 654
Flour, Filling barrels with	B. Bowman and A. Kauffman	Franklin County, Pa	Nov. 7, 1848	5, 907
Flour for bread-making, Preparation of	H. Jones	Bristol, Great Britain	May 1, 1849	6, 418
Flour for confectionery, &c., Preparing	W. G. Dean	Brooklyn, N. Y	Apr. 18, 1871	113, 859
Flour for exportation, Preserving	E. Hord and B. Browning	Fleming County, Ky	Mar. 12, 1825	....
Flour from becoming sour, Preserving	W. Wood, jr	Saint Clairsville, Ohio	Nov. 4, 1824	....
Flour from bran, Machine for separating	W. W. Huntley and A. Babcock	Silver Creek, N. Y	Apr. 12, 1870	101, 736
Flour from bran, &c., Machinery for separating	E. and J. M. Clark	Lancaster, Pa	Apr. 17, 1849	6, 335
Flour from bran, Machinery for separating	I. Frost and J. Monroe	Albion, Mich	Feb. 27, 1849	6, 148
Flour from bran, Machinery for separating	J. Johnston	Wilmington, Del	Apr. 17, 1849	6, 366
Flour, &c., Hopper-filler for bolting	A. Hershe	Lancaster, Pa	Jan. 15, 1814	....
Flour in barrels, Machine for packing	J. Bartholomew	Union, N. Y	Nov. 1, 1859	25, 940
Flour in casks, &c., Machine for packing	J. Hinman	Hartley Township, Pa	Mar. 2, 1835	....
Flour, Machine for manufacture of	T. Carr	Bristol, Great Britain	Nov. 25, 1873	144, 830
Flour, Machine for preparing	L. S. Chichester	Brooklyn, N. Y	Jan. 7, 1873	134, 513
Flour, Machinery for dressing	C. Learned and S. Hughes	Indianapolis, Ind	Nov. 27, 1849	6, 932
Flour-making	G. Motley	Rochester, N. Y	Mar. 28, 1871	113, 079
Flour, Manner of mixing the middlings with the chops in the process of making.	A. D. Worman	Fredericktown, Md	July 23, 1841	2, 189
Flour, Manufacture of	L. G. Binkly	Baughman, Ohio	Feb. 6, 1872	123, 446
Flour, Manufacture of	C. Colgate	Lancaster, Ohio	Mar. 31, 1863	38, 033
Flour, Manufacture of	W. Freudenau	Saint Louis, Mo	Feb. 1, 1870	99, 427
Flour, Manufacture of	E. S. Hutchinson	Baltimore, Md	Feb. 21, 1871	112, 046
Flour, Manufacture of corn	C. Jones and W. Standing	De Soto, Ill	Jan. 5, 1869	85, 592
Flour, Manufacturing	D. R. Clem	Edinburgh, Va	Oct. 19, 1869	95, 987
Flour, Manufacturing	J. Rich	Madison County, New York	Jan. 27, 1812	....
Flour, meal, and other farinaceous substances, Process and apparatus for treating.	J. J. Ridge	St. John's, Southwark, England.	Aug. 31, 1869	94, 341
Flour, meal, &c., Treating cereals for the manufacture of.	E. Weise	Basle, Switzerland	Dec. 22, 1868	85, 261
Flour, Method of dressing	B. Barter	Faribault, Minn	Apr. 9, 1872	125, 518
Flour-mill	W. B. Allen	Winona, Minn	Dec. 10, 1872	133, 819
Flour-mill	J. M. Clark	Philadelphia, Pa	Jan. 10, 1860	26, 751
Flour-mill	H. Cutler	Ashland, Mass	June 22, 1869	91, 612
Flour-mill	J. Dean	New Baltimore, N. Y	June 3, 1873	139, 553
Flour-mill	J. B. Gendebien and A. Honyet.	Brussels, Belgium	Jan. 5, 1847	4, 920
Flour-mill	R. M. Thomas	Brady, Pa	Apr. 23, 1872	126, 101
Flour-mill bran-duster	J. E. Weaver	Nether Providence Township, Pa.	Sept. 28, 1869	95, 293
Flour-mill, Cutting	J. Burdge	Cincinnati, Ohio	June 10, 1856	15, 060
Flour-mill, Friction-bolt	L. S. Reynolds	Indianapolis, Ind	Mar. 29, 1859	23, 394
Flour-mill ventilator	C. Moegling	Milwaukee, Wis	Dec. 17, 1867	72, 317
Flour-mills, Hopper-boy for	W. F. Cochrane	Springfield, Ohio	Sept. 30, 1862	36, 583

Index of patents issued from the United States Patent Office from 1790 *to* 1873, *inclusive*—Continued.

Invention.	Inventor.	Residence.	Date.	No.
Flour, &c., mixing-machine	J. B. Peterson	Brooklyn, E. D., N. Y	June 30, 1868	79, 386
Flour-packer	J. Beall	Berlin, Ill	May 19, 1863	38, 546
Flour-packer	I. Cook	Saint Louis, Mo	Apr. 26, 1864	42, 463
Flour-packer	I. Cook	Saint Louis, Mo	Sept. 12, 1865	49, 859
Flour-packer	I. Cook	Saint Louis, Mo	May 29, 1866	55, 063
Flour-packer	C. Custer	Philadelphia, Pa	June 23, 1868	79, 211
Flour-packer	S. Hewit	Seneca Falls Village, N. Y	Apr. 28, 1868	77, 374
Flour-packer	N. Kinman	Buffalo, N. Y	Oct. 30, 1849	6, 830
Flour-packer	N. Kinman	Lewiston, N. Y	Mar. 23, 1852	8, 826
Flour-packer	J. Musser	Frizellburgh, Md	June 26, 1866	55, 885
Flour-packer	A. H. Nordyke	Richmond, Ind	Dec. 13, 1870	110, 155
Flour-packer	O. Place	Brooklyn, N. Y	July 24, 1866	56, 605
Flour-packer	S. Taggart	Indianapolis, Ind	Dec. 30, 1873	146, 107
Flour-packer	L. W. Teeter	Hagerstown, Ind	Nov. 20, 1866	59, 872
Flour-packer	C. E. Timmerman	Frederick, Md	Aug. 13, 1872	130, 461
Flour-packer	G. A. Warner	Portland, Oreg	Sept. 25, 1866	58, 325
Flour packing and pressing machine	O. Jewell	Rochester, N. Y	Mar. 30, 1837	156
Flour-packing machine	J. Banta, jr	Utica, N. Y	Aug. 2, 1839	1, 271
Flour-packing machine	H. A. Barnard	Moline, Ill	July 30, 1867	67, 249
Flour-packing machine	W. Bashoe	Johnson City, Tenn	June 28, 1870	104, 817
Flour-packing machine	B. F. Bashor	Carter's Depot, Tenn	Aug. 30, 1870	106, 912
Flour-packing machine	A. Brown	Mifflinville, Pa	Apr. 29, 1862	35, 075
Flour-packing machine	S. A. Clapp	Hamilton, Ill	June 5, 1860	28, 561
Flour-packing machine	J. Mattison	Oswego, N. Y	Mar. 9, 1858	19, 572
Flour, Preparation of	T. Byrne	Baton Rouge, La	Sept. 4, 1860	29, 859
Flour-pressing machine	S. Hathaway	Massillon, Ohio	Feb. 13, 1832	....
Flour, Process of manufacturing middlings	G. T. Smith	Minneapolis, Minn	Apr. 1, 1873	137, 495
Flour-sack	J. M. Hurd	Auburn, N. Y	Dec. 26, 1865	51, 722
Flour-sack packer, Hand	J. Detweiler	West Liberty, Ohio	Jan. 23, 1872	123, 000
Flour-sacks, Apparatus for filling	J. C. Philbrook	East Sanbornton, N. H	July 29, 1862	36, 023
Flour-sacks, Machine for making	J. M. Hurd	Auburn, N. Y	Aug. 9, 1864	43, 773
Flour-sacker	C. B. Horton	Sand Bank, N. Y	Mar. 16, 1869	87, 930
Flour, Self-raising	W. C. Hughes	Scio, Mich	Feb. 25, 1868	74, 824
Flour-separator	S. Hughes	Hamilton, Ohio	Apr. 17, 1860	27, 907
Flour-separating machine, Power vibrating	B. Calver	Glastonbury, Conn	Oct. 6, 1830	....
Flour, starch, and spirit from wheat, &c., Making	E. Perkins	Shrewsbury, N. J	Feb. 26, 1811	....
Flour, Stone facing to admit cool air to	R. C. Stephens	Hackettstown, N. J	Feb. 18, 1834	....
Flour, Sweet-potato	C. K. Marshall	New Orleans, La	June 22, 1869	91, 554
Flour, Worm for cooling	J. Smelzer	Adams County, Pa	May 6, 1813	....
Flouring and bolting	J. Stouffer, P. Brough, and J. W. Barr.	Chambersburgh, Pa	July 11, 1854	11, 312
Flouring and grist mill	E. Clark	Lancaster, Pa	Jan. 14, 1862	34, 129
Flouring and grist mills, Alarm-indicator for	E. Clark	Lancaster, Pa	Jan. 14, 1862	34, 130
Flouring and grist mills, Mode of preventing the destruction of bolting-cloth in.	W. McKain	Conoy Township, Pa	Dec. 24, 1861	34, 002
Flouring-apparatus	J. M. Clark	Lancaster, Pa	May 13, 1851	8, 089
Flouring-mill	W. Bowman	Craig's Mills, Va	May 10, 1870	103, 003
Flouring-mill	R. J. Brown	Perry, Pa	Aug. 3, 1858	21, 062
Flouring-mill	E. Clark	Lancaster, Pa	Jan. 5, 1858	19, 016
Flouring-mill	E. Clark	Lancaster, Pa	May 25, 1858	20, 329
Flouring-mill	E. and J. M. Clark	Lancaster, Pa	June 6, 1854	11, 015
Flouring-mill	T. Crane	Fort Atkinson, Wis	Jan. 22, 1856	14, 132
Flouring-mill	J. Durling	Sparta, N. J	Apr. 21, 1842	2, 579
Flouring-mill	A. F. Menefee	Rappahannock County, Va	Mar. 12, 1850	7, 174
Flouring-mill	C. Rands	Peoria, Ill	May 25, 1858	20, 370
Flouring-mill	J. Thompson	Ashtabula, Ohio	July 7, 1830	....
Flouring-mill	D. S. Wagener	Penn Yan, N. Y	Sept. 25, 1855	13, 610
Flouring-mill	J. Weis	Bordentown, N. J	Jan. 29, 1856	14, 179
Flouring-mill	S. Wolff	Vicksburgh, Miss	July 20, 1858	20, 972
Flouring-mill	J. L. Yule	New Orleans, La	Jan. 9, 1855	12, 223
Flouring-mill bolt	S. Godfrey	Peoria, Ill	Oct. 17, 1865	50, 466
Flouring-mill bolt	S. Godfrey	Peoria, Ill	Jan. 9, 1866	51, 939
Flouring-mill cleaning-bolt	W. Cann	Black Rock, N. Y	June 6, 1854	11, 039
Flouring-mills, Distributing-apparatus in	A. T. Clark	Lancaster, Pa	June 30, 1857	17, 667
Flouring-mills, Distributing-apparatus in	J. M. Clarke	Lancaster, Pa	Nov. 10, 1857	18, 574
Flouring, Process of	D. P. Bonnell	Tecumseh, Mich	Aug. 14, 1849	6, 648
Flower, Artificial	C. A. Schaller	Philadelphia, Pa	Sept. 2, 1873	142, 353
Flower-bracket	W. Hichborn	Charlestown, Mass	July 4, 1871	116, 708
Flower-casket	J. M. Hess	Philadelphia, Pa	Oct. 25, 1870	108, 592
Flower-casket	J. M. Hess	Philadelphia, Pa	Mar. 5, 1872	124, 207
Flower-frame	C. Hochbrunn	New York, N. Y	June 23, 1868	79, 122
Flower-pot	E. Baldwin	Washington, D. C	July 16, 1872	129, 451
Flower-pot	O. Eberhardt	Brooklyn, N. Y	Feb. 5, 1861	31, 306
Flower-pot	M. B. Gould	Buffalo, N. Y	Jan. 28, 1873	135, 271
Flower-pot	T. Griffin	Roxbury, Mass	July 30, 1861	32, 942
Flower-pot	J. Hively	Dayton, Ohio	Jan. 17, 1860	26, 849
Flower-pot	A. D. Judd	New Haven, Conn	Sept. 26, 1871	119, 272
Flower pot	M. Ludlum	Williston, Vt	Mar. 1, 1870	100, 300
Flower-pot	M. Ludlum	Middlebury, Vt	July 30, 1872	129, 972
Flower-pot	T. J. Mayall	Roxbury, Mass	Sept. 3, 1861	33, 205
Flower-pot	C. R. Penfield	Lockport, N. Y	Apr. 26, 1870	102, 311
Flower-pot	W. H. Pugh	Chicago, Ill	Oct. 15, 1872	132, 178
Flower-pot	B. W. Putnam	Boston, Mass	Oct. 26, 1869	96, 144
Flower-pot	C. L. Steele	Boston, Mass	Sept. 20, 1870	107, 558
Flower-pot	F. C. A. Von Levetzow	Kiel, Prussia	Apr. 23, 1872	126, 112
Flower-pot	E. Whitman	Fitchburgh, Mass	Sept. 8, 1868	82, 052
Flower pot and tub	J. Booher	Dayton, Ohio	Mar. 12, 1867	62, 728
Flower-pot bracket	M. D. Jones	Boston, Mass	Jan. 14, 1873	134, 751
Flower-pot support	T. Prince	Roxbury, Mass	Jan. 23, 1866	52, 200
Flower pot, vase, and basket	T. McClunie	Hartford, Conn	Sept. 6, 1870	107, 073
Flower-pots and other pottery, Machine for molding.	F. Herrmann	Milwaukee, Wis	June 18, 1872	128, 039
Flower-pots, Green-glaze for	J. E. Brooks	Yarmouth, Me	Mar. 21, 1871	112, 776
Flower-pots, Hook for hanging	I. A. Lovejoy	Lynn, Mass	May 27, 1873	139, 254
Flower-pots, Machine for cleaning	S. W. Curtis	Stoughton, Mass	July 25, 1865	48, 912
Flower-pots or vases for plants, &c., Construction of.	J. Adams	Boston, Mass	Sept. 3, 1840	1, 761
Flower-shears	J. W. Barbour	Winooski Falls, Vt	Oct. 11, 1870	108, 091

Index of patents issued from the United States Patent Office from 1790 to 1873, inclusive—Continued.

Invention.	Inventor.	Residence.	Date.	No.
Flower-stand	E. T. Cobb	Conway, Mass	Sept. 12, 1871	118, 844
Flower-stand	E. D. Castelow	Meriden, Conn	Feb. 7, 1871	111, 608
Flower-stand	H. J. Coster	Chicago, Ill	July 17, 1860	29, 145
Flower-stand	J. Crawford	Roxbury, Mass	Dec. 2, 1862	37, 070
Flower-stand	A. C. Dakin	Clinton, Mass	Feb. 11, 1873	135, 696
Flower-stand	G. Erkson	Brooklyn, N. Y	Mar. 28, 1871	113, 035
Flower-stand	C. J. Hauck	Williamsburgh, N. Y	Jan. 7, 1868	73, 005
Flower-stand	H. H. Kendrick	Fulton, N. Y	Nov. 8, 1870	109, 130
Flower-stand	C. T. Lee	Taunton, Mass	June 27, 1871	116, 459
Flower-stand	P. B. Sheldon	Prattsburgh, N. Y	May 9, 1865	47, 664
Flower stand and holder, Metallic	H. Miller	Cranston, R. I	July 6, 1869	92, 203
Flower-stand f r windows	F. W. Test	Chicago, Ill	Dec. 19, 1871	121, 972
Flower-stand, Revolving	T. Leslie	Brooklyn, N. Y	Oct. 17, 1871	120, 078
Flowers and fruit, Composition for wax	A. A. Hinkley	Boston, Mass	Feb. 16, 1869	86, 921
Flowers, Artificial stem for cut	J. B. Craig	Perrysville, Pa	Nov. 11, 1873	144, 446
Flowers, Case for preserving	E. M. Stigale	Philadelphia, Pa	Nov. 24, 1868	84, 445
Flowers, Compound for the manufacture of wax	M. J. McColl	Chicago, Ill	Mar. 8, 1870	100, 540
Flowers, Cutting wax for artificial	M. J. McColl	Chicago, Ill	Feb. 15, 1870	99 928
Flowers, Machine for branching artificial	A. Giraudat	New York, N. Y	Nov. 9, 1869	96, 582
Flowers, Manufacture of artificial	O. E. Fillion	Paris, France	May 10, 1870	102, 798
Flowers, Manufacture of artificial	C. E. Howard	San Gabriel, Cal	Mar. 1, 1870	100, 293
Flowers, Manufacture of artificial	C. C. Nichols	Providence, R. I	Oct. 17, 1848	5, 867
Flowers, Manufacture of artificial and preservation of natural.	E. S. Harris	Philadelphia, Pa	Nov. 9, 1869	96, 587
Flowers, Preserving natural	P. T. Vining	Springfield, Mass	June 27, 1871	116, 375
Flowers, Process for preserving and restoring natural.	A. J. Knox	Boston, Mass	Feb. 7, 1865	46, 247
Flowers, Process of bleaching, &c., dried natural	J. W. and M. L. Ware	Philadelphia, Pa	Jan. 7, 1873	134, 714
Flowers, &c., Transplanting	E. G. Nichols	Beaufort, S. C	Nov. 5, 1867	70, 457
Flue	N. Fouché	New Orleans, La	Oct. 4, 1870	108, 014
Flue and setting of open boilers	J. Chilcott	Brooklyn, N. Y	Jan. 9, 1866	51, 922
Flue-block	J. Binns	Oskaloosa, Iowa	June 9, 1868	78, 717
Flue-bottom of steam-boilers, Adjustable	A. M. Sprague	Mobile, Ala	May 9, 1854	18, 897
Flue-brazier, Portable upright	W. Grunert and G. E. Bingham	Milwaukee, Wis	Mar. 24, 1868	75, 899
Flue-cleaner	N. W. Wheeler	Brooklyn, N. Y	Nov. 28, 1865	51, 249
Flue-cleaner, Revolving	G. E. Bingham	Milwaukee, Wis	Dec. 4, 1866	60, 128
Flue-cleaner, Steam	W. Doty	Circleville, Ohio	Aug. 29, 1871	118, 596
Flue-contractor and chimney-valve for fire-places and grates.	H. Batchelder	Beverly, Mass	Jan. 8, 1842	2, 418
Flue-expander	I. S. Hamilton	Hamilton, Ohio	Dec. 5, 1871	121, 514
Flue for buildings	E. T. Gould	Mont Clair, N. J	July 29, 1873	141, 219
Flue-stopper	H. Smith	Southington, Conn	May 25, 1869	90, 401
Flues and dampers of cooking-apparatus, Arrangement of.	J. A. Elder and W. J. Thorn	Westbrook, Me., and Hollister, Mass.	Dec. 4, 1855	13, 868
Flues, Construction of	R. F. O'Brien	Boonville, Mo	May 15, 1860	28, 295
Fluid and mode of generating the same, Imponderable.	M. Ziegler	Mulhouse, France	Jan. 1, 1867	60, 986
Fluid, Burning	E. Howe	Brooklyn, N. Y	Sept. 24, 1850	7, 667
Fluid-can	J. Clements	Ann Arbor, Mich	Aug. 12, 1862	36, 190
Fluid, Compound illuminating	N. A. Dyar and J. F. Augustus	Medford and Boston, Mass	Sept. 6, 1859	25, 302
Fluid-distributing apparatus	J. W. Middleton	Philadelphia, Pa	Sept. 12, 1854	11, 675
Fluid-elevator, Rotary	S. P. Ruggles	Boston, Mass	July 7, 1868	79, 781
Fluid-evaporator	C. S. Wheeler	Flowerfield, Mich	Mar. 8, 1859	23, 209
Fluid-forcing apparatus	T. W. Malone	Mason City, W. Va	Sept. 5, 1871	118, 776
Fluid-gate or faucet	J. W. Smith	Hartford, Conn	Mar. 10, 1857	16, 810
Fluid-indicator	J. Cordnan	Brooklyn, N. Y	Mar. 31, 1868	76, 166
Fluid-meter	L. Allen	New York, N. Y	Mar. 10, 1868	75, 342
Flui -meter	N. Aubin	Albany, N. Y	July 8, 1862	35, 806
Fluid-meter	E. J. Baker	Philadelphia, Pa	Apr. 19, 1864	42, 337
Fluid-meter	C. W. Baldwin	Boston, Mass	May 25, 1869	90, 479
Fluid-meter	P. Ball and B. Fitts	Worcester, Mass	July 20, 1869	92, 691
Fluid-meter	S. J. Burr	Brooklyn, N. Y	Apr. 21, 1857	17, 127
Fluid-meter	L. F. Buschmann	New York, N. Y	Jan. 17, 1871	111, 040
Fluid-meter	E. A. Chameroy	Paris, France	Dec. 1, 1868	84, 476
Fluid-meter	J. Cochrane	New York, N. Y	Mar. 31, 1857	16, 945
Fluid-meter	R. Crewzbaur	Williamsburgh, N. Y	Jan. 24, 1871	111, 179
Fluid-meter	H. A. Desper	Worcester, Mass	Nov. 18, 1873	144, 747
Fluid-meter	J. Dooling	Boston, Mass	May 14, 1872	126, 626
Fluid-meter	J. H. A. Gericke	Hoboken, N. J	Apr. 16, 1872	125, 805
Fluid-meter	W. Hamilton	Toronto, Canada	Oct. 26, 1869	96, 105
Fluid-meter	J. Harris	Boston, Mass	Jan. 5, 1869	85, 656
Fluid-meter	A. Heaton	Bridgeton, Conn	Apr. 6, 1869	88, 709
Fluid meter	H. B. Herbert	New York, N. Y	Aug. 1, 1871	117, 628
Fluid-meter	J. O. Johnson	New York, N. Y	May 6, 1873	138, 657
Fluid-meter	H. B. Leach	Boston, Mass	Feb. 23, 1869	87, 104
Fluid-meter	H. B. Leach	Boston, Mass	Nov. 23, 1869	97, 097
Fluid-meter	W. B. Leonard	New York, N. Y	Nov. 1, 1853	10, 198
Fluid-meter	W. H. Lindsay	New York, N. Y	Feb. 20, 1849	6, 130
Fluid-meter, &c	W. H. Lindsay	New York, N. Y	June 22, 1852	9, 060
Fluid-meter	J. R. Maxwell	Cincinnati, Ohio	June 2, 1857	17, 443
Fluid-meter	C. Moore	New York, N. Y	June 29, 1869	92, 082
Fluid-meter	C. Moore	New York, N. Y	Jan. 24, 1871	111, 233
Fluid-me er	C. E. Moore	Elizabethport, N. J	Apr. 28, 1868	77, 307
Fluid meter	W. Park	Norwich, Conn	Aug. 11, 1868	80, 996
Fluid-meter	W. C. Perrine	New York, N. Y	May 4, 1858	20, 169
Fluid-meter	T. Poore	Scranton, Pa	May 18, 1869	90, 123
Fluid-meter	J. Powers and J. B. Van Deusen.	New York, N. Y	Mar. 17, 1868	75, 644
Fluid-meter	H. C. Sergeant	Newark, N. J	May 24, 1870	103, 509
Fluid-meter	J. Sheffield	Williamson, N. Y	Nov. 3, 1863	40, 504
Fluid-meter	J. Sheffield	Buffalo, N. Y	Feb. 23, 1869	87, 118
Fluid-meter	G. Sickles	Boston, Mass	Feb. 16, 1869	86, 949
Fluid-meter.	C. W. Siemens	London, England	Dec. 14, 1858	22, 315
Fluid-meter	D. B. Spooner	Syracuse, N. Y	Sept. 5, 1871	118, 755
Fluid-meter	C. Stein	Philadelphia, Pa	Mar. 10, 1868	75, 313
Fluid-meter	J. Taggart	Roxbury, Mass	May 15, 1855	12, 887
Fluid-meter	J. B. Van Deusen	New York, N. Y	June 29, 1869	91, 989
Fluid-meter	F. Wagner	New York, N. Y	June 29, 1869	91, 991

Index of patents issued from the United States Patent Office from 1790 *to* 1873, *inclusive*—Continued.

Invention.	Inventor.	Residence.	Date.	No.
Fluid-meter	F. Wagner	New York, N. Y	Nov. 15, 1870	109, 359
Fluid-meter	E. D. Weatherbee	Worcester, Mass	July 20, 1858	20, 979
Fluid meter	J. W. Weller	Cleveland, Ohio	Feb. 25, 1868	74, 778
Fluid-meter, Diaphragm	J. H. Darlington and W. Piper	New York, N. Y	Nov. 11, 1856	16, 049
Fluid-meter, Diaphragm	R. L. Hawes	Worcester, Mass	Apr. 15, 1856	14, 692
Fluid-meters by hand, Device for operating	W. Mason	Warren, Mass	Dec. 23, 1856	16, 284
Fluid-meters, Propeller-wheel for	W. Van Auden	Poughkeepsie, N. Y	Apr. 9, 1872	125, 506
Fluid-motor, Rotary	H. Q. Hawley	Albany, N. Y	July 1, 1873	140, 367
Fluid-motor, Rotary	H. Q. Hawley and E. Anthony	Albany, N. Y	July 30, 1872	129, 943
Fluid or grain elevator	R. Christy	Jefferson County, Va	Nov. 21, 1812	....
Fluid-pressure regulator	W. J. Fay and T. A. Cairns	Denver, Colo	July 16, 1872	129, 015
Fluid-regulator	W. A. Simonds	Boston, Mass	May 1, 1866	54, 424
Fluids, Apparatus for compressing elastic	J. Jameson	Gateshead, England	Feb. 15, 1859	22, 956
Fluids, Apparatus for expanding and compressing elastic.	J. Jameson	Gateshead, England	Dec. 11, 1860	30, 924
Fluids, Apparatus for raising	J. Parker	Camberwell, Great Britain	Nov. 19, 1867	71, 050
Fluids, Apparatus for raising and forcing	M. Alden	Philadelphia, Pa	Feb. 1, 1859	22, 773
Fluids, Cooling	W. Thornton	Washington, D. C	July 31, 1827	....
Fluids, Gage for measuring the pressure of	V. Beaumont	New York, N. Y	June 14, 1859	24, 365
Fluids, Machine for raising or projecting	D. Tomlinson	Brookfield, Conn	May 27, 1805	....
Fluids, Pipe for transmission of	E. P. Vaux	Washington, D. C	Oct. 15, 1867	69, 869
Fluids, Retention and discharge of	B. Seymour	Westmoreland, N. Y	Nov. 10, 1827	....
Fluids under pressure, Device for controlling	J. Atkins	Washington, D. C	Mar. 30, 1869	88, 431
Flush-bolt	W. B. Carness	Roxbury, Mass	May 22, 1860	28, 346
Flush-bolt	J. M. Hopkins	New York, N. Y	May 1, 1866	54, 350
Flush-bolt	C. E. Lattin	Birmingham, Conn	Oct. 29, 1867	70, 340
Flute	T. Berteling	New York, N. Y	Apr. 7, 1868	76, 389
Flute	C. G. Christman	New York, N. Y	Dec. 25, 1849	6, 968
Flute, &c	S. C. Goodsell	New Haven, Conn	Sept. 11, 1866	58, 022
Flute	J. Pfaff	Philadelphia, Pa	Apr. 14, 1857	17, 054
Flute	O. J. C. Wardrum	Chicago, Ill	Sept. 14, 1869	94, 795
Flute, German	W. Schaffer	New York, N. Y	June 6, 1814	....
Fluted cutters, Machine for grinding cylindrical	A. G. Coes	Worcester, Mass	Oct. 19, 1869	95, 988
Fluted rollers, Machinery for making	W. Weild	Manchester, Great Britain	Nov. 14, 1865	50, 997
Fluting and plaiting machine	M. E. Wilson and A. J. Perry	Galesburgh, Ill	June 24, 1873	140, 331
Fluting and puffing iron	A. M. Thorne	Syracuse, N. Y	Feb. 9, 1869	86, 711
Fluting and quilling, Apparatus for	G. R. Houghton	Flint, Mich	Aug. 31, 1869	94, 211
Fluting and sad iron	C. Hyatt	Buffalo, N. Y	Aug. 30, 1870	106, 828
Fluting and sad iron	M. H. Knapp	Bay City, Mich	Aug. 2, 1870	105, 953
Fluting and sad iron, Combined	A. S. Mann	Pittsburgh, Pa	Oct. 29, 1872	132, 590
Fluting-apparatus	G. B. Arnold, A. H. Price, and A. S. Urner.	New York, N. Y	July 24, 1860	29, 337
Fluting-apparatus	F. B. Perkins	Elgin, Ill	June 18, 1872	128, 168
Fluting-iron	S. D. Hubbard	Pittsburgh, Pa	Nov. 19, 1872	133, 104
Fluting-machine	H. B. Adams	New York, N. Y	Apr. 6, 1869	88, 598
Fluting-machine	H. B. Adams	New York, N. Y	Dec. 14, 1869	97, 751
Fluting-machine	S. W. Babbitt	West Meriden, Conn	Apr. 4, 1871	113, 242
Fluting-machine	A. Burbank	Rochester, N. Y	Jan. 10, 1871	110, 895
Fluting-machine	S. G. Cabell	Quincy, Ill	Nov. 10, 1868	83, 924
Fluting-machine	S. G. Cabell	Washington, D. C	Mar. 1, 1870	100, 371
Fluting-machine	S. G. Cabell	Washington, D. C	Sept. 27, 1870	107, 657
Fluting-machine	M. P. Carpenter	San Francisco, Cal	June 28, 1870	104, 825
Fluting-machine	H. H. Cole	New York, N. Y	June 12, 1866	55, 469
Fluting-machine	C. F. Corbett	Boston, Mass	Apr. 20, 1869	89, 028
Fluting-machine	W. D. Corrister	New York, N. Y	Dec. 8, 1868	84, 799
Fluting-machine	E. M. Deey	New York, N. Y	Mar. 22, 1870	100, 989
Fluting-machine	E. M. Deey	New York, N. Y	Apr. 4, 1871	113, 271
Fluting-machine	E. M. Deey	New York, N. Y	Nov. 28, 1871	121, 235
Fluting-machine	E. M. Deey	New York, N. Y	Aug. 13, 1872	130, 413
Fluting-machine	E. M. Deey	New York, N. Y	Aug. 19, 1873	141, 923
Fluting-machine	C. Dion	New York, N. Y	Oct. 18, 1870	108, 336
Fluting-machine	J. F. Hayen	Buffalo, N. Y	Jan. 9, 1872	122, 607
Fluting-machine	F. Hewitt	Bloomfield, N. J	Dec. 14, 1869	97, 774
Fluting-machine	E. P. Holley	Lockport, N. Y	May 6, 1873	138, 650
Fluting-machine	C. E. L. Holmes	New York, N. Y	Mar. 1, 1870	100, 405
Fluting-machine	A. Y. Hubbell	Elmira, N. Y	Nov. 29, 1870	109, 738
Fluting-machine	G. E. King	New York, N. Y	Feb. 26, 1867	62, 492
Fluting-machine	S. Knox and W. D. Corriston	New York, N. Y	Apr. 3, 1866	53, 633
Fluting-machine	S. R. Knox	New York, N. Y	Nov. 20, 1866	59, 913
Fluting-machine	S. Leavitt and E. L. Howard	Malden, Mass	Mar. 8, 1870	100, 645
Eluting-machine	H. Lucbs	Washington, D. C	Nov. 16, 1869	96, 820
Fluting-machine	J. W. Madden	Buffalo, N. Y	Nov. 7, 1871	120, 591
Fluting-machine	J. W. Madden and J. Dodsworth	Buffalo, N. Y	June 18, 1872	128, 156
Fluting-machine	E. J. Manville	Waterbury, Conn	Feb. 23, 1869	87, 182
Fluting-machine	E. J. Manville	Waterbury, Conn	May 17, 1870	103, 063
Fluting-machine	W. P. McKee	Cincinnati, Ohio	Nov. 22, 1870	109, 535
Fluting-machine	H. Sauerbier	Newark, N. J	Nov. 22, 1870	109, 456
Fluting-machine	D. R. Saunders	Houston, Tex	Jan. 14, 1873	134, 936
Fluting-machine	C. Schortau	New York, N. Y	July 6, 1869	92, 374
Fluting-machine	H. C. Sergeant	Newark, N. J	Nov. 23, 1869	97, 125
Fluting-machine	H. Sommer and C. Bauer	Newark, N. J	May 23, 1871	115, 251
Fluting-machine	C. A. Sterling	New York, N. Y	Aug. 21, 1866	57, 403
Fluting-machine	T. Stockmarr	New York, N. Y	Mar. 25, 1873	137, 258
Fluting-machine	C. W. Thompson	Chicago, Ill	Aug. 1, 1871	117, 578
Fluting-machine	T. M. Tucker	Newark, N. J	Feb. 7, 1871	111, 588
Fluting-machine	T. M. Tucker	Newark, N. J	July 25, 1871	117, 487
Fluting machine	W. Weitling	New York, N. Y	Aug. 27, 1872	130, 962
Fluting, Machine for straight and spiral	J. January	Greenville, Ky	Mar. 3, 1829	....
Fluting-machine roller	H. G. Pearson	New York, N. Y	Dec. 21, 1869	98, 103
Fluting rollers, Machine for	W. Weild	Manchester, Great Britain	Oct. 4, 1864	44, 585
Fluting sad-iron	E. A. Franklin	Brenham, Tex	Nov. 14, 1871	120, 869
Fluting-tongs	H. Gerecke	Carlstadt, N. J	May 17, 1870	103, 039
Fluting-tongs	J. B. Mersereau	Binghamton, N. Y	May 17, 1870	103, 224
Fluting-tongs	J. C. Robie	Binghamton, N. Y	Jan. 31, 1871	111, 475
Fluting-tongs	E. R. Shepard	Binghamton, N. Y	Nov. 28, 1871	121, 428
Fluting trimmings, Apparatus for	S. E. Totten	Brooklyn, N. Y	Jan. 31, 1865	46, 157
Flutter-wheels, Application of water to	J. Stewart	Muloy's Post Office, Tenn	Oct. 24, 1828	....
Flutter-wheels, Letting water on	J. Smith	Queen's County, N. Y	July 1, 1817	....

Index of patents issued from the United States Patent Office from 1790 to 1873, inclusive—Continued.

Invention.	Inventor.	Residence.	Date.	No.
Flutter-wheels. Method of applying water to compound buckets of.	D. Rankin	Augusta County, Va	July 11, 1854	11, 255
Flux for working metals and minerals	S. W. Kirk	Philadelphia, Pa	Nov. 8, 1870	109, 021
Fly and musquito bar	J. H. Jennings	New Bedford, Mass	Mar. 13, 1866	53, 149
Fly and musquito bar for windows	F. D. Wright	Jordan, N. Y	July 2, 1867	66, 272
Fly-catcher	L. Bartlett	Yarmouth, Me	Feb. 18, 1873	135, 961
Fly-catcher	H. A. Farnam	South Bend, Ind	Jan. 31, 1871	111, 332
Fly-catcher	J. Olson	Chicago, Ill	Nov. 5, 1872	132, 733
Fly-catcher	C. E. Penny	Fort Wayne, Ind	Nov. 12, 1872	132, 977
Fly-catcher	W. H. Rice	Oberlin, Ohio	Nov. 12, 1872	133, 056
Fly-driver	R. H. Fauntleroy	New Harmony, Ind	Aug. 13, 1834	......
Fly-expelling compound	J. Baquol	Baltimore, Md	Feb. 25, 1873	136, 203
Fly-exterminator	A. K. Walker	Hampden, Me	Jan. 31, 1871	111, 497
Fly-flap	T. Royer	Lancaster, Pa	Aug. 21, 1866	57, 384
Fly-frame	J. G. Luscomb	Taunton, Mass	June 8, 1869	91, 032
Fly-frame flyer	J. S. Streeter	Providence, R. I	Aug. 4, 1868	80, 783
Fly-killing machine	A. Glendening	Loudoun County, Va	Sept. 9, 1824	......
Fly or balance wheel	R. Rice	Mineral, Ill	Sept. 3, 1867	68, 530
Fly-protector	I. Daugherty	Rocky Station, Va	June 3, 1873	139, 552
Fly-screen for animals	B. F. Adams	Bangor, Me	Feb. 2, 1869	86, 342
Fly-string cutter and rounder	S. W. Sheller	Mount Carroll, Ill	July 6, 1869	92, 377
Fly-switch	L. S. Welch	Canaan, N. H	May 6, 1873	138, 719
Fly-trap	S. Arnold	Wilson County, Tenn	Aug. 5, 1856	15, 464
Fly-trap	S. Arnold	Green Hill, Tenn	Sept. 23, 1856	15, 752
Fly-trap	B. Atwater	Berlin, Conn	Oct. 5, 1858	21, 646
Fly-trap	S. B. Bacheller	McDonough, N. Y	Jan. 14, 1873	134, 833
Fly-trap	N. P. Bassett	Fulton, N. Y	Apr. 28, 1863	38, 277
Fly-trap	V. D. Beach	Battle Creek, Mich	May 28, 1872	127, 297
Fly-trap	E. D. Blakeman	New Lebanon, N. Y	Mar. 29, 1859	23, 422
Fly-trap	A. Bristol	Constantine, Mich	Dec. 24, 1867	72, 446
Fly-trap	M. V. Bulla	South Bend, Ind	May 14, 1872	126, 671
Fly-trap	P. A. Burgess	Butler, Mo	Apr. 30, 1872	126, 180
Fly-trap	A. M. Chapel and J. G. Hubbard	Pittsfield, Mass	Nov. 26, 1872	133, 354
Fly-trap	H. L. Chapman	Marcellus, Mich	Dec. 2, 1873	145, 093
Fly-trap	J. B. Childs	Lee Centre, Ill	July 16, 1872	129, 317
Fly-trap	W. B. Clark	South Bend, Ind	Oct. 1, 1872	131, 848
Fly-trap	I. S. Clough and S. R. Burrell	Brooklyn and New York, N. Y.	June 14, 1859	24, 375
Fly-trap	J. J. Craig	Knoxville, Tenn	Sept. 7, 1869	94, 569
Fly-trap	E. N. Cummings	Colebrook, N. H	Jan. 16, 1866	52, 034
Fly-trap	A. J. Davis	Hartford, Mich	Aug. 5, 1873	141, 495
Fly-trap	S. S. Day	New York, N. Y	Nov. 13, 1860	30, 619
Fly-trap	W. De Puy	Polk Station, Pa	Oct. 1, 1872	131, 813
Fly-trap	A. Eames	Kalamazoo, Mich	Nov. 1, 1859	25, 961
Fly-trap	G. W. Eicholtz	New Berlin, Ill	Dec. 23, 1873	145, 791
Fly-trap	W. Elwell	Gardiner, Me	Nov. 1, 1859	25, 997
Fly-trap	J. Emery and J. E. Gott	Bucksport, Me	May 22, 1866	55, 007
Fly-trap	G. W. Ernst and I. Lucas	Fremont, Ohio	May 13, 1873	138, 797
Fly-trap	D. and S. K. Flanders	Parishville, N. Y	Apr. 18, 1854	10, 801
Fly-trap	J. Fletcher	Cleveland, Ohio	Dec. 17, 1872	133, 931
Fly-trap	S. Friend	Decatur, Ill	Dec. 3, 1872	133, 579
Fly-trap	J. B. Fuller and G. W. Pierce	Worcester, Mass	Apr. 16, 1850	7, 288
Fly-trap	G. Gilbert	Westville, Conn	Oct. 7, 1856	15, 848
Fly-trap	B. Glasscock	Hillsborough, Ohio	Apr. 27, 1869	89, 305
Fly-trap	L. M. Gould	Chicago, Ill	Mar. 26, 1872	124, 951
Fly-trap	J. O. Greene	New Albany, Ind	July 9, 1872	128, 874
Fly-trap	L. Grim	Fort Branch, Ind	Sept. 12, 1871	118, 852
Fly-trap	C. R. Hardy	Lexington, Ind	Apr. 4, 1871	113, 515
Fly-trap	J. M. Harper	El Paso, Ill	Sept. 3, 1872	131, 098
Fly-trap	D. Henderson	North Bridgewater, Mass	Feb. 20, 1872	123, 897
Fly-trap	J. Hoover	Gratis, Ohio	Dec. 8, 1868	84, 825
Fly-trap	P. D. Horton and E. T. Bryan	Marengo Township, Mich	Feb. 21, 1871	111, 936
Fly-trap	J. Hyter	Kent, Ind	July 22, 1856	15, 378
Fly-trap	J. R. Johnson	Benton Harbor, Mich	Aug. 19, 1873	141, 931
Fly-trap	J. H. and J. Kiplinger	North Manchester, Ind	Mar. 23, 1869	88, 044
Fly-trap	D. Lake	Smith's Landing, N. J	June 21, 1864	41, 212
Fly-trap	D. Lake	Smith's Landing, N. J	Jan. 10, 1865	45, 839
Fly-trap	D. Lake	Smith's Landing, N. J	Mar. 20, 1866	53, 310
Fly-trap	T. Lane	Whitesburgh, Tenn	Dec. 16, 1873	145, 507
Fly-trap	G. E. Le Roy	South Bend, Ind	July 16, 1872	129, 350
Fly-trap	B. J. Leslie	Irvine, Ky	Aug. 22, 1871	118, 373
Fly-trap	M. Little	Ashley, Ill	Jan. 18, 1870	98, 984
Fly-trap	S. F. McGown	Rockville, Ind	Oct. 31, 1871	120, 449
Fly-trap	M. Merk	Rochester, N. Y	Aug. 2, 1870	105, 963
Fly-trap	R. P. and W. I. Miller	Lineville Station, Pa	May 27, 1873	139, 412
Fly-trap	A. C. Mills	Oaktown, Ind	Aug. 3, 1869	93, 329
Fly-trap	C. Packard and S. Standish	Eureka, Nev., and Pacheco, Cal.	Nov. 25, 1873	144, 860
Fly-trap	J. Parker	Dubuque, Iowa	Nov. 22, 1870	109, 444
Fly-trap	M. Patzaner	New York, N. Y	May 3, 1870	102, 585
Fly-trap	N. Pike	Brooklyn, N. Y	Feb. 20, 1866	52, 794
Fly-trap	H. H. Potter	Carthage, N. Y	Jan. 8, 1867	61, 096
Fly-trap	M. M. Preble	Kokomo, Ind	Jan. 22, 1867	61, 358
Fly-trap	W. Riley	Madison County, Miss	Apr. 27, 1858	20, 091
Fly-trap	H. H. Robertson	Kingston, Mo	July 3, 1860	29, 008
Fly-trap	C. S. Rouse	Dowagiac, Mich	Oct. 7, 1873	143, 423
Fly-trap	G. T. Savary	Reading, Mass	Sept. 27, 1864	44, 486
Fly-trap	T. M. Scott	La Grange, Ga	Feb. 16, 1858	19, 382
Fly-trap	R. Shaler	Madison, Conn	Feb. 1, 1859	22, 840
Fly-trap	W. T. Shannon	Greensborough, Ga	July 14, 1857	17, 811
Fly-trap	W. Shreve	Elkton, Ky	Aug. 22, 1848	5, 726
Fly-trap	J. C. Skeen	Barton Township, Ind	July 16, 1872	128, 982
Fly-trap	S. W. Smith and H. Bigelow	Brooklyn and New York, N. Y.	Feb. 15, 1859	22, 986
Fly-trap	W. Smith	Alexandria, Ind	May 25, 1869	90, 402
Fly-trap	H. Snow and L. T. Smart	Lowell, Mass., and Campton, N. H.	July 29, 1851	8, 252
Fly-trap	A. Snyder	Jackson, Mich	Mar. 10, 1868	75, 480

Index of patents issued from the United States Patent Office from 1790 *to* 1873, *inclusive*—Continued.

Invention.	Inventor.	Residence.	Date.	No.
Fly-trap	A. Standinger	Saint Louis, Mo	Oct. 19, 1869	96, 050
Fly-trap	F. Stengel	New York, N. Y	July 23, 1872	129, 763
Fly-trap	J. E. Stone	Erving, Mass	Mar. 16, 1869	87, 801
Fly-trap	G. J. Swingle	Knoxville Ill	Apr. 14, 1868	76, 673
Fly-trap	A. Veling	Pana, Ill	Nov. 26, 1872	133, 507
Fly-trap	E. Victor	Fort Branch, Ind	July 25, 1871	117, 489
Fly-trap	T. H. Whiting	Grand Haven, Mich	June 24, 1873	140, 176
Fly-trap	T. Whitmore and J. Beebe	Waterloo, Iowa	June 25, 1872	128, 444
Fly-trap	S. R. Wilmot	Watertown, Conn	Sept. 22, 1857	18, 261
Fly-trap, Automatic	F. L. Rosentrater	Des Moines, Iowa	Sept. 5, 1871	118, 747
Fly-wheel	D. Eldridge	Philadelphia, Pa	Mar. 21, 1865	46, 890
Fly-wheel	H. Gerner	New York, N. Y	Sept. 23, 1873	143, 009
Fly-wheel	J. W. Keely	Philadelphia, Pa	Aug. 15, 1871	118, 022
Fly-wheel	C. Root	Cleveland, Ohio	July 18, 1871	117, 115
Fly-wheel and crank-shaft, Combined	E. B. Jucket	Roxbury, Mass	Oct. 23, 1866	59, 032
Fly-wheel, Compensating	A. H. Smith	Charlton, N. Y	June 30, 1868	79, 403
Fly-wheel for rolling-mill machinery	J. Geyser	Allegheny, Pa	Mar. 22, 1859	23, 299
Fly-wheel press	D. Evans	Philadelphia, Pa	Aug. 26, 1831	....
Fly-wheel, Sectional	H. L. Farr	Indianapolis, Ind	Feb. 8, 1870	99, 659
Fly-wheels, Construction of	J. Bryant	Brooklyn, N. Y	Sept. 22, 1863	40, 011
Fly-wheels, Mechanical movement for regulating the action of.	A. C. Frederick	Clarendon, N. Y	Dec. 1, 1857	18, 734
Fly-wheels, Method of arranging	H. B. Peck	Wolcott, N. Y	Apr. 2, 1861	31, 935
Fly-wheels to multiply their motion, Manner of actuating.	C. Johnson	Amity, Ill	Oct. 11, 1841	2, 295
Flyer	E. C. Johnson	Lowell, Mass	Dec. 12, 1854	12, 063
Flyer	D. F. Smith	Manchester, N. H	Dec. 3, 1861	33, 866
Flyer for roving, &c	T. Marquis	New York, N. Y	Oct. 31, 1848	5, 892
Flyer guides, Machine for manufacturing	D. L. Hill	Lowell, Mass	Jan. 19, 1864	41, 297
Flyers and spindles, Arrangement of	J. Dermond	Paterson, N. J	Feb. 12, 1850	7, 081
Flyers, Compresser for	W. B. Thompson and R. H. Plummer.	Biddeford, Me	July 19, 1853	9, 865
Flying-apparatus	W. F. Quinby	Wilmington, Del	Sept. 10, 1867	68, 789
Flying-apparatus	W. F. Quinby	Wilmington, Del	Oct. 8, 1872	132, 022
Flying-horse	E. S. Scripture	Green Point, N. Y	June 4, 1850	7, 419
Flying-machine	W. F. Quinby	Wilmington, Del	Oct. 5, 1869	95, 513
Flying-machine	J. Wootton	Boonton, N. J	May 22, 1866	54, 992
Fodder-cutter	J. Eiberweiser	Cincinnati, Ohio	July 20, 1869	92, 946
Fodder-cutter	T. Hazard	Wilmington, Ohio	May 22, 1866	54, 899
Fodder-cutter	A. R. Reese	Phillipsburgh, N. J	Nov. 20, 1860	30, 697
Fodder-cutter	E. F. Varner	Harveysburgh, Ohio	Oct. 27, 1868	83, 571
Fodder-cutter and corn-husking machine, Combined	M. C. Jeffers	New York, N. Y	Feb. 11, 1868	74, 370
Fodder, Cutting and crushing corn	R. Miller	York, Pa	Oct. 3, 1844	3, 775
Fodde , Cutting and crushing corn	H. A. Pitts	Winthrop, Me	May 1, 1845	4, 024
Fodder cutting and grinding machine	I. Fulton	Madison, Pa	Aug. 15, 1865	49, 396
Fodder cutting and grinding machine	J. Jessop, J. Wanbaugh, G. W. Ilgenfritz, and J. C. Baker.	York, Pa	Feb. 20, 1846	4, 391
Fodder cutting and grinding machine	J. Royer	Uniontown, Md	Mar. 12, 1845	3, 938
Fodder-cutting machine	P. S. Clinger	Conestoga Centre, Pa	Aug. 14, 1860	29, 572
Fodder-cutting machine, Corn	J. Elgar	Baltimore, Md	June 19, 1847	5, 159
Fodder-grating machine	J. Lusk	Fredonia, Mich	Mar. 9, 1869	87, 573
Fodder, hay, straw, and potato cutter	W. A. Hamilton	Albany, N. Y	Nov. 19, 1833	....
Fodder, hay, straw, and potato cutter	A. Russell and N. Davis	Syracuse, N. Y	Nov. 19, 1833	....
Fodder-stand	J. Antram and E. B. Mullin	Franklin, Ohio	Jan. 31, 1871	111, 301
Fog-alarm	J. R. Anderson	Brooklyn, N. Y	July 7, 1868	79, 538
Fog-alarm	S. G. Cabell	Quincy, Ill	Aug. 8, 1871	117, 861
Fog-alarm	C. L. Daboll	New London, Conn	June 26, 1860	28, 837
Fog-alarm	G. Hull	Wallingford, Conn	Sept. 19, 1865	50, 004
Fog-alarm	J. C. Lyons	New York, N. Y	Sept. 3, 1867	68, 763
Fog-alarm	C. and G. M. Stevens	Boston, Mass	July 29, 1873	141, 396
Fog-horn	J. R. Anderson	Brooklyn, N. Y	Aug. 8, 1871	117, 717
Fog-signal	F. Brown	New York, N. Y	July 23, 1867	66, 942
Fog-signal	G. P. Goulding, D. Clark, and T. Dickinson.	Buffalo, N. Y	Nov. 13, 1866	59, 589
Fog-signal	G. C. Pattison	Baltimore, Md	Nov. 25, 1873	145, 008
Fog-signal	W. A. Stewart	Bethel, Me	Dec. 23, 1873	145, 915
Fog signal	I. Van Trump	Wilmington, Del	Jan. 29, 1867	61, 643
Fog-signal machine	J. D. Custer	Morristown, Pa	Oct. 5, 1858	21, 656
Folding and extension table	G. Mayer	Sullivan, Ill	Dec. 21, 1869	98, 079
Folding and reclining chair	G Hunzinger	Brooklyn, N. Y	Sept. 15, 1863	39, 995
Folding arm-chair	H. S. Golightly and C. S. Twitchell.	New Haven, Conn	Oct. 6, 1863	40, 210
Folding-bench	T. S. Lewis	Kendall's Mills, Me	Dec. 21, 1858	22, 371
Folding-boat	J. Hegeman	Vischer's Ferry, N. Y	July 16, 1872	129, 026
Folding-box	M. and J. Erpelding	Chicago, Ill	May 23, 1871	115, 183
Folding-box	C. C. Moore	New York, N. Y	June 6, 1871	115, 764
Folding-case	J. C. Barker	Chicago, Ill	Feb. 18, 1873	135, 878
Folding-chair	E. Bartels	New York, N. Y	Oct. 18, 1870	108, 314
Folding-chair	B. Beach	Meriden, Conn	Dec. 21, 1869	98, 141
Folding-chair	P. Born	New York, N. Y	Oct. 6, 1868	82, 791
Folding-chair	A. C. Boyd	Grafton, Mass	Oct. 13, 1868	83, 034
Folding-chair	A. C. Boyd	Worcester, Mass	Aug. 2, 1870	105, 898
Folding-chair	A. C. Boyd	Worcester, Mass	Apr. 22, 1873	138, 124
Folding-chair	C. Brada	New York, N. Y	July 4, 1871	116, 676
Folding-chair	H. E. Braunfeld	Philadelphia, Pa	Aug. 1, 1871	117, 509
Folding-chair	W. E. Cameron	Taunton, Mass	Aug. 2, 1870	105, 903
Folding-chair	A. Collignon	Closter, N. J	Sept. 29, 1868	82, 493
Folding-chair	A. Collignon	Closter, N. J	Nov. 24, 1868	84, 344
Folding-chair	A., C. O., and N. Collignon	Closter, N. J	June 10, 1873	139, 776
Folding-chair	C. O. and N. Collignon	Closter, N. J	Sept. 29, 1868	82, 494
Folding-chair	N. and C. O. Collignon	Closter, N. J	Nov. 16, 1869	96, 778
Folding-chair	N., C. O., and A. Collignon	Closter, N. J	July 11, 1871	116, 811
Folding-chair	F. Colton	Brooklyn, N. Y	Dec. 27, 1870	110, 438
Folding-chair	T. B Comins, jr	Lowell, Mass	Jan. 11, 1870	98, 743
Folding-chair	T. R. Comins, jr	Lowell, Mass	Nov. 8, 1870	108, 973
Folding-chair	J. C. Compton	Clarksville, N. J	May 28, 1872	127, 221
Folding-chair	J. Cram	Boston, Mass	Aug. 21, 1855	13, 479
Folding-chair	N. Cross	New York, N. Y	July 29, 1862	35, 993

Index of patents issued from the United States Patent Office from 1790 *to* 1873, *inclusive*—Continued.

Invention.	Inventor.	Residence.	Date.	No.
Folding-chair	J. C. Crummy and A. A. Parsons	Pittsburgh, Pa	Mar. 15, 1870	100, 733
Folding-chair	I. N. Dann	New Haven, Conn	Feb. 6, 1866	52, 488
Folding-chair	I. N. Dann	New Haven, Conn	Oct. 29, 1867	70, 323
Folding-chair	I. N. Dann	New Haven, Conn	Dec. 6, 1870	109, 876
Folding-chair	J. A., W. F., and I. A. Dann	New Haven, Conn	Jan. 6, 1863	37, 277
Folding-chair	C. Dietrich	West Roxbury, Mass	Apr. 13, 1869	88, 776
Folding-chair	A. Eliaers	Boston, Mass	Nov. 22, 1864	45, 146
Folding-chair	F. B. Fabri	New York, N. Y	Dec. 3, 1872	133, 576
Folding-chair	W. Gardner	Glen Gardner, N. J	Oct. 10, 1871	119, 754
Folding-chair	K. Geisler	New York, N. Y	Aug. 12, 1873	141, 784
Folding-chair	H. S. Golightly and C. S. Twitchell.	New Haven, Conn	Mar. 10, 1863	37, 864
Folding-chair	H. S. Golightly and C. S. Twitchell.	New Haven, Conn	Feb. 25, 1868	74, 910
Folding-chair	E. Hambujer	Detroit, Mich	Sept. 4, 1866	57, 709
Folding-chair	P. J. Hardy	New York, N. Y	Dec. 22, 1863	41, 001
Folding-chair	P. J. Hardy	New York, N. Y	Aug. 13, 1867	67, 759
Folding-chair	B. J. Harrison	New York, N. Y	July 29, 1873	141, 271
Folding-chair	B. J. Harrison and J. Condie	New York, N. Y	July 17, 1866	56, 410
Folding-chair	F. M. Holmes	Boston, Mass	June 28, 1870	104, 851
Folding-chair	F. M. Holmes	Boston, Mass	July 5, 1870	105, 079
Folding-chair	F. M. Holmes	Boston, Mass	Jan. 24, 1871	111, 209
Folding-chair	F. M. Holmes	Boston, Mass	Jan. 31, 1871	111, 455
Folding-chair	F. M. Holmes	Boston, Mass	Feb. 21, 1871	112, 040
Folding-chair	F. M. Holmes	Boston, Mass	Feb. 21, 1871	112, 041
Folding-chair	D. Howarth	Portland, Me	Apr. 16, 1867	63, 897
Folding-chair	G. Hunzinger	New York, N. Y	May 13, 1873	138, 892
Folding-chair	J. Hyde	Troy, N. Y	May 7, 1867	64, 535
Folding-chair	J. Hyde	Troy, N. Y	July 23, 1867	67, 119
Folding-chair	C. A. Jackson	Boston, Mass	Oct. 10, 1871	119, 849
Folding-chair	C. A. Jackson	Boston, Mass	Apr. 23, 1872	126, 059
Folding-chair	H. James	North Adams, Mass	Apr. 2, 1872	125, 195
Folding-chair	T. Johnson	Portland, Me	Jan. 16, 1872	122, 834
Folding-chair	F. Kilian	New York, N. Y	Apr. 5, 1870	101, 628
Folding-chair	B. Koechling	New York, N. Y	Feb. 26, 1867	62, 428
Folding-chair	M. Lechler	New York, N. Y	July 5, 1870	104, 965
Folding-chair	R. M. Lytle, W. I. Ashton, and L. W. True.	Williamson County, Tenn	Dec. 14, 1858	22, 297
Folding-chair	C. Marcher	New York, N. Y	Feb. 20, 1872	123, 832
Folding-chair	S. E. Mason and E. Downe	Bangor, Me	Aug. 13, 1867	67, 780
Folding-chair	G. McAleer	Worcester, Mass	Nov. 3, 1868	83, 720
Folding-chair	G. McAleer	Worcester, Mass	Apr. 19, 1870	102, 022
Folding-chair	G. McAleer	Worcester, Mass	July 19, 1870	105, 472
Folding-chair	J. D. Merriam	Ashburnham, Mass	Jan. 6, 1863	37, 324
Folding-chair	G. Miller and P. Hannah	Rochester, N. Y	Mar. 28, 1871	113, 077
Folding-chair	G. F. Mitchell and A. A. Sheafe	South Boston, Mass	Feb. 6, 1872	123, 412
Folding-chair	E. P. More and S. J. Anderson	Cazenovia, N. Y	Sept. 6, 1870	107, 094
Folding-chair	W. Morstatt	New York, N. Y	May 24, 1870	103, 358
Folding-chair	W. Morstatt and F. Kipps	New York, N. Y	Sept. 20, 1870	107, 525
Folding-chair	J. Nicolai	Boston, Mass	Nov. 19, 1867	71, 045
Folding-chair	J. Nicolai	Boston, Mass	Aug. 4, 1868	80, 656
Folding-chair	J. Nicolai	Boston, Mass	Sept. 27, 1870	107, 708
Folding-chair	J. Nicolai and J. P. Rinn	Boston, Mass	Oct. 26, 1869	96, 139
Folding-chair	P. W. Nolan	New York, N. Y	Aug. 5, 1873	141, 456
Folding-chair	P. W. Nolan	New York, N. Y	Aug 5, 1873	141, 457
Folding-chair	H. T. Pratt	Fitchburgh, Mass	Dec. 4, 1860	30, 858
Folding-chair	E. C. Ranks	Boston, Mass	Dec. 28, 1869	98, 415
Folding-chair	F. W. Richardson	New York, N. Y	Apr. 25, 1871	114, 199
Folding-chair	A. M. Rodgers	Brooklyn, N. Y	Mar. 30, 1869	88, 513
Folding-chair	A. M. Rodgers	Brooklyn, N. Y	July 12, 1870	105, 253
Folding-chair	C. C. Schmitt and R. Wodrich	New York, N. Y	Oct. 6, 1868	82, 755
Folding-chair	D. N. Selleg	Newburgh, N. Y	Oct. 14, 1873	143, 721
Folding-chair	A. W. Stewart	Glasgow, Scotland	Feb. 22, 1870	100, 209
Folding-chair	A. W. Stewart	Boston, Mass	Apr. 19, 1870	102, 178
Folding-chair	A. W. Stewart	Boston, Mass	Apr. 19, 1870	102, 179
Folding-chair	A. W. Stewart	Boston, Mass	Apr. 19, 1870	102, 180
Folding-chair	A. W. Stewart	Boston, Mass	Aug. 23, 1870	106, 633
Folding-chair	A. W. Stewart	Boston, Mass	Aug. 6, 1872	130, 327
Folding-chair	J. H. Swan	New York, N. Y	Sept. 13, 1859	25, 452
Folding-chair	J. H. Swan	New York, N. Y	Aug. 21, 1860	29, 750
Folding-chair	J. H. Travis	Charlestown, Mass	Mar. 22, 1870	101, 186
Folding-chair	J. H. Travis and E. H. Mahoney	Charlestown and Boston, Mass.	Nov. 26, 1872	133, 503
Folding-chair	G. Trinks	New York, N. Y	July 30, 1867	67, 378
Folding-chair	G. Trinks	New York, N. Y	June 29, 1869	92, 125
Folding-chair	C. S. Twitchell	New Haven, Conn	Sept. 24, 1867	69, 276
Folding-chair	E. W. Vaill	Worcester, Mass	Apr. 7, 1863	38, 132
Folding chair	E. W. Vaill	Worcester, Mass	Sept. 17, 1867	69, 050
Folding-chair	E. W. Vaill	Worcester, Mass	Sept. 24, 1867	69, 145
Folding-chair	E. W. Vaill	Worcester, Mass	Nov. 3, 1868	83, 744
Folding chair	E. W. Vaill	Worcester, Mass	Oct. 12, 1869	95, 856
Folding-chair	P. B. Viele	Rochester, N. Y	May 7, 1872	126, 595
Folding-chair	P. B. Viele	Rochester, N. Y	July 9, 1872	128, 767
Folding-chair	N. Waterman	Toledo, Ohio	Apr. 23, 1867	64, 173
Folding-chair	E. Watkins and A. McConnell	Philadelphia, Pa	Aug. 29, 1871	118, 500
Folding-chair	A. D. Whitmore	Housatonic, Mass	Nov. 3, 1863	40, 526
Folding-chair	G. E. Whitmore	Housatonic, Mass	June 4, 1867	65, 520
Folding chair	C. A. Wiedemann	New York, N. Y	June 29, 1869	92, 133
Folding-chair and life-preserver	J. M. Rudiger	New York, N. Y	July 18, 1871	117, 209
Folding-chair, bed, and ottoman combined	E. Fauh	New York, N. Y	Jan. 14, 1873	134, 875
Folding-chair for pews	M. S. Beach	Brooklyn, N. Y	Oct. 13, 1857	18, 377
Folding-chair, Iron	J. Lauer	Chicago, Ill	June 11, 1872	127, 899
Folding-chair, Iron	G. Wilson	Chicago, Ill	June 27, 1871	116, 384
Folding-chair, Iron	G. Wilson	Chicago, Ill	July 4, 1871	116, 784
Folding-chair, Iron	G. Wilson	Chicago, Ill	Nov. 14, 1871	121, 034
Folding-chair or lounge	J. Sutter	New York, N. Y	Nov. 3, 1865	40, 512
Folding-chair or table	F. Lüdke	New York, N. Y	Jan. 31, 1865	46, 121
Folding convertible chair	W. B. Kimball	Peterborough, N. H	Apr. 5, 1870	101, 472

Index of patents issued from the United States Patent Office from 1790 *to* 1873, *inclusive*—Continued.

Invention.	Inventor.	Residence.	Date.	No.
Folding-frame for boats, Sectional	W. M. Ducker	Brooklyn, N. Y	Aug. 19, 1873	141, 860
Folding-gate	C. A. Ackerson and W. D. Harrah.	Bath, N. Y., and Davenport, Iowa.	July 16, 1867	66, 668
Folding-gate	I. Meritt	North West Bridgewater, Mass.	Dec. 18, 1849	6, 957
Folding gates, Method of opening and closing vertico-lateral.	F. Thrasher and H. B. Horton	Akron, Ohio	Sept. 29, 1857	18, 308
Folding-guide	A. Douglas	New York, N. Y	Oct. 5, 1858	21, 659
Folding ironing-table	J. H. Mallory	La Porte, Ind	Mar. 1, 1870	100, 430
Folding knife and fork	H. Schumacher	Philadelphia, Pa	Mar. 4, 1873	136, 552
Folding or ironing table	M. G. Briggs	Boston, Mass	June 9, 1868	78, 642
Folding or knock-down chair	J. K. Coolidge and N. H. Hill	Cincinnati, Ohio	Sept. 20, 1870	107, 455
Folding or lunch box	G. B. Mershon	Philadelphia, Pa	Nov. 26, 1867	71, 511
Folding or spiral spring for carriages	J. Armour, jr	Baltimore, Md	June 27, 1808	....
Folding-screen	M. G. Lazarus	Pittston, Pa	May 6, 1873	138, 507
Folding-seat	C. J. Everickx	Paris, France	Apr. 9, 1872	125, 556
Folding-seat	C. A. French	Lowell, Mass	Aug. 30, 1870	106, 805
Folding-seat	J. H. Hall	Chicago, Ill	Oct. 28, 1873	143, 979
Folding-seat	G. W. King	Oswego, N. Y	July 12, 1870	105, 222
Folding-seat	D. H. Nation	Saint Louis, Mo	May 18, 1869	90, 183
Folding-seat	A. M. Olds	New York, N. Y	May 14, 1867	64, 694
Folding-seat	W. W. Parker	Minneapolis, Minn	May 20, 1873	139, 021
Folding-seat	T. Reeve and M. B. Swezey	Brooklyn, N. Y	Apr. 19, 1859	23, 708
Folding-seat	C. W. Sherwood	Chicago, Ill	Mar. 26, 1867	63, 315
Folding-seat	G. Sherwood	Chicago, Ill	Oct. 15, 1867	69, 850
Folding-seat	J. M. Swain	Peekskill, N. Y	Sept. 19, 1871	119, 060
Folding-seat and arm	F. J. Dibble	Chicago, Ill	July 23, 1867	67, 107
Folding-seat for carriage-bodies	R. F. Briggs	Amesbury, Mass	Oct. 1, 1867	69, 397
Folding-table	A. C. Ballard	Winooski, Vt	Feb. 20, 1872	123, 806
Folding-table	J. F. Birchard	Milwaukee, Wis	Feb. 18, 1873	135, 881
Folding-table	J. P. Brown	Boston, Mass	Aug. 6, 1867	67, 406
Folding-table	J. H. Bush	Bone Creek, W. Va	Feb. 26, 1867	62, 391
Folding-table	S. V. Cornell	New Haven, Conn	Apr. 8, 1873	137, 658
Folding-table	D. Doty	Detroit, Mich	July 16, 1867	66, 813
Folding-table	F. W. Heublein	Hartford, Conn	June 10, 1873	139, 673
Folding-table	J. Johnson	New York, N. Y	Feb. 5, 1861	31, 353
Folding-table	C. Lammrich	New York, N. Y	Dec. 14, 1858	22, 294
Folding-table, &c	H. Lorth	Philadelphia, Pa	May 13, 1873	138, 934
Folding-table, &c	T. P. I. Magoun	Worcester, Mass	Feb. 25, 1873	136, 167
Folding-table	F. Mohr	Fond du Lac, Wis	May 1, 1866	54, 386
Folding-table	P. Munde	East Hampton, Mass	Aug. 5, 1873	141, 453
Folding-table	G. W. Nellis	Richmondville, N. Y	Oct. 2, 1866	58, 462
Folding-table	J. Juevedo	Brooklyn, N. Y	Apr. 9, 1872	125, 484
Folding-table	G. G. Small	New York, N. Y	Oct. 24, 1865	50, 664
Folding-table	J. W. Smith	Charlestown, Mass	Apr. 13, 1869	88, 988
Folding-table	W. Smith	Cincinnati, Ohio	Sept. 22, 1868	82, 360
Folding-table	J. Sutter	New York, N. Y	Nov. 3, 1863	40, 513
Folding-table	J. Sutter	New York, N. Y	Dec. 24, 867	72, 562
Folding-table	J. W. Wayne and J. R. Miller	Cincinnati, Ohio	July 12, 1864	43, 538
Folding-table	C. H. Wheeler	Saint Louis, Mo	Aug. 26, 1873	142, 306
Folding-table	A. Windeck	Peoria, Ill	Aug. 30, 1870	106, 906
Folding-table and toilet-glass	H. W. Eastman	Baltimore, Md	Oct. 18, 1864	44, 714
Folding table or bench	R. Carter, jr	Lawrence, Mass	Aug. 22, 1865	49, 500
Folding-table, Portable	C. D. Barnitz	Baltimore, Md	July 29, 1856	15, 407
Folding-table support	J. Daly	Troy, N. Y	June 20, 1871	116, 164
Folding-table top	C. W. Mills	Chicago, Ill	Apr. 4, 1871	113, 548
Folding-tub	C. H. Hudson	New York, N. Y	Jan. 26, 1869	86, 159
Fomentations, Preparing and applying	T. L. Jennison	Cambridge, Mass	Aug. 30, 1832	....
Food and diet from cerealines, Article of	J. E. Brown	Philadelphia, Pa	June 14, 1864	43, 091
Food, Article of	G. G. Campbell	Oswego, N. Y	Jan. 28, 1873	135, 204
Food, Article of	W. J. and A. Coleman	Bury St. Edmunds and London, England.	Dec. 22, 1868	85, 070
Food, Article of	L. S. and M. G. Johnson	Cortland, N. Y	Feb. 25, 1873	136, 165
Food, Article of	J. R. Weed	New York, N. Y	July 30, 1872	130, 091
Food, Artificial	H. C. Morris	Richmond, Va	Mar. 4, 1873	136, 447
Food, Cattle	J. Christie and H. G. Dayton	Atlanta, Ill., and Maysville, Ky.	Mar. 2, 1869	87, 397
Food, Cattle	J. T. Harris	Tyngsborough, Mass	Nov. 2, 1869	96, 317
Food, Composition or paste for articles of	R. M. Livingston	Mobile, Ala	June 4, 1867	65, 494
Food-compound	L. S. Chichester	Brooklyn, N. Y	Feb. 25, 1873	136, 302
Food-compound	L. S. Chichester	Brooklyn, N. Y	Feb. 25, 1873	136, 303
Food-compound	L. S. Chichester	Brooklyn, N. Y	Feb. 25, 1873	136, 304
Food, Compound for cattle	W. Marsden	Newburgh, N. Y	May 31, 1870	103, 761
Food, Concentrated	J. H. Schenck	Saint Louis, Mo	Nov. 22, 1864	45, 180
Food, Cooked vegetable	E. C. Frost	Highland Nurseries, N. Y.	Mar. 31, 1863	38, 039
Food for animals	J. S. Kirk	Pittsburgh, Pa	Dec. 29, 1868	85, 313
Food for animals, Machine for cutting	R. Fanslan	New Haven, Conn	Jan. 28, 1873	135, 326
Food for cattle, Composition for	E. Payne	London, England	Dec. 1, 1868	84, 574
Food for domestic animals	M. S. Bringier	Ascension Parish, La	Mar. 16, 1869	87, 821
Food for infants from cereals	L. S. Chichester	Brooklyn, N. Y	Nov. 11, 1873	144, 508
Food for stock	D. Embree	Dayton, Ohio	Dec. 31, 1867	72, 827
Food for the sick, Article of	A. Meyer-Berck	Frankfort-on-the-Maine, Prussia.	Aug. 18, 1868	81, 190
Food for the table, Device for forming articles of	J. Blaettler	Philadelphia, Pa	Mar. 19, 1872	124, 782
Food from algae or sea mosses, Article of	W. J. Rand, jr	Brooklyn, E. D., N. Y	Apr. 4, 1871	113, 562
Food from cereals	L. S. Chichester	Brooklyn, N. Y	Feb. 25, 1873	136, 305
Food from cider, Article of	S. W. Mahan	Middlebury, Vt	Oct. 21, 1873	143, 918
Food from oyster-juice, Article of	B. G. Noble	New York, N. Y	July 16, 1867	66, 732
Food from potatoes, Article of	C. K. Marshall	New Orleans, La	May 19, 1868	77, 995
Food from pumpkins and squashes, Article of	E. W. and M. C. Ayer	South Waterford, Me	Aug. 31, 1869	94, 375
Food from wheat and process of preparing the same	E. H. Murray	Saint Paul, Minn	June 3, 1873	139, 600
Food, Horse and cattle	E. H. Clowser	Boston, Mass	Jan. 18, 1870	98, 849
Food made from beans, Article of	S. R. Andres	Troy, N. Y	July 23, 1861	32, 853
Food made of sweet potatoes, Article of	S. R. and S. Andres, and M. Bucklin.	Troy and New York, N. Y	Feb. 11, 1862	34, 389
Food, Method of preparing and preserving	J. M. Call and B. G. Sloper	London and Walthamstow, England.	Dec. 20, 1864	45, 569
Food or beef-tea, Concentrated	E. S. Muringer	Philadelphia, Pa	Mar. 11, 1862	34, 642

Index of patents issued from the United States Patent Office from 1790 to 1873, inclusive—Continued.

Invention.	Inventor.	Residence.	Date.	No.
Food or pearl wheat, Article of	J. E. Weaver	Havelock, Pa	Jan. 9, 1872	122, 543
Food or sauce	F. A. Friscia	Brooklyn, N. Y	Dec. 16, 1873	145, 562
Food, Preparation of wheat for	W. S. Brewster	Chicago, Ill	Jan. 28, 1870	104, 700
Food prepared from fish and potatoes, Article of	W. D. Cutler	Philadelphia, Pa	Nov. 10, 1868	83, 836
Food, Preparing	J. Bouis	Baltimore, Md	Jan. 19, 1826	....
Food, Preparing farinaceous	E. N. Horsford	Cambridge, Mass	Mar. 16, 1869	87, 850
Food, Preparing tomatoes and other fruits and vegetables to be used as.	C. Alden	Newburgh, N. Y	Apr. 5, 1870	101, 562
Food, Preparing wheat and other cereals for	G. W. Waitt	Philadelphia, Pa	June 25, 1872	128, 342
Food, Preparing wheat for	M. H. Kollock	Philadelphia, Pa	July 23, 1872	129, 835
Food, Process for preparing fish for	I. L. Stanley	New York, N. Y	May 21, 1872	127, 115
Food, Process of preparing Iceland and Irish moss for use in.	W. J. Rand	Brooklyn, N. Y	Aug. 10, 1869	93, 477
Food, Sauce for	A. P. Agresta and A. Meuecci	NewYork and Clifton, N.Y	Aug. 26, 1873	142, 071
Food, Treating vegetables for	W. Adamson and C. F. A. Simonin.	Philadelphia, Pa	Apr. 2, 1872	125, 247
Food-warmer	E. Bevan and A. Fleming	Birkenhead and Shipston, England.	Apr. 7, 1868	76, 390
Foot-ball covering	H. A. Alden	Matteawan, N. Y	Dec. 31, 1867	72, 772
Foot-bath	I. A. Isaacs	Cleveland, Ohio	Dec. 18, 1866	60, 521
Foot-boards to splints, Attachment of adjustable	J. Gruol	New York, N. Y	Jan. 5, 1858	19, 025
Foot-cleaner	A. McKeachnie	New York, N. Y	May 25, 1858	20, 359
Foot-cleaner	R. Shaler and C. B. Rogers	Madison and Deep River, Conn.	July 31, 1860	29, 443
Foot-comforter	G. W. Rothrock	Mifflin, Pa	June 22, 1869	91, 567
Foot-light for theaters	C. Defries	London, England	June 2, 1868	78, 580
Foot-lights, Mode of constructing and arranging theater.	G. W. Lloyd	Detroit, Mich	June 24, 1862	35, 696
Foot-mill, Vertical cylindrical	S. Fowks	Catskill, N. Y	Sept. 13, 1824	......
Foot or bed warmer	L. M. Roby	Leesville, Ohio	Oct. 12, 1869	95, 728
Foot-power	E. Hutson	Brockport, N. Y	Dec. 17, 1867	72, 300
Foot-power	G. B. Kirkham	New York, N. Y	Dec. 5, 1871	121, 525
Foot-power apparatus	E. and H. Harding	Delevan, Minn	Aug. 19, 1873	141, 928
Foot-power machine	F. S. Stoddard	Litchfield, Conn	May 17, 1859	24, 064
Foot-press	J. N. Smith	Jersey City, N. J	Nov. 13, 1866	59, 669
Foot-press	N. C. Stiles	West Meriden, Conn	Mar. 27, 1866	53, 499
Foot-press	W. M. Warren	Watertown, Conn	Sept. 16, 1862	36, 491
Foot-rest	C. Adams	Pittsburgh, Pa	Oct. 1, 1867	69, 298
Foot-rest	C. S. Adams	Hillsdale, Mich	July 11, 1865	48, 638
Foot-rest	I. Van Hagen	Chicago, Ill	Feb. 19, 1867	62, 167
Foot-rest	F. M. Watson and H. H. Clough	Warner, N. H	May 26, 1863	38, 718
Foot-rest	E. Wilkins	Warner, N. H	May 19, 1863	38, 619
Foot-rest and boot-jack, Combined	D. H. James	Cincinnati, Ohio	Dec. 20, 1870	110, 240
Foot-rest and kneeling-board	H. Morrison	Steubenville, Ohio	Feb. 26, 1867	62, 434
Foot-rest for chairs	T. A. Johnson	Portland, Me	Mar. 11, 1873	136, 734
Foot-rest for chairs, &c., Extension	J. H. Travis	Charlestown, Mass	Oct. 22, 1872	132, 503
Foot-rest, grate, and fire-brick base, Combined	J. H. Keyser	New York, N. Y	Aug. 11, 1868	80, 971
Foot-shield	D. C. Winans	New York, N. Y	Feb. 23, 1864	47, 735
Footstool for churches, &c	W. G. Brown	Monmouth, Me	Mar. 22, 1870	100, 971
Footstool, Nursery	L. Burnell	Milwaukee, Wis	Oct. 4, 1870	107, 869
Foot-straightening reel	G. Goodrich	Portland Harbor, N. Y	July 22, 1833	....
Foot-warmer	J. J. Andrews	Clyde, Ill	Dec. 19, 1865	51, 534
Foot-warmer	D. Austin	Sheldon, Vt	Aug. 24, 1869	94, 000
Foot-warmer	N. H. Bruce	Forge Valley, Westford, Mass.	Sept. 17, 1867	68, 944
Foot-warmer	J. B. Craig	Perrysville, Pa	Nov. 11, 1873	144, 445
Foot-warmer	A. Eckert	Trenton, Ohio	Mar. 7, 1865	46, 649
Foot-warmer	C. R. Everson	Palmyra, N. Y	Nov. 6, 1866	59, 374
Foot-warmer	H. Forncrook	Elbridge, N. Y	Dec. 4, 1855	13, 871
Foot-warmer	W. Heissenbuttel	Brooklyn, N. Y	Oct. 28, 1873	144, 095
Foot-warmer	H. Hock and J. Zilz	Philadelphia, Pa	Sept. 26, 1865	50, 123
Foot-warmer	S. Hunt	Danville, Ind	July 22, 1862	35, 936
Foot-warmer	J. W. Merrill and J. H. Rowe	Boston, Mass	June 10, 1862	35, 532
Foot-warmer	A. Palmer	Hudson, Mich	Aug. 15, 1865	49, 433
Foot-warmer	C. L. Palmer	Brookline, Mass	Apr. 18, 1865	47, 327
Foot-warmer	J. H. Parsons	Quincy, Mich	Feb. 13, 1866	52, 593
Foot-warmer	H. G. Seekins, sr., and H. G. Seekins, jr.	Elyria, Ohio	Dec. 15, 1857	18, 868
Foot-warmer	G. W. Smith	Aurora, Ind	Aug. 31, 1858	21, 376
Foot-warmer	N. Waterman	Boston, Mass	Nov. 27, 1855	13, 859
Foot-warmer and reflecting-lamp, Combined	C. S. Merwin and C. A. Metcalf	Dubuque, Iowa	Oct. 2, 1866	58, 453
Foot-warmer, Electric	C. V. Littlepage	Austin, Tex	May 17, 1870	103, 061
Forage-ration	M. Fletcher	Louisville, Ky	Dec. 15, 1863	40, 922
Forceps, Surgical	J. G. Loomis	Philadelphia, Pa	Nov. 21, 1854	11, 982
Forceps, Tubular	G. W. Wooley	New York, N. Y	Nov. 25, 1862	37, 023
Forces, Machine for applying and measuring	H. T. Stanard	Wayne, Mich	July 23, 1867	67, 144
Fore-arm, Artificial	B. F. Palmer	Philadelphia, Pa	Jan. 11, 1859	22, 575
Fore-iron for shoemakers	S. A. Shurtleff	North Carver, Mass	Nov. 15, 1859	26, 129
Fore-part irons	J. Blease	Richmond, Ind	Apr. 28, 1868	77, 246
Forebays, Gate for	J. J. Meeker and L. Cortright	Columbia County, Pa	June 26, 1866	55, 882
Forebays, Regulating	H. Mallow	Pendleton County, Va	Mar. 13, 1849	6, 172
Forge	G. Campbell	North Buffalo, N. Y	Mar. 22, 1870	100, 975
Forge	J. Howe	Alna, Me	Apr. 16, 1834	....
Forge	W. T. Kosinski	Philadelphia, Pa	July 25, 1871	117, 303
Forge	C. V. Queen	Peekskill, N. Y	Nov. 18, 1845	4, 273
Forge	C. N. Taylor and E. J. Holmes	Upton and Dedham, Mass	Apr. 25, 1865	47, 467
Forge and applying bellows thereto	R. Green	Brunswick, N. Y	May 31, 1834	....
Forge and bellows for blacksmiths, jewelers, &c	J. C. Conklin	Peekskill, N. Y	June 19, 1835	....
Forge and furnace blowing apparatus	J. A. Stewart	Springfield, Tenn	Aug. 18, 1840	1, 724
Forge and furnace water-back	W. McEwen	Norristown, Pa	Nov. 10, 1841	2, 349
Forge and furnace water-back and tuyere	A. Blood	Cohocton, N. Y	Sept. 29, 1825	....
Forge and other furnaces, Application of air to	S. W. Watson and C. Robinson	Ashtabula, Ohio	Sept. 26, 1835	....
Forge-back	F. Avery	Hamilton, N. Y	Feb. 12, 1833	....
Forge-back	T. Bush, jr	Springport, N. Y	Apr. 12, 1833	....
Forge-back	A. Graham	Hamilton, N. Y	Feb. 26, 1833	....
Forge back, Blacksmith's	I. Sawyer	Hallowell, Me	Feb. 13, 1835	....
Forge-bellows	C. McMurtry	New Marlborough, Mass	July 8, 1811	....
Forge, Blacksmith's	T. S. Clark	Lena, Ill	Dec. 29, 1868	85, 283

Index of patents issued from the United States Patent Office from 1790 *to* 1873, *inclusive*—Continued

Invention.	Inventor.	Residence.	Date.	No.
Forge, Blacksmith's	J. H. Gould	Cincinnati, Ohio	Mar. 14, 1865	46, 792
Forge, Blacksmith's	J. R. Hobbs	Huntsville, Ala	Sept. 15, 1846	4, 760
Forge, Blacksmith's	W. T. Kellogg	Troy, N. Y	Nov. 25, 1873	144, 986
Forge, Blacksmith's	J. Knickerbacer	La Porte, Ind	Sept. 26, 1835	....
Forge, Blacksmith's	C. Richardson	Greenfield, N. H	Mar. 12, 1836	....
Forge, Blacksmith's	M. Scott	Fairfield, Iowa	Jan. 30, 1872	123, 202
Forge, Blacksmith's	F. A. Stuart	Catharine, N. Y	July 1, 1844	3, 647
Forge, Blacksmith's portable	J. F. Bridge	Deadwood, Cal	Mar. 29, 1864	42, 068
Forge, Blacksmith's portable	M. De La Montanya	San Francisco, Cal	Oct. 15, 1861	33, 479
Forge-bonnet	W. Dunkerly	Woonsocket, R. I	May 17, 1870	103, 160
Forge-bonnet	W. Dunkerly	Woonsocket, R. I	Apr. 25, 1871	114, 115
Forge-chimneys, Flue-casing for	H. S. Wilcox	Nevada, Ohio	Aug. 26, 1873	142, 311
Forge fire	J. Evans	New Haven, Conn	Mar. 24, 1863	37, 958
Forge-fire	W. Rodgers and A. Bannon	Bellefonte, Pa	Apr. 1, 1856	14, 575
Forge fire, Hot-blast blomary	P. A. Sabbaton	Reading, Pa	Feb. 24, 1845	3, 922
Forge for manufacturing wrought iron, Blomary	S. Guilford	Lebanon, Pa	Dec. 27, 1843	3, 390
Forge-furnace	B. Hotchkiss and H. Shattuck	New Haven and Hamden, Conn.	Sept. 25, 1866	58, 346
Forge-hearth	R. W. Clark	Pittsburgh, Pa	Jan. 21, 1868	73, 502
Forge-hearth	J. Coubach	Middletown, Pa	Nov. 10, 1841	2, 348
Forge-hearth, Hot-air	L. V. Badger and R. Walker	Portsmouth, N. H	Nov. 30, 1835	....
Forge, Hollow-fire	S. Collins	Springfield, Mass	Sept. 11, 1822	....
Forge, Mode of producing the blast for blacksmith's	W. and H. W. Sharp	Catharine, N. Y	Aug. 2, 1839	1, 270
Forge, Portable	J. B. Bolinger	Detroit, Mich	Nov. 17, 1868	84, 048
Forge, Portable	J. M. Cayce	Franklin, Tenn	Aug. 20, 1867	67, 845
Forge, Portable	J. H. Dickerson	Cincinnati, Ohio	Jan. 17, 1865	45, 911
Forge, Portable	W. G. Hyndman	Cincinnati, Ohio	Nov. 17, 1857	18, 643
Forge, Portable	S. Rohrer	Palmyra, N. Y	Dec. 27, 1864	45, 678
Forge, Portable	P. H and F. M. Roots	Connersville, Ind	Nov. 1, 1870	108, 941
Forge, Queen's portable	C. V. Queen	Peekskill, N. Y	Sept. 19, 1848	5, 782
Forge, Smith's	A. Bissey	Point Pleasant, Pa	June 23, 1838	803
Forge, Smith's	J. W. Crannel	Olivet, Mich	Feb. 3, 1857	16, 531
Forge, Smith's	W. E. Risher	Austin, Tex	Feb. 12, 1867	62, 072
Forges and furnaces, Back for	L. Wilder	Leominster, Mass	Mar. 17, 1838	645
Forges, Bellows-box for blacksmith's	C. Foster	Rochester, N. Y	May 11, 1841	2, 088
Forges, Blowing wind for	D. Strobel, jr	Washington, D. C	May 9, 1831	....
Forges, Driving-gear for portable	L. R. Fitch	Chicago, Ill	Nov. 14, 1871	120, 957
Forges, Fire-box for	H. Sayler and J. Bair	Saint Paris, Ohio	Sept. 10, 1867	68, 657
Forges, Gas-chamber and valve for	J. V. Karr	Goshen, Ind	June 4, 1867	65, 490
Forges, &c., where a blast is required, Back for	A. Graham	Hamilton, N. Y	Dec. 15, 1832	....
Forgery, Means to prevent	R. Willcox	New York, N. Y	Sept. 19, 1823	....
Forging and punching machines, Drop and die	S. Andrews	Perth Amboy, N. J	Apr. 4, 1824	10, 220
Forging and stamping machine	W. Ball	Chicopee, Mass	Jan. 18, 1870	98, 839
Forging apparatus	J. G. N. Alleyne	Alfreton, Great Britain	Nov. 27, 1866	59, 940
Forging-apparatus	D. Davies	Crumlin, England	Sept. 15, 1868	82, 093
Forging-apparatus	T. B. De Forest	Birmingham, Conn	Sept. 24, 1867	69, 080
Forging-apparatus	A. J. Grainger	Wilmington, Ill	Feb. 26, 1867	62, 407
Forging-apparatus	R. S. Lawrence	Hartford, Conn	Feb. 18, 1862	34, 434
Forging-apparatus	E. F. McFarland	Worcester, Mass	Jan. 17, 1865	45, 928
Forging-apparatus	N. Peterson and G. W. Jones	Antioch, Cal	June 9, 1868	78, 825
Forging-apparatus	J. Price	New York, N. Y	June 18, 1867	65, 941
Forging-apparatus	E. A. Raymond	Brooklyn, N. Y	Nov. 28, 1865	51, 267
Forging-apparatus	A. Rix	San Francisco, Cal	Feb. 6, 1866	52, 447
Forging-apparatus, Blacksmith's	L. and I. Andrews	Biddeford, Me	Dec. 18, 1866	60, 458
Forging bolts and round iron	C. Rentgin		Nov. 17, 1796	....
Forging, drawing, swaging, or forming spindles, rollers, bolts, &c., in metal, Machine for.	W. Rider	Bolton, England	Aug. 26, 1843	3, 235
Forging, Furnace for heating wrought-iron wheels for.	W. R. Thomson	Cleveland, Ohio	May 1, 1855	12, 800
Forging, Heating wrought-iron wheels for	W. R. Thomson	Cleveland, Ohio	June 12, 1855	13, 053
Forging iron, &c., Blacksmith's striker for	E. Brooks	Ridgeville, Va	Feb. 16, 1843	2, 956
Forging-machine	J. Copley, jr	Allegheny City, Pa	June 16, 1868	78, 862
Forging-machine	L. L. Crane	Cleveland, Ohio	May 7, 1867	64, 408
Forging-machine	W. H. Defrees	Andover, Mass	May 26, 1868	78, 266
Forging-machine	J. C. Jewell	Boston, Mass	July 4, 1865	48, 560
Forging-machine	W. T. Leach	East Wareham, Mass	Mar. 20, 1860	27, 550
Forging-machine	D. Noyes	Abington, Mass	Aug. 14, 1855	13, 434
Forging-machine	J. Pipes	Ripley, W. Va	Apr. 18, 1871	113, 922
Forging-machine	S. S. Putnam	Boston, Mass	May 29, 1855	12, 961
Forging-machine	G. H. Richards	West Roxbury, Mass	Sept. 14, 1852	9, 266
Forging-machine	E. Schlanker	Buffalo, N. Y	Mar. 29, 1859	23, 400
Forging-machine	J. Stone	Chicago, Ill	Feb. 5, 1867	61, 888
Forging machine, Iron	S. S. Putnam	Boston, Mass	Dec. 9, 1856	16, 186
Forging metal ic sockets, Machine for	G. Fitch and P. Shaffer	Etna, Pa	Dec. 17, 1872	134, 045
Forging metals, Apparatus for	T. Shaw	Philadelphia, Pa	Feb. 15, 1870	99, 958
Forging metals, Drop for	E. K. Root	Hartford, Conn	Nov. 9, 1858	22, 034
Forging metals, &c., Machinery for	W. Field	Providence, R. I	Dec. 14, 1852	9, 471
Forging, shearing, and punching device	J. E. Emerson	Trenton, N. J	June 5, 1866	55, 263
Forging wrench-bars, Die for	L. Coes	Worcester, Mass	Nov. 25, 1873	144, 832

Fork:

See Agricultural fork.
Band-cutting fork.
Barley-fork.
Barley or gavel fork.
Convertible fork.
Cook-fork.
Culinary fork.
Dung-fork.
Flesh-fork.
Four-tined fork.
Fruit-fork.
Gavel-fork.
Gaveling-fork.
Gold-digger's fork.
Grain-fork.
Grappling-fork.
Grate-fork.
Green-corn fork.
Hay-fork.
Hay-elevating fork.
Hoisting-fork
Horse-bag fork.
Loom-filling fork.
Manure-fork.
Parer-fork.
Pickle-fork.
Pitch-fork.
Plate-handling fork.
Potato-fork.
Steel-spring fork.
Table-fork.
Toasting-fork.
Tuning-fork.
Turning-fork.
Wire fork.

Index of patents issued from the United States Patent Office from 1790 *to* 1873, *inclusive*—Continued.

Invention.	Inventor.	Residence.	Date.	No.
Fork	S. C. Blodgett	Philadelphia, Pa	Feb. 19, 1856	14, 275
Fork and band-cutter combined	J. H. Beffemmyer	Enterprise, Pa	Feb. 13, 1872	123, 671
Fork and band-cutter, Combined	M. Wenger	Upper Leacock Post-Office, Pa.	Aug. 23, 1870	106, 758
Fork and cake-lifter	P. L. Suine	Shirleysburgh, Pa	Dec. 18, 1866	60, 650
Fork and pick, Combined	D. Mater, jr	Bellmore, Ind	Aug. 13, 1872	130, 517
Fork and sharpener, Combined	F. C. Beach	Stratford, Conn	Dec. 5, 1865	51, 285
Fork-bending machine	J. G. Batcheller	Wallingford, Vt	Aug. 30, 1870	106, 769
Fork-blank	J. C. Richardson	Ilion, N. Y	Nov. 24, 1868	84, 377
Fork-blank	J. C. Richardson	Ilion, N. Y	Dec. 29, 1868	85, 400
Fork-blank	J. C. Richardson	Ilion, N. Y	June 15, 1869	91, 367
Fork-guard	H. D. P. Cunningham	Alverstroke, England	July 23, 1872	129, 796
Fork, hoe, &c	S. Sheble	Philadelphia, Pa	Mar. 28, 1871	113, 212
Fork-making machinery	H. B. Kinney	Leonardsville, N. Y	Aug. 7, 1866	56, 954
Fork, shovel, and hoe combined	J. A. Heald	Columbus, Miss	Aug. 18, 1868	81, 166
Fork-tine	W. H. Rodden	Toronto, Canada	Oct. 31, 1871	120, 458
Fork-tines, Die for punching	L. S. White	Hartford, Conn	June 2, 1857	17, 475
Fork-wrench	D. Witt	Hubbardston, Mass	July 16, 1872	129, 302
Forks and rakes to their handles, Mode of securing the tines of.	J. P. W. Riley	Montrose, Pa	May 28, 1867	65, 277
Forks and spoons to knives, Means of attaching	N. Ames	Saugus Centre, Mass	Nov. 19, 1861	33, 730
Forks, Machine for forming shoulders on	J. C. Batcheller	Wallingford, Vt	Mar. 20, 1866	53, 258
Forks, Making	H. Whipple and E. Denio	Baldwinsville, N. Y	Sept. 8, 1868	81, 965
Forks, Making four-tined	G. Martin	Waterbury, Conn	June 13, 18[illegible]3	....
Forks, Manufacture of	S. H. Gilman	Boston, Mass	Oct. 16, 1845	4, 235
Forming and planing machines, Carriage for	E. Allen	Newark, N. J	Nov. 11, 1862	36, 884
Forming and punching articles of irregular form	L. Dodge	Waterford, N. Y	Mar. 12, 1861	31, 660
Forms, Machine for cutting tapering	L. E. Phillips	Bristol, N. Y	Apr. 26, 1864	42, 504
Fort	E. Clark	Philadelphia, Pa	Apr. 2, 1812	....
Forts, &c., by means of inflammable liquid, Destroying.	A. Berney	Jersey City, N. J	Apr. 26, 1864	42, 458
Forts, Construction of iron	E. G. Woodman	Lowell, Mass	Jan. 27, 1843	2, 928
Fortification	J. W. Reid	New York, N. Y	Jan. 27, 1863	37, 519
Fortification	A. Roff	Bridgeport, Conn	Apr. 7, 1863	38, 127
Fortifications, Constructing field	P. Jamain	Bordeaux, France	Oct. 6, 1863	40, 213
Foundations, Constructing subaqueous	J. B. Eads	Saint Louis, Mo	Feb. 13, 1872	123, 685
Foundations, Construction of subaqueous	J. B. Eads	Saint Louis, Mo	Jan. 23, 1872	123, 002
Foundations, Forming sub	C. Pontez and C. L. McAlpine	New York, N. Y	Nov. 11, 1862	36, 913
Founder's cleansing-mill	S. D. Horton	Peekskill, N. Y	Sept. 11, 1866	57, 907
Founder's flask	A. L. Robinson, M. M. Donnelly, and D. H. Kruna.	Cincinnati, Ohio	Apr. 21, 1863	38, 243
Founding	A. H. Emery	New York, N. Y	Jan. 27, 1863	37, 497
Founding-apparatus	C. Warner	Louisville, Ky	Dec. 2, 1851	8, 570
Foundery-press, Double	W. Blake	Boston, Mass	Apr. 29, 1833	....
Foundery purposes, Venting-core for	H. Tucker	Newton, Mass	Nov. 13, 1866	59, 684
Fountain: *See* Crystal fountain. Drinking-fountain. Ink-fountain. Lamp-fountain. Parlor-fountain. Pen-fountain. Portable fountain. Portable refreshment-fountain. Rotating fountain. Self-feeding fountain. Soda-fountain. Soda-water fountain. Wash-boiler fountain.				
Fountain	H. Broezel	Mauston, Wis	Dec. 5, 1871	121, 580
Fountain	G. Finley	Pittsburgh, Pa	Aug. 27, 1872	130, 798
Fountain	G. Polyblank and J. Parkin	Cleveland, Ohio	Sept. 19, 1871	119, 046
Fountain	J. Ross	Greenville, Mich	Mar. 19, 1867	63, 099
Fountain	H. H. Sawtell	Randolph, N. Y	Nov. 14, 1871	120, 902
Fountain	L. Schoeney	New York, N. Y	May 9, 1871	114, 718
Fountain	J. Storer	Hammersmith, England	Feb. 7, 1871	111, 697
Fountain	A. P. Yates	Syracuse, N. Y	May 31, 1870	103, 814
Fountain and aquarium	J. Moore	Brooklyn, N. Y	Oct. 7, 1873	143, 456
Fountain and cooler combined	C. Lauby	Brodhead, Wis	Jan. 9, 1872	122, 617
Fountain and evaporator, Combined	G. H. Thatcher	Albany, N. Y	July 22, 1851	8, 232
Fountain and pump combined	J. J. Sink	Philadelphia, Pa	Aug. 5, 1873	141, 600
Fountain-comb	W. Kerr, jr., and J. A. Robbins	Boston, Mass	Dec. 29, 1868	85, 311
Fowl fetter or clog	S. J. Baker	Madison Centre, Me	Jan. 3, 1871	110, 621
Fowl-perch	L. T. Stetson	Randolph, Mass	Nov. 21, 1871	121, 067
Fowl, Trapping wild	A. Brear	Saugatuck, Conn	Nov. 27, 1866	59, 953
Fractured thigh, Apparatus for	S. Wolston	Vincentown, N. J	July 2, 1836	....
Fractures and dislocations, Apparatus for treating	E. H. Barnes	Marathon, N. Y	Apr. 7, 1868	76, 382
Fractures and displacements, Apparatus for treating.	J. S. McClelland	Crawfordsville, Ind	Dec. 17, 1867	72, 215
Fractures, Apparatus for	T. Burr	Battle Creek, Mich	Apr. 30, 1861	30, 229
Fractures, Apparatus for	W. Mills and M. Hoar	New Athens, Ohio	Nov. 8, 1845	4, 255
Fractures, Apparatus for	L. Post	Lodi, N. Y	Dec. 16, 1844	3, 859
Fractures, Apparatus for	L. Roe	White Plains, N. Y	Nov. 6, 1844	3, 810
Fractures, Apparatus for	J. Whitten	Boston, Mass	Feb. 19, 1861	31, 501
Fractures, Apparatus for the cure of	O. M. Allaben	Middletown, N. Y	Dec. 12, 1839	1, 428
Fractures, Apparatus for treatment of	Z. Hussey	Chillicothe, Ohio	Dec. 14, 1852	9, 467
Fractures, Instrument for supporting	S. B. Tucker	Saint Louis, Mo	Mar. 19, 1867	62, 982
Fractures of the lower jaw, Apparatus for the treatment of.	J. Stowe	Lawrence, Mass	Aug. 2, 1870	106, 091
Frame: *See* Advertising-frame. Alphabet-frame. Arithmetical frame. Artist's stretching-frame. Awning-frame. Bag-frame. Baking-frame. Barrow-frame. Bed-frame. Bed-bottom frame. Bridge-truss frame. Bonnet-frame. Canopy-frame. Car-frame. Car-body frame. Car-seat frame. Car-seat end frame. Carpet-bag frame. Carriage-top frame. Caster-frame. Chair-frame. Chair-seat frame. Cheese-frame. Clothes-frame. Comb-frame. Diking-sheet frame. Door-frame.				

Index of patents issued from the United States Patent Office from 1790 *to* 1873, *inclusive*—Continued.

Invention.	Inventor.	Residence.	Date.	No.
Frame—Continued. *See* Drawing-frame. Dress-frame. Dressing-frame. Drying-frame. Electroplating-frame. Fender-frame. Filling-frame. Flax and hemp drying frame. Flower-frame. Fly-frame. Folding-frame. Fruit-drying frame. Furnace-door frame. Gilt-frame. Glass-frame. Grate-frame. Grate-bar frame. Grindstone-frame. Harrow-frame. Harvester-frame. Hat-frame. Heddle-frame. Hinged frame. Hoop-skirt frame. Hop-frame. Hop-vine frame. Ivory frame. Kite-frame. Lace-drying frame. Looking-glass frame. Mattress-frame. Mica-frame. Milk-stool frame. Mirror-frame. Mirror and picture frame. Necktie-frame. Net-frame. Oval frame. Pants-stretching frame. Photographic frame. Photographic-paper frame. Photographic-printing frame. Piano-frame. Picture-frame. Pier-glass frame. Pillow-frame. Pillow-spread frame. Porcelain-printing frame. Printing-frame. Quilting-frame. Revolving-frame. Rock-drilling-machine frame. Roller-frame. Roofing-frame. Roving-frame. Sample-frame. Sash-frame. Saw-frame. Settee-frame. Ship-frame. Shutter-blind frame. Skirt-frame. Slate-frame. Spectacles-frame. Spinning-frame. Spool-frame. Staging-frame. Stool or ottoman frame. Stove-door frame. Stripper-frame. Tatting-frame. Tender-frame. Tent-frame. Throstle-frame. Traveling-bag frame. Trunk-caster frame. Tub-washer frame. Umbrella-frame. Vehicle-seat frame. Vertical-engine frame. Wardrobe-frame. Warp-setting frame. Warping-frame. Watch-frame. Wheelbarrow-frame. Winding-frame. Window-frame. Window and door frame. Window-screen frame.				
Frame	B. A. Stevens	Toledo, Ohio	Oct. 8, 1872	132, 114
Frame, bottle, &c., Composition for	J. T. Peet	Cincinnati, Ohio	Aug. 1, 1865	49, 147
Frame-joints, Method of securing	C. F. Linscott	New York, N. Y	Jan. 24, 1871	111, 128
Frame or caissons of breakwater, &c	E. H. Tracy	New York, N. Y	Apr. 27, 1859	20, 105
Frame, Standing-press	B. F. Brown	New York, N. Y	Mar. 2, 1822	....
Framing-joint	J. Newton	New York, N. Y	July 4, 1871	116, 623
Freeing-tool, screw, and jewel-setter combined	C. E. Evard	Leesburgh, Va	May 4, 1869	89, 568
Freezer, Artificial	N. M. Johnson	Philadelphia, Pa	Sept. 9, 1843	3, 254
Freezer, Ice-cream	E. P. Torrey	New York, N. Y	Sept. 19, 1861	31, 497
Freezing-apparatus	J. B. Toselli	Paris, France	May 19, 1868	78, 159
Freezing-apparatus, Process of forming vacuum in	E. S. Boynton	Meriden, Conn	Aug. 9, 1870	106, 251
Freezing-box for fish, &c	W. Davis	Detroit, Mich	Jan. 19, 1869	85, 913
Freezing fish, meat, &c., Device for	D. Y. Howell	Toledo, Ohio	Dec. 6, 1870	109, 820
Freezing liquids, Apparatus for	J. Baptiste, J. Mignon, and S. H. Rouart.	Paris, France	Sept. 26, 1865	50, 212
Freight, Device for unloading or storing	H. A Whitney	Brooklyn, N. Y	June 20, 1865	48, 330
Freight-elevator	W. F. Morrow	Shippensburgh, Pa	Jan. 30, 1872	123, 189
Freight or merchandise, Unloading	R. Bragg	San Francisco, Cal	June 2, 1863	38, 725
Freight, Receiving and discharging	N. A. Patterson	Kingston, Tenn	Sept. 4, 1866	57, 825
Freight-transferring mechanism	J. H. James, jr	Urbana, Ohio	Jan. 12, 1869	85, 829
Friction-brake	R. Kitson	Lowell, Mass	June 2, 1863	38, 749
Friction-brake for machinery	J. C. Clapp	Boston, Mass	Aug. 15, 1871	118, 107
Friction brake or clutch	A. G. Waldo	Milwaukee, Wis	June 6, 1871	115, 792
Friction-coupling	A. and F. Brown	New York, N. Y	Nov. 4, 1862	36, 832
Friction-coupling	J. Mattison	Oswego, N. Y	Apr. 10, 1866	53, 846
Friction-coupling, Double	J. Hendy	San Francisco, Cal	Oct. 11, 1859	25, 733
Friction-furnace for generating heat without the consumption of fuel.	J. W. Cochran	Lowell, Mass	Nov. 19, 1833	....
Friction-heater for mill, &c	D. H. Ball	Enterprise, Pa	Jan. 26, 1869	86, 270
Friction in machinery, Reducing	J. J. Reckers	Baltimore, Md	June 13, 1831	....
Friction in mill-gudgeons, Reducing	F. Eichelberger	Creagerstown, Md	June 29, 1833	....
Friction-joint, Hydrodynamic	T. E. Sandgren	Wilmington, Del	July 24, 1855	13, 324
Friction, Mode of diminishing	C. Badin	Paris, France	Aug. 29, 1869	49, 685
Friction of axles, mandrils, &c., Reducing	I. Cooper	Baltimore, Md	Sept. 28, 1831	....
Friction-roller	D. Baldwin	Queensbury, N. Y	Oct. 1, 1830	....
Friction-roller	W. Brown	Portsmouth, England	Dec. 6, 1870	109, 866
Friction-roller	J. Patterson	Franklinville, N. Y	Aug. 9, 1853	9, 926
Friction-roller	C. W. Pierce	Albany, N. Y	Jan. 7, 1868	73, 117
Friction-roller	J. M. Totten	Peoria, Ill	Sept. 10, 1859	7, 639
Friction-roller, Adjustable	J. and T. Sweeney	Birmingham, Pa	Apr. 10, 1855	12, 701
Friction-roller bearing	C. M. Daboll	New London, Conn	May 10, 1870	102, 779
Friction-roller, Elastic	A. A. Moss	Philadelphia, Pa	July 5, 1859	24, 653
Friction-roller for machinery	I. Clowes	Norfolk, Va	Sept. 9, 1834	....
Friction-roller for machinery	B. Stancliffe	Philadelphia, Pa	Dec. 31, 1833	....
Friction-roller support or bearing	S. W. Eaton	Farmington, Me	May 21, 1867	64, 958
Friction-rollers, Mode of applying	R. Dickson and S. G Merriman	Southington, Conn	Mar. 26, 1838	657
Friction-rollers to gudgeons, Applying	M. C. Forrist	Foxborough, Mass	Nov. 16, 1841	2, 364

Index of patents issued from the United States Patent Office from 1790 *to* 1873, *inclusive*—Continued.

Invention.	Inventor.	Residence.	Date.	No.
Friction rolling	G. Danforth	Centreville, Ill	May 17, 1833	....
Friction-spindles, Reducing	F. Fredley	Logan, Pa	Mar. 10, 1834	....
Friction-wheel	T. Hotchkiss	Stratford, Conn	Apr. 2, 1867	63, 520
Friction-wheel and oil-chamber	A. I. Ambler	Chicago, Ill	Mar. 21, 1865	46, 867
Friction-wheel for driving machinery	J. Hinkley	Norwalk, Ohio	Apr. 14, 1863	38, 165
Friction-wheel for gearing	W. D. Andrews	New York, N. Y	Mar. 15, 1870	100, 839
Friction-wheel or roller for machinery	J. D. Cobb	Lebanon, Ohio	June 22, 1832	....
Frictional-brake	P. W. Yarrell	Garysburgh, N. C	Apr. 2, 1872	125, 158
Frilling and crimping machine	C. O. Crosby and H. Kellogg	Hartford, Conn	Dec. 2, 1862	37, 033
Frilling, Double	C. O. Crosby and H. Kellogg	New Haven, Conn	Apr. 28, 1863	38, 289
Fringe	J. E. Gillespie	Norwich, Conn	Feb. 27, 1872	124, 051
Fringe-cutting machine	W. J. Horstmann	Philadelphia, Pa	Apr. 7, 1857	16, 977
Fringe, Machinery for twisting shawl	M. D. Whipple	Lowell, Mass	Nov. 27, 1849	6, 911
Fringe-making machine	E. Doran	Philadelphia, Pa	Aug. 18, 1868	81, 073
Fringe-making machine	L. D. Valetton	New York, N. Y	Apr. 2, 1861	31, 916
Fringe of shawls, &c., Machine for twisting	J. Nesmith and W. Sawyer	Lowell and Dracut, Mass	Oct. 13, 1851	8, 424
Fringe on textile fabrics, Machine for forming	T. Henderson	Glasgow, North Britain	Jan. 23, 1872	123, 017
Fringe-twister	H. Howard	Leeds, N. Y	May 9, 1871	114, 562
Fringe-twisting machine, Bullion	E. Barton	Paterson, N. J	Mar. 9, 1869	87, 620
Fringed fabric, Woven	P. Cocker	Philadelphia, Pa	Dec. 13, 1870	110, 012
Frog. Self-acting guard	C. A. Postley	Spring Garden, Pa	June 24, 1851	8, 171
Frowers, Die for forging	C. Konold	Pittsburgh, Pa	Jan. 21, 1873	134, 993
Fruit and berry basket	G. W. Swan and W. Finch	San Francisco, Cal	Aug. 26, 1873	142, 299
Fruit and berry box or basket	J. H. Marvil	Laurel, Del	May 2, 1871	114, 456
Fruit and clothes drier	T. B. Carroll	Indianapolis, Ind	July 20, 1869	92, 700
Fruit and ice house combined	J. S. Ross	Hiram, Ohio	Jan. 8, 1867	61, 107
Fruit and lard press	W. H. Davis	Lexington, Ind	Sept. 2, 1873	142, 329
Fruit and meat drying apparatus	H. Endemann	New York, N. Y	Oct. 24, 1871	120, 253
Fruit and poultry box	D. B. Spinning	Brooklyn, N. Y	June 25, 1867	66, 183
Fruit and preserve jar	J. S. and T. B. Atterbury	Pittsburgh, Pa	June 30, 1863	39, 027
Fruit and vegetable crate	E. B. Georgia	Clifton Station, Va	July 16, 1872	129, 332
Fruit and vegetable cutter	W. H. Trissler	Lima, Ind	May 22, 1860	28, 419
Fruit and vegetable desiccating apparatus	J. A. Miller	New York, N. Y	Sept. 13, 1864	44, 260
Fruit and vegetable preserver	P. Kephart	Uniontown, Md	Sept. 24, 1844	3, 758
Fruit and vegetable press	C. Parham	Philadelphia, Pa	Oct. 18, 1864	44, 742
Fruit annually, Method for growing	F. Clymer	Galion, Ohio	Feb. 9, 1869	86, 733
Fruit, Apparatus for cooking and preserving	W. Janney	Martinsville, Ohio	Mar. 19, 1867	62, 960
Fruit, Apparatus for packing	R. Law	Lockport, N. Y	July 12, 1859	24, 779
Fruit-bag	W. I. Ludlow	Cleveland, Ohio	Apr. 28, 1868	77, 201
Fruit-basket	R. S. Bartlett	Northampton, Mass	Jan. 23, 1872	122, 984
Fruit-basket	S. D. Bedell	New York, N. Y	May 6, 1873	138, 605
Fruit-basket	L. W. Beecher	New Haven, Conn	Apr. 29, 1862	35, 073
Fruit-basket	L. W. Beecher	New Haven, Conn	May 31, 1864	42, 923
Fruit-basket	L. W. Beecher	New Haven, Conn	Dec. 17, 1872	134, 027
Fruit-basket	W. H. Burridge	Cleveland, Ohio	Jan. 31, 1865	46, 177
Fruit-basket	H. Carpenter	New York, N. Y	Sept. 20, 1864	44, 280
Fruit-basket	H. Carpenter	Williamsburgh, N. Y	Nov. 7, 1871	120, 620
Fruit-basket	N. S. Clement	New Britain, Conn	Sept. 29, 1868	82, 601
Fruit-basket	W. Clement	Charlestown, Ill	May 29, 1866	55, 061
Fruit-basket	E. Colby	Brockport, N. Y	May 31, 1870	103, 570
Fruit-basket	S. B. Conover	New York, N. Y	Oct. 1, 1872	131, 851
Fruit-basket	C. C. Converse	Dubuque, Iowa	Aug. 30, 4864	43, 974
Fruit-basket	C. C. Converse	Dubuque, Iowa	Sept. 27, 1864	44, 400
Frult-basket	D. Cook	New Haven, Conn	July 12, 1859	24, 723
Fruit-basket	A. Dean	Otto, Ind	July 30, 1872	130, 025
Fruit-basket	J. H. Doolittle	Derby, Conn	Aug. 15, 1865	49, 390
Fruit basket	I. C. Gleason	Middletown, Conn	June 26, 1866	55, 851
Fruit-basket	J. S. Hoard and C. M. Milese	Vineland, N. J	May 23, 1865	47, 822
Fruit-basket	E. A. Jeffery	New Haven, Conn	Aug. 22, 1865	49, 590
Fruit-basket	H. C. Jones	Dowagiac, Mich	Aug. 6, 1872	130, 299
Fruit-basket	O. Macdaniel	New York, N. Y	May 19, 1868	78, 110
Fruit-basket	R. Mitchell	Smyrna, Del	Aug. 23, 1870	106, 605
Fruit-basket	C. Moore	St. atford, Conn	Nov. 17, 1868	84, 207
Fruit-basket	G. Munger	New Haven, Conn	Oct. 17, 1865	50, 486
Fruit-basket	O. A. North	New Britain, Conn	Aug. 27, 1872	130, 937
Fruit-basket	J. K. Park	Marlborough, N. Y	June 12, 1866	55, 530
Fruit-basket	S. D. Payne	Kasota, Minn	Aug. 23, 1870	106, 719
Fruit-basket	E. F. Percival and N. S. True	Hammonton, N. J	Aug. 18, 1868	81, 205
Fruit-basket	D. H. Priest	Watertown, Mass	May 8, 1866	54, 594
Fruit-basket	P. B. Sheldon	Prattsburgh, N. Y	May 1, 1866	54, 422
Fruit-basket	D. Sherwood and G. D. Dudley	Lowell, Mass	Mar. 16, 1869	87, 7[illegible]7
Fruit-basket	M. L. and O. A. Stray	Willoughby, Ohio	Mar. 25, 1862	34, 792
Fruit-basket	M. L. and O. A. Stray	Willoughby, Ohio	Oct. 30, 1866	59, 290
Fruit-basket	O. Stoddard	Busti, N. Y	Oct. 27, 1863	40, 436
Fruit-basket	W. D. Trissler	Dunkirk, N. Y	Feb. 11, 1873	135, 737
Fruit-basket	W. H. Trissler	Dunkirk, N. Y	July 9, 1872	128, 927
Fruit-basket	P. B. Viele	Rochester, N. Y	Feb. 11, 1868	74, 456
Fruit-basket	C. Wheat and C. Bunge	Geneva, N. Y	Aug. 7, 1866	57, 024
Fruit-basket	G. H. White	Huntington, N. Y	Dec. 6, 1870	109, 983
Fru.t-basket	W. R. Wilcox	Saint Joseph, Mich	Nov. 4, 1873	144, 376
Fruit basket and crate	A. F. Newell	Warren, Ohio	Oct. 21, 1862	36, 723
Fruit-basket cover	A. S. Dyckman	South Haven, Mich	Nov. 28, 1871	121, 238
Fruit-basket, Paper	A. Adams and J. F. Jewett	Chagrin Falls and Cincinnati, Ohio.	July 26, 1870	105, 619
Fruit-basket platform or handle	J. Knapp	Coloma, Mich	Nov. 21, 1871	121, 055
Fruit-baskets, Cutter for cutting the bodies of	B. D. Whitney	Winchendon, Mass	May 24, 1870	103, 533
Fruit-baskets, Machine for bottoming	B. D. Whitney	Winchendon, Mass	May 24, 1870	103, 532
Fruit-baskets, Machine for cutting out the bodies of	H. Mellish	Walpole, N. H	Apr. 2, 1867	63, 414
Fruit-baskets, Machine for cutting the bottoms of.	H. Mellish	Walpole, N. H	Mar. 26, 1867	63, 280
Fruit-baskets, Machine for making	H. Mellish	Walpole, N. H	Mar. 26, 1867	63, 279
Fruit-baskets, Tool for fitting bottoms to	A. S. Parks	Winchendon, Mass	May 24, 1870	103, 493
Fruit-box	C. A. Blair	New Britain, Conn	Dec. 19, 1871	121, 926
Fruit-box	C. A. Blair	New Britain, Conn	May 7, 1872	126, 440
Fruit-box	E. P. Bothwell	McArthur, Ohio	Jan. 21, 1873	134, 973
Fruit-box	I. F. Brown	New London, Conn	Sept. 17, 1867	68, 943
Fruit-box	C. Colby and H. C. Ward	Benton Harbor, Mich	Aug. 23, 1870	106, 663
Fruit-box	I. Copeland	North Bridgewater, Mass	Jan. 14, 1868	73, 300
Fruit-box	T. B. Doolittle	Ansonia, Conn	June 19, 1866	55, 631

Index of patents issued from the United States Patent Office from 1790 *to* 1873, *inclusive*—Continued.

Invention.	Inventor.	Residence.	Date.	No.
Fruit-box	W. H. Earle	Vineland, N. J	Oct. 16, 1866	58, 939
Fruit-box	J. H. Fisher	Chicago, Ill	Dec. 7, 1869	97, 493
Fruit-box	L. L. Gilliland	Dayton, Ohio	June 7, 1870	104, 116
Fruit-box	H. H. and M. L. Gridley	Auburn, N. Y., and Burlington, N. J.	Apr. 9, 1867	63, 629
Fruit-box	N. Hallock	Flushing, N. Y	Sept. 7, 1858	21, 415
Fruit-box	J. W. Hayes	Newark, N. J	Aug 12, 1858	15, 514
Fruit-box	W. Huey	Galena, Md	July 2, 1867	66, 346
Fruit-box	T. B. Jones	Radnor, Ohio	Oct. 27, 1868	83, 504
Fruit-box	J. H. Marvil	Laurel, Del	Oct. 10, 1871	119, 872
Fruit-box	E. Morris	Burlington, N. J	Jan. 10, 1865	45, 848
Fruit-box	E. Morris	Burlington, N. J	Sept. 12, 1865	49, 908
Fruit-box	A. F. Newell	Warren, Ohio	Jan. 5, 1864	41, 168
Fruit-box	W. Nicklin	Marlborough, N. Y	July 16, 1872	129, 047
Fruit-box	J. M. Perkins	Plainfield, N. J	Sept. 22, 1868	82, 438
Fruit-box	S. W. Phelps	Sandusky, Ohio	Nov. 28, 1871	121, 412
Fruit-box	C. Reese	Baltimore, Md	June 19, 1866	55, 709
Fruit-box	A. T. Robinson and J. Shepard	Bristol, Conn	Mar. 16, 1869	87, 875
Fruit-box	J. T. Severns	Burlington, N. J	Oct. 16, 1866	58, 899
Fruit-box	J. Shepard	Bristol, Conn	Feb. 20, 1873	123, 941
Fruit-box	J. Shepard and B. B. Lewis	Bristol, Conn	May 8, 1866	54, 614
Fruit-box	J. S. Shields	Medora, Ind	Nov. 17, 1868	84, 139
Fruit-box	J. Vincent	Newfane, N. Y	Feb. 9, 1869	86, 886
Fruit-box	C. W. Weston	San Francisco, Cal	Oct. 10, 1871	119, 816
Fruit-box	C. W. Weston	San Francisco, Cal	Aug. 27, 1872	130, 963
Fruit-box	C. W. Weston	San Francisco, Cal	Nov. 12, 1872	132, 942
Fruit-box	C. W. Weston	San Francisco, Cal	Aug. 12, 1873	141, 842
Fruit-box	J. White	Cleveland, Ohio	Aug. 20, 1867	68, 019
Fruit-box	J. F. and O. B. Whitney	Milton, N. Y	Sept. 3, 1867	68, 401
Fruit-box	W. R. Wilcox	Saint Joseph, Mich	July 16, 1867	66, 925
Fruit-box	H. B. Willcox	Troy Mills, Pa	Nov. 26, 1867	71, 435
Fruit-box crate	J. White	Cleveland, Ohio	Nov. 16, 1869	96, 856
Fruit-box fastening	H. T. Barker	Napa, Cal	June 12, 1866	55, 455
Fruit-box, Folding	J. H. Hollingsworth	Philadelphia, Pa	Jan. 26, 1869	86, 157
Fruit-box handle, Adjustable	C. Peebles	Santa Clara, Cal	Mar. 19, 1867	63, 086
Fruit-box lock	C. Colby	Madison, Wis	Mar. 10, 1868	75, 372
Fruit box or basket	J. H. Doolittle	Ansonia, Conn	Sept. 12, 1865	49, 866
Fruit-boxes, Case for conveying	R. H. Baker	Jamestown, N. Y	Jan. 5, 1864	41, 049
Fruit-can	M. Bray	Newton, Mass	Nov. 11, 1873	144, 380
Fruit-can, &c	C. Becker, J. A. Ross, and J. Steuernagel.	Allegheny City, Pa	July 14, 1868	79, 889
Fruit-can	H Callahan	Dayton, Ohio	Aug. 29, 1871	118, 586
Fruit-can	B. F. Ells	Dayton, Ohio	July 17, 1866	56, 390
Fruit-can	R. G. Farnham	Elbridge, N. Y	Jan. 3, 1871	110, 757
Fruit-can	O. F. Fitch	Morristown, Ind	Mar. 11, 1862	34, 627
Fruit-can	J. Grimes	Portsmouth, Ohio	Jan. 2, 1872	122, 455
Fruit-can	J. Haines	West Middleburgh, Ohio	Aug. 13, 1867	67, 754
Fruit-can	G. E. Heinig	Louisville, Ky	July 19, 1870	105, 572
Fruit-can	L. E. Holden	Cleveland, Ohio	Apr. 21, 1868	76, 917
Fruit-can	I. Kling	Seymour, Ind	Mar. 22, 1870	101, 024
Fruit-can	S. Lutz	Philadelphia, Pa	May 10, 1870	102, 952
Fruit-can	W. W. Lyman	West Meriden, Conn	Dec. 28, 1858	22, 436
Fruit-can	W. W. Lyman	West Meriden, Conn	June 10, 1862	35, 529
Fruit-can	A. J. McMillen	Ravenswood, W. Va	Dec. 7, 1869	97, 669
Fruit-can	J. F. Merrill	Cincinnati, Ohio	July 5, 1870	105, 109
Fruit-can	H. Mitchell	Osborne, Ohio	Apr. 27, 1869	89, 327
Fruit-can	J. Neuberger and P. J. Illig	Buffalo, N. Y	Apr. 11, 1865	47, 216
Fruit-can	P. Nemsen	Baltimore, Md	Mar. 3, 1868	75, 189
Fruit-can	M. O'Connor	New Brunswick, N. J	Sept. 2, 1873	142, 503
Fruit-can	W. and G. Pollyblank	Cleveland, Ohio	Feb. 27, 1872	124, 156
Fruit-can	J. S. Shaneman and J. S. Hoon	Beaver Falls, Pa	Feb. 21, 1871	112, 082
Fruit-can	C. F. Spencer	Cleveland, Ohio	Feb. 27, 1872	124, 171
Fruit-can	L. J. Wicks	Bridgeton, N. J	Oct. 23, 1866	59, 111
Fruit-can	A. A. Wilcox	Philadelphia, Pa	Mar. 19, 1872	124, 710
Fruit-can	J. R. Williamson	Bethlehem, N. J	May 26, 1868	78, 346
Fruit-can	J. B. Wilson	Fislerville, N. J	Jan. 26, 1864	41, 417
Fruit can and jar	J. K. Chase	Brooklyn, N. Y	June 18, 1872	128, 112
Fruit-can bodies, Manufacturing	J. Pfau	Cincinnati, Ohio	June 2, 1868	78, 605
Fruit-can cover	T. Earle	Smithfield, R. I	Dec. 22, 1863	40, 996
Fruit-can fastening	G. H. Hammer	Newville, Pa	June 26, 1866	55, 953
Fruit-can manufacture	C. Becker, J. A. Ross, and J. Steuernagel.	Allegheny City, Pa	July 14, 1868	79, 890
Fruit-can opener	W. W. Lyman	West Meriden, Conn	May 22, 1866	54, 929
Fruit-can opener	A. McClanahan	Bath, Ill	Nov. 19, 1872	133, 108
Fruit-can-opening tool	H. Holt	New York, N. Y	Dec. 10, 1867	72, 042
Fruit-can-sealing apparatus	T. M. Ferguson	Rainsborough, Ohio	July 28, 1868	80, 401
Fruit-can, Self-sealing	T. Parker	Germantown, Pa	Dec. 18, 1866	60, 547
Fruit-can, Sheet-metal	C. F. Sturgis	Buena Vista, Ala	Mar. 28, 1871	113, 111
Fruit-can tongs	A. T. Atherton	Lowell, Mass	Oct. 17, 1871	119, 912
Fruit-can top	A. Stewart	Cincinnati, Ohio	Oct. 2, 1866	58, 502
Fruit-cans and cleaning off the tops, Machine for filling.	L. J. Wicks	Bridgeton, N. J	Dec. 26, 1871	122, 298
Fruit-cans and other cylindrical packages, Machine for varnishing and labeling.	A. C. Platt	Sandusky, Ohio	Aug. 23, 1870	106, 724
Fruit-cans, Apparatus for exhausting the air from	L. C. Cooley	Albany, N. Y	June 24, 1873	140, 247
Fruit-cans by steam, Mode of exhausting air from	D. Beardsley	Ithaca, N. Y	Jan. 29, 1867	61, 506
Fruit-cans, Closing	N. S. Gilbert	Lockport, N. Y	Aug. 25, 1863	39, 643
Fruit-cans, Closing	W. Webster	Middletown, Ohio	Sept. 8, 1863	39, 853
Fruit-cans, Closing	W. Webster	Middletown, Ohio	Feb. 16, 1864	41, 657
Fruit-cans, Machine for closing	G. C. Grodhaus	Jamestown, Ohio	Sept. 3, 1872	130, 989
Fruit-cans, Machine for making	I. Kling	Seymour, Ind	Mar. 15, 1870	100, 775
Fruit-cans, Machine for making tin	A. Kollenberg	Owensborough, Kentucky	May 22, 1866	54, 923
Fruit-cans, Making tin	J. M. Francis	Waldo, Ohio	June 26, 1866	55, 845
Fruit-cans, Sealing	E. K. and J. M. Bruce	Wilkins, Pa	Nov. 20, 1866	59, 816
Fruit-cans, Sealing	J. M. Cooper and W. L. Haller	Chambersburgh and Carlisle, Pa.	Aug. 7, 1860	29, 544
Fruit-cans, Sealing	H. S. Fisher	Newburgh, Pa	Mar. 22, 1864	41, 985
Fruit-cans, &c., Sealing	W. K. Lewis and J. W. Bailey	Boston and West Brookfield, Mass.	Apr. 24, 1866	54, 182

Index of patents issued from the United States Patent Office from 1790 *to* 1873, *inclusive*—Continued.

Invention.	Inventor.	Residence.	Date.	No.
Fruit-cans, Sealing	C. F. Spencer	Rochester, N. Y	Nov. 19, 1867	71, 239
Fruit-cans, Tongs for lifting	A. H. Johnson	Bridgeport, Conn	Jan. 7, 1873	134, 604
Fruit, Canning	J. R. Matthews	Cincinnati, Ohio	Feb. 18, 1873	135, 927
Fruit, Canning	C. J. Paine	Young America, Ill	Sept. 3, 1867	68, 384
Fruit-canning ladle	R. D. Baker	Syracuse, N. Y	Aug. 8, 1871	117, 723
Fruit-canning machine	J. H. Ellis	Peoria, Ill	June 21, 1870	104, 438
Fruit-carrier	J. W. Weston	New York, N. Y	Nov. 3, 1868	83, 678
Fruit-carrying box	G. A. Lloyd	San Francisco, Cal	Sept. 6, 1870	107, 070
Fruit-case	C. Doolittle and A. Carson	Oswego and New York, N. Y.	Oct. 9, 1860	30, 303
Fruit collecting and drying apparatus	S. N. Thomas	Auburn, N. Y	June 9, 1863	38, 848
Fruit-coring knife	A. L. Harris	Kent, Ohio	July 5, 1870	104, 954
Fruit-cover	O. W. Alexander	Osage, Tex	Dec. 17, 1872	133, 914
Fruit-crate	G. Clapp	Geneva, N. Y	Nov. 15, 1870	109, 175
Fruit-crate	W. H. Clarkson	Bridgeville, Del	Mar. 18, 1873	136, 968
Fruit-crate	D. Crane	Saginaw, Mich	Aug. 26, 1873	142, 148
Fruit-crate	G. M. Fenley	Medora, Ind	Aug. 17, 1869	93, 693
Fruit-crate	W. G. Goodale	Centralia, Ill	Aug. 18, 1868	81, 153
Fruit-crate	H. and E. W. Humphreys	Salisbury, Md	Dec. 24, 1872	134, 205
Fruit-crate	L. A. Lindsey and J. F. O'Sullivan.	Jackson, Miss	Apr. 6, 1869	88, 647
Fruit-crate	T. Mabbett, sr	Vineland, N. J	Apr. 21, 1868	77, 060
Fruit-crate	J. H. Marvil	Laurel, Del	Mar. 5, 1872	124, 366
Fruit-crate	L. Selling	Detroit, Mich	July 29, 1873	141, 389
Fruit-crate	F. R. Van Dake	Jackson, Miss	Sept. 21, 1869	95, 169
Fruit, Crate for carrying	W. Gilbert	Catskill, N. Y	Mar. 27, 1866	53, 437
Fruit-crates, Hasp for fastening	F. R. Baird	Norfolk, Va	Feb. 8, 1870	99, 620
Fruit, Device for boiling and stirring	M. G. Collins	Baltimore, Md	May 12, 1868	77, 870
Fruit, Device for quartering, coring, and stringing	S. T. Sanford	Fall River, Mass	Sept. 15, 1863	39, 963
Fruit-dryer	J. Allen	Everett, Mo	July 18, 1871	117, 029
Fruit-dryer	J. Allen	Everett, Mo	July 2, 1872	128, 521
Fruit-dryer	R. N. Allen	Cleveland, Ohio	Nov. 20, 1866	59, 806
Fruit-dryer	S. C. Barth	Indianapolis, Ind	Mar. 19, 1872	124, 658
Fruit-dryer	H. Beamer	Smithburg, Pa	Oct. 9, 1860	30, 285
Fruit-dryer	J. S. Biddle and T. S. Lingenfelter.	Pattonville, Pa	Mar. 14, 1871	112, 532
Fruit-dryer	J. I. Boone	West Milton, Ohio	Jan. 2, 1866	51, 792
Fruit-dryer	D. K. Boswell	Columbus, Ohio	Jan. 28, 1868	73, 691
Fruit-dryer	J. K. Boswell	Richmond, Ind	Apr. 23, 1867	64, 065
Fruit-dryer	C. A. Boynton	Vineland, N. J	Apr. 23, 1872	125, 929
Fruit-dryer	J. W. Brooks and H. Rudoff	Ashley, Ill	July 27, 1869	93, 048
Fruit-dryer	W. R. Clark	Indianola, Ill	Nov. 23, 1869	97, 168
Fruit-dryer	N. C. Cooley	Wyoming, Del	June 21, 1870	104, 559
Fruit dryer	I. B. Cottrell	Bridgeville, Del	Aug. 26, 1873	142, 147
Fruit-dryer	E. Dilday	South Pass, Ill	Nov. 23, 1869	97, 174
Fruit-dryer	E. Duncan	West Hilton, Ohio	June 18, 1861	32, 597
Fruit-dryer	D. Durfee	Fort Seneca, Ohio	Dec. 17, 1867	72, 377
Fruit-dryer	A. Edwards	New Haven, Conn	Jan. 7, 1873	134, 528
Fruit-dryer	B. F. Ells	Dayton, Ohio	Feb. 21, 1871	112, 022
Fruit-dryer	O. P. Fence	Des Moines, Iowa	Oct. 4, 1870	108, 048
Fruit-dryer	W. D. Fisher and W. Holly	Freeport, Ill	Sept. 11, 1866	57, 885
Fruit-dryer	M. W. Florer	Bracken County, Ky	Dec. 24, 1867	72, 471
Fruit-dryer	J. Harvey	Martinsville, Ind	Oct. 19, 1869	95, 900
Fruit-dryer	W. Heaton	Greene County, Pa	Mar. 16, 1858	19, 635
Fruit-dryer	H. Henley	Shoals Station, Ind	June 22, 1869	91, 626
Fruit-dryer	H. Henley	Shoals, Ind	Aug. 16, 1870	106, 484
Fruit-dryer	J. Hildebrand	Taneytown, Md	May 31, 1870	103, 744
Fruit-dryer	I. Hogeland	Indianapolis, Ind	Aug. 17, 1869	93, 885
Fruit-dryer	C. Leavitt	Cleveland, Ohio	May 14, 1867	64, 678
Fruit-dryer	A. C. Lewis	Burlington, Mich	July 31, 1860	29, 390
Fruit-dryer	D. Lippy	Mansfield, Ohio	July 4, 1865	48, 570
Fruit-dryer	M. E. Lloyd	New York, N. Y	May 25, 1869	90, 369
Fruit-dryer	R. A. Lucas and L. S. Lehman	Wooster, Ohio	Dec. 29, 1868	85, 459
Fruit-dryer	C. H. Martin	Chapinville, N. Y	Dec. 12, 1871	121, 795
Fruit-dryer	J. B. May	Magnolia, Ohio	Mar. 15, 1870	100, 914
Fruit-dryer	J. V. R. Miller	Richmond, Ind	Jan. 31, 1871	111, 467
Fruit-dryer	J. Mongene	Vincennes, Ind	Apr. 26, 1870	102, 298
Fruit-dryer	R. S. Morse	East Dixfield, Me	Jan. 2, 1855	12, 167
Fruit-dryer	G. R. Nebinger	Lewisberry, Pa	Aug. 7, 1866	56, 982
Fruit-dryer	G. R. Nebinger	Philadelphia, Pa	May 6, 1873	138, 516
Fruit-dryer	J. B. Okey	Indianapolis, Ind	Oct. 11, 1870	108, 289
Fruit-dryer	A. Paige and G. Wilkinson	Chicago, Ill	Aug. 27, 1872	130, 861
Fruit-dryer	J. L. Post	Ashley, Ill	Mar. 11, 1873	136, 670
Fruit-dryer	J. W. Pyne	Danville, Ill	Oct. 20, 1868	83, 313
Fruit-dryer	I. Randall, 2d	Claremont, N. H	June 19, 1860	28, 775
Fruit-dryer	S. D. Rogers and F. C. Selby	Allegan, Mich	June 22, 1869	91, 671
Fruit-dryer	B. L. Ryder	London, Pa	Nov. 12, 1872	133, 060
Fruit-dryer	M. A. Shepard	Bridgeport, Ill	Apr. 7, 1868	76, 532
Fruit-dryer	R. H. Sipes and D. Denbaugh	Bloody Run, Pa	Oct. 19, 1869	95, 942
Fruit-dryer	A. J. Smith	Decorah, Iowa	June 29, 1869	92, 113
Fruit-dryer	M. P. Smith	Baltimore, Md	Sept. 3, 1872	131, 125
Fruit-dryer	A. Snyder	Clyde, Ohio	July 11, 1865	48, 733
Fruit-dryer	J. Spear	Carbondale, Ill	Sept. 29, 1868	82, 654
Fruit-dryer	H. Speer and J. L. Harlow	Chelsea, Mich	Nov. 17, 1863	40, 646
Fruit-dryer	G. M. Sternberg	Fort Riley, Kans	June 28, 1870	104, 788
Fruit-dryer	G. W. Stevens and J. Gray	San Francisco, Cal	Apr. 16, 1872	125, 703
Fruit-dryer	J. Stevenson	Sparta, Ill	Apr. 8, 1873	137, 634
Fruit-dryer	J. H. L. Tuck	Saint Charles, Ill	Aug. 11, 1863	39, 5[illegible]9
Fruit-dryer	W. Vogel	Chelsea, Mich	June 28, 1864	43, 354
Fruit-dryer	T. L. West	West Salem, Wis	June 7, 1864	43, 058
Fruit-dryer	J. Williams	South Haven, Mich	Oct. 21, 1873	143, 949
Fruit-dryer and food-warmer	S. Richmond	Annapolis, Md	Mar. 21, 1871	112, 963
Fruit, Drying	I. Lynde	Marathon, N. Y	Apr. 19, 1864	42, 386
Fruit, Drying and preserving	J. Lowe	Guilford County, N. C	July 4, 1871	116, 729
Fruit-drying frame	C. Gardner	Freedom, Ohio	Sept. 26, 1865	50, 113
Fruit-drying house	J. Billings	Dayton, Ohio	Oct. 10, 1865	50, 414
Fruit-drying house	J. F. Winchell	Springfield, Ohio	Jan. 8, 1867	61, 1[illegible]0
Fruit-drying machine	D. Rice	Shelburne Falls, Mass	Sept. 3, 1867	68, 4[illegible]9

Index of patents issued from the United States Patent Office from 1790 *to* 1873, *inclusive*—Continued.

Invention.	Inventor.	Residence.	Date.	No.
Fruit-fork	I. C. Draper	New York, N. Y	Feb. 18, 1873	135, 975
Fruit-frame	S. T. Emerson	Seville, Ohio	July 28, 1868	80, 468
Fruit-frame	C. Stone	Ravenna, Ohio	Feb. 11, 1868	74, 252
Fruit-gatherer	G. Aldridge	Henderson City, Ky	July 11, 1871	116, 789
Fruit-gatherer	J. S. and A. M. Barry	Sheridan Township, Mich	Aug. 15, 1871	117, 966
Fruit-gatherer	J. Bowles	Augusta, Ga	Aug. 17, 1869	93, 667
Fruit-gatherer	A. W. Brinkerhoff and A. T. Barnes.	Upper Sandusky, Ohio	Sept. 2, 1862	36, 334
Fruit-gatherer	N. H. Bruce	Shirley, Mass	Aug. 2, 1861	32, 973
Fruit-gatherer	M. L. Byrn and G. Clark	New York, N. Y	Feb. 26, 1861	31, 527
Fruit-gatherer	I. T. Carpenter	Thompsontown, Pa	Aug. 28, 1866	57, 473
Fruit-gatherer	D. P. Chamberlin	Hudson, Mich	Jan. 3, 1860	26, 651
Fruit-gatherer	P. Collyer	Hunter, N. Y	June 12, 1847	5, 156
Fruit-gatherer	J. H. Colthar	Hamersville, Ohio	Oct. 29, 1872	132, 634
Fruit-gatherer	P. Conver	Farmington, Ill	Mar. 5, 1872	724, 334
Fruit-gatherer	J. C. Counts	Cross Roads, Ohio	May 14, 1867	64, 749
Fruit-gatherer	M. Darling	Blodgett's Mills, N. Y	July 16, 1867	66, 807
Fruit-gatherer	J. A. Daum	Canton, Ohio	May 15, 1866	54, 696
Fruit-gatherer	O. R. Dinsmore	Auburn, N. H	Sept. 4, 1866	57, 685
Fruit-gatherer	W. Doty	South Hartford, N. Y	Oct. 27, 1857	18, 503
Fruit-gatherer	J. Evans	Newark, N. J	Nov. 4, 1862	36, 834
Fruit-gatherer	T. Flagler	Grass Lake, Mich	Oct. 22, 1867	69, 980
Fruit-gatherer	L. Fleckenstine	Manor Township, Pa	July 30, 1867	67, 279
Fruit-gatherer	J. Franz	Selbysport, Md	Mar. 5, 1867	62, 623
Fruit-gatherer	C. W. Gage	Homer, N. Y	Apr. 7, 1868	76, 320
Fruit-gatherer	E. Gilliam	Allegheny City, Pa	May 8, 1866	54, 527
Fruit-gatherer	F. Goodwin	Astoria, N. Y	Nov. 10, 1857	18, 582
Fruit-gatherer	J. B. Haines	Millersville, Pa	Apr. 23, 1867	64, 096
Fruit-gatherer	R. S. Hall	Hamburgh, Mich	June 9, 1868	78, 662
Fruit-gatherer	O. C. Hamilton and H. McKinney.	Turtle Creek, Pa	July 14, 1868	79, 827
Fruit-gatherer	F. L. Hicks	New Haven, Conn	Feb. 13, 1872	123, 630
Fruit-gatherer	N. E. Hinds	Cooperstown, N. Y	Mar. 19, 1872	124, 743
Fruit-gatherer	J. C. Kearns	Lewistown, Pa	July 4, 1871	116, 718
Fruit-gatherer	H. Kelsey	Ottawa, Kans	May 6, 1873	138, 565
Fruit-gatherer	Z. S. Kelsey	Huntington, Ohio	Sept. 4, 1866	57, 731
Fruit-gatherer	J. Kisor	Nevada, Ohio	Feb. 18, 1873	136, 072
Fruit-gatherer	J. Lane	Chicago, Ill	Feb. 27, 1872	124, 000
Fruit-gatherer	C. F. Lang	Venedy, Ill	Oct. 20, 1868	83, 178
Fruit-gatherer	J. A. Little	Danville, Ind	Mar. 21, 1865	46, 916
Fruit-gatherer	M. Lounsbury	Seymour, Conn	Dec. 3, 1861	33, 843
Fruit-gatherer	V. H. Lyon	Plainfield, Ind	Mar. 3, 1868	75, 035
Fruit-gatherer	F. A. Maxfield	East Spring Hill, Pa	Apr. 19, 1864	42, 387
Fruit-gatherer	A. McWilliams	Washington, D. C	Mar. 13, 1844	3, 478
Fruit-gatherer	S. Mellinger, jr	Mount Pleasant, Pa	Aug. 7, 1866	56, 972
Fruit-gatherer	M. A. and D. F. Morton	Angola, N. Y	June 4, 1867	65, 416
Fruit-gatherer	I. L. Myers and I. Corl	Agricultural College, Pa	July 2, 1872	128, 648
Fruit-gatherer	H. W. Neal	Sidney, Ohio	Apr. 28, 1868	77, 400
Fruit-gatherer	E. H. Newcomb	New York, N. Y	May 29, 1866	55, 150
Fruit-gatherer	C. Ostrander	Poughkeepsie, N. Y	Mar. 14, 1871	112, 622
Fruit-gatherer	L. M. Parker	Shirley Village, Mass	Feb. 19, 1861	31, 475
Fruit-gatherer	O. B. Parker	Hopkinston, Mass	Nov. 17, 1863	40, 638
Fruit-gatherer	H. Perry	Manlius, N. Y	Mar. 23, 1869	88, 071
Fruit-gatherer	C. H. Phillips and D. F. Briggs	Providence, R. I	Mar. 5, 1872	124, 384
Fruit-gatherer	F. I. Rausschert	Buffalo, N. Y	Sept. 4, 1866	57, 766
Fruit-gatherer	C. R. Roberts and J. S. Hartzell	Addison, Pa	Dec. 4, 1866	60, 249
Fruit-gatherer	H. L. Scott	Plessis, N. Y	Dec. 18, 1866	60, 565
Fruit-gatherer	W. Sedgwick and J. Brooks	Poughkeepsie, N. Y	Oct. 3, 1846	4, 792
Fruit-gatherer	A. Sclover	Brooklyn, Ohio	Mar. 28, 1865	47, 044
Fruit-gatherer	Y. W. Smith	Bristol, N. Y	Sept. 4, 1866	57, 785
Fruit-gatherer	W. H. Stone	Saint John's, Mich	Aug. 7, 1866	57, 008
Fruit-gatherer	G. Tanner	Freetown, N. Y	Sept. 15, 1868	82, 177
Fruit-gatherer	D. W. Thompson	Saint Joseph, Mo	Aug. 2[illegible], 1872	130, 769
Fruit-gatherer	B. Tukey	Fairfield, Me	June 24, 1862	35, 717
Fruit-gatherer	J. Vail	Newfield, N. Y	Nov. 15, 1864	45, 095
Fruit-gatherer	W. H. Wakeman	North Fairfield, Ohio	Oct. 15, 1872	132, 190
Fruit-gatherer	J. Waters	West Sutton, Mass	Mar. 12, 1872	124, 464
Fruit-gathering bag	N. B. Dixon and M. W. Sprague	Rochester, N. Y	Nov. 23, 1869	97, 061
Fruit, grain, &c., Mill for grinding	M. N. Whitely, J. Tassler, and O. S. Kelly.	Springfield, Ohio	Dec. 15, 1863	40, 937
Fruit-house	N. Cope	New Waterford, Ohio	Oct. 12, 1869	95, 657
Fruit-house	E. C. Roberts	Salem, Mich	Oct. 13, 1863	40, 282
Fruit-house ventilator	J. S. Houghton and C. B. Rees	Philadelphia, Pa	Oct. 20, 1868	83, 163
Fruit in barrels, &c., Machine for pressing	E. S. Holmes	Wilson, N. Y	Mar. 12, 1861	31, 689
Fruit, Instrument to loosen dried	J. F. Schmeltzer and J. M. Roberts.	Winona, Minn	Oct. 28, 1873	144, 147
Fruit-jar	H. U. Allen	North Bennington, Vt	Dec. 26, 1871	122, 143
Fruit-jar	J. C. Baker	Mechanicsburgh, Ohio	Aug. 14, 1860	29, 557
Fruit jar	T. J. Bargis and J. C. Underwood.	Richmond, Ind	Dec. 7, 1869	97, 588
Fruit-jar	T. E. Batterson	Rochester, N. Y	May 5, 1868	77, 570
Fruit-jar	E. Bennett	Philadelphia, Pa	Feb. 6, 1866	52, 379
Fruit-jar	E. Bennett	Baltimore, Md	Nov. 16, 1869	96, 869
Fruit-jar	L. F. Betts	Philadelphia, Pa	July 23, 1872	129, 780
Fruit-jar	M. R. Bissell	Kalamazoo, Mich	Feb. 7, 1871	111, 607
Fruit-jar	J. Borden	Bridgeton, N. J	Dec. 18, 1866	60, 468
Fruit-jar	I. Buckman, jr	Williamsburgh, N. Y	Mar. 8, 1870	100, 496
Fruit-jar	G. W. Buffington	Mechanicsburgh, Ohio	Mar. 5, 1867	62, 603
Fruit-jar	N. C. Burnap	Argusville, N. Y	Dec. 3, 1872	133, 518
Fruit-jar	T. B. Carroll	Indianapolis, Ind	May 20, 1873	139, 115
Fruit-jar	T. A. Clark and H. C. Mascroft	Worcester, Mass	Sept. 20, 1870	107, 449
Fruit-jar	W. F. Corpe	Windsor Locks, Conn	Apr. 24, 1866	54, 117
Fruit-jar	E. Croft	Philadelphia, Pa	Sept. 20, 1870	107, 598
Fruit-jar	R. M. Dalbey	Springfield, Ohio	June 5, 1866	55, 248
Fruit-jar	W. H. Daniels	Bryan, Ohio	Feb. 15, 1870	99, 763
Fruit-jar	E. M. Davis	Pittsburgh, Pa	Oct. 27, 1868	83, 367
Fruit-jar	H. S. Draper	Rochester, N. Y	June 22, 1869	91, 726
Fruit-jar	T. Earle	Valley Falls, R. I	June 28, 1870	104, 839

Index of patents issued from the United States Patent Office from 1790 *to* 1873, *inclusive*—Continued

Invention.	Inventor.	Residence.	Date.	No.
Fruit-jar	A. E. Fife	Rochester, N. Y	Feb. 8, 1870	99, 5[illegible]0
Fruit-jar	J. Focer	Glassborough, N. J	June 12, 1866	55, 581
Fruit-jar	W. Galloway	Philadelphia, Pa	Feb. 8, 1870	99, 662
Fruit-jar	H. C. Gaskill	Mount Holly, N. J	Feb. 25, 1873	136, 148
Fruit-jar	T. P. Gibbons	Philadelphia, Pa	June 21, 1870	104, 574
Fruit-jar	T. Gibson	Rochester, N. Y	July 28, 1868	80, 472
Fruit-jar	W. T. Gillinder and E. Bennett	Philadelphia, Pa	Aug. 8, 1865	49, 256
Fruit-jar	C. A. Gregory	Stratford, Conn	Aug. 17, 1869	93, 820
Fruit-jar	J. F. Griffen	New York, N. Y	Oct. 7, 1862	36, 612
Fruit-jar	J. Haines	West Middleburgh, Ohio	Mar. 1, 1870	100, 396
Fruit-jar	E. G. Haller	Carlisle, Pa	Feb. 25, 1873	136, 240
Fruit-jar	E. G. Haller	Carlisle, Pa	July 15, 1873	140, 916
Fruit-jar	W. L. Høller	Carlisle, Pa	Feb. 5, 1867	61, 827
Fruit-jar	W. L. Høller	Philadelphia, Pa	Jan. 4, 1870	98, 586
Fruit-jar	L. B. Harberger	Philadelphia, Pa	Nov. 30, 1869	97, 293
Fruit-jar	B. I. Harris	Harrisburgh, Pa	Aug. 7, 1866	56, 934
Fruit-jar	E. Harris	Boston, Mass	Feb. 9, 1864	41, 575
Fruit-jar	R. Hemingray	Cincinnati, Ohio	June 27, 1865	48, 399
Fruit-jar	G. W. Hempell	Millville, N. J	Mar. 18, 1873	136, 996
Fruit-jar	H. Hering	Philadelphia, Pa	Mar. 4, 1873	136, 513
Fruit-jar	W. Hicks	Trenton, N. J	Mar. 24, 1863	39, 962
Fruit-jar	P. M. Hinman	Rochester, N. Y	Jan. 19, 1869	85, 932
Fruit-jar	D. I. Holcomb	Henry County, Iowa	Dec. 14, 1869	97, 920
Fruit-jar	E. D. Holman	Buffalo, N. Y	July 2, 1867	66, 237
Fruit-jar	T. and H. H. Houghton	Philadelphia, Pa	Dec. 14, 1869	97, 922
Fruit-jar	H. Howson	Philadelphia, Pa	Sept. 3, 1872	131, 003
Fruit-jar	H. Howson	Philadelphia, Pa	Feb. 4, 1873	135, 430
Fruit-jar	D. Hughes, H. E. Shaffer, and W. S. Thompson.	Rochester, N. Y	Mar. 30, 1869	88, 296
Fruit-jar	W. Hunt	New York, N. Y	July 31, 1866	56, 755
Fruit-jar	C. G. Imlay	Philadelphia, Pa	May 23, 1865	47, 834
Fruit-jar	C. G. and W. L. Imlay	Philadelphia, Pa	Nov. 29, 1870	109, 625
Fruit-jar	C. G. and W. L. Imlay	Camden, N. J	July 16, 1872	129, 235
Fruit-jar	J. Johnson	New York, N. Y	May 16, 1865	47, 731
Fruit-jar	J. Johnson	New York, N. Y	Mar. 13, 1866	53, 151
Fruit-jar	J. Johnson	New York, N. Y	July 10, 1866	56, 226
Fruit-jar	A. T. Jones	Clinton, Wis	June 3, 1873	139, 580
Fruit-jar	A. T. Jones	Clinton, Wis	July 1, 1873	140, 508
Fruit-jar	J. M. W. Kitchen	New York, N. Y	Jan. 7, 1868	73, 187
Fruit-jar	J. M. W. Kitchen	Brooklyn, N. Y	Sept. 21, 1869	95, 025
Fruit-jar	J. Letchworth	Philadelphia, Pa	June 12, 1866	55, 512
Fruit-jar	W. A. Loder	Rochester, N. Y	July 14, 1868	79, 843
Fruit-jar	J. R. and N. E. Lupton	Stafford, Ohio	May 29, 1866	55, 128
Fruit-jar	W. W. Lyman	West Meriden, Conn	July 28, 1868	80, 296
Fruit-jar	W. W. Lyman	Meriden, Conn	Oct. 12, 1869	95, 819
Fruit-jar	J. B. Lyon	East Cleveland, Ohio	Aug. 4, 1868	80, 554
Fruit-jar	J. L. Mason	New York, N. Y	Jan. 19, 1869	86, 089
Fruit-jar	J. L. Mason	New York, N. Y	Jan. 19, 1869	86, 090
Fruit-jar	J. L. Mason	New York, N. Y	Feb. 23, 1869	87, 274
Fruit-jar	J. L. Mason	New York, N. Y	Mar. 1, 1870	100, 306
Fruit-jar	J. L. Mason	New York, N. Y	May 10, 1870	102, 913
Fruit-jar	J. L. Mason	New York, N. Y	Sept. 24, 1872	131, 695
Fruit-jar	J. L. Mason	New Brunswick, N. J	Apr. 1, 1873	137, 461
Fruit-jar	R. McCully	Philadelphia, Pa	Apr. 19, 1870	102, 024
Fruit-jar	A. D. McMaster	Rochester, N. Y	Mar. 17, 1868	75, 639
Fruit-jar	T. McSpedon and J. Steger	New York, N. Y	May 7, 1872	126, 561
Fruit-jar	H. B. Morton	Rochester, N. Y	June 2, 1868	78, 474
Fruit-jar	G. H. Myers	Philadelphia, Pa	Dec. 22, 1868	85, 236
Fruit-jar	T. G. Otterson	Millville, N. J	Oct. 28, 1862	36, 853
Fruit-jar	P. Pallissard	Saint Anne, Ill	Sept. 19, 1865	50, 027
Fruit-jar	S. J. Parker	Ithaca, N. Y	Feb. 9, 1864	41, 532
Fruit-jar	T. C. Purdy	Janesville, Wis	Apr. 5, 1870	101, 505
Fruit-jar	N. Raymer	New Sterling, N. C	Nov. 17, 1868	84, 214
Fruit-jar	G. A. Reynolds	Rochester, N. Y	Oct. 9, 1866	58, 674
Fruit-jar	F. Rohrbacher and F. Hormann.	Philadelphia, Pa	Aug. 18, 1868	81, 296
Fruit-jar	S. B. Rowley	Philadelphia, Pa	Dec. 14, 1869	97, 964
Fruit-jar	G. H. Russell	Dickinson, Pa	Apr. 3, 1866	53, 685
Fruit-jar	H. E. Shaffer	Rochester, N. Y	Aug. 31, 1869	94, 248
Fruit-jar	H. E. Shaffer	Rochester, N. Y	Nov. 2, 1869	96, 490
Fruit-jar	A. Sherwood	Auburn, N. Y	Sept. 26, 1865	50, 172
Fruit-jar	C. S. Siddons	Rochester, N. Y	Mar. 24, 1868	75, 993
Fruit-jar	C. F. Spencer	Rochester, N. Y	Aug. 27, 1867	68, 319
Fruit-jar	C. F. Spencer	Rochester, N. Y	Jan. 28, 1868	73, 846
Fruit-jar	C. F. Spencer	Rochester, N. Y	Aug. 18, 1868	81, 116
Fruit-jar	J. J. Squire	Windsor Locks, Conn	Mar. 7, 1865	46, 720
Fruit-jar	J. J. Squire	New London, Conn	Sept. 26, 1865	50, 181
Fruit-jar	D. Stone	Rochester, N. Y	Apr. 14, 1868	76, 846
Fruit-jar	H. Stone	Cleveland, Ohio	July 21, 1868	80, 234
Fruit-jar	L. C. Straub	Pittsburgh, Pa	July 18, 1871	117, 121
Fruit-jar	W. S. Thompson	Rochester, N. Y	Aug. 31, 1869	94, 452
Fruit-jar	W. S. Thompson	Rochester, N. Y	Apr. 12, 1870	101, 944
Fruit-jar	J. Weidig	Philadelphia, Pa	May 5, 1868	77, 555
Fruit-jar	E. B. Whitmore	Rochester, N. Y	Jan. 14, 1868	73, 271
Fruit-jar	B. B. Wilcox	New Haven, Conn	Mar. 26, 1867	63, 193
Fruit-jar	B. B. Wilcox	New Haven, Conn	June 21, 1870	104, 676
Fruit-jar	E. R. Willi ms	Rochester, N. Y	Sept. 1, 1868	81, 856
Fruit-jar	G. Williams	West Middlebury, Ohio	Nov. 13, 1866	59, 699
Fruit-jar	J. F. Winchell	Springfield, Ohio	Sept. 18, 1866	58, 185
Fruit-jar	L. Worcester and J. S. Brown	Lowell, Mass	May 5, 1868	77, 559
Fruit-jar and clamp	A. J. H. Hilton	Boston, Mass	Apr. 21, 1868	76, 915
Fruit-'ar and preserving-vessel	A. Warner	Williamsburgh, N. Y	Mar. 24, 1868	76, 008
Fruit-jai cap	R. Gray and R. Hemingray	Covington, Ky	June 9, 1863	38, 820
Fruit-jar cap	N. P. Whittelsey	West Meriden, Conn	May 19, 1863	38, 617
Fruit-jar cap	H. Wright	Pittsburgh, Pa	Mar. 22, 1870	101, 074
Fruit-jar clamp	I. Buckman, jr	Williamsburgh, N. Y	Nov. 28, 1871	121, 232
Fruit-jar cover	T. B. and J. S. Atterbury	Pittsburgh, Pa	Nov. 20, 1860	30, 662
Fruit-jar cover	F. A. Bunnell	Syracuse, N. Y	Feb. 13, 1866	52, 525

Index of patents issued from the United States Patent Office from 1790 *to* 1873, *inclusive*—Continued.

Invention.	Inventor.	Residence.	Date.	No.
Fruit-jar cover	T. A. Clark and H. C. Mascroft.	Worcester, Mass	Sept. 6, 1870	107, 003
Fruit-jar cover	J. L. Mason	New York, N. Y	Apr. 1, 1873	137, 462
Fruit-jar cover	H. C. Nicholson	Mount Washington, Ohio	Apr. 15, 1862	34, 976
Fruit-jar cover	T. G. Otterson	Port Elizabeth, N. J	Dec. 19, 1865	51, 613
Fruit-jar cover	S. B. Rowley	Philadelphia, Pa	Dec. 31, 1872	134, 400
Fruit-jar cover	J. Siddons	Rochester, N. H	Oct. 6, 1868	82, 884
Fruit-jar covers, Screw-fastening for	S. B. Rowley	Philadelphia, Pa	Mar. 2, 1869	87, 515
Fruit-jar fastening	E. Boorse	Philadelphia, Pa	Nov. 16, 1869	96, 873
Fruit-jar fastening	W. Galloway	Philadelphia, Pa	Apr. 5, 1870	101, 606
Fruit-jar fastening	T. F. Woodward	Winslow, N. J	Apr. 12, 1870	101, 958
Fruit-jar fastening	T. F. Woodward	Winslow, N. J	Nov. 29, 1870	109, 703
Fruit-jar holder	C. G. Imlay	Philadelphia, Pa	Oct. 3, 1865	50, 301
Fruit-jar holder	W. P. Walter	Philadelphia, Pa	Apr. 26, 1870	102, 453
Fruit-jar lifter	S. R. Pinckney	New York, N. Y	Mar. 21, 1871	112, 955
Fruit-jar safety-case	J. Carter	Towanda, Pa	Dec. 20, 1870	110, 340
Fruit-jar screw-cap and ring	J. L. Mason	New York, N. Y	June 6, 1871	115, 754
Fruit-jar stopper	W. Chrysler	Lockport, N. Y	Nov. 21, 1865	51, 020
Fruit-jar stopper	C. R. Doane	Spotswood, N. J	Nov. 7, 1865	50, 806
Fruit-jar stopper	W. W. Lyman	West Meriden, Conn	Jan. 2, 1866	51, 844
Fruit-jar stopper	T. T. Prosser	Fond du Lac, Wis	May 19, 1863	38, 600
Fruit-jar stopper	J. M. Whitall	Philadelphia, Pa	Apr. 11, 1865	47, 238
Fruit-jars and other vessels, Process of manufacturing enameled.	H. Reed	Jersey City, N. J	Feb. 3, 1863	37, 591
Fruit-jars, &c., Closing	R. M. Dalbey	Springfield, Ohio	Jan. 12, 1864	41, 202
Fruit-jars, &c., Closing	J. Harbster	Reading, Pa	Aug. 4, 1863	39, 441
Fruit-jars, Closing	W. L. Imlay	Philadelphia, Pa	Jan. 28, 1868	73, 724
Fruit-jars, Closing	W. L. Imlay	Philadelphia, Pa	Mar. 10, 1868	75, 275
Fruit-jars, Closing	C. Newman	Pittsburgh, Pa	May 12, 1863	38, 536
Fruit-jars, Constructing	G. M. Ramsy	New York, N. Y	Apr. 17, 1866	54, 015
Fruit-jars for receiving written labels, Compound to be applied to.	G. W. Doty	Wooster, Ohio	Aug. 31, 1869	94, 405
Fruit-jars, Instrument for extracting air from	J. H. Parrish	Talladega, Ala	Mar. 19, 1872	124, 758
Fruit-jars, Instrument for tightening and loosening screw-caps of.	A. French	Philadelphia, Pa	Sept. 21, 1869	95, 102
Fruit-jars, Machine for grinding glass	M. Neckermann	Pittsburgh, Pa	Dec. 15, 1868	85, 022
Fruit-jars, Manufacture of locking-rings for closing	L. R. Boyd	New York, N. Y	Jan. 21, 1868	73, 571
Fruit-jars, Sealing	R. S. Manning	Trenton, N. J	May 20, 1873	139, 170
Fruit-jars, Sealing	E. Purdy	Ithaca, N. Y	July 30, 1867	67, 215
Fruit-jars, Securing the tops of	W. Galloway	Philadelphia, Pa	Nov. 22, 1870	109, 507
Fruit-jelly	C. Alden	Newburgh, N. Y	July 11, 1871	116, 912
Fruit-knife	H. Soggs	Columbus, Pa	Dec. 17, 1872	134, 106
Fruit-knife	G. W. Stevens	San Francisco, Cal	Apr. 1, 1873	137, 501
Fruit-knife and nut-picker	G. Mayland	Brooklyn, N. Y	June 13, 1865	48, 194
Fruit, Knife for seeding stone	S. S. Marques	Mason, Ill	Aug. 17, 1869	93, 896
Fruit-knife gage	C. R. Howe	Minneapolis, Min	Nov. 12, 1872	133, 031
Fruit lifter, Pressed	E. A. Raymond	Waterloo, Iowa	Mar. 21, 1871	112, 959
Fruit loosener, Dried	H. W. Holman	Waterloo, Iowa	Nov. 11, 1873	144, 542
Fruit loosener, Dried	C. Ragan	Waterloo, Iowa	Apr. 8, 1873	137, 622
Fruit-masher and lemon-squeezer	W. W. Armington	Lowell, Mass	Sept. 26, 1865	50, 199
Fruit-mill	E. Greenlee	Rundells, Pa	Feb. 2, 1869	86, 391
Fruit-mill	G. S. Hull	Washington, Iowa	Feb. 11, 1868	74, 365
Fruit-mill and press	H. A. Holderman	North Manchester, Ind	Feb. 11, 1868	74, 361
Fruit or grain dryer	C. W. Davis	Newark, N. J	Mar. 25, 1856	14, 494
Fruit-package	D. Snedeker	New York, N. Y	Aug. 5, 1873	141, 605
Fruit-packer	M. E. Lewis	Mansfield, Ohio	July 1, 1873	140, 511
Fruit-packing box	E. D. Lewelling	San Lorenzo, Cal	Oct. 10, 1871	119, 776
Fruit-packing implement	C. C. Roberts	Perrysburgh, Ohio	Apr. 2, 1872	125, 146
Fruit-packing press	T. J. Jones	Rochester, Mich	Feb. 18, 1868	74, 543
Fruit-paring machine	W. H. Williams	Canton, Ohio	Mar. 1, 1870	100, 548
Fruit-peeling machine	C. Lehman	Hartford, Conn	June 15, 1869	91, 238
Fruit-picker	J. H. Adams	Martinsville, Ind	June 22, 1869	91, 698
Fruit-picker	J. Bally	Deposit, N. Y	May 7, 1867	64, 472
Fruit-picker	A. T. Barnes	Tiffin, Ohio	Aug. 27, 1867	68, 030
Fruit-picker	W. Brown	Worcester, Mass	Feb. 5, 1867	61, 709
Fruit-picker	L. D. Cogswell	Lowell, Mass	Nov. 30, 1869	97, 275
Fruit-picker	P. and S. Conver	Yates City, Ill	Dec. 31, 1867	72, 804
Fruit-picker	E. Evans	Sparta, Ohio	Aug. 14, 1866	57, 106
Fruit-picker	R. Evans	Brant, N. Y	June 30, 1868	79, 455
Fruit-picker	E. W. Gurnee	Haverstraw, N. Y	July 30, 1867	67, 296
Fruit-picker	L. Hotchkiss	Torrington, Conn	July 14, 1868	79, 906
Fruit-picker	N. G. Hughes	Waynesburgh, Pa	Aug. 11, 1868	80, 864
Fruit-picker	J. A. Knight	Durham, Me	July 28, 1868	80, 288
Fruit-picker	J. H. and D. A. Lament	Troy, Pa	June 23, 1868	79, 292
Fruit-picker	C. M. and W. F. Lunt	Biddeford, Me	Sept. 4, 1866	57, 741
Fruit-picker	J. Melendy	Southbridge, Mass	June 27, 1854	11, 170
Fruit-picker	H. Mewes	Binghamton, N. Y	May 20, 1873	139, 015
Fruit-picker	O. B. Moore	Walled Lake, Mich	Feb. 4, 1868	73, 989
Fruit-picker	J. Neff, jr	Pultney, N. Y	Aug. 28, 1866	57, 553
Fruit-picker	T. Nutting	Georgiaville, R. I	June 15, 1869	91, 256
Fruit-picker	S. Page	McAllisterville, Pa	July 9, 1867	66, 517
Fruit-picker	G. J. Parham	Harrodsburgh, Ind	Aug. 3, 1869	93, 338
Fruit-picker	B. C. Phelps	Weathersfield, Conn	Apr. 18, 1865	47, 364
Fruit-picker	L. Richards and D. Lincoln	Orangeville, N. Y	Nov. 13, 1866	59, 655
Fruit-picker	G. S. Richardson	Stow, Ohio	Jan. 15, 1867	61, 257
Fruit-picker	O. P. Rogers	Roxbury, Mass	May 28, 1867	65, 279
Fruit-picker	J. F. Saiger and A. Davis	Shelby, Ohio	Dec. 18, 1866	60, 561
Fruit-picker	J. Schroy	Fortville, Ind	Oct. 13, 1868	83, 098
Fruit-picker	W. L. Shaw	Etna, Pa	Jan. 17, 1871	111, 0[illegible]9
Fruit-picker	D. F. Slane	Chillicothe, Ohio	Jan. 4, 1870	98, 639
Fruit-picker	A. S. Stevens	Attica, N. Y	June 2, 1868	78, 549
Fruit-picker	I. Tower	Milford, Mich	Sept. 24, 1867	69, 144
Fruit-picker	S. W. Valentine	Bristol, Conn	July 6, 1869	92, 235
Fruit-picker	E. Ward	Urbana, Ohio	Aug. 31, 1869	94, 457
Fruit-picker	J. T. Warren	Lee Roy, N. Y	Jan. 26, 1869	86, 333
Fruit-preserving can	W. H. Hammond	Syracuse, Mo	Jan. 14, 1873	134, 799
Fruit-press	G. Jenkins	Queensburgh, N. Y	May 26, 1863	38, 682
Fruit-press	J. Meurow	Sacramento, Cal	Dec. 1, 1863	40, 762
Fruit-press	O. Metcalf	Mitchell, Ind	Apr. 15, 1873	137, 787

Index of patents issued from the United States Patent Office from 1790 to 1873, inclusive—Continued.

Invention.	Inventor.	Residence.	Date.	No.
Fruit-press	D. T. Robinson	Boston, Mass	Nov. 27, 1866	60, 060
Fruit-press	G R. Rust	Chester, Ill	July 15, 1862	35, 896
Fruit-press	G. J. Wells	South Vineland, N. J	Feb. 28, 1871	112, 304
Fruit-pulp, Apparatus for separating seed from	R. H. Mayo	Paris, Tex	Mar 29, 1870	101, 289
Fruit-renovator	J. E. Weaver	Lancaster, Pa	Aug. 6, 1872	130, 167
Fruit-seeder	S. A. Russell	Huntington, Conn	Nov. 19, 1867	71, 069
Fruit-stand	A. Greenman	East Kendall, N. Y	June 15, 1869	91, 330
Fruit stem cutter	A. Strong and J. A. Dadmun	South Boston, Mass	Aug. 20, 1867	68, 011
Fruit-stoning machine	R. McCormick	Greenville, Va	June 26, 1869	28, 881
Fruit-straining apparatus	M. E. Grigsby	Putnamville, Ind	July 12, 1870	105, 196
Fruit-transportation box	W. Shaw	Newfane, N. Y	Mar. 8, 870	100, 676
Fryer and boiler, Combined	G. Smith	Williamsburgh, N. Y	Oct. 28, 1873	144, 151
Frying-pan	G. H. Knight	Cincinnati, Ohio	July 9, 1867	66, 503
Frying-pan	S. B. Sexton	Baltimore, Md	Sept. 20, 1864	44, 346
Frying-pan	F. P. Warren	East Court Cosham, Great Britain.	Feb. 13, 1872	123, 753
Frying-pan	R. C. Whitehouse	Booth Bay, Me	Mar. 3, 1868	75, 095
Frying-pan and kettle	C. Avery	Ashtabula, Ohio	Aug. 30, 1864	43, 965
Frying-rack, Reversible	F. Bucknam	Portland, Me	Jan. 28, 1868	73, 692
Fuel	I. Bicknell	Cincinnati, Ohio	June 29, 1869	92, 003
Fuel, also improved stove, Mode of preparing	T. Joice	Camberwell, England	Nov. 12, 1838	1, 005
Fuel and for compressing conglomerate substances into masses. Machine for the manufacture of artificial.	A. Dietz	New York, N. Y	Nov. 30, 1869	97, 279
Fuel, and method of burning same, Artificial	A. Berney	Jersey City, N. J	May 27, 1873	139, 288
Fuel and other purposes, Composition of matter for	J. S. Lipps	Brooklyn, N. Y	Jan. 1, 1867	60, 755
Fuel, Apparatus for economizing	W. Levin	Saint Louis, Mo	Apr. 8, 1862	34, 891
Fuel, Apparatus for the combustion of	J. Bührer	Munich, Bavaria	Aug. 6, 1867	67, 492
Fuel, Apparatus for using mineral oils as	D. Dick	Meadville, Pa	Oct. 28, 1862	36, 769
Fuel, Artificial	J. E. Atwood	Trenton, N. J	Nov. 19, 1867	71, 119
Fuel, Artificial	R. B. Bayard	Philadelphia, Pa	July 4, 1865	48, 596
Fuel, Artificial	W. D. Beaumont	Mobile, Ala	June 12, 1855	13, 056
Fuel, Artificial	A. W. Buckland and A. M. Daniels.	Hartford, Conn	Apr. 21, 1868	76, 887
Fuel, Artificial	W. Budd and J. L. Husband	Philadelphia, Pa	July 12, 1864	43, 475
Fuel, Artificial	P. Binson	New York, N. Y	Apr. 5, 1864	42, 163
Fuel, Artificial	J. F. Bulkley	Brooklyn, N. Y	Apr. 10, 1866	53, 779
Fuel, Artificial	J. Cornell	Brooklyn, N. Y	Nov. 8, 1864	44, 994
Fuel, Artificial	R. Courtney	Albany, N. Y	Sept. 9, 1856	15, 688
Fuel, Artificial	H. Cutler	Springfield, Mass	Mar. 12, 1872	124, 553
Fuel, Artificial	A. M. Daniels	Hartford, Conn	Dec. 24, 1867	72, 460
Fuel, Artificial	A. De Lentilhac	Tamaqua, Pa	Feb. 6, 1866	52, 397
Fuel, Artificial	F. C. Epting	Schuylkill Haven, Pa	Jan. 2, 1872	122, 447
Fuel, Artificial	M. A. Febrey and T. Smith	Washington, D. C	Jan. 9, 1872	122, 590
Fuel, Artificial	T. M. Fell	Brooklyn, N. Y	Dec. 15, 1863	40, 920
Fuel, Artificial	R. Fish	Washington, D. C	Mar. 27, 1866	53, 431
Fuel, Artificial	G. R. Gladding	Providence, R. I	Apr. 18, 1865	47, 296
Fuel, Artificial	G. Gray	Temperanceville, Pa	Jan. 8, 1867	61, 006
Fuel, Artificial	W. Halsted	Trenton, N. J	Jan. 17, 1865	45, 922
Fuel, Artificial	W. and O. S. Halsted, jr	Washington, D. C., and Newark, N. J.	June 14, 1864	43, 112
Fuel, Artificial	T. Hooker and W. D. Beaumont	New Orleans, La	May 8, 1855	12, 847
Fuel, Artificial	S. D. Hovey	Chicago, Ill	Oct. 24, 1865	50, 588
Fuel, Artificial	S. D. Hovey	Chicago, Ill	Jan. 2, 1866	51, 833
Fuel, Artificial	J. H. Hubbard	Hartford, Conn	Dec. 1, 1863	40, 753
Fuel, Artificial	J. Kircher	New York, N. Y	Mar. 5, 1872	124, 363
Fuel, Artificial	C. Korff	New York, N. Y	July 4, 1865	48, 564
Fuel, Artificial	E. Loiseau and C. F. Reguin	Nashville, Tenn	June 16, 1868	78, 982
Fuel, Artificial	E. F. Loiseau and C. F. Reguin.	Nashville, Tenn	June 21, 1870	104, 471
Fuel, Artificial	H. S. Lucas	Chester, Mass	Aug. 2, 1864	43, 695
Fuel, Artificial	M. Mann	Syracuse, N. Y	May 27, 1862	35, 427
Fuel, Artificial	P. M. McGill	Washington, D. C	Jan. 11, 1870	98, 786
Fuel, Artificial	P. M. McGill	Washington, D. C	Nov. 15, 1870	109, 231
Fuel, Artificial	E. Miannay	New York, N. Y	Dec. 22, 1857	18, 920
Fuel, Artificial	F. C. Payne	New York, N. Y	Jan. 17, 1865	45, 935
Fuel, Artificial	B. F. Penny	Rochester, N. Y	Feb. 7, 1871	111, 565
Fuel, Artificial	H. Realich	Chicago, Ill	June 27, 1865	48, 439
Fuel, Artificial	J. A. Roth	Philadelphia, Pa	Apr. 18, 1865	47, 337
Fuel, Artificial	H. Seymour	Dartmoor, Great Britain	Aug. 26, 1862	36, 305
Fuel, Artificial	E. Sharpe	Paris, France	May 15, 1866	54, 832
Fuel, Artificial	J. and R. C. Walrath	Chittenango, N. Y	Feb. 5, 1867	61, 778
Fuel, Artificial	C. D. Williams	Saint Paul, Minn	May 17, 1870	103, 266
Fuel, Artificial	C. D. Williams	Saint Paul, Minn	Feb. 20, 1872	123, 962
Fuel, Artificial	H. Wilverth	Caseyville, Ky	Dec. 20, 1859	26, 541
Fuel, Artificial	H. Wurtz	New York, N. Y	Feb. 8, 1870	99, 738
Fuel-box and washing-apparatus with settees, Combination of.	M. Bishop	Washington, D. C	May 13, 1862	35, 210
Fuel-burning furnace, Metal-heating	T. J. Leigh	London, England	May 12, 1868	77, 822
Fuel, Burning oil for	R. A. Chesebrough	New York, N. Y	Oct. 2, 1866	58, 379
Fuel, Burning wet	J. F. Manahan	Lowell, Mass	Jan. 8, 1856	14, 063
Fuel by the aid of calcarious cement, Preparing a composition for.	J. Allen	New York, N. Y	Mar. 17, 1838	643
Fuel, Combustion of	R. Coad	Kensington, England	May 8, 1849	6, 446
Fuel, Composition	E. Bellenger	Mohawk, N. Y	Dec. 1, 1857	18, 729
Fuel, Composition	F. N. Hopkins	Baltimore, Md	Nov. 23, 1869	97, 087
Fuel, Composition	J. Newton	Providence, R. I	Mar. 28, 1871	113, 083
Fuel, Composition	E. H. Richter	Taunton, Mass	June 27, 1871	116, 489
Fuel, Composition	H. Slatter	Covington, Ky	Jan. 15, 1867	61, 271
Fuel, Composition for	S. O. Doris	Philadelphia, Pa	Jan. 2, 1855	12, 159
Fuel, Composition for	W. Stickney and N. B. Chase	Lockport, N. Y	Jan. 21, 1868	73, 553
Fuel, Composition for	F. Stoker	Lyons, France	May 1, 1866	54, 477
Fuel, Consolidating coal-dust for	W. Footner	Chicago, Ill	May 19, 1868	77, 970
Fuel-dumper	J. Haines	West Middleburgh, Ohio	Sept. 25, 1866	58, 248
Fuel-economizing and smoke-consuming furnace	F. P. Dimpfel	New York, N. Y	May 9, 1839	1, 148
Fuel for glass-furnaces, Drying	J. Lee	Philadelphia, Pa	Jan. 14, 1811	....
Fuel for metallurgic purposes	C. E. Lester	New York, N. Y	Oct. 26, 1869	96, 243
Fuel for producing heat and light, Process and apparatus for using liquid.	T. S. Dickerson and R. M. Whipple.	Chicago, Ill	May 3, 1870	102, 662

Index of patents issued from the United States Patent Office from 1790 *to* 1873, *inclusive*—Continued.

Invention.	Inventor.	Residence.	Date.	No.
Fuel from anthracite coal-dust, Manufacture of	E. G. Markley and G. H. Bardwell	Sunbury and Philadelphia, Pa.	Apr. 30, 1867	64, 243
Fuel from brush-wood and twigs, Manufacture of granular.	R. Daniels	Woodstock, Vt	June 15, 1852	9, 015
Fuel from coal-dust and fresh-water peat, Preparing.	H. S. Lucas	Chester, Mass	Apr. 30, 1867	64, 233
Fuel from coal-dust, &c., Manufacture of	A. Kloezewski and D. Mindeleff.	Washington, D. C	July 2, 1872	128, 636
Fuel from coal dust or slack, Manufacture of	H. M. Smith	Chicago, Ill	Oct. 1, 1872	131, 794
Fuel from coal-dust, Solidified	E. D. Williams	Philadelphia, Pa	Mar. 6, 1860	27, 401
Fuel from coal-waste, Manufacture of	J. R. Hayes	Washington, D. C	Mar. 4, 1873	136, 375
Fuel from spent tan-bark	B. Irving	New York, N. Y	Oct. 13, 1868	83, 066
Fuel, Generating and burning vapor	A. J. Works and A. J. Daniels	New York, N. Y., and Washington, D. C.	Jan. 10, 1871	110, 946
Fuel into blocks or bricks, Machine for pressing	J. B. Collen	Philadelphia, Pa	Jan. 22, 1867	61, 318
Fuel, Machine for making peat	G. Weissenborn	New York, N. Y	Dec. 24, 1867	72, 573
Fuel, Machine for preparing peat for	J. H. Ames	New York, N. Y	July 2, 1867	66, 277
Fuel, Machine for preparing peat for	S. Marden	Newton, Mass	Dec. 5, 1865	51, 390
Fuel, Machine for preparing peat for	A. M. Sawyer	Athol, Mass	Oct. 1, 1867	69, 370
Fuel, Machinery for manufacturing artificial	M. L. Keen	Royer's Ford, Pa	Aug. 16, 1859	25, 124
Fuel, Manufacture of	D. E. Breinig	Brooklyn, N. Y	Apr. 16, 1872	125, 656
Fuel, Manufacture of	M. Rae	Upball, North Britain	Feb. 25, 1873	136, 263
Fuel, Manufacture of artificial	D. Barker	Northfleet, England	July 1, 1873	140, 452
Fuel, Manufacture of artificial	W. A. Bradley and J. Bigelow	Washington, D. C	Dec. 28, 1868	22, 410
Fuel, Manufacture of artificial	G. H. Bronson	New York, N. Y	Sept. 15, 1868	82, 079
Fuel, Manufacture of artificial	J. F. Cranston, J. H. Banks, and J. M. Ingersoll.	Springfield, Mass	Apr. 12, 1870	101, 828
Fuel, Manufacture of artificial	H. G. Dayton	Maysville, Ky	Nov. 20, 1866	59, 791
Fuel, Manufacture of artificial	E. J. De Smedt	New York, N. Y	May 31, 1870	103, 580
Fuel, Manufacture of artificial	C. Du Lin	Mans, France	Mar. 9, 1869	87, 650
Fuel, Manufacture of artificial	S. D. Gilson	Oswego Falls, N. Y	Sept. 11, 1866	57, 890
Fuel, Manufacture of artificial	W. Ho sted	Trenton, N. J	Sept. 4, 1866	57, 708
Fuel, Manufacture of artificial	C. Saffray	New York, N. Y	June 5, 1866	55, 367
Fuel, Manufacture of peat	J. Webster	Malden, Mass	Jan. 29, 1867	61, 586
Fuel, Means of utilizing fine	E. Thayer	Worcester, Mass	Sept. 13, 1864	44, 262
Fuel, Non-fusible	W. Budd	Philadelphia, Pa	Dec. 1, 1863	40, 791
Fuel, Pine resin as	R. L. Wood	Philadelphia, Pa	Sept. 10, 1828	....
Fuel, Preparation of artificial	H. A. Archereau	Paris, France	Feb. 22, 1859	23, 005
Fuel, Preparation of peat for	A. Betteley	Boston, Mass	Nov. 21, 1865	51, 004
Fuel, Preparing artificial	D. E. Contardt	New York, N. Y	Mar. 8, 1864	41, 832
Fuel, Preparing artificial	W. H. and E. Cory	Notting Hill, England	Nov. 5, 1872	132, 751
Fuel, Preparing peat	E. H. Ashcroft and A. Betteley	Lynn and Boston, Mass	Sept. 6, 1864	44, 062
Fuel, Preparing peat and other substances for	L. S. Robbins	New York, N. Y	Dec. 4, 1866	60, 248
Fuel, Preparing peat for	A. Betteley	Boston, Mass	Aug. 8, 1865	49, 218
Fuel, Preparing peat for	L. W. Boynton	Hartford, Conn	Feb. 26, 1867	62, 469
Fuel, Preparing peat for	N. F. Potter	Providence, R. I	May 2, 1865	47, 564
Fuel, Preparing peat for	N. C. Sawyer	Boston, Mass	Sept. 20, 1864	44, 342
Fuel, Preparing peat for	H. Winter and F. W. Newton	Williamsburgh, N. Y., and South Orange, N. J.	Oct. 2, 1866	58, 528
Fuel-press	T. M. Mitchell	Philadelphia, Pa	June 7, 1870	103, 913
Fuel, &c., Process of forming blocks and slabs from green grasses for.	C. L. Fleishmann	Washington, D. C	July 2, 1872	128, 478
Fuel, Saving	Z. Phinney	Cairo, N. Y	Oct. 31, 1812	....
Fuel size-indicator	J. Gibson, jr	Albany, N. Y	Aug. 25, 1868	81, 490
Fullers' nap and card machine	J. Groff	Rapho, Pa	Feb. 10, 1830	....
Fulling-mill	W. and F. Bates	Sowerby Bridge, Halifax, England.	June 28, 1870	104, 819
Fulling-mill	G. M. Coppo	Paris, France	May 12, 1863	38, 469
Fulling-mill	C. P. Ladd	Bloomfield, N. J	June 4, 1872	127, 489
Fulling-mill	R. Hunt and J. H. Waite	Orange, Mass	July 29, 1862	36, 005
Fulling-mill	S. E. Coleman	West Haven, Vt	June 11, 1841	2, 126
Fulling-mill	E. Dams	Newark, N. J	Sept. 21, 1869	95, 094
Fulling-mill	A. Danielson	Otsego, N. Y	May 16, 1815	....
Fulling-mill	R. Eickemeyer	Yonkers, N. Y	Nov. 25, 1873	144, 841
Fulling-mill	E. Gessner	Ane, Saxony	June 9, 1868	78, 660
Fulling-mill	W. B. Lodge	Danbury, Conn	July 27, 1869	93, 100
Fulling-mill	T. J. Mayall	Roxbury, Mass	Nov. 24, 1863	40, 700
Fulling-mill	J. McKenzie and J. C. Millar	Troy, N. Y	July 29, 1862	36, 013
Fulling-mill	J. C. Millar	Springfield, Mass	Aug. 20, 1850	7, 579
Fulling-mill	S. M. Pike	Providence, R. I	May 28, 1872	127, 267
Fulling-mill	W. E. Underwood	Middlefield, Mass	Dec. 21, 1852	9, 492
Fulling-mill	J. H. Waite	Orange, Mass	Mar. 16, 1869	87, 806
Fulling-mill and power-loom	A. Atwood	Salem, N. Y	Oct. 1, 1830	....
Fulling-mill and washing-machine	J. Kennion	Dutchess County, N. Y	Mar. 26, 1806	....
Fulling-mill called the double-crank, Construction of the.	L. Osborne	....	July 12, 1804	....
Fulling-mill stock, Propelling	E. S. Norris	Monmouth, Me	July 7, 1835	....
Fulling-stock	W. B. Lodge	Danbury, Conn	June 25, 1867	66, 095
Fulling vegetable and other textures, Chemical process for.	J. Mercer	Oakenshaw, England	Aug. 19, 1851	8, 303
Fulminating-composition	G. Boldt	Chicago, Ill	July 10, 1866	56, 167
Fulminating-compound	J. Goldmark	Brooklyn, N. Y	Sept. 24, 1867	69, 206
Fulminating-compound	H. B. Stockwell	Brooklyn, N. Y	June 27, 1865	48, 469
Fulminating-powder for needle-guns	H. Büchner and F. Ebertz	New York, N. Y	Aug. 13, 1867	67, 714
Fulminating-powder, Manufacture of	J. S. Lipps	Brooklyn, N. Y	Sept. 6, 1864	44, 143
Fumiductor	W. A. Baron	New York, N. Y	Sept. 10, 1812	....
Fumigating-apparatus	K. P. Kidder	Burlington, Vt	Apr. 19, 1864	42, 380
Fumigating plants, Machine for	D. S. Brown	Surrey County, England	Sept. 24, 1850	7, 663
Fumigator	S. Andrews	Perth Amboy, N. J	Sept. 3, 1872	131, 075
Fumigator	A. R. Delinger	Gordonville, Pa	Nov. 25, 1873	144, 962
Fumigator	I. Hutchins, jr	Wellington, Me	Oct. 23, 1866	59, 025
Fumigator	R. Kerr	Boston, Mass	Apr. 21, 1868	76, 923
Fumigator	A. W. Todd	Chicago, Ill	Aug. 2, 1864	43, 723
Fumigator	S. Vanstone	Providence, R. I	Oct. 31, 1865	50, 752
Fumigator for destroying vermin	J. R. Hamilton	Portland, Oreg	Aug. 27, 1867	68, 188
Fumigator for smoking bees, &c	G. W. Hughes	Bloomington, Ill	Sept. 27, 1864	44, 427
Fumigator, Hospital, &c	T. J. Mayall	Boston, Mass	Oct. 14, 1873	143, 583
Funnel	J. I. Beaumont	Saint Paul, Minn	June 29, 1869	91, 899

Index of patents issued from the United States Patent Office from 1790 *to* 1873, *inclusive*—Continued.

Invention.	Inventor.	Residence.	Date.	No.
Funnel	F. Catlin	Watertown, Conn	June 25, 1867	66, 127
Funnel	W. B. Crowther	Philadelphia, Pa	July 1, 1873	140, 350
Funnel	L. P. Edwards	Hamlinton, Pa	Feb. 7, 1871	111, 525
Funnel	B. French	Rochester, N. Y	Nov. 7, 1871	120, 637
Funnel	J. Goudoin	New York, N. Y	Nov. 26, 1867	71, 378
Funnel	G. F. Herrick	Sharon, Minn	June 7, 1864	43, 075
Funnel	J. Q. Hill	Worcester, Mass	Aug. 22, 1865	49, 522
Funnel	C. Jones	Brooklyn, N. Y	Dec. 12, 1865	51, 515
Funnel	H. F. Lawrence	Vallejo, Cal	July 6, 1869	92, 321
Funnel	H. F. Lawrence	New York, N. Y	Aug. 6, 1872	130, 302
Funnel	W. E. Ledmun	Bridgeville, Del	Mar. 1, 1870	100, 420
Funnel	C. L. Lochman	Carlisle, Pa	Feb. 7, 1865	46, 255
Funnel	C. L. Lochman	Carlisle, Pa	Aug. 21, 1866	57, 347
Funnel	P. H. Niles	Boston, Mass	May 10, 1870	102, 855
Funnel	S. W. O'Laughlen	Baltimore, Md	June 4, 1872	127, 506
Funnel	N. L. Price	Lynchburgh, Va	Aug. 15, 1871	118, 651
Funnel	C. Ruf	New York, N. Y	May 10, 1870	102, 974
Funnel	C. Schneider	Washington, D. C	May 4, 1852	8, 928
Funnel	T. W. Slade	Manchester, Mass	Mar. 3, 1868	75, 065
Funnel	J. D. Smedley	Chicago, Ill	Oct. 6, 1863	40, 193
Funnel	A. Warth	Stapleton, N. Y	Nov. 15, 1870	109, 360
Funnel	C. G. Way	Boston, Mass	Jan. 28, 1873	135, 391
Funnel, Air-escape	J. I. Beaumont	Saint Paul, Minn	July 7, 1868	79, 799
Funnel, Air-escape	H. F. Hildebrand	Baltimore, Md	Sept. 14, 1869	94, 742
Funnel, Alarm	J. Sholl and J. Collins	Burlington, N. J	June 12, 1866	55, 544
Funnel and cock, Combined	A. G. Wilson	Chicago, Ill	Mar. 6, 1866	53, 074
Funnel and grater	E. A. Goodes	Philadelphia, Pa	Mar. 17, 1868	75, 541
Funnel, Beer	W. Golden	Flint, Mich	June 21, 1870	104, 575
Funnel, Bung	J. Buck	Baltimore, Md	Aug. 22, 1871	118, 337
Funnel can-filler	N. L. Brundage and B. Downing	Pittston, Pa	Mar. 15, 1870	100, 851
Funnel can-filler	T. Scantling	Evansville, Ind	Apr. 19, 1870	102, 050
Funnel, Filtering	J. H. Goodfellow	Troy, N. Y	May 25, 1869	90, 523
Funnel for canning fruit	S. B. Hertwig	Cincinnati, Ohio	Nov. 26, 1872	133, 445
Funnel for filling vessels with fluid	P. Apple	Philadelphia, Pa	July 13, 1808	....
Funnel, Indicating	J. D. Smedley	Chicago, Ill	Mar. 22, 1864	42, 024
Funnel-measure	C. W. Fuller	Earlville, Ill	Aug. 28, 1866	57, 494
Funnel-measure	G. A. Keene	Newburyport, Mass	Aug. 5, 1862	36, 095
Funnel, Measuring	C. Chinnock	Brooklyn, N. Y	Sept. 15, 1868	82, 087
Funnel, Measuring	J. W. Clarke	Kingston, Wis	July 31, 1866	56, 710
Funnel, Measuring	W. B. Cleves	Binghamton, N. Y	Jan. 22, 1867	61, 398
Funnel, Measuring	J. K. Cohic and D. H. Shartzer	West Hempfield Township, Pa.	June 3, 1873	139, 496
Funnel, Measuring	T. E. Cropper	Suffolk, Va	Mar. 25, 1873	137, 182
Funnel, Measuring	J. H. Elward	Mendota, Ill	May 14, 1867	64, 825
Funnel, Measuring	J. M. Estabrook	Worcester, Mass	Sept. 5, 1865	49, 739
Funnel, Measuring	R. F. Fisher and G. F. Waldron	Boston, Mass	July 4, 1871	116, 580
Funnel, Measuring	W. E. Keene	Lynn, Mass	Oct. 23, 1866	59, 034
Funnel, Measuring	J. Lloyd	Springfield, Ohio	Apr. 10, 1866	53, 841
Funnel, Measuring	G. B. Massey	New York, N. Y	May 25, 1869	90, 457
Funnel, Measuring	G. W. McCann	Springfield, Ohio	Mar. 12, 1867	62, 866
Funnel, Measuring	N. Otis	Cook County, Ill	May 10, 1864	42, 684
Funnel, Measuring	W. H. Rodgers	Brooklyn, N. Y	Sept. 24, 1867	69, 129
Funnel, Measuring	A. H. Whitney	Portland, Me	June 26, 1866	55, 941
Funnel, Measuring	H. J. Wolters	Salem, Mass	Mar. 9, 1869	87, 745
Funnel, Pendent measuring	G. A. Keene	Newburyport, Mass	June 17, 1862	35, 613
Funnel, Safety measuring	F. H. Smith	Burke, Vt	July 26, 1870	105, 857
Funnel, Sorghum	A. Bare	Mexico, Ohio	May 1, 1866	54, 279
Funnel with a vent	D. Clark	West Stockbridge, Mass	Apr. 9, 1810	....
Funnels, Manufacture of	L. R. Comstock	Baltimore, Md	June 17, 1873	139, 873
Funnels, Mode of connecting the sections of metallic	J. W. Cochran	New York, N. Y	Mar. 23, 1858	19, 685
Fur-band, Elastic	J. W. Gay	Brooklyn, N. Y	Jan. 5, 1864	41, 145
Fur-blower	W. B. Rotch	New Bedford, Mass	Mar. 9, 1824	....
Fur-blower	R. Wildman	Danbury, Conn	Mar. 6, 1866	53, 071
Fur-blowing machine	S. Whitman	New Albany, Ind	Mar. 22, 1834	....
Fur-box	H. Braunhold	New York, N. Y	June 20, 1871	116, 145
Fur-box	M. Fitzgibbons	New York, N. Y	Mar. 2, 1869	87, 334
Fur-box	S. C. Nichols	Buffalo, N. Y	Sept. 19, 1871	119, 168
Fur-cleaning machine	W. Woodworth	New York, N. Y	Apr. 19, 1831	....
Fur-coated fabrics, Manufacture of	H. Kellogg	Milford, Conn	Sept. 23, 1873	143, 163
Fur cuff	E. H. Hart	New York, N. Y	May 5, 1868	77, 483
Fur-cutting and cloth-shearing machine	B. Martial and D. Johnson	Concord, N. H	Dec. 7, 1816	....
Fur-cutting machine	D. Beard	Guildford, N. C	Apr. 30, 1816	....
Fur-cutting machine	M. Petre	Womelsdorf, Pa	Dec. 20, 1827	....
Fur-cutting machine, Reciprocating	C. M. Sampson	New York, N. Y	Feb. 5, 1835	....
Fur, Dyeing	P. Norden and H. Mischo	New York, N. Y	Sept. 27, 1870	107, 800
Fur, Dyeing and coloring	A. Müller	San Francisco, Cal	June 20, 1871	116, 211
Fur for the use of hatters, Machine for cutting	N. Young		May 14, 1802	....
Fur from hair, Machine for separating	C. and R. Lockwood and J. Arnold.	Fairfield County, Conn	Dec. 4, 1832	....
Fur from pelt, Machine for cutting	D. Williams	New York, N. Y	Oct. 25, 1832	....
Fur from peltry, Cutting	J. Witherle	Boston, Mass	May 28, 1811	....
Fur from peltry, Machine for cutting	E. Cutter	Walpole, N. H	Feb. 4, 1813	....
Fur from peltry, Machine for cutting	W. Jackson	Burlington, N. J	Feb. 2, 1815	....
Fur from peltry, Machine for cutting	E. Sprague	Danbury, Conn	May 9, 1810	....
Fur from peltry, Machine for pulling	W. Jackson	Burlington, N. J	Feb. 2, 1815	....
Fur from skins and pelts, Machine for cutting	M. Clark	New York, N. Y	Apr. 21, 1810	....
Fur from skins, Machine for cutting	C. C. K. Beach	Portland, Me	Nov. 10, 1827	....
Fur from skins, Machine for cutting	J. Hubbard	Jamestown, N. C	Nov. 4, 1826	....
Fur, Machine and process for blowing or cleaning.	I. W. Cochran	New York, N. Y	Nov. 4, 1842	2, 842
Fur, &c., Manufacture of vegetable	P. Baumgras	Syracuse, N. Y	Apr. 12, 1864	42, 326
Fur muffler	G. W. and W. F. Parker	Kalamazoo, Mich	Apr. 21, 1868	77, 085
Fur, Process of treating	A. C. Brush	Darien, Conn	Jan. 23, 1866	52, 133
Fur-set box	J. Crane	Bloomfield, N. J	Feb. 6, 1872	123, 333
Fur-set box	J. Crane	Bloomfield, N. J	Feb. 6, 1872	123, 334
Fur-set box	C. W. Frazer	Brooklyn, N. Y	Dec. 27, 1870	110, 615
Fur-set box	B. F. Porter	Nashau, N. H	Nov. 14, 1871	120, 897
Fur-set box	E. H. Smith	Bergen Heights, N. J	Sept. 19, 1871	119, 095
Fur-skins, Machine for extracting hair from	S. Graham	Farmington, Me	Mar. 27, 1835	....

Index of patents issued from the United States Patent Office from 1790 *to* 1873, *inclusive*—Continued.

Invention.	Inventor.	Residence.	Date.	No.
Fur-substitute for dressed fur-skin	A. Belden	Hudson, N. Y	Apr. 22, 1835	....
Fur tassel	J. Schmid	Boston, Mass	Mar. 12, 1872	124, 633
Fur, wool, &c., Mode of cleaning	D. Vail	Philadelphia, Pa	Feb. 21, 1821	....
Furs, clothes, &c., from injury by moths, &c., Preserving.	J. Crane	Bloomfield, N. J	July 6, 1869	92, 274
Furnace:				

See Air-furnace.
Air-heating furnace.
Annealing-furnace.
Bagasse-furnace.
Barrel-pitching furnace.
Blast-furnace.
Blast-heating furnace.
Boiler-furnace.
Boiler and stove furnace.
Boiling-furnace.
Bone-black furnace.
Bone-black reburning and ore-reducing furnace.
Broiling-furnace.
Charcoal-furnace.
Chimney-furnace.
Cider-clarifying furnace.
Coal-furnace.
Coking-furnace.
Cooking-furnace.
Crucible and metal-heating furnace.
Cupola furnace.
Decarbonizing-furnace.
Dentist's furnace.
Deodorizing-furnace.
Deoxidizing-furnace.
Desulphurizing-furnace.
Drying-furnace.
Evaporating-pan furnace.
Evaporator-furnace.
Fire-proof furnace.
Fixing, puddling, and boiler furnace.
Forge-furnace.
Friction-furnace.
Fuel-burning furnace.
Fuel-economizing and smoke-consuming furnace.
Gas-furnace.
Gas-burning furnace.
Gas-generating furnace.
Gas-producing furnace.
Gas-retort furnace.
Gypsum-calcining furnace.
Glass-furnace.
Glass-melting furnace.
Hatter's furnace.
Hatter's iron-furnace.
Heating-furnace.
Heating and puddling furnace.
Hot-air furnace.
House-warming furnace.
Iron furnace.
Iron and steel furnace.
Iron boiling and puddling furnace.
Iron-finishing furnace.
Iron-galvanizing furnace.
Iron-heating furnace.
Iron heating and puddling furnace.
Iron-manufacturing furnace.
Iron-melting furnace.
Iron melting and refining furnace.
Iron-plating furnace.
Iron-remelting furnace.
Iron-smelting furnace.
Iron-working furnace.
Kiln-furnace.
Lead-smelting furnace.
Lime-burning furnace.
Lime-burning and ore-smelting furnace.
Locomotive-furnace.
Locomotive-boiler furnace.
Melting-furnace.
Melting and smelting furnace.
Metal-heating furnace.
Metal-melting furnace.
Metal-plate-heating furnace.
Metal-treating furnace.
Metallurgic furnace.
Metallurgic gas-furnace.
Ore-furnace.
Ore-calcining furnace.
Ore-oxidizing furnace.
Ore-reducing furnace.
Ore-roasting furnace.
Ore roasting and treating furnace.
Ore-smelting furnace.
Ore-treating furnace.
Oven-heating furnace.
Pipe-welding furnace.
Portable furnace.
Puddling-furnace.
Pyrite-burning furnace.
Quicksilver-furnace.
Radiating-furnace.
Refuse-burning furnace.
Regenerator-furnace.
Retort-furnace.
Reverberatory furnace.
Reverberatory and cupola furnace.
Roasting-furnace.
Salt-furnace.
Salt-boiling furnace.
Sand-drying furnace.
Saw-dust-burning furnace.
Saw-heating furnace.
Scythe-heating furnace.
Shaft-furnace.
Small-coal furnace.
Small coal or culm furnace.
Smelting-furnace.
Smoke-burning furnace.
Smoke-condensing furnace.
Smoke-consuming furnace.
Soldering-furnace.
Spider-furnace.
Steam-furnace.
Steamboat-furnace.
Steam-engine furnace.
Steam-generating furnace.
Steam-generator furnace.
Steel heating and tempering furnace.
Steel, iron, &c., melting furnace.
Steel-melting furnace.
Steel-tempering furnace.
Stove-furnace.
Sugar-juice-evaporating-furnace.
Summer-furnace.
Tailor's furnace.
Tank-furnace.
Tinman's furnace.
Tinner's furnace.
Tinsmith's furnace.
Tire-heating furnace.
Tire sprinkling and removing furnace.
Tube-heating furnace.
Zinc-furnace.

Index of patents issued from the United States Patent Office from 1790 *to* 1873, *inclusive*—Continued.

Invention.	Inventor.	Residence.	Date.	No.
Furnace	J. Albee	Boston, Mass	Oct. 4, 1864	44, 497
Furnace	T. and J. Aldridge	Hudson City, N. J	Oct. 27, 1857	18, 491
Furnace	M. Battel	Albany, N. Y	Sept. 18, 1860	30, 040
Furnace	C. F. Baxter	Boston, Mass	June 19, 1860	28, 730
Furnace	B. F. Blood	Port Jackson, N. Y	Dec. 29, 1857	18, 951
Furnace	J. Case and I. Soules	Amsterdam, N. Y	Oct. 20, 1857	18, 432
Furnace	E. B. Cherevy	New York, N. Y	June 28, 1859	24, 599
Furnace	I. Clute and J. Seabury	Cohoes, N. Y	Dec. 5, 1842	2, 875
Furnace	C. F. Cory	Lebanon, Ill	Nov. 27, 1860	30, 724
Furnace	N. F. B. De Chodzko	Paris, France	June 16, 1863	38, 885
Furnace	J. H. Duhme	Cincinnati, Ohio	June 28, 1859	24, 547
Furnace	B. W. Dunklee	Boston, Mass	Oct. 11, 1859	25, 729
Furnace	W. Duryea and W. Ennis	Glen Cove, N. Y., and Hudson, N. J.	Mar. 24, 1868	75, 881
Furnace	J. Ekin	Xenia, Ohio	Mar. 18, 1862	34, 714
Furnace	W. Ennis	New York, N. Y	May 29, 1866	55, 079
Furnace	W. Ennis	Hudson, N. J	Jan. 1, 1867	60, 867
Furnace	B. D. Evans	Mount Vernon, Ohio	Mar. 20, 1860	27, 541
Furnace	S. E. Foster	Fitchburgh, Mass	Oct. 25, 1864	44, 835
Furnace	D. Hargar	Des Moines, Iowa	Nov. 5, 1867	70, 557
Furnace	M. L. Horton	Worcester, Mass	Feb. 18, 1868	74, 536
Furnace	J. B. Hoyt	Stamford, Conn	Feb. 8, 1870	99, 570
Furnace	J. Leeds	Philadelphia, Pa	May 20, 1865	47, 963
Furnace	D. G. Littlefield	Albany, N. Y	Oct. 9, 1860	30, 333
Furnace	P. Low	Cincinnati, Ohio	Apr. 3, 1860	27, 724
Furnace	M. F. Magliocco	Philadelphia, Pa	Oct. 18, 1864	44, 772
Furnace	J. McCracken	Bloomfield, N. J	Apr. 13, 1858	19, 942
Furnace	J. T. McDougall	San Francisco, Cal	Dec. 4, 1866	60, 219
Furnace	J. H. Mearns	Philadelphia, Pa	Oct. 16, 1866	58, 863
Furnace	J. R. Morris	Houston, Tex	Apr. 12, 1870	101, 965
Furnace	B. Palazot	Bordeaux, France	July 7, 1863	39, 168
Furnace	S. Pierce	Troy, N. Y	Jan. 18, 1859	22, 670
Furnace	R. B. Pullan	Cincinnati, Ohio	Jan. 24, 1860	26, 920
Furnace	G. E. Reynolds	Philadelphia, Pa	May 1, 1866	54, 409
Furnace	C. Schacher and L. Feret	Paris, France	Dec. 16, 1873	145, 689
Furnace	G. Schreyer	Columbus, Ohio	Mar. 10, 1868	75, 300
Furnace	T. P. Scripter	Des Moines, Iowa	May 23, 1871	115, 111
Furnace	J. Sholl	Burlington, N. J	Aug. 6, 1867	67, 457
Furnace	J. W. Smith	Chicago, Ill	Jan. 30, 1872	123, 300
Furnace	L. Solomon	New York, N. Y	July 19, 1859	24, 828
Furnace	T. S. Speakman	Camden, N. J	Feb. 22, 1870	100, 205
Furnace	J. L. Stevens	Kennington, England	Nov. 21, 1854	11, 975
Furnace	W. Stevens	Bloomington, Ill	Oct. 1, 1867	69, 505
Furnace	R. R. Taylor	Reading, Pa	May 8, 1860	28, 214
Furnace	W. D. Thomas	Morristown, Vt	Sept. 4, 1860	29, 925
Furnace	C. W. Trotter	Rochester, N. Y	June 18, 1867	65, 967
Furnace	J. I. Vinton and E. John	Ironton, Ohio	Oct. 4, 1859	25, 694
Furnace	B. H. Washington	Hannibal, Md	July 6, 1858	20, 836
Furnace	R. Wells	Baltimore, Md	Sept. 30, 1856	15, 832
Furnace	D. T. Woodrow	Cincinnati, Ohio	Aug. 28, 1860	29, 840
Furnace air and boiler-water heater	Z. C. Robbins	Saint Louis, Mo	Oct. 16, 1844	3, 796
Furnace and bake-oven	C. E. Russell	Philadelphia, Pa	Feb. 13, 1835	....
Furnace and boiler	H. McClure	Terre Haute, Ind	Oct. 2, 1866	58, 552
Furnace and boiler combined	A. Harrison	New Haven, Conn	Mar. 2, 1836	....
Furnace and cooking-range	J. Brown and L. Bridges	Chicago, Ill	Oct. 2, 1860	30, 203
Furnace and cupola	Z. Ellis	Philadelphia, Pa	Nov. 15, 1864	45, 030
Furnace and furnace-bar	E. R. Austin	Norwalk, Conn	Oct. 31, 1871	120, 361
Furnace and furnace-door	B. R. Hawley	Normal, Ill	Mar. 4, 1873	136, 509
Furnace and range, Combined	E. Edwards	South Boston, Mass	Sept. 13, 1870	107, 347
Furnace and steam-boiler, Combined	L. Disbrow	New York, N. Y	May 6, 1833	....
Furnace and steam-generator combined	O. W. Ketchum	Toronto, Canada	June 10, 1873	139, 795
Furnace and steam-generator, Combined	F. Morth	Vienna, Austria	Aug. 10, 1869	93, 468
Furnace and steam-generator for heating, &c	B. R. Hawley	Normal, Ill	Mar. 4, 1873	136, 510
Furnace and stove	C. B. Sawyer	Fitchburgh, Mass	June 7, 1859	24, 332
Furnace and stove draft-regulator	F. E. Chatard, jr	Baltimore, Md	Dec. 26, 1871	122, 105
Furnace and tea-kettle combined	C. L. Taylor and G. C. Setchell	Greenville, Conn	Aug. 30, 1870	106, 889
Furnace and ventilator	C. B. Sawyer	Fitchburgh, Mass	Aug. 30, 1859	25, 279
Furnace baker	G. Chilson	Boston, Mass	June 10, 1840	1, 627
Furnace-blower tube	B. W. Reynolds	Evansville, Ind	July 18, 1871	117, 206
Furnace-boiler	J. Seabury	New York, N. Y	July 31, 1847	5, 213
Furnace, Combined	L. Disbrow	New York, N. Y	May 6, 1833	....
Furnace dead-plate	A. C. Rand	Aurora, Ill	Mar. 26, 1872	125, 080
Furnace-door	D. Auld, jr	Glasgow, North Britain	Dec. 16, 1873	145, 608
Furnace-door	J. M. Clark	Louisville, Ky	Dec. 2, 1873	145, 150
Furnace-door	W. W. Crane	Philadelphia, Pa	Sept. 22, 1868	82, 294
Furnace-door	L. F. Johnson	Buffalo, N. Y	Oct. 6, 1868	82, 721
Furnace-door	J. Philips and D. Keeley	Phœnixville, Pa	Sept. 28, 1869	95, 263
Furnace-door	N. L. Sibley and B. Shiverick	Waltham and Weston, Mass.	July 25, 1865	49, 041
Furnace-door	J. Wickersham	Baltimore, Md	Dec. 19, 1865	51, 638
Furnace-door fastening	P. E. Shear	Saugerties, N. Y	Apr. 21, 1868	77, 112
Furnace-door for boilers	J. Penketh	Chicago, Ill	Feb. 14, 1865	46, 423
Furnace-door frame	P. A. Sabbaton	Albany, N. Y	June 21, 1859	24, 493
Furnace-door frame	D. H. Young	Manchester, N. H	Oct. 5, 1869	95, 550
Furnace-door latch	J. L. Reilly	Chester, Pa	Mar. 3, 1868	75, 053
Furnace-door-opening device	H. Fessler and H. Maxell	Canton, Ohio	Oct. 16, 1866	58, 709
Furnace door-regulator	O. A. Dodge	Burlington, Vt	Feb. 20, 1866	52, 695
Furnace-doors, Constructing	J. Watson	Buffalo, N. Y	Nov. 26, 1867	71, 433
Furnace draft-regulator	A. H. Mershon	Philadelphia, Pa	May 27, 1866	55, 138
Furnace draft-regulator	J. F. Neall and W. Myers	Philadelphia, Pa	Apr. 21, 1868	77, 081
Furnace draft-regulator, Boiler	W. E. Pearson	East Boston, Mass	May 16, 1871	114, 965
Furnace draft-regulator, Steam-boiler	T. H. Moore	Alexandria, Va	Nov. 28, 1871	121, 398
Furnace for burning as fuel tar, oil, &c	J. C. Love	Pittsburgh, Pa	June 30, 1863	39, 057
Furnace for burning coal-dust, small fuel, &c	J. Tissot	Paris, France	Jan. 28, 1873	135, 298
Furnace for burning edgings, saw-dust, &c	I. O. Smith	Muskegon, Mich	Feb. 15, 1870	99, 793
Furnace for burning pulverized fuel	T. R. Crampton	London, Great Britain	Feb. 7, 1871	111, 616
Furnace for burning pulverized fuel under steam-boilers, evaporators, &c	J. D. Whelpley and J. J. Storer	Boston, Mass	Feb. 7, 1871	111, 705

Index of patents issued from the United States Patent Office from 1790 *to* 1873, *inclusive*—Continued.

Invention.	Inventor.	Residence.	Date.	No.
Furnace for burning shavings	L. Crandell	New York, N. Y	Dec. 13, 1870	110, 118
Furnace for burning wet fuel	M. Thompson	Henrico County, Va	Apr. 10, 1855	12, 678
Furnace for heating metallic bars, tubes, &c	S. P. M. Tasker	Philadelphia, Pa	Feb. 11, 1873	135, 674
Furnace for liberating and using the gaseous products of coal.	T. T. Prosser	Chicago, Ill	Apr. 20, 1869	89, 239
Furnace for producing hydrocarbon and treating ores.	J. R. Morris	Houston, Tex	Mar. 28, 1871	113, 191
Furnace-grate bar	J. Cone and W. K. Kelly	Bristol, Pa	Feb. 8, 1870	99, 642
Furnace-grate bar	C. Hoffman	New York, N. Y	Jan. 23, 1872	123, 018
Furnace-heater	G. W. Wilson	Chelsea, Mass	Sept. 13, 1864	44, 246
Furnace, Heating	M. F. Magliocco	Philadelphia, Pa	Oct. 8, 1867	69, 568
Furnace, Heating	W. Von Faber du Faur	Würtemberg	Apr. 16, 1842	2, 558
Furnace-lining	B. A. Haycock	Richland, Iowa	Apr. 7, 1868	76, 442
Furnace-lining, retorts, &c., Plastic compound for.	S J. Payne	Charlton, England	May 6, 1873	138, 688
Furnaceman's clamp	A. P. Briggs	Taunton, Mass	Mar. 6, 1866	52, 958
Furnace-mold clamp	E. Card	Providence, R. I	Apr. 2, 1867	63, 468
Furnace or oven and tempering-die combined	H. Disston	Philadelphia, Pa	Sept. 20, 1870	107, 599
Furnace or stove, Economical	J. Pondrell	New York, N. Y	Apr. 6, 1808	....
Furnace-pot	J. Ballou	Boston, Mass	June 6, 1871	115, 677
Furnace-raking-attachment	J. Rice	Owego, N. Y	July 12, 1870	105, 249
Furnace-register	E. Barrows	New York, N. Y	May 28, 1846	4, 538
Furnace-regulator for hot-water apparatus	T. T. Tasker	Philadelphia, Pa	Dec. 5, 1854	12, 039
Furnace-shield	E. S. Collins	United States Navy	Jan. 22, 1867	61, 401
Furnace smoke-stack	B. F. Smith	New Orleans, La	Sept. 12, 1871	118, 883
Furnace, stove, &c	S. Rolph	Wales, N. Y	Nov. 8, 1826	....
Furnace with reflectors	J. Hurd, jr	Boston, Mass	Nov. 10, 1829	....
Furnaces, Apparatus for burning liquid fuel to heat	W. C. Wren	Brooklyn, N. Y	Oct. 1, 1872	131, 804
Furnaces, Apparatus for distributing and feeding powdered fuel to.	T. R. Crampton	London, Great Britain	Feb. 7, 1871	111, 615
Furnaces, Apparatus for increasing the draft of	I. B. Martin	Wilmington, N. C	Feb. 1, 1859	22, 814
Furnaces, Apparatus for supplying gases to	S. C. Salisbury	New York, N. Y	Aug. 27, 1867	68, 119
Furnaces, Apparatus for supplying saw-dust to	H. Doty	Cardington, Ohio	Nov. 22, 1859	26, 169
Furnaces, Apparatus for utilizing heat from	S. Bennett	Newcastle, Pa	Oct. 24, 1865	50, 551
Furnaces, &c , Blasts by steam-jets for	P. W. Mackenzie	Blauveltville, N. Y	Apr. 25, 1871	114, 163
Furnaces, Bridge-wall for	S. C. Sturtevant	Cleveland, Ohio	Nov. 11, 1873	144, 421
Furnaces, Checking draft in	J. C. Bagnall	Saint Louis, Mo	June 11, 1867	65, 630
Furnaces, crucibles, &c., Composition for lining	A. E. Bates	Monroe, Mich	Dec. 9, 1873	145, 326
Furnaces, Door for reverberatory and other	C. H. Burgess, 2d	Sandwich, Mass	Feb. 18, 1862	34, 401
Furnaces, Feeding	S. M. Fales	Baltimore, Md	May 16, 1846	4, 527
Furnaces, Feeding fuel to	G. F. Deacon	Liverpool, England	June 20, 1871	116, 165
Furnaces, Feeding fuel to	H. Delano	Syracuse, N. Y	Mar. 20, 1855	12, 546
Furnaces, Feeding fuel to	J. Honington	Richmond, Ind	Apr. 14, 1857	17, 039
Furnaces, Feeding fuel to	C. P. Leavitt	Newark, N. J	Aug. 12, 1873	141, 650
Furnaces, Feeding fuel to	J. G. McCormick	Louisville, Ky	July 14, 1868	79, 914
Furnaces, Feeding fuel to	J. Y. Smith	Pittsburgh, Pa	Oct. 17, 1871	120, 007
Furnaces, Feeding fuel to	J. Y. Smith	Pittsburgh, Pa	Nov. 7, 1871	120, 680
Furnaces, Feeding fuel to	A. M. Sprague	Mobile, Ala	Apr. 15, 1856	14, 674
Furnaces, Feeding fuel to	J. D. Whelpley and J. J. Storer	Boston, Mass	Nov. 13, 1866	59, 695
Furnaces, Feeding pulverized fuel to	T. R. Crampton	London, Great Britain	Feb. 7, 1871	111, 614
Furnaces, Feeding pulverized fuel to metallurgical and other.	J. Y. Smith	Pittsburgh, Pa	Oct. 17, 1871	120, 008
Furnaces, Feeding saw-dust to	A. J. Emlaw	Grand Haven, Mich	Oct. 17, 1870	120, 052
Furnaces, Feeding saw-dust to	J. A. McClelland	Vernon, Ind	Aug. 4, 1868	80, 647
Furnaces, Feeding saw-dust to	J. P. Wigal	Henderson, Ky	May 8, 1860	28, 226
Furnaces, Fire-chamber for	S. Smith	Worcester, Mass	Apr. 16, 1867	63, 956
Furnaces, Machine for feeding fuel to	A. Rogers and E. Tarrant	Muskegon, Mich	Mar. 14, 1871	112, 636
Furnaces, Means for directing blast in	B. H. Washington	Hannibal, Mo	Nov. 7, 1854	11, 914
Furnaces, Method of promoting combustion in	C. Fisher	Trenton, N. J	Sept. 25, 1866	58, 239
Furnaces, Mode of making	G. W. Robinson	Attleborough, Mass	Aug. 19, 1822	....
Furnaces, Mode of producing hot-blast in	T. McDowell	Light Street, Pa	Mar. 10, 1868	75, 442
Furnaces of steam-engines, &c., Supplying air to	P. Robinson	Waterloo, N. Y	Apr. 20, 1844	3, 555
Furnaces, Protecting hearths of	H. W. Ellicott	Baltimore, Md	Jan. 3, 1871	110, 639
Furnaces, Protecting heated parts of	E. G. Scovil	St. John's, New Brunswick	Oct. 22, 1867	70, 031
Furnaces, Removing slag from	J. Thomas	Hokendauqua, Pa	Feb. 14, 1871	111 789
Furnaces, Restoring waste heat from	W. Gorman and J. Paton	Glasgow, Great Britain	July 16, 1872	129, 403
Furnaces, safes, &c., Lining for	A. C. Hamlin	Bangor, Me	Apr. 23, 1872	125, 951
Furnaces, Saw-dust feeder for	M. Garland	West Eau Claire, Wis	May 28, 1872	127, 335
Furnaces, Saw-dust feeder for	S. Sykes	Chippewa Falls, Wis	June 15, 1869	91, 384
Furnaces, Self-regulating hot-blast for	C. Schinz	Camden, N. J	Dec. 4, 1855	13, 887
Furnaces, Straw-feeding attachment for	D. Morey	Watsonville, Cal	Feb. 11, 1873	135, 659
Furnaces, Straw-feeding attachment to	D. Morey	Watsonville, Cal	May 20, 1873	139, 075
Furnaces, Treating cinder for fixing	A. McDonald	Allegheny, Pa	Mar. 31, 1868	76, 223
Furnaces, Utilizing slag of	W. H. Smith	Philadelphia, Pa	Dec. 7, 1852	9, 459
Furnaces, Ventilating	H. Ruttan	Coburg, Canada	May 20, 1851	8, 109
Furnaces with hot-air, Apparatus for supplying	C. Fletcher	Cincinnati, Ohio	Aug. 16, 1859	25, 159
Furnaces with hot-air, Supplying	C. Fletcher	Cincinnati, Ohio	June 12, 1855	13, 031
Furnaces with hydrocarbon liquids, Heating	J. K. Caldwell	Philadelphia, Pa	Mar. 19, 1872	124, 791
Furnaces with pulverized metal, Apparatus for supplying.	E. Schmitz	New York, N. Y	Jan. 23, 1855	12, 286
Furniture and other purposes, Composition for	J. J. Wiggin	Cincinnati, Ohio	Dec. 4, 1866	60, 309
Furniture-attachments	J. B. Haupt	Philadelphia, Pa	July 16, 1872	129, 556
Furniture, Barber's	O. Stoelker	Montgomery, Ala	Aug. 16, 1870	106, 425
Furniture-button	J. H. Howcroft	Cincinnati, Ohio	Mar. 12, 1872	124, 577
Furniture, Cabinet	J. D. Browne	Cincinnati, Ohio	Aug. 16, 1859	25, 089
Furniture, Construction of	A. D. Brown	Glasgow, North Britain	Jan. 19, 1858	19, 127
Furniture-drawer	C. Brada	Newton, Mass	Sept. 24, 1867	69, 068
Furniture-drawer	E. B. Johnson	Milwaukee, Wis	May 25, 1869	90, 452
Furniture-drawer	G. F. Joyce	Boston, Mass	May 10, 1870	102, 826
Furniture-drawer	J. W. Warth	New York, N. Y	July 16, 1872	129, 377
Furniture-drawer and fastening	J. Koch	Brookline, Mass	Mar. 17, 1868	75, 553
Furniture, Drawer for cabinet	L. Burnell	Milwaukee, Wis	Nov. 8, 1870	109, 110
Furniture-edge	F. Hütwohl	New York, N. Y	Mar. 24, 1868	75, 920
Furniture, &c., Elastic tip for	W. S. Paddock	Albany, N. Y	July 13, 1869	92, 639
Furniture, Extensible	J. M. Dennis	Galesburgh, Ill	Dec. 5, 1871	121, 596
Furniture-fastening	L. A. Johnson	Candor, N. Y	Aug. 23, 1870	106, 590
Furniture fender	G. R. Willmot	Meriden, Conn	Feb. 20, 1872	123, 965
Furniture fender or cushion	G. R. Willmot	Meriden, Conn	Apr. 11, 1871	113, 605
Furniture Floor-attachment for	H. Cole	Cincinnati, Ohio	Mar. 27, 1866	53, 415

Index of patents issued from the United States Patent Office from 1790 *to* 1873, *inclusive*—Continued.

Invention.	Inventor.	Residence.	Date.	No.
Furniture, Folding	A. Tracy	United States Army	June 26, 1860	28, 921
Furniture for vessels	S. F. Pratt	Roxbury, Mass	May 21, 1867	65, 007
Furniture, House, ship, and camp	E. Clibborn	Cincinnati, Ohio	Sept. 12, 1831	....
Furniture, Joint for folding	N. Thompson	Brooklyn, N. Y	Dec. 12, 1871	121, 735
Furniture-leg	J. C. Orr and J. M. Baird	Wheeling, W. Va	July 22, 1873	141, 071
Furniture-legs, Elastic tip for	E. S. Torrey	New York, N. Y	Jan. 15, 1867	61, 282
Furniture-lock, Automatic	J. T. Brown and I. Hird	Cincinnati, Ohio	Nov. 1, 1870	108, 874
Furniture, Marine	J. Foster	Sandwich, Mass	May 21, 1867	64, 962
Furniture, Marine	E. Gallier	Saint Louis, Mo	Apr. 6, 1869	88, 622
Furniture, Marine	L. D. Newell	New York, N. Y	Apr. 5, 1870	101, 495
Furniture, Means for attaching elastic tips to legs of	E. S. Torrey	New York, N. Y	Jan. 1, 1867	60, 967
Furniture, Means for attaching hooks to	A. Moutleart and W. Tent	Mildmay Park and London, England.	Feb. 9, 1864	41, 528
Furniture, Method of manufacturing	J. H. Belter	New York, N. Y	Feb. 23, 1858	19, 405
Furniture-nail die	W. H. Van Gieson	Waterbury, Conn	Sept. 5, 1865	49, 808
Furniture, Ornamenting	J. E. Rogers	Chelsea, Mass	Mar. 12, 1872	124, 630
Furniture-pad	D. H. Clark and H. Winson	New Haven, Conn	Mar. 14, 1871	112, 686
Furniture-pad	J. E. Earle	New Haven, Conn	Nov. 6, 1866	59, 371
Furniture-pad	W. B. Moses	Washington, D. C	Apr. 5, 1870	101, 648
Furniture-polish	J. L. Brabyn	New York, N. Y	Aug. 19, 1856	15, 550
Furniture-polish	C. A. Libby	La Cygne, Kans	Apr. 29, 1873	138, 262
Furniture-polish	A. Sabatier	New York, N. Y	June 19, 1860	28, 779
Furniture polish and restorer	G. Bricker, sr	Newville, Pa	Jan. 1, 1867	60, 679
Furniture, Printers'	T. J. House	Pittsburgh, Pa	Mar. 2, 1869	87, 339
Furniture-protector	G. F. Boyden	Providence, R. I	Dec. 29, 1868	85, 361
Furniture-rocker	A. Strawbridge	Covington, Ky	Nov. 29, 1864	45, 302
Furniture rubber or brush	B. Y. Conklin	Brooklyn, N. Y	Oct. 29, 1872	132, 522
Furniture, School	J. M. Johnson	Chillicothe, Ohio	June 14, 1870	104, 161
Furniture, School	J. L. Riter	Brownsville, Ind	Mar. 4, 1873	136, 548
Furniture-spring	W. T. Doremus	New York, N. Y	Dec. 17, 1872	133, 971
Furniture-spring	W. T. Doremus	New York, N. Y	Apr. 8, 1873	137, 600
Furniture-spring	W. T. Doremus	New York, N. Y	June 24, 1873	140, 188
Furniture-spring	W. T. Doremus	New York, N. Y	June 24, 1873	140, 189
Furniture-spring	D. Hawkins	Derby, Conn	Oct. 17, 1865	50, 471
Furniture-spring	J. M. Kirkpatrick	Utica, Ohio	Jan. 19, 1869	85, 938
Furniture-spring	C. F. and J. W. Tillman	La Crosse, Wis	Dec. 15, 1863	40, 963
Furniture-spring	F. Tyleo	Cleveland, Ohio	Mar. 22, 1864	42, 053
Furniture-spring	W. C. Wyckoff	Brooklyn, N. Y	Dec. 19, 1865	51, 644
Furniture, Spring-guard for legs of	D. F. Hartman	Charles City, Iowa	May 16, 1871	114, 812
Furniture-spring, Japanned	J. J. Eagleton	New York, N. Y	Dec. 19, 1871	122, 001
Furniture-springs, Method of manufacturing	J. L. Haigh	New York, N. Y	Feb. 13, 1872	123, 627
Furniture, Stationary	A. D. Hibbs	Trenton, N. J	Apr. 26, 1870	102, 398
Furniture-tip	J. F. Akerstein	Chicago, Ill	June 27, 1871	116, 392
Furniture-tip	O. B. Collins	Carthage Landing, N. Y	Dec. 22, 1868	85, 071
Furniture, Triangular stand for	T. W. Currier	Lawrence, Mass	Feb. 22, 1859	23, 013
Furniture, Upholstering	F. Mathesius	New York, N. Y	May 17, 1853	9, 730
Furniture, Wall-guard for	J. L. Brander	Boston, Mass	Feb. 6, 1872	123, 377
Furrow in land, Machine for dressing	J. Whitehead	Manchester, Va	June 2, 1857	17, 467
Furrow-staff	G. H. Comer	Indiana, Canada	Nov. 12, 1872	132, 952
Furrowing and dropping corn, Machine for	M. and I. Nichols	Otsego County, N. Y	Oct. 12, 1809	....
Furrowing-device	W. S. Riggs	Hightstown, N. J	Oct. 11, 1864	44, 659
Furrowing-machine	F. M. Birdsall	Martinsville, Ohio	May 22, 1866	54, 842
Furrowing-machine	P. Jotter	Monroe, Ohio	Dec. 3, 1872	133, 537
Furrowing-machine	W. H. Rutledge	Hamilton, Ohio	Aug. 26, 1873	142, 283
Furrowing-machine	J. I. Wilson	Abingdon, Ill	Feb. 6, 1866	52, 482
Fuse, Blasting, &c	R. Bacon	Simsbury, Conn	Feb. 5, 1847	4, 957
Fuse, Blasting, &c	J. S. Bickford	Tuckingmill, Great Britain	May 9, 1865	47, 677
Fuse, Blasting	S. H. Daddow	Saint Clair, Pa	Oct. 8, 1872	132, 061
Fuse, Blasting	S. H. Daddow	Saint Clair, Pa	Dec. 24, 1872	134, 128
Fuse, Blasting	T. P. Shaffner	Louisville, Ky	Aug. 17, 1869	93, 755
Fuse, Blasting	T. P. Shaffner	Louisville, Ky	Dec. 28, 1869	98, 428
Fuse, Blasting	T. H. Walton	Ashland, Pa	Jan. 3, 1865	45, 774
Fuse, Blasting	R. Wren	Santa Cruz, Cal	Apr. 25, 1871	114, 233
Fuse, Combined time and concussion	C. Arick	Saint Clairsville, Ohio	Sept. 6, 1864	44, 061
Fuse, Combined time and concussion	W. F. Goodwin	Powhatan, Ohio	Nov. 1, 1864	44, 861
Fuse, Combined time, percussion, and concussion	A. Merriman	New York, N. Y	Oct. 4, 1864	44, 546
Fuse-composition	W. H. Rogers	Brooklyn, N. Y	June 7, 1870	103, 931
Fuse composition, Safety	E. Gomez and W. Mills	New York, N. Y	Sept. 15, 1857	18, 199
Fuse, Concussion	E. A. Dana	Brookline, Mass	Apr. 20, 1869	89, 204
Fuse, Electric	C. A. and I. S. Browne	Adams, Mass	July 16, 1872	128, 945
Fuse, Electric	G. M. Mowbray	North Adams, Mass	June 10, 1873	139, 686
Fuse, Electric	T. P. Shaffner	Louisville, Ky	Dec. 18, 1866	60, 569
Fuse, Electric	H. J. Smith	Boston, Mass	June 23, 1868	79, 268
Fuse, Electric	H. J. Smith	Boston, Mass	Nov. 23, 1869	97, 241
Fuse, Electric	H. J. Smith	Boston, Mass	Mar. 21, 1871	112, 859
Fuse, Electric blasting	C. A. and I. S. Browne	North Adams, Mass	Oct. 18, 1870	108, 324
Fuse for conveying fire in blasting rocks, &c., Machine for making safety.	W. Lewis	New York, N. Y	Oct. 26, 1838	991
Fuse for explosive projectiles, Concussion	J. L. Henry	United States Army	June 2, 1863	38, 797
Fuse for explosive projectiles, Safety concussion	J. P. Schenckl	Boston, Mass	Oct. 15, 1861	33, 495
Fuse for explosive shell	F. Alger	Boston, Mass	Sept. 2, 1862	36, 329
Fuse for explosive shell	C. Arick	Saint Clairsville, Ohio	Oct. 11, 1864	44, 588
Fuse for explosive shell, &c	J. F. Clew	New York, N. Y	Nov. 15, 1864	45, 024
Fuse for explosive shell	J. McIntyre	New York, N. Y	Oct. 20, 1863	40, 350
Fuse for explosive shell	J. McIntyre	New York, N. Y	Oct. 4, 1864	44, 581
Fuse for explosive shell	B. F. Sturtevant	Boston, Mass	July 29, 1862	36, 037
Fuse for explosive shell	B. F. Sturtevant	Boston, Mass	July 29, 1862	36, 038
Fuse for explosive shell	B. F. Sturtevant	Boston, Mass	July 29, 1862	36, 039
Fuse for explosive shell, Combined time and percussion.	S. and A. M. Sawyer	Fitchburgh, Mass	Aug. 12, 1862	36, 172
Fuse for explosive shell, Concussion	W. S. Beebe	Philadelphia, Pa	Apr. 16, 1867	63, 834
Fuse for explosive shell, Concussion	G. P. Ganster	New York, N. Y	June 13, 1865	48, 167
Fuse for explosive shell, Concussion	B. B. Hotchkiss	Sharon, Conn	June 17, 1862	35, 611
Fuse for explosive shell, Concussion	J. P. Schenckl	Boston, Mass	Aug. 19, 1862	36, 236
Fuse for explosive shell, Concussion	A. J. Simpson and J. J. Janezeck.	Philadelphia, Pa., and Washington, D. C.	July 9, 1867	66, 644
Fuse for explosive shell, Percussion	J. W. Cochran	New York, N. Y	Jan. 6, 1863	37, 275
Fuse for explosive shell, Percussion	J. W. Cochran	New York, N. Y	Feb. 17, 1863	37, 675

Index of patents issued from the United States Patent Office from 1790 *to* 1873, *inclusive*—Continued.

Invention.	Inventor.	Residence.	Date.	No.
Fuse for explosive shell, Percussion	J. A. Curran	United States Army	May 23, 1865	47, 803
Fuse for explosive shell, Percussion	B. B. Hotchkiss	Sharon, Conn	Sept. 16, 1862	36, 465
Fuse for explosive shell, Percussion	R. P. Parrott	Cold Spring, N. Y	Mar. 15, 1864	41, 937
Fuse for explosive shell, Percussion	J. P. Schenkl	Boston, Mass	Sept. 30, 1862	36, 576
Fuse for explosive shell, Percussion	J. F. Shearman	Brooklyn, E. D, N. Y	Apr. 17, 1866	54, 027
Fuse for explosive shell, Time	M. McDevitt	Beloit, Wis	Aug. 23, 1864	43, 922
Fuse for explosive shell, Time	G. Wright	Washington, D. C	Dec. 6, 1864	45, 381
Fuse for explosive shell, Time	G. Wright	Washington, D. C	Mar. 21, 1865	46, 965
Fuse for explosive shell, Time and percussion	B. B. Hotchkiss	New York, N. Y	Dec. 24, 1867	72, 494
Fuse for shell	E. Estabrook	Jersey City, N. J	Jan. 24, 1865	45, 986
Fuse for shell, Combined time and concussion	C. Arick	Saint Clairsville, Ohio	Nov. 22, 1864	45, 128
Fuse for shell, Combined time and percussion	F. Alger	Boston, Mass	Sept. 30, 1862	36, 553
Fuse for shell, Combined time and percussion	J. P. Schenkl	Boston, Mass	Aug. 25, 1863	39, 682
Fuse for shell, Combined time and percussion	W. S. Smoot	Washington, D. C	Oct. 28, 1862	36, 806
Fuse for shell, Combined time and percussion	C. W. Stafford	New York, N. Y	Aug. 30, 1864	44, 023
Fuse for shell, Concussion	W. F. Goodwin	New York, N. Y	No 15, 1864	45, 035
Fuse for shell, Concussion	W. H. Hubbell	Philadelphia, Pa	Sept. 30, 1862	36, 566
Fuse for shell, Concussion	S. R. Russell	Middletown, Ohio	Dec. 16, 1862	37, 200
Fuse for shell, Concussion	I. P. Tice	New York, N. Y	June 23, 1863	38, 994
Fuse for shell, Igniting	C. W. Smith	Evans, N. Y	Aug. 9, 1864	43, 801
Fuse for shell, Igniting time	A. M. Sawyer	Fitchburgh Mass	May 26, 1863	38, 699
Fuse for shell, Percussion	A. H. Emery	New York, N. Y	Dec. 8, 1863	40, 828
Fuse for shell, Percussion	G. P. Ganster	New York, N. Y	Apr. 5, 1864	42, 185
Fuse for shell, Percussion	B. B. Hotchkiss	Sharon, Conn	Feb. 24, 1863	37, 756
Fuse for shell, Percussion	W. F. Patterson	Somerset, Ky	Dec. 8, 1863	40, 885
Fuse for shell, Time	B. B. Hotchkiss	Sharon, Conn	May 10, 1864	42, 660
Fuse for shell, Time and concussion	J. P. Schenkl	Boston, Mass	July 15, 1862	35, 897
Fuse head, Electric	H. J. Smith	Boston, Mass	June 14, 1870	104, 217
Fuse heads, Electric and other	E. A. L. Roberts	Titusville, Pa	Mar. 21, 1871	112, 850
Fuse-hood for explosive shell	T. Taylor	Washington, D. C	Apr. 11, 1865	47, 231
Fuse-hood for shell	S. Sawyer	Fitchburgh, Mass	Dec. 24, 1861	34, 040
Fuse-lock, Miners'	G. Hagenmeyer	Big River, Cal	Oct. 9, 1866	58, 639
Fuse-making machine	A. F. Andrews	Avon, Conn	July 28, 1857	17, 863
Fuse-manufacturing machine	T. Richards	Medford, Mass	Aug. 18, 1868	81, 291
Fuse of shells and other projectiles	N. Scholfield	Norwich, Conn	Dec. 15, 1857	18, 866
Fuse or slow-match for igniting under water	T. K. Anderson	Hornellsville, N. Y	Jan. 28, 1862	34, 233
Fuse, Percussion	W. Gardner	San Francisco, Cal	May 31, 1870	103, 599
Fuse, Safety	A. F. and J. H. Andrews	Avon, Conn	Dec. 26, 1865	51, 679
Fuse, Safety	J. H. Andrews	Avon, Conn	Dec. 27, 1864	45, 572
Fuse, Safety	J. E. Chase and J. Foy	Simsbury, Conn	Nov. 22, 1864	45, 140
Fuse, Shell	J. D. Bacon	New York, N. Y	June 22, 1869	91, 701
Fuse, Shell	J. G. Butler	United States Army	July 30, 1872	129, 929
Fuse, Shell	J. G. Butler	United States Army	July 30, 1872	129, 930
Fuse, Shell	E. Drake	Stoughton, Mass	Feb. 14, 1871	111, 823
Fuse, Shell	J. Eggo	Jersey City, N. J	Dec. 20, 1870	110, 219
Fuse-stock for bomb-shells	A. Powell, jr	Mare Island, Cal	June 26, 1855	13, 138
Fuse, Tape	P. Bacon	Simsbury, Conn	May 8, 1855	12, 810
Fuse, Tape	J. E. Chase and J. Foy	Simsbury, Conn	June 30, 1863	39, 033
Fuse to shell, Applying	R. P. Parrott	Cold Spring, N. Y	Nov. 5, 1861	36, 662
Fuses, Apparatus for casting	G. Wright	Washington, D. C	Apr. 28, 1863	38, 352
Fuses by electricity, Firing	F. E. Beardslee	College Point, N. Y	Aug. 18, 1863	39, 542
Fuses, Compound for priming electric	G. M. Mowbray	Titusville, Pa	Nov. 2, 1869	96, 465
Fuses, Compound for priming electric	G. M. Mowbray	North Adams, Mass	June 25, 1872	128, 241
Fuses, Concussion-bulb for	G. P. Gauston and I. S. Schuyler	New Nork, N. Y	Mar. 29, 1864	42, 082
Fuses, Construction of trains or	E. Gomez	New York, N. Y	Jan. 7, 1862	34, 057
Fuses for explosive shell, Percussion-igniter of time	B. B. Hotchkiss	Sharon, Conn	Aug. 30, 1864	43, 993
Fuses, Machine for making	A. F. Andrews	Avon, Conn	May 25, 1852	8, 963
Fuses, Machinery for manufacturing safety	R. Uren, T. Dunstone, and J. Blight	Eagle Harbor, Mich	Dec. 2, 1862	37, 079
Fuses, Manufacture of	G. F. James	Manchester, England	May 7, 1872	126, 462
G.				
Gaff-check for vessels	J. C. Cottingham	Philadelphia, Pa	July 6, 1869	92, 271
Gaff-fastening	J. H. David	Damariscotta, Me	Sept. 24, 1872	131, 508
Gaff for ships' spars	G. C. Pattison	Baltimore, Md	Apr. 2, 1867	63, 555
Gaff for vessels' sails	W. H Conway	Harrison, Md	Sept. 17, 1861	33, 295
Gag-runner	W. Robotham	Newark, N. J	Feb. 14, 1860	27, 158
Gag runner and buckle	S. Siebold	Syracuse, N. Y	Mar. 29, 1870	101, 386
Gag-swivel	W. Greacen	Newark, N. J	Oct. 4, 1864	44, 579
Gag-swivel	C. B. Payne	Clinton, Ill	Nov. 3, 1868	83, 787

Gage:

See Auger-gage.
Axle-gage.
Belt-lacing gage.
Bilge-water gage.
Bill-folding gage.
Boiler-gage.
Boiler alarm-gage.
Boiler safety-gage.
Boot and shoe gage.
Boot and shoe heel gage.
Button hole-cutter gage.
Button-shank gage.
Carpenter's gage.
Carriage-axle gage.
Cart-gage.
Changeable gage.
Clapboard-gage.
Clock-work-turning gage.
Cloth-gage.
Cock-gage.
Cock and last gage.
Collar-gage.
Compound gage.
Countersink-gage.
Depth-gage.
Diamond-gage.
Dowel-gage.
Drill-gage.
Edge gage.
Embossing-press gage.
Feather-edging gage.
Feed-gage.
Floor-gage.
Fruit-knife gage.
Gas-fitter's gage.
Grain-gage.
Gun-hammer gage.
Harness-maker's gage.
Index-gage.
Joiner's gage.
Key-way gage
Lamp-wick gage.
Leather-gage.
Leather-splitting gage.
Liquid-gage.
Lumber-slitting gage.

Index of patents issued from the United States Patent Office from 1790 *to* 1873, *inclusive*—Continued.

Index of patents issued from the United States Patent Office from 1790 *to* 1873, *inclusive*—Continued.

Invention.	Inventor.	Residence.	Date.	No.
Galvanic battery	T. A. Edison	Newark, N. J	Sept. 23, 1873	142, 999
Galvanic battery	E. J. Fraser	Chicago, Ill	Nov. 3, 1863	40, 537
Galvanic battery	G. W. Freed	Lancaster, Pa	June 7, 1864	43, 014
Galvanic battery	A. C. Garratt	Boston, Mass	July 7, 1868	79, 567
Galvanic battery	E. Grenet, jr	Paris, France	Sept. 20, 1859	25, 503
Galvanic battery	H. Highton	Putney, England	Oct. 1, 1872	131, 878
Galvanic battery	E. A. Hill	Galesburgh, Ill	Aug. 18, 1863	39, 571
Galvanic battery	E. A. Hill	Chicago, Ill	Apr. 25, 1871	114, 006
Galvanic battery	J. Hill	New York, N. Y	May 24, 1870	103, 331
Galvanic battery	J. Kidder	New York, N. Y	Oct. 25, 1870	108, 602
Galvanic battery	J. Kidder	New York, N. Y	June 27, 1871	116, 451
Galvanic battery	J. Kidder	New York, N. Y	Oct. 10, 1871	119, 855
Galvanic battery	G. L. Leclanché	Paris, France	June 5, 1866	55, 441
Galvanic battery	E. J. Leland.	Worcester, Mass	Nov. 7, 1871	120, 651
Galvanic battery	C. A. Linke	Pittsburgh, Pa	July 16, 1872	129, 148
Galvanic battery	R. M. Lockwood	New York, N. Y	Apr. 8, 1873	137, 556
Galvanic battery	E. D. McCracken	New York, N. Y	Aug. 16, 1870	106, 383
Galvanic battery	J. R. McPherson	Beloit, Wis	Dec 14, 1869	97, 949
Galvanic battery	A. L. Nolf	New York, N. Y	Sept. 2, 1873	142, 502
Galvanic battery	A. Olmstead	Easton, Pa	Apr. 17, 1849	6, 362
Galvanic battery	G. M. Phelps	Brooklyn, N. Y	Aug. 20, 1872	103, 593
Galvanic battery	J. Plumbe, jr	Boston, Mass	Mar. 4, 1843	2, 984
Galvanic battery	J. W. Powell	New York, N. Y	May 30, 1871	115, 519
Galvanic battery	E. Provost	New York, N. Y	Sept. 19, 1871	119, 175
Galvanic battery	J. A. Robbins	Medford, Mass	Oct. 24, 1871	120, 327
Galvanic battery	J. A. Robbins	Medford, Mass	July 2, 1872	128, 660
Galvanic battery	E. Seaver	Boston, Mass	Jan. 26, 1858	19, 209
Galvanic battery	W. J. Wilder	Cleveland, Ohio	Nov. 12, 1872	132, 997
Galvanic battery adapted to medical purposes	P. Coad	Philadelphia, Pa	Mar. 28, 1842	2, 521
Galvanic-battery connection	H. Splitdorf	New York, N. Y	Feb. 13, 1866	52, 617
Galvanic battery for remedial uses	H. Fitz	Cleveland, Ohio	Mar. 19, 1867	63, 032
Galvanic-battery switch	G. Little	Rutherford, Park, N. J	June 13, 1871	115, 966
Galvanic-battery switch	E. M. Pierson	Newark, N. J	Oct. 18, 1870	108, 513
Galvanic chains, bands, &c., Electro	I. L. Pulvermacher	London, England	Nov. 7, 1871	120, 772
Galvanic chains, Fluid for exciting	F. T. Bakker	Chicago, Ill	June 30, 1868	79, 432
Galvanic electricity applied to cure disease	D. Harrington	Philadelphia, Pa	Mar. 31, 1835	....
Galvanic electricity applied to surface of the body	D. Harrington	Philadelphia, Pa	Apr. 8, 1835	....
Galvanic fluid for curing certain diseases	D. Harrington	Philadelphia, Pa	July 22, 1833	....
Galvanic fluid to cure diseases	D. Harrington	Philadelphia, Pa	Jan. 27, 1834	....
Galvanic instrument	D. Harrington	Philadelphia, Pa	Sept. 2, 1845	4, 176
Galvanic plate for medical use	J. Hill	Brooklyn, N. Y	Oct. 9, 1860	30, 317
Galvanic plate for remedial purposes	C. Maray	New York, N. Y	Jan. 19, 1869	86, 088
Galvanic register for steam-boilers	A. Dunn	Dalston, England	May 28, 1850	7, 394
Galvanic ring, belt, &c	D. C. Moorhead	New York, N. Y	Aug. 26, 1845	4, 167
Galvanism, Apparatus for treating diseases by means of.	J. B. Hatting	New York, N. Y	June 21, 1870	104, 587
Galvanism for salivating, &c	W. Phœbus	New York, N. Y	June 9, 1807	....
Galvanized nails, Cleansing and separating	W. Blake	Boston, Mass	Aug. 21, 1860	29, 664
Galvanizing metals, Process for	C. B. Miller	Wilmington, Del	May 30, 1854	10, 976
Galvano-electric machine	J. R. Palmenberg	New York, N. Y	Nov. 9, 1858	22, 029
Galvano-plastic process for precipitating iron on molds, &c.	M. H. Jacobi and E. Klein	St. Petersburg, Russia	Sept. 29, 1868	82, 525
Galvanometer, Reflecting	W. Thomson	Glasgow College, Scotland.	July 6, 1869	92, 228
Game	C. B. Barlow	Portsmouth, N. H	Oct. 19, 1869	95, 969
Game	J. Brandl	New York, N. Y	Dec. 24, 1872	134, 125
Game	E. J. Brooks	New York, N. Y	Mar. 19, 1872	124, 786
Game	J. M. Fletcher	Clifton, N. Y	Apr. 16, 1872	125, 671
Game	D. F. Hale	Chicopee, Mass	Oct. 25, 1870	108, 587
Game	H. Jackson	New York, N. Y	Feb. 11, 1868	74, 368
Game	G. Krotzinger	New York, N. Y	Dec. 3, 1867	71, 626
Game	B. E. Mead	Peekskill, N. Y	Jan. 3, 1865	45, 731
Game	J. B. Murray	Newark, N. J	Aug. 6, 1872	130, 234
Game	R. Patterson	New Santa Fé, Mo	July 30, 1872	129, 983
Game	J. M. Rix	Warren, N. H	Mar. 26, 1872	124, 915
Game	A. G. Slagle	Memphis, Tenn	Mar. 30, 1869	88, 421
Game	N. J. Vander Weyde	Franklin, N. H	June 14, 1870	104, 379
Game	W. H. Wilson	Providence, R. I	Sept. 22, 1868	82, 370
Game and rat trap	B. F. Tatom	Memphis, Tenn	Nov. 7, 1871	120, 683
Game-apparatus.	R. E. Bean	Franklin, N. H	Dec. 9, 1873	145, 385
Game-apparatus	J. N. Sawkins	Langport, England	Dec. 23, 1873	145, 757
Game-apparatus	A. M. Smith	Chicago, Ill	Feb. 4, 1873	135, 494
Game-apparatus	F. W. Smith	Bridgeport, Conn	Dec. 23, 1873	145, 914
Game-apparatus	P. West and G. S. Lee	Worcester, Mass	Sept. 23, 1873	143, 047
Game-apparatus	P. West and G. S. Lee	Worcester, Mass	Oct. 21, 1873	143, 799
Game-apparatus	J. C. Wilhelm	Shaver's Creek, Pa	Dec. 16, 1873	145, 706
Game, Arithmetical	S. A. Emery	Boston, Mass	Nov. 10, 1868	83, 946
Game ball	E. A. Barrett	New York, N. Y	Feb. 6, 1872	123, 442
Game-board	J. C. Arms	Northampton, Mass	Feb. 25, 1873	136, 200
Game-board	A. F. R. Arndt	Detroit, Mich	Dec. 9, 1873	145, 271
Game-board	H. C. Drexel	Baltimore, Md	Jan. 23, 1872	123, 001
Game-board	J. T. Edson	Stowe, Mass	Apr. 25, 1865	47, 491
Game-board	G. R. Elliott	Boston, Mass	Feb. 18, 1873	136, 048
Game-board	F. P. Holmes	North Bridgewater, Mass	July 22, 1873	141, 053
Game-board	G. W. Kintz	Rochester, N. Y	Aug. 22, 1871	118, 249
Game-board	C. Krath and G. H. Moll	Saint Louis, Mo	Sept. 6, 1870	107, 065
Game-board	J. Smith and E. M. Nutter	Feltonville, Mass	May 23, 1865	47, 867
Game-board	G. Wentz	Cincinnati, Ohio	Aug. 19, 1873	142, 066
Game board, Top	D. Wight	New London, Conn	Apr. 7, 1868	76, 572
Game-box	S. F. Brooks	Weston, Mass	June 19, 1860	28, 733
Game-box for ten-pins	G. B. Fowler	Brooklyn, N. Y	Sept. 6, 1870	107, 030
Game called vinco	J. Carlin	New York, N. Y	Dec. 29, 1868	85, 281
Game-card	C. W. Saladee	Paducah, Ky	Feb. 9, 1864	41, 587
Game-counter	A. A. Griffing	Lexington, Mass	Feb. 16, 1869	86, 919
Game-counter	F. H. Richardson	Brooklyn, N. Y	July 9, 1872	128, 910
Game-counter	E. Schellhorn	Urbana, Ohio	Feb. 9, 1869	86, 781
Game entitled "Talisman"	J. W. Wilson	New York, N. Y	Apr. 27, 1869	89, 535
Game for pastime	C. Richardson	Richmond, Va	Apr. 23, 1867	64, 149

Index of patents issued from the United States Patent Office from 1790 *to* 1873, *inclusive*—Continued.

Invention.	Inventor.	Residence.	Date.	No.
Game, Geographic	L. Branson	Raleigh, N. C	Jan. 19, 1869	85, 990
Game, Letter	J. E. Wheat	Rochester, N. Y	Feb. 4, 1868	74, 022
Game, Miniature-war	C. Portillo	New York, N. Y	Feb. 21, 1871	111, 969
Game, Musical	G. W. Dawson	New Haven, Conn	Dec. 7, 1869	97, 612
Game of battle war chess	C. Richardson	Richmond, Va	Dec. 4, 1866	60, 247
Game of cards	M. Bradley	Springfield, Mass	Nov. 26, 1872	133, 296
Game of chance	V. Bareau	Paris, France	July 16, 1872	128, 941
Game of colors	C. H. Douglas	Hartford, Conn	Dec. 15, 1868	84, 865
Game, Parlor	G. A. Coffin	Cincinnati, Ohio	June 6, 1871	115, 576
Game, Parlor	C. N. Hoyt	Providence, R. I	June 8, 1869	91, 022
Game, Parlor	A. W. Smith	Birmingham, Pa	May 11, 1869	89, 894
Game, Parlor	E. Trump	Cincinnati, Ohio	Apr. 6, 1869	88, 756
Game, Parlor	H. M. White	East Hartford, Conn	Feb. 2, 1869	86, 479
Game-register	J. Enright	Louisville, Ky	Apr. 23, 1867	64, 085
Game-register	E. H. Keith	Peoria, Ill	Mar. 22, 1870	101, 133
Game-register	J. W. Wormald	Buffalo, N. Y	Oct. 29, 1872	132, 553
Game register, Card	C. W. Saladee	Paducah, Ky	Mar. 1, 1864	41, 820
Game-register for cards	J. W. Sheppard	New York, N. Y	Oct. 7, 1873	143, 536
Game-signal	W. M. Tileston	New York, N. Y	June 20, 1871	116, 117
Game, Social	M. Bradley	Springfield, Mass	Apr. 3, 1866	53, 561
Game-table	E. Brunswick	Chicago, Ill	Sept. 26, 1871	119, 262
Game-table	R. R. Crawford	Wytheville, Va	Nov. 18, 1873	144, 659
Game-table	H. R. Heyl	Philadelphia, Pa	Jan. 16, 1872	122, 830
Game-table	W. Keil	Hastings, Minn	July 21, 1868	80, 185
Game-table	L. A. Powers	West Meriden, Conn	Feb. 18, 1873	136, 092
Game-table	L. Raymond	Rockland, Del	Nov. 5, 1867	70, 469
Game-table	S. S. Schindler	West Meriden, Conn	May 27, 1873	139, 425
Game-table	F. Uebel	Cedar Rapids, Iowa	May 13, 1873	138, 961
Game-table top	G. G. Thomson	New Haven, Conn	Mar. 25, 1873	137, 113
Game-target	J. C. Schooley	New York, N. Y	Jan. 3, 1871	110, 792
Game-trap	E. M. Day	Elkhart, Ill	Dec. 7, 1869	97, 747
Game-trap, Self-setting	A. Wilkin	McConnellsville, Ohio	Nov. 12, 1867	70, 929
Games, Adjustable ball-holder for	F. A. Spofford and M. G. Raffington.	Columbus, Ohio	Feb. 4, 1868	74, 164
Games, Alley-board for ball	C. Robinson	Boston, Mass	Sept. 20, 1870	107, 545
Games, Apparatus for playing	H. Plumb	Philadelphia, Pa	May 31, 1870	103, 774
Games, Combination apparatus for	C. N. Hoyt	Providence, R. I	Aug. 8, 1871	117, 780
Games of chance, Selecting balls for	M. Nelson	New York, N. Y	June 18, 1861	32, 581
Games, Scoring	W. B. O. Peabody	Boston, Mass	Apr. 21, 1868	76, 940
Garancine, Preparation of	S. Borden	Fall River, Mass	Nov. 22, 1870	109, 489
Garbage and ash box	C. W. Stafford	Saybrook, Conn	Apr. 9, 1867	63, 664
Garbage-box	M. Bacharach	New York, N. Y	Nov. 5, 1872	132, 788
Garbage-box	E. D. Clapp	Washington, D. C	Aug. 6, 1872	130, 190
Garbage-box	J. W. Evans and G. F. Godley	New York, N. Y	Mar. 16, 1869	87, 918
Garbage-box	M. Gilbert	New York, N. Y	Mar. 12, 1867	62, 836
Garbage-box	T. Jarvis	New York, N. Y	Sept. 24, 1872	131, 617
Garbage-box	J. L. Mason	New York, N. Y	Sept. 8, 1868	81, 919
Garbage-box	J. J. Slevin	New York, N. Y	June 26, 1866	55, 920
Garbage-box	D. D. Templeton	New York, N. Y	May 14, 1867	64, 810
Garbage can or vessel	W. Shires	Cincinnati, Ohio	Jan. 7, 1868	73, 130
Garbage or ash box	C. W. Stafford	Saybrook, Conn	Apr. 9, 1867	63, 665
Garbage, &c., Process of deriving useful products from.	W. E. Johnson	Chicago, Ill	Mar. 23, 1869	88, 258
Garbage-tub	S. B. Munson, jr	Chicago, Ill	July 1, 1873	140, 527
Garden-bed border	J. E. Dickson and S. Richmond	Annapolis, Md	Mar. 28, 1871	113, 145
Garden-digger	R. R. Frohock	Boston, Mass	May 15, 1866	54, 711
Garden, Elevated and suspended	F. O. Rogers	Boston, Mass	Apr. 12, 1870	101, 918
Garden-engine, Portable	W. B. Robins	Middlesex County, England	July 23, 1872	129, 750
Garden, Geographical	G. W. Cherry	Derby, Conn	May 27, 1825	....
Garden-implement	J. Armstrong	Bucyrus, Ohio	July 7, 1868	79, 540
Garden-implement	F. Fuller	New York, N. Y	Sept. 1, 1868	81, 619
Garden-implement	J. M. Lunguest	Atlanta, Ga	Dec. 30, 1873	146, 083
Garden-implement	H. Miller	Roadside, Va	Aug. 24, 1869	94, 125
Garden-implement	H. Miller	Roadside, Va	Dec. 7, 1869	97, 542
Garden-implement	D. S. Wilhoit	Madison Court-House, Va	Aug. 15, 1871	118, 088
Garden-implement and weeder	W. Somers	Bridgeport, Conn	May 18, 1869	90, 319
Garden-implement handle	A. A. Porter	Griffin, Ga	May 30, 1871	115, 352
Garden-line	C. Richel	Cleveland, Ohio	Oct. 22, 1867	70, 022
Garden-rake	M. G. Baker	New Burlington, Ohio	Aug. 14, 1866	57, 066
Garden-rake	L. Sisson	North Easton, Mass	May 10, 1870	102, 979
Garden-rake	S. N. and W. F. Stillman	Leonardsville, N. Y	Feb. 13, 1855	12, 396
Garden-roller	J. B. Brown	Peekskill, N. Y	Nov. 17, 1868	84, 167
Garden-roller for destroying insects	H. Gray	Sugar Creek, Wis	Mar. 27, 1866	53, 439
Garden-sprinkler	J. E. Spear	San Francisco, Cal	May 2, 1871	114, 362
Garden-sprinkler, Portable	J. Gibson	San Francisco, Cal	July 16, 1872	129, 125
Garden-syringe	A. F. Hammond	Houston, Ohio	Mar. 19, 1867	62, 955
Garden-syringe	W. J. Johnson	Newton, Mass	July 4, 1871	116, 599
Garden-tool	J. Lane	Chicago, Ill	Feb. 27, 1872	124, 001
Garden-tool	H. Von Unwerth	Salem, Mass	Feb. 23, 1858	19, 457
Garden-tools, Combined	L. and F. Perrot and C. H. Bates.	Greenville and Appleton, Wis.	Nov. 29, 1870	109, 657
Garden-walk cleaner	P. Boice	Chatham Village, N. Y	Feb. 21, 1871	112, 012
Gardening-implement	R. W. Porter and J. F. Spalding.	Nashua and Hudson, N. H	Oct. 3, 1865	50, 305
Garlic from wheat, Separating	S. Fahrney	Boonsborough, Md	Oct. 26, 1842	2, 835
Garlic-machine	S. Fahrney	Boonsborough, Md	Dec. 5, 1843	3, 367
Garlic-separator	W. C. Grimes	York, Pa	July 26, 1843	3, 197
Garment-clasp	W. Wright	Bloomfield, N. J	June 2, 1868	78, 505
Garment-dummy	A. M. Davis	Washington, D. C	Apr. 5, 1870	101, 591
Garment-fastener	M. H. N. Kendig	Washington, D. C	Apr. 16, 1867	63, 906
Garment-fastening	C. W. Baldwin	Boston, Mass	July 3, 1860	29, 031
Garment-fastening	E. G. Belknap	Spring Garden, Pa	June 15, 1852	9, 011
Garment-fastening	J. W. Bliss	Hartford, Conn	June 2, 1857	17, 416
Garment-fastening	W. G. Cook	New York, N. Y	May 29, 1866	55, 064
Garment-fastening	J. E. Dallon	Brooklyn, N. Y	Aug. 30, 1870	106, 920
Garment-fastening	T. J. Harris, jr	New York, N. Y	Oct. 3, 1854	11, 749
Garment-fastening	E. Howe, jr	Cambridge, Mass	Nov. 25, 1851	8, 540
Garment-fastening	R. Oliver	New York, N. Y	Oct. 10, 1854	11, 792

Index of patents issued from the United States Patent Office from 1790 *to* 1873, *inclusive*—Continued.

Invention.	Inventor.	Residence.	Date.	No.
Garment-fastening	F. I. Palmer	Springfield, Mass	Mar. 27, 1866	53, 472
Garment-fastening	R. S. Pickett	New Haven, Conn	Mar. 20, 1866	53, 331
Garment for ladies, Interlined under	C. L. Morehouse	Cleveland, Ohio	Feb. 28, 1865	46, 575
Garment for travelers, Sleeping	V. P. Corbett	Washington, D. C	Apr. 5, 1864	42, 168
Garment-hanger and size-ticket holder combined.	I. Desky and S. A. Jennings	Seneca Falls, N. Y	Jan. 4, 1870	98, 476
Garment having body and sleeves	H. Osler	Philadelphia, Pa	June 2, 1863	38, 757
Garment-holder	B. V. Taylor	Newark, N. J	Nov. 8, 1870	109, 156
Garment, Hooded	A. Keating	Boston, Mass	Dec. 20, 1870	110, 242
Garment-hook	M. Fowler	North Branford, Conn	Jan. 12, 1864	41, 213
Garment, Lady's accouching	H. R. Esterling	Bennettsville, S. C	Jan. 30, 1872	123, 249
Garment-pattern, Adjustable	S. Shawcross	Freeport, Ill	Mar. 22, 1870	101, 052
Garment-pressing apparatus	J. W. Thorp	South Weare, N. H	Dec. 16, 1851	8, 598
Garment-pressing machine	W. B. Walker	Boston, Mass	Feb. 27, 1872	124, 177
Garment, Skin under	J. H. Andrus	New York, N. Y	Mar. 28, 1871	113, 128
Garment-strap, Adjustable and detachable	S. L. Clemens	Hartford, Conn	Dec. 19, 1871	121, 992
Garment-strap, Adjustable and detachable	H. C. Lockwood	Baltimore, Md	Dec. 19, 1871	122, 038
Garment-support	J. L. Kendall	Foxborough, Mass	Apr. 20, 1869	89, 152
Garment-supporter	H. M. Clemence	Worcester, Mass	Nov. 19, 1867	71, 136
Garment, Under	O. P. Flynt	Boston, Mass	Nov. 18, 1873	144, 609
Garments, Apparatus for cutting	T. H. Moore	Boston, Mass	Mar. 25, 1862	34, 766
Garments, Apparatus for fitting and laying out	W. H. Mayer	Newark, N. J	Dec. 5, 1871	121, 642
Garments, Apparatus for laying off the scye in cutting.	P. Spilman	Richmond, Va	July 18, 1854	11, 339
Garments, Applying measurement to and laying out.	J. J. Miller	McAlevy's Fort, Pa	July 12, 1870	105, 355
Garments, Attachment for fastening overlapping parts of.	B. J. Greely	Boston, Mass	Dec. 7, 1869	97, 629
Garments, Attachment for protecting cuff and sleeve of.	J. C. Reed	Boston, Mass	Oct. 24, 1871	120, 324
Garments, Brace for supporting	D. Minthorn	New York, N. Y	June 5, 1855	13, 011
Garments, Cutting	O. Madison	Troy, N. Y	Aug. 18, 1829	....
Garments, Cutting	D. N. Sipperly	Troy, N. Y	July 8, 1843	3, 160
Garments, Cutting	S. B. Stilwell	Brooklyn, N. Y	June 20, 1845	4, 083
Garments, Drafting	W. L. Leete	Oswego, N. Y	Sept. 6, 1870	107, 068
Garments, Drafting and cutting	J. H. Chappell	Chillicothe, Ohio	Jan. 18, 1834	....
Garments, Drafting and measuring	C. Lucas	Charlottesville, Va	June 13, 1848	5, 635
Garments, Hook for fastening	G. A. Watkins	Springfield, Vt	Feb. 24, 1863	37, 783
Garments, Machine for cutting out	W. A. McLaughlin	New York, N. Y	Nov. 10, 1868	83, 870
Garments, Machine for drafting	J. M. Weston	Chesterfield, N. Y	Feb. 2, 1858	19, 271
Garments, Manufacturing seamless felt	D. W. Gitchell and L. W. Badger	Matteawan, N. Y	Oct. 20, 1857	18, 487
Garments, Marking off and cutting out	G. Beard, jr	West Whiteland Township, Pa.	Aug. 5, 1833	....
Garments, Marking off and cutting out	B. J. Lewis	Mount Vernon, Ohio	Nov. 19, 1833	....
Garments, Mode of constructing	T. S. Lambert	Peekskill, N. Y	Feb. 18, 1862	34, 464
Garments, Pattern for cutting	S. A. Millwee	Greenwood, S. C	May 14, 1872	126, 825
Garments, Pattern for laying out	W. M. Michael	Indiana, Pa	Dec. 7, 1869	97, 672
Garments, Sleeve of knitted	W. H. Abel	Greenville, R. I	Aug. 4, 1868	80, 697
Garments, Spring-hook fastening for	D. M. Smith	Springfield, Vt	June 16, 1863	38, 920
Garments, Spring hook for fastening	A. Putnam, jr	Chester, Vt	Nov. 11, 1862	36, 933
Garments, Square for cutting	J. G. Wilson	New York, N. Y	Feb. 28, 1827	....
Garments, System of cutting	A. Wiswell	Exeter, N. H	July 11, 1837	256
Garments, System of laying out	J. A. Shreckengaust	Chillicothe, Ohio	July 16, 1872	129, 603
Garments, Tailor's instrument and mode of measuring	L. Fleuner	Philadelphia, Pa	Nov. 10, 1841	2, 341
Garments, Tailor's instrument for drafting	E. J. Axford	Philadelphia, Pa	Mar. 30, 1839	1, 113
Garments to hooks, Securing	G. Woodward and F. S. Hathaway.	Keene, N. H	Feb. 15, 1859	22, 996
Garments, Uniting bats for making seamless felt.	D. W. Gitchell	Rahway, N. J	Sept. 26, 1854	11, 739
Garments without spinning or weaving, Manufacturing woolen.	J. Foster and J. Stoudenburgh	Greene County, N. Y	Apr. 20, 1830	....
Garter	E. F. Burrows	Mystic River, Conn	July 24, 1866	56, 524
Garter	C. Coester, jr., and J. L. Moore	Bridgeport, Conn	Aug. 16, 1870	106, 328
Garter	J. P. Fuller	New York, N. Y	June 26, 1860	38, 841
Garter	H. A. House	Bridgeport, Conn	Nov. 29, 1870	109, 617
Garter	H. A. House	Bridgeport, Conn	Nov. 29, 1870	109, 736
Garter	H. A. House	Bridgeport, Conn	Nov. 29, 1870	109, 737
Garter	H. A. House	Bridgeport, Conn	Mar. 11, 1873	136, 599
Garter and belt, Coil-spring	J. M. Ellis	Bridgeport, Conn	Dec. 2, 1873	145, 160
Garter, Metallic	H. A. House	Bridgeport, Conn	Mar. 7, 1871	112, 344
Garter, Metallic	W. H. McCoy and A. Wheeler	Charlestown, Mass	Oct. 29, 1867	70, 238
Gas-alarm	P. H. Vander Weyde	New York, N. Y	Mar. 22, 1864	42, 032
Gas and heating buildings, Apparatus for generating.	S. C. Salisbury	New York, N. Y	Mar. 23, 1869	88, 079
Gas and heating dwellings, Apparatus for generating.	T. S. C. Lowe	Morristown, Pa	Aug. 13, 1872	130, 381
Gas and illuminating street and other cars, Production of.	A. Barbarin	New Orleans, La	Sept. 22, 1868	82, 273
Gas and in application of the same, Process of generating.	J. T. Rich	Philadelphia, Pa	Feb. 4, 1868	74, 001
Gas and liquid meter	H. H. Stuart	Jamaica, N. Y	Dec. 11, 1866	60, 437
Gas and liquid regulator	T. H. Dodge	Nashua, N. H	June 27, 1854	11, 154
Gas and oil, Apparatus and process for obtaining light from.	J. Kidd	New York, N. Y	Aug. 31, 1869	94, 219
Gas and oil from coal, Apparatus for manufacturing.	J. Shoemaker	Putneyville, Pa	Nov. 19, 1867	71, 233
Gas and other heater	J. Q. Birkey	Philadelphia, Pa	Mar. 17, 1868	75, 516
Gas and other lights, Apparatus for igniting	W. Klinkerfues	Göttingen, Prussia	May 16, 1871	114, 950
Gas and other liquids, Device for igniting	W. H. Smith	New York, N. Y	May 30, 1871	115, 373
Gas and other products, Manufacture of illuminating.	J. Absterdam	New York, N. Y	Dec. 15, 1868	84, 981
Gas and smoke consuming apparatus	G. Marlow	Chicago, Ill	Oct. 24, 1871	120, 299
Gas and steam fittings	A. Hallowell	Lowell, Mass	Nov. 17, 1868	84, 112
Gas and vapor from petroleum, Apparatus for generating.	A. I. Ambler	Washington, D. C	May 14, 1872	126, 770
Gas and water fittings, Machine for tapping	A. D. Laws	Bridgeport, Conn	Sept. 23, 1873	143, 168
Gas and water mains, Coupling for	W. Kilburn	Napa, Cal	July 15, 1873	140, 834
Gas and water meter	G. R. Moore	Philadelphia, Pa	June 1, 1869	90, 678
Gas and water meter register	J. J. Squire	New Haven, Conn	Mar. 3, 1863	37, 832

Index of patents issued from the United States Patent Office from 1790 *to* 1873, *inclusive*—Continued.

Invention.	Inventor.	Residence.	Date.	No.
Gas and water pipe	E. H. Austin	New York, N. Y	Mar. 18, 1873	136, 952
Gas and water pipe	W. B. Guy	Boston, Mass	Dec. 20, 1864	45, 491
Gas and water pipe	A. Wyckoff	Elmira, N. Y	Nov. 22, 1864	45, 201
Gas and water pipe coating	N. Clute	Schenectady, N. Y	Mar. 21, 1871	112, 786
Gas and water pipe joint	C. W. Isbell	New Haven, Conn	July 24, 1860	29, 281
Gas and water pipe joint	J. E. Quinn	Chicago, Ill	Apr. 26, 1859	23, 811
Gas and water pipe plug	E. P. Schutt	Cortland, N. Y	Mar. 1, 1870	100, 456
Gas and water pipes, Casting packing-rings in	R. C. Robbins	New York, N. Y	Jan. 26, 1864	41, 413
Gas-apparatus	A. L. Bogart	New York, N. Y	Jan. 3, 1871	110, 729
Gas-apparatus	J. W. Brown and H. B. West	Butlerville, Ind., and Put in Bay, Ohio.	Apr. 29, 1873	138, 377
Gas-apparatus	C. H. Childs	Cleveland, Ohio	May 26, 1868	78, 185
Gas-apparatus	R. T. Coverdale	Circleville, Ohio	July 23, 1867	66, 950
Gas-apparatus	C. Deavs	New York, N. Y	June 25, 1867	66, 004
Gas-apparatus	W. Foster, jr., and G. P. Ganster.	New York, N. Y	Mar. 9, 1869	87, 556
Gas-apparatus	J. S. Gallaher, jr, and J. W. Smith.	Washington, D. C	Dec. 11, 1855	13, 904
Gas-apparatus	D. M. Graham	Evansville, Ind	Sept. 3, 1867	68, 435
Gas-apparatus	E. J. Manville and S. G. Blackman.	Waterbury, Conn	June 1, 1858	20, 438
Gas-apparatus	H. S. Maxim	Brooklyn, N. Y	Jan. 9, 1872	122, 625
Gas-apparatus	J. McCleish	New York, N. Y	May 26, 1868	78, 307
Gas-apparatus	R. Morton	London, England	Sept. 12, 1871	118, 967
Gas-apparatus	A. Myers	Philadelphia, Pa	June 7, 1864	43, 079
Gas-apparatus	G. Olney	Brooklyn, N. Y	Jan. 16, 1872	122, 733
Gas-apparatus	A. Pierce	Philadelphia, Pa	Feb. 27, 1849	6, 145
Gas-apparatus	E. A. Pond and M. S. Richardson.	Rutland, Vt	Mar. 27, 1866	53, 482
Gas-apparatus	J. Ponton	Buffalo, N. Y	May 19, 1868	78, 006
Gas-apparatus	R. Porter and T. Lane	London, England	Aug. 13, 1872	130, 388
Gas-apparatus	J. E. Richard	Columbia, S. C	Nov. 1, 1870	108, 937
Gas-apparatus	C. Seeger	Quincy, Ill	Mar. 19, 1872	124, 766
Gas-apparatus	J. F. Spence	Williamsburgh, N. Y	Feb. 5, 1867	61, 887
Gas-apparatus	J. H. Steiner	Cincinnati, Ohio	Apr. 9, 1872	125, 496
Gas-apparatus	O. Tirrill	Burlington, Mass	June 5, 1866	55, 395
Gas-apparatus	H. H. Wainwright	Philadelphia, Pa	Feb. 4, 1873	135, 455
Gas-apparatus	A. Walker, jr	Burke, Vt	Aug. 7, 1849	6, 626
Gas-apparatus	W. Warner and E. S. Redstreake.	Philadelphia, Pa	Aug. 7, 1866	57, 020
Gas apparatus and carbureter, Portable	J. MacDougall	New York, N. Y	Nov. 26, 1867	71, 514
Gas apparatus and carbureter, Portable	M. A. Root and J. D. Custer	Philadelphia and Norristown, Pa.	Nov. 23, 1869	97, 122
Gas-apparatus, Automatic air-holder for	H. L. McAvoy	Baltimore, Md	Nov. 22, 1864	45, 205
Gas apparatus, Coal	E. Jones	Boston, Mass	Dec. 19, 1871	122, 024
Gas, Apparatus for broiling or roasting by	W. F. Shaw	Boston, Mass	June 19, 1860	28, 781
Gas, Apparatus for carbonizing	W. H. Laubach	Philadelphia, Pa	Apr. 21, 1868	77, 156
Gas, Apparatus for carbureting and regulating the pressure of.	T. G. Springer	New York, N. Y	Sept. 2, 1873	142, 525
Gas, Apparatus for collecting marsh and other	C. S. Hunt and J. B. Knight	Terre Bonne Parish and New Orleans, La.	May 19, 1868	77, 982
Gas, Apparatus for compressing	W. H. Gwynne	New York, N. Y	Aug. 7, 1860	29, 481
Gas, Apparatus for condensing and purifying	A. Hendrickx	New York, N. Y	Aug. 3, 1858	21, 072
Gas, Apparatus for domestic manufacture of	J. W. Brown	Wooster, Ohio	Sept. 15, 1868	82, 080
Gas-apparatus for domestic use	W. Mills and O. H. Burdett	New Athens, Ohio	July 7, 1863	39, 159
Gas, &c., Apparatus for exhausting	R. Laidlaw and J. Thomson	Glasgow, Great Britain	Apr. 25, 1871	114, 156
Gas, Apparatus for exhausting and purifying	P. Munzinger	Philadelphia, Pa	Aug. 29, 1871	118, 472
Gas, Apparatus for exhausting and washing	C. H. Brown and J. J. Thomas.	Philadelphia, Pa	Mar. 25, 1873	137, 174
Gas, Apparatus for generating and burning	W. Stewart	Steubenville, Ohio	July 5, 1870	105, 012
Gas, Apparatus for generating and carbureting	C. F. Dunderdale	New York, N. Y	June 1, 1869	90, 644
Gas, Apparatus for generating and carbureting hydrogen.	J. B. Terry	Brooklyn, N. Y	Sept. 12, 1871	118, 983
Gas, Apparatus for generating carbonic-acid	S. T. Bacon	Boston, Mass	Jan. 29, 1867	61, 596
Gas, Apparatus for generating carbonic-acid	J. Matthews	New York, N. Y	June 25, 1872	128, 234
Gas, Apparatus for generating carbonic-acid	J. D. O'Donnell	Washington, D. C	Aug. 8, 1871	117, 805
Gas, Apparatus for generating carbonic-acid	T. Warker	New York, N. Y	Apr. 27, 1859	20, 110
Gas, Apparatus for generating carbonic-acid	O. Zwietusch	Milwaukee, Wis	July 30, 1872	130, 001
Gas, Apparatus for generating carbonic-acid and other.	F. M. Ruschhaupt	Philadelphia, Pa	Apr. 19, 1864	42, 447
Gas, Apparatus for generating, carbureting, and burning hydrogen.	B. Sloper	Saint Louis, Mo	May 30, 1871	115, 369
Gas, Apparatus for generating illuminating	M. P. Coons	Brooklyn, N. Y	Nov. 22, 1859	26, 163
Gas, Apparatus for generating illuminating	D. Davison	New York, N. Y	Feb. 15, 1870	99, 860
Gas, Apparatus for generating illuminating	C. N. Tyler	Washington, D. C	Dec. 28, 1858	22, 463
Gas, Apparatus for generating oxygen	B. R. Smithson	New York, N. Y	Dec. 3, 1867	71, 657
Gas, Apparatus for making illuminating	O. Collins	New York, N. Y	Aug. 22, 1865	49, 505
Gas, Apparatus for making water	W. H. Gwynne	Brooklyn, N. Y	Mar. 11, 1862	34, 632
Gas, Apparatus for manufacturing	J. Absterdam	Boston, Mass	June 15, 1858	20, 534
Gas, Apparatus for manufacturing	W. Beaumont	Paterson, N. J	June 15, 1858	20, 541
Gas, Apparatus for manufacturing	R. Carkhuff	Lewisburgh, Pa	Aug. 2, 1864	43, 668
Gas, Apparatus for manufacturing	B. F. Caston	Washington, D. C	July 26, 1847	5, 210
Gas, Apparatus for manufacturing	J. C. Clapp	Homer, N. Y	July 16, 1867	66, 676
Gas, Apparatus for manufacturing	E. Jones	Boston, Mass	Dec. 19, 1871	122, 025
Gas, Apparatus for manufacturing	W. Maynard	Salem, Mass	Feb. 18, 1873	136, 081
Gas, Apparatus for manufacturing	S. C. Salisbury	New York, N. Y	May 30, 1865	47, 986
Gas, Apparatus for manufacturing	W. H. Spencer	New York, N. Y	July 22, 1873	141, 090
Gas, Apparatus for manufacturing	G. Symes	London, England	Aug. 6, 1872	130, 164
Gas, Apparatus for manufacturing coal	S. B. Darwin	Shrewsbury, England	Feb. 13, 1872	123, 682
Gas, Apparatus for manufacturing coal	W. Gibson	Cambridge, Mass	Sept. 19, 1871	119, 135
Gas, Apparatus for manufacturing coal	A. M. Giles	Boston, Mass	Mar. 26, 1872	125, 043
Gas, Apparatus for manufacturing coal	D. H. Irland	Fayette, N. Y	May 26, 1868	78, 209
Gas, Apparatus for manufacturing coal	E. Jones	Boston, Mass	Feb. 11, 1873	135, 647
Gas, Apparatus for manufacturing heating and illuminating.	J. A. Bassett	Salem, Mass	Sept. 8, 1868	81, 974
Gas, Apparatus for manufacturing hydrocarbon	E. J. L. Caillot	Barcelona, Spain	Dec. 10, 1872	133, 829
Gas, Apparatus for manufacturing hydrocarbon	J. Kidd	New York, N. Y	Aug. 29, 1871	118, 459
Gas, Apparatus for manufacturing hydrogen	W. L. Imlay	Philadelphia, Pa	Nov. 11, 1873	144, 543
Gas, Apparatus for manufacturing illuminating	R. Alsop	Philadelphia, Pa	June 22, 1869	91, 588

Index of patents issued from the United States Patent Office from 1790 to 1873, inclusive—Continued.

Invention.	Inventor.	Residence.	Date.	No.
Gas, Apparatus for manufacturing illuminating	J. Dailey	Saint Louis, Mo	June 7, 1870	103, 994
Gas, Apparatus for manufacturing illuminating	J. Jennings	New York, N. Y	Feb. 1, 1865	46, 473
Gas, Apparatus for manufacturing illuminating	E. Jones	Boston, Mass	June 27, 1871	116, 450
Gas, Apparatus for manufacturing illuminating	H. G. Ludlow	Troy, N. Y	Sept. 6, 1870	107, 208
Gas, Apparatus for manufacturing illuminating	J. G. and W. Müller	Dayton, Ohio	Dec. 23, 1873	145, 810
Gas, Apparatus for manufacturing illuminating	H. B. Myer	Philadelphia, Pa	June 25, 1872	128, 321
Gas, Apparatus for manufacturing illuminating	S. Nowlan	New York, N. Y	Aug. 30, 1859	25, 275
Gas, Apparatus for manufacturing illuminating	F. W. Ofeldt and A. W. Almqvist.	New York, N. Y	Aug. 18, 1868	81, 198
Gas, Apparatus for manufacturing illuminating	A. P. Pitkin	Hartford, Conn	Mar. 25, 1862	34, 773
Gas, Apparatus for manufacturing illuminating	T. Sabbaton	New York, N. Y	Feb. 20, 1866	52, 751
Gas, Apparatus for manufacturing illuminating	S. Short	Buffalo, N. Y	June 12, 1860	28, 720
Gas, Apparatus for manufacturing illuminating	J. H. Spang	Dayton, Ohio	May 7, 1872	126, 587
Gas, Apparatus for manufacturing illuminating	L. Stevens	Washington, D. C	Apr. 14, 1868	76, 841
Gas, Apparatus for manufacturing illuminating	J. E. Thomson	Buffalo, N. Y	Oct. 7, 1862	36, 627
Gas, Apparatus for manufacturing illuminating	J. C. Tiffany	Portsmouth, N. H	Nov. 26, 1872	133, 391
Gas, Apparatus for manufacturing illuminating	P. H. Vander Weyde	New York, N. Y	Aug. 18, 1868	81, 232
Gas, Apparatus for manufacturing water	W. H. Gwynne	New York, N. Y	Sept. 10, 1861	33, 249
Gas, Apparatus for mixing	A. Walton	Philadelphia, Pa	Apr. 15, 1862	34, 994
Gas, Apparatus for naphthalizing	W. H. Gwynne	New York, N. Y	Apr. 30, 1861	32, 222
Gas, Apparatus for naphthalizing	E. H. Kendall	New York, N. Y	Mar. 19, 1861	31, 720
Gas, Apparatus for preparing nitrous-oxide	C. H. Moseley	Brooklyn, N. Y	May 1, 1866	54, 389
Gas, Apparatus for producing and carbureting hydrogen.	J. H. Steiner	Philadelphia, Pa	Dec. 28, 1869	98, 442
Gas, Apparatus for producing illuminating	C. F. Dunderdale	New York, N. Y	Nov. 30, 1869	97, 284
Gas, Apparatus for producing light and heat from	R. d'Hurcourt	Paris, France	Feb. 23, 1869	87, 130
Gas, Apparatus for producing olefiant	W. Elmer	New York, N. Y	Aug. 4, 1863	39, 387
Gas, Apparatus for purifying	A. Dickinson	Claremont, N. H	June 28, 1859	24, 543
Gas, Apparatus for purifying	A. Walker	Claremont, N. H	Dec. 21, 1858	22, 391
Gas, Apparatus for purifying	W. Wigston	New York, N. Y	Aug. 30, 1853	9, 981
Gas, Apparatus for purifying illuminating	D. H. Chamberlain	West Roxbury, Mass	Mar. 6, 1855	12, 498
Gas-apparatus for railway-cars	J. B. Olney	Brooklyn, N. Y	Aug. 19, 1873	141, 886
Gas-apparatus for railway-cars, &c	J. S. Wood	Philadelphia, Pa	July 26, 1870	105, 756
Gas-apparatus for railway-cars, &c	J. S. Wood	Philadelphia, Pa	July 26, 1870	105, 757
Gas-apparatus for railways, &c	W. Foster, jr., and G. P. Gauster.	New York, N. Y., and Reading, Pa.	July 19, 1870	105, 561
Gas, Apparatus for regulating the pressure of	W. A. Simonds, A. H. Silvester, and C. Caldwell.	Boston and Chelsea, Mass	Mar. 22, 1864	42, 023
Gas, Apparatus for roasting and boiling by	J. B. Blake	Worcester, Mass	Mar. 18, 1856	14, 437
Gas, Apparatus for the preparation and administration of nitrous-oxide.	A. M. Leslie	Saint Louis, Mo	May 7, 1867	64, 431
Gas, Apparatus for treating air and hydrocarbon vapor for illuminating.	L. Stevens	Fitchburgh, Mass	June 11, 1867	65, 705
Gas, Apparatus for turning on	W. P. Wage	Barre Centre, N. Y	Dec. 10, 1867	71, 927
Gas, Apparatus for washing	H. Guild	New Orleans, La	Sept. 27, 1859	25, 566
Gas apparatus, Hydrocarbon	L. Maring and E. Mertz	Basle, Switzerland	Feb. 4, 1873	135, 568
Gas apparatus, Hydrocarbon	M. H. Strong and W. I. Reid	Brooklyn, N. Y	Mar. 21, 1871	112, 981
Gas apparatus, Illuminating	R. Foulis	Saint John's, New Brunswick.	Oct. 12, 1852	9, 318
Gas apparatus, Illuminating	C. B. Warring	Poughkeepsie, N. Y	Sept. 15, 1857	18, 216
Gas-apparatus, Portable	W. Foster, jr., and G. P. Ganster	New York, N. Y	Dec 15, 1868	84, 941
Gas-apparatus, Portable	G. H. Kitchen and S. C. Nash	New York and Brooklyn, N. Y.	Nov. 24, 1868	84, 283
Gas-apparatus, Portable	G. Lowden	Brooklyn, N. Y	Nov. 7, 1871	120, 590
Gas-apparatus, Portable	J. H. Miller and S. Albright	Grafton, Va	Nov. 8, 1859	26, 042
Gas-apparatus, Portable	M. E. Stebbins	Springfield, Mass	Oct. 27, 1868	83, 419
Gas-apparatus, Portable	W. and M. Stratton	Philadelphia, Pa	Feb. 1, 1853	9, 568
Gas apparatus, Portable water	C. Harasythy	San Francisco, Cal	May 21, 1861	32, 362
Gas-apparatus, Sealing dip-pipe of	R. B. Chapman	Waltham, Mass	Aug. 1, 1871	117, 6.2
Gas-apparatus, Sealing dip-pipe of	J. R. Farnum	Waltham, Mass	May 21, 1872	127, 035
Gas as a motive-power, Utilizing	O Bolton, jr	Chartiers Township, Pa	Oct. 28, 1873	143, 954
Gas, Attachment for heating kettles and boilers by	M. Van Vranken	Washington, D. C	Mar. 5, 1867	62, 707
Gas-bracket	J. F. Goldthwait	Boston, Mass	S pt. 23, 1873	143, 138
Gas-bracket	J. R Hunter	Baltimore, Md	Oct. 30, 1855	13, 739
Gas-bracket fender	W. H. Miller	Philadelphia, Pa	Sept. 26, 1871	119, 236
Gas-bracket, lamp-stand, &c., Self-sustaining	C. Robb	Montreal, Canada	June 11, 1872	127, 798
Gas-brackets, Connecting-joint and cock of	L. Hull	Charlestown, Mass	Sept. 5, 1871	118, 722
Gas blow-pipe	A. H. Wood	Boston, Mass	Oct. 20, 1863	40, 376
Gas burning apparatus	R. W. Hoit	Boston, Mass	Oct. 9, 1860	30, 319
Gas-burning furnace	J. Green	Philadelphia, Pa	May 23, 1871	115, 193
Gas-burning furnace	C. Schinz	Offenburg, Baden	Feb. 21, 1865	46, 536
Gas by atomized liquid, Purifying illuminating	B. E. Chollar	Leavenworth, Kans	Oct. 1, 1872	131, 740
Gas by electricity, Switch for turning on and off and lighting.	S. Gardiner, jr	Washington, D. C	Feb. 27, 1872	124, 126
Gas by electricity, Turning on and shutting off	S. Gardiner, jr	New York, N. Y	Sept. 4, 1866	57, 097
Gas by means of a spirit-lamp, Generating	S. Andrews	Perth Amboy, N. J	May 5, 1831	....
Gas-carbonizing attachment for street and other lights.	S. Whitney	Newark, N. J	Sept. 27, 1870	107, 743
Gas, Chemical compound for the manufacture of medicated.	A. H. Carpenter	New York, N. Y	Oct. 30, 1866	59, 179
Gas, Clay retort for manufacture of	F. C. Krause	New York, N. Y	Dec. 20, 1870	110, 249
Gas, Combining carbonaceous matters for the manufacture of.	G. McKenzie	Glasgow, Scotland	Apr. 18, 1871	113, 905
Gas, Combining hydrogen and wood	W. C. Choate and C. N. Tyler	Washington, D. C	Feb. 24, 1857	16, 682
Gas-compensator	P. W. McKenzie	Jersey City, N. J	Mar. 4, 1862	34, 582
Gas-compensator	A. Smith	New York, N. Y	Sept. 22, 1863	40, 085
Gas, Composition for purifying	P. B. Goddard	Philadelphia, Pa	Dec. 7, 1858	22, 233
Gas, Composition for purifying	I. C. G. Howitz	Copenhagen, Denmark	Mar. 3, 1863	37, 815
Gas, Composition for purifying illuminating	S. P. Parham	New York, N. Y	Nov. 4, 1873	144, 284
Gas, Composition for purifying illuminating	W. H. St. John and P. Cartwright.	New York, N. Y	Apr. 7, 1868	76, 544
Gas, Composition-fuel for manufacture of	I. C. Sellars	Birkenhead, England	Dec. 10, 1872	133, 894
Gas, Compound for the manufacture of illuminating	G. McKenzie	Glasgow, Scotland	Mar. 1, 1870	100, 433
Gas, Compound oil for producing	J. Butler	New York, N. Y	Aug. 10, 1869	93, 411
Gas, Condenser for manufacture of illuminating	P. T. Burtis	Chicago, Ill	Aug. 5, 1873	141, 543
Gas condenser, scrubber, and washer	T. B. Burtis	Chicago, Ill	Apr. 30, 1867	64, 194
Gas-consuming furnace	J. Green	Philadelphia, Pa	June 3, 1856	15, 009

Index of patents issued from the United States Patent Office from 1790 *to* 1873, *inclusive*—Continued.

Invention.	Inventor.	Residence.	Date.	No.
Gas, Converting waste into combustible	B. Todd	Newcastle-upon-Tyne, England.	Dec. 24, 1872	134, 332
Gas cooking-apparatus	M. Germann	Cincinnati, Ohio	Apr. 7, 1868	76, 321
Gas cooler and washer	R. Salter	Cincinnati, Ohio	Mar. 30, 1869	88, 590
Gas-engine	G. B. Brayton	Boston, Mass	Apr. 2, 1872	125, 166
Gas-engine	P. Hugon	Paris, France	Jan. 19, 1864	41, 299
Gas-engine	P. Hugon	Paris, France	Aug. 8, 1865	49, 346
Gas-engine	M. Isnard	New York, N. Y	Dec. 11, 1824	....
Gas-engine	O. H. Kratze	Leipsic, Saxony	Aug. 4, 1863	39, 448
Gas-engine	W. H. Laubach	Philadelphia, Pa	Jan. 28, 1868	73, 816
Gas-engine	C. P. Leavitt	New York, N. Y	Aug. 15, 1871	118, 028
Gas-engine	F. Milion	Paris, France	Apr. 2, 1867	63, 416
Gas-engine	S. Perry	New York, N. Y	Oct. 7, 1846	4, 800
Gas-engine	S. L. Wiegand	Philadelphia, Pa	Oct. 4, 1864	44, 572
Gas-engine, Explosive	A. Drake	Philadelphia, Pa	Apr. 17, 1855	12, 715
Gas, Engines for the utilization of ammoniacal	J. Frot	Orleans, France	Dec. 18, 1866	60, 500
Gas-engine without steam	S. Brown	London, England	Mar. 2, 1824	....
Gas-engines, Arrangement of	J. C. F. Saloman	Baltimore, Md	May 4, 1858	20, 172
Gas-engines, Method of actuating	O. Hammel	Jersey City, N. J	June 18, 1867	65, 808
Gas-engines, Electrical apparatus for lighting	W. M. Storm	New York, N. Y	Sept. 25, 1855	13, 598
Gas-exhausters, &c., Governor for	R. Koch	New York, N. Y	Mar. 25, 1873	137, 215
Gas explosive engine for condensing air	B. T. Babbitt	New York, N. Y	July 14, 1868	79, 938
Gas explosive engine for condensing air	B. T. Babbitt	New York, N. Y	July 14, 1868	79, 939
Gas-extinguisher	D. M. Reynolds	Port Deposit, Md	Dec. 2, 1873	145, 243
Gas-extinguisher and cut-off, Automatic	G. R. Pierce	Grand Rapids, Mich	Aug. 27, 1872	130, 940
Gas-fitter's clamp	J. Peace	Camden, N. J	June 27, 1865	48, 431
Gas-fitter's gage-attachment	H. Getty	Hoboken, N. J	Aug. 29, 1871	118, 603
Gas-fitter's hook-blank	E. P. Gleason	New York, N. Y	Aug. 8, 1865	49, 257
Gas-fitter's pressure-gage	R. B. Donaldson	Washington, D. C	July 2, 1867	66, 227
Gas-fitter's tool	J. Himmer	Hartford, Conn	Sept. 29, 1868	82, 620
Gas-fitter's use, Rod of connected hook-blanks for	J. Fellows and J. W. Lyon	Brooklyn, N. Y	Mar. 16, 1869	87, 919
Gas-fitter's wrench	G. B. Phillips	Albany, N. Y	May 3, 1859	23, 857
Gas-fittings	G. Rosenthal	Pittsburgh, Pa	Oct. 24, 1871	120, 329
Gas-fittings, Device for boring and turning	M. Walty	Buffalo, N. Y	Apr. 29, 1873	138, 456
Gas-fittings, Machine for drilling and tapping	R. T. Crane	Chicago, Ill	Mar. 15, 1870	100, 731
Gas-fittings, Machine for finishing	J. W. Lyon	Brooklyn, N. Y	Oct. 30, 1860	30, 536
Gas-fittings, Machine for reaming and tapping	H. A. Chapin	Springfield, Mass	July 1, 1856	15, 219
Gas-fixture	N. L. Bradley and J. A. Evarts	West Meriden, Conn	Oct. 20, 1868	83, 246
Gas-fixture	E. McClintock	New Brunswick, N. J	Mar. 31, 1868	76, 222
Gas-fixture	D. Milne	Norwich, N. Y	Sept. 6, 1870	107, 191
Gas-fixture	C. A. Shaw	Biddeford, Me	Feb. 16, 1864	41, 644
Gas-fixture	G. G. Sheldon	Chicago, Ill	May 13, 1873	138, 766
Gas-fixture attachment	B. Jacobs	New York, N. Y	May 22, 1866	54, 915
Gas-fixture, Extension	H. Coester	New York, N. Y	Aug. 2, 1870	105, 911
Gas-fixture, Extension	H. Krüger	New York, N. Y	Mar. 29, 1870	101, 369
Gas-fixture, Oxyhydrogen	A. W. Wilkinson	New York, N. Y	Feb. 6, 1872	123, 535
Gas-fixture socket-coupling	T. L. Reed	Providence, R. I	July 17, 1866	56, 448
Gas-fixtures, Device for raising and lowering	J. F. Pond	Cleveland, Ohio	June 14, 1870	104, 197
Gas-fixtures, Extension-slide for	J. Horton	New York, N. Y	June 15, 1869	91, 443
Gas-fixtures, Lock-coupling for	T. L. Reed	Providence, R. I	Jan. 7, 1868	73, 039
Gas-fixtures, Trap-attachment for	J. B. Hyde	New York, N. Y	Sept. 13, 1870	107, 264
Gas-flame expander	H. Whitney	Watertown, Mass	Oct. 17, 1871	120, 139
Gas for fuel, illumination, &c., Manufacture of	W. Elmer	New York, N. Y	Feb. 23, 1869	87, 156
Gas for fuel, &c., Manufacture of inflammable	W. Elmer	New York, N. Y	Aug. 23, 1870	106, 569
Gas for head-lights, Apparatus for generating	H. S. Maxim	New York, N. Y	Feb. 15, 1870	99, 927
Gas for heating and illuminating, Apparatus for the manufacture of.	J. H. Connelly and J. McLure	Wheeling, W. Va	May 23, 1871	115, 028
Gas for heating and illuminating buildings and for other purposes, Manufacture of.	T. Arnold	New York, N. Y	Aug. 15, 1865	49, 358
Gas for heating and illuminating purposes, Method of applying.	C. Pepper	Albany, N. Y	Dec. 14, 1858	22, 331
Gas for heating and illumination, Generating	J. Arbos	Barcelona, Spain	Dec. 8, 1863	40, 804
Gas for heating and lighting, Producing	T. G. Springer	Clinton, Iowa	May 4, 1869	89, 802
Gas for illuminating and heating, Manufacture of	G. Eveleigh	Peckham, Great Britain	Jan. 30, 1872	123, 255
Gas for illuminating, heating, &c., Manufacture of	R. M. Whipple and J. G. Blunt	Chicago, Ill., and Leavenworth, Kans.	Apr. 1, 1873	137, 521
Gas for illuminating, &c., Manufacture of pneumatic.	J. W. Stow	San Francisco, Cal	Apr. 4, 1871	113, 702
Gas for illumination, Apparatus for purifying	D. Garnet	Richfield, N. Y	June 27, 1840	1, 656
Gas for illumination, &c., Manufacture of	J. Kidd	New York, N. Y	Aug. 23, 1870	106, 699
Gas for illumination, Manufacture of coal	J. W. Smith	Washington, D. C	Dec. 13, 1864	45, 460
Gas for illumination, Treating	W. A. Simonds and S. Warner	Boston and East Hampton, Mass.	Mar. 24, 1863	38, 017
Gas for illumination, &c., Treating	L. Stevens	Fitchburgh, Mass	July 3, 1866	56, 116
Gas for light-houses, Generating and burning	B. F. Coston	Washington, D. C	Jan. 31, 1845	3, 894
Gas for lighting and heating purposes, Manufacture and purification of.	G. Eveleigh	London, Great Britain	Jan. 30, 1872	123, 093
Gas for lighting railway-cars, Apparatus for generating and carbureting.	J. H. Steiner	Saint Louis, Mo	July 6, 1869	92, 391
Gas for metallurgic and other purposes, Apparatus for burning.	C. M. Tessié du Motay	Paris, France	Mar. 2, 1869	87, 476
Gas for motive-power	J. Arbos	Barcelona, Spain	Dec. 8, 1863	40, 805
Gas for motive-power for extinguishing fire and for other purposes, Generating.	C. G. Wheeler	Chicago, Ill	Aug. 24, 1869	94, 157
Gas for motive-power, Generating	D. E. Somes	Washington, D. C	Sept. 4, 1866	57, 787
Gas for the production of heat, light, &c., Process of burning.	S. Stevens	New York, N. Y	July 24, 1866	56, 629
Gas for various purposes, Manufacture and application of.	P. Salmon	London, England	Dec. 15, 1868	84, 967
Gas from anthracite coal, Generating inflammable	M. Ward and R. W. Hall	Baltimore, Md	Jan. 19, 1828	....
Gas from bitumen, Manufacture of illuminating	A. Gesner	Halifax, Nova Scotia	Jan. 29, 1850	7, 052
Gas from bituminous coal, Purifying and condensing illuminating.	W. H. St. John and P. Cartwright.	New York, N. Y	Aug. 13, 1872	130, 545
Gas from blast and puddling furnaces, Apparatus for collecting and forcing.	D. H. Geiger	Saint Clair, Pa	May 25, 1869	90, 440
Gas from coal and other materials, Manufacture of illuminating.	G. McKenzie	Glasgow, Scotland	Mar. 1, 1870	100, 432
Gas from coal, Apparatus for producing	T. O'Meara	Brooklyn, N. Y	Aug. 30, 1870	106, 863

Index of patents issued from the United States Patent Office from 1790 *to* 1873, *inclusive*—Continued.

Invention.	Inventor.	Residence.	Date.	No.
Gas from coal-tar, Manufacture of illuminating	J. Kidd	New York, N. Y	Mar. 12, 1872	124, 441
Gas from fuel, Process of producing	J. H. Burgin	Philadelphia, Pa	Sept. 17, 1867	68, 840
Gas from gasoline, Apparatus for making illuminating.	H. S. Maxim and J. Radley	New York, N. Y	May 4, 1869	89, 588
Gas from hydrocarbon liquids, Generating	M. S. Richardson and E. A. Pond.	Rutland, Vt	Oct. 1, 1867	69, 483
Gas from hydrocarbon vapors, Method of generating fixed.	J. Butler	Brooklyn, N. Y	Nov. 24, 1868	84, 259
Gas from hydrocarbons, Apparatus for making	J. T. Tyler and J. J. Johnston.	Pittsburgh and Allegheny City, Pa.	June 15, 1869	91, 499
Gas from hydrocarbons, Apparatus for the manufacture of.	J. Rigby	Portsmouth, Ohio	Feb. 11, 1873	135, 666
Gas from hydrocarbons, Apparatus for the manufacture of.	J. H. Smith	Newark, Ohio	Dec. 6, 1870	109, 848
Gas from hydrocarbons, Generating	J. R. Smedberg	San Francisco, Cal	Nov. 22, 1870	109, 460
Gas from hydrocarbons, Manufacture of illuminating.	H. H. Eames and C. J. Eames	Philadelphia, Pa., and New York, N. Y.	Oct. 15, 1872	132, 265
Gas from hydrocarbons, Producing	X. Moussard	Paris, France	Mar. 28, 1871	113, 192
Gasfrom hydrocarbons, Retort for the manufacture of.	B. Sloper and R. M. Potter	New York, N. Y., and Jersey City, N. J.	Apr. 23, 1872	126, 098
Gas from naphtha, &c., Apparatus for generating and burning.	D. H. Lowe	Boston, Mass	Feb. 23, 1869	87, 272
Gas from oil, Apparatus for the manufacture of	M. J. Barry	Washington, D. C	May 7, 1872	126, 510
Gas from oil, Apparatus for the manufacture of	C. and F. A. G. Gearing	Pittsburgh, Pa., and Houston, Tex.	June 18, 1872	128, 199
Gas, &c., from oil, Generating	S. Andrews	Perth Amboy, N. J	Apr. 15, 1831	....
Gas from oil-vapor, hydrogen, and air, Manufacture of illuminating.	T. G. Springer	New York, N. Y	Dec. 17, 1872	134, 109
Gas from oils, Apparatus for making	S. H. Goldthorp	Pittsburgh, Pa	July 15, 1873	140, 911
Gas from peat, Manufacture of illuminating	J. B. Hyde	Newark, N. J	July 19, 1864	43, 585
Gas from peat, Method of making	J. B. Hyde	Newark, N. J	Oct. 18, 1859	25, 866
Gas from petroleum and other hydrocarbons, Apparatus for generating.	G. W. Thompson and J. Foster	Bordentown, N. J	May 5, 1863	38, 429
Gas from petroleum and other wells, Device for collecting.	H. M. Hamilton	Franklin, Pa	June 21, 1864	43, 201
Gas from petroleum, Apparatus for generating	A. I. Ambler	Washington, D. C	Aug. 29, 1871	118, 575
Gas from petroleum, Apparatus for generating	A. I. Ambler	Washington, D. C	Sept. 10, 1872	131, 240
Gas from petroleum, Apparatus for generating	D. M. Graham	Evansville, Ind	May 9, 1865	47, 634
Gas from petroleum, Apparatus for manufacturing	H. H. Edgerton	Fort Wayne, Ind	Apr. 23, 1872	125, 941
Gas from petroleum, Apparatus for manufacturing	W. C. Wren and W. Barker	Brooklyn, N. Y	July 31, 1866	56, 843
Gas from petroleum, Apparatus for producing	H. Hirzel	Leipsic, Saxony	May 14, 1867	64, 672
Gas from petroleum, Apparatus for separating	J. Smith and A. Greig	Tarville, Pa	Mar. 29, 1864	42, 121
Gas from petroleum, Apparatus for separating and collecting.	I. H. Hobbs	Philadelphia, Pa	Sept. 27, 1864	44, 421
Gas from petroleum-distilleries, Mode of utilizing waste.	H. W. C. Tweddle	Pittsburgh, Pa	Dec. 6, 1864	45, 363
Gas from petroleum, Generating	W. M. Sloane	Buffalo, N. Y	Feb. 23, 1869	87, 210
Gas from petroleum, Manufacture and application of.	T. S. Dickerson	Chicago, Ill	Oct. 12, 1869	95, 665
Gas from petroleum, Manufacture of	L. Stevens	Washington, D. C	Feb. 22, 1870	100, 208
Gas from petroleum, Manufacture of	G. W. Wren	Brooklyn, N. Y	Feb. 9, 1869	86, 793
Gas from petroleum, Manufacture of illuminating	R. H. Smith	Pittsburgh, Pa	Aug. 12, 1873	141, 732
Gas from petroleum, Manufacture of illuminating	W. H. Spencer	Brooklyn, N. Y	Feb. 20, 1872	123, 950
Gas from petroleum, Manufacture of illuminating	W. C. and G. W. Wren	Brooklyn, N. Y	Oct. 31, 1871	120, 409
Gas from petroleum, Method of generating	C. Carpenter	Buffalo, N. Y	Aug. 18, 1868	81, 136
Gas from petroleum, naphtha, &c., Apparatus for generating and burning.	M. E. Hanson	Newport, Me	Aug. 28, 1866	57, 502
Gas from resin, Apparatus for making	A. Schmidt	New York, N. Y	Sept. 27, 1859	25, 610
Gas from retorts, &c., Apparatus for exhausting	J. Kidd	New York, N. Y	Jan. 23, 18ˆ2	122, 894
Gas from retorts, Apparatus for exhausting	S. Trumbore	Easton, Pa	June 6, 1871	115, 788
Gas from solid carbons, Producing	L. Stevens	Washington, D. C	Feb. 21, 1871	112, 088
Gas from the ignition of explosive compounds applied to machinery.	H. Rogers	New York, N. Y	June 29, 1833	....
Gas from volatile liquids, Manufacture of	C. A. Seely	New York, N. Y	Nov. 17, 1868	84, 219
Gas from volatile oils, &c., Machine for making	J. E. Schwippel	Saint Joseph, Mo	Feb. 23, 1869	87, 299
Gas from wood, Apparatus for making	A. Schmidt	New York, N. Y	Sept. 27, 1859	25, 609
Gas from wood, Making	L. R. Breisach	New York, N. Y	Sept. 6, 1859	25, 316
Gas from wood, Making	A. Schmidt	New York, N. Y	Sept. 4, 1860	29, 941
Gas from wood, Making illuminating	W. P. McConnell	Washington, D. C	Sept. 26, 1854	11, 740
Gas from wood, Retort for the manufacture of	M. Levy	New York, N. Y	Apr. 9, 1861	31, 986
Gas-furnace	J. Jordan	Liverpool, England	Sept. 12, 1871	118, 947
Gas-furnace	L. Stevens	Washington, D. C	July 22, 1873	141, 179
Gas-furnace	L. Stevens	Washington, D. C	July 22, 1873	141, 180
Gas furnace and forge	J. R. Morris	Houston, Tex	Nov. 7, 1871	120, 764
Gas-furnace for heating metals, &c	Z. S. Durfee	New York, N. Y	Sept. 17, 1872	131, 333
Gas, &c., Furnace for the manufacture of	F. Carroll	New Orleans, La	Nov. 11, 1873	144, 506
Gas-furnace, Metallurgic	H. Frank	Pittsburgh, Pa	Feb. 11, 1873	135, 639
Gas-furnace, Metallurgic	J. M. Hartman	Philadelphia, Pa	July 22, 1873	141, 002
Gas-furnace, Metallurgic	C. W. Siemens	Westminster, England	Nov. 8, 1870	109, 064
Gas-furnace, Metallurgic	J. Thomas	Middlesborough, England	June 10, 1873	139, 834
Gas-furnace, Metallurgic	W. C. Wren	Brooklyn, N. Y	July 8, 1873	140, 006
Gas, &c., Gage for measuring the pressure of explosive.	T. Shaw	Philadelphia, Pa	May 3, 1864	42, 627
Gas, Gas-works for making coal	A. Babbett and W. W. Binney	Auburn, N. Y	June 8, 1869	91, 066
Gas-generating and blast-heating apparatus for metallurgic and other purposes.	J. D. Whelpley and J. J. Storer	Boston, Mass	Jan. 24, 1871	111, 288
Gas generating and carbureting machine, Hydrogen	H. I. Hoyt	Norwalk, Conn	May 24, 1870	103, 465
Gas, Generating and charging liquid with	J. H. Laning	Davidson County, Tenn	Dec. 23, 1824	....
Gas, Generating and supplying illuminating	E. A. Pond and M. S. Richardson.	Rutland, Vt	June 5, 1866	55, 359
Gas-generating apparatus	Z. S. Durfee	New York, N. Y	Jan. 2, 1872	122, 311
Gas-generating furnace, Portable	W. M. Sloane	Buffalo, N. Y	Nov. 5, 1867	70, 477
Gas-generating furnace, Steam	J. M. Sanders	New York, N. Y	July 6, 1869	92, 212
Gas, Generating heat by hydrogen	L. A. Hall	Newark, N. J	June 3, 1843	3, 121
Gas, Generating hydrogen and hydrocarbon	J. S. Wood	Philadelphia, Pa	Dec. 7, 1869	97, 580
Gas, Generating hydrogen and hydrocarbon	J. S. Wood	Philadelphia, Pa	Apr. 5, 1870	101, 558
Gas, Generating illuminating	A. Hamar	Philadelphia, Pa	Dec. 7, 1869	97, 632
Gas, Generating illuminating	F. King	Richmond, Va	Jan. 14, 1868	73, 252

Index of patents issued from the United States Patent Office from 1790 to 1873, inclusive—Continued.

Invention.	Inventor.	Residence.	Date.	No.
Gas, Generating steam	E. A. Lester	Boston, Mass	Mar. 10, 1828	... ...
Gas-generator	N. Aubin	Albany, N. Y	Sept. 26, 1854	11, 714
Gas-generator	N. Aubin	Albany, N. Y	June 23, 1857	17, 614
Gas-generator	J. Bagot	New York, N. Y	Oct. 24, 1865	50, 548
Gas-generator	J. A. Bassett	Salem, Mass	Oct. 13, 1868	83, 026
Gas-generator	C. F. Brown	Baltimore, Md	Feb. 26, 1850	7, 115
Gas-generator	J. A. Bruce	Baltimore, Md	May 12, 1857	17, 309
Gas-generator	J. Butler	Brooklyn, N. Y	Sept. 15, 1857	18, 184
Gas-generator	J. Butler	New York, N. Y	Jan. 24, 1871	111, 174
Gas-generator	S. Chamberlaine	Philadelphia, Pa	Apr. 10, 1860	27, 775
Gas-generator	M. P. Coons	Brooklyn, N. Y	May 3, 1859	23, 828
Gas-generator	M. P. Coons	Brooklyn, N. Y	Sept. 4, 1866	57, 682
Gas-generator	E. Doty	Janesville, Wis	May 10, 1870	102, 784
Gas-generator	J. J. Ensley	New York, N. Y	Aug. 28, 1866	57, 491
Gas-generator	M. Faloon	Bloomington, Ill	Oct. 29, 1867	70, 184
Gas-generator	T. B. Fogarty	New York, N. Y	May 17, 1870	103, 036
Gas-generator	J. W. Fox and D. H. Irland	Chicago, Ill	Apr. 23, 1872	125, 888
Gas-generator	A. M. Giles	Boston, Mass	Mar. 17, 1857	16, 830
Gas-generator	J. Hansor	Wardsworth Road, England.	Feb. 3, 1857	16, 544
Gas-generator	A. A. Hayes	Boston, Mass	June 16, 1857	17, 574
Gas-generator	J. G. Hock	Newark, N. J	Mar. 30, 1858	19, 777
Gas-generator	C. A. Howard	Pontiac, Mich	Oct. 28, 1856	15, 973
Gas-generator	D. H. Irland	Hudson, Mich	Apr. 22, 1873	138, 160
Gas-generator	P. Kelly	Dayton, Ohio	July 6, 1869	92, 317
Gas-generator	F. King	Richmond, Va	Feb. 11, 1868	74, 230
Gas-generator	H. Lyles	Washington, D. C	Aug. 10, 1858	21, 142
Gas-generator	R. J. Malcolm	Cincinnati, Ohio	June 2, 1868	78, 600
Gas-generator	A. L. McKay	Bolton, Miss	Apr. 26, 1870	102, 293
Gas generator	J. McWilliams	Pittsburgh, Pa	June 5, 1866	55, 328
Gas-generator	M. Pettenkofer and C. Ruland	Munich, Bavaria	May 20, 1856	14, 926
Gas-generator	A. Pierce	Philadelphia, Pa	June 27, 1846	4, 604
Gas-generator	A. Pollock	Washington, D. C	Aug. 11, 1857	17, 981
Gas-generator	D. W. Ranke	Limestoneville, Pa	June 9, 1868	78, 828
Gas-generator	S. C. Salisbury	New York, N. Y	Aug. 6, 1872	130, 318
Gas-generator	D. F. Scheaf	Dayton, Ohio	Jan. 7, 1868	73, 124
Gas-generator	A. Schwaninger	Milwaukee, Wis	July 24, 1860	29, 318
Gas-generator	G. W. R. Seal	Winchester, Va	July 13, 1858	20, 897
Gas-generator	S. Skinner	Yonkers, N. Y	Oct. 13, 1857	18, 414
Gas-generator	W. M. Sloan	Buffalo, N. Y	Apr. 7, 1868	76, 535
Gas-generator	J. W. Smith	Washington, D. C	June 30, 1857	17, 704
Gas-generator	J. H. Steiner	Kansas City, Mo	Jan. 19, 1869	85, 972
Gas-generator	C. A. Stevens	New York, N. Y	Jan. 2, 1872	122, 499
Gas-generator	W. N. Taylor	Philadelphia, Pa	May 4, 1858	20, 177
Gas-generator	A. K. Tupper	Milford, Mich	May 22, 1860	28, 421
Gas-generator	P. H. Vander Weyde	Philadelphia, Pa	Feb. 12, 1867	62, 095
Gas-generator	J. Watson and E. Cart	Hull, England	Sept. 18, 1849	6, 729
Gas-generator	E. W. Whitehead and J. L. Conklin.	Newark, N. J	June 16, 1857	17, 599
Gas-generator	A. B. Wilson	Waterbury, Conn	Oct. 26, 1858	21, 914
Gas-generator	J. S. Wood	Brooklyn, N. Y	May 13, 1873	138, 778
Gas-generator and burner	C. B. Loveless	Syracuse, N. Y	Dec. 21, 1869	98, 174
Gas-generator and burner	C. N. Tyler	Washington, D. C	July 24, 1860	29, 328
Gas-generator and carbureter	C. F. Dunderdale	New York, N. Y	Nov. 9, 1869	96, 565
Gas-generator and carbureter	J. B. Olney	New York, N. Y	Dec. 22, 1868	85, 239
Gas-generator and carbureter	J. H. Steiner	Cincinnati, Ohio	May 14, 1872	126, 652
Gas-generator and carbureter	A. Stevens	Fitchburgh, Mass	Dec. 21, 1869	98, 118
Gas-generator and carbureter	W. Thompson	Cleveland, Ohio	Apr. 30, 1867	64, 382
Gas generator and carbureter, Hydrogen	J. S. Wood	Philadelphia, Pa	Apr. 5, 1870	101, 557
Gas generator and carbureter, Illuminating	A. Stevens	Fitchburgh, Mass	Nov. 30, 1869	97, 457
Gas generator, Carbonic-acid	P. and F. Hinkel	New York, N. Y	Apr. 11, 1865	47, 205
Gas generator, Carbonic-acid	J. W. Stanton	Brooklyn, N. Y	Apr. 1, 1873	137, 330
Gas generator, Carbonic-acid	F. W. Wiesebrock	New York, N. Y	Nov. 18, 1873	144, 719
Gas-generator, Compressed	J. Gros	Paris, France	Apr. 3, 1866	53, 758
Gas-generator for heating purposes	L. Stevens	Washington, D. C	Oct. 11, 1870	108, 302
Gas generator, Illuminating	S. N. Chamberlin	Abington, Mass	Feb. 27, 1866	52, 946
Gas generator, Illuminating	G. P. Ganster	New York, N. Y	Mar. 31, 1868	76, 182
Gas generator, Illuminating	H. B. Myer	Philadelphia, Pa	Aug. 28, 1866	57, 551
Gas-generator, Portable	C. B. Loveless	Syracuse, N. Y	Feb. 23, 1869	87, 271
Gas-generator, Portable	W. A. Simonds	Boston, Mass	Sept. 1, 1857	18, 109
Gas-generator, Portable	W. Snodgrass	Macomb, Ill	Feb. 22, 1870	100, 080
Gas generator, Steam	H. S. Maxim	New York, N. Y	Nov. 26, 1867	71, 400
Gas generator, Steam petroleum	R. M. Whipple and A. L. Ambler.	Chicago, Ill	July 13, 1869	92, 687
Gas generator, Wood	W. D. Porter	New York, N. Y	Aug. 22, 1854	11, 560
Gas generator, Wood	C. F. Werner	New York, N. Y	June 2, 1857	17, 465
Gas-generators, Feed-apparatus to	S. Meredith	Erie, Pa	Sept. 6, 1853	9, 994
Gas-generators, Feeding	C. B. Loveless	Syracuse, N. Y	June 2, 1857	17, 435
Gas-generators, Method of cleansing	S. Coates	New York, N. Y	Mar. 23, 1858	19, 686
Gas-governor	E. Beggs	San Francisco, Cal	May 5, 1868	77, 572
Gas-governor and by-pass	P. Munzinger	Philadelphia, Pa	June 3, 1873	139, 514
Gas-heater	A. Adams	Sturgis, Mich	June 21, 1870	104, 531
Gas-heater	B. Allen	Boston, Mass	Sept. 7, 1869	94, 538
Gas-heater	J. Bannihr	Hempstead, N. Y	Nov. 9, 1869	96, 559
Gas-heater	E. Barnes	London, England	Nov. 5, 1872	132, 793
Gas-heater	J. Q. Birkey	Philadelphia, Pa	Oct. 31, 1865	50, 678
Gas-heater	A. L. Bogart	New York, N. Y	July 27, 1869	92, 931
Gas-heater	C. Burnham	Philadelphia, Pa	May 19, 1868	78, 053
Gas-heater	C. C. Burt	Jackson, Mich	May 24, 1870	103, 297
Gas-heater	L. Bush	Boston, Mass	Apr. 26, 1870	102, 258
Gas-heater	J. Comly	Philadelphia, Pa	May 17, 1870	103, 017
Gas-heater	J. E. Cone	Chicago, Ill	July 12, 1870	105, 305
Gas heater	S. G. Dare	New York, N. Y	Nov. 1, 1870	108, 888
Gas-heater	S. Darling	Bangor, Me	Feb. 4, 1868	73, 957
Gas-heater	L. A. and W. G. Duval	Charleston, S. C	Jan. 12, 1869	85, 804
Gas-heater	O. C. Fox	Georgetown, D. C	June 16, 1868	78, 951
Gas-heater	C. Geisse	Taycheedah, Wis	July 10, 1866	56, 204
Gas-heater	R. George	Kilburn, England	Oct. 25, 1870	108, 583

Index of patents issued from the United States Patent Office from 1790 *to* 1873, *inclusive*—Continued.

Invention.	Inventor.	Residence.	Date.	No.
Gas-heater	J. T. Greenwood	Beloit, Wis	Sept. 8, 1868	81, 892
Gas-heater	D. G. Haskins	Cambridge, Mass	Nov. 19, 1867	71, 002
Gas-heater	D. G. Haskins	Cambridge, Mass	Jan. 11, 1870	98, 767
Gas-heater	D. G. Haskins	Cambridge, Mass	Nov. 21, 1871	121, 170
Gas-heater	J. P. Hayes	Philadelphia, Pa	Oct. 10, 1871	119, 761
Gas-heater	J. S. Hull	Cincinnati, Ohio	Mar. 31, 1868	76, 195
Gas-heater	J. H. Jones	New York, N. Y	Apr. 25, 1865	47, 426
Gas-heater	W. Jones	Chelsea, Mass	June 23, 1868	79, 230
Gas-heater	D. Kellogg	Jackson, Mich	Mar. 10, 1868	75, 429
Gas-heater	A. Komp	New York, N. Y	Sept. 10, 1872	131, 280
Gas-heater	H. Y. Lazear	New York, N. Y	July 14, 1868	79, 989
Gas-heater	H. Y. Lazear and J. L. Sharp	New York, N. Y	July 6, 1869	92, 322
Ga -heater	D. H. Lowe	Boston, Mass	Dec. 15, 1868	84, 889
Gas-heater	J. Lundgren	New York, N. Y	Aug. 2, 1870	106, 070
Gas-heater	S. T. McDougall	Brooklyn, N. Y	May 5, 1868	77, 635
Gas-heater	G. F. Meiggs	Boston, Mass	May 17, 1870	103, 222
Gas-heater	A. H. Mershon	Philadelphia, Pa	May 7, 1872	126, 473
Gas-heater	H. B. Musgrave	Cincinnati, Ohio	Oct. 26, 1869	96, 260
Gas-heater	C. H. Prentiss	Cleveland, Ohio	Mar. 4, 1873	136, 383
Gas-heater	O. M. Reynolds and D. T. Kitchell.	Oil City, Pa	Apr. 4, 1871	113, 567
Gas-heater	E. O. Schartan	Philadelphia, Pa	Nov. 9, 1869	96, 623
Gas-heater	P. Schreyer	New York, N. Y	Apr. 14, 1868	76, 828
Gas-heater	W. F. Shaw	Boston, Mass	Jan. 23, 1855	12, 267
Gas-heater	J. Sheedy	New York, N. Y	Apr. 12, 1870	101, 928
Gas-heater	G. Smith	Ayer, Mass	Apr. 16, 1872	125, 850
Gas-heater	W. C. Trowbridge	New York, N. Y	Feb. 16, 1869	87, 014
Gas-heater	H. F. W. Wesche	New York, N. Y	June 6, 1871	115, 666
Gas-heater and petroleum-stove	A. T. Boon	Galesburgh, Ill	Mar. 19, 1867	63, 004
Gas-heater boiler	C. Geisse	Taycheedah, Wis	Oct. 16, 1866	58, 807
Gas-heater, Drum	W. H. Towers	New York, N. Y	Dec. 27, 1864	45, 655
Gas-heater for cooking, &c	J. S. Hull	Cincinnati, Ohio	July 3, 1866	56, 052
Gas heating and cooking apparatus	R. S. Andrews	Baltimore, Md	May 12, 1857	17, 251
Gas heating and cooking apparatus	F. A. Jacquet	Paris, France	June 1, 1869	90, 846
Gas heating and lighting apparatus for locomotive and railway cars.	J. H. Connelly	Wheeling, W. Va	May 23, 1871	115, 027
Gas-heating apparatus	P. S. Devlan	Camden, N. J	Jan. 26, 1858	19, 185
Gas-heating apparatus	C. M. Guild	Brooklyn, N. Y	July 11, 1854	11, 244
Gas-heating apparatus	D. G. Haskins	Cambridge, Mass	Apr. 10, 1866	53, 820
Gas-heating apparatus	W. F. Shaw	Boston, Mass	Feb. 26, 1856	14, 325
Gas-heating apparatus	S. L. Wiegand	Philadelphia, Pa	Nov. 10, 1863	40, 591
Gas heating or cooking apparatus	W. F. Shaw	Boston, Mass	Mar. 11, 1856	14, 414
Gas heating or cooking apparatus	W. F. Shaw	Boston, Mass	Nov. 4, 1856	16, 031
Gas, Heating, warming, and cooking by	W. Boggett and G. B. Pettit	Westminster, England	Apr. 18, 1854	10, 793
Gas-holder	S. Hill and W. I. Wood	Rochester, N. Y	Nov. 6, 1855	13, 754
Gas-holder	C. A. Stebbins	Springfield, Mass	Apr. 20, 1869	89, 090
Gas-holder	T. R. White	Philadelphia, Pa	Aug. 6, 1872	130, 346
Gas-holder, Dry	N. Aubin	Albany, N. Y	July 2, 1861	32, 676
Gas-holder, Portable	O. L. Lawson	New York, N. Y	June 26, 1860	28, 873
Gas-holder, Portable	J. McFarlan	Brooklyn, N. Y	Sept. 27, 1859	25, 607
Gas, Illuminating	W. Elmer	New York, N. Y	Jan. 17, 1865	45, 915
Gas, Illuminating	C. S. Hunt and J. B. Knight	Terre Bonne Parish and New Orleans, La.	May 19, 1868	77, 983
Gas-illuminator	M. Andrew	New York, N. Y	Sept. 5, 1871	118, 669
Gas-illuminator	J. B. Van Patten	Newark, N. J	Mar. 4, 1873	136, 565
Gas in apparatus for diving, Regulating the flow of.	B. Bouquayrol	Paris, France	Nov. 6, 1866	59, 529
Gas in fire-extinguishers, &c., Composition for generating.	J. F. Babcock	Boston, Mass	Sept. 29, 1868	82, 582
Gas in fu naces, Method of burning	J. C. Tiffany	Portsmouth, N. H	Dec. 2, 1873	145, 257
Gas, In the preparation of materials to be used in the purification of.	A. A. Croll	London, England	Apr. 4, 1865	47, 160
Gas into furnaces, retorts, converters, &c., Introducing oxygen.	O. M. Phillips	New York, N. Y	Jan. 26, 1869	86, 247
Gas, iron, and steel from the ore, Process and furnace for making.	T. J. Chubb	Williamsburgh, N. Y	Nov. 19, 1872	133, 202
Gas-jets, Device for igniting	G. W. Parke and J. G. Stowe	Bloomington, Ill	July 16, 1872	129, 363
Gas-lamps, &c., Apparatus for lighting street	J. W. Beard	St. John's, New Brunswick	Dec. 10, 1867	71, 842
Gas-light and pressure-indicator	W. W. Goodwin	Camden, N. J	Apr. 22, 1873	138, 016
Gas-light apparatus	J. Crutchett	Cincinnati, Ohio	May 6, 1844	3, 573
Gas-light globe	C. Collier	Selma, Ala	Nov. 29, 1870	109, 589
Gas light globe	T. Trudeau	Ottawa, Canada	July 25, 1871	117, 486
Gas-light-governor case	N. Tufts	Boston, Mass	May 25, 1869	90, 609
Gas-light multiplier	J. F. Boynton	Syracuse, N. Y	Sept. 5, 1865	49, 705
Gas-light multiplier	J. F. Boynton	Syracuse, N. Y	Oct. 8, 1867	69, 621
Gas-light shade	W. Fullagar	Brooklyn, N. Y	June 7, 1870	103, 865
Gas-lights, Apparatus for lighting and extinguishing.	N. S. Manross	Forestville, Conn	Feb. 5, 1861	31, 322
Gas-lights from cotton-seed, Manufacture of	D. Olmstead	New Haven, Conn	July 21, 1827	....
Gas-lights, Means of extinguishing	C. H. Harwood	Salem, Mass	Aug. 22, 1871	118, 239
Gas-lights, Means of extinguishing	O. S. Judd	New Britain, Conn	June 10, 1862	35, 525
Gas-lights, Mode of extinguishing	H. K. Symmes	Newton, Mass	Feb. 14, 1860	27, 170
Gas-lights, Packing for sliding	G. Clay	New York, N. Y	Nov. 8, 1859	26, 015
Gas-lighter	W. B. Johns	United States Army	Aug. 16, 1859	25, 122
Gas-lighter	E. D. McCracken	New York, N. Y	Feb. 18, 1873	136, 084
Gas-lighter	W. Wiler and L. Moss	Philadelphia, Pa	June 26, 1855	13, 134
Gas-lighter, Automatic	A. N. Allen and R. H. Dewey	Pittsfield, Mass	Oct. 24, 1871	120, 226
Gas-lighter, Electric	A. N. Allen and R. H. Dewey	Pittsfield, Mass	Nov. 28, 1871	121, 308
Gas-lighter, Electric	E. J. Frost and G. A. Lawrence	Springfield, Mass	Aug. 8, 1865	49, 254
Gas-lighter, Fulminate	H. B. Stockwell	Brooklyn, N. Y	June 27, 1865	48, 459
Gas, Lighting	A. Barbarin	New Orleans, La	Nov. 20, 1866	59, 754
Gas, Lighting	A. Barbarin	New Orleans, La	Apr. 30, 1867	64, 188
Gas, Lighting	W. W. Batchelder	New York, N. Y	May 14, 1867	64, 738
Gas, Lighting	W. W. Batchelder	New York, N. Y	Nov. 3, 1868	83, 593
Gas, Lighting	E. D. McCracken	New York, N. Y	Oct. 17, 1871	120, 082
Gas, Lighting and extinguishing	M. G. Farmer	Salem, Mass	Dec. 24, 1867	72, 616
Gas lighting and extinguishing apparatus	A. N. Allen and R. H. Dewey	Pittsfield, Mass	Apr. 12, 1870	101, 806
Gas lighting and extinguishing apparatus, Automatic.	E. P. Russell	Manlius, N. Y	June 25, 1867	66, 044
Gas lighting and extinguishing apparatus, Electric	J. Vansant	San Francisco, Cal	Apr. 4, 1871	113, 370

Index of patents issued from the United States Patent Office from 1790 *to* 1873, *inclusive*—Continued.

Invention.	Inventor.	Residence.	Date.	No.
Gas lighting and extinguishing, Automatic machine for.	H. R. Richardson	Manlius, N. Y	June 26, 1866	55, 909
Gas lighting and extinguishing by electricity, Apparatus for.	E. E. Bean	Boston, Mass	June 1, 1869	90, 629
Gas lighting and extinguishing by electricity, Apparatus for.	F. Bean	Somerville, Mass	Oct. 18, 1870	108, 434
Gas lighting and extinguishing by electricity, Apparatus for.	J. P. Tirrell	Charlestown, Mass	Nov. 28, 1871	121, 301
Gas lighting and extinguishing by electricity, Apparatus for.	J. P. Tirrell	Charlestown, Mass	Nov. 28, 1871	121, 302
Gas lighting and extinguishing by electricity, Apparatus for.	J. Vansant	San Francisco, Cal	Mar. 19, 1872	124, 773
Gas-lighting apparatus	A. Barbarin	New Orleans, La	Sept. 1, 1868	81, 735
Gas-lighting apparatus	H. G. Fiske	Springfield, Mass	May 25, 1869	90, 519
Gas-lighting apparatus	E. D. McCracken	New York, N. Y	Oct. 17, 1871	120, 083
Gas-lighting apparatus	A. Potter	Philadelphia, Pa	July 8, 1873	140, 591
Gas-lighting apparatus, Automatic	F. Korwan	Mannheim, Germany	Mar. 11, 1873	136, 739
Gas-lighting apparatus, Electric	C. N. Ealer	Opelousas, La	Sept. 20, 1870	107, 465
Gas-lighting apparatus, Electrical	J. Vansant	San Francisco, Cal	June 10, 1873	139, 692
Gas-lighting apparatus, Electro-magnetic	A. N. Allen and R. H. Dewey	Pittsfield, Mass	Oct. 3, 1871	119, 492
Gas-lighting apparatus, Electro-magnetic	F. Heyl and P. Diehl	East New York, N. Y	June 20, 1871	116, 054
Gas-lighting apparatus, Electro-magnetic	A. W. Scharit, L. A. Hudson, and D. Lyman.	Saint Louis, Mo., Syracuse, N. Y., and Parkman, Ohio.	Nov. 2, 1869	96, 488
Gas-lighting apparatus, Magneto-electric	A. N. Allen and R. H. Dewey	Pittsfield, Mass	July 4, 1871	116, 660
Gas-lighting by electrical sparks, Apparatus for	J. Vansant	San Francisco, Cal	May 21, 1872	127, 000
Gas-lighting by electricity, &c	A. N. Allen	Pittsfield, Mass	Feb. 6, 1872	123, 439
Gas-lighting by electricity	E. E. Bean and W. H. Mumler	Boston, Mass	June 4, 1867	65, 406
Gas-lighting by electricity	A. L. Bogart	New York, N. Y	Oct. 3, 1871	119, 561
Gas-lighting by electricity	R. Cornelius	Philadelphia, Pa	June 4, 1861	32, 471
Gas-lighting by electricity	R. Cornelius	Philadelphia, Pa	May 19, 1863	38, 562
Gas-lighting by electricity	R. Cornelius	Philadelphia, Pa	May 19, 1863	38, 563
Gas-lighting by electricity	S. Gardiner, jr	New York, N. Y	Dec. 22, 1857	18, 945
Gas-lighting by electricity	S. Gardiner, jr	New York, N. Y	Mar. 30, 1858	19, 766
Gas-lighting by electricity	S. Gardiner, jr	New York, N. Y	Nov. 29, 1864	45, 239
Gas-lighting by electricity	S. Gardiner, jr	New York, N. Y	Nov. 29, 1864	45, 240
Gas-lighting by electricity	S. Gardiner, jr	New York, N. Y	Nov. 29, 1864	45, 241
Gas-lighting by electricity	S. Gardiner, jr	New York, N. Y	June 19, 1866	55, 641
Gas-lighting by electricity	J. M. Higgins	Saint Louis, Mo	Nov. 19, 1867	71, 005
Gas-lighting by electricity	G. G. Percival	Brooklyn, N. Y	Jan. 15, 1867	61, 247
Gas-lighting by electricity	R. G. Pike	New York, N. Y	Sept. 4, 1866	57, 761
Gas-lighting by electricity	W. A. Pitt	New York, N. Y	June 10, 1873	139, 811
Gas-lighting by electricity	A. Wilson	New York, N. Y	Aug. 16, 1859	25, 167
Gas-lighting by electricity, Apparatus for	A. Barbarin	New Orleans, La	June 1, 1869	90, 626
Gas-lighting by electricity, Apparatus for	W. W. Batchelder	Boston, Mass	Sept. 7, 1869	94, 545
Gas-lighting by electricity, Apparatus for	W. W. Batchelder	Boston, Mass	May 17, 1870	103, 127
Gas-lighting by electricity, Apparatus for	W. W. Batchelder	Boston, Mass	June 7, 1870	103, 831
Gas-lighting by electricity, Apparatus for	S. Gardiner, jr	New York, N. Y	Feb. 19, 1867	62, 125
Gas-lighting by electricity, Apparatus for	W. H. Kelly	New York, N. Y	Mar. 15, 1870	100, 773
Gas-lighting by electricity, Apparatus for	W. Klinkerfues	Göttingen, Germany	Jan. 2, 1872	122, 389
Gas-lighting by electricity, Apparatus for	W. J. Morris and W. J. Reid	New York, N. Y	Apr. 5, 1870	101, 491
Gas-lighting by electricity, Apparatus for	H. T. Robbins	Boston, Mass	Sept. 6, 1870	107, 105
Gas-lighting by electricity, Apparatus for	T. P. Tirrell	Charlestown, Mass	Aug. 20, 1872	130, 770
Gas-lighting by electricity, Apparatus for	J. Vansant	San Francisco, Cal	Oct. 31, 1871	120, 469
Gas-lighting by electricity, Instrument for	R. Cornelius	Philadelphia, Pa	Oct. 18, 1864	44, 708
Gas-lighting by electro-galvanic battery, Method of	A. Wilson	Boston, Mass	Feb. 23, 1858	19, 460
Gas-lighting by frictional electricity, Method of	W. W. Batchelder	New York, N. Y	Jan. 31, 1860	26, 964
Gas-lighting by galvanic electricity, Method of	W. W. Hopkins	Amelia, Ohio	Feb. 15, 1859	22, 952
Gas-lighting, Construction of instrument for	A. Damarin and G. C. Brower	New Orleans, La	Apr. 24, 1860	27, 971
Gas-lighting device	E. P. Gleason	New York, N. Y	Dec. 8, 1868	84, 689
Gas-lighting device	J. G. Harper	New York, N. Y	July 25, 1865	48, 932
Gas-lighting, &c., Distributing electricity for	S. Gardiner, jr	New York, N. Y	Apr. 9, 1872	125, 387
Gas-lighting, Electric apparatus for	F. Bean	Boston, Mass	Jan. 28, 1868	73, 868
Gas-lighting, Electric torch for	W. W. Batchelder	New York, N. Y	Apr. 30, 1872	126, 251
Gas-lighting, Electrical	C. G. Mueller and H. Meier	Hanover, Germany	June 3, 1873	139, 599
Gas-lighting, Electrical apparatus for	R. Cornelius	Philadelphia, Pa	May 24, 1864	42, 840
Gas-lighting, Electrical apparatus for	S. B. H. Vance	New York, N. Y	Feb. 5, 1861	31, 359
Gas-lighting, Implement for	T. W. Houchin	Morrisania, N. Y	Dec. 10, 1867	71, 880
Gas-lighting instrument	T. W. Houchin	Morrisania, N. Y	Apr. 11, 1865	47, 207
Gas-lighting instrument	A. Shipley and W. T. Mersereau	Newark, N. J	May 12, 1868	77, 771
Gas, Lighting street	E. P. Russell	Manlius, N. Y	Oct. 29, 1867	70, 272
Gas-lighting torch	E. P. Gleason	Brooklyn, N. Y	June 24, 1873	140, 191
Gas-lighting torch	C. H. Roberts	Troy, N. Y	Feb. 18, 1873	136, 006
Gas-lighting torch, Electric	W. W. Batchelder	New York, N. Y	Mar. 5, 1872	124, 317
Gas-lime, &c., Obtaining bisulphide or carbon from	J. Kircher	New York, N. Y	May 6, 1873	138, 504
Gas-lime, &c., Obtaining sulphur, sulphuric acid, and sulphurets of sodium and potassium from.	J. Kircher	New York, N. Y	Apr. 8, 1873	137, 692
Gas-machine	S. R. Ball	Hyde Park, Ill	Jan. 4, 1870	98, 462
Gas-machine	N. W. Bancroft	Worcester, Mass	Oct. 6, 1868	82, 786
Gas-machine	W. W. Binny	Auburn, N. Y	June 14, 1870	104, 253
Gas-machine	E. H. and W. H. Covel	New York, N. Y	Nov. 24, 1868	84, 460
Gas-machine	T. B. Fogarty	Brooklyn, N. Y	June 6, 1871	115, 591
Gas-machine	T. B. Fogarty	Kings County, N. Y	June 6, 1871	115, 592
Gas-machine	T. B. Fogarty	Brooklyn, N. Y	June 6, 1871	115, 593
Gas-machine	T. B. Fogarty	Brooklyn, N. Y	June 6, 1871	115, 594
Gas-machine	T. B. Fogarty	Brooklyn, N. Y	June 6, 1871	115, 595
Gas-machine	T. B. Fogarty	Brooklyn, N. Y	June 6, 1871	115, 596
Gas-machine	T. B. Fogarty	Brooklyn, N. Y	June 6, 1871	115, 597
Gas-machine	T. B. Fogarty	Brooklyn, N. Y	Sept. 26, 1871	119, 227
Gas-machine	T. B. Fogarty	New York, N. Y	Feb. 18, 1873	135, 980
Gas-machine	J. P. Gallagher	Saint Louis, Mo	July 12, 1870	105, 190
Gas-machine	D. M. Graham	Evansville, Ind	July 28, 1868	80, 404
Gas-machine	J. W. Groat	Fremont, Ohio	May 25, 1869	90, 445
Gas-machine	C. C. Hare	Kansas City, Mo	May 18, 1869	90, 259
Gas-machine	J. Kaufmann	Jackson, Miss	May 28, 1872	127, 245
Gas-machine	P. H. Lawler and W. H. Gibson	Rochester, N. Y	Dec. 22, 1868	85, 104
Gas-machine	H. S. Maxim	New York, N. Y	Sept. 8, 1868	81, 922
Gas-machine	H. S. Maxim	Brooklyn, N. Y	Oct. 24, 1871	120, 302

Index of patents issued from the United States Patent Office from 1790 to 1873, inclusive—Continued.

Invention.	Inventor.	Residence.	Date.	No.
Gas-machine	H. S. Maxim and J. F. Lockwood.	New York, N. Y	June 2, 1868	78, 465
Gas-machine	W. T. McMillen	Richmond, Ind	Nov. 14, 1871	120, 824
Gas machine	I. Prichard	Terre Haute, Ind	Feb. 4, 1868	74, 132
Gas-machine	W. A Simonds	Boston, Mass	May 2, 1871	114, 358
Gas-machine	A. R. Spang and D. F. Scheaf	Dayton, Ohio	Sept. 21, 1869	94, 982
Gas-machine	J. D. Spang	Dayton, Ohio	Dec. 22, 1868	85, 185
Gas-machine	T. G. Springer	Clinton, Iowa	Dec. 7, 1869	97, 748
Gas-machine	T. G. Springer	Saint Louis, Mo	Mar. 8, 1870	100, 684
Gas-machine	T. G. Springer	Saint Louis, Mo	Mar. 21, 1871	112, 975
Gas-machine	T. G. Springer	Fayette City, Pa	Oct. 3, 1871	119, 663
Gas-machine	W. Thompson	Cleveland, Ohio	Nov. 10, 1868	84, 021
Gas-machine	H. Tilden	Boston, Mass	Nov. 23, 1869	97, 247
Gas-machine	H. Tilden	Philadelphia, Pa	May 6, 1873	138, 715
Gas-machine	J. H. Van Houten	Newark, N. J	Nov. 22, 1870	110, 568
Gas-machine	H. Wain	Ravenna, Ohio	Oct. 20, 1868	83, 344
Gas machine, Air	P. Werni	Newark, N. J	Aug. 19, 1873	141, 973
Gas machine, Electro-hydrocarbon	H. J. Smith	Boston, Mass	Mar. 22, 1870	101, 171
Gas, Machine for generating and carbureting	C. F. Dunderdale	New York, N. Y	July 20, 1869	92, 943
Gas machine, Pneumatic	D. Boyle	San Francisco, Cal	June 7, 1870	103, 836
Gas-machine, Portable	B. Sloper	New York, N. Y	Oct. 7, 1873	143, 426
Gas-machines, Adjustable pulley for	E. F. Van Houten	Newark, N. J	Aug. 19, 1873	141, 967
Gas machines and carbureters, Safety-apparatus for	J. F. Boynton	Syracuse, N. Y	Sept. 18, 1866	58, 055
Gas-main	I. N. Stanley	Brooklyn, N. Y	Aug. 7, 1866	57, 006
Gas-main pipes, Condensing liquids in	J. Walton	Louisville, Ky	June 30, 1857	17, 711
Gas-mains, Leveling hydraulic	P. Munzinger	Philadelphia, Pa	May 25, 1869	90, 379
Gas-mains, Straddle-pipe for hydraulic	P. Munzinger	Philadelphia, Pa	May 4, 1869	89, 592
Gas, Making	J. Hansor	Wardsworth Road, England.	Feb. 10, 1857	16, 591
Gas, Making	J. McGeary	Salem, Mass	Apr. 7, 1868	76, 338
Gas, Making and application of combustible	W. Garnet	New York, N. Y	Dec. 27, 1822	....
Gas, Making and using nitrous-oxide	P. H. Vander Weyde	Philadelphia, Pa	Feb. 12, 1867	62, 094
Gas, Making carbureted hydrogen	B. Kugler	Philadelphia, Pa	Apr. 23, 1816	....
Gas, Making illuminating	H. W. Adams	New York, N. Y	Aug. 10, 1852	9, 175
Gas, Making illuminating	N. Aubin	Albany, N. Y	Jan. 8, 1856	14, 045
Gas, Making illuminating	G. Danré, P. Nicolas, and F. Loperz.	Marseilles, France	Dec. 28, 1852	9, 501
Gas, Making illuminating	R. Grant	Brooklyn, N. Y	Jan. 27, 1857	16, 480
Gas, Making illuminating	J. L. Graves	Springfield, Mass	June 4, 1872	127, 411
Gas, Making illuminating	L. L. Hill	Hudson, N. Y	June 17, 1862	35, 610
Gas, Making illuminating	J. Howarth	Salem, Mass	May 17, 1864	42, 771
Gas, Making illuminating	A. C. Rand	Union Mills, Pa	June 25, 1867	66, 041
Gas, Manufacture of	J. H. Connelly	Wheeling, W. Va	Sept. 18, 1866	58, 221
Gas, Manufacture of	J. H. Connelly	Wheeling, W. Va	May 21, 1867	64, 845
Gas, Manufacture of	J. Crutchett	Stroud, England	Mar. 12, 1867	62, 823
Gas, Manufacture of	L. D. Gale	Washington, D. C	Nov. 8, 1859	26, 028
Gas, Manufacture of	L. D. Gale	Washington, D. C	Nov. 8, 1859	26, 030
Gas, Manufacture of	D. C. Knab	Paris, France	Mar. 9, 1858	19, 575
Gas, Manufacture of	T. S. C. Lowe	Norristown, Pa	Aug. 13, 1872	130, 382
Gas, Manufacture of	S. T. McDougall	New York, N. Y	Mar. 13, 1860	27, 460
Gas, Manufacture of	G. Michiels	Paris, France	Oct. 3, 1846	4, 789
Gas, Manufacture of	C. Noble	New York, N. Y	July 11, 1865	48, 714
Gas, Manufacture of	R. H. Patterson	Hammersmith, England	Apr. 8, 1873	137, 713
Gas, Manufacture of	J. T. Rich	Philadelphia, Pa	July 30, 1867	67, 217
Gas, Manufacture of	F. A. Sabbaton	Troy, N. Y	May 20, 1873	139, 083
Gas, Manufacture of	H. Skoines	London, Great Britain	Nov. 25, 1873	145, 021
Gas, Manufacture of	J. L Stewart	East Boston, Mass	June 1, 1858	20, 453
Gas, Manufacture of	C. N. Tyler	Washington, D. C	June 21, 1859	24, 506
Gas, Manufacture of carbon-black for natural carbureted hydrogen.	J. Howarth	Salem, Mass	Sept. 17, 1872	131, 446
Gas, Manufacture of coal	J. A. Bassett	Salem, Mass	Aug. 29, 1871	118, 579
Gas, Manufacture of coal	D. Davison	New York, N. Y	Oct. 24, 1871	120, 151
Gas, Manufacture of coal	W. Gibson	Cambridge, Mass	Oct. 5, 1869	95, 459
Gas, Manufacture of coal	W. H. Gwynne	New York, N. Y	Dec. 15, 1863	40, 925
Gas, Manufacture of hydrocarbon	J. A. Bassett	Salem, Mass	Jan. 3, 1860	26, 644
Gas, Manufacture of hydrocarbon	J. Calkins	Hudson, N. Y	Jan. 3, 1860	26, 649
Gas, Manufacture of hydrocarbon	F. A. Sabbaton	Troy, N. Y	July 11, 1871	116, 994
Gas, Manufacture of illuminating	J. A. Bassett	Salem, Mass	July 8, 1862	35, 807
Gas, Manufacture of illuminating	J. A. Bassett	Salem, Mass	Aug. 19, 1862	36, 254
Gas, Manufacture of illuminating	J. A. Bassett	Salem, Mass	June 25, 1867	66, 070
Gas, Manufacture of illuminating	J. A. Bassett	Salem, Mass	June 25, 1867	66, 071
Gas, Manufacture of illuminating	J. A. Bassett	Salem, Mass	Oct. 20, 1868	83, 239
Gas, Manufacture of illuminating	J. Boston	New York, N. Y	Feb. 11, 1831	....
Gas, Manufacture of illuminating	A. S. Cameron and W. E. Everett.	New York and Rye, N. Y.	May 9, 1871	114, 642
Gas, Manufacture of illuminating	C. Carpenter	Buffalo, N. Y	Mar. 2, 1869	87, 466
Gas, Manufacture of illuminating	D. Davison	New York, N. Y	Sept. 26, 1871	119, 329
Gas, Manufacture of illuminating	C. F. Dieterich and A. Schüssler.	New York, N. Y	July 23, 1872	129, 720
Gas, Manufacture of illuminating	C. F. Dunderdale	New York, N. Y	Aug. 31, 1869	94, 297
Gas, Manufacture of illuminating	W. Elmer	New York, N. Y	Sept. 15, 1863	39, 905
Gas, Manufacture of illuminating	W. Elmer	New York, N. Y	Feb. 2, 1864	41, 431
Gas, Manufacture of illuminating	W. Elmer	New York, N. Y	June 11, 1867	65, 733
Gas, Manufacture of illuminating	W. Elmer	New York, N. Y	Aug. 5, 1873	141, 500
Gas, Manufacture of illuminating	J. J. Ensley	New York, N. Y	Feb. 4, 1868	74, 063
Gas, Manufacture of illuminating	R. M. and A. R. Fryer	New York, N. Y	Jan. 21, 1868	73, 521
Gas, Manufacture of illuminating	G. P. Ganster	New York, N. Y	June 16, 1868	78, 870
Gas, Manufacture of illuminating	C. Gearing	Pittsburgh, Pa	June 24, 1873	140, 264
Gas, Manufacture of illuminating	H. D. Green	Portland, Oreg	Aug. 14, 1866	57, 123
Gas, Manufacture of illuminating	H. D. Green	Portland, Oreg	Oct. 23, 1866	59, 004
Gas, Manufacture of illuminating	W. H. Gwynne	White Plains, N. Y	July 29, 1862	36, 032
Gas, Manufacture of illuminating	W. H. Gwynne	White Plains, N. Y	Jan. 6, 1863	37, 289
Gas, Manufacture of illuminating	W. H. Gwynne	White Plains, N. Y	July 14, 1863	39, 227
Gas, Manufacture of illuminating	A. W. Hall	New York, N. Y	Nov. 22, 1870	109, 510
Gas, Manufacture of illuminating	G. W. Harris and H. P. Allen	Elizabeth, N. J., and New York, N. Y.	July 30, 1872	129, 951
Gas, Manufacture of illuminating	G. W. Harris and H. Holdrege	Elizabeth, N. J., and New York, N. Y.	Sept. 7, 1869	94, 596

Index of patents issued from the United States Patent Office from 1790 *to* 1873, *inclusive*—Continued.

Invention.	Inventor.	Residence.	Date.	No.
Gas, Manufacture of illuminating	S. Hevner	San Francisco, Cal	May 9, 1871	114, 559
Gas, Manufacture of illuminating	E. R. Hopkins	Newark, N. J	Dec. 16, 1873	145, 655
Gas, Manufacture of illuminating	J. Kidd	New York, N. Y	Sept. 19, 1871	119, 034
Gas, Manufacture of illuminating	F. King	Washington, D. C	Aug. 1, 1871	117, 645
Gas, Manufacture of illuminating	M. Levy	New York, N. Y	Dec. 9, 1862	37, 101
Gas, Manufacture of illuminating	J. S. Lipps	New York, N. Y	Dec. 29, 1868	85, 458
Gas, Manufacture of illuminating	C. B. Loveless	Syracuse, N. Y	Dec. 1, 1868	84, 636
Gas, Manufacture of illuminating	W. L. Lowrey	Saratoga Springs, N. Y	July 23, 1867	67, 127
Gas, Manufacture of illuminating	W. L. Lowrey	Saratoga Springs, N. Y	Aug. 4, 1868	80, 642
Gas, Manufacture of illuminating	E. P. McCarthy	San Francisco, Cal	May 17, 1870	103, 218
Gas, Manufacture of illuminating	W. P. McConnell	Washington, D. C	July 28, 1863	39, 350
Gas, Manufacture of illuminating	E. D. McCracken	New York, N. Y	July 12, 1870	105, 351
Gas, Manufacture of illuminating	E. D. McCracken	New York, N. Y	Aug. 13, 1872	130, 437
Gas, Manufacture of illuminating	G. A. McIlhenny	Washington, D. C	June 18, 1867	65, 927
Gas, Manufacture of illuminating	G. McKenzie	Glasgow, Great Britain	July 9, 1867	66, 511
Gas, Manufacture of illuminating	T. N. Miller	Pittsburgh, Pa	June 17, 1873	139, 910
Gas, Manufacture of illuminating	A. Millochau	New York, N. Y	Oct. 2, 1866	58, 553
Gas, Manufacture of illuminating	E. A. Pond	Rutland, Vt	Oct. 10, 1865	50, 385
Gas, Manufacture of illuminating	E. A. and G. H. Pond and M. S. Richardson.	Rutland, Vt	Sept. 27, 1870	107, 809
Gas, Manufacture of illuminating	A. C. Rand	Union Mills, Pa	Feb. 26, 1867	62, 363
Gas, Manufacture of illuminating	A. C. Rand	New York, N. Y	Apr. 13, 1869	88, 982
Gas, Manufacture of illuminating	A. C. Rand	New York, N. Y	Mar. 8, 1870	100, 668
Gas, Manufacture of illuminating	W. D. Seal	Washington, D. C	Feb. 27, 1866	52, 893
Gas, Manufacture of illuminating	B. Silliman	New Haven, Conn	Oct. 19, 1869	95, 941
Gas, Manufacture of illuminating	B. Sloper and R. M. Potter	New York, N. Y., and Jersey City, N. J.	Jan. 23, 1872	123, 052
Gas, Manufacture of illuminating	J. W. Smith and T. H. Phillips	Washington, D. C	Oct. 8, 1867	69, 594
Gas, Manufacture of illuminating	J. Somerville and R. Elsdon	Maidstone, Great Britain	Apr. 14, 1868	76, 837
Gas, Manufacture of illuminating	A. P. Southwick	Buffalo, N. Y	Aug. 26, 1873	142, 289
Gas, Manufacture of illuminating	W. H. Spencer	Brooklyn, N. Y	July 9, 1872	128, 918
Gas, Manufacture of illuminating	W. H. Spencer	Brooklyn, N. Y	Sept. 3, 1872	131, 035
Gas, Manufacture of illuminating	T. G. Springer	Fayette City, Pa	Dec. 5, 1871	121, 679
Gas, Manufacture of illuminating	T. G. Springer	Fayette City, Pa	Dec. 17, 1872	134, 108
Gas, Manufacture of illuminating	J. W. Stanley	Brooklyn, N. Y	Jan. 31, 1871	111, 486
Gas, Manufacture of illuminating	L. Stevens	Washington, D. C	Jan. 7, 1868	73, 057
Gas, Manufacture of illuminating	L. Stevens	Washington, D. C	Jan. 26, 1869	86, 187
Gas, Manufacture of illuminating	L. Stevens	Washington, D. C	Feb. 23, 1869	87, 123
Gas, Manufacture of illuminating	J. B. Terry	Hartford, Conn	Dec. 10, 1867	72, 118
Gas, Manufacture of illuminating	J. E. Thomson	Buffalo, N. Y	May 20, 1862	35, 336
Gas, Manufacture of illuminating	P. H. Vander Weyde	New York, N. Y	Apr. 9, 1872	125, 633
Gas, Manufacture of illuminating	A. Walton and J. L. Kite	Philadelphia, Pa	Jan. 14, 1862	34, 185
Gas, Manufacture of illuminating	S. L. Wiegand	Philadelphia, Pa	May 5, 1863	38, 438
Gas, Manufacture of illuminating	S. L. Wiegand	Philadelphia, Pa	Aug. 18, 1863	39, 605
Gas, Manufacture of illuminating	S. L. Wiegand	Philadelphia, Pa	Aug. 18, 1863	39, 606
Gas, Manufacture of illuminating	A. W. Wilkinson	New York, N. Y	Feb. 6, 1872	123, 538
Gas, Manufacture of illuminating	A. W. Wilkinson	New York, N. Y	June 17, 1873	140, 104
Gas, Manufacture of illuminating	W. C. Wren	Brooklyn, N. Y	Apr. 8, 1873	137, 750
Gas, Manufacture of illuminating	W. Young and P. Brash	Magdalen Bridge and Leith, Scotland.	Sept. 27, 1870	107, 848
Gas, Manufacture of oxygen	O. M. Phillips	New York, N. Y	Jan. 26, 1869	86, 248
Gas, Manufacture of oxygen	J. Webster	Birmingham, England	June 24, 1862	35, 742
Gas, Manufacture of pneumatic	H. Bloomfield	San Francisco, Cal	June 6, 1871	115, 684
Gas, Manufacture of vapor	C. L. Cohen	Philadelphia, Pa	July 22, 1873	141, 119
Gas, Manufacture of vapor	C. A. Seely	New York, N. Y	June 29, 1869	92, 105
Gas, Manufacture of water	W. H. Gwynne	White Plains, N. Y	Aug. 11, 1863	39, 480
Gas, Manufacture of water	E. J. Jerzmanowski	New York, N. Y	Dec. 9, 1873	145, 350
Gas-meter	T. Brattan	Birkenhead, England	Feb. 1, 1870	99, 285
Gas-meter	C. F. Brown	Baltimore, Md	June 22, 1842	2, 687
Gas-meter	S. Clegg	Great Britain	Sept. 22, 1838	942
Gas-meter	S. Clegg	Putney, County Surrey, England.	Apr. 16, 1861	32, 049
Gas-meter	A. A. Croll	London, England	Feb. 22, 1853	9, 591
Gas-meter	D. De Castro and R. Burton	Mortlake, Surrey, and London, England.	July 29, 1873	141, 263
Gas-meter	J. S. Elliott	Philadelphia, Pa	Sept. 15, 1863	39, 904
Gas-meter	J. E. Fisk	Salem, Mass	Oct. 5, 1858	21, 663
Gas-meter	T. B. Fogarty	Charleston, S. C	Dec. 13, 1859	26, 423
Gas-meter	D. Forrest	Eastport, Me	Nov. 26, 1867	71, 375
Gas-meter	E. R. Hallam and T. B. Barnard	New Haven, Conn., and Brooklyn, N. Y.	Feb. 8, 1853	9, 580
Gas-meter	J. Hemming	Great Britain	Nov. 4, 1842	2, 837
Gas-meter	H. J. Hyams	Pittsburgh, Pa	Sept. 13, 1870	107, 380
Gas-meter	H. H. and J. F. G. Kromschroeder.	Regent's Park, Hanover	Oct. 13, 1863	40, 266
Gas-meter	G. Laidlaw	New York, N. Y	Nov. 2, 1852	9, 367
Gas-meter	T. W. Lane	Woburn, Mass	Oct. 8, 1850	7, 703
Gas-meter	J. Long	Chicago, Ill	Mar. 5, 1850	7, 154
Gas-meter	J. W. Mahlon	Brooklyn, N. Y	Apr. 28, 1868	77, 298
Gas-meter	H. Robinson	Boston, Mass	Mar. 10, 1831	....
Gas-meter	J. Schatt	Philadelphia, Pa	July 24, 1860	29, 323
Gas-meter	J. T. Scholte	Paris, France	Aug. 14, 1866	57, 268
Gas-meter	T. Shaw	Philadelphia, Pa	Apr. 27, 1858	20, 130
Gas-meter	A. W. Smith	Birmingham, Pa	Mar. 17, 1868	75, 653
Gas-meter	W. A. Telling and S. Johnson	London, England	Sept. 30, 1873	143, 390
Gas-meter	N. Tufts, jr	Boston, Mass	Aug. 14, 1860	29, 639
Gas-meter	G. J. Willson and D. H. Fox	Reading, Pa	Aug. 21, 1860	29, 740
Gas meter and regulator	C. C. Lloyd	West Philadelphia, Pa	June 20, 1854	11, 128
Gas-meter, Dry	D. Alcorn	New York, N. Y	July 21, 1863	39, 266
Gas-meter, Dry	A. W. Almqvist and F. W. Ofeldt.	New York, N. Y	June 6, 1871	115, 557
Gas-meter, Dry	L. Boore	Buffalo, N. Y	July 9, 1861	32, 747
Gas-meter, Dry	F. Darracott	Boston, Mass	Dec. 5, 1854	12, 045
Gas-meter, Dry	S. Down	New York, N. Y	May 24, 1859	24, 108
Gas-meter, Dry	J. E. Fisk	Salem, Mass	Mar. 18, 1862	34, 678
Gas-meter, Dry	J. E. Fisk	Salem, Mass	Sept. 15, 1863	39, 907
Gas-meter, Dry	W. W. Goodwin	Camden, N. J	Apr. 21, 1868	76, 908
Gas-meter, Dry	R. H. Gratz and C. C. Lloyd	Philadelphia, Pa	Oct. 23, 1860	30, 524

Index of patents issued from the United States Patent Office from 1790 *to* 1873, *inclusive*—Continued.

Index of patents issued from the United States Patent Office from 1790 *to* 1873, *inclusive*—Continued.

Invention.	Inventor.	Residence.	Date.	No.
Gas, Process and apparatus for generating combustible.	C. M. Tessié du Motay	Paris, France	Mar. 2, 1869	87, 478
Gas, Process and apparatus for making	T. S. C. Lowe	Norristown, Pa	Aug. 13, 1872	130, 383
Gas. Processes and compositions for the manufacture of illuminating.	W. H. Sterling	San Francisco, Cal	Sept. 16, 1873	142, 959
Gas producer or furnace	C. W. Siemens and F. Siemens.	Westminster, England, and Berlin, Prussia.	May 10, 1864	42, 717
Gas-producing apparatus for use in metallurgy and glass-making and for other purposes.	J. Green	Norristown, Pa	Feb. 2, 1869	86, 529
Gas-producing furnace	W. Gerhardt	New York, N. Y	Feb. 8, 1870	99, 554
Gas, Producing illuminating	W. Elmer	New York, N. Y	Aug. 4, 1863	39, 388
Gas, Production of illuminating	J. M. Sanders	Cincinnati, Ohio	July 27, 1858	21, 027
Gas, Purification of coal	A. A. Croll	London, England	June 18, 1867	65, 880
Gas, Purification of coal	E. McMillen	Ironton, Ohio	Mar. 1, 1870	100, 309
Gas, Purification of illuminating	W. H. St. John	New York, N. Y	Sept. 2, 1873	142, 358
Gas-purifier	R. C. Bocking	Indianapolis, Ind	July 3, 1866	55, 994
Gas-purifier	P. Fontain	Philadelphia, Pa	June 28, 1859	24, 551
Gas-purifier	J. T. Goodfellow and F. A. Sabbaton.	Troy, N. Y	June 17, 1873	140, 034
Gas-purifier	P. Munzinger	Philadelphia, Pa	Mar. 30, 1869	88, 326
Gas purifier and regulator	J. A. Enos	Peabody, Mass	May 20, 1873	139, 131
Gas-purifier, Dry	E. Duffee	Haverhill, Mass	May 2, 1871	114, 275
Gas purifier, Dry lime	C. F. Werner and C. Deutschmann.	New York and Buffalo, N. Y.	July 1, 1856	15, 267
Gas-purifier screen	T. G. Arnold	New York, N. Y	Oct. 16, 1866	58, 749
Gas-purifier screen	E. Duffee	Haverhill, Mass	July 17, 1866	56, 490
Gas-purifier screen	E. Duffee	Haverhill, Mass	Aug. 6, 1872	130, 190
Gas purifier screen, Coal	G. W. Day	Haverhill, Mass	June 11, 1872	127, 856
Gas purifier screen, Coal	E. Duffee	Haverhill, Mass	Dec. 12, 1871	121, 764
Gas purifier screen, Coal	J. Hale	Georgetown, Mass	June 18, 1872	127, 973
Gas-purifier screen, Dry	E. Duffee	Haverhill, Mass	Oct. 2, 1866	58, 393
Gas-purifiers, Mode of forming connection of	R. Briggs	Philadelphia, Pa	June 8, 1869	90, 917
Gas-purifiers, Tray for	P. Munzinger	Philadelphia, Pa	Oct. 11, 1870	108, 167
Gas-purifiers, Tray or grating for	J. L. Cheesman	New York, N. Y	June 10, 1873	139, 702
Gas, Purifying	W. T. Kosinski	Philadelphia, Pa	May 14, 1872	126, 717
Gas-purifying apparatus	W. F. Danowsky	Allentown, Pa	Aug. 10, 1858	21, 121
Gas-purifying apparatus	A. F. Havens	Brooklyn, N. Y	Aug. 29, 1871	118, 609
Gas-purifying apparatus	A. Longbottom	New York, N. Y	Feb. 3, 1852	8, 705
Gas-purifying apparatus	A. Walker	Claremont, N. H	Aug. 3, 1858	21, 095
Gas-purifying apparatus	W. T. Walker	London, England	July 30, 1872	129, 997
Gas-purifying apparatus	J. Waterhouse	Little Falls, N. Y	Aug. 3, 1858	21, 096
Gas, Purifying carbonic-acid	A. P. Meylert	New Britain, Conn	Jan. 21, 1873	135, 001
Gas, Purifying carbonic-acid	A. P. Meylert	New Britain, Conn	Apr. 8, 1873	137, 615
Gas, Purifying coal	J. A. Sabbaton	Albany, N. Y	July 30, 1850	7, 534
Gas, Purifying illuminating	F. J. De Cavaillon	Paris, France	May 6, 1851	8, 081
Gas, Purifying illuminating	R. J. Everett	Bridgeport, Conn	Apr. 23, 1872	125, 943
Gas, Purifying illuminating	A. Ruthel	Savona, Italy	Oct. 29, 1872	132, 642
Gas, Purifying illuminating	P. Spence	Manchester, England	Oct. 27, 1868	83, 417
Gas, Purifying illuminating	W. H. St. John and P. Cartwright.	New York, N. Y	Nov. 15, 1870	109, 268
Gas-purifying machine	W. C. Turnbull	New York, N. Y	Sept. 11, 1866	58, 002
Gas-reflector	W. J. McLea	Buffalo, N. Y	Apr. 14, 1868	76, 789
Gas-regulator	L. Abbott	Boston, Mass	Dec. 10, 1861	33, 873
Gas-regulator	S. D. Baldwin	Milwaukee, Wis	Apr. 12, 1859	23, 540
Gas-regulator	J. Battin	Philadelphia, Pa	Sept. 18, 1847	5, 300
Gas-regulator	S. Bidwell	Chicago, Ill	Sept. 21, 1858	21, 544
Gas-regulator	J. E. Boyle	Brooklyn, N. Y	Apr. 19, 1864	42, 430
Gas-regulator	F. W. Brocksieper	Bridgeport, Conn	Nov. 17, 1863	40, 602
Gas-regulator	F. W. Brocksieper	Bridgeport, Conn	Feb. 16, 1864	41, 599
Gas-regulator	F. H. Brown	Chicago, Ill	Nov. 18, 1862	36, 940
Gas-regulator	S. W. Brown	Lowell, Mass	May 29, 1855	12, 943
Gas-regulator	S. W. Brown	Lowell, Mass	July 10, 1855	13, 210
Gas-regulator	S. W. Brown	Lowell, Mass	Aug. 7, 1855	13, 377
Gas-regulator	T. Champion and C. Champion.	Washington, D. C., and El Dorado County, Cal.	July 24, 1860	29, 246
Gas-regulator	J. S. Conant	Lowell, Mass	Dec. 9, 1851	8, 578
Gas-regulator	J. B. Coolidge	Boston, Mass	Oct. 31, 1871	120, 416
Gas-regulator	J. H. Cooper	Philadelphia, Pa	Feb. 17, 1857	16, 639
Gas-regulator	J. H. Cooper	Philadelphia, Pa	June 30, 1857	17, 671
Gas-regulator	J. H. Cooper	Philadelphia, Pa	Aug. 18, 1857	18, 008
Gas-regulator	J. H. Cooper	Philadelphia, Pa	June 22, 1858	20, 625
Gas-regulator	R. Cornelius	Philadelphia, Pa	Apr. 21, 1857	17, 079
Gas-regulator	R. Cornelius	Philadelphia, Pa	May 19, 1857	17, 317
Gas-regulator	R. Cornelius	Philadelphia, Pa	May 19, 1863	38, 561
Gas-regulator	E. H. Covel	New York, N. Y	May 31, 1859	24, 199
Gas-regulator	C. M. Cresson	Philadelphia, Pa	Apr. 11, 1865	47, 189
Gas-regulator	O. Dean	Richmond, Va	May 2, 1871	114, 272
Gas-regulator	J. C. Dickey	Saratoga Springs, N. Y	Oct. 23, 1855	13, 700
Gas-regulator	G. B. Dixwell and J. A. Dorr	Boston, Mass., and New York, N. Y.	Apr. 18, 1854	10, 786
Gas-regulator	J. Edson	Boston, Mass	May 6, 1862	35, 146
Gas-regulator	C. H. Edwards	Chicago, Ill	Aug. 26, 1873	142, 155
Gas-regulator	G. M. Eldridge	Philadelphia, Pa	Apr. 23, 1872	125, 942
Gas-regulator	J. Foster	Richmond, Va	Oct. 16, 1860	30, 399
Gas-regulator	H. Gerner	New York, N. Y	June 20, 1871	116, 176
Gas-regulator	H. Giroud	Paris, France	Nov. 3, 1868	83, 706
Gas-regulator	W. Grover	Holyoke, Mass	Sept. 2, 1862	36, 343
Gas-regulator	C. J. Halsted and J. Coeyman	New York, N. Y	Mar. 31, 1857	16, 951
Gas-regulator	C. L. Herring	Saint Louis, Mo	Jan. 22, 1861	31, 168
Gas-regulator	J. W. Hoard	Providence, R. I	Mar. 13, 1855	12, 509
Gas-regulator	C. F. Holzer	Philadelphia, Pa	July 27, 1858	21, 048
Gas-regulator	H. G. Hubert	New York, N. Y	Dec. 24, 1867	72, 643
Gas-regulator	C. T. Judkins	Boston, Mass	Feb. 25, 1862	34, 507
Gas-regulator	J. Keeling	New York, N. Y	Oct. 24, 1871	120, 280
Gas-regulator	P. Keller	New York, N. Y	Jan. 11, 1870	98, 776
Gas-regulator	P. Keller	New York, N. Y	Oct. 4, 1870	108, 029
Gas-regulator	P. Keller	New York, N. Y	June 27, 1871	116, 321
Gas-regulator	P. Keller	New York, N. Y	Apr. 1, 1873	137, 454

Index of patents issued from the United States Patent Office from 1790 *to* 1873, *inclusive*—Continued.

Invention.	Inventor.	Residence.	Date.	No.
Gas-regulator	W. Kidder	Lowell, Mass	Oct. 12, 1852	9, 325
Gas-regulator	W. Kidder	Lowell, Mass	Oct. 12, 1852	9, 326
Gas-regulator	W. Kidder	Lowell, Mass	Oct. 12, 1852	9, 327
Gas-regulator	G. H. Kitchen	New York, N. Y	Oct. 18, 1859	25, 834
Gas-regulator	J. G. Leffingwell	Newark, N. J	Oct. 16, 1860	30, 415
Gas-regulator	W. B. Leonard	New York, N. Y	Feb. 10, 1852	8, 725
Gas-regulator	C. C. Loyd and R. M. Potter	Philadelphia, Pa., and New York, N. Y.	Mar. 15, 1864	41, 930
Gas-regulator	W. Mallerd	Bridgeport, Conn	Oct. 12, 1858	21, 765
Gas-regulator	S. F. Mathews	Mechanicsburgh, Pa	May 26, 1868	78, 305
Gas-regulator	J. S. Merriken	Baltimore, Md	May 9, 1871	114, 699
Gas-regulator	S. P. Mervine, jr	Philadelphia, Pa	Jan. 19, 1869	86, 027
Gas-regulator	J. H. Norton	Boston, Mass	June 10, 1862	35, 538
Gas-regulator	E. T. Orne	Boston, Mass	Mar. 27, 1860	27, 659
Gas-regulator	S. P. Parham	Trenton, N. J	Apr. 10, 1855	12, 692
Gas-regulator	A. H. Phillippi	Reading, Pa	Sept. 24, 1872	131, 701
Gas-regulator	C. C. Place	Boston, Mass	June 27, 1871	116, 349
Gas-regulator	R. M. Potter	Jersey City, N. J	Oct. 8, 1872	132, 103
Gas-regulator	J. H. Powers	Newark, N. J	Sept. 1, 1857	18, 103
Gas-regulator	J. H. Powers	Newark, N. J	July 27, 1858	21, 022
Gas-regulator	T. Powers	Philadelphia, Pa	May 14, 1861	32, 312
Gas-regulator	S. P. Ruggles	Boston, Mass	Aug. 14, 1855	13, 437
Gas-regulator	H. Schutte	Kansas City, Mo	Apr. 25, 1871	114, 206
Gas-regulator	H. C. Sergeant	Cincinnati, Ohio	Apr. 15, 1862	34, 985
Gas-regulator	W. A. Simonds	Boston, Mass	Aug. 15, 1865	49, 449
Gas regulator	W. A. Simonds	Boston, Mass	Dec. 19, 1865	51, 664
Gas-regulator	W. A. Simonds	Boston, Mass	Mar. 3, 1868	75, 210
Gas-regulator	A. Smith	Brooklyn, N. Y	Aug. 26, 1862	36, 306
Gas-regulator	G. H. Smith	Rochester, N. Y	June 25, 1861	32, 670
Gas-regulator	W. G. Sterling	Bridgeport, Conn	Nov. 11, 1856	16, 073
Gas-regulator	W. G. Sterling	Bridgeport, Conn	Aug. 24, 1858	21, 281
Gas-regulator	S. O. Trudell	Detroit, Mich	Sept. 6, 1870	107, 127
Gas-regulator	H. Waterman	Hudson, N. Y	May 13, 1856	14, 893
Gas-regulator	D. Wheeler and I. Little	Fairfield and Bridgeport, Conn.	May 31, 1859	24, 253
Gas-regulator	M. Wheeler	Honesdale, Pa	June 3, 1856	15, 028
Gas-regulator	H. Wheelock	Boston, Mass	June 5, 1855	13, 020
Gas-regulator	S. H. Whitaker	Cincinnati, Ohio	June 12, 1860	28, 722
Gas-regulator	A. H. Wood	Boston, Mass	Jan. 29, 1867	61, 593
Gas-regulator	J. S. Wood	Philadelphia, Pa	Aug. 1, 1865	49, 188
Gas-regulator	J. S. Wood	Philadelphia, Pa	Aug. 21, 1866	57, 425
Gas-regulator	J. S. Wood	Philadelphia, Pa	Aug. 13, 1867	67, 694
Gas-regulator	G. B. Woodruff and J. N. Palmer	New Haven, Conn	May 8, 1855	12, 844
Gas regulator and purifier	P. Fontain	New York, N. Y	Jan. 27, 1863	37, 500
Gas-regulator, Dry	J. B. Hoffman	Philadelphia, Pa	Dec. 3, 1867	71, 757
Gas-regulator for blow-pipes, Automatic	J. H. Snow	Providence, R. I	June 15, 1869	91, 376
Gas-regulator for nitrous-oxide apparatus, Mercurial.	J. B. Coolidge	Boston, Mass	Nov. 23, 1869	97, 051
Gas-regulator for railway-cars	A. H. Phillippi	Reading, Pa	July 31, 1860	29, 401
Gas-regulator, Stop-cock	O. L. Lawson and A. A. Starr	New York, N. Y	Aug. 4, 1857	17, 936
Gas-retort	W. P. Battey and W. N. Taylor	Utica, N. Y., and Philadelphia, Pa.	Aug. 5, 1862	36, 065
Gas-retort	W. Beaumont	Paterson, N. J	June 28, 1859	24, 531
Gas-retort	H. P. M. Birkinbine	Philadelphia, Pa	Apr. 17, 1855	12, 711
Gas-retort	J. Butler	New York, N. Y	Mar. 5, 1872	124, 250
Gas-retort	J. Butler	New York, N. Y	Aug. 27, 1872	130, 842
Gas-retort	M. L. Callender	New York, N. Y	Dec. 8, 1868	84, 679
Gas-retort	S. Coates	New York, N. Y	Sept. 8, 1857	18, 134
Gas-retort	C. M. Cresson	Philadelphia, Pa	Oct. 3, 1854	11, 742
Gas-retort	J. Davis and S. Chaddock	Boston, Mass	Feb. 14, 1860	27, 113
Gas-retort	D. Davison	New York, N. Y	Oct. 4, 1870	108, 009
Gas-retort	D. Davison	New York, N. Y	Mar. 14, 1871	112, 557
Gas-retort	D. Davison	New York, N. Y	Aug. 1, 1871	117, 610
Gas-retort	D. Davison	New York, N. Y	Oct. 14, 1873	143, 675
Gas-retort	E. Duffee	Haverhill, Mass	Feb. 27, 1866	52, 929
Gas-retort	H. H. Edgerton	Fort Wayne, Ind	Oct. 3, 1871	119, 586
Gas-retort	J. M. Gallacher	Roxbury, Mass	Apr. 30, 1861	32, 219
Gas-retort	J. Green	Saint Louis, Mo	July 16, 1872	129, 276
Gas-retort	R. C. Harrington	Newark, N. J	Mar. 20, 1860	27, 543
Gas-retort	G. W. Harris	Elizabeth, N. J	Dec. 4, 1866	60, 183
Gas-retort	G. W. Harris	Elizabeth, N. J	Mar 14, 1871	112, 593
Gas-retort	J. D. Higgins	Rome, N. Y	Sept. 12, 1871	118, 936
Gas-retort	J. J. Holden and S. J. Best	London, England	Dec. 3, 1867	71, 617
Gas-retort	A. S. King	Commerce, Mich	Feb. 4, 1862	34, 333
Gas-retort	W. H. Lauback	Philadelphia, Pa	Dec. 28, 1858	22, 434
Gas-retort	A. Marsh	Detroit, Mich	Aug. 10, 1858	21, 169
Gas-retort	A. Marsh	Detroit, Mich	May 17, 1859	24, 038
Gas-retort	E. D. McCracken	New York, N. Y	July 11, 1870	105, 350
Gas-retort	G. A. McIlhenny	Washington, D. C	Dec. 16, 1873	145, 672
Gas-retort	M. I. Miller	Saint Louis, Mo	Feb. 17, 1857	16, 651
Gas-retort	J. D. Patton	Trevorton, Pa	June 3, 1873	139, 605
Gas-retort	J. Rigby and P. A. Palmer	Marietta, Ohio	June 7, 1870	103, 929
Gas-retort	C. A. Robbe	Augusta, Ga	Aug. 9, 1859	25, 046
Gas-retort	W. A. Simonds	Chelsea, Mass	June 1, 1858	20, 448
Gas-retort	I. T. Sloan, V. Smith, M. Hoover, and R. M. Briggs.	Jackson, Cal	May 25, 1858	20, 375
Gas-retort	J. H. Smith	Newark, Ohio	May 16, 1871	114, 872
Gas-retort	J. W. Smith	Washington, D. C	June 21, 1859	24, 524
Gas-retort	T. G. Springer	Fayette City, Pa	May 28, 1872	127, 381
Gas-retort	W. Stratton	Philadelphia, Pa	July 5, 1859	24, 670
Gas-retort	H. K. Symmes	Newton, Mass	Aug 16, 1859	25, 225
Gas-retort	J. C. Tiffany	Boston, Mass	Aug. 13, 1872	130, 453
Gas-retort	J. C. Tiffany	Portsmouth, N. H	Dec. 2, 1873	145, 256
Gas-retort	A. K. Tupper	Pontiac, Mich	July 9, 1861	32, 802
Gas-retort	A. K. Tupper	Pontiac, Mich	Dec. 10, 1861	33, 921
Gas-retort	C. N. Tyler	Washington, D. C	June 22, 1858	20, 671
Gas-retort	E. Walcott	Providence, R. I	June 21, 1859	24, 510

Index of patents issued from the United States Patent Office from 1790 *to* 1873, *inclusive*—Continued.

Invention.	Inventor.	Residence.	Date.	No.
Gas-retort	J. H. Walker and J. Walker	Milwaukee, Wis., and South Bend, Ind.	Dec. 10, 1872	133, 731
Gas-retort	S. H. and M. C. Walker	Boston, Mass	Apr. 9, 1861	32, 019
Gas-retort	D. L. Weatherhead	Philadelphia, Pa	Mar. 29, 1859	23, 433
Gas-retort	C. Wooster	New York, N. Y	May 22, 1860	28, 431
Gas-retort	J. Wotherspoon and W. Foulis	Glasgow, North Britain	Dec. 2, 1873	145, 267
Gas-retort and apparatus for charging	L. F. Blair	Painesville, Ohio	May 28, 1872	127, 144
Gas-retort and heating-furnace	G. H. Pond	Rutland, Vt	Dec. 27, 1870	110, 496
Gas-retort benches, Arrangement of	J. G. Hock	Newark, N. J	June 3, 1856	15, 010
Gas-retort charger	T. F. Rowland	Green Point, N. Y	Apr. 1, 1873	137, 487
Gas-retort charges, Apparatus for filling	T. F. Rowland	Brooklyn, N. Y	Dec. 31, 1872	134, 399
Gas-retort, Clay	J. P. Kennedy	Trenton, N. J	Mar. 13, 1860	27, 451
Gas-retort cleaner	S. H. and M. C. Walker	Lancaster, Pa	May 20, 1856	14, 934
Gas-retort closings	G. A. McIlhenney	Washington, D. C	Apr. 8, 1873	137, 704
Gas-retort, Composite	J. Cochrane	New York, N. Y	Sept. 14, 1869	94, 714
Gas-retort cover	A. F. Havens	Brooklyn, N. Y	Dec. 26, 1871	122, 250
Gas-retort fastening	J. G. Hock	Newark, N. J	May 20, 1856	14, 913
Gas-retort fastening, Copper-ring	W. H. St. John	New York, N. Y	Nov. 11, 1856	16, 075
Gas, Retort for generating	J. H. Irwin	Chicago, Ill	Sept. 11, 1866	57, 915
Gas, Retort for generating	W. H. Laubach	Philadelphia, Pa	June 15, 1858	20, 567
Gas, Retort for the manufacture of coal	W. J. Cochran	Baltimore, Md	June 1, 1869	90, 819
Gas, Retort for the manufacture of illuminating	A. Millochau	New York, N. Y	Dec. 18, 1866	60, 537
Gas-retort furnace	W. C. Wren	Brooklyn, N. Y	Apr. 15, 1873	137, 811
Gas-retort mouth-piece	P. Munzinger	Philadelphia, Pa	Nov. 25, 1873	144, 857
Gas-retort mouth-piece	T. F. Rowland	Brooklyn, N. Y	Oct. 28, 1873	143, 998
Gas-retort, Portable	J. W. Smith	Washington, D. C	Mar. 16, 1858	19, 655
Gas-retort, Portable	D. L. Weatherhead and J. T. Henry	Philadelphia, Pa	Apr. 6, 1858	19, 900
Gas-retorts, Air-tight joint for	C. F. Dieterich and A. Schüssler	New York, N. Y	June 6, 1871	115, 586
Gas-retorts, Air-tight joint for	C. F. Dieterich and A. Schüssler	New York, N. Y	June 18, 1872	127, 965
Gas-retorts and other like purposes, Apparatus for charging and drawing	S. J. Best and J. J. Holden	London, England	Jan. 15, 1867	61, 144
Gas-retorts, Apparatus for charging	A. F. Havens	Brooklyn, N. Y	Dec. 17, 1872	134, 055
Gas-retorts, Apparatus for charging	A. F. Havens	Brooklyn, N. Y	Dec. 17, 1872	134, 056
Gas-retorts, Apparatus for charging	A. F. Havens	Brooklyn, N. Y	July 8, 1873	140, 624
Gas-retorts, Apparatus for charging	T. F. Rowland	Green Point, N. Y	Apr. 1, 1873	137, 485
Gas-retorts, Apparatus for charging	J. F. Snediker and W. F. Bailey	Bristol, Pa	Mar. 10, 1868	75, 308
Gas-retorts, Apparatus for charging	J. Somerville and J. Robinson	Dublin, Ireland	Sept. 23, 1873	143, 039
Gas-retorts, Apparatus for charging and discharging	J. J. Holden	Bermondsey, England	May 9, 1871	114, 682
Gas-retorts, Apparatus for charging and drawing	W. Foulis	Glasgow, North Britain	Nov. 11, 1873	144, 526
Gas-retorts, Apparatus for raking	T. F. Rowland	Green Point, N. Y	Apr. 1, 1873	137, 486
Gas-retorts, Binder for closing	A. Fulton	Albany, N. Y	May 18, 1869	90, 102
Gas-retorts, Casting	A. Pevey	Lowell, Mass	Dec. 22, 1857	18, 926
Gas-retorts, Casting	A. Pevey	Lowell, Mass	Apr. 15, 1862	34, 980
Gas-retorts, Cleaning	C. A. Bush	New London, Conn	Oct. 26, 1869	96, 197
Gas-retorts, Cleaning	S. W. Carpenter	Yonkers, N. Y	Dec. 1, 1857	18, 791
Gas retorts, Closing	N. Aubin	Albany, N. Y	Apr. 21, 1857	17, 068
Gas-retorts, Closing	G. A. McIlhenney	Washington, D. C	Aug. 26, 1873	142, 253
Gas-retorts, Coating	A. R. Terry	Detroit, Mich	June 20, 1854	11, 142
Gas-retorts, Composition for luting	J. Chilcott	Brooklyn, N. Y	Aug. 30, 1864	43, 970
Gas-retorts, Compound for	G. F. Kreischer and L. A. Tartiere	New York, N. Y	Apr. 15, 1873	137, 934
Gas-retorts, Compound for cleaning	W. L. Pitkin and C. J. Gleason	Montpelier, Vt	July 8, 1873	140, 590
Gas-retorts, Cover for	B. H. Bartol	Philadelphia, Pa	July 9, 1867	66, 444
Gas-retorts, &c., Enameling	D. W. Clark	Chicago, Ill	May 16, 1871	114, 763
Gas-retorts, Feeding-apparatus for	N. Aubin	Albany, N. Y	June 3, 1856	14, 996
Gas-retorts, Feeding hydrocarbon liquids to hot	T. G. Springer	Saint Louis, Mo	Nov. 15, 1870	109, 264
Gas retorts, furnaces, &c., Cover or door for	W. Matthews and J. Moore	Philadelphia, Pa	Dec. 29, 1868	85, 463
Gas-retorts, Machine for charging	T. F. Rowland	Green Point, N. Y	Sept. 24, 1872	131, 564
Gas-retorts, Machine for charging	N. O. J. Tisdale	New Orleans, La	Aug. 24, 1869	94, 045
Gas-retorts, Machine for making fire-clay	J. S. Heartt and S. English	Troy, N. Y	Oct. 29, 1861	33, 623
Gas-retorts, Method of preventing deposition of carbon in	A. Marsh	Detroit, Mich	Oct. 11, 1859	25, 790
Gas-retorts, Method of removing carbon from	J. A. Bassett and O. C. Smith	Salem, Mass	July 28, 1868	80, 438
Gas-retorts, Method of removing carbon from	B. E. Chollar	Leavenworth, Kans	Oct. 29, 1867	70, 166
Gas-retorts, Method of removing incrustation from	A. J. White	New York, N. Y	Aug. 8, 1865	49, 329
Gas-retorts, Mode of constructing head, neck, and connection of	J. Chilcott	Brooklyn, N. Y	Aug. 8, 1865	49, 231
Gas-retorts, Mode of securing lid on	J. R. Thomas	Williamsburgh, N. Y	May 29, 1860	28, 519
Gas-retorts, Securing lids to	S. Holman	London, England	Aug. 1, 1871	117, 631
Gas-retorts, Setting	T. Curley	Wilmington, Del	May 31, 1870	103, 579
Gas-retorts, Setting	A. Weber	New York, N. Y	Aug. 5, 1862	36, 119
Gas-retorts, Stand-pipe of	M. Combs, jr	Youngstown, Ohio	Nov. 28, 1871	121, 276
Gas-retorts with liquids, Device for supplying	E. L. Norfolk	Salem, Mass	Sept. 22, 1863	40, 058
Gas-seal, &c	R. M. Caffall	Alton, England	Nov. 11, 1873	144, 504
Gas service-pipes for automatically cutting off the gas in case of fire, Attachment to	W. Humphreys	Waterford, N. Y	Apr. 25, 1871	114, 144
Gas-socket	G. Mooney	Providence, R. I	Dec. 15, 1868	84, 961
Gas-socket	T. L. Reed	Providence, R. I	Jan. 7, 1868	73, 040
Gas-stand, Portable	B. Allen and J. Riddell	Boston, Mass	June 12, 1866	55, 447
Gas, steam, and fluid regulator	E. C. Maldant	Paris, France	Mar. 9, 1869	87, 575
Gas, steam, &c., Method of drawing from manufacturing inclosures waste	R. F. Brower	Bloomfield, N. J	Sept. 9, 1856	15, 716
Gas stopper or cork	N. D. Whitin	New York	Apr. 29, 1842	2, 593
Gas-tar and ammoniacal liquors, Apparatus for separating	E. D. McCracken	New York, N. Y	Oct. 18, 1870	108, 499
Gas-tar, Apparatus for burning	A. Smith	Niagara Falls, N. Y	Sept. 2, 1873	142, 357
Gas through pipes, Mode of facilitating the flow of illuminating	J. F. Russell	Washington, D. C	Oct. 29, 1867	70, 365
Gas to be used for motive-power, Process of generating	D. E. Somes	Washington, D. C	Apr. 3, 1866	53, 695
Gas-torch	W. A. Lawton	New York, N. Y	Feb. 4, 1868	74, 009
Gas-tube	E. L. Perry	New York, N. Y	Apr. 28, 1868	77, 314
Gas-tube, Extension	C. Monson	New Haven, Conn	Sept. 8, 1857	18, 154
Gas-tube, Flexible	J. Butler	Brooklyn, N. Y	June 12, 1860	28, 647
Gas-tube for chandelier, Extensible	H. L. McAvoy	Baltimore, Md	Feb. 22, 1870	100, 171
Gas-tube joint	C. Monson	New Haven, Conn	Jan. 19, 1858	19, 150
Gas-tube support, Flexible	A. Housinger	Chicago, Ill	Mar. 26, 1872	124, 897

Index of patents issued from the United States Patent Office from 1790 *to* 1873, *inclusive*—Continued.

Invention.	Inventor.	Residence.	Date.	No.
Gas-tubes, Flexible joint for	A. Stratton	Brooklyn, N. Y	July 10, 1860	29, 113
Gas-tubes, Manufacture of flexible	T. J. Mayall	Roxbury, Mass	Sept. 4, 1860	29, 898
Gas-tubing, Flexible	A. W. Hale	New York, N. Y	July 16, 1872	129, 405
Gas-tubing, Manufacture of flexible	G. L. Burnham	Providence, R. I	Dec. 3, 1872	133, 500
Gas, water, &c., Machine for making laminated pipes for.	J. S. Patric	Rochester, N. Y	May 13, 1873	138, 814
Gas with vapor of hydrocarbon liquids, Charging	C. M. Williams	New York, N. Y	Nov. 3, 1868	83, 748
Gas-works, Apparatus for regulating the exhauster in.	J. A. Harris	Philadelphia, Pa	Mar. 26, 1867	63, 155
Gas-works, By-pass for	P. Munzinger	Philadelphia, Pa	Nov. 11, 1873	144, 408
Gas-works, Center-seal for	P. Munzinger	Philadelphia, Pa	Nov. 22, 1870	109, 540
Gas-works, Center-seal for	P. Munzinger	Philadelphia, Pa	June 6, 1871	115, 632
Gas-works, Condensing-apparatus for	H. H. Edgerton	Fort Wayne, Ind	July 23, 1872	129, 723
Gas-works, Dip-pipe in hydraulic main for	J. Hannan	Gallipolis, Ohio	Apr. 16, 1872	125, 733
Gas-works, Exhaust-apparatus for	P. W. McKenzie	Blauveltville, N. Y	May 30, 1871	115, 334
Gas-works, Exhausting-apparatus for	S. R. Brick	Philadelphia, Pa	Mar. 29, 1870	101, 348
Gas-works, Hydraulic main for	P. T. Burtis	Chicago, Ill	Apr. 8, 1873	137, 655
Gas-works, Hydraulic main for	C. Collier	Selma, Ala	Oct. 17, 1871	119, 919
Gas-works, Hydraulic main for	W. Farmer	New York, N. Y	Jan. 14, 1873	134, 874
Gas-works, Hydraulic main for	J. R. Floyd and J. A. Sabbaton.	New York, N. Y	Apr. 21, 1868	76, 904
Gas-works, Mode of deodorizing the spent lime of	A. Millochau	New York, N. Y	Apr. 6, 1869	88, 658
Gas-works, Purifier, condenser, &c., for	A. Fulton	Albany, N. Y	Feb. 14, 1871	111, 737
Gas-works, Regulator for exhauster in	A. S. Cameron	New York, N. Y	Oct. 3, 1871	119, 505
Gas-works, Seal for dip-pipes in	W. Cartwright	Oswego, N. Y	Dec. 10, 1872	133, 756
Gas-works, Seal for dip-pipes in	G. Douty	Columbus, Ohio	Jan. 31, 1871	111, 439
Gas-works, Seal for dip-pipes in	G. Douty	Columbus, Ohio	Jan. 31, 1871	111, 440
Gas-works, Seal for dip-pipes in	A. F. Havens	Brooklyn, N. Y	Aug. 29, 1871	118, 608
Gas-works, Seal for hydraulic mains for	A. Odiorne	Springfield, Ill	June 6, 1871	115, 634
Gas-works, Seal for hydraulic mains of	S. Trumbore	Easton, Pa	Apr. 18, 1871	113, 946
Gas-works, Sealing and unsealing dip-pipes in hydraulic mains of.	W. E. Grenelle	New York, N. Y	Aug. 8, 1871	117, 880
Gas-works, Sealing dip-pipes of	H. H. Edgerton	Fort Wayne, Ind	Apr. 1, 1872	137, 425
Gas-works, Sealing dip-pipes of	E. Jones	Boston, Mass	Nov. 18, 1873	144, 619
Gas-works, &c., Superheater for	M. L. Callender	Brooklyn, N. Y	Oct. 18, 1870	108, 328
Gas-works, &c., Treating ammoniacal liquor of	H. H. Eames and C. J. Eames	Philadelphia, Pa., and New York, N. Y.	Oct. 15, 1872	132, 264
Gasalier	J. W. Kerr	Pittsburgh, Pa	May 22, 1860	28, 377
Gasalier	J. H. Seaman	Brooklyn, N. Y	June 27, 1871	116, 358
Gasalier	J. H. Seaman	Brooklyn, N. Y	June 27, 1871	116, 359
Gasalier	J. H. Seaman	Brooklyn, N. Y	June 27, 1871	116, 360
Gasalier and cigar-lighter combined	W. C. Lester	New York, N. Y	Nov. 13, 1866	59, 617
Gasalier drop-light	J. Horton	New York, N. Y	Jan. 16, 1872	122, 721
Gasalier extension	L. Hull	Charlestown, Mass	Oct. 21, 1873	143, 765
Gasalier-extension apparatus	L. Hull	Charlestown, Mass	Jan. 23, 1872	123, 022
Gasalier, Sliding center-light extension	S. B. H. Vance	New York, N. Y	Apr. 30, 1872	126, 241
Gasalier smoke-bell	C. Deans	New York, N. Y	Aug. 12, 1873	141, 634
Gasaliers and drop-lights, Means of suspending	S. B. H. Vance	New York, N. Y	Nov. 5, 1867	70, 653
Gaseous bodies, Machinery for compressing	W. A. Royce	Newburgh, N. Y	May 26, 1857	17, 394
Gases, Apparatus for liquefying nitrous-oxide and other.	W. F. and W. A. Johnston	Brooklyn, N. Y	Nov. 14, 1871	120, 977
Gases, Apparatus for mixing	W. D. Parrish	Philadelphia, Pa	May 12, 1863	38, 499
Gases, Apparatus for naphthalizing	E. H. Ashcroft	Boston, Mass	June 5, 1860	28, 549
Gases for the purpose of elevating water, Method of applying heat to dilate.	J. W. Middleton	Philadelphia, Pa	Sept. 12, 1854	11, 671
Gases from furnaces, Collecting, separating, and purifying the.	J. H. Connelly and J. McLure	Wheeling, W. Va	May 31, 1870	103, 572
Gases from oils, Retort for generating	S. C. Salisbury	New York, N. Y	Apr. 24, 1866	54, 214
Gases from petroleum and water, Apparatus for producing and burning.	A. J. Griffin	Lowell, Mass	July 3, 1866	56, 143
Gases, &c., in furnaces, Apparatus for separating	W. D. Jones	Hagaman's Mills, N. Y	May 25, 1858	20, 351
Gases, Method of collecting and separating carbonic acid from mixtures of.	J. S. Baldwin	New York, N. Y	May 29, 1866	55, 038
Gases of smelting-furnaces, Apparatus for collecting the waste.	B. Branon and G. H. Baldwin	Sharon, Pa	June 29, 1869	92, 006
Gasoline for heating and illuminating, Vaporizing and burning.	H. Gilbert	Philadelphia, Pa	Feb. 12, 1867	61, 021
Gasometer	J. Bogardus	New York, N. Y	Oct. 7, 1834	....
Gasometer	J. Butler	New York, N. Y	Feb. 27, 1872	123, 977
Gasometer	J. E. Hobbs	North Berwick, Me	Jan. 26, 1869	86, 155
Gasometer	G. W. Kraft	Philadelphia, Pa	Oct. 26, 1858	21, 867
Gasometer	T. F. Rowland	Green Point, N. Y	Mar. 8, 1870	100, 559
Gasometer	H. B. Williams	Baltimore, Md	June 11, 1830	....
Gasometer or gas-holder	J. C. Tiffany	Portsmouth, N. H	Jan. 21, 1873	135, 172
Gasometer, Portable	J. H. Hayward	New York, N. Y	Mar. 29, 1864	42, 085
Gasometer, Portable	J. H. Hayward	New York, N. Y	Aug. 10, 1869	93, 435
Gasometers, Method of counterpoising	P. T. Burtis	Chicago, Ill	July 27, 1858	20, 988

Gate:

See Approach-opening gate.
Automatic gate.
Balance-gate.
Bridge-gate.
Bridge turning gate.
Canal-lock gate.
Cattle-gate.
Change-gate.
Chute-gate.
Double gate.
Double sliding gate.
Elastic gate.
Farm-gate.
Fence-gate.
Field-gate.
Flexible gate.
Flood-gate.
Fluid-gate.
Folding gate.
Grain-gate.
Hanging gate.
Hatchway safety-gate.
Molasses-gate.
Molder's gate.
Nursery-gate.
Operating-gate.
Railway-gate.
Railway cattle-gate.
Railway-crossing gate.
Rising gate.
Road-gate.
Safety-gate.
Saw-mill gate.
Self-acting gate.
Self-operating gate.
Sliding gate.
Sliding and swing-ing gate.
Sluice-gate.

Index of patents issued from the United States Patent Office from 1790 *to* 1873, *inclusive*—Continued.

Invention.	Inventor.	Residence.	Date.	No.
Gate—Continued. *See* Snow-gate. Stock guard-gate. Suspension-gate. Swing-bridge gate. Swinging gate. Tilting gate. Turbine-gate. Turbine-motor gate. Turnpike-gate. Wagon end-gate. Waste-gate. Water-gate. Water-wheel gate.				
Gate	P. M. Ackerman	Webster, N. Y	Oct. 9, 1866	58, 566
Gate	P. M. Ackerman	Webster, N. Y	June 4, 1867	65, 326
Gate	H. Adams	Seattle, Wash	Oct. 23, 1866	58, 965
Gate	J. Adams	Pontiac, Mich	May 5, 1868	77, 564
Gate	R. Adams	Ottawa, Ill	Jan. 14, 1868	73, 277
Gate	J. B. Alexander	Washington, D. C	June 4, 1867	65, 327
Gate	W. J. Alexander	Rolling Prairie, Ind	Dec. 3, 1867	71, 675
Gate	S. S. Allen	Belvidere, N. Y	Jan. 5, 1869	85, 555
Gate	S. Allington	West Dresden, N. Y	Oct. 5, 1858	21, 645
Gate	T. Andrews	Warren, Wis	Aug. 30, 1870	106, 763
Gate	S. E. Anthony	Stillwater, N. Y	Apr. 2, 1867	63, 455
Gate	W. D. and W. I. Armstrong	Harlem, Ill	Apr. 9, 1867	63, 687
Gate	W. I. Armstrong	Rockford, Ill	Aug. 21, 1866	57, 432
Gate	J. Atkins	Mokena, Ill	Feb. 4, 1868	74, 034
Gate	V. Babcock	Marshall, Mich	July 31, 1866	56, 693
Gate	D. B. Baker	Rollerville, Ohio	May 8, 1866	54, 641
Gate	D. D. Baker	West Alexandria, Ohio	June 25, 1867	66, 113
Gate	G. E. Baker	Waukegan, Ill	July 24, 1860	29, 234
Gate	F. Ball	Cleona, Iowa	Mar. 28, 1865	46, 985
Gate	H. F. Balschmiter	Davenport, Iowa	Sept. 10, 1867	68, 684
Gate	H. Barber	Milpitas, Cal	Feb. 19, 1861	31, 435
Gate	J. F. Barrow	Baltimore, Md	Sept. 17, 1872	131, 417
Gate	U. N. Beardsley	Goshen, Ind	July 16, 1867	66, 778
Gate	A. Becraft	Jacksonville, Ill	Apr. 5, 1870	101, 570
Gate	J. Behel	Rockford, Ill	Apr. 13, 1869	88, 770
Gate	J. S. Benedict	Bedford, Ohio	Sept. 19, 1871	119, 110
Gate	I. C. Bennett	Clinton, Ill	Jan. 18, 1870	98, 841
Gate	J. H. H. Bennett	Hunt's Hollow, N. Y	Oct. 23, 1860	30, 460
Gate	E. L. Bergstresser	Sunbury, Pa	Jan. 1, 1867	60, 828
Gate	A. H. Betts	Cleveland, Ohio	Nov. 14, 1871	120, 932
Gate	J. Bickhart	Harlan, Ind	Dec. 9, 1862	37, 083
Gate	G. W. Bishop	Stamford, Conn	Mar. 3, 1868	75, 116
Gate	J. Blinn	Rockford, Ill	Feb. 4, 1873	135, 463
Gate	A. Blood, sr	Janesville, Wis	Nov. 22, 1864	45, 132
Gate	F. F. Blood	Janesville, Wis	Dec. 15, 1863	40, 902
Gate	C. S. Bonney	Syracuse, N. Y	Feb. 15, 1870	99, 822
Gate	A. T. Boon	Galesburgh, Ill	Mar. 20, 1866	53, 263
Gate	D. Bordner	Canton, Ohio	Apr. 30, 1867	64, 190
Gate	R. A. Boulware	Doniphan, Kans	Feb. 6, 1872	123, 447
Gate	G. C. Bovey	Cincinnati, Ohio	Oct. 31, 1871	120, 484
Gate	J. Bowers	Clinton, Wis	Mar. 10, 1868	75, 356
Gate	R. T. Bowne	Fallston, Md	Apr. 25, 1871	114, 101
Gate	C. D. Brewer	Williamsport, Pa	May 18, 1869	90, 074
Gate	J. R. Brisel	Middletown, N. Y	Jan. 1, 1867	60, 678
Gate	L. D. Brooks	Syene, Wis	Apr. 13, 1869	88, 773
Gate	H. Brouse	Wellington, Ohio	May 21, 1872	126, 928
Gate	F. C. Brown and C. Allen	Palmyra, N. Y	May 25, 1869	90, 421
Gate	L. F. Brown	Keokuk, Iowa	Oct. 8, 1867	69, 535
Gate	R. T. Browne	Fallston, Md	Nov. 29, 1870	109, 713
Gate	E. and A. Buckman	Greenbush, N. Y	Dec. 8, 1868	84, 729
Gate	J. Budd	Pittsford, N. Y	Apr. 30, 1867	64, 193
Gate	J. A. Burchard	Beloit, Wis	May 21, 1867	64, 945
Gate	J. A. Burchard and R. Tattershall.	Beloit, Wis	June 23, 1868	79, 201
Gate	T. I. Burhyte	Fond du Lac, Wis	Mar. 19, 1867	63, 008
Gate	J. P. Butz and A. McFarland	Enterprise, Ind	May 19, 1868	77, 956
Gate	J. P. Cadman	Freeport, Ill	July 10, 1866	56, 174
Gate	S. W. Chamberlain	Three Oaks, Mich	Dec 20, 1859	26, 477
Gate	J. D. Chambers	Williamsport, Ind	June 21, 1870	104, 555
Gate	J. D. Chambers	Williamsport, Ind	June 21, 1870	104, 556
Gate	I. A. Clark	Marion, N. Y	Sept. 21, 1869	95, 083
Gate	B. Clough	Amherst, Ohio	Sept. 18, 1866	58, 218
Gate	D. M. Cochran and L. A. Hawkins.	Richmond, Ind	May 23, 1871	115, 167
Gate	R. Conway	Volga, Ind	Feb. 26, 1867	62, 396
Gate	R. R. Cool	Millen's Bay, N. Y	Mar. 1, 1864	41, 760
Gate	W. Cooley	Tafton, Wis	Nov. 19, 1867	70, 963
Gate	J. S Corbin	Ann Arbor, Mich	Nov. 17, 1863	40, 609
Gate	J. B Cottom	Dayton, Ohio	Mar. 28, 1871	113, 020
Gate	J. S. Covell	Salt River, Mich	Nov. 1, 1870	108, 764
Gate	W. H. Cowley	Cleveland, Ohio	Dec. 22, 1868	85, 072
Gate	H. B. Crandall	Brocton, N. Y	Jan. 31, 1871	111, 322
Gate	P. S. Crawford	Union, Ill	Mar. 21, 1871	112, 904
Gate	P. S. Crawford	Union, Ill	July 25, 1871	117, 263
Gate	D. Creighton	Vacaville, Cal	Nov. 7, 1871	120, 573
Gate	J. Curry	South Bend, Ind	Nov. 5, 1872	132, 809
Gate	G. G. Curtis	Rochester, N. V	Mar. 12, 1867	62, 735
Gate	A. Dambacher	New York, N. Y	July 16, 1872	129, 538
Gate	S. A. Darrach	Newburgh, N. Y	Oct. 3, 1871	119, 509
Gate	J. R. Davis	Covington, Ga	Nov. 16, 1869	96, 783
Gate	S. S. Davis	Edgerton, Wis	Oct. 13, 1868	83, 046
Gate	L. S. Deming	Newington, Conn	June 22, 1869	91, 723
Gate	D. A Denison	Troy, Mich	Apr. 2, 1867	63, 270
Gate	S M Denniston	Hudson, Wis	Oct. 8, 1867	69, 649
Gate	J. Dicnason	Vevay, Ind	June 4, 1867	65, 354
Gate	B. F. Dickey	Marshall Township, Mich.	May 10, 1870	102, 783
Gate	B. F. Dickey	Marshall, Mich	May 31, 1870	103, 583
Gate	A. J. Dimick	Berlinville, Ohio	Jan. 3, 1871	110, 750
Gate	A. O Divine	Cambria Mills, Mich	Apr. 30, 1867	64, 289
Gate	C. Dixon and S. H. Close	Port Byron, N. Y	July 3, 1866	56, 019

Index of patents issued from the United States Patent Office from 1790 *to* 1873, *inclusive*—Continued.

Invention.	Inventor.	Residence.	Date.	No.
Gate	E. R. Dobbs	Poughkeepsie, N. Y	Apr. 9, 1867	63, 710
Gate	O. Dowd	Dansville, N. Y	Nov. 12, 1867	70, 819
Gate	W. R. Dugdale	Penn Township, Ind	July 9, 1867	66, 572
Gate	E. Duncan	West Milton, Ohio	Oct. 30, 1866	59, 196
Gate	R. R. Earnest	Springfield, Ohio	June 5, 1866	55, 259
Gate	C. Edgar	Dayton, Ohio	Sept. 10, 1872	131, 257
Gate	C. H. Eggleston	Marshall, Mich	Feb. 22, 1870	100, 129
Gate	S. Elliott	Richmond, Ind	Aug. 24, 1869	93, 977
Gate	T. Ellison	Abingdon, Ill	Mar. 15, 1870	100, 739
Gate	C. H. Embree	West Dresden, N. Y	Jan. 28, 1868	73, 704
Gate	S. F. Emerson	Seville, Ohio	July 17, 1866	56, 392
Gate	J. B. Erwin	Pittsburgh, Pa	Apr. 4, 1871	113, 282
Gate	L. Essig	Canton, Ohio	Jan. 14, 1868	73, 312
Gate	F. Ewer	Honeoye Falls, N. Y	Jan. 29, 1867	61, 526
Gate	B. H. Fairchild and E. Sadler	Farmington, Mich	June 4, 1867	65, 359
Gate	S. G. Farnham	East Hartford, Conn	Nov. 10, 1863	40, 557
Gate	J. Fausett	Leonardtown Md	Dec. 19, 1871	122, 003
Gate	D. E. Fenn	Tallmadge, Ohio	Aug. 28, 1860	29, 774
Gate	S. L. Fisher	Brimfield, Ill	Aug. 29, 1865	49, 615
Gate	B. F. Fisk	Fredonia Township, Mich	Apr. 27, 1869	89, 301
Gate	J. E. Fitts	Candia Village, N. H	Nov. 6, 1866	59, 378
Gate	G. C. Flagg	Tanktown, Ohio	Apr. 9, 1861	31, 965
Gate	D. Flint	Sacramento, Cal	Oct. 15, 1867	69, 788
Gate	W. G. Franklin	Shelbina, Mo	Jan. 24, 1871	111, 190
Gate	P. Freeman	Benton County, Iowa	June 12, 1866	55, 481
Gate	S. Fleet	Upper Strasburgh, Pa	Nov. 30, 1869	97, 288
Gate	F. Friedrich and C. H. Allen	Platteville, Wis	Apr. 23, 1872	125, 947
Gate	D. Fuller	Oakwood, Mich	Sept. 10, 1867	68, 726
Gate	A. Gaskill	Neoga, Ill	Jan. 16, 1872	122, 764
Gate	W. Gause and J. C. Curryer	Indianapolis and Thorntown, Ind.	Nov. 15, 1870	109, 198
Gate	E. Gemberling	Elkhart, Ind	Nov. 29, 1870	109, 609
Gate	R. Gidley	La Grange, N. Y	Dec. 24, 1867	72, 477
Gate	R. Gidley	La Grangeville, N. Y	Jan. 3, 1871	110, 646
Gate	R. Gidley	Moore's Mill, N. Y	July 25, 1871	117, 403
Gate	R. J. Gilbert	Hanover, Wis	Dec. 4, 1866	60, 171
Gate	R. J. Gilbert	Hanover, Wis	Oct. 1, 1867	69, 336
Gate	S. M. Gillett	Homer, N. Y	Sept. 12, 1865	49, 873
Gate	J. and W. B. Goff	Hornellsville, N. Y	Apr. 30, 1867	64, 303
Gate	W. H. Goodale	Colton, N. Y	July 13, 1869	92, 524
Gate	S. A. Gould	Aberdeen, Ind	Feb. 16, 1869	87, 040
Gate	G. S. Granger and W. Northop	Wayland, N. Y	May 28, 1867	65, 210
Gate	J. H. Graves	Rochester, N. Y	July 3, 1866	56, 039
Gate	I. J. Gray	Seville, Ohio	Nov. 20, 1866	59, 743
Gate	R. D. Green	Columbia, Mo	May 21, 1867	64, 860
Gate	W. W. Green, jr	Janesville, Wis	Sept. 15, 1868	82, 112
Gate	B. Greenside	Fort Dodge, Iowa	July 16, 1867	66, 832
Gate	A. L. Grinnell	Des Moines, Iowa	Jan. 9, 1866	51, 940
Gate	S. Grinnell, G. Bez, and H. C. Stoll.	Mokena, Ill	Sept. 5, 1865	49, 753
Gate	W. H. Griscom	Salem, N. J	Mar. 16, 1869	87, 841
Gate	I. H. Gustin	Middletown, Ind	July 5, 1870	105, 067
Gate	D. Hague	Balville Township, Ohio	Feb. 26, 1867	62, 412
Gate	U. W. Hardy	Abingdon, Ill	Dec. 29, 1868	85, 306
Gate	U. W. Hardy	Abingdon, Ill	Apr. 4, 1871	113, 294
Gate	J. H. Hardy	Penn Township, Pa	Sept. 13, 1870	107, 254
Gate	J. Harpster	Clyde, Ohio	Oct. 19, 1869	96, 002
Gate	N. Harrier	Muscatine, Iowa	June 29, 1869	91, 932
Gate	J. K. Harris	Springfield, Ohio	Jan. 24, 1871	111, 201
Gate	H. P. Haskin	Roscoe, Ill	Dec. 22, 1868	85, 091
Gate	H. P. Haskin	Roscoe, Ill	May 18, 1869	90, 261
Gate	H. R. Haskins	Harlan, Ind	Dec. 20, 1870	110, 363
Gate	R. Hatch, jr	Traverse City, Mich	Oct. 26, 1869	96, 106
Gate	W. Hathaway	Northbridge, Mass	Sept. 19, 1871	119, 141
Gate	C. P. Hawley and E. B. Murdock	East Galway, N. Y	July 17, 1866	56, 412
Gate	J. Hays	Fostoria, Ohio	Mar. 15, 1870	100, 759
Gate	B. S. Healy	Cohocton, N. Y	Sept. 4, 1866	57, 713
Gate	N. B. Helm	Aldin, Ill	May 21, 1872	126, 958
Gate	H. A. Henderson	Avoca, N. Y	Aug. 25, 1868	81, 501
Gate	S. Henry	Chenoa, Ill	Apr. 19, 1870	102, 003
Gate	L. Hermance	Hudson, N.Y	Oct. 15, 1867	69, 914
Gate	J. Hibbard	Prospect Lake, Mich	Feb. 5, 1867	61, 832
Gate	E. Hickman	Red Bluff, Cal	Dec. 2, 1873	145, 104
Gate	F. M. Hickman	Rolling Prairie, Ind	Mar. 31, 1868	76, 190
Gate	E. Higgins	Sacramento, Cal	July 25, 1871	117, 418
Gate	W. Holdredge	Oxford, N. Y	Apr. 30, 1867	64, 317
Gate	W. C. Hooker	Abingdon, Ill	June 2, 1868	78, 452
Gate	W. C. Hooker	Abingdon, Ill	Nov. 1, 1870	108, 786
Gate	J. J. and J. T. Hoss	Tipton County, Ind	Feb. 20, 1872	123, 802
Gate	H. A. House	Brooklyn, N. Y	Aug. 21, 1860	29, 696
Gate	R. H. Hudgin	Fairfield, Canada	Jan. 24, 1871	111, 124
Gate	R. H. Hudgin	Fairfield, Canada	Feb. 13, 1872	123, 700
Gate	R. H. Hudgin	Fairfield, Canada	July 2, 1872	128, 490
Gate	G. Hungerford	Union, Ill	July 23, 1872	129, 733
Gate	H. Hunt	Delavan, Wis	Dec. 24, 1867	72, 495
Gate	H. Hunt	Delavan, Wis	Apr. 21, 1868	76, 980
Gate	H. Hunt	Delavan, Wis	May 12, 1868	77, 735
Gate	J. H. Hunter	Versailles, Ind	Nov. 2, 1869	96, 436
Gate	A. B. Hurd	Watkins, N. Y	Apr. 23, 1867	64, 108
Gate	C. B. Huixthal and J. Lee	Bolivar, Ohio	Oct. 2, 1860	30, 223
Gate	J. L. Janeway	Flemington, N. J	Mar. 10, 1868	75, 276
Gate	J. L. Janeway	Flemington, N. J	Mar. 31, 1868	76, 081
Gate	H. J. Johnson	Saint Peter, Minn	Oct. 1, 1867	69, 443
Gate	J. Johnson	Geneseo, N. Y	Mar. 6, 1860	27, 397
Gate	S. S. Kappel	Woodhull, Ill	Nov. 6, 1866	59, 405
Gate	C. Kark	Huntington, Ohio	Aug. 27, 1867	68, 084
Gate	R. Kelly	Tuscola, Ill	Jan. 31, 1865	46, 112
Gate	E. Kemper	Thorn Township, Ohio	June 24, 1862	35, 689

Index of patents issued from the United States Patent Office from 1790 *to* 1873, *inclusive*—Continued.

Invention.	Inventor.	Residence.	Date.	No.
Gate	E. Kemper	Thornville, Ohio	July 16, 1867	66, 852
Gate	M. F. Kent	West Union, Iowa	Aug. 11, 1868	80, 969
Gate	S. Kepner	Pottstown, Pa	Oct. 4, 1870	108, 031
Gate	J. H. King	Smithfield, Ind	Sept. 15, 1868	82, 229
Gate	W. H. Kosht	Ashland, Ohio	July 25, 1871	117, 431
Gate	S. A. Kroner	Doylestown, Pa	Jan. 15, 1867	61, 215
Gate	A. Larrowe	Cohocton, N. Y	Nov. 6, 1866	59, 416
Gate	A. Larrowe	Cohocton, N. Y	May 21, 1867	64, 987
Gate	J. Lee	Massillon, Ohio	June 2, 1868	78, 598
Gate	W. Leonard	Orleans, Ind	Sept. 14, 1869	94, 900
Gate	F. Livings	East Enterprise, Ind	Oct. 18, 1870	108, 368
Gate	F. Livingston	Marathon, N. Y	Apr. 21, 1868	76, 930
Gate	M. E. Livingston	Manchester, Ill	Aug. 8, 1871	117, 901
Gate	J. C. Long	Eaton, Ind	Mar. 12, 1872	124, 600
Gate	N. Long	Muncie, Ind	June 20, 1871	116, 202
Gate	M. Loomis	Liberty Centre, Ohio	Dec. 9, 1873	145, 434
Gate	W. I. Ludlow	Cleveland, Ohio	Nov. 21, 1871	121, 181
Gate	C. Mack	Leipsic, Ohio	Oct. 1, 1867	69, 455
Gate	C. Mack	Leipsic, Ohio	July 6, 1869	92, 329
Gate	G. W. and G. S. Mackey	Lathrop, Pa	Nov. 18, 1873	144, 780
Gate	H. Mansfield	Warsaw, Ind	Sept. 24, 1867	69, 108
Gate	S. L. Marsden	New Haven, Conn	Apr. 6, 1869	88, 575
Gate	J. Martin	New Oxford, Pa	May 1, 1866	54, 381
Gate	J. W. Martin	Washington, D. C	Mar. 19, 1867	63, 067
Gate	M. Martin	Rockford, Ill	Dec. 26, 1871	122, 125
Gate	H. Z. Mast	Fork Meeting-House, Md	Dec. 10, 1872	133, 788
Gate	E. A. Matthiessen	Cornwall, N. Y	July 2, 1867	66, 368
Gate	C. F. Mawbey	Woodbridge, N. Y	Dec. 24, 1867	72, 657
Gate	H. Maxell	Canton, Ohio	June 5, 1866	55, 322
Gate	J. M. May	Janesville, Wis	Aug. 8, 1865	49, 286
Gate	J. M. May	Janesville, Wis	Dec. 17, 1867	72, 213
Gate	W. McAfee	Summerville, Mich	Aug. 21, 1860	29, 706
Gate	O. C. McCarty	Haysville, Ohio	Oct. 23, 1866	59, 045
Gate	P. McCollum	Fayette, Md	Nov. 10, 1868	83, 867
Gate	J McCreary	Middletown, Pa	May 7, 1867	64, 548
Gate	F. H. McGeorge	Corning, N. J	Dec. 14, 1869	97, 947
Gate	E. R. McKinney	Lacon, Ill	Apr. 30, 1867	64, 239
Gate	G. McKnight	Hebron, N. Y	Jan. 29, 1867	61, 676
Gate	J. H. McKnight	Oakwood, Mich	Sept. 1, 1868	81, 662
Gate	I. H. McOmber	El Paso, Ill	Sept. 3, 1867	68, 376
Gate	A. W. Meek	Waterloo City, Ind	Sept. 22, 1868	82, 336
Gate	J. L. Meredith	Bloomingsburgh, Ind	Apr. 25, 1871	114, 177
Gate	R. C. Mighell	Plano, Ill	Sept. 8, 1868	82, 021
Gate	L. Miller	Johnsville, Ohio	May 26, 1868	78, 389
Gate	P. L. Miller	Mechanicsburgh, Pa	May 7, 1867	64, 551
Gate	P. L. Miller	Mechanicsburgh, Pa	Mar. 17, 1868	75, 642
Gate	J. H. Morgan	Warsaw, Ind	Aug. 6, 1872	130, 306
Gate	J. D. Morrison	Richfield, Ill	Nov. 21, 1871	121, 188
Gate	G. Mott	Big Run, Ohio	June 13, 1871	115, 883
Gate	G. Mott, J. Morris, jr., and D. Lupton.	Big Run, Ohio	Sept. 14, 1869	94, 704
Gate	T. Munger	Cedar Falls, Iowa	July 16, 1867	66, 870
Gate	T. Munger	Jaynesville, Iowa	Nov. 26, 1867	71, 503
Gate	E. M. Naramore	North Underhill, Vt	Apr. 14, 1868	76, 800
Gate	M. Neudgent	Hartland, Mich	Jan. 12, 1869	85, 755
Gate	V. C. Newland	Sparta, Wis	Dec. 5, 1871	121, 654
Gate	W. E. Nichols	Baldwin, Mo	Aug. 18, 1868	81, 196
Gate	P. O'Neil	Murfreesborough, Tenn	Jan. 24, 1871	111, 238
Gate	H. S. Otis	Prescott, Wis	Jan. 5, 1869	85, 607
Gate	C. N. Owen	Salem, Ohio	Feb. 28, 1871	112, 174
Gate	M. Packard	Clarendon, N. Y	Oct. 23, 1866	59, 060
Gate	C. H. Paine	Providence, R. I	Apr. 16, 1867	63, 932
Gate	C. H. Paine	Providence, R. I	June 11, 1867	65, 591
Gate	B. F. Palmer	Baraboo, Wis	Apr. 4, 1871	113, 334
Gate	N. Parker	Trimble County, Ky	Mar. 21, 1871	112, 843
Gate	J. M. Peirce	Mokena, Ill	Apr. 28, 1863	38, 331
Gate	J. J. Pellett	Oconomowoc, Wis	Apr. 21, 1868	77, 088
Gate	W. A. Penny	Morrisville, N. C	Nov. 7, 1871	120, 770
Gate	O. and C. Perry	Ortonville, Mich	Feb. 18, 1868	74, 716
Gate	E. Petteys	Chestertown, N. Y	July 23, 1867	67, 135
Gate	E. Petteys and T. C. Leggett	Chestertown, N. Y	Dec. 18, 1866	60, 551
Gate	A. H. Phillips	Pontiac, Mich	Aug. 27, 1872	130, 938
Gate	W. H. Phillips	Staunton, Md	Mar. 19, 1872	124, 508
Gate	C. H. Platt	North Fairfield, Ohio	Dec. 31, 1867	72, 897
Gate	N. M. Platt	North Fairfield, Ohio	Dec. 22, 1868	85, 127
Gate	J. Pool	Elizabeth City, N. C	Feb. 7, 1871	111, 676
Gate	J. Potter	Pierceton, Ind	July 14, 1868	79, 857
Gate	J. B. Powell and S. H. Everett	Macedon, N. Y	June 25, 1867	66, 171
Gate	S. Puffer	Oxford, N. Y	Sept. 11, 1866	57, 967
Gate	C. Purdy	Bedford, Ohio	May 8, 1866	54, 596
Gate	H. R. Raub	Pymatuning, Pa	July 21, 1868	80, 220
Gate	F. Raymond	Cleveland, Ohio	Apr. 12, 1870	101, 765
Gate	F. Raymond and A. Miller	Cleveland, Ohio	Nov. 10, 1868	83, 881
Gate	C. D. Reed	Polo, Ill	Oct. 25, 1870	108, 628
Gate	S. Regan and E. Mensy	La Motte, Iowa	Oct. 11, 1870	108, 186
Gate	E. Reynolds	Metomen, Wis	Sept. 17, 1867	69, 024
Gate	W. W. Riley	Columbus, Ohio	Mar. 24, 1868	75, 792
Gate	J. F. Rodgers	South Bend, Ind	Oct. 27, 1868	83, 550
Gate	W. H. Rogers	Harlem, Ill	Jan. 7, 1868	73, 049
Gate	H. Root	Union City, Ind	Aug. 22, 1871	118, 393
Gate	E. Roth	New Oxford, Pa	Mar. 31, 1868	76, 251
Gate	E Roth and G. Shane	New Oxford, Pa	Apr. 23, 1867	64, 150
Gate	N. Rue	Harrodsburgh, Ky	Dec. 29, 1868	85, 479
Gate	C. W. Saladee	St. Catharine's, Canada	Feb. 14, 1871	111, 780
Gate	C. Saxton	Fredonia, Ohio	Dec. 21, 1869	98, 194
Gate	E. B. Scattergood	Saint John's, Mich	Feb. 23, 1869	87, 206
Gate	E. B. Scattergood	Saint John's, Mich	June 14, 1870	104, 210
Gate	M. Schneider	Rochester, Minn	Aug. 27, 1872	130, 946

Index of patents issued from the United States Patent Office from 1790 *to* 1873, *inclusive*—Continued.

Invention.	Inventor.	Residence.	Date.	No.
Gate	P. Schwebel	Quincy, Ill	Mar. 19, 1872	124, 858
Gate	L. M. Scothorn	Findley, Ohio	Nov. 5, 1867	70, 626
Gate	C. Seefeld	Lomira, Wis	Oct. 23, 1866	59, 084
Gate	W. Serviss	Sidney, Ohio	Oct. 1, 1867	69, 494
Gate	J. Shartle	Lima, Ind	Dec. 24, 1867	72, 549
Gate	C. Shepard	Binghamton, N. Y	Sept. 10, 1867	68, 658
Gate	F. R. Sherman	Dowagiac, Mich	Jan. 7, 1868	73, 129
Gate	L. W. Sibley	Ames, Iowa	June 22, 1869	91, 677
Gate	L. W. Sibley	Ames, Iowa	Jan. 24, 1871	111, 266
Gate	G. W. Sigerfoos, J. J. Sands, and G. Fry.	Potsdam, Ohio	Sept. 4, 1866	57, 782
Gate	S. H. Sill	Geneva, N. Y	May 8, 1860	28, 205
Gate	J. W. Singleton	Quincy, Ill	Jan. 1, 1867	60, 798
Gate	G. W. Sizer	Springvale, Wis	May 14, 1867	64, 802
Gate	G. A. Slater	Benton Harbor, Mich	Jan. 3, 1871	110, 687
Gate	L. and D. Slinger	Carmi, Ill	June 18, 1872	128, 183
Gate	J. A. Smith	Lacon, Ill	Sept. 29, 1868	82, 648
Gate	L. Smith	Easton, Mass	May 29, 1849	6, 488
Gate	S. Smith and A. Persels	Rockford, Ill., and Beloit, Wis.	Sept. 10, 1867	68, 801
Gate	W. B. Smith	Copper Creek, Ill	Dec. 10, 1872	133, 807
Gate	S. Smyth	East Bridgewater, Pa	Oct. 3, 1871	119, 661
Gate	J. Snell	Evans' Mills, N. Y	June 22, 1869	91, 783
Gate	B. Snyder	Clinton, Wis	Sept. 26, 1871	119, 421
Gate	W. W. Sowles	Manlius, N. Y	Apr. 13, 1869	88, 818
Gate	S. Spoor	Phelps, N. Y	Nov. 20, 1866	59, 930
Gate	S. Spoor	Phelps, N. Y	Dec. 11, 1866	60, 435
Gate	G. S. Spragg and G. Mott	Tabor, Iowa	Jan. 23, 1872	122, 973
Gate	G. P. Stebbins	Sparta Centre, Mich	Jan. 7, 1868	73, 206
Gate	E. Stevens	New Carlisle, Ind	June 25, 1872	128, 259
Gate	G. Stovel	Chicago, Ill	Mar. 21, 1865	46, 954
Gate	W. W. Sutliff	Town Line, Pa	Jan. 8, 1867	61, 115
Gate	J. M. Swift	Shelbyville, Ill	Sept. 10, 1867	68, 804
Gate	W. Tallman	Manteno, Ill	June 20, 1865	48, 322
Gate	A. Tandy	Columbia, Mo	Oct. 1, 1867	69, 509
Gate	R. Tattershall and J. A. Burchard.	Beloit, Wis	June 25, 1867	66, 108
Gate	T. D. Taylor	Hartleton, Pa	Dec. 3, 1872	133, 682
Gate	G. L. Templeton	Pierceton, Ind	Nov. 12, 1867	70, 762
Gate	J. W. Thompson	Greenfield, Mass	Dec. 10, 1867	72, 120
Gate	W. Tobey	Naples, N. Y	Sept. 14, 1858	21, 526
Gate	J. J. Tofflemire and J. D. Linnell.	Rockford, Ill	Sept. 20, 1870	107, 638
Gate	C. Trexler	La Grange, Ill	July 2, 1867	66, 421
Gate	G. W. Tucker	Elba Township, Ill	May 5, 1868	77, 682
Gate	I. C. Tunison and A. Reeve	Roodhouse and Pike County, Ill.	Sept. 3, 1872	131, 039
Gate	H. Turner	Ripon, Wis	July 2, 1867	66, 423
Gate	J. Vail	Beloit, Wis	May 21, 1867	64, 924
Gate	C. H. Van Eps	Farmington, Iowa	Apr. 2, 1867	63, 444
Gate	H. B. Van Voorhis	Pittsburgh, Pa	June 11, 1867	65, 619
Gate	W. B. Waldo	Johnsville, N. Y	Apr. 19, 1864	42, 422
Gate	W. S. Wandell	Battle Creek, Mich	Mar. 17, 1868	75, 607
Gate	H. M. Ward	Stone Church, N. Y	May 15, 1866	54, 796
Gate	D. R. Warfield	Muscatine, Iowa	Jan. 27, 1863	37, 536
Gate	D. R. Warfield	Muscatine, Iowa	Mar. 15, 1864	41, 951
Gate	N. Waterbury	Fond du Lac, Wis	Nov. 8, 1859	26, 063
Gate	S. H. Wheeler	Dowagiac, Mich	June 18, 1867	65, 974
Gate	E. B. Whitaker	Bel Air, Md	Dec. 17, 1872	133, 960
Gate	S. Whitman	Wayland, N. Y	Sept. 6, 1864	44, 132
Gate	A. D. Wilcox	Manlius, N. Y	Apr. 13, 1869	88, 828
Gate	T. P. Wilcox	Hebron, Ind	Apr. 9, 1872	125, 511
Gate	M. S. G. Wilde	Somerville, Mass	July 27, 1869	93, 027
Gate	S. P. Williams	Sheridan, N. Y	Mar. 23, 1869	88, 249
Gate	J. F. Winchell	Springfield, Ohio	Sept. 18, 1866	58, 161
Gate	J. Wineganer	Gratiot, Ohio	June 25, 1872	128, 269
Gate	G. Winteringer	Fredericktown, Ohio	Apr. 21, 1868	76, 963
Gate	D. D. Wisell	Zanesville, Ind	July 23, 1872	129, 702
Gate	H. S. Wolf	Rolling Prairie, Ind	Apr. 16, 1867	63, 974
Gate	E. R. Wolfe	Plymouth, Pa	July 23, 1867	67, 094
Gate	E. J. Wolfgang and J. M. Kenreigh.	Salem, Ohio	Mar. 23, 1869	88, 108
Gate	J. A. Wood	Crosswicks, N. J	June 27, 1871	116, 526
Gate	J. A. Wood and E. V. Marbaker.	Crosswicks, N. J	Dec. 7, 1869	97, 745
Gate	R. J. Wood	Hancock, Mich	Oct. 24, 1871	120, 358
Gate	S. G. Wood	Rochester, N. Y	Sept. 19, 1871	119, 101
Gate	J. Woodward	Wilmot, N. H	Oct. 28, 1862	36, 817
Gate	W. J. Wooster	Harvard, Ill	Sept. 3, 1872	131, 043
Gate	W. Worth	Jackson, Mich	Aug. 11, 1863	39, 520
Gate	C. Wright	Mason, Ill	Mar. 14, 1871	112, 762
Gate	J. Wright	Versailles, Ill	Nov. 29, 1870	109, 704
Gate	E. Young	Camden Centre, Mich	July 9, 1867	66, 663
Gate	I. N. Young	Swan, Ind	Dec. 31, 1867	72, 957
Gate, Adjustably-hinged	E. M. George	Three Rivers, Mich	Feb. 25, 1873	136, 149
Gate and barn-door fastening	E. Pea	Mechanicsburgh, Ill	Dec. 3, 1867	71, 636
Gate and door closing device	G. Turner	Lansing, Mich	Mar. 15, 1864	41, 948
Gate and door spring	J. Bliss	Cleveland, Ohio	Oct. 15, 1872	132, 133
Gate and door spring	A. T. Boon and L. Mills	Galesburgh, Ill	July 11, 1871	116, 800
Gate and door spring	J. C. Gould	Oxford, N. J	Nov. 26, 1867	71, 478
Gate and door spring	M. Harrington	Waupun, Wis	Nov. 22, 1870	109, 512
Gate and door spring	J. Palmer	Cincinnati, Ohio	July 16, 1872	129, 584
Gate and door spring	B. F. Whitaker	Whitestown, Ind	Mar. 10, 1868	75, 324
Gate and door swing	F. W. Kroeber	Forbestown, Cal	Oct. 9, 1860	30, 327
Gate and fence combined	J. W. Sanford	Bath, N. Y	Aug. 20, 1867	67, 915
Gate and gate post	G. W. Balding	Pleasant, Ind	Nov. 20, 1866	59, 753
Gate, Approach-opening	A. Iske and J. B. Erbe	Lancaster and Conestoga Township, Pa.	Aug. 9, 1859	25, 018
Gate, Approach-opening	J. S. Lloyd	Philadelphia, Pa	Sept. 20, 1859	25, 515

Index of patents issued from the United States Patent Office from 1790 *to* 1873, *inclusive*—Continued.

Invention.	Inventor.	Residence.	Date.	No.
Gate, Approach-opening	E. C. Rowland	Phelps, N. Y	Oct. 19, 1858	21, 851
Gate, Approach-opening	C. Winegar	Union Springs, N. Y	Dec. 7, 1858	22, 261
Gate-attachment	H. M. Long	Williamsville, N. Y	Dec. 29, 1868	85, 390
Gate-catch	W. W. Robinson	Ripon, Wis	Oct. 6, 1863	40, 187
Gate-closing device	W. Gilfillan	Syracuse, N. Y	Oct. 14, 1862	36, 647
Gate-closing device	L. Kolloff	Brooklyn, N. Y	Nov. 25, 1862	37, 001
Gate-fastener	J. H. Nichols	La Fayette, Ill	Dec. 9, 1873	145, 362
Gate-fastener	P. Philippi	Beardstown, Ill	Sept. 18, 1866	58, 130
Gate-fastener	H. S. Shisler	Manheim Township, Pa	May 11, 1869	89, 893
Gate-fastening	J. D. Bourne	De Witt, Iowa	Feb. 5, 1867	61, 800
Gate-fastening	W. Broomhall	Circleville, Ohio	Sept. 12, 1865	51, 417
Gate-fastening	J. Bull	Galesburgh, Ill	Dec. 3, 1867	71, 694
Gate-fastening	S. E. James	Smithfield Station Post-Office, Ohio.	Feb. 19, 1867	62, 136
Gate-fastening	J. C. Kellogg	Thorntown, Ill	Jan. 2, 1866	51, 838
Gate-fastening	W. Kimball	Salem, Ohio	Sept. 10, 1867	68, 752
Gate-fastening	H. Last	West Lebanon, Ind	Nov. 22, 1864	45, 162
Gate-fastening	R. A. Leeds	Stamford, Conn	Sept. 25, 1866	58, 268
Gate-fastening	J. Lintner	Indianapolis, Ind	May 31, 1870	103, 629
Gate-fastening	M. B. Markham	Grass Lake, Mich	Sept. 29, 1868	82, 537
Gate-fastening	G. McCoy	Antioch, Cal	Nov. 19, 1867	71, 195
Gate-fastening	C. Seymour	La Porte, Ind	Apr. 23, 1867	64, 153
Gate-fastening	J. P. Woodcock	Bedford, N. Y	Sept. 5, 1865	49, 819
Gate-fastening	S. Young	Milton, N. Y	Oct. 14, 1856	15, 911
Gate-flume	H. Frink	Chautauqua County, N. Y	Feb. 25, 1836	.....
Gate opening and closing apparatus	S. G. Dugdale	Richmond, Ind	Oct. 11, 1853	10, 105
Gate opening and closing apparatus	E. Woolman	Damascoville, Ohio	Dec. 2, 1851	8, 572
Gate opening and closing device	J. H. Nevin	Ogdensburgh, N. Y	Feb. 28, 1860	27, 304
Gate opening and closing device	C. Winegar	Union Springs, N. Y	Aug. 14, 1855	13, 445
Gate-operating device	D. G. Goodall	Beloit, Wis	Mar. 16, 1869	87, 839
Gate or door spring	J. W. Briggs	Cleveland, Ohio	Sept. 24, 1861	33, 332
Gate-post	A. Fishburn	Carlisle, Pa	Feb. 2, 1869	86, 383
Gate-post	G. O. Hutson	Iowa City, Iowa	Sept. 19, 1855	50, 005
Gate-post	W. F. Veber	Perrysburgh, Ohio	Mar. 3, 1868	75, 224
Gate-post attachable to any panel of its corresponding field-fence.	J. G. Hunt	Cincinnati, Ohio	Apr. 7, 1857	16, 978
Gate-post, Non-swagging	I. Johnson	Alliance, Ohio	Oct. 29, 1861	33, 590
Gate-post, Portable	W. A. Dillon	Middletown, Mo	Dec. 3, 1872	133, 571
Gate purchase, Labor-saving rotary	J. Musser and L. B. Gitchel	Canton, Ohio	Feb. 11, 1832	....
Gate-spring	W. W. Sutliff	Town Line, Pa	Nov. 19, 1867	71, 083
Gates and presses, Locking device for	W. Welch	Bridgeport, Conn	Sept. 3, 1867	68, 540
Gates, Arrangement of weight and pulley for closing.	W. Twitchell	Syracuse, N. Y	Aug. 7, 1849	6, 632
Gates, &c., Closing and opening	C. Winegar	Union Springs, N. Y	May 22, 1855	12, 930
Gates, Construction and hanging of	J. Healy	South Dansville, N. Y	Mar. 7, 1865	46, 667
Gates, doors, &c., Hanging	S. Oberholzer	Terre Hill, Pa	May 6, 1856	14, 826
Gates, &c., Hanging	N. W. Cilley	Nottingham Township, N. Y.	May 16, 1854	10, 928
Gates, Hanging	A. Hotchkin	Schenevus, N. Y	Mar. 7, 1854	10, 619
Gates, Hanging	T. S. Minniss	Meadville, Pa	Feb. 14, 1865	46, 377
Gates, Hanging and operating	T. Parkinson	Naples, N. Y	Aug. 6, 1850	7, 548
Gates, Hanging for	P. Rasar and D. J. Mayes	Illiopolis, Ill	July 28, 1868	80, 305
Gates, Opening	J. A. Ayres	Hartford, Conn	Feb. 8, 1859	22, 845
Gates, Opening	F. B. Betts	Brownhelm, Ohio	Mar. 29, 1859	23, 345
Gates, Opening and closing	B. R. Cole	Geneva, N. Y	Oct. 18, 1859	25, 808
Gates, Opening and closing	W. T. Merritt	Hart's Village, N. Y	Nov. 1, 1853	10, 199
Gates, Opening and closing	W. G. Philips	Newport, Del	Mar. 7, 1854	10, 593
Gates, Operating	J. L. Betts	Archbold, Ohio	Apr. 9, 1872	125, 375
Gathered fabrics	H. S. Brown	New York, N. Y	Aug. 23, 1864	43, 943
Gavel-fork	T. R. George	West Dryden, N. Y	Nov. 16, 1869	96, 794
Gavel-fork	B. Wright and W. C. Park	Cardiff, N. Y	Apr. 25, 1871	114, 080
Gear, Changing	W. M. Davis	Gardiner, Me	July 17, 1847	5, 192
Gear, Chill for casting toothed	R. T. Davis	Canton, Ohio	May 10, 1870	102, 781
Gear-cutter	C. Evotte	Paris, France	Mar. 16, 1869	87, 766
Gear-cutter	H. N. Keables	Worcester, Mass	July 2, 1867	66, 354
Gear-cutter	E. Parker	Middletown, Conn	July 3, 1866	56, 149
Gear-cutter	W. Sellers	Philadelphia, Pa	Feb. 1, 1870	99, 356
Gear-cutters, Machine for shaping and cutting	F. A. Pratt	Hartford, Conn	Mar. 7, 1871	112, 379
Gear-cutters, Making	L. F. Grant	Thomaston, Conn	July 17, 1866	56, 495
Gear-cutting	A. T. Boon	Galesburgh, Ill	Nov. 10, 1863	40, 550
Gear-cutting engine	H. Pfarrer	New York, N. Y	Oct. 11, 1859	25, 759
Gear-cutting machine	R. Cairns	Waterbury, Conn	Aug. 6, 1872	130, 188
Gear-cutting machine	J. W. Foster	Pawtucket, R. I	Mar. 4, 1873	136, 429
Gear-cutting machine	J. J. Greenough	Syracuse, N. Y	Jan. 28, 1873	135, 218
Gear-cutting machine	C. Van Haagen	Philadelphia, Pa	Dec. 20, 1870	110, 406
Gear-cutting machine, Adjustable scroll-index for	W. M. Galusha	Arlington, Vt	Apr. 14, 1868	76, 741
Gear-cutting tool	J. Harrington	New London, Conn	Sept. 22, 1868	82, 402
Gear-cutting tool	H. R. Taylor	Westport, Conn	Mar. 3, 1868	75, 219
Gear-cutting wheel	T. B. Russell	Salem, Mass	July 30, 1867	67, 219
Gear elevator, Differential	D. Hussey	Nashua, N. H	Nov. 17, 1868	84, 123
Gear for vehicles, Running	S. J. Edwards	New Berlin, N. Y	Nov. 19, 1867	70, 980
Gear for wagons, Front	A. Finley	Bainbridge, Ind	July 20, 1869	92, 948
Gear, Friction	F. Simmons	New Orleans, La	Apr. 29, 1873	138, 444
Gear, Friction driving	W. W. Tunis	Easton, Md	Jan. 14, 1873	134, 825
Gear, Machine for cutting teeth of beveled	G. H. Corliss	Providence, R. I	Mar 10, 1849	6, 161
Gear, Machine for cutting wood	T. F. Freeman	Brooklyn, N. Y	Oct. 29, 1867	70, 192
Gear, Machinery for cutting bevel	C. E. Roper	Canton, Ohio	Aug. 6, 1867	67, 587
Gear or pulley mechanism	A. M. Damon	Lowell, Mass	Feb. 1?, 1872	123, 618
Gear or universal joint, Spherical	T. Weaver	Harrisburgh, Pa	Dec. 2, 1873	145, 075
Gear power machine, Differential	H. F. Shaw	West Roxbury, Mass	Mar. 10, 1868	75, 304
Gear press, Power	W. and R. Skene	Louisville, Ky	June 28, 1859	24, 585
Gear, Proportional scales for the construction of toothed.	J. Walker	Philadelphia, Pa	Feb. 21, 1871	112, 097
Gear, Reversing	G. Juengst	New York, N. Y	Sept. 9, 1856	15, 697
Gear, Shifting	C. D. Rogers	Utica, N. Y	Jan. 10, 1865	45, 864
Gear, Spherical	T. Weaver	Harrisburgh, Pa	Aug. 1, 1871	117, 706
Gear, Universal bevel	J. Lewis	Burlington, Vt	Nov. 29, 1838	1, 025
Gear-wheel	W. H. Ward	Auburn, N. Y	May 24, 1870	103, 398

Index of patents issued from the United States Patent Office from 1790 *to* 1873, *inclusive*—Continued.

Invention.	Inventor.	Residence.	Date.	No.
Gear-wheel, Adjustable	W. H. Ward	Auburn, N. Y	Oct. 18, 1870	108, 539
Gear-wheel and pulley	G. I. Washburn	Worcester, Mass	Mar. 8, 1864	41, 896
Gear-wheel, Stop-motion	J. H. Whitney	Rochester, Minn	Nov. 8, 1870	109, 164
Gear-wheel teeth	J. Letzkus	Allegheny City, Pa	July 28, 1868	80, 291
Gear-wheels, Cutter for cutting	J. R. Brown	Providence, R. I	Nov. 29, 1864	45, 294
Gear-wheels, Cutting teeth of	G. W. Bigelow	New Haven, Conn	Nov. 20, 1855	13, 813
Gear-wheels, Manufacture of	J. Comly	Williamsburgh, N. Y	Nov. 12, 1872	132, 899
Gear-wheels, Molding	W. Rowell	New York, N. Y	Nov. 24, 1868	84, 305
Gear-wheels, Pattern for curved-tooth	R. Oliver	Buffalo, N. Y	Nov. 26, 1872	133, 384
Gear-worm	D. Harrigan and J. Whitney	Winchester, Mass	Jan. 7, 1868	73, 095
Gearing	B. Arnold	East Greenwich, R. I	Oct. 30, 1849	6, 821
Gearing	A. M. Beard	Hillsborough, N. H	Feb. 18, 1868	74, 488
Gearing	E. G. Chormann	Philadelphia, Pa	Jan. 7, 1873	134, 642
Gearing	P. D. Cummings	Portland, Me	June 5, 1860	28, 631
Gearing	F. Emmerich	New York, N. Y	July 8, 1873	140, 690
Gearing	G. P. Ganster	Reading, Pa	Nov. 23, 1858	22, 116
Gearing	E. A. Goodes	Philadelphia, Pa	Nov. 23, 1858	22, 118
Gearing	J. J. Greenough	Syracuse, N. Y	Dec. 16, 1873	145, 499
Gearing	S. W. and J. F. Palmer	Auburn, N. Y	May 8, 1866	54, 589
Gearing	A. Sibley	Pawtucket, R. I	July 7, 1868	79, 605
Gearing	H. M. Street	Denmark, Tenn	Aug. 14, 1860	29, 634
Gearing and self-adjusting shaft	G. B. Hamlin	Willimantic, Conn	Aug. 16, 1870	106, 360
Gearing and ungearing pinions and wheels	J. Skinner	Hadley, Mich	Feb. 28, 1871	112, 187
Gearing, Anti-friction	T. Chase	Washington, D. C	July 19, 1870	105, 426
Gearing, Belted friction	J. D. Whelpley	Boston, Mass	Apr. 3, 1866	53, 717
Gearing, Changeable	J. Evans and J. H. Thompson	Paterson, N. J	Apr. 24, 1847	5, 085
Gearing, Cog	J. A. Bazin	Canton, Mass	Aug. 22, 1854	11, 585
Gearing, Cog	L. R. Faught	Philadelphia, Pa	Oct. 3, 1871	119, 683
Gearing, Device for adjusting	G. S. Barton	Worcester, Mass	Apr. 6, 1869	88, 691
Gearing, Device for increasing the friction of helical.	G. Lindsay	Belfast, Ireland	July 22, 1873	141, 149
Gearing, Differential	W. D. Andrews	Brookhaven, N. Y	June 25, 1872	128, 352
Gearing, Differential wheel	C. F. Cooke and J. Standfield.	York and Lambeth, Great Britain.	Nov. 5, 1867	70, 416
Gearing, Driving	G. B. Hamlin	Willimantic, Conn	Apr. 12, 1870	101, 872
Gearing for connecting feed or pressure rollers	W. E. Cornell and C. W. Brown	Boston, Mass	July 17, 1847	5, 191
Gearing for driving agricultural machinery, Arrangement of.	T. Salisbury	Albion, Pa	Sept. 14, 1869	94, 844
Gearing for driving machinery	M. Young, jr	Frederick, Md	July 2, 1861	32, 733
Gearing for driving machinery, Arrangement of	J. Urmy	Wilmington, Del	Feb. 6, 1838	593
Gearing for grinding-rollers	W. E. Sibley	Weston, Mass	Mar. 13, 1866	53, 236
Gearing for twisting-apparatus, &c., Differential	J. and J. H. Webster	Boston, Mass	Mar. 25, 1873	137, 207
Gearing for machinery	S. P. Gary	Oshkosh, Wis	Dec. 16, 1862	37, 165
Gearing for machinery	T. M. Millet, sr	Savannah, Ga	Dec. 13, 1870	110, 151
Gearing for machinery	W. Webster	Jefferson County, Wash	June 22, 1858	20, 672
Gearing for machinery, Extension	H. P. Minot	Chicago, Ill	Dec. 24, 1872	134, 304
Gearing for machinery, Friction	F. P. Dimpfel	Philadelphia, Pa	Mar. 12, 1861	31, 659
Gearing, Frictional	D. H. Chamberlain	West Roxbury, Mass	Mar. 22, 1870	100, 977
Gearing, Gin	H. R. Easterling	Bennettsville, S. C	Jan. 30, 1872	123, 248
Gearing, Intermittent and expansive	L. B. Potter	Putnam, Conn	Oct. 23, 1866	59, 064
Gearing, Machine	R. J. Gatling	Indianapolis, Ind	Sept. 18, 1860	30, 059
Gearing, Machine	A. Hitchcock	New York, N. Y	Feb. 12, 1867	61, 938
Gearing, Mill	J. C. Cunningham	Oglethorpe, Ga	Nov. 19, 1867	70, 970
Gearing, Mill	J. H. Glover	Glasgow, Ky	Jan. 8, 1861	31, 078
Gearing, Mill	J. Shickel	Harrisonburgh, Va	Sept. 10, 1867	68, 799
Gearing, Mill	H. Shoemaker and J. A. McClintock.	Perry, Ill	Nov. 8, 1870	109, 063
Gearing, Mill	H. M. Smith	Peoria, Ill	June 28, 1870	104, 793
Gearing mills	C. Coleman	Barry's Bridge, Va	Aug. 27, 1835	....
Gearing, Mode of increasing, reducing, and communicating motion in machinery to be used as a substitute for cog.	F. S. Barnard	New York, N. Y	Sept. 10, 1839	1, 318
Gearing, Multiplying	F. Dibben and L. Bollman	New York, N. Y	Aug. 9, 1853	9, 914
Gearing, Pivot	J. J. Duchesne	Lacon, Ill	Dec. 10, 1867	72, 003
Gearing, Spiral	U. Haskins, jr	Pittsburgh, Pa	Mar. 17, 1868	75, 544
Gearing, Spur or bevel	C. Neer	Waterford, N. Y	Mar. 9, 1827	....
Gelatine-factories, Mode of recovering useful products from the waste liquor of.	F. Bihn and W. Schrader	Frankford, Pa	Dec. 15, 1868	84, 934
Gelatine from algæ, Manufacture of vegetable	W. J. Rand, jr	Brooklyn, N. Y	June 25, 1872	128, 248
Gelatine from bones, horn, pith, &c., Obtaining	N. B. Rice	East Saginaw, Mich	May 9, 1871	114, 602
Gelatine from fish-heads, Process of obtaining	B. Robinson	East Gloucester, Mass	May 19, 1868	78, 016
Gelatine from impure solution, Manufacture of	B. F. Shaw	Cambridge, Mass	Dec. 10, 1872	133, 896
Gelatine or glue, Treating liquors containing	O. Lugo	Baltimore, Md	Mar. 8, 1870	100, 647
Gelatine, Preparation of portable	P. Cooper	New York, N. Y	June 20, 1845	4, 084
Gelatine, tannin, and cellulose, Compound of	A. K. Eaton	Brooklyn, N. Y	July 16, 1872	129, 217
Gelatine, Treating marine plants to obtain	G. Bourgade	New York, N. Y	Mar. 14, 7871	112, 535
Genealogy, chronology, &c., Representing by lines	A. Bostwick	New York, N. Y	Aug. 2, 1826	....
Generating coal-oil, Apparatus for	W. T. Barnes	Buffalo, N. Y	Aug. 2, 1859	24, 921
Generator: *See* Acid-generator. Gas-generator. Hydrogen-generator Ozone-generator. Steam-generator. Steam and vapor generator. Vapor-generator.				
Geometrical interest-table	G. Cobb	Boston, Mass	Sept. 7, 1808	....
Geometrical interest-table	G. Cobb	Boston, Mass	Apr. 24, 1809	....
Geometrical lines, centers, &c., Machinist's instrument for determining.	R. B. Light	Dunkirk, N. Y	Apr. 9, 1861	31, 987
Geometrical lines, Instrument for drawing	W. Ritchie	Wilmington, Ill	Feb. 22, 1870	100, 072
Geometrical protractor and tablet	J. Pool, jr	Easton, Mass	June 16, 1830	....
Gib	A. H. Rhodes	Fall River, Mass	June 9, 1868	78, 761
Gib and self-oiler	C. B. White	Port Richmond, N. Y	July 28, 1868	80, 376
Gib for cross-heads	W. R. Bishop	Sherwood, Wis	July 3, 1866	55, 992
Gib, Self-lubricating	W. A. Devon	Port Richmond, N. Y	Nov. 19, 1867	71, 145
Gig for cloth	O. M. Stillman	Westerly, R. I	Feb. 11, 1868	74, 443
Gig-mill	E. Gessner	Aue, Saxony	May 21, 1867	64, 859
Gig-mill	R. Kershaw	Philadelphia, Pa	Dec. 24, 1861	34, 038
Gig-mill	J. C. Miller	Troy, N. Y	Sept. 23, 1862	36, 550
Gig-mill	J. Shaw	Manayunk, Pa	Aug. 28, 1860	29, 828

Index of patents issued from the United States Patent Office from 1790 to 1873, inclusive—Continued.

Invention.	Inventor.	Residence.	Date.	No.
Gig mold, Mackerel	G. Bassett	Taunton, Mass	Aug. 2, 1870	105, 887
Gig-tree	E. A. Cooper	Lancaster, N. Y	Apr. 3, 1866	53, 578
Gigs, phaetons, and other carriages, Fall-top of	J. Eberts	Philadelphia, Pa	Sept. 8, 1815	....
Gilding and ornamenting surfaces, Process of	M. W. Brown	New York, N. Y	Feb. 20, 1866	52, 673
Gilding and silvering mica and glass	W. M. Marshall	Philadelphia, Pa	Aug. 4, 1868	80, 754
Gilding, Apparatus for preparing elliptical frames for.	R. I. Marcher	New York, N. Y	Sept. 7, 1858	21, 430
Gilding, Compound for	A. L. D. Vries	Cleveland, Ohio	Apr. 9, 1872	125, 383
Gilding copper, brass, &c., Process for	G. R. Elkington	Birmingham, England	May 17, 1838	741
Gilding-machine	J. Lick	San Francisco, Cal	Apr. 6, 1869	88, 646
Gilding moldings, &c., Composition for	D. Wright	Boston, Mass	June 9, 1868	78, 780
Gilding on glass, Mode of protecting	P. V. Mathews	Philadelphia, Pa	Apr. 27, 1858	20, 078
Gilding or plating fibrous substances, Process for	A. Hock	Paris, France	Mar. 14, 1854	10, 637
Gilding preparations to oval frames, Device for applying.	D. Garrison	Philadelphia, Pa	June 1, 1869	90, 658
Gilding, Preparing frames for	J. W. Campbell	New York, N. Y	Aug. 10, 1858	21, 173
Gilding, Preparing oval frames for	L. Reinauer	Cincinnati, Ohio	Mar. 20, 1866	53, 338
Gilding, Processes of coloring tin, zinc, &c., to resemble.	J. Kintz	West Meriden, Conn	July 16, 1872	129, 284
Gilding, silvering, &c., in dead colors	D. Davis, jr	Boston, Mass	Mar. 21, 1843	3, 015
Gilt frames, Manufacture of partly	W. Wallick	Philadelphia, Pa	Dec. 28, 1869	98, 450
Gimlets, &c	W. M. Fowler	North Branford, Conn	Apr. 28, 1836	....
Gimlet	C. L. Griswold	Chester, Conn	Nov. 26, 1872	133, 440
Gimlet	E. L'Hommedieu	Chester, Conn	Mar. 10, 1836	627
Gimlet	A. Pell	New York, N. Y	Mar. 24, 1863	37, 973
Gimlet	C. C. Tolman	Shelburne Falls, Mass	Dec. 4, 1855	13, 897
Gimlet-handle	C. L. Griswold	Chester, Mass	Sept. 23, 1873	143, 142
Gimlet-handle	H. S. Shepardson	Shelburne, Mass	Aug. 12, 1873	141, 671
Gimlet-handle	G. H. Talbot	Boston, Mass	Oct. 14, 1856	15, 907
Gimlet-manufacturing	J. Mix	West Cheshire, Conn	Mar. 3, 1868	75, 182
Gimlet, Twisted screw	J. Broad	Salisbury, Conn	June 25, 1813	....
Gimlet-ventiduct	J. F. Peacock	Reno, Nev	Sept. 17, 1872	131, 408
Gimlets, Forging	D. Fowler	Wallingford, Conn	July 2, 1836	....
Gin-cordial called Hollands	A. Boucherie	Philadelphia, Pa	Jan. 31, 1809	....
Gin-feeder	J. Eubank, jr	Glasgow, Ky	July 29, 1828	....
Gin, Making	E. V. Freeman	....	Apr. 10, 1811	....
Ginger-snap and cracker making machine	J. McCollum and J. Parr	New York, N. Y	June 22, 1869	91, 759
Ginger-snap, &c., making machine	D. M. Holmes	Williamsburgh, N. Y	Aug. 25, 1868	81, 505
Girder	Z. S. Ayres	New York, N. Y	Oct. 24, 1871	120, 228
Girder	W. G. Cutler	Milwaukee, Wis	Nov. 26, 1872	133, 306
Girder	P. H. Jackson	New York, N. Y	May 7, 1872	126, 396
Girder bridge, Truss	D. Hammond and J. Abbott	Canton, Ohio	Apr. 26, 1870	102, 394
Girder for bridges, etc, Tubular-arch	D. Hammond and J. Abbott	Canton, Ohio	Apr. 26, 1870	102, 392
Girder, Iron	C. H. Latrobe	Baltimore, Md	Oct. 8, 1872	132, 087
Girder, Iron truss	J. W. Murphy	Philadelphia, Pa	May 8, 1860	28, 240
Girder, Trussed compound	J. A. Roebling	Trenton, N. J	Aug. 28, 1860	29, 825
Girder, Tubular-arch	D. Hammond and J. Abbott	Canton, Ohio	Apr. 26, 1870	102, 393
Girder, Wrought-iron	T. G. Gaylord	Cincinnati, Ohio	Mar. 16, 1858	19, 630
Girders, Apparatus for testing	P. H. Jackson	New York, N. Y	Jan. 7, 1873	134, 549
Girders, beams, &c., Homogeneous metals for casting.	W. F. Brooks	New York, N. Y	Aug. 22, 1871	118, 336
Girt	W. C. Hays and J. S. Pancake	Sharonville, Ohio	Aug. 29, 1871	118, 610
Glass: *See* Drinking-glass. Eye-glass. Jelly-glass. Looking-glass. Opera glass. Photographic monocular glass. Pier-glass. Spy-glass. Vault-glass. Wine-glass.				
Glass and in protecting the same, Silvering	H. B. Walker	New York, N. Y	Dec. 14, 1869	97, 838
Glass and "moils," Mode of removing metallic scale from.	W. P. Parrott and J. J. Bordman.	Boston, Mass	May 12, 1868	77, 834
Glass and other vessels, Metallic base for	G. C. White, jr	Brooklyn, N. Y	Aug. 17, 1869	93, 935
Glass and polishing metallic wares, Compound for cleaning.	H. P. Marquam	Harrisburgh, Pa	July 9, 1867	66, 509
Glass-annealing apparatus	G. F. Neal and L. Amede	South Boston, Mass	Apr. 30, 1867	64, 244
Glass, Apparatus for the manufacture of window	W. W. Pilkington	St. Helen's, England	Jan. 14, 1873	134, 926
Glass, Application of bronze and gilding to plate	E. Ingraham	Bristol, Conn	Apr. 18, 1871	113, 772
Glass articles, Manufacture of	C. A. Moore	Westbrook, Conn	Nov. 29, 1870	109, 646
Glass articles, Preparing surface of	W. A. Fischer	Allegheny, Pa	Apr. 16, 1872	125, 670
Glass articles, Process of forming orifices and necks on.	J. Wing	Boston, Mass	Oct. 21, 1873	143, 863
Glass-blowers, Chimney-tool for	J. G. Mustin	Pittsburgh, Pa	Nov. 18, 1873	144, 628
Glass-blower's mold	S. R. Bowie	New Bedford, Mass	Apr. 2, 1872	125, 165
Glass-blower's mold	S. R. Bowie	New Bedford, Mass	July 23, 1872	129, 709
Glass-blower's mold	O. P. Shinkle	Covington, Ky	May 8, 1866	54, 617
Glass-blower's molds, Machine for opening	D. Jarves	Boston, Mass	Feb. 2, 1821	....
Glass-blower's spring-clamp	T. Wightman	Pittsburgh, Pa	May 10, 1870	102, 899
Glass-blower's tool, Machine for holding	B. F. Turner	Bridgeton, N. J	June 4, 1872	127, 530
Glass-blowing apparatus	B. F. Cloud	Philadelphia, Pa	Apr. 20, 1869	89, 127
Glass-blowing machine	T. and J. P. Bakewell	Pittsburgh, Pa	Feb. 8, 1834	....
Glass-blowing machine	S. L. Fleishman	Pittsburgh, Pa	Sept. 16, 1873	142, 845
Glass-blowing machine	J. Laird	Pittsburgh, Pa	Dec. 14, 1832	....
Glass-blowing machine	J. Stouvenel and F. A. Martin	Philadelphia, Pa	Sept. 16, 1833	....
Glass-board and apparatus for cutting glass	F. Bowly	Winchester, Va	Mar. 9, 1869	87, 626
Glass by exposure to heat, Method of preventing the breaking of.	E. Thayer	Worcester, Mass	Aug. 1, 1865	49, 171
Glass case	E. D. Kimmey and C. Wright	Philadelphia, Pa	July 11, 1865	48, 693
Glass case	T. W. Whitly	Paterson, N. J	Apr. 21, 1836	....
Glass, Casting plate	E. Cossaboom	Lenox, Mass	Oct. 3, 1871	119, 451
Glass-cleaner	J. B. Dunlop	Meriden, Conn	Apr. 16, 1867	63, 870
Glass, Combination of molds in forming	G. and P. C. Dummer and J. Maxwell.	Jersey City, N. J	Oct. 16, 1827	....
Glass, Composition for writing on	W. Davidson	New York, N. Y	May 8, 1840	1, 588
Glass, Composition of	W. Price	Pittsburgh, Pa	Apr. 30, 1816	....
Glass-cutter	J. Collmann and H. Feenders	Freeport, Ill	Nov. 27, 1860	30, 722
Glass-cutter	P. Jennet	Meadville, Pa	Apr. 30, 1872	126, 302
Glass-cutter	M. Kleeman	Columbus, Ohio	Dec. 18, 1860	30, 973
Glass cutter and knife, Steel	T. Spenard	Coaticoke, Canada	Jan. 24, 1871	111, 269

Index of patents issued from the United States Patent Office from 1790 *to* 1873, *inclusive*—Continued.

Invention.	Inventor.	Residence.	Date.	No.
Glass-cutting, Graved rule and self-adjusting diamond for.	J. Dickinson	Brooklyn, N. Y	Oct. 1, 1861	33, 380
Glass-cutting machine	W. Vom Hofe	New York, N. Y	Dec. 31, 1872	134, 498
Glass-cutting machinery	J. P. Colné	New York, N. Y	Aug. 26, 1851	8, 323
Glass-cutting, polishing, dressing, and ornamenting machine.	T. J. W. Robertson	New York, N. Y	June 7, 1864	43, 042
Glass-cutting tool	S. G. Monce	Bristol, Conn	June 8, 1869	91, 150
Glass-decoration	W. Nielson	New York, N. Y	July 23, 1872	129, 856
Glass, Device for cutting	A. S. McClure	New Buffalo, Pa	Sept. 20, 1864	44, 331
Glass, Embellishment for	E. Ingraham	Bristol, Conn	Nov. 29, 1870	109, 626
Glass, Fire-polishing	J. S. Gilliland	Brooklyn, N. Y	Jan. 11, 1853	9, 533
Glass, Flattening	J. J. Adams	Washington, D. C	Apr. 21, 1832	....
Glass, Flattening and annealing	S Rickards	Philadelphia, Pa	Apr. 6, 1843	3, 035
Glass, Flattening and tempering window	J. J. Adams	Winslow N. J	Oct. 17, 1842	2, 820
Glass-flattening furnace and leer	J. Clabby	Lenox, Mass	Mar. 7, 1871	112, 322
Glass, Flexible fastening for	W. H. Taylor	Stamford, Conn	Feb. 28, 1871	112, 193
Glass for windows, Flattening-cylinder for	W. Coffan, jr	Hammonton, N. J	Oct. 1, 1830	....
Glass frame for looking-glass, &c	J. Scott	Philadelphia, Pa	Apr. 6, 1831	....
Glass from cylinders, Manufacturing plate	W. P. Walter	Philadelphia, Pa	July 10, 1855	13, 245
Glass, Frosting plates of	I. Taylor	New York, N. Y	Nov. 11, 1851	8, 519
Glass-furnace	E. Bayard and B. A. Mason	New York, N. Y	Mar. 18, 1873	136, 957
Glass-furnace	J. Carroll	Longacoming, N. J	July 25, 1865	48, 903
Glass-furnace	H. R. De Monthureux	Birmingham, Pa	Nov. 19, 1872	133, 083
Glass-furnace	J. W. Ells and J. J. Deabold	Pittsburgh, Pa	July 9, 1872	128, 716
Glass-furnace	G. W. and C. W. Foster	Charlestown, Mass	July 23, 1872	129, 657
Glass-furnace	N. Granger	Saratoga, N. Y	Aug. 4, 1868	80, 623
Glass-furnace	J. Green	Philadelphia, Pa	Nov. 7, 1854	11, 890
Glass-furnace	J. Green	Norristown, Pa	Mar. 26, 1867	63, 241
Glass-furnace	A. K. Hay	Winslow, N. J	Nov. 7, 1854	11, 893
Glass-furnace	A. K. Hay	Winslow, N. J	May 20, 1862	35, 314
Glass-furnace	J. B. Hay	Winslow, N. J	July 24, 1860	29, 342
Glass-furnace	J. Henderson	Wheeling, W. Va	Jan. 18, 1870	98, 963
Glass-furnace	D. Jarves	Boston, Mass	Oct. 3, 1846	4, 783
Glass-furnace	T. Leighton	Cambridge, Mass	Sept. 19, 1846	4, 770
Glass-furnace	W. Leighton, jr	Wheeling, W. Va	Aug. 19, 1873	141, 935
Glass-furnace	S. Oakman	Boston, Mass	Mar. 23, 1869	88, 066
Glass-furnace	A. Pocheron	Paris, France	Aug. 12, 1873	141, 666
Glass-furnace	S. Richards	Philadelphia, Pa	June 3, 1856	15, 018
Glass-furnace	S. Richards	Philadelphia, Pa	July 22, 1856	15, 389
Glass-furnace	S. Richards	Philadelphia, Pa	Aug. 25, 1857	18, 059
Glass-furnace	S. Richards	Philadelphia, Pa	Mar. 12, 1867	62, 887
Glass-furnace	F. Rohrbacher and F. Hormann	Philadelphia, Pa	Aug. 6, 1872	130, 154
Glass-furnace	F. Schaum	Baltimore, Md	Apr. 25, 1854	10, 830
Glass-furnace	C. W. and F. Siemens	Westminster, England, and Dresden, Saxony.	June 11, 1872	127, 806
Glass-furnace	J. Stanger and D. H. Miller	Philadelphia, Pa	Aug. 16, 1815	....
Glass-furnace, kiln, &c	J. Green	Norristown, Pa	Feb. 23, 1869	87, 255
Glass furnaces, and pots, Manufacture of	E. Wells	Covington, Pa	Dec. 21, 1858	22, 393
Glass-furnaces, Mode of feeding resin in the fires of	B. Shiverick	North Sandwich, Mass	Feb. 1, 1853	9, 569
Glass furniture, Method of making	J. P. Bakewell	Pittsburgh, Pa	Sept. 9, 1825	....
Glass, Gilding on	V. Schwarzenbach	Berne, Switzerland	Aug. 12, 1873	141, 670
Glass-globe-cutting apparatus	J. T. H. Richardson	Tutbury, England	July 18, 1871	117, 208
Glass-goblet mold	A. J. Sweeney	Wheeling, Va	July 3, 1860	29, 017
Glass goblets, glasses, &c., Mold for making	J. Magoun	East Cambridge, Mass	Sept. 10, 1867	68, 633
Glass grinding and polishing machine	A Hathaway	Lenox, Mass	May 28, 1872	127, 344
Glass grinding, cutting, and engraving machine	T. J. W. Robertson	New York, N. Y	June 7, 1864	43, 041
Glass-heating table for silvering	H. B. Walker	New York, N. Y	Oct. 18, 1870	108, 413
Glass-holder	B. H. Badger	New York, N. Y	Dec. 31, 1867	72, 776
Glass-house pot	T. Scanlon	Birmingham, Pa	Aug. 17, 1869	93, 839
Glass in molds, Pressing	J. Magoun	East Cambridge, Mass	Dec. 6, 1845	4, 297
Glass into molds, Pressing melted	D. Jarves	Boston, Mass	Dec. 1, 1828	....
Glass-jar	W. M. Kirchner	Pittsburgh, Pa	May 30, 1871	115, 326
Glass-jar mold	R. Hemingway	Covington, Ky	Sept. 18, 1860	30, 063
Glass jars, Machine for grinding	A. W. Kelly and J. B. Samuel	Philadelphia, Pa	Dec. 28, 1869	98, 270
Glass jars, Machine for removing the "blow-over" on	J. Chambers	Birmingham, Pa	Jan. 25, 1870	99, 160
Glass jars, Means for attaching covers to	D. C. Ripley	Pittsburgh, Pa	June 29, 1869	91, 871
Glass jars, Mode of grinding the mouth-edges of	O. O. G. Elliott	Philadelphia, Pa	Mar. 13, 1866	53, 218
Glass jars, Process of forming smooth tops on	F. Rohrbacher and F. Hormann	Philadelphia, Pa	Aug. 23, 1870	106, 624
Glass jars, Tool for forming mouths of	G. M. Keeffer	East Birmingham, Pa	Dec. 20, 1870	110, 243
Glass jars, Tool for forming screw-threads on	W. M. Kirchner	Pittsburgh, Pa	Dec. 6, 1870	109, 825
Glass, Kiln for annealing	T. B. Atterbury	Pittsburgh, Pa	June 28, 1864	43, 278
Glass, Kiln for annealing	T. Lowry	Pittsburgh, Pa	Mar. 1, 1870	100, [illegible]24
Glass, Ladling of molten	W. P. Walter and J. Green	Philadelphia, Pa	May 6, 1856	14, 838
Glass-lamp mold	D. C. Ripley	Birmingham, Pa	June 14, 1870	104, 205
Glass letters, numbers, &c., Making	O. Stietz	New York, N. Y	May 14, 1867	64, 807
Glass light	W. A. Demuth	New York, N. Y	Sept. 22, 1868	82, 389
Glass light for ship and building	J. Oakes	Boston, Mass	May 11, 1822	....
Glass, &c., Machine for cutting and polishing	J. P. and C. Colné	Washington, D. C	Nov. 19, 1872	133, 204
Glass, Machine for grinding	A. H. Hook	New York, N. Y	Nov. 15, 1859	26, 103
Glass, &c., Machine for marking designs on	H. A. Wassell	Stourbridge, England	Feb. 4, 1873	135, 610
Glass, Machine for making sheet	S. S. Ferries	New York, N. Y	Nov. 10, 1868	83, 841
Glass, Machine for mixing "batch" for	W. T. Gillinder	Philadelphia, Pa	Dec. 13, 1870	110, 029
Glass, &c., Machinery for grinding and polishing	A. Broughton	Malone, N. Y	May 29, 1860	28, 532
Glass, Machinery for polishing	P. Burgess	New York, N. Y	Nov. 18, 1856	16, 085
Glass, &c., Machinery for polishing	A. Lindsay	Malone, N. Y	Mar. 9, 1858	19, 569
Glassmaker's mold	D. Jarves	Boston, Mass	May 28, 1830	....
Glassmaker's pot	W. H. Capewell	Westville, N. J	Dec. 3, 1867	71, 578
Glass, Making	W. Price	Pennsylvania	Mar. 4, 1816	....
Glass-making pot	E. Dithridge	Pittsburgh, Pa	Jan. 1, 1861	31, 011
Glass-making, Tank-furnace for	G. Leuffgen	Charlottenburg, Prussia	May 17, 1870	103, 208
Glass, Manufacture of	W. H. Balmain	St. Helen's, Great Britain	June 20, 1871	116, 137
Glass, Manufacture of	L. Bémelmans and L. De Give	Atlanta, Ga	July 14, 1868	79, 892
Glass, Manufacture of	L. Bémelmans and L. De Give	Atlanta, Ga	July 14, 1868	79, 893
Glass, Manufacture of	J. Best	Pittsburgh, Pa	Jan. 10, 1865	45, 809
Glass, Manufacture of	J. L. Gilliland	Brooklyn, N. Y	Jan. 5, 1864	41, 065
Glass, Manufacture of	C. H. Jenkins	Boston, Mass	Apr. 12, 1870	101, 737
Glass, Manufacture of	H. Napier and J. J. Hollins	Elizabeth, N. J	Dec. 5, 1865	51, 343
Glass, Manufacture of	D. C. Ripley	Pittsburgh, Pa	Mar. 17, 1868	75, 577

Index of patents issued from the United States Patent Office from 1790 *to* 1873, *inclusive*—Continued.

Invention.	Inventor.	Residence.	Date.	No.
Glass, Manufacture of	H. Trumbull	Jersey City, N. J	July 3, 1860	29, 020
Glass, Manufacture of	R. Washburn	Monsey, N. Y	Feb. 27, 1866	52, 917
Glass, Manufacture of	S. Wetherill	Bethlehem, Pa	Oct. 16, 1860	30, 459
Glass, Manufacture of	T. A. Zellers	East Birmingham, Pa	July 2, 1867	66, 274
Glass, Manufacture of black bottle	J. F. McCully	Gonzales, Tex	Sept. 2, 1856	15, 665
Glass, Manufacture of crystal	O. Wuth	Pittsburgh, Pa	Oct. 12, 1869	95, 752
Glass, Manufacture of plate	J. J. Greenough	Boston, Mass	June 14, 1853	9, 791
Glass, Manufacture of plate	P. Stenger	Philadelphia, Pa	Aug. 7, 1855	13, 411
Glass, Manufacture of plate and window	T. Clark	Pittsburgh, Pa	June 8, 1852	8, 994
Glass, Manufacture of window	C. F. Carstens and T. H. Schwenck.	Chicago, Ill	Mar. 5, 1872	124, 195
Glass, Manufacturing	J. M Brookfield and E. V. White	Honesdale, Pa	June 14, 1853	9, 789
Glass-manufacturing process	S. Richards	Philadelphia, Pa	May 29, 1866	55, 159
Glass, Material for the manufacture of	P. E. Minor	Schenectady, N. Y	Dec. 31, 1867	72, 878
Glass, Melting and fusing	T. W. Dyott	Philadelphia, Pa	Sept. 10, 1828	
Glass-melting furnace	L. B. Goodhue	Saint Louis, Mo	May 5, 1868	77, 479
Glass-melting pot	J. Dougherty	Somerville, Mass	Jan. 14, 1873	134, 789
Glass-melting pot	C. Newman	San Francisco, Cal	May 7, 1867	64, 558
Glass, Metallic molds for molten	W. Pountney	Brooklyn, N. Y	June 21, 1864	43, 224
Glass, Method of lettering and ornamenting	J. B. Shaw	Pittsburgh, Pa	Aug. 12, 1856	15, 532
Glass, Method of preventing the corrosion or staining of the surface of.	W. B. Richards	New York, N. Y	Mar. 28, 1865	47, 040
Glass, Mode of applying crystal frosting to	H. B. Kimball	Charlotte, Mich	Dec. 8, 1868	84, 699
Glass, Mode of frosting	J. Levy and C. Jones	New York, N. Y	Dec. 7, 1852	9, 453
Glass-mold	H. Brooke	New York, N. Y	Jan. 5, 1869	85, 637
Glass-mold	H. Brooke	New York, N. Y	Aug. 10, 1869	93, 591
Glass-mold	W. Brooke	Jersey City, N. J	Aug. 15, 1854	11, 515
Glass-mold	E. W. Cooper	Williamstown, N. J	Nov. 24, 1868	84, 412
Glass-mold	T. G. Otterson	Philadelphia, Pa	Mar. 2, 1869	87, 506
Glass-mold	C. H. Over, J. Robinson, and H. Faupel.	Bellaire, Ohio	July 23, 1872	129, 679
Glass-mold	J. H. Reighard	Wheeling, W. Va	Nov. 19, 1867	71, 216
Glass-mold	J. C. Schaffer	Rochester, N. Y	Mar. 16, 1869	87, 795
Glass-mold	G. W. Scollay	Saint Louis, Mo	Sept. 18, 1860	30, 093
Glass-mold	C. Stadelmann	Pittsburgh, Pa	May 30, 1871	115, 377
Glass-mold	C. Stadelmann	Pittsburgh, Pa	Apr. 23, 1872	126, 099
Glass-mold	M. Sweeney, J. E. Mathews, and T. Hartley.	Wheeling, W. Va	Jan. 30, 1866	52, 338
Glass-mold	D. Turpie	Sandwich, Mass	Mar. 17, 1868	75, 604
Glass-mold	C. H. Warner	Brooklyn, N. Y	Apr. 10, 1860	27, 873
Glass-mold	F. A. Weise	Baltimore, Md	Apr. 2, 1872	125, 234
Glass-mold	H. Wickham	Chicago, Ill	Feb. 4, 1873	135, 502
Glass-mold and press	W. M. Kirchner	Birmingham, Pa	July 16, 1872	129, 036
Glass-mold carriage	D. Bennett, M. Krebs, and J. Haley.	Baldwin Township and Pittsburgh, Pa.	Apr. 29, 1873	138, 368
Glass-mold for making argand-lamp fountain	E. B Horn	Boston, Mass	Aug. 1, 1848	5, 684
Glass, Mold for pressing	H. Dillaway	Boston, Mass	Aug. 21, 1841	2, 226
Glass, Mold for pressing	J. Magoun	East Cambridge, Mass	Sept. 25, 1847	5, 303
Glass, Mold for pressing	T. Shaw	Philadelphia, Pa	June 7, 1859	24, 360
Glass, Mold for working	A. N. N. Aubin and J. P. Colné	Portland, Conn., and Washington, D. C.	Dec. 3, 1872	133, 515
Glass-mold from gas-carbon or graphite	J. B. Lhote	Paris, France	June 29, 1869	91, 946
Glass-mold, Machine for operating	W. C. King	Pittsburgh, Pa	May 9, 1871	114, 569
Glass-mold plunger	J. McCord	East Birmingham, Pa	Apr. 5, 1870	101, 485
Glass-molds, Method of treating	S. Lydiatt	Montreal, Canada	Sept. 9, 1873	142, 573
Glass-molder's press	F. Klinck	Philadelphia, Pa	Aug. 8, 1871	117, 785
Glass, Molding	J. Magoun	Cambridge, Mass	Oct. 24, 1848	5, 875
Glass, Molding and pressing	J. Magoun	East Cambridge, Mass	Sept. 25, 1847	5, 302
Glass-molding press	W. O. Davis	Pittsburgh, Pa	Jan. 31, 1854	10, 470
Glass-molding tool	D. Challinor	Birmingham, Pa	June 6, 1871	115, 569
Glass, Ornamental window	C. Frederici	New York, N. Y	Aug. 12, 1873	141, 782
Glass-ornamentation	W. G. Webb	Wordsley, Great Britain	Dec. 5, 1871	121, 696
Glass, Ornamenting	S. M. Adams	New York, N. Y	July 29, 1873	141, 305
Glass, Ornamenting	J. S. Miles	Ann Arbor, Mich	Oct. 26, 1858	21, 896
Glass, Ornamenting	J. C. Millward	New York, N. Y	Oct. 29, 1867	70, 240
Glass, Ornamenting	C. Schüssler	New York, N. Y	Aug. 26, 1873	142, 125
Glass-ornamenting composition	J. J. H. Brainchon	Paris, France	Jan. 18, 1859	22, 620
Glass-ornamenting machine	T. J. W. Robertson	New York, N. Y	June 7, 1864	43, 043
Glass pipes, Mold for making	G. Scott	Albany, N. Y	Sept. 4, 1849	6, 694
Glass plates, &c., Machine for grinding	J. Kendall and A. Hathaway	South Framingham and Lenox, Mass.	June 23, 1868	79, 131
Glass-polish	J. M. Warren	Boston, Mass	Oct. 10, 1865	50, 406
Glass-polishing machine	A. H. Hook	New York, N. Y	July 26, 1859	24, 908
Glass-polishing machine	J. Kendall and A. Hathaway	South Framingham and Lenox, Mass.	June 23, 1868	79, 132
Glass, porcelain, &c., Attaching metal caps to	C. B. Jenkins	New York, N. Y	June 17, 1873	139, 961
Glass-pot	D. McAfee	Pittsburgh, Pa	Nov. 21, 1865	51, 068
Glass-press	A. P. Brooke	New York, N. Y	July 11, 1871	116, 926
Glass-press	A. P. Brooke	New York, N. Y	June 25, 1872	128, 280
Glass-press	A. P. Brooke	New York, N. Y	July 16, 1872	129, 095
Glass-press	W. O. Davis	Pittsburgh, Pa	Aug. 25, 1863	39, 698
Glass-press	H. Dillaway	Sandwich, Mass	Aug. 21, 1866	57, 296
Glass-press	J. Haley	Allentown, Pa	July 30, 1872	130, 039
Glass-press	J. Haley	Pittsburgh, Pa	May 13, 1873	138, 750
Glass-press	W. C. King	Pittsburgh, Pa	Dec. 17, 1872	134, 070
Glass-press	W. C. King	Pittsburgh, Pa	Dec. 17, 1872	134, 071
Glass-press	H. J. Leasure	Wheeling, W. Va	Mar. 5, 1872	124, 364
Glass-press	A. M. Smith	Brooklyn, N. Y	Jan. 28, 1873	135, 292
Glass-press, Cooling	H. J. Leasure and J. S. Gill	Wheeling, W. Va	Dec. 4, 1866	60, 203
Glass-pressing machine	G. J. Capewell	West Chesire, Conn	July 7, 1868	79, 635
Glass-pressing machine	F. McKee and C. Ballinger	Pittsburgh, Pa	Mar. 29, 1864	42, 143
Glass-pressing machine	M. Sweeney	Wheeling, W. Va	July 1, 1868	79, 786
Glass-pressing mold	P. C. Dummer	Jersey City, N. J	Oct. 16, 1827	
Glass, process for the manufacture of	H. M. Baker	Rochester, N. Y	Dec. 4, 1866	60, 119
Glass, Process of forming letters, characters, and ornaments on.	C. M. Strauss	Memphis, Tenn	Oct. 5, 1869	95, 617
Glass, Removing stains from	J. G. Pohle and J. N. Crow	Morrisania and Mott Haven, N. Y.	Mar. 24, 1863	37, 975
Glass shades and globes, Mode of ornamenting	R. Guthrie and J. Shearer	New York, N. Y	Nov. 5, 1867	70, 554

Index of patents issued from the United States Patent Office from 1790 *to* 1873, *inclusive*—Continued.

Invention.	Inventor.	Residence.	Date.	No.
Glass shades, Machine for grinding	C. C. P. Waterman	Sandwich, Mass	Aug. 27, 1861	33, 175
Glass, silver-ware, &c., Composition for cleaning	W. H. Rosevelt	Rochester, N. Y	Aug. 12, 1873	141, 819
Glass, Silvering	H. B. Walker	New York, N. Y	Dec. 20, 1870	110, 408
Glass-smelting pot	R. Combs and H. J. Leasure	Wheeling, W. Va	May 3, 1870	102, 502
Glass, soluble silicates, hydrochloric acid, and bleaching-powder, Process to be used in the manufacture of.	W. R. Stace and H. M. Baker	Rochester, N. Y	Aug. 27, 1867	68, 254
Glass, Staining	E. A. Goodes	Philadelphia, Pa	Mar. 14, 1871	112, 703
Glass-staining composition	H. V. Edmond	Norwich, Conn	July 6, 1869	92, 292
Glass stoppers for bottles, &c., Apparatus for making.	T. R. Hartell	Philadelphia, Pa	Oct. 19, 1858	21, 831
Glass, Tool for manufacture of	G. Matthewman	Williamsburgh, N. Y	Oct. 10, 1865	50, 373
Glass, Transparent and flexible materials, designed as a partial substitute for.	C. Sussegger	New York, N. Y	July 14, 1863	39, 265
Glass tubes for philosophical apparatus, Joint around.	A. B. Latta	Cincinnati, Ohio	Mar. 16, 1852	8, 801
Glass, Use of the alkalies obtained from the spent lye of soap-makers as a flux in the manufacture of.	G. H. Burgin	Philadelphia, Pa	Apr. 3, 1829	....
Glass-vessel covers, Screw-collar for	J. Cook	New York, N. Y	Feb. 23, 1869	87, 146
Glass vessels, Attachment of covers to	R. D. Bryce	East Birmingham, Pa	Aug. 21, 1860	29, 666
Glass vessels, Attachment of hinged covers of	J. H. Reighard and C. L. Knecht.	Birmingham, Pa	Aug. 21, 1860	29, 718
Glass vessels, Fastening for metallic covers to	J. Bird	Birmingham, Pa	Aug. 21, 1860	29, 743
Glass vessels to metal base, Mode of securing	A. French	Philadelphia, Pa	July 5, 1870	105, 061
Glass-ware and metal stem connections	C. L. Knecht and T. Adams	Saint Clair and Stow Township, Pa.	Dec. 13, 1870	110, 049
Glass-ware, Annealing	E. Dithridge	Pittsburgh, Pa	June 16, 1863	38, 930
Glass-ware, Cooling-stand for	J. Osterling	Wheeling, W. Va	Mar. 5, 1872	124, 378
Glass-ware holder	H. Dillaway	Sandwich, Mass	Aug. 11, 1857	17, 9 0
Glass-ware in bas-relief, Manufacture of hollow	J. S. and T. B. Atterbury and J. Reddick.	Pittsburgh, Pa	June 3, 1862	35, 429
Glass-ware makers, Snap for	O. B. Brigham	Cambridge, Mass	Nov. 26, 1867	71, 447
Glass-ware, Manufacture of	J. S. and T. B. Atterbury	Pittsburgh, Pa	Mar. 3, 1868	75, 110
Glass-ware, Manufacture of	J. S. and T. B. Atterbury	Pittsburgh, Pa	Apr. 20, 1869	89, 005
Glass-ware, Manufacture of	A. H. Baggs	Bridgeport, Ohio	Dec. 2, 1873	145, 144
Glass-ware, Manufacture of	J. P. Pears	Birmingham, Pa	Oct. 13, 1868	82, 983
Glass-ware, Manufacture of	D. C. Ripley	Birmingham, Pa	Oct. 20, 1868	83, 210
Glass-ware, Manufacture of graduated	J. H. Hobbs	Wheeling, W. Va	Oct. 15, 1872	132, 208
Glass-ware, Manufacture of hollow	J. S. and T. B. Atterbury and J. Reddick.	Pittsburgh, Pa	Feb. 11, 1862	34, 345
Glass-ware, Manufacture of hollow	J. S. and T. B. Atterbury and J. Reddick.	Pittsburgh, Pa	June 3, 1862	35, 430
Glass-ware, Manufacture of silvered	J. W. Haines	Somerville, Mass	May 30, 1865	47, 948
Glass-ware, Manufacture of stemmed	J. Oesterling	Wheeling, W. Va	Oct. 15, 1872	132, 216
Glass-ware, Manufacture of stemmed	J. Oesterling	Wheeling, W. Va	Oct. 21, 1873	143, 778
Glass-ware, Method and mold for manufacturing	J. S. and T. B. Atterbury	Pittsburgh, Pa	June 17, 1873	139, 993
Glass-ware mold	D. Ashworth	East Cambridge, Mass	July 16, 1872	129, 306
Glass-ware mold	J. S. Atterbury, J. Reddick, and T. B. Atterbury.	Pittsburgh, Pa	Mar. 4, 1862	34, 555
Glass-ware mold	H. Dillaway	Sandwich, Mass	July 7, 1868	79, 737
Glass-ware mold	R. E. Haines	Cambridge, Mass	Apr. 30, 1867	64, 312
Glass-ware mold	G. H. Lomax	Somerville, Mass	Oct. 14, 1873	143, 629
Glass-ware mold	J. B. Lyon	Pittsburgh, Pa	Dec. 13, 1870	110, 056
Glass-ware mold	J. H. Reighard	Wheeling, W. Va	Mar. 26, 1872	125, 083
Glass-ware mold	A. E. Young	Dorchester, Mass	May 11, 1869	90, 040
Glass-ware, Mold for forming blown	H. Dillaway	Sandwich, Mass	Feb. 22, 1870	100, 127
Glass-ware mold, Sectional	R. D. Haines	Cambridge, Mass	June 8, 1869	91, 118
Glass-ware mold, Solid	R. D. Haines	Cambridge, Mass	June 8, 1869	91, 119
Glass-ware molds, Cooling	H. Dillaway	Sandwich, Mass	July 7, 1868	79, 738
Glass-ware-molding press	J. Bird	Philadelphia, Pa	Sept. 14, 1869	94, 863
Glass-ware press	H. Dillaway	Sandwich, Mass	Oct. 1, 1867	69, 325
Glass-ware press	J. Haley	Cambridge, Mass	Oct. 1, 1867	69, 426
Glass-ware press	C. H. Hersey and W. E. Hawes	Boston, Mass	June 8, 1869	91, 132
Glass-ware press	J. Myers	Dorchester, Mass	Jan. 15, 1867	61, 233
Glass-ware, Process of manufacturing silvered	E. Dithridge	Pittsburgh, Pa	Oct. 29, 1867	70, 325
Glass-ware with handles, Manufacturing	J. S. and T. B. Atterbury	Pittsburgh, Pa	June 30, 1868	79, 298
Glass with platinum, Method of coating	L. P. Angenard	New York, N. Y	Mar. 14, 1865	46, 767
Glasses for orreries, &c., Preparing luminous	M. J. Gardiner	York, Pa	Apr. 30, 1832	....
Glasses for plants, hot-beds, &c., Folding	J. St. John	Stamford, Conn	Dec. 3, 1867	71, 812
Glazier's diamonds, Mounting	J. Dickinson	Brooklyn, N. Y	Sept. 3, 1861	33, 188
Glazier's diamonds, Mounting	P. Sinsz	Baltimore, Md	Apr. 23, 1867	64, 157
Glazier's pins, Machine for cutting	J. G. Baker	New Brunswick, N. J	June 15, 1858	20, 539
Glazier's points, Machine for cutting	W. Eaton	Carbondale, Pa	May 16, 1854	10, 925
Glazier's points, Machine for cutting	J. M. Jay	Canton, Ohio	Feb. 18, 1868	74, 693
Glazier's points, Tool for driving	A. Woodworth and E. W. Warren.	Cambridge, N. Y	June 28, 1870	104, 915
Glazier's tool	S. G. Monce	Bristol, Conn	July 1, 1873	140, 426
Glazing, Composition for	T. and E. Parker	Orangeville, Pa	Feb. 20, 1844	3, 443
Glazing, Heating calender-rollers for	J. Brimhall and T. Keyes, jr	West Boylston, Mass	Apr. 1, 1826	....
Glazing pottery-ware	C. W. Fenton	Bennington, Vt	Nov. 27, 1849	6, 907
Globe	G. D. Abbott	New York, N. Y	Aug. 11, 1868	80, 891
Globe	E. Bascom	New York, N. Y	Oct. 16, 1866	58, 757
Globe	J. Monteith	New York, N. Y	July 24, 1860	29, 291
Globe	G. Vale	New York	Oct. 28, 1843	3, 318
Globe, Automatic terrestrial time	F. S. Barnard	New York, N. Y	Aug. 28, 1860	29, 755
Globe, Clock-work	L. J. N. Mouret	Paris, France	June 17, 1873	140, 065
Globe, Concentric celestial and terrestrial	H. Williamson	New York, N. Y	Dec. 3, 1867	71, 830
Globe for teaching geography	E. Oram	New York	Jan. 12, 1831	....
Globe, Geographical	E. Perce	Brooklyn, N. Y	Mar. 15, 1864	41, 938
Globe-holder	T. Hay	Newark, N. J	Jan. 26, 1869	86, 224
Globe-holders, Manufacture of	C. H. Barney	Providence, R. I	Oct. 14, 1873	143, 656
Globe-joint	J. F. Hollister	Plano, Ill	June 23, 1868	79, 124
Globe, School	J. R. Agnew	Philadelphia, Pa	July 24, 1860	29, 229
Globe, School	J. R. Agnew	Mercersburgh, Pa	June 10, 1862	35, 498
Globe, School	J. R. Agnew	Mercersburgh, Pa	Sept. 9, 1862	36, 387
Globe, School	J. R. Agnew	Mercersburgh, Pa	June 16, 1863	38, 875
Globe, School	E. Weissenborn	Hudson City, N. J	Nov. 24, 1868	84, 398

Index of patents issued from the United States Patent Office from 1790 *to* 1873, *inclusive*—Continued.

Invention.	Inventor.	Residence.	Date.	No.
Globe, Terrestrial	G. P. Clarke	New York, N. Y	Oct. 1, 1867	69, 408
Globes, Apparatus for roughening the outer surface of.	T. W. Mellor	Philadelphia, Pa	Aug. 13, 1872	130, 520
Globes, Making artificial	W. B. Annin	Boston, Mass	May 4, 1826	....
Globes, maps, &c., for schools, Construction of	J. D. Brinkerhoff and J. Duthie.	Morrisania, N. Y	Nov. 29, 1870	109, 581
Globes, Method of relieving geographical outlines on molded elastic.	H. B. Goodyear	New Haven, Conn	Feb. 5, 1861	31, 311
Globes, Method of suspending school	J. Monteith	New York, N. Y	July 24, 1860	29, 292
Globes, Mold for making school	J. R. Agnew	Lancaster, Pa	July 5, 1864	43, 379
Globes, Mounting	S. Cornell	Rochester, N. Y	July 5, 1845	4, 098
Glossing and fluting iron	C. W. Monroe	Chicago, Ill	Dec. 12, 1871	121, 885
Glove	E. W. and A. A. Avery	Plymouth, N. H	Apr. 25, 1871	114, 091
Glove	O. Bartlit and G. D. Edson	Rockford, Ill	Aug. 31, 1869	94, 380
Glove	C. J. Brown	Plymouth, N. H	May 14, 1872	126, 781
Glove	C. J. Brown	Plymouth, N. H	July 2, 1872	128, 536
Glove	R. D. Burr	Kingsborough, N. Y	Aug. 4, 1868	80, 707
Glove	R. D. Burr	Kingsborough, N. Y	May 30, 1871	115, 277
Glove	R. D. Burr	Kingsborough, N. Y	July 29, 1873	141, 203
Glove	G. Chant	Port Jervis, N. Y	Oct. 8, 1872	131, 998
Glove	S. J. Clute and D. M. Durfee	Rockwood, N. Y	July 30, 1872	129, 934
Glove	T. G. Foster	Gloversville, N. Y	Nov. 18, 1873	144, 665
Glove	S. Goge	Brooklyn, N. Y	June 8, 1869	91, 113
Glove	D. S. Hulett	Gloversville, N. Y	July 26, 1870	105, 687
Glove	H. Z. and A. J. Kasson	Gloversville, N. Y	Dec. 5, 1871	121, 630
Glove	T. Kehoe	Poughkeepsie, N. Y	Nov. 26, 1872	133, 319
Glove	J. F. Mason	Johnstown, N. Y	Nov. 26, 1872	133, 376
Glove	J. I. McMartin	Johnstown, N. Y	Dec. 17, 1872	133, 998
Glove	J. H. Putnam	Gloversville, N. Y	Apr. 5, 1870	101, 506
Glove	J. H. Putnam	Gloversville, N. Y	Apr. 4, 1871	113, 695
Glove	A. J. Stevens	Rumney, N. H	Jan. 2, 1872	122, 413
Glove	W. S. Tooker	Kingsborough, N. Y	Nov. 1, 1870	108, 849
Glove	W. S. Tooker	Kingsborough, N. Y	Nov. 1, 1870	108, 850
Glove	E. V. Whitaker	Gloversville, N. Y	Dec. 19, 1871	122, 091
Glove	E. V. Whitaker	Gloversville, N. Y	Feb. 18, 1873	136, 115
Glove	W. W. Whitaker	Gloversville, N. Y	Mar. 28, 1871	113, 230
Glove	W. W. Whitaker	Gloversville, N. Y	Dec. 12, 1871	121, 832
Glove	W. W. Whitaker	Gloversville, N. Y	Dec. 12, 1871	121, 833
Glove	J. L. Whitten	Essex, Vt	May 31, 1870	103, 696
Glove-clasp	J. L. Weir	Indianapolis, Ind	May 14, 1872	126, 657
Glove-cleaning composition	M. J. Pulte	Cincinnati, Ohio	June 24, 1862	35, 706
Glove, Corn-husking	P. N. Harts	French Grove, Ill	Apr. 15, 1873	137, 918
Glove, Corn-husking	A. W. Preston	Mazon, Ill	June 18, 1867	65, 827
Glove-fastener	I. Cole	Brooklyn, N. Y	June 9, 1868	78, 649
Glove-fastener	P. Courvoisier	Paris, France	Nov. 10, 1868	83, 935
Glove-fastener	L. Ferris	San Francisco, Cal	Nov. 4, 1873	144, 197
Glove-fastener	M. B. Foote	Northampton, Mass	Aug. 1, 1871	117, 530
Glove-fastener	L. Meyers	New York, N. Y	Aug. 5, 1873	141, 580
Glove-fastener	H. R. Minns	Bristol, England	July 30, 1872	129, 900
Glove-fastening	H. P. Carver	Binghamton, N. Y	July 8, 1873	140, 613
Glove-fastening	D. A. Cooper	Worcester, England	June 10, 1873	139, 703
Glove-fastening	T. Deschamps	Paris, France	May 25, 1869	90, 348
Glove-fastening	M. B. Foote	Northampton, Mass	July 7, 1868	79, 746
Glove-fastening	C. H. Hall and R. Knott	Trenton, N. J., and Brooklyn, N. Y.	Aug. 5, 1873	141, 555
Glove, Gauntlet	F. Farrant	Gloversville, N. Y	Dec. 2, 1873	145, 099
Glove, Gauntlet	V. Price	New York, N. Y	Oct. 3, 1871	119, 642
Glove, Gauntlet	I. B. Whipple	Gloversville, N. Y	Apr. 15, 1873	137, 988
Glove, Husking	J. H. Titus	Independence, Iowa	Jan. 5, 1869	85, 707
Glove, Husking and shelling	E. Cohen	Washington, D. C	Jan. 5, 1858	19, 018
Glove, Swimming	D. Campbell	New York, N. Y	Aug. 21, 1855	13, 455
Glove-turning machine	F. Vanderpool	Mayfield, N. Y	Dec. 30, 1873	146, 111
Gloves, Dyeing kid	J. T. Reed	Charlestown, Mass	Mar. 29, 1864	42, 111
Gloves, Dyeing kid	J. T. Reed	Charlestown, Mass	Apr. 11, 1865	47, 221
Gloves, Machine for cutting out	H. J. Dickerson	Gloversville, N. Y	Nov. 22, 1864	45, 145
Gloves, Machine for cutting out	J. H. Harlan and T. Pomeroy	Denver City, Colo	Dec. 17, 1867	72, 197
Gloves, Manufacturing knit	J. Peatfield	Ipswich, Mass	July 13, 1858	20, 893
Gloves, &c., Mode of coloring kid	S. C. Chase	Charlestown, Mass	Jan. 19, 1864	41, 279
Glucose and white lead, Manufacture of	R. Rowland	New York, N. Y	June 6, 1865	48, 099
Glucose, Manufacture of	W. H. Keyt	Madison, Ind	June 4, 1872	127, 418
Glucose, Manufacture of	G. R. Percy	New York, N. Y	Feb. 28, 1865	46, 585
Glucose-manufacture, Process in	G. Riley	New York, N. Y	Mar. 5, 1850	7, 148
Glue	W. Adamson	Philadelphia, Pa	June 18, 1867	65, 785
Glue	E. Goddard	New York, N. Y	Oct. 4, 1864	44, 528
Glue and paint pot	J. J. Wilson	New York, N. Y	Nov. 18, 1870	109, 090
Glue and water heater	J. Edgecomb	Worcester, Mass	Sept. 20, 1864	44, 294
Glue-can	W. F. Muchmore	Astoria, N. Y	Mar. 31, 1868	76, 233
Glue-cement	S. Krewson	Springfield, Ohio	Feb. 9, 1869	86, 843
Glue, Clarifying	W. Adamson	Philadelphia, Pa	Jan. 30, 1855	12, 304
Glue-cutting machine	T. Brown, jr	South Danvers, Mass	Aug. 7, 1860	29, 541
Glue-dryer	J. J. Manning	Rockport, Mass	Aug. 8, 1871	117, 905
Glue-drying apparatus	M. Newbauer and P. Adelmann.	New York, N. Y	June 7, 1859	24, 325
Glue-drying apparatus	C. Wahl	Chicago, Ill	July 21, 1868	80, 248
Glue-drying, Holder for	W. Adamson	Philadelphia, Pa	Jan. 14, 1868	73, 220
Glue-drying machine	C. Wahl	Chicago, Ill	July 21, 1868	80, 249
Glue-drying machine	C. Wahl	Chicago, Ill	July 21, 1868	80, 250
Glue from the pith of horns, Manufacture of	J. Winward	East Cambridge, Mass	July 13, 1869	92, 683
Glue, gelatine, and size, Bleaching and clarifying	N. J. Wells	Holyoke, Mass	June 18, 1872	128, 000
Glue, Heating	R. Jackman	New York, N. Y	Aug. 9, 1864	43, 774
Glue into grooves, Machine for putting	J. A. Danforth	Potsdam, N. Y	Oct. 15, 1872	132, 257
Glue, Liquid	C. F. Binder	Philadelphia, Pa	July 24, 1866	56, 665
Glue, Liquid	W. Horwitz	New York, N. Y	Nov. 8, 1870	109, 010
Glue, Manufacture of	W. Adamson	Philadelphia, Pa	June 18, 1867	65, 787
Glue, Manufacture of	W. Adamson	Philadelphia, Pa	Aug. 16, 1870	106, 448
Glue, Manufacture of	C. W. Cooper	Brooklyn, N. Y	Aug. 6, 1861	32, 979
Glue, Manufacture of	A. Dietz	New York, N. Y	June 7, 1870	103, 852
Glue, Manufacture of	H. Fleck	Dresden, Saxony	May 18, 1869	90, 160
Glue, Manufacture of	O. S. Follett	Mont Clair, N. J	Apr. 15, 1873	137, 835

Index of patents issued from the United States Patent Office from 1790 to 1873, inclusive—Continued.

Invention.	Inventor.	Residence.	Date.	No.
Glue, Manufacture of	G. Guenther	Chicago, Ill	Dec. 14, 1869	97, 771
Glue, Manufacture of	J. A. and R. Lighthall	Brooklyn, N. Y	Apr. 28, 1868	77, 388
Glue, Manufacture of	J. H. Mark	Philadelphia, Pa	Oct. 3, 1822	....
Glue, Manufacture of	H. and C. McDougall	Chicago, Ill	Aug. 6, 1872	130, 230
Glue, Manufacture of	W. Plumer	Lexington, Mass	July 29, 1873	141, 379
Glue, Manufacture of	L. Reid and J. Rogers	New York, N. Y	Feb. 28, 1860	27, 310
Glue, Manufacture of	B. F. Shaw	Cambridge, Mass	Dec. 9, 1873	145, 454
Glue, Manufacture of	G. Upton	South Danvers, Mass	Jan. 1, 1867	70, 968
Glue, Manufacture of aërated	W. Adamson	Philadelphia, Pa	June 18, 1867	65, 786
Glue, Manufacture of liquid	W. C. Watson	Paterson, N. J	Oct. 30, 1866	59, 326
Glue, Manufacturing	P. Cooper	New York, N. Y	Apr. 29, 1830	....
Glue, Manufacturing	J. Morgan	Portland, Me	Sept. 18, 1835	....
Glue, Manufacturing	H. G. C. Paulsen	New York, N. Y	Feb. 28, 1842	2, 474
Glue, Mode of drying	G. Guenther	New York, N. Y	June 4, 1867	65, 377
Glue or cement	N. S. Whipple	Detroit, Mich	June 21, 1870	104, 520
Glue or gelatine and other materials called durogel, Composition of.	H. Wurtz	New York, N. Y	Jan. 1, 1867	60, 984
Glue-pot	J. I. Baringer	Germantown, N. Y	Sept. 19, 1871	119, 002
Glue-pot	J. Bragdon	Boston, Mass	July 14, 1868	79, 945
Glue-pot	T. C. Howes	Troy, N. Y	Apr. 16, 1872	125, 680
Glue-pot	H. C. Stewart	Cincinnati, Ohio	Jan. 1, 1867	60, 958
Glue-pot	J. Tinney	Westfield, N. Y	Feb. 9, 1869	86, 788
Glue-pot	J. Turner	Cambridgeport, Mass	Jan. 24, 1860	26, 957
Glue, Preparation of	J. M. Hunter	New York, N. Y	Aug. 14, 1860	29, 596
Glue, Prepared	J. F. Peting	Rochester, Ind	Nov. 14, 1871	120, 996
Glue, Process of making	D. A. James	Cincinnati, Ohio	July 26, 1853	9, 877
Glue, Process of treating	A. Dietz	New York, N. Y	July 7, 1868	79, 736
Glue-stock and other products from animal substances, Preparation of.	D. K. Tuttle and O. Lugo	Baltimore, Md	May 4, 1869	89, 709
Glue-stock, Preparation of	W. Adamson	Philadelphia, Pa	June 23, 1868	79, 178
Glue-stock, Preparing	O. Rich	Cambridge, Mass	Nov. 24, 1857	18, 724
Glue-stock, Treating	C. W. Cooper	Brooklyn, N. Y	Aug. 15, 1865	49, 383
Gluing and cementing machine	M. H. Merriam and E. L. Norton.	Charlestown, Mass	June 5, 1866	55, 335
Gluing-hopper	J. W. Campbell	New York, N. Y	Nov. 22, 1870	109, 494
Gluing-hopper	J. W. Campbell and W. J. Miller.	New York, N. Y	June 15, 1869	91, 414
Gluing-press	M. H. Merriam and E. L. Norton.	Charlestown, Mass	June 5, 1866	55, 334
Gluing-table	S. P. Groocock and W. G. Brasington.	Clifton, N. J., and Brooklyn, N. Y.	Dec. 5, 1871	121, 510
Glycerine from soap-makers' spentlyes, Process of obtaining.	B. T. Babbitt	New York, N. Y	Sept. 13, 1870	107, 324
Glycerine, Manufacture of	O. Laist	Cincinnati, Ohio	Mar. 24, 1868	75, 929
Glycerine, Manufacture of nitro	T. P. Shaffner	Louisville, Ky	Dec. 28, 1869	98, 425
Glycerine, Preparation of	J. F. Wisnewski	Cincinnati, Ohio	Aug. 9, 1859	25, 072
Goblet	T. Leach	Taunton, Mass	Jan. 12, 1869	85, 934
Goggles, Strabismus	A. Lake	Flatbush, N. Y	Nov. 4, 1842	2, 838
Gold, amalgam, and quicksilver, Apparatus for saving.	G. R. Evans	Virginia City, Nev	Feb. 2, 1869	86, 379
Gold, amalgam, and quicksilver saving device	O. H. Young and D. J. Vaughn.	Wisconsin Hill, Cal	Feb. 7, 1871	111, 713
Gold and amalgam saving apparatus	G. R. Evans	Virginia City, Nev	July 18, 1871	117, 162
Gold and other metals from ores, Reducing and separating.	C. M. Nes	Baltimore, Md	Apr. 16, 1872	125, 835
Gold and other precious metals from foreign substances, Machine for separating.	E. N. Kent	New York, N. Y	Feb. 26, 1856	14, 316
Gold and other precious metals from their ores, Extracting.	H. Wurtz	New York, N. Y	June 27, 1865	48, 499
Gold and silver, Amalgamated plate for collecting	M. Attwood and J. Roach	San Francisco, Cal	Feb. 23, 1869	87, 132
Gold and silver amalgamator	W. M. Fuller	Chicago, Ill	Sept. 1, 1868	81, 767
Gold and silver from base metals, Process for separating.	E. Lundquist	Grass Valley, Cal	Apr. 1, 1873	137, 375
Gold and silver from lead, Separating	C. Roswag and A. N. De Pauville.	Paris, France	May 13, 1873	138, 938
Gold and silver from mineral and other substances, Process for separating.	G. N. Jennings	Virginia City, Nev	Mar. 21, 1865	46, 909
Gold and silver from ores by means of the vapor of mercury, Mode of extracting.	R. Spencer	New York, N. Y	Nov. 22, 1864	45, 188
Gold and silver from ores, earth, &c., Mill for grinding, washing, and separating.	W. H. Folger	Charlotte, N. C	Feb. 13, 1828	....
Gold and silver from ores, Separating	E. Brown	Chicago, Ill	Nov. 27, 1866	59, 955
Gold and silver from quartz, Separating	E. A. Hyde	Ann Arbor, Mich	Feb. 8, 1870	99, 571
Gold and silver from solutions, Apparatus for precipitating.	W. S. Laighton	Norwich, Conn	Oct. 11, 1870	108, 158
Gold and silver from sweepings, washings, &c., Method of collecting.	J. H. Rae	Syracuse, N. Y	Mar. 12, 1867	62, 776
Gold and silver from their ores, Extracting	J. W. Kidwell	Washington, D. C	Oct. 27, 1868	83, 582
Gold and silver from their ores, Method of extracting.	J. Tunbridge	Newark, N. J	Dec. 22, 1868	85, 258
Gold and silver, Machine for collecting and amalgamating.	E. B. Prater	Washoe County, Nev	Dec. 6, 1864	45, 341
Gold and silver, Machine for grinding and amalgamating.	W. H. Hepburn and G. K. Peterson.	San Francisco, Cal	Apr. 19, 1864	42, 371
Gold and silver ores, Apparatus for roasting and treating.	A. B. Crosby and R. L. Thompson.	Gilpin County, Colo	Oct. 18, 1864	44, 767
Gold and silver ores, Machinery for washing	D. Asbury	Colburn's Post-Office, N.C	May 2, 1846	4, 496
Gold and silver ores, Method and means for treating.	L. E. Rivot	Paris, France	Jan. 28, 1868	73, 838
Gold and silver ores, Process of treating	L. E. Rivot	Paris, France	June 9, 1868	78, 831
Gold and silver ores, Treating	J. Kallmes	San Francisco, Cal	May 6, 1873	138, 500
Gold and silver, Process of collecting	A. F. W. Partz	Oakland, Cal	June 8, 1869	90, 955
Gold and silver, Refining	N. A. F. Brewer	Camden, S. C	July 11, 1848	5, 663
Gold and silver, Sluice and blanket for collecting	E. Coleman	San Francisco, Cal	July 27, 1869	93, 060
Gold and silver washing apparatus	J. Hendy	San Francisco, Cal	Feb. 27, 1866	52, 850
Gold, &c., Apparatus for disintegrating gravel containing.	I. B. Cox	San Francisco, Cal	Aug. 4, 1868	80, 606
Gold, Apparatus for saving	C. Schofield	Kernville, Cal	May 10, 1870	102, 870
Gold, Apparatus for saving floating	D. Gay, jr	Vallejo, Cal	Feb. 2, 1869	86, 388

Index of patents issued from the United States Patent Office from 1790 *to* 1873, *inclusive*—Continued.

Invention.	Inventor.	Residence.	Date.	No.
Gold, Apparatus for washing and amalgamating	J. C. Dickey	Saratoga Springs, N. Y	July 19, 1864	43, 574
Gold-beater, Mechanical	R. B. Ruggles and L. W. Serrell	New York, N. Y	Jan. 6, 1852	8, 642
Gold-beating apparatus	T. C. Robbins	Philadelphia, Pa	Aug. 21, 1866	57, 380
Gold beating machine	M. Hastings	Philadelphia, Pa	June 27, 1865	48, 394
Gold-beating machine	W. Vine and J. H. Ashmead	Hartford, Conn	Aug. 6, 1850	7, 552
Gold-beating machinery	W. Vine	Hartford, Conn	May 11, 1852	8, 945
Gold bullion to toughen and refine it, Process of treating	F. B. Miller	Sidney, Colony of New South Wales	Mar. 10, 1868	75, 289
Gold, &c., by amalgamation, Method of obtaining	M. A. Bertolet, L. Kirk, and A. M. De Hart	Reading, Pa	Dec. 28, 1852	9, 499
Gold by a vibrating circular cylindrical trough, Separating	R. King	McIntosh County, Ga	Oct. 1, 1830	....
Gold-cleaner	J. Bogardus	New York, N. Y	Apr. 7, 1834	....
Gold-collector	J. Perry	New York, N. Y	Dec. 12, 1854	12, 069
Gold-digger's fork	L. Teese and Son	San Francisco, Cal	Feb. 20, 1855	12, 453
Gold, Digging and procuring	H. Jordan	Lexington, Ky	Oct. 1, 1830	....
Gold-digging apparatus	D. Tisdale	Des Moines, Iowa	Sept. 7, 1869	94, 669
Gold, Double-acting rocker for washing	A. Buffum and P. Thorp	New York, N. Y	Oct. 1, 1850	7, 678
Gold-dust, &c., Machine for washing, cleaning, and separating	R. Lee	Erwinsville, N. C	July 8, 1829	....
Gold from earth, &c., Machine for separating	S. H. Mead	Saint Andrew's, N. Y	Sept. 10, 1861	33, 257
Gold from earth, &c., Machine for separating	G. B. Palmer	Pendleton, N. C	Apr. 23, 1831	....
Gold from foreign matter, Apparatus for extracting	A. W. Hall	New York, N. Y	Dec. 27, 1864	45, 670
Gold from impurities, Machine for separating	J. Sullivan	Gold Region, N. C	Feb. 27, 1847	4, 988
Gold from its ores, Machine for extracting	N. Bosworth	Philadelphia, Pa	June 6, 1835	....
Gold from its ores, Process of extracting	R. D'Heureuse	San Francisco, Cal	Apr. 7, 1868	76, 413
Gold from ores, Collecting	A. F. W. Partz	Oakland, Cal	Jan. 4, 1870	98, 518
Gold from pyrites, Apparatus for extracting	G. F. Deetken	Nevada, Cal	Jan. 6, 1863	37, 278
Gold from river-bottoms, Collecting	J. Johnson	Saco, Me	Apr. 2, 1867	63, 394
Gold from sand and gravel, Machine for washing	C. Bechtler	Rutherfordton, N. C	Oct. 5, 1831	....
Gold from sand and pounded ores, Machine for washing	C. Bechtler	Rutherfordton, N. C	Oct. 5, 1831	....
Gold from sand, Apparatus for separating	D. F. Hawkes	Timbuctoo, Cal	Oct. 5, 1869	95, 472
Gold-leaf condenser	J. F. Adams	Worcester, Mass	Apr. 20, 1869	89, 002
Gold-leaf condenser	J. F. Adams	Worcester, Mass	May 18, 1869	90, 062
Gold, Machine for collecting and amalgamating fine particles of	A. B. Crosby and J. Ladd	Greene, Me., and Boston, Mass	Sept. 30, 1862	36, 557
Gold, Machine for excavating and washing	S. Johnson	New York, N. Y	Apr. 13, 1858	19, 930
Gold, Machine for separating and collecting	W. H. Folger	Spartanburgh District, S. C	Feb. 13, 1828	....
Gold, Machinery for separating	I. Babbitt	Boston, Mass	May 2, 1848	5, 545
Gold, Magnetic machine for washing and separating	S. Gardiner, jr	New York, N. Y	Mar. 8, 1853	9, 610
Gold mineral, Reducing	W. Longmaid	London, England	Aug. 10, 1852	9, 187
Gold-ores and alluvial auriferous earth, Machine for washing	J. Powell	Salisbury, N. C	Apr. 1, 1831	....
Gold-ores and alluvial soil, Washing-machine for	V. De Rivafinoli, C. Harslebin, and W. Davis	London, England, and Great Britain	Nov. 1, 1830	....
Gold, Process for dissolving	C. F. Spieker	New York, N. Y	Feb. 10, 1852	8, 729
Gold, Process for preparing	A. J. Watts	Utica, N. Y	Apr. 26, 1853	9, 691
Gold, Process for refining	J. C. Booth	Philadelphia, Pa	Sept. 24, 1850	7, 661
Gold, &c., roasting and smelting furnace	J. W. Shaeffer	Red Wing, Minn	July 14, 1868	80, 020
Gold, &c., Saving float or fine	E. J. Fraser	San Francisco, Cal	Jan. 30, 1872	123, 096
Gold, Separating and grinding	S. Whisler and J. Smith	Rockingham County, Va	Jan. 15, 1830	....
Gold, Separating and grinding flint-rock	A. Carson	Kingston, Tenn	Jan. 29, 1833	....
Gold-separator	G. Aughinbaugh	Portland, Oreg	Apr. 23, 1867	63, 981
Gold-separator	J. Dobson	Burke County, N. C	Aug. 21, 1834	....
Gold-separator	R. H. Dunning	North San Juan, Cal	Feb. 7, 1860	27, 041
Gold-separator	W. T. Duvall	Georgetown, D. C	Oct. 15, 1867	69, 784
Gold-separator	M. C. Gritzner	Washington, D. C	Nov. 29, 1853	10, 272
Gold-separator	D. Jones	Granville, N. C	Nov. 3, 1830	....
Gold-separator	W. H. Long	Mountain City, Colo	May 2, 1865	47, 557
Gold-separator	D. Pierce	Woodstock, Vt	Jan. 10, 1854	10, 414
Gold-separator	R. L. Reaney	Philadelphia, Pa	Jan. 10, 1860	26, 784
Gold-separator	F. D. Sanno	Philadelphia, Pa	Dec. 24, 1830	....
Gold-separator	T. Seay	Columbia County, Ga	May 4, 1841	2, 078
Gold-separator	E. L. Seymour	New York, N. Y	Sept. 19, 1854	11, 712
Gold-separator	E. L. Seymour	New York, N. Y	Apr. 7, 1857	16, 999
Gold-separator	W. C. Stiles	Nevada City, Cal	Nov. 12, 1867	70, 914
Gold-separator	C. F. Testman	Portland, Oreg	July 24, 1866	56, 636
Gold-separator	J. A. Veatch	San Francisco, Cal	Oct. 2, 1860	30, 273
Gold separator, amalgamator, and washer	J. L. Montandevert	Charlotte, N. C	Apr. 30, 1831	....
Gold, silver, and copper, Process for parting	G. A. Scherpf	Hoboken, N. J	Jan. 30, 1866	52, 325
Gold, silver, and other ores, Smelting	W. O. Davis	Pittsburgh, Pa	Dec. 17, 1872	133, 927
Gold, silver, and plated ware, Mode of manufacturing	H. G. Reed	Taunton, Mass	Feb. 21, 1871	112, 077
Gold-size, Composition for	C. Bartholomae	New York, N. Y	May 8, 1866	54, 488
Gold-swinging riddle	O. Willis	Morgantown, N. C	Sept. 5, 1832	....
Gold-washer	W. Ball	Chicopee, Mass	June 19, 1849	6, 535
Gold-washer	H. Barnard	Morristown, N. Y	Feb. 16, 1858	19, 338
Gold-washer	M. Bradley	Empire Ranch, Cal	Oct. 1, 1861	33, 376
Gold-washer	J. Canfield	Sabula, Iowa	Mar. 25, 1862	34, 738
Gold-washer	N. D. Clark	Bentonsport, Iowa	Mar. 7, 1865	46, 641
Gold-washer	W. Davis	Fauquier County, Va	Nov. 22, 1832	....
Gold-washer	M. English	Lagro, Ind	Aug. 28, 1849	6, 676
Gold-washer	L. Jennings	New York, N. Y	May 1, 1849	6, 410
Gold-washer	W. H. Jennison	New York, N. Y	Apr. 3, 1849	6, 267
Gold-washer	L. Lacharme	St. Leger de Feugeret, France	Oct. 2, 1849	6, 771
Gold-washer	M. Nelson	New York, N. Y	Oct. 4, 1859	25, 667
Gold-washer	I. F. Quinby	Rochester, N. Y	July 16, 1867	66, 736
Gold-washer	C. Ringel	San Francisco, Cal	Dec. 20, 1859	26, 524
Gold-washer	H. M. Ritterband	New York, N. Y	Nov. 1, 1853	10, 190
Gold-washer	T. Rives, sr	Hall County, Ga	Feb. 3, 1832	....
Gold-washer	H. Roberts	Mormon Island, Cal	July 26, 1859	24, 889
Gold-washer	P. Summey	Lincoln, N. C	Jan. 30, 1830	....
Gold-washer	J. H. Ward	Sonora, Cal	Oct. 4, 1853	10, 090
Gold-washer	O. Willis	Burke County, N. C	Dec. 21, 1831	....

Index of patents issued from the United States Patent Office from 1790 to 1873, inclusive—Continued.

Invention.	Inventor.	Residence.	Date.	No.
Gold-washer and alluvial separator	T. W. A. Sumter	Poplar Grove, N. C	May 22, 1830	......
Gold washer and amalgamator	J. S. Addison	New York, N. Y	Jan. 16, 1855	12, 237
Gold washer and amalgamator	M. Battel	Albany, N. Y	Jan. 6, 1863	37, 268
Gold washer and amalgamator	A. Buffum	New York, N. Y	May 31, 1853	9, 759
Gold washer and amalgamator	J. C. Dickey	Saratoga Springs, N. Y	Aug. 28, 1860	29, 771
Gold washer and amalgamator	J. C. Dickey	Saratoga Springs, N. Y	Nov. 20, 1860	38, 670
Gold washer and amalgamator	W. S. Pierce	North Attleborough, Mass	Aug. 12, 1856	15, 524
Gold washer and amalgamator	A. F. Potter	Boston, Mass	Jan. 25, 1853	9, 561
Gold washer and amalgamator	T. V. Tavnay	San Francisco, Cal	July 7, 1857	17, 758
Gold-washer, Concentric centrifugal	J. H. Bull	New York, N. Y	Apr. 3, 1849	6, 268
Gold-washer, Cylinder and trough	T. M. Collins	Marion, Ark	May 14, 1850	7, 361
Gold-washer, Rotary	H. Parry	Pittsburgh, Pa	Apr. 10, 1849	6, 308
Gold-washer, Vertical cylindrical	R. King	McIntosh County, Ga	Oct. 1, 1830	......
Gold-washers, Arrangement of the conductors in centrifugal.	L. P. Jenks	Boston, Mass	Oct. 2, 1849	6, 763
Gold-washers, Method of connecting sections of	R. Burton	Rome, N. Y	Mar. 26, 1850	7, 209
Gold-washers, Rocker for	T. I. Green	Jamaica Plain, Mass	Oct. 16, 1849	6, 801
Gold, Washing	P. L. Dauvergne	Clarkesville, Ga	Sept. 17, 1842	2, 783
Gold washing and amalgamating machine	A. Barclay	Newark, N. J	June 22, 1852	9, 045
Gold washing and amalgamating machine	G. C. Wheeler	Graysville, Ga	July 5, 1859	24, 706
Gold washing and separating machine	W. H. Folger	Charlotte, N. C	Sept. 10, 1829	......
Gold-washing machine	H. Bourne	Elberton, Ga	Sept. 14, 1843	3, 267
Gold-washing machine	W. B. Eltonhead	Philadelphia, Pa	July 13, 1869	92, 594
Gold-washing machine	S. S. Lewis	San Juan, Cal	Mar. 31, 1857	16, 948
Gold-washing, Riffle for	O. G. Auld and J. S. Whiting	Stockton, Cal	May 13, 1856	14, 847
Gong	V. B. Starr	East Hampton, Conn	Nov. 8, 1851	8, 537
Gong, Door	D. Liebrich	Philadelphia, Pa	Dec. 3, 1867	71, 627
Gong, Electro-magnetic alarm	C. Williams, jr., and J. Redding	Somerville and Charlestown, Mass.	Oct. 25, 1870	108, 743
Gong or bell for signals	I. F. Woodward	Philadelphia, Pa	May 24, 1859	24, 173
Gong-striking apparatus	J. W. Bliss	Hartford, Conn	Dec. 13, 1859	26, 411
Gongs or bells, Mode of striking	T. G. Estes	Fall River, Mass	Aug. 13, 1867	67, 640
Gongs, Striking-mechanism for	S. S. Chandler	Chelsea, Mass	Dec. 4, 1860	30, 800
Goniometer	W. W. Cooper	Washington, D. C	July 3, 1866	56, 013
Goods, Apparatus for delivering	J. D. Sinclair	Brooklyn, N. Y	Dec. 31, 1867	72, 924
Goods, Machine for packing	J. Clark and E. Evans		July 20, 1803	......
Goods, Machinery for raising and lowering	W. Bradbury	Newton, Mass	June 29, 1869	91, 819
Gopher-trap	J. Bowman	Santa Cruz, Cal	Feb. 20, 1872	123, 807
Gopher-trap	W. W. McKay	Frankville, Iowa	Jan. 23, 1872	122, 953
Gopher-trap	D. N. Smith	San Bernardino, Cal	Oct. 26, 1869	96, 159
Gouge	J. F. Wood	Philadelphia, Pa	Apr. 26, 1870	102, 459
Gouges, Making	M. M. Brainard	Great Barrington, Mass	Mar. 4, 1836	......
Governor	H. Allen	Brattleborough, Vt	Aug. 22, 1848	5, 718
Governor	W. Bahme	New Media, Pa	Jan. 22, 1867	61, 381
Governor	W. Bellis	Richmond, Ind	June 9, 1868	78, 782
Governor	W. F. Burden	Troy, N. Y	Apr. 21, 1863	28, 215
Governor	J. P. Burnham	Chicago, Ill	Feb. 23, 1864	41, 679
Governor	D. A. Clary	Pittsfield, Mass	Mar. 14, 1865	46, 778
Governor	G. H. Corliss	Providence, R. I	June 10, 1851	8, 148
Governor	J. Degnon	Cleveland, Ohio	Aug. 7, 1866	56, 908
Governor	J. B. Duff	New York, N. Y	Apr. 8, 1873	137, 662
Governor	M. Gally	Rochester, N. Y	Feb. 4, 1873	135, 423
Governor	R. W. Gardner	Quincy, Ill	May 20, 1873	139, 055
Governor	W. Gardner	New York, N. Y	June 10, 1851	8, 151
Governor	J. H. A. Gericke	Hoboken, N. J	Sept. 10, 1872	131, 161
Governor	J. E. Gillespie	Hartford, Conn	July 28, 1868	80, 403
Governor	J. W. Hayes	Kittery, Me	July 21, 1868	80, 173
Governor	C. Hindle	Brooklyn, N. Y	May 28, 1867	65, 221
Governor	J. S. Howell	Portsmouth, N. H	Dec. 23, 1862	37, 230
Governor	J. E. Hugon	Richmond, Ind	Nov. 4, 1873	144, 205
Governor	W. F. Keeler	La Salle, Ill	Apr. 4, 1865	47, 109
Governor	O. A. Kelly	Slaterville, R. I	Mar. 12, 1867	62, 853
Governor	W. A. L. Kirk	Hamilton, Ohio	Feb. 26, 1867	62, 343
Governor	E. H. Knight	Washington, D. C	Nov. 6, 1866	59, 411
Governor	E. H. Knight	Washington, D. C	Nov. 6, 1866	59, 412
Governor	E. H. Knight	Washington, D. C	Nov. 6, 1866	59, 413
Governor	T. S. La France	Elmira, N. Y	May 9, 1865	47, 648
Governor	W. B. Le Vau	Philadelphia, Pa	July 16, 1872	129, 040
Governor	P. Louis	New York, N. Y	Sept. 20, 1864	44, 325
Governor	T. B. McConaughey	Newark, Del	May 7, 1867	64, 435
Governor	T. B. McConaughey	Newark, Del	Oct. 1, 1867	69, 458
Governor	T. B. McConaughey	Newark, Del	Jan. 7, 1868	73, 111
Governor	E. L. McNett	Canton, Pa	Oct. 8, 1867	69, 687
Governor	E. Morris	New York, N. Y	Feb. 10, 1852	8, 726
Governor	F. J. Nutz and P. Estes	Leavenworth, Kans	July 9, 1867	66, 617
Governor	J. T. Rich	Rahway, N. J	Dec. 20, 1864	45, 522
Governor	E. P. Rogers	Corning, N. Y	Feb. 25, 1868	74, 852
Governor	H. F. Shaw	West Roxbury, Mass	Dec. 19, 1871	121, 968
Governor	R. Spear	New Haven, Conn	Nov. 30, 1869	97, 324
Governor	J. L. Todd	Newburgh, N. Y	Nov. 1, 1870	108, 848
Governor	E. Towns	Cisne, Ill	June 3, 1873	139, 631
Governor	J. Tremper	Buffalo, N. Y	Oct. 12, 1852	9, 336
Governor	D. J. Wolfe	Liverpool, England	Mar. 19, 1872	124, 871
Governor	J. L. Warren	Fishkill-on-the-Hudson, N. Y.	Mar. 12, 1872	124, 523
Governor and cut-off device for steam-engines, Automatic.	C. Moore	New York, N. Y	June 27, 1871	116, 340
Governor, Atmospheric	B. Mackerley	Paint Post-Office, Ohio	May 31, 1864	42, 956
Governor, Atmospheric	B. Mackerley	Paint, Ohio	May 29, 1866	55, 134
Governor, Automatic	C. H. Jones and H. D. Hall	North Bennington, Vt	Feb. 20, 1872	123, 911
Governor, Automatic cut-off steam-engine	J. W. Thompson	Salem, Ohio	July 16, 1872	128, 986
Governor, Centrifugal	J. C. Clime	Philadelphia, Pa	Feb. 10, 1863	37, 609
Governor, Centrifugal	J. M. Dillon	Wheeling, Va	June 17, 1862	35, 589
Governor, Centrifugal	T. R. Pickering	New York, N. Y	Oct. 7, 1862	36, 621
Governor, Centrifugal	J. Tremper	Buffalo, N. Y	Dec. 2, 1862	37, 064
Governor, Combination of speed and resistance	W. H. Elliot	Plattsburgh, N. Y	Mar. 27, 1855	12, 586
Governor-connections for steam-engines	T. Carpenter	Providence, R. I	Apr. 8, 1862	34, 877
Governor cut-off	H. H. Meyer	Denver, Colo	Feb. 6, 1872	123, 500

Index of patents issued from the United States Patent Office from 1790 *to* 1873, *inclusive*—Continued.

Invention.	Inventor.	Residence.	Date.	No.
Governor-cut-off gear	H. H. Meyer	Denver, Colo	Sept. 2, 1873	142, 491
Governor, Electro-magnetic speed	G. M. Phelps	Troy, N. Y	Jan. 5, 1858	19, 042
Governor, Engine	E. Buss	Buckan Magdeburg, Prussia.	July 1, 1873	140, 467
Governor, Engine	W. J. Hallefas	Brooklyn, N. Y	May 1, 1866	54, 336
Governor, Engine	J. F. Haskins	Fitchburgh, Mass	June 4, 1872	127, 602
Governor, Engine	J. Hendy	San Francisco, Cal	July 1, 1873	140. 414
Governor, Engine	W. S. Henson	New York, N. Y	Oct. 13, 1868	83, 060
Governor, Engine	F. W. Howe	Newark, N. J	July 28, 1857	17, 879
Governor, Engine	R. K. Huntoon	Boston, Mass	May 2, 1871	114, 296
Governor, Engine	B. S. Lawson	Brooklyn, N. Y	Nov. 14, 1871	120, 982
Governor, Engine	J. D. Lynde	Philadelphia, Pa	Feb. 21, 1871	112, 058
Governor, Engine	R. Stewart	Elmira, N. Y	June 4, 1867	65, 444
Governor for direct-acting engines	A. S. Cameron	New York, N. Y	Mar. 7, 1871	112, 415
Governor for direct-acting engines	A. S. Cameron	New York, N. Y	Mar. 7, 1871	112, 416
Governor for electro-motors	T. A. Eddison	Newark, N. J	Jan. 24, 1871	111, 112
Governor for engines, water-wheels, &c	J. P. Sibley and A. Walsh	Bennington, Vt	Oct. 6, 1868	82, 758
Governor for machinery	G. M. Phelps	Troy, N. Y	Dec. 22, 1857	18, 927
Governor for marine and other engines, Differential	C. N. Clow	Port Byron, N. Y	June 17, 1856	15, 122
Governor for marine or other enginery	J. Atkins	Washington, D. C	Jan. 12, 1869	85, 779
Governor for mill-wheels, steam-engines, &c	H. Burt	Boston, Mass	Aug. 31, 1844	3, 722
Governor for regulating the speed of steam-engines	T. Silver	Philadelphia, Pa	Apr. 26, 1859	23, 790
Governor for regulating the work of windmills, &c	E. Allen	Worcester, Mass	July 28, 1857	17, 862
Governor for side-wheel ocean-steamers, Engine	W. B. Godfrey	Auburn, Iowa	May 27, 1856	14, 954
Governor for steam and other enginery	J. Bell	Cincinnati, Ohio	Feb. 15, 1870	99, 751
Governor for steam and other enginery	T. Gill	Waltham, Mass	July 27, 1869	92, 956
Governor for steam and other enginery	W. J. and C. A. Kesselmeyer and E. H. Nacke.	Manchester, England, and Als-Schoenfeld, Saxony.	Oct. 5, 1869	95, 481
Governor for steam and other enginery	J. T. Lassen	Wurzburg, Bavaria	Oct. 27, 1868	83, 516
Governor for steam and other enginery	B. Mackerley	Paint, Ohio	Dec. 22, 1868	85, 113
Governor for steam and other enginery	D. F. Mosman	Chelsea, Mass	Mar. 30, 1869	88, 406
Governor for steam and other enginery	M. Murphy	Charlotte, N. C	Nov. 9, 1869	96, 608
Governor for steam and other engines	C. P. Bowen	Silver City, Idaho	Oct. 31, 1871	120, 366
Governor for steam and other engines	W. Clark	Plumstead, England	June 4, 1872	127, 572
Governor for steam and other engines	J. A. Marden	Boston, Mass	May 4, 1869	89, 780
Governor for steam and other engines	H. D. Snow	Rochester, N. Y	Oct. 11, 1859	25, 769
Governor for steam-engines, Centrifugal	C. T. Porter	New York, N. Y	June 18, 1861	32, 583
Governor for steam-engines, Centrifugal	J. Wheelock	Worcester, Mass	July 3, 1860	29, 025
Governor for steam-engines, Fan	I. Y. Chubbuck	Roxbury, Mass	Dec. 13, 1859	26, 414
Governor for steam-engines, Instantaneous	W. W. H. Mead	Chestertown, N. Y	May 27, 1856	14, 967
Governor for steam-engines, Marine	J. L. Cathcart	Georgetown, D. C	Apr. 26, 1859	23, 755
Governor for steam-engines, Throttle	H. Camp and G. W. McIntosh	Rouseville, Pa	Sept. 26, 1871	119, 315
Governor for steam-engines, &c., Vane	F. Gustine	Medford, Mass	June 23, 1857	17, 623
Governor for steam-engines, Vane	C. Whittier	Roxbury, Mass	Nov. 3, 1857	18, 563
Governor for steam-engines, Water	G. Aab	Brooklyn, N. Y	Oct. 3, 1871	119, 490
Governor for steam-heating apparatus	S. J. Olsson	Chicago, Ill	June 24, 1873	140, 156
Governor for water, steam, and other powers	N. Scholfield	Norwich, Conn	July 21, 1857	17, 847
Governor for water-wheels, &c	W. M. Bailey	Matteawan, N. Y	July 23, 1872	129, 707
Governor, Hydraulic	J. E. Gillespie	Trenton, N. J	Jan. 7, 1862	34, 055
Governor, Hydraulic	J. E. Gillespie	Boston, Mass	Aug. 28, 1866	57, 630
Governor, Hydraulic	S. M. Hunter	Terrysville, Conn	Dec. 18, 1866	60, 632
Governor, Hydro-pneumatic	A. Harris	Philadelphia, Pa	Dec. 21, 1869	98, 162
Governor, Marine	H. J. Behrens	New York, N. Y	Mar. 24, 1863	37, 944
Governor, Marine-engine	J. Sullivan	South Boston, Mass	Dec. 17, 1867	72, 239
Governor, Marine steam	J. B. Cullen	Philadelphia, Pa	Mar. 24, 1868	75, 868
Governor, Marine steam engine	O. Marland	Boston, Mass	Apr. 29, 1873	138, 420
Governor, Marine steam-engine	T. Silver	Philadelphia, Pa	July 3, 1855	13, 202
Governor, Marine steam-engine	E. M. Troth	New York, N. Y	Dec. 31, 1867	72, 939
Governor or hydraulic regulator	S. T. Thomas	Gilford, N. H	Dec. 24, 1872	134, 328
Governor, Power	J. Judson	New York, N. Y	Mar. 4, 1851	7, 960
Governor, Steam	G. W. Clark	Council Bluffs, Iowa	Nov. 14, 1871	120, 856
Governor, Steam	W. L. Collamore	Warren, R. I	Jan. 21, 1868	73, 578
Governor, Steam	R. D. Jacobus	Newark, N. J	Apr. 20, 1858	19, 995
Governor, Steam	A. Matson	Quincy, Ill	July 16, 1872	129, 287
Governor, Steam	G. E. Noyes	Washington, D. C	Nov. 6, 1866	59, 442
Governor, Steam	E. H. Parker	Bucksport, Me	Nov. 3, 1868	83, 655
Governor, Steam	A. F. Reeder	Normal, Ill	July 26, 1870	105, 847
Governor, Steam	R. Sanderson	Cleveland, Ohio	Jan. 15, 1867	61, 266
Governor, Steam	R. Sanderson	Cleveland, Ohio	May 14, 1867	64, 712
Governor, Steam	H. D. Snow	Bennington, Vt	Oct. 1, 1867	69, 499
Governor, Steam	J. Tremper	Wilmington, Del	Feb. 11, 1868	74, 454
Governor, Steam-engine	C. D. Allen	New York, N. Y	Dec. 28, 1869	98, 216
Governor, Steam-engine	T. Alsop	Elkhart City, Ill	Aug. 25, 1868	81, 455
Governor, Steam-engine	A. Anderson	Lancaster, Ohio	Aug. 3, 1858	21, 056
Governor, Steam-engine, &c	J. and E. Arthur	New Brunswick, N. J	Aug. 14, 1855	13, 415
Governor, Steam-engine	W. Ashby	Timber Township, Ill	Jan. 5, 1869	85, 632
Governor, Steam-engine	C. H. Bacon	Boston, Mass	May 19, 1868	77, 948
Governor, Steam-engine	H. Bilgram	Philadelphia, Pa	Nov. 19, 1872	133, 192
Governor, Steam-engine	H. Boardman	Port Richmond, N. Y	Mar. 15, 1870	100, 847
Governor, Steam-engine, &c	J. M. Bottum	New York, N. Y	Apr. 8, 1873	137, 652
Governor, Steam-engine	J. Broughton	New York, N. Y	Apr. 19, 1859	23, 660
Governor, Steam-engine	A. Brown	New York, N. Y	Nov. 7, 1865	50, 793
Governor, Steam-engine	C. P. Buckingham	Mount Vernon, Ohio	Aug. 7, 1860	29, 459
Governor, Steam-engine	J. S. Camac	Shickshinny, Pa	May 28, 1872	127, 305
Governor, Steam-engine	D. L. F. Chase	Boston, Mass	Mar. 17, 1868	75, 523
Governor, Steam-engine	J. C. Clime	Philadelphia, Pa	Apr. 17, 1866	54, 057
Governor, Steam-engine	C. A. Condé	Indianapolis, Ind	June 29, 1869	91, 915
Governor, Steam-engine	C. A. Condé	Indianapolis, Ind	Mar. 7, 1871	112, 420
Governor, Steam-engine	C. G. Cross	Chicago, Ill	Aug. 4, 1868	80, 533
Governor, Steam-engine	G. W. Davis and G. A. Rollins	Nashua, N. H	May 7, 1867	64, 500
Governor, Steam-engine	T. S. Davis	Jersey City, N. J	June 18, 1867	65, 885
Governor, Steam-engine	R. Defrees	Newark, N. J	Nov. 23, 1869	97, 056
Governor, Steam-engine	J. L. Dickinson	Dubuque, Iowa	Aug. 18, 1868	81, 072
Governor, Steam-engine	F. Douglass	Norwich, Conn	Sept. 8, 1863	39, 799
Governor, Steam-engine	C. Duclos	New Harmony, Ind	Aug. 24, 1869	94, 091
Governor, Steam-engine	J. B. Duff	Patchogue, N. Y	Apr. 23, 1872	126, 039
Governor, Steam-engine	J. Eddy	Barnesville, Ohio	Sept. 3, 1867	68, 495
Governor, Steam-engine	E. C. Edmonds	Buffalo, N. Y	Oct. 23, 1866	58, 996

Index of patents issued from the United States Patent Office from 1790 *to* 1873, *inclusive*—Continued.

Invention.	Inventor.	Residence.	Date.	No.
Governor, Steam-engine	R. Eickemeyer	Yonkers, N. Y	Aug. 28, 1866	57, 490
Governor, Steam-engine	L. Eikenberry	Philadelphia, Pa	Sept. 15, 1863	39, 903
Governor, Steam-engine	J. Farcot	St. Ouen, (Seine,) France	Feb. 16, 1869	87, 034
Governor, Steam-engine	W. C. Freeman	Louisiana, Mo	Aug. 13, 1872	130, 422
Governor, Steam-engine	L. F. Fuller	Providence, R. I	Mar. 31, 1868	76, 071
Governor, Steam-engine	R. W. Gardner	Quincy, Ill	Aug. 14, 1860	29, 579
Governor, Steam-engine	R. W. Gardner	Quincy, Ill	Dec. 27, 1864	45, 599
Governor, Steam-engine	R. W. Gardner	Quincy, Ill	Sept. 16, 1873	142, 846
Governor, Steam-engine	W. W. Gilbert	New York, N. Y	Jan. 5, 1869	85, 580
Governor, Steam-engine	J. W. Gray	Clermont County, Ohio	Apr. 7, 1868	76, 322
Governor, Steam-engine	J. L. Hastings	Towanda, Pa	Apr. 26, 1864	42, 478
Governor, Steam-engine	A. A. Henderson	Norfolk, Va	Dec. 18, 1866	60, 629
Governor, Steam-engine	J. C. Hoadley	Lawrence, Mass	Oct. 28, 1873	144, 098
Governor, Steam-engine	W. H. Howland	San Francisco, Cal	June 29, 1869	92, 051
Governor, Steam-engine	J. E. Hugon	Richmond, Ind	Nov. 4, 1873	144, 204
Governor, Steam-engine	J. D. Humphreys	London, England	Dec. 1, 1863	40, 754
Governor, Steam-engine	R. K. Huntoon	Boston, Mass	Dec. 4, 1866	60, 192
Governor, Steam-engine	R. K. Huntoon	Boston, Mass	Nov. 19, 1867	71, 015
Governor, Steam-engine	R. K. Huntoon	Boston, Mass	Dec. 3, 1867	71, 761
Governor, Steam-engine	R. K. Huntoon	Boston, Mass	May 4, 1869	89, 581
Governor, Steam-engine	R. K. Huntoon	Wakefield, Mass	Nov. 8, 1870	109, 013
Governor, Steam-engine	R. K. Huntoon	Boston, Mass	July 4, 1871	116, 596
Governor, Steam-engine	J. Judson	Rochester, N. Y	Nov. 19, 1861	33, 743
Governor, Steam-engine	O. A. Kelly	Slatersville, R. I	Dec. 17, 1867	72, 204
Governor, Steam-engine	O. A. Kelly and E. Lamb	Slatersville, R. I	Jan. 31, 1865	46, 111
Governor, Steam-engine	A. K. Kline	Readington, N. J	Nov. 21, 1871	121, 109
Governor, Steam-engine	T. S. La France	Elmira, N. Y	Aug. 7, 1866	56, 956
Governor, Steam-engine	H. H. Lamont	San Francisco, Cal	Sept. 10, 1872	131, 282
Governor, Steam-engine	J. P. T. Lang	Washington, D. C	May 14, 1867	64, 775
Governor, Steam-engine	C. M. Lancley	Lowell, Mass	Aug. 1, 1871	117, 548
Governor, Steam-engine	A. P. and B. F. Lanterman	Prairie City, Ill	Jan. 30, 1866	52, 298
Governor, Steam-engine	A. Lawrence	Lowell, Mass	Feb. 20, 1866	52, 789
Governor, Steam-engine	B. S. Lawson	Brooklyn, N. Y	July 11, 1871	116, 968
Governor, Steam-engine	J. F. Letellier	Grand Rapids, Mich	July 20, 1869	92, 818
Governor, Steam-engine	T. J. Lovegrove	Philadelphia, Pa	June 20, 1865	48, 344
Governor, Steam-engine	J. A. Lynch	Boston, Mass	Feb. 28, 1871	112, 159
Governor, Steam-engine	J. A. Lynch and R. K. Huntoon	Boston, Mass	Sept. 22, 1868	82, 332
Governor, Steam-engine	J. D. Lynde	Philadelphia, Pa	Oct. 11, 1870	108, 162
Governor, Steam-engine	J. D. Lynde	Philadelphia, Pa	Aug. 8, 1871	117, 903
Governor, Steam-engine	J. A. Marden	Boston, Mass	Oct. 6, 1868	82, 729
Governor, Steam-engine	J. A. Marden	Boston, Mass	Mar. 30, 1869	88, 495
Governor, Steam-engine	J. A. Marden	Boston, Mass	Mar. 30, 1869	88, 496
Governor, Steam-engine	J. A. Marden	Boston, Mass	Mar. 30, 1869	88, 497
Governor, Steam-engine	J. A. Marden and C. E. Abbott	Boston, Mass	Mar. 30, 1869	88, 498
Governor, Steam-engine	A. Matson	Quincy, Ill	Aug. 26, 1863	142, 167
Governor, Steam-engine	H. D. McMaster and A. Dale	Guilford, Ireland	Apr. 5, 1870	101, 487
Governor, Steam-engine	S. H. Miller	Hanoverton, Ohio	Sept. 11, 1860	29, 986
Governor, Steam-engine	T. Moore	Brooklyn, N. Y	Mar. 15, 1870	100, 785
Governor, Steam-engine	D. F. Mosman	Cambridge, Mass	Dec. 31, 1867	72, 882
Governor, Steam-engine	W. Nichols	Elmira, N. Y	Sept. 11, 1866	57, 953
Governor, Steam-engine	W. Ord	Brooklyn, Ohio	May 6, 1873	138, 521
Governor, Steam-engine	J. Parlane	Brooklyn, N. Y	May 18, 1869	90, 294
Governor, Steam-engine	G. T. Parry and H. W. Evans	Philadelphia, Pa	Mar. 1, 1859	23, 110
Governor, Steam-engine	A. J. Peavey	Boston, Mass	Aug. 16, 1870	106, 400
Governor, Steam-engine	T. R. Pickering	New York, N. Y	Oct. 24, 1865	50, 624
Governor, Steam-engine	W. H. Place	New York, N. Y	July 26, 1870	105, 841
Governor, Steam-engine	J. H. Pomeroy	Jordan, N. Y	Dec. 10, 1861	33 903
Governor, Steam-engine	C. T. Porter	New York, N. Y	July 13, 1858	20, 894
Governor, Steam-engine	G. F. Pottle	Boston, Mass	Feb. 7, 1871	111, 677
Governor, Steam-engine	G. T. Pracy	San Francisco, Cal	Jan. 12, 1869	85, 763
Governor, Steam-engine	G. W. Rains	Newburgh, N. Y	May 29, 1860	28, 502
Governor, Steam-engine	J. H. and C. E. Randall	Boston, Mass	Oct. 6, 1868	82, 874
Governor, Steam-engine	J. M. Rees	Scott, Ohio	Oct. 17, 1865	50, 496
Governor, Steam-engine	E. Reynolds and N. G. Herreshoff	Providence, R. I	Mar. 26, 1872	125, 084
Governor, Steam-engine	S. P. Ruggles	Boston, Mass	Sept. 16, 1873	142, 860
Governor, Steam-engine	C. R. Rungvist	Stockholm, Sweden	Oct. 14, 1873	143, 642
Governor, Steam-engine	I. S. Schuyler	Brooklyn, E. D., N. Y	Feb. 20, 1872	123, 939
Governor, Steam-engine	H. C. Sergeant	Columbus, Ohio	Dec. 21, 1858	22, 380
Governor, Steam-engine	J. W. Shirley and W. H. Fasig	Terre Haute, Ind	June 11, 1867	65, 697
Governor, Steam-engine	D. Shive	Philadelphia, Pa	May 1, 1866	54, 423
Governor, Steam-engine	T. Silver	New York, N. Y	Oct. 2, 1866	58, 491
Governor, Steam-engine	B. B. Smith	Nashville, Tenn	Apr. 8, 1873	137, 573
Governor, Steam-engine	W. Smith	Philadelphia, Pa	June 1, 1869	90, 696
Governor, Steam-engine	W. Smith	Philadelphia, Pa	Feb. 22, 1870	100, 203
Governor, Steam-engine	H. D. Snow	Rochester, N. Y	Sept. 27, 1864	44, 466
Governor, Steam-engine	J. H. Springer	Philadelphia, Pa	July 21, 1868	80, 096
Governor, Steam-engine	G. S. Stearns and W. Hodgson	Cincinnati, Ohio	Aug. 31, 1852	9, 236
Governor, Steam-engine	F. Taggart	Brooklyn, N. Y	Nov. 27, 1866	60, 084
Governor, Steam-engine	H. N. Throop	Pultneyville, N. Y	Dec. 29, 1857	18, 997
Governor, Steam-engine	S. Trumbore	Easton, Pa	Nov. 24, 1868	84, 396
Governor, Steam-engine	J. H. Wait	Portsmouth, Ohio	Dec. 26, 1865	51, 764
Governor, Steam-engine	A. F. Ward	Louisville, Ky	July 14, 1857	17, 817
Governor, Steam-engine	C. Waters	Boston, Mass	Jan. 3, 1871	110, 703
Governor, Steam-engine	H. B. Weaver	Hartford, Conn	June 20, 1871	116, 248
Governor, Steam-engine	J. V. Weitz	Cleveland, Ohio	Feb. 26, 1867	62, 457
Governor, Steam-engine	M. Wheeler	Honesdale, Pa	June 10, 1856	15, 095
Governor, Steam-engine	W. Wickersham	Boston, Mass	Oct. 5, 1869	95, 543
Governor, Steam-engine	J. Wood	Brooklyn, N. Y	Apr. 16, 1867	63, 976
Governor, Steam-engine	W. W. W. Wood	Philadelphia, Pa	Sept. 7, 1858	21, 475
Governor, Steam-engine	J. H. Wooster	Strykersville, N. Y	Aug. 20, 1867	67, 936
Governor stop-valve	J. Crawley	Perrysville, Ind	July 10, 1866	56, 186
Governor stop-valve for steam-engines	C. A. Condé	Indianapolis, Ind	May 25, 1869	90, 427
Governor-valve	R. Andrews and E. Armstrong	Allegheny, Pa	June 2, 1868	78, 410
Governor valve	W. W. Gilbert	New York, N. Y	Apr. 27, 1869	89, 399
Governor-valve for steam-engines	W. A. Cogswell	Rochester, N. Y	Aug. 13, 1872	130, 480
Governor-valve for steam-engines	W. A. Cogswell	Rochester, N. Y	Aug. 13, 1872	130, 481
Governor-valve for steam-engines	W. H. Cowles	Erie, Pa	Apr. 23, 1872	125, 937

Index of patents issued from the United States Patent Office from 1790 *to* 1873, *inclusive*—Continued.

Invention.	Inventor.	Residence.	Date.	No.
Governor-valve, Steam	C. H. Burton	Cleveland, Ohio	Aug. 27, 1872	130, 790
Governor valves, Casting casings for steam	W. A. Cogswell and J. Judson	Rochester, N. Y	Aug. 13, 1872	130, 482
Governor-valves for steam-engines, Operating	W. G. Crutchfield	Dayton, Ohio	Feb. 28, 1860	27, 275
Governor-valves, Milling-head machine of	W. A. Cogswell	Rochester, N. Y	Aug. 22, 1871	118, 200
Governor, Vibrating	E. Towns	Moreland's Grove, Ill	Nov. 20, 1866	59, 877
Governor, Water	H. Curtner	Anna, Ohio	Nov. 16, 1869	96, 895
Governor, Water	A. W. Woodward	Rockford, Ill	May 31, 1870	103, 813
Governor, Water-wheel	J. A. Whitman	Auburn, Me	Nov. 2, 1869	96, 522
Governor, Windmill	D. Halladay	Ellington, Conn	Aug. 29, 1854	11, 629
Governor with a slide-valve, Combination of a	R. Gornall	Baltimore, Md	Sept. 14, 1858	21, 493
Governors and other valves, Bushing for	D. W. Payne and H. Tabor	Corning, N. Y	Dec. 31, 1872	134, 483
Governors, Equalizing the action of springs in	H. W. Evans	Philadelphia, Pa	Aug. 20, 1861	33, 123
Governors of steam-engines, &c., Method of constructing.	L. Lizé	France	Nov. 25, 1841	2, 374
Governors, Safety-appliance for	J. Gaskell	Bridgeport, Conn	Nov. 25, 1873	144, 973
Governors to horse-power, Method of applying	J. Arnold	Freeport, Ill	Sept. 12, 1848	5, 769
Governors, Variable eccentrics for steam-engine	S. Stanton	New York, N. Y	Apr. 4, 1871	113, 701
Governors with gates of water-wheels, Method of connecting.	J. W. Pitt	North Adams, Mass	Mar. 15, 1864	41, 939
Grab for clearing conduits	J. Ingram	New York, N. Y	Jan. 5, 1858	19, 030
Grab for self-closing hook	J. P. James	Pepin, Minn	July 23, 1861	32, 872
Grace-hoop, Return	F. Munson	Cincinnati, Ohio	Jan. 8, 1867	61, 087
Grade-delineator	O. H. Bogardus	Syracuse, N. Y	July 30, 1861	32, 959
Grade-delineator	G. R. Clarke and S. Adams	Antioch, Cal	Mar. 31, 1857	16, 902
Grader, Road	E. L. Foreman	Rantoul, Ill	Nov. 30, 1869	97, 378
Grader, Road	J. M. Ragsdale	McCoy's Station, Ind	Oct. 27, 1868	83, 547
Gradients, Apparatus for descending	S. Marsh	Chicago, Ill	Nov. 8, 1864	44, 965
Grading and ditching machine	J. W. Fawkes	Maroa, Ill	Sept. 5, 1871	118, 707
Grading and ditching machine	A. A. Maxwell	Pratt, Ohio	Dec. 17, 1867	72, 411
Grading and ditching machine, Road	G. Trump	Second Fork Village, Pa	Sept. 19, 1871	119, 064
Grading and dressing roads	G. W. Sayre	Pisgah, Ohio	Mar. 3, 1863	37, 829
Grading and excavating machine	W. T. Grant	Jacksonville, Ill	Mar. 11, 1862	34, 662
Grading and excavating machine	T. C. Hammond	Nicolaus, Cal	Dec. 3, 1867	71, 747
Grading and excavating machine	A. Keith	Lisbon, Ill	Jan. 28, 1862	34, 256
Grading-instrument	S. L. Donnell	South Carroll, Tenn	Sept. 11, 1860	29, 955
Grading-instrument	S. L. Donnell	Spring Creek, Tenn	Dec. 11, 1866	60, 346
Grading-machine	W. C. Bartlit and J. M. Merryman	Aledo and Moline, Ill	Apr. 14, 1868	76, 698
Grading-machine	J. F. Hanna	Momence, Ill	Sept. 26, 1871	119, 353
Grading-machine	J. Preston	Atchison, Kans	May 3, 1870	102, 706
Grading-machine	W. Spalding	Port Clinton, Ohio	Mar. 3, 1863	37, 831
Grading-machine, Railway	C. Foster	Prairie City, Ill	Apr. 5, 1864	42, 183
Grading streets and roads, Apparatus for	R. Fish	New York, N. Y	Nov. 9, 1839	1, 403
Graduated cutter for cloth and other substances	H. D. Walcott	Boston, Mass	July 27, 1852	9, 158
Graduated cutter for cloth and other substances	H. D. Walcott	Boston, Mass	May 17, 1853	9, 734
Grafting	C. E. Symonds	Salem, Mass	July 22, 1873	141, 092
Grafting	D. S. Wagener	Poultney, N. Y	Nov. 21, 1871	121, 222
Grafting-machine	J. W. Crawford	Rockport, N. Y	Nov. 13, 1860	30, 617
Grafting, Method of	D. S. Wagener	Poultney, N. Y	Sept. 13, 1870	107, 427
Grafting-tool	J. Maddy	Clearfield, Pa	Nov. 14, 1871	120, 986
Grafts, Machine for cutting root	S. S. Rockwell	Vermontville, Mich	Oct. 5, 1858	21, 700
Grahamite called irisine, Preparation from	H. Wurtz	New York, N. Y	Jan. 28, 1868	73, 861
Grahamite called viscosine, Preparation from	H. Wurtz	New York, N. Y	Jan. 28, 1868	73, 862
Grahamite, Chemical product called fused or anhydrous.	H. Wurtz	New York, N. Y	Feb. 8, 1870	99, 741
Grahamite, Manufacture of refined	H. Wurtz	New York, N. Y	Jan. 28, 1868	73, 859
Grahamite, Preparation of	H. Wurtz	New York, N. Y	Jan. 28, 1868	73, 860
Grahamite, Preparing anhydrous	H. Wurtz	New York, N. Y	Feb. 8, 1870	99, 740
Grailing-machine	P. Pratt	Meriden, Conn	Feb. 12, 1828	....
Grain and apple grinding mill	C. B. Hutchinson	Auburn, N. Y	Aug. 7, 1860	29, 490
Grain and berries, Screening	M. N. Armstrong and W. H. King.	New York, N. Y	Dec. 2, 1834	....
Grain and cooling, bolting, and conveying flour Machine for cleaning, scouring, and conveying.	A. Ball	Caroline, N. Y	Jan. 16, 1840	1, 474
Grain and cooling millstones, Machine for cleaning	W. H. Akins and D. Babcock	Dryden, N. Y	June 12, 1860	28, 643
Grain and destroying insects, Machine for cleaning	J. Morgan	Baltimore, Md	Feb. 20, 1819	....
Grain and flour bags for shouldering, Raising	J. Kinman	Mifflinburgh, Pa	Mar. 15, 1834	....
Grain and fruit cleaner	S. A. Slocomb	Philadelphia, Pa	Nov. 29, 1870	109, 680
Grain and fruit drier	C. A. Haskins and G. Macardle	New York, N. Y	Nov. 23, 1858	22, 144
Grain and grass by horse-power, Cutting	E. Ambler	Root, N. Y	Dec. 23, 1834	....
Grain and grass, Cutting	R. French and J. T. Hawkins		May 17, 1803	....
Grain and grass, Cutting and gathering	J. Comfort	Bucks County, Pa	Feb. 26, 1811	....
Grain and grass seed collector	D. Ashmore and J. Peck	Jefferson County, Tenn	Sept. 18, 1835	....
Grain and grass seed separator	J. B. Wallace	Franklin, Ohio	June 20, 1865	48, 329
Grain and hay elevator	J. Dennis	Oswego, N. Y	Sept. 21, 1869	95, 006
Grain and hay elevator	H. Keck	Canaan, Ohio	June 23, 1868	79, 130
Grain and hay rake	J. M. and B. B. Brown	Marits Post-Office, Ohio	May 29, 1847	5, 132
Grain and malt cleaner and crusher	N. Thielen	Sacramento, Cal	Dec. 9, 1873	145, 314
Grain and other material, Reservoir for	G. H. Johnson and B. Kriescher	New York, N. Y	Mar. 21, 1871	112, 927
Grain and rice huller	B. Maltby and M. Fowler	New Haven, Conn	Feb. 26, 1819	....
Grain and rice hulling machine	M. Fowler	New Haven, Conn	July 28, 1820	....
Grain and seed, Apparatus for protecting	J. M. Joannides	London, England	Mar. 4, 1873	136, 437
Grain and seed cleaner	N. M. Bowen	Knightstown, Ind	Oct. 4, 1870	107, 860
Grain and seed cleaner	J. Sattison	Ripley Township, Ohio	Oct. 1, 1867	69, 489
Grain and seed cleaning machine	W. H. Peabody	Woodbury, Conn	June 8, 1810	....
Grain and seed drill	G. M. Shirkittle	Belleville, Mich	Oct. 4, 1870	107, 980
Grain and seed drill	J. H. Shreiner	Wilmington, Del	Aug. 12, 1873	141, 730
Grain and seed, Machine for screening	B. F. Watson and C. H. Tinkel	Bridgeport, Ill	Apr. 27, 1869	89, 526
Grain and seed, Machine for separating	G. M. Brown	Northumberland County, Va.	Mar. 19, 1812	....
Grain and seed separator	J. Boozer	Potter's Mills, Pa	Dec. 26, 1871	122, 148
Grain and seed separator	R. Hawkins	Sugar Creek, Ind	July 19, 1870	105, 451
Grain and seed separator	B. S. Hyers	Pekin, Ill	Aug. 2, 1864	43, 693
Grain and seed separators, Fan-case for	C. L. Allen	Flat Rock, Mich	July 12, 1870	105, 158
Grain and seeds for sowing, Coloring	J. C. H. Claussen	Charleston, S. C	Jan. 10, 1872	122, 757
Grain and similar substances, Drying	D. C. Rand and M. Wadhams	Perinton, N. Y	June 3, 1862	35, 469
Grain and straw carrying attachment for separators	B. and B. F. Jackson	Woodland, Cal	Mar. 8, 1870	100, 532
Grain and straw separator	H. Berdan	Plymouth, Mich	Oct. 9, 1847	5, 322
Grain and straw separator	L. H. Davis	Newark, Del	Dec. 17, 1867	72, 374

Index of patents issued from the United States Patent Office from 1790 *to* 1873, *inclusive*—Continued.

Invention.	Inventor.	Residence.	Date.	No.
Grain and straw separator	S. Huson	Jacksonville, N. Y	Sept. 16, 1862	36, 467
Grain and straw separator	A. Major	Lebanon, Pa	Jan. 27, 1863	37, 549
Grain and straw shaker	W. H. and P. Bott	West Manchester Township, Pa.	July 18, 1871	117, 040
Grain, &c., Apparatus for collecting and transporting.	J. and G. Richards	Philadelphia, Pa	Sept. 30, 1873	143, 254
Grain, Apparatus for dampening	J. Shellabarger	Decatur, Ill	Aug. 11, 1868	81, 016
Grain, Apparatus for decorticating	S. Dodson	Jersey City, N. J	Nov. 26, 1872	133, 309
Grain, &c., Apparatus for decorticating, separating, and drying.	A. J. Glas	London, England	Sept. 20, 1870	107, 480
Grain, Apparatus for preserving	L. M. F. Doyére	Paris, France	Dec. 20, 1859	26, 481
Grain, &c., Apparatus for preventing overheating of	T. A. Hoffmann	Beardstown, Ill	Mar. 8, 1870	100, 628
Grain, Apparatus for washing, boiling, and fermenting.	E. F. Prentiss and R. A. Robertson.	Philadelphia, Pa	Aug. 1, 1865	49, 151
Grain-bag	J. W. H. Campbell	San Francisco, Cal	July 19, 1864	43, 567
Grain-bag	W. B. Carlock	Worshiam, Va	Oct. 21, 1873	143, 876
Grain-bag holder	W. P. Leland	Mendon, Mich	May 16, 1871	114, 952
Grain-band and bag-tie	E. Foote	East Bloomfield, N. Y	Feb. 18, 1873	135, 899
Grain-bands, Device for securing	J. Nelson	Rockford, Ill	May 2, 1865	47, 603
Grain-basket	G. P. Coan	Wyandotte, Mich	Oct. 28, 1873	144, 018
Grain-bin	D. D. Badger and W. S. Sampson.	New York, N. Y	June 14, 1869	24, 424
Grain-bin	L. S. Chichester	Brooklyn, N. Y	Apr. 2, 1872	125, 169
Grain-bin	G. H. Johnson	New York, N. Y	Dec. 9, 1862	37, 134
Grain-bin	S. Marsh	Roxbury, Mass	Oct. 23, 1860	30, 486
Grain-bin	C. W. Mills	Brooklyn, N. Y	May 18, 1869	90, 116
Grain-bin	O. I. Porter	Hudson, Ohio	Jan. 8, 1867	61, 095
Grain-bin	F. Raymond	Cleveland, Ohio	July 12, 1870	105, 367
Grain bin	F. Raymond	Cleveland, Ohio	Aug. 30, 1870	106, 961
Grain-bin	F. Raymond and A. Miller	Cleveland, Ohio	Dec. 21, 1869	98, 190
Grain-bin	W. S. Sampson	New York, N. Y	Jan. 14, 1862	34, 164
Grain-bin	W. S. Sampson	New York, N. Y	Dec. 9, 1862	37, 139
Grain-bin	W. S. Sampson	New York, N. Y	Aug. 3, 1869	93, 352
Grain-bin	C. D. Woodruff	Toledo, Ohio	Aug. 31, 1869	94, 265
Grain-bin, Fire-proof	G. H. Johnson	Buffalo, N. Y	Mar. 9, 1869	87, 568
Grain-bin for storing and drying	J. Royal	White Rock, Ill	Feb. 6, 1872	123, 424
Grain-bins, Operating discharge-valve for	G. H. Johnson	Buffalo, N. Y	Feb. 16, 1869	86, 928
Grain-binder	J. F. Appleby	Mazo Manie, Wis	June 1, 1869	90, 807
Grain-binder	J. Baker	Fairbury, Ill	July 27, 1869	93, 035
Grain-binder	W. P. Barker	Grand Rapids, Mich	Dec. 9, 1862	37, 123
Grain binder	W. P. Barker	Grand Rapids, Mich	Mar. 21, 1865	46, 869
Grain-binder	C. L. Beamer	Cambria, N. Y	June 15, 1869	91, 204
Grain-binder	J. Bebel	Earlville, Ill	Feb. 16, 1864	41, 661
Grain-binder	J. Bebel	Rockford, Ill	Aug. 3, 1869	93, 165
Grain-binder	C. W. Bowron	Chicago, Ill	Jan. 16, 1872	122, 803
Grain-binder	H. S. L. Bryan	Kearney, Mo	Oct. 22, 1872	132, 436
Grain-binder	J. K. Bull	Buckingham, Iowa	Sept. 8, 1868	81, 875
Grain-binder	W. W. Burson	Yates, Ill	June 26, 1860	28, 830
Grain-binder	W. W. Burson	Atkinson, Ill	Aug. 11, 1863	39, 463
Grain-binder	W. W. Burson	Rockford, Ill	Oct. 4, 1864	44, 513
Grain-binder	W. W. Burson	Rockford, Ill	July 25, 1865	48, 900
Grain-binder	S. D. Carpenter	Madison, Wis	Dec. 22, 1868	85, 209
Grain-binder	S. D. Carpenter	Madison, Wis	Dec. 22, 1868	85, 210
Grain-binder	E. Chapman	Rochester, Minn	May 7, 1872	126, 520
Grain-binder	E. H. Clinton	Iowa City, Iowa	July 13, 1869	92, 517
Grain-binder	E. H. Clinton	Iowa City, Iowa	Apr. 30, 1872	126, 129
Grain-binder	C. G. Dickenson	Poughkeepsie, N. Y	May 30, 1871	115, 284
Grain-binder	C. H. Durkee	Hartford, Wis	Nov. 22, 1859	26, 171
Grain-binder	N. B. Fassett	Saint Louis, Mo	May 21, 1872	127, 036
Grain-binder	N. F. Gilman	Rochester, Minn	Aug. 24, 1869	93, 985
Grain-binder	W. F. Goodwin	Washington, D. C	Mar. 13, 1866	53, 138
Grain-binder	J. F. Gordon	Kalamazoo, Mich	May 12, 1868	77, 878
Grain-binder	J. F. Gordon	Rochester, N. Y	July 15, 1873	140, 822
Grain-binder	J. B. Greenhut	Chicago, Ill	Sept. 8, 1868	81, 891
Grain-binder	W. D. Harrah	Davenport, Iowa	Dec. 22, 1863	41, 002
Grain-binder	W. D. Harrah, I. M. Gifford, and E. T. Johnston.	Davenport, Iowa	May 10, 1870	102, 815
Grain-binder	H. Harrier	Indianapolis, Ind	Sept. 4, 1866	57, 710
Grain-binder	V. Hayes, C. G. Waldo, and H. A. Main.	Tekonsha, Mich	Dec. 8, 1868	84, 693
Grain-binder	J. F. Hemperly and C. Barns	West Liberty, Iowa	Sept. 5, 1865	49, 756
Grain-binder	J. S. Hickey	Pike, Ill	July 17, 1860	29, 170
Grain-binder	S. T. Holly	Rockford, Ill	Aug. 14, 1866	57, [illegible]38
Grain-binder	S. T. Holly	Rockford, Ill	Sept. 11, 1866	57, 904
Grain-binder	S. T. Holly	Rockford, Ill	June 11, 1867	65, 746
Grain-binder	A. S. Hoyt	Winona, Minn	Dec. 13, 1870	110, 138
Grain-binder	A. S. Hoyt	Winona, Minn	Aug. 5, 1873	141, 507
Grain-binder	S. Judevine and Z. Shaw	Roxbury, Wis	July 14, 1863	39, 234
Grain-binder	H. Kaller	Perry, Ill	June 5, 1860	28, 584
Grain-binder	I. Lancaster	Baltimore, Md	Jan. 23, 1866	52, 175
Grain-binder	I. Lancaster	Baltimore, Md	Apr. 24, 1866	54, 177
Grain-binder	I. Lancaster	Baltimore, Md	Nov. 19, 1867	71, 023
Grain-binder	S. D. Locke	Janesville, Wis	Dec. 19, 1865	51, 599
Grain-binder	S. D. Locke	Janesville, Wis	Dec. 19, 1865	51, 600
Grain-binder	S. D. Locke	Janesville, Wis	July 24, 1866	56, 580
Grain-binder	S. D. Locke	Janesville, Wis	Sept. 4, 1866	57, 739
Grain-binder	S. D. Locke	Janesville, Wis	Dec. 4, 1866	60, 208
Grain-binder	S. D. Locke	Janesville, Wis	Dec. 7, 1869	97, 531
Grain-binder	S. D. Locke	Janesville, Wis	Dec. 7, 1869	97, 532
Grain-binder	S. D. Locke	Janesville, Wis	Dec. 7, 1869	97, 533
Grain-binder	S. D. Locke	Janesville, Wis	Dec. 7, 1869	97, 534
Grain-binder	S. D. Locke	Janesville, Wis	Dec. 7, 1869	97, 535
Grain-binder	S. D. Locke	Janesville, Wis	Dec. 7, 1869	97, 536
Grain-binder	S. D. Locke	Janesville, Wis	Jan. 17, 1871	111, 069
Grain-binder	S. D. Locke	Janesville, Wis	Nov. 28, 1871	121, 2[illegible]0
Grain-binder	S. D. Locke	Hoosick Falls, N. Y	Feb. 11, 1873	135, 826
Grain-binder	S. D. Locke	Hoosick Falls, N. Y	May 20, 1873	139, 008
Grain-binder	W. Lottridge	Charles City, Iowa	Aug. 10, 1869	93, 458

Index of patents issued from the United States Patent Office from 1790 *to* 1873, *inclusive*—Continued.

Invention.	Inventor.	Residence.	Date.	No.
Grain-binder	W. Lottridge	Charles City, Iowa	Oct. 4, 1870	107, 933
Grain-binder	G. W. Loveless and C. H. Shaffer.	Charles Hill, Ind	Nov. 16, 1869	96, 933
Grain-binder	W. D. May	Baltimore, Md	Feb 16, 1869	87, 056
Grain-binder	J. M. McMaster	Rochester, N. Y	June 29, 1869	91. 860
Grain-binder	D. McPherson	Caledonia, N. Y	Sept. 27, 1870	107, 797
Grain-binder	J. H. Morse	Peoria, Ill	Dec. 17, 1872	134, 089
Grain-binder	J. H. Mudgett	Camanche, Iowa	Oct. 12, 1869	95, 714
Grain-binder	W. B. Oglesby	Ridge Prairie, Ill	June 21, 1870	104, 487
Grain-binder	W. H. Paine	Janesville, Wis	Aug. 2, 1870	105, 974
Grain-binder	L. Parker	Davenport, Iowa	Dec. 27, 1870	110, 492
Grain-binder	L. F. Parker	Davenport, Iowa	Aug. 31, 1869	94, 436
Grain-binder	J. Pearson	West Milton, Ohio	Apr. 9, 1872	125. 481
Grain-binder	P. A. Perry	Perth Amboy, N. J	Apr. 18, 1871	113, 792
Grain-binder	A. Philippi	Saint Louis, Mo	Sept. 26, 1871	119, 241
Grain-binder	A. Phillippi	Saint Louis, Mo.	Aug. 19, 1873	142, 040
Grain-binder	F. W. Randall	Tekonsha, Mich	Dec. 27, 1870	110, 498
Grain-binder	M. T. Ridout	Sun Prairie, Wis	Nov 14, 1871	120, 828
Grain-binder	O. B. Ross	Bowen's Prairie, Iowa	Sept. 12, 1871	118, 975
Grain-binder	Q. A. Scott	Pittsburgh, Pa	June 17, 1873	140, 083
Grain-binder	G. A. Scribner	Rochester, N. Y	Sept. 27, 1870	107, 823
Grain-binder	G. B. Shafer	Delta, Ohio	Mar. 23, 1869	88, 087
Grain-binder	W. Siverd, jr	Geneseo, N. Y	Feb. 27, 1872	124, 020
Grain-binder	A. J. Smith	New York, N. Y	Jan. 15, 1867	61, 272
Grain-binder	W. W. Snell	Bushford, Minn	Feb. 23, 1869	87, 215
Grain-binder	G. H. Spaulding	Rockford, Ill	May 31, 1870	103, 673
Grain-binder	A. S. Stone	Plain View, Minn	Mar. 3, 1868	75, 215
Grain-binder	O. O. Storle	Norway, Wis	Dec. 3, 1867	71, 660
Grain-binder	O. O. Storle	Norway, Wis	June 15, 1869	91, 282
Grain-binder	M. Summers and S. B. Lane	Zionsville, Ind	Oct. 3, 1871	119, 668
Grain-binder	J. Waddington	New Philadelphia, Ohio	Aug. 26, 1873	142, 504
Grain-binder	S. J. Wallace	Carthage, Ill	Apr. 12, 1864	42, 322
Grain-binder	S. J. Wallace	Carthage, Ill	Jan. 10, 1865	45, 885
Grain-binder	G. Warner	West Liberty, Iowa	July 30, 1867	67, 389
Grain-binder	J. H. Whitney	Rochester, Minn	Apr. 2, 1872	125, 366
Grain-binder	C. B. Withington	Janesville, Wis	Feb. 20, 1872	123, 967
Grain-binder	J. Youll	Manchester, Iowa	Aug. 15, 1871	118, 091
Grain-binder, Automatic	R. D. Brown	Covington, Ind	Apr. 7, 1863	38, 093
Grain-binders, Band-tuck for	J. Beall	Defiance, Ohio	Dec. 24, 1872	134, 192
Grain-binders' reel	S. D. Locke	Janesville, Wis	Feb. 20, 1866	52, 722
Grain-binders' reel	S. D. Locke	Janesville, Wis	Nov. 17, 1868	84, 065
Grain-binding apparatus	J. F. Barrett	North Granville, N. Y	Apr. 28, 1857	17, 135
Grain-binding apparatus	G. W. Chandler	Mason, N. H	Feb. 1, 1870	99, 404
Grain-binding machine	D. W. Ayres	Middleport, Ill	May 22, 1860	28, 338
Grain-binding machine	J. F. Black	Lancaster, Ill	Sept. 22, 1857	18, 231
Grain-binding machine	W. W. Burson	Yates City, Ill	Feb. 26, 1861	31, 526
Grain-binding machine	T. Courser	Princeton, Ill	July 10, 1860	29, 063
Grain-binding machine	T. Fowler	Tottensville, N. Y	June 7, 1870	103, 861
Grain-binding machine	T. Fowler	Tottensville, N. Y	June 7, 1870	103, 862
Grain-binding machine	A. Goodyear, 2d	New Haven, Conn	Nov. 7, 1865	50, 814
Grain-binding machine	S. T. Holly	Rockford, Ill	Jan. 26, 1864	41, 377
Grain-binding machine	S. T. Holly	Rockford, Ill	Jan. 26, 1864	41, 378
Grain-binding machine	I. Keyes	Putney, Vt	July 17, 1839	1, 251
Grain-binding machine	W. F. Pagett	Stone Bridge, Va	July 29, 1856	15, 436
Grain-binding machine	L. D. Phillips	Chicago, Ill	Dec. 29, 1857	18, 988
Grain-binding machine	S. Reynolds	Richmond, R. I	Feb. 12, 1861	31, 402
Grain-binding mechanism	A. Sherwood	Auburn, N. Y	Aug. 30, 1859	25, 308
Grain, Bushing-screen for cleaning	E. Tisdall	Windham, Conn	July 17, 1815	....
Grain by blowing, Machine for raising	J. Bailey	Chester County, Pa	Mar. 5, 1810	....
Grain by hand or horse power, Grinding or cracking	B. Hinkley	New York, N. Y	Mar. 10, 1834	....
Grain by horse-power, Machine for cutting	L. Durham and J. S. Pleasants	Halifax County, Va	July 28, 1827	....
Grain by sulphurous acid, Bleaching	J. M. Clark	Philadelphia, Pa	Apr. 17, 1860	27, 887
Grain-carrier	O. M. Gould	Montreal, Canada	Dec. 12, 1871	121, 867
Grain-carriers, Construction of	A. Linhart and S. McClain	Fulton, Ohio	Sept. 25, 1849	6, 749
Grain-cleaner	W. Ager	Washington, D. C	July 13, 1869	92, 556
Grain-cleaner	J. E. Anderson	Boiling Springs, Pa	Oct. 27, 1868	83, 438
Grain-cleaner	G. B. Bailey	Greenfield, Ind	Dec. 2, 1862	37; 031
Grain-cleaner	C. F. Baylor	Clinton, N. J	Aug. 7, 1866	56, 880
Grain-cleaner	E. Bradfield	Rochester, N. Y	Sept. 19, 1840	1, 794
Grain-cleaner	G. Clark	Sandusky, Ohio	Apr. 21, 1863	38, 258
Grain-cleaner	J. H. De Force	Healdsburgh, Cal	June 11, 1872	127, 680
Grain-cleaner	W. S Deisher	Hamburgh, Pa	Feb. 16, 1864	41, 609
Grain-cleaner	P. C. Fritz	Barrytown, N. Y	May 1, 1860	28, 071
Grain-cleaner	A. Gaar	Richmond, Ind	Mar. 13, 1860	27, 497
Grain-cleaner	J. A. Hall	Greenfield, Ind	May 28, 1867	65, 074
Grain-cleaner	T. Hancock and J. H. Leaman	Richmond, Va	Jan. 28, 1868	73, 803
Grain-cleaner	W. Houghton	Great Grimsby, England	Nov. 11, 1873	144, 455
Grain-cleaner	A. Hunter	Rockford, Ill	Oct. 29, 1872	132, 664
Grain-cleaner	J. Hutchison	Three Rivers, Mich	Dec. 8, 1863	40, 840
Grain-cleaner	C. Jones	De Soto, Ill	Jan. 1[illegible], 1870	98, 975
Grain-cleaner	J. A. Krake	Alden, N. Y	May 7, 1872	126, 400
Grain-cleaner	G. Leach	Owego, N. Y	Mar. 13, 1855	12, 512
Grain-cleaner	J. P. Leonard	Five Mile, Ohio	Nov. 12, 1872	133, 041
Grain-cleaner	W. A. Lewis	Joliet, Ill	June 22, 1869	91, 549
Grain-cleaner	E. Mantz	Frederick, Md	Feb. 9, 1864	41, 519
Grain-cleaner	J. McTaggart	Rochester, N. Y	Apr. 2, 1867	63, 410
Grain-cleaner	L. and J. Miller	Canton, Ohio	Dec. 17, 1861	33, 956
Grain-cleaner	J. Montgomery	Baltimore, Md	Dec. 29, 1868	85, 325
Grain-cleaner	S. Moore	Rochelle, Ill	May 27, 1873	139, 257
Grain-cleaner	M. T. Nesbitt	Colora, Md	Apr. 4, 1871	113, 686
Grain-cleaner	G. W. Osborn	Centreville, Mich	Mar. 13, 1860	27, 467
Grain-cleaner	C. Perry	Rochester, N. Y	June 7, 1870	103, 922
Grain-cleaner	C. Perry and J. E. Wheat	Rochester, N. Y	Mar. 1, 1870	100, 441
Grain-cleaner	P. Provost	Rochester, Minn	Oct. 15, 1872	132, 319
Grain-cleaner	N. Reece	Hemlock Township, Pa	Aug. 1, 1871	117, 681
Grain-cleaner	H. D. Reynolds	Pendleton, Ind	June 19, 1855	13, 103
Grain-cleaner	F. P. Root	Sweden, N. Y	Nov. 15, 1843	3, 341
Grain-cleaner	J. Simpson and W. Hayden	Tecumseh, Mich	Oct. 14, 1862	36, 676

Index of patents issued from the United States Patent Office from 1790 *to* 1873, *inclusive*—Continued.

Invention.	Inventor.	Residence.	Date.	No.
Grain-cleaner	W. B. Smith	Clayton, Ill	July 6, 1869	92, 385
Grain-cleaner	J. Sternberg	Webster City, Iowa	Feb. 21, 1871	112, 087
Grain-cleaner	W. H. Stevens	Salem, Ill	July 7, 1846	4, 624
Grain-cleaner	G. Stevenson	Zionsville, Ind	Apr. 9, 1867	63, 763
Grain-cleaner	G. Stevenson and J. J. Crider	Zionsville and Greenfield, Ind.	May 29, 1866	55, 174
Grain-cleaner	J. Stroop	Joliet, Ill	Nov. 9, 1869	96, 630
Grain-cleaner	B. T. Trimmer	Parma, N. Y	Apr. 3, 1855	12, 657
Grain-cleaner	I. Wait	Watertown, N. Y	Oct. 11, 1859	25, 777
Grain-cleaner	A. T. Waldo	Dryden, N. Y	Mar. 13, 1860	27, 489
Grain-cleaner	J. H. Weaver	Gap, Pa	June 20, 1871	116, 122
Grain-cleaner	W. B. Webster	Foxville, Va	May 1, 1860	28, 119
Grain-cleaner	J. E. Wheat	Rochester, N. Y	Jan. 26, 1869	86, 194
Grain-cleaner and fertilizer-sifter	J. A. Green	Mill Dale, Va	Mar. 7, 1871	112, 334
Grain cleaner and scourer	E. H. Kellogg	Milwaukee, Wis	May 9, 1871	114, 688
Grain cleaner and separator	G. S. Carter	Lewisburgh, Pa	Jan. 2, 1872	122, 436
Grain cleaner and separator	W. A. Cockrill	Zanesville, Ohio	June 6, 1871	115, 707
Grain cleaner and separator	W. Gardner	Catalpa, Ky	Jan. 28, 1870	104, 728
Grain cleaner and separator	J. W. Patterson	Monticello, Minn	Dec. 15, 1863	40, 942
Grain cleaner and separator	J. H. Redfield	Salem, Ind	Feb. 6, 1872	123, 361
Grain cleaner and separator	B. T. Trimmer	Rochester, N. Y	May 29, 1866	55, 179
Grain cleaner and separator	R. Ward	Edinburgh, Ind	Aug. 26, 1856	15, 630
Grain cleaner and separator	F. Wegmann	Naples, Italy	Oct. 18, 1870	108, 541
Grain cleaner and smut-machine	J. Ferguson	Fall River, Mass	July 20, 1869	92, 809
Grain, Cleaning	R. Redfield	Salem, Ind	Feb. 27, 1866	52, 882
Grain, Cleaning	M. Urfler	Upper Milford, Pa	Oct. 1, 1830	....
Grain, Cleaning and dressing	G. Arnold	Angelica, N. Y	June 17, 1830	....
Grain cleaning and drying machine	H. N. Black	Philadelphia, Pa	Aug. 1, 1854	11, 458
Grain cleaning and hulling machine	J. M. Mayer	New York, N. Y	Feb. 14, 1865	46, 374
Grain cleaning and winnowing machine	Z. Rice	Lyons, N. Y	Apr. 24, 1841	2, 067
Grain-cleaning device	P. G. B. Westmacott	Elswick, Newcastle-upon-Tyne, England.	July 16, 1867	66, 759
Grain, Cleaning, hulling, and drying	E. Cole	Dryden, N. Y	June 23, 1863	38, 948
Grain-cleaning machine	B. Barney	Tune, Ill	Sept. 18, 1866	58, 048
Grain-cleaning machine	J. D. Beers	Philadelphia, Pa	Dec. 10, 1841	2, 384
Grain-cleaning machine	S. Bentz	Boonsborough, Md	July 23, 1841	2, 193
Grain-cleaning machine	J. N. Bird and E. D. Weld	Trenton, N. J	Mar. 28, 1842	2, 513
Grain-cleaning machine	J. L. Booth	Cuyahoga Falls, Ohio	Dec. 18, 1855	13, 937
Grain-cleaning machine	G. W. Bowers	Leitersburgh, Md	Sept. 24, 1850	7, 662
Grain cleaning machine	D. H. Cole	Portland, Me	July 17, 1838	846
Grain-cleaning machine	P. Cook	Westfield, N. Y	Jan. 17, 1842	2, 423
Grain-cleaning machine	W. Crotzer	Spruce Creek, Pa	Nov. 20, 1860	30, 704
Grain-cleaning machine	J. De Rush	Saint Mary's, Ohio	May 11, 1858	20, 196
Grain-cleaning machine	M. Eckley	Olney, Ill	May 5, 1868	77, 468
Grain-cleaning machine	W. T. Fisher	Cleaveland, Tenn	Oct. 5, 1858	21, 662
Grain-cleaning machine	H. Fitts	Somerset, Mich	Apr. 12, 1859	23, 641
Grain-cleaning machine	D. Flickenger and S. Krim	Hanover, Pa	May 28, 1842	2, 649
Grain-cleaning machine	J. R. Gates	Eckmansville, Ohio	May 19, 1857	17, 325
Grain-cleaning machine	T. C. Gleason	Rochester, N. Y	May 3, 1859	23, 838
Grain-cleaning machine	I. G. Goshon and W. Bowers	Mercersburgh and Chambersburgh, Pa.	June 1, 1858	20, 422
Grain-cleaning machine	M. L. Hall	Bridgeport, Conn	June 1, 1858	20, 425
Grain-cleaning machine	C. B. Horton	Elmira, N. Y	Nov. 18, 1856	16, 088
Grain-cleaning machine	G. H. Johnson	Johnsonburgh, N. Y	Dec. 15, 1838	1, 039
Grain-cleaning machine	G. Mann, jr	Lockport, N. Y	June 29, 1839	1, 211
Grain-cleaning machine	R. C. Mauck	Harrisonburgh, Va	Dec. 18, 1860	30, 978
Grain-cleaning machine	T. McCrea	Anne Arundel County, Md.	Aug. 9, 1839	1, 280
Grain-cleaning machine	J. Nott	West Hempfield, Pa	Aug. 11, 1841	2, 220
Grain-cleaning machine	W. H. Orr	Martin's Ferry, Ohio	July 13, 1858	20, 923
Grain-cleaning machine	J. Outram	Elmira, N. Y	Oct. 30, 1860	30, 540
Grain-cleaning machine	W. Partridge and G. W. Shaw	Ellicott's Mills, Md	June 15, 1858	20, 581
Grain-cleaning machine	T. Reese	Baltimore, Md	July 20, 1831	....
Grain-cleaning machine	J. Rood	Beaver Dam, Wis	Sept. 28, 1869	95, 269
Grain-cleaning machine	N. H. Sherburne	Campton, Ill	July 13, 1858	20, 899
Grain-cleaning machine	S. Spangler	Stoney Creek, Pa	May 19, 1840	1, 608
Grain-cleaning machine	E. Sweetland	South Bend, Ind	Mar. 27, 1866	53, 502
Grain-cleaning machine	G. E. Throop	Syracuse, N. Y	Feb. 11, 1873	135, 675
Grain-cleaning machine	B. T. Trimmer	Rochester, N. Y	July 27, 1858	21, 036
Grain-cleaning machine	J. P. Tunison	Ovid, N. Y	Sept. 18, 1860	30, 099
Grain-cleaning machine	J. Tyler	Claremont, N. H	May 18, 1827	....
Grain-cleaning machine	W. H. Waldby	Cooperstown, N. Y	Aug. 19, 1862	36, 250
Grain-cleaning machine	H. Wallace and W. Mellon	North Sewickley, Pa	Mar. 8, 1859	23, 205
Grain cleaning, scouring, and decorticating machine	J. A. Maloney	Georgetown, D. C	Nov. 14, 1871	120, 987
Grain-cleaning screen, Revolving	E. P. Fitzpatrick	Mount Morris, N. Y	Nov. 14, 1835	....
Grain, &c., Cleansing	I. Honeywells	Hillsdale, N. Y	Apr. 27, 1816	....
Grain, coffee, and rice cleaner	A. and I. D. Crawford	Wilkesbarre, Pa., and Bloomington, Ill.	Jan. 31, 1871	111, 323
Grain-conveyer	D. L. Bartlett	Rockford, Ill	Jan. 12, 1869	85, 782
Grain-conveyer	D. W. Bryant	Chicago, Ill	Mar. 21, 1865	46, 876
Grain-conveyer	O. C. Dodge	New York, N. Y	Feb. 10, 1863	37, 615
Grain-conveyer	J. Gardiner	Philadelphia, Pa	Nov. 23, 1869	97, 070
Grain-conveyer	O. Johnson and C. O. Wall	Galva, Ill	Feb. 22, 1870	100, 154
Grain-conveyer	C. Lazarevitch	Brooklyn, N. Y	Dec. 2, 1873	145, 112
Grain-conveyer	J. M. Rush	Marengo, Iowa	Apr. 7, 1868	76, 529
Grain-conveyer	S. W. Wood	Cornwall, N. Y	Dec. 4, 1866	60, 313
Grain-conveyer for elevators	D. C. Chester	Ogdensburgh, N. Y	Apr. 13, 1869	88, 849
Grain-conveying apparatus	H. G. Yates	Kalamazoo, Mich	Nov. 11, 1873	144, 589
Grain-conveying machine	S. W. Wood	Cornwall, N. Y	May 28, 1867	65, 149
Grain-cooler	S. A. Stebbins	Toledo, Ohio	Apr. 19, 1870	102, 175
Grain-cooler	G. D. Woodworth	Chicago, Ill	July 3, 1866	56, 136
Grain cooler and sifter	Armstrong and King	New York, N. Y	May 9, 1835	....
Grain cooler and ventilator	C. D. Clark	Chicago, Ill	Aug. 24, 1858	21, 245
Grain-cradle	J. Babcock	Rensselaerville, N. Y	Mar. 24, 1823	....
Grain-cradle	D. D. Devoe	Ilion, N. Y	Apr. 5, 1864	42, 173
Grain-cradle	D. Duesler	Coldwater, Mich	Dec. 30, 1873	145, 933
Grain-cradle	M. R. Flanders	Parishville, N. Y	June 28, 1859	24, 550
Grain-cradle	C. Goss	Madrid, N. Y	Feb. 16, 1843	2, 955
Grain-cradle	I. T. Grant and D. H. Viall	Schaghticoke, N. Y	Oct. 15, 1850	7, 720

Index of patents issued from the United States Patent Office from 1790 *to* 1873, *inclusive*—Continued.

Index of patents issued from the United States Patent Office from 1790 *to* 1873, *inclusive*—Continued.

Invention.	Inventor.	Residence.	Date.	No.
Grain-drill	B. Kuhns	Dayton, Ohio	Nov. 16, 1869	96, 926
Grain-drill	B. Kuhns	Dayton, Ohio	Feb. 14, 1871	111, 853
Grain-drill	B. Kuhns	Dayton, Ohio	July 4, 1871	116, 719
Grain-drill	E. Lake	Davisburgh, Mich	Sept. 17, 1867	68, 996
Grain-drill	G. Leigh	Clinton Station, N. J	Oct. 13, 1863	40, 270
Grain-drill	M. T. Lowth and T. J. Howe	Owatonna, Minn	Oct. 6, 1868	82, 853
Grain-drill	J. T. Lynam	Jeffersonville, Ind	Oct. 27, 1868	83, 517
Grain-drill	S. Markham	Flat Rock, Kans	Aug. 29, 1871	118, 621
Grain-drill	R. Marks and A. C. Behne	Connersville, Ind	July 4, 1871	116, 612
Grain-drill	A. Maschka	Chicago, Ill	Feb. 23, 1864	41, 713
Grain-drill	P. P. Mast and C. O. Gardiner	Springfield, Ohio	Apr. 2, 1872	125, 314
Grain-drill	J. McDonald	Hardin, Ill	Sept. 25, 1866	58, 274
Grain-drill	D. E. McSherry	Dayton, Ohio	Jan. 24, 1871	111, 132
Grain-drill	D. E. McSherry	Dayton, Ohio	July 18, 1871	117, 191
Grain-drill	D. E. McSherry	Dayton, Ohio	Jan. 16, 1872	122, 729
Grain-drill	D. E. McSherry and J. H. Landis.	Dayton, Ohio	Dec. 5, 1871	121, 648
Grain-drill	T. S. Mills	Iberia, Ohio	Apr. 19, 1864	42, 390
Grain-drill	J. Milton	Hillsborough, Va	May 14, 1872	126, 826
Grain-drill	W. H. Moore, jr	Blooming Grove, Ind	Nov. 16, 1869	96, 825
Grain-drill	H. A. and L. B. Myers	Elmore, Ohio	June 25, 1861	32, 641
Grain-drill	H. B. and G. A. Myers	Schoolcraft, Mich	Nov. 3, 1863	40, 495
Grain-drill	M. L. Nickels	Dunlapsville, Ind	June 9, 1868	78, 682
Grain-drill	S. R. Nye	Winchendon, Mass	Feb. 18, 1873	135, 932
Grain-drill	H. Paddack and C. Hollar	Abington, Ind	Apr. 27, 1869	89, 333
Grain-drill	A. Palmer	Brockport, N. Y	June 19, 1849	6, 536
Grain-drill	C. E. Patric	Macedon, N. Y	Dec. 29, 1868	85, 472
Grain-drill	C. E. Patric	Springfield, Ohio	Nov. 5, 1872	132, 889
Grain-drill	C. E. Patric	Springfield, Ohio	Feb. 25, 1873	136, 260
Grain-drill	C. E. Patric and L. Bickford	Macedon, N. Y	Nov. 26, 1867	71, 528
Grain-drill	W. P. Penn	Belleville, Ill	May 24, 1864	42, 871
Grain-drill	W. P. Penn, J. Geiss, and J. Brosius.	Belleville, Ill	June 27, 1865	48, 432
Grain-drill	O. M. Pond	Independence, Iowa	Oct. 20, 1863	40, 359
Grain-drill	D. J. Powers	Madison, Wis	Nov. 18, 1862	36, 966
Grain drill	A. Pritz	Dayton, Ohio	Aug. 17, 1858	21, 212
Grain-drill	H. Pulse	Saint Paul, Ind	Feb. 12, 1867	62, 066
Grain-drill	H. Pulse	Saint Paul, Ind	Nov. 12, 1867	70, 896
Grain-drill	H. Pulse	Waldron, Ind	Mar. 8, 1870	100, 555
Grain-drill	G. A. Pursly	Pittsfield, Ill	June 3, 1873	139, 610
Grain-drill	A. Putnam	Owego, N. Y	June 19, 1866	55, 707
Grain-drill	B. Regan	Miamisburgh, Ohio	Mar. 14, 1865	46, 821
Grain-drill	D. Rentchler	Belleville, Ill	Apr. 4, 1871	113, 564
Grain-drill	M. Rich	Horicon, Wis	Dec. 1, 1863	40, 770
Grain-drill	J. L. Riter	Brownsville, Ind	May 25, 1869	90, 582
Grain-drill	J. L. Riter	Brownsville, Ind	Oct. 11, 1870	108, 294
Grain-drill	J. L. Riter	Brownsville, Ind	May 30, 1871	115, 523
Grain-drill	W. Ross	Oshkosh, Wis	Mar. 29, 1864	42, 112
Grain-drill	J. R. Rude	Liberty, Ind	Feb. 5, 1867	61, 765
Grain-drill	J. R., S. B., and G. W. Rude	Liberty, Ind	Oct. 5, 1869	95, 607
Grain-drill	P. J. Schmitt	Carlinville, Ill	Apr. 20, 1869	89, 247
Grain-drill	P. J. Schmitt	Carlinville, Ill	July 13, 1869	92, 658
Grain-drill	P. and P. J. Schmitt	Waterloo, Ill	Apr. 24, 1866	54, 219
Grain-drill	P. and P. J. Schmitt	Waterloo, Ill	Feb. 5, 1867	61, 879
Grain-drill	S. C. Schofield	Freeport, Ill	Oct. 20, 1863	40, 365
Grain-drill	J. Scovil	Hamburgh, N. Y	Dec. 22, 1863	41, 023
Grain-drill	U. H. Shockley	Litchfield, Ill	Mar. 29, 1864	42, 116
Grain-drill	J. H. Shreiner	Camp Hill, Pa	May 12, 1868	77, 924
Grain-drill	J. H. Shreiner	Camp Hill, Pa	Aug. 25, 1868	81, 547
Grain-drill	B. F. Smith	Unity, Iowa	Oct. 27, 1863	40, 435
Grain-drill	J. Smith	Tiffin, Ohio	June 17, 1862	35, 634
Grain-drill	J. Smith	Tiffin, Ohio	Nov. 18, 1862	36, 969
Grain-drill	E. Steacy	Strasburgh, Pa	June 5, 1849	6, 497
Grain-drill	C. Street	Barre Centre, N. Y	May 29, 1855	12, 973
Grain-drill	J. H. Thomas	Springfield, Ohio	July 26, 1870	105, 866
Grain-drill	J. H. Thomas	Springfield, Ohio	Feb. 28, 1871	112, 299
Grain-drill	J. H. Thomas and P. P. Mast	Springfield, Ohio	Oct. 17, 1865	50, 545
Grain-drill	J. H. Thomas and P. P. Mast	Springfield, Ohio	June 19, 1866	55, 742
Grain-drill	J. H. Thomas and P. P. Mast	Springfield, Ohio	Dec. 7, 1869	97, 729
Grain-drill	J. H. Thomas and P. P. Mast	Springfield, Ohio	Feb. 21, 1871	112, 093
Grain-drill	J. H. Thomas, P. P. Mast, and C. O. Gardiner.	Springfield, Ohio	Aug. 3, 1869	93, 369
Grain-drill	J. H. Thomas, P. P. Mast, and C. O. Gardiner.	Springfield, Ohio	Aug. 3, 1869	93, 370
Grain-drill	W. H. Trimmer	Round Hill, Pa	Oct. 5, 1869	95, 619
Grain-drill	W. W. Tuttle	Gratiot, Wis	Dec. 1, 1863	40, 780
Grain-drill	S. E. Tyler	Horicon, Wis	May 31, 1864	42, 975
Grain-drill	J. G. Vale	Cumberland County, Pa	Dec. 10, 1867	72, 127
Grain-drill	E. Wagoner	Westminster, Md	Nov. 27, 1866	60, 096
Grain-drill	L. N. Warren	Milwaukee, Wis	May 29, 1866	55, 184
Grain-drill	T. W. Watts	Rushville, Ill	Apr. 19, 1864	42, 424
Grain-drill	W. Weusthoff	Dayton, Ohio	July 13, 1869	92, 678
Grain-drill	W. Weusthoff	Dayton, Ohio	July 13, 1869	92, 679
Grain-drill	W. Weusthoff	Dayton, Ohio	Oct. 19, 1869	96, 064
Grain-drill	W. Weusthoff and T. G. Troup	Dayton, Ohio	Mar. 19, 1872	124, 707
Grain-drill	S. H. Wheeler and W. Tuttle, jr	Dowagiac, Mich	Feb. 5, 1867	61, 903
Grain-drill	L. Wight and O. G. Ewings	Whitewater, Wis	Dec. 26, 1871	122, 299
Grain-drill and broadcast sower	J. Ingels	Milton, Ind	Jan. 25, 1870	99, 198
Grain-drill and corn-cultivator, Combined	D. B. Platt	Jeffersonville, Ind	Feb. 7, 1871	111, 675
Grain-drill and corn-dropper	J. D. Sater and T. Barns	Greensburgh, Ind	Mar. 9, 1869	87, 716
Grain-drill and corn-planter, Combined	T. Short	Fairmount, Ill	Dec. 6, 1864	45, 350
Grain-drill and cultivator combined	E. Badlam	Ogdensburgh, N. Y	Oct. 17, 1865	50, 438
Grain-drill and land-roller, Combined	H. D. Palmer	Volena Township, Mich	Sept. 28, 1869	95, 375
Grain-drill attachment	S. Bowman	Camp Hill, Pa	Feb. 2, 1869	86, 354
Grain-drill feed	J. L. Riter	Liberty, Ind	Jan. 25, 1870	99, 238
Grain-drill feeder	M. L. Nickels	Dunlapsville, Ind	Aug. 30, 1870	106, 950
Grain-drill grass-seed attachment	J. P. Fulghum	Dublin, Ind	July 8, 1873	140, 694
Grain-drill-lifting apparatus	C. E. Patric	Macedon, N. Y	Dec. 17, 1867	72, 323

Index of patents issued from the United States Patent Office from 1790 *to* 1873, *inclusive*—Continued.

Invention.	Inventor.	Residence.	Date.	No.
Grain-drill roller	O. F. Momany	Dowagiac, Mich	June 1, 1869	90, 770
Grain-drill, seed-sower, and corn-planter, Combined.	D. Evans	Newton, Iowa	June 29, 1869	91, 925
Grain-drill shoe	P. and P. J Schmitt	Waterloo, Ill	Aug. 4, 1868	80, 671
Grain-drill teeth	L. Brickford	Macedon, N. Y	Apr. 19, 1870	102, 081
Grain-drill teeth	I. H. Palmer	Lodi, Wis	Nov. 3, 1863	40, 497
Grain-drill teeth	C. E. Patric	Macedon, N. Y	Feb. 1, 1870	99, 467
Grain-drill teeth	F. Villard	Mount Eaton, Ohio	Feb. 15, 1870	99, 981
Grain-drill teeth	J. D. Welsh	Farmland, Ind	Jan. 21, 1873	135, 186
Grain-drill tube	S. K. Lighter and T. Harding	Hamilton, Ohio	Nov. 6, 1866	59, 422
Grain-drill tube	S. K. Lighter, T. Harding, and J. Curtis.	Hamilton, Ohio	Aug. 13, 1867	67, 660
Grain-drills, Adjustable drag-bar for	J. D. Jones	Pittsburgh, Pa	Sept. 12, 1865	49, 883
Grain-drills, &c., Cup for	J. P. Zeller	South Bend, Ind	May 2, 1871	114, 384
Grain-drills, Drag-bar and teeth for	J. D. Jones	Pittsburgh, Pa	Sept. 26, 1865	50, 135
Grain-drills, Drag-bar for	J. H. Thomas and P. P. Mast	Springfield, Ohio	June 6, 1865	48, 112
Grain-drills, Fastening tubes in	F. Gardner	Carlisle, Pa	May 3, 1870	102, 531
Grain-drills, Feed-roller for	J. H. Thomas	Springfield, Ohio	Apr. 25, 1871	114, 227
Grain-drills, Seed-box for	C. H. Godfrey	Stewartsville, N. J	June 4, 1867	65, 374
Grain-drills, Seed-coverer for	J. S. Gage	Dowagiac, Mich	Aug. 26, 1862	36, 291
Grain-drills, &c., Seed-feeding device for	A. Schopp	Belleville, Ill	Sept. 21, 1869	95, 149
Grain-drills, Seed-wheel for	W. Weusthoff	Dayton, Ohio	Oct. 19, 1869	96, 063
Grain-drills, Seed-wheel for	W. Weusthoff and C. Schmidt	Dayton, Ohio	July 13, 1869	92, 680
Grain-drills, Vulcanized-rubber tube for	J. R. Bird	Brooklyn, N. Y	May 2, 1871	114, 394
Grain-drilling machine	J. Ingels	Milton, Ind	July 26, 1870	105, 960
Grain-dryer	E. A. Abbott	Baltimore, Md	Mar. 9, 1869	87, 613
Grain-dryer	L. Abbott and J. A. Sherburne	Lewiston, Me., and Boston, Mass.	Jan. 24, 1871	111, 163
Grain-dryer	J. W. Adams	Elyria, Ohio	Oct. 8, 1867	69, 530
Grain-dryer	S. V. Appleby	Spotswood, N. J	Oct. 3, 1871	119, 493
Grain-dryer	J. Babillion	Detroit, Mich	Sept. 13, 1864	44, 150
Grain-dryer	A. H. C. Barber	Clinton, Ill	Jan. 1, 1867	60, 666
Grain-dryer	H. H. Beach	Philadelphia, Pa	June 2, 1863	38, 723
Grain-dryer	H. H. Beach	Rome, N. Y	Nov. 7, 1865	50, 789
Grain-dryer	H. H. Beach	Rome, N. Y	July 17, 1866	56, 348
Grain-dryer	A. Bigelow	Adrian, Mich	May 16, 1848	5, 574
Grain-dryer	H. H. Bingham and J. C. Hunt	Terre Haute, Ind	Mar. 24, 1868	75, 844
Grain-dryer	W. Blakey	Baltimore, Md	Oct. 5, 1869	95, 556
Grain-dryer	W. Blakey	Brooklyn, N. Y	Apr. 18, 1871	113, 840
Grain-dryer	H. Boden	Olney, Ill	July 30, 1867	67, 256
Grain-dryer	D. Bonnell	Oswego, N. Y	Sept. 29, 1868	82, 589
Grain-dryer	A. T. Boon and C. L. Stevens	Galesburgh, Ill	Nov. 7, 1865	50, 792
Grain-dryer	C. H. Booth	Dubuque, Iowa	Jan. 19, 1864	41, 273
Grain-dryer	J. Buckingham	Wethersfield, Conn	Feb. 28, 1871	112, 118
Grain-dryer	J. S. Buell and S. A. W. Marsh	Buffalo, N. Y	Oct. 4, 1864	44, 512
Grain-dryer	J. S. Buell and S. A. W. Marsh	Buffalo, N. Y	Dec. 20, 1864	45, 471
Grain-dryer	H. G. Bulkley	Kalamazoo, Mich	Mar. 2, 1852	8, 769
Grain-dryer	H. G. Bulkley	New York, N. Y	Aug. 20, 1872	130, 564
Grain-dryer	J. Burns	New York, N. Y	May 30, 1871	115, 431
Grain-dryer	J. Burt	Westport, Mass	July 9, 1867	66, 559
Grain-dryer	W. L. Card	Kankakee, Ill	July 9, 1872	128, 707
Grain-dryer	C. F. Chichester	Brooklyn, N. Y	Dec. 5, 1871	121, 588
Grain-dryer	L. S. Chichester	New York, N. Y	Aug. 25, 1863	39, 630
Grain-dryer	L. S. Chichester	Brooklyn, N. Y	Mar. 15, 1864	41, 905
Grain-dryer	L. S. Chichester	Brooklyn, N. Y	May 2, 1865	47, 596
Grain-dryer	L. S. Chichester	Brooklyn, N. Y	Aug. 15, 1865	49, 470
Grain-dryer	L. S. Chichester	Brooklyn, N. Y	June 18, 1867	65, 793
Grain-dryer	L. S. Chichester	Brooklyn, N. Y	Feb. 25, 1868	74, 893
Grain-dryer	L. S. Chichester	Brooklyn, N. Y	Oct. 20, 1868	83, 255
Grain-dryer	L. S. Chichester	Brooklyn, N. Y	Jan. 10, 1871	110, 896
Grain-dryer	G. Clark	Buffalo, N. Y	Apr. 19, 1864	42, 348
Grain-dryer	G. Clark	Buffalo, N. Y	Apr. 3, 1866	53, 575
Grain-dryer	G. Clark	Buffalo, N. Y	July 31, 1866	56, 708
Grain-dryer	C. R. Coe	Bloomington, Ill	Nov. 26, 1872	133, 410
Grain-dryer	M. C. Cogswell and A. G. Williams.	Buffalo, N. Y	Feb. 18, 1862	34, 405
Grain-dryer	M. C. Cogswell and A. G. Williams.	Buffalo, N. Y	Aug. 11, 1863	39, 466
Grain-dryer	J. De Bary	Offenbach, Germany	Mar. 10, 1868	75, 386
Grain-dryer	W. H. Dole and D. R. Fraser	Chicago, Ill	Sept. 1, 1863	39, 722
Grain-dryer	M. R. Dudley	New Orleans, La	Apr. 30, 1850	7, 321
Grain-dryer	T. W. Eaton	Kankakee, Ill	June 13, 1871	115, 833
Grain-dryer	J. R. Evertson	Mount Vernon, Ind	Nov. 27, 1866	59, 989
Grain-dryer	J. R. Evertson	Mount Vernon, Ind	Oct. 15, 1867	69, 785
Grain-dryer	E. S. Forgy	Dayton, Ohio	Apr. 8, 1873	137, 606
Grain-dryer	S. Godfrey	Peoria, Ill	Mar. 20, 1866	53, 293
Grain-dryer	R. Grotz	Chicago, Ill	Aug. 31, 1869	94, 308
Grain-dryer	J. Guardiola	Chocola, Central America	May 7, 1872	126, 455
Grain-dryer	H. B. Hebert	New York, N. Y	Dec. 28, 1869	98, 374
Grain-dryer	R. Heneage	Buffalo, N. Y	Aug. 29, 1865	49, 626
Grain-dryer	R. Heneage	Buffalo, N. Y	Sept. 25, 1866	58, 254
Grain-dryer	H. Henley and J. A. Reinhart	Shoals and Loogootee, Ind	Dec. 15, 1868	85, 007
Grain-dryer	J. Hollingsworth	New York, N. Y	Sept. 24, 1872	131, 682
Grain-dryer	J. R. Hoopes	West Philadelphia, Pa	Aug. 27, 1850	7, 601
Grain-dryer	W. Hull and C. W. Hammond	Baltimore, Md	Sept. 28, 1869	95, 351
Grain-dryer	G. H. Johnson and G. Milsom	Buffalo, N. Y	Jan. 1, 1869	90, 847
Grain-dryer	S. C. Kenaga	Kankakee, Ill	Dec. 7, 1869	97, 650
Grain-dryer	E. Knaur and S. Beaver, jr	Valley Forge and Great Valley, Pa.	Apr. 18, 1848	5, 517
Grain-dryer	C. W. T. Krausch	Chicago, Ill	Mar. 10, 1863	37, 869
Grain-dryer	S. Marsh	Chicago, Ill	May 31, 1864	42, 957
Grain-dryer	S. Marsh	Chicago, Ill	July 4, 1865	48, 573
Grain-dryer	A. W. J. Mason	New Orleans, La	Sept. 12, 1871	118, 954
Grain-dryer	H. Merrill	Brooklyn, N. Y	Nov. 22, 1870	109, 536
Grain-dryer	F. H. C. Mey	Buffalo, N. Y	Apr. 12, 1864	42, 333
Grain-dryer	F. H. C. Mey	Buffalo, N. Y	May 28, 1872	127, 256
Grain-dryer	F. H. C. Mey and H. W. Dopp	Buffalo, N. Y	Dec. 3, 1872	133, 590
Grain-dryer	R. Milbourne and T. Browning	Whitechapel, Great Britain	July 26, 1870	105, 709
Grain-dryer	C. W. Mills and L. S. Chichester	Brooklyn, N. Y	Sept. 22, 1868	82, 432
Grain-dryer	W. F. Morgan	Buffalo, N. Y	July 22, 1873	141, 160

Index of patents issued from the United States Patent Office from 1790 *to* 1873, *inclusive*—Continued.

Invention.	Inventor.	Residence.	Date.	No.
Grain-dryer	J. J. Munger	Syracuse, N. Y	Feb. 2, 1869	86, 436
Grain-dryer	I. Y. Munn	Chicago, Ill	Apr. 12, 1870	101, 759
Grain-dryer	J. Norton, 3d	Chicago, Ill	July 10, 1866	56, 255
Grain-dryer	J. H. Pattee and E. S. Cleveland	Galva, Ill	Dec. 5, 1865	51, 348
Grain-dryer	R. S. Reynolds	New Haven, Conn	June 23, 1863	38, 985
Grain-dryer	A. Robert	Paris, France	May 23, 1871	115, 240
Grain-dryer	A. W. Roper	Glasgow, Mo	Sept. 17, 1872	131, 464
Grain-dryer	P.C. Schuyler and S.W. Warren	New York, N. Y	June 2, 1863	38, 790
Grain-dryer	S. Schuyler	Brooklyn, N. Y	Jan. 22, 1861	31, 191
Grain-dryer	H. H. Scoville	Chicago, Ill	Sept. 26, 1848	5, 816
Grain-dryer	C. S. Snead	Louisville, Ky	Oct. 1, 1850	7, 690
Grain-dryer	A. Soper	New York, N. Y	Nov. 18, 1873	144, 710
Grain-dryer	J. Souter	Chicago, Ill	June 28, 1859	24, 589
Grain-dryer	H. Spendelow and R. Heneage	Buffalo, N. Y	Sept. 15, 1868	82, 170
Grain-dryer	J. R. Stafford	Cleveland, Ohio	Apr. 18, 1848	5, 518
Grain-dryer	J. R. Stafford	Cleveland, Ohio	Apr. 18, 1848	5, 519
Grain-dryer	J. R. Stafford	Cleveland, Ohio	Apr. 18, 1848	5, 524
Grain-dryer	W. Standing	Cairo, Ill	July 7, 1868	79, 699
Grain-dryer	W. Stark and J. G. Fisher	Toledo, Ohio	Mar. 28, 1871	113, 219
Grain-dryer	S. M. Stevens	Elwood, Ill	Oct. 5, 1869	95, 616
Grain-dryer	J. E. Strode	Litchfield, Ill	Feb. 19, 1867	62, 233
Grain-dryer	B. F. Sturtevant	Jamaica Plain, Mass	Feb. 22, 1870	100, 212
Grain-dryer	B. F. Sturtevant	Jamaica Plain, Mass	Feb. 22, 1870	100, 235
Grain-dryer	R. T. Sutton	Rochester, N. Y	Dec. 22, 1863	41, 028
Grain-dryer	R. T. Sutton	Rochester, N. Y	Mar. 15, 1864	41, 947
Grain-dryer	R. T. Sutton	Rochester, N. Y	Jan. 2, 1866	51, 880
Grain-dryer	W. H. Sutton and J. J. Gibson	Bantford, Canada	Sept. 29, 1863	40, 130
Grain-dryer	E. Trenholm	Washington, D. C	May 19, 1863	38, 614
Grain-dryer	H. Walker	Detroit, Mich	Jan. 26, 1869	86, 192
Grain-dryer	T. Wallace	Chicago, Ill	Oct. 6, 1863	40, 219
Grain-dryer	T. E. Weed	Williamsburgh, N. Y	Feb. 24, 1852	8, 764
Grain-dryer	J. B. Wheeler	Bolton, Mass	Apr. 14, 1863	38, 191
Grain-dryer	R. J. Williams	Ottumwa, Iowa	Aug. 26, 1873	142, 184
Grain-dryer	H. Wood, G. A. Fourdinier, and R. Haselden.	Montreal, Lyn, and Montreal, Canada.	Feb. 23, 1864	47, 748
Grain-dryer	M. H. Wright	Chicago, Ill	Feb. 5, 1867	61, 909
Grain dryer, cooler, and scourer	L. S. and C. F. Chichester	Brooklyn, N. Y	Dec. 12, 1871	121, 847
Grain-dryer furnace	M. C. Coggswell and A. G. Williams.	Buffalo, N. Y	Sept. 29, 1863	40, 090
Grain-dryer, Vacuum	G. Clark	Buffalo, N. Y	Dec. 10, 1867	71, 981
Grain-dryers, Endless bands for	J. Massey	New York, N. Y	Apr. 17, 1849	6, 322
Grain, Drying	J. Babillion	Detroit, Mich	Mar. 3, 1863	37, 800
Grain, Drying	J. H. Patten	New York, N. Y	June 19, 1849	6, 550
Grain, Drying	H. Quinn	New Alexandria, N. J	Mar. 10, 1849	6, 163
Grain drying and cleaning machine	A. Tonnar	Prussia, Germany	July 31, 1866	56, 868
Grain drying and cooling machine	J. B. Wheeler	Chicago, Ill	Oct. 23, 1860	30, 512
Grain drying and renovating process	G. H. Johnson and G. Milsom	Buffalo, N. Y	Feb. 9, 1869	86, 758
Grain-drying apparatus	C. W. T. Krausch	Chicago, Ill	Mar. 31, 1863	38, 048
Grain, &c., drying apparatus	S. Marsh	Chicago, Ill	Feb. 10, 1863	37, 632
Grain-drying apparatus	T. F. Rowland J. Stephens, and W. H. Mason.	Brooklyn, N. Y	May 22, 1855	12, 922
Grain-drying machine	E. I. Bodrio	Saint Louis, Mo	Oct. 2, 1860	30, 196
Grain, &c., drying machine	C. C. Custer	Philadelphia, Pa	Sept. 8, 1859	18, 137
Grain-drying machine	R. Else	Middlesex County, England	Aug. 14, 1839	1, 286
Grain-drying machine	T. H. McCulloch	Peoria, Ill	Apr. 17, 1860	27, 917
Grain-drying machine	S. B. Robinson	Oswego, N. Y	June 20, 1854	11, 140
Grain-drying machine, Wet	S. V. Appleby	New York, N. Y	Apr. 8, 1856	14, 588
Grain-dump	W. M. Hall, jr	Bloomington, Ill	Sept. 6, 1870	107, 040
Grain, Dumping	J. Sypes	Fairbury, Ill	Oct. 10, 1871	119, 799
Grain elevating and bagging apparatus	J. S. Hasbrouck	Tyre, N. Y	Mar. 15, 1870	100, 887
Grain elevating, cleaning, and bagging machine	I. A. Stafford	Essex, N. Y	Oct. 23, 1860	30, 506
Grain, Elevating, conveying, storing, and shipping	H. I., P. F., and E. D. Chase	Peoria, Ill	May 20, 1873	138, 994
Grain-elevating machine	J. Bruckshaw, H. Bruckshaw, and W. S. Underhill.	Oakley, Market Drayton, and Newport, England.	Nov. 5, 1861	33, 634
Grain elevating, measuring, registering, and bagging machine.	P. Barker	North Adams, Mich	June 1, 1858	20, 399
Grain-elevator	T. H. Green	Fond du Lac, Wis	Sept. 4, 1860	29, 881
Grain-elevator	C. W. T. Krausch	Chicago, Ill	Mar. 24, 1863	38, 004
Grain-elevator	H. Merrill	Brooklyn, N. Y	Apr. 22, 1873	138, 175
Grain-elevator	J. F. Moulton	Chicago, Ill	June 21, 1864	43, 222
Grain-elevator	J. Nichols	Fond du Lac, Wis	Dec. 20, 1864	45, 515
Grain-elevator	A. B. Nimbs	Buffalo, N. Y	Dec. 6, 1864	45, 336
Grain-elevator	A. B. Nimbs	Buffalo, N. Y	Dec. 6, 1864	45, 337
Grain-elevator	J. T. Parlour	Buffalo, N. Y	May 15, 1866	54, 822
Grain-elevator	F. Taggart, L. S. Chichester, and C. W. Mills.	Brooklyn, N. Y	June 27, 1865	48, 495
Grain elevator and dryer, Floating	J. W. Sykes	Chicago, Ill	Apr. 15, 1862	34, 992
Grain elevator and dumping apparatus	M. Eldridge and F. A. Reed	Alexandria, Va	Apr. 23, 1867	64, 002
Grain elevator and feeder	B. F. Sherman	San Francisco, Cal	Oct. 22, 1867	70, 126
Grain-elevator, Floating	A. B. Nimbs	Buffalo, N. Y	Aug. 12, 1862	36, 193
Grain elevator, Pneumatic	S. W. Wood	Cornwall, N. Y	June 16, 1868	79, 044
Grain elevator, Portable wet	D. W. Kellogg and J. W. McKee.	Buffalo, N. Y	May 10, 1864	42, 733
Grain-elevator, Adjustable gate for	S. Brown	Utica, Ohio	Apr. 27, 1869	89, 284
Grain-elevators, Clearing guard of	G. Mann, jr	Ottawa, Ill	May 12, 1857	17, 289
Grain-elevators, Yoke for	T. E. Jewell	Brooklyn, N. Y	Nov. 12, 1867	70, 855
Grain-fan and corn-sheller	H. E. Smith	Philadelphia, Pa	Jan. 18, 1859	22, 689
Grain-fan blast	J. and W. H. Butterworth	Trenton, N. J	Apr. 13, 1869	88, 843
Grain fanning and assorting machine	R. Nutting	Randolph, Vt	Aug. 10, 1858	21, 144
Grain fanning and separating machine	J. I. Smith and W. H. Nicodemus.	Frederick, Md	June 28, 1870	104, 784
Grain-feeder, Revolving	M. Decamp	South Bend, Ind	Apr. 24, 1866	54, 126
Grain feeding and scouring apparatus	J. W. Ardinger	Mount Pulaski, Ill	Jan. 26, 1869	86, 199
Grain, Fermenting alcoholic liquors from	J. Ellinwood	Owensborough, Ill	Nov. 1, 1870	108, 773
Grain, Filling bags with	L. Eggleston	Battle Creek, Mich	Oct. 28, 1862	36, 772
Grain, Finger for lifting lodged	S. Manning	San José, Cal	Sept. 17, 1867	69, 004
Grain, flour, &c., Apparatus for drying	J. R. Stafford	Cleveland, Ohio	Aug. 14, 1847	5, 238
Grain for distillation, Mashing	M. Thompson	Saint Louis, Mo	July 20, 1869	92, 901

Index of patents issued from the United States Patent Office from 1790 to 1873, inclusive— Continued.

Invention.	Inventor.	Residence.	Date.	No.
Grain for distillation, Preparing	T. Sim and E. S. Hutchinson	Baltimore, Md	Mar. 16, 1869	87, 980
Grain for distillation, Preparing	H. Tauszky	New York, N. Y	Nov. 16, 1869	96, 998
Grain for distillation, Preparing and treating	M. Thompson	Saint Louis, Mo	June 7, 1864	43, 047
Grain for distillation, Process for preparing	J. Chilcott	Brooklyn, N. Y	Apr. 25, 1865	47, 394
Grain for distillation, Process of preparing	J. Fleischman	New York, N. Y	Jan. 3, 1865	45, 793
Grain for flouring, Preparing	I. W. Howlet and F. M. Walker	Greensborough, N. C	Oct. 14, 1846	4, 813
Grain for food, Preparing	R. B. Fitts	Philadelphia, Pa	June 13, 1871	115, 947
Grain for food, Preparing wheat, corn and other	R. B. Fitts	Philadelphia, Pa	July 18, 1871	117, 165
Grain for grinding, Apparatus and process for preparing.	A. S. Sackett	Rochester, Minn	July 30, 1872	129, 906
Grain for grinding, Preparing	L. S. Chichester	New York, N. Y	Apr. 2, 1872	125, 170
Grain for grinding, Process of preparing	A. E. Wells	Jamestown, N. Y	Sept. 17, 1872	131, 379
Grain, &c., for malting, Preparing	S. Weidenfield	New York, N. Y	Apr. 28, 1863	38, 347
Grain for manufacture into flour, Process for preparing.	O. F. Cook	Grand Island, Cal	Dec. 23, 1873	145, 846
Grain for mashing, Process of preparing	F. W. De Spessbourg	Normandy, France	Sept. 7, 1869	94, 479
Grain-fork	W. W. Bryan	Schaghticoke, N. Y	Aug. 23, 1870	106, 656
Grain-fork	E. G. Bullis	Manchester, Iowa	Dec. 10, 1867	71, 971
Grain-fork	H. M. and W. W. Bruson	Atkinson, Ill	Aug. 11, 1863	39, 464
Grain-fork	A. Clow	Port Byron, N. Y	Sept. 3, 1867	68, 352
Grain-fork	M. C. Remington	Auburn, N. Y	July 10, 1866	56, 328
Grain fork and rake	M. M. Wells	Hartwick, N. Y	Feb. 25, 1873	136, 347
Grain fork, Loose	H. Gary	Croton, N. J	Nov. 23, 1869	97, 187
Grain from garlic, Machine for separating	H. Staub	Shepherdstown, Va	Nov. 11, 1837	460
Grain from smut, Machine for cleansing	L. Lee and C. Maston	Penn Yan, N. Y	Apr. 25, 1826	....
Grain from straw, &c., Machine for clearing	W. Tunstall	....	June 30, 1804	....
Grain from straw, Machine for extracting	C. Hoxie	....	Aug. 20, 1801	....
Grain from straw, Machine for separating	M. and C. B. Packard	Clarendon, N. Y	Nov. 18, 1844	3, 832
Grain, &c., from vessels, Apparatus for discharging	J. Pagin	Buffalo, N. Y	May 8, 1847	5, 101
Grain from wagons, Apparatus for unloading	C. S. Dole	Chicago, Ill	Jan. 5, 1869	85, 573
Grain-gage	H. Haak	Myerstown, Pa	Oct. 30, 1866	59, 213
Grain-gate	G. Seitzinger	Ottawa, Ill	Aug. 21, 1866	57, 445
Grain-gatherer	W. Herries	Fayette, N. Y	Mar. 13, 1849	6, 183
Grain gathering and binding machine	M. L. Baker	Mannsville, N. Y	Apr. 15, 1862	34, 934
Grain, grass, &c., Machine for cutting	C. Taylor	McKeesport, Pa	June 26, 1855	13, 143
Grain, grass-seed, rice, &c., from straw, Separating	A. Look and W. Coleman, jr	Fredericktown, Md	Mar. 21, 1832	....
Grain-grinder, Conical	D. and J. Fitzgerald	New York, N. Y	Oct. 30, 1834	....
Grain grinder, scourer, and huller	D. Parmelee and J. Mooers	New Troy, Pa	June 12, 1832	....
Grain, Grinding	J. Bicknell	Buckfield, Me	Dec. 11, 1822	....
Grain, Grinding	M. W. Chapman	Girard, Pa	June 1, 1833	....
Grain, Grinding	B. and J. C. Langdon, and J. Trash	Troy, N. Y	Sept. 26, 1823	....
Grain, Grinding	D. Parmelee and J. C. Shoemaker	Kingston, Pa	Apr. 16, 1833	....
Grain-grinding machine	O. Wyman	East Cambridge, Mass	Dec. 20, 1837	531
Grain, hemp, &c., Band for binding	A. Ralston	West Middletown, Pa	Apr. 5, 1859	23, 496
Grain-huller	W. C. Grimes	Philadelphia, Pa	Feb. 20, 1866	52, 706
Grain-huller	M. Hoffmann	Munich, Bavaria	Apr. 18, 1871	113, 770
Grain-huller	B. Maltby and M. Fowler	New Haven, Conn	Feb. 28, 1818	....
Grain-huller	J. H. Thompson	Hoboken, N. J	June 20, 1865	48, 326
Grain-huller	R. W. Van Peyma	Lancaster, N. Y	Feb. 20, 1866	52, 774
Grain huller and cleaner	O. Lull	Otsego, N. Y	Aug. 25, 1832	....
Grain hulling and cleaning machine	J. Cross	Centre Liste, N. Y	Oct. 8, 1838	968
Grain hulling and cleaning machine	G. H. Rice	Kingston, Pa	June 25, 1872	128, 424
Grain hulling and scouring machine	T. F. Wagoner	Trenton, N. J	June 28, 1859	24, 595
Grain hulling, cleaning, and grinding machine	C. F. Campbell	Chenango, N. Y	Sept. 24, 1861	33, 336
Grain hulling cotton-seed, rubbing down whetstones, &c., Grinding.	B. N. Fyler	Bradford, Vt	Apr. 15, 1830	....
Grain-hulling machine	C. O. Bullot	Santa Rosa de los Andes, Chili.	Aug. 1, 1865	49, 205
Grain-hulling machine	S. Gardner and A. B. Howe	New York, N. Y	Dec. 12, 1865	51, 445
Grain-hulling machine	W. J. Hart	Talmadge, Ohio	May 21, 1824	....
Grain-hulling machine	F. Henckel and W. Seck	Munich, Bavaria	Nov. 20, 1866	59, 838
Grain-hulling machine	A. Hubbell	Sharon, Conn	Mar. 24, 1868	75, 761
Grain-hulling machine	J. A. Welsh	Xenia, Ohio	Aug. 28, 1866	57, 605
Grain in a vessel's hold, Apparatus for leveling	H. Milsom, H. Spendelow, and G. V. Watson.	Buffalo, N. Y	Mar. 28, 1865	47, 030
Grain in bulk, Treating and preserving	C. F. Parrott	New York, N. Y	July 26, 1870	105, 720
Grain in bundles, Machine for binding	J. D. Osborn	Constantine, Mich	June 14, 1859	24, 400
Grain in bundles or sheaves, Mode of securing	J. P. Manny	Rockford, Ill	July 6, 1858	20, 809
Grain in elevator-bins, Device for distributing	W. O. Strong	Detroit, Mich	Feb. 11, 1862	34, 379
Grain in mills, &c., Distributing	C. S. Hamilton	Fond du Lac, Wis	June 21, 1864	43, 200
Grain in process of grinding, Steaming	J. F. Lawton	Venedy, Ill	Sept. 20, 1864	44, 322
Grain in the mass, Apparatus for drying	J. C. Pedrick	Washington, D. C	Dec. 16, 1856	16, 259
Grain into flour and meal, Machinery of mills for the manufacture of.	W. Parkinson	Wheeling, Va	July 31, 1829	....
Grain into gavels, Device for gathering	W. M. Waggoner	Middletown, Ind	Jan. 18, 1859	22, 682
Grain-kiln	R. Andrews	Fleming County, Ky	Nov. 7, 1822	....
Grain-kiln	I. S. Stover	Erwinna, Pa	Nov. 11, 1851	8, 518
Grain, Kiln for drying	J. Abraham	Middlesex, N. J	Dec. 20, 1805	....
Grain, Kiln for drying	W. W. Alcott	Boston, Mass	Sept. 26, 1846	4, 774
Grain, Kiln for drying	T. Cook	New Hope, Pa	Nov. 30, 1835	....
Grain, Kiln for drying	J. Deneale, jr	....	July 10, 1800	....
Grain, Kiln for drying	A. Greenleaf, jr., and T. C. Vice	Brooklyn, N. Y., and New Haven, Conn.	May 5, 1863	38, 382
Grain, Kiln for drying	H. Y. and A. Haupt, jr	Bucks County, Pa	Dec. 5, 1842	2, 867
Grain, Kiln for drying	S. Howard	Adrian, Mich	Sept. 26, 1846	4, 777
Grain, Kiln for drying	W. Poole	Wilmington, Del	Dec. 20, 1805	....
Grain, Kiln for drying	N. F. Potter	Providence, R. I	Dec. 11, 1847	5, 391
Grain, Kiln for drying	J. H. Tower	Kirkland, N. Y	June 20, 1848	5, 638
Grain, Kiln for drying	N. Wallaster	Detroit, Mich	Oct. 23, 1866	59, 102
Grain, Machine for cleaning and separating garlic, &c., from.	J. Heygel	Salisbury, Pa	Sept. 25, 1841	2, 270
Grain, Machine for cutting the bands of	A. J. Luckey	Bradford, Wis	Apr. 15, 1862	34, 973
Grain, Machine for decorticating and drying	E. Skelly	Plaquemine, La	Aug. 23, 1870	106, 627
Grain by wind power, Machine for grinding	D. McColler	Hudson, Ohio	May 2, 1829	....
Grain, Machine for registering measured	A. Rakestraw and W. Colwell	Chillicothe, Ill	Dec. 13, 1864	45, 436
Grain, Machine for separating	L. Butler	Cobleskill, N. Y	June 3, 1837	225
Grain, Machine for separating and scouring	D. S. Mackey	Batavia, N. Y	Sept. 18, 1860	30, 072
Grain, Machine for separating garlic from	P. C. Fritz	Barrytown, N. Y	Dec. 21, 1858	22, 359

Index of patents issued from the United States Patent Office from 1790 *to* 1873, *inclusive*—Continued.

Invention.	Inventor.	Residence.	Date.	No.
Grain, Machine for separating garlic from	W. C. Grimes	York, Pa	Sept. 13, 1840	1,763
Grain, Machine for separating straw from	E. S. Snyder	Charlestown, Va	June 3, 1848	5,630
Grain, Machine for sowing and drilling	G. A. Titus	Mantorville, Minn	July 20, 1869	92,903
Grain, malt, &c., Apparatus for drying	S. R. Andres, S. Andres, and M. Bucklin.	Troy and New York, N. Y	Jan. 18, 1859	22,614
Grain, malt, &c., Drying	S. Marsh	Chicago, Ill	Jan. 13, 1863	37,403
Grain, Malting	R. D'Heureuse	New York, N. Y	Feb. 8, 1870	99,541
Grain mash, wort, and beer after fermentation	N. Eisendrath	Chicago, Ill	June 1, 1869	90,827
Grain, meal, &c., Elevating	J. Baily	Kennett's Square, Pa	June 19, 1812	......
Grain-meter	T. Brockett and J. J. Brown	Davenport, Iowa	Nov. 16, 1869	96,878
Grain-meter	F. G. Chesman	Lemont, Ill	July 19, 1870	105,427
Grain-meter	J. T. Keeling	Hibernia, Mo	May 24, 1870	103,470
Grain-meter	A. McBride	Fayette, Pa	July 16, 1872	129,045
Grain-meter	H. Pooley, T. Roberts, and E. O'Brien.	Liverpool, England	Apr. 9, 1872	125,612
Grain-meter	R. Rutherford	Belleville, Ill	May 14, 1872	126,749
Grain-meter	W. S. Sampson	New York, N. Y	Apr. 17, 1866	54,072
Grain-meter	W. Schnebley	Hackensack, N. J	Aug. 28, 1866	57,580
Grain meter	J. C. Walker	Waco Village, Tex	Sept. 3, 1867	68,472
Grain, Method of unloading	I. H. Palmer	Lodi, Wis	June 18, 1867	65,826
Grain-mill	E. H. Austin	Scott's Hill, Tenn	Sept. 5, 1871	118,672
Grain-mill	G. W. Grader and B. F. Cowan	Memphis, Tenn	Dec. 19, 1854	12,096
Grain-mill	J. J. Johnston	Allegheny, Pa	Feb. 2, 1858	19,251
Grain-mill	H. Mellish	Walpole, N. H	Aug. 22, 1854	11,558
Grain-mill	J. Norman	New Orleans, La	Sept. 7, 1869	94,635
Grain-mill	P. Perry	Troy, N. Y	Feb. 23, 1858	19,441
Grain-mill	J. C. Smith	Lacon, Ill	Sept. 25, 1837	397
Grain-mill	E. G. Ward	New York	Feb. 20, 1841	1,988
Grain-mill	W. Westrup	Wapping, England	June 6, 1854	11,011
Grain-mill	J. W. Wheeler	Cleveland, Ohio	Feb. 21, 1860	27,259
Grain-mill	O. Wyman	Watertown, Mass	July 1, 1836	....
Grain, Mill for cutting	W. Gerrish	Portsmouth, N. H	Jan. 11, 1836	....
Grain, Mill for hulling, grinding, and sifting	T. Ellicot	Pennsylvania	Feb. 17, 1816	....
Grain-mill, Portable	C. Leavitt	Quincy, Ill	July 6, 1852	9,096
Grain-mill, Portable	C. Leavitt	Quincy, Ill	Feb. 27, 1855	12,461
Grain-mills, Dress of grinding-surfaces for	O. W. Stanford	Cincinnati, Ohio	Aug. 11, 1857	17,985
Grain-mills, Feeder for	M. Decamp	South Bend, Ind	Dec. 10, 1867	71,857
Grain-mills, Feeding and cooling device for	J. Nairn	Milton, Ind	Oct. 6, 1868	82,741
Grain-mills, Shoe for	H. Mellish	Walpole, N. H	May 29, 1855	12,959
Grain-moistener	L. J. Adams and J. H. Esale	Avon, Ill	Sept. 8, 1868	81,861
Grain-mover	W. Moses	Buffalo, N. Y	Jan. 30, 1866	52,309
Grain, nuts, &c., Machine for cleaning	J. Johnson	New York, N. Y	May 27, 1873	139,248
Grain of wood, Transferring the natural	J. R. Cross	Morrisania, N. Y	July 2, 1872	128,468
Grain, paints, &c., Machine for grinding	H. Averill	Richland, N. Y	Apr. 30, 1829	....
Grain, plaster, &c., for sowing, Apparatus for carrying.	O. W. Smith	Flint, Mich	Aug. 9, 1870	106,216
Grain, Portable mill for grinding	E. Arnold	Otego, N. Y	Mar. 9, 1844	3,468
Grain preparatory to grinding, Steaming	B. F. Broomell	London Grove, Pa	May 14, 1850	7,358
Grain, Preparing and washing	C. H. Frings	Centreton, Mo	Apr. 25, 1871	113,997
Grain, Process for mashing	E. J. Hainault	Belgium	Dec. 9, 1856	16,179
Grain-rake	W. Baldwin	Plymouth, Conn	July 7, 1868	79,720
Grain-rake	W. Gates	Barre Centre, N. Y	Dec. 20, 1843	3,386
Grain-rake	D. Harkness	Raisin, Mich	Mar. 14, 1846	4,422
Grain-rake	E. Palmer	Solon, N. Y	Aug. 27, 1867	68,227
Grain-rake	B. F. Partridge	Onondaga, N. Y	Mar. 13, 1844	3,482
Grain-rake	E. G. Warner	Union Township, Ohio	July 4, 1865	48,606
Grain-rake	R. Warnock and C. Abbey, 2d	Ridgeville, Ohio	July 28, 1868	80,523
Grain-rake	M. M. Wells	Hartwick, N. Y	May 5, 1868	77,556
Grain-rake	M. M. Wells	Hartwick, N. Y	Dec. 27, 1870	110,613
Grain rake and loader	G. S. Dudley	Dixon, Cal	May 27, 1873	139,303
Grain raking and binding apparatus	T. K. Griffith	Redstone, Pa	Aug. 16, 1870	106,357
Grain raking and binding machine	A. S. Harding	Mount Hope, N. Y	Apr. 15, 1862	34,999
Grain raking and binding machine	J. E. Heath	Warren, Ohio	July 22, 1850	7,520
Grain, Reaping	C. H. McCormick	Rockbridge County, Va	June 21, 1834	....
Grain, Reaping and cutting	O. Hussey	Cincinnati, Ohio	Dec. 31, 1833	....
Grain reaping and thrashing machine	L. B. Lathrop	San José, Cal	May 25, 1869	90,561
Grain-reaping machine	S. Adams	....	Dec. 28, 1805	....
Grain-register	G. D. Denison	Troy, Ohio	Jan. 7, 1862	34,052
Grain-register	L. O. Hayworth	New Cumberland, Ind	Mar. 12, 1867	62,845
Grain-register	L. W. Hines, G. Saterlee, and S. W. Harden.	Quasqueton, Iowa	Sept. 30, 1862	36,565
Grain-register	W. C. Howard	Belle Plaine, Iowa	July 27, 1869	92,971
Grain-register	S. Hudson	Milford, Mich	May 26, 1868	78,208
Grain-register	C. Lamb	Binghamton, N. Y	Nov. 22, 1870	109,522
Grain-register	G. W. Nesmith	Metamora, Ill	Oct. 7, 1873	143,527
Grain-register	M. W. and G. W. Nesmith	Metamora, Ill	Mar. 3, 1868	75,187
Grain-register	J. S. Price and P. Miller	Champaign County and Clarke County, Ohio.	Jan. 14, 1873	134,928
Grain-register	S. Ramer	Winona, Minn	Feb. 11, 1873	135,845
Grain-register	B. Taylor	Forestville, Minn	July 28, 1868	80,372
Grain-register	W. Z. Taylor	Burlington, Iowa	Dec. 27, 1870	110,605
Grain-register	T. N. Wheeler	Rio, Wis	July 29, 1862	36,045
Grain-register	J. T. Wiley	Clayton, Iowa	Sept. 5, 1865	49,817
Grain-registering device	W. H. Stinson	Newbern, Iowa	May 9, 1871	114,723
Grain-regulator	E. W. Hitchings	Potsdam, N. Y	Feb. 25, 1868	74,824
Grain, rice, coffee, &c., Machine for hulling and scouring.	L. H. Whitney	Washington, D. C	Sept. 20, 1870	107,644
Grain-riddle	A. Rowe	Atalissa, Iowa	Dec. 4, 1860	30,840
Grain, Riddle for separating	M. M. Cooper and J. W. Donaldson.	Fairfield, Cal	Nov. 29, 1870	109,716
Grain-sacking device	P. Van Lackum	Saint Charles, Minn	Apr. 16, 1867	63,967
Grain-sampler	J. J. Bois	Rantoul, Ill	Oct. 28, 1873	143,953
Grain-scale, Automatic	A. Stevely	Fond du Lac, Wis	Apr. 14, 1863	38,185
Grain-scourer	I. N. Harshbarger	Bloomington, Wis	Sept. 20, 1870	107,486
Grain-scourer	C. B. Horton	Waterloo, N. Y	Nov. 25, 1873	144,980
Grain-scourer	G. S. Newman	Liberty Mill, Va	May 7, 1872	126,567
Grain-scourer	D. M. Richardson	Detroit, Mich	Aug. 6, 1872	130,315
Grain-scourer	T. Shively	North Lansing, Mich	Feb. 4, 1873	135,602

Index of patents issued from the United States Patent Office from 1790 *to* 1873, *inclusive*—Continued.

Invention.	Inventor.	Residence.	Date.	No.
Grain-scourer	A. Smith	Valmont, Colo	Dec. 20, 1870	110, 301
Grain-scourer	G. E. Throop	Chicago, Ill	Dec. 22, 1863	41, 031
Grain-scourer	V. Weismantel	Belleville, Ill	Apr. 12, 1870	101, 950
Grain scourer and cleaner	A. B. Paige	Washington, D. C	Jan. 2, 1872	122, 330
Grain scourer and huller	L. S. Chichester	Brooklyn, N. Y	Apr. 2, 1872	125, 171
Grain scourer and separator	S. Canby	Ellicott's Mills, Md	May 26, 1857	17, 363
Grain scourer and separator	S. H. Hinsdell, H. W. Drake, and C. B. Way.	Camillus, N. Y	Apr. 4, 1871	113, 296
Grain scourer and separator	C. B. Horton	Waterloo, N. Y	July 16, 1872	129, 346
Grain scourer, smutter, and separator	J. C. Hunt and W. W. Ingraham	Chicago, Ill	Aug 27, 1872	130, 804
Grain, Scouring	P. Pettis	Middlebury, Ohio	July 2, 1830	
Grain, Scouring and cleaning	J. Sitzenbergor	Philadelphia, Pa	Nov. 24, 1823	....
Grain, Scouring and cleaning	B. T. Trimmer	Rochester, N. Y	Sept. 23, 1862	36, 541
Grain scouring and hulling machine	J. N. Treadwell	Reading, Conn	Mar. 1, 1859	23, 127
Grain scouring and separating machine	M. Bartholomew	Enterprise, Pa	July 24, 1860	29, 237
Grain scouring and thrashing machines, Cylinder for.	J. A. Welsh	Xenia, Ohio	Mar. 4, 1862	34, 617
Grain-scouring apparatus	P. H. Massey	South Bend, Ind	Apr. 7, 1868	76, 486
Grain scouring, cleaning, and polishing machine	G. P. Plant and J. Raith	Saint Louis, Mo	Sept. 18, 1860	30, 090
Grain-scouring machine	J. Bergstresser	Berrysburgh, Pa	Jan. 20, 1863	37, 430
Grain-scouring machine	W. McLaughlin	Jersey City, N. J	Aug. 9, 1870	106, 184
Grain-scouring machine	W. P. Robinson	Buffalo, N. Y	Jan. 16, 1872	122, 782
Grain-scouring machine	B. T. Trimmer	Rochester, N. Y	Apr. 12, 1870	101, 946
Grain-screen	J. E. Anderson	Boiling Springs, Pa	Sept. 28, 1869	95, 303
Grain-screen	G. B. Bailey	Greenfield, Ind	May 10, 1864	42, 635
Grain-screen	C. F. Baylor	Trenton, N. J	Sept. 18, 1866	58, 050
Grain-screen	S. Blair	New Wilmington, Pa	Feb. 23, 1869	87, 239
Grain-screen	D. A. and S. Church	Friendship, N. Y	June 27, 1846	4, 600
Grain-screen	J. J. Crider	Greenfield, Ind	Nov. 24, 1868	84, 345
Grain-screen	J. Hatfield and J. Wall	Ogden, Ind	Oct. 11, 1864	44, 625
Grain-screen	R. Hawkins	Palestine, Ind	July 2, 1867	66, 333
Grain-screen	W. G. Hoag	Hoosick, N. Y	Mar. 24, 1863	39, 963
Grain-screen	J. Long	Morristown, Ind	Oct. 2, 1866	58, 551
Grain-screen	C. F. and J. B. Messinger	Logansport, Ind	Aug. 15, 1865	49, 429
Grain-screen	H. Ogborn	Richmond, Ind	Jan. 3, 1865	45, 740
Grain-screen	H. Ogborn	Richmond, Ind	May 29, 1866	55, 152
Grain-screen	W. Rowan and J. M. H. Gill	Freeport, Pa	Oct. 21, 1862	36, 733
Grain-screen	D. D. Schamp	Pleasant Run, N. J	May 7, 1872	126, 493
Grain-screen	W. Tullock	Lantern Mills, Orange Court-House, Va.	Oct. 28, 1806	....
Grain-screen	J. H. H. Wiseheart	Shawneetown, Ill	Aug. 25, 1868	81, 567
Grain screen and sieve	H. B. Thomas	Chicago, Ill	Nov. 15, 1864	45, 125
Grain-screen, Revolving	D. Loeffel	Mount Vernon, Ind	July 6, 1869	92, 327
Grain-screen, Revolving	F. Mills	Mount Vernon, Ind	Aug. 30, 1870	106, 949
Grain-screen, Rotary	D. Pease, jr	Floyd, N. Y	Oct. 29, 1850	7, 744
Grain, seed, &c., Machine for hulling and scouring	O. P. Stevens	Cleveland, Ohio	July 1, 1856	15, 269
Grain-separator	S. Adams	Boston, Mass	Feb. 16, 1864	41, 660
Grain-separator	A. J. Alexander	Chicago, Ill	June 11, 1867	65, 716
Grain-separator	J. R. Allen	Edinburgh, Ind	Dec. 7, 1869	97, 584
Grain-separator	W. B. Allen	Winona, Minn	Feb. 11, 1873	135, 746
Grain-separator	J. Allonas	Mansfield, Ohio	Apr. 9, 1872	125, 513
Grain-separator	P. I. Aukney and D. McGreery	New Lexington, Ohio	Sept. 20, 1859	25, 478
Grain-separator	S. K. Ayers	Delton, Wis	June 13, 1865	48, 233
Grain-separator	S. K. Ayres	Delton, Wis	May 2, 1871	114, 251
Grain-separator	C. F. Babcock	Chicago, Ill	June 8, 1869	91, 067
Grain-separator	F. A. Balch	Hingham, Wis	Aug. 15, 1871	118, 094
Grain-separator	S. Ballard, sr	Sullivan, Ind	June 8, 1869	90, 981
Grain-separator	J. B. Barcalo	Mount Morris, N. Y	Dec. 9, 1862	37, 082
Grain-separator	M. J Barcalo	Mount Morris, N. Y	June 23, 1863	38, 937
Grain-separator	M. J. Barcalo	Mount Morris, N. Y	Jan. 12, 1864	41, 188
Grain-separator	P. Barker	Battle Creek, Mich	Apr. 6, 1869	88, 690
Grain-separator	A., C., and H. K. Barkholder	Clear Spring, Pa	June 15, 1869	91, 412
Grain-separator	H. A. Barnard	Moline, Ill	July 25, 1865	48, 890
Grain-separator	C. R. Barnes	Muncy, Pa	Aug. 4, 1863	39, 374
Grain-separator	C. Bates	Hardin, Iowa	Nov. 24, 1863	40, 670
Grain-separator	H. H. Beach	Philadelphia, Pa	Sept. 10, 1861	33, 231
Grain-separator	F. A. Begole	Jackson, Mich	Oct. 4, 1870	107, 856
Grain-separator	J. Benner	Allegheny, Pa	Apr. 12, 1859	23, 546
Grain-separator	C. Bergen	Farmer, N. Y	July 31, 1860	29, 352
Grain-separator	C. Bergen	Covert, N. Y	May 6, 1862	35, 134
Grain-separator	J. Bergey	Wadsworth, Ohio	Oct. 5, 1852	9, 293
Grain-separator	D. Best	Yuba, Cal	Apr. 25, 1871	114, 097
Grain-separator	C. A. Bikle	Hagerstown, Md	Aug. 10, 1869	93, 586
Grain-separator	J. Bluo	Covert, N. Y	Nov. 8, 1853	10, 202
Grain-separator	J. S. Bodge	Bath, N. Y	Nov. 10, 1863	40, 548
Grain-separator	J. S. Bodge	Bath, N. Y	Dec. 26, 1865	51, 687
Grain-separator	J. S. Bodge	La Porte, Ind	Sept. 18, 1866	58, 052
Grain-separator	J. L. Booth	New York, N. Y	Mar. 8, 1859	23, 153
Grain-separator	J. L. Booth	Cuyahoga Falls, Ohio	July 12, 1859	24, 714
Grain-separator	J. L. Booth	Cuyahoga Falls, Ohio	Sept. 20, 1859	25, 484
Grain-separator	J. L. Booth	Rochester, N. Y	Nov. 4, 1862	36, 830
Grain-separator	J. C. Bowden	Farmington, Cal	Mar. 5, 1872	124, 244
Grain-separator	J. W. Breese	Canandaigua, Mich	Sept. 9, 1873	142, 672
Grain-separator	J. Brightbill	Lebanon, Pa	June 22, 1869	91, 710
Grain-separator	G. E. Bringman	Gettysburgh, Pa	Jan. 19, 1869	85, 992
Grain-separator	J. D. Brunner	Doylestown, Pa	July 4, 1871	116, 549
Grain-separator	J. D. Brunner and E. R. J. Ueberroth.	Doylestown, Pa	Sept. 6, 1870	106, 994
Grain-separator	M. Bugher	New Philadelphia, Ohio	Sept. 18, 1860	30, 047
Grain-separator	H. Burdick	Monroe, Wis	Feb. 15, 1870	99, 835
Grain-separator	H. K. Burkholder	Clear Spring, Pa	Dec. 28, 1869	98, 346
Grain-separator	M. Burr	Plymouth, Mich	Dec. 16, 1862	37, 148
Grain-separator	W. T. Chaffee	Richmond, Va	Mar. 17, 1868	75, 520
Grain-separator	W. C. Chamberlain	Dubuque, Iowa	May 17, 1864	42, 747
Grain-separator	J. H. Chase and J. M. Tiffany.	Montgomery, Ill	July 10, 1866	56, 177
Grain-separator	D. Claude, jr	Annapolis, Md	Feb. 24, 1843	2, 974
Grain-separator	J. N. Clees	Darbyville, Ohio	July 5, 1864	43, 390
Grain-separator	J. Clum and G. A. Fisher	Shelby and Alabama, N. Y	July 12, 1864	43, 478

Index of patents issued from the United States Patent Office from 1790 to 1873, inclusive—Continued.

Invention.	Inventor.	Residence.	Date.	No.
Grain-separator	J. A. Cohoon	Toledo, Ohio	Mar. 19, 1872	124, 793
Grain-separator	H. Cook	Dillsburgh, Pa	Sept. 13, 1870	107, 338
Grain-separator	L. B. Corbin	Dryden, N. Y	Feb. 28, 1860	27, 274
Grain-separator	J. W. Cormack and F. C. Walker	Quincy, Ill	Oct. 14, 1856	15, 879
Grain-separator	W. R. Cox	Delhi, Iowa	Nov. 2, 1858	21, 945
Grain-separator	J. B. Crist	Evansville, Ind	May 10, 1859	23, 903
Grain-separator	J. F. and H. D. Cummings	Fremont, N. Y	Dec. 22, 1863	40, 995
Grain-separator	A. Curtis	Lena, Ill	July 7, 1857	17, 728
Grain-separator	A. Curtis	Warren, Ill	Oct. 8, 1867	69, 545
Grain-separator	J. L. Custer	Bonaparte, Iowa	May 14, 1872	126, 683
Grain-separator	G. A. Dabney	San José, Cal	Mar. 26, 1872	125, 027
Grain-separator	E. Davis	Almond, N. Y	Mar. 1, 1870	100, 379
Grain-separator	E. Davis and A. Palmer	Hudson, Mich	Mar. 5, 1861	31, 591
Grain-separator	J. Davis	Allegheny City, Pa	Nov. 14, 1865	50, 913
Grain-separator	L. H. Davis	Newark, Del	July 14, 1868	79, 813
Grain-separator	S. Daw	Corvallis, Oreg	Nov. 25, 1873	144, 836
Grain-separator	M. Decamp	South Bend, Ind	Jan. 27, 1857	16, 471
Grain-separator	J. A. Denton, D. W. Shannon, and E. Lucas.	Winslow, Ind	Jan. 12, 1869	85, 801
Grain-separator	W. W. Dingee and A. B. Farquhar.	York, Pa	June 17, 1862	35, 590
Grain-separator	A. H. Dixson	San Francisco, Cal	Nov. 5, 1861	33, 636
Grain-separator	J. W. Donaldson	Fairfield, Cal	Dec. 27, 1870	110, 445
Grain-separator	E. L. Dorsey	Winslow, Ind	Mar. 3, 1868	75, 133
Grain-separator	E. Doud	Oshkosh, Wis	June 9, 1857	17, 498
Grain-separator	J. F. Dunham	Fayette, Iowa	July 10, 1866	56, 194
Grain-separator	A. Durrs	San Francisco, Cal	Oct. 11, 1870	108, 120
Grain-separator	T. Earheart	Donelson, Tenn	July 24, 1860	29, 256
Grain-separator	J. Esse	Redwood City, Cal	Feb. 6, 1872	123, 387
Grain-separator	J. G. Evans	Orville, Ohio	Oct. 25, 1870	108, 577
Grain-separator	O. J. Everson	Lake City, Minn	July 22, 1873	141, 130
Grain-separator	J. H. Fairchild	East Highgate, Vt	Apr. 3, 1866	53, 735
Grain-separator	A. Fanebouer	Schoolcraft, Mich	Jan. 15, 1861	31, 114
Grain-separator	J. Fargusson	Dubuque, Iowa	Nov. 5, 1861	33, 639
Grain-separator	J. Fargusson and C. S. Burt	Dubuque, Iowa, and Dunleith, Ill.	June 30, 1863	39, 093
Grain-separator	J. Faulkner	Dansville, N. Y	Feb. 20, 1863	37, 440
Grain-separator	J. Felsing	Granville, Wis	Apr. 1, 1862	34, 824
Grain-separator	P. Flickinger	Hanover, Pa	May 16, 1871	114, 789
Grain-separator	A. Foster	Quincy, Ill	Oct. 26, 1858	21, 877
Grain-separator	F. R. Foster	Brandon, Wis	Oct. 12, 1869	95, 674
Grain-separator	S. W. Foster	Scio, Mich	Dec. 4, 1849	6, 920
Grain-separator	J. W. Free	Richmond, Ind	Feb. 27, 1866	52, 841
Grain-separator	A. Gaar	Richmond, Ind	June 21, 1870	104, 571
Grain-separator	D. Garver	Ringgold, Md	May 9, 1871	114, 546
Grain-separator	W. E. Gaunt and B. B. Hinman	Keokuk, Iowa	Mar. 19, 1861	31, 711
Grain-separator	D. Geiser	Waynesborough, Pa	Aug. 9, 1864	43, 766
Grain-separator	P. Geiser	Smithsburgh, Md	Oct. 19, 1852	9, 341
Grain-separator	P. Geiser	Smithsburgh, Md	Oct. 9, 1855	13, 644
Grain-separator	H. N. Goodrich	Aurora, Ill	Jan. 24, 1865	45, 993
Grain-separator	A. Gordon	Rochester, N. Y	Oct. 7, 1862	36, 611
Grain-separator	J. Gray	Milwaukee, Wis	Dec. 22, 1863	41, 000
Grain-separator	J. Green	Norwalk, Ohio	June 26, 1866	55, 952
Grain-separator	J. C. Gregg	Hillsborough, Ohio	July 17, 1860	29, 161
Grain-separator	P. Griswold	Hudson, Mich	May 22, 1866	54, 895
Grain-separator	P. Griswold	Hudson, Mich	Mar. 7, 1871	112, 447
Grain-separator	P. Griswold and H. H. Seeley	Hudson, Mich	Nov. 22, 1859	26, 181
Grain-separator	A. Hall	Dansville, N. Y	Jan. 19, 1858	19, 140
Grain-separator	C. S. Hall	Rochester, N. Y	Nov. 7, 1871	120, 582
Grain-separator	J. H. Hamaker	Frease's Store, Ohio	Apr. 25, 1865	47, 417
Grain-separator	G. F. Harlan	Elkton, Md	May 18, 1869	90, 260
Grain-separator	S. Harris	Springfield, Mass	Mar. 10, 1868	75, 417
Grain-separator	T. Harrison and W. C. Buchanan.	Belleville, Ill	Sept. 12, 1865	49, 876
Grain-separator	G. Harrowsmith	Lockport, N. Y	July 10, 1860	29, 045
Grain-separator	D. Hathaway	Wyoming, Wis	Nov. 3, 1868	83, 630
Grain-separator	G. Heberling	Quincy, Ill	Jan. 20, 1857	16, 439
Grain-separator	S. Heflebower and J. M. Reed	Alexandria and Loudoun County, Va.	Dec. 18, 1866	60, 513
Grain-separator	A. Higley	Sand Creek, Minn	Dec. 3, 1861	33, 838
Grain-separator	A. Higley	Chicago, Ill	Jan. 7, 1864	43, 026
Grain-separator	O. Holmes	New Lenox, Ill	Jan. 21, 1868	73, 605
Grain-separator	H. A. Hummer	Frenchtown, N. J	Feb. 15, 1870	99, 903
Grain-separator	A. Hunter	Solano County, Cal	Apr. 9, 1861	31, 981
Grain-separator	A. Hunter	Solano County, Cal	Oct. 20, 1863	40, 340
Grain-separator	A. Hunter	San Francisco, Cal	June 1, 1869	90, 844
Grain-separator	S. S. Hurlbut	Cordova, Ill	May 5, 1868	77, 490
Grain-separator	C. B. Hutchings	Rochester, N. Y	Nov. 20, 1860	30, 679
Grain-separator	C. B. Hutchings	Rochester, N. Y	Nov. 15, 1864	45, 120
Grain-separator	B. S. Hyers	Pekin, Ill	Dec. 22, 1863	41, 041
Grain-separator	T. W. Irvin	Marion County, Ind	Nov. 18, 1862	36, 980
Grain-separator	L. P. Josse	Paris, France	Dec. 1, 1863	40, 756
Grain-separator	C. Kathan	Hardin, Iowa	Oct. 14, 1862	36, 653
Grain-separator	J. Kefer	Hamilton, Ohio	May 17, 1864	42, 820
Grain-separator	E. L. Kelly	Reading, Mich	Aug. 1, 1871	117, [illegible]45
Grain-separator	J. B. King and O. N. Cronkite	Sacramento, Cal	Dec. 3, 1872	133, 648
Grain-separator	J. Koons	New Auburn, Minn	Sept. 23, 1873	143, 081
Grain-separator	D. Ladd	Chicago, Ill	Jan. 25, 1870	99, 093
Grain-separator	G. Landers and H. Lampman	Atton, N. Y	Oct. 16, 1860	30, 413
Grain-separator	J. L. La Rose	Leavenworth, Kans	Oct. 29, 1872	132, 674
Grain-separator	W. H. Lawrence	Baltimore, Md	Oct. 24, 1871	120, 285
Grain-separator	G. Leach	Elmira, N. Y	May 27, 1862	35, 421
Grain-separator	S. F. Lefler	Racine, Wis	Apr. 5, 1864	42, 205
Grain-separator	S. Lessig, sr	Reading, Pa	Nov. 14, 1871	120, 983
Grain-separator	S. Lessig, sr	Reading, Pa	Nov. 4, 1873	144, 211
Grain-separator	A. J. and H. Linebarger	Jackson, Ill	July 10, 1866	56, 237
Grain-separator	A. W. Lockhart	Sacramento, Cal	July 16, 1867	66, 859
Grain-separator	L. Low	San Francisco, Cal	June 28, 1864	43, 318

Index of patents issued from the United States Patent Office from 1790 *to* 1873, *inclusive*—Continued.

Index of patents issued from the United States Patent Office from 1790 *to* 1873, *inclusive*—Continued.

Invention.	Inventor.	Residence.	Date.	No.
Grain-separator	H. B. Thomas	Chicago, Ill	May 3, 1864	42, 628
Grain-separator	J. Thompson	Chili, N. Y	Apr. 6, 1852	8, 864
Grain-separator	J. D. Tiff	Cuyahoga, Ohio	Aug. 31, 1858	21, 383
Grain-separator	W. Todd	Ottawa, Ill	Dec. 27, 1864	45, 654
Grain-separator	J. Tomlinson	Newburgh, Wis	July 4, 1865	48, 603
Grain-separator	J. P. Tostevin	Racine, Wis	Aug. 17, 1869	93, 926
Grain-separator	B. T. Trimmer	Rochester, N. Y	Feb. 14, 1860	27, 171
Grain-separator	B. T. Trimmer	Rochester, N. Y	Jan. 3, 1865	45, 772
Grain-separator	B. T. Trimmer	Rochester, N. Y	Apr. 18, 1865	47, 346
Grain-separator	G. B. Turner and J. A. Vaughn	Cuyahoga Falls, Ohio	Apr. 9, 1861	32, 017
Grain-separator	J. Turner	Sunapee, N. H	Apr. 6, 1858	19, 899
Grain-separator	W. E. Turner	Neosho Falls, Kans	Aug. 12, 1873	141, 676
Grain-separator	E. R. J. Weberroth	Doylestown, Pa	Nov. 12, 1872	133, 070
Grain-separator	J. S. Upton	Battle Creek, Mich	Apr. 28, 1868	77, 419
Grain-separator	A. J. Vandegrift	Lexington, Ky	June 8, 1858	20, 522
Grain-separator	A. J. Vandegrift	Saint Louis, Mo	July 24, 1860	29, 335
Grain-separator	A. J. Vandegrift	Cincinnati, Ohio	Dec. 12, 1865	51, 495
Grain-separator	J. Van Horne	Magnolia, Ill	Sept. 4, 1855	13, 532
Grain-separator	J. Van Houten	Mount Morris, N. Y	Dec. 22, 1863	41, 032
Grain-separator	A. J. Vantuyl	Hector, N. Y	July 2, 1861	32, 729
Grain-separator	J. Vaughn	Magnolia, Ill	May 10, 1859	23, 965
Grain-separator	J. A. Vaughn	Cuyahoga Falls, Ohio	Apr. 24, 1860	28, 026
Grain-separator	D. S. Wagener	Penn Yan, N. Y	Nov. 29, 1859	26, 311
Grain-separator	W. M. Watson	Tonica, Ill	Oct. 29, 1861	33, 617
Grain-separator	J. V. A. Wemple	Chicago, Ill	Nov. 1, 1853	10, 195
Grain-separator	J. V. A. Wemple and G. Westinghouse.	Mohawk and Schoharie, N. Y.	July 13, 1844	3, 663
Grain-separator	G. Westinghouse	Schenectady, N. Y	Apr. 17, 1860	27, 941
Grain-separator	H. L. Whitman	Saint Louis, Mo	May 2, 1871	114, 500
Grain-separator	W. Wicken	Muscoda, Wis	Jan. 28, 1862	34, 279
Grain-separator	L. Wilcox	Hudson, Mich	Aug. 17, 1858	21, 227
Grain-separator	J. N. Williams, jr	Saint Paul, Minn	Oct. 22, 1867	70, 060
Grain-separator	M. D. Williams	Lawton, Mich	Aug. 25, 1868	81, 448
Grain-separator	W. Wilmington	South Bend, Ind	May 23, 1848	5, 595
Grain-separator	W. Wilmington	Toledo, Ohio	Nov. 29, 1859	26, 316
Grain-separator	S. M. Wirts	Hudson, Mich	Sept. 11, 1860	30, 017
Grain-separator	S. M. Wirts and F. Swift	Medina, Mich	Oct. 9, 1866	58, 707
Grain-separator	S. M. Wirts and L. Swift	Hudson, Mich	June 22, 1869	91, 805
Grain-separator	S. M. Wirtz and F. Swift	Hudson, N. Y	Apr. 16, 1861	32, 099
Grain-separator	D. Woodbury	Perkinsville, Vt	Mar. 27, 1849	6, 235
Grain-separator	J. Woolerver	Peoria, Ill	July 10, 1866	56, 316
Grain-separator	B. Wright and J. Bean	Hudson, Mich	Oct. 16, 1855	13, 688
Grain-separator	D. S. Yeakel	Dillingersville, Pa	July 7, 1868	79, 715
Grain-separator	E. Youngs	Tuscarora, N. Y	June 30, 1863	39, 090
Grain-separator	E. Youngs	Tuscarora, N. Y	Jan. 24, 1865	46, 044
Grain-separator	W. Zimmerman	Quincy, Ill	July 21, 1857	17, 853
Grain-separator	A. Zwiebel	Burlington, Wis	June 18, 1872	128, 197
Grain separator and bagger	J. J. Bradner	Pine Creek, N. Y	Mar. 26, 1872	125, 014
Grain separator and cleaner	W. M. Arnall	Sperryville, Va	May 1, 1860	28, 046
Grain separator and cleaner	W. M. Arnall	Sperryville, Va	June 26, 1866	55, 800
Grain separator and cleaner	D. W. Harshbarger	Myersburgh, Pa	July 7, 1863	39, 146
Grain separator and cleaner	S. Howes and G. E. Throop	Silver Creek, N. Y., and Chicago, Ill.	Mar. 16, 1858	19, 637
Grain-separator and clover-cleaning machine	E. L. Kelly	Reading, Mich	Aug. 10, 1869	93, 450
Grain separator and conveyer	J. Lyndall	Santa Clara, Cal	Nov. 18, 1856	16, 103
Grain separator and fan	R. T. Merrill	Bloomfield, Mich	Apr. 8, 1851	8, 031
Grain separator and fanning mill	S. S. Hammond and J. S. Paden	North East, Pa	Feb. 28, 1871	112, 141
Grain separator and mixer	J. J. Crowley	San Francisco, Cal	June 8, 1869	90, 932
Grain separator and scourer	S. W. Andrews and L. Godfrey	Greeneville, Tenn	Nov. 4, 1873	144, 180
Grain separator and scourer	W. P. Clifford	West Jersey, Ill	Sept. 30, 1873	143, 331
Grain separator and scourer	W. C. Knox	Jacksonville, Ill	June 29, 1869	92, 061
Grain separator and scourer	W. C. Knox	Jacksonville, Ill	Aug. 9, 1870	106, 177
Grain-separator and straw-carrier	C. Van Derzee	Albany, N. Y	Feb. 24, 1857	16, 698
Grain-separator and straw-carrier, Combined	A. T. Dunbar and A. McNaught	Alba, Pa	Feb. 5, 1867	61, 816
Grain, Separator for cleaning	G. B. Turner	Cuyahoga Falls, Ohio	Aug. 5, 1873	141, 524
Grain-separator, Rotary	H. Moore	Green Lake, Wis	Oct. 1, 1872	131, 771
Grain-separators, Blast-governor for	I. Hoge	Washington, D. C	May 6, 1873	138, 563
Grain-separators, Blast-regulator for	A. W. Fox	McConnellsburgh, Pa	Oct. 1, 1872	131, 870
Grain-separators, Elevator and table for feeding	D. C. Matteson and T. P. Williamson.	Stockton, Cal	Feb. 2, 1869	86, 564
Grain-separators, Governor attachment to	L. D. Lane	Freeport, Ill	July 17, 1860	29, 178
Grain-separators, Hopper for	F. H. Schroeder	Bushnell, Ill	Mar. 21, 1865	46, 947
Grain-separators, Metallic sieve for	J. A. Maloney	Georgetown, D. C	Oct. 3, 1871	119, 626
Grain-separators, Platform-attachment for	J. Whiteside	Salina, Cal	Jan. 11, 1870	98, 829
Grain-separators, Riddle for	G. A. Wells	Oskaloosa, Iowa	Dec. 15, 1868	85, 043
Grain-separators, Screen for	A. Gaar	Richmond, Ind	Oct. 20, 1857	18, 444
Grain-separators, Shoe for	H. Aldridge	Michigan City, Ind	May 24, 1859	24, 084
Grain-separators, Sieve for	E. Dond	Oshkosh, Wis	Aug. 12, 1873	141, 637
Grain-shovel	B. E. Miles	Washington, D. C	July 12, 1864	43, 519
Grain-shovel	D. B. Rogers	Pittsburgh, Pa	May 10, 1859	23, 949
Grain-shovel	G. V. Watson, G. Milson, and Spendelow.	Buffalo, N. Y	Nov. 22, 1864	45, 197
Grain-shovel	E. P. Williams	Buffalo, N. Y	Aug. 8, 1865	49, 350
Grain-shovel handler	F. Clark	Marcellus, N. Y	Mar. 26, 1867	63, 139
Grain-shoveling apparatus	T. D. Hawley	Detroit, Mich	June 15, 1869	91, 440
Grain Sifting and bagging	E. L. Seymour	New York, N. Y	Aug. 12, 1862	36, 176
Grain smutter, scourer, and separator	J. C. Hunt and W. W. Ingraham	Terre Haute, Ind., and Chicago, Ill.	Dec. 28, 1869	98, 266
Grain, snuff, paint, &c., Grinding	W. S. Johnson	New York	June 26, 1835	....
Grain-spout	A. D. Foote	Berlin, Wis	May 1, 1866	54, 322
Grain-spout	J. O. Frost	Candor, N. Y	Aug. 1, 1871	117, 531
Grain-spout	G. H. Johnson	Buffalo, N. Y	Feb. 16, 1869	86, 925
Grain-spreading device	H. H. Beach	Philadelphia, Pa	July 22, 1862	35, 916
Grain-steaming apparatus	J. H. Ebert and E. Pitts	Decatur, Ill	Aug. 19, 1873	142, 068
Grain stirring and delivering apparatus	S. Marsh	West Roxbury, Mass	Oct. 11, 1859	25, 745
Grain stirring and drying apparatus	T. C. Vice	New Haven, Conn	Jan. 20, 1863	37, 467
Grain, Stirring, conveying, and cooling	J. B. Wheeler	Bolton, Mass	May 13, 1862	35, 271
Grain-storehouse	G. Clark	Buffalo, N. Y	Mar. 9, 1869	87, 634

Index of patents issued from the United States Patent Office from 1790 to 1873, inclusive—Continued.

Invention.	Inventor.	Residence.	Date.	No.
Grain-storer	R. M. Mitchell	Fort Atkinson, Wis	Sept. 22, 1868	82, 339
Grain-stripper	J. O. King and H. A. Rice	Louisiana, Mo	Dec. 14, 1869	97, 932
Grain-tallying machine	A. Harter	Delphi, Ind	Oct. 30, 1866	59, 217
Grain, Tallying-machine for measured	S. Hudson	Milford, Mich	Jan. 10, 1865	45, 829
Grain, Teeth for lifting lodged	W. M. Jackson	Woodland, Cal	June 11, 1867	65, 750
Grain-tester, Pocket	B. Martin	Prairie du Chien, Wis	Jan. 14, 1868	73, 356
Grain to burr-millstones, Mode of cleaning and feeding.	S. G. Morrison	Williamsport, Pa	June 18, 1861	32, 578
Grain to flour or meal, Apparatus for reducing	J. J. Webster	Magog, Canada	Sept. 17, 1872	131, 485
Grain to millstones, Cleaning and feeding in	S. Shearman	Goshen, Ind	Aug. 1, 1854	11, 443
Grain to millstones, Feeding	M. and C. Painter	Owing's Mills, Md	June 2, 1857	17, 446
Grain to mills, Feeding	M. H. Ferguson	Sunfish, Ohio	Sept. 11, 1860	29, 961
Grain to obtain extractive matter for coloring and flavoring spirits, Treating.	S. H. Gilman	Galveston, Tex	June 14, 1870	104, 138
Grain to prevent smut, Composition to be applied to	A. N. Overton	Knoxville, Iowa	Oct. 1, 1861	33, 400
Grain-toller	S. R. and B. A. Peden	Franklin, Ky	Jan. 5, 1869	85, 610
Grain-tolling apparatus	J. Armstrong	Bucyrus, Ohio	Sept. 15, 1868	82, 193
Grain-tolling apparatus	W. S. Widger and W. M. Reed	Fairfield, Iowa	Oct. 27, 1868	83, 428
Grain-transferer, Railway	J. W. Sykes	Chicago, Ill	Oct. 12, 1869	95, 747
Grain, &c., Transporting and storing	S. F. Schoomaker	New York, N. Y	May 12, 1868	77, 768
Grain, &c., Treating and storing	C. Alden	Newburgh, N. Y	Nov. 3, 1868	83, 753
Grain, Ventilating	B. Dunwiddie	Monroe, Wis	May 20, 1873	139, 126
Grain, Ventilating	J. Shone	Blackwoodtown, N. J	May 22, 1866	54, 969
Grain-vessels, Ventilating	W. S. Sampson	New York, N. Y	Oct. 17, 1871	120, 108
Grain-washer	G. and G. W. Feaga	Frederick, Md	Jan. 4, 1853	9, 517
Grain-washing machine	G. Copeland	Denver, Colo	May 7, 1872	126, 523
Grainer's tool	R. A. Adams	Indianapolis, Ind	Feb. 12, 1861	31, 363
Graining and ornamental painting, Process for	W. J. Potter	Chicago, Ill	May 5, 1863	38, 412
Graining-apparatus	W. H. Kay	Lemont, Ill	May 11, 1869	90, 004
Graining-instrument	W. Russell	Beloit, Wis	Apr. 18, 1865	47, 339
Graining-machine	W. H. Berger	Pittsburgh, Pa	Oct. 12, 1869	95, 760
Graining-machine	G. Geiger	Cleveland, Ohio	Nov. 26, 1872	133, 311
Graining-machine	B. M. Hall	South Bend, Ind	Aug. 13, 1867	67, 755
Graining-machine	W. H. Smith	New York, N. Y	May 11, 1869	90, 056
Graining, Method of	J. J. Callow	Cleveland, Ohio	July 5, 1870	104, 929
Graining or imitating wood	J. Johnston	New York, N. Y	Jan. 21, 1873	135, 039
Graining, printing, &c., Flexible forms for	H. Tubesing	Pittsburgh, Pa	Mar. 7, 1865	46, 736
Graining process	J. R. Cross	Morrisania, N. Y	Oct. 29, 1872	132, 638
Graining-tool	W. J. Potter and W. H. Arnold	Chicago, Ill	Sept. 15, 1863	39, 953
Grains of wood, Process and composition for printing.	J. Bongardt	New York, N. Y	Dec. 8, 1868	84, 728
Grammatical key	J. Brown	Newark, N. J	Mar. 3, 1817	....
Granaries and other buildings, Cooling, drying, and ventilating.	D. E. Somes	Washington, D. C	Mar. 21, 1865	46, 950
Granary	A. C. L. Devaux	London, England	June 30, 1863	39, 030
Granary	E. Ford	Spring Cottage, Miss	Oct. 24, 1854	11, 830
Granary	T. Hermans	Mitchellsville, Tenn	Oct. 13, 1863	40, 261
Granary	C. T. Moorman, jr	Jamestown, Ohio	Nov. 19, 1872	133, 244
Granary	B. M. Nice	Cleveland, Ohio	Oct. 3, 1865	50, 267
Granary	J. Walsh	Valley Town, Ill	Jan. 1, 1867	60, 971
Granary and fruit-house	S. R. Beckwith	Cleveland, Ohio	Nov. 7, 1865	50, 790
Granary, Fire-proof	G. H. Johnson	Buffalo, N. Y	Mar. 9, 1869	87, 679
Granary, fruit-house, &c	S. R. Beckwith	Cleveland, Ohio	Mar. 13, 1866	53, 101
Granary to preserve wheat, &c., Construction of	J. Harmony	Chambersburgh, Pa	Aug. 20, 1835	....
Granite and stone cutting and dressing machine	W. C. Poland and E. Blossom	Portland, Me	Nov. 11, 1837	458
Granite-cutting machine	J. W. Maloy	Boston, Mass	Oct. 16, 1866	58, 853
Granite-dressing machine	J. D. Buzzell	Cape Elizabeth, Me	June 2, 1836	....
Granite, Hammering and dressing	W. Morse	Corinna, Me	Sept. 5, 1836	....
Granite, Machine for dressing or hammering	W. Morse	United States	Sept. 5, 1836	21
Grape and flower picker	C. W. H. Delano	Cedar Rapids, Iowa	Nov. 25, 1873	144, 837
Grape-box	O. Mallory	Rochester, N. Y	June 13, 1865	48, 192
Grape-box	S. P. Talman	Perrysburgh, Ohio	Jan. 23, 1872	123, 060
Grape-crusher	F. B. Schoenstein and A. Klein	San Francisco, Cal	Oct. 31, 1871	120, 409
Grape crusher and stem separator	T. C. Purington	Lincoln, Cal	Mar. 30, 1869	88, 329
Grape crusher and stem separator	T. C. Purington	Lincoln, Cal	Nov. 30, 1869	97, 313
Grape crusher and stemmer	O. Hyde	Oakland, Cal	Sept. 17, 1872	131, 352
Grape crusher and stoner	G. Johnston and W. F. Johnson	Sacramento and Folsom, Cal.	Apr. 2, 1872	125, 197
Grape-frame	S. O. Cross	Kingsbury, N. Y	June 27, 1854	11, 153
Grape-gatherer, Self-relieving	C. Wadsworth	Madison, Ohio	Sept. 3, 1867	68, 399
Grape-mill	A. Hemminger	Sandusky, Ohio	Nov. 22, 1864	45, 156
Grape-picker	G. A. Warner	San Francisco, Cal	Oct. 3, 1871	119, 485
Grape-pressing machine	H. Krause	New York, N. Y	July 20, 1858	20, 947
Grape vine cutter	L. W. Mayer	Sonoma, Cal	Feb. 9, 1869	86, 681
Grape-vine protector	J. S. Davis	La Porte, Ind	May 1, 1866	54, 302
Grape-vine protector	J. Walter	Princeton, Ill	Nov. 27, 1866	60, 099
Grape-vine support	F. B. Green	Seneca Falls, N. Y	Apr. 25, 1865	47, 415
Grape-vines, Mode of cultivating	G. Perry	Georgetown, Conn	Feb. 11, 1868	74, 417
Grape-vines, Propagating	W. Griffeth	North East, Pa	May 14, 1867	64, 760
Grape-vines, Training	G. S. Salsbury	Clarendon, N. Y	Sept. 4, 1866	57, 777
Grapes, apples, &c., Grinding and pressing	C. B. Hutchinson	Auburn, N. Y	Feb. 3, 1863	37, 579
Grapes, Implement for harvesting	J. F. Single	Painesville, Ohio	May 26, 1868	78, 241
Grapes, Machine for stemming and crushing	C. Wadhams	Los Angeles, Cal	Sept. 10, 1872	131, 316
Grapes, Mill for compressing and grinding	Z. C. Robbins	Washington, D. C	Aug. 14, 1855	13, 448
Graphite in reducing metals, Using	J. Weisman	Philadelphia, Pa	Mar. 16, 1858	19, 668
Graphodometer, Automatic mechanism for operating surveyor's.	J. M. Wampler	Baltimore, Md	July 13, 1858	20, 908
Graphotype	J. McElheran	Brooklyn, N. Y	Mar. 23, 1858	19, 707
Grapnel	N. P. and N. E. Allen	Salem, Mass	Dec. 20, 1870	110, 329
Grapple	J. H. Brinton	Thornbury, Pa	Aug. 10, 1869	93, 590
Grapple	J. Burkhart	Brookville, Ind	Apr. 8, 1873	137, 592
Grapple	E. G. Crandal	Belfast, N. Y	Mar. 14, 1871	112, 690
Grapple	S. B. Dexter	Mason City, Iowa	Mar. 25, 1873	137, 130
Grapple	C. La Dow	South Galway, N. Y	Sept. 19, 1871	119, 157
Grapple	S. Rogers	Pittsburgh, Pa	Mar. 1, 1870	100, 330
Grapple	J. F. Thomas	Ilion, N. Y	Aug. 3, 1869	93, 247
Grapple	H. Whitehall and J. Burson	Philadelphia, Pa., and Yates City, Ill.	Oct. 10, 1871	119, 729

Index of patents issued from the United States Patent Office from 1790 *to* 1873, *inclusive*—Continued.

Invention.	Inventor.	Residence.	Date.	No.
Grapple and excavator	A. T. Morris	Bloomfield, N. J	Jan. 5, 1869	85, 602
Grapple for raising stone	M. M. Cass and L. R. Bigelow	Watkins, N. Y	Feb. 19, 1856	14, 282
Grapple for raising sunken bodies	G. A. Wilbur	Skowhegan, Me	Aug. 19, 1856	15, 586
Grapple for raising sunken vessels	J. T. Martin	New York, N. Y	July 11, 1854	11, 291
Grapple, Spring	O. Warner and C. S. Gaylord	Gaylord's Bridge, Conn	Oct. 8, 1850	7, 709
Grapple, Store and household	J. Seltzer	Philadelphia, Pa	Apr. 12, 1870	101, 772
Grappling-apparatus, Naval	S. Riggs	Blanchester, Ohio	Sept. 5, 1865	49, 790
Grappling-fork	G. Hunziker	Summit, Miss	July 16, 1872	129, 032
Grappling-hook	E. Harter	Dowagiac, Mich	Dec. 28, 1869	98, 259
Grappling-hook	H. H. Hatheway	Clockville, N. Y	Dec. 7, 1869	97, 635
Grappling-hook	E. J. Riker	Lewiston, Me	Dec. 1, 1868	84, 510
Grappling-hook	E. Ziegler and C. Cable	Harmony, Pa	Mar. 28, 1871	113, 126
Grappling-iron	J. H. Chapman	Utica, N. Y	Aug. 28, 1866	57, 476
Grappling-iron	W. H. Hawley	Utica, N. Y	Oct. 22, 1867	69, 992
Grappling-iron	W. H. Hawley	Utica, N. Y	Oct. 6, 1868	82, 832
Grappling or dredging machine	A. Stoner	Mount Joy, Pa	Mar. 24, 1857	16, 886
Grappling-tool	N. W. Green	Cortland Village, N. Y	Dec. 11, 1866	60, 361
Grass and grain cutting machine	W. Manning	Plainfield, N. J	May 3, 1831	....
Grass-burner	J. A. Craig	Columbia, Ark	Feb. 3, 1852	8, 701
Grass-cutter	S. W. Sears	New York, N. Y	Sept. 20, 1870	107, 632
Grass-cutter	Sturdivant and Holmes	Portland, Me	June 19, 1835	....
Grass cutter and cradling machine	E. Badlam, jr	Chester, Vt	Sept. 18, 1835	....
Grass-cutting machine	W. Boone	New Hope, Mo	Nov. 21, 1848	5, 931
Grass-cutting machine	C. H. McCormick	Chicago, Ill	Sept. 21, 1858	21, 573
Grass-cutting machine, Flower-maker's	T. and J. Millot	New York, N. Y	Nov. 25, 1873	144, 916
Grass, &c., Extracting fiber from China	J. Steart	Bermondsey, England	Oct. 30, 1866	59, 331
Grass, Implement for destroying quack	C. W. Moseley	Onondaga, N. Y	Nov. 2, 1869	96, 464
Grass, Mode of destroying cocoa	H. B. Kenner	New Orleans, La	Oct. 6, 1843	3, 296
Grass. Mowing	J. P. Chandler	Wilton, Me	Aug. 17, 1835	....
Grass or grain cutter and rake	A. Rundel	Verona, N. Y	Apr. 22, 1835	....
Grass-renovator	J. Gould	Lexington, Mass	May 11, 1869	89, 983
Grass-seed-cleaning machine	H. Child	Canton, Me	Jan. 11, 1823	....
Grass-seed huller	H. P. Byram	Louisville, Ky	Oct. 11, 1853	10, 102
Grass-seed, &c., Machine for hulling	T. Blake	Paris, Me	July 12, 1822	....
Grass-seed separator for mangers	D. B. Dixon	Unionville, Mo	Aug. 23, 1870	106, 562
Grass under water, Apparatus for cutting	P. J. Stone	Athens, Pa	Aug. 2, 1870	105, 996
Grass under water, Machine for cutting	J. Hinds	Hindsburgh, N. Y	Sept. 5, 1840	1, 772
Grasshopper-exterminating composition	S. Green	Arapahoe County, Colo	Aug. 8, 1865	49, 258
Grate	J. L. Babbitt	Glen Cove, N. Y	Mar. 24, 1868	75, 830
Grate	J. Bennett	New York, N. Y	May 14, 1836	....
Grate	E. Bosdevex	Philadelphia, Pa	June 23, 1868	79, 195
Grate	J. S. Clark	Philadelphia, Pa	Feb. 12, 1867	62, 005
Grate	J. C. Cochrane	Rochester, N. Y	Feb. 26, 1867	62, 316
Grate	B. W. Dunklee	Boston, Mass	June 1, 1869	90, 645
Grate	F. Glick and U. Keck	Allentown, Pa	Oct. 4, 1870	107, 899
Grate	G. W. Griswold	Carbondale, Pa	July 25, 1854	11, 371
Grate	R. Ham	Troy, N. Y	Aug. 17, 1869	93, 712
Grate	C. Hires	Salem, N. J	May 15, 1866	54, 725
Grate	C. Hunt	New York, N. Y	Mar. 17, 1812	....
Grate	W. Keiser	Stroudsburgh, Pa	June 4, 1867	65, 392
Grate	S. J. Kelly	Pemberton, N. J	Oct. 20, 1863	40, 341
Grate	S. Kepner	Pottstown, Pa	Dec. 2, 1873	145, 212
Grate	D. Lister	Glasgow, Great Britain	Jan. 12, 1864	41, 225
Grate	C. B. Loveless	Syracuse, N. Y	Aug. 5, 1862	36, 098
Grate	L. G. Marshall	Mokena, Ill	Jan. 17, 1865	45, 948
Grate	W. L. McDowell	Philadelphia, Pa	Apr. 28, 1863	38, 317
Grate	J. H. Meissner	New York, N. Y	Oct. 22, 1867	70, 102
Grate	J. Miller	Saint Louis, Mo	June 27, 1865	48, 425
Grate	H. Mulford	Philadelphia, Pa	Feb. 8, 1870	99, 584
Grate	P. Murray	Milwaukee, Wis	Dec. 12, 1865	51, 472
Grate	P. Murray	Philadelphia, Pa	Dec. 29, 1868	85, 470
Grate	J. Old	Pittsburgh, Pa	Mar. 16, 1869	87, 790
Grate	P. A. Palmer	Troy, N. Y	Nov. 5, 1867	70, 462
Grate	J. F. Phelps	Huntsville, Ala	May 30, 1871	115, 515
Grate	B. Pike	New York, N. Y	Mar. 11, 1835	....
Grate	N. Prymer	Troy, N. Y	July 23, 1867	67, 136
Grate	E. S. Renwick	New York, N. Y	Feb. 23, 1869	87, 112
Grate	G. L. Smith	Brooklyn, N. Y	Mar. 29, 1864	42, 118
Grate	G. L. Smith	Brooklyn, N. Y	Aug. 21, 1866	57, 396
Grate	P. Smith	Fall River, Mass	Apr. 12, 1859	23, 621
Grate	S. Smyth	East Bridgewater, Pa	Oct. 21, 1873	143, 856
Grate	S. Stevens and J. P. Smith	Pittsburgh, Pa	Sept. 15, 1863	39, 969
Grate	J. Tiberi	Saint Louis, Mo	Sept. 6, 1859	25, 352
Grate	T. Tomkinson	Philadelphia, Pa	Aug. 17, 1869	93, 925
Grate	W. J. Towne	Newton, Mass	May 30, 1865	48, 000
Grate	J. Watson, jr	Louisville, Ky	Oct. 13, 1863	40, 315
Grate	M. D. Wellman	Allegheny City, Pa	Nov. 19, 1867	71, 253
Grate	J. S. Williams	Saint Louis, Mo	Sept. 13, 1859	25, 462
Grate	C. J. Woolson	Cincinnati, Ohio	Apr. 14, 1863	38, 194
Grate	C. J. Woolson	Cleveland, Ohio	Jan. 1, 1867	60, 981
Grate	W. Wright	South River, N. J	Mar. 17, 1863	37, 933
Grate	J. H. Yocum	Ashland, Pa	Jan. 28, 1868	73, 767
Grate, Adjustable stove	R. Moss	Philadelphia, Pa	Oct. 24, 1865	50, 613
Grate, Agitating coal	A. Keeney	Carlisle, Pa	Apr. 2, 1850	7, 245
Grate and andiron, Portable fire	J. H. Coate	West Milton, Ohio	Nov. 27, 1866	59, 968
Grate and ash-sifter in cooking-stoves	D. E. Paris	Troy, N. Y	June 9, 1868	78, 685
Grate and back for cooking-stoves	J. B. Slusser and W. H. Meech	Roanoke, Ind	June 7, 1870	104, 070
Grate and blower for coal	S. C. Mott and W. Holmes	New York	Nov. 26, 1826	....
Grate and cooking-stove	J. J. Giraud	Baltimore, Md	Feb. 10, 1836	....
Grate and door of open-grate or parlor stove	E. Brown	Philadelphia, Pa	Mar. 5, 1872	124, 325
Grate and fire-place	E. Conger	Newark, N. J	July 22, 1837	288
Grate and fire-place, Adjustable hood for coal	W. T. Fester	Jeffersonville, Ind	Oct. 22, 1867	69, 982
Grate and fire-place for anthracite coal	W. M. Russell	Boston, Mass	Feb. 8, 1833	....
Grate and fire-place register and air-box	A. Pollock	Boston, Mass	Mar. 3, 1837	137
Grate and fire-pot for heating-stoves	P. J. Schopp	Louisville, Ky	June 14, 1870	104, 212
Grate and grate-bar	J. C. Grant	Salem, Mass	Aug. 29, 1871	118, 604
Grate and grate-bar	W. B. Treadwell	Albany, N. Y	Mar. 6, 1866	53, 059
Grate and stove-bar	J. L. Mott	New York	Oct. 14, 1835	....

Index of patents issued from the United States Patent Office from 1790 to 1873, inclusive—Continued.

Invention.	Inventor.	Residence.	Date.	No.
Grate and stove, Coal	C. K. Marshall	New Orleans, La	July 14, 1868	79, 845
Grate and stove for warming apartments	E. H. Dixon	New York, N. Y	Aug. 8, 1837	347
Grate and stove, Parlor and kitchen	E. Ingalls	Providence, R. I	Apr. 22, 1835	....
Grate, Anthracite-coal stove	E. Nott	Schenectady, N. Y	June 29, 1833	....
Grate-bar	H. Ball	New York, N. Y	Nov. 29, 1870	109, 711
Grate-bar	H. K. Bates	North La Crosse, Wis	June 19, 1866	55, 603
Grate-bar	H. L. Budd	New York, N. Y	Apr. 30, 1867	64, 191
Grate-bar	J. Buzby	Moorestown, N. J	Oct 11, 1859	25, 720
Grate-bar	G. H. Clarke	Brooklyn, N. Y	Aug. 26, 1873	142, 146
Grate-bar	G. H. Clarke and C. Van Wagenen.	New York, N. Y	Oct. 30, 1866	59, 311
Grate-bar	H. Collinson	Boston, Mass	May 5, 1868	77, 458
Grate-bar	H. Collinson	Dorchester, Mass	Feb. 8, 1870	99, 640
Grate-bar	H. Collinson	Boston, Mass	July 11, 1871	116, 812
Grate-bar	A. F. Crowell	Hyannis, Mass	Sept. 30, 1873	143, 224
Grate-bar	T. S. Davis	Lancaster, Pa	Feb. 22, 1870	100, 016
Grate-bar	J. Easterly	Albany, N. Y	Apr. 5, 1859	23, 456
Grate-bar	W. Ferrel	Charleston, S. C	Apr. 25, 1843	3, 059
Grate-bar	A. Fickett and C. C. Benton	Rochester, N. Y	Jan. 17, 1871	111, 047
Grate-bar	A. C. Fletcher	New York, N. Y	Apr. 17, 1866	53, 966
Grate-bar	A. C. Fletcher	New York, N. Y	Jan. 29, 1867	61, 615
Grate-bar	A. C. Fletcher	New York, N. Y	Feb. 18, 1868	74, 526
Grate-bar	A. C. Fletcher	New York, N. Y	Apr. 14, 1868	76, 734
Grate-bar	A. C. Fletcher	New York, N. Y	July 7, 1868	79, 743
Grate-bar	A. C. Fletcher	New York, N. Y	Aug. 18, 1868	81, 155
Grate-bar	A. C. Fletcher	New York, N. Y	Nov. 7, 1871	120, 733
Grate-bar	A. W. Foster, jr	Pittsburgh, Pa	Oct. 24, 1871	120, 188
Grate-bar	C. A. Greenleaf	Indianapolis, Ind	Nov. 16, 1869	96, 798
Grate-bar	P. Griffith	Philadelphia, Pa	Aug. 5, 1862	36, 083
Grate-bar	J. W. Griswold and E. L. Thomson.	Philadelphia, Pa	Aug. 18, 1868	81, 161
Grate-bar	S. Harrison	Philadelphia, Pa	Sept. 25, 1866	58, 252
Grate-bar	A. Hartupee	Pittsburgh, Pa	Apr. 21, 1868	77, 038
Grate-bar	H. Hartwig	Covington, Ky	Jan. 2, 1872	122, 400
Grate-bar	M. Helnling	Allegheny, Pa	Mar. 9, 1869	87, 564
Grate-bar	W. E. Hill	Brooklyn, N. Y	Dec. 12, 1865	51, 455
Grate-bar	M. Hodgson	East Saginaw, Mich	Aug. 2, 1870	105, 942
Grate-bar	D. Housten	New York, N. Y	May 1, 1866	54, 349
Grate-bar	R. A. Hutchinson	Jersey City, N. J	July 30, 1872	130, 053
Grate-bar	R. A. Hutchinson	Bergen, N. J	Sept. 2, 1873	142, 471
Grate-bar	W. Kearney	Belleville, N. J	Aug. 2, 1870	105, 948
Grate-bar	H. C. Kerstine	Cleveland, Ohio	Sept. 23, 1873	143, 079
Grate-bar	H. King	Waterbury, Conn	May 26, 1868	78, 292
Grate bar	C. Kingsland	Allegheny, Pa	Oct. 16, 1849	6, 799
Grate-bar	J. S. Kirk and W. H. Elliot	Plattsburgh, N. Y	Mar. 27, 1855	12, 597
Grate-bar	L. F. Lakey and W. B. Hayte	Quincy, Ill	Oct. 12, 1869	95, 812
Grate-bar	D. Lasher	Brooklyn, N. Y	Sept. 11, 1860	29, 977
Grate-bar	W. S. Mackintosh	Allegheny City, Pa	Oct. 13, 1868	82, 965
Grate-bar	W. W. Marsh	Alton, Ill	Sept. 18, 1860	30, 074
Grate-bar	J. T. Marshall	Wilmington, Del	Jan. 24, 1871	111, 223
Grate-bar	J. McDonald	Cincinnati, Ohio	Mar. 29, 1864	42, 099
Grate-bar	W. McMannies	Brooklyn, N. Y	Feb. 8, 1870	99, 582
Grate-bar	J. A. Miller	Providence, R. I	Sept. 12, 1871	118, 962
Grate-bar	R. Montgomery	New York, N. Y	Aug. 21, 1866	57, 358
Grate-bar	W. Müir and P. Butler	Archibald and Carbondale, Pa.	June 20, 1871	116, 080
Grate-bar	J. T. Osborn	New Orleans, La	Jan. 22, 1856	14, 142
Grate-bar	B. F. Penny and J. Jones	Rochester, N. Y	July 6, 1869	92, 351
Grate-bar	C. W. Pierce	Albany, N. Y	Oct. 2, 1866	58, 474
Grate-bar	A. D. Puffer	Somerville, Mass	Mar. 21, 1865	46, 939
Grate-bar	W. Randall	Salem, Mass	Feb. 9, 1869	86, 862
Grate-bar	M. L. Roucout	Paris, France	May 31, 1853	9, 758
Grate-bar	S. T. Savage	Albany, N. Y	Nov. 23, 1858	22, 134
Grate-bar	H. B. Scofield	New York, N. Y	May 1, 1866	54, 415
Grate-bar	J. Sherman	Burlington, N. J	May 28, 1867	65, 289
Grate-bar	J. A. Sinclair	Bridgeport, Ohio	Feb. 4, 1873	135, 447
Grate-bar	J. R. Smith	Salem, Mass	Nov. 5, 1867	70, 638
Grate-bar	S. Smith	Salem, Mass	Oct. 2, 1866	58, 494
Grate-bar	J. W. Stanton	Barnesville, Ohio	Feb. 13, 1872	123, 739
Grate-bar	O. H. Taylor	Brooklyn, N. Y	Aug. 4, 1868	80, 574
Grate-bar	L. B. Tupper	New York, N. Y	June 14, 1864	43, 143
Grate-bar	L. B. Tupper	New York, N. Y	Feb. 27, 1866	52, 913
Grate-bar	L. B. Tupper	New York, N. Y	Aug. 21, 1866	57, 411
Grate-bar	P. Umholtz	Tremont, Pa	Nov. 4, 1873	144, 372
Grate-bar	P. and A. Umholtz	Tremont, Pa	Sept. 24, 1872	131, 641
Grate-bar	S. Vansyckel	Little York, N. J	Aug. 23, 1853	9, 958
Grate-bar	S. Vansyckel	Little York, N. J	Oct. 31, 1854	11, 879
Grate-bar	J. Yocum, jr	Philadelphia, Pa	Mar. 30, 1869	88, 355
Grate-bar	J. Yocom, jr	Philadelphia, Pa	Nov. 15, 1870	109, 285
Grate-bar, Air-conducting	R. G. Orwig	Des Moines, Iowa	Apr. 9, 1872	125, 404
Grate-bar and bearer	W. Kearney	Belleville, N. J	Nov. 1, 1870	108, 796
Grate bar and grating, Furnace	J. Cuthbert	Pittsburgh, Pa	Apr. 26, 1870	102, 233
Grate-bar for boiler and other furnaces	G. A. Eyars	Meriden, Conn	May 18, 1869	90, 248
Grate-bar for boilers	D. Byard	Sharon, Pa	Sept. 7, 1869	94, 561
Grate-bar for boilers	E. Thayer	Worcester, Mass	Mar. 28, 1865	47, 052
Grate-bar for furnaces and heaters	J. Reynolds	Philadelphia, Pa	May 11, 1869	89, 888
Grate-bar for furnaces, Hollow	G. S. Nevins	Bushnell, Ill	Jan. 23, 1866	52, 189
Grate-bar for steam and other enginery	M. and C. H. Morse	Franklin, Mass	Oct. 26, 1869	96, 138
Grate-bar for steam-boilers, Hollow	B. L. Griffith	Reading, Pa	Aug. 30, 1859	25, 258
Grate-bar for steam-generators	E. G. Blakeslee and A. Manser	Sing Sing, N. Y	Oct. 10, 1865	50, 327
Grate-bar frame, Hollow	G. E. Turner	Chicago, Ill	Dec. 28, 1869	98, 321
Grate bar, Furnace	F. Armstrong	New Orleans, La	Feb. 17, 1852	8, 732
Grate bar, Furnace	C. C. Bemis	San Francisco, Cal	Dec. 4, 1866	60, 125
Grate bar, Furnace	W. C. Cambridge	Bristol, Great Britain	Nov. 3, 1868	83, 689
Grate bar, Furnace	G. H. Clarke	Brooklyn, N. Y	Jan. 21, 1868	73, 436
Grate bar, Furnace	E. Dugdale	Burlington, N. J	Aug. 18, 1857	18, 010
Grate bar, Furnace	J. H. Fellows	Cincinnati, Ohio	Mar. 27, 1847	5, 035
Grate bar, Furnace	H. Gerner	New York, N. Y	Oct. 11, 1864	44, 622

Index of patents issued from the United States Patent Office from 1790 *to* 1873, *inclusive*—Continued.

Invention.	Inventor.	Residence.	Date.	No.
Grate bar, Furnace	R. C. Graves	Barnesville, Ohio	Feb. 11, 1873	135, 799
Grate bar, Furnace	J. Kymer	Caermarthen, South Wales	July 18, 1844	3, 671
Grate bar, Furnace	W. S. Low	Albany, N. Y	June 7, 1859	24, 316
Grate bar, Furnace	W. Mellor	Paterson, N. J	Mar. 26, 1872	124, 966
Grate bar, Furnace	A. Rawson	Des Moines, Iowa	June 4, 1872	127, 428
Grate bar, Furnace	A. Rawson	Des Moines, Iowa	July 23, 1872	129, 862
Grate bar, Furnace	A. Rawson	Des Moines, Iowa	Aug. 19, 1873	141, 890
Grate bar, Furnace	J. C. Schlough	Easton, Pa	May 29, 1855	12, 967
Grate bar, Furnace	W. H. Settle	Louisville, Ky	July 23, 1872	129, 756
Grate bar, Furnace	G. O. Tupper	New York, N. Y	Apr. 10, 1866	53, 903
Grate bar, Furnace	J. Vandercar	Brooklyn, N. Y	May 24, 1864	42, 888
Grate bar, Furnace	B. C. Vanduzen	Cincinnati, Ohio	May 30, 1854	10, 996
Grate bar, Furnace	R. Wicks	New York, N. Y	May 15, 1855	12, 883
Grate bar, Furnace	J. Williams, J. Forgie, and J. Edwards.	New York, N. Y	Mar. 24, 1868	76, 023
Grate-bar, Hollow	N. Shaw	West Eau Claire, Wis	Aug. 31, 1869	94, 345
Grate-bar, Revolving	G. C. Waggonner	Hamilton, Ill	Oct. 22, 1872	132, 423
Grate-bar, Rocking	J. Jones	Rochester, N. Y	May 30, 1871	115, 482
Grate-bar, Rotary	D. Byard	Sharon, Pa	Oct. 18, 1870	108, 327
Grate bar, Steam-generator	J. Mahony	Newport, R. I	June 29, 1869	91, 949
Grate bar, Steam-generator	M. D. Wellman	Allegheny County, Pa	Apr. 12, 1870	101, 795
Grate bar, Stove	G. W. Gardner	Albany, N. Y	Nov. 18, 1851	8, 523
Grate-bar supporter	W. F. Morgan and F. C. Bartlett.	New York, N. Y	Sept. 19, 1865	50, 023
Grate bar, Tubular	W. H. Farris	Cairo, Ill	May 2, 1871	114, 280
Grate bar, Water	W. H. Farris	Cairo, Ill	Mar. 28, 1871	113, 037
Grate-bars, Agitating	A. D. Spoor	Troy, N. Y	Apr. 15, 1851	8, 043
Grate-bars, Construction of	F. P. Dimpfel	Philadelphia, Pa	Mar. 16, 1852	8, 799
Grate-bars for furnaces, Casting	J. A. Miller	New York, N. Y	Jan. 31, 1865	46, 127
Grate-bars, Interlocking	S. Vansyckel	Jersey City, N. J	Oct. 9, 1855	13, 669
Grate, Brick-kiln	J. Maltpress	Edgerton, Wis	Dec. 1, 1868	84, 639
Grate called caloret, Fire	C. M. Graham	New York	Nov. 10, 1821	....
Grate, Coal	C. O. Greene	West Troy, N. Y	Jan. 1, 1850	6, 985
Grate, Coal	W. T. McMillen	Saint Louis, Mo	May 22, 1860	28, 390
Grate, Coal	I. Pickard	Lena, Ill	Dec. 13, 1870	110, 157
Grate, Coal-stove	S. G. Morrison	Williamsport, Pa	Aug. 5, 1873	141, 452
Grate, Coal-vault	G. W. Scott	Greencastle, Ind	Oct. 11, 1870	108, 298
Grate combination	J. Wallace	Louisville, Ky	Nov. 12, 1867	70, 924
Grate, Common fire	J. Atwater	New Haven, Conn	Oct. 25, 1832	....
Grate, Cooking	T. Vinton	Philadelphia, Pa	Oct. 31, 1829	....
Grate, Drip-receiving	W. N. Reed	Arlington, Va	Nov. 22, 1870	109, 452
Grate-fender	S. S. Bent	Port Chester, N. Y	July 12, 1870	105, 295
Grate-fender	G. Buchanan	Washington, Pa	Mar. 9, 1869	87, 629
Grate-fender	G. Buchanan	Washington, Pa	Nov. 7, 1871	120, 571
Grate, Fire	J. Atwater	New Haven, Conn	Jan. 9, 1833	....
Grate, Fire	W. S. Bronson	Hartford, Conn	May 5, 1868	77, 445
Grate, Fire	W. H. Farris	Cairo, Ill	Aug. 12, 1873	141, 780
Grate, Fire	W. D. Guseman	Morgantown, W. Va	June 30, 1863	39, 043
Grate, Fire	J. Habermehl	Wheeling, W. Va	May 30, 1865	47, 947
Grate, Fire	G. R. Moore	Philadelphia, Pa	Apr. 18, 1871	113, 908
Grate, Fire	M. Peckham	Utica, N. Y	Aug. 16, 1870	106, 502
Grate, Fire	W. H. Pulver	Troy, N. Y	Aug. 7, 1847	5, 232
Grate, Fire	H. Speeler	Trenton, N. J	Jan. 21, 1868	73, 662
Grate, Fire	J. Tiberi	Saint Louis, Mo	Apr. 2, 1861	31, 914
Grate, Fire	J. Vandercar	Brooklyn, N. Y	Aug. 11, 1868	80, 844
Grate, Fire	R. F. Weller	Albany, N. Y	Sept. 5, 1871	118, 762
Grate, Fire	G. Wellhouse	Akron, Ohio	Mar. 7, 1871	112, 399
Grate, Fire	G. Williamson	Milwaukee, Wis	May 4, 1869	89, 720
Grate, Fire-place	S. S. Bent	Port Chester, N. Y	July 12, 1870	105, 296
Grate, Fire-place	S. S. Bent	Port Chester, N. Y	July 12, 1870	105, 297
Grate, Fire-place	L. Bertsche, jr	Allegheny City, Pa	June 22, 1869	91, 597
Grate, Fire-place	F. S. Bissell	Pittsburgh, Pa	Aug. 30, 1870	106, 772
Grate, Fire-place	J. Caven	Indianapolis, Ind	Oct. 31, 1871	120, 490
Grate, Fire-place	G. Chilson	Boston, Mass	June 4, 1850	7, 411
Grate, Fire-place	J. A. Crawford	Newcastle, Pa	Jan. 28, 1870	104, 836
Grate, Fire-place	G. W. Everhart	Louisville, Ky	Dec. 21, 1869	98, 045
Grate, Fire-place	W. H. Garrett	Cannonsburgh, Pa	Apr. 18, 1871	113, 757
Grate, Fire-place	J. Goldenburgh	Cincinnati, Ohio	Oct. 7, 1846	4, 801
Grate, Fire-place	A. Greenaway and H. J. Needham.	New Albany, Ind	June 27, 1871	116, 438
Grate, Fire-place	J. Hackett	Louisville, Ky	Sept. 20, 1870	107, 483
Grate, Fire-place	G. W. Hinman	Paducah, Ky	June 29, 1869	92, 049
Grate, Fire-place	M. C. Hull	New York, N. Y	Sept. 15, 1863	39, 928
Grate, Fire-place	G. H. McElevey	Newcastle, Pa	Feb. 8, 1870	99, 581
Grate, Fire-place	E. D. Merrick	New Brighton, Pa	Mar. 29, 1870	101, 296
Grate, Fire-place	E. Norman	New Orleans, La	July 12, 1870	105, 234
Grate, Fire-place	M. Obmer	Dayton, Ohio	June 11, 1872	127, 916
Grate, Fire-place	J. Old	Pittsburgh, Pa	Nov. 2, 1869	96, 342
Grate, Fire-place	D. Pangle	Belmont, Ohio	Dec. 19, 1871	122, 050
Grate, Fire-place	W. Pulsfort	Louisville, Ky	Feb. 21, 1871	111, 971
Grate, Fire-place	C. S. Rankin	Cincinnati, Ohio	June 30, 1868	79, 391
Grate, Fire-place	J. S. Runyan	Columbus, Ohio	Nov. 22, 1870	109, 550
Grate, Fire-place	J. S. Runyan	Columbus, Ohio	Sept. 2, 1873	142, 514
Grate, Fire-place	R. P. Sause	Louisville, Ky	Mar. 19, 1872	124, 699
Grate, Fire-place	J. W. Thornily	New Brighton, Pa	Mar. 21, 1871	112, 986
Grate, Fire-place	M. S. Watkins	Memphis, Tenn	Nov. 14, 1871	120, 917
Grate, Fire-place	W. E. Whitehurst	Norfolk, Va	Feb. 1, 1870	99, 384
Grate, Fire-place	W. S. Withers	Atlanta, Ga	Aug. 17, 1869	93, 939
Grate, Fire-place	J. E. Wood	Huntington, W. Va	Dec. 2, 1873	145, 141
Grate, Fire-place	J. M. Woodcock	Bridgeport, Ohio	Apr. 15, 1873	137, 993
Grate, Fire-place	W. Young	London, England	Nov. 19, 1867	71, 260
Grate, fire-place, and furnace	J. H. Sherwood	New York, N. Y	Mar. 11, 1873	136, 775
Grate, fire-place, and hot-air furnace	C. S. Rankin	Cincinnati, Ohio	Feb. 13, 1872	123, 727
Grate, Fire-place and stove	B. Franklin	Indianapolis, Ind	Mar. 26, 1872	125, 040
Grate for admitting air to sides and body of the fuel-stove.				
Grate for base-burning stoves, Plate or	L. W. Harwood and C. D. Newton.	Troy, N. Y	Jan. 19, 1869	86, 069

Index of patents issued from the United States Patent Office from 1790 to 1873, inclusive—Continued.

Invention.	Inventor.	Residence.	Date.	No.
Grate for burning coal, Open	J. Atwater	New Haven, Conn	Nov. 9, 1838	1,001
Grate for burning coal-screenings	G. W. Hildreth	Lockport, N. Y	Feb. 28, 1871	112,246
Grate for burning fuel, Suspension	T. Pearson	Monroe Works, N. Y	July 17, 1837	270
Grate for burning petroleum and other liquid fuel	J. D. Smedley	Chicago, Ill	Oct. 28, 1862	36,805
Grate for coal-stoves	J. Easterly	Albany, N. Y	Sept. 7, 1858	21,410
Grate for coal-stoves	C. Isbister	Allegheny City, Pa	Apr. 17, 1849	6,358
Grate for coal-stoves and furnaces	W. Hailes	Albany, N. Y	Nov. 18, 1862	36,950
Grate for cooking-stoves	J. G. Clarke	Cincinnati, Ohio	July 11, 1865	48,773
Grate for cooking-stoves	J. T. Davy	Troy, N. Y	Apr. 16, 1850	7,284
Grate for cooking-stoves	L. Emmons	Hamilton, Ohio	Jan. 28, 1868	73,705
Grate for cooking-stoves	D. P. Foster	Shelburne Falls, Mass	July 25, 1865	48,923
Grate for cooking-stoves	J. H. Roelker	Evansville, Ind	Mar. 23, 1869	88,213
Grate for cooking-stoves	W. H. Whitehead	Chicago, Ill	Oct. 15, 1867	69,879
Grate for cooking-stoves, Portable summer	S. Spoor	Troy, N. Y	July 30, 1872	129,907
Grate for fire-places, Revolving	A. Brase and L. Salladey	Sciotoville, Ohio	May 17, 1870	103,134
Grate for furnaces, Basket	J. J. Heindl	New York, N. Y	Apr. 7, 1868	76,444
Grate for furnaces, Circular	G. L. Smith	Brooklyn, N. Y	Sept. 24, 1867	69,134
Grate for furnaces, Drop	W. Shepherd	New York, N. Y	Aug. 15, 1871	118,062
Grate for furnaces, stoves, &c	P. W. Pratt	Abington, Mass	June 4, 1872	127,514
Grate for furnaces, Water	R. L. Walker	Globe Village, Mass	Nov. 19, 1867	71,251
Grate for heating stoves	G. Nimmo	Jersey City, N. J	Oct. 23, 1866	59,057
Grate for locomotive-engines	J. W. Pole	Philadelphia, Pa	July 27, 1858	21,021
Grate for steam-boiler furnaces	G. L. Smith	Brooklyn, N. Y	June 27, 1865	48,455
Grate for steam-boiler furnaces	J. Zeh	Vienna, Austria	June 13, 1865	48,247
Grate for steam-boilers	F. A. Hull	Belvidere, Ill	Sept. 11, 1860	29,974
Grate for steam boilers	J. Montgomery	Brooklyn, N. Y	July 27, 1858	21,013
Grate for steam-boilers, Fire	R. Eaton	Lee, England	Jan. 1, 1867	60,706
Grate for steam-boilers, Hollow	C. E. Hutson	Commerce, Mo	Mar. 8, 1870	100,631
Grate for steam-boilers, Tubular	S. C. Sturtevant	Cleveland, Ohio	June 11, 1861	32,541
Grate for steam-boilers, Water	T. Stone	Carbondale, Ill	Oct. 24, 1871	120,342
Grate for steam-engines	R. Winans	Baltimore, Md	Apr. 6, 1858	19,890
Grate for steam-generator and other furnaces	B. T. Babbitt	New York, N. Y	June 29, 1869	91,999
Grate for steam-generators, Circulating	J. Braden	Indianapolis, Ind	Nov. 2, 1869	96,354
Grate for stoves and fire-places	W. B. Sutor	Indiana, Pa	Apr. 8, 1873	137,733
Grate for stoves and furnaces	N. A. Boynton	New York, N. Y	May 14, 1872	126,777
Grate for stoves and furnaces	J. B. McIntosh	Erie, Pa	Sept. 28, 1869	95,250
Grate for stoves and furnaces	J. J. Richardson	Brooklyn, N. Y	Aug. 19, 1873	141,891
Grate for stoves and furnaces	G. Vander Heyden	Troy, N. Y	Dec. 1, 1863	40,781
Grate for stoves, Basket	F. H. Root	Buffalo, N. Y	Apr. 27, 1869	89,347
Grate for stoves, ranges, and heaters	R. Whiting and A. Hamilton	New York, N. Y	Aug. 4, 1868	80,689
Grate for stoves, Revolving	E. Draper	Oskaloosa, Iowa	Feb. 13, 1866	52,548
Grate-frame, Base for summer-pieces and	A. Brown and W. Patterson	Brooklyn, E. D., N. Y	Feb. 8, 1870	99,631
Grate-front and oven, Combined	J. W. Gillespie and W. Hughes	Alliance, Ohio	June 14, 1870	104,136
Grate, Furnace	A. Adams	Stamford, Conn	Apr. 2, 1867	63,354
Grate, Furnace	J. Alexander	Green Point, N. Y	Jan. 1, 1867	60,842
Grate, Furnace	A. J. Allen and W. S. Hudson	Paterson, N. J	May 25, 1858	20,316
Grate, Furnace	I. R. Barbour	Hannibal, Mo	July 13, 1869	92,562
Grate, Furnace	C. F. Cory	Lebanon, Ill	July 24, 1860	29,248
Grate, Furnace	R. W. and D. Davis	Flushing and Long Island City, N. Y.	Apr. 17, 1866	54,064
Grate, Furnace	R. C. Graves	Barnesville, Ohio	Apr. 30, 1872	126,285
Grate, Furnace	T. T. Holdsworth	Brooklyn, N. Y	Aug. 18, 1863	39,573
Grate, Furnace	R. A. Hutchinson	Bergen, N. J	Sept. 27, 1870	107,780
Grate, Furnace	C. Kugler	Barnesville, Ohio	Apr. 23, 1872	126,060
Grate, Furnace	E. Langen	Cologne, Prussia	Nov. 14, 1865	50,996
Grate, Furnace	D. Lasher	Brooklyn, N. Y	Jan. 7, 1862	34,064
Grate, Furnace	W. B. LeVan	Philadelphia, Pa	Aug. 19, 1873	141,936
Grate, Furnace	E. I. McCarthy	Saugerties, N. Y	July 19, 1859	24,815
Grate, Furnace	G. R. Moore	Philadelphia, Pa	Apr. 4, 1871	113,324
Grate, Furnace	C. M. Northrup	New York, N. Y	July 25, 1871	117,319
Grate, Furnace	A. L. Pennock	Upper Darby, Pa	Sept. 27, 1870	107,715
Grate, Furnace	T. E. Purchase	Danville, Pa	Feb. 14, 1860	27,155
Grate, Furnace	J. Reynolds	Philadelphia, Pa	July 9, 1867	66,628
Grate, Furnace	M. M. Rounds	New Haven, Conn	Mar. 12, 1861	31,676
Grate, Furnace	H. Ryder	Somerville, Mass	Mar. 11, 1873	136,673
Grate, Furnace	W. H. Short	Brooklyn, N. Y	Jan. 3, 1865	45,760
Grate, Furnace	B. F. Smith	New Orleans, La	Sept. 12, 1871	118,884
Grate, Furnace	G. L. Smith	Brooklyn, N. Y	Nov. 24, 1863	40,712
Grate, Furnace	E. F. Steele	Wallingford, Conn	July 11, 1871	117,009
Grate, Furnace	T. Von Bolzano	Schlan, Austria	Jan. 28, 1873	135,390
Grate, Furnace	R. Van Velthoven	Philadelphia, Pa	Apr. 19, 1859	23,729
Grate, Furnace	C. Van Wagenen	New York, N. Y	May 28, 1872	127,203
Grate, Furnace	A. B. Weeks	Rockland, Me	Oct. 4, 1870	107,987
Grate, Furnace	C. Whittier	Roxbury, Mass	Jan. 23, 1866	52,235
Grate, Furnace	S. L. Wiegand and W. B. Le Van	Philadelphia, Pa	Jan. 5, 1864	41,181
Grate, Furnace	W. A. Wilson and J. Smith	Liverpool, England	Aug. 27, 1867	68,139
Grate, Furnace	A. Winterburn	Albany, N. Y	Nov. 3, 1863	40,532
Grate, Furnace	J. Withington	Blossburgh, Pa	Aug. 19, 1873	142,068
Grate, Furnace and fire-place	G. Warriner	Little Ilford, England	Feb. 12, 1867	61,964
Grate furnace for locomotive-boilers, Multiple	F. Harbach	Cleveland, Ohio	Jan. 30, 1849	6,076
Grate, Hot-air	T. F. Randolph	Cincinnati, Ohio	Dec. 22, 1863	41,019
Grate, Hot-air-furnace	E. S. Rennick	New York, N. Y	Aug. 19, 1868	81,109
Grate in cooking-stoves, Apparatus for raising the	B. K. Maltby	Cleveland, Ohio	June 18, 1850	7,442
Grate in heating-stoves	G. Moody	Falmouth, Me	May 11, 1869	89,880
Grate, Kitchen	L. Disbrow	New York	Nov. 22, 1830	......
Grate, Locomotive and furnace	M. E. Brown	Buffalo, N. Y	Apr. 26, 1864	42,526
Grate, Locomotive-fire	R. Eaton	Lee, England	Oct. 30, 1866	59,329
Grate, Locomotive-furnace	G. R. Comstock	Manheim, N. Y	Jan. 29, 1856	14,153
Grate, Open	J. Easterly	Troy, N. Y	May 16, 1842	2,627
Grate, Open coal	C. Crawford	East Cleveland, Ohio	May 29, 1866	55,065
Grate or furnace, Anthracite coal-stove	J. Atwater	New Haven, Conn	Aug. 23, 1833	......
Grate or lining of fire-pot, Fire	D. H. Dean	Lowell, Mass	June 9, 1857	17,540
Grate or parlor-stove, Open	O. Jenks	Albany, N. Y	Nov. 16, 1841	2,357
Grate or portable fire-place	J. Williamson	Washington, D. C	Nov. 8, 1836	......
Grate, Parlor	W. Anderson	New York, N. Y	June 25, 1836	......
Grate, Parlor	D. Lamoureux	New York, N. Y	Sept. 6, 1859	25,338
Grate, Parlor	J. Wilson	New York, N. Y	Sept. 13, 1845	4,191

Index of patents issued from the United States Patent Office from 1790 *to* 1873, *inclusive*—Continued.

Invention.	Inventor.	Residence.	Date.	No.
Grate, Pendulum	N. Winslow	Portland, Me	July 2, 1836	....
Grate, Portable camp	L. D. Gavitt	Los Angeles, Cal	Jan. 17, 1871	110, 967
Grate, Quadrant hinged	G. H. Thatcher	Albany, N. Y	Aug. 5, 1851	8, 277
Grate, Reverberating	R. Mayo	Richmond, Va	Nov. 1, 1825	....
Grate, Revolving	P. J. Boris	Fairfax, Nova Scotia	Jan. 10, 1865	45, 895
Grate, Revolving	C. Evans	Charlestown, Mass	Dec. 25, 1855	14, 007
Grate, Revolving and sifting	E. B. M. Hughes	New Haven, Conn	July 29, 1837	312
Grate, Revolving coal	J. B. Chollar	West Troy, N. Y	Aug. 27, 1850	7, 593
Grate, Revolving horizontal coal	J. F. Weishampel	Baltimore, Md	June 19, 1849	6, 541
Grate, Rocking	J. Seddon	Susquehanna Depot, Pa	Sept. 23, 1873	143, 034
Grate, Rotary stove	A. Harrison	Philadelphia, Pa	Oct. 5, 1852	9, 297
Grate, Sliding	J. C. Howard	Hampton, Conn	Feb. 13, 1836	....
Grate, Sliding	G. W. Walker	Boston, Mass	Feb. 25, 1862	34, 536
Grate, Sliding-flue	D. Desmond	New York, N. Y	Dec. 26, 1837	541
Grate, Steam-boiler	A. M. Searles	Cincinnati, Ohio	Sept. 30, 1856	15, 825
Grate, Steam-furnace	E. H. Jones	West Albany, N. Y	June 20, 1865	48, 286
Grate, Stove	A. J. Arnold	Columbus, Nebr	Dec. 24, 1872	134, 238
Grate, Stove	D. S Baker	West Bloomfield, N. Y	May 12, 1868	77, 707
Grate, Stove	M. R. Barr	Erie, Pa	June 27, 1871	116, 396
Grate, Stove	P. Boyden	Amsterdam, N. Y	May 23, 1871	115, 021
Grate, Stove	L. Bridge	Philadelphia, Pa	June 14, 1870	104, 258
Grate, Stove	A. Brown	Troy, N. Y	Mar. 25, 1862	34, 731
Grate, Stove	A. Brown	Troy, N. Y	Dec. 11, 1866	60, 334
Grate, Stove	E. Card	Pawtucket, R. I	Dec. 7, 1869	97, 477
Grate, Stove	G. Chilson	Boston, Mass	Apr 7, 1868	76, 302
Grate, Stove	G. Chilson	Boston, Mass	June 30, 1868	79, 312
Grate, Stove	J. Churchman	Burlington, N. J	May 16, 1871	114, 762
Grate, Stove	W. Craven	Cincinnati, Ohio	Aug. 18, 1868	81, 139
Grate, Stove	S. P. Davis	Constantine, Mich	June 13, 1871	115, 827
Grate, Stove	P. Dempsey	Erie, Pa	May 24, 1870	103, 307
Grate, Stove	E. Dewitt	Belvidere, N. J	Jan. 21, 1873	135, 095
Grate, Stove	E. Dewitt	Belvidere, N. J	Jan. 21, 1873	135, 096
Grate, Stove	W. Doyle	Albany, N. Y	Nov. 28, 1871	121, 236
Grate, Stove	W. Doyle	Albany, N. Y	June 11, 1872	127, 684
Grate, Stove	S. Duncan	Syracuse, N. Y	Feb. 4, 1873	135, 471
Grate, Stove	G. W. Eltonhead	Saint Louis, Mo	Oct. 7, 1873	143, 443
Grate, Stove	M. P. Farnham	Janesville, Wis	Mar. 26, 1867	63, 150
Grate, Stove	D. A. Flood and D. W. Brown	Woodbridge, N. J	June 6, 1871	115, 590
Grate, Stove	C. O. Foley	Troy, N. Y	Sept. 26, 1871	119, 343
Grate, Stove	C. Fulton	Rochester, N. Y	Apr. 27, 1869	89, 304
Grate, Stove	J. Glass	Troy, N. Y	Aug. 8, 1865	49, 344
Grate, Stove	W. A. Green	Brooklyn, N. Y	Nov. 21, 1871	121, 097
Grate, Stove	W. Hagerty	Philadelphia, Pa	Dec. 2, 1873	145, 172
Grate, Stove	W. Hailes	Albany, N. Y	May 11, 1869	89, 863
Grate, Stove	L. F. Hake	Salem, Ohio	Feb. 19, 1867	62, 265
Grate, Stove	R. Ham	Troy, N. Y	Aug. 9, 1870	106, 154
Grate, Stove	E. Harrington	Boston, Mass	Nov. 18, 1862	36, 952
Grate, Stove	A. M. Harris	Columbus, Ga	Feb. 18, 1873	135, 909
Grate, Stove	T. Hartley	Bridgeport, Ohio	Nov. 28, 1871	121, 363
Grate, Stove	C. R. Harvey and J. H. Foote	New York, N. Y	May 2, 1871	114, 298
Grate, Stove	L. W. Harwood	Troy, N. Y	Nov. 13, 1860	30, 620
Grate, Stove	L. W. Harwood	Troy, N. Y	Sept. 8, 1863	39, 811
Grate, Stove	D. Hathaway	Troy, N. Y	Sept. 13, 1864	44, 188
Grate, Stove	D. Hathaway	Troy, N. Y	Nov. 9, 1869	96, 588
Grate, Stove	D. Hathaway	Troy, N. Y	Dec. 21, 1869	98, 059
Grate, Stove	B. F. Holbrook and E. B. Rumrill	Boston, Mass	Sept. 8, 1868	81, 904
Grate, Stove	W. J. Keep	Troy, N. Y	June 3, 1873	139, 583
Grate, Stove	H. G. Leonard	Taunton, Mass	May 7, 1867	64, 430
Grate, Stove	E. C. Loud	Springfield, Mass	Mar. 8, 1870	100, 536
Grate, Stove	J. Magee	Boston, Mass	Dec. 10, 1861	33, 919
Grate, Stove	A. J. Magoon	Providence, R. I	Aug. 4, 1868	80, 645
Grate, Stove	H. C. March	Lawrenceville, Pa	July 29, 1862	36, 055
Grate, Stove	W. L. McDowell	Philadelphia, Pa	Oct. 14, 1862	36, 662
Grate, Stove	W. McIlvain	Philadelphia, Pa	Oct. 3, 1865	50, 258
Grate, Stove	H. Miner	Green Island, N. Y	Apr. 19, 1870	102, 143
Grate, Stove	E. Mingay	Boston, Mass	May 1, 1860	28, 102
Grate, Stove	E. Monense and L. Duparquet	New York, N. Y	July 7, 1868	79, 570
Grate, Stove	G. R. Moore	Philadelphia, Pa	July 18, 1871	117, 194
Grate, Stove	G. R. Moore	Philadelphia, Pa	Sept. 12, 1871	118, 874
Grate, Stove	G. R. Moore	Philadelphia, Pa	Dec. 9, 1873	145, 360
Grate, Stove	J. Moran	Washington, D. C	Sept. 7, 1869	94, 627
Grate, Stove	R. Moss	Philadelphia, Pa	Nov. 14, 1871	120, 992
Grate, Stove	D. H. Nation	Albany, N. Y	July 24, 1860	29, 300
Grate, Stove	D. E. Paris	Troy, N. Y	Dec. 31, 1867	72, 754
Grate, Stove	J. W. Parnell	Troy, N. Y	Sept. 25, 1860	30, 182
Grate, Stove	H. W. Pell	Rome, N. Y	Nov. 26, 1872	133, 477
Grate, Stove	G. A. Philip	New York, N. Y	Sept. 4, 1847	5, 277
Grate, Stove	G. H. Philips and W. H. Johnson	Troy, N. Y	Sept. 29, 1863	40, 146
Grate, Stove	J. A. Price	Scranton, Pa	Oct. 10, 1871	119, 787
Grate, Stove	W. Quay and E. M. Hinsdale	Troy, N. Y	Sept. 6, 1870	107, 197
Grate, Stove	S. H. Ransom and B. Burton	Albany, N. Y	June 11, 1872	127, 795
Grate, Stove	H. J. Ruggles	West Poultney, Vt	Nov. 8, 1851	8, 535
Grate, Stove	W. Sanford	Brooklyn, N. Y	Dec. 12, 1871	121, 733
Grate, Stove	J. J. Savage	Troy, N. Y	July 16, 1867	66, 743
Grate, Stove	I. Smith	Albany, N. Y	Nov. 27, 1860	30, 769
Grate, Stove	I. Smith	Albany, N. Y	Dec. 16, 1862	37, 204
Grate, Stove	J. C. Smith	Troy, N. Y	July 21, 1868	80, 233
Grate, Stove	S. Smyth	East Bridgewater, Pa	June 24, 1873	140, 224
Grate, Stove	R. Solliday	Allentown, Pa	May 17, 1870	103, 098
Grate, Stove	S. B. Stewart	Brush Valley, Pa	Dec. 3, 1867	71, 659
Grate, Stove	J. R. Stone	Round Grove, Kans	Feb. 11, 1873	135, 735
Grate, Stove	W. H. Stryker	Syracuse, N. Y	Oct. 7, 1873	143, 541
Grate, Stove	D. Stuart and L. Bridge	Philadelphia, Pa	Dec. 2, 1873	145, 253
Grate, Stove	L. Stuck	Bryan, Ohio	May 10, 1870	102, 880
Grate, Stove	W. Teamer	Evansville, Ind	July 12, 1870	105, 384
Grate, Stove	J. M. Thatcher	Bergen, N. J	Dec. 6, 1870	109, 968

Index of patents issued from the United States Patent Office from 1790 *to* 1873, *inclusive*—Continued.

Invention.	Inventor.	Residence.	Date.	No.
Grate, Stove	W. S. Thomas	Kendallville, Ind	Jan. 31, 1871	111, 493
Grate, Stove	G. Troh	Philadelphia, Pa	Feb. 22, 1870	100, 024
Grate, Stove	C. Truesdale	Cincinnati, Ohio	July 20, 1869	92, 906
Grate, Stove	C. Truesdale	Cincinnati, Ohio	Nov. 9, 1869	96, 743
Grate, Stove	J. S. Van Buren	Troy, N. Y	June 17, 1873	139, 934
Grate, Stove	G. Vander Hayden	Troy, N. Y	Jan. 10, 1865	45, 881
Grate, Stove	G. W. Walker	Boston, Mass	Jan. 10, 1865	45, 883
Grate, Stove	R. Ward	Edinburgh, Ind	Aug. 16, 1870	106, 521
Grate, Stove	C. Waters and H. A. Brown	Poughkeepsie, N. Y	Nov. 26, 1867	71, 345
Grate, Stove	M. D. Welman	Allegheny City, Pa	Jan. 18, 1870	99, 041
Grate, Stove	R. Wilson	Half Moon, N. Y	June 27, 1848	5, 652
Grate, Stove	G. A. Wing	Albany, N. Y	Feb. 2, 1869	86, 616
Grate, Stove	A. Winterburn	Albany, N. Y	June 14, 1870	104, 242
Grate, Stove	G. D. Woodworth	Chicago, Ill	Oct. 20, 1868	83, 232
Grate, Stove	J. H. Yocum	Ashland, Pa	July 7, 1868	97, 716
Grate, Stove and furnace	J. V. B. Carter	Albany, N. Y	July 24, 1860	29, 245
Grate, Stove and furnace	W. T. Coggeshall	Fall River, Mass	Oct. 20, 1857	18, 434
Grate, Stove and furnace	J. W. Griswold	Philadelphia, Pa	Jan. 28, 1868	73, 800
Grate, Stove and furnace	B. Gommenginger and C. W. Trotter.	Rochester, N. Y	July 28, 1868	80, 280
Grate, Stove and furnace	H. W. Pell	Rome, N. Y	Oct. 29, 1872	132, 688
Grate, Stove-furnace	G. A. Wing	Albany, N. Y	Aug. 17, 1869	93, 781
Grate, Stove or furnace	G. A. Wing	Albany, N. Y	Aug. 16, 1870	106, 442
Grate, Stove-oven	W. G. James	Richland Centre, Wis	Feb. 14, 1871	111, 850
Grate, Stove-pipe	J. O. Malley	Montreal, Canada	Nov. 8, 1870	109, 043
Grate, Tubular	B. Garvin and R. J. Pettibone	Oshkosh, Wis	Feb. 12, 1867	61, 022
Grate, Tubular	B. Garvin and R. J. Pettibone	Oshkosh, Wis	Sept. 13, 1870	107, 356
Grate, Tubular	E. Thayer	Worcester, Mass	Mar. 28, 1865	47, 053
Grate, Union or double	J. Wilson	New York	Sept. 12, 1834	....
Grate, Water	W. A. L. Kirk	Hamilton, Ohio	Oct. 23, 1866	59, 130
Grate, Water	J. Ryan	Saint Louis, Mo	Jan. 31, 1871	111, 387
Grates and dampers for chimneys, Arrangement of	J. Cohen	New York, N. Y	Apr. 15, 1856	14, 650
Grates and stools, Fire-back for	J. Habermehl	Wheeling, W. Va	Nov. 26, 1867	71, 297
Grates, Apparatus for raising	J. W. Allyn	Philadelphia, Pa	Nov. 1, 1864	44, 844
Grates, Ash-sifting device for	J. Beesley	Philadelphia, Pa	Jan. 22, 1867	61, 386
Grates, Casting fire	H. Anshutz	Allegheny, Pa	Jan. 14, 1873	134, 832
Grates, Coal-stirrer for furnace	W. R. Nichols and B. C. Boyes	Philadelphia, Pa	Apr. 23, 1850	7, 306
Grates, Constructing and arranging stove	G. Chilson	Boston, Mass	Sept. 11, 1841	2, 246
Grates, &c., Draft and ventilating device for open	J. M. Crockett	Newbern, Va	Dec. 3, 1867	71, 711
Grates, Construction of grates for lime-kilns	W. B. Hill	Bellevue, Mich	July 30, 1841	2, 206
Grates, Hoisting	G. Stowe	Braceville, Ohio	July 14, 1868	79, 873
Grates, Raising and lowering stove	J. Dutcher	New York, N. Y	June 30, 1838	822
Grates, Shade and draft-blower for	F. McCarthy	Chicago, Ill	Jan. 7, 1873	134, 556
Grates, Shaker-bar of stove	G. W. Gardner	Troy, N. Y	Feb. 3, 1857	16, 538
Grater	N. Amas	Saugus, Mass	Oct. 13, 1857	18, 422
Grater	G. Booth	Philadelphia, Pa	Apr. 22, 1873	138, 122
Grater	J. A. Hard	Lawrence, Kans	July 9, 1872	128, 796
Grater	W. Kinyon and J. Maxson	Scott, N. Y	Mar. 22, 1870	101, 023
Grater	J. A. Latham	New Haven, Conn	Mar. 24, 1868	75, 931
Grater	L. Schmidt	Lancaster, Pa	Mar. 15, 1870	100, 809
Grater	J. M. Smith	Seymour, Conn	June 7, 1870	104, 071
Grater	H. Stone	Williamsburgh, N. Y	Aug. 27, 1867	68, 256
Grater	E. B. Strong	Buffalo, N. Y	Aug. 27, 1835	....
Grater	H. C. White	Philadelphia, Pa	Apr. 25, 1871	114, 070
Grater and egg-beater	W. A. Bemis	Spencer, Mass	June 26, 1866	55, 807
Grater and slicer	C. W. Saladee and J. H. Hall	Newark, Ohio, and Pittsburgh, Pa.	June 2, 1868	78, 612
Grater, Apple	U. Emmons	New York	Feb. 13, 1828	....
Grater, Apple, &c., revolving	D. Flagg, jr	New York	Dec. 20, 1830	....
Grater, Cider-mill	W. Barr	Ypsilanti, Mich	May 20, 1873	139, 105
Grater, Cocoa-nut	W. H. McCall	Philadelphia, Pa	July 16, 1872	129, 238
Grater, Corn	G. C. Richards, jr	Philadelphia, Pa	Apr. 30, 1872	126, 333
Grater, Corn	B. Taylor	Philadelphia, Pa	Feb. 12, 1856	14, 259
Grater, Corn and apple	C. Moore	Guilford County, N. C	Dec. 30, 1826	....
Grater for carrots, &c	E. Stimson	Montpelier, Vt	Aug. 14, 1866	57, 213
Grater for spice and fruit	H. S. Shepardson	Shelburne Falls, Mass	Sept. 5, 1865	49, 836
Grater, Green-corn	G. L. Witsil	Philadelphia, Pa	Nov. 16, 1869	97, 019
Grater, Nutmeg	H. J. Amerling	Erie, Pa	Apr. 9, 1872	125, 428
Grater, Nutmeg	L. V. Badger	Chicago, Ill	Jan. 8, 1867	61, 037
Grater, Nutmeg	H. H. Barstow	Chicago, Ill	July 21, 1868	80, 116
Grater, Nutmeg	G. Blanchard	New York, N. Y	July 15, 1856	15, 325
Grater, Nutmeg	W. Bradley	Lynn, Mass	July 25, 1854	11, 351
Grater, Nutmeg	W. Bradley	Lynn, Mass	Jan. 29, 1867	61, 511
Grater, Nutmeg	H. Carsley	Lynn, Mass	Nov. 20, 1855	13, 834
Grater, Nutmeg	R. H. Chinn	Washington, D. C	July 16, 1867	66, 675
Grater, Nutmeg	J. L. and D. H. Coles	New York, N. Y	July 28, 1868	80, 456
Grater, Nutmeg	C. A. Durgin	New York, N. Y	July 16, 1867	66, 689
Grater, Nutmeg	C. L. Gilpatric	South Dedham, Mass	Oct. 9, 1866	58, 632
Grater, Nutmeg	E. A. Goodes	Philadelphia, Pa	July 28, 1868	80, 347
Grater, Nutmeg	H. H. Herrick	Boston, Mass	Nov. 1, 1864	44, 865
Grater, Nutmeg	J. A. Hooper	South Berwick, Me	Mar. 5, 1867	62, 542
Grater, Nutmeg	J. Lofoendahl	Boston, Mass	June 13, 1865	48, 237
Grater, Nutmeg	T. Marriatt	Detroit, Mich	Dec. 23, 1873	145, 884
Grater, Nutmeg	W. W. Owen and D. Kelly	Muskegon, Mich	Dec. 17, 1867	72, 223
Grater, Nutmeg	A. L. Platt	Bloomington, Ill	Apr. 22, 1873	138, 191
Grater, Nutmeg	G. C. Richards, jr	Philadelphia, Pa	July 16, 1872	129, 426
Grater, Nutmeg	J. Riddle and B. Allen	Boston, Mass	Oct. 30, 1866	59, 266
Grater, Nutmeg	J. G. Roth	New York, N. Y	Apr. 14, 1868	76, 820
Grater, Nutmeg	A. S. Skillin and G. W. Reed	Portland, Me	Sept. 3, 1867	68, 463
Grater, Nutmeg	L. Von Froben	Washington, D. C	Aug. 6, 1867	67, 616
Grater, Nutmeg	D. C. Warner	Chicago, Ill	Jan. 24, 1871	111, 284
Grater, Nutmeg	R. W. Whitney and J. P. Davis	South Berwick, Me	July 23, 1867	67, 010
Grater, Nutmeg	G. L. Witsil	Philadelphia, Pa	May 6, 1862	35, 192
Grater, Nutmeg	C. Worden	Binghamton, N. Y	Sept. 24, 1867	69, 150
Grater, Revolving	S. S. Wilcox and E. J. Colegrove.	Lincklaen, N. Y	Jan. 18, 1870	99, 042
Grater, Rotary vegetable	W. E. Knight	Shrewsbury, Vt	Oct. 19, 1869	95, 913
Grater, Spice	H. W. Oliver	New Haven, Conn	July 9, 1867	66, 619

Index of patents issued from the United States Patent Office from 1790 *to* 1873, *inclusive*—Continued.

Invention.	Inventor.	Residence.	Date.	No.
Grater, Vegetable	G. Booth	Philadelphia, Pa	Apr. 22, 1873	138, 123
Grater, Vegetable	T. W. Houchin	Morrisania, N. Y	Apr. 30, 1872	126, 144
Grater, Vegetable	J. Keagy	Newark, Ohio	Dec. 3, 1872	133, 585
Grater, Vegetable	S. A. McGill	Cincinnati, Ohio	Mar. 6, 1866	53, 021
Grater, Vegetable	A. S. McNeir and W. D. Stockton.	Philadelphia, Pa	May 20, 1873	139, 173
Grater, Vegetable	C. R. Peirce	Philadelphia, Pa	Aug. 8, 1871	117, 924
Grater, Vegetable	J. Wehrle and W. Wittlinger	Cincinnati, Ohio	Mar. 21, 1871	112, 872
Grater, Vegetable	S. M. Wilson	New York, N. Y	Jan. 11, 1870	98, 832
Grating for stove, furnace, &c., Supplementary	B. F. Foering	Philadelphia, Pa	Mar. 4, 1856	14, 356
Grating, Illuminating	J. K. Ingalls	Brooklyn, N. Y	Mar. 18, 1856	14, 456
Grating machine, Vegetable	H. Arthur	Martinsburgh, N. Y	Oct. 8, 1867	69, 607
Grating, sifting, and slicing machine	J. F. Shepard	Hampton Falls, N. H	May 24, 1870	103, 378
Grave-cover, Terra-cotta	C. C. W. Morgan	Holly Springs, Miss	Nov. 5, 1872	132, 851
Grave-covering	J. R. Abrams	Greenville, Ala	Nov. 4, 1873	144, 300
Grave-guard	A. Rank	Salem, Ohio	July 8, 1873	147, 728
Grave-mound	J. Mcley	Trenton, Tenn	Oct. 13, 1868	83, 077
Grave-mound cover	B. Hunter	Philadelphia, Pa	Nov. 11, 1873	144, 392
Grave-stone, monument, &c., Composition	E. A. Locke	Boston, Mass	Sept. 3, 1872	131, 010
Gravel and sand heater	P. Le Goullon	Pittsburgh, Pa	Jan. 10, 1871	110, 861
Gravel-heater	W. A. Gay	Newark, N. J	Jan. 25, 1870	99, 077
Gravel-heating apparatus	W. D. Andrews	Brookhaven, N. Y	June 25, 1872	128, 351
Gravel-pan	H. Franke	Brooklyn, N. Y	Mar. 15, 1870	100, 745
Gravel-spreader, Railway	J. C. Casement and J. Elliott	Cleveland, Ohio, and Erie, Pa.	Mar. 9, 1869	87, 542
Graver	R. S. Mershon	Zanesville, Ohio	Dec. 24, 1867	72, 521
Graver	F. R. Stockton	New York, N. Y	Feb. 20, 1866	52, 769
Gravimotometer	J. W. Whetmore	Erie, Pa	Feb. 16, 1858	19, 392
Grease and oils from animal and vegetable substances, Extracting.	J. Besso	Philadelphia, Pa	June 25, 1867	66, 119
Grease-cup	G. Hagenmeyer	Big River, Cal	Aug. 8, 1865	49, 259
Grease-cup	G. Hagenmeyer	Big River, Cal	Apr. 17, 1866	53, 973
Grease from cloth, &c., Composition for removing	S. Guess	Boston, Mass	Aug. 26, 1845	4, 161
Grease from slush, Apparatus for separating	D. H. Kaufman	Kokomo, Ind	July 4, 1865	48, 559
Grease or sizing	G. and R. Birtwistle	Fall River, Mass	Feb. 11, 1868	74, 288
Grease-trap	E. Whiteley	Cambridge, Mass	Aug. 3, 1869	93, 258
Green-brier, Obtaining useful products from the berries of the.	P. Baumgras	Syracuse, N. Y	May 17, 1864	42, 814
Green-houses, Portable steam-apparatus for	E. Whiteley	Cambridge, Mass	Aug. 3, 1869	93, 380
Green, Manufacture of Paris	T. Schwartz	New York, N. Y	Apr. 17, 1849	6, 327
Grenade, Hand	G. P. Ganster	New York, N. Y	Apr. 19, 1864	42, 363
Grenade, Hand	G. P. Ganster and I. S. Schuyler	New York, N. Y	Feb. 16, 1864	41, 615
Grenade, Hand	W. F. Ketchum	Buffalo, N. Y	Aug. 20, 1861	33, 089
Grenade, Igniting hand	J. S. Adams	Taunton, Mass	Jan. 10, 1865	45, 806
Griddle	W. Bennett	New York, N. Y	May 26, 1857	17, 361
Griddle	T. D. Gail	Waukegan, Ill	Feb. 14, 1871	111, 835
Griddle	B. Gilbert	Pittsburgh, Pa	Oct. 11, 1853	10, 118
Griddle	E. A. Jeffery	Trappe, Md	Aug. 27, 1867	68, 202
Griddle	S. Kennedy	Allegheny City, Pa	Aug. 26, 1873	142, 164
Griddle	G. W. Pittock	Union Mills, N. Y	Sept. 11, 1860	30, 028
Griddle	C. Wilson	New York, N. Y	Feb. 20, 1855	12, 419
Griddle-greaser	W. H. Bixler	Easton, Pa	July 22, 1873	140, 992
Griddle-greaser	L. Ward	Poughkeepsie, N. Y	July 18, 1871	117, 130
Griddle-lifter	M. D. Murphy	Watkins, N. Y	July 4, 1871	116, 739
Griddle or cooking-utensil	E. J. Smith	Washington, D. C	Jan. 22, 1867	61, 478
Gridiron	W. Andrews	Alleghany County, Md	Mar. 3, 1868	75, 107
Gridiron	D. Ball	Ballston Spa, N. Y	Aug. 29, 1822	....
Gridiron	A. Bataille	New York, N. Y	Mar. 18, 1873	136, 955
Gridiron	W. Bennett	New York, N. Y	Sept. 30, 1856	15, 799
Gridiron	E. C. Brewster	Bristol, Conn	Feb. 9, 1864	41, 475
Gridiron	J. S. Brooks and L. B. Grover	Rochester, N. Y	July 24, 1860	29, 238
Gridiron	F. Bush and L. Pratt	Meriden, Conn	July 21, 1832	....
Gridiron	A. Clark	Berlin, Conn	Mar. 28, 1834	....
Gridiron	I. Damon	Northampton, Mass	Jan. 30, 1841	1, 960
Gridiron	C. Denn	Frankford, Pa	June 23, 1868	79, 056
Gridiron	W. A. Greene and J. G. Treadwell.	Albany, N. Y	Mar. 29, 1859	23, 367
Gridiron	J. Hawkins	West Windsor, N. J	Mar. 26, 1845	3, 973
Gridiron	G. B. Isham	Burlington, Vt	Feb. 16, 1869	86, 923
Gridiron	C. H. Mock	Quincy, Ill	Aug. 11, 1868	80, 831
Gridiron	C. Noble	Philadelphia, Pa	Oct. 31, 1871	120, 528
Gridiron	M. V. Nobles	Elmira, N. Y	Nov. 23, 1869	97, 217
Gridiron	J. T. Page	Rochester, N. Y	Feb. 26, 1867	62, 437
Gridiron	E. B. Phelps	New York, N. Y	Dec. 8, 1868	84, 758
Gridiron	J. Powers	Lansingburgh, N. Y	Aug. 10, 1829	....
Gridison	E. P. Russell	Manlius, N. Y	Apr. 9, 1867	63, 753
Gridiron	J. Shavor and A. C. Corse	Troy, N. Y	Feb. 19, 1861	31, 482
Gridiron	J. G. Treadwell	Albany, N. Y	Dec. 20, 1859	26, 539
Gridiron	N. Waterman	Boston, Mass	May 1, 1847	5, 092
Gridiron	E. Webster	Hartford, Conn	Feb. 14, 1860	27, 176
Gridiron and spider	A. and G. Sizer	Meriden, Conn	Nov. 14, 1836	....
Gridiron and spider, Combined	A. and G. Sizer	Meriden, Conn	Nov. 14, 1836	78
Gridiron-case	M. V. Nobles	Elmira, N. Y	Apr. 5, 1870	101, 652
Gridiron-cover	R. Shaler	Madison, Conn	June 11, 1867	65, 614
Gridiron, Folding	J. H. Thomas	Newark, N. J	Aug. 10, 1858	21, 157
Gridiron, Gas-burning	E. D. Willard	Washington, D. C	July 17, 1855	13, 283
Gridiron, Hollow or guttered	T. Mussey	New London, Conn	Mar. 6, 1820	....
Gridiron, Rotary	K. Strong	Meriden, Conn	Oct. 28, 1820	....
Gridiron, Sheet-metal	G. Booth	Philadelphia, Pa	Aug. 22, 1865	49, 581
Gridirons, Construction of	F. Bush and L. Pratt	Meriden, Conn	Sept. 17, 1834	....
Grinder, Card	J. S. Dronsfield	Olham, Great Britain	Apr. 26, 1870	102, 236
Grinder, Cutter	N. F. Stone	Chicago, Ill	Apr. 17, 1866	54, 036
Grinder, Flock	R. Aldrich	Forestdale, R. I	Jan. 25, 1870	104, 813
Grinder or hone for razors, penknives, &c., Metallic.	C. Veltenair		Aug. 10, 1804	....
Grinder, Percussion	A. P. Stevens	Brooklyn, N. Y	Feb. 28, 1865	46, 597
Grinders, Method of forming teeth upon cast-iron	E. Ripley	Troy, N. Y	Aug. 12, 1851	8, 293

Index of patents issued from the United States Patent Office from 1790 *to* 1873, *inclusive*—Continued.

Invention.	Inventor.	Residence.	Date.	No.
Grinding and abrading surfaces, Method of employing Franklinite pig-metal for making.	T. Selleck	Greenwich, Conn	May 1, 1860	28, 107
Grinding and amalgamating machine, Shoe and die for.	F. G. Belknap	Washoe, Nev	Jan. 16, 1866	52, 015
Grinding and bolting machines, Combining	J. M. Clark	Lancaster, Pa	Jan. 1, 1850	6, 982
Grinding and bolting mill	J. Hollingsworth	Zanesville, Ohio	Nov. 18, 1851	8, 527
Grinding and chopping mill, Grain	P. Pope	Washington Township, Pa	Aug. 17, 1825	....
Grinding and crushing mill	W. Frost	New York, N. Y	Nov. 19, 1850	7, 782
Grinding and crushing mill	P. Perry	Troy, N. Y	Apr. 19, 1859	23, 702
Grinding and crushing mill	G. Sanford	Poughkeepsie, N. Y	Jan. 4, 1859	22, 515
Grinding and crushing mills, Ore-feeder for	C. P. Stanford	San Francisco, Cal	June 3, 1873	139, 523
Grinding and cutting machine	F. B. Hunt	Richmond, Ind	June 8, 1858	20, 490
Grinding and hulling mill, Universal	J. Bogardus	New York	July 29, 1841	2, 194
Grinding and polishing composition	N. A. Buhle	New York, N. Y	Aug. 7, 1866	56, 896
Grinding and polishing cylindrical concave surfaces, Apparatus for.	W. C. Hicks	New York, N. Y	Dec. 24, 1867	72, 636
Grinding and polishing knives	J. Dodge	Waterford, N. Y	Oct. 12, 1858	21, 746
Grinding and polishing machine	D. Lovejoy and G. F. Butterfield.	Lowell, Mass	Oct. 27, 1857	18, 509
Grinding and polishing machine	T. Prosser	New York, N. Y	June 18, 1867	65, 942
Grinding and polishing machine, Metal	J. H. and J. S. Lane	Akron, Ohio	Nov. 1, 1870	108, 822
Grinding and polishing machine, Metal	J. A. Whelpley	Greenwich, New Brunswick.	Dec. 31, 1867	72, 957
Grinding and polishing machine, Tool	J. A. Hendrick	Providence, Pa	Dec. 8, 1863	40, 838
Grinding and polishing metal	M. A. and J. H. Diedrichs	Baltimore, Md	Sept. 17, 1867	68, 854
Grinding and polishing metal	J. Dodge	Waterford, N. Y	May 2, 1865	47, 527
Grinding and polishing metallic surfaces, Machinery for.	R. M. Hoe	New York	May 30, 1842	2, 656
Grinding and polishing tools, Machine for	J. Vaughan, jr	Union, Me	Dec. 11, 1849	6, 949
Grinding and pounding mill	A. D. Moore	New Haven County, N. C	Aug 7, 1813	....
Grinding and shaping metal, Apparatus for	S. Darling	Bangor, Me	Aug. 30, 1853	9, 976
Grinding-apparatus	A. Assman	Linden, N. J	Oct. 15, 1872	132, 231
Grinding-apparatus	W. L. Washburn	New York, N. Y	July 12, 1870	105, 392
Grinding artificial granite, &c., Facing-beds for	B. Hardingo	New York, N. Y	May 8, 1855	12, 820
Grinding-cylinder	J. Bridges	Troy, N. Y	July 24, 1832	....
Grinding cylinder, Toothed	B. Mackerley	New Petersburgh, Ohio	May 18, 1858	20, 282
Grinding device, Tool	D. W. Ayres	Sheldon, Ill	June 23, 1868	79, 049
Grinding edge-tools	L. Zimmerman	Wakeshma, Mich	July 27, 1869	93, 031
Grinding edged tools, Device for	H. K. Trask	Beaver Dam, Wis	Apr. 6, 1869	88, 679
Grinding edge-tools, Machine for	J. D. Smith	Greig, N. Y	Feb. 23, 1869	87, 212
Grinding ledger and fly blades, planer-knives, &c.	C. Hardy	Biddeford, Me	June 21, 1870	104, 584
Grinding-machine	W. Battell and M. E. Worrell	Quincy, Ill	Apr. 9, 1872	125, 434
Grinding-machine	G. T. Chattaway and J. Dickinson.	Brooklyn and New York, N. Y.	Dec. 21, 1869	98, 028
Grinding-machine	P. D. Cummings	Portland, Me	Dec. 16, 1873	145, 488
Grinding-machine	J. Flint	Rochester, N. Y	Dec. 22, 1868	85, 081
Grinding-machine	G. W. Libbey	Philadelphia, Pa	Dec. 24, 1872	134, 296
Grinding-machine	J. L. Otis	Leeds, Mass	Oct. 27, 1868	83, 405
Grinding-machine	T. H. Worrall	East Blackstone, Mass	Apr. 5, 1870	101, 559
Grinding-machine for the knives of mowing-machines.	B. F. Davis	Auburn, N. Y	Feb. 23, 1869	87, 150
Grinding machine, Metal-plate	A. R. Reynolds	Auburn, N. Y	Mar. 5, 1867	62, 566
Grinding-machinery for knives which have warped surfaces.	W. Hovey	Worcester, Mass	Dec. 18, 1847	5, 398
Grinding metal articles, Machine for	J. P. Curtiss	New Britain, Conn	Sept. 1, 1868	81, 608
Grinding metal plates, Device for	E. A. White	Rock Island, Ill	Oct. 19, 1869	96, 066
Grinding, Method of removing and discharging dust produced by.	T. Fairbanks	Saint Johnsbury, Vt	May 26, 1843	3, 105
Grinding-mill	H. Albright	Cranesville, W. Va	June 8, 1869	90, 978
Grinding-mill	G. N. Annan	Buffalo, N. Y	Sept. 1, 1868	81, 725
Grinding-mill	A. Arnold	Troy, N. Y	Sept. 15, 1857	18, 178
Grinding-mill	J. Aubin	Paris, France	June 19, 1866	55, 792
Grinding-mill	J. G. Baker	Philadelphia, Pa	June 21, 1870	104, 537
Grinding-mill	J. G. Baker	Philadelphia, Pa	Oct. 21, 1873	143, 867
Grinding-mill	J. W. Baldwin	Sidney, N. J	May 8, 1866	54, 486
Grinding-mill	S. A. Bantz and W. Andrew	Frederick, Md	Dec. 4, 1849	6, 916
Grinding-mill	A. Barber	Stephentown, N. Y	June 5, 1847	5, 143
Grinding-mill	L. B. Bealay	Lebanon, N. H	Sept. 17, 1872	131, 385
Grinding-mill	J. H. Bear	York, Pa	Jan. 29, 1867	61, 599
Grinding-mill	B. A. Beardsley	Waterville, N. Y	June 29, 1858	20, 692
Grinding-mill	T. Bennett	New York, N. Y	Jan. 4, 1859	22, 479
Grinding-mill	C. P. Benoit	Detroit, Mich	Oct. 23, 1866	58, 977
Grinding-mill	C. Bollinger	Harrisburgh, Pa	Sept. 8, 1863	39, 793
Grinding-mill	C. Bollinger	Harrisburgh, Pa	Sept. 4, 1866	57, 667
Grinding-mill	R. W. Bowman	Orangeville, Pa	Oct. 5, 1869	95, 557
Grinding-mill	D. E. Breinig	Philadelphia, Pa	Apr. 6, 1858	19, 826
Grinding-mill	A. Briggs	Harrison, Ohio	Sept. 14, 1869	94, 808
Grinding-mill	E. Brisson	Orleans, France	Feb. 10, 1863	37, 605
Grinding-mill	J. Broughton	New York, N. Y	Dec. 13, 1859	26, 412
Grinding-mill	W. Broughton	London, England	Apr. 25, 1846	4, 473
Grinding-mill	C. W. Brown	Boston, Mass	Jan. 15, 1850	7, 016
Grinding-mill	C. W. Brown	Boston, Mass	Aug. 23, 1859	25, 173
Grinding-mill	J. Bryant	Brooklyn, N. Y	Feb. 14, 1860	27, 102
Grinding-mill	C. P. Buckingham	Mount Vernon, Ohio	Dec. 6, 1859	26, 332
Grinding-mill	J. Burns	New York, N. Y	Sept. 24, 1867	69, 174
Grinding-mill	J. Burns	New York, N. Y	Jan. 16, 1872	122, 811
Grinding-mill	N. Burr	Batavia, Ill	Aug 24, 1869	94, 072
Grinding-mill	T. B. Burtis	Chicago, Ill	Dec. 19, 1865	51, 551
Grinding-mill	D. A. Caldwell	Jacksonville, Ill	Dec. 23, 1873	145, 786
Grinding-mill	J. Carl	Grenada, Miss	Aug. 23, 1859	25, 176
Grinding-mill	T. A. Chandler	Rockford, Ill	July 10, 1849	6, 583
Grinding-mill	E. Clark	Lancaster, Pa	Nov. 11, 1862	36, 893
Grinding-mill	G. W. Clark and E. Butterfield	Lowell, Mass	Oct. 3, 1848	5, 824
Grinding-mill	J. M. Clark	Lancaster, Pa	Dec. 16, 1862	37, 151
Grinding-mill	D. R. Clem	Front Royal, Va	Feb. 5, 1867	61, 714
Grinding-mill	E. Coleman	Philadelphia, Pa	June 23, 1857	17, 619
Grinding-mill	W. P. Coleman	New Orleans, La	Oct. 1, 1850	7, 679
Grinding-mill	M. Cosgro	Peoria, Ill	Apr. 2, 1867	63, 479

Index of patents issued from the United States Patent Office from 1790 *to* 1873, *inclusive*—Continued.

Invention.	Inventor.	Residence.	Date.	No.
Grinding-mill	E. H. Cotton	Manchester, N. H	Nov. 21, 1865	51, 022
Grinding-mill	A. Crease	Cleveland, Ohio	Apr. 16, 1872	125, 791
Grinding-mill	H. P. Crouse	Hartland, Mich	Nov. 8, 1864	44, 942
Grinding-mill	J. Culbertson	Covington, Ky	Jan. 6, 1857	16, 325
Grinding-mill	W. H. Culver	West Troy, N. Y	Oct. 10, 1871	119, 746
Grinding-mill	C. F. Dean	Saint Johnsbury, Vt	Oct. 9, 1866	58, 719
Grinding-mill	R. Denison and J. B. Moon	Grand Rapids, Mich	Nov. 7, 1865	50, 805
Grinding-mill	J. Donaldson	Rockford, Ill	Oct. 15, 1867	69, 903
Grinding-mill	J. F. Drummond	New York, N. Y	Dec. 10, 1867	72, 002
Grinding-mill	H. V. Duryea	Fult n, N. Y	Feb. 9, 1858	19, 289
Grinding-mill	G. Eberius and F. A. Heinig	Washington, Mo	Aug. 18, 1863	39, 558
Grinding-mill	S. T. Eck	Taneytown, Md	July 5, 1870	104, 946
Grinding-mill	J. Ellston	Cleveland, Ohio	Mar. 3, 1868	75, 135
Grinding-mill	G. Erkson	New York, N. Y	July 20, 1858	20, 941
Grinding-mill	P. Evans	New York, N. Y	Oct. 21, 1873	143, 816
Grinding-mill	L. Fagin	Cincinnati, Ohio	Oct. 30, 1849	6, 827
Grinding-mill	A. Felton	Troy, N. Y	Jan. 2, 1855	12, 181
Grinding-mill	J. Fickinger	Kingsville, Ohio	Apr. 9, 1867	63, 712
Grinding-mill	J. A. Forsman	Jamestown, Ohio	Nov. 3, 1863	40, 467
Grinding-mill	J. A. Forsman	Chicago, Ill	Sept. 13, 1870	107, 353
Grinding-mill	M. Foster	Cleveland, Ohio	Sept. 21, 1869	94, 952
Grinding-mill	S. Godfrey	Peoria, Ill	Apr. 3, 1866	53, 603
Grinding-mill	R. D. Granger	Philadelphia, Pa	Mar. 9, 1858	19, 559
Grinding-mill	T. Grey	Clarence, N. Y	Dec. 3, 1867	71, 606
Grinding-mill	Z. Griffin	Montgomery, Ala	Oct. 3, 1848	5, 829
Grinding-mill	D. Halladay	Batavia, Ill	July 19, 1870	105, 448
Grinding-mill	C. A. Harper	Canterbury, N. H	Nov. 8, 1864	44, 950
Grinding-mill	E. Harrison	New York, N. Y	Nov. 20, 1847	5, 374
Grinding-mill	E. Harrison	New Haven, Conn	June 6, 1854	11, 040
Grinding-mill	E. Harrison	New Haven, Conn	May 8, 1866	54, 535
Grinding-mill	E. Harrison	New Haven, Conn	Sept. 1, 1868	81, 780
Grinding-mill	E. Harrison	New Haven, Conn	Dec. 29, 1868	85, 444
Grinding-mill	J. T. Harvey	Murrysville, Pa	Feb. 25, 1873	136, 321
Grinding-mill	P. Hauser	Cincinnati, Ohio	Nov. 7, 1835	....
Grinding-mill	M. W. Helton and J. H. Redfield.	Bloomington, Ind	Jan. 1, 1867	60, 724
Grinding-mill	F. M. Hemphill	Newport, Ky	Mar. 29, 1859	23, 372
Grinding-mill	F. M. Hemphill and R. H. Knox.	Washington, Ohio	Oct. 10, 1848	5, 836
Grinding-mill	H. Hensley	Elysianfield, Tex	May 9, 1871	114, 558
Grinding-mill	S. S. Howard	Milton, N. Y	June 18, 1861	32, 565
Grinding-mill	S. S. Howard	Milton, N. Y	Sept. 22, 1863	40, 078
Grinding-mill	G. W. Hubbard and S. A. Smith.	Philadelphia, Pa	Mar. 10, 1868	75, 273
Grinding-mill	T. E. Hunt	Louisville, Ky	Jan. 3, 1860	26, 738
Grinding-mill	J. Hutchison	Three Rivers, Mich	June 26, 1866	55, 872
Grinding-mill	E. J. Hyde	Philadelphia, Pa	Oct. 16, 1860	30, 407
Grinding-mill	S. Hyde	Malone, N. Y	Nov. 26, 1835	....
Grinding-mill	C. and A. Kaestner	Chicago, Ill	Apr. 17, 1866	53, 989
Grinding-mill	F. Kaiser	Buffalo, N. Y	Sept. 29, 1868	82, 532
Grinding-mill	J. Kemp	Brooklyn, N. Y	Dec. 19, 1865	51, 596
Grinding-mill	B. Kenoyer	Edina, Mo	Sept. 1, 1863	39, 735
Grinding-mill	F. Klinkerman	Farmer's Retreat, Ind	Aug. 30, 1864	44, 000
Grinding-mill	P. Kraus	Augusta, Ga	May 31, 1870	103, 626
Grinding-mill	F. W. Krause and G. W. Strong	Chicago, Ill	June 18, 1861	32, 570
Grinding-mill	J. G. and W. J. Lane	Mill-brook, N. Y	Apr. 9, 1872	125, 399
Grinding-mill	F. H. La Port	Clarinda, Iowa	Apr. 4, 1871	113, 534
Grinding-mill	J. A. Lechler	Philadelphia, Pa	Feb. 2, 1864	41, 439
Grinding-mill	B. W. Leonard	Bridgeport, Conn	Jan. 12, 1858	19, 093
Grinding-mill	E. D. and E. C. Little	Shabbonas Grove, Ill	Mar. 28, 1871	113, 179
Grinding-mill	G. W. Lay and F. C. Baker	Jefferson, Tex	July 23, 1872	129, 741
Grinding-mill	J. C. Lyon and H. F. Phillips	Auburn and Seneca Falls, N. Y.	May 3, 1859	23, 850
Grinding-mill	J. C. Lyon and H. F. Phillips	Auburn and Seneca Falls, N. Y.	June 21, 1859	24, 473
Grinding-mill	D. Marsh and E. B. Nichols	Fairfield, Conn	Oct. 30, 1849	6, 834
Grinding-mill	I. and W. D. Mayfield	Mayfield, Ky	Jan. 10, 1871	110, 927
Grinding-mill	P. G. McCulla	Philadelphia, Pa	Aug. 14, 1860	29, 612
Grinding-mill	J. W. Miles	Hubbardstown Village, Mich.	July 10, 1866	56, 246
Grinding-mill	J. M. Miller	Hamilton, Ohio	Dec. 11, 1866	60, 404
Grinding-mill	S. M. Miller	Beaver Mill, Pa	Nov. 6, 1866	59, 435
Grinding-mill	G. Mitchell	Philadelphia, Pa	Aug. 9, 1870	106, 271
Grinding-mill	C. Moegling	Milwaukee, Wis	Mar. 19, 1867	62, 966
Grinding-mill	J. A. Montgomery	Crawford, N. J	Aug. 25, 1868	81, 526
Grinding-mill	J. P. Moore	Morning View, Ky	June 9, 1868	78, 814
Grinding-mill	S. Moore	Wellsburgh, Va	June 12, 1860	28, 681
Grinding-mill	J. R. Morrison	East Springfield, Ohio	Dec. 22, 1857	18, 923
Grinding-mill	E. Munson	Utica, N. Y	Apr. 3, 1860	27, 735
Grinding-mill	W. Newlove	Utica, N. Y	Oct. 14, 1851	8, 425
Grinding-mill	O. Nichols	Lowell, Mass	Oct. 12, 1852	9, 330
Grinding-mill	A. L. Norcross	Hallowell, Me	Aug. 20, 1835	....
Grinding-mill	A. H. Nordyke and D. W. Marmon.	Richmond, Ind	Aug. 1, 1871	117, 667
Grinding mill	A. H. Nordyke and D. W. Marmon.	Richmond, Ind	Aug. 1, 1871	117, 668
Grinding-mill	E. and A. H. Nordyke	Richmond, Ind	Sept. 4, 1866	57, 754
Grinding-mill	W. B. North	Jersey City, N. J	Oct. 3, 1848	5, 831
Grinding-mill	L. Norton	Madison, Conn	Oct. 3, 1848	5, 826
Grinding-mill	H. P. and P. Nuchols	Barren County, Ky	Jan. 21, 1835	....
Grinding-mill	G. and H. O'Connor	Mishawaka, Ind	July 19, 1870	105, 592
Grinding-mill	F. Olds	Providence, R. I	Dec. 29, 1857	18, 985
Grinding-mill	J. Ormsby and T. Cohoon	Washington, D. C	Jan. 4, 1816	....
Grinding-mill	A. Orvis	Niagara, N. Y	May 31, 1859	24, 266
Grinding-mill	J. F. Ostrander	New York, N. Y	Apr. 25, 1846	4, 478
Grinding-mill	D. Paddack	Pontiac, Mich	Nov. 28, 1848	5, 944
Grinding-mill	L. Paige	Cavendish, Vt	Jan. 29, 1856	14, 164

Index of patents issued from the United States Patent Office from 1790 *to* 1873, *inclusive*—Continued.

Invention.	Inventor.	Residence.	Date.	No.
Grinding-mill	R. and S. Patterson	Newcastle-upon-Tyne, England.	Oct. 14, 1873	143, 710
Grinding-mill	W. Peck	Rockford, Ill	May 3, 1870	102, 588
Grinding-mill	J. Peirce	Buffalo, N. Y	Sept. 18, 1847	5, 298
Grinding-mill	E. Peugeot and J. B. C. Laurent.	Paris, France	Nov. 6, 1866	59, 528
Grinding-mill	J. Platt	Bridgeport, Conn	Dec. 26, 1845	4, 334
Grinding-mill	S. W. Powell	Tuscarora Valley, Pa	Dec. 4, 1849	6, 926
Grinding-mill	A. Prosens	Philadelphia, Pa	Jan. 11, 1859	22, 580
Grinding-mill	D. Read	Hamilton, N. Y	Aug. 7, 1860	29, 521
Grinding-mill	J. C. Reed	Mount Vernon, Ohio	June 6, 1854	11, 045
Grinding-mill	E. Ripley	Troy, N. Y	Apr. 21, 1857	17, 116
Grinding-mill	C. H. Roberts	Evansville, Ind	Apr. 12 1870	101, 917
Grinding-mill	J. C. Roberts	Adamstown, Md	Oct. 3, 1865	50, 274
Grinding-mill	J. C. Roberts	Adamstown, Md	Jan. 1, 1867	60, 789
Grinding-mill	J. Rogers, jr	Jackson, Mich	Dec. 17, 1850	7, 844
Grinding-mill	S. G. Rollins	Boston, Mass	Aug. 20, 1872	130, 750
Grinding-mill	J. Ruof, A. Heupel, and F. Leuthy.	Lancaster, Pa	July 3, 1860	29, 010
Grinding-mill	J. H. Rusk	Philadelphia, Pa	Dec. 20, 1870	110, 397
Grinding-mill	G. Sanford	Poughkeepsie, N. Y	Mar. 9, 1858	19, 587
Grinding-mill	W. Scarlett	Kenosha, Wis	June 29, 1858	20, 734
Grinding-mill	A. H. Searfoss	Newark, N. J	Feb. 24, 1863	37, 793
Grinding-mill	G. Selsor	Philadelphia, Pa	Mar. 29, 1859	23, 431
Grinding-mill	G. Selsor	Philadelphia, Pa	Feb. 21, 1871	112, 080
Grinding-mill	H. Shaw	Cincinnati, Ohio	Aug. 17, 1869	93, 913
Grinding-mill	C. W. Shedd	Addison, Ala	Oct. 30, 1860	30, 552
Grinding-mill	O. Sherwood, jr	Independence, Iowa	Oct. 28, 1862	36, 804
Grinding-mill	N. Shoemaker	Montrose, Pa	Nov. 28, 1865	51, 227
Grinding-mill	T. J. Sloan	New York, N. Y	Apr. 24, 1866	54, 260
Grinding-mill	T. J. Sloan	New York, N. Y	Apr. 24, 1866	54, 261
Grinding-mill	T. J. Sloan	New York, N. Y	Apr. 24, 1866	54, 262
Grinding-mill	F. Smith	Evans, N. Y	Mar. 18, 1835	....
Grinding-mill	J. B. Smith	Bowensburgh, Ill	Dec. 12, 1871	121, 819
Grinding-mill	T. F. Smith	Ohio County, W. Va	Nov. 13, 1866	59, 674
Grinding-mill	E. S. Snyder	Charlestown, Va	Feb. 10, 1846	4, 382
Grinding-mill	J. Snyder	Hart's Mills, Ind	Feb. 4, 1868	74, 161
Grinding-mill	H. Southwick	Little Cooley, Pa	Mar. 2, 1858	19, 521
Grinding-mill	J. R. Stafford	Cleveland, Ohio	June 18, 1850	7, 447
Grinding-mill	O. W. Stanford	Cincinnati, Ohio	Feb. 14, 1860	27, 164
Grinding-mill	W. H. Starry	Franklin, Ohio	Aug. 9, 1864	43, 802
Grinding-mill	W. Stauffer	Middlebury, Ind	Sept. 8, 1857	18, 163
Grinding-mill	W. Stewart	Philadelphia, Pa	Mar. 20, 1860	27, 579
Grinding-mill	G. M. Stone	Saint Louis, Mo	Nov. 12, 1867	70, 916
Grinding-mill	J. J. Storer and J. D. Whelpley	Boston, Mass	Sept. 30, 1862	36, 580
Grinding-mill	T. B. Stout	Keyport, N. J	Dec. 16, 1856	16, 249
Grinding-mill	H. P. Straub	Cincinnati, Ohio	Mar. 20, 1866	53, 358
Grinding-mill	I. Straub	Cincinnati, Ohio	June 27, 1854	11, 181
Grinding-mill	I. Straub	Kenton County, Ky	May 28, 1867	65, 133
Grinding-mill	B. Swift	Washington, N. Y	Aug. 16, 1845	4, 149
Grinding-mill	C. N. Taylor	Cookstown, N. J	Sept. 3, 1867	68, 539
Grinding-mill	A. Thwing and C. H. Fowler	Hopedale and West Roxbury, Mass.	May 4, 1869	89, 609
Grinding-mill	G. Todd	Saint Louis, Mo	Apr. 26, 1859	23, 799
Grinding-mill	C. Tripp	Ann Arbor, Mich	Nov. 10, 1857	18, 610
Grinding mill	C. T. Umfrid	Stuttgart, Würtemberg	Aug. 27, 1867	68, 263
Grinding-mill	A. J. and G. W. M. Vandegrift	Cincinnati, Ohio	May 17, 1870	103, 106
Grinding-mill	S. Vascou and A. Guirand	Cincinnati, Ohio	May 18, 1858	20, 310
Grinding-mill	A. Verbeck	Sterling, Ill	Sept. 20, 1870	107, 640
Grinding-mill	E. H. Vining	Govington, Ga	Mar. 15, 1870	100, 824
Grinding-mill	A. H. Wagner	Chicago, Ill	Feb. 24, 1863	37, 796
Grinding-mill	A. H. Wagner	Chicago, Ill	June 2, 1863	38, 795
Grinding-mill	A. H. Wagner	Staunton, Va	June 2, 1868	78, 624
Grinding-mill	J. N. Walker	Cincinnati, Ohio	Dec. 24, 1850	7, 862
Grinding-mill	G. T. Walters	Nicholasville, Ky	Feb. 12, 1844	3, 434
Grinding-mill	J. W. Webb	Ledyard, N. Y	Jan. 29, 1850	7, 062
Grinding-mill	D. Weimer	Gettysburgh, Ohio	Sept. 28, 1869	95, 396
Grinding-mill	J. M. Westmoreland	Danville, Tex	Nov. 15, 1870	109, 361
Grinding-mill	C. T. Weston	Scranton, Pa	Oct. 24, 1865	50, 646
Grinding-mill	J. D. Whelpley and J. J. Storer	Boston, Mass	Nov. 8, 1864	44, 990
Grinding-mill	G. L. Witsil	Philadelphia, Pa	Nov. 27, 1866	60, 105
Grinding-mill	T. B. Woodward	Kensington, Pa	July 11, 1854	11, 309
Grinding-mill	C. D. Young and J. McLean	Waterloo, N. Y	July 24, 1866	56, 659
Grinding mill, Barley	J. Mackay	Dundas, Canada	Mar. 4, 1873	136, 527
Grinding-mill bolt	R. Denison	Grand Rapids, Mich	Nov. 22, 1864	45, 142
Grinding mill, Bone	A. and E. Lister	Nowark, N. J	Sept. 6, 1870	107, 184
Grinding-mill, Cast-iron	J. Russell	Troy, N. Y	May 17, 1859	24, 058
Grinding-mill, Conical	A. W. Sweet	Cincinnati, Ohio	Feb. 21, 1860	27, 246
Grinding-mill cooler	P. C. Fritz	Barrytown, N. Y	Nov. 6, 1866	59, 382
Grinding mill, Corn	J. J. Johnston	Allegheny, Pa	Jan. 25, 1870	99, 205
Grinding mill, Corn	R. Medley	Bloomfield, Ky	Sept. 5, 1828	....
Grinding mill, Cracker and	C. Parker	Meriden, Conn	Sept. 21, 1869	95, 131
Grinding-mill crushing and hulling attachment	G. C. Hohenstein and C. T. Glaeser.	Cincinnati, Ohio	Jan. 17, 1871	111, 061
Grinding-mill, Family	P. M. Wright	New York	Apr. 14, 1835	....
Grinding mill, Feed	M. S. Harsha	Batavia, Ill	Mar. 19, 1872	124, 737
Grinding-mill feed	G. Parker	Poughkeepsie, N. Y	Oct. 12, 1869	95, 829
Grinding-mill feed-apparatus	J. D. Whelpley and J. J. Storer	Boston, Mass	May 16, 1870	102, 987
Grinding-mill feed-mechanism	H. L. Bennett	Geneva, Ill	Oct. 19, 1869	95, 973
Grinding-mill feed-regulator	E. H. Austin	Scott's Hill, Tenn	Sept. 30, 1873	143, 315
Grinding-mill feed-regulator	J. C. Dunlap	Moffat's Creek, Va	Apr. 29, 1873	138, 384
Grinding-mill feeding-shoe	J. C. Andrew	Seventy-Six, Ky	Mar. 9, 1869	87, 615
Grinding-mill for coffee, spices, &c	J. Garfield	Ayer's, Mass	Aug. 8, 1871	117, 879
Grinding-mill for grain	J. Brown	Utica, N. Y	Dec. 19, 1865	51, 549
Grinding-mill for grain	P. Davis	North Providence, R. I	May 17, 1838	738
Grinding-mill for grain	V. Fouchier	Paris, France	Sept. 17, 1861	33, 301
Grinding-mill for grain	J. Grant	Providence, R. I	Aug. 19, 1834	....
Grinding-mill for grain	E. Holton	Westminster, Vt	Apr. 3, 1835	....

Index of patents issued from the United States Patent Office from 1790 *to* 1873, *inclusive*—Continued.

Invention.	Inventor.	Residence.	Date.	No.
Grinding-mill for grain	W. H. Hope	Washington, D. C	Feb. 1, 1859	22, 807
Grinding-mill for grain, &c	J. Ives	New York	Dec. 2, 1825	......
Grinding-mill for grain	E. B. Nichols and D. Marsh	Fairfield, Conn	Mar. 13, 1844	3, 479
Grinding-mill for grain	H. Pearce	Cincinnati, Ohio	July 29, 1839	1, 266
Grinding-mill for grain	F. Price	New York, N. Y	Feb. 20, 1843	2, 962
Grinding-mill for grain	E. Ripley	Troy, N. Y	Dec. 25, 1855	13, 996
Grinding-mill for grain	J. R. Sleeper	Philadelphia, Pa	Jan. 27, 1835	......
Grinding-mill for grain	J. Ware	Farmington, Ohio	July 20, 1842	2, 733
Grinding-mill for grain, Cast-iron	H. Bailey	Hartford, Conn	May 14, 1825	......
Grinding-mill for grain, Cylindrical	J. Groat	Troy, N. Y	July 11, 1844	3, 658
Grinding-mill for mustard, &c	C. Walker	Brooklyn, N. Y	Aug. 28, 1847	5, 262
Grinding-mill hopper	M. Replogle	Moulton, Iowa	June 17, 1873	139, 973
Grinding mill hopper	G. S. Thompson	Philadelphia, Pa	Apr. 22, 1873	138, 212
Grinding-mill hopper and casing	J. M. Finch	Cedar Falls, Iowa	Apr. 1, 1873	137, 429
Grinding-mill-hopper attachment	D. C. Walters	Warsaw, Ind	Jan. 7, 1868	73, 142
Grinding-mill, Metallic	G. Palmer	Littlestown, Pa	Apr. 22, 1862	35, 036
Grinding-mill, Metallic	H. B. Stevens	Buffalo, N. Y	Apr. 1, 1873	137, 503
Grinding-mill, Portable	L. Scott	Saint Louis, Mo	May 16, 1854	10, 931
Grinding-mill, Portable	A. W. Straub	Philadelphia, Pa	Feb. 25, 1868	74, 774
Grinding-mill regulator	A. B. Hamaker	Salunga, Pa	Aug. 25, 1863	39, 648
Grinding-mill spindles, Bush for	J. H. Teahl	Eberly's Mills, Pa	May 14, 1867	64, 809
Grinding mill, Sumac	R. G. Chase	Alexandria, Va	Jan. 12, 1869	85, 726
Grinding-mills, Apparatus for delivering grain, ore, &c., into.	J. D. Whelpley and J. J. Storer	Boston, Mass	Feb. 7, 1871	111, 593
Grinding-mills, Attachment for preparing corn in the ear for.	J. M. Seely and W. E. Tomlinson.	Lockport, Ohio	May 21, 1850	7, 386
Grinding-mills, Dress of metallic hemispherical	A. Atwood	Troy, N. Y	Sept. 9, 1856	15, 680
Grinding-mills, Feeding-device for	S. Middleton	Dunkirk, Ind	Oct. 28, 1873	143, 989
Grinding-mills, Flour-distributing bolt for	W. W. Hamer	Cincinnati, Ohio	Nov. 17, 1857	18, 637
Grinding-mills, Operating	J. Holben	Allentown, Pa	June 3, 1862	35, 444
Grinding-mills, Tram-staff for	W. Ring	Gosport, Ind	Oct. 29, 1867	70, 266
Grinding-mills, Tramming-bolt for	J. T. Noye	Buffalo, N. Y	Sept. 16, 1873	142, 809
Grinding objects cylindrical, Machine for	J. M. Poole	Wilmington, Del	Aug. 20, 1872	130, 741
Grinding objects cylindrically, Machine for	J. M. Poole	Wilmington, Del	Jan. 18, 1870	99, 000
Grinding or hulling mills, Grinding or hulling plates for.	H. Shaw	Cincinnati, Ohio	Nov. 9, 1869	96, 736
Grinding or polishing implement	N. A. Buhle	New York, N. Y	Feb. 19, 1867	62, 110
Grinding-pan and amalgamator	W. H. Thoss	West Point, Cal	Mar. 7, 1871	112, 395
Grinding-plate	E. S. Howland	Batavia, Ill	Apr. 4, 1871	113, 432
Grinding-plate	E. S. Howland	Batavia, Ill	Aug. 20, 1872	130, 719
Grinding-plate	P. M. Randall	San Francisco, Cal	Nov. 22, 1864	45, 175
Grinding-plate, Iron	D. Halladay and B. H. Ruggles	Batavia, Ill	May 25, 1869	90, 531
Grinding, scouring, and polishing machine	A. B. Walters	Philadelphia, Pa	Feb. 4, 1873	135, 456
Grinding-surface in mills	C. Ross	Rochester, N. Y	Oct. 17, 1854	11, 811
Grinding-surfaces, Roll for	O. I. Foster	Salem, N. H	Dec. 10, 1872	133, 843
Grinding-tool, hammer, sadiron, &c	D. Welch	Canaan, N. H	Jan. 10, 18[illegible]3	......
Grinding tools, Device for	S. Bennett	Wilkesbarre, Pa	Feb. 2, 1869	86, 352
Grinding tools, &c., Machine for	N. B. Reynolds	Auburn, N. Y	Aug. 28, 1866	57, 571
Grinding tools, Machinery for	W. Hovey	Worcester, Mass	Sept. 23, 1845	4, 204
Grinding tools, Rest for	J. H. Brown	Berea, Ohio	Mar. 26, 1867	63, 207
Grindstone	C. Burkholder	Sterling, Ill	July 30, 1872	130, 014
Grindstone	J. F. and S. H. Green	Haverstraw, N. Y	July 15, 1873	140, 823
Grindstone	T. Loring	Blackwoodtown, N. J	Nov. 23, 1869	97, 098
Grindstone	W. P. Miller	New York, N. Y	May 21, 1867	64, 893
Grindstone	J. F. Shillaber	Portsmouth, N. H	Sept. 12, 1865	49, 928
Grindstone, Artificial	G. G. Griswold	Chester, Conn	Nov. 29, 1864	45, 243
Grindstone-axle	J. W. Ligon	Marion, Ky	June 4, 1872	127, 492
Grindstone-cutting machine	J. P. Gillespie	Louisville, Ky	Apr. 1, 1873	137, 435
Grindstone-dresser	R. Barkley and L. Semple	Philadelphia, Pa	May 17, 1864	42, 738
Grindstone-frame	B. Bisbee	North Waterford, Me	Oct. 12, 1869	95, 639
Grindstone-frame	G. L. Cummings	New York, N. Y	Dec. 31, 1872	134, 363
Grindstone-frame	J. W. Douglas	Middletown, Conn	Sept. 1, 1868	81, 611
Grindstone-frame	I. L. Lord	Chester, Conn	Aug. 15, 1854	11, 526
Grindstone-hanger	S. L. Bignall	Chicago, Ill	Oct. 28, 1873	143, 952
Grindstone journal-box	T. W. Brown	Reading, Pa	June 22, 1869	91, 514
Grindstone journal-box	P. P. Child	Saint Louis, Mo	Sept. 5, 1871	118, 688
Grindstone journal-box	J. L. Haven	Cincinnati, Ohio	Jan. 12, 1869	85, 819
Grindstone journal-box	J. B. Sargent	New Haven, Conn	Aug. 16, 1870	106, 510
Grindstone or tool-sharpener	U. Farris and A. Miller	Red Rock, Iowa	Sept. 27, 1870	107, 768
Grindstone, Parlor	J. M. Simpson	Oshkosh, Wis	Aug. 16, 1870	106, 413
Grindstone-rest	F. M. Stearns	Berea, Ohio	Dec. 27, 1864	45, 650
Grindstone, Self-sharpening	J. Pannabecker	Elizabeth Township, Pa	Jan. 20, 1852	8, 676
Grindstone trough and support	C. P. Richardson	Groveton, N. H	Mar. 18, 1873	136, 939
Grindstone turning and grinding machine	P. Leonard	Sharon, Pa	June 29, 1869	91, 944
Grindstones, Apparatus for supplying water to	F. Blauss	New York, N. Y	Mar. 24, 1868	75, 725
Grindstones, Device for holding tools against	E. Fernald	Turner, Me	July 28, 1868	80, 344
Grindstones, Device for wetting	D. Cumming, jr	Jersey City, N. J	Nov. 25, 1873	144, 891
Grindstones, Dressing	G. C. Howard	Philadelphia, Pa	Feb. 5, 1867	61, 738
Grindstones, Dressing	J. F. Schuyler	Philadelphia, Pa	June 5, 1860	28, 639
Grindstones, Gearing for	F. Howlett and C. R. Sherman	West Rupert, Vt., and Salem, N. Y.	Oct. 13, 1868	83, 064
Grindstones, Hanging	H. M. Church	Brunswick, Ohio	Sept. 6, 1870	107, 002
Grindstones, Hanging	D. B. Herrington	Detroit, Mich	Sept. 17, 1867	68, 876
Grindstones, Hanging	D. Hinman	Berea, Ohio	June 24, 1856	15, 180
Grindstones, Machine for cutting out	J. E. Mitchell	Philadelphia, Pa	June 7, 1870	103, 912
Grindstones, Machine for facing	J. Bidwell	New York, N. Y	June 2, 1863	38, 782
Grindstones, Machine for facing	R. B. Matthews	Fitchburgh, Mass	Apr. 28, 1868	77, 303
Grindstones, Machine for making	J. Baldwin, jr	Berea, Ohio	Jan. 14, 1862	34, 124
Grindstones, Machine for making	C. Foss	Painsville, Ohio	Apr. 24, 1849	6, 399
Grindstones, Machine for splitting	J. McDermott	Cleveland, Ohio	May 3, 1870	102, 693
Grindstones, Machine for turning off	J. Thierry	Aurora, Ill	June 10, 1862	35, 553
Grindstones Method of holding edged tools on	P. V. Dunn	Calamus, Wis	Mar. 19, 1867	62, 945
Grindstones, minerals, &c., Machine for dressing	P. Leonard	Sharon, Pa	July 14, 1868	79, 990
Grindstones, Mode of forming the center for the shaft of.	D. Hinman	Berea, Ohio	July 31, 1860	29, 375
Grindstones, Mode of packing	F. M. Stearns	Berea, Ohio	June 20, 1865	48, 319
Grindstones, Operating	H. Pray	Sharon, Conn	Nov. 30, 1869	97, 441
Grindstones, Tools for dressing	C. Arthur	Keeseville, N. Y	Aug. 26, 1845	4, 160

Index of patents issued from the United States Patent Office from 1790 *to* 1873, *inclusive*—Continued.

Invention.	Inventor.	Residence.	Date.	No.
Grindstones, Tool-holder for	P. Leonard	Sharon, Pa	Dec. 7, 1869	97, 656
Grindstones, Tool-rest for	W. H. Mesteller	Sharonville, Ohio	Apr. 26, 1870	102, 420
Grindstones, Tool-rest for	W. H. Straham	Philadelphia, Pa	Oct. 2, 1866	58, 504
Grindstones, Truing	C. E. Wilson	Boston, Mass	July 6, 1869	92, 242
Griping-block for press	G. W. Swinebroad	Bolivar, Tenn	Sept. 24, 1872	131, 640
Grist and coffee mill	J. Stroub	Charleston, S. C	Sept. 6, 1833	....
Grist and flour mill	I. Straub	Northumberland County, Pa.	May 9, 1834	....
Grist and saw mill combined	N. Porter	Boston, Mass	Nov. 17, 1831	....
Grist-mill	R. W. Adams	Marlborough, Vt	Dec. 8, 1818	....
Grist-mill	W. Adams	Guilford, N. C	July 18, 1827	....
Grist-mill	J. Amell and J. Gallery	Brooklyn, N. Y	Aug. 21, 1844	3, 711
Grist-mill	J. F. Anderson	Louisville, Ky	May 3, 1831	....
Grist-mill	A. Bacon	Windsor, N. Y	June 4, 1832	....
Grist-mill	C. Badger	Edgerton, Wis	May 22, 1860	28, 434
Grist-mill	A. Barnes	Colesville, N. Y	Apr. 27, 1832	....
Grist-mill	J. Demis	Worcester, Mass	Nov. 17, 1826	....
Grist-mill	W. Benbow	Guilford County, N. C	Jan. 19, 1827	....
Grist-mill	A. Bencine	Caswell County, N. C	Jan. 16, 1827	....
Grist-mill	E. Bigelow	Georgetown, D. C	Feb. 11, 1831	....
Grist-mill	E. Brees	Kingston, Pa	Sept. 28, 1831	....
Grist-mill	M. L. Chase	Frankfort, Me	Dec. 23, 1829	....
Grist-mill	A. and S. Coe	Guilford, N. C	July 21, 1827	....
Grist-mill	W. Coleman	Euclid, Ohio	Feb. 25, 1830	....
Grist-mill	J. Copes	Georgetown, Del	May 2, 1805	....
Grist-mill	J. Crail	Warren, Ohio	June 19, 1828	....
Grist-mill	J. W. Dart and W. and H. Webster.	Truxton, N. Y	July 20, 1831	....
Grist-mill	A. Delap and A. Coe	Guilford County, N. C	May 31, 1827	....
Grist-mill	W. W. Forwood	Harford County, Md	June 15, 1827	....
Grist-mill	J. C. Gentry	Philadelphia, Pa	July 14, 1832	....
Grist-mill	E. Goodell and O. P. Stevens	Port Lawrence, Ohio	Oct. 10, 1838	974
Grist-mill	E. Gray	Ulysses, N. Y	Mar. 25, 1840	1, 523
Grist-mill	C. B. Gregory	Danbury, Conn	Feb. 16, 1843	2, 952
Grist-mill	E. Griswold	Truxton, N. Y	Oct. 16, 1830	....
Grist-mill	E. Hale	Haverhill, Mass	Feb. 22, 1807	....
Grist-mill	S. M. Handy, J. Albee, and E. B. Cutts.	Hallowell, Me	June 6, 1834	....
Grist-mill	F. Harris and J. Wilson	Albany, N. Y	June 9, 1826	....
Grist-mill	E. Harrison	New Haven, Conn	Jan. 9, 1872	122, 605
Grist-mill	E. Harrison	New Haven, Conn	Jan. 16, 1872	122, 827
Grist-mill	J. and D. Hascall	Sikay, N. Y	Mar. 9, 1822	....
Grist-mill	S. Holland	Hanover, Ohio	Mar. 1, 1828	....
Grist-mill	J. W. Holly	....	Mar. 27, 1802	....
Grist-mill	G. Hotchkiss	Windsor, N. Y	Jan. 27, 1832	....
Grist-mill	C. Kaestner	Chicago, Ill	July 4, 1871	116, 717
Grist-mill	R. Kendall	Wilkes County, Ga	Nov. 19, 1833	....
Grist-mill	E. C. L. Kunnecke	Dayton, Ohio	Aug. 15, 1871	118, 136
Grist-mill	C. Sangford	Claridon, Ohio	July 8, 1830	....
Grist-mill	S. Lawing and J. Monteith	Statesville, N. C	June 11, 1827	....
Grist-mill	O. N. May	Hancock, N. Y	May 5, 1832	....
Grist-mill	W. and J. McCreight	Winnsborough, S. C	Feb. 5, 1836	....
Grist-mill	M. Mendenhall	Greensborough, N. C	Oct. 20, 1826	....
Grist-mill	T. Newman	Guilford County, N. C	Feb. 6, 1827	....
Grist-mill	A. L. Norcross	Hallowell, Me	Dec. 21, 1833	....
Grist-mill	J. Northorp	Woodbridge, Conn	July 31, 1826	....
Grist-mill	L. Olds	Otsego, N. Y	May 18, 1833	....
Grist-mill	B. Overman	Greensborough, N. C	Feb. 28, 1827	....
Grist-mill	J. P. Phipps and J. Holliday	Wilmington, Del	May 12, 1831	....
Grist-mill	I. Platt	Weston, Conn	Sept. 28, 1843	3, 283
Grist-mill	A. Porter	New London, Ind	Mar. 10, 1830	....
Grist-mill	J. Robinson	Buckskin Township, Ohio	Dec. 11, 1827	....
Grist-mill	I. Ryon	Bridgewater, Mass	June 29, 1826	....
Grist-mill	A. Sawyer	Chester, Vt	July 20, 1813	....
Grist-mill	J. Smith and W. Sapp	Mount Vernon, Ohio	Sept. 9, 1828	....
Grist-mill	J. C. Smith	Wheeling, Va	Jan. 9, 1830	....
Grist-mill	M. Stockman	Hampton, N. H	Apr. 18, 1826	....
Grist-mill	W. L. Taylor	McMinn County, Tenn	Jan. 28, 1828	....
Grist-mill	R. S. Thomas	Rockingham, N. C	June 4, 1827	....
Grist-mill	W. A. Turner	Plymouth, N. C	June 27, 1827	....
Grist-mill	B. Tyler	....	Feb. 20, 1800	....
Grist-mill	D. D. Wagener	Pittsburgh, Pa	Jan. 8, 1839	1, 065
Grist-mill	A. H. Wagner	Chicago, Ill	June 6, 1871	115, 791
Grist-mill	A. Warren	Saugerties, N. Y	Mar. 12, 1828	....
Grist-mill	C. T. Weston, S. Broadbent, and W. B. Culver.	Scranton, Pa	June 14, 1870	104, 384
Grist-mill	B. Whitney	New Brunswick, N. J	Oct. 27, 1868	83, 574
Grist-mill	J. Wickersham and T. Crozer	East Fairfield, Ohio	Aug. 29, 1829	....
Grist-mill	I. Wilson	New London, Conn	Feb. 23, 1830	....
Grist-mill	O. Wyman	East Cambridge, Mass	Apr. 18, 1839	1, 125
Grist-mill	J. Yeamans	Ashtabula, Ohio	Mar. 8, 1831	....
Grist-mill alarm	J. D. Irwin and B. I. Seward	Corydon and Bloomington, Ind.	Jan. 28, 1868	73, 896
Grist-mill and cotton-seed huller combined	J. W. Smith	Columbus, Ga	Apr. 25, 1871	114, 215
Grist-mill and horizontal spiral water-wheel	A. Temple	Brookfield, Ohio	Dec. 11, 1829	....
Grist-mill bush	G. M. Copeland	Genoa, Ohio	Oct. 11, 1841	2, 313
Grist-mill, Conical	S. Sheldon	Cincinnati, Ohio	Sept. 11, 1841	2, 251
Grist mill, crusher, and sheller	J. G. Morse	Randolph County, N. C	Mar. 20, 1827	....
Grist-mill for grain, &c	J. Ambler, jr., and D. C. Ambler.	New Berlin, N. Y	June 13, 1831	....
Grist-mill for grinding grain	J. Platt	Weston, Conn	Oct. 9, 1841	2, 282
Grist-mill-gate pressure	S. Prentiss	New York	June 4, 1832	....
Grist-mill grinding-plate	H. Shaw and W. D. Leavitt	New Orleans, La	July 14, 1868	79, 865
Grist-mill-hopper shoe	W. E. Wyche and Y. P. Dickson.	Brookville, N. C	July 7, 1868	79, 620
Grist-mill, Portable	M. Riech	Wheeling, W. Va	Nov. 5, 1872	132, 777
Grist-mill, Portable	S. Sheldon	Cincinnati, Ohio	Sept. 12, 1854	11, 681
Grist-mill, Portable	I. Straub	Cincinnati, Ohio	Feb. 18, 1840	1, 491

Index of patents issued from the United States Patent Office from 1790 to 1873, inclusive—Continued.

Invention.	Inventor.	Residence.	Date.	No.
Grist-mill, Portable	H. Weed	Sandwich, N. H	Jan. 10, 1831	....
Grist-mill, Portable iron-husk	H. W. Shipley and Z. Blair	Mount Vernon, Ohio	Aug. 16, 1859	25, 144
Grist-mill, Pressure or weighted	J., jr., and D. C. Ambler	New Berlin, N. Y	Dec. 6, 1830	....
Grist-mill, Screw	J. L. Miller	Brookfield, N. Y	Mar. 28, 1810	....
Grist-mill, "Self-stopper"	R. McCormick, jr	Augusta County, Va	Apr. 20, 1831	....
Grist-mill, spindle, and bush	J. Barber	Phelps, N. Y	Feb. 28, 1844	....
Grist-mill spindle, Cast-iron	W. Rice	Athens, Pa	Oct. 1, 1823	....
Grist-mill spindle, Apparatus for lubricating	C. Brown, sr	Richmond, Ind	May 6, 1856	14, 791
Grist-mill toll-collector	F. Klinkerman	Aurora, Ind	Feb. 23, 1869	87, 176
Grist-mill toll-collector	T. R. Van Gelder	Damascus, Pa	Mar. 20, 1860	27, 582
Grist-mill toll-gathering machine	J. Bartholomew	Dundee, N. Y	June 15, 1858	20, 540
Grist-mill toll-taker	W. W. McCauley	Fancy Farm, Ky	Oct. 15, 1872	132, 302
Grist-mill toll-taking machine	C. F. Keller	Nevada, Ohio	May 19, 1868	78, 099
Grist-mills, Automatic alarm for	M. W. Helton and J. H. Redfield.	Bloomington, Ind	Jan. 14, 1868	73, 247
Grist-mills, Mode of constructing bales and divers for.	E. R. Benton	Ohio City, Ohio	Mar. 31, 1840	1, 533
Grist-mills, Motive-power cut-off in	J. Hough	West Chester, Pa	July 5, 1864	43, 409
Grist-mills, &c., "Wry-fly" which may be applied by wind or water to	B. Tyler	....	Mar. 19, 1804	....
Grist, paint, and plaster mill	C. Manning	Littleton, Mass	Apr. 2, 1835	....
Grocer's can	J. Adair	Kilbuck Township, Pa	July 9, 1872	128, 837
Grocer's canister	W. H. Smith	Portland, Conn	May 2, 1871	114, 360
Grommet	W. Brown	Middletown, Conn	July 2, 1867	66, 296
Grommet	J. W. Norcross	Boston, Mass	Dec. 15, 1868	84, 900
Grommet, Metallic	J. Allender	New London, Conn	June 20, 1854	11, 108
Grommet, Metallic	J. Mair	Philadelphia, Pa	July 6, 1869	92, 199
Grommet, Metallic	E. H. Penfield	Middletown, Conn	Sept. 19, 1848	5, 779
Grommet, Strap	E. F. Southward	Wellfleet, Mass	Oct. 8, 1850	7, 7[illegible]8
Grooved-roll-shaping die	A. Reese	Pittsburgh, Pa	Nov. 19, 1867	71, 062
Grooved rollers, Pattern for casting	J. Herald	Unadilla, N. Y	Feb. 21, 1871	111, 931
Grooved wheel or pulley	J. H. Barnes	Brooklyn, N. Y	Jan. 1, 1867	60, 668
Grooves and slots, Machine for cutting	R. F. Underhill	Indianapolis, Ind	May 26, 1857	17, 398
Grooves, Device for casting circle-plates, roses, &c., with dovetailed.	N. Matthews	Pittsburgh, Pa	Apr. 20, 1852	8, 898
Grooves in the necks of cans, Machine for forming.	J. D. Willoughby	Petersburgh, Va	Aug. 21, 1860	29, 739
Grooves, Machine for boring circular	W. Wright	Rochester, N. Y	June 10, 1845	4, 076
Grooves on metallic rods, Machine for forming spiral.	T. T. Prosser	Chicago, Ill	June 20, 1871	116, 218
Grooving boards, Device for	G. C. Fisk	Dansville, N. Y	Aug. 8, 1854	11, 478
Grooving-machine	W. H. Bond and G. G. Lee	Syracuse, N. Y	Oct. 20, 1868	83, 128
Grooving-machine	D. D. Hanson	Weare, N. H	June 29, 1833	....
Grooving-machine	T. Holt	Brooklyn, N. Y	June 22, 1869	91, 635
Grooving-machine	W. G. Raoul	Independence, La	Feb. 1, 1870	99, 350
Grooving-machine	J. W. Smith	Hartford, Conn	Nov. 1, 1870	108, 943
Grooving-machine	J. L. Taylor	New York, N. Y	Oct. 15, 1861	33, 501
Grooving-machine and planing-bit	J. Shugert	Lawrenceville, Pa	Nov. 19, 1833	....
Grooving machine, Sheet-metal	C. H. Raymond	Southington, Conn	Feb. 8, 1870	99, 592
Grooving-tool	J. Dill	Grand Rapids, Mich	Dec. 13, 1870	110, 123
Grooving-tool	C. Van Haagen	Philadelphia, Pa	Dec. 20, 1870	110, 407
Ground-roller	C. D. Roberts	Jacksonville, Ill	Sept. 4, 1866	57, 773
Ground-roller and stalk-cutter	P. H. Tompkins and E. Dougal	Van Buren, Iowa	June 22, 1869	91, 581
Grout-conductor	W. S. Folensbee	Janesville, Wis	Nov. 19, 1867	71, 155
Grub and stump machine	A. McKinney	Maumee, Ohio	Apr. 17, 1866	54, 000
Grub-hook	J. W. Goodall	Eldred, Pa	Dec. 21, 1869	98, 159
Grubbing-implement	J. Sattazahn, jr	Pine Grove Township, Pa	May 17, 1870	103, 086
Grubbing-machine	J. B. Ash	Elkton, Md	Aug 21, 1860	29, 659
Grubbing-machine	C. Ball	Augusta, Mich	Nov. 29, 1864	45, 216
Grubbing-machine	C. Ball and J. W. Houghtelin	Detroit, Mich	Aug. 14, 1866	57, 067
Grubbing-machine	C. E. Chase and B. T. Devendorff.	Wyoming Township, Mich	Dec. 22, 1868	85, 069
Grubbing-machine	O. A. Cheney	Orleans Township, Mich	Mar. 6, 1866	52, 967
Grubbing-machine	J. H. Flanagan and W. Lanning	Chicago, Ill., and Stoughton, Wis.	Jan. 19, 1864	41, 287
Grubbing-machine	J. Frey	Battle Creek, Mich	Feb. 3, 1863	37, 574
Grubbing-machine	D. I. Hall	Dowagiac, Mich	Dec. 3, 1867	71, 608
Grubbing-machine	A. McKenney	Maumee City, Ohio	Feb. 18, 1862	34, 4[illegible]9
Grubbing-machine	C. R. Moffett	Philadelphia, Pa	June 20, 1865	48, 298
Grubbing-machine	D. C. Payne	Elkhart, Ind	July 29, 1862	36, [illegible]22
Grubbing machine	Y. W. Short	Oglethorpe County, Ga	Jan. 28, 1840	1, 480
Grubbing-machine	W. W. St. John	Saint Louis, Mo	Aug. 28, 1866	57, 593
Grubbing-machine	T. C. Wood	Charleston, Mich	Nov. 9, 1858	22, 047
Grubbing-machine and for working on roads	E. Fraser	Hector, N. Y	Dec. 31, 1833	....
Grubbing-machine capstan	B. B. Newell	Centreville, Mich	June 30, 1868	79, 380
Guano and other fertilizers, Machine for distributing	E. Wagner	Westminster, Md	Nov. 30, 1858	22, 212
Guano and seed distributer	J. H. Boyd	Plain, S. C	Nov. 4, 1873	144, 2[illegible]0
Guano and seed drill	L. M. Rhodes	Warrenton, Ga	Apr. 18, 1871	113, 797
Guano and the manufacture of fertilizer, Treatment of.	C. Morfit	New York, N. Y	Apr. 30, 1870	106, 851
Guano-distributer	J. D. Coxwell	Gibson, Ga	June 15, 1869	91, 434
Guano-distributer	N. Foster	Palmyra, N. Y	Apr. 14, 1868	76, 621
Guano-distributer	W. E. Martin	Oconee, Ga	Oct. 4, 1870	107, 937
Guano-distributer	E. R. Stedman	Sparta, Ga	Oct. 4, 1870	107, 975
Guano-distributer and seed-sower	B. F. Hinkley	Baltimore, Md	Oct. 11, 1870	108, 262
Guano-distributing machine	H. L. and C. P. Brown	Manchester, N. Y	May 25, 1869	90, 493
Guano-distributing machine	G. W. Sizer and W. M. Owen	New Orleans, La	Sept. 6, 1870	107, 111
Guano, &c., distributing machine	J. F. Thomas	Adamstown, Md	Feb. 11, 1868	74, 448
Guano, Drying	E. P. Baugh	Philadelphia, Pa	May 3, 1870	102, 648
Guano, phosphate, &c., bag	B. R. Croasdale	Philadelphia, Pa	Nov. 23, 1869	97, 169
Guano, Process of treating Navassa	R. B. Potts	Camden, N. J	Mar. 7, 1865	46, 700
Guano. Restoring de-ammoniated	A. A. Hayes	Boston, Mass	Feb. 16, 1864	41, 663
Guano, Restoring phosphate	L. Harper	Brooklyn, Mass	Feb. 2, 1864	41, 428
Guano-spreader	I. J. Saunders	Sparta, Ga	Feb. 12, 1861	31, 409
Guano, Treating and preparing "Navassa"	G. A. Liebig	Baltimore, Md	Mar. 22, 1864	42, 006
Guano, Treating phosphatic	L. D. Gale	Washington, D. C	Mar. 31, 1863	38, 040
Guard: *See* Ankle or knee guard. Ax-handle guard. Bed or cradle guard. Foot-strap guard.				

Index of patents issued from the United States Patent Office from 1790 *to* 1873, *inclusive*—Continued.

Invention.	Inventor.	Residence.	Date.	No.
Guard—Continued. *See* Bridge-guard. Candle-guard. Car safety-guard. Carriage-guard. Carriage-spring guard. Carriage-wheel guard. Catamenial guard. Cattle-guard. Damper-guard. Door-guard. Door and window guard. Door-key guard. Door-knob guard. Dress-guard. Ferry-boat guard. Finger-guard. Fork-guard. Grave-guard. Hame-guard. Harvester-guard. Hat and coat guard. Hatchway-guard. Hatchway safety-guard. Heel-guard. Heel-shaving guard. Horse's elastic heel-guard. Insect-guard. Key-guard. Key-hole guard. Key-hole key-guard. Knife-guard. Knob-guard. Lantern-guard. Lock-guard. Loom-shuttle guard. Mining-shaft safety-guard. Mowing-machine guard. Musquito-guard. Mustache-guard. Paint-guard. Pistol safety-guard. Plow-guard. Pocket-book guard. Railway cattle-guard. Railway safety-guard. Rein-guard. Roof-guard. Roof snow-guard. Safety-guard. Saw-guard. Sawing-machine guard. Screen-guard. Shoe-knife guard. Spool-thread guard. Spring-guard. Steam-boiler safety-guard. Thill-guard. Thread-guard. Trunk-guard. Watch-guard. Weather-guard. Window-guard. Window safety-guard.				
Gudgeon-box, Self-oiling	J. Shugert	Elizabeth, Pa	Apr. 1, 1842	2, 527
Gudgeon, Wing	M. Wilder	Princeton, Mass	Apr. 9, 1850	7, 278
Gudgeons, journals, and wheel-boxes, Iron	S. Reynolds	Guilford, N. Y	June 13, 1829	....
Gudgeons, Oiling	P. S. Devlin, J. Hancock, and C. S. Wood.	Philadelphia, Pa	Aug. 8, 1846	4, 686
Guide and sign board	S. Carter	Raynham, Mass	Nov. 25, 1829	....
Guide-post	R. C. Maners	Boston, Mass	Aug. 13, 1833	....
Guitar	R. Knaffl	Nashville, Tenn	Jan. 7, 1873	134, 679
Guitar	G. D. Reed	Springfield, Vt	Dec. 2, 1873	145, 241
Guitar	E. N. Sherr	Philadelphia, Pa	Oct. 6, 1831	....
Guitar	W. B. Tilton	New York, N. Y	Jan. 3, 1854	10, 380
Guitar	W. B. Tilton	New York, N. Y	Mar. 1, 1856	14, 378
Guitar	W. H. Towers	Philadelphia, Pa	May 16, 1854	10, 934
Guitar-banjo	L. Brown	Baltimore, Md	Oct. 17, 1865	50, 444
Guitar-head and capio d'astra	J. Ashborn	Wolcottville, Conn	Apr. 16, 1850	7, 279
Guitars, Bracing the sounding-board of	J. E. Biui	Mount Vernon, N. Y	Dec. 24, 1867	72, 591
Guitars, Tuning-attachment for	H. Seehausen	Memphis, Tenn	Sept. 24, 1867	69, 259
Gum and palate, Artificial	J. A. Cummings	Boston, Mass	June 7, 1864	43, 009
Gum, Chewing	T. Adams	Hudson City, N. J	Feb. 14, 1871	111, 798
Gum, Chewing	W. W. Kilbourn	Sanford, N. Y	Sept. 27, 1870	107, 693
Gum, Chewing	W. F. Semple	Mount Vernon, Ohio	Dec. 28, 1869	98, 304
Gum, Chewing	N. Wood	Portland, Me	Dec. 17, 1872	134, 022
Gum compound, Chewing	A. H. Tyler	Toledo, Ohio	July 27, 1869	93, 141
Gum-elastic: (*See* India rubber.)				
Gum-elastic braces	R. Warner	New York, N. Y	Mar. 18, 1836	....
Gum-elastic-cloth making	H. G. Tyer and J. Helm	Ballard Vale, Mass., and New Brunswick, N. J.	May 6, 1856	14, 814
Gum for coating and water-proofing, Artificial	R. O. Lowrey	Salem, N. Y	Aug. 4, 1868	80, 641
Gum from machinery, Composition for removing	S. Maxwell	Baltimore, Md	Apr. 24, 1860	28, 061
Gum, Process of purifying spruce	H. B. Esty	Houlton, Me	Aug. 21, 1866	57, 3[illegible]4
Gum, Treating waste and inferior	J. Murphy	New York, N. Y	Jan. 3, 1860	26, 698
Gun	A. Boyden	Newark, N. J	Jan. 10, 1824	....
Gun, Air	G. W. B. Gedney	New York, N. Y	Sept. 24, 1861	33, 344
Gun, Air	P. Giffard	Paris, France	Feb. 9, 1864	41, 500
Gun, Air	E. Lindner	New York, N. Y	Dec. 16, 1862	37, 173
Gun, Air repeating	P. Giffard	Paris, France	Feb. 25, 1873	136, 315
Gun, Alarm	C. J. Beasley	Petersburgh, Va	Feb. 22, 1870	100, 106
Gun, Alarm	M. C. Heptinstall	Enfield, N. C	June 29, 1869	91, 935
Gun, Alarm	A. Johnson and S. E. Allen	Raleigh, N. C	Jan. 1, 1867	60, 897
Gun, Alarm	T. A. Marable and G. Utley	Petersburgh, Va	May 14, 1867	64, 682
Gun and bayonet battery	J. W. Andrews	Norristown, Pa	Nov. 19, 1861	33, 731
Gun and blasting powder	C. F. Fuchs and A. Clement	Boston, Mass	Aug. 6, 1872	130, 123
Gun and blasting powder	G. A. Neumeyer	Altenburg, Germany	July 2, 1867	66, 378
Gun and blasting powder	G. B. Weistling	Oxford Furnace, N. J	Sept. 22, 1863	40, 070
Gun and fire-arm	J. Shaw	Philadelphia, Pa	May 7, 1829	....
Gun and percussion-lock, Revolving four-barreled	H. Rogers	Middletown, Ohio	May 7, 1829	....
Gun and pistol, Air	E. H. Hawley	Kalamazoo, Mich	June 1, 1869	90, 749
Gun and pistol bayonet, Combined	R. K. Colvin	Lancaster, Pa	Oct. 25, 1864	44, 784
Gun and pistol lock	J. Marsh	East Dorset, Vt	July 1, 1836	....
Gun and pistol, Percussion	J. Finch	New York, N. Y	Apr. 12, 1823	....
Gun and rifle	F. Oswan	Harper's Ferry, Va	Feb. 25, 1815	....
Gun and rifle, Convertible shot	S. McCulloch	Yellow Springs, Ohio	Dec. 10, 1867	72, 063
Gun, Arrow	C. Robinson	Boston, Mass	Aug. 17, 1869	93, 908
Gun-barrel	E. Allen	Worcester, Mass	June 20, 1865	48, 249
Gun-barrel	R. R. Moore	Cortland, N. Y	Dec. 26, 1871	122, 187
Gun-barrel scraper	E. L. Pratt	Boston, Mass	Apr. 11, 1865	47, 260
Gun-barrels, Cleaning the bores of	P. F. Carr	Wyalusing, Pa	Feb. 9, 1864	41, 481
Gun-barrels, Coloring	J. S. Howard	Mansfield, Mass	Aug. 30, 1870	106, 823
Gun-barrels, Expanding scraper for	A. L. Bausman	Minneapolis, Minn	Sept. 11, 1866	57, 8[illegible]6
Gun-barrels, &c., from Bessemer steel, Process of making.	J. Thompson	Bilston, England	Nov. 28, 1865	51, 281

Index of patents issued from the United States Patent Office from 1790 *to* 1873, *inclusive*—Continued.

Invention.	Inventor.	Residence.	Date.	No.
Gun-barrels, Heating and soldering	E. Allen	Worcester, Mass	June 19, 1866	55, 596
Gun-barrels, Instrument for cleaning	W. E. Turner	Fort Snelling, Minn	June 3, 1873	139, 633
Gun barrels, locks, &c., Plating	J. Fowler	Lancaster, Pa	Jan. 4, 1810	....
Gun-barrels, Machine for boring	N. Fobes	....	Dec. 31, 1804	....
Gun-barrels, Machine for draw-grinding	T. Dakin	Harper's Ferry, Va	July 28, 1820	....
Gun-barrels, Machine for rifling	W. and C. Sellers	Philadelphia, Pa	Mar. 7, 1865	46, 714
Gun-barrels, Machine for rolling	J. Yates	Mott Haven, N. Y	Nov. 7, 1865	50, 869
Gun-barrels, Machine for turning	S Nash	Harper's Ferry, Va	Apr. 11, 1818	....
Gun-barrels, Machine for turning	S. Youngs	Hartford, Conn	May 1, 1810	....
Gun-barrels, Manufacture of	W. Baker	Ilion, N. Y	Feb. 23, 1864	41, 669
Gun-barrels, Manufacture of	J. H. Burton	Jefferson County, Va	Mar. 20, 1860	27, 539
Gun-barrels, Manufacture of	R. A. Douglas	Orange, N. J	Apr. 14, 1863	38, 201
Gun-barrels, Manufacture of	S. Hiler	Harlem, N. Y	Apr. 15, 1862	34, 961
Gun-barrels, Manufacture of	J. Thompson	Bilston, England	May 10, 1864	42, 718
Gun-barrels, Manufacturing	A. Waters	Millbury, Mass	Oct. 25, 1817	....
Gun-barrels, Manufacturing plates for	H. Mills	Springfield, Mass	July 12, 1834	....
Gun-barrels, Means of attaching the fore-end stock to	J. Deeley and J. S. Edge, jr	Yardley, England	July 1, 1873	140, 482
Gun-barrels, Process for making twisted	T. Warner	Chicopee, Mass	Sept. 6, 1853	9, 999
Gun-barrels, Scarfing and rolling the scalp for	J. Bruce	Springfield, Mass	Oct. 15, 1824	....
Gun-barrels, Scraper for cleaning	M. G. Crane	Charlestown, Mass	July 19, 1864	43, 573
Gun-barrels, System of rifling	O. F. Winchester	New Haven, Conn	June 25, 1872	128, 446
Gun-barrels to stocks, Attaching	N. R. Davis	Freetown, Mass	Aug. 25, 1868	81, 348
Gun-barrels, Turning	A. Waters	Millbury, Mass	Dec. 19, 1818	....
Gun, Battery	W. Douglas	Corry, Pa	Aug. 23, 1864	43, 903
Gun, Battery	W. Fields	Wilmington, Del	Apr. 25, 1871	113, 996
Gun, Battery	R. J. Gatling	Indianapolis, Ind	May 9, 1865	47, 631
Gun, Battery	A. E. Miltimore	United States Army	Dec. 2, 1873	145, 224
Gun battery, Many-barreled	J. Brett	Matteawan, N. Y	May 3, 1864	42, 552
Gun battery, Repeating	E. Ripley	Troy, N. Y	Oct. 22, 1861	33, 544
Gun, Blast	C. Kirchhof	Newark, N. J	Apr. 21, 1868	76, 925
Gun-boat	S. D. Carpenter	Madison, Wis	Jan. 31, 1865	46, 074
Gun-boat	L. M. Van Sickle	Woodbridge, N. J	Apr. 28, 1862	38, 344
Gun-boats, Drilling bolt-holes in turrets of	T. F. Rowland	Green Point, N. Y	May 19, 1863	38, 605
Gun, Breech-loading	E. Lindner	New York, N. Y	May 6, 1856	14, 819
Gun, Breech-loading	C. Sharps	Philadelphia, Pa	Nov. 11, 1856	16, 072
Gun, Breech-loading and magazine	B. and W. G. Burton	Brooklyn, N. Y	Oct. 14, 1873	143, 614
Gun, Burglar-alarm	P. Swisher	Versailles, Ohio	Jan. 1, 1867	60, 960
Gun, Burglar-alarm	J. Wilson	Anderson Court-House, S. C.	July 9, 1867	66, 662
Gun, Cane	A. Davis	Shelbyville, Ind	Aug. 21, 1860	29, 676
Gun, Cane	A. Karutez	Brooklyn, N. Y	Apr. 9, 1872	125, 460
Gun, Cane	J. F. Thomas	Ilion, N. Y	Feb. 9, 1858	19, 328
Gun, Cane	W. H. Werner	Nazareth, Pa	June 7, 1870	104, 087
Gun-cap	J. C. Bandle and E. J. Christner	Cincinnati, Ohio	July 25, 1871	117, 367
Gun-cap	J. Talbott	Albany, Ga	July 6, 1869	92, 398
Gun-capper	H. Buffington	South Coventry, Conn	June 1, 1869	90, 634
Gun-capping implement	E. D. Seely	Brookline, Mass	Oct. 29, 1861	33, 626
Gun-carriage	G. Birkbeck, jr	New York, N. Y	Oct. 4, 1864	44, 506
Gun-carriage	L. W. Broadwell	New Orleans, La	June 1, 1869	90, 814
Gun-carriage	T. Coughlan	Newton, Mass	Nov. 15, 1870	109, 181
Gun-carriage	J. B. Eads	Saint Louis, Mo	Aug. 17, 1869	93, 691
Gun-carriage	J. B. Eads	Saint Louis, Mo	May 23, 1871	115, 181
Gun-carriage	J. B. Eads	Saint Louis, Mo	June 18, 1872	128, 130
Gun-carriage	J. Ericsson	New York, N. Y	June 28, 1864	43, 298
Gun-carriage	J. Ericsson	New York, N. Y	Mar. 8, 1870	100, 514
Gun-carriage	J. Ericsson	New York, N. Y	July 23, 1872	129, 804
Gun-carriage	W. C. Fuller	London, England	July 9, 1861	32, 762
Gun-carriage	S. Hawkins	New York, N. Y	Feb. 19, 1806	....
Gun-carriage	J. C. Honel and F. L. F. Caillet	Paris, France	Jan. 4, 1870	98, 595
Gun-carriage	J. R. Kelso	Freedom, Mo	June 15, 1869	91, 345
Gun-carriage	J. Laurens	Charleston, S. C	July 1, 1856	15, 244
Gun-carriage	J. B. Lyons	Litchfield, Conn	June 9, 1863	38, 831
Gun-carriage	A. Moncrieff	Woolwich, Conn	Nov. 10, 1868	83, 873
Gun-carriage	A. F. Potter	Oakland, Cal	Sept. 6, 1870	107, 099
Gun-carriage	T. R. Timby	Tarrytown, N. Y	Oct. 31, 1871	120, 553
Gun-carriage	C. S. Tyson	Old Point Comfort, Va	May 19, 1868	78, 030
Gun-carriage	G. J. Van Brunt	Dedham, Mass	June 15, 1858	20, 597
Gun-carriage	J. J. Walsh	New York, N. Y	Sept. 25, 1860	30, 186
Gun-carriage	M. Wappick	Sacramento, Cal	Mar. 10, 1863	37, 882
Gun-carriage	G. R. Wilson	Washington, D. C	Feb. 9, 1869	86, 720
Gun-carriage	J. W. Wilson	New York, N. Y	Mar. 1, 1870	100, 482
Gun-carriage, Counterpoise	J. G. Foster	Nashua, N. H	July 13, 1869	92, 597
Gun-carriage, Counterpoise	J. G. Foster	Boston, Mass	May 2, 1871	114, 430
Gun-carriage, Counterpoise	J. G. Foster	Boston, Mass	Oct. 17, 1871	119, 924
Gun-carriage for naval and other purposes	W. Smith	Washington, Ky	July 19, 1838	847
Gun-carriage for ships of war	J. Bubier	Marblehead, Mass	Oct. 20, 1837	432
Gun carriage, Pivot	L. M. Laighton	Portsmouth, N. H	Nov. 29, 1814	....
Gun-carriages, Operating	S. J. Ashley	San Francisco, Cal	Dec. 15, 1863	40, 893
Gun-carriages, Operating	A. L. Caswell	Lansingburgh, N. Y	Oct. 18, 1859	25, [illegible]06
Gun-carriages, Operating	J. Ericsson	New York, N. Y	Dec. 15, 1863	40, 919
Gun-carriages, Operating	J. Ericsson	New York, N. Y	Jan. 23, 1866	52, 1[illegible]0
Gun-carriages, Operating	R. H. Long	Philadelphia, Pa	Aug. 4, 1863	39, 449
Gun-carriages, Operating	I. Rindge	Cincinnati, Ohio	June 21, 1864	43, 228
Gun-carriages, Pile or fagot for shoe-rails for	J. L. Lewis	Pittsburgh, Pa	Aug. 19, 1862	36, 223
Gun-carriages, Quoins for	D. D. Porter	United States Navy	Dec. 21, 1858	22, 377
Gun-carriages, &c., Wheel for	C. F. Brown	Warren, R. I	July 10, 1860	29, 055
Gun, Centrifugal	C. S. Dickinson	Cleveland, Ohio	Aug. 9, 1859	24, 997
Gun, Centrifugal	G. C. Eaton and S. W. Turner	Cleveland, Ohio	Dec. 16, 1862	37, 159
Gun, Centrifugal	W. Joslin	Cleveland, Ohio	May 17, 1859	24, 031
Gun, Centrifugal	C. B. Thayer	Boston, Mass	Aug. 3, 1858	21, 109
Gun, Centrifugal spring	R. Shaler	Madison, Conn	Nov. 18, 1862	36, 968
Gun-charger	H. Kahn	Troy, N. Y	Oct. 18, 1870	108, 359
Gun-cleaner	M. G. Crane	Charlestown, Mass	Nov. 15, 1864	45, 027
Gun-cleaner	C. G. Gould	Windham, Vt	Sept. 23, 1873	143, 139
Gun, Combined piston-breech and firing-cock repeating	W. Hunt	New York, N. Y	Aug. 21, 1849	6, 663
Gun-cotton	B. W. Lenk	Vienna, Austria	June 14, 1864	43, 166

Index of patents issued from the United States Patent Office from 1790 *to* 1873, *inclusive*—Continued.

Invention.	Inventor.	Residence.	Date.	No.
Gun-cotton and lint, Manufacture of	J. P. McLean	Brooklyn, N. Y	Apr. 18, 1865	47, 316
Gun-cotton, Making solutions of	M. Newton	Boston, Mass	June 25, 1872	128, 416
Gun-cotton, Manufacture of	F. A. Abel	Woolwich, Great Britain	Nov. 20, 1866	59, 888
Gun-cotton, Manufacture of	S. J. Mackie	Westminster, England	Aug. 12, 1873	141, 654
Gun-cotton, Manufacture of	J. J. Révy	Vienna, Austria	Sept. 19, 1865	50, 082
Gun-cotton, Manufacture of	J. J. Révy	London, England	Sept. 19, 1865	50, 083
Gun-cotton, Manufacture of	T. P. Shaffner	Louisville, Ky	Dec. 18, 1866	60, 571
Gun, Eight-barreled percussion	S. L. Faries	Middletown, Ohio	Oct. 10, 1829	....
Gun, Faucet-breech	A. D. Perry	New York, N. Y	Dec. 11, 1849	6, 945
Gun for driving stock from railroad-track, Steam	F. G. Smith	Columbia, Tenn	Nov. 28, 1865	51, 239
Gun-hammer gage	W. T. Round	Middletown, Conn	July 2, 1867	66, 399
Gun-lock	J. Albright	Pleasant View, Mo	June 27, 1871	116, 252
Gun-lock	S. Belden and J. F. Crabtree	Visalia, Cal	Apr. 14, 1868	76, 587
Gun-lock	W. N. Bennett	Illyria, Iowa	July 25, 1871	117, 245
Gun-lock	W. Briggs	Norristown, Pa	Aug. 30, 1859	25, 244
Gun-lock	E. F. Burrows	Mystic River, Conn	Oct. 1, 1872	131, 845
Gun-lock	J. J. Byers	Delta, N. Y	June 18, 1872	128, 015
Gun-lock	J. J. Byers	Delta, N. Y	Sept. 24, 1872	131, 598
Gun-lock	P. F. Charpie	Mount Vernon, Ohio	Aug. 16, 1853	9, 934
Gun-lock	J. F. and W. N. Crabtree	Visalia, Cal	Mar. 10, 1868	75, 248
Gun-lock	S. Cromwell	Edgecomb, Me	Feb. 3, 1827	....
Gun-lock	J. C. Dane	La Crosse, Wis	Mar. 26, 1872	124, 939
Gun-lock	W. Dashner	Point Pleasant, W. Va	Aug. 10, 1869	93, 420
Gun-lock	J. Deutz	San Antonio, Tex	Aug. 16, 1870	106, 337
Gun-lock	W. R. Evans	Thomaston, Me	Sept. 19, 1871	119, 020
Gun-lock	R. H. Fauntleroy	Posey County, Ind	Aug. 17, 1833	....
Gun-lock	E. Gilbert	Rochester, N. Y	Apr. 3, 1829	....
Gun-lock	C. Gordon	Goswell Road, England	Apr. 22, 1873	138, 142
Gun-lock	J. B. Gray	Fredericksburgh, Va	Oct. 7, 1834	....
Gun-lock	L. Hailer	Washington, D. C	July 26, 1870	105, 790
Gun-lock	R. D. Hay	Crooked Creek, N. C	Nov. 22, 1870	109, 514
Gun-lock	R. D. Hay and J. M. Hill	Crooked Creek, N. C	June 8, 1869	91, 014
Gun-lock	E. B. Hendee	San Francisco, Cal	Dec. 20, 1870	110, 360
Gun-lock	C. B. Holden	Worcester, Mass	Nov. 8, 1870	109, 128
Gun-lock	P. W. Hoyt	Danbury, Conn	Mar. 10, 1838	629
Gun-lock	J. Hults	Berlin Township, Ohio	May 16, 1854	10, 927
Gun-lock	A. Judson	New Lebanon, N. Y	June 13, 1831	....
Gun-lock	J. Kelsay	Richmond, Mo	Jan. 5, 1869	85, 672
Gun-lock	E. C. Kirk	Baltimore, Md	Mar. 20, 1866	53, 306
Gun-lock	N. C. Lock	Salem, Mass	Jan. 11, 1870	98, 781
Gun-lock	J. A. Sowe	New York, N. Y	Feb. 8, 1859	22, 881
Gun-lock	W. W. Marston	New York, N. Y	June 5, 1849	6, 514
Gun-lock	T. J. Massie	Arrington, Va	Oct. 31, 1871	120, 388
Gun-lock	A. Miller	Daleville, Ala	Sept. 26, 1871	119, 386
Gun-lock	J. C. Miller	Danville, Ky	Mar. 30, 1869	88, 319
Gun-lock	E. Monroe	Charlestown, Mass	Mar. 25, 1856	14, 513
Gun-lock	W. J. Morris	New York, N. Y	Apr. 1, 1873	137, 381
Gun-lock	S. Morrison	Milton, Pa	Feb. 10, 1836	....
Gun-lock	J. Phin	Rochester, N. Y	Nov. 20, 1855	13, 825
Gun-lock	W. Rudolph and A. Braun	San Francisco, Cal	Apr. 17, 1866	54, 021
Gun-lock	W. Rudolph and A. Braun	San Francisco, Cal	June 19, 1866	55, 716
Gun-lock	N. Saltonstall	New London, Conn	May 29, 1828	....
Gun-lock	F. Schenck	San Antonio, Tex	Sept. 11, 1866	57, 978
Gun-lock	C. W. Scott	Constantia, Ohio	Oct. 25, 1864	44, 827
Gun-lock	J. H. Shapley	Exeter, N. H	Aug. 11, 1863	39, 501
Gun-lock	J. H. Smith	Browster's Station, N. Y	Sept. 24, 1861	33, 371
Gun-lock	E. T. Starr	New York, N. Y	Dec. 19, 1865	51, 629
Gun-lock	J. Stokes	Springfield, Mass	Nov. 24, 1868	84, 314
Gun-lock	M. Tromly	Mount Vernon, Ill	Aug. 14, 1855	13, 442
Gun-lock	M. Tromly	Washington, D. C	Nov. 17, 1868	84, 233
Gun-lock	G. B. Warren	Prospect, Pa	June 13, 1871	115, 993
Gun-lock	F. Wesson	Worcester, Mass	Apr. 9, 1872	125, 640
Gun-lock	E. West	....	July 6, 1802	....
Gun-lock	A. Young	Philadelphia, Pa	Feb. 23, 1869	87, 316
Gun-lock cover	J. B. Leverich	New York, N. Y	June 3, 1862	35, 456
Gun-lock, Double-acting	E. Brey	Pennsburgh, Pa	June 29, 1858	20, 757
Gun lock, Lever percussion	J. Ambler, jr	South New Berlin, N. Y	Oct. 16, 1827	....
Gun lock, Magazine percussion	J. B. Lowry	Mayville, N. Y	Sept. 11, 1827	....
Gun lock, Percussion	J. Caswell	Manlius, N. Y	May 8, 1828	....
Gun lock, Percussion	M. Davis	Mayville, N. Y	July 10, 1827	....
Gun lock, Percussion	W. A. Hart	Fredonia, N. Y	Feb. 20, 1827	....
Gun lock, Percussion	J. Lawrence	New Berlin, N. Y	May 24, 1828	....
Gun lock, Percussion	J. Shattuck	Jefferson County, Ohio	Nov. 10, 1827	....
Gun-lock, Rotary-tumbler	T. W. Harvey	New York, N. Y	June 19, 1849	6, 537
Gun-lock, Safety	C. Bowlen	Milwaukee, Wis	Dec. 10, 1867	71, 963
Gun-lock, Safety	W. F. Kussmaul	Baltimore, Md	Oct. 15, 1867	69, 919
Gun-lock, Safety	D. H. Mapother	Louisville, Ky	Jan. 28, 1873	135, 233
Gun-lock, Safety	J. E. McBeth	New Orleans, La	Oct. 2, 1866	58, 443
Gun-lock, Self-priming	F. H. Bell	Washington, D. C	Apr. 12, 1859	23, 545
Gun-lock, Self-priming	J. S. Butterfield and S. Marshall	Philadelphia, Pa	June 14, 1859	24, 372
Gun-lock, Self-priming	M. I. Gallagher	Savannah, Ga	July 7, 1857	17, 733
Gun-lock, Self-priming	R. S. Lawrence	Hartford, Conn	Apr. 12, 1859	23, 590
Gun-lock, Self-setting hair-triggered	J. Altman	Armstrong County, Pa	Feb. 17, 1857	16, 634
Gun-lock springs, Forging	G. P. Foster	Bristol, R. I	Feb. 3, 1857	16, 537
Gun lock, Water-proof self-priming percussion	S. L. Faries	Middletown, Ohio	Aug. 29, 1828	....
Gun-locks, Safety-stop for	W. G. Oliver	Buffalo, N. Y	June 12, 1866	55, 588
Gun, Machine	L. Christopher and J. Montigney	Brussels, Belgium	Nov. 28, 1871	121, 277
Gun, Machine	W. B. Farwell	New York, N. Y	Apr. 1, 1873	137, 428
Gun, Machine	W. A. Miles	Salisbury, Conn	July 30, 1872	129, 976
Gun, Machine	C. Stensland	Negaunee, Mich	Oct. 14, 1873	143, 729
Gun, Machine	M. Wood	Lewisburgh, W. Va	July 30, 1872	130, 098
Gun, Magazine	N. H. Ambler	East Cleveland, Ohio	Aug. 9, 1870	106, 246
Gun, Magazine	F. Brady and J. C. Noble	Washington, Pa	Jan. 14, 1862	34, 126
Gun, Magazine	A. Burgess	Owego, N. Y	June 25, 1872	128, 208
Gun, Magazine	A. Burgess	Owego, N. Y	July 16, 1872	129, 523
Gun, Magazine	H. J. Drew	Dixon, Ill	Mar. 14, 1871	112, 563
Gun, Magazine	W. R. Evans	Thomaston, Me	Dec. 8, 1868	84, 685

Index of patents issued from the United States Patent Office from 1790 *to* 1873, *inclusive*—Continued.

Invention.	Inventor.	Residence.	Date.	No.
Gun, Magazine	E. H. Graham	Biddeford, Me	Oct. 4, 1853	10,084
Gun, Magazine	E. H. Graham	Biddeford, Me	May 16, 1854	10,944
Gun, Magazine	C. R. Stickney	Ilion, N. Y	July 2, 1872	128,671
Gun, Magazine	A. Swingle	San Francisco, Cal	Apr. 1, 1873	137,392
Gun, Magazine, repeating, and needle	E. Lindner	New York, N. Y	June 27, 1854	11,197
Gun, Many-barreled	E. A. Mejia	Mexico	Feb. 19, 1867	62,281
Gun, Method of manufacturing ribs and bolsters for double-barrel.	D. B. Wesson and J. H. Blaze	Springfield, Mass	Dec. 31, 1867	72,949
Gun, Needle	G. A. Blittkowski and F. W. Hoffman.	New York, N. Y	Mar. 25, 1856	14,488
Gun, Needle	W. Burghart	Lawrence, Mass	Jan. 12, 1858	19,068
Gun, Needle	A. A. Chassepot	Paris, France	Jan. 1, 1867	60,832
Gun, Needle	T. Twickeler	Boston, Mass	Mar. 18, 1862	34,706
Gun-nipple protector	J. Haskins	Roxbury, Mass	May 27, 1862	35,418
Gun-nipples, Safety-guard for	C. T. Moore	Gilmanton, N. H	Aug. 17, 1869	93,733
Gun or rifle	O. Stith	Brunswick County, Va	Mar. 16, 1819	....
Gun or rifle, Double-shooting	S. Mosher and N. White	Hamilton, N. Y	May 5, 1828	....
Gun, Percussion	J. Shaw	Philadelphia, Pa	June 19, 1822	....
Gun, Percussion	J. Tyrer	Petersburgh, Va	June 3, 1825	....
Gun, Repeating	C. H. Palmer	Lakeville, Conn	Dec. 2, 1862	37,052
Gun, Repeating	A. Wheeler	Concord, Mass	June 10, 1818	....
Gun-rest, Hinged	J. Hawkins	West Windsor, N. J	May 14, 1867	64,765
Gun, Revolving battery	R. J. Gatling	Indianapolis, Ind	Nov. 4, 1862	36,836
Gun, Revolving battery	R. J. Gatling	Indianapolis, Ind	Feb. 28, 1871	112,138
Gun, Revolving battery	R. J. Gatling	Hartford, Conn	Apr. 9, 1872	125,563
Gun, Rifle or plain barrel	A. Wheeler	Massachusetts	Feb. 19, 1819	....
Gun-scraper, Adjustable	E. L. Pratt	Boston, Mass	Jan. 31, 1865	46,140
Gun-scrubber holder	L. Fleckenstine	Manor Township, Pa	Jan. 7, 1868	72,993
Gun, Self-loading battery	T. J. Cranmer	Vallicita, Cal	Mar. 3, 1868	74,994
Gun, Shot	G. Buckel and E. Dorsch	Monroe, Mich	Apr. 8, 1856	14,597
Gun, Shot	D. Smith	Springfield, Mass	May 30, 1871	115,370
Gun-shot wounds and extracting bullets, Instrument for treating.	S. J. Howell	Orange, Mass	Jan. 19, 1869	86,016
Gun-sight	H. B. Barber	Scott, N. Y	Apr. 5, 1870	101,568
Gun-sight	F. A. Churchill	Pittsfield, Mass	Feb. 28, 1871	112,124
Gun-sight	M. W. Harrington	Homestead, Iowa	Feb. 25, 1873	136,159
Gun-sight	J. T. La Rue	Pleasant Post-Office, Ind	June 18, 1872	128,049
Gun-sight	F. N. Martin	Covington, Ky	Jan. 5, 1864	41,162
Gun-sight	H. A. Schottky and T. Simendinger.	Hartford, Conn	Jan. 14, 1873	134,772
Gun-sight, Telescopic	D. Wood	Rochester, N. Y	May 31, 1864	42,983
Gun, Sighting	E. A. Stevens	Hoboken, N. J	Jan. 6, 1863	37,365
Gun, Spring	J. E. Blythe	New York, N. Y	Jan. 3, 1865	45,789
Gun, Spring	A. Gemunder	Springfield, Mass	Jan. 12, 1858	19,086
Gun, Spring	W. W. Hannah	Hudson, N. Y	June 11, 1872	127,873
Gun-stock	C. R. Alsop	Middletown, Conn	May 22, 1860	28,433
Gun-stock	W. Burnett	Boston, Mass	Jan. 7, 1862	34,103
Gun stock and barrel attachment	D. C. Thresher	Freetown, Mass	May 8, 1866	54,624
Gun-stock and spade combined	W. E. Blake	New York, N. Y	Feb. 11, 1873	135,624
Gun-stock, Canteen	S. Colt	Hartford, Conn	Jan. 18, 1859	22,627
Gun-stock machine	E. S. Wright and E. Allen	New York, N.Y., and Newark, N. J.	Nov. 17, 1863	40,665
Gun-stock machine	E. S. Wright and E. Allen	New York, N.Y., and Newark, N. J.	Nov. 17, 1863	40,666
Gun-stock machine	E. S. Wright and E. Allen	New York, N.Y., and Newark, N. J.	Nov. 17, 1863	40,667
Gun-stocks, Machine for making	H. W. Oliver	New Haven, Conn	July 1, 1862	35,775
Gun-stocks, &c., Machine for turning	T. Blanchard	Middlebury, Mass	Sept. 6, 1819	....
Gun-stocks, &c., Machine for turning	A. Woolworth	Waterbury, Conn	June 15, 1820	....
Gun-stocks, Machinery for carving and drilling	J. G. Pusey	New York, N. Y	Feb. 17, 1863	37,705
Gun-stocks, Mode of crooking	J. Schirer	Charleston, S. C	Apr. 12, 1826	....
Gun-stocks, Sawing	A. Myers	Boonsborough, Md	Nov. 9, 1832	....
Gun-stocks to pistols, Mode of attaching	E. B. Savage	Cromwell, Conn	Apr. 9, 1861	32,003
Gun-stocks with pistols, Mode of coupling	S. Colt	Hartford, Conn	Jan. 18, 1859	22,626
Gun, Submarine steam	W. W. W. Wood and J. L. Lay	Philadelphia, Pa., and Buffalo, N. Y.	July 18, 1865	48,862
Gun-swab	P. M. Hendrick and J. J. Chattaway.	Springfield, Mass	July 24, 1866	56,559
Gun traversing-mechanism, Machine	R. J. Gatling	Hartford, Conn	Dec. 16, 1873	145,563
Gun-trucks, Machine for cutting	R. Rose	Washington, D. C	Aug. 6, 1821	....
Gun-wad	C. W. Lovett, jr	Boston, Mass	June 25, 1872	128,231
Gun, Walking-stick	R. R. Beckwith	New York, N. Y	Mar. 23, 1858	19,674
Gun, Walking-stick	I. Buckman, jr	New York, N. Y	Aug. 4, 1857	17,915
Gun-wiper	H. Berdan	New York, N. Y	Sept. 12, 1865	49,848
Gun-wiper	C. F. Gillette	Sparta, Wis	Feb. 8, 1870	99,557
Gun-wiper	H. Greve	Sparta, Wis	Apr. 19, 1870	101,907
Gun-worm	H. C. Bascom	La Crosse, Wis	Mar. 19, 1867	62,994
Guns and gun-towers, Operating	J. B. Eads	Saint Louis, Mo	Mar. 31, 1863	38,038
Guns and gun-turrets, Operating	J. B. Eads	Saint Louis Mo	Feb. 7, 1865	46,223
Guns, Apparatus for unspiking	T. J. Dobbs	Weehawken, N. J	Apr. 6, 1869	88,615
Guns by adjustable ports, Directing	R. Trussell	Brooklyn, N. Y	Jan. 12, 1864	41,245
Guns, &c., Combining barrels of	J. Griswold	Chambers County, Ala	Feb. 1, 1842	2,441
Guns, Constructing large	R. F. Loper	Philadelphic, Pa	July 30, 1844	3,685
Guns, Detachable muzzle for shot	S. H. Roper	Roxbury, Mass	July 14, 1868	79,861
Guns exhausted of air, Muzzle-cap for	R. Gibbons	Oakland, Cal	Aug. 2, 1864	43,680
Guns, Flexible rammer for turret	J. B. Walker	Elizabeth, Pa	Sept. 10, 1867	68,813
Guns in turrets, Operating	J. B. Eads	Saint Louis, Mo	Feb. 7, 1865	46,222
Guns, Lock of double-barreled	H. Barnes	Wilson, N. C	Jan. 19, 1858	19,121
Guns, Machine for battery	B. B. Hotchkiss	New York, N. Y	Aug. 13, 1872	130,501
Guns, Machine for elevating heavy	L. and W. H. Bell	Fortress Monroe, Va	Dec. 8, 1829	....
Guns, Machine for finishing the cascabel of	E. Kaylor	Pittsburgh, Pa	Sept. 26, 1865	50,139
Guns, Machinery for rifling	W. H. Gwynne	Brooklyn, N. Y	Dec. 10, 1861	33,884
Guns, Making rifle	E. Strong and C. Killogg	New Hartford, Conn	Aug. 31, 1810	....
Guns, Maneuvering heavy	K. Stewart	San Francisco, Cal	Nov. 26, 1861	33,803
Guns, Manufacture of breech-plates for	W. Baker	Ilion, N. Y	Mar. 23, 1869	88,003
Guns, Manufacturing	D. G. Colburn	Canton Canal, N. Y	June 29, 1833	....
Guns, Means for operating heavy	A. Moncrieff	Culfargie, Scotland	Oct. 28, 1873	144,120

Index of patents issued from the United States Patent Office from 1790 *to* 1873, *inclusive*—Continued.

Invention.	Inventor.	Residence.	Date.	No.
Guns, &c., Method of attaching bits eccentrically to arbors for stocking	S. D. Sizer	Springfield, Mass	May 12, 1843	3, 090
Guns, Method of preventing accidental discharge in the Prussian.	J. Wurfflein	Philadelphia, Pa	Apr. 30, 1850	7, 334
Guns, Mounting heavy	J. B. Newman	Milford, Pa	June 28, 1864	43, 330
Guns, Muzzle for shot	J. Fry	Latrobe, Pa	Dec. 15, 1868	84, 942
Guns, Muzzle for shot	J. A. McKenzie	Galesburgh, Ill	Jan. 19, 1869	85, 949
Guns, Operating heavy	P. F. Jones	New York, N. Y	Dec. 10, 1861	33, 891
Guns, Operating machine	G. O. Kinne	Hartford, Conn	Nov. 7, 1871	120, 588
Guns, Operating ships'	J. H. Ward	United States Navy	May 3, 1864	42, 630
Guns, Percussion-lock for	R. Beale	Washington, D. C	Feb. 20, 1835	....
Guns, Percussion-lock for	T. Daplyn	Dover, Ohio	Feb. 20, 1835	....
Guns, pistols, and other fire-arms	G. Stocker and J. Bentley	Birmingham, England	Apr. 8, 1840	1, 544
Guns, Piston for muzzle-loading	J. T. Foster and J. J. Banta	Jersey City, N. J	Mar. 17, 1857	16, 860
Guns, Planing the rim-bases of	E. Kaylor	Pittsburgh, Pa	July 12, 1864	43, 510
Guns, Priming for needle	C. H. F. Thieme	North Vernon, Ind	Aug. 11, 1868	81, 038
Guns, Removing spikes from	A. Lafever	Battle Creek, Mich	Sept. 22, 1863	40, 051
Guns, Rifled muzzle for smooth-bored	C. R. Alsop	Middletown, Conn	Dec. 16, 1862	37, 193
Guns, Rifling of	J. B. Atwater	Ripon, Wis	Sept. 30, 1862	36, 592
Guns, Shot-charge for measuring shot in charging	G. W. Dobbin	Baltimore, Md	Mar. 23, 1838	654
Guns, Target for air	C. A. Demling	New York, N. Y	Jan. 1, 1867	60, 862
Gunnery, Repeating	J. C. Chambers	West Middletown, Pa	Mar. 23, 1813	....
Gunpowder	E. B. Dodson	Reading, Pa	Feb. 10, 1857	16, 580
Gunpowder	L. Du Pont	Wilmington, Del	May 19, 1857	17, 321
Gunpowder	L. H. G. Ehrhardt	Baywater, England	June 19, 1866	55, 795
Gunpowder	L. H. G. Ehrhardt	London, England	Jan. 28, 1868	73, 786
Gunpowder	A. Molfino	New York, N. Y	Aug. 15, 1871	118, 040
Gunpowder	J. F. E. Schultze	Potsdam, Prussia	June 2, 1863	38, 789
Gunpowder	T. Taylor	Washington, D. C	Dec. 7, 1869	97, 567
Gunpowder, &c	C. M. Wetherill	La Fayette, Ind	Mar. 22, 1864	42, 056
Gunpowder and blasting-powder, Manufacture of	G. A. Neumeyer	Altenburg, Saxe-Altenburg.	Sept. 1, 1868	81, 670
Gunpowder and lamp-black, Application of Grahamite in the manufacture of.	P. H. Vander Weyde	New York, N. Y	Mar. 2, 1869	87, 382
Gunpowder and other explosive substances, Method of blasting with.	T. P. Shaffner	Louisville, Ky	Aug. 17, 1869	93, 757
Gunpowder, Apparatus for graining	P. A. Oliver	Wilkesbarre, Pa	Dec. 31, 1872	134, 438
Gunpowder, Apparatus for the manufacture of	C. M. Wetherill	La Fayette, Ind	Mar. 22, 1864	42, 057
Gunpowder-canister	O. Scott	Bennington, Vt	Dec. 31, 1867	72, 916
Gunpowder, &c, Composition for	E. Harrison	New York, N. Y	Feb. 9, 1864	41, 576
Gunpowder, Composition for	H. Leibert	Norristown, Pa	Jan. 6, 1863	37, 296
Gunpowder corning or graining machine	L. T. Swett	Canton, Conn	Nov. 16, 1841	2, 362
Gunpowder, Cylinder for polishing	R. H. Cunningham	Schaghticoke, N. Y	Aug. 26, 1862	36, 320
Gunpowder, Drying	E. E. Hendrick	Carbondale, Pa	Nov. 19, 1867	71, 004
Gunpowder, Drying and glazing	J. Smith	Kingston, N. Y	Feb. 7, 1865	46, 275
Gunpowder-engine	J. S. Foster	Salem, Mass	Jan. 30, 1872	123, 095
Gunpowder, Granulating	R. Crosbie	Newark, N. J	Feb. 17, 1812	....
Gunpowder, Granulating	C. Dalmas	Wilmington, Del	Apr. 26, 1816	....
Gunpowder, Granulating	G. Fulton	Philadelphia, Pa	Aug. 21, 1819	....
Gunpowder, Granulating	D. Rogers	Newburgh, N. Y	Aug. 26, 1818	....
Gunpowder, Granulating	J. Worseley	Berne, N. Y	Feb. 21, 1815	....
Gunpowder, Machine for granulating	E. J. Du Pont de Nemours		Nov. 23, 1804	....
Gunpowder, Machine for granulating	W. H. Richardson	Baltimore, Md	Aug. 3, 1822	....
Gunpowder, Machinery for the manufacture of	P. A. Oliver	New York, N. Y	Apr. 7, 1868	76, 510
Gunpowder-making	J. M. Merrow and R. McKee, jr	East Hartford, Conn	Apr. 19, 1822	....
Gunpowder, Making charcoal for manufacturing	F. Parker	Prince George's, Md	July 25, 1815	....
Gunpowder, Manufacture of	F. S. Allen	New York, N. Y	Oct. 9, 1866	58, 567
Gunpowder, Manufacture of	F. Burney	Faversham, Great Britain	Dec. 2, 1873	145, 149
Gunpowder, Manufacture of	C. W. Curtis	London, England	Nov. 14, 1871	120, 862
Gunpowder, Manufacture of	H. E. Drayson	Edgeworth Lodge, England	Sept. 13, 1864	44, 269
Gunpowder, Manufacture of	L. and E. Du Pont	New Castle County, Del.	Dec. 3, 1872	133, 522
Gunpowder, Manufacture of	L. H. G. Ehrhardt	London, England	Jan. 5, 1869	85, 576
Gunpowder, Manufacture of	W. H. Jackson	Salem, Mass	June 23, 1868	79, 229
Gunpowder, Manufacture of	V. L. Maxwell	Wilkesbarre, Pa	Dec. 27, 1859	26, 602
Gunpowder, Manufacture of	F. G. Murray	Washington, D. C	June 20, 1865	48, 303
Gunpowder, Manufacture of	R. I. L. Witty	Lowell, Mass	Apr. 2, 1838	669
Gunpowder, Manufacturing	T. Ewell	Georgetown, D. C	Dec. 7, 1813	....
Gunpowder, Manufacturing	H. Keyser	....	Aug. 10, 17 1	
Gunpowder-mill	B. Potter, jr	Hubbardston, Mass	Jan. 24, 1860	26, 922
Gunpowder, mining-powder, &c	H. Hochstalter	Hesse-Darmstadt, Germany.	Mar. 22, 1864	42, 047
Gunpowder, Mode of keeping	J. Gale, jr	Devonshire Terrace, England.	Oct. 3, 1865	50, 313
Gunpowder, Mode of preparing vessels for holding	A. T. Rand	New York, N. Y	Mar. 13, 1866	53, 184
Gunpowder, Plate for pressing	L. Du Pont	Wilmington, Del	Sept. 26, 1865	50, 104
Gunpowder, Preparation of cotton-wool, &c., as substitutes for.	C. F. Schoenbein	Basel, Switzerland	Dec. 5, 1846	4, 877
Gunpowder, Press for pressing	L. Du Pont	Wilmington, Del	Oct. 24, 1865	50, 568
Gunpowder, Substitute for	A. Noble	Hamburg	Oct. 24, 1865	50, 617
Gunpowder to flat projectiles, giving them rotation, Application of.	E. O. C. Ord	United States Army	Feb. 14, 1860	27, 147
Gunpowder to form cartridges, Treating	R. O. Doremus and B. L. Budd	New York, N. Y	Mar. 18, 1862	34, 724
Gunpowder to serve as charge for fire-arms, Preparation of granulated.	J. H. Brown	Ramsey, England	Aug. 20, 1861	33, 069
Gutta-percha and caoutchouc, Covering with	C. Goodyear	New Haven, Conn	Oct. 11, 1853	10, 106
Gutta-percha and caoutchouc, Dissolving and softening.	C. F. Durant	Jersey City, N. J	Apr. 25, 1848	5, 539
Gutta-percha and India rubber, Manufacturing	C. Goodyear and R. Haering	New Haven, Conn	Apr. 12, 1853	9, 668
Gutta-percha, Apparatus for cleaning	J. Reynolds	New York, N. Y	May 27, 1856	14, 972
Gutta-percha, Apparatus for covering wire with	J. Reynolds	New York, N. Y	July 29, 1856	15, 439
Gutta-percha boats, Making	E. B. Larchar	Baltimore, Md	July 24, 1855	13, 315
Gutta-percha by molding, stamping, or embossing, Making articles of.	R. A. Brooman	London, England	May 23, 1848	5, 592
Gutta-percha cord, Making	J. Reynolds	New York, N. Y	Dec. 9, 1856	16, 215
Gutta-percha, &c., Desulphurizing	W. E. Rider and J. Murphy	New York, N. Y	Nov. 7, 1854	11, 906
Gutta-percha fabrics in imitation of patent-leather, Preparing.	H. H. Day	Jersey City, N. J	May 2, 1848	5, 543

Index of patents issued from the United States Patent Office from 1790 *to* 1873, *inclusive*—Continued.

Invention.	Inventor.	Residence	Date.	No.
Gutta-percha, Feed-apparatus for working	J. Reynolds	New York, N. Y	June 10, 1856	15, 087
Gutta-percha, Process for purifying	R. Haering	New York, N. Y	May 5, 1857	17, 214
Gutta-percha, Process for treating	J. Murphy	New York, N. Y	May 30, 1854	10, 977
Gutta-percha, Process of manufacturing	J. Rider	New York, N. Y	June 1, 1852	8, 992
Gutta-percha, Process of working	S. T. Armstrong and C. J. Gilbert.	New York, N. Y	Sept. 17, 1850	7, 643
Gutta-percha tubing and covering wire. Machine for.	J. Reynolds	New York, N. Y	Apr. 22, 1851	8, 051
Gutter-fastening	W. L. Rogers	Rochefort, Mo	Aug. 29, 1871	118, 556
Gutter, Iron	E. Whitehead	Cincinnati, Ohio	Nov. 20, 1866	59, 804
Gutter, Metallic	T. McClunie	Hartford, Conn	May 27, 1873	139, 324
Gutter-strap	A. B. Schulz	Baltimore, Md	Aug. 15, 1871	118, 061
Gutter, Street	H. O. Ames	New Orleans, La	Sept. 24, 1872	131, 588
Gutter-sweeping machine	W. H. King	Philadelphia, Pa	Aug. 19, 1856	15, 566
Gutter-sweeping machine	R. I. Smith	Philadelphia, Pa	Oct. 23, 1855	13, 709
Gutter-trough, Tinners'	J. N. Woolwin	Mechanicsburgh, Ohio	July 20, 1869	92, 922
Gutters, Beading rain	W. H. Henderson	Franklin, Ind	May 28, 1861	32, 420
Gutters for buildings, Machine for making	A. K. P. Buffum	Gardiner, Me	July 25, 1871	117, 255
Gutters, Machine for forming tubular beads on sheet-metal.	O. W. Stow	Plantsville, Conn	Mar. 10, 1868	75, 487
Gutters to buildings, Mode of sustaining	W. Yapp	Cleveland, Ohio	Oct. 28, 1862	36, 876
Gymnasium, Equestrian	E. S. Scripture	Williamsburgh, N. Y	July 30, 1872	129, 988
Gymnasium, Portable	W. G. Hanlon	New York, N. Y	Oct. 29, 1861	33, 583
Gymnastic apparatus	G. W. Bacon	London, England	Oct. 22, 1867	69, 956
Gymnastic apparatus	D. P. Butler	Boston, Mass	Jan. 19, 1869	85, 996
Gymnastic apparatus	W. Hanlon	New York, N. Y	Jan. 4, 1870	98, 587
Gymnastic apparatus	W. Hanlon	New York, N. Y	Jan. 4, 1870	98, 588
Gymnastic apparatus	J. Smith	Saint Paul, Minn	Oct. 18, 1870	108, 401
Gymnastic apparatus	J. Smith	Philadelphia, Pa	May 6, 1873	138, 590
Gymnastic apparatus	F. Veerkamp and F. Leopold	Philadelphia, Pa	Jan. 1, 1861	31, 059
Gypsum-calcining furnace	B. Fowler	Lubec, Me	June 18, 1850	7, 439
Gypsum-calcining furnace	F. Godfrey	Grand Rapids, Mich	Sept. 11, 1866	57, 892

www.ingramcontent.com/pod-product-compliance
Lightning Source LLC
LaVergne TN
LVHW021056110826
845150LV00001B/89

* 9 7 8 1 4 2 5 5 5 7 7 0 6 *